ENCYCLOPAEDIA JUDAICA

ENCYCLOPAEDIA JUDAICA

SECOND EDITION

VOLUME 2
ALR–AZ

FRED SKOLNIK, *Editor in Chief*
MICHAEL BERENBAUM, *Executive Editor*

MACMILLAN REFERENCE USA
An imprint of Thomson Gale, a part of The Thomson Corporation

IN ASSOCIATION WITH
KETER PUBLISHING HOUSE LTD., JERUSALEM

THOMSON
GALE

Detroit • New York • San Francisco • New Haven, Conn. • Waterville, Maine • London

THOMSON GALE

ENCYCLOPAEDIA JUDAICA, Second Edition

Fred Skolnik, *Editor in Chief*
Michael Berenbaum, *Executive Editor*
Shlomo S. (Yosh) Gafni, *Editorial Project Manager*
Rachel Gilon, *Editorial Project Planning and Control*

Thomson Gale
Gordon Macomber, *President*
Frank Menchaca, *Senior Vice President and Publisher*
Jay Flynn, *Publisher*
Hélène Potter, *Publishing Director*

Keter Publishing House
Yiphtach Dekel, *Chief Executive Officer*
Peter Tomkins, *Executive Project Director*

Complete staff listings appear in Volume 1

For more information, contact
Macmillan Reference USA
An imprint of Thomson Gale
27500 Drake Rd.
Farmington Hills, MI 48331-3535
Or you can visit our internet site at
http://www.gale.com

LIBRARY OF CONGRESS CATALOGING-IN-PUBLICATION DATA

Encyclopaedia Judaica / Fred Skolnik, editor-in-chief ; Michael Berenbaum, executive editor. -- 2nd ed.
v. cm.
Includes bibliographical references and index.
Contents: v.1. Aa-Alp.
ISBN 0-02-865928-7 (set hardcover : alk. paper) -- ISBN 0-02-865929-5 (vol. 1 hardcover : alk. paper) -- ISBN 0-02-865930-9 (vol. 2 hardcover : alk. paper) -- ISBN 0-02-865931-7 (vol. 3 hardcover : alk. paper) -- ISBN 0-02-865932-5 (vol. 4 hardcover : alk. paper) -- ISBN 0-02-865933-3 (vol. 5 hardcover : alk. paper) -- ISBN 0-02-865934-1 (vol. 6 hardcover : alk. paper) -- ISBN 0-02-865935-X (vol. 7 hardcover : alk. paper) -- ISBN 0-02-865936-8 (vol. 8 hardcover : alk. paper) -- ISBN 0-02-865937-6 (vol. 9 hardcover : alk. paper) -- ISBN 0-02-865938-4 (vol. 10 hardcover : alk. paper) -- ISBN 0-02-865939-2 (vol. 11 hardcover : alk. paper) -- ISBN 0-02-865940-6 (vol. 12 hardcover : alk. paper) -- ISBN 0-02-865941-4 (vol. 13 hardcover : alk. paper) -- ISBN 0-02-865942-2 (vol. 14 hardcover : alk. paper) -- ISBN 0-02-865943-0 (vol. 15: alk. paper) -- ISBN 0-02-865944-9 (vol. 16: alk. paper) -- ISBN 0-02-865945-7 (vol. 17: alk. paper) -- ISBN 0-02-865946-5 (vol. 18: alk. paper) -- ISBN 0-02-865947-3 (vol. 19: alk. paper) -- ISBN 0-02-865948-1 (vol. 20: alk. paper) -- ISBN 0-02-865949-X (vol. 21: alk. paper) -- ISBN 0-02-865950-3 (vol. 22: alk. paper)
1. Jews -- Encyclopedias. I. Skolnik, Fred. II. Berenbaum, Michael, 1945-
DS102.8.E496 2007
909'.04924 -- dc22
2006020426

ISBN-13:

978-0-02-865928-2 (set)
978-0-02-865929-9 (vol. 1)
978-0-02-865930-5 (vol. 2)
978-0-02-865931-2 (vol. 3)
978-0-02-865932-9 (vol. 4)
978-0-02-865933-6 (vol. 5)
978-0-02-865934-3 (vol. 6)
978-0-02-865935-0 (vol. 7)
978-0-02-865936-7 (vol. 8)
978-0-02-865937-4 (vol. 9)
978-0-02-865938-1 (vol. 10)
978-0-02-865939-8 (vol. 11)
978-0-02-865940-4 (vol. 12)
978-0-02-865941-1 (vol. 13)
978-0-02-865942-8 (vol. 14)
978-0-02-865943-5 (vol. 15)
978-0-02-865944-2 (vol. 16)
978-0-02-865945-9 (vol. 17)
978-0-02-865946-6 (vol. 18)
978-0-02-865947-3 (vol. 19)
978-0-02-865948-0 (vol. 20)
978-0-02-865949-7 (vol. 21)
978-0-02-865950-3 (vol. 22)

This title is also available as an e-book
ISBN-10: 0-02-866097-8
ISBN-13: 978-0-02-866097-4
Contact your Thomson Gale representative for ordering information.
Printed in the United States of America

10 9 8 7 6 5 4 3 2

TABLE OF CONTENTS

Initial "A" at the opening of the Book of Judith in a bible from Citeau, Eastern France, 1109, showing Judith decapitating Holofernes. Dijon, Bibliothèque Municipale, Ms. 14, fol. 158.

Alr–Az

ALROY, DAVID (**Menahem**; 12th century), leader of a messianic movement in *Kurdistan. Alroy was born in Amadiya, east of Mosul. His personal name was Menahem b. Solomon, but he called himself David as befitted his claim to be king of the Jews. "Alroy" (אַלְרוֹאִי) and "al-Rūḥī" (אֶל־רוּחִי) are evidently corruptions of al-Dūjī, his family name in Arabic. The available information about the movement and its initiators is contradictory and tendentious. The movement probably started among the "mountain Jews" of northeast Caucasus before 1121, although some sources and historians place its beginnings in the second half of the century. It gathered momentum from the ferment that accompanied the struggle waged between Christendom and Islam in the wake of the First Crusade, and during the wars preceding the second. The tribulations of the period and massacres in which they were the victims appeared to many Jews as the pangs heralding the advent of the Messiah. The principal leader of the movement was initially Solomon, Alroy's father, who claimed to be the prophet Elijah. An important role was played by one Ephraim b. Azariah, called "the Jerusalemite." The young Menahem was declared the Messiah, a claim assisted by his personal charm. He was of fine appearance, had excelled in his studies in the Baghdad academy, was acquainted with Muslim customs, learned in Jewish mysticism, and skilled in sorcery. To announce their intentions, the leaders of the movement addressed a missive "to all Jews dwelling nearby or far-off and in all the surrounding countries" announcing that "the time has come in which the Almighty will gather together His people Israel from every country to Jerusalem the holy city." They emphasized penitential preparation by fasting and praying. Their opponents viewed such propaganda as dangerous, and shortly afterward the movement was suppressed. Alroy, however, reestablished his center in Amadiya on the route leading then from Khazaria to the Crusader kingdom. Its strategic position as a Muslim base for operating against Edessa (Urfa) had been strengthened by fortifications constructed by Zangī, ruler of Mosul. Alroy now proposed to capture Amadiya. He was encouraged by the contemporary Muslim sectarians (Yezidis) who also sought to gain control of the stronghold and its surroundings, aided by the superstitious awe with which its inhabitants regarded miracle workers and mystics. Rumors were circulated that when imprisoned by the Seljuk sultan, then overlord of the local rulers, Alroy had magically freed himself. Alroy then invited the Jews of the vicinity as well as those living in Azerbaijan, Persia, and the Mosul region, to Amadiya. They were to come with weapons concealed in their garments to witness how he would obtain control of the city. According to an anti-Jewish tradition, rumors of his activities reached Baghdad. Two impostors had forged a letter from Alroy in which he promised to convey the Jews of Baghdad to Jerusalem by night, on the wings of angels. Alroy, therefore, acquired many adherents in Baghdad, and those who waited up all night for the promise to be fulfilled became a laughingstock. Before Alroy managed to do more, he was murdered – according to one version by order of the authorities – according to another, by his father-in-law, who had been bribed. A number of his followers in Azerbaijan who continued to believe in him after his death became known as Menahemites. Alroy's death probably occurred long before the date recorded by Benjamin of Tudela (c. 1160). The character in Benjamin Disraeli's novel, *Wondrous Tale of Alroy* (1839), is largely fictional as he is depicted there as a conquerer.

BIBLIOGRAPHY: A.N. Poliak, *David Alro'i* (Heb., 1958); idem, *Khazaria* (1951^3), 232–4; Baron, Social 2:5 (1957), 202–5.

[Abraham N. Poliak]

ALSACE, former province of the Germanic (Holy Roman) Empire, and from 1648, of *France, including the present department of Haut-Rhin and Bas-Rhin.

Middle Ages

The first evidence of Jews in Alsace is reported by *Benjamin of Tudela who mentions (c. 1170) Jews in Strasbourg. From the beginning of the 13th century, Jews are also mentioned in Haguenau, Obernai, and Rosheim, and later, during the same century, in Wissembourg, *Guebwiller, Colmar, Marmoutier, *Rouffach, *Ensisheim, Molsheim, Mulhouse, and Thann. Probably many refugees expelled from France in 1306 went to Alsace. Jews are henceforward found residing in some 40 additional localities there, notably, *Ribeauvillé, *Sélestat, Bouxwiller, Kaysersberg, and *Saverne. The Jews of some 20 communities in Alsace were victims of the *Armleder massacres, principally at the beginning of 1338. Further anti-Jewish persecutions affected the communities of Colmar, Sélestat, Obernai, Rosheim, Mulhouse, Kaysersberg, Turckheim, and Munster in 1347. Later, the Jews were accused of spreading the *Black Death, even before the epidemic began to ravage Alsace. A gathering of nobles and representatives of the imperial cities of Alsace discussed the subject in *Benfeld at the beginning of 1349, and the city of Strasbourg alone defended the Jews. Subsequently, the Jews were cruelly put to death in some 30 towns in Alsace. After the artisans gained control of the municipal council of Strasbourg, having eliminated the patricians, the important Jewish community of this city met the same fate. These events left their mark on the folklore and the toponyms of Alsace. The Jews reappeared in several towns of Alsace after a short while, apparently with an improved legal status. They were admitted as citizens in Colmar from 1361, in Sélestat from the end of the 14th century, and in Mulhouse from 1403, with almost the same rights as the Christian citizens.

End of 15th Century to Middle of 17th Century

Jews were able to settle in the villages of Alsace when expelled from its cities. They mainly engaged in moneylending. Jews were admitted into Strasbourg during the day to carry on trade, but were compelled to leave the city at nightfall. Regular contact and traffic existed between the Jews of Alsace and those in western Germany, Switzerland, Holland, and Lorraine. Alsace Jewry, basically Ashkenazi, developed individual characteristics, in certain ritual matters, for instance, in the choice of *seliḥot* ("penitential prayers"). The Alsatian rite (*Minhag Elzos*), has been published several times in at least ten editions (for the first time in Frankfurt, 1725). Communal leadership was centralized and authoritarian. The outstanding personality in Alsace Jewry during the Renaissance period was the *shtadlan* ("interceder") *Joseph (Joselmann) of Rosheim. The works of Joselmann's older contemporary, Johanan Luria, show that Alsace Jews at this period were much influenced by Christian society, ideas, and manners; their social and religious life shows on this evidence much variety, and indicates the social tensions and patrician tendencies in certain circles.

The aristocracy and citizenry found the Jews a profitable source of income and oppressed them in every way. In places where Jews were not granted the right of residence, they had to pay exorbitant transit tolls. Whenever Alsace was ravaged by war, the Jews were the first victims of the soldiers. The Jews living in Alsace were subjected to many restrictions. These extended to the wearing of the Jewish *badge, the humiliating form of *oath, and to family life. (Every Jewish marriage was submitted for authorization, and illegitimate children were forcibly baptized.) Jews were not permitted to own land or any building except their place of residence. Newcomers were excluded unless they obtained special authorization.

Under France (the Ancien Regime)

Although a new tax, the *Leibzoll* ("body-tax") was imposed on Alsace Jewry by the French, Jews continued to enter Alsace, and in certain cities their numbers rapidly increased. There were 522 Jewish families living in Alsace in 1689, 1,269 families in 1716, and 2,125 in 1740. The "General Enumeration of the Jews Tolerated in the Province of Alsace" of 1784, published in Colmar in 1785, shows that Jewish communities were scattered throughout the province, numbering 3,910 families (nearly 20,000 persons). The principal settlements were often near main towns, from which the Jews had been expelled but into which they were temporarily admitted for purposes of trade under differing regulations. Communities existed in *Bischheim, a suburb of Strasbourg (473 persons), Haguenau (325), Marmoutier (299), Westhoffen (282), Mutzig (307), Rosheim (268), Wintzenheim, near Colmar (381), Bergheim (327), Ribeauville (286), Bisheim (256), *Hegenheim, near Basle (409), Niederhagenthal (356), Oberhagenthal (271), Durmenach (340), Zillisheim (332), and Rixheim (243).

Economic conditions for the Jews in Alsace were precarious. Many engaged in moneylending almost always on a small scale, frequently to peasants. A few Jews acquired wealth as army contractors. The majority consisted of hawkers and dealers in livestock, grain, and scrap iron. In most of the villages where they were living, the Jews kept the butcher shops. The chief communities of Bouxwiller, Haguenau, Mutzig, and Niedernai wielded extensive jurisdiction according to the administrative division of Alsace. The inflexible piety of the Jews and their distinctive Judeo-Alsatian language distinguished them clearly from their neighbors, although in many aspects they blended into the Alsatian environment.

In 1735 Jews were forbidden to draw up their accounts in Hebrew characters and they were ordered to keep registers of civil status in 1784. Efforts were made to reduce their numbers by preventing Jews from other countries from settling in Alsace and severely limiting Jewish marriages. Tensions built up toward the end of the 18th century: in 1777 a band of criminals, egged on by the bailiff François-Joseph of Hell, forged a mass of false receipts which they sold to peasants indebted to Jews, purportedly freeing them from their obligations. Although the culprits were eventually executed, this affair aggravated the economic difficulties of the Jews and inflamed the Christian populace against them. In 1775 Herz Mendelsheim *Cerfberr of Bischheim, a wealthy purveyor to the king, obtained permission to reside in Strasbourg permanently with his family, although this was opposed by the municipality. Cerfberr was

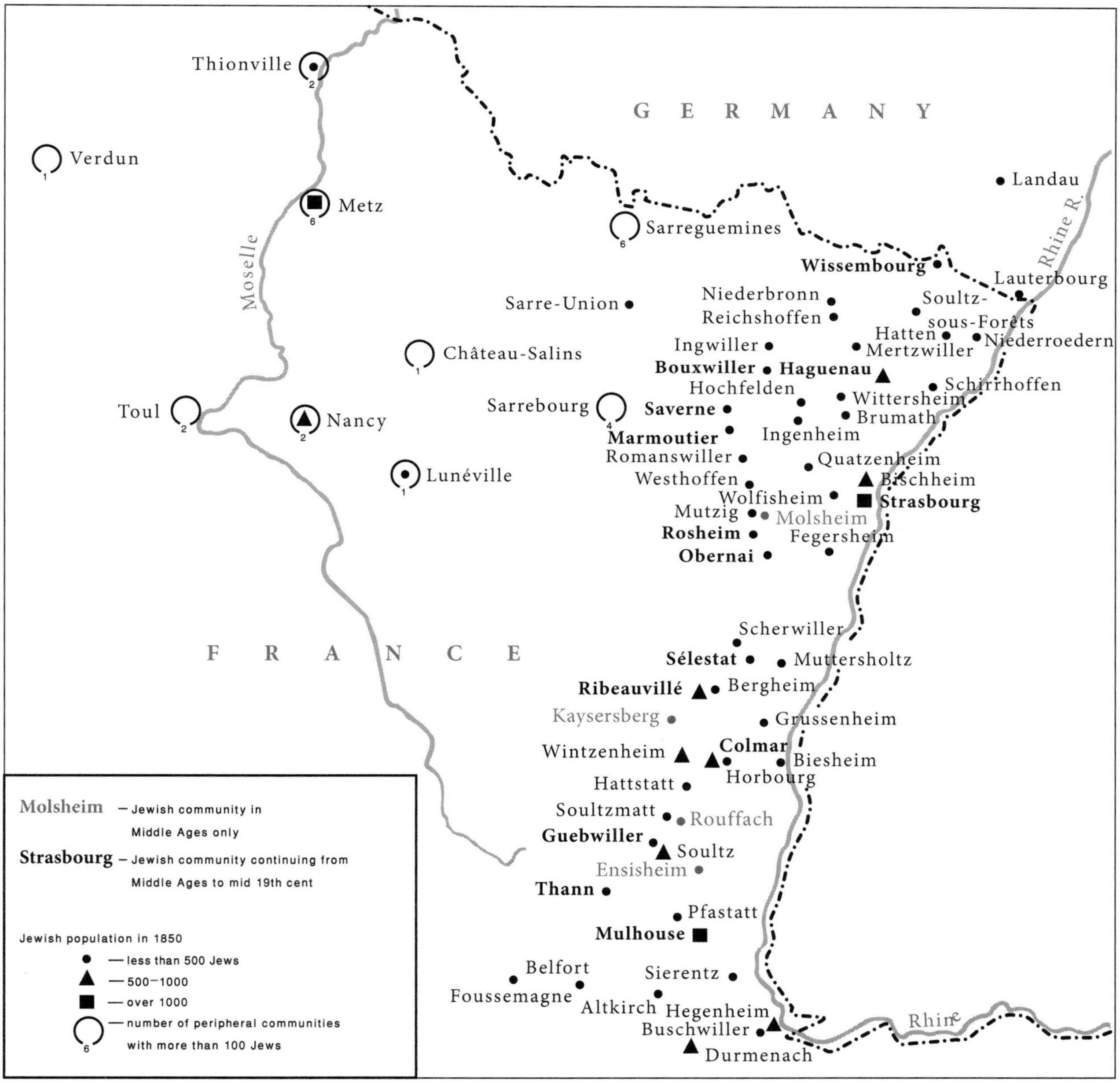

Jewish communities of Alsace, including those of the Middle Ages.

in contact with Christian Dohm who advocated reform of the Jewish status. Cerfberr appealed also to Louis XVI for its amelioration. An edict was issued in 1784 repealing the *Leibzoll*. Subsequent letters patent brought some security to the Jews, although reinforcing other restrictions. A commission presided over by *Malesherbes was considering the position of the Jews in Alsace, when the French Revolution swept away the *Ancien Régime*.

The Emancipation (1789–1844)

Despite the efforts of Jewish notables, such as Cerfberr, Isaiah *Beer-Bing of Metz, and Berr Isaac Berr of Turique, supported by *Mirabeau, Robespierre and, above all, by Abbé Grégoire, a change in the status of the "German" Jews was strenuously and successfully opposed in the first years of the Revolution by the deputies from Alsace and Lorraine. They claimed that such a move would provoke riots and massacres in their districts. Even when the equality of the Jews before the law was proclaimed on Sept. 27, 1791, people in the eastern provinces became used to it only gradually. These districts of France became in practice, and in formulation of anti-Jewish theory, the hotbed of opposition to Jewish emancipation. Many attacks were made on Jews in Alsace-Lorraine. While the Jews themselves were not overly eager to integrate there, they gladly used their newly won rights, especially concerning freedom of settlement. The Jewish population of Strasbourg, for instance, grew in about ten years from less than 100 Jewish inhabitants to over 1,000. *Napoleon I tried to force the Jews of Alsace-Lorraine to integrate, first on the basis of the document formulated by the *Assembly of Jewish Notables and the *Sanhedrin of 1807, and later by the edict of March 17, 1808, called by the Jews the "infamous decree" (*Décret infâme*).

The repayment of debts owed to Jews by Christian peasants was deferred, trading by Jews was subjected to special authorization, and the possibilities of finding replacements for the army draft were restricted. The regulations were theoretically aimed at Jews throughout the country but were implemented only in Alsace and Lorraine. Napoleon's requirement that Jews should adopt family *names, and the creation of the consistorial organization (see *Consistory), compelled, even the Jews most opposed to reforms, to conform to the general legal and economic structure of the country despite attempts at resistance. The discriminatory regulations were not renewed in 1818, and the Jewish religion was recognized by the July Monarchy in 1831 as one of the three religions supported financially by the state. This more liberal policy finally succeeded in turning the Jews of Alsace, like their French coreligionists, into loyal citizens of the realm. An *Ordonnance*, issued on May 17, 1849, supplied French Jewry with a strong constitution as one of the "spiritual families" of the French nation. In that framework the Jews from Alsace and Lorraine became a significant element in French Jewry because of their number and the tenacity of their Jewish religious identification.

The Expansion (1844–1871)

The Jews rapidly adapted themselves to the modern society. They retained strong roots in the villages. In about 1900 there were still some 30 official rabbinical posts in Alsace, apart from those in Strasbourg and Colmar which with the seats of consistorial chief rabbis. However, the Jewish population increased in the large towns, such as Strasbourg, Metz, Nancy, Mulhouse, Colmar, Belfort, Sélestat, and Saverne. A considerable number moved to Paris, or emigrated mainly to North and South America. Many became wealthy through wholesale trade and industry, and soon large numbers entered the liberal professions. The Jewish communal elementary schools, which after the emancipation increasingly replaced the *ḥeder* system and private teaching, provided a complete education, giving religious and preponderantly secular instruction. Those who could afford it preferred the state secondary schools to the Jewish vocational schools opened in the main towns (Metz, Strasbourg, Mulhouse, and Colmar) so as to direct the young toward handicrafts and agriculture. Jews also distinguished themselves in the universities. Local writers, such as Alexandre *Weill (1811–95) of Schirrhoffen and Lémon Cahun of Haguenau (1841–1900), achieved some literary fame. In the rural areas religious life continued nearly as in the past and Alsatian villages provided rabbis for the whole of France, Algeria, and some other countries. A great part of the urban population, however, tended to seek other more unorthodox means in which to express their Jewish faith or Jewish identification. This took the form of a tendency to mild religious reform (opposed only by the leader of French Orthodoxy, the chief rabbi of Colmar Solomon-Wolf *Klein), and of Jewish social activity outside the scope of religion in the narrower sense of the work, such as the founding of Jewish newspapers and periodicals. There were also cases of discreet withdrawals from Judaism and of some notorious conversions, such as those of the Strasbourg-born rabbi David *Drach (1791–1865), son-in-law of the chief rabbi of France, E. Deutz; and the brothers *Ratisbonne, who were the sons of the first president of the Lower Rhine consistory.

Under Germany (1871–1918)

The annexation to Germany of a part of Lorraine and the whole of Alsace (except Belfort) after the Franco-Prussian War of 1870–71, found the Jews of this region so rooted in French life that many families preferred emigration to accepting German nationality. Thus a number of textile enterprises belonging to Jews were transferred to Normandy (Elbeuf), while the Epinal, *Lyons, Paris, and many others were vastly increased by newcomers from Alsace and Lorraine. In the climate of opinion of the Third Republic, political activity, as well as the sciences and the arts, were open to Jews. The army also, despite the *Dreyfus affair, was an attractive career for many young Jews of Alsatian origin.

A group of the Jews who had remained in Alsace-Lorraine accepted the new situation and were strengthened by a large influx of Jews from the eastern side of the Rhine. The local community thus also reflected a German orientation but most of the Jews there maintained a distrustful attitude toward Germany and welcomed the return to France in 1918.

After 1918

Although the Concordat with the papacy had been abolished in France in 1905, it was maintained in the recovered territories in order to conciliate the Catholic Church, which continued to receive financial support from the state. For this reason the Jewish consistories, which were administered under the same system, continued as official institutions, and officiating rabbis and ministers received their salary from the state. This situation remained unchanged after World War II.

The Nazi Period

In June 1940 the Germans again appropriated Alsace and Lorraine and commenced to make them *judenrein*. Jews who had not been previously evacuated to the interior of France were expelled and synagogues and cemeteries were desecrated. New communities grew up in the center and south of France in which those coming from Alsace-Lorraine cooperated with their coreligionists of all origins; like the rest, they were persecuted. A large number of young Alsatian Jews were active in the underground movement, and many were deported and perished, among them the chief rabbi of Strasbourg René *Hirschler, the youth chaplain Samy Klein, and the young mathematician Jacques Feldbau. Soon after the Allied victory, many of the survivors returned to Alsace and Lorraine. Most of the village communities, which had already decayed before the war, were not reinstituted, but Jewish life was renewed in the large cities, especially in Strasbourg.

Postwar Conditions

In 1970 the Jewish population of Alsace and Lorraine numbered about 50,000, including newcomers from Algeria who arrived in France in 1962. Still the seat of a consistory, Strasbourg had an Orthodox, an Eastern European, and subsequently an Algerian-Moroccan *kehillah*, several officiating rabbis, and various educational and philanthropic institutions. There were officiating rabbis in the region for Bischheim (a suburb of Strasbourg), Bischwiller, Erstein, and Obernai (all three rabbis resident in Strasbourg); Haguenau, Saverne, and Sélestat for the Lower Rhine; Colmar, Mulhouse, Dornach (a suburb of Mulhouse, with a rabbi resident in Strasbourg), and Saint-Louis (French suburb of Basle) for the Upper Rhine; and Metz and Sarreguemines for the Moselle district. Of the 67 other communities only 41 had officiating ministers (some only for the High Holidays).

By the 1970s local traditions of the Jews of Alsace-Lorraine were dying out, and only a few elderly people still dimly remembered them. Large sections of the Jewish population were becoming indifferent to their Jewish identity and mixed marriages were common. However, the Jewish school in Strasbourg, where over 15,000 Jews lived in the early 21st century, other forms of religious instruction, as well as the influence of the State of Israel helped keep alive some knowledge of Judaism and an interest in Jewish affairs among elements of the Jewish population.

BIBLIOGRAPHY: Germ Jud, 1 pt. 2 (1963), 96; 2 pt. 1 (1968), 202ff. (includes bibliography); X. Mossmann (ed.), *Cartulaire de Mulhouse* (1883), 211–4; L. Sittler (ed.), *Listes d'admission à la bourgeoisie de Colmar* (1958), nos. 1, 2, 55, 103, 109, 114; C. Pfister, *Juifs d'Alsace sous le régime français* (1927); R. Anchel, *Juifs de France* (1946), ch. 18; H.H. Ben-Sasson, in: *Zion*, 27 (1962), 166–98; idem, in: HTR, 59 (1966), 369–90; E. Scheid, *Histoire des juifs d'Alsace…* (1887); Z. Szajkowski, *Economic Status of the Jews in Alsace, Metz and Lorraine: 1648–1789* (1954); M. Lévy, *Coup d'oeil historique sur l'état des Israélites en France et particulièrement en Alsace* (1836); A. Cahen, *Le Rabbinat de Metz pendant la période française, 1567–1871* (1886); A. Glaser, *Geschichte der Juden in Strassburg* (1894); M. Bloch, *L'Alsace juive depuis la révolution de 1789* (1907); S. Halft, *La fidélité française des Israélites d'Alsace et de Lorraine, 1871–1918* (1921); E. Schnurmann, *La population juive en Alsace* (1936); *Bulletin de nos communautés: organe du judaïsme d'Alsace et de Lorraine* (1945–1968), since Feb. 1968 *Tribune Juive*. **ADD. BIBLIOGRAPHY:** G. Weill, "L'Alsace," in: *Histoire des Juifs en France* (1972); V. Caron, *Between France and Germany* (1988).

[Bernhard Blumenkranz / Moshe Catane]

ALSCHULER, ALFRED S. (1876–1940), U.S. architect. Alschuler was a native of Chicago and a prolific architect whose commercial, industrial, and synagogue buildings dotted the greater Chicago landscape between 1910 and 1930. He worked his way through the Armour Institute of Technology (now the Illinois Institute of Technology) and the School of the Art Institute of Chicago. His most famous building, the London Guarantee and Accident Company Building, now a designated landmark, stands proudly at the corner of Wacker Drive and North Michigan Avenue and is better known today simply as 360 North Michigan Avenue. Located on the site of Fort Dearborn, a log-built outpost established by Thomas Jefferson in 1803, the property became valuable real estate when the Michigan Avenue Bridge was built. Work began on this remarkable 21-story structure in 1921. The building was viewed at the time as a permanent "civic" contribution to Chicago's cityscape, akin to the monuments of ancient Greece and Rome. Alschuler turned the irregular property line to advantage. The slight curve of the façade softens the rigor of the tall building. The classical Greco-Roman details that accent the arched entrance speak "power" as they did in ancient Rome. Four massive Corinthian columns hold up a pediment that bears the name of the building. Over the three-story arch, two reclining figures, Ceres and Neptune, gracefully make the transition from the arch to the horizontal pediment. Heraldic shields soften the windows on the third story. Centered over the pediment a spread eagle hovers over the entrance adding to the power icons of the entrance. The rhythmic colonnade of Corinthian columns near the top of the building as well as the cupola serve to add to the buildings height and its unity of design. Throughout the building there are also icons of corporate power and history. Alschuler built The Chicago Merchandise Mart ("The Merc") in 1927. It was an impressive limestone structure located at 100 N. Franklin

Street. Alschuler's design was classical, similar to the London Guarantee with arched windows and limestone sculptures depicting farmers' products. When it became known that the building was scheduled to be demolished by the Crown family real estate interests, Preservation Chicago launched a campaign to save it. The campaign failed and the Merc was demolished in 2003.

BIBLIOGRAPHY: Catalogue, *Architecture in Context*, Art Institute of Chicago (1981); R.H. Alschuler (ed.), *Oral History Interview with Rose Haas Alschuler* (1985).

[Betty R. Rubenstein (2nd ed.)]

ALSCHULER, SAMUEL (1859–1939), lawyer and judge. Alschuler was appointed by President Woodrow Wilson to the U.S. Federal Court of Appeals in 1915 and served until 1936, part of the time as presiding judge. He practiced law in Aurora, Ill. Alschuler was a Democratic candidate for the U.S. Congress in 1892 and for governor of Illinois in 1900. He served in the Illinois House of Representatives from 1896 to 1900. From 1901 to 1915 he practiced law in Chicago. Appointed federal arbitrator in labor disputes between the packers and their employees, he also served on the U.S. Coal Commission under President Harding.

ALSHEIKH, RAPHAEL BEN SHALOM (1881–1957), Yemenite scholar, teacher, and communal worker; the descendant of a family of sages and leaders in San'a. During the great famine in the years 1900–03, Alsheikh fled to Aden and from there migrated to Jerusalem. He studied at the yeshivot and earned his living by working as a scribe. After World War I he was asked to serve as head of the Yemenite community school in Tel Aviv and taught there until his final years. Alsheikh also served as a rabbi and religious instructor. In his later life he was appointed rabbi of Tel Aviv's Yemenite community and represented it in the Asefat ha-Nivḥarim, the *Va'ad ha-Le'ummi, and the local religious council and burial society.

BIBLIOGRAPHY: Y. Ratzaby and I. Shivtiel (eds.), *Harel, Sefer Zikkaron R. Alsheikh* (1962).

[Yehuda Ratzaby]

ALSHEIKH, SHALOM BEN JOSEPH (1859–1944), rabbi of the Yemenite community of Jerusalem. Alsheikh preached and taught at the Alsheikh Great Synagogue in San'a. He left his hometown in 1888 and in early 1891 reached Jerusalem. There he first devoted himself to studying in various yeshivot. However, he became involved in the leadership of the community of Yemenite immigrants in Jerusalem, founding educational and charitable institutions for them. In 1893 Alsheikh was elected to the administrative committee of the Yemenite community; in 1895 he was one of the founders of the kabbalist yeshivah Reḥovot ha-Nahar; and in 1908 he was chosen chief rabbi of the Yemenite community of Jerusalem. He left several works in manuscript form, including a kabbalistic commentary on the Torah, sermons, commentary on Yemenite liturgy, and various liturgical poems. In his unfinished *Divrei ha-Yamim le-Adat ha-Teimanim bi-Yrushalayim* ("Chronicles of the Yemenite Community in Jerusalem"), he describes the tremendous awakening of San'a Jewry to the idea of immigration to Ereẓ Israel and the beginning of the actual emigration in 1881–82.

BIBLIOGRAPHY: Y. Ratzaby, in: *Din ve-Ḥeshbon shel ha-Va'ad ha-Kelali le-Adat ha-Teimanim* (1946), 19–29; A. Yaari, *Masot Ereẓ Yisrael* (1946), 640–50, 781–2; Tidhar, 1 (1947), 151.

[Avraham Yaari]

ALSHEKH, MOSES (d. after 1593), rabbi and Bible commentator, born in Adrianople. He studied in Salonika under Joseph *Taitaẓak and Joseph *Caro, and then emigrated to Ereẓ Israel, settling in Safed, where he gained prominence as an halakhic authority, a teacher in two talmudic academies, and a preacher. He was active in communal affairs and was a member of the rabbinical court of Joseph Caro, who conferred upon him the full *ordination which had been reintroduced by R. Jacob *Berab. In turn, in 1590, Alshekh ordained Ḥayyim Vital, who was his disciple in *halakhah*. His major field of interest was *halakhah* but, acceding to requests to preach on Sabbaths, in the course of preparing his sermons he occupied himself also with Bible exegesis. He also engaged in the study of the Kabbalah, from which he derived the fundamentals of his religious philosophy. According to one tradition, Isaac *Luria sought to dissuade him from pursuing kabbalistic studies.

About 1590 Alshekh visited the Jewish communities of Syria and Turkey, and perhaps also of Persia, in the interests of Safed Jewry. He also sent an appeal on behalf of the Safed community to Italy and other countries. The last information about him was from Damascus. He participated there in a rabbinical court session in the spring of 1593. He died soon after at a venerable age.

Alshekh reworked his sermons into commentaries to most of the books of the Bible. Several of these commentaries appeared during his lifetime: *Ḥavaẓẓelet ha-Sharon* (Constantinople, 1563; Venice, 1591) on Daniel; *Shoshannat ha-Amakim* (Venice, 1591) on the Song of Songs; *Rav Peninim* (*ibid.*, 1592) on Proverbs; and *Torat Moshe* (Constantinople, c. 1593) on Genesis. Alshekh's commentary on the Book of Psalms under the title of *Tappuḥei Zahav* appeared in Constantinople in 1597–98. This edition was criticized by Alshekh's son Ḥayyim in the introduction to his own edition of his father's commentary on the Psalms. Ḥayyim Alshekh averted that the manuscript of *Tappuḥei Zahav* had been stolen from him and represented a first draft only of his father's commentary.

Between 1600 and 1607, Ḥayyim Alshekh reissued in Venice some of the commentaries published by his father and printed those which had remained in manuscript. They were *Torat Moshe* on the whole of the Pentateuch, *Einei Moshe* on Ruth, *Devarim Neḥumim* on Lamentations, *Devarim Tovim* on Ecclesiastes, *Masat Moshe* on Esther (all 1601); *Ḥelkat Meḥokkek* on Job (1603) and *Marot ha-Ẓove'ot* on the early and Later Prophets, with the exception of Ezekiel (1603–07); and *Romemot El* on the Psalms (1605).

Alshekh's exegetical approach was to present numerous questions that were followed by answers that delved into the syntactic, thematic, and linguistic unity of the biblical text. Alshekh's spiritual world consisted of rabbinic *aggadah* with kabbalistic elaborations. Nevertheless, he was keenly attuned to the stylistic nuances of the biblical text. Alshekh assumed that the biblical characters conducted their affairs using rigorous logic and deliberate thinking. In addition, the Bible had to be viewed as a faithful record of the thoughts, actions, and speeches of the biblical characters.

Alshekh's commentaries, which are permeated with religious, ethical, and philosophical ideas supported by ample quotations from talmudic and midrashic sources, became very popular and have often been reprinted. Some of the commentaries appeared also in abbreviated versions. Ḥayyim Alshekh also published his father's responsa (Venice, 1605). Alshekh was the author of a dirge on the "exile of the *Shekhinah*," which became part of **Tikkun Ḥaẓot*. Never published and subsequently lost were *She'arim*, a book of a religious-philosophical nature; a commentary on *Genesis Rabbah*; and a talmudical work. The commentaries on *Avot* and on the Passover *Haggadah* printed under the name of Alshekh are not original works but compilations from his commentaries on the Bible.

BIBLIOGRAPHY: Rosaries, Togarmah, 3 (1938), 276 ff.; S. Shalem, *Rabbi Moshe Alshekh* (Heb., 1966), incl. bibl. by N. Ben-Menahem; A. Yaari, *Ha-Defus ha Ivri be-Kushta* (1967), nos. 165, 232, 329. **ADD. BIBLIOGRAPHY:** K. Bland in: *The Bible in the Sixteenth Century* (1990) 5–67; A. van der Heide, in: *Jewish Studies in a New Europe* (1998), 365–71.

[Tovia Preschel / David Derovan (2nd ed.)]

ALSHVANG, ARNOLD ALEKSANDROVICH (1898–1960), musicologist and composer. Born in Kiev, Alshvang became involved in political activities and was exiled to northern Russia in 1914. On his return in 1915 he studied composition, theory, and piano at the Kiev Conservatory with Reingold Glier, Boleslav Yavorsky, and Heinrich Neuhaus. Graduating in 1920, he accepted a teaching post there in 1923. In 1930 he was appointed professor at the Moscow Conservatory. Having abandoned teaching after a serious illness, he devoted himself to writing. Among his works are books on Debussy (1935), Musorgsky (1946), Tchaikovsky (1951, 1959²), and Beethoven (1952, 1977²), articles on Scriabin and piano playing, and compositions: *Symphony* (1922), *Symphonic Poem on Ukrainian Folk Themes* (1927), piano pieces, songs, and choral works.

BIBLIOGRAPHY: NG², s.v.; V. Del'son, in: *Sovetskaya muzyka*, 2 (1960), 187–9; B. Bernandt and I.M. Yampol'sky, *Kto pisal o muzyke* ("Writers on Music," 1971).

[Marina Rizarev (2nd ed.)]

°**ALT, ALBRECHT** (1883–1956), German Bible scholar. In 1908 he visited Palestine for the first time as a student in the Palaestina-Institut, directed by G. *Dalman. In 1913 he was appointed as one of the directors of the Deutsches Evangelisches Institut in Jerusalem. In 1921–23 he headed the German Evangelical community in Jerusalem and served as visiting director of the Institut until its activities were ended in 1938. Alt served as professor of Bible at the universities of Greifswald, Basle, Halle, and Leipzig. During World War II he resided in Leipzig and was rector of the university in that city for some time until he retired in 1953.

Alt's first book was *Israel und Aegypten* (1909). Noteworthy among his other publications are: *Die griechischen Inschriften der Palaestina Tertia westlich der Aruba* (1921); *Der Gott der Vaeter* (1929); and *Die Staatenbildung der Israeliten in Palaestina* (1930). He also published many works on the geographical history of Israel during its various periods. Much of his research, published in the form of articles in the *Palastinajahrbuch* and in the *Zeitschrift des Deutschen Palaestina-Viereins*, was collected in *Kleine Schriften zur Geschichte des Volkes Israel* (3 vols., 1953–59). In Alt's works one can discern a trend toward illuminating the history of the occupation of localities, the political and administrative history of Palestine, and the role of the great powers in the Palestine area. He thereby created a scientific method that is adhered to by some of the most important contemporary researchers on ancient Israel. But the specific name the "Alt School" or the "Alt-Noth trend" generally refers to the scholars, mostly German, who subscribe to Alt's (and M. *Noth's) views on the nature of the traditions in Joshua 2–9, and on the period of the documents in Joshua 15–19. Alt prepared a revised edition of R. *Kittel's *Biblia Hebraica* (1937³), together with O. Eisfeldt. Beside his many articles on the biblical period, he excelled in his knowledge of later periods of the history of Palestine down to and including the Byzantine era, and made important contributions to research on the Negev and Roman times. A number of his books and articles were translated into English by R.A. Wilson in Alt's *Essays on Old Testament History and Religion* (1966), including *Staatenbildung…* and *Der Gott der Vaeter*.

BIBLIOGRAPHY: W.F. Albright, in: JBL, 75 (1956), 169–173; idem et al., *Geschichte und Aires Testament* (1953), 211–23; *Festschrift A. Alt* (1953), 174–5.

[Michael Avi-Yonah]

ALTAR (Heb. מִזְבֵּחַ, *mizbe'aḥ*, derived from the root *zbḥ* (זבח), meaning "to slaughter [as a sacrifice]"), originally the place where sacrificial slaughter was performed (e.g., the sacrifice of Isaac in Gen. 22). According to biblical law however, animal slaughter was never upon the altar but nearby. Moreover, the altar was not restricted to animal offerings; it also received grain, wine, and incense offerings. Thus, whatever the original intention of the word altar, it was extended to designate the place for offering all oblations. Finally, this definition does not mention all the uses of the altar, since non-sacrificial functions are also attested: testimony (e.g., Josh. 22:26–29) and asylum (see below).

Typology

Altars are found everywhere in the ancient Near East. They were constructed from three kinds of material: stone, earth, and metal. The choice depended on such factors as permanence, cost, and, in Israel, on whether the altar was alone or attached to a sanctuary. This discussion will naturally be limited to Ereẓ Israel.

Stone altars are not corroded by time and archaeological excavations have unearthed abundant pre-Israelite specimens. Their form ranges from unworked, detached rocks, to slightly hollowed surfaces, to hewn natural stone, and to completely man-made structures. Some undisputed examples are at Gezer, Hazor, Megiddo, Nahariyyah, and Arad. At Arad, the Israelite sanctuary contains an altar three cubits square and five cubits high (the exact dimensions of the Tabernacle altar in Ex. 27:1) and is built of earth and small unworked stones (in accordance with Ex. 20:22; see below). The Bible also speaks of the same types of stone altars, namely, natural rock (Judg. 13:19–20; I Sam. 6:14; 14:33–35; I Kings 1:9) and artificial heap (Gen. 31:46–54; Josh. 4:2–8, 20ff.; I Kings 18:31–32). All biblical altars, with the exception of those in sanctuaries, seem to have been built of stone.

Altars of earth are explicitly commanded in Exodus 20:24 (cf. II Kings 5: 17), but because earthen altars would not survive the ravages of time, none have been found. Nor, for that matter, were any of the altars mentioned in the Bible built of earth. These, the simplest and least pretentious of all altars, were exclusively the creation of the common folk. Brick, technically also earth, so common a material in Mesopotamia, is not evidenced in Israel; a Canaanite brick altar, however, has been found (*Beth-Shean, stratum IX).

The shape of the Israelite stone and earth altars thus far discussed seems to have been simple, no doubt because of the prohibition against the hewn stone and steps (Ex. 20:22–23). The Arad altar, though in a sanctuary, is indicative of this simplicity. It is a square structure. In contrast to stone and earth altars, metal altars, associated exclusively with the central sanctuary of Israel, differ profoundly in shape and function.

THE TABERNACLE. Israel's desert sanctuary had two altars: the bronze, or burnt-offering, altar standing in the courtyard, and the gold, or incense, altar within the Tent. The courtyard altar was for sacrifices. Its name, *'olah* ("whole-offering"), is taken from its most frequent sacrifice, required twice daily (Ex. 29:38–43) and on every festival (Num. 28–29); it was also the only sacrifice entirely consumed upon the altar (see: *Sacrifice). The name "bronze" stems from its plating. Actually, it was made of acacia wood and its dimensions, in cubits, were 5 × 5 × 3. Its form is minutely described, though the meaning of all the terms used is not certain (Ex. 27:1–8; 38:1–7).

The most important feature of the bronze altar was its *keranot* (*qeranot*) or "horns," seen on small altars found in Israel. Refugees seeking asylum seized the altar horns. The altar was purified by daubing the blood of the *ḥaṭṭ'at*, or "purification offering," on the altar horns (Ex. 30:12; Lev. 4:25–30). Horns were an essential element of all the altars in the Jerusalem Temple. The origin of the horns is still unknown.

Beneath the horns was the *karkov* ("rim" or "border") which seems to have been a projecting rim, and is exemplified by many small altars in Ereẓ Israel. The *mikhbar* ("net" or "grating") was a bronze mesh that covered the upper half of the altar beneath the rim but neither its appearance nor its function is understood.

Since the altar was part of a portable sanctuary, it was fitted with four rings and two staves. Moreover, it was hollow and hence not burdensome. The altar was only a portable frame, since, in contradistinction to the incense altar (Ex. 30:3) there is no mention of a roof, and at each encampment it would, therefore, be filled with earth and rocks (in actual conformity with Ex. 20:21ff.). The same system of hollowed altars is known from some Assyrian samples.

SOLOMON'S TEMPLE. In the account of the building of the First Temple (I Kings 6–7), there is no mention of the sacrificial altar although the building of an altar, 20 × 20 × 10 cubits in size, is mentioned in II Chronicles (4:1). There are also allusions to the sacrificial altar in the construction account (I Kings 9:25) under the name of "the bronze altar" (I Kings 8:64; II Kings 16:14–15). The silence of I Kings 6–7 may be due to textual corruption.

More is known about its replacement, the altar constructed by King Ahaz (II Kings 16:10–16). It was a copy of the altar in the main temple of Damascus, probably that of Hadad-Rimmon (5:18). It was called the "great altar" (16:15), and was therefore larger than Solomon's altar. It had to be ascended (16:12); it was not made of bronze, since that name was reserved for Solomon's altar. It may have been the model for Ezekiel's altar (below). Ahaz had Solomon's altar moved to the northern part of the courtyard, where it was reserved for his private use (16:14, 15b).

Ezekiel's Altar

Ezekiel's vision of a new Temple (Ezek. 40:48) comprises a minute description of its sacrificial altar (43:13–17). It consists of four tiers, each one cubit less per side than the tier below. Since the uppermost tier had a horizontal 12 × 12 cubits, the ones underneath were respectively 14 × 14, 16 × 16, and 18 × 18 cubits. The height of the respective tiers, from top to bottom, is given as 1 + 2 + 4 + 4, to which another cubit must be added for the horns (*ibid.* 43:15). Thus, the total height of the altar is 12 cubits. Because the long cubit is used (app. 20½ inches), the altar was about 20½ feet tall, even higher than the altar attributed to Solomon by the Chronicler (II Chron. 4:1). It was ascended by a flight of stairs on its eastern side. The edges of two of its tiers were apparently shaped into troughs for collecting the sacrificial blood, the one at the base being called "the *ḥeik* [*ḥeiq*; Heb. חֵיק] of the earth" and the other, in the middle, "the *ḥeiq* of the ledge" (Ezek. 43:14, 17). Their purpose was to collect the blood of the *ḥaṭṭ'at*, which was daubed at these points (43:20; see below). If rabbinic tradition for the Second Temple holds good for Ezekiel, then even the remaining *ḥaṭṭ'at* blood was collected into the middle gutter, for it was dashed on the upper part of the altar walls (see Mid. 3:1).

It has been suggested that Ezekiel's altar corresponded to the one he remembered from the First Temple, in which case it would be an exact description of Ahaz' altar. Supporting this view is the Syrian-Mesopotamian influence upon certain of its features. It is known that Ahaz copied a Damascene altar. Its storied structure resembles the ziggurat temple-tower. The uppermost tier is called *'ari'el* or *har'el;* the latter may mean "God's mountain." Perhaps Isaiah's symbolic name for Jerusalem, *Ariel*, has its origin in this altar (Isa. 29:1–2, 7).

Ezekiel also envisions inside the Temple an incense altar, which he calls "the table that is before the Lord" (41:22). That it is of wood may reflect the reality of 597 B.C.E., when Nebuchadnezzar stripped all the Temple cult implements of their gold (II Kings 24:13).

Sanctity and Theology

The altars are legitimate only in the Promised Land. This is not because the power of Israel's God is spatially limited – He controls the destiny of all nations and can be addressed in prayer everywhere (e.g., I Kings 8:33ff.) – but because of the basic concept of the sanctity of Israel's territory: it is the Holy Land. This principle underlies the argument against the erection of a Transjordanian altar (Josh. 22:19), as well as the legal fiction of taking Israelite soil abroad, adopted by the Aramean Naaman (II Kings 5:17) and, perhaps, by his Israelite townsmen (cf. I Kings 20:34). The sanctity of the altar is evidenced by the theophany which concluded the week-long consecration rites for the Tabernacle: "The presence of the Lord appeared to all the people. Fire came forth from before the Lord and consumed the whole offering and the suet pieces on the altar. And all the people saw, and shouted, and fell on their faces" (Lev. 9:23–24). It is an assumption common to biblical tradition that a sanctuary is not fully consecrated – or is not divinely sanctioned – unless it has a tradition of a theophany upon its altar (I Kings 18:38; II Chron. 7:1), or that its altar is built on the site of one. The altar has mediating powers; it may bring God to earth, and it enables humans, through worship, to reach heaven. This is nowhere more evident than in Solomon's dedicatory prayer for the Temple, when he proclaims that even in a foreign land Israel's armies or exiles need but turn to the Temple and their prayer will travel to God along a trajectory that passes through their land, city, Temple, and then, at the altar, turns heavenward (I Kings 8:44, 48; cf. 31, 38). The altar, then, is the earthly terminus of a Divine funnel for man's communion with God. It is significant that later Judaism carried the tradition that the air space above the altar was an extension of its sanctity. The sanctity of the altar is evidenced by the asylum it provided anyone who "seized its horns" (e.g., I Kings 1:50–51). An early law, however, stipulated that this privilege was not to be extended to murderers (Ex. 21:14). On this basis, the altar provided no safety for Joab (I Kings 2:28–34); even then, Solomon tried at first to remove Joab who "seized the altar horns" (verse 34) from the altar before he had him killed (verse 30). The altar is consecrated with the "oil of anointment" (Ex. 40:10); it is the only object outside the Tent to fall into the category of the "most sacred" (Ex. 29:37), though not to the same degree as the Holy of Holies inside it. For example, the non-priest is prohibited from viewing the inner sancta (Num. 4:20) but is only barred from touching the altar (Ex. 29:37); the disqualified priest is barred from contact with the sanctuary Holy of Holies, but in regard to the altar, as the verb *karav* (*qrv*) or *niggash* ("encroach") shows, he is forbidden only to officiate at it but is free to touch it (Ex. 28:43; 30:20; Lev. 21:23). The composition of the Holy of Holies also bespeaks this sanctity differential: the inner sancta are plated with gold, the altar with bronze; in transit the former are covered with a blue cloth, the latter with a purple cloth (Num. 4:4–14). Laymen were permitted access only to a corridor within the sanctuary enclosure to perform the required preliminary rituals with their animal oblation (the presentation, laying of hands, slaughter, and flaying of the animal; Lev. 1:3–6), and to assemble there as spectators (Lev. 8:3–4; 9:5). Only the high priest may bless the people from the altar (Lev. 9:22, "and he descended"). Solomon, who performed this function, did so in front of the altar (I Kings 8:64–65).

The sacrificial altar must not only be consecrated by an application of the anointing oil but by a week-long ceremonial, during which the altar horns are daubed with the blood of a purification offering (Lev. 8:15) each day of the week (Ex. 29:36–37). The meaning of this consecration can be deduced through a series of analogies with other uses of sacrificial blood, such as the purification rite of a healed leper (Lev. 14:14–17, 25–28); the investiture of new priests (Ex. 29:20; Lev. 8:23–24); the reconsecration rites for defiled altars (Lev. 4:25, 34; 5:9); and the smearing of the lintel and doorposts with blood of the paschal sacrifice (Ex. 12:7, 22). The things which receive the blood are extremities; i.e., the very points of the object which a hostile force would strike first in attacking it. In the ancient Near East, temples were periodically smeared with supposed potent substances at precisely the same vulnerable points, in order to expel the malefic power from the object and to protect it against future incursions. The blood rites therefore had a purgative and an apotropaic function. It is not too difficult to deduce that in Israel these rituals had the same dual purpose; i.e., to purge the altar of any uncleanliness and to protect it from future evil influence. The verbs used in regard to purification apply to the altar but never to man. The blood for each stems from a different sacrifice: for the altar the *ḥaṭṭ'at* is used but not for humans. Indeed in the case of humans the ritual purification has already taken place by previous ablution (for the leper, Lev. 14:2–9; for the priest, Ex. 29:4). The function of the blood rite therefore is to ward off evil; it is an apotropaic act (cf. the paschal sacrifice, Ex. 12:23). The consecration of both priest and altar was performed, however, by the anointing oil (Ex. 29:21; Lev. 8:11).

The blood of sacrifices must terminate on the altar, if not on its horns, then upon its walls and base. This leads to another equally significant function of the altar: the blood prohibition. Israelites and non-Israelites alike are constrained from eating blood, because it is the life of the animal (Gen. 9:4). The blood must be drained and returned to the Creator. There is only one legitimate place where this can be done: at the altar of the central sanctuary. The altar, then, is the instrument by which the animal's life is restored to God. Indeed, in Leviticus occurs the clear, unambiguous statement that whoever slaughters an ox, sheep, or goat elsewhere but at the sanctuary altar is guilty of murder (Lev. 17:3–4). It is permitted to kill animals and eat their flesh but the blood must not be tampered with; it must be returned to God via the altar, if the animal is sacrificeable, and via the earth if brought down in the hunt (Lev. 17:13–14). Thus, the sanctuary altar legitimates animal slaughter; it is the divinely-appointed instrument of effecting expiation for taking animal life (Lev. 17:11).

The prohibition of making steps on the altar "that your nakedness be not exposed upon it" (Ex. 20:23) is another evidence for the sanctity of the altar. The early altar at the sanctuary of Arad, with a step to it, illustrates that the prohibition was practical, not theoretical. For this reason, once Israelites adopted trousers, a Persian invention, the priests were required to wear breeches (Ex. 28:42–43).

Incense Altar

All the biblical accounts of the sanctuary speak not only of the sacrificial altar but also of an incense altar within the sanctuary building. The incense altar of the Tabernacle is described in detail (Ex. 30:1–10; 37:25–28). Its dimensions were 1 × 1 × 2 cubits. Like the sacrificial altar, it contained horns, rings, and staves for carrying, and was made of acacia wood. However, it differed from it in being plated with gold, not with bronze; also, the plating extended over the top for it was solid and had a roof, in contrast to the sacrificial altar. Its place was directly in front of the curtain, flanked by the two other golden objects, the candelabrum (Ex. 25:31ff.) and table (23ff.). Incense was burned upon it twice daily at the time of the *tamid*, or "daily," offering. No other offering but the prescribed incense was tolerated (9b).

Reference to the incense altar of Solomon's Temple is found in the construction account (I Kings 6:20–22; 7:48) and in the incense offering ascribed to King Uzziah (II Chron. 26:16). In his blueprint for the new Temple (Ezek. 41:22), Ezekiel may have been thinking of the incense altar he saw in the Temple (as a priest, he had access to it).

The historicity of these accounts has been called into question since the critical work of J. *Wellhausen in the late 19th-early 20th centuries on the assumption that the burning of incense was not introduced into Israel until the Second Temple (see I Macc. 1:54). However, many small altars have been found in Ereẓ Israel dating back to the Bronze Age, too small for animal offerings. Some actually approximate the dimensions of the Tabernacle altar and are even equipped with horns, e.g., at Shechem and Megiddo. An incense altar, identified as such by its inscription, has been recently excavated in Khirbet Mudayna in Jordan at a site dating to the early eighth century B.C.E. Thus, the incense altar was standard equipment for neighboring temples and cannot be denied to Israel.

Since there is no reason to deny that there was an incense altar in Solomon's Temple, there remains only the question of the incense altar ascribed to the Tabernacle. Scholars have been nearly unanimous in declaring it an anachronistic insertion based upon the Temple. Their suspicion is strengthened by the placement of its description not in the text containing the rest of the inner sancta (Ex. 26), but after the description of the entire Tabernacle and its paraphernalia (Ex. 30:1–10) – an afterthought, as it were. The objection is fallacious. The fact that it is not found in its "logical" place is in itself reason to suspect that another kind of logic obtained there. Functionally, the incense is outside the carefully graded sanctity outside of chapters 28–29; as such its description appropriately follows those chapters.

[Jacob Milgrom]

In *Halakhah*

In talmudic sources the word "altar," when unqualified, refers to the outer altar (Yoma 5:5), which stood in the Temple Court in the open, a distance of 22 cubits from the corner of the porch (Mid. 5:1). Most of it was in the southern sector (Yoma 16a; but see the opinion of R. Judah, *ibid.;* see also Zev. 58b). For building the altar for the Second Temple prophetical testimony was needed to determine the exact required location (Zev. 62a). This altar is also called "the altar of bronze" because of its bronze cover (Hag. 3:8) and "the altar of the burnt offering," because daily burnt offerings and other sacrifices were offered upon it (Men. 4:4).

According to talmudic sources the altar was ten cubits high (but Jos., Wars, 5:225 has 15 cubits). It was a structure of stones joined together with earth (Mekh. Sb-Y. Yitro 20; Epstein, ed., 156) and consisted of four square layers formed of stones, plaster, and a filling of mortar (Zev. 54a), the wider stones being placed below and the narrower above, as described later (Suk. 45a; Mid. 3:1; Zev. 54a). These dimensions made the altar four cubits larger on all four sides than the altar of Solomon's Temple (II Chron. 4:1; Mid. 3:1). The first layer was 32 × 32 cubits (according to Jos., *ibid.*, 50 × 50), and one cubit high. The second layer was 30 × 30 cubits and five cubits high. The lower projection of one cubit each on the north and at the northeast and southwest corners, which were one cubit higher than the ground (Tosef. Zev. 6:2; Mid. 3:1), was called the base. There was no base in the southeast corner (Zev. 54a). In the southwest corner there were several narrow apertures through which the blood flowed down to the water channel, and from there to the brook of Kidron (Mid. 3:2; Yoma 5:6). Five cubits from the ground, i.e., in the middle of the altar, a red line, the "*hut shel sikrah*," encircled it, indicating the place for the upper and the lower sprinkling of the blood (Mid. 3:1; Tosef. Zev. 6:2). The third layer was 28 × 28 cubits, and three cubits high. The cubit-wide projection which encircled the middle of the altar was called the *sovev* ("surround"). The priest walked along it, to offer up the burnt offering of a bird (Zev. 6:5), and to sprinkle the blood of the sacrifices upon the altar with his finger (Zev. 5:3). The fourth layer constituted the "horns" of the altar. They were four stones, one cubit by one, placed at the four corners of the altar. After deducting the breadth of the horns (one cubit) and another cubit within, used as a path for the priests (*karkov*, "border"; Tosef. Shek. 3:19; Zev. 62a) when removing the ashes, an area of 24 × 24 cubits remained which was assigned as the place of the fire. The larger fire was in the southeast corner (Tam. 2:4) and the smaller, for incense, opposite it in the southwest corner (Tam. 2:5). Although open to the sky, it is stated that the rain never extinguished the wood fire, nor did the wind disturb the column of smoke (Avot 5:5). In the center of the altar there was an enormous heap of ashes called *tappu'ah* ("apple"), because of its round shape (Tam. 2:2).

According to R. Meir, the dimensions of the projections of the base, of the surround, and of the horns, were measured by the larger cubit, which was six handbreadths (Kelim 17:10; Tosef. Kelim, BM 6:12–13; see Men. 97b). On top of the altar there were two bowls, either of silver or limestone, into which the water and the wine of the water libation were poured during Tabernacles (Suk. 4:9). During the rest of the year the wine libation was poured into the bowl on the east (Tosef. Suk. 3:14; Sif. Num., Shelah 107). From the bowls the wine flowed through a gutter in the floor of the court (Tosef. Suk. 3:14) into the pits (foundations of the altar) in the southwest corner (Mid. 3:3). The wine was absorbed in the pit or congealed inside the pipe between the porch and the altar, and the pipe consequently had to be cleaned. In the opinion of R. Yose, the pit penetrated to the abyss (Tosef. Suk. 3:15; Suk. 49a).

The stones of the altar were smooth (Zev. 54a), taken from the virgin soil of the valley of Beth Cherem (Mid. 3:4). The use of iron was forbidden in its erection. The stones were plastered over twice yearly, at Passover and at Tabernacles, and, according to Judah ha-Nasi it was plastered with a cloth every Sabbath eve (Mid. 3:4; Maim., Yad, Beit ha-Behirah 1:16). In the times of the Hasmoneans the Syrians placed the "Abomination of Desolation" upon the altar (I Macc. 1:54). When the Temple was subsequently cleansed they were doubtful whether it could be used, and hid the stones (*ibid.* 4:44; Meg. Ta'an. 9; Av. Zar. 52b) in a chamber in the *Bet ha-Moked* (Chamber of the Hearth; Mid. 1:6). The dedication of the altar (I Macc. 4:53–59) became the central feature of the festival of Ḥanukkah. One reason given for the Ḥanukkah celebration lasting eight days is that it took this much time to build the altar and plaster it (Meg. Ta'an. 9, 25th Kislev). At the southern side of the altar there was a stone ramp, 32 cubits long and 16 wide, enabling the priests to reach the top of the altar without transgressing the prohibition contained in Exodus 20:26 (Mekh. Yitro, Ba-Hodesh, 11; see above). There was a space between the end of the ramp and the altar (Zev. 62b).

Altar and ramp together were 62 cubits long (Mid. 5:2), the ramp overhanging the lower part of the altar. From the large ramp two smaller ones branched off, one on the east side in the direction of the surround, and the other on the west in the direction of the base (Zev. 62b and Rashi *ibid.*). The existence of a ramp to the surround is mentioned explicitly only by the *amora* Judah b. Ezekiel. Usually one ascended the altar from the right-hand side of the ramp and descended from the left one (Zev. 6:3).

Lack of precision in the aforementioned dimensions of the altar and the ramp did not disqualify them from use (Tosef. Men. 6:12), but the absence of the horns, the base, the surround, the ramp, the lack of a square appearance, or the slightest flaw in the altar would disqualify the sacrifice (Tosef. Suk. 3:16; Zev. 62a and 59a).

Only the slaughter of birds took place on the actual altar (Zev. 6:4–5); other sacrifices were slaughtered to the north of it (Zev. 5:1–2; Mid. 3:5). If the slaughtering took place on the altar, however, the sacrifice was acceptable (Zev. 6:1).

During the Second Temple period no fire descended from heaven (Yoma 21b) as it did in the First Temple (Zev. 61b). A tradition was preserved that the fire of the First Temple was concealed in a well and was brought out in the days of Nehemiah (II Macc. 1:19–24).

Whenever the altar was not in use for regular sacrifices additional burnt-offerings were offered (Tosef. Shek. 2:8). These are referred to as the *keiz ha-mizbe'ah* ("summer fruit" of the altar; Shek. 4:4). A special regulation "for the benefit of the altar" was enacted to ensure continual sacrifice on the altar (Git. 5:5; Git. 55a). The altar fire continued to burn even at night so that the portions of the sacrifice which it had not been possible to burn during the day would be consumed (Ber. 1:1; Tam. 2:1). The priests would rise early in the morning and undergo ablution in order to be privileged to remove the ashes (Tam. 1:2; Yoma 1:8; 2:1). After ascending to the top of the altar they cleared away the ashes (Tam. 1:4) and shoveled them on to the ash heap (*ibid.* 2:2). When the heap was overfull the ashes were removed, but during the three Pilgrim Festivals they remained there as they were considered ornamental (*ibid.*).

Priests alone were permitted to approach the altar and minister (Zev. 116b) and proof that a person had "stood and ministered at the altar" (Yev. 7:6) was accepted as evidence of his priestly lineage (Kid. 4:5; cf. Ter. 8:1; Jos., Ant., 9:160). The altar and ramp made sacred whatever was prescribed for them. Even if disqualified sacrifices were placed upon them, they were not removed (Zev. 9:1–7; Tosef. Mak. 5:4; and Tosef. Tem. 1:14). A vow made "to the altar" was considered as referring to the altar sacrifices (Ned. 1:3; Tosef. Ned. 1:3).

In the talmudic era the principle that the altar because of its sanctity served as a refuge for murderers who seized hold of its horns was restricted (Mak. 12a; Num. R. 23:13; cf. TJ Kid. 4:1, 65c).

The altar played an important role in the festival ceremonies. During Tabernacles a daily circuit with palm branches or willow branches (Suk. 43b) was made of the altar and verses of *Hallel* were recited. On the seventh day the circuit was made seven times (Suk. 4:5), and the people took their leave of the altar with expressions of laudation, "Beauty is thine, O Altar! Beauty is thine, O Altar!" (*ibid.*).

During Passover, so large was the number of paschal lambs sacrificed in the Temple court, that the sprinkling of the blood against the base of the altar was performed by successive rows of priests (Pes. 5:5). The *omer* was waved on the east side of the altar and offered on the west side (Men. 5:6); so also with the waving of the two loaves on Shavuot (*ibid.*). The baskets of first fruits were placed at the side of the altar (Bik. 3:6; Tosef. Sanh. 3:6).

The golden altar (Yoma 5:5), also called the inner altar (Tam. 3:1), stood in the center of the center of the sanctuary (Yoma 33a–b), opposite the *parokhet* ("curtain") which separated the sanctuary from the Holy of Holies (Tosef. *ibid.* 2:2). Incense was burnt (Men. 4:4) and the sacrificial blood was sprinkled upon its sides (Men. 3:6; Lev. 5:1–2; Yoma 5:7). The measurements of the golden altar were the same as those used in the Tabernacle of Moses (Ex. 30:1–10) except that the larger cubit of six handbreadths was used (Kelim 17:10).

In the *Aggadah*

The altar as a symbol of atonement recurs again and again in rabbinic literature (Tosef. BK 7:6). Johanan b. Zakkai explains the prohibition against the use of iron in erecting the altar, because the sword (iron) represents catastrophe, and the altar, atonement (*ibid.*), its whole (*shelemot*) stones "bringing peace (*shalom*) between Israel and their Father in Heaven" (*ibid.* 7; Mekh. end of Yitro). In line with this homily, the Mishnah taught: "It is not right for that which curtails life to be lifted up against that which prolongs it" (Mid. 3:4). The word *mizbe'aḥ* ("altar") is interpreted as suggesting, by assonance, the four words *mezi'aḥ, mezin, meḥabbev, mekhapper* ("removes evil decrees, sustains, endears, atones"; Ket. 10b); or as a **notarikon*, its four letters being the initials of *Meḥilah-Zekhut Zikkaron – Berakhah-Ḥayyim* ("forgiveness-merit (memorial) – blessing-life"; Tanh. Terumah 11). Because of the merit of the altar, blessing accrued to Israel (Tosef. Ma'as. Sh. 5:29), and because of it, the Holy One blessed be He will punish the kingdom of Edom (Tanḥ. Terumah 11). Its dimensions and its parts are also interpreted symbolically (*ibid.* 10; Mid. Tadshe 11).

According to one aggadic opinion, Adam was formed from earth taken from the site of the altar, in order that the site of his atonement should give him power to endure (Gen. R. 14:8; TJ Naz. 7:2, 56b).

According to a late *aggadah* the altars of the ancients – Adam, Cain, Abel, Noah – were erected on the site of the altar where also Isaac was bound (PdRE 31), and it was from them that Jacob took the stones that he placed at his head at the ford of the Jordan (Gen. 35).

According to R. Isaac Nappaḥa the fact that the Temple was built on the site of the **Akedah* (Zev. 62a) is the basis of the saying that "whoever is buried in the land of Israel is as if he were buried beneath the altar" (Tosef. Av. Zar. 4:3; ARN[1] 26:41; S. Lieberman, *Hellenism in Jewish Palestine* (1950), p. 163). The idea of the Sanctification of the Divine Name implicit in the binding of Isaac also gave rise to the metaphorical use of "building an altar" as an expression for such an act (Lam. R. 1:16, 50; Git. 57b). The more usual metaphor is "… as if he built an altar," used with reference to one observing the commandments of Judaism (Ber. 15a; Suk. 45a–b; Men. 110a).

By interpreting scriptural verses the aggadists coined such expressions as, "as if an altar was erected in his heart" (*Otiyyot de-Rabbi Akiva*, 8), and "the altar shed tears" (Sanh. 22a). Plagues afflicting a person are merely "an altar of atonement for all Israel" (Ber. 5b, see Rabbinovicz, DIK, 50F, 1, 14).

After the destruction of the Temple, a Jew's table is regarded as taking the place of the altar (cf. Tosef. Sot. 15:11–13), and it was said that "now that there is no altar, a man's table atones for him" (Ber. 55a; Men. 97a). The halakhic authorities explain many table customs on this basis (*Shibbolei ha-Leket*, Buber's ed., 141; *Sefer Ḥasidim*, 102).

[Bialik Myron Lerner]

BIBLIOGRAPHY: de Vaux, Anc Isr, 406–14, 527 (incl. bibl.); Haran, in: EM, 4 (1962), 763–80 (incl. bibl.); idem, in: *Scripta Hierosolymitana*, 8 (1961), 272–302; Aharoni, in: BA, 31 (1968), 2–32; J. Milgrom, *Studies in Levitical Terminology*, 1 (1969), 37–41; Maim. Yad., *Beit ha-Beḥirah* 1:13–2:18; Barth, JJLG, 7 (1909), 129–130; J. Doktorovitz, *Middot ha-Battim* (5697 – 1936/7), 45–54; M. Weiss, *Beit ha-Beḥirah* (5706 – 1945/6), 11–27, 101–3; Ginzberg, Legends, index; Bialoblocki, in: *Alei Ayin, S. Schocken Jubilee Volume* (5712 – 1951/2), 51–52, 55; S. Lieberman, *ibid.*, 81; idem, *Hellenism in Jewish Palestine* (1950); idem, *Tosefta ki-Feshutah* 4 (1962), 684, 710, 871, 879–83; C. Albeck, *Mishnah* [5], *Seder Kodashim* (5719 – 1958/9), 313, 324–7, 424–5, 433–5; Safrai, *Ereẓ Yisrael*, 5 (1958), 212; S. Scheffer, *Beit ha-Mikdash* (5722 – 1961/2), 25–29; D. Conrad, *Studien zum Altargesetz* (1968). **ADD. BIBLIOGRAPHY:** S. Japhet, *I & II Chronicles* (1993), 564; Z. Zevit, in: D. Wright (ed.), *Pomegranates and Golden Bells* (FS Milgrom; 1995), 29–38; C. Meyers, in: M. Fox (ed.), *Texts, Temples and Traditions* (Harran FS; 1996), 33–46; K. Smelik, in: M. Vervenne (eds.), *Deuteronomy and Deuteronomic Literature* (Brekelmans FS; 1997), 263–78; N. Na'aman, in: VT, 48 (1998), 333–49; S.D. Sperling: in, R. Chazan et al. (eds.), *Ki Baruch Hu* (Levine FS; 1999), 373–85.

ALTARAS, Spanish family which originated in Castile, and spread to Italy, Turkey, and Ereẓ Israel. To MOSES (c. 1500) was attributed, probably erroneously, a Ladino translation of the Shulḥan Arukh, printed in Latin characters under the title *Libro de Mantenimiento de la Alma* (Venice, 1609, 1713). Apparently it was written for the Marranos who could not read the work in the original. According to Steinschneider this work was written by a certain Meir, and Altaras was merely its patron. Three generations of this family were printers. SOLOMON ALTARAS THE ELDER supervised the publication of the Sephardi prayer book which appeared in Venice in 1685. His son, DAVID B. SOLOMON, known as *Devash* ("honey"), an acronym of his name, lived in Venice between 1675 and 1714. He wrote *Kelalei ha-Dikduk* ("Principles of Grammar") which was printed at the beginning of the Venice edition of the *Mikra'ot Gedolot* (1675–78). From 1675 he printed Hebrew books, including a prayer book (1696) and the Mishnah with annotations (1756–60). His signature appears on a variety of halakhic rulings along with those of other rabbis of Venice, and he gave approbations to various books. His last will and testament and an elegy on his death appear in *Ẓuf Devash* (Venice, 1714). In an addendum to his testament "*Devash*" he emphasizes "that one must conspire craftily and with cunning in order to fear God and observe his commandments." David's son SOLOMON published books in Venice during the 18th century, among them a prayer book containing the *minhag* ("custom") of Corfu, entitled *Leket ha-Omer* (1718).

BIBLIOGRAPHY: Steinschneider, Cat Bod, 1777, no. 6432 (on Moses); 3029, no. 9082 (on Solomon the Elder); 856, no. 4787; 2869, no. 7969; Ghirondi-Neppi, 83 (on David b. Solomon); S.D. Luzzatto, *Prolegomena to a Grammar of the Hebrew Language* (1836), 60; H.B. Friedberg, *Toledot ha-Defus ha-Ivri*²... (1956²); Zedner, Cat, 45.

[Yehoshua Horowitz]

ALTARAS, JACQUES (Jacob) ISAAC (1786–1873), French merchant, shipbuilder, and philanthropist. Born in Aleppo, Syria, Altaras spent his early years in Jerusalem, where his father was a rabbi. In 1806 Altaras settled in Marseilles, and there prospered in shipbuilding and the Levant trade; he became an influential member of the Marseilles Chamber of Commerce. A member of the French Consistoire and president of the Marseilles Jewish community, he founded a Jewish school in Marseilles and was a member of the Legion of Honor. In 1846 Altaras visited Russia to negotiate the resettlement of Russian Jews in Algeria. The project failed because of the harsh Russian terms – the payment of 60 rubles in taxes and fines for each Jew.

BIBLIOGRAPHY: S. Dubnow, *Neueste Geschichte des juedischen Volkes*, 2 (1920), 206.

[Joachim O. Ronall]

ALTARAS, JOSEPH (16th century), *ḥazzan* and poet. Born in Damascus, he settled in Aleppo. He was praised by the Hebrew poet Israel *Najara as the "... highest of heavenly heights above all his contemporaries in the sweetness of his voice" (*Zemirot Yisrael*, 142–144, 147). Najara also praised his poetry. Joseph's son Nissim was also a poet. It may be assumed that the poems attributed to "Joseph" and "Nissim" scattered throughout the *siddur* of Aleppo (Venice, 1520, 1560) were written by these two. These poems are also included in the collection *Shirei Yisrael be-Ereẓ ha-Kedem* (1921).

BIBLIOGRAPHY: M.D. Gaon, *Yehudei ha-Mizraḥ be-Ereẓ Yisrael*, 2 (1938), 50; Rosanes, Togarmah, 3 (1938), 230.

[Simon Marcus]

AL-TARĀS, SĪDĪ IBN (end of 11th century), Karaite scholar in Castile. According to Abraham ibn Daud and Joseph b. Ẓaddik, Al-Tarās went in his youth from Castile to Ereẓ Israel, where he became a pupil of the Karaite Abu al-Faraj (probably *Jeshua b. Judah). When he returned to Andalusia, he brought back his teacher's book with him and not only attempted to circulate it among the *Karaites, but also tried to gain adherents for Karaism among the *Rabbanites. After Al-Tarās' death, his wife, who is referred to by the Karaites as *al-Muʿallima* ("the teacher") and was considered by them an authority on religious practice, continued to spread the tenets of Karaism. Abraham ibn Daud indicates that their propaganda prompted the leaders of the Rabbanites to vigorous action, and Joseph *Ferrizuel "Cidellus" (Alkabri), a Jewish favorite of Alfonso VI, obtained authority to expel the Karaites from all the Castilian towns except one.

BIBLIOGRAPHY: Steinschneider, in: JQR, 11 (1899), 624, n.755; Mann, Texts, 2 (1935), 3, 39; L. Nemoy (ed.), *Karaite Anthology* (1952), xxi (introd.), 124; Z. Ankori, *Karaites in Byzantium* (1959), 359n.; Ibn Daud, Tradition, XLVI, 94–95, 164–5; J. Rosenthal, *Meḥkarim u-Mekorot* (1967), 238; Baer, Spain, 1 (1966), 65, 390–1.

[Moshe Nahum Zobel]

ALTAUZEN, YAKOV (Dzhek) MOYSEYEVICH (1907–1942), Russian poet. The son of a Siberian gold prospector, Altauzen ran away from home at the age of 11 and wandered through China and the Soviet Far East. His works include *Yakutyonok Oleska* (1927), children's verse; and *Bezusy entuziast* ("A Juvenile Enthusiast," 1929) and *Pervoye pokoleniye* ("First Generation," 1933), poems about young Communists in the industrialization drive. He died in action against the Nazis.

ALTENBERG, PETER (pseudonym of **Richard Englaender**; 1859–1919), Austrian author. The son of a merchant, Altenberg studied law and medicine in Vienna and worked briefly in the book trade. Eventually, he chose the life of a bohemian and became a familiar, picturesque figure in Viennese coffee houses and in the turn-of-the-century circles of "Young Vienna." In 1894, Altenberg published his first sketches. Fourteen volumes of his prose vignettes appeared. His subjects were Viennese characters and scenes and he portrayed them with delicacy, insight, and wit. His attitude towards Judaism was highly ambivalent. Among his major works are *Wie ich es sehe* (1896), *Maerchen des Lebens* (1908), and *Vita ipsa* (1918).

BIBLIOGRAPHY: E. Friedell (ed.), *Altenbergbuch* (1921); A. Ehrenstein, in: G. Krojanker, *Juden in der deutschen Literatur* (1922), 193–97; E. Randak, *Peter Altenberg* (Ger., 1961); R.J. Klawitzer, in: *Modern Austrian Literature*, 1 (Winter 1968), 1–55. **ADD. BIBLIOGRAPHY:** A. Caspary, in: A. Kilcher (ed.), *Metzler Lexikon der deutsch-juedischen Literatur* (2000), 12–14.

[Harry Zohn / Marcus Pyka (2nd ed.)]

ALTENSTADT (now **Illereichen-Altenstadt**), village in Bavaria, Germany. A few Jewish families lived there from the late 17th century. A community was founded in 1719 when five Jewish families from the neighborhood were granted rights of residence and permission to open a cemetery and build a synagogue. This was erected in the Jews' street in 1722. In 1834 the 56 Jewish families (403 persons), living in 35 houses, constituted almost the entire village. Subsequently many Jews left for cities in Germany or emigrated to the United States. The rabbinate of Altenstadt, which served the neighboring Jewish community of Osterberg as well, ceased to exist in 1869. There were 250 Jews living in Altenstadt in 1859 and 28 in 1933. The impressive synagogue built in 1803 was desecrated in 1938. About half the Jews left by 1939 and 13 were deported to Izbica in Poland in April 1942. The synagogue was torn down in 1955.

BIBLIOGRAPHY: H. Boehm, in: *Illereichen-Altenstadt* (1965), 52–62; H. Rose, *Geschichtliches der israelitischen Kultusgemeinde Altenstadt* (1931). **ADD. BIBLIOGRAPHY:** K. Sommer, in: P. Fassl (ed.), *Geschichte und Kultur der Juden in Schwaben* (1994), 93–104.

[Ze'ev Wilhem Falk / Stefan Rohrbacher (2nd ed.)]

ALTER, ELEANOR B. (1938–), U.S. divorce lawyer. Born in Slingerlands, N.Y., the daughter of Charles *Breitel, chief judge of New York State's Court of Appeals, Alter graduated from the University of Michigan and earned her law degree from Columbia University. She worked for several law firms in New York City before becoming a specialist in divorce law. Over more than 35 years, she oversaw the termination of more than 2,000 marriages, including two of her own. Her famous clients included Joy Silverman, the ex-inamorata of Sol *Wachtler, New York's former top judge, and Mia Farrow, Woody *Allen's former companion.

When she began matrimonial work in the mid-1960s, divorce law had a tawdry reputation because the only legal cause for divorce in New York then was adultery. But the law changed and Alter's practice prospered and her reputation grew. An early first marriage, which produced two sons, was to William D. Zabel, who would become a dean of the trust and estates bar. In addition to her practice, she taught at several law schools and lectured widely.

[Stewart Kampel (2nd ed.)]

ALTER, ISRAEL (1901–1979), *ḥazzan* and composer. Born in Lvov, Alter studied music in Vienna. A powerful tenor with a wide range, he began his career as *ḥazzan* at Vienna's Brigittenauer Tempel-Verein when he was 20. In 1925 he moved to Hanover, where he remained for ten years before becoming chief *ḥazzan* of the United Hebrew Congregation in Johannesburg, South Africa. He went to the U.S. in 1961, and became a faculty member of the School of Sacred Music of Hebrew Union College. Alter published his cantorial compositions in *Shirei Yisrael* (2 vols., 1952–57; vols. 3 and 4 were subsequently published by the Cantors' Association of Montreal, Canada) and *Cantorial Recitatives for Hallel, Tal, Geshem* (1962), and his musical settings of Yiddish poems in *Mayne Lider* (1957). He also edited some of David Eisenstadt's liturgical works in *Le-David Mizmor* (n.d.). A phonograph record of his compositions was issued in 1973. In 1978 the Cantors' Assembly of New York issued Alter's "*Ribono Shel Olam*" for *Seliḥot* according to the order of services adopted by the Rabbinic Assembly.

[Akiva Zimmerman (2nd ed.)]

ALTER, ROBERT B. (1936–), U.S. literary critic. Born in the Bronx, New York, Alter taught at Columbia University from 1962 to 1966. In 1967, he joined the faculty of the University of California at Berkeley teaching Hebrew and Comparative Literature.

Alter has published works on English, French, and American literature. A specialist in modern Jewish literature and culture, he has written numerous articles for the *New York Times Book Review*, the *Times Literary Supplement*, and *Commentary*.

In *After the Tradition: Essays on Modern Jewish Writing* (1969), Alter explores the meaning of tradition in post-Holocaust Jewish literature, examining the works of such writers as Elie Wiesel, Saul Bellow, S.Y. Agnon, and Bernard Malamud. In *Defenses of the Imagination: Jewish Writers and Modern Historical Crisis* (1977), he saw Jewish writing as emerging from the problems of the 20th century and concentrated on Jewish writers such as Gershom Scholem and Osip Mandelshtam. He has also explored the profound influence of 20th-century wars on such writers as Norman Mailer and Joseph Heller, and the influence of historical forces on such writers as Saul Bellow.

Alter has also been deeply concerned with biblical narrative. *The World of Biblical Literature* (1978), *The Art of Biblical Poetry* (1981), and *The Art of Biblical Narrative* (1985) show how literary scholarship can be utilized in the study of the Bible as both a literary and religious document. His translations include *Genesis* (1996), *The David Story* (2000), and *The Five Books of Moses* (2004), each with an extensive commentary.

[Susan Strul (2nd ed.)]

ALTER, VICTOR (1890–1941), leader of the *Bund in Poland. Alter was born in Mlawa, Poland, into a wealthy ḥasidic family. He graduated as an engineer in 1910, in Liège, Belgium. In 1912 he became active in the Bund in Warsaw. Exiled to Siberia for his political activities, he later escaped. During World War I, Alter found employment in England, as a laborer and then as an engineer. He returned to Poland after the February Revolution in 1917 and became a member of the central committee of the Bund. Between 1919 and 1939 Alter was one of the prominent leaders of the Bund and Jewish trade unions in Poland. He was a Warsaw city councilor for almost 20 years, and after 1936 a member of the board of the Jewish community. After the Germans invaded Poland in September 1939, Alter escaped to the Russian-occupied zone. However, he was soon arrested with his associate, Henryk Erlich. They were both executed on December 4, 1941, in Kuibyshev. Alter wrote *Tsu der Yidnfrage in Poiln* ("The Jewish Problem in Poland," 1927) and *Anti-semitizm w Swietle Cyfr* ("Anti-Semitism in the Light of Statistics," 1937).

BIBLIOGRAPHY: LNYL, 1 (1956), 95ff.; American Representation of General Jewish Workers Union of Poland, *The Case of Henryk Erlich and Victor Alter* (1943).

[Ezekiel Lifschutz]

ALTERMAN, NATHAN (1910–1970), Israeli poet. Alterman, who was born in Warsaw, settled in Tel Aviv in 1925. He published his first poem in 1931. Alterman achieved distinction as a poet on two levels: as the author of popular satirical verse which reflected the political aspirations of the *yishuv* in its struggle against the policies of the British authorities in the 1940s, and as a sophisticated modern poet who was recognized as one of the leaders of the country's literary avant-garde.

His role as a poetic spokesman for the national struggle began in 1934 when he became a regular contributor of political verse to the daily *Haaretz*. In 1943 he switched to the Labor daily *Davar* where, in his weekly feature *Ha-Tur ha-Shevi'i* ("The Seventh Column"), he attacked the British authorities, and described the struggle of the Haganah and the Palmaḥ to break the embargo on Jewish immigration and gain national independence. Many of these verses became part of Israel's patriotic repertoire; poems banned by the British censors were passed from hand to hand by an eager public. Alterman also wrote lyrics that were set to music and were popular features of the program of Matateh and other satirical theaters.

After 1948 internal social and political themes became the dominant feature in Alterman's public verse. Following the 1967 Six-Day War, he advocated the views of the Movement for an Undivided Ereẓ Israel, expressing them in prose rather than poetry. Alterman's literary reputation rests upon his more aesthetic works. Originally associated with the A. Shlonsky group of modernist poets, and influenced by both French and Russian symbolists, he soon became the leading "imagist" poet of his generation. Characterized by brilliant wit and imagery, his idiom followed the rhythms of spoken Hebrew.

Alterman constructed a mythical world of his own, subject to its own rules, and made up of two components. One is the poet's lost Eden, a primeval land in which wild beasts and primordial forces of nature rage in a violent blaze of color and sound, from which he was expelled for some unknown original sin and into which he is forever striving to regain entry. In contrast to this elemental landscape stands his mythical city, mechanized, hostile, and decadent, and at the same time morbidly alluring with its aura of catastrophe and death. A central motif of Alterman's poetry is the inevitable clash between these two components which can only be resolved in a final moment of awareness at the very brink of death and oblivion.

Alterman's love poetry is also expressed within the context of this romantic agony. The women he depicts are either idealized ethereal products of a primordial Eden, or jaded daughters of the city, or a combination of both. Again, fulfillment or reconciliation can only occur at the brink of death.

Alterman's first poems show signs of a dichotomy in his conception of poetry. On the one hand, there is the realization that poetry is incapable of penetrating the essence of things, often expressed by the declaration that it is perhaps better to cease writing; on the other hand, some of Alterman's verse suggests that poetry is so powerful it can prevail over the paradisaic world's elemental forces and accurately depict them. Hence poetry must be built upon fixed rules and regulations. Alterman, therefore, considers symmetrical repetition the supreme value of order and beauty. Each of his poems has a fixed number of stanzas and sentences, a rhyme scheme, and a constant number of feet.

Simḥat Aniyyim ("Joy of the Poor," 1941) signaled a radical change in Alterman's poetry both in language and conception. The most marked innovations in this collection are the figures of speech, symbols, and allusions taken from traditional Jewish literature, folklore, and liturgy. The primordial forest and the timeless city are now superseded by images drawn from the Jewish folk tradition of Eastern Europe. Alterman makes no attempt to conceal the affinity between his poetry and the collective national experience, with its clear historical indications of impending disaster. The central poetic idea is that the barriers ordinarily separating the living from the dead through love and trust can be broken. These two attributes offer the hope of rebirth out of doom and destruction only if one courageously confronts death.

In the *Shirei Makkot Miẓrayim* ("Plagues of Egypt," 1944), Alterman continues to develop his historiosophic views, applying them not only to the Jewish people but also to humanity. The poet intentionally removes the biblical Ten Plagues from their historical and national context, and turns them into a prototype of the eternal and cyclical history of mankind with its wars and renewal. The main innovation in *Ir ha-Yonah* ("Wailing City," 1957) is the application of the abstract concept of history to one particular and fateful chapter in the history of the Jewish people – the years of the Holocaust, illegal immigration to Israel, and the struggle for national independence. Alterman's diction here is often prosaic and even relies on slang. At the same time he also uses the ballad form more typical of his earlier poetry and characterized by dramatic monologues and theatrical flourishes.

Alterman's plays include *Kinneret, Kinneret* (1962); *Pundak ha-Ruḥot* ("The Inn of the Ghosts," 1963), a poetic drama concerning the artist between the opposing worlds of life and death, home and inn, and art and life; *Mishpat Pythagoras* ("Pythagoras' Law," 1965), about a computer with human sensibilities; and *Ester ha-Malkah* ("Queen Esther," 1966). Alterman also wrote *Ḥagigat Kayiẓ* (1965), a collection of poems, and a book of critical essays entitled *Ha-Massekhah ha-Aḥaronah* (1968). Alterman's translations of Molière's plays appeared in three volumes in 1967. He also translated some of Shakespeare's plays. His collected works appeared in four volumes called *Kol Shirei Alterman* (1961–62). For English translations of his poems, see B. Hrushovsky, in S. Burnshaw, et al. (eds.), *The Modern Hebrew Poem Itself…* (1966), 109–19; *Ariel*, no. 14 (1966), 43–55; *Poetry*, 92 (1958), 236ff. A detailed list of translations into English appears in Goell, Bibliography, 2–5.

[Matti Megged]

All 15 published volumes of Alterman's works have now been republished and have achieved great popularity. In the field of literary criticism *Mivḥar Ma'amarim shel Yeẓirato shel*

Alterman ("A Selection of Works by Alterman") edited by A. Baumgarten (1971) has appeared, as well as *Ha-Ḥut ha-Meshulash*, a collection of articles edited by M. Dorman (1971, 1975), and *Maḥberot Alterman* (1977–81), which includes hitherto unpublished material, a bibliography of his work, and studies on him. Recent years have seen new editions of his poetry, such as the collection *Shirim mi-she-Kevar* (1999), a new edition of four plays (*Maḥazot*, 2002), in addition to various reprints of his translations of classical plays. A bilingual Hebrew-English collection, "Selected Poems," was published in 1978, followed in 1981 by "Little Tel Aviv." Individual poems have been published in 20 languages.

[Anat Feinberg (2nd ed.)]

BIBLIOGRAPHY: A. Ukhmani, *Le-Ever ha-Adam* (1953), 169–75; Y. Zmora, *Sifrut al Parashat Dorot*, 2 (1950), 225–64; S.Y. Penueli, *Sifrut ki-Feshutah* (1963), 249–58; D. Kenaani, *Beinam le-Vein Zemannam* (1955), 220–54; D. Miron, *Arba Panim ba-Sifrut Bat Yameinu* (1962), 13–108; D. Sadan, *Bein Din ve-Ḥeshbon* (1963), 124–30; B. Kurzweil, *Bein Ḥazon le-Vein ha-Absurdi* (1966), 181–257; M. Shamir, *Be-Kulmus Mahir* (1960), 99–117; Zach in: *Akhshav*, 3:4 (1959), 109–22; Ẓuri, in: *Massa*, 2, no. 11 (1952); 3, no. 17 (1953); 4, nos. 1, 2 (1954); Waxman, Literature, 5 (1960), 22–24. **ADD. BIBLIOGRAPHY:** Z. Mendelson, *Natan Alterman* (1973); Y. Nave, *Biblical Motifs Representing the "Lyrical Self" in the Works of Scholem Aleichem, Natan Alterman, Lea Goldberg, Ariela Deem, and Shulamit Har-Even* (1987); M. Shamir, *Natan Alterman: ha-Meshorer ke-Manhig* (1988); M. Dorman, *Alterman vi-Yeẓirato* (1989); Z. Shamir, *Od Ḥozer ha-Niggun: Shirat Alterman bi-Rei ha-Modernizm* (1989); A. Schiller, *Caminante en su tiempo: la poesia de Natan Alterman* (Spanish, 1991); M. Dorman, *Natan Alterman: Pirkei Biyografyah* (1991); R. Kartun-Blum, *Ha-Leẓ ve-ha-Ẓel* (1994); M.E. Varela Morena, *Literatura hebrea contemporanea*, 9 (Spanish, 1994); H. Shaham, *Hedim shel Niggun* (1997); Y. Ben Tolila and A. Komem (eds.), *Konkordanẓyah shel Natan Alterman* (1998); Z. Shamir, *Al Et ve-al Atar: Poetikah u-Politikah be-Shirat Alterman* (1999); H. Barzel, *Avraham Shlonski, Natan Alterman, Lea Goldberg* (2001); D. Miron, *Parpar min ha-Tola'at* (2001); D. Ider, *Alterman-Baudelaire, Paris-Tel Aviv, Urbaniyut u-Mitos* (2004).

ALTHEIMER, BENJAMIN (1850–1938), U.S. banker and philanthropist. Altheimer, who was born in Darmstadt, Germany, immigrated to the United States in 1868 and settled in St. Louis, Missouri. He built up a successful banking and investment business, was a founder and trustee of Temple Israel, and became a leading figure in St. Louis philanthropic and cultural organizations. In 1918 he proposed the institution of Flag Day to President Wilson. He served as treasurer of the National Jewish Hospital for Consumptives, Denver, for more than 30 years. Moving to New York in 1916, Altheimer served as president of Temple Beth El and treasurer of the New York executive of the Union of American Hebrew Congregations.

[Sefton D. Temkin]

AL TIKREI (Heb. אַל תִּקְרֵי; "Do not read"), term used to denote a change in the masoretic reading of Scripture in order to give a meaning to a phrase, other than the literal one. The object of its application was not to abrogate the accepted reading or deny its literal meaning, since there is a rule that "a verse never loses its ordinary meaning." The intention of the scholars was to reveal additional meanings supporting their interpretation of the *halakhah* or the *aggadah*. The sages used various methods in applying the *al tikrei*:

(1) Changes in Punctuation

Biblical text is unvocalized. Hence the traditional reading can be altered by changing the punctuation, and in this way the word is given a new meaning. For example: (a) The reading in Exodus 32:16 of "*ḥarut*" ("graven") upon the tablets is changed to "*ḥerut*" ("freedom"); this enables the rabbis to derive the ethical lesson that true spiritual freedom can be attained only by fulfilling the commandments, i.e., "freedom is in the tablets." (b) The moral that "a man does not commit a transgression unless the spirit of folly enters him" is derived from turning the letter *sin* of *tisteh* ("go aside"; Num. 5:12) into a *shin*, making the reading "*tishteh*" ("shall commit folly"; Sot. 3a).

(2) Transposition of Letters

Such transposition is not unknown in the text of the Bible, e.g., *kesev* and *keves* ("sheep"), *simlah* and *salmah* ("garment"). The rabbis however extended this principle to add a new meaning to a verse. For example, by transposing the letters' of *kirbam* ("their inner thought") to *kivram* ("their grave") in Psalms 49:12, they concluded that there is no resurrection for the wicked since "their home is their grave" (MK 9b).

(3) Change of Letters

Some of the *al tikrei* involve change in the letters, particularly homorganic ones such as *alef* and *ayin*, *ḥet* and *he*. Thus, by reading "*al*" for "*el*" in Numbers 11:2, the verse is made to read "and Moses prayed against the Lord" upon which R. Eleazar bases the statement that man spoke presumptuously to God. In this case the transposition is justified in that "in the school of R. Eliezer b. Jacob they read *alef* as *ayin* and *ayin* as *alef*" (Ber. 32a). An example that involves both transposition of letters and change of vowels is the reading of *hadrat* ("majesty") as *ḥerdat* ("reverence") in Psalms 29:2. The lesson derived is that one should not stand up to pray except in a reverent frame of mind (cf. Ber. 30b).

BIBLIOGRAPHY: I. Heinemann, *Darkhei ha-Aggadah* (1954²), 127–9; Z.H. Chajes, *Mevo ha-Talmud* (1845), 52–53; A. Rosenzweig, *Die Al-tikre-Deutungen* (1911); enlarged offprint of the article in *Festschrift… Lewy* (1911), 204–53.

[Abraham Arzi]

°**ALTING, JACOBUS** (1618–1679), Dutch theologian and Hebraist. Born in Heidelberg, Alting studied Oriental languages and theology in Groningen, Utrecht, and Leiden. In Emden (1638–39) he read Jewish literature with a Jewish teacher named Gumprecht b. Abraham. During his journey to England (1641–43) he was ordained priest of the Church of England and studied Arabic at Oxford with *Pococke. In 1643 he succeeded Gomarus as professor of Oriental languages at the University of Groningen, where in 1667 he became professor of theology. His works (*Opera Omnia*, 5 vols., ed. by his friend and disciple Balthasar Bekker, Amsterdam, 1687) include a manual of Syriac and Aramaic (Groningen, 1676) and a – didactic rather than descriptive – Hebrew grammar (*Fundamenta punctationis linguae sacrae*, 1654; Dutch translation, 1664) dedicated to *Buxtorf II and *Hottinger, with whom he conducted a scholarly correspondence. As a theologian Alting advocated a purely biblical theology based on the interpretation of Hebrew Scripture. This approach brought him into a long-standing conflict with his scholastic-dogmatic colleague Samuel Maresius. For information on Jewish antiquities Alting drew on post-biblical Jewish sources.

BIBLIOGRAPHY: A.J. van der AA., *Biografisch Woordenboek der Nederlanden*, 1 (1852), 214–18; W. van Bekkum, in: G. Veltri and G. Necker (eds.), *Gottes sprache in der philoloigschen Werkstatt. Hebraistik vom 15. bis zum 19. Jahrhundert* (2004), 49–74; J.P. de Bie and J. Loosjes, *Biographisch woordenboek van protestantsche godgeleerden in Nederland*, 1 (1907), 107–27; W. van Bunge et al., *The Dictionary of Seventeenth and Eighteenth-Century Dutch Philosophers* (2003), 18; W. Gesenius, *Geschichte der hebraeischen Sprache und Schrift* (1815), 122ff.; P.C. Molhuysen et al., *Nieuw Nederlandsch Biografisch Woordenboek*, 1 (1911), 96f.; P.H. Roessingh, *Jacobus Alting. Een bijbelsch Godgeleerde uit het Midden der 17e Eeuw* (1864); I.E. Zwiep, in: J. Noordgraaf and F. Vonk (eds.), *Five Hundred Years of Foreign Language Teaching in the Netherlands 1450–1950* (1993), 40–45.

[Irene E. Zwiep (2nd ed.)]

ALTMAN, ARYEH (1902–1982), Zionist Revisionist leader. Altman was born in Balta, Russia, where his father, Menasheh, a Hebrew teacher, was head of the local Zionist movement, and after the Revolution of 1917, head of the Jewish community and deputy mayor of the town. In 1919 the family moved to Odessa, where Aryeh Altman was imprisoned on various occasions by the Soviet authorities for Zionist activity. He was one of some 300 leading Zionists belonging to all political parties who were arrested by the Bolshevik authorities in 1924. Altman traveled to Moscow to intercede with the authorities to allow them to immigrate to Israel instead of being exiled to Siberia. After months of negotiation between the Russian and British authorities he finally received the required permission for *aliyah,* with the Zionists and their families finally departing on a special boat.

From 1927 to 1935 Altman resided in the United States, where he received his doctorate, and headed the Zionist Revisionist movement. On his return to Ereẓ Israel he held the same position and was instrumental in the formation of the *Irgun Ẓeva'i Leummi in 1937 and was appointed by V. *Jabotinsky as chairman of the triumvirate that headed the organization. After the death of Jabotinsky he was appointed head of the New Zionist Organization. From 1948 to 1950 he was a member of the Provisional Government Council. Altman was a member of the Second through the Fifth Knesset. In 1972 the honor of Yakir Yerushalayim was conferred upon him and in 1976 he was appointed vice chairman of the Israeli-American Friendship Society.

ALTMAN, BENJAMIN (1840–1913), U.S. merchant, art collector, and philanthropist. Altman was born on New York's Lower East Side. Altman and his brother Morris opened a store in 1865. After Morris's death in 1876 Altman assumed sole control over the business, which he developed into a large, high-quality department store. When Altman moved the business, known as "B. Altman and Co.," to Fifth Avenue in 1906, it became the first large store in New York to be established in a residential area. At the same time Michael *Friedsam became his partner and contributed considerably to the growth of the establishment. After Benjamin's death and until its closing, the store was run by the Altman Foundation, a philanthropic trust donating funds to many charities, including Jewish organizations. Altman was also a pioneer in the provision of social, medical, and recreational facilities for employees. Altman's art collection, appraised upon his death at 15 million dollars, was bequeathed to the Metropolitan Museum of Art.

BIBLIOGRAPHY: DAB, 1 (1928); New York Metropolitan Museum of Art, *Handbook of The Benjamin Altman Collection* (1915).

[Hanns G. Reissner]

ALTMAN, MOISHE (1890–1981), Yiddish poet and novelist. Altman, who was born in Bessarabia, was partly self-educated. He lived in Romania and the Soviet Union. In 1920 he began writing poems and literary articles for the Czernowitz weeklies *Frayhayt* and *Dos Naye Leben*. In 1930 he immigrated to Argentina but after a year he returned to Romania and settled in Bucharest. During WWII he lived in the U.S.S.R. After World War II Altman was sent, with other Soviet Yiddish writers, to a Siberian forced labor camp (1949–52), but he survived and resumed his literary work. His prose includes two volumes of short stories, *Blendenish* (1926) and *Di Viner Karete* (1935), and the novels *Midrash Pinkhas* (1936) and *Shmeterlingen* (1939). His selected works *(Geklibene Verk)* were published in New York in 1955, with a biographical and critical introduction by S. Bickel, and in Bucharest (*Oysgeveylte shriftn*, 1974). His last books, *Baym fenster* and *Di viner karete un andere dertzeylungen*, were published in Moscow in 1980.

BIBLIOGRAPHY: LNYL, 1 (1956), 92–94.

[Shlomo Bickel]

ALTMAN, NATHAN (1889/90–1970), Russian painter, graphic artist, sculptor, stage designer. Altman was born in Vinnitsa. As a child, he studied in a *ḥeder* and then at a Russian elementary school in Vinnitsa. In 1902–7, he attended classes in painting and sculpture at the Odessa Art School. During these years, he got close to Jewish intellectuals and writers, among them Ḥayyim Naḥman *Bialik. He first showed his work at the exhibit of the Association of Southern Russia Artists in Odessa. In 1910–11, Altman lived in Paris, where he attended M. Vasilyeva's art studio at the Russian Academy. During this period, he met many Jewish artists then living in Paris, among them Marc *Chagall and David *Shterenberg. In 1911, Altman exhibited at the Salon des Beaux-Arts in Paris.

Later in 1911, he returned to Vinnitsa, and then moved to Petersburg in 1912 where he became known as a leading Russian artist and bohemian figure. In his works of this period, Altman combined elements of cubism with the decorative features and linearity of modern art (as in the portrait of Anna Akhmatova, 1914; Gosudarstvenny Russki Muzei, St. Petersburg). In 1913–14, Altman participated in exhibits of various art associations in Moscow and Petrograd, ranging from moderately modernist ones (like "World of Art") to overtly radical ones (like "The Jack of Diamonds") and avant-garde groups (like "The Youth Union" or "0.10"). Starting from his earliest works and throughout his life, Altman placed great emphasis on Jewish subjects when selecting themes for his works. Prior to World War I, he had become the first among Jewish artists in Russia to pursue a goal of forging a "contemporary Jewish art." Seeking the foundations of this new art, Altman copied tombstone reliefs at Jewish cemeteries in the Ukraine. In 1914, he executed a graphic series, "The Jewish Graphics," incorporating the relief motifs, its first printed edition dedicated to Bialik. In his "Jewish works" of this period, Altman strove to combine the archaic plastics of the Ancient Middle East with the latest achievements of European Modernism (as in the sculpture *A Portrait of a Young Jew* (Self-Portrait, 1916, State Russian Museum, St. Petersburg)). Altman was a founder and a member of the executive committee of the Jewish Society for the Encouragement of the Arts, established in 1915 in Petrograd. He was commissioned to design the emblem of the Society and participated in its exhibits (1916, 1917, Petrograd; 1918, Moscow). In 1916, Altman designed a Hebrew-language textbook. After the Bolsheviks came to power, he was appointed both director of the Petrograd Department of Fine Arts at the People's Commissariat of Education and director of the Museum of Artistic Culture (1918). He was one of leaders of Communist-Futurist (ComFut) Association. In 1919, Altman moved to Moscow and started working for Jewish theaters. In 1920, he executed stage and costume designs for the Habimah Theater production of *The Dibbuk*. At the same time, he became the principal stage designer for the Moscow Jewish Theater (GOSET), where he designed sets for a number of productions. Being active in Kultur-Lige, Altman was its Moscow branch chairman and participated in its exhibit together with Chagall and Shterenberg (1922), At this exhibit, he showed non-figurative futurist works as examples of his new "Jewish art." In the early 1920s, he collaborated with Jewish publishers and designed books in Yiddish. He participated in all major exhibitions in Moscow and Petrograd as well as in international exhibitions in Berlin (Van Diemen Gallery, 1923), Paris, and Venice. His first one-man show took place in Moscow in 1926. From 1928, Altman lived in Paris. In 1929, he participated in Ausstellung juedischer Kuenstler in Zurich. In the early 1930s, he exhibited in Paris and the U.S.S.R. In 1932–33, Altman executed series of graphic works treating biblical themes. His main genres of this period were still lifes and landscapes that established him as a virtuoso master of color and composition. In 1936, Altman returned to Leningrad. In the 1940s, he designed books by *Sholem Aleichem and stage designs for several productions at Jewish theaters in Moscow and Kiev. In the 1940s–1960s, Altman was active mostly in book and stage design while continuing painting and sculpturing. Not long before he died he had a one-man show in Leningrad.

BIBLIOGRAPHY: A. Efros, *A Portrait of Nathan Altman* (1922); B. Arvatov, *Nathan Altman* (1924); B. Aronson, *Modern Jewish Graphic Work* (1924), 80–84; *Nathan Altman. The Retrospective Show of Works*. Exh. Cat. Leningrad (1968); *Nathan Altman*. Exh. Cat. Moscow (1978) – all in Russian; M. Etkind, *Nathan Altman* (1984).

[Hillel Kazovsky (2nd ed.)]

ALTMAN, OSCAR LOUIS (1909–1968), U.S. economist and treasurer of the International Monetary Fund. Altman, who was born in New York, was educated at Cornell University and at the University of Chicago. He began to work as an economist for the Securities and Exchange Commission in 1936 and was its senior economist from 1938 to 1940. During World War II he was the principal economist of the National Resources Planning Board and served as an officer in the United States Air Force. After heading the analysis and planning office of the French Supply Council, he joined the International Monetary Fund, and in 1966 was appointed the Fund's treasurer. Altman's main interest was international liquidity problems, and he was one of the first economists to understand the significance of the Eurodollar market. He published numerous papers on both these issues.

[Joachim O. Ronall]

ALTMAN, SIDNEY (1939–), research biologist and educator. Altman, born in Montreal, Canada, received his doctorate in biophysics from the University of Colorado in 1967. He joined the department of biology at Yale University in 1971, becoming a professor in 1980 and serving as chairman of the department 1983–85. He was the dean of Yale College in 1985. In 1989 he shared the Nobel Prize in chemistry with Thomas Cech of the University of Colorado for similar discoveries they made in the 1970s and early 1980s while working independently. They found that in its role as a chemical catalyst, the RNA subunit of RNase P from bacteria can cleave some transcripts of genetic information.

[Bracha Rager (2nd ed.)]

ALTMANN, ADOLF (1879–1944), rabbi, historian, philosopher. Born in Hunsdorf, Hungary, Altmann studied at the yeshivot of Hunsdorf and Pressburg, and graduated as doctor of philosophy from Berne University. An early follower of Herzl, he worked for the acceptance of religious Zionism in the face of hostility on the part of the Hungarian Orthodox rabbinate. He was a delegate to the First Mizrachi Congress in Pressburg, correspondent for *Die Welt* (1905), and editor of the *Ungarische Wochenschrift* (1904).

He served as rabbi in Salzburg (1907–1915) where he wrote the two-volume *Geschichte der Juden in Stadt and Land*

Salzburg (1913, 1930), which is still the authoritative work on the subject, and in Merano. In World War I he served as senior chaplain in the Austro-Hungarian Army, receiving the Golden Cross of Merit; in witness to Jewish service in the war he collected testimonials from military commanders on the conduct of their Jewish soldiers. From 1920 to 1938 he served as chief rabbi – the last one – of Trier, one of the oldest Jewish communities in Germany. The results of his historical research into the community's origins were published in *Das Früheste Vorkommen der Juden in Deutschland; Juden in romischen Trier* (1931), which threw new light on the subject, dating the settlement of Jews in Trier to the end of the 3rd and early 4th century C.E. He contributed the entry on the history of German Jews to the *Jüdisches Lexikon* (1927). He was a leading delegate to the Association of Jewish Communities (Preussischer Landesverband Jued. Gemeinden) and as prolific author and orator participated widely in Jewish cultural life in Germany. In 1938 he immigrated to Holland and met his death in Auschwitz in 1944 with his wife Malwine, née Weisz, their daughter Hilda van Mentz and family, and their son Dr. Wilhelm Altmann. He was survived by three sons: Professor Alexander *Altmann, Dr. Erwin Altmann, and Dr. Manfred Altmann. A street was named after him in Trier in 1956 and in 1979 in commemoration of the centenary of his birth a special ceremony was held in the Town Hall of Trier. An illustrated brochure, *Dr. Adolf Altmann zum Gedenken* was published by the City of Trier on the event.

BIBLIOGRAPHY: A complete list of Adolf Altmann's works, 166 items, is in: *Zeitschrift fuer die Geschichte der Juden*, 8 (1971), 149–57; ON ALTMANN: A. Altmann, in: *Leo Baeck Yearbook*, 26 (1981), 145–76: H. Gold, *Geschichte der Juden in Oesterreich* (1971), 149–57: M. Karin-Karger, *Salzburg's wiedergeabaute Synagoge* (1968): AJR Information, Sept. and Nov. 1979: S. Dasberg, in: *Nieuw Israelitisch Weekblad* (Sept. 1, 1939): H. Istor, in: *Allgemeine Juedische Wochenzeitung* (Aug. 31, 1979).

ALTMANN, ALEXANDER (1906–1987), rabbi, teacher, and scholar. His father was Adolf *Altmann (1879–1944), a Hungarian-born rabbi who officiated in Trier in 1920–38 and wrote a history of the Jews there and in Salzburg. He died in Auschwitz, together with his wife and other members of his family. Alexander commemorated them in "A Filial Memoir," which appeared in the *Leo Baeck Yearbook*, 26 (1981). In 1931, Altmann received both a doctorate in philosophy from Berlin University and ordination from the Hildesheimer Rabbinical Seminary in Berlin, where he taught from 1932. He served as rabbi in Berlin from 1931 and established there the Rambam Lehrhaus, a public institute for adult education, in 1935. Altmann was obliged to flee Germany in 1938, and was then appointed communal rabbi in Manchester, England, serving in that capacity until 1959. In 1954 he founded the Institute of Jewish Studies in Manchester, serving as its director until his departure from England, when the Institute moved to University College, London, under the watchful eyes of his devoted brother, Manfred. In 1959, Altmann was appointed Lown Professor of Jewish Philosophy and History of Ideas at Brandeis University, where he taught until his retirement in 1976. He established the Lown Institute for Advanced Judaic Studies at Brandeis and directed it from 1960 to 1965. Altmann's scholarship was primarily in the fields of medieval Jewish philosophy and mysticism, as well as in the writings of Moses *Mendelssohn. His initial German essays were theological and contemporary in nature and appeared in translation as *The Meaning of Jewish Existence* (1992). Altmann's work includes *Des Rabbi Mosche Ben Maimon More Newuchim* (abridged German translation, 1935); *Saadya Gaon: The Book of Doctrines and Beliefs* (1946, abridged English translation and commentary); *Isaac Israeli* (together with S.M. Stern, 1969); *Moses Mendelssohns Fruehschriften Zur Metaphysik* (1969); *Studies in Religious Philosophy and Mysticism* (1969); *Moses Mendelssohn: A Biographical Study* (1973); *Essays in Jewish Intellectual History* (1981); *Moses Mendelssohn, Jerusalem or On Religious Power and Judaism* (introduction and commentary; translation by Allan Arkush, 1983); *Von der Mittlealterlichen zur Modernen Aufklaerung: Studien Zur Juedischen Geistesgeschichte* (1987). Altmann was the editor of *Scripta Judaica* (jointly with J.G. Weiss) and the *Journal of Jewish Studies* (1954–58); of *Studies and Texts* of the Lown Institute (four volumes, 1963–67); and editor in chief of the *Moses Mendelssohn Gesammelte Schriften Jubilaeumsausgabe* from 1970 until his death in 1987. In that period, he was sole editor of five volumes in that series and part editor of five more. A complete bibliography of Altmann's work is found in *Perspectives on Jewish Thought and Mysticism*, edited by A.L. Ivry, E.R. Wolfson, and A. Arkush (1998). An appreciation of his manifold contributions to scholarship is given in the *Leo Baeck Yearbook*, 34 (1989) and in the Hebrew publication *In Memory of Alexander Altmann* (1990), published by the Israel Academy of Sciences and the Hebrew University of Jerusalem.

[Alfred L. Ivry (2nd ed.)]

ALTONA, major port, suburb of Hamburg, Germany; until 1864 part of Denmark. The Portuguese Jews living in Hamburg were prohibited from burying their dead there, and acquired land for a cemetery in Altona in 1611. Thirteen Portuguese families from Hamburg settled in Altona in 1703, augmenting the small Portuguese settlement already in existence. They organized a community known as Bet Ya'akov ha-Katan (later Neveh Shalom). A synagogue was built in 1770. The Sephardi community, however, remained a branch of the community in Hamburg. Greater importance was attained by the community established by Ashkenazi Jews, who first arrived in Altona around 1600. In 1641, they received a charter from the king of Denmark to found a community and build a synagogue. After the Russian-Polish War of 1654/55, Jewish refugees from Lithuania expelled from Hamburg settled in Altona. At the same time numerous families, while formally remaining Danish subjects and members of the Altona community, had established themselves in Hamburg, where they formed a semi-independent subcommunity. In 1671 the Altona community amalgamated with the community of Hamburg, and afterward with that of Wandsbek, to form a single community, known by the initials AHW (אה"ו), under Chief Rabbi *Hillel b. Naphtali Ẓevi. The chief rabbinate, as well as the attached yeshivah and *bet din*, was situated in Altona. It had jurisdiction over the Ashkenazi Jews in all three communities as well as *Schleswig-Holstein. In the 18th century the community in Altona overshadowed that of Hamburg, in both scholarship (having a series of eminent rabbis and scholars) and affluence. It was in Altona that the acrimonious *Emden-*Eybeschuetz amulet controversy took place. Altona was also an important center of Hebrew printing (see below). The Chief Rabbinate existed until 1863, its *bet din* being the last institution of Jewish jurisdiction to function autonomously in Germany.

The three communities remained united until 1811, when Hamburg was occupied by French forces. In 1815 a number of Jews moved from Hamburg to Altona after the emancipation granted by the French was annulled. The Jews in Altona engaged in commerce, some being shareholders of ships employed in the South American trade and, especially in the 18th century, whaling. Special economic privileges were granted to them by the Danish kings. Hamburg Jews frequently helped to finance these activities. After the annexation of the area to Prussia in 1866, the Hamburg community grew rapidly and eclipsed that of Altona. In 1938 Altona was officially incorporated into Hamburg. Rabbis of the independent community of Altona were Akiva Wertheimer (1816–35); the eminent halakhist Jacob *Ettlinger (1835–71); Eliezer Loeb (1873–92); Meyer *Lerner (1894–1926); and Joseph Carlebach (1927–37). The Jewish population of Altona numbered 2,350 in 1867 (out of a total of 50,000), around 2,000 in 1900, and around 5,000 in 1925 (out of 186,000). (See also *Hamburg.)

Hebrew Printing in Altona

In 1727 Samuel S. Popert of Koblenz established a printing press in Altona, having learned the craft in nearby Hamburg where he had published a few books. He did the printing himself, assisted by the wandering typesetter Moses Maarsen of Amsterdam. Until 1739 Popert published various works in Hebrew and Judeo-German. In 1732 the wealthy Ephraim Heckscher set up a printing house which a year later passed into the hands of his assistant Aaron b. Elijah ha-Kohen, who was called Aaron Setzer ("setter"). He continued printing until 1743, when he became the manager of the press set up by Jacob Emden, where later many of Emden's polemical writings against Jonathan Eybeschuetz were printed. In 1752 they separated, as Aaron had sided with Eybeschuetz. Another assistant in Emden's printing works, Moses Bonn, set out on his own in 1765, and this business was operated for many years by his sons and grandsons as Brothers Bonn.

BIBLIOGRAPHY: E. Duckesz, *Ivoh le-Moshav* (Heb. and Ger., 1903); idem, *Ḥakhmei AHW* (Heb. and Ger., 1908); W. Victor, *Die Emanzipation der Juden in Schleswig-Holstein* (1913); H. Kellenbenz, *Sephardim an der unteren Elbe* (1958); O. Wolfsberg-Aviad, *Die Drei-Gemeinde* (1960). **ADD. BIBLIOGRAPHY:** H.M. Graupe, *Die Statuten der drei Gemeinden Altona, Hamburg und Wandsbek*, 2 vols. (1973); G. Marwedel, *Die Privilegien der Juden in Altona* (1976). HEBREW PRINTING: Shunami, Bibl, index; Steinschneider, in: ZGJD, 1 (1887), 281ff.; Ch. D. Friedberg, *Toledot ha-Defus ha-Ivri… be-Augsburg…* (1935), 105–8. **ADD. BIBLIOGRAPHY:** B. Brilling, in: *Studies in Bibliography and Booklore*, 9 (1971), 153–66; 13 (1980), 26–35.

[Akiva Posner]

ALTSCHUL(ER; Perles), family probably originating in Prague. Its descendants were found throughout Central and Eastern Europe. The name Altschul first occurs as the surname of ABRAHAM EBERLE, a lay leader of Prague who died toward the close of the 15th century. His son MOSES (c. 1542) became a *parnas* of the Bohemian community of Cracow after the Jews were driven out of Prague. HANOKH BEN MOSES ALTSCHUL (1564–1633), *shammash* and secretary of the Prague community, was sentenced to be hanged in connection with the theft of a Gobelin tapestry from a palace, but was saved when it was revealed that he was the middleman in a legitimate business transaction. Ḥanokh described his hardships in *Megillat Purei ha-Ketayim* and for centuries his family celebrated "Purim Altschul" or "Purim Fuerhang" (see Special *Purims) on the 22nd of Tevet. His son MOSES (d. 1643) succeeded his father and was the author of the unpublished *Zikhron Bayit*. ELEAZAR BEN ABRAHAM ḤANOKH PERLES (d. c. 1635) wrote a commentary to Elkanah b. Jeroham's *Keneh Ḥokhmah Keneh Binah* (1610–11) giving the kabbalistic principles to be discerned in the *Shema*, and esoteric explanations of the commandments. This was very popular and was added to many editions of the prayer book. He is thought to have been the author or editor of the unpublished Hebrew grammar, *Dikdukei Yiẓḥak*. ISAAC, the son of Eleazar, included biographical notes on his father in the latter's *Tikkunei Moẓa'ei Shabbat* (1650). JUDAH AARON MOSES BEN ABRAHAM ḤANOKH (early 17th century), the brother of Eleazar, was rabbi of Kromau. He wrote *Va-Yeḥal Moshe* (Prague, 1613), an ethical treatise giving practical advice to repentant sinners. NAPHTALI HIRSCH BEN ASHER (late 16th century) lived in Lublin and Zhitomir and was in Constantinople in 1607. He was the author of *Ayyalah Sheluḥah*, a digest of earlier commentaries on the Prophets and Hagiographa (Rabbinical Bible, Cracow 1593, Amsterdam 1740). He also published a biblical concordance *Imrei Shefer* (Lublin, 1602) arranged in 32 sections. ABRAHAM BEN ISAAC PERLES (d. c. 1690) published *Tikkunei Shabbat* (1678), and wrote an unpublished kabbalistic commentary on the Pentateuch. MOSES MEIR BEN ISAAC ELEAZAR PERLES (1666–1739) lived in Prague and was the author of a commentary on the book of Esther, *Megillat Sefer* (Prague, 1710). AARON BEN MOSES MEIR PERLES (d. 1739) wrote an unpublished commentary, *Tohorat Aharon* on the section of Isaac b. Abba Mari's *Ittur* which deals with porging. In 1725 he published a pamphlet in Yiddish on the same subject. ZE'EV WOLF BEN DOV BAER (d. 1806) published *Zeved Tov* (1793), a commentary on the description of the Temple in Ezekiel 40–48, together with an account of the pedestals for the lavers made by Solomon (I Kings 7:17–35);

and *Ḥamishah Ḥallukei Avanim* (1794), containing commentaries on Ruth and Song of Songs. His son ELIAKIM (GOTTSCHALK) BEN ZE'EV WOLF (first half of the 19th century) wrote commentaries to the 1814 edition of his father's *Zeved Tov*.

BIBLIOGRAPHY: Zunz, Gesch, 289 no. 154; 291 no. 168; K.Z. Lieben, *Gal Ed* (1856), 57 no. 106; Kisch, in: *Graetz-Jubelschrift* (1887), 48–52; idem, in: MGWJ, 37 (1893), 131; S. Hock, *Die Familien Prags* (1892), 280–2, n.1; J. Cohen-Zedek, in: *Der Yesharim* 20–21 (= *Ha-Goren*, 1 (1898), 2nd pagination); Flesch, in: JJLG, 17 (1926), 59; Gaster, in: *Jewish Studies in memory of G.A. Kohut* (1935), 272–7; Assaf, in: *Reshumot*, 4 (1947), 131–43; 5 (1953), 62–77; Zinberg, Sifrut, 4 (1958), 80–82; Michael, Or, Nos. 209, 490, 956; Sadek, in: *Judaica Bohemise*, 4 (1968), 73–78.

[Yehoshua Horowitz]

ALTSCHUL, AARON MEYER (1914–1994), U.S. nutrition expert. He was born in Chicago, where he obtained his doctorate in 1937. He joined the Southern Regional Research Laboratory of the U.S. Department of Agriculture in 1941, and was named head of its protein and carbohydrate division in 1949 and of its oilseed section in 1952. He became successively chief research chemist of the Seed Protein Pioneering Research Laboratory in 1958, a professor at Tulane University in 1964, lecturer on nutrition at Massachusetts Institute of Technology, and professor emeritus of nutrition at Georgetown University Medical School from 1971 to 1983. His main interest was nutrition improvement, nationally and internationally. Among other appointments, he was a member of the President's Science Advisory Committee and a United Nations consultant. In 1967 he was given special responsibility for improving protein quality and supply in domestic and international programs. He published the authoritative *Proteins, Their Chemistry and Politics* (1965), and his numerous honors included the Charles Spencer Award for achievements in food chemistry (1965). He was active in many Jewish communities, especially in New Orleans.

[Michael Denman (2nd ed.)]

ALTSCHUL, EMIL (Elias, Uri; 1797–1865), physician in Prague; professor of homeopathy at Prague University from 1849, author of medical and pharmaceutical works, and editor of a homeopathic periodical from 1853. Altschul attended the yeshivah of Bezalel Ronsburg and wrote a eulogy on him in Hebrew. In his *Kol Kore, Kritisches Sendschreiben ueber das bisherige Verfahren mit dem Sterbenden bei den Israeliten*, published in 1846, Altschul criticized certain established methods in Jewish practice concerning death and burial, stating that it was his intention to "harmonize modern ideas of medical science with the classic talmudic rulings" (xii). Altschul considered that the customary procedure of the *ḥevra kaddisha* when establishing death was hurried and inadequate, and that death should be certified only by a properly qualified physician. He also advocated the establishment of mortuary chambers at cemeteries. His suggestions influenced Jewish public opinion and were instantly adopted by the French *consistoire, which addressed to him a grateful message. His suggestions were also adopted in 1858 by the Prague *ḥevra kaddisha*.

BIBLIOGRAPHY: AZDJ, 10 (1846), 339–40; 12 (1848), 195–7; 22 (1848), 608–9; C. von Wurzbach, *Biographisches Lexikon des Kaisertums Oesterreich*, 1 (1856), 21–22.

[Meir Lamed]

ALTSCHUL, FRANK (1887–1981), U.S. banker. Altschul was born in San Francisco and served as captain in the U.S. Army in Europe during World War I. He entered banking in New York, and became director of Lazard Frères Inc. and the General American Investors Corporation as well as of several other investment and insurance companies. He was a member of the executive committee of the American Jewish Committee, director of the Woodrow Wilson Foundation, and vice chairman of the National Planning Association. Altschul wrote *Toward Building a Better America* (1949), in which he proposed a master plan for U.S. economic expansion, and *Let No Wave Engulf Us* (1941).

[Edward L. Greenstein]

ALTSCHUL, JOSEPH (1839–1908), *ḥazzan* and improviser of synagogue songs. Altschul, who was commonly known as Yosh(k)e Slonimer, was born in Vilna. He went to Courland for talmudic studies, and there became a successful singer (solo soprano) with a local *ḥazzan*. He was appointed cantor, but preferred to perfect his singing and became apprentice to the famous *ḥazzan* Yeruham *Blindman at Berdichev. Altschul is said to have copied the latter's style for some years but developed his own when he was town *ḥazzan* (*ḥazzan de-mata*) at Slonim (1870–88). Altschul gained wide popularity, attracted pupils from Lithuania and Poland, and was noted for his rabbinic knowledge. From 1888 until his death, Altschul served as a *ḥazzan* at Grodno.

Only four small works which Altschul noted down for Eduard *Birnbaum, a small fraction of his numerous compositions and improvisations, have been preserved. Some of these include easily mastered, almost popular tunes in 6/8 time which are inserted into the cantorial recitative, a predominant Lithuanian feature. The popular trend is also evident in his melodies for congregational singing.

BIBLIOGRAPHY: Idelsohn, Melodien, 8 (1932), v, xxiii (introd.) and nos. 254–7; E. Zaludkowski, *Kulturtreger fun der Yidisher Liturgie* (1930), 130–3.

[Hanoch Avenary]

ALTSCHUL, LOUIS (1870–1943), U.S. businessman and philanthropist. Altschul, who was born in Poland, immigrated to the U.S. when he was 21, and settled in New York City. He worked for a while in the fur business and then started a highly successful career in real estate in the Bronx and Westchester County. Active in several Jewish organizations, Altschul was a founder of the Bronx division of the New York Federation of Jewish Philanthropies, director and president of the Bronx Hospital, and a prominent figure in the United Palestine Appeal. In 1941 he incorporated the Altschul Foundation, which disburses funds for charitable purposes.

[Edward L. Greenstein]

ALTSCHUL, MOSES BEN ḤANOKH (c. 1546–1633), early Yiddish writer. He was the author of the *Brant Shpigl* ("The Burning Mirror"), the first original comprehensive book of ethics in Yiddish. Printed by Conrad Waldkirch in Basle in 1602, it was based upon Altschul's earlier Hebrew ethical tract *Mar'ah ha-Sorefet* (1577). *Brant Shpigl* was part of the cycle of Yiddish didactic works appearing in the late 16th and early 17th centuries addressed primarily to women who could not read Hebrew. Altschul's volume emphasized women's duties and ideal moral behavior, and included chapters on such subjects as "how a modest woman should behave at home" and "how a woman should treat her domestic help." Three editions were published during the author's lifetime; it continued to be reprinted until 1706 and became particularly popular among German Jews. Other books followed in imitation of Altschul; for example, the *Tsukht Shpigl* ("Mirror of Modesty"), a rhymed, versified compendium of proverbs alphabetically arranged, selected by Seligman Ulma from holy texts (1610, and frequently reprinted); and *Kleyn Brant Shpigl* ("The Smaller Burning Mirror") edited by Judah b. Israel Regensburg. Its original title in 1566 had been *Mishlei Khakhomim*, but it was renamed as a result of the popularity of *Brant Shpigl.*

BIBLIOGRAPHY: I. Zinberg, *Geshikte fun der Literatur bay Yidn*, 6 (1943), 179–82; J. Prijs, *Die Basler hebraeischen Drucke* (1964), 283 ff.; M. Erik, *Geshikhte fun der Yidisher Literatur* (1928), 287–99.

[Sol Liptzin]

ALTSCHULER, DAVID (18th century), Bible exegete. Altschuler lived in Jaworow, Galicia. In order to promote the study of the Bible, he planned an easy-to-read commentary on the Prophets and Hagiographa, based on earlier commentators. Altschuler's commentary on Psalms, Proverbs, and Job was published in Zolkiew in 1753–54. JEHIEL HILLEL (18th century), continued his father's work. He visited Jewish communities in Germany, Holland, and Italy. In 1770 he published in Berlin his father's commentary on the Latter Prophets, which he had completed (two vols.). Five years later his own work, *Binyan ha-Bayit*, appeared in Zolkiew. It describes Ezekiel's vision of the future Sanctuary. The treatise contains a poem by Solomon *Dubno and talmudic novellae by the author. In 1780–82 he printed in Leghorn the entire completed commentary on the Prophets and Hagiographa together with a new edition of his own *Binyan ha-Bayit* (five vols.). The commentary consists of two parts, called respectively *Meẓudat Ẓiyyon* ("Fortress of Zion") and *Meẓudat David* ("Fortress of David"). The former explains individual words. The latter elucidates the meaning of the text. The commentary attained great popularity and has been reprinted frequently.

BIBLIOGRAPHY: Azulai, 2 (1852), 18, no. 100; M.Z. Segal, *Parshanut ha-Mikra* (1952^2), 110–1.

[Tovia Preschel]

ALTSCHULER, MODEST (1873–1963), violoncellist and conductor. Born in Mogilev, Russia, Altschuler studied cello at Warsaw Conservatory with J. Hebelt (1884–86) and at the Moscow Conservatory with W. Fitzenhagen (until 1890) and other disciplines with A. Arensky, V. Safonov, S. Taneyev, and others (graduating in 1894). In 1895 he immigrated to the United States and founded the Russian Symphony Society (with the orchestra, in New York), which he directed and conducted in 1903–18, presenting works by Russian composers. He performed with Rachmaninoff, Prokofiev, Micha *Elman, Joseph Levin, and Scriabin. With the latter he was associated by close friendship and performed all his symphonic works, many of them for the first time in the United States, including the world première of *Poème de l'Extase* (1908). He also wrote recollections on the composer published by L. Stanley. After 1925 he taught in Los Angeles, continued conducting, wrote transcriptions, including an orchestral version of Tchaikovsky's *Trio*, and published his *Memoirs* (1956).

BIBLIOGRAPHY: L. Stanley, "Scriabin in America," in: *Musical America* 15/2 (1954); J. Soroker, *Rossiyskie muzykanty evrei, Bio-Bibliograficheskiy Lexikon*, part 1, Jerusalem (1992), 37–8.

[Marina Rizarev (2nd ed.)]

ALUMMOT (Heb. אֲלֻמּוֹת; "sheaves"), kibbutz in Israel, 1½ mi. (2 km.) W. of the Jordan outlet from Lake Kinneret. Alummot, affiliated with Iḥud ha-Kevuẓot ve-ha-Kibbutzim, was originally founded in 1939 by a religious group. In 1947 it was taken over by immigrants from Central and Eastern Europe, who had, three years earlier, set up a village on the nearby Poriyyah Ridge. The site, also called Bitanyah, had served *PICA (Palestine Jewish Colonization Association) as a fruit tree nursery. Alummot's economy was based on irrigated field and garden crops, bananas and other tropical fruit, carp ponds, and dairy cattle. The kibbutz also rented family vacation apartments. In 2002 its population was 247.

[Efraim Orni]

ALVA (Allweiss), SIEGFRIED (Solomon; 1901–1973), painter. He was born in Berlin, but lived in Galicia until the age of ten, and was given a strict Jewish education. Alva studied music and later drawing and after a period of travel in Europe studied painting in Paris. Shortly before the outbreak of World War II he settled in England. His works include an illustrated and decorated version of the first chapter of Genesis, a series of studies of the Prophets in lithograph, serigraphs, and oil paintings on several subjects from Jewish life in Eastern Europe. Some of his paintings are symbolist and abstract. Characteristic of his style is the use of a distinctive brush stroke and aerial perspective. He wrote an autobiography, *With Pen and Brush: The Autobiography of a Painter* (1973).

BIBLIOGRAPHY: *Alva: Paintings and Drawings* (1942), introduction by M. Collis; R. Gindertael, *Alva* (Fr., 1955); Y. Haezraḥi, *Alva* (Heb., 1954).

ALVAN BEN ABRAHAM (10th–11th century), rhetorician, poet, and *paytan* who lived in Syria. His *piyyutim* and poems were collected in a *divan* of which only a few pages were found in the Cairo *Genizah*. Evidently Alvan was also a *ḥazzan*: various *piyyutim* from the *Genizah* which bear the signature "Alvan Ḥazzan" may be his. Several of his nonreligious poems are in the form of letters written to patrons in various cities in Syria. These letters express the author's longing and respect for those to whom they are addressed. The language of the poem is generally marked by simplicity, but occasionally the poet incorporates ancient paytanic expression, as was customary among the poets of the time. The name Alvan is biblical (Gen. 36:23) and was used exclusively in Syria.

BIBLIOGRAPHY: Davidson, in: JQR, 2 (1911), 221–39; Ḥ. Schirmann, *Shirim Ḥadashim min ha-Genizah* (1966), 53–57.

[Abraham Meir Habermann]

ALVARES (Alvarez), Sephardi family of Marrano descent. The first known to bear the name was SAMUEL DIOS-AYUDA (= Joshua?) of Astorga, baptized as Garcia Alvarez Delcón, probably at the time of the persecutions of 1391. He is sneeringly referred to as "the delight and ornament of Jewry" in an anti-*Converso satire preserved in the Cancionero de Baena.

There were many martyrs of the Inquisition of the name both in the New World and the Old. FERNANDO ALVAREZ (c. 1620–1640) of Bordeaux and later Leghorn, who had returned to Judaism under the name of Abraham de Porto, was one of the few Marranos burned by the Roman Inquisition. DUARTE HENRIQUES was treasurer of the customs in the Canary Islands before escaping in 1653 to England, where, as Daniel Cohen Henriques, he became active in the synagogue. His effigy was burned by the Inquisition in 1658, but seven years later he was denounced again by his own son. ISAAC (died 1683) alias Isaac Israel Nuñes, court jeweler, headed the London Sephardi Community immediately after the Plague and Fire of London: his tombstone, still legible, is written in English alexandrine couplets and praises him because "his far-gain'd knowledge in mysterious gems/ sparkled in the European diadems." Joseph Israel Nunez, alias Antonio Alvarez, a jeweler of French origin, lived in Amsterdam in the second half of the 17th century. Isaque Alvares lived in Bayonne in the 17th century. We find Rodrigo Alvarez in Cologne and Emanuel Alvares in Hamburg in the 16th century. In America, the name figures in the Jewish community from the beginning of the 18th century (SOLOMON, distiller in New York in 1703). The English musician ELI PARISH-ALVARS (1808–1849) presumably belonged to this family. The Alvares Correa family lived in Brazil.

BIBLIOGRAPHY: L. Wolf, *Jews in Canary Islands* (1926), index; J. Caro Baroja, *Los Judíos en la España moderna* (1962), index; Rosenbloom, Biogr. Dict. 7; Roth, Marranos, index; JHSET and JHSEM, index volume. **ADD. BIBLIOGRAPHY:** R. Barnett and W. Schwab (eds.), *The Western Sephardim* (1989), index.

[Cecil Roth]

ALVAREZ, ALFRED (1929–), British poet, critic, and writer. Educated at Oxford University, Alvarez served as an editor on the *Observer* newspaper, and has written many well-regarded works of poetry, among them his collected *Poems* (1978) and *Day of Atonement* (1991), which explore the interaction of public and private forces on individual behavior. Alvarez has also written many works of criticism and non-fiction, as well as an autobiography, *Where Did It All Go Right?* (1999).

[William D. Rubinstein (2nd ed.)]

ÁLVAREZ GATO, JUAN (1445?–1510?), Spanish poet. Álvarez Gato flourished in the reigns of Henry IV and of Ferdinand and Isabella. A member of the Converso bourgeoisie of Madrid, he eventually became Isabella's keeper of the royal household. Álvarez Gato wrote amorous, religious, and satirical verse. His love poetry, the best and most lyrical part of his output, includes many of the gallant trivialities typical of the period, but it also contains some of the subtle irony which gives it his personal stamp. In his religious poetry Álvarez Gato frequently used popular forms and refrains. During the last years of Henry IV's reign, the tone of his poetry underwent a radical change and through it he bitterly reproached the monarch for the calamities of his rule. Alvarez Gato's short treatises and letters on moral questions shed light on the attitudes and problems of the Spanish Conversos at the end of the 15th century.

BIBLIOGRAPHY: J. Artiles Rodriguez (ed.), *Obras Completas de Juan Álvarez Gato* (1928); J. Márquez Villanueva, *Investigaciones sobre Juan Álvarez Gato* (1960).

[Kenneth R. Scholberg]

ALZEY (Heb. אלזא, אלזיי, אלזייא), town near *Worms, Germany. Jews living in Alzey are first mentioned in 1260, and again in 1348 during the *Black Death massacres. They were expelled from the town with the other Jews of the Palatinate in 1391. Although there were Jews living in Alzey in the 16th century, an organized community was not established until about 1700. Notable in Alzey was the Belmont family: Jessel (d. 1738) served as the first *parnas*, and Elijah Simeon built the synagogue in 1791. A new synagogue was consecrated in 1854. There were nine Jewish households in Alzey in 1772 and 30 in 1807. In 1880, 331 Jews were living there (approximately 6% of the total population); in 1926, 240; in 1933, 197; and by **Kristallnacht* (Nov. 1938), when the synagogue was burned down, there were fewer than 100 as a result of emigration. The last 41 were deported to the extermination camps of Eastern Europe in 1942–43.

BIBLIOGRAPHY: L. Loewenstein, *Geschichte der Juden in der Kurpfalz* (1895). **ADD. BIBLIOGRAPHY:** O. Boecher, in: *Alzeyer Geschichtsblaetter*, 5 (1968), 131–46; idem, in: *1750 Jahre Alzey* (1973), 196–206; D. Hoffmann, in: *Geschichte in Wissenschaft und Unterricht*, 43 (1992), 79–92.

ʿAMADIYA, town in the mountains of Kurdistan, N.E. of Mosul; birthplace of David *Alroy. *Benjamin of Tudela in the 12th century estimated the number of Jews in Amadiya at approximately 2,000 (another manuscript gives the figure as 25,000). He claimed that they were descendants of Israelites from the Assyrian captivity, exiled by Shalmaneser, and that they spoke Aramaic. Other sources mention 1,000 Jewish families there. ʿAmadiya maintained its leading position among the Jewish communities in Kurdistan, as attested by letters and documents from the 16th century and later. These show the influence exercised by the rabbis of ʿAmadiya throughout Kurdistan and *Azerbaijan. There were two synagogues in ʿAmadiya; the inscription on the "upper synagogue," dated about 1250, is still legible. The Jewish traveler David d'Beth Hillel, who visited ʿAmadiya around 1828, found wealthy merchants, workmen, and cattle owners among the 200 Jewish families there, who still spoke Aramaic. In 1933, there were some 1,820 Jews in Amadiya; since then all have emigrated.

BIBLIOGRAPHY: Mann, Texts, 1 (1931), 477–549; S. Assaf, *Be-Oholei Yaʿakov* (1943), 116–44; Fischel, in: *Sinai*, 7 (1940), 167–77; idem, in: JSOS, 6 (1944), 195–226; E. Brauer, *Yehudei Kurdistan* (1947); J.J. Rivlin, *Shirat Yehudei ha-Targum* (1959); A. Ben-Jacob, *Kehillot Yehudei Kurdistan* (1961), 71–81; Benayahu, in: *Sefunot*, 9 (1965), 111–17.

[Walter Joseph Fischel]

AMADO LÉVY-VALENSI, ELIANE (1919–), French Jewish philosopher. Amado Lévy-Valensi was born in Marseilles, to an old Jewish family of Italian origin. Her studies were interrupted by World War II but were resumed in Paris in 1950. She was appointed to the Centre National de la Recherche Scientifique and later became a lecturer at the Sorbonne. The subject of her doctoral thesis (1963) already indicated the direction of her interest, the Jewish reply to the problems of the West, and she became increasingly a kind of Jewish counterpart to Henri *Bergson, as profoundly Jewish as Bergson was de-Judaized. She evolved a practical and theoretical system wherein the Jewish and the general human points of view were indissolubly linked. A psychoanalyst who opposed the closed nature of psychoanalytical societies, she founded in 1965, together with Dr. Veil and Professor Sivadon, an interdisciplinary center for psychoanalysis. Ever sensitive to the concept of Jewish existence she was, with André *Neher, the moving spirit behind the *Colloque des Intellectuels Juifs de langue française*, whose proceedings, important contributions to French Jewish thought on contemporary problems, she edited, together with Neher and Jean Halpérin (*La conscience Juive*, 5 vols., 1963–1973).

Amado Lévy-Valensi immigrated to Israel in 1968 and was appointed professor of Jewish and universal philosophy at Bar-Ilan University. After settling in Israel she published, in addition to fundamental works, articles on topical problems about which she felt intensely, seeking to reveal the psychoanalytical and Jewish substrata which could help in the search for concrete solutions to the important political problems facing Israel, particularly the Israeli-Arab dialogue.

Among her important works are *Les niveaux de l'Etre, la connaissance et le mal* (1963); *La racine et la source (essais sur le Judaisme)* (1968); *Isaac gardien de son frere?* (1969); *Les voies et les pieges de la psychanalyse* (1971); *Le grand désarroi* (1973); *La onzième épreuve d'Abraham ou De la Fraternité* (1981); *Le Moïse de Freud ou la Référence occultée* (1984); *A la gauche du Seigneur ou l'illusion idéologique* (1987); *Job, réponse à Jung* (1991); *La poétique du Zohar* (1996); and *Penser ou et rêver: mécanismes et objectifs de la pensée en Occident et dans le judaïsme* (1997).

[Andre Neher / Dror Franck Sullaper (2nd ed.)]

°**AMADOR DE LOS RIOS, JOSE** (1818–1878), Spanish literary critic and historian. In addition to works on general Spanish literary history, Amador wrote *Estudios históricos, políticos y literarios sobre los Judíos de España* (1848, repr., 1942), which was one of the first serious studies on Spanish Jews. This work earned him a chair at Madrid University. Included in his book are numerous quotations from works by Sephardi authors, especially poets, thus introducing them to the Spanish public. His *Historia social, política y religiosa de los judíos de España y Portugal* (3 vols., 1875, repr. 1943) is the first comprehensive history of the Jews in Spain based on documentary sources. Though there are errors of fact and tendentious interpretations, his works are of fundamental importance.

ADD. BIBLIOGRAPHY: D. Gonzalo Maeso, in: *Boletín de la Real Academia de Córdoba*, 99 (1978), 5–27.

[Kenneth R. Scholberg]

AMALEKITES (Heb. עֲמָלֵק), people of the Negev and the adjoining desert, a hereditary enemy of Israel from wilderness times to the early monarchy (Exod. 17:8–16; Judg. 3:13; 6:3; 10:12; I Sam. 14:48; ch. 15; ch. 30). Amalek, a son of Esau's son Eliphaz (Gen. 36:2), was presumably the eponymous ancestor of the Amalekites.

Amalek and Israel

According to the Bible, Amalek was the first enemy that Israel encountered after the crossing of the Sea of Reeds. Inasmuch as contemporary archaeology has convinced most biblicists that the biblical traditions of enslavement in Egypt, wilderness wandering, and conquest of the land are unhistorical, traditions about Amalek and Israel in the pre-settlement period probably reflect later realities. In effect, by setting encounters with Amalek in the days of Moses and Joshua, the writers of the Bible were saying that hostilities existed from time immemorial. Among these traditions we find that Amalekites attacked the Israelites in a pitched battle at Rephidim, which, to judge by the Bible (Ex. 17:6, 7, 8–16; 18:5), is in the neighborhood of Horeb; if the locality Massah and Meribah (17:7) is to be found in the region of Kadesh-Barnea or is identical with it (Num. 20:1–14, 24; Ezek. 47:19), then this battle was waged in the northern part of the Sinai Peninsula. The Book of Exodus relates that Joshua fought against Amalek under the inspiration of Moses, who was supported by Aaron and Hur, and that he mowed them down with the sword. Amalek was not destroyed, however, and at the end of this war Moses was ordered to write in a document, as a reminder, that the Lord would one day blot out the memory of Amalek from under the heaven. In commemoration of the victory, Moses built an altar which he called "YHWH-Nissi," and proclaimed that "The Eternal will be at war against Amalek throughout the ages." This implies that Israel is commanded to wage a holy war of extermination against Amalek (Deut. 25:12–19), for in the early days "the wars of Israel" and the "wars of the Lord" were synonymous expressions (cf., e.g., Judg. 5:23).

In the biblical traditions, Israel, after sinning through cowardice and lack of faith as a result of the discouraging report of the spies, turned around and "defiantly marched to the crest of the hill country" (Num. 14:44–45) against the divine command and was punished by sustaining a shattering blow at the hands of the Amalekites and Canaanites who inhabited the hill country, the former no doubt being confined to its southernmost end (Num. 14:45). In this particular case, therefore, YHWH, who according to Exodus 17:16 had sworn eternal enmity to Amalek, permitted Amalek to defeat Israel, but, since He had specifically warned Israel against this particular undertaking, there is no real contradiction between Exodus 17:16 and Numbers 14:45. It is possible that this tradition is based on abortive attempts by Israel to expand its holdings in the South during the premonarchic period (see Num. 13:29; 21:1–3, 4–34; Deut 1:44). More closely historical than the Pentateuch's accounts of Amalek are the traditions set in the period of the Judges and the monarchy. During the period of the Judges, the Amalekites participated with other nations in attacks on the Israelite tribes. Together with the Ammonites, they joined Moab against Israel and were among those who captured "the city of palms" – apparently Jericho or the pasture lands of Jericho (Judg. 3:12–13). It seems probable that the wanderings of the Amalekites, or of a particular part of them, extended as far as Transjordan in the neighborhood of Moab or Ammon. (Some scholars (Edeleman in Bibliography) have argued that there was a northern Amalekite enclave adjoining Ephraimite territory.) The Amalekites and the people of the East joined the Midianite raids on the Israelites in the time of *Gideon, and, like true desert tribes, undoubtedly participated in the destruction of the crops, as related in the Book of Judges (6:1–7). The Amalekites took part in the battles in the valley of Jezreel (6:33; 7:12) and perhaps also in the Jordan Valley, but there is no evidence that Gideon also fought with the Amalekites in his pursuit of the Midianites in Transjordan. In no case did the Amalekites as a whole suffer decisive defeat at this time and their center in the Negev was not harmed.

The decisive clash between Israel and Amalek came only with the advent of the monarchy, in the famous Amalekite war of *Saul. According to the biblical account, the war began as a result of a divine command of the Lord to Saul through Samuel to smite Amalek and destroy it, infant and suckling, ox and sheep, camel and ass" (I Sam. 15:3). Although Samuel alludes to Amalek's provocation of Israel, "in opposing them on the way, when they came up out of Egypt" (15:2), there is no mention of the battle of Rephidim and of the victorious war of Moses and Joshua. Samuel's words more closely parallel the narrative about the attack of Amalek in the Book of Deuteronomy (25:17–19), which relates that the Amalekites attacked the Israelites on their way out of Egypt, "when you were famished and weary," and cut down the stragglers in the rear, without mentioning any victorious Israelite counteraction. Deuteronomy explicitly admonishes the Israelites to remember Amalek and blot out its memory from under heaven, whereas in the Exodus version this can only be inferred (see above). The command imposed on Saul to subject the Amalekites to the ban (*ḥerem), however, conforms to the version in Deuteronomy. The dispute between Samuel and Saul with regard to the *ḥerem* was not over the command itself, but the extent to which it had been put into effect. Saul's act of extermination was not absolute, for he spared the best of the sheep and cattle – setting aside part for a sacrifice to God – and *Agag, king of Amalek. It should be noted that even the deuteronomic *ḥerem*, though it does not allow for the sparing of persons (such as Agag), except for particular ones (like *Rahab) specified in advance, permits the taking of booty (e.g., Deut. 2:34–5; Josh. 8:26–27) except in special cases (Deut. 13:13ff.; Josh. 6:17ff.). Despite the "pre-deuteronomic" literary framework of chapter 15 and its prophetic-ideological aim, embedded in it is an ancient historical tradition about a war of extermination that reflects Saul's war against Amalek. This may be seen in the record of Saul's wars in which the war of Amalek receives special mention: "He did valiantly, and smote the Amalekites, and delivered Israel out of the hands of those who plundered them" (I Sam. 14:48). The matter was, therefore, a war of rescue as were the wars of the Judges, and it seems that because of its difficulty Saul vowed that in the event of success he would devote the spoil to the Lord by *ḥerem*.

From the scanty information in I Samuel 15, it may be concluded that Saul achieved victory over the Amalekites and advanced all the way to their headquarters, "the city of Amalek." The battle (or the main one) was waged in "the wadi," by which is perhaps meant the Wadi of Egypt (cf. Num. 34:5; Josh. 15:4; Ezek. 47:19). Accordingly, the main Amalekite center was on the Sinai Peninsula in the region of "the waters of Meribath-Kadesh," which may have been in the vicinity of Kadesh-Barnea, as the Amalekite attack at Rephidim was also in the same area. The term "city of Amalek" is not to be understood literally, and it is possible that it means a fortified camp. Neither does the title "king," applied to Agag, necessarily imply an organized kingdom as customarily found in settled regions, and it may be presumed that Agag was a type of tribal chief called a king, like the kings of Midian (Num. 31:8; Judg. 8:5, 12; cf. Num. 25:18; Josh. 13:21) and the kings of Ḫana in *Mari, whose main function may have been a military one.

According to I Samuel 15:7, "Saul defeated the Amalekites from Havilah all the way to Shur, which is east of (or close to) Egypt." However, Saul himself can hardly have advanced as far as the borders of Egypt (and if this Havilah is the same as that in Gen. 10:7, 29 – Arabia as well). Perhaps the author merely wishes to define the normal range of the nomadic Amalekites in the time of Saul. A similar expression occurs in the description of the much wider range of the Ishmaelites: "From Havilah, by Shur, which is east of (or close to) Egypt, etc." (Gen. 25:18). The magnitude of the Amalekite defeat in the days of Saul is apparently reflected in the pronouncement of *Balaam: "Their (i.e., Israel's) king shall rise above Agag, their kingdom shall be exalted" (Num. 24:7). It is related that when Samuel put Agag to death he said "As your sword has bereaved women, so shall your mother be the most bereaved of women" (I Sam. 15:33). This may indicate that Agag's military success was proverbial. The Amalekites were not completely destroyed by Saul, since at the end of his reign they were still raiding the Negev of the Cherethites, of Judah, and of Caleb, and the town of Ziklag, that had been assigned by King Achish of Gath to David (I Sam. 30:14).

Although the story of David's victory over the Amalekites is intended to add to his glory, it need not be doubted that it reflects an historical truth about David's wars against the desert tribes in his premonarchial period, being distinguished by exact topographical indications, by correct military-legal conduct, and the division of booty among the cities of Judah and of the Negev (30:9, 21–31). After the victories of Saul and David the Amalekites ceased to be a factor of any influence in the border regions of Judah and the Negev, just as the Midianites had after the war of Gideon. In I Chronicles 4:42–43, some obscure information has been preserved about the remnant of Amalek. These verses relate that some of the Simeonites went to Mt. Seir, killed the survivors of Amalek, and settled there. It is difficult to imagine that Mt. Seir means Edom, in light of the fact that the concept "Seir" may be applied to a variety of regions (e.g., Josh. 15:10; and perhaps also Judg. 3:26) and the areas mentioned in the previous verses (I Chron. 39–42); it seems most likely that the reference is to the western Negev, where the Amalekites roamed from early times. According to the allusion in verse 41, it is possible to say that the destruction of the survivors of Amalek took place during the reign of *Hezekiah.

Land and People

The name Amalek is not mentioned in writings outside the Bible. The proposed identification of the Amalekites with the Amaw or the Shasu of Egyptian sources is untenable. In the biblical genealogical system (see *Genealogy) Amalek is the son of Esau's son Eliphaz by Eliphaz's concubine Timna (Gen. 36:12). On the analogy of the genealogies of the sons of Nahor by concubinage (Gen. 22:24) and of Abraham's sons by Keturah and Hagar it may be surmised that Amalek's genealogy was intended to imply his special status as a nomad as distinct from the sedentary Edomites, in the same way as the Ishmaelites or the children of Keturah were distinct from the sedentary descendants of Abraham. There may be geographical significance in the listing of Amalek after Edom in the Song of Balaam (Num. 24:18, 20).

The Amalekites and the Kenites

Those among the Amalekites who lived in the border regions maintained a relationship to the Kenites, who certainly lived near the permanent settlements (I Sam. 15:6). Whereas the Kenites passed into permanent settlement during the First Temple period and were assimilated in Judah (I Chron. 2:55), the Amalekites did not deviate from their desert nomadic character until they ceased to exist. Some believe that this Amalekite patronage of the Kenites is also mentioned in Judges 1:16, reading (in accordance with a few Septuagint manuscripts and the Latin Vulgate version) "and they settled with the Amalekite" instead of "and they settled with the people." However, such an interpretation contradicts the meaning of the chapter – whose purpose is to relate how various tribes and families became annexed to Judah, i.e., "the people." This reading which occurs only in secondary versions of the Septuagint and not in original ones can be explained as an attempt to interpret a difficult passage in the light of I Samuel 15:6, i.e., the verse in the Song of *Deborah where it says of Ephraim "they whose root is in Amalek" (Judg. 5:14). Without raising the possibility of textual reconstruction in detail, it may be established, by drawing a parallel with the element "people," which appears repeatedly in this song, that the name Amalek in the masoretic text is the authentic one. Hence the meaning of the name in this context is not merely geographic (Judg. 12:15), but serves to indicate the warlike nature of Ephraim, beside Benjamin. It is unimaginable that such a juxtaposition would have been possible after the consciousness of the divine war of extermination against Amalek had taken root in Israel.

[Samuel Abramsky / S. David Sperling (2nd ed.)]

In the *Aggadah*

Amalek, "the first of the nations" (Num. 24:20), had no wish to fight alone against Israel but rather, with the help of many nations (Mekhilta, ed. by H.S. Horovitz and I.A. Rabin (1960^2), 176; Jos., Ant., 3:40). At first these nations were afraid to join Amalek, but he persuaded them by saying: "Come, and I shall advise you what to do. If they defeat me, you flee, and if not, come and help me against Israel."

Moses appointed Joshua to lead the Israelite army not because of his own weakness or advanced years but because he wished "to train Joshua in warfare" (Mekhilta, 179; Ex. R. 26:3). After he defeated the Amalekites, Joshua refrained from the common practice of abusing the bodies of the slain and instead "treated them with mercy" (Mekhilta, 181). The war with Amalek did not end with their defeat, and the Israelites were commanded always to remember the deeds of Amalek (Deut. 35:17). In rabbinic literature, the reasons for the unusual eternal remembrance of Amalek are the following: (1) Amalek is the irreconcilable enemy and it is forbidden to show mercy foolishly to one wholly dedicated to the destruction of Israel (PR 12:47). Moreover, the attack of the Amalekites upon the Israelites encouraged others. All the tragedies which Israel suffered are considered the direct outcome of Amalek's hostile act (PdRK 27). (2) The injunction "Remember" does not enjoin us to recall the evil actions of others but rather our own. For "the enemy comes only on account of sin and transgression" (*ibid.*). (3) The verse "Remember…" is meant to remind all men of "the rule which holds good for all generations, namely, that the scourge [the staff of God's indignation] with which Israel is smitten will itself finally be smitten" (Mekhilta, 181). In the course of time this biblical injunction became so deeply rooted in Jewish thought that many important enemies of Israel were identified as direct descendants of Amalek. Thus the tannaitic *aggadah* of the first century B.C.E. identifies Amalek with Rome (Bacher, Tann, 1 (1930[2]), 146). The most outstanding example is "Haman the Agagite" (Esth. 3:1) who is regarded as a descendant of Agag (I Sam. 15:8) the Amalekite king (Jos., Ant., 11:209).

[Elimelech Epstein Halevy]

BIBLIOGRAPHY: G.B. Gray, *The Book of Numbers* (ICC, 1912[2]), 373–6; S.R. Driver, *The Book of Deuteronomy* (ICC, 1895), 186–288; H.P. Smith, *The Book of Samuel* (ICC, 1899), 128–43; Kaufman Y., Toledot, 1 (1960), index; 2 (1960), index; idem, *Sefer Shofetim* (1964), 81–83, 154–5; M.Z. Segal, *Sifrei Shemu'el* (1964[2]), 117–27; Th. Noeldeke, in: *Encyclopaedia Biblica*, 1 (Eng., 1899), 128ff.; E. Meyer, *Die Israeliten und ihre Nachbarstaemme* (1906), 389ff.; A. Reuveni, *Shem, Ḥam ve-Yafet* (1932), 144–5; Abel, Geog, 1 (1933), 270–3; S. Abramsky, in: *Eretz Israel*, 3 (Heb., 1954), 119–20; Aharoni, Ereẓ, 255–57; Z. Kallai, in: J. Liver (ed.), *Historyah Ẓeva'it shel Ereẓ Yisrael* (1964), 140–1; Landes, in: IDB, 1 (1962), 101–2. **ADD. BIBLIOGRAPHY:** D. Edelman, in: JSOT, 35 (1986), 71–84; P. Stern, *The Biblical Herem* (1991), 165–78.

AMALFI, Italian port on the Gulf of Salerno, S.E. of Naples. The first information about Jews living in Amalfi dates from the tenth century. According to the Chronicle of *Ahimaaz, two of his great-uncles, Shabbetai and Papaleone, went on a mission some time in the tenth century on behalf of the lord of Amalfi to the emir of Kairouan, bearing gifts to their kinsman Paltiel, who held a high position at the emir's court. The Jews of Amalfi formed a relatively small community, engaged in trade, silk manufacture, and garment dyeing. Jewish presence in Amalfi is also attested by letters from the Cairo **Genizah*. In a letter from the beginning of the 11th century a young Jewish scholar of Italian origins who passed through Amalfi on his way to Palermo and then to Egypt mentioned meeting two local Jews, Hannanel and Menahem, who helped him deal with the local traders. Other letters of the *Genizah*, from the middle of the 11th century, mention trade in silk, textiles, and honey from Amalfi. The *Genizah* letters indicate that the Jews were involved to some extent in the commerce between Amalfi, Sicily, and Egypt during the 11th century. The medieval Jewish traveler *Benjamin of Tudela found some 20 Jewish families there in about 1159. A Jew is mentioned among ten bankers who loaned money to Charles I of Anjou in 1269. In 1292, after measures were taken to force the Jews to convert to Christianity throughout the kingdom of *Naples, more than 20 families of "neofiti" (converts) remained in Amalfi. The Jewish community, reconstituted in 1306, ceased to exist when the Jews were banished from the kingdom of Naples in 1541.

BIBLIOGRAPHY: Kaufmann, Schriften, 3 (1915), 32ff.; Cassuto, in: *Hermann Cohen Festschrift* (1912), 389–404; Roth, Italy, index; Milano, Italia, index; Dark Ages, index; N. Ferorelli, *Ebrei nell' Italia meridionale* (1915); M. Ben Sasson, *The Jews of Sicily 825–1068* (1991); M. Gil, *In the Kingdom of Ishmael*, vols. 2, 3 (1997); S. Simonsohn, *The Jews in Sicily*, 1 (1997).

[Nadia Zeldes (2nd ed.)]

AMANA (Heb. אֲמָנָה), mountain mentioned in Song of Songs 4:8. As it is referred to together with the Senir and Hermon mountains, it was apparently situated in southern Syria and should be distinguished from Mount Amanus farther to the north. Its marble or alabaster was already known at the end of the third millennium B.C.E., being mentioned in the inscriptions of Gudea, the Sumerian ruler of Lagash. The same stone and cedars were later imported to Assyria by Tiglath-Pileser III, Sargon II, and Sennacherib. In Roman times, a road-station called Amana still existed on the Damascus-Palmyra road. Amana is usually identified with Jabal az-Zevedani (5,900 ft. [1,800 m.] high), which forms part of the Anti-Lebanon chain N.W. of Damascus.

Amanah is also the name of a river flowing from the above, and one of the two rivers of Damascus mentioned in II Kings 5:12 (written Avanah but corrected to Amanah in the *keri*). It was called *Chrysorhoas* in Hellenistic literature and is now named Nahr Barada.

BIBLIOGRAPHY: Abel, Geog, 1 (1933), 343ff., 347, 486ff.; EM, s.v.; Press, Ereẓ, 1 (1951[2]), 26.

[Michael Avi-Yonah]

AMAR, LICCO (1891–1959), violinist. Born in Budapest, a pupil of Henri Marteau, Amar became second violinist of the Marteau Quartet, and concertmaster of the Berlin Philharmonic Orchestra (1915–20) and of the National Theater at Mannheim (1920–23). In 1922 he organized the Amar Quartet, which included Paul Hindemith, and was active until 1929 in the promotion of contemporary music. In 1935 he became professor of violin at the Conservatory of Ankara, Turkey. After 1957 he taught at the Musikhochschule in Freiburg.

AMARILLO, AARON BEN SOLOMON (1700–1772), halakhic authority and kabbalist. Amarillo was born and spent his whole life in Salonika. He studied under David Serero, one of the great Salonikan halakhic authorities of his day. On the death of Isaac b. Shangi in 1761, he was appointed one of the three chief rabbis of Salonika (as his father had been before him), serving together with R. Benvenisti Gatigno and R. Eliezer Raphael Naḥmias. His responsa *Penei Aharon* (1796) were published by his son Moses. Some of his responsa were published in the *Ashdot ha-Pisgah* of Joseph Naḥmuli (Salonika, 1790). He edited *Kohelet Ben David* (Salonika, 1749) of David Ḥazzan, appending to it a eulogy and elegies on the death of his brother Ḥayyim Moses. During a severe economic crisis in 1756, he proposed a moratorium on all debts. This was adopted by the community and led to an improvement in the economic situation.

BIBLIOGRAPHY: D.A. Pipano, *Shalshelet Rabbanei Saloniki ve-Rabbanei Sofia* (1925); I.S. Emmanuel, *Maẓẓevot Saloniki*, 2 (1968), nos. 1603, 1604.

AMARILLO, ḤAYYIM MOSES BEN SOLOMON (1695–1748), halakhic authority and preacher; brother of Aaron *Amarillo. Born in Salonika, Ḥayyim Moses studied under his father Solomon, who before his death appointed him his successor as preacher in the Talmud Torah congregation. The community, however, opposed this appointment and on the death of Solomon they prevailed upon *Joseph David, author of *Beit David*, to accept the position. Ḥayyim Moses filled many posts in Salonika, teaching in his father's yeshivah and enacting local *takkanot*. With the outbreak of plague in 1724 he fled. In 1733 he was in Constantinople. Upon Joseph David's death in 1736, Ḥayyim Moses was appointed one of the three chief rabbis. Amarillo was a prolific writer and the following of his works have been published: 1) *Devar Moshe* in three parts (Salonika, 1742, 1743, 1750), responsa. The laws of divorce, which constituted sections of parts 1 and 3, were published as *Simḥat Moshe* (Leghorn, 1868); (2) *Halakhah le-Moshe* in two parts (Salonika, 1752), on the fourth book of Maimonides' *Yad, Nashim*. At the end of each chapter he gives a précis of the laws with explanations; (3) *Yad Moshe* (*ibid.*, 1751), sermons. He also edited his father's books, *Penei Shelomo* (1717) and *Kerem Shelomo* (1719), and also wrote an introduction to the responsa, *Edut be-Ya'akov* (Salonika, 1720), of Jacob di *Boton.

BIBLIOGRAPHY: D.A. Pipano, *Shalshelet Rabbanei Saloniki ve-Rabbanei Sofia* (1925), 7a; M.S. Molcho, *Be-Veit ha-Almin shel Yehudei Saloniki*, 2 (1932), 15; Rosanes, Togarmah, 5 (1938), 23–24; M. Benayahu, in: *Aresheth*, 1 (1958), 226; I.S. Emmanuel, *Maẓẓevot Saloniki*, 2 (1968), nos. 1445, 1517.

AMARILLO, SOLOMON BEN JOSEPH (1645–1721), Salonikan halakhic authority and preacher, father of Aaron and Ḥayyim *Amarillo. While still a youth, he wrote responsa, and in 1666, he began to preach in various Salonikan congregations. On the death of his teacher, Isaac b. Menahem ibn Ḥabib (before 1685), Amarillo was appointed to replace him until Ibn Ḥabib's son became old enough to assume the position. Amarillo was an outstanding halakhist. Communities from all parts of Turkey turned to him with their problems. In 1691, following the death of Aaron ha-Cohen *Peraḥyah, he was appointed one of the three chief rabbis of Salonika. In 1716 his *bet ha-midrash* was in the old Sicilian synagogue. He was the author of *Penei Shelomo* (Salonika, 1717), sermons, mainly eulogies, to which are appended notes on the Pentateuch, and *Kerem Shelomo* (Salonika, 1719), responsa. Some of his responsa under the title *Olelot ha-Kerem* were published by his son, Ḥayyim Moses, at the end of the *Torat Ḥayyim*, pt. 3 (Salonika, 1722) of Ḥayyim Shabbetai and also at the end of the responsa *Devar Moshe*, pt. 2 (Salonika, 1743) of his son Ḥayyim Moses. In the introduction to *Kerem Shelomo*, his son Ḥayyim Moses refers to his father's novellae on the *Ḥoshen Mishpat*.

BIBLIOGRAPHY: D.A. Pipano, *Shalshelet Rabbanei Saloniki ve-Rabbanei Sofia* (1925), 6–7a; Rosanes, Togarmah, 4 (1935), 220–3; I.S. Emmanuel, *Maẓẓevot Saloniki*, 2 (1968), nos. 1218, 1499, 1593.

AMARKAL (Heb. אֲמַרְכָּל), an anonymous halakhic compendium written in the 13th–14th century by a pupil of *Asher b. Jehiel, whose first name seems to have been Baruch. The work embodies valuable halakhic and literary material dating from the previous two centuries, particularly concerning the distinctive ritual of the German and French communities. The author quotes decisions of his father and reports his own observation and experience. Shalom b. Isaac of Vienna (14th century) already quotes the *Amarkal*. About the same time Ḥayyim b. David, the copyist of Isaac b. Meir *Dueren's *Sha'arei Dura*, used the work in his annotations. A manuscript, written before 1440, from which N. Coronel published a selection (*Likkutim me-Hilkhot Mo'adim* in *Ḥamishah Kunteresim*, 1864) is at Jews' College library (London). J. Freimann published the section *Yein Nesekh* in *Festschrift… D. Hoffmann* and M. Higger published *Hilkhot Pesaḥ* in *A. Marx Jubilee Volume*.

BIBLIOGRAPHY: J. Freimann, in: *Festschrift… D. Hoffmann* (1914), 421–32 (Ger. section), 12–23 (Heb. section); M. Higger, in: *A. Marx Jubilee Volume* (1950), 143–73; idem, in: *Talpiot*, 5 (1950), 196–200.

AMASA (Heb. עֲמָשָׂא), military commander of *Absalom's army in his rebellion against his father David (II Sam. 17:25) and of Judah after the rebellion of Absalom (II Sam. 20:5; I Kings 2:32). Amasa was the son of Jether or Ithra the Ishmaelite, and Abigail the sister of David (II Sam. 19:14; I Chron. 2:17). According to II Samuel 17:25, he was the son of Ithra the Jesraelite (LXX–Jezreelite) and Abigail the daughter of Nahash.

Amasa can probably be identified with Amasai (Heb. עֲמָשַׂי), the leader of the 30 "mighty men" who joined David at Adullam (I Chron. 12:18). This makes it necessary, however, to assume that Jether the Ishmaelite married Abigail the daughter of Jesse long before David came to the court of Saul, and that Amasa was later deposed from his position in the service of David, since in the list of those who arrived with David in Ziklag, it is Ishmaiah the Gibeonite who commands the 30 "mighty men" (I Chron. 12:4); but it has the advantage of offering an explanation for Amasa's siding with Absalom against David – he was embittered over the fact that David had removed him from his duties. Absalom appointed Amasa military commander because he was a relative and a doughty warrior. After defeating Absalom, David tried to reconcile Amasa and any hostile elements in Judah by appointing Amasa as his commander instead of Joab, who had aroused his anger by killing Absalom (II Sam. 19:14). After his appointment, Amasa regained the loyalty of all Judah to David's side (*ibid.* 19:15).

Amasa was then ordered to assemble the men of Judah to subdue the rebellion of *Sheba the son of Bichri (*ibid.* 20:4–5). He did not succeed in this, and David therefore placed *Abishai at the head of his servants to suppress the rebellion. The latter was then joined by Joab and David's "mighty men" (*ibid.* 20:7). On their way, in Gibeon, Joab encountered Amasa and treacherously slew him (*ibid.* 20:9–10). This murder aroused David's anger, and in his last days he ordered Solomon to take revenge on Joab for this act (I Kings 2:5).

[Josef Segal]

In the *Aggadah*

Amasa, together with Abner, refused to be a party to the massacre of the priests of Nob (I Sam. 22:17); and he said to Saul: "What more do we owe you than our arms and insignia, which you have given us? Here they are at your feet" (TJ Sanh. 10:2, 52b). He did however accompany Saul to the witch of Endor (Lev. R. 26:7). He vigorously defended David's legitimacy, despite his descent from Ruth the Moabitess, challenging his opponents with the words: "Whoever will not obey the following *halakhah* will be stabbed with the sword; I have this tradition from Samuel the Ramathite: 'An *Ammonite*, but not an Ammonitess, a *Moabite*, but not a Moabitess,' are excluded from the congregation of Israel" (Yev. 76b).

His piety brought about his death. When challenged by Solomon at the heavenly court, Joab pleaded that he murdered Amasa because he had been tardy in obeying David's order to gather an army (I Sam. 20:4–5). The real reason for the delay, however, was that Amasa was loath to interrupt the studies of those whom he was to summon, considering that study overrode his duty to obey the royal command (Sanh. 49a).

BIBLIOGRAPHY: Bright, Hist, 188f.; De Vaux, Anc Isr, 161; Mazar, in: *Sefer David Ben-Gurion* (1964), 251ff. (includes bibl.); M.Z. Segal, *Sifrei Shemu'el* (1964), 341ff.; S.R. Driver, *Notes on the Hebrew Text of the Books of Samuel* (1913), 372.

AMASIYA, chief district town in northern Turkey. The Turks found a small Greek-speaking (*Romaniot) Jewish community in Amasiya. After 1492 exiles from Spain settled there in a separate street, where they were merchants and craftsmen. In their neighborhood lived Greeks, and Armenians, popularly called "Amalekites." The Jewish community was small but organized, with a recognized leadership, and there is information about the regulations of the community and some disputes among its members. A document from 1683 mentions 73 Jews in the town and another document from 1576 mentions 63 Jews. Amasiya was an important town during the rule of Sultan *Suleiman I the Magnificent (1520–66). His son Mustafa was *sanjakbey* ("district governor") and was known for his hatred of the Jews. In 1553 a *blood libel was spread by Christians when an Armenian woman reported seeing the slaughter of a Christian boy by the Jews in order to use his blood at the Passover feast. Several Jews were imprisoned and tortured and some "confessed" to the crime and were hanged. Finally, the Armenian who supposedly was murdered was found and the government punished the accusers. Moses *Hamon, the sultan's personal physician, succeeded in then obtaining from him a firman which prohibited governors and judges to judge cases of blood libel, and ordered these to be brought before the sultan himself. Jewish merchants from Amasya traveled to Tokat and Persia in the 16th century. In 1590 the Jews of Amasya suffered from the Cellali gangs of bandits. Many frightened Jews fled from the city and only in 1608 was the community renewed. During the 17th century most of Amasiya's Jews moved to Tokat and Ankara. In 1672 there existed a Jewish court of law. At the beginning of the 18th century only a few Jewish families remained in Amasiya. There is no longer a Jewish community there.

BIBLIOGRAPHY: Rosanes, Togarmah, 2 (1938), 283f.; Heyd, in: *Sefunot*, 5 (1961), 137–49; F. Babinger, *Hans Dernschwams Tagebuch einer Reise nach Konstantinopel…* (1923), 117; A. Galanté, *Histoire des Juifs d'Anatolie*, 2 (1939), 285–9. **ADD. BIBLIOGRAPHY:** U. Heyd, in: *Sefunot*, 5 (1961), 135–50; E. Bashan, *Sheviyah u-Pedut* (1980), 99; M.A. Epstein, *The Ottoman Jewish Communities and Their Role in the Fifteenth and Sixteenth Centuries* (1980), 200; Y. Barnai, in: *Pe'amim*, 12 (1982), 50; H. Gerber, *Yehudei Ha-Imperi'ah Ha-Otmanit ba-Me'ot ha-Shesh Esrei ve- ha-Sheva Esrei: Ḥevrah ve-Kalkalah* (1983), 159.

[Abraham Haim / Leah Bornstein-Makovetsky (2nd ed.)]

AMATEAU, ALBERT JEAN (1889–1996), communal activist, businessman. Amateau was born in Milas, a town in rural Turkey. His family was part of the westernized middle class elite of the Turkish Jewish community. His father, a lawyer, was the son of the French consul in Izmir. His maternal grandfather, Rabbi Moses *Franco, originally from Rhodes, served as chief rabbi of the Sephardi community in Palestine. Amateau received his primary and secondary education from Jewish schools in Milas and Smyrna. In 1908 he graduated from the Presbyterian American International College with a basic teacher's diploma and, probably more importantly, the means to escape compulsory military service. Following the Young Turks Revolution in 1908, teachers were exempted from conscription. Teaching part-time, Amateau studied law at the University of Istanbul. In 1910, the government altered its conscription policy, prompting Amateau to flee the country. After a brief stint working as a dishwasher in Naples to raise money for his onward journey, Amateau arrived in New York in August 1910. His early employment in New York mirrored his experience in Naples, moving between a string of jobs that included selling lemonade, delivering bread, and giving English lessons to fellow immigrants. Polylingual and literate, Amateau's language abilities translated into more stable employment, and he got jobs as an interpreter for the Court and on Ellis Island, and later working for the Industrial Removal Office.

Even while struggling to support himself, Amateau became involved in the leadership of the Sephardi community of New York. Together with Joseph Gedalecia, Amateau founded the Federation of Oriental Jews of America in 1912 with the intention of coordinating the activities of the mutual aid societies within the disparate Sephardi community, an initiative spurred by the mass immigration of Jews from the Balkans and Turkey. Amateau became increasingly involved in Jewish communal life, working for the Society for the Welfare of the Jewish Deaf and, in his spare time, as an activist for the Federation, the Oriental Jewish Community of New York (a looser confederation of Sephardi groups), and the Sephardic Brotherhood of America, a mutual aid society. He also took classes in social work at Columbia University and in rabbinics at the Jewish Theological Seminary, receiving his ordination from the latter in 1920. He served as the rabbi of the first congregation of the deaf, delivering sermons and leading services using sign language. Amateau volunteered for the United States Army during World War I and was wounded while serving in Europe. In the mid-1920s, Amateau went into private business, only to be left unemployed by the Great Depression. He retrained as a lawyer, and worked in the insurance industry. At about the same time, Amateau became disillusioned with the failings of Sephardi communal life and began to devote much of his free time and organizational abilities working on behalf of the Democratic Party. In a further career shift, he left New York for Los Angeles in 1940, trading on his language skills to start a company which provided foreign language dubbing for Hollywood films. Amateau was active in both Sephardi and civic organizations in this new setting. He retained a fierce lifelong attachment to Turkey, publicly defending it against the accusation that it had orchestrated the Armenian genocide.

BIBLIOGRAPHY: J. Papo, *Sephardim in Twentieth Century America: In Search of Unity* (1987); *New York Times* (Feb. 29, 1996).

[Adam Mendelsohn (2nd ed.)]

AMATUS LUSITANUS (João Rodrigues de Castelo Branco; 1511–1568), physician; one of the greatest Jewish figures in medical literature in the first half of the 16th century. Amatus Lusitanus was born to Marrano parents in the town of Castelo Branco, Portugal. His parents were only outwardly Christians and from them Amatus Lusitanus inherited his attachment to Jewish tradition and a knowledge of Hebrew. He studied medicine in Spain at the University of Salamanca, and received his degree in about 1530. He returned to Portugal to pursue his practice, but when the situation of the Marranos worsened, and hostility toward Marrano doctors increased, he moved to Antwerp (1533). Three years later he published his first book on medicinal botany (*materia medica*), the *Index Dioscorides* – the only book he published under his baptismal name, Joannus Rodericus. His other works were written under the name "Amatus Lusitanus." "Amatus" was probably derived from his family name, which may have been Ḥaviv ("beloved"). It is probable that he established his connections with the *Nasi family during this period and he dedicated one of his *centuriae* to Joseph Nasi.

Because of Amatus Lusitanus' great fame as a physician and scientist, the duke of Ferrara, Ercole II d'Este, in 1540 appointed him lecturer in medicine at the University of Ferrara, a city where there existed both religious freedom and freedom for scientific research. Among his friends were the physician Brassavola (who wrote about medicinal plants), the anatomist, Canano, and the botanist, Falconer. Lusitanus worked with Canano on dissecting corpses. In one of the *centuriae*, he wrote that he performed 12 dissections of corpses (*dissecare fecimus*), a large number for this early stage of anatomy, in order to clarify one single detail of the structure of veins. He carried out other experiments on corpses to prove the possibility of performing certain operations (*Centuriae* 1, *curatio* 61).

While in Ferrara, Amatus declined an offer to become court physician to the king of Poland, Sigismund II. Instead, he accepted the invitation of the free republic of Ragusa (today Dubrovnik), to become the town physician. In 1547 Amatus Lusitanus left Ferrara, and went to Ancona to await his official letter of appointment. Here he was called upon to cure the sister of Pope Julius III, and became permanent physician to several monasteries (in *Centuriae* 4 and 5, he describes the illnesses of the monks). In 1549 he finished his first *centuria*, in which he collected 100 medical case histories and described their treatment and results. Many of the cases (*curationes*) are accompanied by learned explanations, clarifying various opinions on these cases, and dealing with the pathology and the treatment of the subject. Between 1549 and 1561 he wrote seven *centuriae*, which established his reputation as a thorough researcher in various fields, including anatomy, internal medicine, dermatology, and mental illness. The *centuriae* are also a mine of information on 16th century medical history, social life, and individual biography.

Amatus' fame was such that he was ordered to Rome several times to treat Pope Julius III. A number of cities invited him to treat their sick. In 1551 he was invited to accept the post of court physician to the ruler of Transylvania, but refused. Amatus finished his commentary on Dioscorides' work on *materia medica* in 1549 and published it in Venice under the title *In Dioscoridis enarrationes* (1553). The book was published six times in this form. In the 1558 edition (Lyons), it covers 800 pages, with 30 excellent illustrations, mainly woodcuts of plants but also of animals and birds. He gives the names of flora and fauna in Greek, Latin, Italian, and Arabic, and sometimes in French and German. This work is among the first ever published on *materia medica*. In it Amatus mentions several mistakes that he found in Matthioli's commentary on Dioscorides, which had been published in 1544. Matthioli, a famous botanist and court physician in Vienna, would not tolerate any criticism. He attacked Lusitanus in insulting and vulgar terms and accused him of heresy. Nevertheless, Amatus' works on *materia medica* won international renown. When Pope Paul IV was elected in 1555 and the *Ancona decrees against Marranos were published, Amatus' home was looted, together with his library and the manuscripts of his works. It was Matthioli's hatred and baseless charge of heresy which were the main reasons for this persecution. Amatus managed to escape first to Pesaro and then in 1556 to Ragusa, where he spent two peaceful years. In 1558 he moved to Salonika, which had a large Jewish community. There Amatus openly practiced Judaism, and mainly treated Jewish patients. It was in Salonika that he died of the plague.

In *Centuria* 1, *curatio* 52, Amatus Lusitanus vividly described his important discovery of the valves in the veins, which direct the bloodstream in one direction and prevent it from flowing back the opposite way. Because of a misinterpretation of the Latin text, the discovery was long attributed to Canano. The discovery of the valves has also been wrongly attributed to Fabricius, who described them at a later date. Amatus also demonstrated that the optic nerves are not hollow, and that the cavity of the human womb is not divided. He described the structure of the mammary gland, and a treatment for inflammation of the lactating breast. He used enemas to feed a man suffering from a stricture of the esophagus. He also gave a precise description of the enlargement of the spleen and the changes in its consistency which are characteristic of chronic malaria.

Amatus Lusitanus' lofty medical ethics are demonstrated in the oath printed at the end of his sixth and seventh *centuriae*. The oath, written after his return to Judaism, is one of the most exalted literary documents in medical ethics. He takes the oath in the name of "the Ten Holy Commandments, which were delivered into the hands of Moses on Mount Sinai for the people who were redeemed from bondage in Egypt." This oath emphasizes the philanthropic side of the art of healing and the need to aid the poor and the needy. In this it differs (as do the Christian oaths) from the professional materialism of the Hippocratic oath. His Latin is fluent and graceful and does not contain the barbarities of style and vocabulary common in medieval Latin. All this helped to popularize the *centuriae* with its readers. Twenty-three different editions of Amatus' works are known (together with that on *materia medica*). They have not yet been fully translated into a modern language, although the first three *centuriae* have been translated into Portuguese (1946–). From the point of view of Jewish history, Lusitanus' life exemplifies the internal struggle and emotional burden to which Marranos were subjected. Despite the necessity of concealing his origins, he emphasizes in his books, long before his open return to Judaism, his attachment to Jewish values. In one of his *centuriae*, he quotes the opinions of Maimonides, with no particular relevance to the context. In his description of the treatment of Azariah dei *Rossi, who was apparently suffering from a gastric ulcer, Amatus Lusitanus described the customs and eating habits of the Jews. There is a figure of Amatus Lusitanus above the door of the medical faculty of the University of Coimbra and he is also represented in the tableau of "Portuguese Medicine" in the medical faculty of Lisbon University.

BIBLIOGRAPHY: Leibowitz, in: *Eitanim*, 1 (1948), 23f.; idem, in: *Ha-Refu'ah*, 39 (1950), 9; idem, in: *Bulletin of the History of Medicine*, 27 (1953), 212–16; idem, in: *Estudos Castelo Branco* (1968); idem, in: *Journal of the History of Medicine and Allied Sciences*, 12 (1957), 189–96; 13 (1958), 492–503; 15 (1960), 364–71; *Proceedings of the 21st International Congress of the History of Medicine, Siena 1968*; E.H.F. Meyer, *Geschichte der Botanik*, 4 (1857), 385–9; M. Salomon, *Amatus Lusitanus und seine Zeit* (1901); M. Lemos, *Amato Lusitano: a sua vida e a sua obra* (Port., 1907); Rudy, in: *Archeion*, 13 (1931), 424 (It.); L. Šik, *Juedische Aerzte in Jugoslawien* (1931), 9–20; H. Friedenwald, *Jews and Medicine*, 1 (1944), 332–80; Lopes Dias (ed.), *Homenagem ao Doutor João Rodrigues de Castelo Branco* (1955).

[Joshua O. Leibowitz]

AMAZIAH (Heb. אֲמַצְיָה(וּ); "YHWH is strong" [or "YHWH adopted"]), the name of two biblical figures.

(1) King of Judah, son of Joash son of Ahaziah. Amaziah reigned for 29 years (II Kings 14:1–20; II Chron. 25) but the synchronism with the reign of Jeroboam II (II Kings 14:23) presents chronological problems. Amaziah's mother was Jehoaddin of Jerusalem (II Kings 14:2; Jehoaddan in II Chronicles 25:1). The period of his ascension to the throne was difficult both for internal and external reasons because of the serious conflicts between King *Joash, his father, and the sons of *Jehoiada the priest, which brought about the murder of Joash (II Chron. 24:20–26). During the first years of his rule he did not have the power to punish his father's murderers. "But when the kingdom was established unto him" he punished the murderers without harming their children or families. II Kings 14:6 and II Chronicles 25:4 stress that Amaziah acted in accordance with "the book of the law of Moses… Parents shall not be put to death for children, nor children be put to death for parents: a person shall be put to death only for his own crime" (cf. Deut. 24:16). This moderation toward his father's murderers, as well as his political acts in which he procured the participation of the family heads in Judah, brought quiet back to Judah. Consequently, aided by the family heads, Amaziah succeeded in raising a powerful force to fight Edom. At first, he wanted the army of Israel to participate in this war, but when he realized the opposition this had aroused among various sectors of the people, he gave up the idea of receiving help from the Israelite army although its mobilization had already cost him dearly; the Israelite regiment returned home embittered (II Chron. 25:6–10).

Amaziah won a great victory in Edom in the Valley of Salt, captured Sela, which he named Joktheel (II Kings 14:7; II Chron. 25:11–13), but did not succeed in conquering all Edom. It is possible that Amaziah, by forgoing the help of the Israelite army in the war against Edom, caused bitter conflicts between Judah and Israel. These were apparently mainly caused by the acts of plunder and murder committed in various settlements in Judah by the Israelite contingent, which was sent back to its own country after its departure from Judah (II Chron. 25:13). It is possible that Amaziah's reaction to these deeds was a result of the influence of public opinion in Judah which displayed excessive sensitivity toward the Israelite actions against Judah in view of the strengthened self-confidence of the Judeans after their victory over Edom. Amaziah proclaimed war against Joash, king of Israel, and though Joash sought to prevent this war, Amaziah went ahead with it. It may even have been impossible for him to act otherwise since the official reply of Joash included the parable of the thistle and the cedar – a parable with a derisive design and humiliating content that was offensive to both Judah and Amaziah (II Kings 14:8–10; II Chron. 25:17–19). In the war between Amaziah and Joash near Beth-Shemesh, Judah was soundly defeated. Amaziah was taken captive, and Joash ordered that a wide breach be made in the northern part of the wall of Jerusalem to facilitate the conquest of Jerusalem by Israel (II Chron. 25:23). Apart from this, Joash looted much treasure from the Temple and the palace of the king, and, to assure the fulfillment of the peace terms that he imposed upon Judah, took hostages. According to II Chronicles 25:14–16, Amaziah was guilty of worshipping the "gods of the children of Seir"; this sin brought about a conspiracy against him in Jerusalem in his last days. He fled to Lachish and was murdered there; his body was later buried in the tombs of the kings in Jerusalem (*ibid.* 15, 16, 27). It can be assumed that for political reasons Amaziah took several images of Edomite idols and set up their cult in Jerusalem. This, combined with the defeat he sustained in the war against Joash, brought about a cooling of relations between the king's court and the family heads. According to II Chronicles (25:25), Amaziah was murdered 15 years after the defeat of Judah in the war at Beth-Shemesh, and it is therefore difficult to regard the murder as a consequence of the defeat alone. It is certain that in the course of time political causes were added which brought about a complete rift between him and the nobles.

[Joshua Gutmann]

In the *Aggadah*

The *aggadah* quotes an ancient tradition that Amaziah was a brother of Amoz (the father of Isaiah; Is. 1:1; Meg. 10b). It was on the latter's advice that the king dismissed the army he had gathered from among the Ephraimites (II Chron. 25:7–10; SOR 20). His method of killing of the 10,000 Edomite captives (II Chron. 25:12) is severely criticized. "Death by the sword was decreed upon the descendants of Noah, but he cast them from a rock." As a result he was exiled (Lam. R. introd. 14).

The chronological difficulties presented by differing scriptural references to the lives and reigns of various kings are solved by the statement that Amaziah did not rule for the last 15 years of his life, the kingdom being administered by his son, Uzziah, who, in turn, left the administration to his son (Jotham) for 20 years (SOR 19).

(2) A priest of the king's sanctuary at Beth-El in the time of *Jeroboam II, son of Joash; one of the opponents of the prophet *Amos (Amos 7:10ff.). Amaziah sent Jeroboam the essence of one of the prophecies of Amos: "Jeroboam shall die by the sword and Israel shall surely be led away captive out of his land." Amaziah accused him of conspiracy and drove Amos away to Judah. Following this decree of expulsion, Amos repeated his prophecy against Israel, and declared the dire fate in store for Amaziah. Apparently the impetus for this conflict between the prophet and the priest came from the prophetic activity of Amos in the northern kingdom which was directed against the worship in the temples of the state, in general, and against that of the temple of Beth-El, in particular (Amos 3:14; 4:4; 5:5–6; 9:1).

[Joshua Gutmann]

BIBLIOGRAPHY: Bright, Hist, 237f.; Tadmor, in: H.H. Ben-Sasson (ed.), *Toledot Am Yisrael bi-Ymei Kedem* (1969), 126f.; Y. Liver (ed.), *Historyah Ẓeva'it shel Ereẓ Yisrael bi-Ymei ha-Mikra* (1964), 201f. (2) Rost, in: *Zahn-Festgabe* (1928), 229–36; R.L. Honeycutt, *Amos and his Message* (1963), 132ff. **ADD. BIBLIOGRAPHY:** M. Cogan and H. Tadmor, *II Kings* (AB; 1988), 154; S. Paul, *Amos* (Heb.; 1994), 121–25; H. Stoebe, in: VT, 39 (1989), 341–54.

AMAẒYAH (Heb. אֲמַצְיָה), moshav shittufi in southern Israel, in the Adoraim Region of the southern Judean foothills, affiliated with the Ḥerut movement. Amaẓyah was founded in 1955 as a border outpost and settled by Israeli-born, South African, and other settlers. Its economy was based on vineyards, deciduous fruit, grain, beef cattle, and poultry. In 2002 its population was 128. The name refers to Amaziah, king of Judah, who asserted his sovereignty over the area.

[Efraim Orni]

AMBERG, city in Bavaria, Germany. Jews had settled in Amberg before 1294, when mention is made in a municipal document of their privileges. Thirteen members of the community were killed in 1298 in the *Rindfleisch massacres; a few escaped. In 1347 six families received permission to reside in Amberg. Sussman, the *Hochmeister* (rabbi) of Regensburg, was permitted to open a yeshivah in Amberg in 1364. In 1403 the community was expelled, and a church was erected on the site of the synagogue. The community was not reestablished until after 1872. The number of Jews increased from a single Jewish resident in 1810 to 101 (0.5% of the total population) in 1900; 64 remained by 1933, and only 31 by 1939. On November 10, 1938, the furnishings of the synagogue, Jewish shops, and homes were demolished by the Nazis. Twelve Jews remained in 1942, of which ten were deported to Piaski and Theresienstadt. A few Jews returned after the Holocaust. The reorganized Jewish community numbered 67 in 1965. As a result of the immigration of Jews from the Former Soviet Union, the number of community members rose from 74 in 1989 to 275 in 2003.

BIBLIOGRAPHY: M. Weinberg, *Geschichte der Juden in der Oberpfalz*, 3 vols. (1909–27), index; Germ Jud, 2 (1968), 13–14; Germ Jud, 3 (1987), 13–15; PK Germanyah. **ADD. BIBLIOGRAPHY:** D. Doerner, *Juden in Amberg, Juden in Bayern* (2003).

AMBRON (Heb. עמרון), **SHABBETAI ISAAC** (17th–18th centuries), Italian scholar who lived in Rome; member of a distinguished Roman family, whose ancestors left Spain after the expulsion of 1492. About 1710 Ambron composed his *Pancosmosophia*, a treatise on the universe, written in Latin. In this, in opposition to the astronomical and cosmological opinions of Ptolemy, Copernicus, and Galileo, but in accordance with beliefs current among Jewish mystics and kabbalists, Ambron maintained that the earth was semi-elliptical and the firmament solid; the hidden side of the world included paradise with its bliss and hell with its torments. The Inquisition in Rome and Venice opposed the publication of the treatise as harmful to Christian beliefs. The work with many engravings was sent to Leipzig to be published, but was lost. Another work by Ambron, containing corrections to the *Bibliotheca Magna Rabbinica* of Giulio *Bartolocci, also disappeared. Ambron was a member of the council (*congrega*) of the Roman community. EZEKIEL AMBRON, banker and literary patron, was active in Roman Jewish affairs in the middle of the 18th century and friendly with Pope Clement XIV, on whose death in 1775 he hurriedly left Rome for Florence. He was perhaps the father of SABBATO ISAAC AMBRON, who wrote in Italian an interesting account of his pilgrimage to Ereẓ Israel (Montefiore Ms. 520, etc.).

BIBLIOGRAPHY: Vogelstein-Rieger, 2 (1896), 279–81, and passim; A. Milano, *Il Ghetto di Roma* (1964), 392–3, and passim; C. Roth, in: REJ, 84 (1927), 7ff.

[Attilio Milano]

°AMBROSE (339–397), church father, bishop of Milan from 374; canonized by the Catholic Church. Nothing in Ambrose's works points to his having had personal relations with Jews, and he seems to have avoided any such contact. One of the reproaches he directed against the anti-Pope Ursinus was that he had had dealings with Jews (Epist. 11:3). Ambrose took up his most violent anti-Jewish position in connection with an incident in Callinicum (Ar-Rakka) on the Euphrates; on August 1, 388 the Christians of that city, at the instigation of their bishop, had pillaged and burned the synagogue. The emperor *Theodosius I thereupon ordered the perpetrators to be punished, and the stolen objects restored, instructing the bishop to pay for rebuilding the synagogue. Ambrose addressed a long letter (Epist. 40) to the emperor to persuade him to withdraw these instructions, asserting that to have the synagogue rebuilt with public or Christian funds would be tantamount to permitting the enemies of Christ to triumph over Christians. The arguments he mustered are that the destruction of the synagogue was a meager vengeance for the many churches or basilicas destroyed by the Jews in the reign of *Julian the Apostate, when objects had also been stolen and never restored. Moreover, Ambrose asks, what precious things could there have been in the synagogue of a remote garrison city? Ambrose declared that the bishop must not be faced with the painful alternative of disobeying the emperor or Christ. There was no necessity to search so far for the guilty since Ambrose would gladly offer himself as a substitute for the bishop of Callinicum. If it were asked why Ambrose did not then set fire to the synagogue in Milan, the answer was that God had spared him that task, as it had been struck by lightning. Despite these assertions, Ambrose did not question the legal right of synagogues to exist, as months before he had not protested when Emperor *Maximus had ordered the rebuilding of a synagogue destroyed by the people of Rome. Theodosius later revised his instructions and directed that the Callinicum synagogue was not to be rebuilt at the expense of the bishop but out of the state or municipal funds, although still demanding that the stolen objects were to be returned and the guilty punished. Sometime later, however, when Ambrose celebrated mass in Milan in the presence of Theodosius he extorted a promise from the emperor, under a thinly veiled threat of excommunication, to suspend further prosecutions in the Callinicum affair (Epist. 41). Several of Ambrose's other missives, dated probably 378, contain anti-Jewish polemics. They include an attack on circumcision because the injunction had been abolished by the death of Jesus (Epist. 72); a disquisition on Old Testament law, to be understood not literally but spiritually (Epist. 73 and 74); and juridical argument to refute the claim of the Jews to be the heirs of the Covenant (Epist. 75). The *Apologia David altera*, a polemic directed against paganism and heresy, which has been attributed to Ambrose, also contains an anti-Jewish section (4). Heretics (mainly Arians) are frequently charged by Ambrose with being Jewish in outlook and manners (*De fide*, 2, 15, 130; 5, 9, 116; *De incarn.*, 2, 9). Ambrose cannot be said to have had any real influence on church policy toward the Jews. His intervention in the Callinicum affair exemplifies the fierce hatred felt by the church against the Jews in the fourth century, but it had little effect on imperial policy.

BIBLIOGRAPHY: G. Figueroa, *Church and the Synagogue in St. Ambrose* (1949); F.H. Dudden, *Life and Time of St. Ambrose* (1935); B. Blumenkranz, *Die Judenpredigt Augustins…* (1946), 37ff.; Wilbrand, in: *Festschrift… J. Hessen* (1949), 156ff.; F.R. Hoare, *Western Fathers* (1954), 165–7, 171.

[Bernhard Blumenkranz]

AMEIMAR (c. 400 C.E.), Babylonian *amora*. Although he acted in a judicial capacity, and also gave halakhic decisions at Maḥoza (Shab. 95a; RH 31b), he was a Nehardean and one of that city's leading sages (BB 31b; et al.). He was also the head of the newly reactivated yeshivah in Maḥoza. On the Sabbath preceding a festival, he came to his seat on the shoulders of his students (Beẓah 25b). In Nehardea he also served as a *dayyan*, and instituted certain regulations (Suk. 55a; et al.). It is not clear who his teachers were, but he transmitted statements in the name of Rava (Kid. 10a), and quoted the views of R. Zevid and R. Dimi, sages of Nehardea (*ibid.*, 72b; Ḥul. 51b), and of the elders of Pumbedita (Er. 79b). Among those who attended his yeshivah were Mar Zutra, later head of the yeshivah of Pumbedita, and R. Ashi, the editor of the Babylonian Talmud (Ber. 44b, 50b; Men. 37b; Beẓah 22a; et al.) The exilarch, R. Huna b. Nathan, was his close friend and quoted *halakhot* he had heard from Ameimar (Zev. 19a; Kid. 72b; Git. 19b). Most of the statements cited in his name deal with halakhic subjects. Of his aggadic interpretations the following are examples: "A sage is superior to a prophet" (BB 12a), and "As a rule a heathen behaves lawlessly," applying to them the statement in Psalms 144:11, "Whose mouth speaketh falsehood, and their right hand is a right hand of lying" (BB 45a). Ameimar's son, Mar, was a pupil of R. Ashi (Suk. 32b).

BIBLIOGRAPHY: Hyman, Toledot, 227–29; Bacher, Bab Amor, 146ff.

[Yitzhak Dov Gilat]

AMELANDER (also **Amlander**), **MENAHEM MANN BEN SOLOMON HA-LEVI** (1698–1767?), Hebrew grammarian, publisher, translator, and historian. He was born in Amsterdam, went to a yeshivah in Prague, and was a student of Moses *Frankfurter, a *dayyan* and publisher in Amsterdam, whose *Mikra'ot Gedolot* edition of the Bible (1724–27) he proofread. In conjunction with his brother-in-law, Eliezer Zussman Roedelsheim, he published a Yiddish translation of the Bible, together with the Hebrew text and a Bible commentary in Yiddish entitled *Maggishei Minḥah* (Amsterdam, 1725–29). He also edited the *Midrash Tanḥuma* (*ibid.*, 1733), together with a commentary consisting mainly of lexicographical glosses, and he published a Bible edition with his own notes, other commentaries, and appended to it *Sefer ha-Ḥinnukh* (*ibid.*, 1767). His commentary *Lada'at Ḥokhmah* was appended to Elijah de Vidas' *Reshit Ḥokhmah* (*ibid.*, 1737). Amelander's most important work, *She'erit Yisrael*, is an addition to the Yiddish translation of **Josippon*. It is written in Yiddish and continues the historical account of the latter with a short history of the Jews from the destruction of the Second Temple to the year 1743. In its first edition (*ibid.*, 1743) the Yiddish translation of *Josippon* is called *Keter Kehunnah* and *She'erit Yisrael* is also entitled *Keter Malkhut*. A third volume, a Yiddish edition of *Tam ve-Yasar*, was planned as *Keter Torah*. Amelander used both Jewish and Christian sources to present a world history of Jewry, interwoven with broader political developments. It was meant for the broader Ashkenazi public and therefore written in Yiddish. *She'erit Yisrael* was very successful and ran into at least 12 editions in Yiddish, 16 in Hebrew (the first in Lemberg, 1804), and one in Dutch (1855). Often the editions were updated to the date of republication. For example, the 1771 Amsterdam edition brings the history up to the year 1770; the publisher Kosman ben Josef Baruch wrote the addition here. Several subsequent chronicles were written to continue Amelander's *magnum opus*. The Amsterdam successors also wrote in Yiddish: Avraham Haim Braatbard on Dutch and Jewish history in the period 1740–52 and Zalman ben Moses Prinz on the impact of the Patriotic coup d'état in the Amsterdam Jewish quarter (1784–88). The Bohemian Abraham Trebitsch from Nikolsburg dealt in his Hebrew *Korot ha-Ittim* with the history of the Habsburg Empire from 1740 until 1801; while a second unpublished volume covered the period until 1833. The chronicle *Lezikorn* (1795–1812) by Bendit ben Ayzek Wing was the last outburst of Yiddish historiography in the Netherlands.

BIBLIOGRAPHY: H. Hominer (ed. and tr.), *Sefer She'erit Yisrael ha-Shalem* (1964), 17–28 (introd.). **ADD. BIBLIOGRAPHY:** L. Fuks, in: *Zeitschrift für Deutsche Philologie*, 100 (1981), 170–86; L. Fuks and R. Fuks-Mansfeld, in: *Studia Rosenthaliana*, 15 (1981), 1, 9–19.

[Ignacy Yizhak Schiper / Bart Wallet (2nd ed.)]

AMEN (Heb. אָמֵן; "it is true," "so be it," "may it become true"), word or formula used as confirmation, endorsement, or expression of hope and wish on hearing a blessing, prayer, curse, or oath. Originally an adjective ("true"; but see Isa. 65:16 for its use as a noun), it became an indeclinable interjection. As such it is found 30 times in the masoretic text of the Bible and an additional three times in the Septuagint (see Tob. 8:8 and 1 QS 1:20, 2:10, 18). It usually stands alone, but is followed by a more explicit prayer formula in I Kings 1:36 and Jeremiah 28:6. In the service of the Second Temple, "Amen" was the response to the songs chanted by the levites (Ps. 41:14; 72:19; 89:53; 106:48; Neh. 8:6; I Chron. 16:36; cf. however Tosef. Ber. 7:22). In the synagogue liturgy, "Amen" was the response to all prayers and blessings. In the vast synagogue of Alexandria the *ḥazzan* signaled with a flag from the central reading platform to the congregation when to respond "Amen" after blessings (Suk. 51b). It may be assumed that in Temple and talmudic times responding "Amen" was the main form of participation in the service, not only because congregations were unfamiliar with the prayer texts (cf. RH 34b) but because public worship mainly took the form that one spoke and the rest responded. The saying of "Amen" is equivalent to reciting the blessing itself, and such religious value has been attached to it, that it has been said to be superior to the benediction that occasioned the response (Ber. 53b; Maim., Yad, Berakhot 1:11). A person should not usually respond with "Amen" to a blessing he himself has recited, the only exception now being the third blessing of the Grace after Meals (Ber. 45a and Tos.). This prohibition may be a reaction to the Christian custom to conclude every prayer with "Amen." The early church borrowed the use of "Amen" together with most of the liturgy, and it is found in the New Testament 119 times, of which 52 are uses different from the Hebrew. In Islam, "Amen" is the response after reciting the first *sura (Surat al-Fatiḥa)* of the Koran.

"Amen" is used as a response to blessings recited both privately and in the synagogue liturgy. The congregation also responds "Amen" after each of the three verses of the Priestly Blessing (Sot. 7:3, 39b). In some rites the response after each verse is *Ken yehi raẓon* ("Let this be [His] will"; cf. Sh. Ar., OḤ 127:2). After each paragraph of the *Kaddish* and after a number of other prayers, such as the *Mi she-Berakh* formulas in the Sabbath morning service, the reader invites the congregation to respond "Amen" by saying *ve-imru Amen*, or *ve-nomar Amen* ("and say Amen" or "let us say Amen"). Numerous rules are given concerning how "Amen" should be recited, e.g., with a strong, clear voice but not too loud; not too quick and not too slow. It describes various types of "Amen," such as "snatched," "mumbled," and "orphaned" (Ber. 47a). Other problems discussed in the Talmud are whether to respond to the blessing of a Samaritan or of a non-Jew (Ber. 8:7; Ber. 51b; TJ Ber. 8:1, 12d). The *aggadah* stresses the great religious value of responding "Amen": it prolongs life (Ber. 47a); the gates of Paradise will be opened to him who responds with all his might (Shab. 119b); his sins will be forgiven, any evil decree passed on him by God will be canceled (*ibid.*); and he will be spared from

Hell (Pseudo SEZ 20, ed. Friedmann (1904), 33:1; Yal. Isa. 429). The Talmud (Shab. 119b; Sanh. 111a) also offers a homiletical etymology of "Amen" by explaining it as made up of the initial letters of *El Melekh Ne'eman* ("God, faithful King"), a phrase by which the reading of the *Shema* is preceded when recited other than in congregational worship. However, in the older prayer orders (Amram, Saadiah, Vitry) the original "Amen" appears before the *Shema*. Even God Himself "nods" "Amen" to the blessing given to him by mortal man (Ber. 7a and Rashi). According to legend, two angels accompany each Jew on Friday evening to his home, where they either bless him for his receiving the Sabbath properly or curse him for neglecting it, and they confirm their curse or blessing with "Amen" (Shab. 119b). Any good wish offered should be answered by *Amen, ken yehi raẓon*, as can be inferred from an incident going back to Second Temple times (Ket. 66b).

In Music

According to the Talmud (Ber. 47a; TJ Ber. 8:10), the "Amen" should be drawn out in pronunciation, an act which is said to prolong life (repeated in the Zohar, *Shelaḥ Lekha*, 162a). Since Eastern chant does not use extended single notes, this very old precept furnished a challenge to elaborate the "Amen" response with ornament and coloratura. The free evolution of an "Amen"-melisma is found in Christian chant as early as the Oxyrhynchos hymn (late third century), in some settings of the *Gloria* and the *Credo* in the Roman mass, and later in figural church music. As to Jewish chant, the *Gemara* already limited the length of the "Amen" pronunciation; therefore, prolonged melodies are restricted to the "Amen" after the Blessing of the Priests (Example 1) and to the solo-part of the precentor (Example 2). In 1696, Judah Leib Zelichover (*Shirei Yehudah*, fol. 13b) disapproved of the excessive lengthening of "Amen"-melodies by some of his fellow singers. The "Amen" of the congregation in general remains a simple repetition, a conclusion or short continuation of the precentor's melody. "Amen"-motives characteristic of a certain feast were derived from its specific musical modes and prayer tunes. In the 19th century synagogue, S. *Sulzer, Hirsch Weintraub, and others attempted an imitation of figural "Amen" composition, but without success.

'AMEN

[Hanoch Avenary]

BIBLIOGRAPHY: E. Blau, in: REJ, 31 (1895), 179–201; H. Graetz, in: MGWJ, 21 (1872), 481ff.; H.W. Hogg, in: JQR, 9 (1896/97), 1ff.; Elbogen, Gottesdienst, 495ff.; F. Heiler, *Gebet* (1921²), 383, 442ff.; D. de Sola Pool, *Kaddish* (1909); L. Jacobs, *Faith* (1968), 199f.; ET, 2 (1949), 46–50. MUSIC: JE, EJ, Adler, Prat Mus, 21, 249; Idelsohn, Melodien, 1 (1914); 4 (1923), 131 no. 26, 137 no. 32; H. Weintraub, *Schire Beth Adonai* (1901²), 82–83 no. 96; J. Freudenthal, *Final Amens and Shabat Shalom* (1963); F. Piket, *Eleven Amens for All Occasions* (1960).

AMENITIES, COMMUNAL. From the beginnings of Jewish communal organization, the Jewish *community "held nothing human to be beyond its ken." Its corporative character and national and social cohesion led to the inclusion of social services, socio-religious amenities, and even socialite institutions and mores, within the sphere of communal activity. Total care had to be taken of the community, especially of the less fortunate members.

To conform to dietary requirements, the community had to provide a *shoḥet* to slaughter animals according to halakhic regulations. It also sometimes provided the means for cooking meat, having a cauldron at the disposal of members for wedding celebrations. Many congregations, particularly in Germany, owned a communal bakehouse, or oven, annually used for baking *mazzot* or for keeping the Sabbath meal of *cholent* warm on Fridays. Wealthy members sometimes paid to use the oven, while the poor could do so without charge. Occasionally baking took place in a building, or bakers' guildhall. Many French and German communities had a large communal hall above the bakehouse or nearby, which probably served both as a hostel and a dancing hall, or *Tanzhaus*. The *Tanzhaus* (as it was known in Germany) was probably identical with the *bet ha-ḥatunot* or marriage-hall.

Direct assistance to the poor (see *Pletten; *Charity), also a long-established tradition of the Jewish community, gave rise to several institutions which may be classified as amenities. The daily distribution of food, the *tamḥui*, soup kitchen, applied not only to contributions of food, such as bread or fruits, but later also to occasional relief, as distinguished from the regular relief afforded by the *kuppah*. The community usually took care of ritual requirements, in particular if these were expensive; it supplied at least one *etrog* ("citron") for general use during the festival of Tabernacles. Israel *Isserlein relates that three tiny settlements in 15th-century Germany, unable to afford an *etrog* each, shared one for the celebration of the festival. In Spain similarly a communal *seder* for the poor was held in the synagogue on Passover. Among other civic duties, sanitary control sometimes had to be undertaken by the community. The communities of Rome, Frankfurt, Cracow, Posen, and other large centers retained paid or honorary officials (*memunnim*) in charge of public safety and sanitation. The budget for sanitation was generally provided by special dues, such as the garbage tax and chimney tax, levied on every member of the community. The communal minutes often mention the problem of garbage collection, the streets of the more affluent residents usually receiving greater attention. The other main concern of the sanitary officials was to keep the water sources and conduits clean and flowing. The community also made provision for a water supply. When necessary a well was dug within the synagogue enclosure, probably to provide the water for the communal baths. These included the *mikveh* ("ritual bath"), usually part of the regular Jewish bathhouse which many communities also had to provide since Jews were often forbidden to bathe in the waters used by Christians. The inventory of property confiscated from the synagogue of Heidelberg in 1391 mentions a "vaulted chamber" which stood near the synagogue and served as the "Jews' bath" (*balneum judeorum*). The Jews of Augsburg also had a segregated public bath. No congregation was without a *mikveh.*

Besides the *mohel* to perform circumcision, some communities retained physicians, surgeons, and midwives, not only to serve in communal hospitals, where these existed, but also to supervise certain general health services (see *Sick Care). The Spanish congregation in London, for instance, appointed as early as 1665 "a Physician of the Hebra who shall be obliged to attend the sick as soon as he shall have been informed… that visiting him he shall prescribe what is needful." The physician or physicians received an annual salary from the community, supplemented by the fees they were allowed to take (according to their contracts) from wealthier members. The deeds of contract and communal regulations repeatedly stress the physician's duty to visit the needy sick, either in a special "house for the sick" (sometimes called **hekdesh*), or at home. The *hekdesh*, also used as a shelter where poor itinerant Jews could stay for a limited number of days, in modern times developed into a regular Jewish hospital, first in Western and Central Europe, and later in other communities.

Later, the community also undertook new and more specialized duties for the benefit of its members. Some followed the example of the Salonika *talmud torah*, which established a circulating library. After introduction of the postal system, Jewish letter carriers in Frankfurt and Hamburg distributed, for a small fee, the mail handled by the Thurn-Taxis Company. With Jewish integration into the larger society, the tendency to retain the communal amenities conflicted with the inclination to leave such functions to the municipality or specific institutions. The change in the attitude of Jews toward this service is linked with the evolution of Jewish society in modern times.

In Muslim Lands

The amenities provided in Muslim countries in the Near East, and in Spain during Muslim rule there, were determined by the form in which the society was organized. Social organization was based on family bonds or common origin; a community consisted of several *kehalim* ("congregations") and it was these that provided most of the amenities for their members. Sometimes even communities that were comparatively small consisted of several *kehalim*, each functioning as an enlarged family. The synagogue not only served as a house of prayer but also as the organizational center of the *kahal.* Rabbinical authorities living in Salonika in the 16th century ruled that "a synagogue is an institution which has officers, a burial society, and persons charged with the collection of taxes and charity for the daily needs and for the synagogue itself" (Adarbi, *Divrei Rivot*, para. 59). "Each *kahal* is a city unto itself" (Samuel de Medina, ḤM, para. 398). Every *kahal* was responsible for providing all the requirements of its members, schools for the children, a teacher for the adults, a rabbinical judge, aid for the needy and the poor, the ransoming of prisoners, the burial of the dead, etc. Samuel de Medina (*ibid.*) points out that a person who was not a member of a *kahal* was not, in fact, included in the local Jewish community and had no institution to appeal to for his needs. The custom observed in the early period of Muslim Spain, of setting up a single *sukkah* in the synagogue and thereby absolving the individual Jew from building his own *sukkah* in his home, a practice which does not have the sanction of rabbinical authorities (*Sha'arei Simḥah*, 1, 88–89), may have its origin in the feeling of unity prevailing among the members of each congregation.

It should be pointed out, however, that in matters of common concern to the entire local community, it was the most respected rabbi who represented the community as a whole before the authorities; this applied, for example (cf. responsa David b. Zimra, 1, para. 74) to the institution of an *eruv* (to enable Jews to carry objects inside the city on the Sabbath), for which permission of the local authorities had to be sought.

BIBLIOGRAPHY: I. Abrahams, *Jewish Life in the Middle Ages* (1932²); Finkelstein, Middle Ages; *Monumenta Judaica* (1963); J.R. Marcus, *Communal Sick Care in the German Ghetto* (1947); Baron, Community.

[Emmanuel Beeri]

°**AMENOPHIS III (Nebmare Amunhotpe**; c. 1405–1367 B.C.E.), Egyptian pharaoh. When Amenophis III assumed the throne just after the middle of the 18th dynasty (c. 1575–1308 B.C.E.), the Egyptian Empire was approaching its zenith. The wars of his predecessors had placed Canaan and the Lebanon under nominal Egyptian control and had brought Egypt deep into southern Syria. Wealth and tribute flowed into Thebes, the Egyptian capital, from every quarter of the ancient Near East, as a result of which Egypt enjoyed an almost unparalleled period of opulence and luxury. There are no records of wars waged by Amenophis III, except for occasional border skirmishes in the south (in Nubia) at the outset of his reign. Instead, the Egyptian records concern themselves with his building accomplishments, his achievements as a sportsman and hunter, and his gifts to the temples. For his political accomplishments outside Egypt one must turn to the information provided in the *El-Amarna letters. These texts, which formed part of the archives of the Egyptian "foreign office," clearly establish that Egypt had become one of the great powers of the ancient world. They show that Amenophis pursued a dual foreign policy in Asia. He avoided warfare with the major leading powers – Ḫatti, Babylon, Mitanni, Assyria, and Cyprus – and entered into trade agreements and alliances, which he frequently cemented with diplomatic marriages. His policy toward his vassal-states in Asia was to leave them virtually autonomous, while playing them off against one another. The policy succeeded for Amenophis, but with the dangerous result that Egyptian prestige lessened and the local Asiatic princes began to turn toward the newly resurgent Hittite Empire. In the sphere of religion, Amenophis III continued to honor Amun-Re and the other traditional deities of Egypt but, simultaneously, brought the disk of the sun, the Aton, into prominence as his personal god. The cult of the Aton, which first appeared in the reign of his predecessor, Thutmose IV, was to play a violent and chaotic role in the reign of his son and successor, *Akhenaton.

The theory that there was a co-regency of Amenophis III with his son Akhenaton has been generally abandoned.

BIBLIOGRAPHY: J.A. Wilson, *The Culture of Ancient Egypt* (1957), 193–5, 201–4, 210–5, 232–5; A. Gardiner, *Egypt of the Pharaohs* (1961), 205–11 (incl. bibl.); D.B. Redford, *History and Chronology of the Eighteenth Dynasty* (1967), 88–169; C. Aldred, *Akhenaton* (1968), 41–63. **ADD. BIBLIOGRAPHY:** D. Redford, *Akhenaten the Heretic King* (1984), 34–54.

[Alan Richard Schulman]

AMERICA. Although recent research has corrected earlier exaggerated statements regarding the number of persons of Jewish birth or ancestry who accompanied Christopher *Columbus on his first voyage of discovery, it is known that the interpreter, Luis de *Torres, the first European to set foot on American soil, was a former Jew who had been baptized the day before the expedition set sail. The *Marranos of Spain and Portugal were quick to realize the potentialities of the new land and to transfer themselves there; some are even known to have accompanied Spanish adventurer Fernando Cortes and his conquistadores in the invasion of *Mexico.

Marranos and the *Inquisition in the New World

Religious intolerance soon manifested itself in the new land. Two Marranos who had served with Cortes were burned as heretics in Mexico as early as 1528. An inquisitional tribunal was set up there in 1571, to be followed before long by others in various provinces of Spanish South America and in the Philippines. In Brazil under Portuguese rule there was no independent tribunal, but the Lisbon Inquisition maintained perpetual vigilance. From the close of the 16th century, Portuguese New Christians of Jewish stock in relatively considerable numbers began to settle throughout Central and South America, attracted not only by the opportunities for economic advancement, but also by the possibility of escape from suspicion in a land where their antecedents were not generally known. Although voluntary emigration from Portugal was often forbidden, deportation to Brazil was one of the penalties imposed by the Portuguese inquisitional tribunals.

Before long, the Marranos of the New World were in an affluent position, and it was alleged that they controlled the import and export trade with Europe. They maintained a loose secret religious organization among themselves, and were in touch with their coreligionists, both concealed and openly, in Europe. It is noteworthy that their religious observance seems to have been somewhat closer to the norms of traditional Judaism than was the case among the Marranos of the Iberian Peninsula. From time to time, however, the Inquisition was stirred to violent action against them, and *autos-da-fé of an intensity similar to those in Spain and Portugal were carried out. In 1634 there began a series of interconnected inquisitional onslaughts on the Marranos throughout Spanish South America, which continued for some years and from which the crypto-Jewish communities never fully recovered. During the Dutch attempt to conquer *Brazil from the Portuguese in the 17th century, many local Marranos openly declared themselves Jews and, in addition, a considerable number of Jews emigrated there from Amsterdam.

Hence, from 1631 to 1654 there was an open, well-organized Jewish community with its ancillary institutions in the capital of Dutch Brazil, Recife, Pernambuco, as well as in a couple of minor centers elsewhere. With the Portuguese reconquest in 1654 these communities broke up, and the refugees were scattered throughout the New World, forming open communities where it was possible. This was in effect the origin of the Jewish communities in the Caribbean area in *Suriname and Curaçao under Dutch rule, in *Barbados, and a little later in *Jamaica under the English. For the next three centuries this nexus of Sephardi communities, wealthy out of proportion to their numbers, played an important role in the Jewish world.

First Settlements in North America

One small band of refugees from Brazil in 1654 sought a home in New Amsterdam (later *New York), then under Dutch rule; after some difficulty, they were allowed to remain. At about the same time, probably, the first Jewish settlers reached *Newport, Rhode Island, and those years saw also the sporadic appearance of individual Jews in various other places throughout the English settlements in North America. The great majority of the earliest settlers were Sephardim of Marrano stock, but they were before long joined by Ashkenazim, arriving mainly from Amsterdam or London. By the second half of the 18th century there were half a dozen organized Jewish communities following the Sephardi rite in the British possessions on the North American mainland, including one in *Montreal, Canada.

In this new land, where the Old World prejudices had waned, they enjoyed a degree of social freedom and eman-

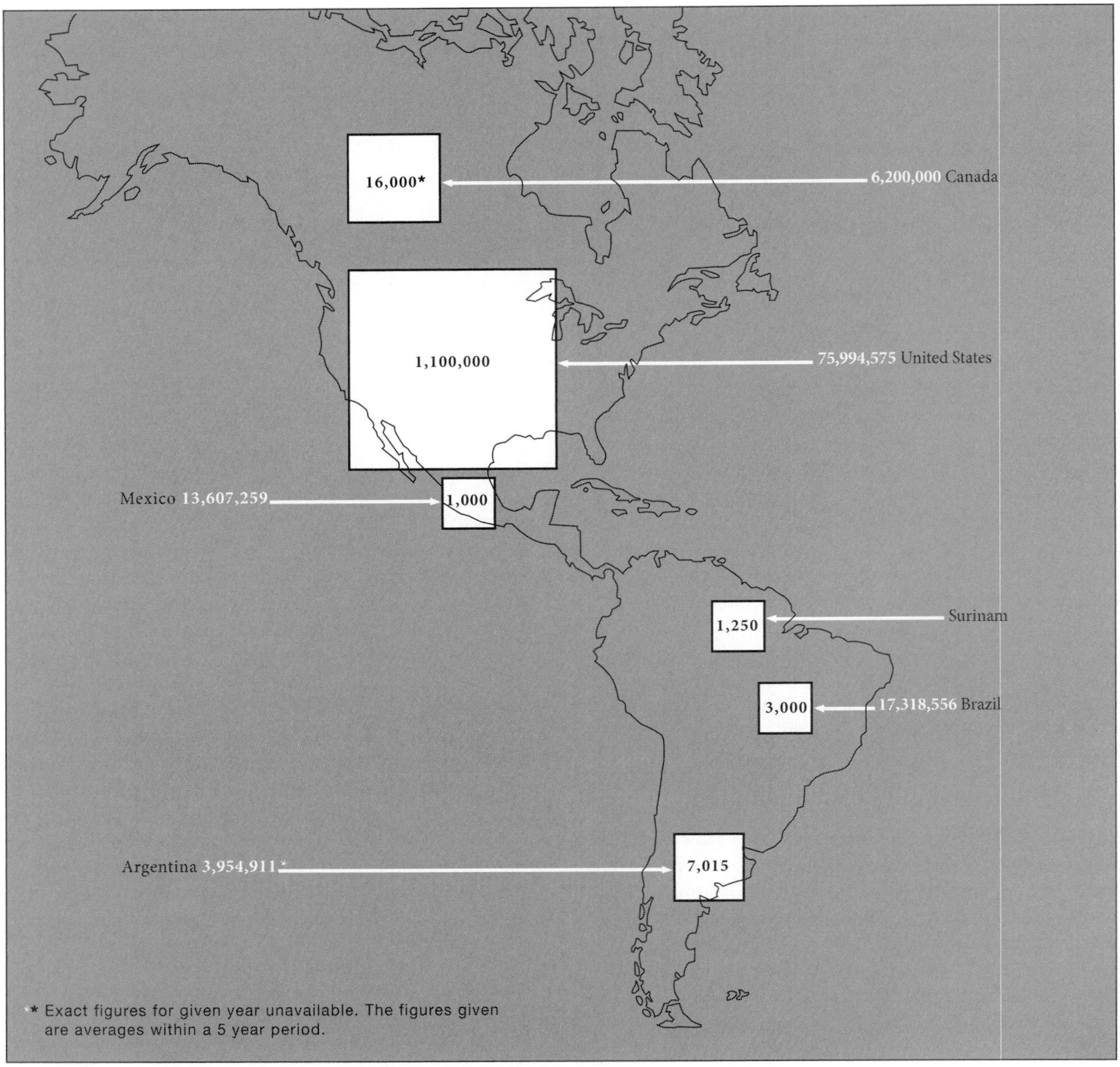

Jewish population of the Americas, 1900. Black numerals: Jewish population. White numerals: Total population.

cipation greater than that in the mother country. America was uniquely tolerant of Jews among western nations in the colonial era and thereafter because the new land needed settlers and, therefore, accepted people of diverse sectarian and regional origins. The need for newcomers created a national impulse toward multi-culturalism.

Another reason for favorable reception of Jews was that America was settled after the passing of the Middle Ages and at the conclusion of the Wars of the Reformation and Counter-Reformation. Hence religious and other conditions which fostered victimization of Jews were absent or much weaker in North America. Consequently, at the time of the American War of Independence, the 2,000 Jews then resident in the 13 colonies were permitted to collaborate freely with their neighbors both in the civil and the military sphere in an unprecedented manner. The Virginia Bill for Establishing Religious Freedom of 1785 was the earliest law in history to grant full equality to all citizens regardless of religion, the Constitution of the *United States, ratified in 1789, stipulated that no religious test should be required as qualification for any federal office, and the first Amendment to the Bill of Rights, adopted in 1791, prohibited a national religious establishment or any other interference with liberty of conscience. Thus, on American soil, except in certain states, which temporarily

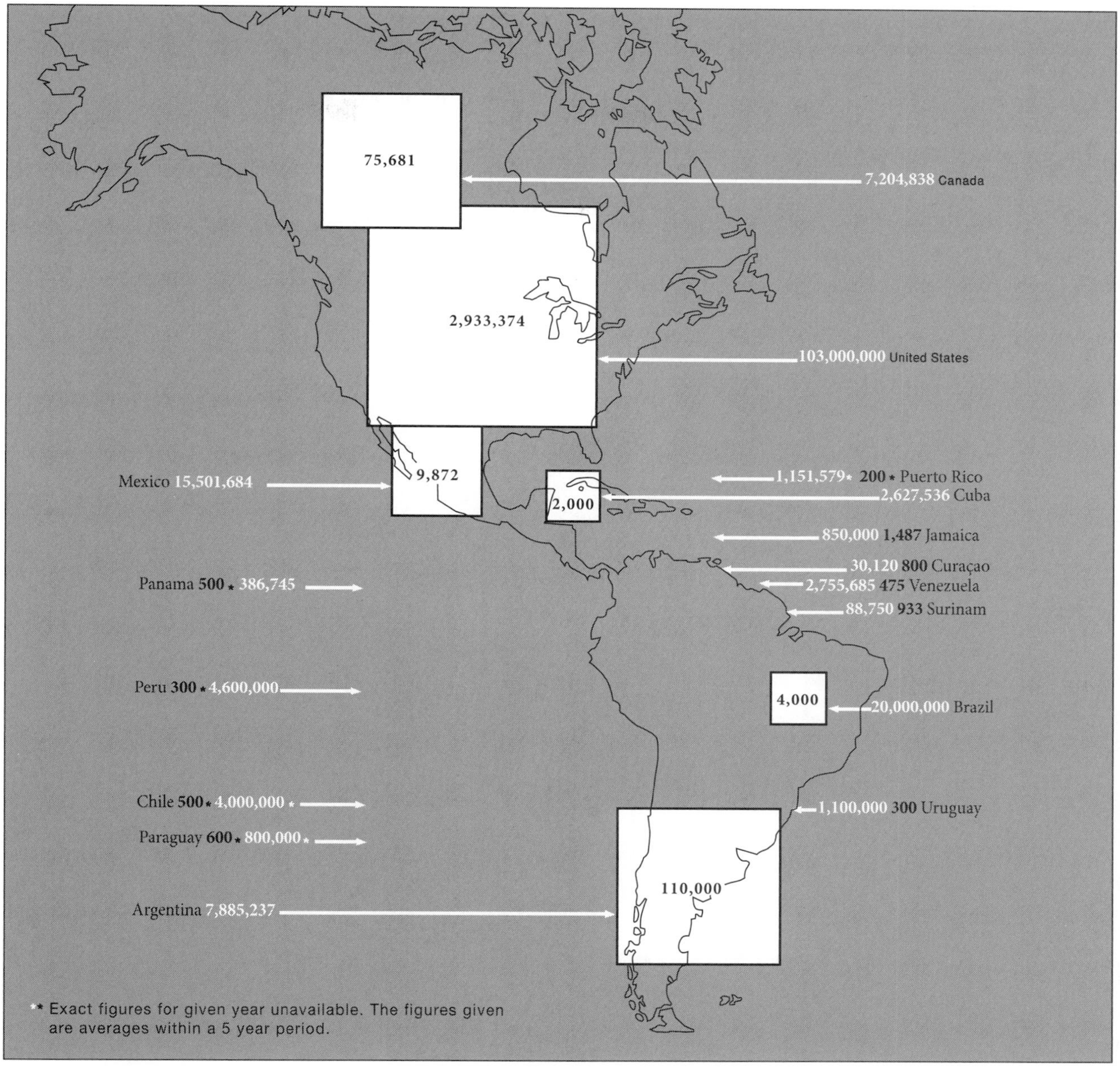

Population figures for 1914. Black numerals: Jewish population. White numerals: Total population.

retained test oaths or funding for Christian denominations, Jewish emancipation was formally established for the first time in history.

In the period after the Revolution Jewish immigration continued on a relatively small scale, and a few more communities were established; the first Ashkenazi congregation was founded in Philadelphia in 1795.

Expansion of United States Jewry in the 19th Century

In the second quarter of the 19th century German Jews, escaping discrimination at home and attracted by the economic opportunities that beckoned ahead, began to immigrate. Mainly merchants and itinerant traders, they spread quickly from the coast inland, founding new communities and synagogues in every new urban center, and playing an important part in opening up the Middle West. The Gold Rush of 1849 brought them to *California and the Pacific. In the new land they felt free from the trammels of tradition, and Reform Judaism became dominant largely through the influence of Isaac Mayer *Wise of Cincinnati, one of the great creative and organizing forces in American Jewish life. In 1843 the Independent Order *B'nai B'rith was founded as a fraternal organization and expanded steadily. By the time of the Civil War there were about 150,000 Jews in the United States and many of these fought with their fellow citizens in both the Federal and Confederate forces. The economic expansion in the North during the war, which occurred particularly in those branches of trade and manufacture in which Jews were active, brought them increased prosperity. Since colonial times Jews had achieved acceptance in prestigious social and charitable organizations, were active in important businesses and activities, won renown in the legal and medical professions, and held public office. Nevertheless, especially with the coming of the Civil War Jews were subject to discriminatory behavior and other forms of aversion. For more than a century after the late 1850s they were excluded from neighborhoods, hotels, country and social clubs, and had stringent quotas imposed upon them in schools, business corporations, and the professions.

Eastern European Jewish immigrants also became relatively numerous and set up their own religious and social organizations. But the intensification of persecution in Russia in the 1880s, coupled with the economic opportunities in America, resulted in a migration on an enormous scale, which within a few years completely changed the face of Jewish life in the United States. The rapid expansion of the needle industries, with which the Jews had long been associated, especially contributed to the radical changes. Between 1881 and 1929

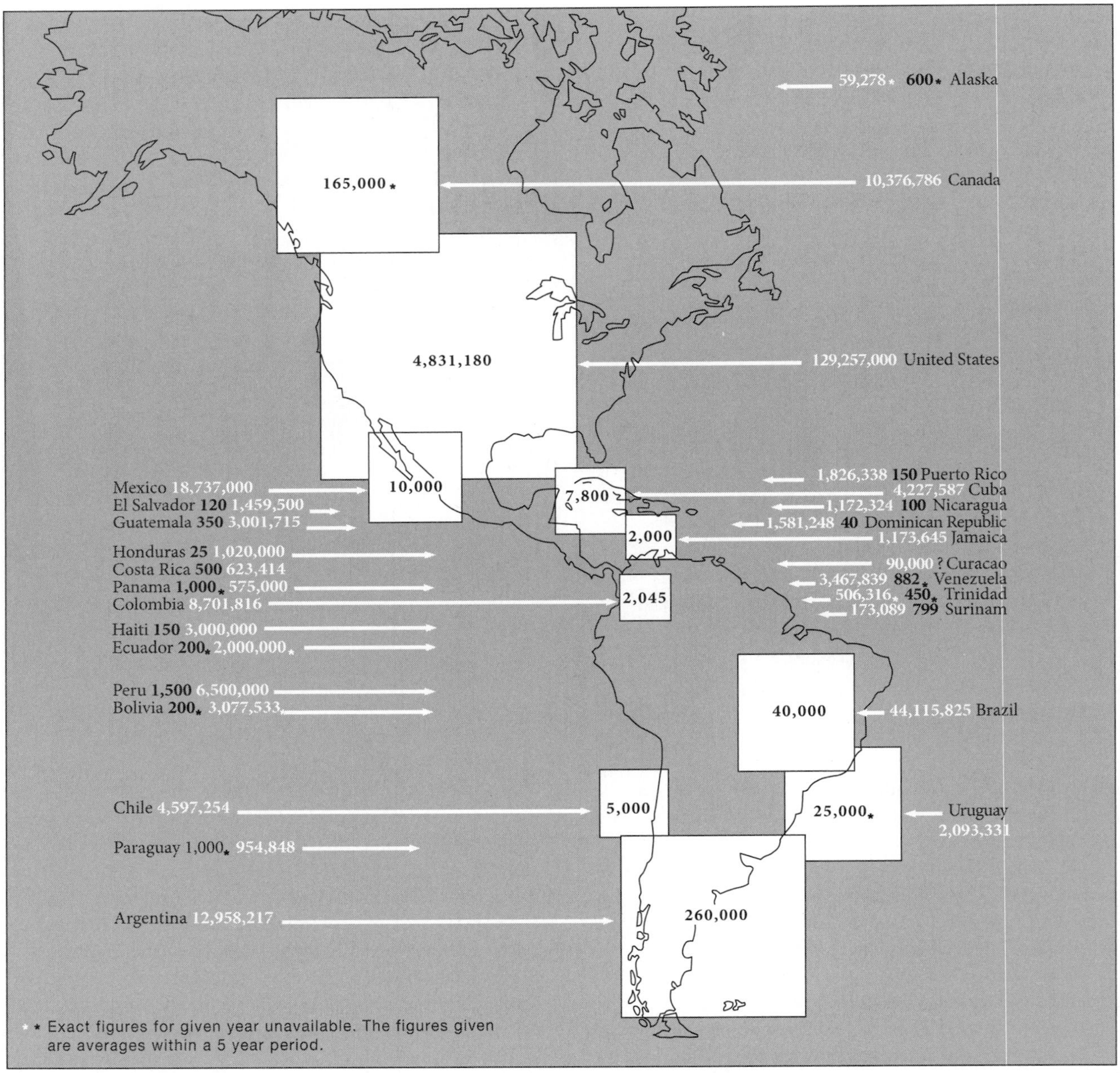

Population figures for 1937. Black numerals: Jewish population. White numerals: Total population.

over 2,300,000 Jews from Eastern Europe landed in American ports. At the same time the Sephardim of the Mediterranean area also founded a number of new Sephardi communities throughout the country. By the middle of the 20th century the Jewish population of the United States alone, excluding other American countries, exceeded 5,000,000. Well before, New York, with more than 2,000,000 Jews, had become by far the greatest urban Jewish center that the world had ever known. (See Map: Jewish Population, America).

North and South American Jewry in the 20th Century

This large immigration changed the outlook as well as the composition of the United States Jewry: it stemmed the once triumphant advance of Reform Judaism, strengthened Orthodoxy as well as the new *Conservative Judaism, temporarily expanded Yiddish culture and journalism, and provided mass support for the Zionist movement. Also as a result of this mass immigration, the role of United States Jewry in world Jewish affairs became significant.

The full strength of American Jewry was manifested for the first time during World War I, when the *American Jewish Joint Distribution Committee took the lead in relief work in Eastern Europe, when American support for Zionism contributed toward securing the *Balfour Declaration, and when

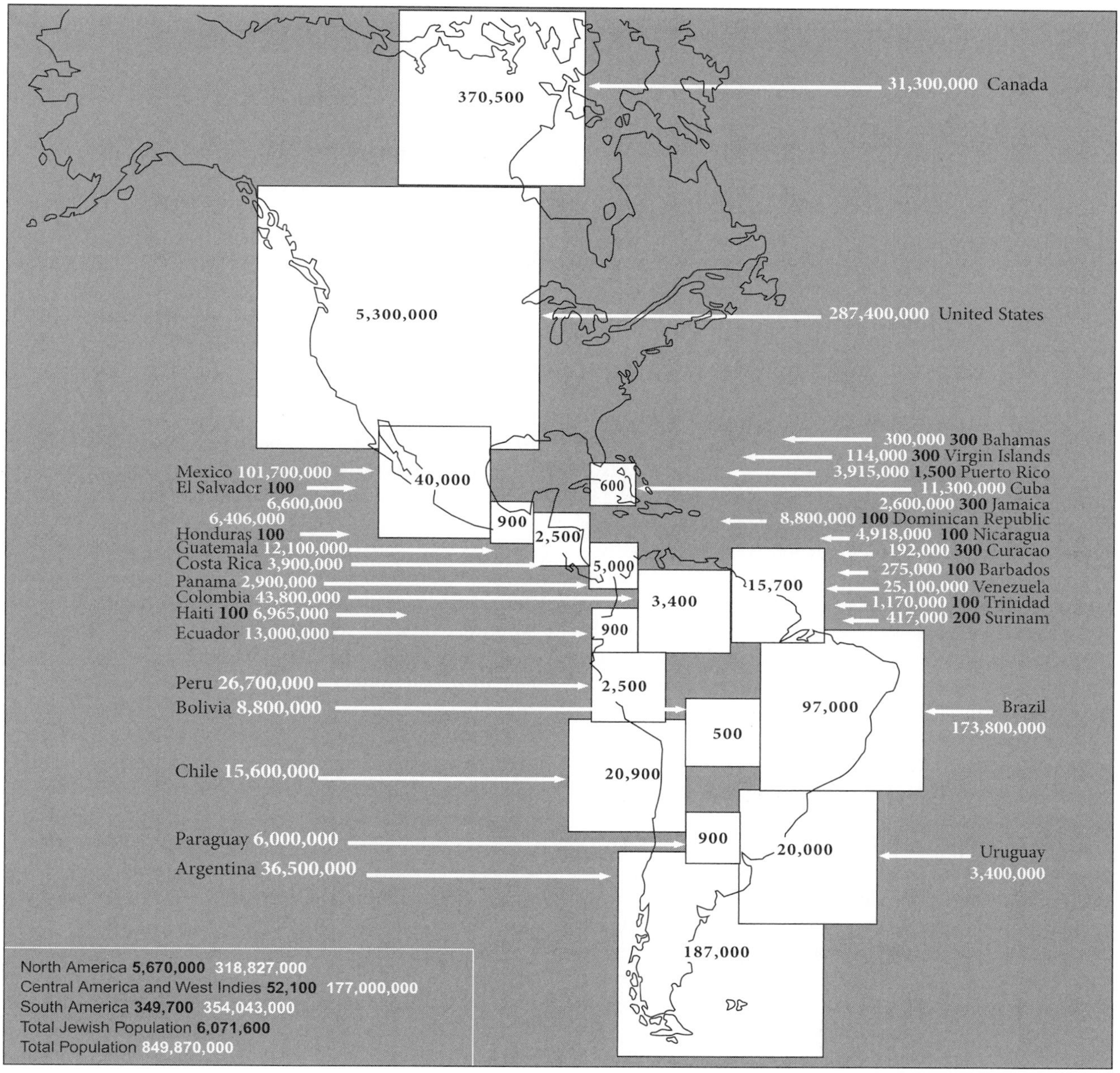

Population figures for 2003. Black numerals: Jewish population. White numerals: Total population.

American Jewish organizations made their voice heard at the Paris Peace Conference.

After World War I Jewish immigration to the United States was stemmed by legislation to some extent, but settlement in other parts of the continent continued by persons seeking new homes. Canada, whose community had developed simultaneously with that in the United States, though on a far smaller scale, found its Jewish population considerably strengthened. *Latin America had previously attracted relatively few settlers, despite the fact that religious exclusiveness had ended with the collapse of Spanish rule, and notwithstanding Baron de *Hirsch's munificently endowed attempts to establish Jewish agricultural colonies in *Argentina. After World War I, however, there was a considerable expansion in that area. The prosperity of its Jewish settlement and the similarity of language proved a powerful attraction, also, to Sephardim from the Mediterranean area who were then being faced with increasing difficulties at home. The Nazi persecution in Germany naturally gave great impetus to immigration to South America, where fewer obstacles were encountered than in almost any other part of the world; this continued during and after the war period. Whereas before 1914 the total number of Jews throughout Latin America did not exceed 50,000, of whom more than one half lived in the Argentine, by 1939 the number exceeded 500,000 and by the second half of the century, 750,000.

World War II made a very considerable difference in the position of American Jewry, due more perhaps to the change in the world's circumstances than to developments within Jewry. By then well-established, the 5,000,000 Jews of the United States played their part on the field of battle and elsewhere to a greater extent than ever before in history. In fact, on a per capita basis, until World War II Jews had served in the armed forces in every war in excess of their percentage of the national population and in 1941–45 served in proportion to their share in the population. Being affluent, they alone were able to shoulder the main burden of relief both during the war and in the years of reconstruction, so that the partial rehabilitation of the Jewish communities in many countries of the Old World would have been impossible without them. Being influential, they were largely responsible for swaying public opinion and the United Nations in favor of the establishment of the State of Israel, which they supported decisively, in the critical period and after. But by this point, the relative position of American Jewry in the Jewish world had changed beyond recognition. With the annihilation of most of Central and a great part of Eastern European Jewry and the enforced isolation of the Jews of Russia, the United States Jewish community was left by far the largest Jewish community of the Diaspora. The change of balance was emphasized even further after the war, when restrictions on immigration were to some extent relaxed. The majority of those refugees from the concentration camps and the hopeless conditions in Europe who did not desire to settle in Israel found their new homes beyond the Atlantic, the Canadian Jewish community in particular receiving a powerful impetus. The number of newcomers was further swelled after 1948 by new immigrants from Egypt, Iraq, and other Arab states, who provided a fresh element in the kaleidoscope of American Jewry. On the other hand, the escape of many Nazi leaders and propagandists to South America led to a recrudescence there, particularly in Argentina, of *antisemitism, which in turn was partly responsible for a migratory movement toward Israel, though on a far smaller scale. The changed circumstances in *Cuba in the late 1950s and 1960s similarly led to the partial disintegration of the Jewish community in that country. Before World War II approximately twice as many Jews lived in Europe as in America. After World War II nearly twice as many lived in the United States alone than in all of Europe, ten times more than in any other country of the Diaspora, with the exception only of Russian Jewry. The communities of Canada, Argentina, and to a lesser degree Brazil were among the world's greatest. Antisemitism peaked in the United States from the Great Depression to World War II and then declined to its lowest point, as measured in public opinion polls in 1998. According to an ADL public opinion survey it has increased in this county by about 5 percent, less than it has in Europe and other sectors of the world. Whether that makes the future problematic for Jews here and elsewhere is an open question but has certainly escalated anxiety in the American and other Jewish communities. In the new millennia the increase of antisemitism is Europe and Islamic countries has led to a heated debate among historians and writers, sociologists and Jewish organizational officials regarding the extent and scope of antisemitism in the United States. Furthermore, the dramatic increase of the Jewish population of Israel, which was but 10% of the American Jewish population when it was established in 1948, has now reached parity and should surpass the United States shortly.

[Cecil Roth]

AMERICA-ISRAEL CULTURAL FOUNDATION, fundraising agency on behalf of educational and cultural institutions in Israel. In 1939 Edward A. *Norman founded the American Palestine Fund, Inc., for the purpose of amalgamating committees that were supporting educational, cultural, and social service institutions in Palestine, which until then were competing with each other in the United States. After changing its name a number of times, in 1957 the organization was renamed the America-Israel Cultural Foundation. However, it was popularly known as the "Norman Fund" for many years. Norman was followed as president of the organization by Frederic R. Mann, Samuel Rubin, the violinist Isaac Stern, and William Mazer. In 2005 Vera Stern was president.

In 1956 the Foundation decided to limit itself to artistic and cultural activities. The America-Israel Culture House in New York, opened in 1966, became the Foundation's headquarters. The house contains an Israel art gallery, an Israeli arts and crafts center, and rooms used for cultural programs. In Israel, the Foundation acts through an advisory board.

In addition to giving financial aid to Israel's cultural institutions, the Foundation provides scholarships to over 900 young Israel artists anually through the Sharett Scholarship Program and helps to take orchestras, theater groups, dance ensembles, and art exhibits to the United States from Israel. It took valuable art collections to Israel from America, including the works for the Billy Rose Sculpture Garden at the Israel Museum in Jerusalem. Building funds support the construction of theaters, music academies, concert halls, and cultural centers in agricultural areas.

AMERICAN, SADIE (1862–1944), U.S. organizational leader. American was born and educated in Chicago. In 1893, in conjunction with the World Parliament of Religions, she was asked to organize the National Council of Jewish Women, an organization she served as executive secretary until 1914. In this capacity, she established the NCJW's Department of Immigrant Aid and Ellis Island programs. She went on to help found Jewish women's organizations in England (1899) and Germany (1904) and was instrumental in forming the International Council of Jewish Women (1923). Sadie American was a leader in the suffragist movement and the fight against white slavery, and a pioneer in establishing vocational schools and public playgrounds. An activist member of many civic and philanthropic organizations, including the General Federation of Women's Clubs and the International Council of Women, she was frequently invited to deliver conference papers and consulted to several governments. American was also involved in the Reform movement, teaching Sunday school at Chicago Sinai Congregation and speaking from the pulpit of other congregations. She supported the Sunday Sabbath and the ordination of women. In speeches on behalf of the NCJW, she called on women to extend their domestic responsibilities outside the home to participate in social reform work for the benefit of society. At the same time, she urged women to carry on Jewish traditions, arguing that their roles as mothers uniquely positioned them to combat assimilation.

BIBLIOGRAPHY: K.M. Olitzky, L.J. Sussman, and M.H. Stern, *Reform Judaism in America: A Biographical Dictionary and Sourcebook* (1993).

[Bezalel Gordon (2nd ed.)]

AMERICAN ACADEMY FOR JEWISH RESEARCH, organization of scholars, rabbis, and interested laymen; formally established in 1920 and incorporated in 1929 under the laws of the State of Maryland. The original officers were Louis Ginzberg, president; Gotthard Deutsch, vice president; Henry Malter, secretary; and Jacob Z. Lauterbach, treasurer.

The Academy's functions include periodic public meetings at which learned papers are read and discussed, joint scholarly ventures, publication of scholarly works, and the establishment of a working relationship with other groups of similar character and aims. An annual meeting is held at the end of each year, at which members and invited guests are asked to present the results of their particular investigations; most of these reports are published in the yearly *Proceedings* (1930–present). Monograph series produced by the Academy are *Ya'acov b. Ela'zar Kitab al Kamil* (N. Allony), *Affricated Sade in Semitic Languages* (R. Steiner), and *Economics & Toleration in 17th Century Venice* (B. Ravid). The Academy also financed and endowed publications of several critical editions of classical texts, such as *Midrash Leviticus Rabbah*, the tractate *Ta'anit* of the Babylonian Talmud, *Yerushalmi Neziqin* with introduction and commentary by Professor Saul Lieberman (first printing 1983; second printing 1986). Among other works published by the Academy are the *Union Catalog of Hebrew Manuscripts and Their Location* (1973) by Aron Freimann and *Le-Toledot Nusah ha-She'iltot* (*Textual History of the She'iltot*, 1991) by R. Brody. It has made numerous grants to promising young scholars. The income of the Academy is derived from membership dues, allocations by welfare boards, special contributions, and bequests. The Academy's membership is composed of fellows, who are nominated and elected by their peers, and associate members who are enrolled upon nomination. Most of its affairs are conducted on a volunteer basis. The Academy's presidents from the late 1960s on have been Salo *Baron (1968–71; 1975–81); Louis Finklestein (1971–75); Harry M. Orlinsky (1981–83); Isaac E. Barzilay (1983–89); David Weiss Halivni (1989–92); Arthur Hyman (1992–96); Robert *Chazan (1996–2000); David *Ruderman (2000–04); and Paula E. *Hyman from 2004.

BIBLIOGRAPHY: *Proceedings of the American Academy for Jewish Research* (1928), secretary's report.

[Abraham Solomon Halkin]

AMERICAN ASSOCIATION FOR JEWISH EDUCATION, organization founded in 1939 to promote the cause of Jewish education by raising the standards of instruction and professional service, to encourage research and experimentation, and to stimulate communal responsibility for local organizations of Jewish educational endeavor. The American Association for Jewish Education stressed the status of Jewish education as a major concern within the entire Jewish community. It introduced, on a national scale, the scientific study of Jewish education, and was instrumental in founding 32 bureaus of Jewish education to coordinate, supervise, and direct local school systems. It pointed to new approaches in the field of pedagogies, including adult education, provided a variety of community services, and fostered lay participation in the Jewish educational endeavor. The Association published the *Pedagogic Reporter* (bi-monthly); *Jewish Education Newsletter* (from 1940, bi-monthly); *Audio-Visual Review* (biannually); and *Jewish Education Register and Directory* (biannually). Lay leaders (presidents) of the organization included Mark Eisner (1939–47), Philip W. Lown (1955–64), and Isadore Breslau (1964–78). Its professional directors included I.S. Chipkin (1944–49), Judah Pilch (1949–60), and Isaac Toubin (from 1960).

In 1981 the American Association for Jewish Education was succeeded by the *Jewish Education Service of North America.

BIBLIOGRAPHY: American Association for Jewish Education, *Its Purposes and Its Service* (1940–48).

[Judah Pilch]

AMERICAN COUNCIL FOR JUDAISM, the only American Jewish organization ever created to fight Zionism and the establishment of a Jewish state. It was founded in 1942 by a group of Reform rabbis led by Louis Wolsey to protest a resolution of the Central Conference of American Rabbis, which supported the establishing of a Jewish Army in Palestine. At its inception the dissidents consisted of 36 rabbis, some of whom sought to revitalize Reform Judaism and some who sought to oppose Zionism. These rabbis were ideological anti-Zionists, and thus from its inception the Council was the most articulate anti-Zionist spokesman among American Jews. Within a year, the leadership was turned over to laymen and the organization, led by Lessing J. Rosenwald, an heir to the Sears Roebuck fortune, and Rabbi Elmer Berger, became a secular anti-Zionist pressure group. The timing of its founding was inauspicious as Jews throughout Europe were being assaulted because they were a "nation" – a race in Nazi terminology; as American Jews were just learning of the existence of Nazi death camps in what became known as the "Final Solution"; and as Zionism, which had been in decline among American Jews, was taking control of the agenda of American Jewry with the *Biltmore Program. The Council sought without success to establish an alliance with the non-Zionist American Jewish Committee, but non-Zionism was rather different from anti-Zionism.

The Council opposed the establishment of Israel and remained critical of what it calls "the Israel-Zionist domination of American Jewish life." In the formative pre-State years it did accept the Report of the Anglo-American Committee of Inquiry for the immigration of 100,000 Jews to Palestine, but not a Jewish state. It was allied with the American foreign policy establishment, which also opposed the concept of a Jewish state for other reasons. It primarily used the mass communications media to publicize its program. Its first president was Lessing Rosenwald. The executive vice president and chief spokesman was Rabbi Elmer Berger until his ouster in 1968.

With the birth of the State of Israel, the Council sought to limit Israel's influence on Diaspora Jewry, to promote integration of Jews, and to establish institutions that were resistant to Zionism. Among its activities are a quarterly journal *Issues*, discontinued from November 1969, a religious education program devoid of "Zionist" influence, and a philanthropic fund separate from the standard Jewish philanthropies, which it feels are under Zionist control. By the end of 1955 the Council had established ten schools for Judaism teaching the positions of classical Reform Judaism.

The Council describes its own ideology as follows: "Judaism is a religion of universal values not a nationality… nationality and religion are separate and distinct… Israel is the homeland of its own citizens only, and not of all Jews." Zionism was a philosophy of despair, without faith in the Enlightenment; it advocated the self-segregation of Jews just when they should be seeking integration. Those who belong to the Council reflect an ideological stance closely akin to some of Reform Judaism's 19th-century founders. The Council has occupied an isolated position in Jewish life in America and has often been accused of advocating the Arab anti-Israel viewpoint. It claimed 20,000 members. The Six-Day War of 1967 led several of its most prestigious lay supporters to abandon the Council for a more or less active participation in efforts to aid Israel. It was one thing to oppose Israel; it was quite another to stand aside as Jews were under attack. Most of the Reform congregations organized under its influence have since denied identification with its viewpoint. In the words of Thomas Kolsky: "In the end the Council failed … the organization became neither a focus for the revival of the classical version of Reform Judaism nor an effective force for fighting Zionism and preventing the establishment of a Jewish state."

BIBLIOGRAPHY: American Council for Judaism, *Formal Policy Statements, 1959–1963* (1963); idem, *Information Bulletin 1943–1947;* idem, *Statement of Views* (1943); E. Berger, *Jewish Dilemma* ($1945–1946^2$); idem, *Judaism or Jewish Nationalism; the Alternative to Zionism* (1957). **ADD. BIBLIOGRAPHY:** T.A. Kolsky, *Jews Against Zionism: The American Council for Judaism 1942–1948* (1990).

[Frank N. Sundheim / Michael Berenbaum (2nd ed.)]

AMERICAN GATHERING OF JEWISH HOLOCAUST SURVIVORS. Immediately after the World Gathering of Jewish Holocaust Survivors in Israel in June 1981, a new organization was established to prepare for another event, the American Gathering of Jewish Holocaust Survivors in Washington, DC, in April 1983. The officers of this "event-geared" organization were Benjamin Meed, Sam Bloch, Ernest Michel, Roman Kent, Norbert Wollheim, Hirsch Altusky, Fred Diament, James Rapp, and Solomon Zynstein.

The event in the American capital attracted 20,000 survivors and their families, where for three days attendees commemorated the Holocaust, attended cultural events, met with politicians, including the president and vice president of the United States, attended seminars, listened to many speeches from survivors and their children, and lobbied for Israel. At the Capital Center, they were addressed by President Ronald Reagan and learned that an umbrella organization for American Jewish Holocaust survivors had been created in the name of the Gathering. The announcement was made by Benjamin Meed, a Warsaw Ghetto survivor, the driving force behind the gatherings, which started as a dream of Ernest Michel, a German survivor, when he was in Auschwitz. The mission of the organization is remembrance, education, and commemoration.

Indeed further gatherings were held in Philadelphia, New York, and Miami and together with the United States Holocaust Memorial Museum in Washington to mark the tenth anniversary of the museum's opening.

The New York City-based American Gathering has a number of ongoing projects tied to its mission statement.

The Benjamin and Vladka Meed Registry of Jewish Holocaust Survivors

The Registry was established by the American Gathering in 1981 to document the lives of survivors who came to the United States after World War II. It was originally created to help survivors search for relatives and friends, and now contains the names of survivors and their families from all over the world. In 1993, the Registry was moved to the United States Holocaust Memorial Museum, where user-friendly computers allow visitors to access the database. There is also a page for the Registry on the Museum's website (www.ushmm.org) and the Gathering continues to seek new registrants via its quarterly newspaper, *Together* (circ. 180,000), and its website, www.americangathering.org.

The Registry now includes over 185,000 records related to survivors and their families and seeks to include the names of all Holocaust survivors, facilitate contacts, collect and display basic information about them, and assist survivors seeking lost relatives (registry@ushmm.org or max@americangathering.org or amgathtogether@aol.com).

Summer Seminar Program

Another important program administered jointly by the American Gathering of Jewish Holocaust Survivors, the Jewish Labor Committee, and the U.S. Holocaust Museum is the Summer Seminar Program on Holocaust and Jewish Resistance, initiated in 1984 by Vladka Meed, who purchased arms for the Warsaw Ghetto Uprising while posing as a Christian Pole during the Holocaust. The program brings teachers to Poland, the Czech Republic, and Washington, DC. Participating scholars come from Yad Vashem in Jerusalem, the Study Center at Kibbutz Loḥamei ha-Getta'ot, and the United States Holocaust Memorial Museum in Washington, DC.

The Teachers Program goals are to advance education in U.S. secondary schools about the Holocaust and Jewish resistance; to deepen knowledge and ability to implement Holocaust studies in the classroom; to teach each new generation about the Holocaust and Jewish resistance, so that they will know, understand, and never forget; to further educational activities which use the lessons of the past as warnings for the present and the future.

The Holocaust & Jewish Resistance Teachers Program is sponsored by the American Gathering of Jewish Holocaust Survivors; American Federation of Teachers; Educators Chapter, Jewish Labor Committee; the Atran Foundation, Inc.; Conference on Jewish Material Claims Against Germany; Caroline and Joseph S. Gruss Funds, Inc.; and the United States Holocaust Memorial Museum.

In 1988, the American Gathering of Jewish Holocaust Survivors became one of only two Holocaust survivor organizations to join the Conference on Material Claims Against Germany. The organization is also a member of the World Jewish Congress, the World Jewish Restitution Organization, and the Conference of Presidents of Major American Jewish Organizations. In that capacity, its mission is to lobby for survivors' rights and restitution.

The effect of the American Gathering on the survivors and on America has had a lasting impact. Survivors now contribute actively to educational programs around the country by speaking in classrooms and religious institutions, writing their memoirs, and pressing their case as eyewitnesses before the sands of time run out on them.

Holocaust education is now mandatory in many states of the union because of the need to teach tolerance. Hate Crimes laws have been enacted around the country because survivors pressed for legislation to outlaw racist acts. Holocaust commemoration and remembrance is carried on in almost every state house in the Union. And because of the survivors and the American Gathering, the Holocaust has even had an influence on American domestic policy and even on foreign policy, particularly in Europe and the Middle East.

The American Gathering held its inaugural "organization" meeting in Philadelphia, Penn., in 1985, where its theme was to speak truth to power and to request that the president of the United States, Ronald Reagan, not place a wreath at the *Bitburg Cemetery in Germany, where the Waffen SS were buried.

In February 2005 the officers of the organization were Benjamin Meed, Roman Kent, Sam Bloch, and Max Liebmann.

BIBLIOGRAPHY: *From Holocaust to New Life: A Documentary Volume Depicting the Proceedings and Events of the American Gathering of Jewish Holocaust Survivors, Washington DC, April 1983–Nissan 5743* (1985).

[Jeanette Friedman (2nd ed.)]

AMERICAN HEBREW, THE, New York Jewish weekly begun in 1879. *The American Hebrew* was published by Philip *Cowen, with editorial responsibility vested in a board of nine members, all of them young. The paper was vigorously written, favoring Orthodoxy over Reform, and concerned with maintaining good literary standards and covering news from all parts of the Jewish world. Though Cowen denied it, the belief persisted that the paper was supported by Jacob Schiff. In 1906 Cowen sold his controlling interest to a group of leading New York Jews that included Isaac *Seligman, Oscar S. *Straus, Cyrus L. *Sulzberger, Nathan *Bijur, and Adolph *Lewisohn. For the next ten years Joseph *Jacobs was editor, succeeded by Herman Bernstein. During the editorship of Rabbi Isaac *Landman (1918–37) *The American Hebrew* often took an anti-Zionist position. It was greatly interested in fostering goodwill between Jews and Christians, and in 1929 instituted an annual award for achievement in this field. Landman was succeeded by Louis H. Biden. In the course of its history *The American Hebrew* absorbed several Jewish weeklies. It ceased to appear as a separate publication in 1956 when it was combined with the *Jewish Examiner* to form the *American Examiner.*

[Sefton D. Temkin]

AMERICAN ISRAELITE, U.S. Anglo-Jewish weekly, founded by Isaac Mayer *Wise in Cincinnati, Ohio, in 1854. *The Israelite* (its name was changed in 1874), edited by Wise until his death, served as a platform for his ideas, and, though run haphazardly, was replete with historical and theological articles as well as news items from all parts of the Jewish world. On Wise's death (1900) his son Leo, business manager from 1875, became editor. In 1928 he was succeeded by Rabbi Jonah *Wise. The family sold the paper in 1930, and its work was then carried on by H.C. Segal (d. 1985). It is the oldest Jewish journal in the U.S., though by the mid-20th century reduced to a local community bulletin. In 1855 Wise had added to *The Israelite* a German supplement, *Die Deborah*. Later published as a separate journal, this paper did not long survive Wise's death.

[Sefton D. Temkin]

AMERICAN ISRAEL PUBLIC AFFAIRS COMMITTEE (AIPAC), U.S. organization often viewed as a synonym for – if not the embodiment of – "the Jewish lobby." Founded in 1951 to ensure the special relationship between the United States and Israel, AIPAC saw the partnership between the two countries as rooted in an understanding that Israel shares with the United States a deep and abiding commitment to democratic principles and institutions and is a reliable partner in defending shared interests.

On this basis, AIPAC built a formidable record over a period of six decades, reflecting the organizational skill of its leadership in mobilizing American Jewry in support of the Jewish state. In its early years, bringing together a popular constituency in support of a political goal was unique and previously unheard of within the national political process. Yet AIPAC benefited from the post-World War II climate in which many Americans and virtually all Jews, appalled by the horrific calamity that had befallen European Jewry, were active (if not always eager) participants in grappling with the issue of what might be done to assure that the Jews never again be confronted with the imminent threat of extermination.

During World War II, spirited debate swirled through the Jewish community over the timing and even the advisability of advocating the establishment of a Jewish state in Palestine. Pro-Zionists argued that no solution other than immediate statehood would allow Jews to achieve full rights and "normalcy" within the world community. Opponents pointed out that, in the midst of war, agitating for a Jewish homeland might be seen as hurting the effort to defeat Nazism. Other anti-Zionists strenuously opposed the state on the grounds that Jews are a religion, not a nationality.

While certain increasingly marginalized groups continued to maintain an anti-Zionist position, the creation of the State in 1948 abruptly ended the discussion of whether there should be a Jewish state and channeled communal energy and passion into the question of what steps needed to be taken to secure Israel against Arab irredentism and also provide the resources required to successfully integrate the huge numbers of refugees from Europe and Arab lands flooding the new Jewish nation.

With Israel's encouragement, the American Zionist Council, which had played a major role in building support for the nascent Jewish state, initiated a project in 1951 to lobby Congress for American aid to resettle Jewish refugees in Israel. It became quickly apparent that the lobbying necessary to win support for Israel could not be sustained by the AZC, constrained by its non-profit status from engaging in substantial lobbying. Thus, in 1954, the American Zionist Committee for Public Affairs was established as a separate lobbying organization. In 1959, recognizing that many non-Zionists supported its work, the organization changed its name to the American Israel Public Affairs Committee and expanded its leadership base to include national and local representatives from other organizations.

Heading the effort from the start was I.L. Kenen, known to everyone as "Si." A soft-spoken, low-profile individual, Kenen was a fierce advocate, imaginative strategist, and thoughtful analyst. He understood from the start that the United States' foreign policy establishment had as a priority extending American influence in the Arab world to preserve, among other goals, access to Middle East oil. Therefore, Kenen insisted that effective advocacy on Israel's behalf needed to be focused on the Congress (the "people's house") and must, in all respects, remain bipartisan. Undergirding that strategy, Kenen shaped arguments presenting the case for assistance to Israel as consistent with American national interests, not as a sop to a special interest. It was not surprising, therefore, to find Kenen, in 1951, supporting economic assistance to the Arab states so that they, like Israel, would have resources to resettle the Arab refugees who had been displaced by the fighting that ensued following the establishment of the State of Israel.

Under Kenen's professional leadership, and with the support and cooperation of many of the national membership organizations, AIPAC achieved remarkable success in winning first economic assistance and later military support for Israel. Its authoritative newsletter, the *Near East Report*, became required reading in Congressional offices, and its periodic publication, *Myths and Facts*, provided the interpretive data with which the pro-Israel case might be made.

AIPAC played an immensely important role in strengthening American assistance during the Six-Day War of 1967 and the Yom Kippur War of 1973. In the aftermath of each, the diplomatic relationship of the two countries mitigated much of the disadvantages that Israel experienced in other parts of the globe, including Europe, Africa, and at the United Nations, where sympathy for the Palestinian cause continued to grow, even as revulsion was often expressed at some of the terrorist tactics of its more militant supporters.

Kenen had understood that lobbying was considered a pejorative to most Americans and therefore kept a low profile for AIPAC. He pointedly observed that, while it was free to do so, AIPAC did not endorse political candidates or contribute to electoral campaigns.

Nevertheless, AIPAC's success with the Congress created hostility that was often expressed not in disagreement on issues but by questioning the organization's loyalty. Despite AIPAC's insistence on a fundamental congruence of Israeli and American interests, opponents argued that the Jewish lobby operated at cross-purposes with the U.S. Arkansas Senator William J. Fulbright was a particularly strident critic of Israel's Capitol Hill supporters. During the 1973 *Yom Kippur War, Fulbright declared on CBS's *Face the Nation* that "Israelis control the policy in the Congress. The emotional and political ties are too strong. On every test, on everything the Israelis are interested in, in the Senate the Israelis have 75 to 80 votes." Although he drew away from the harsher inferences of this rant, Fulbright's views found resonance in later comments by General George S. Brown, who in 1974 told a Duke University audience that Jews controlled the banks and newspapers and that Americans "may need to get tough-minded enough to set down the Jewish influence in this country and break that lobby." (Brown's comment, which he came to regret, has become a staple on antisemitic websites.) Perhaps the most startling and notorious expression of that "dual loyalty" sensibility came in 1991 when President George H.W. Bush characterized activists gathered in Washington, D.C., to support loan guarantees for Israel as "a thousand lobbyists" opposed to him and, inferentially, U.S. policy. The remark caused an uproar throughout the community and is generally acknowledged to have permanently strained the president's relationship with the Jewish community.

When Kenen retired in 1974, AIPAC underwent a dramatic transformation. First under Morris J. Amitay and then Tom Dine, the organization was revamped and professionalized. The revamping of AIPAC was triggered by two developments: the post-Watergate reforms which decentralized power in Congress and required AIPAC to develop relationships with more than a handful of key legislators such as Senators Henry Jackson, Jacob Javits, and Hubert Humphrey and Representatives Benjamin Rosenthal and Charles Vanik, and the need to fight arms sales to Arab countries hostile to Israel. In response, it expanded its research department, increased the number of lobbyists who worked on the Hill, enhanced its presence on university campuses, and dramatically strengthened its outreach to the community through more vigorous resource development and the establishment of regional offices (there were nine in the early 2000s). AIPAC made a conscious effort to bring legislators as well as senior aides to Israel. It also joined with local Jewish organizations to strengthen pro-Israel support among grassroots and statewide political activists. These efforts accelerated after 1988, when a coalition led by the Reverend Jesse Jackson and a number of Arab groups managed to bring forward a plank to the Democratic Party platform committee that was viewed as hostile by the pro-Israel forces; it was defeated, but only following a roiling debate.

More systematically than had been done heretofore, AIPAC built and utilized its system of "key contacts" to assure ready access to members of Congress through local supporters. In 2005, AIPAC boasted a membership of 65,000 people in all 50 states.

Attesting to the ongoing influence of AIPAC is the continuing strong, bipartisan support for Israel on Capitol Hill. There is still a robust commitment to the special relationship between the two countries, and Israel is generally acknowledged as a partner in the struggle against terrorism and Islamic fanaticism – a partnership reflected in a multibillion dollar mostly military assistance package.

Since the 1980s AIPAC has made a conscious effort to work closely with the executive branch. Ironically, though AIPAC often found itself at odds with the Department of State, it came to be seen as an important instrument in winning support for the nation's larger foreign assistance program. With assistance to Israel a dominant part of the foreign aid package, that support is often leveraged by the administration to assure adoption of the entire bill. Since Americans in general oppose foreign aid, the energy of the well-organized pro-Israel constituency became the engine for gaining support for the whole program.

Despite its vaunted effectiveness, AIPAC finds itself operating in a more fractious climate than ever before. Increasingly, a broader range of positions was held – and expressed – on vital issues related to Israel's security and the role of American Jewry in supporting the Jewish state. Not only has the consensus eroded, but organizational discipline has loosened as well. It is no longer rare to find organizations publicly lobbying members of Congress both to AIPAC's political left and right on such issues as Israel's settlement policy, an independent Palestinian state, and many other issues.

The divisions within the Israeli body politic are mirrored within the organized Jewish community. It is noteworthy that the growth of AIPAC's membership and the expansion of its reach into the community occurred during a period when the government of Israel was dominated by the right wing *Likud. Thus, activists attracted to join an organization supportive of Israel's government would tend to be right wing themselves. It is therefore not surprising that AIPAC's members who joined after 1977 and staffers who came politically of age at that time appear to be more comfortable with the historic positions of the hard-line Likud of Menaḥem *Begin, Yitzhak *Shamir, and Benjamin *Netanyahu rather than with the more dovish views of Labor's Yitzhak *Rabin, Shimon *Peres, and Ehud *Barak. Consequently, after the signing of the Oslo Accords in 1993, diplomats of the Rabin government were often critical of the American Jewish lobby for not actively and publicly supporting the peace process. Shortly after becoming prime minister, Rabin let it be known that he did not need American intermediaries – i.e., AIPAC – to speak to the American administration for Israel.

The public tension was eventually resolved, but the private misgivings remained. Former Likud officials who had served in the Israeli embassy and some of their American Jewish supporters used their contacts to lobby against the peace process.

Within the American context, AIPAC activists also appeared to be comfortable with the Middle East policies of President George W. Bush.

Chants of "four more years, four more years" greeted the president at the 2004 AIPAC Policy Conference, creating the semblance of a partisan atmosphere. Some observers felt this was particularly unsettling given the support that all presidents, Democrat as well as Republican, professed for Israel.

An AIPAC past president observed that the immediate past president, Bill Clinton, a Democrat, had been "pluperfect" on the Israel issue.

While the post-Kenen AIPAC publicly followed the organizational commitment to remain above partisan politics, the perception grew that behind the scenes it quietly directed Jewish money to favored candidates. When he left AIPAC Amitay doled out large amounts of campaign money as the head of an influential Political Action Committee (PAC), and many other AIPAC leaders took visible roles in campaigns and even administrations. The inference that AIPAC was not a simple bystander to partisan politics was bolstered when, to its embarrassment and regret, a president of the organization was forced to resign after boasting to a potential contributor about the lobby's ability to elect friends and defeat enemies.

In the late 1980s AIPAC was investigated extensively by the F.E.C. (Federal Elections Commission), accused of directly forwarding the contributions of pro-Israel PACS. AIPAC was exonerated. AIPAC's leaders do participate vigorously and generously in political campaigns and were credited with the defeat in 1984 of the then-chairman of the Senate Foreign Relations Committee Charles Percy (R-IL) and in 2002 of Cynthia McKinney (D-GA), who ran again and was elected in 2004.

Other missteps, more central to AIPAC's core mission, have come to light. In 1981, for example, the Jewish community took on the Reagan administration, which sought Congressional approval to sell sophisticated Airborne Warning and Control System (AWACS) aircraft to Saudi Arabia. The increasingly bitter and public battle, pitting the so-called Jewish lobby against the president, became increasingly nasty. When Congress voted to approve the controversial sale, some saw it not simply as a defeat for AIPAC but a sign of its weakness. A more sober analysis, however, suggests that the AWACS campaign revealed AIPAC's limits in seeking to overturn a presidential initiative in foreign relations, an area where historically the White House has been able to rely on the principle that partisanship ends at the water's edge.

The episode gave birth to the key contact system and the outreach to every senator and virtually every congressman. In addition AIPAC repositioned and became an advocate for maintaining Israel's qualitative military edge over its enemies. Future sales to Arab neighbors would be offset with increased military aid to Israel.

More damaging to AIPAC's reputation was its role during the early 1990s in the effort to secure for Israel $10 billion in loan guarantees for the resettlement of Soviet Jews immigrating to Israel in record numbers. Although the Congress seemed more inclined to support the initiative, the George H.W. Bush administration refused to budge without some assurances from the Israelis about limiting settlement development in the territories. Either hubris or a serious miscalculation of the administration's resolve caused AIPAC to reassure the Israelis that it could overcome the administration's reservations and move the loan guarantees forward in the Congress without compromising Israel's unpopular settlement policy. Others, including the Anti-Defamation League and the Jewish Council for Public Affairs, told the Israelis that they could have loan guarantees or settlements, not both. Again, Israel had been given advice on the American political process that was flawed. Ultimately Israel got the loan guarantee package issued over a five-year period with amounts spent in settlements deducted from that year's installment. In the end, it also did not use the guarantee.

Following a period of some turbulence and two changes at the professional top of the organization, AIPAC seemed to have righted the ship in the mid-1990s. Howard Kohr, a longtime AIPAC professional who became the director in 1996, had worked for Republicans yet had respect among Democrats. In a sense, his lower profile better served the needs of the organization. Dine had been unceremoniously dumped in 1993 after making remarks that were thought insensitive to Orthodox Jews, and Neal Sher, his successor, had had a rough three-year tenure. It seemed to be a good time to take a deep breath. However, AIPAC found itself thrust on the front pages again in 2003 and 2004 when the FBI launched an investigation following allegations that top AIPAC officials had passed along to Israel classified State Department information about Iran.

Whether ultimately proven or not, the charges are redolent of the old "dual loyalty" canard, an aroma that does not easily disperse in the political atmosphere of the nation's capital.

In a profound if paradoxical way, the September 11, 2001, attack on America strengthened the relationship between Israel and the United States. With the terrorist attacks in New York and Washington, DC, Americans now experienced directly what the Israelis had themselves been shouldering for decades. Pro-Israel advocacy was energized by mutual anguish and loss. For others, however, the linkage was found not in shared victimization but in joint complicity. In a painful and in some ways puzzling reversal, Israel and the United States were branded by many around the world as co-collaborators in a failed global policy that led to the occupation of Arab and Muslim lands – by the United States in Afghanistan and Iraq, and by Israel in the territories. Thus, in a grim and grotesque way, cataclysmic world events conspired to demonstrate the common interests of the United States and Israel – the very assumption upon which AIPAC has built its program for over more than half a century.

[Lawrence Rubin (2nd ed.)]

AMERICAN JEWESS, monthly magazine published between April 1895 and August 1899. It was the first English-language periodical intended for American Jewish women. Indicative of newly emerging public identities for Jewish women, the *American Jewess* offered health, household, and fashion tips; discussion of women's demands for synagogue membership; early expressions of American Zionism; short fiction; and reflections on the propriety of women riding bicycles. Rosa Sonneschein, the creator and editor of the *American Jewess*, was a Hungarian immigrant who divorced her rabbi husband in St. Louis. Her successful participation in the Press Congress and Jewish Women's Congress that were both part of 1893's World's Columbian Exposition in Chicago inspired her to create the *American Jewess*.

Like the *National Council of Jewish Women, which also emerged from the Jewish Women's Congress, the *American Jewess* was intended to represent the aspirations of America's prosperous and acculturated Jewish women who believed that the national and religious aspects of their identity were not in conflict. Thoroughly American and thoroughly Jewish, the "American Jewess" felt fully at home in her overlapping worlds of American and Jewish culture. Working initially from Chicago and later from New York, Sonneschein echoed NCJW's calls for female synagogue membership and leadership. Through her magazine, she was able to offer the first sustained critique, by a Jewish woman, of gender inequities in Jewish worship and organizational life. In addition, by publishing a veritable portrait gallery of locally prominent Jewish women (often those serving their communities as NCJW officers), Sonneschein altered expectations of what American Jewish leaders should look like. Male and female authors within the magazine offered differing views on Jewish women's public roles within the Jewish and general communities, but all were engaged in making sense of new collective and individual identities for women.

At its height, the magazine claimed a circulation of 31,000. Deflected by both business and health setbacks, however, Sonneschein yielded control to an unidentified group of publishers in the summer of 1898. Despite Sonneschein's continued contributions as a correspondent, the publication suffered from the loss of her editorial vision and energy. When the new publishers were unable to revive the magazine's financial fortunes, the *American Jewess* shifted from a monthly to a quarterly publication in 1899; it concluded its run with a "valedictory" issue in August 1899.

BIBLIOGRAPHY: J. Rothstein, "The American Jewess," in: P.E. Hyman and D. Dash Moore, *Jewish Women in America* (1997), 39–42.

[Karla Goldman (2nd ed.)]

AMERICAN JEWISH ARCHIVES (AJA), archives founded in 1947 by the historian Jacob Rader Marcus (1896–1995) on the Cincinnati campus of the Hebrew Union College-Jewish Institute of Religion. Marcus established the AJA in the aftermath of the European Holocaust, when American Jews inherited a primary responsibility of preserving the continuity of Jewish life and learning for future generations. The AJA functions as a semi-autonomous organization to collect, preserve, and make available for research materials on the history of Jews and Jewish communities in the Western Hemisphere, primarily in the United States. The term "history" is construed in its broadest aspect to embrace data of a political, economic, social, cultural, and religious nature.

In its collections, the AJA attempts to assemble data describing the American Jew, both as a Jew and as an American. In this sense, the AJA probably possesses the largest collection of source materials found anywhere documenting the history of the Jewish community of a country. Important accessions to the collection are listed annually in the *American Jewish Archives Journal* and in the successive volumes of the *National Union Catalogue of Manuscript Collections*. The AJA began with a small assortment of congregational and societal minute books and a few collections of private papers. By the dawn of the 21st century, it contained more than 12,000 linear feet of manuscripts and archival records.

The collection includes the papers of famous Reform rabbis such as Isaac Mayer *Wise, David *Philipson, and David *Einhorn; scholars Trude *Weiss-Rosmarin, Horace M. *Kallen, and Maurice *Samuel; scientists and physicians Abraham *Flexner and Robert C. Rothenberg; lawyers and politicians Anna M. *Kross, Samuel Dickstein, and Fanny E. Holtzmann; and philanthropists and Jewish leaders Louis *Marshall, Jacob *Schiff, Felix *Warburg, among many others. The holdings also include documents and letters of prominent colonial and Civil War era Jews such as Aaron *Lopez, Raphael J. *Moses, Judah P. *Benjamin, and the *Gratz and *Franks families. In its collections are the records of district and local B'nai B'rith lodges, women's synagogue auxiliaries, and organizations such as the American Jewish Alternatives to Zionism, the Intercollegiate Menorah Association, the World Union for Progressive Judaism, the American Council for Judaism, and the Socialist Labor Party of America. The records of the New York office of the World Jewish Congress (WJC), one of the AJA's largest archival holdings, contain data relating primarily to the WJC's activities during and after World War II.

In 1998, the AJA was designated as the official repository of the historical records of the Union for Reform Judaism (formally the Union of American Hebrew Congregations). These materials compliment the records of the Hebrew Union College, the Jewish Institute of Religion, and the combined Hebrew Union College-Jewish Institute of Religion as well as the records of the Central Conference of American Rabbis.

The AJA is divided into several departments: manuscripts and typescripts, "nearprint," photographs, indices, publications, and programs. The "nearprint" collection subsumes all ephemeral material in the vast zone between letters and books: throwaways, news releases, broadsides, mimeograph announcements and advertisements, newspaper and magazine clippings, brochures, etc. The collection's broad recorded tape holdings consist of over 6,500 cassettes of oral histories, lectures, religious services, and music. In addition, a photograph collection of well over 15,000 images is used by scholars, publishers, filmmakers, among others, to illustrate books, articles, movies, and television programs. All manuscript collections have been catalogued; indices have been made of important 19th-century magazines like *Sinai, Israel's Herold, Occident, Deborah,* and *Menorah Monthly.* One of the AJA's most important publications is the *American Jewish Archives Journal* (est. 1948), which appears semi-annually. The institution has also published a wide-ranging series of monographs, including Malcolm H. Stern's *Americans of Jewish Descent* (1960), which marked a milestone in the study of American Jewish genealogy. This monumental volume was updated and revised in 1991, appearing under the title *First American Jewish Families: 600 Genealogies, 1654–1988.* An online version of Stern's classic text is available on the institution's website (www.AmericanJewishArchives.org). The AJA also offers a series of enrichment programs for scholars, educators, and the public at large.

Closely associated with the American Jewish Archives is the American Jewish Periodical Center (AJPC), which microfilms all American Jewish serials to 1925 with selected periodicals after that date. AJPC catalogues have been published; microfilm copies of all listed entries are available on interlibrary loan.

Jacob R. Marcus directed the American Jewish Archives from its founding in 1947 until his death in 1995, when the institution was renamed The Jacob Rader Marcus Center of the American Jewish Archives. Gary P. Zola became the second director of the American Jewish Archives in 1998.

[Gary P. Zola (2nd ed.)]

AMERICAN JEWISH COMMITTEE (**AJC**), oldest Jewish defense organization in the United States, established in 1906 "to prevent the infraction of the civil and religious rights of Jews, in any part of the world." It was formed as one response to the search for a basis upon which a central representative organization of American Jews could be built and as a direct outgrowth of concerns about conditions in Czarist Russia, especially the 1905 Kishinev pogrom. The Committee initially consisted of a small group drawn from the established German-Jewish community, who had migrated in large numbers to the United States beginning in 1820. They were well established and viewed their purpose as being able to mobilize American Jews to respond to matters of concern. Its founders included Jacob *Schiff, Mayer *Sulzberger, Louis *Marshall, Oscar *Straus, and Cyrus *Adler, men who represented the prominent German stratum within the Jewish community, and who, out of a sense of noblesse oblige, combined philanthropic activities and *hofjude* ("court Jew") diplomacy on behalf of their fellow Jews. The Committee was their attempt to guard against the rise of what they considered to be more radical popular agencies based on mass membership and employing extensive publicity. Oligarchic in design, the Committee – literally a "committee" – limited its membership to 60 American citizens (expanded by 1931 to 350), with offices in New York, and remained a small group for many years. AJC was self-selected, and had a sense of the "elitism" of the German-Jewish community, then the regnant Jewish population in America.

Much enlarged after 1943, the AJC developed into a highly-professional organization in which the leadership have played the critical role in decisionmaking, and the agency has been an effective voice on intergroup and, in recent decades, in public policy issues. The AJC has traditionally had a special interest in ethnicity, pluralism, and Jewish family life, in Israel and the Middle East, and in a broad range of interreligious affairs, and is significantly active in these areas. In recent years with the perception of declining antisemitism and full acceptance of Jews into American society, the AJC's agenda has expanded beyond matters of "defense" to include questions of Jewish "continuity" deemed essential after the 1990 Jewish population survey.

During the 1960s and 1970s, under the stewardship of executive leaders John Slawson and especially Bertram Gold, the AJC resembled not a single agency but a collection of related "fiefdoms," each directed by a leader in his respective field, who collectively contributed to the shaping of the contemporary community relations agenda: Rabbi Marc Tanenbaum in interreligious relationships; Yehuda Rosenman in Jewish communal affairs; Milton Himmelfarb, who shaped AJC's research agenda and who edited the *American Jewish Year Book*; Hyman *Bookbinder, the highly-visible director of AJC's Washington office, who was instrumental in shaping the agency's public affairs agenda.

The AJC has since the early 1980s undergone a necessary process of redefinition of mission and function within the community. This process culminated in 1990, with David Harris as the new executive director – this following a period of institutional and financial instability, in which there were four chief executives within a very few years – with the AJC turning aggressively toward activity in the international arena, positioning itself as an "international diplomatic corps for the Jewish people." The American Jewish Committee's joining the *Conference of Presidents of Major American Jewish Organizations in 1991 signified more than a symbolic affiliation; the AJC, by its membership in the Presidents Conference (the designated spokesman of the American Jewish community to the American administration on Israel and other international issues), asserted that international affairs now had primacy on the AJC's agenda.

The plight of Russian Jewry before World War I prompted the AJC's strong defense of a liberal American immigration policy. The AJC contributed to the defeat of a literacy test requirement for immigrants in 1907 and 1913 by lobbying, propaganda, and publicity. In 1911 the Committee conducted a successful campaign for the abrogation of the Russo-American treaty of 1832. Not only did the AJC object to the Russian discrimination against the entry of American Jews into Russia, which it considered a violation of the treaty, but it hoped that by its abrogation Russia would inevitably be compelled to free her own Jews.

On the outbreak of World War I, the American Jewish Committee sparked the organization of the American Jewish Relief Committee, which set up a central relief fund for Jewish war victims. Opposed to the idea of a democratic and nationalist American Jewish movement presenting the Jewish demands to the Paris Peace Conference in 1919, the Committee joined the first *American Jewish Congress under pressure of public sentiment. However, the minority rights secured for Jewry in the new, succession states of Europe were largely the result of the work of Julian *Mack, Louis Marshall (who served as AJC president from 1906–29), and Cyrus Adler who operated as individual intercessors in Paris. The Committee welcomed the *Balfour Declaration but underscored the provision that it would in no way prejudice the liberties of Jews in other lands. Louis Marshall's post-war correspondence with Chaim Weizmann led in 1929 to an enlarged *Jewish Agency composed of Zionists and non-Zionists. The AJC's stance was a "non-Zionist" one until the creation of the State of Israel in 1948.

During the 1920s the Committee centered its attention on the United States. It fought the popular "Jew-Communist" charge circulated in the infamous "Protocols of the Elders of Zion" and further propagated in Henry Ford's *Dearborn Independent.* Marshall, as president of the Committee, formulated the terms for Ford's retraction in 1927. The approach of the Committee, both strategically and tactically, differed sharply from that of the American Jewish Congress, which was more confrontational and which relied – especially after 1945 – on litigation as a primary vehicle for social action. AJC's approach reflected the Louis Marshall idea that discreet lobbying would best serve the interests of American Jews. This non-confrontational strategy reflected the fear that AJC would be perceived as a "Jewish lobby" with interests at odds with those of other Americans.

The rise of Nazism led to intensified activities on two fronts. In an effort to ameliorate the situation of German Jewry, the American Jewish Committee applied pressure upon the Roosevelt administration, the Vatican, the League of Nations, and even individual German officials. The objective of halting the Nazis by an aroused public opinion failed, and Committee members turned increasingly to plans of rescue and emigration for German Jews. The outbreak of the war halted independent operations, leaving the fate of Jewry contingent upon the Allied war effort. Upon learning of the mass murders, the Committee with other American organizations staged protest meetings and appealed for concrete assistance from the *Bermuda Conference on Refugees (1943). The Committee also cooperated in the efforts of the *War Refugee Board.

Simultaneously, the Committee fought the alarmingly sharp rise in organized antisemitism in America, with an emphasis on education and "prejudice-reduction" programs. In developing new techniques both to measure and to influence general and Jewish opinion, the Committee discarded the traditionally apologetic Jewish reaction to antisemitism and asserted and demonstrated that antisemitism is a device to undermine the foundations of democratic society. The Committee also investigated the operations of the virulent hate groups and disclosed their connections with the Nazi regime. The AJC pioneered an approach to combating antisemitism in the communities, using as a model the idea that every Jewish community in the U.S.A. needed to have a "volunteer fire brigade" countering antisemitism. In 1941 the AJC and the *Anti-Defamation League joined forces in the Joint Defense Appeal, to raise funds for both agencies' domestic programs.

While the American Jewish Committee joined the Zionists in protesting British curtailment of immigration into Palestine as a result of the British White Paper, it denounced the concept of "Diaspora nationalism" inherent in the programs of the American Jewish Congress and *World Jewish Congress. It opposed the Zionists' Biltmore *Program of 1942 and, in protest against Zionist tactics, left the *American Jewish Conference in 1943. It hoped that the future of Jewry would be secured by universal recognition of human rights to be protected by the United Nations; and it lobbied in 1945 at the San Francisco Conference, at which the charter for the United Nations was prepared, for an international commitment to that principle. By 1946 the Committee realized that the problem of the displaced persons could be solved only by the creation of a Jewish state, and it cooperated with the Zionists in pushing the cause of Palestine partition. After 1948 the Committee filled a dual function with respect to the State of Israel; it worked consistently to insure American sympathy and diplomatic aid, and by agreement with Israeli statesmen, it officially kept Israel's interests distinct from those of Diaspora Jewry. This dynamic was exemplified in the 1950 "entente" between Israeli Prime Minister David Ben-Gurion and AJC President Jacob Blaustein, following reports that Ben-Gurion had called for large-scale immigration to Israel by American Jewish youth; Ben-Gurion acknowledged that American Jews "have only one political attachment, to America," and in effect admitted that the "ingathering of exiles" as a central Zionist principle did not apply to American Jewry.

The American Jewish Committee also assumed a role in several extended projects relating to the Holocaust: prosecution of Nazi war criminals, material restitution by Germany to the Jewish community, and rehabilitation of Jewish cultural life within Europe. The Committee concentrated in the postwar period on combating the persecution of Jews within the Soviet orbit; it was active in disclosing the character of Kremlin-inspired antisemitism in documented form. The eruption of antisemitism in two other areas, the Muslim countries and South America, involved the Committee in tasks of relief and emigration with respect to the former, and self-defense with respect to the latter.

After World War II the Committee expanded markedly in size and function. A chapter plan adopted in 1944 slowly changed the oligarchic cast and elitist control of the organization. The AJC's strategic approaches to participating in litigation as a vehicle for achieving its goals underwent a marked change as well in the post-war years. In its early years the AJC, parting company from the Anti-Defamation League, did promote advocacy against anti-immigration measures. But the Committee had long believed that litigation was confrontational and would damage the constructive relationships that Jews had built up in the interfaith arena. Louis Marshall's view was that individuals, not groups, were constitutionally protected from prejudicial action. (The ADL, conversely, believed that Jews had every right to oppose the insult of group defamation.) Taking upon itself the obligation of strengthening the foundations of a pluralistic democratic society, the Committee took an active interest in the rights and liberties of non-Jews as well as Jews. The AJC's strategy of working with diverse non-Jewish organizations, especially in the Christian religious community, reflected the Committee's concerns both with legal matters (such as the separation of church and state) and social relations. A turning point came in 1943 with the appointment of John Slawson as AJC executive, who believed that, consistent with the AJC tradition of viewing rights for Jews as part of the larger struggle for rights for all minorities, AJC needed to be transformed into a vibrant civil rights agency. From 1947 AJC actively participated, through litigation, educational campaigns, and community projects, in the struggle of the blacks for equal rights. Work to break down the barriers in education, housing, employment, and public accommodations led to pioneer efforts against anti-Jewish discrimination in clubs, fraternities, and the "executive suite." The American Jewish Committee's focus on human relations resulted in new approaches to intergroup cooperation and intercultural education. In that area it labored successfully for the revision of prejudiced teachings about Jews in Christian textbooks and for the historic declaration on the Jews approved by the *Vatican Council in 1965. The Committee consistently emphasized the need for research in the behavioral sciences to guide it in plotting its action program. It sponsored the multivolume *Studies in Prejudice and Other Sociological Studies*. The watershed volume *The Authoritarian Personality* (1950) emphasized the psychological, rather than the socioeconomic, forces at work in group prejudice.

Through surveys of American Jewish and general communities, and through conferences and other programmatic initiatives, the AJC has also explored new ways to understand intergroup dynamics and to strengthen Jewish identity within the United States. The annual *Survey of American Jewish Public Opinion*, conducted by the Market Facts agency, provides valuable data for social scientists and policymakers. Numerous studies on a range of issues have emerged from the AJC over the past 40 years.

In 2005 the AJC had a membership of approximately 150,000 people organized in 33 chapters around the United States. Operating in 2005 on a budget of approximately $37,000,000 – the AJC's budget in 1979 was $8 million, on par with the Anti-Defamation League – the agency maintains offices in Brussels, Berlin, Geneva, and Jerusalem, and has a presence in Paris, Bombay, and Warsaw, in addition to its New York headquarters.

The Committee's orientation has long been that of a thoughtful and deliberative organization. Indeed, it traditionally viewed itself as being the "think tank" of the Jewish community. In addition to its regular sponsorship of a range of studies and conferences, an influential periodical, **Commentary*, is produced under the AJC's auspices, with a completely independent editorial policy. (*Present Tense*, a bimonthly, ceased publication in the early 1990s.) Since 1900 the AJC has published the annual *American Jewish Year Book*, which over the years has become the "document of record" for American Jewry.

BIBLIOGRAPHY: N. Schachner, *The Price of Liberty* (1948); M.D. Waldman, *Nor by Power* (1953). **ADD. BIBLIOGRAPHY:** J.A. Chanes, "The Voices of the American Jewish Community," in: *Survey of Jewish Affairs 1991* (1991); N.W. Cohen, *Not Free to Desist: The American Jewish Committee, 1906–1966* (1972); G. Ivers, *To Build a Wall: American Jews and the Separation of Church and State* (1995); S. Svonkin, *Jews Against Prejudice: American Jews and the Fight for Civil Liberties* (1997).

[Naomi W. Cohen / Jerome Chanes (2nd ed.)]

AMERICAN JEWISH CONFERENCE, representative American organization established in 1943 at the initiative of B'nai B'rith to deal with the problems of Palestine and the European Holocaust. Originally composed of representatives of all major Jewish groups and delegates from local Jewish communities, the Conference was given direction from Zionist bodies which sought a pro-Zionist declaration by a body representing American Jewry as a whole. Such a declaration was overwhelmingly adopted at its New York assembly in August 1943. As a result, the American Jewish Committee seceded from the Conference. Nevertheless, the organization submitted a series of pro-Zionist statements to official national and international bodies and waged a public relations campaign until its dissolution in 1949.

AMERICAN JEWISH CONGRESS (AJCongress), one of the central agencies in American Jewish community relations. The origins of the American Jewish Congress, founded in 1918, provide an important lesson in the dynamics of American Jewry. The AJCongress was established by a group that felt dissatisfaction with the *American Jewish Committee. This group, largely of East European origin, felt that the "aristocratic" German-Jewish leadership of the Committee was a self-appointed, self-perpetuating body with no mandate from American Jewry, and that the AJC was paternalistic in its dealings with East Europeans. The debate, largely between East European and German Jews and between Zionists and anti-Zionists, was primarily over the establishment of a congress that would represent American Jewish interests at the peace conference following World War I. The result was an ad hoc "congress" that would act as an "umbrella" for Jewish groups and represent Jewish interests. Institutionally, the American Jewish Congress was an outgrowth of the first American Jewish Congress, which assembled in Philadelphia in December 1918. A written agreement entered into by a number of organizations stipulated that the Congress was to dissolve as soon as it fulfilled its task of formulating a postwar program of the Jewish people, named a delegation to the Peace Conference in Versailles, and received its report. This agreement was implemented at the second and last session of the Congress in Philadelphia in 1920. However, some delegates from religious, Zionist, and fraternal organizations, and from *Landsmannschaften*, reassembled the next day under the chairmanship of Stephen S. *Wise and laid the foundation for the present American Jewish Congress, which was fully organized in 1928. The initial constituency of the American Jewish Congress was mainly Zionist, other voices coming into the body following the 1928 reorganization. In sum, while the American Jewish Committee and other organizations wanted the Congress to go out of business – and indeed it did formally dissolve itself in 1920 – the pressure for a permanent representative organization resulted in the formation of the present Congress, which came into being in 1922, originally as a council of agencies. (The AJCongress evolved into a membership organization in the 1930s.)

The American Jewish Congress began with two goals, which together molded the agency's subsequent ideology: providing humanitarian relief for European Jews in the aftermath of World War I and restoring a political Jewish presence in Palestine. The American Jewish Congress is the only community-relations agency that has been pro-Zionist throughout its history, and, on a number of issues (for example, a boycott of German goods in the 1930s), was arguably more representative of the views of the grassroots of American Jewry than the other "defense" and community-relations agencies. The early AJCongress leaders, Louis *Brandeis and Stephen S. *Wise, believed that only a democratic structure would make possible maximum participation in Jewish affairs by Jews, and not just by German Jews. Moreover, they fervently rejected the belief that Jews should not organize along ethnocentric lines, that Jews ought not restrict their lobbying efforts to "behind the scenes," and that Jews ought not engage in vigorous advocacy. The American Jewish Congress's view of pluralism was different from that of the American Jewish Committee or the *Anti-Defamation League: the AJCongress articulated the view that group and not individual interests needed to be advocated through appropriate organizational channels, and not merely through a few well-connected individuals. Stephen S. Wise especially offered a vision of American Jewry as both religious and ethnic, and, as a people possessing a distinct cultural history, needing openly to advocate its interests.

The AJCongress set goals related to American Jewish affairs, as well as to Palestine and the world Jewish scene. In the 1930s the AJCongress emerged as a leading force in the anti-Nazi movement and in efforts to aid the victims of Hitlerism. It sought to arouse American public opinion and to combat antisemitic manifestations in America. With the *Jewish Labor Committee, the AJCongress organized the Joint Boycott Council directed against German goods and services. The AJCongress was a founder of the short-lived General Jewish Council and of the National Community Relations Advisory Council (NCRAC, later National Jewish Community Relations Advisory Council, NJCRAC; now *Jewish Council for Public Affairs, JCPA).

In the mid-1930s the AJCongress led in the formation of the *World Jewish Congress, and shortly thereafter changed itself from a body representing organized groups into one based on individual membership. National Jewish organizations found that group affiliation alongside individual membership was untenable, and withdrew in order to form the American Section of the World Jewish Congress, of which the American Jewish Congress is also an affiliate.

The American Jewish Congress pioneered the use of law and social action as tools in combating prejudice and discrimination. This strategy – opposed by other Jewish communal groups, especially the American Jewish Committee and the Anti-Defamation League, which believed in quiet diplomacy and social relations – led to the creation in the 1930s of a number of "commissions" within the agency to examine the utility of litigative action to secure constitutional protection of equal rights. While the image of the AJCongress was one of a creative and aggressive advocate for Jewish interests, there was little substantive difference between the AJCongress and the ADL and AJC until after World War II.

In 1945 the AJCongress embarked on a program based on proposals submitted by Alexander H. Pekelis, in which the character of the agency was matured. Proceeding from the premise that the well-being of Jews depended on a liberal political and social climate, the AJCongress became increasingly involved in the promotion of social legislation and in activities designed to strengthen American democracy, eliminate racial and religious bigotry, and advance civil liberties. The AJCongress created its Commission on Law and Social Action (CLSA, a merger of two commissions, on discrimination and law and legislation) to implement this premise. The CLSA was created for the purpose of engaging the direct-action strategies that would encompass legislative and judicial measures to redress constitutional grievances of American Jews. The CLSA began implementing a vision of advocacy that had been fermenting within the AJCongress for some years. The underpinnings of CLSA advocacy were that the AJCongress ought not limit its work to attacking governmental infringements on the rights of Jews, but should fight discriminatory practices by large, private organizations, such as universities and corporations, and in doing so enter into coalition with like-minded groups such as the NAACP and the ACLU. Moreover, the direct-action method – law and litigation – would concentrate on fighting legal discrimination, and not prejudicial attitudes. This approach was a major departure from the strategic stances of the ADL and the AJC, both of which were committed to education programs and goodwill campaigns to educate Americans about Jewish interests, and to "quiet diplomacy" to redress grievances. Indeed, the creation of the CLSA created shock waves that reverberated throughout these American Jewish organizations. Contributing to the widening gap between the AJCongress's commitment to legal reform and the ADL's and AJC's preference for the "social-relations" model was the towering figure of Leo *Pfeffer, for many years the director of CLSA. Pfeffer's uncontested emergence as the Jewish community's chief strategist on church-state matters was accompanied by his exercise of almost complete authority over the Jewish community's litigation agenda.

CLSA activity over the years has led to the AJCongress having viewed itself as being the "lawyer" for the American Jewish community; indeed, it took a pioneering stance and leading role in Jewish community involvement in landmark Supreme Court cases on First Amendment (especially church-state separation) and civil rights issues. Major advocates such as Alexander Pekelis, David Petegorsky, and Will Maslow, and above all Leo Pfeffer, put their stamp on the AJCongress's agenda, and, beyond the agency, on American Jewish communal activities in the First Amendment and civil rights arenas.

In Zionist affairs the Congress has adopted a pro-Israel position, and indeed is the only American Jewish group (aside from Zionist organizations) to be pro-Zionist from its beginnings. It has organized annual "dialogues" in Israel with the participation of U.S. and Israeli intellectuals and has sponsored regular tours of its members to Israel. Nuanced changes with respect to Israel emerged under the professional leadership of Henry Siegman in the 1980s and 1990s, and the AJCongress veered sharply to the "left" on Israel-related issues, departing in some cases radically with consensus positions of the Jewish community on issues such as settlements and the peace process. Viewed as being relatively "liberal" on most social justice issues and on Israel-Palestinian matters, the AJCongress in the 21st century is re-examining a number of its stances, including its strong "separationist" position in church-state affairs.

The AJCongress is a membership organization with approximately 40,000 members; in 2005 it operated out of 15 chapters, with offices in Jerusalem and Paris, and a presence in Moscow and Brussels. Its 2005 budget was $6.5 million, raised from membership dues, independent campaigns, allocations from Jewish federations, and other sources. The small budget – relative to its sister defense agencies, the Anti-Defamation League and the American Jewish Committee – is deceptive. While many predicted the demise of the AJCongress during the 1990s – particularly after merger talks with the AJC broke down – and while it is clearly in the "second tier" of defense agencies, the AJCongress in the first decade of the 21st century is hardly moribund. The core of its operation, CLSA, is active, and the AJCongress has added an Office of Jewish Life. The AJCongress holds national conventions annually, and is administered by a Governing Council. The publications *Congress Monthly* and the scholarly *Judaism*, which for many years was one of the premier intellectual journals in American Jewish life, are produced under American Jewish Congress auspices.

BIBLIOGRAPHY: American Jewish Congress, *Reports… to the National Convention* (1949–51); idem, *Confidential Congress Reports* (1943–44); *American Jewish Congress, What It Is and What It Does* (1936); *Fortnightly Newsletter* (1959–61). **ADD. BIBLIOGRAPHY:** G. Ivers, *To Build a Wall: American Jews and the Separation of Church and State* (1995); S. Svonkin, *Jews Against Prejudice: American Jews and the Fight for Civil Liberties* (1997); J.A. Chanes, "The Voices of the American Jewish Community," in: *Survey of Jewish Affairs 1991* (1991); M. Fommer, "The American Jewish Congress: A History," Ph.D. dissertation, Ohio State University (1978).

[Jerome Chanes (2nd ed.)]

AMERICAN JEWISH HISTORICAL SOCIETY, scholarly organization founded in 1892. An interest in the Jewish experience on the American continent was brought into a formal framework with the founding of the Society on June 7, 1892, in New York City.

The need to collect and preserve the records of the native Jewish population and their forebears, as well as those of subsequent Jewish immigrants, became the serious concern of Abram S. *Isaacs, Bernhard *Felsenthal, Leo N. Levi, and, especially, Cyrus *Adler, then of the United States National Museum. To study American Jewry required research materials and thus it was necessary to begin a serious collection of books, manuscripts, pamphlets, periodicals, newspapers, and historical memorabilia and objects of art. The Society's first president Oscar S. *Straus declared at the initial meeting of the American Jewish Historical Society, "Every nation, race, and creed, which contributed toward the building of this great continent and country, should from motives of patriotism gather up its records and chronicles, so that our historians may be able to examine and describe the forces of our national and political existence." In 1966 the objectives of the Society were restated as "… the collection, preservation, exhibition, publication, and popularization of material of every kind having reference to the settlement, history, and life of Jews on the American continent, and the promotion and encouragement of research in, and the study of, Jewish history in general, and particularly in its relation to American Jewish history, and in connection with the causes and nature of Jewish emigration from various parts of the world to this continent."

For over half a century the American Jewish Historical Society was housed in the buildings of the Jewish Theological Seminary of America in New York City. In 1968, after a few years in rented quarters in the same city, it moved to its own building on the campus of Brandeis University in Waltham, Mass.; the new building was financed by the bequest of Lee Max *Friedman, the Society's fourth president. The holdings of the Society consist of the collections and writings of some of the pioneers of Jewish historical research, such as A.S.W.

*Rosenbach, Max J. *Kohler, George Alexander *Kohut, Philip *Cowen, Samuel Oppenheim, Jacques Judah *Lyons, Bernhard Felsenthal, N. Taylor Phillips, and Leon Huehner, as well as the theater and music collection of Abram Kanof.

The Society published 58 volumes of its *Publications*, which became a quarterly with volume 38, and assumed the title *American Jewish Historical Quarterly* with volume 51. Selected studies from these publications were reprinted in *The Jewish Experience in America* (5 vols. (1969), ed. by A.J. Karp). The Society's official publication is now called *American Jewish History*. The contents of this journal for the years 1893–1979 are available on ADAJE, an electronic repository of digitized American Jewish periodicals. The Society's quarterly newsletter is called *Heritage*. The Society also issues a monograph series, *Studies in American Jewish History*, and the *American Jewish Communal Histories* series. Each spring it sponsors American Jewish History Week; it also aids in the arrangement of exhibitions of American Jewish history and the publication of various bibliographies and literature. The Society's presidents have included Oscar S. Straus, Cyrus Adler, A.S.W. Rosenbach, and Lee Max Friedman and, more recently, Salo W. *Baron, Abraham Kanof, Bertram W. *Korn, Jacob R. *Marcus, Leon J. Obermayer, David de Sola *Pool, Abram Vossen Goodman, and Sidney Lapidus.

BIBLIOGRAPHY: I.S. Meyer, in: *Journal of Jewish Bibliography*, 4, nos. 1–2 (1943), 6–24; American Jewish Historical Society, *Report of Organization* (1892); Appel, in: JSOS, 23 (1961), 3–20; N.M. Kaganoff, *A Preliminary Survey of the Manuscript Collections found in the American Jewish Historical Society* (1967).

[Isidore S. Meyer]

AMERICAN JEWISH JOINT DISTRIBUTION COMMITTEE (known as JDC or **The Joint**), independent, non-political American Jewish relief and welfare organization dedicated to providing both emergency aid and long-term assistance to individual Jews and Jewish communities throughout the world outside North America. In 2004, after 90 years of service, JDC was operating in over 60 countries, from the former Soviet Union and Eastern Europe to South America, Asia, North Africa, and the Middle East. Nearly one in 10 Jews outside Israel and the United States and one out of four in Israel were benefiting from JDC programs.

In World War I

JDC was founded in 1914 shortly after the outbreak of World War I to send aid to the Jews of Palestine and Eastern Europe who were in danger of starvation. The first call for help came in a telegram sent in August 1914 by United States Ambassador to Turkey Henry *Morgenthau to prominent American Jewish leader Jacob *Schiff, requesting $50,000 for the Jews of Palestine. Subsequent pleas for help from Jewish communities in Eastern Europe led to the formation of both the Central Relief Committee by American Orthodox Jews and the American Jewish Relief Committee by prominent German-American Jews. On November 27, 1914, the two groups agreed to coordinate the distribution of relief shipments to Jews overseas within a common framework – the Joint Distribution Committee of American Funds for the Relief of Jewish War Sufferers – under the chairmanship of Felix M. *Warburg. The socialist People's Relief Committee joined them in 1915. The diversity of the three groups comprising the JDC ensured that JDC would assist Jews of every religious and political persuasion. By the end of World War I, JDC's leaders had concluded that rescue and relief to Jews in need would not be sufficient. JDC should also undertake to rebuild Jewish communities in Eastern Europe destroyed by the war. Thus, Rescue, Relief and Reconstruction began to emerge as the threefold mission of JDC.

During the course of World War I, JDC raised more than $16,000,000 (equivalent to $236,000,000 in 2005) for relief supplies. These funds were distributed overseas by local committees in Europe and Palestine.

Interwar Period

Immediately following World War I, in coordination with the American Relief Administration, JDC sent convoys of trucks with food, clothing, and medicines to Jewish communities in Eastern Europe which had been devastated by the war and by the subsequent regional conflicts and pogroms. Teams of JDC representatives brought in these supplies and established soup kitchens to ward off starvation. The situation in Poland and Russia at that time was still unstable and private militias roamed the countryside. In 1920 a Red Army militia murdered two JDC workers, Rabbis Israel *Friedlander and Bernard *Cantor.

At the same time that immediate relief needs were being addressed, JDC turned its attention to the rebuilding of Jewish communities in Eastern Europe. In the area of health care, JDC financed the repair of damaged Jewish hospitals, provided medical equipment and supplies, and sent more than 100 doctors, social workers, and public health experts from the United States, under the direction of Dr. Boris Bogen, to institute health programs and train local medical personnel. In 1921, JDC initiated the founding of a local medical society in Poland, *TOZ (Towarzystwo Ochrony Zdrowia Ludnosci Zydowskiej, Society for Safeguarding the Health of the Jewish Population) to supervise these medical activities. JDC also supported *OZE, the Russian Jewish Health Organization.

More than 200,000 Jewish children in Eastern Europe had been orphaned by the war. To care for them and for children whose parents could not support them, JDC established orphanages, kindergartens, and summer camps, and provided food supplements and medical and dental treatment for children in need. In 1923 JDC founded *CENTOS (Federation for the Care of Orphans in Poland), an orphan care group that functioned in Poland until World War II.

One of JDC's priorities was the restoration of Jewish religious and cultural life in Eastern Europe. JDC rebuilt community institutions such as synagogues and ritual baths, which had been destroyed during the war, and provided aid to Jewish schools and yeshivot.

To foster economic recovery in Jewish communities in Eastern Europe, JDC joined together with the Jewish Colonization Association in 1924 to found the American Joint Reconstruction Foundation. The Foundation set up a network of cooperative credit institutions – *loan kassas* – that provided low-interest loans to Jewish craftsmen and small businessmen in towns and villages throughout Eastern Europe. Interest-free loans were granted to the poorer families. In cooperation with *ORT (the Society for Crafts and Agricultural Labor among Jews in Russia, later known as the Organization for Rehabilitation through Training), JDC established vocational training courses for young adults. These measures eased the economic crisis for hundreds of thousands of Jewish families.

In Palestine, once urgent postwar relief needs had been met, JDC began to implement economic, social, and cultural reconstruction programs. In the area of medical care, JDC funded the Malaria Research Unit, which helped combat malaria in Palestine. JDC helped finance the American Zionist Medical Unit sent to Palestine by *Hadassah in 1921, the forerunner of the Hadassah Medical Organization in Palestine.

To care for some 5,000 children orphaned as a result of World War I, JDC established the Palestine Orphan Committee, which supervised these children from 1919 to 1929 until they could become self-supporting. In the area of education, JDC supported schools and yeshivot and provided funds to the newly established Hebrew University of Jerusalem.

In 1922, JDC, in cooperation with the Jewish Colonization Association, established the Central Bank of Cooperative Institutions, which financed agricultural projects in Palestine such as the developing citrus industry. JDC helped establish the Palestine Economic Corporation in 1925 to promote economic development in Palestine, provided subsidies to the Rutenberg Hydroelectric Association, and created a Kuppat Milveh which granted small loans. JDC spent more than $8 million in Palestine during the years 1914–32.

One of JDC's best-known and most innovative projects, the Agro-Joint, was created by JDC during the 1920s in the newly established communist Soviet Union. In 1924, with the consent of the Soviet government, JDC set up the American Jewish Joint Agricultural Corporation (Agro-Joint) to promote agricultural settlement among Jews. Agro-Joint's purpose was fully supported by the Soviet authorities, who favored redirecting Jewish economic activity from commerce to manual labor. Agro-Joint also sought to solve the problem of Jews who were left without a livelihood when the communists outlawed their professions as tradesmen or religious officials. Between 1924 and 1938, under the direction of Russian-born agronomist Dr. Joseph *Rosen (1877–1949), Agro-Joint helped settle more than 100,000 Jews in agricultural colonies in the Crimea and the Ukraine.

In the late 1930s, however, the Soviet government under Stalin became increasingly suspicious of foreign organizations, and a number of Agro-Joint staff members were arrested and executed. In 1938, faced with growing hostility on the part of the Soviet authorities, Agro-Joint disbanded its operations in the Soviet Union. During World War II, the colonies established by Agro-Joint were overrun by the German armies and most of the colonists were murdered.

By the mid-1920s, JDC, which had been created as an ad hoc body, had begun to function as a major international Jewish relief organization. Some JDC leaders believed that with the basic relief and reconstruction of Jewish life in Eastern Europe under way, JDC's goals had been achieved and the organization should disband. This opinion was expressed again during the Depression years when JDC's income declined drastically.

However, recurring crises in Eastern and Western Europe and the continuing needs of Jewish communities in Palestine, the Soviet Union, and elsewhere showed the need for a permanent organization. In 1931, JDC was officially incorporated in New York State as the American Jewish Joint Distribution Committee.

The rise of Hitler in 1933 confronted JDC with new challenges. In addition to its reconstruction programs in Eastern Europe, JDC now provided support to the Jewish community of Germany, which became increasingly impoverished under Nazi rule. From 1933 to 1939, JDC spent $5 million in Germany, subsidizing medical care, Jewish schools, welfare programs, and vocational training. With the German invasion of Austria and its incorporation of Czechoslovakia in 1938 and 1939, JDC extended its support to the Jewish communities in those countries as well. Following the rise of Hitler, JDC transferred its European headquarters from Berlin, where it had been since 1922, to Paris.

JDC's primary efforts from 1933, however, were directed toward assisting the tens of thousands of German, Austrian, and Czech Jews who sought desperately to emigrate from German-occupied countries and to find safe havens abroad. JDC helped the emigrants with travel expenses, provided them with food, shelter, and medical care when they were stranded en route, assisted them in obtaining berths on ships and places on trains, helped them in obtaining visas and paid landing fees so that they could enter countries of refuge. In 1939, when the German ship *St. Louis*, with more than 900 Jewish passengers fleeing from Germany aboard, was denied permission to land in Cuba, JDC arranged for the passengers to be accepted by England, Holland, Belgium, and France, so they would not have to return to Germany. Most passengers, not only those in England, survived.

After the Dominican Republic offered to take in refugees at the *Evian Conference in 1938, JDC founded the Dominican Republic Settlement Association (DORSA), which established an agricultural settlement for refugees in Sosua. In 1941, when 2,000 Polish Jewish refugees in Lithuania received visas to Japan, JDC subsidized their travel expenses. When over 1,000 *"illegal" immigrants bound for Palestine were stranded in Kladovo, Yugoslavia, in 1940, JDC supported them for an entire year while they waited for a ship to take them to safety. The ship did not arrive before the German invasion of Yugoslavia in 1941, and the Germans subsequently murdered most of the refugees.

By 1939, JDC had helped more than 100,000 refugees emigrate from Germany. In 1940, JDC was assisting refugees in transit in more than 40 countries in Eastern and Western Europe, Asia, and Latin America.

In World War II

After the outbreak of World War II, until the United States entered the war, JDC could still function legally in German-occupied countries. In Poland, for example, JDC opened shelters and soup kitchens for the thousands of Jewish refugees who crowded into the cities. In the spring of 1940, JDC shipped tons of foodstuffs to Poland for Passover. JDC continued to support hospitals, child-care centers, and educational and cultural programs in occupied Poland. After the establishment of the Warsaw ghetto in November 1941, JDC-Warsaw supported the soup kitchens, the Jewish hospitals, and the educational and cultural programs in the ghetto. In Cracow, JDC supported the Jüdische Soziale Selbsthilfe (JSS), which distributed food, clothing, and medicines to ghettos and labor camps in the area of the *General gouvernment* (German designation for occupied Central Poland). Of the three million Jews in Poland in 1941, some 600,000 were receiving assistance from JDC.

With the entry of the United States into the war in December 1941, JDC – an American organization – could no longer operate legally in enemy countries. In countries such as Poland and France, local JDC representatives now had to operate underground. Furthermore, JDC could no longer transfer funds to enemy countries because U.S. State Department regulations prohibited such transfers and stipulated that a U.S. Treasury Department license must be obtained for any transfer of funds overseas, even to neutral countries. In response, JDC authorized local representatives in German-occupied countries to borrow money locally from wealthy Jews on the promise of repayment by JDC after the war (*loans après*).

JDC representatives responded in different ways to the regulations imposed by the American government. The JDC administration in New York, headed by Chairman Edward M.M. Warburg, advocated strict adherence to the State Department guidelines. However, the overseas professional staff, headed by Morris Troper, the director of European Affairs, and his deputy and successor, Dr. Joseph Schwartz, sought greater flexibility. Schwartz, in particular, who headed JDC's European headquarters in Lisbon from 1940 until the end of the war, supported illegal rescue and resistance activities in German-occupied Europe. As a rule, those in the United States were more sensitive to the requirements of American regulations and would not jeopardize the JDC's standing. Those on the ground in Europe were confronted more directly with the desperation of the situation and were more willing to employ extra-legal means.

In June 1940, shortly before the Germans occupied Paris, Troper and Schwartz left Paris and transferred JDC's European headquarters to neutral Lisbon. There, Schwartz leased every available ship to enable the thousands of refugees arriving in Lisbon to proceed to safe havens in North and South America. Schwartz provided funds to legal and illegal Jewish organizations in France, including the Jewish underground resistance organization L'Armée Juive, whose treasurer, Jules Jefroykin, became the JDC representative in France in 1941.

In neutral Switzerland Saly *Mayer, the local JDC representative, channeled JDC funds to Jews throughout Occupied Europe and, on Schwartz's instructions, smuggled funds to France as well. Schwartz authorized the use of funds smuggled into France by couriers, or raised by means of loans, to support 7,000 Jewish children in hiding in France and to smuggle over 1,000 children to Switzerland and Spain. In 1944, JDC spent more than $1 million on rescue in France alone.

After the United States' entry into the war, the JDC representatives in the Warsaw ghetto – Isaac Giterman, David Guzik, Leib Neustadt, and the historian Emanuel *Ringelblum – continued their activities underground. By means of loans, they secretly supported the soup kitchens, the "house committees" that provided food and educational programs for children, the underground schools and newspapers, and the underground cultural activities. In 1943, Guzik used JDC funds to help finance preparations for the Warsaw ghetto revolt.

In Shanghai, where JDC was providing daily meals to 8,000 impoverished Jewish refugees from Central and Eastern Europe, the United States' entry into the war in December 1941 threatened the continued existence of the soup kitchens. Laura Margolis, the JDC representative in Shanghai, persuaded the Japanese, who had occupied Shanghai, to allow her to continue operating the soup kitchens by means of loans from members of the local Jewish community. Interned as an enemy alien in February 1943, Margolis was later released in a prisoner exchange.

JDC relief and rescue activities continued during 1943–44. JDC sent relief parcels to concentration camps by way of Lisbon, and to Polish Jewish refugees in the Soviet Union via Teheran. JDC helped finance the activities of the War Refugee Board (WRB), established by the United States Government in 1944. Through the WRB, JDC transmitted $100,000 to Swedish diplomat Raoul *Wallenberg to facilitate the rescue of tens of thousands of Jews in Hungary.

With the limited resources at its disposal, JDC made valiant efforts to provide relief and rescue to the Jews of Europe during the Holocaust period. From a welfare agency engaged in temporary relief and reconstruction primarily in Eastern Europe and Palestine, it emerged as the only Jewish organization involved in immigration, refugee aid, and rescue operations in virtually every part of the globe. JDC was not able to save the overwhelming majority of Europe's Jews, but there is no doubt that hundreds of thousands of Jews who escaped from Nazi Europe, owed their lives to JDC.

Early Postwar Period

During the war, JDC's income was limited. Expenditures fell from $8.4 million in 1939 to $5.7 million in 1941, and totaled only $52 million for the entire war period. Following the war, there was a dramatic increase in JDC income – from $25 million in 1945 to more than $70 million in 1948. In 1947, more than one half the survivors in Europe – some 700,000 Jews – received help from the JDC.

During the years from 1945 to the early 1950s, JDC cared for over 200,000 Jews in Displaced Persons camps in Europe, providing them with food supplements, medical care, and clothing, and setting up schools and religious and cultural programs. JDC food shipments to Romania and Hungary saved hundreds of thousands of Jews there from starvation. Throughout liberated Europe, JDC aided in the care of child survivors, in the tracing of relatives, in the reestablishment of Jewish religious and cultural life, and in the immigration of survivors to North and South America, Australia, and countries in Western Europe.

Under the influence of Joseph Schwartz, JDC supported the *Beriḥah, the "illegal" movement of Jews from Eastern to Western Europe, and from there to Palestine. Thousands of Jewish *"illegal" immigrants interned by the British on Cyprus were cared for by JDC, which provided medical, educational, and social services to the Jewish detainees.

During the years following World War II, JDC invested heavily in the reconstruction of Europe's Jewish communities. With the aid of funds from the *Conference on Material Claims Against Germany, JDC helped rebuild synagogues, hospitals, schools, and community centers in France, Italy, Belgium, Holland, and other countries. In 1949, JDC founded the Paul Baerwald School of Social Work in Paris to help war-torn Europe's survivors rebuild their lives. In France, JDC helped establish the Fonds Social Juif Unifié (FSJU) the chief fund-raising body of the French Jewish community. In the 1950s and 1960s, JDC helped the French Jewish community meet the challenge of absorbing more than 100,000 Jewish immigrants to France from Morocco, Tunisia, and Algeria.

JDC became involved in North Africa itself during World War II, when camps for Jewish refugees were established in Morocco. From the 1950s on, JDC has supported educational, social, medical, and welfare programs for Jews in Morocco, Tunisia, Algeria, Ceuta, and Melilla. JDC supports medical programs conducted by OSE (Oeuvre de Secours aux Enfants) and educational programs conducted by the *Alliance Israélite Universelle, Lubavitch, Ozar Hatorah, and ORT. Beginning in 1949, JDC established similar programs in Iran.

After the establishment of the State of Israel in 1948, JDC subsidized the immigration of hundreds of thousands of Jews to the fledgling state from Europe and from countries in North Africa and the Middle East. In 1949 JDC financed Operation Magic Carpet, the airlift of some 50,000 Yemenite Jews from Aden to Israel, and Operation Ezra and Nehemia, which brought thousands of Iraqi and Kurdish Jews to the Jewish state.

Many new immigrants to Israel, among them Holocaust survivors, were handicapped or suffering from chronic illnesses. The young state of Israel was not equipped to provide the long-term care they needed. In 1949 therefore, JDC in cooperation with the Jewish Agency and the Israeli government, founded *MALBEN to provide institutional care and social services to handicapped and chronically ill immigrants. MALBEN, which from 1951 was financed solely by JDC, established hospitals, clinics, and old-age homes and fostered the development of private and public organizations in Israel for the care of the handicapped. From 1957, MALBEN cared for veteran Israelis as well as new immigrants. In 1958 JDC established the Paul Baerwald School of Social Work at The Hebrew University of Jerusalem to address the social problems of the new Jewish state.

At the end of 1975 JDC transferred its MALBEN institutions to Israeli government authorities. In 1976, JDC established JDC-Israel and moved its Israel headquarters from Tel Aviv to Jerusalem. Henceforth, JDC-Israel would develop social service programs for populations in need in Israel through partnerships with Israeli government and non-profit agencies.

In Eastern Europe

Dramatic changes in JDC activities during the second half of the 20th century occurred in Eastern Europe and the Soviet Union. Immediately following World War II, JDC was active in East European countries, helping survivors and aiding in the reconstruction of Jewish communities. After the Communist takeover in Eastern Europe, JDC was expelled from Poland, Romania, and Bulgaria in 1949, from Czechoslovakia in 1950, and from Hungary in 1953. Only in Yugoslavia was JDC permitted to continue its activities.

In 1957, JDC was readmitted to Poland to care for 19,000 repatriates from the Soviet Union but was expelled again in the wake of the 1967 Six-Day War. That same year, however, JDC was readmitted to Romania, where it supported Jews in need and provided kosher food and religious services through the Federation of Jewish Communities of Romania (FEDROM). In August 1967, Charles *Jordan, JDC's executive vice chairman, was murdered in Prague under mysterious circumstances.

In 1980, through the efforts of JDC's Executive Vice President Ralph I. Goldman, JDC resumed direct operations in Hungary, and in 1981, in Czechoslovakia and Poland. JDC concentrated initially on aid to elderly Holocaust survivors in these countries and on the establishment of kosher canteens, support for cultural activities, and the provision of religious books and supplies. JDC subsequently expanded its activities to include educational programs for children and the development of local Jewish community leadership.

With the opening of the gates to Jewish emigration from the Soviet Union in the 1970s and 1980s, JDC set up transit centers for the transmigrants in Vienna, and in Rome, Ostia, and Ladispoli. To help absorb over 840,000 immigrants who arrived in Israel from the Soviet Union during the 1980s and 1990s, JDC established vocational training courses, youth programs, and special projects for the immigrants, particularly those from Bukhara and the Caucasus.

Ethiopian Jewry

With the arrival of Ethiopian Jews in Israel through Operation Moses in 1984–85, JDC established vocational training courses, health education projects, family counseling, and youth projects to aid in their absorption. In the 1980s JDC initiated medical and agricultural assistance programs in Ethiopia and, in 1990–91, provided food and medical and social services to Ethiopian Jews waiting in Addis Ababa to immigrate to Israel. JDC played a major role in facilitating Operation Solomon, the airlift of some 14,000 of these Ethiopian Jews to Israel in 1991. Among the innovative programs designed by JDC for the Ethiopian immigrants was PACT (Parents and Children Together) – begun in 1998 in partnership with American Jewish Federations and Israeli agencies – which supports early-childhood education for Ethiopian-Israeli preschoolers.

In Israel

During the 1970s, 1980s, 1990s, and 2000s, JDC-Israel continued its assistance to weak and disadvantaged populations in Israel. Programs for the care of the elderly were initiated and developed by ESHEL, the Association for the Planning and Development of Services to the Aged in Israel, founded in 1969 in partnership with the Israeli government. Research in the areas of health, aging, immigration, children and youth, and disabilities was carried out by the Brookdale Institute of Gerontology and Human Development, established in 1974 in partnership with the Israeli government and renamed the Myers-JDC-Brookdale Institute in 2003. During the 1970s, JDC took part in the development of a network of community centers in Israel and, in 1976, initiated the Joseph Schwartz Program to train senior staff for these centers. Through the Center for Social Policy Studies in Israel, established in 1982 and renamed the Taub Center in 2003, JDC provides data on economic and social trends in Israel to national decision makers. ELKA, the Association for the Advancement and Development of Manpower in the Social Services, founded in 1984, conducts training courses for managers in Israel's civil service.

Beginning in the 1950s, JDC placed special emphasis on programs for children in Israel. JDC supported voluntary agencies for handicapped children including AKIM for the mentally retarded, MICHA and SHEMA for the deaf and hearing-impaired, and ILAN for children with neuro-muscular disorders. JDC-Israel's Mifneh program, created in 1987, encouraged potential school dropouts to remain in school, while subsequent programs introduced innovative teaching methods into Israeli schools. During the 1990s, JDC-Israel helped found a network of emergency centers for abused children and, in 1998, together with the government of Israel and the UJA-Federation of New York, JDC established Ashalim to coordinate the development of programs in Israel for children at risk. In 2002, in the wake of the outbreak of terror attacks in Israel, JDC-Israel, with funding from the United Jewish Communities/Federation Israel Emergency Campaign, provided summer camps for 300,000 Israeli children.

Since the 1990s, JDC has placed increasing emphasis on programs to promote employment among Arabs, the ultra-Orthodox, and the handicapped. In 2005 JDC launched a partnership with the Israeli government to promote employment among these and other underemployed populations.

Throughout its history, JDC has recognized the importance of Jewish tradition and education. JDC was an important source of support for yeshivot in Europe and Palestine during the 1920s and 1930s. Following World War II, JDC played a major role in rebuilding yeshivot, which had been destroyed during World War II, and in supporting Jewish educational institutions in Jewish communities throughout the world.

In the Former Soviet Union

In 1988, after an absence of 50 years, JDC returned to the Soviet Union. During its official absence, JDC had provided aid to Soviet Jews in need by indirect means. In 1988, however, Ralph Goldman negotiated JDC's resumption of open operations in what was soon to become the Former Soviet Union (FSU).

JDC faced a double challenge in the FSU: how to reawaken Jewish identity in a Jewish population that had been cut off from the religious, cultural, and intellectual sources of Jewish life for 70 years, and how to create a Jewish community infrastructure where none existed. To strengthen Jewish knowledge and identity, JDC sent Judaica libraries (sets of Jewish texts in Russian translation) to Jewish communities in the FSU. By 2005 there were more than 180 libraries in over 100 communities. JDC encouraged the development of university courses on Jewish subjects, subsidized the Moscow Cantorial Academy and the Mekor Chaim Judaic Studies educational center in Moscow, and provided Russian translations for the Jewish prayer book, the Passover *Haggadah*, the Pentateuch, and other Jewish texts. JDC created educational materials for Jewish children, including a Russian-language version of *Sesame Street*, subsidized Jewish schools, and organized summer camps. JDC sent ritual items and kosher food for the holidays, and organized communal *seders* and other religious activities.

To meet the needs of indigent elderly Jews, many of them Holocaust survivors, JDC established community-based welfare centers called Heseds to supply kosher food and medical care. By 2005, there were 174 Hesed centers serving 233,000 elderly Jews across the FSU. In addition to providing food, medical assistance, and home care, these centers distributed fuel for heating and blankets for the cold Russian winters.

To foster community development in the FSU, JDC established a network of 184 Jewish community centers, sent Russian Jewish activists to leadership training courses in Israel, and helped establish 27 Hillel centers for Jewish students and young adults. In late 2002, JDC began creating Jewish family services modeled on those in the United States. By the end of the 1990s, JDC's program in the FSU was the single largest JDC program, with local offices in 15 cities across the FSU.

Additional Activities

JDC's programs since the 1990s address the changing needs of Jewish communities all over the world. In Western Europe, JDC has concentrated on strengthening community development and fostering inter-community cooperation. JDC supports the European Council of Jewish Communities and the European Union of Jewish Students, and in 1994 established the European Center for Jewish Leadership (LEATID-EUROPE).

In Eastern Europe, JDC has concentrated on strengthening Jewish education and Jewish identity among Jewish youth. In Poland, JDC conducts seminars at the summer camp at Srodborow and has established a resource center for educational materials in Warsaw. JDC supports the Association of Holocaust Children in Poland, whose 500 members were hidden as children during the Holocaust. In Hungary, JDC subsidizes the Anne Frank High School in Budapest and supports the Ronald S. Lauder Foundation/American Jewish Joint Distribution Committee International Summer Camp at Szarvas. The camp hosts 2,000 youngsters per year from 25 countries in central and Eastern Europe and the Former Soviet Union.

JDC continues to see its role as providing rescue and relief in emergency situations. The outbreak of fighting in Yugoslavia in 1992 led JDC to undertake rescue efforts there. Through its connections with the Yugoslav welfare agency La Benevolencija, and its good relations with all sides in the war, JDC was able to send food and medications for distribution in beleaguered Sarajevo. As fighting intensified, JDC organized an airlift from Sarajevo and then a series of bus convoys from the city, which brought over 2,000 individuals (about half of them non-Jews) to safety. JDC aided in the immigration of the refugees to Israel and elsewhere, and in rebuilding the former Yugoslavia's remaining Jewish communities.

The economic crisis in Argentina in 2000 led to an emergency JDC welfare initiative to assist tens of thousands of Jews who were suddenly impoverished. At its peak in 2003, this initiative provided relief to over 36,000 people. JDC had been active in South America since the 1930s, when JDC sought havens there for Jewish refugees from Europe. JDC has supported Jewish education and community programs in Argentina and in other communities, such as Chile and Uruguay. In 1987 JDC established the Latin America Training and Research Center for the Development of Jewish Communal Leadership (LEATID), and in 1991 renewed its activities in Cuba after an easing of restrictions there.

Changes in the political climate have enabled JDC to resume activities in a number of Arab and Moslem countries. JDC was able to provide direct assistance to Jews in Egypt from 1982, to aid the Jews in Yemen from 1990, and, in the 1990s, played a pivotal role in the departure of most of the remaining 4,000 Jews from Syria. In 1992, JDC resumed activities in Turkey. JDC has developed an extensive program in India and assists the small numbers of Jews in other Asian countries.

JDC receives a major part of its funding for overseas activities from the North American Jewish community.

JDC's global activities include non-Jews as well as Jews. In 1986, JDC established the International Development Program (IDP), to meet the urgent needs of populations around the world following natural or other disasters. JDC-IDP has provided aid to 50 countries worldwide, including Armenia and Turkey following earthquakes, and Rwanda, Bosnia, and Kosovo following civil war, and has established a Palestinian-Israeli healthcare program in the West Bank and Gaza. It provided relief and reconstruction to South Asian communities devastated by the tsunami in 2004.

In the 21st century, JDC continues to define its mission as Rescue, Relief, and Rehabilitation. In the pursuit of these goals, JDC seeks to strengthen Jewish identity, to build Jewish communities, and to preserve the Jewish cultural heritage.

BIBLIOGRAPHY: H. Agar, *The Saving Remnant: An Account of Jewish Survival* (1960); Y. Bauer, *My Brother's Keeper: A History of the American Jewish Joint Distribution Committee 1929–1939* (1974); idem, *American Jewry and the Holocaust: The American Jewish Joint Distribution Committee 1939–45* (1981); idem, *Out of the Ashes: The Impact of American Jews on Post-Holocaust European Jewry* (1989); M. Beizer and M. Mitsel, *The American Brother: The "Joint" in Russia, the USSR and the CIS* (2005); O. Handlin, *A Continuing Task: The American Jewish Joint Distribution Committee 1914–1964* (1964); S. Kadosh, "Joint Distribution Committee," in: W. Laqueur, *The Holocaust Encyclopedia* (2001); J. Neipris, *The American Jewish Joint Distribution Committee and its Contribution to Social Work Education* (1992); E. Somers and R. Kok (eds.), *Jewish Displaced Persons in Camp Bergen-Belsen 1945–1950: The Unique Photo Album of Zippy Orlin* (2004); T. Szulc, *The Secret Alliance: The Extraordinary Story of the Rescue of the Jews Since World War II* (1991).

[Sara Kadosh (2nd ed.)]

AMERICAN SEPHARDI FEDERATION (ASF). The American Sephardi Federation was founded in 1973. In 2002 it affiliated with Sephardic House to create one, stronger organization. With its main office in New York City, and regional offices in Miami, Seattle, and Los Angeles, the American Sephardi Federation with Sephardic House is a national Jewish organization dedicated to ensuring that the history, legacies, and traditions of the great Sephardi communities throughout the world be recorded, remembered, and celebrated as an integral part of the Jewish heritage. The Sephardim were the first Jews to settle in the Western Hemisphere, and the ASF/SH seeks to educate the broader American Jewish and non-Jewish communities about the unique history and values it perpetuates, while revitalizing a sense of affiliation and commitment among the younger Sephardi generations. ASF/SH endeavors to foster understanding and cooperation with significant members of the non-Jewish community of the countries where Sephardim lived in peace and harmony for so many generations.

The activities of the American Sephardi Federation with Sephardic House include a Sephardi library, publications, and cultural and educational programming dealing with the Sephardi experience, including the International Sephardi Film Festival, the only permanent Sephardi exhibition gallery, its unique publication, the *Sephardi Report,* and a scholarship program for Sephardi studies. Since its arrival at the Center for Jewish History, New York, which is the joint home of YIVO, The Leo Baeck Institute, Yeshiva University Museum, and the American Jewish Historical Society, the archival holdings and library of ASF have been enriched with valuable records of personal and community history.

[Esme E. Berg (2nd ed.)]

AMERICAN SOCIETY FOR JEWISH MUSIC (ASJM), organization founded in New York in 1974. Its precursors included the *Makhon Eretz Yisraeli le-Mada'ei ha-Musikah* (MAILAMM; 1932–39), established in 1932 by Miriam Zunzer and which, in 1934, became affiliated with the Hebrew University of Jerusalem; and the Jewish Music Forum (1939–63), created by Abraham Wolf Binder and which reemerged as the Jewish Liturgical Music Society of America (1963–74). Evolving from the latter, the ASJM earned increasingly greater international stature under the leadership of Albert *Weisser, its first president, who envisioned much wider goals for the society – expansion into folk, popular, and art music as well as the publication of a scholarly journal, *Musica Judaica* (issued almost annually since 1975), which he and Israel J. *Katz coedited. The ASJM's membership includes cantors, composers, educators, musicologists, performers, and interested laymen. The society presents a variety of annual public programs, sponsors seminars and workshops at which scholars and composers discuss and analyze works in progress, and organizes concerts, recitals, and conferences relating to cantorial issues and other music of Jewish interest. Upon Weisser's untimely death, Paul Kavon succeeded him as president (1982–91), followed by Jack Gottlieb (1991–97), Hadassah Markson (1997–2003), and Michael Leavitt (2003–). Following Katz as editor of the journal were Neil Levin and Alexander V. Knapp (vols. 11–13), Irene *Heskes (vol. 14), and Israel J. Katz and Arbie *Orenstein (vols. 15–).

BIBLIOGRAPHY: M. Leavitt, "President's Greetings," in: *Musica Judaica*, 17 (2003–04), iv–vii.

[Israel J. Katz (2nd ed.)]

AMERICAN ZIONIST MOVEMENT (AZM), umbrella organization for American Zionist organizations. AZM is composed of 21 Zionist membership organizations and agencies. It was created to be a programming, educational, and information arm for American Zionism. AZM is the successor organization of the American Zionist Emergency Council (organized in 1939), the *American Zionist Council (1949), and the American Zionist Federation (May 1970). Each successive organization was generated by changing political and social circumstances in the United States and the Middle East.

Established in 1993, AZM set out to heighten the profile and relevancy of organized Zionism in the U.S. through greater activism on a wide range of political and social issues of concern to American Jews. Like all members of the WZO, AZM's unifying principles are those of the Jerusalem Program.

The American Zionist Movement has its own mandate for action in the United States. It has set our own goals and objectives to involve more Jews in Zionism and to take an activist posture on the Jewish scene. AZM defends Israel's cause with vigor and confidence. It offers the next generation of young Zionists opportunities for leadership and action in the Zionist cause; it attempts to link young Jewish students confronting the problems on American campuses today and to strengthen the links between Jewish faculty and students. It promotes and enhances creative Jewish continuity and aims at forging stronger bonds between American Jews and Israel that result from personal contact with Israel.

AMÉRY, JEAN (Hans (Chaim) Maier); 1912–1978), Austrian writer and essayist. Born in Vienna, Améry started his career as a bookseller and thereafter studied philosophy and literature in Vienna. His first publications appeared under the name Hanns Mayer; together with Ernst Mayer, he published the journal *Die Bruecke* in 1934. In 1935 he wrote *Die Schiffbruechigen*, a novel favorably reviewed by Thomas Mann and Robert Musil. In this work Améry created an alter ego: the novel's protagonist, Eugen Althager, an unemployed Jewish intellectual. In 1939 he fled Austria for Belgium and was detained in South France in 1940. A year later Améry illegally returned to Belgium and became a member of the Communist resistance movement. Améry was captured by the Gestapo in 1943 and sent to Auschwitz, Buchenwald, and later Bergen-Belsen. After being liberated from Bergen-Belsen in 1945 he returned to Brussels. It was in Brussels where his wife died, and where he started writing political and literary essays under his pseudonym Hans Mayer for various Swiss and Dutch journals. After 1955 he published under his anagrammatic nom de plume Jean Améry, a name that symbolized his admiration for the humanitarian French ideals of liberty and equality. Known primarily for his essay writing, Améry was influenced by existentialism. He was particularly fond of the writings of Jean-Paul Sartre, whom he met in 1945. One of Améry's first essays was entitled *Tortur*. It described and analyzed his experiences under Nazi interrogations and in concentration camps. *Jenseits von Schuld und Suehne* was a survivor's testimony against the Nazi regime that railed against oblivion. With the help of Helmut Heissenbuettel, Améry published his most important texts commencing in the mid-1960s: *An den Grenzen des Geistes* (*At the Mind's Limits*, 1980), which depicted the limits of the intellectual's mind in the process of losing its basic quality of transcendence; *Ueber das Altern* (*On Aging*, 1994), and *Unmeisterliche Wanderjahre*. This trilogy was favorably received by intellectuals like Alfred Andersch and Elias Canetti, who praised it for the intersection of autobiographical and contemporary historical perspectives. Jean Améry's writing career also included works of fiction. His most famous literary work *Lefeu oder der Abbruch*, published in 1974, detailed the life of a Holocaust survivor. His final piece of fiction appeared in 1978 and bore the title, *Charles Bovary, Landarzt*. The subject of suicide appeared in his 1976 publication *Hand an sich legen. Diskurs ueber den Freitod* (*On Suicide*, 1999), and in 1978, Améry took his own life in a Salzburg hotel room.

Améry was a member of the *Akademie der Kuenste Berlin*, corresponding member of the *Deutsche Akademie fuer Sprache und Dichtung*, and a member of the German PEN-

Club. The *Jean-Améry-Preis*, an award for essay writing, was awarded for the first time in 1982.

BIBLIOGRAPHY: I. Heidelberger-Leonhard, *Jean Améry. Revolte in der Resignation* (2004); S. Steiner, *Jean Améry (Hans Maier)* (1996); S. Wolf, *Von der Verwundbarkeit des Humanismus: ueber Jean Améry* (1995); D. Lorenz, *Scheitern als Ereignis: der Autor Jean Améry im Kontext europaeischer Kulturkritik* (1991); *Text u. Kritik*, 99 (1988).

[Ann-Kristin Koch (2nd ed.)]

°AMERY, LEOPOLD CHARLES MAURICE STENNETT (Mauritz; 1873–1955), pro-Zionist British statesman. In 1917 Amery assisted Vladimir *Jabotinsky in obtaining official consent for the formation of the *Jewish Legion and, as assistant secretary to the war cabinet (1917–18), drafted one of the formulas which eventually became the *Balfour Declaration. From 1924 to 1929, when Amery was secretary of state for the colonies, Palestine enjoyed a peaceful period and in his memoirs, *My Political Life*, 3 vols. (1953–55), he takes pride in this achievement. As a member of Parliament, he fought the anti-Zionist policies of the British government and voted against the White Paper of 1939. In 1946 Amery testified in the same spirit before the Anglo-American Committee of Inquiry on Palestine. Amery's famous speech in the House of Commons in May 1940 helped to bring Winston Churchill to power as prime minister. In 1950 Amery was one of the first major British politicians to visit the new state of Israel.

Many years after Amery's death, historical research revealed that Amery's mother, Elisabeth Leitner (*née* Sapher or Sapier), was Jewish, a member of a prominent Budapest family which had converted to Protestantism about 1840 and whose members moved to Britain from about 1850 on. Amery had concealed his Jewish background all his life, while working in an influential way on behalf of Zionist causes. Amery's background made all the more mysterious the actions of his eldest son JOHN (1912–1945), who, during World War II, resided in Germany and tried to recruit British prisoners of war to fight for Germany against the Soviet Union. As a result, John Amery was hanged for treason in 1945. Amery's younger son JULIAN (1919–1996) was a Conservative member of Parliament from 1950 until 1992 and was a prominent minister in the Macmillan and Heath governments. He was given a life peerage in 1992 as Baron Amery of Lustleigh.

BIBLIOGRAPHY: J.B. Schechtman, *Vladimir Jabotinsky Story*, 2 vols. (1956–61), index; Ch. Weizmann, *Trial and Error* (1949), index. **ADD. BIBLIOGRAPHY:** W.D. Rubinstein, "The Secret of Leopold Amery," *Historical Research* (2000); A. Weale, *Patriot Traitors: R. Casement, John Amery and the Real Meaning of Treason* (2001); ODNB online.

[Oskar K. Rabinowicz / William D. Rubinstein (2nd ed.)]

AMES (Añes), 16th century *Marrano family living in the British Isles. GEORGE AÑES settled in London in 1521 but later returned to Portugal, where he died. In 1541 his wife and sons, FRANCISCO and GONSALVO, fled to England to escape the Inquisition. Francisco, soldier and administrator in Ireland, became mayor of Youghal. Gonsalvo (Dunstan) Añes (d. 1594), a successful merchant and financial agent, was purveyor to Elizabeth I and served as an intelligence agent, conveying secret mail on his ships. His eldest daughter, SARAH, married Roderigo *Lopez. Of his sons, JACOB settled in Constantinople and lived openly as a Jew; another, William, was an English soldier and intelligence agent. The English branch of the family became complete Christians.

BIBLIOGRAPHY: Wolf, in: JHSET, 11 (1924–27), 12–17; Roth, England, index.

[Vivian David Lipman]

AM HA-AREẒ (Heb. עַם־הָאָרֶץ; lit., "people of the land").

Bible

In biblical Hebrew, the signification of the term varies in accord with its context. (a) Generally, it denotes "population," whether Israelite (II Kings 16:15; 25:3; Ezek. 39:13; 45:22) or non-Israelite (Gen. 42:6 – of Egypt; Num. 14:9 – of Canaan; Ezra 4:4 – of the province of Judah). (b) In the plural (Heb. עַמֵּי־הָאָרֶץ/הָאֲרָצוֹת) it denotes foreign (= heathen) populations, e.g., of the world at large (Deut. 28:10; I Kings 8:43ff.) or of a specific country (Esth. 8:17), but more particularly, in post-Exilic texts, the natives in and about Palestine who threatened and harassed the returning Jewish exiles (Ezra 3:3; 9:11; 10:2; Neh. 10:29, 31–32). (c) Much debated is the meaning of the term in contexts referring to an operative element of the population (e.g., II Kings 11:18ff.; 21:24; 23:30; Jer. 34:19). In such contexts the term has been interpreted variously as an ancient Hebrew "parliament"; the landed nobility; the free, male, property-owning citizenry; and the like. Some representative body of the population is evidently intended, though as a general, rather than a specific term (cf. the vague "all the people of Judah" who enthroned King Azariah, II Kings 14:21).

[Moshe Greenberg]

Second Temple and Mishnah

Some scholars derive the term *am ha-areẓ* (in the singular) from the plural form found in Neh. 10:29, where it designates the heathen inhabitants of Palestine (Rabin, 61). The rabbinic use of the term, however, seems to derive from the Torah (Lev. 4:27), where it designates ordinary Israelite citizens. The Midrash (Sifra, ḥovah, parashah 7, 6–7) interprets the words *me-am ha-areẓ* to exclude the *nasi* (leader) and the *mashi'aḥ* (priest), on the one hand, and the apostate, on the other. Already here we can see that the term *am ha-areẓ* does not designate any specific group within the Jewish people. It merely refers to ordinary Jews, who are distinguished neither by any exceptionally positive (*nasi*, *mashi'aḥ*) nor by any exceptionally negative qualities (apostate). Contrary to the impression made by later rabbinic and post-rabbinic usage, the term, in its tannaitic beginnings, has no clear pejorative connotations. In Tosefta *Avodah Zarah* (3:10) *Simeon ben Nethanel (a disciple of Rabban *Johanan ben Zakkai) is mentioned as an example of an *am ha-areẓ*. In the (unpublished *genizah*) version of a previous *halakhah* (3:8) a scribe who is described as an *am ha-areẓ* is opposed to a scribe who is called an expert (*mumḥeh*). From this it seems that the term *am ha-areẓ* is semantically analogous to the term *hedioṭ*, also used in tannaitic literature in opposition to the *nasi*, the *mashi'aḥ*, and the *mumḥeh*. Like the term *hedioṭ*, it has no specific content of its own, but rather indicates the absence of some particular quality which is to be found only in some exceptional individual or group of individuals.

In the main stratum of tannaitic literature, the term *am ha-areẓ* is used regularly to refer to the ordinary Jewish population which did not belong to the religious and intellectual elites of the *ḥaverim* (companions) and *ḥakhamim* (sages). The *ḥaverim* were distinguished as a group by the observance of special restrictions, mostly concerning food. These restrictions fell into two categories: restrictions concerning tithes and restrictions concerning purities. The details of these restrictions, which also govern to a large extent the interaction between the *ḥaver* and the *am ha-areẓ*, are spelled out in different tractates in the Mishnah, especially *Demai* and *Toharot*. The *ḥakhamim* were an intellectual elite devoted to the study of Torah and committed to the notion that true piety and true godliness could only be achieved through the study of Torah and personal association with the *ḥakhamim*. This conviction is reflected throughout tractate *Avot*, especially in the famous statement (2:5): "The uncultivated man (*bur*) cannot be godfearing, nor can the *am ha-areẓ* be pious (*ḥasid*)." Here, the term *am ha-areẓ* primarily indicates the absence of education (parallel to "uncultivated"). The saying as a whole is directed against those who would attempt to achieve spiritual excellence (fear of God, piety), without the guidance of the sages and the discipline of their teachings. Another example of this criticism is found further on in *Avot* (5:10), where the *am ha-areẓ* is ridiculed for espousing a simplistic communism ("what's mine is yours and what's yours is mine"), in opposition to the enlightened communism of the *ḥasid*, who renounces selfish exclusivity over his own property while respecting the rights of the other ("what's mine is yours and what's yours is yours").

Since the term *am ha-areẓ* is used primarily in opposition to groups like the *ḥaverim* and the *ḥakhamim*, if we wish to define the *am ha-areẓ* further, we must examine the relationship between the *ḥaverim* and the *ḥakhamim*. On the one hand, they do not seem to be identical. On the other hand, they do not seem to be totally distinct. For example, in Tosefta *Demai* (2:13), we are told that even a disciple of a *ḥakham* needs to be officially admitted into the *ḥavurah*. On the other hand, a *ḥakham* is automatically considered a *ḥaver*. Similarly in Mishnah *Demai* (2:3) Rabbi Judah considers "service in the house of study" as one of the formal conditions for acceptance into the *ḥavurah*. Therefore scholars who have suggested that the *am ha-areẓ* "with respect to tithes and purities" and the *am ha-areẓ* "with respect to Torah study" were separate and distinct phenomena have probably introduced an artificial distinction which is not borne out by the sources.

This connection between ritual restrictions and devotion to Torah study in the ideal definition of the rabbinic elite finds confirmation in an earlier stratum of religious tradition still preserved in tannaitic literature. Tosefta *Demai* 2:11 may be one of those rare cases in which the later tannaitic sources preserve a halakhic tradition from the late Second Temple period relatively intact. There are three considerations which point in this direction. First, this *halakhah* uses terminology otherwise unknown in rabbinic sources: *kenafayim* (wings) as a category designating a group of people. Second, this *halakhah* is the subject of a dispute between the House of *Shammai and the House of *Hillel (2:12), and therefore apparently is older than the earliest literary level of the main stratum of tannaitic literature. Finally, scholars (Lieberman, Rabin) have pointed out similarities between the content of this *halakhah* and certain parallel passages in the Dead Sea Scroll *Manual of Discipline*.

This Tosefta sets down two stages for acceptance to the *ḥavurah* – the first is called "wings" (*kenafayim*) and the second "purities" (*toharot*). In the following *halakhah toharot* seems to be further subdivided into drinks and clothing. As indicated, these phenomena find close but not exact parallels in the *Manual of Discipline*. The term *kenafayim* itself has received special attention (Rabin, 19). Various interpretations have been suggested, almost all based on later rabbinic sources. On the other hand, this very term is found in the *War Scroll*, and Yadin in his edition (p. 176) suggests that it refers to the auxiliary forces which are positioned in the wings, i.e. on the periphery. If this is the meaning here, then this Tosefta represents an early precedent (and an earlier terminology) for the two-tiered structure of the rabbinic elite described in the main stratum of tannaitic literature (Mish. Demai 2:2–3). According to the Mishnah, between the *ḥaverim* (defined by *toharot* restrictions) and the *am ha-areẓ*, there was a third intermediate group – the "trustworthy" (*ne'emanim*) – who observed the restrictions concerning tithes, but not *toharot*.

The community described in the *Manual of Discipline*, while defined formalistically by a rigorous discipline of purity rules and a primitive communism (cf. the *ḥasid* of *Avot* 5:10), was at the same time deeply committed to Torah study and other forms of personal piety. It is clearly impossible to isolate the intellectual and spiritual content of membership from the formalistic ritual and economic conditions of membership. So also the attempt to separate the *ḥaverim* and the *ḥakhamim* into two separate and distinct ideal elites may be an arbitrary abstraction, posited by scholars to deal with apparent contradictions between different rabbinic sources that will be dealt with below.

Developments in Later Talmudic Literature

We possess no sources which can testify directly to the attitudes or practices of the *am ha-areẓ*. Moreover, the *am ha-areẓ* in all likelihood did not exist as an organized or even an identifiable group. As a result, the varying rabbinic descriptions and testimonies which either describe or characterize the *am ha-areẓ* should be understood as reflecting variations in the self-perception and self-definition of the rabbinic elite. These differences may indeed reflect significant changes in the attitudes or practices of the *am ha-areẓ* themselves, but we have no way of either confirming or rejecting such an hypothesis.

How then do our rabbinic sources describe the relations between the rabbinic elite (*ḥaverim* and *ḥakhamim*) and the general community (*am ha-areẓ*)? Different answers emerge from different sources. Even within a given source, radically differing opinions may be expressed. Within tannaitic literature we find a strict approach which tends to exclude the *am ha-areẓ* almost totally from any significant social contact with the rabbinic elite. We also find within tannaitic literature a much more lenient, inclusive approach. Most early amoraic literature reflects this lenient, conciliatory attitude. In the later literary levels of the Babylonian Talmud, however, we find a new and radically different attitude. This attitude goes far beyond the strict approach found in early tannaitic literature, reflecting a new and virulent contempt and even hatred for the *am ha-areẓ*, going so far as to describe the *am ha-areẓ* as subhuman, as an animal – even less than an animal – who may be slaughtered without even the courtesy of a blessing (TB Pes. 49b). In order to define the place of this approach in the history of rabbinic tradition, it is necessary to take into account a methodological principle of talmudic criticism.

By now it is fairly well understood and accepted that the anonymous literary stratum of the Babylonian Talmud – the *stam ha-talmud* – often radically alters the original intent of the amoraic statements which form the foundations of the talmudic *sugya* (discussion). It is therefore crucial for the correct understanding of the development of the talmudic *sugya* to isolate the amoraic literary level and to interpret it in its own right before proceeding to examine the way in which the anonymous editors of the Talmud interpreted it. It is not so well known that the anonymous editors of the Babylonian Talmud often integrated their interpretive comments into the very fabric of the older traditions. In such cases, it is only possible to separate tradition from commentary by comparing the version of a tradition found in the Babylonian Talmud to an earlier or at least an independent version of the same tradition, found, for example, in the Tosefta or the Jerusalem Talmud.

Thus we find that in the Babylonian Talmud statements of *amoraim* who favored the lenient and conciliatory attitude toward the *am ha-areẓ* are reinterpreted by the *stam ha-talmud*, so that they now seem to reflect the strict and exclusionist approach. Older traditions which are either neutral toward or merely mildly critical of the *am ha-areẓ* are reformulated by the later editors of the Babylonian Talmud, thereby putting into the mouths of *tannaim* and early *amoraim* positions and attitudes that they never dreamed of, and which sometimes even stand in direct contradiction to their explicit statements as preserved in earlier Palestinian rabbinic traditions (Wald, *Pesahim III;* Wald, *Sin'ah ve-Shalom*).

Most historians who have written on this topic (see bibliography) have taken these traditions at face value, without seriously questioning their historical authenticity. In order to reconcile the blatant contradictions between different families of sources describing the same historical period (Palestine in the second to third centuries), some have posited a distinction between two different kinds of *am ha-areẓ* – the *am ha-areẓ* "with respect to tithes and purities" and the *am ha-areẓ* "with respect to Torah study." Others have attempted to assign these different traditions to different geographical locations, positing a special form of "Galilean" *am ha-areẓ*. Understanding these violently hate-filled traditions to reflect early Palestinian tradition, some have seen in them evidence of late Second Temple period class struggle, and others repercussions of the rise of Christianity. After determining, however, that this unique and particularly virulent strain of anti-*am ha-areẓ* polemic in all likelihood reflects a much later Babylonian tradition, it is possible to outline the development of the rabbinic traditions concerning the *am ha-areẓ* in a somewhat more straightforward fashion.

As stated above, within tannaitic sources we can detect two distinct tendencies. One reflects an almost separatist, even a sectarian, ethos. Shared meals are forbidden, not only between the *am ha-areẓ* and the *ḥaver*, but even between the *am ha-areẓ* and the *ne'eman* (Mish. Demai 2:2; Tosef. Demai 2:2, Rabbi Meir). One may not say a blessing, nor participate in a *zimun* (cf. Mish. Berakhot 7:1), nor answer amen to an *am ha-areẓ* who does not observe the rules of purity with regard to food (Tosef. Demai 2:22, 24). Marriage between *ḥaverim* and *amei ha-areẓ* are virtually banned (Tosef. Avodah Zarah 3:9, Rabbi Meir). A *ḥaver* who leaves the *ḥavurah* is treated as a traitor, and may never be readmitted (Tosef. Demai 2:9, Rabbi Meir), a view reflected also in the *Manual of Discipline* (VII, 22–25).

But there is also a more lenient view in tannaitic literature. For example, Rabbi Judah relates that a *ne'eman* may eat in the house of an *am ha-areẓ* without compromising his official status (Mish. Demai 2:2; Tosef. Demai 2:2). The Mishnah in *Berakhot* (7:1) states unequivocally that one may perform a *zimun* with one who has eaten *demai*, i.e., an *am ha-areẓ*. The sages mentioned in Tosefta *Avodah Zarah* 3:9 accept in principle that marriage between *ḥaverim* and *amei ha-areẓ* may be subject to some restrictions, but these restrictions are minimized as much as possible. Further on in the same source (3:10), another view (also referred to as of "the sages") totally rejects the assumption that there are any limitations whatsoever on marriage between a *ḥaver* and one who does not observe the rules of purity concerning food. To the extent that they recognize the *halakhah* transmitted above by Rabbi Meir, they interpret it as referring to marriage between members of the community at large and those few who "do not tithe their food" at all. Food which has not been tithed is considered *tevel*, and the punishment for eating it is "death by the hands of heaven." In the main stratum of tannaitic literature, the *am ha-areẓ* is only suspected of eating *demai*, not *tevel*. Therefore the position of the sages in Tosefta *Avodah Zarah* 3:10 removes all limitations on marriage between *ḥaverim* and *amei ha-areẓ* (as the term is ordinarily understood). This lenient view is reflected also in the anonymous position found in Tosefta *Demai* 2:16–17. Finally, in Tosefta *Demai* 2:9 Rabbi Judah seems to have heard the tradition which forbids readmission of *ḥaverim* who leave the *ḥavurah*, but limits it to those who by their deceitful behavior undermine their credibility. Rabbi Simeon and Rabbi *Joshua ben Korḥa reject this tradition in its entirety. All three of them, as opposed to Rabbi Meir, view the *ḥavurah* as a voluntary organization that one may openly leave if one wishes, without compromising eligibility for readmission in the future.

We find therefore two very different views of the rabbinic religious elite in tannaitic sources. One is separatist, exclusivist, unconditional, allowing for virtually no social interaction between insiders and outsiders. The other assumes a much larger degree of social interaction. According to this latter view, there are no prohibitions on sharing common meals, beyond the technical ones of assuring that the insiders' food has been properly tithed and prepared in accordance with the rules of purity. There are no insurmountable obstacles to marriage between insiders and outsiders, and perhaps no such limitations whatsoever. The elite is structured in a way which permits movement across the boundary lines which separate insiders from outsiders in both directions, without fear of recriminations.

These two views may represent competing tendencies, current during the end of the tannaitic period. On the other hand, the separatist position is found primarily in anonymous *halakhot* and in *halakhot* transmitted in the name of Rabbi Meir, and may reflect an older tradition whose roots lie in the sectarian atmosphere of the late Second Temple period. In any case, the more lenient, socially integrated view predominates in the later strata of tannaitic literature, as well as in the main body of Palestinian amoraic literature and in the early strata of the Babylonian Talmud. The situation begins to change in the fourth generation of Babylonian *amoraim*. Two examples will suffice: TB *Berakhot* 47b quotes a brief and anonymous **baraita*, which states: "One may not participate in a *zimun* with an *am ha-areẓ*." This *baraita* is probably a paraphrase of the anonymous *halakhah* found in Tosefta *Demai* 2:24, which concerns an *am ha-areẓ* who does not observe the rules of ritual purity. As stated above, this apparently contradicts the tendency of the *halakhah* in Mishnah *Berakhot* to permit a *zimun* not only with one who has eaten *demai* (= *am ha-areẓ*), but even with a Samaritan. *Abbaye (fourth generation Babylonian *amora*) accepted the strict opinion of the *baraita*. *Rava affirmed the lenient position of the Mishnah. He reinterpreted the *baraita* in line with the lenient position of the sages in Tosefta *Avodah Zarah* 3:10. By so doing, Rava limited the prohibition in the *baraita* to one who ate *tevel*, not *demai*. In Rava's view it is permitted to participate in a *zimun* with an *am ha-areẓ*, as that term is ordinarily understood.

Further on in the same passage, Rami bar Ḥama refused to participate in a *zimun* with Menashya bar Taḥlifa, because Menashya bar Taḥlifa did not "serve in the house of study." Mishnah *Demai* (2:3) lists "service in the house of study" as one of the formal conditions for acceptance into the *ḥavurah*, perhaps the only one still applicable in Babylonia. Rami bar Ḥama's actions therefore should be seen as putting into practice the strict position articulated by Abbaye. Thus it is not surprising that Rava again rejects this position. Rava's strong language is indicative of his vehement disapproval of Rami bar Ḥama's actions: "Rami bar Ḥama died [as a young man] because he refused to participate in a *zimun* with Menashya bar Taḥlifa!" If we relate only to the amoraic component of the passage we must conclude that in the fourth generation of *amoraim* in Babylonia the older tannatic or pre-tannaitic separatist or sectarian view was revived, first theoretically by Abbaye, then put into practice by Rami bar Ḥama. However, Rava (at least on the amoraic literary level) had the last word, rejecting Abbaye's theoretical position and condemning Rami bar Ḥama's actions.

Some time later, the *stam ha-talmud* added an additional interpretive layer to the end of the *sugya*, turning Rava's words on their head. According to the *stam ha-talmud* even Rava agrees that one may not participate in a *zimun* with one who does not "serve in the house of study," i.e. one who is not a member of the inner circle of the rabbinic elite in Babylonia. We are now to understand that Rami bar Ḥama was criticized for not participating in a *zimun* with Menashya bar Taḥlifa only because Menashya bar Taḥlifa actually did "serve in the house of study," and so was indeed an active adherent of the Babylonian rabbinic elite. Rami bar Ḥama foolishly and wickedly misjudged Menashya bar Taḥlifa, and for this he was punished. This interpretation clearly is not consistent with Rava's own position, and reflects a not uncommon phenomenon in the Babylonian Talmud: a minority view which is raised and rejected by the *amoraim* themselves is then adopted by the *stam ha-talmud*, and used to reinterpret the words of the *amoraim*.

A similar phenomenon occurs in TB *Pesaḥim* 49a. The Talmud relates a lively discussion between *amoraim* concerning the advisability of marriage between the families of *ḥakhamim* and *kohanim* (priests). Some *amoraim* are in favor, others against. Examples are given in favor and against. None of the *amoraim* and none of the examples even mention the topic of marriage to an *am ha-areẓ*. Nevertheless, the *stam ha-talmud* manages to reinterpret the entire passage such that all the *amoraim* agree that marriage between families of *ḥakhamim* and *kohanim* is unquestionably appropriate and advantageous, whereas marriage between families of *ḥakhamim* and *amei ha-areẓ* is an abomination. Here again the latest literary level of the Babylonian Talmud has resurrected an ancient tradition, presented in one source (Tosef. Avodah Zarah 3:9) as a minority position, explicitly rejected by the other sages there and simply ignored in another source (Tosef. Demai 2:16–17). It then reinterprets the words of all the *amoraim* appearing in the *sugya*, as if they all explicitly agreed with the notion that marriage to an *am ha-areẓ* is an abomination.

The evidence thus points to the latter half of the amoraic period in Babylonia as the time and the place in which ancient separatist traditions began to be revived, when rigid social boundaries preventing ordinary interaction between members of the rabbinic and social elite and "outsiders" began to form. It points also to the end of this period and the early post-amoraic period as the time in which these tendencies first gained the upper hand, at least in those circles responsible for the redaction of the Babylonian Talmud.

But, as indicated above, this later editorial approach did not limit itself merely to "reviving" authentic ancient positions, nor did it limit itself to augmenting the authentic statements of *amoraim* with editorial comments of its own. Two examples will suffice in order to clarify this point.

Tosefta *Avodah Zarah* 3:9 relates the following simple *halakhah*: "It is forbidden to give them [= *am ha-areẓ*] daughters [in marriage], irrespective of whether they are grown up, or still children – these are the words of Rabbi Meir." This *halakhah* probably provided the ideological foundation for the radical reinterpretation of the amoraic statements quoted in TB *Pesaḥim* 49a. In fact, on the very next page (49b) we find the following *baraita:* "Rabbi Meir used to say: Anyone who marries his daughter to an *am ha-areẓ* is as if he has bound her in front of a lion – just as a lion attacks and devours without the slightest bit of shame, so also an *am ha-areẓ* beats [his wife] and has intercourse [against her will] without the slightest bit of shame." Boiled down to its halakhic "essentials" this *baraita* corresponds exactly to the simple statement of Rabbi Meir found in Tosefta *Avodah Zarah* 3:9. But in its present form it reflects an interpretation which is quite unwarranted in the original context. Indeed most of the many extreme statements concerning the *am ha-areẓ* found in *Pesaḥim* 49b can be shown to be late Babylonian interpolations of earlier tannaitic and amoraic material (Wald, *Pesahim III*). Thus we read there: "Rabbi Samuel bar Naḥmani said in the name of Rabbi Jonathan: It is permissible to tear an *am ha-areẓ* open like a fish; Rabbi Samuel bar Yiẓḥak added: And from the back." When one compares these brutal lines to their original form and context in TB Ḥullin 21a, one can only conclude that these two *amoraim* never dreamed of the use to which some later anonymous editor would eventually put them. A similar process of tendentious reinterpretation and interpolation is evident in another important *sugya* (TB BB 8a), concerning Rabbi Judah ha-Nasi and his refusal to support an *am ha-areẓ* during a time of famine (Wald, *Sin'ah ve-Shalom*).

The present state of scholarship probably does not permit a convincing explanation for this radical turn of events toward the end of the talmudic period. It is clear that by the geonic period and the early period of the **rishonim*, most of the excesses of this late literary level were largely repudiated, (Alfasi, *Pesaḥim*, ed. Hyman, pp. 88–93, 327–34). It is possible that it reflects the internal social development of the Babylonian Jewish community, or perhaps the external influence of certain social changes which may have been going on in Sassanian society at the same time (*Cambridge History of Iran*, 3(1), pp. xl–xlii, 3(2), pp. 632–33).

[Stephen Wald (2nd ed.)]

In Later Times

The term came to designate a person without adequate knowledge of the Scriptures and of traditional Jewish literature and consequently one who is ignorant of the rules of Jewish ritual and ceremonial customs, as opposed to the *talmid ḥakham* ("disciple of the wise") or *ben Torah.* In common usage, *am ha-areẓ* is the equivalent of ignoramus or boor (pl.: *amaraẓim*).

In ḥasidic folktales the *am ha-areẓ* tends to mean a naive, but God-loving simpleton. God Himself "wishes his heart" (Sanh. 106b), because it is full of good intentions, and his prayer is more efficacious than that of many a learned scholar.

BIBLIOGRAPHY: BIBLE: M. Sulzberger, *Am-Haaretz in the Old Testament* (1909); M. Weber, *Das Antike Judentum* (1921), 30–31; S.E. Wuerthwein, *Der 'am ha'areẓ im Alten Testament* (1936); Nicholson, in: JSS, 10 (1965), 59–66; S. Talmon, in: *Beit-Mikra*, 31 (1967), 27–55. SECOND TEMPLE AND MISHNAH: L. Finkelstein, *Pharisees*, 2 (1962^3), 754–62 and index; Geiger, Urschrift, 121ff.; A Buechler, *Der galilaeische 'Am ha'Areṣ des zweiten Jahrhunderts* (1906); idem, *Political and Social Leaders... Sephoris* (1909), index s.v. *'Amha'areṣ*; Zeitlin, in: JQR, 23 (1932/33), 45–61; Klausner, Bayit Sheni, index; C. Rabin, *Qumran Studies* (1957), index; Kaufman Y., Toledot, 4 (1957), 183–5; Alon, Meḥkarim, 1 (1957), 148–76; Alon, Toledot, 1 (1958^3), index; 2 (1961^2), 80–83; Baron, Social 2, index; S. Klein, *Ereẓ ha-Galil* (1967^2). **ADD. BIBLIOGRAPHY:** S. Lieberman, *Texts and Studies* (1974), 200–7; A. Oppenheimer, *The 'Am Ha-Aretz* (1977); S. Wald, *Pesahim III* (2000), 211–39; idem, in: A. Bar-Levav (ed.), *War and Peace* (2005); J. Rubenstein, *The Culture of the Babylonian Tamlud* (2003), 123–42. FOLKFORE: Heller, in: HUCA, 4 (1927), 365–407; A. Scheiber, in: *Yeda Am*, 4 (1956), 59–61; Noy, in: *Maḥanayim*, 51 (1960), 34–35; Schwarzbaum, *ibid.*, 55 (1961), 116–22; S. Talmon, in: *Papers of the Fourth World Congress of Jewish Studies*, 1 (1967), 71–76.

AMIA (Asociación Mutual Israelita Argentina), organization of the Buenos Aires Ashkenazi community. On Sept. 26, 1893, representatives of the four Jewish organizations in *Buenos Aires, among them the Congregación Israelita de la República Argentina (CIRA), met and decided to form the Sociedad de Entierros (Burial Society). On July 22, 1894, the Chevra Keduscha Ashkenazi (Ashkenazi Burial Society) was formed, headed by Henry *Joseph, rabbi of CIRA. The purpose of the society was to ensure that both members and nonmembers receive a Jewish burial. At first the Burial Society leased graves in the Protestant cemetery, while simultaneously endeavoring to obtain its own burial ground. These efforts encountered many financial and legal difficulties, in addition to hostile public opinion. Only in 1910, due to the efforts of its president, Naum Enkin, was the first burial ground acquired in the suburb of Liniers. The Chevra Kedusha had unwritten agreements with the Sephardic burial societies, allowing each to bury only its own ethnic group. The monopoly on an indispensable religious service made the cemetery a source of community funds for those seeking financial assistance. In the 1920s it partially financed public institutions, increasing these activities in the 1930s. After it had acquired a larger cemetery site in Tablada in 1934, it helped found in 1935 the Va'ad ha-Ḥinnukh (Education Committee), which was responsible for organizing Jewish education in Greater Buenos Aires, and founded the Rabbis' Committee. It then became a mutual association called the Asociación Mutual Israelita Argentina (AMIA) on Dec. 17, 1940. During the 1940s, AMIA gradually extended the scope of its community activities and, on March 31, 1949, under the presidency of Moshe Slinin, designated itself the Kehila de Buenos Aires. In September 1952, on the initiative of its president, Moises Goldman, AMIA established the Va'ad ha-Kehillot (Communities' Committee), which united all the communities of Argentina (36 communities in 1952, 130 in 1964). AMIA played a dominant role in this committee and also supplied most of its funds. On April 16, 1956, AMIA changed its statutes. Thenceforth, 90 members were elected to its council, under a system of proportional representation, from a list of eight parties; most of them were from the Zionist parties that generally had their counterparts in the Israeli party system. From among its members, the council chose a president and an executive committee of 24 members.

From 85 members in the year of its foundation, the membership of AMIA gradually rose until in July 1968 it registered 51,798. Since membership is registered by families, this figure represents a much larger number of individuals. The number of associated families is estimated in 2004 as close to 16,000, preserving the traditional position of AMIA as the largest Argentinean Jewish institution, and in latter years there was a membership increase of close to 3,000, probably as a result of its welfare and aid programs. In the 1960s more than 50% of the total budget was spent on the Jewish education system through the Central Education Committee (Vaad ha-Ḥinukh ha-Mercazi). It also covered most of the budget of the institutions of higher learning, Ha-Midrashah ha-Ivrit, the rabbinical seminary, and also a secondary day school, Rambam. But this support to Jewish education was reduced drastically in the 1990s and many of these institutions were closed. In recent years, a new coalition was established by AMIA, the Joint Distribution Committee (JDC), and the Jewish Agency for Israel for the economic rationalization and support of the school network. This new organization – Central Agency of Jewish Education – gives financial assistance and provides organizational planning for all the associated schools in the country, embracing nearly 17,000 pupils. In the 1960s and 1970s the Youth Department of AMIA ran a network of youth centers in Buenos Aires and a central course for youth leaders in conjunction with Sociedad Hebraica Argentina and since the 1970s with the World Zionist Organization. Today AMIA supports many youth centers and programs on a basis of partnership. Its Cultural Department organizes weekly lectures, films and theater exhibitions, etc. Until the 1980s it sponsored an annual "Jewish Book Month," during which thousands of books in Spanish, Yiddish, and Hebrew on Jewish subjects were sold. In 1986 AMIA founded a publishing house – Editorial Mila – which has published hundreds of books in Spanish including literature, essays, testimonies, and research studies.

AMIA has a rabbinical department headed by Chief Rabbi Shlomo Benhamu. Rabbi Benhamu was born in Tetuán (1936) and studied in a yeshivah in Great Britain. After serving as head of a yeshivah in Tetuán, he arrived in 1962 to Argentina as the principal of the schools of Agudat Israel (Hechal Hatorah and Beth Yaakov). In 1965 AMIA sent him to complete his rabbinical studies in Israel, and he entered AMIA's rabbinical department. He was appointed as chief rabbi in 1976.

The social welfare department has many assistance programs in Buenos Aires and in cooperation with Vaad ha-Kehillot also in the provinces, all of them co-sponsored by JDC. In 2004 these programs gave monthly support for the distribution of food, medicines, clothing, and housing to approximately 5,000 people in Buenos Aires and 6,500 in the provinces (Program Mezonot together with the Argentinean welfare association Tzedaka), and subsidized meals for about 2,000 children (Program Meitiv) all over the country. Other functioning programs, with the support of the Inter-American Development Bank, provide employment for Jews and non-Jews. AMIA also established a network of educational and social centers for people with special needs which serves 200 people, and centers for the aged with 2,500 users.

For several years AMIA had an arbitration department that dealt with business and other disputes, which in many cases replaced litigation. AMIA also had (from 1962) a department for social research – CEHIS – engaged mainly in summarizing demographic statistics on Argentinean Jewry, but it was closed in 1995.

The community building of AMIA, built in the mid-1940s and which housed the DAIA, the Va'ad ha-Kehillot, the Va'ad ha-Ḥinuch, and the Jewish Scientific Institute (YIVO), with its library and archives, was destroyed in a terrorist bombing on July 14, 1994. In this tragic attack 85 people, Jews and non-Jews, were killed and hundreds wounded. The new AMIA building, dedicated in 1999, houses the above-mentioned institutions and the offices of the Jewish Agency. Since the statutes of AMIA were revised in the 1950s, it has been run by a coalition of most of the Zionist parties. However, there has been a constant decline in the number of voters, a fact that worries the community's leaders.

ADD. BIBLIOGRAPHY: AMIA. Comunidad Judía de Buenos Aires 1894–1994 (1995), at: www.amia.org.ar.

[Haim Avni / Efraim Zadoff (2nd ed.)]

AMICHAI, YEHUDA (1924–2000), Israeli poet and novelist. Born in Germany, Amichai went to Palestine in 1936, settled in Jerusalem, and served with the Jewish Brigade in World War II. In the latter part of the 1940s he began to publish poetry. The appearance of his first volume *Akhshav u-ve-Yamim Aḥerim* (1955) marked the emergence of a new school of Hebrew poetry. Amichai's poetry reflected the drastic changes which had taken place in the Hebrew language during World War II and the War of Independence. It had become enriched with new idioms and had adopted syntactical elements derived from the new slang. Amichai's familiarity with the wit and irony of modern English poetry as well as its use of understatement and prose phrasing aided him in working this new Hebrew vernacular into his verse.

Amichai introduced airplanes, tanks, fuel trucks, and administrative contracts into a Hebrew poetry which had hitherto avoided these modern terms in order not to mar the beauty of its classic texture. The worlds of technology and law, which became the raw materials for his metaphors, replaced the earlier sacral phrasing. The result was either ironic or tragic and represented an eschewal of history – a mawkish, obdurate, and pathetic version of biblical myth. He was awarded the Israel Prize in 1982. His volumes also include *Be-Merḥak Shetei Tikvot* (1958); *Ba-Ginnah ha-Ẓibburit* (1959); and his collected poems, *Shirim… 1948–1962* (1963). Amichai's novel, *Lo me-Akhshav, Lo mi-Kan* (1963; *Not of This Time, Not of This Place*, 1968), and his short stories are written in a prose style which tends to be confessional, reflective, and redolent of poetic illumination. The novel focuses upon an Israeli seeking revenge upon the Germans who participated in the extermination of his native town and presents a picture of men in spiritual and physical flight. Amichai also wrote *Massa le-Nineveh* (1962), a retelling of the story of Jonah, staged by Habimah in 1964; a number of radio sketches, including *Pa'amonim ve-Rakkavot* (Eng. "Bells and Trains" in *Midstream*, Oct. 1966, 55–66); and a book for children, "Numa's Fat Tail" (1978). Among his other poetry volumes are *Lo Rak Lizekor* ("Not Only to Remember," 1971), *Zeman* ("Time," 1977), and *Sh'at ha-Ḥen* ("Hour of Grace," 1982), as well as *Patuaḥ, Sagur, Patuḥ* ("Open, Closed, Open," 1998). Amichai's poetry has been translated into 33 languages. Available in English translation are, among others, *Achziv, Caesarea and One Love* (1996); *Amen* (1977); *Even a Fist Was Once an Open Palm with Fingers* (1991); *Great Tranquility, Questions and Answers* (1983; 1997); *Poems of Jerusalem and Love Poems* (1992). The *Collected Poems of Amichai* appeared in 2004 in five volumes.

BIBLIOGRAPHY: A. Cohen, *Soferim Ivriyyim Benei Zemannenu* (1969), 259–65; S. Zemach, *Sheti va-Erev* (1960), 216–35, "Friend," in: S. Burnshaw et al. (eds.), *The Modern Hebrew Poem Itself* (1965), 160–7. **ADD. BIBLIOGRAPHY:** B. Arpaly, *Ha-Peraḥim ve-ha-Agartal: Shirat Amichai 1948–1968* (1986); G. Abramson, *The Writing of Yehuda Amichai: A Thematic Approach* (1989); N. Gold, *Lo ka-Brosh* (1994); G. Abramson (ed.), *The Experienced Soul* (1997); E. Hirsch, *Responsive Reading* (1999); M.L. Sethi, *Knowing by Heart: The Sweetness and Pain of Memory in the Poetry of Yehuda Amichai and Mahmud Darwish* (2002); Z. Avran and M. Itzhaki (eds.), *Hommage à Yehuda Amichai* (French, 2002); E. Negev, *Close Encounters with Twenty Israeli Writers* (2003). **WEBSITE:** www.ithl.org.il.

[Dan Tsalka]

AMIDAH (Heb. עֲמִידָה; "standing"), the core and main element of each of the prescribed daily services. In talmudic sources it is known as *Ha-Tefillah* ("The Prayer" *par excellence*). As its name indicates, the *Amidah* must be recited standing. Other names for this prayer include *Shemoneh esreh*, for the number of its benedictions (presently 19), and *Tefillat laḥash*, because of the obligation to recite it silently.

Types, Manner, and Nature

The *Amidah* is recited individually during each of the daily services – **Shaḥarit* (Morning Service),**Minḥah* (Afternoon Service) and **Arvit* (Evening Service); on Sabbaths and the festivals it is recited also for **Musaf* ("Additional Service") and on the Day of Atonement, a fifth time, for *Ne'ilah* ("the Concluding Prayer"). In congregational prayer, i.e., when there is a *minyan* (a quorum of at least ten male adults), the reader repeats the *Amidah* aloud and a number of additions are made (see below). The original purpose of the repetition was to enable uneducated persons, who did not know the prayers, to fulfill their duty by listening to the recital and responding "Amen" after each benediction. There are various forms of *Amidah*. On weekdays, the *Amidah* originally comprised 18 benedictions (later 19); on fast days one more is added in the repetition by the reader, and in ancient times, on some public fasts, six were added to the regular 18 (Ta'an. 2:2–4). On Sabbaths and festivals, there are only seven benedictions, except in the *Musaf* of *Rosh Ha-Shanah, when there are nine. In cases of emergency or illness, the intermediate blessings of the weekday *Amidah* may also be combined into one (see below *Havinenu*). The various forms have in common the first three and the last three benedictions; the former are devoted to the praise of God, the latter, to closing and leave-taking. On weekdays, the intermediate benedictions are petitions, and the daily *Amidah* is, therefore, predominantly a prayer of supplication. The pronoun "we" is used throughout the *Amidah* (even when it is recited silently by the individual), both in praise and in petition, indicating that it was always conceived as a communal prayer. Even the individual worshiper recites it not on his own behalf but as a member of the congregation.

The *Amidah* was fashioned in the form of an interpersonal dialogic encounter between the worshiper and God. The language of the prayer addresses God in the second person, and the order of the benedictions – praise, petition, closing and leave-taking – is consistent with how a slave approaches his master (Ber. 34a). Consequently, the worshiper stands throughout the recitation of the prayer and bows at its beginning and end (T. Ber. 1:8). At its conclusion, the worshiper bows again and takes leave of the divine presence with backward steps (Yoma 53b). The further obligation to face the locus of the Temple (T. Ber. 3:15) is grounded in the notion that, while praying, the worshiper stands directly in the presence of the *shekhinah*. After the destruction of the Temple, even though some sages opined that the *shekhinah* had left Jerusalem, based on other national-religious considerations, worshipers continued to face the place of the Temple. But they directed their hearts to the *shekhinah*, wherever its locus: "He who prays should regard himself as if the *Shekhinah* were before him" (Sanh. 22a; see also T. Ber. 3:14). To facilitate achieving this elevated spiritual state, the rabbis forbade the worshiper to divert his thoughts from the *tefillah* (M. Ber. 5:1), and some prohibited recitation of the Prayer when of unsettled mind (Erub. 65a).

Evolution and Redaction of the Amidah

Scholarly opinion is divided as to the origins of statutory prayer in general, and of the *Amidah* in particular. Even the talmudic sources reflect such diverse opinions as the one attributing the formulation of the *Amidah* to the Men of the Great Assembly (Meg. 17b), namely to the early Second Temple period, as opposed to one that explicitly ascribes the arrangement of the prayer to the activity of Rabban Gamliel in the post-destruction era at Jabneh (Ber. 28b). Scholarly opinion spans these two poles: some scholars date the origins of the Prayer to the final centuries preceding the destruction of the Temple; others date it as late as the era of Rabban Gamliel at Jabneh. From the welter of sources and opinions, the following likely scenario emerges. As a means of religious expression, prayer gained in importance during the late Second Temple period. Qumran literature provides rich testimony to fixed prayer among circles that opposed the Temple. Rabbinic sources indicate that, at the same time, some Pharasaic circles began to make use of fixed prayer ceremonies and to recite prayers on special occasions. For example, there is attestation to set benedictions recited by the priests in the Temple, of which some partially parallel *Amidah* benedictions (M. Yoma 7:1; M. Tamid 5:1). Explicit testimony from the Tosefta (Rosh Ha-Shanah 2:17) indicates the practice of prayer on Sabbaths and holidays among the sages of Beit Shammai and Beit Hillel. But it is only in the wake of the destruction, from the period of Rabban Gamliel and onward, that we have testimony for the institutionalization of prayer as a mandatory communal, and individual, obligation. The requirement to recite the *Shemoneh Esreh* daily dates only from the time of Rabban Gamliel and his contemporaries.

The exact nature of the fixing of the prayer by Rabban Gamliel at Jabneh also remains a debated point among scholars. Until the late 1980s the prevailing view was that Rabban Gamliel did not mandate the precise wording of the benedictions but rather their number, main motif, and concluding formula, giving worshipers and prayer leaders leeway to formulate the wording of the benediction as they saw fit. Over time, whether by natural processes or rabbinic fiat, certain versions came to predominate. Only in geonic Babylonia did the versions of the prayer achieve greater uniformity, but even then, variants were not entirely eliminated. In the early 1990s a different viewpoint was proposed, according to which Rabban Gamliel not only set the general principles governing the *Amidah* but also its precise wording, which he sought to impart to all Jewish communities. Over time, because of alterations in the worshipers' outlook and esthetic taste, this primary version underwent changes. The scattering of the Jewish people in various diasporas, and the lack of a central leadership, fostered the creation of different branches of the text in the diverse Jewish communities.

For the first centuries of its development, due to the absence of a complete version of the *Amidah* in talmudic literature, we have only vague testimony to its language. The first full witnesses to the wording of the prayer come from *siddurim* in use in the late first/early second millennium C.E. – the *siddurim* of Rav Amram Gaon and Rav Saadiah Gaon as well as thousands of *genizah* fragments – namely, from texts compiled centuries after the fixing of the *Amidah*. Among the *siddurim* preserved in the Cairo *Genizah*, it is possible to distinguish two main branches: a Palestinian and a Babylonian rite. Despite many differences of detail, the *Amidah* as preserved in both rites retains an inherent linguistic kinship. With the thinning out of the Jewish settlement in Palestine in the early second millennium C.E. and the growing influence of the Babylonian yeshivot on most of the Jewish world, the Palestinian rite disappeared and the Babylonian rite became the progenitor of all versions of the *Amidah* to the present.

The Weekday Amidah

The sequence of the benedictions of the weekday *Amidah* is as follows:

(1) Refers to God as the God of the *avot* ("patriarchs"), and extols Him as great, mighty, and awesome (Deut. 10:17); it concludes with *Barukh … Magen Avraham* ("Blessed … Shield of Abraham").

(2) Praises God for His deeds of *gevurot* ("power and might"). Among the manifestations of God's power are his providing sustenance for all living creatures and His causing the rain to fall in the rainy season. Special stress is laid on the revival of the dead and the benediction which concludes with *Barukh… meḥayyeh ha-metim* ("Blessed … He Who revives the dead") is therefore also known as *Teḥiyyat ha-Metim* ("Resurrection of the Dead").

(3) Speaks of God's holiness, and is, therefore, called *Kedushat ha-Shem*. It concludes with *Barukh … ha-El ha-Kadosh* ("Blessed … is the Holy God").

(4) Petitions God to grant wisdom and understanding. It concludes with *Barukh … ḥonen ha-da'at* ("Blessed … gracious giver of knowledge").

(5) Entreats God to cause a return to His Torah and to His service. It concludes with *Barukh… ha-roẓeh bi-teshuvah* ("Blessed… Who delights in repentance").

(6) Beseeches forgiveness for all sins, concluding with *Barukh … ḥannun ha-marbeh lisloaḥ* ("Blessed … Who are gracious and abundantly forgiving").

(7) Implores God to redeem. It concludes with *Barukh … go'el Yisrael* ("Blessed … redeemer of Israel").

(8) Requests God to heal the sick and concludes with *Barukh … rofe ḥolei ammo Yisrael* ("Blessed … Who heals the sick of Your people Israel").

(9) Supplicates God to bless the produce of the earth and grant a good (fertile) year; It is, therefore, called *Birkat ha-Shanim* ("Blessing of the Years") and concludes with *Barukh … mevarekh ha-shanim* ("Blessed … Who blesses the years").

(10) Is a request for the ingathering of the exiles, concluding with *Barukh … mekabbeẓ niddeḥei ammo Yisrael* ("Blessed … Who gathers the banished ones of Your people, Israel").

(11) Appeals to God to restore righteous judges and reign Himself over Israel. It concludes with *Barukh ... Melekh ohev ẓedakah u-mishpat* ("Blessed ... King Who loves righteousness and judgment").

(12) Asks God to destroy the *malshinim* ("slanderers" or "informers"), all His enemies, and to shatter the "kingdom of arrogance" (see below). The text of this benediction, called in the Talmud *Birkath ha-Minim ("Benediction Concerning Heretics"), underwent many changes. It concludes with *Barukh ... shover oyevim u-makhni'a zedim* ("Blessed ... Who breaks the enemies and humbles the arrogant").

(13) Supplicates God to have mercy upon the righteous, the pious, the proselytes, and all those who trust in Him; it concludes with *Barukh ... mishan u-mivtaḥ la-ẓaddikim* ("Blessed ... the support and trust of the righteous").

(14) Solicits God to rebuild Jerusalem and dwell there. It concludes with *Barukh ... boneh Yerushalayim* ("Blessed ... Who rebuilds Jerusalem").

(15) Seeks the reestablishment of the kingdom of David. It concludes with *Barukh ... maẓmi'ah keren yeshu'ah* ("Blessed ... Who causes the horn of salvation to flourish").

(16) Is a general plea to hearken to (i.e., accept) prayers. It concludes with *Barukh ... shome'a tefilah* ("Blessed ... Who hearkens unto prayer").

(17) Begs God to reinstate the *avodah* ("the Temple service"), and to return the Divine Presence to Zion. It concludes with "*Barukh ... ha-maḥazir Shekhinato le-Ẓiyyon* ("Blessed ... Who returns the Divine Presence unto Zion").

(18) Gives thanks to God for all His mercies. The benediction is called *Hodayah* ("Thanksgiving") and concludes with *Barukh ... ha-tov shimkha u-lekha na'eh lehodot* ("Blessed ... whose name is good and to whom it is fitting to give thanks").

(19) Is a petition for peace. It is called *Birkat ha-Shalom* ("Blessing of Peace") and on some occasions is preceded by the Priestly Blessing, recited by the worshipers of priestly descent (see below). The latter concludes with the word *shalom* ("peace") and the benediction is a kind of response to the blessing. It is, therefore, also called *Birkat Kohanim* (Priestly Blessing; RH 4:5) and concludes with *Barukh ... ha-mevarekh et ammo Yisrael ba-shalom* ("Blessed ... Who blesses Your people Israel with peace").

The 13 petitions (4–16) may be subdivided into two distinct groups: Benedictions 4 to 9 are concerned with general human, everyday needs, both spiritual and material; benedictions 10 to 15 give expression to specific Jewish-national aspirations, all concerned with various aspects of messianic redemption.

The above description of the daily *Amidah* essentially portrays most of the details of the accepted prayer rites that are the continuation of the early Babylonian rite. The *Amidah* of the early Palestinian rite differed somewhat in several, some important, details. Of these, the most striking is that in Palestinian *siddurim* the *Amidah* has only eighteen, not nineteen, benedictions. The Palestinian rite has no separate benediction for the restoration of the kingdom of David (benediction 15 in the Babylonian rite), and this request is incorporated in the benediction regarding Jerusalem (14 in the Babylonian rite). The reason for this distinction between the rites, already found in talmudic times, is not entirely clear. Some link it to the development of *Birkat ha-Minim*, which was added to the *Amidah* at Jabneh after the full redaction of the *Shemoneh Esreh*. In Palestine, seeking to preserve the number eighteen, the benedictions on Jerusalem and the Davidic kingdom were united. Another change in the early language of the *Amidah* came with the deepened awareness of *galut* and the concomitant aspiration for redemption. An outstanding example is the seventeenth benediction, whose closing formula is based on the notion that the *shekhinah* had departed Jerusalem in the wake of the destruction. This conception is missing from the early Palestinian versions of the benediction, which concludes with *she-otekha be-yir'ah na'avod* ("we worship you with awe"). The twelfth benediction as well underwent significant alteration. Its early version did not encompass a request to destroy the *malshinim* (slanderers), but was rather directed at Jewish separatists who endangered internal Jewish unity, explicitly mentioning the early Nazarenes, as well as against the "evil kingdom," namely, Rome. Because of historical circumstances, changed worldviews, and Christian censorship, this benediction underwent manifold changes, the most significant of which was the expunging of the word *noẓerim* from the benediction (see **Birkat ha-Minim*). With modernity, in some streams of Judaism wide-ranging changes have been made in the wording of the benedictions, including alterations related to awareness of women's status.

Additions

When the *Amidah* is recited aloud in the congregational service, some additions are made within the above-mentioned framework. Different customs prevail regarding the recitation of the Priestly Blessing which is interpolated before the last benediction. In the Diaspora it is customarily recited in Ashkenazi communities only in the *Musaf* of festivals. In the Eastern communities it is recited in every *Shaḥarit* service (and at *Minḥah* on fast days). In Ereẓ Israel the Sephardim do the same, and the Ashkenazi communities in most places. While the reader intones *Modim* (the 18th benediction) the congregation recites *Modim de-Rabbanan*, a different prayer of thanksgiving, in an undertone. The most striking addition to the congregational recitation of the *Amidah* is the **Kedushah*. This is an expanded version of the third benediction and comprises the exalted praise of God by the angels (quoted in Isa. 6:3 and Ezek. 3:12). Other additions to the *Amidah* are made on specific occasions, also in the individual recitation. In the rainy season mention is made in the second benediction of God's power which causes the rain to fall; in the ninth, rain is prayed for. On the New Moon and intermediate days of festivals, the significance of the occasion is mentioned in the **Ya'aleh ve-Yavo* prayer, inserted into the 17th benediction. The miracles performed on Ḥanukkah and Purim are described in the *Al ha-Nissim* prayer which is added to the 18th benediction. On public fast days, a special supplication, *Anenu*, is inserted into the 16th benediction in the silent recitation; the reader recites this as a separate benediction between the seventh and eighth benedictions. On the Ninth of *Av, the 14th benediction is elaborated with a lamentation on the destruction of the Temple. During the *Ten Days of Penitence, petitions that God may grant life are inserted into the first two and the last two benedictions while the third concludes with *ha-Melekh ha-Kadosh* ("the Holy King) and the 11th with *ha-Melekh ha-Mishpat* ("the King of Judgment"). These changes are not found in the early Palestinian rite. In the evening service, after the conclusion of the Sabbath, a **Havdalah* is inserted into the fourth benediction. Additions may be made to the standard framework by a worshiper as long as these are appropriate to the general theme of the particular benediction to which they are added (Sh. Ar., OḤ 119:1–3).

Sabbath and Festivals

In the Sabbath and festival *Amidah*, as well as in the *Musaf* on New Moon, all petitions (4–16) are omitted, and one central benediction, *Kedushat ha-Yom* ("the sanctification of the day"), expressing the special character of the holy day in question, is recited instead. For festivals, the text of this benediction is uniform, only the name of the festival being changed (an exception being at the *Musaf Amidah;* see below). The benediction concludes with *Barukh … mekaddesh Yisrael veha-Zemannim* ("Blessed … Who sanctifies Israel and the festive seasons"). On Rosh Ha-Shanah this is expanded to read *Barukh … Melekh al kol ha-areẓ mekaddesh Yisrael ve-Yom ha-Zikkaron* ("Blessed … King over all the earth who sanctifies Israel and the Day of Memorial"); on the Day of Atonement, *Barukh … Melekh moḥel ve-sole'aḥ le-avonoteinu… mekaddesh Yisrael ve-Yom ha-Kippurim* ("Blessed … King Who pardons and forgives our iniquities… who sanctifies Israel and the Day of Atonement"). On all the festivals it begins with thanks to God for choosing Israel from among all the peoples (*Attah Beḥartanu*) sanctifying them through His Torah and *mitzvot* and giving them "festivals and seasons of joy" with the mention of the particular festival; *Ya'aleh ve-Yavo*, in which the name of the festival recurs, follows and it concludes with a brief petition for the blessing of the festivals. The same version is used for all services, except for *Musaf*, where *Attah Beḥartanu* is followed by a prayer for the restoration of the Temple *(U-mi-Penei Ḥata'einu)* and of the pilgrimages and the sacrificial cult; this is followed by the appropriate Bible verses (taken from Num. 28–29) containing the instructions for the sacrifices of the day in question and a more elaborate and solemn petition for speedy redemption and the rebuilding of the Temple. The conclusion is again as above. On New Moons a different text, stressing the character of the day as one of atonement, is used, concluding with *Barukh … mekaddesh Yisrael ve-Rashei Ḥodashim* ("Blessed … Who sanctifies Israel and New Moons"). On festivals and special Sabbaths poetical prayers are often inserted and said by the congregation during the reader's repetition. These are known as *Kerovot* and are to be found added to the various benedictions. Special poems concerning the 613 commandments and known as **azharot*, are added in the Shavuot prayers, usually in the *Musaf Amidah*.

On the Sabbath, the introduction of the fourth benediction varies in each *Amidah*. In *Arvit* the Sabbath is presented as a "memorial of creation," followed by the recital of Genesis 2:1–3; in *Shaḥarit* the Sabbath is associated with the giving of the Torah at Sinai and presented as the symbol of the Covenant between God and Israel; in *Minḥah* the Sabbath is extolled as the day of complete rest, anticipating, as it were, the perfect peace and rest of the messianic age. The above texts seem to have been chosen intentionally to express three different, yet complementary, aspects of the Sabbath: creation – revelation – redemption; a triad of concepts, occurring elsewhere in Jewish thought and liturgy. Other introductions to this benediction are also known and used: for *Musaf, Tikkanta Shabbat* ("You did institute the Sabbath") in the Ashkenazi version and *U-le-Moshe Ẓivvita* ("You did command Moses") in the Sephardi, both of which mention the sacrifices; for *Arvit, U-me-Ahavatekha* ("Out of Thy Love"; Tosef., Ber. 3:11, used in the Italian rite); for *Minḥah, Hannaḥ Lanu* ("Grant us Rest" – see the *siddurim* of Rav Amram Gaon and of Rav Saadiah Gaon). The versions of the Sabbath prayers found in the Cairo *Genizah* indicate that this variety is a secondary development and that the benediction for the day was originally uniform as for the festival prayer.

The only festival *Amidah* which diverges from the general pattern of seven benedictions is that of *Musaf* of Rosh Ha-Shanah which has three intermediate benedictions, making a total of nine. This special structure probably came into being in order to provide three separate occasions for sounding the **shofar*, as required by the Mishnah (RH 4:9), at the end of each of the three intermediate benedictions. According to Sephardi custom the *shofar* is blown both in the silent as well as the reader's repetition of the *Amidah*, whereas the Ashkenazim sound it only in the latter. The text of each of them, therefore, relates to one of the special aspects of the day. In addition to the usual "sanctification of the day" (fourth blessing), the fifth benediction was devoted to **Zikhronot* ("Remembrances") as Rosh Ha-Shanah is the "Day of Remembrance," and the sixth to *Shofarot* ("the blessing of the *Shofar*") to express the *shofar* aspect of the festival. A third aspect of the day, "the Kingship of God" was made the subject of *Malkhuyyot*, probably at a later stage. *Malkhuyyot* was not allocated a separate benediction, but was combined with the "sanctification of the day" (RH 4:5). On Rosh Ha-Shanah and the Day of Atonement, the third benediction is recited in a more elaborate version which contains the prayer *u-Vekhen Ten Paḥdekha* ("Now therefore impose Your awe"), an ancient petition for the eschatological Kingdom of God. On the Day of Atonement, the silent recital of the *Amidah* is followed by the *viddui* ("confession of sins"), which is not written as a benediction. In the repetition by the reader, however, the *viddui* is inserted into the fourth benediction. Two confessions, one short and one long, are recited; both are arranged in alphabetical form. Sins, which might have been committed during the year, are enumerated. In common with other community prayers, they are formulated in the "we"-style: "we have trespassed, etc." (see *Confession of Sins).

[Uri Ehrlich (2nd ed.)]

Havinenu

Shortened form of the *Amidah*. An abbreviated form of the *Amidah* (known as *Havinenu* ("give us understanding") from its initial word) may be recited instead of the *Amidah* in cases of emergency, e.g., when a person is hurried or is ill and unable to concentrate for any length of time. The *Havinenu* prayer consists of a shortened version of the 13 intermediary benedictions of the *Amidah* and concludes with the blessing "Blessed are You, O Lord, who hearkens unto prayer." It is preceded by the three introductory benedictions of the *Amidah* and concludes with the last three blessings of the *Amidah*. There are several versions of the *Havinenu* (Ber. 29a; TJ, Ber. 4:3, 8a, see also B.M. Lewin, *Oẓar ha-Ge'onim*, 1 (1928), Teshuvot 72, no. 184 and A.I. Schechter, *Studies in Jewish Liturgy* (1930), 71). The version from the Babylonian Talmud (Ber. 29a), ascribed to Mar *Samuel, is the commonly accepted text in the daily liturgy. *Abbaye scorned those who substituted the shortened *Havinenu* version for the full *Amidah* (Ber. 29a). The law, however, permits such a substitution, except during the evening service at the termination of the Sabbath, when the fourth benediction (*Attah Ḥonen*) is supplemented by a special prayer marking the distinction between Sabbath and the weekdays (*Havdalah*); and during the winter season when the petition for rain (*ve-ten tal u-matar*) must be said in the sixth benediction of the *Amidah* (Ber. 29a; see Sh. Ar., OḤ 110:1).

Music

In Ashkenazi tradition, the first benediction of the *Amidah* is sometimes distinguished by a particular melody that contrasts with the subsequent cantillation in the *tefillah*-mode. On the occasion of the *Tal*, *Geshem*, and **Ne'ilah* prayers, the special *Avot* tunes employ merely the motive material of the preceding **Kaddish*. A more conspicuous and peculiar melody appears in the morning prayers of the High Holidays. It is considered among the unchangeable **Mi-Sinai* tunes. Like the majority of the latter, the *Avot* melody starts with a theme of its own, while the continuation draws from the thematic stock in use for this kind of synagogue song. The characteristic *Avot* themes show a relatively late European tonality. They develop by means of sequential progression, and are followed by a typical synagogue motive. After repetition of this section the melody uses themes known from **Aleinu le-Shabbe'ah* and **Kol Nidrei*. Like several other tunes from the *Mi-Sinai* cycle, the basic *Avot* melody sometimes underwent elaboration and extension into a "cantorial fantasia." This was done by Aaron *Beer in 1783, and in the local tradition of Frankfurt and other communities until late in the 19th century. Examples of the basic melody can be found in: S. Naumbourg, *Zemirot Yisrael* (1847), no. 54; Idelsohn, Melodien, 7 (1932), pt. 1, no. 150a; pt. 3, no. 146; I. Schorr, *Neginot Baruch Schorr* (1928), no. 81; and others. Examples of the cantorial fantasia can be found in: Idelsohn, Melodien, 6 (1932), pt. 2, no. 5; 7, pt. 1, nos. 150b–c; F. Ogutsch, *Der Frankfurter Kantor* (1930), no. 177; M. Deutsch, *Vorbeterschule* (1871), no. 269.

[Hanoch Avenary]

BIBLIOGRAPHY: GENERAL: **ADD. BIBLIOGRAPHY:** U. Ehrlich, *The Nonverbal Language of Prayer: A New Approach to Jewish Liturgy* (2004); idem, "The Earliest Versions of the Amidah – The Blessing about the Temple Worship" in: J. Tabory, ed., *From Qumran to Cairo: Studies in the History of Prayer*, 17–38 (Heb., 1999); I. Elbogen. *Jewish Liturgy: A Comprehensive History*. tr. R.P. Scheindlin (1993), 24–66; L. Finkelstein. "The Development of the Amidah," in: JQR, 16 (1925–1926), 1-43, 127-70. (Reprint, J.J. Petuchowski (ed.), *Contributions to the Scientific Study of Jewish Liturgy* (1970), 91–177); E. Fleischer, *Eretz-Israel Prayer and Prayer Rituals* (Heb., 1988), 19–159; idem, "Le-kadmoniyyut Tefillot ha-Ḥovah be-Yisrael," *Tarbiz*, 59 (1990), 397–441, idem, "Tefillat Shemoneh Esreh: Iyyunim be-Ofya, Sidra, Tokhna, u-Megamoteha," *Tarbiz*, 62 (1993), 179–223; J. Heinemann, *Prayer in the Talmud: Forms and Patterns* (1977), 13–76, 218–50; L.I. Levine, *The Ancient Synagogue: The First Thousand Years* (2000), 151–59, 510–19; Y. Luger, *The Weekday Amidah in the Cairo Genizah* (Heb., 2001); B. Nitzan, *Qumran Prayer and Religious Poetry*. (1994); S. Reif, *Judaism and Hebrew Prayer* (1993), 53–87. HAVINENU: ET, 8 (1957), 120; Hertz, Prayer, 158–60, text and Eng. tr. MUSIC: Idelsohn, Melodien, 7 (1932), xxxiii; idem, in: *Zeitschrift fuer Musikwissenschaft*, 8 (1926), 445, 465; Avenary, in: *Yuval*, 1 (1968), 65–85.

AMIDAR, the Israeli national immigrant housing company. It was established in 1949 by the Israeli government, in order to build housing projects for the masses of new immigrants. The government controlled 75% of its shares, and the *Jewish Agency held 25% of its shares. With the steady rise in immigration, however, construction was transferred to the Labor division. Amidar was given the task of proprietor and administrator of public housing: assignment of tenants to the housing projects, maintenance and improvement of the houses, rental and sales of apartments, and organization of community activities. In 20 years Amidar handled approximately 250,000 housing units, placing more than a million people in over 200 housing projects. Amidar's first task was the initial absorption of the immigrants. At first, it even assumed basic municipal functions. It instilled in tenants a sense of initiative in taking care of property and the concept of the citizen's responsibility toward property upkeep. Since housing construction in the early 1950s proceeded according to quantitative rather than qualitative needs, Amidar employed various means to allay premature deterioration and to improve neighborhoods. As a nonprofit institution, Amidar fixed rents according to an immigrant's means at the rate of 7–10% of his average monthly earnings during his first years in Israel. When the immigrant became better established, he was encouraged to buy his apartment with a down payment of 10–20%, and the rest on a mortgage with an interest rate of 3.5–4.5% annually for a period of 25 years. The encouragement of property ownership, initiated in 1955, led by the late 1960s to the purchase of tens of thousands of housing units by their tenants.

At the beginning of the 21st century the tenants in Amidar's apartments were a mix of old and new immigrants. The company managed 60,000 apartments in 200 settlements, among them 2,200 for the elderly located in 30 sites all over Israel. It continued to be responsible for renting empty apartments, rent collection, maintenance, registration, etc. In this same period there was much public agitation among tenants owing to the high price of apartments, which prevented them from realizing their right to buy them.

[David Tanne / Shaked Gilboa (2nd ed.)]

AMIEL, MOSHE AVIGDOR (1883–1946), rabbi, religious thinker, and author. Amiel studied under his father and at the Telz yeshivah. From there he proceeded to Vilna where he studied under R. Ḥayyim *Soloveichik and R. Ḥayyim Ozzer *Grodzinski. At the age of 22 Amiel became rabbi of Swieciany, and in 1913, rabbi of Grajewo. One of the first rabbis to join the Mizrachi movement, he began publishing articles, noted for their lucid literary style, on communal and national questions and presenting his outlook on Judaism and the ideology of religious Zionism. In 1920 Amiel was elected rabbi of Antwerp, where his initial public appearance at the Mizrachi convention immediately established him as one of the chief ideologists of religious Zionism. In Antwerp Amiel created a wide network of educational and communal institutions from Jewish day schools to a yeshivah, where he lectured. In 1936 Amiel was elected chief rabbi of Tel Aviv where he found further scope for his varied activities. He established the modern high school yeshivah "Ha-Yishuv he-Ḥadash," now named after him. The school combined talmudic and secular studies and was the first of its kind in Ereẓ Israel. Amiel's first halakhic publication was *Darkhei Moshe* followed by his three-volume *Ha Middot le-Ḥeker ha-Halakhah.* A renowned preacher, he published the homiletical works *Derashot el Ammi* and *Hegyonot el Ammi.* Amiel was a regular contributor to the religious press.

BIBLIOGRAPHY: J.L. Fishman, *Anashim shel Ẓurah* (1947), 212–23; D. Halaḥmi, *Ḥakhmei Yisrael* (1957), 408; Kerstein, in: L. Jung (ed.), *Guardians of Our Heritage* (1958), 661–72. A bibliography of his works was published in *Sefer Yovel… M.A. Amiel* (1943).

[Mordechai Hacohen]

AMIGO, Sephardi family prominent in Temesvár, Hungary (now Timișoara, Romania). Its founder, MEIR AMIGO, who was born in Constantinople, settled there together with four other Sephardi Jews in 1736, by a special authorization obtained for them by Diego D'*Aguilar, who held the tobacco monopoly in Austria and appointed Amigo as his agent. Amigo became the organizer and leader of the combined community of Ashkenazi and Sephardi Jews which was subsequently established. He was nicknamed "*rey chico*" (little king) because of his wealth. Amigo maintained contacts between his community and the Sephardi community in Vienna. The Vienna community also enlisted his help in preventing the impending expulsion of the Jews from *Bohemia in 1745.

Members of the Amigo family continued to play a leading role in Temesvár. ISAAC AMIGO, who headed the community from 1784 to 1788, afforded great assistance to the Jews from *Belgrade who sought refuge in Temesvár in 1791. The last member of the family to serve as head of the community was JOSEPH MEIR AMIGO, who held office from 1808 to 1810.

BIBLIOGRAPHY: M. Loewy, *Skizzen zur Geschichte der Juden in Temesvár* (1890), 71–84; *Magyar Zsidó Lexikon* (1929), 34.

[Yehouda Marton]

AMIGO, ABRAHAM (c. 1610/15–c. 1683), rabbi and author. Amigo was born in Constantinople, or Adrianople – where he was a pupil of Elijah Obadiah. He immigrated to Ereẓ Israel about 1655, settled in Jerusalem, and was a member of the *bet midrash* of Jacob *Ḥagiz. The rabbis of Egypt and Turkey referred questions to him and his opinion was decisive. He also studied Kabbalah and joined the circle of Jacob b. Ḥayyim Ẓemaḥ. Among his disciples in Jerusalem were David ha-Kohen Rapaport, author of *Da'at Kedoshim,* and Ḥayyim Abulafia the Younger. Amigo was also a distinguished preacher and moralist and his homilies were transmitted by his pupils even after his death. He opposed Shabbetai Ẓevi and strove to have him banished. The rabbis of Constantinople wanted to appoint him as one of the "four great men in Israel" who were to go to Gaza to investigate *Nathan of Gaza. His works are *Peri Hadash*, on the Shulḥan Arukh *Oraḥ Ḥayyim*, from the laws of Passover to the end; and responsa, decisions, and novellae on the Talmud, mentioned by Ḥayyim Joseph David *Azulai (part now in the Benayahu Collection). Some of his responsa were printed in the work of his colleague Samuel Garmison, *Mishpetei Ẓedek* (nos. 78, 99), and in *Naharot Dammesek* by Solomon Camondo (ḤM, no. 13).

BIBLIOGRAPHY: M. Benayahu, in: *Sinai*, 17 (1945), 309–13.

AMINA (pen name of **Binyamin ben Mishael**; 1672–after 1732/33), prolific Jewish poet of Iran. Our only information about Amina's life is contained in his poetic work entitled *Sargozasht-e Aminā bā hamsarash* (Library of the Hebrew University, Jerusalem, microfilm #19874), where he addresses each of his seven children and complains about his wife after 25 years of marriage. A recent study of Judeo-Persian manuscripts in the libraries of the Hebrew University, Ben Zvi Institute in Jerusalem, the Jewish Theological Seminary of New York, the Hebrew Union College in Cincinnati, and the British Museum in London has shown that Amina composed approximately 40 poetic works, most of which are short. His longest works are about Esther and Mordechai (based on the Book of Esther), the sacrifice of Isaac according to the Midrash of Judah b. Samuel b. Abbas (a poet and preacher of 12th-century Tunisia and Syria), and *Tafsir-e azharot* or commentary on the "Commandments and Prohibitions" of Solomon ibn *Gabirol (the famous poet and philosopher of 11th-century Spain). Each of these works contains 300 to 400 verses. He also composed a 92-verse poem in Hebrew.

BIBLIOGRAPHY: A. Netzer, "The Jewish Poet Amina of Kashan and His Sacred Poems," in: S. Shaked and A. Netzer (eds.), *Irano-Judaica*, 5 (2003), 68–81.

[Amnon Netzer (2nd ed.)]

AMIR (Heb. עָמִיר; "ear of corn"), kibbutz in northern Israel, in the Ḥuleh Valley, affiliated with Ha-Kibbutz ha-Arẓi. Amir was founded in 1939 by immigrants from Poland, Lithuania, and other countries, near the *Ḥuleh swamps. It was the settlement most prone to the dangers of flooding and of malaria. In 1968 Amir's economy was based on intensive irrigated farming (apples and other deciduous fruit, and field crops in partnership with kibbutz *Sedeh Neḥemyah and kibbutz *Shamir), and dairy cattle. Later on, the kibbutz set up a successful enterprise producing disposable diapers and other sanitary products, but in 2004 it was sold to a private company when the kibbutz ran into economic difficulties. Amir's population was 579 in 2002.

[Efraim Orni / Shaked Gilboa (2nd ed.)]

AMIR, AHARON (1923–), Israeli writer, translator, and editor. Amir, who was born in Kovno, immigrated to Palestine in 1935. He studied Arabic language and literature at the Hebrew University. A member of the anti-British underground organization Leḥi, he served on the editorial board of its daily, *Mivrak*, and edited its literary supplement (1948). Amir was also a founding member of the Canaanite movement, which saw Hebrew culture as defined by geographical location rather than by religious affiliation. He edited *Alef* (from 1948–50 with Yonathan *Ratosh, and from 1950 on his own), the periodical of the *Canaanites. His publications include *Kaddim* ("Sirocco," poetry, 1949) and *Saraf* ("Fiery Angel," poetry, 1957); *Ahavah* ("Love," stories, 1952); *Ve-lo Tehi la-Mavet Memshalah* ("And Death Shall Not Rule," novel, 1955); the trilogy *Nun* (1969–89); *Matteh Aharon* ("Aaron's Rod," poetry, 1966); and *Ha-Nevalim* ("The Villains," 1998). Amir also edited several books and anthologies. He translated many books into Hebrew, from English, French, and American literature. In 1959 he founded and became editor of *Keshet*, a literary and political quarterly.

BIBLIOGRAPHY: Kressel, Leksikon, 1 (1965), 122–3. **ADD. BIBLIOGRAPHY:** G. Shaked, *Ha-Sipporet ha-Ivrit*, 4 (1993), 103–4.

[Gitta (Aszkenazy) Avinor]

AMIR (Pinkerfeld), ANDA (1902–1981), Hebrew poet. She was born in Galicia, into an assimilated family. Her father worked as an architect for the Austro-Hungarian government. She completed secondary school in Lvov, and published a book of verse in Polish at the age of 18, her first poem being the prayer of a Polish child for the liberation of his country. After studying at the universities of Leipzig and Lvov, she immigrated to Palestine in 1923. In 1921 she published another volume of verse in Polish, *Piesni życia* ("Songs of Life"). Thereafter, under the influence of Uri Ẓevi *Greenberg, she began writing in Hebrew. The themes of her verse are love of nature, romantic love, and the joys of motherhood. Her long poem "*Aḥat*" ("One," 1953) describes a young Jewish girl who immigrates to Israel after surviving the Holocaust and dies fighting for Israeli independence. Among her books are *Yamim Dovevim* ("Days Tell," 1929); *Yuval* (1932); *Geisha Lian Tang Sharah* (1935); *Gittit* (1937); *Duda'im* ("Mandrakes," 1943); *Gadish* ("Grain Heap," 1949); *Kokhavim bi-Deli* ("Stars in a Bucket," 1957).

Anda Amir was the first poet to write poetry in Hebrew specifically for children and distinguished herself in this field. Her first collection of such poetry, *Al Anan Kevish* (1933), was edited by H.N. Bialik, while her *Shirei Yeladim* (1934) was awarded the Bialik Prize for poems for children. In 1978 she received the Israel Prize for children's literature.

BIBLIOGRAPHY: A. Cohen, *Soferim Ivriyyim Benei Zemannenu* (1964), 186–9; Kressel, Leksikon, 2 (1967), 560–1. **ADD. BIBLIOGRAPHY:** I. Yaoz-Kest, "*Im Anda, Monolog bi-Shenayim*," in: Z. Beilin (ed.), *Anda* (1977), 131–36; H. Hever, "*Shirat ha-Guf ha-Le'ummi: Nashim Meshorerot be-Milḥemet ha-Shiḥrur*," in: *Te'oriyah u-Vikoret*, 7 (1995), 99–123; Y. Oppenheimer, *Nashim u-Le'ummiyut, Shirei Anda Pinkerfeld bi-Shenot ha-Arba'im*; Y. Berlovitz, "'*Me-Olam, Demuyot mi-Kedem' le-Anda Pinkerfeld Amir: Haẓa'ah le-Narativ Mikra'i Nashi*," in: M. Shilo, R. Kerk, and G. Hazan-Rokem (eds.), *Ha-Ivriyot ha-Ḥadashot* (2002), 368–82.

[Yohanan Twersky]

AMIR, ELI (1937–), Israeli novelist. Amir was born in Baghdad, Iraq, and came to Israel in 1950. He was sent to study at a kibbutz. His career began as a messenger in the Prime Minister's Office, and he worked his way up to Arab affairs advisor to the prime minister. Later he became director of the Youth Immigration Division of the Jewish Agency. He won the Yigal Allon prize for outstanding pioneering service to Israeli society. His first novel, *Tarnegol Kaparot* ("Scapegoat," 1987), is a semi-autobiographical novel depicting the integration of an Iraqi Jewish youth in an Israeli transit camp shortly after 1948. This novel is included in Israel's secondary school syllabus. Other novels by Amir are *Mafri'aḥ ha-Yonim* (1992; "Farewell Baghdad," Ger., 1998), *Ahavat Sha'ul* ("Saul's Love," 1998), and *Yasmin* (2005).

BIBLIOGRAPHY: A. Zehavi, in: *Yedioth Ahronoth*, Feb. 3, 1984; N. Berg, "*Sifrut Ma'abarah*: Literature of Transition," in: K.W. Avruch (ed.), *Critical Essays on Israeli Society, Religion and Government* (1997), 187–207; R. Snir, "*Ha- Ẓiyyonut bi-Re'i ha-Sifrut ha-Yafah ha-Aravit ve-ha-Ivrit shel Yehudei Irak*," in: *Pe'amim*, 73 (1998), 128–46; Y. Manzur, "*He'arot Lashon: E. Amir*," in: *Leshonenu la-Am*, 50:2 (1999), 80–92.

[Anat Feinberg (2nd ed.)]

AMIR, MENAHEM (1930–), Israeli criminologist; considered one of the founding fathers of the field of criminology in Israel and specializing in rape, victimology, organized crime, police, and terror. In 1953 he graduated in sociology and education from the Hebrew University of Jerusalem and in 1958 he received his M.A. degree in sociology and psychology there. In 1965 he received his Ph.D. in criminology from University of Pennsylvania in Philadelphia. From 1966 until 1969 he served as a lecturer in criminology at the Hebrew University. In 1971–72 he was a senior lecture at Tel Aviv University, returning to the Hebrew University in 1972. From 1977 until 1982 he served as the head of the Center of Criminology at the Hebrew University. He also held this position 1983–84 and 1989–91. In 1989 he became full professor at the Hebrew University and in 1999 professor emeritus. During these years Amir also taught at universities abroad in the U.S., Canada, and Australia, and at the same time he participated in public action, such as the founding of Al-Sam, the anti-drug organization, serving as its chairman in Jerusalem. He was also a member of public committees dealing with prostitution and organized crime and chairman of the prisoner rehabilitation program. He was awarded the Human Rights Association Founders Prize, the Israeli Criminologist Association Prize, and the Ford Fund for Researches Prize. He received the Israel Prize for criminology in 2003 with a citation that pointed to his work as a rare combination of theory, empirical research, and practical application. Amir published more than 90 articles and wrote or edited eight books, including *Patterns in Forcible Rape* (1971); *Organized Crime: Uncertainties and Dilemmas* (1999) with S. Einstein; and *Police Security and Democracy: Theory and Practice*, 2 vols. (2001) with S. Einstein.

[Shaked Gilboa (2nd ed.)]

AMIRA, BINYAMIN (1896–1968), Israeli mathematician. Born in Mogilev-Podolsk, Russia, Amira was taken to Palestine in 1900. He founded the Institute of Mathematics at the Hebrew University, Jerusalem. He also founded the *Journal d'analyse mathématique*, which appeared in 17 volumes from 1955 to 1966.

AMIRAN, DAVID (1910–2003), Israeli geographer. Amiran was born in Berlin, Germany. After studying in Berne, Switzerland, he immigrated to Palestine in 1935 and became librarian of the geological department of the Hebrew University of Jerusalem. During World War II he was an officer in the Royal Engineers, and on his discharge joined the Palestine Meteorological Service. In 1949 he began teaching geography at the Hebrew University and was appointed a full professor in 1963. From 1956 to 1959 Amiran was director of the Research Council of Israel and of the Negev Institute for Arid Zone Research. In 1961 he founded the Israel Geographic Society and served as its president until 1977. From 1962 to 1968 he was acting chairman of the International Geographical Union's Commission on the Arid Zone and in 1968 became a member of the Union's Commission on Man and Environment. From 1965 to 1968 he was vice president of the Hebrew University. In 1978 he established the Jerusalem Institute for Israel Studies and served as its director until 1984. In 1977 he was awarded the Israel Prize in the social sciences.

Amiran directed the compilation of the *Atlas of Israel* (Hebrew edition, 1956–64; English enlarged edition, 1970) and together with A.P. Schick wrote *Geographical Conversion Tables* (1961). He edited the 1963 edition of R. Roericht's *Bibliotheca Geographica Palestinae* and for UNESCO *Land Use in Semi-arid Mediterranean Climates* (*Arid Zone Research*, vol. 26, 1964). Amiran published over 120 books and articles in various fields of geography, among them several which summarized the whole field. His work contributed to the discipline in diverse areas, such as physical and human geography. One of his major fields of study was the desert, which he studied in Israel as well as in other places around the world. His specialization in desert studies led the governments of Peru and Brazil to invite him to carry out studies for them. His wife RUTH (1914–), an archaeologist, served as a staff member of the Hazor expedition (1955–58) and also excavated tumuli west of Jerusalem (1953), Tell Nagila (1962–63), Arad (with Y. Aharoni; 1962–66), the Citadel of David in Jerusalem (1968–), etc. She is a coauthor of *Hazor*, 3 vols. (1958–61) and published *Ancient Pottery of the Holy Land* (1970), a comprehensive study of ancient pottery in Ereẓ Israel. She was appointed field archaeologist to the Israel Museum. In 1982 she was awarded the Israel Prize for archaeology.

AMIRAN (formerly **Pougatchov**), **EMANUEL** (1909–1993), composer and teacher. Born in Warsaw, Amiran went to Palestine in 1924, and after study in London, returned to teach music in schools and teachers' seminaries. He was co-founder and director of the Music Teachers Training College in Tel Aviv (1944–55), and in 1955 became supervisor of musical education in the Ministry of Education and Culture. His songs, which are among the most important contributions to the Israeli folk style, include *Emek Emek Avodah, El ha-Ma'ayan Ba Gedi Katan, Mayim Mayim, Ki mi-Ẓiyyon, Uru Aḥim ve-Na'aleh Har Ẓiyyon, Ha-Zore'im be-Dimah*, and *Halleluyah-Kumu ve-Na'aleh*. He also wrote choral, orchestral, and piano music.

AMIRIM (Heb. אֲמִירִים; meaning "summits," referring to the beautiful local scenery), moshav in northern Israel, near Mt. Meron in Upper Galilee. Amirim was founded in 1950, and taken over in 1956 by a group of vegetarians and naturalists (Israeli-born and others). Amirim had no livestock but grew fruit (apples, apricots, peaches, various kinds of nuts) and vegetables, supplying the settlers' dietary requirements. The moshav offered the public a wide array of alternative health cures, from reflexology to holistic massage as well as restaurant and vacationing facilities. Amirim's population was approximately 380 in the mid-1990s, growing to 458 in 2002.

[Efraim Orni / Shaked Gilboa (2nd ed.)]

AMISHAI-MAISELS, ZIVA (1939–), art scholar. Amishai-Maisels was born Maxine Maisels in Brooklyn, N.Y., the daughter of Moses Ḥayyim (Misha) *Maisels (M.H. Amishai). Her family moved to Israel in 1959, and in the 1963 academic year, she began teaching at the Hebrew University's Department of Art History. She is known for her work on religious, historical, and personal symbolism in modern art, including problems of identity and depictions of the other. She concentrated especially on Modern Jewish Art and the work of Chagall, Steinhardt, Lipchitz, and Bezem. Among her most important contributions to the field is her work on the influence of the Holocaust on modern art among both Jews and Christians. She divided their reactions between depictions of the Holocaust's events and the way they have been symbolized in traditional and personal terms, explaining how the resulting images have become archetypes for representations of catastrophe. For this work, she received the Israel Prize in art history in 2004. She wrote many articles, and the books she published include *Chagall at the Knesset* (1973); *Jakob Steinhardt: Etchings and Lithographs* (1981); *Gauguin's Religious Themes* (1985); *Naftali Bezem* (1986); *Depiction and Interpretation: The Influence of the Holocaust on the Visual Arts* (1993); *Jewish Art* (with Gabrielle Sed-Rajna et al., 1995, 1997).

AMIT (Mizrachi Women's Organization of America), U.S. organization founded in 1925 by Bessie Goldstein *Gotsfeld to give religious Zionist women an independent role in the development of Palestine as a Jewish homeland. Prior to the group's formation, women participated in the *Mizrachi movement through auxiliary organizations that raised funds for projects administered by men. When they decided to implement their own programs, the new American Mizrachi women confronted resistance from a male leadership accustomed to controlling movement coffers. In the face of the men's unrelenting claims to their members' resources, the Mizrachi women struggled in their first decade to maintain institutional integrity. In 1934, the group declared its complete autonomy from the men and stands today as the largest religious Zionist organization in the United States.

The Mizrachi Women's Organization has been guided by the principle that the establishment of the land of Israel by the Jewish people should be in the spirit of Israel's Torah. Its initial projects focused on ensuring that young Jewish girls in Palestine would receive training and preparation for productive and spiritual lives. Beit Zeiroth Mizrachi, a technical school and cultural center for adolescent girls in Jerusalem, opened its doors in 1933, welcoming both German refugee and native girls for training in technical, secular, and religious subjects. A second school in Tel Aviv included a Beth Chalutzoth where young working women could reside. The American Junior Mizrachi Women broadened their mother's initial endeavors to take on the creation and support of day nurseries. The religious Zionist women also built an agricultural training school and a teacher's seminary for young women, as well as homes for orphaned and neglected children.

Mizrachi women made a critical contribution to *Youth Aliyah rescue through its establishment of children's residences and youth villages for refugees from traditional backgrounds. These included the Motza Children's Home, where the first of the "Teheran children" were received, the Mosad Aliyah Children's Village in Petaḥ Tikvah, and Kfar Batya in Ra'ananah. Throughout the ensuing decades, Mizrachi women have housed and educated the needy children of each generation of new Israeli immigrants, from countries as diverse as Russia, Iran, Kazakhstan, France, and Ethiopia.

The Mizrachi Women's Organization continues its commitment to vocational education and teacher training. In 1983, the group adopted the name AMIT, and was designated as Israel's official network for religious technological secondary education. Today, AMIT cares for more than 15,000 youngsters in more than 60 schools, youth villages, surrogate homes, and child care facilities throughout Israel. The organization raises funds for all the major Israel campaigns and is a member of both the World Zionist Organization and the Conference of Presidents of Major American Jewish Organizations.

BIBLIOGRAPHY: L.M. Goldfeld, *Bessie* (1982); *Mizrachi Women's Organization of America: Its Aims and Accomplishments* (n.d.); A. Kahn, "Gotsfeld, Bessie Goldstein," in: P.E. Hyman and D. Dash Moore (eds.), *Jewish Women in America: An Historical Encyclopedia*, 1 (1997), 545; R. Raisner, "AMIT," *ibid.*, 48–49.

[Tracy Sivitz (2nd ed.)]

AMIT (Slutzky), MEIR (1921–), Israeli military commander and politician. Member of the Ninth Knesset. Amit was born in Tiberias. From 1939 to 1952 he was a member of kibbutz *Alonim. He joined the *Haganah in 1936, and from 1940 to 1945 served in the supernumerary police. In 1947 Amit participated in the battles for *Mishmar ha-Emek and the *Jezreel Valley. In 1948 he joined the IDF and participated in the battle for the liberation of the Lower Galilee and Operation Hiram (see *War of Independence). In 1950 he was appointed commander of the Golani Brigade and in 1951 commander of the Training Command, and chief of operations on the General Staff. After spending a year in an officers' course in England, he was appointed IDF chief of operations in 1954, commander of the Southern Command in 1955, and again chief of operations in 1956, in which capacity he coordinated the planning team for the *Sinai Campaign of 1956. In 1958 he became commander of the Northern Command. In 1959 he took time off to study business administration at Columbia University in New York. In 1961 he was appointed head of the Intelligence Section of the IDF. From 1963 to 1968 he was head of the Mossad (Israel's intelligence services). From 1968 to 1977 Amit was director-general of Koor Industries, the Histadrut's industrial conglomerate. In 1977 he resigned from Koor to join the Democratic Movement for Change and was elected to the Ninth Knesset on its list. In October of that same year he was appointed minister of transportation and communications but resigned in September 1978 after the DMC disintegrated, and joined the Shinui ve-Yozmah parliamentary group. He later left Shinui to join the Israel Labor Party. After 1978 Amit held various senior management positions in various hi-tech companies.

[Susan Hattis Rolef (2nd ed.)]

AMITSUR, SAMSON ABRAHAM (1921–1994), mathematician. Born in Jerusalem, Amitsur studied at the Hebrew University, where he received his doctorate in 1949. From 1951 to

1954 he was a member of the Institute for Advanced Studies at Princeton, U.S.A., and was appointed professor at the Hebrew University in 1960. He was awarded the Israel Prize for exact sciences in 1953.

AMITTAI (c. 800), Hebrew liturgical poet in *Oria, southern Italy; father of the liturgical poet *Shephatiah of Oria. According to tradition, the family was exiled to Italy by *Titus, after the destruction of the Temple. The *Ahimaaz chronicle describes Amittai as "a sage, learned in the Torah, a poet and scholar, strong in faith." Several *piyyutim* signed simply Amittai may probably be credited to him, including the touching *pizmon Ezkerah Elohim ve-Ehemayah* ("Lord I remember Thee and am sore amazed") which is included in the Concluding Service for the Day of Atonement according to the Ashkenazi rite, as well as *Eikh Narim Rosh be-Ereẓ Oyevim* ("How shall we raise our heads in a hostile land"). Some authorities however ascribe the former *piyyut* to his grandson *Amittai ben Shephatiah. The compositions breathe the spirit of the ancient Palestinian religious poetry.

BIBLIOGRAPHY: B. Klar (ed.), *Megillat Aḥima'aẓ* (1944), 12, 206f.; Davidson, Oẓar, 4 (1933), 368; Zunz, Lit Poesie, 256; Roth, Italy, 50ff.; Schirmann, in: Roth, Dark Ages, 250.

[Abraham Meir Habermann]

AMITTAI BEN SHEPHATIAH (late ninth century), liturgical poet in Oria, S. Italy, grandson of *Amittai; he succeeded his father *Shephatiah as leader of the community in Oria, evidently exercising his authority in an arbitrary manner. Over 30 of Amittai's liturgical poems have been published, and several were incorporated into the Italian and Ashkenazi liturgies. Although following the traditions of the Hebrew poetry of the Orient, Amittai often makes use of rare or novel word forms. Amittai's poems contain references to the persecutions to which the Jews of his day were subjected, in particular lamenting the forced conversions imposed by the Byzantine emperor *Basil I (867–86). Allusions to religious *disputations between Jews and Christians also appear in his work. In one poem he employs the dialogue form for a disputation between the Congregation of Israel and its enemies, possibly chanted by two groups of worshipers, or by the precentor and congregation alternately. Another poetical dialogue, also possibly recited in synagogue, is a debate between the vine and other trees discussing the merits of drinking and abstinence. Amittai also composed hymns and poems for special occasions; his epithalamium on the marriage of his sister Cassia to Hasadiah b. Hananeel served as a model for subsequent compositions in France and Germany. He was able to improvise, and recited a lament over the bier of a wayfarer which he saw being conveyed through the streets. The incident was parodied by a teacher named Moses (later of Pavia) who incurred Amittai's resentment, and had to leave Oria. In general his poems consist of equal stanzas each with its own rhyming key, varying from distiches to decastiches, sometimes with a repetend at the end of each strophe. Y. David's critical edition of Amittai's poems contains 46 poems collected on the basis of 100 manuscripts in addition to the work by B. Klar, *Megillat Aḥima'aẓ*.

BIBLIOGRAPHY: Schirmann, Italyah, 2–11; idem, Roth, Dark Ages, 252–6; B. Klar (ed.), *Megillat Aḥima'aẓ* (1944), 36–37, 72–119; Davidson, Oẓar, 4 (1933), 368–9; Zunz, Lit Poesie, 166–8; Y. David, *The Poems of Amittay, Critical Edition with Introduction and Commentary* (1975).

[Abraham Meir Habermann]

AMMATHA (**Hamta, Ammatu, Ammatus**), ancient town located east of the Jordan, 21 Roman mi. south of *Pella. Ammatha was a fortified city in the period of the Second Temple, when it was captured by Alexander Yannai, who seized there the treasures of Theodore, the son of Zeno, ruler of Philadelphia (Jos., Ant. 13:356; Wars 1:86–87). When Alexander later resumed his campaign in Transjordan, he found that Theodore had razed the abandoned city to the ground (Jos., Ant. 13:356; Wars 1:86–89). A royal palace, nevertheless, still existed there in the time of Herod (Jos., Ant., 17:277).

Ammatha was the capital of one of the five districts, each with its own council (*synhedrion*), into which Gabinius divided Judea (Jos., Ant. 14:91; Wars 1:170). In Byzantine times it was still the headquarters of a fiscal district. It is mentioned several times in rabbinic sources as Ammatu, Hamtan, or Hamata, which would indicate a place possessing hot springs (TJ, Shev. 6:1, 39d; Mid. Ps. to 92:11). In the Arab period, Ammatha continued to be an important center of agriculture (cereals, indigo) and industry (arrowheads). The Arab geographer al-Idrīsī (1154) mentions it along with Jericho and Beth-Shean as one of the finest towns of the Jordan Valley. Ammatha is identified with Tell ʿAmmātā, northeast of the confluence of the Jabbok and Jordan rivers.

BIBLIOGRAPHY: Glueck, in: AASOR, 15 (1935), 95ff.; Avi-Yonah, Geog, 165.

[Michael Avi-Yonah]

AMMERSCHWIHR (Ger. **Ammerschweier**), town in eastern France, 5 mi. N.W. of *Colmar. Jewish residents in Ammerschwihr are mentioned in 1534 when *Joseph (Joselmann) ben Gershom of Rosheim notified them of complaints made by the Colmar magistracy that they were contravening its regulations by introducing foreign currency into the city and selling new clothes there. The municipal regulations of 1561–63, which refer to the text of a former regulation (of 1440), specify the conditions governing Jewish residence in Ammerschwihr. The Jews were required to make an annual payment of 16 florins to the city and city guilds and were prohibited from leaving their homes during the week preceding Easter, and from fetching water from the wells on Sundays and Christian holy days. Outside their homes they were to wear the Jewish *badge. Sale of goods was forbidden to Jews at any place other than in front of the "Stockbrunnen"; they could, however, engage in peddling, and sell their wares at the annual fair; all Jewish visitors to Ammerschwihr had to pay three *deniers* for each day they spent in the city, and an additional six *deniers* if they remained overnight. Jewish residence ceased from the end of the 16th century; the toll was still imposed between 1625 and 1630 on transients (Archives Municipals. BB 17 fol. 82, 103). The "rue des Juifs" was located between the Colmar gate and the market place.

BIBLIOGRAPHY: Hoffmann, in: *Documents inédits*, 1 (1904), 81–82 (published by the *Revue d' Alsace*); Loeb, in: REJ, 5 (1882), 95.

[Bernhard Blumenkranz]

AMMI'AD (Heb. עַמִּיעַד), kibbutz in northern Israel, on the Tiberias–Rosh Pinnah highway. Ammiad, affiliated with Iḥud ha-Kevuẓot ve-ha-Kibbutzim, was founded in 1946 by a group of Israeli-born youth, who were later joined by immigrants. The rocky ground allocated to the settlement had to undergo thorough land reclamation to enable the development of farm branches, which included an avocado plantation, deciduous fruit orchards, intensive field crops, and beef cattle. Its factory produced filtration and fertilization systems. The kibbutz also operated a winery and vacation resort. In 2002 it numbered 429 residents. Remnants of a wayfarers' hostel from the Middle Ages have been unearthed there.

[Efraim Orni]

°**AMMIANUS MARCELLINUS** (c. 330–400), last of the great Latin pagan historians of antiquity. He speaks of Jews in four separate passages of his history. The first refers to Pompey's conquest of Jerusalem (14, 8:11–12); in the second he quotes the disparaging remarks of Marcus Aurelius on the Jews (22, 5:5). Most important is the third passage which contains a description of the attempt of *Julian the Apostate to rebuild the Temple in Jerusalem (23, 1:2–3). He ascribes this not to sympathy with the Jews, but to the emperor's desire to leave a memorial to his reign. According to Marcellinus, the project was entrusted to a certain Alypius of Antioch, but it could not be executed because of an explosion of balls of fire on the Temple Mount. The fourth passage mentions a city on the Euphrates deserted by its Jewish inhabitants during Julian's campaign against the Persians (24, 4:1–2). Marcellinus does not express his personal opinion with regard to the proposed rebuilding of the Temple, but from his quotation from Marcus Aurelius he does not seem to have been well disposed to the Jews.

BIBLIOGRAPHY: Reinach, Textes, 351–5.

[Menahem Stern]

AMMI BAR NATHAN (end of third century), Palestinian *amora*. Ammi and his colleague, R. Assi, were the most outstanding of the Palestinian *amoraim* of the period. They were referred to as "the renowned Palestinian *kohanim*" (Meg. 22a) and "the Palestinian magistrates" (Sanh. 17b). Apparently, while still in Babylonia, Ammi studied under Rav (Ned. 40b–41a). In Palestine he studied under Oshaya and Ḥanina, and also transmitted statements in the names of R. Yannai, R. Joshua b. Levi, and R. Judah ha-Nasi II. However, like his colleague R. Assi, his main teacher was R. Johanan. Both Ammi and Assi studied at Johanan's yeshivah in Tiberias (Shab. 119a; Git. 40a). When Johanan died, Ammi observed the mourning customary for a father (MK 25b). He also studied under Resh Lakish who once ransomed him from captivity (TJ, Ter. 8:10, 46b). Ammi seems to have been both a pupil and a colleague of Eleazar and apparently also of R. Isaac Nappaḥa. Ammi and Assi are frequently mentioned in conjunction. They were ordained together, and at their ordination a song was sung in their honor, commencing: "Ordain us men like these!" (Ket. 17a). After the death of R. Johanan and R. Eleazar in the year 279, both headed the yeshivah at Tiberias, but Ammi was the more important (*Iggeret R. Sherira Gaon*). Both were praised for their piety and stories were told of miracles which happened to them (Ber. 62a), of their scrupulousness in honoring the Sabbath, of their preparation of *eruv tavshilin for all the inhabitants of Tiberias (Beẓah 16b), and of their good works (TJ, Ḥag. 1:7, 76c), especially the redemption of captives. It is also stated that although there were 13 synagogues in Tiberias, they used to pray "between the pillars" in their place of learning (Ber. 8a, 30b). Ammi and Assi would interrupt their studies and announce "Let anyone who has a lawsuit enter" (that the case could be heard in the presence of both litigants; Shab. 10a). Together with R. Ḥiyya b. Abba, Ammi and Assi were appointed by R. Judah ha-Nasi II as inspectors of education in the towns and villages of Palestine, with authority to introduce necessary reforms (TJ, Ḥag. 1:7, 76c). Ammi accompanied Judah ha-Nasi II to Hammath-Geder (TJ, Av. Zar. 2:2, 40d and 5:15, 45b). There is also a record of his visit to the court of Zenobia, queen of Palmyra, to intercede for the release of a scholar who had been taken prisoner (TJ, Ter. 8:10, 46b). Despite his closeness to the *nasi* and his household, Ammi did not refrain from criticizing their actions when he disapproved of them; as in the case of the appointment of magistrates in consideration of monetary payment (TJ, Bik. 3:3, 65d). As long as R. Huna, head of the yeshivah of Sura, in Babylonia, was still alive, Ammi and Assi continued to be subject to his authority (Meg. 22a). The reference in Bava Batra 11b, "R. Huna asked R. Ammi" is taken by some to allude to another, earlier Ammi, and by others to another, later R. Huna (see Tos. *ibid.*). However, after the death of R. Huna in the late third century, Ammi seems to have been the outstanding authority of his generation. On one occasion the preamble to the publication of a certain practical halakhic decision of his read: "From me, Ammi b. Nathan, the Torah goes forth to all Israel" (Git. 44a). Among those who addressed halakhic inquiries to Ammi were R. Abbahu, head of the yeshivah at Caesarea in Ereẓ Israel (TJ, Yev. 4:11, 6a) and R. Naḥman and Rava, heads of the yeshivah at Maḥoza in Babylonia (Git. 63b). Ammi probably returned to Babylonia for some time, since halakhic discussions are reported between him and R. Naḥman (Ber. 47b) and R. Ḥisda (Yev. 21b).

BIBLIOGRAPHY: Hyman, Toledot, 219–25; Frankel, Mevo, 63ff.; Halevy, Dorot, 2 (1923), 348ff.; Bacher, Pal Amor.

[Zvi Kaplan]

AMMINADAV (Heb. עַמִּינָדָב), moshav S.W. of Jerusalem. It was founded in 1950 as a work village whose settlers were primarily employed as laborers for *Jewish National Fund land reclamation. The settlers came from Turkey, Morocco, or were Israeli-born. The village economy was based on hillculture (vineyards, deciduous fruit, vegetables) and poultry. In the vicinity the John F. Kennedy Memorial was built and a great deal of afforestation work done. Amminadav's population in the mid-1990s was approximately 400 but due to its location near Jerusalem many new families settled there, bringing the population up to 595 in 2002. The moshav's name derives from a prince of the Judah tribe, the father of Nahshon.

[Efraim Orni]

AMMON, AMMONITES, ancient people. The Ammonites are one of the many tribes that emerged from the Syrio-Arabian desert during the second millennium B.C.E. and eventually established a national kingdom in Transjordan. In the Bible they are usually called "*Benei ʿAmmon*" ("Children of Ammon"), while Akkadian inscriptions have them as *Bīt Am-ma-na-aia* and their land as *māt Ba-an-am-na-aya.* As is now known from Ammonite inscriptions of the seventh century B.C.E. their self-appelation was *bnʿmn* written as one word, with no *yod* following the nun. According to Genesis 19:38, the Ammonites are named for their ancestor Ben-Ammi (*ben ʿammi*, "son of my kin"), who was so named by Lot's younger daughter because he was born of her incestuous relations with her father. Since Lot was a nephew of Abraham, the story attests the Israelites' belief that the Ammonites were related to them. However, Deuteronomy 23:4 forbids participation by Ammonite and Moabite aliens in the Israelite cultic community.

The Land

At the end of the 15th century B.C.E., the Ammonites settled along the upper and central Jabbok River and in the area of its tributaries. Their eastern border was the desert, with the central Jabbok constituting their northern boundary (e.g., Deut. 3:16; Josh. 12:2). It was supposed that their western and southern boundaries were marked by the so-called *rujm malfūf* (sing.). These were massive structures built of large, rough stones. Some of the structures are circular and up to 16 meters in diameter, while others are rectangular or square. Their massive construction and strategic location, within sight of one another, indicate that these buildings were used for guarding and defense purposes. But a recent excavation in *rujm malfūf* west of Rabbath-Ammon (Amman) showed it to be from the Roman period, as no earlier remains were found there. It is possible then to reconstruct the Ammonite borders approximately in light of biblical data and topographical conditions. The northern boundary ran from the central part of the Jabbok River (which flows east to west) to the point where Wadi al-Rumaymīn enters the Jabbok. The western border extended from the Jabbok Wadi at Rumaymīn confluence southward along the Wadi Umm al-Danānīr, which originates

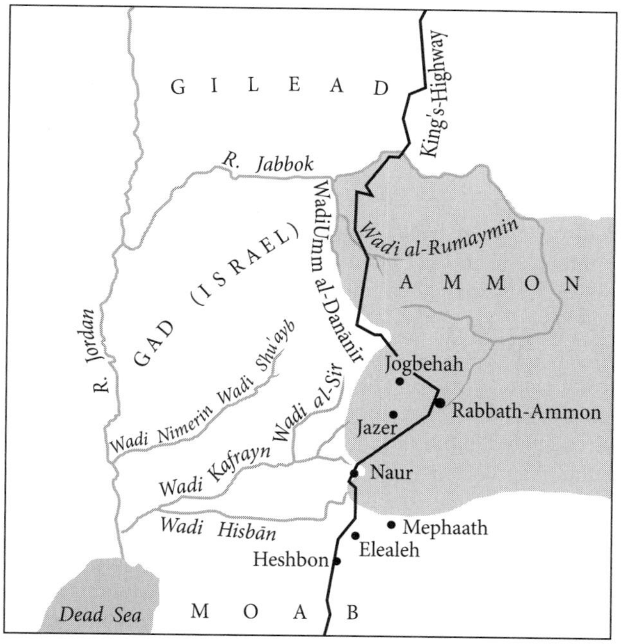

Ammonite region and towns.

in the Sahl al-Bugay'a Valley. The ridge of mountains divides the upper Jabbok tributaries from the upper beds of Wadi Shu'ayb, Wadi al-Sīr, Wadi Kafrayn, and Wadi Ḥisbān. Important settlements along the western boundary were at Jogbehah (al-Jubahyat), Jazer, and Nāʿūr. On the south, at Nāʿūr, the border turned eastward, passing north of the Israelite settlements at Elealeh and Mephaath. The most important of the Ammonite settlements was *Rabbath-Ammon, whose location made it ideal as the royal city and the capital of the country. The city is situated alongside the source of the Jabbok (II Sam. 12:27) and enjoys natural protection. It drew its wealth from the agricultural surroundings and from international trade conducted along the main north-south road of the Transjordanian highlands – the "King's Highway." As a border city, Rabbath-Ammon lay in the path of the caravan trade between Arabia and the major centers of the Fertile Crescent. But the country was equally open to incursions of nomads who lived by raising sheep, goats, and camels, and by raiding the settled population (as well as each other). An exploration headed by N. Glueck discovered a network of fortresses along the eastern border of the Transjordanian states. It has become clear that these communities were destroyed by invasions of desert nomads in the second quarter of the first millennium B.C.E.

Culture

The transition from the nomadic life to permanent settlement in the Jabbok region caused changes in the social order, economy, and government of the Ammonites. They adopted a way of life and form of government which was an amalgam of nomadism, in which they had been rooted for generations, and the customs of the urban and agricultural civilizations.

The Ammonites were organized along the lines of a centralized national monarchy (I Sam. 12:26). It was dynastic (II Sam. 10:1) and based upon a ramified administration (II Sam. 10:3 = I Chron. 19:3; Jer. 49:3; Amos 1:15). Ammonite seals testify to the existence of high officials with the title *ʿbd* ("servant"), such as *lʾDnnr ʿbd ʿMndb* "belonging to Adoni-Nur, servant of Amminadab," and *lʾDnplṭ ʿbd ʿMndb* "belonging to Adoni-Phelet, servant of Amminadab." The statuette of an important Ammonite bears the legend *Yrḥʿzr rb rkshn* "Yaraḥʿazar, Overseer of the Horses." Seals of Ammonite women indicate that they were also appointed to the administrative staff or owned property. It is fairly certain that the higher officialdom was selected from the Ammonite nobility. Luxurious stone-carved burial caves containing tools and expensive jewelry, undoubtedly reserved for noble families, have been found in Rabbath-Ammon and its environs.

Most of the population supported itself by farming (grain crops and orchards) and grazing (Num. 32:1–4; Jer. 48:32; II Chron. 27:5). There were extensive tracts of arable land and settlements were usually situated near wells and streams, which were used to irrigate the fields by means of man-made channels. In areas unsuited for agriculture, mainly in the east, the inhabitants lived as seminomads in temporary quarters, such as tents and huts. In times of danger they could find shelter in the fortresses that dotted the borders. The Ammonite material culture, as far as can be determined from finds (mostly from the eighth and seventh centuries), was influenced by several centers of culture. The local imitations were marked by design and workmanship inferior to those of Ammon's northern and western neighbors. Architectural style was simple and massive, and lacked any decorative elements. Ceramic artifacts, however, indicate that Ammonite potters achieved a high level of technical proficiency and adapted Assyrian, Phoenician, and Israelite styles. Stone sculpture reveals a mixture of Egyptian, Phoenician, Syrian, and Assyrian elements. The two most common forms of seals – the scarab-shaped and the cone-shaped – are represented. The engraving on seals tends to be crude and does not represent the work of consummate artists. The designs engraved on the seals are rich in art motifs taken from Phoenicia, Egypt, Aram, and Assyria. Most of the objets d'art that have been recovered came from well-planned and spacious rock-hewn family burial caves. Some of these caves have ledges upon which the corpses were placed. Many ceramic, metal, and glass objects were found near the bones in these tombs. The discovery of a tenth- or ninth-century cover of an anthropoid coffin from Sahab is worth note, as it appears to have been widespread in Egypt and Philistia; during the eighth and seventh centuries, the Ammonites buried their dead in Assyrian-type coffins (cf. the tomb of Adoni-Nur). (For Ammonite mourning customs, see Jer. 49:3.)

Comparatively little is known of the Ammonite religion. The national god was Milcom (e.g., I Kings 11:5), whose name appears on two seals from the neo-Babylonian and Persian periods. The custom of burning children for *Moloch is mentioned several times in the Bible, but it is not clear if the references are to the Ammonite cult and its god Milcom, and there is no positive evidence that the sacrifice of human beings to Milcom was practiced in Ammon. It is also unclear if the various theophoric elements appearing in private Ammonite names, such as Yaraḥʿazar, or the motifs engraved on seals, such as the crescent on the seal of Mannu-ki-Inurta, indicate religious syncretism. Like most of the tribes whose descent is traced to *Eber, the Ammonites were circumcised, as is apparent from Jeremiah 9:24–25.

Evidence about the Ammonite script and language is available from many names and a few epigraphic discoveries. The Ammonites used the Canaanite alphabet, which displayed the substantial influence of Aramean lapidary writing. The Ammonite language was no doubt a North-West *Semitic language, as may be seen from personal names (e.g., Nahash, Hanun, Shabel, Amminadab, Hananel, Menahem, Abihaz, Elisha) and words (e.g., *bn*, "son"; *bt*, "daughter"; *ʿbd*, "servant"; *ʾmh*, "maidservant"; *naʿar*, "young man"). However, Arabic elements can also be discerned in the Ammonite onomasticon. These South-Semitic elements must have entered the language at a later stage, when the Ammonites entered into trade with Arabia, which received its first impetus beginning in the tenth century and intensified during the Assyrian period.

Ammon and Israel

The Ammonites' finest hour came at the end of the period of the Judges. *Nahash, their king, conquered Israelite territories bordering Ammon and even succeeded in crossing the Jabbok to the north and besieging Jabesh-Gilead (I Sam. 11). His degrading demand upon the inhabitants of Jabesh-Gilead testifies to Ammonite power and self-confidence; it was a challenge to all the tribes of Israel, as was the seven-day period given to the population of the city to find a savior (I Sam. 11:3). The unexpected appearance of *Saul at the head of a unified Israelite army completely altered the balance of power between Ammon and Israel and brought about the Ammonite withdrawal from Israelite territory in Gilead. Saul did not enslave the Ammonites, as he was so occupied with ending internal feuds and wars with Israel's neighbors (I Sam. 14:47–48). Nahash the Ammonite remained on his throne and even passed the kingdom on to his son Hanun (II Sam. 10:1; I Chron. 19:1). Hanun's provocation of King David's goodwill delegation (II Sam. 10), which was probably instigated by the Arameans, led to war between Ammon and David (II Sam. 10–12; I Chron. 19–20). Aramean military aid to Ammon was not sufficient to prevent David's conquest of the entire country. The intent of II Samuel 12:30 (= I Chron. 20:2), regarding the crown that David removed from the head of the Ammonite king, is not clear: it may mean either that David crowned himself king of the Ammonites or that he only took the crown as spoil but left the kingdom in the hands of Shobi, the son of Nahash, who became his vassal (II Sam. 17:27).

Ammon was subjugated to Israel during the reigns of David and Solomon. Although David subjected the Ammonites to a corvée (II Sam. 12:31), he also appointed some of them to important positions in the kingdom (II Sam. 23:37; = I Chron. 11:39). *Solomon had Ammonite wives, some of whom brought the worship of their god, Milcom, to Jerusalem (I Kings 11:5–8; II Kings 23:13). Moreover, Solomon's son *Rehoboam, the heir apparent, was born of an Ammonite mother (I Kings 14:21). This fact might have been reason for some affinity between Ammon and Jerusalem, but it did not prove sufficient to create a firm alliance with either Judah or Israel after the division of the kingdom. The split in Solomon's kingdom, the wars between Rehoboam and Jeroboam, *Shishak's campaign into Ereẓ Israel, and the rise in strength of *Aram-Damascus all encouraged the Ammonites to cast off the Israelite yoke and become independent. The kings of Aram-Damascus, who sought hegemony over Palestine, encouraged the Transjordanian states to act against the kingdoms of Israel and Judah.

Ammon's fate was largely dependent upon the relative military strengths of Aram, Israel, and Judah and the political ability of its own rulers to exploit developments in Syria and Palestine for their own ends. It seems that the Ammonites did not participate in the 12-party pact of the kings of Syria, Phoenicia, and Palestine against Assyria. It is most probable that Baasha son of Rehob of Aman who is mentioned among the allies who fought against Shalmaneser III at Karkar in 853 (Pritchard, Texts, 279), was from Mount Amana in Syria, and not from the land of Ammon. II Chronicles 20 contains a description of an invasion of Judah by Moab and Ammon during *Jehoshaphat's time, but the geography of the account is difficult. It is almost certain that the Ammonites exploited the strong Aramean pressures on Israel to extend their borders in Gilead at Israel's expense (Amos 1:13). During the reigns of *Jeroboam son of Joash, *Uzziah, and *Jotham, there was a change in the balance of power in Palestine and Syria. Jeroboam is credited with ruling over Damascus and Hamath (II Kings 14:28), while Uzziah subjugated the Ammonites, who paid a tax and tribute to him and his son Jotham (II Chron. 26:8; 27:5). Some believe that during the period families moved from Judah to Transjordan and established large estates in Gilead, and that among them was the family of Tabeel (Isa. 7:6), which is later called the family of Tobijah. If II Chronicles 27:5 is to be understood literally that the king of the Ammonites paid a tax to Jotham in the second and third years of his reign, it is possible to assume that he rebelled against Jotham and ceased to pay his levy in the fourth year. This cessation of the tax may be explained against the background of II Kings 15:37, where the hostile activities of *Rezin and *Pekah against Judah during Jotham's reign are mentioned. Even though Ammon liberated itself from Judah's domination during this period, Tiglath-Pileser III does not list the king of Ammon among Assyria's enemies. As far as can be seen, the Ammonites did not join the anti-Assyrian alliance of Rezin and Pekah.

Under Assyrian and Babylonian Rule and the End of the Kingdom

The campaign of Tiglath-Pileser III into Palestine in 734–732 B.C.E. drew all the states of the area, including Ammon, into the Assyrian orbit. Subjection to Assyria took the form of periodic payment of taxes, occasional tributes, a corvée, and military aid to the Assyrian king. The tax records of Tiglath-Pileser III mention Sanipu of Ammon (Pritchard, Texts, 282). An Assyrian letter from the last third of the eighth century discovered at Nimrud (Calah) mentions a delegation from the land of the Ammonites (*māt Ba-an-am-ma-na-aia*) that came to Calah together with delegations from other countries bearing tributes to the Assyrian king. Buduilu (Puduil), king of Ammon, did not join *Hezekiah's rebellion against Assyria in 701, but declared his allegiance to the Assyrian monarch by rendering a tribute to him (Pritchard, Texts, 287). In 676, Buduilu is mentioned along with "the kings of Ḫatti, the seashore, and the islands," who were obliged to supply cedar and pine beams from the Lebanon and Sirion mountain ranges for the construction of Esarhaddon's palace at Nineveh (Pritchard, Texts, 291). Amminadab (Amminadbi), the Ammonite king who was contemporary with Esarhaddon and Ashurbanipal, is mentioned together with "22 kings of provinces of the shore, the islands, and the mainland" who paid heavy tributes to the two Assyrian kings and sent their armies to the Assyrian war against Egypt in 667 (Pritchard, Texts, 294). Two Assyrian documents that mention a tax paid by the Ammonites and other nations to Assyria probably come from this period.

The Ammonite kings submitted to Assyrian domination because they saw in it a guarantee of their security against desert marauders and a position within the Assyrian imperial framework was beneficial to commercial activities and economic growth (Jer. 49:4). This considerable economic activity is attested to by the large number of seals and other finds from the period of Assyrian rule. Archaeological evidence also testifies to the growth of local Ammonite production, alongside substantial import of jewelry and other luxury items. The war conducted by Kamashaltu, king of Moab, against the king of Kedar (Pritchard, Texts, 298) and Ezekiel's prophecy regarding Ammon (Ezek. 25:4–5) indicate the serious dangers that the wandering bands posed to the peoples of Transjordan. Only with the aid of Assyria, which held substantial interests in international trade and waged numerous wars against the desert tribes, were the Transjordanian states able to fortify their desert borders and repulse the nomadic marauders. The Assyrians for their part had an interest in strengthening the border states and tying them into the empire's defense system. It is even possible that Ammon was able to extend its borders in Gilead under Assyrian auspices (Zeph. 2:8).

There is no evidence that the transition from Assyrian to Babylonian rule at the end of the seventh century brought about any immediate changes in Ammon's political or economic situation. When Nebuchadnezzar fought Ashkelon in 604–603 B.C.E., "all the kings of the land of Heth" paid a tribute to the Babylonian king, and it appears that the king of

Ammon was counted among this group. Ammonite troops served with the Chaldeans in suppressing *Jehoiakim's rebellion (II Kings 24:1–2), and perhaps in return for this service the Ammonites were given a free hand in Gilead (Jer. 49:1) and their territory was extended westward to the Jordan, as was also the case with the later Babylonian and Persian province of Ammon. A few years later, however, Ammon was disaffected against Babylonia. An Ammonite king is mentioned among the rulers who sent messengers to *Zedekiah in 594–593, in connection with the organization of a general rebellion against Babylonia (Jer. 27:3), but there is no detailed evidence about the fate of the rebellion or about Ammon's participation. There are, however, several suggestions of Ammonite participation in the 589–586 rebellion, namely the representation of Nebuchadnezzar as stopping to decide whether to advance on Rabbath-Ammon or on Jerusalem in Ezekiel 21:23–27, Zedekiah's evident attempt to flee to Transjordan (I Kings 25:4–5), the refugees from Judah who found asylum in Ammon (Jer. 40:11), and the involvement of Baalis', king of Ammon, perhaps the initiator of the anti-Babylonian policy, in the plot to murder *Gedaliah son of Ahikam, the Babylonian deputy in Judah. A Babylonian punitive expedition against Ammon followed several years later. Josephus (Ant., 10:181–2) relates that five years after the destruction of Jerusalem, during the 23rd year of his reign (in 582 B.C.E.), Nebuchadnezzar conducted a military campaign against Syria and Transjordan. As there is no clear and irrefutable indication about the existence of an independent or semi-independent Ammonite nation after the end of the neo-Babylonian period it may be assumed that it was in the course of Nebuchadnezzar's above-mentioned campaign, or shortly thereafter, that Ammon was reorganized as the province, reaching down to the Jordan, which was known in the Hellenistic times as Ammonitis.

The disintegration of the Assyrian Empire toward the end of the seventh century and the political upheavals in Palestine during the neo-Babylonian period led to the collapse of the defense system along Ammon's desert border. Transjordania was invaded by Arabian tribes which destroyed the community. N. Glueck's archaeological survey of Transjordan reveals that sedentary occupation of Transjordan was terminated in the middle of the sixth century; cultivated lands became the territory of desert nomads (cf. Ezek. 25:4–10). Later mention of Ammon or Ammonites does not refer to the country or people as such, but to the province of Ammon and its population. About "Tobiah the Ammonite servant" (e.g., Neh. 2:10; 3:35) there are divergent opinions. According to one view he was not a true Ammonite but a Jew from the family of Tobijah who served in an important role in the Persian administration. He was called an Ammonite by reason of his residence in that territory. But others maintain that just as Sanballat was a Horonite (of Horonaim in Moab?) but a Samarian by residence, so Tobijah was an Ammonite by descent but a Samarian by residence, and like the other Samarians a Yahwist by religion. During the Hellenistic period, the area of Ammon was reduced to its eastern section and its urban center, Philadelphia (Rabbath-Ammon). The western part, which had a large Jewish population, was known as Perea (Peraea) and was annexed by the Hasmonean kingdom under Jonathan.

[Bustanay Oded]

In the *Aggadah*

Ammonites are linked with Moabites throughout the *aggadah* and *halakhah*. The *aggadah* explains the especially severe decree against Ammonites and Moabites: "They shall not enter the congregation of the Lord" (Deut. 23:4). It says that these tribes did not show gratitude to the Israelites, whose ancestor, Abraham, had saved Lot, the father of Ammon and Moab. Instead, they committed four hostile acts against Israel. They sought to destroy Israel by hiring Balaam. They waged open war against them at the time of Jephthah and of Jehoshaphat. Finally they gave full rein to their hatred against Israel at the destruction of the First Temple. As a result, God appointed four prophets – Isaiah, Jeremiah, Ezekiel, and Zephaniah – to proclaim their punishment (Lam. R. 1:10, ed. Buber (1899), 74). When they heard Jeremiah foretell the destruction of Jerusalem, the Ammonites and Moabites hastened to report it to Nebuchadnezzar and persuaded him to attack the capital (Sanh. 96b). At the capture of the city, instead of seeking booty, they seized the Scroll of the Law in the Temple in order to erase the decree against them (Lam. R. 1:10; Yev. 16b). According to another view, they seized the two cherubim from above the Ark of the Covenant and displayed them in order to prove that Israel, too, was worshipping idols (Lam. R. Proem 9, ed. Buber (1899), 8). The original attitude toward the Ammonites and Moabites was certainly positive as can be seen from the biblical prohibition against attacking them: "Be not at enmity with Moab, neither contend with them in battle; for I will not give thee of his land for a possession" (Deut. 2:9) and "when thou comest nigh over against the children of Ammon, harass them not, nor contend with them, for I will not give thee of the land of the children of Ammon for a possession; because I have given it unto the children of Lot for a possession" (Deut. 2:19). The latter legends stem from deep disappointment; the Ammonites and Moabites could have been expected to be the natural allies of Israel because of their close relationship through Lot, instead of which they became their enemies.

In the *Halakhah*

The rabbis made two significant and far-reaching reservations to the injunction "an Ammonite and a Moabite shall not enter into the congregation of the Lord forever." The first was the halakhic ruling contained in the Mishnah (Yev. 8:3) restricting the prohibition to males. There was scriptural justification for this since not only did Boaz marry Ruth the Moabitess, but Rehoboam the son of Solomon was the son of an Ammonite woman (I Kings 14:21, 31). The *aggadah* (Yev. 76b–77a; cf. Ruth R. 4:6) tells in great detail the dramatic story of the dispute concerning David's claim to the throne on account of his descent from Ruth. The dispute was solved by Ithra the Israelite (II Sam. 17:25) "who girt himself with a sword like an Ishmaelite" (since he is called Jether the Ishmaelite in I Chron. 2:17), and threatened to put to death anyone who disputed the *halakhah* which he had received from the *bet din* of Samuel that the law applied only to males.

Equally dramatic were the circumstances which led to the second ruling, the complete abolition of the restriction. On the day when R. Gamaliel was deposed and R. Eliezer b. Azariah appointed *nasi*, "Judah, an Ammonite proselyte," came to the *bet midrash* and asked whether the prohibition applied to him. Joshua b. Hananiah declared himself in favor of his being accepted since the inhabitants of these countries at that time were not descended from the Ammonites and Moabites of the Bible, as "Sennacherib had long ago mixed up all nations." His view was accepted as the *halakhah* (Ber. 28a; cf. Maim., Yad, Issurei Bi'ah 12:25)

[Louis Isaac Rabinowitz]

BIBLIOGRAPHY: G. Landes, in: IDB, 1 (1962), 108–14 (incl. bibl.); idem, in: BA, 24 (1961), 66–88; B. Oded, in: EM, vol. 6, pp. 254–271 (incl. bibl.); N. Glueck, *The Other Side of the Jordan* (1940); idem, in: D. Winton-Thomas (ed.), *Archaeology and Old Testament Study* (1967), 429–53 (incl. bibl.); H.L. Ginsberg, in: *A. Marx Jubilee Volume* (Eng., 1950), 347–68; Noth, in: ZDPV, 68 (1949), 36–45; W.F. Albright, in: *Miscellanea Biblica… B. Ubach* (1954), 131–6 (Eng.); H. Gese, in: ZDPV, 74 (1958), 55–64; H.G. Reventlow, *ibid.*, 79 (1963), 127–37; N. Avigad, in: IEJ, 11 (1952), 163–4; 15 (1965), 222–8. **ADD. BIBLIOGRAPHY:** W. Aufrecht, *Corpus of Ammonite Inscriptions* (1989); S. Ahituv, *Handbook of Ancient Hebrew Inscriptions* (1992), 219–46; B. Macdonald and R. Younker (eds.), *Ancient Ammon* (1999). IN THE AGGADAH: Ginzberg, Legends, index. IN THE HALAKHAH: L. Loew, *Gesammelte Schriften*, 3 (1893), 118–20; Freund, in: *Festschrift… Schwarz* (1917), 180–1.

AMNON (Heb. אֲמְנֹן, אַמְנוֹן, אַמִינוֹן; from the root אמן (*'mn*); "to be firm or trustworthy"), eldest son of King David, born in Hebron of Ahinoam the Jezreelitess (II Sam. 3:2). Becoming infatuated with his beautiful half-sister Tamar, he acted on a ruse devised by his friend Jonadab, "a very clever man," and son of David's brother Shimah, lured her to his bedside on the pretext of illness, raped her, and then cast her out. She then took refuge in the home of her full brother *Absalom. The king did not punish Amnon (II Sam. 13:21). Two years later Absalom invited Amnon to his estate in Baal-Hazor, together with the other royal princes, for a sheep shearing celebration, and ordered his men to kill him while Amnon was merry with wine. (It appears from II Sam. 13:32–33 that Jonadab had now cast his lot with Absalom.) Since David's second son evidently either died young or was incapacitated, Absalom, the third son, now had the strongest claim to the succession on the score of seniority. Recent work from the standpoint of the Bible as literature and feminist criticism has questioned whether Tamar was, in fact, raped. Another trend has been to compare Amnon's actions toward Tamar with David's actions toward Bathsheba.

According to rabbinic tradition (Sanh. 21a), Amnon could have married Tamar as she was conceived prior to her mother's conversion. This tragic incident prompted the rabbis to forbid an unmarried girl to remain alone with a man in a room (*ibid.* 21a–b). The affair of Amnon and Tamar is stigmatized in *Avot* 5:16 as the prototype of selfish love prompted by lust. For reasons of propriety, the Mishnah excludes the story from public reading in synagogue, whether in the original or in Aramaic translation (Meg. 4:10).

BIBLIOGRAPHY: S. Yeivin, *Meḥkarim be-Toledot Yisrael ve-Arẓo* (1960), 196; Ginzberg, Legends, 4 (1913), 118–9. **ADD. BIBLIOGRAPHY:** P. Trible, *Texts of Terror* (1984); T. Reis, in: JANES, 25 (1997), 43–60.

AMNON OF MAINZ (tenth century), martyr and legendary figure. Amnon is known mainly through *Isaac b. Moses of Vienna (12th–13th century) who quotes *Ephraim b. Jacob (12th century) as speaking of Amnon as "a leader of his generation, wealthy, of distinguished ancestry, and pleasing appearance." The legend is that after Amnon resisted repeated attempts by the bishop of Mainz to persuade him to accept Christianity, he was barbarically mutilated. He was brought back to his home, and on Rosh Ha-Shanah was carried into the synagogue. As the *Kedushah* prayer was about to be recited Amnon asked the *ḥazzan* to wait while he "sanctified the great name (of God)," and thereupon recited the hymn "*U-Netanneh Tokef Kedushat ha-Yom*" ("Let us tell the mighty holiness of this day"), after which he died. Three days afterward, he appeared in a dream to *Kalonymus b. Meshullam and taught him the entire prayer, asking him to circulate it throughout the Diaspora for recital in synagogues on Rosh Ha-Shanah. This legend, which gained wide credence during the time of the Crusades, inspired many to martyrdom. In Johanan *Treves' commentary on the Roman *maḥzor* (Bologna, 1540) and in various editions of the Ashkenazi rite, the story is repeated with slight changes. In the Ashkenazi liturgy of Rosh Ha-Shanah (and in its eastern branch, of the Day of Atonement also), the recital of the hymn is invested with great solemnity. It has been adapted by many Sephardi communities of the Mediterranean, in some of which it is recited before *Musaf* in a Ladino translation. *U-Netanneh Tokef* is actually older; for it is found in old liturgical manuscripts and in *genizah* fragments. It apparently derives from a very early Palestinian prayer which was later attributed to Amnon.

BIBLIOGRAPHY: Germ Jud, 1 (1963), 204. **ADD. BIBLIOGRAPHY:** I.G. Marcus, in: *Studien zur juedischen Geschichte und Soziologie* (Festschrift Carlebach, 1992), 97–113.

[Abraham Meir Habermann]

AM OLAM, Russian Jewish society formed to establish agricultural colonies in the United States. The organization took its name from Perez *Smolenskin's famous Hebrew essay "*Am Olam*, ("The Eternal People"), and was founded in Odessa in 1881 by two young utopian idealists, Mania Bakl and Moses Herder, who called for the settling of Jews on the land in America in the form of socialist communes. Coming at a time of rising Jewish emigration and interest in national and social renewal such as motivated the Bilu movement as well, their appeal fell on fertile ground and Am Olam chapters were quickly formed in a number of Russian cities. The first contingent of 70 Jewish craftsmen, artisans, and students left for America from Yelizavetgrad in the spring of 1881 and was followed in 1881–82 by additional groups totaling several hundred people from Kiev, Kremenchug, Vilna, and Odessa. Many of the immigrants never proceeded beyond New York, where they eventually drifted apart, but four colonies were ultimately established. The first of these, consisting of 32 families led by Herman *Rosenthal, settled on over 1,000 acres at Sicily Island, Louisiana, in the spring of 1882 but was soon forced to abandon the site as a result of a disastrous Mississippi River flood. Twelve of these families then went with Rosenthal to South Dakota, where they founded a second colony called "Crimea" in September 1882. Another settlement, "Bethlehem of Judea," was established the same year a few miles away. Both lasted until 1885, when debt and other difficulties led to their liquidation.

The longest-lived of the Am Olam colonies, as well as the most intensely communistic, "New Odessa," was established by some 70 persons near Portland, Oregon, in 1882. Led by the socialist Pavel Kaplan and the non-Jewish disciple of Comte's "religion of humanity," William Frey, the settlement flourished for a while until internal bickering and demoralization set in, bringing about its demise in 1887. Some of the survivors, led by Kaplan, sought to reorganize as an urban commune, first in San Francisco and then in New York, but by 1890 they too had disbanded and the last vestiges of Am Olam had ceased to exist. Many of its former members, however, continued to play an active role as individuals within New York's Jewish socialist community.

BIBLIOGRAPHY: A. Menes, in: A. Tcherikover, *Geshikhte fun der Yidisher Arbeter-Bavegung in di Fareynikte Shtaten*, 2 (1945), 203–38; A. Litvin, in: *Yidisher Kemfer* (Dec. 6, 1935); A. Cahan, *Bleter fun Mayn Lebn*, 2 (1926), 115–8 (on Mania Bakl), 157–8 (on Pavel Kaplan), 84–87, 123–8 (on William Frey), 296–305 (on New Odessa).

[Hillel Halkin]

AMON (Heb. אָמוֹן, אָמֹן), son of *Manasseh; became king of Judah (642–640 B.C.E.) at the age of 22. The author of Chronicles considered the "transgressions" of Amon to have been "more numerous" than those of his father Manasseh (II Chron. 33:23). The reasons for Amon's assassination by members of his court are not explained in the Bible, but the conspirators were put to death by the *am ha-arez* (i.e., "the people of the land," probably the large landowners). They enthroned his young son Josiah. It has been argued that the conspirators were opponents of the pro-Assyrian policies of Manasseh and Amon, while the *am ha-arez* were pro-Assyrian. Support for the hypothesis is based on synchronizing Amon's reign with the period of a rebellion in Syria against Ashurbanipal, king of Assyria, which is reported in Assyrian sources. On this analysis, Amon, who is said to have followed the ways of his father Manasseh (II Kings 21:20–21), would have remained loyal to the Assyrian régime and opposed this rebellion, while the intervention of the *am ha-arez* and their crowning of the eight-year-old Josiah were intended to forestall eventual complications after the suppression of the rebellion by the Assyrians. But a revised chronology of Ashurbanipal's inscriptions militates against the suggested synchronism.

In the *Aggadah*

Talmudic tradition considers Amon, in the light of what is said in Chronicles, as the worst of Judah's kings and concludes that his sins surpassed those of Ahaz and Manasseh. Ahaz put his seal on the Torah to prevent the reading of it; Manasseh erased the names of God from the Torah; while Amon ordered all of the Torah scrolls burned. Only one Torah scroll, which was found during the reign of Josiah, managed to escape his decree. The sins of Amon in the interruption of the Temple cult were also extremely severe (Sanh. 103b; SOR 24). Nevertheless, Amon is not enumerated among the kings (Jeroboam, Ahab, and Manasseh) who do not have a portion in the World to Come. This was a consequence of the merit of his son Josiah (Sanh. 104a).

BIBLIOGRAPHY: Malamat, in: *Tarbiz*, 21 (1949/50), 123ff.; idem, in: IEJ, 3 (1953), 26–29; Bright, Hist, 294–5; M. Streck (ed.), *Assurbanipal*, 1 (Ger., 1916), ccclxiff.; EM, s.v. (includes bibliography); S. Yeivin, *Meḥkarim be-Toledot Yisrael ve-Arẓo* (1960), 254, 289, 317. **ADD. BIBLIOGRAPHY:** M. Cogan and H. Tadmor, *II Kings* (1988), 275–76. IN THE AGGADAH: Ginzberg, Legends, 4 (1947), 281; 6 (1946), 267, 376.

AMORA (Aram. אָמוֹרָא; "sayer," "spokesman"), a term which designates the "interpreter," who communicated audibly to the assembled pupils the lessons of the rabbinic teacher. It is also used as a generic term for the rabbis of the post-mishnaic period, whose activities were centered on the interpretation of the Mishnah (see *Amoraim). The *amoraim* as teachers would often employ an *amora* as their spokesman. The *amora* stood by the teacher when he lectured. It was primarily to him that the rabbi spoke and he, in turn, conveyed those words to the audience. The Talmud (Yoma 20b) states that *Rav, who himself had served as an *amora* to R. Shila, appointed an *amora* when he wished to address a large assembly. There are instances both of the scholar communicating his words to the *amora* in Aramaic (Gen. R. 10) and of the *amora* addressing the pupils in Hebrew (Sanh. 7b).

The *Amora* is mentioned during the talmudic period both in Palestine and in Babylonia. Avdan is mentioned as the *amora* of R. Judah ha-Nasi (TJ, Ber. 4:1, 7c), while R. Pedat served as the *amora* of R. Yose (TJ, Meg. 4:10, 75c). Even Mar b. R. Ashi, one of the last of the *amoraim*, used to employ an *amora* at his addresses (Kid. 31b). Sometimes the *amora* was given considerable latitude in his expositions (Sot. 40a). Resh Lakish once told his *amora* Judah ben Naḥman, to utter words of comfort on his behalf to mourners whom they both visited (Ket. 8b). On occasion, questions by the students would be addressed to the *amora* who would prepare them for submission to the rabbi. At times he would make the concluding remarks after the delivery of an aggadic discourse or public discussion (TJ, Ber. 4:3, 7c). Sometimes when the assembly was exceptionally large, several *amoraim* were employed, Rav Huna on one occasion employing no less than 13 simultaneously (Ket. 106a). On one occasion when the *nasi* appointed a judge, who though wealthy was of doubtful erudition, Judah b. Naḥman was appointed as his *amora*. In the course of his discourses, Judah made sarcastic references to his ignorance, and criticized the *nasi* for appointing him (Sanh. 7b). References are found to *amoraim* who delivered the discourse in an unnecessarily loud voice, thus minimizing the effect of the original address, spoken in a soft and gentle tone (Eccl. R. 9:17; Ber. 56a). The institution of the *amora* continued as late as the 12th century, and is mentioned by Pethahiah of Regensburg under the name *meturgeman* (A. Benisch (ed.), *Travels of Rabbi Petachia* (1856), 16–17).

BIBLIOGRAPHY: Guttmann, Mafte'aḥ, 3 (1924), 182–4; S.J.L. Rapoport, *Erekh Millin* (1852), 115–21.

[Shmuel Safrai]

AMORAIM (Aram. אָמוֹרָאִים), designation of the scholars in the Land of Israel and Babylonia who succeeded the *tannaim* and preceded (in Babylonia) the **savoraim* and *geonim*. (See Table: Heads of Academies.) The composition of the Mishnah by R. Judah ha-Nasi in the beginning of the third century, and its subsequent dissemination and gradual acceptance in the academies of the Land of Israel and Babylonia led to a break between scholarly activity of the earlier period and the halakhic and aggadic activity of later scholars. These scholars are the "*amoraim*," whose words constitute most of the attributed material in the Talmudim and the amoraic midrash-compilations. The word "*amora*" means "speaker" or "interpreter," and the application of this term to these scholars likely stems from their work in interpreting and deriving *halakhah* from the Mishnah and contemporaneous *beraitot*. Already in both Talmudim, we find references to the *amoraim* as a group distinct from *tannaim*: R. Levi and R. Simon are described as "two *amorin*" (TJ Berakhot 1:1, 2c), and the Babylonian Talmud (Bavli) explicitly distinguishes *tannaim* from *amoraim* (TB Eruvin 7a; TB Sanhedrin 6a and 33a). At times, the Babylonian Talmud also calls attention to *amoraim* it describes as "*amora'ei be-ma'arava*" ("*amoraim* in the West," meaning the Land of Israel; e.g., TB Shabbat 21b, 96a; TB Ketubot 80a).

Many Palestinian *amoraim* (and the *tannaim* before them) conventionally bear the title "Rabbi"; the equivalent title of recognition for Babylonian *Amoriam* is "Rav." A number of *amoraim* in both centers hold neither title. The traditional view is that the title "Rabbi" was only conferred on a scholar after ordination by the patriarch and Sanhedrin in Palestine. Modern scholars have suggested that the difference between these titles is actually a linguistic feature marking separate dialects.

The Generations of the Amoraim

The *amoraim* were active between approximately 220 C.E. (the traditional date of the redaction of the Mishnah) and 360 or 370 in the Land of Israel, and between 220 and approximately

Heads of the Academies of Ereẓ Israel (Palestine) and Babylon.

Ereẓ Israel	Babylon
First Generation 220 C.E.–250 C.E.	
R. Ḥanina b. Ḥama: head of the Council of Sepphoris Oshaiah Rabbah: head of the academy at Caesarea R. Yannai R. Joshua b. Levi: head of the Academy at Lydda	Rav (Abba b. Aivu): founder and head of the Academy of Sura Samuel: head of the Academy of Nehardea Karna: "Dayyan of the Golah" Mar Ukba: the Exilarch
Second Generation 250 C.E.–290 C.E.	
R. Johanan: head of the Academy at Tiberias R. Simeon b. Lakish: (Resh Lakish) R. Eleazar b. Pedat: Head of the Academy at Tiberias	R. Huna: head of the Academy of Sura R. Judah b. Ezekiel: head of the Academy of Pumbedita R. Hamnuna
Third Generation 290 C.E.–320 C.E.	
R. Ammi b. Nathan: head of the Academy at Tiberias R. Assi: head of the Academy at Tiberias R. Abbahu: head of the Academy at Caesarea R. Zeira	R. Ḥisda: head of the Academy of Sura Rabbah b. Huna: head of the Academy of Sura Rabba b. Naḥmani: head of the Academy of Pumbedita R. Joseph B. Ḥiyya: head of the Academy of Pumbedita
Fourth Generation 320 C.E.–350 C.E.	
R. Jonah: head of the Academy at Tiberias R. Yose: head of the Academy at Tiberias R. Jeremiah R. Haggai	Abbaye: head of the Academy of Pumbedita Rava b. Joseph: founder and head of the Academy of Maḥoza Rami b. Ḥama R. Zeira
Fifth Generation 350 C.E.–375 C.E.	
R. Mani: head of the Academy at Tiberias R. Yose b. Avin R. Tanḥuma b. Abba	R. Papa: founder and head of the Academy at Naresh R. Huna b. Joshua R. Zevid: head of the Academy at Pumbedita
Sixth Generation 375 C.E.–425 C.E.	
	Rav Ashi: head of the Academy of Sura in Matah Mehasya Ravina Mar Zutra Ameimar
Seventh Generation 425 C.E.–460 C.E.	
	Mar b. Rav Ashi (Tabyomi): head of the Academy of Sura R. Yeimar: head of the Academy of Sura R. Geviha of Bei-Katil: head of the Academy of Pumbedita
Eight Generation 460 C.E.–500 C.E.	
	Ravina ii b. Huna: head of the Academy of Sura R. Yose: head of the Academy of Pumbedita Aḥai b. Huna

500 in Babylonia. Rabbinic tradition credits Rav, a student of R. Judah ha-Nasi, with bringing the Mishnah to Babylonia and thus inaugurating the amoraic period in Babylonia. It is customary to divide the amoraic period into generations. In most cases such a division is artificial, since many of the scholars can be assigned to two successive generations. The first five generations consist of both Palestinian and Babylonian *amoraim*. The last two to three generations, however, are limited to Babylonian *amoraim*. It is not easy to identify all the *amoraim* mentioned in the Talmud and Midrash since the same *amora* often appears under different names, whereas two *amoraim* from two different generations can bear the same name. Moreover, many names have been transmitted incorrectly. Over 2,000 *amoraim*, however, can be identified with tolerable certainty. See the table of the more prominent of the *amoraim* of the different generations.

THE PROBLEM OF AMORAIC ATTRIBUTIONS AND BIOGRAPHY. Up to and throughout much of the 20th century, scholars generally assumed that amoraic statements preserved in the Talmudim and midrash-compilations accurately represented the positions held by the sages to whom they were attributed, and that narratives purporting to relate information about the lives of individual *amoraim* reflected reliable biographical traditions about the *amoriam* as real, historical figures. Both of these views have undergone radical revision, and we must attend to these issues before proceeding further with the portrayal of the *amoriam* as set out in rabbinic literature.

Jacob Neusner and his students called the reliability of amoraic attributions into question, partly on the ground that there is no source external to rabbinic literature that can be used to verify them, and partly on the basis of a comparison of parallel traditions which testify to an internal literary development within the rabbinic sources themselves. Skepticism about the reliability of attributions is justified in part by the Babylonian Talmud itself, which sometimes notes that an *amora* did not explicitly state a view attributed to him, but that the attributed view was inferred from the *amora*'s conduct in a particular instance ("*lav be-ferush itamar ela me-kelala itamar*"; e.g., Bava Batra 40b, 126a). In the Jerusalem Talmud as well, Shimon b. Ba was said to have doubted R. Abbahu's attribution of a particular view to R. Yohanan (TJ Shabbat 6:1, 7d), again demonstrating amoraic awareness that not all amoraic attributions may be accurate.

Few, if any, scholars still maintain the view that amoraic attributions are in all circumstances to be presumed reliable. Recent studies by Richard Kalmin have demonstrated that one must also be cautious about leaping to the opposite conclusion: that attributions are in all circumstances to be presumed unreliable. Kalmin demonstrated the existence of patterns in statements attributed to particular *amoriam* or to the *amoriam* of particular generations, and concluded that these patterns are indicative of real historical differences in the amoraic scholarly enterprise. Thus, while the accuracy of a discrete amoraic statement may be impossible to verify, the statements of an *amora* or of a generation, when taken together, may indeed yield information that may be used for historical reconstruction. Other research – such as Z.M. Dor's work on Rava's and Rav Papa's engagement with Palestinian learning, and David Kraemer's finding that the later Babylonian amoraic generations are more likely to preserve argumentation – buttresses that conclusion. But it remains difficult to determine whether or not a given amoraic statement was actually uttered by the sage to whom it is attributed, or whether the statement as transmitted preserves a form of the tradition which remains relatively close to the original, without a detailed examination of all of the parallel versions of the tradition, and all the relevant manuscript material. As a result, references in this article to what a sage said or did should be understood as references to what he *is represented* to have said or done.

Rabbinic literature also contains narratives, many of which present details about the lives of particular rabbis in the course of telling other stories. Other narratives purport to relate entire episodes from rabbis' lives. Throughout the 19th and most of the 20th centuries, scholars viewed these narratives as sources for rabbinic biography, and some scholarly work was done to draw together the scattered details from disparate rabbinic sources in order to construct rabbinic "biographies." To the extent that narratives contained accounts of supernatural events, scholars resorted to the technique of the "historical kernel": ignoring the fantastic elements of narratives in order to recover the kernel of historical information the story was thought to yield about the sage. This project was problematic because for most, if not all *amoraim*, the Talmudim and midrash-compilations leave large gaps in the chronology of their lives, which could only be supplemented by guesswork and creative extrapolation – hardly the stuff of scholarly biography. The seminal work of Jacob Neusner, William Scott Green, Shamma Friedman, Richard Kalmin, Jeffrey L. Rubenstein and other scholars has led to a complete rethinking of the project of "rabbinic biography." Scholars now recognize that rabbinic narratives are literary creations formulated to serve the purposes of their narrators and/or of the redactors of the compilations in which they are now found; they present edifying moral lessons, or teach about the rabbinic way of life, but are not meant to be straightforward presentations of history or biography and must not be utilized as such. Therefore, alleged discrete biographical details must not be lifted out of rabbinic narratives; the narratives must be carefully studied as whole compositions in order to discern the overall message the storytellers or redactors wished to convey. All of these methodological considerations complicate the project of presenting the lives and activities of the *amoraim*, but the resulting presentation benefits from the rigorous examination of the sources that these methodological considerations require.

Organization of Amoraic Torah Study and Teaching

The major study-centers in amoraic Palestine were Caesarea, "the South" (most likely Lydda), Sepphoris, and Tiberias. In Babylonia, the principal study-centers were Sura, Pumbedita,

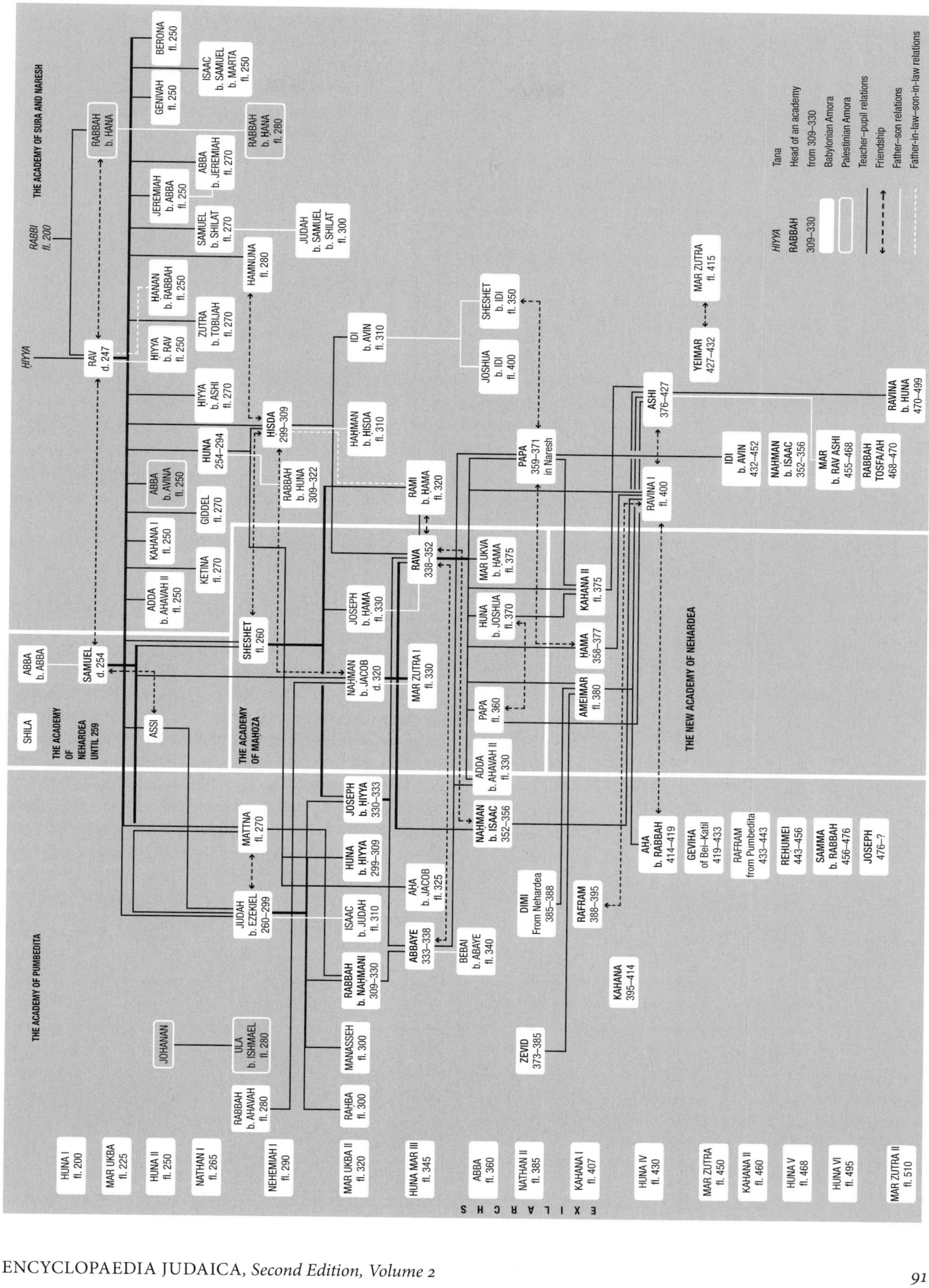

The principal Amoraim *of the Babylonian academies.*

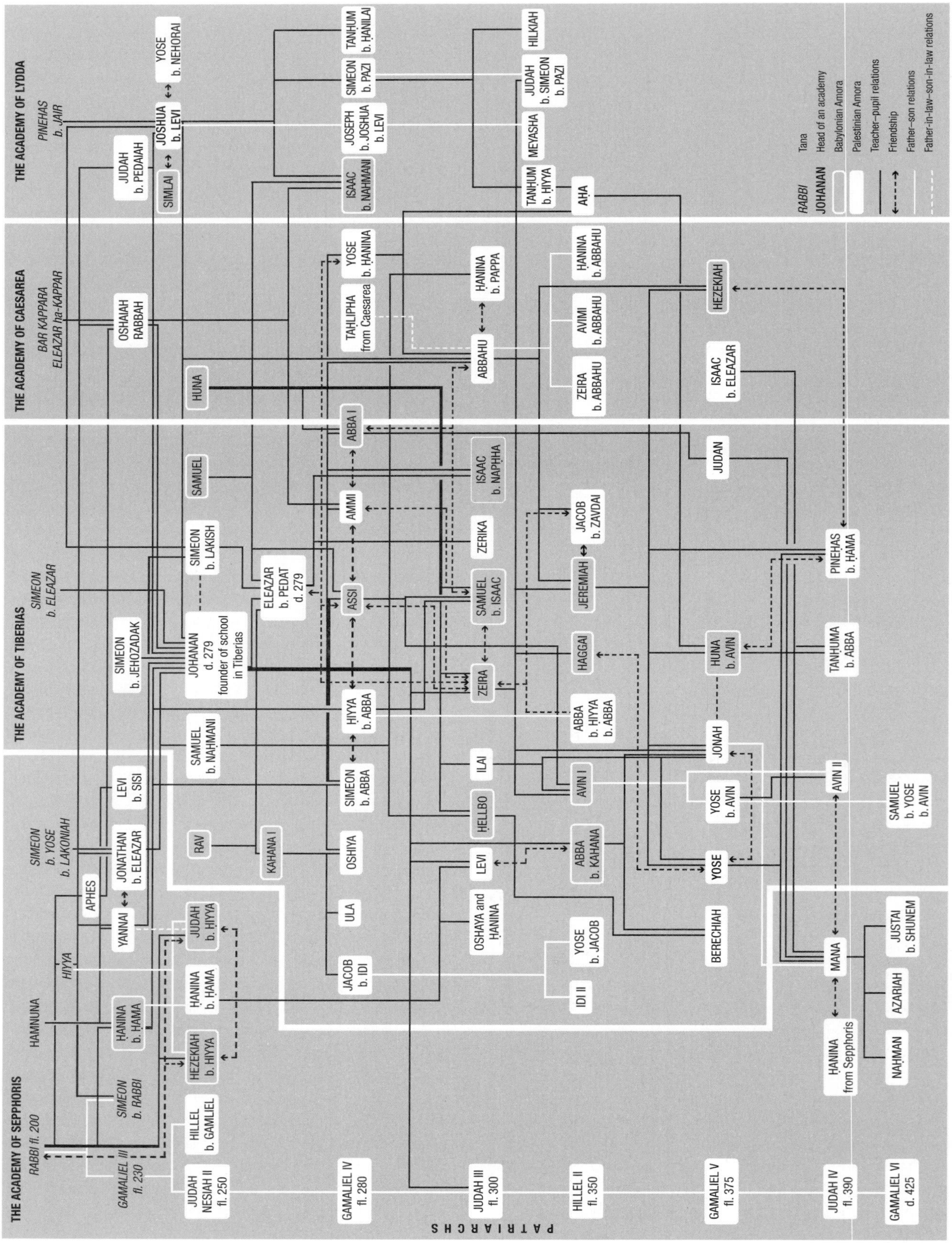

The principal Amoraim *of the Palestinian academies.*

Nehardea (destroyed and eventually transplanted), Mahoza, and Naresh.

Most likely these cities were not the sites of organized academies. Rather, groups of rabbinic disciples would gather around a teacher, with whom they studied Torah and whom they personally served as part of their initiation into the rabbinic way of life.

Memorization and constant recitation of one's learning were stressed as the cultural ideal in the rabbinic centers of both the Land of Israel and Babylonia. Although some *amoraim*' allegedly kept written notes (e.g., TJ Kilayim 1:1, 27a; TJ Ma'aserot 2:4, 49d), and may even have consulted books of *aggadah* (TJ Shabbat 16:1, 15c), orality, rather than writing, was the primary and favored mode of study and teaching. Rav Sheshet was said to have reviewed his learning every 30 days (TB Pesaḥim 68b). Rava advised that one should always recite one's learning, even if one tended to forget, and even if one did not know the meaning of what was recited (TB Avodah Zarah 19a; see also TB Shabbat 63a). Recitation was to be done in a melodious chant (TB Megillah 32a).

The emphasis on memorization coexists in the Babylonian Talmud in tension with a growing Babylonian amoraic emphasis on dialectic and argumentation. R. Yohanan is represented as claiming that there was a Tannaitic dispute as to whether "Sinai" (the scholar who had memorized much Torah) or the "uprooter of mountains" (a sharp thinker) was preferable. According to the Babylonian Talmud Palestinian scholars resolved this question in favor of "Sinai." Nevertheless, Rav Yosef – described as "Sinai" – was said to have deferred to Rabbah, the "uprooter of mountains," as academy head (TB Horayot 14a). This story illustrates the growing Babylonian preference for skill in argument. Similarly, Rav reported that the people Israel forgot hundreds of *halakhot* after Moses' death, but, according to R. Abbahu, these *halakhot* were restored through the dialectical creativity of Othniel b. Kenaz (TB Temurah 16a). Thus, although the accumulation of knowledge is lauded because "everyone needs the master of wheat" (TB Horayot 14a, referring to one who possesses much memorized knowledge), the Babylonian *amoraim* moved in the direction of ascribing at least equal weight to the achievement of analytic ability and dialectical skill.

Relations Between the Land of Israel and Babylonia During the Amoraic Period

The presence of Palestinian amoraic traditions in the Babylonian Talmud and of Babylonian amoraic traditions in the Jerusalem Talmud testifies to a significant degree of interaction between these two centers of learning during the first four generations of the *amoraim*. While much of this activity involved the transmission of traditions from Palestine to Babylonia, the Jerusalem Talmud does call attention to the halakhic traditions of "the rabbis of there [Babylonia]," who are contrasted with "the rabbis of here [Palestine]" (e.g., TJ Berakhot 1:9, 3d; 9:4, 14a). The Babylonian Talmud also describes the activities of scholars known as the "*naḥote*" ("those who descended"), who carried learning with them from the Land of Israel to Babylonia and back. Two of the best-known *naḥote* were R. Dimi (= Avudimi, of the fourth Palestinian amoraic generation) and Rabin (= Avin or Avun, of the third and fourth Babylonian amoraic generations), who eventually moved to the Land of Israel. *Naḥote* typically brought discrete halakhic traditions (called "*memrot*"), stories, halakhic *sugyot,* and aggadic traditions to Babylonia; their activity is often introduced by the formulaic "When Rabbi X came [to Babylonia]" (e.g., Ket. 17a, AZ 11b). Rabin is also described as writing letters to Babylonian *amoraim* (TB Ketubot 49b, TB Bava Meẓi'a 114a), as are other Palestinian *amoraim* (TB Bava Meẓi'a 41b; TB Sanhedrin 29a; TB Ḥullin 95a).

The Babylonian Talmud also highlights halakhic information brought from Palestine by use of the introductory phrase *shalḥu mitam* ("they [= the Palestinian scholars] sent from there [Palestine]"). Among these communications were some that cautioned the Babylonians to be careful to observe the second day of the Festival (TB Beẓah 4b), to be careful to treat Rav Ahai with respect, who is described as "lighting up the eyes of the Exile" (TB Ḥullin 59b), and some that corrected and expanded their halakhic knowledge in particular areas (e.g., TB Bava Batra 165b, TB Menaḥot 43a).

The two rabbinic centers are not portrayed as being of equal authority or as having equal prestige during the amoraic period. Babylonia and its scholars are portrayed as subordinate to the authority of the Land of Israel. Abbaye claims that since "we are subordinate to them, we do as they do" (TB Pesaḥim 51a). The Babylonian Talmud also describes Babylonian judges as being the "agents" of the scholars of the Land of Israel who are only empowered to adjudicate certain types of cases that do not require expert, ordained judges only found in the Land (TB Bava Kamma 84b; see also TB Sanhedrin 14a). Abbaye, speaking to Rav Yosef, thus referred to them both as "laypeople" (*hedyotot*), presumably because they had not been ordained in Palestine (TB Gittin 88b).

The Palestinian *amoraim* are also portrayed as ridiculing Babylonian halakhic traditions (TB Pesaḥim 34b, TB Yoma 57a, TB Zevaḥim 60b). R. Yohanan explained that Babylonia is called "Bavel" because scripture, mishnah, and talmud are all mixed up ("*balul*") in it (TB Sanhedrin 24a). This ridicule may simply reflect the natural tensions between competing rabbinic centers rather than a real evaluation of Babylonian amoraic capabilities, since we can also observe sharp intra-Palestinian polemics between sages in northern and southern Palestine (TJ Sanhedrin 1:2, 18c; TJ Avodah Zarah 2:9, 41d). There is further support for this conclusion in a tradition about Palestinian appreciation of the scholarly competence of the Babylonian rabbis. Contrary to earlier Palestinian doubts about Babylonian competence with regard to bills of divorce, the "Scholars" (*ḥavrayya*) said in the name of R. Yehoshua b. Levi: "Now that scholars are found outside the Land, they are considered 'experts' [with regard to bills of divorce]" (TJ Git. 1:1, 43b).

The fourth generation Babylonian Amora Rava is the last Babylonian Amora mentioned in the Jerusalem Talmud (TJ Beẓah 1:3, 60b). The absence of the rest of the fourth generation (not to mention the fifth–seventh), from the Jerusalem Talmud is evidence that the final redaction of the Jerusalem Talmud was being brought to a close during this time. Some post-Jerusalem Talmud Palestinian scholars do appear in the Babylonian Talmud (e.g., TB Shabbat 107a; TB Ḥullin 59b).

Amoraim as Aggadists

Amoraim in both centers studied both *halakhah* and *aggadah*, although the latter is noticeably less of a Babylonian project. The Jerusalem Talmud itself contains relatively little *aggadah*, but Palestinian *amoraim* are richly represented in the great amoraic midrash-collections: **Bereshit Rabbah*, **Vayikra Rabbah*, and **Pesikta de-Rav Kahana*. The Babylonian Talmud contains much *aggadah* (in keeping with its encyclopedic nature), but most of this material is Palestinian in origin.

The greater Palestinian contribution to *aggadah* is also reflected in the scholarly profiles of some *amoraim*. Among Babylonian *amoraim*, Rav is noteworthy as a scholar of both *halakhah* and *aggadah*, while among Palestinian *amoraim*, there are several scholars renowned for *aggadah* alone – R. Levi, R. Shmuel b. Nahman, R. Tanhuma, and other great aggadists who rarely formulated halakhic statements. No Babylonian Amora is identifiable as an expert on *aggadah* alone. The Palestinian rabbinic compilations alone also refer to certain scholars as *rabanan d'aggadeta* ("the rabbis of aggadah"; TJ Yevamot 4:2, 5c; TJ Ma'aserot 1:2, 48d), or as *ba'alei aggadah* ("masters of aggadah"; Bereshit Rabbah 94:5; Leviticus Rabbah 31:1). The historical reason for the greater Palestinian engagement with *aggadah* is unclear, but R. Isaac is credited with the notion that a greater emphasis on the study of scripture and *aggadah* is characteristic of periods of economic deprivation and social oppression, such as that imposed by the "wicked kingdom," Rome (Pesikta de-R. Kahana 12:3).

The Talmudim also indicate that there may have been some tension, or at least competition, between scholars of *halakhah* and *aggadah*. In the Jerusalem Talmud, R. Zeirah is said to have chided R. Abba b. Kahana and R. Levi, claiming that aggadic works are "books of divination," presumably because *aggadah* at times interprets scriptural verses in highly creative, counterintuitive ways (TJ Ma'aserot 3:10, 51a). According to the Babylonian Talmud, the public left R. Ḥiyya b. Abba's lecture on *halakhah* in order to attend R. Abbahu's discourse on *aggadah* (TB Sotah 40a).

The Amoraim as Authorities and Sources of Guidance for Non-Rabbis

Palestinian sources describe rabbis as providing guidance on legal and other matters for non-rabbis, including on questions of choosing local religious leadership (TJ Shevi'it 6:1, 36d). But this should not be taken as indicative of non-rabbis' complete, unconditional acceptance of the *amoraim* as religious leaders, because non-rabbis are also portrayed as ignoring rabbinic directives when these were perceived as too draconian (e.g., TJ Shevi'it 4:3, 35b). Rabbis are also described as modifying the Sabbatical year laws in order to bring them in line with what people were already doing, even if they perhaps might not have considered those behaviors ideal (ibid; TJ Shevi'it 4:2, 35a).

Palestinian sources (and sources about Palestinian *amoraim*) portray rabbis giving public discourses attended by non-rabbis (TJ Horayot 3:7, 48b; TB Sotah 40a). As to Babylonia, Rav Ashi alluded to a twice-yearly gathering of people in Mata Mehasya, presumably for the purpose of hearing discourses about holiday law (TB Berakhot 17b). This may be related to the Babylonian institution of the "*pirka*" (lit. "chapter"), which was a lecture delivered before a large audience containing non-scholars as well as scholars. The institution of the *pirqa* probably stems from the fourth century.

The Amoraim as Holy Men and Medical Experts

Scholars of late antiquity have identified certain kinds of stories and forms of behavior as characteristic of the period's signature "holy man". Similar stories and forms of behavior are also characteristic of many *amoraim* (Kalmin, *Saints and Sages*). *Amoraim* are represented as being visited by heavenly beings, including the prophet Elijah (e.g., TB Berakhot 29b), angels (TB Nedarim 20a; TB Menaḥot 41a), and spirits (TJ Peah 8:9, 21b). *Amoraim* are portrayed as speaking to the Angel of Death (TB Ḥagigah 4b–5a) and even outmaneuvering him for a time through Torah study (TB Mo'ed Katan 28a). Rav Judah is portrayed as being thanked by a dead man for easing his pain in the hereafter (TB Shabbat 152b). It is said about the rabbis collectively that wherever they cast their eyes, death or poverty results (TB Nedarim 7b). Sages in the Land of Israel were particularly sought out for the all-important activity of rain-making (e.g., TJ Ta'anit 3:4, 66c). In a related vein, *amoraim* are also portrayed as giving advice about health, including remedies for various ailments (e.g., TB Shabbat 81b; TB Avodah Zarah 28a–29a).

Communal Roles of the Amoraim and their Socioeconomic Status

Leading Babylonian *amoraim*, notably Rav, Rav Huna, Rava, and Rav Papa are portrayed as wealthy men. While few Babylonian *amoraim* are explicitly described as poor, the Babylonian Talmud does at times portray Palestinian *amoraim* as such (e.g., R. Johanan at TB Ta'anit 21a). Scholars were not to receive payment for teaching Torah (TB Nedarim 37a), and they are portrayed as engaging in commerce (TB Bava Metsia 83a), trade, agriculture, and other callings. Nevertheless, economic reversals and the demands of study could result in hardship. Some Palestinian sources show the *amoriam* encouraging people to support rabbis by giving the ancient agricultural tithes to scholars rather than to priests (TJ Ma'aser Sheni 5:5, 56b; Pesikta de-R. Kahana 10:10; see also TB Nedarim 62a).

Leading Palestinian and Babylonian *amoraim* are portrayed as playing active roles in communal collection and distribution of *ẓedakah*, notably R. Jacob b. Idi and R. Isaac b. Nahman (TJ Pe'ah 8:9, 21b), R. Hiyya b. Abba and Resh Lakish (TJ Horayot 3:6, 48a), Rav Huna (TB Megillah 27a–b), Rabbah (Bava Batra 8b), and Rav Ashi (Bava Batra 9a). The Jerusalem Talmud equates *ẓedakah* and acts of kindness (*gemilut ḥasadim*) to all the other *mitzvot* of the Torah (TJ Pe'ah 1:1, 15c), while the Babylonian Rav Huna is even represented as claiming that, regarding one who only engages in Torah to the exclusion of acts of kindness, it is as if he has no God (TB Avodah Zarah 17b). In a related vein, both Talmudim represent *amoraim* as judging cases and being sought out to administer justice (e.g., TB Ketubot 49b; TB Sanhedrin 27a–b). But the Babylonian Talmud also indicates that people did not always necessarily receive the justice they sought (TB Shabbat 55a; TB Sukkah 31a).

The Jerusalem Talmud portrays *amoraim* – under the direction of the Patriarch – as being in charge of setting up schools and hiring instructors (TJ Ḥagigah 1:7, 76c), while the Babylonian Talmud, although not portraying Babylonian *amoraim* in the same way, does show Rava setting down guidelines for the hiring and retention of teachers (TB Bava Batra 21a). Both Talmudim portray Palestinian *amoraim* as traveling around, observing Jewish communities' religious practice, and reporting halakhic violations to more senior rabbis (e.g., TJ Shevi'it 8:11, 38b–c; TB Avodah Zarah 59a), and they are in general described as being more integrated with their communities than their Babylonian counterparts (D. Levine, E. Diamond). Taken all together, these traditions point towards a Palestinian amoraic community that was – or at least portrays itself as – more highly organized and bureaucratic than its Babylonian counterpart.

Although, as noted, scholars were not to receive payment for teaching Torah, Babylonian *amoraim* did see themselves as entitled to certain allowances by virtue of their rabbinic status. Rava rules that when Torah scholars are litigants, their cases should be heard first (TB Nedarim 62a), and that they are entitled to tax exemptions (TB Nedarim 62b). Rava is also portrayed as allowing R. Josiah and R. Obadiah a commercial privilege not provided by law, which the Babylonian Talmud explains as a necessary allowance so that their studies would not be interrupted (TB Bava Batra 22a). A close reading of the sources about amoraic tax exemptions (TB Nedarim 62b; TB Bava Batra 7b–8a) supports the conclusion that the *amoraim* were likely making arguments in favor of their receiving such exemptions in these sources rather than straightforwardly reporting the historical reality of such exemptions.

BIBLIOGRAPHY: Frankel, Mevo; Halevy, Dorot, 2; Weis, Dor, 3; Bacher, Bab Amor; Bacher, Pal Amor; Bacher, Trad; G.F. Moore, *Judaism in the First Century of the Christian Era*, 2 (1927); H.L. Strack, *Introduction to the Talmud and Midrash* (1931); M. Mielziner, *Introduction to the Talmud* (1925); Hyman, Toledot; Margalioth, Ḥakhmei; J.N. Epstein, *Mevo'ot le-Safrut ha-Amora'im* (1962); **ADD. BIBLIOGRAPHY:** M. Beer, *The Babylonian Amoraim: Aspects of Economic Life* (Heb., 1982); M. Elon, *Jewish Law: History, Sources, Principles* (1994); R. Kalmin, *Sages, Stories, Authors, and Editors in Rabbinic Babylonia* (1994); idem, *The Sage in Jewish Society of Late Antiquity* (1998); idem, "Saints and Sages in Late Antiquity," in: *Continuity and Change*, ed. Lee I. Levine (Hebrew) (2004); Lee I. Levine, *The Rabbinic Class of Roman Palestine in Late Antiquity* (1990); Jacob Neusner, *A History of the Jews in Babylonia* (1965–1970); Jacob Neusner, "The Present State of Rabbinic Biography," in: G. Nahon & C. Touati (eds.), *Hommage á Georges Vajda* (1980), 85–91; Y. Breuer, in: Tarbiz, 61 (1997), 41–59; D. Levine, *Ta'aniyyot Ẓibbur u-Derashot ha-Ḥakhamim – Halakhah u-Ma'aseh bi-Tekufat ha-Talmud* (2001); E. Diamond, in: USQR, 48 (1994), 29–47.

[Alyssa M. Gray (2nd ed.)]

AMORITES (Heb. אֱמֹרִי; Emori), the pre-Israelite inhabitants of the land of Israel. The word appears approximately 85 times in the Hebrew Bible and is used to designate all or part of that population. The Semitic derivation of the word, and possibly also the biblical usage of the term, can be illuminated to some extent from extra-biblical sources.

Extra-biblical Sources

In Sumero-Akkadian and Eblaite texts from the period from 2400 to 1600 B.C.E., Sumerian *MAR.TU*, Eblaite *Martu(m)*, and Akkadian *Amurru* occur as a geographical term meaning literally "the West." The area extended westward from the Euphrates River as far as the Mediterranean Sea. It specifically embraced the great Syrian desert, the Orontes River valley, and the Amanus Mountains. In later Assyrian texts, *Amurru* was an established name for Syria-Palestine.

References to "the people of *Amurru*," in contrast with the more common geographical allusions, are largely from the period prior to 2000 B.C.E. and come from the Akkadian and Ur III periods. A date formula of the Old Akkadian king Shar-kali-sharri (ca. 2200) refers to the defeat of the MAR.TU in Basar, identified by scholars with Jebel Bishri, a mountain range in central Syria west of the Euphrates. It seems that the people so named, after having overthrown or weakened Sumero-Akkadian dynasts, and in some cases having founded their own regimes, either quickly amalgamated with the Sumero-Akkadian population or passed on beyond the Tigris River to resume their habitual semi-nomadic type of life. The use of the term in an ethnic sense soon disappeared from the texts.

Strictly speaking, the extra-biblical usage of the name Amorites was applied almost exclusively to people who came from southern Mesopotamian locations prior to 2000 B.C.E. It is clear, however, that people with the same language were present along the mid-Euphrates at *Mari in the 20th century, at Babylon about 1830, and at Asshur on the Tigris River about 1750 B.C.E. That they were even present in Palestine is witnessed by the Egyptian Execration Texts of the 20th and 19th centuries. Their language did not survive in writing, but when they took over Akkadian Old Babylonian, they transliterated their names (which were often theophorous, for example, the elements *'am* "people"; *'ab* "father"; *'aḥ* "brother," were combined with names of deities such as El and Hadad) and employed words, forms, and linguistic usages most closely paralleled in later West Semitic languages. These wide-ranging peoples belonging to a common linguistic stock have commonly been called "Amorites," by extension of the Sumero-Akkadian geographical term, but not exclusively so. T. Bauer proposed "East Canaanites" to stress their affinities with the Syro-Palestinian or West Canaanites. M. Noth for a time preferred "Proto-Arameans" to underscore their connections with later Arameans. A. Caquot opted for "early West Semites" to emphasize their distance from any of the later West-Semitic subdivisions. It is still a matter of considerable scholarly dispute whether the language of this group was the direct predecessor of Canaanite-Hebrew or Aramaic, or whether it was rather an early development without immediate ties to any of the later, better attested West-Semitic tongues. Indeed, the discovery of *Ebla (Tell Mardikh) some 40 miles south of Aleppo, brought to light the Eblaite language, a previously unknown Semitic language of the third millennium and has complicated the entire classification system of ancient Semitic. For further information, see *Alphabet (North-West Semitic); *Aramaic; *Hebrew Language (Pre-Biblical); and *Semitic Languages.

If one draws together all the evidence from the sources which are "Amorite" in the broad sense, the bearers of the name appear originally as ass nomads who came out of the Syrian desert and settled unevenly over parts of Syria-Palestine and Mesopotamia, overthrowing existing political regimes and frequently establishing substitute dynasties. Only at Mari, near their desert home, do they seem to have formed the bulk of the populace. They rapidly adopted Sumero-Akkadian or Syro-Palestinian culture; in Mesopotamia they soon lost their original language, whereas in Palestine they may have retained it while it gradually developed over the centuries into the later Canaanite-Hebrew dialects of West Semitic. There is no evidence that they called themselves "Amorites"; instead, they were known as such only to some Sumero-Akkadians, who viewed them as "Westerners." In fact, no ethnic term is known which they applied to themselves.

The life style of the Amorite before settling down is attested, perhaps in exaggerated manner, in a Sumerian hymn: "The Weapon (is his) companion… / Who knows no submission, / Who eats uncooked flesh, / Who has no house in his life-time, / Who does not bury his dead companion" (E. Chiera, *Sumerian Religious Texts*, 1 (1924), 24; *Sumerian Epics and Myths* (1934), no. 58, rev. col. 4, lines 26–29). That this semi-nomadic cultural level was abandoned once the newcomers gained a foothold in settled lands is well attested by the hostile policies of Amorite dynasts at Mari toward troublesome nomads in their own kingdom. No inclusive "Amorite" cultural or religious loyalties held the invaders together for long; the newly established Amorite city-states were soon vigorously at war with one another in the familiar Sumero-Akkadian fashion. Similarly, in Canaan the Execration Texts suggest that, within a century of their arrival, the Amorites were split into contending city-states, with single dynasts replacing the initial tribal rule by a cabal of sheikhs or elders. From an 18th century B.C.E. letter to King Zimri-Lim of Mari comes the earliest testimony to a country in Syria called Amurru. Localized non-biblical usage of *Amurru* appears next in 14th–13th century B.C.E. Syro-Palestinian texts referring to a kingdom located in the mountains and along the coast of northern Lebanon. The relation of the regional political term to earlier usages of *Amurru* is unknown. Conceivably it was merely intended to herald that Syrian kingdom as the most important political entity in "the West."

Biblical References

The biblical occurrences of Emori are of two types with three sub varieties of one of the types: (1) Amorites are the pre-Israelite inhabitants of the occupied land in general (e.g., Gen. 15:16; Josh. 7:7). This meaning occurs characteristically in the E source of the Pentateuch (in contrast to J's "Canaanites"), in the conquest narratives, and in the Deuteronomic traditions; and (2) Amorites are a particular subgroup of the pre-Israelite inhabitants of the occupied land: one of several peoples itemized in lists of dispossessed ethnic or political groups (including variously: Canaanites, Hittites, Perizzites, Girgashites, Jebusites, Hivites-Horites, etc.; Gen. 10:16; Ex. 3:8; I Chron. 1:14); inhabitants of the Transjordanian kingdoms of Og and *Sihon (e.g., Num. 21:13; Josh. 2:10; 9:10; Judg. 10:8); and inhabitants of the mountainous regions of West Jordan (in contrast to the Canaanites on the coast and in the plains; e.g., Deut. 1:19ff., 27, 44; Josh. 10:5ff.). It is now impossible to draw a direct link between the Sumero-Akkadian term *Amurru* from 2000 B.C.E. and the Israelite term Amorite in use after 1200 B.C.E. Hebrew Amorite is never a geographical term the way *Amurru* largely is (save in Josh. 13:4–5 where the kingdom of *Amurru* in the Lebanon is likely meant). It is impossible to draw a direct link between the Hebrew usage of the name Emori and the Sumero-Akkadian *Amurru*, which died away one thousand years before the Israelites arose in Ereẓ Israel. It is assumed on geographical and chronological grounds, that some of the elements in the local population, perhaps the rulers of the kingdoms of Og and Sihon, were offshoots of the Syrian city-state of *Amurru*. However, there is no positive evidence in favor of the hypothesis and, even if it were granted for want of a better alternative, it does not explain how the localized usage was extended to refer either to all the pre-Israelite populace in the hill country of Cisjordan or to the peoples of Canaan in toto.

A comparison of the biblical and extra-biblical ethnic usages of Amorite and *Amurru* shows that groups of Semites with linguistic affinities were called "Amorites" at opposite ends of the Fertile Crescent at periods almost a millennium apart. Beyond that, the peculiarities and disjunctions in the geographical and ethnic references in the two contexts, the uncertainties of relationship between the early Amorite language and the later Canaanite-Hebrew, as well as the vast time gap between the compared terms, frustrate any attempt to determine the precise meaning or meanings of the biblical term Amorites.

[Norman K. Gottwald]

Talmudic References

The Talmud applies the term *darkhei ha-Emori* ("the ways of the Amorite") to superstitious heathen practices not covered by specific prohibitions but subsumed under the general prohibition of "neither shall you walk in their statutes" (Lev. 18:3). The verse actually refers generally to the prohibition against "the doings of the land of Canaan" in general. The Mishnah (Ḥul. 4:7) forbids as "Amorite practices" the burial at the crossroads of the afterbirth of the first born of an animal which had been set aside for an offering, or hanging it on a tree, and the wearing of such charms as "a locust's egg, a fox's tooth, or a nail from the gallows of an impaled convict" (Shab. 6:10). Chapters 6 and 7 of Tosefta *Shabbat* give a comprehensive list of such prohibitions, and are referred to as "the chapter on Amorite practices" (Shab. 67a where other examples are given). Nevertheless, the rabbis held that whatever is done for medicinal purposes is not prohibited as Amorite practice (*ibid.*).

BIBLIOGRAPHY: Albright, Stone, 151–6, 163–6; T. Bauer, *Die Ostkanaanaeer* (1926); E. Dhorme, *Recueil Edouard Dhorme* (1951), 81–165; Gibson, in: JNES, 20 (1961), 220–4; K. Kenyon, *Amorites and Canaanites* (1966); Noth, in: ZAW, 58 (1940–41), 182–9; Gelb, in: JCS, 15 (1961), 27–42; Lewy, in: HUCA, 32 (1961), 32–72; Tur-Sinai, in: JQR, 39 (1949), 249–58; Mazar, in: EM, 1 (1955), 440–6; Tur-Sinai, *ibid.*, 446–8; H.B. Huffmon, *Amorite Personal Names in the Mari Texts* (1965); Aharoni, Land, index s.v. *Amurru.* **ADD. BIBLIOGRAPHY:** J. van Seters, in: VT, 22 (1972), 64–81; G. Mendenhall, in: ABD, 1, 199–202; M. Anbar, *Les Tribus amurrites de Mari* (1991); R. Whiting, in: CANE, 2, 1231–42.

AMOS (Heb. עָמוֹס; eighth century B.C.E.), prophet in the northern kingdom of Israel. The Book of Amos is the third book of the 12 Minor Prophets according to the Hebrew order (between Joel and Obadiah) and the second according to the Septuagint (between Hosea and Micah). Amos is considered the earliest of the Latter Prophets and by some is considered the first of the writing prophets.

The Prophet, His Place and Time

According to the superscription of the book, Amos was a herdsman (*noqed*) from Tekoa who prophesied concerning Israel in the days of *Uzziah, king of Judah, and *Jeroboam, son of Joash, king of Israel, "two years before the earthquake" (1:1). The title *noqed* is applied again in the Bible to *Mesha, king of Moab, who is said to have been a sheepmaster (II Kings 3:4). Amos also attributes this employment to himself when he says that he was primarily not a prophet but a *noqed* (in the masoretic text *boker* (*boqer;* "cowherd"), it seems necessary to read the word *noqed*, with the help of the LXX) and a dresser of sycamore trees who was taken from following the flock to prophesy concerning Israel (7:14–15). The term *rb nqdm* is cited in the Ugaritic writings along with the title *rb khnm*, i.e., "chief priest" (C.H. Gordon, *Ugaritic Text-Book*, 62:54–55), where it is explained as one of the temple functionaries who was responsible for the flocks ("chief herdsman"). Some scholars therefore deduce that *noqed*, as connected with Amos, also has a sacral meaning and that even before becoming a prophet, Amos was directly concerned with the service at the Temple in Jerusalem (Haldar, Kapelrud, et al.). However, this supposition is far from certain.

Amos' birthplace, *Tekoa, was located to the south of Bethlehem near the Judean Desert, and was known for its wise men (II Sam. 14:2–21). This has led to the conclusion that Amos' origin was in Judah. But it is striking that there is no hint of denigration of calf worship in his prophecies, despite the fact that he does not refrain from condemning cultic sins (2:7, 12). In his silence on the matter of the calves, he is similar to the northern prophets *Elijah and *Elisha. Furthermore, Tekoa of Judah is not a sycamore-growing locale; sycamores grew in the Shephelah. Therefore, there may be truth in the explanation first suggested by David Kimḥi and since adopted by several modern scholars, such as Graetz, Oort, and Schmidt, that Amos' Tekoa was in fact a northern city. A Galilean Tekoa is known from talmudic literature. The verse, "The Lord roars from Zion, and utters his voice from Jerusalem" (1:2), is a formulaic image (cf. Joel 4:16; Jer. 25:30). The mention of Zion in 6:1 is not decisive, since the prophecy is intended for the northern kingdom. The oracle on the restoration of the house of David (9:11ff.) is doubtful and perhaps not to be attributed to Amos (see below), while the words of *Amaziah to Amos may not testify to the origin of the prophet, for Amaziah does not tell him to return to Judah, but rather: "… go, flee away into the land of Judah, and there eat bread…." A priest of Beth-El could issue such an order even to a northern prophet, particularly during the period of Jeroboam II and Uzziah, when peaceful relations between the two kingdoms flourished. Amos' prophetic activity took place within the northern kingdom only. There are several allusions in his prophecies to events concerning the northern kingdom and mention is made of Samaria (3:12; 4:1; 6:1; cf. 3:9), and the northern shrine cities, with Beth-El at their head (3:14; 4:4; 5:5–6; 8:14; cf. 9:1). It appears that Samaria, and especially the sanctuary of Beth-El, were actually the scenes of his activity, as is confirmed by the narrative on his encounter with Amaziah (7:10–17).

His prophetic activity began two years before the earthquake (1:1) and continued for some time afterward. This earthquake, which occurred during the reign of Uzziah, is mentioned again in Zechariah 14:5. Impressions of it were recorded by a number of prophets who were active during that period, including Amos himself (see below). Also reflected in Amos are the great political and military changes that took place during the 41-year reign of Jeroboam son of Joash (II Kings 14:23); they provide the chronological framework of the prophet's career.

The earliest of Amos' oracles are the "prophecy against the nations," at the beginning of the book (1:2–2:6), and the prophecy of visions (7:1–9; 8:1–3). Both precede the earthquake, impressions of which are not yet recognized therein (except for 1:2, where a formulaic usage serves as the superscription for the first prophecy). The situation reflected in the "prophecy against the nations" is that of the early years of Jeroboam's reign, before Transjordan was returned to Israelite sway. In this instance the prophet cries out against the injustices of Israel's neighbors, reminding them of their acts of violence and oppression, particularly against Israel. In the prophecy of visions he even refers to Jacob as "so small" (7:2, 5), an attribute that would hardly be appropriate after Jeroboam's extensive gains in Syria. Some claimed that the oracle of visions was Amos' inauguration prophecy (Wellhausen, Budde, et al.). There is nothing in its form or content, however, to justify this claim, though the prophecy does belong to an early stage of Amos' career.

In contrast, the moral reprimands (2:7–6:14; 8:4–14) belong to his later prophecies and reflect the later period of Jeroboam's reign, when *Damascus and *Hamath were already under the hegemony of Israel. The conquest of Transjordan is alluded to in these reprimands (6:13), "the kine of Bashan" who are said to dwell on Mount Samaria (4:1), and Israel's territory is described as stretching from Lebo-Hamath to the Brook of the Arabah (6:14; cf. 3:12). Life in Samaria is characterized by luxury, complacency, and frolic (3:12, 15; 5:23; 6:1, 4–6; 8:10). The inflictions of hunger, locust, and drought are mentioned as part of the past (4:6–9; cf. 8:10). Even the earthquake is recalled in these reprimands as a foregone matter (4:11), while the shocking experiences that came in its wake serve to perceive the impending catastrophe (2:13–15; 3:14–15; 4:3; 6:9 ff.). Still another event alluded to in the moral rebukes, and serving to fix their upper chronological limits, is the solar eclipse, which, according to the Assyrian eponym lists, took place in Sivan 763 B.C.E. This event also serves the prophet as a fitting figure of the punishment to come (8:9).

Thus, although the prophecies of Amos that survived and were collected in the book bearing his name are few, they range over a relatively long period. Variations of character and diction among them lend support to the conclusion that Amos' prophetic output was far greater than what has been preserved in his book.

In the narrative section 7:10–17, a conflict between Amos and Amaziah, the priest, is recorded. Amaziah, who apparently had no authority to punish the prophet, complains about him to Jeroboam, the king: "Amos has conspired against you in the midst of the house of Israel" (7:10). Since there is no royal response the king deemed the matter unimportant. The priest himself tries to drive Amos out of Beth-El by derision (7:12–13), to which Amos responds with emphatic pride about his mission (7:14–15). He ends with a fearful prediction of Amaziah's own future and a renewed pronouncement of Israel's exile (7:16–17). Even in his response Amos says nothing about the king, reinforcing the impression that the quarrel was between him and the priest. Nor are there any further details on the progress or resolution of this clash. This excerpt may pertain only to an extraordinary and provocative event, which did not necessarily occur at the end of Amos' career.

The Structure and Editing of the Book

1. The Book of Amos falls into four divisions, in each of which all or most of the prophecies are of one kind: a prophecy against the nations (1:2–2:6), prophecies of the punishment of Israel (2:7–6:14), "stories" about the life experiences of the prophet (7:1–9:6), and a prophecy of comfort for Israel (9:7–15). The remaining prophetic books of the Bible are built upon the same four categories, but they are not necessarily arranged in the same order and not every one has left prophecies in all four categories. The editors of the Book of Amos chose the above-mentioned order so that the "prophecy against the nations" opens the book, and the prophecy of consolation brings it to a close. The beginning and end divisions each contain only a single unit, since the editors did not find any more than that, whereas the remaining divisions have clusters of prophecies that could be considered as small scrolls in their own right.

The classification of the prophecies was not a priori but rather as viewed in retrospect by the editors. There are prophecies that could have been classified in a category other than the one into which they are now placed. The editors, however, found a justification for such placement. The first prophecy (1:2–2:6), for instance, is not really an oracle against the nations, since it concludes with Judah and Israel; but since its greater part deals with the neighbors of Israel, the editors could view it as a prophecy against the nations as well. The larger part of the third division does not contain actual stories but visions spoken by the prophet in the first person. From the point of view of their content they could be considered among the judgment prophecies. In the Book of Jeremiah similar visions are in fact included among the judgment prophecies (cf. Jer. 1:11–14; 24:1–3). However, since they are stamped with an autobiographic and narrative form, they could serve in the hands of the editors as a narrative division. One such fragment has already been established among these visions, the incident in the sanctuary of Beth-El (7:10–17), which heightens the narrative character of the entire division through its biographic style. At the same time, a small group of rebukes, similar to those in division two, has been found here (8:4–14). Yet the editors could not allow themselves to transfer it; neither was it significant enough to alter the character of this division as a whole. Similar instances are to be found elsewhere in the Prophets, where the editors did not smooth over inconsistencies for the sake of absolute uniformity.

2. The scope of the isolated prophecies is a subject of disagreement among critics. According to one theory (Koehler, Weiser, Robinson, et al.) the text is divided into the smallest units, each ranging from two to seven verses, with some even limited to a single verse. According to this theory, it was the redactors who combined the original utterances into small collections, thus giving them a more substantial scope. According to another theory (Driver, Sellin, et al.), the prophecies are themselves integral compositions of sizable scope, sometimes being divided into subsections and secondary parts. It can be said that scholars are in agreement on the size and scope of the smallest, indivisible units. The dispute is over whether the smallest units are prophecies in their own right or are links or segments of larger pericopes (and from here on the question

is how the segments join to make up the larger pericopes). The second method seems more likely because many of the tiny segments do not have a unity of thought unless they are attached to the adjacent segments. It appears, then, that the complete prophecies are actually built up by joining the single links together. The single links, which are like strophes of a poem, vary in length, and each one can open with an introductory formula or close with a concluding verse, as if it stood alone. Nonetheless, they are connected to each other by association and continuity of thought. Consequently, the formal structure of the prophecies is rather weak, yet they cannot be understood except as literary wholes. Moreover, within a single prophecy, a prophet sometimes expresses a certain idea in two different ways, without providing real justification for splitting the prophecy in two (for the structure of the single prophecies and the associative connections within their parts, see below.)

3. Verses of a unique type are found in the following places in the Book of Amos: 4:13; 5:8–9; 8:8; 9:5–6. Except where the verses interrupt the continuity (5:8–9), they fit fairly well into the context. Yet, they are distinct in content, language, and literary form. Their subject is words of praise to God and the description of his power as revealed in nature. Since scholars apprehended their specific character as cosmic hymns to God, the term "doxologies" has been applied to these verses. The distinctiveness of these verses in the Book of Amos has caused many scholars to claim that these are later additions (Wellhausen, Nowack, Stade, Driver, Sellin, et al.). Various suppositions have been expressed concerning their function; for example, that they served as conclusions to chapters that were read as cultic liturgy (Weiser, et al.), or conclusions to prophetic collections that were absorbed into the Book of Amos (Fohrer, et al.). After the hymnic character of these verses had been noted, the supposition was raised that these are fragments of one hymn that were scattered throughout the Book of Amos, and some attempts have even been made to reconstruct that hymn in its entirety (Budde, Horst, et al.). On the other hand, there were scholars who never denied the authenticity of these verses, and even after their hymnic quality was determined, assumed that the prophet expressed himself here by means of a formulaic style (Robinson, Hammerschaimb, Botterweck, et al.). There were also scholars who attempted to maintain both assumptions at once, i.e., that these verses are both authentic and fragments of a hymn written by Amos (Kaufmann), or of a hymn which Amos interlaced with his own words (Watts, similarly Farr).

Even though these verses are set in a hymnic die, they differ in the Bible, and some of the praises to God contained in them have no example elsewhere in the Bible. Apparently this hymnic style is not that of psalms. In other words, in contradiction to the psalmodic hymns, these did not serve as prayers, but as mere literary clichés. Hymnic passages which do not belong to the psalmodic genre are also found in the Book of Hosea (12:6, and in a slightly different tone 13:4–5 (in LXX there are additional verses nonexistent in the Masoretic Text)) and intertwined with the speeches of the Book of Job (5:9–16; 9:4–10 (the closest to the hymnic verses of Amos); 12:7–25; 26:6–13), and to a certain degree similar verses are found in the words of Deutero-Isaiah (Isa. 40:22; 42:5; 44:24; 45:18, et al.). But then Amos' verses probably reflect an early phase of this literary type. The fitting of most of these verses in their context makes it not impossible that they are of the prophet's pen and that Amos availed himself of them to conclude some of his oracles, with the exception of one instance where the verses were not inserted in their proper place (Amos 5:8–9). Furthermore, in the descriptions of the trembling of the earth, its rising and sinking "as the river of Egypt," and the pouring out of the sea over the face of the earth (5:8; 8:8; 9:5–6), one may hear an echo of the earthquake, whose impression is recorded in the other prophecies of Amos as well (see above).

4. In the first prophecy of the book (1:2–2:6) various scholars denied the authenticity of the sections concerning the Philistines (1:6–8), Tyre (1:9–10), Edom (1:11–12), and Judah (2:4–5). However, their claims are not decisive, and the opinion of the commentators who consider these sections an integral part of the body of the prophecy should be preferred. Doubts have also been raised concerning Amos 6:2, which mentions the destruction of Calneh, Greater Hamath, and Philistine Gath – cities which were conquered by *Tiglath-Pileser III and *Sargon many years after the reign of Jeroboam. But it is possible that the verse refers to earlier catastrophes that overwhelmed these cities. The statement in 1:5 – "the people of Aram shall go into exile to Kir" – appears to correspond too faithfully to reality according to II Kings 16:9, so that the mentioning of Kir in one of these two passages seemed suspect. In addition, it is not customary for Amos to mention by name the place to which a nation will be exiled. However, the mention of Kir in another passage as the provenance of the Arameans (9:7) is an argument in favor of the authorities in the prophecy of exile, which is comparable to the threat in other books that Israel will return to Egypt (Deut. 28:68; Hos. 8:13).

The prophecy of comfort at the end of the book has also been taken to be late. Indeed, it does contain late expansions (see below). Perhaps in the course of time, some late idioms have found their way into the words of Amos, even in places where there is no reason to deny the authenticity of the passage in general. Of this type seem to be the references to the deities Siccuth, Chiun, and Kokhav (star god) in 5:26, and Ashimah of Samaria in 8:14. Siccuth (Succoth-Benoth) and Ashimah are mentioned in II Kings 17:30 as deities which were worshipped by the men of Babylon and the men of Hamath who were settled in Samaria after the exile of Israel. However, there are some who think that the cult of these deities had gained a foothold in Israel, even prior to the exile of the northern tribes. Possibly, a few Deuteronomic idioms also became attached to various places in the text of Amos. Such is the idiom "I will set my eyes upon them for evil and not for good" (9:4), to which Jeremiah 21:10; 24:6; 39:16, et al., can be compared. There are those who find Deuteronomic impressions in the section on Judah (2:4–5) as well. But even if this assumption were certain, it would still not be sufficient to invalidate the reliability of the core of this section.

Content of the Prophecies

THE FIRST DIVISION. The "prophecy against the nations" (Amos 1:2–2:6) begins with a formulaic call (1:2) and contains a series of sections in a stereotyped structure, the subject of which is the neighbors of Israel, concluding with Judah and Israel themselves. To them all, the prophet promises exile and destruction. The utterances to Judah and Israel serve as an apex of this prophecy; hence it appears that this is actually not a prophecy against the nations, though in the main it does speak against Israel's neighbors. Many scholars believe that its conclusion coincides with the end of chapter two (2:16). However, all that is said after 2:6 is already stamped with the mark of the moral reproofs of the second division, and it is doubtful whether it constitutes a suitable continuation to the first prophecy. Probably the section on Israel (2:6), which lacks the typical conclusion, "So I will send a fire… and it shall devour the strongholds of…" has not been preserved in its entirety, but this prophecy was cut short at the end, and the editors then attached to it the scroll of reproofs to Israel. Thus the section on Israel, and thereby all of the "prophecy against the nations," was stitched to the moral reproofs of the second division. This is one of Amos' earliest prophecies; the period of time reflected in it is the beginning of Jeroboam's reign, before Transjordan was recovered by Israel (see above).

THE SECOND DIVISION. This division is made up exclusively of prophecies of reproof. The first is 2:7–16, the first part of which is probably lost, for it lacks a formal opening (see above). It is divided into three segments: a description of the moral and cultic corruption (7–8), the past grace of God to Israel (9–12), and a description of the impending catastrophe (13–16). 3:1–15 opens with the call "Hear this word." It is divided as follows: a statement about the relation of the election of Israel and the greater responsibility placed upon it (1–2), a proverb on the connection between cause and effect and on the significance of the prophetic word (3–8), descriptions of catastrophes and reminders of sins (9–12), and a statement on the day of punishment and the destruction of Israel for its transgressions (13–15). The prophecy 4:1–13 again begins with the call "Hear this word." It is divided into four segments: a description of the corruption and punishment of the "kine of Bashan which are on the mountain of Samaria" (1–3), a denunciation of the worship in the temples (4–5), a series of afflictions that came upon Israel but were not sufficient to return the people to God (6–11), and a call to the people to prepare to meet their God, concluding with hymnic verse (12–13). The prophecy 5:1–17 also opens with "Hear this word" and is divided into the following segments: a lament on the downfall of Israel (1–2) and a description of calamity (3); an accusation against the worship in temples and a warning of exile and destruction (4–6); a description of the moral corruption and its attendant punishment (7, 10–13), in which two hymnic verses are inserted (8–9); a call to repentance (14–15) and a depiction of mourning as a result of the coming catastrophe (16–17).

The prophecy 5:18–27 opens with the call "Ah!" (Heb. *Hoi*). It is divided into three segments: a description of the terrors of the Day of the Lord (18–20), a denunciation of the worship in the temples and a call to repentance (21–25), and a promise of exile to Israel (26–27). The following prophecy, 6:1–14, also begins with the exclamation "Ah!" and is divided into four segments: a call to Israel not to be tranquil about its future, since it is no better than other kingdoms that were also destroyed (1–2); a description of the serene and luxurious life and a warning of exile (3–7); God's oath to bring destruction upon Israel and descriptions of calamities (8–11); and a reproof on the moral corruption and a warning of catastrophe (12–14).

THE THIRD DIVISION. The prophecy of visions (7:1–9; 8:1–3) is divided into two pairs of sections, which are of a similar structure. All the sections begin with the words "Thus has the Lord God shown unto me, and behold…," a specific vision being mentioned in each one. In the first two sections the prophet sees visions of disasters – locusts (7:1–3) and drought (4–6). He begs for mercy until God repents the evil decree and cancels it. In the last two sections the prophet sees symbolic visions: "The Lord stands upon a wall made by a plumbline, with a plumbline in his hand" (7–9) and "a basket of summer fruit," that is, figs that ripened late (8:1–3). These two visions are explained to him as symbols of the destruction of Israel, and the prophet does not even attempt to void the decision. Both conclude with poetic sentences depicting the destruction. This prophecy belongs to the two years at the beginning of Amos' activity, before the earthquake (cf. above). The opinion of Sellin, Rost, and others that this prophecy should be fixed at the end of Amos' work does not stand to reason.

A fragment of a story on an incident that occurred to Amos at the temple of Beth-El (7:10–17) has been inserted into the midst of the prophecy of visions. According to the story, the priest of Beth-El complained to Jeroboam about Amos and even attributed to the prophet intentions of rebellion against the king, quoting from his words: "Jeroboam shall die by the sword, and Israel shall surely be exiled away from his land" (11). Throughout all of Amos' prophecies Jeroboam is mentioned by name only at the end of the third section of the prophecy of visions (7:9). This was judged a sufficient reason to insert the narrative at this point, thereby separating the two last sections of the prophecy of visions. Also attached to the prophecy of visions is a group of prophetic sayings whose content is close to the prophecies of the second division (8:4–14). It comprises two or three fragments: a prophecy divided into two links, or two pieces that have been joined together – a description of the moral corruption, God's oath not to forget the deeds of Israel, with a hymnic verse (4–8), and a description of the terrors of the Day of the Lord (9–10); and a piece consisting of sayings concerning the future hunger and thirst for the words of God (11–14).

Chapter 9, verses 1–6 is a vision of the destruction of Israel. Similar to the prophecy of visions, this unit is also related in the first person, which caused many scholars to believe that it is a direct continuation and climax of the preceding visions. However, it is more likely that it is a self-contained literary unit. At the same time it is possible that the editors found this vision in the continuation of the scroll of "stories" that contains the prophecy of visions, with the fragments inserted in, and attached to it. The literary structure of this vision differs from that of the former visionary prophecy. At the beginning of this unit the prophet remarks that he saw the Lord standing beside the altar and ordering the execution of the catastrophe. There is no exchange of words between the prophet and the Lord, and from the opening the vision immediately proceeds to depict the catastrophe. The work of destruction begins with Beth-El, and from there it spreads out enveloping the entire people, without leaving them any place of refuge. The vision is concluded by two hymnic verses.

THE FOURTH DIVISION. This is a single prophecy of comfort to Israel, divided into four segments (9:7–15): in the eyes of God, Israel is not considered to be more important than other nations (9:7); therefore, God is about to destroy the sinning kingdom, but it will not be completely destroyed – He will scatter Israel among all the nations, and the sinners in its midst who were indifferent to the coming calamity will perish (8–10); afterward God will raise up the fallen tabernacle of David, and His people will inherit the remnants of Edom and other nations (11–12); Israel will return to its land and rebuild it, without being exiled from it again (13–15). Thus, the first two segments essentially express a message of calamity, whereas the last two, a message of salvation. Most scholars are of the opinion that the last two segments are not of Amos, whereas a minority views them as authentic. The opinion of the former appears to be the more plausible. However, the editors of the Book of Amos found this prophecy in its expanded form, i.e., when both last segments were already contained in it and attributed to Amos. Consequently, they took it to be a prophecy of comfort and placed it as a division on its own. Even though the last two segments seem to be later expansions of the words of Amos, it does not imply that he was only a prophet of woe and did not compose prophecies of comfort. Among the extant prophecies in the book bearing his name, however, there is no prophecy of comfort except this one.

His Personality and Prophetic Message

Amos testifies that he "was taken from following the flock" to prophesy to Israel (7:15). Nevertheless, one cannot conceive of him as a common person, whose power lies in spiritual inspiration and insight alone. His writings also demonstrate qualities of education and erudition. His polished and highly artistic style could not be attained without literary training, since such a style serves as an obvious indication of the creativity of a man of letters. Amos is well acquainted with the life of the social elite, has a clear perception of all the military and political occurrences on Israel's perimeter (1:3–2:3; 4:10; 5:27; 6:13–14, et al.), and displays an outlook that encompasses even the fates of nations throughout the Near East (1:3–5; 6:2; 9:7, et al.). Moreover, among his compositions are found a few prophecies explicitly molded in an autobiographic form (see above), as are to be found also in other prophets, and they suffice to verify that Amos, similar to the rest of the Latter Prophets, was also a writer. His other prophecies even though not of an explicit autobiographical mold, are first and foremost literary creations, which he himself, as an artist and poet, shaped. It cannot be told for certain whence this prophet, who was taken from following the flock, received his erudition and literary training. It could have been in his city, Tekoa, which was known for its wise men (cf. above). He could also have attained this stage later on in life.

Amos' prophetic creation is undoubtedly rooted in literary tradition and his compact and superior style may prove that others preceded him in crystallizing words of prophecy in writing. A few formulaic traits are already discernible in his language. Amos surely did not invent these, but received them ready-made. It is even possible that in some places prophetic words prior to those of Amos have found their way into the books in our possession, but the names of their authors are lost. Amos, however, is the first whose name has been preserved on prophetic writings that were collected in a special book and whose prophetic personality transpires from this book.

The major part of his message is devoted to promises of catastrophe to befall Israel, expressed in several ways. Often the terrors of the earthquake serve him to make the coming catastrophe perceptible (2:13–16; 3:14–15; 4:3; 6:11; 9:1). In other places he depicts scenes of siege, the conquering of a city, and the despoiling of palaces (3:9–11; 4:2–3; 6:8). He also promises Israel the tragedy of exile (5:5, 27; 6:7; 9:9). Amos is the first to express the threat of exile in the Bible, just as he is the first to use explicitly in this connection the Hebrew verb *galah*. Apparently, in this instance his words reflect the Assyrian system, i.e., to uproot and transfer nations from their homelands. In portraying the impending calamity, Amos avails himself of the concept of the *Day of the Lord. This concept primarily denoted a day of salvation for Israel and stringent judgment upon its enemies. This is its significance in the words of several prophets as well as in the passage of consolation appended at the end of the Book of Amos (9:11). Even Amos himself probably fashioned his "prophecy against the nations" after the model of the Day of the Lord oracles (1:3–2:3), though he tacked on to it words of punishment to Judah and Israel. At the same time, Amos reverses the meaning of the Day of the Lord, conceiving it as a day of calamity and judgment upon Israel itself. His usage of this popular concept in reversed fashion is clearly indicated in several verses (see 5:18, 20; also 8:3, 9–10). From the latter passages it can be inferred that in other connections also, when Amos cries out a lamentation and depicts scenes of mourning, a multitude of corpses, and silence everywhere (5:1–2, 15–17; 6:9–10), it is possibly the horrible image of the Day of the Lord that hovers before his eyes.

These various expressions of the message of catastrophe sometimes contradict each other on certain points. Yet, they should not be measured by principles of harsh logic, for the prophet himself undoubtedly did not mean to express his visions in formal, systematic concepts. The poetic images served him only as a means to portray the terror of the impending crisis. Similarly, he often describes the calamity as decided and absolute, allowing no living remnant to survive (see especially 9:2–4). But on the other hand, he speaks of exiling the people from the country, and sometimes assumes that a remnant will be preserved (3:12; 5:3, 15). Furthermore, those who are destined to die are only the sinners who do not believe that evil will befall them (9:10). Contradictions of this nature can be found even within the same prophecy: from Israel will be preserved remnants (5:3), but even so the people are liable to burn in a fire which no one will be able to extinguish (5:6); they will be exiled from their land (6:7), but even so God will raise up against them a nation who will oppress them from Lebo-Hamath to the Brook of the Arabah (6:14). Thus in the first prophecy to all the nations enumerated there the prophet promises burning by fire and destruction, but to a few of those he adds a promise of exile (1:5, 15). Real contradictions exist in these words for those who conceive of them in the framework of contemplative and methodical thought. But in the agitated images of a prophet their purpose is only to complement and strengthen each other. Likewise, the prophet will often describe the catastrophe as inevitable, as a predetermined decree of fate, but he also calls for repentance, thereby pointing the way to life. This occurs even in the midst of the depictions of catastrophe (5:4–6, 14–15). Hence, in the depictions of the decreed catastrophe, he does not exactly "mean" what he says. His words are rooted in a despair of repentance, or their true meaning is that of a threat only.

The promises of doom are explained by Amos, as well as by other prophets, as the result of the people's social and moral corruption: robbery of the poor, extortion of judgments, cheating in business, acts of plunder and violence by the ruling elite (2:7–8; 3:9–10; 4:1; 5:7, 10–12, 15; 6:4–6). At the same time he denounces the life of luxury and enjoyment (3:12, 15; 4:1; 5:11; 6:4–6; 8:3), and here too he is a partner in the prophetic ideal of simple and innocent life (Isa. 2:12–17; 3:16–23; Hos. 8:14; 13:5–6; Zeph. 3:11–12, et al.). The comforts and great happiness in the lives of the rulers evoke hostility in Amos, for the additional reason that they indicate apparent security and disbelief in the impending calamity (4:1–2; 6:3–7; 9:10). Therefore, he mocks the happiness of the people for their military conquests, which, according to his outlook, will turn to nought (6:13–14). He also defies the worship in the temples, which accompany an abundance of sacrifices, rapturous assemblies, and shouts of joy (4:4–5; 5:5, 21, 23). The people do not sense that all these exhibitions of abundance and pomp will not erase the decree of destruction of the places of worship (5:5; 7:9; 9:1). Rescue will come by seeking the Lord, which is the seeking of the good and is intertwined with a moral and social purification (5:4–6, 14–15, 24). In this connection, the prophet does not hesitate even to state that the Lord despises the cult practiced in His honor in the temples (5:21–23). Furthermore, he claims that even in the desert, Israel did not worship the Lord with sacrifices and offerings (5:25). This claim reflects the view of the early Pentateuchal sources (JE), according to which Israel made some sacrifices before they left Egypt (Ex. 12:21–27) and when they were encamped by Mount Sinai (Ex. 3:12; 17:15; 18:12; 24:4–8; 32:5–6), but no mention is made of their sacrifices along the journey from Sinai to Canaan. Similarly Jeremiah asserts that when God brought Israel out of Egypt he neither spoke to Israel nor commanded them concerning burnt offerings and sacrifices (Jer. 2:22–23).

Although Amos appears to invalidate the worship in the temples, he does not do it because of the cult as such, but only to accentuate the significance of social ethics. Cultic acts are not important enough to him when they are bound with moral corruption and oppression of the poor (2:7–8). The demand to remove the noise of songs and the melody of harps serves him as an introduction to the positive demand: "and let justice roll down like waters, and righteousness like an everflowing stream" (5:23–24). Similarly, the call to refrain from coming to the temples is related by him to the call to seek the Lord in order to be saved from the catastrophe and to live (5:5–6). Therefore, one should not attribute to Amos a decisive invalidation of the value of the cult (as, e.g., Weiser tended to do), for this invalidation is decreed by him not for its own sake, but rather serves as a kind of rhetorical-polemic means to a greater emphasis on the value of ethics. However, the very perception that the people's fate is determined solely by its social and moral perfection, found in Amos its first exponent in biblical literature. Afterward, it recurs in various degrees of accentuation in the books of some of the great prophets who succeeded him. But Amos and the other prophets were hardly conscious of the uniqueness of this notion, in which an exceedingly revolutionary idea is hidden. To them it looked like a fundamental principle of the ancient belief in YHWH, in whose name they spoke to the people and by whose authority they made ethical demands. Consequently, it also would not be accurate to say (as did, e.g., Cramer), that in fact Amos did not introduce any new religious idea. The unique innovation of Amos (and of the prophets after him) was in a new apprehension of the inner significance of the Yahwistic belief with its ancient tradition. But this innovation was hardly perceptible to its exponents.

Many scholars assert that Amos is also superior to his contemporaries in his perception of God, for he emphasizes the power of YHWH over the fates of many nations besides Israel (9:7; cf. 6:1). The people of Israel are no more important to YHWH than are the Ethiopians (9:7); their election from among all the families of the earth only burdens them with a greater moral responsibility (3:2). Amos' prophecies were one of the turning points in moving Yahwistic religion in the direction of monotheism. Although this view was challenged by such outstanding scholars as *Albright and *Kaufmann, our increased knowledge of ancient Israelite religion indicates that the road to monotheism was a long one, and that Amos was a significant signpost on that road.

BIBLIOGRAPHY: COMMENTARIES: J. Wellhausen, *Die kleinen Propheten* (1893[2]); W.R. Harper (ICC, Eng., 1905); S.R. Driver (Eng., 1915[2]); W. Nowack (Ger., 1922[3]); E. Sellin (Ger., 1929[2, 3]); T.H. Robinson (Ger., 1954[2]); N.H. Snaith (Eng., 1956); E. Hammershaimb (Danish, 1958[2]); R.S. Cripps (Eng., 1960[3]); A. Weiser (Ger., 1964[5]); J.L. Mays (Eng., 1969); H.W. Wolf (Ger., 1969, incl. bibl., 139–44). **ADD. BIBLIOGRAPHY:** Idem, *Joel and Amos* (Hermeneia; 1977); F. Andersen and D.N. Friedman, *Amos* (AB; 1989); S.M. Paul, *Amos: A Commentary* (Hermeneia; 1991); G. Jeremias, *Amos: A Commentary* (1998). SELECTED BIBLIOGRAPHY: H. Schmidt, in: BZAW, 34 (1920), 158–71; K. Budde, in: JBL, 43 (1924), 46–131; 44 (1925), 63–122; A. Weiser, *Die Profetie des Amos* (1929); K. Cramer, *Amos-Versuch einer theologischen Interpretation* (1930); L. Koehler, in: *Theologische Rundschau*, 4 (1932), 195–213; R. Gordis, in: HTR, 33 (1940), 239–51; J. Morgenstern, *Amos Studies* (1941) = HUCA, 11 (1936), 19–140; 12–13 (1937–38), 1–53; 15 (1940), 59–305); idem, in: *Tribute... Leo Baeck* (1954), 106–26; idem, in: HUCA, 32 (1961), 295–350; H.H. Rowley, in: *Festschrift... O. Eissfeldt* (1947), 191–8; E. Wuerthwein, in: ZAW, 62 (1950), 10–52; A. Neher, *Amos. Contribution à l'étude du Prophétisme* (1950); M. Bič, in: VT, 1 (1951), 293–6; V. Maag, *Text, Wortschatz und Begriffswelt des Buches Amos* (1951); J.P. Hyatt, in: ZAW, 68 (1956), 17–24; S. Jozaki, in: *Kwansei Gakuin University Annual Studies*, 4 (1956), 25–100 (Eng.); J.D.W. Watts, *Vision and Prophecy in Amos* (1958); G. Botterweck, in: BZ, 2 (1958), 161–76; Y. Kaufmann, Toledot, 3 (1960), 56–92; A.H.J. Gunneweg, in: ZTK, 57 (1960), 1–16; M.J. Dahood, in: *Biblica*, 42 (1961), 359–66; A.S. Kapelrud, *Central Ideas in Amos* (1961[2]); idem, in: VT Supplement, 15 (1966), 193–206; S. Terrien, in: *Essays... A. Muelenburg* (1962), 108–15; G. Farr, in: VT, 12 (1962), 312–24; H. Gese, *ibid.*, 417–38; H. Reventlow, *Das Amt des Propheten bei Amos* (1962); S. Cohen, in: HUCA, 32 (1962), 175–8; 36 (1965), 153–60; R. Fey, *Amos und Jesaja* (1963); H.W. Wolf, *Amos' geistige Heimat* (1964); M. Weiss, in: *Tarbiz*, 34 (1965), 107–28, 303–18; W. Schmidt, in: ZAW, 77 (1965), 168–92; H. Gottlieb, in: VT, 17 (1967), 430–63; S. Segert, in: *Festschrift... W. Baumgartner* (1967), 279–83; M. Haran, in: VT, 17 (1967), 266–97; idem, in: IEJ, 18 (1968), 201–12; idem, in: *Tarbiz*, 39 (1970) 126–36. ON THE "DOXOLOGIES": K. Budde, in: JBL, 44 (1925), 106–8; T.H. Gaster, in: *Journal of Manchester Egyptian and Oriental Society*, 19 (1935), 23–26; G.R. Driver, in: JTS, 4 (1953), 208–12; J.D.W. Watts, in: JNES, 15 (1956), 33–39; F. Horst, *Gottes Recht* (1961), 155–66; G. Farr, in: VT, 12 (1962), 321–4; W. Brueggemann, *ibid.*, 15 (1965), 1–15; J.L. Grenshaw, in: ZAW, 79 (1967), 42–52. **ADD. BIBLIOGRAPHY:** R.F. Melugin, in: *Currents in Research*, 6 (1998), 65–101; I. Jaruzelska, *Amos and the Officialdom in the Kingdom: The Socio-Economic Position of the Officials in the Light of the Biblical, the Epigraphic and Archaeological Evidence* (1998); M.D. Carroll Rodas, *Amos-the Prophet and his Oracles: Research on the Book of Amos* (2002).

[Menahem Haran]

AMRAM (Heb. עַמְרָם; "the Divine Kinsman is exalted"), father of Aaron, Moses, and Miriam (Ex. 6:18, 20; Num. 26:58–59). Amram married his aunt Jochebed (Ex. 6:20), which is contrary to biblical law (Lev. 18:12–13; 20:19–20). He was the son of Kohath, the grandson of Levi, and his name frequently appears in genealogical lists of the tribe of Levi (Num. 3:19; I Chron. 5:28–29; 6:3; 23:12–13; 24:20). Amram was also the father of the Amramites, a Kohathite branch of the tribe of Levi (Num. 3:27; I Chron. 26:23).

In the *Aggadah*

The *aggadah* relates that Amram was "head of the Sanhedrin" (Ex. R. 1:13), and describes him as "the leader of his generation" (Sot. 12a). When Pharaoh decreed the death of all the male Jewish children, Amram divorced Jochebed, his wife, declaring: "We labor in vain." His example was followed by all the men in Israel. His daughter, Miriam, however, criticized his action declaring that his example was worse than Pharaoh's decree. Amram heeded her words, and remarried Jochebed. All the men of Israel, thereupon remarried their wives (Sot. 12a).

Amram's piety is described as being partly responsible for bringing the divine presence closer to earth (PdRK 1). It is also recorded that he was one of the four personalities (the others were Benjamin, Jesse, and Chileab), who died untainted by sin (Shab. 55b; BB 17a).

BIBLIOGRAPHY: H.H. Rowley, *From Joseph to Joshua* (1950), 57–108; Ginzberg, Legends, 2 (1910), 258–61; I. Ḥasida, *Ishei ha-Tanakh* (1964).

[Elimelech Epstein Halevy]

AMRAM, name of two Babylonian *amoraim*. AMRAM I (third century). His preceptors were Rav and R. Assi, whom Amram quotes both in *halakhah* and *aggadah* (Pes. 105a; Ned. 28a; et al.). He was once requested by his colleagues to relate "those excellent sayings that you once told us in the name of R. Assi" (Er. 102a). Among his aggadic statements are "[There are] three transgressions which no man escapes for a single day: sinful thought, calculation on [the results of] prayer, and slander" (BB 164b). On Psalms 112:1 ("Happy is the man that feareth the Lord") he comments, "happy is he who repents while he is still a man," i.e., while he is still in the prime of life (Av. Zar. 19a). AMRAM II (early fourth century) was a pupil of R. Sheshet, whose halakhic rulings he quotes (Yev. 35a, et al.). Sheshet affectionately called him "My son Amram" (Av. Zar. 76a). Once when Amram was guilty of hairsplitting, Sheshet remarked: "Perhaps you are from Pumbedita where they try to make an elephant pass through the eye of a needle?" (BM 38b). Only a few sayings are transmitted in his own name (e.g., Nid. 25b), as he generally quotes *halakhah* in the name of others such as R. Isaac (Zev. 6b); R. Naḥman (Ber. 49b); Ulla (Git. 26b); and Rabbah b. Bar Ḥana (Yoma 78a). He engaged in discussions on *halakhah* with Rabbah and R. Joseph (Sot. 6a). According to the *aggadah*, in one of these, Rabbah expressed himself so sharply when opposing Amram that a pillar in the academy cracked (BM 20b).

BIBLIOGRAPHY: Hyman, Toledot, 983.

[Yitzhak Dov Gilat]

AMRAM (late 14th century), *nagid of the Jewish communities in Egypt. Amram is mentioned as *nagid* in a document of 1377 and in a letter written in 1380, probably by Joseph b. Eliezer Tov Elem of Jerusalem. The name *Amram*, appearing without the epithet *nagid* in a partially preserved document dated 1384, may refer to him. His name also appears in a Hebrew letter which states that rumors of the exodus of the Ten Tribes have spread through Italy, and emissaries have been sent to the East to check their veracity.

BIBLIOGRAPHY: Ashtor, Toledot, 2 (1951), 21–26; Assaf, in: *Zion*, 6 (1940/41), 113–8.

[Eliyahu Ashtor]

AMRAM, DAVID (1930–), French horn player, pianist, composer. A man of many parts, the Philadelphia-born Amram has written and performed in almost every conceivable musical context. He studied composition at Oberlin College, then did his U.S. Army service as part of the Seventh Army Symphony, where he played with Sonny Rollins and Charles Mingus. Upon leaving the army he stayed on in Paris briefly, where he led a jazz quintet, which recorded there. The mix of jazz and classical runs through his entire career, as might be expected from a French horn player who jammed with Dizzy Gillespie, among others. He scored and appeared in the famous underground film *Pull My Daisy*, then film director John Frankenheimer brought him to Hollywood to score *All Fall Down* (1961); his stay was relatively brief but did result in the memorable soundtrack to Frankenheimer's *The Manchurian Candidate* (1962), one of the most successful jazz-influenced scores of the period, and two excellent scores for Elia Kazan, *Splendor in the Grass* (1962) and *The Arrangment* (1969). Amram is a prolific composer with over 100 orchestral and chamber works and two operas to his credit, including the Holocaust-themed TV opera *The Final Ingredient* (1965), *Native American Portraits* (1976), and *Symphony: Songs of the Soul* (1986–87). His compositions draw tellingly on Native American, Latin jazz, Middle Eastern, and other folkloric influences. *Vibrations*, an autobiography, was published in 1968.

BIBLIOGRAPHY: "David Amram," in: MusicWeb Encyclopaedia of Popular Music, at www.musicweb.uk.net; B. Priestly, "David Amram," in: *Jazz: The Rough Guide* (1995).

[George Robinson (2nd ed.)]

AMRAM, DAVID WERNER (1866–1939), U.S. jurist, community leader, scholar; son of Werner David Amram, Philadelphia businessman and owner of the first *mazzah* bakery in Philadelphia. Amram practiced law from 1889 to 1903 when he was appointed a bankruptcy referee to the U.S. District Court. In 1908 he became lecturer in law and from 1912 to 1925 he was professor of jurisprudence at the Law School of the University of Pennsylvania. Active in community affairs, he was on the Board of Governors of *Gratz College and the publication committee of the *Jewish Publication Society. He was chairman of the Philadelphia Zionist Council and editor of its official publication, the *Maccabean*. Amram first began to study Talmud when already an adult, under Marcus *Jastrow, and was deeply influenced by him in his attitude toward Jewish life and thought.

Amram wrote articles on Jewish law in the Bible and Talmud for the Anglo-Jewish press as well as for the *Jewish Encyclopedia*. Among his books on Jewish law are *Jewish Law of Divorce According to the Bible and Talmud* (1896, repr. 1968) and *Leading Cases in Biblical Law* (1905). Amram also published *genizah* legal documents (in *The Green Bag, an Entertaining Magazine of Law*, vol. 13, 1901), books on law and legal practice in Pennsylvania, and studies in Mexican and Peruvian textile designs and on Aztec pottery. His special interest in Hebrew books and printing led him to write *Makers of Hebrew Books in Italy* (1909, repr. 1963), which contains important descriptions of Hebrew printing in Italy from the 15th–17th centuries and remains the best introduction in the English language to the subject.

BIBLIOGRAPHY: AJYB, index to vols. 1–50 (1967), s.v.

[Abraham Meir Habermann]

AMRAM, NATHAN BEN ḤAYYIM (1805–1870), rabbi and emissary of Ereẓ Israel. Born in Safed, Amram was sent to Egypt in 1825 on behalf of the community of Tiberias. He remained in Alexandria until 1835, when he left for Europe as an emissary of Hebron. Accused of misappropriating funds from a mission, he wrote a pamphlet called *Iggeret ha-Emunah ve-ha-Tiferet* (1843) to justify his accounts. He returned to Alexandria by 1851 and was appointed rabbi there in 1863, serving until his death. Amram was interested in the sciences, medicine, economics, and mysticism and wrote scores of small books on *halakhah*, philosophy, and Kabbalah, some of which were published. In 1853 he began the publication of his major work, *No'am ha-Middot*, concerning philosophical and moral topics, arranged alphabetically (pt. 1, 1855; pt. 2, 1865; pt. 3, 1869). He appended to it *Hitnasse'ut ha-Mishar*, a discussion of the development of the economy of Europe and its ethical and social significance. His novellae on the Scriptures and Talmud, sermons, and letters survive in manuscript form.

BIBLIOGRAPHY: S. Hazzan, *Ha-Ma'alot li-Shelomo* (1894), 114b; Yaari, Sheluḥei, 687–90; M. Benayahu, in: *Oẓar Yehudei Sefarad*, 3 (1960), 106, 109–10; N. Allony and E.(F.) Kupfer, *Reshimat Taẓlumei Kitvei ha-Yad ha-Ivriyyim ba-Makhon*, 2 (1964), 78, no. 877.

AMRAM BEN SHESHNA (**Amram Gaon**; d. c. 875), *gaon* of Sura noted for his responsa and the oldest surviving order of prayer. According to the epistle of *Sherira Gaon, Amram was given the title of *gaon* even during the lifetime of his predecessor Natronai b. Hilai, although the circumstances which led to this are unknown. The precise period during which he served in the gaonate is uncertain; however it is clear from one of his responsa that by 858 he was already acting in that capacity. More than 200 of Amram's responsa are extant, some in collections of geonic responsa such as *Sha'arei Ẓedek* and *Sha'arei Teshuvah*, others of the earlier rabbinic authorities; still others having been discovered in the Cairo *Genizah*. His responsa include both practical halakhic decisions and comments on the Talmud. In one of them he states that it is prohibited to lend money to a non-Jew on interest, and even though indirect interest (*avak ribbit*) is permitted, scholars should shun it (*Sha'arei Ẓedek* (Salonika, 1792), 40a). Amram's fame, however, rests primarily on his *Seder* (commonly called his *siddur*), "the order of prayers and blessings for the entire year… according to the tradition which we possess, as laid down by the *tannaim* and *amoraim*." The *Seder*, known also as "*Yesod ha-Amrami*" and as "*Maḥzor de-Rav Amram*," originated in a responsum which was seemingly sent to the community of Barcelona. From there it spread throughout Spain and to other countries. The *Seder R. Amram* is the oldest order of Jewish prayers extant. It contains the text of the prayers for the entire year, as well as the laws and customs pertaining to the different prayers. Although Amram's predecessor Natronai had written a responsum (mentioned at the beginning of Amram's *Seder*) to the community of Lucena explaining how the rabbinic injunction to recite 100 blessings daily should be fulfilled and had established the sequence of weekday prayers, Amram was the first to compose a systematic arrangement including prayers for the whole annual cycle as well as the pertinent laws. Amram's sources, in addition to the Talmud, were the works of the *geonim* and the rites of the Babylonian yeshivot. The *Seder* enjoyed a very wide circulation and was extensively quoted by the leading scholars of Spain, Provence, France, and Germany. It served as the basis for later orders of service, such as *Siddur Rashi, Maḥzor Vitry*, and especially the liturgy of countries which came under Babylonian influence.

In a responsum to Meshullam b. Nathan of Melun, Jacob b. Meir *Tam (12th century) states: "Whoever is not well-versed in Rav Amram's *Seder* and in *Halakhot Gedolot*… dare not alter the words of the early authorities or their customs, for we must rely upon them wherever they do not contradict our Talmud but [merely] add to it. Many customs we observe originated with them" (*Sefer ha-Yashar*, 619). Three different manuscripts of the *Siddur* are extant, and additional fragments have been discovered in the Cairo *Genizah*. The present work is not that written by Amram and contains later interpolations. Moreover, a thorough study of the *Seder*, as well as a comparison between it and passages cited from it by the earlier rabbinic authorities, show that in the course of time changes were introduced into Amram's original text, both in the sections comprising the prayers and in those dealing with the laws. Some scholars even maintain that Amram sent to Spain only the "order" of the prayers and blessings together with the relevant laws but not the actual text of the prayers and blessings, which were added later. Some contend that the *Seder* was basically composed not by Amram but by Ẓemaḥ b. Solomon, the *av bet din* at the time.

The *Siddur* has been edited by N. Coronel, *Seder R. Amram Ga'on* (in two parts; 1865); by A.L. Frumkin, *Seder Rav Amram ha-Shalem* (1912); and by D. Hedegard, *Seder R. Amram Ga'on* (only the weekday prayers; 1951). A. Marx published additions and corrections to Coronel's edition under the title of *Untersuchungen zum Siddur des Gaon R. Amram* (1908). A critical edition of the *Seder R. Amram* based on manuscripts and old editions was published by Daniel S. Goldschmidt (Jerusalem, 1971).

BIBLIOGRAPHY: Graetz-Rabbinowitz, 3 (1894), 259; 464; Weiss, Dor, 4 (1904⁴), 107–10; Halevy, Dorot, 3 (1923), 243–6, 258–9; B.M. Lewin, *Iggeret R. Sherira Ga'on* (1921), 115; J.N. Epstein, in: *Kovez J.N. Simḥoni* (1929), 122–41; Assaf, Ge'onim, 180–4; L. Ginzberg, *Geonica*, 1 (1909), 119–54; 2 (1909), 301–45; Elbogen, Gottesdienst, 358–60, 564–5; D. Goldschmidt, in: KS, 29 (1953/54), 71–75.

[Tovia Preschel]

AMRAM DARAH (fourth century C.E.), Samaritan poet who wrote in Aramaic and whose poems form a central part of the Samaritan basic prayer book, the *Defter*, to this day. He is believed to be the priest (or high priest) Amram b. Sarad mentioned in the Samaritan chronicles of *Abu al-Fat and the *New Chronicle*. According to these sources, Bāba Rabbah appointed him, together with a layman, as head of the fourth district of the reorganized Samaritan province in the fourth century C.E. The *Tolidah* identified him with Tūta, the father of the famous poet Markah, which would make him one of the early revivers of the Samaritan liturgy in an age of political renaissance. His epithet, Darah, meaning the ancient one, differentiates him from later priests called Amram. Amram Darah's style is primitive, and his poems lack a standard number of lines and a fixed line length. Twenty-nine poems in the *Defter* are attributed to him, the greater part under the heading "Verses of Durran," i.e., verses by Darah or in the style of Darah. A smaller section bears the designation "Verses of Markah" because of their stylistic affinity to the poems of his son.

BIBLIOGRAPHY: A.E. Cowley, *Samaritan Liturgy*, 1 (1909), 21, 27–29, 38–47, 62, 341; 2 (1909), 491, 670; Z. Ben-Ḥayyim, *Ivrit ve-Aramit Nusaḥ Shomeron*, 3, pt. 2 (1967), 12–15; idem, in: *Eretz-Israel*, 4 (1956), 119–27.

[Ayala Loewenstamm]

AMRAM ḤASIDA (Aram. "the Pious"; c. third century), a prominent member of the Jewish community in Nehardea. It is reported that he applied the punishment of lashes to anyone who followed lenient opinions regarding the sowing of *kilayim* ("mixed seeds") in a vineyard, even outside the Land of Israel (Shab. 130a). He attached *ẓiẓit* to a garment worn by his wife (Suk. 11a). He was physically maltreated by the house of the exilarch (because according to Rashi, "he was pious and strict and therefore imposed numerous restrictions upon them") and he became ill. (Git. 67b). The Talmud tells of his struggle against temptation in which he publicly admitted his weakness. When the sages said to him, "You have shamed us", he replied, "It is better that you be ashamed of the house of Amram in this world, than that you be ashamed of it in the world to come" (Kid. 81a). For the phenomenon of talmudic stories concerning saintly figures who live on the periphery of established rabbinic circles, see Kalmin (2004).

BIBLIOGRAPHY: Hyman, Toledot, s.v. R. Kalmin, in: *Continuity and Change* (Hebrew), ed. L.I. Levine (2004) 210–232.

[Zvi Kaplan]

AMRAM OF MAINZ, legendary medieval figure. According to the story R. Amram, who was born in Mainz, taught later in Cologne. He requested his pupils to send his body to Mainz for burial after his death. His corpse arrived in an unmanned boat on the Rhine but was seized by Christians who buried him as a Christian saint in a church named after him. A similar legend was current among Christians about the arrival of the corpse of the martyr St. Emmeram at Regensburg. The Jewish legend which originated at the end of the 16th century identifies Emmeram with Amram.

BIBLIOGRAPHY: M. Gaster (tr.), *Ma'aseh Book: Book of Jewish Tales and Legends*, 2 (1934), 641–3; J.J. Schudt, *Juedische Merckwuerdigkeiten*, 1 (1714, repr. 1922), 441–4; R. Strauss, *Urkunden und Aktenstuecke zur Geschichte der Juden in Regensburg* (1960), nos. 111–2, 29–30.

AMRAN, town in Yemen, about ten hours' walk northwest of San'a, with a large Jewish community in a separate walled quarter. Jacob Sappir visited it in 1859 and brought out a first account (*Massa Teiman*, 174–80). There were about 100 Jewish families in Amran at the time, led by the rabbi and president Slayman al-Tanimi, who had reversed the previously gloomy spiritual situation. There were two synagogues and the majority of Jews made good livings as tailors, farmers, blacksmiths, and silversmiths. Many of them had fled from San'a because of its unstable political situation. The Muslims of Amran were considered anti-Jewish. In 1900 most of the houses in the Jewish quarter were very severely damaged in a big flood (*sayl*) and about 40 Jews were killed (Koraḥ, p. 62). Abraham *Arusi wrote a special poem to commemorate this event (Gamlieli, 1978, 435–38). B. Stevenson, who studied Amran in 1978–79, collected important data about the Jews there. According to local tradition the Jews came to Amran about 300 years earlier from nearby villages seeking the protection of the sheikh. They were allowed to settle in Amran in return for scattering the ashes from the public baths on his fields. A few Jews were rich landholders, and many rented stalls or owned shops in the market. As opposed to other places they were not remembered as skilled artisans or craftsmen. When they left for Israel (1948–51) there were 500–600 people living in 121 houses. The houses and the farmland of the Jews (100 acres) and the synagogues were sold for very low prices. Most of these were changed architecturally, so there is very little evidence in the town of Jewish existence there.

BIBLIOGRAPHY: J. Sappir, *Massa Teiman* (ed. A. Ya'ari; 1945); S.D. Goitein, *From the Land of Sheba* (1947), 15–33; A. Koraḥ, *Sa'arat Teiman*, (1953); N.B. Gamlieli, *Ḥadrei Teiman*, (1978); T.B. Stevenson, *Social Change in a Highlands Town* (1985).

[Yosef Tobi (2nd ed.)]

AMRAPHEL (Heb. אַמְרָפֶל), king of Shinar. Amraphel is one of the monarchs who according to Genesis 14:1–9 accompanied King *Chedorlaomer of Elam on his campaign against the rebellious cities of the Sodom region. The identification of Amraphel is uncertain. The old view that Amraphel is the Hebrew reflex of *Hammurapi king of Babylon is philologically impossible. (A fanciful talmudic derivation of the name as composed of *amar*, "decreed," and *pol*, "leap," identified Amraphel with Nimrod, who in Jewish legend ordered Abraham to leap into the fire. See Er. 53a.) At the same time, biblical Shinar designates or includes the country around Babylon in the context of Genesis 11:2 and Zechariah 5:11. The biblical identification of Shinar with Babylon is corroborated by the 15th century B.C.E. cuneiform place name Shanharu, which may itself go back to the name of a Kassite tribe during the period that the Kassites ruled Babylonia. Nothing further is recorded in the Bible about Amraphel, and the invasion of Canaan in which he participated has not so far been attested in extra-biblical sources. Some scholars have, nonetheless, argued that Genesis 14 has the features of a genuine chronographic account.

BIBLIOGRAPHY: N.M. Sarna, *Understanding Genesis* (1966), 110–9 (includes bibliography). **ADD. BIBLIOGRAPHY:** C. Cohen, in: K.L. Younger et al. (eds.), *The Biblical Canon in Comparative Perspective* (1991), 67–107; R. Zadok, in: ZA, 74 (1984), 240–44.

[Nahum M. Sarna]

AMSHEWITZ, JOHN HENRY (1882–1942), British artist. He was born in Ramsgate and studied in London. He was best known for his historical murals. He painted four frescoes for the Liverpool town hall and in 1910 was commissioned to paint a historical panel for the Royal Exchange, London. His interest in acting took him to South Africa in 1916, where he remained until 1922 as cartoonist for the *Rand Daily Mail* and *Sunday Times*. He was a vital influence in South African art and his later murals were mainly done as South African commissions (e.g., South Africa House, London, in 1934; Witwatersrand University in 1936; and Pretoria City Hall in 1938). He painted many portraits and illustrated an edition of the *Haggadah* and works by *Zangwill.

BIBLIOGRAPHY: S.B. Amshewitz, *The Paintings of J.H. Amshewitz* (1951).

AMSTERDAM, constitutional capital of the *Netherlands.

Ashkenazim until 1795

DEMOGRAPHY AND ECONOMY. *The beginning.* The first Ashkenazim arrived in Amsterdam from the end of the 1610s onwards. They left the German countries owing to the Thirty Years War, which devastated the economy and resulted in anti-Jewish measures. At first they depended socially and economically on the Sephardi community, but were in the same position as to legal status.

The first Ashkenazi synagogue services were organized for Rosh Ha-Shana and Yom Kippur 1635. Until then the growing group of Ashkenazim had visited the Sephardi synagogue. From 1636 they hired a room to serve as a synagogue, which resulted in the establishment of an independent Ashkenazi *kehillah* in 1639. Its first rabbi was Moses ben Jacob Weile of

Prague. The community acquired its own cemetery in Muiderberg in 1642.

While the first Ashkenazim were of German descent, a second group of Ashkenazi immigrants settled in Amsterdam in the wake of the *Chmielnicki pogroms of 1648–49 in Poland and the Russian invasion in Lithuania in 1655–56. These Polish Jews brought with them their own *minhagim* and soon established their own *minyan*. Although the existing Ashkenazi community was opposed to it, they formed their own *kehillah* with a rabbi and cemetery in 1660. The Polish community maintained ties with the *Council of the Four Lands. In 1670 the Polish *kehillah* numbered 70 members versus the 238 of the so-called High German *kehillah*. Only by pressure of the local authorities were the two communities unified in 1673. From then on, only the chief rabbi was allowed to have a *minyan*; Chief Rabbi Saul *Loewenstamm followed the Polish rite. After his death in 1790 this Polish *minyan* was allowed to be held in a room under the Uilenburgerstraatshul. From the beginning of the 18th century the Ashkenazi community called itself Talmud Torah.

Demography. The Jewish population clustered in the eastern quarters of the city. While the Ashkenazim kept growing in numbers, the Sephardim had stabilized. The great migration from Eastern Europe started after 1726. In 1674 there were 5,000 Ashkenazim. This number quadrupled in the next century. In 1795 Amsterdam counted 22,000 Ashkenazi inhabitants.

Ashkenazi Jews from Amsterdam, in their turn, founded communities in England and the New World. The communities in Surinam, Curaçao, and London were considered daughters of the Amsterdam one. The London Great Synagogue was therefore called the "Dutch Jews' Synagogue."

Economy. Ashkenazi Jews were active in those parts of economic life that were not organized via the guilds. On the whole, the Amsterdam government was not very strict in the enforcement of protective laws, which enabled Jews to work on the edge of privileged jobs. They worked in the markets, were peddlers, opened small shops and were active in the money business, the diamond industry, the silk industry, the tobacco industry and in sugar refining. The majority of the Ashkenazi Jews were very poor. In 1795 87% of them lived on poor relief, while the city average was only 37%. There was a small elite consisting of wealthy businessmen such as Ruben Gompertssohn, Abraham Auerbach, and Benjamin *Cohen. Much of their business was with Germany and Poland, where they could exploit their Ashkenazi network. In London, too, branches of Amsterdam Ashkenazi firms were established by the firms of Cohen, Goldsmid (Goldsmith), Preger (Salomons), Diamantschleifer, and Van Oven. The economic crises of 1763 and 1772–73, which affected Dutch economy as a whole, also damaged the Amsterdam Ashkenazi community.

ORGANIZATION. *Parnassim.* The economic elite supplied the *kehillah* with community leaders. The most wealthy members were elected to be *parnassim*. This oligarchy ruled the community with a firm hand. They were in close contact with both the local authorities and the Sephardi *mahamad*. Within the city the Ashkenazim enjoyed the status of a semi-autonomous "High-German Jewish Nation." This meant that the community could handle all internal affairs, including justice. The *parnassim* took care of relief for the poor, taxed the members and represented the *kehillah* outside the Jewish community. They could even put someone in jail or exile him from Amsterdam, and they were allowed to have a small police force.

Religious establishment. Just as in the Sephardi community (after which the organization was modeled), the rabbis were subordinated to the *parnassim*, which was a source of regular tensions. The religious establishment was headed by the chief rabbi, who presided over the local *bet din*. Until 1749 two *dayyanim* supported him in this task; from that year on, the members of the Beth ha-Midrash Ets Haim (erected 1740) supplied the two other members. The community had two *ḥazzanim* and two upper-wardens in its service. A whole range of *melammedim*, school teachers, educated the Ashkenazi youth. There were several schools, such as Lomde Torah for boys up to 13, the school of the orphanage Megadle Jethomim (since 1738) and *talmud torah* for the youngest children. Many *ḥevrot* (membership associations) organized lessons for adults. At least once a week the *ḥevrah* rabbi gave a lesson.

Synagogues. The Great Synagogue was erected by Elias Bouman in 1671. It had place for 399 men on the ground floor and 368 women on the balconies. In 1730 it was joined by the Neie Shul, which was built next to the Great Synagogue. The latter was replaced by a much larger synagogue in 1750–52, in which 596 men and 376 women could follow the service. The complex of synagogues in the heart of the Jewish quarter was completed by two smaller ones, the Obbene Shul (1685) and the Dritt Shul (1700, completely rebuilt 1778). These two synagogues were attended by people from the lower social classes, while the more prominent and wealthy members attended both the Great Synagogue and the Neie Shul. From 1766, the Jewish inhabitants of the Uilenburg-quarter could visit their own synagogue, the so-called Uilenburgerstraatshul.

Rabbis. Most chief rabbis were from Poland. Some of them were important Talmudic scholars and prominent *dayyanim*, such as David ben Aryeh Leib *Lida (1679–1684). The most famous personality, Zevi Hirsch ben Jacob Ashkenazi (who obtained his title Ḥakham Ẓevi in Amsterdam), served the community from 1710 until 1714. He left the *kehillah* after a conflict with the *parnassim*, being succeeded by Abraham Berliner from Halberstadt (1714–1730). After a period in which the community was split into factions over the choice of a new chief rabbi, the local authorities decided that Eleazar ben Samuel of Brody should be entrusted with the task (1735–1740). The son-in-law of the Ḥakham Ẓevi, Aryeh Leib ben Saul *Loewenstamm from Rzeszów, thereupon became Amsterdam's chief rabbi (until 1755). He became the founder of the Dutch rabbinical Loewenstamm dynasty: his son Saul ben Aryeh Leib Polonus succeeded him and served until 1793, when his grandson Moses Saul Loewenstamm took over (until 1815).

Politics. The economic position of the Jews in the city was endangered by the 1748 Doelist Revolt. The Doelists advocated the expansion and enforcement of the protective laws and wished to secure the position of the guilds. Had the local government adopted the Doelist position, the Jews would have suffered grave economic losses. Thanks to the stadholder William IV, however, order was restored in the city and the Doelist coup aborted. In the second half of the 18th century the Amsterdam Jews gradually politicized. Although they did not participate in local government, they became more and more involved in the political battle between the enlightened Patriot faction and the Orangist faction. The *parnassim* tried to secure the neutrality of the community, but the great majority of the members supported the Orangists. In the 1787 Patriot Revolution, which also caused regime change in Amsterdam, Ashkenazi Jews battled on the streets with Patriotic mobs. When stadholder William IV was reinstalled with the help of his brother-in-law, the king of Prussia, Amsterdam Jewry celebrated this victory extensively.

CULTURE AND INTELLECTUAL LIFE. *Language.* The vernacular of the Amsterdam Ashkenazim was West-Yiddish, which was brought in by the first settlers from Germany. The influx of Polish immigrants did not change the predominance of the West-Yiddish dialect. From the end of the 17th century this language was spiced up with a growing number of hollandisms. Hebrew was taught at the Jewish schools and by private teachers. Only at the end of the 18th century did a small part of the community, its elite, use Dutch as its vernacular. But in the lower social classes too, the language contacts between Dutch and Yiddish were extensive.

Printing. During the 18th century Amsterdam was widely know in the Ashkenazi world as the capital of Hebrew and Yiddish printing. Amsterdam was renowned for its quality of printing and the typesetting of Hebrew letters, known as *otiyyot Amsterdam*. Besides Christian and Sephardi printers, some of whom also printed Yiddish books, Ashkenazim too were very active in this field.

*Uri Phoebus started his printing firm in 1658, moving to Zolkiev in 1692. R. Moses ben Simon *Frankfurt (1678–1768), besides a printer also *dayyan*, published many classical Hebrew works and Yiddish translations. He believed the classics of Hebrew literature should also be accessible to the Yiddish reading public. The most prominent Ashkenazi printer was Samuel Proops (1702–1734), who printed many *siddurim*, *maḥzorim*, and halakhic works as well as *musar* literature for the entire Ashkenazi world. In 1730 he published *Appiryon Shlomo*, the first sales catalogue of Hebrew books. The firm was continued by his family until 1849.

Yiddish literature. Of especial importance were the two Yiddish Bible translations. Jekuthiel ben Isaac Blitz's translation was published in 1676–79, while the rival work by Joseph Witzenhausen was printed in 1678. Numerous translations of Hebrew books into Yiddish were printed, including *Sefer *Josippon*, *Manasseh ben Israel's *Mikveh Israel*, the travelogue of *Benjamin of Tudela and *Menorat ha-Ma'or* of *Aboab. But original works in Yiddish were printed, too. One of the bestsellers became the universal Jewish history book *She'erit Yisro'el* by Menahem Mann ben Shlomo *Amelander. Contemporary history was presented in a number of chronicles. In the years 1686–87 (and possibly over a longer period), the Amsterdam Ashkenazim could read the news in the oldest known Yiddish newspaper, the *Dinstagishe un Freitaghishe Kurantn.*

Intellectual life. Besides the traditional patterns of religious learning, a number of Amsterdam Jews developed new intellectual activities, often parallel to contemporary Christian developments. In the 18th century some studied at the universities of Leiden and Harderwijk. Hartog Alexander van Embden (Herz Levi Rofe) obtained the rank of doctor in medicine at Harderwijk University in 1716. Active as a physician, Hebrew printer and keeper of a bookshop, he was part of a small group of Jewish intellectuals, interested in science and scholarly debates. In 1775 David ben Phoebus Wagenaar translated *Mendelssohn's *Phaedon* into Hebrew, which remained unpublished. Salomon *Dubno, the grammarian, teacher, and friend of Mendelssohn, spent the last years of his life in Amsterdam and had profound influence on a circle of young Ashkenazim. Eleasar Soesman was active as a publicist for both Jewish and Christian audiences and therefore wrote both in Hebrew and Dutch. He was in contact with various Christian scholars, especially theologians and Hebraists, for whom he wrote his Hebrew grammar *Mohar Yisrael* (1742).

Like the Sephardim, the Amsterdam Ashkenazim were great lovers of the theater. Yiddish theater not only blossomed during Purim, when all kinds of *Purimshpiln* were produced and performed, but also on a more regular basis. From 1784 onwards, Jacob H. Dessauer led a Jewish opera- and theater-group, which also included women. This group was very active and performed many contemporary plays for a Jewish audience.

[Bart Wallet (2nd ed.)]

Sephardim until 1795

After the northern provinces of the Netherlands proclaimed their independence of Catholic Spain (Union of Utrecht, 1571), *Marranos of Spanish and Portuguese origin became attracted to Amsterdam where little inquiry was made as to their religious beliefs. Portuguese Jewish merchants began to settle in Amsterdam, in about 1590, but did not openly reveal themselves as Jews. In 1602 a group of Sephardi Jews arrived with Moses Uri ha-Levi of Emden, and apparently held religious services in a private home. Prominent in the community were Samuel Palache, the ambassador of Morocco to the Netherlands, and his family, who lived in Amsterdam as professing Jews, and did much to assist Jews to settle in the country. Subsequently, increasing numbers of Marranos from Spain and especially Portugal took refuge in Amsterdam, which was now becoming one of the most important international commercial centers. The legal status of these Jews long remained unclarified. While the Reform Church opposed Jewish settlement in Amsterdam, the civic authorities favored it. In consequence, the newcomers, though not formally recognized as citizens, enjoyed religious freedom and protection of life and property, especially in relation to foreign powers. Until the Jews officially attained civic *emancipation, they were debarred from practicing all trades organized in guilds, but the municipality rejected any attempt to ban Jews from other professions.

From 1607 religious services had been held at the home of Jacob *Tirado, who organized a congregation under the name Beth Jaäcob (Casa de Jacob) with 15 fellow-Jews. In 1614 they erected a synagogue with the permission of the authorities. Another congregation, Neveh Shalom, was organized in 1608 by a group of wealthy Marranos with Isaac Uziel (d. 1622) as rabbi. Both congregations cooperated in the establishment of a society for providing dowries to poor brides, in 1615, and a school called Talmud Torah in 1616.

The religious and intellectual life of the community in Amsterdam became marked by tensions between the strict authoritarian orthodoxy of the rabbis and the majority of communal leaders on the one side and the critical libertarian, individualist views of influential intellectuals on the other. This conflict was all the more acute as it was the consequence of the underground existence which the Marranos had formerly led, and their sudden freedom in an open society. A split developed in the Beth Jaäcob congregation, apparently because of a bitter religious controversy. The more orthodox wing, under the leadership of the *ḥakham* Joseph *Pardo, seceded in 1619 to found the Beth Jisrael congregation, while a freethinking physician Abraham Farrar, led the Beth Jaäcob congregation. The Beth Jaäcob synagogue was awarded by the municipality all the property of the congregation and three-fifths of its capital. However, the three congregations continued to cooperate in the central institutions. In 1639 they reunited under the name KK (Kahal Kadosh) Talmud Torah and services were henceforward conducted in one place of worship. The magnificent synagogue dedicated in 1675 became the model for Sephardi synagogues in many other places.

The intellectual life of the community, in both its religious and secular aspects, attained a high level. As a center of Jewish learning throughout the Marrano Diaspora, Amsterdam Jewry wielded a powerful influence and became a focus of intellectual ferment. The Talmud Torah school was celebrated for the breadth of its syllabus and excellence of its teaching, covering not only talmudic subjects, but also Hebrew grammar and poetry, and in the upper classes Hebrew only was spoken. It flourished during the 17th century under the leadership of Saul Levi *Morteira, and subsequently under the *ḥakham* Isaac Aboab de *Fonseca. Its pupils officiated as rabbis in numerous Sephardi communities in Western Europe and the Mediterranean countries, and it produced Hebrew writers and poets. Most of the religious literature in Spanish and Portuguese intended for the guidance of the Sephardi communities was composed and printed in Amsterdam. The first Jewish printer there was *Manasseh ben Israel, who began printing in 1627 and produced more than 70 books. Other Sephardi printers included Joseph *Athias and David de *Castro Tartas. Their publications were sold locally and throughout the Spanish-speaking Jewish Diaspora, and even in Eastern Europe and Asia, The community included such diverse personalities as the rabbis Manasseh ben Israel, Jacob *Sasportas, the physicians Abraham Zacutus *Lusitanus and Ephraim *Bueno, the kabbalist Abraham Cohen *Herrera, the playwright Antonio *Enriquez Gomez, the physician and thinker Isaac *Orobio de Castro, the poet Daniel Levi de *Barrios, and the rebel-philosophers Uriel da *Costa and Baruch *Spinoza, instancing all the manifold trends in the intellectual life of the Amsterdam community. Jewish attachment to messianic hopes and yearning for a change from exile existence were powerfully demonstrated in the ferment aroused by *Shabbetai Ẓevi in the middle of the 17th century. The majority of the community in Amsterdam became ardent followers of the pseudo-messiah and only a minority vigorously opposed him. The leadership of the community remained for a long period in the hands of former Shabbateans, including the rabbis Isaac Aboab de Fonseca, Moses Raphael *Aguilar, and Benjamin *Mussaphia. Even in the early 18th century when Solomon *Ayllon was the Portuguese *ḥakham* a controversy arose over the Shabbatean work of Nehemiah Ḥayon. The chief rabbi of the Ashkenazi community, Ḥakham Ẓevi *Ashkenazi, who joined in the dispute, was excommunicated by the Portuguese congregation in 1713.

The role of the Jewish Portuguese merchants in the economic life of Amsterdam remained modest until the end of the war against Spain in 1648. Subsequently many other ex-Marranos settled in Amsterdam, and became extremely prosperous. Jewish merchants in Amsterdam were one of the first groups to engage in recognizably modern capitalist-type activities. Their foreign interests included trade with the Iberian peninsula, England, Italy, Africa, India, and the East and West Indies. Jews in Amsterdam also engaged in industry, especially in the tobacco, printing, and diamond industries; the last eventually passed almost entirely into Jewish hands. By the end of the 17th century many Portuguese Jews in Amsterdam were active in the stock market, owning a quarter of the shares of the East India Company. They thus became prominent on the stock exchange and helped to organize and develop it. *Confusion de Confusiones* by Joseph *Penso de la Vega (Amsterdam, 1688) is the first work written on the subject. The claim of certain writers that the wealth of Amsterdam was mainly due to Jewish economic activity is, however, an exaggeration. The economic position of the Sephardi Jews was jeopardized during economic crises in the republic, especially critical in 1763. The community *parnas*, Isaac *Pinto, the banker-philosopher, arranged for tax relief on food and fuel for the poor members of the community and for their emigration overseas, but it soon became evident that the community could not carry the burden. After the French conquest of the Netherlands in 1794, the Sephardi community became even poorer: two-thirds of the 3,000 members depended on relief. In 1799, 36.7% of the general population in Amsterdam and 54% of the Sephardi community were living on relief. Few of the wealthier families managed to retain their property.

[Jozeph Michman]

Emancipation, Stabilization and Integration, 1795–1870

EMANCIPATION IN THE BATAVIAN-FRENCH PERIOD. *Politics.* In 1795 the Dutch Republic was replaced by the Batavian Republic, a satellite state of the revolutionary French Republic established by joint forces of Dutch Patriots and French invaders. This regime change had massive impact on the country, because the Orangist elite was replaced by new Patriotic authorities and new laws created gradually a different type of state. From a federal republic it became a central state. Also in Amsterdam the local government was reformed, however, initially without a change of attitude towards the Jewish community. The regime change led to fights on the streets between radical Patriots and Jewish Orangists. Continuation of these fights was prevented by the establishment of waiters of the Jewish quarter at the end of August 1795. The local authorities entrusted the *parnassim* the control of the quarter in order to maintain order.

A small group of Jewish intellectuals influenced by the ideas of the Enlightenment and Dutch Patriotism founded a club, *Felix Libertate. Although also open for non-Jews, two-third of its members were Jewish. The club wanted to gain citizenship for Jews in the Batavian Republic and the introduction of democracy within the Jewish community. On September 2, 1796, Felix Liberate was successful in its first task: the national government decreed the emancipation of the Jews. This meant equal rights for Jews in politics and before court. One of the first fruits of the emancipation decree was the right of the Amsterdam Jews to vote. Also Jews were appointed to public offices, such as Moses Salomon Asser who became a member of the judicial committee of the city in 1798.

Split in the community. An internal change within the Ashkenazi *kehillah* appeared to be much more difficult. After the emancipation decree was issued, Felix Libertate asked for new regulations. The members of the club wanted instead of the oligarchic *parnassim* a new, democratic elected board of directors, which could reorganize the *kehillah* and issue social improvements. The *parnassim* rejected their proposals, because it would reduce their power and influence. They were backed by the local authorities, for whom the *parnassim* were one of the pillars to keep order and silence in the city. As a result, the enlightened members decided to secede from the *kehillah*, using the new religious freedom laws to found a new community. On April 8, 1797, the Neie Kille, as the new community was called in Amsterdam Yiddish, had its first synagogue service. Its official name became Adat Jesurun. Appointed as its rabbi was Isaac Ger Graanboom (1738–1807), one of the *dayyanim* of the *kehillah*. It acquired a cemetery as well, in Overveen. The Neie Kille introduced small changes in liturgy, such as the use of Dutch for making announcements. Only a tiny minority of the Amsterdam Ashkenazim joined the Neie Kille: in 1799 there were 108 paying members and a total of 700 individuals involved in it. From 1799 the Neie Kille had its own synagogue at the Rapenburgerstraat.

Although the vast majority, consisting of circa 20,000 people, remained faithful to the Alte Kille, the *parnassim* considered the new community as a serious threat to their power. Both sides were heavily engaged in a propaganda war, which was fought over in a series of competing pamphlets: the Yiddish *Diskursn* (July 1797–March 1798). Things radically changed when on both the national and local level a coup brought into power a radical enlightened regime. In the few months in 1798 during which the radicals ruled the city, the balance of power within the Ashkenazi community also changed. The *parnassim* were fired and replaced by enlightened "provisional directors." This new board wanted re-unification with the Neie Kille and an accommodation of the whole community to the innovations of the enlightened group. But after a new coup brought into power a more moderate group, the *parnassim* were re-installed and the troubled relationship between the two Ashkenazi *kehillot* was continued.

Only pressure from King Louis Napoleon, who ruled over the Kingdom of Holland from 1806 until 1810, could bring together both communities in 1808. The terms for the re-unification were the abrogation of all innovations of the Neie Kille, but a relatively large representation of the enlightened faction within the influential strata of the *kehillah*. Thanks to the existence of the Neie Kille for a couple of years, the enlightened Jews could acquire a grip on the policy of the entire *kehillah* following the re-unification.

The Sephardi community. The Sephardi community remained relatively detached from the frictions between conservative and enlightened Jews. Some of the Sephardim were active in Felix Libertate but were already part of the establishment of the Portuguese *kehillah*. They could work from within the community for changes. One of them, Dr. Immanuel Capadoce, served as well as the private doctor of King Louis Napoleon. The *parnassim* of both the Sephardi and Ashkenazi community continued mutual consultations regarding the position of the Jews in the city. In 1810 they agreed on a concordat dealing with mixed marriages and its consequences for membership rules.

New situation. After the annexation of the Kingdom of Holland to the French Empire, the discontent with the political situation grew in Dutch society. Also the vast majority of Amsterdam Jewry, traditionally an Orangist stronghold, opposed the French rulers. This became all the more clear when the compulsory recruiting of Jewish boys into Napoleon's army resulted in riots in the Jewish quarter. This could not hinder a number of young Amsterdam Jews from serving in the army.

After the defeat of Napoleon the son of the last stadholder returned to Holland, becoming as William I the first king of the Kingdom of the Netherlands. The Amsterdam Jews widely celebrated his return. In the Ashkenazi community a number of French regulations regarding the liturgy were immediately abrogated, resulting in the reintroduction of Yiddish to the synagogue. The new political situation did not, however, result in a return to the pre-Batavian period, which meant that the political emancipation remained in force.

DEMOGRAPHY AND ECONOMY. *Demography.* The period 1795–18. 0 was both from a demographic and economic point of view a period of stagnation. The migration to Amsterdam from Central and Eastern Europe declined greatly in the 18th century. America was the new favorite migration destination for many Jews. Because of the poverty in Amsterdam Jews even left the city, but many of them stayed within the Netherlands. Because of the emancipation decree they could settle in small provincial towns and villages. In 1795 3,000 Sephardim and 22,000 Ashkenazim lived in the city. This number diminished to 2,534 Sephardim and 18,910 Ashkenazim in 1809. In particular, Sephardi community shrank in this period. The total number of Amsterdam Jews grew from 25,156 in 1849 to 29,952 in 1869. Throughout the period Jews made up 10% of the city's total population.

Economy. Most of the Amsterdam Jews were poor. The economic crises of the late 18th century and the introduction of the Continental System in 1805 by the French, which forbade all economic contacts with England and cut Holland off from its colonies, affected the economy of Amsterdam, and its Jews as well. In 1820 no less than 78% of the city's Ashkenazim depended on welfare for the poor. This percent diminished gradually to 55% in 1849. Also within the Sephardi community poverty rose to high numbers: in 1849 63% received aid to the poor. The number for the total population was much better: less than 20%. Most Jews lived in the Jewish quarters, only 3.5% wealthy Jews lived in other quarters.

A consequence of the abrogation of the guilds in 1809 was that all jobs were open for Jews. But in fact, many Jews stayed within the old patterns and only a small group benefited from the new situation. In the second half of the 19th century the economic situation improved. The Jews profited from the improved education and the economic recovery of the city after 1860. Jewish peddlers and keepers of small shops founded the first warehouses. Also intellectual positions, such as journalist, lawyer, and doctor, together with governmental jobs provided a growing number of Jews their daily bread.

ORGANIZATION. *Sephardi community.* The social. nfrastructure of the Amsterdam Sephardim remained largely intact in the period 1795–1870. Community life was concentrated around the Esnoga. The economic crises at the end of the 18th century and during the Batavian-French period had seriously affected the Sephardim, resulting in a growing number of poor members. The social differences within the community widened. Relatively easily the more well-to-do Sephardim integrated into Amsterdam society, using the opportunities created by the emancipation. Within the community Sephardi identity was nourished, especially to stress the difference from the Ashkenazi community, with which they forced into a joint national organization.

Ashkenazi community. The Ashkenazi *kehillah* was led by a small elite, consisting of rich businessmen and the newly emerging intellectual elite. Many of these intellectuals had their roots in the former Neie Kille. The largest part of the community, however, consisted of poor people. They did not have the money to rent a seat in one of the official synagogues. Therefore a number of *chevreshuls* provided in their religious needs. Although from 1827 personal *minyanim* were forbidden, in 1850 no less than seven *chevreshuls* were accepted within the community. The gap between the elite, striving for integration in Dutch society, and the vast majority of the community, attached to the Jewish quarter, grew immensely.

In contrary to many German Jewish communities, Reform did not take hold in Jewish Amsterdam. A small group, united in Shokharee De'a, strove in the 1850s for the introduction of Reform-like changes in synagogue liturgy. When on their invitation a German Reform rabbi, Dr. Isaac Loeb Chronik, came to Amsterdam, riots broke out in the Jewish quarter. Chronik subsequently left for Chicago. Only in 1861 did Shokharee De'a achieve a little success: the introduction of a choir in the Great Synagogue. This inspired two Jewish musicians, Aharon Wolf Berlijn (1817–1870) and Isaac Heymann (called the Gnesener Chazzen, 1827–1906), to compose new melodies for the synagogue liturgy. Also the atmosphere in synagogue changed, with the introduction of measures to encourage decorum. In 1867 an experiment began for having sermons in Dutch in the synagogue once every two weeks, which led to the decision to replace Yiddish completely by Dutch in 1872.

Religious leaders. Rabbis and schoolteachers for the Ashkenazi community were trained at the reorganized Dutch Israelite Seminary (from 1836), while the Portuguese Israelite Seminary Ets Haim continued to deliver well-trained rabbis and teachers for Amsterdam and the Sephardi diaspora. Until 1822 Daniel Cohen d'Azevedo served as the Sephardi chief rabbi, but after his death no successor was appointed until 1900. After the death of Chief Rabbi S.B. Berenstein in 1838, a period without a chief rabbi began for Ashkenazi Amsterdam as well. No suitable candidate was found in the Netherlands, while the leaders were hesitant to have a chief rabbi from the German countries. They did not want to import along with the chief rabbi a division between Reform and Orthodoxy. Finally, Dr. Joseph Hirsch *Duenner (1833–1911) became the new chief rabbi in 1874, besides being rector of the Seminary following his appointment in 1862.

Social Work. Due to the poverty of the majority of Jewish Amsterdam, special importance was given to social work. In

1825 the Dutch Israelite Poor Relief (Nederlandsch Israelitisch Armbestuur) was founded and given the responsibility for the Ashkenazi poor, which had previously been a task of the *parnassim*. The organization was funded both by the government and the Jewish community. In the 1830s half of Amsterdam's Jewry depended on its welfare. It operated a hospital for the poor, which had existed since 1804. In 1845 a separate Doll House was founded. The Sephardim had their own hospital from 1820. There were as well houses for the elderly. The Sephardim had their Old Men's House, Mishenet Zeqenim, from 1750 and an Old Women's House, Mesib Nefes, from 1833 on the Rapenburg. The Ashkenazi Old Women's House, Rechoboth, was located at the Nieuwe Keizersgracht.

Education. The Jewish schools were generally known for their low quality. The schools that were active as early as the 18th century continued their existence in the first half of the 19th century, until the School Law of 1857 turned the Jewish schools into state schools. This was part of a policy of national integration and improvement of education. Religious instruction was since then given after school and on Sundays. Only the Sephardi schools managed to survive a bit longer, until 1870.

But even before the new law, many Jewish children attended private schools or were given education by private teachers; some also attended Christian schools. In 1797 no less than 320 Jewish children were enrolled in church schools. That was nearly one-third of the total of 1,000 Jewish children receiving education. After 1870, many Jewish children did not go to religious schools anymore, because of finances or out of lack of interest. This resulted in loosening ties with Hebrew and the Jewish tradition.

INTEGRATION AND POSITION IN THE CITY. *Jewish politicians.* After the emancipation decree Jews were able to take part in local politics. Jewish participation in the city council was nearly continuous. Until the constitutional changes of 1848 it was primarily Sephardim who were chosen as representatives of the city's Jewish communities: Abraham Mendes de Leon, Immanuel Capadoce, Jacob Mendes de Leon, and Samuel Teixeira de Mattos. After 1848 Ashkenazim, too, obtained seats, such as Ahasveros S. van *Nierop, who represented the liberal faction.

Jewish philanthropists. Two men acquired a special position within the city. Samuel Sarphati (1813–1866), a Sephardi doctor, initiated and developed many institutions for better education, poor relief and the promotion of labor and industry. He was a thriving force behind the modernization of Amsterdam and built the Amstel Hotel and the Palace for People's Industry. He was faithful to the Jewish tradition and also served the Sephardi community in a number of functions. His idealism inspired others to work for the general good. After his death a park and a street were named after him. His friend and, to some degree, successor was Abraham Carel Wertheim (1832–1897). The Ashkenazi Wertheim, a banker, was a philanthropist and politician as well. He was especially interested in culture and sponsored the local theater. Although he was a freemason and did not observe Shabbat and *kashrut*, he was a leading figure in Jewish Amsterdam and served as a *parnas* of the Ashkenazi *kehillah* for many years.

Jewish elite. The politicians and philanthropists were part of the elite of Amsterdam's Jewry, which consisted of old business dynasties, such as the De Jongh (Rintel) family. Also bankers were well represented within this circle. The families Bisschofsheim, Koenigswaerter, Raphael, Hollander and Lehren had branches of their firms all over Europe. Some of them left the Netherlands before 1850, but others took their places (Rosenthal, Wertheim, Lippmann). Also lawyers obtained a position within the elite. J.D. *Meyer, the members of the *Asser family, and M.H. *Godefroi all enjoyed prestigious positions within both general society and the Jewish community. A large part of the elite integrated in Dutch society and became detached from the majority of the Jewish community, but they did not completely assimilate because they developed a specific Dutch-Jewish patrician culture. Marriage partners were found among themselves and in Germany. Only a tiny minority converted to Christianity, as did Isaac da *Costa, Abraham Capadoce, and S.Ph. Lipman. Some families remained strictly Orthodox, such as the *Lehren family. The brothers Zevi Hirsch (1784–1853), Meyer (1793–1861), and Akiba (1795–1876) Lehren had an extensive network all over the Jewish world. They led the Pekidim and Amarkalim organization, which helped and controlled the *yishuv*. They alos supported the struggle of German Orthodoxy against the Reform movement.

CULTURE AND INTELLECTUAL LIFE. *Language.* The process of using the vernacular, which started already in the 18th century among the elite, spread in the 19th century over the whole community. The knowledge of the Iberian languages dropped dramatically within the Sephardi community. Although the language was maintained in same parts of the synagogue liturgy, Dutch entered relatively easily in the Sephardi domain. In the early 1850s Dutch replaced Portuguese as the language of the sermon, because most people left the synagogue when a Portuguese sermon was preached. The replacement of Yiddish by Dutch was more difficult. The proletariat, including Sephardim, spoke Amsterdam Yiddish. Gradually this language was replaced through a combined effort of the government and the Jewish elite. The closing of the Jewish schools was a major step, because since then Jewish children were educated only in Dutch.

Intellectual life. In the first half of the 19th century a circle of Jewish intellectuals advocated the Hebrew language. In 1808 the society Chanog lanangar ngal pi darko was founded in order to promote Hebrew. Mozes Lemans, Hirsch Zwi Sommerhausen and Mozes Cohen *Belinfante played an important role in this society. They published several textbooks and prepared a translation of Tenakh into Dutch. A new society was founded with a common objective in 1816, Tongelet. The members devoted themselves to writing poetry in Hebrew.

They published two volumes with their work. Circa 50 members were involved. Samuel Israel *Mulder, Gabriel *Polak and Abraham Delaville (1807–1877) were its most prominent members. Within the Dutch Jewish community they served in several functions; they had as well an extensive network in the European Jewish intellectual world. A third society, Reshit Chochma, was founded in 1813. Within this body traditional Jewish study was the objective, but Mendelssohn's *Be'ur* was included in the curriculum as well. Until the middle of the 19th century the yearly meetings were conducted in Hebrew.

[Bart Wallet (2nd ed.)]

1870–1940: Rapid Growth and the Creation of an Amsterdam Dutch-Jewish Sub-Culture

1870 has been widely accepted in Dutch and Dutch-Jewish historiography as the beginning of a new period (see *Netherlands). The general economic. Social and political developments which caused the change, affected Amsterdam, as the capital and as a major harbor, especially, and Jewish society in this city was deeply affected too.

DEMOGRAPHY AND PROFESSIONAL OCCUPATIONS. This period was first of all characterized by rapid demographical growth of the Jewish community in Amsterdam – from 30,039 (almost 11% of a total population of 281,502) in 1869, through 59,117 (11+% out of 531,733) in 1899 and 65,558 (8.5% out of 768,409) in 1930, to 79,497 "full Jews" according to the German racial census, plus almost 7,000 "half-" and "quarter"-Jews) (about 10% out of 803,073) in 1941. Amsterdam Jewry's importance within Dutch Jewry grew even more: from 44% in 1869, to about 60% in 1920, and almost 57% in 1941. The growth resulted from several sources: high birth rates (between 1869 and1889; but between 1905 and 1932, a sharp decline occurred, dropping more than 40%, from 164 births per 1,000 to 87.2 births per 1,000) and low mortality rates.

The major reasons for the growth of Amsterdam Jewry were internal migration from the little communities in the countryside to the capital because of economic, cultural, educational and religious motivations; and the immigration from abroad – a limited number of Eastern European Jews at the turn of the 19th to 20th century, a considerable number of Jews from Germany in the 1920s, and many thousands of refugees from Germany after the rise of the Nazi party to power in 1933. Until 1870 most Jews were living in the central and eastern neighborhoods. But when the size of the community grew and an affluent middle class emerged, Jews settled also in Amsterdam-south and later in the neighboring "new-south" neighborhood (in the 1930s many German-Jewish refugees concentrated in this area too). The older neighborhoods remained centers of the Jewish proletariat, which made up for a major part of Amsterdam Jewry. Though during the 1930s less than 10% of the city's Jewish population still lived in the so-called "Jewish quarter," this area continued to have a dominantly Jewish character.

Jews worked in a variety of professions, but concentrated mainly in a limited number of them (about 75%): diamond cutters (2,095; 5.8%, vs. 2% among the general city population in 1941); textile and cleaning (7,229; 20% vs. 7.8%); commerce (11,668; 32.4% vs. 20.9%); free profession (6,523; 18.1% vs. 8.3). On the other hand, Jews were extremely lowly represented in the construction, food, transportation, banking and housekeeping professions.

The Jewish proletariat. Apart from the small class of wealthy Jews, the majority of the community in Amsterdam in the first half of the 19th century were in serious economic straits and still lived in cramped quarters. Their position improved after 1867 with the development of the diamond industry, which became a "Jewish" profession involving many diamond workers and traders as well (called "The profession" among Amsterdam Jews). When in 1876 the industry underwent a serious crisis, the diamond workers established a strong trade union, under the leadership of Henri *Polak, the first such organization in Holland. Socialism gained ground among the Jewish proletariat, the diamond trade union became the corner stone of the Social Democratic Workers Party, and Polak one of its leaders.

JEWISH SOCIAL INSTITUTIONS. The size of the Amsterdam community together with the extent of poverty created the necessity for the establishment of a network of Jewish social services, which transformed a strong Jewish tradition of *ẓedakah* into modern modes. This network included country-wide organizations whose headquarters were in the capital, such as the Dutch-Jewish Organization for the Poor (Nederlandsch-Israëlitisch Armbestuur), and health care institutions such as the Joodsche Invalide and the Nederlandsch Israëlitisch Ziekenhuis (hospital). In the 1920s a (pro-Zionist) Union of Jewish Women was established, which focused on welfare activities. Many organizations dealt especially with youth. Many of those institutions were supported by rich assimilated Jews.

JEWISH POLITICS BETWEEN SOCIALISM AND ZIONISM. As mentioned, as from the 1860s socialism and its varieties found strong inroads in Jewish society, and the Amsterdam socialist organizations were known for their pronounced Jewish color. Through socialism and the Social-Democratic youth movement many lower middle class and lower class Jews became involved in city and countrywide politics. Among the middle class, Jews were already prominent in municipal activities in the beginning of the second half of the 19th century, and contributed to the modernization process of the city; as time proceeded, many became active in the Liberal party and represented it both on the municipal and provincial level. Several Jews in various political parties served for long periods on the municipal council; when in 1933 four of the six city counselors (wethouders) were Jewish, albeit from different parties, served council, antisemitic voices protested "Jewish dominance."

Political Zionism found support in Amsterdam from its inception. Among those who welcomed the movement was

Chief Rabbi Dr. Joseph Hirsch *Duenner; on the occasion of the first Zionist Congress in 1897 he held a sermon titled with the biblical quotation: "For this child we prayed." In the early 20th century the movement found some adherents among students in Amsterdam, but for a long time Zionist support was confined to intellectual and orthodox circles. After World War I, a strong Zionist youth movement was formed. The number of youths in the Zionist movement grew from 350 in 1929 to 800 in 1939. However, other Jewish political parties, as were activive in Eastern Europe, found no ground here.

JEWISH DAILY LIFE AND FOLKLORE. Amsterdam Jewry was the nucleus of Dutch Jewry, and because of its size established a clear sub-culture. As part of the "Hollandization" process, Jews turned to speaking Dutch instead of Yiddish around the beginning of the second half of the 19th century. On the other hand, however, many Yiddish words made their way into local slang (until today). A pronounced expression of the special features of Amsterdam Jewishness was to be found in the Waterlooplein market. The peculiarities of Amsterdam Jewish life at the turn of the 19th century has been depicted in literature, especially by Herman Heijermans in some of his critical stories ("The Diamond City," "The Ghetto").

RELIGIOUS DENOMINATIONS AND SECULARIZATION. The two separate communities of Amsterdam Jewry – the Ashkenazim who were the great majority, and the Sephardim, who were a tiny minority – continued to exist, but cooperation intensified.

The appointment of Dr. Joseph Hirsch *Duenner to the directorship of the rabbinical seminary (Nederlandsch-Israëlitisch Seminarium), and in 1874 as chief rabbi of Amsterdam and the province of North-Holland, inaugurated a marked change. Although strictly preserving the Orthodox character of the community, he raised the academic level of the seminary and educated a group of rabbis who achieved a high standard of scholarship. He also included representatives from all sectors in the leadership of the Ashkenazi community, even the nonobservant such as the banker A.C. *Wertheim. In this way, Duenner prevented religious dissension towards Reform Judaism, which had started some time before his coming. He also built a basis for a nucleus of Modern Orthodoxy (the seminary became its stronghold); however, he could not stop the general process of secularization, caused by the enormous economic and social changes. Consequently, the majority of Amsterdam Jewry became non-observant and hardly visited the synagogues; yet they continued keeping to some basics of Judaism thus creating a clear Jewish sub-group. Mixed marriages between Jews and non-Jews expanded (the number of mixed marriages increased from 6.02% in 1900 to 16.86% in 1930) but still remained quite low until as compared to other western European countries. In the 20th century, with the relocation of affluent Jews to new neighborhoods, some new (Ashkenazi) synagogues were built in them.

Liberal (Reform) Jewry was finally introduced in Amsterdam only in 1932, through an outside initiative by the World Union for Progressive Judaism. It succeeded in rooting in the city as a result of the influx of German Jewish Refugees as from 1933; it thus became a predominantly "German-Jewish" phenomenon. One of the refugees joining this community was Otto Frank, the father of Anne.

EDUCATION AND CULTURE. The Education Act of 1857, enacted in the spirit of separation of church and state, withheld subsidies for religious schools. This brought in its wake the rapid decline of Jewish schools for the poor, and the transition of Jewish children to the general school system. The law foresaw the closure on Sabbath of schools with more than 50% Jews, and in the 1920s this was the case with 20 schools. Only one Ashkenazi school for the poor, *Talmoed Touro*, could be preserved, as well as a high school. Special Jewish education, especially on Sundays, was unable to cope with the consequent decline in Jewish knowledge. Only at the beginning of the 20th century could a change for the better be made, and an organization for Special Jewish Education (Joodsch Bijzonder Onderwijs) was established. After the enactment of the new constitution in 1917, new efforts were undertaken and several new schools were established in the 1920s. But in 1932 still only about 800 children learned at Jewish day schools.

From the end of the 19th century, Amsterdam became a foremost cultural center of the Netherlands. Jewish writers, painters, theatrical artists, and others took an active part in Dutch cultural life. Writers included the above-mentioned Herman Heijermans (1864–1924); Israel *Querido (1872–1932); Jacob Israel de Haan (1881–1924), who went to Ereẓ Israel, changed sides and joined the anti-Zionist ultra-Orthodox community in Jerusalem, and was murdered against this background; and his sister Carry van Bruggen de *Haan (1881–1932). The jurist, Prof. Tobias M.C. *Asser (1838–1913) won the Nobel Prize.

REFUGEES FROM NAZI GERMANY AND THE THREAT OF THE 1930S. The rise of Nazism to power in Germany made a considerable and immediate impact on the Jewish communities in surrounding countries, including the Netherlands. Amsterdam became a major refuge: thousands of Jews (as well as non-Jewish political refugees) settled in the city for shorter or longer periods between 1933 and the German invasion in May 1940. At the moment of invasion more than 7,000 such refugees were staying in the city. Their presence during the pre-war years caused the establishment of a Committee for Jewish Refugees, headed by Prof. David *Cohen, backed by the Jewish community organizations and prominent Jews. Due to its many activities, its considerable budget, and the contacts it developed with the Dutch authorities and international organizations (Jewish and non-Jewish), this committee became the most important and powerful Jewish organization in the 1930s. The Nazi threat and the refugees also strengthened the Zionist movement and the tiny community of Liberal (Reform) Jews. Two local publishers, Querido and Allert de Lange, published *Exilliteratur*. Two cabaret-groups were established by well-known Jewish refugee cabaretiers from

Germany, and others influenced the still young Dutch film industry. On the other hand, for antisemitic groups the Jewish refugee "invasion" became a major issue through which they strengthened their rows; consequently, many local Jews showed an ambivalent attitude towards those Jews.

1939–1945: The Holocaust

Being the capital and hosting a Jewish community of more than 80,000 souls made Amsterdam the main target for anti-Jewish policies; many of the general measures were tried out and took shape first in Amsterdam, and focal institutions of persecution were established in it. Therefore, the impact of persecutions was intensely felt in this city. Only 25% of Amsterdam Jews survived the Holocaust. (For an account of the general picture of the Holocaust in the Netherlands, see *Netherlands.)

FIRST ANTI-JEWISH MEASURES. Amsterdam was conquered immediately after the German invasion of the Netherlands on May 10, 1940. As Dutch Jews, especially in Amsterdam, had followed the developments in Germany in the 1930s carefully, the awareness of the dangers awaiting ahead were well understood by many (even though the Final Solution, which was not yet decided upon, was not foreseen). Some 128 Amsterdam Jews consequently committed suicide during the first days of German rule, even though persecutions had not yet started. In the fall of 1940 and the beginning of 1941 a series of discriminating decrees were enacted, defining Jews, firing Jews who worked in the bureaucracy (including universities and the legal system), registering Jews and Jewish enterprises. This started a process of legal segregation which immediately affected also the economic situation of many Jews. But the Jewish communities as well as other Jewish organizations resumed their activities, and even books could be published (but Jewish newspapers, except for a minor one, were prohibited in the fall of 1940).

JOODSCHE RAAD VOOR AMSTERDAM (JEWISH COUNCIL). The Nazi governor of the Netherlands, Reichskommissar Arthur Seyss-Inquart, had appointed a special supervisor (*Beauftragte*) for the city of Amsterdam, Senator. H. Böhmcker, who was also in charge of anti-Jewish policies. Under his auspices, an idea of establishing a ghetto in Amsterdam was raised in January 1941. However, this idea was never realized, accept for the installation – together with the establishment the Jewish Council in February – of sign-posts with the word *Judenviertel* (Jewish neighborhood) on them around the "Jewish quarter" in the center of the city. This non-ghetto has therefore been nicknamed "the optic ghetto."

On February 9 clashes between youngsters belonging to the militia (WA) of the Dutch National-Socialist Movement (NSB), who wanted to carry out a pogrom in the Jewish quarter, and some organized Jews, resulted in the death of one Dutch Nazi. German forces reacted by closing that Jewish quarter on February 12 for a short while; Böhmcker ordered on that same day the establishment of a Jewish Council for Amsterdam, according to the model of the *Judenräte* which had been established in Poland in 1939–1940. In a mode unparalleled in the entire Nazi-occupied Europe and North Africa, *two* chairpersons were appointed to the Council: the diamond industrial, politician and head of the Amsterdam Ashkenazi community Abraham Asscher; and the Zionist activist, university professor and chairperson of the Jewish Refugee Committee David Cohen. They were officially assisted by a committee of representatives of the Jewish population, but this committee had hardly any influence on the policies. The competences and authority of the *Joodsche Raad* gradually expanded to encompass the entire Jewish population in the country (through a network of representatives). It published a weekly, *Het Joodsche Weekblad*, serving to inform the Jewish population of anti-Jewish measures and of internal issues; and as from the fall of 1941 administered the segregated Jewish education system as well as cultural activities. It was used by the Germans to impose many of the persecutions. As such, the Council employed thousands of employees.

In April 1941, in the wake of the establishment of the *Joodsche Raad*, a branch of Adolf Eichmann's office (named *Zentralstelle für jüdische Auswanderung*) was established in the city, to supervise the activities of the Council. It later on served as the main authority carrying out the deportations.

"FEBRUARY STRIKE". On February 22–23, 1941, the Germans for the first time carried out a round-up ("razzia") in the "Jewish quarter" and arrested 425 men. They were assembled in a square, brutally treated, and later deported to Mauthausen, where they all died. The round-up caused protests by the non-Jewish population, which resulted in a two-day strike in Amsterdam and its surroundings (February 25–26), a unique occasion in Europe (which was never repeated in the Netherlands too, even when systematic deportations to the death camps started). The German authorities suppressed the strike with force; additionally, Seyss-Inquart reacted with a threatening speech on March 12 in the Amsterdam Concertgebouw, stating that the Jews were declared enemies of Germany, and whoever supported them would have to bear the consequences. And indeed, no retreat in anti-Jewish policies was felt; on the contrary: in June 1941, still a year before the beginning of the Final Solution in the Netherlands, another 300 Jews were rounded-up in Amsterdam and once again sent to Mauthausen, where they died.

CONCENTRATION OF JEWS IN AMSTERDAM, DEPORTATIONS AND HIDING. Between January 1942 and April 1943, most parts of the country were declared as forbidden for Jews to live in; their Jewish inhabitants were mostly evacuated to Amsterdam. Additionally, many decrees limited the possibility of Jews to move around (such as the use of public transportation, cars and even bicycles). As from the beginning of May 1942 Jews had to wear a Yellow Star with the word *Jood* on it. Jewish bank accounts and assets were channeled to the Lippmann-Rosenthal bank in the Sarphatistraat, a cover institution created by the German authorities. A first deporta-

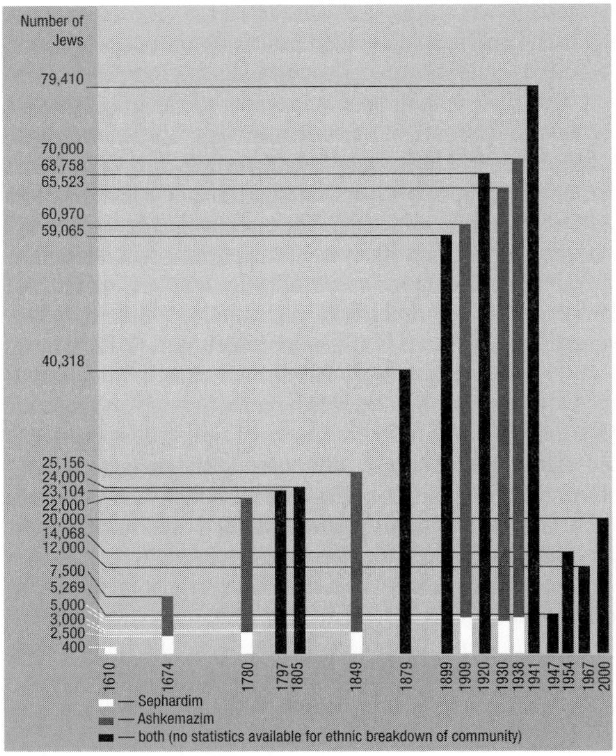

Amsterdam's Jewish population.

tion train left the Amsterdam Central Railway Station with 962 persons to the transit camp Westerbork in eastern Holland in the night of 14–15 July. An assembling center for the Amsterdam Jews was created in the Joodsche (formerly: Hollandsche) Schouwburg (i.e. theatre), in the Jewish quarter; this site serves today for the commemoration of the Holocaust of Dutch Jewry. Deportations came to a close on September 29, 1943, on the eve of Rosh Hashana 5704; the last Jews officially living in Amsterdam, including the chairpersons of the *Joodsche Raad*, were arrested and sent away.

RELIGIOUS LIFE. In view of the harsh persecutions and the disastrous number of murdered Jews, it is amazing to note that religious life could go on relatively unhindered during this whole period. True, in the very beginning kosher slaughtering – without prior stunning – was prohibited, but when a solution was found for that by the Amsterdam rabbis, slaughtering continued as long as meat was available. *Maẓẓot* for Passover were distributed even in 1943. Official prayers went on, and Jews were not arrested in synagogues. Synagogues were partially plundered during the last stage of the war, but never desecrated. Thus, all synagogues, including the impressive Sephardi and Ashkenazi ones in the center of the Jewish quarter, remained in tact, and could be reopened after the war.

REACTIONS OF NON-JEWISH NEIGHBORS. The reactions of the non-Jewish citizens cannot be generalized. On the one hand, expressions of solidarity were expressed at different stages of the persecutions. The February strike of 1941 was a genuine such expression. When the Yellow Star was imposed, some Amsterdammers wore yellow flowers. Other helped in helping Jews to find shelter or flee. A special such case was the smuggling of hundreds of Jewish children, brought to the Joodsche Schouwburg and smuggled out on the initiative of Jewish employees and the assistance of a German guard, to the neighboring kindergarten ("crèche"), from where the children were directed to hiding addresses throughout the country.

On the other hand, Dutch city officials were instrumental from an early stage in registering Jews, the local police played a major role in arresting and deporting the Jews, streetcar drivers worked additional hours during the round-ups, and others denunciated hiding Jews.

Altogether, Amsterdam Jewry was so badly hit in the Holocaust, that the colorful and sparkling Jewish life which had existed in the city for more than three hundred years, was almost entirely disrupted. After the war Amsterdam became once again the major Jewish community in the Netherlands, but never returned to its former importance, both for the Jewish world and for Dutch society.

[Dan Michman (2nd ed.)]

Contemporary Period

Jewish survivors, who returned to Amsterdam after the Holocaust, continued prewar patterns and mostly resettled in its southern neighborhoods. This was even intensified since the postwar Jewish population had a very different socio-economic structure. The proletariat, lacking the social networks and the money one needed to go into hiding, was nearly completely wiped out. Their quarters, known as the original Jewish neighborhoods in the center of Amsterdam, were demolished by the municipality in the interest of renovation and traffic requirements. In time, middle- and upper-middle class Jews spread out into several new suburbs like Amstelveen and Diemen, but the majority still lives in Amsterdam itself, especially in Buitenveldert. This "Greater Amsterdam area" comprised some 20,000 Jews in the year 2000. They represent less than half of the total Jewish population in the Netherlands, estimated at 43,000. Of these only 70% have a Jewish mother and fewer than 25% are connected with the official Jewish community. The "Greater Amsterdam" community is still by far the largest Jewish concentration in the Netherlands and also the most conscious one when it comes to Jewish identity. Most Amsterdam Jews (56%) still have two Jewish parents, while elsewhere the average is much lower (37%). Jews who are in need of community services such as schools, synagogues, kosher food, tend to move to Amsterdam, the only place in the Netherlands offering all those services. Jews, who do not need them, tend to move out of Amsterdam. Over the years, the original Dutch Jewish community in Amsterdam was not able to keep its numbers from deteriorating, but it was resupplied by several thousands of foreign Jews, many of them Israelis and younger than the original community. The prewar Jewish weekly *Nieuw Israelietisch Weekblad* is the oldest weekly in the Netherlands (since 1862), and it preserved its central place in the organized Jewish community. Immediately after the war, efforts were undertaken to unite the different congregations in Amsterdam into one *Grossgemeinde*. These efforts failed and the different prewar communities all continued their independent existence.

THE ASHKENAZI ORTHODOX COMMUNITY. The four Ashkenazi synagogues in the center of Amsterdam were sold to the Amsterdam municipality in 1955, followed by the ones in Uilenburgerstraat and Rapenburgerstraat. A smaller synagogue replaced the one in Linnaeusstraat, but it was ultimately closed down in the 1990s for lack of worshippers. In Amsterdam South the prewar synagogue in the Lekstraat was found too large. It continued to be in use but part of it was turned into the Resistance Museum. The synagogues on the Jacob Obrechtplein, in Gerard Doustraat and Kerkstraat continued to be in use, as did the one that is part of the Dutch Israelite Seminary in Gerrit van der Veenstraat. There continued to be a synagogue in use in Amsterdam West. However, in 1965 a new synagogue was opened in the new Buitenveldert neighborhood on the southern municipality border. Its establishment was soon followed by a new Orthodox synagogue in nearby Amstelveen. These areas had become the central Jewish area of Amsterdam. In 1970 the Central Dutch Israelite Synagogue (NIHS) bought a complex of buildings in Buitenveldert and transformed it into a Jewish Cultural Center including a synagogue, classrooms, community center and offices. None of the Ashkenazi Rabbis of Amsterdam had survived the Holocaust. Rabbi Justus Tal from Utrecht was nominated chief rabbi of Amsterdam in 1951 and from 1954 Rabbi Aaron *Schuster dominated the scene as chief rabbi and as director of the Rabbinical Seminary. He was educated at the prewar Rabbinical Seminary and preserved the traditions of the prewar community. After he left in 1972, the Ashkenazi community went through a number of changes leaving little of its original character. The Netherlands Israelite Rabbinical and Teachers Seminary in Amsterdam no longer produced rabbis after the war. This made the community dependent on foreign-educated rabbis, who, in general, were much stricter in their interpretation of *halakhah*. Rabbi Meir Just from Switzerland, already in the country from 1962, became more dominant after 1972. Later rabbis were educated in the ultra-orthodox Rabbinical School of Gateshead, such as Rabbi Frank Lewis (1990s). At the same time the Lubavitch movement started to have an impact on the community. As a result halakhic decisions were increasingly taken without reference to Dutch customs. All these different Orthodox streams stayed united in the Nederlands Israelietisch Kerkgenootschap (NIK). The combined membership of the Amsterdam congregations was 5,202 in 1951, but has dwindled over the years. Already in the 1970s it was clear that the real membership was below 4,500 and it further plunged to 2,821 in the year 1998. From 1955 the Ashkenazi Orthodox community of Amsterdam published its own journal *Hakehillah*, which in the 1990s was renamed *Hakehilloth* and extended to the whole country.

THE PORTUGUESE COMMUNITY. Portuguese Jews still use their 17th century synagogue building in the old Jewish neighborhood in the center of Amsterdam where the traditions of the old community are more or less preserved, but since many of the Portuguese moved to Amstelveen they opened a new congregation there in 1995. Only some 800 Portuguese Jews had survived the Holocaust and the community dwindled down to about 450 in 2000. That number includes new immigrants from Morocco, Iraq, and Israel who have joined the community. The Portuguese Rabbi, S.A. Rodrigues-Pereira, survived the war. In 1968 the community for the first time in its history nominated an Ashkenazi-educated rabbi, Barend Drukarch. Working together with the congregation's president, Dr. Jacques Baruch, Rabbi Drukarch adjusted very well. Both men served the Portuguese community for many decades and preserved its tolerant Orthodox attitude. From 1947 the community published its own journal, *Habinyan*, stressing its independence. It also reopened its famous Ets Haim library as early as 1947 and the part of the library that was sent to Israel as a permanent loan was returned to the Netherlands in recent years and reintegrated in the precious collection. The small community has continuous problems in preserving its prestigious synagogue building and its other historical treasures.

THE LIBERAL CONGREGATION. Liberal Jews in Amsterdam had a very small congregation of about 130 members left in 1946, which consisted mainly of German refugees. They had no synagogue building and efforts to revive the community seemed to bear no fruit. It was on the verge of disappearance when, in 1954, the Union of Liberal Religious Jews in the Netherlands nominated a Dutch Rabbi, Jacob *Soetendorp, who was a former student of the prewar Orthodox Rabbinical Seminary. He had not finished his studies since he had started to have doubts about the kind of Judaism he was learning. In 1955, Dr. Leo Baeck officially ordained him a rabbi and he stayed with the Amsterdam congregation until 1972. Together with its president, Dr. Maurits *Goudeket, Soetendorp succeeded to revive the community and to guide it through a period of explosive growth during the 1960s and early 1970s. From a mainly German community they also succeeded to mold it into a solid Dutch one. The Liberal congregation opened its own synagogue and community center in 1966, in the south of Amsterdam. In 1954 the community established a journal, *Levend Joods Geloof* ("Living Jewish Faith"). After Rabbi Soetendorp, Swedish-born Rabbi David Lilienthal served the congregation for 32 years until the end of 2003. A young rabbi, Menno ten Brink, born and raised in the community itself, took over. The Amsterdam congregation had a membership of 1,700 in 2005.

BETH HACHIDDUSH. This new, *havurah*-like congregation, is not linked up with any of the world's mainstreams of Judaism nor with the official Dutch Jewish community. It grew out of the gay community in town and started off in 1996 as very progressive when it came to the status of women or homosexuals in Judaism. It attracted many Americans who were used to this type of community in the United States and did not adjust well to the established congregations in the Netherlands. Beth Hachiddush found a permanent home in the renovated synagogue in Uilenburgerstraat, after which it appointed a female Rabbi.

EDUCATION. Amsterdam is the only place in the Netherlands with Jewish day schools. Since the Holocaust, the regular Orthodox schools (Rosh Pina and Maimonides), from nurseries up to high school have been functioning. They are in the hands of a private foundation, Joods Bijzonder Onderwijs (JBO), representing in fact the traditional Ashkenazi community. They attract several hundreds of pupils, many from families who do not have a strictly Orthodox lifestyle. Since 1975 there is a *ḥeder* as well, founded by the Lubavitch community. It grew with the years into a complete educational system. Both school systems attract quite a lot of Israeli children. A *kolel*, a strictly Orthodox center of Talmud study was opened in Amsterdam in 1976. The Netherlands Israelite Rabbinical and Teachers Seminary in Amsterdam, from the 1990s presided over by Rabbi Raphael Evers, trains teachers, Torah-readers, and *shliḥei ẓibbur* and it offers the adult education the community was asking for, but it trains no rabbis. In 2003 the Liberal community set up the Mr. Robert A.*Levisson Institute for the training of its own rabbis, having Rabbi David Lilienthal as its first dean. Along with the program of the Institute itself, the students take required studies at the University of Amsterdam and at Crescas, a countrywide Jewish Institute for adult education since 1999.

WOMEN'S ORGANIZATIONS. During the first decades after the war, women were mostly active in the Dutch branch of the Women International Zionist Organization, but in 1964 women in the Liberal congregation of Amsterdam founded a special group of a more emancipatory brand. Frieda Menco-Brommet was its chairperson for many years and shaped its character. The group was striving for more equality in the administrative structure of the congregation and also in its services. It created international contacts with other women's groups and activities were extended beyond Amsterdam by founding the Federation of Liberal Religious Women. It received support from both the board and the rabbinate. In later years Annie van Dantzig-Hagenaar took over and the group, having largely achieved its goals, became very much involved with social matters and serious Jewish education for women. In the meantime the Orthodox women had founded their own group, "Deborah." in 1978. Deborah was chaired for 15 years by Dr. Blume Evers-Emden. In spite of its activities and its progress, women were still barred from being elected to the board of the Amsterdam congregation, even in the early years of the 21st century. On a national level and in several other congregations in the country, they were fully integrated as board members. The failure to achieve anything in Amsterdam is quite exemplary for the restrictive influence of both Rabbi Meir Just, Rabbi Frank Lewis, and the Lubavitch movement on the Amsterdam congregation. Deborah found a partner however in the Federation of Liberal Jewish Women, when it discovered that this group already was a member of the International Council of Jewish Women (ICJW). Each country could have only one representative. Together with Annie van Dantzig-Hagenaar, who was eager to cooperate with the Orthodox women, the Dutch National Council of Jewish Women (NCJW) was founded in which the Liberal Women and Deborah are equally represented. This NCJW became the new Dutch member of the ICJW.

SOCIAL WELFARE FOUNDATION. Next to the religious congregations the Jewish Social Welfare Foundation (JMW), founded in 1947, took up a central position in the organized community. Most Jewish organizations including all religious communities are represented in it. JMW over the years developed into a highly professional institution taking care of Holocaust victims, refugees and the old-aged. The last group is disproportionally large. A system of domestic help for the elderly was set up in Amsterdam alone, in addition to the old-age home Beth Shalom, located in Amstelveen. Several previous Jewish old-age homes were concentrated in Beth Shalom as a result of the centralizing policy of the government. JMW also offers community work and alternative frameworks for Jews who are no longer interested in a religious expression of their identity. Among them is a considerable group of Israelis, who are brought together in at least one yearly event. Jewish soccer, also organized by JMW, became very popular during the 1990s and the yearly *Jom Ha-Voetbal* (Jewish Football day) attracts the largest number of spectators to any annual Jewish event.

REMEMBERING THE HOLOCAUST. During the first decades after the war, Jews joined non-Jews in the general Dutch remembering of the victims of the Second World War on May 4. More than half of these victims were Jewish. Jews also attended the remembrance of the February Strike each year together with the population of Amsterdam. Later on, from the 1970s, separate Jewish memorial ceremonies became more accepted, stressing the specific Jewish character of most victims and getting the function of bringing more Jews together on these sensitive occasions. The Hollandse Schouwburg where some 80,000 Amsterdam Jews were concentrated before their deportation to Westerbork, underwent extensive renovation and a permanent exhibition was placed in it. Thus it was transformed into the monument where each year on Yom Hashoah a Jewish ceremony takes place, attended by non-Jews as well. This development from "general Dutch" to "specifically Jewish" also resulted in the new Auschwitz monument which in the beginning of the 1990s was placed in the Wertheim public garden, a few hundred meters from the Hollandse Schouwburg: a large Star of David constructed of glass plates by sculptor Jan Wolkers. A small monument for the Jews in the Resistance was erected in the late 1980s, also stressing their specific identity while in previous decades this had not been the case. Although the famous Anne Frank house draws some 600,000, mostly foreign, visitors each year, this institution is not in Jewish hands and it plays a minor role in the community.

THE PERIPHERY. Most Jews in Amsterdam are not connected with the community and freely mix with non-Jews including for marriage purposes. Part of them, however, are the founders of many unofficial Jewish or semi-Jewish frameworks that came to life over the years and usually disappeared again after some time. Some took the form of café's like Gotspe, a café for young Jews in 1973, and Betty's Coffee Shop, Naches and Blanes in the 1980s. In the 1970s Jewish lesbians and homosexuals founded Shalhomo, an organization that continued to exist for 30 years. Other young Jews started debating clubs or groups around the conflict in the Middle East, ranging from defenders of Israel to groups that barely identify with the Jewish State and voice criticism. In the 1990s the Jewish "Women in Black," demonstrated against the occupation of the West Bank and Gaza in the center of Amsterdam every second Friday of the month showing that younger generations of Jews had become more critical of Israel. This is especially true about a group called "Another Jewish Voice," active since the end of the 1990s and apparently seeking to become more accepted by their non-Jewish surroundings by criticizing Israel in a rather unbalanced way.

RELATIONS WITH THE SURROUNDINGS. The relation with the authorities was very positive over the years and although Jews have become a very small minority in Amsterdam, the city had no less than four Jewish mayors nominated (Dr. Ivo Samkalden, Wim Polak, Ed van Thijn, Dr. Job Cohen). After a short difficult period immediately after the war, antisemitism barely existed in Amsterdam and was limited to incidents. If they occurred they were usually followed by large anti-racist demonstrations. The Ajax Amsterdam soccer club was identified with Jews and always attracted antisemitic shouts and incidents in the stadium. From 1997 to 2002, the number of antisemitic incidents rose as a result of frictions with the large Muslim community in Amsterdam. In those years the population of immigrants from Third World countries, mainly Muslims, had risen to about 10% of the Dutch population, and they are concentrated in the large cities. They have become the majority of pupils in many Dutch elementary schools in the larger cities. If incidents took place, they were limited to verbal abuse, but some ended with harassment and stone throwing. As a result mayor Job Cohen started a program for improvement of relations between the different communities. In 2003 and 2004 the situation stabilized.

CULTURE. Many Jews in Amsterdam work in the free professions. They are well represented among Amsterdam's journalists, authors and artists and in spite of their small numbers succeeded to continue a Jewish flavor in these fields. Many nostalgic books were published about the prewar Jewish neighborhoods or even certain streets, Jewish life in Amsterdam before the Holocaust and the like. "Jewish Amsterdam," now greatly reduced to a myth, still plays a role in literature and plays. Authors like Siegfried van Praag and Judith Herzberg, who made themselves felt up to the 1980s and 1990s, are followed by a younger generation still seeking to express itself in a recognizable Jewish way. During the first decades after the war the expressions of Jewish culture were rather modest, but during the 1980s and 1990s interest in Jewish culture only seemed to grow and was not limited to Jews at all. Some of it even has become Jewish culture without Jews, e.g., several *klezmer* groups became popular, most of them, like "Di Gojim," consisting entirely of non-Jewish musicians. At the end of the 1970s a special Commission for Dutch Jewish history was founded within the Royal Academy of Sciences. It organizes international symposia every six years in Amsterdam while symposia of the same kind take place in-between in Jerusalem. The interest in Dutch Jewish history has been growing ever since among Jews and non-Jews alike and the symposia attract hundreds of people. At the University of Amsterdam a special chair for modern Jewish history was created, also by the same Commission in the early 1990s. The first one to occupy it was Prof. Dr. Rena Fuks-Mansfeld. While Yiddish has disappeared from the streets of Amsterdam, there is an amazing revival of interest in Yiddish on a more academic level. The interest in Yiddish is a phenomenon completely unknown to Amsterdam before 1940. In the 1990s two Yiddish festivals were organized in Amsterdam mainly by Mira Rafalowicz, a champion of Yiddish culture in the Netherlands. From the early 1990s students of Semitic languages at the University of Amsterdam were required to attend courses in Yiddish during their second year. The centenary of the Bund, which had no more than a handful of members left in the Netherlands, was celebrated by a new Jiddisjer Krajz group with the participation of an equally new Haimish Zajn choir in 1997. All events are attended by Jews and many non-Jews. Also in 1997 the Menashe ben Israel Institute was established. It coordinates Jewish Studies at the University of Amsterdam and at the Free University (also in Amsterdam) and it organizes well-attended international study days. In the fall of 2000 the first issue of *Di Grine Medine* appeared, published by the recently founded Society for the promotion of Yiddish in the Netherlands. This is the country's first Yiddish periodical in two centuries. Another quite recent phenomenon is the great interest in *ḥazzanut* and especially the reproduction of prewar *ḥazzanut*. In 1986 the Amsterdam Synagogue Choir, consisting of male singers only, was reestablished. A Lewandowski Choir, came into being as well. It has some 40 singers both male and female. Greatly adding to all this with publications, catalogues and exhibitions is the Jewish Historical Museum, first reopened on the Nieuwmarkt, but in 1987 it moved to the four great Ashkenazi synagogues in the center of Amsterdam opposite the monumental Portuguese Esnoga. The project of the reestablishment of a much larger and modern museum in those buildings was in the hands of Judith Belinfante, its director for 25 years until1998, and Ted Musaph-Andriesse, chair of the board for an equally long term up to 2000. A special exhibition for children, now known as the Children's Museum, created by Petra Katzenstein, added much to the permanent exhibition. The Jewish Historical Museum of Amsterdam is the one place visited by the largest number of Dutch Jews in the Netherlands and as such it has a positive influence on Jewish identity and identification.

[Wout van Bekkum and Chaya Brasz (2nd ed.)]

Musical Life in the 17th and 18th Centuries

There is much evidence of an intensive musical life during the 17th and 18th centuries, especially within the Sephardi community in Amsterdam. These descendants of the *Marranos who had lived in cultural assimilation in their country of origin for generations, retained the cultural and literary expression of their previous way of life, even after they had returned to a strict observance of Judaism. It is known from contemporary sources that many local rabbis had a good knowledge of music and played musical instruments. From the late 17th and throughout the 18th centuries, there were many musical events in synagogues, within the framework of the "academies" or the various societies, or in celebration of some family occasion. The Sephardi synagogue in Amsterdam was dedicated in 1675 to the music of an orchestra and choir. This event made an impression on the life of the community, and the anniversary became a regular festival, accompanied by musical offerings. The choral rendering of *Ḥeshki Ḥezki* was one of the most beautiful compositions written for this occasion in the first half of the 18th century by Abraham *Caceres. The festival of *Torah served as another occasion for the poets and composers in the congregation to present their works. The *ḥatan Torah* and *ḥatan Bereshit* were honored in an elaborate ceremony. Among the compositions written for the celebration, particular mention should be made of the cantata *Le-El Elim* (words by Moses Ḥayyim *Luzzatto, music by A. Caceres), first performed in 1738 and often repeated. During the 18th century there flourished in Amsterdam, as in Italy, many societies at whose celebrations musical compositions were heard. Another prominent musical occasion was the contest for the appointment of a new **ḥazzan* for the synagogue, at which candidates were called upon to prove their musical talents. Family events, and particularly weddings, were often accompanied by musical plays. The Jews of the 18th century made a notable contribution to the development of Dutch musical life in general; their influence was particularly strong in opera. Among the Jewish activities in this field one of the most noteworthy is the attempt by Sephardi Jews in the mid-18th century to establish a theater which would also play French opera. There was also the important enterprise of a member of the Ashkenazi community from Amsterdam, Jacob Dessauer, who in 1784 founded a German theatrical and operatic troupe, the first of its kind in Amsterdam, in which all the members – actors, singers, and the 23 members of the orchestra – were Jews.

[Israel Adler]

BIBLIOGRAPHY: J.C.H. Blom, R.G. Fuks-Mansfeld and I. Schöffer (eds.), *The History of the Jews in The Netherlands* (2002); M.H. Gans, *Memorbook* (1977); Y. Kaplan and C. Brasz, *Dutch Jews as Perceived by Themselves and Others* (2001); J. Michman, H. Beem, and D. Michman, *Pinkas: Geschiedenis van de joodse gemeenschap in Nederland* (1999); J. Michman (ed.), *Dutch Jewish History* vols. 1–3 (1984–1993); J. Michman, *Dutch Jewry during the Emancipation Period, Gothic Turrets on a Corinthian Building, 1787–1815* (1995); B. Moore, *Victims and Survivors* (1997); *Studia Rosenthaliana*, 1–76 (1967–2005); H. van Solinge and M. de Vries (eds.), *De joden in Nederland anno 2000, demografisch profile en binding aan het jodendom* (2001); R.G. Fuks-Mansfeld (eds.), *Aspects of Jewish life in the Netherlands, a selection from the writings of Leo Fuks* (1995); J. Meijer, *Hoge hoeden, lage standaarden, de Nederlandse joden tussen 1933 en 1940* (1969); D. Michman, *Het liberale jodendom in Nederland, 1929–1943* (1988); J. Michman and M. Aptroot, *Storm in the Community, Yiddish Polemical Pamphlets of Amsterdam Jewry 1797–1798* (2002); Daniel M. Swetschinski, *Reluctant Cosmopolitans, the Portuguese Jews of Seventeenth-Century Amsterdam* (2004); R.G. Fuks-Mansfeld, *De Sefardim in Amsterdam tot 1795, aspecten van een joodse minderheid in een Hollandse stad* (1989). MUSICAL LIFE: Adler, Prat Mus, 1 (1966), 191–236; 2 (1966), 173–230; J. Fransen, *Les comediens français en Hollande au 17e et 18e siècles* (1925); D.F. Scheurleer, *Het muziekleven in Nederland in de tweede helft der 18e eeuw...* (1909); Shatzky, in: YIVO *Bleter*, 21 (1943), 302–22.

AMSTERDAM, BIRDIE (1901–1996), U.S. lawyer and judge. Amsterdam was born on the Lower East Side of Manhattan, New York City into a first generation Jewish American family. She was the second of six children, all of whom pursued professional careers. A graduate of Hunter College High School at age 17, she studied accounting and banking at the City College of New York while waiting to reach the age for admission to law school. Amsterdam worked days and studied in the evening at New York University Law School; she was awarded a LLB in 1922 and admitted to the bar the following year. Amsterdam practiced law independently before forming a partnership with her brother-in-law, Milton Sanders. The firm of Amsterdam and Sanders was dissolved when Amsterdam became a judge. Amsterdam was called the "First Lady of the Judiciary" because of her prominence and her record of "firsts" as a woman in the legal profession. She was the first woman to sit on the Municipal Court in New York County, where she served from 1940 to 1954. She became the first woman judge of the City Court to which she was appointed in 1954. In 1955 she won a full term. In 1958 Amsterdam was elected to the New York State Supreme Court, again a first for a woman. Amsterdam served two terms on the State Supreme Court before retiring in 1975. She was approached in the course of her career to accept an Appellate Court appointment. She declined, preferring to remain a trial judge. Amsterdam received many honors. In 1960 *Who's Who of American Women* named her "Outstanding Woman of the Year in the Legal Field." A leader in the Democratic Party, she was often endorsed in elections by other parties, civic groups, and labor organizations. Active in numerous legal, religious, political, and charitable causes, she also encouraged aspiring women lawyers. She credited her experiences as a lifelong resident on the immigrant and poor Lower East Side with sensitizing her to social needs. Amsterdam's special concerns included slum clearance, medical care, summer camps for poor children, tuition assistance, and housing for the aged and handicapped.

BIBLIOGRAPHY: *Current Biography Yearbook* (1940; obituary, 1996); *New York Times* (obituary, July 10, 1996); D. Thomas, *Women Lawyers of the United States* (1957).

[Libby White (2nd ed.)]

AMULET. From earliest times, man has tried to protect himself from misfortune by the use of objects which he considered holy or otherwise (e.g., magically) potent. One of the ways of doing this was to keep the object close to his person, frequently wearing it as an article of clothing, or as an ornament. It was felt that the evil spirits which cause misfortune would not dare to attack one so protected. It has been suggested that this desire for protection is the source of man's habit to adorn himself with jewelry and other ornamentation; the female being weaker – and consequently in greater danger – has the greater need for protection. The custom developed for people to have on their persons pieces of paper, parchment, or metal discs inscribed with various formulae which would protect the bearer from sickness, the "evil eye," and other troubles. The use of inscription as a means to ward off evil spirits stemmed from a belief in early times in the holiness and in the power of words. Such artifacts are known as amulets (for other types of charms and protective items, see *Magic). It is not known whether amulets were used in the biblical period. Presumably they were, but there is no direct evidence to prove it. Traditional Judaism does not consider *tefillin* and *mezuzah* – whatever their original antecedents may have been – to be amulets. The purpose of *tefillin* is stated to be "for a sign upon thy hand" (Deut. 6:8) and from the immediate proximity of the verse regarding *mezuzah* it would seem that its purpose is the same. While one biblical rite involving the doorposts (Ex. 11:7, 13) had an apotropaic function and the current translation for *tefillin* ("phylacteries") suggests the same purpose, the traditional interpretation of the "sign" was that of a reminder of God's commandments and of the duty of the Jew to bear witness to his God.

Amulets are frequently mentioned in talmudic literature. The term used is *kame'a* or *kami'a* (pl. *kemi'ot* or *kemi'in*), a word whose origin is obscure. It is possible that it derives from a root meaning "to bind" (cf. Rashi to Shab. 61a), but it might come from an Arabic root meaning "to hang." In either case, the reference is clearly something that is bound or hung on the person (cf. Kohut, Arukh, 7 (1926²), 123). The Talmud mentions two sorts of *kemi'ot*: a written one and the *kame'a shel ikrin*, a *kame'a* made from roots of a certain plant. The written *kame'a* was a parchment inscribed with one or more quotations from a variety of sources, including the Scriptures (cf. Shab. 61b). The question arose whether the amulets were invested with the holiness of the scriptural scrolls and whether they should, therefore, be saved from a conflagration occurring on the Sabbath. A *baraita* is quoted which specifically states that they are not holy and that they, together with other texts which contain scriptural quotations (lit. *berakhot*), should be left to burn (*ibid.*). In the original Tosefta text, however, no mention is made of *kemi'ot* (Tosef. Shab. 13:4). Unfortunately, there is no record in the Talmud of the inscriptions in the amulets (but see Yoma 84a). Later amulets were inscribed with quotations relevant to their specific purpose. The text of the *Priestly Blessing (Num. 6:24–26) was considered effective against the "evil eye." Permutations and combinations of the letters of the different names of God were frequently used; names of angels were also very common. The simplest amulet had an inscription of the name of God on a piece of parchment or metal, usually made of silver; ה (*He*), יה (*YaH*), and שדי (*Shaddai*, "Almighty") being very popular. These still feature prominently on pendants worn by Jewish women today. The efficacy of the amulet depended not only on the inscription but also on the person who wrote it; the more pious the author the more effective was the amulet.

The Talmud differentiates between "expert" (or proven, *min ha-mumḥeh*) amulets and others. The former had proved its effectiveness by curing a sick person on three different occasions or three sick persons, and hence one may wear such an amulet outside the home on the Sabbath (Shab. 6:2).

The Talmud (Shevu. 15b) states that it is forbidden to recite verses of the Torah for the purpose of curing an existing illness but it is permitted "to guard" against possible future sickness (see also Maim, Yad, Avodat Kokhavim 11:12). This distinction was equally applied to amulets. During the Middle Ages, the rabbinic attitude to amulets varied considerably. *Maimonides, following the precedent of *Sherira Gaon and his son *Hai, opposed the use of amulets and came out very strongly against the "folly of amulet writers" (Guide, 1:61; Yad, Tefillin 5:4). He also opposed the use of religious objects, such as the Torah scroll and *tefillin*, for the curing of sickness (Yad, Avodat Kokhavim 11:12). On the other hand, both Solomon b. Abraham *Adret and *Naḥmanides permitted the use of amulets. Earlier magical traditions, including the use of amulets, magic charms, names of angels, combinations of Hebrew letters, etc. subsequently merged with the *Kabbalah and came to be known as "practical Kabbalah." Many mystical texts, such as the *Sefer Yeẓirah* and the *Sefer Razi'el*, contain instructions for the preparation of amulets and other charms, for a variety of purposes. After the expulsion of the Jews from Spain, the belief in the efficacy of amulets spread to Eastern Europe. In Ereẓ Israel, it spread from Safed, the center of Kabbalah, to all parts of the country.

One of the most vehement controversies in Jewish history was caused by amulets. Jonathan *Eybeschuetz, the rabbi of Hamburg, was accused by Jacob *Emden of having used the name of the false messiah Shabbetai *Ẓevi in amulets which he had prepared. Eybeschuetz vigorously denied the charge. It is interesting that the validity of writing amulets was not questioned in the controversy. The congregational burial society of Hamburg officially endorsed the efficacy of Eybeschuetz' amulets. In a particularly sharp attack against Maimonides' rationalism in these matters, *Elijah b. Solomon Zalman, the Gaon of Vilna, a bitter opponent of Ḥasidism, also endorsed the use of amulets (to Sh. Ar., YD 179). The belief in amulets gradually diminished with the emancipation of European Jewry, although in Eastern Europe it remained widespread until World War II. *Kemi'ot*, in particular, were worn during pregnancy to prevent miscarriage; amulets called *Kimpet-Tsetl, Shir Hamalos-Tsetl*, and *Shmine-Tsetl* were also placed above the head and under the pillow of a woman in labor, to ward off the evil demon *Lilith. Among Oriental communities, amulets are still widely used. Many amulets were inscribed on small discs of silver or other metal and worn as a pendant around the neck. Amulets being small in size, biblical verses and names were indicated by their initial letters, with the result that the inscription is frequently very difficult to decipher. The Samaritan community uses names of angels unknown in Jewish tradition.

For specific laws regarding amulets see Shulḥan Arukh (OḤ 301:24–27; 305:17; 334:14; and YD 179:12).

[Raphael Posner]

Amulets for Safe Childbirth and Protection of Infants

Amulets and talismans intended to protect women in childbirth and their newborns were a significant part of Jewish folk religion in Christian Europe and the Islamic world. The late ninth to early tenth century *Alphabet of Ben Sira* promulgated the legend of *Lilith, the "first Eve," who claimed that she had been created to harm newborn babies. According to this folk tradition, Lilith was convinced by three angels, Sanoi, Sansanoi, and Semangalof, that she would be unable to enter a house to harm either a baby or its mother wherever she saw their images illustrated or their names written on an amulet. *Sefer Raziel* (first printed Amsterdam, 1701), a compilation of magic, cosmology, and mystical teachings popular among both Ashkenazi and Sephardi communities, contained a recipe for an inscribed amulet to protect a laboring woman as well as for an amulet for a newborn specifically directed against Lilith. Polish and Russian Jews put the book itself under the pillow of women in childbirth; in Iraq it was put on the Chair of Elijah, an object believed to have protective powers which was placed in the center of the birthing room.

In Europe, amulets to protect mothers and infants were generally written or printed on paper, sometimes with illustrations. In the Muslim realm, protective objects made of metal, especially gold and silver, were preferred and also functioned as jewelry for women and for small children. The mystical texts and formulas inscribed on these amulets did not differ significantly in east or west.

[Judith R. Baskin (2nd ed.)]

Childbirth Amulets in Art

While the Hebrew texts inscribed on Jewish amulets in the different countries, East and West, often share similar formulae, names, and selection of biblical verses, the images drawn on those which are ornamented vary greatly, reflecting folk beliefs and traditions, visual ideas and ideals, and the influence of local folk arts. This is best exemplified by childbirth amulets – the most prevalent category of extant amulets produced in Europe and the lands of Islam from the 17th century on, reflecting the high mortality rate of children before the modern era.

Paper German childbirth amulets are often printed with small, crude figurative woodcuts expressing the ideal roles expected for the newborn when he/she grows up. For example, the amulets for a male newborn depict a boy holding an open book from which he reads, while those for a female show her kindling the typical star-shaped Sabbath lamp used by German Jews. The proselyte *Abraham ben Jacob working for the acculturated Dutch community decorated his popular amulet with a biblical image, which he copied from a Christian Bible, depicting a nude Eve and Adam in Paradise. In Poland handmade colorful papercut amulets were preferred, featuring intricate designs, including a wide selection of animals, such as a pair of rampant lions, which symbolize ideal human qualities ("be strong as the lion ..." Pirkei Avot 5:23). Images of leading rabbinical authorities, known for their righteous conduct, may appear on East European amulets as a sign of blessing and protection. In amulets of the Old Yishuv on the other hand the preferred "protective" images were conventional pictures of the holy sites (Temple Mount, Rachel's Tomb). Italian Jews created for the amulets of their children attractive silver cases decorated with appliqués of the Temple implements. In Islamic lands silver amulets and jewelry were very common, not only for newborn babies but also for children and women, considered weak and susceptible to the evil eye. Prevalent images included the hand (*ḥamsa*) mentioned above and fish. Both were interpreted by local *ḥakhamim* (e.g., *Joseph Ḥayyim of Baghdad) as symbols imbued with deep Jewish meanings. The *ḥamsa*, as well as the closely related number five, were viewed as bearing potent magical powers based on Jewish textual sources (for example, five is associated with the monogrammaton, *he*, the holy single-letter name of God, which is often inscribed in the center of amulets). Persian Jews also depicted a fantastic image of *Lilith, usually shown "in chains." In modern Israel some of the designs, the *ḥamsa* and *ḥai* [חי], in particular, have been revived and enjoy widespread popularity. Images of rabbis considered holy, both Sephardi and Ashkenazi, are common in modern Israeli amulets as well.

[Shalom Sabar (2nd ed.)]

"Illuminated Amulets"

Illuminations on amulets are seldom applied for purely decorative purposes. The various designs, symbols, and letters were believed to be efficacious in warding off the evil eye, disasters, or sickness. They consist of magical triangles, squares, rectangles, and other geometrical features, e.g., the Hexagram ("Star of David") and the Pentacle ("Star of Solomon"). The *menorah* with its seven branches, as well as an outstretched hand, is often used. More rarely, birds, animals, human figures, Satan, and the angel Metatron may appear. Letters which are not as yet completely understood and which are known as "kabbalistic writing" have also figured on amulets.

MAGICAL TRIANGLES. By gradually reducing the size of an inscription, the evil spirit is eased out of its victim and its influence is thus diminished. Magical triangles therefore serve a useful purpose and when used in writing amulets it is with this idea in mind.

SQUARES AND RECTANGLES. These are divided into several boxes each of which contains one or more letters. In this way acrostics may be formed in which powerful inscriptions may be secretly placed in the amulets to exert their beneficent influence without the knowledge of the uninitiated. The squares vary from those of nine boxes to those of 64 or even 100 boxes. The rectangles are usually small and often contain hidden verses from the Bible. Their use and influence naturally depend on the particular biblical verse inscribed.

THE HEXAGRAM. The Star of David as a silver amulet is one usually made by the Jerusalem group of amulet makers. The six points of the hexagram often contain the letters ירושלים or מלך דוד, the latter obviously alluding to the city of David. Hexagrams may also appear in written amulets.

THE MENORAH. The 7-branched candlestick is often found on the *shivviti* amulets from Persia. In the silver amulets only the initial letters of the words are used but in the parchment ones the verses are written out in full. These are so called because tradition states that King David's shield was shaped like these silver amulets, and headed with the words "I have set (*shivviti*) the Lord always before me" (Ps. 16:8).

THE HAND. A frequent occurrence is a hand inscribed on the paper or parchment amulets. Silver amulets made in the form of hands are common and are usually North African in origin and the hand is supposed to ward off the "evil eye." It is considered by some to be the hand of Fatima, who was Muhammad's daughter, but hands have appeared on North African amulets since the times of the Carthaginians and these people antedate the Muslim tradition by more than a thousand years. The tradition of using hands on amulets still persists strongly in Morocco, Tunis, and Algeria, as well as throughout the Muslim world.

THE DISC, CRESCENT, AND CROSS. The cross and the crescent are rare. The disc and crescent represent Baal and Tanit respectively and may be found as pendants on silver amulets from North Africa. They carry on the traditions of the Semitic colonization of Carthage and its neighboring countries.

THE KABBALISTIC LETTERS. Mysterious and unexplained to this day, the interpretation of these letters has long aroused controversy. Letters of this type are found on ancient amulets before they appeared on Jewish amulets, e.g., on a magic plate discovered in Pergamon from the tannaitic period. There is no proof that they were made in Jewish circles but apparently they were adapted to the needs of Jewish magic. Some scholars derive the origin of these signs from cuneiform writing. Moses *Gaster considered that there were variant forms of Samaritan (i.e., Old Hebrew) writings and in support of this opinion he cites *Rashi (TB, Sanh. 21b), who called them *Ketav Libbona'ah* and also thought they were of Samaritan origin. However, the Samaritan script bears little resemblance to these curious characters. It may well be that these letters are Hebrew writing in code form. The manuscript "Alphabet of Metatron" in the British Museum is one of the codes that enables the deciphering of some of these letters but much more research is necessary before all the kabbalistic writing can be interpreted. Many manuscripts of practical Kabbalah include alphabets of angels, each alphabet belonging to a different angel, according to the pattern of this writing. It is quite possible that some amulets can be deciphered by the use of such angelic alphabets. Although these characters are often used for ornamental purposes, they should not be dismissed as mere ornamentations. In Hebrew books on magic, many examples and formulas of amulets are published. These sources include *Ta'alumot u-Mekorot ha-Ḥokhmah* (Venice, 1664); *Derekh Yesharah* (Fuerth, 1697); *Toledot Adam* (Zolkiew, 1720); *Mifalot Elohim* (Zolkiew, 1727; the latter in many editions); *Refu'ah ve-Ḥayyim* by Ḥayyim Palache (Smyrna, 1874).

[Theodore Schrire]

BIBLIOGRAPHY: T. Schrire, *Hebrew Amulets, Their Decipherment and Interpretation* (1966), includes bibliography; J. Trachtenberg, *Jewish Magic and Superstition* (1939), index. **ADD. BIBLIOGRAPHY:** N. Behrouzi (ed.), *The Hand of Fortune: Khamsas from the Gross Family Collection and the Eretz Israel Museum Collection* (2002); E. Deitsch (ed.), *Kabbalah: Mysticism in Jewish Life*, Exhibition catalog, Museum of Judaica, Congregation Emanu-El, New York (2003); *Living Khamsa: Die Hand zum Gluek / The Hand of Fortune*, Exhibition catalog, Museum im Prediger Schwäbisch Gmünd (2004); H. Matras, "Jewish Folk Medicine in the 19th and 20th Centuries," in: N. Berger (ed.), *Jews and Medicine: Religion, Culture, Science* (1995), 1133–5; S. Sabar, "Childbirth and Magic: Jewish Folklore and Material Culture," in: D. Biale (ed.), *Cultures of the Jews: A New History* (2002), 6707–22; idem, "The Judaization of the Khamsa: The Motif of the Magic Hand in the Thought and Folklore of the Jews in the Lands of Islam," in: *Mahanaim*, 14, (2002), 1922–03 (Heb.); Y. Stillman, "The Middle Eastern Amulet as Folk Art," in: I. Ben-Ami and J. Dan (eds.), *Studies in Aggadah and Jewish Folklore* (1983), 951–01.

AMULETS, SAMARITAN. Samaritan amulets are rare because there were no more than 200 members of this sect by the beginning of the 20th century, when (in 1905) M. *Gaster acquired a number of amulets which are now housed in the British Museum. They have been most comprehensively described by Gaster in his *Studies and Texts.* E.A.W. Budge enumerates six forms of these Samaritan amulets: (1) a square sheet of parchment representing practically an entire goat's skin; (2) a scroll varying in length and width; (3) a booklet, probably carried in a case; (4) a scrap of paper; (5) a metal disc like a coin or medal; and (6) inscribed stones.

In other respects, the Samaritan amulets resemble ordinary Hebrew amulets with a few changes made in conformity with the Samaritans' own angelology, esoteric beliefs, and particularly their own text of the Bible.

The construction of Samaritan amulets follows the standard Jewish practice. God is invoked by means of the Tetragrammaton and the 72-letter Name. The name of their archangel, *Penuel*, is often inscribed on them as are the names of specifically Samaritan angels: (1) *Kevala*, derived from Num. 4:20, which they translate as "lest they see *Kevala* alongside the Holy Place and perish"; (2) *Nasi*, derived from Ex. 17:15, read in their own pronunciation as "and Moses built an altar and called the name of it *Jehovah-Nasi*"; (3) *Anusah*, derived from Ex. 14:25; (4) *Yat*, an angel whose name derives from the first word of Ex. 14:21, which verse is itself involved in the formation of the 72-letter Name.

Although demons are known among the Samaritans, none has yet been found depicted on one of these amulets. They are (1) *Zir'ah* (צרעה), deriving from Ex. 23:21 and Deut. 7:20, which is said to be an anagram of *yezer ha-ra* (יצר הרע); (2) *Belial*; and (3) *Azazel*.

BIBLIOGRAPHY: M. Gaster, *The Samaritans* (1925), 81; idem, *Studies and Texts* (1925–28), 1, 387; 3, 109; E.A.W. Budge, *Amulets and Talismans* (1961), 262; T. Schrire, in: IEJ, 20 (1970), 111; idem, in: *ibid.*, 22 (1972), 154; I. Ben-Zvi, *Sefer ha-Shomronim* (1935), 160, no. 6.

[Theodore Schrire]

°**AMULO** (d. 852), archbishop of Lyons from 841 in succession to *Agobard whose anti-Jewish prejudices he shared. The Church Council of Meaux and Paris held in 845–46 passed, probably at Amulo's suggestion, a number of regulations excluding Jews from public office, forbidding them to appear in public during Easter, and prohibiting Christians from having contact with them. Amulo subsequently addressed a lengthy epistle (*Liber contra Judaeos*) to Charles the Bald in 846, trying to persuade him that such segregation was justified. This had a wide circulation and asserted that the Jews blasphemed Jesus and the Christians, and by a play on words referred to the apostles as "apostates," and to the Gospels (*Evangelion*) as *aven gilyon*, i.e., "a sheet of iniquity." Amulo quotes at length from the Hebrew **Toledot Yeshu* already circulating among the Jews. He also states that the Jews employed Christian servants and forced them to observe the Jewish laws while transgressing Christian precepts. A further charge was that Jewish tax collectors persuaded ignorant Christians to renounce Christianity with promises to reduce their taxes. Amulo's efforts were unsuccessful, however, as Charles refused to ratify the anti-Jewish canons passed by the council.

BIBLIOGRAPHY: B. Blumenkranz, in: *Revue historique de droit français et étranger*, 33 (1955), 229 ff., 560 ff.; idem, *Juifs et chrétiens dans le monde occidental…* (1960), passim; Roth, Dark Ages, index.

[Bernhard Blumenkranz]

AMUSIN, JOSEPH (**Iosip**; 1910–1984), Russian historian, specialist in *Qumran studies. Amusin was born in Vitebsk and lived in Leningrad from 1924. He was persecuted for Zionist activities, imprisoned, and exiled to Siberia (1926–33). After returning from exile he worked as a bookkeeper. In 1935–38 he studied history at Leningrad University. During the Great Terror of the Stalinist years Amusin was once again arrested (1938) but released the same year and continued his studies. In 1945–50, after serving at the front during the war, he was an instructor at Leningrad University and the Leningrad Pedagogical Institute. When the campaign against the so-called "cosmopolitans" was unleashed, Amusin displayed courage defending his teacher S. *Lurie. Consequently he had to leave Leningrad, teaching for a while at the pedagogical institutes of Ulyanovsk and Gorky. After the death of Stalin he returned to Leningrad (1954), working from 1960 at the Leningrad department of the Institute of Oriental Studies of the Soviet Academy of Sciences. In 1965 he was awarded a doctor's degree in history.

Most of Amusin's work was devoted to the history of the Jews and biblical studies. He published a translation of Qumran texts into Russian with an extensive preface and historical as well as linguistic commentaries (1971). Other important works of his were *Rukopisi Mertvogo mor'a* ("The Dead Sea Scrolls," 1960), *Nakhodki u Mertvogo mor'a* ("The Dead Sea Finds," 1964), the seminal study *Kumranskaya obshchina* ("The Qumran Community," 1983), and numerous papers on the history and ideas of the Qumran community as well as on various aspects of the history of ancient Greece, ancient Rome, and the Hellenistic world. A collection of his papers under the title *Problemy sotsialnoy struktury obshchestva drevnego Blizhnego Vostoka (1-e tys´acheletie do n.e.)* ("Problems of the Social Structure of the Ancient Near East in the First Millennium B.C. according to Biblical Sources") was published posthumously in 1993.

[Naftali Prat (2nd ed.)]

AMZALAK, ḤAYYIM (1824–1916), notable of the Jewish community in Ereẓ Israel. Amzalak, who was born in Gibraltar, went to Jerusalem with his parents in 1830. He became a grain merchant and banker, settled in Jaffa, and was appointed British vice consul for that town. He advised and guided the first emissaries of the Ḥovevei Zion (*Hibbat Zion) associations who came to Ereẓ Israel in 1882 from Russia, and was elected honorary president of the Committee of the Yesud ha-Ma'alah pioneers. This committee had been established in Jaffa by Z.D. *Levontin to organize the activities of the settlers' associations. In 1882 when Jews of Russian origin were forbidden to purchase land in Ereẓ Israel, the Rishon le-Zion land was registered in Amzalak's name. At the beginning of World War I, Amzalak refused to renounce his British nationality and was exiled to Egypt.

BIBLIOGRAPHY: Z.D. Levontin, *Le-Ereẓ Avoteinu*, 1 (1924), 48, 115; M.D. Gaon, *Yehudei ha-Mizraḥ be-Ereẓ Yisrael*, 2 (1938), 105–6; Tidhar, 2 (1947), 816; I. Klausner, *Be-Hitorer Am* (1962), index.

[Yehuda Slutsky]

AMZALAK, MOSES BENSABAT (1892–1978), Portuguese scholar and economist. Amzalak was born and educated in

Lisbon, combined a successful business career with encyclopedic academic activity, became professor of philosophy and later dean of the Lisbon School of Economics and Finance, and was president of the Portuguese Academy of Sciences and chancellor of the Lisbon Technical University. His main interests were economic history, history of economic thought, and marketing. A devoted Jew, he headed the Lisbon Jewish community for an entire generation. His publications are extensive, extending beyond economics to Oriental languages, Jewish history, bibliography, and related subjects. He wrote on rare works of Judaica of the 17th and 18th centuries in Spanish and Portuguese, which he reproduced in facsimile from the copies in his own extensive library. He wrote works on several economists of Marrano extraction, such as Joseph *Penso de la Vega, Duarte Gomez Solis, and Isaac de *Pinto. The bibliography of Amzalak's publications exceeds 300 entries including *Do Estudo da Evolução das Doutrinas Económicas em Portugal* (1928), *História das Doutrinas Económicas da Antiga Grécia* (12 vols., 1942–), and *História das Doutrinas Económicas da Antiga Roma* (6 vols., 1953–).

BIBLIOGRAPHY: A. Elmaleh, *Professeur Moses Bensabat Amzalak* (1962). **ADD. BIBLIOGRAPHY:** G. Nahon, in: REJ, 138 (1979), 487–8; J.B. Glass and R. Kark, *Sephardi Entrepreneurs in Eretz Israel: The Amzalek Family, 1816–1818* (1991).

[Menahem Schmelzer]

ANAB (**Anav**; Heb. עֲנָב), city in the southern hill district of Judah that is mentioned in the Bible next to Eshtemoah (Josh. 15:50). In another reference Joshua "cut off the Anakim ('giants') from Hebron, Debir, and Anab" (*ibid.* 11:21). Eusebius (Onom. 26:8) places it in the area of Eleutheropolis (Bet-Guvrin). It has been identified with Khirbat ʿAnāb al-Ṣaghīra (Heb. Tel Rekhesh) 1 mi. (1.5 km.) west of al-Ẓāhiriyya on the Hebron–Beersheba road, where Iron Age pottery has been discovered.

BIBLIOGRAPHY: Abel, Geog, 2 (1938), 243; Press, Ereẓ, 4 (1955), 141–2. **ADD. BIBLIOGRAPHY:** P. Benjamin, ABD, 1, 219.

[Michael Avi-Yonah]

°**ANACLETUS II, PETER PIERLEONE** (c. 1090–1137), in the official church view an anti-pope, outside the apostolic succession. His great-grandfather Benedict (originally probably Baruch), adopted Christianity and married a Christian noblewoman of Roman lineage. The family eponym, "Pierleone," combines the names of Benedict's son Leo and his grandson Peter. Wealth and powerful connections made the Pierleone family highly influential in Rome. In the turbulent politics of the day they sided with the Reform party in the church. The family's personal ambitions were advanced when Peter (son of Peter) was created a cardinal around 1120. In 1123 he represented Pope Calixtus II as legate to France, where he presided over councils held at Chartres and Beauvais. On the death of Pope Honorius II in 1130 the cardinals, fearing an outbreak of the popular rioting which often accompanied the election of a new pope, decided to keep the death of the pope and the impending election secret for a few days, presumably until Neapolitan troops could arrive to maintain order. A number of them, however, were hostile to the possible election of Peter Pierleone, broke their promise of delay, and elected one of their own number, who assumed the name Innocent II. The other cardinals, more numerous than their rivals, thereupon elected Pierleone, who took the name Anacletus. The schism shook Christendom. *Bernard of Clairvaux, the most influential churchman of his time, sided with Innocent II. Among his other objections to Anacletus, he expressed horror that a scion of Jews should occupy the Throne of St. Peter. Most of the monarchs and peoples of Europe heeded Bernard. Among the hostile rumors that circulated about Anacletus were charges of incest and of robbing churches with the aid of the Jews. The fickle Roman population eventually also turned against him, and he could maintain himself in Rome only with the help of Roger II, king of Naples. Anacletus remained in control of Rome until his death; only then did Innocent take possession of the city and gain universal recognition. Most church historians continue to write about Peter Pierleone with vehement contempt. In Jewish tradition he gave rise to a number of legends about a Jewish pope.

BIBLIOGRAPHY: Roth, Italy, 73ff.; Vogelstein-Rieger, index; Baron, Social², index.

[Solomon Grayzel]

ANAHARATH (Heb. אֲנָחֲרַת), Canaanite city in the eastern part of Lower Galilee. It is mentioned in the list of cities conquered by Thutmosis III in approximately 1469 B.C.E. (no. 52). It was the most distant place captured in the second campaign of his successor Amenhotep II (c. 1430 B.C.E.), and the booty there included captives, chariots, and cattle. Anaharath later became part of the territory of Issachar (Josh. 19:19). The village of al-Nāʿūra, north of the Jezreel Valley and east of the Hill of Moreh, may preserve the ancient name and has been suggested for its identification. It lacks, however, suitable archaeological remains, as does the nearby Tell al-ʿAjjūl which has also been proposed. The only other possible site in the vicinity is Tell al-Makharkhas, a prominent tell 5 mi. (8 km.) north of al-Nāʿūra and 4 mi. (7 km.) east of Mount Tabor, which dominates the upper part of Wadi al-Bīra and contains remains dating from the end of the fourth millennium up to about the tenth century B.C.E.

BIBLIOGRAPHY: EM, s.v.; Press, Ereẓ, 1 (1951²), 28; Aharoni, in: JNES, 26 (1967), 212–5; Aharoni, Land, index.

[Yo. A.]

ANAK, ANAKIM (Heb. עֲנָק, עֲנוֹק, עֲנָקִים), son of Arba (Josh. 15:13; 21:11), and a giant people of southern Ereẓ Israel (called *Anakim*, *Benei ʿAnak*, and *Benei ʿAnakim*). According to Joshua 14:15, Arba, to whom the city of *Hebron owed its ancient name of Kiriath-Arba, was the greatest of the Anakim, and according to Joshua 15:13 he was the father of "the Anak."

From the time when the Israelite spies explored the region of Hebron to the time when it was conquered by Caleb, it was inhabited by *Ahiman, Sheshai, and Talmai, who were "born of the Anak" (*yelidei ha-ʿAnak*, Num. 13:22; or "children of the Anak," Josh. 15:14). The Anakim are described as *Nephilim (Num. 13:33), a term which is probably used here virtually as a common name for giants (cf. Gen. 6:4), much as titan(s) is used today. In Deuteronomy 2:21 (cf. 1:28) the great stature of Anakim is referred to. Such traditions about an ancient race of giants were apparently current in Israel, Ammon, and Moab (see *Rephaim).

Most biblical references connect the Anakim with Hebron (Num. 13:22; et al.), but Joshua 11:21–22 indicates that they occupied a wider area. It is not known whether the *Iy-ʿnq* of the Egyptian Execration Texts (first half of the second millennium B.C.E.) are connected with the biblical Anakim. The three rulers of the former bear Semitic names (Pritchard, Texts, 328), whereas the names of Ahiman, Sheshai, and Talmai have exact affinities with Hurrian names (cf. de Vaux, in RB, 55 (1948), 326, no. 1). The term *anak* is used in Modern Hebrew for a giant.

BIBLIOGRAPHY: W.F. Albright, in: JPOS, 8 (1928), 223–56; Wright, in: JBL, 57 (1938), 305–9; B. Mazar, in: *Sefer Dinaburg* (1949), 321; Albright, in: JPOS, 8 (1928), 223–56. **ADD. BIBLIOGRAPHY:** O. Margalith, in: *Beit Mikra*, 25 (1986), 359–64.

ANAMMELECH (Heb. עֲנַמֶּלֶךְ), deity worshiped by the people of *Sepharvaim (II Kings 17:31), who were settled in Samaria (II Kings 17:24; Isa. 36:19), probably by Shalmaneser V or by *Sargon II. The people of Sepharvaim (possibly Sibraim in Syria [cf. Ezek. 47:16; II Kings 17:24; 18:34], or Sipra'ani, a Chaldean locale) continued to worship their gods, Anammelech and *Adrammelech, and maintain the worship of the God of Israel. According to II Kings 17:31, the cult of Anammelech was accompanied by the sacrifice of children (see *Moloch). The identity of this deity raises some difficulties, as no Assyrian or Babylonian deity bearing this name is known. The "Ana" element in the name has been variously explained as referring to Anu, the sky god, who was the head of the old Babylonian trinity (Anu, Bel, and Ea) and as a male counterpart of the well-known goddess *Anat. The "Melech" element has been explained as meaning "king" or "prince" (*melekh*), or as referring to human sacrifice to Moloch, or to a god bearing that name (cf. de Vaux, Anc Isr, 446).

BIBLIOGRAPHY: E. Ebeling and B. Meissner (eds.), *Reallexikon der Assyriologie*, 1 (1932), 115–7; A. Jirku, *Altorientalischer Kommentar zum Alten Testament* (1923), 180ff.; Maisler, in: JPOS, 16 (1936), 152–3; Pohl, in: *Biblica*, 22 (1941), 35 (Ger.); Albright, Arch Rel, 162ff., 220ff.; de Vaux, Anc Isr, 529 (incl. bibliography). **ADD. BIBLIOGRAPHY:** M. Smith, in: JAOS, 95 (1975), 477–79; A. Green, *The Role of Human Sacrifice in the Ancient Near East* (1975); S. Kaufman, in: JNES, 37 (1978), 109–18; R. Zadok, in: JANES, 8 (1976), 115–16; M. Cogan and H. Tadmor, *II Kings* (1988), 212; A. Millard, DDD, 34–5.

ANAN (mid-third century), Babylonian *amora*. He was also called Anan bar Rav. A pupil of *Samuel, Anan transmitted many statements in his teacher's name as well as in the name of *Rav. Anan was a judge in Nehardea, and frequented the house of the exilarch Mar Ukva (Ket. 69a, 79a). His colleague was Hanan (Kid. 39a), and R. Naḥman consulted him on halakhic matters (BM 70a). He disputed points of *halakhah* with *Huna (BM 65b); nevertheless, Huna, who regarded himself as Anan's teacher, was deeply offended when Anan addressed him as "Huna our colleague" (Ket. 69a). References are made to his piety, which expressed itself particularly in the way he honored the Sabbath and in his scrupulous incorruptibility.

According to a talmudic *aggadah*, the prophet Elijah used to visit him and instruct him in the *Seder Eliyahu*, but stopped, because of an incident in which Anan unwittingly caused a miscarriage of justice. After Anan fasted and prayed for mercy, Elijah resumed his visits, but Anan was afraid of him. As a result of this fear, Anan would sit in a box when Elijah was teaching him, until the *Seder Eliyahu* was completed. According to the *aggadah*. this explains why the work is divided into two parts – the *Seder Eliyahu Rabbah* ("major" *Seder Eliyahu*), the part composed before this occurrence, when Anan faced Elijah directly; and the *Seder Eliyahu Zuta* ("minor" *Seder Eliyahu*), composed when Anan was sitting in the box (Ket. 105b–106a; see **Tanna de-Vei Eliyahu*).

BIBLIOGRAPHY: Hyman, Toledot, 284–5.

[Zvi Kaplan]

ANAN, SON OF ANAN, high priest of the family of *Anan the son of Seth. Appointed to the office by *Agrippa II in 62 C.E., Anan officiated for three months only. He used the interval between the death of the procurator *Festus and the arrival of his successor *Albinus to convene the Sanhedrin and have several persons condemned to death, including James, brother of Jesus. The people resented Anan's audacity and successfully persuaded Agrippa and Albinus to depose him. Anan was elected to the government constituted after the defeat of Cestius Gallus in the autumn of 66. He played a central role at the beginning of the war against the Romans when he was entrusted with defending the walls of Jerusalem. However, he was not wholeheartedly in favor of the war. Anan tried to hold on to the reigns of government even when his conciliatory policy toward the Romans was no longer popular. When the *Zealots prevailed in Jerusalem, mistreating the pacifists among the local aristocrats and appointing an illegitimate high priest, Anan, with other heads of government, decided to suppress them by force. He convened an assembly of the people and hoped to incite them against the Zealots, whom he condemned for converting the Temple into a fortress and for abusing its ritual purity. Claiming that the Zealots' deeds were worse than those of the Romans, he blamed the people for allowing them to come to power. Many answered his call. Though Anan hesitated to use the Temple precincts as a battleground, his men captured the Temple courtyard where they besieged the Zealots. In this struggle *John of Giscala played an important role. At first he belonged to Anan's camp and tried to mediate between both parties. Finally convinced that Anan was collaborating with Romans, John went over to the Zealots. Upon his suggestion, the Zealots solicited the aid of the Idumeans, whose forces decided the conflict. Anan was a victim of the ensuing wholesale massacre in the city. Josephus once criticized Anan as a willful conceited Sadducee, but later eulogized him by saying that, had he lived, the city would have been saved and peace achieved between the Jews and Romans. Anan is identified by some scholars with the "Wicked Priest" of the Dead Sea Scrolls.

BIBLIOGRAPHY: Jos., Ant., 20:197ff.; Jos., Wars, 2:563, 648, 651; 4:160ff., 314ff., 508; Jos., Life, 38, 39, 44, 60; Schuerer, Gesch, 1 (1904[4]), 581ff., 618ff.; 2 (1907), 273; Graetz, Hist, 6 (1898), 168f. (index).

[Lea Roth]

ANAN BEN DAVID (eighth century), ascetic sage in Babylonia, founder of the sect of Ananites (Heb. עֲנָנִיִּים, *Ananiyyim*; Ar. *ʿAnāniyya*) and regarded by the *Karaites as their founder. A tenth-century Karaite account, related by al-*Kirkisani, places his appearance between 754 and 775. The report states that Anan was "the first to bring to light a great deal of the truth about the scriptural ordinances. He was learned in the lore of the Rabbanites… The Rabbanites tried their utmost to assassinate him, but the Almighty prevented them from doing so." Kirkisani always refers to him as the Exilarch (*ra's al-jālūt*). In the second half of the ninth century there were *Rabbanites who saw Anan as a heresiarch "who said to those who strayed… after him, 'Forsake ye the words of the Mishnah and of the Talmud, and I will compose for you a Talmud of my own'" (attributed to *Natronai Gaon). With various permutations, this tradition persists in the *Sefer ha-Kabbalah* of Abraham *Ibn Daud (1161) which adds that Anan was descended from the Davidic line, but as he showed heretical tendencies he was not named *exilarch. A more detailed version of this story is quoted by the 12th-century Karaite *Elijah b. Abraham who ascribes it to 10th century Rabbanites (probably Saadia). In this version the exilarchate was given to Anan's younger brother. Anan thereupon rallied a group of sectarians who set him up as their own exilarch. This led to his arrest. He was sentenced to death for defying the caliph's confirmation of his brother in the office. A fellow prisoner, identified in another Karaite work as the Muslim jurist-theologian Abū Ḥanīfa (d. 767), founder of the Hanafite school of Muslim jurisprudence, advised him to bribe the officials and to obtain a hearing before the caliph in order to claim that he represented a different faith distinct from that of his brother, and therefore was not guilty of the crime ascribed to him. According to this version, Anan stressed before the caliph that in matters pertaining to calculation of the calendar his method was akin to the Muslim system, namely it was based on observation and not on perpetual calculation. He was thus released. The last account may well be mixed of factual and legendary elements. The only proven historical fact about Anan's life seems to be that he was a learned Rabbanite of aristocratic descent, who for some reason founded a sect of his own. A reliable authority, although of a later period, states that Anan lived in Baghdad. Other facts combine to date the founding of his sect between 762 and 767.

Anan's immediate followers, the Ananites, were never numerous. Not many remained by the mid-tenth century. By the tenth century they had probably developed a modest corpus of legal works written in Judeo-Arabic. Such are quoted by al-Kirkisani. None of them survived. The Ananites steadily decreased in number and were absorbed into the later Karaites. However, Anan's prestige among the Karaites increased until he was acknowledged by them as the founder of the Karaite sect itself. Anan's descendants claimed Davidic lineage. At some time during the tenth century they had been acknowledged by the Karaites as their leaders and accorded the honorific of *nasi* (which in the Middle Ages always indicated Davidic lineage). Individual Karaite scholars often criticized or rejected Anan's views on various matters of law. These somewhat contradictory attitudes arise from the recognition that Anan was the first learned and aristocratic figure to lend his prestige to Jewish groups who had been opposed to the authority of the Babylonian yeshivot. In addition, at some point in late tenth century, his major work, *Sefer ha-Mitzvot* ("Book of Precepts"), came to occupy an important place in Karaite literature. The *Sefer ha-Mitzvot* is a manual of religious law according to Anan's own teaching and his interpretation of the Torah, written in *Aramaic. As such it was a novelty, being an attempt to put to writing a systematic alternative to talmudic law. The portions so far discovered contain concise, if dry, expositions of the law on various subjects, as well as some homiletic sections.

The guiding principles later ascribed to Anan's teaching include rejection of the talmudic tradition, a return to Scripture as the sole source of Divine Law, and repudiation of the authority of the geonic and exilarchic leadership. However, his extant writings demonstrate attempts to adapt the ancient biblical legislation to the changed circumstances of his day. His Rabbanite training ensured that his methods of biblical exegesis, as well as of formulation and interpretation of the law, were much the same as those adopted by the Talmud. But his conclusions were in some cases innovatory, in others he adopted positions ascribed to talmudic sages that had been rejected in the Talmud. His preferred method of deduction was by analogy (Heb. *hekkesh*; Arabic *qiyās*), also frequently applied in Muslim jurisprudence. Anan, however, applied it not only to situations in law, but also to single words or even letters of the biblical text. In line with talmudic exegetical tradition, Anan held that the rules of rhetoric and syntax do not apply to Scripture. If two biblical texts seemingly describe the same situation, but in slightly different words, or employing somewhat varying grammatical constructions, a new and variant rule must be applied to construe the second text.

Anan's procedure often seems to be a deliberate construction of proof, by forced interpretation of Scripture, for an Ananite preformulated rule. His rigorous, ascetic approach moved him to postulate the principle that the strict and prohibitive must always take precedence over the lenient and permissive, wherever both alternatives are equally admissible. Accordingly Anan also championed the *rikkuv* ("restrictive catenary") theory of forbidden marriages (extending the forbidden degrees of marriage), a 70-day fast (from the 13th of Nisan to the 23rd of Sivan evidently involving daytime fasting only, in the manner of the Muslim fast of Ramadan), and prohibition of the practice of medicine as incompatible with faith in the Divine healing power. There is no evidence that Anan insisted on basing the calculation of the calendar on lunar (or other) observation. The reference to such a position in the reports on his secession may be a back-projection of later polemicists, Rabbanites and Karaites. From the surviving sections on liturgy it emerges that Anan saw the synagogue as an imitation of the Temple.

Various earlier and contemporary rigoristic and ascetic trends may have influenced Anan. His teaching indicates the inception of institutions for the separate existence of his sect. Rabbanite writers often accused Anan of leaning toward the doctrines of the *Sadducees, but since the available information is meager and partly contradictory, the extent of Sadducean influence, if any, remains in doubt. The same uncertainty also prevails regarding his probable espousal of religious customs current among certain Jewish groups in the talmudic period. These had been subsequently dropped in favor of those approved by the majority and incorporated in the Talmud. References to some such superseded customs seem to be discernible in the talmudic discussions, and are paralleled in some of Anan's rulings. Certain of Anan's doctrines coincide with those upheld by nearly all other schisms. They presumably represent a long-persisting dissident Jewish tradition, possibly harking back to pre-mishnaic times. An example is the rule that the festival of Shavuot should always fall on a Sunday, and perhaps also the prohibition on having any fire burning on the Sabbath (which had later become a hallmark of Karaites) and the literal interpretation of the *lex talionis* ("an eye for an eye"). It has been suggested that there is some connection between Anan's teaching and that found in the *Dead Sea Scrolls. The picture of Anan as an inflexible ascetic presented by his teaching may be modified to some extent in the light of the maxim ascribed to him, "Search diligently in Scripture, and rely not on my opinion." The earliest attestation of this maxim is found in a commentary by *Japheth ben Eli (late tenth century), where only the first half (in Aramaic) is quoted. It may well be that this half is original, while the second half represents tenth-century Karaite tendencies (notably *Daniel al-Qumisi). While Anan preached engagement in the study of the Torah and its interpretation he considered his interpretation to be definitive. Some modern scholars find parallels between the central position given by Anan to the biblical text, as a source of law and a subject of study, and the attitudes of some Muslim groups ("scripturalists") towards the Koran. Accordingly it is not a coincidence that Anan emerged at his particular period of time.

Later reports that Anan acknowledged the prophetic mission of Jesus and Muhammad and accepted the doctrine of transmigration of souls seem to lack any factual basis. The text of *Sefer ha-Mitzvot le-Anan* was published by A. Harkavy, in: *Studien und Mitteilungen*, 8 (1903; with Hebrew translation, repr. 1970); S. Schechter, *Sectaries*, 2 (1910); Mann, in: *Journal of Jewish Lore and Philosophy*, 1 (1919), 329–53.

BIBLIOGRAPHY: L. Nemoy, *Karaite Anthology* (1952), index (bibliography, 395); idem, in: HUCA, 7 (1930), 328–9, 383–6; idem, in: *Semitic Studies in Memory of Immanuel Loew* (1947), 239–48; Ibn Daud, Tradition, index; Z. Ankori, *Karaites in Byzantium* (1959), index; J.N. Epstein, in: *Tarbiz*, 7 (1935/36), 283–90. **ADD. BIBLIOGRAPHY:** H. Ben-Shammai, in: B. Lewis and F. Niewoehner (eds.), *Religionsgespräche im Mittelalter (Wolfenbütteler Mittelalter-Studien)*, vol. 4 (1992), 11–26; M. Gil, *Palestine during the First Muslim Period (634–1099)*, (1992), index; M. Polliack (ed.), *Karaite Judaism: A Guide to Its History and Literary Sources* (2003), index; Y. Erder, *The Karaite Mourners of Zion and the Qumran Scrolls* (2004), index.

[Leon Nemoy]

ANAN BEN MARINUS HA-KOHEN (first half of 11th century), rabbi and poet. He lived in Siponto in southern Italy. According to Zedekiah b. Abraham *Anav, Anan handed down decisions concerning the order in which people should be called to the reading of the Torah, and ruled that a kohen might be called when there was no Levite, and a Levite when there was no kohen (*Shibbolei ha-Leket ha-Shalem*, ed. S.K. Mirsky (Section 34:233)), and concerning the laws of **shofar* (*Shibbolei ha-Leket*, 34:292).

He is known as the composer of a poem to be recited at the termination of the Sabbath. This was a lyrical appeal to Elijah to come without delay, since the appointed time of the coming of the Messiah, 1,000 years after the destruction of the Temple, had already passed, and the enemy was oppressive.

BIBLIOGRAPHY: Luzzatto, in: *Oẓar Tov*, 2 (1878), 37; Schirmann, Italyah, 68ff.; A.M. Habermann, *Ha-Piyyut* (1968), 33ff.; Zunz, Geseh, 163; Vogelstein-Rieger, 2 (1896), 224, 355; in Idelson, Jewish Liturgy (1930), 115; Davidson, Oẓar, 4 (1933), 460.

[Yonah David]

ANAN BEN SETH (Σεθί), high priest from 6 to 15 C.E. Anan was appointed by *Quirinius, governor of Syria, to succeed *Joezer b. Boethus but was deposed by *Valerius Gratus, procurator of Judea. During his high priesthood, the Samaritans succeeded in penetrating into the Temple during Passover and desecrated it by scattering bones in the porticoes (Zev. 113a; Tosef. Eduy. 3:3). Entrance to the Temple was thereupon forbidden and a strict watch imposed. Many of Anan's family served as high priests, including his five sons: Eleazar, Jonathan, Theophilus, Matthias, and Anan. Joseph Caiaphas, the high priest in the time of Jesus, was his son-in-law. Evidently Anan was an important figure in Jerusalem even after his deposition, since Jesus was first sent to him for interrogation after his arrest. The family of Anan (Bet Ḥanin) is one of the high-priestly families censured in the Talmud (Pes. 57a) for extortionate practices.

BIBLIOGRAPHY: Jos., Ant., 18:26, 29–30, 34; John, 18:13 ff.; Acts, 4:6; Schuerer, Gesch, 2 (1907[4]), 270.

[Lea Roth]

ANANIAS AND HELKIAS, two brothers, sons of *Onias IV, who were generals in the army of Cleopatra III, queen of Egypt (116–110 B.C.E.). They commanded the Jewish military colony at Heliopolis. Their loyalty to Cleopatra III (Josephus' reference to which is based on the testimony of Strabo) in her wars against her son Ptolemy Lathyrus for the throne of Egypt won for them great influence (Jos., Ant., 13:284–7). In these wars Ananias and Helkias were in command of the Egyptian army that advanced into Ereẓ Israel to drive out Ptolemy Lathyrus who had consolidated his position there after defeating Alexander Yannai, the Hasmonean king (103–102 B.C.E.). The growing strength of Lathyrus in Ereẓ Israel posed a threat not only to Alexander Yannai's position but also to Cleopatra's rule of Egypt. Ptolemy Lathyrus was defeated in battle and forced to withdraw from Ereẓ Israel, and while in pursuit of him, Helkias died (*ibid.*, 13:348–51). After her victory over her son, Cleopatra was advised by some of her counselors to occupy the Hasmonean kingdom but Ananias warned her against this, pointing out its injustice, as well as the enmity that an attack upon Alexander Yannai would arouse among the latter's fellow Jews in Egypt, her subjects. Because of Ananias' warning Cleopatra did not harm Alexander Yannai and even made a pact with him (*ibid.*, 13:352–5). Helkias, or perhaps his son, is probably mentioned in an Egyptian inscription of 102 B.C.E. as the *strategos* (commander) of the *nome* (province) of Heliopolis. It is very doubtful whether the account in Justinus (39:4) of a Ptolemaic general who permitted Lathyrus to escape from Egypt refers to Helkias.

BIBLIOGRAPHY: R. Marcus in Jos., Ant., 13:87, n.f. (and literature cited there); Pauly-Wissowa, 2 (1894), 2056 (1); Schuerer, Gesch, 1 (1901[4]), 278; 3 (1909[4]), 132 n.39; Klausner, Bayit Sheni, 3 (1950[2]), 148; Tcherikover, Corpus, 3 (1964), 144–5 n. 1450.

[Uriel Rappaport]

ANANIAS BEN NEDEBEUS (Heb. חֲנַנְיָה בֶּן נְדָבָאִי), high priest at the end of the Second Temple period. Ananias served as high priest for 12 years (47–59 C.E.), longer than any other high priest after the fall of the Hasmonean dynasty, with the exception of Joseph *Caiaphas. He was the second high priest appointed by Herod of Chalcis, succeeding Joseph b. Kimḥit. As a result of the conflict between the Samaritans and the Jews, he was arrested by Quadratus, the procurator of Syria, and sent to Rome to report to Claudius. As the investigation in Rome ended in a victory for the Jews, Ananias probably did not remain long. He rather returned to Judea and to his office at the same time that *Felix was appointed procurator of Judea (52). About 59, Agrippa II appointed *Ishmael b. Phabi II high priest, but Ananias continued to exercise a powerful influence over developments in Judea because of his extraordinary wealth and his firm ties with the Roman administration. He was especially close to the procurator Albinus (62–64), whom he bribed with gifts, as he did the high priest, Joshua b. Damnai. Josephus states that Ananias was highly regarded by the citizens of Jerusalem and was greatly honored by them, a statement consistent with two talmudic passages (Pes. 57a; Ker. 28a). On the other hand, Josephus writes that Ananias set a bad example for other high priests by having his servants take tithes from the granaries by force, thus depriving other priests of their shares. In the period immediately preceding the destruction of the Temple, his great wealth made it possible for him to hire mercenaries who took a leading part in the street battles in Jerusalem. An example of Ananias' influence was the appointment of his son, Eleazar, as captain of the Temple. The *Sicarii considered Ananias one of the major Roman collaborators; they kidnapped Eleazar's secretary, and offered to exchange him for ten Sicarii whom Albinus held imprisoned. Ananias persuaded the procurator to agree. This set a precedent for similar occurrences. At the outset of the revolt, Ananias became a target for the hatred of the extreme elements led by *Menahem b. Judah the Galilean and his home was burnt down together with the palaces of Agrippa II and Berenice. He was subsequently put to death, together with his brother Hezekiah. Ananias was apparently not a member of the oligarchic high-priestly families of the time (Boethus, Ḥanin, Phabi, and Cantheras). He was probably a member of the House of Guryon (or Garon).

BIBLIOGRAPHY: Jos., Ant., 20:103, 131, 179, 205 ff.; Jos., Wars, 2:243, 426, 441; Shab. 1:4; Mekh., ed. by H.S. Horowitz and I.A. Rabin (1960[2]), 229; Schuerer, Gesch, 2 (1907[4]), 272; Derenbourg, Hist, 232 ff.; Graetz, Gesch, 3, pt. 2 (1906[5]), 723 ff.

[Menahem Stern]

ANANIAS OF ADIABENE (early first century C.E.), Jewish merchant who was instrumental in the conversion of *Izates and the royal family of *Adiabene. Izates, son of King Monabaz and Queen Helena of Adiabene, was sent as a youth to Charax Spasinu, capital of the tiny kingdom of Charakene between the mouths of the Tigris and the Euphrates. Izates was converted to Judaism by Ananias, a Jewish merchant who had previously converted the wives of the local ruler. After he became king of Adiabene, Izates learned that his mother had also converted to Judaism; consequently he wished to complete his own conversion by having himself circumcised. However, both his mother and Ananias rejected this idea, the latter on the grounds that "the king could worship God even without being circumcised if indeed he had fully decided to be a devoted adherent of Judaism, for this counted more than circumcision."

BIBLIOGRAPHY: Jos., Ant., 20:34 ff.; Josephus, *Works* (Loeb ed.), 9 (1965), 410–1, 586.

[Isaiah Gafni]

ANANIAS SON OF ZADOK, a prominent Pharisee of the first century. With the outbreak of the Roman war in 66 C.E., the Roman garrison in Jerusalem was forced to retreat to the royal towers of Hippicus, Phasael, and Mariamne. The force was incapable of prolonged resistance and finally offered to surrender. The besiegers agreed, and sent three envoys, among them Ananias, to take the necessary oaths and guarantee fair treatment. The Roman commander Metilius marched his men out, unarmed, only to have them surrounded and massacred to a man. Metilius himself, however, was spared after promising to convert to Judaism. Ananias was also a member of another delegation. After receiving reports from the supporters of *John of Giscala denouncing *Josephus, the Jewish leaders in Jerusalem decided to relieve the latter of his command in Galilee. For this purpose they dispatched four prominent emissaries, including Ananias, with a force of 2,500 men. Josephus, however, succeeded in capturing the deputies, and they were sent back to Jerusalem under armed escort.

BIBLIOGRAPHY: Jos., Wars, 2:451, 628; Jos., Life, 197ff., 290ff., 316, 332; Graetz, Gesch, 3 pt. 2 (1906[5]), 462, 491; Klausner, Bayit Sheni, 5 (1963[5]), 149, 178.

[Isaiah Gafni]

ANANYEV (**Ananiev**), city in Odessa district, Ukraine. Ananyev was founded in 1753. Jews began to settle there in the beginning of the 19th century. In the 1820s the community owned a synagogue and cemetery; it numbered 532 in 1856 and 992 in 1864. A *talmud torah* operated from 1880. Mob attacks in a pogrom that took place on April 27, 1881, destroyed 175 Jewish homes and 14 shops; the poorer Jewish sector in the outskirts suffered most. A second, less damaging pogrom broke out on Oct. 17, 1905. Another pogrom, carried out by Ukrainian soldiers, occurred in February 1919, with many killed. On May 22, the marauding antisemitic Grigoryev gang killed 44 Jews and pillaged much property. In early 1920, in a battle with the Tutyunyuk gang, the Jewish *self-defense unit lost 220 of its 300 fighters.

The Jewish population numbered 3,527 in 1897 (out of a total population of 16,684), 4,810 in 1910 (out of 22,157), and 3,516 in 1926 (out of 18,230). Between the world wars Jews worked in a textile cooperative and in a Jewish *kolkhoz*. Their number dropped to 1,779 by 1939 (total population 5,918). Ananyev was occupied by the Germans on August 7, 1941. Three hundred Jews were murdered on August 28, and later another 600. On September 1, Ananyev was made part of Transnistria under Romanian rule and a ghetto was established for the remaining 300 Jews. In early October they were ordered to set off for *Dubossary but were murdered on the way near the village of Mostovoye. In 1990 there were 30 Jews in Ananyev.

BIBLIOGRAPHY: *Judenpogrome in Russland*, 2 (1909), 134–7; *Yevrei v SSSR*, 4 (1929); PK Romanyah, 398, Ukrainah, s.v.

[Shmuel Spector (2nd ed.)]

ANAPA, Black Sea port and resort, Krasnodar territory, Russia. Jews settled there during the rule of King *Mithridates (first century C.E.). It came under the rule of the *Khazar Kingdom, and subsequently under that of the Turks. When the Russians occupied Anapa in 1828 no Jews were living there. The law of Dec. 15, 1846, allowed only Jewish craftsmen to settle, and in 1892 almost all Jews were banned from the Kuban territory, which included Anapa. There were 19 Jews in the town in 1897. During the German occupation (1942–43), Anapa was almost totally destroyed.

ANASCHEHON (**Anaschichun**), Spanish family which settled in Ereẓ Israel and in Turkey after the expulsion from Spain in 1492. Joseph *Sambari lists Meir Anaschehon among the exiles who settled in Jerusalem and in Safed. He was known to have spent some time in Aleppo in 1525. At the end of the 16th and during the 17th century several scholars of the Anaschehon family lived in Ereẓ Israel. They all wrote books which remained in manuscript and none was ever published. Josiah *Pinto, in his book *Nivḥar mi-Kesef* (Par. 74, p. 145b) speaks of "the perfect scholar, the outstanding *dayyan*" JOSEPH ANASCHEHON who died in 1632. There are manuscripts of the correspondence between Anaschehon and Jonathan Galante at the Jewish Theological Seminary of America (Enelow Collection 462–469). A relative, the kabbalist Meir Anaschehon II, lived in Ereẓ Israel and Egypt at the same period. He was a younger contemporary of Ḥayyim *Vital, knew the latter's students and writings, and apparently moved in the circle of Benjamin ha-Levi and Elisha Vestali. He wrote a copious and important commentary on the *Idra* which Samuel *Vital edited and included in a collection of commentaries by the disciples of his father, Ḥayyim Vital, and of Isaac *Luria. Meir Poppers wrote strictures on that commentary which appear in many manuscripts (e.g., Adler 2254). Meir transcribed a homiletical manuscript on the symbolic *Adam Kadmon* ("Primordial Man," Ms. Parma 93). Among Meir II's colleagues in Jerusalem were Jacob *Ẓemaḥ and Samuel *Garmison. A halakhic responsum addressed to him by the latter is found in *Mishpetei Ẓedek* (Par. 117). JOSEPH II, grandson of Joseph I, grew up in Safed and was educated by his grandfather. In the manuscript of his works he cites many novellae of "my teacher and mentor, Joseph, my grandfather." He also studied with his maternal grandfather, Mordecai ha-Kohen Ashkenazi, whose oral teachings he quotes, as he does the many remarks that he recalls from Josiah Pinto of Damascus. He taught at the yeshivah, and Pinto's son, Daniel, was among his disciples. He lived in Turkey and moved among the greatest rabbis there. In 1675 he served as rabbi in *Tokat, Turkey, where he is also known to have lived in 1684. An extensive work of Joseph is to be found in the library at Columbia University. This is a collection of novellae on the aggadic dicta of the rabbis, on halakhic remarks by the tosafists, and on *Rashi's commentary to the Pentateuch. This work is evidence that he was also a kabbalist. He makes numerous references in it to his work, *Likkutei Shoshannim*. Other manuscripts, not extant but known to have existed because of reference to them in this book, are *Yad Yosef*, *Pe'er Yosef*, and *Rosh Yosef*. The last was apparently a commentary on the Talmud, for Joseph writes "… in the book of novellae which I wrote and which I entitled *Rosh Yosef* … on the tractate *Kiddushin*."

BIBLIOGRAPHY: J.M. Toledano, *Sarid u-Falit* (1945), 46, 52; G. Scholem, in: KS, 22 (1945/46), 307–8; M. Benayahu, *ibid.*, 23 (1946/47), 75–76.

ANATH (Heb. עֲנָת), a major goddess of the Western Semites (Amorites-Canaanites, Arameans) worshiped over a wide area of the Near East (in Mesopotamia, Syria-Ereẓ Israel, Anatolia, and Egypt). The earliest evidence of a cult devoted to Anath comes from the literary remains of the Amorites at *Mari on the Euphrates near the beginning of the second millennium B.C.E.

Cult

The cult of Anath had considerable vogue in Egypt, where it was introduced at least as early as the Hyksos period, since *ʿnt* is attested as the theophorous element in a few Hyksos names. Some rulers of the New Kingdom were apparently devotees of the goddess. An Egyptian magical papyrus relates the sexual assault of Anath by Seth (Baal), who copulated with her in fire and deflowered her with a chisel. Her character is vividly revealed in the mythological texts of *Ugarit from the middle of the second millennium.

Name

Scholarly speculation has been provoked as to whether the goddess' name is a possible clue to her nature. It has been connected with the root *ʿny*, from which the meaning "destiny" or "providence" was deduced. The Hebrew *ʿet* ("time") and Akkadian *ettu* (< *ittu*, "sign," "omen") have also been correlated with the supposed sense of "destiny, purpose, active will." Anath has been presumed to be the personification or hypostatization of the will of Baal, but the Ugaritic texts indicate that she had a strong will of her own. In Arabic the root *ʿanat* is connected with fornication, coercion, belligerency, obstinacy, stubborn zeal, and the like, qualities and activities that comport with the dominant character of the goddess in the Ugaritic myths. The standard name of the goddess in the Ugaritic myths is "Virgin Anath" (*btlt ʿnt*) and she retains this attribute despite copulation with her consort (though the interpretation of Ugaritic texts as describing Anat's sexual activity has been challenged). She is also called "Girl Anath" (*rḥm ʿnt*), or simply "Girlish" (*rḥmy*). She is once called Anath *Itn* (i.e., Leviathan), presumably by reason of her conquest or collaboration with Baal in the defeat of that monster, and once is also called "Anath Destroyer" (*ʿntḥbly*). She is occasionally designated simply "Lady" (*št*).

Mythology

A few highlights of Anath's activities in the myths may be mentioned: she mourns and buries her dead consort, Baal, and avenges his death by pulverizing his slayer Mot ("Death"). She launches a sudden and unexplained assault on humankind, wading hip deep in blood and gore, piling up the heads and hands of her victims and adorning herself with a necklace of heads and a girdle of hands. She ceases the slaughter as abruptly as she had begun, bathes and performs her toilet, and subsequently receives a message from Baal commending peace and inviting her to hasten to him and hear his secret plans for a splendid shrine on his holy mountain. Anath's warlike character may be reflected in the Hebrew *bn ʿnt* arrowheads which indicate the association of the surname *bn ʿnt* with military families. For all her violent ways, however, Anath has occasional gentle moments.

Anath and *Ashtoreth are kept apart in the Ugaritic mythological texts, in which Ashtoreth plays a very minor role. In a text that introduces the gods in order of their rank and mentions the abode of each, however, Anath and Ashtoreth are combined (*ʿnt wʿṯtrt*) and their common abode (*ʾinbb*) is elsewhere attributed to Anath. An Egyptian plaque presents a single nude goddess identified by three names – Qudšu, Ashtoreth, Anath – thus attesting the blending of the three major West Semitic goddesses (*Quadšu;* "Holiness" is a title of *Asherah). Later in Hellenistic-Roman times, Anath and Ashtoreth are probably combined in reverse order in the compound Atargatis. The equation of Anath with Athena is made in a Phoenician-Greek bilingual inscription of the fourth century B.C.E. from Cyprus, in which the Semitic goddess is called "Anath Strength of Life" (*ʿnt mʿz ḥym*), while the Greek equivalent is *Athena Soteira Nike*. Anath/Asthoreth/Ishtar is thus the prototype of Athena and the Winged Victory. A number of beautiful and/or armed and/or winged goddesses appear in ancient Oriental iconography, and some of them doubtlessly represent Anath.

In Israel

Although not explicitly mentioned as a goddess in the Bible, the name Anath is preserved in the place names *Beth-Anath and *Anathoth, and in the personal name *Shamgar the son of Anath. Perhaps due to her martial qualities, the cult of Anath apparently enjoyed a renewed vogue in the fifth century B.C.E. in the Jewish military colony at Elephantine, Egypt, where oaths were sworn on the names *ʿnt*-Beth-El and *ʿnt*-YHWH. Some savants sought to eliminate the association of the God of Israel with a goddess – and especially one of such unsavory repute – by construing the element *ʿnt* as a common noun meaning "providence" or "abode" rather than the name of the goddess, but their efforts have not been wholly convincing.

BIBLIOGRAPHY: W.F. Albright, *Yahweh and the Gods of Canaan* (1968), 105ff., 112ff.; idem, in: AJSL, 41 (1925), 73–101, 283–5; 43 (1927), 223–6; Barrelet, in: *Syria*, 32 (1955), 222–60; U. Cassuto, *The Goddess Anath* (1970); A.W. Eaton, "The Goddess Anat…" (dissertation, Yale, 1964); A.S. Kapelrud, *The Violent Goddess* (1969); Meyer, in: ZDMG, 31 (1877), 716–41; Pope, in: H.W. Haussig (ed.), *Woerterbuch der Mythologie*, 1 (1965), 235–41; S.E. Loewenstamm and S. Ahituv, in: EM, s.v.; R. Stadelmann, *Syrisch-palaestinensische Gottheiten in Aegypten* (1967), 88ff.; Pritchard, Texts, 129ff. **ADD. BIBLIOGRAPHY:** M. Heltzer, in: *Al-Haperek* (1994), 1–3; P. Day, in: DDD, 336–43 (with extensive bibliography).

[Marvin H. Pope]

ANATHOTH (Heb. עֲנָתוֹת, עֲנָתֹת).
1. Levitical city in the territory of *Benjamin (Josh. 21:18; I Chron. 6:45; 7:8; Jer. 1:1; Neh. 11:32). It was the birthplace of two of David's "mighty men" (II Sam. 23:27; I Chron. 11:28; 12:3). *Abiathar, one of David's two "priests to the king," owned an estate there, to which he was subsequently banished by Solomon (I Kings 2:26). *Jeremiah was also "of the priests that were in Anathoth" and probably moved to Jerusalem only when his townsmen became dangerously hostile to him (Jer. 11:21). During the siege of Jerusalem by Nebuchadnezzar in 588–87 B.C.E., he purchased land in Anathoth from his uncle in order to preserve the family patrimony (cf. Lev. 25:25), thus demonstrating his faith in the eventual return of the Judeans to their land (Jer. 32:7ff.). Among the Jews who took advantage of *Cyrus' permission to settle in the province of Judah were 128 "men of Anathoth" (Ezra 2:23; Neh. 7:27). The location of Anathoth is mentioned in Isaiah (10:30) along with Gallim and Laish as being in the vicinity of Jerusalem. Josephus states (Ant. 10:144) that it was 20 *stadia* (2½ mi.) from Jerusalem. According to Eusebius (Onom. 26:27), it was 3 mi. (4.8 km.) north of Jerusalem. The name is preserved in the village of ʿAnt, 2½ mi. (4 km.) north of Jerusalem. Ancient remains have been discovered on Ra's al-Ḥarrba, a hill southwest of ʿAnt. In 1968 ʿAnt had 1,260 Arab inhabitants, while in 2003 its population was 9,067. Its economy was based on the cultivation of olives, vineyards, field crops, and sheep breeding.

2. Settlement located in the Judean Hills, east of Mount Scopus. A group of Jews wishing to set up a secular settlement in the desert founded it in 1982. The population included people of various age groups, native Israelis as well as newcomers. Most worked in nearby Jerusalem. In 2004 the population of Anathoth included about 160 families.

BIBLIOGRAPHY: G.A. Smith, *Historical Geography of the Holy Land* (1931[25]), 314; Neubauer, Géogr, 154; Alt, in: PJB, 22 (1926), 23–24; Bergman (Biran), in: BASOR, 62 (1936), 22ff.; idem, in: BJPES, 4 (1936/37), 13ff.; N. Ha-Reuveni, *Or Ḥadash* (1950), 8–26; Abel, Geog, 2 (1938), 243–4. **WEBSITE:** www.anatot.co.il.

[Michael Avi-Yonah / Shaked Gilboa (2nd ed.)]

ANATOLI, JACOB BEN ABBA MARI BEN SAMSON (13th century), physician, homilist, and translator. He married a daughter of Samuel ibn *Tibbon. Samuel taught him mathematics. At the suggestion of friends in Narbonne and Béziers, Anatoli began translating Arabic works on astronomy and logic into Hebrew. However, before completing them, he left France for Naples where he is mentioned in 1231. There Emperor Frederick II employed him as a physician and enabled him to devote himself to scholarly work. In Naples Anatoli became a close associate of another favorite of the emperor, the learned Michael Scot, who had translated works by Aristotle and Averroes from Arabic into Latin. It is doubtful that Anatoli assisted Scot in his translations, as some scholars maintain. Anatoli translated the following works: (1) Averroes' *Intermediate Commentary* on the first five books of Aristotle's *Logic*. The first three books were translated into Latin by Jacob Mantino from Anatoli's Hebrew translation and printed, together with other works by Averroes, in the editions published between 1550 and 1553; (2) the *Almagest* of Ptolemy; (3) the astronomical work of al-Farghānī, its full title in later manuscripts being *The Elements of Astronomy*. This book was translated by Anatoli from a Latin version but was corrected on the basis of the original Arabic text. Specimens of this translation were published by Campani (RSO, 3 (1910), 205–52); (4) the *Compendium of the Almagest* by Averroes. This translation was begun in Naples in 1231. According to a note in the Vienna manuscript no. 195, 1, the work was completed in Padua, and it is not clear whether this was by Anatoli or by someone else. Other translations have been erroneously ascribed to Anatoli.

Anatoli was also an active preacher. In his discourses, he employed allegorical and philosophical exegesis. Generally, he followed Maimonides, and his sharp public rebuke of the latter's detractors made him many enemies. This was, probably, one of the reasons which caused him to leave France. In Naples he also encountered opposition. Anatoli collected his homilies in a book which he called *Malmad ha-Talmidim* (Lyck, 1866, "A Goad to Scholars"), which follows the order of the weekly scriptural portions. The work argues that observance of the commandments must rest on knowledge of the reasons underlying them and on an adequate understanding of the biblical texts as well as of the prayers. The author sharply castigates the superficial reader of the Bible and endeavors both to demonstrate the ethical value of the biblical stories and to disclose the hidden philosophical truth which, in his opinion, is inherent in the language of Scripture. Yet his sermons also contain practical admonitions. For example, he reproaches those who, like the non-Jews, permit their daughters to sing love songs, and those who indulge in incantations to obtain answers to various questions in dreams. He was an enemy of superstition and of outward piety. He quotes thinkers such as Plato, Aristotle, and Averroes. He also refers to the Vulgate and cites the biblical interpretations of such contemporaries as Michael Scot and Emperor Frederick II.

Anatoli contributed greatly to the dissemination of philosophical knowledge among the Jews of Italy. The *Malmad ha-Talmidim* was widely read in the 13th century; parts of it are quoted almost verbatim in the works of Zerahiah b. Isaac Gracian and *Immanuel of Rome. It was also well-known beyond Italy. When Solomon b. Abraham *Adret issued his famous ban against philosophy and philosophers, he named *Malmad ha-Talmidim* as a dangerous work which should be proscribed. Some scholars also attribute *Ruʾaḥ Ḥen*, an introduction to Maimonides' *Guide*, to Anatoli. However, according to one manuscript, the author was Anatoli's son, Anatolio, also a philosopher and disciple of Maimonides. Anatolio was the teacher of R. Moses b. Solomon of Salerno, the commentator on the *Guide*. R. Moses often mentions Anatolio in his commentary. One manuscript of *Ruʾaḥ Ḥen* was transcribed by a grandson of Anatoli, who refers to himself as "Jacob b. Samson b. Anatoli b. Jacob, author of *Malmad ha-Talmidim*."

BIBLIOGRAPHY: C. Roth, *Jews in the Renaissance* (1959), 67–80; I. Bettan, in: HUCA, 11 (1936), 391, 424; Steinschneider, Cat Bod, 1180 and add.; Steinschneider, *Uebersetzungen*, index; Munk, Mélanges, 145, 488; A. Neubauer and E. Renan, *Les rabbins francais* (1887), 580–9; J.L.A. Huillard-Bréholles, *Historia Diplomatica Friderici Secundi*, 1 (1852), DXXVI (introd.); Perles, *R. Salomo b. Abraham b. Adereth* (1863), 13–15, 67–70 (German section), 56–61 (Hebrew section); S. Assaf, *Mekorot le-Toledot ha-Ḥinnukh be-Yisrael*, 2 (1931), 44–45.

[Umberto (Moses David) Cassuto]

ANATOLI BEN JOSEPH (late 12th and early 13th century), *dayyan* at Alexandria. Apparently from Lunel in Languedoc, he was one of the European scholars who settled in Alexandria in the days of *Maimonides. Toward the end of his life he lived in Fostat (now Cairo). He was apparently the uncle of *Abraham b. Nathan ha-Yarḥi, author of *Ha-Manhig* (ed. Warsaw, (1885), 90b, no. 156). Anatoli was widely renowned as a halakhist, communities from various countries turning to him with halakhic problems and requesting his assistance in different matters. When, on one occasion, the Jews of Syracuse submitted a problem to him, he was unwilling to answer himself and asked Maimonides to decide the issue. Maimonides' reply shows the high esteem in which he held Anatoli (*Responsa*, ed. by J. Blau, 2 (1960), 620–3). Anatoli's *Iggeret Mehallelim* ("The Epistle of Those who Praise"), addressed to Maimonides, expresses his great desire for knowledge and to be in close contact with him (*Ḥemdah Genuzah*, ed. Z.H. Edelman, 1856, 1, 23a–24a). He also corresponded on halakhic subjects with Maimonides' son Abraham who addressed him as "the illustrious *dayyan*, our teacher and master, the eminent Anatoli" (*Responsa*, ed. by A. Freimann (1937), 161–72). Several *piyyutim* and *seliḥot* are ascribed to him and he also wrote secular poems, including wine songs (see Anatoli's *Mikhtamim al ha-Yayin*, ed. A.M. Habermann, 1940). His *Diwan* is extant in manuscript in the Firkovitch Collection in Leningrad.

BIBLIOGRAPHY: Mann, Egypt, 1 (1920), 247ff.; 2 (1922), 324ff.; Mann, Texts, 1 (1931), 412–5; B.Z. Halper, in: *Ha-Tekufah* (1923), 209; J. Braslavi, in: *Eretz Israel*, 4 (1956), 156–8.

[Yehoshua Horowitz]

ANATOMY. There is no systematic account of the anatomy of the human body in the Bible, although abundant use is made there of anatomical facts, metaphors, and expressions. Biblical anatomy is factual, empirical in the good sense of the word, and based on correct observation. Talmudic anatomy is inestimably richer; it is not free from fanciful distortions, but it reaches further and supplants the Greek theory of the "humors" with a rational explanation of the normal and pathological structure of the body. The details are sometimes astonishing in their accuracy, as in the description of the small cartilage rings in the structure of the trachea, discovered by Western anatomists only in the 18th century. At the same time, talmudic anatomy is deficient by omission, apparently because the subject was not studied systematically but only incidentally as far as it was necessary for the solving of halakhic problems. Side by side with fanciful notions, there are to be found in the Talmud the beginnings of a scientific method using postmortem examination and dissection of the bodies of animals. Like Greek anatomy, talmudic anatomy shows lack of precision in terminology, which is sometimes expressed through analogy and figures of speech. Graphic illustration is also lacking, since drawing was introduced in the study of anatomy only during the period approaching the Renaissance.

As in all ancient anatomical works, numerous terms are cited in the Bible for the bones: the lower part of the spinal column is called *aẓeh* (Lev. 3:9); the upper part of the pelvis *kesalim*; the loins are given a plural (*ibid.* 3:4), in accordance with their dual structure; the upper (cervical) part of the spinal column is described as *mafreket* (I Sam. 4:18) with its anatomical location, explaining the sudden death resulting from its fracture. Joints mentioned are the *berekh* ("knee"); *karsol* ("ankle," "malleolus"; Ps. 18:37; II Sam. 22:37); the term *kaf ha-yarekh* ("the hollow of the thigh") and its topographical connection with the *gid ha-nasheh* ("sinew of the thigh"; Gen. 32:33) have not been sufficiently defined. The term thigh entered Vesalius' *Tabulae Anatomicae* (Table 5), where it is labeled as the *yarekh*, femur, and also *paḥad ha-yarekh* (Table 6, according to Job 40:17). Even in Vesalius' time it was felt that the biblical word *yarekh* was used in various meanings and was not altogether clear.

The Bible makes frequent mention of internal organs of the body such as the pharynx (*lo'a*), the gullet (*garon*), the heart (*lev*), the liver (*kaved*) with the gallbladder (*marah*), the womb (*reḥem*), the stomach (*kevah*), the entrails (*me'ayim*), and the kidneys (*kelayot*). The *yoteret ha-kaved* or *ha-yoteret al ha-kaved* (in connection with the liver) is difficult to identify (Lev. 3:4), although the reference is probably to the mesentery, called by Tobias *Cohn the Physician "the covering membrane." The *gidim* ("sinews") in the Bible, as in Greek anatomy, denote both nerves and ligaments and sometimes even vessels. The *gid ha-nasheh* ("nerve of the thigh") is usually identified with the ischiadic nerve. The muscles are recognized as the parts furnishing power and movement: "his strength is in the muscles of his belly" (Job 40:16).

Talmudic scholars were much occupied with the regulations concerning ritually unclean meat, with physical disfigurement that disqualified a man for the priesthood, and with rules concerning the menstruous woman, defilement, and the like. This accounts for the anatomical knowledge so widespread among talmudists. The dissection of animal carcasses to ascertain their ritual fitness revealed important facts and prevented the development of fantastic notions. The Talmud even assumes the possibility of the investigation of the human body for forensic purposes (Ḥul. 11a). In *Bekhorot* 45a, Samuel relates that "the disciples of R. Ishmael boiled the corpse of a prostitute who had been condemned by the king to be burned; upon examination, they found that she had 252 [bones]." This investigation was carried out in order to ascertain the number of bones in the human body, since the remains of corpses defile an abode only if they constitute more than half the skeleton, i.e., most of the bones. The sages carried out the examinations themselves or relied on the testimony of a qualified physician (cf. Tosef. Oho. 4:2; Naz. 52a, "Todos the physician entered and all the physicians with him").

The Skeleton

The enumeration of 248 (רמ״ח) members (bones) in the human body is famous in rabbinic tradition (Oho. 1:8). This number does not correspond to the number of bones in the body of an adult, which amounts only to 200. From the number counted by Ishmael's pupils it may be inferred that the body they examined was that of a girl of 17. Supporting this explanation is the figure "six [members] of the key of the heart," i.e., the breastbone (sternum), of which there is only a single unit in an adult but which contains six points of ossification. The term "key of the heart" is to be explained by the inclusion of the two superior ribs in the morphological description of the breastbone: these two superior ribs are shorter and rounder, and their junction with the breastbone actually resembles a key. Accordingly, the rabbis of the Mishnah enumerate only 11 ribs instead of 12, the upper being already included in the "key of the heart." The figure 248 for the number of bones in the body also occurs in the writings of Abu-l-Qasim, the famous surgeon of the tenth century. It would seem that in this detail the Arabs were influenced by the Talmud rather than by the Greeks, since Hippocrates cites figures which are widely inaccurate (101, including the nails), while Galen gives no figure at all. The nomenclature of the bones in the Talmud is precise in its anatomical differentiation. The Mishnah distinguishes bet ween the foot (*pissat ha-regel*), the leg (*shok*), and the thigh or thighbone (*yarekh, kulit*). Corresponding to these are three joints by which the bones are joined to each other: the ankle (*karsol*), the knee joint (*arkuvah*), and the hip joint (*katlit*). Besides these precise anatomical details, mention is also made of the legendary bone known as the *luz* (the medieval *os resurrectionis*) said to be situated at the bottom of the spinal column. According to the legend, it could not be dissolved in water or burned by fire, "and from it man will blossom forth at the resurrection" (Eccles. R. 12:5, no. 1; Gen. R. 28:3).

The Digestive Organs

A remarkable passage is that which compares the salivary glands to springs of water and refers to them as "the conduit (*ammat ha-mayim*) that passes beneath the tongue" (Lev. R. 16:4). This is most interesting in view of the fact that the ducts of the salivary glands were not described with precision in scientific literature until the 16th and 17th centuries. The tongue (*lashon*) is described as enclosed by two walls – the jawbone (*leset*) and the flesh of the cheek (*leḥi*; Ar. 15b). The topography of the windpipe (*kaneh*) and the esophagus (*veshet*) is described correctly ("lest the food enter the windpipe before it reaches the esophagus" – Ta'an. 5b; Pes. 108a). In the esophagus two membranes were accurately distinguished: the outer or red muscular membrane, and the inner or white mucous one (Ḥul. 43a). Many structural details of the maw of the ruminants were also known to talmudists (Ḥul. 3:1). The digestive tract of the human being is described in a pseudo-scientific manner: "Ten organs minister to the body in the following phases of food absorption: from the mouth to the esophagus; from there to the first stomach where the food is ground; from there to the lower digestive tract of the maw; from there to the stomach; from there to the small intestine; from there to the *colon ascendens*; from there to the *colon transversum*; from there to the *colon descendens*; from there to the anus, and thence outward." This defective account, which is to be found in several midrashic versions (Lev R. 3:4; Eccles. R. 7:19, no. 3; et al.), is patently influenced by findings in animals. The liver was regarded as one of the ruling parts of the human body (Zohar, IV, 153a), the other two being the brain and the heart. The *tarpesh* above the liver, according to Maimonides, designates the diaphragm. The *ḥaẓẓar ha-kaved* ("courtyard of the liver"; Yoma 8:6) according to Preuss, is the part known as the *lobus caudatus* [?]. The *eẓba ha-kaved* ("finger of the liver"; Tam. 4:3) is identified by J.L. Katzenelsohn as the pancreas, although that structure was unknown in ancient anatomy as a special organ. The spleen is described in its various parts (Ḥul. 93a), its convex side being called *dad ha-teḥol* ("nipple of the spleen"). The membrane and the blood vessels of the *hilus lienalis* are also mentioned. The removal of the spleen by surgery is referred to in the Talmud (Sanh. 21b).

The Respiratory Organs

The upper part of the windpipe is called the *gargeret* (Ḥul. 3:1); the windpipe is composed of rings (*ḥulyot*), and sub-rings are also referred to, i.e., the ligaments joining the cartilage rings. There are descriptions of the ring cartilage called "the large ring," of the thyroid cartilage, called the *kova* ("helmet") together with its protruding part, *ḥud ha-kova* ("the point of the helmet"), an d of its lower parts, *shippu'ei kova* ("the slopes of the helmet"). Identification was also made of the two small cartilages called *ḥitin* ("protuberances") at the end of the large ring. (These cartilages were not discovered in the West before Santorini in the 18th century.) The talmudists also correctly recognized the existence of three lobes in the right lung and two in the left. (Hippocrates enumerated three on each side.) They also described the serous membranes of the lung and of the bronchial tubes.

The Heart

The Talmud contains few details on the anatomy of the heart, since a wound in the heart generally caused the death of the animal before slaughtering. The position of the heart is given as on the left side of the body (Men. 36b), in contrast to Galen's statement that it was in the exact center of the chest. The heart is divided into chambers (Ḥul. 45b), but there is no trace of Aristotle's erroneous view, supported by Avicenna, of the existence of three chambers in the heart. The aorta is mentioned under the name of *keneh ha-lev* ("pipe of the heart") in *Ḥullin* 45b, and Maimonides adds *mizrak gadol* ("the aorta is the great fountain"). The two auricles are mentioned in *Tikkunei Zohar* (69): "There are two houses (*battim*) and two ears (*udenin*) in the heart."

The Genital Organs

IN THE MALE. The special terms for the *membrum virile* are *eiver* (BM 84a), *ezba* (Pes. 112b), *gid, ammah* (Shab. 108b), *shammash* (Nid. 60b), etc. The term *atarah* ("crown") designating the part projecting behind the glans of the penis passed to Western anatomy as *corona glandis.* The (erroneous) view that "there are two ducts in the male, one to emit urine and the other semen, separated by a thin tissue" (Bek. 44b) was widely held in the Middle Ages, also among the Arabs, and was corrected only in the 16th century by Vesalius. The rabbis described the two membranes of the testicles (Ḥul. 45a) and the *vas deferens* (*ḥutei beiẓah*; Yev. 75b) and knew of the connection between erection of the penis (*kishui*) and the spinal cord, where disease prevents cohabitation.

IN THE FEMALE. Because of their attention to regulations concerning the menstruous woman, the talmudic scholars treated the female genitalia much more extensively. The language they used (for reasons of propriety) to designate them frequently causes great difficulty in understanding the anatomical details referred to. The Mishnah (Nid. 2:5) lists the chamber (*ḥeder*), antechamber (*perozedor*), upper chamber (*aliyyah*), and fallopian tube (*adnexa*). "The blood of the chamber defiles (the blood of the upper does not); that found in the antechamber defiles on account of uncertainty, since it is strongly probable that it comes from the source (uterus)." The *Gemara* (Nid. 17b) explains: "The chamber is within and the antechamber without, and the upper chamber is built over both and there is an open passage (*lul*) between the upper chamber and the antechamber; consequently, from the *lul* inward the blood in case of doubt (*sefeko*) is defiling; from the *lul* outward, it is in a state of purity." Ever since modern medical historiography came into existence, scholars have struggled to explain these *halakhot.* Abraham Hartog Israels identifies the "upper chamber" with the fallopian tube; Rosenbaum (see bibl.) identifies it with the *adnexa uteri* and the broad ligaments. Leibowitz' identification is that the "chamber" is the womb; the "antechamber" is the part nearest the cervix. But Preuss holds that the "antechamber" is the exterior portion of the female genitalia (*vulva*); the "upper chamber" is the vagina, which in present day Hebrew is called *nartik.* This conjecture is irreconcilable with the talmudic passage as a whole, since the *vulva* everywhere in the Talmud is called *bet ha-toref, bet ha-setarim, bet ha-ḥizon* (exterior chamber; hidden chamber; outer chamber), which also includes the *labia.* Katzenelson would identify the parts of the "antechamber" with the *septum vesico-vaginale* and the *septum recto-vaginale.* Nor is it at all clear what is meant by the term *lul*; it is perhaps to be identified with the cavity in the upper vagina: "from the *lul* inward" denotes the upper parts near the cervix; "from the *lul* outward," the lower parts of the vagina. In the anatomy of the female genitalia there is a place called in the Jerusalem Talmud *bein ha-shinnayim* ("between the teeth") or *bet ha-shinnayim* ("abode of the teeth"), which Rosenbaum identifies as the *collum*; Rashi says "within the womb are fleshy protuberances like teeth."

Other Organs

The Talmud does not deal much with the normal anatomy of the kidneys, but gives numerous accounts of kidney diseases. It contains descriptions of the membranes of the kidney, and refers to *hilus renalis* as *ḥariẓ* (Ḥul. 55b). It describes the outer and inner membranes (meninges) of the brain and recognizes the existence of motor centers in the spinal column. The Talmud records examinations of the spinal cord and of injuries to its membranes and marrow (Ḥul. 45b); it describes various kinds of morbid changes in the tissue and important details in its pathology such as softening (*hamrakhah*), dissolution (*hamsasah*), and softening (*hitmazmezut*) of the marrow; and mentions the fontanel: "the place where an infant's brain is soft" (*rofes*; Men. 37a). It recognized two hemispheres of the cerebellum over the large aperture at the base of the cranium "like two beans (*polim*) lying at the aperture of the cranium" (Hul. 45a–b). These are also described by R. Jeremiah in the case of a fowl: "He examined a fowl and found objects resembling two beans placed at the aperture of the cranium" – a fine example of comparative anatomy.

Middle Ages

In the Middle Ages and the Renaissance period, the Jewish physicians shared the anatomical opinions of their neighbors. Vesalius was, however, assisted in his work of the compilation of his Anatomical Tables in the 16th century by the Jew Lazarus (Lazaro) de *Frigeis. The reluctance of Jews to submit bodies for dissection led to complications and ill-feeling in the universities (e.g., at *Padua in the 17th–18th centuries; Eastern Europe in the 20th). The most outstanding Jewish physician of the Renaissance was *Amatus Lusitanus, who in the 16th century participated in the teaching of anatomy at the university at Ferrara. He first described the valves of the veins, exemplified on the azygos vein. Lusitanus identified these valves through opening 12 bodies, although he did not show their connection with the circulation of the blood.

Modern

Outstanding in the modern study of anatomy was Friedrich Gustav Jacob *Henle (1809–1885) who did important research on the skin, the intestinal tract, and the kidneys. Another important figure was Benedict *Stilling (1810–1879) who did pioneer research on the spinal cord.

BIBLIOGRAPHY: M. Perlmann, *Midrash Refu'ah* (1926); J.L. Katzenelson, *Ha-Talmud ve-Ḥokhmat ha-Refu'ah* (1928); A.H. Israels, *Dissertatio historico-medica exhibens collectanea ex Talmude Babylonico* (1845); R.J. Wunderbar, *Biblisch-talmudische Medicin*, 2 vols. (1850–60); J.L. Katznelson, *Die normale und pathologische Anatomie des Talmuds* (1896); E. Rosenbaum, *L'anatomie et la physiologie des organes génitaux de la femme* (1901); J. Preuss, *Biblisch-talmudische Medizin* (1911).

[Joshua O. Leibowitz]

ANAU (**Anav**; Heb. מן הענוים), ancient Italian family. Most of its members lived in Rome, although some moved to other towns in Italy. According to family tradition, the Anaus were descended from one of four aristocratic families of Jerusalem whom Titus brought from Jerusalem to Rome after the destruction of the Temple. It is the first Jewish family living in Rome to be known by a surname, which is found also in the Italian forms Delli Mansi, Delli Piatelli, or Umano. Branches of the Anau family are the ancient Roman Bozecco family, and the Min ha-Keneset (מן הכנסת) or Mi-Bet El (מבית אל; De Synagoga) families. The well-known Tuscan families of Da Pisa, Da San Miniato, and Da Tivoli who engaged in loan banking toward the end of the 14th century were also offshoots of the Anau family. The accompanying genealogical chart indicates the main ramifications of the family and its most distinguished members between the 9th and 14th centuries.

Especially noteworthy was JEHIEL B. ABRAHAM (d. 1070), head of the yeshivah of Rome and liturgical poet. The most important of his sons, *NATHAN B. JEHIEL, was author of the *Arukh*. Jehiel's other two sons were DANIEL BEN JEHIEL (d. before 1101), teacher in the yeshivah of Rome, liturgical poet, and commentator on the Mishnah, and ABRAHAM BEN JEHIEL, teacher in the yeshivah of Rome. He founded a synagogue in Rome in 1101 with his brother Nathan. DANIEL (12th century), rabbi, is mentioned by *Benjamin of Tudela (c. 1159) as a leader of the Jewish community of Rome. JEHIEL, a nephew or grandson of Nathan B. Jehiel, is described by Benjamin of Tudela as a leader of the community and major domo of Pope Alexander III. BENJAMIN and ABRAHAM BEN JEHIEL (beginning of the 13th century) were both physicians and talmudists. JUDAH B. BENJAMIN *ANAV (d. after 1280) was a talmudist and liturgical poet. One of the most eminent members of the family was BENJAMIN B. ABRAHAM *ANAV (mid-13th century), scholar and poet, one of the most versatile scholars of his day. MOSES BEN ABRAHAM, liturgical poet, wrote two *seliḥot* expressing his consternation at the condemnation of the Talmud (1240). His younger brother ZEDEKIAH B. ABRAHAM *ANAV (1225–1297), a noted talmudist, was author of the halakhic compendium, *Shibbolei ha-Leket*. JEHIEL B. JEKUTHIEL *ANAV (second half of the 13th century), liturgical poet, ethical writer, and copyist, was author of the popular ethical work *Beit Middot* (later published as *Ma'alot ha-Middot).* Significant members of the family in later generations included ABRAHAM BEN JACOB ANAV (18th century), poet and rabbi in Rome, and PHINEHAS ḤAI *ANAU (known as Felice Umano; 1693–1768), rabbi in Ferrara. SALVATORE was active in the Italian Risorgimento and a member of the provisional government at Ferrara in 1848 and a year later in Rome.

BIBLIOGRAPHY: Milano, Italia, index; Roth, Italy, index; Vogelstein-Rieger, 1 (1896), index.

[Attilio Milano]

ANAU (Piattelli), PHINEHAS ḤAI BEN MENAHEM (1693–1768), rabbi in Ferrara. A member of the *Anau family, he was also known as Felice Umano. He was a pupil at the yeshivah of Isaac *Lampronti, and brother-in-law of Jacob Daniel *Olmo. An extremely fierce dispute among the rabbis in Ferrara was sparked off in 1715 when Isaac Lampronti published in Venice a periodical containing the halakhic rulings of his pupils. The second number, entitled *Tosefet Bik-*

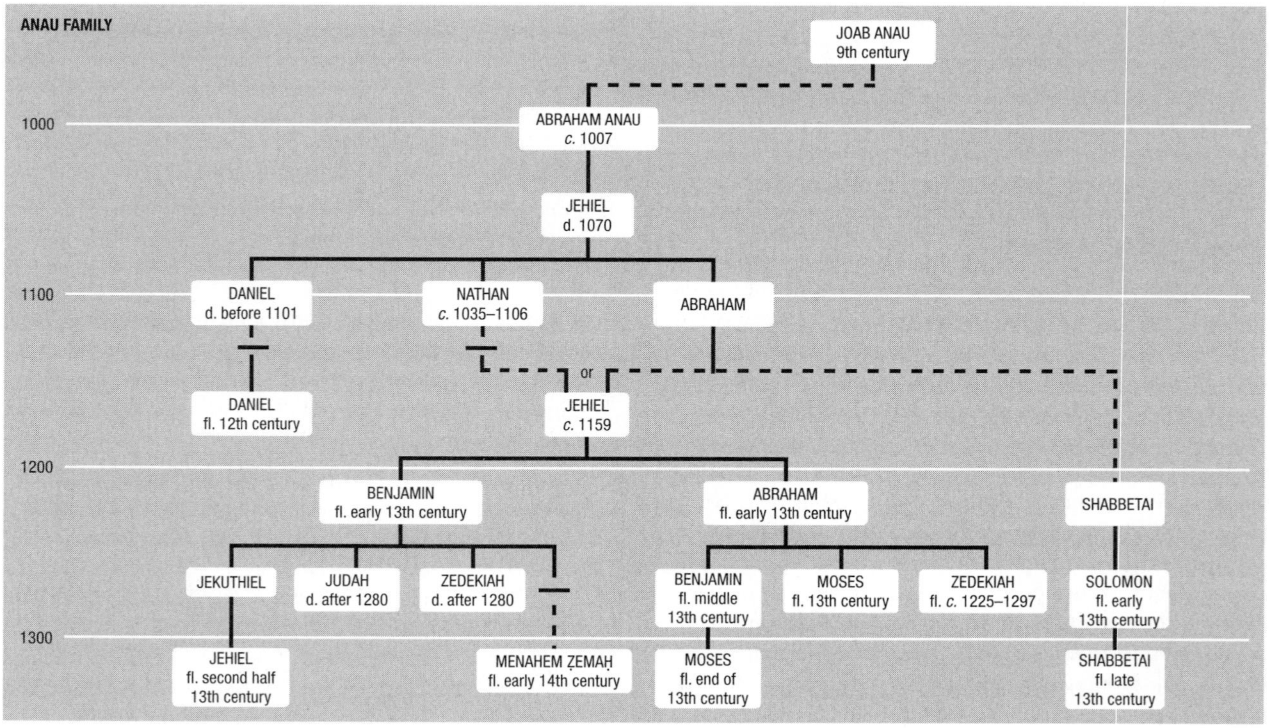

kurei Kazir, included a ruling by Anau deciding in favor of the Ashkenazi custom of stressing the words of the Priestly Blessing on the last syllable and against the view of Nehemiah ha-Kohen and his followers who wished to stress the words on the penultimate syllable. Nehemiah regarded this ruling as a personal insult and complained about Anau to Mordecai Zahalon. The latter, who refused to recognize Isaac Lampronti as chief rabbi of Ferrara, came to the defense of Nehemiah in his work *Meziz u-Meliz* (Venice, 1715) which deplored the insult to Nehemiah and denigrated all those rabbis, including Lampronti, who supported Phinehas Ḥai Anau's ruling. Anau wrote *Givat Pinḥas*, a collection of responsa which has remained in manuscript. Some of his responsa were published in the book *Paḥad Yizḥak* of Isaac Lampronti.

BIBLIOGRAPHY: I.B. Ha-Levi, in: *Ha-Maggid*, 16 (1872), 519–20; B. Cohen, in: *Sefer ha-Yovel li-Khevod... A. Marx* (1943), 55; I. Sonne, in: *Horeb*, 6 (1951), 80, 92; Yaari, Sheluḥei, index; S. Simonsohn, *Toledot ha-Yehudim be-Dukkasut Mantovah*, 1 (1962), 332–4; Milano, Italia; Vogelstein-Rieger, 1 (1896), index. **ADD. BIBLIOGRAPHY:** H.A. Sosland, *A Guide for Preachers on Composing and Delivering Sermons* (1987), 65.

[Abraham David]

ANAV, BENJAMIN BEN ABRAHAM (c. 1215–c. 1295), Italian scholar and poet. Anav's teachers included the poet Meir b. Moses of Rome, and Joab, Daniel, and Isaac of Camerino. His main interest was in *halakhah*, but he had a thorough knowledge of mathematics and astronomy, and was among the most esteemed liturgical poets of his age. The bulk of his poetry, which he began writing in 1239, is still in manuscript. The part that has been published reveals him as a poet sensitive to the events of his time and to the suffering of his people, which he mourns in his many *seliḥot*. The themes of his poetry are historical. Thus, he wrote *kinot* when the apostate Nicholas *Donin made his onslaught on the Talmud (1239); when the Talmud was burned in Italy (1244); when the scrolls of the Torah were torn and the Jews compelled to wear the *badge of shame on their clothing (1257); and when the Jewish cemetery in Rome was desecrated (1267). Many of his *kinot* and *seliḥot* were included in the *maḥzor* of the Italian rite.

His works include *Massa Gei Ḥizzayon* – a satire in sprightly rhymed prose on the arrogance of the wealthy and noble which reflects the life of the affluent Jewish families in his city, Rome (Riva di Trento, 1560; repr. 1860, 1967); *Perush Alfabetin* ("Alphabetical Commentary"), on the Aramaic *piyutim* for the Feast of Weeks (**Akdamut*) – the commentary reveals the poet's knowledge of Italian, Latin, Greek, and Arabic; *Sefer Yedidut* – a book of legal decisions, which has been lost; *Sha'arei Ez Ḥayyim* – a lyrical composition on morals and good character, in 63 stanzas (Prague, 1598; and in *Kobez al Jad* (1884), 71–74; the poem was also included in Moses b. Jekuthiel de Rossi's *Sefer ha-Tadir*); notes on *Rashi's commentary to the Torah; rules on making a calendar; responsa to R. Avigdor b. Elijah Ha-Kohen: a prayer book, which included laws of ritual slaughter, and which has been lost; *Sod* or *Seder ha-Ibbur* (on intercalation), written between the years 1276 and 1294, found in various manuscripts of the *maḥzor* according to the Roman rite; and glosses on the commentary of Solomon b. Shabbetai Anav and on the *She'iltot* of R. *Aḥa.

BIBLIOGRAPHY: Vogelstein-Rieger, 1 (1896), 235–8, 240, 244, 277, 379–82, 452; A. Berliner, *Geschichte der Juden in Rom*, 1 pt. 2 (1893), 34, 50, 54; Steinschneider, in: HB, 4 (1861), 57ff.; Halberstamm, in: *Kobez al-Jad*, 4 (1888), nos. 4, 6, 11, 12, 13; S.D. Luzzatto, *Mavo le-Maḥzor ke-Minhag Benei Roma* (1856), 22; idem, *Iggerot Shadal* (1882), 664ff., 669; idem, in: *Ozar Tov*, 3 (1880), 19; Steinschneider, Cat Bod, no. 4544; Guedemann, Geseh Erz, 2 (1884), 201; S. Bernfeld, *Sefer ha-Dema'ot*, 1 (1924), 263ff.; Davidson, Ozar, 4 (1933), 372; Waxman, Literature, 2 (1960^2), 74–75.

[Yonah David]

ANAV, JEHIEL BEN JEKUTHIEL BEN BENJAMIN HAROFE (second half of 13th century), author, copyist, and *paytan;* a member of the Anau family of Rome. Little is known of his life. He was the author of a significant work, first published at Constantinople (1512) under the title of *Beit Middot* and later in a different version at Cremona (1556) under the title of *Ma'alot ha-Middot*, on which subsequent editions were based. The book, dealing with 24 "steps" with ethical conduct, is based on talmudic, midrashic, and other sources. It begins and ends with a poem. The work enjoyed great popularity (nearly 40 manuscripts are extant). It was often reissued and was translated into Ladino. Entire chapters of it were included by Jacob *Emden in his *Migdal Oz* (1748). In 1968 the work was republished from a manuscript written in 1287 by the author. Jehiel also wrote *Hilkhot Sheḥitah* on the laws of ritual slaughter (in manuscript).

Some manuscripts which Jehiel copied have been preserved. The number of errors which they contain is not at all surprising in view of the great speed at which he worked. The only complete extant manuscript of the Jerusalem Talmud, now in the Leiden Library, from which the 1523–24 Venice edition was published, was copied by him in 1289. He completed the orders of *Nashim* and *Nezikin* in a month and 12 days. This manuscript has proved of great importance for research into the text of the Jerusalem Talmud. It contains his own notes and emendations, as do other manuscripts which he copied (in some instances he inserted various annotations into the text itself). His share, if any, in *Tanya Rabbati* (Mantua, 1514) has not been convincingly demonstrated, and there are divergent views on this score. There are also differences of opinion concerning the similarity between large sections of this work and the *Shibbolei ha-Leket*, written by his relative Zedekiah b. Abraham *Anav. There are two principal views on this subject. S.H. Kook maintains that *Tanya Rabbati* is the first edition of *Shibbolei ha-Leket*, which Jehiel copied and into which he inserted his own notes and incorporated passages from a later edition of the *Shibbolei ha-Leket* as known today. S.K. Mirsky regards Jehiel as the author of *Tanya Rabbati* and attributes the similarities in the two works to the fact that both Jehiel and Zedekiah received the teachings of Jehiel's uncle, Judah b. Benjamin Anav. In addition to the poems mentioned above, Jehiel wrote another at the end of the Jerusalem Talmud manuscript and a *kinah* on the destruction of a synagogue and of 21 Torah scrolls in a fire that broke out in Trastevere, Rome, in 1268 (*Kobez al Jad*, 4 pt. 2 (1888), 26, 29ff.). Other *piyyutim* are ascribed to him (see Davidson, Oẓar, 4 (1933), 409).

BIBLIOGRAPHY: Guedemann, Gesch Erz, 2 (1884), 196–201, 327–8; S. Buber (ed.), *Shibbolei ha-Leket ha-Shalem* (1886), 24–31 (introd.); Vogelstein-Rieger, 1 (1896), 393ff.; Frankel, Mevo, 141b–143a; Epstein, in: *Tarbiz*, 5 (1933/34), 257–72; 6 (1934/35), 38–55; S. Lieberman, *Ha-Yerushalmi ki-Feshuto* (1934), 15ff. (introd.); idem, in: *Sefer ha-Yovel… H. Albeck* (1963), 283–305; S.H. Kook, *Iyyunim u-Meḥkarim*, 2 (1963), 268–73; S.K. Mirsky (ed.), *Shibbolei ha-Leket ha-Shalem* (1966), 40–49 (introd.).

[Shlomoh Zalman Havlin]

ANAV, JUDAH BEN BENJAMIN HA-ROFE (13th century), author, copyist, and *paytan;* member of the *Anau family of Rome. He was also known as Judah Ya'aleh (initial letters of *Yehudah Anav le-Mishpaḥat ha-Anavim*, an allusion to Judg. 1:2). Of his personal life, little is known. He studied under Meir b. Moses of Rome and may be approximately dated by means of a Ms. (Paris 312; of the *Hilkhot ha-Rif* on *Seder Moed*), copied by him in 1247, and from a *piyyut, "El Mi Anusah le-Ezrah,"* written by his cousin and pupil, Benjamin b. Abraham, in 1239, occasioned by Nicholas *Donin's denunciation of the Talmud. In 1280 he completed his work on the laws of ritual slaughter with special reference to the customs of Rome and fixed the formula of a *get* ("bill of divorce") for Rome. He was apparently the initiator of the communal synod in the same year (Ms. Hamburg 193, Ms. Oxford 633).

Among his works are a commentary on the tractate of *Shekalim* (published in the Vilna ed. of the Talmud), and on the *Hilkhot ha-Rif* of Isaac *Alfasi (Ḥ.J.D. Azulai saw a manuscript of this latter commentary which covered most of Alfasi's work). The only extant manuscripts, however, are on *Berakhot, Seder Mo'ed, Yevamot, Ḥullin*, and on *Hilkhot Tumah, Sefer Torah, Mezuzah, Tefillin*, and *Ẓiẓit*. The only ones published are those on *Pesaḥim* (1955), *Sukkah* (in: M. Herschler (ed.), *Ginzei Rishonim*, 1962), *Rosh Ha-Shanah, Yoma, Ta'anit* ((1963); also in *Sefer Yovel I. Elfenbein*, 1963), and *Berakhot* (1967). His work on the laws of ritual slaughter *(Hilkhot Sheḥitah)* has been published in the introduction to *Shibbolei ha-Leket* (ed. by S.K. Mirsky (1966), 50–74). He also completed Solomon b. Shabbetai Anav's commentary on Aḥa of Shabḥa's *She'iltot* (from *"Ki Tavo"* onward; *She'iltot*, ed. S.K. Mirsky, 1 (1960), 38–9). His halakhic questions addressed to Avigdor b. Elijah of Vienna and the latter's replies are quoted in *Shibbolei ha-Leket*, written by his cousin and most outstanding pupil Zedekiah b. Abraham, and containing much of his teachings. He is not the author of *Tanya Rabbati* as some erroneously contend but the work was influenced by his writings. Of Judah's *piyyutim*, a *zulat* to *parashat "Shekalim"* is extant.

BIBLIOGRAPHY: Azulai, 1 (1852), 98, no. 287 (RIF); 170, no. 49 (Shelomo mi-Trani); S.D. Luzzatto, *Iggerot*, 5 (1882), 669, no. 269; S. Buber (ed.), *Shibbolei ha-Leket ha-Shalem* (1886), 6–7, 11; Vogelstein-Rieger, 1 (1896), 277ff., 377–8, 504 (index); S.K. Mirsky (ed.), *Perush R. Yehudah b. Binyamin Anav al-ha-RIF, Massekhet Pesaḥim* (1966), introd.; idem, *Shibbolei ha-Leket ha-Shalem* (1966), 35–74 (introd.).

[Shlomoh Zalman Havlin]

ANAV, ZEDEKIAH BEN ABRAHAM (13th century), Italian talmudist; author of the compendium, *Shibbolei ha-Leket* ("The Gleaned Ears"), which can perhaps be considered the first attempt in Italy at the codification of Jewish law. Although Zedekiah's exact dates are unknown, he was alive at the time of the burning of the Talmud in Paris, which he describes as having taken place in 1244 (*Shibbolei ha-Leket*, 263), although most historians place the event in 1242. At the time he wrote, Zedekiah lived in Rome, as is obvious from the many references to "the custom here in Rome." He received some of his education in Germany, where he was a pupil of Jacob of Wuerzburg. He also may have studied for a time with *Meir b. Baruch of Rothenburg.

The *Shibbolei ha-Leket* is a major halakhic compendium on the liturgy (with copious explanations of individual prayers, and a complete commentary on the Passover *Haggadah* and the laws regarding the Sabbath, holidays, and fasts). The work is extant in several manuscripts, with only minor variant readings. A comprehensive edition, containing sections on the laws of circumcision, *tefillin*, mourning, and ritually unclean food as found in the various manuscripts (but lacking in source references and notes), was first published by S. Buber in 1886. The first volume of a new critical edition by S. Mirsky, based on a 1260 manuscript in the Sassoon collection, appeared in 1966. A second work by Zedekiah, mistakenly thought by some to be a continuation of the first, is the *Sefer Issur ve-Hetter* ("Book of Prohibitions and Permissions"). Only 136 of its 173 chapters were published in a mimeographed edition from a deficient manuscript (Segullah, Jerusalem). This work deals with the dietary laws and with the laws of oaths, marriage and divorce, menstruating women, judges and witnesses, commerce (including partnership, loans, and usury), and inheritance.

Zedekiah's method is to state a particular case (or problem) and to cite the authorities, both ancient and contemporary, who have dealt with it. He then proceeds to discuss their points of view and, when required, refers to the talmudic source, often quoting novel interpretations. Only rarely does he give his own explanations and hardly ever does he render a decision. The two works are of great importance both in themselves and as sources of earlier material. Zedekiah quotes with equal facility from both the Occidental and the Oriental schools, citing more than 230 authorities by name in addition to references to the *geonim* and to anonymous sources. He cites in particular the decisions of *Isaiah b. Mali di Trani and the responsa of Avigdor b. Elijah.

The *Shibbolei ha-Leket* is arranged in 13 *arugot* ("rows"), i.e., sections, and 372 *shibbolim* ("ears"), i.e., chapters. *Sefer Issur ve-Hetter* is arranged straightforwardly in 173 chapters divided into several sections, some of which are introduced by poems usually bearing the author's name in acrostic as does the whole work. A shortened version of the *Shibbolei ha-Leket* was first printed in Venice in 1546 and achieved great popularity. There were at least two other abbreviated versions of the work, which was also plagiarized under the name of *Tanya Rabbati* (see *Anav, Jehiel b. Jekuthiel).

According to Ḥayyim Joseph David Azulai, Zedekiah also wrote notes to Isaiah di Trani's commentary to the Pentateuch. *Immanuel of Rome puts Zedekiah and his three sons among the prominent scholars and saints whom he meets in Paradise (canto 28, ed. D. Jarden, 2, 1957) and also addresses a dirge to him (canto 24) mourning the death of two of his sons within a month.

BIBLIOGRAPHY: Schorr, in: *Zion*, 1 (1840/41), 93–98, 110–5; Guedemann, Gesch Erz, 2 (1884), 192–4; S. Buber (ed.), *Shibbolei ha-Leket ha-Shalem* (1886), introduction; S.K. Mirsky (ed.), *Shibbolei ha-Leket ha-Shalem* (1966), introduction; Vogelstein-Rieger, 1 (1896), 273, 382–6, 438; Gross, in: ZHB, 13 (1909), 87ff.; Michael, Or, no. 1169; Waxman, Literature, 2 (1960), 130–2.

[Raphael Posner]

ANČERL, KAREL (1908–1973), conductor. He studied composition and conducting at the Prague Conservatory with J. Křička and A. Habá, and finally became a pupil of V. Talich and H. Scherchen. He conducted at the theater (1931–33), the Symphony Orchestra of Prague Radio (1933–39), and also performed in festivals abroad. Forbidden to work by the Nazis, Ančerl was sent to Theresienstadt, were he played as a violinist and conducted a camp orchestra. In 1944 he conducted the premiere of Pavel Hass's *Study* for string orchestra. In late 1944 he was transported to Auschwitz. He was the only member of his family to survive the concentration camps. After the war, he dedicated all his efforts to renewing the musical life of Prague. In 1945 he was appointed conductor at the opera, resumed his post at the Prague Radio Symphony Orchestra (1947–50), and held a post as professor at the Prague Academy (1948–51). He took over the directorship of the Czech Philharmonic Orchestra (1950–68) and in spite of the Communist constraints he restored its international fame. Ančerl received the State Prize (1958) and was named National Artist (1966). While he was conducting in Tanglewood, the Russians invaded Prague. Ančerl immigrated to Canada and took over the leadership of the Toronto Symphony Orchestra, a post he retained, despite ill health, until his death. He was held in great esteem for his idiomatic interpretations of music from his homeland and his remarkable insight into masterworks of the 20th century. He made many recordings, which reflect his concentration, reflection, intuition, and musical warmth.

BIBLIOGRAPHY: *Grove Dictionary* (2001); *MGG2; Baker's Biographical Dictionary* (1997); T. Potter, "Time's Arrow: Karel Ančerl (1908–73)," in: *Gramophone*, 81 (Aug. 2003), 30–31.

[Naama Ramot ((2nd ed.)]

ANCHEL, ROBERT (1880–1951), French historian. An archivist-paleographer, he worked from 1912 until 1940 in the Archives Nationales in his native Paris. His major work was *Crimes et châtiments au XVIIIe siècle* (1934). Anchel devoted much of his scholarly activity to Jewish history. His principal contributions are *Napoléon et les Juifs* (1928), *Notes sur les frais du culte juif de 1815 à 1831* (1928), and *Les Juifs de France* (1946), a fragmentary but useful work. An objective, scrupulous historian, Anchel's work is characterized by the painstaking precision of an archivist, accompanied by the broad perspective of a historian. His presentation, however, is sometimes influenced by his desire to demonstrate the antiquity of the Jewish settlement in France and its continuity from the Middle Ages until the contemporary period, sometimes on the basis of slender evidence.

BIBLIOGRAPHY: Feuerwerker, in: REJ, 112 (1953), 53–56; *Livret de L'Ecole des Chartes* (1936), 143; *Revue Historique*, 158 (1928), 296–383; Mathiez, in: *Annales historiques de la révolution Française*, 5 (1928), 372–83.

[Georges Weill]

ANCIENT OF DAYS. The King James Version of the Bible rendered both *attik yomin* in Daniel 7:9 and *attik yomayya* in verses 13 and 22 by the phrase "the Ancient of days," i.e., with the definite article *the* and with a capital *A*, hence with the clear implication that this was an appellation or epithet of God (like, e.g., "the God of heaven" in Dan. 2:18, 19, etc.); just as it rendered *kevar enash* in Daniel 7:13 by the phrase "one like the *Son of man," likewise with a capital letter preceded by the definite article, with the clear implication that the reference was to "the Son of man" of the Gospels, i.e., Jesus. All revisions of the King James Version, however – the Revised Version, the American Standard Version, and the Revised Standard Version (see *Bible Translations, English) – have recognized that this is precluded not only by the context but also by the very grammar of biblical *Aramaic and have consequently rendered *attiq yomin* in Daniel 7:9 by "one that was ancient of days"; *attiq yomayya* in Daniel 7:13, 22 by "the ancient of days" but without a capital *a* – *the* in this case meaning not "the well-known" but "the aforementioned" – and *kevar enash* in Daniel 7:13 by "one like unto a son of man" (with *a*, not *the*). For, of course, these expressions – exactly like "great beasts" in verse 3, "lion" and "eagle" in verse 4, "bear" in verse 5, etc. – do not purport to be designations of objective realities but only descriptions of figures seen in a dream. To be sure, the figures symbolize objective realities; and that the reality that corresponds to the figure of one of advanced age, with fleece white hair and snow white raiment, who sits on a throne of fire, surrounded by millions of attendants, and determines the fates of kingdoms and nations is God Himself, is so obvious that, unlike other features of the dream, it is not specifically interpreted in the second half of the chapter. One cannot, therefore, ask, "Why is God called the Ancient of Days in Daniel 7?" because He is not, but only, "Why is God represented in the vision of Daniel 7 by the figure of an ancient of days?" As for the explanation, no further one than His role there as the Lord of history is necessary, but an additional factor has been suggested. A vague recollection of a Canaanite tradition has been surmised on the basis of one of the epithets of El, the head of the Ugaritic pantheon, namely, *mlk ab šnm,* which is commonly interpreted as "the King, Father of Years." Such a connection would be possible, but not certain, even if the correctness of the rendering "Father of Years" for the Ugaritic *ab šnm* were certain. But in the first place, "years" is elsewhere in Ugaritic (as in Phoenician) not *šnm* but *šnt*; and in the second place, "father of" in the sense of "possessing" or "characterized by" is strictly an Arabic idiom. (That is why H.L. Ginsberg formerly translated "King Father Shunem," guessing that El was identified with the God Shunem who is known from the Ugaritic ritual texts – which has its difficulties. So has another possible solution: that *šnm* in this title is a doublet of *nšm* "men, people," so that *ab šnm* would be synonymous with El's other epithet *ab adm* "Father of Man[kind].")

That "ancient of days" is not an epithet of God in Daniel 7 does not constitute an objection to the liturgical use of it as such in English (in which it has a solemn and singularly beautiful ring), even if it probably is in large measure a result of the mistranslations of the King James Version cited above (see the Book of *Daniel).

BIBLIOGRAPHY: H.L. Ginsberg, *Studies in Daniel* (1948), 15–18, 70–71; J.A. Montgomery, *The Book of Daniel* (ICC, 1949^2), 297–8; A. Bentzen, *Daniel* (Ger., 1952^2), 61–62. **ADD. BIBLIOGRAPHY:** B. Becking, in: DDD, 44–45.

[Harold Louis Ginsberg]

ANCONA (Marche), Adriatic seaport in Italy. According to Early Christian legends, the first bishop of Ancona was no less than the Great Rabbi of Jerusalem, who took the Christian name of Quincus after baptism. Jews were living near Ancona in 967. In that year a document attests that Peter, the archbishop of Ravenna, gave land in perpetual rent to the Jew Eliahu, son of Justus. In the Codex De Rossi, dated to the tenth century, there is a reference to Nathan, son of Machir, son of Menahem of Ancona. It seems that there was already a synagogue in Ancona, destroyed in the earthquake of 1279, as the *paytan* Solomon ben Moses ben Yekutiel De Rossi of Rome wrote a *seliḥah* on the subject.

By about 1300, there was an organized Jewish community in the city on whose behalf the poet *Immanuel of Rome sent a letter to the Rome community intimating that as the Ancona community was in economic straits and suffered from persecution, it should not be subjected to heavy taxation (*Maḥberet* 24). Most of the Jews who settled in Ancona came from the Muslim East. Jews probably engaged in moneylending in Ancona in the first half of the 15th century. There were also many merchants engaged in maritime trade with the Eastern Mediterranean. In 1427 the Franciscan Giacomo della Marca, an enthusiastic disciple of *Bernardino da Siena, tried to force the Jews in Ancona to wear the Jewish *badge and to restrict Jewish residence to a single street. He was in part successful, as the city senate indeed passed restrictive measures. Around 1450 the Jewish population of Ancona numbered 500 persons, representing 5% of the city's population. Both in 1456 and 1488 Jews were accused of ritual murder.

The arrival of refugees from the Iberian Peninsula opened a new chapter in the history of the Ancona Jewish community. The first to arrive, in 1492, were refugees from *Sicily. They were joined in 1497 by refugees from Portugal, and after 1510 by others from the Kingdom of *Naples. An order to wear the badge was again issued in 1524, but was revoked four years later. Solomon *Molcho visited the community in 1529 and stimulated messianic enthusiasm there. The assumption by the papal legate of authority in Ancona in 1532 had mixed results for the community. As Ancona was declared a free port, many Jewish merchants took advantage of its excellent harbor facilities to trade with the Levant. At first mercantile interests prevailed in papal policy and Pope Paul III invited merchants from the Levant to settle there regardless of their religion. In 1541 he encouraged the settlement of Jews expelled from Naples and in 1547 extended the invitation to Marranos, whom he promised to protect against the Inquisition. *Julius III renewed these guarantees, and about 100 Portuguese Marrano families apparently settled in Ancona. Jews from Germany also arrived in this period. Thus, around 1550 the Jewish community numbered around 2,700 persons.

In 1555, however, *Paul IV began to institute anti-Jewish measures in the Papal States. The Papal *Bull of July 12, 1555, was implemented in full in Ancona. The Jews were segregated in a ghetto, built the following year, prohibited from owning real property, and restricted to trade in second-hand clothing. Papal opposition to the Marranos proved particularly implacable, and a legate was sent to Ancona to take proceedings against them. Some managed to escape to Pesaro, Ferrara, and other places, but 51 were arrested and tried. Twenty-five were burned at the stake between April and June 1555. The horrors of the tragedy, mourned throughout the Jewish world, inspired touching elegies, still recited locally on the Ninth of Av. The event moved Dona Gracia *Nasi to organize a boycott of Ancona. The boycott, however, caused dissension within Jewry, some rabbis supporting the action while others opposed it, fearing that the pope might retaliate against Jews living under his jurisdiction.

Still, the legal position of Ancona Jewry changed more than once during the second half of the 16th century. It temporarily improved under Pius IV, but again deteriorated under Pius V in 1567. Ancona was one of the cities in the Papal States (together with Rome and Avignon) from which the Jews were not expelled by the Pope in 1569, being tolerated because of their utility in the Levant trade; nevertheless many decided to leave. Some amelioration was afforded by the favorably disposed Sixtus V in 1586 and Ancona was again exempted when *Clement VIII renewed the decree of expulsion in 1593. However by the beginning of the 17th century, the Ancona community was reduced to a state of debility that lasted through two centuries. Any temporary improvement that occurred was prompted by economic considerations. It is interesting that in 1659, when Pope Alexander VII ordered the closing of shops outside the ghetto, the city senate opposed him on the grounds that this would adversely affect the economic situation of the city. The decree was revoked. A local Purim was observed on Tevet 21 to commemorate the deliverance of the community from an earthquake that occurred on December 29, 1690.

In the 18th century the Ashkenazi community slowly began to emerge. The *Morpurgo family was the most important of the Ashkenazi families. In 1763 there were 1,290 Jews living in Ancona. As late as 1775 Pius VI again enforced all the most extreme anti-Jewish legislation.

During the occupation of Ancona by the army of *Napoleon between 1797 and 1799, the Jews were fully emancipated. The gates of the ghetto were removed, and two Jews, Ezechia and Salvatore Morpurgo, sat on the new municipal council, although the Jews, as well as the local population, were obliged to contribute heavy war levies. In 1814, after Napoleon's downfall, Ancona reverted to the Papal States, and in part the former discriminatory legislation was reimposed by Pope Leo XII. The revolutionary activity of 1831 resulted in the destruction of the gates of the ghetto. However, only in 1848 was obligatory residence in the ghetto abolished. Various Jews contributed to the Italian Risorgimento, such as David Almagià, Giuseppe Coen Cagli, and Pacifico Pacifici. Ancona Jews paid a high price for their participation in the Italian Risorgimento. In 1860 the pontifical general Lamoriciére demolished the Levantine synagogue to punish the Jewish community. The Jews obtained complete civic rights in 1861, when Ancona was annexed to the Kingdom of Italy. After the unification the richest elements of the community took part in the municipal life of the city. In 1869 Gioacchino Terni was called upon to direct the Chamber of Commerce, and from 1924 to 1927, Mario Iona. The Jewish population of Ancona numbered approximately 1,600 in the 19th century.

The size of the community and its widespread connections attracted many noted rabbis and scholars throughout the centuries, including the humanist *Judah Messer Leon (15th century), the physician *Amatus Lusitanus, and Moses *Basola (16th century), Mahalalel Hallelyah of Civitanova, Hezekiah Manoah Provenzal, Joseph Fermi (17th century), Samson *Morpurgo, Joseph Fiammetta (18th century), Jacob Shabbetai *Sinigaglia, Isaiah Raphael Azulai, David Abraham Vivanti, Isaac Raphael Tedeschi (19th century), and H. Rosenberg, who published several monographs on local history.

In 1938 there were 1,177 Jews in Ancona. During World War II, persecution was more individual than collective in character. The Germans, and eventually the Italian Fascists, demanded tributes to allow the Jews to live. In 1944 soldiers of the Jewish Brigade arrived in Ancona, and helped the community get back on its feet. In 1967, there were 400 Jews in Ancona. In 2004 the figure was around 200, with two synagogues in operation, the Levantine and the Italian, in the same building on Via Astagno. The original Levantine synagogue, originally erected in 1549 by Rabbi M. Bassola, was demolished in 1860, rebuilt in 1861 and inaugurated in 1876, utilizing elements of the previous synagogue.

BIBLIOGRAPHY: Milano, Bibliotheca, index; C. Ciavarini, *Memorie storiche degli Israeliti in Ancona* (1898²); C. Roth, *House of Nasi: Doña Gracia* (1947); I. Sonne, *Mi-Paulo ha-Revi'i ad Pius ha-Ḥamishi* (1954); Roth, Italy, index; Milano, Italia, index. **ADD. BIBLIOGRAPHY:** E. Ashtor, *Gli ebrei di Ancona nel periodo della republica*, *"Atti e Memorie"* (1977); M. Corvatta and M.L. Moscati, "Vicende degli ebrei marchigiani," in: *Storia delle Marche* (1985); M.L. Moscati-Beningni, *Marche Itinerari ebraici, I luoghi, la storia, l' arte* (1996), 22–43; H. Rosembergh, *Cenni bibliografici di Rabbini e Letterati della Comunita' Israelitica di Ancona* (1932); H.V. Volterra, *Ashkenaziti in Ancona* (1989), 126.

[Attilio Milano / Samuel Rocca (2nd ed.)]

ANCONA (D'Ancona), Italian family whose members were active in the Italian Risorgimento. ALESSANDRO (1835–1914), patriot, philologist, and literary critic. Born into a wealthy Pisa family, Alessandro studied at Pisa University. In these early years he joined the liberal circles in Tuscany seeking the liberation and unification of Italy. In 1854 he wrote his first essay, on the philosophy of the political reformer Tommaso Campanella, which brought him to the attention of the Liberal Party in Tuscany. He joined the staff of two Pro-Risorgimento newspapers in Florence, the *Genio* and the *Spettatore Italiano*. In 1854–59, he went to Turin, ostensibly to study law. In fact he played an important role in the liberal movement, acting as a liaison between Cavour, prime minister of the Kingdom of Sardinia, and the Liberal Party of Tuscany. Ancona became friendly with the Tuscan patriot Farini, and in 1859, when Tuscany was annexed to the Kingdom of Sardinia, he assumed the post of secretary of the Second Army Corps of Central Italy. Between 1859 and 1860, he promoted the cause of the Italian nationalists as editor of the liberal newspaper, *La Nazione*.

In 1860, Ancona gave up politics for literary scholarship; through the efforts of his friend Salvagnuoli, he was appointed deputy-professor of Italian literature at the University of Pisa (1861). The official occupant of the chair was no less than the celebrated critic De Sanctis. Later on he received the Chair of Italian Literature, a post he held until 1900. He was also vice president and director of the Regia Scuola Normale Superiore of Pisa and a member of the Academia Reale delle Scienze. In 1904 he became a member of the Italian Senate. A typical representative of the positivist trend in the study of Italian literature, Ancona made an important contribution to the study of medieval Italian literature as one of its first philologists. His philological research included the study of folklore material. He unearthed and edited many important documents and encouraged others to publish critical editions of 13th- and 14th-century texts. Ancona himself produced one of the most important anthologies of 13th-century Italian poetry, *Le antiche rime volgari, secondo la lezione del Codice Vaticano 3793* (1875). In *La poesia popolare italiana* (1878), he tried to prove that Italian poetry was developed mainly from popular verse. Other books dedicated to the early development of Italian popular literature were the *Canti del popolo reggino* (1881) and *Poemetti popolari italiani* (1889). In his attempt to trace the origin of medieval Italian prose tales, Ancona engaged in comparative research that involved the whole of European literature. Examples of this pioneering work are his study of the motif of the *Wandering Jew *La leggenda dell' Ebreo errante* (in *saggi di letteratura popolare*, 1913) and his examination of the development of religious theater in medieval Italy, *Le sacre rappresentazioni dei secoli XIV, XV, e XVI* (1873), a collection of old mystery plays with notes and commentary, on which he based his *Origini del teatro in Italia* (3 vols., 1877, 1891^2; 2 vols., 1966). It was in the second edition of the latter that he included a chapter on his important discoveries concerning the Jewish Renaissance Theater at Mantua (vol. 2, pp. 403–22 and 578–84). From his work published in the *Rivista Storica Mantovana* (1, p. 183) he revealed that there was at Mantua a company of Jewish actors who had won considerable fame in the 16th century and were obliged to play before the Dukes of Gonzaga between 1525 and 1597. About the same time, the playwright Leone (Judah) di *Sommo Portaleone was active. Ancona showed that at Venice, too, plays on Jewish themes and even one operetta were presented by Jews at intermittent periods between 1531 and 1607. Ancona surveyed the role and importance of Jews as actors and stage directors in the Italian Renaissance Theater. He also wrote many articles on Jewish literary personalities.

Ancona's contribution to the study of Italian literature includes his critical edition of Dante's *Vita Nuova* (1872) as well as the book *I precursori di Dante* (1874). His most important critical studies dedicated to individual Italian literary figures are those on the *Contrasto di Cielo d'Alcamo* (1884), the *Odi* of Giuseppe Parini (1884), and *Il Tesoro di Brunetto Latini* (1889).

Ancona founded the literary periodical *Rassegna bibliografica della letteratura italiana*, which he edited until 1912; his own articles appeared in leading scholarly journals.

His son PAOLO (1878–1964) was a celebrated art historian and educationalist. He was born in Pisa. In 1909 he was appointed professor of the history of medieval and modern art at the University of Milan. He was also a member of the Fine Arts Council of the Italian Ministry of Education. Among his publications are *Modigliani, Chagall, Soutine, Pascin, aspetti dell' expressionismo* (1952; Eng. translation, 1953); works on Italian miniature painting; and studies on the masters of the Italian Renaissance, including Piero della Francesca (1951) and Paolo Uccello (1959).

Alessandro's brother, SANSONE (1814–1894), born in Pisa, was an important journalist and politician in the Italian Risorgimento. In his youth, like his brother, he wrote for Tuscany's Liberal newspapers, the *Spettatore* and the *Nazione*. In 1859 he was appointed to the financial commission of the provisional government. He was chosen to write a report on the financial situation of the provisional government under the leadership of Ricasoli. Later, after the annexation, he was called upon by Cavour, the prime minister of the United Kingdom of Italy, to direct the "Department of Finances, Commerce, and Public Works" of Tuscany.

With two other Jews he sat in the parliament of united Italy in 1861, where he represented the moderate liberals, and in 1882 he was appointed a life member of the senate, on the floor of which he died in 1894.

His younger brother was the painter Vito d'*Ancona.

BIBLIOGRAPHY: ALESSANDRO: *In memoriam Alessandro D'Ancona* (1915); L. Russo, *La critica letteraria contemporanea* (1942), index; Coppola, in: *Nuova Antologia*, 88 (1953), 435–56; G. Laras and R. Elia, in: *Scritti… G. Bedarida* (1966); L. Ferrari et al., *Bibliografia degli scritti di Alessandro d'Ancona* (1915). **ADD. BIBLIOGRAPHY:** S. Foà, *Gli ebrei nel Risorgimento italiano* (1978). SANSONE: *Vessillo Israelitico*, (1894), 403–5. **ADD. BIBLIOGRAPHY:** S. Foà, *Gli ebrei nel Risorgimento italiano* (1978).

[Joseph Baruch Sermoneta / Samuel Rocca (2nd ed.)]

ANCONA, CESARE D' (1832–1901), Italian geologist. D'Ancona was born in Pisa and studied geology under Meneghini. He was appointed professor of paleontology at the University of Florence in 1874. D'Ancona reorganized the section of tertiary malacology of the Central Italian Collection of Paleontology over a period of several years, and as a result, the Italian Geological Committee asked him to prepare a comprehensive, systematic survey of the malacology of the Italian pliocene and early quaternary. This survey, the first since the early study of G.B. Brocchi in 1808, was published in 1871–73 and became the standard work on the subject. In 1894 d'Ancona published a paper on the evolution of the horse, which earned him election to the Italian Royal Geological Association. He was cofounder and secretary of the Italian Botanical Society. His major publications are: *Sulle Neritine fossile dei terreni terziari superiori dell' Italia centrale* (1889); *Malacologia pliocenica italiana* (in *Memorie per servire all descrizione della carta geologica d'Italia*, 1 (1871), 305–63; 2 (1873), pt. 1, 171–264); *Gli antenati della vigna vinifera* (in *Atti della Accademia dei Georgofili di Firenze*, 13, 1890); *Storia genealogica del cavallo* (*ibid.*, 17, 1894).

[Yakov K. Bentor]

ANCONA, MARIO (1860–1931), Italian baritone singer. Born in Leghorn, Ancona was a lawyer and diplomat before he began to study singing. He made his debut in Trieste in 1890; and in 1892 he was taken to London by Lago for a short season at the Olympic Theatre. Engaged by Covent Garden in 1893, he sang regularly there until 1901, playing Tonio in the first London performances of Leoncavallo's *I Pagliacci* (1893). He sang regularly both in Italy and in New York – at the Metropolitan (1893–97), then with the Manhattan Opera for one season (1906–07). After World War I, he retired to Florence, where he taught singing until his death.

[Max Loppert (2nd ed.)]

ANCONA, VITO D' (1825–1884), Italian painter of the "Macchiaioli" School. He studied engraving with Samuele Jesi and then at the Florence Academy. In 1856 he left Florence for

Venice, where he lived for a long period. Back in Florence, he produced his first well-known painting, *Le Maschere*, clearly inspired by his Venetian stay. His painting *L'abbandonata* is dated to the year 1860 and the *Portico* to 1861. By then D'Ancona had adopted analytic composition. However, contrary to most of the Macchiaioli painters, who depicted contemporary subjects, Ancona favored in this period historical subjects. Thus, his best-known painting is the *Esilio di Giano della Bella* (1864), with a clear historical character. Towards the end of the decade he moved to Paris, where he was at home in the literary and artistic world, which included other Italian painters living there. In this period he painted mainly female nudes and scenes of domestic life. Back in Florence in 1875, he opened a studio at Borgo di Pinti. Already quite ill, he still found the strength to participate in the National Exhibition of painting at Naples in 1877, where he won a gold medal with the painting *A porte chiuse: figura di donna nuda*. In 1879, owing to his sickness, he had to give up painting completely.

BIBLIOGRAPHY: S., Bietoletti, *I Macchiaioli, la storia, gli artisti, le opere* (2001), 112–21; I. Ciseri, *Vito D'Ancona*, Soncino (1996).

[Samuel Rocca (2nd ed.)]

ANDERNACH, city in the Rhineland, district of Coblenz, Germany. A Jewish community lived there toward the end of the 12th century under the protection of the archbishop of Cologne, who acquired Andernach in 1167. The ritual bathhouse, built in the 14th century, still exists. In 1287 the Jews were expelled, and the populace destroyed and pillaged the houses in the *Judengasse;* the archbishop, however, compelled the burghers to restore all property to the Jews and to expel the rioters from the city. The Jews again appear to have been driven out of Andernach in the first half of the 15th century, but evidently remained close to its walls. They were permitted to take refuge inside the city during emergencies, especially during the wars of 1573–1655. The community increased from a single Jewish resident in 1860 to about 140 by 1925. In 1939, only 45 Jews remained in Andernach. At least 11 died in the Holocaust. No Jews have lived there since World War II.

BIBLIOGRAPHY: Germ Jud, 1 (1965), 11ff.; 2 (1968), 14–17; Salfeld, Martyrol, 68, 90, 841.

[Zvi Avneri]

ANDERS, GUENTHER (Stern; 1902–1992), German philosopher, political writer, and novelist. Born in Breslau as the second child of psychologist William Stern and his wife, Clara, Anders was raised in an assimilatory milieu, or, in his own words, a "tradition of anti-traditionalism." In 1919, he began to study philosophy in Freiburg with Edmund *Husserl, who also supervised his Ph.D. thesis in the field of logic. In 1929 he married Hannah *Arendt (they were divorced eight years later). Two months after Hitler's election, Anders fled the Gestapo to Paris for three years. There he wrote his novel *Die molussische Katakombe*, a fierce examination of the conditions of thinking and story-telling under dictatorship (the manuscript was reworked several times and finally published after Anders' death in 1992). In 1936 he was awarded the Amsterdam Prize of Emigration for his novel *Der Hungermarsch*. In the same year he immigrated to the United States, where he developed the focus of his later thought: the status of man in the age of self-iterating technology. Far from being a question of "evolution," under Anders' argument the 20th century locates mankind at a crucial point of its development, i.e., within a process of industrial revolutions that sets up structures inevitably leading to the destruction of life and marginalizing man as a willing executor of his own agony. The triumph of technology over life presupposes the transformation of man into raw material. Herein the final significance of Auschwitz can be seen, a thought not least explicitly formulated in Anders' open letter to the son of Adolf Eichmann (*Wir Eichmannsoehne*, 1964). In his system of negative anthropology, Eichmann represents man under the reign of technical totalitarianism, willingly fulfilling the demands of the killing machinery and unable to recognize the monstrous consequences of his own deeds. (His guilt remains, since despite his blindness, people are always able to defy the progress of monstrosity.)

Thus the rise of technology, its manifestation as historical protagonist, must be viewed from the perspective of catastrophe. The scenery Anders chose for his principal work, *Die Antiquiertheit des Menschen* (Part 1, 1956; Part 2, 1980), is Hiroshima; the invention of the atom bomb – a product not answering any economic need, created to end all needs – becomes an initial proof of his apocalyptic reading of cultural history. After returning to Europe (Vienna) in 1950, Anders dedicated most of his efforts to political realities. While his philosophical approach seemed too unorthodox and isolated to enable an academic career (he was recommended by Ernst *Bloch for a professorship at the University of Halle, GDR), Anders was strongly committed to the protest against the Vietnam War (*Visit Beautiful Vietnam*, 1968) and proceeded to become one of the most prominent activists against military and civil uses of nuclear power (*Die atomare Drohung*, 1981; *Hiroshima ist ueberall*, 1982).

Along with several literary awards, Anders received the Deutscher Kritikerpreis (1967), the Österreichischer Staatspreis für Kulturpublizistik (1979), and the Theodor-W.-Adorno-Preis (1983).

BIBLIOGRAPHY: W. Reimann, *Verweigerte Versöhnung: zur Philosophie von Günther Anders* (1990); *Text u. Kritik*, 115 (1992); K.P. Liessmann, *Guenther Anders: Philosophieren im Zeitalter der technischen Revolutionen* (2002); L. Luetkehaus, *Schwarze Ontologie: ueber Guenther Anders* (2002²).

[Phillipp Theisohn (2nd ed.)]

ANDRADE, EDWARD NEVILLE DA COSTA (1887–1971), British physicist and author, who established "Andrade's Laws," concerning the flow of metals. Andrade was born and educated in London, and graduated from University College. He worked in Manchester with Rutherford, measuring the wavelength of gamma rays. In 1935 he was elected a Fellow of the Royal Society. He served as an artillery officer in World War I and after the war became professor of physics at the Artillery College, Woolwich, and later head of the physics department of University College, London. In 1950 he was appointed director of the Royal Institution and of its Davy-Faraday Research Laboratory. He resigned in 1952 after basic differences with the governing body. He carried out research at the Imperial College of Science on the electrical properties of flames and on radioactivity, and on the viscosity of liquids (here, too, a law bears his name). He was a noted historian of science, with special interest in Isaac Newton and Robert Hooke. His books, both scientific and popular, include *Structure of the Atom* (1923), *The Mechanism of Nature* (1930), *The Atom and Its Energy* (1947), *Sir Isaac Newton* (1954), *Physics for the Modern World* (1963), *Rutherford and the Nature of the Atom* (1964), and *Poems and Songs* (1949).

[Samuel Aaron Miller]

ANDRADE, VELOSINO JACOB DE (1639–1712), physician and philosophical author. Andrade was born in Pernambuco, Brazil, then under Dutch rule, the son of Portuguese parents who fled there when the Inquisition persecuted *Marranos. After the Portuguese recapture of Pernambuco in 1654, Andrade went to Holland where he first settled in The Hague and subsequently in Antwerp. In both places he devoted himself to the practice of medicine. After the death of *Spinoza in 1677, Andrade wrote a polemical work entitled *Theologo religioso contra o Theologo Politico de Bento de Espinosa que de Judeo sefez Atheista* directed against the latter's *Tractatus Theologico-Politicus*. A manuscript of Andrade's work may still be extant. It may be assumed that he joined the circle of S.L. *Morteira, who had participated in Spinoza's excommunication, and that his work reflects the views of that group.

Andrade also composed a six-volume work entitled *Messias restaurado: contra el libro de M. Jaquelot… intitulado Dissertaciones sobre el Messias*. This presents the Jewish view concerning the Messiah and is directed against a book in which Isaac Jaquelot, a minister of the Dutch Reformed Church, tried to substantiate Jesus' messianic claims from passages in Hebrew Scripture. Andrade translated Morteira's *Torat Moshe* from Hebrew into Portuguese under the title *Epitome de la verdad de la Ley de Moyses*.

BIBLIOGRAPHY: A. Kohut, in: AJHSP, 3 (1895), 108–9; M. Kayserling, *Geschichte der Juden in Portugal* (1867), 296; Kayserling, Bibl. 12–13; idem, in: HB, 3 (1860), 58–59.

[Joseph Elijah Heller]

°**ANDREWES, LANCELOT** (1555–1626), Anglican bishop, one of the principal translators of the King James Version of the Bible (1611). Andrewes studied at Cambridge where he became a fellow in 1576, took his orders in 1580, and became master of Pembroke Hall in 1589. He was bishop of Chichester (1605), of Ely (1609), and of Winchester (1618). Andrewes knew many languages and it was said of him that he qualified as "interpreter general at Babel." Andrewes opposed the Puritan tendency to place less emphasis on ritual. He had a working knowledge of biblical Hebrew, but it is difficult to assess the depth of his Hebrew knowledge.

BIBLIOGRAPHY: M.F. Reidy, *Bishop Lancelot Andrewes, Jacobian Court Preacher…* (1955), includes bibliography; H. Hunger, *Die biblischen Gebete des Lancelot Andrewes* (1960); Schmidt, in: RGG, 3:1 (1957), 369.

°**ANDREW OF RINN** (Ger. **Anderle von Rinn**), alleged victim of a ritual murder (see *Blood Libel) on July 12, 1462. The murder was reputedly committed on the "Judenstein" in the neighborhood of Rinn near Innsbruck, Austria, in the diocese of Bressanone (Brixen). The perpetrators were said to be four Jewish travelers who had purportedly bought the child from his uncle. The cult of Andrew was introduced in Rinn in 1620, following the cult of Simon of Trent. Pope *Benedict XIV approved his equivalent beatification in 1752 but in 1755 refused to authorize Andrew's canonization and stated that the Roman Church did not formally venerate him. Despite repeated prohibitions by the Catholic Church and the Austrian government, there is an antisemitic cult of Andrew in Rinn up to the present time.

ADD. BIBLIOGRAPHY: W. Kunzenmann (ed.), *Judenstein* (1994); B. Fresacher, *Anderl von Rinn. Ritualmordkult und Neuorientierung in Judenstein 1945–1995* (1998).

[Bernhard Blumenkranz / Marcus Pycka (2nd ed.)]

°**ANDREW** (or **Andreas**) **OF SAINT-VICTOR** (c. 1110–1175), Christian Hebraist, probably English by birth; died as abbot of Wigmore (Herefordshire). Andrew was the pupil, in Paris, of Hugh of Saint-Victor (d. 1141), who was interested in Jewish biblical exegesis. Andrew acquired some proficiency in Hebrew, engaged in prolonged oral discussion with Jews, and was the first exegete after *Jerome to introduce Jewish material into a Christian Bible commentary on a substantial scale. His works cover Genesis through Kings, the Prophets (including Daniel), Proverbs, and Ecclesiastes (the last is the only one available in a printed edition; ed. by G. Calandra, 1948). The Vulgate is collated with the Hebrew text, and an embryonically critical attitude is adopted toward the sources, patristic and Jewish alike. Andrew's lack of concern with Christian theological tradition even allowed him to interpret the "Suffering Servant" of Isaiah 53 not as Jesus, but as Israel, or Isaiah himself. As an innovator, he was at first fascinated by his newfound Jewish sources and recited them indiscriminately. Later he assessed them more critically, though primarily from a rationalist rather than a theological standpoint. He evinced interest in biblical chronology and geography. His work parallels matter found in *Rashi and Joseph *Bekhor Shor. Andrew's work circulated quite widely, and in about 1271–72, Roger *Bacon, while commending his resort to the Hebrew text, deplored the prestige enjoyed by his "literalist" commentaries.

BIBLIOGRAPHY: B. Smalley, *The Study of the Bible in the Middle Ages* (1952²), 112–95; R. Loewe, in: JHSET, 17 (1951/52), 238–40; H. Hailperin, *Rashi and the Christian Scholars* (1963), index; Mahoney, in: *New Catholic Encyclopedia*, 1 (1967), 496 (incl. bibl.).

[Raphael Loewe]

ANDROGYNOS (Gr. ἀνδρός man, γυνή woman), animal or individual having both male and female characteristics and organs, a hermaphrodite. Both the actual and the legendary androgynos are known in talmudic literature. The legal position and disabilities of the androgynos and a description of his abnormalities are collated in a number of *beraitot* in Tosefta *Bikkurim* 2. In many editions of the Mishnah that chapter is reproduced as chapter 4 of tractate *Bikkurim*, although there are noticeable differences between the two texts. In talmudic literature, the androgynos is nearly always mentioned together with the *tumtum*, a creature whose sex cannot be determined. According to the majority opinion, the laws relating to the androgynos are determined by the fact that it is doubtful whether it is male or female. As a result, in certain matters "it has the status of a male, in others that of a female, or of both, or of neither" (Bik. 4:1). R. Yose, however, is of the opinion that an androgynos is a "creature of its own," i.e., belonging to a third sex (cf. also Yev. 83a). Most of the laws affecting the androgynos are based upon the oft-repeated comment on the word "*zakhar*" ("male") occurring in Scripture, which is interpreted "(specifically) as 'male,' but not a *tumtum* or an androgynos" (cf. Naz. 2:7). The Midrash (Gen. R. 8:1) takes the verse "male and female" (Gen. 1:27) as referring to the creation of a single individual. Whereas R. Jeremiah b. Eleazar says that it refers to the creation of an androgynos, R. Samuel b. Naḥman says "It means that he created them with a double face (*du-parẓufin*) which was then severed in two." In the Talmud, however, only the latter view is found (Er. 18a, Ber. 61a). This view is similar to that mentioned in Plato's *Symposium* (190b), with the difference that Plato speaks of three types of "double-faced" creatures, masculine-masculine, feminine-feminine, and masculine-feminine, whereas only the third type is mentioned in rabbinic literature. Nevertheless the view of R. Jeremiah is quoted by the Christian Fathers, who were at pains to refute this "Jewish fable." Augustine, in his commentary *De Genesi ad Litteram* 3:22, refers to it, and Strabo declared it to be "one of the damnable fables of the Jews."

BIBLIOGRAPHY: Guttmann, Mafte'aḥ, 3 pt. 1 (1924), 217–23; ET, 2 (1949), 55–60; S. Lieberman, *Tosefta ki-Feshutah*, 2 (1955), 834–46; Ginzberg, Legends, 5 (1955), 88–89.

[Bialik Myron Lerner / Stephen G. Wald (2nd ed.)]

ANDRONICUS SON OF MESHULLAM (Messalamus), Alexandrian sage. He lived during the reign of Ptolemy VI Philometor (180–145 B.C.E.). Andronicus acted as the spokesman of the Jews in a dispute that arose between the Jews and Samaritans in Alexandria. The Samaritans claimed that the sanctuary on Mt. Gerizim and not that of Jerusalem had been built according to the Law of Moses and demanded a public disputation between them and the Jews in the presence of Ptolemy Philometor. In the discussion, he demonstrated that the genuine high-priestly succession had been retained by the priests in charge of the Temple in Jerusalem, and that the sanctity of the Temple was unquestionable (since it was famous throughout the world and many kings had offered sacrifices). The king acknowledged the justice of Andronicus' arguments and sentenced his Samaritan opponents to death. According to Samaritan tradition, however, the Samaritan spokesmen, Sabbaeus and Theodosius, gained the day. They proved that before his death Moses had established Mt. Gerizim as the sole holy place from which the priests could bless the people (Deut. 27), but that this was not recognized by the Jews whose text of the Bible was later. According to the Samaritans, their argument was approved by Ptolemy Philometor, and he prohibited the Jews from going up Mt. Gerizim, on penalty of death.

BIBLIOGRAPHY: Jos., Ant., 13:74ff.; J.A. Montgomery, *Samaritans* (1907), 76ff.; Graetz, Gesch, 3 (1905–065), 44ff., 651ff.

[Abraham Schalit]

ANER, ESHKOL, AND MAMRE (Heb. עָנֵר, אֶשְׁכֹּל, וּמַמְרֵא), three Amorite brothers, allies of Abraham (Gen. 14:13). They participated in Abraham's campaign against *Chedorlaomer, king of Elam, and his confederates who had waged battle against Sodom and other cities and had captured Lot and his family. After the victory Abraham refused any share in the spoils, but declared that Aner, Eshkol, and Mamre should receive theirs (Gen. 14:24). The *Genesis Apocryphon* (22:6; Aner is called there ענרם) explicitly accords the three brothers an active role in the battle with these kings.

The names Eshkol and Mamre are associated with Hebron. A wadi in the vicinity of the city is named Eshkol (Num. 13:23–24; 32:9; Deut. 1:24); and the particular spot near Hebron where Abram pitched his tent is called "the terebinths of Mamre" (Gen. 13:18; 14:13; 18:1). In Genesis 23:19 (cf. 35:27) Mamre is spoken of loosely as a former name of Hebron as a whole. According to B. Mazar, the ancient name of Hebron, Kiriath-Arba, implies that the city was a member of four neighboring confederated settlements in which the families of Mamre, Eshkol, and Aner resided, around the citadel of Hebron. However, these locations have not yet been identified archaeologically.

BIBLIOGRAPHY: Maisler (Mazar), in: *Sefer Dinaburg* (1949), 316–20; idem, in: JPOS, 16 (1936), 152ff.; Albright, in: JSOR, 10 (1929), 231–69; Benzinger, in: BZAW, 41 (1925), 21–27; Boehl, in: ZAW, 36 (1916), 65–73.

ANFINSEN, CHRISTIAN BOEHMER (1916–1995), U.S. biochemist and Nobel laureate. Anfinsen was born in Monessen, Pennsylvania, the son of Norwegian immigrants, and converted to Judaism in 1980.

After moving to Philadelphia, he received his B.Sc. in chemistry at Swarthmore College (1937) and his M.Sc. in organic chemistry from the University of Pennsylvania (1939).

A research fellowship in Copenhagen was cut short by the onset of World War II. He received his Ph.D. in biological chemistry from Harvard (1943), where he worked until 1950. He worked at the National Institutes of Health (1950–80) where he became head of the Laboratory of Chemical Biology (1963). Anfinsen's research mainly concerned the relationship between protein structure and function but he had broad scientific interests, notably the molecular basis of evolution and protein purification. He was awarded the Nobel Prize for chemistry in 1972 (jointly with Stanford Moore and William *Stein) for proving that the three-dimensional, folded structures of protein chains depend partly on the amino acid sequences which make up protein chains and partly on the physiological milieu (the "thermodynamic hypothesis"). Later he applied the technique of affinity chromatography to protein isolation and purification, which enabled the production of large quantities of interferon and opened the way to advances in anti-viral and anti-cancer therapy. He also worked on the structure of enzymes related to the infectious properties of the bacterium staphylococcus. In 1982 he became professor of biology at Johns Hopkins University, Baltimore, where he worked on extraordinary bacteria that thrive at high temperature on ocean floors, a property which may have practical applications. Anfinsen's many honors included election to the U.S. National Academy of Sciences (1963) and awards from the Hebrew University of Jerusalem (1985) and Bar-Ilan University (1990). He had a long association with the Weizmann Institute, where he was an honorary fellow (1962), a member of the Board of Governors (from 1962), and chairman of the Scientific Advisory Council (1974). Anfinsen's many activities arising from his broad social concerns included his protest with other Nobel laureates against U.S. budget cuts for biomedical research (1976), protests on behalf of political prisoners (in 1981, necessitating travel to Argentina), and criticism of the potential misuses of biotechnology.

[Michael Denman (2nd ed.)]

ANGARIA, transportation corvée. A postal system was introduced under the Achaemenian monarchy (see *Persia) for the transaction of official business between the various states in the Persian Empire and the imperial court. Herodotus (7:98) describes how the Persians divided the principal routes of the empire into stages, none of which exceeded a day's journey.

Although there are no data in the sources, the angaria must have been introduced in Ereẓ Israel by the Persians at the beginning of the Second Temple period, since the main coastal route to Egypt, then ruled by the government of the Persian king Cambyses, passed through it. The first mention of the angaria in Ereẓ Israel, however, dates from the Hasmonean period: release from it being included in the immunities which Demetrius II of Syria offered to the Jews (I Macc. 10:33). There is no mention of the angaria being imposed under the Hasmoneans. During the Roman period the highway between Sidon and Jerusalem was considered a principal route for the purposes of angaria, while the cities of Acre, Caesarea, Samaria, and Beth-El were important stations along it. The Jerusalem-Antipatris highway was also a principal route, its important stations being Emmaus and Lydda. Although the original institution of the angaria was as a postal service, the term came to mean impressment for nearly any public service. Not only were animals requisitioned, but men were conscripted to perform tasks quite unrelated to the *cursus publicus*. Thus, R. Zeiri (third-fourth centuries) relates that he was forced *be-angaria* to bring myrtles to the palace (TJ, Ber. 1:1, 2d). It is related of Eleazar b. Ḥarsom, a member of a high-priestly family, that his servants failed to recognize him when they encountered him with a sack of flour on his shoulder traveling to study the Torah and seized him for the duty of angaria (Yoma 35b). The third century was a period of economic and administrative breakdown, and the angaria served as a pretext for the imposition of all manner of burdens, levies, and confiscations (e.g., Lev. R. 12:1). In this period animals were requisitioned, but never returned (BM 78a–b); but this may have been a purely Babylonian phenomenon, as it is not mentioned in the parallel Jerusalem Talmud (BM 7:3, 11a; cf. TB, BM 49b). As a result, in rabbinic literature, the term came to mean any act done unwillingly; cf. the statements that Israel accepted the Torah *be-simḥah* ("joyfully") and not *be-angaria* (PR 21:99) and that the sun runs its daily course with delight, and not *be-angaria* (Mid. Ps. to 12:12), though here there is a subtly pointed allusion to the original connotation, the *cursus publicus*.

BIBLIOGRAPHY: Pauly-Wissowa, 2 (1894), 2184–85, s.v. *Angaria* and *Angarium*; 8 (1901), 1846–63, s.v. *Cursus publicus*; Rostowzew, in: *Klio*, 6 (1906), 249–58; Preisigke, *ibid.*, 7 (1907), 241–77; Krauss, Tal Arch, 2 (1911), 327, 374, 461 (no. 340), 502 (no. 748), 677 (no. 162); O. Seeck, *Geschichte des Untergangs der antiken Welt*, 2 (1921[2]), 289 ff.; Supplement, 2 (1901), 550 ff.; Guttmann, Mafte'aḥ, 3 pt. 1 (1924), 216–7; M.P. Charlesworth, *Trade-routes and Commerce of the Roman Empire* (1926[2]); Allon, Toledot, 2 (1958[3]), 189–90; I. Hahn, in: *Acta Antiqua*, 7 (Budapest, 1959), 155; R.N. Frey, *The Heritage of Persia* (1966), ch. 3, no. 74, ch. 5, notes 65, 67; D. Sperber, in: *Antiquité Classique*, 38 (1969), 164–8.

[Joshua Gutmann and Daniel Sperber]

ANGEL, AARON (1913–1996), Sephardi rabbi in Argentina. Angel was born in Komotine, Greece. He graduated from the Rabbinical Seminary of Rhodes and studied philosophy at the Hebrew University of Jerusalem. In 1940 he was named chief rabbi of Alexandria and a member of the *bet din* (rabbinical court) of Egypt. Following the Sinai War in 1956 the Jews were compelled to emigrate from Egypt. Angel was one of the last to leave. In 1958 he settled in Buenos Aires, Argentina, and from then until his death served as chief rabbi of the Asociación Comunidad Israelita Sefaradí de la Argentina – the Ladino-speaking community. In his 42 years in Buenos Aires he was the spiritual and social leader of the Sephardi community and active in strengthening formal Jewish education. He taught in the Midrasha Haivrit and founded the Maimonides Jewish primary school, serving as its principal until 1989.

In 1988 he received the Jerusalem Award for Jewish education in the Diaspora from the World Zionist Organization and the Jewish Agency for Israel.

[Efraim Zadoff (2nd ed.)]

ANGEL, BARUCH (1595–1670), talmudist, preacher, and kabbalist of Salonika. Angel, head of the Talmud Torah Yeshivah, was one of the outstanding scholars of his age. His disciples included David *Conforte, Solomon b. Samuel Florentin, and Isaac Florentin. In 1651 he was one of the seven foremost scholars of the city. He signed a regulation dealing with a tax on clothing. He was invited to accept the appointment of rabbi of Smyrna but refused, because he was unwilling to encroach upon the domain of the incumbent rabbi. His published works are *Ḥiddushei ha-Rav Barukh Angel* (Salonika, 1716), on selected chapters of various tractates, and responsa (*ibid.*). His glosses to the Shulḥan Arukh, *Ḥoshen Mishpat*, are included in the *Doresh Mishpat* (Salonika, 1650) of his disciple, Solomon Florentin. A work on the tractates *Ketubbot* and *Shevu'ot* exists in manuscript form at the Israel National Library.

BIBLIOGRAPHY: I.S. Emmanuel, *Maẓẓevot Saloniki*, 1 (1963), 371–2, no. 840.

ANGEL, MARC D. (1945–), U.S. Sephardi rabbinical leader and scholar. Angel was born in Seattle, Wash., the son of Sephardi immigrants from Rhodes and Tekirdag, Turkey, and nephew of veteran Sephardi rabbi Solomon Maimon. Angel received his B.A., Ph.D., and rabbinical ordination from Yeshiva University in New York, with an M.A. in English literature from the City College of New York. From 1969 he served as rabbi of the Shearith Israel Spanish and Portuguese Synagogue in New York.

Angel wrote about 20 books on Sephardi history, tradition, and customs; mourning; rabbinic thought; and ethics, and many scholarly and popular articles. He won the 1988 National Jewish Book Award in the category of Jewish thought. His doctorate on the history of the Jews of Rhodes was a pioneering study in the field.

Angel also served as president of the Rabbinical Council of America, was founder, president, and honorary president of Sephardic House, and subsequently became vice president of the American Sephardi Federation and chairman of the Rabbinic Advisory Committee of the Jewish National Fund. He was a board member of the New York Federation of Jewish Philanthropies, the HealthCare Chaplaincy, CancerCare, and many other organizations. He was on the Board of Governors of the Orthodox Union (OU) and a member of the editorial board of *Tradition*.

Angel received the National Rabbinic Leadership Award of the Orthodox Union, the Bernard Revel Award of Yeshiva University for Religion and Religious Education, and the Finkle Prize of the New York Board of Rabbis.

Representing the Spanish and Portuguese Synagogue founded in 1654, Angel developed sympathy for the American Indian and in 1993 delivered a eulogy at Wounded Knee for the Native Americans killed there by soldiers of the United States Army.

[Yitzchak Kerem (2nd ed.)]

ANGEL, MEIR BEN ABRAHAM (c. 1564–c. 1647), rabbi and preacher. Angel was born in Sofia, where his father was a communal leader. His family immigrated to Safed in his youth and there he studied under Samuel *Uceda, Eleazar Ascari, and Ḥayyim *Vital; he also mentions Israel *Saruk as his teacher. Angel returned to his native town where he was appointed rabbi and preacher. He later served in other communities, including Belgrade. He visited Constantinople before 1620. His sermons were unique in form, as they were based on a homiletical explanation of the *Masorah Magna* of the Bible. He followed and developed the homiletic system of Jacob b. Asher and of Moses Alshekh, with his own kabbalistic comments. Angel published *Masoret ha-Berit* (Cracow, 1619), a commentary on more than 600 masoretic readings in alphabetical order, which was immediately in very great demand and was rapidly sold. He thereupon published *Masoret ha-Berit ha-Gadol* (Mantua, 1622) on 1,650 readings. His *Keshet Neḥushah*, an ethical work in rhymed prose, was published at Belvedere near Constantinople in 1593 by the press of Donna Reyna, the widow of Don Joseph Nasi. According to Conforte, Angel returned to Safed after 1622 and died there. The high esteem in which Angel was held by his contemporaries can be seen in the eulogy of Solomon Algazi (printed in *Ahavat Olam* (1643), sermon 20).

BIBLIOGRAPHY: Conforte, Kore (1846[2]), 51b; Ghirondi-Neppi, 252–3.

ANGEL, SHEMAYAHU (1810–1874), Turkish banker, merchant, and philanthropist. Angel provided generous support for the Jews of Syria and other Jewish communities throughout the Levant. He was born in Rosetta, Egypt, and settled in Damascus in 1832 after Muhammad ʿAli's occupation of Syria. There he used his wealth, reputation, and influence with the Ottoman authorities to help the local Jewish community, which suffered from the 1840 *Damascus Affair and the 1860 Druze revolt. Angel provided material assistance for the Ottoman troops engaged in suppressing the revolt and successfully extricated many Jews from alleged involvement in the uprising. Sultan Abdül Aziz decorated him and a guard of honor was present at his funeral. Angel's writings include "Les Biens de Mainmorte de la Communauté Israélite," in: *Hamenorah*, 4, no. 5 (May 1926), 133–44.

BIBLIOGRAPHY: M. Franco, *Essai sur l'histoire des Israélites de l'Empire Ottoman* (1897), 209–10.

[Joachim O. Ronall]

ANGEL OF DEATH (Heb. מַלְאַךְ הַמָּוֶת, *malakh ha-mavet*). The polytheistic concept of a specific deity of *death who is responsible for the origin and constant occurrence of death on earth (cf. the Canaanite idea of the god *Moth*) was rejected by Jewish monotheism. According to the Bible, God is the master of death and of life. The origin of death is motivated not by the actions of an anti-human supernatural being, but through man's own sin (cf. the formulation of Adam's punishment in Gen. 3:22–23). Death, however, is often personified in the Bible; the fact that he has emissaries and a host of angels alludes to his independence of God (cf. Prov. 16:14; Hos. 13:14). These allegorical notions, probably survivals of a polytheistic influence on the Bible, are dominated by the more pervasive concept that only God possesses the power to return mortal man to dust (cf. Job 10:9). This power He delegates to a "messenger" (*malakh*), one of His many angel servants. A cruel snatcher of souls, the "Angel of the Lord" who "smites" and "destroys" human beings (cf. II Sam. 24:16; Isa. 37:36) is called the destroyer (Ex. 12:23; II Sam. 24:16) and is described as standing between earth and heaven, with a drawn sword in his hand (I Chron. 21:15–16). The Bible only refers to a temporary messenger and the instances in the Bible in which death is personified (Prov. 16:14; 17:11; 30:12; Ps. 49:15; 91:3; Job. 18:14) do not point to a constant sacred power or to a permanent angel whose function it is to terminate life on earth.

Only in post-biblical times did the concept of an Angel of Death who acted independently emerge. In popular belief, he was conceived as an amalgam of forms and concepts which had their biblical associations with death, cruelty, and wretchedness. The Angel of Death was also identified with the horrifying and dreadful ogres and demons described in the oral tradition, in the literature of the ancient Near East, and in the literatures of medieval Europe ("devil" and "Satan"). An active supernatural being, interested not only in fulfilling God's orders, but also on his own initiative, in fighting, harming, and destroying man, the Angel of Death is identified in the Talmud (BB 16a) with *Satan ("Samael") and with *yeẓer ha-raʿ* ("evil inclination"). He symbolizes the demoniac forces, which were responsible for Adam's fall and which continue to fight his descendants.

In folklore, the Angel of Death is described allegorically: He is full of eyes (nothing escapes him), a diligent reaper (cf. Jer. 9:20), an old man holding a sword dripping poison into the mouths of mortals, etc. (cf. Av. Zar. 20b; Ar. 7a). But mostly he appears disguised as "a fugitive and wanderer" (cf. Gen. 4:12 on Cain, the first being to take another man's life), a beggar, a peddler, and an Arab nomad. Since the Angel of Death is only a messenger in Jewish tradition, his powers are limited and depend on his master's (God's) decrees and orders. Thus there are remedies to overcome the Angel of Death and weapons against him. In general folk literature, the combatants of death endeavor to find the "herb of life" (cf. the Gilgamesh epics), or go in quest of magic means to attain *immortality. In normative Jewish legends, the study of the Torah, or some exceptional act of piety or benevolence, replaces the magic weapons generally used against death (cf. the folk exegesis on Prov. 10:2; 11:4 – Charity delivers from Death). There are, therefore, many heroes, most of them biblical, who defeated the Angel of Death with their efficacious prayer, constant study, and outstanding acts of charity for a short or longer period. In the numerous versions of the legend about the death of *Moses (*Midrash Petirat Moshe*), Moses succeeds in chastising Samael who comes to fetch his soul. Only God's promise that He Himself would take the soul induces Moses to lay down his staff with the engraved Ineffable Name which had made the Angel of Death flee in terror. One of the post-biblical heroes who defeated the Angel of Death was R. *Joshua b. Levi. He seized the slaughtering knife and even came close to abolishing death forever. Only God's intervention brought about the sage's surrender (Ket. 776).

Several of the animals that achieved immortality, among them the *milḥas* or *ziz* birds (aggadic equivalents of the phoenix), as well as many of the persons who entered Paradise alive, "without tasting death" (cf. Ginzberg, Legends, 5 (1925), 96), reached their goal after a successful confrontation with the Angel of Death. The confrontation of mortals with the Angel of Death is a theme prevalent in folk literature and in popular traditions. The three main types of narrative in which the motif is found reflect man's ambivalent attitude toward death:

(1) Where the Angel of Death is defeated, mainly by means of deception. Legends of this kind have mostly a humorous tone, as the cheated and fooled Angel of Death is a grotesque and stupid character. Man's victory reflects his wishful thinking and longing to alter his mortal fate, or at least to postpone his time of death. The heavenly decree of death and the determination of each man's span of life are, indeed, irrevocable; since the executor, however, is not God Himself, the possibility exists to escape the messenger and to extend at least the span of life, if immortality in life itself cannot be attained. This narrative is associated with many motifs found in the universal tales of the "stupid ogre" and the "beaten devil." The Angel of Death is tricked into missing the right moment for taking the soul. He is fooled by the change of the doomed mortal's name (a tale still found in current folk literature in all Jewish communities); fails to identify the man whose soul he is supposed to fetch; marries a termagant who torments him and is at a loss to comprehend the queer conduct of Jews, etc. Already at creation the Angel of Death is cheated by the fox and the weasel: he thinks their reflections which he sees in the sea to be them. This fable in the Alphabet of *Ben Sira, which is similar to Far Eastern tales that originated in India, has been the subject of much comparative research and investigation.

(2) The cruel and stubborn Angel of Death as hero of tales of horror and magic. In this narrative, mortals upon meeting the terrible Angel of Death accept his authority submissively with their heart full of fear. In the Talmud, R. Naḥman is reported as having said: "Even if the Almighty were to order me back upon earth to live my life all over again, I would refuse because of horror of the Angel of Death" (MK 28a; see Rashi *ibid.*). In this narrative, the Angel of Death cannot be induced to swerve from his course; he is also the source of

magic knowledge, including medicine. In the stories belonging to this type of narrative, the Angel of Death is a physician of excellent repute (or an assistant to a physician). He controls sickness, diseases, and plagues (his messengers). Sly, he takes man's life prematurely, frightens and harms people, and is merciless and brutal. In the Book of Jubilees (10:1–13), Noah prays that the wicked spirits will not destroy him and his sons, and God answers his prayer. However, He allows only one tenth of the "malignant ones" to remain, ruling that Noah be taught all of the medicines for their diseases so that he might cure them with herbs.

(3) The compassionate Angel of Death is the outgrowth of man's optimism and wishful thinking. In this narrative the Angel of Death, though inherently cruel, can be moved to mercy and concession by a mortal's exceptional deed. The narrative includes the numerous Jewish versions of the Greek Alcestis (Indian Savitri) motif (cf. A. Jellinek, *Beit ha-Midrash*, 5 (1938^2), 152–4) where the wife offers the Angel of Death her own life as substitute for that of her husband or fiancé. In one of the versions (cf. M. Gaster, *The Exempla of the Rabbis* (1968^2), no. 139), the Angel of Death, seeing the devotion and readiness of self-sacrifice of the bride of Reuben the Scribe's son (after his parents had refused to serve as substitute), sheds a "tear of mercy." The Almighty then grants the couple 70 additional years of life, proclaiming: "If he who cruelly kills souls [i.e., the Angel of Death] has been filled with mercy for them, shall not I who am 'merciful and gracious' [Ex. 34:6] show compassion toward them?" To this narrative belong also the stories of the helpful Angel of Death who rewards a benevolent man, consoles people after a disaster, etc.

In most of the legends in the three types of narratives, the encounter between the mortal and the Angel of Death takes place on the mortal's wedding night when either bride or bridegroom is doomed to die and opposes the executor. The evil demon Asmodeus (or Ashmedai) slays the seven husbands of Sarah so that she can become a wife to Tobias, in the apocryphal book of Tobit (3:8, 17). In another post-biblical work, the Testament of Solomon, Asmodeus informs the king that his object is to plot against the newly married and bring calamities upon them. Solomon learns how to subdue him (as in Tobit 8:2) and harnesses him for work in the building of the Temple. Jewish preachers and storytellers associated either the defeat or the concession of the Angel of Death, occurring specifically on that occasion, not only with the "wedding versus death" motif which intensifies the contrast in the narrative but also with the biblical prophecy, "And then shall the virgin rejoice in the dance, and the young men and the old together, for I will turn their mourning into joy" (Jer. 31:12). Homiletic interpretation of this verse could easily associate it with the motifs extant in the "Angel of Death at the wedding" stories. The motif of a young girl unsuccessfully imploring the Angel of Death (an aged, white-haired gentleman) not to take her life is very common in Yiddish folk ballads (cf. N. Priluzki, *Yidishe Folkslider*, 2 (1913), 1–42: Songs and Tales of Death). Unlike the folktales, the ballads end tragically.

The Angel of Death played also an important role in the Jewish dance of death, where he capered with sinners (mostly misers) of all classes and professions. His movements, mostly grotesque, as was the whole dance (performed by wandering troupes of paupers), highlighted the feeling of "memento mori" (cf. Ecclus. 7:38). The performances given mostly on festive and gay occasions (weddings, Purim meals, etc.) offset the surrounding glamour, joy, and splendor. The dancing Angel of Death often recited or sang; in his song he stressed the vanity of mortal and perishable values and contrasted them to everlasting and immortal merits and piety.

In many of the Jewish folk customs related to death, *burial, *mourning, and folk medicine, the traditional acts are directed against the unseen source of the disaster, the Angel of Death. Practices which do not seem to bear a direct affinity to the Angel of Death (closing the eyes of the dead, pouring out the water in a house where death had occurred, breaking pots, mourners' meals, narrating *theodicy folktales, etc.) go back to old folk beliefs in which the Angel of Death, or demons affiliated with him, played a dominant role. Most of these beliefs are no longer current. A comparison of past and present mortuary and funeral customs, traditions, and beliefs in Eastern and Western Jewish communities and those in the culture areas of these communities can contribute toward a reconstruction of the original affinities between belief and rites with regard to the Angel of Death.

The impersonation of the Angel of Death led to the extension of his traits and characteristics to the members of his family and servants etc. Indeed, in Jewish-Islamic folk legends, Azrail (the name of the angel who removes the soul from the dying body) is married, has children, sends emissaries (diseases, old age), etc. This also holds true for Samael in East Europe who is often identified with the Angel of Death himself. He is married to *Lilith, who, beside her Satanic functions of luring and seducing men, also performs duties on behalf of her husband, the Angel of Death: she kills babies, harms pregnant women and those giving birth, etc. She fights life and human attempts to continue its successive chain in the same way as the Angel of Death. In many folktales, the Angel of Death is tormented by his wife (cf. Eccles. 7:26; where "death" became personified), his sons often suffer (one of them usually accepts his father's advice and becomes a physician), and all the family members suffer from various disasters and calamities. The motifs in these tales are mainly man's revenge on the Angel of Death and the consolation that man finds in this revenge; the concept being that as long as man has no other means to overcome his eternal and, in the end, always successful adversary, his only way out is through ridicule and irony.

BIBLIOGRAPHY: C. Barth, *Die Errettung vom Tode* (1947); Key, in: JBR, 32 (1964), 239–47; J. Zandee, *Death as an Enemy* (1960); Ginzberg, Legends, 7 (1938), 31; J. Rabbinowicz, *Der Todtenkultus bei den Juden* (1898); JQR, 12 (1899/1900), 20; J. Trachtenberg, *Jewish Magic and Superstition* (1961), 335; T.H. Gaster, *The Holy and the Profane* (1955), 242–7; H. Chayes, in: YIVO, *Filologishe Shriftn*, 2 (1928), 281–328; Zelkovitsh, in: *Lodzher Visnshaftlekhe Shriftn*, 1 (1938),

149–90; D. Noy, in: *Haifa Yorbukh*, 5 (1969), 177–224; Schwarzbaum, *Studies in Jewish and World Folklore* (1968), 430, 501–2; E.R. Lange, *Sterben und Begraebnis im Volksglauben zwischen Weichsel und Memel* (1955); S. Thompson, *Motif Index of Folk Literature*, 6 vols. (1955–58), D 1725, F 833, R 185, Z 111.

[Dov Noy]

ANGELS AND ANGELOLOGY. The entry is arranged according to the following outline:

Bible
- TERMINOLOGY
- ANGELS AS A GROUP
- THE ANGEL OF THE LORD
- IN THE HAGIOGRAPHA
- SILENCE OF THE PROPHETS
- EZEKIEL AND ZECHARIAH
- DANIEL

Apocrypha
- AMONG THE JEWISH SECTS
- FUNCTIONS OF ANGELS
- FALLEN ANGELS

Angels in the Talmud and Midrash
- ORIGIN OF ANGELS
- CLASSIFICATION OF ANGELS

In the Liturgy
- MOVEMENTS OPPOSING THE VENERATION OF ANGELS

Mysticism

In Jewish Philosophy
- PHILO
- MAGHĀRRĪYA AND KARAITES
- SAADIAH GAON
- ABRAHAM IBN EZRA
- MAIMONIDES
- AVICENNA AND AVERROES

Modern Period

Bible

Many biblical writers assume the existence of beings superior to man in knowledge and power, but subordinate to (and apparently creatures of) the one God. These beings serve as His attendants, like courtiers of an earthly king, and also as His agents to convey His messages to men and to carry out His will.

TERMINOLOGY. These beings are clearly designated by the English word "angel." The terminology of biblical Hebrew is not so exact. *Mal'akh* (מַלְאָךְ), the word most often used, means "messenger" (cf. Ugaritic *lak* "to send"). It is applied frequently to human agents (e.g., Gen. 32:4) and is sometimes used figuratively (e.g., Ps. 104:4). This term was rendered in the Greek Bible by *angelos* which has the same variety of meanings; only when it was borrowed by the Latin Bible and then passed into other European languages did it acquire the exclusive meaning of "angel." Post-biblical Hebrew employs *mal'akh* only for superhuman messengers, and uses other words for human agents. Apparently for greater clarity, the Bible frequently calls the angel the *mal'akh* of God; yet the same title is occasionally applied to human agents of the Deity (Hag. 1:13; Mal. 2:7). Elsewhere angels are called *'elohim* (usually "god" or "gods"; Gen. 6:2; Job 1:6), more often *bene 'elohim* or *bene 'elim* (lit. "sons of gods") – in the general sense of "divine beings." They are also known as *kedoshim (qedoshim*; "holy beings"; Ps. 89:8; Job 5:1). Often the angel is called simply "man." The mysterious being who wrestled with Jacob is first called a man, then *'elohim* (Gen. 32:24 (25), 28 (29), 30 (31)), but Hosea refers to him also as a *mal'akh* (Hos. 12:5). As a result of this diversity, there are some passages where it is uncertain whether a human or superhuman messenger is meant. The Bible also speaks of winged creatures of angelic character called *cherubim and seraphim, who serve a variety of functions. A further ambiguity is due to the fact that the Bible does not always distinguish clearly between God and His messenger. Thus, Hagar encounters an angel, but later addresses "the Lord that spoke unto her" (Gen. 16:7, 13; similarly 21:17ff.). It is God who commands the sacrifice of Isaac; later Abraham is addressed by the angel of the Lord from heaven (Gen. 22:1ff., 11-18). The angel of the Lord appears to Moses in the burning bush (Ex. 3:2), but through the rest of the story Moses converses with the Deity. So, too, in the Gideon story, Gideon speaks sometimes with God, sometimes with the angel of God (Judg. 6:11ff.). Some scholars infer from this phenomenon that the angel was not regarded as an independent being, but simply as a manifestation of the Divine power and will. Others suppose that in the earliest version of these stories a human being was confronted directly by God, and that later scribes toned down the boldness of this concept by interposing an angel.

ANGELS AS A GROUP. Micaiah describes a vision in which the Lord is seated on His throne, with the host of heaven standing by on His right and left (I Kings 22:19; II Chron. 18:18). But frequently the phrase "host of heaven" means the heavenly bodies (Deut. 4:19; Jer. 8:2, etc.). Similarly, Isaiah (ch. 6) sees the Deity enthroned while the seraphim proclaim His holiness and majesty. One of the seraphim purifies Isaiah by a symbolic act, so that, unlike Micaiah, he becomes not a witness to but a participant in the ensuing deliberation of the council (cf. Zech. 3:7b), and when the Lord, as in Micaiah's vision, calls (like El in the council of the gods in the Ugaritic Epic of Keret) for a volunteer, Isaiah responds. In the ancient cosmic hymn Psalms 89:1–3, 6–19, the goodness of God is praised by the assembly of the holy beings because, the psalmist emphasizes, He is incomparably greater than they and they stand in awe of Him (Ps. 89:6–9). This last is similarly stressed in two other early compositions (see Ex. 15:11 and Ps. 29). Not improbably, the motif arose in an age when it was not yet a platitude that "the assembly of the holy beings" or "the company of the divine beings" (Ps. 29:7) is not a pantheon of real gods. So, no doubt, did the practice of representing those beings as standing before God, who alone is seated (I Kings 22:19; Isa. 6:2; Zech. 3:1–7, especially 3:7 end; Job 1:6; 2:1). The exception, Isaiah 14:13, only confirms the rule: the speaker there is a pagan. Despite the masoretic pointing *dina'* ("the Tribunal") in Daniel 7:10, 20, the scruple may have persisted into the second century C.E., since the context favors rather the interpretation of the consonantal graph דינא as *dayyana'* ("the Judge"). Related to the deuteronomic idea that the Lord actually assigned the heavenly bodies and the idols to the Gentiles but chose Israel to worship him (Deut. 4:15–20; 29:25) is the remarkable passage (Deuteronomy 32:8–9): "When the Most High gave nations their homes and set the divisions of men, He fixed the borders of peoples according to the numbers of the divine beings (בְּנֵי אֵל; so a Qumran fragment, in agreement with the Septuagint). But the Lord's own portion is His people, Jacob His own allotment." The masoretic reading בְּנֵי יִשְׂרָאֵל "the children of Israel" for the reading of the Qumran fragment and the Septuagint cited above is a conflation of the latter and of a variant שָׂרֵי אֵל, "the ministers of God." This variant is not attested directly, but its existence may be deduced from the fact that it would account both for the masoretic reading in Deuteronomy 32:8 and for the use of שַׂר, "minister" in Daniel 10:20 twice, 21; 12:1. For these passages are obviously nothing but a bold development of Deuteronomy 32:8–9. Their doctrine is that the fates of nations are determined by combats among the celestial "ministers" to whom they have been assigned and that (despite Deut. 32:9) Israel also has a "minister," Michael, who is assisted by another angel, Gabriel. In Job, the divine beings appear before God as a body, perhaps to report on the performance of their tasks and to obtain fresh orders; one of them is the Satan, who carries out his functions under God's directions (Job 1:6ff.; 2:1ff.). The angels seen by Jacob ascending and descending the ladder (Gen. 28:12) seem to be messengers going forth on their several errands and coming back to heaven to report.

THE ANGEL OF THE LORD. The narrative books offer many instances of an angel – rarely, two or more – delivering a message or performing an action, or both. The angel appears in human form, and sometimes is not immediately recognized as an angel. The appearance of an angel to Hagar (Gen. 16:7ff.; 21:17ff.) and to Abraham at Mount *Moriah (Gen. 22:11ff.) was noted above. Further, three "men" visit Abraham to announce the birth of Isaac; two of them go on to Sodom to warn Lot to flee and to destroy the city (Gen. 18:1ff.; 19:1, 13ff.). The angel of God appears to Jacob in a dream, says "I am the God of Beth-El," and bids him return to his home (31:11ff.). The angel of God plays a role, not entirely clear, in the events at the Sea of Reeds (Ex. 14:19ff). In the *Book of the Covenant, God promises to send His angel to lead the Israelites and to overcome the obstacles to their entrance into the promised land. God's name is in the angel, who must be faithfully obeyed (23:20ff.). When Balaam accedes to Balak's plea for help, the angel of the Lord comes as an adversary to the enchanter. The angel is visible to the she-ass, but Balaam cannot see the angel until the Lord opens his eyes (Num. 22:22ff.). When the "captain of the host of the Lord" appears to Joshua, the latter does not at first realize that his visitor is an angel (Josh. 5:13). The *mal'akh* of the Lord in Judges 2:1ff., 10 and 5:23 may be a prophet; but the visitor who summons Gideon to leadership and performs wonders is clearly an angel (*ibid.* 6:11ff.). The same is true of the emissary who foretells the birth of Samson, and whose angelic nature is made manifest only when he ascends to heaven in the altar flame (*ibid.* 13:2ff., esp. 16, 20). An angel with a drawn sword is the agent of the pestilence in the days of David (II Sam. 24:16–17; I Chron. 21:15ff.; the drawn sword is mentioned also in the Balaam and Joshua incidents). The old prophet pretends he has received a revelation from an angel (I Kings 13:18). An angel appears once in the Elijah stories (*ibid.* 19:5ff.). The army of Sennacherib is destroyed by the angel of the Lord (II Kings 19:35; Isa. 37:36; II Chron. 32:21). The angel of the Lord appears two times in Psalms: in 34:8, he protects the righteous; and in 35:5–6, he brings doom upon the wicked.

IN THE HAGIOGRAPHA. Other references to angels in the Psalms are scattered throughout the book. In a few places, angels are called on to join with the rest of creation in praising God (Ps. 29:1; 103:20–21; 148:2; cf. 89:6ff.; in 96:7, the phrase "families of the nations" is substituted for the "sons of God" of 29:1; Ps. 78:49 and 104:4, most probably refer to forces of nature that perform God's will). In Psalms 91:11–12, God commands His angels to protect the faithful from harm. The other Hagiographa have little to say about angels. The only possible allusion, in Proverbs 30:3, is doubtful. In Job, aside from the references to the "sons of God," angels are mentioned only by the three friends and Elihu. The friends point out that even the angels, the holy ones, are not flawless, and that man is still further from perfection (Job 4:18; 5:1; 15:15). Elihu speaks of an angelic intercessor for man (*ibid* 33:23–24), but the passage is obscure. The subject matter of the Five Scrolls is such that no special significance need be attached to their silence on the subject of angels (Eccles. 5:5 is hardly relevant).

SILENCE OF THE PROPHETS. The prophets, except Ezekiel and Zechariah, say almost nothing about angels. In all pre-Exilic prophecy, there are just two passages in which angels are mentioned. One is the rather obscure reference to the Jacob story in Hosea (12:5–6; contrast v. 14). It has been explained as a satirical attack on the cult of the angel (or divinity) Beth-El (see Ginsberg, in: JBL, 80 (1961), 343–7; cf. Gen. 31:11–12). The other is Isaiah's initial vision (6:1ff.), in which the winged seraphim have a prominent part. Thereafter, Isaiah makes no mention of angels (33:7 is obscure and probably not Isaianic). Jeremiah is completely silent on the subject; so is (according to the critical theory) the roughly contemporaneous Book of Deuteronomy. In the Exilic period, Deutero-Isaiah does not mention angels (Isa. 63:9 does mention the "angel of His presence," but the Greek reads – probably correctly: "No messenger or angel; it was His presence that saved them"). Special significance is attached to the fact that Haggai calls himself (1:13) "the messenger of the Lord with the message of the

Lord" (*mal'akh 'Elohim be-mal'akhut 'Elohim*) – apparently to stress the thought that God's emissary to man is a prophet, not a supernatural being. Malachi's attitude is not entirely certain. His name (meaning "My messenger") may be a pseudonym, and he asserts that the priest is the *mal'akh* of the Lord of Hosts (Mal. 2:7). The *mal'akh* of the Covenant (*ibid.* 3:1–2) may, however, be an angel, though the phrase might also refer to the returning Elijah (*ibid.* 3:23–24). Finally, it should be noted that the priestly code (regarded by many scholars as post-Exilic, though others consider it very ancient) does not allude to angels, except for the provision that cherubim are to be depicted on the Ark cover. This array of facts cannot be dismissed as mere accident, especially since angels appear so often in the narrative portions of the Pentateuch, in the historical books, and in the prophetic writings of Ezekiel and Zechariah. Perhaps David Neumark overstressed this disagreement as a major issue of biblical thought (see: e.g., his *Essays in Jewish Philosophy* (1929), 104ff.). But the issue was certainly not unimportant.

EZEKIEL AND ZECHARIAH. In the theophanies described by Ezekiel, the Divine Presence is seated on a throne supported by four fantastic creatures, called in chapter 1 *ḥayyot* ("living beasts" or "beasts"), but identified in chapters 8–11 as cherubim. In the latter section, moreover, the destruction of Jerusalem is a task assigned to six armed "men," while a "man clothed in linen with a scribe's inkhorn on his side" is to mark the foreheads of such righteous individuals as are to be saved (9:1ff.). Later, this same man in linen takes live coals from the fire between the cherubim, to be used in setting the city afire (10:1ff.). Chapters 11–39 of Ezekiel do not mention angels. But in the visions of the rebuilt Temple (ch. 40–48), the prophet is guided by a man "who shone like copper" (40:3) and who goes about measuring the various courts and buildings and explaining their functions. During the vision Ezekiel also receives instruction directly from God; and after chapter 47:12 the "man" is not mentioned again.

In Zechariah, angels are almost constantly present. The book consists largely of symbolic visions, explained to the prophet by "the angel that spoke with me" (1:9, 14; 2:1–7; 4:1–5; 5:5–10; 6:4–5). The "angel of the Lord" appears several times; he intercedes with God on behalf of Israel (1:12–13); he presides over the rehabilitation of Joshua and rebukes the Satan for accusing the latter (3:1ff.). A number of other angels are reported to be standing by. Zechariah also applies the term "man" to angelic beings (1:8ff.; 2:5ff.; the two women with stork-like wings, 5:9, seem to be symbolic figures rather than angels). For the first time in the Bible the angels in Zechariah appear to be acquiring an independent life on their own.

DANIEL. The Book of Daniel repeats much about angels which is found in earlier parts of the Bible. It tells of innumerable attendants around the Divine throne (7:10), and reports that an angel saved the three men in the furnace (3:25, 28) and Daniel from the lions (6:23). It sometimes calls an angel "man"; one angel is described as a man clad in linen (10:5; 12:7; cf. above on Ezekiel). But Daniel has strong affinities with the extra-biblical apocalypses, and so presents many new features in regard to angels. The revelations received by Daniel are either symbolic visions, which an angel interprets (ch. 7, 8), or they are revealed in their entirety by an angel (ch. 10–12). Zechariah, too, had visions which an angel explained. But he also delivered prophecies received directly from God; such a thing never occurs in Daniel. In the latter book, too, angels do not merely carry out orders, but have some powers of initiative: "The matter has been decreed by the ever-wakeful ones, the sentence is by the word of the holy ones" (4:14). Moreover, the angels now have proper names: *Gabriel (8:16; 9:21) and *Michael (10:13; 12:1). This is the only biblical book in which angels have distinct personalities. Finally, the idea that each nation has an angelic patron, whose actions and destinies are bound up with those of his nation, is encountered for the first time. Mention is made of the patrons of Persia and Greece (10:13, 20); and Michael is the champion of Israel (12:1; on this concept cf. Isa. 24:2).

[Bernard J. Bamberger]

Apocrypha

In post-biblical literature angels frequently manifest themselves as independent beings, distinguishable by their own names and individual traits. Contrary to the general impression gained from the Bible, certain allusions contained in it lead to the assumption that in the earlier periods of Jewish history angels played a more independent role in popular mythology than in the post-biblical period. It was not, however, until the Hellenistic period of Jewish history that the conditions existed for a special doctrine of angels.

During the Second Temple period it was assumed that only the great prophets of earlier times had had the privilege of direct communication with God while in later generations mysteries of the end of days and of man's future could be discovered only through the intermediary of angels. This led to attempts to explore the nature and individual character of the angels. Furthermore, Jewish literature of this period sought to teach the mysteries of nature, of heaven, of the end of days, etc.; revelation no longer served as the point of departure for the acquisition of knowledge, but as corroboration of the validity of existing doctrines – on medicine (Jub. 10:10ff.), botany (1 En. 3:1), astronomy, cosmology, etc. This type of apocalyptic wisdom literature assumed that the secrets of the universe could be found only beyond the range of earthly surroundings – by means of angels. The development of the concept of angels was also deeply influenced by the syncretism which characterized the Hellenistic Age. By means of the wisdom of the Chaldeans (which enjoyed great prestige among the Diaspora Jewry, see Dan. 1:4), the Jews had become familiar with many of the old Babylonian myths – the creation, the deluge, the early generations of man, etc. – and they sought to harmonize the myths with the biblical reports of these events. Old Babylonian tales of intercourse between gods and legendary heroes, and of books containing heavenly wisdom, were thus made to concur with Jewish legends; however, in order to avoid contradiction with the monotheistic character of Judaism, they were ascribed to the world of angels. One such example was Enoch, a figure created under the influence of Babylonian concepts, who appears as the bearer and creator of human culture, and as the transmitter of heavenly wisdom to the early generations of man; his authority is derived exclusively from his constant communication with angels. Various sources treat Noah and Abraham in the same manner, ascribing their wisdom to their intimate knowledge of the world of angels. In addition, various religious concepts accepted by the Jewish people under the influence of pagan magic and demonology – insofar as they were not in direct contradiction to monotheism – were eventually incorporated into the doctrine of angels.

AMONG THE JEWISH SECTS. The doctrine of angels was not evenly spread among the various parts of the Jewish people. The apocalyptic wisdom teachers imparted the knowledge that they had secretly acquired through their contact with angels, only to a narrow circle of the specially initiated. Consequently, the doctrine of angels found its widest distribution among the secret societies of the Essenes. The latter (Jos., Wars, 2:142) carefully guarded the secret list of angels' names. The Qumran scrolls testify to an organized system of angelology, in which the "Prince of Light" and other heavenly princes were expected to fight alongside the Sons of Light on the "last day," and they thought them present at meetings of the Qumran sect. A certain dualism is seen in the struggle for power between the forces of evil (Belial) and those of goodness over the sons of man (1QM 13:11). The Pharisees, on the other hand, showed little interest in these problems. The Sadducees, who were opposed to any kind of mysticism, are described by the Acts of the Apostles (23:8) as denying the very existence of angels; this however, was undoubtedly a false assumption, derived from the Sadducees' rejection of apocalyptic teachings. Among Jewish magicians and sorcerers, the concept of angels was particularly confused, influenced as they were by the pagan literature on the subject, where the angels usually appear in the company of pagan gods, to combat disease. In some literary sources biblical figures, such as Solomon, are mentioned as having been in possession of secret formulas or means whereby they were able to induce angels to come to man's aid. The Greek "Testament of *Solomon" cites a number of angels with whose activities Solomon became acquainted only with the help of demons. A similar manipulation of angels through the use of magic is found in the *Sefer ha-*Razim*. Angels appearing in post-biblical literature may be divided into several classes. The angel appearing in one of the visions of Zechariah (1:9) is not mentioned by name, but his active advocacy of the cause of Israel indicates that he was not a "messenger" in the strict sense of the term. In the Book of Daniel (8:16; 9:21) the angel Gabriel appears as an interpreter of Daniel's vision. In later apocalyptic writings various angels appear as interpreters of symbolic visions, such as Uriel (I En. 19:1; 27:2), Raguel (23:4), Raphael (32:6), and Michael (60:4ff.; *Testament of Abraham*, ed. James, passim). A group of seven angels is frequently described as heading the world of angels; also designated as "archangels," they have "entry to the presence of the glory of the Lord" (Tob. 12:15). They are Uriel, whose function is to lead the angelic host and guard the underworld (Sheol); Raphael, who is in charge of the spirits of humans; Raguel, who takes revenge upon the world of lights; Michael, who watches over Israel; Sariel, whose duties are not defined; Gabriel, who rules Paradise; Jeremiel (IV Ezra 4:38), who according to a later apocalyptic composition (*Apocalypse of *Elijah;* Ger., ed. by Steindorff, p. 10) guards the souls of the underworld (I En. 20). These seven angels are always in the proximity of God and are the ones that are always called upon to carry out tasks of special significance for world history, such as the punishment of the fallen angels, or of the 70 angels who act as princes of the peoples of the earth (I En. 90:21ff.), the elevation of Levi to the priesthood (Test. Patr., Levi 8), the transmission of heavenly wisdom to Enoch (I En. 81:5ff.), etc. A similar list is preserved in the *Serekh Shirot Olot le-Shabbat* (Angelic Liturgy) from Qumran (in VT Suppl. 7, pp. 318–45), in which the heavenly tasks of each of seven angels is recorded. Their names, however, were omitted. The War Scroll describes two angels of prime importance: "The Prince of Light" and "The Angel of Darkness," with whom were associated "the sons of righteousness" and "the sons of darkness" respectively (1QM 13:10–12). These angels were in perpetual conflict and thought to fight on the sides of the two armies at the "last battle," when the Angel of Darkness and his army would be destroyed. This is likewise expressed in the Manual of Discipline (1QS 3:20–22), "In the hand of the Prince of Light is the dominion of all the sons of righteousness… and in the hand of the Angel of Darkness is the dominion of the sons of evil." Some have supposed that the Prince of Light was Uriel but others think he was Michael, for he is described in the War Scroll (1QM 17:6) as being sent by God in "eternal light" (cf. Dan. 10:13, "Behold Michael, one of the leading princes has come"). The Angel of Darkness seems to have been Belial: "But for corruption you have made Belial, an angel of hatred and his dominion is in darkness" (1QM 13:11).

Related to the group of seven is a group of four angels, most of whose names appear also among the seven; designated as "the angels of the Presence" (*Malakhei ha-Panim*) they are in Enoch: Michael, Gabriel, Raphael and Phanuel (sometimes Raphael and Gabriel are interchanged). They have an important role in the punishment of the fallen angels (I En. 9:1; 10:1ff.; 54:6). Their place is on each of the four sides of God's throne (40:2ff). Contrary to all other angels, they move freely in and out of the Palace of God – the "Heaven of Heavens" – to serve "the *Ancient of Days" (i.e., God: I En. 71:5ff.). In the *Book of Adam and Eve*, however, and in rabbinic literature the four are Michael, Gabriel, Uriel, and Raphael. The names of a similar group of angels (Michael, Gabriel, Suriel, and Raphael) were to be inscribed on the battle-towers at the "last battle" (1QM 9:15). Another special group of angels are the 70 "princes of the peoples," appointed over each of the 70 peoples of the earth. They are first mentioned in the Septuagint to Deuteronomy 32:8 – without their number being given – from which it may be gathered that at this time the number of all angels was thought not to exceed the number of peoples. Ben Sira (Ecclus. 17:17) quotes the figure 70; the Hebrew Testament of Naphtali (Test. Patr., Naph. 8–9) regards them as the 70 ministering angels (*Malakhei ha-Sharet*). The latter source relates that at the time of Peleg (cf. Gen. 10:25) God descended from Heaven with the 70 angels in order to teach the peoples of the earth their respective languages. Later, Michael, at the behest of God, asked each people to choose its patron angel, and each people chose the angel who had taught it its language, with the exception of Israel, which chose God Himself as its patron. According to a concept found in the Book of I Enoch (89:59ff; 90:22, 25), at the time of the destruction of the First Temple, these 70 angels were appointed to rule over Israel (whom God had rejected) until the Day of Judgment.

Another category of angels are the "guardians." Like the general concept of angels (cf. the Ba'almalakh in CIS, vol. 1, part 1, no. 182, verse 2; part 2, no. 1373, verse 4), "guardian angels" seems to have been a religious concept common to the entire Semitic world, a fact which supports the identification of guardians with Ζωφασημιν (equivalent to the Hebrew *ẓofei shamayim*) by Philo Byblos (Eusebius, *Praeparatio Evangelica*, 1:10, 3). At times the title of guardian, similar to the title "he who never sleeps," is employed to designate all angels (I En. 61:12; 39:12) for it is their function to be on guard before God at all times; the same was later also said of angels whose function it is to supervise the actions of man (see I En. 100:5). The guardians are also regarded as a superior category of angels, although not equal to the "angels of the Countenance." They are at all times in the proximity of God and must not leave Him by day or by night. Due to their special importance, they are also designated as "the holiest of the holy" (I En. 14:23). Many scholars see a connection between the guardian angels and the "Irin" (עִירִין, Aram. "watchers") mentioned in the Book of Daniel (4:10, 14, 20). A reference to the "Irin" has been found in the *Genesis Apocryphon* in which Lamech expresses concern over the conception of Noah, who, he fears, was a child "of the watchers (*Irin*), the holy ones, or the fallen angels" (1QA poc. 2:1). In the *Genesis Apocryphon* (1QA poc. 2) the term refers to "the sons of God" in Genesis 6:2ff. (cf. I En. 6:8). Perhaps the divine cherubim described by Ezekiel (10:12) are also to be regarded as "guardians" in the sense that the term is used in apocalyptic literature. According to the Book of Jubilees, they descended from Heaven at the time of Jared (cf. Gen. 5:15–20) to teach mankind the practice of law and justice (4:15ff.); they were seduced by the daughters of men and thus the fallen angels came into being. As a result, the guardian angels are sometimes identified with the fallen angels (see I En. 10:9; 12:4; 13:10; 14:1ff.; and passim); other sources, however, make a clear distinction between the two (Slavic Book of II Enoch 7:8; 35:2). Apart from these angels, who were thought to resemble man, the stars were also assumed to be living entities and regarded as angels (Isa. 34:4; 40:26; 45:12; Jer. 33:22; Ps. 33:6; I En. 18:13ff.; 21:3ff.). However, the more widely accepted version was that certain angels rule the stars (Jub. 19). Connected with this was the concept of the spirits of elements (a concept which came into being under pagan influence), e.g., the angels of the spirit of fire, of the spirit of the wind, the clouds, darkness, snow and hail, thunder, and lightning (Jub. 2:2ff.; I En. 60:11ff.; 65:8; Or. Sybill. 7:33ff., etc.). This category also includes the angels of the seasons of the year, all of which – with hardly any exception – bear Semitic names (I En. 82:10ff.). A foreign influence may also be discerned in the concept of angels functioning as the originators and inventors of human civilization. Thus in "The Life of Adam and Eve," Michael appears as Triptolemus (in the mythology, the hero who taught man grain cultivation) teaching Adam how to work the soil. In addition to the angelic hosts mentioned in the Bible and Apocrypha under generic names, such as cherubim, seraphim and *ofannim*, there are also angels of power, and angels of dominion; angels who serve as patrons of individual human beings (already alluded to in Ps. 91:11); angels of peace (I En. 52:5; 53:4; 54:4; 56:2; Test. Patr., Ben. 6), and angels serving as intercessors (*malakh meliẓ*, Test. Patr., Levi 5). Beside the Angels of Light, Darkness and Destruction (see above) there also occur in the Dead Sea Literature Angels of Holiness (1QM 7:6).

FUNCTIONS OF ANGELS. Offering praise to God is regarded as the major function of angels (I. En. 40; Test. Patr., Levi 4). Their functions as intermediaries between God and man were, however, also of special importance. As early as the Book of Tobit (3:16; 12:12, 15) Raphael is depicted as one of the seven angels charged with bringing the prayers of man before God's throne (compare Test. Patr., Dan 6). At times, an angel is ordered by God to accompany a man on his travels in order to ward off dangers that may beset him, or, as in the Greek Apocalypse of Baruch, to guide Baruch through the seven heavens and explain the sights. More frequent is the angels' role as intercessors, pleading for man before God (I En. 9:4ff.; 15:2; etc.); sometimes man pleads with the angels to transmit his prayers to God (*ibid.* 9:2). Angels also appear in opposition to evil angels who wish to act as prosecutors before the throne of God. It is significant, that in spite of Exodus 33:11 ("God would speak to Moses face to face"), the prevailing opinion of later traditions is that at the giving of the Law the angels acted as intermediaries between God and Moses (Jos., Ant., 15:136; Jub. 1:27ff.; Gal. 3:19; Heb. 2:2). Specific mention of the presence of angels at the right hand of God, during the Revelation on Sinai, is made in the Septuagint, Deuteronomy 33:2.

Although no traces of a cult of angels were retained in normative Judaism, in the *Sefer ha-Razim* angels seem to be used for purposes of magic. Formulas for influencing the angels, stars, and the moon by means of incantations over flasks of wine and blood, by burning incense, sacrifices, and other methods all appear in *Sefer ha-Razim.* Likewise the names of the angels, when coupled with those of Greek gods and magic phrases, were efficacious for incantations (*Sefer ha-Razim*, ed. Margaliot, 1:123–6; 2:99; introduction, 8–9). Testament of Levi 5 makes mention of an appeal to an angel; the passage, however, does not imply that an angel can be venerated as an independent being, for the context makes it clear that the angel acts only as an intermediary between God and Israel. The imperfect nature of angels is frequently stressed. Although they are regarded as immortal (I En. 15:6), their existence did not precede the Creation; they were created on the First Day (Jub. 2:1 ff.), or, according to another version (Slavic Book of II En. 29), on the Second Day. Nor are they omniscient; sometimes they are incapable of answering questions put to them and have to confess their ignorance (IV Ezra 4:51). It follows from this that communication between God and man by means of angels is regarded only as a temporary situation. Before the First Temple was built, communication between God and Israel was by means of an angel, but afterward God and Israel communicated directly, without an intermediary (Job. 1:27 ff.). This concept of the nature of angels permitted the view that no unbridgeable gulf existed between the material world and the world of angels, and some righteous men could be transformed into angels (I En. 51:4). Similarly, in the fragments of the pseudepigraphal "Prayer of Joseph," Israel, known to mankind as Jacob, declared that in reality he was "the archangel of the power of the Lord" and no mere mortal (Origen, Commentary to John, II, 84, 15). Even the people of Israel as a whole, by virtue of its covenant with God, was in some ways regarded as being equal to angels; in consequence, while other peoples are in the custody of angels, Israel is under the protection of God Himself and is independent of angels (Jub. 15:27 ff.). A further development of this view gives Israel the privilege of participating in the heavenly choir of the angels; at the time that the angels praise the glory of God – as they do at certain hours of the day – the praise by the people of Israel is also heard before the heavenly throne (Ḥul. 91b; *Constitutiones Apostolicae*, 8:35). This idea may be similar to the concept found in Coptic texts and the Prayer of Joseph of an angel "Israel" who serves God in heaven.

[Joshua Gutmann]

FALLEN ANGELS. A special category are the so-called Fallen Angels, frequently mentioned in post-biblical literature. This concept is also common to all Semitic peoples; the idea of vanquished gods or demons, who then appear as accursed and damned, is one that prevailed among all the peoples of antiquity. It is found in a special form in earlier versions of the story of the creation, in which Rahab appears in the role of the vanquished god. Although for a variety of reasons little trace has remained of the ideas upon which the Rahab legends are based, the dualistic concepts of paganism have nevertheless exerted a profound influence upon Judaism, and the concept of the existence of good and evil powers, contradicting as they did the idea of monotheism, found their way into Judaism through the story of the Fallen Angels. It must be pointed out, however, that the passage Genesis 6:1 ff., although usually quoted as the basis of all subsequent legends of Fallen Angels, has in fact little to do with this concept, as it later developed. Not only is the interpretation of "Nephilim" as Fallen Angels of a doubtful nature (see Num. 13:33), but the text contains no denouncement of the "*Benei Elohim*" who had married the daughters of men; on the contrary, it stresses that the children of these connections were "the heroes of days gone by, the famous men." It was only at a later stage, when the dualistic belief in the existence of evil demons had become a firm component of popular religion, that attempts were made to find biblical authority for this concept, contradictory as it was to monotheism.

The earliest report of Fallen Angels is found in the Book of Enoch (6 ff.): The sons of heaven, who belonged to the "guardian" angels, had lusted for the beauty of the daughters of men and in the time of Jared decided to descend upon Mt. Hermon to carry out their plans from there. There were two hundred of them and their leader was Shemhazai; he made them swear an oath (*ḥerem*) to adhere to their purpose and it was this oath that gave the mountain its name – Hermon. They consorted with the daughters of men, who gave birth to a generation of giants who set about mercilessly destroying human beings. The Fallen Angels also taught man the use of weapons and other tools promoting immorality and crime. In this manner a demonic wisdom came into being, in addition to Divine wisdom, and this led to the corruption of mankind. Moved by man's outcry, the four archangels appealed to God and were given the order to punish the Fallen Angels. Later there is a resumé of this episode in chapter 69, where the Fallen Angel Jeqôn was blamed for the downfall of all the angels. Each of the Fallen Angels taught mankind a particular evil or perversion, thus destroying mankind's innocence (69:1 ff.). The story of Fallen Angels, in the same spirit, appears in the Book of Jubilees (4:15; 5:1 ff.), with the difference that here the angels are said to have descended to earth to instruct mankind how to order society, and when they arrived on earth they were seduced by the daughters of men. A hint at this latter idea is preserved in the additional chapter at the end of the Book of Enoch (106), called the Fragment of the Book of Noah. Here the angels are feared for having taken to themselves the daughters of man. In the Qumran *Genesis Apocryphon* (the Birth of Noah), Noah is suspected of being the offspring of an evil angel and a daughter of Man (1QA poc. 2:1–26).

Apart from the punishment meted out to them before the Deluge, final sentence on them would be passed on the day of the Last Judgment (I En. 16:1 ff.; see also *Azazel). Talmudic sources contain a different version of the legend of the Fallen Angels. According to *Midrash Avkir* (see Smaller *Midrashim), the leaders of the Fallen Angels, named Shemhazai and Asael (as in the Book of Enoch), heaped scorn upon the sinfulness of the generation of man after the Deluge. God submitted that if they were on earth, they would also commit sins, and in response to this challenge they offered to descend to earth. They did so and were at once seduced by the beauty of the daughters of men; they revealed the secret Name of God to a girl named Istehar, who by virtue of this knowledge was able to escape from the hands of Shemhazai and ascend to heaven. This experience did not have any effect upon Shemhazai and his associates. They took wives unto themselves who gave birth to two sons, Hiva and Hiya, whose names (the syllables Hi-va and Hi-ya) henceforth became the cries of pain uttered by suffering men. Thus, this version is closer to the story told in the Book of Jubilees, for in it the Fallen Angels commit their sin only after their descent to earth. Other versions in talmudic literature contain even more far-reaching variations from the story as told in the Book of Enoch: in these versions, it was only after the angels had assumed the nature of man that they committed sin (PdRE 22, et al.). Some talmudic circles attacked the interpretation of Genesis 6:1 in the sense that it is found in the Book of Jubilees. On one occasion, R. *Simeon b. Yoḥai interpreted the term *"Benei Elohim"* as "sons of the judges" and condemned those who gave it the meaning of "sons of God" (Gen. R. 26:5). Similarly, *Midrash ha-Ne'lam* (on this passage) interprets the term "Nephilim" as referring, not to the Fallen Angels, but to Adam and Eve who had come into being on earth without having had a father and a mother. Maimonides also states that the term *"Elohim"* as used in this instance should be taken in its profane sense (*ḥol*), the reference being to "the sons of rulers and judges" (M. Gaster, in: *Devir*, no. 1 (1923), 196). This opinion was also shared by other Jewish scholars in the Middle Ages. Related to the concept of Fallen Angels is another concept found in apocryphal literature, that of the 70 angels whom God had charged with the power over Israel after the destruction of the First Temple and who abused this power by persecuting Israel (I En. 53:3; 62:11; 63:1; 89:59; 90:22, 25). By these deeds the angels violated God's will and came to be regarded as rebellious angels to whom punishment would be meted out. It was under the influence of this concept that Satan – who in the Bible appears either as a punishing angel of God or as an angel testing the sincerity of the Righteous – came to be regarded as an independent evil demon. According to an apocryphal source, his fall followed immediately upon the creation of Adam: the angels were ordered to bow before Adam, but Satan refused and was deposed (Adam and Eve, 12 ff.). Other concepts of Satan appear to have come about under the influence of Parsiism (see *Satan). Satan was also known by two other titles, *Belial and *Samael. The former was frequently identified as the spirit of evil, and in the Dead Sea Scrolls he stood at the head of the forces of darkness. The latter appears as a prime foe of Michael.

Angels in the Talmud and Midrash

In the talmudic age, belief in angels was general, among both scholars and laymen. There were, however, differences of opinion among the sages as to the nature of angels. Some maintained that a new group of angels was created every day, who praised God on that day and then sank in the river of fire (*nehar di-nur*). Others accepted this opinion and added that only two angels, Michael and Gabriel, permanently serve God while all other angels sing their hymn of praise on the day of their creation and then disappear (Ḥag. 14a; Gen. R. 78:1). The distinction between eternal angels and those created for a specific purpose only seems to have been widely accepted among talmudic sages engaged with problems of religious philosophy; Ben Azzai mentions the two categories of angels as though their existence was a generally acknowledged fact (Sifra 1:1). The Mishnah makes no mention at all of angels and this may be due to the tendency to minimize their significance. Other tannaitic sources, while containing references to angels, rarely mention those angels who bear proper names. It is also significant that even eternal angels are said to be incapable of viewing the glory of God.

ORIGIN OF ANGELS. The Talmud and Midrash contain a variety of opinions on the origin and nature of angels. The angels were created on the second or the fifth day of creation (R. Johanan and R. Ḥanina, Gen. R. 1:3 and parall.; S.A. Wertheimer, *Battei Midrashot*, 1 (1950^2), 25; cf. also R. Kirchheim in *Oẓar Neḥmad*, 3 (1860), 59, ed. J. Blumenfeld). Creation of angels is continuous since every pronouncement by God results in the creation of angels. Angels walk upright, speak Hebrew, and are endowed with understanding; they can fly in the air, move from one end of the world to another, and foretell the future (Ḥag. 16a). Thus angels have something in common with both men and demons. They have the shape of man, but consist half of fire and half of water (TJ, RH 2; PdRK, ed. Mandelbaum, 6; Song R. 3:11, 15). The angels enjoy the splendor of the *Shekhinah* and are free of the *yeẓer ha-ra* ("evil inclination"; Gen. R. 48:11); they have no needs (Yoma 4b; Mid. Ps. to 78:25; cf. also LXX and Targum, Ps. 78:25; MGWJ, 22 (1873), 113); they are classified according to countries and as a result there are angels who must not leave Ereẓ Israel (Tanḥ. B., Gen. 178); no angel may carry out more than one mission at a time (BM 86b; Gen. R. 50:2; Justin Martyr, *Dialog.* 56c); and they are capable of error (Eccles. R. 6:10, no. 1: cf. Adam and Eve 13–05). According to one concept the size of an angel is equal to a third of the world (R. Berechiah, PR 83:12; Gen. R. 68:12).

CLASSIFICATION OF ANGELS. Angels are divided into angels of peace and evil angels; the former dwell near God, while the latter are remote from Him (R. Johanan, Tanh. B., Lev. 39). There are also angels of life and angels of death (R. Samuel b. Isaac, Gen. R. 9:10). The number of angels is countless; they are classified into groups of higher and lower angels. Like apocryphal literature, the *aggadah* regards Gabriel, Michael, Raphael, and Uriel as the archangels and refers to them as the ministering angels (*malakhei ha-sharet*); the angels Sandalfon, Zagzagael, and Suriel appear only rarely. The angel *Metatron assumes great importance in the Midrash. There are angels who control such matters as prayers, hail, rain, anger, Gehinnom, birth and pregnancy, and other matters. The names of angels, according to talmudic sources, became known to Israel only after the return from the Babylonian exile. The *aggadah* elaborates upon the concept already developed in the apocryphal literature of the guardian angels of the nations of the earth and of individual kings. The former are regarded as hostile to Israel and have to be put in chains to prevent their doing harm to Israel (Ex. R. 42:1; Gen. R. 56:11). When their nations fall, the guardian angels fall with them, and when they are punished the angels also suffer punishment (Mekh. SbY to 15:1; Deut. R. 1:22). A similar concept of guardian angels is, incidentally, also found with Christian Neoplatonists (see A.F. Daehne, *Geschichtliche Darstellung der juedisch-alexandrinischen Religions-Philosophie...* 2 (1834), 62ff.; C. Bigg, *The Christian Platonists of Alexandria*, 1913²). Dubiel, the guardian angel of the Persians, was known by name to the rabbis (Yoma 77a); the guardian angel of Edom is also mentioned (Mak. 12a; A. Jellinek, *Beit ha-Midrash*, part 3 (1855), 70); in some instances, the guardian angel of a people pleads on its behalf in order to avert Divine punishment. At the time of the Exodus from Egypt, the guardian angels of all the nations were summoned by God to discuss His quarrel with Egypt. During the discussions, the angel Gabriel, acting upon orders from Michael, produced a portion of the wall which the Israelites had been forced to build for the Egyptians. When it was found to contain the body of an Israelite child, punishment was meted out – first to the guardian angel of Egypt and then to the Egyptians themselves (Yal., Ex. 243). Other *aggadot* tell of the guardian angels of all the nations accusing Israel of being no better than all others (PdRK, ed. Mandelbaum, 221). Kings are also said to have guardian angels; Nebuchadnezzar's angel bore the name of Kal (Ex. R. 21:5). The sea has its own guardian angel (BB 74b; Ex. R. 15:22; 24:2). Frequent mention is made of the angel or "Prince" (שַׂר) of the world (Ex. R. 17:4; Ḥul. 60a). The angels' relationship to God is described as dependence upon Him. They must take no step without His command (Tanḥ. B., Ex. 115). Their main purpose is to sing hymns in praise of God and to proclaim His sanctity (*ibid.* 120; Sif. Deut. 306). They are incapable of viewing the glory of God and do not know their own dwelling place (Yal., Deut. 825; Mekh. SbY to 15:2). God may forbid them to sing, as He did when the Egyptians were cast into the sea (Meg. 10b; Ex. R. 23:7). God consults the angels on occasion, as He did before the creation of man (Gen. R. 8:5). Angels are quoted as posing questions regarding contradictions found in the Bible. From the third century, the expression of God's "familia" (*Pamalya*) or the heavenly court of justice is found in the sources. God takes no action without prior consultation with the "familia"; such consultation should be assumed in all instances where the expression "and God" appears in the biblical text. The *Angel of Death (*malakh ha-mavet*) plays a special role among the guardian angels and is regarded as the most evil among the wicked angels (*malakhei ḥabbalah*).

The above data leads to the conclusion that angels were generally regarded as being superior to mortal man. On this point, however, the *aggadah* contains divergent views. Thus it is asserted that the righteous are superior to the ministering angels. Other sages, for whom this claim was too excessive, granted the righteous a status equal to that of the ministering angels; every man has the capability of becoming equal to angels and of resembling them. A third version restricts this capability to Israel as the people of God. Yet another view is that equality to angels can be achieved only after death. There is also the opinion that at the end of days the righteous will rank above the angels and that the angels will learn the mysteries of heaven from the righteous (TJ, Shab. 6:10, 8d). These varied views found in the *aggadah* were apparently influenced by contemporary trends. Heretical influences can also be discerned in the view of the archangels' participation in the creation of man and in the giving of the law; the *aggadah* combats such theories by various means and on all these occasions makes angels appear as opposing the Divine will. Nevertheless, by its extensive use of angelology as a means of interpreting the story of the Bible, the *aggadah* may well have contributed more to the intensification of the belief in angels than all the heretics and angel worshipers combined.

The *aggadah* contains numerous examples of actions carried out by angels in the biblical and post-biblical periods. As mentioned above, God consulted the angels before creating man (Sanh. 38a; Gen. R. 8:5; Justin Martyr, *Dialog.* 62c); at Adam's wedding to Eve, Michael and Gabriel acted as sponsors (*shoshevinin*, R. Abbahu, Gen. R. 8:15; PdRE 12, 16). Angels attended Adam in the Garden of Eden (Sanh. 59b; ARN 151), but they later became his accusers (PdRE 13). The angel Samael made Eve pregnant (Targ. Jon., Gen. 4:1; PdRE 21). Enoch is removed from earth and ascends to heaven, where he is given the name of Metatron (Gen. R. 25:1 and parall. Targ. Jon., Gen. 5:24); an angel leads the animals into Noah's Ark (Zev. 116; Gen. R. 32:8; PdRE 23; Targ. Jon., Gen. 6:20). God converses with the ministering 70 angels who correspond to the 70 tongues and 70 nations (see ZDMG, 57 (1903), 474; ZAW, 19 (1899), 1–14; 20 (1900), 38ff.; 24 (1904), 311; REJ, 54 (1907), 54). Angels are subject to punishment and are expelled from heaven (Gen. R. 50:13; 68:18; 78:3) for betraying its secrets (Targ. Jon., Gen. 28:12). On special occasions, angels assume the shape of men or animals (Targ. Jon., Gen. 32:25; 37:15; see also the miraculous story of R. Ḥanina b. Dosa (Eccles. R. 1:1; Song R. 1:1, 4, et al.) of R. Yose b. Ḥanina and the two brothers of Ashkelon (Song R. 7:3, 8; Deut. R. 2:20; Ex. R. 1:36, et al.)). The angel who wrestled with Jacob seeks to return to heaven in time for the morning hymns of praise (Gen. R. 78:2). God spoke to Sarah through an angel (Gen. R. 53:5); angels argue with God over Isaac's sacrifice (Gen. R. 56:7; Targ. Jon., Gen. 22:10) and rescue Abraham from Nimrod's fiery furnace (Pes. 118a); angels bear Isaac to Shem and Eber's house of learning (Targ. Jon., Gen. 22:19). An angel with a drawn sword appears before Laban in his dream (Targ. Jon., Gen. 31:24). Gabriel approaches Joseph in the shape of a man (Targ. Jon., Gen. 37:15). The angel Zagzagael reveals himself to Moses in the Burning Bush; angels make their appearance at the Sea of Reeds and at the giving of the Law on Mount Sinai. Michael or Metatron call on Moses to ascend to God; in heaven, the angels attempt to take Moses' life. The angels join God in wailing over the death of Moses, and over the destruction of the Temple. Angels try to shut the windows of heaven, to prevent Manasseh's prayer from being heard (TJ, San. 10:2, 28c). Gabriel saves the three youths in the furnace (PdRE 33). Michael smites Sennacherib's army (Ex. R. 18:5). Ministering angels also gather in the post-biblical period, to listen to the discussions between R. Johanan b. Zakkai and R. Eleazar b. Arakh (TJ, Meg. 2:1, 77a); or to engage scholars in conversation (MK 28a; Men. 41a); they accompany and protect the Righteous (Shab. 119b, et al.; see Reitzenstein, Poimandres 13). God ordains that angels be ready at all times to help man (Gen. R. 65:15).

In the talmudic age, like in earlier periods, no traces of angel worship are to be found, in spite of the Church Fathers' assertion to the contrary. One talmudic passage (Sanh. 38b) may imply that angel worship was practiced by certain sects who were close to Christianity, but the talmudic sages took strong exception to this practice (see TJ, Ber. 9:1, 13a); the claims of Christian writers regarding angel worship among Jews may well refer to these sects.

[Arthur Marmorstein]

In the Liturgy

The concepts concerning angels, as developed in the *aggadah*, have also been incorporated into the liturgy. This is especially true of the idea of angels singing hymns in praise of God; different groups of such angels appear in the *kedushot* hymns of the *tefillah* and the *yoẓer*, each in a role of its own. Thus, in the *tefillah*, it is the seraphim (*Sarfei Kodesh*) which are given prominence, while in the *yoẓer* it is the *ofannim, Ḥayyot ha-Kodesh*, and the cherubim (the mention of the latter being based on Isa. 6:3; Ezek. 3:12). It was presumably in the early geonic period that the doctrine of angels was given increasing prominence in the daily prayers, under the influence of mystical movements, especially the "*Yoredei Merkavah.*" Prime examples are the introductory and connecting passages of the *Kedushah* and the hyperbolic descriptions of the *yoẓer.* Both these portions of the prayers afterward inspired numerous *piyyutim*, which reveal a growing speculation about angels and introduce new designations and functions for them. The very name of the *piyyutim* of the *yoẓer* – "*ofan*" – points to their preoccupation with angels; in the course of the centuries the *piyyutim* became more and more extravagant and detailed in their descriptions. The hymns inserted between the various passages of the *Kedushah* describe the adoration of the angels with an infinite variety of images and terms. Of a similar nature are certain portions of the *Siddur* of *Amram b. Sheshna Gaon, in which several angels appear in apocalyptic visions, the prayer *mi-ymini El u-mi-semoli Uzzi'el*, and others (see *Seder R. Amram*, 13b, 54a and passim). In several of the *Seliḥot* angels appear in yet another role, that of independent beings whose task it is to transport the prayer of man to God, so that He may have mercy upon the petitioner (*malakhei raḥamim makhnisei raḥamim*). This idea also has its origin in apocryphal literature, the Talmud, and the Midrash. Special concepts of the role of certain angels were held by the group of mystics who lived in Safed in the 16th century and were first led by Isaac *Luria and later by Ḥayyim *Vital. This group ascribed to the daily prayer a special redemptive significance, for it was the prayer that achieved the perfection of world order; it regarded the angels as the leaders of the heavenly spheres who would accept only those prayers which are consecrated to a certain name of God, by means of prescribed preparations and concentrations. This implies a special appeal to the angels. According to this concept, the angel Sandalfon weaves a crown for the infinite God out of the prayers that have been accepted, and the angel Metatron rewards the petitioner for his prayer by granting him the heavenly blessing. By virtue of its doctrine and its strict way of life, the Safed group gained great influence among the Jewish people. Its continued efforts to introduce new prayers into the liturgy expressing its doctrine gained wide acceptance.

MOVEMENTS OPPOSING THE VENERATION OF ANGELS. To counteract this movement, an opposing trend developed whose aim it was to entirely exclude angels from the liturgy. One of the most outspoken opponents of appealing to angels was *Maimonides (see his commentary of Sanh. 10). Joseph *Kimḥi (12th cent.) made the following observation on the practice of appealing to angels: "True penitence does not stand in need of intervention by the saints; feigned penitence will not be helped by either the dead or the saints, by man or angel" (*Sefer ha-Berit* in *Milḥemet Ḥovah, p.* 33a). Isaac *Abrabanel agrees with Maimonides' view decrying appeals to angels (*Rosh Amanah*, ch. 12). Yom Tov Lipmann *Muelhausen (14–15th century) opposed the practice in the following terms: "Our sages rejected any intermediation between man and the Creator; appeals to intermediaries lead to devilry and idolatry" (*Sefer ha-Nizzaḥon*, no. 132). Among the opponents of appealing to angels there were such who did not reject outright the terms *malakhei raḥamim makhnisei raḥamim* (angels of mercy, introducers of mercy), but rather made amendments to the text that avoided any implication of pleading with angels for their intervention (see "*Netivot Olam,*" *Netiv ha-Avodah*, ch. 12, by *Judah Loew b. Bezalel of Prague; *Ḥatam Sofer,* OḤ, no. 166). Those authorities who did not introduce any amendments to the text of the prayers, felt themselves obliged to justify why they did not regard these passages as contradicting pure monotheism (*Shibbolei ha-Leket*, no. 282 and others). Yet in spite of the rejection of the practice of appealing to angels, popular belief has clung to this doctrine and the prayer book has retained traces of it. It was only when the *siddur* by Benjamin Ze'ev Wolf *Heidenheim was published (c. 1800) and a new era of prayer book literature was inaugurated, that a regression of the doctrine of angels took place, accompanied by a general rejection of mystical ideas. Although passages of mystical contents may even be found in *siddurim* of the Reform movement, the present tendency calls for a total exclusion of such prayers from the prayer book.

[Dov Shmuel Flattau (Plato)]

Mysticism

Mysticism distinguishes several categories of angels: ministering and corrupting angels, angels of mercy, and angels of severe judgment. Furthermore, angels with masculine characteristics are distinguished from those with feminine qualities (Zohar 1:119b; 2:4b). The angels stemming from the highest light came into being on the first Day of Creation and enjoy eternal life; the others, having rebelled against God and consequently having been consumed by fire, were formed on the second Day of Creation (*ibid.* 1:17b, 46a). The angels consist of fire and water or, according to another account, of four heavenly elements: mercy, strength, beauty, and dominion, corresponding to the four earthly elements: water, fire, earth, and air (*Sefer Yeẓirah* ("Book of Creation"), ch. 1, 7; *Pardes Rimmonim*, sect. 24, ch. 10f.). The angels represent spiritual powers of the finest, ethereal substance. When fulfilling their functions on earth, they manifest themselves sometimes in human form and sometimes as spirits (Zohar, 1:34a, 81a, 101a; *Pardes Rimmonim*, sect. 24, ch. 11). The strength of the angels lies in the emanation of the Divine light which becomes manifest in them and because of which they are described as elements of the heavenly throne (*Pardes Rimmonim, ibid.*). The notion, already found in apocalyptic literature, that the ministering angels daily sing hymns before God and praise His wisdom, was enlarged upon in later Jewish mysticism. The Zohar (1:11 to 45) says that the angels live in the seven heavenly halls (*heikhalot*). A special hall is set aside for a certain type of angel that mourns the destruction of the Temple (the so-called *Avelei Ẓiyyon;* "Mourners of Zion"; *ibid.* 2:8b). The ministering angels may only begin to sing in heaven when Israel commences to praise God on earth. The angel Shemiel carries the prayers of the Jews from their synagogues up to the Temple, whereupon the hosts of ministering angels, suffused in streams of light, descend to earth only to return to the Divine throne to intone their hymns to God (*Pirkei Heikhalot*, in Eisenstein's *Oẓar ha-Midrashim*, 1 (1915), 123). Of the ministering angels, those serving God Himself are called youths (*baḥurim*), and those serving the **Shekhinah* are called virgins (*betulot;* J. Israel, *Yalkut Ḥadash* (1648), nos. 63, 93). The angels led by archangels are arranged in four groups before the throne of God. *Uriel's group stands in front of the throne, Raphael's group behind it; Michael's group is to the right, and to the left is Gabriel's (*Massekhet Heikhalot*, Eisenstein, op. cit., p. 109). The first encounter between the angels and man is supposed to have taken place when at God's behest the mysterious Book of the Heaven was handed to Adam through *Raziel, Hadarniel, and Raphael (Zohar 1:55b). The angels know all men's futures; their fate is made known in heaven by a herald. Every day angels in raiments of light are dispatched to the lower world with special assignments: some serve the human body, others the soul (Zohar 2:10a, 11a, h, 94a, 118b). In each human being there lives a good angel and a wicked one (1:144b); man's every step is accompanied by good and bad spirits (3:48b). Even in the hereafter the angels accompany man where, depending upon his life on earth, he is received either by the angels of peace or by the angels of destruction (*Zohar Ḥadash* to Ruth (1902), 89a). In the service of the unclean of the *sitra di-semola* ("left side") stand the angels of destruction (*Malakhei Ḥabbalah*), corresponding to the ministering angels of the holy *sitra di-ymina* ("right side"). In accordance with God's command, the latter bring man either good or evil, but with the angels of destruction malice is a natural characteristic. These angels, too, live in seven halls and are subject to certain "superiors." They swarm through the air, mingle with humans in order to seduce them, and later report their sinful acts to their leaders so that the latter can present the indictments before God (*Pardes Rimmonim*, sect. 26, chs. 1–7). The huge army of the angels of destruction, the counterpart to God's entourage, constitutes the family of the unclean "other side," the so-called *kelippah*.

[Samuel Abba Horodezky]

In Jewish Philosophy

PHILO. Philo identified the angels of Scripture with the demons of the Greek philosophers (Gig. 2:6; I Sonn. 142). They were, according to him, incorporeal and immortal souls hovering in the air and ascending to heaven, which having "never felt any craving after the things of the earth," never descended into bodies. They were intermediaries between God and men, hence they are represented as "ascending and descending" in Jacob's dream. Unlike the Stoic philosopher Posidonius (b. c. 135 B.C.E.), who saw in the demons the necessary link between the upper and lower stages of being, Philo considered the angels merely as instruments of Divine Providence, whose services could on occasion be dispensed with when God chose to address men directly. There were, however, "evil angels" also, who were not messengers of God and hence "unworthy of their title." Evidently, Philo was thinking of the "fallen angels" of Jewish apocalyptic literature.

MAGHĀRRĪYA AND KARAITES. Philonic and gnostic influences were combined in the angelology of al-Maghārrīya, a Jewish sect that flourished in Egypt during the first centuries of the common era. As attested by al-*Kirkisānī, Karaite dogmatist and exegete, and al-Shahrastānī (1076 or 1086–1153), Muslim historian of religion and philosopher, the Maghārrīya interpreted all anthropomorphic passages in the Bible as referring to an angel, rather than God Himself, and claimed that it was the angel who created the world and addressed the prophets. According to al-Kirkisānī the writings used by this sect included a work by "the Alexandrian," a reference, no doubt, to Philo. The angel-demiurge of the Maghārrīya, therefore, represents a distorted and gnostically inspired version of Philo's *logos. This doctrine has no parallels in either the sectarian Qumran writings or in the Greek literature describing the Essenes. It is, however, closely akin to the view held by the Karaite theologian Benjamin *Nahawendi in the first half of the tenth century, as was already noted by al-Kirkisānī. Judah *Hadassi, the 12th-century Karaite teacher, followed Nahawendi in predicating the appearance of angels in all instances of prophecy, including that of Moses, to whom the highest angel is said to have appeared.

SAADIAH GAON. *Saadiah Gaon rejected the Karaite view that the anthropomorphic terms in the Bible refer to angels.

He explained the passages describing Divine revelations to Moses and the other prophets by his theory of the "created glory" (*kavod nivra*) and "created speech" (*dibbur nivra*). The "created glory," identified by him with the rabbinic concept of *Shekhinah* ("Divine Presence"), is a manifestation of light accompanying the "created speech" and proof that the voice heard is of Divine origin. The angels, too, are created and luminous, but rank below the *kavod*. Nevertheless, Saadiah does admit that prophetic revelation may also take place through the mediacy of angels.

ABRAHAM IBN EZRA. Abraham *Ibn Ezra understood Saadiah's views as asserting the superiority of men over angels and attacked his notion. Man, according to him, is far below the angels, since all his knowledge is imperfect; only under certain conditions may his soul be admitted to the rank of the angels in the afterlife. This disagreement stemmed from different conceptions of the angelic nature. For Saadiah, the angels, although more refined in substance than man, are still corporeal beings, while in Ibn Ezra's view, they are identical with the immaterial or simple substances of Neoplatonic ontology. They represent the "supernal world," which is "all glory" and consists of the "supernal forms" of all things below (cf. Ibn Ezra's commentary on Genesis 1:1, which is more explicit in the first recension, J. Blumenfeld (ed.), *Ozar Neḥmad*, 2 (1857), 210ff.; cf. also M. Friedlaender, *Essays on the Writings of Abraham ibn Ezra* (1877), 115). This Neoplatonic view of the world of angels is poetically described in Ibn Ezra's Hebrew paraphrase of *Ḥai ibn Yaqẓan* by the Muslim philosopher Avicenna, which he called *Ḥai ben Mekiẓ* (in D. Rosin's *Reime und Gedichte des Abraham ibn Ezra* (1885–94), 196). Avicenna identified the angels of the Koran with the "separate intelligences," which, following Aristotle, he assumed to be the external movers of the spheres.

MAIMONIDES. The equation of the "separate intelligences" (Ar. *ʿuqūl Mufāraka;* Heb. *sekhalim nifradim* or *sekhalim nivdalim*) with angels became the accepted doctrine in Jewish Aristotelianism. Declaring that the angels are incorporeal, *Maimonides writes, "This agrees with the opinion of Aristotle; there is only this difference – he used the term 'intelligences' and we say 'angels' instead" (Guide, 2:6). This view marks a radical departure from the traditional view of angels as corporeal beings. The assertion of their incorporeality raised the questions of how they could be visibly perceived and what could be meant by the biblical descriptions of them as flying, winged, and so on. Maimonides answered that all such attributes should be understood as figurative expressions (Guide, 1:49). At the same time he considered the word "angel" a homonymous term denoting not only the separate intelligences, but all natural and psychic forces, both generic and individual. Thus, the formative power which produces and shapes the limbs of an embryo may be called an angel; the libidinous disposition aroused by the sight of a beautiful woman may be spoken of as "an angel of lust" (as in Gen. R. 85:8); the spheres and elements, too, may be referred to as "angels" (Guide, 2:6–7). The rabbinic statement "Every day God creates a legion of angels; they sing before Him and disappear" (Gen. R. 78:1) was taken by him to describe the natural and psychic forces in transient individuals.

AVICENNA AND AVERROES. Jewish Aristotelians were greatly influenced by the divergent views of the Muslim philosophers *Avicenna and *Averroes, who identified angels with the moving principles of the celestial spheres. According to Avicenna (c. 980–1037), the motions of the spheres were due to two kinds of movers, the intelligences and the celestial souls. The intelligences moved the souls by virtue of being their objects of contemplation, and the souls, in turn, moved their respective celestial spheres. Avicenna identified the hierarchy of the intelligences with the cherubim and that of the celestial souls with the ministering angels. This doctrine and the complicated theory of emanation supporting it were criticized by Averroes, who eliminated the angelic hierarchy of celestial souls and preserved only the angelic hierarchy of intelligences. He interpreted the "soul of the sphere" in the sense of "nature of the sphere."

Abraham *Ibn Daud and Maimonides followed Avicenna, while Jewish Averroists like Isaac *Albalag adopted Averroes' angelology. Ibn Daud (*Emunah Ramah*, ed. by S. Weil (1919), 58–62) demonstrated the existence of angels from the motions of the heavens, which were caused by the celestial souls' desire to imitate the intelligences. This is a clear restatement of Avicenna's dual hierarchy with the important difference, however, that the celestial souls are not specifically designated as angels. Maimonides also accepted Avicenna's dual hierarchy but reserved the term "angel" for the intelligences, the rank of an angelic order being in proportion to its capacity to conceive of God (Yad, Yesodei ha-Torah 2:5–8). Isaac Albalag, on the other hand, followed Averroes in opposing Avicenna's position and even exceeded Averroes' critique by denying the need for an internal principle of motion in the spheres. He proposed instead a dual hierarchy of intelligible and natural forces, or angels. Philosophers who rejected the doctrine of separate intelligences in its entirety and the angelology based on it were *Judah ha-Levi (Kuzari, 5:21; cf., however, 4:3, where he refuses to pronounce either for or against this view), Ḥasdai *Crescas (*Or Adonai*, 1:2, 15; 4:3), and Isaac *Arama (*Akedat Yizḥak*. 2). Both Avicennians and Averroists agreed that the separate intelligences (i.e., angels) were simple substances or pure forms without matter. A different view was held by Jewish Neoplatonists, such as Isaac *Israeli who described the hypostasis of intellect as composed of spiritual matter and form, and Solomon ibn *Gabirol, who held that the intelligible substances or angels are composed of matter and form. Abraham Ibn Daud (and Thomas Aquinas in his *De ente et essentia*) attacked Gabirol's view. Isaac *Abrabanel, in his commentary on the Book of Kings (ch. 3), quotes Gabirol's doctrine and offers an elaborate survey of the views advanced on the subject. For the role of angels in prophecy according to the Jewish Aristotelians see *Prophecy.

[Alexander Altmann]

Modern Period

The modern Jewish attitude to angels tends to regard the traditional references and descriptions as symbolic, poetic, or representing an earlier world-concept. Contemporary movements such as Reform Judaism and certain sections of the Conservative Movement have either completely expunged from the liturgy all references to angels or where they remain have understood them in poetic or mythological terms. They feel that a belief in their existence is out of keeping with a modern approach to the world and God and cannot be reconciled with modern rationalism.

The attitude prevailing among many of the Orthodox is ambiguous. They have retained the relevant liturgical passages and accept the appropriate biblical and rabbinic references, but nevertheless modern Orthodoxy tends to demythologize them and reinterpret them without compromising the belief in their ontological status. Angels are interpreted symbolically and belief in their existence is not denied altogether. The degree of literalness of this belief varies from sub-group to sub-group. It is only among the small fundamentalistic sections, such as some of the Ḥasidim as well as the Oriental Jewish communities, that the literal belief in angels, which for so long characterized Jewish thought, is still upheld.

BIBLIOGRAPHY: BIBLE: G. Davidson, *A Dictionary of Angels* (1967), introd.; L. Koehler, *Old Testament Theology* (1957), 157–60; F. Stier, *Gott und sein Engel im Alten Testament* (1934); Kaufmann Y., Religion, 63–67. APOCRYPHA, TALMUD AND MIDRASH: Jos., Wars, 2:142; Y. Yadin, *A Genesis Apocryphon…* (1956), 280–9; J. Neusner (ed.), *Religions in Antiquity… in Memory of E.R. Goodenough* (1968), 254–95; G.R. Driver, *The Judean Scrolls* (1965), s.v. *Angelology:* M. Margalioth, *Sefer ha-Razim* (1967), 14, 19, 20, 53; J. Strugnell, in: VT, suppl. 7 (1959), 318–45; A.R.C. Leaney, *The Rule of Qumran and its Meaning* (1966), index; E.E. Urbach, *Ḥazal: Pirkei Emunot ve-De'ot* (1969), 115–60 (bibl. 682–3). JEWISH PHILOSOPHY: A. Altmann, in: E.I.J. Rosenthal (ed.), *Saadya Studies* (1943), 17ff.; S. van den Bergh (ed. and tr.), *Averroes Tahafut al-Tahafut*, 1 (1954), 104ff.; H. Corbin, *Avicenne, Le récit visionnaire*, 2 (1954), 49–54, 66–67, 105; idem, *Avicenna and the Visionary Recital* (1960), 46–47; M. Friedlaender, *Ibn Ezra Literature, Essays on the Writings of Abraham Ibn Ezra* (1877, repr. 1964), 17, 115; N. Golb, in: JAOS, 80 (1960), 347–59; idem, in: JR, 41 (1961), 38–50; R. Margulies, *Malakhei Elyon* (1945, repr. 1964); A. Schmiedl, *Studien uber juedische… Religionsphilosophie* (1869), 67–88; G. Vajda, *Isaac Albalag* (Fr., 1960), 172–211; idem, *Recherches sur la philosophie et la kabbale dans la pensée juive du Moyen Age* (1962), 76–91 (= REJ, 3, 1962); H.A. Wolfson, *Philo*, 1 (1947), 218–21, 366–423; idem, in: *Dumbarton Oaks Papers*, 16 (1962), 67–93. MYSTICISM: G. Seholem, *Major Trends in Jewish Mysticism* (1941), 41, 268; idem, *Jewish Gnosticism, Merkabah Mysticism, and Talmudic Tradition* (1965); R. Margulies, *Malakhei Elyon* (1945, repr. 1964); A. Jellinek, *Beitraege zur Geschichte der Kabbala* (1852); idem, *Auswahl kabbalistischer Mystik* (1853); M.J. bin Gorion, *Sagen der Juden* (1913), 259ff.

ANGERS (Heb. אנג׳יירש), capital of the Maine-et-Loire department, western France, and of the ancient province of *Anjou. Jews probably resided in Angers from the 12th century. They were expelled by Charles II in 1289. The Jews who evidently resettled in Angers during the 14th century became the victims of bloody persecutions and humiliating restrictions. In 1394, soon after Anjou was reunited with France (1390), the Jews of Angers were again expelled, with the rest of the Jews of the kingdom (see *France). Jews subsequently visited Angers on business, but in 1758 the municipal council prohibited them from entering the market. The present "Rue de la Juiverie," bordering on the modern part of the city, is not the site of the medieval Jewish quarter. A number of Hebrew inscriptions may be seen on four covings above the portal of the Cathedral of Angers, describing the attributes of the savior, taken mainly from Isaiah 9:5. In 1968 there were 250 Jews in Angers.

BIBLIOGRAPHY: Brunschvicg, in: REJ, 29 (1894), 229–41; Joubert and Delacroix, in: Société d'agriculture, science et arts d'Angers, *Memoires* (1854), 129ff.

[Bernhard Blumenkranz]

ANGLO-ISRAEL ARCHAEOLOGICAL SOCIETY, founded in 1961 by Alec Lerner, Leon Shalit (at that time both on the staff of Marks and Spencer), and Richard Barnett, who was Keeper of Western Asiatic Antiquities at the British Museum. It is likely that they were influenced by both positive and negative considerations.

Positively, there was much popular interest at the time in what has often been called "Biblical Archaeology," and this same group had already been active in seeking to gain material support for excavations in Israel. During 1961–62, Yigal *Yadin was spending a year in London. In preparing for his excavations at *Masada, where the system of using volunteer labor was first introduced, he was in close touch with his three friends about the logistical problems involved. It is thus no surprise that he should have given the Society's inaugural lecture in November 1961 to an audience of some 700.

Negatively, it is likely that Barnett, who was also involved with the much older *Palestine Exploration Fund, was disappointed at the lack of interest being shown in academic circles in the work specifically of Israeli archaeologists and that he was anxious to foster a greater exchange of ideas and the dissemination of the important work that they were doing.

All these concerns led to the formulation of the main aims of the Society, which have continued to the present, namely public lectures (about ten per annum) on the archaeology of Israel and surrounding countries, and the support by grants of students going to join excavations in Israel and similar projects or of Israeli students who need to visit Britain for archaeological research. In recent years, these aims have been further developed by the introduction of museum visits, the provision of lectures in Manchester as well as London, joint lectures with other societies (including the PEF) and in particular by the publication of an annual *Bulletin* which, under the editorship of Shimon Gibson, has become established as a mainstream academic journal for archaeological and related research as well as continuing to provide summaries of the society's activities and lectures.

The society has had three chairman in its 25-year history; Barnett himself, who steered it with a very personal touch until 1985, then more briefly J.B. Segal, and since 1991 H.G.M. Williamson, who has sought to develop the role of the executive committee. Honorary presidents have been Lord Segal and currently Viscount Allenby of Megiddo, the great-nephew of the distinguished field marshal.

The charitable society has no religious or political affiliation, and its modest membership is open to all with an interest in the subjects it seeks to promote.

BIBLIOGRAPHY: D. Barag, "*In Memoriam* R.D. Barnett," in: *Bulletin of the Anglo-Israel Archaeological Society,* 5 (1985–86), 4–6; B. Barnett, "The Anglo-Israel Archaeological Society – Forty Years On," ibid., 18 (2000), 9–15. **WEBSITE:** www.aias.org.uk.

[H.G.M. Williamson (2nd ed.)]

ANGLO-JEWISH ASSOCIATION (AJA), British organization originally founded for the protection of Jewish rights in backward countries by diplomatic means. Its objectives and activities were patterned after those of the *Alliance Israélite Universelle. It was established in 1871 with Jacob Waley as its first president; five Jewish members of Parliament served as vice presidents. By 1900 it had 36 branches, 14 in British colonies. In 1871 it was instrumental in securing the creation of the Romanian Committee and in 1882 collaborated in establishing the Russo-Jewish Committee. From 1878 it cooperated with the *Board of Deputies of British Jews in the Conjoint (Joint) Foreign Committee. The AJA undertook educational work among "underdeveloped" Jewish communities, maintaining schools in Baghdad, Aden, Mogador, Jerusalem (the Evelina de Rothschild School), and other places. In 1893 it became associated with the direction of the *Jewish Colonization Association (ICA). As its president, Claude *Montefiore condemned the *Balfour Declaration. After the Board of Deputies became overwhelmingly Zionist in 1940, the AJA under Leonard J. *Stein became a rallying point of non-Zionist sentiment; as a result, ostensibly because it was not a democratically elected body, its representation on the Joint Foreign Committee was reduced and then abolished. After the establishment of the State of Israel, it modified its attitude toward Zionism. Circumstances have reduced its overseas interests. It published the *Jewish Monthly* (1947–52), and the *AJA Review* (1944–55) which was superseded by the *AJA Quarterly,* and more recently by *AJA Today.* In recent years it has awarded student scholarships and holds cultural events, but it has also continued to represent the Jewish community on government and international bodies.

BIBLIOGRAPHY: *AJA Annual Report* (1870–to date); *Year Book of the Anglo-Jewish Association* (1950–51).

[Cecil Roth]

ANGOFF, CHARLES (1902–1979), U.S. novelist and editor. Born in Russia, Angoff was taken to the U.S. as a child and began his writing career in the 1920s. He assisted H.L. Mencken, whose attitudes about Jews were variable, in editing the *American Mercury* and in 1934 succeeded him as editor. Angoff's first book, *Literary History of the American People* (2 vols., 1931), surveyed the period from 1607 until 1815, but his qualities were best revealed in his fiction. He first ventured into this field with a series of short stories based on his own experiences: *Adventures in Heaven* (1945), *When I was a Boy in Boston* (1947), and *Something about My Father and Other People* (1956). Only in the 1950s, however, did Angoff emerge as a writer of real significance, recording the saga of East European immigrant Jewry's integration into American society. His most notable achievement was a series of autobiographical novels centering on his alter ego, David Polonsky: *Journey to the Dawn* (1951), *In the Morning Light* (1952), *The Sun at Noon* (1955), *Between Day and Dark* (1959), *The Bitter Spring* (1961), *Summer Storm* (1963), *In Memory of Autumn* (1968), *Winter Twilight* (1970), and *Season of Mists* (1971). With sympathy and fidelity Angoff weaves into the story of his hero a whole gallery of American-Jewish types, ranging from the Yiddish-speaking immigrants at the turn of the century to their Americanized descendants of the post-World War II era, stung to new Jewish awareness by the Holocaust and Israel. He also wrote a book of poems entitled *The Bell of Time* (1967) and a volume of essays, *The Tone of the Twenties* (1966). In 1957 Angoff became an editor of the *Literary Review.* He wrote a frank treatment of a former literary idol and his old associate in *H.L. Mencken: A Portrait from Memory* (1956). He also published *Prayers at Midnight,* consisting of 26 original prayers in the form of "prose poems." In 1969 Angoff was elected president of the Poetry Society of America and subsequently reelected for a second term as president. In 1970, he published, with Meyer Levin, an important anthology of selections from American-Jewish novels, *The Rise of American Jewish Literature.*

BIBLIOGRAPHY: S. Liptzin, *Jew in American Literature* (1966), 199–209.

[Sholom Jacob Kahn]

ANGOULÊME, capital of the department of Charente, western France. It seems from a missive addressed by Pope Gregory IX in 1236 to the bishop of Angoulême and other prelates that the crusaders had committed excesses against the Jews there. In about 1240 Nathan b. Joseph *Official engaged in a controversy with the bishop of Angoulême. The Jewish cemetery was situated between the city wall and the abbey, and the synagogue near the present Place Marengo. The "Rue des Juifs" (now Rue Raymond-Audour) began at Rue des Trois-Notre-Dame and ended at the Place du Palet. A second "Rue des Juifs" in Faubourg l'Houmeau is mentioned for the first time in 1811. The community seal represents a crescent moon and a six-pointed star with the encircling inscription *S[igillum] Iudaeorum.*

BIBLIOGRAPHY: Gross, Gal Jud, 62–63; A.F. Lièvre, *Angoulême* (Fr., 1885), 132–3; Blumenkranz, in: *Archives Juives*, 2, no. 4 (1966), 2; S. Grayzel, *Church and the Jews in the XIIIth Century* (1933), 226–9.

[Bernhard Blumenkranz]

ANGRIST, ALFRED ALVIN (1902–1984), U.S. pathologist. Angrist, who was born in Brooklyn, held various teaching posts at the New York Medical College from 1929 to 1954, when he became professor of pathology at the Albert Einstein College of Medicine of Yeshiva University, New York, retiring from there in 1969. He was also director of laboratories of the Bronx Municipal Hospital Center and consultant pathologist to many New York City hospitals. Angrist made many important contributions to the knowledge of endocarditis. One of his favorite subjects, however, was the importance of the autopsy, both for the advancement of medical knowledge and for teaching. He campaigned vigorously on the matter, and dealt with it in many of his scientific papers. Angrist was a member of the committee that produced the standard nomenclature of pathology and for over 20 years was on the committee on medical education of the New York Academy of Medicine. He was a strong supporter of "controversial" scientists in the McCarthy era. Among other posts, he served as president of the Queens County Medical Society and New York Pathology Society. Angrist was also a director of the Health Insurance Plan of Greater New York and president of the Queensboro Council for Social Welfare.

[Fred Rosner / Bracha Rager (2nd ed.)]

ANHALT, former German state, now part of the Land of Saxony-Anhalt, Germany; until the 12th century part of the duchy of Saxony, later becoming an independent principality. Jews living in the towns of Bernburg, Aschersleben, Koethen, and Zerbst in Anhalt are mentioned in sources from the 14th century. Communities existed in the first two towns during the 15th century when the rabbi of Aschersleben was Isaac Eilenburg, mentioned in the responsa of Israel Isserlein. No further Jewish settlement in Anhalt is recorded from the end of the 15th century to the beginning of the 17th. Afterward, the mercantilist policies of the absolutist regime encouraged Jewish traders and financiers to settle in the principality. They formed a well-to-do group which soon engaged in cultural activities.

Hebrew printing presses were established in Koethen in 1621. Moses Benjamin Wolff, the court Jew, set up a Hebrew press in 1695 in Dessau (which was active till 1704) as well as in Koethen and Jessnitz where Israel b. Abraham, who was a proselyte, was active for many years. He printed Maimonides' Code with commentaries (1739–42) and his *Guide of the Perplexed* with the standard commentaries in 1742. In 1742 too, Benjamin Moses Wolff's son Elijah restored his father's press for one year, producing the *Sifra* and the Jerusalem Talmud, *Seder Mo'ed*. In the period of Enlightenment Moses *Philippson (1775–1814) established a Hebrew press in Dessau; David (b. Moses) *Fraenkel printed there the first Judeo-German monthly *Sulamith* (1806–33).

A synagogue was built at Dessau in 1687. The characteristic relationship of this period between the German princes and the rich Jews they patronized, a mixture of exploitation, oppression, and socializing, was also found in Anhalt. Thus, permission was given to build a synagogue in the famous gardens of Woerlitz, and a Jewish wedding was held at the palace. Anhalt Jewry played an important role in the Enlightenment (*Haskalah) and acceptance of German culture. Moves toward Jewish emancipation were initiated in the community of Dessau early in the 19th century. In 1804 the "body" tax levied on Jews was abolished in Anhalt, and Jews were required from 1810 to adopt surnames. Full political rights were granted in 1867. In 1831 the civil authorities appointed S. *Herxheimer chief rabbi of Anhalt, contributing half of his salary. Prominent among Anhalt Jews were the philosophers Moses *Mendelssohn, Hermann Heyman *Steinthal, and Hermann *Cohen, the historian Isaac Marcus *Jost, the theologian Ludwig *Philippson, and the mathematician Ephraim Solomon Unger. The Jewish population, numbering 3,000 in 1830, decreased to 1,140 by 1925. The synagogues of Anhalt were burned in November 1938; the 1,000 Jews still living there were murdered during World War II.

BIBLIOGRAPHY: E. Walter, "Die Rechtsstellung der israelitischen Kultusgemeinden in Anhalt" (Dissertation, Halle-Wittenberg, 1934); *German Jewry* (Wiener Library Catalogue, Series no. 3, 1958), 35; M. Freudenthal, *Aus der Heimat M. Mendelssohns* (1900), passim. **ADD. BIBLIOGRAPHY:** B. Bugaiski (ed.), *Geschichte juedischer Gemeinden in Sachsen-Anhalt* (1997); J. Dick (ed.), *Wegweiser durch das juedische Sachsen-Anhalt* (1998).

[Zvi Avneri]

ANHALT, ISTVÁN (1919–), composer. Anhalt was born in Budapest where he studied with Zoltán Kodály at the Franz Liszt Academy of Music in 1937–41. Conscripted into a forced-labor unit of the Hungarian army in 1942, Anhalt escaped in 1944 and was hidden by Pater Janos Antal and Theresa de Kerpelz, whom he sponsored for recognition by Yad Vashem.

At war's end Anhalt went to Paris where he studied conducting at the Conservatoire with Louis Fourestier; piano with Soulima Stravinsky; and composition with Nadia Boulanger. During this time he lived on a stipend from the Union des étudiants juifs de France and led the vocal quartet at a Paris synagogue. He immigrated to Canada as the only musician among 64 displaced intellectuals who were fellows of the Lady Davis Foundation (1949–52). Anhalt spent the rest of his career at McGill University's Faculty of Music (1949–71) and Queen's University's School of Music (1971–84). His students included composers Jack Surilnikoff and William Benjamin.

Among Canadian composers, Anhalt was a leading figure in the postwar avant-garde. Seemingly self-taught in Arnold Schoenberg's 12-tone technique, he employed an idiosyncratic form of serialism that culminated in his *Symphony*. Anhalt conducted the premiere of this, his first large-scale instrumental piece, at a 1959 Montreal concert sponsored by the Canadian Jewish Congress to commemorate the 200th anniversary of the first Jewish community in Canada. A turning point in his career, the *Symphony* helped secure Anhalt a tenured position at McGill and resulted in international exposure. Other works of this period are *Seu Sheorim* (1951) for chorus and organ to a traditional text, and Psalm XIX (1951) for baritone and piano, to a text by A.M. Klein, for Otto Steieren, cantor of Montreal's Temple Emanuel.

Also a pioneer in electronic music, Anhalt spent his summers in the late 1950s and early 1960s at Canada's National Research Centre, the Columbia-Princeton Center, and Bell Labs. In 1964 he established Canada's first electronic music studio at McGill. These experiments resulted in *Electronic Compositions 1–4* (1959–61) and such mixed-media works as *Foci* (1969). As in other post-1960 pieces, Anhalt himself wrote *Foci*'s text, which contains kabbalistic references and requires extended vocal techniques. In his 1995 opera *Traces* (*Tikkun*), a single singer enacts many characters in Anhalt's libretto, which is influenced by the Kabbalah, the Exodus story, and the writings of Martin Buber, Gershom Scholem, and Isaac Luria. *The Tents of Abraham* (*A Mirage – Midrash*), which Anhalt has characterized as "a dream of peace between Judaism and Islam," was awarded Canada's Juno Award for best classical composition in 2005. Anhalt was named an Officer of the Order of Canada in 2003.

BIBLIOGRAPHY: R. Elliott and G.E Smith (eds.), *István Anhalt: Pathways and Memory* (2001).

[Jay Rahn (2nd ed.)]

ANIELEWICZ, MORDECAI (1919–1943), commander of the Warsaw ghetto uprising. Anielewicz, who was born into a Jewish working-class family in Wyszków, Poland, was for a short time a member of *Betar. He later joined *Ha-Shomer ha-Ẓa'ir and at the outbreak of World War II, was one of the leaders of its Warsaw branch. When the German army approached Warsaw, he fled eastward in an attempt to reach Palestine but was caught at the Romanian border. He went to Vilna, then Soviet-occupied, where many members of the Zionist youth movements found refuge but returned to Warsaw in order to reestablish his movement in German-occupied Poland. He was instrumental in founding an urban kibbutz in a house in the Warsaw ghetto, in organizing educational activities for small groups, and in publishing an underground paper *Neged ha-Zerem* ("Against the Stream"). He was outside the ghetto in Western Poland during the *Aktion* of July–September 1942 (see *Warsaw, Ghetto) in which more than 265,000 Jews were shipped to Treblinka, where they were gassed. Consequently, he was less ridden by guilt and self-loathing for the failure to resist than his comrades who had remained in Warsaw. Anielewicz had long advocated armed resistance against the Germans, and upon the formation of the Żydowska Organizacja Bojowa or Z.O.B. ("Jewish Fighting Organization"), he was named its commander. He was the sole survivor of the Ha-Shomer ha-Ẓa'ir force, which he led at the time of the *Aktion* on January 18, 1943, in which Jews openly resisted the German deportations, which were halted after four days. The Z.O.B. believed that their resistance had halted the deportations and doubled their efforts. Thereafter Anielewicz prepared both the Z.O.B. and the entire ghetto, now effectively under his control, for the final uprising in April 1943. He deeply sensed the historic importance of his mission. On April 23, he wrote to Yitzhak Zuckerman, a unit commander on the Aryan side:

> What we have experienced cannot be described in words. We are aware of one thing only: what has happened has exceeded our dreams. The Germans ran twice from the ghetto…I have the feeling that great things are happening, that what we have dared is of great importance.
>
> Keep well, my dear. Perhaps we shall meet again. But what really matters is that the dream of my life has become true. Jewish self-defense in the Warsaw ghetto has become a fact. Jewish armed resistance and retaliation have become a reality. I have been witness to the magnificent heroic struggle of the Jewish fighters.

On May 8, the Germans sent gas inside the bunkers at Z.O.B. command headquarters at Mila 18. Anielewicz died as he expected, as his wished, fighting the Germans. In the underground Anielewicz used three aliases: "Marian," "Aniol" (Polish for angel), and "Malakhi," all variations of either his first name or family name. Kibbutz Yad Mordekhai is named after him.

BIBLIOGRAPHY: P. Friedman (ed.), *Martyrs and Fighters* (1954), index; M. Barkai (ed.), *Fighting Ghettos* (1962), index; E. Ringelblum, *Ksovim fun Geto*, 2 (1963), 141–50; Y. Guttman, *Mered ha-Neẓurim – Mordekhai Anielewicz u-Milḥemet Getto Varshah* (1963); B. Mark, *Oyfshtand in Varshever Geto* (1963), index (Ger., 1959³, Fr., 1955, Pol., 1963). **ADD. BIBLIOGRAPHY:** Y. Zuckerman, *A Surplus of Memory: Chronicles of the Warsaw Ghetto Uprising* (1993); I. Gutman, *The Jews of Warsaw 1939–1943* (1982); idem, *Resistance* (1994).

[Shaul Esh / Michael Berenbaum (2nd ed.)]

ANILAEUS AND ASINAEUS (first century C.E.), two Babylonian Jewish brothers who founded a robber state in Babylon and ruled it for 15 years (c. 20–35). Natives of Nehardea, Anilaeus and Asinaeus had been apprenticed by their mother to learn the weaving trade. Punished by their master for laziness, the brothers fled and were joined by other young discontented Jews in the area of the Euphrates. These they armed, and, acting as their leaders, the brothers forced the surrounding herdsmen to pay a tribute from their flocks, and threatened violence to all who refused. Eventually they established a robber state and thus came to the attention of the Parthian satrap of Babylonia. The latter, however, was defeated in battle by the two brothers after miscalculating that the Jews would not defend themselves if attacked on the Sabbath. When news of the battle reached the Parthian king, Artabanus III (c. 12–38 C.E.), he decided "to use the prowess of the Jewish brothers as a curb to ensure the loyalty of his satrapies, for some of them were in rebellion, and some were considering whether to rebel" (Jos., Ant., 18, 9, 330). As a result, they were formally appointed rulers of those regions of Babylonia which they already controlled. On reaching his own territory, Asinaeus fortified the land and in general "held sway from now on over all Mesopotamia, and for 15 years the brothers' prosperity kept on increasing."

Only with the appearance of a certain Parthian general in the area did the situation begin to deteriorate. Anilaeus, having fallen in love with the general's wife, forced him into battle, secured his death, and married his widow. By tolerating her idolatry Anilaeus aroused great dissension among his Jewish followers. When Asinaeus brought their protests before his brother and urged him to send the woman away, he was poisoned by her. Thus began the downfall of the small Jewish kingdom. Anilaeus assumed control of the army and managed to defeat Mithridates, a Parthian governor and son-in-law of Artabanus. Mithridates, captured and humiliated by Anilaeus, was eventually released. He thereupon gathered a greater force, and "the followers of Anilaeus suffered a disgraceful rout" (Jos., Ant., 18:366). Anilaeus himself managed to escape, and for a while succeeded in plundering villages near Nehardea. He was finally discovered and trapped by the Babylonians, who, after killing him, unleashed a violent wave of terror against the Jews of Babylonia.

BIBLIOGRAPHY: Jos., Ant., 18:310–79 (on the nature of this source see Schalit, in *Annual of the Swedish Theological Institute*, 4 (1965), 163–88); Jos., Ant., 20:567–8; Neusner, Babylonia, 1 (1965), 50–54.

[Isaiah Gafni]

ANI MA'AMIN (Heb. אֲנִי מַאֲמִין; "I believe"), a short creed based, as is the **Yigdal* hymn, on the Thirteen *Articles of Faith formulated by *Maimonides. Each article begins with the words *Ani ma'amin be-emunah shelemah* ("I believe with complete faith"). The author is unknown. The credo character of the formula and the custom of reciting this creed may both be due to Christian influence. The catechistic formula "I believe with perfect faith…," reminiscent of early Christian creeds, has no basis in the Arabic original of Maimonides' thirteen principles, which are stated apodictically, although the medieval Hebrew translation by Solomon b. Joseph ibn Ya`aqub frequently interpolates "to believe" (*le-ha'amin*) or "that we believe" (*she-na'amin*).

The *Ani Ma'amin* is found, in a somewhat enlarged version, in a 15th-century manuscript (Parma, 1753 (997)) of miscellaneous prayers with the superscription: "These are the 13 principles of religion, faith, and ethics, and denying one of them is equivalent to denying the whole Torah. They should be recited daily after prayer, for whosoever recites them daily, will come to no harm all that day." The Ashkenazi prayer book, printed in Mantua in 1558, is apparently the first to incorporate the *Ani Ma'amin*. It appears after the *Hallel* prayer and the superscription in High German reads: "Some have the custom to recite this also in the morning." It can now be found in most Ashkenazi prayer books at the end of the morning service. Unlike the **Yigdal* hymn, however, the more creedal *Ani Ma'amin* never became part of the liturgy. The recital of the *Ani Ma'amin* is concluded by the three words of Genesis 49:18 repeated three times in different order, in Hebrew and Aramaic, as in the Night Prayer, a custom based on Kabbalah. The 12th article, expressing belief in the coming of the Messiah, became the Martyrs' Hymn during the Nazi Holocaust, when it was sung to a haunting melody by those taken to their death in the extermination camps and thereafter was frequently sung in their memory. For a *piyyut* based on *Ani Ma'amin*, see Davidson, Oẓar, s.v.

BIBLIOGRAPHY: Abrahams, Companion, ciiff.; Hertz, Prayer, 248ff.; D. Neumark, *Toledot ha-Ikkarim*, 2 (1923), 161; L. Jacobs, *Principles of Jewish Faith* (1964), 17–18. **ADD. BIBLIOGRAPHY:** M.D. Gaon, "*Keriat Yod Gimmel ha-Ikkarim*," in: *Yeda Am*, 3 (1955), 39–41; A. Cosman, "*Yod Gimmel ha-Ikkarim la-Rambam be-'Ferush ha-Mishnah,' be-'Yigdal,' u-ve-'Ani Ma'amin,'*" in: Itamar Warhaftig (ed.), *Minḥah le-Ish* (1991), 337–48; M. Shapiro, *The Limits of Orthodox Theology: Maimonides' Thirteen Principles Reappraised* (2004).

[Marc B. Shapiro (2nd ed.)]

ANIMALS, CRUELTY TO (Heb. צַעַר בַּעֲלֵי חַיִּים, *ẓa'ar ba'alei ḥayyim*; lit. "pain of living things"). Moral and legal rules concerning the treatment of animals are based on the principle that animals are part of God's creation toward which man bears responsibility. Laws and other indications in the Pentateuch and the rest of the Bible make it clear not only that cruelty to animals is forbidden but also that compassion and mercy to them are demanded of man by God. According to rabbinic tradition, interpreting the biblical record, mankind was not allowed to eat meat until after the Flood, although the sacrifice of animals to God had been previously allowed (Gen. 1:29; 9:3). Once permitted, the consumption of meat remained surrounded with many restrictions (see *Dietary Laws). According to the rabbis, the Hebrew word for "desireth" in the verse, "When the Lord thy God shall enlarge thy border and thou shalt say: 'I will eat flesh,' because thy soul desireth to eat flesh…" (Deut. 12:20), has a negative connotation; hence, although it is permitted to slaughter animals for food, this should be done in moderation. It has been suggested that the Jewish method of slaughter, particularly the laws that the knife be exceedingly sharp and without the slightest notch, were motivated by consideration for the animal because this method is the most painless. The biblical Sabbath laws also suggest consideration for animals ("Thou shall not do any manner of work… nor thine ox, nor thine ass, nor any of thy cattle" (Ex. 20:10; Deut. 5:14); "but on the seventh day thou shalt rest; that thine ox and thine ass may have rest" (Ex. 23:12)), as do the prohibitions against muzzling an ox as it threshes (Deut. 25:4), and slaughtering an animal and its young on the same day (Lev. 22:28). One reason for the commandment to let the fields lie fallow in the Sabbatical year is that "the poor of thy people… and the beast of the field" may eat from them (Lev. 25:6–7). This same idea is inherent in the commandment "If thou see the ass of him that hateth thee lying under its burden…. thou shalt surely release it with him" (Ex. 23:5), and in the requirement to release the parent bird before taking the young (Deut. 22:6–7). (However, there is a difference of opinion in the Talmud as to the reason for these last *mitzvot* (see below).) Indications of the same consideration appear in the narrative sections of the Bible. The angel rebuked Balaam for smiting his ass (Num. 22:32), and God Himself admonished Jonah "and should not I have pity on Nineveh, that great city, wherein are more than sixscore thousand persons… and also much cattle?" (Jonah 4:11). God is also praised as the One who satisfied all living creatures (Ps. 145:9–16), and for giving the beasts and the birds their food (Ps. 147:9).

In view of all this, the rabbis based a great deal of their legislation and interpretation on the principle of *ẓa'ar ba'alei ḥayyim*. As one the seven *Noachide Laws, the prohibition to eat the flesh of a living animal, applies also to non-Jews (Sanh. 56a–57a, 59a–b; Tosef. Av. Zar. 8:4–6). The dietary laws limiting the killing of animals are discussed at great length, and the rabbis recommend moderation in eating even permitted meat. The rabbis were not completely opposed to killing animals – giving priority to human needs – but they were entirely against wanton killing as they were against causing pain to animals. It is forbidden to inflict a blemish on an animal (Ḥul. 7b). Many acts otherwise forbidden on the Sabbath are permitted when their purpose is to relieve animals' pain on the grounds that cruelty to animals is biblically prohibited (Shab. 128b). The accepted (although not unanimous) view is that the commandment to help unload (Ex. 23:5, see above) is motivated by consideration for animals, which is thus regarded as a principle of biblical force (Maim., Yad, Roẓe'aḥ u-Shemirat Nefesh 13; Tur, ḤM 272) and thus it is permitted to unload a burden from a laboring animal even on the Sabbath (Maim., Yad, Shabbat 21:9–10). It is permitted to ask a non-Jew to milk cows on the Sabbath – an act that would be otherwise forbidden. The rabbis ordained that one should not recite the festive benediction *She-Heḥeyanu* before the act of ritual slaughter or before putting on new leather shoes because the enjoyment is at the cost of the animal. On the basis of the verse "I will give grass in thy fields for thy cattle, and thou shalt eat and be satisfied" (Deut. 11:15), the rabbis decided that "it is forbidden for a man to eat before he has fed his animal because the animal is mentioned first" (Ber. 40a). This decision accordingly passed into the *halakhah* and was subsequently codified (Maim., Yad, Avadim 9:8). Out of the same consideration they also legislated that "a man is not permitted to buy animals unless he can properly provide for them" (TJ, Yev. 15:3, 14d; TJ, Ket. 4:8, 29a). The principle of kindness to animals played no less a part in the *aggadah* than it did in the *halakhah*. It is as though God's treatment of man will be according to the latter's treatment of animals. This is suggested by the juxtaposition of the promise of long life with the *mitzvah* of sending the parent bird away before taking the young (Deut. 22:6–7). R. Judah ha-Nasi was divinely punished because he did not show mercy to animals, and the punishment was removed only when his attitude improved, and Moses and David were considered fit to be leaders of Israel only after they had been shepherds (TJ, Kil. 9:3, 32a; BM 85a). In later rabbinic literature, both halakhic and ethical, great prominence is also given to demonstrating God's mercy to animals, and to the importance of not causing them pain (see R. Margaliot (ed.), *Sefer Ḥasidim* (1957), 589, 667, 668, 670; M. Cordovero, *Palm Tree of Deborah* (1966), ch. 2–3). Even the necessary inflicting of pain is frowned upon as "cruel."

The rabbinical attitude toward hunting is entirely negative. Harsh things are said about those who hunt even for a living. R. Ezekiel Landau said that "the only hunters we know of (in the Bible) are Nimrod and Esau; it is not the way of the children of Abraham, Isaac, and Jacob."

Medieval Jewish philosophers used the principle of *ẓa'ar ba'alei ḥayyim* to explain various *mitzvot*. It was suggested that the reason for not plowing with an ox and an ass together (Deut. 22:10) is that the ox, being the stronger, would cause pain to the ass (Ibn Ezra, *ibid.*). Philosophers from R. Joseph *Albo to R. Abraham Isaac *Kook discussed the question of why it is permitted to eat meat at all and, indeed, from the talmudic statement that "the *am ha-areẓ* (i.e., "the boor") is forbidden to eat meat" (Pes. 49b), it would seem that its authors were also sensitive to the problem (see D. Cohen, in: *La-Ḥai Ro'i* (Memorial A.Y. Raanan Kook; 1961), 201–54).

BIBLIOGRAPHY: I.A. Dembo, *Jewish Method of Slaughter* (1894); Wohlgemuth, in: *Jeschurun*, 14 (1927), 585–610; 15 (1928), 245–67, 452–68; S.H. Dresner, *Jewish Dietary Laws, their Meaning for Our Time* (1959); S.D. Sassoon, *Critical Study of Electrical Stunning and the Jewish Method of Slaughter* (1955[3]); E. Bar-Shaul, *Mitzvah va-Lev* (1960), ch. 1; A. Chafuta, in: *No'am*, 4 (1961), 218–25; N.Z. Friedman, *ibid.*, 5 (1962), 188–94.

[Zvi Kaplan]

ANIMALS OF THE BIBLE AND TALMUD. Although no basic changes have occurred in the faunistic composition of Ereẓ Israel since biblical times, an examination of the names of the animals mentioned in the Bible and in talmudic literature reveals that a number of wild animals have disappeared from the country's landscape in fairly recent times. This applies particularly to cloven-hoofed ruminant wild animals. Of the nine such animals referred to in the Bible as permitted for food, namely, the deer, gazelle, and fallow deer, the addax, bison, and oryx, the wild goat, wild ox, and ibex, there survive today in Israel and in the neighboring countries only the gazelle and the ibex. Whereas the wild ox had already disappeared from the confines of the country in early times, the rest of these wild animals were to be found in Ereẓ Israel and neighboring countries until the end of the 19th century. The main reason for the subsequent disappearance of these animals, which were eagerly hunted for their tasty meat, their excellent skins, and their horns, has been the improved means of hunting, particularly the use of the long-range rifle. This has also led to the elimination of the large carnivorous animals – the lion, the bear, the leopard, and the cheetah (though specimens of the last two have survived in the country). The presence of these carnivorous animals in Ereẓ Israel in biblical times has been interpreted as indicating that the country was then sparsely populated and extensively forested. But these animals were also found in Ereẓ Israel in mishnaic and talmudic times, when the country was densely populated. Their dens were the thickets of the Jordan (Jer. 49:19), the Lebanese mountains (Song 4:8), the Syrian desert and the Negev (Isa. 30:6), from which they descended upon populated places. In Crusader times the lion was still to be found in the Negev. Of the Syrian bear some specimens have survived in Syria and in the Lebanese mountains, from where leopards occasionally make their way into Upper Galilee. Whereas the hippopotamus disappeared from the region in very early days, some *crocodiles survived in the western rivers of Ereẓ Israel up to the beginning of the 20th century. The ostrich became extinct in Ereẓ Israel and in the neighborhood several decades ago, and the last wild asses were exterminated in the Syrian desert at the end of the 19th century.

Most domestic animals were domesticated as early as in the pre-biblical period. Prehistoric engravings of camels and cattle have been found on the rocks of Kilweh in Transjordan, and clay images representing cattle, goats, sheep, and pigs dating from the fifth millennium B.C.E. have been uncovered in Jericho. There were domesticated cats in Egypt in the period of the First Dynasty, and images of cats were discovered in an Egyptian temple at Beth-Shean. The Bible makes no mention of the cat, which was apparently not bred to any great extent in Ereẓ Israel. Even in mishnaic times, when the cat was doubtless known in the country, other animals (the mongoose, etc.) were reared for the purpose of catching mice in the home. Several breeds of dogs appear in ancient drawings uncovered in Ereẓ Israel. It is not clear what strains of cattle were raised in Ereẓ Israel in biblical times, but drawings from the mishnaic period depict long-horned, humped cattle, resembling the present-day Zebu cow. There are pictures dating from the 15th century B.C.E. of the black long-eared goat. The broad-tailed sheep was also to be found in Ereẓ Israel and in the neighboring lands in ancient times. The horse was not much used in the country, the donkey and the mule having been preferred instead. The dove was domesticated in very olden days. The raising of fowl is attested by a seal which dates from the period of the kingdom of Israel and on which a cock is engraved. For royal and princely courts playful and ornamental animals, such as monkeys, elephants, and peacocks, were imported.

There are some 120 names of animals (excluding synonyms) in the Bible, mammals, birds, and reptiles being well represented. (See Table: Animals in the Bible.) Of the 86 mammals, 359 birds, and 76 species of reptiles of Ereẓ Israel about 37, 38, and 12 respectively are specified by name in the Bible. It must be stressed that it is only by chance that animals (and also flora) are described in the Bible. The biblical books were written by men who were close to nature and drew their inspiration from it in the consciousness that all these are the works of the Almighty, the expression of His providence over all creation. The portrayal of nature, although generally poetic and allegoric, is organically associated with the real landscape of Ereẓ Israel. In talmudic literature – the Mishnah, the Tosefta, the two Talmuds, and the Midrashim – there are scores of additional names of animals, but the numbers are small compared with the hundreds of names of plants. The reason for this paucity in the animals mentioned in talmudic literature is that the *halakhah* mentions them in the main only for the laws of *sheḥitah* and *terefot*, while the *aggadah* employed similes from the animal world of the Bible.

Classification of the Animals in the Bible and Talmud

MAMMALS. The Bible uses two terms to denote a mammal. The usual one is בְּהֵמָה (*behemah*), which refers to both domestic and wild mammals, seven species of the latter being included among the *behemah* permissible as food (Deut. 14:5). The other is חַיָּה (*ḥayyah*), which is a term sometimes incorporating domestic and wild animals (Lev. 11:2). Another passage however speaks of "hunting any beast (*ḥayyah*) or fowl" (Lev. 17:13), where the word refers specifically to a wild mammal. In talmudic literature *ḥayyah*, a wild mammal, and *behemah*, a domestic mammal, are clearly distinguished from each other, with different laws applying to each. Whereas the domestic mammal (if belonging to the category of clean animals) may be offered as a sacrifice, has some prohibited fat (*ḥelev*), and its blood is not required to be covered after slaughter, the wild animal (even though it is permitted for food) is ineligible as a sacrifice, has no prohibited fat, and its blood must be covered after slaughter. The distinction between a *ḥayyah* and a *behemah* applies to forbidden animals also. Thus the sages held divergent views on whether a dog is a *ḥayyah* or a *behemah* (Kil. 8:6; Tosef. Kil. 5:7). There was some doubt about which category certain animals belonged to. According to one opinion the כוי (*koi*, also pronounced *kavi* or *kevi*), which is "doubtfully a *behemah* or a *ḥayyah*," is a hybrid of both (Ḥul. 80a). Similarly with regard to the *shor ha-bar*, the wild ox, there was uncertainty whether it had always been a wild animal so that the laws of a *ḥayyah* applied to it or had originally been a domestic animal which had become wild and to which therefore the laws of a *behemah* would refer. In later generations a similar question arose with regard to the water buffalo. Among the wild animals prime importance was attached to the permissible cloven-hoofed ruminants, which were the choicest game. Of these the Pentateuch (Deut. 14:5) enumerates seven: the *deer, *gazelle, fallow deer, wild goat, addax antelope, bison (*buffalo), and *antelope. Two additional permitted wild animals are mentioned in other biblical passages: the wild ox (*cattle) and the *ibex. As permitted domestic animals, the Bible names *sheep, *goats, and cattle; as prohibited ones, the *horse, *ass, *mule, *camel, and *pig. The ass was the most valuable work animal, and the camel of great importance in areas adjoining desert regions. The mule was used for riding and as a beast of burden, and the horse only for limited purposes. The fierce beasts of prey, although they did not usually inhabit Ereẓ Israel, sometimes penetrated its populated areas from neighboring countries. The *lion, *leopard, *bear, and *wolf, frequently mentioned in biblical parables and allegories as symbols of strength, cruelty, and

The Animals Listed in the Bible and in the Talmud

English Name	Scientific Name	Order or Family	Hebrew Name	Reference
Addax	Addax nasomaculatus	Ruminantia Artiodactyla	יַחְמוּר	Deut. 14:5; I Kings 5:3
Ant	Messor semirufus	Formicidae	נְמָלָה	Prov. 6:6–8; 30:25
Ass	Equus asinus	Equidae	חֲמוֹר	Gen. 12:16; 24:35; etc.
			עַיִר	Gen. 32:16; Judg. 5:10; etc.
			אָתוֹן	Gen. 32:16; 49:11; etc.
Bat	Chiroptera	Chiroptera	עֲטַלֵּף	Lev. 11:19; Isa. 2:20
Bear, Syrian	Ursus arctus syriacus	Ursidae	דֹּב	I Sam. 17:34–7; Hos. 13:8; etc.
Bee	Apis mellifica	Hymenoptera	דְּבוֹרָה	Deut. 1:44; Judg. 14:8; etc.
Beetle	Cerambyx; Capnodis	Coleoptera	תּוֹלַעַת	Deut. 28:39; Jonah 4:7
			חִפּוּשִׁית	Par. 9.2
Bison, European	Bison bonasus	Artiodactyla Ruminantia	תְּאוֹ	Deut. 14:5
			תּוֹא	Isa. 51:20
Boar, Wild	Sus scrofa	Artiodactyla non Ruminantia	חֲזִיר מִיַּעַר	Ps. 80:14
Buffalo, Water	Bos bubalus	Artiodactyla Ruminantia	מְרִיא	II Sam. 6:13; Isa. 1:11
Bug	Cimex lactularis	Rhynchota	פִּשְׁפֵּשׁ	Ter. 8:2
Buzzard	Buteo sp.	Falconiformes	אַיָּה	Lev. 11:14; Deut. 14:13; Job. 28:7
			רָאָה	Deut. 14:13
			גַּס	Hul. 3:1
Camel	Camelus dromedarius	Tylopoda	גָּמָל	Gen. 12:16; Lev. 11:4; etc.
			בֶּכֶר, בִּכְרָה	Isa. 60:6; Jer. 2:23
			נַאֲקָה	Shab. 5:1; Kelim 23:2
Cattle	Bos taurus	Artiodactyla Ruminantia	בָּקָר	Gen. 13:5; 18:7; etc.
			שׁוֹר	Gen. 32:6; Ex. 20:17; etc.
			אֲלָפִים	Deut. 7:13; 28:4; etc.
			אַבִּירִים	Isa. 34:7; Jer. 46:15; etc.
			פָּר, פָּרָה	Gen. 32:16; Judg. 6:25; etc.
			עֵגֶל, עֶגְלָה	Gen. 15:9; Lev. 9:2; etc.
Centipedes	Scolopendra; Eraphidostrephus	Myriapoda	מַרְבֵּה רַגְלַיִם	Lev. 11:42
			נָדָל	Mik. 5:3
Chameleon	Chamaeleon vulgaris	Chamaelonidae	תִּנְשֶׁמֶת (שֶׁרֶץ)	Lev. 11:30
Cheetah	Acinonyx jubatus	Felidae	בַּרְדְּלָס	B.K. 1:4; Sanh. 1:4
Cobra	Naja haje	Elapinae	פֶּתֶן	Deut. 32:33; Isa. 11:8
			שָׂרָף	Num. 21:6; Isa. 14:29; etc.
Cock	Gallus gallus domesticus	Galliformes	שֶׂכְוִי ?	Job. 38:36
			זַרְזִיר מָתְנַיִם (?)	Prov. 30:31
Corals	Corallium rubrum	Coralliacae	פְּנִינִים	Lam. 4:7; Prov. 8:11; etc.
Crane	Grus grus	Gruidae	עָגוּר	Isa. 38:14; Jer. 8:7
Cricket, Mole	Gryllotalpa gryllotalpa	Orthoptera	צְלָצַל	Deut. 28:42
Crimson Worm	Kermes biblicus	Ryncotidae	תּוֹלַעַת שָׁנִי	Ex. 25:4; Num. 4:8; etc.
			כַּרְמִיל	II Chron. 2:6; 3:14
Crocodile	Crocodilus vulgaris	Crocodilia	תַּנִּין	Ex. 7:9; Jer. 51:34; etc.
			לִוְיָתָן	Job. 40:25–41:26
Deer, Fallow	Cervus dama dama	Artiodactyla Ruminantia	יַחְמוּר	Deut. 14:5; I Kings 5:3
Deer, Roe	Cervus capreolus	Artiodactyla Ruminantia	אַיָּל, אַיָּלָה	Deut. 14:5; Jer. 14:5; etc.
Dog	Canis familiaris	Canidae	כֶּלֶב	Ex. 22:30; Judg. 7:5; etc.
Dove	Columba sp.	Columbiformes	יוֹנָה	Gen. 8:8; 8:12; Isa. 38:14; etc.
Eagle	Aquila sp.	Falconiformes	עַיִט	Gen. 15:11; Isa. 18:6; etc.
Earthworm	Lubricus sp.	Vermes	תּוֹלַעַת	Isa. 14:11; 41:14; etc.
Elephant, Ivory	Elephas africanus	Proboscidae	פִּיל	Kil. 8:6
			שֶׁנְהָב	I Kings 10:22; II Chron. 9:21
			שֵׁן	I Kings 10:18; 22:39; etc.

The Animals Listed in the Bible and in the Talmud (continued)

English Name	Scientific Name	Order or Family	Hebrew Name	Reference
Fish	Pisces	Pisces	דָּג דָּגִים	Gen. 9:2; Jonah 2:1; etc.
			דָּגָה	Gen. 1:26; Ex. 7:18; etc.
Flea	Pulex irritans	Aphantiptera	פַּרְעֹשׁ	I Sam. 24:14; 26:20; etc.
Fly	Musca domestica	Dyptera	זְבוּב	Isa. 7:18; Eccles. 10:1
Fly, Drosophila	Drosophila	Dyptera	יַבְחוּשׁ	Nid. 3:2
Fox	Vulpes vulpes	Canidae	שׁוּעָל	Lam. 5:18; Ps. 63:11; etc.
Frog	Rana esculenta	Amphibia	צְפַרְדֵּעַ	Ex. 7:27; Ps. 78:45; etc.
Gazelle	Gazella sp.	Artiodactyla Ruminantia	צְבִי	Deut. 12:15; Song 4:5; etc.
Gecko	Hemidactylus; Ptyodoctylus	Geckoidae	אֲנָקָה	Lev. 11:30
			שְׂמָמִית	Prov. 30:28
Gnat	Culex; Anopheles	Dyptera	עָרוֹב	Ex. 8:17; Ps. 78:45; etc.
Goat	Capra hircus	Artiodactyla Ruminantia	עֵז	Lev. 7:23; Song 4:1; etc.
			שָׂעִיר	Gen. 37:31; Lev. 4:28; etc.
			תַּיִשׁ	Gen. 30:35; Prov. 30:31; etc.
			עַתּוּדִים	Gen. 31:10; Jer. 50:8; etc.
Goat, Wild	Capra aegagrus	Artiodactyla Ruminantia	אַקּוֹ	Deut. 14:5
Goose	Anser anser domesticus	Anseriformes	בַּרְבּוּר	I Kings 5:3
			אַוָּז	Bek. 7:4; Shab. 24:3; etc.
Grasshopper, Longhorned	Tettigonidae	Orthoptera	חַרְגּוֹל	Lev. 11:22
Grasshopper, Shorthorned	Acrididae	Orthoptera Orthoptera	חָגָב	Num. 13:33; Isa. 40:22; etc.
			סָלְעָם	Lev. 11:22
Gull	Larus sp.	Laridae	שַׁחַף	Lev. 11:16; Deut. 14:15
Hare	Lepus sp.	Leporidae	אַרְנֶבֶת	Lev. 11:6; Deut. 14:7
Hawk	Accipiter nissus	Falconiformes	נֵץ	Lev. 11:16; Job. 39:26; etc.
Heron	Egretta sp.; Ardea sp.	Ardeidae	אֲנָפָה	Lev. 11:19; Deut. 14:18; etc.
Hippopotamus	Hippopotamus amphibius	Artiodactyla non Ruminantia	בְּהֵמוֹת	Job. 40:15–23
Horse	Equus caballus orientalis	Equidae	סוּס	Gen. 47:17; Ex. 9:3; etc.
			פָּרָשׁ	Isa. 28:28; Ezek. 27:14; etc.
Hyena	Hyaena hyaena	Hyaenidae	צָבוֹעַ	I Sam. 13:18
Hyrax, Syrian	Procavia syriaca	Hyracoidea	שָׁפָן	Lev. 11:5; Ps. 104:18; etc.
Ibex	Capra nubiana	Artiodactyla Ruminantia	יָעֵל, יַעֲלָה	Ps. 104:18; Job 39:1; etc.
Jackal	Canis aureus	Canidae	שׁוּעָל	Judg. 15:4; Ps. 63:11; etc.
			אִיִּים (?)	Isa. 13:22;
Kestrel	Falco tinnunculus	Falconiformes	תַּחְמָס	Lev. 11:16; Deut. 14:15
Kite	Milvus sp.	Falconiformes	דָּאָה	Lev. 11:14
			דַּיָּה	Deut. 14:13; Isa. 34:15
Leech	Hirudo; Limnatis	Hirudinae	עֲלוּקָה	Prov. 30:15
Leopard	Felis pardus tullianus	Felidae	נָמֵר	Isa. 11:6; Jer. 13:23; etc.
Lion	Felis leo	Felidae	אֲרִי	Isa. 38:13; Amos 3:12; etc.
			אַרְיֵה	Gen. 49:9; Job. 4:10; etc.
			כְּפִיר	Ezek. 19:3; Job. 4:10; etc.
			לָבִיא	Gen. 49:9; Isa. 5:29; etc.
			לַיִשׁ	Job. 4:11; Prov. 30:30; etc.
			שַׁחַל	Hos. 5:14; Job 4:10; etc.
Lizard	Lacerta sp.	Lacertidae	לְטָאָה	Lev. 11:30
Lizard, Dab	Uromastix aegyptius	Agamida	צָב	Lev. 11:29
Lizard, Monitor	Varanus griseus niloticus	Varanidae	כֹּחַ	Lev. 11:30
Locust	Schistocerca gregaria	Orthoptera	אַרְבֶּה	Ex. 10:11–19; Deut. 28:38; etc.
			גָּזָם	Amos 4:9; Joel 1:4; 2:25
			גּוֹבַי	Amos 7:1; Nahum 3:17
			חָסִיל	I Kings 8:37; Joel 1:4; etc.
			יֶלֶק	Jer. 51:14; Joel 1:4; etc.

The Animals Listed in the Bible and in the Talmud (continued)

English Name	Scientific Name	Order or Family	Hebrew Name	Reference
Louse	Anoptura	Rhynchoidae	כֵּן כִּנִּים כִּנָּם	Isa. 51:6; Ex. 8:12 Ex. 8:13–14; etc
Mackerel	Scomber scomber	Scombridae	קוֹלְיַאס הָאִסְפַּנִין קוֹלְיַאס	Shab. 22:2
Maggot	Lucilia sp.; Drosophila sp.	Dyptera	רִמָּה	Ex. 16:24; Job 7:5; etc.
Mole Rat	Spalax ehrenbergi	Rodentia	חֲפַרְפָּרוֹת אִשׁוּת	Isa. 2:20; Kelim, 21:3; M.K. 1:4
Mongoose	Herpestes ichneumon	Viverridae	נְמִיָּה	B.B. 2, 5
Monkey	Simia	Anthropoidea	קוֹף	I Kings, 10:22; II Chron. 9:21
Moth, Carpenter	Cossidae	Lepidoptera	נִסֵס	Isa. 10:18
Moth, Clothes	Microlepidoptera	Lepidoptera	סָס עָשׁ	Isa. 51:8 Isa. 50:9; 51:8; etc.
Mouse	Microtus guenthri Mus musculus	Rodentia	עַכְבָּר	Lev. 11:29; Isa. 66:17; etc.
Mule	Equus asinus mulus	Equidae	פֶּרֶד, פִּרְדָּה רֶכֶשׁ (?)	Isa. 66:20; I King 1:38; etc. Mic. 1:13; Esth. 8:10; etc.
Nightingale	Luscinia megarhynchos;	Passeres Passeres	זָמִיר	Song 2:12
Onager, Arabian Wild	Equus hemionus onager	Equidae	עָרוֹד	Job. 39:5
Onager, Syrian Wild	Equus hemionus hemihippus	Equidae	פֶּרֶא	Jer. 14:6; Job 6:5; etc.
Oryx	Oryx leucoryx	Artiodactyla Ruminantia	זֶמֶר (?)	Deut. 14:5
Ostrich	Struthio camelus	Struthionidae	יָעֵן כְּנַף רְנָנִים	Lam. 4:3 Job. 39:13–18
Owl, Barn	Tyto alba	Striges	תִּנְשֶׁמֶת (עוֹף)	Lev 11:18; Deut. 14:16
Owl,Eagle	Bubo bubo aharonii	Striges	אֹחַ	Isa. 13:21
Owl, Eagle Desert Dark	Bubo bubo ascalaphus	Striges	בַּת-יַעֲנָה	Lev. 11:16; Isa. 34:13; etc.
Owl, Eagle Desert Pale	Bubo bubo desertorum	Striges	תַּנִּים (?)	Isa. 34:13; Mal. 1:3; etc.
Owl, Fish	Ketupa zeylonensis	Striges	שָׁלָךְ	Lev. 11:17; Deut. 14:17
Owl, Little Dark	Athene noctua glaux	Striges	כּוֹס	Lev. 11:17; Ps. 102:7; etc.
Owl, Little Desert	Athene noctua saharae	Striges	קָאָת	Lev. 11:18; Isa. 34:11; etc.
Owl, Longeared	Asio otus	Striges	יַנְשׁוּף	Lev. 11:17; Isa. 34:11; etc.
Owl, Scops	Otus scopus Screech	Striges	שָׂעִיר	Isa. 13:21; 34:14
Owl, Shorteared	Asio flammeus	Striges	קִפּוֹד קִפּוֹז (?)	Isa. 14:23; Zeph. 2:14; etc. Isa. 34:15
Owl, Tawny	Strix aluco	Striges	לִילִית	Isa. 34:14
Ox, Wild	Bos primigenius	Artiodactyla Ruminantia	רְאֵם; רִים	Num. 23:22; Job 39:9–10; etc.
Partridge, Chuckar	Alectoris graeca	Galliformes	חָגְלָה	Num. 26:33; 27:1; etc.
Partridge, See-see	Ammoperdix heyi	Galliformes	קֹרֵא	I Sam. 26:20; Jer. 17:11
Peacock	Pavo cristatus	Galliformes	תֻּכִּי	I Kings 10:22; II Chron. 9:21
Porcupine	Erinaceus; Hemiechinus	Erinaceidae	קוּפָּד	Kil. 8, 5; Shab. 5, 4
Quail	Coturnix coturnix	Galliformes	שְׂלָו	Ex. 16:13; Num. 11:31; etc.
Rat	Rattus rattus	Rodentia	חֹלֶד חוּלְדָּה	Lev. 11:29 Kelim 15. 6; Par. 9.3
Raven	Corvus sp.	Corvidae	עוֹרֵב	Gen. 8:7; Lev. 11:15; etc.
Sardine	Sardinella maderensis Sardinella aurita	Clupeidae Clupeidae	טָרִית חִילָק	Ned. 6, 4; Av. Zar. 2.6 Av. Zar. 2.6
Scorpion	Scorpio sp. Buthus sp.	Scorpionidae	עַקְרָב	Deut. 8:15

The Animals Listed in the Bible and in the Talmud (continued)

English Name	Scientific Name	Order or Family	Hebrew Name	Reference
Sheep	Ovis vignei platyura	Artiodactyla Ruminantia	צֹאן	Gen. 4:2; I Sam. 25:2; etc.
			אַיִל	Gen. 22:13; 31:38; etc.
			רָחֵל	Gen. 32:15; Isa. 53:7; etc.
			כֶּבֶשׂ, כִּבְשָׂה	Ex. 12:5; Lev. 14:10; etc.
			כֶּשֶׂב, כִּשְׂבָּה	Lev. 3:7; 5:6; etc.
			טָלֶה	I Sam. 7:9; Isa. 65:25; etc.
Sheep, Wild	Ovis musimon	Artiodactyla Ruminantia	כּוֹי (?)	Bik. 2.8; Bek. 1.5; etc.
Skink	Eumeces sp; Chalcides sp.	Skincidae	חֹמֶט	Lev. 11:30
Snake	Ophidia	Serpentes	נָחָשׁ	Gen. 3:1; Amos 5:19; etc.
Sparrow	Passer domesticus biblicus	Ploceidae	צִפּוֹר דְּרוֹר	Lev. 14:4; Ps. 84:4; etc.
Spider	Araneida; Solifugae	Arachnoidae	עַכָּבִישׁ	Isa. 59:5; Job 8:14
			עַכְשׁוּב	Ps. 140:4
Stork	Ciconia ciconia	Ciconidae	חֲסִידָה	Lev. 11:19; Jer. 8:7; etc.
Swift	Apus sp.	Apodidae	סִיס	Isa. 38:14; Jer. 8:7; etc.
Swine	Sus domestica	Artiodactyla non Ruminantia	חֲזִיר	Lev. 11:7; Prov. 11:22; etc.
Tahash	Dugong; Giraffa?		תַּחַשׁ	Ex. 36:19; Num. 4:6; etc.
Turtle dove	Streptopelia turtur	Columbiformes	תּוֹר	Gen. 15:9; Jer. 8:7; etc.
Viper, Carpet	Echis sp.	Viperidae	אֶפְעֶה	Isa. 30:6; Job 20:16; etc.
Viper, Horned	Cerastes sp.	Viperidae	שְׁפִיפוֹן	Gen. 49:17
Viper, Palestinian	Vipera palaestina	Viperidae	צֶפַע	Isa. 14:29
			צִפְעוֹנִי	Isa. 11:8; Jer. 8:17; etc.
Vulture, Bearded	Gypaetus barbatus	Vultures	פֶּרֶס	Lev. 11:13; Deut. 14:12
Vulture, Black	Aegypius monachus	Vultures	עָזְנִיָּה	Lev. 11:13; Deut. 14:12
			עוֹז	Kelim 17, 4
Vulture, Egyptian	Neophron percnopterus	Vultures	רָחָם; רָחָמָה	Lev. 11:18; Deut. 14:17; etc.
Vulture, Griffon	Gyps fulvus	Vultures	נֶשֶׁר	Lev. 11:13; Deut. 32:11; etc.
Wasp	Vespa orientalis	Hymenoptera	צִרְעָה	Ex. 23:28; Deut. 7:20; etc.
Whale	Balenoptera; Physeter	Cetacea	לִוְיָתָן	Ps. 104:26; Isa. 27:1; etc.
Wolf	Canis lupus	Canidae	זְאֵב	Isa. 11:6; Jer. 5:6; etc.

agility, consort with domestic animals in Isaiah's vision of eternal peace (Isa. 11:6–7). The wild beasts include the *dog. The *fox and *jackal are types of creatures that inhabit ruins and deserted places. Of the small mammals, the hyrax and *hare are mentioned among the animals prohibited as food, the statement that they chew the cud (Lev. 11:5–6) being due to their having characteristics similar to those of ruminants. An animal whose identity is uncertain is the **taḥash*. To the mammals belong also animals included in the Bible in other groups. Thus, for example, the Pentateuch mentions, among the unclean birds, the *bat (Lev. 11:19); among the swarming things, the *mouse and the *rat (Lev. 11:29) which by reason of their short legs appear to creep along the ground. The term "leviathan" sometimes refers to an aquatic mammal, while the "great fish" that swallowed Jonah may have been intended by the author of the Book of Jonah to denote a species of whale (see *Leviathan).

BIRDS. Of the birds, which are called by the collective name of צִפּוֹר (*ẓippor*) or עוֹף (*of*), there are more than 350 species in Israel, some of them non-migratory, remaining in Israel all year round, others migratory, remaining only in winter or summer, and others transmigratory, staying no more than a short time. The Talmud (Ḥul. 63b) declares that "there are innumerable species of clean birds," that is, the overwhelming majority of the birds of Ereẓ Israel are permitted, which is the reason given for the fact that whereas the Pentateuch enumerates the clean mammals, of the birds only the unclean ones are listed (20 in Lev. 11; an additional one in Deut. 14). Constituting as they did an important source of food, birds were much hunted, for which purpose various types of hunting equipment were used. The snaring of birds is frequently referred to in the Bible in an allegorical representation of someone who becomes entangled in difficulties. The eggs of wild birds were also collected for food (cf. Deut. 22:6; Isa. 10:14). The Bible makes no mention of the breeding of birds except *doves, which together with *turtledoves and *sparrows were used as sacrifices (the last in the purification rites of the leper (Lev. 14:4)). Descriptions, parables, and allegories taken from bird life occur in the Bible: mention is made of the exact timing of the migrations of the *stork, turtledove, *swift, and *crane; the beauty and purity of the dove are portrayed, as are the cruelty of the *eagle, and the concern for its young shown by the griffon *vulture; desolation and destruction are symbolized by the *owl, a species designated by many names; the strange habits of the *ostrich receive special attention. To the 37 birds mentioned in the Bible, the Talmud adds many more, in particular in a discussion of the features which determine their ritual fitness as food. The post-biblical period saw the increased breeding in Ereẓ Israel of poultry, fowl, geese, and ducks in addition to several species of doves, while in wealthy homes ornamental birds – *peacocks and *pheasants – were raised.

REPTILES AND "CREEPING THINGS." The Pentateuch defines reptiles as "every swarming thing that swarmeth upon the earth… whatsoever goeth upon the belly, and whatsoever goeth upon all fours" (Lev. 11:41–42). This embraces all species of reptiles, including *snakes, crocodiles, as well as species of the lizard, gecko, skink, chameleon, and monitor. Of these last five genera, the Pentateuch enumerates six species of swarming things to which particularly severe laws of uncleanness apply (Lev. 11:29–39). Among the reptiles, the crocodile and snakes are extensively described. Although all reptiles are forbidden as food, they are an important source of proteins for the Bedouin who also eat their eggs. The Talmud distinguished between the egg of a reptile and that of a bird, the former being rounded at both ends with the white and the yolk mixed (Ḥul. 64a). Several times the Bible mentions gigantic legendary animals named *tannin* and *livyatan* that were said to have rebelled against the Creator who was compelled to declare war upon them and kill them (cf. Isa. 51:9; Ps. 74:13–14; Job 7:12; 3:8). The Midrashim preserve such legends which are common to the myths of people of the east and which may have been suggested by the remains of bones belonging to species of prehistoric reptiles that stirred the imagination of the aggadists.

FISH AND AMPHIBIA. Fish are often mentioned in the Bible, where they are referred to by the collective terms of דָּגָה (*dagah*) and by its plural דָּגִים without specifying any by name. A distinction is made only between those that have fins and scales and are therefore permitted as food and those without these features (see *Dietary Laws). In Ereẓ Israel, with its seashores, fish constituted an important food, reference being made to their increasing number in the "Great Sea" (Ezek. 47:10). In Jerusalem one of the gates was called the Fish Gate (Zeph. 1:10; Neh. 3:3). Egypt is rich in fish, these being mentioned among the food for which the Israelites longed when wandering in the wilderness (Num. 11:5). The rapid multiplication of fish gave rise to a verb *dagah* (דָּגָה; "to teem"; Gen. 48:16). Although it does not mention any fish by name, the Bible has more than a dozen terms for fishing implements. The importance of fish in the economy of Ereẓ Israel is reflected in Ezekiel's vision of the desalination of the waters of the Dead Sea: "And it shall come to pass, that fishers shall stand by it from En-Gedi even unto En-Eglaim; there shall be a place for the spreading of the nets" (Ezek. 47:10). In describing the destruction of the earth, prophets spoke of the extinction of fish (Hos. 4:3; Zeph. 1:3). Talmudic literature contains the names of dozens of fish, these being mentioned particularly in the Babylonian Talmud, since fish were plentiful in the Euphrates and Tigris. Seven species of amphibia are found in Israel, of which only the *frog is mentioned in the Bible. The *aggadah* refers to the salamander as a remarkable creature unaffected by fire (Ḥag. 27a; Sanh. 63b).

INVERTEBRATES. This is the richest group of animals in the number of its species and in the variety of their forms. The vast majority of them are small animals. Although they occupy a comparatively meager place in the ancient literature, except for insects which are frequently mentioned in the Bible and talmudic literature, the insects comprise almost three-quarters of the species in the world. The great majority of them are injurious to vegetation and carriers of diseases. Of the insects, the most important place in the Bible and in talmudic literature is occupied by the *Orthoptera*, to which belong the *grasshopper and the *locust. Notorious for the ravages they cause to agriculture, they were also permitted as food. Among the common agricultural pests are mentioned insects that belong to the species of beetles, fruit flies, and *ants. Species of the *moth are injurious to clothing; troublesome to man are the *fly, *gnat, *louse, and *flea (to which talmudic literature adds the bug and mosquito). The *hornet and the *bee were regarded as dangerous to human beings, who however benefit from the latter's honey. From the *crimson worm, a prized dye was extracted. Of the other *Arthropoda*, "whatsoever hath many feet" are mentioned: centipedes and millipedes, the *spider, and the *scorpion; of the *Mollusca*, the snail. The gland in the body of purple snails (murex), yielded blue and purple dye (see **tekhelet*). Of the *Vermes* group, the *worm is mentioned, the Hebrew for which, תּוֹלַעַת (*tola'at*), refers to various insects, and also to the earthworm. The *leech is mentioned only once in the Bible (Prov. 30:15) and several times in the Talmud. Creatures lower than the invertebrates that were known to the ancients were the *corals, which however they thought to be wood.

The identification of the animals in the Bible has given rise to divergent views, some contending that it is possible to identify them in a few cases only. Others, however, hold that this can be done in most instances. While the problem of their identification has been raised in the separate articles on them, the above list gives only the most probable identification of the animals mentioned in the Bible and in the Mishnah.

BIBLIOGRAPHY: F. Hasselquist, *Iter palaestinum* (Stockholm, 1757); Tristram, Survey; Tristram, Nat Hist; Lewysohn, Zool; S. Bodenheimer, *Prodromus faunae palaestinae* (1937); idem, *Animal and Man in Bible Lands* (1960); J. Feliks, *The Animal World of the Bible* (1962); S. Avrahamoviẓ, *Toledot ha-Teva* (1862); Y. Aharoni, *Torat ha-Ḥai* (1924); idem, *Zikhronot Zoʾolog Ivri* (1943); J. Margolin, *Zoʾologyah*, 2 vols. (1943–48); M. Dor, *Leksikon Zoʾologi* (1965).

[Jehuda Feliks]

ANIMAL TALES, stories in which animals are the principal characters, with the plot revolving around them and the setting mainly in the animal world. A man in an "animal tale" is an intruder in a strange world inhabited, ruled, and dominated by animals. One of the oldest forms of the narrative folktale, the animal tale is found at all culture levels in all periods. Very often it was used by later narrators and writers as an exemplum in fable form in which the social background and the animal traits reflect those extant in the human world. Animal tales and animal characters were used as a vehicle to protest against and expose immediate local conditions, ethnic or social conflicts, and human behavior in general, and the narrator remained immune from censorship, while the audience grasped and understood what the tale really intended to convey.

Bible

Many metaphorical and allegorical animal references in different literary forms are to be found in the Bible: Numbers 24:8–9 speaks of "God… is for them like the horns of the wild ox; they shall devour enemy nations, crush their bones… they crouch, they lie down like the lion; like the king of beasts"; Ezekiel 17:3–12 contains the prophetic *parable (*mashal*) and the riddle (*ḥidah*) about the two great eagles with great wings and long pinions; Ezekiel 19:2–3 is an allegorical lament (*kinah*) about a lioness among lions that reared her whelps: "And she brought up one of her whelps, he became a young lion… and they brought him with hooks unto the land of Egypt." In Proverbs the animal portraiture serves mostly to teach exemplary behavior: "Go to the ant, thou sluggard; consider her ways, and be wise" (Prov. 6:6–8); ants, rock-badgers, locusts, spiders are seen as small animals which are exceedingly wise (Prov. 30:24–28); the lion, the greyhound, and the he-goat are stately in their march (Prov. 30:29–31). They are also depicted in riddles not necessarily prophetic (the lion in the Samson story, Judg. 14:12ff.). There are also full-length "true" animal tales in the Bible as well, including two plant tales related as fables by Jotham (Judg. 9:8–15) and by King Jehoash (II Kings 14:9).

Talmud and Midrash

In talmudic and midrashic literature the 36 preserved Hebrew and Aramaic animal tales are designated as "fox fables," though the fox features in only 11, mostly as a clever and sly trickster. Probably, the fox was the main character in many of the oral animal tales of the tannaitic period which for various reasons were not written down. Rabban Johanan b. Zakkai (Suk. 28a) is said to have included "fox fables" in the realms of his studies, yet none adapted or written by him is known. Similarly, only three of the "300 fox fables" associated with R. Meir (Sanh. 38b) were known three generations after the sage's death. The name of each (a biblical verse) is recorded in the Talmud, but not the plot or the gist of the tale. They were retold in a different way by later interpreters such as Hai Gaon and Rashi. The fact that the animal tales of R. Meir (see Sot. 9:15, "When R. Meir died there were no more makers of parables") have not survived is in contrast to the fact that so many of his other statements have. Even if one regards the number as exaggerated and formalistic (see the numerous references to the number 300 in the *aggadah*, in the index of Ginzberg, Legends, 7 (1938), 474), an explanation is nevertheless needed. The opposition of R. Meir's contemporaries to the Greek literary heritage, including the rich Aesopian fable tradition, may be one reason.

The obscure phrase מִשְׁלֵי כ(ו)בְסִים, *mishlei k(o)vesim*, in the panegyric to Johanan b. Zakkai's extensive knowledge has led to a variety of interpretations centering around the animal tale and its nature. The word כ(ו)בְסִים, *k(o)vesim*, has been explained as "washermen" (vulgar stories popular among people dealing with "unclean" matters) and as "Kybises" (referring to the famous first-century Libyan fabulist). The word has also been identified with כְּבָשִׂים, *kevasim* ("sheep"). The latter has its roots in the hypothesis that aggadic animal tales are structurally based mainly on the confrontation between the cunning and unscrupulous clever fox and the naive and gentle (foolish) sheep. The hypothesis is not corroborated by textual evidence of "fox-and-sheep fables," but might have been among the suppressed and lost material (cf. the Aesopian fables of the wolf and the sheep, ed. Chambry, nos. 217, 218, 220–2, 230–1; ed. Span, indicating Hebrew parallels, nos. 45–46, 52–54, 56–57).

Most of the animal tales found in the *aggadah* are also extant in the fable collections of India (the *Jataka*: the birth stories of the Buddha, and the *Panchatantra*), and in Greek fables (Aesop's fables as formulated by the later Latin fabulists Phaedrus and Babrius). Where narrative parallels exist between Indian, Greek, and aggadic fables, the Jewish version is closer to the Indian one; e.g., the animal tale used by R. Joshua b. Hananiah (Gen. R. 64:10) as a means to persuade the Jews not to rebel against Rome, has for its hero the lion, like "Javasakuma" in the *Jataka*, whereas the hero in the Aesopian parallel is a wolf (Phaedrus 1:8; ed. Chambry, 224, ed. Span, 41).

Middle Ages

Throughout the Middle Ages, animal tales were current among European Jews. These had reached them in three ways: (1) through the Jewish and local oral tradition; (2) through the traditional aggadic compilations; and (3) through West European "bestiaries" or beast epics (Roman de Renart) and Latin (Avianus, Romulus) or Old French fables (the *Fables of Marie de France*, written around 1170–80), the adaptations of ancient Greek texts, and of European translations of *Kalila and Dimna*. The threefold influence is evident in the 119 *Mishlei Shu'alim* ("Fox Fables") of *Berechiah ha-Nakdan (12th- or 13th-century fabulist) which is the main source of the later Yiddish animal tale (see Moses b. Eliezer *Wallich). The direct Hebrew rendering of Aesopian fables (*Mishlei Ysopeto*, printed in Constantinople, 1516) had no essential effect on the Jewish animal tales, neither on their literary formulations by Hebrew (see J.L. *Gordon) and by Yiddish (see E. *Steinbarg) fabulists, nor on the oral tradition current among Jewish storytellers in the East and in the West.

Modern Period

Among the 8,000 Jewish folktales collected from oral tradition in Israel and preserved in the Israel folktale archives, there are only 140 animal tales, a percentage lower than in any national archive, or in any current non-Jewish folktale collection. Similarly, in the Yiddish collection of 540 East European folktales of Naphtali Gross (New York, 1955), only 24 are animal tales. Of the 300 international animal-tale types only 40 are represented in Jewish oral tradition. Five of the types are Jewish oikotypes (local ethnic narrative type), the most common among them being no. 184 (see bibl., Aarne-Thompson): in it man insults the animal (camel) which later avenges itself (six versions).

Many animal tales still bear their etiological character and have not been transformed into fable. The tale of the camel that asked for horns and lost his ears (Sanh. 106a) is, for example, moralistic and didactic, directed against discontent, haughtiness, overweening ambitions, and immoderate and unreasonable requests; at the same time, however, it explains the origin of the camel's short ears. Most of the animal tales combine the explanatory and didactic motifs.

It is difficult to determine the dividing line between the literary and the oral (folk) animal tale. Literary tales as those of the *aggadah* have been drawn from, and then again become part of, the oral tradition. An analysis of their contents proves that the main line of distinction is functional. The original oral animal tale was meant either to entertain or to satisfy the intellectual curiosity of mankind interested in the animal world. It reflected the fantasy of the masses, but it can also be seen as an early stage of the study of zoology. The literary animal tale tends to be a fable and is essentially didactic and moralizing, reflecting the ideas of the normative leadership and of the ruling elite.

BIBLIOGRAPHY: A. Aarne and S. Thompson, *The Types of the Folktale* (1961); Brunner-Traut, in: *Saeculum*, 10 (1959), 124–85; N. Gross, *Mayselekh un Mesholim* (1955); T. Gutman, *Ha-Mashal bi-Tekufat ha-Tannai'im* (1949²); Harkort, in *Fabula*, 9 (1967), 87–99; D. Noy, *Ha-Mashal be-Sifrut ha-Aggadah* (1960); idem, in: *Maḥanayim*, 79 (1963), 50–61; 91 (1964) 34–40; 105 (1966), 116–21; 121 (1969), 126–39; H. Schwarzbaum, in: *IV International Congress for Folk-Narrative Research, Athens, 1964, Lectures and Reports* (1965), 467–83; S. Span, *Mishelei Aisopos* (1961²).

[Dov Noy]

ANIM ZEMIROT (Heb. אַנְעִים זְמִירוֹת; "Let me chant sweet hymns"), also called *Shir ha-Kavod* ("Song of Glory"); synagogue hymn ascribed to *Judah he-Ḥasid, of Regensburg (d. 1217) and, with less probability, to a number of other medieval authors. The hymn is an alphabetical acrostic of 31 lines, the first and last four being a prologue and epilogue respectively. Each line consists of two half-lines which rhyme. The first three of the last four lines may not be part of the original poem.

The theme is a fervent paean of God's greatness and might, drawing upon Bible and Midrash but also showing the influence of philosophical ideas. The metaphors used are bold to the point of anthropomorphism. The hymn is recited in Ashkenazi rites at the end of the Sabbath and festival *Musaf* service, though in some synagogues it is said before the Reading of the Law after *Shaḥarit*. The custom to recite it daily is disappearing, although it has appeared at the end of the daily *Shaḥarit* in most editions of the prayer book since that of Venice in 1547 (see also Singer, Prayer (1962), 81ff.). *Anim Zemirot* and all the Songs of Unity (*Shir ha-Yiḥud*) are recited at the conclusion of the **Kol Nidrei* service in some Orthodox synagogues. Objections against the recital of *Anim Zemirot* in general were voiced by Solomon Luria, and against its daily use by Mordecai *Jaffe, *Judah Loew of Prague, Jacob *Emden, and *Elijah b. Solomon of Vilna, because these considered it an extremely holy poem. It is customary to open the Ark for *Anim Zemirot*, and in most synagogues the hymn is sung antiphonally. There are a variety of tunes.

A Purim parody of the hymn was composed by Aryeh Leib Cordovero of Torczyn (d. 1721; Davidson, Oẓar, 1 (1924), 310, no. 6828). The custom has developed of having *Anim Zemirot* recited by a child at the close of the Saturday morning service.

BIBLIOGRAPHY: Baer S., Seder, 250; Abrahams, Companion, xc, clxviii; Simonsen, in: MGWJ, 37 (1893), 463ff.; A. Berliner, *Randbemerkungen*, 1 (1909), 72ff.; A.M. Habermann, *Shirei ha-Yiḥud* (1948), 46–51.

ANINUT (Heb. word from the root אוֹנֵן, *onen*), status of a bereaved person in the period between the death and the burial of a close relative. The *onen* is exempted from fulfilling certain religious duties such as reciting the *Shema* and the daily prayers, or wearing *tallit* and *tefillin* so as to enable him to make burial arrangements. The *onen* eats in solitude and should abstain from meat and wine (MK 23b; Sh. Ar., YD 341:1). During Sabbaths and festivals, however, the *onen* participates in the customary ceremonials such as *Kiddush*. *Aninut* is terminated with the burial which commences the official mourning period.

BIBLIOGRAPHY: H. Rabinowicz, *A Guide to Life* (1964), 30–33.

ANISFELD, BORIS (**Ber**; 1878–1973), painter, graphic artist, sculptor, and stage designer. Born in Beltsy, Bessarabia, Anisfeld started his art education at the Odessa Art School (1895–1900). In 1901–9, he studied at the St. Petersburg Academy of Arts, where his tutors were I. Repin and D. Kardovsky. In 1903, he participated in the Summary Exhibition at the Academy of Arts, and in 1906–10 showed his works at exhibitions of the Union of Russian Artists in St. Petersburg and Kiev. In 1905–8, Anisfeld drew political cartoons for satirical magazines. Later he focused mainly on painting and stage design. He exhibited at the Salon in Paris in 1906, at the Vienna Secession in 1908, as well as at international exhibitions in Milan and London. In 1910, he joined "World of Art" and participated in all the exhibitions arranged by this association.

His works of this period feature highly sophisticated painting techniques, subtlety of color, and symbolic content. Anisfeld created several works inspired by biblical themes. From 1907, he was active as a stage designer. In 1912–14, he designed sets for S. Diagilev's Ballet Troupe productions and for ballets performed on the foreign tours of such leading dancers as A. Pavlova, V. Nijinsky, and V. Fokin. Anisfeld's designs for the sets and costumes of the ballet *Islamey* composed by M. Balakirev (Mariinsky Theater, St. Petersburg, 1912) brought him well-deserved recognition. In 1915, Anisfeld joined the Jewish Society for the Encouragement of the Arts and participated in its exhibits in Petrograd and Moscow (1916, 1917). In 1918, Anisfeld and his family settled in New York. His one-man show at the Brooklyn Museum in the same year brought him fame and success in America. In the 1920s, he continued working as a stage designer and created sets for several productions at the Metropolitan Opera. He collaborated with Jewish cultural organizations and associations, lectured at the Educational Alliance Art School, and published prints of his works in the American Yiddish press. In 1924 and 1926, he had one-man shows in New York. In 1928, Anisfeld moved to Chicago and exhibited his works at another one-man show at the Art Institute. In the early 1930s, Anisfeld all but ceased working for theater and focused mainly on painting. He also taught at the Chicago Art Institute until 1958. His later works feature a wide variety of themes and artistic techniques, from realistic landscapes to symbolic paintings executed in the expressionist manner. Big retrospectives of Anisfeld's works were held in Pittsburgh (1946), New York (1956), Chicago (1958), and Washington (1971).

BIBLIOGRAPHY: *Boris Anisfeld. Retrospective Exhibition.* Catalogue, Art Institute of Chicago (1958); *Boris Anisfeld: Twenty Years of Designs for the Theatre.* Catalogue of the Exhibition. Washington City (1971).

[Hillel Kazovsky (2nd ed.)]

ANISIMOV (Nissim-Oglu), ILYA SHERBATOVICH (b. 1862), ethnographer of Caucasian Jewry. He was born in Tarka (Dagestan). His father was the first "*mountain Jew" to study at the *Volozhin yeshivah, becoming rabbi of Tarka, and later of Temir Khan Shura, also in Dagestan. Anisimov studied engineering in Moscow and later worked in the Rothschild Naphtha Company in the Caucasus. He drew the attention of Russian philologists to the Tat language spoken by the Caucasian mountain Jews. In 1886 he was sent by the Moscow Archaeological Society to the Caucasus where he visited 88 localities and gathered a vast amount of ethnological and statistical material on the Jews there. His study on the Caucasian Jews, published in 1888, is of great ethnological value.

BIBLIOGRAPHY: S.A. Vengerov, *Istochniki slovarva russkikh pisateley*, 1 (1900), 75; *Voskhod*, 9 no. 1–2 (1889), 92–110; 9 no. 3 (1889), 49–64; I. Ben-Zvi, *The Exiled and the Redeemed* (1961^2), 39–48.

ANJOU (Heb. אנ׳ו), ancient province and former duchy in western France. In the Middle Ages the Jews of Anjou lived mainly in *Angers, the capital, and in Baugé, Saumur, Segré, and perhaps also in the hamlets called Rue-Juif, 3 mi. (5 km.) northeast of Saumur, and La Juiverie, 3 mi. (5 km.) west of Baugé. Near Fontevrault there was a "Jew's mill." The principal occupations of the Jews of Anjou, commerce and pawnbroking, are referred to in the customs tariffs of Saumur in 1162 and of Les Ponts-de-Cé near Fontevrault in 1177, and in the 13th-century custumal of Anjou. Records from the middle of the 11th century show that Joseph b. Samuel *Bonfils (Tov Elem) had the title "rabbi of the communities of Limousin and Anjou." Some rabbis of Anjou took part in a synod convened in the middle of the 12th century by Jacob b. Meir (Rabbenu *Tam) and *Samuel b. Meir. In 1236 many of the Jews of Anjou, *Poitou, and *Brittany were massacred during a wave of persecutions; others consented under threat of violence to convert to Christianity (see **anusim*). In 1269 and later, Charles I, count of Anjou, exacted considerable sums of money from the Anjou communities, then numbering less than one thousand persons, represented by Moses, their "syndic and commissioner." On the whole, however, the position of the Jews in Anjou was favorable. They were exempted from wearing the Jewish *badge, permitted to live in any place with more than 120 households, to engage in commerce, and to give loans on interest, using deeds stamped with the court seal. However on Dec. 8, 1289, shortly after his accession, Charles II ordered the expulsion of the Jews from Anjou and from Maine. It was alleged that they practiced usury in a scandalous manner, had sexual relationships with Christian women, and were turning Christians from their faith. In compensation for the loss of revenues involved, Charles levied an indemnity from the province. The Jews apparently returned to Anjou after 1359 (cf. custumal of 1385), in particular to Angers, staying there until the general expulsion of the Jews from France in 1394.

BIBLIOGRAPHY: Gross, Gal Jud, 64ff; Brunschvicg, in: REJ, 29 (1894), 229ff.; P. Marchegay, *Archives d'Anjou*, 2 (1849), 263, 257; C.J. Beautemps-Beaupré, *Coutumes… Anjou* 1, pt. 1 (1877), 52, 151ff., 335; Ibn Verga, *Shevet Yehudah*, ed. by A. Shohet and Y. Baer (1947), 148; A. de Bouard, *Actes… Charles Ier* (1926), 25, 83ff., 173ff., 258ff.; P. Rangeard, *Histoire Universelle d'Angers*, ed. by A. Lemarchand, 2 (1877), 183ff.

[Bernhard Blumenkranz]

ANKARA (Turk. **Engürü**, Rom. **Ancyra**, med. **Angora**), capital of the Republic of Turkey since 1923. A trading center on the trade route to Persia and the Far East, it was a way station for Jewish merchants. A few settled there permanently. After the expulsion from Spain and Portugal, the number of Jewish settlers increased. Exiles in large numbers arrived in Ankara, and on their initiative two organized communities (Spanish and Portuguese), which also included the city's previous Jewish inhabitants, were established. The two communities united in the mid-16th century. They numbered 231 Jews in the 1520s and 747 in the 1570s. The Jews of Ankara engaged in the silk trade, ordering wares from Persia and selling them throughout Turkey, and some merchants became wealthy.

The rabbis of Safed decided that the rabbis in Ankara could not be depended on in profound matters of *halakhah* requiring detailed knowledge, but Moses de Boton and David ha-Kohen, who were consulted by several communities in the vicinity, were exceptions. The community dwindled as a result of the plague of 1672. In the 18th century, when prosperity returned, a permanent religious court which also supervised communal arrangements was established; business expanded and commercial ties were formed between Ankara and other commercial towns. In the 19th century there were no decisive changes in the economic situation, but the intellectual level of the community declined, and many Jews left the town. Migration after World War II reduced the Jewish population from 1,500 to 800. There was a certain subsequent increase and in 1968 it numbered 1,000, but in 2005 it was estimated that only 700–800 Jews live there.

BIBLIOGRAPHY: A. Galanté, *Histoire des Juifs d'Anatolie*, 2 (1939), 275ff.; idem, *Appendice à l'Histoire des Juifs d'Anatolie* (1948), 25–29. **ADD. BIBLIOGRAPHY:** A. Galanté, "Les Juifs d'Ankara," in: *Hamenora*, 11 (Oct.–Dec. 1933), 240–48; B.L. Bahar, "Tarihde Ankara Yahudileri," in: *Salom* (Mar. 4–July 22, 1964), 854–74; S.J. Shaw, *The Jews of the Ottoman Empire and the Turkish Republic* (1991), index; F. Ilter, "Ankara'nin eski kent dokesunda Yahudi mahallesi ve sinagog" in: *Belleten*, 60 (Dec. 1966), 734–43; B.L. Bahar, *Efsaneden tarihe Ankara Yahudileri* (2003).

ANKAWA, ABRAHAM BEN MORDECAI (b. 1810), rabbi and kabbalist. Ankawa was born in Salé (Morocco). His family, probably of Spanish origin, had settled in Tlemcen (Algeria) and in Salé, where his father, Mordecai, was president of the community for a time. After serving as *dayyan* in his native town, Ankawa traveled to Leghorn about 1838 to arrange the printing of his first works. On his return he journeyed to many towns in Morocco and the Oran district, seeking material for his halakhic works. He was particularly interested in the unpublished research and rulings of old Castilian and North African rabbis, making extensive use of these and the works of authoritative European writers. His visits were usually short, but he stayed three years in Tlemcen and founded a talmudic academy there. He made a second trip to Leghorn in 1858.

The following works by Ankawa have been published: *Zekhor le-Avraham* (Leghorn, 1838), the rules of *terefot* in verse form, with a commentary based mainly on manuscripts by authoritative Fez writers, and an appendix containing four liturgical poems for the New Year by Spanish poets; *Ḥukkat ha-Pesaḥ* (1843), an Arabic paraphrase of memorial verses for *seder* nights; *Kol Teḥinnah* (1843), prayers for fasts and a few elegies; *Ḥesed le-Avraham* or *Sha'ar ha-Shamayim* (1845), a prayer book for the whole year arranged in accordance with the teachings of Isaac *Luria, containing the "*Idra Zuta,*" various mystical prayers, formulas, directions, and explanations: this prayer book was later published in several revised editions and under various titles (*Kol Bo, Limmudei ha-Shem*, etc.); *Ḥomer ha-Dat he-Attik* (1844), a summary of *Shefa Tal* by Shabbetai Sheftel *Horowitz, printed as an appendix to Ḥayyim *Vital's *Oẓerot Ḥayyim; Zevaḥim Shelamim*, a double commentary to Maimonides' rules of ritual slaughter, together with the *Maggid Mishneh*, with source references by Judah Alkalaz: included in this volume were *Get Mekushar* and *Seder Ḥaliẓah*, on the arrangements for the bill of divorce and for *ḥaliẓah* by Judah ibn *Attar and Jacob *Ibn Ẓur; *Yuẓẓa la-Rabbim* (1858) concerning a dispute between Ankawa and some Algers rabbis; *Kerem Ḥemed* (1869–71), responsa in two volumes arranged according to the four parts of Shulḥan Arukh: the second volume also contains *Sefer ha-Takkanot*, the statutes of the Castilian communities in Fez (since 1492) and *Et Sofer*, on legal documents. The *Sefer ha-Takkanot* is based on a copy which was completed by Jacob ibn Ẓur in 1698, and also contains *Kiẓẓut Takkanot*, after the version of Raphael *Berdugo (no. 196). Unpublished works of Ankawa include: *Oẓar Ḥokhmah*, an abstract of Ḥayyim Vital's *Oẓerot Ḥayyim; Afra de-Avraham* and *Millel le-Avraham*, homilies; *Seivat Avraham*, novellae to a few talmudic tractates; and a Hebrew translation of the Arabic paraphrase of the Decalogue, formerly ascribed to *Saadiah Gaon.

BIBLIOGRAPHY: Zedner, in: HB, 1 (1858), 113; Steinschneider, *ibid.*, 16 (1876), 25, 33–35; Steinschneider, Arab Lit, 268; J.M. Toledano, *Ner ha-Ma'arav* (1911), 209; J. Ben-Naim, *Malkhei Rabbanan* (1931), 17a; Davidson, Oẓar, 4 (1933), index.

[Heinrich Haim Brody]

ANKAWA, RAPHAEL BEN MORDECAI (1848–1935), Moroccan rabbi. Ankawa was born in Salé, a descendant of an illustrious Sephardi family. He received an excellent traditional religious education from his father-in-law, Issachar Asseraf, the chief rabbi of Salé. His great authority made him the uncontested leader of Moroccan Jewry. In 1880 Ankawa was appointed *dayyan* in Salé. In 1918 he became president of the Supreme Rabbinical Court in Rabat, the supreme court of Moroccan Jewry, after the reorganization of Moroccan Jewish communities by French Protectorate authorities. Ankawa held this post until his death. In 1929 he was made a Chevalier of the Legion of Honor. His tomb in the Salé cemetery became a shrine for Moroccan Jewish pilgrims. He wrote the following halakhic works: *Karnei Re'em* (1910), *Pa'amonei Zahav* (1912), and *To'afot Re'em* (1930), and a book of talmudic glosses entitled *Ḥadad ve-Teima* (in manuscript form).

BIBLIOGRAPHY: J. Ben-Naim, *Malkhei Rabbanan* (1931), 108a.

[Haim Zafrani]

ANKORI, ZEVI (1920–), scholar and writer on Karaite history. Born in Tarnow, Poland, Ankori graduated from the Hebrew University, Jerusalem, and Columbia University, New York. He taught at Tel Aviv University, the Hebrew University, Ohio State University, and Columbia University where (in 1970) he became professor of Jewish history. His published work includes *Karaites in Byzantium* (1959), a major contribution to Karaite studies, and articles on Karaism in various periodicals. He co-edited *Madrikh Bibliografi le-Toledot Am Yisrael* (1961), a bibliographical guide to the history of the Jewish people in the Middle Ages.

ANNA BE-KHO'AḤ (Heb. אָנָּא בְּכֹחַ), prayer hymn ascribed to the *tanna* R. Neḥunya b. ha-Kanah, but probably composed in the circle of the 13th-century Spanish kabbalists. The hymn, originally part of a group of kabbalistic prayers known under the title *Tefillat ha-Yiḥud*, gives expression to the longing of Israel for deliverance from the Diaspora and implores God's support and protection. It consists of seven verses of six words each, the initials of which form the 42-lettered Holy Name of God and similar mystical combinations (e.g., the initials of the second verse form the sentence קְרַע שָׂטָן (*Kera Satan*; "Rend Satan"), i.e., silence the adversary of Israel. The prayer is recited, according to some rites, in the order of sacrifices contained in the daily morning prayer and on the Sabbath eve before the hymn *Lekhah Dodi*. Among the rites of Eastern Europe influenced by the Kabbalah it is recited in the counting of the **Omer*.

ANNA BE-KORENU (Heb. אָנָּא בְּקָרְאֵנוּ), a *seliḥah* in the Sephardi rite, recited on the eve of the *Day of Atonement. It was composed by David b. Eleazar *Ibn Paquda (12th century). The prayer, its eight stanzas spelling the acrostic *David Ḥazak* ("David, be strong!"), consists of a plaintive theme developed by the cantor and punctuated frequently by the congregation singing either "Hear, O Lord!" or "Pardon, O Lord!" The chorus, from which the name is derived, reads, "To the voice of our supplication when we call Thee, Hear, O Lord! Through Thy mercy, the sins caused by our selfish ambition, Pardon, O Lord!"

ANN ARBOR, city in Michigan, U.S. The present-day Jewish community of Ann Arbor – comprising over 3,000 family units in 2005 – traces its roots to the turn of the century with the arrival of the Lansky family in 1895 and Mr. Osias Zwerdling, furrier, in 1904. Although the Lanskys had heard that Jews had previously lived in the area, there were no signs of the existence of an earlier community. It was not until 1980 – with the serendipitous discovery of a tombstone, beautifully engraved in Hebrew script and dated 1858, and the efforts to determine its original resting place – that the picture of a viable Jewish life in Ann Arbor from the 1840s to the 1880s began to emerge. These first Jews of Ann Arbor, the Weils and their extended family members and friends, arrived from Bohemia and began their lives as farmers and peddlers, then traded furs and skins and finally opened a successful tannery business.

As a result of the information garnered during this discovery process, it was possible to ascertain that the first Jewish cemetery in the state of Michigan existed at the northeast corner of the grounds of what today is the Horace H. Rackham School of Graduate Studies at the University of Michigan. Dedication of a Historical Marker, commemorating the establishment of the first organized Jewish community in Michigan, took place in 1983. Appropriately, this site also became the location for the Holocaust Memorial sculpture by Leonard Baskin that was dedicated in 1994.

William and Hattie Lansky originally had set up a grocery/general store and, as the Jewish community began to grow, it was this family that undertook a leadership role. The Lanskys were joined in this endeavor by Osias Zwerdling, who served as president of Beth Israel Congregation from 1918 to 1958. By 1902, the landmark Lansky junkyard was established and, as extended family members joined the early pioneers, more Jewish families were attracted to the area: Abraham Levy, shoemaker; Thomas Cook, who made his mark by establishing a foundry business with an African-American partner; Israel Friedman, scrap iron business; Jacob Ingber, auto parts; Mark Ross, furniture store; and Joseph Lampe, retired carpenter, who crafted the *aron kodesh* for Beth Israel Congregation that still exists in its small chapel. His son, Isadore Lampe, was among the first Jewish faculty members at the University of Michigan Medical School. Following his studies, in 1936, Dr. Lampe was named director of the Division of Radiation Therapy, the first full division in the country. His lasting legacy was the training of over 200 radiation oncology physicians, many of whom went on to leadership positions in other universities. Also on the faculty, from 1913 to 1954 in the Department of Economics, was I. Leo Sharfman who became chair in 1928. Prof. Sharfman, uncle of Mike *Wallace, a U-M graduate himself, enlisted William Haber to the department in 1936, and he later became chair and subsequently dean of the College of Literature, Science and Arts. Additional early faculty members of note include Kasimir Fajans, physical chemist, renowned for his pioneering work on radioactive isotopes; Reuben Kahn, originator of the Kahn Test for syphilis; and Jonas *Salk, developer of the polio vaccine. Another famous graduate of the university's College of Architecture and Design was Raoul *Wallenberg, in 1935. In his honor, the College holds an annual Wallenberg Lecture series. Additionally, an endowment was established at the university by members of the Jewish and non-Jewish communities to fund an annual Lecture and Medal series. Invited guests are those who personify the Wallenberg ideals of bravery, stamina and integrity, and who imbue in the students the fact that one person can make a difference.

As the University of Michigan grew, so grew the influx of Jewish faculty – in all disciplines. In the 1950s and 1960s, with the population growth, a split developed between town and gown. At that time, Beth Israel was the only formal congregation in the city. A new B'nai Brith Hillel-Beth Israel building was dedicated in 1951 and Beth Israel changed its name to Beth Israel Community Center. In 1964, bursting at the seams, Beth Israel embarked on a fundraising campaign to build its own building. Subsequently, a faction of the membership broke off and began the Reform congregation, Temple Beth Emeth. The Conservative Beth Israel returned to its former name and remained joined in the Hillel Building until its own new facility was built in 1978 under the leadership of Rabbi Allan D. Kensky, spiritual leader of the congregation from 1971 to 1988. Membership in the two congregations, led by Rabbi Robert Dobrusin at Beth Israel since 1988, and Rabbi Robert Levy at Beth Emeth since 1984, comprised over 1,200 family units. The rift between town and gown was bridged at the outbreak of the Six-Day War, when the community came together in support of Israel, and was cemented at the time of the Yom Kippur War. The thriving Jewish community today, in addition to the aforementioned congregations and Hillel, includes Congregation Chabad, led by Rabbi Aharon and Esther Goldstein since 1975, the Jewish Cultural Society, the Ann Arbor Orthodox Minyan, and the Ann Arbor Reconstructionist Havurah. There is a Jewish Community Center, Jewish Federation, Jewish Family Services organization, Hadassah and Women's American ORT chapters, a Yiddish group and Hebrew Day School.

The most recent wave of major Jewish influx in Ann Arbor began in 1979 with the arrival of the first "New Americans," refugees from the Former Soviet Union. Their population today approximates 200 families, and most of them have become involved in various aspects of the Jewish community.

Enriching the community is the Samuel and Jean Frankel Center for Judaic Studies, established at the University of Michigan in 1988, co-directed by Professors Zvi Gitelman and Todd *Endelman. The Center superseded the University's Program in Judaic Studies, established in 1971 with a grant from the Jewish Welfare Association in Detroit. The Program was co-directed by Professors Zvi Gitelman and Edna Coffin, and it brought Professor Yehuda Reinharz, now president of Brandeis University, to the Ann Arbor campus to teach Jewish history. In 2005, Stanley and Judy Frankel, son and daughter-in-law of Samuel and Jean, donated $20 million to the University of Michigan to establish the Frankel Institute for Advanced Judaic Studies. The Frankel Center coordinates programs and teaching; the Frankel Institute will have 15 faculty members, 40 courses, and 10–14 visiting scholars, teaching 800–1,200 students per year. The total population at the University numbers 36,000, of which 24,000 are undergraduates; it is estimated that ⅓ of the student body is Jewish. Thus, two percent of all Jewish students in North America study at the University of Michigan and the Jewish community of Ann Arbor swells while the university is in session. The students are served by the B'nai Brith Hillel Foundation, the second largest student organization at the University of Michigan, whose modern, new facility was built in 1989, under the leadership of its long-time and current executive director, Michael Brooks. The University of Michigan is a major feeder school for the Hebrew Union College, Jewish Theological Seminary, and AIPAC's Young Leadership Cabinet.

[Helen Aminoff (2nd ed.)]

ANNENBERG, WALTER H. (1908–2002), editor and diplomat; publisher of the oldest U.S. daily newspaper, the *Philadelphia Inquirer*; head of one of America's largest communications chains. Born in Milwaukee, Wisconsin, Walter was the son of Moses L. Annenberg (1878–1942), a newspaper publisher who had added the *Inquirer* to his chain in 1936. Walter became president of Triangle Publications Inc. in 1942. Subsequently he also acquired the holdings of another Philadelphia newspaper, the tabloid *Daily News*, six radio and television stations, and two mass circulation national magazines: *Seventeen* and *TV Guide* – which reached a circulation of 17 million per issue, making it a competitor with *Reader's Digest* as the magazine with the largest circulation. The horse racing daily, the *Daily Racing Form,* also came under his control. In 1969 he sold the *Philadelphia Inquirer* and the *Philadelphia Daily News* to the Knight-Ridder chain, while the Triangle Publications communications empire was sold to Australian media magnate Rupert Murdoch in 1988 for $3 billion. A public benefactor with a wide range of philanthropic and civic interests, Annenberg founded and became president of the M.L. Annenberg School of Communications at his alma mater, the University of Pennsylvania. He also became president of the M.L. Annenberg Foundation and of the Annenberg Fund, charitable foundations devoted to supporting higher education, medical research, music, and community welfare. In 1969 he was appointed U.S. ambassador to the United Kingdom.

In 1977 Annenberg underwent a hip replacement operation at Philadelphia's Pennsylvania Hospital. He was so pleased with the outcome of the surgery that he gave the institution $2 million to found a hip replacement institute, named after his physician Dr. Richard Rothman. Generous to many of his friends, Annenberg paid most of the bills to add a bowling lane in the White House during Richard Nixon's years and installed a swimming pool at Chequers, the English country home of the prime minister of Great Britain. Annenberg donated more than $17,500,000 to refurbish Philadelphia's Academy of Music, and an additional $10 million to endow the chair of Music Director Wolfgang Sawallisch, conductor of the Philadelphia Orchestra. In 1981 Annenberg was elected trustee emeritus of the board of the Metropolitan Museum of Art in New York, which he had joined in 1974. In 1991 he made the decision to bequeath his collection of French Impressionist and Post-Impressionist art, valued at some $1 billion, to the Museum; this constituted the largest gift of its kind in some 50 years. His $50 million contribution to the United Negro College Fund in 1990 represented the largest single donation ever given to African-American higher education in the United States. In 1993 his foundation donated a total of $365 million – then the largest one-time gift ever given to private education in America – to the universities of Harvard, Southern California, and Pennsylvania, and to his prep school, the Peddie School in New Jersey. He also made a major donation to *Dropsie University (formerly Dropsie College), the center for Jewish learning in Philadelphia, which in 1986 became the Annenberg Research Institute.

In 1986 Annenberg was awarded the nation's highest civilian honor, the Medal of Freedom. He also won the George

Foster Peabody Award in 1987. In 1992 he was inducted into the Broadcast Pioneers Hall of Fame. In 2001 the Annenberg Foundation gave $100 million each to the communications schools named after him at the University of Pennsylvania and the University of Southern California. At the same time, the Annenberg Foundation gave the Philadelphia Art Museum a cash gift of $20 million, the largest gift in the institution's 125-year history.

BIBLIOGRAPHY: F. Lundberg, *Imperial Hearst* (1936), 151ff.; W.A. Swanberg, *Citizen Hearst* (1961), 27.

[Irving Rosenthal / Rohan Saxena and Ruth Beloff (2nd ed.)]

ANOINTING. The anointing of persons and objects with oil was widespread in ancient Israel and its environment for both practical and symbolical reasons. Its most practical usage was cosmetic, and for medicinal purposes (see *Cosmetics).

Aside from its cosmetic and therapeutic functions, anointment was an important component of ritual formularies. The anointment of vassals was not a mere ceremonial trapping: "As oil penetrates your flesh, so may they [the gods] make this curse enter into your flesh" (D.J. Wiseman, *The Vassal-Treaties of Esarhaddon* (1958), lines 622–4, p. 78; cf. Ps. 109:18; for the use of oil in the making of a covenant, see Hos. 12:2; see McCarthy in bibl.). The main role of symbolic anointment in the ancient Near East, however, was to solemnize formally an elevation in legal status: the manumission of a slave woman, the transfer of property, the betrothal of a bride, and the deputation of a vassal. Israel continued the Syrian and Anatolian practice of anointing the king (El Amarna Letter 51:4–9, see below). The consecration of a priest involved anointing, a practice attested at Emar in Central Syria in the thirteenth century B.C.E. The Bible also requires anointing for the rehabilitation of persons afflicted with certain skin diseases. The above cases indicate that in Israel symbolic unction took place in the cult but not in legal proceedings. The attribute *mashi'aḥ* ("anointed") came to designate the king and the high priest and, by extension, other divinely appointed functionaries who were not anointed at all, e.g., the prophets (I Kings 19:16b, 19b; Isa. 61:1), the patriarchs (Ps. 105:15), and even foreign kings (I Kings 19:15; Isa. 45:1; cf. II Kings 8:7). This figurative use of *mshḥ* is not a late development since it is already attested in Ugaritic (76:11, 22–23; cf. Ps. 89:21 and 25). Eventually it was applied to the messiah (the very word being taken from the Hebrew "anointed").

In Israel, anointment conferred upon the king the *ru'aḥ* YHWH ("the spirit of the Lord"), i.e., His support (I Sam. 16:13–14; 18:12), strength (Ps. 89:21–25), and wisdom (Isaiah 11:1–4; see *Messiah). The king absorbs divine attributes through unction. The anointment of the high priest served an entirely different function. It conferred neither *ru'aḥ* nor any other divine attribute. Moses, for example, transferred his powers (by hand-laying) upon a *ru'aḥ*-endowed Joshua (Num. 27:18–20), but when he transfers the high priest's authority from Aaron to his son Eleazar, these spiritual features are conspicuously absent (Num. 20:25ff.). The high priest's anointment is otherwise designated by the verb *kadesh* (*qaddesh*; "to sanctify"). Indeed, the anointment "sanctifies" the high priest by removing him from the realm of the profane and empowering him to operate in the realm of the sacred, i.e., to handle the sancta, such as the oracle. The high priest was anointed in conjunction with the cult objects (Ex. 40:9–15), and the latter practice is found in the oldest portions of the Bible (anointment of pillars, Gen. 28:18; 31:13; 35:14). The story of Solomon's anointment by the high priest Zadok (I Kings 1:39) leads us to the assumption that the royal unction is a derivative of the unction of the high priest. The story could not be an interpolation of the priestly editors, since the latter would by their own laws have condemned Zadok to death (by God) for the crime of anointing a *zar,* a non-priest (Ex. 30:33). On the contrary, this incident complements the image of the king in the historical narratives: since he may officiate at the sacred altar like a priest (e.g., I Kings 3:4; 8:63–64), why should he not be similarly anointed with the sacred oil?

According to the priestly source, the sons of Aaron were anointed along with him. Though the word *mashaḥ* is used in Exodus (e.g., 40:15a), it means only that they received the sacred oil and implies nothing about the manner of its application. Indeed, the respective ceremonies differ sharply: the sons were sprinkled (*hzh*) after the sacrificial service (Ex. 29:21), whereas Aaron's head was doused (*yẓk*) separately, before the service (v. 7). Furthermore, whereas each succeeding high priest was anointed while his father was still in office (Lev. 6:15), the anointing of the first priests was never repeated; it was to be valid for their posterity (Ex. 40:15b). This concept is proven to be ancient, for it is found in the El-Amarna letters (51:4–9), where a vassal stakes his authority on his grandfather's anointment.

The leper was anointed on the eighth and concluding day of his purification ritual, but the oil was not sacred. The "waving" and the sevenfold sprinkling of the oil "before the Lord" (Lev. 14:12, 16), even before it can be used on the leper, are not rites of consecration but of purification; moreover, the indispensable verb *mshḥ* is tellingly absent. Perhaps even the "change of status" is operative: the ostracism of the erstwhile leper is ended, and he is free to reenter society. However, an apotropaic function may also be present.

[Jacob Milgrom]

In the Talmud

According to the Talmud the anointing oil was compounded only once in Jewish history, by Moses (Ex. 30:31–33), and the supply made by him sufficed for the whole period from the anointing of Aaron and his sons until the residue was hidden away by Josiah. Anointing oil was therefore not used for the kings and high priests after Josiah, and it was one of the five appurtenances used in the First Temple but not in the Second.

After the anointment of Aaron and his sons only high priests and the priest anointed for war (the appellation of the

Talmud for the priest mentioned in Deut. 20:2ff.; Mishnah Sotah 8:1) were anointed. Every high priest and "priest anointed for war" was anointed, the former even if he succeeded his father as high priest.

On the other hand, from Solomon onward only kings of the Davidic dynasty whose succession was disputed or was in doubt were anointed (as was Jehu, see below). Where the succession was natural and undisputed no anointing took place. Thus Solomon was anointed on account of the rival claims of Adonijah (I Kings 1:39), Joash because of Athaliah (II Kings 11:12), and Jehoahaz because Jehoiakim was his senior by two years (II Kings 23:30).

This anointing of David and his descendants was by oil poured from a horn. For Saul, the only non-Davidic king to be anointed with oil, a cruse was used (I Sam. 16:13) since "his kingdom was not a lasting one."

The kings of the northern secessionist kingdom of Israel were not anointed with oil but with balsam, as was Jehoahaz of Judah since Josiah had hidden away the anointing oil. The statement that Jehu was anointed (with balsam) because of his dispute with Joram would appear to suggest that even in the case of the kings of Israel anointing took place only in the case of disputed succession but it would, of course, have applied to each usurping king and founder of a dynasty, though not to his descendants (cf. Ker. 5b with Hor. 11b).

In the anointing of kings the whole head was covered with oil ("in the shape of a wreath") whereas in the case of priests it was "in the shape of a *chi*." What is meant by "the shape of a *chi*?… the shape of Greek X" (the printed texts have "a Greek *kaph*," probably because of the opposition to the sign of the cross).

All the above data except where otherwise stated are to be found in *Horayot* 11b and 12a, and more compactly in the Jerusalem Talmud, *Horayot* 3:4, 47c.

[Louis Isaac Rabinowitz]

BIBLIOGRAPHY: E. Cothenet, in: DBI, supplément 6 (1960), 701–32; E. Kutsch, *Salbung als Rechtsakt* (BZAW, 87, 1963); K.R. Veenhof, in: BOR, 23 (1966), 308–13; J. Licht, in: EM, 5 (1968), 526–31; S. Paul, in: JNES, 28 (1969), 48–53; D.J. McCarthy, in: VT, 14 (1964), 215–21. **ADD. BIBLIOGRAPHY:** D. Fleming, *The Installation of Baal's High Priestess at Emar* (1992).

ANOKHI, ZALMAN YIẒḤAK (pseudonym of **Z.I. Aronsohn**; 1878–1947), Hebrew writer. Anokhi was born in Lyady, Russia. His first story, *"Ha-Yenukah,"* written in Hebrew, was published in *Ha-Shilo'aḥ* (12 (1903), 52–64). He soon began to write in Yiddish and published two collections of stories, *Tsvishen Himel un Erd* ("Between Heaven and Earth," 1909) and *Reb Elkhonon* (1910). His *Reb Abbe* (1911), the monologue of an aging, naive, and pious Ḥasid, won wide acclaim. In 1911 Anokhi visited Palestine and recorded his impressions in *Unzer Land* ("Our Country," 1919). After a brief stay in Argentina (1923) he settled in 1924 in Palestine and reverted to writing in Hebrew. He translated *Reb Abbe* into Hebrew (1927) and published two dramas. His collected stories, *Bein Shamayim va-Areẓ* ("Between Heaven and Earth," 1945), appeared shortly before his death in Tel Aviv. Nearly all of his stories are sentimental, romantic vignettes of Jewish life in Eastern Europe.

BIBLIOGRAPHY: D. Sadan, *Avnei Zikkaron* (1954), 303–13; Kressel, Leksikon, 1 (1965), 127; Rejzen, Leksikon, 1 (1928), 119–22; LNYL, 1 (1956), 126–8.

[David Zakay]

ANSBACH, city in Middle Franconia, Germany; formerly capital of the Margravate of Ansbach. Its Hebrew designation אנולצבך, אנשבאן, אונשפך retains the older form Onolzbach. Records of a Jewish community in Ansbach date from the beginning of the 14th century and many Jews were massacred during the *Black Death in 1349. A Jews' Street is again mentioned in the second half of the 15th century, but the Jews were expelled from Ansbach in 1561, although readmitted in 1609. The communities in the margravate were organized in a *Landesjudenschaft. During the 17th century members of the Model and Fraenkel families played an important role as *court Jews in the economy and administration as well as leading the Jewish communities of the margravate. Two of these court Jews, however, were dismissed and sentenced to life imprisonment. The synagogue of Ansbach was built by the Italian architect Leopold Retty in 1745–46. In 1836 a conference of rabbis, teachers, and communal leaders was held at Ansbach to oppose liturgical reforms in Bavaria. Rabbis of Ansbach included Abraham Merzbacher and Phinehas (Pinchas) *Kohn, both of *Agudat Israel. The Jewish community declined from 385 persons in 1809 to 220 (1.5% of the total population) in 1880 and 197 (0.9%) in 1933. On Nov. 10, 1938, when the Nazis destroyed many German synagogues, the mayor of Ansbach saved the synagogue there by staging a mock fire. By the outbreak of World War II, after emigration and expulsions, only 10 Jews remained in the city. After the war a displaced persons camp was established at Ansbach. The ancient synagogue was completely restored, but Jewish community life was not reestablished.

BIBLIOGRAPHY: *Sefer Yovel… Y. Baer* (1960), 351–73; S. Haenle, *Geschichte der Juden im ehemaligen Fuerstentum Ansbach* (1867); D.Y. Cohen, in: *Koveẓ al Yad*, 6 (1966^2), 457ff.; Wiener Library, London, *German Jewry* (1958), 35; Ger Jud, 2 (1968), 17–18; BJCE; R. Wischnitzer, *Architecture of the European Synagogue* (1964), 157, 169. **ADD. BIBLIOGRAPHY:** A. Biernoth, "Die Ansbacher juedische Gemeinde im 19. Jahrhundert," Ms. (1995).

[Zvi Avneri]

ANSELL, DAVID ABRAHAM (1834–1914), Canadian businessman, Jewish community leader. Ansell was born in London and arrived in Montreal via Queensland, Australia, in 1866. He went into business as an importer of glassware and representative of a firm headed by his father in Frankfurt, Germany. He also became very involved in the Montreal Jewish community and was soon one of the most prominent Montreal Jews of his era. When he arrived in Montreal he joined the fledgling Young Men's Hebrew Benevolent Association, which in 1891 was renamed the Baron de Hirsch Society in honor of its most generous benefactor. Ansell served as the society's president for many years. As a member of the *Jewish Colonization Association he became a promoter of Jewish farm settlement in Western Canada. Keenly interested in issues of education, Ansell helped establish a free school for children in the Jewish community and was prominent in pressing provincial authorities for legislation granting equal rights to Jews in the Quebec elementary educational system.

In politics Ansell supported the Conservative Party and maintained an active correspondence with Prime Minister John A. Macdonald and other prominent political figures. In letters to newspapers and speeches Ansell advocated on behalf of British imperial federation and free trade. He also served as consul-general for Mexico in Canada from 1888 to 1913 and worked to increase trade between Canada and Mexico.

BIBLIOGRAPHY: G. Tulchinsky, *Taking Root* (1993).

[Gerald Tulchinsky (2nd ed.)]

ANSELM (Anshel) HA-LEVI (15th century), German rabbi and communal leader; active in Cologne, Andernach, and Worms. Anselm was highly reputed as a scholar among his contemporaries, and even among the secular authorities. Hence in 1435, he was appointed supreme rabbi of the Holy Roman Empire by Conrad von Weinsberg, hereditary chamberlain of Emperor Sigismund and acting on his authority. His seat was in Worms and his nominal jurisdiction extended over a wide area of Germany, France, Switzerland, and the Netherlands. A similar appointment had been made by King Rupert in 1407, when Israel b. Isaac was appointed *Hochmeister* of the Jews of Germany (see *Chief Rabbinate). The creation of this rather high-sounding office was doubtless an act of expediency to facilitate the collection of taxes from the Jewish communities. The appointment of Anselm is not mentioned in Jewish sources, and it can be assumed that it was as unpopular with the Jews as was that of Israel b. Isaac. Such an appointment by an outside authority would have been regarded by the Jews as an unwarranted intervention in their internal affairs. Joseph b. Moses, author of the *Leket Yosher*, was Anselm's pupil.

BIBLIOGRAPHY: A. Kober, *History of Jews in Cologne* (1940), 31, 366; J. Freimann (ed.), *Leket Yosher*, 2 (1904), xxii–xxiii; Guedemann, Gesch Erz, 3 (1888), 35ff.

°**ANSELM OF CANTERBURY** (c. 1033–1109), abbot of Bec (Normandy) from 1078 and archbishop of Canterbury from 1093; theologian and philosopher, perhaps canonized by the Catholic Church though there is some uncertainty about this. The Jew appears as the imaginary adversary in his most important work *Cur Deus Homo*, which is about the theology of atonement. The composition may have been influenced by the Judeo-Christian dialogue which Gilbert *Crispin had dedicated to him. He was among the church reformers whose opposition to William II (Rufus) may have been stimulated by the king's reputed friendliness to the Jews. Anselm favored Christian missionary activities among the Jews. In a letter he sent to two English clerics Anselm commends to them a certain Robert and his family who had recently been converted, asking them to assist him "so that he should not suffer from want, but should rejoice that he has left perfidy for the true faith."

BIBLIOGRAPHY: N.F. Cantor, *Church, Kingship and Lay Investiture in England 1089–1135* (1958), 126ff.; R.W. Southern, *St. Anselm* (Eng., 1959, 1990²), 88ff. **ADD. BIBLIOGRAPHY:** Eadmer, *Vita Anselmi*, ed. and tr. R.W. Southern (1962).

[Bernhard Blumenkranz / Shimon Gibson (2nd ed.)]

ANSHEL (Asher) OF CRACOW (first half of 16th century), putative author of *Mirkevet ha-Mishneh*, an alphabetical concordance and glossary of the Bible, with references and Yiddish translations of the words. Two editions were published. The one published in Cracow, 1534, was the first book printed in Yiddish. The title page states that the work "was composed in two languages, the holy language and German, the language prevalent among us." The second, and better-known, edition was published under the title *Sefer shel R. Anshel* (Cracow, 1584). Some suggest a polemical background to its composition, pointing out that *Luther's German translation of the Bible was also published in 1534 and that the Jews were interested in publishing this concordance to counterbalance Luther's translation. A possible factor was the desire to facilitate the study of the Bible for uneducated Jews, particularly women and children. The identity of Anshel has given rise to many conjectures and theories. He has been erroneously identified with Asher Anshel b. Joseph Mordecai of Posen, who translated the festival prayer book into Yiddish, and with Asher of Cracow, grandfather of Meir b. Gedaliah of Lublin, author of the kabbalistic book *Emek Berakhah*. Steinschneider conjectured that he might possibly be Asher b. Ḥayyim Halicz, one of the brothers who printed the first edition. Some date the work earlier than the 16th century because the German words used by the author belong to an earlier period, some going back as far as the 14th and 15th centuries. The simple title of the second edition, *Sefer shel R. Anshel* ("R. Anshel's Book"), has led many scholars to suggest that the author must have been well known, either as a scholar or as a communal leader.

BIBLIOGRAPHY: Zunz, Schr, 3 (1876), 85; J. Perles, *Beitraege zur Geschichte der hebraeischen und aramaeischen Studien* (1884), 33, 100, 117–9; J. Meisl, *Geschichte der Juden in Polen und Russland*, 1 (1921), 296; Waxman, Literature, 2 (1960), 637–8; Steinschneider, Handbuch, 14; Szlosberg, in: *YIVO Bleter*, 13 (1938), 313–24; H.D. Friedberg, *Toledot ha-Defus ha-Ivri be-Folanyah* (1950²), 1; Zinberg, Sifrut, 4 (1958), 30, 245. **ADD. BIBLIOGRAPHY:** C. Shmeruk, *Sifrut Yiddish be-Polin* (1981), 25–26, 75–76.

[Yehoshua Horowitz]

AN-SKI, S. (pseudonym of **Shloyme-Zanvl Rappoport**; 1863–1920), author and folklorist. An-Ski was born in Tshashnik, Belorussia, where his father was a landowner's agent and his mother an innkeeper. An-Ski attended a traditional Jewish *heder*. In 1878, at the age of 16, he became a close friend of Chaim *Zhitlowsky and soon discovered Hebrew and Russian literature. Attracted by the doctrines of the Haskalah, and the Narodniki (a group committed to revolutionizing the Russian peasants), he went to live among Russian peasants and miners, and worked as a blacksmith, bookbinder, factory hand, and teacher. On the advice of the Russian writer Gleb Uspensky, he returned from south Russia to St. Petersburg and wrote for the Narodniki's monthly publication. Compelled to leave Russia in 1892, he stayed briefly in Germany and Switzerland before settling in Paris in 1894. There he worked for six years as secretary of the revolutionary and philosopher Piotr Lavrov, while writing short stories about Jewish radicals. Returning to Russia in 1905, he joined the Social-Revolutionary Party, circulated his 1902 *Bund hymn "*Di Shvue*" ("The Oath"), and wrote folk legends and stories about Jewish poverty. Until 1908 An-Ski wrote chiefly in Russian, switching to Yiddish after meeting Peretz. An-Ski brought to Yiddish literature a deep appreciation of Jewish folk values. As head of the Jewish ethnographic expedition financed by Baron Gunzberg he traveled through the villages of Volhynia and Podolia from 1912 to 1914, collecting material. His knowledge of folklore inspired his famous play *The *Dybbuk* (written and reworked by An-Ski between 1912 and 1917 in both Russian and Yiddish, the latter originally called *Tsvishn Tsvey Veltn*), which was first produced in Yiddish by the Vilna troupe (1920), and then, in the Hebrew translation of Bialik, by the Habimah company in Moscow, Tel Aviv, and New York. Bialik translated *The Dybbuk* into Hebrew in *Ha-Tekufah*, vol. 1 (1918). An-Ski subsequently lost the Yiddish original *en route* from Russia to Vilna and thus revised and retranslated it into Yiddish from Bialik's Hebrew version. This latter version was the one performed by the Vilna Theater group. Productions in numerous languages followed; the Italian composer L. Rocca based an opera on the play; musical versions by Renato Simoni and David Temkin appeared in New York, and movie versions in Poland (1938) and Israel (1968). Pulitzer Prize-winning author Tony *Kushner rewrote *The Dybbuk* in 1998. The play is An-Ski's masterpiece, combining folkloristic aspects with universal themes of love, suffering, and the search for an authentic self. During World War I, An-Ski devoted himself to organizing relief committees for Jewish war victims. He would later recount his experiences during the war in his extraordinary chronicle *Khurbn Galitsye* ("The Destruction of Galicia"). In 1917 he was elected to the All-Russian Constituent Assembly as a Social-Revolutionary deputy and in 1918 he helped to reorganize the Vilna community. In 1920, when the Polish legion took over Vilna and began attacking the Jewish population, An-ski reluctantly moved to Warsaw, where he founded a Jewish ethnographic society. He died soon thereafter and was buried in the Warsaw Jewish cemetery next to Peretz.

BIBLIOGRAPHY: Sh. An-Ski, *The Dybbuk* (1926[1], 1937[2], 1953[3]); Rejzen, Leksikon, 1 (1926), 125–41; LYNL, 1 (1956), 131–4; Bibliography by E.H. Jeshurin, in: *Ilustrirte Yom-Tov Bleter* (Winter, 1951), 38–41, 52; Rozenhak, in: *Karmelit*, 9 (1963). **ADD. BIBLIOGRAPHY:** *Dos Yidishe Etnografishe Program; Oysgabe fun der Yidisher Etnografisher Ekspeditsye inem Nomen fun dem Baron Herts Guntsberg* (1914); Sh. An-Ski, *Gezamlte Shriftn in Fuftsn Bend* (1920–28); D. Roskies (ed.), *The Dybbuk and Other Writings by S. Ansky* (2002).

[Yitzhak Maor / Leah Garrett (2nd ed.)]

AN-SKI COLLECTIONS, Jewish collections of the State Ethnographic Museum in St. Petersburg. For many years the existence of the legendary An-Ski collections was doubted outside the Soviet Union, even maybe outside the walls of the State Ethnographic Museum. All that was known about them was the description of the ethnographical expeditions of 1910–16, headed by the well-known dramatist S.Z. Rappoport (An-Ski), written by one of its members, Abraham Rechtman. He gave a list of their finds: 700 ceremonial objects, 2,000 photographs, music recorded on 500 wax cylinders, and many folktales, articles of everyday life, and documents. Due to the consequences of the Russian Revolution, two world wars, and official Soviet antisemitism, only a fraction of these items survived in the Russian collection. In 1992, 90% of these remnants, approximately 330 objects, were shown for the first time outside Russia, in Amsterdam, in the Jewish Historical Museum.

The State Ethnographic Museum and the Jewish Historical Museum joined forces to register, describe, photograph, and publish these traces of the once important center of Jewish culture and history: the Pale of Settlement in Czarist Russia.

The history of the Jewish collection in the State Ethnographic Museum in St. Petersburg began early in the century. The scale of collection and completion of material relating to the Jewish culture and way of life has varied greatly at different times – after all, it had to deal with no fewer than six million people who lived within the Pale of Settlement.

The first entries related to the subject date from 1904 to 1912, when the cultural heritage of the peoples inhabiting the vast territories of the Russian Empire attracted special interest. It was a time when there were thorough studies of the way of life among national minorities, when ethnographical expeditions were undertaken, and folklore collected. The enlightened section of the Russian intelligentsia appreciated that rapid urbanization was taking place throughout the country and feared the consequent destruction of traditional forms of folk life, including that of the Russian Jews. Among this group were F.K. Volkov, an expert in Ukrainian ethnography, A.K. Serzhputovsky, a researcher in Byelorussian ethnography, and A.A. Miller, a specialist in the people of the Caucasus, the one who made the first contribution to the Jewish collections.

The second fruitful period for the Jewish collections was during the 1930s when the Jewish section of the St. Petersburg (Leningrad) Museum was headed by I.M. Pulner. His aim was not only to expand the collection but also to form a comprehensive exhibition entitled "The Jews in Czarist Russia and the U.S.S.R." This exhibition opened in 1939 and turned out to have a rather propagandistic character, which only seemed natural in those years.

After World War II the purposeful collection of ethnographical data related to Russian Jews was virtually finished. The Pale of Settlement was now past history, while the years of brutal fascist occupation of the Ukraine, Belorussia, and Lithuania destroyed vast quantities of cultural material.

There was also strongly anti-religious propaganda, which became the policy of the Soviet Union and destroyed the last vestiges of spiritual life – that is, the Jewish religious communities.

During the postwar years the collections were mostly augmented with gifts from other museums as well as rare purchases and private donations. A large collection from the former Moscow Museum of the Peoples of the U.S.S.R., which was passed on to the St. Petersburg Museum in 1948, should be mentioned in this respect.

The S.A. Rappoport (An-Ski) Collection is held to be the heart of the Ashkenazi collection. An-Ski headed a number of ethnographical expeditions during 1911–12, working in the provinces of Podolia, Volhynia, and Kiev. The items collected were intended for exhibition in the Jewish Museum formed as a section of the St. Petersburg Society of History and Ethnography. The *Evreskaya Starina* ("Jewish Antiquity") magazine, the published organ of the society, printed articles on the collecting activities of the museum. In 1914–16 An-Ski was known to be working in the front lines of Galicia, helping to evacuate historical valuables. This mission was formed by the State Duma (the Russian Parliament), and the data he collected while there were delivered to St. Petersburg. In 1917–18 *Evreskaya Starina* reported that "robbery and pogroms have been taking place since autumn 1917, which force us to close the museum and pack its exhibits into boxes to be kept in a safe place." From the published An-Ski will it is known that "five boxes and suitcases with exhibits were given to be kept in the Alexander III Museum," now the State Ethnographic Museum.

As we now have no precise documents or lists it is quite difficult to identify whether certain An-Ski exhibits date back to 1911–12 or to the times of his expeditions of 1914–16. Unfortunately, the documents relating to these expeditions are lost and it proves impossible to identify the geographical source of objects. Indirect indications helping to date the items can be found when deciphering the inscriptions and also in the writings of A. Rechtman. We can, however, only make guesses as to the routes An-Ski followed and the places where he found his exhibits.

The Jewish Ashkenazi collections of the State Ethnographic Museum present a historical and cultural heritage, covering the period from the late 18th to the early 20th century. In terms of geography it embraces most of the area where the Pale of Settlement was introduced after 1795 (the third partition of Poland).

The Judaica occupy a central place in the museum's collection, together with household objects and personal belongings.

The Czarist policy towards the Jews was ambivalent. It forced the Jews to live in the Pale of Settlement, where they formed 5% of the population. On the other hand, it tried to assimilate the Jews in their culture. Hundreds of measures were taken to achieve these goals, but without success. The Jews, speaking their own language, keeping their own religion and its traditions, resisted this policy.

But, as in all other communities, their material culture was heavily influenced by the Russian surroundings. The most exciting examples are the so-called Lubok paintings, Russian folk art used for decoration at home, but also as amulets to keep evil out of the house. In Judaica, often made by Jewish craftsmen, Russian folk elements like deer, birds, lions, and flowers decorated the Ḥannukah lamps, spice boxes, and *rimmonim*. The Czarist crown can be seen on covers for synagogue arks.

Another important part of the collection is clothing: the specific "*brustichel*" for women, and the headgear for men, both decorated with the so-called "*spanjerwerk*," gold embroidery. There are also the simple homemade wooden chess set, Ḥannukah cards, and the models of cookies, specific for the Jewish kitchen like the bridal cake in a Star of David form.

The remnants of the An-Ski Collection, modest as they are in number, should be treasured for the wealth of background they give of a poor man's deeply felt Jewish culture of bygone days. And we hope that through the exhibitions and through the publications of the material (see the catalogue *Tracing An-Ski: Jewish Collections from the State Ethnographic Museum in St. Petersburg* with excerpts from A. Rechtman and articles by Igor Krupnik and by Ludmilla Uritskaya, 1992) new generations can benefit from its resurgence.

[Judith Belinfante and Ludmilla Uritskaya]

ANSORGE, MARTIN CHARLES (1882–1967), U.S. congressman, attorney, and corporate director. One of Mark Perry and Jenny (Bach) Ansorge's seven children, Martin was born in Corning, New York, where his father was a successful clothing manufacturer. In 1885, the family relocated to New York City, where Martin and his siblings were educated. In their prosperous home, the Ansorge family's *lingua franca* was German. The senior Ansorge eventually became the owner of Ansorge Brothers and Company in Scranton, Pennsylvania. One of his sons, Herbert, would become president of the Wholesale Clothing Manufacturers Association.

After attending New York public schools, Martin Ansorge earned both a B.A. and a law degree from Columbia University. Ever resourceful, he earned a handsome living while attending Columbia by selling advertising space in the school paper, the *Columbia Spectator*. After practicing law in New York City for six years, Ansorge ran as a Republican for the United States Congress in 1912. He came in third in a three-man race. Ansorge also lost Congressional elections in 1914 and 1916. After serving in the Transportation Corps in World War I, he was finally elected to Congress in 1920. During his one term in the House of Representatives (1921–23), the Republican Ansorge floor-managed passage of the resolution establishing the New York Port Authority. He also gave strenuous vocal support to two anti-lynching proposals. Running for reelection in 1922, Ansorge lost by ten votes. Returning to New York City, he resumed to the practice of law.

In 1927, auto magnate Henry Ford retained Ansorge to negotiate out-of-court settlements in the much-publicized Ford-Sapiro libel case. The suit, brought by Sapiro, alleged that Ford had severely libeled him in the pages of the mogul's newspaper, the *Dearborn Independent*. That the antisemitic Ford should hire a Jewish attorney struck many as being incongruous. Following a mistrial, Ford hired Ansorge, who successfully negotiated an out-of-court settlement for an undisclosed amount, plus a public retraction from Ford. In 1934, Ansorge became a director of United Airlines, a position he held until 1961.

BIBLIOGRAPHY: K.F. Stone, *The Congressional Minyan: The Jews of Capitol Hill* (2000), 8–9; *The Reminiscences of Martin Ansorge*, Special Collections Department, Columbia University (1950).

[Kurt Stone (2nd ed.)]

ANSPACH, PHILIPPE (1800–1875), French lawyer and politician. Anspach, who was born in Metz, practiced law in Paris. He took an active part in the 1830 revolution and was appointed a deputy procurator in the department of Seine-et-Marne by the government of Louis Philippe. It was the first step in a brilliant career. Anspach successively became judge deputy of the Court of Justice in Paris, section president of the Court of Appeals, and counselor to the Court of Cassation. He was the first Jew in France to attain this position. Anspach combined the qualities of a practical jurist with the erudition of a law theoretician. Active in Jewish life, he served as a member of the Paris Consistory and was selected to the Central Consistory in 1845.

ANT (Heb. נְמָלָה, *nemalah*). The ant most frequent in Israel is the "harvest ant," the *Messor semirufus*. It is this ant which is described as the symbol of diligence and wisdom, preparing for the future by storing food during the harvest, and having no "guide, overseer, or ruler" (Prov. 6:6–7; 30:24–25). Rabbinic literature contains further details of their habits. They gnaw at the corn to extract the ears (Pe'ah 2:7). They cause extensive damage to harvested grain, and as a result R. Simeon b. Gamaliel permitted the destruction of antheaps during the intermediate days of festivals. He put forward an original method for their destruction: "Soil is brought from one heap, placed in the other, and they strangle one another" (MK 6b). This procedure is based on the belief that every antheap has its own peculiar odor which acts as a deterrent to the entry of ants from other heaps. *Simeon b. Ḥalafta also refers to their developed sense of smell. Undertaking experiments to determine their social life, he came to the conclusion that one ant does not take an ear of corn dropped by another since it recognizes its smell (Ḥul. 57b; Yal., Prov. 938). Large amounts of grain are gathered in their nests; according to one statement "three hundred *kor*" were once found (*ibid.*). The antheap consists of three chambers; the grain is stored in the upper one and the insects live in the middle, while the lower one is their summer habitat. The same Midrash actually refers to these compartments, but regards the middle one as the storehouse.

BIBLIOGRAPHY: Lewysohn, Zool, 328–30; Tristram, Nat Hist, 319–21; S. Bodenheimer, *Ha-Ḥai be-Arẓot ha-Mikrah*, 2 (1956), index; J. Feliks, *Animal World of the Bible* (1962), 122. **ADD. BIBLIOGRAPHY:** Feliks, Ha-Ẓome'aḥ, 252.

[Jehuda Feliks]

ANTEBI, ALBERT (**Avraham**; 1869–1918), leader of the Jewish community in Ereẓ Israel. Antebi was born into a prosperous rabbinical family in Damascus and was educated at the Alliance Israélite Universelle school there. He was sent by the Alliance to further his education in Paris. In 1896 he was appointed chief assistant to Nissim *Behar, director of Alliance institutions in Ereẓ Israel, and replaced Behar when the latter retired in 1898. Antebi served as director of the Alliance trade school and established a workshop for hand-weaving in Jerusalem. He was also instrumental in the establishment of new quarters in the city and was elected to the Jerusalem District Council. Antebi was later appointed representative of I.C.A. (Jewish Colonization Association) in Ereẓ Israel and represented the Palestine office of the Zionist Organization in its contacts with the Ottoman authorities. Because of his knowledge of the Turkish language and way of life, he was well liked by the Turkish officials, who regarded him as the chief spokesman of the Jewish community. On the outbreak of World War I, Antebi succeeded in persuading the commander in chief in Syria, Jamal Pasha, to commute the sentence of banishment passed against leaders of the Jewish community to 14 days confinement to Tiberias. In 1916 he was exiled to Damascus and two years later he went to Constantinople to plead for the refugees and exiles from Ereẓ Israel. He was unsuccessful in this mission, and was sent as an enlisted soldier to the eastern Anatolia front. There he caught typhoid fever and was transferred to Constantinople, where he died.

BIBLIOGRAPHY: M. Dizengoff, *Im Tel Aviv ba-Golah* (1931), 87–95; M.D. Gaon, *Yehudei ha-Mizraḥ be-Ereẓ Yisrael*, 2 (1937), 521f.; M. Smilansky, *Mishpaḥat ha-Adamah*, 2 (1954^2), 158–62.

[Yehuda Slutsky]

ANTELOPE. In ancient times various species of antelope of the group *Hippotraginae* existed in Ereẓ Israel and surrounding countries. They have completely disappeared from Israel and are found only in the Arabian Peninsula and in Africa. Sundry species of antelope have been identified with some of the seven clean animals, cloven-hooved ruminants, enumerated in Deuteronomy 14:5. Apparently the *dishon* is the antelope, since the Septuagint renders it πύγαργος, i.e., pygargos, which means "having a white rump," the reference being to the *Addax nasomaculatos* (a large antelope with hollow horns, with black spots on its neck and head, but otherwise white).

Some also identify the *zemer* (*AV* "chamois") with a species of antelope, the *Oryx leucoryx*, but others say that it refers to a species of wild sheep. The *re'em* mentioned in Psalms 92:11 as having long horns has also been identified with the *Oryx*. It was this animal, depicted in profile, which gave rise to the legend of the unicorn. In other passages, however, the *re'em* seems to be the wild ox (see *Wild Bull).

BIBLIOGRAPHY: S. Bodenheimer, *Ha-Ḥai be-Arẓot ha-Mikra*, 1 (1950), 79; J. Feliks, *Animal World of the Bible* (1962), 9, 13, 18; Lewysohn, Zool, 114, 149.

[Jehuda Feliks]

ANTHEDON, Hellenistic city in the vicinity of Gaza. Anthedon in Greek means "Flower City." It is first mentioned as a daughter city of Gaza, captured by Alexander Yannai (Jos., Ant., 8:357). Pompey "freed" it but the actual work of rebuilding was left to his successor Gabinius (*ibid.*, 14:88; Wars, 1:166). Together with the entire coastal area it passed to Cleopatra, and later Augustus presented it to Herod (Ant., 15:217; Wars, 1:396). Herod embellished the town and named it Agrippias in honor of M. Vipsanius Agrippa, Augustus' general and son-in-law. During the Jewish War (66–70 C.E.) Anthedon was attacked by the Zealots but the attack was repulsed and it remained a hellenized city. Paganism was deeply rooted in Anthedon, flourishing there until the fifth century (Sozomenus, Eccl. Hist., 5:9), when it became a Christian Episcopal see. The site has been identified with Tell Iblakhiye, on the sea shore 1½ mi. (2 km.) north of the port of Gaza; a hill farther north is still called Teda (= Anthedon). The Arab geographer el-Idrisi (12th century) called the harbor of Gaza "Tida."

BIBLIOGRAPHY: Gatt, in: ZDPV, 7 (1884), 5ff.; Pythian-Adams, in: PEFQS (1923), 14ff.; Schuerer, Gesch, 2 (1907^4), 118ff.; Avi-Yonah, Land, index, s.v. *Agrippas*. **ADD. BIBLIOGRAPHY:** Y. Tsafrir, L. Di Segni, and J. Green, *Tabula Imperii Romani. Iudaea – Palaestina. Maps and Gazetteer.* (1994), 63.

[Michael Avi-Yonah]

ANTHONY, JOSEPH (Deuster; 1912–1993), U.S. director and actor. Born in Milwaukee, Anthony appeared in many stage productions including *Peer Gynt, Camino Real*, and *Anastasia*, as well as a few motion pictures, such as the 1941 comedy *Shadow of the Thin Man*. He also directed movies. These films include the 1956 classic *The Rainmaker*, starring Burt Lancaster and Katharine Hepburn, as well as *The Matchmaker* (1958), *Career* (1959), *All in a Night's Work* (1961), and *Tomorrow* (1983).

Anthony made his Broadway debut in 1937, and in the years following was the dance partner of dancer and choreographer Agnes de Mille, the niece of director Cecil B. de Mille. Anthony worked as a set designer on films and dabbled as a film actor. His main interest, however, was the stage, and he became one of Broadway's most accomplished directors. He was nominated six times for a Tony award as best director for his productions of *The Lark* (1956); *A Clearing in the Woods* (1957); *The Most Happy Fella* (1957); *The Best Man* (1960); *Rhinoceros* (1961); and *110 in the Shade* (1964).

Anthony made numerous television appearances as an actor on such shows as *The Defenders*, *The Untouchables*, *Suspense*, *Kraft Television Theatre*, and *Danger*, and directed for TV as well, becoming the house director of the 1960s crime series *Brenner*.

[Ruth Beloff (2nd ed.)]

ANTHROPOLOGY, literally "an account of man," is the comparative study of human societies and cultures. Anthropology has four major subfields: *archaeology, the study of past cultures through an examination of material remains; biological (physical) anthropology, the study of humankind from a biological and evolutionary perspective; cultural anthropology, the study of contemporary cultures and societies and the study of human behavior that is learned rather than genetically transmitted; and linguistic anthropology, the study of human languages and the relationship between culture and communication. Due to the diversity of its subfields and the various approaches to its study, anthropology is variously considered a science, a social science, or a part of the humanities. Anthropology as a field of study in universities began in the latter part of the 19th century. Jews played a significant role in the founding and development of cultural anthropology. An early Jewish name in anthropology is that of the Frenchman, Marcel *Mauss (1872–1950), who became the leading figure in French sociology after his uncle, Emile *Durkheim, a sociologist by training who was a powerful influence in anthropology. He helped Durkheim in the establishment of the journal *L'Année Sociologique* and contributed important articles to it. Mauss' main interest was in comparative religion or the sociology of religion. His most influential work is *The Gift*, written in 1925, which focused on his theory of "gift exchange" and explored the religious, legal, economic, mythological, and other aspects of giving, receiving, and repaying in different cultures. Another French Jew and a colleague of Durkheim's at the Sorbonne was Lucien *Lévy-Bruhl (1857–1939) who wrote a series of ethnological works on various aspects of preliterate culture, the purpose of which was to demonstrate the nature of "primitive" mentality or "how natives think." In his posthumously published notebooks, he retracted his evolutionary interpretation of native thought. He came to realize that so-called prelogical thought was not limited to preliterate societies but was rather characteristic of human thought which did not exclude logical thought to meet the practical demands of the natural environment. Lévy-Bruhl's interpretation of native thought was especially influential in the fields of literary and art criticism.

The most influential Jewish anthropologist was Franz *Boas, who played a key role in the establishment of anthropology as an academic discipline in the United States. Popularly considered to be the "father of American anthropology," Boas trained most of the first generation of American anthropologists including Ruth Benedict and Margaret Mead. Boas was born in Germany in 1858, moved to the United States in 1886, and became professor of anthropology at Columbia (New York City) in 1899. He did extensive field research in North America rather than "armchair" anthropology and helped to make "fieldwork" a hallmark of anthropology. His theory of Historical Particularism stresses the biological and "psychic unity" of man and explains cultural diversity by appealing to specific culture histories and environments. He rejected the theories of the 19th-century cultural evolutionists and instead introduced the concept of cultural relativism which holds that cultures cannot be evaluated on an evolutionary scale. Cultures are equal and cultural characteristics should be examined in relation to the culture in which they are found. His "Limitations of the Comparative Method of Anthropology" was the first exposition of cultural relativism, a concept that continues to be a powerful concept in anthropology. With the rise of Hitler, Boas spoke out forcefully against racism and intolerance and wrote and lectured widely in opposition to the Nazis. Boas trained many outstanding American teachers and researchers in anthropology. Most of his students specialized in cultural anthropology, though a few became linguists, physical anthropologists, and archaeologists. One of his disciples, Robert H. *Lowie, was one of the best ethnographers and ethnologists of his day and did extensive field work among a great variety of Indian tribes. Another of Boas' pupils, Alexander A. *Goldenweiser, was not interested in field work and made only one trip to the Northern Iroquois of Canada. His major interest was in social theory and in theoretical aspects of ethnology, such as issues related to totemism, evolution, diffusion, and culture history. He was a significant figure in the development of anthropological thought in America during the first quarter of the 20th century. Leslie *Spier was also deeply influenced by Boas' canons of scientific method and the conviction that the understanding of culture depended upon an inquiry into historical antecedents. In his extensive writing he manifested his belief in the essential unity of anthropology as a general science of humankind. Edward *Sapir was perhaps the most creative and brilliant of Boas' students. He did major linguistic and ethnographic work among the Indians of the Canadian Northwest and Vancouver Island. Toward the end of his life he became interested in the ethnological and linguistic study of the Talmud. The research of Paul Radin, who was also a student of Boas, lay predominantly in ethnology, and within this area, in religion and mythology. His principal field work was done among the Winnebago Indians of Wisconsin. Melville J. *Herskovits completed his doctorate under Boas with a dissertation on "The Cattle Complex in East Africa." He was the recognized dean of African studies in the United States and trained most of the Africanists in that country. He made Northwestern University virtually the center of African studies in the United States and stimulated widespread interest in Africa among American anthropologists. Ruth *Bunzel (1898–1990), among the earliest of American Jewish women to receive a doctorate in anthropology (1929), worked as a secretary for Boas. With the encouragement of Boas and Ruth Benedict, Bunzel received her Ph.D. from Columbia, where she later taught. Her many books, including *The Pueblo Potter* (1929) and *Zuni* (1935), focused on Zuni ceremonialism. Another student of Boas and Benedict was Ruth *Landes (1903–1991). The daughter of Russian Jewish immigrants, Landes did pioneering work on race and gender, issues that define central current concerns in anthropology. Her field research among the Ojibwa resulted in her masterpiece study, *The Ojibwa Woman* (1938). Her field research in Brazil resulted in her landmark *The City of Women* (1947).

In Britain, Jews have played a role predominately in social/cultural anthropology. Meyer *Fortes (1906–1983), professor of social anthropology at Cambridge University, immigrated to England from South Africa. He worked among the Tallensi and Ashanti in Africa and his major contributions were in lineage theory, studies of religion, and ancestor worship. His 1940 seminal work (with Evans-Pritchard), *African Political Systems*, influenced a generation of anthropologists. Max *Gluckman also went to England from South Africa, where he had done a great deal of field work among the Zulu and Barotse of Africa and shorter surveys of Rhodesian tribes. Gluckman was a political activist. Publicly anti-colonial, he wrote and lectured about the abuses of colonialism and racism. A.L. Epstein did research on problems of urbanization and social change in emerging urban communities in Northern Rhodesia, Central Africa, and Melanesia. Maurice Freedman specialized in the social anthropology of Southeast Asia and China. Hortense *Powdermaker (1896–1970), although born and raised in the U.S., studied anthropology at the London School of Economics with the influential Bronislaw Malinowski, receiving her Ph.D. in 1928. Her books include *Life in Lesu* (1933), *After Freedom* (1939), *Copper Town* (1962), and *Stranger and Friend: The Way of an Anthropologist* (1966).

Claude *Lévi-Strauss, born in 1908 in Brussels, was the most distinguished social anthropologist in 20th-century France. His most original and significant contribution is his theory of structural anthropology which is heavily influenced by linguistics and assumes that the most effective way to understand human societies is to investigate the structures, rather than the content, of its organization. Among his strongest early influences were Sigmund Freud and Karl Marx. His *The Elementary Structures of Kinship*, published in 1949, quickly came to be regarded as one of the most important works on anthropological kinships. Lévi-Strauss was elected to the Académie Française in 1973, France's highest honor for academics and intellectuals. He was a prolific writer and his works include *Tristes Tropiques* (1955), *The Savage Mind* (1962), *Totemism* (1962), *Structural Anthropology*, (2 vol., 1958–73), *The Raw and the Cooked* (1964), *From Honey to Ashes* (1967), *The Origin of Table Manners* (1968), *The Naked Man* (1971), *The View from Afar* (1983), and *The Jealous Potter* (1985).

Other Jewish anthropologists of France included Paul Levy, who was director of studies at Ecole Pratique des Hautes Etudes (Sorbonne) and specialized in the culture of India and

Southeast Asia. David Cohen was attaché, Centre National de la Récherche Scientifique in Paris. He specialized in the social anthropology of North Africa and the Near East. Marcel *Cohen was honorary professor at the École des Langues Orientales in the Sorbonne and was an authority on Ethiopian and Hamito-Semitic linguistics. Simone Dreyfus was also connected with the Centre National de la Récherche Scientifique in Paris and pursued research in ethnomusicology and among the Indians of Brazil.

In East Germany, Heinz Israel was connected with the Museum fuer Voelkerkunde of Dresden. He was a specialist on the ethnology and archaeology of the circumpolar peoples, especially the Eskimo of Canada, Alaska, and the peoples of North Siberia.

Robert Heine-Geldern taught ethnology, prehistory, and art history of Asia at the University of Vienna. His main publications dealt with ethnology, archaeology, and the art of Southeast Asia and Oceania. He was especially concerned with problems of ancient Asiatic influences on America.

In Soviet Russia, M.G. Levin was deputy director of the Institute of Ethnography of the Academy of Sciences and head of its section for physical anthropology. He co-edited with L.P. Potapov the monumental *Historical and Ethnographic Atlas of Siberia* (Russ., 1961). He authored *Principles of Physical Anthropology* (Russ., 1955) and *Ethnic Origins of the Peoples of Northeastern Asia* (Engl., 1963) and was one of the editors and principal authors of *Peoples of Siberia* (Russ., 1956).

In South Africa, Phillip V. *Tobias specialized in physical anthropology and prehistory and was closely associated with L.S.B. Leakey in connection with the discoveries of fossil man in Tanganyika.

Moshe *Stekelis taught prehistoric archaeology at the Hebrew University of Jerusalem. He carried out extensive and important field research on the prehistoric archaeology of Israel. Henry Rosenfeld, who also taught at the Hebrew University, did research on the Bedouin and on village and urban Arabs.

Among Jewish psychoanalysts in the United States who have taken an active role in promoting the integration of psychology and cultural anthropology, Géza *Róheim, Abram *Kardiner, Theodor *Reik, and Erich *Fromm distinguished themselves. Modern studies of personality and culture owe much to their pioneering research. Róheim's *The Eternal Ones of the Dream* (1945) was a psychoanalytical interpretation of the origin and meaning of Australian myths and rituals. Abram Kardiner's *The Individual and His Society* (1939) was a pioneer theoretical analysis of the relation of the individual to his culture from a psychological point of view. Reik wrote works on the psychoanalytical interpretations of myths and rituals. Erich Fromm discussed the relation of psychology to current problems of religion and ethics. Fromm, in particular, was concerned with the problem of freedom and responsibility and the hard facts of individual alienation in contemporary culture. Marvin K. Opler published *Culture, Psychiatry and Human Values* (1956), which treated personality differences in various cultures. Iago Galdston edited and participated in a series of symposia on the interrelations of medicine and anthropology.

Among contemporary Jewish cultural anthropologists in America, Sol *Tax was president of the American Anthropological Association. David Bidney of Indiana University published *Theoretical Anthropology* (1953), which was a pioneer work dedicated to basic theory in the history of anthropological thought. Morris Opler of Cornell University was president of the American Anthropological Association and did extensive field work among North American Indians and in rural India.

Harry L. *Shapiro was chairman of the department of anthropology at the American Museum of Natural History and professor of anthropology at Columbia University.

Alexander Spoehr of the University of Pittsburgh was another Jew who served as president of the American Anthropological Association.

Oscar *Lewis published studies of life in a Mexican village, in northern India, and of a family in Puerto Rico and New York. Barbara *Myerhoff (1935–1985) was a renowned scholar, popular professor, prolific writer, and filmmaker, whose influences extended beyond the academy. Her works include *Peyote Hunt* (1974), *Number Our Days* (1978), and the autobiographical film *In Her Own Time* (1985). Sherry Ortner (1941–) of Columbia University has focused her work among the Sherpa people of Nepal and, more recently, in the United States. She helped establish the sub-discipline of feminist anthropology and has made significant contributions to social, cultural, and feminist theory. She is a prolific writer whose works include *Sherpas Through Their Rituals* (1978), *Making Gender: The Politics and Erotics of Culture* (1996), *Life and Death on Mt. Everest: Sherpas and Himalayan Mountaineering* (1999), and *New Jersey Dreaming: Capital, Culture and the Class of '58* (2003).

Jules Henry of Washington University in St. Louis published *Culture Against Man* (1963), a critical analysis of contemporary American culture with special reference to the interconnections among American institutions, values, and personal character among adolescents. Melville Jacobs taught anthropology at the University of Washington in Seattle. He specialized in the folklore of the North American Indians.

In the field of anthropological linguistics there was a distinguished group of Jewish scholars. Joseph Greenberg, of Stanford University, specialized in the linguistics of African peoples and wrote numerous articles on linguistic theory. Zellig S. Harris of the University of Pennsylvania published *Methods in Structural Linguistics* (1951). Stanley Newman of the University of New Mexico specialized in the languages of North American Indians. George L. Trager of the University of Buffalo was a well-known specialist in American Indian languages. Wolf Leslau, professor of Semitic and Ethiopic linguistics at the University of California at Los Angeles, did field research in Ethiopia. Roman Jakobson of Harvard University was the recognized dean of contemporary linguists in

America and was a distinguished authority on Russian language and folk literature.

M.F. Ashley *Montagu was a prolific writer who did much to popularize anthropology in the English-speaking world. While specializing in physical anthropology, he also published a number of popular books on cultural anthropology.

Raphael *Patai published a number of ethnological works on the Near East. James S. Slotkin (d. 1958) was professor of anthropology at the University of Chicago. His study of Peyote religion was the result of active participation in the native Indian church. Rena Lederman of Columbia University does research in the highlands of Papua New Guinea, focusing on the political economy of gift exchange, on inequality and leadership, on gender roles and ideologies. Her books include *What Gifts Engender* (1986). Karin Brodkin of UCLA explores gender, race, work, kinship, and migration in contemporary North American Jews. Her book, *How Jews Became White Folks and What That Says About Race in America* (1999), examines the relationships among Jewishness, gender, and class in the structuring of social identity. Riv-Ellen Prell's research also focuses on Jews in the U.S., with an emphasis on community, gender relations, and religious life. She is the author of *Fighting to Become Americans: Jews, Gender and the Anxiety of Assimilation* (1999) and *Prayer and Community: The Havura in American Judaism* (1989). Ruth Behar of the University of Michigan was born in Havana, Cuba. She has explored her Jewish identity and its relationship with her anthropological research. She is a prolific writer, essayist, poet, and filmmaker. Among her best-known works are *Translated Woman: Crossing the Border with Esperanza's Story* (2003) and *The Vulnerable Observer: Anthropology That Breaks Your Heart* (1997). Sandra Morgen is professor of anthropology at the University of Oregon. Her books include *Into Our Own Hands: The Women's Health Movement in the U.S. 1969–1990* (2002).

[David Bidney / Diane Baxter (2nd ed.)]

ANTHROPOMORPHISM, the attribution to God of human physical form or psychological characteristics. Anthropomorphism is a normal phenomenon in all primitive and ancient polytheistic religions. In Jewish literary sources from the Bible to the *aggadah* and Midrashim, the use of anthropomorphic descriptions and expressions (both physical and psychical) is also widespread. Yet at the same time it is accepted as a major axiom of Judaism, from the biblical period onward, that no material representation of the Deity is possible or permissible. The resolution of this apparent contradiction requires consideration and understanding of virtually every anthropomorphic expression. In every instance it should be asked whether the expression is an actual, naively concrete personification of God, or a fresh and vital form of religious awareness resorting to corporeal imagery, or an allegorical expression, in which the anthropomorphism is not merely an aesthetic means for the shaping of a particular perception or utterance, but is rather a conscious method of artificially clothing spiritual contents in concrete imagery.

The evolutionary approach to the study of religion, which mainly developed in the 19th century, suggested a line of development beginning with anthropomorphic concepts and leading up to a more purified spiritual faith. It argued, among other things, that corporeal representations of the Deity were more commonly found in the older portions of the Bible than in its later books. This view does not distinguish between the different possible explanations for anthropomorphic terms. It especially fails to account for the phenomenon common in the history of all cultures, that sometimes a later period can be more primitive than an earlier one. In fact, both personifications of the Deity as well as attempts to avoid them are found side by side in all parts of the Bible. The paucity of anthropomorphisms in certain works is not necessarily proof of any development in religion, but may well be due to the literary characteristics and intentions of certain biblical narratives, e.g., the narratives designed to express the growing distance between God and man through describing His relationship to Adam, the patriarchs, and the early and late prophets, etc.

In The Bible

An obviously anthropomorphic expression is found in Genesis: *ẓelem Elohim* ("the image of God"), and there are references to actually "seeing" God (Ex. 24:10–12; Num. 12:8). The limbs of the human body frequently serve as allegorical descriptions of the acts of God as perceived by man. Thus divine providence is referred to as "the eyes of the Lord" and "the ears of the Lord" (very common in Prophets and Psalms); "the mouth of the Lord" speaks to the prophets (both in Torah and Prophets); the heavens are the work of His fingers (Ps. 8:4), and the tablets of the covenant are written by the finger of God (Ex. 31:18). Striking figurative expressions are *af* ("nose"; i.e., "the wrath of the Lord"), "His countenance" (which He causes to shine or, alternatively, hides), *yad*, ("hand," "His right hand," "His arm," "His sword"). At times the personification is startlingly extreme: God (or His voice) "walks about in the garden" (Gen. 3:8); He "goes down" in order to see what is being done on the earth (Gen. 11:5; 18:21) or in order to reveal Himself there (Ex. 19:18; 34:5), and He "goes up again" (Gen. 17:22; 35:13); He goes through the land of Egypt and passes over the houses of the Israelites (Ex. 12:12–13); He sits on a throne (Isa. 6:1), causes His voice to be heard among the cherubim who are over the ark of the tabernacle (Num. 7:89), dwells in Zion and in Jerusalem (Ps. 132:13; 135:21); the hair of His head is as wool (Dan. 7:9); Moses sees "His back" (Ex. 33:23). Anthropomorphic expressions abound in the song at the Red Sea (Ex. 15) and in the song of David (II Sam. 22; Ps. 18).

More important from a theological perspective are the anthropopathisms, or psychical personifications of the Deity. Scripture attributes to God love and hate, joy and delight, regret and sadness, pity and compassion, disgust, anger, revenge, and other feelings. Even if one explains these terms as being nothing but picturesque expressions, intended to awaken within man a sense of the real presence of God and His works, nonetheless they remain personifications. The basis for such terms is the conception of God as a Being who wills in a personal (though not exactly in a human) way. This personalized conception of the Deity, in conjunction with the axiomatic belief in His absolute transcendence, leads to unusual boldness in the use of anthropomorphic imagery.

Ultimately, every religious expression is caught in the dilemma between, on the one hand, the theological desire to emphasize the absolute and transcendental nature of the Divine, thereby relinquishing its vitality and immediate reality and relevance, and on the other hand, the religious need to conceive of the Deity and man's contact with Him in some vital and meaningful way. Jewish tradition has usually shown preference for the second tendency, and there is a marked readiness to speak of God in a very concrete and vital manner and not to recoil from the dangers involved in the use of apparent anthropomorphisms.

However, this anthropomorphic style is frequently accompanied by mitigating expressions indicating reservations. The basic opposition to all such personifications is decisively formulated in the Decalogue. In addition, it finds expression in many verses which maintain that nothing can be compared to God, who has no form or shape, cannot be seen, is eternal and without end (very frequent in the Pentateuch, Former and Latter Prophets, Psalms, Job, and Chronicles). Yet, many of these verses appear to contradict others which describe God in corporeal terms (for example, Ex. 20:4; Deut. 4:15, as against Gen. 1:26; Num. 23:19 and 1 Sam. 15:29 as against Gen. 6:6; 1 Kings 8:27 as against Ex. 25:8, and other such examples). These verses emphasize the transcendent nature of the Divine, not in philosophical abstractions but in vivid descriptive expressions. In other places one finds attempts to avoid such personifications and to substitute less daring imagery; if it is said, on the one hand, that the Lord dwells in His sanctuary (Ex. 35:8), and also appears in the cloud over the cover of the ark (Lev. 16:2), on the other hand there are verses which speak instead of God's *kavod* ("glory") or *Shemo* ("His name"; Ex. 24:16–17; Lev. 9:23; Num. 14:10; Deut. 12:5, 11; 16:2, 6; 1 Kings 8:11). Some scholars (S.D. Luzzatto and Geiger) argued that the present vocalization of Exodus 34:24 "to appear before the Lord" was emended by the masoretes from original לִרְאוֹת (*lirot*; "to see") to לֵרָאוֹת (*leraʾot*; "to be seen"), to avoid an objectionable anthropomorphism.

There is no evidence of any physical representation of God in Jewish history (in contradistinction to the worship of Canaanite and other foreign gods by Israelites). Even the golden calves of Jeroboam represented, according to the view of most scholars, only a footstool for the invisible God. In archaeological excavations no images of the God of Israel have been unearthed. Biblical Hebrew is the only fully developed language which has no specific term for the notion "goddess."

The Targumim

The method of mitigating offensive anthropomorphisms by means of small emendations, described by the *tannaim* as "biblical modifications of expression," is also prevalent in the early translations of Scripture. *Onkelos often renders the name of the Lord in such substitutes as "the glory of the Lord," "the Word of the Lord," and "fear of the Lord." Similarly, he translates "He saw" or "He knew," referring to the Deity as "it was revealed before Him"; "He went down" becomes "He revealed Himself"; "He heard" becomes "it was heard before Him," and other similar examples. If the same verb is used in the Bible to describe an action of God and of man, Onkelos uses two different words in order to distinguish clearly between the Divine and the human (Gen. 32:29; 40:8; Ex. 14:31; and others). He is less hesitant, however, about attributing man's psychical qualities to God, and he translates such expressions as hatred, love, anger, and the like without making any changes except for those words which indicate regret and sadness on the part of God (for example, Gen. 6:6). Yet Onkelos is not consistent in his treatment of anthropomorphism as Maimonides already observed (*Guide of the Perplexed* 2:33), and it has been suggested that he prepared his translation with the simple worshiper in mind: expressions whose metaphorical meaning was obvious, were translated literally; where misunderstanding and error were likely, his translation circumvents the anthropomorphism by a paraphrase. The other Aramaic translators follow a similar course, although the Targum known as "Yerushalmi" goes even further in avoiding anthropomorphisms than do Onkelos and the Targum Jonathan to the Prophets.

The same generally applies to the Greek translations. For instance, *temunah* ("likeness") is always translated in the Septuagint as μορφή ("form") or ὁμοίωμα ("likeness"), and, if it refers to the Deity (Num. 12:8), it is rendered δόξα ("that which appears"). The Septuagint is extremely careful with God's "wrath," "anger," and similar terms, which the Aramaic Targumim never hesitate to translate literally. Yet even within the Septuagint one finds no consistency in handling anthropomorphisms. Among the other Greek translations, of which only fragments are extant, Symmachus is the most consistent in avoiding personifications of the Deity. For example, in Genesis 1:27, he separates the terms "in the image of God," reading instead: "in the image – God created him" (the Targum Yerushalmi attributed to Jonathan treats this verse similarly).

Hellenistic Philosophy

Aristobulus deals in a systematic way with the "true" (that is, the allegorical) interpretation of anthropomorphic verses in Scripture, basing himself on Greek thinkers and poets. The consistent avoidance of any personification of God led Philo of Alexandria to the concept of a Deity who neither acts nor creates, who is without attributes or qualities and hence no kind of positive relationship to this world could be attributed to him. At the same time Philo could not be unaware of the dynamic vitality and activity of God as portrayed in the Bible. This contradiction caused him to posit an intermediate being between God and the world. His biblical exegesis is an allegorization of Scripture in this direction. Hence the *memra* ("word") of Onkelos and the *logos* of Philo, despite their terminological similarity cannot be equated.

Aggadic Literature

Rabbinical *aggadah* essentially follows the biblical manner of boldly using anthropomorphic imagery, while at the same time qualifying it. The number of substitute terms for God increases. To the *memra* of the Targum are now added other names and circumlocutions, such as *gevurah* ("strength"), *shamayim* ("heaven"), *makom* ("place"), etc. Sentences in which personifications occur are softened by means of the qualifying term *kivyakhol* ("so to speak," "as it were") or by means of sayings such as "if it were not written in Scripture, it would be impossible to utter it." Occasionally, anthropomorphic personifications of God are justified for didactic reasons and by the need to make divine truth accessible to human understanding: "The Torah speaks in the language of men." At times the rabbis resort to anthropomorphic language in order to drive home a moral lesson. Thus God's "descent" on Mount Sinai is used for the following exhortation: "Let a man always learn from his Creator, for here the Holy One blessed be He forsook all of the mountains and high hills and caused His presence to rest on the lowly Mt. Sinai" (Sot. 5a). Similarly, on the third day after the circumcision of Abraham, "the Holy One blessed be He said to the ministering angels: Let us go down and visit the sick man."

However, definite attempts to qualify anthropomorphic tendencies are evident in other homilies on the revelation at Sinai: "The Divine Presence never descended, nor did Moses and Elijah ever ascend to heaven" (Suk. 5a; Mekh. Ha-Ḥodesh 4). The commandment to cleave to the Lord is explained in the Talmud in this way: "As He is compassionate, so should you be compassionate; as He visits the sick, so should you visit the sick" (Shab. 133b; Sot. 14a). But the original version of the Midrash read: "As He is called compassionate and gracious, so you be compassionate and gracious," thereby avoiding the potential personification involved (Sif. Deut. 11:22). The rabbis did not recoil from such terms whenever they thought them useful to impress man with an awareness of the existence of God, His love and His fear, and, hence, aggadic literature abounds in statements to the effect that the Holy-One-blessed-be-He studies the law (Ḥag. 15b), puts on *tefillin* (Ber. 6a), weeps over the destruction of the Temple, and the like.

In the Middle Ages

The proper explanation of the anthropomorphic passages in biblical and aggadic texts became a major problem in Jewish theological thought. Generally one may discern three main trends of thought, although there are no clear lines of demarcation, and the number of intermediate positions is considerable: (1) Allegorization: every anthropomorphic description of the Deity is explained simply as a metaphor. This approach developed chiefly through the influence of Greek and Arabic philosophy. (2) Talmudic orthodoxy: a well-nigh literal understanding of the sayings of the rabbis. Philosophical, i.e., allegorical, exegesis was considered a danger to religion, since the whole biblical, halakhic, and aggadic tradition might easily evaporate into allegorical ideas. (3) The mystical view: there are intermediate beings between God and the world (or stages of God's self-manifestation), and all anthropomorphic expressions refer to these emanations from the Deity. Further support for this line of thought is found in the Targumim and *aggadah*, which make frequent use of such names as *Shekhinah* ("Divine Presence").

Philosophy

The medieval Jewish philosophers aimed at purifying the concept of the Deity of any trace of anthropomorphism. *Saadiah Gaon held that all corporeal references to God refer to noncorporeal matters, and that strictly speaking only the attribute of existence could be ascribed to God. The forms which the prophets saw in their visions were not actually the Deity but His *Shekhinah* ("Presence") – viz. the divine light or *kavod* ("glory") created by Him. Later thinkers developed Saadiah's views, although many of them defended the unlettered, simple believers who were intellectually incapable of properly understanding Scripture and approaching God without material notions (Joseph b. Ẓaddik, Baḥya ibn Paquda; Abraham b. David of Posquières' gloss to Maimonides' Yad, Teshuvah 3:7). Judah Halevi even saw a logical justification and a didactic value in such anthropomorphisms (compare his comment on the golden calf episode (Kuzari 1:97)). Discussion of the problem reached its zenith in the philosophical work of Maimonides, who insisted upon a nonliteral, allegorical understanding of all anthropomorphic expressions, both physical and psychical, and ruled that every anthropomorphism was outright heresy.

The violence of Maimonides' polemic against anthropomorphic beliefs and doctrines suggests that these were fairly widespread, and that a great many people were affected by "the *aggadot* ("homilies") which confuse one's mind" (so Abraham b. David of Posquières, loc. cit.). The influence of Maimonides, however, was both powerful and lasting. Even against the vehement opposition of more conservative thinkers of his day, his "*Guide*" determined what was to become the Orthodox concept of God within Judaism for a long time. There is evidence (Jedaiah ha-Penini of the 13th century, Moses Alashkar of the 15th) to show that it was the writings of Maimonides which finally did away with all anthropomorphic notions among Jews. Whereas in his lifetime Maimonides' orthodoxy was suspected because of his opposition to anthropomorphic beliefs, Spinoza was equally strongly denounced in the 17th century for his rejection of Maimonides' principles of exegesis and for his contention that scriptural anthropomorphisms were originally meant to be taken literally.

[R.J. Zwi Werblowsky]

In the Kabbalah

The talmudic *Merkabah (the heavenly throne-chariot) mysticism taught the ascent of the ecstatic soul into the realm of the divine throne. A description of the revelation of the divine majesty in the form of a human figure (following Ezekiel 1:26) became the focal point of this vision. This description is found in fragments of a tract called *Shi'ur Komah*, literally "the measure of the body," i.e., the body of God as He appears, revealing Himself in this form. The text, attributed to the two mishnaic rabbis R. *Ishmael and R. *Akiva, gives enormous figures for the measurement of each organ of that divine primordial man on the throne. Such measurements are preserved, for example, of God's right and left eyes, of His lips, and other parts. The description of God's organs is designedly linked with the description of the beloved one in the Song of Songs 5:11–15, and it is certainly connected with some esoteric doctrine about the Song of Songs as a mystical text. It constitutes a major piece of theosophy, no longer clear, evolved precisely within the circle of strict rabbinical Orthodoxy. The age of these fragments, which were forcefully attacked by the *Karaites as a profanation and degradation of the religious concepts about God, was long debated. Some philosophic apologists of the Middle Ages, for whom the existence of these doctrines was a source of embarrassment, tried to explain them away as late forgeries. Judah Halevi justified the *Shi'ur Komah* "because it brings the fear of God into the souls of men" (*Kuzari* 4:3). Later Maimonides ruled that it was unquestionably an idolatrous work and should be destroyed (*Teshuvot Rambam*, ed. Freimann, nos. 373, 694). Scholars like *Graetz assumed that they were due to the influence of an anthropomorphic school in early Islam. These opinions are no longer tenable. The term *Shi'ur Komah* appears as the keyword of an esoteric doctrine connected with the Song of Songs in the hymns of Eleazar ha-Kallir, which are pre-Islamic. The existence of an esoteric doctrine about the Song of Songs is attested in the third century by the church father Origen who lived at Caesarea. By this he cannot have meant the openly accepted allegorization of the Song of Songs as the relationship between God and Israel, but rather as a doctrine about the appearance of God in the form of the beloved one, such as is taught by the *Shi'ur Komah*. Saul *Lieberman has shown that in the earlier *aggadah* the revelation of God on His Merkabah at the exodus from Egypt and the revelation on Mount Sinai are in fact attested in a manner which fits into the traditions of the *Shi'ur Komah*. However it is clear from the extant fragments that this extreme form of anthropomorphism was not really meant to describe the Divine Being as corporeal. The description here is of a visionary apparition, however exotic, but not the appearance of God Himself. In kabbalistic literature, *Shi'ur Komah* was interpreted as a symbol for the revelation of the Divinity in the *Sefirot* (Divine Emanations) and therefore it was favorably appraised. Important parts of the *Zohar, in particular the Great and Small *Idras*, represent a kind of kabbalistic adaptation or imitation of the *Shi'ur Komah*. In them, the theosophic beliefs of the kabbalists are quite consciously expostulated in the form of concrete descriptions of the features of the head of the Divinity, in order to doubly stress their symbolic character. Parallels to the *Shi'ur Komah* are also found in the second century in the *gnostic literature of Christian heretics who had a knowledge of Aramaic, such as Marcion. His description of the "Body of Truth" comes particularly close to the traditions of the *Shi'ur Komah*.

[Gershom Scholem]

In Jewish Art

Although Jews have speculated on the anthropomorphic nature of God, visible representation of the Deity was clearly forbidden by the Mosaic law. In spite of this injunction, the Deity has sometimes been represented in Jewish art. In the synagogue frescoes of *Dura Europos (third century C.E.), there are representations of the Hand of God stretching forth from heaven. In certain cases where they depict the visions of Ezekiel the representations might be justified as an illustration of a biblical text (e.g., the prophet said, "the hand of the Lord was upon me"; Ezek. 37:1). No such justification, however, can be used to explain the fact that at Dura Europos and at *Bet Alfa there are representations (as in contemporary Christian art) of the Divine Hand extending from heaven to prevent Abraham from sacrificing his son (it is specifically stated in the Bible that the patriarch was restrained by the voice of an angel). The anthropomorphic tradition was continued in medieval Jewish illuminated manuscripts. In the Sarajevo *Haggadah* there is a figure of a man in repose which according to one opinion illustrates God taking rest after the labor of creation. Later, the theme was taken up in documents and printed books. One of the vignettes to *Jacob b. Asher's *Arba'ah Turim* published by Ḥayyim Schwarz (with his son and son-in-law) in Augsburg in 1540 shows the Deity engaged in the work of the sixth day of creation and in the creation of Eve. The Deity was also depicted in small vignettes of scenes from the Vision of Ezekiel on the engraved title page of the *Minḥat Shai* (Mantua, 1742); on the engraved border of an Italian **ketubbah* of the 17th century; and in a representation of the Vision of Jacob at Bethel on the title page of the *Ir Binyamin* by Benjamin Ze'ev Wolf Romaner (Frankfurt on the Oder, 1698). There is a depiction in relief of God appearing to the infant Samuel (1 Sam. 3:10) on the gravestone of Samuel Senior Texeira in the Oudekerk cemetery of the Sephardi Jewish community in Amsterdam (1717). This is especially remarkable in view of the biblical prohibition of graven images. The accumulated evidence shows that it is even possible that the cast figure of Jupiter Fulgur, incorporated in the perpetual lamp of at least two 18th-century German synagogues, was also intended to represent the Deity. It is clear that the prevalent idea that medieval Jewish art would not brook anthropomorphism is certainly incorrect.

[Cecil Roth]

BIBLIOGRAPHY: IN KABBALAH: M. Gaster, *Studies and Texts in Folk-lore...* 2 (1960), 1130–53; A. Schmiedl, *Studien ueber juedische, insbesondere juedisch-arabische Religionsphilosophie* (1869), 239–58;

G. Scholem, *Jewish Gnosticism…* (1960), 36–42, 118–26 (appendix by S. Lieberman); idem, *Von der mystischen Gestalt der Gottheit* (1962), 7–48 (*On the Mystical Shape of the Godhead* (1991), 15–55); Scholem, Mysticism, 63–67; S. Mussayoff (ed.), *Merkavah Shelemah* (1921), 30a–44b (for the time being the best available texts of the *Shi'ur Komah* fragments). IN ART: A. Grabar, in: *Cahiers Archéologiques*, 16 (1964), 245–8; Morton Smith, in: BJRL, 40 (1957–58), 473–572. **ADD. BIBLIOGRAPHY:** IN KABBALAH: D. Abrams, "The Dimensions of the Creator – Contradiction or Paradox? Corruptions or Accretions to the Manuscript Witness," in: *Kabbalah*, 5 (2000), 35–53; *The Shi'ur Qomah: Texts and Recensions*, ed. Martin Samuel Cohen (1985); J. Dan, "The Concept of Knowledge in the "*Shi'ur Qomah*," in: *Studies in Jewish Religious and Intellectual History in Honor of A. Altmann* (1979), 67–73; A. Farber-Ginat, "Inquiries in Shi'ur Qomah," in: M.I Oron and A. Goldreich (eds.), *Massu'ot, Studies in Kabbalistic Literature and Jewish Philosophy in Memory of Prof. Ephraim Gottlieb* (1994), 361–94, Heb.; M. Idel, "Une figure d'homme au-dessus des *sefirot* (A propos de la doctrine des "eclats" de R. David ben Yehouda he-Hassid et ses developments)," in: *Pardes*, 8 (1988), 131–50; idem, "The World of Angels in Human Shape," in JSJT (*Jerusalem Studies in Jewish Thought*) = J. Dan and J. Hacker (eds.), *Studies in Jewish Mysticism, Philosophy and Ethical Literature Presented to Isaiah Tishby* (1986), 1–66; Y. Lorberbaum, "Nahmanides' Kabbalah on the Creation of Man in the Image of God," in: *Kabbalah*, 5 (2000), 287–325 (Hebrew); Ch. Mopsik, "La datation du *Chi'our Qomah* d'apres un texte neotestamentaire," in: *Revue des Sciences Religieuses*, no. 2 (April 1994), 131–44; E. Wolfson, "Anthropomorphic Imagery and Letter Symbolism in the *Zohar*," in: JSJT (*Jerusalem Studies in Jewish Thought*), 8 (1989), 161–63; idem, "Metatron and *Shi'ur Qomah* in the Writings of Haside Ashkenaz," in: K.-E. Groezinger and J. Dan (eds.), *Mysticism, Magic and Kabbalah in Ashkenazi Judaism*, (1995), 60–92.

ANTIBI, family of rabbis in Aleppo, Egypt, and Ereẓ Israel. The name is derived from Ain Tab, in southern Turkey. Its members include: ISAAC BEN SHABBETAI (d. 1804), of Aleppo, author of *Ohel Yiẓḥak*, sermons; *Beit Av*, novellae on Maimonides' *Yad ha-Ḥazakah* and Joseph Caro's *Beit Yosef*; and various responsa. These works were published by his son Abraham b. Isaac *Antibi. JACOB (d. 1846), born in Aleppo. He was rabbi of Damascus for 40 years and a halakhic authority. He corresponded with the chief rabbi of Jerusalem, Raphael Joseph Ḥazzan, who endorsed his decisions. The great publicity given the *Damascus Affair (1840) and the world reaction to it were largely due to him. In February 1840, he was imprisoned and cruelly tortured, but following the intercession of Moses *Montefiore, Adolph *Crémieux, and Solomon *Munk, he was released that September. Upon Montefiore's request he wrote a detailed account of his imprisonment. After his release he moved to Jerusalem (1841) and was reckoned among that city's important scholars, residing there until his death. He is the author of *Abbir Ya'akov*, novellae, at the end of which is a description of the Damascus blood libel, appended to Ḥayyim Kafusi's *Be-Or ha-Ḥayyim* (1929). Some of his responsa are extant (Ben Zvi Institute, no. 403; Benayahu Collection), and several appear in the works of his contemporaries. He was also a poet. One of his poems, composed on his release from prison, deals with his salvation from the blood libel. Some of his *pizmonim* were recited in the synagogues of Damascus although they were never published. ḤAYYIM JUDAH SHABBETAI RAPHAEL (1808–1888), son of Jacob, also known as "Mashi'aḥ," was a wealthy philanthropist. He aided the rehabilitation of Safed after the 1837 earthquake, and also built a synagogue which bore his name. Later he was appointed rabbi and member of the *bet din* in Cairo. He died there in 1888. His son, ELIJAH RAḤAMIM (1852–1920), born in Safed, wrote *Ara de-Rabbanan*, sermons; *Derash Eliyahu*, funeral orations; *Tuv Ta'am*; and *Imrei Shabbat*, all of which are still in manuscript.

BIBLIOGRAPHY: M.D. Gaon, *Yehudei ha-Mizraḥ be-Ereẓ Yisrael*, 2 (1937), 523–4; D.Z. Laniado, *Li-Kedoshim asher ba-Areẓ*, 1 (1952), 8f., 40, 72; Steinschneider, in: JQR, 40 (1898/99), 488.

[Haim J. Cohen]

ANTIBI, ABRAHAM BEN ISAAC (1765–1858), Syrian talmudist. Antibi, who was born in Aleppo, studied under his father, Isaac Berakhah, and Isaiah Dabah. A scholar of great erudition and acumen, he wrote books on a variety of topics. He ruled his community with a firm hand, making regulations, opposing the inroads of the wealthy, and criticizing the failings of his generation. When his father died he succeeded him, acting as rabbi of Aleppo and head of the *bet din*. He served approximately 40 years. Antibi studied Kabbalah, and speculated on the date of redemption. His ethical publications established his reputation as a moralist. He also wrote poems, most of which expressed the yearning for redemption and for the revelation of the Divine Presence. In Aleppo some of these were sung on Sabbath eves and on festive occasions, being included in the *Bakkashot* books. His learning was acknowledged in Ereẓ Israel, and *Israel b. Samuel of Sklov solicited from him a commendation for his book *Pe'at ha-Shulḥan* (1836). Antibi was host to visiting Ashkenazi scholars and emissaries from Ereẓ Israel and his works incorporated his learned discussions with them. His son Isaac was also a distinguished scholar in Aleppo. Antibi is the author of (1) *Yoshev Ohalim* (Leghorn, 1825). This work includes *Ohel Avraham*, sermons on the pentateuchal passages, on the Exodus, and on Passover; *Penei ha-Bayit*, a treatise on the *Torat ha-Bayit* of Solomon b. Abraham *Adret; and *Ohel Yiẓḥak*, some sermons of his father. (2) *Mor ve-Aholot* (Leghorn, 1843), responsa of Antibi and his father. (3) *Ohel Yesharim* (Leghorn, 1843), moral discourses and homilies to which are appended some 50 *piyyutim*. (4) *Penei ha-Bayit* (Leghorn, 1849), on the Shulḥan Arukh, ḤM, together with *Bet Av* by his father. (5) *Ḥokhmah u-Musar* (Leghorn, 1850), on ethical conduct, to which is added *Derekh Ḥukkekha*, laws of the festivals, which also contains *Ḥukkei Nashim*, matrimonial law based chiefly on the responsa of *David b. Solomon Abi Zimra. (6) *Penei Ohel Mo'ed* (Jerusalem, 1959), homiletical discourses for the special Sabbaths. His works are an important source for the cultural, social, and economic life of the Jews of Syria. To this day legends are current in praise of him and the wonders which he performed.

BIBLIOGRAPHY: D.Ẓ. Laniado, *Li-Kedoshim asher ba-Areẓ*, 1 (1952), 8, 40; J. Avadi Shayev (ed.), *Ḥokhmah u-Musar* (1962), 5–8 (introd.).

ANTICHRESIS (ἀντίχρησις) in Greco-Roman law an arrangement whereby a creditor may, under certain conditions, enjoy the use and fruits of property (land or chattels) given to him as security. In talmudic literature, such an arrangement appears under various designations such as *mashkanta di-Sura, nakhyata, kiẓuta* (see *Loans, *Pledge, *Property, *Usury), while the word *antichresis* (אנטיכרסים) itself appears only once in the Talmud (TJ BM 6:7, 11a; another passage in TJ Git. 4:6, 46a has אנטריס which might be a corruption of *antichresis* (אנטיכרסים) – see Epstein, in: *Tarbiz*, 8 (1937), 316–8). In Greco-Roman sources too, though antichretic transactions must have been widespread, the word *antichresis* appears only rarely, and it is difficult to ascertain its exact meaning. The glossator Cujacius (Observations 3:35) restricts the term to an arrangement whereby the usufruct is in lieu of interest (*in vicem usurarum*). A. Manigk, rejecting this narrow definition, argues that in Roman, Assyro-Babylonian, Greco-Egyptian, Syrian, and other laws, arrangements whereby usufruct was granted in partial or total amortization of the principal debt were also included in *antichresis*: hence Manigk speaks of "amortization-*antichresis*" as distinct from "interest-*antichresis*" (F. Stier-Somlo and A. Elster (eds.), *Handwoerterbuch der Rechtswissenschaft*, 1 (1926), s.v.). By allowing a token deduction from a principal debt, actual interest-*antichresis* can be made to appear as amortization-*antichresis* (which is what *mashkanta di-Sura* or *nakhyata* really were). This was a means of evading the prohibition of usury. It is thus difficult to say whether the terse statement in the Talmud, which explicitly denounces *antichresis* as usury, refers to pure interest-*antichresis* or also to amortization-*antichresis* of the fictitious kind. The Mishnah discussing it deals with loans on pledge and quotes a saying of Abba Saul allowing amortization-*antichresis* under certain circumstances ("a poor man's pledge").

In Christian countries in the Middle Ages, when all interest on loans was forbidden, *antichresis* was linked with the evasion of usury (see C.F. Glueck, *Ausfuerliche Erlaeuterung der Pandecten*, 14 (1813), 47ff.). Economically justified interest rates having become permissible, the significance of *antichresis* faded away and is not found in modern legislation.

BIBLIOGRAPHY: A. Gulak, *Toledot ha-Mishpat be-Yisra'el bi-Tekufat ha-Talmud*, 1 (1939); *Ha-Ḥiyyuv ve-Shi'bbudav*, 72, 76, 80, 121, 152; B. Cohen, in: *Alexander Marx Jubilee Volume* (1950), 179–202, reprinted in his *Jewish and Roman Law*, 2 (1966), 433–56, addenda 784–5; Ehrman, in: *Sinai*, 54 (1963/64), 177–84.

[Arnost Zvi Ehrman]

ANTICHRIST, Gr. Ἀντιχριστος, a term first occurring in the Johannine epistles in the New Testament (I John 2:18, 22; 4:3; II John 7). It refers to an eschatological figure, the opponent of God, the pseudo-messiah who will be revealed at the end of days as the great enemy of Jesus. According to II Thessalonians 2:2–4 the second coming will be preceded by apostasy, and the "man of lawlessness" will be revealed, the "son of perdition" so evil that "he shall sit in the Temple of God, showing himself to be God." Perhaps this figure too is to be identified with Antichrist, and he is destroyed by "the breath of the Messiah's mouth" (cf. Isa. 11:4, Targ. *ibid.*, and many other places in Jewish writings).

The background to this figure lies in Jewish eschatology, where the ideas of the wicked king of the last generation and of the rise of evil to the highest point preceding salvation are found at an early period (cf. Ezek. 28:2; Dan. 7:24–25; 11:36; cf. 9:27). Another form of the same idea can be found in the eschatological battle in which the forces of evil and their leader are finally to be overcome (QM xviii:1; 1QS iv:18–19; Test. Patr., Levi 3:3, et al.). Peculiar to the Christian form of this tradition in which the term Antichrist developed is the anti-messianic aspect of the figure. Thus, in a later Christian apocalypse he is described in the following terms: "His knees are unbending, he is crippled in his eyes, with wide eyebrows, crooked [sickle] fingered, with a pointed head, gracious, boastful, wise, sweet in laughter, visionary, clever, sober, gentle, mild, worker of signs, bringing close to him the souls of the corrupt, bringing forth bread from stones, [making] the blind to see, the lame to walk, he will move mountains from place to place…" (Seventh Vision of Daniel, ed. Z. Kalemkian, 1892, pp. 25ff.). The description of his ugly physical appearance is similar to those found in other Christian apocalypses, such as *Testamentum Domini*, the Greek Esdras Apocalypse and others. But in the Daniel Apocalypse quoted, certain of the characteristics of Antichrist are directly inspired by those of the Christ. Descriptions of the physical form of this figure also occur in later Jewish apocalypses such as *Sefer Zerubbavel* (ed. Ibn Shemu'el, 79ff.), there ascribed to *Armilus.

Another element which entered into this complex of ideas is that of *Nero redivivus*. Here the eschatological wicked ruler took on the characteristics of the Roman emperor who represented the very epitome of all conceivable evil. The idea of *Nero's eschatological reappearance developed and is to be found in the Sibylline Oracles (e.g., 4:119–39) which constitute the most extensive early source for this idea. In this book the demonization of the Nero figure is complete (5:361–70) and it is very clear further (5:28–34), where of his return it says (33f.): "Then he shall return, making himself equal to God, but [God] shall convince him that he is not." The same concept is also to be found in Revelation 13:17. There, too, the antidivine arises in the form of a dragon, the "primordial serpent called Satan" (12:9), and of two beasts, one of which is generally associated with Nero (13:17–18). The Church Fathers also speculated about Antichrist, but their interest was more in his theological aspects than in the mythical features dear to the apocalyptic writers. So, for example, both Irenaeus in his treatise *Adversus haereses* and Hippolytus in his "On Christ and Antichrist" and his fragmentary commentary on Daniel reflect this interest and for them II Thessalonians 2:2–4 is most important. The later developments of this legend are complex. One particular form, basing itself on Jewish traditions (see Test. Patr., Dan. 5:6), makes the Antichrist a Jewish pseudo-messiah of the tribe of Dan.

In the Antichrist figure of Christianity, therefore, elements of Jewish thought were given particular formulations as they crystallized. The idea of the rise of evil to its height before the coming of salvation, the embodiment of this evil in the eschatological king (cf. Test. Patr., Dan. 11:36, 37; Ass. Mos. 8), the overweening pride and blasphemy of the figure (Test. Patr., Dan. 7:11, 20; II Thess. 2:2–4, etc.), all these are old Jewish motifs. Their combination in the figure of the wonder-working pseudo-messiah or Antichrist is apparently a Christian development, and one which, in turn, may have influenced later Jewish ideas. It is clearly possible that this Christian formulation, which often bears distinct anti-Jewish traits, grew in part from the reaction of Christianity to continuing Jewish messianic hopes. It might be added that Jewish tradition about this eschatological figure may have been more highly developed and earlier than is generally recognized, as the primarily Jewish material in the fragmentary Coptic Elijah apocalypse indicates.

BIBLIOGRAPHY: Boehmer, in: *Jahrbuecher fuer deutsche Theologie*, 4 (1859), 405–67; W. Bousset, *The Antichrist Legend* (1896); L. Ginzberg, in: JE, 1 (1901), 625–7, s.v. (contains bibliography); J. Kaufmann, in: EJ, 2 (1928), 906–10, s.v. (contains bibliography); B. Rigaux, *L'antéchrist et l'opposition au royaume messianique* (1932); D. Flusser, in: EH, 4 (1952), 466–9, s.v. (contains bibliography).

[Michael E. Stone]

ANTI-DEFAMATION LEAGUE (ADL). The Anti-Defamation League (originally "The Anti-Defamation League of B'nai B'rith") was founded in 1913 in reaction to the crude and overt antisemitism of the period, specifically to the Leo *Frank case. The ADL's goal, as stated in the charter that established the League, is "to end the defamation of the Jewish people … to secure justice and fair treatment for all citizens alike."

Originally headquartered in Chicago, the offices of the League are in New York City. The ADL works out of 31 regional offices located throughout the United States. The ADL has as well a cooperative relationship with the B'nai B'rith Canadian office, an office in Jerusalem, and representation in Rome and Moscow.

The ADL is governed by a National Commission of 700. Unlike the *American Jewish Congress, *American Jewish Committee, and other community relations organizations, the ADL is not a membership organization. It has evolved from being a commission of its parent body to an organization with independent board and fundraising structures, and in reality is fully autonomous. The ADL is staffed by career professionals who are specialists in various disciplines related to community relations: religions, law, communications, promotion, education, labor, foreign affairs (especially Israel and the Middle East), social sciences, politics (national and local), and government.

The ADL recognizes threats to Jewish security coming from an antisemitism that appears in new forms and guises, such as anti-Israel activity and radicalism of the right and left. The League views itself as being an "active" organization, responding in a timely manner to what are perceived to be threats to the rights and security of Jews. It sees itself as taking a pragmatic, rather than an ideological, approach to issues. The ADL, by virtue of its budget and its varied activity, is considered to be a significant voice among the community relations agencies.

The ADL's initial efforts focused on the blatant antisemitism of the pre- and post-World War I period, which included restricted neighborhoods and resorts, jobs, and schools that rejected Jews. (For example, model legislation drafted by the ADL helped unmask the Ku Klux Klan and drastically diminish its power.) The ADL's focus, however, in its early decades was not on legal remedies against discrimination but on countering defamation of Jews. For example, the League exposed the vicious antisemitism of the *Dearborn Independent*, which printed and circularized the infamous *Protocols of Zion*, and extracted an apology and retraction from its publisher, Henry Ford. Throughout the 1930s the League fought and exposed the many hate groups which sprang up during the Depression and the Hitler period, such as the Christian Front, the Silver Shirts, and the German-American Bund.

Particularly in the post-World War II period, the ADL was successful in advocating on behalf of legislation against such discrimination. It also dealt with vulgar stereotypes and caricatures of Jews on the stage and in communication media and with incidents of antisemitic vandalism, and played a role in strengthening interfaith and interracial relationships.

In the 1960s, the ADL played a role in the successful coalitional effort that resulted in the passage of the Civil Rights Act of 1964, and of subsequent fair-housing and voting-rights laws. The ADL's sponsorship of a comprehensive study of the roots of prejudice (the seven-volume University of California Five-Year Study of Antisemitism in the United States – the "Berkeley Studies") helped create a new climate of interreligious understanding and ecumenism, and was a factor in the deliberations of Vatican II that led to the watershed document *Nostra Aetate*, which re-defined the Catholic Church's attitude toward Jews.

On the international scene, advocacy on behalf of the State of Israel and other involvement in Middle East issues became, especially after 1967, an ADL priority. The League carries out an education and action program to help mold public opinion and exposes and counteracts Arab propaganda; ADL led the effort which resulted in the passage of anti-boycott legislation and worked within the European Economic Community to counter the boycott. The League is also active in protecting and securing the rights of Jews wherever they are in danger, and played an important role in the Soviet Jewry movement. Interreligious activities as well have been an important part of the ADL agenda.

During the 1970s, in response to what it then characterized as "the new antisemitism," which derived less from overt expression and more from apathy and insensitivity to Jews and to Jewish concerns and problems, including Israel, the ADL re-contoured its approaches to antisemitism. A major prejudice-reduction program, "A World of Difference," has been an ADL centerpiece since the early 1990s, as has been Holocaust education. Convinced that preferential treatment will destroy equality of opportunity and selection based upon merit, the League's position on affirmative action is nuanced in terms of ADL's opposition to the re-emergence of quotas.

The ADL's traditional ideology was that aggressive use of litigation and other legal remedies to counter discrimination and church-state violations was too confrontational and would ultimately damage the constructive relationships that Jews had built up with other faith communities over the years. From its earliest years the ADL, unlike its sister "defense" agencies, rejected advocating on behalf of antidiscrimination legislation, and instead focused on combating prejudice and defamation. The League's national director until 1947, Richard E. Gustadt, articulated the view that held that intergroup negotiation and education programs emphasizing cultural pluralism offered the best chances to remedy societal abuses. Certain societal evils could not, in the view of the ADL, be eliminated, only tempered. This view (shared in large measure by the American Jewish Committee) marked a fundamental ideological difference with the American Jewish Congress, which believed in direct legal action.

From the late 1940s until the late 1970s the ADL was led by a tandem of Benjamin Epstein and Arnold Forster, who together began aggressively prosecuting a civil rights agenda for the League. Beginning in the early 1980s, however, with a marked shift in the national public policy agenda back to church-state and other First Amendment matters, there was again a shift in the priorities of the ADL. During the tenure of national director Nathan Perlmutter additional legal expertise and resources were added to the agency's staff (the ADL's litigation capacity dated back to the late 1940s and was a result of the decision by the American Jewish Congress to organize its Commission on Law and Social Action), and the League became an aggressive "player" in the church-state arena. During this period there was a certain degree of de-emphasis of the traditional civil rights agenda, resulting in large measure from antisemitism within some black civil rights groups.

Even with a new emphasis placed on church-state separation and other legal matters, the ADL always viewed church-state concerns to be but one of several major civil rights and liberties issues on its organizational palette, which includes countering racial supremacist organizations, judicial remedies for "hate crimes," and discrimination and harassment. Changes within the organization arising out of exogenous factors did not mean that the ADL intended to abandon its charter purpose of public response to anti-Jewish defamation.

From the mid-1980s, under the stewardship of Abraham H. *Foxman, the ADL has become one of the most "visible" national Jewish organizations on the American – and indeed international – scene. Although viewed as increasingly conservative in some areas of activity, the reality is that the ADL has carved a highly nuanced political path, especially on Israel-related issues, threading its way skillfully between agencies such as the rightist Zionist Organization of America and Jewish groups of the left. This "centrist" approach has been evident in a range of domestic public affairs issues as well. Newer areas of activity for the ADL include threats of global antisemitism, "hate" activity on the Internet, working with law-enforcement agencies, a new generation of church-state situations, and balancing traditional civil liberties concerns with those of national and local security. The ADL has commissioned a series of public opinion surveys, both in the United States and in Europe, which have elicited valuable data on antisemitic attitudes and on attitudes toward Israel.

The core mission of the ADL – to combat antisemitism – remains as it has been. The related mission of the League – working for justice for all – has in the view of the ADL not only intrinsic value but instrumental value as well, as it assists in the ADL's core mission.

In terms of institutional considerations, until the early 1980s the leading "defense" agency, in terms of budget and stature, was the American Jewish Committee; the annual budgets of the two agencies were at approximate parity, at around $12 million. The ADL budget ($5.5 million in 1971) began increasing in the 1980s at approximately $3 million per year in that decade, and soon far outstripped the other "defense" agencies, reaching some $30 million by the early 1990s and approximately $60 million by 2005. The League's staff and programmatic initiatives have increased commensurately.

Also important in terms of institutional dynamics is the ADL's relationship with *B'nai B'rith. The ADL began life as a commission of B'nai B'rith, but tensions developed between the two agencies as B'nai B'rith was reshaping itself from being primarily a fraternal and service organization to one that addresses community relations issues. In the mid-to-late 1990s the issue with B'nai B'rith came to a head, with B'nai B'rith – itself seeking finally to reshape its own identity – asserted that its community relations and "defense" agenda would be pursued aggressively. The ADL, maintaining that it was B'nai B'rith's "defense" arm, in effect severed its ties with its erstwhile parent. (The ADL does retain a *de jure* legal connection with B'nai B'rith.)

BIBLIOGRAPHY: N.C. Belth, *A Promise to Keep: A Narrative of the American Encounter with Anti-Semitism* (1979); J.A. Chanes, "The Voices of the American Jewish Community," in: *Survey of Jewish Affairs 1991* (1991); A. Forster, *Square One: The Memoirs of a True Freedom Fighter's Life-long Struggle against Anti-Semitism, Domestic and Foreign* (1988); G. Ivers, *To Build a Wall: American Jews and the Separation of Church and State* (1995); S. Svonkin, *Jews Against Prejudice: American Jews and the Fight for Civil Liberties* (1997).

[Jerome Chanes (2nd ed.)]

ANTI-FASCIST COMMITTEE, JEWISH, a group of Jewish public figures and intellectuals in the Soviet Union organized during World War II on the initiative of the Soviet government to mobilize world Jewish support for the Soviet war effort against Nazi Germany. When the Germans invaded the Soviet Union, the Soviet government felt the need to organize a Jewish body among the many organizations set up to arouse world opinion to aid embattled Russia. On Aug. 24, 1941, a meeting of "representatives of the Jewish people" was held in Moscow and it was addressed by Solomon *Mikhoels, Ilya *Ehrenburg, David *Bergelson, and others, who called on "our Jewish brethren throughout the world" to come to the aid of the Soviet Union. This appeal made a great impression on Jews in countries free of the Nazi yoke. In the U.S. the Jewish Council for Russian War Relief was established, headed by Albert *Einstein; in Palestine, a reply to the call from Moscow was broadcast in Hebrew on Sept. 28, 1941, on behalf of the *yishuv*. A public committee to aid the Soviet Union's fight against fascism, which was later known as "League V," was also established.

At the same time, two representatives of the *Bund in Poland, Henryk *Erlich and Victor *Alter, who had been released from Soviet imprisonment in September 1941, suggested to the Soviet government that it establish an anti-fascist committee. When the two were executed in December 1941, it appeared that the proposal had been rejected; however, the serious situation on the war fronts led the Soviet government to recognize the need for propaganda directed toward Jews throughout the world. It was decided to establish a Jewish Anti-Fascist Committee within the *Sovinformbureau*, which served Soviet war propaganda. On April 7, 1942, the Committee published its first appeal to "Jews throughout the world," signed by 47 people, including writers, poets, actors, doctors, and Jewish soldiers who had distinguished themselves in battle against the Germans (General Jacob *Kreiser, the submarine commander Israel Fisanovich, and others). The Committee was headed by Solomon Mikhoels, and its secretary was the journalist Shakhne Epstein. On May 24, the second meeting of the "representatives of the Jewish people" was held and broadcast an appeal to Jews throughout the world to collect contributions for the acquisition of 1,000 tanks and 500 airplanes for the Red Army. **Eynikeyt*, the Yiddish journal of the Committee, was first published on July 6, 1942, at Kuibyshev and appeared three times a month. The Committee organized radio broadcasts four times a week in Yiddish for the Jews in the U.S. and Great Britain and collected information on Nazi atrocities in Nazi-occupied Soviet areas that was published in *Eynikeyt* and sent outside the Soviet Union for publication in Jewish newspapers. The Committee also collected a total of 3,300,000 rubles in their fundraising campaign among Jews in the Soviet Union for the purpose of setting up a tank unit to be called "Soviet Birobidzhan." In February 1943, the Committee met in plenary session, at which Mikhoels delivered a shocking report of the fate of Jews in areas liberated by the Red Army. He also gave details on the Jewish role in the struggle against the Nazis. Ehrenburg denounced the wave of antisemitism then spreading through the country, whose slogan was that "one does not see Jews at the front," and urged that all circles of the Soviet public be supplied with information on the participation of Jews in the battles against the Germans. In the second half of 1943, Mikhoels and the poet Itzik *Fefer were sent by the Committee on a propaganda tour to the U.S., Canada, Mexico, and Great Britain and were enthusiastically received by almost all sections of the Jewish public. This visit was regarded as the first step in renewing the contact between Soviet Jews and world Jewry that had been severed since October 1917.

The third meeting of "representatives of the Jewish people" in the Soviet Union took place in April 1944, including for the first time a representative of religious Jewry, Rabbi Solomon *Schliefer of Moscow. When Germany was defeated in May 1945, the Anti-Fascist Committee published a declaration emphasizing that during the war "a basis for increasing unity was created" between Jews of various countries and the Jews of the Soviet Union.

When the war ended, the activities of the Anti-Fascist Committee centered mainly around the periodical *Eynikeyt*, which appeared three times a week after February 1945. The Committee planned to publish two books, *The Black Book* on Nazi atrocities in occupied territories and *The Red Book* on Jews as armed fighters against the Nazis; their publication was banned, however. In late 1946, Itzik Fefer declared in *Eynikeyt* that "we have never affirmed all-Jewish (*klal Yisroel*) unity, but only anti-Fascist unity." Ehrenburg resigned from the Committee in time, while its chairman Mikhoels was murdered by the secret police in January 1948. In late November 1948, the Anti-Fascist Committee was liquidated together with all the remaining Jewish institutions, and most Jewish writers and public figures were arrested.

From the first, the Anti-Fascist Committee had been established as a Soviet propaganda tool operating under the guidance and supervision of the government. But after the war, when Jewish refugees began returning from the eastern regions of the U.S.S.R. to their former residences in the Ukraine and Belorussia and faced difficulties in regaining possession of their homes and getting their jobs back, they turned to the Committee for help. The Committee, and especially Mikhoels, frequently interceded with the authorities on their behalf. It seems that the Committee also sent a memorandum to Stalin demanding that the renewed symptoms of antisemitism be stamped out and that an area be set aside for the settlement of Jewish refugees in the Crimea. These activities, in which the Committee overstepped the limits of its official assignment, were the official cause of its dissolution and the execution of its chairman on January 12, 1948, in a staged car accident in Minsk. The Committee was dissolved on November 20, 1948 and the Jewish publishing house Der Emes was closed. In 1952, at a secret trial, its leading members were accused of being Western (American) spies and, as Jewish nationalists and Zionists, traitors, and of conspiring to separate the Crimea from the Soviet Union and to convert it into a Jewish bourgeois republic that would serve as a military base for the enemies of the U.S.S.R. (the "Crimea Affair"). All the accused – S. Lozovskii, J. Juzefovich, Prof. B. Shimeliovich, I. Fefer, L. Kvitko, P. Markish, D. Bergelson, D. Hofstein, B. Zuskin, L. Talmi, I. Vatenberg, E. Teumin, and Ch. Vatenberg-Ostrovska – were executed on Aug. 12, 1952. Prof. Lina Stern was sentenced to 3½ years of prison and then deportation to Kazakhstan. In related measures, another 110 Jews were tried, 10 were executed, and the others were sentenced to various prison terms.

BIBLIOGRAPHY: S. Redlich, *Propaganda and Nationalism in Wartime Russia: The Jewish Antifascist Committee in the USSR, 1941–1948* (1982); S. Schwarz, *Jews in the Soviet Union* (1951), 201–16; B.Z. Goldberg, *Jewish Problem in the Soviet Union* (1961), index; Litvak, in: *Gesher*, 12, nos. 2–3, (1966), 218–32; *Brider Yidn fun der Ganster Velt* (Moscow, 1941); *Antifashistisher Miting fun di Forshteyer funem Yidishn Folk, Tsveyter Miting* (Moscow, 1942); *Dos Yidishe Folk in Kamf kegn Fashizm* (Moscow, 1945); Redlich, in: JSOS, 31 (1969), 25–36. **ADD. BIBLIOGRAPHY:** G. Kostyrchenko, *V plenu krasnovo faraona* (1994).

[Yehuda Slutsky / Shmuel Spector (2nd ed.)]

ANTIGONUS (c. 135–104 B.C.E.), Hasmonean prince; son of John *Hyrcanus and younger brother of Judah *Aristobulus. Antigonus and Aristobulus were put in command of the siege of Samaria by their father. They succeeded in capturing and destroying the city after defeating Antiochus IX Cyzicenus of Syria and the army of Ptolemy Lathyrus of Egypt which had been sent to aid the besieged town. When Judah Aristobulus succeeded to the throne, he imprisoned his mother and his younger brothers, but appointed Antigonus commander of the army and his associate in the administration of the state. During the war, Upper Galilee, southern Lebanon, and part of northern Transjordan were captured, and the Itureans were compelled to adopt Judaism.

Josephus' account of the death of Antigonus contains several contradictions. He states that Aristobulus, ridden by suspicion and fear of assassination, issued an order forbidding anyone to enter his palace armed. Subsequently, Antigonus returned after the war on the Itureans. On appearing in the Temple during the Feast of Tabernacles dressed in his splendid new armor, he was loudly acclaimed by the people. When the king heard this he sent a messenger to his brother commanding him to appear before him unarmed. Antigonus' enemies, however, bribed the messenger to tell Antigonus the opposite and when he reached Strato's Tower on his way to the palace, he was killed by the guards. This tale is linked with another relating the "prophecy" of a certain Essene who foresaw that Antigonus would be slain that day.

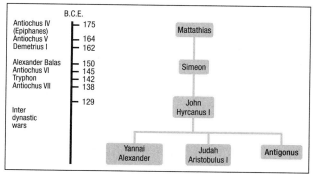

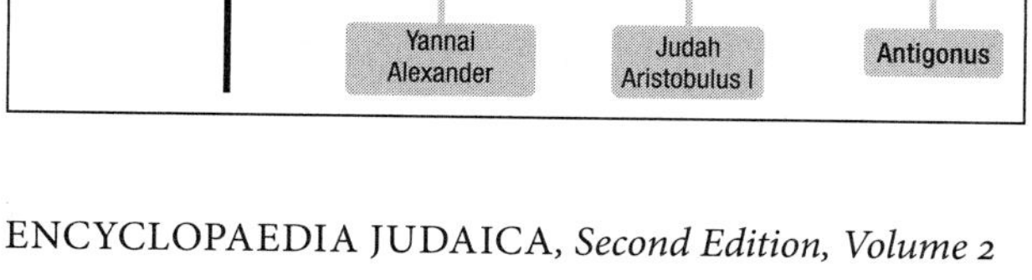

BIBLIOGRAPHY: Jos., Ant., 13:276–81, 301–13; Jos., Wars, 1:64ff., 70ff.; Klausner, Bayit Sheni, 3 (1950[2]), 141ff.; Schuerer, Gesch, 1 (1901[4]), 267ff., 274; Meyer, Ursp, 2 (1921), 273ff.

[Abraham Schalit]

ANTIGONUS II (Mattathias), last king of the *Hasmonean dynasty, reigned 40–37 B.C.E.; youngest son of Aristobulus *II. After the conquest of Jerusalem by Pompey (63 B.C.E.) Antigonus was taken to Rome with other members of the royal family. In 57 he escaped with his father, but was sent back to Rome by *Gabinius. Eventually Aristobulus' children received permission from the Senate to return to Judea. After the death of his father and his brother Alexander (49), Antigonus and his sisters went to Chalcis to Ptolemy, son of Mennaeus (see *Alexandra, daughter of Aristobulus II). In 47 he argued before Julius Caesar the case for his right to rule over Judea, over which *Antipater II, father of Herod, was in control. Caesar, however, preferred Antipater who was more useful to his plans in the East. After the assassination of Caesar (44), Antigonus tried to enter Galilee in an attempt to advance on Jerusalem and seize the throne, but he was repulsed by Herod and returned to Chalcis. After the Parthians conquered Syria (40), Antigonus allied himself with them, and broke through to Jerusalem at the head of an army of Hasmonean supporters. Herod with his men retreated to the royal palace while Antigonus remained on the Temple Mount, awaiting the Parthian troops who were moving on Jerusalem. Against Herod's wishes, his brother *Phasael and ex-king Hyrcanus II were persuaded to go to the Parthian headquarters in Galilee for a conference and were arrested. Herod thereupon escaped from Jerusalem with Mariamne the Hasmonean and her mother Alexandra. Antigonus' men pursued the fugitives and overtook them south of Jerusalem at the spot where Herod afterward built his fortress palace Herodium. They were repulsed and Herod brought his family and the remnant of his force to Idumea, entrusting them to his brother Joseph, who settled them in *Masada. There are contradictory accounts as to the fate of Phasael; it is probable that he committed suicide or was killed while attempting to escape. The Parthians cut off Hyrcanus' ears, on the advice of Antigonus, who desired thereby to disqualify him from the high priesthood. Antigonus was now designated king over Judea by the Parthians and also assumed the high priesthood. This appointment bound him to the Parthians and from then on he was regarded by Rome as a declared enemy. Antigonus besieged Masada but failed to conquer it. Herod, who had arrived in Rome, succeeded in being appointed king of Judea, and immediately left for the East. He arrived in Judea at the end of 40 or early in 39, and immediately began hostilities against Antigonus. However, Ventidius,

Antony's legate (later the victor of the Parthian War), gave him no substantial support, and left Judea soon after, probably having been bribed by Antigonus. Herod meanwhile succeeded in liberating Masada, after which he marched on Jerusalem, and attempted to take the city in a surprise attack. The attempt failed, and Herod retreated. The war continued throughout the winter of 39–38 and Herod succeeded in subduing the whole of Galilee, while Antigonus remained in Jerusalem, unable to assist his partisans in the north. Nevertheless Herod would not have got the upper hand if Ventidius had not decisively defeated the Parthians (38). As a result of this victory, Roman forces were freed for action. Even then they did not cooperate with Herod who journeyed to Mark Antony's camp to seek his full support. During Herod's absence from Palestine Antigonus defeated Herod's brother Joseph, who was killed in battle. A general rising followed in Galilee, whose inhabitants seized partisans of Herod and drowned them in the Sea of Galilee; the revolt even spread to Idumea. Herod, returning at the head of a considerable Roman force, crushed the uprising. Antigonus then committed a fatal error: instead of concentrating all his forces against Herod, he dispatched a large part of them against the Roman troops in Samaria, and his army was defeated at Jeshanah. Only the approach of winter prevented Herod from besieging Jerusalem. In 37 Herod was reinforced by a large Roman army, 11 legions (about 50–60,000 men), sent by Mark Antony and commanded by Sosius. The siege lasted five months and the distress in the city was particularly acute, as that year was a sabbatical year and food was in short supply. Two sages in the besieged city, whose names are given by Josephus as Sameas (Shammai or Shemaiah) and Pollion (Hillel or Avtalyon), recommended that the city gates be opened, not out of love for Herod, but in the belief that this was a heaven-sent punishment which must be endured. Josephus' statement that the city fell on a fast day has been wrongly understood to refer to the Day of Atonement; it was probably a communal fast customarily proclaimed in time of danger. Antigonus and his forces fortified themselves on the Temple Mount, and when this was taken by storm by the Romans, Antigonus surrendered to Sosius. He was sent to Antioch to Mark Antony, who ordered him to be beheaded. This was the first time that the Romans executed a legitimate king in such a way, probably to show that they did not recognize him as such.

BIBLIOGRAPHY: Jos., Wars, 1:239–40; 248–353; Jos., Ant., 4:297–300; 330–491; 15: 1–10; Klausner, Bayit Sheni, 3 (1950²), 262–73; A. Schalit, *Hordos ha-Melekh* (1960), 47–59, 370–3, 507–11; Schuerer, Gesch, 1 (1904⁴), 354ff.; R. Laqueur, *Der juedische Historiker Flavius Josephus* (1920), 186ff.

[Abraham Schalit]

°ANTIGONUS OF CARYSTUS (fl. 240 B.C.E.), an Athenian biographer and bronze-worker who labored under Attalus I at Pergamum. He cites Callimachus, who, in turn, cites Zenophilus (Xenophilus), on the phenomena of the Dead Sea.

[Louis Harry Feldman]

ANTIGONUS OF SOKHO (early second century B.C.E.), sage. Antigonus represents the link in the chain of tradition between *Simeon the Just, his teacher, and the **Zugot* ("pairs"). His Greek name indicates the extent of Hellenistic influence in this period. Only one of his statements has been preserved: "Be not like servants who minister to their master in order to receive a reward, but be like servants who minister to their master not in order to receive a reward; and let the fear of Heaven be upon you" (Avot 1:3). It is not clear, whether this saying has any actual background specifically typical of Antigonus' age. Antigonus did not thereby intend to deny the doctrine of future reward, but according to rabbinic tradition, his dictum was misinterpreted by his pupils, Zadok and Boethus, who saw in it a denial of the afterlife. As a result, they founded the sects known as the *Sadducees and *Boethusians who denied the doctrine of the world to come. "They (Zadok and Boethus) taught their disciples who repeated it to their disciples… and said to them, 'what caused our forefathers to say this? Is it possible that a laborer should toil all day and not receive his reward in the evening?' Therefore, had our forefathers known of the existence of the world to come and the resurrection of the dead they would not have said this" (ARN^1 5, 13; cf. ARN^2 10, 13). It is hard to say what historical basis there is to this legend. Some scholars find significance in the fact that the first recorded controversy among the Pharisees themselves (over the issue of *semikhah* "the laying of hands on the head of a sacrificial animal") started in the days of Antigonus' disciples.

BIBLIOGRAPHY: Geiger, Mikra, 41, 71f., 86; Weiss, Dor, 1 (1904⁴), 94f.; Frankel, Mishnah, 9, 31f.; Halevy, Dorot, 1 pt. 3 (1923), 371–3; L. Finkelstein, *Ha-Perushim ve-Anshei Keneset ha-Gedolah* (1950), 40–45, 77–79.

[Moshe David Herr]

ANTIN, MARY (1881–1949), Polish-born U.S. author. Antin immigrated to Boston in 1894, publishing her first poem in the *Boston Herald* while still at elementary school and her first book, *From Plotsk to Boston* (1899), at age 18. An eloquent Progressive whose books also included the classic immigrant autobiography *The Promised Land* (1912) and *They Who Knock at Our Gates* (1914), Antin saw herself as the social representation of those who had likewise fled from persecution to freedom. Her life exemplified the increasing elasticity of Jewish identity in modern American culture. Antin married Amadeus W. Grabau, a German-American Lutheran geologist and paleontologist, in 1901 and the couple had one child. Antin had to relinquish her goal of attending Radcliffe College when her husband assumed a professorship at Columbia University; she studied at Columbia's Teachers College and at Barnard College but did not complete a degree, apparently due to illness and the realities of domestic life that made it difficult for women of her time to combine marriage and motherhood. The marriage later collapsed over Grabau's support for Germany in WWI and conflict generated by Antin's national celebrity and financial success. Antin was an eclectic thinker who maintained a Jewish identity and some Jewish practices while exploring other forms of spirituality. Initially enthralled by the writings of Thoreau, Emerson, and Darwin, in later life she was attracted to Christian mysticism and spent parts of her final years as a disciple of Meher Baba and Rudolf Steiner. Her popularity as a writer and lecturer waned and her success was followed by writer's block and years of hardship, when she supported herself by doing social work.

BIBLIOGRAPHY: A. Mazur, *A Romance in Natural History: The Lives and Works of Amadeus Grabau and Mary Antin* (2004); P.S. Nadell, "Introduction," to Mary Antin, *From Plotzk to Boston* (1986); E. Salz (ed.), *Selected Letters of Mary Antin* (2000); W. Sollors, "Introduction" to Mary Antin, *The Promised Land* (1997).

[Keren R. McGinity (2nd ed.)]

ANTINOMIANISM (from Greek *anti*, "against," and *nomos*, "law"), opposition to the law and, more especially, a religiously inspired rejection and abolition of moral, ritual, and other traditionally accepted rules and standards. Antinomianism in the narrow sense has usually been applied to one of the main trends in the early church which, in the wake of Paul's disparagement of the Mosaic Law in favor of the law of the "New Covenant," asserted that those who are saved may "do evil that good may come" (Rom. 3:8). Paul himself indignantly repudiated this accusation (*ibid.* 3) though he held that the Mosaic Law was no longer valid after the coming of Christ. In a wider sense the term is used to designate doctrines asserting that at certain times (e.g., in the messianic era when the old things have passed away and a new order is established) or for certain individuals or groups (e.g., those who have attained higher knowledge, salvation, or initiation into certain mysteries) men are no longer bound by constricting rules and norms applicable to less perfect times or individuals. It is not surprising, therefore, that the problem of antinomianism should have posed itself mainly in connection with Gnostic, mystical, or messianic movements. Licentiousness seems to have been characteristic of some Gnostic sects, even as the doctrine of the "freedom of the children of light" or Luther's teachings regarding justification by faith only, without regard to works, contributed to manifestations of antinomianism among the Anabaptists and among some 17th-century English sects. Antinomian tendencies in Judaism often based themselves on arbitrary interpretations of rabbinic statements to the effect that in the "world to come" all ritual prohibitions would be abolished (see also *Gnosticism).

On the other hand, ritual and customs were an integral part of the Torah, the "divine law," and like the Torah itself, were said to possess eternal and absolute validity. Post-Exilic Judaism took great pains to observe every single precept contained in the Torah. Pharisaic Judaism, although it regarded all commandments as equally sacred, did sense a difference between ritual laws and moral laws, as well as between reasonable laws and such that could not be rationally justified. A *baraita* (Yoma 67b) makes a distinction between *mishpatim*, i.e., commandments which "even if they had not been written down, would have been written down as a matter of course," such as the prohibitions of idolatry, incest, murder, etc., and *ḥukkot*, i.e., commandments "which the Satan always urges one to transgress," such as the consumption of pork, the use of cloth that is part wool and part linen, levirate marriages, etc. The *baraita* goes on to say: "You might argue that this (i.e., the *ḥukkot*) is of no account; therefore it is written 'I am God' (Lev. 18:4) – I, God, have fixed the laws and you have no right to question them." This passage in the *baraita* amounts to a clear rejection of antinomian freedom of judgment and clearly expresses the attitude of observant Judaism of all periods to the problem of ritual laws. It was not, however, a solution designed to satisfy the inquisitive mind. The need to find meaning and purpose in the ritual laws seems to have been felt first in the Hellenistic period, when it became indispensable for the propagation of Judaism among the pagans, especially the learned among them. It was necessary to explain to them not only the ancient traditions and legends and adapt them to the Greek way of thinking but above all to justify the law itself. Hellenistic Judaism conceived the Torah as *nomos*, the law being the supreme expression of Jewish religious distinctiveness; it was of the utmost importance to explain to the pagans the inner meaning of Jewish religious laws. Attempts were made to give the laws a symbolic interpretation and thereby to bring out their profound meaning (Aristobulus, the letter of Aristeas, Philo, Josephus, etc.). At the same time, an antinomian trend also made itself felt; the attempt to explain the law had the natural result of a relaxation in its observance. Philo testifies to this trend when he states: "There are, however, people who regard the written law as images of spiritual concepts, take great pains in exploring the latter, while neglecting the former. These are people that I must censure. For one must be careful to do both: to explore the hidden meaning and to practice the plain meaning. Even though the commandment on Sabbath observance contains the hidden meaning that action is the prerogative of God and His creatures should remain passive, this does not absolve us of the obligation to observe the sanctity of the Sabbath. Similarly, although the holy days and festivals are only images of our spiritual joy and our gratitude to God, we are not permitted to renounce the customary ceremonies and rituals. Circumcision may essentially only mean the removal of all passion, lust, and godless thought, yet we are not permitted to disregard the custom, as it is commanded; for if we were to adhere only to the higher meaning of the law, we would also have to give up sanctification in the Temple and untold other essential ceremonies" (cf. Philo, Migration, 89 ff.; Wolfson, *Philo*, 1 (1948), 66–71). A similar danger of the erosion of ritual practice and the observance of the law was felt as a result of the rise and spread of Graeco-Arab philosophy among the Jews after the tenth century.

In medieval Jewish thought, antinomian tendencies appeared in three different manners: (a) in allegorical exegesis of the commandments, which regarded them as symbolic of rational and scientific attainment; (b) in spiritualistic interpretation of worship as the supreme human goal; (c) in astrological antinomianism. Antinomian allusions began to appear regularly in Abraham *Ibn Ezra's Bible commentaries. For instance, Ibn Ezra maintained that worship of images was legitimate outside the Holy Land, but was prohibited within the Land of Israel on account of its special astrological status (viz., Commentary to Deut. 31:16). Maimonides laid the foundations for allegorical interpretation of biblical and talmudic sources, although he generally refrained from applying such allegorical interpretation to the commandments. Nevertheless, he suggested that the Torah teaches an abstract form of worship of God (*Guide for the Perplexed* 3:32). In the controversy over philosophy which erupted in the 13th century, the conservative faction accused the rationalists of antinomian attitudes and behavior, based on their alleged allegorization of the commandments, charges which continued to be leveled despite repeated and strenuous denials by the rationalists, such as *Levi b. Abraham b. Hayyim. Such Jewish attacks on rationalism and accusations of antinomianism parallel and reflect the suppression by the Church of the "heresy" of the rationalist Albigensians (from Albi, in southern France), who had begun in the 11th century to interpret Scripture allegorically, and who denied the literal interpretation of the miraculous events in the life and resurrection of Jesus that are central to Catholic doctrine, allegorization allegedly resulting in laxity in morals. The rationalist threat was met by repeated Church bans (1209, 1210, 1215) on the study of the works of Arabic philosophy and science, and of Aristotle. These bans were renewed in 1231 by Pope Gregory IX, who then established the permanent Inquisition under the Dominicans, with the aim of eradicating the heresy.

In the 14th century, many rationalists did, in fact, display antinomian attitudes, in some cases in their supercommentaries to Ibn Ezra, arguing that "the essence of the worship of God is in the heart" (Samuel ibn Zarza, *Mikhlol Yofi*, Ms. Paris, f. 729–730; Sec. 2, f. 207a). Much additional evidence to antinomian attitudes leading to laxity or abandonment of ritual observance may be found in medieval Jewish sources, although it is not at all clear whether these sources are proof of concrete cases of antinomian behavior, or only of a certain type of homiletical style.

The allegorical interpretations of the philosophical meanings of the laws clearly encouraged laxity among those who thought that the outer observances were merely a means for expressing philosophical truths. Philo's remarks incidentally suggest that the antinomians found no fault with the Temple and the cult of animal sacrifice; in general, however, it was precisely the rejection of the cult of sacrifice which was a cardinal point of many antinomian groups. Epiphanius (*Adversus Haereses* 1:18) mentions a pre-Christian Jewish sect, the Nazarenes, which rejected the Pentateuch, regarding it as a forgery; they observed most Jewish customs but did not accept the cult of animal sacrifice (cf. Meyer, Urspr, 2 (1921), 408ff.; Harnack, *The Mission and Expansion of Christianity*, 1 (1961), 402f.). Similar views were also held by many Judeo-Christian sects. Some scholars claimed to find allusions to antinomianism and Gnosticism in several of the books of the Bible and the Talmud (M. Friedlaender, *Der vorchristliche juedische Gnosticismus* (1898), 71ff.). The rejection of the ceremonial law by the modern *Reform movement can be regarded as a form of antinomianism, but in recent years there can be detected a distinct tendency toward at least a partial return to ceremonial observance.

[Dov Schwartz (2nd ed.)]

In Kabbalah

Since the Kabbalah's basic aim was to strengthen the Jewish religious tradition, it is in general far removed from antinomian tendencies. Its attitude to the *halakhah* is positive but it endeavors to endow the precepts with symbolic value. For this reason we find in the early Kabbalah phenomena which may be regarded only as latent antinomianism. There are three such occurrences: (1) The doctrine of *Sefer ha-*Temunah* (first printed in 1784) on the changes of the reading of the Torah due to new combinations of its letters in the various stages of the cosmic cycle. Each such stage is called *shemittah* and what is forbidden in the *shemittah* during which we live may become permitted, and even considered a commandment, during another *shemittah*. Adherents to this doctrine also held that in actual fact the alphabet contained 23 letters, but that one letter became "unseen" in our *shemittah*; its revelation in the next *shemittah* will, of course, deeply change our manner of understanding the Torah. (2) The doctrine of the book *Ra'aya Meheimna* ("The Faithful Shepherd," part of the *Zohar dealing with the interpretation of the commandments): during the period of exile the Torah derives from the *Ez̥ ha-Da'at* ("the Tree of Knowledge") and for this reason it contains purity and defilement, things that are permitted and things that are prohibited, and so on. At the time of *redemption, however, the Torah will be revealed from the *Ez̥ ha-Ḥayyim* ("the Tree of Life") and with the annihilation of the *yez̥er ha-ra* ("evil inclination"), prohibitions and limitations will no longer be necessary. Thus, its secret (i.e., mystic) knowledge, the pure spirituality which is its essence, will become manifest and people will act according to it. This spiritual Torah which is concealed in our revealed Torah is called *Torah de-Az̥ilut* ("Torah of the Higher World"). (3) The doctrine of the books *Peli'ah* and **Kanah* (written around 1340–80), according to which there is no literal meaning in the Talmud and in the *halakhah*; the secret (mystic) knowledge itself is the literal meaning. One should observe the halakhic values for this reason only; for, if one should suppose that these values have the literal, customary meaning, then there is no need to keep many of them, since it is possible to prove through inner criticism of the *halakhah* and by the way of talmudic discussion itself that numerous essential halakhic rules do not apply in exile and that most of the ritual precepts are not observed in it at all.

Common to all three doctrines is the fact that in actual reality, in our time, there is no place for antinomianism. But the existence of the halakhic world is always dependent on a certain esoteric condition, and with the change of this condition the value of the talmudic *halakhah* will also change, although the absolute value of the Torah as a divine revelation will not change at all. Actual antinomianism became manifest only in the radical groups of the Shabbatean movement. However, it was based on the three above-mentioned doctrines. Since they believed that redemption had already come they reached the conclusion that the *Torah de-Beri'ah* ("the Torah in its present form"), which is the material Torah of traditional Judaism, should be abolished and one should act according to the esoteric Torah, *Torah de-Aẓilut*. This antinomianism was a revolutionary element in the Shabbatean sect and brought in its wake destructive phenomena in the lives of the radical Shabbateans. Serious sins were considered meritorious, and particularly those sins punishable with *karet* ("divine punishment by premature death"), such as adultery. Antinomian activities were also introduced as a special religious rite (reading the traditional phrase *matir assurim* as "who permits what is forbidden" rather than as "who frees prisoners"). It attained its most extreme form with the Frankists (see Jacob *Frank). This antinomianism of the Shabbateans and the Frankists was connected with their messianic claims and was based on the talmudic statement that in the messianic period all commandments would be abolished, "all sacrifices would disappear, except for the sacrifice of thanksgiving" (Lev. R. 9: 7; 27: 12), and that all fasts would be converted into feasts.

[Gershom Scholem]

One of the main sources of kabbalistic antinomianism is the astrological theory of changes of law which depend on Saturn and Jupiter. The rule of a certain planet over a certain period of time, a cosmic cycle, and the corresponding nature of the law that governs during this cycle, has been transferred by some kabbalists to the rule of a certain *Sefirah*, whose specific nature is reflected in the structure of the Torah.

[Moshe Idel (2nd ed.)]

BIBLIOGRAPHY: Scholem, in: *Keneset*, 2 (1937), 347–92; M. Balaban, *Le-Toledot ha-Tenu'ah ha-Frankit*, 1 (1934), 18–72; Dubnow, in: *Ha-Shilo'aḥ*, 7 (1901), 314–20; J.M. Rosenthal, *Perspectives in Jewish Learning*, 3 (1969), 48–53. **ADD. BIBLIOGRAPHY:** I. Twersky, *Introduction to the Code of Maimonides (Mishneh Torah)* (1980), 392–97; D. Schwartz, *The Philosophy of a Fourteenth Century Jewish Neoplatonic Circle* (Heb., 1996), 246–49; I. Ta-Shma, in: *Jewish Law Annual* 18–19 (1992–94), 479–95.

ANTIOCH (Turk. **Antakya**), city in southern Turkey, on the lower Orontes (Asi) near the Syrian border. Population (2004): 158,400. Part of Syria under the French mandate, it was annexed to Turkey in 1939 along with the district of Alexandretta (*Iskenderun) and made into the capital of the province of Hatay.

Antioch was founded by Seleucus Nicator in 300 B.C.E. and became the capital of the Seleucid Empire. In antiquity Antioch was an important Jewish center, and from its foundation full rights were bestowed upon the Jews. When the inhabitants rebelled against Demetrius II in 142 B.C.E., the soldiers of *Jonathan the Hasmonean were sent to quell the revolt and set the city in flames. There must have been a considerable number of Jews in Antioch by the second century B.C.E. Josephus praises the beauty of its great synagogue, and there were doubtless a number of other places of worship. Antioch had no special Jewish quarter as had *Alexandria, Jews being apparently dispersed throughout the city. *Hannah and her seven sons are said to have been buried in Antioch and it is possible that the martyrdom recounted in the Second and Fourth books of the Maccabees occurred in Antioch; IV *Maccabees could in fact be, in essence, the oration of a Jew of Antioch in memory of these martyrs. The Christians too, later honored the martyrs' grave, which, according to them, was situated in the Kerataion quarter, near the synagogue. The franchise of the Jews in Antioch was engraved on bronze tablets set up in a public place in the city. During the Roman period the Jewish population grew and was augmented by many proselytes. After the Roman war of 66–70 the inhabitants of Antioch asked Titus to expel the Jews from the city, and to destroy the tablets on which the Jewish privileges were inscribed, but he refused. Nevertheless, according to later chroniclers, the Romans erected a splendid memorial to celebrate their victory and set up the *cherubim taken from the Temple in Jerusalem on one of the western gateways of the city, which was conse-

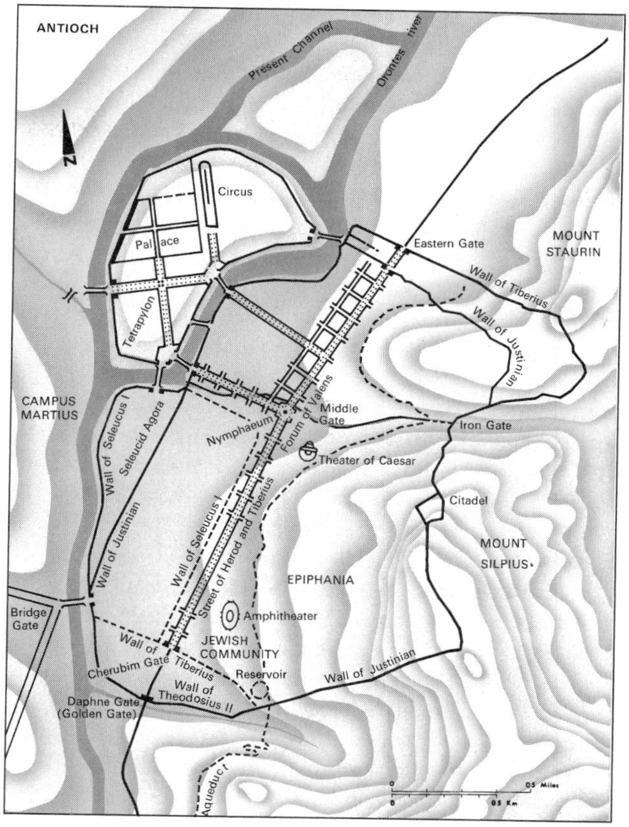

Plan of ancient Antioch.

quently called "The Gate of the Cherubim." This, however, appears to be a late legend. The Jewish community of Antioch maintained permanent commercial ties with Palestine and took an interest in the spiritual life of their coreligionists there. In the second century, Abba Judah of Antioch contributed liberally to the maintenance of the Palestinian scholars, many of whom visited Antioch.

Antioch played an important role in the history of Christianity. Here for the first time, in the days of the Apostles, the members of the new faith were called "Christians" (Messianists). The first Christians were, of course, Jews, but already in the days of Paul, pagans also joined their ranks. Barnabas visited Antioch, where he dwelt together with Paul. When the apostle Peter came to Antioch he ate with the pagans, but when messengers arrived from James, the brother of Jesus, who was a Nazarene, Peter felt ashamed and withdrew from the pagan society, Barnabas following suit. According to a tradition of the church fathers, Peter headed the Christian church of Antioch for seven years.

Antioch became a center of Christian learning and the Antiochian school of theology, which flourished in the third and fourth centuries C.E., was particularly renowned. Unlike the school of Caesarea, which interpreted the Bible allegorically and in accordance with speculative philosophy, the Antiochian school expounded the Scriptures in conformity with their historical and literal meaning. The biblical commentaries composed by this school in the fourth and fifth centuries C.E. are of great importance. In Antioch, various means were used to counteract the great influence which the Jews had upon the local Christians. The synod of Antioch (341) forbade the Christians to celebrate Easter when the Jews were observing Passover, and John Chrysostom of Antioch, in his six sermons (c. 366–387), vituperatively denounced those Christians in Antioch who attended synagogues and resorted to the Jewish law courts.

When Christianity became the state religion, the position of the Jews of Antioch deteriorated. The Jews of Imnestar were accused of having crucified a Christian boy on the feast of Purim, and the Antiochian Christians destroyed the synagogue (423 C.E.). When the emperor Theodosius II restored it, he was rebuked by Simon Stylites and refrained from defending the Jews. In the brawls between the sport factions known as the "blues" and the "greens," many Jews were killed.

When the Persians threatened the *Byzantine Empire, Emperor Phocas attempted to force the Jews of Antioch to convert to Christianity. In revenge the Antiochian Jews are alleged to have attacked the Christians (608 C.E.) and killed the patriarch Anastasius. When the rebellion was suppressed, many Jews were slain or exiled. From this date on there is little further information about the Jews of Antioch. *Benjamin of Tudela (c. 1171) found only about ten Jewish families there, most of whom were glass manufacturers.

Under Ottoman rule (1516–1918) there was always a Jewish community in Antioch, and it was reinforced by immigrants from *Corfu and *Aleppo. By the middle of the 18th century there were 40 Jewish families and several rabbis in residence. The community followed the Sephardi rite. However, when the English traveler A. Buckingham visited Antioch around 1816 he found only 20 Jewish families, who met for prayers in a private house on the Sabbath. The Jewish population seems to have increased later on and by 1894 there were three to four hundred Jews.

Under the Turkish Republic many Jews left and the community dwindled once again. In 1977 there were only 164 Jews living in the city, divided among three large families. Most of them were textile merchants. There was one synagogue in operation, but no rabbi.

BIBLIOGRAPHY: S. Krauss, in: REJ, 45 (1902), 27–49; A.Y. Brawer, *Avak Derakhim*, 1 (1944), 69 ff.; M. Schwabe, in: *Tarbiẓ*, 21 (1950) 112f.; V. Tcherikover, *Hellenistic Civilization and the Jews* (1959), index; G. Downey, *History of Antioch in Syria from Seleucus to the Arab Conquest* (1961); A. Cohen, *Anglo-Jewish Scrapbook* (1943), 39. **ADD. BIBLIOGRAPHY:** EIS² under Antakiya, 1 (1960), 516–17; W.A. Meeks and R.L. Wilken, *Jews and Christians in Antioch in the First Four Centuries of the Common Era* (1978); P.R. Trebilco, *Jewish Communities in Asia Minor* (1991); S. Tuval, *"Ha-Kehillot be-Turkiya ka-Yom,"* in: *Pe'amim*, 12 (1982), 127–28.

[Abraham Haim / David Kushner (2nd ed.)]

°**ANTIOCHUS**, name of 13 Seleucid monarchs who ruled Syria for the greater part of two and a half centuries. They include:

(1) ANTIOCHUS I SOTER (b. 324 B.C.E.), son of Seleucus I Nicator, ruled from 281 to 261. Although unsuccessful in his attempt to capture *Coele-Syria (276–72) from *Ptolemy II of Egypt, Antiochus nevertheless pursued his father's policy of founding Greek cities throughout the empire, and was even erroneously credited in late rabbinic and Roman literature with the founding of the capital, Antioch.

(2) ANTIOCHUS II THEOS, son of Antiochus I, ruled from 261 to 246 B.C.E. Antiochus recaptured those parts of Syria and Asia Minor lost by his father in the First Syrian War. His confrontations with the Egyptian king, and the intrigues of his wives (which eventually caused his death) are alluded to in the Book of Daniel 11:16 ff. Scholars have pointed to a passage in Josephus (Ant., 12:125–7) as proof that Antiochus II granted special rights and even full citizenship to the Jews of certain Greek cities. (For discussion, see Josephus, Loeb edition, vol. 7, 741 ff. For selected literature on the early Seleucid rulers and the Jews, see p. 737.)

(3) ANTIOCHUS III, THE GREAT (b. c. 242 B.C.E.), son of Seleucus II Callinicus (244–26). Antiochus became king after the murder of his brother Seleucus III Soter (223) and immediately succeeded in stabilizing and strengthening the Seleucid Empire. With his accession, however, the long period of peace in Judea came to an end. For 20 years, until 198, the country constantly changed hands. The young king's second expedition through Coele-Syria was particularly successful. By 217 he reached the southernmost parts of Palestine only to suffer a crushing defeat at the hands of *Ptolemy IV near

Rafi'aḥ (Rafa; south of Gaza), in one of the fiercest battles of the Hellenistic period. Antiochus was forced to relinquish the conquered areas, and according to Josephus, the Jews "were in no way different from a storm-tossed ship which is beset on either side by heavy seas, finding themselves crushed between the successes of Antiochus and the adverse turn of his fortunes" (Ant., 12:130). By 198 B.C.E. the Jews of Palestine had become disenchanted with Ptolemaic rule, and they opened the gates of Jerusalem to Antiochus, and assisted in the expulsion of its Egyptian garrison. Antiochus rewarded the Jews for their "splendid reception" by restoring those parts of Jerusalem destroyed by the war, freeing its citizens from taxes for three years and supplying funds for the Temple, and in general by permitting "members of the nation to have a form of government in accordance with the laws of their country" (κατὰ τοὺς πατρίους νόμους). It was also forbidden to bring to Jerusalem animals forbidden for consumption by Jews (Jos., Ant., 12:129–53). The victories of Antiochus brought him to the attention of the Romans who were advancing through Greece. In 190 Antiochus suffered his greatest defeat near Magnesia and was forced into a degrading settlement by the victorious Romans. Sensing this, the eastern provinces of the Seleucid Empire revolted and Antiochus, determined to finance his recent setback at their expense, died while trying to sack one of the Temple treasuries of Elymais (187; I Macc. 8:6–16; Jos., Loeb edition, vol. 7, p. 743ff., App. D; M. Stern, *Ha-Te'udot le-Mered ha-Ḥashmona'im* (1965), 28–46; Schalit, in: JQR, 50 (1959/60), 289–318).

(4) ANTIOCHUS IV EPIPHANES, son of Antiochus III, ruled from the death of his brother *Seleucus IV in 175 B.C.E. until his death in 164. His reign marks a turning point in Jewish history. Striving vigorously to restore the strength of the Seleucid Empire, Antiochus founded more new Greek cities than all his predecessors. He became the champion of an intense Hellenization, more as a result of personal tendencies than as a means of reunifying the divided kingdom. To this end Antiochus paid particular attention to the Jews of Palestine. *Onias III, the high priest, was replaced in 173 by *Jason who had strong leanings toward the Hellenistic party in Jerusalem. In time the character of the Jewish capital itself was altered, with Jason undertaking "to register the Jerusalemites as citizens of Antioch" (II Macc. 4:9; on the legal status of Jerusalem under the government of the Hellenizers see V. Tcherikover, *Hellenistic Civilization and the Jews* (1959), 161ff.). Jason was eventually outbid for the office of high priest by Menelaus, who proved even more servile and prepared to carry out the most extreme Hellenization of Judea. In 168 Antiochus set out on his second expedition to Egypt. Wishful thinking probably promoted the spread of false rumors regarding the king's death, and as a result, Jason, who had fled to Transjordan, returned to Jerusalem and tried to reestablish his rule. On returning from Egypt, Antiochus, convinced that a rebellion had broken out against him, stormed the city, killed thousands of Jews, and sold thousands more into slavery. In their place, and especially in the citadel of Jerusalem (*Acra) which was erected on the instructions of Antiochus, a Greek community was set up, thus outwardly transforming the city into a foreign *polis* (city-state). By 167 the enforced Hellenization of the Jews reached its peak; the Jews were compelled, under penalty of death "to depart from the laws of their fathers, and to cease living by the laws of God. Further, the sanctuary in Jerusalem was to be polluted and called after Zeus Olympius" (II Macc. 6:1, 2). The nature of these decrees has puzzled most scholars and students of the Hellenistic period. Ancient polytheism for the most part was tolerant, and this particular brand of Hellenization was not applied by Antiochus to any segment of the non-Jewish population under his rule. It would seem, therefore, that religious oppression appeared to Antiochus to be the only means of achieving political stability in Palestine, since it was that country's religion, if anything, that was out of place in a predominantly Hellenized empire. It would be wrong, however, completely to disregard the nature of the king himself. His strange behavior, causing contemporaries to refer to him as *Epimanes* ("madman") instead of Epiphanes, obviously played a major part in the formation of such violent policies. In any case, Antiochus did not personally oversee the implementation of these policies. He died in the city of Tabae (Isfahan). He was succeeded by his nine-year-old son Antiochus V Eupator (Polybius 26:10; 31:3–4; Livius 41:19, 20; Diodorus 29:32; 31:16; for a summation of modern literature on Antiochus IV see Tcherikover, op. cit., 175–203).

(5) ANTIOCHUS V EUPATOR reigned only two years before being murdered by his cousin Demetrius, the son of Seleucus IV.

(6) ANTIOCHUS VII SIDETES (b. 164 B.C.E.), the son of *Demetrius I Soter and younger brother of *Demetrius II Nicator. During the early years of his reign (138–129) Antiochus was forced to overcome the usurper Tryphon. His confirmation, therefore, of the privileges granted by his predecessors to the Jews and Jerusalem (I Macc. 15:1ff.; Jos., Ant., 13:223ff.) was an obvious attempt to solicit the help of *Simeon the Hasmonean, the high priest. When it was clear, however, that he would defeat Tryphon, the king immediately relented and demanded the return of Jaffa, Gezer, and the citadel in Jerusalem to Seleucid rule. To enforce these demands, Antiochus sent the general Cendebaeus to Judea, but the latter was defeated by Judah and John, the sons of Simeon the Hasmonean. Antiochus probably instigated Simeon's murder in 134 by *Ptolemy the son of Abubus, for immediately afterward he laid siege to Jerusalem. The Jews, led by John *Hyrcanus, managed to hold out for two years, but were finally compelled to accept the harsh terms set by Antiochus. The king was thereupon free to turn eastward, and in his expedition against the Parthians, in which soldiers of John Hyrcanus also participated, met his death (129; Tcherikover, op. cit., 240–1, 250–1; Stern, op. cit., 122–4, 139–43).

(7) ANTIOCHUS IX CYZICENUS, son of Antiochus VII and half-brother of Antiochus VIII Grypus, with whom he competed for the Seleucid throne from 113–95 B.C.E. Cyzicenus was unsuccessful in two attempts to rescue the Samari-

tans from John Hyrcanus. In 107 *Samaria fell to the sons of Hyrcanus, *Antigonus and *Aristobulus I, and the two pursued Cyzicenus as far as *Beth-Shean (Scythopolis), where he finally succeeded in eluding them. The second attempt by the Syrian king to subdue the armies of Hyrcanus, this time with the aid of Ptolemy VIII Lathyrus of Egypt, was similarly rebuffed, and Antiochus retreated to Syria. In 95 B.C.E. Cyzicenus was defeated by Seleucus VI, the son of Grypus, and took his own life (Jos., Ant., 13:270ff.).

BIBLIOGRAPHY: Klausner, Bayit Sheni, index; Schuerer, Gesch, 1 (1901), 175ff.

[Isaiah Gafni]

ANTIPAS, HEROD (b. 20 B.C.E.), son of Herod by his Samaritan wife Malthace. Antipas was educated in Rome with his older brother *Archelaus. As the age difference between the two was not great, both were sent to Rome together to complete their education. Antipas was designated crown prince in place of Antipater, Herod's eldest son. Herod, however, changed his will shortly before his death and left to Antipas only Galilee and the Jewish portion of Transjordan. According to the final version of the will, Antipas was to have been subject to the authority of Archelaus, who received the kingship and dominion over all parts of the kingdom. After Herod's death, however, Antipas appealed to Augustus against the legality of this will and claimed the throne. Augustus confirmed Antipas as ruler over Galilee and Judean Transjordan and also confirmed the title, "*tetrarch," which had been given to him by Herod. Antipas rebuilt and fortified Sepphoris, which had been burnt in the war of Varus in 4 B.C.E., and made it his chief capital. In Transjordan he rebuilt Betharamphtha (biblical Beth-Haram, Bethramtha in the Talmud) which had also suffered seriously in the war, and named it Livias. After Augustus' death in 14 C.E. he renamed it Julias, in honor of the deceased emperor's wife Julia, who took this name as her husband had ordained in his will. He named his new capital, on the western shore of the Sea of Galilee, Tiberias, in honor of the emperor Tiberius. The city was splendidly built and the tetrarch paid no attention to the protests of his Jewish subjects, who regarded it as a place of defilement since it was built on the site of a cemetery. Tiberias was organized as a Hellenistic city with a city council. The exact date of the founding of Tiberias is unknown, although probably it was shortly after Tiberius' appointment as emperor (c. 14 C.E.), with a view to currying favor with him. Josephus states explicitly that there were close relations between Herod

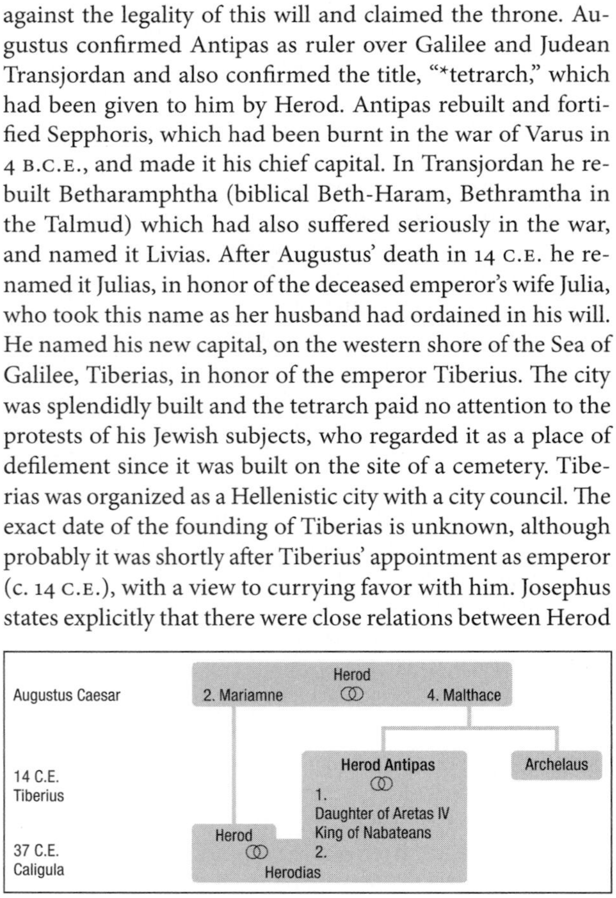

Antipas and Tiberius which were maintained until his death. The forbidden marriage (Lev. 18:16) of Antipas to Herodias, the wife of his brother Herod, the son of Mariamne, the high priest's daughter, stirred the resentment of the people against him. When John the Baptist dared to denounce this marriage publicly, he was executed in Machaerus at the command of Antipas. According to Josephus, however, the principal reason for the execution was Antipas' fear of political disturbances in the wake of John's appearance. His marriage to Herodias also led to war with *Aretas IV, king of the Nabateans, in 36 C.E. Antipas had previously married a daughter of Aretas, who fled to her father when she heard of the impending marriage between her husband and Herodias. In this war Antipas was defeated, and when Tiberius heard the news, he ordered Vitellius, governor of Syria, to go to Antipas' aid. In the spring of 37 C.E. Vitellius set out with his army to fight the Nabateans at Petra; at the request of the Jews he avoided passing through Judea. After the dismissal of the procurator, Pontius Pilate, he and Antipas set out alone for Jerusalem to ascertain the state of events there. Tiberius died four days later, and Vitellius interrupted his preparations for war against the Nabateans. Antipas had been the mediator between Rome and the Parthians. When a peace treaty between Rome and Artaban III, king of Parthia, was signed, Antipas informed Caesar before Vitellius, and thus aroused the wrath of the latter. With the accession of Caligula, the influence of Agrippa, Antipas' enemy, in Rome increased. Agrippa accused Antipas before the emperor of preparing for a war against Rome with Parthian assistance. Antipas came to Rome and tried in vain to prove to Caesar that this information was incorrect. He was exiled to Lugdunum and his property was confiscated. His domain was attached to Agrippa's kingdom.

BIBLIOGRAPHY: Jos., Ant., 18:27–28, 36–38, 102–5, 109–26, 240–55; Jos., Wars, 1:646, 664; 2:94–95, 182–3; Matt. 14:1–12; Mark 6:14–28; Luke 9:7–9; 13:31–32; 23:7–12; Acts 13:1; Klausner, Bayit Sheni, index; Schuerer, Gesch, 1 (1904[4]), 431ff.; F.W. Madden, *Coins of the Jews* (1881), 118ff.

[Abraham Schalit]

ANTIPATER (first century C.E.), the eldest son of Herod by his first wife Doris. After his marriage to Mariamne the Hasmonean, Herod sent Doris and Antipater away. But when Mariamne had been condemned to death and tension grew between her sons and Herod's other sons, Herod restored Antipater to court. From the moment he returned to his father's house, Antipater sought to annihilate the sons of Mariamne in order to attain the throne. As long as he was in Jerusalem, he informed on them to his father. He continued to inform against his half brothers even when he was sent by his father to Rome already as the designated crown prince (13 B.C.E.). This activity only ceased for a time when Augustus brought about a reconciliation between Herod and his sons, but in the end Antipater and his allies gained their object: Alexander and Aristobulus were executed on Herod's order and Antipater was designated as heir apparent (7 B.C.E.). But just as he had al-

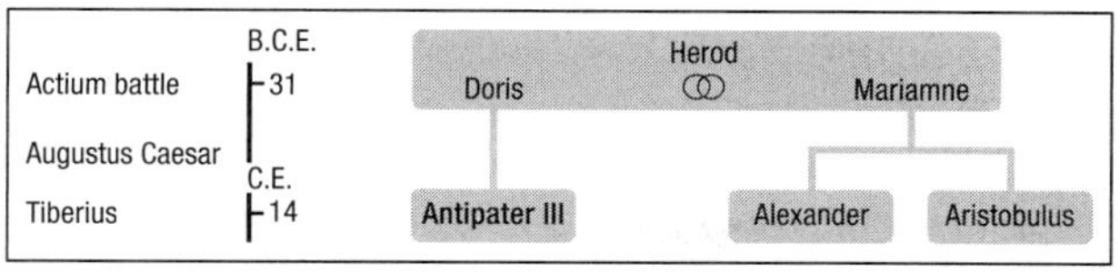

most reached his objective, his plot to murder the aged Herod was discovered. Antipater was condemned to death and the sentence carried out five days before Herod's own death.

BIBLIOGRAPHY: Jos., Ant., books 16–17; Jos., Wars, 1:552ff.; Klausner, Bayit Sheni, 4 (1963[5]), 153–69; Schuerer, Gesch, 1 (1901[4]), 407–14; H. Willrich, *Das Haus des Herodes* (1929), index.

[Abraham Schalit]

ANTIPATER II or **ANTIPAS** (d. 43 B.C.E.), governor of Edom in the time of Alexander Yannai and Salome Alexandra, son of Antipater I, and father of *Herod. Josephus states that Antipater I belonged to a distinguished Edomite family, the members of which had embraced Judaism in the days of John Hyrcanus. The statement of the historian, Nicholas of Damascus, that the family was descended from Jews who had returned from the Babylonian Exile is denied by Josephus. The Church Fathers give differing accounts of his origins. Eusebius states that Antipater was the son of a female slave in Ashkelon, that he was kidnapped as a child and carried off to Idumea where he was brought up as a Jew after the forced conversion of the Edomites in the reign of John Hyrcanus. It is probable that Josephus' account is to be preferred. Josephus depicts Antipater II as an ally of *Hyrcanus, son of Alexander Yannai, and as an opponent of the latter's brother *Aristobulus. Aristobulus was dependent on the military aristocracy which was directly opposed to Edomite influence. Even before the death of Salome Alexandra, Aristobulus had attempted to put his supporters in key governmental positions and this certainly aroused opposition. It seems clear, too, that Antipater feared that his position would be endangered in the event of Aristobulus coming to power. When Aristobulus drove Hyrcanus from the throne, Antipater, with Nabatean help, won a victory over Aristobulus who was forced to retreat to the Temple Mount. In return for their assistance Antipater promised to restore to the Nabateans 12 cities conquered by Alexander Yannai. Although Scaurus, one of Pompey's generals, intervened on the side of Aristobulus, Antipater's political position was not substantially changed, for he had previously been the mediator between the Romans and the Nabateans and had negotiated the reparations that the latter were to pay to Rome. During the rebellions of Alexander, the son of Aristobulus, Antipater supported the Roman governor Gabinius

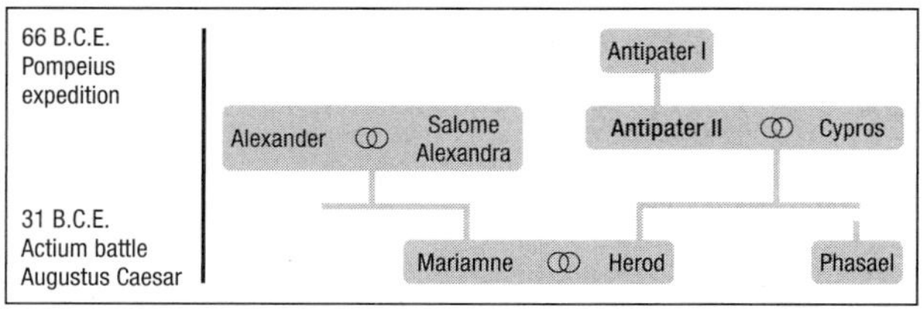

and held the position of "agent" or, according to another version, "overseer" of taxes in Judea. After Julius Caesar's defeat of Pompey, Antipater immediately aligned himself with the victor, and hastened to recruit Jewish and Nabatean soldiers to fight for him. He prevailed upon the Jews of Egypt to support Caesar, thus hastening his triumph over Egypt. When Caesar went to Syria in 47 B.C.E., he appointed Antipater regent of Judea, rejecting Mattathias Antigonus' claims to the throne of his fathers. Antipater thus became, in effect, the ruler of Judea, a position of power which he freely exercised. He gave his sons the most important offices of state: *Phasael was appointed governor of Jerusalem while Herod was sent to Galilee. With the arrival of Cassius in Syria, to wage war against Caesar's successors, Antipater placed himself at his disposal. He and his sons, Herod in particular, tried to raise the huge sums that Cassius required in the country. In 43 B.C.E. Antipater was poisoned but his policies were continued by his sons. Antipater was a cautious statesman who never presumed to act independently of his master, Hyrcanus, despite the fact that the government of the state was wholly in his hands.

BIBLIOGRAPHY: Jos., Ant., 14; Jos., Wars, 1; Juster, Juifs, 1 (1914), 135ff.; Schuerer, Gesch, 1 (1901[4]), 291ff.; R. Laqueur, *Der juedische Historiker Flavius Josephus* (1920), 148ff.; Klausner, Bayit Sheni, 3 (1950[2]), 215–7, 240–1, 251–7; A. Schalit, *Hordos ha-Melekh* (1964[3]), 13ff.

[Abraham Schalit]

ANTIPATRIS (Gr. Αντιπατρις), ancient Palestinian city in the valley of Kefar Sava on the coastal plain, close to the important route *Via Maris*. This was the site of biblical *Aphek, known also as Pegae in Hellenistic times, and perhaps as Arethusa from the time of Pompey. It was eventually rebuilt by Herod the Great in memory of his father Antipater (Jos., Ant., 16:142ff.). In Roman times Antipatris stood at the junction of important highways leading to Jerusalem, Caesarea, and Jaffa, and is often mentioned as a military campsite or as a stopover for travelers (Acts 23:31). It was the northern boundary of the territory of Judea (Git. 7:7). A vivid picture of Jewish life in Antipatris in the days of R. Johanan b. Zakkai is portrayed in *Derekh Ereẓ Rabbah*, 6. During the war against Rome, the Romans left Antipatris unharmed and Vespasian regulated its affairs much as he had done in Jabneh, Lydda, Timnah, and other places whose inhabitants had remained loyal to Rome. In the fourth century Antipatris declined in importance and is referred to as "a half-ruined townlet." In the Arab period it was known by the name of Abu Fuṭrus and during the period of transition from Umayyad to Abbasid rule, it achieved prominence as one of the towns that remained loyal to the Umayyads in 750.

Antipatris is today situated close to the modern town of *Rosh ha-Ayin (Ras al-ʿAyn), 3½ mi. (5 km.) east of Petaḥ Tikvah. Its many springs serve as sources of the *Yarkon River, for which reason Ras al-ʿAyn is also identified with the Hellenistic customs-post known as Πηγαί ("The Springs"). The castle erected there by the Crusaders was similarly called Le Toron aux Fontaines Sourdes. The ruins of a Turkish fort erected in the 17th century can still be seen. Earlier excavations at the site in 1961 revealed Roman and Hellenistic remains, and a Roman mausoleum as well. Extensive excavations were conducted at the site by M. Kochavi between 1975 and 1985, revealing part of a defensive system from the Early Bronze Age, a series of palaces from the Middle Bronze Age (IIA), destroyed in a conflagration in the mid-16th century B.C.E., two city walls from the Middle Bronze Age, a palace from the Late Bronze Age, remains of a Philistine settlement from the 12th century B.C.E., and Iron Age dwellings from the 10th and 8th centuries B.C.E. These excavations also brought to light important remains dating from the time of the city of Antipatris, including a street lined with shops that led to the forum, rebuilt at the time of Herod Agrippa I with the establishment of workshops instead. Following the Great Revolt the city fell into decline until the second century C.E.; the latter excavations have revealed segments of the *cardo maximus* street with an odeon situated at its southern end, as well as signs of a marketplace and a residential quarter. The city fell victim to a massive earthquake in the year 363 C.E.

BIBLIOGRAPHY: Avi-Yonah, Geog, 65, 128ff.; Press, Ereẓ, 1 (1951), 28ff. **ADD. BIBLIOGRAPHY:** M. Kochavi, *Aphek-Antipatris: Five Thousand Years of History* (1989); Y. Tsafrir, L. Di Segni, and J. Green, *Tabula Imperii Romani. Iudaea – Palaestina. Maps and Gazetteer.* (1994), 63.

[Michael Avi-Yonah / Shimon Gibson (2nd ed.)]

ANTISEMITISM, a term coined in 1879, from the Greek ἀντί = anti, and Σημ = Semite by the German agitator Wilhelm *Marr to designate the then-current anti-Jewish campaigns in Europe. "Antisemitism" soon came into general use as a term denoting all forms of hostility manifested toward the Jews throughout history. It is often qualified by an adjective denoting the specific cause, nature or rationale of a manifestation of anti-Jewish passion or action: e.g., "economic antisemitism," "social antisemitism," "racial antisemitism," etc.

In Antiquity

Prejudice against Jews appeared in antiquity almost exclusively in those countries which later became part of the Roman Empire. Some manifestations were noted in the Parthian Empire, which contained Babylonian Jewry, but such hatred never attained serious proportions. Josephus states it as a well-known fact that in the lands of the Babylonian exile antisemitism did not exist (Apion 1:71). In those countries that afterward formed part of the Roman Empire, a distinction must be drawn between Ereẓ Israel and the Diaspora.

IN EREẒ ISRAEL. Even in the days of David and Solomon the land of Israel contained a substantial Gentile population. In Hellenistic times it was primarily concentrated in the coastal towns and in certain districts of Transjordan, but the boundaries between the Jewish and non-Jewish regions were not fixed and the seeds of friction were ever present. Of particular importance, however, was the difference in occupations between the Jews and Gentiles of those areas. The Jewish population engaged principally in agriculture, particularly in small-scale farming; the non-Jewish population occupied itself primarily with commerce. The transit and sea trade was almost entirely in the hands of the inhabitants of the coastal cities, or of the Transjordanian cities situated along the routes that connected Syria, Asia Minor, and the regions of the Euphrates with the Arabian countries. The inhabitants of Ereẓ Israel who engaged in commerce, with connections abroad, were thus mainly non-Jewish. These Gentiles were therefore in close contact with the foreign powers in the region and were confident of their support; in Ereẓ Israel they were contemptuous of the Jewish population, whom they regarded as an isolated people that eschewed civilization and refrained from all contact with the outside world. Moreover, the non-Jews who dwelt in Ereẓ Israel knew that the Jews looked upon that land as their divine inheritance, and upon themselves as a unique and elevated people. In the eyes of the Jews, as these Gentiles knew, their pagan religions and practices rendered them "unclean"; intermarriage with them was forbidden and, as a consequence of the dietary laws, no real social intercourse was possible.

In normal times these two segments of the population dwelt alongside each other without any undue hostility. In time of crisis, however, relations deteriorated sharply. The first serious manifestation of antisemitism in history was the concentrated attack on the Jewish religion in the days of *Antiochus Epiphanes (175–164 B.C.E.). The immediate cause was anger by the Seleucids at the fact that the vast majority of Jews traditionally sided with the Ptolemies against the Seleucids. Tension was exacerbated still further by the image that Hellenistic rulers such as Antiochus had of themselves. Their role was not only political; they were also to be torchbearers of the ideals of *Hellenism within their dominions. The seeming unfriendliness of the Jews toward all Gentiles, and their refusal to adopt any other religion, was therefore seen as an obstacle to the realization of this cultural mission. An echo of this attitude can be seen in the account of the negotiations that took place outside Jerusalem in 133 B.C.E., when John Hyrcanus was compelled to yield to Antiochus Sidetes after the latter had besieged the capital for a year. Antiochus Sidetes' officers counseled him to seize the opportunity to conquer the city and completely destroy the Jewish people, since the Jews were the only people in the world that refused to associate with other peoples. Pressing the point, they reminded Antiochus Sidetes of the course taken by Antiochus Epiphanes, who undertook to abrogate those laws of the Torah that he regarded as inimical to humanity. To this end, he had sacrificed a swine on the altar at Jerusalem and ordered that juices from the sacrificial flesh be sprinkled over the books containing the statutes that were directed against the Gentile world (Diodorus, *Bibliotheca* 34:1, 1ff.).

This reiterated insistence on the alleged antipathy of the Jews to other nations is best understood against the background of the peculiar conditions and circumstances obtaining in the Hellenistic period. No other nation at that time denied the gods of its neighbors; on the contrary, it recognized them, identifying them with its own deities. This pan-religiosity was used with considerable success by the Hellenistic ruling authorities to create a social bond between the various peoples in their domains. None of the peoples refrained from dining at one table with their neighbors and from partaking of the sacrifices offered to their gods, except the Jews. None of the peoples refused to send gifts to its neighbors' temples, except the Jews. None of the peoples was unequivocally hostile to intermarriage, except the Jews. They characterized it as a misanthropy in general, and as a flagrant denial of the Hellenic principle of the unity of mankind in particular.

As the Hasmonean kingdom expanded and established its dominion over the whole land, its kings occasionally adopted a policy of political and religious oppression vis à vis the inhabitants of the pagan cities of Palestine, who had sided earlier with Antiochus Epiphanes and had joined the war of Antiochus Sidetes against the Jews. Against this background, libels began to circulate, denying that the Jews had any right to remain in the land. Underlying these libels were Egyptian legends concerning shepherd kings who had once ruled over Egypt and oppressed its people but who had subsequently been expelled. There were also stories about a leprous or unclean people who had been banished from Egypt so that the land and its temples, which they had defiled, might be purified. These legends were now related to the biblical tale of the Exodus; the composite version was that the Jews had been expelled from Egypt because of their uncleanliness and had continued to separate themselves from the other nations in Ereẓ Israel. If such was their origin and the reason for their present habits, they had no legitimate claims on this or any other land, or on being unique and elevated.

Descriptions of the Jews as homeless wanderers are found in the allegations of Antiochus Sidetes' officers, who regarded their nomadic status as justification for destroying them. The general motif, however, is undoubtedly much older, having been employed by non-Jews to counter the Jewish claim that Ereẓ Israel was the inheritance of the Lord and that idolaters had no share in it. However, if in the period preceding the Hasmonean conquests this Jewish conception of Ereẓ Israel made little practical difference to its non-Jewish inhabitants, in the Hasmonean epoch it became the justification for eradicating idolatry from the land, and not idolatry alone. The sins of the Canaanites, as they are enumerated in the Wisdom of Solomon (12:3ff.), an apocryphal book composed in this period, were depicted as so offensive to the Holy Land that their perpetrators would have to be cast out if they did not mend their ways and conduct themselves in a manner compatible with the sanctity of Ereẓ Israel. This view, in turn, aroused more animosity against the Jews.

With the consolidation of Roman rule in Palestine there was apparently little reason for the Jews of Palestine to obstruct the policy pursued by Rome on its eastern borders. Even the attempts at such obstruction in the time of *Antiochus II (e.g., his approach to the Parthians), and by the war party during the war which led to the destruction of the Second Temple, constituted no great danger to Rome. Any anti-Judaism which then was associated with Roman foreign policy was not caused by militancy or even by revolt on the part of Palestinian Jewry. Even in the relations between the Jewish and non-Jewish settlements in Palestine, or Palestina, as the Romans named the region. Rome created a kind of equilibrium, and clashes on any large scale between the two sides ceased completely. Fresh fuel for antisemitic excesses, however, was provided by emperor-worship, which had begun to assume the form of a permanent political institution in all the countries of the Roman Empire from the time of Augustus onward. From the views of contemporaries to this worship, it appears not to have been regarded as an act of religious homage to the emperor but as an expression of loyalty to the state, which was itself endowed with religious sanctity. The refusal by the Jews to accept the imperial cult in any form was thus equated in the minds of many Romans with a refusal to recognize the authority of the state, and as a result, the belief gradually began to take hold in the pagan world that the Jews had no respect for whatever was held in esteem by the rest of humanity. For example, when the Jews were ordered by Caligula to erect and worship an image of the emperor in Jerusalem, but his assassination spared the Jews of Palestine and other parts of the Roman Empire a bitter conflict with the imperial authorities.

IN THE DIASPORA. The Jews of the Roman Empire (unlike their later-day descendants in the late Middle Ages) were not, as a rule, restricted in regard to place of residence; according to the testimony of reliable sources, there was no part of the empire where Jews were not to be found. The Jews formed up to 10–12 percent, approximately, of the population of the empire, and since an appreciable portion of the Jews in the Diaspora were found in the cities, it follows that they played an important role in the economic life of the countries in which they lived (Jos., Ant. 14:115). It would also seem that the Jews were as unrestricted in their choice of occupation as they were in their choice of residence. In regard to their legal position, no discrimination was made between them and the other citizens of the empire, the extent of their rights being dependent, as a rule, on the class to which they belonged. In some cases Jews even received favored treatment in deference to their religious needs. The observance of Sabbath and the fulfillment of other religious precepts led them to seek exemptions from certain civic obligations which were imposed upon the rest of the populace. According to Josephus (Ant. 14:187, 190ff.), the prerogatives granted the Jews were protected by special decrees of the kings of Persia and Macedonia, and even the Roman rulers honored them, without thereby arousing popular resentment. Still, it should be taken into consideration that Jews maintained the same habits outside Ereẓ Israel as well.

About the first century B.C.E., however, several factors brought about a radical change. In Egypt, particularly in Alexandria, strong opposition to Roman rule became manifest, for many reasons. The upper strata of Alexandrian Egyptians had particular cause for complaint. They had directed the country's policies during the reign of the Ptolemies but they were now, under Rome, out of power. They were thus reduced to a level no higher than that of the Jews, who were now competing with the former ruling class for Roman favor. Relations inevitably deteriorated.

Illuminating in this respect are the orders issued by the emperor Claudius soon after the restoration of quiet in Alexandria, following the turbulence resulting from the riots organized by the Greeks against the Jewish community there. In his injunction to the citizens of Alexandria and the Syrian cities (Jos., Ant. 19:279ff.) Claudius fully confirms the original privileges granted to the Jews to allow them to keep the precepts of the Torah without let or hindrance. However, in his edict to all the countries of the empire, in which Claudius addresses himself to the Jews as well, after reaffirming their privileges, he declares: "I enjoin upon them also by these presents to avail themselves of this kindness in a more reasonable spirit, and not to set at nought the beliefs about the gods held by other peoples, but to keep their own laws" (Ant. 19:286ff., especially 290). Claudius, in an edict to the Alexandrians which has been preserved in a papyrus (published by Idris Bell), is even more explicit. In it, after stating that the Jews are completely at liberty to observe the injunctions of the Torah, Claudius warns that if they will not content themselves with the rights accorded them, he will employ against them all such means as should be used against people who spread "a general plague throughout the world."

Despite the friction between Judaism and the centers of Hellenistic-Roman culture in Egypt, Syria, and cities of the Roman Empire, where intellectual and economic circles were adverse to the Jews, no change was made in the Roman legal code. However, Judaism and the Jews were increasingly described in those circles as flouting not only the law, but all of human society. Though the elements of such characterizations had all already appeared during the struggle between the Hasmonean kings and their adversaries in Palestine, in the first century C.E. they were arranged into a kind of connected rationale of anti-Jewishness.

In common with the courtiers of Antiochus Sidetes two centuries earlier, many Greek authors of the first century C.E. portrayed the Jewish people as the descendants of a mob of lepers, a contaminated rabble, whom the Egyptians had cast out to purge themselves of their defilement and who had continued to pursue in Judea, their adopted home, the pattern that accorded with their degenerate and outcast state. Thus, the portrayal went on, as unclean people who had been afflicted with leprosy they shunned the flesh of swine, this creature being more prone than others to contract this disease. The observance of the Sabbath and the worship of God by the Jews in general were interpreted in a similar vein. No stranger was permitted to approach the Temple in Jerusalem because human beings were sacrificed there. A number of writers of the first century C.E. attempted to portray Jewish life in this manner, the most prominent among them being *Chaeremon, Nero's teacher; *Lysimachus of Alexandria, the head of the library at Alexandria, and *Apion, who surpassed all the others in the crudeness of his fabrications. The destruction of the Second Temple added fuel to the fire. In the period immediately preceding this event, visions of the redemption of the world from the Roman yoke in a form closely corresponding to that of Jewish eschatology began to spread within sections of pagan society. The attraction of the idea of redemption, with its attendant liberation from the ruling power, was a great boon to the propagation of the message of Judaism, the recognition of the unity of God being inextricably interwoven with the redemptive vision. The destruction of the Temple at this juncture produced a sharp counterreaction to this ferment, many of the Jewish adversaries seizing upon it and upon the catastrophe that befell Judea and the Jewish communities in Alexandria, Antioch, and Cyrene as evidence that the Jews were hated by God and had received their due punishment at His hands. According to a story from an antisemitic source (Philostratus, *Vita Apolloni*, 6:29), when representatives of the peoples living in proximity to Judea came and presented to Titus a wreath of victory for his destruction of Jerusalem, he declined to accept it, saying that he had only lent a hand to God, who had revealed his wrath against the Jews. Of what worth was a doctrine of world redemption propagated by a nation forsaken by its god?

The same period saw a deterioration in the attitude of a number of the representatives of the Roman aristocracy toward Jews and Judaism. The factors responsible for this change stemmed, on the one hand, from the conditions prevailing in Rome and among its ruling classes, and, on the other, from the continuing influence, even after the year 70, exerted by Judaism upon some sections of Roman society. Emperors of the type of Nero and Domitian snuffed out the last glimmer of freedom. Sycophancy and subservience dominated the atmosphere. As they dreamt of a purer past which ought to be restored, many Roman intellectuals felt hampered by the multiplicity of foreign cults in imperial Rome and by the powerful influence of Judaism, which appeared to them as subversive of the entire life pattern of Rome. The Jewish community in Rome had already felt the barbs of a number of Roman writers (e.g., *Horace, *Martial), but the first Roman authors to deal with the Jews did not rise to unusual heights of invective. Even *Cicero, the first writer to discuss the Jews seriously (in his speech on behalf of Lucius Valerius Flaccus, the proconsul of Asia Minor, in 62 B.C.E., he attacked the Jews of Palestine and the Diaspora, and, in particular, those of Rome), did not carry his criticism of the Jews beyond the bounds customary among the pleaders in Rome who tried to discredit a litigant in the interests of their client. It may be well to point out here that Cicero, in attacking the Gauls in defense of one of his clients, leveled such grave charges against them and their religion that, by comparison, the accusations he made against the Jews were not unduly severe (cf. the fragments of Cicero's speech *Pro Pontio*).

The end of the first century C.E. witnessed a radical change. Those who saw Rome's salvation in the resuscitation of civic liberty, in the revival of the Roman attribute of *virtus*, and in the renewal of the ancient Roman ideals of heroism and justice, pointed to the danger inherent in the Jewish attempt to swamp the lower and middle classes with new ideas. They sought to rally the public to their standard by declaring the struggle against the propagators of such ideas a life and death necessity. One of the most capable and outspoken of these agitators was Cornelius *Tacitus. He cited all the libelous fabrications against Jews to be culled from Greek anti-Jewish literature. His presentation of the subject as an inquiry into the various accounts of the Jews and their doctrines to the end of discovering that most consonant with historic reality is but a futile attempt to mask his single, overriding purpose, to prove the Jews a mere rabble, hateful to the gods and men alike, and capable of gaining adherents for their degenerate cause only in a Rome that had become a breeding ground for all that was vile and abhorrent (Tacitus, *Historiae* 5:1–13; cf. also his *Annales* 15:44).

*Juvenal followed closely in the footsteps of Tacitus. In one of his poems he portrayed a convert to Judaism as estranged from Roman society and from the members of his family, as unprepared to guide a person who has lost his way if he is not an observer of the Law of Moses, and as unwilling to give a thirsty man a drink if he is uncircumcised (Juvenal, *Saturae* 14:96ff.). General Roman policy toward the Jews was not greatly affected by the diatribes of writers such as Tacitus or Juvenal. It is not inconceivable, however, that the emperor Hadrian's anti-Jewish policy, which represented only a brief episode in the history of Roman legislation in regard to the Jews, was influenced to a certain extent by the circles in which Tacitus and his associates moved.

[Joseph Heinemann / Joshua Gutmann]

The Early Christian Period

The anti-Judaism of the pagan world, whether expressed in outbreaks of violence and rioting or in ideological diatribes and libels, did not hold such fateful consequences for Jews as that which later crystallized within Christianity. The crucial factor here was not so much Christianity's refusal to countenance any other faith, as its commitment to an idea of redemption so manifestly in opposition to that of the Jews as to render their mutual coexistence inconceivable. With the political triumph of Christianity, the old pagan image of the Jews as a people hated by God was resuscitated, but the reasons for God's hatred were changed to suit the new circumstances. Under the stigma of this image, the Jews were gradually excluded from every sphere of political influence and their political and civic rights were increasingly denied them, until in the end such rights were almost entirely a thing of the past.

Since Christianity originated as a dissident Jewish sect, certain judgments of Judaism in the New Testament must be examined in this light. Such, for instance, is the case with the writings of Saul (Paul) of Tarsus. In his Epistle to the Romans he protests against the idea of God's rejection of the Jews: "They are beloved for the sake of their forefathers" (Rom. 11:28): "I myself am an Israelite, a descendant of Abraham, a member of the tribe of Benjamin" (Rom. 11:1). Of the Gospels – easily the most popular writings in the New Testament – the last chronologically, namely Matthew and John, are the most hostile to Judaism, which they criticize from the standpoint of an outsider. In addition, these Gospels already contain the two cardinal themes appearing later in Christian antisemitism: the Jews themselves are made to admit their collective responsibility for the crucifixion of the son of God ("Then answered all the people and said, His blood be on us, and on our children": Matt. 27:25), and are identified with the powers of evil ("Ye are of your father the devil, and your will is to do your father's desires": John 8:44).

Regarded by the Jews as members of a heretical sect, the first Christians stood aloof from the Jewish struggle against Rome. The Gospels' description of the crucifixion, in minimizing the role of Pilate, attests a desire to gain the goodwill of the Roman authorities, while the destruction of Jerusalem in 70 C.E. provided obvious proof of the divine anger and chastisement. In sum, the evolution of Christian anti-Judaism reflects the spread of the new faith among pagan circles and a progressive withdrawal from the ancient faith. The growing hostility was also fed by the rivalry for proselytes. Since traditional Judaism continued to attract pagan elements, the newly Christianized groups were highly susceptible to its influence. The young church, therefore, which declared itself to be the true Israel, or "Israel according to the spirit," heir to the divine promises, found it essential to discredit the "Israel according to the flesh," to prove that God had cast away His people and transferred His love to the Christians. From the outset, therefore, Christian anti-Judaism was an original manifestation: it differed from the traditional tensions between Israel and the nations and did not merely reflect them. Obliged to contest Israel's historic heritage and title, and confronted in addition by a vigorous rabbinical counter-propaganda, the church unremittingly concentrated its attention on the Jews and Judaism. The anti-Jewish theories developed by the *Church Fathers are preeminently variations or extensions of the first accusations leveled in the Gospels. They are developed with particular vehemence by the Greek Fathers who exercised their apostolic authority in regions where the Jewish population was large and influential. Certain polemics already afford an insight into the psychology of the early bishops, whose judeophobia was on the same scale as their religious fervor. To Gregory of Nyssa and John Chrysostom, love of Jesus and hatred for his presumed executioners were indistinguishable. These polemics also testify to the existence of a Jewish population which mixed with its Gentile neighbors on an equal footing. In the fourth century, John Chrysostom characteristically reproached these Jews with extravagance, gluttony, and dissolute living, as well as with deicide.

After Christianity became the official religion of the Roman state (in 321 C.E.) the emperors began to translate the concepts and claims of the theologians into practice. The ancient privileges granted to the Jews were withdrawn, rabbinical jurisdiction was abolished or severely curtailed, and proselytism was prohibited and made punishable by death, as were relations with Christian women. Finally, Jews were excluded from holding high office or pursuing a military career. The rapid disintegration of the Roman Empire in the fifth century, however, postponed the principal effects of this legal forfeiture of rights. As the model that was to inspire the clerical and lay legislators of the Middle Ages, its repercussions on Judeo-Christian relations only become apparent centuries later. The persistence of Judaism, seemingly a contradiction of the Christian conception of the church as *Verus Israel*, "the true Israel," led the great theologians, notably *Augustine, to elaborate the doctrine that represents the Jews as the nation which was a "witness" to the truth of Christianity. Their existence was further justified by the service they rendered to the Christian truth in attesting through their humiliation the triumph of the church over the synagogue. "Unintelligent, they possess intelligent books"; they are thus condemned to perpetual servitude. A further variation, reversing a biblical image, depicts the Jews as Esau and the Christians as Jacob. They are also Cain, guilty of fratricide, cursed and marked with a sign for eternity. However, the hostility of this allegorization also implies a nascent tendency on the part of the church to protect the Jews, since "if someone killed Cain, Cain would be revenged sevenfold." Thus the ideological arsenal of Christian antisemitism was completely established in antiquity. However, from the social standpoint the deterioration of the Jewish position was only beginning, and it seems clear that in the early period virulent judeophobia was mainly limited to the clergy.

In Early Islam

From the theological standpoint, the Koran also contained attacks against the Jews, as they refused to recognize Muhammad as the prophet sent by God. In certain respects, Muhammad utilized the Bible in a manner similar to that of the Christian theologians, since he found in it the announcement of his own coming, but at the same time he also used the New Testament in the same way. As a result, Jews and Christians, although "infidels," are both regarded by the Koran as "Peoples of the Book," "possessing Scriptures."

Since Islam spread by force of arms rather than by spiritual propaganda, it did not generally aspire, at least initially, to conquer souls. Therefore, it displayed greater tolerance than Christianity. The religions of the two "Peoples of the Book" were officially recognized, and a special status combining subjection and protection was evolved for them. Apart from the distinguishing colors of their insignia, the *dhimmi* ("protected") Jews and Christians were subjected to the same measures and were obliged to pay the same tax. On various occasions they were included in the same persecutions. But in the regions where Islam reigned, the forms of anti-Judaism and anti-Christianity each evolved in their own way. When Islam began to spread, the majority of the subjected territories were Christian, and in them Greek remained the official language for some time. One source of antisemitism in Islam, therefore, may derive from ancient Christian anti-Judaism. The celebrated controversialist Al-Jahiz (mid-ninth century) cites in an anti-Christian polemic four reasons why the faithful held a better opinion of the Christians than of the Jews: the Christians wielded power in Byzantium and elsewhere; unlike the Jews, they engaged in secular sciences; they assimilated more easily and adopted Muslim names, and they engaged in more respectable occupations. In the same period the historian Al-Tabari observed that "the Christians bear witness against the Jews morning and night." Thus, a number of anti-Jewish traditions and legends from Christian folklore penetrated, with appropriate adaptations, into that of Islam.

However, the concepts relating to ritual purity and dietary laws, of similar inspiration for both Jews and Muslims, as well as the observance of circumcision, drew them together in that they excluded or lessened certain inhibitory phobias such as the fear of pollution. In addition, Muslim revelation was not founded on the biblical canon and could not become a ground of contention, thus excluding one source of polemics and oppression. In sum, the term antisemitism, which becomes a particularly blatant semantic misnomer when used in connection with the Arab world, also regarded as "Semitic" can be employed only with qualifications in reference to Islam.

From the 12th century, the expeditions of the Crusades aggravated the condition of Christians in the Orient. Persecutions were followed by forced mass conversions to Islam. In many regions the Jews remained the only "infidels" with exceptional status, so that their situation became more vulnerable. In North Africa and Muslim Spain they were also fiercely persecuted (period of the *Almohads). Yet it is from this period that the position of the Jews in western Christendom progressively deteriorated, and until the modern era, Jewish migration usually proceeded from Christian to Islamic countries. But migratory phenomena, like the frequency or intensity of persecutions, are imperfect indicators of a collective attitude, and literature provides a better conspectus: Although in Islamic literature and folklore the Jew is often depicted in an unfavorable light – frequently accused of malevolence toward non-Jews, or even of plotting their damnation – he is only in exceptional cases invested with the satanic character and attributes frequent in Christian literature. There are Islamic literary sources in the medieval age in which the contemporary Jew is endowed with positive characteristics. In the modern period the position of the Jew in Islamic countries, although varying according to region and historical circumstance, has tended to deteriorate. The most notorious persecutions, in *Yemen in 1697, and in *Meshed, Iran in 1839, were perpetrated by Shi'ites. The *Yahud* confined to his ghetto – until recently in Yemen and even up to the 1970s in certain *mellahs* in Morocco – appeared to the Muslim an object of contempt rather than of hatred.

The Middle Ages

Jews had appeared in Western Europe from the beginning of the Christian era. At the commencement of the Middle Ages, no sign of particular animosity toward them was discernible. The clerical anti-Jewish polemics of the period deplored the influence the Jews exerted on the simple people and pointed to the existence of cordial, sometimes intimate, Judeo-Christian relations. Characteristic are the epistles of the ninth-century Christian reformer Archbishop *Agobard: "Things have reached a stage where ignorant Christians claim that the Jews preach better than our priests… some Christians even celebrate the Sabbath with the Jews and violate the holy repose of Sunday… Men of the people, peasants, allow themselves to be plunged into such a sea of errors that they regard the Jews as the only people of God, and consider that they combine the observance of a pure religion and a truer faith than ours."

The *Church Councils continually legislated to prevent these contacts. Ecclesiastical propaganda seems to have produced its first fruits at the beginning of the 11th century, when persecutions and expulsions were recorded in Rouen, Orleans, Limoges, and Mainz. A persecution inflicted at the time on Christians in the Orient was used as a pretext, and, apparently dating from the same period is the fable depicting the Jews as legionaries of the Anti-Christ. However, the crucial event was the First Crusade (1096). Religious excitation commingled with greed for gain. As bands of crusaders set out to recapture the sepulcher of Jesus they were prompted to wreak vengeance on Jesus' legendary enemies and killers and attacked the Jewish quarters of German and French towns along their way. The massacres perpetrated during the summer of 1096 made a lasting impression on both Christians and Jews. The tradition of sacrifice, **Kiddush ha-Shem*, was expressed in collective suicides to avoid forced conversion.

European economic life began to revive in the 12th century. Although the Christian guilds which began to flourish in the cities did not admit Jews, an action which had unfavorable repercussions on their commercial activities, the economic resurgence in Europe considerably increased credit operations, against which the church began to adopt measures. The church regarded the practice of *usury as endangering the eternal salvation of its flock, and opposed the overt and authorized practice of usury, i.e., the acceptance of pledges, with particular severity. Being inevitable in contemporary economic conditions, however, the church subsequently endorsed the practice of usury by the Jews, for according to the prevalent opinion their souls were lost in any case. The doctrine and practice which thus spread constituted a major source of antisemitism for, in general, agrarian societies tended to leave the practice of usury to foreigners (those who were not "brothers"). The Jew, already stigmatized as an infidel and deicide, was now regarded by most as the direct antagonist of the Christian, and thus began to symbolize the hostile stranger *par excellence*. The process of differentiation was slow, as shown by the legend of a miraculous conversion around 1220 which places the following question in the mouth of a little girl: "Why is it that the Jews and the Christians have different names since they speak the same language and wear the same clothes?" Thus the Jew was distinguished primarily by his name, and in contemporary idiom the verb "to judaize" meant both to be a heretic and to lend money on interest.

Secular princes and church prelates were in fact the Jews' silent partners in the practice of usury. Although this partnership multiplied the sources of internal antagonism among Christians, the Jews were assured of an influential protection justified by patristic doctrines: the monarchs of the Holy Roman Empire regarded the Jews as serfs of the chamber (*servi camerae). Thomas *Aquinas considered them condemned to perpetual servitude because of their crime, but they were not to be deprived of the necessities of life. As a later scholastic, Angelo di Chivasso (1411–1495), said: "to be a Jew is a crime, not, however, punishable by a Christian."

Each renewed preaching for the Crusades roused anti-Jewish excesses, despite the protection afforded by the ecclesiastical and lay authorities. Religious consciousness in the masses intensified, and the evolution of theological thinking tended to emphasize and particularize the Jewish role as the scapegoat of Christianity. The 12th and 13th centuries saw the crystallization of the doctrine of transubstantiation, whereby the flesh and blood of Christ become present in the consecrated Host and wine – a doctrine definitively stated at the Fourth Lateran *Council (1215). As a result, the eucharistic cult acquired concrete character. Miraculous tales in connection with the Host, proliferated, frequently of *Host desecration by the Jews, and the *blood libel also began to inflict its ravages. These two closely connected allegations both relate to the delusion that a criminal conspiracy was being fabricated by the Jews against Jesus and the Christians. Psychologists have explained this suspicion as the transference of a guilt complex on the part of Christian communicants who attacked Jews. In partaking of the flesh and blood, they sought to identify themselves with the God-man who had taken upon himself the sins of the world, but they were unable to attain this identification satisfactorily. The resultant feeling of culpability could well be projected onto the "witness" people: the Jews were the people of God, but the only group to remain outside the universal communion of Christians.

The Fourth Lateran Council also promulgated a canon requiring the Jews to wear a distinguishing mark: the decision was intended to make any intimate relations between Jews and Christians impossible. The form of mark was not specified. In practice, the Jews in Latin countries were made to adopt a disk sewn onto their clothing, and in the Germanic countries a distinctive hat. Characteristically, contemporary iconography also depicts the biblical patriarchs, as well as Christian heretics of all kinds, in this dress. The appearance of the Jewish *badge also helped to propagate fables that showed the Jews as physically different from other men. The badge, or patch, became popularly known as the yellow badge, yet colors and forms varied in the Christian as well as in the Muslim world, where markings to distinguish the non-Muslim seem to have been introduced as early as the eighth century. Other features ascribed include a tail and horns – the attributes of the devil – and a distinctive smell (*foetor judaicus*), the converse of "the odor of sanctity."

During the 13th century the economic position of the Jews, and consequently the protection from which they benefited, was impaired by the development of finance on an international scale in Italy by, e.g., the Florentine and Siennese banks, and by the Lombards in France. The kings of England found that they could now dispense with the services of the Jews, and expelled them in 1290. In 1306 the first general expulsion from France took place. *Expulsions and massacres also followed in the German towns. The mass expulsions helped to perpetuate the image of Jewish homelessness, of the *Wandering Jew condemned to roam from country to country, in the eyes of the masses. At the beginning of the 14th century the specter of conspiracy against Christianity found new expression in the popular belief that the wells were being poisoned by the Jews. It is necessary to draw a distinction between these myths of a popular demonology, which the church itself did not endorse, but on the contrary combated, and the clerical anti-Jewish tradition. Apart from the religious and economic factors referred to above, persistent agencies of religious excitation were the development of a literature written in the vernacular and the growing popularity of the "Passion plays," which reenacted the crucifixion. Passion plays took place annually, lasted several days, and presented the cruelty and perfidy of the Jewish executioners in a highly realistic fashion.

Very often the established lay and ecclesiastical authorities continued to protect the Jews The most implacable adversaries of the Jews were now recruited among the rising middle class, and particularly among the mendicant Franciscan and Dominican orders. The Italian anti-Jewish Franciscan preachers John of *Capistrano and *Bernardino da Feltre, at whose instigation the institution of the *Monte di Pietà spread rapidly, and the Dominican Vincente *Ferrer in Spain, were especially vituperative. In Spain, the slow pace of the Christian reconquest – a process lasting from the 11th to the 15th centuries – enabled the Jews to continue to benefit from a privileged situation. Thus the conceptions current in the rest of Europe took time to spread to the Peninsula. It was not until the end of the 14th century that the preaching of Archdeacon Fernando Martinez of Seville set in motion a wave of bloody persecutions. The numerical and social importance of Spanish Jewry resulted in a different evolution, particularly the phenomenon of Crypto-Judaism practiced by the *Conversos. The Castilian *Inquisition was founded in 1478 to eradicate it. In 1492 Jews of the faith were expelled from Spain after a preliminary blood libel trial – the case of Nino de la Guardia – had been staged.

Poland, where a Christian middle class was slow to develop, became the principal country of refuge for European Jewry at the end of the Middle Ages. Russia, however, followed a different course in consequence of a religious schism which menaced Russian Orthodoxy at the end of the 14th century. This "judaizing heresy" predicated in an extreme form the tendencies of return to the Old Testament present in the Reformation movements of Western Europe. It acquired followers at the court of Moscow but was rapidly stifled. As a result, access to Russia was barred to Jews hereafter. Religious struggle was thus the starting point for the traditional judeophobia of the ruling Russian dynasties.

In general, popular susceptibility to antisemitism developed in the Middle Ages. It was henceforth perpetuated by linguistic usage and religious instruction. In all languages the term "Jew" and its derivatives had assumed a derogatory significance. Religious instruction by the catechism, practically the only form of popular education until a later period, instilled hostility against the "executioners of Christ" into the souls of children. "If it is incumbent upon a good Christian to detest the Jews, then we are all good Christians," Erasmus stated ironically at the beginning of the 16th century.

The Reformation

The Reformation had important complex and even contradictory repercussions on the evolution of antisemitism. One branch of Protestantism, namely Calvinism and the sects or movements influenced by it, proved less judeophobic than Catholicism until the 20th century. The other branch, Lutheranism, became increasingly antisemitic. How may this divergency be explained? It is as difficult to give a complete answer as it is to establish the exact relationship – a problem posed by Max *Weber and his school –between the "Protestant ethic" and "the capitalist spirit" or modern mentality. From the outset Calvinism and its derivatives emphasized individual responsibility, embracing social values and energetic moral action. To Lutheranism, on the other hand, justification by faith implied a renunciation of civic responsibility, and hostility to active faith (or "salvation through works"), which Luther himself described as *juedischer Glaube* ("Jewish faith"). At the end of his life the German reformer vilified the Jews in violent pamphlets which could not fail to exert their influence. Conversely, the role played by the Old Testament in Calvinism led the Puritan sects to identify themselves with the Jews of the Bible and reflected favorably on their attitude toward contemporary Jewry. The French Calvinists were a special case: themselves persecuted until the French Revolution, their sympathies were traditionally pro-Jewish, an outlook retained to a considerable extent to the present day.

An immediate consequence of the Reformation was to aggravate the position of the Jews in regions which remained Catholic. The popes of the Counter-Reformation were determined to restore ecclesiastical usages and the strict application of canon law. One result was that from the second half of the 16th century ghettos were introduced, at first in Italy and afterward in the Austrian Empire. This segregation then served as a convenient additional demonstration of the error of Judaism: "A Jewish ghetto is a better proof of the truth of the religion of Jesus Christ than a whole school of theologians," declared the 18th-century Catholic publicist G.B. Roberti. In France, the celebrated Bossuet had expressed analogous views in the 17th century. With the advent of the Counter-Reformation, therefore, the theses of Augustine and Thomas Aquinas regarding the Jews were applied to the letter. However, in the Low Countries, which had been freed of Spanish domination, the Jews could settle freely. They also began to settle in Great Britain and its colonies, and in particular North America, from the time of Cromwell.

Spain after 1492

Traditional Christian conceptions condemned the Jews because their faith was erroneous and strenuous efforts were made to convert them, but the mass conversion in Spain in the 15th century resulted in transference of the customary hostility to the converts and to their real or suspected descendants, the New Christians. In other words, religious antisemitism, far from disarmed by the disappearance of Jews of the faith, transformed itself into racial antisemitism. The Inquisition gradually stamped out Crypto-Judaism. However, statutes promulgated in Spain made "purity of blood" (*limpieza de sangre*) a new criterion to bar entry of the New Christians whose faith was suspect, to certain guilds, and to certain military and religious orders. This discrimination, sanctioned by Emperor Charles v, spread to the military academies and universities and persisted until the Napoleonic Wars. The law involved detailed genealogical research and contributed to the obsession with the code of honor and hidalgoism characteristic of old-time Spain. Since New Christians were traditionally concentrated in productive and commercial occupations and in crafts, the contempt with which they were held was connected with these callings. Such an attitude can be considered a major cause of Spanish economic decline in modern times. Vestiges of this attitude toward the New Christians still persist in the Balearic islands, affecting the *Chuetas of Palma de Majorca. Needless to say, the determinant of "purity of blood" was not based on actual religious, cultural, or even biological differences, but on the illusion fostered by the Old Christians that such a difference existed.

[Leon Poliakov]

The Enlightenment

For as long as Christianity held unchallenged sway in Europe, Jews could exist only on the margin of European social life. With the coming of the 18th-century Enlightenment, however, their isolation slowly began to crumble. A new class of bourgeois intellectuals – the *philosophes* – denounced Christianity in the name of Deism, or "natural religion," and ushered in the secularism of the modern era. As a result of their efforts, for the first time in centuries the status of the Jews became a matter for widespread debate. Many *philosophes* found it only natural to sympathize with the Jews. Not only were Jews the oppressed people *par excellence* in a century which prided itself on its concern for justice, but they were also the most notorious victims of Christian intolerance, which the Enlightenment was sworn to destroy. Accordingly, protests against the persecution of Jews – and especially against the Inquisition, the Enlightenment's *bête noire* – became one of the standard set pieces of 18th-century rhetoric. Led by Charles Louis *Montesquieu, Gotthold Ephraim *Lessing, and Jean Jacques *Rousseau, Enlightenment writers everywhere preached that Christian and Jew shared a common humanity and common human rights. Relatively few of these men foresaw the Emancipation, which for most of the 18th century remained a distant prospect. But emancipation was proposed as early as 1714 by the English freethinker John Toland, and it drew increasing support from *philosophes* as the century went on. When, at last, the Jews of France were emancipated in 1791, it was largely the authority of the Enlightenment which overcame the objections of churchmen and gentile economic interests.

Despite its achievements, however, the Enlightenment's pro-Jewish agitation was not so purely humanitarian as it appeared. Much of the indignation which Jewish suffering aroused was calculated not to comfort the Jews, but to exploit their plight for the purpose of condemning Christianity. Admiring accounts of the Jewish religion, such as those favored by Lessing, were also intended to discredit Christianity – often so blatantly that, like Lessing's famous *Nathan der Weise*, they expounded Judaism as a religion for *philosophes* to make Christianity seem backward by comparison. In short, when the Enlightenment chose to defend the Jews, it did so largely for reasons of its own; and it dealt with them, in consequence, not as real individuals, but as a useful abstraction. The sole novelty of its approach was that, whereas the Jews had once been a witness to the truth of Christianity, now they were expected to demonstrate its error. The actual Jews, meanwhile, were usually regarded with suspicion and distaste. The Judaism which they practiced, after all, was a religion much like Christianity and hence considered by Enlightenment thinkers as a "superstition" to be eradicated. What was still more serious, Judaism was often considered a particularly anti-social religion, one which nurtured a stubborn sense of particularism, perpetuated ancient, fossilized habits, and created grave divisions within the state. These opinions were so widely held by Enlightenment writers that even friends of the Jews continually urged them to abandon their traditions and observances. Only Montesquieu, of all the 18th century's great thinkers, showed any willingness to accept the Jews without reforming them into something else. Indeed, the most common argument for emancipation, as conceived by Christian Wielhelm von *Dohm, Honore-Gabriel-Victor Riqueti, Comte de *Mirabeau, and others, was precisely that it would convert the Jews to the majority culture, thus expunging their most obnoxious traits. This view was ultimately upheld by the French revolutionaries, who declared, when they emancipated the Jews in 1791: "To the man, everything; to the Jew, nothing." Though as a citizen the Jew was to receive full rights, as a Jew he was to count for nothing.

Even so, this program of compulsive emancipation did not fully reflect the intense Jew-hatred of the more extreme *philosophes*. Though it is surprising to recall the fact, among this group were some of the leading minds of the 18th century, including Denis*Diderot, Baron Paul Heinrich Dietrich d'*Holbach, and *Voltaire. Despite their intellectual stature, these men launched scurrilous attacks on the Jews which far surpassed the bounds of reasoned criticism. Many of their polemics were not only intolerant, but so vicious and spiteful as to compare with all but the crudest propaganda of the 1970s or the late 1990s. To some extent, this anti-Jewish fervor can be understood as merely one aspect of the Enlightenment's war on Christianity. Diderot, d'Holbach, Voltaire, and their followers were the most radical anti-Christians of their time, and – in contrast to the more moderate Deists who praised the Jews – they did not hesitate to pour scorn on Christianity by reviling its Jewish origins. This tactic was all the more useful because Judaism, unlike Christianity, could be abused in print without fear of prosecution; but even the fact that the Jews made a convenient whipping-boy cannot explain all the hostility which they excited. Diatribes written against Jews by Enlightment thinkers were often so bitter, so peculiarly violent, that they can only have stemmed from a profound emotional antagonism – a hatred nourished not only by dislike of Jewish particularism, refurbished from ancient Greco-Roman sources, but also by unconscious Christian prejudice and resentment of Jewish economic success. Voltaire, in particular, detested the Jews with vehement passion. A large part of his whole enormous output was devoted to lurid tales of Jewish credulity and fanaticism, which he viewed as dangerous threats to European culture. At times, Voltaire actually pressed this argument so far as to imply that Jews were ignorant by nature, and could never be integrated into a modern society.

To be sure, prejudices of this kind made little headway against the ingrained egalitarianism of the Enlightenment. Neither Voltaire nor any other pre-Revolutionary thinker seriously denied that Jews could be assimilated, so that in this sense, at least, antisemitism was hardly known. Still less respectable were outright fantasies like the blood libel, which most Enlightenment writers firmly repudiated. Yet the fact remains that, for all their resistance to racism and other delusions, some of the leaders of the Enlightenment played a central role in the development of antisemitic ideology. By declaring the Jew an enemy of the modern secular state, they refurbished the religious anti-Judaism of the Middle Ages and set it on an entirely new political path. In so doing, moreover, they revealed a depth of feeling against Jews which was wholly disproportionate to the Jews' supposed faults, and which would continue to inspire antisemitism even when the Jews' secularism was no longer open to question.

[Paul Weissman]

Emancipation and Reaction

ACHIEVING EMANCIPATION. The newer 19th-century version of antisemitism arose on a soil which had been watered for many centuries in Europe by Christian theology and, more important, by popular catechisms. The Christian centuries had persecuted Jews for theological reasons, but this "teaching of contempt" had set the seal on the most ancient of all antisemitic themes: that the Jews were a uniquely alien element within human society. In every permutation of European politics and economics within the course of the century, the question of the alienness of the Jew reappeared as an issue of quite different quality from all of the other conflicts of a stormy age. Jews themselves tended to imagine that their troubles represented the time-lag of older, medieval Christian attitudes, of the anger at "Christ-killers" and "Christ-rejecters," which would eventually disappear. It was not until the works of Leo *Pinsker and Theodor *Herzl, the founders of modern Zionism were published, that the suggestion was made that antisemitism in all of its varieties was, at its very root, a form of xenophobia, the hatred of a stranger – the oldest, most complicated, and most virulent example of such hatred –and that the end of the medieval era of faith and politics did not, therefore, mean the end of antisemitism.

As a result of both the French and the American revolutions there were two states in the world at the beginning of the 19th century in which, in constitutional theory, Jews were now equal citizens before the law. In neither case was their emancipation complete. In the U.S. certain legal disabilities continued to exist in some of the individual states and the effort for their removal encountered some re-echoes of older Christian prejudices. The Jews in America were, however, at the beginning of the 19th century a mere handful, less than 3,000 in a national population approaching 4,000,000, and there was therefore no contemporary social base for the rise of a serious antisemitic reaction. The issues were different in Europe. In France there had been more than a century of economic conflict between Jewish small-scale moneylenders, illegal artisans, and petty credit and their Gentile clients and competitors. The legal emancipation of the Jews did not still these angers but, on the contrary, exacerbated them. The spokesmen of the political left in eastern France during the era of the Revolution and even into the age of *Napoleon argued, without exception that the new legal equality for the Jews would not act to assimilate them as "useful and productive citizens" into the main body of the French people but, rather that it would open new avenues for the rapacity of these aliens. Napoleon's own activities in relation to the Jewish question, including the calling of his famous French *Sanhedrin in 1807, were under the impact of two themes: the desire to make the Jews assimilate more rapidly and the attempt, through a decree that announced a ten-year moratorium on debts owed to Jews in eastern France, to calm the angers of their enemies.

On the other hand, Jews were visibly and notoriously the beneficiaries of the Revolution. It was, indeed, true that a number of distinguished émigrés had been helped to escape by former Jewish associates, and it was even true that the bulk of the Jewish community, at least at the very beginning of the Revolution and a few years later during the Terror, feared rather than favored the new regime. Nonetheless, in the minds of the major losers, the men of the old order and especially of the church, the Jews were the chief, or at the very least the

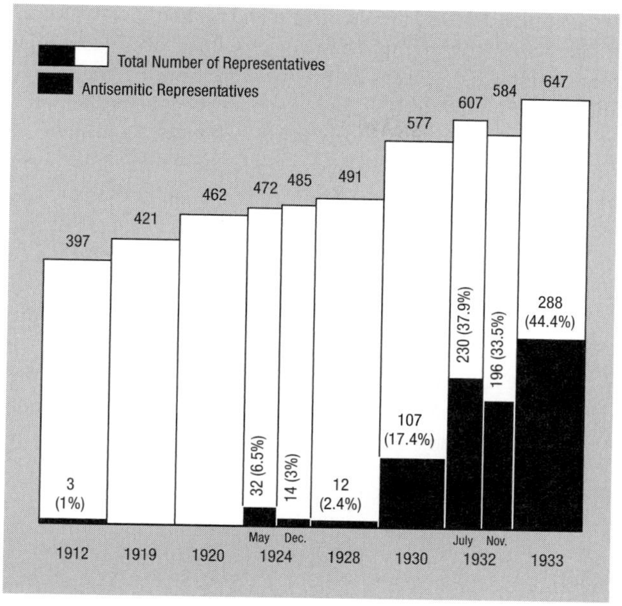

Antisemitic representatives in the German Reichstag from 1912 to 1933.

most obvious, winners during the era of the Revolution. The association of French antisemitism with counterrevolutionary forces, with royalist-clericalist reaction, throughout the next 150 years was thus begun very early. In the demonology of antisemitism it was not difficult to transform the Sanhedrin in Paris in 1807 into a meeting of a secret society of Jews plotting to take over the world. This connection was made in that year by Abbé *Barruel in his book *Mémoire pour servir a l'histoire du jacobinisme*. This volume is the source of all of the later elaborations of the myth of the Elders of Zion.

In Europe as a whole a new kind of antisemitism was evoked by the new kind of war that the revolutionary armies, and the far more successful armies of Napoleon, were waging against their enemies.

Between 1790 and 1815 the armies of France appeared everywhere not, as they announced, as conquerors holding foreign territory for ransom or for annexation, but as liberators of the peoples from the yoke of their existing governments in order to help them regenerate themselves in a new state of freedom. Wherever the Revolution spread, its legislation included, in places as far-flung as Westphalia, Italy, and even briefly, Ereẓ Israel, equality for Jews. It was entirely reasonable on the part of the Austrian police, and the secret services of some of the other European powers, to suspect that some of the Jews within their borders were really partisans of Napoleon. In the wake of his defeat the emancipation of the Jews remained on the books in France, but it was removed elsewhere, with some modifications in favor of Jews, as an imposition of a foreign power. The battle for Jewish equality had to begin again; it became part of a century-long battle in Europe to achieve the liberal revolution everywhere. This struggle had not yet ended by the time of World War I, for at that moment the largest Jewish community in the world, that in the Russian Empire, was not yet emancipated and had, indeed, suffered grievously throughout the century.

In the early and middle years of the 19th century the most important battleground between Jews and their enemies was in Germany. Capitalism was rapidly remaking the social structure and Jews were the most easily identifiable element among the "new men." The victims of the rising capitalist order, especially the lower-middle classes, found their scapegoat in the most vulnerable group among the successful, the Jews. In a different part of society, and from a nationalist perspective, the most distinguished of German historians of the day, Heinrich *Treitschke, was insisting toward the end of the century that the acculturated and legally emancipated Jews, who thought in their own minds that they had become thoroughly German, were really aliens who still had to remake themselves from the ground up and to disappear inconspicuously. Not long after the turn of the century Werner *Sombart (*Die Juden und das Wirtschaftsleben*, 1911) was to express his own ambivalence about capitalism as a whole by insisting, against Max Weber, that it was the Jews, and not the Protestants, who had always been, even in biblical days, the inventors and bearers of the capitalist spirit. Such identification between the Jews and the spirit of capitalism had been made, to their discredit, seven decades earlier, in 1844, by the young Karl *Marx in his essay "On the Jewish Question." For antisemites of both the political right and the left, who struggled against capitalism for different reasons, such identification was one of the sources and rationales of Jew-hatred throughout the modern era, well into the Nazi period.

On the surface of events modern German antisemitism began with riots by the peasants in 1819, using the rhetoric of older Christian hostility. This attitude toward Jews was soon transformed by the rising romanticism and the nationalist reactions to the Napoleonic wars into an assertion that the true German spirit, which had arisen in the Teutonic forests, was an organic and lasting identity in which the Jew could not, by his very nature, participate. For this purpose the work of Count Joseph-Arthur de *Gobineau on race was pressed into service to make the point that the Jews were a non-Aryan, Oriental element whose very nature was of a different modality. Richard *Wagner insisted on this point not only in his overt antisemitic utterances but also indirectly in his operas, in which he crystallized the Teutonic myths as a quasi-religious expression of the authentic German spirit. In Wagner's footsteps there appeared the work of his son-in-law, Houston Stewart *Chamberlain (*The Foundations of the Nineteenth Century*, 1899), which pronounced the presence of Jews in German society to be radically inimical to its very health. In the popular mind these theorists of national culture were understood within a situation in which the intellectual importance of Germany in Europe was not equaled by its political significance, for the scandalous division of the country lasted until 1870. To be united and German was the dominant ideal.

The very difficulties in realizing the unity of Germany brought the existence of Jews into unfriendly focus. Very few elements in mid-19th century Germany society, even among their friends, were willing to regard Jews as true Germans. Jews were asking for political equality more in the name of the universal rights of man – that is, as partisans of the cosmopolitan principle – than as sons of the German people. As a result, the ultimate attainment of equality, first in Prussia in 1859 and ultimately in all of Germany in the aftermath of the unification of the country in 1870, had a quite narrow social base. It was identified with the rise of the bourgeois liberalism, but this element never dominated in mid-19th-century Germany as it did in contemporary England. What was worse, from a Jewish perspective, was that as a middle-class element the Jews were themselves in competition with the very class which had facilitated their entry into society. Toward the end of the century the German middle class itself was shifting its political alignment from liberalism to romantic conservatism. To be sure, the main thrust of German liberalism continued to regard antisemitism as reactionary, just as the main body of German Socialism would have no truck with the identification of all Jews with the capitalist oppressors of the working class. Nonetheless, antisemitism was sufficiently potent for all its themes to coalesce into the image of the successful, non-national, unproductive foreigner, whose power resided in money, in his mastery of the legerdemain of modern manipulation, and his cosmopolitan contacts. This "Jew" was a lineal descendant of the Jewish maker of love potions in Greco-Roman demonology and the poisoner of wells of the medieval myths, but the new version was very up to date and answered to contemporary frustrations and angers.

In the last quarter of the 19th century, antisemitism became an acceptable element in German political life to be manipulated at opportune moments by political leaders seeking popular lower-middle-class support. The very term antisemitism had been invented by Wilhelm Marr in 1879 and it was in that year that the court chaplain, Adolph *Stoecker, had made his first public antisemitic speech, "What We Demand of Modern Jewry," and had then turned his Christian Socialist Party in overtly anti-Jewish directions. With the rise of German imperialism toward the end of the century and the sense of success it gave Germany, political antisemitism waned, but social distance continued unaltered.

In France, Jews had not been an issue of any considerable importance after the restoration of the Bourbons to power in 1815. There alone Jewish political gains had been safeguarded without question, because the fundamental social changes which had been introduced by the Revolution could not be radically altered by the return of the émigrés. Nonetheless, Jews remained one of the most visible symbols of these very changes, and the attacks upon Jews, both from the extreme right and the extreme left, were sufficiently overt to provide the spark for greater difficulties in the second half of the century. Two of the greatest theorists of Socialism in France, Pierre-Joseph *Proudhon and Charles *Fourier, were anti-Jewish on the ground that Jewish capitalist interests stood counter to those of the peasants and the workers, and that the Jewish spirit as a whole was antithetical to their vision of a reformed humanity living the life of unselfish social justice. In France, too, the changes being brought about by capitalism and the Industrial Revolution made many people feel helpless, as their lives were being remade for the worse. The power of the *Rothschilds was very evident in France, especially in the age of Louis Napoleon, and some of the anger at the new age came to expression in attacks on them by left-wingers such as Alphonse *Toussenel. In the time of conflict which followed the fall of France in 1870 major elements among all forces contending for power after the debacle could blame their troubles on the Jews.

In the renewed political battles of the 1870s and 1880s the overwhelming majority of the Jewish community in France was associated with the liberal republican forces against the conservative Catholics, who were enemies of the Republic. From 1879 to 1884 republican anti-clericals dominated in parliament and succeeded in freeing French education from clerical control. One of the building blocks of the almost successful counterrevolution of 1888, in which General Boulanger very nearly made an end of the Republic, was antisemitism. The myth that the small handful of Jews in France had enormous and highly dangerous economic power had been broadcast two years before in perhaps the single, most successful antisemitic and counterrevolutionary book ever published, Edouard *Drumont's *La France Juive*, which went through innumerable editions. Late in 1894 antisemitism became the central issue of French society and politics for at least a decade and the reechoes of the positions taken in those years can still be heard. Captain Alfred *Dreyfus, the first Jew to become a member of the general staff of the French army, was accused of spying for Germany. The outcry against Dreyfus was joined not only by the clerical-royalist right but also by some elements of the French left. His ultimate vindication was the result of the exercise of the moral conscience in the service of truth by a number of individuals more concerned about the preservation of the Republic than about the rights of Jews.

[Arthur Hertzberg]

ANTISEMITIC POLITICAL PARTIES AND ORGANIZATIONS. A distinction must be made between organizations that temporarily adopted antisemitic attitudes and those founded with the express purpose of fighting alleged negative Jewish influences. Into the first category fall some originally liberal groups, especially in Austria and Romania, as well as most of the clerical parties. For example, the German Catholic Center Party blamed Bismarck's *Kulturkampf* on the Jews but later relented and even protected Jewish religious interests. Many conservative groups vacillated in a similar fashion as did certain socialist movements, like the Fourierists in France, some disciples of F. *Lassalle in Germany, and the Narodniki in Russia. Even the Social-Democrat parties later rid themselves, though rather tardily, of antisemitic tendencies. The groups that called themselves Christian-Social were steeped in antisemitism, although for some of them anti-Judaism served

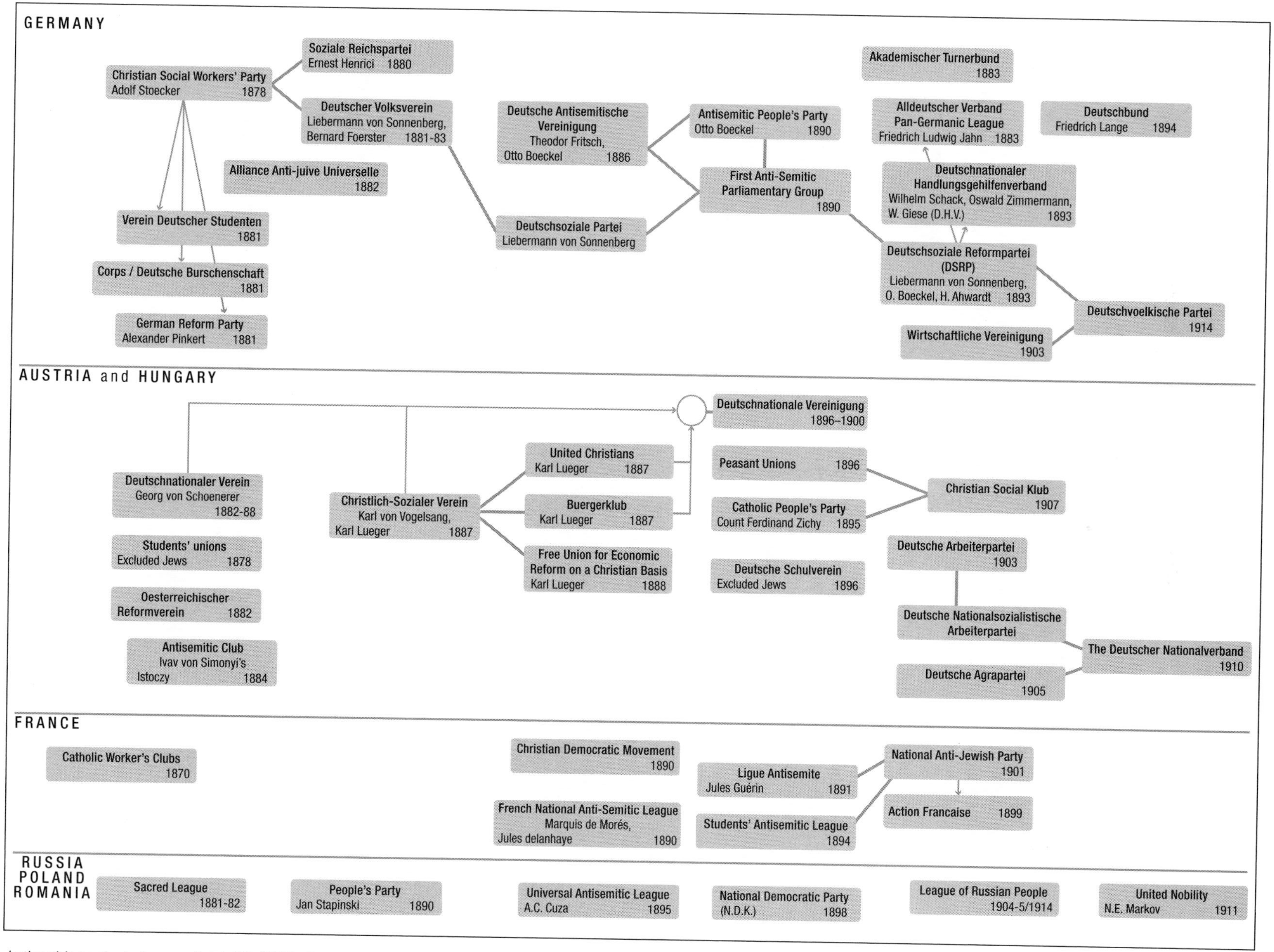
GERMANY
Christian Social Workers' Party
Adolf Stoecker 1878
Soziale Reichspartei
Ernest Henrici 1880
Deutscher Volksverein
Liebermann von Sonnenberg,
Bernard Foerster 1881-83
Alliance Anti-juive Universelle
1882
Verein Deutscher Studenten
1881
Corps / Deutsche Burschenschaft
1881
German Reform Party
Alexander Pinkert 1881
Deutsche Antisemitische Vereinigung
Theodor Fritsch,
Otto Boeckel 1886
Deutschsoziale Partei
Liebermann von Sonnenberg
Antisemitic People's Party
Otto Boeckel 1890
First Anti-Semitic Parliamentary Group
1890
Akademischer Turnerbund
1883
Alldeutscher Verband
Pan-Germanic League
Friedrich Ludwig Jahn 1883
Deutschbund
Friedrich Lange 1894
Deutschnationaler Handlungsgehilfenverband
Wilhelm Schack, Oswald Zimmermann,
W. Giese (D.H.V.) 1893
Deutschsoziale Reformpartei
(DSRP)
Liebermann von Sonnenberg,
O. Boeckel, H. Ahwardt 1893
Deutschvoelkische Partei
1914
Wirtschaftliche Vereinigung
1903
AUSTRIA and HUNGARY
Deutschnationale Vereinigung
1896–1900
Deutschnationaler Verein
Georg von Schoenerer
1882-88
Students' unions
Excluded Jews 1878
Oesterreichischer
Reformverein 1882
Antisemitic Club
Ivav von Simonyi's
Istoczy 1884
Christlich-Sozialer Verein
Karl von Vogelsang,
Karl Lueger 1887
United Christians
Karl Lueger 1887
Buergerklub
Karl Lueger 1887
Free Union for Economic
Reform on a Christian Basis
Karl Lueger 1888
Peasant Unions 1896
Catholic People's Party
Count Ferdinand Zichy 1895
Deutsche Schulverein
Excluded Jews 1896
Christian Social Klub
1907
Deutsche Arbeiterpartei
1903
Deutsche Nationalsozialistische
Arbeiterpartei
The Deutscher Nationalverband
1910
Deutsche Agrapartei
1905
FRANCE
Catholic Worker's Clubs
1870
Christian Democratic Movement
1890
French National Anti-Semitic League
Marquis de Morés,
Jules delanhaye 1890
Ligue Antisemite
Jules Guérin 1891
Students' Antisemitic League
1894
National Anti-Jewish Party
1901
Action Francaise 1899
RUSSIA
POLAND
ROMANIA
Sacred League
1881-82
People's Party
Jan Stapinski 1890
Universal Antisemitic League
A.C. Cuza 1895
National Democratic Party
(N.D.K.) 1898
League of Russian People
1904-5/1914
United Nobility
N.E. Markov 1911

Antisemitic parties in Europe, 1870 to World War I.

mainly as a means of vote-catching and of competing with all-round antisemitic parties, while for others it constituted an integral part of their program. Since it is difficult to separate them, all parties which displayed anti-Jewish tendencies are included here.

The appearance of anti-Jewish parties and organizations, whether they were based on economic, religious, or *voelkisch* (Aryan nationalist) ideologies or a combination of all three, constitutes the most important distinguishing mark of modern antisemitism, which came to the fore after the political reshuffle of Europe following the wars of 1866 and 1870–71, and particularly after the general economic crisis of 1873. All antisemitic organizations aspired to influence public life by means such as mass movements and parliamentary pressure groups. Although before World War I most of them were short lived and failed to acquire mass support, they registered local victories and accumulated valuable political experience. Moreover, by their incessant propaganda they infected large parts of the population with a latent antisemitism. Germany and Austria were the first countries to experience organized antisemitism, preceding Hungary and Poland. France on the one hand, and Russia and Romania on the other, constitute separate categories.

Germany. In the mid-1870s certain antisemitic social reform groups of artisans, small traders, and clerks began to form local organizations. A prominent instance in Saxony was Ernst Schmeitzner's Society for the Protection of Artisans and Traders. Rural advocates of social reform also gathered in small societies. Groups like the Antisemitic League of Wilhelm *Marr (1879) occupied themselves less with economic reform than with *voelkisch* issues. Thus, from the outset of organizational activities, two main trends in political antisemitism asserted themselves: the social and the racist trends. It must be added, however, that both were complex: there was a radical and a conservative trend in the reform associations, as well as rather radical and ultraconservative wings in the racist groups. This divergence, originating in the multifaceted and even contradictory image of the Jew, caused incessant splits and re-formations in political antisemitism, rendering it more or less ineffective until the end of World War I.

The first political organizer to use antisemitism as a lever for a mass movement was the court preacher Adolf *Stoecker in Berlin. Stoecker failed to attract followers to his Christian Socialist Workers' Party (1878) on a platform of Christian ethics and reconciliation between state and workers through state intervention in economics. In 1879, however, he hit upon antisemitism as a vote-catcher for artisans and other members of the lower-middle classes in his speech "Our Demands on Modern Judaism." His activities inspired the founding of the antisemitic students' movement, Verein Deutscher Studenten (1881). This was not powerful in itself, but it imbued the old students' organizations – the Corps and the Deutsche Burschenschaft – with the spirit of racial intolerance, so that finally they excluded all Jews from membership. Meanwhile, Stoecker was elected, with Conservative help, to the Prussian Diet (1879) and to the Reichstag. Stoecker's initial success was paralleled in Saxony, where the First International Anti-Jewish Congress convened in Dresden in 1882, assembling during the blood libel of the *Tisza-Eszlar trial, convened delegates from Germany, Austria, and Hungary. A standing committee decided on the founding of an Alliance Anti-Juive Universelle (an allusion to the *Alliance Israélite Universelle) and fixed a second congress to be held the following year in Chemnitz. This congress attracted additional delegates from Russia, Romania, Serbia, and France but no lasting unity was established. Later antisemitic congresses (Kassel 1886, Bochum 1889) were strictly German, and they too accomplished close to nothing.

During 1880 and 1881, some of Stoecker's most vociferous racist allies broke away. The first was Ernst Henrici, who headed the radical anti-conservative Soziale Reichspartei for about three years. Next was the ultraconservative Max Liebermann von Sonnenberg, who in conjunction with Friedrich *Nietzsche's brother-in-law, Bernhard Foerster, established the Deutscher Volksverein (1881–83). Both parties remained weak, and their endeavors to win general support by presenting to Bismarck their joint antisemitic petition asking for the abolition of Jewish equality gained them only fleeting success. Although they collected 225,000 signatures, they failed at the polls. When in 1883 the *Conservative Party severed all connections with them, the center of political antisemitism shifted for a time from Berlin to small towns and rural districts and to other German states. This happened in 1886 when Theodor *Fritsch of Leipzig, one of the most rabid racists, joined with the "Hessian King of Peasants," Otto Boeckel, and others in the Deutsche Antisemitische Vereinigung. Boeckel was immediately elected to the Reichstag as the first antisemite per se. Before the elections of 1890 he founded his own Antisemitic People's Party (renamed in 1893 Deutsche Reformpartei), enjoying a certain measure of cooperation with Liebermann von Sonnenberg's reshuffled Deutschsoziale Partei. Thus in 1890 Von Sonnenberg, Boeckel, and three of Boeckel's followers were elected to the Reichstag, the latter forming the first antisemitic parliamentary group. The 1893 elections showed even more striking gains: 16 antisemitic candidates were elected, half of them in Hesse.

This increase was brought about by the public reaction to Jewish emancipation, by a definite antisemitic turn in the Conservative Party, which adopted an openly anti-Jewish paragraph in its so-called Tivoli Program (1892), and by the entrance of the feudal-agrarian Bund der Landwirte ("Agrarian League") into the political arena as an ultraconservative and antisemitic pressure group. Finally, there emerged in Berlin a new rabble-rouser, Hermann *Ahlwardt, the "headmaster of all the Germans." Ahlwardt's triumphs were, however, short lived. In 1894 he was received into the parliamentary faction of the later-united wings of Liebermann Von Sonnenberg and Boeckel's Deutschsoziale Reformpartei (DSRP), but was soon excluded again. Boeckel himself lost his seat in 1903 to a candidate from a Protestant group. Nevertheless, 11 antisemites were elected in 1903, and three more joined them at by-elections. However, the realignments within their ranks continued. Von Sonnenberg's Deutschsoziale joined forces with the Agrarian League, the Christian-Socialists, and the Bavarian Peasant Party. Thus a parliamentary alignment, Wirtschaftliche Vereinigung, was established. Only the remnants of the DSRP held aloof, commanding six seats in 1907 and three in 1912, while the Wirtschaftliche Vereinigung secured 19 and ten respectively. On the eve of World War I, although again amalgamated into a Deutschvoelkische Partei (1914), party antisemitism seemed to be declining, but other previously non-antisemitic groups had been deeply infected by its vociferous activities. Even the left-wing liberal parties (alternately called Fortschritt, Freisinn, and again Fortschritt), which had staunchly defended Jewish equality, began making election agreements with antisemites or otherwise alienating their Jewish followers. It was therefore not surprising that various club-like right-wing groups openly pursued an anti-Jewish line. Such groups, mostly pan-Germanic and imperialist in outlook, comprised beside the already mentioned Students' and Agrarian Leagues, the Akademischer Turnerbund (from 1883), other gymnastic clubs imbued with Friedrich Ludwig Jahn's exclusive nationalism, the Alldeutscher Verband ("Pan-Germanic League"), a small but effective organization of influential right-wing personalities, the somewhat similar Colonial Society, and many others. Of another hue was the Deutschnationaler Handlungsgehilfenverband – DHV (from 1893), which became Germany's largest white-collar union, combining trade-union activities with conservative-nationalist and antisemitic policies. In 1933 the DHV merged with the Nazis in the National Socialist Labor Front. Among the small, lodge-like organizations were the Deutschbund of Friedrich Lange (1894), the Deutsche Volksbund of Boeckel (1907), the Germanen und Waelsungenorden (1912), whose activities were coordinated with Fritsch's Reichs-Hammerbund, and many others.

Austria and the Hapsburg Dominions. Although there are many similarities in the development of the German and Austrian antisemitic organizations, there remain two main differences. Christian-Socialist antisemitism played a leading part in Catholic Austria and even included the conservatives, while in Germany Protestant conservatism never relinquished its predominance over the Christian-Social movement. Secondly, racial antisemitism in Austria partly derived from the liberal camp, because of the essentially German nationalism of Austrian liberalism which denied the various minorities the right of self-determination. Yet the minorities themselves were often antisemitic, regarding Jews as proponents of Hapsburg domination. On the other hand, pan-German racism antagonized the minorities and did not attain the same influence as in Germany. Chronologically, students' unions led the way, excluding Jews as early as 1878. Soon the first Societies for the Protection of the Artisans (from 1880) amalgamated in the Oesterreichischer Reformverein (1882), which, under the leadership of Franz Holubek, was temporarily the main antisemitic organization. Later also the Deutsche Schulverein, supporting German schools in non-German territories, excluded Jews (1896), as did the nationalist Turnverein, cycling clubs, and the Deutsch-Oesterreichischer Alpenverein, which, however, adopted antisemitism only at the end of World War I.

The way for antisemitism as a force in party politics was paved by Georg Ritter von *Schoenerer, who gradually shifted from liberalism to the extreme nationalist pan-Germanic wing, his movement probably influencing the young Adolf Hitler. In 1888, when Von Schoenerer was sentenced to prison for assault, his Deutschnationaler Verein began to dissolve, and the road was clear for the ascendancy of the Christian-Social movement. Karl von *Vogelsang was its ideological mainspring and Karl *Lueger its leading personality. They first attached themselves to the Christlich-Sozialer Verein (founded in 1887). Lueger, although still associated with a Jew (Julius Mandl), gradually identified himself with a newly formed anti-Jewish and anti-liberal election alignment, the United Christians (from 1887). In Vienna he formed a special antisemitic city branch (Buergerklub), and in the Austrian Reichsrat he led the Free Union for Economic Reform on a Christian Basis. These Christian-Social organizations backed him for the mayoralty of Vienna, although the nationalist elements broke away and formed the short-lived Deutschnationale Vereinigung (1896–1900). He also enlarged the Christian-Social field of action outside the capital by means of Peasant Unions; he was helped by an able organizer, Msgr. Joseph Scheicher. Thus, in the elections of 1902 all 51 antisemitic members of the lower Austrian Diet were Christian-Socialists.

Catholic conservatives (united since 1895 in the Catholic People's Party) also wanted Lueger; when the introduction of a general ballot in 1907 raised the number of Christian-Social members in the Reichsrat to 67, about 29 conservatives joined with them in a parliamentary *Klub*, thus establishing the Christian-Social movement as the protagonist of Austrian conservatism also. Only the radicals, continuing Von Schoenerer's pan-Germanic racism, went their separate way, mainly among the German elements in the Czech Sudetenland. Here the Deutsche Arbeiterpartei (1903, later called Deutsche Nationalsozialistische Arbeiterpartei) and the Deutsche Agrarpartei (1905), with their anticlerical, anti-Jewish, and anti-Czech attitude, registered considerable gains. However, antisemitism in the Hapsburg countries was not a German monopoly. Czech, Polish, and Ruthenian nationalists were sporadically as anti-Jewish as they were anti-German, or anti-Russian and anti-Polish, all regarding the Jews as part of rival nationalism, or decrying them as entirely foreign.

Hungary. Győzo (Victor) *Istóczy, from the liberal benches of the Diet, started local antisemitic cells, similar to Marr's Antisemitic League. He boasted that in 1880 there were already 78 such cells, which he hoped to amalgamate into a Union of Non-Jews. After the riots and pogroms which followed the

Tisza-Eszlar blood libel, Istóczy and Ivan Simonyi, a "national-social" antisemite, founded the Antisemitic Club for the elections of 1884. They gained 17 seats and captured the majority in the Pozsony (Bratislava) municipality but quarreled among themselves and dissolved again. Later, Count Ferdinand Zichy's Christian-Social movement (Catholic People's Party, founded in 1895) attracted much antisemitic support, but was not to the taste of radical-nationalists, although it spread vicious anti-Jewish propaganda.

Poland. While antisemitism in Czechoslovakia and Hungary was more or less sporadic, it was endemic in Galicia and Russian Poland. Already in the 1880s it had found a spokesman in Teofil Merunowicz, who advocated anti-Jewish legislation in the Galician Diet. During the 1890s, the Polish Catholic People's Party, led by Jan Stapiński, which sponsored social measures like rural producers' and consumers' cooperatives, also supported anti-Jewish *boycott measures. When the Jesuit Father Stojalowski took over the direction of propaganda, this Christian Social movement even initiated a wave of pogroms during the by-elections of 1898, in which Father Stojalowski was returned to the Diet. At the same time, the National Democratic Party (NDK, *Endecja) organized the radical national forces, mainly in Russian Poland. The National Democrats and their propaganda were instrumental in transferring antisemitism into the new Polish state founded after World War I.

France. In the abovementioned countries, with the exception of Russian Poland, political antisemitism emerged as an immediate reaction to the granting of Jewish emancipation. French Jewry had already been emancipated for 80 years when it was hit by the organized forms of Jew-hatred. The chaotic conditions after the French defeat by Germany in 1871, the bloodbath of the Paris Commune, and the birth pangs of the unloved Third Republic formed the background for anti-liberalism, anti-parliamentarism, and antisemitism. Even socialists, influenced by the teachings of Charles *Fourier, Pierre Joseph *Proudhon, and Alphonse *Toussenel, quickly adopted the image of Rothschild as the symbol of financial capitalism. But in the main, French feelings against the Jews, whether of a conservative or of a democratic and social type, were perhaps inspired mostly by Catholicism. In its fight against liberalism and socialism Catholicism was looking for a scapegoat; this it found first in *Freemasonry and finally in a "Jewish plot," allegedly exploiting the Masonic order to attain "world domination."

Paralleling Austrian developments, the French-Social-Catholic movement started in the 1870s with rather conservative Catholic Workers' Clubs; their antisemitism gradually increased, especially after the collapse of the Catholic bank Union Générale in 1882. However no mass organization emerged until about 1890, with the formation of the Christian Democratic movement by forces that took their inspiration from Edouard *Drumont's book *La France Juive* (1886). Such a movement also served as a refuge for the disillusioned remnants of General Boulanger's supporters. Certain Boulangists and Boulangist organizations, like Paul Déroulède's Patriotic League, had already dabbled in antisemitism, as had Jacques de Biez, one of the first followers of Drumont, who in 1886 attended the founding ceremony of the Alliance Anti-Israélite Universelle in Bucharest. It was only during the course of elections of 1890, however, that the French National Antisemitic League took shape, under the leadership of the Marquis de Morès and Jules Delahaye, as an election alignment for Boulangists and adherents of Drumont. It quickly disintegrated, its candidates being defeated at the polls. An attempt by Morès to organize the Paris street mob into strong-arm brigades did not help, but it invited imitations (see below). The Christian Democrats became more republican and radical, and most violently antisemitic during the *Dreyfus Affair. Typical of this development are the utterances of the anti-monarchist Father Hippolyte Gayraud at the first Christian Democratic Congress in Lyons (1896). Gayraud held that the church had always been antisemitic "on a high moral plane," and that "all social excrement, especially the Jews" should be expelled from France. The movement quickly disintegrated after the pardon of Dreyfus in 1906. Meanwhile, however, antisemitism prospered, not only in Paris, but also in the provincial towns where antisemitic small businessmen's and salesmen's organizations sprang up in Lyons, Poitiers, Dijon, Nancy, and other places, and finally in Algiers, where Max Régis instigated anti-Jewish atrocities, gaining for himself the mayoralty and for Drumont a seat in the Chamber of Deputies. In Paris itself, the most important local group before 1897, when Jules Guerin renewed the Ligue Antisémite and organized the mob into anti-Dreyfusard and anti-Jewish commandos, was the Students' Antisemitic League (1894), which remained active in the streets and at the university during the Dreyfus Affair. Several of its founders later formed a National Anti-Jewish Party (1901), but finally joined l'*Action Française. This extreme chauvinist and royalist group (founded in 1899), which sponsored a conservative "landed antisemitism," remained a political force for more than 40 years, until Hitler's conquest of France.

Romania. In Romania and czarist Russia, antisemitism was to a large extent government-sponsored. Within the borders of constitutional Romania parliamentary parties flourished and vied among themselves in sponsoring anti-Jewish measures, turning the parliament itself into the main stage for antisemitic propaganda and for discriminative legislation against the "foreigners," in flagrant violation of international commitment (see Congress of *Berlin). In this, the so-called Liberal Party under John Bratianu surpassed the conservatives, as the land-owning boyars were to a certain extent interested in protecting "their" Jews. In 1886, under the influence of Edouard Drumont, Bucharest served as the center for a new departure in international antisemitism: the Alliance Anti-Israélite Universelle was founded by Romanian, Hungarian, and French intransigents, Drumont being unanimously elected president. But this time, too, the international organization very quickly proved abortive. About ten years later (1895), the Romanians organized their own Universal Antisemitic League with A.C. *Cuza, the deputy N. Jorga, and other members of parliament and high officials in leading positions. It established branches in many towns, pledging itself "to make life intolerable" for Jews and to force them out of the country. In the following years pogroms in Romania were numerous and vicious, culminating in rural anti-Jewish riots that led to a general peasant uprising, which in 1907 had to be quelled by the army. On the eve of World War I, the so-called "Culture-League" continued the pogrom propaganda in derision of its name, vowing to create a situation in which "Russia with its pogroms and blood libels would seem to be a Promised Land to the Jews."

Russia. Although Russia was the land of the most violent antisemitism, it had perhaps the fewest organizations devoted to it, for Russian autocratic patterns of government did not allow even antisemitic groups. Thus, the first known reactionary antisemitic organization, the Sacred League, which sprang up after the assassination of Czar Alexander II in March 1881, was clandestine, although arch-reactionary high officials and even ministers seem to have furthered it. In their eyes the Jews were the source of all rebellion, and they themselves used terror and violence to destroy the "leaven of revolution." It is generally believed that the Sacred League was instrumental in fomenting the pogroms of 1881 and 1882. It was dissolved at the end of that year. Toward the end of 1904, when the Japanese war was going badly for Russia, and early in 1905, when the revolution broke out, another antisemitic organization was formed, the *Union of the Russian People, rather similar in character and aims to its predecessor. This league was openly recognized, and even furthered by the czar and his government, together with its secret fighting squads, the "Black Hundreds," which were largely responsible for the pogroms of 1905 and for counterrevolutionary political assassinations. The Union of the Russian People, acting in the open, continued in existence until World War I, and inspired the formation of several similar "patriotic" organizations. Perhaps its most reactionary offspring was the United Nobility (1911), one of its leading spirits being N.E. Markov. This party openly advocated the complete expulsion of the Jews from the country, and did much to spread blood libels against the Jews which finally culminated in the *Beilis case. Even during the war, government-sponsored antisemitism scarcely abated and was responsible for the allegation of an act of Jewish high treason against the Russian Army in the village of Kuzhi (1915), which was given wide publicity by every Russian newspaper.

[Jacob Toury]

RUSSIA AND CENTRAL EUROPE. There was a radical difference between the situation in Western Europe in the 19th century and that which prevailed in the Russian Empire. At least in theory the West European states were not anti-Jewish. Despite occasional liberalizations, the czarist regime as a whole regarded it as its duty to protect the bulk of its population against the spread of Jewish economic influence or even of Jewish population. A few attempts in the course of the century at the assimilation of the Jews did not alter the basic outlook of the state, that Jews were dangerous aliens. The czar continued to derive the validation of his absolutism from theology, from the identification of the Caesar and Jesus by the Orthodox faith; antisemitism based on Christian religious prejudice thus remained alive and virulent. Whatever hopes the Jews had in the course of the 19th century for improvement in their status rested in the hopes for the evolution of czarist absolutism toward parliamentary democracy. Repeated repressions made such hopes clearly illusory, and younger Jews in increasing numbers turned to helping to prepare revolution. This served to enrage the government, and the reactionary circles which supported it, even further. The regime kept imposing more economic disabilities on the Jews, keeping them in the least secure of middlemen occupations such as petty shopkeepers, innkeepers, and managers of estates for absentee landlords; in these capacities Jews were in direct, often unpleasant, contact with the poorest of the peasants. The government made it its business to use these resentments to draw attention away from the seething angers which pervaded the whole of the social system. Antisemitism was thus encouraged and fostered as a tactical tool for preserving czarist absolutism.

The critically important event in the history of Russian antisemitism took place in 1881, when a wave of pogroms occurred involving outbreaks in some 160 cities and villages of Russia. The occasion for these outrages was the assassination of Czar Alexander II by revolutionary terrorists on March 13, 1881. Among the assassins was one Jewish girl who played quite a minor role, but reactionary newspapers almost immediately began to whip up anti-Jewish sentiment. The government probably did not directly organize these riots, but it stood aside as Jews were murdered and pillaged, and the regime used the immediate occasion to enact anti-Jewish economic legislation in 1882 (the *May Laws). The situation continued to deteriorate to such a degree that in the next reign Czar *Nicholas II financially supported the antisemitic organization, the Black Hundreds, and made no secret of his personal membership, and that of the crown prince, in that organization (see *Union of Russian People). This body was associated with the government in directly fomenting pogroms during the revolutionary years of 1903 and 1905; in that latter year the libel known as the Protocols of the *Elders of Zion was first published under the auspices of the secret police by the press of the czar, although he himself believed the work to be a fraud. The ordeal of Mendel *Beilis arose within the hysterical atmosphere of disintegrating czarism. He was accused in 1911 in Kiev of ritual murder, and the full weight of government power was put behind the prosecution. His acquittal at the trial in 1913 was the culmination of two years of battle between the regime and the Jews and their supporters in liberal humanitarian circles in Russia and throughout the world.

It was, indeed, in such circles, which were the Russian parallel to the forces which had created western parliamentary democracy and social and intellectual liberalism, that the Jews found support during a tragic period. When these elements came briefly to power in the revolution of February 1917 the Jews were immediately given the rights of equal citizens.

Nonetheless, despite this later, brief, and abortive victory of liberalism, after 1882 this current seemed too weak and divided to afford the Jews much hope for the future. Men like Ivan Sergejevitch Turgenev had mixed feelings about Jews and even Lev Nikolajevitch Tolstoy did not always hasten to support them when they were under attack. The political left was even more ambiguous. Even some of the Jews within the general revolutionary movements saw the Jewish petty bourgeoisie not as a victim but as an oppressor. The anger of the peasants and the urban poor was, therefore, regarded as merited, and their pogrom activities were even viewed as positive stirrings toward the ultimate revolution. This was, for example, the stand of the Narodniki, the pro-peasant populist group, with regard to the pogroms of 1881. More fundamentally, the revolutionary groups in Russia had even less patience with specifically Jewish problems, or with any desires on the part of Jews to continue their own communal identity, than was to be found in the European left as a whole. The young Lenin was an opponent of antisemitism, and he held that the problems of the Jews would disappear along with that of all other people in Russia in a new socialist order. On the other hand, Lenin insisted that Jews would have to undergo a more radical and cultural transformation than any other element in Russia and that any Jew who opposed assimilation was "simply a nationalist philistine" ("The Position of the Bund in the Party," in *Iskra*, Oct. 22, 1903). Any form of Jewish national feeling had already been pronounced to be a form of particularly obnoxious reaction. The stage was thus set for the ultimate questioning by Stalin of the loyalty of even Communist Jews.

These difficulties in the Russian Empire in the decades right before and after 1900 had their parallels in the buffer countries between Germany and Russia. In Romania, despite promises that had been made in the Berlin Convention of 1878, Jews were systematically excluded from most walks of life. Even the native-born were declared to be foreigners, so that very few Jews held citizenship. There was little that Jews could do except attempt to flee in large numbers. In the Austro-Hungarian Empire the blood libel was revived in 1899 in Bohemia, but this was only the most sensational case of a series that had begun in *Tisza-Eszlar, a small Hungarian village, in 1882. Much Jewish energy went into the defense against such charges. What was being debated was not so much the blatant lie of the blood accusation but rather the more fundamental issue of the moral integrity of Judaism and the Jew. This was, essentially, still medieval antisemitism, but more contemporary currents were running strong. There were deep national tensions within the multinational Austro-Hungarian Empire, and the Jews were caught in the middle of all of the most embittered of these situations. In Bohemia they identified with the ruling Germans, to the chagrin and anger of Czech nationalists, but the local Germans nevertheless rejected the Jews as not true members of the *Volk*. In Galicia, the poorest and most medieval of the Austro-Hungarian provinces, the dominant Poles could claim a majority over the Ukrainians only by counting the Jews as Poles, but that did not induce them to accept even those Jews who were Polonizing themselves. The masses of Galician Jewry, almost a million at the turn of the century, were living in poverty that was abject even by Russian and Romanian standards, with no hope of betterment.

BETWEEN EAST AND WEST. Those years, of the last quarter of the 19th century and the beginning of the 20th, were the crucial turning point, the hinge on which modern Jewish history, the era of the emancipation, turned into contemporary Jewish history, the age of unparalleled virulence of antisemitism, the virtual end of European Jewry, and the rise of the American Jewish community and the State of Israel. Between 1880 and 1914 it became clear that the dominant response to the growing difficulties and dangers in Central and Eastern Europe was for Jews to attempt to flee westward; at first westward in Europe itself, to Vienna in the Austro-Hungarian Empire, to Germany, to France, and to England. In all of these countries quite small Jewish populations were, on the average, at least doubled between 1882 and 1914. In the United States, however, during that very same period, the Jewish population increased nearly fifteen fold, from a quarter of a million to three and a half million; Jews were some 8 percent of the total that arrived between 1880 and 1914. In the main, the reasons for this great increase were economic as America was then expanding rapidly in economic dynamism and through the settling of its large territories, and was thus in need of large numbers of new immigrants.

However, a partial reason was the increasing lack of hospitality to Jews in Western Europe. Antisemitism was growing, and so was the increased fear of it on the part of the older Jewish residents in Germany, France, and England. In Vienna the 1890s were marked by the repeated reelection as mayor of the city of Karl *Lueger on an avowedly antisemitic platform. Lueger appealed to the impoverished lower-middle classes, who envied the success of Jews in Vienna's economic and cultural life. The emperor refused to confirm his first four elections, but on the fifth such occasion, in 1897, he finally gave in. It was Lueger to whom the very young Adolf Hitler listened when he came to Vienna to try to become a painter; it was Lueger whom Theodor Herzl had in mind when, watching the degradation of Alfred Dreyfus in Paris, he came to the conclusion that antisemitism which could become a major political issue in the two most enlightened cities in Europe could no longer be regarded as a passing phenomenon. Even in England, the country which had been freest of all forms of antisemitism in the middle third of the 19th century, it reappeared after 1881, as relatively large numbers of Yiddish-speaking new immigrants continued to arrive. The moral qualities and working habits of these Jews were debated and investigated by parliamentary commissions and, after years of tension, an Aliens Act putting restrictions on further immigration became law in 1906.

In England, and even in France during the Dreyfus affair, anti-Jewish arguments and attitudes rested on a purely national premise, that is, on the supposed need to protect the integrity of national traditions. So, for example, the problem for Charles *Maurras, the central figure of French integral nationalism, was whether the Jews would be regarded, along with Bretons, Normans, etc., as one of the valid "families of France." It was, indeed, to the nationalist forms of antisemitism that Pinsker and Herzl were responding by suggesting that the cure for such tensions could come through the establishment of a normalized Jewish national identity parallel to that of all other nations. In those years, however, new forms of antisemitism were arising. These were no longer rooted in real or supposed defense of national integrity. The ideologies of both Pan-Germanism and Pan-Slavism were politically conceived in international terms (both movements were in being in 1890). In the realm of metaphysics their sense of the Teutonic or Slavic traditions as the prime bearers of human culture reflected, and conflicted with, biblical notions about the chosenness of the Jews. The distance from either of these ideologies to racism, to the insistence that the superiority of the Slav or the German inhered not in his history but in his very biological type, was not very large. Gobineau, who had been half forgotten, was again being read in the 1890s, especially in Germany. The first international meeting of all the antisemitic parties of Europe had taken place as early as 1882; by 1900 antisemitism was clearly an international movement in which objection to the Jews had become the unifying premise for groups as disparate and clashing as the anti-Dreyfusards and the nationalists of the very Germany for which Alfred Dreyfus had been accused of spying. This paradox made a certain kind of antisemitic sense. Jews were heavily identified in the major capitals of European culture with the most modern, critical, cosmopolitan supra-national spirit, and thus with the very cultural force which the newest ideologies of the radical right were trying to destroy. The leading figure of the Enlightenment, Voltaire, had not believed that Jews could ever really become *philosophes*, and he had, therefore, been less than a staunch proponent of their equality. Little more than a century later the newest forms of national antisemitism were attacking the Jews as harmful to society precisely because they were regarded, with considerable truth, as the most significant single element among the bearers of the tradition of the European Enlightenment. In this task Jews continued to be important in Europe after 1900, but their position was already clearly embattled.. By that year the Jewish masses on the move had already made a crucial decision that the future of most of the migrants was to be found in the United States. The ideologists and earliest pioneers of Zionism had moved eastward, out of the European arena to the creation of a renewed Jewish national identity in Ereẓ Israel.

For the first two centuries of the United States' national history antisemitism as an active force was practically nonexistent. Certain remnants of exclusion on Christian grounds from public office did exist in the early years of the 19th century, but these were all ultimately removed on the grounds of constitutional logic. As a population the Jews were an insignificant handful; the social structure of the country as a whole was largely fluid. The serious conflicts within the United States until after the Civil War had almost nothing to do with Jews, and they played so little role that none of the contenders could use them as scapegoat. A certain amount of endemic social prejudice reappeared in the 1870s, especially in the sight of the rapid economic rise of the first generation of German Jews to affluence. This was one expression of the process by which newly rich gentile elements were asserting their social positions by manufacturing exclusiveness. The serious tensions which did arise were a concomitant of the mass immigration from 1881 to 1914, as gentiles fled from – or battled to retain – neighborhoods becoming filled with masses of very foreign Jews from Eastern Europe. There was substantial discrimination in housing and educational opportunities at the colleges and universities, and especially in jobs in the highly structured bureaucracies of heavy industry, insurance, and banking. This new immigration provided in the first third of the century many of both the leaders and the followers of what little there was of left-wing politics in the big cities, and their role was well remembered in the reaction to the Russian Revolution and later, to the Great Depression of 1929, when there appeared a substantial amount of overt American antisemitism. The memory was carried further in the 1930s under the impetus of Nazism and its American wing, the German-American Bund. Native-born American radicalism, the populist tradition with its suspicions of the big cities, the intellectuals and, above all, of the Wall Street bankers, had its own antisemitic component. It looked for a moment in the 1930s as if antisemitism might become a substantial force in the United States, but that moment was superseded by World War II. As a whole, American antisemitism has been one of the least serious of all its manifestations in the Western world, at least in part because the United States has had, during the last century, phenomenal economic expansion and was absorbing a variety of immigrants and their cultures.

The Inter-War Period

In Europe, however, the 20th century brought with it the most violent forms of antisemitism in all of history, worse even then the outbreaks during the Crusades or in the 17th century. The border wars in Russia and Poland in the days immediately after World War I were attended by pogroms in which many thousands were killed and hundreds of thousands were robbed and rendered homeless. The major force which perpetrated these murders was the army of the Ukrainian Democratic Republic under Simon *Petliura, which made blood baths of as many as 500 places. The justification that was advanced, insofar as any rationale was offered at all, was that the Jews were supposedly partisans of the Bolsheviks. Under the impact of these horrors and the pressure mounted by the world Jewish community on the peacemakers at Versailles, minority rights for Jews, along with those for other national minorities, were written into the treaties which created such newly independent states as Poland, Lithuania, and Czechoslovakia. In the interwar period these arrangements became a source both of some protection for Jews and of considerable friction. Especially in Poland, where Jews were 10% of the population and particularly conspicuous in the cities, the essential trend between 1919 and 1939 was toward driving the Jews out of their economic positions, and toward emigration, in a world in which almost all doors were increasingly closed. The scare of Bolshevism provided the impetus for an American isolationist campaign in 1921 to close the doors of the United States to further unrestricted immigration, especially from Eastern Europe, which ended with the Monroe Law of 1924, that intentionally closed the doors to Jews. Even though some migration from Poland continued in this period and a relatively large number of Central European Jews did escape from Hitler after 1933, the European Jewish community as a whole had to face its destiny in Europe after World War I without the possibility of the kind of migrations which could make a radical difference. The only exception was Ereẓ Israel, where Jewish population grew from relatively negligible numbers to over half a million in this interwar period, and the foundations of the future State of Israel were laid.

The great and virulent outbreak of antisemitism in the Nazi era and its culmination in the Holocaust of most of European Jewry is discussed in detail elsewhere (see *Holocaust). Nazism succeeded in the backwash of German defeat in World War I and the creation of the Weimar Republic and subsequent economic disaster, all of which paved the way for nationalist-racist pan-German ideology and Third Reich hallucinations. Jews were prominent in the very founding of Weimar and in the anti-traditional culture of the Weimar period. They were thus identified with the most "un-German" era of modern German history. This was the situation within which Nazism appealed, especially to the petty bourgeoisie who envied the seemingly ever more successful Jews, but the question of what were the ultimate roots and sources of the Nazi horrors remains a matter of controversy. The most debatable issue is whether it was a demonic aberration in which the underside of human nature broke all the bonds of civilization, or whether Nazism arose from a joining together of all of the forms, of old and modern antisemitism and a need for calculated modernization in an outbreak armed with the most advanced technical tools of mass murder. To survey the whole history of antisemitism suggests that the demonic element in Nazism was not so unprecedented and that its appearance is related to a long past for which Western history cannot disclaim moral responsibility.

The Early Postwar Period

As a result of mass murder in World War II and of the emigration caused by the heightened tensions with the Arab world attending the creation of the State of Israel, Jewish residence in the classic centers of antisemitism, Christian Europe and the Islamic Middle East, was enormously reduced. The primary centers of Jewish population in the wake of the war were in the United States, the Soviet Union, and Israel.

In the post-World War II era, the Jews of America rose rapidly to very close to the top of American economic, political, and intellectual life. This has been attended by remarkably few conflicts. Some social antisemitism remained, for, as repeated studies have shown, the Jews are the only white group in the United States for whom social rank is consistently lower than economic status. Nonetheless, quotas in the colleges and universities and in certain professions, and exclusion from the highest posts of political life, have well-nigh ended. The visible difficulties that exist are noticeable in the black community. The Jew has generally been the last occupant of the neighborhoods in which blacks now live in the large cities and Jews are therefore still quite visible as landlords and storekeepers in the black neighborhoods. In addition, some Jews have felt that they have been resented for being too prominent in what some blacks would like to regard as their own revolution, which other people are taking away from them in the very act of participating in it. Nevertheless, antisemitism in postwar America was generally regarded as a minor problem.

The mood of Christians in the aftermath of World War II was overwhelmingly that of contrition. World Protestantism in its international meetings immediately after World War II, at Amsterdam and New Delhi (1948, 1961), was at great pains to condemn antisemitism and to express contrition for not having acted more strongly during the Nazi era. It was in this mood, despite ongoing theological problems with the question of whether the church continues to need to convert Jews in order to be true to itself, and the further problems of understanding, from the perspective of Christian theology, the right of the Jews to the Holy Land, that there was substantial Christian support in the late 1940s, especially among Protestants, for Zionist efforts toward the creation of the State of Israel.

In Catholic circles, Pius XII began the process of dissociating himself from Nazism after World War II by maintaining public neutrality during the battle for the creation of the State of Israel and insisting only on the internationalization of Jerusalem. The radical changes in Catholic-Jewish relations took place in the reign of John XXIII, with his excision of certain objectionable anti-Jewish references from the Good Friday liturgy, such as the term perfidy and with his setting into motion the revision of the church's basic attitude on the Jews. This crystallized in the declaration on the subject at the Vatican Council of 1965, that clearly stated: "True, the Jewish authorities and those who followed their lead pressed for the death of Christ; still, what happened in His Passion cannot be charged against all the Jews, without distinction, then alive, nor against the Jews of today." And: "Although the Church is the new people of God, the Jews should not be presented as rejected by God or accursed, as if this followed from the

Holy Scriptures." This historic theological revolution made necessary further rethinking on the part of Catholics on a whole host of theological doctrines, a process of review that is still going on. A document in which the religious significance of the Holy Land for Judaism, if it be understood in its own terms, is warmly hailed, was discussed within the highest instances of the Catholic Church. There have been since the 1950s cooperative efforts between Jews and Christians of many persuasions toward the removal of antisemitic elements in church textbook material.

Nonetheless, the significance of the "ecumenical age" could be overestimated at the time. Christianity was no longer considered the dominant spiritual force in the West during the 1960s or the 1970s that it was two centuries ago, nor has the antisemitism of the last modern age been primarily Christian. Therefore Christian ecumenism could indeed be considered less than an absolute deathblow to antisemitism. The increased friendship and understanding between Jews and Christians involved the most Western, modern, and intellectual elements: yet large parts of the Christian community remained unaffected. More important, following the Six-Day War of 1967 between Israel and its Arab neighbors, the Christian churches, and most especially the Protestant ones, in many places in the world, evidenced an increasing hospitality to Arab anti-Israel propaganda. Much of this has emanated from the Christian churches of the Arab world. Such material has often been careful to make a distinction between antisemitism, which is ruled out, and anti-Zionism and opposition to Israel, which is affirmed. Nonetheless this distinction was not always maintained. In place of the old stereotype of the Jews as accursed of God for rejecting or killing Jesus, the weak and cringing figure held in contempt, a new stereotype became prevalent in some Christian circles of the Jews as arrogantly victorious and ruthless toward the Arabs.

In the aftermath of June 1967, General de Gaulle, then president of France, angered by the support the Jews of France had given to Israel, which was contrary to his political line and wishes, pronounced the Jews to be an "elitist, self-confident, and domineering people." Here and there older antisemitic stereotypes were used in reaction to the newest phenomena, the appearance of the Israeli Jew and his effect on the Jewish mentality throughout the Diaspora. In the course of the short period of its existence, Israel has produced for the world the Jew who is unconcerned with what opinions others hold of him and who insists on his personal and national autonomy and sovereignty. This "new Jew" has elicited admiration, but also resentment. The newest forms of antisemitism have responded to the new Jewish stance by attacking what is in their eyes the elements of power. In the late 1960s and 1970s considerable left and-radical left-wing opinion in the world was strongly opposed to Israel and to the Jewish involvement in it. There was within this movement the paradox, but not an unprecedented one, of the presence of considerable numbers of leftist Jewish youngsters who were indifferent or even hostile to all forms of contemporary Jewish identity and survival (see *New Left, and "New Antisemitism" below).

The existence of Jews, the Jewish community, Judaism, and Jewish identity – whatever may be their self-definitions – as a people apart inevitably carries with it the prospect of that attack upon them which is termed antisemitism. The hatred of the unlike is an all too human phenomenon. Add to it dimensions of supposedly demonic powers; of many centuries of damnation of Jews by Christianity as the enemies of God; of the need for scapegoats in times of turmoil or defeat – and there then appears antisemitism, the most lasting expression in Western history of the hatred of the man who is regarded as alien, and therefore even possibly inhuman. Have that alien maintain, or have once maintained, or be believed to maintain, his own religious or cultural superiority – and thus appear to be a threat in the midst of elements of the majority– and the "great hatred" has arisen. Antisemitism has been less fashionable after the horror of Hitler, but it was too hopeful to believe in the post-war decades that its day is over.

[Arthur Hertzberg]

In Arab Countries

Postwar Arab antisemitism was influenced by European antisemitic literature (mainly French) published in Arabic in the second half of the 19th century, particularly in connection with the *Damascus Affair. In about 1869, Neophytos' *Destruction of the Jewish Religion* was published in Arabic in Beirut. In 1890 H. Fāris published in Cairo a book on the blood libel entitled *The Cry of the Innocent in the Horn of Freedom* (reissued in 1962 in the UAR official series of "National Books" under the title *Talmudic Human Sacrifices*). August *Rohling's *The Talmud Jew* was published in Cairo in 1899 and was cited as a source in such publications as the Arab version of the *Protocols of the of the Elders of Zion* published (c. 1967) by Shawqī ʿAbd al Nāṣir, President *Nasser's brother.

The publication of antisemitic literature became a spate as a result of the Arab-Israel conflict. Antisemitic themes and arguments were developed by Arab propaganda as a weapon against the *yishuv* during the Mandate period (1917–48) and even more so against the State of Israel. The radical objective of liquidating the Jewish state as a political entity induced Arab writers and officials to present the State of Israel as both aggressive and inherently evil, and the need to substantiate the wickedness of Israel led them to trace the sources of its evil to the history, culture, and religion of the Jewish people. Despite attempts to differentiate between Zionism and Judaism, it has been stressed repeatedly that Zionism – which is presented in such writings as a sinister, racist colonialism-originated from, and is a continuation of, Judaism. Zionism is also frequently characterized as "the executive mechanism" of Judaism. For example, H. al-Hindī and M. Ibrahim wrote in their *Isrāīl: Fikra, Ḥaraka, Dawla* ("Israel: Thought, Movement, State," Beirut, 1958, p. 113): "We fight against the imperialist regime and the Jewish people, whose invading vanguard in Palestine, called Israel, is preparing for a further leap." Though Arab antisemitism did not cause the Arab-Israel conflict, but rather was stimulated by it, it has aggravated Arab hostility.

The amount and vehemence of antisemitic literature in Arabic has no parallel in the post-World War II era. In addition to its quality and tenor, the fact that much of it has emanated from official publishing houses and government agencies makes it all the more significant, as it does not originate on the fringes of Arab society but rather at the center. The *Protocols of the Elders of Zion* has been translated into Arabic several times and been recurrently referred to, summarized, and quoted by various Arab authorities, including Nasser himself (see e.g., the official English volume of his speeches and press interviews, 1958, part 2, p. 30). Antisemitic themes and abstracts from the *Protocols* have been included in Arab secondary school textbooks, as e.g., in Dh. al-Hindāwī's *al-Qaḍiyya al-Falisṭīnyya* ("The Palestine Problem"), published in 1964 by the Jordanian Ministry of Education, and in indoctrination material of the armed forces, as in Ḥasan Ṣabrī al-Khūlī's *Qaḍiyyat Filasṭīn* ("The Palestine Problem"), published by the Indoctrination Directorate of the UAR (United Arab Republic) Armed Forces. The concept of a Jewish world conspiracy, as described in the *Protocols*, was the main theme adopted by Arabs from European antisemitism as early as the 1920s. It later may have served the psychological need of alleviating Arab self-reproach for failures and defeats by asserting that the Arabs fought not only against Israel, but against "those who are behind her" – imperialism and world Jewry.

That Arabs have not hesitated to exploit antisemitic themes, despite their witnessing the moral havoc wrought by Nazi antisemitism in Germany, proves the vehemence of Arab hostility. In Arab political literature, the Nazi extermination of the Jews has been justified. It has been suggested that others will follow this example, and Adolf *Eichmann has been hailed as a martyr (see, e.g., Abdallah al-Tal's *Khaṭr al-Yahūdiyya ʿAlā al-Islām wa-al-Masīḥiyya* ("The Danger of World Jewry against Islam and Christianity") and M.A. ʿAlūba's *Filasṭīn wa-Ḍamīr al-Insāniyya* ("Palestine and Humanity's Conscience"), both published in Cairo in 1964). Thus, antisemitism has served Arab political and intellectual leaders as a psychological tool to prepare their people for the violent liquidation of Israel.

The quibble that the Arab anti-Jewish attitude cannot be defined as antisemitism because "the Arabs themselves are Semites" is sometimes used by Arab spokesmen, particularly in statements addressed to the outside world. Arabs have distributed antisemitic literature in European languages in various countries, and antisemitic groups in Europe and America have collaborated with Arab representatives, as the Arab states can offer them such instrumentalities as support and asylum. The affiliation between Arabs and Western antisemites is manifested by the tendency of post-World War II antisemitism, especially on the left, to support the Arab case against Israel. Arab leaders are aware of the dilemma that by helping to propagate antisemitism they may endanger the position of the Jews in various countries and thereby induce further Jewish migration to Israel, but their emotions and their belief that the Arab struggle is a global one directed against world Jewry often override other considerations. The very meagerness of the remnants of the Jewish communities in most Arab countries, apart from *Morocco, has been a factor limiting the development of social antisemitism. However, there was clearly an element of antisemitism in the persecution of Jews in *Syria and *Iraq. After the Six-Day War there appeared in the Arab press condemnations of the excessive use by Arabs of antisemitic themes, specifying the damage caused by extremism to the Arab cause The frequency of antisemitic publications subsequently abated somewhat. A later book is Bint al-Shāṭiʾ (Dr. ʿAʾisha ʿAbd al-Raḥman), *Aʿda al-Bashar* declaring the Jews the enemies of humanity), published by no less than the UAR Government – The Higher Council of Islamic Affairs, 1964.

[Yehoshafat Harkabi]

In the Soviet Bloc

THEORY AND PRACTICE. Antisemitism, according to Communist doctrine, is an extremely negative social phenomenon; it could only be part of reactionary, capitalist, and pre-capitalist regimes, in which hatred of the Jews is exploited for the gain of the ruling classes. Lenin, along with the other revolutionaries in czarist Russia, was a sincere and resolute opponent of antisemitism and of any form of oppression, discrimination, and persecution of Russian Jewry. However, after the consolidation of the Soviet regime, principally under *Stalin's one-man rule, a distinctly anti-Jewish policy was sometimes planned and implemented in the Soviet Union. This policy consciously exploited the traditional antisemitism of the people in the Ukraine and in other parts of Russia, who viewed the Jews as a foreign element, "rootless in the homeland," who tended to conspire with the country's enemies, to evade dangerous defense duties in time of war, and who quickly profited by illicit economic manipulations and by exploiting the toiling masses. The word "Jew" itself has been mentioned relatively rarely in Soviet antisemitic propaganda, precisely in order to avoid breaking an ideological taboo; the antisemitic intent, however, was clear to everybody through the use of thinly disguised, conventional terms, such as "*Cosmopolitans," "Zionists," "people without a fatherland," etc. The aim was mostly "a so-called educational" one: to produce tangible evidence that certain popular tendencies which the regime tried to eradicate (such as interest in Western life and culture, or illicit manufacturing and marketing of goods) were initiated and conducted by foreign, traitorous, "rootless" elements, i.e., the Jews. A further stimulus arose during the Cold War years, when the system of suspecting and supervising whole groups of the population by the security organs reached its peak. Every Jew was thus regarded as a real or potential security risk because of his family ties with Jews in the U.S. or other Western countries, and because of his sympathy, open or hidden, for the young State of Israel. This "cosmopolitanism," presumably an inherent characteristic of every Jewish body, was considered dangerous from the security point of view and warranted the liquidation of all Jewish institutions and organizations, with the exception of only a few synagogues which were placed under constant supervision by the security police. A further stage in Soviet antisemitism was reached in the late 1960s when the Soviet Union adopted an extreme anti-Israel policy, particularly after the Six-Day *War in June 1967. Soviet propaganda started a campaign grotesquely inflating the image of Zionism as a sinister international conspiracy spread over the whole world, very similar to that propounded in the *Protocols of the Elders of Zion*.

AFTER THE OCTOBER REVOLUTION. During and immediately after the October Revolution, antisemitism served as one of the prime weapons of the Russian counterrevolution, when the White forces depicted the Bolshevik regime as executing the enslavement of Mother Russia by the Jews. Lenin saw antisemitism not only as a socio-political evil, in accord with his ideological outlook, but also as a formidable factor which he had to combat in his struggle for saving the revolution. He attacked antisemitism in his statements and speeches, including the well-known resolution of the Soviet government which defined perpetrators and instigators of pogroms as enemies of the revolution who had to be outlawed (*Izvestiya*, July 27, 1918). This atmosphere existed in the Soviet Union for years, at least up to the consolidation of Stalin's dictatorship toward the end of the 1920s. Among the masses antisemitic feelings continued in the 1920s, particularly during the NEP ("New Economic Policy"), sometimes even increasing, as when a large influx of Jews from the townlets came to the industrial and administrative centers, where they competed for the available jobs. Antisemitism also increased among the peasants as Jews received land in southern Russia and Crimea for agricultural settlement. But, despite popular antisemitism and the official persecution of the Jewish religion and the Zionist and Jewish Socialist movement (carried out to a large extent by Jewish Communist party members), vast numbers of Jews in the U.S.S.R. enjoyed (during the 1920s and most of the 1930s) considerable geographic and social mobility, with no obstacles of an antisemitic nature standing in their way.

The turning point began toward the end of the 1930s with the Great Purges, during which the Soviet government discontinued denouncing and punishing expressions and outbursts of popular antisemitism. At this time, the government initiated a systematic liquidation of Jewish institutions and leading figures. Then, however, it was possible to view this as part of the general processes designed to secure Stalin's dictatorship, since there still were significant numbers of Jews holding middle and higher positions of power in the party hierarchy and in vital branches of government, such as the political secret police. From 1939 onward, after the signing of the Nazi-Soviet Pact (Ribbentrop-Molotov Non-Aggression Pact) and the outbreak of World War II in the West, the Soviet press and radio systematically concealed reports about the anti-Jewish character of the Nazi regime and about the oppression and murder of Jews after the invasion of Poland. In this respect, there was a considerable improvement following the German attack on the U.S.S.R. in June 1941. However, in the many detailed accounts of Nazi atrocities in the Soviet press and radio there was still a discernible tendency to cover up the fact of the genocide of the Jewish people, which was mostly described in vague terms, as the murder of "peaceful, innocent citizens." This systematic concealment continued even more strongly after World War II. Anyone attempting to emphasize the special suffering of the Jewish people under the Nazi occupation of the U.S.S.R. (as, e.g., Yevgeny Yevtushenko) was strongly criticized by official spokesmen.

THE BLACK YEARS 1948–1953. The Black Years began for Russian Jewry when the anti-Jewish line became the active policy of the highest government echelon. These were the last four or five years of Stalin's regime (1948–53). The secret police murdered Solomon *Mikhoels, director of the Jewish State Theater in Moscow and chairman of the Jewish *Anti-Fascist Committee, thus touching off what became the systematic liquidation of all Jewish cultural institutions which were remnants of the 1930s or established during the war. At the end of 1948 and the beginning of 1949 Soviet newspapers and journals opened an anti-Jewish campaign, condemning the alleged cosmopolitan rootless elements in intellectual life. This campaign was the first undisguised expression of the wide exploitation of popular antisemitism for Soviet government aims. The ingrained hatred and suspicion of Jews – as a foreign element liable to treason – served here as a powerful demagogic means of educating the nation against "westernizing" tendencies and for seclusion behind the wall of Russian nationalism. The closing down of the Jewish Anti-Fascist Committee; the arrests and execution of Jewish writers, artists, and public figures; the "Crimea Affair" trial behind closed doors; the Slansky *trial in Prague (initiated and run by emissaries from the Soviet Union); the *Doctors' Plot; the dismissal of many thousands of Jews from their work; and the portrayal of the State of Israel and of the Zionist movement as instruments of an anti-Soviet American spy network, were all part of the anti-Jewish program of the "Black Years." Antisemitism served as one of the principal tools of Stalin's regime and policy during the Cold War years both in the U.S.S.R. and in the satellite countries. According to reliable testimony, Stalin intended, following the Doctors' Plot trial," to initiate a mass deportation of the Jewish population from the principal cities of the U.S.S.R. to Eastern Siberia, but he died in March 1953, before he could carry out his plan.

THE KHRUSHCHEV PERIOD. The period following Stalin's death was inaugurated by an apparent reversal of the anti-Jewish policy through the official retraction of the "Doctors' Plot" accusation, but expectations that the Jewish institutions would be reinstated and that there would be a vigorous campaign against popular antisemitism were frustrated. Nikita Khrushchev, who in a closed session of the 20th Congress of the Soviet Communist Party (February 1956) denounced

Stalin and his methods, completely ignored the anti-Jewish aspect of the defunct dictator's rule, and silence on this subject was regarded as ominous for Soviet Jewry. Khrushchev himself, who was the supreme party and government representative in the Ukraine during and after World War II, was apparently deeply impressed by the immense power of popular antisemitism as a socio-political factor. Upon becoming prime minister and first secretary of the Communist Party of the U.S.S.R., he more than once expressed his own anti-Jewish thoughts and feelings in talks with foreign personalities, delegations, and newsmen and once even spoke out in defense of Stalin's stand in the "Crimea Affair," thus indirectly vindicating the liquidation of the Jewish Anti-Fascist Committee and its members.

Khrushchev's antisemitic policy was moderate in comparison with that practiced in Stalin's last years. It took the form not only of a consistent concealment of the genocide inflicted on the Jews during the Nazi invasion, but also of using Jews for show trials in the campaign against "economic crimes." This campaign was carried out by the security police from May 1961 until Khrushchev was removed from office in 1964. The Jews accused of "economic crimes" were picked out from a large number of people engaged in illicit economic activities and assigned the role of alleged initiators, instigators, and organizers of transgressions and other "crimes" against the Soviet laws in matters of production, marketing, and foreign currency regulations. Jews were the majority of those found guilty. Many of them received the death penalty, and their being Jews was emphasized in various ways in the press. During Khrushchev's office, books and pamphlets appeared which strongly denounced not only Zionism and the State of Israel, but also Judaism as such, as an extremely negative historical, cultural, and religious phenomenon. These publications were sometimes accompanied by crude antisemitic cartoons (as in the book by the Ukrainian antisemite Trofim Kychko, *Judaism without Embellishment*, published by the Academy of Sciences of the Ukrainian Soviet Republic, Ukrainian, 1963). A new effort to eradicate organized Jewish life in the U.S.S.R. was made under Khrushchev through the closing of many synagogues, often following a smear campaign by the local newspapers in which the synagogues were described as hangouts where criminals met for their sinister purposes. Synagogue leaders were arrested; *minyanim* in private homes were brutally dispersed; and the baking of *maẓẓot* for Passover was gradually abolished. In some places, burial of Jews in separate Jewish cemeteries was discontinued. In these years, popular antisemitism made itself felt in several outbursts, as, e.g., the arson of the synagogue and murder of the Jewish cemetery's *shammash* in the town of Malakhovka near Moscow, accompanied by the posting of antisemitic proclamations in the streets (Rosh Ha-Shanah 1959); the burning of the synagogue in Tskhakaya, Georgia, in 1962; anti-Jewish street riots, at times incited by blood libels (in Tashkent and in Tskhaltubo in 1962); public tension created by a blood-libel story in Vilna in 1963; and in one instance, the publication of an anti-Jewish blood libel in the official organ of the Communist Party (in the town Buinaksk, Dagestan, in the local newspaper on August 9, 1961, where a few days later an official apology of sorts was printed).

In widespread circles of the Russian intelligentsia opposition to the official and popular antisemitic clime was expressed in several ways, but for the most part by hints and implications rather than by overt criticism. It reached its climax in Yevtushenko's poem *Babi Yar published in *Literaturnaya Gazeta* in 1961 and in the fact that Dmitri Shostakovich included the poem in one of the movements of his 13th symphony. The poem immediately aroused severe criticism, with antisemitic overtones, on the part of official literary critics and even from Khrushchev himself. A clear hint was given that any public declaration on behalf of the Jews was in contradiction to official policy. At the same time Jews of the U.S.S.R. were affected by systematic discrimination in many spheres. Jews almost completely disappeared from the foreign service, from commanding posts in the army, from positions as representatives of the government, the party hierarchy, the judiciary, etc. The number of Jews in local, republican, or Soviet government bodies fell far below the percentage of Jews, not only in the cities (where about 95% of the Jews reside), but in the population as a whole. Young Jews met with increasing difficulties in getting accepted in higher institutions of learning in the main cities of Russia and the Ukraine, particularly in those fields of study which usually lead to positions of power or to classified fields.

UNDER KOSIGIN-BREZHNEV. When Khrushchev was demoted in October 1964, and the "collective leadership" headed by Alexei Kosigin and Leonid Brezhnev initiated, there were signs of slight improvement in the attitude to Soviet Jewry. The campaign against "economic crimes" and the synagogues ceased; baking of *maẓẓot* was to a certain extent renewed; Jews were mentioned as victims of the Nazi Holocaust on Soviet soil; and even a public denunciation of antisemitism as one of the evils of society was once made in a speech by Prime Minister Kosigin. Following this, editorials in the same spirit were published in several leading newspapers in 1965. However, after the Six-Day War in June 1967 between Israel and the Arab states, a most severe anti-Jewish campaign in the Soviet press and propaganda media was unleashed again. Its declared aim was to condemn Israel and Zionism, but its general spirit and the caricatures accompanying it were markedly antisemitic. The Ukrainian style of antisemitism, which represents Judaism as a criminal religious tradition from ancient times, educating its followers in racial superiority and hatred of other peoples, began reappearing in widely diffused publications, as well as in tracts written by Trofim Kychko who reappeared on the scene after having had to remain silent for a few years, as his 1963 book had caused a world-wide scandal even in Communist parties in the West. In the new campaign, "Zionism" was assigned a central place: it was depicted as a powerful instrument or a main ally of "imperialism," serving its sinister global aims, such as enslaving nations and exploiting them, undermining Socialism, and, of course, manipulating Israel for criminal aggression against the progressive Arab states. These descriptions of Zionism closely resembled the description of the world Jewish conspiracy in the *Protocols of the Elders of Zion*. It created an atmosphere of depression and deep apprehension in Soviet Jewry, who again were led to fear for their physical and economic security. However, no persecutions of Jews in the manner of the "Black Years" of Stalin are known to have taken place; it seems that the government took steps to prevent any outbursts of popular antisemitism such as those which occurred in Khrushchev's time.

POLAND AND CZECHOSLOVAKIA. Popular expression of antisemitism in Poland became overt when Wladislaw Gomulka's government rose to power in October 1956. One of its sources was hatred of the overthrown Stalinist higher echelon, which in Poland included a number of Jews in key positions (e.g., Jacob *Berman and Hilary *Minc). However, Gomulka's regime was expressly opposed to antisemitism. In the framework of repatriation of former Polish citizens, it made possible the return of many Jews from the U.S.S.R. and their further migration to Israel. It did not interfere with the exodus of the remnant of Polish Jewry to Israel and other countries. However, its policy underwent a marked change following the Six-Day War in June 1967, becoming extremely anti-Israel, in line with Soviet policy. Gomulka even went a step further, when he publicly warned the Jews in Poland against becoming a "fifth column" by expressions of sympathy for Israel. Following this stand, a number of books and articles appeared that sharply attacked Israel and Zionism, with distinctly antisemitic overtones. This paved the way for wide anti-Jewish purges in the ranks of the government, universities, and other fields in the spring of 1968, when government circles blamed "Zionists" for mass demonstrations held by students and professors in the universities. The anti-Jewish purge and propaganda campaign was directed and exploited by one of the party factions for political ends. This faction, known as the "Partisans," was headed by the minister of the interior and head of the security police, Mieczysław Moczar.

In Czechoslovakia, where traditional antisemitism has no deep roots, as in the Ukraine and in Poland, Antonin Novotny, president of the republic and secretary of the Communist Party, ruled continuously from the period of the (Rudolf) Slansky Trial until early in 1968. When he was ousted by the liberal wing of the Communist Party, there was a general improvement in the atmosphere. Jewish cultural and religious life was favorably affected. But, during the sharp controversy between the Soviet government and the liberal regime in Prague that led to the invasion of Czechoslovakia by the Soviet army in August 1968, Soviet and Polish propaganda used anti-Jewish allusions (e.g., that "Zionists" had pulled the strings of the "counterrevolution" in Czechoslovakia). Following the invasion, Jewish figures in the liberal Czechoslovak regime, such as Eduard *Goldstuecker, Ota Šik, and others, were forced to disappear or even to leave the country. In the Czechoslovak crisis, as in the anti-Jewish purges in Poland that year, antisemitism, mostly disguised as "anti-Zionism," was one of the prime elements in the influence exerted by Soviet agencies in Soviet bloc countries; it naturally served even more the needs of the anti-Israel campaign conducted by the Soviet government and propaganda media in Arab countries.

[Binyamin Eliav]

In the United States

IDEALS AND REALITY. In the United States the fate of the Jewish community has been more fortunate than in almost any other country. Jews in general experienced wider tolerance and greater civil and political equality than in the countries they had left, and Judaism was accepted by most Americans as one of the great religions. The U.S. government has exemplified George Washington's famous words accepting the formula of the Newport Hebrew Congregation to give "to bigotry no sanction, to persecution no assistance." American Jews, unlike many European compatriots, did not live as an autonomous community, or with a separate legal system for running the affairs of a ghetto.

Jews benefited not only from the absence of official governmental hostility, pogroms, or serious restrictions, and of an established religion that might encourage discrimination against other faiths, but also from the social, economic, and political traits of American life: the pluralistic society with its opportunities for social and geographic mobility, ability to participate in political activity, political parties as broad coalitions in which ethnic groups could compete and also be mutually protected, constitutional protection of civil rights in most cases, the competitive economic system, and the decentralized congregational structure permitting different expressions of the Jewish faith. Some legal restrictions of the civil and political rights of Jews to vote and hold office were almost all eliminated by the early 19th century. No systematic antisemitic ideology has been advocated by any mainstream political leader or group; overt antisemitism has, with rare exceptions, been associated with fringe or non-political elements. Indeed, care must be taken to distinguish the application to Jews of the normal intergroup tensions and conflicts in America from genuine antisemitism.

Nevertheless, anti-Jewish sentiment, social prejudice, and hatred motivated by religious, economic, and racial considerations, has been a constant presence in American life. Sometimes it has taken the form of violence. The Jewish community has suffered from discrimination in many forms: housing, employment, admission to resort hotels, business, college quotas, membership of social clubs. Negative images of Jews in popular literature and culture have persisted. Stereotypes – killers of Christ, criminals, Shylocks, uncouth *nouveaux riches* responsible for social disintegration, ethnic and cultural aliens, clannish conspirators, financial exploiters, revolutionaries or radicals – have been rife. For long periods Jews were rarely portrayed positively or realistically.

Antisemitic rhetoric and behavior have been more pronounced in some periods of American history than in others. During the Civil War the most discriminatory act against Jews was the official order of General Grant in December 1862, expelling them from military territories in the border states for alleged illegal trading; the order was immediately revoked by President Lincoln. In the 1880s and 1890s, the agrarian and Populist movements in the Middle West gave vent to some antisemitic utterances. Anxiety at the influx of East European Jews, and of others held undesirable, led to the imposition of quotas, and the virtual end of Jewish immigration by 1918. Jewish residents also experienced an increase in social antisemitism.

American constitutional ideals, liberal traditions, and pluralistic society and politics, were normally sufficient to prevent extreme antisemitic behavior. Yet ugly incidents did occur, the most dramatic being the unjust conviction in 1913, and the lynching by a mob in 1915, of Leo Frank, a Jewish factory superintendent in Atlanta for the alleged murder of a female employee. In the 1920s, the most influential expressions of antisemitism emanated from publications financed by the industrialist Henry Ford, *The International Jew* and the *Dearborn Independent*, with a circulation of 700,000, and reprinting of the *Protocols of the Elders of Zion*. Before World War II demagogues, such as Senator Theodore Bilbo and Congressman John Rankin, attacked international Jewry in general and New York Jews in particular as aggressive capitalists, communists or radicals, or polluters of American culture. Over a hundred organizations, mostly small and local in character, seeing Jews as mainly or partly responsible for social ills appealed to different social classes and ethnic groups.

Of these organizations, five were particularly active: The German-American Bund, the Silver Shirts, the Christian Front led by Father Coughlin, Gerald L.K. Smith's Committee of One Million, and the Protestant Defenders of the Christian Faith.

Since the end of World War II, polls and surveys, though differing on the exact figures, have suggested a considerable decline in antisemitic attitudes, though about half of American Jews believed that antisemitism is a serious problem and two-thirds feared it could be serious in the future. Moreover, in the U.S., negative attitudes have rarely led to serious manifestations of prejudice. In its 1989 audit of antisemitic incidents in the United States, the Anti-Defamation League of B'nai B'rith reported 845 incidents of vandalism and desecration, ranging from arson to swastika daubings of Jewish institutions and property, and over 580 assaults, threats, and harassments against Jews or Jewish institutions. Over 85 percent of those arrested for the incidents were under 21.

Though it significantly declined from 1944 to the late 1960s, antisemitism persisted during these years notwithstanding the determined efforts of Jewish organizations and political action to counter it, despite elimination of many hostile references to Jews in Christian religious books and increased interfaith activity and institutes on Judaism, civil rights legislation, federal and state laws, continuing revulsion about Nazi crimes against Jews, the breaking down of social barriers in the post-War era, and in spite of the changed nature of the American Jewish community.

That community is a well-educated, affluent, highly urban, liberal, Democratic, politically active, mobile, adaptable, aging and gradually becoming less religiously observant group. In the late 1970s it amounted to 2.5% of the total population, and still declining, it has achieved an unparalleled social, political, and economic status, occupying prominent positions in education, government, business, the professions, and the cultural world. The very fact that intermarriage of Jews with members of other faiths rose so dramatically – by some calculations to 40% of Jewish males and 10% of females – itself indicated the increased acceptance of Jews. In 1981 only 14% of non-Jews objected strongly, and another 14% somewhat, to a mixed marital relationship.

In post-World War II America, until the 1980s at least, open advocacy, let alone ideological formulation, of antisemitism was not respectable. The symbol of the Holocaust; the moderate political climate; the absence of any mass dissatisfaction with the prevailing socio-economic system; the decline in Christian religious orthodoxy; the modifications of doctrine and attitude by churches, especially by the Catholic Church at Vatican Council II; and the growth of the economy and in the standard of living all helped lessen tension between Jews and non-Jewish whites.

Besides the decline in unofficial anti-Jewish prejudice in areas such as housing and employment, state laws increasingly forbade discrimination, and the courts removed restrictive covenants on housing. In universities, the quota system imposing limitations on Jews was largely ended. Overt discrimination appeared confined to a few exclusive cooperatives, athletic or golf clubs, and law firms.

Public opinion polls tried to measure the attitudes of Americans towards Jews in the postwar years. Survey findings sometimes showed widely differing results and must be treated with care. Yet, they were a valuable way to assess the degree of prejudice since American antisemitism was then largely attitudinal and not usually translated into either ideological coherence or concrete actions.

The index of 11 antisemitic beliefs proposed by Selznick and Steinberg in 1969 has been a useful benchmark for later studies. Between 1964 and 1981, negative beliefs in the index declined by about 14 percentage points. Americans were then less likely to see Jews as dishonest businessmen, clannish, in control of international banking or the media, television, or the movies, as having a lot of irritating faults, or as willing to choose money over people.

Yet, significant numbers of Americans between 1978 and 1985 still accepted negative stereotypes of Jews in general. They saw Jews as pushy, aggressive (25%), clannish (40%), going out of their way to hire only Jews (57%), controllers of movie and television (25%), willing to use shady practices (33%), choosing money over people (34%), and control over international banking (43%).

In 1981, over 80% would vote for a qualified Jew as president. A 1988 Gallup poll shows that only 3% did not want Jews as neighbors; 13% disliked black and 9% disliked Hispanic neighbors. In a 1981 Gallup poll, about 40% had a "highly favorable" opinion of Jews while only 2% were "highly unfavorable." The highly antisemitic attitudes declined from 37% in 1964 to 23% in 1981. Negative stereotypes existed about Jews but they were held even more strongly against evangelical or fundamentalist Protestants, and against oil companies and big business.

Accompanying the decline in negative images is an increase in positive ones. Jews are seen as hard working, talented, intelligent, warm and friendly, as contributing much to American cultural life, as philanthropic, and as good family members. A 1982 Roper poll found that 59% thought it was "a good thing" that Jews had immigrated to the U.S.

On some issues, negative attitudes increased over the 1960s and 1970s. In 1981, 35% thought Jews had too much power in the business world, 20% that they had too much power in the U.S. (11% in 1964) and more were concerned about the loyalty of Jews to Israel. Polls show that between a quarter and a third of the population believed Jews "are more loyal" to Israel than to America. In a poll in April 1987, 28% thought Jews placed the interests of Israel ahead of the U.S.

ANTISEMITIC GROUPS. Few in post-war America have ventured antisemitic remarks in public. Generalizations, however, can be made on the basis of certain factors: educational level, income, age, race, religion, place of birth, and geographical location. Those holding antisemitic beliefs tended to hold other prejudiced, intolerant, or undemocratic views in general. They were most widespread among the uneducated and poorer members of American society.

Education is a key variable. The least educated scored highest in antisemitic attitudes, except for blacks. Decline in negative images of Jews, as well as in general intolerance, could be correlated during the 1970s and 1980s with the higher level of education of the community. More knowledge of minorities, possession of cognitive skills to think rationally, and understanding of the virtues of tolerance and civil rights have meant less negative images of Jews. Antisemitism was found to be highest in the working class and lowest among professionals and the middle class.

Antisemitism was higher among Protestants than among Catholics. About 80% of Southern Baptists and 70% of Missouri Synod Lutherans agreed that Jews remained unforgiven for the death of Christ. Religion has been a powerful reinforcement of antisemitic views; 45% of all American antisemites get their antisemitic ideas from religious indoctrination or from some religious influence. The number of prejudiced among fundamentalists is some 7% greater than among nonfundamentalists.

Older people tend to be more antisemitic than younger individuals. This might be explained by lower educational level, by the fact that antisemitism was more prevalent when the older people were themselves young, and by the possibility that the aging process might have led to greater feelings of insecurity and intolerance.

Foreign-born Americans in general, partly because they tend to be older and less well educated than the average, hold stronger antisemitic views than the native born. Rural residents, especially in the South and Midwest, tend to be more antisemitic than urban residents. There appears to be little difference in beliefs between the sexes.

The greater degree of antisemitism among blacks than among the white population is disenchanting for those with memories of Jewish sympathy for the plight of blacks, and of actions, even at cost of life, to remedy that plight. Jews have always been more concerned about the state of blacks than have members of other religions, and given disproportionate support and financial aid to civil rights organizations. Black prejudice, often inherited from the Christian fundamentalism imbibed in youth, essentially stemmed from disparaging economic stereotypes of Jews as money grubbers, callous storekeepers and landlords, uncaring employers of black domestics, and as individuals who would use their economic power to degrade blacks.

Moderate black leaders, such as Martin Luther King, Jr., praised "the contribution that Jewish people have made toward the Negro's struggle for freedom." They acknowledged the Jewish help and alliance in black organizations and in the campaigns in the South with their freedom riders and voter registration teams.

However, from the 1960s on, the alliance had become strained. The Student Non-Violent Coordinating Committee (SNCC), formed in 1960 with Jewish help, within a decade, under the leadership of Stokely Carmichael, began attacking "the Rothschilds" as well as "Zionist Jewish terrorists." Malcolm X denounced Jews as part of the white exploitative majority and wrote, "I don't care what a Jew is professionally, doctor, merchant, housewife, student or whatever – first, he or she thinks Jew," and talked of "Jews who sapped the very lifeblood of blacks." The extremist Black Panthers, the Black Muslims, believing in a Jewish conspiracy to control the world, and some black intellectuals were vocal in anti-Jewish sentiment.

All polls and surveys of the time, as well as other empirical evidence, showed that black antisemitism was considerably higher than that of whites at every educational level. Two-fifths of blacks, compared with one out of five whites, could then be characterized as having high or moderate antisemitic beliefs.

Looking at the surveys of black antisemitism, five features seemed significant. The first was that it increased relative to that of whites. Secondly, black antisemitism was higher in the urban North than in the more rural South. Thirdly, it was manifested more on economic than on other issues. Those blacks who had economic dealings with or who perceived economic mistreatment by Jews recorded a higher level of antisemitism than those who do not. Blacks remained more opposed than did whites to political antisemitism and to social discrimination, but negative beliefs on some noneconomic matters, especially on Israel, also increased. Fourthly, blacks who had personal contact with Jews, mostly in a subordinate role, were likely to be more antisemitic than those who did not, the reverse of the relationship between adult whites and Jews.

Most significant, it was younger blacks and the better educated who exhibited the strongest negative attitudes. This may be the consequence of the competition with or envy of Jews by aspiring black professionals. The antisemitic level of elite black leaders was about double that of blacks as a whole. Assertions of black consciousness and power from the 1960s, greater racial pride and solidarity, meant rejection of white, primarily Jewish, control of black organizations. For many black leaders, the politics of integration changed to the politics of confrontation.

That confrontation took the form of disputes over political goals and the exercise of power. But also the dismissal in 1979 of Andrew Young as American ambassador to the United Nations for meeting with a PLO official, the abusiveness of Nation of Islam leader Louis Farrakhan's remarks about Judaism as a "gutter religion" and his declared admiration for Hitler, the references to New York City as "Hymietown" by presidential candidate Jesse Jackson in 1984, the injection of black-Jewish animosity into the 1988 Democratic party primary in New York, all inflamed passions on both sides. Blacks held about 10% less favorable attitudes to Israel than do whites. Jews and blacks have strongly differed on questions of open enrollment in New York City colleges and, above all, on the issues of quotas for employment. Yet, the old black-Jewish liberal coalition, with its mutual support for electoral office and for policies favoring integrated schools, civil rights, and vitality of urban areas on the one hand, and issues significant to Jews, especially the security of Israel on the other, did not break down.

Besides a few radical left groups, most contemporary vitriolic antisemitism stems from a wide diversity of extremist right-wing hate groups, small in size, essentially anti-democratic and estranged from political and social reality, Identity Church groups and neo-Nazi organizations, living with the memories of Adolf Hitler, and limited to between 400 and 450 members, and the various, small Ku Klux Klan bodies. Some of these groups have engaged not only in hate rhetoric against minorities and racist ideology, but also in crimes, from synagogue bombings to armed robbery and murder, and fanciful conspiracies to overthrow the U.S. government.

These groups, whose members are often disaffected and frustrated, share overlapping beliefs: hostility to government which is seen as illegitimate; enmity toward Jews and non-whites; attacks on Jewish interests supposedly controlling government, finance, and the media; and purported Christian concepts by which white Protestants are seen as the "chosen people."

The better known of the hate groups are the Aryan Nations, the Christian Defense League, the Posse Commitatus, the Covenant, the Sword, and the Arm of the Lord, and the Christian-Patriots Defense League.

Probably the most aggressive of the non-religious hate groups are the "skinheads," gangs of shaven-headed youths who glorify violence, and have been responsible for an increasing number of assaults as well as antisemitic bigotry.

The Liberty Lobby, the most active and the best financed antisemitic organization in the country, describes itself as "a pressure group for patriotism," and maintains close connections with a number of members of Congress. Its weekly newspaper, *The Spotlight*, started in 1975 and now, with a circulation of over a quarter of a million, is the most widely read right-wing extremist paper in the country. Among its favorite targets are Zionism, and people defined euphemistically as "dual loyalists" or "international bankers."

The Institute for Historical Review was created in 1979. Its chief concern has been to deny or minimize the reality of the Holocaust and explore Jewish "atrocity propaganda" through a number of books and materials with antisemitic themes and by annual conventions.

To conclude: Extreme groups in the U.S. remained small and outside the political mainstream, and their membership appeared to have declined even further. American politics embodies and public opinion coheres around a consensus of political moderation in which antisemitic expressions are not respectable.

The country, with certain qualifications, exhibited a lower level of overt prejudice and bigotry than ever before in racial and religious matters. Jews as a group were no longer blamed, except by a fringe element, for the nation's problems or condemned for not being truly American. Indeed, in the working of the American political system today, Jews both as political activists and participants, and as elected and appointed officials have played a prominent role.

Yet, the portrait of antisemitism is a composite of conflicting traits. If most churches no longer insist on Jewish responsibility for the Crucifixion, those of an orthodox or particularist persuasion are inclined to do so. An appreciable minority, between one-fifth and one-quarter, still believed in the 1980s that Jews have too much power. Some remain obsessed by the idea of Jewish domination of the media and banking.

Two other major problems remained. Black antisemitism, stemming from religious teachings and economic stereotypes, exacerbated by the politics of confrontation and, to a lesser degree, a rise in adherence to Islam, was a troubling issue. The issue of Israel, support for its policies, aid for its security, and Jewish relations with the state did not lead to an increase in antisemitism. But about a quarter of non-Jews were highly unfavorable to Israel, and young people are more likely to be so than are older people.

Appropriate anxiety should be shown for the rhetoric and the potential for violence of those extreme groups which have antisemitism high on their agenda, though their membership is small and declining. But that anxiety should not be excessive. Even admitting a significant minority of the population can be regarded as having antisemitic attitudes, Jews have not been made scapegoats for economic or social problems. What is finally important is that the antisemitic beliefs that existed until the late 1980s did not lead to an organized movement with any serious support for violence against Jews.

[Michael Curtis]

Trends in the 1970s

FROM NAZISM TO NEO-NAZISM. In the post-Holocaust period, there have been attempts in Western countries to revive Nazi organizations with antisemitic ideologies. Still, the "swastika plague." that swept West Germany and other countries in 1959–60, accompanied by a wave of antisemitic incidents, was found to have been orchestrated by the Soviet Union, in order to embarrass West Germany, and subsided shortly thereafter. Indeed, the efforts to set up an international organization of neo-Nazi groups were centered in Belgium, where a group called *Nation Europa* tried to get a foothold in the 1960s. In the U.S., a small body was set up by Gerhard Lauck in Lincoln, Nebraska, which kept the old label of the NSDAP (National Socialist German Workers' Party) and still acts as a main supplier of ideological guidance to neo-Nazi groups. Other propaganda centers exist in Switzerland, Denmark, Spain, Britain, Belgium and elsewhere. In Germany, the weekly *Deutsche National-Zeitung* (cir. 100,000 in 1977; 130,000 in 1978) served as a rallying point. After various groups tried to form a neo-Nazi party in the 1950s, the NPD (National-demokratische Partei Deutschlands) emerged; Jewish issues were not on the whole central, but the 1953 Luxembourg agreements on German *restitution were attacked, German war-guilt was rejected, and the Holocaust either minimized or denied. This last tendency became especially marked after the appearance in the U.S. in 1975 (German edition, 1977) of Arthur R. Butz's *The Hoax of the Twentieth Century*. However, the vote received by the NPD in Federal elections fell from 0.3% in 1976 to 0.2% (68,096 out of 38 million) in 1980. The total average editions of all right-wing periodicals in Germany added up to 324,000 in 1983, of which 17,000 represent neo-Nazi publications (according to the ADL the Anti-Defamation League of B'nai B'rith). The total readership would therefore indicate a slightly higher percentage of sympathizers than actual voters. Membership in the NPD declined from 21,000 in 1970 to 6,500 in 1983, but the *Deutsche Volksunion*, headed by the editor of the *Deutsche National-Zeitung*, claimed 10,000 members. Other German right-wing and neo-Nazi groups rejected the legalistic approach of the NPD and, from about the mid-1970s, increasingly leaned towards extra-legal and terrorist activities. The main targets were the democratic institutions of the German Federal Republic, but antisemitism is part and parcel of the ideological baggage of these groups. They numbered about 70 in 1977, with fewer than 20,000 members. Overall, public opinion polls revealed a marked decline in antisemitic sentiments, which are now prevalent mainly among older people, whereas the younger generation appeared to be very much less prone to antisemitism. The decline in antisemitic sentiment was accompanied, paradoxically, by increased violence on the part of the minuscule neo-Nazi movement. Group hatred was directed mainly towards Turkish and other foreign workers ("Gastarbeiter").

A similar picture emerges in other countries. In Britain, the neo-Nazi National Front was declining steadily after initial successes. In 1977, it polled over 5% (119,000 votes) in the Greater London council elections; by 1978 it had dropped to 34,000 votes, with the downward trend continuing in subsequent years. Its antisemitism, while very marked ("the Jewish question" is "a central issue in the struggle for the salvation of British nationhood," in *Spearhead*, February 1977), was overshadowed by its opposition to black and Asian immigration to Britain. In the early 1980s, the NF split into four groups. Some of the more extreme splinters (such as the British Movement and Column 88) have evinced an inclination to terrorist action.

In France, a May 1977 enquiry (by the Paris *Le Matin*) showed that about 5% of Frenchmen exhibited clear antipathy to Jews, while 29% were against the idea of a Jew as French president (as opposed to 60% in 1966). French group animosity was directed largely towards foreigners (92% dislike Arab North Africans). Right-wing extremist political groups came and went, but they did not poll, until the late 1970s, more than 1% in national elections. An extreme terrorist group (FANE) was banned in 1980.

The Italian neo-fascist party, MSI (Movimento Sociale Italiano), was a force to be reckoned with, despite a split in December 1976. Openly antisemitic views, however, were expressed only in marginal groups such as Ordine Nuovo or Ordine Nero. The MSI polled 8.6% in 1972 parliamentary elections and 5.3% in 1979. In Belgium, a militant Flemish nationalist group, the VMO (Vlaams Militante Orde), was instrumental in several attempts to coordinate neo-Nazi activities on an international scale. In Spain, a similar group called Fuerza Nueva was accused of being linked to a December 1976 bomb attack on the Madrid synagogue. The European country with the strongest antisemitic popular feelings appears to have been Austria, where 50% of Viennese were found to have negative attitudes to Jews in 1977.

In the U.S., Ku Klux Klan groups reappeared occasionally. Their membership numbered about 10,000 in 1980 (but 50,000 in 1967); however, ADL estimates of Klan sympathizers run to about 100,000. A Nazi party was active, under the leadership of Lincoln Rockwell, but has declined considerably. According to polls conducted in the U.S. and Western Europe, popular antisemitism was generally on the decline. Yet at the same time, the shrinking extreme right-wing and neo-Nazi groups had become more violent and terror-prone. In the U.S. the number of acts of vandalism, mail and phone threats, and harassment of Jews and Jewish institutions increased.

In France and Belgium, terrorist attacks were aimed at Jewish targets, such as the January 1978 attack on Jewish communal buildings in Paris, the October 3, 1980, attack on the rue Copernic synagogue in Paris, the July 1980 murder of Jewish children at Antwerp, the August 1982 attack on the Goldenberg restaurant in Paris, and many more. Similar occurrences took place in Austria and Italy, while less serious incidents were recorded in Britain and other countries. The security organs in all these countries largely failed to uncover the culprits. At least some of these attacks appear to have been perpetrated by Arab terrorists; they were clearly antisemitic, as they were directed against Jews as Jews and not against Israeli targets. Other attacks may have been carried out by right-wing or left-wing extremists, by themselves or in collusion with Arab groups. All this must be seen against the background of the general increase in terrorist activity throughout the Western world, with antisemitic terror playing some, but not a large part. Terror may have the effect of disrupting organized Jewish life, and various Jewish groups have attempted to counteract it by legal action and other means. Laws against racial incitement were legislated in most European countries and in the U.S., sometimes with a salutary effect.

In Germany, the Statute of Limitations on Nazi crimes was abolished in July 1979; however, only 6,342 individuals were sentenced for Nazi crimes in Germany between 1945 and 1978, out of 84,403 indicted by public prosecutors.

THE DENIAL OF THE HOLOCAUST. A new phenomenon in the antisemitic discourse was the denial of the Holocaust. While before World War II extreme antisemites demanded the annihilation of the Jews, increasingly influential groups of pseudo-intellectuals argued in its aftermath that six million Jews were not in fact killed. While immediately after the war it was argued that Jews exaggerated the number of victims, this was done by people on the fringes of society and in the gutter press. The situation changed with the writings of Paul Rassinier (*Le Mensonge d'Ulysse*, 1961; *Le Drame des Juifs Européens*, 1964), a former French socialist and resistance fighter who spent some time in a Nazi concentration camp. Identifying with the SS aggressors, he saw great merit in Nazi Germany, argued that the Nuremberg trials had been a sham, and that "only" a few hundred thousand Jews had been killed. Towards the end of his life, he began to doubt the existence of the gas chambers.

The theme was picked up in the U.S. by students and followers of historian David Hogan, and more so of Harry E. Barnes, an American isolationist historian who opposed America's participation in the European Allies' war against Germany. His anti-Communist leanings led him to take the position that Nazi Germany should have been an ally against the U.S.S.R. Academics, many of them of German ancestry, developed his thinking into an attack on American democracy in general and American participation in the Nuremberg trials, which were seen as kangaroo courts dispensing the victors' justice against tortured Nazis forced to confess to crimes they never committed. Jews were seen as the conspiratorial element behind this unfortunate American involvement.

A number of influential publications helped spread the idea. Former SS-man Thies Christophersen published "The Auschwitz Lie" in Germany in 1973, a term that became a code name for Holocaust denial. Richard E. Harwood (or Verral), a known member of the British National Front, published in 1974 the brochure "Did Six Million Really Die? The Truth at Last." Arthur Butz's 1975 book *The Hoax of The Twentieth Century* became a focal intellectual event: Butz, a Northwestern professor of electrical engineering, was supported by his colleagues on freedom of speech grounds. In 1978 an Institute of Historical Review was founded at Torrance, California, publishing the *Journal of Historical Review*, which is still largely devoted to the denial of the Holocaust. It was founded by extreme rightist Willis A. Carto, publisher of the antisemitic *Spotlight* and head of the so-called Liberty Lobby. International conferences have brought together the French, American, and other branches of what became an international group of activists, with most of its members holding academic degrees from respectable institutions or being lawyers (such as Nazi veteran Wilhelm Staeglich, author of the 1979 *Der Auschwitz Mythos*, or Robert Faurisson, a Lyon university professor of literature).

The tack was to deny the genuineness of Jewish and Allied documentation, regard all trials of Nazi criminals as based on confessions obtained by torture, deny the existence of gas chambers, brush aside testimonies of survivors as lies (Anne Frank's diary was declared to have been forged, for instance), and see a Jewish-Israeli conspiracy as threatening the West. Some Jews, such as Dr. Alfred Lilienthal, an extreme anti-Zionist, and Dr. Howard Stern, a medical psychiatrist, supported this group of intellectuals. Prof. Noam *Chomsky of MIT defended its right to be heard. Other Jews admired by the Institute include Yehudi *Menuhin, Rabbi Elmer *Berger and the leaders of *Neturei Karta.

The purpose, consciously or otherwise perceived, seemed to be an attack on Western institutions and systems of justice, in order to create a moderate picture of Nazi Germany and its crimes, by presenting the west as no less responsible for World War II: the Jews pushed Germany into the war and were the reason for the fight to the bitter end. Discrediting the Jews was a means to achieving this purpose. Some of the propaganda was very cleverly aimed at young intellectuals in the West. At least some of the authors appeared to believe their own lies. Their influence appeared to have increased in the 1970s and 1980s: in high schools and some universities the literature of these so-called "revisionist" historians entered into the curriculum. Activities directed against these groups included law suits (such as the one pursued by Mel Mermelstein in Los Angeles, which resulted in a judicial statement acknowledging as a fact that the Holocaust occurred) and attempts at legal measures (in the German Federal Republic) that would make the denial of the Holocaust a punishable offense. This denial was obviously a new form of antisemitism, because it saw the Jewish mind as capable of fabricating such a horror, and it was attuned to the psychology of Western post-Holocaust society.

In countries such as France, antisemitic sentiment and activity was connected in one way or another with the denial of the Holocaust. While French popular feeling appeared to be veering away from antisemitism, new forms, especially among small groups of the intelligentsia, appeared to be spreading. Groups variously known as the "Nouvelle Droite" or "Nouvelle Ecole" propagated a sophisticated racism directed against non-Europeans such as the North African workers who are the equivalent of the "Gastarbeiter" in Germany. The supposedly destructive influence of these non-French elements was linked to the Jews. The groups mentioned were anti-Christian as well as anti-Jewish, and propounded an integral French nationalism based on "new scientific" insight ("sociobiology"). A group led by the poet Alain de Benoist and associated with the Nouvelle Ecole was prominent in the Sunday *Figaro Magazine*. A group of Rassinier's followers gathered around *La Vielle taupe*, a leftist source of publications. Their influence on French intellectual life seemed to be greater than its apparently small numbers would warrant. In 1980 the group organized itself as GRECE (Groupement de recherche et d'études pour la civilisation européene), with about 10,000 adherents.

LATIN AMERICA. It was not easy to clarify the situation in Latin America during the reign of the military juntas. Undoubtedly, the terror initiated by the generals turned with special venom against Jews, and Jewish victims were especially maltreated; the number of Jewish victims (reportedly about 2,500) was out of proportion to the number of Jews involved in political strife in Argentina. Indeed, it is difficult to accept the view of editor Jacobo Timmerman, for instance, that the junta was a Nazi group whose main purpose was to attack and eliminate Jews, because South American antisemitism would rather seem to be a reaction to economic and political crises based on traditional antisemitic prejudices that are revived as the crises get worse. But the impact of the Nazis who reached Argentina after the war, and of Fascist ideologies, on parts of the military and political high echelons of Latin America cannot be ignored. In Argentina, some outrages continued into the post-junta period despite efforts of the new democratic government to stop them. Bombs were thrown at Jewish centers elsewhere as well, for instance, in August–September 1982 alone, there were incidents in Quito (Ecuador), Guatemala City, Guadalajara (Mexico) and Maracaibo (Venezuela). However, violent antisemitic incidents in Latin American countries were few, and the intensity of verbal expressions was far lower than that of European countries.

(For more on Holocaust denial, see below.)

SOVIET ANTISEMITISM. The major antisemitic threat during the 1970s was from the Soviet Union. With the tightening of the Stalinist dictatorship came an increasingly anti-Jewish tendency, reviving pre-Bolshevik anti-Jewish stereotypes as butts of propaganda in a crisis-ridden society. Culminating in the mass murder of the leaders of Jewish culture in the U.S.S.R. in 1949–50 and the so-called "Doctors' Plot" of early 1953, this tendency caused Jews as a group to be seen as the protagonists of an imperialist campaign designed to topple the Communist regimes in Eastern Europe. Loyal Communists of Jewish descent were tortured into admitting impossible deeds of treachery as part of the regime's efforts to strengthen its hold over the satellite nations. Stalin's death on March 7, 1953, prevented the tragedy of a mass expulsion of Soviet Jews to Siberia. Under Stalin's immediate successors, the anti-Jewish campaign abated. After the Six-Day War in 1967, and the consequent breaking off of diplomatic relations between Israel and the Soviet bloc, a new campaign started.

In literally hundreds of publications, some with very high circulation (up to quarter of a million copies), and at what must have been a tremendous cost, Soviet writers and journalists, some of whom of Jewish descent, focused on a number of Jewish questions: first, the theme of an inherently evil Jewish culture, whose central text, the Bible, was presented as the source of racism, as the expression of the vilest human qualities, and as endangering the human race through its nefarious cultural influence (V.Y. Begun, *The Creeping Counterrevolution*, Minsk, 1974; T. Solodar, *The Wild Woodworm*, Moscow, 1980, and many others). The second and perhaps major theme was that of a Jewish world conspiracy which managed to gain effective power in the West, where it controls Western imperialism. Writers such as Yuri Ivanov, Lev Korne'ev, and others represented the "Zionist clique" dominating the West as equivalent to the traditional concept of the Devil. Continuing a tradition that started in Christian antisemitism long ago and was perpetuated via the Protocols of the Learned *Elders of Zion (1903) and on through Nazi writings, contemporary Soviet writers did not actually accuse Soviet Jewry of being part of an international conspiracy. The accusation was directed against a nebulous entity, interchangeably described as Zionist or Jewish, which controlled the levers of economic and political power in the West. By comparison, attacks on Israel's policies were relatively rational, obviously reflecting Soviet political, strategic and economic interests as perceived by the ruling oligarchy.

In a large number of Soviet publications, then, Jews, Judaism and Zionism (the terms are interchangeable) were seen as the greatest danger to the Communist world. This view was echoed, among East European states, mainly in Czechoslovakia, which excelled in the most violent antisemitic propaganda in its major newspapers. The impact of all this on the general public in the U.S.S.R. and Czechoslovakia was difficult to gauge, but it could be assumed that government-organized antisemitic propaganda could have catastrophic consequences for the remnants of the Jewish populations at some future date; there appeared, however, to be some opposition among Soviet intellectuals, including some close to official circles, to the excesses of Soviet antisemitic propaganda (e.g., G. Martynov).

Antisemitic writings were rife indeed: the bibliography runs into hundreds of items for the years since 1967, including pseudo-scientific writings in a number of disciplines, fiction (including science fiction), and journalism. Little was done to distribute these publications in other countries. They were mainly intended for home consumption and appeared to answer a deep-seated need for an explanation of the failures of the regime in the economic, social and political spheres.

ANTISEMITISM AND ANTI-ZIONISM. The campaign to identify Zionism with racism, which reached its apogee in 1975 with the resolution at the UN equating the two, was initiated and orchestrated by the U.S.S.R., in cooperation with Arab and Third World countries, as a direct consequence of its antisemitic campaign. The aim seemed to be the delegitimization of the Jewish State, which was increasingly being forced into the position of a pariah within the international community, reminiscent of the situation of the individual Jew in antisemitic societies in pre-modern times.

The 1970s Soviet antisemitic propaganda denied without exception that it was antisemitic. It was everywhere claimed that the attack was against Zionism. Some observers, and especially certain Israeli politicians, have argued that all so-called anti-Zionism is antisemitic, because Israel is representative of Jewish endeavors and therefore every attack on any Israeli interest is anti-Jewish. Others (e.g., Shlomo Avineri) have argued that criticism of Israeli policies is hardly antisemitic, as practically all Israeli citizens have at one time or another been opposed to their government, and if such opposition were anti-Zionist or antisemitic, these terms would lose all meaning. Anti-Zionism should therefore be defined as denying the existence of a Jewish people as such and their right to an independent state, and not as criticism of policies or acts. Such anti-Zionism is then considered to be antisemitic, when antisemitism is equated with anti-Judaism. Jewish anti-Zionists, with some exceptions (such as those who align themselves with the deniers of the Holocaust), are regarded as collective self-haters, though some will admit a category of Jewish antisemites.

The attempt to differentiate between criticism of Israel and anti-Zionism in principle is especially important in the study of Arab and Third World antisemitism, on the other hand, and Western liberal and left-wing antisemitism on the other.

The study of Arab antisemitism – as contrasted with anti-Israeli attitudes, including opposition to Jewish national aspirations – is problematic, as the elements are obviously intertwined. However, a case study of Egypt might well show this differentiation because of the Egyptian-Israeli peace treaty (1978), which was accepted as a fact by some of the more extreme antisemitic writers in the pro-government camp (e.g., Anis Mansur). In mass publications such as *Akhbār al-Yawm* or the government party's ideological periodical, *October*, articles were published lauding Hitler's attitude to the Jews, quoting the Protocols of the Learned Elders of Zion as a basic historical text, and comparing Israeli (interchangeable with Jewish) actions on the West Bank and in the Lebanon with the Holocaust. Stereotyped descriptions of Jews as controlling the wealth of the world, as exploiters and usurers, as a morally defective community were abundant. Fanatic Sunni writers opposed to the peace treaty repeated these accusations but combine them with the view that the Jews are enemies in principle of Islam from its inception; the idea of independent Jewish political existence is totally unacceptable as it would mean relinquishing territory within *Dār al-Islam*, the area of Islam, to a subject people viewed as the enemy of Islamic traditions. This is the view of the Muslim Brotherhood (e.g., Sayyid Qutb, *Al Yahud, al Yahud*, Riyad, 1970), just as it is of the Khomeinite Shiʿa movement, whose anti-Jewish ideology increasingly penetrated into Sunni countries (Syria) and areas with large Shiʿite populations (Iraq, Lebanon).

The Palestine Arab Nationalist organizations fighting Israel with terrorism are an entirely different case. The Palestine National Covenant of 1968 (article 20) states that "Judaism, in its character as a religion of revelation, is not a nationality with an independent existence. Likewise, the Jews are not one people with an independent personality." Article 22 sees Zionism as "aggressive, expansionist and colonialist in its aims; and Fascist and Nazi in its means. Israel is the tool of the Zionist movement and a human and geographical base for world imperialism." These statements are clearly antisemitic, and even genocidal, in two respects: first, because the destruction of Israel clearly implies the destruction of its Jewish population, despite the declaration in article 6 that Jews who were living in Palestine before 1917 could remain (not many of these were still alive in 1968, and even fewer later); second, because the majority of Jews see Israel as an expression of their nationality or ethnicity and not only their religious beliefs. All other national or ethnic groups are likely to have such sentiments recognized by the international community, including, presumably, the Palestine Liberation Organization. The non-recognition, in principle, only of the Jewish case is therefore not merely antisemitic but genocidal by implication. However, from the mid-1970s, the PLO took great care to avoid any antisemitic statements or propaganda, with the important exception of refusing to budge from the original statements included in the 1968 Covenant.

In the West, the apparent ease with which anti-Israeli criticism can turn into clearly antisemitic statements was exemplified in the 1982 media attack on Israel's entry into Lebanon. Beyond political or moral opposition to a military move, which in itself cannot be termed antisemitic, the following was characteristic of media criticism of Israel's action: the Jews (not Israel) are "said to be God's chosen people; at all times and in all countries and with every means they have stolen the property of others" (*Ostersunds-Posten*, Sweden, June 1982); the ritual murder story was revived: "A child disappeared" (in Lebanon) "and was found a few days afterwards in a crevice, shot in his head, ritually executed" (*Aftonbladet*, 25.9.82). Respectable papers compared the attack on Lebanon with the Holocaust and then joined the deniers of the Holocaust: "How ironic it is that the word 'holocaust,' now synonymous with the deaths of supposedly 6 million Jews in Nazi concentration camps, is the only word that can describe what is now going on in Lebanon… there is much controversy going on now about the accuracy of that 6 million figure… perhaps it was a type-setter's error that was repeated" (*The Barrie Examiner*, Canada, 3.7.82). British papers and many Continental journals published similar material. Alongside political or moral criticism of Israel's government, which in itself is certainly not antisemitic, traditional antisemitic themes were introduced – Jewish world conspiracy, ritual murder, flawed Jewish character, including racial superciliousness – all directed against the Jewish people as a whole and not just an Israeli government. It would appear that the Lebanese war only served as a pretext for these outbursts.

Anti-Jewish feelings, often masquerading as opposition to Israeli policy, could be found in liberal circles, among which media was but one example. In another context, the 1983 Assembly of the World Council of Churches – founded by Willem A. Visser t'hooft, who was active in efforts to rescue Jews during World War II – declared its support for PLO participation in Middle East negotiations and lamented the rift in the ranks of the Palestinians and the loss of consensus among Arab nations.

Dangerous tendencies could be discerned in New Left circles. Thus, for instance, the National Union of Students in Britain attempted to ban university and polytechnic Jewish societies on the grounds that as they were pro-Israel and as Zionism was racism they should be denied platforms and union facilities (House of Commons, Hansard, 25.22.1977, cols. 2058–2072).

On the other hand, there is no consensus regarding the many Protestant groups on the American Right, loosely described as Fundamentalist or Evangelical. Many, though by no means all, are ardent supporters of Israel, and many also abjure any kind of anti-Jewish stance. Some may have different views, but no in-depth investigation or self-analysis was attempted during the 1970s.

The increase in antisemitic expressions since the late 1960s justifies calling it a wave. "Classical" antisemitism was gradually declining, but what is more important is that new configurations were cropping up, though here too a clear continuation from previous periods can be shown: the emphasis was on Jewish world conspiracy and rule and the Jewish state as the embodiment of the flawed Jewish character and as the center of the conspiracy.

OPPOSITION TO THE ANTISEMITIC WAVE. During the 1970s and the early 1980s the fight against antisemitism was not carried out by Jews alone, though of course Jewish defense organizations bore the brunt of the struggle. In the U.S., the ADL fought manifestations of the phenomenon not only locally but increasingly in Europe and Latin America as well. The American Jewish Congress concentrated more on attacking the Arab boycott of Israel. The American Jewish Committee emphasized the defense of Jewish communities in the political and cultural spheres.

The World Jewish Congress was active on the international scene fighting antisemitism at the UN and elsewhere. Its research institution, the Institute of Jewish Affairs in London, was a major source of information about contemporary antisemitism. In Berlin, the Center for Research on antisemitism at the Technische Universität, specialized mainly, but not exclusively, in Central and West European antisemitism in the last two centuries. National Jewish bodies such as the Board of Deputies in Britain, and the CRIF (Conseil Representatif des Institutions Juives de France) in France acted against antisemitism locally; in France, a research group associated with CRIF, CERAC (Centre d'Etudes et de Recherche sur l'antisemitisme Contemporain), was engaged in a study of French antisemitism. In Jerusalem, the Hebrew University's International Center for the Study of Antisemitism is currently engaged in a broad historical and contemporary investigation of antisemitic phenomena.

In the Christian world, there came about an increased awareness of the importance of fighting antisemitism. Following the Vatican's historic decisions in 1965 (see before), the Catholic Church was making efforts to combat antisemitism among its adherents. In 1973, the pastoral Instructions of the French Catholic bishops' Conference called for a repudiation of "pseudo-theological arguments" used to reject Judaism. The Protestant World Council of Churches established a Commission on the Church and the Jewish People, headed by Prof. Krister Steadhal, working for better interfaith understanding. The bond between the Jews and the Land of Israel is recognized in the Guidelines for Christian-Jewish Dialogue of the WCC (1982). In May 1981, the Assembly of the Church of Scotland declared "its belief in the continuing place of God's people of Israel within the divine purpose," and the Lutheran World Federation consultation of August 1982 stated that "we Christians must purge ourselves of any hatred of the Jews and any sort of teaching of contempt for Judaism." The Rhineland-Westphalia Synod of the evangelical church in Germany proclaimed the continued validity of Judaism, and the Catholic Church established an International Liaison Committee for itself and the International Jewish Committee for Interreligious Consultations in 1971. A German bishops' declaration of April 1980 was rather weak and apologetic regarding German Catholic responses to the Holocaust, but it acknowledged the Catholic debt to Judaism and opposed the "deicide" accusation. Apart from these official bodies, important Christian leaders are working to fight antisemitism. Franklin H. Littell (Methodist Church) set up the conferences on the Holocaust and the Church Struggle (Detroit, 1970); Father John Pawlikowski and a number of other Catholic leaders in North America have helped fight antisemitism in their Church; in Rome, August Cardinal Bea (d. 1968) was a major influence in the same cause.

Public figures and leaders in the arts, literature and science and in secular movements in the West were concerned with the phenomenon. From Jean-Paul Sartre to Daniel Patrick Moynihan and from President François Mitterand to Ambassador Jeane Kirkpatrick, strong opposition to antisemitic attitudes and actions was expressed and the danger to Western society from antisemitism was recognized.

The term antisemitism (or rather "anti-Semitism"), as a catch-all phrase denoting anti-Jewish attitudes or acts of all types, is misleading. Casual expressions of dislike as well as murderous hatred are subsumed under one term; but in the absence of a differentiating terminology the term continues to be used. As there is no "Semitism" to which "anti-Semites" object, the term being used to denote haters of Jews as Jews, it should indeed properly be written antisemitism rather than anti-Semitism.

Partly as a reaction to antisemitism, Jewish antagonism to non-Jews, sometimes of a violent and even terrorist nature, has no name, but belongs to the same general category of group hate. Originally a protective psychological defense mechanism, it has burgeoned in the last few decades into a recognizable stance among some radical religious and nationalist Jewish groups in Israel and in the Jewish Diaspora.

[Yehuda Bauer]

In the 1980s

In the Western world, the decade of the 1980s began with a wave of antisemitism sparked off by the Lebanon war. There followed a decline in public expressions of it until the late 1980s when economic recession took hold, far-right parties made significant advances, and newer forms of antisemitic expression gained ground. The resurgence of grassroots antisemitism in Eastern Europe, following the collapse of Communism, gave encouragement to antisemitic groups in the West, and by 1992 it was clear that a wave of resurgent antisemitism was under way.

THE WEST: NEW FORMS OF ANTISEMITIC EXPRESSION. In the United States and Germany, anti-Jewish sentiment, as measured by opinion polls, declined steadily, and in other countries no marked increases in antisemitic sentiment were recorded. However, even in countries where polls indicated decreasing levels of antisemitism, the number of antisemitic incidents appeared to rise steadily and become more violent and abusive. A particularly gruesome example was the desecration in May 1990 of the Jewish cemetery in Carpentras, France, where a corpse was dug up. This shocked many and a huge demonstration led by President Mitterrand, took to the streets of Paris.

In the U.S., skinhead groups were thought to be responsible for the rise in antisemitic incidents in the mid-1980s which continued until 1992, when there was a reported decrease in such incidents for the first time in six years. Skinhead groups were also a source of concern in the United Kingdom, Italy, France, Germany, and Canada, where they were thought to be behind the increase in antisemitic attacks over the decade.

Many neo-Nazi groups were formed during the 1980s. Most remained electorally marginal, although some were thought to be responsible for the more violent attacks. There was increased international co-operation between extremist groups in terms of the publication and distribution of propaganda and the organization of conferences and speaking tours.

By the mid-1980s, disillusionment with established political parties, rising nationalism, ethnic conflicts, and an influx of immigrants and asylum-seekers from Eastern Europe led to increased electoral gains for far-right parties in Western Europe. These parties were principally anti-immigrant but their leaders used antisemitic innuendo to make it clear to supporters that antisemitism was part of the fundamental ideological outlook. Antisemitism was far more open at local party level. Racial violence was directed mostly at blacks, Asians, Turks – anyone seen as a "foreigner" – and not at Jews. Yet antisemitic slogans and rhetoric often seemed to be employed by those perpetrating such violence.

In France, the Front National consistently achieved between 9 and 15 percent of the vote. By the late 1980s far-right parties such as the German Republikaner Partei, the Belgian Vlaams Blok, and the Austrian Freiheits Partei also won seats at local and national levels. In 1984, for the first time, the far-right parties had sufficient numbers in the European Parliament to form the Group of the European Right, entitling them to EC funding.

In the U.S., David Duke, the former Ku Klux Klan leader, and Pat Buchanan, known for anti-Jewish comments, were candidates for the 1992 Republican Party's presidential nomination. Although both failed, there was considerable unease at the willingness of the American body politic to embrace these candidates.

Black antisemitism was a serious concern through the 1980s in the U.S. Two of its principal sources were Louis Farrakhan, leader of the Nation of Islam Movement, and the Reverend Jesse Jackson, the black contender for the 1988 Democratic Party presidential nomination. Further tension was caused when, in 1991, a black child was run over by a Ḥasidic driver in the Crown Heights district of New York and a seminary student was murdered in riots which followed.

The "Pollard affair," in which Jonathan Pollard, a Jewish U.S. citizen was convicted of spying for Israel, caused anxiety in the Jewish community. However, fears that the affair would result in the traditional antisemitic accusation of dual loyalties were allayed by opinion polls which indicated that it had little negative effect.

Antisemitism in Latin America was marginal during the period, except in the case of Argentina. Under the Argentine military junta, antisemitism had been a factor in the violent campaign waged against perceived political enemies. When democracy was restored after the Falklands/Malvinas war, expressions of antisemitism in publications increased markedly. However, by the end of the decade, even in Argentina, antisemitism appeared to be decreasing in significance.

In South Africa, Australia, New Zealand, and other countries in the Asia-Pacific region, antisemitism remained essentially marginal, although overtly antisemitic groups existed and their activities were occasionally cause for concern.

While significant efforts were made to curb antisemitism throughout the period, the start of the first intifada in December 1987 reignited tensions. Interfaith dialogue played an important role in countering antisemitism in the Christian churches, particularly among the clergy, but did not appear to have sufficient impact on their charges.

POST-COMMUNIST ANTISEMITISM IN EAST-CENTRAL EUROPE. These years could be characterized as a time of transition from institutionalized to grassroots antisemitism. Indeed, the early 1980s were for the Soviet Union a transitional phase between the bureaucratic stagnation of the Brezhnev era and the reformism of the Andropov-Gorbachev regimes. Beginning around the years 1982–83, there was a shift away from the state-sponsored ideological and political media campaign against Zionism and Israel which had begun in the late 1960s in response mainly to the emigration movement of Soviet Jewry. The campaign had been expressed in Marxist-Leninist terms but elements of it had been marked by transparent anti-Jewish imagery, in particular the invocation of an alleged "Zionist"-Masonic world conspiracy against Moscow and the Soviet Bloc.

As the political wind changed, some writers, propagandists and activists who had specialized in this form of propaganda paid lip service to *perestroika*, others joined the burgeoning chauvinistic and antisemitic groups which had sprung up in Russia, yet others disappeared from view.

With the failure of reform, the economic, political, and social fabric of the Soviet Union deteriorated. This was accompanied by ethnic strife in a number of republics. In December 1992 the Soviet Union finally collapsed and was replaced in part by the shaky Commonwealth of Independent States; the three Baltic states had earlier successfully sued for independence from Moscow.

By the beginning of the 1990s, the situation with regard to antisemitic expression in Central and Eastern Europe had changed radically. In not a single country was antisemitism tolerated as a state policy. On the contrary, Jewish culture was undergoing an unimpeded renaissance, emigration was virtually unrestricted, and the leaders of the new states were concerned both with combating xenophobia, racism, and antisemitism by political and legal means and with maintaining good relations with Israel.

At the same time, the collapse of the Communist system was accompanied in several of the countries by the rise of grassroots anti-Jewish movements of varying degrees of importance. One particular source of danger was tactical alliances between "unreconstructed" Communists and extreme nationalists. Another source of concern, in particular in the Baltic countries, was the rehabilitation of accomplices of the Nazis in implementing the "Final Solution."

At the turn of the decade, the principal danger spots in post-Communist Central and Eastern Europe appeared to be Russia, where the far right embraced both the would-be respectable National Salvation Front and numerous Pamyat-style neo-Nazi and neo-fascist groups; Hungary, where the far-right parliamentarian and writer Istvan Csurka had been expelled from the governing party and had started up a party of his own; and Romania, where the governing coalition depended on the support of a number of xenophobic parties. While there appeared to be relatively little popular prejudice against Jews in any of the post-Communist countries-there was no shortage of ethnic scapegoats – the economic, political, and social dislocation which followed the collapse of Communism remained serious cause for alarm. The bitter warfare in the former Yugoslavia, with its abhorrent practice of "ethnic cleansing," served as a solemn reminder of the depths to which ethnic strife could descend.

ANTI-ZIONISM AND ANTISEMITISM. Much expression of antisemitism at the beginning of the 1980s was disguised as anti-Zionism. Although by no means all anti-Zionists were antisemites, many groups across the political spectrum, but particularly on the extreme left, couched their antisemitism in anti-Zionist rhetoric. For some Communist countries too, anti-Zionism was a convenient tool for concealing state-sponsored antisemitism. The 1975 UN General Assembly resolution 3379, which equated Zionism with racism, was a principal tool of the antisemitic anti-Zionist campaign, which reverberated for a number of years, well into the 1980s, with over 200 denunciations of Israel or the Jewish people or both in national and international forums.

The Israeli invasion of Lebanon in 1982 sparked off a wave of antisemitism which was closely related to negative images of Israel. In the following few years, criticism of Israel provided effective cover for expressions of antisemitism, generating considerable debate as to the relationship between anti-Zionism and antisemitism. Some believed that since anti-Zionism denied the rights of Jews on a collective level, it was the equivalent of denying the Jew individual rights – a classic element of antisemitism.

As the 1980s wore on, however, anti-Zionism began to diminish. The Third World forums in which anti-Zionist rhetoric was constantly featured declined in importance as many of the participants saw that it brought them no benefit. The collapse of the Soviet empire led to an end to Communist state-sponsored anti-Zionism. Far-right groups which utilized anti-Zionism continued to do so but, as anti-Zionism became less of an acceptable notion on the international political stage, it became less useful to those seeking a "respectable" front for their antisemitism. In addition, as socialism appeared to be discredited, far-left antisemitic anti-Zionism declined markedly.

In many Arab countries antisemitism was used in the continuous fight against Zionism and the State of Israel. Much of this antisemitism was imposed from above since practically all Arab governments exercised strict control of the media. However, in some countries, Egypt in particular, there was clear evidence of antisemitism becoming increasingly a grassroots phenomenon, linked to the rise of Islamic fundamentalism.

Antisemitism from Islamic fundamentalist sources became a cause of increasing concern during the period, with extremist groups in certain Western countries propagating violent anti-Jewish rhetoric and using traditional far-right Christian antisemitic themes. Much of this activity was encouraged by Iran and although it resulted in little actual violence against Jews outside of the Middle East, the potential for violence was certainly increasing at the end of the period under review.

THE DENIAL OF THE HOLOCAUST. During the 1980s, Holocaust-deniers sought to depict denial as a scholarly endeavor, issuing "research" purporting to prove that the Holocaust was a hoax. Their main focus was on the gas chambers, particularly at Auschwitz.

Fred Leuchter, who invented the lethal injection system used for executions in some American states, was commissioned to analyze the gas chambers "scientifically." Leuchter's work, which claimed to prove the gas chambers a physical impossibility, was disseminated widely by Holocaust-deniers, although it was found to contain fundamental scientific errors and historical inaccuracies. In Britain, the so-called Leuchter Report was published by the far-right historian David Irvin, whose influence in Neo-Nazi circles worldwide increased parallel to the escalation of his tone and arguments, and his moderate portrayal of Hitler.

Other Holocaust-deniers who continued to provide the "conceptual" framework for the deniers' arguments were Robert Faurisson, in France and Arthur Butz in the U.S. (see above).

Young people were targeted by deniers in an attempt to spread doubt about the Holocaust and the veracity of such works as the *Diary of Anne Frank*. They continually placed advertisements denying the Holocaust in American campus newspapers. A significant number of papers accepted the ads, contending that they represented "ideas" and "points of view" which, however odious, deserved to be heard. In addition, the deniers strenthened their ties with extremist groups worldwide.

Certain countries tried to use the courts as a means of controlling Holocaust-denial activities. However, such legal measures are often difficult to sustain. In 1992, the Canadian Supreme Court overturned the conviction of prominent Holocaust-denier Ernst Zundel, ruling that the prohibition against spreading false news likely to cause injury to a public interest was too vague and possibly restricted legitimate forms of speech

[Hadas Altwarg / Antony Lerman / Julia Schopflin / Howard Spier]

IN JAPAN. Beginning in late 1986, a marked increase in antisemitic literature surfaced in Japan. Antisemitic literature had been popular in Japan previously, most notably in the 1930s.

In Japan, the image of the Jew that has developed over the past century is a warped and distorted one due to inaccurate sources of information: the anti-Bolshevik White Russian officers of the 1920s, the translation of the *Protocols of the Elders of Zion*, Nazi propaganda in the 1930s and 1940s, and American antisemitic writing in the 1950s and 1960s. But, ironically, although the intention of many of these sources of misinformation is antisemitic it has not led to antisemitic acts by the Japanese. This is because the Japanese have a different value system from that of the West. While they have accepted the image of the Jew as "smart and rich" this has not led to dislike. On the contrary as the Japanese respect "smart and rich" people, they believe that the Jews should be admired and emulated.

However, during the 1980s there were dozens of other works published about Jews and Judaism, including Japanese translations of authors such as David Ben-Gurion and Elie Wiesel. In addition, Japanese scholars have written on Jewish subjects. It is important to emphasize that these, as well as antisemitic books, have also been published in Japan.

The antisemitic literature can be divided into two general categories. The first describes the extraordinary intelligence and financial wizardry of the Jews. These kinds of books are not necessarily intended to slight or insult the Jews. On the contrary they extol the Jews for their great business acumen and, propose that the Japanese should emulate the so-called "Jewish way of business." These books usually led not to a dislike of Jews but a peculiarly Japanese kind of admiration.

The second category is based on *The Protocols of the Elders of Zion* and uses *The Protocols* to explain the troubled economic situation. They blame the rising value of the Japanese yen on a world-wide Jewish conspiracy to control Japan. One "proof" of this is that multinational companies are a "Jewish invention." IBM, Exxon, Ford, and Chrysler as well as other leading companies, are Jewish-owned; Rockefeller, George Shultz, and Stalin are Jewish; and Korea's economy was planned by the Jews to beat Japan. Jews are also held responsible for the Tanaka-Lockheed scandal (charges of corruption involving the Japanese prime minister Nakoi Tanaka and the American aircraft company in 1976), the Chernobyl nuclear accident, and the pillage of the Incas in the 15th century. The most important "fact" in these arguments is that the Jews control the United States and whoever controls the U.S. controls the world.

The "evidence" is as absurd as the allegations. For example, the Lockheed scandal is seen as an act of retaliation by the Jewish world conspiracy. The "Jew" Rockefeller had planned to have the "Jew" Kissinger open China to the U.S. in order to procure off-shore oil rights. Similarly Tanaka had to be eliminated lest the Japanese endanger the "Jewish world conspiracy" to gain off-shore oil rights.

The leading "Jewish conspiracy" theorist is Masami Uno whose four books have sold well over 1,000,000 copies. Uno also lectures extensively on this subject and has written several articles for various publications. In the April 1987 issue of *Big Man*, a popular monthly, he wrote the following passage:

> How does the international Jewish capital, which effectively controls the U.S. assess America? Jews have gradually been taking their money out of the U.S. for the past several years.
>
> The concept of multinational enterprise, which can move like an amoeba all over the world in search of profits, is typically Jewish.
>
> While Japan is struggling with problems arising from loans made to the Third World countries and massive investment in the U.S., these multinational enterprises have removed far more massive assets from the U.S. to elsewhere and are looking for next investment targets. What will be their next investment target? I'm sure that they will invest their money in buying up Japanese enterprises. When will they start their action? It will be when debtors in the Third World declare a moratorium and stocks plummet simultaneously.
>
> The Great Depression calls to mind scenes of people in bread lines, but these pictures only show one side of things. The other side of the Depression was that the Jewish capital groups, such as Rockefeller, Mellon and Morgan in the U.S. and Rothschild in Europe, accumulated massive fortunes during that period. They kept buying massive banks and companies that went bankrupt. There is no guarantee that the same thing will not happen in Japan.

Among other things these books also trivialize the Holocaust. Uno claims that it was physically impossible for 6,000,000 Jews to have been killed and also states that Hitler had no choice but to eliminate the Jews. Another writer, Toru Kawajiri, estimates that only 200,000 Jews died.

During the late 1980s a total of approximately 1,500,000–2,000,000 antisemitic books in both categories were bought in Japan. These books' popularity is an outgrowth of the tremendous concern in Japan about current economic conditions. The recent leap in the value of the yen has hurt Japanese exports. Many Japanese perceive themselves as gravely threatened and are fearful of the future.

Thus, when a book claims it has answers for the economic situation it has great appeal. Many people who bought books with such titles as *If You Understand the Jews, You Understand the World* were primarily interested in what was said about economic matters and had only a vague curiosity about the Jews. Thus the fact that two million copies of the above book were sold should not be regarded as a sign of a rise in antisemitism.

There is another explanation for the recent popularity of antisemitic books. Japan is very concerned with preserving its sense of national identity. Historically, it has always been fearful of foreigners, with large numbers believing that Japan is only for the Japanese. Such a concern can lead to varying degrees of xenophobia and a tendency to blame the outsider in times of trouble. Thus the recent popularity of antisemitic literature can be understood as a reaction against foreigners in general. It has even been suggested that in reality antisemitic books are attacking America, but since America is too important to Japan it is more politic to blame the Jews.

Other groups have also been blamed for Japan's economic problems. This includes the Rockefellers, Illuminati, and Freemasons.

There is, however, a fundamental difference between Western antisemitism and Japanese attitudes to Jews. In the West Jews are blamed as such but in Japan the word "Jew" is often used as a pseudonym for Americans and even possibly for all foreigners. Furthermore, Japanese do not generally distinguish between one white Westerner and another but see all Westerners as a large group with only minor differences between them. These attitudes reflect a sense of xenophobia in general rather than any specific hostility towards the Jews.

These antisemitic books are believable to the Japanese for several reasons. First, the books are popular in form and language. They are aimed at the low- and middle-level white-collar workers. Such people have had little contact with or understanding of the West and have no reason to doubt the "facts" presented to them. Furthermore the Japanese are great respecters of the printed word.

Until March 1987 these antisemitic publications went basically unopposed both in Japan and abroad. The *New York Times* on March 12, 1987, carried an article, "Japanese writers critical of Jews," which detailed the rise in popularity of the Jewish conspiracy books. This article was followed by others in the Western press.

Subsequently, the Japanese press published several essays debunking the Jewish conspiracy theory. The first of these appeared in the April edition of the intellectual monthly *Bungei Shunju.* This article, by Professor Herbert Passin, a leading Japanologist, detailed the inaccuracies of such theories and scoffed at their credibility. Other eminent writers also published articles in this vein included Professor Go Muramatsu, Y. Teshima, and Shuichi Sato. Masahiro Miyazaki, former lecturer at Waseda University and author of several books on economics, published *If You Mind the Jews, You Will Lose Sight of the World* which parodied the three of Uno's books and explained point by point why the claims made against the Jews are baseless.

On a political level, U.S. Senator Arlen Specter and Rep. Charles Schumer called on Prime Minister Yasuhiro Nakasone to take action against the spreading of antisemitic feeling. On March 19, 1987, Mr. I. Umezu, director of the Japan Information Center in New York, wrote a letter to the *New York Times* which contained the following reassurances: "Anti-Semitism has no roots in Japan's cultural history. The Japanese government and people are firmly opposed to any form of discrimination, whether ethnic, religious or other grounds, and we are firm in our determination to uphold that position."

On March 23, 1987, a delegation from the Anti-Defamation League of B'nai B'rith met with the Japanese ambassador to the U.S., H.E. Nobuo Matsunaga, to protest to the Japanese government about the antisemitic literature being published in Japan. Matsunaga responded that while Japan guarantees freedom of speech these publications did not reflect the view of the Japanese government or people.

On September 4, 1987, in response to a question in a session of the Japanese Diet, then Foreign Minister Tadashi Kuranari stated: "I must say that the argument that the problems Japan faces today are due to a global conspiracy of the Jews is totally untrue and irresponsible." While this statement should have helped to delegitimize antisemitic literature, its value and importance were severely limited by the fact that the statement received almost no Japanese press coverage.

On February 3, 1988, the American Jewish Committee held a consultation on Japanese-Jewish relations. It can be said that world Jewish organizations were slowly coming to the realization that Japan as a growing economic and political power could no longer be ignored by world Jewry. While this antisemitic literature has not led to any significant acts of antisemitism, such misinformation left unchecked might ultimately be harmful both to Jews and to the Japanese. In light of this, an effort was made to establish a Yudaya Bunka Center, a Jewish cultural center, to provide accurate and basic information about Jews to the Japanese.

[Michael J. Schudrich]

The 1990s and After

WAVES OF ANTISEMITISM AND THEIR CAUSES. Antisemitic activities and expressions were on the rise from the beginning of the 1990s: during the first Gulf War world Jewry, especially the U.S. communities, were accused of pushing their countries into a war that was in Israel's interests. This accusation served to bolster the "conspiracy theory" that was already in place and according to which the Jewish desire for world domination manipulates global events. Moreover, the waves of immigrants and foreign workers caused by the fall of the Soviet Bloc and the globalization process exacerbated problems of defining and relating to ethnicity, nationality, and the rights of newcomers arriving from the poor Southern Hemisphere to the richer Northern one – all bearing on attitudes to Jews, the symbol of the eternal other. Indeed, the year 1994 was by far the worst of the decade – more than 300 cases of violence against Jews were registered worldwide. Violence doubled in Western Europe, most notably in Germany, and increased in Russia. Great Britain remained the most violent country with respect to racist and antisemitic activities for the third year running.

Additional reasons for these developments were the considerable increase throughout the Western world of the role of extremist Muslim groups and movements affiliated to fundamentalist organizations in North Africa and the Middle East. The extreme right, reacting to the growing presence of immigrant minorities, escalated its response to Jews as well, and even more so, having at their service the skinheads, youth devoid of ideology and of institutionalized frameworks. New and constantly improving techniques, the Internet first and foremost, that facilitated the dissemination of antisemitic propaganda and the cooperation among extremist groups, defied government efforts to impose bans and legal constraints. Worst of all was the impact of public debates on World War II (see below), the gradual dissolving of former taboos and the filtering of instigation by hard-core extremists down to the general public.

In 1995 these developments prompted government agencies, police and parliaments included, to increase anti-terrorist and anti-racist legislative and enforcement efforts. Their unequivocal response to these few years of rising violence against foreigners and Jews resulted in a sharp decline in such violence for the following two years, until 1998, especially in Western Europe, Canada, and the U.S., but not in Russia. However, use of the Internet by extremists was not hampered and served as a vehicle to disseminate their views, especially the "world Jewish domination" notion that was still prevalent in Japan at the time and was enhanced by additional claims made by U.S. Nation of Islam leader Louis Farrakhan: having been slave traders, the Jews fabricated a Holocaust story to divert public attention from the suffering of the blacks, and distorted their image through Jewish control of Hollywood and the media. The ongoing globalization, resulting in rampant unemployment, cuts in welfare spending, and subsidization of newcomers' needs, caused public dissatisfaction. The extreme right-wing parties were not slow in exploiting the situation, and their leaders – Jorg Haider in Austria, Filip Dewinter in Belgium, and Jean-Marie le Pen in France, made impressive electoral gains in 1995–97. A few years later, Corneliu Vadim Tudor in Romania, Christoph Blocher in Switzerland, and Istvan Churka in Hungary would follow. While such parties became stronger, extra-parliamentary extremist groups weakened.

After three relatively quiet years, 1998 and 1999 were years of great concern and unease as violence became more severe and each attack caused more damage and underscored the enhanced local and international organizational capacities of the perpetrators. The first signs of cooperation between Islamic extremists, active even during the years of the Oslo Accord, and ultra-rightists or -leftists surfaced in a number of countries. They were coupled to attempts by the right-wing organizations to compensate for their weakness through regional or even European reorganization, and to maintain "leaderless cells of resistance" that were harder to identify and monitor. Indeed, the far right orchestrated a violent summer in the U.S. in 1999, and German authorities warned that the number of such groups whose members are prepared to use arms is on the rise, and that some areas in slowly adjusting East Germany were closed off by hooligan youngsters even to the police. Moreover, violence spread to countries hitherto quiet in this respect, not to speak of overt and uncurbed use of antisemitic motifs and an atmosphere of violence in Russia that kept intensifying each year, with the beating of rabbis on the streets of Moscow, Buenos Aires, and London – blatant acts unknown for decades. Violence was accompanied by a no less troubling proliferation of graffiti, slogans, personal insults, threats, and harassment, together with a host of verbal, electronic, and visual anti-Jewish expressions.

Following two difficult years, the year 2000 ushered in a new century with cautious hope. At the Stockholm Conference some 45 countries declared their commitment to embarking on a less violent century by implementing the lessons of the Holocaust. Pope *John Paul II visited Yad Vashem, and Holocaust denier David *Irving lost his lawsuit against American Jewish historian Deborah Lipstadt with an unequivocal condemnation by a British court that upheld the contention that he had falsified truth and facts – all dealing Holocaust denial a severe blow and creating a new atmosphere. But within a few months, in October 2000, with the outbreak of the second Intifada, an unprecedented wave of violence against Jews swept Western Europe, the U.S., and Canada. Young immigrants from Muslim countries perpetrated most of the 180 or so incidents of violence within a few weeks, during the High Holidays. From then until 2005 a number of waves occurred, each more violent than the previous one, primarily targeting the young and old who looked Jewish on the streets and in educational institutions, but not abandoning the desecration of cemeteries and synagogues. The Durban, South Africa, U.N. World Conference against Racism, held in September 2001, originally assembled to address acute world problems of discrimination, xenophobia, and intolerance originating in the migration process, turned into a wholesale attack that singled out Israel and the Jewish people from among 160 countries and nations. Together with the September 11 events, for which American Jews and Israel were immediately blamed, the conference opened a new wave of virulent antisemitism, later followed by another in 2002, with the opening of Operation Defensive Shield, and another with the invasion of Iraq led by the U.S.

Fueling the fire were the concurrence of interests between radical Islam and the European left; deep-seated anti Americanism and pacifism, combined with anti-globalization movements, associating rich Jews operating in the global economy and the State of Israel with both their bugbears; post-nationalist and post-colonial discourse in a unifying and repentant Europe when the Jewish people exercised a unique kind of nationality; the unspoken wish to shake off the heavy shadow of the Holocaust and the Jewish demand to be compensated for its property looted during the war. Violence against persons has been perpetrated in countries with a large immigrant population, most notably a Muslim one (France, Great Britain, and Canada), while attacks on property and communal sites are more evident in countries where the far right is active (U.S., Russia, and Germany). Thus, the left, gradually realizing that millions of frustrated immigrants have not really been integrated, and are being used in the industries of aging countries, are stricken with guilt feelings toward them, but not toward the Jews. Since the liberal left comprises a considerable part of academia, the media, and government, the scene was set for hostility towards the Jewish communities and the Jewish state.

WORLD WAR II AND HOLOCAUST-RELATED ISSUES. Ceremonies held in 1994–96 all over the world, commemorating the 50th anniversary of events that took place during the final stages of the Holocaust and World War II, brought relations between Christians and the Jewish people to the fore. The impact of these ceremonies on public debate and extremist activities was especially marked in Eastern Europe and the former Soviet Union, where most of the Holocaust victims had lived and were killed. The central issues were: compensation for Jewish property; rewriting of the dark history of the past in terms more flattering to local collective memory; rehabilitation of war criminals who became anti-Communist national heroes; cooperation of the local population with the Nazis, which is still being equated with Jewish support of Communism. Every commemoration and new monument or financial agreement – themselves Jewish achievements – took their toll in anti-Jewish terms.

Compensation for Jewish property came to the fore when archives were opened in the Western world in accordance with the 50-year archive laws, and in the former Soviet Bloc after its collapse. While governments, mainly in the West, supported the demands of Jewish organizations, bolstered by American pressure, and even hailed the courageous fight for lost rights and property, grassroot attitudes, especially in Eastern Europe, were different: they clung to the notion of Jewish domination of the world and the image of the rich manipulating Jew first found in the *Protocols of the Elders of Zion*, imagining a Jewish grip so strong that the Jews can sell the world any horror story, blackmail it, and get paid for it twice, even 50 years later. Holocaust denial thus became an even more convenient solution, exonerating former generations. The first example was the "Swiss Gold" affair, which pointed to a large number of countries that benefited either from Jewish assets or from transactions with the Nazi regime, in effect collaborating with and supporting, it. Indeed, antisemitism in Switzerland, long dormant, was openly expressed on the individual and even the official level. Another example was Hungary, where a rise in antisemitic violence was registered with the passage of the 1996 law recognizing Jewish rights. Jewish demands generated resentment especially then, when the majority of the Jews were seen a residing in wealthy countries while millions suffered poverty and human rights abuses worldwide.

As the century drew to a close, World War II was increasingly perceived as the major event that shaped it, and other issues accentuated the pivotal role of the Jewish people: the political and economic crisis in Russia highlighted the alleged role of the Jews in the pre- and post-Communist regimes; Pope John Paul II's epistle to his Catholic flock worldwide, "We Remember: Reflections on the Holocaust," summarized two millennia of Jewish-Christian relations and admitted that Church antisemitism had paved the way to the Holocaust. Right-wing organizations, especially in Germany and Austria, were cautious in formulating their messages, taking into account the resonance of World War II-related issues in public opinion. Their caution paid off in electoral gains, which encouraged the extra-parliamentary extremists. Germany struggled to find a way to remember its past with a new generation in government office. This was evident in a continuing controversy over the erection of a central Holocaust memorial in Berlin, and the first voices among intellectuals doubting that the centrality of Auschwitz in public life is still justified.

While the 50th anniversaries and commemorations of World War II brought to the fore the negative image of the Jewish people and resentment of the Jews' role as an eternal reminder of sins that people preferred to forget, the opposite occurred 10 years later, during the 60th anniversary. A special event dedicated to the liberation of Auschwitz at UN headquarters in New York, not to mention a ceremony in the camp itself, with the participation of leading international figures and hosts of declarations and speeches, might be explained either as a form of compensation for the antisemitic violence that had not yet been suppressed by these same leaders; or as the use of Auschwitz as a symbol of human suffering as such, and not only Jewish suffering.

THE NEW ANTISEMITISM AND ANTI-ZIONISM. The new antisemitism is a term that surfaced after the events of October 2000, to distinguish it from late 19th century political antisemitism and post-World War II antisemitism. It is characterized by increasing violence mainly against the person of the Jews, mostly in Western Europe, where France is the biggest trouble spot, and North America and Russia; it is marked by a transfer of initiative from the Christian world to the Muslim one for the first time in the long history of antisemitism. Virulent propaganda keeps spreading from Arab countries, especially those in the Middle East, into the Western world, and Muslim immigrants, numbering about 15 million in 2005 in Europe, have become an electoral and economic asset overshadowing the Jewish communities and Israel. The basic negative characteristics of the collective image of the Jew as they accumulated throughout history have not changed, and traditional and even primitive antisemitism is still put to use. What has changed is the sharpening of the image and the degree of vilification as well as the intensity of the political use that is being made of it. The new antisemitism is political, serving as a tool in the war of the radical Muslim world against the West, and first and foremost against the U.S., a war in which Israel and the Jews represent modernity, a primary enemy in the radical Muslim worldview. And it is political as a convenient fusion of antisemitism and anti-Zionism based on the contention that Israel and the Jewish people are one entity, each responsible for the other and for the whole.

One might say that while part of the antisemitism in Christian countries in recent decades has turned into anti-Zionism, in the Muslim world anti-Zionism appears to be turning into anti-Jewishness, thus broadening a political and territorial conflict into a clash of ideological and religious world views. The use of Christian and secular European antisemitic motifs in Muslim publications has been on the rise, yet at the same time Muslim extremists are turning increasingly to their religious sources, first and foremost the Koran, as a primary anti-Jewish source. Indeed, in the media and in public meetings in Arab countries antisemitic motifs ranged from absurd accusations that Israel and the Jews engage in the spreading of AIDS and corruption in order to dominate the Middle East, to the extensive use of Nazi motifs, the blood libel and the Protocols of the Elders of Zion, with a hero's welcome to the French Holocaust denier Roger Garaudy.

Two of the most debated issues in this regard are the correlation between antisemitic events and the Middle East conflict and the question of when anti-Zionism becomes, if indeed it does, antisemitism.

While some of the antisemitic waves and incidents were clearly connected to the Middle East, many others were not connected to the outbreak of violence between Israelis and Palestinians, especially those which occurred during the years of the Oslo Accords or following the death of Chairman Yasser Arafat, when a process of rapprochement between the parties seemed to be underway. Also, many of the Muslim immigrants come from countries not necessarily connected to the Middle Eastern conflict, such as those from India and Pakistan in the U.K., from Turkey in Germany, or from central Africa and the Caribbean Islands in France and Canada. Indeed, by 2004 this correlation, previously considered a basic tenet, was being reconsidered because of the growing awareness that the results of immigration are basically a European and global problem, and that the declared correlation with the Middle East is a convenient way to blame the situation on external factors.

While there is general agreement that criticism of Israel's policies is not necessarily antisemitism, there is also agreement, among non-Jews as well, that there are forms of anti-Zionism which are not just criticisms of Israel's policies but an objection to its very existence, thus becoming antisemitism: (a) when the language and images used and the character traits attributed to Israel are imbued with known antisemitic stereotypes, and Israel becomes the collective Jew, or the Jew among the nations; (b) when Israelis and Jews are depicted as a cosmic evil, are blamed for worldwide disasters, and are compared to the Nazis, the ultimate evil; (c) when Israelis and Jews supporting the State of Israel are singled out and attacked, and are treated out of all proportion to the issue at hand and in comparison with the response to the actions of other nations; the often mentioned higher expectations from Israel as a democratic state are at the same time a way to avoid confrontations with despotic regimes, certainly the Muslim ones, spawning such phenomena as a ban only against Israeli universities; (d) when the very existence of a Jewish people, and/or its right to have a national movement and a state are doubted or delegitimized; the Merriam-Webster dictionary stated in 1966 that antisemitism is "opposition to Zionism; sympathy with opponents of the State of Israel"; (e) when the Holocaust is denied, distorted, and made a political weapon, and when the Jews are blamed for allegedly misusing it to extort financial support and to make political capital. While Jewish communities perhaps pay the price for the Middle East conflict, Israel pays for the image of the Jew: "in polite company," wrote a London *Sunday Times* observer, "one uses 'Israel' when hesitating to use the word 'Jew.'"

REACTIONS TO THE WAVES OF ANTISEMITISM. "We are back in the 1930s," was the reaction of most spokespersons of Jewish organizations and many individuals to the waves of antisemitism that started in October 2000. Though originating in calls of "death to the Jews" in the streets and in the numerous cases of arson against synagogues during the High Holidays, which reoccurred in 2001 as well, these developments belonged to an era that cannot be compared with the Nazi period: In the 2000s, the antisemitic waves notwithstanding, Jewish organizations and communities are on the alert, well-organized, pinpointing the recent processes and fighting against them, and applying history's lessons. The clear stance of the U.S., of the late Pope John Paul II (1978–2005), and of Israel, coupled with the desire of countries to be members of international bodies by demonstrating their commitment to human rights, are all postwar developments. There is today no state-orchestrated antisemitism, and the billion-plus Muslim believers comprise a variety of sects, beliefs, and ways of life. Moreover, European and North American countries admit today that the ideal of a multicultural society advanced from the 1990s, especially by human rights-oriented NGOs which believed in the idea of gradual assimilation, is being replaced by a growing awareness that immediate steps should be taken to calm inter-community tensions, the most prominent form of which is antisemitism. These steps include general education, education for the democratic system, legislation, law enforcement, operative definitions and comprehensive databases and monitoring. A long series of conferences and seminars, accompanied by public opinion polls and reports, initiated by the UN, the OSCE (Organization for Security and Cooperation in Europe), the European Union, and individual countries, was devoted to the struggle against antisemitism, and partly against Islamophobia. Intellectuals, Jews and non-Jews alike, joined the debates and condemned racism of all kinds, first and foremost antisemitism.

Two parallel phenomena thus characterize the antisemitism of the 2000s: violence accompanied by hostile verbal and visual outpourings and growing awareness and the practical response of the national and international communities.

[Dina Porat (2nd ed.)]

BIBLIOGRAPHY: S.S. Cohen (ed.), *Anti-Semitism: an Annotated Bibliography*, vol. 1 (1987); R. Singerman, *Antisemitic Propaganda: an Annotated Bibliography and Research Guide* (1982). ANTIQUITY: Reinach, Textes; A. Leroy-Beaulieu, *Israel Among the Nations* (1895); M. Radin, *Jews among Greeks and Romans* (1915); H.I. Bell, *Jews and Christians in Egypt* (1924); Pauly-Wissowa, Suppl. 5 (1931); J.W. Parkes, *Conflict of the Church and Synagogue: A Study in the Origins of anti-Semitism* (1934); idem, *anti-Semitism, A New Analysis* (1964); M. Simon, *Verus Israel* (1948); A. Tcherikover, *Hellenistic Civilization and the Jews* (1961); J. Isaac, *Teaching of Contempt: Christian Roots of Anti-Semitism* (1964). MIDDLE AGES: J.C. Wagenseil (ed.), *Tela ignea Satanae* (Lat., 1681); A.L. Williams, *Adversus Judaeos* (Eng., 1935); J.W. Parkes, *Jew in the Medieval World* (1938); C. Roth, in: I. Davidson (ed.), *Essays and Studies… Linda R. Miller* (1938), 171–90; J. Trachtenberg, *The Devil and the Jew* (1943); G. Kisch, *Jews in Medieval Germany* (1949); B. Blumenkrantz, *Juifs et Chrétiens dans le monde occidental 430–1096* (1960). MODERN TIMES: B. Lazare, *Anti-Semitism, its History and Causes* (1903); J. Katz, *From Prejudice to Destruction: Antisemitism, 1700–1933* (1980); J. Reinharz (ed.), *Living with Antisemitism: Modern Jewish Responses* (1987); H. Coudenhove-Calergy, *anti-Semitism Through the Ages* (1935); H. Valentin, *anti-Semitism Historically and Critically Examined* (1936); J. Maritain, *A Christian Looks at the Jewish Question* (1939); J. Graeber and S.H. Britt (editors), *Jews in a Gentile World* (1942); K.S. Pinson (ed.), *Essays on anti-Semitism* (1946^2); M. Hay, *The Foot of Pride: the Pressure of Christendom on the People of Israel for 1900 Years* (1950); N.W. Ackerman and M. Jahoda, *Anti-Semitism and Emotional Disorder, A Psychological Interpretation* (1950); P.F. Bernstein, *Jew-Hate as a Sociological Problem* (1951); R. Loewenstein, *Christians and Jews: a Psychoanalytic Study* (1951, 1963); G.W. Allport, *Nature of Prejudice* (1954); F. Lovsky, *Anti-sémitisme et mystére d'Israël* (1955); L. Poliakov, *Harvest of Hate* (1955); idem, *Histoire de l'antisémitisme*, 3 vols. (1956–68, *History of anti-Semitism*, vol. 1, 1965); Y. Gilboa, *The Black Years of Soviet Jewry* (1971); G. Langmuir, *From Xenophobia to Prejudice* (1957); J.H.E. Fried, in: *Yad Vashem Studies*, 3 (1959), 17–24; A. Bein, *ibid.*, 7–15; idem, *The Jewish Parasite…* (1964, offprint from YLBI, vol. 10); idem, *The Jewish Question in Modern Anti-Semitic Literature…* (offprint from *In the Dispersion*, 4 (winter 1964/65), 126–54); idem, in: *Between East and West: Essays… Bela Horovitz* (1958), 164–93; C.J. Pulzer, *Rise of Political Anti-Semitism in Germany and Austria* (1964); E.H. Flannery, *Anguish of the Jews* (1965); J.P. Sartre, *Anti-Semite and Jew* (1965); Ch. Y. Glock and R. Stark, *Christian Belief and Anti-Semitism* (1966); M. Meyer, in: YLBI, 11 (1966), 137–70; N. Cohn, *Warrant for Genocide* (1967); S. Esh, in: *Yad Vashem Studies*, 6 (1967), 83–120; A.A. Hertzberg, *The French Enlightenment and the Jew* (1968); U. Tal, *Yahadut ve-Naẓrut ba-Reich ha-Sheni* (1970); American Jewish Committee, *Selected Bibliography of Anti-Semitism* (1942); E. Reichman, *Hostages of Civilization* (1950); G. Mosse, *The Crisis of German Ideology* (1964); P. Massing, *Rehearsal for Destruction* (1949); D. Strong, *Organized Anti-Semitism in America* (1941); R. Byrnes, *Anti-Semitism in Modern France* (1950); H. Arendt, *The Origin of Totalitarianism* (1951); J. Higham, in: AJHSP, 47 (1957–58), 1–33; S. Almog, *Nationalism and Anti-Semitism in Modern Europe, 1815–1945* (1990). ANTISEMITIC POLITICAL PARTIES AND ORGANIZATIONS: S.W. Baron, *The Russian Jew Under Tsars and Soviets* (1964); H. Bender, *Der Kampf um die Judenemanzipation in Deutschland…* (1939); R.F. Byrnes, *Anti-Semitism in Modern France* (1950); N. Cohn, *Warrant for Genocide* (1967); Dubnow, Hist Russ, 2 (1918), 3 (1920), index; J. Frumkin and G. Aronson (eds.), *Russian Jewry 1860–1917* (1966); L. Greenberg, *Jews in Russia*, index; Mahler, in: K. Pinson (ed.), *Essays on Anti-Semitism* (1946), 145–73; Vishniak, *ibid.*, 121–45; P.W. Massing, *Rehearsal for Destruction* (1949); P.G.J. Pulzer, *Rise of Political Anti-semitism in Germany* (1964); I. Schapira, *Der Anti-semitismus in der franzoesischen Literatur* (1927); K. Schickert, *Die Judenfrage in Ungarn* (1937); E. Sterling, *Er ist wie Du* (1956); Stern-Taeubler, in: HUCA, 23 (1950/51), 171–97; V. Eichstaedt, *Bibliographie zur Geschichte der Judenfrage*, 2 (1938, no more published); E. Silberner, *Ha-Sozializm ha-Ma'aravi u-She'elat ha-Yehudim* (1955); J. Toury, *Mehumah u-Mevukhah be-Mahpekhat 1848* (1968); U. Tal, *Ha-Antishemiyyut ba-Reich ha-Germani ha-Sheni* (1969); Y. Katz, *Bonim Ḥofshiyyim vi-Yhudim* (1968); N. Katzburg, *Ha-Antishemiyyut ha-Politit be-Hungaryah* (dissert., Jerusalem, 1962); N. Rotenstreich, *Ha-Yahadut u-Zekhuyyot ha-Yehudim* (1959); Z. Szajkowski, *Anti-semitizm in der Frantsoizisher Arbeiter Bavegung* (1948). ARAB ANTISEMITISM: S.G. Haim, in: JSOS, 17 (1952), 307–12;

idem, *Arab Nationalism, an Anthology* (1962); Y. Harkabi, *Bein Yisrael le-Arav* (1968); idem, *Emdat ha-Aravim be-Sikhsukh Yisrael Arav* (1968). IN THE U.S.S.R.: Jewish Library, London, *Yevrei i Yevreyskiy Narod* (1960–), photostat of material from Soviet daily and periodical press; R.L. Braham, *Jews in the Communist World: A Bibliography 1945–1960* (1961); P. Meyer et al., *Jews in the Soviet Satellites* (1953); S.M. Schwarz, *Jews in the Soviet Union* (1951); idem, *Anti-Semitism in the Soviet Union* (1952); idem, *Yevrei v Sovetskom Soyuze* (1966); *Jews in Eastern Europe*, a periodical survey of events affecting Jews in the Soviet bloc (1958–); B.Z. Goldberg, *Jewish Problem in the Soviet Union* (1961); S.W. Baron, *The Russian Jew under Tsars and Soviets* (1964). **ADD. BIBLIOGRAPHY:** N. Levin, *The Jews in the Soviet Union since 1917* (1988); Sh. Ettinger, (ed.), *Anti-Semitism in the Soviet Union* (1986); A.S. Lindemann, *The Jew Accused: Three Anti-Semitic Affairs (Deyfus, Beilis, Frank), 1894–1915* (1991); W. Korey *The Soviet Cage* (1974). MODERN AND NEW ANTISEMITISM: D. Porat and R. Stauber (eds), *Anti-Semitism Wordlwide*, Roth Institute for the Study of Anti-Semitism and Racism, Tel Aviv University Annual (1994–2004); *Anti-Semitism World Report*, Institute for Jewish Policy Research and AJC (1992–); W.Bergman and J. Wetzle, *Manifestations of Anti-Semitism in the European Union* (2003); *Manifestations of Anti-Semitism in the European Union, 2002–2003*, EUMC (2004): A. Finkielkraut, *Au nom de l'Autre, Reflexions sur l'antisémitisme qui vient* (2003); P.-A. Taguieff, *Rising from the Muck, The New Anti-Semitism in Europe* (2004); R.S. Wistrich, *Anti-Zionism and Antisemitism in the Contemporary World* (1990); idem, *The Longest Hatred* (1992); G. Schoenfeld, *The Return of Anti-Semitism* (2003); D. Matas, *Anti-Zionism: A Human Rights Violation* (2003); R. Rosenbaum (ed.), *Those Who Forget the Past: The Question of Anti-Semitism* (2004); A. Bein, *The Jewish Problem: Biography of a World Problem* (1990). HOLOCAUST DENIAL: D. Lipstadt, *Denying the Holocaust: the Growing Assault on Truth and Memory* (1994); K.S. Stern, *Holocaust Denial* (1993); S. Rembiszewski, *The Final Lie: Holocaust Denial in Germany – A Second Generation Denier as a Test Case* (1995).

ANTOINE, NICOLAS (1603–1632), French pastor who converted to Judaism. Antoine, who was born into a Catholic family in Briey (Lorraine), became a Protestant c. 1624 and studied theology in Geneva. A few years later, during a stay in Metz, his faith in Christianity was shaken by discussions with Jews of that city. Subsequently he went to Venice where he asked the rabbis of the city to circumcise him, but they were afraid to do so. When he returned to Geneva he assumed various functions, including that of pastor of Divonne, although convinced of the truth of Judaism. He followed Jewish observances, and avoided making reference to the New Testament, or explaining Christian dogmas in his sermons and in the exercise of his other pastoral duties. This might have passed unobserved by the Protestant community of Divonne had he not one Sunday in February 1632, in a sermon on Psalm 2, contradicted the Christian interpretation of the text, openly declaring that it referred not to Jesus, but to David. At first he was declared insane and treated as such, but he was later summoned to court. The trial was conducted summarily. Although several French pastors advocated clemency, he was condemned to death and executed at Place du Plainpalais in Geneva in April 1632.

BIBLIOGRAPHY: Weill, in: REJ, 36 (1898), 163–96; 37 (1898), 161–80; P.F. Geisendorf, *Les Annalistes genevois*… (1942), 700.

[Bernhard Blumenkranz]

ANTOKOLSKI, MARK (Mordecai; 1843–1902), Russian sculptor. Antokolski was born in Vilna to poor parents. As a child he studied in a *ḥeder*. He later served as an apprentice to a haberdasher, and then to a wood-carver, and through this medium his artistic talent was discovered. Antokolski was accepted in 1862 at the Academy of Art in St. Petersburg. Two years later, he won the Great Silver Medal for his wood bas-relief, *The Jewish Tailor*. In 1865 he executed the ivory bas-relief *The Miser*, in 1867, *The Kiss of Judas Iscariot*, and in 1869, *The Talmudic Debate*. In 1869 he completed the bas-relief *Inquisition*, on which he worked for six years. When he returned to Russia after a study-trip to Berlin, he ceased treating Jewish subjects and began choosing themes from Russian history. His statue *Ivan the Terrible* (1871) brought him his first great publicity. It was purchased for the Hermitage by Czar Alexander and resulted in Antokolski's election to the council of the Academy. Due to a disease of the lungs he moved to Rome in 1872. Antokolski sculpted *Peter the Great*, a large marble statue, which was placed in Peterhof. He executed three bronze statues, *Jaroslav the Wise*, *Dmitri Donskoi*, and *Ivan the Third*, and in 1874, *Jesus in Chains*. In 1875 Antokolski returned to St. Petersburg and did sculptures of the royal family, L.N. Tolstoi, and I. Turgeniev. Noteworthy among his sculptures in this period are the ivory statue *Mephisto*, the tombstone of Princess Obolenskaya (1875), *The Death of Socrates*, and *Jesus, the Crucified* (1876). International fame came at the Paris World Exhibition in 1878.

Antokolski's noteworthy sculptures between 1881 and 1891 include *Yermak* and *Nestor*. Most of his works were exhibited in the Tretyakow Museum in Moscow and the Russian Museum in Leningrad.

Even in his early works, he departed from the artistic methods of the official academic school generally accepted in the early 19th century. This school viewed classical sculpture and that of the Christian church as a model. Antokolski became associated with the Russian school of artists, the "Peredvizhniki" (the "transmitters"), which saw as its prime object not artistic expression as such, but rather the social ideal, humanity, and an exaggerated realism. Indeed, Antokolski liked to have sculptures embody a social and humane ideal. As long as this school prevailed in Russia (until the 1890s) Antokolski enjoyed much popularity. Later, however, he had many admirers both in Russia and in Western Europe who saw in him a great artist in whose statues the principle was not outward plastics, but rather the lines of the soul which they embodied.

Antokolski became famous during the antisemitic wave in Russia, prior to the pogroms of the 1880s. At that time, the Russian nationalist press opened an attack on him, describing him as a "Jew" who had no right to portray the heroes of Russian history and Jesus and John the Baptist because it was not possible for him to comprehend them and the spirit of Christianity. His fame was attributed to the influence of influential Jewish bankers (mainly Baron Horace Guenzberg). Turgeniev and the art critic Stasov defended Antokolski; but the artist was severely affected by the antisemitic attacks, and, full of bitterness, he left Russia permanently for Paris. There, in the last years of his life, he lived alone and created almost nothing, with the exception of a large marble statue, *Spinoza*. Antokolski observed Jewish traditions and was interested in spreading art among the Jews. He supported young Jewish artists and envisaged a Jewish artistic school. In *Teḥiyyat ha-Ru'aḥ* ("Renewal of the Spirit"), Aḥad Ha-Am accused Antokolski of choosing to depict the monk Nestor, instead of Elijah, the Gaon of Vilna, as a figure aloof from the world, though the Gaon and the artists were natives of the same town. Despite this, however, Aḥad Ha-Am recognized the particular Jewish character of Antokolski's artistic work, in which the statue is not a body but the dress for the spirit and idea embodied in it.

Antokolski wrote many essays on artistic problems and an autobiography, which was published in the Russian monthly, *Vestnik Yevropy* (1887; full manuscript in the Leningrad Public Library). His correspondence, edited by his colleague Stasov, has been published.

BIBLIOGRAPHY: M. Grunwald, *Mark Antokolski* (Ger., 1926); Wininger, Biog, 1 (1925), 134–5.

[Karl Schwarz / Abba Ahimeir]

ANTOKOLSKI, PAVEL GRIGOREVICH (1896–), poet. Trained as a lawyer, Antokolski was for a time associated with Vakhtangov's theatrical studio but turned to literature. The settings of Antokolski's poems range from the medieval France of *François Villon* (1934) to the 19th-century Russia of *O Pushkine* (1960). He also published Russian translations of Georgian and Ukrainian verse.

°ANTONESCU, ION (1882–1946), Romanian soldier and politician. Following a dispute with King Carol II in 1934, Antonescu resigned his post as chief of staff. When Goga and *Cuza formed an antisemitic government late in 1937, Antonescu, an antisemite, was appointed minister of defense, and the Germans established contact with him. On September 4, 1940 he became prime minister, with dictatorial powers. Two days later Antonescu forced King Carol II to abdicate, formed a government together with the *Iron Guard, and called himself *conducator* ("leader") of Romania. Antonescu disapproved of the violent methods of the Iron Guard, fearing that they would lead to Romania's economic ruin. On January 21 and 22, 1941, the Iron Guard made its revolt against Antonescu the occasion for a pogrom. Hitler took Antonescu's part, since he needed the Romanian army for his planned invasion of Russia. After Romania entered the war against Russia on June 22, 1941, the Germans and Romanians conquered Bessarabia and Northern Bukovina, and massacred the Jewish population. Antonescu ordered the Odessa massacre (November 23, 1941), which cost between 25,000 and 30,000 Jewish lives. In the autumn of 1942, the Jewish leadership in Bucharest enlisted the aid of local politicians, neutral diplomats, and the papal nuncio, who applied pressure on Antonescu, and succeeded in preventing the deportation of the entire Jewish population of Romania to concentration camps. After the German defeat at Stalingrad, Antonescu became increasingly lenient toward the Jews. Late in 1943, negotiations began between Jewish leaders and Antonescu's government for the return of those Jews deported to *Transnistria and for their emigration to Palestine. At the same time, Antonescu began negotiating for a separate peace. The Transnistria deportees began to return only in the spring of 1944, when the Russians reconquered the area. Antonescu was sentenced to death by a Bucharest People's Court and executed on June 6, 1946.

BIBLIOGRAPHY: A. Hillgruber, *Hitler, Koenig Carol und Marschall Antonescu* (1954); M. Carp, *Cartea Neagrā*, 3 vols. (1946–48), index; *Gutachten des Instituts fuer Zeitgeschichte*, 1 (1958), 102–83; T. Lavi, *Yahadut Romanyah be-Ma'avak al Hazzalatah* (1965), passim.

[Theodor Lavi]

°ANTONESCU, MIHAI (1907–1946), Romanian lawyer and politician. In 1940 Antonescu, as minister of justice, formulated several anti-Jewish laws. He was the legal representative of Ion *Antonescu (to whom he was unrelated). Upon the outbreak of war with the Soviet Union in June 1941 Antonescu was appointed deputy prime minister and foreign minister. He ordered the persecution and forcible deportation of the Jewish population of Bessarabia and Bukovina in order to achieve "ethnic purity." In July 1942 Antonescu concluded an agreement with Gustav Richter, Adolf *Eichmann's representative in Romania, to deport all Romanian Jews to Poland, but this plan was frustrated by the intervention of diplomats from neutral countries who acted on the initiative of Romanian Jewish leaders. Early in 1944 Antonescu established contact with the officially non-existent Jewish organizations, and particularly with A.L. Zissu, chairman of the Zionist Executive Committee. In June 1944 he permitted the Palestine Office to operate legally and supply identity cards to refugees bound for Palestine from Hungary, Poland, and Slovakia. After the war he was tried with Ion Antonescu by a Bucharest People's Court. They were sentenced to death and executed.

BIBLIOGRAPHY: See Antonescu, Ion.

[Theodor Lavi]

ANTONIA, fortress situated on a rocky prominence on the north side of the Temple Mount in Jerusalem. It replaced a number of earlier fortresses at this location: (1) the *birah* (the "Citadel") from the time of Nehemiah (Neh. 2:8; 7:2); (2) the Hellenistic *acropolis* or *acra* (2 Macc. 4:12, 27–28; 5:5–6) – not to be confused with the later **acra* of the Seleucids, which was situated to the south of the Temple Mount; and (3) the *baris* of the Hasmonean period (Josephus, Antiquities XV, 403; Wars I, 75). A rock-cut tunnel leading from the direction of the later Struthion Pool probably fed a number of cisterns belonging to the Hellenistic/Hasmonean fortress at this location. A rock-cut fosse or ditch originally separated the area of the earlier fortresses from the enclosed temple area itself and was mentioned by Strabo (16, 2:40) and Josephus (Antiquities, 14: 61); it was eventually filled in by Pompey in 63 B.C.E. This rock-cut ditch (118 ft. in width and 20 ft. deep) was still visible to 19th-century explorers. As part of the major landscape changes to the area of the Temple esplanade in Jerusalem, Herod the Great decided to refortify the fortress and rename it in honor of Mark Antony. According to Josephus, it was situated at the corner of the northwestern colonnade of the Temple Mount, which meant that Herod was forced to reduce the area of the fortress quite substantially. Josephus relates that it stood on a rock 50 cubits (82 ft.) high, and its walls reached a height of 40 cubits. Inside the fortress were a palace, courtyards, bath houses, and cisterns. From three of its corners rose ornamental towers 50 cubits high, and from the fourth (southeastern) corner, a tower 70 cubits high. The fortress is believed to have stood at the junction of the "second" defensive wall of Jerusalem with the northwest angle of the Temple Mount, but archaeological proof of this has not yet been forthcoming; a deep rock-cut moat apparently protected it from the north, with underground stairs and passages connecting it to the south with the Temple area. This key position was captured by the Zealots on the 15th of Av, 66 C.E. During the siege of Titus the breach through which the Romans penetrated into the Temple area passed through Antonia. Earlier investigators believed that remains of the Antonia fortress could be detected in the grounds of the present convent of Notre Dame de Sion and that combined with the remains seen at the northwest angle of the Temple Mount area, it was deemed possible to reconstruct the plan of the entire fortress. New archaeological studies indicate this is no longer the case and that the area of the Antonia Fortress was restricted almost entirely to the rocky prominence (295 ft. × 131 ft.) at the northwest angle of the Temple Mount, with a flight of steps leading up to it from the south. Several Christian commentators have maintained that Antonia was the site of *gabbatha* (the stone pavement) mentioned in John (19:13) as the place where Pontius Pilate sat when Jesus was brought before him for judgment. However, it is now believed that the trial of Jesus occurred at the Praetorium, which was the same as the Old Palace of Herod the Great situated in the Upper City and to the south of the crucifixion area. The Antonia Fortress was apparently razed following the capture of the city by the Romans in 70 C.E. The Capitoline Temple may have been built at this location at the time of Hadrian, overlooking the northern market of Aelia Capitolina.

BIBLIOGRAPHY: L.-H. Vincent and A.M. Steve, *Jérusalem de l'Ancien Testament*, 1 (1954), 193ff.; Marie-Aline de Sion, *La Forteresse Antonia à Jerusalem et la Question du Prétoire* (1955). **ADD. BIBLIOGRAPHY:** D. Bahat, "The Western Wall Tunnels," in: H. Geva (ed.), *Ancient Jerusalem Revealed* (1994); G.J. Wightman, "Temple Fortresses in Jerusalem. Part II: The Hasmonean *Baris* and Herodian Antonia," in: *Bulletin of the Anglo-Israel Archaeological Society*, 10 (1990–91), 7–35; J. Wilkinson, *Jerusalem as Jesus Knew it* (1979); D.M. Jacobson, "The Plan of Herod's Temple," in: *Bulletin of the Anglo-Israel Archaeological Society*, 10 (1990–91), 36–66; S. Gibson and D.M. Jacobson, *Below the Temple Mount in Jerusalem* (1996).

[Michael Avi-Yonah / Shimon Gibson (2nd ed.)]

°**ANTONINUS PIUS**, Roman emperor (ruled 138–161); the successor of *Hadrian. Antoninus Pius generally continued the policies of his predecessor. His most notable achievement was in the field of law which he insisted be administered impartially. In regard to the Jews, and particularly in Judea, Hadrian's harsh policies were repealed. Although still not allowed to proselytize, those born as Jews were freely permitted their traditional methods of worship, and the schools and the synagogues were openly reestablished.

[Alan Richard Schulman]

In Talmud and *Aggadah*

A Roman emperor named Antoninus forms the subject of a number of aggadic statements, dialogues, and stories in the Talmud and the Midrashim, in all of which he is described as in the company of R. *Judah ha-Nasi. The talmudic sources refer to more than one emperor; they distinguish, for instance, between Antoninus senior and Antoninus junior (Eccl. R. 10:5), but the attempts of scholars to fit these accounts into the historic framework of the period of the Antonines have proved unsuccessful. The discussions with Antoninus include dialogues on the relationship between the body and the soul, the power of the evil inclination, and matters of state. They contain no data by which it would be possible to determine with certainty the attitude of the dialogists to the problems that were constantly discussed in the philosophical schools in the period of the Antonines. In the dialogues and stories, the Jewish patriarch excels the Roman emperor in wisdom and in moral stature, but the two are good friends and show complete trust in, and respect for, each other. Antoninus' attitude to Judaism is one of reverence. A rabbinic dictum has also been preserved according to which Antoninus would be the first righteous proselyte to be accepted in the messianic era (TJ, Meg. 3:2, 74a).

Underlying the talmudic and midrashic stories there is undoubtedly an element of historic truth; they testify to the good relations that were established for a time in the period of the Antonines between the Roman authorities in Palestine and the Jewish sages. The form of government in the Roman Empire, which in the second century C.E. was to a certain extent federal, made it possible for the people of the different countries of the Empire to express their views before the emperor not only on the form of government, but also on religious and ethical questions.

The tales about Antoninus and R. Judah ha-Nasi were widely current among the people. A number of them, as, for example, the parable of the lame man and the blind (Sanh. 91a–b) are found in comparatively early works of Jewish literature (see the Ezekiel Apocryphon 1; cf. James, in: JTS, 15

(1914), 236) and are derived from the treasury of folk wisdom. Accounts of disputations and conversations of a similar nature (between other rabbis and Roman dignitaries) have been preserved in talmudic and midrashic literature. There are also extant (non-Jewish) Greco-Roman texts containing disputations and dialogues of this type between various individuals and Roman emperors.

[Joshua Gutmann]

BIBLIOGRAPHY: Hoffmann, in: MWJ, 19 (1892), 33–55, 245–55; S. Krauss, *Antoninus und Rabbi* (1910); R. Leszynsky, *Loesung des Antoninusraetsels* (1910); S. Lieberman, *Greek in Jewish Palestine* (1942), 78ff.

°**ANTONIO**, known as the "Prior of Crato" (1531–1595), claimant to the throne of Portugal which, on the death of childless Henry II in 1580, had been seized by Philip II of Spain. Antonio was the grandson of King Manuel (who had been responsible for the expulsion of the Jews from Portugal in 1496–97) through an illegitimate union between the latter's son Luis and a beautiful *New Christian woman, Yolante Gomez. It was therefore hoped that if he succeeded to the throne he would curb the activities of the Portuguese Inquisition. Partly for this reason, partly because of their inveterate hatred of Spain, the Portuguese Marrano communities strongly favored his cause. Among his principal supporters was Solomon *Abenaes, who endeavored to secure Anglo-Turkish support for him. In London, the ill-fated Roderigo *Lopes was his personal physician. Dom Antonio proved a weak and unreliable character and the Marrano group later broke with him, while he retaliated by accusing them of treachery. This quarrel ultimately led to the execution of Lopes, who did not turn down a Spanish suggestion that he should poison the pretender and was also suspected of having similar designs on Queen Elizabeth I.

BIBLIOGRAPHY: Wolf, in: JHSET, 11 (1924–27), 1–91; C. Roth, *House of Nasi: The Duke of Naxos* (1948), 205–13; J. Veríssimo Serrão, *Dom Antonio* (Port., 1962); idem, *O reinado de Dom Antonio, Prior do Crato* (1956).

[Cecil Roth]

°**ANTONIUS DIOGENES** (c. 100 C.E.), author of a fictional romance on Thule, quoted in Porphyry's "Life of Pythagoras." He quotes the tradition to the effect that the philosopher was influenced by the peoples of the East. According to Antonius, Pythagoras visited the Egyptians, Arabs, Chaldeans, and Hebrews, and learned from them the accurate interpretation of dreams.

°**ANTONIUS JULIANUS** (late first century C.E.), author of a book on the Jews mentioned only by the third century Christian Minucius Felix (Octavius, 33:4). Antonius is generally assumed to be identical with the procurator of Judea in 70 C.E. of the same name, who took an active part in the Council of War convened by Titus to debate the fate of the Temple (Jos., War, 6:238).

BIBLIOGRAPHY: Schuerer, Gesch, 1 (1904⁴), 58; E. Norden, in: *Neue Jahrbuecher fuer das klassische Altertum*, 31 (1913), 664ff.; A.M.A. Hospers-Jansen, *Tacitus over de Joden* (1949), 172ff.; E. Paratore, *Tacito* (It., 1962²), 664ff.

[Menahem Stern]

ANTUÑES, Marrano family. HEITOR (HECTOR) sailed for Brazil from Portugal in 1557; he was tried posthumously by the Lisbon Inquisition. His widow, Ana Rois, died in prison. Several members of the family were tried by the Inquisition in the 17th century and the name figures also in the records of the Mexican Inquisition. In the auto-da-fé at Valladolid in 1725, a family from Portugal comprising two brothers and two sisters named Antuñes were reconciled to the church.

David was among the Amsterdam poets who collaborated in the volume in memory of the inquisitional martyr Abraham Nuñez *Bernal in 1655. AARON, rabbi in Amsterdam and Naarden, was in correspondence with contemporary German talmudic scholars and left some works in manuscript, including a commentary on *Avot*. It is questionable whether he is the same Aaron b. Solomon Antuñes who was active as a printer in Amsterdam 1716–20. GABRIEL, who left Suriname with the British in 1675, settled in Barbados. The family of Antuñes Paredes was numerous in Curaçāo.

BIBLIOGRAPHY: AJHSP, index to volumes 1–20 (1914); I.S. Emmanuel, *Precious Stones of the Jews of Curaçao…* (1957), index; A. Wiznitzer, *Jews in Colonial Brazil* (1960), index.

[Cecil Roth]

ANTWERP, Belgian port and commercial center. Although a few Jews are mentioned in Antwerp before the 15th century, the first substantial community was established with the arrival of *Marrano merchants and others from the Iberian penninsula. On March 30, 1526, Emperor *Charles V issued a general safe-conduct to the Portuguese "New Christians" in Antwerp, and numerous Marranos were enabled to settle there, and engage in business. The Marranos in Antwerp, however, were spared from the activities of the Inquisition, which had not been authorized in the southern Low Countries, although under Spanish rule. Nevertheless, the anomaly of Marrano existence under a Catholic prince remained, and they were suspected of aiding the Reformation agitation. Wealthy Marranos, such as the *Mendes family, used the Spanish Netherlands for transit to Muslim countries. These factors, combined with political and economic fluctuations, influenced the sovereigns to revise their attitude to the Marranos in the Spanish Netherlands several times. Toward the mid-16th century it was decided to expel from Antwerp all Marranos who had arrived there before 1543. Attempts by the municipality to avert the expulsion failed. The edict was renewed in 1550 and most of the Marranos were forced to leave, although a group of families continued to reside in Antwerp without rights of domicile. After the Peace of Westphalia (1648), Marranos were able to resettle in Antwerp, and even established a modest place of worship there. For their religious needs, however, they mainly attached themselves to the community in *Amsterdam. Population figures for the "Portuguese nation" in Antwerp in this period indicate that 85 families and 17 individuals were living there in 1571, and 47 families and 20 widows in 1591; 46 names are mentioned in 1619, and 38 males and 27 females in 1666.

By the Treaty of Utrecht (1713), Antwerp passed under Austrian rule. The Jewish community was able to emerge from hiding, and certain privileged Jews of Ashkenazi origin obtained the right of residence in Antwerp. By the end of the 18th century civic rights had been granted to a number of individual Jews. After the occupation of the Low Countries by the French revolutionary forces in 1794, Jews were able to settle freely in Antwerp, and the Ashkenazi element eventually predominated. Antwerp was again attached to the Netherlands before becoming part of independent *Belgium in 1830. The first synagogue was built in 1808 and a cemetery established in 1828. There were 151 Jews in Antwerp in 1829, and 373 in Antwerp province in 1846.

After the beginning of the 20th century the Antwerp community enjoyed unprecedented prosperity through a combination of two chance circumstances: during the 1880s the port of Antwerp became the major embarkation point for the mass Jewish migration to America from Eastern Europe; at the same time there was a spectacular development in the *diamond industry through the discovery of the South African mines. Many of the intending emigrants decided to settle in Antwerp and take up new skills as diamond cutters and polishers or dealers. The occupation became central to the community, and Jewish enterprise made Antwerp the capital of the industry in Europe. The Jewish population in Antwerp increased from 8,000 in 1900 to 25,000 in 1913, 35,000 in 1927, and 55,000 in 1939 (about 20% of the total population). In 1928 several thousand Jews were employed in the diamond industry, 25% of the total workers and 75% of employees in the industry being Jewish. The number of Jewish emigrants passing through Antwerp and afforded relief by the community was 2,300 in 1897, 7,478 in 1900, 19,448 in 1903, 24,479 in 1905, and 23,656 in 1920–21.

[Simon R. Schwarzfuchs]

The Holocaust Period (1939–1945)

When the Germans invaded Belgium, there were about 50,000 Jews in Antwerp, only 10% of whom were Belgian citizens. Most of the Jews escaped to France at the start of hostilities. However, after the Belgian surrender (May 28, 1940), approximately 30,000 Jews returned to the city.

No special measures were taken against the Jews at the beginning of the occupation. The military authorities were more interested in keeping the country quiet, and in reviving the diamond industry, which had been almost entirely owned by Jews. According to the first anti-Jewish decrees, on Oct. 28, 1940, more than 13,000 Antwerp Jews were registered on the *Judenregister*, and Jewish businesses were marked with trilingual signboards. Further decrees forbade Antwerp Jews to leave their homes between 7 P.M. and 7 A.M., enter public parks, or dwell in places other than Brussels, Antwerp, Liège, and Charleroi. On April 14, 1941, Jewish shops were destroyed, two main synagogues looted, and Torah scrolls burnt in the streets by pro-German Flemings. The Gestapo carried out the first confiscation in the diamond bourse on August 18, 1941. According to the German census of October 1941, 17,242 Jews now remained in the city.

The final phase of Nazi persecution began with the introduction of the yellow-star *badge on May 27, 1942. On July 22, Jews traveling on trains between Antwerp and Brussels were arrested, sent to the transit camp at Mechelen, and then deported to the death camps. On Friday night, August 28, 1942, most of Antwerp's Jewish families were arrested in a sudden *Aktion*, and sent to the transit camp. Deportations, first to forced labor camps in France (mostly for the Todt organization) and then to Auschwitz, continued until September 4, 1943, when the remaining Jews (Belgian citizens and the protected Judenrat) were arrested. However, when the city was liberated a year later, some 800 Antwerp Jews emerged from hiding, where they had been supplied with food and other essentials by the organized Jewish resistance. HISO (Hulp aan Joodse Slachtoffers van de Oorlog – Help for Jewish War Victims) was at once organized to aid returned and displaced persons.

[Ephraïm Schmidt]

Contemporary Period

In 1969, the number of Jews was believed to be 10,500, many of whom were occupied in the diamond industry; almost 80% of the membership of the diamond exchange was Jewish. Several factors contributed to the unity of the Antwerp community. Antwerp Jews were not professionally nor residentially dispersed as were the Jews of Brussels, so that their concentration within certain parts of the city and within a limited number of professions had an impact on the religious and social life of the community. Most of the Jews of Antwerp were of Polish origin, oriented toward either orthodoxy or ultra-orthodoxy. These orientations were represented by the Shomre Hadass and Machsiké Hadass congregations, respectively. There were six small ḥasidic communities, with a joint membership of 11–12% of the total number of Jewish households. The Sephardi community had dwindled to a few dozen families maintaining their own synagogue. It was estimated that 90% of the children received a Jewish education, this percentage probably being one of the highest in Europe. The congregations controlled four day schools and a yeshivah, which together had 2,200 students. The two largest schools were Tachkemoni of the Shomre Hadass community and the Jesodé Hatora of the Machsiké Hadass community, both recognized and subsidized by the state. Their curricula conformed to official requirements, but they also provided Jewish studies, according to their religious orientation. The ḥasidic congregations also established day schools where a minimum amount of secular subjects were taught. A central fundraising and welfare organization, Het Central Beheer van Joodse Weldadigheid en Maatschappelijk Hulpbetoon, provided medical, youth, social, and financial services for the benefit of the community and transients. In addition, the Forum oder Joodse Organisaties, founded in 1994, represented Flemish-speaking Jews before the authorities, and like the Coordinating Committee of Belgian Jewish Organizations it was represented in the Consistoire Centrale.

In the ensuing decades the Orthodox character of Antwerp's Jews was strengthened, with the city's Jewish population reaching a level of around 15,000 in 2002 while Belgium's Jewish population as a whole dropped to a little over 30,000. The two big Orthodox schools accommodated over 3,000 children and nearly 2,000 others attended Modern Orthodox, ḥasidic, and other schools. Around 30 synagogues were in operation. The majority of the city's Jews remained connected with the diamond industry, where Yiddish was still the dominant language, and the city's weekly *Belgisch Israelitisch Weekblad* was the country's biggest Jewish newspaper.

[Max Gottschalk / Willy Bok]

BIBLIOGRAPHY: S. Ullmann, *Studien zur Geschichte der Juden in Belgien bis zum 18. Jahrhundert* (1909); I.A. Goris, *Etudes sur les colonies marchandes méridionales… à Anvers de 1488 à 1567* (1925); Revah, in: REJ, 123 (1963), 123–47; Gutwirth, *ibid.*, 125 (1966)' 365–84; idem, in: JJS 10 (1968), 121–38; C. Roth, *House of Nasi: Doña Gracia* (1947), 21–49; E. Schmidt, *Geschiedenis van de Joden in Antwerpen* (1963; French, 1969), includes bibliography. **ADD. BIBLIOGRAPHY:** PK; AJYB (2003).

ANUSIM (Heb. אֲנוּסִים; "forced ones"), persons compelled by overwhelming pressure, whether by physical threats, psychological stress, or economic sanctions, to abjure Judaism and adopt a different faith (in contradistinction to *meshummadim*, or voluntary apostates – see *Apostasy). Here attention will be directed only to instances of group compulsion. An edict or systematic attempt to force Jews to convert to another faith is termed in Hebrew *gezerat shemad* ("edict of apostasy"). In Jewish sources, the term *anusim* is applied not only to the forced converts themselves, but also to their descendants who clandestinely cherished their Jewish faith, attempting to observe at least vestiges of the **halakhah*, and loyalty to their Jewish identity. Both the elements of compulsion and free will enter the psychological motivation of the forced convert. The concept denoted by the term *anusim*, therefore, is fluid, bordering on that applying to apostates and even to *Marranos; it has been the subject of much discussion.

Early Middle Ages

The vituperation heaped on Jews by Christian ecclesiastics, and the violent methods employed by the church in the fourth century (see Jewish *History, Middle Ages), led to many forced conversions. There is clear evidence that *anusim* existed in the Frankish kingdoms of the sixth century, for the typical pattern of mass violence combined with threat of expulsion is already present in the mass conversion of many Jews to Christianity in *Clermont-Ferrand in 576. The almost inevitable result of the creation of a Jewish "underground" within the Christian society is also clearly visible. The events in Clermont were set in motion after a Jew, who had voluntarily adopted Christianity, was molested by other Jews during a religious procession. The participants in the procession then made an attack "which destroyed [the synagogue] completely, razing it to the grounds." Subsequently, Bishop *Avitus directed a letter to the Jews in which he disclaimed the use of compulsion to make them adopt Christianity, but announced at the end of the missive: "Therefore if ye be ready to believe as I do, be one flock with us, and I shall be your pastor; but if ye be not ready, depart from this place." The community hesitated for three days before making a decision. Finally the majority, some 500, accepted Christianity. The Christians in Clermont greeted the event with rejoicing: "Candles were lit, the lamps shone, the whole city radiated with the light of the snow-white flock" (i.e., the forced converts). The Jews who preferred exile left for *Marseilles (Gregory of Tours, *Histories*, 5:11) The poet Venantius Fortunatus composed a poem to commemorate the occasion. In 582 the Frankish king Chilperic compelled numerous Jews to adopt Christianity. Again the *anusim* were not wholehearted in their conversion, for "some of them, cleansed in body but not in heart, denied God, and returned to their ancient perfidy, so that they were seen keeping the Sabbath, as well as Sunday" (*ibid.*, 6:17).

Persistent attempts to enforce conversion were made in the seventh century by the Visigoths in Spain after they had adopted the Roman Catholic faith. Comparatively mild legal measures were followed by the harsh edict issued by King Sisibut in 616, ordering the compulsory baptism of all Jews. After conversion, however, the *anusim* evidently maintained their Jewish cohesion and religious life. It was undoubtedly this problem that continued to occupy Spanish sovereigns at the successive Councils of Toledo representing both the ecclesiastical and secular authorities; it is difficult to conceive that the term *Judaei*, employed in the texts of the canons subsequently promulgated by the councils, actually refers to professing Jews; the restrictive measures adopted against the *Judaei* only make sense if directed at the devoted underground. Thus, steps were taken to secure that the children of converts had a Christian religious education as well as to prevent the older generation from continuing to observe the Jewish rites or from failing to observe the Catholic ones. A system of strict supervision by the clergy over the way of life and movements of the *anusim* was imposed. The attitude of the victims is seen in a letter addressed to the Visigothic king Recceswinth in 654, in which they promised to live as faithful Christians but pleaded not to be compelled to eat pork against which they felt physical revulsion.

Later Middle Ages

Attempts from the beginning of the eighth century to compel Jews in the *Byzantine Empire to accept Christianity similarly resulted in the creation of *anusim* leading a crypto-Jewish existence. According to the chronicler Theophanes, when in 722 the Emperor *Leo III "compelled the Jews and the Montanists to undergo baptism, the Jews, although unwilling, accepted baptism and then washed it off" (*Chronographia*, ed. by De Boor, 1 (1963), 401). At the end of the ninth century and in the first half of the tenth, attempts were made to convert Jews to Christianity in the Byzantine Empire by physical threats, missionary *disputations, and the offer of rewards to the converts. *Basil I is particularly notorious in Jewish chronicles for these attempts.

Compulsory conversions took place in the Rhineland in the tenth century, and during the Crusades amid the anti-Jewish attacks after 1096 (see also *Kiddush ha-Shem*). The action of Emperor *Henry IV, who later permitted the victims to return to their former faith, was violently resented by the Pope and the Christian populace, hence Henry's successors did not always follow this policy. In Spain and North Africa in the 12th century, the Muslim *Almohads forced both their Jewish and their Christian subjects to convert to Islam, apparently by terrorization rather than legislative measures. The converts from Judaism and their descendants remained isolated from their environment and humiliated by society. All the evidence points to them having led a crypto-Jewish existence.

At the close of the 13th century the Jews in southern Italy were given the choice of baptism or death, and there followed a wave of forced conversions under which the Jewish population in *Apulia completely disappeared. Many were driven to simulate Christianity to save their lives. The *neofiti* (neophytes), or *mercanti* as they were called because of their commercial activities, remained a recognizable and unpopular group suspected of retaining their fidelity to their ancestral faith for over two centuries. In 1453 Pope *Nicholas V wrote of them: "their forefathers were Jews who adopted Christianity 150 years ago, rather from compulsion than of their own free will."

[Haim Hillel Ben-Sasson]

THE IBERIAN PENINSULA. Forcible conversion of Jews occurred in many lands throughout the ages, but nowhere was this phenomenon more consequential and widespread than in the Iberian Peninsula, in the Kingdoms of Castile, Aragon, and Portugal. Crypto-Judaism in Sepharad began in 1391 as a result of the massacres that broke out in Seville and spread throughout the peninsula in the summer of that year. The attack against the Jews was perpetrated following a venomous anti-Jewish campaign that was initiated by Ferran Martinez, the archdeacon of Ecija. During the massacres thousands of Jews were killed, thousands fled, and thousands were forcibly converted. Following the massacres, a very strong anti-Jewish campaign was conducted by churchmen. Particularly effective was the campaign led by Vicent Ferrer at the beginning of the 15th century. Many Jews converted to Christianity and joined the ranks of the *New Christians or *conversos*. The Tortosa Disputation in the years 1413–14 initiated by Jerónimo de Santa Fé, Joshua Halorqui before his baptism, proved disastrous to the Jews of the Kingdom of Aragon. Numerous Jews were baptized following in the footsteps of their leaders who had been held like hostages, away from their communities, during long months of the disputation.

Many *conversos* found their way to the financial and administrative top open. Many occupied important positions in the governments of the Hispanic kingdoms, thus arousing the envy and antagonism of many Christians. In any case, among the Old Christians many doubted the sincerity of the *conversos* and did not accept their conversion under duress as an irrefutable proof of their Christianity. The economic, social and political achievements of some of the New Christians strengthened the already existing opposition to their integration into Christian society. In fact, those who were baptized, whether in 1391 or in later years, did not form a homogeneous group. Some were real *anusim* or Crypto-Jews who continued to identify themselves as Jewish and observed Judaism secretly as much as possible. This group must have been large since it is reasonable that many thousands of Jews who converted forcibly or out of fear did not change their faith and their identity overnight. Others might have accepted their fate, and in their despair decided they would put an end to their tragic existence by facing reality and try to become part of the majority society. A third group consisted of Jews who had been somewhat alienated from Jewish tradition and practice and might have found it easier to turn from being Jews "without a synagogue" into Christians "without a church." Another group was composed of true Christians whose conversion was an act of faith. Even if their baptism came in times of persecution, it was the result of religious conviction. Such were Pablo de Santa María, formerly Solomon Halevi, or his disciple Joshua Halorqui. Members of the last group proved to be the greatest persecutors of the Jews.

If the boundaries between these groups sometimes disappeared or were blurred, it was primarily due to the Christian refusal to accept the *conversos* as true Christians and to the prevalent Christian notion that all *conversos* maintained their Jewish identity.

Many New Christians left behind them in the Jewish camp spouses, brothers and sisters, sons and daughters or other relatives or friends and did not cut off their relations with them. Under Vicent Ferrer's influence, Castile decided in 1412 to compel the Jews to live in different quarters and be separated from Old and New Christians. After the Tortosa Disputation various measures were taken to put pressure on the Jewish communities and prevent Jewish influence on the *conversos*. Gradually Christian antagonism towards the *conversos* assumed an ethnic and racial character. The concept of the *limpieza de sangre* (purity of blood) barred the New Christians' integration within Christian society. More and more violence was perpetrated against the *conversos*. The armed rebellion of the *conversos* in Toledo in 1449 was the result of the Old Christians' growing pressure and venomous campaign against them. In 1473 widespread violent attacks were perpetrated against the *conversos* throughout Castile. The demand by churchmen that tough measures be taken against insincere converts led to the establishment of the *Inquisition in 1480 in the Kingdoms of Castile and Aragon. The Inquisition was meant to eradicate heresy among the New Christians. From 1481 onwards the Inquisition conducted a systematic war against the *conversos*. The latter were accused of secretly observing Jewish practices while the Jews were blamed for providing them with the information and material that were necessary to maintain their Jewish identity. The official reason for the Expulsion of 1492 was the influence Jews had on the New Christians. In 1492, the *conversos* were joined by a large group of Jews who decided to convert rather than leave the country. Many expellees were destined to return and be baptized after they had found no haven.

The records of the Inquisition show that the Expulsion did not put an end to the *converso* problem and that for generations to come descendants of New Christians would be tried and condemned for Judaizing. The Chuetas from Majorca remained a segregated group and suffered humiliation and persecution beyond the 18th century.

The largest group of Castilian Jews found refuge in Portugal. When the Portuguese king wished to marry the Castilian princess, the Catholic monarchs laid down one condition to their approval: the Expulsion of the Jews from Portugal. Manuel's edict of Expulsion for 1496 remained a dead letter, since Manuel, who did not wish to lose the Jews, decided to convert them all forcibly in 1497. All these converts were forcible converts, many of whom had left Castile to retain their Judaism. Many kept Judaism secretly and were the target of the Inquisition that was created in 1540. The number of converts in Portugal was high compared to the less than one million people who lived in the country around 1500. Only through flight could any of the Portuguese Crypto-Jews leave the Iberian Peninsula and live as Jews or as Christians away from the Inquisition. The result was the Portuguese communities which were established in Western Europe and the New World and those which were founded in the Ottoman Empire.

It is difficult to generalize about all descendants of *conversos*. Naturally, no "*marrano" Judaism existed in the Peninsula. Various customs and different prayers developed among different groups. In certain areas, however, a very strong "Jewish" identity remained until almost modern times. That is why we have recently witnessed the return of many Crypto-Jews in Belmonte, in northern Portugal, to Judaism and why so many descendants of *conversos* left Spain and Portugal and joined existing Jewish communities or formed their own after their return to normative Judaism.

[Yom Tov Assis (2nd ed.)]

Crypto-Jewish Women

Not all conversas were Crypto-Jews. Those women who chose to identify with the Jewish people instead of the Catholic Church faced considerable risks. Following the establishment of the Inquisition, Jewish observance by New Christians became dangerous as well as difficult. Even the woman's domain was no longer a safe refuge since every home had servants who were potential informants. Once the Jewish community had been expelled, however, the home became the only remaining institution where observance was possible. Women's roles were magnified in importance as they became teachers as well as practitioners of Judaism. The Inquisition was aware of the centrality of women in maintaining Crypto-Judaism and arrested and tried numerous conversas. The most frequent accusations against women which appear in trial transcripts concern observance of the Sabbath and the dietary laws. These Jewish practices would be easily noticed, especially by anyone working in the household. In addition, many conversas observed the fast of Yom Kippur in the hope of attaining salvation. Fasting on Mondays and Thursdays was revived during the messianic fervor between 1497 and 1503 when Inés, a young woman from Herrera, had visions of redemption. She, along with two other converso prophets, spread messianic expectation among the conversos of Extremadura.

Other holiday observances preserved in secret included Passover, although the traditional *seder* disappeared from most homes in Spain fairly quickly. Prior to 1492, *mazzah* was obtained from Jews; afterwards, numerous Judaizing women baked it. The most outstanding example of women baking *mazzah* can be found in the community of Belmonte in Portugal where the women dressed in white and recited lengthy prayers as they ceremonially prepared the *mazzah* while the men stood guard outside. Birth and purity rituals were also observed in secret. One unique ritual was the *hadas*, a celebration including singing on the eighth night after the birth of a male or female child; the infant was dressed in white and a collation was served. In some homes, the de-baptism ritual was another Crypto-Jewish creative addition. On a more traditional note, many women bathed after childbirth and after menstruation, in place of the required visit to the *mikveh*. Death and burial rituals also played a substantial role in Crypto-Jewish life; while they ranged from the halakhic to the superstitious, all were based on past Jewish practices. These customs reflect some of the Crypto-Jewish women's observances; others may emerge from the tens of thousands of trials, especially in the archives of Portugal, that have not yet been read and analyzed. In addition, there were Judaizing conversas in the New World including women from the *Carvajal family in Mexico.

[Renée Levine Melammed (2nd ed.)]

Modern Times

Later instances of forced conversion occurred in *Persia. From 1622 to 1629 the Jews of *Isfahan were compelled to accept Islam, and in 1656 Abbas II issued a decree ordering all Persian Jewry to convert, despite open protest and petitions. The specific ceremonies attending their acceptance into Islam and the name by which they were known, *Jadid al-Islam (New Muslims), show that a typical *anusim* existence and society was created there. In 1839 the entire Jewish community of *Meshed was forced to convert in similar circumstances. Outwardly devout Muslims, they meticulously continued to observe the

Jewish rites in secret, as did their descendants, who were also known as the Jadid al-Islam.

The lot of European Jews, particularly Jewish children, who outwardly embraced Christianity in order to save their lives during the Nazi persecution between 1939 and 1945 was in many ways similar to that of the *anusim* of former ages. It has proved impossible to assess the number of conversions among the Jewish people in this period. Research into this question has been further complicated by emotion and anger on the part of Jews against those who tried "to steal souls" during the *Holocaust on the one hand, and on the other, of gratitude to those who had endangered their lives to save the children.

[Haim Hillel Ben-Sasson]

BIBLIOGRAPHY: C. Roth, *A History of the Marranos* (1941); Y. Baer, *A History of the Jews in Christian Spain* (1966), vol. 2; H. Beinart, *Conversos on Trial*, (1981); idem, *Records of the Trials of the Spanish Inquisition in Ciudad Real* (1974–1985), 4 vols; B. Netanyahu, *The Marranos of Spain*, (1966); S. Schwartz, *Os Cristãos Novos em Portugal no seculo XX* (1925). **ADD. BIBLIOGRAPHY:** M.E. Giles (ed.), *Women in the Inquisition: Spain and the New World* (1999); R.L. Melammed, *Heretics or Daughters of Israel? The Crypto-Jewish Women of Castile* (1999); idem, "Life Cycle Rituals of Spanish Crypto-Jewish Women," and "Visionary Experiences among Spanish Crypto-Jewish Women" (translations with commentary), in: L. Fine (ed.), *Judaism in Practice* (2001), 143–54; 348–52.

APAM (Heb. אַפָּם), initial letters of *Asti, *Fossano, and *Moncalvo, three towns in Italy. The term (more correctly, Afam) denotes the special ritual of prayers that was used by the Jews of these communities who came there originally in the 14th century after the expulsion from France.

BIBLIOGRAPHY: Bernstein, in: *Tarbiz*, 10 (1938/39), 13–25; Disegni, in: *Scritti... Sally Mayer* (1956), 78–81; Goldschmidt, in: KS, 30 (1954/55), 118–36, 264–78; Markon, in: *Meḥkarim le-Zikhron... G.A. Kohut* (1935), 89–101; Rau, in *Emet le-Ya'akov Freimann* (1937), 128–48; D. Sassoon, *Ohel Dawid*, 2 (1932), 829–31, no. 969.

APAMEA, city in lower Phrygia, near the sources of the Maeander River (today: the Turkish town of Dineir, on the Smyrna-Egerdir railway). The city was founded by Antiochus I Soter (280–262 B.C.E.) and Jews probably resided there before the early second century B.C.E. when Antiochus III transported 2,000 Jewish families from Babylonia and places in Phrygia (Jos., Ant., 12:147ff.). In 62 B.C.E. the praetor Flaccus confiscated 100 pounds of gold gathered by the Jews of Apamea for the Temple in Jerusalem (Cicero, *Pro Flacco* 28, 68). The biblical stories and local legends of Noah and Enoch were extremely popular in Apamea and coins depicting the Flood and bearing the name of Noah were minted there from the fourth century C.E. One possible reason for this tradition was the additional name given Apamea: ἡ Κιβωτός, "the ark." There is no evidence, however, that this name (first mentioned by Strabo, about 19 C.E.) was derived from the story of Noah.

BIBLIOGRAPHY: W.M. Ramsay, *Cities and Bishoprics of Phrygia*, 1 pt. 2 (1897), 396–483, 667ff.; Schuerer, Gesch, 3 (1907^4), 18–20; Juster, Juifs 1 (1914), 191, n. 19.

[Isaiah Gafni]

APE (Heb. קוֹף), animal enumerated among the precious articles that Solomon imported (I Kings 10:22, II Chron. 9:21). The word *kof* derives from the Sanskrit *kapi*, meaning a tailless ape. In rabbinic literature, however, it refers both to the tailed and the tailless species. Mention is made of the fact that they were employed to keep houses free of creeping things (Tosef., BK 8:17), and they were even trained for domestic uses (Tosef., Er. 3:12). The *Sifra* (51:4), basing itself upon Leviticus 11:27, enumerates it among the animals forbidden to be eaten. In the Mishnah (Kil. 8:5) there is discussion of whether the laws of ritual uncleanness which apply to a human corpse also apply to creatures called *adonei ha-sadeh* ("the lords of the field") which some scholars have identified with chimpanzees.

BIBLIOGRAPHY: Lewysohn, Zool, 64ff.; F.S. Bodenheimer, *Ha-Ḥai be-Arẓot ha-Mikra*, 2 (1956), index; J. Feliks, *Animal World of the Bible* (1962), 49. **ADD. BIBLIOGRAPHY:** Feliks, Ha-Ẓome'aḥ, 275.

[Jehuda Feliks]

APEL, WILLI (1893–1988), musicologist. Born in Konitz, Germany, Apel studied mathematics at the universities of Bonn and Munich (1912–14) and at the University of Berlin (1918–22). From 1925 he devoted himself to musicology and received his doctorate in Berlin in 1936 for a dissertation on 15th- and 16th-century tonality. In that year (1936) he immigrated to the United States. He was a lecturer at Harvard University (1938–42) and professor of musicology at the University of Indiana, Bloomington (1950–70). Apel's main field of research was medieval and Renaissance music. His publications include reference works such as the *Harvard Dictionary of Music* (1944; 1960^{12}); *The Notation of Polyphonic Music 900–1600* (1942, 1953^5), which has served since it was first published as an essential tool for young scholars; and *Historical Anthology of Music*, edited with A.T. Davison, two volumes (1946, 1950^5). These three contributions were major agents in changing higher music education in the U.S. and abroad. His other works include *French Secular Music of the Late Fourteenth Century* (1950), *Gregorian Chant* (1958), *Geschichte der Orgel- und Klaviermusik* (1967), where Apel reviewed the entire body of keyboard music up to 1700. He was also the general editor of the *Corpus of Early Keyboard Music* and in 1983 published his last major study, a collection of essays on violin music and composers of 17th-century Italy.

BIBLIOGRAPHY: H. Tischler (ed.), *Essays in Musicology: A Birthday Offering for Willi Apel* (1968), incl. C.G. Rayner, "Willi Apel: A Complete Bibliography," 185–91.

[Israela Stein (2nd ed.)]

APELOIG, YITZHAK (1944–), Israeli chemist and president of the *Technion. Apeloig was born in Russia and immigrated to Israel in 1947. Specializing in quantum chemistry, Apeloig received his Ph.D. from the Hebrew University of Jerusalem in 1974 and then did postdoctoral work at Princeton University in 1974–76. In 1976 he joined the faculty of chemistry at the Technion, becoming a professor in 1988 and serving as dean of the faculty of chemistry from 1995 to 1999. In 1996 he established the Lise Meitner Center for Computational Chemistry together with Professor Sason Shaik of the Hebrew University and served as its co-director. In 2001 he was named president of the Technion. He received the Alexander von Humboldt Research Award, the Japan Society for the Promotion of Science Visiting Professor Award, and the Technion Award for Academic Excellence and Excellence in Research. He was a visiting professor in several universities and a member of many scientific advisory committees and the editorial boards of a number of scientific journals. He has over 140 publications to his credit and edited several books.

[Shaked Gilboa (2nd ed.)]

APHEK (Heb. אֲפֵק), name of three places mentioned in the Bible and named after nearby riverbeds (Heb. *afikim*), in which swiftly flowing streams rise after heavy rainfalls.

(1) A Canaanite royal city (Josh. 12:18) east of Jaffa in the Sharon which is possibly referred to in the Egyptian Execration Texts (early 18th century B.C.E.). It appears in the list of cities conquered by Thut-mose III (c. 1469 B.C.E.; No. 66 between Ono and Socoh) and was the first city captured by his successor, Amenhotep II, in his second campaign (c. 1430 B.C.E.). Aphek became a stronghold on the Philistines' northern border, serving them as an important base in their campaigns against the Israelites. They camped there before defeating the Israelites and capturing the ark of the covenant in the days of Samuel (I Sam. 4:1) and also before the final battle against Saul (I Sam. 29:1). In 671 B.C.E., King Esarhaddon of Assyria conquered "Aphek in the land of Samaria" on his way to Egypt. The name Aphek was preserved as late as the period of Roman rule in Migdal Aphek (Jos., Wars, 2:1) but from the time of Herod, Aphek itself became known as *Antipatris. It is today Tell Ras el-Ain (Rosh ha-Ayin) at the source of the Yarkon River. Archaeological excavations were conducted at the site between 1975 and 1985 by Tel Aviv University, bringing to light numerous remains from the Early, Middle, and Late Bronze Ages, including fortification walls and palaces, which help support the identification of this site as biblical Aphek. Remnants of a Philistine city were also uncovered, as well as of dwellings from the Iron Age (i.e. from the tenth to eighth centuries B.C.E.

(2) The place mentioned in I Kings 20:26–30 and II Kings 13:14–17 where Aram defeated the Israelites in the days of Ahab and again in those of Joash. The name has survived in the name of the village Fiq in the Golan, in the region of Susita (Hippos) near the Damascus-Beth-Shean highway east of the Sea of Galilee. A column incised with a *menorah* and a Jewish-Aramaic inscription were found among the ruins of a settlement there dating from the fourth century; however, so far no older remains have been discovered at the site. At Kibbutz Ein Gev on the shore of the Sea of Galilee, a large fortified city of the tenth to eighth centuries B.C.E. exists (known as Khirbet el-Asheq); its identification with the Aramean Aphek has been suggested since it is only 3½ mi. (6 km.) from Fiq. Excavations that were conducted at this tell in 1961 and again in the early 1990s brought to light Iron Age strata on the lower tell and Iron Age, Persian, and Hellenistic strata on the acropolis. The Iron Age II strata (tenth-eighth centuries B.C.E.) included the remains of defensive walls, dwellings, public pillared storehouses, and a variety of pottery and small objects, notably a storage jar bearing an inscription *lsqy* (i.e. "cup-bearer"). The town was apparently destroyed by Tiglath Pileser III in 732 C.E.

[Michael Avi-Yonah / Shimon Gibson (2nd ed.)]

(3) A Canaanite city allotted to the tribe of Asher (Josh. 19:30), which did not, however, succeed in driving out its inhabitants (Judg. 1:31). It is evidently one of the major tells in the Plain of Acre and its most acceptable identification is with Tell Kurdana, at the foot of which rises Nahr Namein (Belus). Pottery and weapons dating from the Middle Bronze to Early Iron Ages have been found at the tell. In Crusader times there were water-mills, known as *Recordane*, at Khirbet Kurdnana near the tell. In 1939 kibbutz Afek (Aphek), affiliated with Ha-Kibbutz ha-Me'uḥad, was founded in the Plain of Acre. It was one of the "tower and stockade" settlements established in 1939 during the Arab riots of 1936–39. When the original plan of developing sea fishing proved impracticable, the kibbutz moved in 1947 to its present site, south of the former site. Afek's settlers came mostly from Eastern and Central Europe. Its economy was based on intensive farming of irrigated field crops, carp ponds, cattle, and a factory for producing pressure meters and other precision instruments. Mego Afek subsequently grew into an international medical and measuring equipment company featuring the Lympha Press for lymphedema treatment. Kibbutz Afek also owned Asiv Textile Industries, supplying garment manufacturers in Israel and abroad, and Hinanit, a sheltered workshop producing soft toys and children's accessories for the local market. In 2002 the population of Afek was 432

[Efraim Orni / Shaked Gilboa (2nd ed.)]

BIBLIOGRAPHY: (1) Albright, in: JPOS, 3 (1923), 50–53; idem, in: BASOR, 11 (1923), 6; Tolkowsky, in: JPOS, 2 (1922), 145–58; Alt, in: PJB, 21 (1925), 50ff.; 28 (1932), 19ff.; Iliffe and Ory, in: QDAP, 5 (1936), 111ff.; 6 (1938), 99ff.; Aharoni, Land, index. **ADD. BIBLIOGRAPHY:** M. Kochavi, *Aphek-Antipatris: Five Thousand Years of History* (1989); Y. Tsafrir, L. Di Segni, and J. Green, *Tabula Imperii Romani. Iudaea – Palaestina. Maps and Gazetteer.* (1994), 63. (2) Alt, in: PJB, 24 (1928), 59; 25 (1929), 41; Saarisalo, in: JPOS, 9 (1929), 38ff.; Maisler (Mazar), in: BJPES, 6 (1939), 151–5. **ADD. BIBLIOGRAPHY:** M.Kochavi, in: IEJ, 39 (1989), 1–17; 41 (1991), 180–84; Y. Tsafrir, L. Di Segni, and J. Green, *Tabula Imperii Romani. Iudaea – Palaestina. Maps and Gazetteer.* (1994), 64. (3) G. Schumacher, *Jaulan* (1888), 136ff.; Albright, in: AASOR, 2–3 (1923), 29ff.; Mazar et al., in: IEJ, 14 (1964), 1–49; Aharoni, *Land*, 304.

APIKOROS, in popular usage, one who negates the rabbinic tradition. The designation *apikoros* first occurs in rabbinic literature in the Mishnah (Sanh. 10:1), enumerated among those who forfeit their "share in the world to come." Although there is no doubt that the name is derived from the Greek Επικουρος (see *Epicureanism), the rabbis seem to have been unaware of, or ignored, the Greek origin of the word and took it to be connected with the Aramaic word *hefker* ("abandoned"; see TJ, Sanh. 10:1, 28b; cf. also Maimonides' introduction to the above Mishnah, which explicitly states that it is an Aramaic word). They extended its meaning to refer generally to anyone who throws off the yoke of the commandments, or who derides the Torah and its representatives. Thus *Korah, who, according to the rabbis, held up the laws of the Torah to ridicule, is referred to as an *apikoros* (TJ, Sanh. 10:1, 27d). The most extensive discussion is to be found in Sanhedrin 99b–100a where different *amoraim* of the third and fourth centuries apply the term variously to one who insults a scholar, who insults his neighbor in the presence of a scholar, who acts impudently toward the Torah, who gibes and says "what use are the rabbis to us, they study for their own benefit," or "what use are the rabbis since they never permitted us the raven nor forbade us the dove" (i.e., who cannot go beyond the dictates of the Torah). Maimonides gives a more precise theological definition of the word. Distinguishing the *apikoros* from the sectarian (*min*), the disbeliever, and the apostate, he defines him as one who either denies prophecy, and therefore the possibility of communion between God and man, or denies divine revelation ("who denies the prophecy of Moses"), or who says that God has no knowledge of the deeds of man (Maim., Yad, Teshuvah 3:8). Later authorities extended the meaning even further to include all those who refuse obedience to the rabbis, even "the authority of a religious work, great or small" (Moses Ḥagiz, *Leket ha-Kemaḥ* YD 103a). In modern parlance, it is popularly used loosely for anyone who expresses a view which is regarded not only as heretical but even as heterodox.

BIBLIOGRAPHY: Guttmann, Mafte'aḥ, 3 pt. 2 (1930), 9–14.

[Louis Isaac Rabinowitz]

°**APION** (first century C.E.), Greek rhetorician; anti-Jewish propagandist in Alexandria, against whom *Josephus wrote his *Contra Apionem*. Evidently of Egyptian origin, Apion was born at the end of the first century B.C.E. or the beginning of the first century C.E. He studied rhetoric and became principal of the Homeric school in Alexandria, lecturing on his interpretation of Homer there and in many places in Greece, which he visited for this purpose. He stayed in Rome during the reign of Tiberius and visited it in the times of Caligula and Claudius.

In scholarly circles Apion was looked upon as a charlatan, spinner of grandiloquent phrases, and gossipmonger. *Pliny the Elder called him *famae propriae tympanum* ("a self-trumpeter"), and Tiberius nicknamed him the "world's drum." His vanity and passion for popularity led him to introduce into his commentaries peculiar or bizarre innovations and some quite unfounded theories. His glosses to Homer were in this category, the excesses of imagination they display comparing unfavorably with the traditional Alexandrian school of criticism. Apion wrote a five-volume *History of Egypt* which was of similar stamp and apparently included a section on the Jews. It is most likely this section that is referred to by Christian writers as his work *Against the Jews*. In it Apion detailed many absurdities about the Jewish people, Judaism, and the Temple in Jerusalem, mainly extracted from the works of earlier antisemitic authors but with his own additions. Josephus' *Contra Apionem* shows that Apion took over the idea that the Jews were expelled from Egypt because they were lepers, from the Egyptian historian *Manetho. The tenets of Judaism obliged the Jews, according to Apion, to hate the rest of mankind. Once yearly, he asserts, they seized a non-Jew, murdered him and tasted his entrails, swearing during the meal to hate the nation of which the victim was a member. In the Holy of Holies in the Temple in Jerusalem there was a golden ass' head which the Jews worshiped – a variation on the fabrication (cf. Mnaseas: see *Greek Literature, Ancient) that the Syrian king *Antiochus Epiphanes had found the statue of a man riding an ass there (see *Ass Worship). In making these statements Apion was not prompted by the type of intellectual curiosity which actuated other Hellenistic ethnographers, such as *Hecataeas of Abdera, who noted down indiscriminately everything he could gather. Apion's method was to give publicity to any disparaging stories he could find about the Jews and to add some from his own imagination. These he used for conducting anti-Jewish propaganda in Alexandria. During an outbreak of anti-Jewish violence in the city during the governorship of *Flaccus, when the Jewish community was forced to fight for its rights and even its existence, Apion was evidently one of the leading rabble-rousers and the most popular with the Alexandrian mob. He tried to show that the Jews were foreigners and had no right to consider themselves citizens; that they were a dangerous element and had always acted to the detriment of the Egyptians. When the Alexandrian Jews sent a delegation to the emperor Caligula, headed by *Philo, Apion joined the opposing delegation. Even if it is assumed that he did not play a major role in these negotiations (Philo and the papyrological sources mentioning only Isidoros and Lampon), there can be no doubt that Apion played a leading role in spreading anti-Jewish propaganda and in provoking agitation, since otherwise Josephus would not have dealt with him at such length in his *Contra Apionem*.

BIBLIOGRAPHY: Schuerer, Gesch, 3 (1909[4]), 538–44; A.V. Gutschmid, *Kleine Schriften*, 4 (1893), 366ff.; Reinach, Textes, 123–34; M. Friedlaender, *Geschichte der juedischen Apologetik* (1903), 372ff.; I. Lévy, in: *Latomus*, 5 (1946), 331–40 (Fr.).

[Abraham Schalit]

APOCALYPSE (Gr. ἀποκαλυψις; "revelation"), term which, strictly speaking, denotes the Jewish literature of revelations which arose after the cessation of prophecy and the Christian writings that derived from this Jewish literature.

The major purpose of apocalyptic writings is to reveal mysteries beyond the bounds of normal knowledge: the secrets of the heavens and of the world order, the names and functions of the angels, the explanation of natural phenomena, and the secrets of creation, the end of days, and other eschatological matters, and even the nature of God Himself.

The term "Apocalypse" as the title of a book first appears in the "Apocalypse of John" and from the second century C.E. Christians applied it to similar writings. In the *baraita*, the term *gillayon* apparently refers to apocalyptic writings: "These writings and the books of the heretics are not to be saved from a fire but are to be burnt wherever found, they and the Divine Names occurring in them" (Shab. 116a). But it is hardly credible that the *tannaim* had such an attitude to Jewish apocalyptic writings such as Syriac (II) Baruch or IV Ezra, which abound in moral and religious piety and the reference is apparently to Christian and Gnostic apocalyptic works. The verb ἀποκαλύπτω is generally used in the Septuagint as a translation of the Hebrew *galeh* ("reveal"), which occurs in Daniel and in the Dead Sea Scrolls in passages where apocalyptic matters are under discussion, e.g., "to conduct themselves blamelessly each man toward his neighbor in all that has been revealed to them" (1QS 9:19). Daniel and the Dead Sea Scrolls also use *ḥazon* ("vision") in the same way (cf. 1QH 4:17f.). The classical period of Jewish apocalypse, a highly developed literary phenomenon in its own right, is from the second century B.C.E. to the second century C.E. Its basic assumption is that prophecy, which had ceased, would be renewed only at the end of days. Therefore, the apocalyptic authors generally attributed their teachings to men who had lived in the period of prophecy, i.e., from Adam to Daniel. The Dead Sea Scrolls, teaching that God made known to "the teacher of righteousness," the leader of the sect, "all the mysteries of the words of his servants the prophets" (1QP Hab. 7:4f.), are an exception to this view. The apocalypse came into being because of its authors' consciousness that theirs was "the last generation" (1QP Hab. 2:5ff.). Consequently, eschatology constitutes one of its central themes. Apocalyptic history divides itself into "this world," subject to the rule of wickedness ("the government of Belial"), and the "next world," in which "wickedness will be forever abolished and righteousness revealed as the sun." The "end of days" is conceived as a cosmic process accompanied by upheavals in nature, and the events on the earth in those days will be a mere echo of the final war between cosmic forces, when "the heavenly host will give forth in great voice, the foundations of the world will be shaken, and a war of the mighty ones of the heavens will spread throughout the world" (1QH 3:34ff.). Thus in the apocalyptic vision Israel's redemption assumes a form much further removed from historical reality than in the prophetic works. The Messiah, for example, often becomes a superhuman figure. Since the apocalyptic vision emphasizes the imminence of the "end," leaving little time for normal historical development, it does not allow for the possibility of the alteration of the course of history through repentance. Of course, a moral lesson is contained in the cosmic vision of the end of days, namely, the final victory of good over evil (the apocalyptic vision having come into being to allay contemporary misfortunes), but this morality finds full expression only in the culmination of the process and not at any one of its earlier stages. This explains the fatalistic mood often manifest in the apocalyptic writings. The apocalyptic vision as a whole is not limited to questions concerning the end of days – rather, universal history becomes a process governed by its own special laws. It speaks not only of the future but also of the distant past. It conceives of world history as a chain of the histories of specific kingdoms, the spans of whose rule are predetermined. Moreover, in many cases it sees the end of days as a return to the events of creation.

In the apocalypses, mysteries are most often revealed by an angel, but occasionally the human hero himself is said to travel in the heavenly realm or to see it in a vision. The mysteries are revealed in the form of strange symbols, and historical personalities are not called by their own names. Some scholars have suggested the Persian influence on Jewish and Christian apocalypse; but basically the Jewish apocalypse is a unique phenomenon, integrally linked with the apocalyptic literature.

The only apocalyptic book included in the Bible is *Daniel. Its apocalyptic portions date from the early days of the Hasmonean revolt, and its visions and symbols became the prototype for all later Jewish and Christian apocalyptic writings. Enoch, Jubilees, and the Testaments of the Twelve Patriarchs (as well as the Dead Sea Scrolls) were apparently written from the time of John Hyrcanus onward. These works reflect the beliefs of a religious apocalyptic movement, which later found expression in the Qumran sect, which was identified by scholars with the *Essenes. Possessing a completely apocalyptic view of life, the movement gave a prominent place in its scheme of history to the war between good and evil (the demonic forces), and also seems to have formulated the myth of the fallen evil angels, and to have developed a psychology and moral code of its own. The works of this movement (particularly the Book of Enoch and the Testament of the Twelve Patriarchs) contain the earliest references to Jewish mysticism.

In the Roman period apocalyptic writings dealing especially with the question of national suffering and redemption appeared in increasing number. The Psalms of Solomon speak of the Romans, of Pompey and his death, and of the messianic kingdom in typical apocalyptic symbols. According to the Assumption of Moses, the Redeemer is none other than the God of Israel. IV Ezra and II Baruch reflect the spiritual upheaval which followed the destruction of the Temple. Apart from those apocalypses, the chief intent of which is national and political, the first two centuries C.E. saw the composition of writings centered on the revelation of the secrets of God and the universe, such as the Slavonic book of Enoch. Similar also are the Greek Apocalypse of Baruch (apparently 150–200 C.E.), the Apocalypse of Abraham, the Testament of Abraham (first or second century C.E.), the Life of Adam and Eve, and the Testament of Job.

There are many points of contact between the apocalyptic and talmudic literatures. The apocalyptic historical and cosmic dualism of this world and the next was accepted by all Israel. Many eschatological views are common to both the Talmud and the apocalypses. Thus the Talmud contains apocalyptic views on Paradise and Hell, the fate of the soul after death, the Messiah, and descriptions of the seven heavens with an angelology – all themes of apocalyptic eschatology. The divine mysteries (*maʿaseh merkavah*) and those of the creation (*maʿaseh bereshit*) became in time topics reserved for groups of mystics, who did not publicize their teachings. In I *Enoch there occurs the earliest description of the "throne of glory," which played a central role in the Merkabah literature. In early Jewish mysticism Enoch himself became an angel and was later identified with Metatron. The *heikhalot* literature contains, beside its central theme, the *maʿaseh merkavah*, various descriptions of the "end of days," the period of Redemption, and calculations of the "end" (see *Merkabah Mysticism). The central figures of these books are the *tannaim*, just as biblical figures were the heroes of earlier pseudepigraphic apocalypses. Apocalyptic works of the type of I Enoch, apparently through translations, exercised an influence on Midrashim, such as *Genesis Rabbati, Midrash Tadsheh, Pirkei de-Rabbi Eliezer,* and *Midrash va-Yissaʿu.* This influence was not restricted solely to apocalyptic matters, and it extended ultimately to the Zohar and the books based on it. (The Book of Enoch is mentioned several times in the Zohar.) The apocalypse is important, therefore, even for an understanding of Kabbalah and Ḥasidism.

BIBLIOGRAPHY: J. Bloch, *On the Apocalyptic in Judaism* (1952); D. Roessler, *Gesetz und Geschichte: Untersuchungen zur Theologie der juedischen Apokalyptik...* (1960); H.H. Rowley, *The Relevance of Apocalyptic: A Study of Jewish and Christian Apocalypses...* (1947^2); D.S. Russell, *The Method and Message of Jewish Apocalyptic...* (1964); D. Flusser, *Mavo la-Sifrut ha Ḥizonit ve-ha-Hellenistit al Ḥazon ha-Keẓ ve-ha-Ge'ullah* (1966); Waxman, Literature, 1 (1960), 25–44; F.C. Burkitt, *Jewish and Christian Apocalypses* (1914). **ADD. BIBLIOGRAPHY:** *The Apocalyptic Imagination: An Introduction to Jewish Apocalyptic Literature* (1998^2).

[David Flusser]

APOCRYPHA AND PSEUDEPIGRAPHA

Definition

Apocrypha and Pseudepigrapha are two separate groups of works dating primarily from the period of the Second Temple. The name "Apocrypha" is applied to a collection of books not included in the canon of the Bible although they are incorporated in the canon of the Roman Catholic and Greek Orthodox churches. In the *Vulgate, in the versions of the Orthodox Church, and in the Septuagint before them, they are found interspersed with the other books of the Old Testament. The Protestant Church denied their sanctity but conceded that they were worthy of reading. Apart from Ecclesiasticus (Wisdom of *Ben Sira), there are no references to these books in talmudic literature.

The pseudepigraphal books, on the other hand, are not accepted in their entirety by any church, only individual books being considered sacred by the Eastern churches (particularly the Ethiopian). The Talmud includes both Apocrypha and

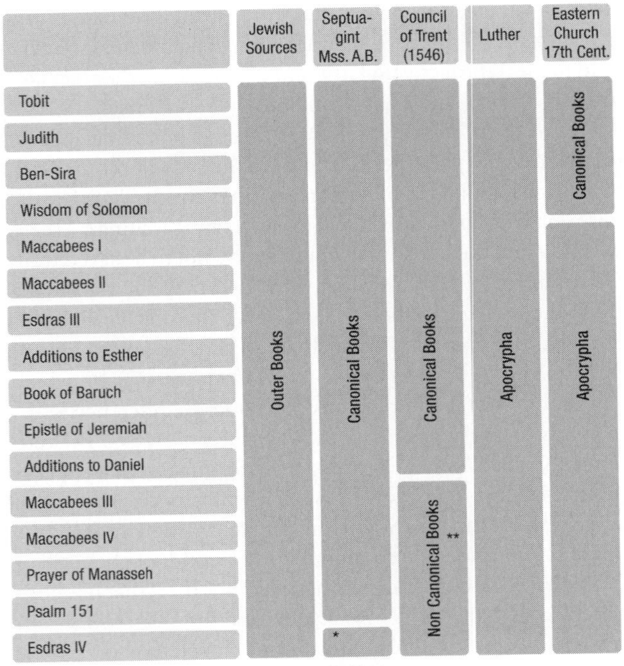

* Non canonical book
** Maccabees IV does not exist in any Latin version.

Diagram showing attitudes to the books of the Apocrypha.

Pseudepigrapha under the name *Sefarim Ḥiẓonim* ("extraneous books"). (See table: Diagram of the Apocrypha.) The Apocrypha, for the most part, are anonymous historical and ethical works, and the Pseudepigrapha, visionary books attributed to the ancients, characterized by a stringent asceticism and dealing with the mysteries of creation and the working out of good and evil from a gnostic standpoint.

Titles and Contents

The number of apocryphal works, unlike those of the Pseudepigrapha, is fixed. Though the church fathers give lists which include many pseudepigraphal works, it is doubtful whether their exact number will ever be known. (IV Ezra 14:46 mentions 70 esoteric books while the Slavonic Book of Enoch attributes 366 books to Enoch.) Many, whose existence was previously unsuspected, have recently come to light in the caves of the Judean Desert.

The books of the Apocrypha are (1) Esdras (alias Greek Book of *Ezra); (2) *Tobit; (3) *Judith; (4) additions to *Esther; (5) Wisdom of *Solomon; (6) Ecclesiasticus (Wisdom of Ben *Sira); (7) *Baruch, with the Epistle of Jeremiah; (8) The *Song of the Three Holy Children; (9) *Susanna; (10) *Bel and the Dragon; (11) The Prayer of *Manasseh; (12) I *Maccabees; (13) II *Maccabees. Esdras is a compilation from II Chronicles 35, 37, Book of Ezra, and Nehemiah 8–9, in an order differing from that of the traditional Bible text and with the addition of a popular story of a competition between youths, the most prominent of whom was Zerubbabel who waited upon Darius I. Tobit tells of a member of one of the ten tribes who was exiled to Assyria, where, because of his merit in burying Sennacherib's victims, he was cured of the blindness which had afflicted him for many years, and saw his son married to one of his kin. Judith tells of a woman of Samaria who ventured into the camp of the soldiers besieging her city, and decapitated their commander, Holofernes, after making him drunk. The Wisdom of Solomon discusses the fate of the righteous and the wicked, with examples from the early history of Israel. Baruch and the Epistle of Jeremiah – additions to the Book of Jeremiah – attack idol worship and are in the form of letters addressed by the putative authors to the exiles in Babylonia. Susanna and the Elders, an addition to the Book of Daniel, is the popular story of a righteous woman who successfully resists the enticements of the city elders and is saved by the youthful Daniel from the death which, on the strength of their slander, had been decreed against her. Bel and the Dragon, which in the Septuagint is another addition to Daniel, is an account of Daniel's ministrations to Nebuchadnezzar, king of Babylon, and Darius the Mede, and of his success in demonstrating to them by various devices the futility of idol worship. The Prayer of Manasseh, an addition to II Chronicles 34:18, is a prayer supposedly recited by King Manasseh while in exile. From the historical point of view, the most important book of the Apocrypha is I Maccabees, the historical account of the *Hasmoneans from the uprising of Mattathias to the death of *Simeon, the first of the Hasmoneans to establish the independence of Judea. II Maccabees confines itself to the wars of *Judah the Maccabee, dealing with them in greater detail. From the literary point of view, by far the most important book in the Apocrypha is the Wisdom of Ben Sira, a book of hymns and proverbs (in the spirit of Proverbs); this work includes an interesting historical sketch down to *Simeon the Just, who lived during the author's youth. The editions of the Vulgate usually append at the end of the book the Apocalypse of *Ezra (or II Esdras), i.e., Salathiel, which contains a theological exposition, in the form of a conversation with an angel, on the fate of Israel.

The books of the Pseudepigrapha are more numerous than those of the Apocrypha, and only the better known will be mentioned here. Probably the most important work in pseudepigraphal literature deals with *Enoch the son of Jared, whom, according to Genesis 5:24, "God took" (i.e., he ascended to heaven). The Book of *Enoch is an account, mainly in the first person, of the visions revealed to him in the heavens. It deals in part with astronomical phenomena, establishing the "correct" calendar at 364 days comprising 52 weeks, and contains some *eschatology on the subject of the preexistent Messiah. Intermingled with the above are stories of how the fallen angels brought evil into the world. The book most similar to it, *Jubilees, is in the form of a conversation between the Angel of the Presence and Moses on Mount Sinai. Unlike Enoch it is a mixture of *halakhah* and *aggadah*, but in a spirit completely different from that of the Talmud. Its *halakhah* is far more stringent than that of the Talmud. The fundamental basis both of the *halakhah* and *aggadah* in the book is its historicism: everything is predetermined in the "heavenly tablets," and was revealed much earlier than the time of Moses, to the patriarchs and even to their predecessors, Noah, Lamech, and the like. The book is presented within a framework of exact dates, reckoned by sabbatical periods and jubilees. It lays special emphasis (even more than Enoch) upon the solar calendar and upon ensuring (as did the Boethusians) that Shavuot always fall on a Sunday. The remaining books are smaller: The Ascension of *Isaiah is an account (also found in the Talmud) of the unnatural death of the prophet. The Assumption of *Moses is a history in retrospect of the Jews, from Moses to the death of Herod and his son. The Book of *Adam and Eve is an *aggadah* concerning their sin and the death of Adam, who is the handiwork of God. The Testaments of the Twelve *Patriarchs is a valuable ethical work in which each of Jacob's sons exhorts his children, particularly against the sin in which he himself has been ensnared. This book is important because of the idea, most fully developed in the *Dead Sea Scrolls, of the coming of two messiahs, one from the tribe of Judah and one from Levi. In addition to these there once existed another large series of books, attributed to Adam, Lamech, Abraham, Joseph, Eldad, Moses, Solomon, Elijah, Zechariah, Ezra, and others.

The Supposed "Canon" of Alexandria

In the old manuscripts of the Septuagint it was the custom to place the books of the Apocrypha, and at times of the Pseudepigrapha, among the Holy Scriptures. In consequence of this and of quotations by the early church writers, who mention details from these books, there arose in the 19th century the theory that at one time – at least in Alexandria – these books were considered part of the canon. There are those who assume that even in Ereẓ Israel the Apocrypha was for a certain period (until the destruction of the Temple in 70 C.E.) considered part of the canon, and that the canon as known later was fixed only in the days of the synod of Jabneh (first century C.E.). All these views, however, are erroneous, based as they are upon a series of faulty premises. Moreover, those scholars were of the opinion that the talmudic discussions about certain books that had to be "hidden away" (Shab. 13b), or about books that do not "render the hands unclean," or Akiva's extreme pronouncement that he who reads *Sefarim Ḥiẓonim* forfeits his share in the world to come (Sanh. 10:1), all indicate that only during their period – following the destruction of the Second Temple – was the traditional canon of 24 books finalized. Against this, however, it may be maintained that the talmudic discussions about "hiding away," and about books that "render the hands unclean" refer to books all of which are in the known canon. Indeed, according to talmudic tradition (BB 14b) the canon was already fixed at the end of the Persian period. This tradition is clearly repeated by *Josephus (Apion, 1:40–41): "From the death of Moses until Artaxerxes… the prophets wrote the events of their time. From Artaxerxes to our own time [i.e., the first century C.E.] the complete history has been written, but has not been deemed worthy of equal credit with the earlier records, because of the failure of the exact succession of the prophets." Indeed, as far as is known, apart from the final Hebrew chapters of the Book of Daniel (which may have been added during the disturbances preceding the Hasmonean uprising), all the scriptural books antedate the Hellenistic period. Furthermore, from the prologue of Ben Sira's grandson to his Greek translation of his grandfather's work, it is clear that the Scriptures had already been translated into Greek in the first generation of the Hasmoneans and that by then the traditional division into three sections – Pentateuch, Prophets, and Hagiographa – was accepted. Although Sira's grandson does indeed speak of "the other books," scholars failed to recognize this term as an alternate name for the Hagiographa. Philo too was acquainted with this division (Cont. 25) as was Luke (24:44) after him. The testimony of Ben Sira's grandson, and that, in particular, of Philo and Josephus (who mentions a fixed number of 22 books, Apion 1:38), who used the Septuagint, shows (1) that the Greek-reading Jews knew no other division of the Bible, and (2) that the canon of that time is identical with the present canon. Philo also draws a clear distinction between the Holy Scriptures and the books written by the *Therapeutae and peculiar to them. It follows that the Apocrypha and Pseudepigrapha were always *Sefarim Ḥiẓonim*, i.e., extraneous to the accepted books (βιβλία), i.e., the Scriptures. It should be added that the authors of the Dead Sea Scrolls wrote a **Pesher* ("interpretation") only on the works comprised in the known canon.

History of the Apocrypha and Pseudepigrapha

Literary activity continued to flourish during the Persian era (probably Tobit, Judith, the additions to Daniel, Song of the Three Children, and III Esdras, for example, can be ascribed to this time) and, more so, during the Hellenistic period. It was during this period that the books of the Apocrypha were composed. The common thread linking all of these works is their concern with Israel as a whole, and their complete ignoring of sectarian schisms. Only later, after the sectarian schism in the beginning of the Hasmonean period (Ant., 13:171ff.), did the composition of the pseudepigraphical works begin to appear. The Book of Jubilees was written (as is indicated by its historical allusions to the conquest of the cities of "Edom" and the coastal region) in the reign of *John Hyrcanus, the essence of Enoch (alluded to in the Book of Jubilees) a little before it, and the Testaments of the Twelve Patriarchs sometime after the above works. In any event, most of the known Pseudepigrapha (both those in Greek or Ethiopian translation, and those from the Qumran caves) originated between this period and the destruction of the Temple. Philo's characterization of the books of the Therapeutae as "allegorical" interpretations, or "psalms" to God, apply in equal measure to the books of the Qumran community.

A fundamental difference between the Apocrypha and the Pseudepigrapha is that whereas the Apocrypha deal mainly with the struggle against idolatry, believing prophecy to have come to an end (cf. Judith 11:17), the pseudepigraphists believed that prophecy continued and that through its agency they could make laws (see *Jubilees) and know the past and future. Because it was generally maintained among the people, however, that prophecy had come to an end, the visionaries attribute their works to the ancients, or feature themselves as permitted to "interpret," to reveal the true meaning of verses which apply to the "end of the days" (the period in which they lived). Past and present are written in the "heavenly tablets." The apocalypist "reads" them and divulges in his book what he has read. Convinced of their knowledge of the future, they also occupied themselves to a considerable extent with the advent of the Messiah, whom they regarded as preexistent (see *Enoch). At the outset, then, the Apocrypha and Pseudepigrapha were differentiated; the former was a collection for Jews, generally, and the latter sectarian. Since the Essenes, from whom much of the Pseudepigrapha may derive, had many devotees both in Israel and in the Diaspora, some of their scriptures too were translated and disseminated. However, it was precisely the importance attached to these prophecies within the sect and their circulation at times of political crisis during the days of Hyrcanus and of the Roman procurators that caused the Pharisee sages to erect a barrier between the Scriptures and everything extraneous to them, even works (like the Wisdom of Ben Sira) which they themselves valued. It is for this reason that the sages decreed that only the canonized Holy Scriptures "render the hands unclean" (Yad. 4:6). These discussions gave rise to the question of whether there might not be books in the Scriptures themselves, which might be exploited for sectarian purposes (e.g., Ezekiel), or which might not accord with the concepts of reward and punishment in the Pentateuch and Prophets (Ecclesiastes). However, though all books outside the canon were rejected outright, the old distinction between books applying to Israel as a whole and sectarian books remained and was taken over by the church. With only a few isolated exceptions all churches rejected the Pseudepigrapha, the difference between the Eastern and Western church consisting only in their official attitude to the Apocrypha. As may be seen from the lists of Melito, Origen, Cyril of Jerusalem, Pseudo-Athanasius, Dialogue of Timotheus and Aquila, etc., the canon of the Eastern church usually numbers (following Josephus) 22 books (although Baruch and the Epistle of Jeremiah are sometimes included in the Book of Jeremiah). The "other" books (τά λοιπά) are either presented as "extraneous" ("Εξω δὲ τούτων, 'Εκτὸς δὲ τούτων, etc.), "contradicted" (άντιλεγόμενα), or called "all the concealed books that are contradicted" (άποκρυφα ὅσα άντιλέγουται; Dialogue of Timotheus and Aquila; Nicephorus' *Stichometry*). In the Roman Church, on the other hand, the apocryphal works are, as a rule, placed at the end, with no visible distinction between them and the canonical books. But lists should not be confused with facts. Even Jerome, who explicitly differentiates between the Holy Scriptures – those in the Hebrew canon – and Apocrypha, translated both. In fact according to the testimony of Augustine these books were accepted by most of the churches (as confirmed by the Latin lists of Ruffinus, Cassiodorus, Innocent I, Isidore of Pelusium, Liber Sacramentorum, etc.). Under the influence of Augustine the councils of Rome (382), Hippo (392), and Carthage (397) officially included the Apocrypha in the canon. The Pseudepigrapha, however, was not accorded great status. Augustine expresses his doubts about Enoch, and in the list of 60 books (of Old and New Testaments), where the Apocrypha is called "extraneous" ("Εξω), the Pseudepigrapha is referred to as ἀπόκρυφα and so in Pseudo Athanasius, *Stichometry* of Nicephorus, Gelasian Decree, and thus as a completely separate group. This too is the cause of the latter's becoming completely lost in the course of time. The final change took place with the *Reformation. This again excluded all books which, according to Jerome, are not part of the canon (i.e., everything not in the Hebrew Scriptures), assigning to them a name and a place outside the books of the Bible.

[Yehoshua M. Grintz]

In Medieval Hebrew Literature

From the first century to the sixth, Hebrew literature (talmudic and midrashic) developed as if the Apocrypha and Pseudepigrapha did not exist. Only very few motifs from this literature were used by the talmudic sages, often in a way far removed from the original context. Even the sayings of Ben Sira were mostly forgotten. Few survived in talmudic literature, but to them were added many popular epigrams, which were quoted as the sayings of Ben Sira, though they are not to be found in the original work.

Only in the Middle Ages did the revival of the apocryphal and pseudepigraphical literature begin within the body of Hebrew literature. This revival was mainly a revival of the contents of that literature, and not of its original form. Thus, there are several medieval versions of the stories of Tobit and Judith, none of which even approaches the original works in length and scope; only the bare skeleton of the plot was preserved, told, and retold by medieval Jewry in various versions. Attempts made by some scholars, especially M. Gaster, to discover in these medieval stories the Hebrew originals of the Greek works utterly failed. Another popular medieval Hebrew story was the *Scroll of Antiochus (*Megillat Antiochus*), which included some of the better-known sections of the Books of Maccabees, but no full translation of these works was known in medieval Hebrew literature. However, the story of the woman whose seven sons refused to worship idols and were martyred, found its way into the Talmud (Git. 57b) and remained as an independent Hebrew tale, and was included in almost every Hebrew medieval collection of stories (see *Hannah and her Seven Sons).

The vast theological and cosmological as well as narrative material included in works like the Books of Enoch and Jubilees reentered Hebrew literature about the time of the conquests of Islam. The first Hebrew work to make use of such material was the **Pirkei de-Rabbi Eliezer*, a work written in the form of a Midrash, but which is, in fact, a retelling of the stories of Genesis, making use both of midrashic material and ideas included in the apocryphal works connected with the Book of Genesis. Some parts of these works survived also independently; thus, the story of the fallen angels from the Book of Enoch was told by medieval Jewry as the story of *Uzza and Azael. To the old Ben Sira which survived until the 13th century, at least with the Eastern Jews, was added a new pseudepigraphic work, the *Alfabet de-Ben Sira*, which, besides a few sayings, has nothing in common with the original work, preserved in Greek.

Only in the Renaissance period did Jewish scholars come into direct contact with the original works of the Apocrypha and Pseudepigrapha. The most important step was made by Azariah dei *Rossi, who translated the Letter of Aristeas into Hebrew, and thus began modern Hebrew scholarship and interest in this field. From then on, increasing numbers of Jewish scholars turned to this material in their quest for Jewish historical and literary material. A new translation of the Apocrypha was made into Hebrew at the beginning of the 16th century but was lost until recently.

[Joseph Dan]

BIBLIOGRAPHY: Charles, Apocrypha; Schuerer, Gesch, index; E. Kautzsch, *Die Apokryphen und Pseudepigraphen des Alten Testaments* (1900); H.B. Swete, *Introduction to the Old Testament in Greek* (1914²); P. Riessler, *Altjuedisches Schrifttum ausserhalb der Bibel* (1928); C.C. Torrey, *Apocryphal Literature: A Brief Introduction* (1948); R.H. Pfeiffer, *History of New Testament Times with an Introduction to the Apocrypha* (1949); Grintz, in: *Sinai*, 32 (1952), 11–43; idem, in: *Beḥinot*, 6 (1954), 85–93; idem, in: *Meḥkarim ba-Megillot ha-Genuzot* (1961), 19–30; idem, in: *Sefer ha-Yovel le-Ḥanokh Albeck* (1963), 123–51; M.H. Segal, *Sefer Ben Sira ha-Shalem* (1958²), 1–69; A.C. Sundberg, *The Old Testament and the Early Church* (1964); Y.L. Bialer in *Min ha-Genazim* 2 (1969), 36–53. **ADD. BIBLIOGRAPHY:** D.J. Harrington, *Invitation to the Apocrypha* (1999); G.W.E. Nickelsburg, *Jewish Literature between the Bible and the Mishna* (1981); J.H. Charlesworth, *The Old Testament Pseudepigrapha*, 2 vols. (1983, 1985).

APOLLONIA, city on the coast of Ereẓ Israel about 9½ mi. (15 km.) N. of Jaffa. Apollonia was apparently founded by Seleucus IV (186–174 B.C.E.). It is today the ruined site of Tel Arshaf (Arsuf). Named after the Greek god Apollo Soter ("Savior"), Apollonia was also known in the Byzantine period as Sozusa ("City of the Savior," in reference to Jesus). The assumption that Apollonia was built on the site of the Canaanite city of Rishpon has not been sustained by archaeological findings. Rishpon was named after the Canaanite deity *Resheph, whom the Hellenized Canaanites presumably identified with Apollo. Apollonia is first mentioned among the cities held by Alexander *Yannai (Jos., Ant., 13:395), but it was probably captured earlier by John *Hyrcanus. In 63 B.C.E., *Pompey detached Apollonia from the territory of Judea. It was one of the cities rebuilt by the Roman governor *Gabinus. After forming part of the realms of Herod and Agrippa I, it became an independent city in the province of Judea (and later, of Syria Palaestina). In the Arab period Apollonia was known as Arsuf (= Resheph). The Crusader king Baldwin captured it in 1101 and under Crusader rule the city (then called Arsur, a corruption of Arsuf) served as a commercial center, especially for the Genoese. Taken by Saladin in 1187, it was recaptured and restored to the Crusaders four years later by Richard the Lion-Hearted. The Egyptian Mamluk sultan, Baybars, captured and destroyed the city in 1265. The remains of a Crusader fortress, castle, and port are visible on the seashore, about 2½ mi. (4 km.) northwest of Herzliyyah. South of these are the ruins of the Greco-Roman city where two Greco-Jewish inscriptions and traces of an ancient glass factory have been discovered. In the 1990s a number of people, mostly well-to-do, built homes near the archeological site, under the name of Arsuf. However, the government did not formally recognize the settlement and did not approve further building in the area, which was planned as a park. In 2002 Arsuf's population was 104.

BIBLIOGRAPHY: S. Klein (ed.), *Sefer ha-Yishuv*, 1 (1939), s.v.; Avi-Yonah, Land, index; Beyer, in: ZDPV, 59 (1936), 3–9, passim; Conder-Kitchener, 2 (1882), 136; Karmon, in: IEJ, 6 (1956), 33–50.

[Michael Avi-Yonah / Shaked Gilboa (2nd ed.)]

°**APOLLONIUS** (third century B.C.E.), finance minister of *Ptolemy II Philadelphus, king of Egypt (285–246 B.C.E.). Apollonius was one of the most efficient administrators of the period. Considerable material on his activities is furnished by the Zeno papyri, particularly on his activities as the owner of estates in the Fayyum. He owned vineyards in Beth-Anath in Judea and also engaged in commerce and manufacture. Several of his agents were stationed in Judea in order to foster trade with Egypt.

BIBLIOGRAPHY: A. Świderek, *W "państwie" Apolloniosa* (1959), with résumé in French; A. Tcherikover, *Hellenistic Civilization and the Jews* (1959), 60, 62f., 157f., 186–89.

°**APOLLONIUS MOLON** (first century B.C.E.), Greek rhetorician and anti-Jewish writer. According to Plutarch (Caesar 3; Cicero 4; cf. Josephus, Apion 2:79) Apollonius settled on the island of Rhodes where he became head of the school of rhetoric. Apollonius criticized the Jews in a pamphlet quoted by Eusebius ("Praeparatio Evangelica") and mentioned by Josephus (Josephus, Apion, 2). He claimed that the Jews were "the worst among the barbarians," lacked any creative talent, did nothing for the welfare of mankind, believed in no divinity, and were commanded by their religion to hate the human race. According to Apollonius, Moses was "an imposter and deceiver." From *Manetho, he borrowed the myth that the children of Israel were banished from Egypt because they were lepers. Apparently, the majority of Apollonius' accusations were not original, but repeated from the writings of antisemites who preceded him.

BIBLIOGRAPHY: Jos., Apion, 2, passim; Eusebius, "Preparatio Evangelica," 9:19; Reinach, Textes, 60–64; Heinemann, in: Pauly-Wissowa, Suppl. (1931) s.v. *anti-Semitismus*; Schuerer, Gesch, 3 (1909^4), 532ff.; F. Susemihl, *Geschichte der griechischen Litteratur in der Alexandrinerzeit*, 2 (1892), 489ff.; Christ-Schmid, *Geschichte der griechischen Literatur*, 2 pt. 1 (1920^6), 457ff.

[Abraham Schalit]

APOLOGETICS. The entry is arranged according to the following outline:

Introduction

Apologetics in Judaism is that literature which endeavors to defend Jews, their religion, and their culture in reply to adverse criticism. The demarcation between apologetics and *disputation is often difficult to draw. The history of Jewish apologetic literature reflects the complicated pattern of relationships between Jews and Gentiles through the generations, and originated in response to the challenges of pagans and subsequently of Christianity. In the Middle Ages Jewish apologetics, termed by Jewish scholars *hitnaẓẓelut*, were intended to defend the spheres of both Jewish religion and Jewish social and national life, past and present, against direct attack and internal doubts arising from comparisons of respective cultures and ways of life. They were also written in the hope of proving to the Gentiles the virtues of the Jewish religion and thereby influencing their outlook on, and attitudes toward, Judaism. In the modern age a new type of Jewish secular apologetics aim at justification of Jewish social and economic conditions in the gentile world. The nonconformist stand adopted by Jewish monotheism against the surrounding polytheism in the ancient world gave rise to aggressive apologetics by the prophets when asserting the supremacy of their faith over "the vanities of the nations" (e.g., Isa. 40:17–21; 42:5–8; 44:6–20; 45:5–7, etc.; Jer. 10:2–5; 14:22; Zech. 8:20–23; 14:9, 16–21).

Against Hellenism

The authors of the Jewish-Hellenistic literature in Greek in the first half and the middle of the third century B.C.E. regarded as their major task the defense of the ideas of Judaism and its historical role. Jewish-Hellenistic historiographers set out to establish argumentation along these lines. *Demetrius, *Eupolemus, and *Artapanus place the Jewish people and Ereẓ Israel at the core of human history. Several Jewish poets expressed these ideas, as attested by extant fragments from compositions of the epic poets Philo the Elder and the Samaritan *Theodotus, while the drama *Exodus* by *Ezekiel the Poet (second century B.C.E.) hints that the dream of Moses beside Mount Sinai and Jethro's interpretation of it relate to the dominion of Israel over the world. The vision of the burning bush, according to this author, symbolizes the historical-universal value of the Revelation at Mount Sinai. Jewish-Hellenistic philosophers interpreted Judaism allegorically as containing all the best in the systems of the great Greek philosophers. The intellectual and material basis of universal civilization was also pioneered by Jews, according to Jewish-Hellenistic writers. Abraham discovered astronomy and astrology and taught these sciences to the Babylonians and the Egyptians. Joseph introduced a well-ordered society in Egypt. Moses invented writing. Jews were the founders of philosophy. According to the philosopher *Aristobulus of Paneas (2nd century B.C.E.), not only Plato but even Homer and Hesiod were influenced by Judaism because parts of the Torah had been translated into Greek before their time. Many of these postulates were later utilized by Christian apologists in their argumentation against the pagans. In the Middle Ages they became Christian axioms and were accepted by Christians as historical truth.

Concomitantly with the general apologetic trend in Jewish-Hellenistic literature, specific apologetic works were also written. Two works of this type are known: *Philo's "Apology on behalf of the Jews" (Ἀπολογία ὑπὲρ Ἰουδαίων, first century C.E.), of which fragments are preserved in the works of *Eusebius, and *Josephus' *Against Apion* (first century C.E.), which summarizes the argumentation used by Jewish-Hellenistic apologetics. The major theme in *Against Apion* is a defense of the refusal of the Jews to participate in the local cults (λειτουργία) in the cities and provinces in which they were living and enjoying rights as citizens. This abstention was considered by their gentile neighbors to constitute either disrespect for religion in general or atheism (ἀθεότης), i.e., denial of the existence of gods. The accusation was repeated by anti-Jewish polemicists from the days of *Apollonius Molon (in the first century B.C.E.) to *Pliny and *Tacitus some two centuries later. Jewish apologists countered by explaining the Jewish belief in one God and the preferability of monotheism, citing Greek philosophers in support (Jos., Apion, 2:22). The apologists continued to denounce idolatry in the prophetic tradition, stressing the baseness of animal and image worship (cf. Arist., 134–9; Wisd., 13–16; Oracula Sibyllina, 3:29–34; Jos., Apion, 2:33–34). The refusal of the Jews to take part in the cult of the Roman emperor was viewed as *lèse majesté* by those antagonistic toward the Jews. In defense, Jewish apologists pointed out that sacrifices were regularly offered in the Temple in Jerusalem for the health of the emperor and that the emperors, satisfied with this arrangement, had granted the Jews special privileges (Philo, *De Legatione ad Caium*, 45; Jos., Apion, 2:6).

Jewish apologists emphasized the humane character of the precepts in the Torah regarding proselytes and Gentiles to counter the widespread accusations that these injunctions demonstrate pride, contempt, and hatred of mankind (Jos., Apion, 2:28–29). They explained reasons for the ceremonial *mitzvot* by way of allegory (see, e.g., Philo's statements on circumcision, Mig., 16); they also pointed out the cruel attitude to strangers and children common in pagan societies (e.g., Philo, Spec., 3:20). Jewish apologetics, although composed in the language of anti-Jewish publicists and adopting their style and mode of thought, contributed little to the understanding of Judaism among the groups who attacked Jews and Jewish law. However, this activity helped to undermine the religious principles of the pagan world, preparing the ground for conversion to Judaism and later on a large scale to Christianity.

In the Talmud and Midrash

The apologetic argumentation found in Hebrew and Aramaic sources is mainly intended to combat Hellenistic influences within the Jewish camp or that of Jewish "Hellenizers" or to oppose heretical sectarians. The Midrash reveals knowledge of the allegation made by ancient authors that the Jews were expelled from Egypt because they were lepers, and in reply demonstrates that leprosy was prevalent among all nations (Gen. R. 88:1). Similarly, the Talmud and Midrash are familiar with the charge that Jews had not contributed to the creation of human cultures, that they were misanthropes, and disregarded the authority of the state (*Beit ha-Midrash*, ed. by A. Jellinek, 1 (1938^2), 9). Consequently, the sages stress the concept that the world was created for Israel's sake and exists thanks to its merit (Shab. 88a; Gen. R. 66:2). On the other hand, they put the blame for Jewish separation on idol worship, to which the Gentiles were addicted, while Jews were enjoined to keep at a distance the customs and cult associated with it.

Apologetics in the Talmud and Midrash take the form of tales, discussions, or exchanges of questions and answers between Jewish sages and Gentiles – philosophers, heretics, matrons, and Roman officials. The opponents of the Jews draw attention to contradictions in Scripture and take issue with anthropomorphic expressions found in the Bible; they censure several principles in the Jewish concept of God and express hostility to the *mitzvot* and laws which appear strange to them. The sages considered it their duty to "know how to answer an **Apikoros*" (a heretic; Avot 2:14). Prominent sages are reported to have participated in these apologetic endeavors, e.g., *Johanan b. Zakkai (TJ, Sanh. 1:4, 19d), *Joshua b. Hananiah (Ḥul. 59b; Nid. 70b), *Gamaliel II, c. 95 C.E. (Sanh. 39a; Av. Zar. 54b), and *Yose b. Ḥalafta (Gen. R. 17:7; Tanḥ. B., Gen. 2). They employ the homiletical method of reasoning (*derush*). Sometimes, however, they did not take the exchanges seriously, and disciples are found asking, "Rabbi, you put him [your opponent] off with a straw, but what will you answer us?" (e.g., TJ, Shab. 3:5, 6a; Ḥul. 27b; Tanḥ. Ḥukkat 8).

In Relation to Christianity

The appearance of a new adversary – the church, which developed and spread its influence through advocating progressive separation from the Jewish fold, inevitably introduced new problems in apologetic argumentation. The pagan polemicist Celsus quotes Jewish opinions in his critique of Christianity, according to *Origen in 231–33 (*Contra Celsum*, 1:28). His statements are repeated by Eusebius and Epiphanius. The

Jews were certain of their ground in understanding Scripture, and asserted that "in all the passages which the *minim* [i.e., Christians] have taken [as grounds] for their [Christian] heresy, their refutation is to be found near at hand" (Sanh. 38b). Therefore, where a verse from Scripture was given a Christological interpretation by exponents of the nascent church, the Talmud supplies an opposing, distinctly anti-Christological exegesis of the continuation of the text. Thus, Simeon bar Yoḥai interprets "sons of God" (Gen. 6:2) as "sons of nobles," as in the old Aramaic versions, and execrated "all who called them the sons of God" (Gen. R. 26:5). Until the beginning of the fourth century the concept of the Trinity was not yet fully accepted in the church. Many statements in Jewish literature recorded from the preceding period, therefore, which appear to some scholars as being directed against the opinions of the Gnostics, or even of the Persian concept of dualism, were in reality formulated against the Christian belief in the Father and Son. Abbahu, unmistakably in reference to Christian beliefs about Jesus, said: "If someone will tell you, 'I am God,' he is a liar; 'I am the son of man,' his end is that he will regret it; that 'I am going to Heaven,' he says this but will not fulfill it" (TJ, Ta'an. 2:1, 65f; see also Ex. R. 29:5). The following homily may be directed against the Christian concept of the divinity of Jesus: "R. Aḥa said: 'God was angry with Solomon when he uttered the verse ["meddle not with them that are given to change" (Prov. 24:21)] which by a play on the Hebrew words was interpreted as meaning "with them that have two gods." God said to Solomon, "Why do you express a thing that concerns the sanctification of My Name by an obscure reference [*notarikon*], in the words 'And meddle not with them that are given to change?'" Thereupon immediately Solomon expressed it more clearly [in the words], "There is one that is alone, and he hath not a second; yea, he hath neither son nor brother" (Eccles. 4:8); "He hath neither son nor brother," but "Hear, O Israel, the Lord our God, the Lord is one"'" (Deut. R. 2:33).

The election of Israel by God also became a topic for apologetics against insistent claims by the church to be the true heir to the election. The sufferings of the Jews, the destruction of the Temple (70 C.E.), and the suppression of the Bar Kokhba revolt (135 C.E.), in contrast to the growth and spread of Christianity, added the elements of visible rejection and punishment of the Jewish nation, while the church was prospering. The same message was repeated by the Church Fathers (second to third centuries) in different forms (Justin, *Dialogus*, 16; Origen, *Contra Celsum*, 4:22; Eusebius, *Historia Ecclesiae*, 2:26). In their attack on the Jews the Christians did not refrain from utilizing arguments used by pagans such as Apion (Jos., Apion, 2:11) and *Cicero (*Pro Flacco*, 28). The "abandonment" of the Jews by God was presented to the Jews with proofs from the Bible. "A certain *min* [Christian] once said to R. Gamaliel: 'You are a people with whom its God has performed *ḥaliẓah* [severed his connections from his sister-in-law], for it is said in Scripture, "with their flocks and with their herds they shall go to seek the Lord, but they shall not find Him; He hath withdrawn from them"' (Hos. 5:6). The other replied: 'Fool, is it written "He hath drawn off for them"? It is written "He hath drawn off from them"; now in the case of a sister-in-law from whom the brother drew off the shoe could there be any validity in the act?'" since the act of *ḥaliẓah* was not valid unless the sister-in-law had removed the shoe of her brother-in-law. Here the image is of God drawing off the shoe, i.e., such a *ḥaliẓah* would be invalid (Yev. 102b; see also Ber. 10a; Sanh. 39a; Av. Zar. 10b). In response to Christian claims that the Old Testament has passed to the church and that Jews have no right to it (Justin, *Apologia*, 1:53; Origen, *Contra Celsum*, 7:26), there is an allusion by the rabbis that the Oral Law alone affirms the truth of the claims of those who uphold the Written Law: "Judah bar Solomon stated that when God said to Moses, 'Write!' Moses also requested that the Mishnah (i.e., the Oral Law) should be given in writing. But God anticipated that the Gentiles would translate the Torah, read it in Greek, and say: We are Israel, and we are the children of God, and henceforth, the scales are balanced. God said to the Gentiles: 'You say that you are My children. I only know that who possess My secret writings are My children. And what are these writings? – the Mishnah'" (Tanḥ. Va-Yera 5; *ibid.* Ki-Tissa 34). In explaining the actions of Jonah who had been sent to gentile Nineveh, it is stressed that he refused to go there (unlike the Christian apostles); this refusal is seen by the *aggadah* as a sign of His love for Israel; Jonah saw that the Gentiles were more inclined to repent "and he did not want to lay his own people open to condemnation. Thus he behaved like the rest of the patriarchs and prophets who offered themselves on behalf of Israel" (Mekh. of Rabbi Ishmael, Pasḥa, 1). The repentance of the Nineveh Gentiles was in reality "a feigned repentance" (TJ., Ta'an. 2:1, 65b). The interpretation served as an answer to the statements of the Church Fathers who stressed that the Gentiles in the time of Jonah obeyed the prophet sent to them, just as the Gentiles in their own time answered the call of the apostles. In contrast, the Jews had refused to obey then, and refuse to do so now, and as a result they are punished (Luke 11:29–30, 32; Justin, *Dialogus*, 107).

Medieval Apologetics

With the predominance of the church and humiliation of the Jews in the Middle Ages, Jewish apologetics had to assume a new character. The religious disputations held between Christians and Jews became acrimonious. The lack of any kind of recognized Jewish statehood or sovereignty had to be explained. The Jews claimed, inter alia, that there still existed a sovereign Jewish state in the East, a claim put forward as early as 633 (Isidore of Seville, *De fide catholica contra Judaeos*, 1:8, para. 2, in: PL, 83 (1862), 464). Medieval Hebrew apologists in the Mediterranean countries also took issue with Jewish sects, such as the *Karaites. Recognizing that Jewish sectarian movements in part drew their inspiration from Christianity and Islam (several Karaite scholars, for instance, accepted the view that Jesus and Mohammed were prophets), Jewish authors felt the necessity of protecting Judaism from within by pointing out the weaknesses of these religions. Apologetics of this type were often combined with presentation of a general philosophical system of Jewish thought. Fragments from the Cairo *Genizah attest to the polemics directed in this period against the Samaritans, Christianity, and Islam, as well as Jewish schismatic sects, apparently from the beginning of the tenth century (Mann, in HUCA, 12 (1938), 427ff.).

David *Al-Mukammiṣ (ninth to tenth centuries), who became converted to Christianity and lived briefly at Nisibis as a Christian, wrote two tractates against Christianity after his return to Judaism, which served as sources for the Karaite scholar al-*Kirkisānī and apparently for *Saadiah Gaon (fragments in JQR, 15 (1903), 684ff.). The latter also directed polemics against Christian philosophers in his *Emunot ve-De'ot*. Concerning the Trinity, Saadiah states, "When I present this refutation I do not have in mind the uneducated among them [the Christians] who profess only a crass corporeal Trinity. For I would not have my book occupy itself with answering such people, since that answer must be quite clear and the task simple. It is rather my intention to reply to the learned who maintain that they adopted their belief in the Trinity as a result of rational speculation and subtle understanding" (*Emunot ve-De'ot*, trans. by S. Rosenblatt (1948), 103). Regarding proofs adduced by Christians in support of the concept of the Trinity from the Bible, Saadiah states: "The misinterpretation of these terms on the part of these individuals who cite them as proof of their theory, is, then, due to unfamiliarity with the Hebrew language" (*ibid.*, 105). In the third section of the work, Saadiah rejects all the arguments adduced by Christians to show that the *mitzvot* and Torah had been abolished with the advent of the New Covenant.

SEFER HA-KUZARI. *Sefer ha-Kuzari* of *Judah Halevi is structured as a work of apologetics, with the subtitle *A Composition in Argumentation and Proof in the Defense of the Despised Faith*. In this work Judah Halevi sets his theory in an historical framework; the conversion of the king of Khazaria and many of his subjects to Judaism, the religion despised by the Gentiles. The Khazars adopted Judaism despite the strictness of its requirements regarding new converts. Judah Halevi elevates the values of human faith in the revealed religion and of Jewish law above those of philosophy, ultimately also opposing the latter. At the basis of his defense of Judaism, he places the history of the Jewish nation and its election by God. The present debased condition of the Jewish people constitutes no reflection on the value of its faith "because the light of God falls only upon humble souls"; humiliation and martyrdom are considered valid signs of proximity to God by all monotheistic religions, even Christianity and Islam, at present powerful in this world. Ultimately, all nations will accept the Torah adhered to by the suffering Jewish people. The religions in which the Gentiles believe at present are merely "a suggestion and an introduction to the anticipated Messiah" (4:22–23).

ISLAM. Comparatively little Jewish apologetic literature is directed specifically against Islam. As *Maimonides states, the claim of Muslim scholars that the Jews have corrupted the text of the Torah, abolishes the common ground on which any effort to explain the Jewish interpretation of the text to Muslims may be based. Muslims taunted Jews less than Christians about the situation implicit in exile. The Islamic conception that Judaism had simply been superseded by Mohammed's message and the law prescribed by him, lacking the element of internal contradiction, also diminished the requirement for apologetics in this sphere. Polemical allusions to Islam appear in the *piyyutim*, late Midrashim (e.g., *Pirkei de-R. Eliezer*), and exegetical and philosophical works, such as those of Saadiah Gaon, the *Emunah Ramah* of Abraham ibn Daud, and Maimonides' *Guide of the Perplexed* (2:32, 39). Identification of the Arabs with various biblical peoples such as *Kedar, Hagarites, or Nebaioth (Gen. 25:13; 28:9; 36:3; Isa. 60:7; Jer. 49:28; I Chron. 1:29) helped Jewish commentators to relate tales disparaging to the Muslims. Derogatory allusions are made to the personality of Muhammad and his actions: he is frequently described as "the madman." A work directed specifically against Islam was the "Treatise on Ishmael" (*Ma'amar al Ishma'el*, 1863) by Solomon b. Abraham *Adret, which rejects the arguments of a Muslim who disparaged inclusion of the stories of Reuben and of Tamar and Judah in the Bible and attacked the Jews for observing *mitzvot* which merited abolition. A detailed critique of Islam is also included in the *Keshet u-Magen* of Simeon b. Ẓemaḥ *Duran. The writer discourses on the attitude in the Koran to Judaism and criticizes the legends related there and its principles of faith and commandments; he points out contradictions found in the Koran, its ignorance of the principles of natural science and philosophical doctrine of the soul, and complains about its obscure style.

SPAIN AND SOUTHERN FRANCE. One of the first works to show the influence of the philosophical method of apologetics employed in Spain and southern France is the *Sefer Milḥamot Adonai* ("Book of the Wars of the Lord," 1170) of *Jacob b. Reuben, where reference is made to Saadiah Gaon, *Abraham b. Ḥiyya, and Abraham *Ibn Ezra. It was written to counter the arguments of an erudite Catholic priest whom the author held in high esteem, and its 12 sections include an imaginary debate between a "monotheist" and a "dissenter." The *Sefer ha-Berit* ("Book of the Covenant") by Joseph *Kimḥi, in similar dialogue form, not only defends the Jewish faith, but also demonstrates the morality and excellence of the Jewish way of life as regulated by the law. The case put by the Jew is as follows:

> I shall now enumerate their good works and you [i.e., the Christian] cannot deny them. To begin with the Ten Commandments… The Jews do not make idols…, there is no people in the world to compare with them in refraining from perjury; none keeps the Sabbath apart from the Jews. "Thou shalt honor thy [father and mother]"; likewise, "Thou shalt not kill; Thou shalt not commit adultery"; likewise, neither murders nor adulterers are found among them [the Jews]. It is known that you will not find robbery and banditry among the Jews as it is among Christians who rob people on the highways, and hang them, and sometimes put out their eyes; these things cannot be said

> of the Jews. The pious Jews and Jewesses… educate their children… in the study of the Torah; when they hear them utter an indecent word they punish them… Their daughters grow up in chastity, you will not see them on the streets, like the daughters of the Christians… Moreover, I tell you that when a Jew stays with a fellow Jew, whether for a day or two or for a year, his host will take no money from him for his board… Thus in every way the Jews in every land behave compassionately toward their brethren. If a Jew sees that his brother is taken captive, he will ransom him; naked – he will clothe him (*Milḥemet Ḥovah*, Constantinople, 1710).

*Meir b. Simeon of Narbonne in the 13th century defended Jewish faith, life, legal status, and economic activity. Thus he justified Jewish moneylending (trans. in JJS, 10 (1959), 51–57). In the draft of a memorandum to the king of France, Meir argues for better treatment of Jews, quoting the Bible on the brotherhood and equality of all men: "Hear me, my Lord King, and all his counselors, sages, and wise men, and all the heads of the Roman faith and its leaders, and follow in the footsteps of the patriarchs, who walked in the ways of the Almighty, for it is His way to hearken to the complaint and outcry of the poor… that all men shall understand that one Creator has created them, of one and same nature and one way of life" (*Milḥemet Mitzvah*, Ms. Parma, 155; Dinur, Golah, 2, pt. 1 (1965), 285–6).

NORTHERN FRANCE. The biblical exegetes in northern France introduced into their commentaries defenses of Jewish law and refutations of the claims of Christians in the homiletical spirit of midrashic apologetics. The commentaries of *Rashi are sometimes intended to refute Christological interpretations of biblical passages (e.g., Isa. 53; Jer. 31, 39; Ps. 2, etc.). In particular, the commentaries of *Samuel b. Meir, Joseph b. Isaac *Bekhor Shor, and *Eliezer of Beaugency contain apologetic explanations for almost all the verses to which Christians gave Christological or figurative interpretations. These explanations in part were prompted by the points raised at the religious disputations. The methods of hermeneutics employed range from literal exegesis of the text (**peshat*) to casuistic interpretation, including the hermeneutical methods of numerology (**gematria*) and abbreviation (*notarikon*), which all the schoolmen used in debate. While some of the disputants on behalf of Christianity were apostates from Judaism, those who replied to the Christian arguments included converts to Judaism or their descendants. Abraham the Proselyte from Hungary studied under Jacob b. Meir *Tam and was familiar with the New Testament and Christian liturgy. The French apologist Joseph ben Nathan Official, a descendant of a family of apologists composed c. 1260 the polemical book *Yosif ha-Mekanneh* (or *Teshuvot ha-Minim*) in the form of a commentary on the Bible. Its main purpose was to refute all Christological interpretations of the church. The book is a collection of such refutations of the French scholars until its own days. The book contains also a detailed criticism of the New Testament. This book, as well as other books patterned after it such as the *Nizzaḥon Vetus* (published by *Wagenseil in his *Tela ignea Satanae*), reflect the increased missionary activity of the church as well as the courageous response of Jewish religious leadership.

14TH- AND 15TH-CENTURY SPAIN. Jewish apologists in 14th-century Spain attempted to protect Judaism from apostates with mystic leanings. Isaac Policar (*Pollegar) came out against *Abner of Burgos in his *Iggeret ha-Ḥarafot* ("Epistle of Blasphemies"), which circulated throughout the Spanish communities. It contains a brief survey of the principles of the "true faith," which are also the principles of rationalism, and an explanation of the Jewish belief in the Messiah who would redeem Israel in the future. At greater length, he discusses these topics in the five dialogues in his *Ezer ha-Dat*. Another apologetic work to counter the influence of apostates was written by Moses (ha-Kohen) of Tordesillas, *Ezer ha-Emunah* (1375). Shem Tov b. Isaac ibn Shaprut's *Even Boḥan* (1385) may be considered a summation of Jewish apologetics in 14th-century Spain. In addition to 14 chapters which include answers to all the arguments raised by Christians, he adds a further chapter specifically directed against the doctrines propounded by Abner of Burgos. One result of the mass conversions of Jews to Catholicism in Spain, which began during the persecutions of 1391 and continued for a considerable time afterward, was the appearance of sharp literary polemics between converts to Christianity and the leaders of Spanish Jewry. Jewish apologetics then revealed outstanding literary talent and expressed new and daring ideas. The leader of Spanish Jewry during this period, the philosopher Ḥasdai *Crescas, wrote an apology in Spanish (translated into Hebrew in 1451 as *Bittul Ikkarei ha-Noẓerim*, "Negation of the Principles of the Christians," and published in Salonika in 1860), in which he turned to gentile intellectuals and demonstrated the grounds for negating the claims made by the Jewish converts to Christianity. A defense of Judaism is also included in his major work *Or Adonai*. Crescas tried to invalidate the view spread by converts, and held by rationalist Jewish apologists, that Judaism is almost identical with philosophical rationalism. He also fought against those who followed the doctrines of *Averroism denying individual providence and free will, the value of fulfilling the *mitzvot*, and the testimony of Jewish history. Ḥasdai set out to prove that Judaism in its original pure form had the power to redeem man through belief and observance of the *mitzvot*.

A colleague and disciple of Ḥasdai Crescas, Profiat *Duran, dedicated himself to the defense of Judaism (see *Disputations). His celebrated satire *Al Tehi ke-Avotekha* ("Be Not Like Your Fathers") is composed in the form of a letter to a friend, Bonet Bonjorn, who became converted to Christianity under the influence of *Pablo de Santa Maria (Solomon ha-Levi of Burgos). Profiat Duran's refined sarcasm, his profound learning, and polished style, were so successful that some Christian apologists took the work seriously as a defense of Christianity. Duran formulates the tenets of Christianity in this epistle with biting irony, using a critical historical method. The disputation of *Tortosa (1413–14) and the difficult circumstances surrounding and following it brought further Jewish apologetics in its wake. Both Joseph *Albo, one of the participants in the disputation, and Simeon b. Ẓemaḥ Duran, wrote works which were to a large degree influenced by the Tortosa disputation. Albo's *Sefer ha-Ikkarim* (1485) includes in its dogmatic formulations much apologetic argumentation on a rationalist basis. Simeon b. Ẓemaḥ Duran's *Keshet u-Magen* (1423) is explicitly an anti-Christian polemical work.

ITALY. The defense of Judaism by the Jewish scholars in Spain influenced the apologetic literature in other countries. In Italy, where there was constant social contact between Christians and Jews, debates on religious matters were held even in the early Middle Ages. The traditions of Jewish apologetic literature in Spain were continued by Jews in Italy in the 16th century after the expulsion from Spain, and included many of the exiles among its proponents. The Renaissance, humanism, and the religious ferment in the Christian world also gave a new impetus to Jewish apologetic literature. In the 16th century Jewish apologists tended to write in languages other than Hebrew to enable their arguments to reach Christian intellectuals. In his *Apologia Hebraeorum* (Strasbourg, 1559), David d'Ascoli challenged the restrictive legislation of Pope Paul IV and was imprisoned for his views. When in 1581 Pope *Gregory XIII renewed the order prohibiting Jewish physicians from treating Christian patients, David de Petals defended the integrity of Jewish doctors in his *De medico Hebraeo enarratio apologetica* (Venice, 1588), at the same time defending the Jewish laws regarding the taking of interest. Leone *Modena, who had frequent discussions with Christians, also engaged in apologetics. He wrote in 1644 the polemical book *Magen va-Ḥerev* ("Shield and Sword"). Modena was probably the first Jew to attempt a historical approach to the personality of Jesus, who was according to him close to the Pharisees. Jesus did not consider himself to be the Son of God. The main tenets of Christianity were crystallized in later centuries as a result of contacts with the pagan world and its beliefs and customs. Simḥah (Simone) *Luzzatto, in his *Discorso circa il stato degli Ebrei* (1638), discusses the character and conduct of the Jews, adverting not only to their positive virtues but also to their weaknesses. Luzzatto's main theme is the role filled by Jews in the economy of the Venetian Republic. He tries to demonstrate that the Jews formed a desirable element of efficient and loyal merchants without other loyalties to distract them from allegiance to a principality that treated them well. Luzzatto also attempts to invest Judaism with certain Catholic attributes.

THE REST OF EUROPE. A new aspect of Jewish apologetics was opened with the beginning of the settlement in Western Europe of Marranos who had left Spain and Portugal because of the pressure of the Inquisition, and their own unsettled religious views, but had not yet found their way to normative Judaism. Jewish scholars of Marrano origin now began propaganda among them to convince them of the truth of Judaism and the moral excellence of the Jews. Among these were, for example, the physician Elijah Montalto in a series of letters addressed to an acquaintance (published in REJ, 87 (1927), 137–65). Similarly, Immanuel *Aboab addressed an appeal couched along these lines to a kinsman in the south of France, replete with historical demonstrations which he used in his *Nomologia* (162. JQR, 23 (1932), 121–62), and were taken over subsequently by *Manasseh Ben Israel in his writings to be described below. Isaac *Cardozo in his *Las excelencias y calunias de los Hebreos* (Amsterdam, 1678) explains the election of the Jews and their mission as the bearers of a universal religion.

In the manner of the Jewish apologetic literature in Italy, there was also literature of this genre among the ex-Marrano Sephardi community in Holland. The most important Dutch-Jewish apologetic work was produced during his mission to England by Manasseh Ben Israel, whose *Vindiciae Judaeorum* was published in London in 1656. In this, Manasseh brings historical evidence in refutation of anti-Jewish libels, primarily of the *blood libel. Also emphasized are the material advantages likely to accrue by accepting the Jews into a state: "Hence it may be seen that God has not abandoned us; for if one persecutes us, another receives us civilly and courteously; and if this prince treats us ill, another treats us well; if one banishes us out of his country, another invites us by a thousand privileges, as various princes of Italy have done, and the mighty duke of Savoy in Nice. And do we not see that those republics which admit the Israelites flourish and much increase in trade?" (*Vindiciae*, sect. 33). His *Esperança de Israel* (1650) discusses the prerequisites for the advent of the Messiah and the return of the Jews to their land. Common to all apologetic compositions of this type are their efforts to achieve the amelioration of the present Jewish status by clarifying the essentials of the Jewish faith and explaining the way of life and character of the Jewish people. Many elements in the *Weltanschauung* of the later Enlightenment (see *Haskalah) movement in the period of Emancipation derive from this apologetic literature.

In Poland and Germany Jewish apologetics developed along different lines. In 1394 a German Jewish convert to Christianity, Pesaḥ-Peter, charged that the content of the prayer *Aleinu (in its original form) – "They bow to vanity and emptiness and pray to a god that does not bring salvation" – was aimed at Christians. Among the Jews consequently imprisoned was Yom Tov Lipmann *Muelhausen. His *Sefer ha-Nizzahon*, written on this occasion, is a defense of Jewish ethics, and of the Bible and Talmud. The work made a profound impact and brought forth responsa by the bishop of Brandenburg, Stephan Bodecker, in 1459. The anti-trinitarian movement which arose in Poland in the 16th century also affected the Jews. Some sectarian leaders were interested in proving to their Catholic opponents who taunted them as being *semi-iudei* the difference between them and the Jews. The Jews in general avoided contacts with the sectarians; but some accepted the challenge. There was a disputation between the Polish Unitarian leader, Marcin Czechowic and the Jew, Jacob of Belzyce. The arguments of Jacob are preserved in the book of answers by Marcin. Of greater importance is the book *Ḥizzuk Emunah* by the Karaite scholar Isaac of *Troki, which was translated into European languages (also into Latin by Wagenseil in his *Tela ignea Satanae*) and exerted an influence on the French encyclopedists in the 18th century. It is a well-organized and clearly written book. Isaac shows a profound knowledge of Christianity and its sources. He was also familiar with contemporary Catholic and sectarian literature. The book contains a thorough and systematic criticism of the New Testament. The main purpose of the book was to prove why Jews refuse to believe in the divinity of Jesus and accept Christianity. In 1759 Jewish representatives in Poland were compelled to defend the Talmud in a public disputation with the *Frankists. Dov Ber *Birkenthal of Bolechov wrote an apology entitled *Divrei Binah* (published by A. Brawer in *Ha-Shilo'aḥ*, 33 (1917), 146 ff.). Jacob *Emden countered the charges of the Frankists in *Sefer Shimmush*, which includes a positive evaluation of Jesus and his activity. Emden also acknowledges that Christianity drove out paganism and obliged its adherents to observe the seven *Noachide laws. He emphasizes that Christians are of good character. They are not bound to observe the *mitzvot* and will not be punished for their belief in the Trinity, but will be rewarded for spreading belief in God among Gentiles who had no knowledge of the God of Israel.

In the 18th Century

Evaluation of Judaism became a factor in the struggle between the old and new in the philosophy of Enlightenment. Despite the anti-Judaic stand taken by many rationalist and deist thinkers (e.g., *Voltaire), there were others who defended Judaism and Jews, such as Roger Williams and John *Toland. The German Christian Wilhelm *Dohm, while insisting in 1781 that Jewish mores and culture must be improved, praised the basic traits in the Jewish character. Gradually Jewish apologetic literature furnished the arsenal and became the battlefield in the struggle to attain Jewish emancipation. Non-Jews increasingly joined Jews in their efforts. Gotthold Ephraim *Lessing and Moses *Mendelssohn frequently turned to apologetics to state the Jewish case. In 1782 Mendelssohn wrote an introduction to Manasseh Ben Israel's *Vindiciae Judaeorum* (in the German translation by Marcus Hertz) in which he advocated Jewish rights. In his *Jerusalem, oder ueber die religioese Macht und Judentum* (1783), he explains Jewish law according to his views, his exposition having an apologetic edge: Mendelssohn here denies the Church the right to use coercion by the arm of the state and argues that no state is justified in withholding civil rights from a group of people because of their religious views.

With the weakening of the influence of religion in the West, the religious grounds for antisemitism were replaced by national, social, and economic arguments. Pro-Jewish apologists therefore had to prove that the Jews constituted an advantageous element from an economic standpoint; that any faults with adverse social consequences, such as the practice of usury, were the result of the economic position into which they had been forced by medieval laws; and that they were loyal to the countries whose national culture they wished to adopt. Preeminent in power and feeling among the defenders of the Jews is the English historian Thomas Babington Macaulay. In his speech in parliament of April 17, 1833, on Jewish disabilities, he dealt with arguments against granting full rights to the Jews, summing up in what may be termed a crescendo of Liberal-Protestant Christian apologetics on behalf of the Jews and their past.

> Such, Sir, has in every age been the reasoning of bigots. They never fail to plead in justification of persecution the vices which persecution has engendered. England has been to the Jews less than half a country and we revile them because they do not feel for England more than half patriotism. We treat them as slaves, and wonder why they do not regard us as brethren. We drive them to mean occupations, and then reproach them for not embracing honorable professions. We long forbade them to possess land and we complain that they chiefly occupy themselves in trade. We shut them out of all the paths of ambition, and then we despise them for taking refuge in avarice. But were they always a mere money-changing, money-getting, money-hoarding race?… In the infancy of civilizations, when our island was as savage as New Guinea, when letters and arts were still unknown to Athens, when scarcely a thatched hut stood on what was afterwards the site of Rome, this condemned people had their fenced cities, their splendid Temple.

In the 19th and 20th Centuries

Jewish apologists in emphasizing the contribution made by Jews to civilization, transformed the conception of *am segullah* ("election") to the concept of *te'udah* ("mission"). They progressively emphasized the universal character of Judaism. Abraham *Geiger defended Judaism in this spirit; he also made a scholarly investigation of apologetics, and published selections from the medieval Jewish apologists in *Proben juedischer Verteidigung des Mittelalters*. An apologist in a similar vein was the historian Isaac Marcus *Jost (1793–1860). Gabriel *Riesser (1806–1863), while advocating Jewish emancipation, compared the subjugation of Jews by Christians to that of the Third Estate by the nobility and of the blacks by whites. When the Protestant theologian E.G. Paulus argued that Jews would have to become converted to Christianity in order to become good citizens, Riesser defended the Jews and Judaism in his *Verteidigung der buergerlichen Gleichstellung der Juden* (1831). Riesser's periodical, *Der Jude*, was of great importance in the arena of apologetics. Leopold *Zunz stated in his introduction to his *Die gottesdienstlichen Vortraege der Juden* that "the Jews in Europe, and especially those in Germany, should be given freedom instead of being granted rights." The Jewish situation in the 19th century continued to stimulate apologetics preoccupied with questions relating to emancipation.

Although the concern of Western Jewry with apologetics considerably diminished with the attainment of emancipation, the recrudescence of antisemitism in Europe during the second half of the 19th century again evoked a renewal of apologetic literature, especially in response to the recurrent blood libels. Joseph Samuel *Bloch (1850–1923) contributed signally to the defense of Jews and Judaism before meetings of workingmen in Vienna and in his activities to combat the accusations made by the Catholic theologian and antisemite, August *Rohling, at the time of the *Tisza-Eszlár blood libel case. In 1884 Bloch founded a periodical *Oesterreichische Wochenschrift*, dedicated to the struggle against antisemitism. His apology *Israel und die Voelker* was published posthumously in 1923.

Adolf *Jellinek (1820–1892), the chief rabbi of Vienna, was active in Jewish defense. His successor Moritz *Guedemann not only combated the bias shown by many scholars on Jewish problems but also prompted a widespread information campaign to defend Judaism in the Viennese press and in public gatherings. Guedemann also wrote a basic study of Jewish apologetics, *Juedische Apologetik* (1906). Among scientists who felt compelled to defend the Jews in the face of contemporary antisemitism was the alienist and criminologist Cesare *Lombroso, an Italian Jew, whose *L'anti-Semitismo e le scienze moderne* (1894) was intended for this purpose.

In Eastern Europe also, Jewish apologetics entered the lists in the struggle for civil rights. Notable among the Jewish apologists active in Poland during the first half of the 19th century were Samuel Baum and Jacob *Tugendhold. The latter followed the model of German Jewish apologetic literature. His *Obrona Izraelitów* ("Defense of the Jews") is a refutation of the blood libel, while he also attacked the manner in which antisemites presented the political and social aspects of the Jewish problem. Among apologists in Russia, Isaac Ber *Levinsohn was prominent. In his *Aḥiyyah ha-Shiloni* (1864) he even renewed apologetics as a form of Christian-Jewish dialogue. *Ta'ar ha-Sofer* (1892), a defense of the Talmud, is directed against the Karaites, and *Efes Damim*, a confutation of the blood libel, was written during the Zaslavl case. In Russia, Jewish apologetics were directed, inter alia, to abolition of the restrictions on Jewish residence outside the Pale of Settlement. They thus emphasized the role of the Jewish merchant in the economy as well as cultural factors. In the 1880s, when individual Jews were accused of taking part in the revolutionary movements, Jewish apologists argued that the overwhelming majority of Jews were conservative in character.

An important turning point in Jewish apologetics was the rise of Jewish nationalism. A conflict developed between Zionists and apologists of the conventional type who still used the arguments employed by the advocates of emancipation, and in countering the humiliating propaganda of the antisemites stressed the merits of the Jews. In contrast, the general tendency of Zionists was to present the Jews as a people like any other nation. Zionism, however, developed its own arguments, including the historic right of the Jews to Ereẓ Israel, which had already been a controversial subject between Jews and Gentiles during the Second Temple period.

The 19th and 20th centuries saw the growth of a specific internal apologetics with the object of bringing Jews back to Judaism. Jewish apologists of this type included spokesmen of neo-Orthodoxy, Samson Raphael *Hirsch (e.g., in *Iggeret Ẓafon*) and Isaac *Breuer (*Der Neue Kusari*, and other works). Of this intention, although in another spirit, were non-Orthodox writers, such as Max *Brod (*Heidentum, Christentum, Judentum*, 1921), Franz *Rosenzweig (*Apologetisches Denken*), Hermann *Cohen, Edmond *Fleg, Leo *Baeck, and others, who advocated a return to Jewish values out of the conviction that these include an original and complete *Weltanschauung* by which a man can live a noble life. Jews in Germany stressed the honorable part they had taken in the German armed forces in World War I. Jewish bodies, such as the Anti-Defamation League (see *B'nai *B'rith), the *Alliance Israélite Universelle, and the *Central-Verein Deutscher Staatsbuerger juedischen Glaubens, devoted themselves to issuing publicity of an apologetic nature. During the Nazi assault on Jewish existence, there developed an anti-racist scientific literature which furnished Jewish apologists with arguments against racism as well as works stressing the prominent role played by Jews in world culture. After the *Holocaust, Jews such as Jules *Isaac went over to the attack and stressed the Christian historic guilt in the annihilation. One of the central problems confronting Jewish apologists, mainly in the modern age, is of a psychological nature. The anti-Jewish calumniator is able to rouse his public by alleging that Jews and Jewish influence are a cause of social evils. Jewish defense, on the other hand, has stressed that Jews are not responsible. By the very negativeness of its argumentation, therefore, modern Jewish apologetics has often failed to demonstrate positive Jewish values to the public.

BIBLIOGRAPHY: Baer, Spain, index, s.v. *disputations*; Urbach, in: *Tarbiz*, 17 (1946), 1–11; 20 (1949), 118–22; Ettinger, in: *Scripta Hierosolymitana*, 7 (1961), 193–219; idem, in: *Zion*, 29 (1964), 182–207; Klausner, Sifrut, 3 (1953), 89–105; G.B. De Rossi, *Bibliotheca judaica anti-Christiana* (1800), 66–67; M. Friedlaender, *Geschichte der juedischen Apologetik* (1903); J. Bergmann, *Juedische Apologetik im neutestamentlichen Zeitalter* (1908); R.T. Herford, *Christianity in Talmud and Midrash* (1903); A.B. Hulen, in: JBL, 51 (1932), 58–70; Urbach, in: REJ, 100 (1935), 49–77; Bergman, *ibid.*, 40 (1900), 188–205; M. Steinschneider, *Polemische und apologetische Literatur in arabischer Sprache* (1877); M. Goldstein, *Jesus in the Jewish Tradition* (1950); O.S. Rankin, *Jewish Religious Polemic* (1956); P. Browe, *Die Judenmission im Mittelalter und die Paepste* (1942); G. Lindeskog, *Die Jesusfrage im neuzeitlichen Judentum* (1938); J. Rosenthal, in: *Aresheth*, 2 (1960), 130–79; 3 (1961), 433–9; idem, in: JBA, 21 (1963), 15–21; idem, in: PAAJR, 34 (1966), 77–93; J. Fleishman, *Be'ayat ha-Naẓrut ba-Maḥashavah ha-Yehudit mi-Mendelssohn ad Rosenzweig* (1964).

[*Encyclopaedia Hebraica*]

APOSTASY, term applied by members of the deserted faith for the change of one faith, set of loyalties, and worship for another. The conception of apostasy could not arise in the atmosphere of polytheism practiced in antiquity before the advent of *Hellenism. The Bible frequently condemns those worshiping other gods, but though this is conceived as a heinous transgression it still lacks the totality of apostasy-conversion.

A product of the spread of Hellenistic culture in Ereẓ Israel was the group of *Mityavvenim* (hellenizers), who according to Jewish sources adopted Hellenistic ways of life and religious worship during the reign of *Antiochus IV Epiphanes in the second century B.C.E. Some scholars take these to be the instigators of his persecution of the Jewish faith. In the Books of the *Maccabees, the Jews who abetted the officials of the Seleucids or joined their armies are described as renegades and apostates. The Tosefta (Suk. 4:28) has preserved the tale of "Miriam of the House of Bilga [a priestly house] who apostatized (שנשתמדה) and married an official of one of the kings of Greece. As the Greeks entered the Temple, Miriam came and struck the top of the altar, saying… 'You have destroyed the property of Israel and did not come to their help in their trouble.'" The woman appears to express disillusionment with the Jewish God. Because of her apostasy, her family was disqualified from certain privileges and symbols of priestly status. *Tiberius Julius Alexander, the nephew of the philosopher *Philo Judaeus, went to the extreme of commanding some of the Roman units during the siege and subsequent destruction of Jerusalem and the Temple. As described in the Talmud, the figure of the second-century scholar and teacher Elisha b. Avuyah, who joined the pagan-philosophic camp, disputed with Jewish scholars, and ridiculed the Jewish religion, has a certain grandeur and is accorded a grudging respect.

After the rise of Christianity apostasy became an accompanying phenomenon of Jewish life, a problem between Jews and their neighbors, and a constant source of irritation to the various religious camps as well as to the apostates themselves. The forlorn hope of Judeo-Christians (see *Jewish-Christian sects) of reconciling the Law with the Cross petered out. By the latter half of the second century it had been rejected both by the vast majority of Christians and by Jews. The parting of the ways between church and synagogue had been reached. Acceptance of Christianity that had forsaken the Law was regarded by Jews as apostasy in the fullest sense. The Christian dogmas of Incarnation and Trinity gave to the acceptance of Christianity an idolatrous character (*avodah zarah*).

The history of ferocious persecutions and systematic humiliations which the Jews subsequently endured for their religion (see *History, Jewish; Church, *Catholic; Jewish *Badge; *Blood Libel; Desecration of the *Host) combined to invest apostasy from Judaism with the character of desertion from the persecuted and a crossing over to the persecuting ruling power. This attitude was enhanced by the fundamental divergence between Jewish and Christian approaches to conversion to the respective faiths, which led Jews to draw a strong moral distinction between apostasy and *proselytism, regarding the two in an entirely different light. As developed in Jewish theory and practice, proselytism to Judaism was made dependent on full and deliberate acceptance of partnership in the Jewish fate and historical consciousness, as well as of belief in its faith and hopes. The attitude to apostasy, however, was conditioned by the Christian missionary approach, which, even when abstaining from the use of threats or forcible coercion, still set out to gain converts by compelling Jews to attend missionary *sermons and involved automatic betterment of the social and legal status of the apostate. This therefore appeared in the Jewish view as a vulgar and essentially nonspiritual attempt to harm souls through moral pressure and promise of material gain. The fear of expulsion or massacre, which always loomed in the background, very often was the root cause of apostasy. Even an apostate whose sincerity was beyond all doubt, like *Abner of Burgos, stated in the 14th century that the starting point for his apostasy was the "revelation" he experienced, in which "I saw the poverty of the Jews, my people, from whom I am descended, who have been oppressed and broken and heavily burdened by taxes throughout their long captivity – this people that has lost its former honor… and there is none to help or sustain them… when I had meditated on the matter, I went to the synagogue weeping sorely and sad at heart. And I prayed… And in a dream, I saw the figure of a tall man who said to me, 'Why dost thou slumber? Hearken unto these words… for I say unto thee that the Jews have remained so long in captivity for their folly and wickedness and because they have no teacher of righteousness through whom they may recognize the truth" (Baer, Spain, 1 (1961), 328–9). To those who gloried in shouldering the burden of the Jewish fate and history, were imbued with love of Jewish culture and way of life, and continued to hope for salvation and the establishment of God's kingdom in the future, such a motivation inevitably appeared the outpourings of a weakling and the self-justification of a traitor. This attitude was strengthened in regard to many apostates who became willing and active virulent enemies of Judaism, like Abner of Burgos himself.

Naturally, apostasy was not always motivated by debased considerations, the historical situation, or meditations of this nature. The autobiography of an apostate of the first half of the 12th century (*Hermannus quondam Judaeus, opusculum de conversione sua*, ed. by G. Niemeyer, 1963; see *Hermanus Quondan Judaeus) demonstrates the effect of gradual absorption of Christian ideas and acclimatization to the Christian mode of life through everyday contacts and conversation. It brought the author, Judah ha-Levi of Cologne, to convert to Christianity and become a Premonstratensian monk.

In the Islamic environment the problems were much the same; some apostates attained prominent positions in Islamic states and society, the outer expressions of tension caused by apostasy being on a smaller scale (see below Apostasy in Islam). In the perpetual conflict and tensions that existed between Jews and Christians in medieval Europe, conversion from one faith to another, although rare, was still more frequent than either side cared to admit clearly. Thus, on the occasion of a halakhic deliberation in the 12th century, the talmudist Jacob b. Meir *Tam reported: "More than 20 letters of divorce from apostates have been written in Paris and France… and also in Lorraine… I have also seen myself the letter of divorce given by the son-in-law of the late noble R. Jacob the Parnas who has apostatized" (*Sefer ha-Yashar*, ed. by S. Rosenthal (1898), 45, no. 25).

Some apostates founded influential families whose Jewish origin was well known among Christians, such as the *Pierleoni family in Rome, the patrician Jud family in Cologne, and the *Jozefowicz family in Poland-Lithuania. Certainly not all apostates from Judaism attempted to injure their brethren. When a number of apostates were asked in 1236 whether there was truth in the blood libel, they denied it categorically. Prominent among the apostates who deliberately set out to attack Judaism were Nicholas *Donin in France, Pablo *Christiani, and Hieronymus de Sancta Fide (Joshua *Lorki) in Spain, and Petrus *Nigri (Schwarz) in Germany. These in the 13th to 15th centuries led the attack on Judaism in the theological *disputations, preached against Judaism, and proposed coercive measures to force Jews to adopt Christianity. Other converts who achieved high rank in the church, like Pablo de Santa Maria (Solomon ha-Levi), who became archbishop of Burgos, did everything in their power to combat Judaism. The most virulent representative of anti-Jewish animus was Abner of Burgos, who initiated the intensified persecution of the Jews in Christian Spain during the 14th and 15th centuries by formulating a complete theory that subsumes the necessity for, and justification of, such persecution. He advised the abolition of Jewish *autonomy, arguing with vicious irony that the Messiah would not come to the Jews "until the Jews possess no authority, not even such petty authority as is exercised over them by their rabbis and communal wardens, those coarse creatures who lord it over the people like kings. They hold out vain promises to them in order to keep them under constant control. Only with the elimination of these dignitaries and judges and officers will salvation come to the masses" (polemical tract, Baer, *op. cit.*, 350). In the name of "many discerning Jews," Abner blamed the pope and Christian monarchs for failing to oppress the Jews adequately. The conditions of salvation for the Jews would come only "when many Jewish communities are massacred and the particular generation of Jews is thereby reduced in numbers, some Jews immediately convert to the dominant Christian faith out of fear, and in that way a handful are saved… and the pain of impoverishment will lead to an increase of shamelessness among them, that is, they will no longer be ashamed to profess the truth openly and convert to Christianity" (Baer, *op. cit.* 353–4). By this means this apostate tried to reinforce his own experience of Jewish weakness and convert it into a terrible reality that would force many more Jews to relinquish their faith.

At the time of the expulsions from Spain and Portugal at the end of the 15th century, a sharp distinction was made by Jews between the renegade apostates, whom they considered an evil and the root cause of the wave of persecutions, and the mass of forced converts, the *anusim or *Marranos, whom they still regarded as brethren, though obliged to practice Judaism clandestinely. However, in realization, the program promoted by Abner of Burgos and others like him created a strong revulsion in Christian society against both the Marranos and genuine converts alike. Political events and social attitudes in Christian Spain in the 15th to 16th centuries fomented the concept whereby the "New Christians" were not to be equated with, and trusted as, the "Old Christians" of "pure Christian blood." Thus it could happen that the second general of the Jesuit order, Diego Lainez, had to face opposition within the order because of his Jewish blood.

In the Renaissance and *Reformation environment apostasy occurred in various circumstances. One type of apostate was the rootless intellectual like Flavius *Mithridates, a translator from Hebrew and an influential expositor of Hebrew works. Others were led to convert to Christianity by their superficial contacts with Renaissance circles and the new importance attached by humanists like Johannes *Reuchlin and *Pico della Mirandola to learning Hebrew from Jewish teachers. The impoverished conditions of late medieval Germany gave rise to the opportunist who could change over at least three times from Judaism to Christianity and back again, and who on one occasion of reconversion quoted a proverb he had heard: "*lasse dich taufen, ich will dir vil Gulden schaffen*" ("Become baptized: I will get you plenty of money"; R. Strauss, *Urkunden und Aktenstuecke zur Geschichte der Juden in Regensburg* (1960), 64–66). The basic attitude of both Jews and Christians toward apostates did not change with the Reformation. Many of the teachers of Hebrew to Christians were Jews, most of them apostates. They also cooperated in bringing out Reformation translations of the Bible. In his later days, Martin *Luther displayed marked distrust of apostates from Judaism. The attacks on the Talmud made by Johann *Pfefferkorn on the eve of the Reformation and the denunciation poured by Anton *Margarita on Jewish ritual practices and way of life continued in new circumstances the tradition of virulent anti-Jewish hatemongering by apostates.

The stimulus provided by 18th-century Enlightenment, stirrings toward *assimilation on the cultural and social plane, and aspirations to attain *Emancipation, inaugurated a trend toward apostasy in the upper circles of Jewish society in Central and Western Europe. A number of Jews opted for Christianity as the basis of European culture and its most sublime expression, despising their Jewish background and traditional way of life as debased and degraded. Typical was a society intellectual like Rachel *Varnhagen von Ense. Others considered apostasy the most facile and ready way of attaining civil equality as an individual before the Jews as such had achieved emancipation. Moses *Mendelssohn was publicly challenged to become converted if he did not refute the testimony advanced in proof of Christianity (see *Disputations). David *Friedlaender proposed in the name of several "Jewish heads of families" to be permitted to accept Christianity without having to subscribe to its "historical dogmas." Jews also left Judaism because they did not find communal obligations or activity to their taste.

Isaac *D'Israeli stated in 1813 to the board of the Bevis Marks congregation in London, as a reason for his refusal to act as warden, that he was "a person who has always lived out of the sphere of your observation; of retired habits of life; who can never unite in your public worship, because, as now conducted, it disturbs, instead of exciting, religious emotions, a circumstance of general acknowledgment; who has only tolerated some part of your ritual, willing to concede all he can in those matters which he holds to be indifferent." This indifference led him to baptize his illustrious son Benjamin in 1817 while formally remaining a Jew himself, a path taken by many others of a similar frame of mind who had their children baptized at the end of the 18th and beginning of the 19th centuries. The attitude of indifference was reinforced by the view that relegated religion to the status of an element in the universal culture or a cell in the social structure.

From the second half of the 18th century the ties linking the individual with the social unit became loosened in the upper strata of European society. Jews then increasingly absorbed the culture and adopted the language of their environment. Baptism was submitted as the visiting card demanded by Christian society for its price of admission. Many able young Jewish intellectuals, among them men outstanding in their field like the jurist Eduard *Gans, Ludwig *Boerne, and the poet Heinrich *Heine, who had first wanted to use their creative activity in the Jewish framework, left Judaism to be able to work within, and contribute to, European culture and society. In some communities, such as Berlin, more than half of the descendants of the old patrician Jewish families adopted Christianity, including the Mendelssohn family. The majority of these did not claim to be drawn by an essential attraction to Christianity or act under rigorous pressure. Apostasy was regarded as a social formality performed for the sake of culture, society, or career. Many of the sensitive among them bitterly regretted their action. Much of Heinrich Heine's work is dominated by a pervasive longing for Judaism, and a biting irony against himself and his fellow apostates, their snobbery and social climbing by means of Christianity.

Karl *Marx, baptized as a child, later professed contempt for and revulsion against Judaism as the representative of Mammon. In his Christian environment Benjamin Disraeli developed a kind of pride in what he considered the destiny and genius of the Jewish "race." The heroine of his novel *Tancred*, Eva, sarcastically asks Tancred: "Pray are you of those Franks who worship a Jewess; or of those others who revile her, break her images, and blaspheme her pictures?" When the Christian refers to the punishment of the Jews for crucifying Jesus, Disraeli's Jewess answers with the ancient argument used by Jews in disputations: "Suppose the Jews had not prevailed upon the Romans to crucify Jesus, what would have become of the Atonement?" When the Christian answers that the Crucifixion was preordained," 'Ah,' said the lady, 'preordained by the creator of the World for countless ages! Where then was the inexpiable crime of those who fulfilled the beneficent intention? The holy race supplied the victim and the immolators.... Persecute us! Why if you believed what you profess, you should kneel to us! You raise statues to the hero who saves a country. We have saved the human race, and you persecute us for doing it.'"

Benjamin Disraeli was representative of a group of apostates who considered themselves deeply Christian in a mythical and social sense and in consequence Jewish in a racial and spiritual sense. In the 19th century they were often active in missions to the Jews, like Bishop Michael Solomon *Alexander in Jerusalem, while at the same time being very responsive to Zionism and its aspirations.

With the granting of emancipation to Jews in most of Western and Central Europe the brutal social pressure for the "visiting card of baptism" moderated. On the other hand, many Jewish scholars and scientists, in particular in Germany and Austria, became baptized for the sake of a university career, which was usually closed to a professing Jew. Some deeply committed apostates like the *Ratisbonne brothers in the 19th century founded special religious orders or groups for the propagation of Christianity among Jews. According to statistics available there were 21,000 aspostates in Poland in the 18th century, and 204,500 throughout the world in the 19th. However these figures are exaggerated since they include the Frankists in Poland and the *Cantonists in Russia.

In czarist Russia, up to 1917, there was relentless pressure for social acceptance through baptism. However, Jewish social and moral cohesion was strong and undeniable, and to a certain degree the Jewish cultural level was superior to that of the surrounding population. Here apostasy of a different type developed: people who accepted Christianity for the sake of a government or university career (a number of apostates were employed for *censorship of Hebrew books) but still retained their ties with Jewish society, and a pride in their Jewish origin, like the orientalist Daniel *Chwolson. Apostates like Jacob *Brafman, however, did much to bring discredit on the institutions of Jewish self-government and to provide fuel for antisemitism.

In the 20th century the phenomenon of apostasy became more complex, with deeper implications. While its effects were more subversive for Judaism, it aroused problems of Jewish nationality and culture which were less prominent previously. Boris *Pasternak is representative of the type of apostate who left Judaism because he rebelled against historical and social realities and obligations. After describing the beatings and humiliations to which the Jews were subjected by the Cossacks of the Christian Russian army in his novel *Dr. Zhivago*, he states concerning the incident he has described, "that, and other incidents like it – of course none of that is worth theorizing about." Having disposed of pogroms and antisemitism by refusing to face them on the intellectual level, he continues that, in regard to "the Jewish question as a whole – there philosophy does enter." The philosophy he perceived – his theory was formulated when World War II was raging and the Jewish people was being systematically destroyed in the *Holocaust – was that Jewish history is a self-inflicted punishment through refusal to heed that in "this new way of life and of communion, which is born of the heart and is called the Kingdom of God, there are no nations, only persons." Having denied the existence of the question of nations and nationality around the year 1941, Pasternak goes on to accuse "the ordinary run of politicians" who like to have "a nicely restricted group" so that they can deliberate and continue "settling and deciding and getting pity to pay dividends. Well now, what more perfect example can you have of the victims of the mentality than the Jews? Their national idea has forced them, century after century, to be a people and nothing but a people – and the extraordinary thing is that they have been chained to this deadening task all through the centuries when all the rest of the world was being delivered from it by a new force which had come out of their own midst… In whose interests is this voluntary martyrdom?… Why don't the intellectual leaders of the Jewish people ever get beyond facile *Weltschmerz* and irony? Why don't they – even if they have to burst like a boiler with the pressure of their duty – dismiss this army which is forever fighting and being massacred, nobody knows for what? Why don't they say to them: 'That's enough, stop now. Don't hold on to your identity, don't all get together in a crowd. Disperse. Be with all the rest. You are the first and best Christians in the world. You are the very thing against which you have been turned by the worst and weakest among you'" (*Dr. Zhivago* (1958), 116–8). Facile antisemitic allusions to the character of the Jewish intellectual, and his looking for gain, are mingled here with a self-righteous denial of Judaism as a religion and an imputation that nationalism is the original and abiding sin of Judaism. Pasternak's resentment toward the religion and community he has abjured is expressed in his poetry on the basis of ancient Pauline symbols, rejecting the "barrenness" of Judaism and substituting another tree for the fertile olive:

Near by stood a fig tree. Fruitless, nothing but branches and leaves. He said to it:

> 'What joy have I of you?
> Of what profit are you, standing there like a post?
> 'I thirst and hunger and you are barren,
> And meeting you is comfortless as granite.
> How untalented you are, and how disappointing!
> Such you shall remain till the end of time!'
> The doomed tree trembled
> Like a lightning conductor struck by lightning,
> And was consumed to ashes.
> If the leaves, branches, roots, trunk,
> Had been granted a moment of freedom,
> The laws of nature would have intervened.
> But a miracle is a miracle, a miracle is God (*ibid.*, 497–8)

Like another apostate, Eugen *Rosenstock-Hussy (for his arguments, see *Disputations), a German of the generation of World War I, Pasternak expresses a categorical and hostile repudiation of Jewish nationalism as the evil archetype of all forms of nationalism. Both men are typical of the modern apostate who joins Christianity as an individual, rejecting communal solidarity as an unwonted yoke, and repudiating Jewish historical continuity, yearning for a mystic penetration of their individuum with the suffering Christian God. In his attitude to Jewish nationalism, Pasternak displays a considerably greater hostility than his German fellow apostate, logical in a man who left Eastern European Jewry in a period of revolution, distress, and annihilation of order.

Another trend in apostasy from Judaism in its modern form is represented by Oswald Rufeisen, who as Brother Daniel entered the Carmelite order in 1945. Born in Poland in 1922, and in his youth an active Zionist, he worked in the wartime underground and saved Jews during the Holocaust. He became a Christian in 1942, but continued to consider himself a Jew. After he became a monk, he wrote to the Polish authorities applying for permission to leave Poland for Ereẓ Israel: "I base this application on the ground of my belonging to the Jewish people, to which I continue to belong although I embraced the Catholic faith in 1942 and joined a monastic order in 1945. I have made this fact clear whenever and wherever it has been raised with me officially… I chose an Order and Chapter in Israel in consideration of the fact that I would receive the leave of my superiors to travel to the land for which I have yearned since my childhood when I was a member of the Zionist youth organization" (*High Court Application of Oswald Rufeisen* v. *The Minister of the Interior* (1963), 54–55). In 1962 Brother Daniel appealed to the Israel High Court to be recognized as a Jew under the terms of the Law of Return, which grants Jews settling in Israel automatic citizenship. This application raised the problem of "Who is a Jew?" in Israel in its full modern implications. For the majority, Judge Silberg refused his petition. The judge admitted that Brother Daniel was a Jew according to *halakhah*, but in rendering judgment stated that the Law of Return is not based on *halakhah* but on the Jewish national-historical consciousness and the ordinary secular meaning of the term "Jew" as understood by Jews. After referring to the "great psychological difficulty" facing the court due to the deep sympathy and sense of obligation felt for the petitioner, the spokesman for the majority stated: "I have reached the conclusion that what Brother Daniel is asking us to do is to erase the historical and sanctified significance of the term 'Jew' and to deny all the spiritual values for which our people were killed during various periods in our long dispersion. For us to comply with his request would mean to dim the luster and darken the glory of the martyrs who sanctified the Holy Name [*kiddush ha-Shem] in the Middle Ages to the extent of making them quite unrecognizable; it would make our history lose its unbroken continuity and our people begin counting its days from the emancipation which followed the French Revolution. A sacrifice such as this no one is entitled to ask of us, even one so meritorious as the petitioner before this court" (*ibid.*, 1–2). The court stated that in order to be declared a Jew from the point of view of the modern Jewish secular conception of Jewish nationality, adherence to the Jewish religion is not essential. At the same time apostasy to Christianity removes that person from this nationality.

Between the two wings representing current tendencies in apostasy exemplified by Pasternak and Rufeisen stands the middle-of-the-road attitude displayed by the Anglican bishop of Kingston, Hugh Montefiore. The bishop acknowledges loyalty to the memory of his fathers and maintains contact with Anglo-Jewish society without adhering to his Jewish national identity. He and others like him would seem to continue in an attenuated form the attitude of Disraeli. On the other hand one wonders if in the hostile attitude to Israel of other apostates there is not the direct continuation of the medieval Jew-hating figure of the apostate.

The issues raised by the Rufeisen decision remain very much at the heart of public deliberation in Israel. Essentially the present time marks a return to the core of the historical Jewish position on unity of faith and nation and to consideration of the apostate from this standpoint. Shortly before the expulsion of the Jews from Spain, Isaac b. Moses *Arama wrote that when "one of the gentile scholars, seeing that Jews were very eager for a letter of divorce to be given by an apostate and he refused… asked… 'Why do you want it from him? As he left his religion it would be proper for them to consider him as if he did not exist. Hence his wife should be considered a widow in every respect…' The answer was: 'Apostasy cannot be of the essence but only accidental, meaning only a change of name or the street where he lives. He cannot change his essence, for he is a Jew… This answer is true according to our religion. This is the meaning of the saying of our Sages, 'Even if he has sinned, he remains of Israel'" (*Akedat Yiẓḥak* (Venice, 1573), 258b no. 97, Ki-Teẓe). The Jewish sage adds that the Christian will not accept this definition since for him religion is the sole criterion. Prevailing halakhic opinion throughout the ages has always considered the apostate a Jew for all purposes of obligations, ties, and possibilities given to a Jew, but denying him some specific legal rights, in particular in the economic sphere, and in the performance of certain honorary or symbolic acts. In terms of conscience and consensus of opinion Jewish society regarded the apostate up to the 18th century as "dead," as proscribed from the Jewish community, considering him as the very essence of desertion and treason.

At the present time extreme individualism or mysticism are the main paths leading some people away from Judaism. Snobbery and careerism, missionary blandishments and promises, still play some role in bringing about apostasy, but this is diminishing. The passive attitude of the majority of believing Christians at the time of the Holocaust, and even more, the conception of many of the courageous minority who risked their lives to save Jews but insisted on "saving their souls" at the same time, often souls of children in their care, threw into relief the harsh and ugly implications in apostasy. The concept of a multi-religious Jewish nation now facing the people of the State of Israel is tied up with and intersected by the problems and phenomena of historical continuity, mutual toleration, and social cohesion of the unique concept of the people of Israel as "a kingdom of priests and a holy nation," forming the cohesive religio-national entity that has united Jews and carried their specific message through the ages.

[Haim Hillel Ben-Sasson]

Decrees of Religious Persecution and Forced Conversion in Jewish Communities in the Diaspora

The periods in history when Jewish communities were the victims of decrees of religious persecution and forced conversions engendered a host of halakhic questions concerning the attitude to Jews who had converted and subsequently returned, or wished to return to the Jewish fold. Jews who abandoned Judaism under duress often expressed a desire to return to their communities.

In Rashi's responsum, (*Teshuvot Rashi*, Y. Alphenbein ed. New York, 5703, s. 70), we find evidence that within the framework of excommunication edicts (*herem*) enacted by Rabbi *Gershom ben Judah Me'or ha-Golah in 11th-century Germany, excommunication was decreed for any individual who reminded a repentant apostate of his past. In the same responsum Rashi himself comments:

> Repentance reaches as high as the Throne of Glory, and even the most righteous individuals do not reach the level of those who repent, as it is written: "peace, peace to the far and to the near" (Isaiah 50 7, 19).

Regarding the actual process of the repentance, divergent approaches may be found. The responsa of Rabbenu Asher (*Rosh*) (32, 8; Rabbi Asher ben Yehiel, Germany – France, 13th–14th centuries) reflects a strict approach. The case concerned a group of women forced into apostasy who subsequently escaped and returned to Judaism. Asheri declares that the act of apostasy committed during a period of religious persecution, i.e., at a time when edicts of forced conversion were imposed on Jews, is graver than the act of conversion when there is no such decree, "because it is considered an act committed in public". Accordingly it is insufficient for the offenders to only return to the community. Rather "they require greater remorse, repentance and acceptance of suffering than those who convert in the absence of such a decree".

Rabbi Israel *Isserlein of 15th-century Germany (*Terummat Haddeshen* 8. 198) adopts a more lenient position: He maintains that a penitent apostate should not be burdened with too many acts of penance and mortification, "because the inclination (of a former apostate) to transgress is greater than the inclination of those who commit other sins," and there is concern that he might "shun his repentance".

A question that gave rise to dispute between halakhic authorities was whether a kohen who became an apostate and subsequently repented, retains his sanctified status as a kohen, entitling him to administer the Priestly blessing and be the first to be called up to the Torah. R. Naturnai Gaon (*Otzar ha-Geonim*, Gittin, 327, 328) and R. Achai Gaon (*ibid.*, Sotah, 259) ruled that he cannot bless the community or be first to bless the Torah. On the other hand, Rabbenu Gershom (Resp. Rabbenu Gershom Me'or ha-Golah, 4) ruled that after his repentance his status was equivalent to that of all other priests, and that he was entitled to administer the priestly blessing and be the first to be called up to the Torah as a kohen. In explaining this ruling R.Gershom states that it is forbidden to remind him of his past deeds, namely the period of his apostasy, due to the prohibition of affliction by words (*Ona'at devarim* (see **Ona'ah*). If he is forbidden to bless the community, "these is no greater affliction than this". Another reason given by R.Gershom is the desire to "avoid weakening the penitents' motivation". Following the ruling of R.Gershom, the Ashkenazic authorities also ruled leniently in this context. On the other hand, the Eastern authorities (Sephardic) tended to the stricter view. Hence Maimonides rules against a kohen performing the priestly blessing even after recanting (Yad, Hilkhot Nesi'at Kappaim, 15.3; see Haghaot Maimuniyyot, *ibid*).

With regard to a repentant *kohen*, Rabbi Jacob "Baal Ha-Turim" (Tur, Orah Hayyim 128) questions whether such individual can administer the priestly blessing. However, with regard to being called up to the Torah, he rules unequivocally that such a kohen may be called up first. Rabbi Joseph Karo rules that we may rely on the opinion of those authorities who permit a kohen who left the faith and subsequently repented to administer the priestly blessing, if only in order "to create an opening for those who would repent". Regarding Maimonides' aforementioned ruling prohibiting such a kohen from performing the priestly blessing even after he has repented, Rabbi Karo maintains that the prohibition does not apply to cases in which the apostasy of the kohen in question was coerced (Bet Yosef, *ibid.*; Sh. Ar. OḤ 128, 37).

Support for this position can be found in an epistle written by Maimonides called "the Epistle of Apostasy." This epistle was written at a time when the Muslim rulers of Spain forced Jews to declare the truth of Muhammad's prophecy, under penalty of death.

Apostasy to Islam

Few of the Jews of Arabia embraced *Islam in the time of Muhammad. Among them *ʿAbdallah ibn Salām was the most distinguished. They contributed to the exacerbation of relations between Jews and Muslims. In the next generation ʿAbdallah ibn Saba', from Yemen, a noted partisan of Ali, is reported to have been a Jewish convert. Two other converts, *Kaʿb al-Aḥbār (companion of ʿUmar b. al-Khaṭṭāb) and *Wahb ibn Munabbih, also from Yemen, were considered authorities on Jewish lore. The affinities of Jewish and Islamic tenets and lore, coupled with the fact that there were Jews among the early converts to Islam, gave rise, among Jews, to the cycle of legends on the Jewish teachers of Muhammad, and, among Muslims, to the allegation that Jewish converts plotted to undermine Islam from within by sowing deviations and heresies. Jews in later times were faced with the complex problem of how to treat the converts to Islam, especially if they claimed to cleave to Judaism in secret (cf. opinions of *Maimonides and his father *Maimon, e.g., in *Iggeret ha-Shemad*).

Substantial group conversions of Jews may have taken place in the era of expansion of Islam, especially in Babylonia, but no definite information seems available. Individual and small group conversions, and occasional forced ones, took place throughout the Islamic world over the centuries. It may be assumed that the recurrent promulgation of sumptuary laws and the agitation against non-Muslims (mostly Christians) were accompanied by waves of conversion, as some people sought to escape the effect of persecution and humiliation, and experienced the disintegration of their ancestral loyalites. In Yemen in the 19th and 20th centuries Jewish orphans were often seized to be brought up as Muslims (i.e., in the "natural" religion of man, unobstructed by "misguided" parents). Some converts turned into denunciators and persecutors (see also *disputations). Certain distinguished figures in Islamic society were known to have been Jewish converts or of Jewish extraction (cf. *Ibn Killis, the poet *Ibn Sahl). *Al-Isrāʾīlī* as a name component is a frequent indication of Jewish origin.

The 12th century was marked by a wave of forced conversions in the wake of the Almohad upheaval (1143) in North Africa and Spain. From the other end of the Islamic world the conversion of a distinguished trio was reported: the philosopher Hibat Allah Abu al-Barakāt, the poet Isaac (son of Abraham) ibn Ezra, and the physician-mathematician *Samau'al b. Judah ibn Abbas. In the 17th century the sect of Muslim crypto-Shabbateans developed (see *Doenmeh) when partisans of the pseudo-messiah *Shabbetai Ẓevi followed the leader's example and embraced Islam. In 1839 the Jews of *Meshed (Iran) were forced to convert, with the result that they continued to live as Jews disguised as Muslims. During the *Damascus Affair (1840), terror and torture forced some to convert. Conversions were festive occasions celebrated inside and outside the mosque, especially if the convert happened to be a prominent person. Conversion stories often laid emphasis on divine intervention and visions as motivations.

[Moshe Perlmann]

In Jewish Law

In Jewish religious law, it is technically impossible for a Jew (born to a Jewish mother or properly converted to Judaism) to change his religion. Even though a Jew undergoes the rites of admission to another religious faith and formally renounces the Jewish religion he remains – as far as the *halakhah* is concerned – a Jew, albeit a sinner (Sanh. 44a). According to *Naḥmanides this attitude derives from the fact that the covenant between God and Israel was made "with him that standeth here with us today before the Lord our God and also with him that is not with us here today" (Deut. 29:14; Naḥmanides *ad loc.*). For the born Jew, Judaism is not a matter of choice and for the proselyte it ceases to be one once he has converted. However, persons who did assume another religion or formally renounced Judaism are treated differently by Jewish law from Jews who, even while sinning, have not taken such actions. These people are known in the *halakhah* as *mumar* (from the root meaning "to change"), or *meshummad* (from the root meaning "to persecute or force abandonment of faith"), or *apikoros* ("heretic"), or *kofer* ("denier"), or *poshe'a Yisrael* ("rebellious Jew"). Since in the technical halakhic sense, apostasy is impossible, the above terms are often used very loosely in rabbinic literature.

According to strict *halakhah* an apostate who reverts to Judaism requires no special ritual since technically he never left it. However, there are authorities who require some symbolic act. He is therefore required to confess his sins and repent of them before a collegium of three rabbis and pronounce that henceforth he will keep the laws of Judaism. Some authorities require ritual immersion in a *mikveh* as in the case of proselytes (Isserles to Sh. Ar., YD 268:12). The law is considerably more lenient with regard to the reversion of the Marranos and other *anusim* who were forced to assume another religion against their will or out of fear for their lives, and they are immediately and automatically reaccepted into the community when they express such a desire (Simeon b. Ẓemaḥ Duran, *Tashbeẓ* (Amsterdam, 1738), 15a–b; Maimonides, *Epistle to Yemen*, ed. and tr. by A.S. Halkin, 1952).

MARRIAGE. A marriage, celebrated in accordance with Jewish law between two apostates or an apostate and a Jew, is valid and the parties are husband and wife according to Jewish law (Yev. 30b; Sh. Ar. EH 44:9; *Tashbeẓ, loc. cit.*; see Mixed *Marriage). Hence, neither of them can contract another marriage with a Jew until their said existing marriage is dissolved by divorce, valid under Jewish law, or death (*ibid.*). If their marriage was celebrated according to the tenets of another faith, they are not considered married in Jewish law (even if they live together as husband and wife), and consequently they do not require a divorce. Nor, in this case, is there any room for applying the presumption that a person does not have licentious sexual intercourse which is the usual basis for the assumption that the cohabitation (*bi'ah*) constituted an act of *kiddushin*, since that presumption applies only in circumstances where there is reason to assume that the parties, in cohabiting together, intended a *kiddushin* to come about thereby in accordance with Jewish law, a possibility excluded in this case in view of the apostate's denial of the Jewish faith and his contracting the marriage according to the tenets of another faith (for differing views on this point, see Israel b. Pethahiah Isserlein, *Terumat ha-Deshen*, 1, 64–65, 83–84; Isaac b. Sheshet, Responsa, no. 11; PDR, 7:35, 39–44 as against 54–56).

STATUS. A child born of an apostate mother is a Jew, regardless of the stage at which she became an apostate, and if he marries a Jewess, even if she is an apostate, the marriage is valid (Maim. Yad, Ishut, 4:15).

DIVORCE. Although generally divorce is considered to be to a woman's detriment, since she is deemed to prefer the married state (Yev. 118b), this factor is disregarded when one of the parties is an apostate. Since an apostate wife is suspected as transgressing all the commandments of the Torah, including adultery, she becomes prohibited to her husband (see *Adultery); and, as a married woman, prohibited to any other man. It can therefore be only to her benefit to be released from the bonds of marriage. Similarly, when the husband becomes an apostate: his wife will prefer a divorce to living with an apostate (Isserles, Sh. Ar., EH 140:5; 154:1; Solomon b. Abraham Adret, Responsa, 1162). Hence, even though, generally, a divorce does not take effect until the *get* ("bill of divorcement") has been delivered to the wife personally, or to an agent appointed by her for this purpose, in accordance with the halakhic rule that "one cannot act to a person's disadvantage without his knowledge or consent" (lit., "in his absence"; Yev. 118b), in this case, however, once the *get* reaches the hands of the agent, appointed not by the wife, but by the court or by her husband, it takes immediate effect, on the grounds of the opposite rule that "one may confer a benefit upon a person without his knowledge or consent" (Sh. Ar., EH 140:5; Isserlein, *Terumat ha-Deshen*, 1, 209, 237; (for Levirate Marriage and *Ḥaliẓah* with regard to an apostate – see *Levirate Marriage).

COMPETENCY AS A WITNESS. Jewish law holds the testimony of an apostate to be unreliable, since he disavows the whole of the Torah and is therefore liable to be untruthful, even though he is considered a Jew from the point of view of his personal status. However, in accordance with the regulations which aim at easing the lot of an *agunah ("deserted wife"), who has to establish death of her husband in order to remarry, the *halakhah* provides that the testimony of an apostate is admissable for this purpose provided that he makes the revelant statement in the course of casual conversation (*"mesi'aḥ lefi tummo"*) and not as formal evidence.

INHERITANCE. In strict law, a son is heir to his father by the mere fact of kinship (Num. 27:8; BB 108a and 111a; and Codes) and accordingly his right is retained by the apostate son and for the same reason his father inherits him. However, the apostate having sinned, the court is authorized, if it so sees fit, to penalize him, excluding him from his father's inheritance by way of his portion passing to heirs who have not apostatized on the strength of the rule of *Hefker bet din hefker* (i.e., the court has the power of expropriation) as well as in order to discourage apostasy (Kid. 18a; and Codes; Asher b. Jehiel, *Piskei ha-Rosh* to Kid. 22). A contrary opinion quoted by Solomon b. Abraham *Adret in the name of *Hai Gaon (Responsa 292) has not been adopted by the majority of the *posekim*.

MOURNING RITES. The general opinion of the codifiers is that mourning rites should not be observed at the death of an apostate (Sanh. 6,6; Sh. Ar., YD 345:5) unless, according to some authorities, he met a sudden death in which case it is assumed that he repented (Isserles to Sh. Ar., YD 340; 5; cf. 157 and ḤM 266:2). It was however customary in some circles to observe the mourning rites at the apostasy of a child.

IN THE STATE OF ISRAEL. The foregoing rules are generally followed in the interpretation of laws with reference to the question of determining the legal status of an apostate, unless the context or the purpose of the law requires a different construction. The question of whether the term "Jew" in the "Law of Return, 1950," which entitled "every Jew" to enter Israel as an immigrant, included an apostate, or whether an apostate could be registered as being of Jewish nationality under the "Registration of Inhabitants Ordinance, No. 50 of 5709 – 1949" (replaced by the "Registration of Population Law, 5725 – 1965"), was decided in the negative by a majority opinion of the Supreme Court (sitting as the High Court of Justice, in the abovementioned case of *Rufeisen* (Brother Daniel); High Court Case 72/62, PD 16:2428–55).

Folklore

Legends of apostates abound in Jewish folktales concerning blood libels. Portrayed as a greater enemy to the Jewish people than the Gentile, the apostate is described as the cause of numerous antisemitic persecutions and Jewish communal disasters. In his attempt to prove his worth to the antisemites, he spreads calumnies against the Jews and leads the attacks on them. It was customary to spit three times on the ground when meeting an apostate, and to recite Isaiah 49:17. The figure of the apostate is also ridiculed in many tales which describe his dilemma in the bathhouse where the contrast between the sign of the circumcision and the cross which he wears in the form of a necklace, is revealed. The problem of the apostate's affinity is finally resolved by the decision that he "belongs to the devil." Tales of the repenting apostate, whose conversion to Christianity was originally insincere, are the basis of the Yiddish proverb "A Jew does not abandon his religion."

[Dov Noy]

Bibliography: HISTORY: Graetz, Hist, 6 (1949), index; A.D. Nock, *Conversion* (1933); S.L. Zitron, *Meshumodim*, 2 vols. (1923); S.M. Ginsburg, *Historishe Verk*, vol. 2 *Meshumodim in Tsarishen Rusland* (1946); Baer, Spain, index; H. Heine, *Confessio Judaica* (Ger., 1925); J. de le Roi, in: *Nathanael*, 15 (1899), 65–118 (Ger.); N. Samter, *Judentaufen im neunzehnten Jahrhundert* (1906); P. Browe, *Judenmission im Mittelalter und die Paepste* (1942). APOSTASY TO ISLAM: I.J. Benjamin, *Acht Jahre in Asien und Afrika* (1858), 74f.; I. Goldziher, in: REJ, 43 (1901), 1ff.; Samauʿal al-Maghrībi, *Ifḥam al-Yahūd*, ed. and tr. into Eng. by M. Perlmann (1964), 115f./85f.; *Revista degli Studi Orientali*, 4 (1911–12), 495; W.J. Fischel, in: *Zion*, 1 (1936), 49–74; idem, in: *Commentary*, 7 (1949), 28–33; I. Ben-Zvi, in: *Zion*, 4 (1939), 250–7; Ashtor, Toledot, 1 (1944), 279–91, 303ff.; 309f.; 2 (1951), 88–95; H.Z. Hirschberg, *Yisrael be-Arav* (1946), 142f., 151f., 174, 176; A.S. Halkin, in: *Joshua Starr Memorial Volume* (1953), 101–10; S.D. Goitein, *Jews and Arabs* (1964²), 77–84; Baron, Social, 3 (1957), 76ff., 96, 111f., 122ff., 290ff.; A. Ben-Jacob, *Yehudei Bavel* (1965), index s.v. *Hitaslemut*, D. Corcos, in: Zion, 32 (1967), 137–60. JEWISH LAW: Levi, in: REJ, 38 (1899), 106–11, 114–6; Weinberg, in: *No'am*, 1 (1958), 1–51; Benedikt, *ibid.*, 3 (1960), 241–58; ET, 1 (1962³), 202; 8 (1957), 443–4; 12 (1967), 162–6; B. Schereschewsky, *Dinei Mishpaḥah* (1967²), 80, 229, 333; M. Elon, *Ḥakikah Datit…* (1968), 52–53; idem, in: ILR, 4 (1969), 128ff.; Eisenstein, Dinim, 23, 206ff.; S.B. Freehof, *Reform Responsa* (1960), 192–9; idem, *Recent Reform Responsa* (1963). 120–37. **ADD. BIBLIOGRAPHY:** M. Elon, *Ha-Mishpat ha-Ivri* (1988), 92, 542, 546, 633, 1111, 1405, 1418; idem, *Jewish Law* (1994), 1:103, 2:660, 664, 784, 3:1674, 1690; M. Elon and B. Lifshitz, M. Elon, B. Lifshitz, *Mafteah ha-She'elot ve-ha-Teshuvot shel Ḥakhmei Sefarad u-Ẓefon Afrikah*, 1 (1986), 247–48, and general index, B. Lifshitz, E. Shohetman, *Mafteah ha-She'elot ve-ha-Teshuvot shel Ḥakhmei Ashkenaz, Ẓarefat ve-Italya* (1997), 179–81, and general index; O. Ir-Shay, "*Mumar ke-Yoresh bi-Teshuvot ha-Ge'onim*," in: *Shenaton ha-Mishpat ha-Ivri*, 11–12 (1984–1986), 435–61; T. Regev, "*Ma'amadam shel Kiddushei Mumar bi-Gezerot Tatnu u-be-Gerush Sefarad*," in: *Geranot*, 1 (2001), 97–108; M. Corinaldi, *Dinei Ishim, Mishpaḥah ve-Yerushah – Bein Dat le-Medinah* (2004), 264–70. FOLKLORE: Schwarzbaum, *Studies in Jewish and World Folklore* (1968), 341–2 and index.

APOSTLE (Gr. "messenger"), in early Christian usage, term applied to the disciples of *Jesus whom he had sent out to preach his message, and occasionally also applied to other missionaries of the early period. Outside the New Testament the noun ἀπόστολος was not common in Greek, though the verb ἀποστέλλω was. The term is equivalent to the Hebrew *shali'aḥ* and some scholars have suggested that the early Christian apostolate was indebted to Jewish precedent (e.g., the custom of sending messengers not singly but in pairs). The alleged similarity between John 20:21 ("As my father has sent me, so I send you") and the rabbinic rule (Ber. 5:5) "A person's messenger is as himself" is more apparent than real. The word "apostle" occurs 79 times in the New Testament. While in a few instances its meaning was an actual messenger, it mainly denoted a person of eminent position and capacity. But even in this latter sense, the precise import was not everywhere the same, and some of the ambiguities have led to scholarly differences of opinion. One of these difficulties was due to the fact that occasionally the term apostle was identical with that of disciple (equivalent to the Hebrew *talmid*). In Christian tradition, the immediate followers of Jesus number 12, most probably a symbolic number signifying the 12 tribes of Israel. The Gospels of Mark, Matthew, and John called these immediate followers disciples, but Mark and Matthew often called them apostles, though without any clear differentiation. In Luke, however, there is a clear distinction, attributing to Jesus countless disciples, of whom 12 were designated apostles. Luke, moreover, contains an account (10:1–17), absent from the other Gospels, that Jesus sent out 70 followers to heal the sick and proclaim the kingdom of God; some explained the number 70 as symbolic of the "nations of the world," as in rabbinic sources. Luke, who thus clearly distinguished among disciples, apostles, and the 70, also emphasized the number 12, by his account of the death of Judas. Mark and John were silent about Judas' death; Matthew 27:5 related that he committed suicide by hanging. According to Luke, who wrote both his Gospel and the Acts of the Apostles, Judas died only after the crucifixion through falling head-long and splitting (Acts 1:17–18). In order to replace Judas and make up again the number 12, two out of the countless disciples were nominated and one of these was elected (Acts 1:23–26).

While many New Testament scholars consider the account in Acts as a somewhat tendentious and idealized portrait of the early Church rather than as an exact historical record, it is generally agreed that apostleship in the strict sense implied a special type of authority. This authority derived from the fact that the apostle was a witness to the life and resurrection of Jesus, and in the case of Paul (who did not know Jesus personally) from the inner experience of a direct calling.

The original association of "The Twelve" with the tribes of Israel, is held by some scholars to have had an eschatological significance (cf. Matt. 19:28: "When the son of man shall sit in the throne of his glory, ye also shall sit upon 12 thrones, judging the 12 tribes of Israel," and Rev. 21:12) which seems to be related to the eschatological symbolism of the Qumran sect. But this eschatological dimension is no longer prominent in Acts which was more concerned with describing the early Church as guided, both in its inner affairs and in its outward expansion, by "apostles." The office of apostle did not endure and the term was confined in Christian writings to the early period. No dignitaries of a later period were called apostles.

The Apostolic Age

The period immediately after Jesus was commonly referred to as the Apostolic Age. During that period the question of the admission of Gentiles to the Church (which still was a Jewish sect) and of the binding character of the Law came to a head. For male Gentiles accepting the Christian message, it was especially the problem of circumcision which required an authoritative ruling. To settle the disputes that had arisen on this subject the "apostles and elders" came together in Jerusalem in what is known as the "Apostolic Council." The account of the meeting which discussed the question of the Jewish *mitzvah* is found in Acts 15, where Peter appears as the advocate of the admission of Gentiles. In Galatians, however, Paul represents himself as the advocate of the Gentiles, who is opposed by Cephas – Peter. James, the brother of Jesus, presided over the meeting and also announced its decision, which is known as the Apostolic Decree. The Decree by implication abrogated the *mitzvot* and enacted instead four prohibitions: food offered to idols, blood, things strangled, and fornication. This list of prohibitions is reminiscent of the rabbinic "seven Noachian laws," but scholarly opinion is divided regarding the nature and significance of this similarity. Some New Testament scholars (see James Moffat, *Introduction to the Literature of the New Testament* (1918^3), 307) completely rejected the historicity of the Council and of the Decree. Such a conclusion, if justified, increases the obscurity about the widening breach between Judaism and early Christianity. The traditional Christian conception of priesthood assumes "apostolic succession," an unbroken continuity in the chain of ordination going back to the apostles and through them ultimately to Jesus. (The basic conception was similar to that underlying the juridical and non-sacerdotal Jewish *semikhah.*) Catholic scholars generally affirm the factual historicity of apostolic succession, but Protestants, except some Anglicans, do not.

BIBLIOGRAPHY: Gavin, in: *Anglican Theological Review*, 9 (1927), 250–9; T.W. Manson, *Church's Ministry* (1948); IDB, 1 (1962), s.v. *Apostle and Disciple*; G. Kittel (ed.), *Theological Dictionary of the New Testament*, 1 (1964), 406–46; Vogelstein, in: HUCA, 2 (1925), 99–123; Flusser, in: C.J. Bleeker (ed.), *Initiation* (1965).

[Samuel Sandmel]

APOSTOMOS, person mentioned in the Talmud, of uncertain identification. According to *Ta'anit* 6:6, on 17 Tammuz Apostomos (or Postemus) burned the Torah and set up (*"ve-he'emid"*) an idol in the sanctuary (*"heikhal"*). *"He'emid"* appears to be the preferable reading, not *"hu'amad"* ("was set up"), a variant suggested in the Jerusalem Talmud *Ta'anit* 4:5, 68d, but unknown to the Babylonian Talmud. (See, however, Epstein, Mishnah, 113–4.) The Jerusalem Talmud adds (*ibid.*) that this took place at the pass of Lydda or Tarlosa. Apostomos does not appear elsewhere in rabbinic literature. His identification has been the source of considerable controversy. The main opinions are as follows: (1) Josephus (Wars, 2:230) relates that in about 50 C.E., an unnamed Roman soldier burned a Torah near Beth-Horon and nearly incited a revolt. However, it seems unlikely that a common soldier would have had the authority to set up an idol in the Temple. (2) Hanina b. Teradyon was wrapped in a Torah scroll and burned, probably around 135 (Av. Zar. 18a). His executioner was a "philosophus" (Sif. Deut. 307). But he too is unlikely to have set up an idol in the Temple area. (3) Louis Ginzberg suggests on the basis of *Ta'anit* 28b that Apostomos refers to Antiochus IV Epiphanes, who set up a statue of Zeus Olympus in the Temple in 168 B.C.E. However, no source which describes the acts of Antiochus mentions a burning of the Torah. Moreover, the statue was set up in the month of Kislev, not Tammuz (I Macc. 1:54). (4) Gedaliah Allon identifies Apostomos with the Syrian procurator Posthumius (see *Syria*, 20 (1939), 53–61) and relates these events to the period of Quietus (c. 116–17 C.E.). According to ancient Christian tradition preserved in *Bar-Saliba*, at that time idols were set up in the Temple area. However, there are chronological difficulties here, as Posthumius seems to have ruled c. 102–3. There have been other suggestions, but none is wholly convincing.

BIBLIOGRAPHY: S.J.L. Rapoport, *Erekh Millin*, 1 (1852), 181; Derenbourg, Hist. 1 (1867), 58–59, n. 2; Halberstam, in: REJ, 2 (1881), 127–9; N. Bruell (ed.), in: *Jahrbuecher fuer juedische Geschichte*, 8 (1887), 9n.; Ginzberg, in: JE, 2 (1907), 21–22; A.M. Luncz, in: *Yerushalayim*, 10 (1913), 151ff.; Kohut, Arukh, 1 (1926^2), 222; Jastrow, Dict, 1 (1950), 101; Allon, Toledot, 1 (1958^3), 258, n. 163; Guttmann, Mafte'aḥ, 3, pt. 2 (1930), 30.

[Daniel Sperber]

APOTROPOS ("Guardian").

The Concept

The term *apotropos* (Heb. אַפּוֹטְרוֹפּוֹס) for guardianship in Jewish law is derived from the Greek ἀπότροπος and means the "father" of minors or the "guardian" or "custodian" of another's affairs (see Maimonides to Mishnah, Bik. 1:5; Obadiah of Bertinoro, ad loc., and Git. 5:4). The need for an *apotropos* arises with persons who are unable to take care of their own affairs, such as minors and adults who are mentally defective or absentees (*ibid.*; *Sha'arei Uziel*, 1 (1944), 1, 2). Halakhic sources deal mainly with an *apotropos* charged with responsibility for the property of his ward, thus taking in activities that in modern times would be the function of the administrator of an estate (see *Succession) or executor of a *will, as well as the trusteeship of consecrated property (*ibid.*; PDR, 2:18, 25). In principle, however, there is nothing in the *halakhah* against appointing an *apotropos* also over the person of another (see PDR, 2:177 and 4:97, 108; Resp. Rosh 82:2; *Sha'arei Uziel*, 4, 1 (1944), 126, 173–6). The halakhic justification for the appointment of an *apotropos* over a person who has not expressed an opinion in the matter and is unable to do so owing to his being an absentee or a minor or incompetent, i.e., legally speaking, absent, is based on the principle that "a benefit may be bestowed on a person in his absence," since the function of an *apotropos* is to act solely in the interests of his ward (PDR 2:181).

Guardianship over Minors

THE IDENTITY OF THE GUARDIAN. Some persons have the legal standing of guardians of others, even if not specifically appointed, such as a father with respect to his minor children (Resp. Rosh 87:1; 96:2; Isserles to Sh. Ar., ḤM 285:8; Resp. Maharashdam, ḤM 308; today the father usually is called natural guardian) or a person who undertakes responsibility for the care and welfare of minors who are dependent on him or who are members of his household, including small children and babes-in-arms (Git. 52a and Rashi, *ibid.; Maggid Mishneh* to Maim., Yad, Naḥalot 11:1; Resp. Rosh 87:1; Tur, ḤM 290:31; Sh. Ar., ḤM 290:24; PDR, 2:168–70, 172–3). Minors are boys under the age of 13 or girls under the age of 12 (PDR, 3:154, 156, 159). Guardianship over minors can also be established by an appointment by their fathers (Git., *loc. cit.*; Sh. Ar., ḤM 290:1) or if they have not done so, by the court, by virtue of its authority as the "father of orphans" (Git. 37a; Resp. Rosh 85:5, 6; 87, 1; Sh. Ar., ḤM 290:1–2).

A mother does not have the legal standing of guardian of her children, unless she is specifically appointed or stands in the same relationship toward them as a householder toward orphans formally part of his household, as mentioned above (Sh. Ar., ḤM 290:1, 24; PDR 2:162, 173). The court is also obliged to appoint a guardian over them if their own father, or the guardian appointed by him, is incapable of taking proper care of the minors, or for any other reason that may be in the interests of the minors (BK 37a; Isserles to Sh. Ar., ḤM 285:8; 290:5; PDR 2: 170, 171:4; 108).

Generally speaking, the court, if guided by the interests of the ward as the overriding consideration, is unrestricted in its choice of guardian. Therefore, the court will seek to appoint someone of personal integrity, who is competent in wordly affairs and able to handle the affairs of orphans (BM 70a; Ket. 109b; Tur and Beit Yosef to Tur, ḤM 290:4; Sh. Ar., ḤM, 2, 6). All other factors being equal, a relative of the ward is preferred over a stranger, he being presumed to take care of the minor's affairs better than a stranger (Beit Yosef and Darkhei Moshe 3 to Tur, ḤM 285:13; Isserles to Sh. Ar., ḤM 285:8, *Sha'arei Uziel*, 1 (1944), 108–9; Resp. Maharashdam, ḤM 312). Talmudic law disapproved of entrusting the immovable property of a minor to the stewardship of a relative who was in line to inherit such property, lest at some future time, when it will be forgotten that the property came into his possession in his capacity as guardian only, he claim that it came to him by inheritance (i.e., by virtue of presumptive possession – see *Ḥazakah; BM 39a and Codes; Resp. Ribash 495), but modern systems of land registration, providing for registration of immovable property in the name of the real owner have rendered this fear groundless, and it is no longer considered a bar to the appointment of a relative as guardian (PDR, 2:364, 367–8; *Sha'arei Uziel, ibid.*).

Talmudic law was also opposed to appointing women as guardians, since they were not regarded as being sufficiently competent or experienced in business matters (Git. 52a and Rashi, *ibid.*, ad loc. Resp. Ribash 495; Sh. Ar., ḤM 290:2). However, some of the *posekim* express the opinion that there is no objection to the court appointing a woman who is experienced in business matters and accustomed to going about in public if the best interests of the minor would thereby be served (Baḥ to ḤM 290:3; Resp. Ribash 495; Sh. Ar., ḤM 285:9; *Sha'arei Uziel* 1 (1944), 109–11). All the authorities agree that the father may appoint a woman to serve as the guardian of his children (Sh. Ar., ḤM 290:1), and a woman may also hold the position of guardian, without being specifically appointed thereto, with respect to members of her household dependent upon her (see above) and, if necessary, such a woman may be appointed guardian expressly by the court (Resp. Ribash 495). These provisions apply particularly to a minor's mother (PDR, 2:172, 173, 177; Resp. Maharashdam, ḤM 236).

Two or more persons may be appointed to serve as co-guardians over a minor, or with a division of functions and powers between them, e.g., separate guardians may be appointed over his person and property respectively, as the best interests of the minor may dictate (Resp. Rosh 82:2). Similarly the court may appoint a guardian to serve together with the minor's father, in a case where the latter is considered incapable of fully discharging his duties toward the child (Resp. Rosh, 82:2; PDR, *ibid., Sha'arei Uziel*, 1 (1944), 126). In case of disagreement, the majority opinion may be followed and, when opinions are divided equally, the court will decide the issue (Resp. Maharashdam, ḤM 434). A person must not be appointed guardian except with his own consent (Rashi, Git. 52b; *Maggid Mishneh* to Maim. Yad, Naḥalot 11:5).

POWERS AND FUNCTIONS. The functions of a guardian are generally defined on his appointment, and he is to be guided by the overriding consideration of the best interests of his ward according to the circumstances. When entrusted with guardianship over the person of his ward, he has the duty of directing the latter's upbringing and education, determining his place of abode, and generally taking care of him (Resp. Rosh, 82:2; Resp. Maharashdam, EH 123; PDR, 2:177; 4:108; *Sha'arei Uziel*, 1 (1944), 126, 173–6). Responsibility for the property of the ward entails careful investment thereof by the guardian, i.e., "near to benefit and far from loss," so that the capital be preserved as far as possible and only the dividends used to de-fray the minor's current expenses, including his maintenance (Git., *loc. cit.*; Sh. Ar., ḤM 290:8–11, 13). Since the guardian has authority only to act for the benefit of his ward, he is generally not entitled to represent the latter as a defendant in judicial proceedings, lest the claimant succeed and the debt be recovered from the minor's property. But when it is clear that the creditor is entitled to recover his debt from the property of the minor – e.g., when the testator had admitted such indebtedness, or if delaying legal proceedings until such time as the latter attains majority would be to his detriment, e.g., in the case of an interest-bearing debt or when the creditor is prepared to waive part of his rights if he will not have to wait with his claim until the minor's majority or in any other case where it is clearly to the benefit of the minor to be represented, as defendant in the proceedings, the guardian will have authority to represent him (Git. 52a and Rashi, ad loc.; Ar. 22a–b; Maim. Yad, Naḥalot 11:7; Malveh ve-Loveh 11:7; Sh. Ar., ḤM 110; 290:12, *Sha'arei Uziel*, 1 (1944), 182–6; PDR, 3:155, 160).

All guardians, including those who have the legal standing of guardians (see above) and including the father of a minor, are subject to supervision by the court (Git. 52a and Codes; *Sha'arei Uziel*, 1:170; PDR, 2:170–1), and the court may set aside any step taken by the guardian as not being in the best interests of his ward and therefore in excess of his powers (PDR, 2:181). In this event the guardian may be held personally liable for any damage suffered by his ward as a result of his actions (BK 39a and Tos. thereto; and Codes), a threat he may avert only by seeking the prior approval of the court to his proposed course of action (Tosef., BB 8:4; Nov. Rashba to Git. 52a; Isserles to Sh. Ar., ḤM 290:13; PDR, 2:180). At any rate, he has to obtain such approval when dealing with the minor's immovable property (Sh. Ar. and PDR, *ibid.*), or making gifts from the latter's property, or waiving any of his rights (Sh. Ar., ḤM 235:26), including also the effecting of any *compromise on his behalf (Isserles to ḤM 110:11).

Guardians are not entitled to any remuneration for their services unless specifically provided for in advance, such services being considered as the fulfillment of a religious duty (*mitzvah*) and therefore presumed to have been undertaken as a *mitzvah* and not for reward (PDR, 5:87–88). No act performed during the subsistence of the guardianship and affecting the rights of a minor is of any legal validity unless undertaken by, or with the approval of, his guardian (Ket. 70a, and Codes).

TERMINATION OF GUARDIANSHIP. A guardianship terminates automatically when the ward attains his majority, since guardians are generally appointed only over minors (BM 39a; Maim. Yad, Naḥalot, 10:8; Sh. Ar., ḤM 290:1, 26). If, however, the father has specifically appointed a guardian over his adult children, guardianship over them will come into force, but will terminate upon their demand (PDR, 3:154, 156–60). The guardian's appointment may also be terminated by his removal from office by the court, a step which will only be taken when deemed in the interests of the minor, e.g., if the guardian has dealt prejudicially with the property of his ward or if his conduct – even in regard to the handling of his own affairs – casts doubt on his personal integrity (Git. 52b, and Codes; PDR, 1:353, 359). It is pursuant to this power that the court may order the removal of a minor from his parents' house and appoint a guardian over his person or property (Beit Yosef to ḤM 290:6; Isserles to Sh. Ar., ḤM 285:8; Resp. Maharashdam, EH 123; PDR, 1:170, 171).

A guardianship may also be terminated on the strength of an application to the court by the guardian asking to be relieved of his appointment, since he cannot be compelled to serve against his will (Beit Yosef, to Tur, ḤM 290:22). But explicit discharge by the court is required, for once undertaken the task of a guardian cannot be abandoned unilaterally (Tosef., BB 8:3; Sh. Ar., ḤM 290:23). The court will not release the guardian from his duties until it has appointed another in his place, so as not to leave the minor or his property without supervision.

Upon the termination of his appointment, the guardian is required to hand over to his successor all the minor's property, to submit a report of his activities and, on the minor's demand, he will also have to take an oath that he has not retained any of the minor's assets (Git. 52a; Beit Yosef, ḤM 290:22–23; Baḥ, *ibid.*, 23 *Sha'arei Uziel*, 1:192–5). When the termination arises because the ward attains majority, he is entitled – even if he is a prodigal – to take possession of his property, unless there is an express instruction to the contrary from his father or the testator (BM 39a; Sh. Ar., ḤM 290:26). Being a prodigal is not sufficient reason for subjecting him to guardianship (Resp. Ribash 20); only if his conduct stems from mental illness will a guardian be appointed over him (see above).

Guardianship over Adults

The court will appoint a guardian over an idiot who, because he is mentally defective or suffering from mental illness, is unable to manage his own affairs, a rule applying also to a *deaf-mute. To such a guardianship apply, generally, the laws of guardianship in respect to minors (Ket. 48a; Maim. Yad, Mekhirah, 29:4; Naḥalot, 10:8; Sh. Ar., ḤM 235:20; Isserles to ḤM 285:2; 290:27). Inability to take care of one's own affairs is also the basis for the court's authority to appoint a guardian (or custodian) over the property of an absentee person, i.e., one who has left his place of residence and whose whereabouts are unknown, if the court deem the appointment necessary for the preservation of his property (BM 39a–b; Maim. Yad, Naḥalot 7:4–10; Tur, Beit Josef and Baḥ, ḤM 285; Sh. Ar., *ibid.; Sha'arei Uziel*, 1:13–23). In this case, unlike that of a minor, the court is not obliged to concern itself with seeking a suitable candidate for the appointment, but has authority to appoint the applicant's nominee, if suitable, as the appointment of a guardian over an adult of full capacity is not in fulfillment of a *mitzvah* (*Maggid Mishneh* to Maim. Yad, Naḥalot 7:5; Isserles to Sh. Ar., ḤM 285:2). However, the court will not appoint a guardian over the assets of an absentee unless his absence is due to duress – e.g., if he is forced to abandon his assets while fleeing for his life. Therefore, a guardian will not be appointed over property voluntarily left, without supervision by its owner – since, had he wanted it, he could have made the appointment himself – except in respect of property which came to him after his departure and without his knowledge, e.g., by way of inheritance (BM 38a–b, 39a–b; Maim. Yad, Naḥalot, 7:4–8; Sh. Ar., ḤM 285:1–4 and Isserles, ad loc., 4; *Sha'arei Uziel*, 1, 13–23).

In the State of Israel, guardianship is mainly governed by the following laws: The Women's Equal Rights Law, 1951; The Capacity and Guardianship Law, 1962; The Administrator General Ordinance, No. 37 of 1944 (as amended); and The Succession Law, 1965. The first of the abovementioned laws (sec. 3) provides that "both parents are the natural guardians of their children; where one parent dies, the other shall be the natural guardian" and further, in conformity with Jewish law, that the said provision does not affect the inherent power of the competent court to "deal with matters of guardianship over the persons or property of children with the interest of the children as the paramount consideration." In the absence of any express provision to the contrary in any of the abovementioned laws, halakhic law is applied.

[Ben-Zion (Benno) Schereschewsky]

The subject of guardianship has been discussed in scholarship as well as in recent rulings of the rabbinic and civil courts in Israel, both substantively and in terms of its connection to the legal system as a whole.

The Explanatory Note to the Capacity and Guardianship draft law (Bill No. 5721–1961, p. 178) emphasized the similarity between the Capacity and Guardianship Law and Jewish Law, stating that: "In substance, its proposals are largely in accordance with Jewish legal rules." In the Knesset debate over the Bill, Justice Minister Pinḥas Rosen explained "the duty and right to care for the needs of minors" (§15 of the Law) as follows:

> From the point of view of the law, the essence of parenthood is the obligation to care for the children. As a practical matter, the parent-child relationship is primarily one that imposes obligations on the parents. This rule has been developed in a long line of Israeli court decisions, and is based upon the principles of Jewish Law.

Among the relevant sources of Jewish Law, the Justice Minister cited inter alia the talmudic passage (Kid. 29a, Rashi *ad loc.*) that enumerates the father's duties towards his son.

Section 67 of the Law provides that: "Where a person acts as a guardian, his duties and liabilities towards the ward shall be in accordance with the provisions of this chapter, even if he was not appointed or there was a defect in his appointment, or he has resigned or been dismissed or his guardianship has expired." In explaining this principle, the minister of justice cited the provision (Sh. Ar., ḤM 290:24) stating that a householder who supports minor orphans at their request is bound to comply in all respects with the legal obligations incident to guardianship.

The law is also based on Jewish Law with respect to the institutions set up in order to deal with guardianship. The law authorized the courts to be assisted by the administrator general in discharging their supervisory role. As the minister of justice observed, this kind of office – the administrator general – is a well-known and venerable institution in Jewish Law and was given the sentimental title of "father of orphans." This role has its source in the regulation enacted by the Council of Lithuania in 1623 (*Pinkas ha-Medinah bi-Medinat Lita* (1925) 9, Enactment §37).

Scholarly literature also cites another institution which is regarded as a kind of guardianship – that of the trustee in public law. In a responsa concerning the prerogatives of the communal leaders to perform legal actions with respect to property, Rashba (*Teshuvot* I, §617) wrote: "The seven good citizens who are frequently mentioned are not seven people who excel in wisdom, wealth, or honor, but seven people chosen by the people and authorized to be administrators of the affairs of the town in general, who act as trustees for their brethren in their locality" (see also *ibid.* III, §443).

Regarding the guardian's right to file an action in the ward's name, as discussed above, the rabbinical court ruled that a father whose divorced wife exploited monies earmarked for the benefit of their daughters (who were in her custody) in a manner that violated their agreement was entitled to sue the wife in the name of the daughters, by virtue of his standing as their natural guardian (PDR 17:260, 289).

In Israel Supreme Court Case Law

The provisions of Jewish Law regarding guardianship were the source of the Israel Supreme Court's ruling in *Moberman* (CA 604/77 *Moberman v. Segal*, 32 (3) PD 83). The Court was required to rule on the validity of an agreement concluded between an executor and a person designated as a beneficiary of the estate. The substance of the agreement involved the beneficiary's waiver of her rights under the will in return for a fixed monthly payment by the executor. The Court found a number of legal defects that tainted the agreement, such as the suspicion of undue influence having been exercised by the executor, which preceded the beneficiary's signing the agreement. Nonetheless, the Supreme Court (Justice Menachem Elon) did not regard this as the only grounds for invalidating the agreement. Under Jewish Law, any act or transaction involving estate assets but performed by the executor for his own personal needs requires the Court's approval prior to its completion. If the executor fails to attain advance judicial approval for the act, then "at least after the agreement was concluded, an examination must be conducted in order to ascertain the reasonability and fairness of the transaction from the perspective of the estate and its beneficiaries" (*ibid.* 97).

The judgment cites various views in Jewish Law regarding the question of whether a guardian can perform a transaction in the estate for his own personal gain. The view of

Rabad (southern France, 12th century), cited in the *Tur* (ḤM 290:15), is that "just as the guardian is permitted to deposit the monies [of the estate] in the hands of a trustee for business purposes, he is also permitted to take them for his own business purposes and take the profit that the other person would have taken, provided however that he gave notice to that effect to the court."

However, the *Tur* (14th century) had reservations regarding this view, stating: "I think it inappropriate for him to take them [the monies] for business purposes, because it may lead to tale-bearing" (*ibid*).

Rabad's opinion was endorsed by the majority of the halakhic authorities (see *ibid.* 99). In his opinion, Justice Elon quotes the comments of R. Joseph *Caro (Spain, 16th century) in *Bet Yosef*, related to the aforementioned view of the *Tur*: "As to the opinion of our Teacher of blessed memory that it is inappropriate for him to take them [the monies] for business purposes because it may lead to tale-bearing, this fear has no basis, inasmuch as he informed the court accordingly." Justice Elon went on to cite R. Moses *Isserles (Rema; Poland, 16th century – Sh. Ar., ḤM 290:8).

Concluding its discussion of Jewish Law, the Court stated:

> From all of the above it follows that, according to the [*Tur*] it is forbidden for the executor to personally conclude any transaction with the estate assets, even if he informed the court. This, despite the fact that the court's approval of the case would obviate the suspicion that the estate's interest would be prejudiced due to a possible conflict of interests on the executor's part. Nonetheless, the situation may still give rise to "tale-bearing," and as such "it is inappropriate." But according to the majority of authorities, among them R. Joseph Caro and the Rema [whose combined rulings comprise the *Shulḥan Arukh*] this suspicion is too remote to warrant consideration, and if the court approved the transaction concluded by the executor with the estate assets, even if for his own purposes, then he is permitted to do so (*ibid.*).

Relying on the above, Justice Elon ruled that the validity of the transaction between the executor and the estate under his management is contingent upon the court's prior approval. In the absence of such approval, the transaction is subject to the court's judicial review, which requires the court to "examine the nature and the essence of the transaction from the perspective of the respondent's best interests" (*ibid.*, 101).

It is interesting to note some other comments made in the judgment (*ibid.*, 97) regarding the interpretation of the law in accordance with Jewish Law: "I find support for this in the laws of estate management set out in the Jewish law. Section 150 of the Palestine Order in Council (the British Mandate legislation that predated Israeli Law) declared that, when there was no conflicting provision in the law itself, the Succession Law should be interpreted first and foremost in accordance with the sources of Jewish Law, thereby establishing its independence from §46 of the aforementioned Order in Council." Indeed, this was also the position of the authors of the Bill, who attested that the Bill was based inter alia "on Jewish Law, which is one of the central assets of our national culture, and we should renew it and continue it… We regard Jewish Law as being the main, but not the only or binding source … regarding the substance of the rules, we attempted wherever possible to anchor our proposal in Jewish Law" (from the introduction to the Explanatory Note to the Bill of the Succession Law, Ministry of Justice, Tammuz 5712 – 1952, 6–7).

Another case in which the Supreme Court ruled in accordance with the guardianship rules of Jewish Law was the *Nagar* case (ST 1/81 *Nagar v. Nagar,* 38 (1) PD 365). Sitting as a Special Tribunal, the Supreme Court was required to decide a question of jurisdiction involving the respective powers of the civil court, on the one hand, and the rabbinical court, on the other, which has jurisdiction in matters of personal status, including guardianship (when both parties gave their consent). The civil court ruled that issue of determination of the minors' education, being disputed by the divorced couple, is within its exclusive jurisdiction. Accordingly, it nullified the ruling of the rabbinical court on this matter, notwithstanding the agreement between the parties, which conferred jurisdiction to the rabbinical court. The civil court relied on the argument that "In fact, *halakhah* does not recognize the institution of guardianship in matters concerning minors, within the meaning of the Legal Capacity and Guardianship Law. Guardianship under Jewish Law exists exclusively with respect to assets, and in relation to a fatherless orphan, and in an exceptional case when the father is alive but caused a depreciation of the minor's assets." Relying on this assumption, the District Court concluded that "in our case the rabbinical court did not adjudicate the question of education as a derivative of guardianship, but rather as a parental right – the father's right under the *halakhah* to fulfill the commandment of teaching Torah" (390–391 of judgment). As such, the matter does not fall within the jurisdiction of the rabbinical court.

The Supreme Court (Justice Elon) clarified that the concept of guardianship in Jewish jurisprudence is a general one, which encompasses both guardianship by appointment and natural guardianship, by virtue of parenthood:

> The central principle in Jewish Law governing the laws of guardianship of children – of any child – derives from the basic rule that the court is the father of all orphans (Git. 37a; BK, 37a). This rule applies to every minor and child, and not just to orphans (*Teshuvot*, Radbaz, §§263, 360; *Sha'arei Uziel*, 1: §§4, 126). Both the parents and any person appointed as guardian of the children serve as quasi-representatives of the court, by virtue of its authority, and in accordance with its instructions, both in concern for the child's health and welfare, in the protection of his property and assets, all in accordance with the meta-principle of the child's best interests. A similar summary of these aspects is provided in the work of the late chief rabbi, and president of the Rabbinical Court, Rabbi Ben-Zion *Ouziel, (*Sha'arei Uziel*, pt. 1):
>
> This is the basis and purpose of guardianship in Israel, which is conferred to the judges of Israel and their courts. The guardianship of the court is the source of the guardianship of

the parents … and they are obligated to guarantee the well-being of their children after them, both in body and in soul, in wisdom and education, and their education in the commandments and decency and the fear of God … (*ibid.*, p. 8) [ibid., pp. 396–97

The court further added that, in Jewish Law, guardianship is not limited to the duty of preserving the minor's assets, but includes the duty to raise and educate him:

> This guardianship too [guardianship of an appointee even if not a parent] in Jewish law, is applicable both with respect to preserving the minor's assets and property and with respect to his education and studies … Its features are expounded upon in talmudic literature (Tosef., Zukermandel: *Terumot* 1:10; BB 8:14; Git. 52a), and the *halakhah* was determined accordingly – that the guardians must "provide the minors with a *lulav* and *sukkah*, *ẓiẓit*, *shofar*, Torah scroll, *tefillin* and *mezuzot* … they are appointed over them in order to educate them" (Maim. Yad, Nahalot, 11:9). This ruling was reaffirmed in the *Shulḥan Arukh* (ḤM 290:15) – again, based on the consideration of "educating them," and I will not elaborate this point here. Summing up, I will quote a passage from the *Talmudic Encyclopedia* (s.v. "Ḥinukh"[Education], Vol. 16, 166f.): "A guardian appointed over minor children is obligated to educate them … it is incumbent upon the educator to educate them in the commandments, for he replaces the father." This matter is quite clear, requiring no further explanation, and as noted by R. Jehiel Michal *Epstein (*Arukh ha-Shulḥan*, ḤM 290:30), "who will educate them if not the guardian?" (*ibid.*).

In view of all the above, the Supreme Court ruled that the duty of education imposed on the parents pursuant to section 15 of the Capacity and Guardianship Law 5722–1962, is the same duty that Jewish law imposes on the parents as guardians. This being the case, when the rabbinical court adjudicates the parents' duty of education *vis-à-vis* their children, it does so within the framework of the aforementioned law, and the matter is within its jurisdiction.

It should be noted that the term *apotropos* was occasionally used in the responsa literature as an appellation for a person who had undertaken to plead in the name of the person he was representing – now known as a "lawyer" (*Resp. Mahar"h Or Zarua*, §222; M. Elon, *Ha-Mishpat ha-Ivri*, 616–20).

[Menachem Elon (2nd ed.)]

BIBLIOGRAPHY: Bloch *Vormundschaft nach mosaisch-talmudischem Recht* (1904); M. Cohn, in: *Zeitschrift fuer vergleichende Rechtswissenschaft*, 37 (1920), 435–45; Gulak, Yesodei, 3 (1922), 106, 146–54; Gulak, Ozar, 140–148; Assaf, in: *Hamishpat ha-Ivri*, 2 (1926–7), 75–81; ET 2 (1949), 121–129; 3 (1951) 35–36, s.v. *Bore'ah*; M. Silberg, *Ha-Ma'amad ha-ishi be-Yisrael* (1964), index and *Milu'im ve-Hashlamot* (1967); B. Sharshewsky, *Dinei Mishpaha* (1967), 403–25; M. Elon, in: ILR, 4 (1969), 121–127; Baker, *Legal System of Israel* (1968), index, s.v. "Guardianship." **ADD. BIBLIOGRAPHY:** M. Elon, *Ha-Mishpat ha-Ivri* (1988), I. 588–89, 617–18; III. 1395–1402; idem, *Jewish Law* (1994), II. 727–729, 763–764; III. 1663–167); A. Shaki, *"Iyyun Meḥudash be-Tivah shel Zekhut ha-Horim le-Mishmoret Yaldeihem ha-Ketinim,"* in: *Iyyunei Mishpat*, 9 (1983–84), 59; Y.Z. Gilat, *Dinei Mishpaḥah* (2000), 301–439; M. Elon and B. Lifshitz, *Mafte'aḥ ha She'elot ve-ha-Teshuvot shel Ḥakhmei Sefarad u-Ẓefon Afrikah*, in: *Legal Digest*, 1 (1986), 16–20; B. Lifshitz and E. Shochman, *Mafte'aḥ ha She'elot ve-ha-Teshuvot shel Ḥakhmei Ashkenaz, Ẓarefat ve-Italyah*, in: *Legal Digest* (1997), 14–19.

APPEAL.

The Problem of the Appeal in Jewish Law

Most modern legal systems comprise a number of judicial forums, organized hierarchically. A litigant dissatisfied with a decision in a lower forum thus has the right to appeal that decision in a higher judicial instance, in the hope that the decision will be altered in his favor. This right of appeal stems from the presumption that the lower forum may conceivably have erred in its ruling, and the aspiration for true justice requires that the litigant be given an additional opportunity to have his claims heard.

On the other hand, in Jewish law the existence of an appellate tribunal is by no means self-evident. Admittedly, according to Jewish law a *bet din* that has erred is duty bound to reexamine its decision and correct it (Sh. Ar. ḤM 25.1–2), and the litigant is entitled to return to the *bet din* after receiving its decision and to attempt to convince it that a mistake was made (Sh. Ar. ḤM 20.1). However, this is clearly not a satisfactory solution. In numerous cases the *bet din* is not convinced that its decision was mistaken. In such cases the litigant will ascribe its position, rightly or wrongly, to the stubbornness of the *dayyanim* who were unwilling to amend their ruling.

It has been claimed that the Sanhedrin itself was a quasi instance of appeal. However, it is highly doubtful whether this claim is substantiated by talmudic sources. An examination of classical halakhic literature indicates that it was indeed possible to submit a ruling for the review of a second *bet din*, but the *bet din* concerned was not officially constituted for the purpose of adjudicating appeals; rather, it was a regular *bet din* whose *dayyanin* were reputed to be of greater expertise than those of the first *bet din*. This law has its source in the Talmud (Sanhedrin 31b), where such a forum was known as the *Bet Va'ad* ("Place of Assembly") or the *Bet Din ha-Gadol* ("High Court"), and it was codified in the Shulḥan Arukh (ḤM 14.1). However, there are *posekim* who ruled that this law does not empower the second *bet din* to reverse or change the original ruling, but merely to express its opinion on its correctness. The power to reverse a ruling resides exclusively with the original *bet din* (for sources, see E. Shochetman, *Seder ha-Din*, 446). Moreover, some of the *posekim* stated that the institution defined as *bet din gadol* does not exist in our times (see Rema, ad loc). According to this view, there is no possibility of review by another court, even if not under the rubric of an appeal.

Instances of Appellate Review in the Past

It would therefore appear that the only means of establishing a permanent institution charged with appellate review of the rulings of other rabbinical courts (*batei din*) is by way of a *takkanah* (see entry on **Takkanah*). Indeed, when the Rabbinical Court of Appeals in Jerusalem was constituted, a controversy ensued regarding the need and /or justification for such an institution (to be discussed below). In this context, R. Simḥa Assaf attempted to prove that appellate tribunals had operated in the past in a number of different times and places and that, "Not only did the Torah scholars of those times not see any prohibition in the matter, but they actually affirmed the regulations pertaining to the procedures for filing the appeal" (Assaf, *Battei Din*, 74–75). However, some of these proofs have been challenged (see Katz, *Masoret u-Mashber*, (Jerusalem, 1964) p. 160, n. 23. As stated, the accepted view in halakhic literature of recent generations is that there is no room for a forum of appeal, and the precedents adduced by R. Assaf did not persuade many of the opponents of such an institution.

Appellate Tribunals in the 20th Century

The establishment of appellate tribunals during the 20th century came about as the result of extrinsic circumstances, such as competition with external judicial institutions, particularly those of foreign governments. In Morocco, a rabbinical appellate court was established in 1918 as a result of the French government's attempt to regulate the functioning of the Jewish rabbinical courts (see M. Amar et al, *Ha-Mishpat ha-Ivri be-Kehillot Morocco* (Jerusalem, 1986), 208, 452). However, the most prominent and influential appellate tribunal with respect to Jewish Law is the Rabbinical Court of Appeals of the Chief Rabbinate, established in Jerusalem in 1921. The establishment of such a tribunal was accompanied by stormy controversy among a number of rabbis in Israel and abroad, the main claim of its opponents being that such an institution was an innovation which contradicted traditional *halakhah*, and as such should be opposed.

Undoubtedly, the Rabbinical Court of Appeals would not have been established had the British rulers not demanded its establishment as a precondition for conferral of jurisdiction to the rabbinical courts in matters of personal status. There were in fact some rabbis who contended that the rule against establishing such an institution was so severe that it justified the waiver of jurisdiction altogether. On the other hand, the founder of the Chief Rabbinate, Rav Kook, chose to accede to the requirement. In his inaugural speech for the Chief Rabbinate he stated that the new tribunal could be established by way of a special enactment of the Torah authorities. Over the years a number of additional justifications were given for the authority of the Rabbinical High Court to hear appeals (see the remarks of Rav Avraham Shapira, 10 *PDR*, 180; Rav Avraham Sherman, "*Mekor ha-Samkhut shel Bet ha-Din ha-Gadol u-Misgeret Samkhuto*," in: 3 *Shurat ha-Din* (1995), 211–220).

Nevertheless, to this day there are *dayyanim* who refuse, for halakhic reasons, to endorse the existence of the Rabbinical Court of Appeals, and by extension see no need to comply with its rulings, so long as they remain convinced that there was no error made in their original ruling. This manner of conduct led in turn to a number of petitions to the High Court of Justice against the "rebellious" rabbinical courts that refused to comply with rulings of the Rabbinical Court of Appeals. The High Court of Justice ruled that, under Israeli law, the Rabbinical court system is a hierarchy in which the regional rabbinical courts are subordinate to the rulings of the Rabbinical Court of Appeals addressed to it (for a survey of these rulings, see Elon, *Jewish Law*, 4:1809–1818).

The establishment of a new appellate tribunal necessitated the creation of procedures regarding the manner of filing an appeal and the procedures for its hearing. To date, there have been three versions of the Rabbinical Courts Procedural Regulations (from the years 1953, 1960, 1993). These regulations and related rulings are discussed at length in *Sidrei ha-Din* (Shochetman, 450–470). It should be emphasized that the establishment of an appellate tribunal produced another innovation in the world of Jewish Law – namely the obligation for the *dayyan* to present the reasons for his judgment in writing, since it is clear that appellate review by another *bet din* is impossible without examining the reasons given by the former instance for its judgment (this practice is already found in the "Place of Assembly" discussed above). A system that confers the litigant a right of appeal against a judgment must also obligate its judges to record the reasons for their judgments. Nevertheless, here too there were *dayanim* who refrained from writing reasoned judgments

BIBLIOGRAPHY: M. Elon, *ha-Mishpat ha-Ivri* (1988), 667–669, 1521–1528; idem, *Jewish Law* (1994), 824–826, 1809–1818; S. Assaf, *Battei Din ve-Sidreihem aḥarei Ḥatimat ha-Talmud* (1924), 74–85; J.D. Bleich, "The Appeal Process in the Jewish Legal System," in:*Tradition*, 28:1 (1993), 94–112; A. Morgenstern, *Ha-Rabbanut ha-Rashit le-Ereẓ Yisrael – Yissudah ve-Irgunah* (1973), 75–76; A. Radzyner, "*Rav Ouziel, Rabbanut Tel-Aviv Yaffo, u-Bet Din ha-Gadol le-Irurim – Sippur be-Arba Ma'arkhot*," in: *Bar-Ilan Studies of Law*, 21 (2004), 129–243; A. Shochetman, "*Ḥovat ha-Hanmaka ba-Mishpat ha-Ivri*," in: *Shenaton ha-Mishpat ha-Ivri*, 6–7 (1979–1980), 319–397; idem, *Sidrei ha-Din* (1988); idem, "*Bet Din ha-Gadol le-Irurim –Ma'amado ve-Samkhuyotav*," in: *Kovez ha-Ẓiyyonut ha-Datit*, 4 (2002), 534–48; Z. Warhaftig, "*Ha-Takdim ba-Mishpat ha-Ivri*," in: *Shenaton ha-Mishpat ha-Ivri*, 6–7 (1979–1980), 105–32.

[Amichai Radzyner 2nd ed.]

APPEL, JUDAH LEIB (1857–1934), one of the first active members of the Ḥovevei Zion movement in Vilna. Appel, who was born in Viekšniai, Lithuania, served as secretary of the Ḥovevei Zion branch in Vilna for almost 25 years. He was also secretary of the *Benei Moshe chapter there. In 1902 Appel and Shealtiel *Graeber established a publishing house which published Zionist periodicals and propaganda literature. In 1921 he went to Palestine and became secretary to Isaac Leib *Goldberg and manager of his estate in Hartuv. Almost all of Appel's valuable archives on Zionism were burned during the 1929 riots. Appel's memoirs of various periods in the history of Ḥibbat Zion and of Zionism in Russia were published in his book, *Be-Tokh Reshit ha-Teḥiyyah* ("In the Beginning of the Rebirth," 1936).

BIBLIOGRAPHY: I. Broides, *Vilna ha-Ẓiyyonit ve-Askaneha* (1939), index; I. Klausner, *Ha-Tenu'ah le-Ẓiyyon be-Rusyah*, 1 (1962), index.

[Yehuda Slutsky]

APPELBAUM (Appelboym, Apfelboym, Applebaum), MOSHE (Maurycy; 1887–1931), painter, graphic artist, and stage designer. Appelbaum was born in Mszsonow in the Warsaw province of Poland and received a traditional Jewish education. His artistic gift manifested itself already in his early childhood. Seeing no way to fulfill his artistic ambitions in a traditional Jewish environment, Appelbaum ran away from home at the age of 15 and found a job in Kalish as an apprentice to a house painter who made signboards. At the same time, he underwent a process of self-education. Soon his work was in greater demand than his employer's. In 1903, he got a job at a local textile mill as a pattern designer. In 1905, he came to Vienna and was admitted to the Academy of Art. However, he had to interrupt his studies due to lack of livelihood. For over a year, he traveled around Germany and Holland on foot. In 1907, he arrived in England and was admitted to an art school in Liverpool, where he studied for two years. In 1910–16, he attended, off and on, the London Academy of Arts. At the end of 1918, his first solo exhibition was on display in London, which brought him recognition. Despite promising prospects of an artistic career in England, he returned to Poland in 1919. Settling in Warsaw, he became very active in Jewish artistic life. He was among the initiators of the Jewish Society for the Encouragement of Artists founded in 1921 and a permanent member of its exhibition committee. He collaborated with Yiddish theaters, among them the Warshawer Yiddisher Kamer-Teater (WIKT), where he designed the settings for several productions staged by Zygmunt Turkow, a leading Jewish theatrical director. Appelbaum was one of the pioneers of the new stage design for the Jewish modernist theater in Poland, into which he incorporated elements of constructivism and expressionism. In the mid-1920s, he produced wall paintings for the synagogue prayer halls in Lomzha and Bedzin (the latter in collaboration with the artists Ḥayyim Hanft and Samuel Tzigler) and executed murals for the assembly hall in the building of the Union of Jewish Writers and Artists in Warsaw. He participated in many European and All-Poland art exhibitions. In the late 1920s, his solo exhibitions were on display in Warsaw, Łodz, Lvov, and Germany. Appelbaum was active in almost every genre (landscape, still life, portrait, etc.), mainly preferring to treat scenes of the Polish-Jewish *shtetl*. His manner features elements of cubism and expressionism and grotesque imagery of characters. In his monumental paintings, especially the synagogue murals, Appelbaum widely used motifs of traditional Jewish art. In the late 1920s, in an attempt to improve his difficult financial situation, he moved to Katowice with his family, where he died of tuberculosis.

BIBLIOGRAPHY: C. Aronson, "Oysshtelung fun Moshe Apelboym," in: *Illustrierte Voch* (Warsaw), 38, 40 (1914), 22–28; O. Schneid, "Mojżesz Applebaum," in: *Miesięcznik Żydowski* (Warsaw), 3 (Feb. 1931), 263–65; Y. Sande, *Yidishe Motiven fun der Foiisher Kunst* (1954), 245–55; J. Malinowski, *Malarstwo i rzeźba Żydow Polskich w XIX i XX wieku* (2000), 369–70.

[Hillel Krakovsky (2nd ed.)]

APPELFELD, AHARON (1932–), Hebrew writer. Appelfeld was born in the province of Bukovina, Romania, to a semi-assimilated Jewish family. In 1941, Germans, accompanied by Romanians, began the destruction of the Jews of Bukovina, killing Appelfeld's mother and grandmother and deporting Appelfeld to a concentration camp. He escaped and roamed through the Ukrainian countryside for years. In 1944, the Russian Army entered the Ukraine and Appelfeld joined them as a kitchen helper, immigrating to Israel after the war. A graduate of the Hebrew University of Jerusalem, Appelfeld served as professor emeritus of Hebrew literature at Ben Gurion University of the Negev. While best known as a prolific novelist, his essays have been published in the *New York Times*, the *New Yorker*, and elsewhere.

At the core of Appelfeld's highly-stylized narratives is the probing of the psyche of characters in a pre- and post-Shoah world. His tales frequently depict fragmented, torn, and sometimes mute people in a state of quest. In his earlier tales, Appelfeld consciously suspended any historical framework, raising his work to a mythic, timeless level while only depicting the Shoah directly in his later works. Throughout, Appelfeld is fascinated by the notion of the Jewish tribe and its various manifestations – Orthodox and converted and particularly the assimilated Jews of Central Europe. Appelfeld's fiction frequently has an autobiographical tone. In *Tzili* (1983), he tells the story of a young girl who like himself spends years in the forest separated from her family while fleeing the enemy. Eventually, like Appelfeld, she joins the hordes of refugees in their journey towards safety. Appelfeld's characters are constantly on the move. Movement is the essence of their being. They are rootless and in a constant quest to repair and to heal. In doing so, Appelfeld has expanded the archetype of the Wandering Jew to include the post-Shoah world of the European wasteland. However, movement does not bring change, instead the Jew continues as an "Other," a stranger hovering like a shadow over an extinct reality. Europe in the post-Shoah period, as Appelfeld has said, is the largest cemetery in history.

Appelfeld's work can roughly be divided into three periods. In the 1960s, he published surreal short fiction with strong fantastic elements. This fiction consists of five books of short stories. Appelfeld made his mark in his second period with the novels *Badenheim 1939* (1980) and *Tor ha-Pela'ot* ("Age of Wonders," 1978). In his third period, the novels of the 1990s and the first years of the new century, the actual Shoah is incorporated into his fiction.

While Appelfeld's narratives are often a fictional recasting of his own autobiography, the importance of the narrator as a chronicler and witness of events gains importance in his later work. His earlier protagonists were often devoid of memory and consequently of historical awareness. In his latest works, a sense of history, continuity, and self-awareness is more apparent. This is clear in the novels *Katerina* (1989) and *Ad Alot ha-Shaḥar* (1995). Until his third period, Appelfeld's stories were geographically situated far from the war and the camps. We encounter the camp for the first time overtly in *The Iron Tracks*, a modern picaresque parable, where Irwin Ziegelbaum (Irwin is Appelfeld's given name) recounts in the 1980s his 40 years of wandering in post-Shoah Europe. A survivor, he continues to move in trains, from south to north and back. Haunted by memories, he nevertheless visits all the stations of his life and those of his parents. He maintains a yearly cycle, like the reading of the Torah in weekly portions, consisting of 22 stations parallel to the number of letters in the Hebrew alphabet. On his way, he redeems various Jewish holy artifacts and fulfills a personal quest by killing the German officer who murdered his parents. In a way Appelfeld transcends the historical limitations of the Holocaust. In a 1986 interview, he said: "I write Jewish stories, but I don't accept the label Holocaust writer. My themes are the uprooted, orphans, the war." An heir to *Kafka, *Celan, *Proust, and *Buber, Appelfeld's voice is at once immediate and removed, historical and transcendent, realistic and postmodern, but always essential.

Appelfeld was awarded the Israel Prize in 1983. Many of his works have been translated into English, including *To the Land of the Reeds* (1986), *Badenheim 1939* (1980), *Beyond Despair* (1993), *The Immortal Bartfuss* (1988), *For Every Sin* (1989), *Katerina* (1992), *The Retreat* (1984), *Age of Wonders* (1981), *The Healer* (1990), *The Iron Tracks* (1998), *Tzili* (1983), *Unto the Soul* (1994), *Lost* (1998), *A Table for One* (with drawings by Meir Appelfeld, 2004). Stories and novellas are included in the following English-language anthologies: G. Ramras-Rauch and J. Michman-Melkman (eds.), *Facing the Holocaust* (1985), G. Abramson (ed.), *The Oxford Book of Hebrew Short Stories* (1996), I. Stavans (ed.), *The Oxford Book of Jewish Stories* (1998), L. Raphael and M.L. Raphael (eds.), *When Night Fell: An Anthology of Holocaust Short Stories* (1999), G. Shaked (ed.), *Six Israeli Novellas* (1999). Mention should be made also of the following English books: E. Sicher, *Holocaust Novelists* (2004), M. Brown and S. Horowitz, *Encounter with Aharon Appelfeld* (2003), and Philip Roth, *Shop Talk: A Writer and His Colleagues and Their Work* (2001).

For detailed information concerning translations into various languages see the ITHL website at www.ithl.org.il

BIBLIOGRAPHY: G. Ramras-Rauch, *Aharon Appelfeld: The Holocaust and Beyond* (1994); Y. Schwartz, *Aharon Appelfeld: From Individual Lament to Tribal Eternity* (Heb., 1996; Eng., 2001); R. Furstenberg, "A. Appelfeld and Holocaust Literature," in: *Jewish Book Annual*, 42 (1984), 91–106; M. Wohlgelernter, "A. Appelfeld: Between Oblivion and Awakening," in: *Tradition*, 35:3 (2001), 6–19; R. Wisse, "A. Appelfeld: Survivor," in: *Commentary*, 76:2 (1983), 73–76; S. DeKoven Ezrahi, "A. Appelfeld: The Search for a Language," in: *Studies in Contemporary Jewry*, 1 (1984), 366–80; G. Shaked, "Appelfeld and His Times," in: *Hebrew Studies*, 36 (1995), 87–100; S. Nash, "Critical Reappraisals of A. Appelfeld," in: *Prooftexts*, 22:3 (2002), 334–54; M.A. Bernstein, "Foregone Conclusions: Narrating the Fate of Austro-German Jewry," in: *Modernism / Modernity*, 1:1 (1994), 57–79; L. Yudkin, "Is A. Appelfeld a Holocaust Writer?" in: *The Holocaust and the Text* (2000), 142–58; E. Miller Budick, "Literature, Ideology and the Measure of Moral Freedom: The Case of A. Appelfeld's 'Badenheim,'" in: *Modern Language Quarterly*, 60:2 (1999), 223–49.

[Gila Ramras-Rauch (2nd ed.)]

APPELMAN, HARLENE (1947–), U.S. Jewish educator. Appelman was born Harlene Winnick in Elmira, New York, where she received her early Jewish education from Rabbi James *Gordon and from *Young Judaea's Camp Tel Yehudah. She earned her B.A. from Northwestern University (1969) and, following three years spent teaching in Jerusalem, her M.A. from the University of California (Berkeley, 1978). Her career as a communal educator began in 1982, when she was appointed director of Family Life Education at Congregation Shaarey Zedek in Southfield, Michigan, where she developed such innovative programs as "Shabbat in a Box" and "So You Want to be a Jewish Parent." After serving as director of Family Programs for the Fresh Air Society of Detroit (1986–90), Appelman became the founding head of Jewish Experiences for Families, under the auspices of metropolitan Detroit's Jewish Community Centers. Under her creative leadership (1991–93), JEFF became a national model in the field of family programming and community building; its success led to Appelman's appointment as the director of Field Services for the Whizin Institute for the Family at the *University of Judaism (1992–95), which was interested in propagating the JEFF paradigm. She continued to serve as senior consultant to Detroit's Agency for Jewish Education (1993–95), introducing *L'Chayim*, A Monthly Jewish Family Supplement, distributed locally by the *Detroit Jewish News*. In 1995, she was named director of Community Outreach and Education for the Jewish Federation of Metropolitan Detroit, remaining with the Federation as executive director of its Alliance for Jewish Education (1999–2001) and Jewish Education Officer.

Appelman's additional accomplishments in Detroit – notably, her development of Shalom Street, a hands-on Jewish children's museum, and the establishment of the Hermelin Davidson Center for Congregation Excellence, a community-wide professional training initiative – gained her an international reputation. She was asked by *Hadassah to join the creative team for the women's organization's acclaimed family program Al Galgalim (Training Wheels), served on the board of directors of the Coalition for the Advancement of Jewish Education, and lectured widely throughout the Jewish world. In 1991, Appelman was the recipient of the first Covenant Award; she was invited to join the Covenant Foundation's Board of Directors in 1994, the same year she won the Madeleine and Mandell Berman Award for Outstanding Jewish Communal Professional. She wrote numerous articles on Jewish education and published *A Seder for Tu B'Shvat* (coauthored with Jane Shapiro, 1985). In 2005, she was named executive director of the New York-based Covenant Foundation, where inter alia she oversaw the funding of initiatives supported by the Jewish Education Service of North America.

[Bezalel Gordon (2nd ed.)]

°**APPIAN OF ALEXANDRIA** (second century C.E.), author of a general history of Rome. Appian mentions the Jews and Jewish history in several places, especially in his books on Syria, Mithridates, and those dealing with the civil wars in Rome. Though he himself shared in the general apprehension during the Jewish uprisings in Egypt in 116 C.E., Appian shows no animosity toward the Jews.

APPLE (Heb. תַּפּוּחַ), mentioned several times in the Bible. In the Song of Songs it is described as a shady tree bearing sweet fruit (2:3). The odor of the beloved is reminiscent of the delicate aroma of the apple (7:9). It was an important product of Palestinian agriculture, and is mentioned as one of the victims of the locust plague described in Joel (1:12). The shapeliness of the golden apple served as a model for artistic ornamentation (Prov. 25:11). The custom of sending apples to the sick is mentioned in rabbinic literature (Tosef., BM 7:4; TJ, Shev. 8:4, 38a). Several localities in Israel bore the name "Tappu'aḥ," giving evidence, incidentally, of its widespread growth and popularity. The *tappu'aḥ* of the Bible has been variously identified as peach, citron, and even mandrake. Yet it undoubtedly refers to the apple – *Pirus malus* (*sylvestris*). This is confirmed by the references to its characteristics in rabbinic literature, for instance, the season of its ripening, the trees on which grafting would be permitted, the preparation of applesauce and apple cider, etc. (see Tosef., Kil. 1:3; TJ, Ma'as. 1:4, 49a; TJ, Ter. 10:2, 47a; Tosef., Ber. 4:2). In Arabic the apple is called *tufaḥ*. In ancient times the aromatic strains apparently were most widely cultivated, and the odor evoked high praise. The verse "the smell of my son is as the smell of a field which the Lord hath blessed" (Gen. 27:27) was interpreted as referring to the smell of an apple orchard (Ta'an. 29b). In art and in later literature the tree of knowledge in Genesis 1 was identified with the apple tree, and the Targum of the Song of Songs renders *tappu'aḥ* as "the aromatic apples of the Garden of Eden." In the Kabbalah, "the orchard of holy apples" signifies the most sublime holiness. In recent times the apple was not cultivated extensively by the Arabs in Palestine. From the middle of the 20th century, however, apples of various strains were grown in many areas of Israel, and are even an export crop.

BIBLIOGRAPHY: Loew, Flora, 3 (1931), 212ff.; J. Feliks, *Olam ha-Ẓome'aḥ ha-Mikra'i* (1968), 60–63. **ADD. BIBLIOGRAPHY:** Feliks, Ha-Ẓome'aḥ, 172.

[Jehuda Feliks]

APPLE, MAX (1941–), U.S. writer. Apple was born in Grand Rapids, Michigan, received a Ph.D. from the University of Michigan in 1970, and taught creative writing at Rice University for 29 years. His fiction began appearing in the middle 1970s and was of that zanily comic character that at the time characterized the work of Tom Robbins (*Another Roadside Attraction*, 1971), William Kotzwinkle (*The Fan Man*, 1974), and Gerald Rosen (*The Carmen Miranda Memorial Flagpole*, 1977). Packed with references to popular American culture, such as Howard Johnson Motels and Major League Baseball, Apple's first stories (collected in *The Oranging of America*, 1976) played a wildly semiotic game with the icons of current life. Whereas Tom Robbins had alternately charmed and shocked readers with the notion of Jesus' mummified body turning up in a hippie-like sideshow redolent of the 1960s, Max Apple offered such delights as Howard Johnson, Colonel Sanders, and other franchised figures rubbing elbows with actual poets (Robert Frost) and politicians (Fidel Castro).

Yet his first novel, *Zip* (1978), suggests how this writer's career would develop, for among the countercultural zaniness of its context (a young radical financing his education as a boxer's manager) and the manipulation of political images (in which Castro and J. Edgar Hoover settle their differences almost literally in the ring) are references to a family of Jewish immigrants making their way in a new world that seems as strange to them as Apple's comic contortions of reality. By the end of the 1990s, readers would know this family as Apple's own.

The stories in Apple's second collection, *Free Agents* (1984), clarify this perspective, that of a young man of the 1960s and 1970s trying to sort out the turbulence of American culture as he has to explain it to his grandparents, who in helping to raise him cannot help but suggest what life was like in the old country. "The American Bakery" is a fiction, but draws on material that would eventually take shape as memoir. Following a novelistic expansion of his Walt Disney mythology in *The Propheteers* (1987), Apple fully embraced the stories of his grandfather and then his grandmother in two heartfelt yet still comic memoirs, *Roommates* (1994) and *I Love Gootie* (1998). Among everything else, Apple says, his grandmother "left me her recipe for stories. You start with a good person and you see what happens next. You listen and you watch. By the end it all adds up to something."

BIBLIOGRAPHY: M. Chenetier, *Beyond Suspicion: New American Fiction Since 1960* (1996); J. Klinkowitz, *Structuring the Void: The Struggle for Subject in Contemporary American Fiction* (1992).

[Jerome Klinkowitz (2nd ed.)]

APPLE, RAYMOND (1935–), Australian rabbi. Born in Melbourne, Australia, and educated there and in London, Apple was a rabbi in London before succeeding Israel *Porush at Sydney's historic Great Synagogue in 1972, retiring in 2004. Apple was one of the leading exponents in Australia of moderate Orthodoxy in the Anglo-Jewish tradition and served as senior rabbi to the Australian Defence Forces and as a member of Sydney's Beth Din. He was often in the public eye as an exponent of Judaism and for his notable interfaith activities, and he was president of the Jewish Historical Society of Australia.

BIBLIOGRAPHY: W.D. Rubinstein, Australia II, index.

[William D. Rubinstein (2nd ed.)]

APPLEBAUM, LOUIS (1918–2000), composer and conductor. Born in Toronto, Applebaum was a composer and conductor for the stage, radio, film, and television. He studied the piano with Boris Berlin, theory and composition with Healey Willan, Ernest MacMillan, and others. He was the musical director of the Canadian National Film Board and produced 250 film scores. In 1955 he established the Stratford Music Festival in Ontario, which he directed until 1960, and composed music for more than 50 productions. During the 1960s he was a musical consultant for the national television network (CBC) and chair of the planning committee for the National Arts Centre, Ottawa. He also served as an executive director of the Ontario Arts Council (during the 1970s) and in 1980 became co-chair of the Federal Cultural Review Committee. His honors include the Canadian Centennial Medal (1967) and appointment to the Order of Canada (1995). Among his works are the ballet suite *Dark of the Moon* (1953); *Suite of Miniature Dances* (1953); Revival Meeting and Finale of "Barbara Allen" (1964); *A Folio of Shakespearean Songs* (1954–87); *King Herod* for choir (1958); *The Last Words of David* for cantor and choir (1980); and *Two Nostalgic Yiddish Folk Songs* for choir (1987).

ADD. BIBLIOGRAPHY: Grove online; W. Pitman, *Louis Applebaum: A Passion for Culture* (2002).

[Israela Stein (2nd ed.)]

APT (Heb. עיר אט or אַט), small town near Avignon, in southern France. Evidence of a Jewish community in Apt dates from a regulation of the second half of the 13th century prohibiting the sale to Christians of meat killed for Jews. In 1348, at the time of the *Black Death, many of the Jews were victims of an anti-Jewish riot. A synagogue existed there in 1416. The tax register of 1420 indicates that 15 Jewish families were then living in Apt, which was, apparently, fourth in order of importance among the Jewish communities in *Provence. The Jewish quarter began near the present-day Place du Postel. Possibly a second one was situated beside the Bouquerie quarter. The Apt community is mentioned by the poet *Isaac b. Abraham ha-Gorni (end of the 13th century). Samuel b. Mordecai of Apt corresponded with Solomon b. Abraham Adret.

BIBLIOGRAPHY: Gross, Gal Jud, 37–38; Hildenfinger, in: REJ, 41 (1900), 65; E. Boze, *Histoire d'Apt* (1813), 156–7, 163ff., 219; F. Sauve, *Monographie... Apt* (1903), 32–33; Schirmann, Sefarad, 2 (1956), 476.

[Bernhard Blumenkranz]

APTA, MEIR (1760?–1831), ḥasidic rabbi and kabbalist. He was born in Apta (now Opatow), Poland. Meir, a pupil of Isaac of Pinczow, served as rabbi in Stobnitsa at an early age, and later in Apta. He was a disciple of *Jacob Isaac ha-Ḥozeh ("the seer") of Lublin, and became his chief successor after his death. His views appear in *Or la-Shamayim* (1850). Meir's doctrine was conservative and contains few innovations. Its main importance was his rejection of the teachings introduced by Jacob Isaac ha-Yehudi ha-Kadosh of *Przysucha and his school. In some respects Meir may be considered the prototype of the ḥasidic traditionalist. He emphasized the central role of the **ẓaddik*, and stressed the principles of piety, reverence, unostentatious performance of religious precepts, and comradely cohesion within the movement, which he regarded as the most important aspects of Ḥasidism. Meir was succeeded by his son Phinehas (died 1837). Phinehas' son, Isaac Menahem of Wolbrom, headed a large ḥasidic congregation; he was succeeded by his son, Alter Meir David (died 1911).

BIBLIOGRAPHY: R. Mahler, *Ha-Ḥasidut ve-ha-Haskalah* (1961), index.

[Adin Steinsaltz]

APTER, DAVID ERNEST (1924–), U.S. political scientist and expert on African political institutions. His book *The Gold Coast in Transition* (1955) received such wide acclaim that it has been reprinted several times as *Ghana in Transition*. Apter's later work on Uganda, *The Political Kingdom in Uganda: A Study in Bureaucratic Nationalism* (1961), considers the nature of secular nationalism in Africa. He constructed a general theory of modernization forecasting changes in the political systems in the African continent and the direction in which they were likely to move.

Apter, who graduated from Princeton University in 1954, was one of the first American doctoral students to focus his research on the African independence movements; and under the Kennedy Administration, he was asked to head up the Peace Corps' first program in Africa. He taught political science at Northwestern University (1955–57) and at the University of Chicago (1957–61). In 1961 he was appointed professor of political science at the University of California at Berkeley, where he served as associate professor (1961–62) and acting director (1964–66) and then director of the Institute of International Studies (1966–67). A fellow of the American Academy of Arts and Sciences, he joined the faculty of Yale University in 1969 and taught there until 2000. He served as director of the Division of Social Sciences (1978–82), chair of the Department of Sociology (1997–99), and chair of the Council on African Studies (1995–99).

During his teaching career, Apter was honored with visiting appointments at major universities in France, Britain, Holland, and Africa. As an international scholar, he also wrote about Latin America, Europe, China, and Japan. Many of his books have been reprinted numerous times and translated into various languages. His prize-winning contributions to social and political theory include his seminal work *The Politics of Modernization* (1965), which set the agenda for an entire generation in the study of comparative democratization. Other books include *Approaches to the Study of Moderniza-*

tion (1968); *Choice and the Politics of Allocation* (1971), winner of the Woodrow Wilson Award of the American Political Science Association for best book of the year in political science and international studies; *Anarchism Today* (1971); *Contemporary Analytical Theory* (1972); *Introduction to Political Analysis* (1977); *Rethinking Development* (1987); *Against the State* (1990); *Political Development and the New Realism in Sub-Saharan Africa* (1994); *Revolutionary Discourse in Mao's Republic* (1994); *Social Protest and Social Change* (1995); *The Legitimization of Violence* (1997); and *The Political Kingdom in Uganda* (1997).

Yale granted Apter emeritus status, naming him the Henry J. Heinz II Professor Emeritus of Comparative Political and Social Development. As such, he is an avid participant of the Henry Koerner Center for Emeritus Faculty. Established in 2003, the Center serves as a base for Yale's retired professors and administrators to bring them back into the mainstream life of the university. Apter believes that his generation of retired professors possesses qualities that other generations lack, as many of his colleagues came to academia after surviving the Depression and World War II. That generation of faculty members, he attests, also brought greater ethnic diversity to a teaching staff that had been "classically Ivy League."

[Ruth Beloff (2nd ed.)]

APTOWITZER, VICTOR (**Avigdor**; 1871–1942), rabbinic scholar. Aptowitzer was born in Tarnopol, Galicia, and studied at the University and the Jewish Theological Seminary of Vienna where, from 1909 to 1938, he taught biblical exegesis, *aggadah*, and religious philosophy, as well as Talmud and Codes. From 1919 to 1938 he also taught Talmud at the Hebrew Teachers' College in Vienna. A confirmed Zionist, he gave his lectures in Hebrew. Although suffering from impaired vision, and completely blind at the end of his life, he remained a productive scholar, who made a strong impression on his students. He investigated, among other things, the biblical quotations in the Talmud and in the Midrash which vary from the masoretic text. Of particular importance in this field is his *Das Schriftwort in der Rabbinischen Literatur* (4 vols., 1906–15). Aptowitzer also sought to clarify the content and literary form of the *aggadah* by comparing it with the Apocrypha and with the commentaries and homilies of the Church Fathers. He established criteria for distinguishing between legends of folk origin and legends created in the academies. He dealt with *aggadah* in his *Kain und Abel in der Agada* (1922), and with both *halakhah* and *aggadah* in his *Parteipolitik der Hasmonaeerzeit im rabbinischen und pseudoepigraphischen Schrifttum* (1927; partly published in Hebrew in *Sefer Yovel... S.A. Poznański*, 1927). Aptowitzer's investigations into the relationship between the legal writings of the Armenians and Syrians and those of the Jews are summed up in his *Beitraege zur mosaischen Rezeption im armenischen Recht* (1907) and *Die syrischen Rechtsbuecher und das mosaisch-talmudische Recht* (1909; Hebrew translation, 1923). In these two works he traces Jewish influence present in these Christian codes. He published an edition of *Sefer Ravyah* by *Eliezer b. Joel ha-Levi, together with textual and explanatory notes (2 vols., 1913–35), with addenda and emendations (2 vols., 1936; new ed. 1965). His comprehensive introduction (1938) is an important source for biographies of medieval Jewish scholars of France and Germany. In 1938 Aptowitzer settled in Jerusalem where, in addition to articles on the history of the *halakhah*, he published *Meḥkarim be-Sifrut ha-Ge'onim* ("Studies in the Literature of the Geonim" (1941)). For many years he reviewed talmudic literature in the *Monatsschrift fuer Geschichte und Wissenschaft des Judentums*.

BIBLIOGRAPHY: J. Klausner, in: KS, 5 (1928/29), 348–55; Albeck, in: *Moznayim*, 16 (1943), 122ff.; Hirschberg, in: Israelitisch-theologische, Lehranstalt, Vienna, *Sefer ha-Zikkaron...* (1946), 46ff.; Waxman, in: S. Federbush (ed.), *Ḥokhmat Yisrael be-Ma'arav Eiropah* (1959), 25ff.

[Moshe Nahum Zobel / Moshe David Herr]

°**APULEIUS, LUCIUS** (second century C.E.), Latin author from N. Africa. Apuleius is best known as the author of the *Metamorphoses*. In his *Apologia* (also known as *De Magia*) he mentions both Moses and Johannes (presumably *Jannes; cf. Numenius) among important magicians who were active after Zoroaster and Hostanes (*Apologia*, 90). In *Florida* 1:6, he refers to the Jews as believers in superstition (*superstitiosi*).

[Jacob Petroff]

APULIA, region in southern Italy, including Calabria until the late Middle Ages. According to an ancient tradition the communities in *Bari, *Oria, *Otranto, and *Taranto were established by captives deported from Judea by *Titus. The constitution of the Western Roman emperor Honorius of 398 confirms that the several Jewish communities in Apulia were liable to the civic burdens. The numerous tombstone inscriptions, many wholly or partly written in Hebrew, found in *Venosa, Taranto, Matera, Bari, Brindisi, Otranto, and Oria attest to the large number of Jews settled in the region, and the wide usage of Hebrew language and names. Inscriptions found in Venosa indicate a remarkable communal organization and Jewish participation in civil life. Emperor *Basil I (867–86) attempted to persuade, and then to force, the Jews of Apulia, then part of the Byzantine Empire, to adopt Christianity; according to the Chronicle of *Ahimaaz, *Shephatiah of Oria obtained the emperor's consent to exempt the Jews of Oria, and possibly also the whole of Apulian Jewry, from this order. Oria was occupied by the Arabs in 925. Many of the Jews there were killed or taken prisoner during the fighting while others escaped to Bari or Otranto. Emperor Romanus I Lecapenus (919–44) again tried to compel the Jews to adopt Christianity. Attacks by the populace to convert them forcibly lasted several days, and many Jews were massacred.

The situation of Apulian Jewry became less precarious in the 11th century, and it was a period of flourishing cultural life.

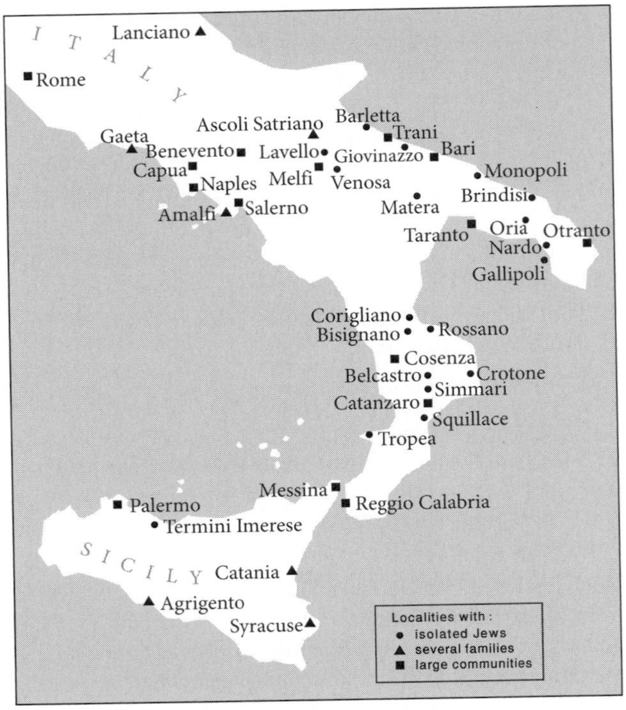

Distribution of Jews in southern Italy in the second half of the 12th century.

Jews in Apulia maintained regular contacts with the centers in Ereẓ Israel. The Chronicle of Ahimaaz (1054) contains many details on Apulian Jewry, and relates both true and legendary tales of pilgrimages to Jerusalem and of Abu Aaron (*Aaron of Baghdad), a miracle-worker and teacher, who established a school and taught mystical lore in Apulia. Hebrew letters and poetry of a high standard were encouraged. Apulian poets of the period include *Silano in Venosa, Shephatiah and his son *Amittai in Oria. Scholars are mentioned from the middle of the tenth century in Oria, Bari, and Otranto. The *Josippon chronicle, composed in about the middle of the tenth century, is a product of the southern Italian Hebrew culture. The physician Shabbetai *Donnolo lived there in the tenth century. South Italian Jewry was the original fount of Ashkenazi culture (see *Ashkenaz). That the Jews of France and Germany recognized their debt to the Apulian center as late as the 12th century is acknowledged in the proverb quoted by the French tosafist Jacob b. Meir *Tam: "For out of Bari goes forth the Law and the word of the Lord from Otranto" (cf. Isaiah 2:3). Noteworthy in the 12th century was the mishnaic commentator *Isaac b. Melchizedek, from the famous academy of *Siponto.

The position of the Jews in Apulia continued to be tolerable until the last decade of the 13th century. Most of the communities were under episcopal jurisdiction. Jews in Apulia acquired land, were occupied in crafts, and practically monopolized the dyeing industry. Thomas *Aquinas, a native of southern Italy, is evidently referring to Jewish economic conditions in Apulia when advising the Duchess of Brabant in 1274 that "it would do better to compel the Jews to work for their living, as is done in parts of Italy, than to allow them… to grow rich by usury." Scholars of the 13th century include *Isaiah b. Mali of Trani the Elder, his grandson *Isaiah b. Elijah di Trani, and Solomon b. ha-Yatom.

The period of toleration came to an end under Charles II of Anjou. Apulian Jewry was all but annihilated between 1290 and 1294 after he gave orders that all the Jews in his realm were to be forcibly baptized. Many fled from this persecution to the Orient; others who resisted were killed, while a large number accepted baptism. Most of the synagogues were converted into churches, and the schools were closed down. A considerable number of the converts led the existence of *anusim*, adhering to the Jewish beliefs and practices in secret; they became known as the *neofiti* (neophytes; see *Crypto-Jews), officially recognized as a distinct group and dealt with accordingly by the authorities. To facilitate their supervision the *neofiti* were frequently forced to live in special quarters. They were regarded by the populace as faithless heretics. In 1311 King Robert directed that those who had relapsed to Judaism were to be severely punished; the order was renewed in 1343 by Joanna I. In the second half of the 15th century the new Christians of Manfredonia were still listed as such in official documents. Both *neofiti* and Jews, who again settled in Apulia in the 15th century, were frequently subjected to mob attacks; anti-Jewish outbreaks occurred in Bari and *Lecce in 1463. The invasion of Otranto by the Ottoman army in 1480 had disastrous consequences for the Jews, who were all killed by the Turks.

The second half of the 15th century saw Jewish immigration into Apulia from other countries. In particular the exiles from Spain and Portugal contributed to a short-lived renascence of Jewish learning. Isaac *Abrabanel and others composed notable works while staying in Apulia. When in 1495 the French king Charles VIII occupied the kingdom of *Naples, however, the Jews of Apulia were again persecuted; looting and war levies dissipated their resources within a few months. The persecutions resulted in widespread conversions and "New Christians who converted since the coming of the French" are mentioned in the laws of 1498 of King Frederick of Aragon. After the return of the Aragonese dynasty to Naples the Jews enjoyed a few years of security, but the conquest of Naples by the Spaniards was followed by renewed suffering. In 1510–11 the Jews were expelled from Apulia and the entire kingdom of Naples, only 200 families being allowed to remain. In 1515 the *neofiti* were also expelled. The grant of limited residential and commercial rights to Jews throughout the Neapolitan provinces in 1520 led to the reestablishment of a few communities. A new decree of expulsion issued in 1533 was canceled shortly before its implementation, but was reissued and finally promulgated in 1540, obliging all Jews to leave Apulia the following year. Apulian Jewry as an historical entity thereby came to an end. Some of them migrated to central and northern Italy. Others settled in Constantinople, Adrianople, Salonika, Arta, Valona, and Corfu, where they founded separate Pugliese (Apulian; Heb. פולִיאסי, פלייסי)

congregations. The dialect long spoken by the Jews of Corfu contained words from old Apulian.

BIBLIOGRAPHY: Milano, Bibliotheca; Milano, Italia, s.v. *Puglia*; Roth, Italy, index; Roth, Dark Ages, index; J. Starr, in: *Speculum*, 21 (1946), 203–11 (*Eng.*); L. Levi, in: *RMI*, 28, nos. 3–4 (1962), 132–53; Cassuto, in: *Judaica, Festschrift H. Cohen* (1912), 389–404; G. Summo, *Gli ebrei in Puglia dall XI al XVI secolo* (1939). **ADD. BIBLIOGRAPHY:** B. Ferrante, "Gli statuti di Federico d'Aragona per gli ebrei del regno," in: *Archivio Storico per le Provincie Napoletane* XCVII (1979); V. Bonazzoli, "Gli ebrei del regno di Napoli all'epoca della loro espulsione. Il periodo aragonese (1456–1499)," in: *Archivio Storico Italiano* CXXXVII (1979), 495–539; C. Colafemmina, *Documenti per la storia degli ebrei in Puglia nell'archivio di stato di Napoli* (1990); idem, "Documenti per la storia degli ebrei in Puglia e nel Mezzogiorno nella Biblioteca Comunale di Bitonto," in: *Sefer Yuhasin*, 9 (1993), 19–43.

[Umberto (Moses David) Cassuto / Nadia Zeldes (2nd ed.)]

AQUILA, town in Abruzzi province, central Italy. The first record of Jews living in Aquila dates from 1294. In 1400, Ladislas, king of Naples, authorized two Jewish families to engage in pawnbroking and trade in Aquila and other towns in the Abruzzi. Queen Joanna II granted a similar license to other Jews in 1420 and in 1423. In 1427 the Franciscan John of *Capistrano obtained its revocation, but the right was restored after the Jews complained to Pope Martin V. However, their situation was precarious when Aquila became the scene of recurrent anti-Jewish preaching by the Franciscan *Bernardino da Siena in 1438, Giacomo della Marca in 1466, and *Bernardino da Feltre in 1488. That year, as a result of the panic caused by renewed preaching by Bernardino da Feltre, only two Jewish families remained in Aquila. The Jews were expelled from the kingdom of Naples, in which Aquila was included, in 1510–11. A few individuals may have returned, but attempts to reside there were finally terminated with the second expulsion of the Jews from the kingdom in 1540–41. A few Jewish families settled there in the 20th century but there was no organized Jewish life.

BIBLIOGRAPHY: Milano, Bibliotheca, index; N. Ferorelli, *Gli ebrei nell' Italia meridionale* (1915); J. Starr, in: JQR, 31 (1940/41), 67–78. **ADD. BIBLIOGRAPHY:** W. Cavalieri, *L'Aquila: dall'armistizio alla Repubblica, 1943–1946: la seconda guerra mondiale all'Aquila e provincia*, (1994); M.R. Berardi, "Per la storia della presenza ebraica in Abruzzo e nel Molise tra Medioevo e prima Età Moderna: dalla storiografia alle fonti," in: C.D. Fonseca, M. Luzzati, G. Tamani, and C. Colafemmina (eds.), *L'ebraismo dell'Italia meridionale Peninsulare dalle origini al 1541 [= Atti del IX Congresso Internazionale dell'Associazione Italiana per lo Studio del Giudaismo., Potenza 1992]* (1996), 267–94; C. Colafemmina, "Documenti per la storia degli ebrei in Abruzzo (III)," in: *Sefer Yuhasin*, 1 (1997), 29–45; W. Cavalieri, *L'Aquila in guerra: il secondo conflitto mondiale sul territorio del capoluogo e delle provincia* (1997).

[Attilio Milano / Manuela Consonni (2nd ed.)]

AQUILEIA, town in Friuli, northern Italy. The earliest evidence of a Jewish presence in Aquileia is an epitaph in Latin, of a certain "Lucius Aiacius Dama, freedman of Publius, a Jew," dated to the late first century B.C.E. There is no other evidence of Jewish settlement in Aquileia until Late Antiquity, with the exception of an epitaph of a Jew, born in Aquileia but living in Rome, dated to the third century C.E. An ancient tradition relates that the Christians set fire to the synagogue in Aquileia in the presence of Ambrose, bishop of Milan in 388. Three African-type lamps decorated with the *menorah* indeed attest the presence of Jews in Late Antiquity.

Excavations conducted in 1948–50 brought to light a place of worship, later transformed into a three-aisled church, with polychrome mosaic flooring, as well as 36 inscriptions. The excavators identified the building as a synagogue, because some inscriptions could be identified as Jewish. However, most scholars today identify the building as a church owned by Syrian Christians.

Jews continued to live in Aquileia in the Middle Ages. A tombstone with a Hebrew epitaph is dated 1140 and another one is undated. R. Menahem, a pupil of *Eleazar b. Judah of Worms (13th century), originated from Aquileia, as did the family of the 18th-century Italian scholar and poet David b. Mordecai *Abulafia.

BIBLIOGRAPHY: F. Luzzatto, in: *Scritti...Riccardo Bachi* (= RMI, 16 (1950), 140–146, second pagination); Milano, Italia, index; L. Ruggini, *Ebrei e orientali nell'Italia settentrionale...* (= *Studia et Documenta Historiae et Juris*, 25 (1959), 186–308), index; Zovatto, in: *Memorie storiche forogiuliensi*, 49 (1960–61), 53–63. **ADD. BIBLIOGRAPHY:** D. Noy, *Jewish Inscriptions of Western Europe*, 1, (1993), xiii–xiv, 11–12.

[Attilio Milano / Samuel Rocca (2nd ed.)]

°**AQUINAS, THOMAS** (1225–1274), most important of the Christian medieval philosophers. Born near Aquino, the son of a count, Aquinas entered a Dominican order at the age of 19 against the will of his family. He studied under the Dominican scholar Albertus Magnus in Cologne and Paris, where he later taught; from 1272 he taught in Naples. His main work, the *Summa theologica* (ST), was designed as an introduction to all problems of doctrine and morals that a friar might meet in his studies for pastoral duties. It shows an intimate knowledge of the works of Jewish philosophers, particularly of Avicebron (Ibn *Gabirol) and *Maimonides. Most of the proofs he adduced for the existence of God may be traced to Jewish sources. A similar systematic exposition, this one addressed to the non-Christian, is contained in his *Summa contra gentiles* (SCG, 1259–64). Aquinas often expressed his opinion about what should be the Christian attitude toward the Jews. In about 1270–71 he wrote a detailed reply, constituting the small treatise *De regimine Judaeorum* (cf. the different editions in E. Gilson, *Christian Philosophy* ... [1956], 422), to a series of questions posed by a duchess of Brabant (probably Margaret, daughter of Louis IX and wife of Jean I of Brabant). These ask whether it is lawful for a Christian prince to exact money from the Jews by means of taxes and fines since this money was the result of usury. Aquinas answered: "It is true, as the Law declares, that Jews in consequence of their sin, are or were destined to perpetual slavery: so that sovereigns of states may treat their goods as their own property, with the sole proviso that they do not deprive them of all that is necessary to sustain life." He did not, however, recommend imposing an overly harsh fiscal policy on the Jews. In addition, since "the Jews in your country appear to possess nothing but what they have acquired by the evil practice of usury," Aquinas advised returning the money to its true owners, the injured Christian borrowers. If these could not be traced, it might be spent on acts of piety or works in the general interest. In Aquinas' view it was preferable "to compel the Jews to work for their living, as is done in parts of Italy, rather than that they should live in idleness and grow rich by usury." They should also be compelled to wear a distinguishing *badge that would make them clearly recognizable from Christians.

Aquinas vehemently condemned the baptism of Jewish and other non-Christian infants against their parents' wishes as violating natural justice (*Summa theol.* 2a, 2ae, qu. 10, c. 12). He considered that the natural order requires that parents should have charge of their children until they reach the age of reason, and only then are they entitled to choose for themselves. Aquinas points out that when children baptized against the wishes of their parents had reached this age, the parents might succeed in convincing them to abandon the faith they had unwittingly received; their apostasy would then certainly be detrimental to the church. He also opposed the argument put forward in Christian circles that as the Jews were legally the slaves of the secular sovereign (see *servi camerae), the latter was therefore entitled to treat the Jews as he wished; Aquinas emphasized that in common law the slave is protected by the moral, natural law and is thus shielded from exaggerated claims by princes. He interdicted, as a general principle, the use of force against non-Catholics to convert them to Christianity. Citing *Augustine, he declared that man is capable of doing certain things against his will, but that faith is given only to him who desires it.

[Bernhard Blumenkranz]

Philosophy

Maimonides has a recognized place among those whose doctrines Aquinas draws on; all attempts to camouflage Maimonides' doctrines, such as the attempts of *William of Auvergne and *Alexander of Hales, have been put aside. "Rabbi Moyses" (Maimonides) appears as a master who has brought together the voluntarism of biblical theology and the Aristotelian theories on the cosmogonic process. Aquinas seems to have been influenced by Maimonides in his account of the relation of faith and reason (SCG, 1:4) and in his proofs of the existence of God (ST, I, qu. 2., a. 3), and he accepts the proposition of Maimonides that the temporal creation of the world cannot be demonstrated or refuted by philosophical argument, but only on the basis of revealed text (ST, I, qu. 46, a. 2). On the other hand, Aquinas opposes Rabbi Moyses' radical denial of all divine attributes, by which humans attempt to explain God's being from their experience in the created world. For Aquinas, analogy remains a means of theological approach to the secrets of divinity (ST, I, qu. 13, 2). Parts of Aquinas' works were translated into Hebrew and some of his views influenced late medieval Jewish philosophers, such as *Hillel of Verona. Aquinas shares the usual ecclesiastical view that the Old Testament is a preparatory stage of revelation. The Mosaic legislation, however, aroused his special interest; it was a source of a type of concrete solution not offered by the New Testament (ST, I–II, qu. 108, a. 2, ad 3). He understood the Sinaitic order of society as a constitution perfectly designed for the preservation of the Hebrew people under given circumstances. For this rationalization he used concepts from Aristotle's *Politics*, which had just been translated from the Greek. Aquinas was also very much stimulated in this task by Maimonides' reflection on the meaning of *mishpatim* (general moral laws); the Latin translation of this term, *praescripta iudicialia*, defined for him all biblical rules that he considered politically or socially relevant. Thus, Aquinas found in the Sinaitic legislation on agrarian property a realization of the Aristotelian theory that private ownership must be justified by responsibility for social cohesion (ST, I–II, qu. 105, a. 2 ad 3). For Aquinas this model constitution was created by divine providence; its appreciation as a product of the Hebrew mind was, of course, quite outside his consideration. Treaties and extracts from the works of Aquinas were translated into Hebrew, notably by Judah *Romano, Eli Habillo, Abraham Nehemiah b. Joseph, and others. Isaac *Abrabanel, who apparently intended to translate one of Aquinas' works, was well acquainted with his writings. The influence of Aquinas is noticeable in medieval and later Jewish works.

[Hans Liebeschutz]

BIBLIOGRAPHY: J. Guttmann, *Das Verhaeltniss des Thomas von Aquino zum Judentum und zur juedischen Literatur* (1891); P. Mandonnet and J. Destrez, *Bibliographie Thomiste* (1960), 80; E.S. Koplowitz, *Abhaengigkeit Thomas… von R. Mose b. Maimon* (1935); K. Foster (ed.), *Life of Saint Thomas Aquinas* (1959); Baron, Social, 5 (1957²), 77–78, 348; Liebeschuetz, in: JJS, 13 (1962), 57–81; Steinschneider, Uebersetzungen, 483–7; E. Gilson, *Christian Philosophy of St. Thomas Aquinas* (1956), incl. bibl.

ʿARA, Muslim-Arab village near the western entrance of the Iron Valley, on the Ḥaderah–Afulah highway. In antiquity the valley was a vital stretch of the Via Maris. In 1967 ʿAra had 1,970 inhabitants. Its economy was based on intensive farming. The village is assumed to be located on the site of Iron, a Canaanite town of the second millennium B.C.E. ("ʾIrn" in the Egyptian reports of Thutmose III's campaign against Megiddo.).

[Efraim Orni]

ARABA (or **Gabara**), place in Israel. It is mentioned by Josephus as one of the three foremost cities in Galilee (after Tiberias and Sepphoris) and as the center of a district (Wars, 3:7, 132). The sages R. Johanan b. Zakkai and R. Ḥanina b. Dosa taught there, and the latter's tomb is said to be at Araba. The Muslim-Arab village of Araba (ʾArrābat al-Baṭṭūf) is located in central Lower Galilee, north of the Bet Netofah Valley. In 1965 it received municipal council status. The town's population was 4,760 in 1967 and 17,900 in 2002, contained within an area of 3.3 sq. mi. (8.5 sq. km.).

[Efraim Orni]

ARABAH, THE (Heb. הָעֲרָבָה, **Aravah**, Ar. **al-ʿAraba**; "[arid] steppe," "desert"), name of two stretches of depressed ground extending north and south of the Dead *Sea. The biblical Arabah, except in one instance, refers to the northern Arabah, i.e., the Jordan Valley from the Sea of Galilee to the Dead Sea (which is also known as the "Sea of the Arabah"). Thus the land conquered by Moses in Transjordan included "the Arabah also, the Jordan being the border thereof, from Chinnereth even unto the sea of the Arabah, the Salt Sea, under the slopes of Pisgah eastward" (Deut. 3:17); or more simply, "and all the Arabah beyond the Jordan eastward, even unto the sea of the Arabah, under the slopes of Pisgah" (Deut. 4:49). It was left to Joshua to conquer "the Arabah" on the other side of the Jordan (Josh. 11:16). Within the northern Arabah, the plains of Jericho are called "the Araboth [plural of Arabah] of Jericho" and those across the stream "the Araboth of Moab." Only in Deuteronomy 2:8 does the Arabah refer to the Rift Valley south of the Dead Sea, but in the course of time the term was applied only to this southern area. It is a deep cleft, 112 mi. (180 km.) long, divided into two parts by a watershed 797 ft. (243 m.) high. The *Negev valleys have created wide deltas of eroded soil in the Arabah. In its center it contains alluvial soil, to a height of 492 ft. (150 m.) below sea level, with Cenomanian-Turonian white cretaceous rocks on the west (except for its southern portion) and pre-Cambrian rocks (including granite and porphyry) on the east and on the west near Elath. The Arabah is now mainly a sandy desert with an average yearly rainfall of up to 1 in. (25 mm.). Oases are few and far between (see *Ḥaẓevah, Gerofit, *Timna, *Yotvatah). The water has a salt content of up to 17% and vegetation is restricted to hardy desert plants such as the tamarisk and acacia. Temperatures vary from 57° F to 93° F (14° C to 34° C) with an average of 73°–75° F (23°–24° C). Traces of ancient agriculture are especially abundant in its northern portion, where the Nabateans irrigated and cultivated large areas near Zoar (Ghawr al-Ṣafiya), Toloha (Qaṣr al-Tilāḥ or al-Tilāḥ), and other places. The cultivation of sections of the Arabah continued into Byzantine times. The copper mines of the Arabah (especially of the Punon (Feinan) region) were exploited as early as the Chalcolithic period (fourth millennium B.C.E.) and were perhaps one of the reasons why the kings of Israel and Judah so often fought over this barren wasteland with the kings of Edom. Another reason was to obtain domination of the Red Sea harbor of Eilat (*Elath) at the southern end of the Arabah. Exploitation of the copper mines was resumed in the Roman and Byzantine periods. The Arabah is now divided between Israel and Jordan; the Sodom-Eilat road passes through its western side. At the beginning of the 21st century, the Arabah area had a population of 4,500, living in five moshavim, ten kibbutzim, and three urban communities. Residents developed special farming techniques suitable to the area's climate and also operated fisheries.

BIBLIOGRAPHY: Alt, in: ZDPV, 58 (1935), 1ff.; F. Frank, *ibid.*, 57 (1934), 191ff.; N. Glueck, *Explorations in Eastern Palestine*, 4 vols. (1934–51); B. Rothenberg, *Ẓefunot Negev* (1967). **WEBSITE:** www.arava.co.il.

[Michael Avi-Yonah / Shaked Gilboa (2nd ed.)]

ARABIA, the Arabian Peninsula. Arabia attained a high level of civilization and culture continuing from antiquity until the rise of Islam in the seventh century C.E. In its southwestern part several developed states existed (see *Ḥimyar); the northern part however was inhabited by a variety of peoples who, whenever circumstances were favorable, raided the countries of the Fertile Crescent – Ereẓ Israel, Syria, and Mesopotamia. There is a theory that northern Arabia was the cradle of the Semitic peoples. The peninsula declined when the majority of the inhabitants left to take part in the great Arab conquest following the rise of Islam in the seventh century. Only Mecca, the birthplace of *Muhammad the Prophet of Islam and the place from where he spread his teachings, maintained its special position – one of the five fundamental duties of the Muslim faith is a pilgrimage to Mecca at least once in a lifetime. *Medina, to which Muhammad fled in 622 and where he was buried in 632, also acquired the status of a holy place. In the 20th century, geopolitical and economic factors restored to the peninsula its historical importance.

The Bible deals extensively with the Arabian Peninsula and its inhabitants. There are lengthy accounts of family ties, relations in war and peace, and trade between the Israelites and the various tribes of the Arabian steppe and the inhabitants of the Red Sea ports, beginning with the era of the patriarchs. In genealogical lists of the sons of Joktan (Gen. 10:26–29), the sons of Abraham (25:1–5) and Ishmael (25:13–16), Esau-Edom (36:11–12), in biblical stories (I Kings 9:26–28; 10:1–13, the stories of the *Queen of Sheba), and in Job 2:11, the names of nomadic tribes, countries, and settlements can be identified, which local sources (inscriptions) and external sources (Assyrian, Babylonian, and Greek) show existed at that time in both the north and south of the peninsula. The relations between the Jews and the Arabs are reflected in the literature of the Second Temple period and the Talmuds. At that time most of the Jews lived in Babylonia, largely in the vicinity of the Arab country of the Lakhmites in northeastern Arabia. Owing to prevailing circumstances many of the Jewish inhabitants of Ereẓ Israel were transferred to wilderness areas in the Negev and in Transjordan, ruled by the *Nabateans and near-Bedouin Arabs.

Any survey of the history of the Jews in the Arabian Peninsula must take into account the great geophysical, anthropological, sociological, and political differences which have always existed between the north – called from the early Muslim period Ḥijāz *(Hejaz), and the southwest – known in the late pre-Islamic period as Ḥimyar and since then as *Yemen.

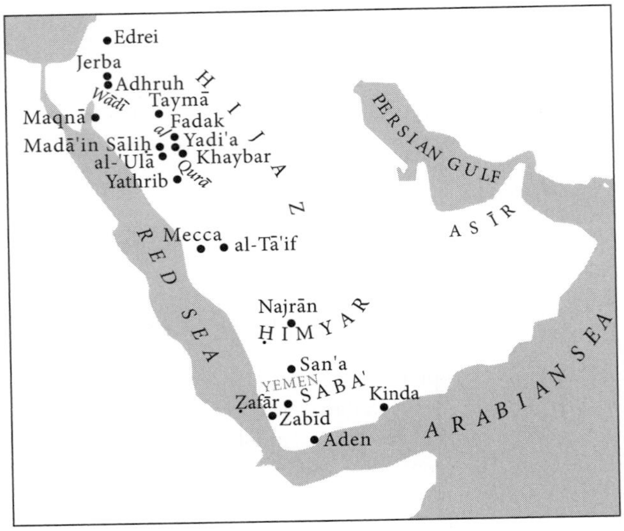

Pre-Islamic Jewish settlement in the Arabian peninsula.

These differences also made their mark on the history of the Jewish communities, and the regional division between north and south is a valid factor in a survey of Jewish history in the peninsula. The north (which for simplicity's sake will be called Ḥijāz) must therefore be discussed separately from the south.

The Jews in Ḥijāz

Arabic historical literature and commentaries (which were written much later) contain many legends about the settlement of the Israelites and the Jews in Ḥijāz. One story dates this settlement as early as Moses' war against the Amalekites (Ex. 17:8–16), while another relates that King David fought against the idol worshipers in Yathrib (Medina). It is related that after the destruction of the First Temple, 80,000 priests who were saved made their way to Arabia and joined those who had settled there previously. Some inscriptions of Nabonidus, king of Babylon (555–539 B.C.E.) – several of which were discovered in 1956 – in which he described the establishment of his capital in Taymāʾ (552–542) from where he conducted his campaigns as far as Yathrib, combined with Nabonidus' Prayer (discovered among the Qumran (Dead Sea) Scrolls) and in which he mentions a Jewish priest and visionary from the Babylonian Diaspora who accompanied him, suggest that some of the Babylonian Jewish exiles settled with him in Taymāʾ and in Ḥijāz. Charles C. *Torrey (*The Jewish Foundation of Islam* (1933), 10, 17–18) thinks that even before that time Jewish traders began to settle in the oases of Ḥijāz. However, definite confirmation of Jewish settlement here appears only with the advent of people who had distinctly Jewish names or were designated as Jews in Aramaic, Nabatean, and Liḥyān inscriptions beginning from the first century B.C.E. or C.E. These tomb inscriptions or *grafitti* were found for the most part in al-ʿUlā (formerly Dīdān: Dedan), Madāʾin Ṣāliḥ (al-Ḥijr), and their environs. Most interesting is the inscription published in 1968: "This was dedicated by ʿAdnōn bar [son of] Ḥani bar Samawʾal resh Ḥijra to his wife Mūnā [the daughter of] ʿAmrū bar Samawʾal resh Taymāʾ, who died in the month of Av 251 [355/56 C.E.] at the age of 38." This Nabatean inscription appears to be the latest dated of those discovered so far. Among the finds at al-Ḥijr there is a sundial with the inscription, "Menashā bar Nathan Shelam." This may have been the name of the craftsman who set up the sundial, or possibly that of the astronomer. The names in these inscriptions are worthy of attention. Among them are the purely biblical Manasseh, Nathan, Zadok, Samuel, Simeon, and Shalom, but several names have changed under the influence of Aramaic (or Arabic?) into forms like Isḥaq and Ismāʿīl (b. Zadok). There are also pre-classical Arabic names such as Shabīt(o), Ha-Yehudi ("The Jew"), Yaḥyā (b. Simeon), and Naʿīm (b. Isḥaq). Though there are only a few of these inscriptions, they reveal a great deal about Jewish life in Ḥijāz.

When Aelius Gallus set out to conquer Yemen in 25 B.C.E. and was delayed in al-Ḥijr, Jews were living there. The task of the auxiliary Jewish contingent sent by Herod as part of this expedition was to act as a link between the Roman army and the Jewish communities in Arabia. Apparently, al-Ḥijr was then an important center and therefore was known in Ereẓ Israel and Babylonia. The Talmud mentions al-Ḥijra a number of times; although there were several places of this name, some of these references undoubtedly mean al-Ḥijr in Ḥijāz (e.g., Anan b. Ḥiyya of Ḥijra; Yev. 116a).

At the end of the fourth century the history of the Jews in Ḥimyar intersects with that of the Jews of Yathrib. According to Arab traditions, Abkarib Asʿad (c. 385–420) embarked on widespread conquests. After Ḥimyar had rid itself of Ethiopian domination during his father's reign, Abkarib conquered Ḥijāz among other places, and laid siege to Yathrib (known as Medina after Muhammad settled there). However, under rabbinical influence he became converted to Judaism. He returned to his country with two sages and began to spread Judaism there. Historians tend to accept these traditions as authentic in the main, but doubts have been aroused by certain Liḥyān inscriptions containing allusions to Jewish scholars and therefore suggesting that a Jewish or proselyte kingdom existed at that time in Ḥijāz.

The names and works of Jewish poets who lived in Arabia a generation before Muhammad and in his day have been preserved in classical Arabic poetry. The most famous of them is *Samuel b. Adiya, called the king of Taymāʾ. Other poets are mentioned in connection with events in Medina. Jewish tribes had lived for generations in this important area. Arab historians mention about 20 tribes who lived in the region, among them the well-known Banu-Naḍīr and Banu Qurayẓa who were called al-Kāhinān, i.e., "Two Tribes of Priests," and the Banu Qaynuqāʿ. Many Jews also lived in Khaybar and in other oases of Wadi al-Qurā ("Valley of the Villages"), such as al-ʿUlā (Dīdān), Madāʾin Ṣāliḥ, al-Ḥijr, Fadak, the Transjordanian plains of Adhruḥ, Jarba, Edrei, and the port of Maqnā on the Gulf of Eilat. Apparently, Jewish refugees from south Arabia also settled in the environs of Ṭā'if after the war of *Yūsuf Dhū Nuwās. The reports from Medina attracted many Arab tribes who settled in this area, in particular two tribes from south Arabia, Banu al-Aws and Banu Khazraj, who from the start were vassals of the Jewish tribes. In the early seventh century they became stronger and the Jews were compelled to seek their protection. This situation is reflected in the pact which Muhammad made with the *al-muhājirūn* ("the emigrants": his first Meccan followers who migrated with him from Mecca to Medina in 622), the Banu al-Aws, Banu Khazraj, and Jewish tribes, and also with his "helpers" (*anṣār*), i.e., those men in Medina who supported him on his arrival.

Muhammad's hopes of converting the Jews of Medina to Islam were disappointed, and at the end of his second year in Medina relations between them began to deteriorate. One after another, Muhammad expelled the Banu al-Aws, Banu Qaynuqāʿ, and the Banu Naḍīr tribes, and had the males of the Banu Qurayẓa put to death. The lands of these tribes were distributed among the *muhājirūn*, thus solving the problem of their livelihood. After the oases of Medina had been acquired by the Muslims, Muhammad was ready to compromise with the Jews living in northern Ḥijāz – Khaybar, Fadak, Taymā', and the other Jewish settlements – and all surrendered to him. The settlers were obliged by contract to set aside a sizeable portion of their agricultural yield or produce for Muhammad and his colleagues. In practice they remained tenants on their lands. These contracts later served as a model for other agreements negotiated with residents of conquered territories who surrendered willingly to the Arabs (see *Kharāj and Jizya).

During the rule of Omar ibn al-Khaṭṭāb (634–44) the conditions of the inhabitants of Ḥijāz took a turn for the worse. At that time, Muhammad's hitherto-unknown will was suddenly discovered, and stated "there must not be two religions in Ḥijāz." On the basis of this spurious will all Jews and Christians were allegedly expelled from the Ḥijāz. But as attested by Arab authors and in the *Genizah* sources, many Jews in fact lived in Wadi al-Qurā, Taymā', and other regions in the 10th and 11th centuries. From the 12th century, concrete information about them disappears and from that time Jews are found only in *Yemen. Like its beginnings, the end of Ḥijāz Jewry is shrouded in legend. Travelers such as *Benjamin of Tudela (12th century); David *Reuveni (early 16th century); the Italian, Ludovico di Varthema (early 16th century), who was converted to Islam and therefore allowed to visit Ḥijāz, and others, have much to tell about the tribes of Israel, and especially the people of Khaybar still inhabiting the Arabian Desert, who were skilled in warfare and courageous. Izhak *Ben-Zvi, the second president of the State of Israel, devoted considerable time to tracing these stories and investigating the kernel of truth they contain.

South Arabia

The history of the Jews in south Arabia from the pre-Islamic period, including isolated information on the Islamic period which in time and source material is related to the history of Ḥijāz, is surveyed below. Because of its essentially different nature, the history from the 12th century to the present day is covered in the article on *Yemen. Various legends, resembling those on the origin of Ḥijāz Jewry, circulated about the beginnings of Jewish settlement in south Arabia. Bible stories of the Queen of Sheba and the ships of Ophir served as a basis for legends about the Israelites traveling in the Queen of Sheba's entourage when she returned to her country to bring up her child by Solomon. Large groups arrived before the destruction of the First Temple and others came afterward. Since the Jews of Yemen ignored Ezra's call to immigrate to Ereẓ Israel, he cursed them; they repaid him by refusing to name their sons Ezra. It may be assumed that Jews reached south Arabia at the latest during the reigns of Ḥimyar, i.e., in the first century B.C.E., some for reasons of trade, others with the legions of Aelius Gallus (25 B.C.E.). Although incontrovertible evidence exists from the early fourth century C.E. at the latest, it serves as a definite proof of the existence of Jewish communities in south Yemen for many decades and even centuries beforehand.

The excavations in 1936 of the central cemetery in *Bet Sheʿarim (near Haifa) of Jews from Ereẓ Israel and the Diaspora from the amoraic period, revealed a series of graves of "the people of Ḥimyar." According to a Greek inscription in one of the chambers, Ḥimyar was the name of south Arabia in the classical world of that time. In another room a Ḥimyarite monogram was drawn, reading: "Menahem the Ḥimyarite Qawl" (classical Ar. Qayl), "the head of a south Arabian tribe." In the same room, the Greek inscription *Menaē presbyteros* (i.e., "Menahem, elder of the community,") was discovered. Whether bodies buried in the Ḥimyarite graves in Bet Sheʿarim were brought from south Arabia or from one of the settlements established by these Jews in northern Arabia, Transjordan, or the Negev is of secondary importance from the point of view of the antiquity of the Jewish community in south Arabia. In any case it is clear that they originated from south Arabia: there is no reason to conjecture that immediately after their arrival in south Arabia the Jews began to wander north to establish settlements. It may be assumed that their settlement there preceded the dates on the graves in Bet Sheʿarim by at least one to two hundred years.

According to Philostorgios, the fourth-century author of a history of the Christian church, the Byzantine emperor Constantine sent Theophilus to south Arabia in the middle of the fourth century to bring Christianity to its inhabitants. Theophilus built two churches, one in Ẓafār and one in Aden, but he did not succeed in converting either the Ḥimyarites or their king. The Jews in the country then conducted propaganda against the Christian missionaries. Theodor Lector states that Christianity gained no converts in Ḥimyar until as late as the reign of the Byzantine emperor Anastasius (491–518), and in fact the majority of the monotheistic inscriptions discovered in Ḥimyar attest to Jewish influence; and only two or three of the latest ones, the work of Ethiopian-Christians (Copts), are of a Christian type. Several of the monotheistic inscriptions were placed there by the kings of Ḥimyar and hence it was concluded that they were converts to Judaism. In other inscriptions the following phrase figures: "The *Raḥmān* ["Merciful One"] who is in the heavens, and Israel and their God, the lord of Judah." One of the tombstone inscriptions includes the characteristically Jewish name Meir (CIS, vol. 4, no. 543).

The last independent king of Ḥimyar, Yūsuf Musuf Asʿar – known by his epithet Dhu Nuwās – was converted to Judaism and waged a prolonged war against his Ethiopian enemies. The Christian communities in Ẓafār and Najrān acted as an Ethiopian fifth column; when Dhu Nuwās was defeated and fell in battle in 525, the country came under Ethiopian rule. At first a native Christian viceroy was appointed, but later a viceroy was sent from Ethiopia. The Jewish community suffered hardship until the Persian conquest of south Arabia in 575. The Jews then prospered and were able to maintain contact with their brethren in Babylonia. In 628 Ḥimyar turned Muslim. In one of his letters to Yemen, Muhammad warned that it is forbidden to force a Jew or a Christian to accept Islam. The spurious will of Muhammad partly enforced in Ḥijāz by the caliph Omar ibn al-Khaṭṭāb (see above) did not include the Jews of Yemen although it severely affected the Christians in Najrān. However, it seems that at that time many of the converts to Judaism of south Arabian origin accepted Islam, and apparently more than a few Jews who were descendants of the exiles. Noteworthy among the converts to Islam are *Kaʿb al-Aḥbār, a contemporary of Omar, and later *Wahb ibn Munabbih.

From Omar's reign on, south Arabian Jewry was not mentioned for several hundred years. Neither Jews nor Christians were permitted to live in Ḥijāz until the discovery of oil in Saudi Arabia in the 20th century. At that time the prohibition against Christians employed in the oil fields was lifted, though it remained in force for Jews.

[Haïm Z'ew Hirschberg]

Modern Period

In 1948, about 54,000 Jews lived in hundreds of small communities in the southern Arabian Peninsula, most of them in Yemen. There were also communities in the British colony of Aden, the Aden Protectorate (including Hadramaut), *Bahrain, Saudi Arabia, and Kuwait. In 1949, 154 Jews gathered in the Najran area in southern Saudi Arabia, near the Yemeni border, and moved to Israel within a year. Kuwait's Jewish population of several dozen was expelled in 1948 and Jews were prohibited to enter the country. In 1968 there were a few hundred Jews left in the entire peninsula area. For Jewish settlements in other areas of Arabia, see by name of area; for relations with Israel, see *Saudi Arabia.

[Hayyim J. Cohen]

BIBLIOGRAPHY: A. Grohmann, *Kulturgeschichte des Alten Orients, Arabien* (1963), in the series *Handbuch der Altertumswissenschaft*; R. Dozy, *Die Israeliten zu Mekka von Davids Zeit…* (1864); C.J. Gadd, in: *Anatolian Studies*, 8 (1958), 77–88; A. Jaussen et al., *Mission archéologique en Arabie*, 1 (1909), 118 ff.; 2 (1914), 231 ff., 428 ff.; J.W. Hirschberg, *Der Dīwān des as-Samauʾal ibn ʿĀdijā* (1931); idem, *Yisrael be-Arav* (1946); Ben Zvi, in: *Eretz Israel*, 6 (1960), 130–48; idem, *The Exiled and the Redeemed* (1958), 167–208; Ryckmans, in: *Miscellanea A. de Meyer* (1946), 194–205; idem, in: *Le Muséon*, 66 (1953), 319–42, RY 507–8; idem, in: *Hebrew and Semitic Studies… G.R. Driver* (1963), 151–2; W. Caskel, *Entdeckungen in Arabien* (1954), 14–26; F. Altheim and R. Stiehl, *Die Araber in der alten Welt*, 4 (1967), 306–17; 5 pt. 1 (1968), 305–9; J.A. Montgomery, *Arabia and the Bible* (1969²).

ARABIC LANGUAGE. According to the generally accepted division of the *Semitic languages, Arabic (also called, more appropriately, North Arabic) belongs to the southwest Semitic branch, although some scholars affiliate it with central Semitic. The affinity between Arabic and Hebrew (which belongs to the northwest Semitic branch) is conspicuous and finds its reflection also in the genealogical tables of the Bible.

Old Arabic (Early Arabic)

Though the Arabs are mentioned in early non-Arabic sources, very little is known of the early Arabic language. While many inscriptions from an earlier period are extant, their limited content conveys only a partial picture of their language. In their epigraphy these inscriptions, mostly graffiti, apparently represent different byforms of the South Arabian alphabet. Their language, however, called Early Arabic, is North Arabic, prima facie differing only slightly from classical Arabic. Yet the method of elucidating them by reference to the Arabic lexicon may make them appear more similar to classical Arabic than they really are. These inscriptions fall into three divisions: the *Thamūdic*, the *Lihyānite*, and the *Ṣafāitic*.

Talmudic literature presents a number of Arabic glosses, *viz.*, statements about the names of various objects in Arabic; most of them written by the Palestinian *amora* Levi b. Laḥma of the third century C.E. Only a part of them, however, can be explained by Arabic; the others belong to Aramaic, which at this period already influenced the Arabic lexicon, and may represent Aramaic loanwords in Arabic.

Classical Arabic

UP TO THE CREATION OF THE ARAB EMPIRE (632 C.E.). The Arabs of the pre-Islamic period, a thinly scattered population in the wide areas of the Arabian Peninsula, no doubt spoke different dialects, as can be deduced from Arabic sources. There is not sufficient evidence for solving the problem as to whether classical Arabic emerged as the language of a particular tribe or was from the beginning an intertribal tongue. The earliest evidence, from the end of the fifth century C.E., shows that classical Arabic was already a supratribal language. Moreover, the differences between the tribal dialects or even between classical Arabic and the tribal vernaculars must not be overestimated. Typologically, it seems they were closely akin, all of them being languages of the synthetic type, tending to express several concepts in a single word, and possessing similar systems of declension and conjugation, so that it was relatively easy to switch from one dialect to another. Nor, presumably, was the speech of the Jews in pre-Islamic Arabic very different. Jewish pre-Islamic poetry, at any rate, did

English	Arabic	Hebrew
ʾ(a)	ا	א
b	ب	ב
t	ت	ת
th	ث	ת׳
j	ج	ג
ḥ	ح	ח
kh	خ	ח׳
d	د	ד
dh	ذ	ד׳
r	ر	ר
z	ز	ז
s	س	ס
sh	ش	ש
ṣ	ص	צ
ḍ	ض	צ׳
ṭ	ط	ט
ẓ	ظ	ט׳
ʿ	ع	ע
gh	غ	ע׳
f	ف	פ
q	ق	ק
k	ك	כ
l	ل	ל
m	م	מ
n	ن	נ
h	ه	ה
w	و	ו
y	ي	י

Arabic alphabet with Hebrew and English transliteration.

not differ from that of heathen contemporaries. Some scholars, however, claim that the more analytic Neo-Arabic lingual type, as characteristic of modern dialects, had already arisen in this period. Sources for the investigation of ancient classical Arabic are pre-Islamic poetry; narrative material, notably on war, as well as proverbial phrases; and the Koran.

The Arabs were almost completely isolated from outer influences, living in the Arabian Peninsula under the same primitive conditions as their ancestors. The absence of any upheaval that might have led to rapid changes accounts for the prima facie astonishing fact that Arabic, though appearing on the stage of history hundreds of years after Hebrew, has in some respects a more archaic character. Thus classical Arabic has preserved almost entirely the Old Semitic stock of phonemes, only *samekh* and *shin* having merged into *s*. As a rule, short vowels have been preserved in every position, including the final ones, which denoted the cases and moods, and the synthetic character of the language has been maintained. On the other hand, the morphology of Hebrew is in many respects more archaic than that of classical Arabic since in the latter, analogic rebuilding is in many aspects much more widespread. While in Hebrew many verbal forms seem to have been derived from roots containing two radical consonants, in Arabic, through analogy, most of the verbal forms are rebuilt according to the pattern of three-radical verbs. Nouns, too, frequently are transferred to the pattern of three-radical nouns, especially in the so-called broken plural. On the other hand, Arabic also preserved archaic features: the use of the dual is much wider than in Hebrew. The chief characteristic of Arabic syntax is the restriction of the large choice of Semitic constructions to a few standardized types, often limiting one construction to one special meaning.

AFTER THE CREATION OF THE ARAB EMPIRE. The creation of the Arab Empire had far-reaching consequences for the development of classical Arabic. In the towns of the new empire, analytic Neo-Arabic dialects soon emerged. Nevertheless, classical Arabic remained the ideal of the Arab society. Since classical Arabic was used in conversation in high society until the beginning of the tenth century, it soon became necessary for the urban population to train themselves in the classical language, and thus an impetus for the beginnings of grammatical studies was given. As a result, the philologists of Basra and Kufa standardized classical Arabic.

Nevertheless, the new Islamic culture with its new scope of ideals changed even classical Arabic. Though the literature, so far as it dealt with pre-Islamic topics, remained unchanged, the language of the classical secular prose writers of the early Abbasid period is different. Its vocabulary avoids the plethora of special Bedouin words, and instead uses general designations, adding the special characteristic by way of circumlocution. In syntax, the new style avoids exclamations and parataxis, instead developing the tendency already found in pre-Islamic Arabic to limit one type of expression to one sense. Through this restriction the Arabic sentence structure becomes admirably accurate and capable of expressing the most complicated range of ideas concisely.

With the lowering of the standard of education and the changes that affected the Bedouin tribes, who were no longer regarded as the best representatives of Arabic speech, classical Arabic ceased to be used in high society conversation after the beginning of the tenth century. From the mid-13th century, after the Mongol invasion and the establishment of Mamluk Egypt, the impact of Middle Arabic, including its Neo-Arabic layer, on literary language increased, and from the 14th century a period of stagnation and decay began, which lasted until the beginning of the 19th century.

NEO-ARABIC, MIDDLE ARABIC AND JUDEO-ARABIC. Neo-Arabic arose as the linguistic consequence of the Arab conquests of the seventh century C.E. As a result of the changes of place and culture and the influence of the indigenous population, this new language type arose in towns as early as 700 C.E.

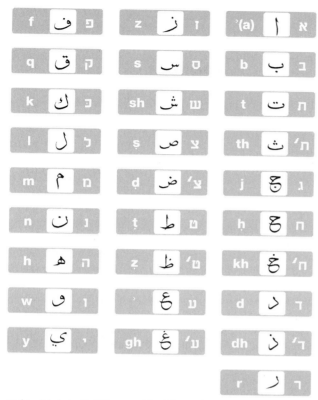

The language of texts in which classical and post-classical features alternate with Neo-Arabic elements, as well as with pseudocorrections including hypercorrections and hypocorrections, is called Middle Arabic. The study of Neo-Arabic as contained in Middle Arabic texts cannot exclusively be based on documents of Muslim provenance. The tremendous influence which classical Arabic as an ideal exerted, as it still does, on Muslim authors meant that their writings did not, until a relatively late date, reflect decisive changes in the character of the language to any marked degree (with the sole exception of early papyri). Consequently, investigation has to concentrate upon the religious minorities of the Arab Empire, who were less devoted to the ideal of classical Arabic than the Muslims. Accordingly, the sources of Neo-Arabic proper are (a) Judeo-Arabic, mainly from the second millennium C.E., written as a rule in Hebrew characters; texts written in phonetic spelling from the second half of the first millennium have been preserved. Jews often preferred writing Arabic rather than Hebrew, even when dealing with the most sacred matters of Judaism. Only poetry was written in Hebrew almost consistently. (b) Christian Arabic texts, especially from southern Palestine, preserved in the Monastery of St. Catherine in Sinai, including the only dated texts from as far back as the ninth century C.E. (c) Middle Arabic translators: As the most important translators were non-Muslims, their works exhibit Neo-Arabic peculiarities, though to a lesser degree.

The linguistic character of ancient Neo-Arabic clearly exhibits all the structural peculiarities that characterize modern Arabic dialects. Since ancient Neo-Arabic and the modern dialects are structurally closely akin, a very short description of the principal features of Judeo-Arabic as compared with classical Arabic may also serve as a summary of the main differences between classical Arabic and the Neo-Arabic as contained both in the other branches of Middle Arabic and the modern dialects (especially the sedentary vernaculars). These ancient Neo-Arabic features must be carefully deduced from Middle Arabic texts full of classical and pseudocorrect elements, since no texts written in pure Neo-Arabic are extant. Before the exploitation of these Middle Arabic texts, Neo-Arabic was only known from modern dialects. The reconstruction of early Neo-Arabic from Middle Arabic texts bridges the gap of more than one thousand years that separated the emergence of the Neo-Arabic lingual type from modern dialects.

Perhaps the most important event in the field of phonetics, an event which determined the very nature of Middle as contrasted with classical Arabic, was the change in the nature of the vowels, caused at least partly by the accent becoming strongly centralized: the vowels were weakened, thus becoming liable to change and elimination. Final short vowels disappeared (this being one, though not the sole, reason for the disappearance of cases and moods), and even in the interior of the word short vowels in open unstressed syllables have been elided. The phonemic structure of the vowels changed, at least in some dialects. Further, the quality of the short vowels has become variable. Diphthongs, it seems, have become simple vowels. In the sphere of the consonants the most important change is the weakening and disappearance of the glottal stop. A great number of assimilations occur and whole words are pronounced in *tafkhīm* (velarized) or *tarqīq* (non-velarized).

As to the linguistic structure of Judeo-Arabic, so far as such different and intricate features may be reduced to a common denominator, the most conspicuous deviation from classical Arabic was that Neo-Arabic detached itself from the synthetic type and approached the analytic type, which generally indicates one concept by one word. The most striking outward sign of this phenomenon is the disappearance of the mood and case endings. The place of the lost flexion is taken by new features: as is general in analytic languages, the subject tends to precede the verb, the direct object to follow it. The verb agrees even with its following subject, thus making distinction between subject and direct object possible (if they are of different gender or number). Apparently under the influence of Aramaic, the direct object is often indicated by *li* and sometimes also referred to by an anticipative pronominal suffix. A further analytic feature is the partial discarding of *status constructus*, while in order to indicate a similar relation not only prepositions, but sometimes also *mataʿ*, *bataʿ* are used. *Status constructus* has greatly changed: two nouns in *status constructus* may govern one noun, the *nomen regens* in the dual or sound masculine plural preserves its *nūn*, thus becoming identical with the *status absolutus*, and words which in classical Arabic as a rule occur in *status constructus* are to be met with in *status absolutus*. The differences between *an*, *anna* ("that"), and *inna* ("behold") have been blurred, and each may occur in syntactical positions proper, according to classical usage, to the others. The *b*-imperfect is rather rare, although it may be found in some early texts. The dual is often replaced by the plural, and the relative pronoun *alladhī* has become invariable (in many cases apparently being a "classical" spelling for vernacular *illī*, which, however, is very rare in Middle Arabic texts). The differences between relative clauses after determinate and indeterminate antecedents, strictly maintained in classical Arabic, are sometimes blurred. Asyndetic clauses occur in every syntactic environment, both in coordination, especially after verbs indicating movement, and in subordination, particularly in object clauses. Indirect questions often take the form of conditional clauses (as in Hebrew and English). The most frequent negation is *mā*, occurring much more often than in classical Arabic. The feminine plural is widely replaced by the masculine, and the passive, formed in classical Arabic by internal vowel change, by reflexive verbal forms. The most far-reaching changes have affected the numerals. Moreover, the fixed and accurate style of classical Arabic is largely replaced by an inconstant and careless language.

Despite the basic linguistic similarity of Judeo-Arabic and other branches of Middle Arabic, there were important differences between them, though mostly not linguistic distinctions proper: Jews, as a rule, wrote Arabic in Hebrew characters, dealt almost exclusively with Jewish topics, and made use of Hebrew (and Aramaic) phrases, thus making their literature virtually unintelligible to Gentiles. One has the feeling that Jews themselves regarded Judeo-Arabic as distinct from other forms of Middle Arabic, as one may infer from special literary traditions in Judeo-Arabic literature.

Modern Literary Arabic

The history of modern literary Arabic, like the modern history of the Arabs, begins with the expedition of Napoleon to Egypt in 1798. The problems confronting Arabic were even greater than those of ordinary living languages facing Westernization. In some respects, classical Arabic had a status comparable to that of Hebrew before its revival in Israel (see *Hebrew Language): both were artificial languages of time-honored civilizations, in which religion occupied a central position. The difficulties which Hebrew had to overcome, were, it is true, even greater than those facing Arabic. Classical Arabic was the language of a coherent population, speaking dialects which, though differing from each other, and all exhibiting a structure different from that of classical Arabic, were nevertheless related to each other and with classical Arabic, and felt as such. By contrast, Hebrew was used by Jews scattered all over the world. On the other hand, since the revival of Hebrew in Ereẓ Israel, the status of Hebrew has become almost "normal" and the Jewish population of Israel is becoming increasingly unilingual. The only important trait distinguishing it from "normal" languages is that it is "open" to a certain degree to classical Hebrew. With the adaptation of classical Arabic to the demands of Western culture, the position of modern literary Arabic has been much less normalized. Its relation to its classical predecessor is, to be sure, similar to that of modern Hebrew to classical Hebrew: modern literary Arabic is open to classical Arabic. The language situation of Arabic, however, is complicated by the existence of the dialects. Whereas the Hebrew linguistic situation is characterized by dichotomy, modern Hebrew versus classical Hebrew, the Arabic linguistic structure is tripartitive at least, consisting of classical Arabic, modern literary Arabic, and the dialects.

The guiding idea of the whole Arabic language movement was the dogma of classical Arabic being the highest authority for linguistic correctness. Later, the emergence of Arabic nationalism conveyed to it additional significance: it was no longer merely a monument of the glorious past, but also the tie binding the Arabs in their various countries into one unit.

The Arabic Dialects

Arabic dialects are spoken by approximately 100 million people. The basic structure of the Arabic dialects, especially of the sedentary vernaculars, is identical with that of ancient Neo-Arabic. The main difficulty of classifying the dialects arises from the necessity of basing classification on both sociological and geographical criteria, though these overlap. According to sociological criteria, the Arabic dialects fall into Bedouin and sedentary vernaculars. According to geographical criteria, the following divisions emerge:

(1) Saudi Arabia, the Syro-Iraqi-Jordanian Gulf;

(2) South Arabic: Yemen, Oman, and Zanzibar;

(3) Iraq;

(4) Syria-Lebanon-Israel-Jordan;

(5) Egypt (excluding Alexandria and certain parts of the population of the Delta, which belong to the Maghrebine dialects);

(6) Sudan and Central Africa; and

(7) Maghrebine Dialects, including Malta. The characteristic of this dialect group is the use of *nqtl* and *nqtlu* for the first person singular and plural respectively of the imperfect.

BIBLIOGRAPHY: EARLY ARABIC: Brockelmann, in: B. Spuler (ed.), *Handbuch der Orientalistik*, 3 (1954), 208–14; Rabin, in: EIS², 1 (1960²), 652–3. TALMUDIC "ARABIC" GLOSSES: A. Cohen, in: JQR, 3 (1912/13), 221–33. CLASSICAL ARABIC: Brockelmann, in: B. Spuler (ed.), *Handbuch der Orientalistik*, 3 (1954), 214–19; J. Fueck, in: Arabiya, 1 (1950); H. Fleisch, *Traité de philologie arabe*, 1 (1961–79). MODERN LITERARY ARABIC: V. Monteil, *L'arabe moderne* (1960). ARABIC DIALECTS: Brockelmann, in: B. Spuler (ed.), *Handbuch der Orientalistik*, 3 (1954), 219–45; Cantineau, in: *Orbis*, 4 (1955), 149–69 (reprinted in J. Cantineau, *Etudes de linguistique arabe* (1960), 257–78); H. Sobelmann, *Arabic Dialect Studies* (1962); Kampffmeyer, in: EIS, 1 (1913), 394–402; Fleisch, in: EIS², 1 (1960²), 574–8; Marçais, *ibid.*, 578–83. **ADD. BIBLIOGRAPHY:** GENERAL: W. Fischer, *Grundriss der arabischen Philologie, I, Sprachwissenschaft* (1982). MIDDLE ARABIC AND JUDEO-ARABIC: J. Blau, *Studies in Middle Arabic and Its Judeo-Arabic Variety* (1982); idem, *A Grammar of Christian Arabic* (1966–67); S. Hopkins, *Studies in the Grammar of Early Arabic* (1984). MODERN LITERARY ARABIC: J. Blau, *The Renaissance of Modern Hebrew and Modern Standard Arabic* (1981).

[Joshua Blau]

ARAB LEAGUE, league of Arab states comprising 22 members. The League was founded in March 1945 in Cairo as a regional organization by the then seven independent or almost independent Arab states (Egypt, Iraq, Transjordan, Syria, Lebanon, Saudi Arabia, and Yemen). Its foundation was a result of two conflicting processes. One was the Pan-Arab ideal, which had gained immense popularity since the 1920s and called for political unity of all Arabic-speaking peoples. The second was the formation and perpetuation of the state system (a "Westphalian order") in the Middle East and the struggle for regional hegemony among these states. Thus, despite the fact that Arab nationalism was the ideological force behind the process that led to the establishment of the League, in practice the League sanctified the existence and sovereignty of the Arab states. Hence, the term "Arab unity" was not even mentioned within the League's charter and decisions did not have binding force among the League's members. It reflected the fact that member-states had conflicting interests which impaired their ability to cooperate politically within the framework of the Arab League and forced them to find the lowest common denominator as grounds for cooperation.

At first the League enjoyed respect. Yet with time and as a result of its inability to coordinate any serious pan-Arab action, it gradually lost prestige. From 1964 the League served as an organizational framework for Arab summit meetings. Although the Council of the Arab League, headed by the member-states' foreign ministers, was scheduled to meet twice a year, Arab summit meetings were irregular and dependent on the problems of the day.

Since its foundation, the League has made Palestine and the Arab-Israeli conflict its most important axis of engagement. The Charter of the League contains a special appendix relating to Palestine, committing its members to support the Palestinians in their national struggle for independence. The League was also involved in coordinating the Arab front in the 1948 war. The Arab defeat in that war symbolized the poor performance of the League and the inability of the Arab states to cooperate successfully even for the Palestinian cause. Palestine remained the most important issue on the League's agenda. Nevertheless, the League was never able to translate its preoccupation with this subject into an effective political agenda.

The attitude of the Arab League towards the Palestinian problem and Israel reflected the changes these two related issues underwent. Until the 1970s the League officially did not recognize the State of Israel and advocated the resolution of the Palestinian problem only within the context of Israel's annihilation. Yet, after the 1967 war and the gradual change in the dynamics of the conflict that led to a slow implicit recognition of Israel, the League started to change its tone as well. Thus, when Egypt signed a peace treaty with Israel in 1979, the League's headquarters were moved from Cairo to Tunisia, and Egypt was stripped of its membership. Yet gradually the League's members reestablished their ties with Egypt and by 1990 the League's headquarters returned to their original location. In addition, the League's official declarations, as manifested in the 2002 Beirut summit, even offered an official Arab peace plan which recognized Israel within its pre-1967 borders in exchange for the establishment of a Palestinian state and a solution to the refugee problem based on UN Resolution 194.

The May 2004 Tunis Arab summit reflected the challenges the League's member-states faced after the American occupation of Iraq. The summit's resolutions reiterated the call for a comprehensive Israeli-Arab peace based on the 1967 borders. They also called for amending the League's charter to improve its effectiveness and to conduct internal political reforms in each state based on universal democratic values. Although the wording of these resolutions was promising, in reality they did not produce major changes either in the League's structure or in the political systems of its member-states.

BIBLIOGRAPHY R.W. MacDonald, *The League of Arab States: a Study in the Dynamics of Regional Organization* (1965); H.A. Hassouna, *The League of Arab States and Regional Disputes: A Study of Middle East Conflicts* (1975); T.Y. Hasou, *The Struggle for the Arab World: Egypt's Nasser and the Arab League* (1985); B. Maddy-Weitzman, *The Crystallization of the Arab State System, 1945–1954* (1993); M.N. Barnett, *Dialogues in Arab Politics* (1998); A. Sela, *The Decline of the Arab-Israeli Conflict: Middle East Politics and the Quest for Regional Order* (1998); M. Hudson, (ed.), *Middle East Dilemma: The Politics and Economics of Arab Integration* (1999).

[Asher Kaufman (2nd ed.)]

ARAB WORLD, 1945–2006. The Arab world is divided into four subregions: the Maghreb (*Morocco, *Tunisia, *Algeria, *Libya, Mauritania), the Nile Valley (*Egypt and Sudan), the Fertile Crescent (*Syria, *Lebanon, *Iraq, *Jordan, and the *Palestinian Authority), and the Arabian Peninsula (*Saudi Arabia, *Yemen, *Kuwait, Qatar, Bahrain, Oman, and the United Arab Emirates). Between 1932 and 1971 these countries became independent nation-states, with the exception of the *Palestinian Authority.

The Maghreb was largely made up of Sunni Arab and *Berber Muslims. Until its independence from European colonialism, aside from a large European settlement (French, Italian, and Spanish), it had sizeable Jewish communities. Morocco gained independence from France and Spain in 1956; Tunisia from France in 1956; Algeria from France in 1962; Libya from Britain in 1951; and Mauritania from France in 1960. Algeria emerged as a presidential republic in 1962, while Tunisia, ruled since 1705 by the Husaynid beylicate, became a republic in 1957. Libya became a monarchy under the Sanusi dynasty in the 1950s and a republic in 1969. Governed by successive military regimes since the 1960s, Mauritania, in the 21st century, is undergoing a process of democratization. Morocco continues to be a monarchy under the Sharifian Alawite dynasty. Authority is vested in the king along with a constitutional government headed by a prime minister and a legislative parliament. The Maghreb's population includes 32 million Algerians; 31 million Moroccans; 8.5 million Tunisians; 4 million Libyans; and 2 million Mauritanians.

Egypt of the post-1945 period comprised a relatively homogeneous population with a Sunni Muslim majority and a sizable Christian Coptic minority estimated at approximately six percent of the total population. The small religious and foreign national minorities, including Jews, Armenians, Italians, British subjects, Syrian Christians, and Greeks departed from the scene during the 1950s and 1960s in the aftermath of Britain's departure. The political system in Egypt until the July 23, 1952, Revolution consisted of a hereditary monarchy (House of Muhammad Ali), a constitutional government, and a parliament. Following the 1952 Revolution, Egypt became a republic (1953) and a one-party state headed by Gamal Abdel *Nasser, the latter having become president in 1956. After Nasser's death (1970), under the presidency of Anwar al-*Sadat (1970–81) and Husni *Mubarak (from 1981), steps were taken to partially democratize the political system, revive the pre-1952 multi-party system, permit the activity of non-governmental organizations, and diversify the press and electronic media. The population grew from 19 million in the 1940s to 70 million in 2005.

Sudan has more than 50 ethnic groups subdivided into at least 500 tribes. While southern Sudan is Christian and pagan black, the main group in the north are Muslims. Nearly half of the population identifies itself as Arab, generally meaning peoples who speak Arabic and reflect its cultural heritage. Half the population speaks Arabic as its native language. Sudan's total population in 2000 was 40 million. The country gained its independence in 1956 after the British and Egyptians had dominated the country for some 57 years. It has been a republic ruled mostly by the army. Since 1989, the military in coalition with Islamist elements have been in control. Sudan has been plagued by civil wars fought between the Muslim north and the Christian south. In January 2005 an agreement was reached to halt the violence.

The Fertile Crescent includes Syria, Lebanon, Iraq, the Hashemite Kingdom of Jordan, and the Palestinian Authority. The combined population of these entities in 2000 was about 45 million. The populations are heterogeneous. With 13 million, Syria is made up of an Arab Sunni majority, different Shiite minorities, the Druze, Christians, and, until recent years, Jews. After independence from the French in 1946, Syria was a republic initially governed by a nationalist bloc. Its leaders were replaced in 1949 by army officers in reaction to the military defeat in the 1948 war against Israel. The traditional politicians returned to power following elections in 1954, but four years later political life in Syria was again dominated by the military and the Syrian-Egyptian Union (United Arab Republic). In the aftermath of the Union's collapse in 1961, the military remained in control of the country. The rise of the leftist nationalist Baʿth (Renaissance) Party in a military-civilian coalition in 1963, to be followed, after another military coup d'état in 1966, by a yet more radical wing of the same political party controlled by the Alawi minority, only solidified the dominance of the army.

Lebanon, a constitutional republic with a population of three million, won its independence from France in 1943. The population is diverse with a large Shiite community (the single largest group), an important Sunni element, several Christian communities, and the Druze. Until the 1970s, a Jewish community existed. The president of the republic is traditionally a Maronite Christian, the prime minister a Sunni, and the speaker of the Parliament a Shiite.

Iraq, with 20 million people, also enjoys population diversity with a substantial Shiite majority (60 percent), though dominated politically by Arab Sunni Muslims until 2003. It won independence from Britain in 1932 and was ruled by the Hashemite monarchy. The latter was removed from power in July 1958 by a group of army officers who transformed Iraq into a republic. Until 2003, the republic's political leadership was vested in the hands of successive administrations propped up by military men belonging mostly to the Sunni Arab minority. This subsequently changed, when the Shiites emerged as the dominant force in local politics after the overthrow of Saddam Hussein's regime by U.S. and western coalition forces. Less than 20 percent are Sunni Arabs; another 20 percent are Sunni Kurds. The Kurds are not Arabs and speak Kurdish. Small minorities include Assyrian Christians, Turkic elements, Marsh Arabs, and a few Jews.

The Hashemite Kingdom of Jordan's population of four million lives largely in the fertile highlands of the *Transjordan Plateau and the Jordan Valley. About 50 percent of the people are Jordanian Sunni Muslim Arabs originating from the land east of the Jordan River. Most of the rest had their roots in *Palestine. Many arrived as refugees during the 1948 war or in the aftermath of the Six-Day War of 1967. In terms of minorities, five percent are Arab Christians, mostly Greek Orthodox. Other ethnic minority groups are even smaller, mainly Armenian Christians and Circassian Muslims.

The Palestinian Authority (PA) was created in the summer of 1994 following the Oslo Declaration of Principles (1993) and the subsequent implementation of the Oslo peace accords. Dominated by the *Palestine Liberation Organization (PLO) and the *Fatah*, until the January 2006 *Hamas parliamentary election victory, the Palestinian Authority governs the towns on the West Bank of the Jordan River, many of the villages surrounding these towns, and *Gaza. The majority of the people are Sunnis.

The Arabian Peninsula countries emerged around family power centers and Western-protected interests. State capabilities have developed in conjunction with oil wealth and the involvement of Western powers. Saudi Arabia, a hereditary monarchy since the mid-1920s, is governed according to the *Shariʿa* (Islamic Law). Its population at the beginning of the 21st century exceeded 25 million. Yemen, with a population of 20 million, gained its independence in 1918 from the crumbling Ottoman Empire. It was governed by a monarchy until its overthrow in September 1962. In 1967, after a five-year civil war, in which Egypt committed troops to prop up the Republican anti-monarchic forces, two separate Yemeni entities emerged: the Yemen Arab Republic; and the Marxist-dominated People's Democratic Republic of Yemen (PDRY). It was only in 1990 that both Yemens merged once again into one nation as the Republic of Yemen. The population in the nominally constitutional monarchy of Kuwait consisted of 2.2 million in 2004, 85 percent of which are Sunni Arab, 30 percent Shiite Arab, while the rest are Hindus and Christians. Qatar, a traditional monarchy, had a population of some 850,000 in 2004, consisting of 40 percent Sunni Arabs, 18 percent Pakistanis, 18 percent Indians, 10 percent Shiite Iranians, and 14 percent classified as "others." Ninety-five percent of the people of Qatar are Sunnis. Bahrain, a constitutional hereditary monarchy, had a population of approximately 680,000 in 2004 that included local Bahraini Arabs, Asians, and Iranians. Seventy percent of the population are Shiite and 30 percent are Sunnis. The Sultanate of Oman had a population of 2.9 million in 2004, made up of Arabs, Beluchis, South Asians, and Africans. Omanis are mostly Sunni with small Shiite and Hindu minorities. The United Arab Emirates (UAE), inhabited by 2.4 million in 2004, is governed by a local hereditary sultanate. Its population consists of 61 percent Sunni Arabs, 22 percent South Asian Muslims and Hindus, and the rest mostly Iranian Shiites.

Inter-Arab Political Rivalries and Efforts toward Unity: 1945–1963

Since 1945, popular political sentiment in the Arab world has been dominated by urgent appeals for Arab unity under the trauma of the military defeat in Palestine, the establishment of the State of Israel, and the exodus of the Palestinian refugees and their resettlement in Arab states. One major manifestation of unity was to be achieved through the creation – with British support – of the League of Arab States (*Arab League) in March 1945. With the exception of the years 1979–90, League headquarters were in Cairo. Sixty years later the League was composed of 22 independent Arab states; Palestine was included as an independent entity. Its multipurpose functions were to strengthen relations between member-states; enhance member-state cooperation and the preservation of Arab sovereignty in the post-colonial era; and promote general Arab interests. The League promotes economic, social, military, and development cooperation among its members. It has been united in its support for Palestine vis-à-vis Israel, though deep divisions existed as to how to deal with Israel. Moreover, all talks of Arab unity and the notion of Pan-Arabism did not translate into reality over many decades. Relations between governments and parties have been dominated by bitter rivalry. Well into the 1960s the idea of Pan-Arabism was inextricably bound up with two concepts: anti-colonialism and revolutionary socialism – the two often overlapping.

Between 1945 and the mid-1950s, the center of the contest for influence in the Arab world was Syria while the main protagonists were Iraq and Egypt. The Arabian Peninsula, the Persian Gulf, and the Maghreb were then either on the margins of Arab affairs, or were still under foreign domination. This competition for power began well before the Egyptian revolution of July 23, 1952, with the decline of European colonialism, and had little to do with ideology. It was geopolitical in nature. With the termination of French domination, Syria had become free to choose her alignment within the Arab world, and other Arab states were free to try and influence her. For sentimental reasons and out of dynastic ambition, as well as the desire to promote Iraqi leadership among the Arabs, the principal Iraqi leaders, the regent, Prince Abdallah, and the powerful prime minister, Nuri al-Saʿid, sought repeatedly to bring about either a Syrian-Iraqi union under the Hashemite monarchy, or at the very least a close alliance. The Egyptians steadfastly opposed them.

Syria was easy prey for the Egyptians and Iraqis, for it lacked political stability from the late 1940s, following the first Arab-Israeli war, and well into the 1950s. A series of domestic and international crises during this period provided the occasions for efforts in and out of Syria to push the country in one direction or the other. A staple ingredient in this process was the chronic involvement of the Syrian army in politics, beginning with three consecutive military coups in 1949. Further coups occurred in the early 1950s. At other times, between 1954 and 1957, military cliques among army officers espousing diverse nationalist ideologies intervened in the affairs of state or carried on struggles against each other to determine which would more successfully manipulate the civilian politicians. At the same time, competing politicians cultivated friends in the army and occasionally encouraged military intervention in support of their own factional interests.

A dominant factor that affected Syria, but equally or more so the domestic and regional politics of the rest of the Fertile Crescent and Egypt, was the effort by Britain and the U.S. to bolster their strategic interests in the Middle East through defense treaties. This was part and parcel of West European and American efforts to block Soviet expansion into the region. Although each of these efforts failed, it exacerbated anti-Western sentiments. In 1951 came the proposal for a combined British, French, American, Turkish, and Egyptian Middle East Defense Organization (MEDO), into which Syria, Iraq, and others would presumably be drawn. The plan came to naught when the Egyptian government rejected it. Four years later, in 1955, Britain, Iraq, *Turkey, *Iran, and *Pakistan created the Baghdad Pact for the purpose of regional defense. Israel was not invited to join the Pact: The British and the Americans did not wish to alienate Iraq since it was impossible for the latter to go along with such an invitation, for this would have meant recognizing the Jewish State. The chief British interest in the Pact was to provide a substitute for the expiring Anglo-Iraqi treaty. The Iraqi authorities were eager to renew their British ties, but they faced the prospect of isolation within the Arab League and condemnation by Arab opinion unless other Arab partners could be brought in. Egypt refused to join the Pact from the outset, claiming to spearhead the notion of non-alignment in the Cold War. Egyptian leader Gamal Abdel Nasser believed that the Pact meant to challenge his leadership in the Arab arena and not thwart Soviet ambitions in the region. Moreover, once it became apparent that the U.S. would not sell fighter planes, heavy artillery, tanks, and light weapons to the Egyptians, Nasser deviated from his non-aligned policy and signed an arms deal with the Soviet Bloc in September 1955. This move weakened the Western strategy of forging defense alliances with Arab states and opened the door to deeper Soviet involvement in the Middle East.

Relentless pressure from the Nasserist regime in Cairo on the Syrians and Jordanians to refrain from joining the Baghdad Pact left Iraq the only Arab country that joined it along with pro-Western Pakistan, Iran, and Turkey. The Sinai-Suez expedition of October-November 1956, when Britain, France, and Israel attacked Egypt following Nasser's nationalization of the Suez Canal, and owing to his support for the Gaza-based Palestinian incursions (against Israel) as well as for the Algerian rebels (against France), reduced prospects for pro-Western defense arrangements with Syria and Jordan even further. The Eisenhower Doctrine of 1957, in which the U.S. declared that the need of the hour was to defend the Middle East against the aggression of "states controlled by international Communism," emerged as a futile attempt after the 1956 war to attract Arab states into the Western fold. The Lebanese, Jordanian, and Saudi governments allowed themselves to become open allies of the U.S. and condemned Cairo and Damascus for allegedly opening the door to the spread of Communism in the area. They were rewarded with American arms and money, but both they and their patrons paid the price of widespread protests. They paved the way for the armed insurrection that plunged Lebanon into anarchy beginning in May 1958 and the army coup that liquidated the Iraqi Hashemite monarchy two months later.

Though Syria did not witness in 1957–58 open unrest like its Lebanese, Jordanian, and Iraqi neighbors, there had been covert signs that both radical leftist and right-wing politicians were undermining its stability. Syria's problems were temporarily solved, or so it seemed at the time, by its union with Egypt in February 1958, in the new framework of the United Arab Republic (UAR). The initiators of the UAR were Egyptian President Gamal Abdel Nasser and the Syrian Baʿth Party. The latter was founded in 1947 by Salah al-Din Bitar and Michel ʿAflaq, two Paris-educated Syrian intellectuals who joined with Akram al-Hawrani, an astute politician who led the Syrian Socialist Party. Together they formed the Syrian Arab Socialist Baʿth Party. By the late 1950s, Baʿthist appeal was not confined to Syria; it branched into Lebanon, Jordan, and Iraq.

Although Nasser agreed to enter into the union with Syria, he laid down his conditions. The UAR should not be a federal but a centralized union. The military had to renounce further involvement in politics. All political parties were to be dissolved. Only the National Union, the sole political party in Egypt, was to serve as an umbrella for guiding the UAR. There were to be two parliaments: one in Cairo and another in Damascus, and one central government, in Cairo, headed by Nasser. These terms were accepted by the Syrian Baʿthists.

Nasser and the Baʿth supported state socialist programs. In Egypt, socialism evolved in the 1950s and early 1960s as a series of improvised programs rather than as an ideology. The military leaders had decreed agrarian, labor, educational, and other reforms in response to specific needs and generally in order to win public support for themselves. The first state incursions into the management of the industrial and commercial economy came as by-products of the international crisis of 1956: the regime found itself in control of the Suez Canal administration and a large number of enterprises sequestered from their British and French owners. In the wake of this experience, Nasser's regime developed a taste for state ownership. When the UAR was created, Nasser felt that state socialism needed to be implemented in Syria too.

Unlike Nasser's socialism, the Baʿth was a mixture of ardent Arab nationalism and Marxist doctrines. Like Nasser, the Baʿthists called for a united socialist Arab nation. The formation of the UAR reduced the pressures of Britain and the U.S. on Syrian domestic affairs. The subsequent Iraqi revolution of July 14, 1958, transforming the country into a military republic, considerably weakened Britain's position in the Fertile Crescent. The landing of American and British troops in Lebanon and Jordan, respectively, soon thereafter, to prevent the possible overthrow of the regimes in those countries, was the last major Western effort to play a vital role in inter-Arab politics for some time.

Once the union was set up, the centralization of Nasser's authority became a reality and the Baʿth soon played second fiddle to him. As time passed, they were further marginalized. Nasser relieved them of ministerial posts. Key Baʿth leaders – notably Akram al-Hawrani, Salah al-Din Bitar, Mustafa Hamdun, and Abd al-Ghani Qannut – resigned at the end of December 1959, thus ending Baʿth collaboration with Egypt. Power now passed in Syria to the pro-Egyptian chief of intelligence, Abd al-Hamid Sarraj.

Tensions gradually brewed within the UAR between Nasser and the Syrians, the latter increasingly resenting Cairo's aggressive meddling in their domestic affairs. Moreover, other Arab states shunned Cairo's efforts to join the union's bandwagon. Iraq, which seemed ripe to join it in the wake of the July 1958 revolution, not only shied away but in effect evinced hostility toward Nasser. The coalition of which the new regime was composed soon faced a struggle in which the Arab nationalists, including the Iraqi branch of the Baʿth Party, lost out to Communists and radical nationalists. The leading Iraqi pro-Nasser Arab nationalist, Colonel Abd al-Salam Arif, found himself in a Baghdad prison under a sentence of death. Nasser reacted and accused Abd al-Karim Qasim, Iraq's commander-in-chief and prime minister, as a traitor to Arab nationalism and a protégé of international Communism. From that time onwards, until February 1963, the situation settled into a tense cold war between Cairo and Baghdad. The problem for Cairo and Damascus was that Qasim was a revolutionary whose behavior defied conventional expectations. On the one hand, he failed to cooperate with the UAR in the march toward Arab unity; on the other hand, he emerged as a hero to the poverty-stricken dwellers of Baghdad.

Iraq's behavior toward Egypt was a slap in the face to Nasser but far worse was the collapse of the union with Syria. By then deep discontent and resentment permeated broad segments of Syria over Egypt's involvement in Syrian politics, economy, and society. On September 28, 1961, this prompted secessionist army officers to overthrow the pro-Egyptian political order and announce Syria's breakaway from the UAR. According to Cairo, the union had been stabbed in the back by Syria's wealthy class, which had been affected by the socialist legislation that Nasser had decreed in summer 1961. These "reactionaries" colluded with the imperialists and the Arab monarchs, then bribed and subverted an opportunistic clique of military officers in order that the *ancien régime* might be restored in Syria.

After the collapse of the union it seemed as if Nasser would attend solely to domestic goals in Egypt in order to enhance his socialist program and the new Arab Socialist Union (ASU), which replaced the previous one-party regime of the Nationalist Union. But Nasser did not detach himself from Arab politics. Egypt's relations with Syria, Saudi Arabia, and Jordan were suspended. No diplomatic ties were maintained between Cairo and Damascus until November 1966. On the other hand, the Yemeni revolution of September 1962 that toppled the Imamate resuscitated in the Egyptian regime a desire for a fresh involvement in a hitherto unknown war. Egypt felt obliged to be drawn into it in the role of the champion of revolutionary progress and committed thousands of troops toward achieving this aim. For their part, the Saudis and Jordanians felt compelled to support the Yemeni Royalists, out of dynastic solidarity. Egypt was thenceforth caught in the complex web of a protracted war (until 1967), facing the anger of a Saudi monarchy that was suspicious of Nasserist hegemonic aims in the Arabian Peninsula. Since the early or mid-1960s, King Faisal also contended that Nasser's agents and supporters had attempted to undermine Saudi monarchical institutions from within.

A major and bloody coup d'état, on February 8, 1963, eliminated Qasim and his regime, bringing to power the Iraqi branch of the Baʿth in a coalition with Nasserists. The Egyptians welcomed the downfall of Qasim, hoping that the new Baʿthi-Nasserite regime would demonstrate a commitment to Pan-Arab causes and to socialism. A month later a coup occurred in Syria. The Egyptians hoped that, unlike the secessionist government of 1961–63, the new government, based on a Baʿthi-Nasserist coalition backed by the army, would help revive Arab unity. Israel, which had benefited from the inter-Arab rivalries of 1961–62, watched the new developments with some anxiety.

Subsequent to the dramatic political changes in Baghdad and Damascus, Nasser hosted unity talks in Cairo between mid-March and mid-April 1963. When the issue of a new Arab union beginning with Egypt, Syria, and Iraq as the pilot experiment was deliberated, Nasser proposed that it be formed in two stages: first Egypt and Syria for a trial period of four months; and then, if successful, with Iraq as third partner. But the search for a unification formula of political leadership was unattainable. It boiled down to the issue of mistrust among leaders, particularly the deep mistrust of Egypt by the Syrian Baʿth. The latter remained bitter over its past experience with Nasser.

In mid-July 1963, the Syrian Baʿth expelled the Nasserists from the government; four months later the Nasserists in Iraq, led by Colonel Abd al-Salam Arif, removed the Baʿthists. The Arab cold war among radical regimes wreaked havoc to the cause of Arab unity and rendered efforts toward a new Arab union obsolete. At the end of 1963 more Arab states were at each other's throats than ever before. Egypt and Saudi Arabia were locked in a struggle for the future of Yemen, where 40,000 Egyptian troops had failed to win a final victory for the republican revolution. Nasser had seized on the revolution in Yemen in September 1962 as an opportunity to break out of his isolation in the wake of Syria's secession from the UAR and regain the initiative in Arab affairs for Egypt on the basis of revolutionary leadership. The struggle with the Yemeni Royalist forces, backed by Saudi Arabia, was soon deadlocked. The longer the Egyptian army remained in Yemen, and the more the Egyptian commitment to consolidate the Yemeni revolution was reiterated, the more difficult it became to disengage. Meanwhile Algeria under the presidency of Ahmad Ben Bella and the regime of the Front de Libération Nationale (FLN) had been involved with Morocco over a border dispute (October 1963) and had another dispute with Tunisia. Tunisia and Morocco had been cool to each other ever since Tunisia had recognized the independence of Mauritania. Moreover, Tunisian President Habib Bourguiba attacked Nasser's Pan-Arab policies. Egypt was hostile to Jordan, and Syria deemed it to be unfriendly to both Jordan and to Morocco. These quarrels pitted revolutionary against conservative or moderate regimes. It left the Arab League ever more powerless.

Toward the end of 1963, at the zenith of Arab disunity, a sudden, albeit temporary, relaxation occurred. The catalyst on this occasion was Israel, which was approaching the completion of its project to divert the waters of the Jordan River for its own needs. Any act by Israel to divert these waters was considered by all Arab states as an act of aggression. Syria seized upon the Israeli initiative to awaken sentiments of Arab unity. Yet nothing materialized from the gestures of solidarity expressed by both conservative and radical Arabs. The disinclination of Egypt and Syria to go to war over Israel's water diversion schemes encouraged the Jewish state to resume its policies.

The Arab Arena: 1964–1970

The year 1964 was a turning point in inter-Arab politics. Added to the role of the Arab League as an all-Arab forum for coordinating economic, social, political, and military endeavors, the Arab states with Egypt at the helm established the Arab Summit Conference. It was meant to iron out differences and solve serious problems in a more efficient way than the League meetings could achieve. The first Arab summit in this spirit was held in Cairo in January. The key issues on its agenda were a negotiated compromise settlement in Yemen after Egypt committed troops and military hardware there and the creation of the *Palestine Liberation Organization (PLO).

As for the first issue, immediate success was achieved. For Nasser, Yemen was not merely a symbol of "revolutionary inevitability" but a foothold in the Peninsula, strategically bordering on both the British-protected South Arabian Federation and the Saudi Kingdom. It was only in August 1965 that Egypt backed down from total commitment to Yemen after Nasser had reluctantly signed an agreement in Jidda, Saudi Arabia, with Saudi King Faisal. The agreement stipulated that the two Yemeni sides – Royalists and Republicans – would convene at the end of the year to arrange for the formation of a mutually acceptable provisional government. The Egyptians and Saudis were to supervise a truce between the two Yemeni forces. But the arrangement did not work out and the Egyptian army remained in the area until 1967. In agreement with the Saudis, and six months after the June 1967 Arab-Israeli war, Egypt withdrew all of its troops and other personnel from Yemen. The Royalists lost out in the end and the Yemen Arab Republic emerged. In 1967, as Nasser was withdrawing his troops from the new Yemeni republic, a second Yemeni republic was established in the former Protectorate of Aden: the People's Democratic Republic of Yemen (PDRY). Once the Egyptians were gone the Saudis were less concerned with the type of regimes in the two Yemens.

As for the PLO and the decision to enable it to create a military unit of its own, most Arab leaders offered their support but with little enthusiasm. They regarded the PLO cynically as a device to enable them to leave the task of confronting Israel to the Palestinians and thereby avoid bearing this responsibility themselves. Even an avid supporter of Palestinian resistance like Nasser believed that tight surveillance had to be imposed on the activity of the PLO throughout the region. Once the PLO was formed, King Hussein's main worries centered on the potential challenges the new organization would pose to the sovereignty of the Jordanian state, almost two-thirds of whose population was Palestinian and whose frontier with Israel was long and difficult to patrol. It was clear that, of all Arab states, Jordan would emerge as the center for PLO activities. In fact, the secret ties forged between the Jordanian king and Israel after 1964 and his meetings with key Israeli diplomats in London were largely related to this mutual concern. Hussein's worries were justified in the course of 1964–65. PLO leader Ahmad Shukeiri expected Jordan to approve the collection of special taxes in the country in order to finance the organization's military activities against Israel. Shukeiri also sought to conscript Jordanian Palestinians into the new Palestine Liberation Army (PLA) and to distribute arms to border villagers.

If tensions arose over Yemen and the status of the PLO, another major difficulty came to the fore: On March 6, 1965, during his trip to the Middle East, Tunisian President Bourguiba, an opponent of Pan-Arabism and an advocate of Arab "state particularism," posed a genuine challenge to Arab leaders in a speech delivered in the Old City of Jerusalem. He publicly urged them to recognize Israel in return for negotiations in the spirit of UN Resolution 181 of November 29, 1947 (partitioning Palestine into two separate states – one Arab and one Jewish) and Resolution 194 of December 1948 (which called for the return to their homes of Palestinian Arab refugees who had fled upon Israel's creation). The next day Bourguiba reiterated these pleas in Jericho before an audience consisting of Palestinian refugees. Yet he neither produced a written proposal nor offered himself as a peace mediator. In 1965 and 1966, his proposals, which were directed more to Arab leaders than to Israel, outlined the following eight major points: (1) the policies of denunciation and rejection embraced by Arab leaders had only led to military confrontations and always ended in Arab defeat at the hands of the Israelis; (2) if Egypt developed a nuclear option, the world would prevent Nasser from using it against Israel; (3) not only was war immoral and counterproductive, but the U.S. would never allow the Arab states to defeat or decimate Israel; (4) prudence and wisdom had to prevail over emotionalism and hatred, for these only made Israel more powerful; (5) the Arabs needed to rid themselves of their feelings of humiliation resulting from past wars, while the Israelis must free themselves from the complex of embattlement and a garrison state mentality; (6) the Arabs would reap far greater benefits if they concentrated their efforts on reaching a negotiated solution to the Arab-Israeli conflict; (7) coexistence with Israel, even de facto recognition, would result in regional stability for all parties involved in the conflict; and (8) negotiations with Israel necessitated direct contacts, with Palestinian representatives leading the process from the Arab side. But Arab leaders would not hear of this. They boycotted Bourguiba and isolated him for some time.

The secret meetings between Israelis and Jordanians, mentioned above, were not unique although they enjoyed continuity into the 1970s and 1980s. Several Arabs leaders, including Jordan's King Abdullah I (Hussein's grandfather), had engaged in back channel contacts with Israel. Even Egypt had had occasional contacts, most of which led nowhere. Egyptian diplomatic emissaries of the Nasser era (like their pre-1952 predecessors) had met Israeli diplomats in Europe or at the UN in New York to discuss various aspects of territorial issues or the implementation of UN resolutions. On a more active level, Israel had maintained secret links with minorities in the Arab world as well as with forces opposed to Nasser's and the Baʿth's Pan-Arab unity ambitions. Thus, in the 1960s and after, Israel's intelligence apparatus, the Mossad, had reportedly assisted the Iraqi Kurds seeking internal regional autonomy against the pro-Nasserist Baghdad regime militarily. Israel apparently offered logistical and other assistance to the Christians in southern Sudan against the Arab regime in the north which was supported by Cairo. Assistance was also supplied to the Maronite Christians in Lebanon. Israel thought that by helping the Lebanese Christians it would help loyal allies to consolidate their political power base in what would become a pro-Western and pro-Israel nation.

More importantly, since the early 1960s, Israel had cultivated ties with Morocco, which opposed Nasserism and Pan-Arab unity and searched for discrete alignments against Cairo. As part of its government's "Periphery Doctrine," in search of allies geographically remote from the Arab-Israeli conflict, such as non-Arab pro-Western Iran and Turkey, Israel also looked for Arab allies with whom to cooperate behind the scenes. It was part and parcel of Israel's efforts to benefit from inter-Arab rivalries and misunderstandings as well as to ease its isolation in the region. Morocco fit neatly into this context. After the death of King Muhammad V in March 1961, Morocco's new king, Hasan II, and the Mossad developed special ties whereby Israel provided intelligence and military assistance and helped stabilize the monarchy, which then encountered strong leftist opposition from the Union Nationale des Forces Populaires (UNFP). Morocco, in turn, provided Israel with vital intelligence data about developments in the Arab arena. These special ties endured for several decades and became diversified in other areas. As Algeria's FLN regime was hostile to Israel, contacts were established with Tunisia's Neo-Destour regime, particularly with President Bourguiba, his son, and diplomatic representatives in Paris and London. After Bourguiba presented his peace plea, the World Jewish Congress, the Israeli embassy in Paris, and the Mossad kept up contacts with the Tunisians. Discussions revolved around discreet joint business ventures, agricultural cooperation, and Jewish tourism. However, Israeli hopes for relations with Tunisia that might become nearly identical to the ties nurtured with Morocco failed to materialize. Bourguiba was unwilling to commit himself as had Hasan of Morocco. Furthermore, in the 1970s Bourguiba seemed to have had a change of heart and espoused strong pro-Palestinian and anti-Israel rhetoric and policies.

Syria in the mid-1960s witnessed far-reaching internal change. There appeared cracks in the Baʿth leadership. A young generation of civilian and military Baʿth-oriented elements had made their appearance on the political scene. Most of them did not belong to the Sunni Muslim majority but rather to the Alawi and Druze religious minorities (formerly Shiite) which together did not constitute more than 15 percent of the Syrian population. Prominent among them within the military were Salah Jadid and Hafez al-Asad; among the civilians there were three physicians: Nur al-Din al-Atasi, Ibrahim Makhus, and Yusif Zuʿayyin. All of them considered the old-style Baʿthi leadership, especially the military dictator, Amin al-Hafiz, as being "too soft" on Israel and insufficiently critical of Arab conservative monarchical regimes. On February 23, 1966, the Syrian government was overthrown by these Neo-Baʿthists. The coup not only forced the old leaders to flee Syria but also shattered the party in other Arab states. The new leadership had injected a heavy dose of Marxist ideology into their political programs, some were even Maoists. Though critical of Cairo for not doing enough to prepare for an Arab military confrontation with Israel, their desire to prevent any coexistence with Arab "reactionary" monarchs propelled them to try and push Egypt into an alliance against the latter. Unlike the previous leadership, the new rulers actively backed a major Palestinian guerilla raid into Israel (November 1966) and engaged their army in skirmishes with Israel along the 1949 armistice line. These moves caused consternation in Cairo. Nasser never ruled out a confrontation with Israel when the propitious moment arose. But 1966 hardly seemed to be a timely occasion. Hoping to restrain the Syrians from dragging themselves along with other Arab states into war and wishing to have a "supervisory role" over Syrian military designs, Nasser invited to Cairo Prime Minister Zuʿayyin on November 7, 1966, to sign a treaty of mutual defense. Diplomatic relations, severed three years earlier, were renewed.

Unlike Syria, which in 1963 ousted the Nasserists from the government, Iraq's leadership was largely Nasserist-oriented under the leadership of President Abd al-Salam Arif and subsequently his brother, Abd al-Rahman. For Nasser this proved vital, given Iraq's strategic position alongside Syria and its major oil reserves. Support for Nasser also came from Algeria, which was geographically remote from the scene. The overthrow of President Ahmad Ben Bella in June 1965, however, and his replacement by Houari Boumedienne at the FLN's helm, was a blow to Egyptian prestige.

Iraq's major problem at the time was the Kurdish struggle for internal autonomy in the northern part of the country, a challenge that kept the Iraqi army on constant alert and weakened its prestige. The Kurdish problem had plagued the economy and contributed to the already tense ethnic and religious rivalries between Sunni Arabs, Shiite Arabs, and Sunni Kurds. In May 1964, Iraq and Egypt had agreed to work toward unification over a two-year period. As time elapsed, this goal proved unattainable owing to Iraq's inability to achieve stability at home. To emulate Egypt's model, the Iraqi government nationalized the private sector of the economy and introduced a charter for the creation of an Iraqi Arab Socialist Union, which would replace existing political parties. But neither of these efforts made much headway.

Changes of Arab regimes occurred after 1967. In July 1968 the pro-Nasser regime was overthrown in Iraq by a military clique led by General Hasan al-Bakr and a group of his fellow Baʿthists, including Saddam Hussein. These were "right-wing" Baʿthists, hostile to the Syrian Neo-Baʿth. In May 1969, a coup was carried out by officers in Sudan led by Jaʿafar Numeiri. The former South Arabian Federation received independence from Britain in 1967 and adopted the title of People's Republic of South Yemen. In September 1969 a coup in Libya deposed King Idris al-Sanusi. A Libyan republic was proclaimed by military officers, headed by Colonel Muʿammar al-Qadhafi. In November 1970, Defense Minister Hafez al-Asad overthrew the Neo-Baʿthists, establishing his own Baʿthi regime. In October 1970, Libya joined with Egypt, Sudan, and Syria in an abortive attempt to form an Arab union.

The Arab-Israeli Conflict: 1948–1970

The Arab-Israel conflict had its origins in Palestine at the end of the 19th century. It gained momentum in the 1890s over Arab opposition to the sale of land to Jews for agricultural settlements and gradually led to violent clashes between Arabs and Jews. The crux of the conflict was the competition between Jewish nationalism (Zionism) and Palestinian Arab nationalism for political control over the area that, in the peace settlement after World War I, became the League of Nations mandated territory of Palestine, held by Britain from 1922 to May 1948. The first major clash occurred in Jaffa in March 1908. Violence escalated in 1920–21, 1929, and 1936–39. Both Arabs and Jews rejected proposals by the 1937 British Royal Commission under Lord Peel to partition Palestine between the two communities, although some Zionist leaders accepted the partition in principle. When Israel was created, the struggle became known as the Arab-Israeli conflict.

With post-1945 international pressure on Britain to remove restrictions on Jewish immigration and land purchases in Palestine (enforced in 1939) following the Holocaust, and for the creation of a Jewish commonwealth, Arab-Jewish tensions brought Palestine to the boiling point. Britain appealed to the UN, which recommended, in the spirit of its General Assembly's Resolution 181 (November 1947), that Palestine be partitioned into Arab and Jewish states with an international enclave containing Jerusalem. The mainstream Zionists accepted the proposal, but a nationalist minority advocated a Jewish state on both banks of the Jordan River.

Palestine Arabs, supported by leaders throughout the

Arab world, rejected partition. The only Arab leader who maintained discreet ties with the Zionist leadership with the aim of resolving the conflict was King Abdullah of Jordan. Clashes then occurred between Palestinians demonstrating against violation of their right to self-determination and Jews celebrating their coming independence; these soon turned into full-scale civil war. Since Britain's mandate was to end on May 14, 1948, a rather disorderly withdrawal of British troops began from disputed areas. By May 1948, as the Jewish community organized its military force, Palestinian Arabs retreated, fled, or were expelled from Israel despite military assistance from several Arab states. Their defeat, uprooting, and dispersion is known as the *nakba* ("catastrophe").

The first Arab-Israeli war lasted until Egypt, Lebanon, Jordan, and Syria signed armistice agreements with Israel in 1949. Iraq refused to sign such an agreement. As a result of the war, Israel extended its frontiers approximately 2,000 square miles beyond the UN partition borders to those of the armistice agreement. The eastern part of Jerusalem fell into Jordanian hands; the Gaza Strip was held by the Egyptians over the next 18 years; and the lines separating Israeli from Syrian territory included several de-militarized zones. Over 700,000 Palestinians became refugees, unable to return to Israel; many lived in refugee camps in the surrounding Arab states, but some moved to the Maghreb, the Gulf states, Europe, or immigrated to the Americas. Territory intended as part of the Arab Palestinian state in the UN Partition Plan, including the West Bank of the Jordan River, came under the control of Israel, Jordan, and Egypt. In July 1951, after King Abdullah of Jordan annexed the West Bank of the Jordan to his kingdom (April 1950), he was assassinated by a Palestinian nationalist. Since the end of the first Arab-Israel war the issues of the Palestinian refugees' rights to return or to compensation, and the status of Jerusalem, along with Arab recognition of Israel, remained unresolved. To grapple with these problems the UN established the United Nations Truce Supervision Organization (UNTSO) to oversee the 1949 agreements between Israel and Egypt, Lebanon, Jordan, and Syria. In 1948 the UN Palestine Conciliation Commission was set up to achieve a peaceful settlement by addressing itself to Middle East economic development and equitable distribution of water between Israel, Jordan, Syria, and Lebanon. For a fuller discussion of the Palestinian refugees, see "Arab Refugees" under *Israel, State of: Historical Survey; and *Intifada.

The birth of modern Israel and her military victories in 1948 led to turmoil in the surrounding Arab states and sparked antigovernment acts. Syria's and Egypt's military setbacks contributed to the army coups of 1949 and 1952, respectively. In Israel, tensions heightened when Egypt's Nasser, who had ended the Egyptian monarchy of King Farouk, was perceived as a growing threat. There was an increase of infiltration into Israel by Palestinian fighters (*fedayeen*) from Egyptian-occupied Gaza across the armistice line. The situation triggered an arms race in the mid-1950s. As noted, Egypt acquired military hardware from the Soviet Bloc. Israel, in turn, obtained aircraft and tanks from the French. Relations between Egypt and Israel also became an integral part of the larger conflict between Egypt, France, and Britain over control of the Suez Canal.

Israel formed a secret alliance with France and Britain to overthrow, or, at the very least, destabilize the Nasser regime after the latter nationalized the Suez Canal Company – dominated largely by European stockholders – on July 26, 1956. After Israel attacked Egypt on October 29, Britain and France occupied the northern Canal Zone and the city of Port Said. In fact, apparently behind the back of the British, Israel and France reached a separate understanding whereby French pilots flew over Israel to prevent possible Egyptian aerial attacks on inland cities, a strategy that would enable Israeli jets to concentrate fully on the war front. The tripartite scheme was stymied by U.S. and Soviet threats of military intervention should the parties fail to pull out their troops from Egypt. In November 1956, the UN General Assembly established the United Nations Emergency Force (UNEF) to supervise the withdrawal of these forces and to act as a peacekeeping apparatus between Israel and Egypt. Anglo-French forces withdrew in December; Israel maintained troops in Egypt until March 1957.

Incidents erupted along other Israeli borders. Palestinian refugee infiltration and guerrilla attacks from Jordan plus clashes with Syria over Israeli projects to divert the Jordan River added obstacles to a peace settlement. The tensions over the use of water reached the boiling point in 1963–64 and resulted in Israeli military actions against Lebanon. Although the Israeli-Egyptian frontier was quiet between 1957 and the decade that followed, the tensions caused by the Jordan River dispute, the escalation of border incidents, especially with Syria and Jordan, and bitter verbal disputes set the stage for the June 1967 War: the third armed Arab-Israeli conflict.

In the aftermath of the signing of the aforementioned November 1966 Syrian-Egyptian defense agreement, achieved through Soviet mediation, and the reestablishment of diplomatic ties between these two states, Israeli-Syrian tensions had heightened. Throughout the early months of 1967 the Soviets and Syrians claimed that Israel had amassed troops along the demilitarized border. Egyptian observers arrived to confirm these developments and found no evidence of such actions. In retrospect, either the Soviets or the Syrians, or both, apparently sought to drag Egypt into a confrontation with Israel.

While many political observers believed that Nasser wished to put Israel's military capabilities to the test, others believed that he did not think that the opportune moment had arrived for him to enter into an armed conflict. Some even pointed out the back channel contacts between Israel's Mossad and General Mahmud Khalil, a close confidant of Nasser, over possible ways of ironing out Egyptian-Israeli differences. Others note that Nasser preferred that the liberation of Palestine be placed on the back burner in favor of the unification of the Arab states and the spread of the socialist revolution. With major units of his army bogged down in Yemen, his treasury empty, and the Anglo-Americans and the Arab monarchs challenging his authority, his primary goal was to consolidate his power base: in Egypt, the Soviet partnership, and his leadership of Arab socialism.

Yet when tensions rose in spring 1967 between Israel and Syria, Nasser's new understanding with the Neo-Baʿth regime placed him in a serious dilemma. If he challenged Israel with a threat of Egyptian military action in response to any move against Syria, he risked war. If he left the Syrians unprotected he would be portrayed in Arab eyes as a weakling. Nasser chose the path of deterrence and embroiled himself, Egypt, Syria, Jordan, and Iraq in the third and most catastrophic Middle East war. To pose a serious deterrent threat he expelled the UNEF from Sinai. He then blockaded Israel's passage through the Straits of Tiran at the southeast edge of the Sinai Peninsula and massed his troops on the border. Once Nasser had got that far, it hardly mattered what his initial purpose had been. His objective now went beyond simply deterring Israel: it was to score a clear political or military victory and then to receive the acclaim of the Arab world.

Israeli leaders responded with a preemptive strike on June 5, 1967, against Egypt and its Syrian, Iraqi, and Jordanian allies which had joined the fighting. After six days of fighting, Israel remained in full control of the military situation and emerged as the dominant power in the region. The Arab states were now thrown into complete disarray, surpassing the disunity of 1961–64. Israel had conquered the Sinai Peninsula up to the east bank of the Suez Canal and the Gaza Strip from the Egyptians; the Golan Heights from the Syrians; and the West Bank and East Jerusalem from the Jordanians. The war aggravated the tensions among the superpowers: the Soviet Union aligned itself with Egypt, Syria, and Iraq more than before, while the U.S. increased its support of Israel. King Hussein lost half his kingdom, whereas the Suez Canal remained closed with Israeli soldiers entrenched on its east bank. While in 1948 some 700,000 Palestinians had become refugees, an additional 300,000 uprooted themselves in an exodus from the West Bank and resettled in Jordan and Syria. Israeli Jewish settlers, mainly religious, created the infrastructure for dotting the West Bank and Gaza Strip with settlements.

Although defeated, the Arab states refused to enter into negotiations with Israel. They demanded that Israel demonstrate largesse by withdrawing to the 1949 (pre-June 5, 1967) lines and allowing the return of the Palestinian refugees to their homes in Israel. At their post-war summit in Khartoum, Arab leaders voted against negotiations, peace, or recognition of Israel. Israel and its U.S. ally advocated direct negotiations with the Arab states in return for which territorial concessions would be forthcoming.

An initiative with long-range implications was UN Security Council Resolution 242, on November 22, 1967, calling for the "withdrawal of Israeli armed forces from territories" conquered in the 1967 war, the end to hostilities, a "just settlement of the [Palestinian] refugee problem," and the "need to work for a just and lasting peace." To inplement the Resolution, the UN chose a special envoy, Dr. Gunnar Jarring, to mediate between the parties. Syria, Iraq, and Algeria rejected the Resolution outright. Jordan and Egypt disagreed over its interpretation. They insisted it meant that Israel had to withdraw from *all* territories occupied in the war. At the same time, Nasser and Hussein became close allies. Both were preoccupied with the same need for political survival and the recovery of lost territory through diplomatic channels. The hostility that had divided them in the late 1950s and early 1960s seemed forgotten. Israel argued that withdrawal should be made "from territories" but not to the armistice lines. Most Arabs, except the Palestinians, no longer expected Israel to withdraw to the 1947 lines. The PLO and the organizations connected to it dismissed Resolution 242 as a sellout. For them it signified Arab acceptance of Israel and relegated the claims of the Palestinians to the level of "a just settlement of the refugee problem."

A new war broke out in March 1969, known as the "War of Attrition." It was initiated by Nasser to try and break the stalemate and force Israel to withdraw from Egyptian territories. The war lasted 17 months. Egypt bombarded Israeli positions on the east bank of the Suez Canal and was supported by Soviet advisers and pilots. Israel retaliated by bombarding targets inside Egypt – demonstrating the might of its air force – including oil refineries and industrial infrastructure. Casualties mounted on both sides. On December 9, 1969, U.S. secretary of state, William Rogers, presented a plan for a comprehensive Middle East peace based on UN Resolution 242. It called for Israel's withdrawal to the pre-June 1967 borders with certain modifications in return for mutual Arab-Israeli security and a solution to the Palestinian refugee problem. Both the Arab and Israeli sides rejected the plan. In light of the escalation of the fighting between April and June 1970, however, Secretary Rogers renewed his efforts. Under a revived plan, the U.S. called for a three-month ceasefire on the Egyptian front, including a plea to all sides to accept UN Resolution 242 as a basis for future negotiations and an immediate request from Israel to negotiate with Egypt and Jordan via the mediation of special envoy Jarring. The Israelis, Egyptians, and Jordanians accepted the terms of the ceasefire, which was implemented in August 1970. For the next three years the potential war arenas in the Middle East remained quiet.

The Palestinians, however, kept fighting, keeping the region in constant tension. As noted above, the PLO, created at the Arab Summit in January 1964, was gradually becoming a potent force by the mid-1960s. In the aftermath of the June 1967 war and Israel's occupation of the West Bank and Gaza, a new Palestinian leadership emerged within that organization. Yahya Hamuda ousted Ahmad Shukeiri. The various guerrilla groups operating at the time with links to the PLO moved in to fill the vacuum created by the military defeat of the Arab states by intensifying their attacks on Israel. Such was the case as early as March 1968 at Karama, Jordan, where Israeli soldiers faced stiff resistance from Palestinian fighters. Karama became a symbol of the struggle against Israel, which many had regarded invincible. These guerrilla groups, especially *al-Fatḥ* ("Triumph"), now won control of the PLO. The PLO Charter was revised in July 1968 to underscore the rejection of the Arab states' interference in Palestinian affairs, the complete liberation of Palestine by Palestinians through armed resistance, and the establishment of a democratic secular state in much of historic Palestine.

The psychological lift the guerrilla fighters received at Karama also paved the way for *al-Fatḥ*'s leader, Yasser *Arafat, to seize control of the PLO. The Fataḥ was the largest fighting group within the PLO, the Palestine Liberation Army, and the Palestine National Council (PNC). The key rivals within the PLO to Fataḥ consisted of the Popular Front for the Liberation of Palestine (PFLP), the Democratic Front for the Liberation of Palestine (DFLP), the Popular Front for the Liberation of Palestine-General Command (PFLP-GC), and *al-Sāʿiqa* ("Thunderbolt"). These operated mainly out of Lebanon, Jordan, and Syria. In the years 1969–73, they caused considerable havoc in Lebanon, contributing to its political and religious instability. The Marxist-oriented PFLP was bent on overthrowing conservative regimes. It challenged King Hussein's authority in September 1970 and ignited a civil war in Jordan that resulted in the death of nearly 4,000 Palestinians, the PLO's defeat, and the relocation of its headquarters to Lebanon.

Inter-Arab Politics in the 1970s

The civil war in Jordan came to a halt thanks to Nasser's mediation between King Hussein and PLO's Arafat. Just as Nasser succeeded in calming tensions temporarily between Palestinians and the government of Lebanon through an emergency summit in November 1969, he was able to arrange for an end to the violence in Jordan, although it was contingent on the PLO's evacuation of the Hashemite kingdom. This was to be Nasser's last initiative on behalf of Arab causes. On September 28, 1970, he succumbed to a massive heart attack. The irony of Nasser's career was that he died while shielding his old enemy Hussein, at the expense of his old clients the Palestinians. Yet Jordan did pay a price for the repression of the Palestinians. The kingdom was ostracized by the all-Arab family well into 1973.

Nasser was succeeded by his vice president, Anwar al-*Sadat, who assumed full authority only in May 1971 after defeating the opposition made up of Nasser's former allies in the government, the heads of the Arab Socialist Union Party, and the military. Sadat then moved to cultivate public support for his presidency. He formulated a new permanent constitution (September 1971) stipulating that the *Shariʿa* (Islamic Law) is a source of legislation (in contradistinction to Nasser's secular policies), pardoned most of the nation's political prisoners, and returned major assets nationalized during the socialist era to their original owners. Simultaneously, he undermined leftist and Nasserist influences by according benefits to the Muslim Brotherhood, a major Islamist movement that had been repressed between the late 1940s and the mid-1950s. The Brotherhood advocated the creation of a universal Islamic nation, beginning with Egypt, in which Islamic Law would be the single source of legislation. Under Nasser they were the main opponents of the regime. They were to become Sadat's counterweights to his secular opponents.

Sadat disengaged himself and his new regime from Nasser's Pan-Arab policies at home and throughout the region. He changed the country's name from the United Arab Republic to the Arab Republic of Egypt, indicating a shift toward state particularism. In July 1972 he ordered all Soviet military advisers and personnel out of Egypt. This was a critical turning point in Egyptian history: the attempt to reverse Nasser's pro-Soviet policies and reduce the dependence on the Kremlin. Sadat also made known his desire to improve ties with Washington, badly damaged during the June 1967 war. After renewing the ceasefire agreement in November 1970 and February 1971, he sought a compromise with Israel. He sent a message to Prime Minister Golda *Meir through Jarring asking for a partial Israeli withdrawal from the Suez Canal to the Ras al-Muhammad line in order to reopen the Canal for navigation. Sadat hinted that a positive gesture from Israel could well constitute a decisive step toward implementing UN Resolution 242. Golda Meir publicly responded in favor of Sadat's approach. Nevertheless, the Egyptian request was finally rejected, apparently due to Sadat's subsequent demands from Israel to return to all pre-June 1967 borders. This was something Israel was unwilling to accept. Realizing that a compromise was not near, Sadat began to consider a limited war, possibly in collaboration with Syria, to regain occupied territories and bring the Suez Canal into operation. In November 1972 he instructed his war minister to begin military preparations for war. Despite the fluctuations in Soviet-Egyptian relations in the wake of the expulsion of Russian military advisers, in spring 1973 a major new arms deal was concluded between Moscow and Cairo, the cost of which was covered by the Saudis and other conservative Arab regimes.

Sadat departed from Nasser's policy of undermining conservative monarchies and republican regimes that disapproved of Pan-Arabism and Egypt's past relations with the Soviet Union. These regimes rewarded Sadat with generous financial assistance. A year later, during and following the October 1973 Arab-Israeli war, the oil-producing monarchies provided Sadat with important leverage: the oil embargo on the West, which was intended to prod the U.S. and Western Europe to pressure Israel into making territorial concessions.

Domestically, in 1974, the Sadat regime implemented economic programs meant to attract considerable foreign investments to Egypt, revive the public sector that had remained dormant under Nasser, and offer significant opportunities for local businessmen. This policy came to be known as *siyāsat al-infitāḥ* – the open door policy to free enterprise. By the late 1970s Sadat allowed formerly outlawed political parties to resume their activity for the first time since 1953. New parties were invited to join in the system under the revised constitution of September 1971. Sadat expected political parties to constitute a loyal opposition and a counterweight to his opponents. With time passing, his harsh treatment of "disloyal" parties and his refusal to permit the Muslim Brotherhood to become a party, with the argument that no religious party had a monopoly over Islam, stirred discontent. Real progress in granting greater political freedom was achieved under Husni *Mubarak, Sadat's successor to the presidency. By the late 1970s, dissatisfaction over Sadat's capitalist policies and the cutting of government subsidies of basic necessities such as foodstuffs also became widespread.

Since 1970 Libya under the radical regime headed by Colonel Qadhafi had become active in inter-Arab affairs. Libyan "socialism" was contradictory: both leftist and Islamic, anti-Communist yet allied with the Soviet Union. Qadhafi pressed for an inter-Arab union in the spirit of Nasserist Pan-Arabism and adopted a militant anti-Israel and pro-Palestinian stance. The British and American military bases that had survived under the Sanusi monarchy were closed, the tiny Italian community was expelled, alcohol was forbidden as were nightclubs, and Christian churches were closed. By the mid-1970s, disappointed with the failure of other Arab rulers to support his pleas for unity, and declining relations with Egypt, Qadhafi plunged into domestic affairs and proclaimed a Libyan Cultural Revolution. The General People's Congress had been created, the country's administration was taken over by committees, and Libya was declared a *Jamāhīriyya*, or "the state of the masses."

Baʿthi Iraq of the post-July 1968 coup under the Hasan al-Baqr and Saddam Hussein regime was active in the inter-Arab arena and the Arab-Israeli conflict. Iraq was in serious contention with Syria for the leading position in the progressive socialist-leftist camp and in the Fertile Crescent. Syria since 1970, under the presidency of Hafez al-Asad, also played a leading role on the inter-Arab scene, though Asad adopted a somewhat more flexible, responsible, and pragmatic stance in the Arab-Israeli conflict by not advocating an immediate war, he opposed UN Resolution 242.

Several inter-Arab rivalries were resolved. Saudi Arabia and Kuwait agreed in 1969 to resolve border disputes between them. Saudi Arabia conceded to Abu Dhabi the disputed Buraimi oasis (1974), obtaining instead an outlet to the sea between Abu Dhabi and Qatar. Other inter-Arab disputes persisted. South Yemen (PDRY) clashed with the Yemen Arab Republic in warlike operations in 1972 and 1979. The PDRY was also in conflict with Oman, where it supported a rebellion in Dhofar. Iraq's border disputes with Kuwait led to clashes in 1973 and 1976. Libya, too, was in conflict with her neighbors: Chad (non-Arab) disputed Libya's annexation of Chadi territory since 1973 and resented Qadhafi's support for rebels. Libya claimed territorial rights from Niger and was frequently accused of meddling in that county's internal affairs. Libya's relations with other West African countries – Mali, Senegal, and Gambia – were tense, as those nations accused Qadhafi of conspiring against their governments. Tensions ran high between Libya and Tunisia. The latter accused Libya of hatching plots and stirring subversion within her borders. In 1977, Libya and Egypt were on the verge of total war following Sadat's accusation that Qadhafi had plotted to assassinate leading Egyptian government officials. Qadhafi's radical actions were also apparent in the assistance he offered the Irish Republican Army in Northern Ireland, Europe's terrorists – rightist and leftist – as well as Muslim rebels in the Philippines and Thailand. Finally, in the Maghreb, border disputes flared throughout the 1970s. A border dispute between Morocco and Algeria was patched up in agreements, mediated by African states. Moroccan-Algerian relations deteriorated once again over Western (formerly Spanish) Sahara. Algeria refused to accept the partition and annexation of that territory by Morocco and Mauritania in 1975. Thus it supported the Saharan rebels (the POLISARIO) and the republic they proclaimed. Algeria offered military aid whereas Israel assisted Morocco.

The Arab-Israeli Conflict in the Early and Mid-1970s

As noted, in 1972 the Egyptians began to lay the groundwork for the fourth major Arab-Israeli war. The war that finally broke out in October 1973 resulted from failure to resolve the territorial disputes arising from the previous conflict. UN Resolution 242 notwithstanding, little progress had been made in its implementation and Israel remained in control of the occupied territories. When Sadat decided to go to war he contacted Syrian President Hafez al-Asad to arrange for a two-front attack on Israel: in the Sinai and the Golan Heights. Despite Sadat's expulsion of Soviet military personnel in summer 1972, he was still dependent on the Russians. Thus, when he approached them for military supplies they stepped up arms deliveries to both Egypt and Syria. The Iraqis entered the war at its inception, as did volunteer fighters from the Maghreb, Kuwait, Sudan, and Saudi Arabia. Jordan dispatched a token military force. The oil-rich monarchies offered financial and diplomatic assistance. In contrast to what had transpired in 1967, Egypt and Syria were reluctant to share precise military plans with King Hussein. The latter visited Israel secretly on September 25, 1973, and, at the Mossad's compound, briefed Prime Minister Golda Meir about Syrian and Egyptian war plans. What he could not do was to pinpoint the exact date of an attack.

The two-front war broke out on October 6, 1973, the Jewish Day of Atonement. It was also the Muslim month of Ramadan and hence the conflict was regarded by the Arabs as the "Ramadan War." Egyptian forces crossed the Suez Canal to the east bank and overran the Bar-Lev Line, built several years earlier to thwart all potential military assault. On the northern front, the Syrians rushed into the Golan Heights and came very close to reaching the June 4, 1967, border with Israel. The war caught Israel completely unprepared, for until then the Israel Defense Forces believed that Egypt and Syria were ill prepared for war and thus would desist from waging it.

On October 10 Sadat requested that the Saudis use the oil weapon as a countermeasure to the American airlift to Israel. On October 16, Arab oil ministers convened in Kuwait and proclaimed an embargo on petroleum shipments to the U.S. and Holland. They said the restrictions would be lifted once

Israel retreated from Arab territories occupied in the 1967 war. The oil ministers then put pressure on other Western governments by reducing oil shipments by five percent a month until the Arabs' terms were met. Algeria, Saudi Arabia, the United Arab Emirates, Qatar, and other Gulf states supported the war effort financially. Algerian President Houari Boumedienne provided the Kremlin with $200 million to finance military assistance to Egypt and Syria.

The fighting was the heaviest since 1948, with major losses of men and war material on both sides. Over 2,800 Israeli and 8,500 Arab soldiers were killed during the battles in the Sinai and the Golan Heights. Israel lost over 100 aircraft and more than 800 tanks while the Arabs lost nearly 400 aircraft and at least 2,500 tanks. Each side was rearmed during the fighting – Egypt by the Soviet Union and Israel by the U.S. Within several days, recovering from the surprise attack, the Israelis launched their counteroffensive. By October 9, the Syrians had been pushed back to their starting point. The Israel Defense Forces then entered Syrian territory and positioned themselves 20 miles outside Damascus. On the Egyptian front, Israeli forces crossed to the west bank of the Suez Canal in mid-October, cutting off the Egyptian Third Army and surrounding it.

The war precipitated an international crisis when the Soviet Union responded to an urgent appeal from Egypt to save its Third Army. Despite the UN Security Council ceasefire resolution, Israeli troops continued to attack. Once the Soviet Union revealed its intentions to dispatch troops to Egypt, Washington called for a worldwide military alert. The crisis subsided after all parties agreed to negotiate an honorable retreat of the Egyptian Third Army. When the belligerents accepted the ceasefire, on October 22, Israel had regained its control of Sinai and its forces were positioned 60 miles from Cairo, though Egyptian forces were still entrenched on the east bank of the Suez Canal. It was then that UN Resolution 338 was passed, calling for the termination of all war activity and the implementation of Resolution 242. Thenceforth, Resolution 338 became an adjunct to 242.

In December 1973 a Middle East peace conference convened in Geneva under the auspices of the U.S., the Soviet Union, and the UN. Israel, Egypt, and Jordan attended it while Syria boycotted it. Apart from opening speeches and brief deliberations over technical matters, the conference failed to reconvene. The U.S. decided to work directly with the Israelis and Egyptians without involving the UN and the Russians. Owing to the mediation efforts of Secretary of State Henry *Kissinger a disengagement agreement was hammered out on January 18, 1974, between Israel and Egypt. Israel withdrew across the Suez Canal and enabled Sadat to reopen and operate it. A second phase of the Israeli pullout from the Sinai, signed on September 4, 1975, entailed, inter alia, an Israeli withdrawal to the east of the Mitla and Gidi Passes and return of the Abu Rudais oil fields to Egypt.

It was far more complicated to work out a disengagement agreement between Israel and Syria. Kissinger was at pains to convince Israel to withdraw its forces from Syrian territory occupied in the 1973 war as well as from the Quneitra area in the Golan Heights that had remained under Israeli control after 1967. A buffer zone was established in the Golan Heights under UN supervision while Damascus agreed to prevent Palestinian fighters from launching attacks into Israel through Syrian territory. The disengagement agreement was signed on May 31, 1974, and remained in place.

The Road to Egyptian-Israeli Peace: 1976–1979

Intertwined with these disengagement agreements, an Arab summit convened in Rabat on October 26, 1974, which only Qadhafi of Libya and President Hasan al-Bakr of Iraq chose to boycott. The outcome amounted to a four-point resolution: (1) extending greater financial assistance to the confrontation states and the PLO; (2) working for a comprehensive peace settlement in the Middle East and opposing separate agreements; (3) recognizing the PLO as "the sole legitimate representative of the Palestinian people," thus stripping Jordan's King Hussein of any real political influence within the West Bank and over its Palestinian population; and (4) offering suggestions for resolving all major political differences that had clouded relations between Arafat and Hussein since 1970, when the PLO was forced out of Jordan.

Meanwhile, President Asad sought to increase his influence in the Middle East by extending Syrian political and military influence into neighboring Lebanon. Some of this related to his claim that Lebanon was an integral part of Greater Syria. The civil war that broke out in Lebanon in April 1975 and lasted into 1990 – resulting from internal ethnic tensions, the PLO's meddling in the country's domestic politics, and its use of Lebanese territory as a launching pad for terrorist actions inside Israel – proved to be timely and advantageous for Asad. The Palestinian issue held dangers for Lebanese religious and political stability, as did the mounting animosities between Shiites, Maronite Christians and their right-wing militias (especially the Phalange), Sunni Muslims, and Druze. These factors were in effect interconnected. While the Lebanese government tried to curb the Palestinian armed presence on its soil, as did right-wing Christian militias, leftist Sunnis expected Lebanon to assist the Palestinians in Beirut as well as in the south, where the latter directed their attacks on Israel. The Sunnis called on the authorities to dispatch the national army to protect southern Lebanon against Israeli retaliatory raids.

The Lebanese civil war led to close collaboration between Israel and Bashir Jumayyil, leader of the Phalange, against the PLO. Simultaneously, Syria seized the opportunity to consolidate her own position by backing the Sunni leftist-Palestinian alliance, though at times she had to restrain the Palestinians, even to the point of military action. Between 1976 and 1984, Syria emerged as the dominant force in the military control of parts of Lebanon and imposed its authority on local politics. Iraq and Libya, too, meddled in Lebanese politics, supplying their radical allies with weaponry and funds.

As these developments occurred, the U.S. encouraged the parties to the Arab-Israeli conflict to convene in Geneva for a Middle East international peace conference. Syria's position on the conference was hazy, but nothing came of the American initiative because both Israel and Egypt expressed misgivings about it. Israel refused to be dragged into a forum where the Soviet Union and Arab leaders might seek to force major territorial and political concessions that would not be acceptable to it. Egypt doubted Syrian flexibility and mistrusted the Soviets. Besides, Sadat concluded that peace ought to be achieved only through direct negotiations with Israel.

It appears that both Egypt and Israel looked for creative solutions to the conflict, with the Americans brought later into the picture. In September 1977, a secret meeting took place in Morocco between Egyptian Deputy Prime Minister Hasan al-Tuhami and Israeli Foreign Minister Moshe *Dayan. It was held in the presence of Moroccan King Hasan. The two men, who met each other with the prior knowledge of their heads of state, discussed the idea of Israel's withdrawal from all occupied Arab territories in return for peace. Much attention, however, was focused on the question of whether Israel would be prepared to return all the rest of the Sinai still under its control. It is difficult at this point to discern what Dayan and the Likud government headed by Prime Minister Menaḥem *Begin could have offered the Egyptians – whether the whole of the Sinai would be returned in return for negotiations and recognition of Israel, or whether the meeting was merely a test of good will and a "warming up session" for future discussions. Apparently, Sadat saw in the event a "green light," an opportune moment for a diplomatic initiative on his part.

In late October and early November 1977 Sadat secretly developed a plan to visit Jerusalem. On November 9, in the course of a speech to the Egyptian People's Assembly, he announced his readiness to go "to the ends of the earth" in order to prevent the outbreak of another war. He then added a sentence, not part of the prepared speech, about his willingness to go to Israel and speak before the Knesset. Yasser Arafat, who was present in the Parliament as a guest during Sadat's speech, was astounded, as was the Carter administration. It took the U.S. two weeks to endorse Sadat's initiative – after he had already visited Jerusalem – and abandon or shelve plans for an international conference.

Sadat's speech drew attention in the Arab world only when Prime Minister Begin responded with a public invitation to Sadat to visit Jerusalem. Before reaching his decision to go to Israel, Sadat visited Asad in an effort to garner wider Arab support for the initiative. When Asad was unable to talk Sadat out of his plan, he even considered arresting him. But Sadat would not budge and visited Jerusalem. He had once again put Egypt's interests above Arab solidarity, as had been the case when he signed the 1974 and 1975 disengagement agreements, setting a precedent for separate initiatives. Sadat spoke in the Knesset on November 20, 1977. While refraining from mentioning the PLO, he urged Israel to evacuate the territories occupied in 1967 and to seek an honorable solution to the plight of the Palestinian people.

Support for Sadat's move was initially forthcoming mostly from Morocco, Sudan, and Oman. Syria and Iraq were furious about it. With Egypt pulling out as an active participant in the Arab-Israeli conflict, the eastern front against Israel, of which Damascus and Baghdad were part, weakened considerably. No large-scale war could now be fought by the Arab states. Algeria, PDRY, and the PLO branded Sadat a traitor to the Arab cause. For the PLO, Sadat's move was most damaging. As far as the Palestinians were concerned, he had backtracked from the formula of an independent Palestinian state, putting forward the concept of Palestinian self-determination as part of a peace settlement with Israel. Libya reacted to the Jerusalem visit by calling for a meeting in Tripoli – without Egyptian participation. The Saudis, backed by Kuwait, Jordan, and Morocco, pressed for Egypt to be invited in order to bring it back into the Arab fold. Only Syria, Iraq, Algeria, PDRY, and the PLO attended the Tripoli meeting on December 5, 1977, and decided to freeze their ties with Egypt, considering moving the Arab League headquarters out of Cairo and reviewing Egypt's membership.

From Israel's point of view a separate peace settlement with Sadat was the preferred solution. The Begin government was not well disposed toward any concessions to the Palestinians and thought that negotiations, even with moderate states like the Kingdom of Jordan, were still premature. Dayan was especially hostile to any concessions to the PLO and made this point plain to Hasan al-Tuhami during their deliberations in Morocco. It was argued in Israel that a separate settlement would reduce significantly the potential of a wide Arab war against the Jewish state, while the status quo in the West Bank and Gaza would be preserved, rendering the thorny issues of Palestinian sovereignty less relevant for some time.

After months of Egyptian-Israeli meetings to overcome political hurdles, top Israeli and Egyptian leaders met at Camp David in September 1978. Under American patronage and mediation an Egyptian-Israeli agreement, known as the Camp David Accords, was signed on September 17, 1978. Like Sadat's visit to Jerusalem the previous year, this development wreaked havoc among Arab leaders. As far as they were concerned, what Sadat had done was to make a separate deal with the Israelis, contrary to the idea of a comprehensive peace settlement agreed upon in October 1974 at the Arab summit in Rabat. In reaction, Iraq convened a summit conference in Baghdad (November 1978) to probe the possibility of imposing sanctions on Egypt. Yet the rivalries that plagued the Arab political scene made it impossible to agree on the sanctions. Iraq, Syria, Algeria, the PLO, and PDRY wanted to isolate Egypt, while the Saudis, Moroccans, and Kuwaitis felt that Egypt was vital to the Arab world. They argued that an attempt to convince Sadat to avoid signing a formal agreement with Israel would perhaps prove more prudent.

But Sadat refused to have anything to do with the radicals and turned down the moderate states' pleas. Thus, Morocco's support for Sadat diminished, and outwardly, at least, King Hasan finally toed the radical Arab line. On March 26, 1979, the Israeli-Egypt peace treaty was signed formally in Washington in the presence of President Jimmy Carter. In April 1982, Israel returned the rest of Sinai to Egypt, and by 1985 the disputed Taba area.

The Arab World and Israel: The 1980s to the Early 1990s

The Israel-Egypt peace treaty of March 26, 1979, and the Islamic revolution in Iran that had toppled the pro-Western Shah Muhammad Reza Pahlavi only several weeks earlier affected the Arab world radically throughout the 1980s. Egypt was expelled from the Arab League, whose headquarter moved from Cairo to Tunis. It is ironic that Tunisian President Bourguiba, who in the 1950s and 1960s had been regarded as the Arab League's most bitter critic, now served as its host. Egypt was further isolated as most Arab states severed their ties with Cairo, which were renewed only in 1987. Meanwhile President Sadat was assassinated by a fanatical Islamist army officer on October 6, 1981, and replaced by his vice president, Husni Mubarak. In the absence of Egyptian leadership in Arab forums, the Arab world fell into disarray and ever-deepening disunity. Iraq, perhaps the most influential Arab country at the time, launched a war against Islamist Iran in September 1980. Iraq's new leader, President Saddam Hussein, having ousted President Hasan al-Bakr in July 1979, took advantage of Iran's difficult internal transition from monarchy to republic in an attempt to weaken it. It is still unclear what motivated the Iraqis to go to war. The standard explanations ranged from the occupation of Iranian territory (the Shatt al-Arab waterway and the oil-rich province of Khuzistan) to the infliction of a decisive defeat on the Iranian revolution and the desire to make Iraq the preeminent Arab and Persian Gulf state. Another plausible explanation is the fear of the predominantly Sunni Arab regime in Iraq that the Iranian Revolution might back the Iraqi Shiite majority and local Kurdish nationalists in an effort to destabilize it. Although caught unprepared, the Iranians demonstrated resilience and fought well into 1988, when the war finally ended with no clear victors.

If Iraq was concerned about the potential of a Shiite-Iranian-Islamist threat in the post-1979 period, the Persian Gulf Arab monarchies were equally anxious. Beside the concern in Bahrain and Qatar, where the Shiites accounted for more than half the general population, that Iran's propaganda efforts would incite them against the political regime, the Gulf monarchies feared possible Iranian territorial expansion into their domain. Syria, on the other hand, improved its relations with Iran, economically and militarily, moving the Gulf states and Saudi Arabia to improve their ties with Iraq.

The Iran-Iraq war proved beneficial to Israel in the short term. Iraq was too busy on the Iranian front to render assistance to radical forces in their struggle against the Jewish state. Two developments suppport this view. First, during the course of the war Israel managed to carry out prolonged military operations inside Lebanon – especially "Operation Peace for Galilee" – and to challenge Syria and the PLO militarily on Lebanese soil with little external interference. Second, Israel hardly encountered Arab opposition when the Knesset approved the Golan Law of December 14, 1981, extending Israeli law to the occupied Golan Heights, which for all intents and purposes signified territorial annexation. Syria itself was in no position to challenge Israel effectively owing to internal upheavals organized by the Syrian Muslim Brotherhood. The latter launched terrorist attacks in the northern part of the country in 1980–82 against the secularist Baʿth and its Alawi leadership elite, prompting Asad to adopt far-reaching repressive measures to quell the unrest.

The aforementioned "Operation Peace for Galilee" represented the clearcut Arab weakness since 1978–80. Throughout the 1978–82 period, the Israel Defense forces were fighting PLO terrorist activity originating from Lebanon inside Israeli territory. The Palestinians also fired Katyusha rockets from Lebanon at Israel's Galilee region. These attacks served as an incentive for the Begin government to decimate the PLO's infrastructure, expel its fighters, eliminate Syria's presence, and implant a Maronite-dominated government led by the Phalange party – Israel's foremost Lebanese ally.

The invasion that was part of "Operation Peace for Galilee," commencing on June 6, 1982, was triggered not by a border incident but by the attempted assassination of the Israeli ambassador in London three days earlier. This was a pretext, though, because the would-be assassin belonged to the anti-PLO Abu Nidal group, which also targeted PLO officials. Initially, "Operation Peace for Galilee" was intended to be limited to a 25-mile security belt south of the Litani River, as Defense Minister Ariel *Sharon had declared. Yet once the operation began and PLO strongholds were eliminated, Sharon and military Chief of Staff Rafael *Eitan instructed the army to proceed to the outskirts of Beirut, a task completed by mid-June. As the Israel Defense Forces were surrounding the Lebanese capital, shelling West Beirut, and engaging in aerial bombardments, they were joined by the Phalange. The pressure was now on the PLO's fighting forces to abandon their West Beirut headquarters and leave the country. The pressure was also directed at the Lebanese government to help carry out the expulsion.

In the aftermath of U.S. diplomatic involvement, the PLO agreed to leave Lebanon in an orderly fashion while an accord was reached wherein a multinational force, including U.S. Marines, would supervise the evacuation procedure. Syria was also required to reduce its military presence in the country. By September 1, over 14,000 PLO fighters and their leaders had left West Beirut for different Arab countries, mainly Tunisia, where Tunis became the PLO's new headquarters. That same day, the Reagan administration announced the Reagan Plan calling for the implementation of UN Resolution 242 and a freeze on building new Israeli settlements in the West Bank and Gaza Strip. The plan refrained from supporting the establishment of an independent Palestinian state but advocated Palestinian autonomy in association with Jordan. Most

Arab states and the PLO rejected the plan outright. Israel, too, regarded it with little enthusiasm.

"Operation Peace for Galilee," Minister of Defense Ariel Sharon's grand plan for a stable Lebanon, turned out to be a tragic illusion. On the one hand, Bashir Jumayyil, leader of the Phalange and Israel's main ally, was elected president of Lebanon on August 23 against Syria's wishes. On the other hand, the longer Israel maintained a military presence in the country, the more the support it initially enjoyed from various segments of the population eroded. This was very much the case with the Shiites in southern Lebanon. In the past they had resented the Palestinians for carrying out terrorist acts against Israel from their territory, for they often paid the price of Israeli retaliatory raids on the ground and from the air. Yet the Israeli entrenchment on Lebanese soil gradually turned the Shiites against them. Then, on September 14, Jumayyil was assassinated, possibly by pro-Syrian elements, shattering any remaining hope for normal life in Lebanon. Israeli forces reacted to the event by taking control of West Beirut and allowing Phalange militiamen to enter the Sabra and Shatila Palestinian refugee camps. The Phalange, seeking revenge for the death of their leader, carried out a horrible massacre among its inhabitants, causing outrage in Israel and throughout the world. A top-level investigative committee was created in Israel to determine the extent of responsibility for the massacre by the government and military. Ariel Sharon was forced to resign from his defense ministry post in February 1983.

Amin Jumayyil succeeded his late brother as Lebanon's president. Following extensive negotiations between Lebanese and Israeli officials under American patronage, a security and peace agreement was concluded on May 17, 1983. It provided Israel with important concessions such as the use of much of Lebanon's air and ground space in the south. It also laid the groundwork for future commercial and tourist activity. In fact, affluent Lebanese families visited Israel in summer 1983. The agreement contained guarantees from Israel to the Reagan administration of a gradual pullout from Lebanon in parallel to the withdrawal of the remaining Syrian armed forces.

An agreement which ignored Syria's interests in Lebanon could not hold up, however. In early fall 1983 Israel did commence a phased evacuation of its forces from Beirut as well as the Shuf area, withdrawing south of the Awali River. Nevertheless, this move and the U.S. and multinational military presence could not maintain the peace. The opposition to the agreement of May 17, 1983, gained momentum. The Lebanese army was torn by factions while small armies consisting of Sunni and Shiite Muslims gained strength and posed serious threats to the continued foreign presence and to Maronite political primacy. They included the Shiite Amal ("Hope") movement and the *Hizbollah ("Party of God"). The latter was founded in 1982 with the help of Iranian agents and gradually became the most potent political and military force in southern Lebanon and the Biqa' Valley. It enjoyed financial and logistical assistance from Iran and Syria. Whereas Amal sought to improve the conditions of the Shiites in south Lebanon within the political realm, Hizbollah sought to establish there an Islamic state on the Iranian model. Both supported a strong Syrian presence in the country (as did the Druze at the time). Hizbollah evinced strong antagonism vis-à-vis Israel, the U.S., and the Lebanese government. It was apparently responsible for the suicide car bomb attacks on Israeli bases, the U.S. embassy in Beirut, and the October 23, 1983, assault on the Marine naval barracks, killing 241 Marines. Hizbollah's actions hastened the withdrawal of multinational forces from Lebanon at the beginning of 1984. For the U.S., sinking in the Lebanese quicksand was perhaps as tragic as for Israel. Syria emerged as the principal beneficiary. Asad seized on these developments to reverse Israel's earlier achievements.

On March 5, 1984, the Israeli-Lebanese agreement was annulled. When Israel withdrew from Lebanon in 1985 – after establishing a six-mile security zone in the south patrolled by local Christian allies –Asad was able to bolster his hegemony over Lebanon. Israel may have eliminated much of Palestinian militancy in Lebanon but gained a more formidable enemy in the radical Islamist Shiites.

Although an Israeli-Lebanese peace agreement could not be implemented in 1983–84, and the Egyptian-Israeli peace treaty did not extend to include other states, there were efforts by several Arab leaders and non-official Israelis and Jews outside Israel, before and after 1983, to initiate peace plans. Attempts had been made by Palestinian leader 'Isam Sartawi and Israeli public figures such Ury *Avneri, Matti Peled, and Ya'akov Arnon to meet secretly and discuss ideas as to how to implement UN Resolution 242 and create an independent Palestinian state alongside Israel. The first meeting over these issues took place in Morocco in the presence of King Hasan and his closest advisers. Nothing came of these meetings. Moreover, Sartawi was assassinated in April 1983, and Avneri and his group wielded little influence inside Israel, as they were politically marginal. A group of Moroccan Jews (Israelis and those living in Morocco and elsewhere) formed in the late 1970s an organization called Identité et Dialogue whose aim was to engage Moroccan Muslims, as well as Israeli and Arab politicians, in peace dialogues. They felt they could serve as a bridge toward Arab-Israeli understanding. They were led by André Azoulay, an economist who served later as chief economic adviser to King Hasan, and later worked in the same capacity under King Muhammad VI. Despite Hasan's support for these efforts, the group accomplished little and by the mid-1980s became invisible.

Of greater significance and seriousness was the effort by the then Saudi Prince Fahd bin Abd al-Aziz ibn Saʿud to revive the Middle East peace process. Two months prior to Sadat's assassination, Fahd proposed a comprehensive settlement to include full Israeli withdrawal from all occupied territories, and dismantling of all the Israeli settlements in the West Bank and Gaza Strip; establishing a Palestinian state with

East Jerusalem as its capital; affirming the right of all nations in the Middle East to coexist peacefully; and guaranteeing the Palestinian rights, with compensation for those refugees and their descendants not interested in returning to their homes inside Israel. The new plan was meant to provide an alternative framework to the Camp David Accords in the hope it might enjoy Arab and international support. King Hasan emerged as the staunchest promoter of the plan.

Hoping to secure some credit from the Saudi plan for himself, Hasan volunteered to host an Arab summit where its contents would be scrutinized. Such a summit did in fact take place in Fez on November 25, 1981. Aside from the affirmation that all states in the region were to coexist in peace, the plan remained fuzzy over the official ending of the Arab-Israeli conflict once the Israelis fulfilled their part of the bargain. It also left out the question of recognition of Israeli sovereignty and the problem of the Palestinian claim of the right of return. The latter was a thorny issue for Israel and would remain so. Excepting Hasan's unequivocal support of the plan and the Gulf states' initial cautious support, in the final analysis the summit's participants studiously avoided any serious discussion of its contents. They focused instead on the issue of extending financial support for Lebanon, ravaged by violence. Not least problematic was the absence at the summit of the presidents of Libya, Syria, Algeria, Sudan, and Tunisia. The banishing of Egypt from the Arab consensus was also a major impediment.

To save face as the summit's host, as well as his personal prestige, and at the same time cover up any possible damage that could be caused to Arab solidarity over the Israeli-Palestinian conflict, Hasan suggested that the plan not be written off completely. The opponents of the plan could not be disregarded either, he averred, and thus the summit should be suspended and reconvened to discuss this issue later on. Arab leaders accepted the compromise. The Fahd plan resurfaced at the second Fez Arab summit of September 1982, which was convened in the aftermath of Israel's "Peace for Galilee" incursion into Lebanon. It also followed the aforementioned Reagan's Middle East proposals of September 1, 1982, calling for the implementation of Resolutions 242 and 338. This time, Syria's Asad attended, as did Iraq's Saddam Hussein, Jordan's King Hussein, and Fahd (now the Saudi king), the rulers of the Gulf emirates, and PLO Chairman Yasser Arafat. Despite Hasan's energetic lobbying among Arab leaders in favor of the Fahd plan, his efforts were only marginally rewarded. The summit did back an Arab peace plan, but it was a considerably altered version of the Saudi initiative that accentuated unequivocally the right of the Palestinians to return to pre-1948 Palestine. Hasan could at least be consoled by his ability to host a relatively widely based Arab forum that debated an issue of such magnitude. In March 2002, after the Saudis laid out a new peace plan at an Arab summit in Beirut, the Moroccan press boasted that the original 1981–82 Fahd plan had been fully endorsed by only one Arab leader: the late King Hasan, a man of "visionary and prophetic" attributes.

In July 1985, Morocco called for a summit meeting in Morocco in order to review once again the contents of the Fahd plan. Syria rejected the proposal while most of the radical Arab states boycotted the summit. So did the PLO leadership in Tunis, which was still steadfastly opposed to U.S. and Israeli demands of direct negotiations, opting instead for the convening of an international conference through which a settlement would be imposed on Israel. Hasan did not give up, however. Trying to break the ice, toward the end of 1985 he invited then Israeli Prime Minister Shimon *Peres to Morocco to further the cause of a comprehensive settlement. At the time the Israeli government consisted of a coalition between the Labor Party and Likud.

On July 22–23, 1986, Hasan hosted Israel's Shimon Peres at his palace in Ifrane, causing considerable consternation in Arab countries. The much publicized meeting produced meager results. Hasan expressed his disappointment that Peres had not been more forthcoming on the Palestinian question. The king posed two questions. First, in return for peace with the Arab world, would Israel agree to withdraw from all Arab territories captured in 1967? Second, would the Israeli government agree to negotiate with the PLO? By asking these questions, Hasan placed his dialogue with Peres within the framework of the Fahd principles of 1981–82. He asserted that the Fahd principles endorsed the Palestinians' right to independence and the PLO as their only legitimate representative body. Peres responded negatively to both questions, for to do otherwise would be unacceptable to both his right-wing Likud partners and to large segments of Israeli public opinion.

In the latter half of 1986, Peres turned over the post of prime minister to Yitzḥak *Shamir, becoming Israel's foreign minister in the coalition's rotation agreement. He continued to oppose the creation of a Palestinian state under the aegis of the PLO, favoring instead the "Jordanian option": Palestinian autonomy in parts of the West Bank under the leadership of moderate local forces subordinate to the Kingdom of Jordan. Attempting to implement this policy, Peres met King Hussein secretly in London in April 1987. Shamir was apprised of the meeting a priori but in the final analysis refused to endorse it.

Given the standstill in solving the Palestine problem, and despite the fact that the senior leadership of the PLO was in exile in Tunis, a younger generation of Palestinians in the West Bank and Gaza Strip decided to rise up actively against the 20-year Israeli presence. The uprising, known as the Intifada, commenced on December 9, 1987. It prompted King Hussein to relinquish his political ambitions in the West Bank and to maintain a low profile as a potential facilitator between Israel and the Palestinians. The uprising did not include the use of weaponry. Those who protested against the ongoing Israeli occupation threw rocks at Israeli soldiers, burned tires in the street, disseminated literature, and engaged in demonstrations. Supporters of the Islamist-oriented Palestinians, known as the Ḥamās (*Ḥarakat al-Muqāwama al-Islāmiyya* = the Islamic Resistance Movement) and the Islamic Jihād organization, as well as the secular supporters of the PLO sub-organizations, were separately involved in the protests. Whereas the senior Islamist leadership was active locally, the pro-PLO protesters lacked leaders, as they had been exiled. Within several months the PLO in Tunis seized control of the pro-PLO protests by remote control.

In spring 1990, an exclusively right-wing government rose in Israel, led by the Likud, which included circles who had little inclination for negotiation. Labor remained now in opposition until the general elections of June 1992. The efforts by President Bush to break the deadlock by pressuring Israel to offer concessions were thwarted by Shamir and proved ineffectual.

Another major event in the Middle East of major proportions that encouraged the Bush administration to seek stability for the region and a solution to the wider Arab-Israeli conflict was the invasion of Kuwait by Iraqi forces on August 2, 1990. Iraq had had long-standing claims to Kuwait since the days the Ottoman Empire ruled over the area. Iraqi-Kuwaiti border disputes and financial disputes over the price of oil aggravated the relationship and contributed to the Iraqi decision to attack. The U.S. opposed the Iraqi-initiated war. President Bush finally gave Saddam Hussein until January 15, 1991, to end it. When Iraq failed to comply, the U.S. and its allied forces, including several Arab armies, began an air attack on Iraq and on Iraqi positions in Kuwait in "Operation Desert Storm." In retaliation Iraq launched SCUD missiles against Israel, damaging many buildings in the Tel Aviv area. Owing to American pressure Israel did not retaliate against Iraq and left the U.S. and its allies to conduct the war against the Iraqis. On February 23, 1991, allied ground forces entered Iraq. On February 27, Kuwait was liberated. During the war, Iraq's national infrastructure was badly damaged while tens of thousands of Iraqi soldiers and civilians were killed, as were hundreds of Kuwaitis. After their liberation, the Kuwaiti authorities vented their anger against the Palestinians residing in their country, accusing them of supporting the Iraqi occupation. The Palestinian community was then reduced through expulsion from 300,000 to 30,000, with many of the new refugees resettling in Jordan.

The Gulf War and the Intifada led to the U.S.- and Russian-sponsored Middle East Peace Conference that convened in Madrid on October 30, 1991. All Arab states were invited to the conference and most attended. The conference outlined a series of bilateral and direct negotiations between Israel and the Syrians, Lebanese, and Jordanian-Palestinian delegations, with multilateral discussions on Middle Eastern refugees, environment, economic development, and water rights. Politically, in 1991 cracks began to appear in Algerian and Libyan hostility toward Israel. In the immediate aftermath of the 1991 Gulf War, Hasan convened a Maghrebi summit in Casablanca, attended by the heads of state of Morocco, Algeria, Tunisia, and Libya. These states, together with Mauritania, had recently founded the new Maghreb Arab Union (AMU), an organization that worked toward coordinating regional and economic development policies and other joint projects. The AMU member states were eager to play a decisive role in Israeli-Palestinian politics. Thus, the Arab-Israeli peace issue dominated the Casablanca summit, beginning with Hasan's welcoming address and following a speech delivered by Tunisia's President Zayn Abidine Ben Ali. The Tunisian president was most explicit regarding the importance of reaching a settlement, saying that a stable Arab world and a stable Maghreb depended on it.

By then, Egypt had already returned to the Arab fold. Most Arab states had renewed ties with Cairo. President Husni Mubarak successfully walked a tightrope. He stuck to Sadat's policy of preserving the peace with Israel (albeit a cold peace) and Cairo's cooperation with the U.S., but, unlike Sadat, he pursued a policy of reconciliation with the Arab world. As Egypt was then receiving financial and military assistance from Washington, reneging on the peace treaty of 1979 with Israel would most certainly have resulted in the loss of U.S. support. Moreover, Egypt was now applying pressure on the Syrians, Israelis, and Palestinians to resolve their age-old conflicts.

Throughout 1992, however, these gestures of goodwill and the post-Madrid Conference Arab-Israeli bilateral/multilateral negotiations, which were moved to Washington, showed little progress. Israel negotiated with the Palestinians as long as they avowed that they were part of the Jordanian delegation, and not the PLO. Yet, the Palestinians who were with the Jordanian delegation were in fact very much part of the PLO. They contacted Tunis regularly for instructions, much to Israel's displeasure, bringing the bilateral Israeli-Palestinian negotiation track to a virtual standstill.

Further, the Syrians were willing to negotiate with Israel bilaterally about occupied territories. Yet when it came to the multilateral talks they shied away, perhaps suggesting to the Israelis they had little inclination of pursuing matters related to the normalization of ties. Little, then, could be accomplished on the Israel-Syria track. In summer 1992, when the Labor Party replaced the Likud in power, Prime Minister Yitzhak *Rabin was prepared to offer generous territorial concessions to the Syrians in return for extensive negotiations. Syria expected Israel to withdraw completely from the Golan Heights to the June 4, 1967 lines. Israel, however, only agreed to a Syrian presence along the international border that had been agreed on between Britain and France in 1923. Though the difference between the two borders was insignificant in terms of territory, for Israel to return to the June 4, 1967 lines meant tolerating Syrian presence along the northeastern shore of the Sea of Galilee and control over al-Hamma south of the lake. Moreover, as before, Syria was unwilling to establish full ties with Israel. Only the Jordanian-Israeli talks made progress.

Israel, the Palestinians, Jordan, Syria, and the Oslo Accords: 1993–2006

From late 1992 or the beginning of 1993, behind-the-scenes discussions were held in Oslo, Norway, in the shadow of the bilateral and multilateral talks that followed the Madrid Conference. Prime Minister Rabin agreed to open a second, secret channel, alongside the other discussions in Washington, insofar as Israeli-Palestinian talks were concerned. By early fall 1993 the Oslo channel became known to the wider public and replaced the deliberations in Washington as the only option for Israeli-Palestinian negotiations. Israel now expressed readiness to negotiate with the PLO and the representatives of its exiled leadership in Tunis. Until then successive Israeli governments had taken legal action against official and non-official Israelis meeting with PLO representatives anywhere. On its part, the PLO had gradually modified its stance toward Israel, a process that had begun at the end of 1988, and gained momentum in the early 1990s following the Madrid Conference. It now claimed to adhere to UN Resolution 242, renounce terrorism, and recognize the State of Israel. The Intifada was over.

On September 13, 1993, Israel and the PLO signed the Oslo Declaration of Principles (DOP) in Washington in the presence of U.S. President Bill Clinton. It outlined a five-year plan for Palestinian self-government, starting with Israel's withdrawal of troops from the West Bank town of Jericho and the Gaza Strip, and the transfer of authority for economic development, education, culture, tourism, tax collection, and welfare. It was agreed that Chairman Arafat and the PLO's exiled leadership in Tunis would be permitted to set up their headquarters in Gaza, a decision implemented in July 1994. The road was paved for the creation of the Palestinian Authority. This was to be followed by the election in 1996 of an interim governing council. Negotiations would then commence (on May 4, 1996) toward a final status agreement on the future of Jerusalem, the 1948 refugees, Jewish settlements in the West Bank and Gaza, and the demarcation of clearly defined borders.

A majority of Israelis and Palestinians were at first favorably disposed to the new accords, even though the Oslo DOP was a peace process, not a peace treaty. The Palestinians were not offered an independent state, in any case not in the initial phases of the process. Most Palestinians were dissatisfied because the hard issues of refugee status, the question of Jerusalem, and the fate of the Jewish settlements were deferred. In Israel, right-wing political figures said they would either work to abrogate the DOP or not honor it. Palestinian radicals, notably Islamists of the Hamas and Jihad movements, as well as secularly oriented radicals within the PLO's Fatah and PFLP, carried out violent actions in the West Bank and Gaza against Jewish settlers and soldiers. Among the Arab states, Syria spearheaded the opposition to the Oslo accords less out of concern about the contents of the DOP than as a protest against the PLO's decision to reach a separate agreement with Israel. The Gulf emirates supported the process as did Egypt, which was active in pushing forward the implementation of the accords. King Hussein not only backed Oslo: on October 26, 1994, he signed a peace agreement with Israel in the Arava Desert region in the presence of official Israeli, Jordanian, U.S., and Russian delegations. The thorniest problem was border demarcation because Israel had expanded its eastern frontier in the late 1960s by an estimated 350 square kilometers, some of which had become farmland. Rabin and Hussein worked out the whole line from Eilat and Aqaba in the south to the point of convergence with Syria in the north. In some areas they agreed to land exchanges. In other areas Hussein allowed Israeli farmers to continue to use the land they had been cultivating after it reverted to Jordanian sovereignty. As for the water, it was decided that Jordan would get 50 million cubic meters a year from Israel. The two countries agreed to cooperate to overcome water shortages by developing new water resources.

Israeli-Palestinian negotiations over the further implementation of the interim process were delayed until the signing in Cairo of Oslo I (May 1994). It was then that Israeli troops withdrew and Palestinian police took control in Jericho and the Gaza Strip. Violence by both sides and postponements diminished support for the accords. Yet the parties reached a number of understandings, including Oslo II, signed at the White House on September 28, 1995, which led to more Israeli concessions in the West Bank.

The Oslo II accord provided for elections to a Palestinian council, the transfer of legislative authority to this council, the withdrawal of Israeli forces from the Palestinian centers of population, and the division of the West Bank into three areas: A, B, and C. Area A consisted of Palestinian towns and cities. Area B referred to Palestinian villages (68 percent of the total Palestinian population in the West Bank). Area C covered areas taken over by Israel for roads and settlements. Area A was placed under exclusive Palestinian control and area C under exclusive Israeli control. In Area B the Palestinians exercised civilian authority while Israel remained in charge of security. Under the terms of Oslo II, Israel conceded to the Palestinian Authority civilian control over one-third of the West Bank. Four percent of the West Bank, mainly the towns of Bethlehem, Hebron, Jenin, Nablus (Shechem), Tulkarem, and Kalkilya, was turned over to full Palestinian control and another 25 percent to administrative-civilian control. In the Gaza Strip, Israel retained control over 35 percent of the land, notably Jewish settlements (*Gush Katif) and roads leading to them. The rest became the responsibility of the Palestinians.

Some setbacks on the Palestinian track loomed large on the horizon following Oslo II. This was several months before the May 4, 1996 deadline for the negotiations over the final status of the occupied territories. Arafat envisaged wresting from Israel in these negotiations a Palestinian state with East Jerusalem as its capital. Israel had reservations regarding Arafat's maximalist approach and, simultaneously, approved the expansion of existing Jewish settlements in the West Bank. But there were other reasons for the indefinite postponement of the final status deliberations. On November 4, 1995, Yigal Amir, a young religious extremist, assassinated Rabin at a Tel Aviv peace rally. Throughout 1995 certain religious elements whose worldview was imbued with messianic tendencies and other ultra-right circles had spearheaded criticism of the government for its decision to concede territories. They insisted that all of the Land of Israel had been promised to the Jews by God and no living person could give up any part of it to foreigners. As far as they were concerned, the Palestinians were aliens. Those who betrayed the Jewish people must be punished and their plans thwarted.

Peres, then foreign minister, succeeded Rabin and vowed to resume the peace process on all fronts, including Syria. To help expedite Israeli-Syrian contacts, the U.S. initiated direct negotiations between the parties at the end of December 1995 at Wye Plantation in Maryland. The Israelis and Syrians focused their attention on issues related to permanent borders, security matters, diplomatic ties, and water. The negotiators met once again toward the end of January 1996 but were deadlocked on most issues. Though secret Israeli-Syrian contacts took place during the Likud's new term in government (May 1996–May 1999), the parties did not meet publicly until 2000.

Peres had no better success with the Palestinians. On February 25, 1996, a Hamas terrorist blew himself up on a bus in Jerusalem, killing all the passengers; suicide bomber attacks followed in Ashkelon, Jerusalem, and Tel Aviv, with more than 60 Israelis killed. The suicide bombings convinced large segments of the Israeli public that Oslo had only wrought havoc. The support that Peres had enjoyed soon eroded. With national elections scheduled for May 29, 1996, the Likud's candidate, Binyamin *Netanyahu, surged ahead of Peres in public opinion polls.

Meanwhile Hizbollah launched Katyusha rockets from Lebanon at settlements in northern Galilee. They also attacked Israeli units and the pro-Israel Christian militias inside the security zone in southern Lebanon. The unwritten agreement brokered by the U.S. in 1993 stipulating that Hizbollah would cease rocket attacks against Israel had been violated. Israel blamed Iran and Syria for backing Hizbollah and took drastic steps to curb the attacks. The Peres government carried out "Operation Grapes of Wrath" in April 1996. It aimed at restoring peace to Galilee and included aerial bombings of Hizbollah guerrilla strongholds in southern Lebanon, the Biqa' Valley, and Beirut. Several hundred thousand people fled Lebanese towns and villages and became refugees. Despite the use of sophisticated weaponry, "Grapes of Wrath" failed to achieve the desired results of subduing Hizbollah. On April 18, due to human error, Israeli shells killed over 100 refugees in the UN base in Qana. Israel now faced condemnation internationally. "Grapes of Wrath" diminished Peres's prospects of retaining his position as prime minister. A month later, Binyamin Netanyahu was elected prime minister, winning by a narrow margin of 30,000 popular votes.

During Netanyahu's first year in office relations with the Arab world reached a new low. Israeli-Syrian relations were characterized by intermittent tensions. Hizbollah became a powerful fighting force in southern Lebanon, capable of operating inside the security zone and killing Israeli and Christian militia soldiers. As before, the Palestinians posed the most difficult challenge to Netanyahu. A crisis of major proportions unfolded in October 1996 over an Israeli government decision to blast open a tunnel in the vicinity of the al-Aqsa Mosque in order to open a second entrance to the tunnel used by the *Hasmoneans in the second century BCE. The project was meant to facilitate the flow of tourists to this site. For the Palestinians the move was interpreted as a ploy to create new facts in East Jerusalem unilaterally, disregarding their interest. An outburst of uncontrollable rioting broke out throughout the West Bank to the point where Palestinian police in the area opened fire on Israeli soldiers. More than a dozen Israeli soldiers and 80 Palestinians were killed.

Anti-Israeli sentiments became more widespread in the Arab world, and even the Clinton Administration did not spare its criticism of Netanyahu's policies. U.S. and international pressure on Israel prompted Netanyahu to offer concessions and return to the spirit of Oslo. The concession came in the context of the Hebron Protocol, signed on January 15, 1997, which divided Hebron into two zones governed by security arrangements. The Palestinian zone (H1) covered 80 percent of Hebron, while the Jewish zone (H2) covered the other 20 percent. In the Jewish zone Israel was to maintain full security control over the hundreds of Jewish settlers and their property until the final status of the territories would be decided. From Oslo I through the Hebron agreement, Israel had maintained complete control of 70 percent of the West Bank (Area C) and still exercised security control over another 23 percent (Area B); the Palestinian Authority exercised full control over only 6 percent (Area A).

Tensions did not abate, however. During 1997 the Netanyahu government resumed its efforts to consolidate Israel's influence within East Jerusalem. The aim was to build housing units for 30,000 Israelis in East Jerusalem's Har Ḥomah district. The Palestinians organized a general strike to oppose the project, which turned violent and exacerbated the already unsteady relations between Israel and the Palestinian Authority. To alleviate tensions, the Clinton Administration invited Netanyahu and Arafat to a summit at Wye Plantation in October 1998. In a two-day period, Clinton brokered an important deal: exchanging Israeli-occupied territory on the West Bank for Palestinian antiterrorist measures to be monitored by the CIA. Jordan's King Hussein, then undergoing treatment for cancer in the U.S., participated in the summit. This was his final involvement in peacemaking. He died several weeks later. The summit's memorandum, signed in Washington on October 23, 1998, sought to invigorate the Israeli-Palestinian Oslo peace process and stimulate intensive negotiations toward permanent peace. Israel agreed to pull back its forces from an additional 13 percent of the West Bank in three stages over a three-month period. This would have given the Palestinians full or partial authority over 40 percent of the West Bank. Arafat agreed to revise the 1968 Palestinian National Covenant by removing all clauses pertaining to Israel's destruction. He carried out the revision reluctantly.

The Israeli pullout as stipulated by the summit memorandum did not take place. Opposition to Netanyahu came from the Likud's coalition partners in the religious and nationalist parties. Netanyahu barely succeeded in getting approval of the agreement in his ruling cabinet. The Knesset, on the other hand, approved it on November 15 by 75 votes to 19, with 19 abstentions. Despite the official decision to honor the agreement, Netanyahu bowed to religious and nationalist lobbyists a month later. He also justified this by blaming the Palestinian Authority for not honoring the security arrangements set forth in the memorandum. The policy of backing away from Wye provoked a crisis in Israel and paved the way for new elections on May 17, 1999.

In the aftermath of a tense election campaign, Ehud *Barak, head of the Labor Party and a former chief of staff in the Israel Defense Forces, was elected prime minister. He formed a coalition government consisting of religious and secular parties before proceeding to continue the peace process with the Palestinians and the Syrians from the point Rabin and Peres had left off. On May 24, 2000, Israel pulled its forces out of the military zone in southern Lebanon and dismantled the local pro-Israeli militia. At that time Barak offered Asad a return to the de facto border of June 4, 1967, along the Jordan River and almost to the shoreline at the northeastern end of the Sea of Galilee. In March 2000, Barak met with Syrian Foreign Minister Faruq al-Sharaʿ in the U.S. in the presence of President Clinton. He then made known his generous offer for territorial concessions to Damascus. The mini-summit was a complete failure. According to Barak, Asad wanted Israel to capitulate a priori to all his demands and then, and only then, would Syria engage in serious negotiations. Some observers thought that Asad was then near death and ill prepared for accepting or providing any political concessions. Others believed that Barak had pushed the Syrians too hard to establish full normal relations with Israel and to withdraw their troops from Lebanon.

As to the Palestinians, an Israeli-Palestinian summit was initiated by Clinton in July 2000 at Camp David. It followed Israel's withdrawal from southern Lebanon. The purpose of the summit was to reach a framework agreement for a permanent settlement. Barak was prepared to grant the Palestinian territorial and political concessions that no previous Israeli prime minister had dared to offer. The summit was attended by Israeli and Palestinian delegations, led by Barak and Arafat, respectively. Barak made an unprecedented offer envisaging a Palestinian state on over 90 percent of the West Bank and all of the Gaza Strip; the establishment of the Palestinian capital in East Jerusalem where some Arab neighborhoods would become sovereign Palestinian territory and others would enjoy "functional autonomy"; Palestinian sovereignty over half the Old City of Jerusalem (the Muslim and Christian quarters) and custodianship – short of sovereignty – over the Temple Mount; and a return of refugees to the Palestinian state, yet with no "right of return" to Israel proper.

Arafat turned down these concessions. He now expected Israel to agree unconditionally to the right of return of all Palestinian refugees who so desired and vehemently opposed Israeli sovereignty over the Western (Wailing) Wall of the Temple Mount. According to Barak, Arafat rejected the two-state solution, which meant putting into question the viability of the State of Israel. After two weeks of talks Clinton ended the summit, placing the blame for its failure squarely on Arafat's shoulders.

The stalemate on the Palestinian track, Arafat's deviation from Oslo, and, perhaps, the feeling in Palestinian political circles that territorial concession could be wrested through violence (e.g., Israel's withdrawal from southern Lebanon was viewed as a sign of weakness) – may have contributed to the outbreak of the second Intifada (*Intifāḍat al-Aqsa*). Some attribute the new Palestinian uprising to the visit to the Temple Mount by Likud party leader Ariel Sharon on September 28, 2000. But this is not what caused it. Sharon's visit had been coordinated in advance with the Palestinian Authority's security apparatus. Sharon's visit was directed against the Barak government – not the Palestinians – to demonstrate that the Likud cared more about Jerusalem than Barak. The visit merely played into Arafat's hand as a pretext for the uprising.

The al-Aqsa Intifada spurred more terrorist attacks against Israel than ever before, directed with equal intensity against the West Bank and Gaza Strip Jewish settlers. These included massive suicide attacks launched by the Hamas and Islamic Jihad movements. Barak was now viewed by Israeli public opinion as a political failure, a leader unable to curb terrorism. Early general elections took place in February 2001. Likud leader Ariel Sharon won a landslide victory and remained in office after a second election victory in February 2003. He was also instrumental in achieving greater security and weakening the Intifada. A good example of his approach could be seen after a devastating terrorist attack in 2002 on Jews attending a Passover *seder* at a hotel in the city of Netanya, with 28 people killed. Sharon responded by ordering a massive military incursion, known as "Operation Defensive Wall," into Nablus, Jenin, Bethlehem, Ramallah, Kalkilya, and Tulkarem. Israeli forces occupied these Palestinian cities for the first time since withdrawing from them under Oslo. Sharon did not stop there. He confined Arafat to his Ramallah compound, virtually placing him under house arrest. Hence, the Palestinian leader became politically irrelevant and isolated from both Arab leaders and the international community until his death in November 2004. Further, Israel began building a wall around the West Bank to prevent the infiltration of Palestinian terrorists into the country.

In 2003, Sharon surprised his leftist critics and rightist supporters when he made it plain that Israel would have to make painful concessions to the Palestinians. While he expressed skepticism regarding overtures made by Bashar al-Asad, who had succeeded his father (who died in June 2000) as president of Syria, regarding a Syrian-Israeli settlement, he made the Palestinian track his first order of priority; he also improved relations with Cairo and Amman.

During the 2002–04 period new proposals for a comprehensive peace settlement emerged. One such proposal was made by Saudi Crown Prince Abdullah bin Abd al-Aziz ibn Saʿud at the Beirut Arab summit of March 2002. The plan called upon Israel to withdraw from all territories occupied in the 1967 war; agree to a "just solution of the Palestinian refugee problem," without specifically mentioning the refugees' right to return or indemnities as stated in UN Resolution 194; and make Arab Jerusalem the capital of a Palestinian state. In return, all the Arab states would agree to end the Arab-Israeli conflict and implement full and normal relations with Israel. The Israelis would have access to the Western Wall but would have to withdraw from East Jerusalem. The plan also advocated the two-state solution and mutual Israeli-Palestinian recognition of the two states in the context of UN Resolutions 242 and 338. At the Algiers summit in March 2005, the Saudi plan resurfaced. King Abdullah of Jordan went so far as to suggest a revision of the plan, whereby the Arab states would grant Israel full recognition prior to the finalizing of Palestinian-Israeli negotiations. The proposal was rejected.

Although Sharon would not go as far as Barak in offering the Palestinians most of the West Bank, and considered negotiations over East Jerusalem as premature, he laid the groundwork for a unilateral Israeli withdrawal from the Gaza Strip, where Jewish settlements still existed, advocating their dismantlement. This policy coincided with a new initiative similar to the Saudi plan, backed by the Quartet (official representatives of the European Union, the UN, Russia, and the U.S.) and known as "the road map." Despite opposition inside his government from right-wing ministers, Sharon accepted major portions of the plan.

The road map as envisaged by the Quartet had been reworked by the U.S. administration of George W. Bush. The revised and more detailed road map was made public in April 2003. It stated that a two-state solution to the Israeli-Palestinian conflict could be achieved only through an end to violence and once the Palestinian people acquired a leadership that acted decisively against terror, willing and able to build a democracy based on tolerance. The settlement would bring about the termination of the Israeli occupation based on the Madrid Conference, UN resolutions, Oslo, and the Saudi plan. This result would promote international efforts to achieve a comprehensive peace on the Syrian-Israeli and Lebanese-Israeli tracks. Specifically, if implemented, the Israeli-Palestinian road map was to consist of three phases according to an as yet unspecified timetable:

Phase One: Ending terror and violence, and building Palestinian institutions; Israeli withdrawal from Palestinian areas occupied from the start of the second Intifada; drafting a Palestinian constitution leading to free and open elections; reforming the Palestinian Authority security apparatuses; nurturing U.S.-Palestinian security cooperation in collaboration with overseers (U.S., Egypt, Jordan); establishing Israeli-Palestinian security cooperation; forming a Palestinian civil society.

Phase Two: Creating an interim Palestinian state under a new leadership as a way station on the road to a permanent status settlement – a phase that would begin after the Palestinian elections. The ties maintained by several Arab states with Israel in the pre-Intifada period (1994–2000) through tourism, trade, and liaison offices (Morocco, Tunisia, and several Gulf states), which were all but severed during the upheavals, would be renewed. Negotiations relating to multilateral engagement on issues including regional water resources, environment, economic development, refugees, and arms control issues would be resumed. The new constitution for a democratic and an independent Palestinian state would be finalized and approved.

Phase Three: Achieving a permanent Israeli-Palestinian status agreement (with final borders) and a fully independent Palestinian state based on UN Resolutions 242, 338, 1397, and a "realistic solution" to the refugee issue, one, however, that excluded the "right of return" to Israel. President Bush highlighted this stipulation in his letter to Sharon from June 2004. The negotiated solution to the status of Jerusalem would take into account the political and religious interests of Jews, Christians, and Muslims. In this phase the vision of two states – Israel and Palestine – living side by side in peace and security would be fulfilled. Henceforth, the Arab states would accept full normal relations with Israel – not mere liaison offices – in the context of a comprehensive Arab-Israeli peace.

Only with the passage of time will one be able to determine if the road map will be implemented and honored. In the early years of the 21st century the Palestinian Authority found itself in the immediate post-Arafat era under the leadership of Chairman Abu Mazin and Prime Minister Abu Ala, both among the architects of the Oslo DOP. Abu Mazin was elected president of the Authority in a democratically held election in January 2005, under the scrutiny of international observers including former U.S. President Jimmy Carter. However, with the victory of Hamas in the January 2006 parliamentary elections and the installation of Ismail Haniyeh as prime minister, Abu Mazin's position was considerably undermined, and the future of the peace process suddenly became highly problematic.

The Maghreb and Israel: A Unique and Fluctuating Relationship

The signing of the Oslo accords in 1993 inspired King Hasan II of Morocco to once again encourage a broader peace between Israel and its Arab neighbors. Moreover, he saw in the revived peace process an opportunity to improve the ailing Moroccan economy through extensive tourism, which would include numerous Moroccan Jews living in Israel, France, and the Americas. This is one of the reasons Hasan appointed the Moroccan-Jewish entrepreneur Serge Bardugo as Morocco's minister of tourism. Hasan then invited Prime Minister Rabin and Foreign Minister Peres to Morocco on their way back from the signing ceremony for the Oslo DOP in Washington. On June 2, 1994, Hasan convened a special session of his cabinet. The ministers who arrived at the meeting were surprised to find Israeli Foreign Minister Peres there, together with Uri Savir (then the Foreign Ministry's director general), Avi Gil (director of the foreign minister's office), and David Dadon – then director of the Middle East Department at the Foreign Ministry and later head of Israel's liaison office in Rabat.

Hasan made known to the visitors his intentions to improve relations between the two nations. Peres also pushed for a Middle Eastern/Maghrebi economic summit in Casablanca, direct telephone connections between the two countries, and liaison offices as the first steps toward full diplomatic relations. It was evident that most Moroccan cabinet members were reluctant to agree to the opening of liaison offices, arguing that the time was not yet ripe for such decisive measures. Yet when the meeting ended, Hasan promised Peres that liaison offices would be established. The opening of the liaison offices in Tel Aviv and Rabat was carried out in November 1994. The raison d'être for establishing liaison offices in Rabat and Tel Aviv was to advance tourism and trade between the two countries. These offices were also to promote cultural and economic exchanges that hitherto had been low-keyed. For the next several years, the liaison office in Tel Aviv busily engaged in issuing tourist visas to Morocco. Postal relations between the two countries, severed on September 22, 1959, had already been established as early as September 1, 1994. The first annual Middle East and North Africa Economic Summit involving senior officials from Israel, numerous Arab states, the United States, Europe, and Japan, as well as representatives of the private business sector, convened toward the end of October 1994 in Casablanca. Leading Moroccan Jews promoted it, while Hasan seized the opportunity to put himself forward as an architect of regional planning. From his standpoint, the summit was a stepping stone for securing aid from the industrialized nations for the Moroccan economy and elevating his own status among Arab leaders. The summit was short on substance, however.

Already before 1995, a number of experimental agricultural farms were launched by Israel in Morocco in conjunction with the U.S. Agency for International Development (USAID) to promote higher yields in Moroccan agriculture. In October 1994, the Israeli Export Institute reported that Israel's export potential to Morocco for the years 1994–97 was estimated at $220 million annually and could include such sectors as agricultural products, irrigation equipment, the building trade, high-tech electronics, processed foods, and professional services for infrastructure development. In 1994–96, the number of Israeli tourists who visited Morocco annually was estimated at approximately 20,000.

The post-Rabin era and the subsequent escalation in Palestinian terrorism inside Israel marked the gradual decline of the more open relationships in several domains. Like the hardships faced by Israeli diplomats in the rest of the Arab world, including Egypt and Jordan, their counterparts in Morocco faced many challenges and limitations, some of which had their inception during Peres' term as prime minister. The Israeli flag was not raised outside the liaison office but was placed inside the building owing to criticism of Israel by Islamic fundamentalist groups and other elements opposed to any kind of Moroccan normalization with the Jewish state.

Following Binyamin Netanyahu's accession to power there were manifestations of pessimism in Morocco. The complaints emanating from Rabat suggested that the Oslo process was in peril, and progress in the Syrian-Israeli negotiations had reached a dead end. But despite the ups and downs, Moroccan-Israeli relations, particularly in the intelligence and defense domains, remained undisturbed. Following his visit to Morocco in late summer 1996, Peres, now the Labor opposition leader, heard from Hasan that Netanyahu's reported "no to Jerusalem," "no to a Palestinian state," and "no to a settlement in the Golan Heights" was reminiscent of the 1967 Arab summit in Khartoum with its own famous three noes.

The 1996 tunnel crisis and the opposition to Netanyahu in the Arab world had a profound effect on Moroccan-Israeli ties. From that time until 1998, the work of the Israelis at the Rabat liaison office was made more difficult owing to media attacks and other obstacles. David Dadon, who headed the office, suffered the same indignity as his counterpart in Egypt, Ambassador Zvi Mazel, by being forced to reduce his visibility. In 1997, to silence mounting opposition locally and in different parts of the Arab world against the ongoing relations with Israel, Hasan canceled the invitation he had extended to Netanyahu and his foreign minister, David Levy, to visit Morocco. Hasan could ill afford to act otherwise, for he chaired the Islamic Conference Organization's Jerusalem Committee for the Glorification of Arab Jerusalem. Morocco, it was said, could not cooperate with an Israeli government that considered Jerusalem as indivisible and ruled by Jews.

As a result of the new political realities, many of the economic projects planned in the early and mid-1990s by Morocco and Israel were later frozen, except perhaps the flow of tourists, which, in any case, remained overwhelmingly one-sided: from Israel to Morocco. Some of the obstacles to large-scale economic cooperation were equally attributable to bureaucratic red tape intermixed with official bias. Certain forces in official Morocco opposed Israel's aspiration to open and fast-paced joint activity.

On May 5, 1999, less than two weeks before the Israeli elections, Hasan called on Moroccan Israelis to make the "choice of peace" and vote for the Labor Party headed by Ehud Barak. Hasan was aware that the majority of Moroccan Jews in Israel remained loyal to the Likud and had played, like the new Russian immigrants, a pivotal role in unseating Peres in 1996. On May 17, 1999, the Moroccan media rejoiced over Barak's election victory. King Hasan passed away on July 23, 1999. The early phase of Muhammad VI's rule did not raise major problems for the relationship. Israeli tourists continued to enter Morocco, as did agronomists and other professionals involved in special agricultural and industrial projects. While Israeli exports to Morocco since 1999 amounted to only several million dollars annually, Moroccan exports to Israel rose markedly at the end of the Hasan era and immediately after Muhammad VI's ascendance to the throne. In the first half of 2000, Israel imported $830 million worth of Moroccan agricultural and textile products, an unprecedented sum for Israel to spend in trade transactions with an Arab state. These figures were to decrease in the wake of renewed Israeli-Palestinian hostilities. To spare the Moroccans embarrassment, from the early 1990s onward Israeli firms – including those specializing in agricultural development, irrigation equipment, and medical products – agreed to be registered by the authorities as foreign companies or worked under the guise of foreign concerns.

The second Intifada, the spate of anti-Israel editorials in the pro-government, independent, and Islamist organs, and pressure attributed to the Arab League and Palestinian Authority forced Morocco, on October 24, 2000, to close the Israeli liaison office in Rabat and recall its diplomats from Tel Aviv. Israeli tourists who thenceforth wished to visit Morocco could only obtain visas at Moroccan consulates in Europe. The Foreign Ministry in Rabat said the decision was justified by the failure of the Middle East peace process following "inhuman acts perpetrated for weeks by Israeli forces against Palestinian civilians." It emphasized that closing down the Israeli liaison office was also related to Morocco's responsibilities to the Jerusalem Committee presided over by King Muhammad VI.

At the end of October 2000, hundreds of thousands of Moroccans marched in the streets of Rabat to show their support for the Palestinians. The marchers included Prime Minister Abd al-Rahman Yussufi and his political party, the Union Socialiste des Forces Populaires (USFP). A competing anti-Israeli rally was organized in Casablanca by the Islamist Parti de la Justice et du Développement (PJD). The rally swelled to 25,000 participants and quickly degenerated into a riot that had to be dispersed with water cannons. This form of protest was repeated on April 7, 2002, in the largest pro-Palestinian demonstrations ever to take place in the Arab world, with nearly half a million demonstrators filling the streets of Rabat.

The Moroccan government did nothing to stop the attacks against Ariel Sharon in public and in the media. Nor did it discourage the publication of press editorials that found a certain justification for the terrorist attacks of 9/11. The Istiqlal Party, represented in the coalition government headed by Yussufi, allowed its press to claim that the crimes of several Muslim terrorists against the U.S. could not be divorced from Israeli arrogance toward the Palestinians. The Bush administration should have taken seriously the warnings by Arab leaders who spoke out against Sharon's policies. Instead the U.S. chose to turn a deaf ear and thus shared the responsibility for the deaths of Americans.

Albeit damaged, Israel's relations with Morocco survived. Particularly intriguing in these troubled times was the decision in 2001 to collaborate in planning and constructing a large casino at Tetuan, a city in northern Morocco. An affluent Jewish family of Moroccan origin living in Barcelona who owned a large tract of land near Tetuan's Mediterranean coast, offered it as a site for the casino. Beside the casino, the $150 million raised by Morocco for the project was also earmarked for a 400-room five-star hotel and a vacation resort. Construction of the casino and resort complex began in 2001 after two leading Moroccan entrepreneurs, the Ligad Group (a private Israeli construction firm), and Sammy Tito, an Israeli architect, signed agreements.

Mauritania, on the margin of the Arab-Israeli conflict and Arab politics, established relations with Israel in 1995 and opened liaison offices in Tel Aviv. It did not sever ties with Israel in the aftermath of the second Intifada.

Algerian-Israeli relations in the Oslo and post-Oslo eras are no less intriguing. During the early and mid-1980s, in the post-Boumedienne period under the presidency of Shadli Ben Jadid, Algeria's FLN regime did not miss any opportunity to discredit Arab-Israeli peace efforts and took an active part in the effort to muster consensual support to isolate Egypt from every Arab forum. It opposed the Saudi peace initiative of 1981–82 and the abortive Lebanese-Israeli peace agreement of 1983. Nonetheless, the FLN no longer displayed the sort of radical zealousness reminiscent of the 1960s and 1970s.

Beginning in summer 1990, Algeria faced deep political divisions and instability, especially as it was striving toward democracy in line with its new constitution, approved on February 23, 1989, which opened the way to a multiparty political system. On June 12, 1990, the country's first free municipal elections took place. Eleven political parties participated in this historic event, among which were the regime's FLN; the religious Islamist Front Islamique du Salut (FIS); the Front des Forces Socialistes (FFS); and the Rally for Culture and Democracy (RCD). The results were stunning: the FIS won a majority of the municipal seats in the country's largest cities – Algiers, Oran, Constantine, and Annaba. The backing of FIS came from the Arab majority; the Berbers boycotted the FIS and supported the secular FFS and RCD. The vote for the Islamists was less an outpouring of massive support for the FIS than a reaction against the FLN's record of authoritarianism and mismanagement. At the end of 1991, the first round of parliamentary elections took place. They delivered a solid victory to the Islamists and raised the possibility of their control of the parliament in a second round. The army canceled the second round and key Islamists were arrested, with the FIS made illegal. In January 1992, Ben Jadid resigned from the presidency, to be replaced by Muhammad Boudiaf. This development ended the domination of the FLN for some time. Violence erupted soon afterwards. In June 1992, after exhibiting an autonomy that the Algerian military had clearly not expected, Boudiaf was gunned down by assassins. In the mid-1990s, under the presidency of Liamine Zeroual and the new government party, the National Democratic Rally (RND), supporters of the FIS and other militant Islamic groups – such as the Groupe Islamique Armé (GIA) – engaged the central government in incessant violence. The upheavals that soon turned into a civil war continued throughout the 1990s and led to Zeroual's resignation in 1999 and to presidential elections.

Abd al-Aziz Bouteflika won the presidency in the April 1999 elections and within two years ended the civil war. His attitude toward Israel was devoid of hostility. In July 1999, Bouteflika met openly with Prime Minister Barak in Rabat during King Hasan's funeral. He promised to mediate between Israel and its Arab neighbors. This unique promise was apparently a result of previous behind-the-scenes contacts. Rumors then circulated that Israel had offered military hardware to Algeria and a deal was in the making. Bouteflika declared that Algeria would be prepared to establish ties with Israel, contingent upon the Israeli withdrawal from all occupied territories, dismantling settlements, and cooperation in creating a Palestinian state.

Contacts between Algeria and Israel had had their roots in the 1980s. Between 1986 and 1988, a close confidant of Ben Jadid and Israeli Foreign Minister Shimon Peres met on several occasions in Paris. Ovadiah Sofer, Israel's ambassador to France, apparently mediated the initiative. For Israel, the contacts seemed important because Algeria was regarded as a key Arab and African state with ample influence at the UN. Israel had hoped that Algeria would tone down its criticism of Israel in Third World forums and thus reduce the hostility against Israeli policies toward the Palestinians. Once Israel rejected the Algerian demand that, in return for continued discreet ties, it should recognize the PLO, the contacts were discontinued.

The secret Algerian-Israeli contacts were revived under Zeroual's presidency, this time in the area of much-needed medical and pharmaceutical supplies from Israel. The Algerians were eager to pursue the contacts following the signing of the Oslo accords, once it seemed as though a major hurdle in the Arab-Israeli conflict had been eliminated. An Israeli delegation led by the minister of health arrived in Algiers to sign the first secret Israeli-Algerian agreement for medical supplies. Thus began the quiet flow of shipments from Israel to Algeria that, as early as July 1994, included 10,000 pregnancy test kits at a cost of $11.34 per unit. These supplies reached Algeria under the fictitious name of Prélude to look like a French product. The Algerian authorities were worried that, in the heat of the civil unrest launched by the Islamists, this form of cooperation would be exposed and subsequently used against the government.

The Israeli-Algerian medical ties endured for several years and included antibiotics, scanners, medications for serious wounds inflicted on victims of Algeria's civil war, and even assistance in hospitalization in parts of rural areas. Algerian medical personnel arrived in Israel to learn techniques of identifying corpses. Moreover, between October 15 and 25, 1999, a high-ranking Israeli delegation visited Algeria secretly in order to reach an undeclared rapprochement between the two countries. The delegation included five Israelis, who were received in Sidi Bel-Abbes, Constantine, and Algiers; they held talks with two of Bouteflika's top aides and discussed bilateral trade and military cooperation and ways to establish liaison offices in Tel Aviv and Algiers. Shortly thereafter Bouteflika reiterated his demand for a full Israeli withdrawal from the territories occupied in the 1967 war.

Although we have no knowledge of what was initially agreed upon behind closed doors, Bouteflika's public declarations did not lead to anything and the various contacts were later broken off. This change was conditioned by the second Intifada. Yet to attribute it only to this is to oversimplify matters. Long before this crisis, Israel had pulled its troops out of Lebanon (May 2000), attempted to negotiate an agreement with the Syrians on the Golan Heights, and, as late as July 2000, the Oslo channel remained viable. It soon became obvious that Bouteflika's domestic political opponents and the intervention of several Arab states, especially Syria, had influenced his policies. One sign of this pressure is evinced by the creation, in November 1999, of the Committee of National Organizations against Normal Ties with Israel. Consisting of representatives of most political parties, it included the Islamist movements Ḥarakat Mujtamaʿ al-Silm (Movement of the Society for Peace), Mouvement Démocratique et Social, and the banned FIS. One FIS leader, Abd al-Qadir Bu Khamkham, addressed a message to Bouteflika in which he advised strongly against "possible recognition of the Jewish Zionist identity on the Arab land of Palestine."

Some attitudes toward Israel changed after the Algerian presidential elections of April 2004, giving Bouteflika a strong majority. Hosting in March 2005 the Algiers Arab summit, Bouteflika openly urged Arab leaders to consider the strategy of recognizing Israel as a top priority in return for an Israeli withdrawal from all occupied territories.

Tunisian-Israeli relations were marred by inconsistencies. The transfer of the Arab League headquarters to Tunis, soon after the signing of the Egyptian-Israeli peace treaty, brought Tunisia into the limelight and bestowed upon its government an aura of importance it had never enjoyed before. Until the mid-1980s, Tunisia joined Algeria in the campaign to ban Egypt from the Arab fold. After the 1982 "Operation Peace for Galilee," Tunisia became an almost permanent sanctuary for PLO headquarters. While the Tunisians appeared outwardly hospitable to the PLO, they were concerned that the presence of the old-time Palestinian leaders in their midst could invite trouble. Bourguiba and his successor, Zayn Abidin Ben Ali, understood what might be at stake: a large Palestinian concentration on Tunisian soil could pose a threat to internal stability, as had been the case with Jordan until 1970 and Lebanon afterwards.

From the inception of the PLO's presence in Tunisia, Israel considered it vital to make every possible effort to counter Palestinian activities there. This was very much the case on October 1, 1985, when Israeli fighter jets strafed PLO headquarters in Tunis. This operation left a number of Tunisians as well as Palestinians dead. Israel claimed that Tunisia conveniently overlooked the PLO's terrorist actions against Israel, purposely ignoring the fact that Palestinian fighters, enjoying sanctuary in Tunisia, were crossing into Algeria, where they underwent military training in the region of Tbessa. Israel arrested many such Palestinian fighters who had sailed to Israel via Tunis and Greece.

As noted, although the first Intifada in the West Bank and Gaza, which began in December 1987, is rightly regarded as a locally inspired Palestinian uprising against Israel's occupation of 20 years, it was soon thereafter aided and partly guided by the exiled leadership in Tunis. Similar to its actions in 1985, Israel once again reacted against the Palestinians in Tunisia. In April 1988, after learning that Palestinian leader Khalil al-Wazir (Abu Jihad) had, from his sanctuary in Tunis, taken command of the PLO's supporters in the Intifada, Israel dispatched a special military commando unit to Tunis and killed al-Wazir in his home.

Bourguiba's removal from power in November 1987 and his replacement by President Zayn Abidine Ben Ali led Tunisia to adopt a more sober attitude toward Israel from the late 1980s. In 1988 and throughout 1989, Tunis was to become an active arena, this time for a diplomatic process to bring the Israelis and the Palestinians to the negotiating table. This materialized after Arafat endorsed the establishment of an independent Palestinian state and UN Resolution 242. Though the Israelis hardly concealed their skepticism over Arafat's declarations at the time, the U.S. entered into talks with the PLO in Tunis through Ambassador Robert H. Pelletreau. The negotiations eventually led to American recognition of the PLO and helped lay the groundwork for the October 1991 Madrid Peace Conference. Arafat's return to Gaza in 1994 and a partial Israeli withdrawal from the West Bank and Gaza served as a stimulant for Tunisia to reassess policies toward Israel.

By endorsing Oslo, however, Tunisia faced double-edged pressure, from local Islamic circles against serious steps toward achieving normalization of ties with Israel and unremitting official Israeli pressure for large-scale joint economic ventures. As to the latter, Tunisian officials preferred that a low profile be maintained in initial trade and other collaborative projects. The sole exception was Israeli and Jewish tourism. After considerable reflection and procrastination, the Ben Ali government finally followed Morocco's initiative and, in April 1996, opened a semiofficial liaison office in Tel Aviv. Its primary function was to promote tourism and arrange for visas. Ben Ali was keenly aware of the benefits his country's tourist industry would reap from this. Israel reciprocated the move by opening a liaison office in Tunis.

Yet as the two countries were on the brink of entering into an era of more serious cooperation, the Israeli elections of May 1996 reduced these prospects radically. According to Muhammad Berrejeb, a high-ranking official at the Tunisian Foreign Ministry, the Netanyahu government's decision to dig the tunnel in the proximity of the Al-Aqsa Mosque aroused as much anger among Tunisians as it did among Palestinians and Muslims generally. As the Oslo process came to a virtual standstill in the first half of 1997, Tunisia recalled its liaison officer from Israel without closing the office altogether. The return of Labor to power in May 1999 led the Tunisians to dispatch a new liaison director to Tel Aviv. On February 6, 2000, Israel's Foreign Minister David Levy met in Tel Aviv with Tahar Sioud, Tunisia's secretary of state. This was the first ever visit to Israel of a high-ranking Tunisian. The two ministers decided to establish a joint committee to study future trade and tourism. Levy assured Sioud that Israel had an unequivocal commitment to the Palestinian track, but advised that it would be pointless for Tunisia to turn every dispute between Israel and the Palestinian Authority into a crisis.

Renewed Israeli-Palestinian hostilities in October 2000 resulted in the complete closure of Israel's liaison office in Tunis and the Tunisian office in Tel Aviv. Tunisia condemned the outgoing Clinton and the new Bush administrations for supporting Israel blindly, while it commended the European Union for backing the Palestinians. At the same time, Tunisia supported the peace plan outlined at the Arab summits of 2002 and 2005. In spring 2005, following seemingly improved ties between Israelis and Palestinians, Tunisia again contemplated reopening the liaison office in Tel Aviv and permitting Israel to do the same in Tunis.

Opposition to Cultural and Economic Globalization: Islamists and Nasserists

Since the Islamic Revolution in Iran (February 1979), the terrorist attack against the World Trade Center in New York and the Pentagon on September 11, 2001, and the following period, radical Islamist movements and political parties sprang up throughout the Arab world. Iran has helped finance both Shiite and Sunni Islamists in the Middle East. Islamic radicalism encouraged blind hatred of Israel as the Jewish state and Zionist entity. It emerged as the foremost enemy of economic and cultural globalization, reforms favoring women's rights, civil society, and secularization, seeing them as modes of "Americanization." In the forefront of the attack against globalization alongside Iran – though separate from it – is the "World Jihad Movement," or *al-Qāʿida* ("Basis"), led by Osama bin Laden and the Egyptian Iman Zawahiri. The latter was in some ways connected with the elements responsible for Sadat's assassination. Not only has al-Qaʿida supported Islamic militancy in different parts of the Muslim world, cultivated terrorists in training camps in Afghanistan (while it was allied there with the Afghani Taliban regime until the latter's overthrow by U.S. forces in 2001) and Sudan, but it also claimed responsibility for 9/11. In a sense, Iran and al-Qaʿida, each on its own, have promoted "Islamist globalization," challenging "modern U.S.-sponsored globalization."

Radical Islam is by no means one-dimensional, but a movement with political ambitions. Its proponents fear that Islam is threatened by Western, mostly American, economic and cultural globalization. Islamists contend that the "trans-nationalism" of modern global capitalist economy, the power of the Internet, and the implantation of multinational corporations in Arab lands would lead to the loss of Islamic identity. Because Arab regimes are eager to sign free-trade agreements with the U.S. and nurture trade and cultural ties with the European Union, the "abode of Islam" could well be overwhelmed by decadence. They believe the external influences will cause a resurgence of *Jāhiliyya* (pre-Islamic barbarism). Most of them define globalization as neo-colonialism spearheaded by the U.S., the World Bank, the International Monetary Fund, the World Trade Organization (WTO), and Zionism.

Most radical currents draw their inspiration from leading Islamist ideologues, among them Hasan al-Banna and Sayyid Qutb (both Egyptians) as well as India's Abu al-Ala Mawdudi. The largest movements became political parties dreaming of a society and government based on the rules of the *Shariʿa* (Law of Islam). These include Lebanon's Hizbollah; al-Jabha al-Islāmiyya al-Sūriyya (the Syrian Islamic Front); the Algerian FIS; the Jordanian Islamic Action Front; Morocco's al-ʿAdāla wa'l Tanmiya (Justice and Development) and al-ʿAdl wa'l Iḥsān (Justice and Beneficence); and Tunisia's al-Nahda (Renaissance) Party. The Tunisian party successfully pressured the regime to build more mosques and allot ample time for media programs on Islam, in a country that already in the 1960s prohibited polygamy and improved women's rights. Of these large entities the Muslim Brotherhood of Egypt is still denied the status of a political party. Egyptian law opposes the formation of political parties that claim a monopoly over religion. Most political movements in Egypt, even secular ones, state in their program that the *Shariʿa* is an acceptable source for legislation. The large political parties of the Arab world include those that advocate the eventual expansion of the abode of Islam from one nation-state to a universal Islamic nation. Others are content with the transformation of their particular society into a state based on Islamic Law. Only a few of these parties wish to accomplish these goals through violence, while others prefer to augment their power base in the society through electoral gains, or by preaching on behalf of Islamic principles (*daʿwa*) and spreading Islamic education. Indeed, not all Islamist parties are opposed to Western-style democratization as a temporary arrangement, for, after all, it could serve their purpose as a stepping-stone to usurp political authority. All of them disapprove of the concept of the secular nation-state as conceived by the colonial power or by regimes in Algeria, Egypt, Syria, Iraq, Lebanon, and the PLO. They see the nation-state as a passing episode in the transition toward the emergence of the Islamic nation. They are also at odds with wide segments of the officially established religious elite (*ʿulamā'*), as the latter usually grants religious legitimacy to secular government policies, such as birth control and family planning as a way to combat large-scale demographic growth. The Islamist parties are vehemently opposed to ending the age-old practice of circumcising girls in Egypt or lifting the veil. Thus far, excepting Iran and Afghanistan (which are beyond the scope of this survey), only in Sudan did an Islamist regime emerge following a military coup in 1989.

In addition to large Islamist parties, there exist two types of Islamist underground currents that consider violence as an avenue to realize their aims: the *jihād-* and *takfīr*-oriented organizations. The first of the two component include the Jihad organization involved in Sadat's assassination, and the Egyptian al-Jamāʿa al-Islāmiyya (Islamic Group) – responsible for the killing of tourists and government officials as a strategy to delegitimize and undermine the National Democratic Party regime. Included in this category are Morocco's Salafiyya Jihādiyya (Salafi Combat) and al-Sirāt al-Mustaqīm (The Right Path) with ties to al-Qaʿida. The latter were responsible for the suicide bombings in Casablanca on May 16, 2003, where Jewish institutions and personalities were also targeted, and for the March 2004 terrorist attacks in Madrid. The same applies to the Algerian GIA. Similar to the large Islamist political parties, they, too, hope to establish a religious state in lieu of the nation-state, with the law of the land based on the *Shariʿa, Sunna* (oral tradition), and the Koran. Some cherish the thought of reviving the Arab caliphate as a source of religious and political power.

Though instrumental in killing government officials and members of the *'ulamā'*, the *takfīr* organizations have a somewhat different outlook on Islam. They are best known under the name al-Takfīr wa'l Hijra. Unlike the Jihad movements, which accuse only the secular Arab leaders of being infidels, the *takfīr* regard much of contemporary Muslim society as deviants from the original Islam in its pristine forms. Their followers point to the Prophet Muhammad and his supporters, who emigrated from Mecca to Medina to create a separate society of true believers. The goal was to augment the number of Islamic adherents and some day return to Mecca victorious and popular. They also identify with the seventh-century *Khawārij* radicals who seceded from the camp of the Caliph Ali because in their eyes he deviated from the right path and exercised authority that had been reserved only to God. The *Khawārij* departed from their milieu and settled in segregated communities in parts of Iraq, Iran, and the Maghreb. They married among themselves and punished by death those suspected of adultery and violation of sacred Islamic principles. Movements espousing such notions operated in Egypt from the 1970s until the 1990s. Originally, members of al-Takfīr wa'l Hijra had planned to immigrate to northern Yemen. But the most that could be realized was the formation of segregated strongholds in Upper Egypt. Eventually they succumbed to government repression. The Moroccan government uncovered a similar movement, but information about it is sketchy. The *takfīr* highlight the notion of *ḥākimiyya*: the rule of God and the rejection of the sovereignty of man. They question the validity of the *Shariʿa* as a reliable religious source but extol the Koran and *Sunna*.

The Pan-Arab Nasserists have been on the defensive in Egypt, Lebanon, Jordan, and Israel's Arab sector, where they still possess influence. Thirty-five years after his death, Nasser's followers are as hostile to globalization as the Islamists; some are in fact more critical of Western democracy. Like the Islamists they regard globalization as a form of American neo-colonialism out to obliterate economic and political nationalism. They insist that Arab identity and Arab culture must be protected against the unrestricted marketing of Americanism as a model for global culture over international communications networks. The Nasserists fear that the encroachment of the forces of globalization on the nation-state will transfer the decision-making process from Arab states to foreign elements and multinational corporations. Hence, to counter these influences would require the formation of a united Arab bloc reminiscent of the Syrian-Egyptian Union of 1958–61.

This latter view has encountered the opposition of most Arab regimes who are opposed to centralized Pan-Arab schemes and prefer local unions, or "common markets," like the Maghreb's AMU. The Gulf states are planning to form an economic union under one currency and lift trade barriers through lowering or eliminating tariffs. They encourage multinational corporations to penetrate their economies and invest. Indeed, it is not unlikely that several separate common markets will emerge in which Israel could participate.

The Struggle for Democracy and the Collapse of Saddam Hussein's Regime

An issue raised frequently since 2000 is the compatibility of democracy with mainstream Islam. It has been said that democratic concepts do not appear in the Koran, or that Western-style democracy is an alien phenomenon to most Muslims. Both arguments are irrelevant to modern-day democracy. Besides, the Koran points to the *shūrā* (consultation) that promotes modes of political coordination as well as some political debate. There are encouraging signs, however, that democratic changes are gradually occurring in the Arab and Muslim world. Changes in the Arab world are not necessarily attributed to visionary leadership. They are often the result of U.S. pressure, a sort of "American visionary approach." The democratic presidential elections in Algeria (April 2004), which had weakened the radical Islamists and gave Bouteflika a second term as president, were encouraged by the U.S. and the Europeans. Bouteflika and the Algerian army generals are eager to purchase American weapons and to mend cultural and economic fences with Washington. Kuwait's decision, in April 2005, to enable women to participate in elections and to be elected to parliament is also a case in point.

The Bush Administration and the Europeans have "nudged" King Muhammad VI to organize freer elections in Morocco, as illustrated by the parliamentary and municipal elections (2002–3). They also encouraged him to grant greater freedom to non-governmental organizations and women's rights, including an end to polygamy and equal rights in financial arrangements relating to divorce and inheritance. Morocco is becoming economically dependent on the U.S. following the signing in April 2004 of a free trade agreement with Washington that would lift tariffs on 95 percent on all import-export products.

The January 2005 elections in the Palestinian Authority after Arafat's death raised some prospects for cautious optimism. The same is to be said of the pro-democracy manifestations in Beirut, seen in the hundreds of thousands of young Christian, Sunni Muslim, and Druze demonstrators in the wake of the assassination, in February 2005, of former Lebanese Prime Minister Rafiq al-Hariri. The demonstrators blamed Syria for the assassination. Al-Hariri, a Lebanese Sunni Muslim billionaire with close political and financial ties to the U.S. and France, was for long an advocate of Lebanese democratization and an avowed opponent of the Syrian military presence. He invested substantial funds to rebuild Beirut after the 1975–90 civil war and won the respect of wide segments of the population, save the Syrian- and Iranian-backed Hizbollah. Hariri and French President Jacques Chirac helped promote UN Security Council Resolution 1559 calling for the evacuation of all "foreign" military forces from Lebanon. Because Israel had pulled out of the southern security zone in 2000, Syria was singled out as the other major foreign force occupying the country. The mass demonstrations after al-Hariri's assassination, combined with U.S. and French insistence on a complete Syrian pullout, intensified. Damascus caved in to the pressure. On April 26, 2005, the last Syrian soldier left Lebanon, though Syrian intelligence personnel stayed behind. On May 29, 2005, national democratic elections were held in Lebanon.

On February 26, 2005, another important development was Husni Mubarak's statement to the French daily *Le Figaro* that, in the Egyptian presidential elections scheduled for fall 2005, more than one candidate will be able to run. Until now only Mubarak had offered his candidacy after being nominated by parliament with the support of the government's powerful National Democratic Party. He was elected through a national referendum whereby Egyptians simply voted "yes" or "no." The 2005 elections were to be conducted through secret ballots and direct elections with international observers supervising them, as had been the case with the Palestinian elections in January the same year. Mubarak acted to implement the reform, particularly by amending Article 76 of the Egyptian Constitution. This revision provides for direct elections via secret ballots and allows an unlimited number of candidates to run for presidential office. There are pressures on Mubarak to amend Article 77 as well, which currently sets no limits on the number of times a president may run for office. Several candidates entered the race, among them Professor Saʿd al-Din Ibrahim, a key civil rights activist who spent time in prison for his advocacy of drastic democratic reforms, and Dr. Nawwal al-Saʿdawi, a leading feminist who strongly favors the separation of religion and state. It appears that a good number of the candidates have no military background, signaling perhaps a departure from a tradition that began in 1952 whereby former army officers held the supreme leadership post. While the reform may be regarded as an evolutionary step toward democracy in Egypt that began after Nasser's death, pressure brought to bear on Mubarak by the Bush administration should not be overlooked. Only several weeks prior to the announcement of the reform initiative, President Bush publicly challenged Mubarak: "The great and proud nation of Egypt, which showed the way toward peace ... can now show the way toward democracy in the Middle East."

There were two fundamental reasons for the second war between the U.S.-led Western coalition and Saddam Hussein's Iraq. First, there was the lingering tension and hostility left over from the Gulf War of 1991, in which Iraqi occupation troops were forced out of Kuwait. As a result of this war, the Iraqi government agreed to turn over or destroy different types of weapons, including SCUD missiles fired at Israel and Weapons of Mass Destruction (WMD). The UN was allowed to send weapons inspectors to confirm the destruction of Iraqi weapons and also to uncover prohibited weapons believed to be hidden. Moreover, "No Fly Zones" were established over northern and southern Iraq for the protection of Iraqi minority groups in opposition to the Baʿthi regime. Over these two zones, Allied aircraft patrolled the skies to prevent Iraqi aircraft from attacking northern Kurds and southern Shiites. As time passed, Iraqi air defense forces fired missiles at U.S. and British planes. In response, Allied planes bombed the air-defense sites and radar installations deep inside Iraq. In 1998, under Iraqi pressure, the UN weapons inspectors left Iraq, angering the U.S. Further, following the terrorist attacks on the U.S. on 9/11, President Bush implied – yet to be proven – that Iraq had intimate ties with al-Qaʿida. Using the potential threat of Iraq's supplying WMD to Islamist terrorists, the U.S. insisted on total Iraqi disarmament. Iraq relented to pressures in 2002 to allow the return of UN weapons inspectors. By early 2003, however, the U.S. and British governments suggested that Iraq was not cooperating with the UN inspectors. On March 17, 2003, Bush issued an ultimatum to Saddam Hussein and his two sons to enter into voluntary exile within two days or face military occupation. The Iraqi leader would not surrender his power.

On March 19, 2003, the U.S. and its Western coalition partners attacked Iraq and occupied it. Saddam Hussein's regime quickly collapsed. Leading military and civilian Baʿthi leaders were later rounded up. Saddam was imprisoned and held for trial. His two sons were killed by Allied forces. Until mid-2004, a representative of the U.S. government governed Iraq. From then until the democratic elections of January 30, 2005, an interim Iraqi government was formed that excluded the Baʿth party. During this time the Allied forces failed to uncover chemical and biological weapons of mass destruction, resulting in major criticism throughout the world of the U.S.-led war and its raison d'être.

On the eve of the U.S.-backed Iraqi democratic elections neighboring nations, especially Syria, Saudi Arabia, and the Gulf states, feared that the changes in Iraq would stir sectarian violence there and spread instability in the region. Kuwait, Jordan, and Saudi Arabia – ruled by Sunni Muslim leaders – were concerned that an Iraq dominated by a Shiite majority after decades of Sunni minority rule, with ties to Shiite Iran, would threaten them. A second Shiite-dominated state in the region, it was argued, might pose serious domestic problems for such countries as Saudi Arabia, Kuwait, and the United Arab Emirates, which have Shiite minorities, and Bahrain, where Shiites are a majority but have no political power under a Sunni government. At the same time, the dominance of the Saudi royal family is connected with the Wahhabi sect, which views Shiites as heretics. Finally, Jordan's King Abdullah feared that the elections might create a "crescent" of Shiite power: contiguous Shiite-controlled territory through Iran, Iraq, and Lebanon. Syria and Turkey fretted that Iraqi Kurds might press for independence, reviving separatist ideas among their own Kurdish populations. On the other hand, the outcome of the war in Iraq and U.S. pressure on Baghdad to commence a process of democratization of political institutions boded well for Israel. The latter became a major beneficiary of the war as the removal of Saddam Hussein eliminated the eastern military front.

The general elections of January 30, 2005 in Iraq and the drafting of a new constitution were seminal events. Doubtless, it is vital for the future evolution of democracies in other Middle Eastern countries. According to the Independent Elections Commission in Iraq, 8,500,000 of the 14 million registered voters including overseas Iraqis cast their ballots. The voters cast two ballots: one for the national assembly and one for one of the 18 provincial councils. The voters in the Kurdish provinces of Dahouk, Erbil, and Sulaymaniyya cast a third ballot for the autonomous 111-seat Kurdish parliament. There were over 100 lists of political parties, coalitions, or individuals, comprising a total of 7,471 candidates who competed for the 275 seats in the National Assembly. The Iraqi Shiite National Alliance consisting of Ḥizb al-Daʿwa al-Islāmiyya (Call for Islam Party), the Supreme Council of the Islamic Revolution in Iraq (SCIRI), and the Iraqi National Congress (INC) won over 48 percent of the vote. The Kurds, aligned with the Shiites, garnered 26 percent of the vote. They were able to tip the scales in favor of candidates amenable to meeting their demands. The Sunni Arabs, whose leaders had ruled Iraq until March 2003, got 25 percent of the vote. Many of them boycotted the elections. In April 2005, Iraq had a new Parliament. The speaker of the Parliament is a Sunni Arab; the Kurdish leader, Jalal Talabani, is president of Iraq. In April, Ibrahim Jaʿafari of the Shiite Daʿwa Party became prime minister and formed a coalition of Shiites, Sunni Arabs, and Sunni Kurdish ministers.

It is uncertain what directions the Arab world will take in the future. Women have made some headway and were elected in significant numbers to the Moroccan parliament (September 2002). Morocco undertook important reforms and Egypt as well as several Gulf emirates introduced legislative measures to do the same. More educated women join the Arab work force. While the struggle for freedom of the press and electronic media, and the empowerment of non-government organizations, has only begun, there is cable and satellite television in several Arab states that enjoy some freedom. Gone are the days when a regime like Nasser's could thrive on government-controlled media alone. The al-Jazeera satellite television channel in Qatar emerged as a critical media tool through its many correspondents stationed in the region. There are independent newspapers throughout the Arab world maintaining ideological party lines and independent thinking, usually privately owned. The newspaper *al-Ḥayāt*, published in London since 1988, is a forum for Arab intellectuals who wish to promote reforms in Arab society. There are overseas Arab television stations (e.g., MBC in London) that offer revolutionary programs for young men and women which are aired in the Arab world. Notwithstanding, the road is still long until freedom of the press and the general media prevails and they have progressive contents. Government-controlled newspapers and television networks in the Palestinian Authority, Saudi Arabia, and Egypt still disseminate antisemitic and not merely anti-Israel propaganda in the spirit of the *Protocols of the Elders of Zion*. There are other outstanding challenges, among them tribal tensions and Arab-Berber confrontations in Algeria and Morocco, with the Berbers struggling for cultural autonomy. Although demographic growth is moderate in most Arab states, this is not the case in Egypt, Algeria, Morocco, Sudan, and the Palestinian Authority. Family planning and reduced birth rates should receive top priority in domestic reforms. This may ease chronic unemployment in these countries. Unemployment will be reduced also through effective economic globalization and industrialization. Rural-agricultural reforms with the help of the West may put an end, or slow down considerably, the waves of rural migration to the urban agglomerations.

It is noteworthy that most Arab states have come a long way in dealing with Israel. This includes post-Saddam Hussein Iraq. They are prepared to recognize Israel and establish full ties with it, including trade relations. Some are in fact cooperating with Israel via back channels. The main stumbling blocks to formalizing ties are the Palestinian crisis and the yet to be implemented UN Resolution 242 in regard to Syria. Shimon Peres envisioned in the early 1990s a "New Middle East" enriched by science and information technology. For many, this seems far-fetched. However, the continued exposure of the Arabs states to globalization, democratization, and demographic reforms is the only viable option. The alternatives offered by Islamists and other extremists can only perpetuate regression and violence: a tragedy of enormous consequences for the Arabs and Israel, as evidenced by the violent fighting in Lebanon between *Hizbollah and Israel in summer 2006.

See also entries on individual Arab countries and the general historical and political surveys under *Israel, State of.

BIBLIOGRAPHY: L.S. Anderson, *The State and Social Transformation in Tunisia and Libya, 1930–1980* (1986); E. Karsh, *The Iran-Iraq War: A Military Analysis* (1987); M.H. Kerr, *The Arab Cold War: Gamal Abd al-Nasir and his Rivals, 1958–1970* (1971); M.M. Laskier, *Israel and the Maghreb: From Statehood to Oslo* (2004); idem, "A Difficult Inheritance: Moroccan Society Under King Muhammad VI," in: *Middle East Review of International Affairs*, 7:3 (Sept. 2003), 1–20; C.G. MacDonald, "League of Arab States" in: *Encyclopedia of the Modern Middle East*, vol. 3 (1996), 1083-85; B. Maddy-Weitzman, "Israel and Morocco: A Special Relationship," in: *The Maghreb Review*, 21:1–2 (1996), 36–48; P. Mattar, "Arab-Israeli War (1982)," in: *Encyclopedia of the Modern Middle East* (1996), 187–88; B. Morris, *The Birth of the Palestinian Refugee Problem* (1988); idem, Interview with Ehud Barak, in: *The New York Review of Books* (June 13, 2002); M.B. Oren, *Six Days of War: June 1967 and the Making of the Modern Middle East* (2002); D. Peretz, "Arab-Israeli Conflict," in: *Encyclopedia of the Modern Middle East* (1996), 179–83; idem, "Arab-Israel War," *ibid.*, 187–89; N. Raphaeli, "Iraqi Elections (VI)," at: memri.org/bun; A. Sela, *The Decline of the Arab-Israeli Conflict: Middle East Politics and the Quest for Regional Order* (1998); Y. Shimoni, *Medinot Arav* (1994); A. Shlaim, *The Iron Wall: Israel and the Arab World* (2000); M.K. Stack and T. Marshall, "Iraqi Election Putting Neighboring Nations on Edge," in: *Los Angeles Times* (Jan. 27, 2005); N. Tal, *Immut mi-Bayit: Hitmodedut Miẓrayim ve-Yarden im ha-Islam ha-Kiẓoni* (1999); M. Tessler, *A History of the Israeli-Palestinian Conflict* (1994).

[Michael M. Laskier (2nd ed.)]

ARAD (Heb. עֲרָד), an important biblical city in the eastern Negev which controlled the main road to Edom and Elath.

Ancient Arad

"The Canaanite, the king of Arad, who dwelt in the South [Negev]" prevented the Israelite tribes from penetrating into Canaan directly from Kadesh-Barnea "by the way of Atharim" (Num. 21:1; 33:40) and he defeated them at neighboring Hormah (Num 14:44–45; Deut. 1:44). Another biblical tradition, however, recounts a second battle between the Israelites and the king of Arad near Hormah. This time the Canaanites were defeated and the victorious Israelites "utterly destroyed them and their cities." The name Hormah ("utter destruction") is derived from this event (Num. 21:2–3). In the list of defeated Canaanite kings in Joshua 12:14, which follows the latter tradition, the kings of Arad and Hormah appear side by side. It is further recorded in the Bible (Judg. 1:16) that "the children of the Kenite, Moses' father-in-law [the Septuagint reads "the children of Hobab the Kenite"] went up out of the city of palm-trees with the children of Judah into the wilderness of Judah, which is in the south [Negev] of Arad, and they went and dwelt with the people" (Heb. *ha-am*; but the Septuagint reads the "Amalekite"; cf. I Sam. 15:6). This account of the settlement of the important Kenite family in the vicinity of Arad acquired special significance after the modern discovery of the sanctuary at Arad. Pharaoh Shishak in listing cities conquered by him in Ereẓ Israel (c. 920 B.C.E.) records the capture of two places in the Negev with the name Arad (No. 107–112), i.e., "the fortresses of Arad Rabbat [Arad the Great] and Arad of the House of Yeroḥam." It seems, therefore, that in the days of Solomon there were two fortresses with the name Arad: a large, main city and a second named for the family of Yeroḥam (probably the biblical Jerahmeelites; and cf. "the South [Negev] of the Jerahmeelites" and "the cities of the Jerahmeelites" in I Samuel 27:10 and 30:29). Eder (Heb.

עֶדֶר), which is mentioned as the second city in the Negev district of Judah (Josh. 15:21) is apparently a corruption of the name Arad. A village called Arad was still known to Eusebius in the fourth century C.E. (Onom. 14:2), 20 mi. from Hebron and four mi. from Malaatha (Moleatha), a description which fits Tell Arad, which is about 18½ mi. (30 km.) E.N.E. of Beersheba. On the *Madaba Map, Arad is erroneously placed south of Beersheba.

Excavations conducted by Y. Aharoni and R. Amiran at Tell Arad from 1962 to 1967 uncovered a large city from the Early Bronze Age II (c. 2900–2700 B.C.E.) which was built over a scattered, unfortified settlement from the Late Chalcolithic period. The Early Bronze Age city was surrounded by a stone wall, 8¼ ft. (2.50 m.) thick, which was strengthened at intervals by semicircular towers. It was a well-planned city which was divided into various quarters by narrow lanes. The houses were built according to a uniform architectural design and were of a typical "broad house" construction – a rectangular room with the entrance on one of the long sides. Of major importance was the discovery of imported pottery from Egypt as well as an abundance of decorated pottery which had previously been known mainly from first dynasty tombs in Egypt (Abydos ware). This pottery is of great chronological value and it proves that commercial ties between Egypt and Arad were already well-developed at that time.

The ancient town was destroyed not later than 2700 B.C.E. and the site remained deserted until some time in the 11th century B.C.E. when a small settlement rose. In the center of the village, a sacred precinct with a *bamah* ("high place") and altar was built. This was undoubtedly the Kenite sanctuary whose priests traced their sacerdotal heritage back to Moses (Judg. 1:16). In the tenth century B.C.E., probably during Solomon's reign, a strong citadel was built on the site which was in existence until close to the destruction of the First Temple. The citadel was destroyed six times during this period. It was followed by a succession of Persian, Hellenistic and Roman fortresses. The latest stratum at Arad dates to the beginning of the Arabic period.

The outstanding discovery at Arad was the temple which stood on the northwestern corner of the Israelite citadel. It is the first Israelite sanctuary to be uncovered in excavations. Its westward orientation, contents, and general layout in many ways recall Solomon's temple in Jerusalem but the temple shows an even more striking resemblance to the biblical description of the Tabernacle in the desert. The sanctuary consists of a main hall from which three steps lead up to the Holy of Holies, in the entrance of which were found two incense altars. In the center of the Holy of Holies were a small *bamah* and a *maẓẓevah* ("stone stele"). Along the eastern side of the hall was a large courtyard which was divided by a stone sill into an outer courtyard and an inner one (porch). Flanking the entrance to the hall were two stone slabs which apparently served as bases of pillars similar to the Jachin and Boaz in the Jerusalem temple (cf. II Chron. 3:17). In the outer courtyard stood an altar for burnt offerings, which was a square of five cubits, the exact measurement of the Tabernacle (Ex. 27:1; cf. II Chron. 6:13), and built of earth and unhewn field stones (cf. Ex. 20:22, 25). Among the various finds and ritual objects discovered in the temple, two ostraca (ink-inscribed sherds) are of interest. These bear the names of Pashhur and Meremoth – two priestly families known from the Bible. A third ostracon contains a list of family names including, among others, "the sons of Korah." The temple was built over the early Kenite high place at the same time as the first citadel, probably during the days of Solomon, and it was destroyed when the last Israelite citadel was erected in the days of Josiah. The destruction of the temple was certainly connected with Josiah's concentration of the religious ritual in Jerusalem which is described in II Kings 22.

In addition to the ostraca found in the temple, numerous others inscribed in Hebrew and Aramaic were also uncovered and these considerably enrich knowledge of ancient Hebrew epigraphy. One group belongs to the archives of "Eliashib, son of Eshyahu," who was a high-ranking official and perhaps the commander of the last Israelite citadel (c. 600 B.C.E.) Most of these contain orders to supply rations of wine and bread to travelers, including the "Kittim," who were apparently a group of mercenaries of Aegean origin. One of the letters mentions Beersheba and another contains a reference to "the house of YHWH," apparently the Temple in Jerusalem. Another ostracon from the same period contains an order for the urgent dispatch of reinforcements from Arad to Ramat Negev ("Ramah of the South," Josh. 19:8; I Sam. 30:27) to head off a threatening Edomite attack. This is possibly a reference to the Edomite invasion during the time of Nebuchadnezzar, hinted at in II Kings 24:2 (reading Edom instead of Aram).

The generally accepted theory that Tell Arad is Arad of the Canaanite period has been refuted by excavation of the site since no traces of settlement from the Middle or Late Bronze Ages were found. Its identification with Israelite Arad, on the other hand, was confirmed, the name even found inscribed on two ostraca. There are two possible solutions to this problem: (1) In the Canaanite period, Arad was the name of a region and not of a specific city; (2) The site of Canaanite Arad is Tell el-Milḥ (present-day Malḥata) 7½ mi. (12 km.) southwest of Tell Arad where strong fortifications dating from the Hyksos period (Middle Bronze Age) have been discovered. This identification is substantiated by the inscription of Pharaoh Shishak according to which it can be assumed that "Arad of the House of Yeroḥam" is the early Arad which was settled by the Jerahmeelite family (cf. I Sam. 27; 30:29) and "Arad Rabbat" (Arad the Great) was the strong citadel established in the days of Solomon in the Negev of Judah on the site of the Kenite sacred precinct.

[Yohanan Aharoni]

Since the writing of the above by one of the excavators of the site, Yohanan Aharoni, considerable research and a number of key publications have appeared furthering our understanding of the development of the Bronze Age and Iron Age settlements at Arad. R. Amiran and her associates, notably O. Ilan, have concentrated their efforts in furthering the publication of the Bronze Age site. Bronze Age Arad is generally regarded as the southernmost bastion of Canaanite culture, although one scholar (Finkelstein) has suggested that it might actually be the other way around, i.e., the site should be viewed as the northernmost cultural manifestation of the desert peoples of the time. It is now clear that the Bronze Age site had five separate strata (I–V): Stratum V representing the remains of a scattered Chalcolithic settlement (c. 4000–3400 B.C.E.); Stratum IV representing an unfortified small hamlet dated to the Early Bronze IB (3200–3000 B.C.E.), with evidence that trade with Egypt had already begun by that time, and with the discovery of a jar fragment with the incised *serekh* of Narmer, the last king of Dynasty O, which provided important synchronism between the Canaanite and Egyptian chronologies; and Stratum III (destroyed in c. 2800 B.C.E.) representing the oldest urban level of the city, with the construction of the city wall, a palace and other public structures, as well as the reservoir. Stratum II, the uppermost urban phase of the Bronze Age city, was the main focus of Amiran's excavations, and seems to have been built not long after the destruction of Stratum III. The urban fabric of the Stratum II was studied in some detail by the excavators: the city was surrounded by a wall (a circumference of 3,858 ft. (1,176 m.) with semi-circular towers and at least two gates and a few posterns; numerous houses of broad room plan with a doorway in the long wall, with benches lining the interior walls and with a ceiling supported by a pillar – of a type now known as the "Arad House" type (a ceramic model of such a house was also found) – were excavated; public and elite areas were also investigated: notably, a market area, a palace, a sacred precinct, and reservoir district. Stratum I represented a sparse settlement (of squatters?) in the ruins of the former Stratum II city. There can be no doubt that Arad was a primary trading center in the Early Bronze Age and was the focal point for much of the region's economic activities.

New information regarding the Iron Age period site, formerly excavated by Y. Aharoni, has also come to light as a result of recent research activities. In addition to this, an important reassessment of the stratigraphy of the site was made by Z. Herzog, who undertook some excavations at the site in 1977. The continued identification of the site as that of biblical Arad (Num. 21:1; 33:40; Josh. 12:14, 15:21; Jud. 1:16) and as the place mentioned as *'Arad n-bt* (i.e. "Greater Arad") in the Egyptian Sheshonq's list of the cities he reached (925 B.C.E.) has also been strengthened by the discovery at the site of a potsherd inscribed with the name Arad four times. It is now clear that the Iron Age site had 12 strata (I–XII): Stratum XII representing the sparse remains of the early Iron Age village (11th century B.C.E.). The original excavator's identification of a cultic temenos with a *bamah* at the site has been reassessed and it would appear that they were ordinary domestic installations instead. Stratum XI (10th century B.C.E.) represents the first fortified fortress 180 × 165 ft. (55 × 50 m.), with a casemate wall and projecting towers, and with a gate on the east side. Strata X–VI represent the major changes that were made to the fortress: the casemate wall was replaced by a solid wall with a glacis reinforcement, and only two gate towers. The water system and the temple were both first constructed during this stage. The defensive wall and the water system continued to be used until the end of Stratum VI with few changes. The suggestion made by the original excavator that a casemate wall replaced the solid wall during Strata VII–VI, appears to be incorrect and the casemate actually represents portions of an unfinished Hellenistic tower. The abolition of the temple at Arad is attributed to the cultic reforms made by King Hezekiah in 715 B.C.E. (see II Kings 18:22). Strata V–I represent the later remains at the site from the Persian, Hellenistic, Roman, Early Islamic, and Ottoman periods. The site was substantially restored for visitors in conjunction with the National Parks Authority of Israel.

[Shimon Gibson (2nd ed.)]

Modern Arad

Modern Arad, town 32 mi. (45 km.) east of Beersheba, 6 mi. (9 km.) east of ancient Arad, situated above the Judean Desert plateau overlooking the Dead Sea, 610 m. above sea level. Arad was founded in 1961 in an area formerly inhabited by nomadic Bedouin tribes. Town planners envisaged Arad as the urban center of an industrial development region. A previous attempt at settlement in the region in 1921, by a group which included Izhak *Ben-Zvi, was unsuccessful.

Designed in six high-density neighborhoods, grouped around the civic center, with a separate industrial sector, resort area and suburbs, Arad was the first Israel development town to be planned by a group of architects and engineers living on the site. The group was responsible, inter alia, for the patio flat, an innovation in public housing, consisting of interlocking four-storey desert apartment buildings, with private courtyards and maximum shade and protection.

The local economy was planned on the region's chemical deposits: potash from the Dead Sea and phosphates and gas located in the area. An industrial complex was constructed to produce fertilizers, chemical and petrochemical products. Employment was also provided by a prefabricated-housing plant and a knitwear factory.

The dry pollen-free climate, the high altitude, and picturesque location combined to attract tourists, and people suffering from respiratory diseases. From the mid-1980s Arad hosted a Hebrew song festival in the summers, attracting many youngsters. However, after three teenagers were crushed to death at a live concerts in 1995, the event was canceled for a few years and never regained its popularity.

In contrast to other development towns, Arad at first drew its population mostly from among Israel-born citizens rather than newly arrived immigrants. Planned as a community of 50,000, the town numbered 4,500 inhabitants in 1968, and only with the arrival of some 12,000 immigrants in the 1990s, mostly from the former Soviet Union, did the town grow significantly, reaching a population of around 18,000 in the mid-1990s, when it received municipal status, and 24,500 in 2002, the municipal area extending over 3.5 sq. mi. (9 sq. km.). Residents continued to be employed mainly in the chemical industry as well as in the hotels of the Dead Sea area.

[Daniel Gavron / Shaked Gilboa (2nd ed.)]

BIBLIOGRAPHY: Abel, Geog, 2 (1938), 248f.; N. Glueck, *Rivers in the Desert* (1959), 50–53, 114f.; Aharoni and Amiran, in: IEJ, 14 (1964), 131–47; idem, in: *Archaeology*, 17 (1964), 43–54; Mazar, in: JNES, 24 (1965), 297–303; Aharoni, in: IEJ, 17 (1967), 233–49; idem, in: *Fourth World Congress of Jewish Studies, Papers*, 1 (1967), 11–13; idem, in: BASOR, 184 (1966), 14–16; idem, in: BA, 31 (1968), 2ff.; idem, in: D.N. Freedman and J.C. Greenfield (eds.), *New Directions in Biblical Archeology* (1969), 25–39 (incl. bibl.); Naor, in: PAAJR, 36 (1968), 95–105; idem, in: *Eretz Israel*, 9 (1969), 10–21; idem, in: *Ariel*, no. 24 (1969), 21–36. **ADD. BIBLIOGRAPHY:** R. Amiran et al., *Early Arad I: The Chalcolithic Settlement and Early Bronze City* (1978); R. Amiran and O. Ilan, *Early Arad II: The Chalcolithic and Early Bronze IB Settlements and the Early Bronze II City* (1996); Y. Aharoni et al., *Arad Inscriptions* (1981); Z. Herzog et al., "The Israelite Fortress at Arad," in: BASOR, 254 (1984), 1–34. **WEBSITE:** www.arad.muni.il.

ARAD, city in Transylvania, western Romania; until 1918 within the borders of Hungary. Jews are first recorded there in 1717. Regulations for the burial society were drawn up in 1750. Jewish occupations during this early period were mainly connected with producing and selling alcoholic beverages and the grain trade. In 1742 the leadership of the local community requested the intervention of the district authorities in order to improve its situation. The small community became important after 1789 with the election as rabbi of Aaron *Chorin, who officiated until his death in 1844. Chorin was born and educated in the Czech provinces of Austria, one of the more prosperous and emancipated regions of the country. He soon came into conflicts with the rabbis of Hungary, who preferred a more conservative and traditional way of life and behavior. Under his leadership, Arad became a center of the nascent *Reform movement in Judaism. He initiated the construction of a synagogue in 1828, established a small yeshivah, and set up an elementary school. He also encouraged Jewish youth to enter productive occupations. Due to his efforts, there were about 100 highly skilled Jewish artisans in Arad in 1841. In 1832, on Chorin's initiative, the first Jewish school was built in Arad, where study of the Hungarian language became compulsory. It was one of the first Jewish schools officially recognized by the Hungarian authorities. Even after Chorin's death, the community in Arad long remained a bastion of extreme Reform. The emancipation of the Jews in 1867 attracted many Jews to take active part in Hungarian economic, political, and cultural life, considering themselves Hungarians of Mosaic religion. The Jews of Arad took an active part in Hungarian public life (one of them, Dr. Ferenc Sarkany, becoming mayor of the city, even volunteered for the army during the World War I). At the end of World War I, however, a considerable number of Orthodox Jews settled there, and established a community. The Neolog rabbis in Arad were early supporters of Magyarization among the Jews; already in 1845 R. Jacob Steinhart delivered a sermon in Hungarian. The Zionist movement found support in Arad, and the "Jewish Party," after Transylvania became a part of Romania in 1919, also obtained many votes in the elections for the Romanian parliament.

Arad Jews shared the fate of the Jewry of Romania between the two world wars, suffering from increasing antisemitism. In the years of the Antonescu government the two Jewish communities – the Orthodox and the Neolog – united to be able to work better for the interests of their membership. The Jewish population numbered 812 in 1839; 4,795 in 1891; 6,430 in 1920; 7,835 in 1941; and 9,402 in 1942 (this last increase was due to the enforced concentration in Arad of Jews from the villages and country towns of the area by the Romanian Fascist authorities in 1941–42). The Jews from the Arad district together with those of the district of Timisoara were slated to be deported to the Belzec extermination camp in 1942, at the very beginning of a massive joint Romanian-German operation which targeted all the Jews from Regat and Southern Transylvania. On October 11, 1942, the order to deport the Jews of Arad was rescinded. Together with the majority of the Jews of Regat and Southern Transylvania the Jews of Arad survived the war.

The Jewish community of Arad numbered 13,200 in 1947. Subsequently, there was a progressive decrease due to emigration from the country, mainly to Israel. In 1969 the Jewish population numbered 4,000. At the outset of the 21st century it numbered a few hundred and continued to decline numerically.

BIBLIOGRAPHY: MHJ, 3 (1937), 180; 7 (1963), 116, 226–31, 694; 11 (1968); 1038, 13 (1970), 193; L. Rosenberg, in: *Jahrbuch fuer die israelitischen Cultusgemeinden* (Arad, 1860), 32–59, 144–52; M. Carp, *Cartea Neagră*, 2 (Rom., 1946), 55, 106, 115, 121, 200, 241–42, 363, 368; 3 (1947), 237, 341; Vágvölgyi, in: *Múlt és Jövö* (Hung., 1917), 296–305; PK Romanyah, 279–85. **ADD. BIBLIOGRAPHY:** J. Ancel, *Documents Concerning the Fate of Romanian Jewry during the Holocaust*, 4, 104–5; R. Ioanid, *The Holocaust in Romania* (1999), 244.

[Yehouda Marton / Paul Schveiger and Radu Ioanid (2nd ed.)]

ARAD, RON (1958–), missing Israeli navigator. Arad grew up in Hod ha-Sharon and lost his father as a teenager. He attended a high school military academy and volunteered for the air force, serving as a navigator and later studying chemical engineering at the Technion. On October 16, 1986, during a flight across the Lebanese border, his Phantom jet was hit. He and his fellow pilot abandoned the plane. The pilot succeeded in reaching the rescue team, but Arad was captured by the terrorist Shiite Amal organization. Amal demanded 200 Lebanese and 450 Palestinians prisoners and $3 million in exchange for Arad. The Israeli government refused to give in to its demands. Subsequently, Arad was in the custody of various organizations, all with connections to Iran. During the first two years of his captivity he sent letters, but from 1987 there was no further information about his fate. Over the years Israel made great efforts to obtain information about him, including the kidnapping of Mustafa Dirani, the Amal security chief who first had custody of Arad. The German government too used its good offices to obtain information about Arad, and his wife, Tami, met with heads of state as Arad's plight became a *cause celebre* and a part of Israel's popular consciousness – but all to no avail. In 2004 the Born To Freedom Foundation, set up to secure his release, offered a $10 million reward for information about his whereabouts. During his captivity, Arad received the rank of lieutenant colonel.

BIBLIOGRAPHY: www.ron-arad.org.il; www.10million.org.

[Shaked Gilboa (2nd ed.)]

ARAD, YAEL (1967–) Israeli judoist, first Israeli to win an Olympic medal. Arad was born in Tel Aviv and began studying judo at the age of eight. At 16 she was the runner-up in the 56-kg class in the German Open for Cadets. Because judo was an underdeveloped and underfinanced sport in Israel, Arad went to Europe and Japan for training, steadily improving before placing second in the German Open in 1988, and third at the European Championships the following year. In 1990, Arad defeated the world no. 1 and no. 2 judoists before losing in the finals, winning the silver medal at a tournament in Germany. She finished second at the 1993 World and European Championships, and placed fifth at the 1995 World Championships. By the 1996 Olympics, Arad had competed in 49 international competitions, winning 24 medals: seven gold, eight silver, and nine bronze, and had been Israeli champion 16 times. But it was her silver medal at Barcelona in 1992 that elevated Arad to a place in Israeli history beyond the world of sports. After 40 years of Olympic competition Israel had finally won a medal, placing Israel on the map of international athletic achievements and uniting the country in a sporting event in a way not seen since the 1977 European basketball championship. Wanting to overcome what she called Israel's "mental barrier" against winning a medal, she took the silver in the half-middleweight class (61-kg) and promptly dedicated it to the victims of the 1972 Munich massacre. Arad competed again at the 1996 Atlanta Games, but she suffered from a viral infection and lost in the bronze medal round and placed fifth. Arad was elected to the Israeli Olympic Committee in 1997 and was a judo coach for Israel at the 2000 Sydney Olympics.

[Elli Wohlgelernter (2nd ed.)]

ARAD, YITZHAK (1926–), ghetto activist, partisan, underground fighter, IDF officer, and historian. Born Isaac Rudnicki in Swieciany, Lithuania, Arad began his underground activities at the age of 15 in his hometown when he was captured by the Germans and put to work cleaning confiscated Soviet weapons. Arad was able to steal a gun and together with a group of friends formed an underground group. In 1943, the group escaped from the ghetto to the forest and joined a contingent of Soviet partisans. After the war, he immigrated to Israel illegally and became active in the underground against the British.

Known by his Russian partisan nickname, "Tulka," he continued to serve in the newly created Israel Defense Forces and as a career officer moved up the ranks in the Armored Corps. Arad's last position in the IDF was chief education officer, retiring from active service with the rank of brigadier general.

Arad served as chairman of the directorate of Yad Vashem from 1972 to 1993, in all likelihood the last survivor to hold that position. Under his leadership, Yad Vashem developed various monuments, including the Warsaw Ghetto Square, with its imposing recreation of Nathan Rapoport's sculptures honoring the Resistance fighters, and the Valley of the Communities, a commemorative sculptural series of walls depicting 5,0000 Jewish communities destroyed in the Holocaust. It opened the Children's Memorial to the Holocaust designed by Israeli architect Moshe *Safdie. Arad was deeply sensitive to the role of Yad Vashem within Israeli society as the conscience of the Shoah and also to its task of Holocaust commemoration.

As a scholar, his expertise was on the Holocaust in the areas of the former Soviet Union. He is the author of the two-volume *History of the Holocaust: Soviet Union and Annexed Territories* (2004); *Belzec, Sobibor, Treblinka: The Operation Reinhard Death Camps* (1987); *Ghetto in Flames: The Struggle and Destruction of the Jews of Vilna* (1982); the memoir *Partisan: From the Valley of Death to Mount Zion* (1979); and *Anthology on Armed Jewish Resistance.* He also served as editor for *The Pictorial History of the Holocaust* (1990), *The Einsatzgruppen Reports: Selections from the Dispatches of the Nazi Death Squads' Campaign against the Jews: 7/41–1/43* (1989), and *Ponary Diary, July 1941–November 1943: A Bystander's Account of a Mass Murder* (2005). He co-edited *Documents on the Holocaust: Selected Sources on the Destruction of the Jews of Germany and Austria, Poland, and the Soviet Union* (1981) and contributed to *The Encyclopedia of the Holocaust.* Arad testified in war crimes trials in Israel and was a consultant for the U.S. Holocaust Memorial Museum.

[Beth Cohen and Yitzchak Mais (2nd ed.)]

ARADUS, Phoenician city (modern Ruad) on a small island off the Syrian coast, about two miles from Tartouse. Aradus was among the many cities to receive a copy of the pact concluded between the Romans and *Simeon b. Mattathias, the Hasmonean (142 B.C.E.). A century later Mark Anthony restored the rights of the Jews in Aradus, as well as in other cities of the area, following the defeat of Gaius Cassius.

BIBLIOGRAPHY: I Macc., 15:23; Jos., Ant., 14:323; M. Stern, *Ha-Te'udot le-Mered ha-Ḥashmona'im* (1965), 131f.

[Isaiah Gafni]

°**ARAFAT, YASSER** (1929–2004), chairman of the *Palestine Liberation Organization (PLO), 1969–2004, a founding father of the Fatah organization (1959), and first chairman of the *Palestinian Authority from its establishment (1994). A distant relative of the prominent Husseini family, Arafat was educated in Egypt and graduated from Cairo University as an engineer. He then established the Palestinian Students Union, centered in Gaza, and was its first chairman. He later became politically active in Kuwait while working there as an engineer 1957–60 (reportedly after briefly serving in the Egyptian Army in 1957).

In the late 1950s, Arafat was a co-founder of the Fatah, as a clandestine Palestinian national liberation movement, which soon had branches among Palestinians residing in Arab states and among students in Europe. In January 1965, shortly after the establishment of the PLO under Egyptian-Jordanian patronage, Fatah embarked on guerrilla activity, launched from Arab territories against Israel.

From the outset Arafat emerged as Fatah's leader although until the early 1990s his status was of *primus inter pares*, sharing a collective leadership with his two main co-founders, Khalil al-Wazir (Abu Jihad) and Salah Khalaf (Abu Iyad). When in mid-1968 the PLO turned into an umbrella-organization of various guerilla groups, popular associations, and voluntary groups, with Fatah gaining effective control of the organization, Arafat was elected spokesman of the PLO. In February 1969 he became chairman of its Executive Committee and the PLO's leader and commander-in-chief. Henceforth, Arafat became the symbol-figure of the Palestinian people, its national cause, and claim for statehood.

As Fatah's leader, Arafat was responsible for the planning and execution of continuous sabotage and terrorist operations committed by this organization in Israel. Shortly after the 1967 war, Arafat failed in his attempt to organize a network of Fatah cells in the West Bank that would implement classical guerrilla warfare against Israel: Arafat himself fled to east Jordan and the newly established guerrilla infrastructure was exposed and eliminated by Israel. As a result, Fatah and other guerrilla organizations that had mushroomed after the 1967 war established themselves in the Jordanian territory from which they fired mortars and rockets against Israel, infiltrated into the West Bank for military purposes, and continued to mobilize people and establish active cells in this area. The growing armed presence of Palestinian armed groups gradually led to the creation of a "state within a state" – which soon began to threaten the Jordanian regime and authority, culminating in the Jordanian monarch's decision to eliminate the armed Palestinian presence on his land, beginning in September 1970. During this period of repeated Palestinian-Jordanian tension, armed clashes and serious violations of Jordanian sovereignty by militant Palestinian groups, Arafat became known for his diplomatic juggling on the inter-Arab level, indecisiveness, poor credibility, and lack of control of the numerous Palestinian factions. Above all, Arafat's main concern was to maintain as wide as possible a consensus with regard to his position as the ultimate Palestinian national leader.

In the wake of the 1967 defeat sustained by the Jordanian army and the loss of its Jordanian territorial base, Fatah expanded its guerrilla operations from 1971 to the Arab and international arena under the name "Black September" (attacks on Jordanian, Israeli, and Western targets, including aviation).

Arafat's early leadership of Fatah was marked by extremely militant and intransigent ideology and action toward Israel – as reflected in the Palestinian National Charter of 1968. He refused to accept any kind of compromise or coexistence with a Jewish state in historic Palestine. His personal inclination was patently conservative, with a measure of Islamist tendencies. However, with the beginning of a peace process in the Middle East following the 1973 war, Arafat emerged increasingly as a pragmatic politician, keen on exploiting opportunities, without losing support of both the right and left wings within his own Fatah organization or the PLO as a whole.

In 1974, amid American mediation efforts aimed at partial Israeli-Arab settlement, Arafat and his mainstream faction ceased to commit hijacking and international terrorism, believing that such operations could harm the PLO's international interest in being included in the diplomatic process over the implementation of UN Security Council Resolution 242.

Henceforth, Arafat led the PLO to a gradual accommodation to the new circumstances of growing international recognition of the acute problem of Palestinian national rights due to the Arab employment of oil as a political weapon in the conflict with Israel.

Arafat was the main force behind the PLO's historic decision at the twelfth session of the Palestinian National Council (June 1974), which decided, *inter alia*, that the PLO would establish a fighting Palestinian national authority in any liberated part of Palestine. This indicated the first shift from a vision of retrieving the whole territory of Palestine to a pragmatic policy acquiescing in the establishment of a Palestinian state in the West Bank and *Gaza Strip. This was followed by the decision of the Arab summit held in Rabat in October 1974 to recognize the PLO as the sole legitimate representative of the Palestinian people. Another indication of the PLO's rising international prestige was Arafat's speech at the UN General Assembly in November of that year in which he combined a message of continued armed struggle with an "olive branch."

During the Lebanese civil war, which erupted in April 1975, Arafat made an effort to remain out of the internal Lebanese conflict, but to no avail. As in the case of Jordan, leftist Palestinian factions dragged Arafat's Fatah into the fray. By early 1976 Arafat became deeply involved in the Lebanese civil war in close alignment with Kamal Junblaṭ, the leading figure of the Lebanese leftist camp. In this capacity, Arafat became increasingly alienated from Damascus and seen as an obstacle to its efforts to put an end to the crisis. Syria's invasion of Lebanon in June, which developed into a full-scale military confrontation with the Palestinian-Lebanese coalition, secured Syrian domination of the Lebanese arena and rendered

Arafat anathema to the Syrian ruling elite. The deep mistrust between the two parties was to motivate future Syrian efforts to replace Arafat by a more tractable Palestinian figure.

Toward the late 1970s, Arafat sanctioned a growing dialogue between the PLO and "progressive" (namely, non-Zionist and later, leftist) Israelis. Such contacts were based, explicitly, on the acceptance of the Jews of Israel as individuals rather than a political community that deserved to be defined in national terms and, implicitly, on the assumption that some settlement between Israel and the Palestinian Arabs was feasible (contrary to the PLO Charter). He refused, however, to commit himself to the recognition of Israel; to renounce terrorism; or to accept Resolution 242, as long as the PLO remained anathema to Israel and the United States.

Israel's invasion of Lebanon in June 1982 was followed by a nine-week siege and bombardment of the Palestinians entrenched in West Beirut. Arafat demonstrated persistent leadership and skillful diplomacy under fire and in the face of growing Arab pressures to accept Israel's demand for full evacuation of the PLO headquarters and military personnel from Lebanon. Eventually, Arafat succeeded in securing a Palestinian exodus under international auspices, thus reaping maximum political benefits from his military defeat. Syria, however, attempted to remove Arafat by encouraging a mutiny within Fatah against their leader. In view of this development and the Reagan Plan for a settlement of the Palestinian problem in which Jordan, not the PLO, was to represent the Palestinians, in October 1983 Arafat and some of his fellow-loyalists returned to Tripoli, Lebanon, and established themselves in an enclave, which included two refugee camps. Arafat's main motive for returning to Lebanon was to retrieve his bargaining position in the regional Arab arena, which he hoped to accomplish by regaining an autonomous territorial base in Lebanon. Arafat's return to Tripoli, however, provoked a strong Syrian military response, which Damascus tried to portray as Palestinian opposition to Arafat. After a few weeks of fighting Arafat was once again expelled from Lebanon, this time by a Syrian-Palestinian military force.

Arafat's sense of political survival was best demonstrated in the wake of the second exodus from Lebanon, when Arafat opted to turn to Egypt, temporarily identifying himself with the American-based peace camp. This step was in line with Arafat's willingness to open a political dialogue with King *Hussein, which led to the Amman Accord of February 1985 by which the two parties were to coalesce toward participating in an international peace conference. A year later, however, King Hussein abrogated the agreement, blaming Arafat for being untrustworthy and unfaithful to the agreement.

The eruption of violence in the West Bank and Gaza in December 1987 confronted Arafat with a new challenge stemming from a young militant local leadership, which by taking the initiative constituted a threat to marginalize the PLO leadership abroad. However, Arafat managed to coopt the uprising and take control of it, primarily due to his control of funds and loyalists in the occupied territories. The Palestinian uprising (*Intifāḍa*) scored significant regional and international achievements for the PLO, which culminated in King Hussein's announcement of disengagement from the West Bank, paving the road to the declaration of an independent Palestinian state by the Palestinian National Council in Algiers in November 1988. A few months later Arafat announced his renunciation of terrorism and acceptance of Resolution 242 in return for U.S. willingness to open a diplomatic dialogue with the PLO. The U.S.-PLO dialogue, however, remained futile mainly because of Arafat's insistence that the PLO should independently represent the Palestinian issue in any future international peace conference. The result was another political shift of PLO policy, this time toward Saddam Hussein's Iraq.

Under the circumstances resulting from the 1991 Gulf crisis – the cessation of financial aid by the oil-rich Arab monarchies to the PLO and the Palestinians and the threatening rise of Hamas in the West Bank and Gaza Strip as a moral and political alternative to the PLO – Arafat was willing to accept Israel's conditions for Palestinian participation in the Madrid Peace Conference (1991) and later on, to sign the Oslo Declaration of Principles (DOP) with Israel, which accounted for mutual recognition between the State of Israel and the PLO. Arafat was the driving force behind the scenes for concluding the agreement and effectively the decisive authority on the Palestinian side. In 1994 Arafat was awarded the Nobel Peace Prize, which he shared with Yitzhak *Rabin and Shimon *Peres.

By the early 1990s, following the killing of Khalil al-Wazir by Israel (1988) and Salah Khalaf by a Palestinian opponent (1991), Arafat came to assume unprecedented authority as the sole decision-maker in the PLO. The solitary and centralized nature of Arafat's leadership became particularly evident with the establishment of the Palestinian Authority (PA) in June 1994 in Gaza and Jericho.

Despite Arafat's election as the Palestine Authority's chairman in January 1996, he preserved his position as chairman of the PLO. In this capacity, Arafat convened the Palestinian National Council (PNC) in Gaza City in May 1996. The PNC was convened to ratify the Palestine Authority's peace policy, and Arafat's official commitment to Rabin to abolish those articles in the Palestinian National Charter calling for the destruction of the State of Israel or contradicting the Rabin-Arafat exchange of letters prior to the signing of the Declaration of Principles. The results of the session were considered successful for Arafat, but in Israel the vague decision made by the PNC regarding the Charter remained very controversial.

Arafat's image as a master of political maneuvers and arch-survivor surfaced following the foundation of the Palestinian Authority, underscoring his paternalistic and indecisive style of state- and nation-building. This was evident in his handling of the political opposition, especially Hamas, and the latter's continued violence against Israel, which contradicted the language and spirit of the Oslo Accords. All through the Oslo years, Arafat persistently refrained from sending a clear message to the Palestinians in general, and to his Fatah fellows in particular, that the armed revolution was over. In fact, Arafat harbored a continued debate within Fatah, by which a resumption of violence against Israel had remained optional. As to the opposition groups, Arafat preferred containment and cooption rather than confrontation, inclusion rather than exclusion, though not at the expense of his own political authority. It was only under extreme circumstances threatening his political authority that he resorted to violent repression, as in the case of the bloody clash with Islamist opponents on November 18, 1994 at the Palestine Mosque in Gaza.

During Prime Minister Ehud *Barak's term, Arafat maintained full control of the negotiations on the Palestinian side, often overlooking his aides' positions and preferences. With the failure of the Camp David summit in July 2000, Arafat was charged with the brunt of responsibility for this failure, which might explain Arafat's effort to canvass wide Arab and Islamic support. With the eruption of the al-Aqsa Intifada in October 2000, Arafat gave it his blessing and made an effort to escalate violence to enlist Arab and international support for his position. The increase and prolongation of violence by various Palestinian factions, including the Islamic opposition, led to the erosion of Arafat's authority and brought about increasing military strikes by Israel on the PA's installations. However, it was only after the terrorist attack on the U.S. on September 11, 2001, that Arafat's personal position began to deteriorate, with the U.S. president giving increasing backing to Israel's pressure on the PA to cease violence against Israel. In December, following the assassination of Israeli minister *Ze'evi by members of the Palestinian Front for the Liberation of Palestine, the Israeli government confined Arafat to his compound of offices in Ramallah, until he arrested the perpetrators. In early 2002, during the al-Aqsa Intifada, while being confined by Israeli troops to his government compound in Ramallah, Arafat expressed his wish to be a "martyr" (*shahid*).

The Israeli government continued its pressure on Arafat, declaring him "irrelevant" and clearly expressing its wish to replace him by another, more pragmatic leader. Arafat's credibility regarding his efforts to stop the violence sustained a serious blow with the seizure in January 2002 by Israel of a Palestinian-owned ship loaded with Iranian weapons earmarked for the PA on its way to the Mediterranean. Arafat's contradictory statements regarding his connection to the ship left a very negative impression on the U.S. administration as well as on European and Arab leaders. The result was a growing American backing for Israel's pressure on Arafat. Yet, despite the destruction of the PA's symbols of power, first and foremost of Arafat's own position, the Israeli pressure resulted in an increasing tendency among Palestinians to rally around his leadership, causing Palestinians, including opposition leaders, to express their allegiance to Arafat.

The Israeli invasion of the PA-controlled areas and siege of Arafat's office, in late March 2002, won him unprecedented worldwide support, particularly in the Arab-Muslim world and the European Union. These responses effectively reconfirmed both his personal status as the paramount legitimate leader of the Palestinian people, as well as serious discontent at the Israeli actions. In November 2004 Arafat died in Paris after his health had rapidly deteriorated, bringing his rule to an end amid rumors and confusion surrounding the diagnosis of his illness and the cause of death. Arafat was buried in Ramallah at a funeral which underscored his historic role as the intiator of organized Palestinian nationalism and the symbol of Palestinian identity.

See also *Arab World; *Palestine Liberation Organization; *Palestinian Authority.

BIBLIOGRAPHY: A. Gowers, *Arafat: The Biography* (1994); A. Hart, *Arafat: A Political Biography* (1994); S.K., Aburish, *Arafat: From Defender to Dictator* (1998); E. Karsh, *Arafat's War: The Man and his Battle for Israeli Conquest* (2003); A. Kapeliouk, *Arafat l'irreductible* (2004).

[Avraham Sela (2nd ed.)]

°ARAGÃO, FERNÃO XIMENES DE (d. 1630), antisemitic Portuguese writer; archdeacon of Braga. In 1624 he embarked on harsh attacks upon Judaism and upon Jewish converts to Christianity who remained faithful to the Jewish religion. His book *Doutrina Catholica para instrução e confirmação dos fieis, extinção das seitas superticiosas e em particular do Judaismo* ("The Catholic Doctrine for the Instruction and Admonition of the Faithful, and the Extinction of Idolatrous Sects and in Particular that of Judaism," Lisbon, 1625) was reissued in 1628 in a second edition, under the title *Extinção do Judaismo* ("The Extinction of Judaism"), and again as late as 1752.

BIBLIOGRAPHY: M. Kayserling, *Geschichte der Juden in Portugal* (1876), 293; Kayserling, Bibl, 114.

[Joseph Kaplan]

ARAKHIN (Aram. עֲרָכִין, "Valuations"), the fifth tractate of the Mishnah, Tosefta, and Babylonian Talmud in the order of *Kodashim*. Mishnah tractate *Arakhin* portrays the system of votive donations that financed the Temple's maintenance – as distinct from the annual collection of a half-shekel per capita (*sheqalim*, discussed in the tractate by that name) that financed the sacrificial cult itself.

The foundation for *Arakhin* is the concluding chapter of Leviticus (27), whose focus is objects consecrated to God. Most objects are not fit for sacrifices, and hence the Bible defines how they are to be redeemed. Specifically, biblical rejection of human sacrifice dictates that a person – consecrated, evidently, by the head of his or her household – is to be redeemed. A human life is evaluated according to a fixed scale (*erekh*), with no individual variation, in a hierarchy from 50 *shekel* for an adult male, down to three for a young girl. Similarly, there is a fixed redemption value for ancestral land, without regard for its quality or market price.

For the rabbis, the notion of human sacrifice had become even more remote, and so the very idea of consecrating a person no longer had any concrete meaning. *Erekh* (plural, *arakhin*) or "valuation" became simply a variant of vows: one can promise to the Temple the price of any object or (say) its weight in gold, but employing the key term "*erekh*" invokes the biblical symbolic scale (M. 5:1–4). The first chapter of Mishnah *Arakhin* introduces these principles by means of an analysis of persons whose status is irregular. For example, while one can vow the market value of a person whose gender is indeterminate, the symbolic value of *erekh* applies only to "either a definite male, or a definite female" (M. 1:1). The format of a range of values, with fixed maximal and minimal – occurring mostly in ritual contexts – is explored in chapter 2. Interestingly, a large sub-unit is devoted to the numbers of instruments and singers who produce the sacral music of the Levites. Chapter 3 again emphasizes the contrast between pronouncing an "*erekh*" and vowing an actual price, along with similar contrasts between payment of a fixed symbolic sum as indemnity and payment of actual damages. The chapter concludes by emphasizing the power of speech.

The various vows and votive promises could create debts toward the Temple, and its treasurers had powers to extract what was owed. The end of chapter 5 and all of chapter 6 deal with the procedures for (and restrictions upon) such collection. The sums received serve for the Temple's maintenance, except where the term "*ḥerem*" was employed – according to "the sages," these go to the priests (M. 8:6).

The last third of the tractate (chapters 7–9) discusses real estate. In the biblical system (Lev. 25:25–34, 27:16–24), sale of ancestral holdings is temporary. At the Jubilee year, they revert to their original owners. Hence the buyer can only consecrate the value of the land's use for the intervening years. Consecration of an ancestral holding can, however, be effected by its original owner. Within its systematic discussion of these laws, the Mishnah also recognizes a historical condition wherein the Jubilee is not operative. In that context, it describes in detail an open auction for "redeeming" the land from the Temple treasury, wherein the original owner has the right of making the opening bid. The concluding chapter is devoted to sale of fields and houses. The Jubilee does not apply to houses in walled towns, except for those of the landless Levites, whose towns constitute their ancestral holdings. In the tractate's penultimate pericope, Rabbi Elazar voices concern lest "Israel's towns be laid waste". The final pericope concludes with the citation, "the Levites shall forever have the right of redemption" (Lev. 25:32), clearly alluding also to the nation's hope for redemption and re-possession of its homeland.

Tosefta *Arakhin* follows the arrangement of the Mishnah rather closely, but adds several distinct short units. 1:7–11 (related to M. 2:2) discusses calendar variations due to the flexibility in the length of a month (29/30 days), with special attention to the festival of Shavuot (Pentecost) which – our text implies – is the day the Torah was given at Sinai. T. 2:3–7 (related to M. 2:3–6, the unit about sacral music) recounts the perfection of several ancient Temple instruments, said to date from the period of Moses: attempted improvements backfired, and restoration was not always possible. Yet whereas the present lyre has seven strings, the Messianic future will herald enhanced versions, first with eight and then with ten strings. Also noteworthy are the Tosefta's systematic explorations of the various, seemingly incongruent, biblical pronouncements regarding *ḥerem* (T. 4:31–34, related to M. 8:4–7); and of the precise definition of a walled town, relevant to several *halakhic* contexts (T. 5:13–16, related to M. 9:5–6).

An important theme in the Tosefta's additions pertains to a person's stewardship of his property. The Mishnah (6:2–5) ordains what possessions should be left in the hands of a person who has (irresponsibly) consecrated all he has. The Tosefta explicitly prohibits such a total giveaway, and cites Rabbi Elazar ben Azaryah, who derives from this that a person is obliged to take care to preserve his property. Specifically, opposition to spendthrift behavior is translated into instructions on adjusting one's spending on food – and in particular, on meat – to one's economic capability (T. 4:23–28).

Perhaps the most striking addition is the homily on the path to destitution. This is introduced by a set of prohibitions: A man may not sell his ancestral land, his daughter, or himself for cash, to be used for business or savings; such sales may be undertaken only in desperation. Then, the several pericopes of Lev. 25 are read as a tale of a person spiraling down into poverty, instigated by the sin of trading in produce of the consecrated Seventh Year. One who commits such greedy sacrilege will be forced to sell first his movable possessions, then his land and home, and finally himself as a slave to pagans (T. 5:6–9).

The infractions regarding the Seventh Year are singled out here from the set of commandments in Lev. 25. This may be an allusion to the following chapter, in which national loss of land and liberty is threatened as divine punishment for violating God's commandments in general, and the Seventh Year observance in particular (cf. Lev. 26:32–35). In its concluding pericopes (5:18–19), the Tosefta addresses the concern "lest the land of Israel [be] laid waste".

[Noam Zohar (2nd ed.)]

TB *Arakhin* contains several noteworthy units, particularly in the first three chapters. At the outset, the lengthy opening *sugya* runs a systematic comparison between the Mishnah's opening clause ("All are fit to value and be valuated: … Priests, Levites and Israelites") and numerous similarly phrased tannaitic statements. Both the term "all" (taken to imply broad inclusiveness) and the items "Priests, Levites, and Israelites" are questioned and placed in their general context, in the larger tannitic corpus. Regarding the differentiation between Priests, Levites and Israelites, the Bavli concludes that distinct halakhic standards apply only in the setting of sacrificial worship. Otherwise, priests' halakhic obligations are no different from those of all other Jews. The theoretical possibility of a separate legal and religious standard for the Priests, suggested by some of the sources examined here, is explicitly rejected.

In chapter 2 the Bavli contains an extended discussion of the Levites and the Temple's musical instruments, exploring connections between the Levites' song and the priests' sacrificial worship; R. Meir invalidates offerings unaccompanied by a levitical song. Since the Levites' song varies daily, the Babylonian Talmud engages in a detailed discussion of calendar and history, including an attempt to determine the exact date and day of the Exile.

The Mishnah's discussion in chapter 3 leads up to an emphasis on the power of speech. The Babylonian Talmud here expands on several matters of language and words. These include the severity of libel, *lashon ha-ra* (Cf., lit., "evil tongue"), citing R. Yosi b. Zimra who compares *lashon ha-ra* to heresy. Another law pertaining to speech is the obligation of rebuke (Lev. 19:10), and an extended *sugya* discusses the manner in which rebukes should be delivered, and the limits of the obligation (15a–16b).

[Yedidah Koren (2nd ed.)]

BIBLIOGRAPHY: Weiss, in HUCA, 16 (1941), 3–9 (Heb. sect.); idem, *Hithavvut ha-Talmud bi-Shelemuto* (1943), 190–1, passim; Epstein, Mishnah, 192, 575, 667, 948–9, passim; Ch. Albeck, *Shishah Sidrei Mishnah, Seder Kodashim* (1956), 191–5; J. Neusner, *A History of the Mishnaic Law of Holy Things* (1978–80).

ARAM, ARAMEANS. The Arameans are a group of western Semitic, Aramaic-speaking tribes who spread over the Fertile Crescent during the last quarter of the second millennium B.C.E. Eleventh and tenth century royal inscriptions from Assyria and Babylonia indicate Aramean movements through the north of the Middle Euphrates and northern Mesopotamia. In other words, the Arameans might be viewed as the successors of the *Amorites of the late third millennium (Dion in Bibliography). These nomads or semi-nomads spread from the Persian Gulf in the south to the Amanus Mountains in the north, and the anti-Lebanon and northern Transjordan in the west.

History

Of the various biblical traditions concerning their place of origin, an obscure reference in Amos 9:7 places it in Kir, whose location is uncertain, but may refer to a locale apparently not far from Emar (modern Tel Meskene), although some locate Kir on the border of *Elam in Iran. The fact that the Table of Nations (Gen. 10:22–23) has the eponymous ancestor Aram (together with Elam and Asshur) only one generation removed from Shem reflects the importance of the Arameans in the Near East during the first third of the first millennium B.C.E. To this Aram the Table assigns four sons, Uz, Hul, Gether, and Mash (I Chron. 1:17; LXX *Meshech*; Samaritan Pent. *Massa*), but the identity and location of the ethnic groups they stand for are uncertain. The Qumran *War Scroll* (1QM 2:10) places them "Beyond the Euphrates." The modest standing of the Arameans prior to their rise is reflected in the genealogical table of the Nahorites, where Aram is a mere grandson of Nahor and a nephew, instead of the father, of Uz (Gen. 22:21). The patriarchal narratives make the Hebrew Patriarchs close kinsmen of the Arameans. Not only is Abraham a brother of the aforementioned Nahor, but Isaac marries a granddaughter of Nahor who is "daughter of Bethuel the Aramean and sister of Laban the Aramean" (Gen. 25:20), and Jacob marries daughters of the same "Laban the Aramean" (cf. Gen. 31:47, where Laban coins an Aramaic equivalent for Gilead (*Galed*)). On one occasion Jacob himself is described as "a wandering-destitute-Aramean" (Deut. 26:5). This tradition conforms to the later Hebrew names for the ancestral home of the Patriarchs in the Haran district: "Paddan-Aram" (Gen. 25:20; 28:2); the "country of Aram" (Hos. 12:13); and "Aram-Naharaim" (i.e., the Jezirah, the region of the Habor and Euphrates rivers; Gen. 24:10).

The existence of the Arameans in the "patriarchal period," however, is not attested by extra-biblical sources – in any case, not as an element important enough to warrant naming the entire Jezirah area after it. Indeed, in the Egyptian and Akkadian sources of the 15th–12th centuries B.C.E. the area is referred to simply as Naharaim (in many different spellings), but never as Aram-Naharaim. Thus, the latter name and the alleged Aramean affiliations of the "Patriarchs" are anachronisms that came into being at the end of the second millennium as a result of the thorough entrenchment of the Aramean tribes in the Jezirah region at that time. The arguments, particularly the linguistic ones, that the "Patriarchs" were "Proto-Arameans" are without substance. The mention of Aram or Aram-Naharaim as the country of origin of Balaam (Num. 23:7; Deut. 23:5) is, perhaps, also an anachronism.

The isolated references to Aram as a place name or personal name between the end of the third and late second millennium B.C.E. are insufficient to establish such an early appearance of the Arameans, especially since, later, the name Aram occurred frequently as an onomastic and toponymic element in entirely non-"Aramean" contexts.

The first, definite extra-biblical mention of the Arameans is found in the annals of Tiglath-Pileser I, king of Assyria (1116–1076 B.C.E.), in the compound name "Aḫlamē Aramāia." However, the identification of the Aḫlamē of the Assyrian sources of the 14th century with the Arameans is untenable; the first appearance of the Arameans should not be traced back to the early documentation of the name Aḫlamē used, like the name Sūtu, for nomad tribes. Moreover, tenth-ninth century royal Assyrian inscriptions mention Aḫlamē Aramāia alongside the Arameans. The close association of the two led to occasional late cuneiform references to the Aramaic language as "Aḫlamē." Tiglath-Pileser I mentions that in his fourth year (1113 B.C.E.) he routed the Aḫlamē Aramāia in the Euphrates region, from the land of Suḫu in the south to Carchemish in the north. At that time the Arameans had already settled in the Mount Bishri district, southeast of the Euphrates bend, where Tiglath-Pileser devastated six of their villages. They are further mentioned as far west as the Tadmor (Palmyra) oasis and even in the foothills of Mount Lebanon. Tiglath-Pileser's son, Ashur-bel-kala (1073–1056 B.C.E.), refers specifically to the land of Aram (*māt Arime*) without connecting it with Aḫlamē. By the time of Tiglath-Pileser I, the Arameans had once penetrated into Assyria proper, and during his son's reign an Aramean usurper, Adad-apal-iddina, managed to seize the throne of Babylonia.

Aramean regions and cities, c. 15th century B.C.E.

Thus, the historical significance of the Arameans began only at the end of the second and beginning of the first millennia B.C.E. At this time independent Aramean states arose in Syria: the biblical Aram-Zobah, Aram Beth-Rehob, Aram-Maacah (II Sam. 10:6), and (slightly later) *Aram-Damascus; and in Mesopotamia: e.g., Bīt-Adini (biblical *Beth-Eden; Amos 1:5) above the Euphrates bend, Bīt-Baḫiāni (capital: *Gozan; cf. II Kings 17:6) and Bīt-Ḫalupē in the Habor region, Ḫindān and Suḫu (biblical Shuah; Gen. 25:2) on the Middle Euphrates, Bīt-Zamāni on the Upper Tigris, and Bīt-Dakuri and Bīt-Iakin near the Persian Gulf. Various Arameans, or closely related tribes, are known to have played an important role in Babylonia; such were the *Chaldeans (though some dispute the extent of their closeness to the Arameans) and the Pekod of the Bible (Jer. 50:21; Ezek. 23:23; Akkadian Puqudu).

For the century spanning the turn of the millennium, the Arameans challenged the very existence of the Assyrian kingdom, which reached its nadir under Ashur-Rabi II and Tiglath-Pileser II. However, at the same time the Aramean expansion itself was being checked in the west by David, who dealt a powerful blow, thrice defeating Hadadezer, king of Aram-Zobah, and his allies, bringing them into vassalage. A few generations later, Ashur-Dan II (934–912 B.C.E.) and Adad-Nirari II (911–891 B.C.E.) were able to relieve the Aramean pressure on Assyria, especially on its western flank. In the next half century, during the reigns of Ashurnaṣirpal II (883–859 B.C.E.) and, particularly, *Shalmaneser III (858–824 B.C.E.), the Assyrians succeeded in subjugating the Aramean states in Syria, on the one hand, and Babylonia, on the other.

The combined evidence of Aramaic documents from the ninth-eighth centuries B.C.E. and Assyrian sources illuminates the structure and political constellation of the various Aramean and neo-Hittite states in Syria – their rivalries and alliances. The outstanding kingdom in southern Syria was Aram-Damascus, while in the north such Aramean states as Hadrach (cf. Zech. 9:1) and, particularly, Arpad (II Kings 18:34; 19:13) rose to power. In the ninth-eighth centuries B.C.E., even in such states of neo-Hittite foundation as Ya'di-Sam'al (capital: modern Zenjirli) in the north and *Hamath in Middle Syria, an Aramaizing process evolved, resulting in the gradual acceptance of Aramaic personal names and script equally with the neo-Hittite. In the second half of the 8th century, *Tiglath-Pileser III (745–727 B.C.E.) reduced the independent Aramean kingdoms to mere vassal states or Assyrian provinces. Still, in 720 B.C.E. revolts in former Aramean lands, such as Damascus, Arpad, and perhaps even Ya'di-Sam'al (with the participation of Samaria), broke out against the rule of Sargon II. In southern Mesopotamia in the later part of the eighth century, various Aramean tribes waged war against Assyria, only to suffer defeat and exile in large numbers.

Culture

The Aramean expansion did not lead to a political or cultural pan-Aramean unity. In Syria, however, political confederations periodically arose, often of considerable extent but of changing leadership: e.g., that of Aram-Zobah, about 1000 B.C.E., whose greatness is known only from the Bible (II Sam. 8:3ff.; 10:16–17); that of Aram-Damascus, mid-ninth century on; and that of Arpad, mid-eighth century. The stature of Arpad is attested in the Aramaic treaty inscriptions from Sefire (south of Aleppo), which contain such indicative terms as "all Aram" and "Upper and Lower Aram." Such confederations were pliant and internally loose, and easily dissolved under pressure from without.

Except for the Aramaic language and script, the Arameans left no manifest traces of their culture among other peoples. The wide spread of the Aramaic language, facilitated by its convenient script, was accelerated by extensive shifts in populations, mass exiles of Arameans and their employ within the Assyrian and Babylonian administration as well as their mercantile activities. The Arameans' widespread settlement along the trade routes, coupled with their inherent wanderlust, brought them to the fore of Middle Eastern commerce from the ninth century on (see also Ancient *Aramaic).

In the sphere of religion, the Arameans were of little influence on others, but instead accepted the local cults of the areas in which they settled. Their principal deity in Syria was the ancient west-Semitic storm god Hadad, the dynastic god of, among others, the Aramean kings of Damascus (cf. the names Bar-Hadad, corresponding to the biblical Ben-Hadad). Evident also from Aramaic inscriptions is their worship of various Canaanite and Mesopotamian deities. In Sam'al the dynastic gods Rakib-el, Baal Ḥamman, and Baal Semed were apparently worshiped by the Arameans, as well as Baal-Haran, whose cultic center was at Haran, home of the ancient moon-god Sin. The worship of female deities is indicated by the pairing on a stela of Rakib-El of Sam'al with the goddess Kubaba of Carchemish, and by the depiction of Astarte as the woman at the window in Aramean ivory plaques found in Assyria at Nimrud (Dion).

Traces of Aramean religion are found in the Hellenistic period at Baalbek and Hieropolis; the latter was the main center for the cult of the female deity Atargatis, whose name combines the Aramaic *ʿatar* (Ashtart) and *ʿata* (Anat). Among the Israelites of the First Temple period, the influence of the Aramean religion was reflected in Ahaz's introduction of a Damascus-style altar at Jerusalem (II Kings 16:10–13; II Chron. 28:22–23), which many believe was accompanied by the introduction of a Damascus cult, and the worship of Hadadrimmon in the plain of Megiddo (Zech. 12:11; cf. II Kings 5:18), and, later, in certain practices of the Jewish colonists at *Elephantine. Conversely, Israelite religious influence on the Arameans is evident in the episode of Naaman, army commander of the king of Aram-Damascus (II Kings 5:15–17), as well as in the names of two kings of (neo-Hittite) Hammath, which contain the theophoric element *yahu*: Joram (II Sam. 8:10), whose name also appears in the form Hadoram (I Chron. 18:10), and Iaʿubidi.

The Aramean material culture, like the religion, was essentially eclectic, being strongly influenced by the specific local environment, e.g., in Syria by the neo-Hittites and the Phoenicians. Though it is difficult to define as Aramean per se particular material remains, it is apparent that the ninth-eighth centuries B.C.E. represent the cultural zenith of the Arameans. Aramean centers during this period included Tell Halaf (Gozan); Arslan Tash (Ḫadatha) and Tell Aḥmar (Til Barsip) in northern Mesopotamia; and Zenjirli (Sam'al), Hamath, and Damascus in Syria. With the continued ascendance of the Assyrian Empire, however, the political and cultural prospects of the Aramean states were extinguished.

BIBLIOGRAPHY: E.G.H. Kraeling, *Aram and Israel* (1918); Forrer, in: E. Ebeling and B. Meissner (ed.), *Reallexikon der Assyriologie*, 1 (1932), s.v. *Aramu*; F. Rosenthal, *Die aramaeistische Forschung* (1939); B. Landsberger, *Sam'al*, 1 (Ger., 1948); R.T. O'Callaghan, *Aram Naharaim* (1948); Bowman, in: JNES, 7 (1948), 65–90; A. Dupont-Sommer, *Les araméens* (1949); idem, in: VT Supplement, 1 (1953), 40–49; A. Malamat, *Ha-Aramim be-Aram Naharaim ve-Hithavvut Medinoteihem* (1953); S. Moscati, *Ancient Semitic Civilizations* (1957), 167ff.; H. Donner and W. Roellig, *Kanaanaeische und aramaeische Inschriften*, 1–3 (1964^2–1967); J.A. Fitzmyer, *The Aramaic Inscriptions of Sefire* (1967); Albright, in: CAH2, 2 (1966^2), ch. 33, 46–53; J.A. Brinkman, *A Political History of Post-Kassite Babylonia* (1968), 267ff.; J. Hoftijzer, *Religio Aramaica* (Dutch, 1968); M. Dietrich, *Die Aramaeer Suedbabyloniens in der Sargonidenzeit* (1970). **ADD. BIBLIOGRAPHY:** P.-E. Dion, CANE, 2, 1281–94; idem, *Les Araméens à l'âge du fer: histoire politique et structures sociale* (1997); R. Hess, ABD, 1 886–87; E. Lipiński, *The Arameans: Their History, Culture, Religion*; V. Matthews, *ibid.*, 345–51; W. Pitard, *ibid.*, 338–41.

[Abraham Malamat]

ARAMA, ISAAC BEN MOSES (c. 1420–1494), Spanish rabbi, philosopher, and preacher. As a young man Arama taught at Zamora and subsequently served the small communities of Tarragona and Fraga in Aragon. He was later appointed rabbi of Calatayud, where he wrote most of his works. In order to counteract the effects of conversionist sermons to which the Jews of Aragon were compelled to listen, Arama delivered sermons on the principles of Judaism. These sermons became the basis of his later works and contain interesting data on the history of the Jews in Spain prior to their expulsion. Arama engaged in several public disputations with Christian scholars. After the expulsion of the Jews from Spain, in 1492 Arama settled in Naples where he died.

Works

Arama is best known as the author of *Akedat Yiẓḥak* ("Binding of Isaac") which exercised great influence on Jewish thought. Written in the form of philosophical homilies and allegorical commentaries on the Pentateuch, the work consists of 105 "Portals." Each portal forms a complete sermon which is divided into two parts: *derishah* ("investigation"), and *perishah* ("exposition"). In the *derishah*, the author examines a philosophical idea in the light of his chosen texts, biblical and rabbinic, with which the sermon opens. In the *perishah*, the Scriptural commentary predominates and the difficulties which seem to appear in the text are solved with the aid of the central idea of the *derishah*. Thus, the gap between the two parts of the sermon is skillfully closed, and they merge into one harmonious whole. First published in Salonika in 1522, the *Akedah* has since been reprinted many times. Among Arama's other works are *Ḥazut Kashah* ("Grievous Vision"; Sabbionetta, 1552), a polemic dealing with the relation of philosophy and religion; a commentary on the Five Scrolls (Riva di Trento, 1561); and *Yad Avshalom* ("Absalom's Memorial"; Constantinople, 1565?), a commentary on the Book of Proverbs, dedicated to the memory of his son-in-law. It should be noted that the commentary on Esther, extant in all editions of *Akedat Yiẓḥak* since Venice, 1573, is actually the work of his son Meir *Arama. Isaac's own commentary on Esther was published in Constantinople, 1518. He also wrote several poems and a commentary on Aristotle's *Ethics*, apparently lost.

Philosophy

Although Arama composed his works in the form of philosophical homilies and commentaries on Scripture rather than as systematic treatises, he nevertheless integrated within this literary framework a treatment of the then-current major philosophical problems: the relation between Scripture and philosophy; faith and reason; the allegorical method; articles of faith; creation and structure of the world; miracles; providence; immortality of the soul; man's free will and God's foreknowledge; prophecy; ethics. Considering the relation of Scripture and philosophy, Arama seeks to demonstrate the superiority of divine truth over human reasoning, and the necessity of subordinating reason to Scripture whenever the two are in conflict. He brings into sharp relief the distinction between religion and philosophy by illustrating the difference between their respective conceptions of God. Discussing the problem of faith and reason, Arama criticizes Maimonides' rationalistic definition of faith, according to which faith is subordinated to reason. Arama describes faith as the voluntary assent to the teachings of Scripture in spite of intellectual uncertainty about them, and he cites the patriarch Abraham's willingness to sacrifice Isaac as an example of this kind of faith. In his interpretation of Scripture, Arama uses the allegorical method, quoting in justification the Zohar's statement that Scripture should not be read literally. In opposition, however, to the extreme allegorical commentators among the philosophers, he emphasizes that the allegorical interpretation of Scripture should not deny its literal meaning. Arama analyzes and criticizes the lists of *articles of faith drawn up by Maimonides, Crescas, and Albo, and he presents six of his own. They are creation, miracles, revelation, providence, repentance, and immortality of the soul. Each of these, according to him, is embodied in a specific Mosaic law. In the case of miracles, Arama maintains that God possesses the power to suspend the laws of nature and perform miracles whenever necessary. He does not hesitate, however, to offer rational explanations of some of the miracles recorded in Scripture, maintaining that man was originally endowed with power over nature and was granted the means of establishing "cosmic harmony." He affirms man's freedom of will and discusses in great detail the nature and history of the problem of man's freedom and God's foreknowledge. He is critical of those philosophers who attempted to escape the dilemma by sacrificing either Divine omniscience or human freedom. He emphasizes that grace must be merited and criticizes the Christian doctrine that grace is given freely by God, a doctrine which, according to him, amounts to a denial of free will. In his treatment of ethics, and his attempt to formulate the Torah's conception of man, Arama assigns a central role to Aristotle's *Ethics*, citing this work with a frequency and intensity of engagement comparable only to his citations of biblical and talmudic literature. Arama declares the teachings of the *Ethics* to be true and in harmony with the Torah.

Akedat Yitzhak includes several important social and political discussions. Along with his discussions of various ideas espoused by preceding Jewish thinkers, Arama's political method also includes innovative elements. His socio-political thought is, for the most part, Maimonidean, yet it also includes neo-republican elements, foreshadowing the line of thought that would later be developed by R. Isaac *Abrabanel.

Concerning the essence of political society, Arama highly regards the existence of the political society, which is founded on law and order. The purpose of this society must be to ensure the personal security of each of its members and to maintain social and judicial justice, which is necessary for the optimal regularization of material life. This regularization is a precondition for the ability to achieve the ultimate goal of any society and state, i.e., enabling every individual to reach spiritual perfection, which Arama considers as the supreme purpose of existence. Any attempt to set a different goal as the purpose of society, such as the political order itself, is bound to fail.

Arama claims that real liberty is only the possession of whomever subordinates himself to a worthy authority. Thus, a truly free person is one who obeys the ideal legal system that the Torah dictates. Arama sees in the latter an eternal and ideal constitution adjusted to the nature of the universe. The Torah dictates social, judicial, and political order as well as how to acquire virtues and moral qualities. It also makes possible the acquisition of intellectual qualities, the immortality of the soul, and the creation of cosmic harmony.

Arama claims the Torah is a foundation for a society that is characterized by mutual aid and cooperation between all of its parts. Nevertheless, he considers certain exceptional deviations from religious law to be an imitation of divine justice. He invests the power to decide on such actions in the hands of the Great Sanhedrin, whose members he regards as gifted with the special qualities and knowledge necessary for making such decisions.

Arama expounds on the issue of social justice, while sharply criticizing injustices in this sphere. He claims that a legal system and an elected leader of a society necessarily reflect the character of their society and stresses the duty of every ruler, by definition, to ensure the well-being of his subjects. Thus, the ruler must enable each and every one of them to realize his or her spiritual and intellectual potential, by creating the optimal physical and material conditions necessary for that purpose. Arama demands that the ruler have noble moral, spiritual, and intellectual qualities, as well as political and administrative wisdom.

Arama stresses the importance of the proper function of the judicial system of any society and imposes its maintenance on the ruler. He also claims it is the public's responsibility, both as a whole and as individuals, to prevent injustices and various improper moral and spiritual phenomena. This responsibility is a necessary condition for the stability of the religio-social and public solidarity and unity, which enable the maintenance of the sovereign political framework.

Arama stresses the importance of peace as an expression of the principle of cosmic harmony, although he supports war against pagan nations. He objects to violence within society, as well as to cruelty during wars.

Arama presents an organic socio-political doctrine, from which derives the natural necessity of a strong central regime with a hierarchic administrative system in which every functionary has a defined role. All citizens are essentially equal, yet they differ from each other in their public function, which determines their social position. A ruler must ensure the existence of an enlightened legal system, the existence of public law and order, and national security. A Jewish king must act according to the "Law of the King" (Deut. 17:14–20) especially, and the laws of the Torah in general. Arama also claims that the Jews must appoint a king for his qualities and capabilities. On the occasion of forming a covenant between God, the king, and his people, the king must act for the good of the people and receive religious and public legitimacy for his reign from all of his subjects. Hence, his appointment will have no validity if he betrays the public mission that has been assigned to him. Therefore, the people may not banish the king as long as he has not betrayed one of the other parties to the covenant. Arama seems to object to the principle of dynastic succession and to support the principle of an elected ruler who must gain the public's confirmation of his appointment at fixed periods of time. Nevertheless, Arama adopts the ideal of the Davidian dynastic reign.

Arama describes the political notion of the messianic king as ideal and, in accord with the aforementioned criteria, giving it socio-political power and international status. Nevertheless, Arama draws a utopian vision of a later perfect period of the End of Days. At that time a change in humanity's nature will enable it to accept the reign of the kingdom of heaven spontaneously and there will no longer be a need for human government.

Arama tries to prove that the laws of Moses are the natural laws of the philosophers; that they are to be identified with the moral and intellectual virtues; that they contain additional virtues not mentioned in any of the lists drawn up by the philosophers; and that they lead to the happiness in which the philosophers find the highest good of man. This happiness consists in a spiritual life in this world and an eternal life in the world to come.

Influence

Arama's sermons met the needs of his own time superbly and influenced the style and character of Jewish preaching through the subsequent centuries. The *Akedat Yiẓḥak* became a classic work in Jewish homiletics and is widely read to the present day.

In the history of medieval Jewish philosophy, Arama's writings represent an attempt to articulate a conservative Jewish philosophy that could withstand the two-fold challenge of radical rationalism and Christianity. His criticism of the former was powerful, yet subtle, selective, and complex. His relation to natural reason is often dialectical as he searches to create a delicate and judicious balance between this reason and the religious faith. Much the same, Arama's attitude towards Maimonides is quite complex. Though he was not a Maimonidean, he knew well that his entire intellectual project would have been impossible without Maimonides.

Arama's philosophical influence is reflected primarily in the writings of Isaac Abrabanel, who incorporated many passages from the *Akedah* in his own writings. The work was also esteemed by Christian theologians. Anthon Julius van der Hardt, professor of theology at the University of Helmstedt, wrote a dissertation on it and translated Portal 62 into Latin (1729).

BIBLIOGRAPHY: S. Heller-Wilensky, *Rabbi Yiẓḥak Arama u-Mishnato ha-Filosofit* (1956), 225–9 (bibl., 26, 225–9); H. Pollack, *Akedat Yiẓḥak*, 1 (1849), introduction; I. Bettan, *Studies in Jewish Preaching* (1939), 130–91; A.M. Habermann, in: *Oẓar Yehudei Sefarad* (1965), 92–104. **ADD. BIBLIOGRAPHY:** Y. Dan, *Sifrut ha-Musar ve-ha-Dreush* (1975), 176–79; M.M. Kelner, "Gersonides and His Cultured Despisers: Arama and Abravanel," in: *Journal of Medieval and Renaissance Studies* 6:2 (1976), 269–96; Ch. Pearl, *The Medieval Jewish Mind* (1971); A. Ravitzki, "Models of Peace in Jewish Thought," in: *Al Da'at ha-Makom* (1991), 13–33 (Heb.); idem, "Has Halakhic Thought Developed a Concept of a Forbidden War?" in: *Ḥerut al ha-Luḥot* (1999), 139–57 (Heb.); Sh. Regev, "Ratio-Mystical Thought in Fifteenth Century Jewish Philosophy, in: *Meḥkerei Yerushalayim be-Maḥshevet Yisra'el*, 5 (1986), 155–89 (Heb.); Sh. Rosenberg, "And Again: According to the Majority," in: E. Belfer (ed.), *Manhigut Ruḥanit be-Yisra'el, Morashah ve-Ya'ad* (1982), 87–103 (Heb.); A. Sagi, *Yahadut: Bein Dat le-Musar* (1998), 142–44 (Heb.); M. Saperstein, *Jewish Preaching* (1989), 2–3, 17–18, 95–96, 263–66, 392–93; D. Schwartz, *Ha-Ra'ayon ha-Meshiḥi ba-Hagut ha-Yehudit Bi-Yemei ha-Beinayim* (1997), 209–10 (Heb.); B. Septimus, "Yitzhak Arama and Aristotle's *Ethics*," in: Y.-T. Assis and Y. Kaplan (eds.), *Jews and Conversos at the Time of Expulsion* (1999), 1–24; H. Tirosh-Rothschild, "Political Philosophy in the Theory of Abraham Shalom: The Platonic Tradition," in: *Meḥkerei Yerushalayim be-Maḥshevet Yisra'el*, 9 (1990), 409–40 (Heb.).

[Sara O. Heller-Wilensky / Michael N. Rony (2nd ed.)]

ARAMA, MEIR BEN ISAAC (1460?–c. 1545), Spanish rabbi, biblical commentator, and philosopher. Born in Saragossa, Arama left Spain, together with his father Isaac *Arama, at the time of the expulsion (1492), and went to Naples. He remained there until compelled to move in 1495 when the French conquered the city, and later that year finally settled in Salonika, where he was appointed rabbi and preacher of the émigré Aragonian congregation. Although the many halakhic decisions he wrote as congregational rabbi and *dayyan* were not preserved, some are mentioned in the works of contemporaries. Arama wrote (1) *Urim ve-Tummim*, a commentary on Isaiah and Jeremiah (Venice, 1603); (2) *Me'ir Iyyov*, a commentary on Job, written in 1506 (Salonika, 1517); (3) *Me'ir Tehillot*, on Psalms, written in 1512 (Venice, 1590); (4) a commentary on the Song of Songs, published in *Likkutei Shoshannim* by Isaac Gershon (1602); and (5) a commentary on Esther, incorrectly attributed to his father, published together with his father's *Akedat Yiẓḥak* (Venice, 1573). Arama also wrote a letter accusing Isaac *Abrabanel of plagiarizing the works of his father (published in *Ha-Maggid*, 1858), and in which he testifies that Abrabanel visited his father's house in Naples and copied his writings. An anthology of aphorisms, *Imrei Kadosh – Zikkukin di-Nurim* (1894), has been attributed to him. Arama's commentaries, in common with those of his father, are written in the form of philosophical allegories, although he opposed the study of philosophy. Moses *Almosnino was on close terms with him and cites his opinions, as does Solomon ha-Levi *Alkabeẓ. His son, Jacob, was a *dayyan* in Salonika. Compendia of biblical commentaries compiled by the 16th-century Turkish scholars, such as that of Joseph *Taitaẓak, include many of Arama's commentaries, which are signed "R.M.A." or "ha-Meiri" (Jewish Theological Seminary Ms. 740/157, Bodleian Library Ms. 969, et al.).

BIBLIOGRAPHY: Conforte, Kore, 30a, 32a, 33b; Sonne, in: KS, 7 (1930/31), 168ff.; A. Tauber, *Meḥkarim Bibliografiyyim* (1932), 83ff.; Rosanes, Togarmah, 2 (1938), 17ff.; Rivkind, in: *Sefer Yovel… A. Marx* (1950), 426ff.; B. Netanyahu, *Don Isaac Abrabanel* (1953), 295ff.; S. Heller-Wilensky, *Rabbi Yiẓḥak Arama u-Mishnato ha-Filosofit* (1956), 28, 32ff., 51ff.; I.S. Emmanuel, *Maẓẓevot Saloniki* (1963), 39ff., 191ff.

ARAMAIC, an ancient northwestern *Semitic language spoken (to some extent) to this day. The entry is arranged according to the following outline:

ANCIENT ARAMAIC AND OFFICIAL ARAMAIC
SOURCES
- Syria and Its Neighboring Countries
- Iraq and Iran
- Egypt

MAIN CHARACTERISTICS
- Biblical Aramaic
- The Aramaic of the Elephantine Documents
- The Aramaic of the Driver Documents

ANCIENT ARAMAIC
OFFICIAL ARAMAIC
THE ORIGIN OF THE ARAMAIC PASSAGES IN EZRA AND DANIEL
THE INFLUENCE OF ARAMAIC ON BIBLICAL HEBREW
MIDDLE ARAMAIC
INSCRIPTIONS FROM NON-ARAMAIC-SPEAKING REGIONS
THE ARAMAIC TARGUMS OF THE PENTATEUCH (ONKELOS) AND OF THE BOOKS OF THE PROPHETS (JONATHAN)
THE ARAMAIC OF THE DEAD SEA SCROLLS
- Aramaic Texts of the Sect
- The Aramaic Bar Kokhbar Letters

JERUSALEM INSCRIPTIONS
ARAMAIC IN THE NEW TESTAMENT
THE URUK INCANTATION TEXT
THE NABATEAN INSCRIPTIONS
THE PALMYREAN INSCRIPTIONS
THE ARAMAIC OF HATRA
THE ARAMAIC OF DURA-EUROPOS
THE ARAMAIC IDEOGRAMS IN PAHLEVI AND OTHER PERSIAN DIALECTS
LATE ARAMAIC
WESTERN ARAMAIC
- Galilean Aramaic
- Palestinian Christian Aramaic
- Samaritan Aramaic

EASTERN ARAMAIC
- Syriac
- Mandaic
- Babylonian Aramaic

THE INFLUENCE OF LATE ARAMAIC ON OTHER LANGUAGES
MISHNAIC HEBREW
CLASSICAL ARABIC
ARAMAIC INFLUENCE ON SPOKEN ARABIC DIALECTS
ARAMAIC IN EUROPEAN LANGUAGES
ARAMAIC IN CONTEMPORARY SPOKEN HEBREW

Aramaic is divided into several dialects which historically fall into five main groups:

Ancient Aramaic
Ancient Aramaic is the language of the ancient Aramaic inscriptions up to 700 B.C.E. (from Upper Mesopotamia, northern Syria, and northern Israel).

Official Aramaic
Official Aramaic was in use from 700 to 300 B.C.E. It includes inscriptions from the Syria-Iraq area; biblical Aramaic (though opinions vary as to its origin in the different biblical passages, see below Ancient and Official Aramaic, and the Origin of the Aramaic Portions in Ezra and Daniel); the *Elephantine documents; the Driver documents; and the Hermopolis documents. This particular Aramaic dialect served not only as the official language of Persia but also as the *lingua franca* of the Near East.

Middle Aramaic
Middle Aramaic was used from 300 B.C.E. to the early centuries C.E. Included are documents, in somewhat corrupt Aramaic, from Persia, India, Afghanistan, and the Caucasus. The Aramaic inscriptions of Jerusalem, Aramaic words found in the New Testament, the Nabatean Aramaic, the Palmyrean Aramaic, that of Hatra, of Dura-Europos, and (partly) the Aramaic ideograms of Middle Persian are all in Middle Ara-

maic. The Onkelos translation of the Bible (see *Targum) also seems to belong to this period, as does the language of most of those scrolls from the *Dead Sea Scrolls written in Aramaic. The Uruk document which dates from this period is the only Aramaic document written in cuneiform. While the common denominator of all these dialects is their effort to imitate Official Aramaic, they also contain elements of Late Aramaic. Most of these versions were apparently not spoken.

Late Aramaic

Late Aramaic may be divided into two dialectal groups: Western Aramaic – including Galilean Aramaic, Palestinian-Christian Aramaic, and Samaritan Aramaic; and Eastern Aramaic – consisting of three dialects: Syriac, the language of the Babylonian Talmud, and Mandaic.

Modern Aramaic

Regarding Modern Aramaic see *Neo-Aramaic.

ANCIENT ARAMAIC AND OFFICIAL ARAMAIC

SOURCES

1) The Aramaic parts of the Bible: Genesis 31:47 (two words); Jeremiah 10:11; Daniel 2:4–7:28; and Ezra 4:8–6:8; and 7:12–26.

(2) Aramaic epigraphical material, spread over an area which extended north to Sardes in Asia Minor; south to the oasis Tēmā in the north of the Arabian Peninsula; southwest to southern Egypt (the Elephantine documents); and east to Persia (The Driver documents). The documents, some of them carved on stone, written on leather, papyrus, ostraca, clay, etc., include memorial inscriptions, contracts, bills, letters, official documents, seals, and legends written on weights, and as "dockets" in Akkadian legal documents, etc. All, except the Uruk document (see Middle Aramaic), are written in an Aramaic alphabet which is a branch of the Canaanite alphabet (see *Alphabet, North-West Semitic – The Rise of Aramaic Script).

Documents were found in the following regions:

Syria and Its Neighboring Countries

The inscriptions from the reigns of kings: PNMW, HAD-YITHʿI, BIR-RKWB, ZKR, and BIRHADAD (HOD), which were all found in northern Syria, a very long inscription discovered in Sefire, an Assyrian-Aramaic bilingual from Tell Fekherye, an inscription from Tell Dan, and two in Asia Minor.

Iraq and Iran

Most of the inscriptions found are short "dockets" written in Akkadian documents; there is, however, one fairly extensive letter (the Assur). There is a document from Bukan in Iranian Azerbaijan.

Egypt

Aramaic papyri as well as a number of ostraca Aramaic papyri were discovered on the isle of Elephantine near Syene (Aswan). The papyri are comprised of bills, letters, official documents (among them parts of a translation of a Behistun inscription), and parts of the Book of *Aḥikar (see *Elephantine). A number of recently published documents also originated in Elephantine. Other Aramaic papyri discovered in Egypt come from Hermopolis; their language, more than that of any of the other material, resembles the language prevalent in Syria during that period. More than a dozen letters, and parts of letters, which were sent from the eastern part of Persia, probably from Shushan and Babylonia to Egypt, were also found in Egypt (see below; most of this material is from the fifth century B.C.E.).

THE MAIN CHARACTERISTICS OF OFFICIAL AND ANCIENT ARAMAIC

Biblical Aramaic

To stress the main characteristics of Official and Ancient Aramaic as they manifested themselves through the history of the language and in the countries in which they were current, a comparative study of some aspects of Aramaic, Hebrew, and Arabic is necessary.

PHONEMICS AND PHONETICS OF ARAMAIC. The consonantal phonemes of Hebrew and Aramaic are identical (though not historically, see below). This is apparently due to the influence which caused Official Aramaic to lose the four additional consonantal phonemes still existing in Ancient Aramaic (see Ancient Aramaic below). In biblical Aramaic, the pronunciation of the phonemes ב'ג'ד' כ'פ'ת' (*bgd kpt*) are governed practically by the same rules as in Hebrew. Traces of this double pronunciation can be detected in the modern dialects. It remains however to be determined which language influenced which.

Consonants. The Hebrew ז, which equals the Arabic ذ (*dh*), corresponds to the Aramaic ד – in Hebrew זהב, in Arabic ذهب (*dhahab*), and in Aramaic דְּהַב ("gold"); the Hebrew צ, which parallels the Arabic ض (*ḍ*), corresponds to the Aramaic ע – in Hebrew אֶרֶץ, in Arabic ارض (*arḍ*), in Aramaic אֲרַע ("land"); the Hebrew צ which parallels the Arabic ظ (*ẓ*), corresponds to the Aramaic ט – in Hebrew עֵצָה, in Arabic عظة (*ʿiẓa*), in Aramaic עֵטָא ("counsel"); the Hebrew שׁ, which equals the Arabic ث (*th*), corresponds to the Aramaic ת – in Hebrew שָׁלֹשׁ, in Arabic ثلاث (*thalāth*), in Aramaic תְּלָת ("three"); the א has become weakened in Aramaic to such an extent that when beside the letter ה it also serves as a mater lectionis.

Vowels. The Hebrew *o* which parallels the Arabic *ā*, is also *ā* in Aramaic – Aramaic שְׁלָם, Hebrew שָׁלוֹם, Arabic سلام *salām* ("peace"). In Aramaic as in Hebrew, the accent may fall either on the penultimate or on the final syllable; the effect in Aramaic however is different from that in Hebrew: a short Proto-Semitic vowel cannot appear in an open non-accented syllable (as opposed to Hebrew where under certain conditions it may be lengthened – cf. the Arabic سلام (*salām*), Aramaic שְׁלָם, Hebrew שָׁלוֹם. It is mainly these characteristics which distinguish Aramaic from Hebrew and from the other Semitic languages.

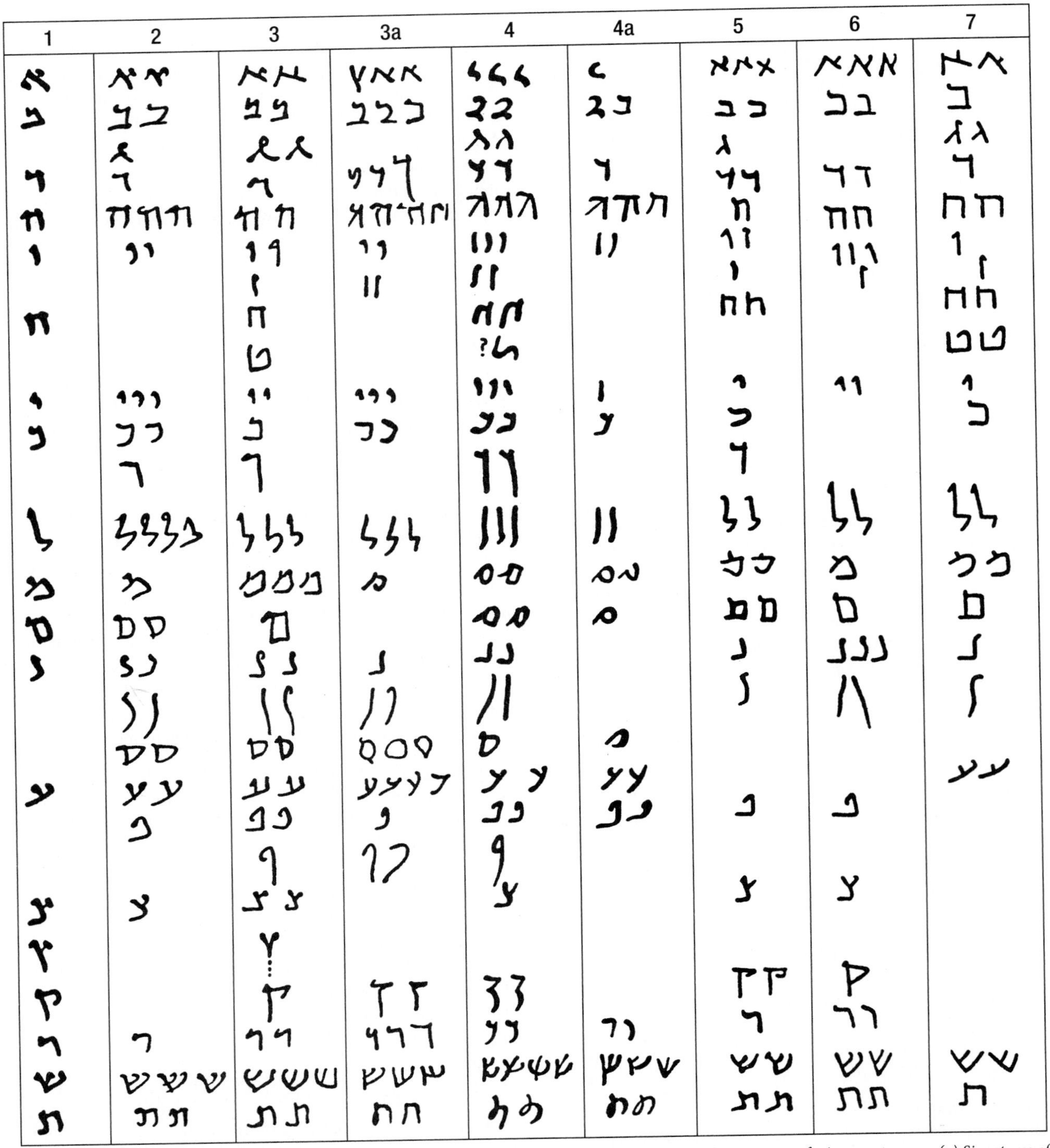

Examples of the Aramaic script. (1) Exodus fragment; (2) Bar Kokhba letter; (3) Bet Mashko letter; (3a) Signatures of witnesses to no. 3; (4) Signatures of witnesses on no. 4; (5) Dura-europos fragment; (6, 7) Bet She'arim tomb inscriptions (1–4a from Wadi Murabba'āt, i.e., before 135 C.E.*; 5–7 of the third century* C.E.*).*

DIFFERENCES IN THE VERB. Aramaic has no *niph'al*. The conjugations *pu'al* and *hoph'al* have practically disappeared, except for the participles. In biblical Aramaic, a few remnants of the internal passive of *pa'al* (*qal*) have survived. Aramaic has the additional conjugation of *hi/'itpə'el* which serves as a passive and a reflexive of *pa'al*. The Aramaic conjugations *pə'al, pa'el*, and *haph'el* correspond to the Hebrew *qal, pi'el*, and *hiph'il*, but they differ in form.

Some archaic forms in biblical Hebrew may be similar to or even identical with forms in Aramaic, e.g., *kətāvā* "they

The Paradigm of the Strong Verb (*Qal*):

	Masculine	Masc./Fem.	Feminine
Perfect			
Singular		כִּתְבֵת	
	כְּתַבְתְּ/תָּ(ה)		not attested
	כְּתַב		כִּתְבַת
Plural		כְּתַבְנָא	
	כְּתַבְתּוּן		not attested
	כְּתַבוּ		כְּתַבָה (כתבו)
Imperfect			
Singular		אֶכְתֻּב	
	תִּכְתֻּב		not attested
	יִכְתֻּב		תִּכְתֻּב
Plural		נִכְתֻּב	
	תִּכְתְּבוּן		not attested
	יִכְתְּבוּן		יִכְתְּבָן
Participle Active			
S.	כָּתֵב		כָּתְבָה
P.	כָּתְבִין		כָּתְבָן
Past Passive			
S.	כְּתִיב		כְּתִיבָה
P.	כְּתִיבִין		כְּתִיבָן
Imperative			
S.	כְּתֻב		כְּתֻבִי
P.	כְּתֻבוּ		not attested
Infinitive		Masc./Fem	
S.		מִכְתַּב	

(fem.) wrote" (cf. Heb. עֵינָיו קָמָה, I Sam. 4:15); כִּתְבַת "she wrote" (compare: אָזְלַת Deut. 32:36; Hebrew יִכְתְּבוּ, תִּכְתְּבוּ =Aramaic יִכְתְּבוּן, תִּכְתְּבוּן), such forms with final *n* ("ן") occasionally appear in the Bible, cf. יֶחֱצוּן (Ex. 21:35) Hebrew תִּכְתֹּבְנָה =Aramaic יִכְתְּבָן but compare וַיֵּחַמְנָה (Gen. 30:38).

The Aramaic passive participle of *pəʿal* is קְטִיל while its infinitive is formed with the prefix מ, e.g., לְמִקְטַל. Instead of a geminated consonant, we quite often find נ + a simple consonant (dissimilation, e.g., תִּתֵּן = תִּנְתֵּן), and even תִּנְדַּע (from the root 'י'ד'ע') instead of תִּדַּע ‡. (The double dagger indicates a reconstructed form.) (See Table: Paradigm of Strong Verb.)

PRONOUNS AND NOUNS. In the pronoun there is the tendency to exchange the final ם for ן (cf. Hebrew אַתֶּם =Aramaic אַנְתּוּן). The demonstrative pronoun of proximity is דְּנָא (masc.), דא (fem.), אֵלֶּ(י)ן, אֵלֶּה, אֵל (plur.). The objective pronouns are attached to the imperfect by inserting a מ or a נ. The definite article has the suffix א; "the king" = מַלְכָּא; "the queen" = מַלְכְּתָא; the plural מַלְכִין "kings" becomes מַלְכַיָּא "the kings" (with a geminated י); "queens" מַלְכָן appears determined as מַלְכָתָא (in the construct state מַלְכַת). The relative pronoun דִּי ("which" and "who") is also employed as a genetive particle. The phrase בֵּית מַלְכָּא ("the king's house") is therefore also found as בֵּיתָא דִּי מַלְכָּא ("the house of the king") and also in the prolepsis form: בֵּיתֵהּ דִּי מַלְכָּא (literally: "his house, of the king").

SYNTAX. Biblical Aramaic is rather free as regards word order (as opposed to Arabic and Hebrew), e.g., מַלְכָּא חֶלְמָא יֵאמַר ("the king the dream will (shall) tell" – Dan. 2:7). (See Table: Biblical Hebrew and Aramaic.)

VOCABULARY. The Aramaic vocabulary resembles the Hebrew more than that of any of the other Semitic languages. This is due to the fact that they are cognate languages (North-Semitic), and to the mutual influence of Canaanite Hebrew and Aramaic on each other. On the other hand, for centuries Aramaic and Akkadian coexisted and vied for dominance in the region known today as Iraq, Aramaic finally gaining ascendancy. The symbiosis led to the mutual influence of the two languages. Official Aramaic, which became the *lingua franca* throughout the Persian Empire (first half of the sixth century B.C.E.), and Eastern Aramaic borrowed many words from Akkadian, e.g., אִגַּרְתָּא ("the letter"), כָּרְסֵא ("a chair"), פֶּחָה ("a high official"). Aramaic also absorbed grammatical elements from Akkadian; it seems that the free word order is also the outcome of Akkadian influence. Since Aramaic was also the official language in Persia, it is not surprising that it comprises some Persian words, e.g., פִּתְגָם ("word").

The Aramaic of the Elephantine Documents

The Aramaic of the Elephantine documents, except for slight differences, resembles biblical Aramaic. The variation in the Aramaic spelling in these documents seems to indicate a more archaic language, but not differences in pronunciation, e.g., instead of ד (*d*) which corresponds to Hebrew ז (*z*) and Arabic *dh*, there is found sometimes זי (דִּי in biblical Aramaic); instead of ʿ which corresponds to the Hebrew צ (*ṣ*) and Arabic *ḍ*, there is sometimes found ק (*q*) (compare אַרְקָא = אַרְעָא "earth" Jer. 10:11); instead of ת (*t*) that corresponds to Hebrew שׁ (*š*) and Arabic *th*, there is sometimes found שׁ (שְׁקֶל *sheqel*). The

A Comparative Table of Biblical Hebrew and Biblical Aramaic Conjugation

Biblical Hebrew	Qal	Pəʿal passive	Niphʿal	Piʿel	Puʿal	Hitpaʿel	Hiphʿil	Hophʿal		
Biblical Aramaic	Pəʿal	Pəʿil	Hitpəʿel Itpaʿel	Paʿel	only participle in məphaʿal	Hitpaʿal	Haphʿel ʾAphʿel	Hophʿal	Shaphʿel	Hishtaphʿel

lack of vocalization (except in biblical Aramaic) and defective spelling (with sparse use of ו and י as matres lectionis) make it difficult to establish the definite structure of this Aramaic dialect. The plural suffix of the masculine noun and participle is usually spelled defectively without the י, e.g., מַלְכִין = מַלְכָן "kings." The rather free word order of biblical Aramaic obtains also in Elephantine Aramaic; however in Elephantine deeds it tends to be: predicate, subject, object. The same is true of Ancient Aramaic.

The Aramaic of the Driver Documents

These documents come from the eastern parts of the Persian Empire and exhibit some traits typical of Late Aramaic dialects which originated and flourished in the very same regions centuries later. The characteristics common to the Driver documents and to Late Eastern Aramaic dialects are (1) free word order (see above Biblical Aramaic and Elephantine); (2) many borrowings from the Persian; (3) the appearance for the first time of the construction שְׁמִיעַ לִי ("I have heard"), the passive participle + ל + possessive suffix (due to Persian influence) eventually led to an entirely different verbal system in Eastern Aramaic which is in use in Neo-Aramaic still today. The construction was discovered later in other texts as well.

ANCIENT ARAMAIC

There are differences between the various documents, particularly in the HDD and PNMW inscriptions, which represent an earlier dialect. In the old inscriptions (cf. Elephantine) an original ḏ is substituted by a ז (אחז)–אחד in Aramaic, אחז "to grasp" in Hebrew; an original ṭ is transcribed by a צ (כיצא)–קיטא in Aramaic, הקיץ ("the summer") in Hebrew; an original ḍ is transcribed by a ק = ע in Aramaic, e.g., ארקא; an original ṯ is transcribed as ש = ת in Aramaic, e.g., אשור = אתור ("Assyria"). Despite these spelling variations, it cannot be said that the Proto-Semitic consonants ḏ, ṭ, ḍ, ṯ changed into ז, צ, ק, ש, but, in the absence of other more suitable consonants, they served to indicate these ancient phonemes. It seems that in the HDD and in the PNMW documents (as in literary Arabic in the singular) the case endings were retained in the plural. It should be noted that in parts of the Sefire documents, the independent infinitive was found to have a similar usage to that of the Hebrew (for emphasis). This is unknown in the Aramaic dialects (except for that of the Onkelos translation). In the Tell Fekherye inscription ṯ is represented by o and the infinitive of *Peal* is מקטל (cf. קטל in Sefire).

OFFICIAL ARAMAIC

When Aramaic documents began to be discovered in Asia Minor, Egypt, etc. (i.e., in countries that had never been inhabited by Arameans), it became clear that Aramaic had been an official language in the Persian Empire and that to some extent it had been a *lingua franca*. Aramaic apparently was also the *lingua franca* of the Assyrian Empire. Thus King Hezekiah's ambassadors implore the Assyrian commander Rab-Shakeh, "Speak, I pray thee, to thy servants in the Aramean language" (i.e., rather than in Hebrew or in Assyrian; Isa. 36:11; II Kings 18:26). This status of Aramaic is also reflected by the fact that the Nabateans, and the Palmyreans, who were Arabs and therefore not likely to use Aramaic as a spoken language, nevertheless wrote their inscriptions (mainly from the first century C.E.) in an Aramaic still based on Official Aramaic (see Middle Aramaic). This also explains why Pahlavi (Middle Persian), which was the official tongue in Persia during the Sassanian dynasty, destroyed by the Arab conquest, employed Aramaic in written ideograms (the words were written in Aramaic, but read as Persian; cf. the English "e.g.," which stands for the Latin *exempla gratia* but reads "for instance"). Some of these ideograms go back to Official Aramaic of the days of the first Persian kings. Forms that originated in Official Aramaic can also be found in Jewish legal deeds that go back to the time of the Talmud and the **geonim*.

THE ORIGIN OF THE ARAMAIC PASSAGES IN EZRA AND DANIEL

S.R. Driver was the first to maintain that Aramaic portions of Ezra and Daniel were written neither in the Aramaic of the fifth and sixth centuries B.C.E. nor in Eastern Aramaic (where they were purported to have come from). Accordingly, he claims that these documents in Ezra must be forgeries. On a basis of comparison with (mainly) the Elephantine texts, the same conclusion was arrived at regarding the Aramaic chapters in Daniel. H.H. Schaeder, however, established that the differences between the Elephantine Aramaic and biblical Aramaic are mainly in the spelling and that in Jerusalem a "modernization" in the spelling of biblical Aramaic had occurred. This modernization accounts for the differences; consequently there is no basis for the assumption of a forgery. Furthermore, it was clarified that at that period many of the characteristics that distinguish Western Aramaic and Eastern Aramaic, dialects of a later period, were not yet in existence. Therefore, neither the date nor the origin of these chapters can be determined. But the free word order possibly points to an Eastern origin.

THE INFLUENCE OF ARAMAIC ON BIBLICAL HEBREW

This influence is mainly prevalent in the vocabulary, morphology, and possibly in the syntax of biblical Hebrew. However, both the dating and the extent of this influence have not yet been sufficiently determined. In the early biblical books, certain roots and grammatical forms which deviate from the standard are not to be regarded as Aramaisms, but rather as representing a common heritage which in Hebrew had survived mainly in poetry and in Aramaic in the everyday (spoken) language. Among these words are אֲתָה "came" (Deut. 33:2), אָזְלַת (יד) (Deut. 32:36; instead of the standard Hebrew אָזְלָה). However, וְשָׁבַת (instead of וְשָׁבָה in Ezekiel 46:17, a book replete with Aramaisms) goes back to Aramaic. It is therefore possible that a certain word or form appearing in an early biblical book, where it is archaic Hebrew, may disappear for a time and reappear in a later biblical book as a result of Aramaic influence. Other Aramaic roots and forms, not to be considered Aramaisms, are to be found in those biblical passages where the author deliberately gives an Aramaic texture to his words – when, for example, he wants to emphasize the "foreignness" of a gentile speaker; e.g., different archaic forms of the verb אתה, which is mainly Aramaic, given as התיו, אתיו as well as the forms בְּעָיו, תִּבְעָיוּן ("demand") which look like pure Aramaic (Isa. 21:11–14; the reference is to the Edomites).

It seems that Aramaic in the Bible was used as a poetic form, e.g., in Deborah's song (Judg. 5:26) there are the words מחק and תנה (*ibid.* 11) – both Aramaic forms: מחק being the presumed Ancient Aramaic parallel of the Hebrew מחץ ("deal a severe blow"; compare Ancient Aramaic), while תנה ("to repeat") is the Aramaic cognate of the Hebrew שנה. The same is true of the Book of Proverbs where the Aramaic בר ("son") appears three times (31:2).

The ordinary Jerusalemite of Isaiah's time did not know Aramaic and only the kings' counselors and ministers understood it (see above). Nevertheless, we find in the Book of Isaiah the Aramaic noun pattern *haqṭālā*: הַכָּרַת (פניהם) "the show" (of their countenance; 3:9), and הֲנָפָה "to sift" (30:28); it is possible that the same is true concerning the noun pattern *qəṭāl*. The existence of an Aramaic element per se in the Bible cannot (as has been shown here) always serve as proof of the late origin of a book. The books in which the Aramaic influence is most obvious are Ezekiel and certain chapters in Psalms, Proverbs, Song of Songs, Ecclesiastes, Esther, Ezra, Nehemiah, and the Books of Chronicles. The influence is recognizable (1) in the usage of certain Aramaic roots, e.g., מחא (Ezek. 25:6), the cognate Hebrew is מחץ ("dealt a severe blow"); טלל (Neh. 3:15), the cognate Hebrew is צלל ("to roof"); שהד (Job 16:19), in Hebrew עד ("witness"); (2) in idioms translated into Hebrew (a loan translation): אֲשֶׁר לָמָּה (Dan 1:10) meaning "why," in Aramaic דִּי לְמָא; זָכָר ("male sheep") instead of the standard Hebrew אַיִל, because of the Aramaic דִּכְרָא which means both "male" and the "male of the sheep"; (3) in an Aramaic noun pattern: e.g., הַשְׁמָעוּת (Ezek. 14:26); and (4) in syntax: perhaps in the regression of the conversive ו in the Books of Chronicles and in Ezra, etc.; and in its final disappearance from mishnaic Hebrew. Other syntactical forms in these books which deviate from standard biblical Hebrew may also be due to the influence of Aramaic.

MIDDLE ARAMAIC

INSCRIPTIONS FROM NON-ARAMAIC-SPEAKING REGIONS

Found mainly in Afghanistan (the edicts of King Aśoka), in Turkmenistan, and in Caucasus (Russia), the language of these inscriptions cannot be considered pure Aramaic; it does contribute however to our knowledge of Aramaic of the period, e.g., in one of the Aśoka inscriptions the first person of the (later) *ittaphʿal* (here spelled *thpʿyl*!), and the ending (*w*)*n* in the perfect plural masculine, are found. The ostraca of Nisá (Turkmenistan) are written in (faulty) Aramaic. Some scholars believe that these had been written in Persian with Aramaic logograms; their assumption is, however, without serious substantiation.

THE ARAMAIC TARGUMS OF THE PENTATEUCH (ONKELOS) AND OF THE BOOKS OF THE PROPHETS (JONATHAN)

Apparently at this period the Aramaic Onkelos translation of the Pentateuch and Targum Jonathan of the Books of the Prophets came into being in more or less the form in which they are known today. The place of origin of Middle Aramaic seems to have been Palestine (according to Dalman, Noeldeke, and Kutscher, as opposed to Kahle), but it was transmitted and vocalized (with the Babylonian vocalization) in Babylonia. Until the discovery of reliable manuscripts from Yemen (other texts are corrupt), no real study of its grammar could be made. Its vocalization apparently reflects some Eastern Aramaic dialect; thus the perfect was reshaped on the basis of the third person singular, e.g., the feminine third person singular "she transmitted" is *məsarat* (as apparently in the Aramaic of the Babylonian Talmud, see below) and not *misrat* as, e.g., in biblical Aramaic. There are other features which it shares with the Eastern Aramaic dialect, e.g., the fact that the determined form which originally was employed apparently correctly (as in the dialects of Western Aramaic) does not function properly any more. Sometimes the Eastern *ē* plural ending (instead of *-ayyā*) is employed. Peculiar to the dialect of the two Targums is the form of the first person singular of the perfect *qal* of the ל״י verbs, e.g., קְרֵיתִי ("I called," instead of קְרֵית); as well as the verbal ending *-an* (instead of *-ayin, -en*, etc., in the other dialects), e.g., קְרַן "the call," תִּקְרַן "you (fem.) will (shall) call" (instead of קְרַיִן – biblical Aramaic; (ן) קְרֵי – Galilean Aramaic; קְרֵן – Syriac).

THE ARAMAIC OF THE DEAD SEA SCROLLS

Among the Dead Sea Scrolls which have been discovered since 1947, there are scrolls, and fragments of scrolls, in Aramaic. These texts are of two types: (1) those which belong to the sect (or its library – texts not written by them), dating from the end of the Second Temple period; and (2) Aramaic letters from the days of Simeon bar Kokhba (the century following the destruction of the Temple); the language is different from the Aramaic of the texts of the sect.

ARAMAIC TEXTS OF THE SECT. These texts, written in biblical Aramaic, include a fragment containing the prayer of the Babylonian king Nabonidus, fragments of various Apocrypha and Pseudepigrapha (e.g., Tobias, the Book of Enoch, The Testament of the Twelve Patriarchs, etc.), and part of a translation of the Book of Job. The language of the last resembles, to some extent, Eastern Aramaic. The longest Aramaic passages from these texts, published to date, are those of the Genesis Apocryphon. The language is indicative of a transitional stage between biblical Aramaic and the later Aramaic dialects. At the same time, many traces of Palestinian Aramaic can be detected, as well as a few of Eastern Aramaic. The Genesis Apocryphon scroll made it possible to establish that Onkelos originated in Palestine, since the Aramaic of the scroll and Palestinian Christian Aramaic closely resemble that of Onkelos. There is also a strong Aramaic influence in the Hebrew of the Dead Sea scrolls, which is evidenced especially in the spelling and in the morphology, e.g., מהסיר in Hebrew מֵסִיר ("takes away"), Isaiah 3:1; and in the vocabulary, e.g., דוכו ("his cleaning"), in Hebrew טהרתו; found in the Manual of Discipline.

THE ARAMAIC BAR KOKHBA LETTERS. These documents are of major linguistic importance for, without a doubt, they represent the spoken Palestinian Aramaic possibly of Judea. A close resemblance was discovered between this Aramaic and Targum Onkelos, another proof that the latter originated in Palestine. Documents written in Nabatean were also discovered among the scrolls of the sect.

JERUSALEM INSCRIPTIONS

The few short Aramaic inscriptions dating from before the destruction of the Second Temple, e.g., the one dealing with transferring King Uzziah's bones, are written in Official Aramaic. The language, however, is already influenced by Late Aramaic.

ARAMAIC IN THE NEW TESTAMENT

Among the few Aramaic words in the New Testament, *rabbūni* reflects the form רבוני, found in the Cairo **Genizah* fragments of the Palestinian Targum (see below).

THE URUK INCANTATION TEXT

This text (second century B.C.E.) found in Iraq and written in cuneiform, gives a glimpse into the "vocalization" of Aramaic of that time (cuneiform writing can clearly indicate several vowel qualities and quantities). Early traits seem to be preserved, e.g., *ś* – spelled as *š*: *šamlat* = שמלה ("garment"), but late forms also appear, e.g., the ending *-ē* for the masculine determined plural, e.g., *rabrabe* רברביא ("elders").

THE NABATEAN INSCRIPTIONS

The *Nabatean inscriptions, mainly on tombs (dating from about 100 B.C.E. to approximately the second century C.E.) are for the most part in Official Aramaic. However, they already contain elements of a Late Aramaic on the one hand, and of Arabic on the other (on the evidence of their names, it is assumed that the Nabateans were Arabs). The use of ית, the accusative particle, which is rare in Official Aramaic, points to a later language, whereas the word עיר, Arabic *ghaira* ("different"), and certain syntactic characteristics, points to Arabic influence.

THE PALMYRENE INSCRIPTIONS

The Palmyrene inscriptions were also written (end of the first century B.C.E.–third century C.E.) in an Aramaic which was based on Official Aramaic. Traces of Arabic, which was the language of the writers, who according to their names are assumed to have been Arabs, are also detected in these inscriptions. The Palmyrean language was also influenced by an Eastern Aramaic dialect, e.g., the plural תגרא "merchants" instead of תגריא (as in the Uruk text).

THE ARAMAIC OF HATRA

These texts, found in Iraq (second century C.E.), show the influence of Eastern Aramaic: ל (instead of י) is prefixed to the third person in the imperfect.

THE ARAMAIC OF DURA-EUROPOS

The Aramaic of these inscriptions (Syria, third century C.E.) was also influenced by Later Aramaic, as evidenced by, e.g., הדן = דנא "this," in Official Aramaic.

THE ARAMAIC IDEOGRAMS IN PAHLEVI AND OTHER PERSIAN DIALECTS

Under the influence of Official Aramaic, many Aramaic ideograms (i.e., words written in Aramaic but read in Persian, e.g., ברה "his son" in Aramaic is *pus* "son" in Persian) were absorbed into the Middle Persian dialects. While they are mostly derived from Official Aramaic, some of them indicate changes, due both to the influence of Late Eastern dialects and to errors made by the Persian scribes who no longer knew the Aramaic language.

LATE ARAMAIC

The two dialectal groups of Late Aramaic – Western Aramaic and Eastern Aramaic – have several common characteristics: (1) דנא "this" (masc.) is replaced by other forms; (2) the prefix ה (+ vowel) of *haphʿel* (and other conjugations) is replaced by א (+ vowel); (3) all the dialects seem to possess the new conjugation *ittaphʿal* – passive of *ʾaphʿel* (see Middle Aramaic); (4) the original form of the relative pronoun has almost entirely disappeared; instead the proclitic 'ד is employed; (5) the internal passives of *qal* and *hophʿal* (see The Main Characteristics of Ancient and Official Aramaic – Differences in the Verb) have disappeared; (6) in all dialects the passive participle קטיל seems to be employed with certain verbs in the active voice (rare in Middle Aramaic), e.g., טעין ("carrying"); (7) in all the dialects, the participle has more or less (in some entirely) replaced the imperfect as the future tense, the imperfect being employed as a subjunctive (after the relative pronoun), a cohortative, and a jussive; (8) the prolepsis form is also found with the verb, e.g., עבדה למלתא literally "he did it the thing," when the object is determined; (9) many borrowings from Greek (less from Latin) are to be found in the dialects of Late Aramaic.

WESTERN ARAMAIC

It was a spoken language until the Arab conquest and even for a time after. (For differences between it, Eastern Aramaic, and Official Aramaic see above.) Differences between Western and

Official Aramaic that do not occur in Eastern Aramaic, or only in some of its dialects, are (1) the third person plural feminine has in all the Western Aramaic dialects the form (ן) קְטַלִי (see below), as opposed to קְטַלָה in Official Aramaic (according to the *qre* – the way it is read), and קְטַלוֹ (according to *ketib* – the way it is spelled); (2) the adverbial construction מִן קְטַל, e.g., מִן קָיֵים ‡ "standing" is common to all of Western Aramaic dialects; (3) tenses (see above): beside עתיד, ל- + infinitive may serve as future tense; (4) vocabulary: e.g., the verb גוב (אגיב) "replied" is used (and not אתיב, תוב); instead (or besides) חזה ("he saw") we have חמה; (5) freedom in the word order, so prevalent in Official Aramaic, seems to be absent here.

Galilean Aramaic

(Only this dialect will be dealt with extensively here.) This is the dialect of the Aramaic parts of the Jerusalem Talmud, of the aggadic Midrashim, the Palestinian deeds, the Aramaic documents of the geonic period (found in the Cairo **Genizah*), and synagogue inscriptions discovered in Ereẓ Israel. The Palestinian Targum and the Targum Pseudo-Jonathan of the Pentateuch are written in a dialect which, for all practical purposes (except for a few details), is that of Galilean Aramaic.

ITS PERIOD. Galilean Aramaic covers a period from the first *amoraim* of the Jerusalem Talmud (third century C.E.) to the last *geonim* (beginning of the second millennium C.E.). It seems (on the evidence of manuscripts), that the Aramaic of the Mishnah also very closely resembles (or is identical to) Galilean Aramaic.

THE NAME. Galilean Aramaic was regarded as an appropriate name because most of the known texts in this dialect originate in the Galilee. The Bar Kokhba letters, originating in Judea, are linguistically closer to the Onkelos Targum, while the Aramaic of synagogue inscriptions, e.g., from Jericho and Noʿaran in Judea, is identical to the language of those of Galilee (cf. the ending of the perfect third pers. plur., which in good texts and in the above inscriptions always appears with a קטלון – in the printed versions this form was "corrected" to קטלו). The קטלו form is employed in the Palestinian Targum fragments published by Kahle. The language of these fragments is yet uncorrected, but since the ל״י verbs even there have a final ן- (in contrast to the printed "corrected" versions of the Palestinian Targum), it seems clear that the Palestinian Targum fragments represent a dialect which is slightly different from Galilean Aramaic. To date, only two inscriptions were found which do not have ן: one at Um-el-ʿAmed, in the north of Galilee, and the other at Maon (near Nir Yiẓḥak), in the south of the country; they, therefore, apparently do not represent the main dialect. This assumption is supported by the fact that the Um-el-ʿAmed inscription has additional linguistic forms alien to Galilean Aramaic, e.g., "the gate" is given as תרא (= תרעא without the ע); "the sky" as שומיא (and not שמיא). Both forms are typical of Samaritan Aramaic where laryngeals have almost completely disappeared and are therefore liable to be dropped in writing altogether. On the basis of most of the inscriptions found outside Galilee, it is possible to assume that at the time when the Jerusalem Talmud was compiled (third–fifth century C.E.) there was one common standard language in almost all of (Jewish) Palestine. However, this cannot be clearly proven since the material is scanty – the name Galilean Aramaic has, therefore, remained, though many today prefer the name Jewish Palestinian Aramaic.

REFERENCE BOOKS. Dictionaries. S. Lieberman's works – including his studies on tannaitic texts (e.g., *Tosefta ki-Feshutah*) – have improved this aspect of the research. See now Sokoloff's dictionary on Jewish Palestinian Aramaic.

GRAMMARS. Dalman's grammar is outdated, Stevenson's work is of little significance, while in Odeberg's work only the chapters dealing with the syntax of *Genesis Rabbah* are useful. Fassberg's grammar deals with the Palestinian Targum Fragments, and Sokoloff's work describes the language of the *Genizah* fragments of **Genesis Rabbah*.

PROBLEMS CONCERNING THE GRAMMAR OF GALILEAN ARAMAIC. Dalman's study is based on the corrupt printed version of the Jerusalem Talmud and Midrash, and is thus unreliable. Copyists and printers, unfamiliar with the Aramaic of the Jerusalem Talmud, had emended it according to the Aramaic of the Babylonian Talmud (and that of Onkelos) – the main source studied by European Jewry. Discoveries in the last few decades have helped to clarify certain points in the research of this dialect. In fragments of the Jerusalem Talmud and of the Midrashim (mainly from the Cairo *Genizah*), the vulgar type vocalization, which substitutes ִ for ֵ and ָ for ַ (and vice versa) is sometimes found. Fragments of the Palestinian Targum also have this vocalization, which is practically identical with that of Galilean Aramaic (see above קטלו). These texts come from the east and therefore cannot be suspected of having been emended by European copyists. A comparison between their language and that of Aramaic inscriptions of Palestine (see Middle Aramaic – Jerusalem Inscriptions) and between the other two Palestinian Aramaic dialects (see below) also proves their reliability. In the following tentative survey, which is mainly based on manuscripts, only those forms whose vocalization is attested to in the sources are vocalized:

A GRAMMATICAL SURVEY. *Spelling.* One of the signs of good Galilean Aramaic manuscripts is the fact that *ā*, at the end of a word, was ordinarily indicated by ה (the same applies to the inscriptions). Spelling tends to be *plene*, especially in the case of ו (*vav*) which indicates even the short vowel 'ו, and sometimes י which also indicates a short vowel; in manuscripts, the א indicates *ā* in the middle of a word. Consonantal ו and י might be spelled וו, יי.

Phonology. (1) Consonants. Contrary to common opinion, only a few examples in the manuscripts hint at the weakening of the laryngeals and pharyngeals. There is however one remarkable shift – the ח may become an ע. The Midrash states clearly: "In Galilee they call a snake (חִוְיָא) עֲוְיָא. That is why Rabbi Judah Ha-Nasi referred to Rabbi Ḥiyya as "עִיָּא. ב (without the *dagesh*) merged with ו (cf., e.g., the spelling of חַבְרָן with חַוְרָן, the name of a country, and the reverse יַבְנֶה = יָוְנֵי (Yavneh), a place name). The final ם (*mem*), may appear as ן, e.g., חכים = חכין ("clever"). An open syllable at the end of a word may be closed with a ן, e.g., כְּמָן (instead of כְּמָה "how many"). (2) Vowels. The vocalization found occasionally in fragments indicates that the short *i* and the short *u* have disappeared almost completely. Instead we find *e* and *o*, e.g., מֶן (= מִן, "from") and גובא (= גֻּבָּא, "pit"). The *e* also appears as a variant of *a*; e.g., יֶמָא (= יַמָּא, "sea"). These phenomena remind us of the Greek transliteration of the Septuagint and of the Hexapla as well as of the Latin transliteration of Jerome from the Hebrew. (There may be remnants of this pronunciation in various manuscripts of Mishnaic Hebrew.) The labials and the ר in a closed preceding syllable tend to turn *a* into *o*, e.g., שׁוּבָּה ‡ (= "Sabbath"); שׁוּרִי ‡ (*paʿel* perfect of < ‡ *šarrī* "he began"). (3) Diphthongs. The diphthong *ay* was preserved rather widely, e.g., בַיתֵה "his house." There also appears the diphthong *aw*, e.g., טַוְרָה, "the mountain" (= טורא in the other dialects).

Morphology. (1) Pronouns. (a) The Independent Pronoun. Besides את "you" (fem. sing.), אתי also survived. The other forms are (?) אַתּוּן, אתין "you" (masc. plur.); אֲנַן "we" (masc. plur.); הִ(י)נוּן, אֱ(י)נוּן, אִ(י)נּוּן "they" (masc. plur.); הינין, אינין "they" (fem. plur.). With various prepositions (prefixes) these pronouns (and others) may undergo change, e.g., ונן "and we." (b) The Objective Pronouns. There is also a third person plural (as opposed to biblical Aramaic and other Aramaic dialects). (c) The Independent Possessive Pronoun. It is formed from the base דִּיד ‡ + the possessive suffix דִּידִי "mine," etc. (d) The Demonstrative Pronoun. The demonstrative pronoun of proximity is הָדֵ(י)ן, דֵּין (masc. sing.); הָדָה, הָדָא (fem. sing.); אִלֵּין, אֵלֵּין, הָאִלֵּין (masc. and fem. plur.), etc. Forms without the ד in the masculine are: אָהֵין, הָהֵ(י)ן, etc.; demonstrative pronouns of distance: masculine ההוא, feminine ההיא. The form אֵלֵּין, etc., is unique in Aramaic; in biblical Aramaic it appears as אִלֵּ(י)ן, in Aramaic inscriptions as אלן. (e) The Interrogative used attributively. The forms of "which" are היידן (sing. masc.), הֵיידָה (sing. fem.), הֵילֵין (masc. and fem. plur.). (f) The relative pronouns. The form ד׳ (rare) and דְּ, דִּ (cf. Syriac) – also written *plene*: דאיתמין ("of orphans"). The presentative is הָא.

(2) The Verbs. (a) The Perfect and Imperfect of *qal*. The perfect of *qal* (mainly of the strong verb) has only two types: פְּעַל, פְּעֵל e.g., כְּתַב, תְּקֵף. In the imperfect the vowel *o* spreads at the expense of *a*, e.g., יִזְבַּן יֶתְקֵף ("he will buy") is a survival of the third type (which has an *i* > *e*). The vocalic structure of the verb resembles, but is not identical with, biblical Aramaic, and is totally different from the Onkelos Targum, e.g., instead of כְּתָבִית (perfect first per. sing. in Onkelos), we find כַּתְבֵת. These forms even look more archaic than those of biblical Aramaic: כְּתְבֵת which seems to go back to כַּתֲבַת.

The third person feminine plural ending is thus identical (except the ן־) to the suffix of Samaritan and Christian Aramaic (and to Syriac). (See Table: Aramaic 1 and Table: Paradigm of *Qal*.)

The Paradigm of Qal – in the Perfect

Masculine	Masc./Fem.	Feminine
	כַּתְבֵת	
כְּתַבְתְּ		כתבת
כְּתַב,סְלֵק		כַּתְבַת
	כְּתַבְנַן	
כְּתַבְתּוֹן (!)	כְּתַבְתּוּן	כתבתין
כתבון, כְּתַבוּ		כְּתָבֵין

The Paradigm of Qal – in the Imperfect

Masculine	Masc./Fem.	Feminine
	אֶכְתוּב, נֶיכְתוּב	
תֶּכְתוּב		תכתבין
יֶכְתוּב		תֶּכְתוֹב
	נֶכְתוּב	
תֶּכְתְּבוּן		תכתבן
יֶכְתְּבוּן		יֶכְתְּבָן

From the present participle a new "tense" has evolved in Galilean Aramaic by prefixing the independent pronoun (as found in *maʿalula*): e.g., אתאָזֵל = "you walk" and וְאָנָה אָמַר = ונמר, etc. In Eastern Aramaic the pronoun is enclitic (see below Eastern Aramaic, par. 1).

(b) The imperative (*O* verbs in the imperfect). The forms are כְּתוּב (masc.), כותבין (masc. plur.). The *-n* is missing in the Palestinian Targum fragments (except for ל״י verbs). The original *o* in other words has been preserved in the first syllable (cf. the Syriac and Mandaic imperative with the pronominal object).

(c) Infinitive. The second vowel is apparently always identical with that of the imperfect, e.g., מעביד, משמע, מֶכְתּוֹב.

(d) Other Conjugations. The infinitive always has the prefix *m* + vowel, as in the *Book of Aḥikar* (cf. Syriac, i.e., *paʿel* מְכַתָּבָה instead of כַּתָּבָה etc.). Note the following forms of ל״י verbs: in the participle we find the form י alongside the form ־יִן (as in biblical Aramaic), e.g., בָּנֵי, בָּנַיִן. The same applies to the imperfect second person feminine singular תבניי, תבנין.

(3) The Declension. As in other Western Aramaic dialects, Galilean Aramaic has preserved the differentiation between the definite and the indefinite forms in gender and in number. (See Table: Noun Declension Wall.)

Note especially the forms שׁוּרֵינַן, שׁורֵיה, שׁורֵיךְ, שׁוּרַן, which differ from biblical Aramaic. The nouns אב, אח appear as אֲבוּ- אֲחוּ- when they are declined and take the plural suffixes, e.g., אֲבוּךְ, אֲבוּהִי, אֲחוּךְ, etc. (but in first person: אֲבָא, אֲחִי(!)).

(4) Prepositions. Prepositions worth mentioning are: כְּוָת ("like") ליד; גב, גבי, לגב, לגבי all = ("to"); קמי, קומי ("before," "in front of") from the root קדם, with the ד apparently assimilated; חורי ("behind," "after"); בְּגֵין ("because").

The Noun Declension ("Wall")

Masculine	Masc./Fem.	Feminine
	Singular	
	שוּרִי	
שוּרָךְ		שוּרִיךְ
שוּרֵ(י)הּ		שוּרַהּ
	שוּרַן	
שוּרכוֹן		שוּרוֹן
שוּרה(וֹ)ן		שוּרהֵ(י)ן
	Plural	
	שוּרַיי	
שוּרֵיךְ		שוּריך
שוּרוֹהִי, שוּרוֹי, שורוה		שוּרֵיה
	שוּרֵינַן	
שוּרֵיכוֹן		
שוּריה(וֹ)ן		שוּרֵיהֵ(י)ן

(5) Adverbs. Worthy of note are כַּדוּן ("now"), תובן ("again"), יומֵדין ("today"), הָכֵן ("so"), הָן, אָן ("where"), and מנן ("from where").

(6) Conjunctions. Conjunctions to be noted are כיון ד- ("since," "because"), בְּזִיל ד-, בְּגֵין ד- ("because"), אוף ("also"), ברם ("but"), and הֶן-אֶן ("if").

Syntax. As in biblical Aramaic, there is, alongside the regular construct, also a construct + ד used often with a proleptic suffix. Before a proper noun, a demonstrative pronoun may appear: הדא טבריה = Tiberias.

Tenses. (See above first paragraph of Late Aramaic.) The participle + conjugated הוה is used in the past and in the future to indicate repetition, durativity, etc. When the direct object is a determined noun (noun with a definite article) ל is added and when a pronoun ית is added, the latter may fuse with the verb and form one word, i.e., חמה יתה = חמתיה ("he saw him"). A proleptic suffix may precede both the direct and the indirect object, e.g., נסתיה לשליחה ("he took the messenger"). A verb may take as an object ם and infinitive: בעי ממרוד ("he wants to rebel"), also an imperfect plus בעי דיזעוף ("he wanted to rebuke"), or a participle שורי בכי ("he started to weep").

Vocabulary. There are borrowings from Akkadian; from Greek, which since the conquests of Alexander the Great became the dominant tongue in the whole Near East especially among the educated ruling classes; from Latin, as a result of the Roman conquest; and from Hebrew. Borrowings from Akkadian are אריסה ("the tenant farmer"), צמת ("to gather"), etc. There are a great number of borrowings from Greek, e.g., אוירה ("the air"), זוגא ("the pair"), טימי ("price"), ליסטם ("robber," misread as לסטים!). Some have given rise to verbs, i.e., ספג ("to dry oneself"). According to Lieberman, Greek was widely employed, even among the sages. Not only single words, but whole sentences in Greek may appear in our sources. Borrowings from Latin mainly belong to the governmental and military spheres, e.g., לגיון ("legion"), איסרטה ("road, way"), מונטה ("coin"), ארנונה (a certain "tax"). It is assumed that these borrowings came into Aramaic from Latin via Greek. The Hebrew influence on Galilean Aramaic is very small (it is felt more in the Palestinian Christian Aramaic, see below), e.g., עצה ("advice") and אציק ("felt sorry") are from the Hebrew. Galilean Aramaic vocabulary resembles that of the other two Western dialects and differs markedly from that of Babylonian Aramaic. Even the very same noun may appear in a different form in these dialects, e.g., דמ(א), in Babylonian Aramaic אדם ("blood"); זעור ("small"); compare Rabbi זעורה in the Jerusalem Talmud as opposed to Rabbi זירא in the Babylonian Talmud. Roots found only in Galilean Aramaic besides חמה ("saw"), are, e.g., אגיב ("answered"), ארתק ("knocked"), גזה ("repaid").

Palestinian Christian Aramaic

This dialect, probably spoken by converted Jews living in Judea, employs one of the Syriac scripts. Texts in this dialect were first discovered in the nineteenth century. The language is attested in texts translated from Greek and in some inscriptions.

Spelling. In contrast to its sister dialects, final *ā* is always indicated by א (influence of the Syriac script!). *Plene* spelling with אוי״ (not with ה!) are to be found both for long and short vowels, and apparently even for half-vowels (שוא נע), e.g., ראב (= רַב ‡ "great"), אילא (= אֶלָּא ‡ "only"), כול (= כֹּל ‡ "all," "every"), טאלין (= טְלָיִן ‡ "boys"), and יכילין (= יָכְלִין ‡ "are able"). The texts are unvocalized, except for dots to indicate the different pronunciations of בג״ד כפ״ת, also to mark the Greek Π and to differentiate between homographic grammatical forms; they may indicate different colors of vowels (e.g., of the *i, e* type, as against *a* type).

The following grammatical sketch does not follow in every case the grammar of Schulthess (which is not always reliable and is now outdated).

Phonology. The pharyngeals and laryngeals are generally well preserved. Labials tend to color neighboring vowels toward *o* (or *u*), e.g., שובא (= שַׁבָּא ‡ "Sabbath"), as in Galilean Aramaic. As sometimes in Galilean Aramaic, *a* in a closed syllable tended apparently to become a kind of *e*, e.g., ניפשה (= נַפְשֵׁהּ ‡ "his soul"). Prosthetic vowels appear (cf. אדרקונא = Greek *drākon*, "dragon").

Morphology. (1) Pronouns. Personal – Note plural אנין etc., and אנה (<אנח "we"). Suffix pronouns – the plural ־נן, etc., also ־נה – (<־נח "our"; see above the independent pronoun). The independent possessive pronoun is based upon ־דיל ‡, e.g., דילי ("mine").

(2) Noun. This is the only Aramaic dialect which has a *qutul* pattern (= *qotel* in Hebrew), e.g.; חוטור ("stick," also חוטר, etc., cf. Hebrew חֹטֶר, and the transliteration of the Hebrew מֹלֶךְ in the Septuagint = *Moloch*).

(3) Verb. Due to lack of vocalization, it cannot be ascertained how, e.g., the perfect of *pe'al* has to be vocalized (cf. biblical Aramaic as against Galilean Aramaic). The third per-

son masculine and feminine plural of the perfect is קטלי, קטלו (rarely + *n*). The imperfect אקטול is very often spelled יקטול. The imperfect frequently has forms that apparently are identical to Hebrew pausal forms, e.g., יכולון (= יְכָלוּן ‡ "they will be able"), apparently influenced by Mishnaic Hebrew. Very rarely are suffixed objective pronouns employed; instead we find ־לי or ־ית (e.g., יתה, לה "him"). The infinitive of the *peʿal* has sometimes the form קטל (obviously=קְטָל ‡), as in Ancient Aramaic (above); in the *paʿel* the form is the same as in Syriac in *apʿel* = Syriac, but also without the prefixed *m*. The infinitive of all the conjugations in Christian Palestinian Aramaic has the prefix *m*- (always in the *peʿal* and the *paʿel*, and sometimes in the *aphaʿel* and the suffix *u* (except in the *peʿal*)).

Vocabulary. Besides borrowings from Greek and Latin, those from Hebrew, e.g., עבר ("to be about"; from mishnaic Hebrew) and from Syriac, e.g., [את]חמת ("he became angry") should be mentioned.

Samaritan Aramaic

Spoken by Samaritans till about the tenth century C.E. (?), this dialect also did not develop a full vocalization system. The studies of Ben-Ḥayyim (who edited texts with transliteration, according to the Samaritan reading tradition), however, have made it possible to reconstruct a grammar of this dialect.

Spelling. It is not very *plene*: final *ā* is indicated only by ה (never by א).

Phonology. The original pronunciations of the different pharyngeals and laryngeals has nearly disappeared; they are therefore constantly mixed up in writing or omitted altogether. ב'ג'ד' כ'פ'ת' have (today) survived only with one pronunciation except for פ, which appears as *b* when geminated and mainly as *f* elsewhere. The *n* appears assimilated only in "old" roots and forms (e.g., אפק "he brought out" from the root נפק), but not in "late" roots and forms. The short *u* has disappeared; the half vowel (שוא נע), where it survives, appears as a full vowel. The old phonemes *(ō-ū, ē-ī)* have merged, and their quality and quantity is conditioned by stress and syllable (open or closed), e.g., *rábbon* ("lord"), but *rabbuni* "my lord." The stress is penultimate.

The Verb. Ben-Ḥayyim's work does not yield enough material to establish beyond any doubt the "vocalization" of certain basic verb forms (e.g., perfect first pers. sing., whether it is קְטַלְת, as in Galilean Aramaic; קִטְלֵת as in biblical Aramaic; or קְטַלִית as in the Onkelos Aramaic). This dialect seems to have been influenced (after it died out as a spoken language?) very much by Hebrew.

EASTERN ARAMAIC

Eastern Aramaic dialects were spoken by Christians, Jews, and Mandeans (a religious sect in southern Iraq) in what today is mainly Iraq. Syriac however was also a literary language used outside this region. Eastern Aramaic dialects were apparently still spoken several hundred years after the Arab conquest. In contrast to Western Aramaic, the differences between Eastern Aramaic and Official Aramaic are quite conspicuous. The main differences are (1) *l*- or *n*- served as the prefix of the third person imperfect; (2) -*e* for common Aramaic -*ayya*, as the ending of the masculine plural determinate (appears already in the *Book of Aḥikar*); (3) the loss of the determinative force of -*a*; (4) the elimination of *n* bearing pronominal suffixes of the imperfect (H.L. Ginsberg); (5) unaccented open syllables at the end of a word tend to disappear, e.g., רַבִּי>רַב; (6)the negation לאו is very common (mainly before nouns); (7) the construction *qətil* (passive participle) + *l*- + the suffix pronoun is employed quite often to express the perfect, e.g., שמיע לי "I have heard" (see The Aramaic of the Driver Documents); (8) the indeterminate active and passive participle may coalesce with an enclitic pronoun of the first and second person singular and plural (rare in Western Aramaic); (9) the word order seems to be much freer than in Western Aramaic; (10) the relative clauses are very conspicuous; (11) all Eastern Aramaic dialects abound in words borrowed from the Akkadian, the language spoken in that territory before the Arameans, and from the Persian, the language of the rulers of most of this area at that time. (Only the dialect of the Jews will be treated extensively here.)

Syriac

Syriac is comprised of two dialects: Western Syriac, current in Syria (as a literary vehicle only?), and Eastern Syriac. The main differences are: the Eastern Syriac vowels *ē, ā, ō* = the Western Syriac vowels *ī, ō, ū*, ח = *ḫ* in Eastern Syriac, but *ḥ* in Western Syriac. They use different (but very similar) scripts and different vocalization systems (which indicate semi-vowels or the vowel zero (as שוא in Hebrew)).

Since Syriac is the only Late Aramaic dialect to have a standardized vocalization (there are two systems, see above), its importance for Aramaic in general, and Eastern Aramaic in particular is very great.

Spelling and Phonology. Long final vowels that disappeared in speech are in certain cases nearly always preserved in writing (*ē, ā, ō*), e.g., רבי̄ pronounced רב "my teacher" (also see verb below). Even the short *u* is spelled *plene*, while the short *i* is on the whole spelled defectively.

Morphology. (1) Pronouns. Note the forms אַנְתְּ, אַנְתי̄, אַנְתּוּן, אַנְתֵּין ("you" in the masc., the fem., the sing. and, the plur.), all to be read *at*, etc. (without *n*). The possessive (and objective) suffixes clearly distinguish between masculine and feminine, singular and plural except for the second person plural with the suffix of the singular (the spelling is different). (See following table.)

(2) Verb. The verbal suffixes of Syriac are closer to earlier Aramaic than those of the sister dialects.

Note: קְטַלְתּוּן in Western Syriac. Final vowels in the third person plural could be preserved by adding *n*. The final *n* stays in the imperfect (dropped in Babylonian Aramaic). The infinitive of all the conjugations in Syriac have the prefix *m* – and, except in the *peʿal*, also the suffix *u*.

דִּין ("judgment") with Possessive Suffixes

Feminine	Masc./Fem.	Masculine
	Singular	
	דִּינִי (read דִּין)	
דִּינֶכִי (read דִּינֶךְ)		דִּינָךְ
דִּינָהּ		דִּינֵהּ
	דִּינַן	
דִּינְכֵין		דִּינְכוֹן
דִּינְהֵין		דִּינְהוֹן
	Plural	
	דִּינַי	
דִּינַיכִי (read דִּינַיכ)		דִּינַיךְ (read דִּינַיכְ)
דִּינֶיהָ		דִּינַוהִ (read דִּינַן)
	דִּינַין	
דִּינַיכֵין		דִּינַיכוֹן
דִּינַיהֵין		דִּינַיהוֹן

Syntax. Syriac has created a past perfect by combining the perfect and the postpositive auxiliary verb הֲוָא ("was"), e.g., דֶאמְרֶית הֲוֵית לכון ("which I had said to you"). This combination as well as that of the imperfect + הֲוָא is also employed in other, sometimes not clearly definable, uses. The word order is quite free: relative sentences abound. The Syriac found in inscriptions has preserved some earlier traits, e.g., the letter *ś (sin* = שׂ) which disappeared nearly entirely from Late Aramaic and the imperfect prefix י*(yod)*, instead of the standard *n*-. (See Table: Eastern Syriac.)

Eastern Syriac

Masculine	Masc./Fem.	Feminine
	Imperfect	
	אֶקטוֹל	
תֶקטלִין		תֶקטוֹל
תֶקטוֹל		נֶקטוֹל
	נֶקטוֹל	
תֶקטלָן		תֶקטלוּן
נֶקטלָן		נֶקטלוּן
	Perfect	
	קֶטלֶת	
קַטַלתִי̄		קַטַלתּ
קֶטלַת		קַטַל
	קַטַלן, קַטַלנַן	
קַטַלְתֵין		קַטַלתּוֹן
קַטַל (קַטַ לִי̄) קַטַלֵין		קַטַלוּ̄, קַטַלוּן

Mandaic

This dialect is close to Babylonian Aramaic.

Spelling. Mandaic has developed *plene* spellings more than any other Aramaic dialect; it uses the letters אהוי"ע both alone and in combination as *matres lectionis*. They indicate long, short, and even semi-vowels (שוא נע), e.g., שאכיב = שְׁכֵב ("lying"), נאכול = נעכול ("he eats"), ליא = לִי ("to me"), שומא = שְׁמָא ("name"). Mandaic is the only Aramaic dialect to have preserved (apparently only as (archaic) spellings) ז for *d* (Ar. *dh*), e.g., זאהבא = דַּהֲבָא ("gold"), and ק for *ḏ* (+ emphatic), e.g., ארקא = אַרְעָה ("earth" see above).

Phonology. The situation is practically identical with that of Babylonian Aramaic, except for the fact that (1) if there are two emphatics in a word, one tends to lose the emphasis, e.g., כושטא = קושטא ‡ ("truth"); (2) instead of a geminate consonant in certain cases we find dissimilation by *n* or *m*, as in Official Aramaic (see above The Main Characteristics of Official and Ancient Aramaic. Differences in the Verb), e.g., מאנדא = מַדָּע ‡ ("knowledge"), קומבא = קוּבָּא ‡ ("vault"), both features go back to the Akkadian substrate. (3) Quite often we find anaptyctic vowels, e.g., עתינסיב = אִתְנְסֵב ‡ ("he was taken"), apparently more often than in Babylonian Aramaic. Prosthetic vowels appear quite often, e.g., אברא = בְּרָא ‡ ("son").

Morphology. (1) Pronouns. אנאת ("you") singular, אנאתון ("you") plural. It distinguishes better between masculine and feminine, and singular and plural of the pronominal suffixes than does Babylonian Aramaic. Note that here also ראב<רַבִּי (= רַב ‡). The demonstrative pronoun: האזין masculine, האזא feminine ("this"); האנאתָה masculine feminine ("that"), masculine האנאתון, feminine האנאתין ("those"). (These forms are as yet unexplained.)

(2) Verb. Due to the apocope of the last (unaccented) vowel, many forms have merged, e.g., נפאק "he-they went out" (masc., fem.). For the last two forms there are to be found (only in Mandaic) the ending יון (masc.), יאן (fem.).

Syntax. The language of the incantation texts of the magical bowls that were found in Iraq and Persia is more or less identical with those of the other texts. Note the ending ־ון of the perfect third person plural masculine.

Babylonian Aramaic

This is the dialect of the Aramaic parts of the Babylonian Talmud, the geonic texts, and the writings of Anan, the founder of the Karaite sect. The language of the incantation texts of Nippur (and other places) is very close (but not quite identical) to it.

PERIOD. It dates back at least to the days of the first *amoraim*, Rav and Samuel (third century B.C.E.), and goes up to the end of the geonic period (11th century C.E.).

COMPOSITION. Considering its duration, it is not surprising to find earlier forms alongside later ones. It is difficult to ascertain why the language (reflecting an earlier stage) of the tractates *Nedarim, Nazir, Me'ilah, Keritot*, and *Tamid* differs from the other tractates; and the language of the *geonim* deviates in certain parts from the language of the Talmud.

REFERENCE BOOKS. (see bibliography). There are very few grammars and dictionaries.

Dictionaries. The earliest surviving complete dictionary is the *Arukh* of R. Nathan of Rome (11th century C.E.; fragments of *Kitab al-Hāwī*, an earlier important dictionary compiled by R. Hai Gaon in the tenth century were discovered in the Cairo *Genizah*, part of them were published by A. Maman, *Tarbiz* 2000). It is important even today both because its material, to a large extent, goes back to geonic sources and because of the good readings preserved in it. The entry system has been followed by all lexicographers up to modern times: i.e., the mishnaic, talmudic, and midrashic vocabulary is all concentrated in one volume, though the material represents at least four different dialects: (1) Mishnaic Hebrew; (2) Galilean Aramaic; (3) Babylonian Aramaic; (4) The Aramaic of the Onkelos (and other) translation. The *Arukh* is a comparative dictionary. Besides Aramaic with its different dialects, it also adduces Arabic, Greek, Latin, and Persian as comparisons with its material. The first modern dictionary is by J. Levy, and it is still of some use today. Arranged according to Hebrew and Aramaic entries, Arabic and Syriac are presented as the main Semitic linguistic parallels; Persian, Greek, and Latin are adduced to interpret borrowings from these languages. The addenda and corrigenda of H.L. Fleischer are still important but often antiquated. The *Arukh ha-Shalem* of A. Kohut, intended as a scholarly edition of the *Arukh* with additions by B. Musafiah (17th century C.E.), and an up-to-date scholarly dictionary, is rich in material but not well organized. Hebrew and Aramaic entries are not separate. Kohut's tendency to look for Persian etymology, even for words found only in Palestinian sources (from a time when there was no Persian rule there) is exaggerated. This tendency was sharply criticized by W. Bacher. In M. Jastrow's dictionary, the material is arranged according to Hebrew and Aramaic entries, but he tries to find Hebrew etymologies for words which obviously are of Greek, Persian, or Latin origin. The first volume of Krauss's work, dealing with the grammar of Greek and Latin loan words, was sharply criticized by S. Fraenkel, a Semitic linguist and expert in Aramaic. The second volume (a dictionary) has however retained its importance to this day due mainly to the addenda and corrigenda by I. Loew, who read the proofs of this volume. The most up-to-date scholarly dictionary is that of M. Sokoloff. Akkadian was deciphered in the 19th century and it has been established (see Zimmern and more recently Kaufman) that there are many Akkadian borrowings, especially in Babylonian Aramaic (see above). To bring the *Arukh ha-Shalem* up to date, the *Tosefet Arukh ha-Shalem* was edited by S. Krauss who was supposed to include the new material discovered since the *Arukh ha-Shalem* was published, especially that of the Cairo *Genizah*. However, this new work was criticized by S. Lieberman in his review (see bibl.), as it did not account for all the new material. Its importance lies in the contribution of an eminent Iranist, B. Geiger, who corrected many of Kohut's "etymologies" and filled in, to a large extent, the cognate material from Akkadian, Arabic, and Mandaic. B.M. Levin's *Oẓar ha-Ge'onim* and Kassovski's *Concordance of the Babylonian Talmud*, both as yet unfinished, are also important to the study of Babylonian Aramaic. Only Loew's work in the field of flora is a full and up-to-date scholarly study (of both Hebrew and Aramaic) – Loew also published many other important articles in the field of realia. There is, however, a great need for a scholarly comparative semantic-historical dictionary, which will comprise all the material, and categorize it – Hebrew and Aramaic (Babylonian Aramaic, Galilean Aramaic, the Targum of Onkelos, and others). S. Fraenkel's study of Aramaic borrowings from Arabic and C. Brockelmann's Syriac dictionary are still very important. Nowadays, however, one must consult Drower-Macuch's Mandaic dictionary (see below).

Grammars. Th. Noeldeke's *Mandaic Grammar* contains many observations which are important for the understanding of Babylonian Aramaic grammar. The unreliability of C. Levias' works (in English and in Hebrew) were shown by the reviews of S. Fraenkel and C. Brockelmann. Margolis' *Grammar* comprises little material and does not give the sources. J.N. Epstein's posthumous book has also been criticized both because of its method and the incompleteness of the material. (For above, see bibl.). On the Yemenite tradition of Babylonian Aramaic see S. Morag on the verb and Morag and Y. Kara on the noun.

THE PROBLEMS OF BABYLONIAN ARAMAIC. The above grammars are defective mainly for two reasons: (1) Not all the authors were linguists; (2) they did not base their studies on good manuscripts, and sometimes used them only in a by-the-way fashion. The printed versions are all corrupt and even manuscripts of European origin are not entirely reliable; there is reason to believe that they (including the Munich Ms.) were, to some extent, "corrected." The only trustworthy manuscripts apparently are those which originated in the east, but their linguistic nature (with the help of certain criteria) needs first to be determined. In an article published in *Leshonenu*, Kutscher identified four new forms in the paradigm of the first (*qal*) conjugation on the basis of these manuscripts. A comparison with Syriac and Mandaic has confirmed these findings. The problem of the grammar of Babylonian Aramaic will only be solved by a series of monographs based upon reliable manuscripts. A thorough study of the Babylonian Aramaic vocalized texts, as begun by Sh. Morag, is highly desirable. Of great importance is the clarification of various contemporary reading traditions, especially that of the Yemenites (dealt with by Morag). However, as long as there is no proof to what extent these reading traditions have preserved their original characteristics, and to what extent they represent internal changes of a later period (mentioned by Morag), their use is as yet problematic.

A SURVEY OF THE GRAMMAR OF BABYLONIAN ARAMAIC. The following tentative survey is based on manuscripts. The main deviating forms of the above tractates and the language of the *geonim* will be noted here, while the standard language of the Talmud will be described in the actual survey.

The salient features of that language are (1) the preservation of the *n* in the suffixes, e.g., להון (instead of להו "to them"); (2) the demonstrative and personal pronouns appear in their earlier form, e.g., הדין (as opposed to האי "this"); (3) certain differences in the vocabulary, e.g., לחמא (=נהמא "bread").

Spelling. Consonantal ו and י are also spelled וו ,יי.

Phonology. (1) The laryngeals א, ה and the pharyngeals ח, ע have weakened, as in Mandaic. (To some extent, the conservative spelling does not reveal this phenomenon, mentioned explicitly by the *geonim.*) These letters are therefore mixed up, e.g., אטמא (<עטמא ‡ = "bone"), הדר (<חדר = "returned"), or dropped altogether: תותי (<תחותי ‡ = "under"), שותא (שעותא ‡= "conversation"). (2) The consonants ר, נ, מ, ד, ב, ל tend to disappear as word finals, e.g., in תו (<תוב "again"), ניבי (<נעבד "we shall make"), אזא (<אזל "went away"), תיקו (<תיקום "it shall stand") אמא (<אמר "he said"). This phenomenon לכו (<לכון "to you," plur.), is especially prominent concerning the *n* of the pronouns, e.g., להו (<להון "to them") and in the verbal suffixes, e.g., תכתבו (< תכתבון "you shall write"). (3) ב (without the *dagesh*) may appear as ו (וו), e.g., אווד (< אבד "got lost"). (4) The accent, it seems, was rather strong; its position was apparently different from the one known to us in biblical Aramaic (see above רַבִּי<רַב first par. Eastern Aramaic).

Morphology. (See following table.) (1) Pronouns. (a) Personal Pronouns. (b) The Copula. Special forms serve as copula: ניהו (masc.),ניהי (fem.), נינהו (masc. plur.), נינהי (fem. plur.). (c) The Demonstrative Pronouns (ordinary): of proximity – האי (masc.), הא (fem.), הני (plur.); of distance – האיך (masc.), הך (fem.), הנך (plur.); ההוא (masc.), ההיא (fem.) הנהו (plur.); אידך (masc. and fem.), אינך (plur.). (d) The relative pronoun is ־ד. (e) The interrogative pronoun is מן ("who"), מאי ("what"). (f) The Possessive Pronoun. The base is ־דיד־, דיל plus suffixes, e.g., דידי, דילי ("mine").

Masculine	Masc/Fem.	Feminine
	אנא	
את		את
הוא, איהו		היא, איהי
	אנן	
אתו(ן)		?
אינהו		אינהי

(2) The Verb. Lately, some new forms were discovered in the basic paradigm (they will be noted with °, see above the Problem of Babylonian Aramaic). (a) It would also seem that the vocalization (of the perfect) is identical to that of the Onkelos tradition which differs from the other Aramaic dialects. In the past of *qal* we found the three types כתב ‡, שכיב ‡, and חרוב ‡ (= יָכֹל, חָפֵץ, כָּתַב in Hebrew). (The paradigm below is only hypothetically vocalized and accentuated.)

Masculine	Masc/Fem.	Feminine
	כתְבִי (ת)	
כְּתַבְתְּ		כְּתַבְתְּ
כְּתַב		כְּתַבַת, כְּתַבָא, כתַב
	כְּתַבן, כְּתַבִינַן, כְּתַבְנַן (?)	
כְּתַבְתּוּ(ן)? כְּתַבִיתוּ(ן)		—
כְּתַבוּ, כְּתוּב, כְתַב (?)		כְּתַבָן, כְּתַב

In the imperfect of *qal* we find mainly the pattern איקטול ‡, איקְטַל ‡ (= אֶשְׁמֹר, אֶשְׁכַּב in Hebrew) and only a few verbs of the pattern אַעֲבֵיד (= the pattern of אֶתֵּן in Hebrew).

Masculine	Masc./Fem.	Feminine
	אִיכתּוֹב	
תִּכְתּוֹב		תִּכְתְּבִי
ל/נִכְתּוֹב		תִּכתּוֹב
	נִכְתּוֹב	
תִּכְתְּבוּ (ן)		—
ל/נִכְתְּבוּ (ן)		ל/נִכְתְּבָן

(b) Imperative, כְּתוֹב (masc. sing.), כְּתוֹבִי (fem. sing.), כְּתוֹבוּ (masc. plur.), כתוב° and (?) כְּתוֹבִין (fem.). (c) Infinitive. מִכְתַּב (and מִכְתְּבָא?). (d) Present and Past Participle. כָּתְבִי(ן) (masc. plur.), כָּתְבָ(א/ן) (fem. plur.) (passive fem. כְּתִיבָ(א/ן)). The forms כתיבא, כָּתְבָא (fem. plur.) are new (the same in Mandaic). As to the other conjugations, the following ought to be noted: The infinitive is formed on the model of כַּתּוֹבֵי in *paʿel*, אַכְתּוֹבֵי in *afʿel*, etc. (The same is true of Mandaic and Palmyrean and the new modern eastern dialects). (e) The weak conjugations. Verbs whose second radical is א are sometimes conjugated like those of ו, e.g., שייל (participle of שאל, "asks"). The ע״ו verbs pattern in *paʿel* as strong roots (the second radical is geminated) and some forms of the ע״ע (geminate) verbs also pattern like that class, e.g., עייל (= < עלל, "he enters"). The *aphʿel* of ע״ו sometimes patterns like that of פ״ו, e.g., אוקים (root קום, "he erected").

(3) The Noun. Few noun patterns (and these are rare) have been added, as those with the derivational suffix ־יסא, ־יזא, e.g., גונדריסא "a small fence" and שופריזא "a small ram's horn."

(4) The Declension. The noun with pronominal suffixes. In a number of persons the plural suffixes are used for the singular as well (and apparently vice versa). This is especially noticeable in the first person singular where חֵילִי < חֵיל (see רַבִּי < רב above), and therefore the form חילאי was taken over from the plural.

Masculine	Masc/Fem.	Feminine
	Singular	
	חילי, חיל, חילאי	
חילך, חיליך, אבוך		חיליך,אבוך
חיליה, כולי,אבוה		חילה, אבוה
	חילין, אבון	
חילכו		?
חילהו		חילהי
	Plural	
	חילאי	
חילך, חיליך		חיליך
חיליה		חילה, חילהא
	חילין	
חילייכו		חילייכי
חילייהו		חילייהי

(5) Particles. (a) Prepositions. (The vocalization is mainly hypothetical) -א (< על, "upon," etc.), קַמֵּי ("before"), בַּהֲדֵי ("with"), בֵּי ("between"), אַטּוּ, אִמְטוּ ל-, אַמְטוּל ("because"), כי ("like"), אֵידָא ("because of," "through").

(b) Adverbs and Conjunctions. לְאַלְתַּר ("immediately"), מִימְּלָא ("at any rate," "from itself"), אַדְּרַבָּא ("on the contrary"), אַכַּתִּי ("still"), כְּלַפֵּי לַיְיא ("with regard to what"), מִי (introducing a question), או, אִי ("if"), הִילְכָּך, הולכך ("therefore"), איכו, כו ("well, then"), איזי, אֵיזו ("well, then"), אלמא ("consequently"), מיה, מיהו, מיהת ("at any rate"), נמי ("also"), נְהִי ("even if").

Syntax. The perfect appears also in the wish form, e.g., שְׁרָא ליה מאריה ("may his master forgive him"). To denote a continuous and a habitual action in the present, the participle is used plus קָא ("he says" = קָא אָמַר). Note the following use of the infinitive: לְמֵיזַל לָא מִבְּעֵי לָךְ לְמֵיזַל ("as for going – you need not go") employed when the verb is the logical subject. The direct and indirect objects are denoted by a prolepsis, that is, besides עַבְדָה לְמִילְּתָא ("he did the thing") one finds also עַבְדָה לַהּ לְמִילְּתָא ("he did it – the thing"). In a nominal sentence, instead of the copula we may find the construction… אֲנַן (e.g., אַטּוּ אֲנַן קַטְלֵי קָנֵי בְאַגְמָא אֲנַן "are we stalk destroyers in a lake, are we?") Relative clauses serve to emphasize the logical subject, as (הא) רבא הוא דאמר ("it is Raba who said"). The relative sentence is very much in use even in cases like עָלְמָא דְאָתֵי ("the world to come" – "the next world"), etc. The verb is negated by לָא, other negations are usually accompanied by לָאו.

Vocabulary. Borrowings from (1) Akkadian (and Sumerian): These are mostly in the fields of building, agriculture, and commerce, etc., e.g., אלפא ("ship"), אַרְדִיכְלָא ("architect"), בָּבָא ("gate"), בִּידְקָא ("gap, flood"), גִּיטָּא (originally "bill," "legal document," but mainly "bill of divorce"), זוּזָא ("a kind of coin"), מָתָא ("city"), נדוּנְיָא ("dowry"), קתא ("handle"), תַּרְבִיצָא ("yard"), שִׁלְדָא ("skeleton"), תרנגלא ("chicken"). (2) Persian, e.g., גוּשְׁפַּנְקָא ("ring"), אפרין ("thanks"), דנקא ("a kind of coin"). (3) Latin, e.g., מִילָא ("mile").

The original vocabulary is, of course, close to that of Mandaic and that of Syriac, e.g., דְּבָבָא ("fly"), Targum Onkelos, but דידבא in Babylonian Aramaic and in Mandaic. On the other hand, this dialect has words which are lacking in Galilean Aramaic, e.g., זוטרא, זוטא ("small"), גזם ("to exaggerate").

THE INFLUENCE OF LATE ARAMAIC ON OTHER LANGUAGES

Mishnaic Hebrew

The Hebrew language continued to absorb Aramaic elements during that period as well.

Morphology. (1) Pronouns, e.g., דְּבָרָךְ ("your word," masc. sing.), דְּבָרֵיךְ ("your word," fem. sing.), אַתְּ ("you," masc. sing.), these suffixes come from Aramaic. (2) Verbs, e.g., אֵרַע ("happened"). (3) Nouns, e.g., סִיעָה ("traveling company," "followers"). (4) Particles, e.g., מִשּׁוּם ("because," Hebrew שם = Aramaic שום).

Changing of Meaning Under Aramaic Influence. Sometimes, under the influence of Aramaic, a cognate Hebrew word might have acquired a different meaning: זָכָר mainly "male" in biblical Hebrew = דְּכַר "male," "ram" in Aramaic; therefore the Hebrew זָכָר "male," quite frequently found in mishnaic Hebrew, has also the meaning of ram (already to be found in biblical Hebrew).

Aramaic Noun Patterns in Hebrew. Nouns built according to Aramaic noun patterns appear more often in mishnaic Hebrew than in biblical Hebrew, e.g., כְּלָל ("general rule"). Syntactic traits such as שֶׁל הָעוֹלָם = רִבּוֹנוֹ שֶׁלָּעוֹלָם "Lord of the world," with the proleptic suffix of ו (רִבּוֹנוֹ) come from the Aramaic. It is possible that the whole mishnaic Hebrew tense system was shaped by Aramaic.

Classical Arabic

Aramaic elements were also absorbed into the vocabulary of classical Arabic. Aramaic words are already found in ancient Arabic poetry and in the Koran, e.g., in religious terms – the word *ʾislām* ("Islam," as well as "Moslem"); the verb *sjd* ("to worship") from which is derived *masjid* ("mosque"); *ʿīd* ("holiday"); *masīḥ* ("Messiah"); *ṣalāt* ("prayer"). Among them are words which Aramaic borrowed from other languages, e.g., *maskīn* ("poor") which comes from the Akkadian, *zawdj* ("pair") which is of Greek origin.

Aramaic Influence on Spoken Arabic Dialects

Aramaic influence on the different Arabic dialects persisted in Syria, Ereẓ Israel, and in Iraq even after the Arab conquest. The local population continued to speak their own language for some time, but at last Arabic superseded Aramaic, and the latter disappeared almost completely. Aramaic elements, however, were retained in the spoken Arabic dialects of these regions. So far, these Arabic dialects have not been thoroughly studied from this point of view (for an exception see Arnold and Behnstedt on Qalamun in Syria), but the influence in the field of vocabulary cannot be denied. In Ereẓ Israel and in Syria, this fact is also of great importance as regards Hebrew since Aramaic had absorbed Hebrew elements and passed them on to Arabic. An example possibly is בעל ("a field watered by rain and not by irrigation"). At times colloquial Arabic inherited from Aramaic a word of European origin, e.g., *furn* ("baking oven"), a word in colloquial Arabic which goes back to the Latin *furnus* ("oven"= "furnace" in English). Aramaic elements in colloquial Arabic have helped to identify especially plant names found in Jewish sources (as shown by I. Loew and G. Dalman).

Aramaic in European Languages

A few Aramaic words reached Europe through Christianity, e.g., אַבָּא ("father" > "monk"), *Abt* in German, abbot in English, etc. Arabic of the Middle Ages gave Europe a few Aramaic words, e.g., *miskīn* (= "poor" from the Akkadian), which passed through Arabic into Italian as *meschino* and into French as *mesquin*, etc. The Semitic root הלוך ("to go") had strange adventures. In Akkadian it is *alāku*, from which the noun *ilku* ("fief") was derived. From here it passed into Aramaic where it took on an Aramaic form: הֲלָךְ in biblical Aramaic. From Aramaic it passed into Persian where it changed its form and returned to the Aramaic of the Babylonian Talmud as כראגא ("head-tax"), passed into Arabic as *harādj* ("land-tax"), from it into Turkish from where it was absorbed by the European languages spoken in the Turkish Empire. It acquired several meanings in Slavic: in Polish e.g., *haracz* ("tax," "tribute"). This is where the Hungarian word *harácsolni* ("to make (grab?) money by dishonest ways") comes from.

Aramaic in Contemporary Spoken Hebrew

Contemporary spoken Hebrew drew on Aramaic elements as the need arose. This refers both to Aramaic words in their original meaning, e.g., אדיש ("indifferent"), and to those whose original meaning has been extended or changed, e.g., אגיב ("he answered," of the Palestinian Aramaic) which is employed in the Hebrew as הֵגִיב ("reacted"); שדר ("to send") has been adapted to the needs of the broadcasting system: שדר ("to broadcast"). Generally, these new words have been morphologically Hebraized, e.g., Aramaic אולפן ("learning"), has become אֻלְפָּן ("center for study of Hebrew by new immigrants"). There are, however, elements, mostly those which passed through Yiddish, which kept their Aramaic form: e.g., הדדי ("reciprocal"). There are also those words and forms which in the beginning had kept their original Aramaic form in Hebrew, yet in time took on a Hebrew form: מִסְתְּמָא ("probably"), today: מִן הַסְּתָם; but אַבָּא ("father") and אִמָּא ("mother"), both already found in mishnaic Hebrew, are not showing any signs of Hebraization.

SELECT BIBLIOGRAPHY: A. All the literature until the mid-1930s may be found in F. Rosenthal, *Die aramaistische Forschung seit Th. Nöldeke's Veröffentlichungen* (1939); review by H.L. Ginsberg, in JAOS, 62 (1942), 229–38 (only a few important titles listed in Rosenthal's work will be mentioned below). **ADD. BIBLIOGRAPHY:** J.A. Fitzmyer and S.A. Kaufman, *An Aramaic Bibliography, Part 1: Old, Official, and Biblical Aramaic* (1992). B. 1. Old Aramaic. (a) Grammar: G. Garbini, *L'aramaico antico* (ANLM series VIII, vol. 7, fasc. 5, 1956), is now outdated. R. Degen, *Altaramäische Grammatik* (in *Abhandlungen für die Kunde des Morgenlandes*, XXXVIII, 3, Wiesbaden 1969). **ADD. BIBLIOGRAPHY:** J.C. Greenfield, "The Dialects of Early Aramaic," in: JNES, 37 (1978), 93–99. For the position of Aramaic among North-Western Semitic languages see: W.R. Garr, *Dialect Geography of Syria-Palestine, 1000–586 B.C.E.* (1985). A very short survey of the scholarly literature may be found in the article by G. Garbini, "Semitico nord-occidentale e aramaico," in G. Levi Della Vida (ed.), *Linguistica semitica: presente e futuro* (1961), 59–60; F.M. Cross Jr. and D.N. Freedman, *Early Hebrew Orthography* (1952), 21–34; also see Fitzmyer (see below), 177–232. (b) Texts: The collections of Aramaic Inscriptions in M. Lidzbarski, *Handbuch der nordsemitischen Epigraphik* (1889) as well as in G.A. Cooke, *A Text-Book of North Semitic Inscriptions* (1903) are still valuable. The material since Rosenthal's volume: J.A. Fitzmyer, *The Aramaic Inscriptions of Sefire* (1995); H. Donner and W. Röllig, *Kanaanäische und aramäische Inschriften*, 3 vols. (1966–69; vol. 1, rev. 2002); J.J. Koopmans, *Aramäische Chrestomatie*, 2 vols. (1962); F. Rosenthal (ed.), *An Aramaic Handbook*, 4 parts (1967, comprises texts from Old Aramaic to New Aramaic dialects). **ADD. BIBLIOGRAPHY:** P.-E. Dion, *La langue de Ya'udi* (1974); J. Tropper, *Die Inschriften von Zincirli* (1993); J.C.L. Gibson, *Textbook of Syrian Semitic Inscriptions, vol. 2: Aramaic Inscriptions* (1975); A. Abou-Assaf et al., *La statue de Tell Fekherye et son inscription bilingue assyro-araméenne* (1982); A. Biran and J. Naveh, "The Tel Dan Inscription: A New Fragment," in: IEJ, 45 (1995), 1–18; M. Sokoloff, "The Old Aramaic Inscription from Bukan," in: IEJ, 49 (1999), 105–115. (c) Dictionaries: J. Hoftijzer and K. Jongeling, *Dictionary of the North-West Semitic Inscriptions* (1995); I.N. Vinnikov, *Slovar arameyskikh nadpisey* ("A Dictionary of the Aramaic Inscriptions"), in *Palestinsky Sbornik*, 3 (1958); 4 (1959); 7 (1962), 9 (1962); 11 (1964); and 13 (1965). 2. Official Aramaic. (a) Grammar: P. Leander, *Laut-und Formenlehre des Ägyptisch-Aramäischen* (1928); H. Bauer and P. Leander, *Grammatik des Biblisch-Aramäischen* (1927); H.B. Rosén, "On the Use of the Tenses in the Aramaic of Daniel," in: JSS, 6 (1961), 183–203. W. Baumgartner, H.H. Schaeder and H.L. Ginsberg (Rosenthal above A, 66–70, 70 note 3) are still important. S. Morag, "Biblical Aramaic in Geonic Babylonia," in *Studies in Egyptology and Linguistics in Honour of H.J. Polotsky*, ed. by H.B. Rosén (1964), 117–31; Z. Ben-Ḥayyim, "The Third Person Plural Feminine in Old Aramaic," in *Eretz-Israel*, 1 (1951), 137–9 (Heb.). Also see F. Altheim and R. Stiehl, *Die aramäische Sprache unter den Achaimeniden* (1963). **ADD. BIBLIOGRAPHY:** T. Muraoka and B. Porten, *A Grammar of Egyptian Aramaic* (2003²); M.L. Folmer, *The Aramaic Language in the Achaemenid Period* (1995); V. Hug, *Altaramaeische Grammatik der Texte des 7. und 6. JH.s.v. Chr.* (1993); F. Rosenthal, *A Grammar of Biblical Aramaic* (1995⁶); E. Qimron, *Biblical Aramaic* (2002²); E.Y. Kutscher, "Aramaic," in: T. Sebeok (ed.), *Current Trends in Linguistics* (1971), vol. 6, 347–412. (b) Texts: A.E. Cowley, *Aramaic Papyri of the Fifth Century B.C.* (1923); E.G. Kraeling, *The Brooklyn Museum Aramaic Papyri* (1953); G.R. Driver, *Aramaic Documents of the Fifth Century B.C.* (1954), a second revised and abridged edition, Oxford 1957. **ADD. BIBLIOGRAPHY:** B. Porten and A. Yardeni, *Textbook of Aramaic Documents from Ancient Egypt* (1986–99); B. Porten and J. Lund, *Aramaic Documents from Egypt: a Keyword-in-Context Concordance* (2002). (Also see above 1b). (c) Dictionaries: (see above 1c) and L. Koehler and W. Baumgartner, *The Hebrew & Aramaic Lexicon of the Old Testament* (2001), vol. 2, 1805–2010; (the Aramaic part compiled by Baumgartner). 3. Middle Aramaic. (a) Grammar. Dead Sea Scrolls: J.A. Fitzmyer, *The Genesis Apocryphon of Qumran Cave 1* (1971²); E.Y. Kutscher, *The Language of the Genesis Apocryphon* (1958), 173–206 (= *Scripta Hierosolymitana*, 4 (1958), 1–35). **ADD. BIBLIOGRAPHY:** K. Beyer, *Die aramaeischen Texte vom Toten Meer* (1984; Ergaenzungsband 1004). Onqəlos type Targumim, see Dalman (below); P. Kahle, *Masoreten des Ostens* (1913), 203–32. **ADD. BIBLIOGRAPHY:** A. Tal, *The Language of the Targum of the Former Prophets and its Position within the Aramaic Dialects* (1975). Uruk: C.H. Gordon, "The Uruk incantation texts," in *Archiv für Orientforschung*, 12 (1938), 105–17, idem, in *Orientalia*, 9 (1940), 29–38. **ADD. BIBLIOGRAPHY:** M.J. Geller, "The Aramaic Incantation in Cuneiform Script (AO 6489-TCL 6,58)," JEOL, 35/36 (1997–2000), 127–46. Nabatean: J. Cantineau, *Le nabatéen*, 1 (1930); Palmyrean: J. Cantineau, *Grammaire du palmyrénien épigraphique* (1935); F. Rosenthal, *Die Sprache der palmyrenischen Inschriften und ihre Stellung innerhalb des Aramäischen* (1936). **ADD. BIBLIOGRAPHY:** D.R. Hillers and E. Cussini, *Palmyrene Aramaic Texts* (1996). Hatra: A. Caquot, in: *Groupe linguistique d'études chamito-sémitiques*, 9 (1960–63), 87–89; R. Degen, in: *Orientalia*, 36 (1967), 76–80. (b) Texts. Various inscriptions: above 1b; Donner-Röllig, Koopmans, Rosenthal. **ADD. BIBLIOGRAPHY:** Y. Yadin et al., *The Documents from the Bar Kokhba Period in the Cave of Letters* (2002); A. Yardeni, *Textbook of Aramaic, Hebrew and Nabataean Documentary Texts from the Judaean Desert*

(2000); S. Abdal-Rahman al-Theeb, *Aramaic and Nabataean Inscriptions from North-West Saudi Arabia* (1993). Onqəlos type Targumim: A. Sperber, *The Bible in Aramaic*, 3 vols. (1959–62; The Pentateuch, the Latter Prophets). Place of origin: Kutscher, *The Language*…, above (a). Dead Sea Scrolls: Fitzmyer, above (a), bibliography, *ibid.*, p. 24, note 67; Nabatean: Cantineau, above (a) 2 (1932); *Revue Biblique*, 61 (1954), 161–81; IEJ, 12 (1962), 238–46. Palmyrene: Rosenthal, above (1b); various publications mainly in the periodicals *Syria* and *Berytus* and *Inventaire des inscriptions de Palmyre*, 11 fascicules, by various editors (1930–). Hatra: Rosenthal, above (1b); Degen above (a), p. 76, note 1. Dura-Europos: Koopmans above (1b) 1 (1962), p. 219; E.L. Sukenik, *The Synagogue of Dura-Europos and its Frescoes* (Hebrew 1947). Nisa: I.M. Diakonov and V.A. Livshitz. *Dokumenty iz Nisi* ("Documents from Nīsa," Moscow 1960); M. Sznycer, in: *Semitica*, 12 (1962), pp. 105–26; *Lešonénu*, 34 (1969/70); Inscriptions of Jerusalem: M. Avi-Yonah (ed.), *Sepher Yerushalayim* 1 (1956), 349–57. Aramaic in the New Testament: H. Ott, in: *Novum Testamentum*, 9 (1967), 1–25 (Ger.; bibliography). Important are G. Dalman, *Die Worte Jesu* (1930^2) and H. Birkeland, *The Language of Jesus* (1954). (c) Dictionaries: Hoftijzer and Jongeling, above (1c); M. Sokoloff, *A Dictionary of Judean Aramaic* (2003). Dead Sea Scrolls: M.G. Abegg et al., *The Dead Sea Scrolls Concordance* (2003), vol. 2, 775–946. Targum: Levy's dictionary of the Targumim is outdated, but G.H. Dalman, *Aramäisch-neuhebräisches Handwörterbuch* (1922) is still important. J. Cantineau, *Le nabatéen* above (a) 2 (1932). Glossaries are to be found in various volumes listed above (a) and (b). 4. New Aramaic. I Western Branch. (a) Grammars. Galilean Aramaic: G. Dalman, *Grammatik des jüdisch-palästinischen Aramäisch* (Leipzig, 1905^2); W.B. Stevenson, *Grammar of Palestinian Jewish Aramaic* (Oxford, 1962^2; not important); H. Odeberg, *The Aramaic Portions of Bereshit Rabba*, part 2 *Short Grammar of Galilaean Aramaic*, in section 1, vol. 36; no. 4 (1940); E.Y. Kutscher, "Studies in Galilaean Aramaic" (Hebrew) in: *Tarbiz*, 21 (1950), 192–205; 22 (1951), 53–63, 185–192; 23 (1952), 36–60. **ADD. BIBLIOGRAPHY:** S.E. Fassberg, *A Grammar of the Palestinian Targum Fragments* (1990). Christian Aramaic of Palestine: F. Schulthess, *Grammatik des christlich-palestinischen Aramäisch* (1924). **ADD. BIBLIOGRAPHY:** M. Bar-Asher, *Palestinian Syriac Studies* (1977); C. Müller-Kessler, *Grammatik des Christlich-Palaestinisch-Aramaeischen* (1991); Samaritan Aramaic: No up-to-date grammar of Samaritan Aramaic exists. See E.Y. Kutscher's short sketch in *Tarbiz*, 37 (1968), 399–403 (Hebrew); A.E. Cowley *The Samaritan Liturgy*^{2} (1909), XXXV–XLI is now outdated. (b) Texts: L. Ginzberg, *Yerushalmi Fragments from the Genizah* (Hebrew), 1 (1909). Other fragments were published mainly by J.N. Epstein in *Tarbiz* (Hebrew) vol. 3 (1932). Several scholarly editions of Midrash used *Genizah* material *(Bereshit Rabbah, Va-Yikra Rabbah, Pesikta de Rav Kahana)*, see respective entries. A. Diez-Macho, *Neophyti*, 1 (1968–79). **ADD. BIBLIOGRAPHY:** M.L. Klein, *Genizah Manuscripts of Palestinian Targum to the Pentateuch* (1986); M. Sokoloff and J. Yahalom, *Jewish Palestinian Aramaic Poetry from Late Antiquity* (1999); M. Sokoloff, *The Geniza Fragments of Bereshit Rabba* (1982). Documents (שטרות) from the *Genizah*: mainly S. Assaf, in: *Tarbiz*, 9 (1938), 11–34. Inscriptions: J.B. Frey, *Corpus Inscriptionum Iudaicarum*, 2 (1952; many misprints); *Sefer ha-Yishuv*, 1, pt. 1 (1939), passim, and various Israel periodicals. As to the importance of most of the texts listed above see Kutscher, above (a). Christian Aramaic of Palestine: M. Black, *A Christian-Palestinian Syriac Horologion* (1954). Samaritan Aramaic: A. Tal, *The Samaritan Targum of the Pentateuch* (1980–83). Very important is Z. Ben-Ḥayyim, *The Literary and Oral Tradition of Hebrew and Aramaic amongst the Samaritans*, 3 pt. 2 (Hebrew, 1967), which contains texts transliterated according to the orally preserved reading tradition of the Samaritans, cf. my review in *Tarbiz* above (a); J. Macdonald, *Memar Marqah*, vol. 1 Text, vol. 2 Translation (1963) (*without* transliteration); cf. review by Z. Ben-Ḥayyim, in *Bibliotheca Orientalis*, 23 (1966), 185–91 (Eng.); Z. Ben-Ḥayyim, *Tibat Marque: A Collection of Samaritan Midrashim* (1988). Also see Z. Ben-Ḥayyim, *Studies in the Traditions of the Hebrew Language* (1954), 112–9 (with the transliteration and English notes). (c) Dictionaries: M. Sokoloff, *A Dictionary of Jewish Palestinian Aramaic* (1990); see also the works of Levy, Jastrow, Kohut, Dalman, and the Additamenta to Kohut. Review of the Additamenta: S. Lieberman, in *Kirjath Sepher* (Hebrew). Important remarks are to be found in various works of J.N. Epstein and S. Lieberman and Yalon. Bibliography: *Tarbiz* 20 (1949), 5–50 (Epstein); *Hadoar* (Heb.), 43 (1963), 381–4; (Lieberman, in: *H. Yalon Jubilee Volume* (1963), 1–14). Very important is I. Löw, *Die Flora der Juden*, 4 vols. (1924–34), see also Rosenthal above (1b), Part 1/2, Glossary. Problems of the lexicography see infra II (c) (Kutscher). Samaritan Aramaic: A. Tal, *A Dictionary of Samaritan Aramaic* (2000); important is the Hebrew-Arabic-Samaritan Aramaic glossary (HMLYS) published by Z. Ben-Ḥayyim, *The Literary and Oral Tradition*… (above b), vol. 2 (Jerusalem 1957), 439–616. Christian Aramaic of Palestine: Only F. Schulthess, *Lexicon Syropalaestinum* (1903), is available and the glossary in his *Grammatik*, above (a). II The Eastern Branch. (a) Grammar. Syriac. Th. Nöldeke's *Kurzgefasste syrische Grammatik* (1898^2) was reprinted by A. Schall (1966), with a few additions (from Nöldeke's copy); J.B. Segal, *The Diacritical Point and the Accents in Syriac* (1953); C. Brockelmann, *Syrische Grammatik* (1960^8); F. Rundgren, "Das altsyrische Verbalsystem" in: *Sprakvetens kapliga Sallskapets i Uppsala Forhandliger* (1958–60), 49–75. **ADD. BIBLIOGRAPHY:** T. Muraoka, *Classical Syriac* (1997). Syriac inscriptions: K. Beyer, ZDMG, 116 (1966), 242–54. **ADD. BIBLIOGRAPHY:** H.J.W. Drijvers and J.F. Healey, *The Old Syriac Inscriptions of Edessa & Osrhoene* (1999). Mandaic: R. Macuch, *Handbook of Classical and Modern Mandaic* (1965), but, Th. Nöldeke, *Mandäische Grammatik* (1875), is still very important. See also E.M. Yamauchi, *Mandaic Incantation Texts* (1967), 69–152. Aramaic of Talmud Bavli: J.N. Epstein, *A Grammar of Babylonian Aramaic* (Hebrew, 1960), cf. E.Y. Kutscher's review in: *Lešonénu* (Hebrew), 26 (1961/62), 149–83. M.L. Margolis, *Lehrbuch der aramäischen Sprache des Babylonischen Talmuds* (1910) is still useful. (There exists also an English edition.); M. Schlesinger, *Satzlehre der aramäischen Sprache des Babylonischen Talmuds* (1928). Also important are the reviews of Levias' both editions (see Rosenthal) by S. Fraenkel, in: *Zeitschrift für hebräische Bibliographie*, 5 (1901), 92–94; C. Brockelmann, in: MGJW, 76 (1932), 173–8. B. Kienast, in: *Münchner Studien zur Sprachwissenschaft*, 10 (1957), 72–76. The Language of the Geonim and Anan: J.N. Epstein, in JQR, 5 (1914/15), 233–51; (1921/22), 299–390. Yemenite Tradition: S. Morag, in: *Phonetica*, 7 (1962), 217–39; *Tarbiz*, 30 (1961), 120–9 (Hebrew), English summary p. 11 of the issue; *Henoch Yalon Jubilee Volume* (1963), 182–220 (Hebrew); *Lešonénu*, 32 (1968), 67–88. **ADD. BIBLIOGRAPHY:** *Babylonian Aramaic: The Yemenite Tradition* (1988); Morag and Y. Kara, *Babylonian Aramaic in the Yemenite Tradition: The Noun* (2002). Incantation texts: W.H. Rossell, *A Handbook of Aramaic Magical Texts* (1953); Epstein in REJ, 73 (1921), 27–58; 74 (1922), 40–82. **ADD. BIBLIOGRAPHY:** J. Naveh and S. Shaked, *Amulets and Magic Bowls* (1985); idem, *Magic Spells and Formulae* (1993). (b) Texts. Syriac. Only inscriptions discovered mainly by J.B. Segal are worth mentioning; E. Jenni in: *Theologische Zeitschrift*, 21 (1965), 371–85 (bibliography pp. 371–7); Segal in BSOS, 30 (1967), 293–304; also see J.A. Goldstein, in: JNES, 25 (1966), 1–16. Mandaic: See the list of Abbreviations of Macuch, supra (a), pp. XXXVII–XLI. Aramaic of Talmud Bavli: S. Sassoon (ed.), *Sefer Halakhot Pesukot* (1950) (Gaonic Literature). As to the Talmud itself: Sh. Abramson has published a manuscript of *Tractate ʿAvodah Zarah* (1957); M.S. Feldblum, *Dikdukei Soferim*, Tractate *Gittin* (1966) continues the series. To *Oẓar ha-Geʾonim*, ed by B.M. Lewin, *Berakhot-Bava Kamma* 1943 (12 vols.) was added part of *Bava Meẓiʿah* (posthumously, no editor and other data are given), as well as Ch. T. Taubes, *Sanhedrin* (1966). (c) Dictionaries. Syriac: No new dictionary has appeared. C. Brockelmann, *Lexicon Syriacum* (1928²) is the best lexicon of any Aramaic dialect. Mandaic: E.S. Drower and R. Macuch, *A Mandaic Dictionary* (1963). The Aramaic of Babylonian Talmud see above (Ic); M. Sokoloff, *A Dictionary of Jewish Babylonian Aramaic* (2002). Problems of a new dictionary of Jewish Aramaic (and Mishnaic Hebrew) dialects: E.Y. Kutscher, in: *Hebräische Wertforschung* ed. by B. Hartmann and others (1967), 158–75; Rosenthal (1b) part 1/2 (Glossary). Ḥ.J. Kassovski, *Thesaurus Talmudis*, Concordantiae Verborum, 18 vols. (1954–). Foreign influences upon Aramaic. Akkadian: H. Zimmern, *Akkadische Fremdwörter als Beweis für babylonischen Kultureinfluss* (1917). **ADD. BIBLIOGRAPHY:** S.A. Kaufman, *The Akkadian Influences on Aramaic* (1974); see also the remarks of B. Geiger in the *Additamenta ad Aruch Completum* above (Ic). Persian: Geiger, *ibid.*; Widengreen Hebrew-Canaanite needs a monograph. Greek and Latin: S. Krauss, *Griechische und lateinische Lehnwörter in Talmud…*, 2 vols. (1898–99) is outdated, but cannot be dispensed with. Reviews: Fraenkel, in: ZDMG, 52 (1898), 290–300; 55 (1901), 353–5 with S. Lieberman, *Greek in Jewish Palestine* (1950), as well as his *Hellenism in Jewish Palestine* (1950), and many other books and articles, see his bibliography in *Hadoar*, 43 (1963), 381ff. A. Schall, *Studien über griechische Fremdwörter im Syrischen* (1960). Aramaic influences upon other languages. Akkadian: W.V. Soden, *Grundriss der akkadischen Grammatik* (1952), 192, 193, 196; idem, in: *Orientalia*, 35 (1966), 1–20; 37 (1968), 261–71. Biblical Hebrew: G.R. Driver, "Hebrew Poetic Diction," in: *Congress Volume*, Supplements to Vetus Testamentum, 1 (1953), 26–39. M. Wagner, *Die lexikalischen und grammatikalischen Aramaismen im Alttestamentlichen Hebräisch* (1966). Also see E. Kautzsch, *Die Aramäismen im A.T.* (1902). Canaanite-Punic: E.Y. Kutscher, in: *Lešonénu*, 33 (1969), 105–7; Dead Sea Scrolls: E.Y. Kutscher, *The Language and Linguistic Background of the Isaiah Scroll* (Hebrew, 1959), 8–13, 141–63. Mishnaic Hebrew: H. Albeck, *Introduction to the Mishnah* (Hebrew, 1959) lists (pp. 134–52) words parallel in both languages. Arabic: S. Fraenkel, *Die aramäischen Fremdwörter im Arabischen* (1886) is still very important. M.T. Feghali, *Etude sur les emprunts syriaques dans les parlers arabes du Liban* (1918); G. Dalman, *Arbeit und Sitte im Palestina* 7 vols. (1928–42) passim. **ADD. BIBLIOGRAPHY:** W. Arnold and P. Behnstedt, *Arabisch-Aramaeische Sprachbeziehungen im Qalamūn (Syrien)* (1993). European languages: K. Lokotsch, *Etymologisches Wörterbuch der europäischen… Wörter orientalischen Ursprungs* (1927), 241; W.B. Henning, in: *Orientalia*, 4 (1935), 291–3; E.Y. Kutscher, *Words and their History* (1961), 13–16. The influence of Aramaic on Modern Hebrew: I. Avinery, *The Achievements of Modern Hebrew* (1946), 72–80. **ADD. BIBLIOGRAPHY:** M. Bar-Asher, in: *Evolution and Renewal: Trends in the Deveolpment of the Hebrew Language* (1996), 14–76.

[Eduard Yecheskel Kutscher]

ARAM-DAMASCUS (Heb. אֲרַם דַּמֶּשֶׂק; RSV, Syria of Damascus), the principal Aramean state during the ninth and eighth centuries B.C.E., centered in Damascus, its capital. As such, it is also referred to as "*Damascus" or simply "*Aram" in the Bible, in Assyrian sources, and in the Aramaic Zakkur inscription (c. 900 B.C.E.). This state extended from the kingdoms of Hamath in the north, to Israel in the south, and between the Syrian desert in the east, and the Phoenician territories on the west. In the earliest known reference Aram-Damascus was a dependency of Hadadezer, king of Aram-Zobah (see *Aram), who enlisted its aid against David. However, David defeated the coalition and annexed both states, or at least Aram-Damascus (II Sam. 8:5–6). In the latter part of Solomon's rule, Rezon son of Eliada threw off the Israelite yoke and established the independent kingdom of Aram-Damascus (I Kings 11:23–25). Aram-Damascus acquired extensive territories and – under the dynasty of Hezion, Tabrimmon, and Ben-Hadad – rose to prominence after the split of the united Kingdom of Israel (I Kings 15:18; cf. the Aramaic Bar-Hadad votive inscription found near Aleppo). Aram, fully exploiting the situation in Palestine and meddling in the disputes between Judah and Israel, continuously threatened the very existence of the northern kingdom. Thus, early in the ninth century B.C.E., *Ben-Hadad I proceeded to wrest eastern Galilee from Baasha, king of Israel, attacking him from the rear after having been bribed by *Asa, king of Judah, to come to his aid (I Kings 15:18–20). Aramean pressure on Israel was further increased during the *Omri dynasty, and territories in northern Transjordan fell to the Arameans. Ben-Hadad II (son of Ben-Hadad I), with 32 of his vassals, was defeated by *Ahab, king of Israel, while attempting an attack on Samaria. He was again defeated at Aphek in the southern Golan and was thus compelled to return the Transjordanian towns conquered by his father and to guarantee Israel preferential mercantile rights in Damascus, such as had been enjoyed by the Arameans in Samaria under Omri (I Kings 20; esp. v. 34; cf. Damascus). This turn of fortune, underscored by the new threat of Assyria during the reigns of Assyrian kings Ashurnaṣirpa II and, especially, Shalmaneser III, forced Ben-Hadad to reconstitute his army and his kingdom, reducing his vassal states to the status of provinces (cf. I Kings 20:24–25). To meet the new menace, Ben-Hadad II (the Adad-Idri of Assyrian sources) joined in forming a league of 12 kings led by himself, the king of Hamath and Ahab, king of Israel. In their first clash in 853 B.C.E. the allies met Shalmaneser III at *Karkar in the land of Hamath – Ben-Hadad with 20,000 infantry, 1,200 horses, and 1,200 chariots. This same coalition, apparently, met Shalmaneser in battle again in 849, 848, and 845 B.C.E. Only after *Hazael had deposed the Ben-Hadad dynasty and after the alliance had fallen apart, did Shalmaneser III defeat Aram-Damascus, in 841 and 838 B.C.E. In the first instance he continued on through Hauran and Galilee, reaching "Mount *Ba'ali-rāsi*" (i.e., "Baal of the summit" *(rosh)*, possibly Mount Carmel). Hazael's rise to the throne reversed Aramean policy toward Israel, and they fought in 842 B.C.E. at Ramoth-Gilead (II Kings 8:28–29). The alleged encounter at this same spot between Ben-Hadad II and Ahab, as related in I Kings 22, seems to reflect this same, or an even later event. After the relaxation of Assyrian pressure, Hazael was able to consolidate his realm. First seizing the entire eastern bank of the Jordan down to the Arnon brook, he later raided western Israel, reducing its army and territory, and reaching the borders of Judah, which he forced to pay a heavy tribute (II Kings 10:32–33; 12:18–19; 13:7, 22). However, after Aramean power reached this peak, the renewal of Assyrian pressure led to its decline under Ben-Hadad III (the "Bar-Hadad" of the Zakkur inscription and possibly the *Mari'* [the Aramaic title "Lord"] of the Assyrian sources). Adad-Nirari III, king of Assyria, conducted several campaigns to Syria in the years 805–802 B.C.E., defeated Ben-Hadad III, and finally besieged Damascus, compelling it to pay a heavy tribute. In a later campaign related in a stele of Adad-Nirari III, found at Tel el-Rimah, the Assyrian king took large quantities of precious metals and fine cloth from the "Land of Damascus," as well as tribute from *Ia'usu Samerinaya*, i.e., *Joash, king of Israel, named here as king of *Samaria. Shalmaneser IV also went up against Damascus in 773 B.C.E.; Joash and *Jeroboam II, kings of Israel, taking advantage of the Arameans' weak position, defeated them several times and freed the Israelite districts beyond the Jordan. Jeroboam even imposed Israelite rule on Damascus (II Kings 13:25; 14:25, 28). Aram-Damascus had one final moment of glory during the reign of *Rezin, the last king, who is first mentioned in about 738 B.C.E. among the vassals of *Tiglath-Pileser III. Rebelling against Assyria, Rezin invaded Israel and annexed Transjordan as far south as Ramoth-Gilead and even raided Elath. He then compelled *Pekah, king of Israel, to join him in an alliance against Ahaz, king of Judah (II Kings 16:6). Ahaz's appeal to Assyria for aid provided Tiglath-Pileser III with a pretense for invading Damascus. In two campaigns in the years 733–732 B.C.E. the Assyrians seized the capital, and then delivered the final blow by putting Rezin to death and exiling many inhabitants (II Kings 15:37; 16:5ff.). The former Aram-Damascus was then split into Assyrian provinces: Damascus at the center, Hauran and Qarnini (biblical Karnaim) in the south, Manṣuate in the Lebanon valley, and Ṣubatu (biblical Zobah) in the north. An unsuccessful rebellion was attempted in Aram-Damascus in 720 (see Aram); sometime later the Assyrians resettled new populations there. Aram-Damascus occupied a prominent place in scriptural prophecy. Nowhere is this more evident than in the *Elisha cycle, where the prophet Elisha's part in the overthrow of the Ben-Hadad dynasty is related, reflecting the heavy pressure applied by Hazael on Israel (II Kings 5–7; 8:7–15). Aramean atrocities against the Israelite inhabitants of Gilead are condemned in Amos' prophecy of doom against Damascus (Amos 1:3–5). Isaiah was firm in his opposition to Aram-Damascus and Samaria at the time of their joint attack against Ahaz of Judah (Isa. 7:1ff.). Indeed, the destruction of Aram-Damascus left a deep impression on Isaiah (17:1–3) and even Jeremiah (49:23–27), as reflected in their oracles.

BIBLIOGRAPHY: E.G.H. Kraeling, *Aram and Israel* (1918); A. Jepsen, in: AFO, 14 (1942), 153–72; W.F. Albright, in: BASOR, 87 (1942), 23ff.; A. Malamat, in: JNES, 22 (1963), 1ff.; idem, in: EM, 1 (1965), 577–80; M.F. Unger, *Israel and the Arameans of Damascus* (1957); B. Mazar, in: BA, 25 (1962), 98–120; H. Tadmor, in: IEJ, 12 (1962), 114–22; J.M. Miller, in: JBL, 85 (1966), 441–54; S. Page, in: *Iraq*, 30 (1968), 139–53. **ADD. BIBLIOGRAPHY:** P-E. Dion, *Les Araméens* (1997), 171–221; for further bibliography see *Aram, *Damascus.

[Abraham Malamat]

ARAN (Aharonowitz), ZALMAN (1899–1970), Israeli politician and labor leader, member of the First to Sixth Knessets. Aran, who was born in Yuzovka, Ukraine, received a religious education and studied agriculture at Kharkov University. As a young man he was active in *Ẓe'irei Zion and when the party split in 1920 joined the Zionist Socialist Party (*Z.S.) and served on its clandestine Central Committee in the years 1924–25. In 1926 he immigrated to Palestine, where he joined the *Aḥdut ha-Avodah party. When *Mapai was founded in 1930 he became its first secretary. From 1931 to 1934 Aran was secretary of the Tel Aviv Labor Council and from 1948 to 1951 secretary-general of Mapai. He was elected to the First Knesset on the Mapai list, and remained a member of the Knesset for 20 years. He served as minister without portfolio in 1953–55 and minister of education and culture from 1955 to 1960 and again from 1963 to 1969. In the latter period he introduced a course in "Jewish Consciousness" into the school curriculum, and was responsible for the expansion of technical education. In 1968 the Knesset endorsed his plan to reform the Israeli school system, establishing junior high schools to bridge primary and high schools.

ʿARʿARA (Ar. عرعرة, *ʿArʿarata*), Israeli Muslim-Arab village near the Iron Valley road connecting Ḥaderah with Afulah (a stretch of the ancient Via Maris). It had 2,450 inhabitants in 1967 and 14,500 in 2002, with an economy based on field and garden crops, tobacco, olives, fruit trees, and sheep. In 1970 it received municipal status. Its area is 3.5 sq. mi. (9 sq. km.).

[Efraim Orni / Shaked Gilboa (2nd ed.)]

ARARAT (Heb. אֲרָרָט; 1QIsa̱, *hwrrṭ*; Akk. *Urarṭu*), name of land and mountains mentioned in the Bible.

The Land of Ararat

The Land of Ararat is mentioned in II Kings 19:37 and Isaiah 37:38 as the land where the sons of Sennacherib fled after murdering their father. From the Bible one would scarcely sense the importance of this ancient nation centering around Lake Van, in Armenia. The major sources of information are the Assyrian records dealing with this kingdom, whose native name was Bia(i)nili though known to the Assyrians as Urarṭu, but a large body of independent data has been obtained from inscriptions found during excavations in Turkey, Iran, and Russia. Urarṭu gradually rose to prominence during the ninth century B.C.E. as a confederation of small kingdoms which became Assyria's major rival. The chief god Haldi, along with Teisheba and Shiwini, is given credit by the Urarṭians for their successes. During the period of Assyrian weakness following the death of Shalmaneser III (858–824 B.C.E.), Urarṭu expanded considerably, reaching its apogee under Sardur III, who effectively severed Assyria from Asia Minor and the littoral by subjugating many city-states west of the Euphrates, including the major city of Aleppo. With the resurgence of Assyrian power under Tiglath-Pileser III (746–727), the Urarṭian Empire in northern Syria was destroyed. At the battle of *Arpad (c. 743 B.C.E.), Tiglath-Pileser decisively defeated the army of Urarṭu, and Sardur fled to Tushpa, his capital. After thoroughly subduing Syria (it is very likely that Isa. 36:18–19 refers to these campaigns, and perhaps Isa. 10:9 also), Tiglath-Pileser invaded Urarṭu, devastated the countryside, and laid unsuccessful siege to the capital. Further weakened by continuing Assyrian pressure from the south and attacks by the Cimmerians (Gomer) in the north, Urarṭu was invaded by Sargon II of Assyria in his eighth campaign (714) and the religious capital Muṣaṣir was taken. Although Urarṭu remained hostile to Assyria, Sargon's campaign marked the end of effective rivalry and open warfare between them; Assyria remained dominant, while Urarṭu was constantly occupied in protecting her northern borders from the invading Cimmerians and Scythians. The last certain reference to an Urarṭian state comes from 643. From Herodotus (I, 74) we know that by 585 the Medes occupied what had been Urarṭian territory. In the Behistun Inscription of Darius the Great (ca. 520), he refers to the territory as Armina (= Armenia), reflective of the newer "Arme" population, but as אררט in the Aramaic, and Uraštu in the Akkadian version.

The Mountains of Ararat

According to the story in Genesis 8:4 Noah's *ark came to rest on the mountains of Ararat. Accordingly, the present form of the story cannot be earlier than the early first millennium B.C.E. when the form "Urarṭu" replaced the previous designations Uruaṭri and Nairi of the Assyrian sources. Although one frequently hears the designation "Mount Ararat," the Bible does not mention any specific mountain. Luther understood Ararat to be the name of the mountain range. Nonetheless, one tradition identifies the particular mountain as Mount Massis, at nearly 17,000 ft. (550 m) the highest peak of Armenia, which is therefore often called Mount Ararat. The Aramaic and Syriac translations of Genesis 8:4 mention Ture Kardu, "the mountains of Kurdistan [Jebel Judi]" southeast of Lake Van, whereas the Book of Jubilees (5:28; 7:1) speaks of Mount Lubar (unidentified). In the Babylonian tradition of the flood, the mountain on which the *ark came to rest is Mount Nimush (sometimes read Niṣir), east of Assyria, now identified as Pir Omar Gudrun.

BIBLIOGRAPHY: A. Goetze, in: *Kulturgeschichte des Alten Orients*, 3 (1957^2), 187–200; B.B. Piotrovskii, *Urartu: the Kingdom of Van and its Art* (1967), ed. and tr. by P.S. Gelling; J.A. Fitzmeyer, *The Aramaic Inscriptions of Sefire* (1966), 26–28, 130–1; Hallo, in: E.F. Campbell and D.N. Freedman (eds.), *Biblical Archaeologist Reader*, 2 (1964), 152–87; A. Heidel, *The Gilgamesh Epic and Old Testament Parallels* (1949^2), 250–1; F.O. Kraeling, in: JAOS, 67 (1947), 181; Speiser, in: AASOR, 8 (1926–27), 17–18. **ADD. BIBLIOGRAPHY:** L. Bailey, in: ABD, 1, 351–53; A. Kuhrt, *The Ancient Near East* (1995), 548–53; P. Zimansky, *Ancient Ararat* (1998); M. Streck, in: RLA, 9, 589–90.

[Tikva S. Frymer / S. David Sperling (2nd ed.)]

ARATON, HARVEY (1952–), U.S. sports columnist. Born and raised in New York, Araton graduated from the City University of New York in 1975. He worked at the *Staten Island Advance* (1970–77), *New York Post* (1977–83), and *New York Daily News* (1983–91), where he was a columnist, before joining the *New York Times* as a sports reporter and national basketball columnist in March 1991. He became a *Sports of the Times* columnist in 1994. He was nominated by the *Times* for the Pulitzer Prize in 1994. Araton also wrote for the *New York Times Magazine, GQ Magazine, ESPN Magazine, Sport Magazine, Tennis Magazine*, and *Basketball Weekly*. He was the winner of the Associated Press Sports Editors award for enterprise reporting in 1992, and in 1997 for column writing. Araton was the winner in the column-writing category of the Women's Sports Foundation journalism awards in 1998. He is the author or co-author of three books: *Alive & Kicking (When Soccer Moms Take the Field And Change Their Lives Forever)* (2001); *Money Players (Inside The New NBA)* (1997); and *The Selling of the Green (The Financial Rise and Moral Decline of the Boston Celtics)* (1992).

[Elli Wohlgelernter (2nd ed.)]

ARAUNAH (Heb. אֲרַוְנָה, אֲוַרְנָה, אֲרַנְיָה; variant in Chronicles: *Ornan* (אָרְנָן)), most probably the last Jebusite ruler of Jerusalem whom David spared after conquering the city. The word Araunah is non-Semitic in origin, probably Hurrian and possibly a title, as it occurs once with the definite article (II Sam. 24:16 and *ibid.* 23 "the king…" cf. Hurrian *ewri*, "governor"). When David offended God by taking a census, plague struck his realm, killing 70,000. In answer to his prayer, it halted outside Jerusalem when the angel of the Lord had reached the threshing floor of Araunah. That day the prophet Gad commanded David to erect an altar to the Lord on this spot. David asked Araunah to sell him the threshing floor, but Araunah offered to give it to him together with his oxen for sacrifice, the threshing boards and ox yokes for firewood, and the wheat for a meal offering. David, however, refused to accept the offer, paid Araunah 50 silver shekels (in I Chron. 21:25 – 600 gold shekels), and then built an altar (II Sam. 24:15ff.; I Chron. 21:15ff.). (There is a certain similarity between this transaction and the purchase of the cave of Machpelah by Abraham; Gen. 23.) Solomon built the Temple on this site (II Chron. 3:1). The same verse connects this location with Moriah where the *Akedah* took place (cf. Jos., Ant., 7:333). It may have been public property, and Araunah, as the ex-ruler of the city, was thus entitled to dispose of it. I Chronicles 21:20 possibly speaks of "his (?) four sons." According to rabbinic tradition Araunah's skull was found on the Temple site in the time of Hezekiah (TJ, Pes. 9:1, 36c) or after the return from Babylon (TJ, Sot. 5:4, 20b). According to the Talmud *Avodah Zarah* 24b, he was a "proselyte of the gate."

BIBLIOGRAPHY: Melamed, in: *Tarbiz*, 14 (1942/43), 13–14; S. Yeivin, *Meḥkarim be-Toledot Yisrael ve-Arẓo* (1960), 199–200; Mazar, in: BIES, 13 (1947), 112–3; EM, 1 (1965), 552–3. **ADD. BIBLIOGRAPHY:** N. Wyatt, in: VT, 40 (1990), 352–60.

ARAZI, YEHUDA (1907–1959), Haganah leader and organizer of "illegal" immigration to Palestine. Arazi was born in Lodz, then Russian Poland, and settled in Palestine in 1923. While serving with the Palestine Police from 1926 until 1934, he passed on information to the *Haganah, helped its prisoners, and engaged in arms smuggling. In 1936–39 Arazi secretly purchased arms from the Polish government which were smuggled into Palestine. During the early part of World War II, Arazi continued to buy arms for the Haganah, particularly from British Army sources in the Middle East and North Africa. His activities were discovered by the British in 1943, but Arazi evaded capture. At the end of the war, he left Palestine illegally, went to Italy and was appointed head of "illegal" immigration activities there. In the spring of 1946 the Italian authorities tried to prevent the departure of two refugee ships, *Eliyahu Golomb* and *Dov Hos*, which were carrying Jewish survivors of the holocaust as "illegal" immigrants. Arazi organized a mass hunger strike of the refugees. The pressure of world opinion forced the British government to permit the entrance of the ships with their passengers into Palestine. In the summer of 1947 Arazi went to the U.S. and organized the purchase and smuggling of light and heavy arms and aircraft to the Haganah. A considerable amount of material reached Palestine.

BIBLIOGRAPHY: Dinur, Haganah, 2 pt. 3 (1963); A. Cohen (ed.), *Be-Ru'aḥ Se'arah* (1966); Tidhar, 5 (1952), 2260. **ADD. BIBLIOGRAPHY:** A. Cohen, *Alon be-Sa'ar* (1973).

[Yehuda Slutsky]

ARBA AMMOT (Heb. אַרְבַּע אַמּוֹת; "four cubits"), a linear and square measure frequently found in halakhic literature. It has both halakhic applications and aggadic implications. (For the length of the cubit, see *Weights and Measures.) The apparent origin of this measurement lies in the observation, "A man's body is three cubits (long) and one cubit is for extending his arms and legs" (Er. 48a). A room that is not four by four cubits in area is unfit for human habitation, and requires neither a *mezuzah* nor a *parapet, and none of the *halakhot* governing homes applies to it (Suk. 3a–b). Analogously, a *sukkah* that does not enclose four by four cubits is unfit for use (*ibid.*). If a man constructs a wall facing his neighbor's window, he must keep four cubits away so as not to block out the light (BB 2:4). According to Jewish law, a man's property "acquires" chattels placed in it (see *Acquisition). A rabbinical enactment established that, in order to avoid disputes, an area of four cubits around a man in a public domain similarly acquires such chattels (BM 10a–b). When praying, one must keep four cubits away from an unclean place (Ber. 3:5). One should walk at least four cubits after each meal (Shab. 41a). The sages were careful not to walk four cubits without keeping their minds on Torah and wearing their phylacteries (Yoma 86a). Among the relevant aggadic statements are: "Whoever walks four cubits in Ereẓ Israel is assured of (his portion in) the world to come" (Ket. 111a); "Since the day the Temple was destroyed, God has nothing in His world except the four cubits of *halakhah*" (Ber. 8a).

BIBLIOGRAPHY: ET, 2 (1956), 28–29, 153.

[Yitzhak Dov Gilat]

ARBA KOSOT (Heb. אַרְבַּע כּוֹסוֹת; "four cups"), four cups of wine drunk by each participant at the *Passover *seder* service. This ceremony is prescribed by the Mishnah as a duty to be observed by even the poorest man (Pes. 10: 1). The four cups are drunk in the following order: (1) the *Kiddush* at the start of the *seder*; (2) at the conclusion of the main part of the **Haggadah* which ends with the **Ge'ullah* ("Redemption") benediction; (3) at the end of the Grace after Meals; and (4) at the conclusion of the *Nishmat* hymn ("*Birkat ha-Shir*"). Only the second and fourth cups were added for the *seder* meal since the drinking of the two other cups forms part of every meal on Sabbaths and holidays. The reason for four cups is based by the rabbis upon the midrashic interpretation of Exodus 6:6–7, where four different terms of deliverance are employed: "I will bring you out … deliver you … redeem you … and will take you to Me for a people," etc. (Ex. R. 6:4). Other symbolic explanations for the four cups are that they correspond to the four cups of Pharaoh mentioned in Genesis, ch. 40, or to the four ancient kingdoms which oppressed Israel and for which God requites Israel with four cups of consolation (TJ, Pes. 10:1, 37b–c). Other examples of the special symbolic significance of the number four in the *Haggadah* are the Four Questions ("*Mah Nishtannah*"). Four Sons, and the four types of food at the *seder* meal: unleavened bread (*matzah*), lamb, bitter herbs, and *ḥaroset*. Some rabbis in the Talmud required a fifth cup of wine for the fifth expression of redemption "I shall bring you" (Pes. 118a, according to the text found in R. Hananel and Alfasi); this became symbolized in the cup of *Elijah on the *seder* table. The four cups of wine should be drunk in a reclined position, as in Roman times reclining was a sign of freedom. Each cup has to contain at least a ¼ log (0.137 liter; Sh. Ar, OḤ 472:9). Red wine is to be preferred but because of the blood accusations in Europe, white wine was often used (see *Blood Libel).

Some feminists have added a Cup of Miriam, containing water to symbolize "Miriam's well" and to be drunk only by women after the second cup of wine.

ARBATOVA, MIA (1911–1990), Israeli ballet dancer and teacher. Arbatova was a soloist at the Riga Opera Ballet for a number of years before settling in Palestine in 1938. She had been a pupil and protégée of Alexandra Federova, artistic director of the Riga Ballet, and was on tour in Europe and the United States when Federova left Riga for America. Arbatova decided to make her home in Tel Aviv and danced and choreographed for the Opera Amamit but in 1943 opened her own ballet studio. By that time she was well known, having performed with her husband, singer-actor Joseph Goland, in various theaters, clubs, hotels, and cabarets. Many young men and women who later became prominent locally and abroad passed through her studio, including Domy Reiter-Soffer, Rina Schenfeld, Noa Eshkol (of the Eshkol-Wachman movement notation system), Moshe Efrati (founder of Kol Demama), and Yonatan Karmon (creator and director of folk dance shows).

Arbatova herself was often invited to serve on the jury of ballet competitions abroad.

A Mia Arbatova Ballet Competition was launched in 1990 in her honor. She attended a benefit performance for this purpose but died before the actual competition took place.

[Dora Leah Sowden (2nd ed.)]

ARBATTA, city mentioned in I Kings 4:10 as Arubboth and in Second Temple sources as Arbatta. On the outbreak of the Hasmonean uprising, in 168 B.C.E., Galilean Jews were threatened by the local gentile population. Hence, Simeon, brother of Judah the Maccabee, set out on an expedition to Galilee with 3,000 men, and thoroughly defeated the opposing forces. On returning to Judea, "he (Simeon) took with him those (Jews) who were in Galilee and in Arbatta (καὶ Ἐν Αρβάττοις) with their wives and children, and everything which was theirs, and brought them into Judea with great rejoicing" (I Macc. 5:21–24). Various attempts have been made to identify Arbatta. Some scholars have identified it with the Arabah mentioned in Deuteronomy 1:7, and Joshua 11:16, 12:8, 18:18, in which case it would be situated in the valley of the Dead Sea, but this seems unlikely. Others follow Eusebius and *Genesis Rabbah* ch. 33, where mention is made of an Araba or Arbu in the vicinity of Beth-Shean. The most reasonable identification is the one proposed by Klein, who read ἐνναρβάττοις and on this basis identified it with Narbatta (cf. Josephus, War II, 291, 509), situated between the southern borders of Galilee and northern Samaria. Recent excavations in this region, at Khirbet el-Hammam, by Adam Zertal, may have succeeding in identifying the site. There are remains at the site belonging to two main periods: from the Iron Age, including a segment of a city wall, and from the Second Temple period (Hasmonean and Herodian) with the remains of a settlement, and a Roman siege ramp and a circumvallation wall from the siege made there by Cestius Gallus in 66 C.E.

BIBLIOGRAPHY: S. Klein, "Narbatta und die jüdischen Siedlungen westlich von Samaria," in: MGWJ, 74 (1930), 369–80; A. Schalit, *Namenwoerterbuch zu Flavius Josephus* (1968), 130ff. **ADD. BIBLIOGRAPHY:** A. Zertal, "The Roman Siege System at Khirbet el-Hammam (Narbata) in Samaria," in: *Qadmoniot*, 14 (1981), 112–18; idem, "Khirbet el-Hammam, 1982," in: *Israel Exploration Journal*, 34 (1984), 52; Y. Tsafrir, L. Di Segni, and J. Green, *Tabula Imperii Romani. Iudaea – Palaestina. Maps and Gazetteer.* (1994), 193.

[I.G./Shimon Gibson (2nd ed.)]

ARBEITER-ZEITUNG ("The Workman's Paper" between 1890 and 1902), a Yiddish socialist weekly published in New York to express the views of the working classes. Under Abraham *Cahan, who edited it for five years, it became an influential newspaper, inaugurating a vital era in Yiddish journalism in America. Cahan wanted to broaden the paper's policy to embrace all labor movements but was opposed by the controlling shareholders, who had a narrower socialistic outlook. Eventually he resigned and the paper split into two rival socialist dailies: *Abendblatt* (1894–1902) and the **Jewish Daily Forward* (1897–), of which Cahan became editor in 1902, serving in that capacity until his death in 1950.

BIBLIOGRAPHY: H. Hapgood, *Spirit of the Ghetto* (1962), 180–5.

ARBEL (**Arbela**; Heb. אַרְבֵּל), name of two sites in Ereẓ Israel (an additional Arbel is also known in Jordan). The first is known principally from the writings of Eusebius (On. 14:20) and was situated nine miles east of Legio in the Jezreel Valley, not far from Afulah. The second and the most important site bearing this name, however, is situated on the east side of Lower Galilee, identified at Khirbet Irbid (Ḥorvat Arbel), to the northwest of Tiberias. The remains of an ancient Byzantine synagogue were explored at the site by Charles Wilson in the 19th century as well as fortified caves which were connected by stairways and situated at a strategic point at the entrance to the valley facing the Sea of Galilee. It is possible that Arbel may be identical with that Beth-arbel which is mentioned in Hosea 10:14 as the site of a historic battle. The Seleucid commander, Bacchides, in his second campaign against Judah Maccabee, captured the "*mesalot* ("steps"?) at Arbel" and executed the inhabitants (I Macc. 9:2; Jos., Ant., 12:421). The reference is apparently to the caves in the vicinity and the connecting stairways. The Zealots who rose against Herod in 39 B.C.E. sought refuge in these caves. Herod routed them by lowering from the escarpment cages containing soldiers who lit fires at the entrances of the caves (Jos., *Ant.*, 14:415–30). During the Jewish War (66–70) against the Romans fortifications were built in this area (probably at Qal'at Ibn Ma'a or Har Nittai) by Josephus, who was a local commander at that time, and he later recorded this in his writings (*Life*, 188). The early Pharisaic leader *Nittai of Arbela (Avot 1:6) may have originated from there. After the destruction of the Second Temple, priests of the House of Jeshua (one of the 24 "courses," i.e., priestly divisions) settled at Arbel. The valley of Arbel was also noted for its agricultural fertility (TJ, Pe'ah 7:4, 20a) and items made of linen were said to have come from Arbel (Gen. R. 19:1). The early Byzantine synagogue discovered there consists of a columned hall entered via a doorway with molded jambs and lintel, and it had an apse in the southern wall, perhaps to contain Torah scrolls. The synagogue was first excavated by Kohl and Watzinger in 1905, and more recently it was investigated by Zvi Ilan between 1987and 1989. The date of the construction of the synagogue has been debated by scholars. What is certain, however, is that the third century C.E. date that was originally proposed for this building based on architectural parallels and carved decorations is no longer accepted by scholars. Near the remnants of this ancient synagogue a *moshav shittufi was established in 1949 by a group of Romanian Jews. In 1968 the economy of the settlement was based on fruit orchards, vegetables, field crops, cattle, and poultry. In the 1990s the population of this moshav grew to some 310 individuals.

BIBLIOGRAPHY: H. Kohl and C. Watzinger, *Antike Synagogen in Galilaea* (1916), 59; Abel, in: RB, 33 (1924), 380ff.; idem, *Les Livres des Maccabées* (1949), 159; Avi-Yonah, Geog, 140; EM, 2 (1954), 68;

Press, Erez, 1 (1951), 34–36; S. Klein (ed.), *Sefer ha-Yishuv*, 1 (1939), 163; Sukenik, in: JPOS, 15 (1935), 143; N. Avigad and H.Z. Hirschberg (eds.), *Kol Erez Naftali* (1967), 98–100. **ADD. BIBLIOGRAPHY:** F. Vitto, "Synagogues in Cupboards," in: *Eretz Magazine*, 52 (1997), 36–42; D. Urman and P.V.M. Flesher (eds.), *Ancient Synagogues*, vol. 1 (1995); Y. Tsafrir, L. Di Segni, and J. Green, *Tabula Imperii Romani. Iudaea – Palaestina. Maps and Gazetteer.* (1994), 168–68; Z. Ilan, *Ancient Synagogues in Israel* (1991), 116–18.

[Michael Avi-Yonah / Shimon Gibson (2nd ed.)]

ARBELL, MORDECHAI (Mario Varssano; 1929–), Israeli diplomat, businessman, and researcher of Sephardi and Caribbean Jewish history. Born in Sofia, Bulgaria, to a prominent Sephardi family, Arbell settled in Tel Aviv in 1941. After serving in the Israeli Air Force in the War of Independence and studying at the Hebrew University of Jerusalem, he entered the Israeli foreign service, holding various positions, including ambassador to Panama and Haiti. In 1977 he became the general manager of International Operations of the Eisenberg Group, consisting of 80 companies in 42 countries.

His studies of the Spanish-Portuguese Jewish communities in the Caribbean and the Guianas began in 1965 and included research trips all over the Caribbean basin. He studied at the Sorbonne in Paris and was a research fellow at the Ben-Zvi Institute in Jerusalem, at the John Carter Brown Library of Brown University and at the American Jewish Archives of the Hebrew Union College.

Among his publications are "*La Nacion*" – *The Spanish and Portuguese Jews of the Caribbean* (1981, an exhibition and catalogue); *Comfortable Disappearance, Lesson from the Caribbean Jewish Experience* (1998); *Spanish and Portuguese Jews in the Caribbean, A Bibliography* (1998); *The Portuguese Jews of Jamaica* (2000); and *The Jewish Nation of the Caribbean* (2002). Arbell also studied Sephardi Jewish history in Vienna, Austria, and Madras, India, the Inquisition in Manila, and the history of the Jews in Vlor (Valona), Albania. He is also an expert in the history of postage stamps featuring Sephardi Jews and has published *Filatelia Sefaradi* (1999).

Active in many communal and research institutes, Arbell was adviser to the World Jewish Congress and chairman of its Research Institute; chairman of Sefarad for the Preservation of the Sephardi Heritage; adviser to the National Council for Ladino and Its Culture and to the Israeli National Council for Foreign Affairs. Among his other activities, he served on the board of directors of the Museum of the Jewish Diaspora, the Institute of Cultural Relations Israel-Iberoamerica, and the Association for Research of Latin American Jewry.

ARBIB, family of North African origin, subsequently spreading to Italy. ISAAC BEN ARROYO (16th century), born in Salonika, author of books of sermons *Tanḥumot El* (1573) and *Makhil Kohelet* (1597), was also called Arbib, but little is known of his life. ESTHER (end of 18th century) played a prominent part in Jewish life in Tripoli and had great influence on the Turkish governor. When the city was in the throes of civil war in 1793, she was tortured in order to extract an enormous ransom. MOSES and VITTORIO were among the leaders of the community in the 19th century. GUSTAVO first introduced printing in Latin characters into Tripoli. ISAIAH, head of the Tripoli community (1774–78), established himself subsequently in Leghorn, and thereafter the family was prominent in Italy. EDOARDO (1840–1906) fought in the Italian-Austrian war of 1859. He was severely wounded a year later in the "Expedition of the Thousand" led by Garibaldi against the kingdom of Naples and was promoted on the field. He then joined the regular army and took part in the war of 1866 against Austria. Later he became editor of the *Gazetta del Popolo* of Florence and founded the daily newspaper *La Libertà* after the liberation of Rome in 1870. He entered political life and was appointed senator. He was also a writer of fiction and a historian of the Italian parliament. ANGELO (1865–1922) entered the Italian army as a professional soldier, commanded an infantry regiment in World War I, and became major general in 1917. Another member of the family, EMILIO (d. 1933), rose to the rank of general in World War I.

BIBLIOGRAPHY: G.V. Raccah, *Appunti per un archivio delle famiglie ebraiche della Libia* (n.d.), s.v.; G. Bedarida, *Ebrei d'Italia* (1950); N. Slouschz, *Travels in North Africa* (1927), 19–20; *Dizionario Biografico degli Italiani*, 3 (1961), 732–4 (includes bibliography); Hirschberg, Afrikah, 2 (1965), 199. **ADD. BIBLIOGRAPHY:** B. Di Porto, "Eduardo Arbib deputato di Viterbo," in: *Rassegna Mensile di Israel*, 40 (1973), 429–43.

[Cecil Roth]

ARBITRATION, method of settling disputes by their submission, voluntarily and with the mutual consent of all parties, for adjudication by a person or institution.

Function of Arbitration

In ancient Greek and Roman law – up to the middle of the third century C.E. – the adjudication of disputes was primarily dealt with by arbitration. But in Jewish law such adjudication from the beginning was based on a system of regular courts, empowered to enforce their judgments on the parties. This is ordained in the Pentateuch (Ex. 18:25–26, and more specifically Deut. 16:18 and 17:8–13). Reference is made to a system of established courts in the time of King Jehoshaphat in the eighth century B.C.E. (II Chron. 19:5–11), and talmudic tradition ascribes to Ezra, in the middle of the fifth century B.C.E., an enactment that courts (*battei dinin*) be held on Mondays and Thursdays (Ket. 1:1; BK 82a) to judge the people whether they wish it or not (Sif. Deut. 144 – contrary to the opinion of B. Cohen, *Jewish and Roman Law*, 2 (1966), 657ff., 796, and Baron, Social², 2 (1952), 266f., that arbitration preceded a system of presiding courts in Jewish law as well; see bibliography below: Gulak, Assaf).

The beginnings of the arbitral institutions are traceable to the middle of the second century C.E., in the period of Hadrian's decrees or even, it has been suggested, to the time of Rabban Gamaliel of Jabneh (first to second century; see G. Alon, below). This was one of the low periods in the history of Jewish judicial *autonomy, in which judicial authority was restricted, even in the field of civil law, i.e., *dinei mamonot* (see **Mishpat Ivri*), as opposed to criminal law (TJ, Sanh. 7:2, 24b), and the prohibition against ordination (*semikhah) was decreed (Sanh. 14a). To ensure the continued existence of Jewish judicial authority, therefore, the institution of arbitration was resorted to, and Jews turned to it of their own free will, prompted by their religio-national feelings. The laws of arbitration are first discussed by R. Meir and other scholars of that period (Sanh. 3:1) and the institution was known and employed mainly in Ereẓ Israel and not in Babylonia, where the Jews enjoyed wide judicial autonomy. For this reason too, the original meaning of the mishnaic term *shetarei berurin* ("deeds of arbitration," MK 3:3; BM 1:8; BB 10:4) was forgotten, and it was interpreted as meaning the statements of the parties, claims, or pleadings (BB 168a), whereas the *amoraim* of Ereẓ Israel adhered to the original meaning of the term, i.e., "*Compromisin*, this one chooses one [arbitrator] and this one chooses another" (TJ, MK 3:3, 82a). The existence in practice of the situation as described, and the background to the creation of arbitration as an institution of Jewish judicial authority, find expression in an order of Honorius in 398 C.E., according to which Jews were rendered subject to Roman law and the regular courts, but permitted, in civil law matters and by mutual consent of the parties, to resort to their own arbitration proceedings, enforceable at the hands of the provincial judges (*Codex Theodosianus*, 2:2, 10; also quoted, with slight changes, in *Codex Justinianus*, 1:9, 8).

At various times and in different countries of the Diaspora, arbitration continued to serve as a substitute for judicial autonomy, in particular where such autonomy had been weakened. But it also fulfilled important functions even where there was autonomy, which was general in the countries of the Diaspora. Thus, it aided in relieving the burden on the regular courts and in speeding up legal proceedings (see e.g., *Or Zaru'a*, BK 10:436) or was employed when the regular court was disqualified from hearing a suit because of its own interest in it (see S. Dubnow (ed.), *Pinkas ha-Medinah* (1925), 6, no. 13 and 307, no. 12) or for other reasons (*Shevut Ya'akov*, vol. 2, no 143).

Composition

Ordinarily, in Jewish law, the arbitral tribunal is composed of three arbitrators. The Mishnah (Sanh. 3:1) records a dispute between R. Meir and other scholars, the former stating that each party chooses one arbitrator and both choose the third, while the other scholars hold that the two arbitrators choose the third. Gulak correctly points out that the scholars sought to lend to arbitration proceedings (at least externally, although the matter is of substantive importance too: see below) the appearance of a Jewish court, composed generally of three judges, in contrast with the single arbiter customary under Roman law. The plain meaning of R. Meir's statement seems to be that the third arbitrator is chosen by the two parties only (so too, TJ, Sanh. 3:1, 21a), but the interpretation of the Babylonian *amoraim* was that all agreed that the consent of the two (arbitrators) is required for the appointment of the third and that R. Meir merely added that the consent of the parties to the third (arbitrator) is also required. The *halakhah* was decided accordingly (Sh. Ar., ḤM 13:1; Maim. Yad, Sanh. 7:1 gives conflicting interpretations). However, the opinion has been expressed that where the arbitrators are empowered to decide not only according to strict law, but also to effect a *compromise (*pesharah*), the two arbitrators may not appoint a third without the consent of the two parties (*Arukh ha-Shulḥan*, ḤM 13:1).

When the two arbitrators are unable to agree on the appointment of the third, the appointment is made by the elders of the city – whose status in various matters is as that of the court (see *Takkanot ha-Kahal; and cf. *Piskei ha-Rosh*, Sanh. 3:2; Sh. Ar., ḤM 13: 1, Isserles *ibid.*) and it was often customary for the rabbi of the city to be the third arbitrator (the "*shalish*"; I. Halperin (ed.)., *Pinkas Va'ad Arba Araẓot* (1945), 111–2, no. 270; 142–3, no. 335; Dubnow, *op. cit.*, 246, no. 932; *Shevut Ya'akov*, vol. 2, no. 143; *He-Avar*, 2 (1918), 73, no. 16). In the Vilna community, where, as in other communities, arbitration was customary despite the existence of regular *battei din*, it was the practice to stipulate in the rabbi's letter of appointment that he would not be required to serve as a third or fifth arbitrator etc., as the case might be (*He-Avar*, 2 (1918), 66, no. 11). The parties to arbitration may agree to a smaller or to a larger number than three (Sh. Ar., ḤM 3:2; Resp. Rosh, 56:1 and 56:7; Resp. Rashba vol. 2, no. 83; Resp. Jacob Weill 11; Naḥmanides, to Deut. 1:12; Isserles to Sh. Ar., ḤM 13:1), a rule carried out in practice (Halperin, *op. cit.*, 85, 308; Dubnow, *op. cit.*, 225, no. 843; 232, no. 888), and in one case cited, ten arbitrators were appointed (Resp. Ritba 85). A party is not heard, however, if an increase in the number of arbitrators is requested as a subterfuge (*Arukh ha-Shulḥan*, ḤM 13:5). When four arbitrators are appointed, the fifth is again chosen by them and not by the parties (*Noda bi-Yhudah, Mahadura Kamma*, ḤM 2).

The plain meaning of R. Meir's statement would allow for either party to reject the other's arbitrator, even if the latter be competent to judge and an "expert" (*mumḥeh*; TJ Sanh. 3:2, 21a). The Babylonian Talmud, however, interpreted R. Meir as conceding that an expert could not be so rejected (Sanh. 23a). The opinion of the scholars who differ from R. Meir is that one party cannot reject the other's arbitrator in the absence of evidence that the latter is a relative of the litigants (or of the other arbitrators: Resp. Rema 104) or not competent to serve as a judge (as detailed in the Mishnah, Sanh. 3:3–4). A bond of friendship between a party and his arbitrator does not of itself entitle the other party to disqualify him (Resp. Maharik 16), but if a defendant wishes to appoint an arbitrator whose integrity is in question, the former is not heard and he is compelled to appear before the regular court. Similarly, the defendant need not appear at arbitration proceedings until the claimant has appointed an honest arbitrator (*Piskei ha-Rosh*, Sanh. 3:2; Sh. Ar., ḤM 13:1). An arbitrator cannot be disqualified merely because he is not "godfearing" (Resp. Ri-Migash 114).

Status and Functions of Arbitrators

The talmudic sages saw a particular advantage in arbitration, in that each party could nominate an arbitrator of his own choice who represented the interests of the party choosing him and therefore a just decision was ensured (Sanh. 23a and Rashi, *ibid.*, cf. TJ, Sanh. 3:1, 21a). In the 13th century, *Asher b. Jehiel pointed out that it was wrong to interpret the above passages as justifying the arbitrator's blind support of the party by whom he was chosen when they should rather be read as meaning that the arbitrators appointed by both parties would thoroughly investigate the facts objectively and negotiate on the respective merits of the litigants' claims – the third arbitrator listening to them and then deciding between them (his Comm. to Sanh. 3:2; see also *Darkhei Moshe* ḤM 13:3 and Resp. Maharik 16).

The status of arbitrators has been described as equivalent in every way to that of *dayyanim* (*Panim Me'irot*, vol. 2, no. 159), and hence an arbitrator is precluded from hearing the contentions of the party appointing him in the absence of the other party, unless this is agreed upon or is local custom (*Arukh ha-Shulḥan*, ḤM 13:4). Arbitrators' fees are payable to the arbitrators chosen by each party, regardless of the outcome, lest the arbitrator be unduly influenced because of his interest in recovering his fees (*ibid.*). To ensure the maximum integrity of the arbitrators, an opinion was expressed that these fees be defrayed from a communal fund especially set up for this purpose and that a ban (*ḥerem) be imposed on both the donor and recipient of any gift beyond the allocation from this fund (*Panim Me'irot, ibid.*), but this far-reaching proposal was apparently not adopted (S. Assaf, *Battei Din...* (1924), 57).

On the other hand, formal legal requirements are relaxed in arbitration proceedings (see e.g., *Resp. Rashba*, vol. 2, no. 64). From the procedural point of view, too, arbitrators act as *dayyanim* and in various places special rules of procedure in arbitration proceedings are provided for. Thus in Cracow, in the 17th century, it was determined that arbitrators were required to commence their hearing within 24 hours of their appointment and to give their decision within three days of the hearing, a limit of nine days being provided for when the issue was complicated (Balaban, in: JJLG, 10 (1912), 333–4).

Agreement to, and the Subject Matter of Arbitration

The Talmud does not deal specifically with the question as to when an agreement to resort to arbitration is considered irrevocable. The problem is touched upon in connection with a case where the parties accepted a relative or other person legally incompetent to act as judge or witness, when it was held that, if accompanied by an act of *kinyan* (see Modes of *Acquisition), such acceptance could not be revoked; if there was no such *kinyan*, either party may revoke its acceptance at any time up to the completion of the litigation, but not thereafter (Sanh. 24a–b). A *fortiori*, where legally competent arbitrators are appointed, there can be no withdrawal from the submission to arbitration if agreed upon by way of a *kinyan*, nor after the conclusion of the proceedings (*Beit ha-Beḥirah*, Sanh. 83–84; Isserles to Sh. Ar., ḤM 13:2).

However, additional ways were sought to enhance the institution of arbitration and to prevent a party's withdrawal of its submission thereto. One such way was the drawing up of a deed of arbitration, referred to already in the Mishnah (above), which can be written only on the decision of both parties, both of whom pay the scribe's fees (BB 10:4 and Codes). The Mishnah also mentions a deed of arbitration as one of the documents permitted to be written on *ḥol ha-mo'ed* ("the intermediate days of a festival"; MK 3:3). Rashi's opinion is that the purpose of a deed of arbitration is to render submission to arbitration irrevocable (BM 20a), since the writing of a document has the same legal effect as a *kinyan* (Nov. Ramban, BM 20a; see also *Nimmukei Yosef*, MK 3:3). Support for the fact that writing a deed is regarded as a *kinyan* is to be found also in the case of providing surety for which *kinyan* is required (Sh. Ar., ḤM 129:4–6; see also Ket. 102a), a view supported in most of the Codes. Other scholars express the view that a deed of arbitration is written "so that the arbitrators should not forget" (cited in *Beit ha-Beḥirah*, Sanh. 84; cf. Maim. Yad, Yom Tov, 7:12) and its mere reduction to writing does not preclude the parties' revocation of the arbitration agreement. Yet another opinion is that the deed is an undertaking by the arbitrators to hear the matter, which they cannot later deny (*Or Zaru'a*, BB 10:232).

A further opinion, accepted in most of the Codes, is that once the parties have commenced their pleas before the arbitrators, they (the parties) can no longer withdraw from the arbitration (*Ha-Ittur*, vol. 1, s.v. *Berurin; Beit ha-Beḥirah, loc. cit; Nimmukei Yosef*, BM 20a. Their reliance on TJ, Sanh. 3:4, 21a and on BK 112b may, however, be considered as not being within the plain meaning of these texts). This view is also quoted by Isserles (to Sh. Ar., ḤM 13:2), who holds that it is generally agreed that where it is not customary for a deed of arbitration to be written, the parties may not withdraw after the commencement of their pleas. Two extreme and contradictory opinions are, firstly, that once the names of the arbitrators have been determined the parties may no longer withdraw, even if no deed has been written and the parties have not yet commenced their pleas (*Or Zaru'a*, Sanh. 3:8), and secondly, that even where there are legally competent arbitrators the parties may withdraw at any time before the proceedings have been concluded, except where the agreement to arbitrate was effected by an act of *kinyan* (Ibn Migash, quoted in *Ha-Ittur, loc. cit.*).

There is a complete consensus of opinion that where the arbitrators are empowered to adjudicate on the basis of a compromise, the parties may withdraw, provided that they had not already performed a *kinyan* or undertaken in writing to observe any such compromise, as the absence of a *kinyan* gives rise to the suspicion of a mistaken release (see *Meḥilah), or *asmakhta (Sh. Ar., ḤM 12:7 and Isserles *ad loc.*). It was customary for most arbitration deeds to be effected with the aid of a *kinyan*, apparently also because the arbitrators were generally empowered to adjudicate both on a strictly legal ruling and by way of compromise (see forms of arbitration deeds in Gulak, Oẓar, 281–6). Similarly it was customary to provide therein for payment of a fixed penalty upon withdrawal, or to deter such withdrawal by the imposition of an oath or ban (*ibid.*).

The subject matter of an arbitration may be an existing dispute between the parties, or one that is likely to arise between them as a result of a particular transaction (as, unlike in the case of real acquisition, a man may obligate himself in respect of something which is not yet in existence, or not quantified (see *Contract; *Leḥem Rav* 82, and see Warhaftig, pp. 516–7)). Similarly, in the opinion of Nissim Gerondi, the issue for arbitration may relate to matters of both civil and criminal law, e.g., "robbery (*gezelot*) and assaults" (Nov. Ran, Sanh. 23a), contrary to the view of Warhaftig, pp. 518–9, that Jewish law permits arbitration in civil cases only. The reason therefore would seem to be that at times the regular courts, required to be composed of expert and professional judges, were themselves obliged to resort to the principle of arbitration, but in practice it was customary only for civil law cases to be referred to arbitration (see e.g., S. Dubnow (ed.), *Pinkas ha-Medinah* (1925), 145, no. 609). An important detail, frequently prescribed in deeds of arbitration, was that the proceedings had to be concluded within a stated period, the arbitrators themselves sometimes being given authority to extend such period at their discretion (Gulak, Oẓar, *loc. cit*; see also above).

Decision of the Arbitral Body

As in the case of the regular court, the decision of the majority prevailed, unless they were authorized to impose a compromise, for which a unanimous decision was required (Sh. Ar., ḤM 12:18). According to talmudic *halakhah*, a party may require the regular court to submit written reasons for its judgment (Sanh. 31b and Codes), but an arbitral body is not obliged to do so, even upon request (Tos., *Yad Ramah, ibid.* and *Beit ha-Beḥirah*, Sanh. 138, *Piskei ha-Rosh*, BM 5:45, Sh. Ar., ḤM 14:4, Isserles). Sometimes however, it is considered desirable to make known the reasons for a judgment – as was held by M.M. Krochmal in the 17th century, in a suit by members of the community of Vienna against the leaders for the return of money allegedly misappropriated, so that "you shall be blameless in the eyes of God and of the people" (see his *Ẓemaḥ Ẓedek* 37).

A decision on a matter not included in the issues submitted to the arbitrators for decision, renders their decision void *pro tanto* (Resp. Rosh 85:5–6, see also Resp. Jacob Berab 27; Resp. Maharashdam, ḤM 4; *Divrei Rivot* no. 155; *Leḥem Rav* 85). A compromise imposed by the arbitrators, when they were not authorized to do so in the deed of arbitration, is also a void decision (Resp. Bera 27). Similarly, their decision is voidable in the event of improper conduct on their part, e.g., if it appears that any one of them was acting for his own benefit (Resp. Maharashdam, ḤM 4) or that they gave their decision without hearing both parties (*Leḥem Rav* 87) or that it was given after the period prescribed in the deed of arbitration had expired (Resp. Rashba vol. 3, no. 209. See also Resp. Ribash 300; Resp. Radbaz 953 (518)). The right of appeal against the arbitrator's decision is coextensive with the right of appeal against judgments of the regular courts (OPD 71ff.), but the parties may stipulate, at the time of the arbitration agreement, that they shall not appeal against or object to the arbitral decision but accept it as final (Resp. Radbaz 953; Gulak, Oẓar, 284–5, no. 306; *Takkanot Moshe Zacuto*; see Assaf, p. 78).

On the role of Arbitration during the Emancipation, see M. Elon, *Ha-Mishpat ha-Ivri* (1988), 1324–29; idem., *Jewish Law* (1994), 1582–88.

In Modern Israel

In the years 1909 to 1910 there was founded in Palestine the *Mishpat ha-Shalom ha-Ivri*, an institution designed to serve the Jewish *yishuv* as a forum for the adjudication of all disputes of a civil law nature, and thus to revive the jurisdiction of Jewish law. From the point of view of the general law of the land, this institution functioned as an arbitral body, reaching the peak of its activities in the years 1920–30. Its presiding arbitrators adjudicated mainly in accordance with general principles of justice, equity, and public order. The rabbinical courts too – whose jurisdiction from the general law viewpoint is confined to matters of personal status only – have had a certain proportion of matters of a civil law nature referred to them for adjudication when sitting in effect as arbitral bodies. This tendency has to a certain extent been intensified in recent years and decisions of this nature of the rabbinical courts carry with them an element of laying down guiding principles with reference to new problems arising in all fields of civil law.

Arbitration in the State of Israel is governed by the Arbitration Law, 5728/1968, based on the recommendations of an advisory committee in 1965. The law deals in detail (*inter alia*) with the manner of appointing arbitrators and their removal from office, their powers and the auxiliary powers of the regular courts, and with the rules of procedure in arbitrations and the manner of confirming or setting aside decisions. The provisions of a common form of agreement between the parties to submit to arbitration, appearing in a schedule to the law, is binding upon them unless they have otherwise agreed. These provisions deal with the composition of the arbitral tribunal, the manner in which it is to be conducted, and its powers vis-à-vis the parties. Several of the provisions of the above law are based on Jewish law.

[Menachem Elon]

As stated, the Arbitration Law deals with the validity of an arbitration agreement, the manner of appointing an arbitrator, the arbitration procedure, and the validity of the arbitration decision. In 1992 the Courts Law [Consolidated Version] 5744–1984 was amended, and a provision was added, establishing recourse to arbitration as an integral part of legal proceeding:

79B Arbitration

(a) A court adjudicating a civil matter may, with the consent of the litigants, submit the matter before it, wholly or partially, to arbitration; and the court is also permitted, with their consent, to define the conditions of the arbitration.

(b) The litigants will, with the approval of the court, appoint an arbitrator; should the litigants fail to agree on an arbitrator the court may appoint him from a list submitted to it by the litigants, or, in the absence of such a list, of its own choice.

The proceeding regulated by this law is an arbitration proceeding to which the litigants are referred after the beginning of the court proceeding. With the litigants' consent the court transfers the proceeding to arbitration, according to the provisions of the Arbitration Law, 5728–1968

See also *Compromise.

[Menachem Elon (2nd ed.)]

BIBLIOGRAPHY: A. Gulak, Yesodei. 4 (1922), 23–32; Gulak, Oẓar, 281–6; S. Assaf, *Battei Din…* (1924), 54–57; Z. Warhaftig, in *Mazkeret…Herzog* (1952), 507–29; G. Alon, Toledot, 1 (1954), 137ff.; idem., Mehkarim, 2 (1958), 30ff., 44ff.; ET, 11, (1965), 684–97; B. Cohen, *Jewish and Roman Law,* 2 (1966), 651–709, 796f.; M. Elon, in ILR, 2 (1967), 528ff.; 3 (1968), 421ff, 434ff. **ADD. BIBLIOGRAPHY:** M. Elon, *Ha-Mishpat ha-Ivri,* 1 (1988), 1:18–31, 574, 668ff.; 2:978, 1254; 3:1324f, 1334, 1340, 1529; idem., *Jewish Law* (1994), 1:19–29; 2:707, 825f.; 3:1182; 4:1582f., 1593–94, 1600, 1818. M. Elon and B.Lifshitz, *Mafte'aḥ ha-She'elot ve-ha-Teshuvot shel Ḥakhmei Sefarad u-Ẓefon Afrikah,* 1:25–27; B. Lifshitz and E. Shochman, *Mafte'aḥ ha-She'elot ve-ha-Teshuvot shel Ḥakhmei Ashkenaz, Ẓarefat ve-Italyah* (1997), 22–23.

°**ARBUÉS, PEDRO DE** (1441–1485), inquisitor of Saragossa. Arbués was appointed inquisitor of the archdiocese of Saragossa by *Torquemada in 1484. The establishment of an inquisitional tribunal in Saragossa aroused vigorous opposition in some aristocratic circles, connected by marriage with *Conversos. On the night of Sept. 14, 1485, Arbués was killed before the high altar in the cathedral. This act was utilized by the Inquisition for intensifying its activities, and many prominent Conversos were condemned for complicity in the crime. Arbués was venerated as a saint, and canonized in 1867.

BIBLIOGRAPHY: Baer, Spain, 2 (1966), 367–71, 376, 379; H.C. Lea, *History of the Inquisition in Spain,* 1 (1906), 244–53; M. Serrano y Sanz, *Origenes de la Dominacion Española en América* (1918), 158–70, 509–20; F. Izquierdo Trol, *San Pedro de Arbués, primer inquisidor de Aragón* (1941); Conde de Castellano, *Un complot terrorista en el siglo XV* (1927).

[Joseph Kaplan]

ARBUS, DIANE (1923–1971), U.S. photographer. The photographer of provocative and unsettling portraits was born in New York to a wealthy Jewish family. Her father, David Nemerov, the son of Russian immigrants, took over Russek's Fur Store owned by his father-in-law and turned it into Russek's of Fifth Avenue, a fashion showplace. Diane (usually pronounced Dee-Ann) was raised with her two siblings (her brother, Howard *Nemerov, was a major poet and critic) in privileged circumstances on Central Park West and Park Avenue in Manhattan. At 13 she met Allan Arbus, who worked in the advertising department of her parents' store, and they married, with her parents' grudging approval, after she turned 18. Trained as a photographer during World War II, Allan put aside his ambitions for an acting career to make a living in fashion photography. Diane became his partner, shaping and styling the shots. With Russek's as their first client, the Arbs, as they were called, got assignments for the fashion magazines *Glamour*, *Seventeen*, and *Vogue*. They worked closely as a team, and they took equal credit on their published photos. The photographic partnership broke up in 1957 when Diane, a victim of recurring depressions, opted out of the business. A year earlier, a photo of theirs was included in the massive "Family of Man" exhibition at the Museum of Modern Art.

The professional separation was followed in 1959 by a marital separation but the Arbuses remained close friends and his laboratory assistants developed her film. Diane enrolled in a course at the New School taught by Lisette Model, a documentary photographer with a flair for the grotesque and exaggerated, and Model became her devoted mentor. Encouraged by Model and her husband, Arbus began to develop her own approach, to register through her lens the "forbidden" subject matter that had always secretly attracted her. She sought out bag ladies, tattooed men and women, nudists, carnival oddities, the deformed, and the retarded. Freaks had "a terrific kind of excitement for me," she said in an oft-repeated quotation. "Most people go through life dreading they'll have a traumatic experience. Freaks were born with their trauma. They've already passed their test in life. They're aristocrats."

By the early 1960s her commercial portraits for magazines like *Esquire* and *Harper's Bazaar* began to assume a distinctive look. Her dream was to photograph everybody in the world. Her edgy, transcendental photographs of peace marches, art openings, circuses, and portraits of the billionaire H.L. Hunt, Gloria Vanderbilt's baby, and Coretta Scott King were memorable. She would spend hours with her subjects, following them to home or office, talking and listening, trying to soften them up. In 1962 she met John Szarkowski, who had replaced Edward Steichen as the curator of photography at the Museum of Modern Art. In 1967 he featured her in the groundbreaking exhibition "New Documents," with images of midgets, transvestites, and nudists, and her fame multiplied. Her depictions of suburban boredom, New Jersey twins in matching dresses and head bands, and shriveled post-celebrity have become archetypes. Photos like "Identical Twins," "A Young Man in Curlers," and, especially, her 1970 "A Jewish Giant at Home With His Parents" (8 ft. Eddie Carmel) remain signatures decades after her death.

In July 1971, after debilitating bouts of depression and hepatitis and her official divorce from Allan Arbus, art director Marvin Israel, her collaborator, critic, and lover, found her with her wrists slit, dead in the bathtub of her apartment. A year after her death the Venice Biennale exhibited ten huge blowups of her human oddities that were the sensation of the American Pavilion. Soon afterward a large retrospective opened at the Museum of Modern Art and was both damned for its voyeurism and praised for its compassion.

Her family put a tight lid on reproductions of her work and insisted on vetting all the textual material that accompanied the photographs. Consequently, very few images were reproduced over the years.

[Stewart Kampel (2nd ed.)]

ARCEL, RAY (1899–1994), U.S. boxing trainer. Arcel is considered the greatest trainer in the sport by virtue of having helped guide 20 boxers to 23 world championships from 1923 to 1982, and was called "the first gentleman of fist fighting" by sportswriter Red Smith. Arcel trained 1,500–2,000 fighters and was the first trainer inducted into the International Boxing Hall of Fame. He was born in Terre Haute, Indiana. His mother died when he was four years old and his father moved the family to New York's Lower East Side and then to East Harlem, primarily an Italian neighborhood. "You had to fight in those days," Arcel said. "We were the only Jewish family there."

After Arcel graduated from Stuyvesant High School in Manhattan in 1917, he began his boxing career as a club fighter and trained at Grupp's Gym, where he learned the trade from old-timer Dai Dollings and veteran Frank "Doc" Bagley. It was Bagley who taught Ray to be a successful "cut man," teaching him how to close the cuts of fighters during the one-minute break between rounds. After professional boxing was legalized in New York City in 1920, Arcel became one of the city's top trainers, and developed his first world champion, flyweight Frankie Genaro, in 1923. Arcel teamed up with Whitey *Bimstein in 1925 to form the most successful training tandem in boxing, a partnership that lasted nine years and handled a number of champions, including Jackie "Kid" *Berg.

Arcel was known as a tough disciplinarian, but a trainer who showed concern for his fighters like a caring father. His strictness was put to the test in 1925, when he had to make Charley Phil Rosenberg lose 37 pounds in 10 weeks to make the 118-pound weight for his bantamweight title challenge. "He hated me," said Arcel. "He used to scream at me, 'You copper!' But he made the weight and went 15 tough rounds," capturing the world bantamweight crown on March 20 by beating Eddie "Cannonball" Martin, to whom he had twice lost previously.

Arcel worked with his hero, Benny *Leonard, when he attempted a failed comeback in 1931, but was otherwise highly successful during that time. In 1934 alone, five of his fighters were world champions. Arcel's first heavyweight was James J. Braddock, whom he trained for his bout with Joe Louis. Braddock lost the fight on June 22, 1937, and became the first of 13 heavyweights Arcel trained who would fall to the Brown Bomber. It earned Arcel the nickname "The Meat Wagon" from Louis, for having to drag each of Louis' victims from the ring. Finally, on September 27, 1950, the Arcel-trained Ezzard Charles won a decision over Louis, who was attempting a comeback.

Arcel was considered a genius for concocting a fight plan and was in great demand, but he dropped out of sight after being hit on the head with a lead pipe in front of a Boston hotel in September 1953. Arcel had been arranging fights for ABC television, but the matches competed with other network television fights run by an organization reputed to have underworld ties, and it was believed the assault was to send Arcel a message.

He returned in the early 1970s and showed he had not lost anything, training Alfonso "Peppermint" Frazier to the junior welterweight championship on March 10, 1972. Arcel then began an eight-year association with Roberto Duran. Arcel trained this Panamanian to the WBA lightweight title on June 26, 1972, and the WBC welterweight championship in his first meeting with Sugar Ray Leonard on June 20, 1980. But Arcel broke with the Panamanian after the famous second bout five months later, on November 25, 1980, when Duran suddenly quit with 16 seconds left in the eighth round by uttering his infamous "*no mas!*" ("no more"). "Duran was never a quitter," Arcel said two years later. "This was one of those things that happen. Who knows what happens to a human being from one moment to the next?"

Arcel worked his last championship bout on June 11, 1982, assisting former student Eddie Futch in Larry Holmes' corner in a successful title defense against Gerry Cooney. In 1982, Ray became the first trainer inducted into *Ring Magazine*'s Boxing Hall of Fame. His world champions were Frankie Genaro (flyweight, 1923), Abe Goldstein (bantamweight, 1924), Charlie Phil Rosenberg (bantamweight, 1925), Jackie "Kid" Berg (welterweight, 1930), Lou Brouillard (middleweight, 1933), Teddy Yarosz (middleweight, 1934), Barney Ross (lightweight and junior welterweight, 1933, and welterweight, 1934), Sixto Escobar (bantamweight, 1934), Bob Olin (light-heavyweight, 1934), James J. Braddock (heavyweight, 1934), Tony Marino (bantamweight, 1936), Freddie Steele (middleweight, 1937), Ceferino Garcia (middleweight, 1939), Billy Soose (middleweight, 1941), Tony Zale (middleweight, 1946), Ezzard Charles (heavyweight, 1950), Kid Gavilan (welterweight, 1951), Alfonso "Peppermint" Frazier (junior welterweight, 1972), Roberto Duran (lightweight, 1972, and welterweight, 1980), and Larry Holmes (heavyweight, 1982).

[Elli Wohlgelernter (2nd ed.)]

ARCHA (Lat. "chest"), name given to the chest or coffer for the deposit of the records ("chirographs") of Jewish financial transactions, set up in England as a result of the regulations concerning the Jews issued in 1194. Their object was to ensure the preservation of the records of Jewish assets for the benefit of the Exchequer, in case of a recurrence of anti-Jewish outbreaks such as those of 1189–90. Loans were required to be registered before two Christians and two Jews, and the record cut down the center with a wavy line. Later tally sticks were used. Originally it was intended that there should be only six or seven centers for the purpose, but ultimately the number rose to over 20. In consequence, the Exchequer became minutely informed of the economic status of every Jew in England, and when extraordinary taxation was levied the *archae* were sent up to Westminster for inspection. The corresponding term used in Norman French was *huche*, in Hebrew *tevah*. The *Exchequer of the Jews coordinated the activities of the local *archae*. The system was reformed in 1239.

BIBLIOGRAPHY: Roth, England, index; K. Scott, in: *Cambridge Law Journal*, 10 (1948–50), 446–55; H.G. Richardson, *English Jewry under Angevin Kings* (1960), index. **ADD. BIBLIOGRAPHY:** H. Rothwell (ed.), *English Historical Documents*, 3 (1975), 305–6; J.M. Rigg, *Select Pleas...*, Selden Society, 15 (1902), index, "chirographers."

[Cecil Roth / Joe Hillaby (2nd ed.)]

ARCHAEOLOGISTS. From the beginning of modern archaeology many Jews have contributed to the work in all aspects of the field.

Classical Archaeology

Classical archaeology developed mainly in the German-speaking parts of Europe, and by the time Jews in these areas were permitted to take up official positions – the middle of the 19th century – archaeology, and especially classical archaeology, had passed its formative stages. The first Jewish names connected with archaeology are those of Heinrich *Heydemann (1842–1895), who cataloged the collections in Naples and Athens, Otto *Hirschfeld (1843–1942), and Gustav Hirschfeld (1847–1895). All three were fellows of the Institute for Archaeological Correspondence in Rome, the most important of the international organizations established early in the 19th century for the scientific study of archaeology. Otto Hirschfeld was a favorite student of the great German historian and archaeologist Theodor Mommsen, and succeeded him as professor at Berlin University. Another, younger, student, the numismatist Behrendt Pick (1860–1940), was destined to hold a Swiss professorship once held by Mommsen, at Zurich University. Two other Jews were among the leading German classical archaeologists of this generation. They were A. Furtwaengler (1853–1907), an unrivaled expert on monuments, and W. Doerpfeld (1853–1940), a master of excavation techniques. Furtwaengler's work on the evaluation of Roman copies of lost masterpieces of Greek art was carried on by W. Klein (1850–1925), professor of archaeology at the University of Prague. He was one of the first men to attempt the reconstruction of the works of Attic vase painters and to identify individual artists among them.

Jews were prominent in the so-called "Vienna School," which established an aesthetic evaluation of archaeology based exclusively on art history. The two outstanding representatives of this school were both Jews: F. Wickhoff (1853–1909) and A. Riegl (1858–1905), who were jointly responsible for introducing a historical-cultural method of interpreting changes in style in various eras and cultures.

In a class by itself between art history and the study of antiquity is the school of the German art historian Aby *Warburg (1866–1929), who founded in Hamburg the Kulturgeschichtliche Bibliothek Warburg, now located in London. This devoted itself to research on the influence of antiquity on the art, culture, and religion of later civilizations, and is probably the most important and most original Jewish contribution to the understanding of the subject. Associated with this research were F. Saxl (1890–1948), the philosopher Ernst *Cassirer, and the art historian Erwin *Panofsky. Together they created a fascinating picture of the influence of classical antiquity on the Middle Ages and the modern age, especially the early Renaissance.

At the end of the 19th and beginning of the 20th centuries there was an upsurge of archaeological activity, which began to look beyond the limits of Greece and Italy and expressed itself in excavation, collection, study, and writing. In this era there were many Jewish scholars of considerable stature who combined detailed knowledge with an understanding of the increasingly global character of their discipline. What until the outbreak of World War I in 1914 had tended to be a specifically Central European field lost its predominantly German character and became international. With the rise of Nazism and World War II, archaeological research gravitated to Western and Northern Europe and the United States, and emigration, especially of Jewish scholars, accelerated this trend. Among those who left Germany were Erwin Panofsky; K. *Lehmann (1894–1960), who went from Heidelberg to New York University; G.M. *Hanfmann, who had only just completed his studies when he went to America in 1934; Berta Segall, a specialist on ancient jewelry; and two numismatists of international renown, W. Schwabacher, who settled in Sweden, and H. Cahn, who spent several years in Switzerland but eventually returned to Germany to teach at Heidelberg University.

Very few Jews had taken part in the 19th-century development of classical archaeology in Western and Northern Europe – mainly Britain, France, and Italy – but in Britain there were two outstanding men: Sir Charles Walston (1856–1927), who taught for many years at Cambridge University and directed the American School of Archaeology in Athens, and Charles Seltman (1886–1957), who also taught at Cambridge and was best known as a numismatist. France's most prominent Jewish classical archaeologist was also a numismatist, H. Cohen (1806– 1880). Cohen, whose great work was a seven-volume manual of Roman coins of the Imperial period, became librarian of the Cabinet des Medailles in Paris. Two other great names in French archaeology are those of the *Reinach brothers, Solomon (1858–1932) and Theodore (1860–1928). Italy produced two important Jewish scholars: A. *della Seta (1879–1944), who directed the Italian School in Athens, and Doro *Levi (1898–1991), a specialist in ancient mythology and the history of religions, and one of the leading figures in contemporary classical archaeology.

Many of the prominent United States archaeologists were refugees from Nazi Europe; but there is a growing number of names to be added to the list of native-born Americans who were active in this discipline, such as Hetty *Goldman and Saul and Gladys Weinberg.

Oriental Archaeology

In the archaeology of Egypt and the Near East (i.e., Syria and Mesopotamia), Jewish scholars began to come to the fore around 1900, and often became leaders in this field. In Egyptology, distinguished names are those of Ludwig *Borchardt (1863–1938), who carried out the excavations at Tell el-Amarna and founded the German Institute of Egyptian Antiquities in Cairo, and Georg Steindorff (1861–1951), who for 40 years was the highly respected professor of Egyptology at the University of Leipzig, until the advent of the Nazis sent him to the United States to continue his work there. Two other leading German-Jewish figures in this sphere were W. Spiegelberg (1870–1930), an authority on demotic papyri; and Elise Jenny *Baumgartel (1892–1975), whose work on Egyptian prehistory came to full flower in England and the U.S.A. The most prominent Jewish scholar in the wide field of non-Egyptian archaeology of the Near East was Henri *Frankfurt (1897–1954), who concerned himself with the entire region – Mesopotamia, Anatolia, and Iran. Ernst *Herzfeld (1879–1948) worked in similar areas. As far as Mesopotamian studies are concerned, Samuel Noah *Kramer (1897–1990), an American of Russian origin, although strictly speaking a philologist, has his place in the context of archaeology because of his indispensable interpretations of Sumerian cuneiform texts. Prominent among the excavators of Mesopotamia was Pinchas Pierre *Delougaz (1901–1975), of the University of Chicago. A British Jew connected with the archaeology of this area, with a special interest in the Nimrud ivories, was Richard David *Barnett (1909–1986), keeper of the Western Asiatic antiquities at the British Museum from 1955 to 1974. Barnett was also the founder of the London-based Anglo-Israel Archaeological Society in 1961. Other distinguished Jewish scholars have been the American, Cyrus H. Gordon (1908–2001), who made an important contribution to the interpretation of Canaanite-Ugaritic mythology and religion, and Max Freiherr von Oppenheim (1860–1946), who excavated Tel Halaf. Stefan Przeworski (1900–1940), who lectured on Anatolian archaeology at the University of Warsaw, was shot by the Nazis. A French Jew, R. *Ghirschman, became one of the most industrious excavators in Iran after World War II.

One of the most unusual figures in the entire history of archaeology was Sir Aurel *Stein (1862–1943), the British scholar whose remarkable explorations in Central Asia were pioneering achievements of enormous scientific value.

Ereẓ Israel

The archaeology of Ereẓ Israel up to the 1920s was conducted mostly by non-Jews, although Jewish biblical scholars were making studies of the antiquities of the country already in the 19th century. Jewish archaeological activity, however, developed systematically with the establishment of the Department of Antiquities of Palestine in 1920 and with the founding of the Hebrew University in 1925. L.A. *Mayer (1895–1959) and M. *Avi-Yonah (1904–1974) worked in the Department of Antiquities for many years. A number of excavations by Jewish archaeologists were initiated very early on, notably the work by N. Slouschz (1871–1966) in Tiberias and in the Kidron Valley in Jerusalem in 1924. The Jewish Palestine Exploration Society (now the Israel Exploration Society) began its work at that time. Significant advances were made in furthering prehistoric research in the country by Moshe *Stekelis (1898–1967). Excavations were carried out in 1936–40 at *Bet She'arim by Benjamin *Mazar (Maisler) (1905–1995) and by Naḥman *Avigad (1905–1992) at the Kidron Valley in Jerusalem. Foremost among the earlier Palestinian Jewish archaeologists was E.L. *Sukenik (1889–1953), who worked on many sites of various periods including *Samaria, Hammath Gader, and the site of the Third Wall of Jerusalem. Sukenik became an expert on Jewish burial caves and synagogues, excavating among other places the *Bet Alpha synagogue. He was also the first person responsible for bringing to light the significance of the *Dead Sea Scrolls when they were discovered by Bedouins in 1947. One should also note that Nelson *Glueck (1900–1971) was one of the leading Jewish American archaeologists working in Israel and its vicinity. His survey of Transjordan (1933–46) was a significant enterprise, and he also carried out major surveys and excavations in the Negev Desert, with research on the *Nabatean civilization, and near Aqaba at Tell el Kheleifeh (which he identified as Ezion-Geber).

Following the founding of the State of Israel in 1948 many Jewish archaeologists began working in the field and because of the popularity of archaeology in Israel this meant many more younger men and women than before. The Israel Department of Antiquities and Museums was established in July 1948 and Shmuel Yeivin became its first director, with numerous archaeologists conducting salvage work in different parts of the country; later directors were Avraham Biran and Avraham Eitan. In addition to the existing Department (later Institute) of Archaeology at the Hebrew University, new departments of archaeology were established at Tel Aviv University and later at Ben-Gurion University in Beersheba and at the University of Haifa. The Israel Exploration Society began supporting archaeological projects in the country, under the supervision of Joseph Aviram, particularly during the 1960s and 1970s. Among the prominent Israeli archaeologists of the 1950s to 1970s were Yigael *Yadin (1917–1984), son of E.L. Sukenik, who excavated many sites including *Hazor and *Masada; Michael Avi-Yonah, who conducted work at Ḥusifa, Beth Shean, Nahariyyah, Bet Yeraḥ, and Caesarea; Yohanan *Aharoni (1919–1976) excavating at *Arad and *Beersheba; Moshe Dothan (1919–1999) digging at *Ashdod and Akko; Avraham Biran working at *Dan; and Ya'akov Kaplan (1910–1989) at *Jaffa and in the Tel Aviv area. Among the prominent women archaeologists who have been working in the field, one must count Ruth *Amiran with her work at Arad, Trude Dothan at Deir el-Balah and Miqne (Ekron), Claire Epstein (1911–2000) on Chalcolithic sites in the Golan, and Miriam Tadmor. Numerous excavations were conducted in Jerusalem during the 1970s and 1980s by Benjamin Mazar, Nahman Avigad, Magen Broshi, and Yigal Shiloh. Younger archaeologists of note working on archaeological sites in Israel during the 1980s and 1990s, and some of them up to the present day, include Ram Gophna, Avraham Negev, Moshe Kochavi, Aharon Kempinski, David Ussishkin, Gideon Foerster, Gabriel Barkay, Eliezer Oren, Yoram Tsafrir, Amnon Ben-Tor, Amichai Mazar, Ehud Netzer, Ephraim Stern, Dan Barag, Israel Roll, Adam Zertal, Arthur Segal, and Israel Finkelstein. The development of prehistoric research in the country has been identified with Ofer Bar Yosef, Avraham Ronen, Tamar Noy, Nigel Goring-Morris, Naama Goren, and Anna Belfer-Cohen. Underwater archaeology has developed under Elisha Linder, Avner Raban, and Ehud Galili. With the establishment of the Israel Antiquities Authority in 1989, replacing the Israel Department of Antiquities, a new generation of archaeologists has been working in different parts of the country, mainly on salvage and emergency operations, notably Amos Kloner, Ronny Reich, Eliot Braun, Vassilios Tzaferis, Zvika Gal, Emanuel Eisenberg, Yosef Porath, Gabi Mazor, Gideon Avni, and others.

ADD. BIBLIOGRAPHY: Y. Ben-Arieh, "Non-Jewish Institutions and the Research of Palestine during the Mandate Period," in: *Cathedra*, 92 (1999), 13–172; 93 (1999), 111–42; S. Gibson, "British Archaeological Institutions in Mandatory Palestine, 1917–1948," in: *Palestine Exploration Quarterly*, 131 (1999), pp. 115–43; R Reich, "The Israel Antiquities Authority," in: *Biblical Archaeology Today*, 1990 (1993), 27–30.

[Penuel P. Kahane / Shimon Gibson (2nd ed.)]

ARCHAEOLOGY. The term archaeology is derived from the Greek words *archaios* ("ancient") and *logos* ("knowledge, discourse") and was already used in ancient Greek literature in reference to "the study of ancient times." In its modern sense it has come to mean the scientific recovery and systematic study of the material remains of ancient human cultures of prehistoric and historic date. Prehistory refers to that part of human existence that preceded the development of writing. To understand what happened in prehistoric periods, the archaeologist is obliged to rely much more on the interpretation of physical remains such as flint tools and cultic objects, habitations and burials, the assessment of the chronological sequencing of remains at sites, while also using an array of scientific techniques to gather information about climatic and environmental changes occurring in the past. Archaeologists dealing with the historic periods, however, are able to rely on a greater variety of artifacts and architectural remains, on the one hand, and on the discovery of written materials (notably inscriptions on durable materials, such as stone or clay tablets, and on ceramic *ostraka*, and to a lesser extent on organic materials, such as scrolls and papyri made of leather skins and parchment) on the other. The study of ancient writing is known as epigraphy, while the study of the development of individual written letter forms is known as paleography (see *Alphabet). The archaeological discipline incorporates within it numerous specialist fields of study, notably the investigation of ceramics (the study of *pottery forms and manufacturing techniques over time), *numismatics (the study of coins), archaeozoology (the study of animal and fish bones), and archaeobotany (the study of plant remains, pollen, and phytoliths). Archaeological data recovered during excavations are often supplemented with information derived from ancient literary sources (such as theological, narrative, or historical writings). Archaeology has an important role in illuminating the cultures of certain peoples referred to for example in the Bible, such as the Hyksos and Philistines (who were not at all boorish as one might think). This is also true of neighboring civilizations such as those of the Egyptians, Sumerians, and Hittites – without archaeology our understanding of these cultures would be very limited. Numerous "historical truths" based on literary sources have had to be re-assessed in the light of irrefutable archaeological finds, for instance the Israelite "conquest" of the Promised Land as recounted in the Bible (see below). Archaeology has much to contribute to the contextual clarification of the later classical and medieval periods as well, and a wealth of data now exists in textbooks and scientific publications. The cut-off period for archaeological investigations in Israel used to be the late medieval period (c. 1750), but recent decades have seen an interest in late Ottoman remains as well and archaeological work has even been conducted on features dating from as late as World War II.

Methods and Approaches

The modern archaeologist uses a variety of methods in gathering information about the ancient past, but surveys (surface explorations) and excavations (methodical digging operations) are two primary methods of recovering data.

In the mid-19th century a shift occurred in terms of the methods used by scholars for understanding the history of the Syria-Palestine region and for the elucidation of biblical writings in particular. Prior to this the field of biblical interpretation was dominated by the writings provided by Jewish travelers and Christian pilgrims, in which uneven accounts of their observations of antiquities in the southern Levant were provided. Much of this information was collated while traveling the country along predetermined routes, under the supervision of local guides, and with the purpose of visiting sites that were primarily of biblical interest. The culmination of all this was the detailed work made by Robinson and Van de Velde, among others. E. Robinson, in particular, crisscrossed the country in 1838 and 1852 and his work ultimately led to the development of the systematic study of place names (topynoms) which was crucial for the identification of places mentioned in the Bible. However, the first systematic overall mapping of the country, with a regional investigation of monuments and sites possessing visible architectural remains from different periods, began with the work of the *Palestine Exploration Fund and undoubtedly one of its greatest achievements was the "Survey of Western Palestine" of the early 1870s. The SWP provided for the first time detailed topographical maps of the country to a scale of one inch to the mile, as well as a number of volumes of memoirs in which were described the sites and landscapes they encountered. The SWP maps have since

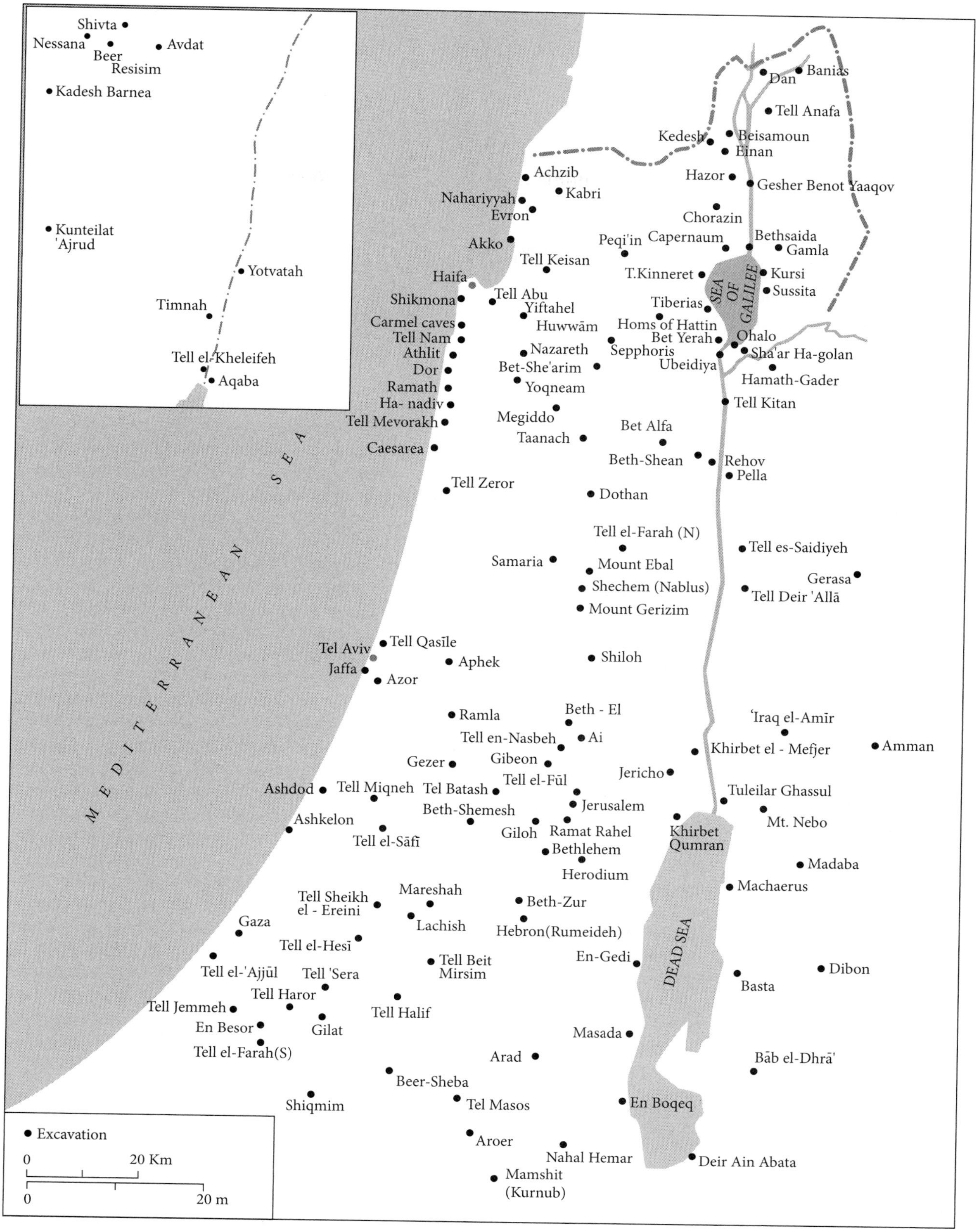
Shivta
Nessana
Beer Resisim
Avdat
Kadesh Barnea
Kunteilat 'Ajrud
Yotvatah
Timnah
Tell el-Kheleifeh
Aqaba
Dan
Banias
Tell Anafa
Kedesh
Beisamoun
Einan
Hazor
Gesher Benot Yaaqov
Achzib
Kabri
Nahariyyah
Evron
Chorazin
Akko
Peqi'in
Capernaum
Bethsaida
Gamla
Tell Keisan
T.Kinneret
Kursi
Sussita
SEA OF GALILEE
Haifa
Shikmona
Tell Abu Yiftahel
Tiberias
Carmel caves
Huwwām
Homs of Hattin
Tell Nam
Bet Yerah
Ohalo
Athlit
Nazareth
Sepphoris
Sha'ar Ha-golan
Dor
Bet-She'arim
Ubeidiya
Ramath Ha- nadiv
Yoqneam
Hamath-Gader
Tell Kitan
Tell Mevorakh
Megiddo
Bet Alfa
Taanach
Caesarea
Beth-Shean
Rehov
Pella
Tell Zeror
Dothan
Tell el-Farah (N)
Tell es-Saidiyeh
Samaria
Mount Ebal
Gerasa
Shechem (Nablus)
Tell Deir 'Allā
Mount Gerizim
MEDITERRANEAN SEA
Tel Aviv
Tell Qasīle
Jaffa
Aphek
Shiloh
Azor
Ramla
Beth - El
'Iraq el-Amīr
Tell en-Nasbeh
Ai
Khirbet el - Mefjer
Amman
Gezer
Gibeon
Jericho
Ashdod
Tell Miqneh
Tel Batash
Tell el-Fūl
Tuleilar Ghassul
Jerusalem
Beth-Shemesh
Mt. Nebo
Ashkelon
Giloh
Ramat Rahel
Khirbet Qumran
Tell el-Sāfī
Bethlehem
Herodium
Madaba
Tell Sheikh el - Ereini
Mareshah
Machaerus
Beth-Zur
Gaza
Lachish
Hebron(Rumeideh)
Tell el-Hesī
DEAD SEA
En-Gedi
Tell Beit Mirsim
Dibon
Tell el-'Ajjūl
Tell 'Sera
Basta
Tell Haror
Tell Jemmeh
Tell Halif
En Besor
Gilat
Masada
Tell el-Farah(S)
Arad
Bāb el-Dhrā'
Beer-Sheba
Shiqmim
Tel Masos
En Boqeq
Aroer
Nahal Hemar
Deir Ain Abata
Mamshit (Kurnub)
Excavation
0
20 Km
0
20 m

Archaeological sites in Ereẓ Israel. (See inset for area south of Dead Sea.)

become an indispensable tool for all new archaeological surveys, even though the information provided was incomplete and by modern archaeological standards defective (e.g., artificial city mounds – tells – were not regarded by the explorers as sites of any archaeological significance). Subsequently, the Survey of Eastern Palestine was made in 1881–82 and then discontinued, the Arabah Survey in 1883–84, surveys east of the Jordan by G. Schumacher in 1885–86, and the Wilderness of Zin survey under T.E. *Lawrence and L. Woolley in 1913–14. An important survey of ancient synagogues in Galilee was undertaken in 1905–7 by H. Kohl, E. Sellin and C. Watzinger, and their book is still a basic textbook for the plans of ancient synagogues in the Holy Land.

Until World War II, surveys conducted in Palestine were fairly basic in terms of the field methodologies and the means of dating that were employed. A "Schedule of Historical Maps and Sites" was prepared and updated by the Palestine Department of Antiquities at regular intervals from the 1920s. A new Archaeological Survey of Palestine was initiated in 1937, but very little progress was made. In July 1964 the Society for the Archaeological Survey of Israel was founded. Surveys were henceforth made within 10 × 10 kilometer maps, with the recording of archaeological remains by making measured plans of architectural remains, photography, and the collection and identification of surface artifacts (notably potsherds, flints, and coins). Since the 1980s Regional Archaeological Surveys have been conducted in various parts of Israel, with excavated tell sites placed within the context of the pattern of archaeological sites known in their specific regions. Site Catchment Analysis or Site Territory Analysis has been particularly useful for the study of the morphological environments of prehistoric sites, particularly in desert areas, and in recent years Landscape Archaeology has come to the fore especially in regard to the investigation of historical landscapes with rural and industrial remains. Historic Mediterranean type landscapes in the southern Levant tend to be regarded by archaeologists as places characterized by an assemblage of features pertaining to a variety of extramural human activities, such as agricultural pursuits (terraces and field systems) and industrial work (stone quarrying and lime and charcoal burning), all of which, of course, necessitated the establishment of a system of communications (roads and paths) so as to form links between farms and villages, and towns and markets. An in-depth study of such remains during a project of Landscape Archaeology can lead to a chronological and contextual understanding of ancient communities and how they adapted themselves to the specific environments they inhabited. The underlying assumption behind this kind of approach, however, is that communities will interact with each other and with the ecology of their environments, in a sensible, harmonious, and stable fashion. Some landscape features, however, reflect their adaptation as a physical means of advancing ideologies and strengthening power struggles and territorial conflicts.

Excavation ("dirt archaeology") is the principal method used by archaeologists in the search for information about ancient cultures. W.F. *Albright once wrote that "excavation is both art and science" and M. Wheeler wrote that "there is no correct method of excavation, but many wrong ones." Numerous factors contribute to the choice of a site for excavation in the Land of Israel, including its historical importance (and biblical identification), chance finds of significance, the impressiveness or accessibility of a site, and observations made during earlier archaeological investigations. The choice of a site chosen for excavation also depends on the budget that the archaeologist and the sponsoring university can raise. The procedure of excavations requires a systematic removal of accumulated earth and debris covering ancient architectural remains, whether belonging to the site of a tell (i.e., a superficial mound created by the accumulation of superimposed layers of ruined ancient towns of different periods) or at the site of a one-period settlement (i.e., a place that was founded on natural land and after a time came to be destroyed or abandoned and never rebuilt). Various techniques of excavation exist and the choice of the techniques employed depends largely on the characteristics of the site being excavated. The first action that is taken in preparation for an excavation at a tell is to lay out a grid-system with iron rods set in cement along a north-south axis across the mound. These rods are used as the baseline for setting out a grid of 5 × 5 meter squares across the area chosen for excavation. By digging squares of 4 × 4 m within the larger grid the excavator is able to leave balks (unexcavated earthen walls) in place as the excavation deepens. Once the first occupation level has been encountered, the balks need to be recorded and taken down so that the general area of excavation will be sufficiently large enough to capture the outlines of more or less complete buildings, otherwise the archaeologist will be left with a series of fragmentary walls scattered within a grid of squares. However, key balks are left at appropriate locations to record the overall stratigraphy of the area under excavation. To ensure that this is properly organized the archaeologist appoints an area supervisor in each field of excavations, and they in turn take charge of monitoring the square supervisors.

The excavating archaeologist is obliged to keep detailed written records of the daily findings, accompanied by photographic dossiers and surveyed architectural maps and drawings, and lists of objects found. The dig director is assisted by a qualified staff: archaeological area supervisors to supervise work in the various fields of excavations, a surveyor and architect, a finds curator/registrar, and an administrator to take care of the tools and budgetary matters. The success of a project often depends on the stamina of an archaeologist in dealing with logistics and organization, and with his/her ability to successfully communicate with people, whether with staff or locals. The archaeological work will include the careful analysis of the strata of a site made on the basis of constant stratigraphical observations of fills of soil and debris, using balks to record the gradual progress of the digging operations, looking at the structural relationships between various phases of building construction, examining foundation-and-robbers' trenches, and looking at post-depositional materials as well. The most difficult problem posed by excavating is that of correctly distinguishing the superimposed layers from the different occupation levels and this inevitably requires a certain amount of interpretation. Features that may be encountered include the lower portions of stone walls, mud-brick walls, robbed-out walls ("ghost walls"), wall foundation trenches, beaten earth or plaster floors, flagstones, silos, pits, hearths and *tabun* (bread oven) installations, and so forth. The fills between the structural remains of the occupation levels may consist of accumulated rubbish, ashes and burnt material, the contents of sunken pits, roof collapse, wall collapse, wind-deposited fills, water-deposited fills, and so forth. Each one of these contexts is ultimately given a locus number to facilitate recording procedures. All changes in soil color, the appearance of walls, installations and other features, are recorded in written and graphic form in the daily field diary with elevations above sea level taken from a fixed benchmark. Hence the professionalism of the field archaeologist is crucial in recognizing all the stratigraphical variables in the field, as well as training inexperienced students, monitoring the work of the surveyor, and keeping a vigilant eye on the volunteers or paid workers digging at the site. At tell sites stone structures or mud-brick buildings are encountered and these two types of materials require different excavation procedures. Having a general idea of the date of the remains to be excavated before the work is commenced may be useful in securing the correctly trained staff ahead of time as well as the appropriate equipment. A site with large fallen blocks of stone will require special lifting equipment that would not at all be useful on a site with mud-brick architecture which will require a lot of trowel-work instead. Sieving of the excavated soils (especially on floors or in pits) is necessary for retrieving small objects such as scarabs, coins, gems, and so forth, as well as very small rodent or fish bones. Soil samples are kept from floor surfaces for flotation in water (for hard and light fraction retrieval) and carbonized wood or seed samples are kept for radiocarbon determinations (short-life materials are preferable; care has also to be taken not to contaminate the sampled materials).

A daily exchange of ideas on matters concerning the interpretation of the stratigraphy at the site between the dig director, site supervisors, and square supervisors is highly recommended while the excavations are in progress, all of which should be recorded as deliberations in available notebooks. Potsherds (and other finds) are collected in numbered buckets with labels identifying the loci they came from and these are recorded in the field diary. The pottery is subsequently washed and sorted. Dipping of sherds is undertaken at sites when *ostraka* (inscribed potsherds) begin appearing. The sorting of the potsherds and small finds in the excavation is an activity undertaken by the finds curator in conjunction with the entire staff on a daily basis. Volunteers or students help with the registering of finds. It is imperative for the success of the expedition that the site supervisors and square supervisors know exactly the date of the pottery coming from their areas. On-the-spot instruction on pottery retrieval may be provided by the finds curator, especially in regard to the excavation of floors where it is suspected that there are crushed vessels that might eventually be mended by a pottery conservator. A draftsperson will prepare drawings of the diagnostic pottery profiles, usually to a scale of 2:5, and these are appended to the finds cards with written descriptions (decorations, slips, glazes, grit inclusions, etc.) and Munsell color readings.

In terms of digging techniques, the 19th century has to be regarded as a time of treasure hunting, to say the least, with Lady Hester Stanhope, for example, digging haphazard holes in the ground at Caesarea in order to extract Roman statues. Although the first tells were excavated in the 1860s by the explorer Charles Warren (at Jericho and Tell el-Ful), this was done without the realization that they in fact contained the ruins of ancient cities. Many explorers at that time excavated in the form of mining shafts, shored up with wooden struts, but this method was not at all conducive to the scientific gathering of data. The first methodological excavation of a tell was made in 1890 by Flinders-*Petrie, the "father of modern Near Eastern archaeology," at Tell el-Hesi in the southern Shephelah, and it was there that he first recognized that by studying the changing forms of ancient pottery vessels and their associated levels, one is able to trace the development of a city and its changing cultures through time. The need for planning and method on a dig was later made clear by Flinders-Petrie in his book, *Methods and Aims in Archaeology* (1904). A trained staff to accompany the chief archaeologist in the field was first employed by Reisner during his work at Samaria in 1908. The wide-scale excavation of tells was subsequently undertaken during the first half of the 20th century by many foreign expeditions, with an attempt to get down to those levels with biblical associations as quickly as possible. This rapid "stripping" of the superimposed city remains at tells – with the exposure of defense walls, gates, temples, administrative buildings, stores, and domestic dwellings – provided enormous amounts of hitherto unknown scientific data, but it also sometimes resulted in great harm to sites (e.g., at Gezer, which was excavated on a wide scale by R.A.S. Macalister with unskilled labor and without a trained backup staff).

During the course of the 20th century scientific techniques of excavations improved considerably, with sensitive area-excavations of a more limited and solid scientific nature being conducted at tells, with careful stratigraphical and architectural observations being made, and with refined material studies of ceramic and environmental remains being initiated. This was the peak of "Biblical Archaeology" and the general public in Israel at that time was fascinated by the discoveries at tells, such as at Hazor, Lachish, and Beersheba. There was also excitement about discoveries relating to sites of Jewish interest from later periods such as at Masada, and in the 1970s in Jerusalem with the excavations close to the Temple Mount and in the Jewish Quarter. Recent decades have seen the development of a much more scientific discipline, with the flourishing of procedures such as radiocarbon and thorium-uranium methods of dating, and with the development of many different areas of specialization amongst archaeologists, not only in terms of the periods studied but also in terms of the interest in specific groups of artifacts (e.g., weapons, stamped seals, beads, glass objects, and so forth). Many smaller one-period sites, such as villages and farms, were also subsequently excavated as part of new project strategies. In the late 1980s and early 1990s there was a boom of archaeological endeavors in Israel, with large-scale excavation projects being undertaken at Beth Shean, Caesarea, and elsewhere. With the growth of scientific specialization and with the clear distancing of the discipline from that of biblical studies since the 1990s and into the 2000s, archaeology, unfortunately, no longer holds the same interest for the general public that it once had. Indeed, archaeology is sometimes perceived as a hindrance to modern development in this Western-oriented country which has limited territorial resources and a growing population possessing higher aspirations for better housing and roads. Conflict has also arisen as a result of objections made by representatives of the religious ultra-Orthodox Jewish community to the scientific excavation of human remains, even when these are under threat of destruction as a result of modern development.

The preparation of a new site for excavation requires the thorough study of the morphology of the site and the mapping of existing remains and surface features, using GPS and other topographical surveying techniques. Having checked on surveys and excavations that might previously have been undertaken at the site in the existing literature, the next step is to check on the site records in archives, such as those at the Palestine Exploration Fund in London, the Israel Antiquities Authority in Jerusalem, and the foreign schools in Jerusalem. Surveys of sites on 10 × 10 km maps have been conducted since 1961 by archaeologists working for the Archaeological Survey of Israel (now the Survey Division of the Israel Antiquities Authority) and information about a site might be available there. Valuable information might also be obtained from geomorphological and geological maps, topocadastral maps, and aerial photographs. The latter are useful when deciding on the location of areas to be opened up on a mound site, with telltale features that might help pinpoint the location of fortification walls, gateways, the internal layout of the final settlement at the site (particularly from the Hellenistic period, or later). Some aerial photographs date back to World War I and may be important if the area around a tell has been substantially developed since then. Modern aerial photographs are useful in monitoring the progress of the dig from season to season. Once the background research has been done and the site has been selected and surveyed, the next stage is to secure the budget for the excavation and a license from the Israel Antiquities Authority. A budget for an excavation may be raised from grant-giving archaeological institutions worldwide or from private sponsors. To obtain the license the director of a potential dig needs to have a recognized academic qualification in archaeology, a pledge of sponsorship from an academic institution (preferably one's own affiliated university), and proof that one has the back-up staff and budget ready to undertake the excavation successfully. The budget has to cover not only the costs of the excavation itself, but also the costs of the conservation of the archaeological remains exposed (e.g., crumbling mosaic floors) and the costs of the post-excavation work (namely, pottery conservation, cleaning of coins, drawing of pottery, anthropological and zoological examination of bones, the identification of plant remains, radiocarbon determinations and other scientific tests).

The preparation of the final archaeological report on the results of an excavation involves much work and time, but ultimately it is the most important part of the exercise. Without it an excavation will not benefit general archaeological research. An excavation may have been carried out with the best available standards but if it remains unpublished then it is close to useless. Thousands of excavations have been carried out in the Land of Israel since the beginning of the 20th century and the sad fact is that only a small percentage of these have actually been *fully* published. Hence, archaeologists nowadays set up classification and recording frameworks while the excavation is still in progress, to ensure a more rapid funneling of material towards publication later on. At a very early stage the various specialists dealing with scientific materials derived from the excavations, among them anthropologists, archaeozoologists, archaeobotanists, metal experts, and petrography experts, are called in to examine materials derived from the excavations. Archaeological experts on pottery, lamps, and coins are also called in, unless of course they are already part of the expedition. To facilitate their research the specialists and experts are provided with the maximum available information on the chronological/stratigraphical significance of the findspots of the materials they will be studying. Much of the preliminary archaeological work for the report consists of sorting through copious field notes and vast amounts of data that accumulated during the course of the excavation: notes on stratigraphy and architecture, notes on chronological considerations, parallels for pottery assemblages that have been drawn and analyzed, specialist lists of identified coins and small finds, identification lists of animal bones, shells, and so forth. In addition, the archaeologist keeps in mind the layout of the report and its structure when planning the necessary illustrative materials (line drawings and photographs). The final report ordinarily begins with a history of previous researches undertaken at the site, followed by a chapter on the environment of the site and its setting, a short summary chapter of the research aims of the new expedition and the methods employed, and, thereafter, the actual report itself with a detailed description of the remains uncovered and all the stratigraphical and architectural considerations. The report on the pottery from the site tends to be one of the most important expert chapters and this because pottery is extremely ubiquitous and ultimately serves as an important dating tool. Specialist reports, appendices, and tables/lists close the excavation report. The best reports are those that are written clearly and simply, with the avoidance of long-winded and complex descriptions. Technical information is placed in tables and kept out of the main text. Archaeologists try to make use of as many illustrations as possible, based on the maxim that a picture, however bad, will always be better than a written account. The drawn pottery is arranged in a sequence of plates, presented chronologically, and according to vessel type, which are depicted in succession from small vessels, such as plates and bowls, to large storage jars and *pithoi*. Some excavators believe (incorrectly) that the final publication of a report should be deferred until such a time that they have undertaken a comprehensive study of all the comparative material available, even if this means waiting for comparative material to come to light from excavations elsewhere. F. Cumont put it quite succinctly in 1926, on the eve of his rapid publication of the amazing *Dura Europas excavations, that he preferred to expose himself to critics "rather than to resemble the dragon in the fable jealously guarding a sterile treasure in its lair."

History of Archaeological Research in Israel

Interest in the antiquities of the southern Levant (present-day Syria, Lebanon, Israel, Jordan, and Palestine) began as early as ancient times. All ancient peoples living in this region would have seen the monuments and ruins that were antecedent to their time and would have shown curiosity in their antiquity. The Jewish historian *Josephus Flavius already remarked in his writings on the evident antiquity of certain monuments and attempted to ascribe to them dates, for example in describing the fortification wall surrounding the Upper City of Jerusalem (the "First Wall") he suggested that it dated back to the time of David and the Israelite kings. While scholars once thought this was nonsense and that the wall was from no earlier than the time of the Hasmoneans (late second century B.C.E.), the subsequent archaeological excavation of portions of this wall in the 1970s revealed that earlier parts of it had indeed been built at the time of the Divided Israelite Monarchy, i.e., in the eighth century B.C.E. Hence, Josephus had got it partly right. One of the earliest descriptions of an excavation in Jerusalem, albeit in a story that may be partly legendary in character, is the one which refers to Helena, mother of Constantine the Great, digging in the early fourth century C.E. in a cistern close to the spot of the crucifixion of Jesus and finding there wooden remnants which she believed were from the holy cross itself. Throughout Late Antiquity the country was visited by numerous Jewish and Christian pilgrims and many of them left written records of their observations regarding the antiquities they came across during their travels. Numerous travelogues and itineraries of pilgrims who came to the Holy Land are extant from the time of the Crusaders onwards, and in the 17th and 18th centuries the pertinent materials were summed up by Quaresmius and Reland, and in the 19th century by T. Tobler and C. Ritter. Some of the important antiquarians of the region in the 19th century were E. *Robinson, V. *Guérin, C. *Schick, G. *Schumacher, among others.

Proper methodical archaeological work in the region began with the work of the Palestine Exploration Fund from the 1860s onwards. Charles *Wilson conducted a survey of Jerusalem and its monuments in 1864–65, and this was followed by excavations in the city by Charles *Warren until the early 1870s with work being conducted especially around the edges of the Temple Mount. The earliest dig at a tell took place by Warren at two places in the 1860s, but the earliest scientific work at a tell was made by Flinders-Petrie at Tell el-Hesi in 1890, followed by the work of his assistant Frederic J. Bliss, who conducted additional work at Tell el-Hesi, as well as work in mining shafts on the slopes of Mount Zion in Jerusalem (together with A.C. Dickie). Together with R.A.S. *Macalister, Bliss also made open area excavation on four tells in the Philistia part of the Shephelah (the western foothills) between 1898 and 1900, and this because the Ottoman Law of Antiquities of that time permitted the granting of an excavation license not just for a single site but for an area of land of about four miles square and all the sites contained therein. The four sites were Tell es-Safi (Gath), Tell Zakariyeh (Azekah), Tell ej-Judeideh (Moresheth Gath), and Tell Sandahanna (Maresha). Most of the work was actually conducted at the latter site, which the excavators correctly identified as biblical Maresha and Hellenistic Marissa. Bliss wanted to expose the acropolis area of the site, layer by layer, but this proved impracticable and only the uppermost Late Hellenistic layer of the city was exposed. Having completed their work at these sites, they covered up their excavation areas in order to return them to the landowners as was required by Turkish law. This was followed by large-scale excavations at the beginning of the 20th century at *Gezer and *Samaria. At Gezer Macalister employed what he thought was a better system of excavations known as the "strip method" in which an area is excavated strip by strip, the rubble from succeeding strips being dumped into the previous ones. Although economical, this did not offer a satisfactory picture of the overall history of the site and much of Macalister's work at Gezer still remains difficult to understand. Excavations were conducted at this time by a number of German and Austrian biblical scholars and architects, at Tell *Taanach by E. Sellin (1902–4), *Megiddo by G. Schumacher (1903–5), and *Shechem by E. Sellin and C. Watzinger (1907–9), but the results were poor owing to the excavators' lack of training and skills in mound excavation. The excavations made at Samaria in 1908 and 1910–11, by D.G. Lyon, C.S. Fisher, and G.A. Reisner, were very important in terms of the careful excavation techniques and recording procedures that were employed there. Many objects from these early excavations – including the important *Siloam Inscription – ended up in the Ottoman Imperial Museum in Constantinople (Istanbul).

With the establishing of the British Mandate over Palestine in 1920 archaeological excavations became much more systematic and scientific. This was the first "golden age" for archaeology in Palestine, between 1920 and 1940. All excavations were regulated by licenses issued in accordance with the new Antiquities Ordinance, prepared by J. *Garstang for the Palestine Department of Antiquities. The Department of Antiquities employed a number of Jewish scholars, notably L.A. *Mayer and M. *Avi-Yonah. In a meeting held in Jerusalem in 1922 the leading archaeologists of that time – J. Garstang, W.J.T. Phythian-Adams, H. Vincent, and W.F. Albright – agreed upon a common classification system of chronological terms in line with systems used elsewhere in Old World Archaeology. A museum of antiquities was also founded in Jerusalem at Way House (later the collection was transferred to the Rockefeller Museum). Important excavations were undertaken by American archaeologists at Megiddo, Beth Shean, Tell el-Ful, and Tell Beit Mirsim, and later by a joint expedition under the direction of J.W. *Crowfoot at Samaria and by Flinders-Petrie and others at Tell el-Farah (south) and at Tell el-Ajjul, and by J.L. Starkey at *Lachish and Garstang at *Jericho. A dominant personality during this period was W.F. Albright. His excavations at Tell el-Ful (1922–23, 1933) and at Tell Beit Mirsim (1926–36) laid the groundwork for the proper study of Iron Age pottery. Studies and excavations were also made at this time on the Nabatean and Byzantine/Early Islamic settlements in the Negev Desert by H. Dunscombe Colt, with the discovery of the now-famous Nessana Papyri. Additional work of importance on later Crusader and medieval remains was made by C.N. Johns. Scholars and archaeologists of the Hebrew University, notably B. Maisler (*Mazar), E.L. *Sukenik, and L.A. Mayer, conducted excavations on remains that were pertinent to the study of the Jewish past, such as the excavation of the Third Wall of Jerusalem dating from the first century C.E., Jewish tombs around Jerusalem and at Beth Shearim, and the remains of synagogues (e.g., at Beth Alpha and at Hammath Gader). Much of this work on Jewish sites was sponsored by the Jewish Palestine Exploration Society (now the Israel Exploration Society) which was founded already in 1914. The climax of archaeological work in Palestine was in the early 1930s – thereafter the outbreak of political disorders in the country disrupted work and slowed down archaeological enterprises. The murder of the archaeologist J.L. Starkey on his way from the excavations at Lachish to the inauguration of the Palestine Archaeological Museum (now the Rockefeller Museum), was a blow to the archaeological community of that time. Jewish archaeologists, notably E.L. Sukenik, played an important part in the recovery and study of the *Dead Sea Scrolls.

With the establishment of the State of Israel in 1948, Jewish archaeologists were cut off from the Palestine Archaeological Museum and the archives of the Department of Antiquities. In July of that year the Israel Department of Antiquities was established, with Shemuel *Yeivin as its first director, and its first archaeological activities were connected with sites under danger as a result of the new building developments in the country. Excavations conducted during these early years included work at Tell Qasile, Jaffa, and Beth Yerah. Large-scale excavations were subsequently conducted by Y. *Yadin at *Hazor during the 1950s and in 1968, and many Israeli archaeologists received their first fieldwork training at this important site. This was the second "golden age" of biblical archaeology in the country. The 1960s saw important excavations at *Arad and *Ashdod, the Judean Desert Caves survey (1961–62), which brought to light important finds from the time of Bar Kokhba, and the expedition to *Masada. Numerous excavations were conducted at tell sites throughout the country during the 1970s and 1980s, from Dan (A. Biran) in the north to Beersheba (Y. *Aharoni) in the south. Following the war in 1967, excavations on a large scale were conducted in various parts of the Old City in Jerusalem: at the foot of the Temple Mount by B. Mazar, in the Jewish Quarter by N. *Avigad, and on Mount Zion by M. Broshi. An emergency survey of the occupied territories (the West Bank and the Golan Heights) was conducted by teams of Israeli archaeologists, and scores of hitherto unknown sites were discovered, including the sites of ancient synagogues.

Israel has five active archaeology departments in Israeli universities: the Institute of Archaeology at the Hebrew University, the Institute of Archaeology at Tel Aviv University, Ben-Gurion University in Beersheba, the Archaeology and Land of Israel Studies at Bar-Ilan University, and the Department of Maritime Civilizations and the Center of Maritime Studies at Haifa University. Numerous archaeological sites have been excavated by the teachers and graduates of these universities from the 1980s to the present day, some projects in cooperation with foreign institutions. Many of the important key sites are described in the five-volume *New Encyclopedia of Archaeological Excavations in the Holy Land*. An Archaeological Congress jointly arranged by the various institutions is held once a year to allow archaeologists to discuss recent discoveries and new approaches. Good relations are maintained between Israeli archaeologists and local foreign archaeological institutions, notably the German Protestant Institute of Archaeology, the Studium Biblicum Franciscanum, the Ecole Biblique et Archéologique Francaise de Jérusalem, the Kenyon Institute (formerly the British School of Archaeology in Jerusalem), and the American W.F. Albright Institute of Archaeological Research. The latter institution, in particular, has always been regarded as a meeting ground for fellows with scholars from Israel, Palestine, and abroad. The early 2000s has seen the independent development of Palestinian archaeological activities within the territories (West Bank and Gaza), with the establishment of a Palestine Department of Antiquities, and with archaeological courses being provided at the universities of Bir Zeit and al-Quds. The focus of Palestinian investigations to date has been on tell archaeology, the investigation of indigenous landscapes, medieval Islamic remains, and cultural heritage.

In 1989 the Israel Department of Antiquities and Museums became the Israel Antiquities Authority under the directorship of Amir Drori, and numerous salvage excavations were conducted throughout the country, as well as larger prestigious projects such as those at Beth Shean and Caesarea, and smaller projects such as those at *Beth Shemesh and *Modi'in. The Antiquities Law of the State of Israel was originally based upon the Antiquities Ordinance of the British Mandate period, with substantial revisions made in 1960, 1978, and 1989. The Israel Antiquities Authority is the official governmental regulatory power for all archaeological activities conducted in Israel: inspecting existing archaeological sites and ensuring their protection, fighting illegal diggings and regulating the trade in antiquities, and issuing licenses for archaeological excavation projects. Many objects from archaeological excavations are exhibited at the Rockefeller Museum (from excavations that predate 1967 because of the status quo), at the Israel Museum in Jerusalem (where many new finds are first exhibited), and at the Eretz Israel Museum in Tel Aviv (particularly the finds from the local site of Tell Qasile). Smaller local museums are scattered throughout the country. The results of excavations and surveys conducted by the various local institutions are frequently published in English and in Hebrew in Israeli scientific journals (such as *Ḥadashot Arkheologiyot, Israel Exploration Journal, Tel Aviv*, etc.) and in popular publications (e.g., *Qadmoniot* and *Ariel*), as well as in local non-Israeli publications (such as the Franciscan *Liber Annuus*) and abroad (*Bulletin of the American Schools of Oriental Research, Palestine Exploration Quarterly*, and *Bulletin of the Anglo-Israel Archaeological Society*, etc.) and in popular magazines (e.g., *Near Eastern Archaeology* and *Biblical Archaeology Review*). Numerous scientific monographs are published in Israel by the respective archaeological departments of the universities and by the Israel Antiquities Authority, as well as by the Israel Exploration Society.

The future of the archaeological discipline in academic circles in Israel looks like it is set to develop along the lines of an elaborate refining of scientific techniques, with project strategies that will entail a greater amount of multidisciplinary work with scientists in related fields than has hitherto been seen. This will undoubtedly improve the contextual understanding of sites and their formation, of dating systems and other approaches to the reconstruction of ancient human and environmental manifestations. The study of regionalism within ancient cultures will be another improvement since there is now a realization that typological classifications of material remains, such as ceramic vessels, are better understood on a regional rather than on a countrywide level. The production of costly scientific monographs will likely be dispensed with and replaced by electronic publication formats. The casualty of this scientific upgrading of the profession is that local lay persons in Israel with a passion for *yedi'at ha-areẓ* (lit. "knowledge of the land") will eventually find themselves slowly dissociated from the subject. On the other hand, the discipline would also seem to be heading towards the establishing of a better system of Contract Archaeology with procedures that will be run on a purely business basis and with financial rather than overt scientific goals. Already academic institutions in Israel are running field units that bid one against the other for tenders to conduct salvage archaeological work at sites being threatened by modern development. At the present time, the Israel Antiquities Authority is the official governmental regulatory power for archaeological work done in Israel – it too bids for tenders to conduct salvage excavations, thus creating a certain amount of conflict of interest.

Archaeology and the Origins of Israel

One has to admit that archaeology has not been very helpful in shedding light on the origins of the Israelites (whose ancestry is traced back to Jacob: Gen 32:32; 49:16, 28; Ex 1:9). Gottwald once pointed out that "origins do not tell us everything, but I believe that in seeking them, we will know more." It has been claimed that the appearance of the name "Israel" on the famous Stele of Merneptah would suggest that there was already an "Israelite" entity in the central hill country well before any "conquest" by Joshua ben Nun. This stele commemorating Merneptah's Syro-Palestine campaign, from 1208 B.C.E., refers to Israel with the determinative indicating a people rather than a land or place: "Israel is laid waste and his seed is not." In the 1950s and 1960s, particularly under the influence of the American scholar W.F. Albright, there was a firm belief that archaeology had much to contribute to the historical understanding of the Patriarchal, Exodus, and Conquest narratives and the Monarchical period (United and Divided). Since then there has been a lot of debate amongst scholars on the subject of the emergence of the people of Israel, where they came from and how they came to settle in the land of Canaan, but no consensus of opinion has yet been reached. There is general agreement, however, that a substantial shift in settlement patterns occurred in the highlands of Palestine (Judah and Ephraim) during the Iron Age I (circa 1200 to the 11th century B.C.E.) in comparison to the preceding Late Bronze Age, with the construction of many small settlements in areas that were not previously inhabited. But the ethnic identity of these new highlanders and their place of origin are still not clear. It is plausible that some of them were Israelites, or, at least, some later *became* Israelites. The new settlements were unfortified, with dwellings in a scattered or grouped layout, and with well-planned storage facilities (silos and very large *pithoi* for water storage). This would suggest that the inhabitants of these Early Iron Age settlements came from an agricultural rather than a nomadic background, but this is not conclusive. The suggestion that these "Israelite" settlements were inhabited by farmers that withdrew from less marginal agricultural lands in the "Canaanite" lowlands, to the west, or from inland valleys, seems reasonable but it does not answer all the questions. In support of the theory of indigenous development, there is evidence for some general continuity in the material culture from the Late Bronze Age to the Early Iron Age. The suggestion that the settlements were inhabited by people from a nomadic background who rapidly became sedentarized by adopting a new agricultural way of life is another possibility but one which is difficult to prove.

The alternative solution is that there was a much more complex symbiosis of Early Iron Age peoples in the highlands, more so than scholars have previously been willing to admit. These "proto-Israelites" may have come from diverse backgrounds, both agricultural and nomadic, from great distances or from regions in Palestine close by. They probably brought with them traditions connected to the Aramean god "El," on the one hand, and to the nomadic god "YHWH," on the other, and these may very well have brought the groups into religious and ideological conflict, but not necessarily to the extent where struggles led to the destruction of settlements. The gelling together of these diverse peoples within rather harsh and restrictive highland environments may have forced the rapid abandonment of earlier lifestyles and the adoption of a fairly simple way of life based on subsistence agriculture. Such a scenario is admittedly difficult to prove archaeologically, but it is a reasonable assumption that the highland cultures of the Early Iron Age were much more variegated than their material artifacts would suggest them to be. What is clear is that the Israelite national entity of the tenth century B.C.E. eventually emerged in precisely the same areas that were formerly occupied by the diverse "proto-Israelites" of the 12th and 11th centuries B.C.E. Archaeology has been able to show strong evidence of the emergence of Israelite statehood in the northern part of the country at the time of the Omride Dynasty, and eventually in the Assyrian period, from no earlier than the eighth century B.C.E., one can trace the emergence of Judah and the consolidation of Jerusalem as an important central city.

Nowadays a dichotomy between the Bible and archaeology no longer exists. Throughout the 1990s and early 2000s serious debates broke out between biblical historians and archaeologists, of both religious and secular backgrounds, regarding the historicity of the Bible. Indeed, Biblical Archaeology, that was so fashionable in the 1950s to 1980s, has few adherents today amongst working academics, and some would even describe themselves simply as the practitioners of a "scientific" archaeology instead, as if any discipline can truly be conducted in a dispassionate and unbiased fashion. Some scholars, notably the so-called "Copenhagen School," regard the Bible as a source of legendary material that has very little antiquity to it (i.e., dating from a time no earlier than the Persian or early Hellenistic periods, fifth to third centuries B.C.E.) and that a true history of ancient Israel cannot be recovered at all. From their perspective, David and Solomon were legendary figures, there were no Patriarchs, the Exodus never took place, and there was no Conquest of Canaan. These revisionists, however, cannot ignore the following evidence that attests to the strength of the biblical traditions: (1) the Neo-Assyrian inscriptions of the ninth to seventh centuries B.C.E. mentioning Israelite and Judaean kings, notably the Black Obelisk showing the Assyrian ruler Shalmaneser III with the Israelite King Jehu bowing down in front of him; (2) the Siloam Tunnel inscription of the eighth century B.C.E. referring to the creation of the water system of Jerusalem under the Judaean King Hezekiah (recent thorium-uranium procedures on the plaster of the tunnel has confirmed the dating of the inscription independently); (3) the Tell Dan stele of the ninth century B.C.E. that refers to the dynasty of the "House of David"; and (4) the Tell Miqne royal dedicatory inscription dating from the second quarter of the seventh century B.C.E., which refers to two kings of Ekron who are also attested in the Neo-Assyrian annals. Ikausu, the builder of the temple at Miqne, is also known from the Assyrian records. In addition to the inscriptional evidence, the student of the Bible must also take into account the undeniable fact of collective memory, with traditions and complete books being transmitted orally from generation to generation. Moreover, in linguistic terms, Classical Hebrew of the First Temple period as it appears in some of the historical books is very different from the Hebrew of the later Persian and Hellenistic periods (e.g., the books of Daniel, Ezra, and others), and this has been confirmed by the recent discovery of written artifacts, notably the text of the Priestly Benediction on a sixth-century B.C.E. silver scroll found at Ketef Hinnom in Jerusalem. Scholars adopting the Julius *Wellhausen approach in the past regarded the books of the Old Testament as a complex fabric of source materials that were written down at different times and by different hands during the First Temple period and also later, and that this process came to an end when the final revisions and canonization eventually took place. However, the extent and date of the historical "kernels" existing within these various sources and how they should be linked to archaeological finds is still very much debated by mainstream scholars.

The Archaeological Periods

Determining an exact chronological terminology for the ancient cultural remains uncovered in the land of Israel has always been a matter of great importance and debate, ever since the days of the explorations of the "Survey of Western Palestine" in the 1870s and up to the present day. The early explorers described the remains they encountered in very general terms, as "rude" (i.e., prehistoric); "Semitic" (Bronze Age); "Jewish" (Iron Age); "Greek" (Hellenistic); "Roman"; "Christian" (Byzantine); "Crusading" (Medieval); and "modern" (Ottoman). Many chronological systems were proposed or adopted by archaeologists at the beginning of the 20th century, but it was only at a meeting held in Jerusalem in 1922 that the leading archaeologists of the time – J. Garstang, W.J.T. Phythian-Adams, H. Vincent, and W.F. Albright – agreed upon a common classification system of chronological terms in line with the Three Age System used in Old World Archaeology. This system is more or less the same as the one used by archaeologists today. However, many of the periods have subdivisions and substages (e.g., EB I A = Early Bronze I stage A), or are sometimes labeled with the names of peoples such as "Canaanite" and "Israelite" (instead of Bronze Age or Iron Age), and in some cases the same period of time may confusingly appear in the archaeological literature under different names (e.g., Middle Bronze I is now called the Early Bronze Age IV or alternatively the Intermediate Bronze Age; or for the later periods the term Herodian is sometimes used interchangeably with Early Roman). In prehistory there has been a tendency to replace the rigid time-line chronological division with a more flexible framework based on the names of identified cultures or names of localities. Although archaeologists dealing with proto-historic and historic periods still adhere to the prevailing chronological system, the realization that cultures in different parts of a country will produce pottery and other objects possessing distinctive traits all of their own is leading researchers more towards a regional appreciation of the chronology of cultures. Much of the relative chronology of the Bronze and Iron Ages is synchronized with the better-established chronologies of Egypt and Mesopotamia. Small objects such as carved and inscribed seals can be useful for dating, but the "heirloom" factor can sometimes be a problem, i.e., objects that are "kept in the family" well beyond the time they represent. With the appearance of coins in Persian times archaeological materials may be better fixed in time, but problems still remain with some coins having a much longer life span than the cultural material in which they are found (e.g., caches of fourth century coins were still being deposited in the fifth century, and Umayyad coins were still the main currency used in the early Abbasid period).

A description of the principal archaeological periods and the main finds is provided below under the following chronological headings: Prehistoric Periods (Palaeolithic to Neolithic); Chalcolithic; Early Bronze Age; Middle Bronze Age; Late Bronze Age; Iron Age and Persian; Hellenistic; Roman; Byzantine; Islamic to Ottoman. Different dating schemes are provided by the relevant authorities and for this the reader is referred to existing publications for comparison purposes (see bibliography below). The following abbreviations have been used: B.P. = Before Present; B.C.E. = Before Common Era; C.E. = Common Era.

PREHISTORIC PERIODS (PALAEOLITHIC TO NEOLITHIC). The earliest human-made artifacts found in the Syria-Palestine region consist of objects made largely from flint and attributed to the Lower Acheulean stage of the Lower Palaeolithic, marking the point in time when the proto-human *Homo erectus* began moving into the region from Africa about 1.4 to 1.0 million years B.P. (= Before Present). Exciting work has been undertaken at Ubeidiya, a key site for understanding the period, which is situated within one segment of the central Afro-Asian rift, in the present-day northern Jordan Valley, with the discovery of large quantities of finds embedded within the local lacustrine and fluvial deposits, some in almost vertical layers owing to the quite substantial natural folding and faulting of the land. Research indicates that the site was originally on the shore adjacent to a sweet-water lake, and an abundance of bones was uncovered in the excavations of mammals, reptiles, fish, and birds. The local hominids survived by hunting and scavenging for meat, notably hippopotamus, deer, and horse. The site yielded scatters of flint core choppers and polyhedrons made from local pebbles, as well as limestone spheroids, and a smaller percentage of handaxes made from basalt, limestone, and flint. Other sites of note belonging to the later Middle or Upper Acheulean of the Lower Palaeolithic period and also reflecting scavenging or hunting activities include the Evron Quarry site in western Galilee where imported flint objects and animal bones were uncovered, and the Gesher Benot Ya'akov site next to the Jordan River which revealed scatters of basalt implements, small fragments of human bones, and numerous bones of large mammals such as elephant, hippopotamus, rhinoceros, and others. The latter site probably dates to around 750,000 years B.P. Upper Acheulean flint tools are also known from Ma'ayan Barukh and Holon as well as further south at Umm Qatafa (Layers E1 and E2), and close to Jerusalem at Baqa and in the Rephaim Valley (mainly handaxes and flakes). The northern and central part of Palestine was characterized in the Upper Acheulean by the Acheulo-Yabrudian lithic industry and is known especially at a number of cave sites, dating to circa 500,000/400,000 to 270,000/250,000 B.P. Fragmentary human remains – a fragment of a *Homo sapiens* skull and a femur – were found at the cave of Zuttiyeh and the cave of Tabun.

The Middle Palaeolithic is characterized by the hunter-and-gatherer Mousterians, who appear to have maintained their scavenging activities as well. Judging by the type of tools they made, the Mousterians were making more refined cutting tools for butchering meat and sawing bones (blades and flakes) and processing animal skins (borers and scrapers). They were also adept in woodworking and hafting flint tools, such as the typical Levallois points to serve as spears for the purpose of hunting medium-sized animals (such as gazelle and fallow deer) that replaced the larger mammals typical of the Lower Palaeolithic. The Tabun cave provided important stratified deposits allowing for the differentiation between the types of Mousterian tool kits: Tabun D dated to 270,000–170,000 B.P.; Tabun C to 170,000 to 90,000/85,000 B.P.; and Tabun B to 90,000/85,000 to 48,000 B.P. Human remains were discovered in the caves of Tabun and Kebara, caves in the Amud Valley, and at Daura in Syria, and represent either a local population of Mediterranean Neanderthals or perhaps a population of Southeast European Neanderthals migrating into the Levant. Skeletal remains of the archaic *Homo sapiens* were found at the Skhul and Qafzeh sites, but whether or not they interacted with the Neanderthals is unclear.

The Upper Palaeolithic coincides with the first half of the Upper Pleistocene, beginning around 43,000 B.P. and ending in about 20,000–18,000 B.P. The period has been subdivided into a number of phases based on various cultures with particular types of flint tools. The Emiran tradition was apparently a transitional Middle to Upper Palaeolithic phase and it had a tool kit characterized by a special type of point, known as the Emireh point, in addition to end-scrapers and blades. This phase is equivalent to Phase A at the Lebanese site of Ksar 'Akil and Boker Taḥtit in the Negev. The locally developed Upper Palaeolithic cultures include the hunter-gatherer-derived Ahmarian tradition, found in the central parts of the Levant and in the Negev and Sinai deserts, as well as in southern Jordan, and typified by its blade industry. The Levantine-Aurignacian tradition, known only from the northern and central Levant, has new types of flint tools, notably the el-Wad points, with the first systematic use of microliths, and a bone industry. During the depreciation of the water level of the Sea of Galilee a site was uncovered (Ohalo II) consisting of the foundations of a settlement of round huts, with flint assemblages *in situ*, with well-preserved plants and animal and fish bones. It is during the subsequent Kebaran that microliths began to predominate and evolve. Human remains are known from Qafzeh, Ksar 'Akil, Naḥal En Gev I (a semi-flexed burial of a woman), Neveh David (Mt. Carmel), and at Kharraneh in Jordan. The country was forested and was particularly suited for game (elk, deer, and boar) which was the object of the hunters. Numerous pounding and grinding stones indicate the processing and consumption of various nuts, grain, and seeds. Hunter-gatherers were also roaming the woodland areas of the central highlands as recent archaeological finds have shown, but their settlements were so temporary and small (estimated at no larger than 150 square meters) that traces have been hard to detect.

Climatic change at the end of the Pleistocene resulted in the emergence circa 12,800 B.C.E. of a sedentary culture known as the Natufian. Natufian sites include 'Ain Mallaha-Eynan, Naḥal Oren Terrace, Hayonim cave, Jericho, el-Wad, and Hatula. Settlement took place in caves or within built complexes of houses, usually curvilinear, with sunken earthen and plastered floors and wall foundations of undressed stones or unbaked bricks. The superstructures of the walls of the dwellings were apparently made of wood, reeds, and other organic materials; postholes found in one large house at Eynan provided evidence regarding roof supports. Houses contained hearths and grinding vessels. Flint tools included sickle blades, borers, and burins, as well as the distinctive production of small bladelets which were used as blanks for tools. The quantity of grinding vessels and sickles from the sites was regarded by some scholars as an indication that the Natufians not only gathered wild cereals but were also proto-farmers. However, convincing evidence for this has not been forthcoming from the plant remains gathered at the sites. Moreover, the grinding stones may have had numerous domestic functions and the sheen visible on sickle blades is easily obtainable from the cutting of wild grasses. Artistic representations include carved heads on sickle hafts, animal and human figurines cut schematically in limestone, and incised geometric designs (such as meanders and zigzags) on everyday objects. Burials were frequently encountered in pits beneath the floors of houses or in adjacent areas, either as single internments (flexed or stretched out) or as collective burials with numerous skulls and bones gathered together. Life expectancy for Natufians was no more than 35 years. Burial goods included necklaces and bracelets and other body decorations that were usually made of shells, notably *Dentalium*, with pendants of stone and bone. In Eynan the discovery that a dog was buried with its presumed owner provides an interesting insight in regard to domestication at that time. The final phase of the Late Natufian uncovered in the more recent excavations at Eynan, with structures, living surfaces, and hearths, may represent the hitherto elusive transition to that of the Pre-Pottery Neolithic A period. Contemporary with the Late Natufian, the Harifian culture emerged in the Negev and Sinai in the southern Levant, with scattered settlement in the lowland areas utilized during the winter months and with additional sites used in the highlands in the summer months. Excavations have brought to light the foundations of huts, with a largely microlithic tool kit dominated by lunates and the Harif point. Grinding stones and stones with cupholes were found in the huts and their vicinity. The occupants were hunters and their prey included gazelle, ibex, and hare.

The subsequent Neolithic has been divided into a pre-pottery period (Early Neolithic, 8500/8300 to 6000/5800 B.C.E.) incorporating the PPNA and PPNB stages, and also at some sites a final PPNC stage (ending around 5500 B.C.E.), and a succeeding pottery period (Late Neolithic, 6000/5800 to 4000 B.C.E.) incorporating the PNA and PNB stages. The Early Neolithic period saw a gradual transformation in the Levant of "Sultanian" communities of hunters (practicing some farming) into "Tahunian" farmers (with the herding of animals) and the eventual emergence of more consolidated permanent villages. PPNA sites were once only known from sites in the Jordan Valley and in the Carmel Hills (notably at Naḥal Oren), but recent work has revealed sites in the western foothills of Palestine (Hatula near Emmaus; Modi'in) and elsewhere at desert sites. Significant remains from the PPNA were uncovered at Jericho (Tell es-Sultan) with the earliest levels possessing "Khiamian" lithic assemblages, defined mainly by el-Khiam type arrowheads and the lower frequencies of microliths, and the later Sultanian assemblages having polished celts of basalt and limestone, flint adzes/axes with single cutting edges and plain sickle blades. An important discovery at Jericho was that of a massive round tower (8.5 m high) with an internal staircase, and an adjacent wall segment fronted by a ditch (3.5 m wide) cut into bedrock. Most scholars believe these architectural features served for defensive purposes (i.e., fortifications) to provide protection for the settlement of curvilinear houses built of plano-convex mud bricks on stone foundations, which had a population estimated at 450 individuals. Others (notably Bar-Yosef) suggest that the wall was used as a barrier to prevent the flooding of the village and that the round tower was the lower part of a mud-brick shrine (no longer extant). At Nahal Oren two PPNA levels were uncovered (IV–III) and the developed settlement consisted of 20 curvilinear structures built on four terraces, with hearths, grinding stones, and cuphole slabs. Important sites in the Jordan Valley include Gilgal and Netiv ha-Gedud, and further afield, close to the Euphrates in Syria, the sites of Mureybet and Abu Hureyra. Various art objects are known made in bone and stone representing animals and humans.

Numerous hamlets or villages from the PPNB period have been excavated: Jericho, Naḥal Oren, Munhata, Kefar ha-Ḥoresh, and Yiftahel (Area C) in Israel, Beidha, Ain Ghazal and Basta in Jordan, and Tell Ramad in Syria. Curvilinear houses were now replaced by rectilinear houses, multi-roomed, with walls of mud brick on stone foundations (as at

Jericho) or completely built of undressed stones (as at Naḥal Oren and at the terraced site of Basta). Floors and interior walls of structures were frequently plastered; a small installation for the burning of lime was uncovered at Ain Ghazal and slag has been found at other sites (e.g., under the PN levels of Yiftahel). Plastered walls were found at Jericho decorated with floral decoration, and at Basta decorated with a representation of twigs and berries. Burials of prone or flexed adults and children (frequently headless) were found beneath floors. The PPNB is characterized by a wealth of clay and plaster statuettes representing humans and animals, as well as numerous plaster-molded human skulls of men, women, and children, with features emphasized with paint and shells, masks and small figurines. Two caches of human statuettes and busts made out of lime-based plaster, molded on lashed reed bundles, were recovered from Ain Ghazal and are dated to 6750/6500 B.C.E. The faces of these statuettes were painted and other features may represent body paint, clothing, or tattooing; polydactyly was evident in a six-fingered toed foot and hand. Such favissae were definitely connected with ritual practices and the statues were originally intended to be displayed in the round. Sixty-one plastered or decorated skulls and crania are known from Syria and the Levant, from the sites of Tell Ramad, Jericho, Beisamoun, Naḥal Hemar (modeled in bitumen), Ain Ghazal and Kefar ha-Ḥoresh. It has been suggested that the human statuettes and plastered skulls represent stylized representations of ancestors, but recent research on the skulls does not support claims that age, sex, or skull shape were domineering factors in the choice of skulls for special treatment. The PPNB lithic industry resembles that of the PPNA except for the fact that heated flint was now used. Blades from naviform (i.e., boat-shaped) cores were used for making arrowheads (the Helwan and Jericho points, and later the Byblos and Amuq points), sickle blades (plain or slightly serrated), and other tools. Bifacial tools are also known. In addition, obsidian (volcanic glass) for making very sharp tools was brought in from eastern Anatolia and indicates the importance of the exchange of commodities at that time. Greenstone was used for making pendants and marine shells were gathered from the Mediterranean and Red Sea. This period also has the earliest attempts at animal domestication and the first systematic cultivation of cereals and legumes (with the earliest known fava beans and lentils at Yiftahel), side by side with the continued practice of hunting and the raising of sheep and goats. The onset of a dry climatic period at the end of the PPNB apparently led to the abandonment of many settlements. At Ain Ghazal the site actually continued expanding in the PPNC (circa 6000 to 5500 B.C.E.) with some changes, such as smaller structures appearing with permanent storage facilities, and sub-floor burials of complete skeletons (breaking the earlier tradition of the headless burials). The PPNC stage has also been noted at the site of Basta in Jordan and at Yiftahel in Israel with the discovery of rectilinear pier houses. Crude attempts at making pottery (sun-dried or low-fired) was found at Ain Ghazal and Basta, and examples of vessels made of White Ware ("vaisselles blanches") are known particularly from the northern Levant.

The succeeding late Neolithic pottery period (6000/5800 to 4000 B.C.E.), incorporating the PNA (typified by "Yarmukian" and Jericho IX) and PNB (typified by Wadi Rabbah) stages, marks a major change with the establishment of new settlements and with a greater sedentary way of life. The early part of this period was once described as characterized by ephemeral settlements of circular sunken huts without solid architecture and rounded pits, based on the results of excavations at Jericho, Sha'ar ha-Golan, Munhata, Tel Aviv sites (e.g., Ha-Bashan Street) and so forth, and that the population was semi-nomadic and pastoral. Recent excavations, however, have shown this to be a misconception and based on faulty data and that there were in fact large and flourishing sedentary villages during this period. Three monumental and solid-built architectural complexes, with rectilinear plans, with courtyards and alleyways, indicating village planning, were uncovered in the 1990s at Sha'ar ha-Golan. Handmade fired pottery – jars, cooking pots, bowls – characterizes the material culture assemblages of this period and the vessels are frequently decorated with red-painted and incised geometric designs (such as chevron and herringbone patterns). The invention of pottery is believed to have taken place first in the northern Levant, together with the plaster-based White Ware, and slowly it began appearing in Palestine as well. At Yiftahel (Stratum III) the White Ware and the early pottery was visually indistinguishable, and some distinctions could only be made by petrographic analysis. Numerous types of female figurines are known made of stone and clay, perhaps representing the Mother Goddess and fertility, as well as incised drawings and symbols on carefully selected river pebbles. The Yarmukian seated female figurines are particularly distinctive; 350 were found at Sha'ar ha-Golan alone. A possible shrine was uncovered at Bikat Uvda, with large animals drawn with stones on the desert floor in its vicinity. Pressure flaking and polishing are two new features of the lithic technology of this period. The lithic tool-kit includes sickle blades, arrowheads in a variety of shapes, and axes/adzes, as well as the normal points, scrapers, and burins. Subsistence was based on cultivation practices, with cereals and legumes, and animal herding (sheep and goats, with pigs and cattle raised in some communities). Groups of hunters and pastoral nomads continued living in the desert fringes.

CHALCOLITHIC. The peak of village development in the southern Levant, with a more permanent agricultural existence and a dependence on livestock and crops, occurred during the Chalcolithic period (4000–3300 B.C.E.). The period is regarded as a complex and stratified society, with clear evidence for trade and craft specialization, maritime pursuits, and the exploitation of marginal environments. Some scholars suggest that the social organization of these communities was in the form of "chiefdoms." This period attests to the widespread use of copper, hence the name of the period (*khalkos* =

copper and *lithos* = stone). Copper extraction was made at the Timna Valley in the southern Arabah, and in Wadi Feinan in southern Jordan. Trade activities were highly developed at this time with raw materials and probable "invisible" products (e.g., textiles) obtained from great distances from all over the Near East. Connections with Egypt were particularly strong with objects of Egyptian provenance appearing at Chalcolithic sites. Important agricultural developments also emerge with evidence for horticultural pursuits and the intensive use of the digging hoe. Specialized olive oil production took place in highland regions, notably in the Golan and in the Palestine highlands. Olive oil plants have been identified at Neballat, Givat Oranim, and at Modi'in consisting of groups of crushing cup-marks and pressing basins. The key site from this period is Tuleilat el-Ghassul situated to the northeast of the Dead Sea with remains of villages extending back to the Late Neolithic perhaps suggesting cultural continuity between the two periods. Important sites in the Negev include Bir es-Safadi, Abu Matar, Naḥal Gerar, Gilat, Shikmim, and Abu Hof. Of the many sites in the Golan, the most important to have been excavated so far is at Rasm Harbush. Settlement in the coastal plain is still hardly understood, though important tombs have been uncovered at Ḥaderah. Smaller villages are known in the highland regions, notably at Sataf west of Jerusalem, with greater quantities of temporary sites or caves in the Judean Desert. Different forms of settlement are known in the southern Levant: permanent villages of houses with stone-built or mud-brick walls, villages with underground loess-cut caves beneath the houses, encampments used by nomadic pastoralists on a seasonal basis, and caves used as temporary dwellings or storage. Houses are usually of broad-room plan, with pits in the floors and various installations, and with large adjoining enclosed courtyards. Parallel lines of structures built on a chain pattern are known from the Golan. Settlements were situated next to springs of water (e.g., Jerusalem) or had wells cut down to groundwater (e.g., Abu Hof). A number of shrines are known, notably the En-Gedi temple, which was close to nearby springs, which may have had a "holy tree" in the external courtyard. The cultic objects from this temple may very well have been hidden in the nearby Naḥal Mishmar cave. This cave produced an amazing cache of 442 different objects made of copper, hematite, stone, and ivory (of hippopotamus and elephant). Another shrine was uncovered at Gilat in the northwestern Negev, with the discovery of an array of cultic objects including a ceramic vessel modeled in the shape of a seated naked woman holding a churn on her head, and another of a ram carrying three cornets on its back. Wall paintings depicting cultic scenes were found at Tuleilat el-Ghassul. Numerous cave burials are known (e.g., Ḥaderah), but the most spectacular find was at Peki'in with numerous types of highly decorated ossuaries and jars for the secondary burial of human bones, as well as "violin" figurines and copper objects. Pottery from the final phases of the Chalcolithic period are extremely diverse and distinctive, especially the churns, cornets, and "v-shaped" bowls which were frequently decorated with bands of red paint, and large storage vessels (*pithoi*). Fine basalt bowls, some on a fenestrated base, are also distinctive of the period, as well as basalt house idols from the Golan. Flint-working continues with a tool-kit of axes/adzes, scrapers, blades, and others. Copper artifacts abound and attest to the artistic and technological expertise of the period, with some objects made in the lost-wax (*cire-perdue*) method. Organic remains have also been preserved, with textiles, mats, and straw artifacts found in caves in the Judean Desert. The reason for the disappearance of the Chalcolithic culture at the end of the fourth millennium B.C.E. remains a mystery, though some have suggested climatic reasons.

EARLY BRONZE AGE. The Bronze Age in the southern Levant is divided into three parts: Early, Middle, and Late, extending from around 3300 B.C.E. to 1200 B.C.E. The Early Bronze Age is itself divided into three parts (EB I to III) with various sub-phases.

The villages of the Chalcolithic were abandoned and replaced by villages of the EB I but these were situated at new locations. The distinctive architecture of the earlier phase of the EB I is represented by dwellings that in plan are curvilinear, oval, or oblong with rounded ends. Originally it was thought the typical dwelling plan of this period was apsidal, largely based on the evidence unearthed at Meser, but this is no longer accepted by scholars. Good examples of early villages of this kind have been unearthed at En Shadud, Tell Teo, and Yiftahel which has the foundations of at least 22 dwellings. Caves used as habitations and temporary settlements with pits have been uncovered at other locations, particularly in the south of the country. Later in the EB I many more villages were founded and these became considerably larger (about 50 acres). This stage also saw the shift to using rectilinear architecture, sometimes with rooms built with slightly rounded corners. An example of a site from this stage was found at Palmaḥim Quarry. Some fortifications from this period may have existed at Jericho and at Tell Shalem. The EB I ceramic material is quite austere compared to the previous Chalcolithic, with an assemblage of plain pottery vessels, with smaller quantities of the highly polished Grey-Burnished ("Esdraelon") ware, some carinated with protrusions along the edges, and jars decorated with the grain-wash or band-slip technique. Later geometric painted wares are also known. Simple seal-impressions have been found on the shoulders of a few ceramic jars, and stone or bone seals are also known. Ground-stone artifacts continued to be made out of basalt, but these differ considerably in technique and design from earlier examples. Small quantities of copper objects, notable adzes or chisels, have been found at sites from this period, some originating from the Feinan mines in southern Jordan. However, the discovery of a workshop for copper working at Ashkelon-Afridar on the coast indicates that metal working was undertaken not just close to the copper sources but throughout the country. Flint tools of ad hoc types continued to be made, with the appearance of the ubiquitous "Canaanean" blade. The social organization of these early communities is uncertain, but some stratification must have emerged between farmers and traders at least in regard to matters of leadership and cooperation. Agricultural activities included new cultivation practices, the introduction of the light plow, the organization of fields and terracing (e.g., at Sataf), herding of animals, and a small amount of specialized hunting. Olive oil and wine surpluses were important commodities used for trade, together with smaller amounts of bitumen and salt from the Dead Sea. Excavations at Ashkelon-Afridar indicate that imported Lebanese cedar was being transported to coastal sites probably by sea, perhaps en route to Egypt. Strong trade networks were set up with parallel traders in Egypt, with their Egyptian representatives living side by side with the local population at sites in southern Palestine. Egyptian-type architecture is known from En Besor (the "residency") and from Tell 'Erani. Stylized renderings of an Egyptian royal symbol (the *serekh*) were also found incised into local wares at Ḥorvat Illin Taḥtit and at Palmaḥim Quarry, corresponding to the proto-historic Dynasty "O" time period in Egypt.

Proper urbanism is characteristic of the second stage of the Early Bronze II (3100–2700 B.C.E.) with the emergence of full-fledged towns with fortifications and city gates, distinct built-up areas set aside for housing, industrial, and mercantile activities, administrative buildings/palaces, temples, and public water systems. The reasons for the development of urbanism at this point in time in the southern Levant are unclear. However, towns are much larger and denser than the previous settlements of the EB I and they appear to have had much more control over their hinterland. The overall number of EB II settlements in the landscapes of Palestine decreased, suggesting a movement of population into the towns. This ultimately led to a differentiation emerging between the status and function of individual villages of different sizes and their interdependence as satellites of the larger dominating towns. Fortifications from the EB II are known from Tell el-Farah (N), Beth Yerah, Aphek, Ai, and Arad. Administrative buildings/palaces have been unearthed at Megiddo and Arad. Temples have been found at Beth Yerah, Megiddo, Ai, and Arad. Arad is a good example of a large fortified town in the eastern Negev Desert. It was a well-planned city, divided into distinct neighborhoods of houses by streets, with shrines (one with a stele depicting deities with upraised arms), public or palace buildings, a water system (more than 15 meters deep), and it was surrounded by a massive fortification wall with projecting semicircular towers. The houses were of distinctive broadroom plan (hence the "Arad house") with the entrance in the long wall. The pottery assemblage from the site includes vessels imported from Egypt, as well as a large quantity of painted and well-burnished local wares that hitherto had been found in quantity in First Dynasty tombs at Abydos. A jar fragment with the *serekh* of Narmer, founder of the First Dynasty of Egypt, provides important synchronism between Egypt and EB II "Canaanite" Palestine. It is believed that the flourishing of EB II sites in the Negev and Sinai was the direct result of the copper trade controlled by Arad. At the end of this period some towns were abandoned: Tell el-Farah (N), Aphek, and Arad.

The Early Bronze III spans about 400 years (2700–2300 B.C.E.), but the reasons why the EB III replaced the EB II are unclear. In terms of material culture new ceramic types emerge, notably the so-called red/black burnished "Khirbet Kerak" wares in the north, and the disappearance of the EB II pottery wares in the south. There can be no doubt that during this period the centralization process of the rural population within cities reached its peak, with the establishment of new fortified towns at Tell Poran, Tell Nagila, and Tell Beit Mirsim. Pre-existing towns at Ai and Yarmut were strengthened and enhanced architecturally and especially in terms of the fortifications, suggesting that dangers of invasion and internecine violence were prevalent at that time. Temples are known from Megiddo and Khirbet Zeraqoun in Jordan. A massive underground water system is known from Zeraquon. The movement of the rural population into towns does not, however, indicate any decline in agricultural production, but quite the contrary. An enormous granary was uncovered at Tell Beth Yerah. Olive oil and perhaps also wine were the chief commodities that were used for trade at this time. Yarmut, situated in the heart of rich agricultural lands in the lowlands of Palestine, was in a key location to affect the control, processing, and marketing of some of the commodities required for trade with Egypt and other parts of the Near East. The town was surrounded by massive fortifications and had an offset gateway, a temple ("White Building"), palatial buildings, and residential quarters.

The gradual abandonment of EB III towns was replaced by the spread of new settlements with a different material culture across the countryside during the Intermediate Bronze Age (also known as the Early Bronze IV, 2300–2000 B.C.E.). Once thought to have occurred as a result of invading "Amorites," it would now appear that there were a number of factors that affected the movement of population away from the towns and into the countryside: the collapse of the trade networks with Old Kingdom Egypt and climatic fluctuations (with possible long-term desiccation) that made specialized cultivation difficult and eventually led to the need for broadening agricultural cultivation instead. Although once regarded as an overall pastoral-nomadic interlude between the Early and Middle Bronze Ages, it would now appear that the pastoral nomads of this period only actually existed in the semi-arid and arid zones (e.g., Be'er Resisim), whereas elsewhere there were flourishing farming communities spread out in large and small villages. Large villages are known in Jordan (Iktanu, Khirbet Iskander – with some fortifications) and in Palestine (Modi'in and Naḥal Rephaim). The abandoned towns were sometimes also used for ephemeral settlement: Hazor, Megiddo, Beth Shean, and Jericho. Numerous burials from this period have been found throughout the country, under cairns in the south, in shaft tombs in the highlands, and within dolmens in the north.

MIDDLE BRONZE AGE. The Middle Bronze Age (2000–1550 B.C.E.) is regarded as a period of renewed urbanism and it reflects the strength of influences emanating from the north and particularly from Syria. Small settlements previously inhabited during the Intermediate Bronze Age were abandoned, particularly along the coastal plain and in some of the inland valleys and were replaced in the MB II A (previously known as the MB I) by a number of urban centers (Tell Aphek, Tell Poleg, Tell Burga), on the one hand, and by a new scatter of villages and campsites (e.g., Dor, Sha'ar ha-Golan), on the other. It is unclear whether the same happened in the highland regions or in the arid zones, and it is quite possible that the Intermediate Bronze Age continued there for a little longer. Clearly the sites closer to the major trade routes, especially in the coastal plain, were the first to be fortified with characteristic wall-and-glacis or earthen rampart defenses. The renewed opening of the trade routes connecting Syria and Egypt probably brought with it an influx of Semitic-speaking and Hurrian groups into the southern Levant and this in turn raised the profile of local elites. At the same time as these changes in the Levant, local Egyptian groups of Western Asiatics ("Hyksos" – foreign rulers) were beginning to establish themselves in Lower Egypt, as has become clear from excavations at Tell ed-Daba. Egyptian texts provide an insight into the character of the Levant at this point in time, notably the story of Sinuhe, who traveled along the coast of Palestine not long after 2000 B.C.E.

Middle Bronze Age material culture was extremely rich and varied. The pottery traditions were almost completely new and many vessels were now made on a fast wheel (replacing the slow tournette). Bronze (an alloy of copper and tin) was now used for making weaponry, implements, and other objects. Religious objects – human and animal figurines and votive objects – some with strong Syrian/Mesopotamian influences, appear at sites and reflect the needs of the elite classes. Cylinder seals decorated with religious and mythological scenes are also typical of the period. Evidence for written tablets in Akkadian indicates that high levels of literacy existed in the towns, particularly among the scribes and temple officials.

The peak of urban development in Palestine took place during the Middle Bronze II B–C with further developments along the coastal plain and with an incredible wave of settlement throughout the highlands, with the establishment of fortified towns, fortresses, and villages. Important village remains have been uncovered at Shiloh, Tell el-Ful, and elsewhere. The key urban centers of this period are Hazor, Dan, Shechem (Tell el-Balata), Megiddo, Jerusalem, Aphek, and Ashkelon. Hazor was enormous (198 acres) and in size it is similar only to towns known from Syria. The fortification systems at these sites became progressively quite elaborate. The city gates uncovered at Dan (with its arches still intact) and Ashkelon are quite impressive. A major MB II tower system was uncovered protecting the Gihon Spring on the lower east slope of the "City of David" in Jerusalem. Temples of *migdal* appearance (i.e., long rooms with massive walls and with altars at one end) are known from Shechem, Megiddo, and Pella. Additional shrines are known from Tell el-Hayat, Tel Kitan, Nahariyyah, Hazor, and an open-air cult place at the unfortified village of Givat Sharett. Palaces have been uncovered at a number of sites and at Kabri elaborate floors with floral-decorated floors and fragmentary wall paintings of Minoan style were found. This discovery may be compared to examples of wall paintings from Tell ed-Daba, Middle Minoan II Phaistos in Crete, and Late Minoan IA Knossos and Thera.

With the expulsion of the Hyksos from the Delta by Ahmose I in about 1540–1525 B.C.E., a few sites of the southern Levant are subsequently destroyed (e.g., Tell el-'Ajjul – ancient Sharuhen). This period of uncertainty continued and eventually led to a series of military campaigns to subjugate the southern Levant undertaken by Thutmosis III.

LATE BRONZE AGE. Palestine during the Late Bronze Age fell under the shadow of Egyptian dominion. Numerous military campaigns were mounted against Western Asia (Syria and Palestine) by the rulers of Egypt, from Thutmosis III and through to the "Amarna" age. The Egyptians also came into conflict with the Hittites and later with the "Sea Peoples," with Syria and Palestine serving for much of that time as a battleground.

The towns of this period were mostly unfortified, but large structures, administrative buildings, and temples are known. Important towns existed along the coast, in the foothills, and within inland valleys. Some sites that were destroyed at the end of the MB were rebuilt in the LB, others were left abandoned, but new settlements were built as well. While highland landscapes became depopulated, a few towns (e.g., Shechem) and small hamlets (e.g., Jerusalem) still existed within these territories. A type of large administrative/palace structure – labeled the "governor's residence" – has been found at sites throughout the country: Beth Shean, Tell es-Sa'idiyeh, Tell Jemmeh, and Tell Sera'. Elaborate temples of different sizes are also known, notably at Hazor, Beth Shean, Megiddo, Tell Mevorakh, and Lachish. Rich finds were found in some of these temples, including carved statues and orthostats. The discovery of large numbers of decorated seals and rich artistic goods of Egyptian and Syrian style (e.g., a thin gold leaf plaque of a goddess standing on a horse from Lachish) is a clear indication of the success of the international trade passing through the region. It would appear that certain elite parts of the population enjoyed prosperity particularly from this trade, while the rest, especially the rural population, suffered hardship and poverty and survived on basic agricultural endeavors. Egyptian officials and tradesmen were situated within some of the towns, and at Deir el-Balah to the south of Gaza anthropoid ceramic coffins in Egyptian style were uncovered within a 13th-century cemetery. LB pottery reflects a continuation of MB pottery traditions, with the addition of foreign vessels, e.g., fine wares imported from Cyprus and the Aegean. A number of tablets inscribed in Akkadian cuneiform attest to the literacy of the period. Bowls bearing texts in Egyptian hieratic script were uncovered at Tell Sera'. The Amarna tablets from Egypt provide a wealth of information about the political landscape of Western Asia at this period. A few inscriptions have been found inscribed with a set of "Proto-Canaanite" symbols, representing an early version of Phoenician and Hebrew alphabets.

Major events towards the end of this period, with the collapse of the Egyptian and Hittite empires, and with the emergence of the "Sea Peoples," led to the breakdown of LB society and the collapse of local city-states.

IRON AGE AND PERSIAN. The Iron Age is divided into two main parts: the Early Iron Age (or Iron Age I, 1200–1000 B.C.E.) and the Late Iron Age (Iron Age II A–C, 1000–586 B.C.E.). During the late 1990s a debate ensued amongst scholars regarding Iron Age chronology with attempts to posit a lower chronology for the accepted mid-twelfth to mid-eighth centuries B.C.E. The matter continued to be debated during the early 2000s with the narrowing of some dates in both the low and high chronologies especially in regard to the dating of Iron Age II A strata at sites, especially as a result of new radiocarbon determinations obtained from sites such as Rehov, but there is now a general acceptance that the extant archaeological evidence points to the emerging process of Israelite "statehood" from as early as the tenth century B.C.E. rather than the ninth century B.C.E. This process culminated in substantial consolidation procedures within the state frameworks during the Omride Dynasty in the ninth century B.C.E. to the north and with the development of the kingdom of Judah with Jerusalem as its capital in the eighth century B.C.E. in the south.

The Early Iron Age saw the disintegration of the entire political and economic framework of the southern Levant and the decline of trade, with the appearance of new groups of people in different parts of the country, among them the "Sea Peoples" (which included the Philistines) along coastal areas, and farmers/herders (some of them undoubtedly Proto-Israelites) in the highland regions and elsewhere, where there was also some intermingling with pre-existing "Canaanite" peoples (see the section "Archaeology and the Origins of Israel," above). Across the Jordan saw the establishment of additional groups of people who eventually became the Ammonites, Moabites, and Edomites. Egyptian and biblical sources document the conflict that ensued between the "Sea Peoples" and the Egyptian Rameses III in his eighth regnal year, particularly with battles in Lebanon and in Egypt. The Egyptian presence in Palestine was maintained until the mid-12th century B.C.E. in some parts of the coastal regions (e.g., at Akko) and in the inland valleys and plains (e.g., Beth Shean, where inscriptions and a statue of Rameses III were found). The subsequent development of the Philistine culture is now well documented owing to a number of key excavations undertaken in the region of Philistia and in surrounding parts, particularly at Ashdod, Ashkelon, Tell Miqne (Ekron), as well as at Tell Qasile, Tell Sera', Tell el-Farah (N) and Tell Batash (Timnah?). The distinctive material culture of the Philistines, which was derived from Aegean traditions, rapidly absorbed foreign (i.e., Egyptian and Cypriot) and local Canaanite influences. In the highland regions surface surveys and excavations attest to the appearance of large numbers of small sites in regions that were hardly occupied in the Late Bronze Age, dating from the 12th century B.C.E. in the central highlands (the territories of Manasseh, Ephraim, and Benjamin) and from the 11th century B.C.E. in the Galilee. Sites include Dan, Hazor, Sasa, Ḥorvat Avot, Ḥorvat Harashim, Mount Ebal, the "bull site," Shiloh, Ai, Khirbet Radaanah, and Giloh. Additional sites are known from the western foothills ('Izbet Sartah) and in the northern Negev (Tel Masos). The period is typified by the emergence of new pottery types (e.g., collared-rim jars), new architecture (e.g., the "four-room" house), and new technologies (e.g., the first use of iron).

The Late Iron Age saw the establishing of Israelite kingdoms, from the time of the United Monarchy of David and Solomon, and the Divided Monarchies of Judah and Israel. Numerous archaeological excavations have uncovered a variety of remains from the Iron Age II reflecting a diverse settlement pattern consisting of urban settlements, smaller towns, and villages/hamlets. Important sites from this period include Dan, Hazor, Megiddo, Jezreel, Rehov, Tell el-Farah (N), Samaria, Tell en-Nasbeh, Jerusalem, Gezer, Beth Shemesh, Lachish, and Beersheba. The cities had strong defense walls and multi-chambered gates, palaces, public administrative buildings, royal enclosures, pillared storehouses, central silos, well-planned streets dividing blocks of houses, cisterns, and subterranean water systems that were reached via sloping stepped tunnels or down vertical stepped shafts. There were also citadels/fortresses (e.g., Arad and Kadesh Barnea), trade outposts (e.g., Vered Jericho), observation towers (Giloh), farmsteads (e.g., Khirbet er-Ras), shrines (e.g., Dan and Arad), and desert cultic centers (e.g., Kuntillet 'Ajrud). Nothing has survived of the central Israelite temple at Jerusalem (I Kings 6–7). Key dates in the chronology of the Iron Age are 925 B.C.E.: the raid of the Egyptian Shoshenq (Shishak) in the country, resulting in the destruction of various sites (Beth Shean, Tel Amal, Megiddo IVB–VA, Gezer VIII, Qasile VIII, sites in the Negev); 735 and 722 B.C.E.: the Assyrian conquest of the northern kingdom (Dan, Hazor V, Megiddo IVA, Yoqneam, and Samaria); 701 B.C.E.: Sennacherib's invasion of Judah (Lachish III, Batash III, Beit Mirsim A, Beersheba II, Arad VIII); 604 B.C.E.: a Babylonian destruction of sites in Philistia; 586 B.C.E.: the Babylonian conquest of Judah (Jerusalem, Ramat Rahel, En Gedi, Lachish, Aroer, Arad VI). A graphic representation of the Assyrian conquest of Lachish was immortalized in a series of monumental carved reliefs found in the palace of Sennacherib in Iraq. Important epigraphic finds from the general region include the Moabite stone, the Dan inscription, the Hadid tablets, the Lachish letters, the Ketef Hinnom amulet, the Miqne inscription, and various inscribed *bullae*. From the eighth century B.C.E. hamlets/small villages (*ḥaẓerim* and *migrashim*) proliferated as never before, particularly in the highlands and foothills regions, and numerous installations for the production of oil and wine are known. There was also a major transformation of the highland regions with the construction of agricultural terracing on a scale that had never been seen before. The countryside was divided up by a network of roads, some of which seem to have been consolidated intentionally by the state, to provide access between the cities and their rural hinterlands. In the seventh century B.C.E. there was a move towards a greater amount of settlement in marginal and arid zones, notably in the Negev and Judean deserts, and along the Dead Sea. Side by side with the Israelite and Judahite kingdoms, there were also additional ethnic entities present in the country, with the Phoenicians to the north (the plain of Akko and the sites of Achziv, Kabri, Keisan, Abu-Hawam) and with the Ammonites, Moabites, and Edomites in Transjordan to the east (Hesban, Dibon, Buseirah, Tawilan, Umm el-Biyara, Tell el-Kheleifeh, with some Edomite presence in the Negev to the south). An interesting Edomite shrine was excavated at Ḥaẓevah in the Negev with the discovery of a very large assemblage of cultic vessels and figurines. Similar finds were also made at the site of Qitmit. The Philistine entity continued to flourish within cities in the southern foothills region as has become particularly clear from the excavations at Tel Miqne (Ekron), Ashkelon, and Ashdod. Ekron had a major economy at this time based on the production and marketing of olive oil.

Difficulties arise in regard to the identification of material remains dating from the time of the Babylonian occupation of the country from 604/586 to 539 B.C.E., as well in regard to the identification of material remains from the earlier phase of the Persian period, at least down to c. 450 B.C.E. when there was the first appearance of imported Greek pottery and *ostraka* written in Aramaic. Some scholars have suggested that the material culture of the Iron Age II C stage in Palestine and Transjordan did not cease with the destruction of Jerusalem in 586 B.C.E. but that it continued at least until 530/520 B.C.E. with others suggesting lowering the terminal date well into the fifth century B.C.E.

The Persian period spans the period from the return from exile of Judeans under *Cyrus in 539 B.C.E. until the coming of *Alexander the Great in 332–31 B.C.E. Following the conquest of Babylon by Cyrus, Judean exiles were allowed back to Jerusalem and permission was given allowing them to rebuild the Jewish Temple destroyed in 586 B.C.E.; the Temple was subsequently completed in 516–15 B.C.E. The Palestine campaign of the Egyptian Cambyses in 525 B.C.E. was probably a direct result of the influx of repatriated peoples into the region. A second wave of returning exiles occurred at the time of *Ezra and *Nehemiah, following the death of *Darius I in 486 B.C.E. At this time the land was part of the district of the larger Persian satrapy of *eber nahari*, "Beyond the [Euphrates] River," and it included various sub-districts: the first included the region of Judah (the province [*phwh*] of *yhd*), Philistia, and Idumea in the south, and the second a part of Galilee, the coastal plain, and Samaria. Recent archaeological work has shown that in the central hilly country of *yhd* there was a settlement pattern of a few large sites with smaller hamlets round about, and this distribution fits in well with the so-called "lists of returning exiles" (Ezra 2:1–34; Neh. 7:6–38; cf. 11: 25–36) which contain the names of settlements in Judah. Judah was surrounded by a mixture of different ethnic entities, with the *Samaritans immediately north, the *Phoenicians (Tyrians and Sidonians) to the far north, the *Ammonites to the east across the Jordan, and with various Arab groups to the south and southeast (eventually replaced by the *Nabateans). In Galilee there is evidence for a Phoenician presence with the capital of this region perhaps situated at Megiddo. Four important sites were situated on the western Galilee coast and south in the area close to modern Haifa: Akhziv (Ecdippa), Akko, Tell Abu Hawam, and Shikmonah. Akko was used as an important military base in 374/373 B.C.E. during the campaigns against the Egyptians. A cargo of Phoenician terracotta figurines, some with representations of the goddess Tanit, was found in the sea next to Shavei Zion, north of Akko. The area of Samaria was governed between the time of Nehemiah and Alexander the Great by the strong local dynastic clan of Sanballat, and this became clear as a result of the papyri finds from Wadi el-Daliyeh. A distribution of some 35 sites, large and small, are known along the coast from Shikmonah to Jaffa. *Dor is an important site on the coastal plain which has yielded many archaeological remains from the Persian period, including fortifications and a two-chambered gate, and an orthogonal city layout with buildings and dwellings. Finds included numerous Greek and Cypriot imported pottery. Some sites along the coast were given by the Persians in the fourth century to the Phoenicians, and this included Dor which, according to the Shamun'azar Sarcophagus, was given together with Jaffa. Further inland are the sites of Nahal Tut and Ein Hofez. There was very little Persian influence on the local material culture of the period, except in terms of some ceramic forms, and in seals and coins with the name of the province *yhd*, including one bearing the name of a governor of the province, Yehezkiah. Aramaic was the *lingua franca* of this period and quite a few epigraphic finds – mainly *ostraka* – have been found at sites throughout Palestine, with a few Greek and Phoenician written finds from the coastal region (e.g., Dor), and some Edomite texts in the south of the country.

HELLENISTIC AND ROMAN. The Hellenistic period is divided into two parts: Early Hellenistic (332–200 B.C.E.) and Late Hellenistic (200–63 B.C.E.). The Hasmonean period is sometimes used by archaeologists in reference to the period extending from the mid-second century B.C.E. to the beginning of the rule of *Herod the Great in 37 B.C.E. The Roman period is divided into two parts: Early Roman (63 B.C.E. to 70 C.E.) and Late Roman (70–325 C.E.). Some scholars suggest a Middle Roman period for the time period 70–200 C.E.

The entire Near East came under the dominion of Alexander the Great following a decisive victory over the Persians in November 333 B.C.E. in the Plain of Issus. With the death of Alexander the Great and the dividing up of the Hellenistic empire amongst his Macedonian successors, Palestine became the springboard for an ensuing conflict between the Ptolemies and Seleucids. From 301 B.C.E. Palestine and Phoenicia were under direct Ptolemaic control. The country was divided up into hyparchies or toparchies for administrative purposes. Military colonies were established at Akko, Philoteria, and perhaps even at Beth Shean/Scythopolis by Ptolemy Philadelphus II (285–246 B.C.E.). Following a major battle held at Banias in 200 B.C.E. between Ptolemy V and *Antiochus III, Palestine came under the rule of the Syrian Seleucids.

Good sources of information exist in regard to Palestine from both Egyptian and Syrian sources. Perhaps the best known of the sources from this period are the Zenon Papyri from the Faiyum in Egypt. These record a visit that was made to Palestine between 260–258 B.C.E. by Zenon the financial minister of Egypt (under Ptolemy II). Places mentioned in the papyri include mostly sites on the *Via Maris* ("way of the sea") route along the coast with a few inland: Gaza, Maresha/Marissa, Ashkelon, Jaffa, Straton's Tower/Caesarea, Adora/Dor, and Akko/Ptolemais. Important archaeological remains of this period have been found at all these sites: fortifications, administrative buildings, palaces, dwellings, as well as pottery and coins. Maresha is referred to in the papyri as a center of the slave trade with Egypt and inscriptions indicate that some of its inhabitants hailed from Sidon and Phoenicia. It was undoubtedly an important city in Idumea. Archaeological work at the site has uncovered a large fortified city with residential quarters, a sacred *temenos*, markets with shops, and subterranean cave complexes. In one of the shops a standard of volumes for liquids that was made under the supervision of two *agoranomes* in 143/142 B.C.E. was found. Excavations conducted at the harbor-city of Dor revealed a city wall with square towers built of ashlars, a dyeing installation with murex shells, large residential buildings, and a structure containing plastered pools. To the north of Dor, off the coast of Athlit, underwater researches brought to light the bronze ram of a warship of the Hellenistic period, decorated with images of a trident, the symbols of Poseidon, the head of an eagle (representing Zeus?) and a helmet of the *Dioscuri*. Hellenistic remains have been found at numerous sites throughout Palestine and a rare and important votive inscription in Greek and Aramaic (to the "God who is at Dan"), dated to circa 200 B.C.E., was discovered during excavations conducted at the High Place of Tell Dan. The enclosed sacred *temenos* of the Samaritans has been uncovered at Mount Gerizim, with the discovery of numerous inscriptions in Greek and Aramaic referring to offerings provided to the temple. The pottery assemblage of this period known at sites in Palestine includes a variety of local vessels that maintain earlier traditions, as well as the appearance of new types of vessels, such as wine amphorae with stamped Greek inscriptions on their handles, brought by ship from the Greek islands (e.g., Rhodes), and a distinctive red-gloss fine ware (*terra sigillata*) which continued to be made into the Roman period.

Despite the cultural influences of Hellenism that existed in the region during this period, very little evidence may be adduced from the material culture of Palestine and Phoenicia at this time to suggest that a purposeful and overall Hellenization process prevailed. On the contrary, it would appear that local traditions were strongly maintained within rural communities as well as in the cities and towns, with some evidence that the elites were borrowing and adapting for their own purposes foreign cultural features of art and architecture, as well as acquiring imported valuable objects and commodities that were derived not only from the Greek world, but also from Syria and Egypt. Tel Anafa is a good example of an extremely wealthy Phoenician-type settlement dating primarily from the second century B.C.E., with buildings, a bath house, mosaic floors, and rich finds. At Tel Kedesh a very large administrative building was unearthed and in it was found a large cache of more than two thousand *bullae*, some bearing portraits of Seleucid monarchs (Antiochus IV to Demetrius I) and Roman Republican merchants, and others decorated with Phoenician symbols (e.g., Tanit). This building was abandoned circa 145 B.C.E.

The Maccabean revolt broke out in 167 B.C.E. and it marks the first manifestation of a Jewish nationalistic struggle against external cultures. It began because of Seleucid attempts to impose upon Jewish religious practices. The struggle that began in the vicinity of the town of Modi'in in the northern foothills of Palestine, northwest of Jerusalem, eventually led in 142 B.C.E. to the establishment of an independent Hasmonean kingdom under *Simeon the Hasmonean, which then expanded considerably under *Alexander Jannaeus (*Yannai; 104–76 B.C.E.) and threatened Nabatean territories in particular (e.g., the Golan and the trade route to Gaza port). Maresha and Gezer were two important sites that were conquered by the Hasmoneans. Important remains of Hasmonean fortified fortresses, palaces, and towns have been found in various parts of the country. The Hasmonean kingdom was considerably weakened with the appearance of the Roman commander Pompey in 63 B.C.E., who captured Jerusalem and took away their dominion over certain cities along the coast and in Transjordan. Henceforth, the Roman governor of Syria held power in the region, with support from the Hasmoneans and Idumeans. Eventually, in 40 B.C.E. the Idumean Antipater's son Herod the Great was declared "King of the Jews" by the Roman Senate, and from 37 to 4 B.C.E. he ruled over much of Palestine. A major source of historical information about this period is derived from the writings of the Jewish historian Josephus Flavius.

An impressive building program was initiated by Herod the Great and it may now be seen to be a direct continuation of the ambitious building projects previously initiated by the Hasmonean rulers. In Jerusalem, Herod undertook numerous building activities, including a massive rebuilding of the Temple Mount and its Jewish Temple, a luxurious palace surrounded by gardens in the Upper City, the fortress of Antonia, the strengthening of the city fortifications and the remodeling of gates, and the construction of a theater. Archaeological remains are known for all these monuments, except for the theater. Building programs were also undertaken at the harbor-city of Caesarea Maritima, with the construction of numerous buildings, a palace, and harbor installations (the foundations of the towers mentioned by Josephus have been uncovered in underwater explorations), and at Samaria (renamed Sebaste in honor of Augustus), with the construction of public buildings and a temple. A sprawling winter palace was built at Jericho, replacing earlier Hasmonean buildings at the site, and fortress palaces were erected at Masada, Herodium, and Machaerus. Under Herod's successors, similar building activities were undertaken at *Tiberias and at Caesarea Philippi (Banias). The city of Tiberias situated on the western shore of the Lake of Galilee was substantially rebuilt by Herod Antipas in 20 C.E. and the remains of a large building (palace?) have recently been uncovered, as well as one small part of an amphitheatre. At Caesarea Philippi, situated at the source of the River Jordan, a large complex palace with enormous underground vaulted chambers was unearthed, probably dating to the time of Philip the Tetrarch. Herod the Great also sponsored the construction of buildings in major cities outside his dominion, presumably to boost his influence. Following Herod's death his kingdom was broken up and divided among his sons. The northern and eastern areas – Galilee and Perea (Transjordan) – were allotted to Herod Antipas. The second son, Philip the Tetrarch, received the region of the Golan Heights and parts of the Hauran in Syria. The central part of the country – Judaea (and Jerusalem), Samaria, and Idumea – passed temporarily into the hands of the third son Herod Archelaus, but because of mismanagement he was deposed and the region came to be known as Provincia Judaea administered by Roman officials based at Caesarea Maritima. Procurators were subsequently appointed to rule over Judea between 44–66 C.E.

Archaeological work has been conducted on a variety of remains dating from the Early Roman period (37 B.C.E. to 70 C.E.). In Jerusalem priestly and aristocratic houses have been unearthed, some adorned with wall paintings and stucco decorations. Synagogues dating from the first century C.E. have been found at Gamla, Herodium, Masada, Jericho, and Modi'in. Numerous farming villages and privately owned *villae* were founded at this time in different parts of the country, with the construction of large areas of terraces in the highlands, regulated co-axial field systems in the lowlands, and large numbers of wine presses. At Qumran a settlement with at least three stages of existence was uncovered close to the caves where the Dead Sea Scrolls were found. However, scholars are still debating whether Qumran was a place inhabited by the Essenes, or whether it had some other primary function, such as a trading center or as an agricultural manor house. Burial customs of the Roman period indicate that the well-off were buried within rock-hewn family caves. A typical cave consists of a small central chamber and *kokhim* (tunnel-like burial recesses) in the walls. Secondary burial was made within limestone ossuaries and some were decorated and even inscribed with the names of the dead. The material culture of this period was quite uniform with a ceramic assemblage of local transport, cooking, and dining wares. Fine wares include a local variety of painted ware, similar in some ways to the Nabatean painted ware, and imported and local versions of red gloss ware (*terra sigillata*). Stone vessels became particularly popular as a result of the Jewish concerns for purity between 50–70 C.E., with the manufacturing of hand-carved and lathe-turned vessels, including mugs, bowls, and large jars, at places around Jerusalem and in Galilee.

Following the Jewish revolt against the Romans from 66 C.E. and the resulting destruction of Jerusalem and the Jewish Temple in 70 C.E., Jews were excluded from Jerusalem but not from the immediate territory as was once thought. Excavations at Tell el-Ful and at Beit Hanina to the north of the city have shown that Jews continued farming the lands around Jerusalem, to maintain the roads and to provide agricultural produce for the occupying Tenth Legion, at least until the second century C.E. Numerous finds have been made connected with the *Bar Kokhba revolt, including large numbers of subterranean hideaways, letters, and manuscripts hidden away in caves in the Judean Desert, and remnants of the final bastion at *Bethar (Battir). Following the Bar Kokhba revolt of 132–35 C.E. Jerusalem became known as the *colonia* of Aelia Capitolina, and Judaea was replaced by the name Syria-Palaestinia. Large tracts of land were distributed by the Roman authorities to members of the army and some of these were maintained by Roman *villae*. One such site was excavated to the southeast of Jerusalem at Ein Yael in the Rephaim Valley, and it included buildings, some with highly decorated mosaic floors, a spring-house, and bathhouses. Similar *villae* existed in the near vicinity at Sataf and Suba. Roman urbanization programs were initiated throughout the country, at Beth Shean/Scythopolis, Sepphoris/Diocaesarea, Shechem/Neapolis, Lod/Diospolis, Beth Guvrin/Eleutheropolis, Emmaus/Nicopolis, and elsewhere. Major features within these cities are the remains of monumental gates, columned streets, marketplaces, temples, shrines, nymphaea, amphitheatres, theaters, and hippodromes. Important discoveries include a lead weight from Ḥorvat Alim inscribed in Hebrew with the name of Shimon Bar Kosba (i.e., Bar Kokhba), an over life-size bronze statue of Hadrian that was found near Beth Shean, a mithraeum – a shrine dedicated to the Iranian mystery god Mithras – at Caesarea, residential buildings with highly decorated mosaic floors at Sepphoris (e.g., the "House of Orpheus"), and a third century C.E. monumental Latin inscription at the fort of Yotvatah in the Aravah. The center of Jewish activities gradually shifted during the second and third centuries B.C.E. to the north, to Galilee and to parts of the Golan, and many villages were founded in these areas. Excavations at the necropolis of Beth Shearim have indicated that it became a center for the burial of prominent Jews, not only from the country but also for people from the Diaspora.

BYZANTINE. The Byzantine period (325 to 638 C.E.) is regarded as one of the richest periods in the archaeology of the country. Some archaeologists distinguish between Early Byzantine (325–500 C.E.) and Late Byzantine (500–638 C.E.).

With Christianity becoming established as one of the official religions of the Roman Empire, paganism was gradually abolished in Palestine with the last pagan temple being shut down in Gaza circa 400 C.E. Jews and Samaritans were tolerated by the authorities and allowed to practice their customs and to maintain their places of prayer in purposefully built synagogues. The country was now regarded as the "holy land" – the place that witnessed the birth, life, and resurrection of *Jesus. Places of worship sprang up throughout the country and Helena, mother of Constantine the Great, according to tradition, made a visit to the country circa 326 C.E. to ascertain the location of some of the sites. In Jerusalem, the site of Jesus' tomb was pointed out below the foundations of the Roman forum and the Temple of Venus, in excavation works supervised by the Bishop Macarius on Constantine's orders. The discovery of Jesus' tomb resulted in the construction of a large *martyrium* basilica on the spot, parts of which are now incorporated into the Church of the Holy Sepulcher. Additional churches were constructed at this time at the Cave of the Nativity in Bethlehem, the Mount of Olives (Church of Eleona), and at Mamre near Hebron. Christianity in Palestine became substantially consolidated during the fifth and sixth centuries C.E., and hundreds of new churches, chapels, and monasteries were constructed all over the country, even at isolated locations. These were adorned with mosaic floors, wall paintings, and portable furnishings made of wood and other materials. The height of these building activities in Jerusalem took place at the time of the Emperor Justinian (mid-sixth century C.E.) with the construction of the southern extension of the Cardo street leading to the entrance to an enormous basilical church called the Nea – foundations of this church were uncovered during excavations in the Jewish Quarter. The church next to the tomb of Jesus and the new church built by Justinian are both depicted on the sixth-century C.E. Madaba mosaic map.

Institutionalized pilgrimage to the Holy Land began in the fourth century. Many pilgrims arrived by boat to the main ports of the country, and at Dor on the north coast, a monumental pilgrimage church was built to accommodate some of their needs. Pilgrimage eventually became an economic mainstay in the country and pilgrims were well catered to by a variety of religious institutions, way stations, hospices, and even hospitals. The existence of so many pilgrims in the country led to the development of a flourishing industry that produced crosses, trinkets, and mementoes (e.g., *eulogia* amulets and *ampullae* flasks), portable art works (e.g., icons), and reliquaries (e.g., with the supposed fragments of the holy cross). The holy sites were scattered at different locations, with pilgrims interested primarily in sites in Jerusalem as their main destination, as well as at places in Judea, Galilee, around the Sea of Galilee, and in the Jordan Valley. One of the earliest of pilgrim accounts is that of the Bordeaux Pilgrim (333 C.E.) and one of the best known is that of Egeria, a nun from western Spain, who visited the country between 381–84 C.E.

Byzantine Palestine was divided into three parts: *Palaestina Prima*, which included the coastal plain, Samaria, Judea, Idumea, and Perea and had its capital at Caesarea; *Palaestina Secunda*, which included Galilee, the Golan, and the Decapolis of Palestine, with its capital at Scythopolis; and *Palaestina Tertia*. During the course of the Byzantine period, settlement extended into marginal regions, particularly in the Negev highlands. Many houses of this period had internal open courtyards, and a few walls were partitioned with so-called "Chorazin" windows, and others had roofs constructed with stone slabs in corbelled fashion, especially in the Negev and in the Golan. Jewish life in Palestine flourished during the Byzantine period and large numbers of synagogues have been uncovered particularly to the north of the country, for example at Khirbet Shema, Meiron, Capernaum, Chorazin, Nabratein, Kefar Baram, and in the Golan. Some of the later examples of synagogues (fifth-sixth centuries C.E.) have a *bema* and ornate mosaic floors depicting the Torah shrine, the *menorah*, and biblical scenes and have dedicatory inscriptions in Hebrew, Aramaic, and Greek. One synagogue from Rehov had a floor decorated with a unique Aramaic inscription with 29 lines of the laws of the *halakhah* pertaining to the sabbatical year. Numerous villages have been investigated in different parts of the country and many of these were identified as being solely Christian, Jewish, or Samaritan, based on the discovery of churches or synagogues. The assumption made by some scholars, however, that a clear-cut ethnic differentiation existed between the ethnic groups at that time is incorrect and without any basis in the extant archaeological finds. During the Persian invasion of 614 C.E. various churches were destroyed in different parts of the country. Large numbers of victims from Jerusalem were buried within a crypt, which was uncovered in excavations close to the Jaffa Gate of today, confirming the writings of the Church Fathers on the subject.

ISLAMIC TO OTTOMAN. With the advent of Islam in the southern Levant in 638 C.E. gradual changes to the settlement pattern of the country and its material culture began to take place, but there was no massive destruction at sites as had once been thought. The Islamic period may be divided into three parts: Early Islamic (638–1099 C.E.), divided into the *Umayyad (638–750 C.E.) and *Abbasid (750–1099 C.E.), and Late Islamic, divided into the Crusader/*Ayyubid (1099–1291 C.E.) and *Mamluk (1291–1517 C.E.). The *Ottoman period extends from 1517 until the invasion of the British in 1917.

Under the Umayyads major construction activities took place in various parts of the country, continuing local architectural trends apparent already in the Late Byzantine period. For a while Byzantine coinage remained in circulation, but eventually was replaced by Umayyad minted coins. In Jerusalem a number of important buildings were built on the Temple Mount (Haram al-Sharif) with the Dome of the Rock, built at the time of the reign of Abd al-Malik, situated at its center, and with the large Aqsa mosque to its south. The Dome of the Rock remains to this day a marvelous gem of Early Islamic architecture. Numerous archaeological remains from this period have been found: fortifications, dwellings and shops in the cities, and pottery kilns. Roads were also repaired as a number of milestones testify. A hoard of 751 gold coins from the first half of the seventh century B.C.E. was uncovered within a large Umayyad residence in Beth Shean. In the baths of Hammath Gader an inscription in Greek testified to the fact that it had been rebuilt at the orders of an Arab governor in 662 C.E. Farms dating from the Umayyad period are known in the Negev, as well as some very early examples of open-air mosques and many rock inscriptions in Arabic. Large building complexes of a kind that is sometimes referred to as the "Umayyad chateau" are known from Khirbet el-Minya on the end of the Sea of Galilee and at Khirbet al-Mafjar close to Jericho. These mansions are richly decorated with mosaic floors and carvings in stone and stucco of a very high order. Coins found at Scythopolis/Beth Shean have shown that this stage of the Early Islamic period came to an end roughly at the same time as a massive earthquake in 749 C.E. The pottery assemblage from the Umayyad period includes common wares that resemble those from the Late Byzantine period, with the addition of a number of new forms and lamps. It would appear that the buff ware that became so distinctive in Abbasid levels already made its appearance towards the end of the Umayyad, i.e., during the century or so preceding the earthquake of 749 C.E., judging by recent finds at Tiberias.

Ramla (*Ramleh) was a new city that was founded in 712–15 C.E. to replace Lod (*Lydda), but major changes and an expansion of the city mainly took place in Abbasid times. The remains of a mosque, dwellings, plastered installations for dyeing, and mosaic pavements have been found, together with large quantities of pottery, artistic objects, inscriptions, and coins. One mosaic floor has one of the earliest representations of a *miḥrab* and also a verse from the Koran. A subterranean reservoir was found with a dated inscription indicating that it was built in 789 C.E. at the time of the reign of Harun al-Rashid. Sources indicate that the town also had a Jewish neighborhood, but remains attesting to this have not yet been found. The pottery from the Abbasid period is quite distinctive, and includes among others mold-made buff jugs and glazed bowls. Umayyad coinage continued in circulation well into the Abbasid phase and this has tended to confuse some archaeological sequences from the early Abbasid (i.e., pre-Fatimid phase). Jewelry hoards from the Fatimid phase have been found during excavations at Ashkelon and Caesarea, and hoards of metal vessels at Tiberias and Caesarea.

Jerusalem was conquered by the Crusaders in 1099 C.E. and thereafter a massive building program of churches and castles took place throughout the Kingdom of Jerusalem. Early castle building was sponsored by Baldwin I (1100–18 C.E.) and Baldwin II (1118–31 C.E.) at Ashkelon on the coast of Palestine, at Shaubak in Transjordan, and on the Isle de Graye in the Gulf of Aqaba. Commercial arrangements were made on behalf of the Genoese, Pisans, and Venetians with the provision of holdings in the port cities. The coinage and metalwork of this period is quite distinctive. Reliquaries with fragments purported to be of the Holy Cross, the bones of John the Baptist, and other relics, were dispersed to churches in the West. The Church of the Holy Sepulcher in Jerusalem was substantially remodeled and redecorated after 1131 C.E., with most of the works completed by the 1140s, and with the dedication taking place in 1149 C.E. Important churches from this period are the Church of the Nativity in Bethlehem, the Church of the Annunciation at Nazareth, and the Church of St John at Sebaste. The *Templer and Hospitaler orders were strengthened and became consolidated during this period. *Saladin (Salah-ad-Din) eventually unified Moslem forces and in 1187 C.E. inflicted a major defeat on the Crusaders at the Horns of Hattin overlooking the Sea of Galilee, reducing the Crusader hold to Tyre and Beirut. In 1191 C.E. the Crusaders managed to regain control over the coastal areas, but they were unable to recapture Jerusalem. In 1219 C.E. in view of an imminent Crusader invasion, the Ayyubid Sultan of Damascus, al-Malik al-Mu'azzem, ordered the razing of the walls of Jerusalem. This self-imposed Ayyubid destruction has been verified in archaeological excavations along the walls of Jerusalem, with the discovery of piles of collapsed ashlars and dedicatory inscriptions in Arabic dating from 1202/1203 C.E. and 1212 C.E. along the western and southern edges of the Old City. Although Frederick II was able to restore control over the holy places in 1229 C.E. through a process of treaty with Sultan al-Kamil, Jerusalem was subsequently captured by the Khwarazmian Turks and access to the holy places was again impossible. The fortifications of Tyre, Acre, and Caesarea were rebuilt at the time of Louis IX, as well as a new castle at Sidon. With the Mamluk capture of the castle of Crac des Chevaliers, the Crusader presence in the Levant was gradually eliminated and the final straw was the Mamluk conquest of Acre (Akko) in 1291. Important archaeological work has been conducted on the churches and secular buildings of the Crusaders throughout the Levant, with work undertaken at Caesarea, Belvoir, and recently at Akko where well preserved and substantial remains of the Crusader city have been uncovered. Numerous monuments attributed to the Mamluk period are known from Jerusalem itself, with markets, baths, and schools (the *madrasas*), and throughout the country as well, notably with the re-use and re-building of castles and towers previously built by the Crusaders. The pottery assemblage from this period includes a variety of glazed bowls and jugs, as well as unglazed green-buff wares, especially jugs with stamped decorations around the necks. Handmade jars and smaller vessels decorated with geometric-painted designs appear during the Ayyubid period and this tradition of pottery making is continued right through the Ottoman period to the early 20th century.

Palestine in the early part of Ottoman period flourished and the city walls of Jerusalem were substantially reconstructed under *Suleiman the Magnificent in the 1540s. Numerous villages were erected in different parts of the country and their remains form the nuclei of present-day Palestinian villages. Forts were erected along the route leading through Jordan to protect pilgrims making their way on the holy pilgrimage (*hajj*) to Mecca. The important towns of this period are Tabaryya (Tiberias), Nablus (Shechem), al-Khalil/Masjid Ibrahim (Hebron), and Acre. In the mid-18th century, a local chieftain, Dahr-al-'Umar, fortified the towns of Acre and Tiberias, and built forts at Sa'sa and Shafr'amr among other places. The country was administered by pashas and towards the 19th century it became the backwater of the Ottoman Empire. Throughout the Islamic to Ottoman periods Jews and Christians were allowed to maintain their communities, to build places of worship and to keep their respective traditions. At the time of the Crusades, however, Jews were excluded from Jerusalem and persecuted together with Moslems. Following the conquest of Jerusalem by Salah ad-Din in 1187, Jews and Christians were allowed to establish their own neighborhoods within the city, and this situation with some changes here and there continued through Ottoman times. Important Jewish communities flourished during the Middle Ages at Tiberias, on the shore of the Sea of Galilee, and at Safed in the hills of Galilee, as well as in adjacent villages. Ottoman rule in Palestine ceased with the arrival of the British in 1917. On entering Jerusalem on December 9, 1917, General Edmund H.H. *Allenby proclaimed martial law and had posters put up on the walls of the city which read: "Since your City is regarded with affection by the adherents of three of the great religions of mankind, and its soil has been consecrated by the prayers and pilgrimages of devout people of those three religions for many centuries, therefore do I make known to you that every sacred building, holy spot, shrine, traditional site, endowment, pious bequest or customary place of prayer, of whatever form of the three religions, will be maintained and protected according to the existing customs and beliefs to whose faiths they are sacred."

BIBLIOGRAPHY: This selected list of books and articles is presented by date of publication and under the relevant sections of the entry. This is only a selection of the vast literature on the subject and readers should check the bibliography contained within the most recent cited books for additional publications. Publications on the archaeology of *Jerusalem are not included here. GENERAL: Y. Aharoni, *The Archaeology of the Land of Israel* (1982); A. Mazar, *Archaeology of the Land of the Bible, 10.000–586* B.C.E. (1990); A. Ben-Tor (ed.), *The Archaeology of Ancient Israel* (1992); W.E. Rast, *Through the Ages in Palestinian Archaeology: An Introductory Handbook* (1992); J. Murphy-O'Connor, *The Holy Land: An Archaeological Guide From Earliest Times to 1700* (1992); E. Stern (ed.), *The New Encyclopedia of Archaeological Excavations in the Holy Land*, 5 vols. (1993–2006); T.E. Levy (ed.), *The Archaeology of Society in the Holy Land* (1995); J.R. Bartlett (ed.), *Archaeology and Biblical Interpretation* (1997); A. Negev and S. Gibson (eds.), *Archaeological Encyclopedia of the Holy Land* (2001). METHODS AND APPROACHES: W.G. Dever, "Two Approaches to Archaeological Method: The Architectural and the Stratigraphic," in: *Eretz-Israel*, 11 (1973), 1*–8*; W.G. Dever, "The Impact of the 'New Archaeology' on Syro-Palestinian Archaeology," in: *Bulletin of the American Schools of Oriental Research*, 242 (1981), 15–29; J.M. Weinstein, "Radiocarbon Dating in the Southern Levant," *Radiocarbon*, 26 (1984), 297–366; A.M. Rosen, *Cities of Clay: The Geoarchaeology of Tells* (1986); R.L. Chapman, "Excavation Techniques and Recording Systems: A Theoretical Study," in: *Palestine Exploration Quarterly*, 118 (1986), 5–26; J.F. Drinkard, G.L. Mattingly, and J. Maxwell Miller (eds.), *Benchmarks in Time and Culture: An Introduction to Palestinian Archaeology* (1988); R. Moorey, *Excavation in Palestine* (1988); A. Kempinsky and R. Reich (eds.), *The Architecture of Ancient Israel: From the Prehistoric to the Persian Periods* (1992); O. Bar-Yosef and A. Khazanov (eds.), *Pastoralism in the Levant: Archaeological Materials in Anthropological Perspectives* (1992); I. Singer, *Graves and Burial Practices in Israel in the Ancient Period* (Heb., 1994); I. Sharon, "Partial Order Scalogram Analysis of Relations – A Mathematical Approach to the Analysis of Stratigraphy," in: *Journal of Archaeological Science*, 22 (1995), 751–67; L.G. Herr, *Published Pottery of Palestine* (1996); E.H.E. Lass, "Lost in the Maze: An Alternative Method of Designing Matrix Diagrams," in: *Bulletin of the Anglo-Israel Archaeological Society*, 15 (1996–97), 41–49; Z. Herzog, *Archaeology of the City* (1997); T.J. Wilkinson, *Archaeological Landscapes of the Near East* (2003); S. Gibson, "From Wildscape to Landscape: Landscape Archaeology in the Southern Levant – Methods and Practice," in: A.M. Maeir, S. Dar, and Z. Safrai (eds.), *The Rural Landscape of Ancient Israel* (2003), 1–25; Y. Elitzur, *Ancient Place Names in the Holy Land* (2004); S. Gitin (ed.), *The Ancient Pottery of Israel and its Neighbors: From the Neolithic through the Hellenistic Period* (2006). HISTORY OF ARCHAEOLOGICAL RESEARCH IN ISRAEL: O. Bar-Yosef and A. Mazar, "Israeli Archaeology," in: *World Archaeology*, 13 (1982), 310–25; P.J. King, *American Archaeology in the Mideast: A History of the American Schools of Oriental Research* (1983); E. Stern, "The Bible and Israeli Archaeology," in: L.G. Perdue, L.E. Toombs, and G.L. Johnson (eds.), *Archaeology and Biblical Interpretation: Essays in Memory of D. Glen Close* (1987); N.A. Silberman, *Between Past and Present: Archaeology, Ideology and Nationalism in the Modern Near East* (1988), 31–40; T. Shay, "Israeli Archaeology – Ideology and Practice," in: *Antiquity*, 63 (1989), 768–72; R. Moorey, *A Century of Biblical Archaeology* (1991); T. Einhorn, "Israeli Law, Jewish Law and the Archaeological Excavation of Tombs," in: *International Journal of Cultural Property*, 6 (1997), 47–79; S. Gibson, "British Archaeological Institutions in Mandatory Palestine, 1917–1948," in: *Palestine Exploration Quarterly* (1999), 115–43; Y. Ben-Arieh, "Developments in the Study of *Yedi'at ha-Areẓ* in Modern Times, up to the Establishment of the State of Israel," in: *Cathedra*, 100 (Heb., 2001), 306–38. ARCHAEOLOGY AND THE ORIGINS OF ISRAEL: R.E. Friedman, *Who Wrote the Bible?* (1987); G. Mendelhall, "Biblical Interpretation and the Albright School," in: L.G. Perdue, L.E. Toombs, and G.L. Johnson (eds.), *Archaeology and Biblical Interpretation: Essays in Memory of D. Glen Close* (1987), 3–14; A. Biran and J. Naveh, "An Aramaic Stele Fragment From Tel Dan," in: *Israel Exploration Journal*, 43 (1993), 81–98; M. Hasel, "*Israel* in the Merneptah Stela," in: *Bulletin of the American Schools of Oriental Research*, 296 (1994), 45–61; I. Sharon, "Demographic Aspects of the Problem of the Israelite Settlement," in: L.M. Hopfe (ed.), *Uncovering Ancient Stones: Essays in Memory of H. Neil Richardson* (1994), 119–34; A. Biran and J. Naveh, "The Tel Dan Inscription: A New Fragment," in: *Israel Exploration Journal*, 45 (1995), 1–18; K.W. Whitelam, *The Invention of Ancient Israel: The Silencing of Palestinian History* (1996); T. Schneider, "Rethinking Jehu," in: *Biblica*, 77 (1996), 100–7; S. Gitin, T. Dothan, and J. Naveh, "A Royal Dedicatory Inscription from Ekron," in: *Israel Exploration Journal*, 47 (1997), 1–16; B.S.J. Isserlin, *The Israelites* (1998); S. Gitin, A. Mazar, and E. Stern (eds.), *Mediterranean People In Transition: Thirteenth to Early Tenth Centuries* B.C.E. (1998); N. Na'aman, "Jehu Son of Omri: Legitimizing a Loyal Vassal by His Lord," in: *Israel Exploration Jour-*

nal, 48 (1998), 236–38; S. Japhet, "In Search of Ancient Israel – Revisionism at all Costs," in: D.N. Myers and D.B. Ruderman (eds.), *The Jewish Past Revisited* (1998); T.L. Thompson, *The Mythic Past: Biblical Archaeology and the Myth of History* (1999); S. Gitin, "The Philistines: Neighbors of the Canaanites, Phoenicians and Israelites," in: D.R. Clark and V.H. Matthews (eds.), *100 Years of American Archaeology in the Middle East* (2000); A. Mazar, *Studies in the Archaeology of the Iron Age in Israel and Jordan* (2001); W.G. Dever, *What Did the Biblical Writers Know and When Did they Know it?* (2001); I. Finkelstein and N. Silberman, *The Bible Unearthed: Archaeology's New Vision of Ancient Israel and the Origin of its Sacred Texts* (2001); K.A. Kitchen, *On the Reliability of the Old Testament* (2003). THE ARCHAEOLOGICAL PERIODS: S. Gitin, "Stratification and its Application to Chronology and Terminology," in: *Biblical Archaeology Today* (1985), 99–107; R.L. Chapman, "The Three Ages Revisited," in: *Palestine Exploration Quarterly*, 121 (1989), 89–111; 122 (1990), 1–20; P. Warren and V. Hankey, *Aegean Bronze Age Chronology* (1989); P. James, I.J. Thorpe, N. Kokkinos, R. Morkot, and J. Frankish, "Centuries of Darkness: Context, Methodology and Implications," in: *Cambridge Archaeological Journal*, 1:2 (1991), 228–35; L.E. Stager, "The Periodization of Palestine From Neolithic Through to Early Bronze Times," in: R.W. Ehrich (ed.), *Chronologies in Old World Archaeology*, vol. 1 (1992[3]), 22–41; O. Bar-Yosef, "Prehistoric Chronological Framework," in: T.E. Levy (ed.), *The Archaeology of Society in the Holy Land* (1995), xiv–xvi. PREHISTORIC PERIODS (PALAEOLITHIC TO NEOLITHIC): O. Bar-Yosef, "Prehistory of the Levant" in: *Annual Review of Anthropology*, 9 (1980), 101–33; O. Bar-Yosef, "The 'Pre-Pottery Neolithic' Period in the Southern Levant," in: J. Cauvin and P. Sanlaville (eds.), *Préhistorie du Levant* (1981), 555–69; A.M.T. Moore, "A Four Stage Sequence for the Levantine Neolithic, ca. 8500–3750," in: *Bulletin of the American Schools of Oriental Research*, 264 (1982), 1–34; O. Bar-Yosef, *A Cave in the Desert: Nahal Hemar* (1985); A.N. Goring-Morris, *At the Edge: Terminal Pleistocene Hunter-Gatherers in the Negev and Sinai* (1987); O. Bar-Yosef and B. Vandermeersch (eds.), *Investigations in South Levantine Prehistory* (1989); O. Bar-Yosef and A. Belfer-Cohen, "The Origins of Sedentism and Farming Communities in the Levant," in: *Journal of World Prehistory*, 3 (1989), 447–98; A. Gopher, T. Tsuk, S. Shalev, and R. Gophna, "Earliest Gold Artifacts in the Levant," in: *Current Anthropology*, 31 (1990), 436–43; K. Wright, "A Classification System for Ground Stone Tools for the Prehistoric Levant," in: *Paléorient*, 17 (1992), 53–81; O. Bar-Yosef and N. Goren-Inbar, *The Lithic Assemblages of 'Ubeidiya: A Lower Palaeolithic Site in the Jordan Valley* (1993); A. Gopher and R. Gophna, "Cultures of the Eighth and Seventh Millennium BP in Southern Levant: A Review for the 1990s," in: *Journal of World Prehistory* (1993), 297–351; Y. Garfinkle, "The Yarmukian Culture in Israel," in: *Paléorient*, 19 (1993), 115–34; D.O. Henry, *From Foraging to Agriculture: The Levant at the End of the Ice Age* (1989); M. Lechevallier and A. Ronen, *Le gisement de Hatoula en Judée Occidentale, Israël* (1994); M. Weinstein-Evron, *Early Natufian el-Wad Revisited* (1998); M. Weinstein-Evron, B. Lang, and S. Ilani, "Natufian Trade/Exchange in Basalt Implements: Evidence From Northern Israel," in: *Archaeometry*, 41 (1999), 267–73; O. Bar-Yosef and A. Belfer-Cohen, "Innovations in Prehistoric Research," in: *Qadmoniot*, 36 (2003), 80–88. CHALCOLITHIC: D. Zohary and P. Spiegel-Roy, "Beginning of Fruit Growing in the Old World," in: *Science*, 187 (1975), 319–27; P. Bar-Adon, *The Cave of the Treasure: The Finds From the Cave in Nahal Mishmar* (1980); S.A. Rosen, "The Adoption of Metallurgy in the Levant: A Lithic Perspective," in: *Current Anthropology*, 25 (1984), 504–5; T.E. Levy, "The Chalcolithic Period," in: *Biblical Archaeologist*, 49 (1986), 82–108; T.E. Levy, "Social Archaeology and the Chalcolithic Period: Explaining Social Organizational Change During the 4th Millennium in Israel," in: *Michmanim*, 3 (1986), 5–20; K. Prag, "Byblos and Egypt in the Fourth Millennium B.C.," in: *Levant*, 28 (1986), 59–74; I. Gilead, "The Chalcolithic Period in the Levant," in: *Journal of World Prehistory*, 2 (1988), 397–443; I. Finkelstein and R. Gophna, "Settlement, Demographic and Economic Patterns in the Highlands of Palestine in the Chalcolithic and Early Bronze Periods and the Beginning of Urbanism," in: *Bulletin of the American Schools of Oriental Research*, 289 (1989), 1–22; S. Sadeh and R. Gophna, "Observations on the Chalcolithic Ceramic Sequence in the Middle Jordan Valley," in *Mitekufat Haeven – Journal of the Israel Prehistoric Society*, 24 (1991), 135–48; S. Shalev and J.P. Northover, "The Metallurgy of the Nahal Mishmar Hoard Reconsidered," in: *Archaeometry*, 35 (1993), 35–47; S. Shalev, "The Change in Metal Production from the Chalcolithic Period to the Early Bronze Age in Israel and Jordan," in: *Antiquity*, 68 (1994), 630–37; Z. Gal, H. Smithline, and D. Shalem, "A Chalcolithic Burial Cave at Peqi'in," in: *Qadmoniot*, 111 (1996), 19–24; S.A. Rosen, *Lithics After the Stone Age. A Handbook of Stone Tools From the Levant* (1997); C. Epstein, *The Chalcolithic Culture of the Golan* (1998); D. Segal, I. Carmi, Z. Gal, H. Smithline, and D. Shalem, "Dating a Chalcolithic Burial Cave in Peqi'in, Upper Galilee, Israel," in: *Radiocarbon*, 40 (1998), 707–12; Y. Garfinkel, *Neolithic and Chalcolithic Pottery of the Southern Levant* (1999). EARLY BRONZE AGE: A. Ben-Tor, *Cylinder Seals of Third-Millennium Palestine* (1978); S. Richard, "Toward a Consensus of Opinion on the End of the Early Bronze Age in Palestine-Transjordan," in: *Bulletin of the American Schools of Oriental Research*, 237 (1980), 5–34; R. Gophna, "The Settlement Landscape of Palestine in the Early Bronze Age II–III and Middle Bronze Age II," in: *Israel Exploration Journal*, 34 (1984), 24–31; E. Braun, "Of Megarons and Ovals: New Aspects of Late Prehistory in Israel," in: *Bulletin of the Anglo-Israel Archaeological Society*, 4 (1985), 17–26; J.W. Hanbury-Tenison, *The Late Chalcolithic to Early Bronze I Transition in Palestine and Transjordan* (1986); A. Ben-Tor, "The Trade Relations of Palestine in the Early Bronze Age," in: *Journal of the Economic and Social History of the Orient*, 29 (1986), 1–27; P. de Miroschedji, *L'urbanisation de la Palestine à l'age du Bronze ancient* (1989); E. Braun, "The Problem of the Apsidal House," *Palestine Exploration Quarterly*, 121 (1989), 1–43; E. Braun, "Basalt Bowls of the EB I Horizon in the Southern Levant," in: *Paléorient*, 16 (1990), 87–96; D. Esse, *Subsistence, Trade, and Social Change in Early Bronze Age Palestine* (1991); A.H. Joffe, "Early Bronze I and the Evolution of Social Complexity in the Southern Levant," in: *Journal of Mediterranean Archaeology*, 4 (1991), 3–58; L. Vinitzky, "The Date of the Dolmens in the Golan and Galilee – A Reassessment," *Eretz-Israel*, 21 (1991), 167–73; R. Gophna, "The Contacts Between 'En Besor Oasis, Southern Canaan, and Egypt During the Late PreDynastic and the Threshold of the First Dynasty: A Further Assessment," in: E.C.M. van den Brink (ed.), *The Nile Delta in Transition: 4th–3rd Millennium BC* (1992); A.H. Joffe, *Settlement and Society in the Early Bronze I and II, Southern Levant* (1993); J. Portugali and R. Gophna, "Crisis, Progress and Urbanization: The Transition From Early Bronze I to Early Bronze II in Palestine," in: *Tel Aviv*, 20 (1993), A. Mazar and P. de Miroschedji, "Hartuv, an Aspect of the Early Bronze I Culture of Southern Israel," in: *Bulletin of the American Schools of Oriental Research*, 302 (1996), 1–40, 164–86; E. Braun, *Yiftahel: Salvage and Rescue Excavations at a Prehistoric Village in Lower Galilee, Israel* (1997); A. Golani, "New Perspectives on Domestic Architecture and the Initial Stages of Urbanization in Canaan," in: *Levant*, 31 (1999), 123–33; E.C.M. van den Brink and E. Yannai (eds.), *In Quest of Ancient Settlements and Landscapes. Archaeological Studies in Honour of Ram Gophna* (2002). MIDDLE BRONZE AGE: P. Gerstenblith, "A Reassessment of the Beginning of the Middle Bronze Age in Syria-Palestine," in: *Bulletin of the American Schools of Oriental Research,* 237 (1980), 65–84; J.N. Tubb, "The MBIIA Period in Palestine: Its Relationship with Syria and its Origin," in: *Levant,* 15 (1980), 49–62; R. Gophna and P. Beck, "The Rural Aspect of the Settlement Pattern of the Coastal Plain in the Middle Bronze Age II," in: *Tel Aviv,* 8 (1981), 45–80; M.F. Kaplan, G. Harbottle, and E.V. Sayre, "Multi-disciplinary Analysis of Tell el-Yahudiyeh Ware," in: *Archaeometry,* 24 (1982), 127–42; P. Gerstenblith, *The Levant at the Beginning of the Middle Bronze Age* (1983); M. Broshi, and R. Gophna, "Middle Bronze Age II Palestine: Its Settlements and Population," in: *Bulletin of the American Schools of Oriental Research,* 261 (1986), 73–90; P. Bienkowski, "The Division of Middle Bronze II B–C in Palestine," in: *Levant,* 21 (1989), 169–79; A. Kempinski, "The Middle Bronze Age in Northern Israel, Local and External Synchronisms," in: *High, Middle or Low? Acts of the Second International Colloquium on Absolute Chronology (The Bronze Age in the Eastern Mediterranean)* (1990), 69–73; M. Bietak, "Egypt and Canaan During the Middle Bronze Age," in: *Bulletin of the American Schools of Oriental Research,* 281 (1991), 27–72; W.G. Dever, "Tell el-Dab'a and Levantine Middle Bronze Age Chronology: A Rejoinder to Manfred Bietak," in: *Bulletin of the American Schools of Oriental Research,* 281 (1991), 73–79; R. Bonfil, "MB II Pithoi in Palestine," in: *Eretz-Israel,* 23 (1992), 26–37, Heb.; W.G. Dever, "The Chronology of Syria-Palestine in the Second Millennium B.C.E.: A Review of Current Issues," in: *Bulletin of the American Schools of Oriental Research,* 288 (1992), 1–25; J.M. Weinstein, "The Chronology of Palestine in the Early Second Millennium B.C.E.," in: *Bulletin of the American Schools of Oriental Research,* 288 (1992), 27–46; M. Artzy and E. Marcus, "Stratified Cypriot Pottery in MB II A Context at Tel Nami," in: G.C. Ionnides (ed.), *Studies in Honour of Vassos Karageorghis* (1992), 103–10; D. Ben-Tor, "The Historical Implications of Middle Kingdom Scarabs Found in Palestine Bearing Private Names and Titles of Officials," in: *Bulletin of the American Schools of Oriental Research,* 294 (1994), 722; M. Artzy, "Incense, Camels and Collared Rim Jars: Desert Trade Routes and Maritime Outlets in the Second Millennium," in: *Oxford Journal of Archaeology,* 13 (1994), 121–47; J.M. Weinstein, "Reflections on the Chronology of Tell ed-Dab'a," in: W.V. Davies and L. Schofield, *Egypt, the Aegean and the Levant: Interconnections in the Second Millennium BC* (1995), 84–90; G. Philip, "Warrior Burials in the Ancient Near-eastern Bronze Age: The Evidence from Mesopotamia, Western Iran and Syria-Palestine," in: S. Campbell and A. Green (eds.), *The Archaeology of Death in the Ancient Near East* (1995), 140–54; D. Ilan, "Mortuary Practices at Tel Dan in the Middle Bronze Age: A Reflection of Canaanite Society and Ideology," in: S. Campbell and A. Green (eds.), *The Archaeology of Death in the Ancient Near East* (1995), 117–37; P. Beck and U. Zevulun, "Back to Square One," in: *Bulletin of the American Schools of Oriental Research,* 304 (1996), 64–75; D. Ilan, "Middle Bronze Age Painted Pottery From Tel Dan," in: *Levant,* 28 (1996), 157–72; M. Bietak, *Avaris the Capital of the Hyksos: Recent Excavations at Tell ed-Daba* (1996); E.D. Oren (ed.), *The Hyksos: New Historical and Archaeological Perspectives* (1997). LATE BRONZE AGE: E.D. Oren, "'Governors' Residencies in Canaan Under the New Kingdom: A Case Study of Egyptian Administration," *Journal of the Society for the Study of Egyptian Antiquities,* 14 (1984), 37–56; R. Gonen, "Urban Canaan in the Late Bronze Age," in: *Bulletin of the American Schools of Oriental Research,* 253 (1984), 61–73; A. Leonard, "The Late Bronze Age," in: *Biblical Archaeologist,* 52 (1989), 4–39; R. Gonen, *Burial Patterns and Cultural Diversity in Late Bronze Age Canaan* (1992); J.M. Weinstein, "The Collapse of the Egyptian Empire in the Southern Levant," in: W.A. Ward and M.S. Joukowsky (eds.), *The Crisis Years: The Twelfth Century B.C.: From Beyond the Danube to the Tigris* (1992); L. Kolska-Horowitz and I. Milevski, "The Faunal Evidence for Socioeconomic Change Between the Middle and Late Bronze Age in the Southern Levant," in: S.R. Wolff (ed.), *Studies in the Archaeology of Israel and Neighboring Lands in Memory of Douglas L. Esse* (2001), 283–305. IRON AGE AND PERSIAN: E. Stern, "Israel at the Close of the Period of the Monarchy: An Archaeological Survey," in: *Biblical Archaeologist,* 38 (1975), 26–54; J.S. Holladay, "Of Sherds and Strata: Contributions Toward an Understanding of the Archaeology of the Divided Monarchy," in: F.M. Cross (ed.), *Magnalia Dei: The Mighty Acts of God* (1976), 253–93; T. Dothan, *The Philistines and Their Material Culture* (1982); D. Ussishkin, *The Conquest of Lachish by Sennacherib* (1982); E. Stern, *The Material Culture of the Land of the Bible in the Persian Period 538–332 B.C.E.* (1982); W.G. Dever, "The Contribution of Archaeology to the Study of Canaanite and Early Israel Religion," in: P.D. Miller, P.D. Hanson, and S.D. McBride (eds.), *Ancient Israelite Religion* (1987), 209–47; J.S. Holladay, "Religion in Israel and Judah Under the Monarchy: An Explicitly Archaeological Approach," in: P.D. Miller, P.D. Hanson, and S.D. McBride (eds.), *Ancient Israelite Religion* (1987), 249–99; I. Finkelstein, *The Archaeology of the Israelite Settlement* (1988); S. Gitin and W.G. Dever (eds.), *Recent Excavations in Israel: Studies in Iron Age Archaeology* (1989); G.J. Wightman, "The Date of Bethshemesh Stratum II," in: *Abr-Nahrain,* 28 (1990), 96–126; G.J. Wightman, "The Myth of Solomon," in: *Bulletin of the American Schools of Oriental Research,* 277–78 (1990), 5–22; D.J. Wiseman, *Nebuchadrezzar and Babylon* (1991); Z. Gal, *Lower Galilee During the Iron Age* (1992); G. Barkay, "The Redefining of Archaeological Periods: Does the Date 588/586 B.C.E. Indeed Mark the End of Iron Age Culture?" in: *Biblical Archaeology Today: Proceedings of the Second International Congress* (1993): B. MacDonald, *Ammon, Moab and Edom* (1994); I. Finkelstein, "The Date of the Settlement of the Philistines in Canaan," in: *Tel Aviv,* 22 (1995), 213–39; 106–9; I. Finkelstein, "The Archaeology of the United Monarchy: An Alternative View," in: *Levant,* 28 (1996), 177–87; L. Stager, "Ashkelon and the Archaeology of Destruction: Kislev 604 B.C.E.," in: *Eretz Israel,* 25 (1996), 61*–74*; S. Bunomovitz and A. Yasur-Landau, "Philistine and Israelite Pottery: A Comparative Approach to the Question of Pots and People," in: *Tel Aviv,* 23 (1996); I. Milevski, "Settlement Patterns in Northern Judah During the Achaemenid Period According to the Hill Country of Benjamin and Jerusalem Surveys," in: *Bulletin of the Anglo-Israel Archaeological Society,* 15 (1996–97), 7–29; D.C. Hopkins, "The Weight of the Bronze Could Not Be Calculated: Solomon and Economic Reconstruction," in: L.K. Handy, *The Age of Solomon: Scholarship at the Turn of the Millennium* (1997), 300–31; S. Gitin, "The Neo-Assyrian Empire and its Western Periphery: The Levant, With Focus on Philistine Ekron," in: S. Parpola and R.M. Whiting (eds.), *Assyria, 1995* (1997), 77–103; A. Mazar, "Iron Age Chronology: A Reply to I. Finkelstein," in: *Levant,* 29 (1997), 157–67; I. Finkelstein, "Bible Archaeology or Archaeology of Palestine in the Iron Age? A Rejoinder," in: *Levant,* 30 (1998), 167–73; A.G. Vaughn, *Theology, History and Archaeology in the Chronicler's Account* (1999); Y. Alexandre, "The Material Culture of Northern Israel at the Time of the Achaemenid Empire (532–332 B.C.) – Two Recent Excavations," in: *Bulletin of the Anglo-Israel Archaeological Society,* 17 (1999), 102–4; A. Faust, The Rural Community in Ancient Israel During the Iron Age II," in: *Bulletin of the American Schools of Oriental Research,* 317 (2000); K. van der Toorn, "Cuneiform Documents from Syria-Palestine: Texts, Scribes, and Schools," in ZDPV, 116 (2000), 97–113; E. Stern, *Archaeology of the Land of the Bible. Vol. II: The Assyrian, Babylonian and Persian Periods 732–332 B.C.E.* (2001); A. Kuhrt, "Greek Contact with the Levant and Mesopotamia in the First Half of the First Millennium BC: A View from the East," in: G.R. Tstskhladze and A.M. Snodgrass (eds.), *Greek Settlements in the Eastern Mediterranean and the Black Sea* (2002), 17–25; S. Gitin (ed.), "The Four-Horned Altar and Sacred Space: An Archaeological Perspective," in: B. Gittlen (ed.), *Sacred Time, Sacred Space: Archaeology and the Religion of Israel* (2002), 95–123; S. Dalley, "The Transition from Neo-Assyrians to Neo-Babylonians: Break or Continuity?" in: *Eretz-Israel,* 27 (2003), 25*–28*; A. Gilboa, and I. Sharon, "An Archaeological Contribution for the Early Iron Age Chronological Debate: Alternative Chronologies for Phoenicia and Their Effects on the Levant, Cyprus and Greece," in BASOR, 332 (2003), 7–80; S. Gitin, "Neo-Assyrian and Egyptian Hegemony over Ekron in the Seventh Century BCE: A Response to Lawrence E. Stager," in: *Eretz-Israel,* 27 (2003), 55*–61*; O. Lipschits, and J. Blenkinsopp (eds.), *Judah and the Judeans in the Neo-Babylonian Period* (2003); N. Franklin, "The Tombs of the Kings of Israel: Two Recently Identified 9th-Century Tombs From Omride Samaria," in: *Zeitschrift des Deutschen Palästina-Vereins,* 119 (2003), 1–11; P. James, "The Assyrian, Babylonian and Persian Periods in Palestine," in: *Bulletin of the Anglo-Israel Archaeological Society,* 22 (2004), 47–68; D. Ussishkin (ed.), *The Renewed Archaeological Excavations at Lachish (1973–1994),* 5 vols. (2004). HELLENISTIC TO ROMAN: D. Sperber, *Roman Palestine 200–400: Money and Prices* (1974); D. Sperber, *Roman Palestine 200–400: The Land* (1978); M. Stern, "Judaea and her Neighbors in the Days of Alexander Jannaeus," in: L.I. Levine (ed.), *The Jerusalem Cathedra I* (1981), 22–46; J.D. Grainger, *The Cities of Seleucid Syria* (1987); K.G. Holum et al., *King Herod's Dream: Caesarea on the Sea* (1988); A. Kasher, *Jews and Hellenistic Cities in Eretz-Israel* (1990); E. Netzer, *Masada III: The Buildings – Stratigraphy and Architecture* (1991); B. Isaac, *The Limits of Empire: The Roman Army in the East* (1992); F. Millar, *The Roman Near East, 31 BC–AD 337* (1993); Safrai, Z., *The Economy of Roman Palestine* (1993); D. Adan-Bayewitz, *Common Pottery in Roman Galilee* (1993); J.B. Humbert and A. Chambon, *Fouilles de Khirbet Qumran*, vol. 1 (1994); D. Barag and M. Hershkovitz, "Lamps," in: *Masada IV: The Yigael Yadin Excavations 1963–1965: Final Reports* (1994); L.Y. Rahmani, *A Catalogue of Jewish Ossuaries in the Collections of the State of Israel* (1994); E. Stern (ed.), *Excavations at Dor, Final Report,* 2 vols. (1995); S. Loffreda, *La Ceramica: di Macheronte e del' Herodion (90 A.C.–135 D.C.)* (1996); A. Kloner, "Stepped Roads in Roman Palestine," in: ARAM, 8 (1996), 111–37; A. Raban and K. Holum, *Caesarea Maritima: A Retrospective After Two Millennia* (1996); M. Fischer, B. Isaac, and I. Roll, *Roman Roads in Judaea II: The Jaffa-Jerusalem Roads* (1996); L.I. Levine, "The Age of Hellenism: Alexander the Great and the Rise and Fall of the Hasmonean Kingdom," in: H. Shanks (ed.), *Ancient Israel: From Abraham to the Roman Destruction of the Temple* (1999); E. Netzer, *The Palaces of the Hasmoneans and Herod the Great* (2001); R. Bar-Nathan, *Hasmonean and Herodian Palaces at Jericho: Vol. III: The Pottery* (2002); J. Magness, The *Archaeology of Qumran and the Dead Sea Scrolls* (2002); A. Kloner, *Maresha Excavations Final Report I* (2003); Y. Magen, *The Stone Vessel Industry in the Second Temple Period: Excavations at Hizma and the Jerusalem Temple Mount* (2002); S. Gibson, "Stone Vessels of the Early Roman Period From Jerusalem and Palestine: A Reassessment," in: G.C. Bottini, L. Di Segni, and L.D. Chrupcala (eds.), *One Land – Many Cultures: Archaeological Studies in Honour of Stanislao Loffreda OFM* (2003), 287–308; R. Rosenthal-Higenbottom (ed.), *The Nabateans in the Negev* (2003); L.I. Levine, "The First-Century Synagogue: Critical Reassessments and Assessments of the Critical," in: D.R. Edwards (ed.), *Religion and Society in Roman Palestine: Old Questions, New Approaches* (2004); Y. Hirschfeld, *Qumran in Context: Reassessing the Archaeological Evidence* (2004). BYZANTINE: R. Rosenthal and R. Sivan, *Ancient Lamps in the Schlossinger Collection* (1978); U. Zevulun and Y. Olenik, *Function and Design in the Talmudic Period* (1979); M. Broshi, "The Population of Western Palestine in the Roman-Byzantine Period," in: *Bulletin of the American Schools of Oriental Research,* 236 (1979), 1–10; A. Ovadiah, *Corpus of the Byzantine Churches in the Holy Land* (1970), with updates in *Levant,* 13 (1981), 200–61 and *Levant,* 16 (1984), 129–65; C. Dauphin, "Mosaic Pavements as an Index of Prosperity and Fashion," in: *Levant,* 12 (1980), 112–34; L.I. Levine (ed.), *Ancient Synagogues Revealed* (1981); D. Urman, *The Golan: A Profile of a Region During the Roman and Byzantine Periods* (1985); K. Russell, "The Earthquake Chronology of Palestine and Northwest Arabia from the 2nd through the Mid-8th Century A.D.," in: *Bulletin of the American Schools of Oriental Research,* 260 (1985), 37–59; R. Hachlili, *Ancient Jewish Art and Archaeology in the Land of Israel* (1988); C.C. Bottini, L. Di Segni, and E. Alliata (eds.), *Christian Archaeology in the Holy Land: New Discoveries* (1990); J.J. Schwartz, *Lod (Lydda), Israel: From Its Origins Through the Byzantine Period, 5600 BCE–640 CE* (1991); Y. Hirschfeld, *The Judean Desert Monasteries in the Byzantine Period* (1992); Y. Tsafrir (ed.), *Ancient Churches Revealed* (1993); J. Magness, *Jerusalem Ceramic Chronology* (1993); Y. Tsafrir, L. Di Segni, and J. Green (eds.), *Tabula Imperii Romani. Iudaea Palaestina: Eretz Israel in the Hellenistic, Roman and Byzantine Periods* (1994); R. Schick, *The Christian Communities of Palestine From Byzantine to Islamic Rule* (1995); D. Urman and P.V.M. Flesher (eds.), *Ancient Synagogues,* 2 vols. (1995); Y. Hirschfeld, *The Palestinian Dwelling in the Roman-Byzantine Period* (1995); F. Vitto, "The Interior Decoration of Palestinian Churches and Synagogues," in: *Byzantinische Forschungen Internationale Zeitschrift für Byzantinistik,* 21 (1995), 283–300; C. Dauphin, "Brothels, Baths and Babes: Prostitution in the Byzantine Holy Land," in: *Classics Ireland,* 3 (1996), 47–72; J. Magness and G. Avni, "Jews and Christians in a Late Roman Cemetery at Beth Guvrin," in: H. Lapin (ed.), *Religious and Ethnic Communities in Late Roman Palestine* (1998), 87–114; B. Isaac, "Jews, Christians and Others in Palestine: The Evidence from Eusebius," in: M. Goodman (ed.), *Jews in a Graeco-Roman World* (1998) 65–74; C. Dauphin, *La Palestine Byzantine: Peuplement et Populations* (1998); M. Fischer, "Marble Studies: Roman Palestine and Marble Trade," in: *Xenia,* 40 (1998); S. Gibson, *The Cave of John the Baptist* (2004); O. Shamir, "Byzantine and Early Islamic Textiles Excavated in Israel," in: *Textile History,* 32 (2001), 93–105; S.A. Kingsley, *Shipwreck Archaeology of the Holy Land: Processes and Parameters* (2004). ISLAMIC TO OTTOMAN: D. Pringle, "The Medieval Pottery of Palestine and Transjordan (A.D. 636–1500): An Introduction, Gazetteer and Bibliography," in: *Medieval Ceramics,* 5 (1981), 45–60; M. Sharon, "The Cities of the Holy Land Under Islamic Rule," in: *Cathedra,* 40 (1986), 83–120; D. Whitcomb, "Khirbet al-Mafjar Reconsidered: The Ceramic Evidence," in: *Bulletin of the American Schools of Oriental Research,* 271 (1988), 51–67; M. Rosen-Ayalon, *The Early Islamic Monuments of Haram al-Sharif: An Iconographic Study* (1989); M. Gil, *A History of Palestine, 634–1099* (1992); W. Khalidi (ed.), *All That Remains* (1992); G.R.D. King, A. Cameron, and L. Conrad (eds.), *The Byzantine and Early Islamic Near East* (1992–95); B.Z. Kedar (ed.), *The Horns of Hattin* (1992); D. Pringle, *The Churches of the Crusader Kingdom of Jerusalem,* vols. 1–3 (1993–); S.A. Rosen and G. Avni, "The Edge of the Empire: The Archaeology of Pastoral Nomads in the Southern Negev Highlands in Late Antiquity," in: *Biblical Archaeologist,* 56 (1993), 189–99; H. Kennedy, *Crusader Castles* (1994); B. Kühnel, *Crusader Art of the Twelfth Century* (1994); J. Folda, *The Art of the Crusaders in the Holy Land, 1098–1187* (1995); R. Ellenblum, "Three Generations of Frankish Castle-Building in the Latin Kingdom of Jerusalem," in: M. Balard (ed.), *Autour de la Première Crois-*

ade (1996), 517–51; N. Luz, "The Construction of an Islamic City in Palestine: The Case of Umayyad al-Ramla," in: *Journal of the Royal Asiatic Society*, 3, 7, 1 (1997), 2754; D. Pringle, *Secular Buildings in the Crusader Kingdom of Jerusalem* (1997); R. Ellenblum, *Frankish Rural Settlement in the Latin Kingdom of Jerusalem* (1998); R. Schick, "Archaeological Sources for the History of Palestine: Palestine in the Early Islamic Period: Luxuriant Legacy," in: *Near Eastern Archaeology*, 61 (1998), 74–108; U. Avner and J. Magness, "Early Islamic Settlement in the Southern Negev," in: *Bulletin of the American Schools of Oriental Research*, 310 (1998), 39–57; A.J. Boas, *Crusader Archaeology: The Material Culture of the Latin East* (1999); S. Rozenberg (ed.), *Knights of the Holy Land: The Crusader Kingdom of Jerusalem* (1999); S. Gibson, *Jerusalem in Original Photographs, 1850–1920* (2003); J. Magness, *The Archaeology of Early Islamic Settlement in Palestine* (2003).

[Shimon Gibson (2nd ed.)]

ARCHANGEL (Rus. **Arkhangelsk**), White Sea port and capital of Archangel district, Russia; excluded from the *Pale of Settlement. The nucleus of the Jewish community was formed between 1828 and 1856 by young Jewish conscripts who had been sent to the *Cantonists' institution in Archangel and were allowed to settle there after being discharged from the army. In 1897 there were 248 Jews in Archangel. After the Pale was abolished in 1917 the number of Jews increased, reaching 850 by 1923. In 1926 there were 1,449 Jews in the entire oblast (0.3% of the total population). In 1939 they numbered 1,346 in the city and 1,858 in the entire district. Between 1939 and 1941 many Jews from the western areas then annexed by the Soviet Union were deported to Archangel and its environs.

[Yehuda Slutsky]

ARCHELAIS, ancient town in the Jordan Valley, north of Jericho. It was founded by Archelaus, the son of Herod, and was later given to Salome, Herod's sister, who in turn bequeathed it in 10 C.E. to Livia, wife of the emperor Augustus. Archelaus built the town as a center for his vast date groves for which he diverted water extending from the springs of Na'aran (Neara; Jos., Ant. 17:1–340). Pliny the Elder (Nat. Hist. v, 44) also refers to the high quality date groves that once grew in this specific region. According to a Roman road map (*tabula Peutingeriana*), Archelais was situated 12 Roman miles N. of Jericho; it is similarly indicated on the *Madaba mosaic Map. It is now identified with Khirbet Beiyudat – as originally suggested by H. Guthe – and excavations conducted there in 1986–91 and 1994–99 by H. Hizmi revealed a large building built of ashlars preserved to a height of 30 ft. (9 m.) and a fifth-century C.E. basilica church with highly decorated mosaic floors and a dedicatory inscription. Substantial remains were uncovered from the Second Temple period (first century C.E.), including ritual bathing pools, residential quarters, and pottery and stone vessels, all lending support to the identification of this site as Archelais. A large inn was apparently built at the site at the time of Herod Agrippa I (41–44 C.E.) and much of its plan was revealed during the recent excavations. It was destroyed at the time of Vespasian's march on Jericho in 67–68 C.E.

BIBLIOGRAPHY: Guthe, in: MNDPV (1911), 65; Abel, in: RB, 22 (1913), 236; Dalman, in: PJB, 9 (1913), 74; Alt, *ibid.*, 23 (1927), 31; 27 (1931), 46; Avi-Yonah, Land, 104, 164. **ADD. BIBLIOGRAPHY:** H. Hizmi, "The Byzantine Church at Khirbet el-Beiyudat – Preliminary Report," in: G.C. Bottini, L. Di Segni, and E. Alliata (eds.), *Christian Archaeology in the Holy Land* (1990); H. Hizmi, "New Discoveries at the Second Temple Period Site of Archelais," in: *Qadmoniot*, 37 (2004), 95–101.

[Michael Avi-Yonah / Shimon Gibson (2nd ed.)]

ARCHELAUS, ethnarch of Judea (4 B.C.E.–c. 6 C.E.), son of Herod by his Samaritan wife Malthace. In his fourth will Herod designated Archelaus king of Judea and Samaria, which constituted the major portion of his kingdom. The testament required confirmation by Augustus. Archelaus prepared to set out for Rome for this purpose immediately after the period of mourning for his father. Before he was able to depart, events in Judea adversely affected his position. At his first meeting in the Temple with the representatives of the people, they demanded relief from the heavy burden of taxation imposed by Herod. Archelaus sought to postpone the matter until his return from Rome in order to allow their passions to cool. However, the extremist elements among the people assembled and decreed mourning for the scholars Judah son of Ẓipporai and Mattathias b. Margalot and their associates, who had been put to death at Herod's command for tearing down the Roman eagle from the Temple gates. The extremists presented additional demands: the punishment of Herod's advisers who had caused the death of these scholars; the appointment of another high priest in place of *Joezer, son of Boethus; and the expulsion of the Greek officials from the royal court. It was the period of the festival of Passover and multitudes of pilgrims were streaming to Jerusalem. Archelaus, fearing disorders, sent a company of troops against the instigators. This act aroused popular anger and, when the soldiers were stoned, Archelaus ordered them to suppress the uprising by force. In the clash which followed approximately 3,000 people were killed. As a result, when Archelaus reached Rome to petition the emperor to confirm his father's testament, a delegation of the people had also arrived there from Judea to request that the authority of the House of Herod be abolished and that Judea be annexed to the province of Syria. The delegation was supported by 8,000 Jews resident in Rome. The Greek cities also sent envoys requesting their transfer to the immediate authority of the imperial legate of Syria. A third deputation of the Herodian family, however, demanded either the equal partition of the entire kingdom among all the sons of Herod, or awarding the throne to Antipas. Meantime, the position in Judea had deteriorated, and the Syrian governor *Quintilius Varus was compelled to suppress the revolt by force. The emperor's decision was influenced in large measure by these disorders in Judea. He did not nullify Herod's will completely, but made one basic change: abolishing the monarchy, and granting Judea, Idumea, and Samaria to Archelaus with the title of ethnarch, promising him the title of king later if he proved successful in his rule. The areas allotted to Herod's other two sons, *Herod Philip and *Antipas, were also confirmed and the title tetrarch bestowed on them. The Greek cities of Gaza, Gadara (Hammath-Gadar), and Susita (Hippos) were annexed to the province of Syria. Meanwhile peace had been restored in Judea after the war with Quintilius Varus. Archelaus ruled with a strong hand, suppressing the rebellious elements in the country with the utmost cruelty and brutality. He replaced the high priest Joezer by his brother Eleazar, who in turn was supplanted by Joshua, son of Seth. He inherited his father's passion for building, and erected the city of Archelais near Jericho, and built a new palace in Jericho in place of that destroyed during the disturbances. He planted the plain with palm trees and installed an irrigation system in it. His bad relations with the people deteriorated further as a result of his marriage to *Glaphyra, widow of his stepbrother *Alexander, by whom she had had children, such a marriage being prohibited by biblical law (Lev. 18:18). In 6 C.E. a delegation of the people again complained of him to Augustus. This time, the emperor dismissed Archelaus from his ethnarchy, exiled him to Vienne in Gaul, and confiscated his property. Judea was annexed to the Syrian province and placed under a procurator responsible to the authority of the governor of Syria. Archelaus died in exile c. 16 C.E.

BIBLIOGRAPHY: Jos., Ant., 17:200–355; Jos., Wars, 1:668 ff.; 2:1–100, 114–6; Matt. 2:22; Klausner, Bayit Sheni, 4 (1950^2), 167, 170 ff.

[Abraham Schalit]

ARCHERD, ARMY (**Armand Archer**; 1919–), U.S. columnist. The son of a textile worker, Armand Archer was born and raised in the Bronx, New York. In 1939, he moved with his family to Los Angeles, where he studied languages at UCLA. After serving on a destroyer in the Navy during WWII, Archerd returned to Los Angeles hoping to pursue a career in writing. He worked in the Hollywood bureau of the Associated Press until he was hired as a "legman" for Harrison Carroll, the Hollywood columnist at the now defunct *Los Angeles Herald Express*. In 1953, Archerd began his iconic career as a columnist for *Daily Variety*. His upbeat "Just for Variety" column presented an assortment of short and unrelated pieces of entertainment news, and he was soon recognized as one of Hollywood's most important opinion-makers and cultural icons. He has won numerous awards for his journalism, most notably the Journalistic Merit Award which he received in 1962 from the Golden Globes. In 1985, Archerd broke the story that Rock Hudson had AIDS and the article contributed to the growing awareness of the epidemic. In addition to his column, Archerd hosted numerous variety shows and movie premieres, the most famous being the red carpet ceremony at the Academy Awards. He also developed a second career as an actor, playing bit parts in over a hundred films and TV shows, often appearing as himself. In 1984, he was given his own star on the Hollywood Walk of Fame to commemorate his iconic status. He is married to actress Selma Archerd.

[Max Joseph (2nd ed.)]

ARCHIPHERECITES, title. In the Novella 145 of *Justinian, of 553, the "elders, archipherecites, presbyters, and those called magistrates" were forbidden to use the power of anathema to prevent the reading of the Scriptures in synagogue in Greek, Latin, or another language other than the original. The title was apparently applied to the intellectual leaders of Palestinian Jewry after the abolition of the patriarchate in 425. It is assumed that the archipherecites mentioned by Justinian was *Mar Zutra III, who was at the head of the Academy of Tiberias, by virtue of which position he was the official leader of Palestinian Jewry. The word archipherecites is apparently a hybrid word formed from the Aramaic פִּירְקָא (*pirka*) and the Greek ἀρχή ("chief") and is thus equivalent to the phrase *resh pirka*, "head of the school" (cf. Kid. 31b).

BIBLIOGRAPHY: J. Parkes, *Conflict of Church and Synagogue* (1934), 292–3; Juster, Juifs, 1 (1914), 399 ff.; 2 (1914), 116 ff.; Mann, Egypt, 1 (1920), 58–97, 269.

ARCHISYNAGOGOS (ἀρχισυνάγωγος; Heb. *rosh ha-keneset*), title used in classical times referring to the head of the synagogue, who served as the leader of the Jewish community. The *archisynagogos* is known from Jewish inscriptions in the period of the Roman Empire and from other sources (Yoma 7:1; Mark 5:22 et al.). His functions were varied and included the arrangement of the service in the synagogue and of everything related to its physical administration as well as supervision of general community affairs. The *archisynagogos* was held in high esteem and it was considered a great honor to marry one of his daughters (Pes. 49b; cf. Git. 60a). For a time it was customary at the consolation meals of mourners to drink a cup of wine in honor of the *archisynagogos*, but this was later abolished (TJ, Ber. 3:1, 6a; cf. Sem. 14, end). *Archisynagogoi* are known in many places: Ereẓ Israel, Syria, Asia Minor, and Rome (see Juster, Juifs, 1 (1914), 450). Outside Ereẓ Israel the *archisynagogos* collected charity funds and donations for Jews in the Holy Land. The manner in which the *archisynagogos* was chosen is not known. The title *archisynagogos* appears also as an honorific, being applied even to women and children. A Roman law of 331 C.E. exempted the *archisynagogos* from physical servitude (to the state, *munus corporale*; Codex Theodosianus 16:8:4), and another law, of 397, exempted them from several state taxes and granted them a legal position equivalent to that of Christian clergymen (Codex Theodosianus 16:8:13). During this period the *archisynagogos* was subject to the **nasi*, who could remove him from office and appoint another in his place (Epiphanius, Panarion, haer. 30:11). According to Finkelstein, however, the *rosh ha-keneset* mentioned in the Mishnah (Sot. 7:7; Yoma 7:1) refers only to the head of a Pharisaic congregation and not to the *archisynagogos* mentioned above.

BIBLIOGRAPHY: S. Krauss, *Synagogale Altertuemer* (1922), 114–21; G.F. Moore, *Judaism*, 1 (1946), 289; 3 (1948), 94 (includes bibliography); L. Finkelstein, *Ha-Perushim ve-Anshei Keneset ha-Gedolah* (1950), 31 ff.; B. Lifshitz, *Donateurs et fondateurs dans les synagogues juives* (1967), index.

[Uriel Rappaport]

ARCHITECTURE AND ARCHITECTS. Archaeology has provided information about "Israelite" architectural practices from the 10th to 6th centuries B.C.E., and to "Jewish" styles of building and decoration from the late Hellenistic period (1st century B.C.E.) and later.

In Antiquity

The planning of isolated dwellings may be traced back to late prehistoric times. Natural geographical and topographical conditions presented early builders with a choice of materials: clay for bricks, stone for walls and wood for ceilings. Structures – circular, curvilinear and rectangular in plan – may be traced back to the Natufian and Pre-Pottery Neolithic periods. Wooden posts supported thatched ceilings. In environments lacking in trees, ceilings were constructed of corbelled stone. Signs of village/town planning with complex architecture, street networks, drainage and water-collecting systems, were already evident within some Neolithic settlements, notably at PPNA Jericho and at PNA Sha'ar Hagolan. Sophisticated architectural planning, however, did not precede the Early Bronze Age. Complex structures used as dwellings (of broadroom or longroom design), palaces, administrative buildings, and temples are known from this period. Although dressed stones appear for the first time as supports for wooden posts in the EB Age temples at Megiddo, most of the walls of this period were built of fieldstones or mudbrick covered with clay plaster and lime. Settlements were surrounded by fortifications, with towers and chambered gates at intervals, and were built on rubble foundations along a predetermined topographical course.

The fortification systems of the Middle Bronze Age were extremely complex engineering feats and were apparently built as a response to the development of sophisticated military sapping equipment. The arch was known in monumental construction from as early as the Middle Bronze Age. At Tel Dan a city gate was unearthed with its outer portal preserved as a true arch with mud-brick voussoirs. Dressed orthostats are known from a number of city gates dating from the Middle Bronze Age, for example at Gezer and Shechem, and further afield at MB sites in Lebanon and Syria.

The efficient architectural planning of Iron Age II cities and towns has become evident as a result of the extensive excavation of a number of Israelite sites, for example at Tell Beit Mirsim, Tell el-Nasbeh and Tell el-Farah (north). Public buildings, dwellings of various sizes and plans, water systems and other underground features are characteristic of such sites. Nothing has survived of the two main buildings constructed by Solomon in Jerusalem – the Temple and the "House of the Forest of Lebanon," both of which were described in the Book of Kings. The description of these buildings suggests that they were large and had walls built of ashlars and with cedar ceiling beams requiring many internal columns for support. The Temple is believed to have been a tripartite structure built on a longitudinal axis and imported cedar beams were utilized; the Bible relates how Hiram, king of Tyre, lent Solomon his builders. The four-room or three-room building units were typical of the dwellings of this period. Dressed stones comprising smoothed or marginal-drafted ashlars are known from the Iron Age II, mainly from the 10th century B.C.E., sometimes laid in alternate courses of headers and stretchers to ensure stability. Wooden beams were sometimes added into the walls horizontally between the courses of stones, to provide elasticity and to minimize damage from earthquakes. Stones were dressed with chisels. The use of the dentate chisel edge is known only from the Persian/Hellenistic period onwards. Windows were occasionally bordered with an indented balustrade (e.g., Ramat Rahel) and the Proto-Aeolic capital – decorated with a triangle flanked by spiraling volutes – was used in doorjambs of important buildings (e.g., Jerusalem, Samaria, Megiddo). Most private houses, however, continued to be built of rubble walls with smoothed mud walls, coated with lime plaster. Complex mud-brick construction was discovered during excavations of Persian-period structures at Tell Jemmeh, with pitched barrel-vaulting in residences and storerooms.

From the Hellenistic period and through the Roman period, architectural planning became much more expansive within cities, while building projects within the rural countryside remained modest and followed on techniques of construction used in previous periods. Various types of mortar and brick construction techniques were introduced into the region in the Roman period. Imported materials, such as marble, were utilized in the construction of palaces and large buildings, especially from the time of Herod the Great in the late 1st century B.C.E. The engineering achievements of the Romans in regard to the construction of roads, bridges and aqueducts, also had its effect on the region. New leisure projects – baths, theaters, amphitheaters – were constructed.

It is hard to define Jewish architecture prior to the Roman period, but from the late 1st century B.C.E. onwards one may point out the existence of tomb architecture with internal decorations (e.g., the tombs at Akeldama in Jerusalem), freestanding tomb monuments (e.g., the Tombs of Absalom and Zachariah in the Kidron Valley in Jerusalem), and public buildings identified as synagogues (e.g., Masada, Herodium, Gamla, Jericho, and Modi'in), which were undoubtedly created by Jewish artisans and architects. The Temple and the esplanade on which it was built was one of the architectural accomplishments from the time of Herod the Great (37–4 B.C.E.). Massive fortifications are known from this period as well. During the Late Roman and Byzantine periods, Jewish architecture continued to be exemplified by various forms of synagogues (e.g., Chorazin, Capernaum, Beth Alpha, etc.) and tombs (e.g., Beth Shearim).

[Shimon Gibson (2nd ed.)]

Modern Period

In modern times there is an abundance of Jewish architects but – except perhaps to a certain extent in Israel – no Jewish architecture to speak of. The men who designed the synagogues for European communities may well have been engaged by their coreligionists for domestic architecture as well. The names of medieval Jewish magnates are frequently associated with stone dwelling-houses, some of which still stand. There is indeed reason to believe that in England – perhaps for reasons of security – it was the Jews who pioneered domestic stone building, a fashion they introduced from the Continent. Notwithstanding such isolated instances, however, it is clear that Jews played little or no part in general architecture before the age of Emancipation. It was only in the 19th century that Jewish architects began to emerge in general practice and to be given civic, monumental, or even ecclesiastical commissions in many countries of Europe without any apparent discrimination. Curiously enough, two of the first Jewish architects to have attained some distinction in the field were both wealthy English Sephardim: the convert to Christianity, George *Basevi, and David *Mocatta. The latter's designs for a series of railway stations in the 1830s and 1840s had a lasting influence. The same tradition of the "gentleman architect" was represented somewhat later by the German Georg Itzig, who designed the princely Palazzo Revoltella in Trieste, and in the same Italian Renaissance style, the Deutsche Reichsbank in Berlin (1879). Around the turn of the century many other Reichsbank branches, designed with the floridity characteristic of German architecture of this period, were built by E. Jacobsthal (1839–1902). In Austria a pioneer in theater architecture was Oscar *Strnad, and in Germany Oskar *Kaufmann worked in the same field, most notably in his Stadttheater in Bremerhaven (1909) and his Komoedie Theater in Berlin (1924). As in other spheres of modern culture, Jews were among the first to break away from conventional forms in architecture. In Germany a pioneer was Alfred Messel, whose Wertheim Department Store in Berlin (1897), a remarkable combination of stone, steel, and glass, is generally considered one of the important influences on modern architecture, notwithstanding its neo-Gothic romanticism. Another modern master was Eric *Mendelsohn, whose expressionistic buildings, such as his Einstein Tower in Potsdam (1919–20), have a highly sculptural appearance. At the turn of the century Budapest was a city vibrating with life. In the feverish building boom of the era, Jewish architects played a considerable role. A new style, Secession (Art Nouveau, Jugendstil), came to the fore, which in Hungary merged folkloristic, and even Oriental motifs, with historicizing styles. In the center of the new architecture stood the non-Jewish architect Ödön Lechner, and many of his helpers and coworkers were Jews or of Jewish descent. His works, and those of other architects of the period were not only neglected, but even frowned upon in later decades only to be restored in the 1970s and 1980s. At present they are highly valued sites of the Hungarian capital. Elsewhere in Europe, among the most influential of modern French architects was Alexandre Persitz (1910–). He was editor of the review *Architecture d'aujourd'hui* and a leading figure in the reconstruction of the city of Le Havre after World War II, as well as the architect of a number of synagogues. Other influential contemporary French architects include Emmanuel Pontrémoli, who taught at the Ecole des Beaux Arts in Paris, Georges Goldberg, Georges Gumpel, and Claude *Meyer-Lévy. In Italy mention should be made of Manfredo d'Urbino and Bruno Zevi, who in addition to being a practicing architect and a writer on the subject was secretary general of the Italian Institute of Town Planning; Julien Flegenheimer (1880–1938), the brother of the author Edmund *Fleg, was architect of the Palace of the League of Nations in Geneva. One of the most interesting and most successful workers' housing projects, the Spaarndammerplantsoen in Amsterdam, was designed by the Dutchman Michel de *Klerk. Indeed, it is perhaps symptomatic of the intense Jewish interest in social welfare and social activism that Jewish architects have tended to be associated with such public developments in disproportionate numbers. One of the most famous of these is the Karl Marx Hof in Vienna, built in 1930 by the partnership of Frank and Wlach. In Russia, particularly since the Bolshevik Revolution, a number of Jewish architects have had prominent public careers. One of the first of these, J.C. Gewuertz, was a leader of the avant-garde even in prerevolutionary times. In the 1920s he won great esteem and became dean of the school of architecture of the Academy. The architect A.I. Gegello (1891–1965) was well known for his House of Culture in Leningrad, reputed to have the best acoustics of any theater in Russia; his Botkin Memorial Hospital for Infectious Diseases is a striking protest against the over-centralization and dehumanization of modern medicine. N.A. Trotski's glass factory "Belyi Bychek," designed in the 1920s, is a bold and masterly integration of diverse elements. His project for the Palace of the Soviets in Leningrad in 1937, however, exhibits a lifeless neoclassicism which may perhaps be attributed to circumstances. A country in the New World in which Jews have been particularly active in the field of architecture is Brazil. A forerunner of modern architecture in Brazil was Russian-born Gregori Warchavchik (1896–1972), who built the first modern house in the country in São Paulo in 1927 and supervised the Brazilian architecture exhibit in the Exhibition of the Modern House which he organized in 1930. Rino Levi (1901–1965) was among the most prolific of Brazilian architects, working in American skyscraper style. In this he was rivaled by Henrique Mindlin (1911–1971), author of *Modern Architecture in Brazil* (1956), whose work has helped to change the skyline of Rio de Janeiro. One of the collaborators in the plans for the new Brazilian capital, Brasilia, as well as a designer of the country's most modern synagogues, was Elias Kaufman (1928–). The versatile Roberto Burle Marx used the luxuriant Brazilian landscape as an integral part of his architecture. The record of distinguished Jewish architects in the United States is long and impressive. The founder of the tradition was German-born Leopold *Eidlitz, an important figure in the Gothic movement, who began his career in America shortly after the middle of the 19th century. He built, besides a number of churches – his Christ Church Cathedral in St. Louis has been called "the most churchly church in America" – the former Temple Emanu-El, one of the most notable buildings in old

New York. Dankmar *Adler, in conjunction with the non-Jew Louis Sullivan, was largely responsible for the evolution of the American skyscraper. Albert *Kahn, creator of the Ford automobile works outside Detroit, has been described as the most influential industrial architect of modern times. Other important Jewish names in 20th-century American architecture are Louis I. *Kahn, who has been called a major form maker; Max *Abramovitz, designer of the Philharmonic Hall in New York; Victor Gruen (d. 1980), who may be said to have invented the suburban shopping center; Albert Mayer (d. 1981) and Percival *Goodman, both well known as city planners as well as architects; Isadore Rosenfield, a leader in functional hospital design; and Gordon *Bunshaft. Ely Jacques *Kahn, Richard J. *Neutra, Paul Friedberg, Lawrence Halprin, Bertrand Goldberg, Rudolph Schindler, Arnold W. *Brunner, Peter D. *Eisenman, Frank O. *Gehry, Robert A.M. *Stern, Daniel *Liebeskind, Stanley *Tigerman, Richard *Meier, and James *Polshek.

In Modern Ereẓ Israel

The architecture in Jewish towns and settlements in modern Ereẓ Israel was conditioned, on the whole, more by the urgent housing requirements of the various *aliyyot* than by any other consideration. The aesthetic aspect mostly reflected the trends prevalent in the architects' countries of origin.

During the Ottoman period two broad categories of buildings were built in the country: Arab village buildings, constructed on the traditional pattern, without architects, using building materials found nearby and in distinctive harmony with the terrain; and town architecture, which was typically Mediterranean, based on southern Italian mixed with traditional Arab styles. In addition, there were buildings erected by the Turkish government, which employed German architects. These were of a high standard, in a pleasant, restrained style. The buildings erected by the Jewish Colonization Association, in a French style, were attractive and less pretentious.

Large-scale Jewish immigration after World War I brought in its wake an acute housing shortage, and there was a rush of building unprecedented in Oriental countries. The building boom provided full employment for the architects and engineers then in the country, but brought about the entry of a number of self-taught technicians into the building field. Many of the buildings of the period were badly designed. During the same period, but on an entirely different level, there was an attempt by creative architects to achieve a modern Oriental style.

The process of introducing a style and working toward its formation was slow and lasted many years. The experiments begun by Alexander *Baerwald and his pupils even before World War I (notably the buildings of the Reali School and the Technion in Haifa, 1912) were not continued. The work of Ze'ev Berlin in Tel Aviv is also noteworthy, but no one continued his work. British government architects also made attempts to invent an original colonial style, most notable being the European-influenced Clifford Holiday, and A. St. B. Harrison, the romanticist, whose small police stations have remained attractive throughout the years. Lastly, there were the architects of Jewish institutions: F. Kornberg, who designed the university campus on Mount Scopus; Eric Mendelsohn, who designed the Hadassah Hospital on the same hill; Leopold *Krakauer and Richard *Kaufmann who both made a particularly valuable contribution to Israel architecture; and Yoḥanan *Ratner, who designed the Jewish agency building in Jerusalem and who dedicated himself to training architects at the *Technion.

During the 1930s Western European architects became prominent in Palestine. They had studied, and in some cases worked, with such great teachers as Gropius and Le Corbusier. Buildings were erected whose architectural style is unquestionably balanced. These include urban workers' housing projects by Aryeh *Sharon and J. Neufeld, and the buildings by Z. *Rechter, Sh. Misteczkin, D. Karmi, and G. Shani. On the other hand, in contrast to the "Orientalists," there were European architects who brought with them European concepts of architecture and made no attempt to adapt them to local topography or climate or to translate them into local terms.

The establishment of the State of Israel in 1948 led to mass immigration and the need for mass housing. In the early 1950s thousands were living in tin huts, wooden prefabs, and tents. Permanent accommodation had to be built quickly and cheaply. Thus the famous "*shikkun*" – quickly constructed housing project – became a feature of many parts of the country. Quantity was the criterion, and the qualitative side was neglected, in regard to the building, the materials, and the efficiency of execution, as well as the architectural and aesthetic aspects. Architectural styles in Israel include the Le Corbusier style, the Brazilian and the Japanese, brutalism, and plasticism. There are also attempts to adapt foreign ideas to specific conditions in Israel, particularly in terms of protection against the sun, and to draw inspiration from ancient Oriental architecture. Here and there one can find regional motifs, such as the use of a vaulted concrete shell, or the mixture of concrete and stone.

Heading the list of noteworthy buildings in Israel are the buildings of the Hebrew University in Jerusalem, the Tel Aviv University, and the new Technion campus in Haifa, as well as the Haifa University (architect: Oscar Niemeyer). The Weizmann Institute at Reḥovot has some good teaching and research buildings; the Hebrew Union College building in Jerusalem (architect: Heinz *Rau) is another excellent structure. Important halls that have been built in the major cities include the Mann Auditorium in Tel Aviv (architects: Rechter-Karmi-Rechter), Binyanei ha-Ummah in Jerusalem (architect: Ze'ev Rechter), and the Haifa Theater (architect: Shelomo Gilead. In Jerusalem the Israel Museum complex is outstanding (architects: Mansfeld-Gad), as is the Knesset building (architects: Y. Klarwein and D. Karmi) and the new Supreme Court building (architects: R. Carmi and A. Carmi Melamed). Housing architecture has also improved considerably; well-built projects are to be found, notably, in the Ramat Aviv district in north Tel Aviv (architect-planners: J. Perlstein-R. Banat).

BIBLIOGRAPHY: G.R.H. Wright, *Ancient Building in South Syria and Palestine*, 2 vols. (1985); R. Hachlili, *Ancient Jewish Art and Archaeology in the Land of Israel* (1988); A. Kempinski and R. Reich (eds.), *The Architecture of Ancient Israel: From the Prehistoric to Persian Periods* (1992); H. Darin, *Public Housing in Israel* (1959); *Contemporary Architecture of the World, 1961* (1961), 34–36; Ministry of Housing, *Shikkun u-Veniyyah…* (1962); A. Sharon, *Tikhnun Fizi be-Yisrael* (1951); B. Tammuz (ed.), *Ommanut Yisrael* (1963), 213–46 pl. 153–225; EIV; A. Reifenberg, *Architektur und Kuntsgewerbe im alten Israel* (1925); Albright, Arch; M. Avi-Yonah and S. Yeivin, *Kadmoniyyot Arẓenu* (1955); M. Avi-Yonah (ed.), *Sefer Yerushalayim* (1956), 176–90, 312–418; Cohen, in: Roth, Art, 121–54; Goodman, *ibid.*, 719–56; Jamilly, in: JHSET, 18 (1958), 127–41; Mayer, Art, index.

ARCHIVES, (a) a place where old records are collected and preserved in an orderly fashion in their entirety, as well as groups of interrelated documents originating from individuals or a public body ("historical archives"); (b) registers and filing units of current documents in an office ("current archive"); (c) collections of material on a specific subject gathered for documentation ("documentary archive"). In this article, wherever Jewish archives are mentioned, the reference is to the more general meaning unless specific reference is made to historical archives.

As a source of Jewish history in the various countries, differentiation must be made between Jewish records, i.e., records accumulated by Jewish authorities and institutions, or by individual Jews, in the course and as part of their work, and records concerning Jews produced by non-Jewish authorities in the course of their administrative activities and preserved in non-Jewish archives. In many instances, however, only one type is available.

This entry is arranged according to the following outline:

BIBLICAL PERIOD
POST-BIBLICAL PERIOD
MIDDLE AGES
MODERN TIMES
- **In the Diaspora**
  - GERMANY
  - RUSSIA
  - POLAND
  - CZECHOSLOVAKIA
  - AUSTRIA
  - ENGLAND
  - FRANCE
  - ITALY
  - GREECE
  - THE NETHERLANDS
  - UNITED STATES OF AMERICA
- **Holocaust Period**
  - UNITED STATES OF AMERICA
- **Major Archives**
  - THE CENTRAL ARCHIVES OF THE HISTORY OF THE JEWISH PEOPLE (CAHJP)
  - CENTRAL ZIONIST ARCHIVES (CZA)
- **Israel**
  - MAJOR ISRAEL ARCHIVES

BIBLICAL PERIOD

When it is used with reference to the ancient Near East, the term archive can be generally defined as a collection of documents (including letters and other functional texts) that were gathered for use in administrative, legal, political, and economic proceedings and activities. However, one should note the functional difference between an archive for documents in current usage, usually attached to a bureau dealing with the subject, and one whose contents were preserved after use for memorial purposes or for the historical value of the material. The latter instance does not require the archive's connection with any particular bureau, though the relationship did exist. The difference between an "archive" and a "library" in the ancient Near East lies in the nature of the material collected in them and their depositors. *Libraries were not so much treasuries as they were repositories for works of an essentially religious and ritualistic character (though not exclusively so), intended for use by people such as priests and scribes, whose interest in and use of the works was continuous and protracted. As a result of the quality of the writing, climatic conditions, and historical developments, all archival finds have been in the northern part of the Fertile Crescent (Mesopotamia, Anatolia, northern Syria, and Phoenicia). In the more southern parts of the Crescent, Palestine, and Egypt, no real archives were found, except for the "archive" of *El-Amarna, which was preserved because its documents are inscribed on clay tablets and which hardly serves as a good example of a typical archive, as it is rather a selection out of an archive. Although it is to be assumed that archives and libraries must have existed, particularly in Egypt, information about them is sporadic and comes secondhand from indirect sources, dating after the Persian period (especially the Hellenistic and later period).

The preservation of epigraphic material in archives accompanies writing from its earliest stages. The earliest epigraphic find, from the beginning of the second half of the fourth millennium, from stratum IV of the city of Uruk, is an archival collection of documents pertaining to the local temple administration, found attached to a structure for storage. Such is the case of finds from Jemdat Nasr (c. 3300 B.C.E.), which were also unearthed near a storeroom. It is possible to conclude that the earliest archives were directly connected storerooms. This conclusion finds some support in the Sumerian terminology, in which the usual terms for "school" and "archive" might be "a sealed house" or a "storehouse," that is, some form of commercial storage area. This is borne out in economic documents from Larsa of the end of the third millennium B.C.E. In addition to this, archaeological evidence from several Sumerian cities, such as Lagash, indicates that the collections of documents at temples were placed in narrow rooms, inaccessible directly from the outside of the building. They had to be entered by ladder or stairs via the second story of the building. These appear to have been archives for the preservation of documents no longer in use. This type of preservation was still in use in the 15th century B.C.E. (*Nuzi), and during the Assyrian period (about the eighth century; *Calneh). The archives of the temple at Sumer also preserved the documents of private parties, who utilized them to store items of personal importance. This custom was maintained in various places for hundreds of years.

Despite clear evidence regarding the existence of archives in the Sumerian period, no such "library" has yet been unearthed, though individual texts that might be expected to have been stored in such libraries have been found. It is nearly certain that the lack of such finds does not indicate the lack of their existence. A number of tablets containing headings of Sumerian compositions in catalog-like form indicate the practical necessity for such an arrangement. Furthermore, the usage of the Sumerian term, whose original meaning was "tablet container" broadened to imply "storage place for tablets," in connection with a temple, i.e., a library.

From the end of the third millennium B.C.E. onward private libraries, distinct from the temple archives which also contained personal documents, begin to appear. The quantity of private material stored in temple libraries also appears to have increased. This development is related to the substantial expansion of the economy, personal contact between individuals and governmental authorities, and the cultivation of commerce on local and international levels. The scope of property and business was the main drive behind the establishment of private and family archives.

In the period of the renewed blossoming and splendor of Sumerian culture, during the Third Dynasty of Ur and the Old Babylonian period, additional basic improvements in the method and criteria for preserving documents were effected. The greatest innovation of the period was the central royal archive, whose appearance was related to the crystallization of kingdoms with broad administrative authority and international political and economic ties. There is no doubt that the period of *Hammurapi's reign (1792–1749 B.C.E.) was the most decisive in this respect, if judged by the number of epigraphic finds rather than the number of archives themselves. The royal archives from *Mari are an illustrative example of an extensive royal archive from about this period. Their structure is indicative of advanced systems of preservation. The archives are spread among conveniently accessible rooms that undoubtedly contained material in current use, in addition to other rooms that served to store tables which had ceased to be functional. The division of archives into such offices on a functional basis is the best proof that the documents were cataloged on the basis of subject. The Mari archives illustrate a new trend in the development of such collections in the ancient Near East, i.e., the preservation of documents of historical value about the history of the kingdom and the royal family. They may not have initiated the process, however, if one considers that Hammurapi's scribes and officials edited and cataloged the documents in these archives, after the Babylonian king had conquered the city, in order to transfer documented material to the center of their kingdom. The Mari archival methods were copied even west of the Euphrates. The royal archives at *Ugarit, preserving epigraphic material of the 15th–12th centuries, are organized along quite similar lines. The discovery of documents in these archives indicates the existence of temporary and permanent archives attached to offices concerned with different levels of government. Even the location of the various offices and archives in the royal complex of buildings was determined on a functional basis: the office and archive concerned with district administration (the Western Archive) was located near the main entrance to the palace, affording easy access to people approaching from outside the city; the archive concerned with metropolitan administration (the Eastern Archive) was located so as to give best access from within the city itself; the archive concerned with the royal household (the Central Archive) was in the center of the palace, and so forth. An interesting phenomenon is the existence of various sorts of instructional texts in the Ugarit archives, which might lead to the conclusion that the offices served as instructional centers for novice scribes. Also of interest is a good deal of archival material in several of the palace rooms at Ugarit. These rooms may have served as offices for high officials who required documents from the nearby archives. The Hittite kingdom also left large royal archives. Excavations at Hattusas – the Hittite capital – (now Boghazköy) have revealed well-developed archival devices and much epigraphic material found in sacred and secular structures in various parts of the city. Fragments of catalogs indicate the existence of an advanced library there that used a subject system to direct its archival arrangements.

From this time on (the end of the third millennium), the royal archives became the most common form of archives in the Near East. The more a country is developed, the larger and more numerous its archives are likely to be and the greater the quality of their material. The royal Assyrian archives, fragments of which have been found in the cities of Assur, Calah, Khorsabad, and Nineveh – capitals of the kingdom at various periods – prove the growing need for archives and libraries, although it is difficult to draw precise conclusions about the system of storing and criteria for selecting and cataloging documents. It is clear, however, that a dual method of classification was employed at Nineveh: according to subject matter and according to the script in the document. Two offices were unearthed at Nineveh: one dealt with material written in cuneiform and the other with documents in Aramaic script. This division results from conditions which required two office staffs – the first specialized in the language of Assyria and Babylonia and the second expert in Aramaic and related tongues. Other types of private archives began to develop in the second, and especially the first, millennium B.C.E. The first type is a sort of combination of a family and a public archive, such as those discovered in the residential quarters of district officials who administered the areas of Arrapha and Nuzi. These contained both administrative material used by the officials in their work and documents related to their families. Another type of collection, which might properly be called a "private professional library," included materials that aided the owner in his daily work. That most of these collections consist of study materials, copy work, and religious and ritual material for sacred works may imply that such "private professional libraries" were owned by priests, scribes, or "academies" for the training of such personnel. In contrast to the existence of public archives, the rather rare phenomenon of public libraries reappears in the second and first millennia. Here again it should be emphasized that despite the almost total absence of finds of such libraries, one should not assume that they did not exist. It seems that the earliest find of such a collection, which was discovered at the temple in the city of Assur and which is clearly definable as a library, belongs to the period of Tiglath-Pileser I (1115–1077), king of Assyria. On the basis of the colophons and the dates of the eponyms that appear on various tablets it may be concluded that the library was already in existence on a limited scale at the time of Tukulti-Ninurta I (1243–1205), though it was Tiglath-Pileser who developed and firmly established it. It included original Babylonian tablets brought to Assur, tablets copied from Babylonian originals by Assyrian scribes, and original Assyrian works. It is known today that some of the texts in this library served as subjects for copy and instructional purposes over many generations. From various pieces of evidence among the tablets, it appears that the canonization of some of the texts in this library was completed during the reign of Tiglath-Pileser I. Some have therefore concluded that far earlier unknown collections must have existed, and attention was given to the thousands of texts unearthed at Nippur at the beginning of the 20th century, most of which belong to the end of the third millennium B.C.E.

The most famous and developed ancient Near Eastern library was that of Ashurbanipal (668–627), king of Assyria at Nineveh. Its size is estimated at about 25,000 tablets, though the number of tablets and fragments thus far recorded does not exceed a few thousand. This library was established by Ashurbanipal, who was a bibliophile with an appreciation for literary creations and was himself able to read and write. It is known from this king's own annals and from several colophons that even before his ascent to the throne various tablets were copied for him. Upon his ascent to the throne he expressed his concern for the expansion of his library by adding many original and copied documents to it from all parts of his kingdom. The administrative staff reported to the king the discovery of desirable texts, not all of which were acquired by pleasant means. In any case, it is known that at Ashurbanipal's order Nineveh established many private libraries, including priestly collections. Widespread copying projects were also initiated at the ancient literary and ritual centers of Babylon, Nippur, etc.

Archaeological and epigraphic evidence were joined together in order to cast light upon the methods of storing and preserving written material. It is known from both Sumerian and Akkadian terminology and archaeological finds themselves that written material was preserved in containers: woven baskets lined with some preservative material, earthenware or clay jugs, and similarly boxes made of earth and especially of wood. These containers were placed on raised stands resembling benches along walls (Calah), in the center of the room that served as an archive, or on shelves and ledges. At Khorsabad, the capital of the Assyrian king Sargon II (722/1–705), the containers were placed in special alcoves in the wall. The various containers held sorted and cataloged materials, and it appears that even the placement of the containers was determined by a predetermined formula. The classification and order is attested to by labels found in such places as Lagash, Mari, Hattusas, and Nineveh. These are small tablets attached to the container by means of a thread or cord and are inscribed with information on the contents of the container, such as the nature of the documents therein, their various subjects, and, in the case of a collection of closely related documents, the earliest and latest dates of the material contained inside. This system of identification was best suited to documents, especially those of an identical nature. It was not suited to relatively longer works, such as literary pieces, subject to frequent use, or to material used by a substantial number of people. Such items were subject to a somewhat different classification system than the labeling method. It appears that in several ancient Near Eastern "libraries," such as the one at Hattusas, the tablets were placed on shelves according to the order in which they were written, but without recourse to containers. The colophons and extratextual notations on many tablets helped in such classification. A complete colophon would contain a statement on the reliability of the contents, a citation of the source (in the case of a canonical work), the name and title of the copyists, and the name of the owner.

This type of colophon usually ended with a warning to and curse upon anyone who might ruin or steal the tablet. Such extratextual notations included indications of whether the text continued and marked it as either a single tablet or part of a series. Occasionally the name of the work was given alongside the number of the tablet within the total work. The "librarians" and scribes were no doubt aided by such information in preventing delays, disorder, and thefts. There appears to have been no consistent method of placing these tablets, as may be seen from their shape and the location of the colophon. While the order among a single series of tablets was carefully adhered to, the tablets themselves were placed either flat or standing on their narrow edges. It should be noted that far more remains unknown than known today about archival methods. There is no information about how material written on organic matter was preserved in the Mesopotamian archives and "libraries." Thus, when the alphabet penetrated into Mesopotamia, following the consolidation of the Arameans in the area, there were undoubtedly essential changes in archival techniques, just as there were substantive changes in the writing materials. Clay tablets were far less suited to alphabet writing, and Aramaic was customarily written on other surfaces, such as parchment.

There is no direct evidence of any sort regarding the existence of archives in Israel. Whatever evidence appears in the Bible relates to royal archives in Persia (Esth. 6:1; Ezra 6:1). However, since writing was known in Israel and there is much biblical evidence about the existence of scribes, including literary and copying activity, and, most important, a highly developed administrative system during the period of the monarchy, it is not unreasonable to conclude that some form of archives existed in Israel. A similar conclusion is reached as a result of the discovery of collections of ostraca, which appear to have been archival "files," in *Samaria, *Lachish, and *Arad. Moreover, one of the basic beliefs of Bible research today is the assumption that a substantial part of the biblical text, particularly in the historiographic works, comes from authentic documents from the royal household and the Temple, including the various lists of officials, and the conflicting descriptions of the Temple and its structure, implements, and decorations, and so forth. If this assumption is correct, it serves as additional proof that archives must have existed. Another proof is the existence of scribal and literary activity in the time of King Hezekiah (Prov. 25:1) which reminds one to some extent of the initiative of Ashurbanipal (see above). Indeed, the Bible hints at the existence of some sort of archive when it mentions the discovery of "the book of the law of the Lord given through Moses" in the Temple during King Josiah's time (II Kings 22:8ff.; II Chron. 34:14ff.). Archaeological evidence, however, is of no help in this area, and current research is unable to indicate that a particular building in an excavation served as an archive. The chief reason that archives and their contents in Ereẓ Israel did not remain preserved is, as stated above, the nature of the writing materials employed, together with climatic conditions which did not allow for the long-term preservation of organic materials. The *Elephantine papyri, also, are the surviving portions of the archive of the Jewish military colony of Yeb on the Upper Nile (fifth century B.C.E.).

[Hanoch Reviv]

POST-BIBLICAL PERIOD

Josephus quotes from the documents relating to the Jews of Ereẓ Israel and the Diaspora which he found in Roman archives, and it may be assumed that copies of such documents were also kept in the Jewish archives in Ereẓ Israel. The repeated references by Josephus to charters of protection, etc., received by the Jews presuppose the existence of some sort of archive where such documents were preserved. Josephus specifically mentions the Jerusalem archives as having been set on fire in 66 C.E., as one of the first acts of the insurgents, in order to destroy the evidence of the debts owed by the Jerusalem poor (Wars, 2:427). According to another tradition, going back to Julius Africanus (third century C.E.) but not otherwise supported, Herod burned the genealogical registers in order to conceal his own Edomite origin (Rosenthal, in MGWJ, 30 (1881), 118ff.). This archive building was finally destroyed by fire during the sack of the city by the Roman soldiery in 70 C.E. (Jos., Wars 6:354). However, even at the last stages of the hostilities in Jerusalem, careful records were kept by the Jews of the numbers of persons buried each day (*ibid.*, 5:567ff.).

Rabbinic sources speak of the Sanhedrin examining the purity of priestly descent, on the basis of genealogical tables (*Megillat* or *Sefer Yuḥasin*) which are known to have been preserved in the Temple (see Mid. 5:4; Tosef. Ḥag. 2:9, 235; Yev. 4:13; Yev. 49a and b). They were guarded with great care and when destroyed by some calamity, were carefully reconstructed on the basis of what remained and the depositions of witnesses (Jos., Apion 1:31). During the Roman period cities in Ereẓ Israel must have maintained local archives which enabled the collection of taxes and the authentication of documents – parallel to the model of the Roman archives; see Josephus, Life, 38, for Tiberias; *Kiddushin* 4:5 for Sepphoris: *Esther Rabba* 1:3 for Gadera. While no administrative documents have been found among the actual *Dead Sea Scrolls, the orders of Bar Kokhba, found recently in a cave in the same region, prove that such documents were obviously carefully preserved; also some other documents of that same period, have been discovered (see Benoit, et al., *Discoveries in the Judaean Desert*, vol. 2, 1961).

In the talmudic period, written records were probably kept in depositories at the academies. The authorities in Ereẓ Israel sent written calendar instructions to outlying communities – to Babylonia in particular; these letters presuppose some method of record keeping (Tosef., Sanh. 2:6; Mid. Tan. 26:13, 174/5; TJ, Meg. 1:7, 71a), *Sherira Gaon must have used records of the Mesopotamian academies for the historical information regarding the succession of exilarchs and *geonim* which he embodied in his famous historical epistle. When inquiries for religious guidance began to be addressed to the Mesopotamian *geonim* from the countries of the Diaspora, the replies (*teshuvot*) seem to have been filed for preservation in the academies, this being the origin of the various ancient collections of the responsa of the *geonim* – apparently official, not personal, collections. Fragments of communal registers, decisions of the *bet din*, official inventories, and contracts, etc., from medieval Egypt in the Fatimid period have been found in the Cairo **Genizah*. In the *Genizah*, too, was found the archive of Nahrai b. Nissim, an 11th-century businessman and communal figure in Egypt (Hebrew University thesis by A.M. Morad, 2 vols.).

MIDDLE AGES

In the pre-emancipation period – before the 16th century in Western Europe, before the 18th in Central Europe, and before the 20th in Eastern Europe – the Jews were regarded as a separate element in the body politic, subject to special regulations and special taxation. Hence there would be in the general archives special sections dealing with Jewish affairs. For the Middle Ages the most important is probably the archive of the Exchequer of the Jews in England (see below). This is, of course, apart from the many scattered documents dealing with Jews, sometimes of the highest importance, which can be found in the general archives. Almost all archives of central, district, and local authorities, as well as religious institutions, in places inhabited by Jews during the Middle Ages, contain a wealth of documents pertaining to Jews. In many countries notarial archives also include important documents on medieval Jewish life. Thus, the notarial archives of *Perpignan have been exhaustively studied by R.W. Emery with rich results; those of *Arles contain records of synagogue seat purchases. The longer the Jews resided in a particular country, the richer its government archives are in documents relating to their history. This applied to countries such as Spain and Portugal, where an abundance of such records may be found in the Central Archives in Madrid, the archives of the crown of Aragon in Barcelona, and the state archives of Simancas and Pamplona, as well as in those of the Inquisition, particularly complete and well organized for Portugal; it also applies to the Italian and German states. In many civic archives in Italy there is a special division dealing with Jewish affairs in the age of the Ghetto – before the French Revolution – e.g., in Venice the *Inquisitorato degli ebrei* which also includes a transcription made for administrative purposes of one entire communal **pinkas* ("register").

Jewish life in the European Diaspora in the Middle Ages was generally organized on a community basis, the synagogues and communal charities being in a way subordinate to the community. The form of the records kept by the communities was the result of an ancient tradition, but it was also influenced and frequently even dictated by the legal requirements and the administrative usage of their environment. Thus, current archives were established in Jewish communities, reaching various stages of development.

MODERN TIMES

In the Diaspora

Files and documents in general archives relating to Jewish life in modern times are much more abundant. Due to the fact that Jewish life was in general subject to a system of laws and regulations, special files relating to Jews dating back to the pre-emancipation period have been preserved in many government archives. Where no such special legislation existed, as in Britain and the United States, almost no special files on Jews were opened. When and where Jews obtained legal equality, special files related only to the status of their religious institutions and their relations with the authorities. From then on, historical records on the participation of Jews in the life of their country are less easy to trace. With the rise of modern antisemitism files dealing with the Jewish problem again appear in the archives of many countries, and their number increases rapidly in countries ruled by the Nazis between 1933 and 1945.

Archival material of Jewish interest is particularly abundant in the records of departments dealing with religion and education, taxation, commerce and industry, legal affairs, police reports, internal migration, and in the reports of diplomatic envoys in countries which had a large Jewish population or where the Jews exerted influence upon economic and political life, e.g., Poland, Turkey, Palestine, and the United States. Only a small part of this documentary material relating to Jewish history which was kept in non-Jewish archives has been published so far, and few detailed reference lists are available. For some years the Central Archives for the History of the Jewish People (CAHJP, see below) in Jerusalem have been engaged in collecting detailed information on archival material of value to the study of Jewish history by conducting surveys in the various countries and collecting lists of the contents of archives.

Archives of Jewish communities have been preserved with a certain degree of continuity in several countries since the 16th and 17th centuries, and with increasing frequency in the following centuries. In the Middle Ages and after pride of place was given to the *pinkas* ("register") in which statutes and regulations governing the community, names of community leaders and officials, minutes of meetings, etc., were recorded. In many instances the *pinkas* also contained decisions of Jewish courts, and copies of notes, letters, and applications submitted to the community board. Out of the main *pinkas* developed auxiliary *pinkasim* for such special purposes as accounts, the *ḥevra kaddisha*, and other religious societies. Other *pinkasim* contained incoming and outgoing correspondence or registered circumcisions – generally however, kept and retained by the *mohel* himself – the distribution of synagogue seats and offices, the distribution of *maẓẓot*, etc. In many countries the Jewish community kept, or had to keep, registers of births, deaths, and marriages, which had legal validity before public registers were introduced by the state.

In the course of time, Jewish community archives also preserved a variety of original documents, similar to the general archives. The systems used in filing and registration of incoming and outgoing documents were largely the same as those prevailing in those archives. In many instances, the civil authorities determined the filing system of the Jewish communities because of the legal importance of the documents and also to facilitate the supervision of the community administration, the collection of taxes, etc. These records have been preserved, with relative continuity, from the time that mass expulsions of Jews ceased; and more in countries with fewer expulsions of Jews than in those where expulsions and persecutions were frequent. Community archives dating back to the second half of the 17th century, and particularly the 18th and 19th centuries, have been preserved mainly in Italy, Great Britain, Western Europe, Austria, Hungary, Czechoslovakia, Germany, and the United States, although even in these countries a great deal of material was lost by lack of care. Those of Recife (Pernambuco) in Brazil were taken back to Amsterdam when the community broke up after the Portuguese reconquest in 1654. In Poland and Russia most of the Jewish records were lost as the result of persecution, fires, and negligence; the archives of many communities in western Poland have been preserved largely because these provinces formed part of Prussia from the end of the 18th century up to 1918. Other Jewish archives which have come into being since the 19th century are those of the national unions of communities, such as the Consistoire in France; of national and international Jewish aid organizations, such as the *Alliance Israélite Universelle in France, the *Hilfsverein in Germany, or the *American Jewish Joint Distribution Committee (JDC) in the U.S.A.; and of national and international political movements and organizations, such as the Zionist movement with its many parties and institutions.

Toward the end of the 19th century historical committees and societies were established in many countries for the purpose of utilizing the material stored in the general archives, and of collecting Jewish historical records. It was not, however, until the beginning of the 20th century that serious efforts were made to establish Jewish historical archives on a scientific basis, first among which was the Gesamtarchiv der deutschen Juden (see below). In 1919 the archives of the World Zionist Organization were set up in Berlin; in 1933 they were moved to Jerusalem, and have since become the Central Zionist Archives. Other archives have been established in Israel (see Ereẓ Israel Archives, below). In the United States, the American Jewish Archives were established in 1947 (see below: U.S.A.). Similar efforts have been under way in recent years in Britain and France. In 1926 the Jewish Scientific Institute (*YIVO) was created in Vilna; it collected significant material on Jewish history, with emphasis on Eastern Europe.

GERMANY. The Gesamtarchiv der deutschen Juden, which had as its task the preservation of files and documents – no longer in use – from Jewish communities, institutions, and societies in Germany, was founded in Berlin in 1906. Its first director was Eugen Taeubler; he was succeeded in 1920 by Jacob Jacobsohn, The Gesamtarchiv succeeded in collecting the *pinkasim* and files of hundreds of Jewish communities in Germany and in the provinces of western Poland which had been part of Prussia from the end of the 19th century until 1918. It also contained the private archives of important personalities; documents, photographs, printed material relating to the history of the Jews in Germany and that of Jewish families, and copies or summaries of documents belonging to government municipal archives. Six volumes of *Mitteilungen des Gesamtarchivs der deutschen Juden* (1908–26) were published, the sixth containing a catalog. When the Nazis came to power, they made extensive use of the *Gesamtarchiv* for their genealogical research and in 1938 took it over in its entirety. At the beginning of World War II part of the archives were sent to eastern Germany for security reasons. In 1950, upon the intervention of the Berlin community, this part of the archives was returned to the Jewish Community in East Berlin, but they were not permitted to transfer it, as intended, to Jerusalem. Important parts of the Gesamtarchiv, however, reached West Germany and were sent to the CAHJP in 1951. The rest – which was in poor condition – was taken to the East German Government Archives in Potsdam. No precise information is available on the amount and condition of this material – or of other records of Jewish organizations which seem to have been added to it by the Nazis. Other community and organizational archives had been deposited from 1933 with German government archives during the Nazi rule, and these were also gradually transferred to Jerusalem, beginning in 1954. The CAHJP now contains parts of the archives of some 800 former Jewish communities in Germany. Other community archives were destroyed by the Nazis or were otherwise lost during the war. In other Diaspora communities no attempt has yet been made to establish comprehensive archives along the lines of the Gesamtarchiv.

[Alexander Bein]

For more than 40 years after the end of World War II and the Holocaust, the tiny Jewish community of the Federal Republic of Germany, never more than about 30,000 individuals, had no central repository to chronicle the complicated and often difficult task of maintaining Jewish life in a nation that before 1933 numbered more than 550,000 Jews.

One of the major obstacles to such an institution was the determination of most of the Jews in Germany, survivors of the Holocaust from Eastern Europe and a few thousand German Jews who managed to survive inside the Nazi state, to ultimately leave a nation "soaked in Jewish blood."

Even those Jews who wanted to stay in post-Holocaust Germany maintained that they were living there with "packed bags," ready to flee at a moment's notice at the first sign of a new organized German antisemitism.

Finally, in 1987, The Central Archives for Research on the History of the Jews in Germany located in Heidelberg, was founded under the auspices of the Central Council of Jews in Germany (Zentralrat der Juden in Deutschland), the umbrella organization that was created in 1950 to represent the interests of Jews in the Federal Republic.

The director of the Central Archives is Peter Honigmann, a Jew from the former German Democratic Republic (DDR). The institution collects documentation from the Jewish communities, associations, and organizations within the borders of what was the Federal Republic, although records are extant for the history of the small Jewish community of the former DDR.

Among the records of the Central Archives are collections on the Central Council of Jews in Germany, the Central Welfare Office of the Jews in Germany, Jewish Student Organizations, and Jewish community records from regions and cities across the former Federal Republic including Berlin, Bremen, Dortmund, Duesseldorf, Frankfurt am Main, Heidelberg, and Lower Saxony.

Individual collections include the papers of Henryk Broder, Rafael Seligmann, Peter Sichrovsky, and Barbara Honigmann, all journalists and authors.

[Abraham J. Peck (2nd ed.)]

RUSSIA. Since Jewish life in Russia, up to the 1917 Revolution, was regulated by a host of special laws and decrees, the archives maintained by the various government departments came to contain many files dealing with Jewish affairs in all their manifestations. It is difficult to estimate how much of this material still exists since it is almost impossible for foreign scholars to obtain access. Jewish and non-Jewish scholars, who began to study the history of Russian Jewry, made use of such material as was accessible to them in government archives under the Czarist regime. In 1908 a Jewish Ethnographical Society was founded in St. Petersburg (Leningrad) by Salvian Goldstein, who directed its archives. After the revolution of 1917, archives were opened to scholars much more liberally. A great deal of material, no doubt, survives, and at least part of the Jewish archives may now be stored in general archives or libraries. The latter may also contain portions of Jewish archives or non-Jewish archives relating to Jews which the Soviets removed from their zones of occupation in East Germany and Poland at the end of the war, although part of this material was returned to its country of origin.

The surviving archives of the Minsk community, 1825–1917, a portion of the rescued Vilna YIVO archives, consisting of 37 folders, have now been catalogued.

POLAND. Many of the archives of the Jewish communities in Poland, in existence in 1939, were destroyed during World War II and its aftermath. The files maintained by the *Lodz community were transferred to the government archives there. The remnants of the *Cracow and Wroclaw (Breslau) archives, and of hundreds of other communities, as well as a vast amount of other material on the history of the Jews and on the Holocaust, were handed over to the Jewish Historical Institute in Warsaw, which was established after the war. In 1968, however, the Institute was closed down, and its archival collection transferred to government and municipal archives. In the past few years some of the material was microfilmed for the CAHJP and Yad Vashem in Jerusalem.

CZECHOSLOVAKIA. The old archive of the *Prague Jewish community was largely preserved until 1689 when it was destroyed in a great fire. The material which had been collected in the 18th century was in turn heavily damaged in the fires of 1754 and 1773. Later, once more, documents and files accumulated in great quantity. The entire archives of the Prague community and all its synagogues and institutions, as well as of several other communities – Budejovice, Dambořice, Holešov, etc. – are now stored in the Jewish Museum in Prague. In 1967 an agreement was concluded for the microfilming of most of this material by CAHJP.

AUSTRIA. The *Vienna community maintained archives and a museum, which had been organized in 1840 by the secretary of the community L.A. *Frankl. These archives contained documents relating to the history of Vienna Jews dating back to the 18th century, as well as the files of the community from its official establishment in 1890. After World War II the entire archives were deposited with the CAHJP which is also cataloging the Jewish historical material in the Austrian government archives. Among the Jewish archives left in Austria are the archives of the *Burgenland communities, which contain protocols and old community *pinkasim* and are now deposited in the government archives in *Eisenstadt.

ENGLAND. Part of the communal records of *Norwich in the form of *shetarot*, probably kept for convenience in the local *archa, were transferred to the capital with other documents and are now among the Muniments at Westminster Abbey (published by M.D. Davis in his *Hebrew Deeds of English Jews*, 1888). A very substantial part of the 13th-century archive of the Exchequer of the Jews, very important for British as well as for Jewish history, is preserved in the Public Record Office in London, the surviving Plea Rolls are in the course of publication by the Jewish Historical Society of England (J.M. Rigg and H. Jenkinson, 3 vols., 1905–29) while the Receipt Rolls have only been cursorily investigated. Among the archives of Anglo-Jewish communities in modern times, the most important is that of the Spanish-Portuguese community; it contains the records of this community from 1663 up to the present time (cf. L.D. Barnett, *Bevis Marks Records*, 2 vols., 1940–49). The regulations of the Sephardi community in London (ed. 1785, p. 33) imposed on the secretary the duty of keeping full records of circumcisions, marriages, and burials. Archives of the major Ashkenazi synagogues in London, dating back to 1690 and up to 1870, are maintained in the offices of the *United Synagogue. The archives of the Western (formerly Westminster) Synagogue, dating back to 1767, were cataloged by C. Roth before their almost complete destruction in a German air raid. The early records of the London *bet din*, dating back to the beginning of the 19th century, are in the Roth and Adler collections, those of the later period are preserved by the *bet din* themselves. The complete archive of the minuscular community of *Penzance in Cornwall, from 1807 down to its extinction in the early 20th century, are in the Roth collection (now in Leeds University). The significant archives maintained by a public institution are those of the *Board of Deputies of British Jews, founded in 1761. The *Jewish Historical Society of England, founded in 1893, seeks to establish a central archive of British Jews (Anglo-Jewish Archives) to supplement the collections of the Mocatta Library (see *Libraries), and has received the archives of the *Anglo-Jewish Association. Archives relating to the history of Zionism in Britain and the World Zionist Organization – when its headquarters were situated in London – form part of the Central Zionist Archives in Jerusalem (in following CZA).

FRANCE. France does not have a central Jewish archive, but La Commission Française des Archives Juives has been active since 1963 and publishes the quarterly *Archives Juives* (editor

B. Blumenkranz). The following important archives are in the possession of Jewish bodies: (a) the archives of the central Jewish *Consistoire and of the *Paris Jewish Consistoire, which contain documents beginning with the year 1808. The archives of the *Lyons Consistoire have also been preserved. On the other hand, the archives of the *Marseilles and *Colmar's Consistoire have been destroyed; little is left of the *Besançon and *Bayonne archives, and only a part of those of Bas Rhin and Moselle. The community archives still in existence generally do not date back beyond the French Revolution or the middle of the 19th century. Sometimes, the Jewish community archives were deposited with the general archives, such as the archives of the *Metz community, in the archives of the department of Moselle, or of *Bordeaux, now in the municipal archives. An outstanding collection was established by the Society for the History of the Jews of *Alsace-Lorraine, now deposited with the archives of the Department of the Bas Rhin in Strasbourg. Various collections and parts of important archives, in original or microfilm, are also kept by the CAHJP; the archives relating to the history of Zionism in France and of French Zionist personalities are deposited with the CZA. (b) From its inception in 1860 the Alliance Israélite Universelle has preserved the correspondence with its branch offices and educational institutions in the Middle East, reports submitted to it, minutes of its board meetings, etc. Its files contain original material which is of importance not only for the history of the Alliance, but also for that of the Jews, especially in Muslim and East European countries. Confiscated by the Nazis during the war, the archives were for the greater part returned to France, put into order, and cataloged. Parts of them were microfilmed by the CAHJP and the CZA.

ITALY. General archives, especially those of north Italian cities, contain important historical records relating to Jews. Jewish community archives were once particularly ample and well-organized. They have suffered however from neglect in some places, and from the effects of war in others. Thus, the very ample archives of the community of *Venice were dispersed through carelessness in the period before World War II; those of *Leghorn were destroyed as a result of bombing in World War II. Some Jewish communities have in their possession various single documents going back to the Middle Ages, and continuous records (*pinkasim*) starting in the 17th and, especially, the 18th centuries. Some of these have been put in order and cataloged – those of *Rome, which cover the period 1536–1627 and are now in the Archivio Urbino in the Capitol (see A. Berliner, *Censur und Konfiskation* … (1891), 4), published by A. Milano and R. Bachi (1929), and those of *Mantua, compiled by Bonaiuoto Isaac Levi from 1782 to 1810 (unpublished). A summary list of documents, preserved in the archives of the Jewish community of Ancona, was published by C. Rosenberg in the *Corriere Israelitico* in 1912–14. Edgardo Morpurgo published in the *Corriere Israelitico* (1910–13; also repr.) a survey of the documents and monuments of the Jews in the province of Venice, indicating the archivistic material – including that in private possession – available for this part of Italy, which once had numerous small communities. A series of registers of contracts drawn up (in Hebrew) by Jewish notaries in Rome in the 15th–17th centuries are preserved in the civic archives (see also Berliner, *Serid me-Ir* in *Kobeẓ-al-Yad*, 5, 1893). A catalog of the archives of the *Florence community, in part deposited in the *Archivio di Stato*, was published by R. Gottheil (REJ, 51–52, 1906), amended and enlarged by U. Cassuto (RI, 3 (1906)). The archives of the *Reggio Emilia community are kept by the municipal archives; material from the *Verona community archives was transferred to the National and University Library in Jerusalem and cataloged by S. Simonsohn (*Zion*, 35, 1960).

GREECE. The bulk of the ancient Jewish archives of *Salonika were destroyed in the great fire of 1917; those of other communities were less significant.

THE NETHERLANDS. Apart from the material contained in the government and municipal archives, the history of Dutch Jews is contained in the records maintained by two major Jewish archives – the archives of the Spanish-Portuguese (Inventory by W.C. Pieterse, 1964) and those of the Ashkenazi communities of Amsterdam. Both are deposited with the Amsterdam municipal archives, and a large part has been microfilmed for the CAHJP. The relations with Ereẓ Israel maintained by Jews in Holland and Germany, from the beginning of the 19th century, find expression in the archives of the *pekidim ve-amarkalim* of which 15 volumes, containing the copies of outgoing letters, have been preserved and are now being published by J. Rivlin.

[Alexander Bein]

UNITED STATES OF AMERICA. In 2004, the American Jewish community celebrated its 350th anniversary with a breathtaking number of lectures, exhibits, and programs across the United States, highlighted by a major exhibition entitled "From Haven to Home: 350 Years of Jewish Life in America" with exhibit materials lent by the Library of Congress, the National Archives and Records Administration, the American Jewish Historical Society, and the Jacob Rader Marcus Center of the American Jewish Archives.

The 2004–5 commemoration was in many respects far different than the two previous national celebrations in 1904, marking the 250th anniversary, and 1954, marking the 300th.

Each of these commemorations was held in the midst of crises within American and general Jewish life. In 1904, anti-immigration forces were already at work seeking to close the doors of America to the millions of persecuted and poverty-stricken East European Jews seeking to enter a land where "the streets were paved with gold."

In 1954, a still traumatized American Jewish community was in the emotional grip of the losses incurred by European Jewry during the Holocaust and the struggles of the recently created State of Israel.

But 2004 was a different story. American Jewry was a secure, affluent, and well-educated community, perhaps the most secure, affluent, and well-educated community in all of Jewish history. American Jewry was less inner-directed and the call in 2004 was for all Americans to celebrate the history of the American Jewish experience.

The history of American Jewish archival institutions also reflected the politics of American Jewish life and identity.

In 1892, a small group of American Jews, already concerned with the negative reactions of many Americans to the growing immigration of Jews from Eastern Europe, created the American Jewish Historical Society (AJHS) in New York. The society was unabashedly "filiopietistic" in its celebration of American Jews as "soldiers and patriots." Its collections and its historical publications reflected the contributions of Jews to the development of the American colonies, the American Revolution, and all the major events of the American experience.

In 1947, Dr. Jacob Rader Marcus, the "father of American Jewish history," founded the American Jewish Archives on the campus of the Hebrew Union College in Cincinnati with a determination to collect and write the history of the Jewish experience in America in a scholarly, unbiased manner, "warts and all."

For nearly 50 years, these two institutions, along with the Leo Baeck Institute, founded in 1955 in New York to chronicle the history of German-speaking Jewry until 1933, and the YIVO Institute, founded in Vilna, Lithuania, in 1925 and moved to New York during World War II, for the history of East European Jewish life and culture, were the foundations of Jewish archival institutions in the United States.

But 2005 not only found an American Jewish community that felt "at home" in the United States, but a much larger group of archival institutions devoted to the Jewish experience in America and beyond.

In 1995, the "feminist revolution" in American and American Jewish life led to the creation of the Jewish Women's Archive in Brookline, Massachusetts. The executive director of the Archive is Dr. Gail Twersky Reimer.

The archive is a leader in utilizing new technologies to transform the practice and knowledge of the history of Jewish women in North America and utilizes an award-winning website to "remember the women who came before us, honor the women among us, and inspire those who will follow us."

On October 26, 2000, the American Jewish archival world witnessed a virtual revolution with the founding of the Center for Jewish History in New York. Called the "Library of Congress of the Jewish People," a consortium of five Jewish archival and cultural organizations joined together to house more than 100 million archival documents and 500,000 books, easily the largest and most important institution of its kind outside of the State of Israel.

The five institutions, the American Jewish Historical Society, the American Sephardi Federation, the Leo Baeck Institue, the YIVO Institute, and the Yeshiva University Museum, seek to create a seamless archival, library and art collection of world-class standards without giving up their individual institutional identities.

The $50 million facility has a state of the art reading room, museum exhibit spaces, and a Jewish genealogy institute. Ultimately, many of the Center's holdings will be digitalized for home access.

Finally, in June 2005, the Jacob Rader Marcus Center of the American Jewish Archives dedicated a $7 million renovation and expansion of its facility and the opportunity to showcase its collection of documents on the American Jewish experience, including the papers of Jacob *Schiff, Louis *Marshall, and Felix *Warburg, outstanding communal leaders of early 20th-century Jewish life in America, and the papers of the World Jewish Congress (WJC) including the chilling telegram sent by the WJC's Gerhard Riegner in 1942 informing the world of the Nazi plans for a "final solution" to the destruction of Jewish life in Europe.

Other institutions of note that house significant Jewish archival collections in the United States include The Magnes Archives in California, The Rocky Mountain Jewish Historical Society in Colorado, The Jewish Museum of Florida, the Jewish Historical Society of Greater New Haven in Connecticut, the Bloom Southwest Jewish Archives in Arizona, the Cleveland Jewish Archives in Ohio, the Chicago Jewish Historical Society in Illinois, the Philadelphia Jewish Archives Center in Pennsylvania, the Feinstein Center for American Jewish History in Pennsylvania, the Ratner Center for the Study of Conservative Judaism in New York, and the Southern Jewish Archives at Tulane University in Louisiana.

[Abraham J. Peck (2nd ed.)]

The Library of the JTSA published *Preliminary Listing of Holdings,* a list of its rare archival collections. Among the items cited in it are some 5,000 prints and photographs from the 17th to the 20th centuries, personal papers of many major Jewish community leaders and scholars, and communal records from Germany, France, Italy, Morocco, Algeria and Palestine.

Holocaust Period

A special significance is attached to archives dealing with the Holocaust period. Even during the war special institutions were established by Jews in the Nazi-occupied territories, such as the Oneg Shabbat Archives by Emmanuel *Ringelblum in Warsaw, whose purpose was to collect evidence on the Holocaust. Similar institutions of this kind were set up after the war. They had both the practical aim of exposing the crimes perpetrated by the Nazi criminals and bringing them to justice, and the scientific-historical aim of preserving as complete as possible a record of this decisive era in the history of the Jewish people.

A great deal of material relating to the persecution and extermination of the Jews during the Nazi period can be found in the archives of the countries directly or indirectly involved and of the Jewish organizations that sought to help the Jews. Of the greatest importance are the archives maintained by the Nazis themselves. The Nazi archives which had fallen into the hands of the Western Allies were, for the most part, returned to Germany – the Foreign Ministry Archives in Bonn and the Bundesarchiv in Coblenz – after most of the files had been microfilmed. Only the Berlin Document Center, made up primarily of the archives of the Nazi Party and its institutions, is still held by the American State Department, and it intends to hand them also back to the Bundesarchiv when they have been microfilmed. Of the archives held by the Russians, important parts have been handed over to the Central East German archives in Potsdam and Merseburg.

Two other (non-Jewish) institutions should be mentioned in this context: (a) The first is the *International Tracing Service (ITS) at Arolsen, established after the war by Supreme Headquarters Allied Expeditionary Force to facilitate the search for missing persons. Its files and 16 million cards contain information on seven to eight million persons. All the ITS material was microfilmed for Yad Vashem in Jerusalem. (b) The Rijksinstituut voor Oorlogsdocumentatie in Amsterdam, established by the Netherlands government in May 1945 and which contains a comprehensive documentary collection, deals primarily with the fate of Dutch Jews during the Holocaust period.

The following are the important archives on the Holocaust period in Jewish hands: (a) The Institute of Jewish Affairs of the *World Jewish Congress in New York, founded in 1940, has built up a systematic collection of documents concerning the Holocaust and related issues. Most of its material, in manuscript and in print, has been transferred to the Institute of Jewish Affairs established by the World Jewish Congress in 1966 in London, to the CZA in Jerusalem, and Beth Hatefutsoth ("House of the Diaspora") at Tel Aviv University. (b) The Institute of Contemporary History and Wiener Library (formerly called simply *Wiener Library) in London founded in 1934 in Amsterdam for contemporary Jewish history, antisemitism, and Nazi persecution, in particular. (c) The *Centre de Documentation Juive Contemporaine in Paris founded clandestinely during the Nazi rule in 1942; this contains a wealth of material, original and photostatic, on the history of Nazi anti-Jewish activities, and of the persecution of Jews in France. Among the significant units held by the Centre are the archives of Alfred *Rosenberg; copies of the documents of the Nuremberg trials; the archives containing the records of the anti-Jewish operations of the German command in France; the archives of the German embassy in Paris and the Gestapo in France; and the archives of various French non-Jewish and Jewish institutions. (d) The archives of the *Jewish Historical Institute in Warsaw include a great amount of documentation on the fate of the Jews in Poland, including the Ringelblum archive. The institute was closed down in 1968 and its archives transferred to Polish government and municipal archives. (e) The archives of the Va'ad ha-Hazzalah ("Rescue Committee"), which the Jewish Agency set up during the war for the rescue of Polish Jewry, collected a great deal of information and reports on the history of the Holocaust, much of it in Poland itself. It is now part of the CZA. (f) The central archives of *Yad Vashem is the major and most comprehensive Jewish archive devoted to the Holocaust era. (g) The Isaac Katznelson Ghetto Fighters' Museum commemorating the Holocaust and the Resistance was established in 1950 at kibbutz Loḥamei ha-Getta'ot in the western Galilee (further information and a comprehensive bibliography of Holocaust documentation and study centers can be found in the *Guide to Jewish History under the Nazi Impact* by J. Robinson and P. Friedman, 1960).

[Alexander Bein]

UNITED STATES OF AMERICA. Jews are a people of memory. They did not forget the exodus from Miẓrayim, from Egypt, and remember it three thousand years later. Jews did not forget those who died in the Holocaust, but it took the better part of several decades before those Jews who had lived in freedom and safety during those years would understand that it was important for all Jews to remember.

In many respects, the 1980 and the 1990s were the "decades of the Holocaust survivor."

From outsiders, on the periphery of American Jewish communal life for the first 25 years after their arrival in America, survivors of the Holocaust became overnight "insiders" as American Jews and America in general became aware of the meaning of the Holocaust for American Jewish and non-Jewish identity.

Suddenly, the Holocaust, and the survivors who were its moral voice, was commemorated in nearly every state capitol and in the Rotunda of the American Congress.

A national Holocaust museum stood on the sacred space of American memory in Washington, D.C., and survivors were the focus of video tapings and participants in countless school lectures.

Even in the Jewish Displaced Persons' camps of Germany, Austria, and Italy telling the story of the Holocaust was a passion that was shared by most survivors.

To tell and to remember: That was a great part of what drove survivors onward. The State of Israel understood this as early as 1942, in pre-State Palestine when the first proposal was made to create a place of commemoration for those Jews who had already died at the hands of the Nazis and their collaborators. The proposal also carried with it the suggestion that it be called Yad Vashem, a "monument and a name."

In 1953, the Israeli parliament, the Knesset, passed the Yad Vashem Law, establishing the Martyrs' and Heroes' Remembrance Authority, and mandating that the authority establish an institution devoted to the murder of six million Jews and the issues that surrounded those murders.

It was not until 1979 when a Jewish media specialist, Laurel Vlock, and a Holocaust survivor and psychiatrist, Dr. Dori Laub, decided that the medium of video was the best instrument to document the personal testimonies of Holocaust survivors at a time when survivors were aging and beginning to die in large numbers. It was also the same year that Americans for the first time learned the extent of the individual and collective evil that led to the destruction of European Jewish life as portrayed in the film "Holocaust."

The Holocaust Survivors Film Project, Inc., located in New Haven, Connecticut, became the grass roots organization that produced the first 200 survivor testimonies.

In 1981, the tapes were deposited at Yale University and, through the generosity of Alan M. Fortunoff, the Fortunoff Video Archive for Holocaust Testimonies became a part of Yale University's Sterling Memorial Library.

Today, the Archive has a collection of over 4,300 videotaped interviews with witnesses and survivors of the Holocaust.

The creation of the Fortunoff Archive coincided with the beginning of an "Americanization of the Holocaust" that linked the events of the Holocaust: the murder of six million Jews, the world's inaction in seeking to save Jews from the Nazi vise, the loss of democratic and human values before and during the Holocaust in large parts of Europe, with the need for Americans to understand their own democratic values and the importance of protecting them against forces similar to those that gave rise to National Socialism.

Not only was the creation of the United States Holocaust Memorial Museum and its Research Institute a reaction to such an "Americanization," but the premiere of the film *Schindler's List*, directed by Steven *Spielberg, allowed American's a glimpse of one of the "Righteous" non-Jews who put their personal safety and careers on the line to save Jewish lives.

A year later, Spielberg financed the creation of the Survivors of the Shoah Visual History Foundation to gather videotaped testimony of Holocaust survivors around the world. Again, Dr. Michael *Berenbaum, so instrumental in the creation of the USHMM's Research Institute, was asked to direct the institution as its president and CEO.

To date, the Shoah Foundation, relying on local staff members and volunteers, has collected nearly 52,000 testimonies in 32 languages in nearly 60 nations around the world.

The phenomenon of the "Americanization" of the Holocaust took on an even greater significance in January 2000, when the first ever "International Forum on the Holocaust" took place in Stockholm, Sweden.

Forty-eight nations along with several multilateral organizations took part in the conference. A total of 600 delegates attended, and most countries sent official delegations comprising official representatives as well as representatives of research and educational communities, staffs from museums and archives, and other experts.

The conference focused on the following fundamental questions: What can politicians and other community forces do to support Holocaust education, remembrance, and research? What lessons can be learned from the Holocaust to alert contemporary society to the dangers of antisemitism, racism, and ethnic conflict, among other expressions of hatred, injustice, and discrimination?

While progress was made in beginning to formulate answers to such questions, the more telling impact of the Conference was that a "globalization of the Holocaust" had now become an established fact. This conclusion was crystallized by the growth of the Association of Holocaust Organizations, headed by Dr. William L. Shulman, established in 1985, and whose membership 20 years later consisted of Holocaust research centers and museums in 39 American states and the District of Columbia as well as 24 other nations as diverse as Japan and South Africa.

In the era of the "globalization of the Holocaust," one research facility stands out among all others in terms of how quickly it has risen to the very top of all institutions devoted to Holocaust-related research.

In 1993, the United States Holocaust Memorial Museum (USHMM) opened its doors on the sacred ground of American history in Washington, D.C. and reflected the "Americanization of the Holocaust" and the phenomenon of Holocaust memory and memorialization.

Its most important scholarly division was the Research Institute of the USHMM directed by Michael Berenbaum. For a number of years before the Museum's opening, teams of microfilmers and researchers from the Research Institute gained access to numerous archives across the length and breadth of Central and Eastern Europe in order to document and ship back to Washington the most important records on the destruction of European Jewry. In 1998 it was restructured as The Center for Advanced Holocaust Studies of the United States Holocaust Memorial Museum, directed by Paul Shapiro, to address the critical challenges affecting the scholarly study of the Holocaust.

Among its many activities, the center has taken the responsibility for collecting and preserving Holocaust-related archival materials on a worldwide basis, making many previously inaccessible sources available to the scholarly community. This project began in the late 1980s at the initiative of the then-unopened United States Holocaust Memorial Museum as the imminent collapse of the Communist regimes presented a unique opportunity and openness toward the microfilming of archival holdings related to World War II and the Holocaust in Eastern Europe. As an American government institution working with governments anxious to improve their relationship with the United States as Soviet-power was waning, the museum used its status to pry open for Western scholars hitherto inaccessible archives, to microfilm their holdings and bring them to the West. Independent projects were undertaken as were joint efforts with Yad Vashem and by the turn of the 21st century, the principle of the exchange between Jerusalem and Washington of Eastern European archival microfilms was firmly established.

As such, the archival branch of the USHMM is today one of the largest and most comprehensive repositories of Holocaust-related records in the world. The collection consists of nearly 20 million pages of records, especially important microform reproductions of materials held by most of the European nations occupied by the German armed forces, including those of the former Soviet Union.

Especially important are the microfilmed holdings of the so-called Osobyi or "Special" Archive that were inaccessible to Western scholars until the end of the Cold War. The USHMM has copied large numbers of files in this archive pertaining to Holocaust-related and other topics. Nearly 400 microfilm reels are available to researchers dealing with previously unknown or missing materials including those on Jewish organizations, both communal and private, in Germany and Austria. The finding aid for the Osobyi Records can be accessed via the catalog of the USHMM.

Online catalogs available to researchers include the Library and Archival Collections (including oral history and film); an Archival Guide to the Collections, which act as an overview of textual records; and a select group of Archival Finding Aids that are detailed inventories and descriptive tools created to help scholars understand the scope and detail of collections.

In addition, the Collections Division of the USHMM contains an oral history collection that is one of the largest and most diverse on Holocaust testimonies. The collection contains over 7,000 interviews, 4,500 of which are video and 2,500 are audio.

The Photo Archives contains 85,000 historical photographs and nearly 14,000 of them are available through an online catalog. The online catalog also contains a small sampling of the more than 10,000 artifacts in the Museum's possession.

[Abraham J. Peck (2nd ed.)]

Major Archives

THE CENTRAL ARCHIVES FOR THE HISTORY OF THE JEWISH PEOPLE (CAHJP). The nucleus of these archives are the Jewish Historical General Archives, founded in 1939 by Joseph *Meisl and taken over in 1944 by the Historical Society of Israel. In 1957 D.J. Cohen became their director. They were set up formally in Jerusalem in 1969 under a resolution of the government of Israel in January 1968, in cooperation with other interested institutions. Only with the establishment of the State of Israel and with the "ingathering of the exiles" was it possible to attempt an "ingathering of the nation's records" in order to perpetuate the collective memory of the Jewish people. Special attention was given to the archives of communities and organizations which had been destroyed or were in the process of disappearing. Thus, all the community records remaining in West Germany after World War II, a large portion of the Gesamtarchiv der deutschen Juden (see above) among them, were brought to Jerusalem.

The archives are engaged in three main activities: the transfer to Israel of community and organizational archives and private collections of prominent Jews, and the preserving, classifying, and placing of them at the disposal of historians and students; photographing documents relating to Jewish history in archives abroad; and compiling a central catalog of all the archival material relating to Jewish history which exists in Jewish and non-Jewish archives all over the world. Accordingly there are three main departments in the CAHJP:

Original Documents. This department contains complete archives and fragments, registers (*pinkasim*), charters and deeds from about 1,300 communities on five continents – mainly from Europe, the Americas, and North Africa – as well as records of many organizations and private papers of families and personalities. The material dates from the 15th century to the present and is arranged according to territorial divisions, following the political borders between the World Wars, with every territorial division preserving, in turn, the original structure of its segments (i.e., archives of communities, organizations, etc.); it also includes a collection of single documents, *Memorbooks* (e.g., Halberstadt, Coblenz, and Kreuznach), and files not necessarily connected with any archival unit.

The following community archives are worthy of special mention:

Austria, Vienna (1812–); *Czechoslovakia*, *pinkasim* from Boskovice, Konice, Mikulov (Nikolsburg), Prostějov, and Trebič (some of them dating from the beginning of the 17th century); *France* (dating from the 16th century), Alsace, Avignon, Bordeaux, Carpentras, Cavaillon, Metz, Nancy, and Paris; *Germany*, Altona-Hamburg-Wandsbeck (from 1669, including the archives of the rabbinical court in Altona, and of the *talmud torah*), Ansbach (1616–), Bamberg (1748–), Bayreuth (1709–), Berlin (1755–), Bingen (1674–), Danzig (1694–), Darmstadt (1663–), Floss (1682–), Frankfurt on the Oder (1736–), Halberstadt (1613–), Koenigsberg (1769–), Mainz (1661–), Offenbach on the Main (1716–), Regensburg (1788–), Worms (1552–), Wuerzburg (1684–), and Zuelz (1627–); *Italy*, the M. and U. Morpurgo and N. Rossi collection (material from Padua and Rovigo), the H.E. Sereni collection (Modena, Pisa, and Rome), the Alliance Israélite Universelle in northern Italy; and *Poland*, Grodzisk, Katowice, Krotoszyn (1747–), Poznań (1595–), and Rawicz.

Special interterritorial subdivisions contain private collections and archives of international organizations. Among them are the records of the Schwarzbard Defense Council set up by the Comité des Délégations Juives in Paris (1926–28); the files of the Jewish Palestinian League of Nations Society (1926–39); Reuben Brainin's diaries; the papers of S. Dubnow; Ismar Freund, (emancipation and legal status of German Jewry); J.L. Magnes (including the records of the *kehillah* of New York City, part of these papers are in the Museum at Berkeley, California); and the following collections: Z. Broches, New England Jewry; P. Diamant, genealogy; N.M. Gelber, Polish Jewry; L. Lamm, Ginsburg family, and the Jews of Swabia; I. Prins, Jews of Holland and Belgium; L. Motzkin, Russian pogroms and emigration; and M. Stern, German and Italian Jewry. A division of special collections – statutes, reports, etc., in print; genealogy; newspaper clippings; photographs; and tape recordings

Microfilm Department. This contains over three million frames from Jewish and non-Jewish archives abroad, beginning with the 12th century: communities of Yugoslavia, Amsterdam (Sephardi and Ashkenazi Congregations, and the *pinkasim* of outgoing letters of the *Pekidim ve-Amarkalim*); Copenhagen; Leghorn; Mantua; Reggio-Emilia; Rome; Venice; Consistoire Central and Alliance Israélite Universelle in Paris; and records from scores of state and municipal archives in Austria, Czechoslovakia, England, France, Germany, Italy, Mexico, Poland, Portugal, Spain, and Switzerland.

Survey Department. This department contains lists of material in archives abroad. Systematic surveys are being carried out in archives of Jewish communities and organizations, which are still located in the places of origin, as well as in state, municipal, ecclesiastical, and private archives in all the European countries in which it has been possible for the Central Archives to operate; mainly Austria, France, Germany, Italy, Spain, and Yugoslavia. There are altogether some 200 catalogs.

An auxiliary library contains reference literature, monographs, and published documents relating to communities and institutions, the records of which are kept in the CAHJP.

[Daniel J. Cohen]

CENTRAL ZIONIST ARCHIVES. The Central Zionist Archives (CZA) are the historical archives of the Zionist Movement and the Zionist Organization which were founded in Berlin in 1919 by G. *Herlitz, who was director of the archives until 1955. In 1933 they were moved to Jerusalem. A. *Bein joined the archives in 1936 and succeeded Herlitz as director in 1955. The 24th Zionist Congress (1956) recognized the CZA as the official historical archives of the Zionist Movement and the Jewish Agency, as well as all their affiliated institutions.

The archives consist of the following major divisions: (a) the official files of the Zionist Organization and the Jewish Agency, and their various institutions from the founding of the Zionist Organization in 1897 to the present day, including those of the national Zionist Federations, the Zionist funds (Jewish National Fund, Keren Hayesod, etc.), and the Land Development Co., Bank Leumi, etc.; (b) archives of the *yishuv* prior to the establishment of the State of Israel. This division includes the archives of the *Va'ad Le'ummi and of its predecessor, the Provisional Council of the Jews of Ereẓ Israel; of the Jewish communities of Jerusalem, Haifa, Aḥuzzat Bayit, and Tiberias; important parts of the *PICA archives, and the archives of various settlers' associations, organizations, and settlements; (c) the archives of the *Ḥibbat Zion movement, of non-official bodies, and various other Jewish national organizations; these include the archives of the central committee of the Ḥovevei Zion society, the British Ḥovevei Zion society, the *Benei Moshe Society, and the Jewish Territorial Organization; Zionist youth and students movements, such as Blau-Weiss, Kadimah, KJV, etc.; and (d) official archives containing only part of the historical documentation and important material being preserved in the private archives of leading Zionist personalities. The CZA have systematically endeavored to acquire such private archives, now about 300 in number, from the Ḥibbat Zion period up to the present. A very significant unit in this collection is the literary and political archive of Theodor *Herzl, a collection of some 5,000 of his letters in original, facsimile, photostat, or transcripts, as well as other documentary material. Other private archives in this division are those of presidents of the Zionist Organization – David Wolffsohn, Otto Warburg, Nahum Sokolow (including his library), Nahum Goldmann – and of other prominent Jews such as: C. Arlosoroff, E. Ben-Yehuda, I. Ben-Zvi, M. Buber (Zionist material only), Z.H. Chajes, F. Frankfurter (Zionist material only), H. Friedenwald, R. Gottheil, M. Hess, Zadoc Kahn, Ẓ. H. Kalischer, S. Levin, M.L. Lilienblum, L. Motzkin, M. Nordau, S.P. Rabinowitz, A. Ruppin, H. Shapira, M. Sharett, H. Struck, H. Szold, J. Trumpeldor, M. Ussishkin, I. Zangwill.

The library of the CZA contains about 60,000 books and booklets in every language and is the most comprehensive collection on Zionism and the *yishuv*. The collection of periodicals and bulletins consists of most of the Zionist newspapers that appeared in Israel and abroad, especially since 1918. The collection of nonperiodical printed items contains many thousands of announcements and placards, leaflets, circulars, etc. The collection of photographs has about 75,000 photographs and negatives of personalities, events, settlements, etc., including the collection of Oron (Oroshkes), the Jerusalem photographer. The microfilm section contains many files and documents on the history of Zionism, photographed in various archives and relevant files of various foreign ministries. The audio division is made up of tape recordings of Zionist Congresses, the Zionist "Actions Committee," etc.

The Herzl Museum, established in 1960 on Mount Herzl in Jerusalem, forms a special division of the Archives. Utilizing the documents in their possession, the CZA are publishing a comprehensive edition of Herzl's letters and writings in Hebrew translation, and assisting in the publication of his writings in other languages. The material for the publication of Moshe *Sharett's writings is also being collected in the Achives.

The CZA publish a bibliographical bulletin, which lists the publications of Zionist institutions and newly published Zionist literature. Other regular publications are its reports to Zionist Congresses, and an annual report on its operations.

Israel

Little information is available concerning the archives of the Jewish communities in Ereẓ Israel after the mishnaic period down to modern times (for ancient times see above [Biblical Period]). Nevertheless, large communities such as Safed and Hebron must have maintained an archive of important documents, such as title deeds and correspondence with the authorities. From the archives of the communities and *kolelim* only a few remnants have been preserved in libraries and private collections. Most of the material was destroyed by fire, lost through negligence, or was otherwise dispersed. Collections of letters addressed to them by the Jewish communities

Safed Landscape, 1950, by Menachem Shemi (1896–1951), Israeli painter. Oil on canvas, 50 x 65 cm. *Collection, The Israel Museum, Jerusalem. Purchased through the Batsheva Fund L'Omanuth v'Haskala. Photo © The Israel Museum.*

Throughout the twentieth century there has been some debate as to what makes a work of art "Jewish." Does the art have to contain Jewish themes and images, or is the fact that the artist is Jewish enough to call it Jewish art? Jewish art that fits either definition is presented here to show its diversity, including a sampler of calligraphic work that was created during the latter part of the twentieth century, when there was a renewed interest in the applications of Hebrew calligraphy.

ART AND CALLIGRAPHY

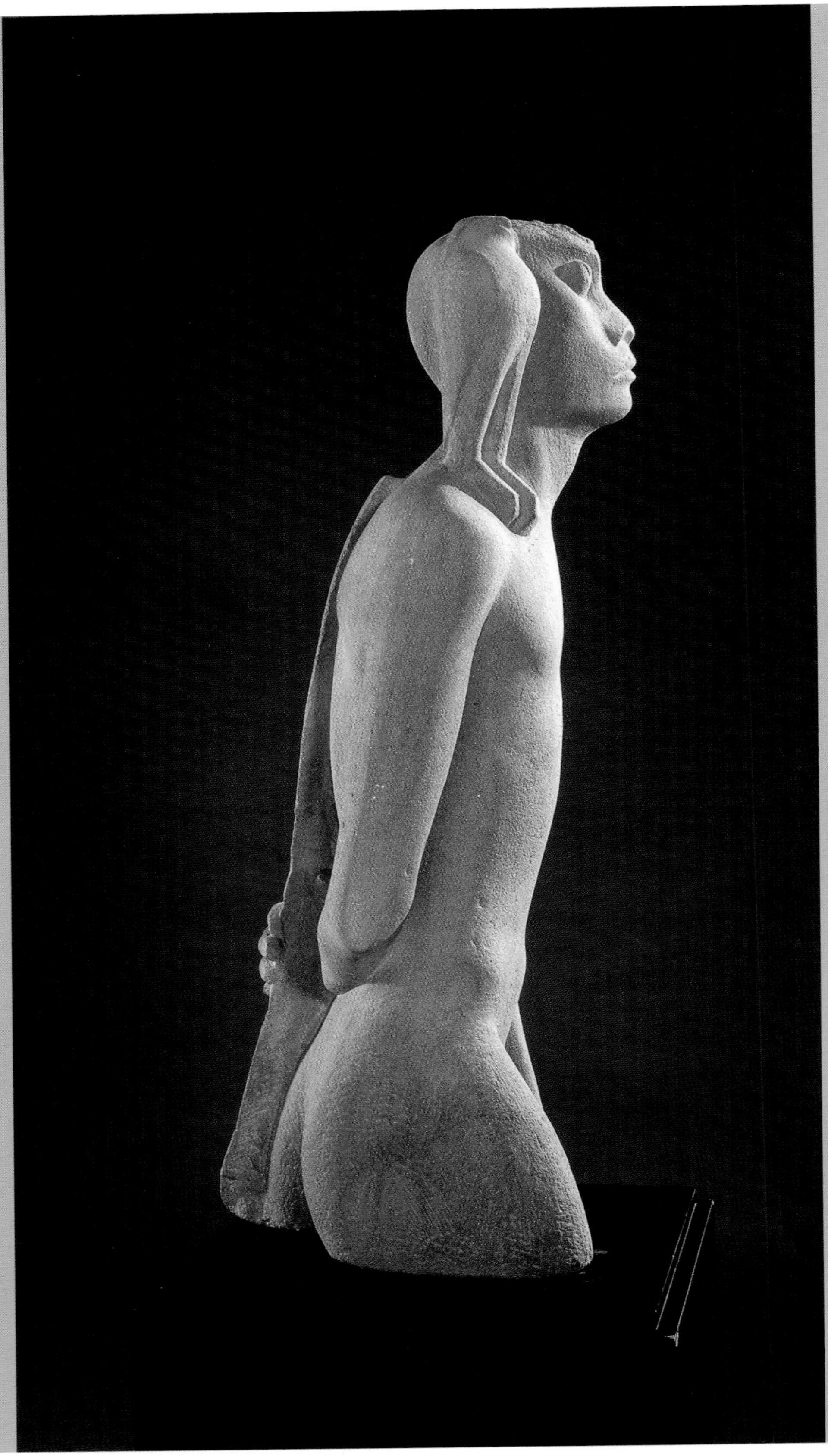

Nimrod, 1939, by Yitshak Danziger (1916–1977), Israeli sculptor, born in Germany. Nubian sandstone, 95 x 33 x 33 cm. *Gift of Dr. David H. Orgeler, Zurich and Jerusalem. Collection, The Israel Museum, Jerusalem. Photo © The Israel Museum, by Nahum Slapak.*

ABOVE:
Proverbs 31. "Woman of Valor" (Eshet Chayil), Hebrew calligraphy, by Kalman Freidus.

LEFT:
***Double Red Yentl, Split (My Elvis)*, 1993, by Deborah Kass (1952–), American painter. Screenprint and synthetic polymer on canvas, 1835 x 1829 cm.** *Courtesy the artist. The Jewish Museum, NYArt Resource, NY.*

RIGHT: **Purim paper cut, 1985, by Daniel Howarth, with a fish, the symbol of the month of Adar, and text from Esther 8:17.** *© Daniel Howarth.*

BELOW: **The main gate of the Knesset, Jerusalem, 1966, by David Palombo (1920–1966), Israeli sculptor.** *Photo: Shlomo Gafni, Jerusalem.*

Self-Portrait, 1918, by Chaim Soutine (1893–1943), born in Russia, active in France. Oil on canvas. © *Corbis.*

Prophecy, 1956, by Lee Krasner (1908–1984), American painter. Oil on cotton duck.

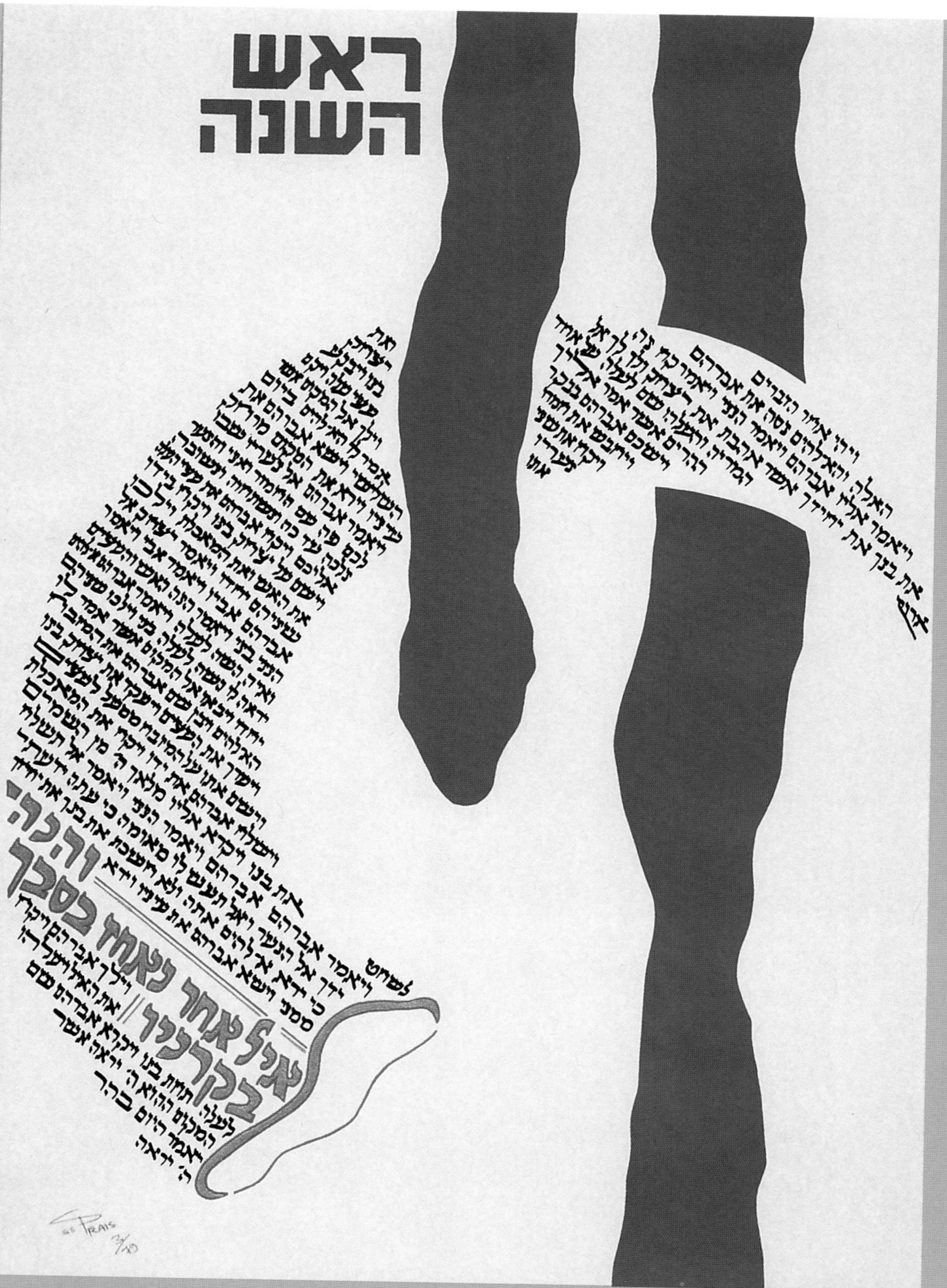

Rosh Ha-Shanah, text of the *Akedah*, the binding of Isaac. *Simon Prais, Birmingham, England, 1986.*

*ABOVE: **Untitled***, 1967, by Mark Rothko (1903–1970), American painter, born in Russia. Oil on paper, mounted on canvas. *© Philadelphia Museum of Art/Corbis.*

TOP RIGHT: Cover of *Maus I: A Survivor's Tale/My Father Bleeds History*, 1986, a graphic novel by Art Spiegelman, American illustrator. *Copyright © 1973, 1980, 1982, 1984, 1985, 1986 by Art Spiegelman.*

*BOTTOM RIGHT: **King Solomon and Asmodeus***, 1920s, by Ze'ev Raban (1890–1970), Israeli painter, born in Poland. Watercolor, pencil, pen and ink on paper, 221 x 219 cm. *Copyright, the Doron Family, Jerusalem. Photo © The Israel Museum, by Meidad Suchowolski.*

in Ereẓ Israel, especially after the beginning of the 19th century, are extant in community archives abroad, as well as in the private archives of outstanding personalities such as Moses Montefiore (see I. Ben-Zvi's publications on the subject, collected in volumes 2 and 3 of his writings, *Meḥkarim u-Mekorot* ("Studies and Sources") and *She'ar Yashuv*).

A decisive change took place in the last quarter of the 19th century, when the first self-supporting Jewish settlements were established. The new situation in which Ereẓ Israel Jews found themselves was mirrored in the structure, contents, and organization of their archives. From the beginning the new settlements took care to preserve the documents, and these reflect not only their community life – as was the custom of the communities in the Diaspora – but touch upon all aspects of the *yishuv*'s life. Many settlements have succeeded in preserving a large part of their files, and documents, including the minutes of the meetings of their administrative bodies from the day of their establishment; nearly all of them have in their archives the files which have accumulated since the end of World War I (during which a great many documents were lost). These archives, however, are only in the first stage of their preparation for scientific study.

The establishment of scientific historical archives, in the modern sense, in Ereẓ Israel, each relating to a well-defined area of interest, dates back to 1933. In that year the Central Zionist Archives (CZA; see above and below), founded in Berlin in 1919, were transferred to Jerusalem, and at about the same time a special archive of the Labor Movement was established in Tel Aviv (see Labor Archives below). In 1939 the General (now Central) Archives for the History of the Jewish People (CAHJP) were set up in Jerusalem.

The establishment of the State of Israel influenced the development of archives in several ways. Since the *yishuv* had now assumed full authority for the conduct of its affairs, the current archives (registries) which were set up by the government ministries and the authorities, reflect the entire range of the country's life. The great *aliyah* movement – "The Ingathering of the Exiles" – also created the demand to gather the documents telling of their past history. An article by A. Bein, "Sources of Jewish History – a National Need" (in: *Zion-New Judea*, no. 1 (1951), 20ff.), inaugurated a systematic effort in this field. New state or public archives were created and existing ones put on a firmer basis. In 1948 the Army Archives were founded, in 1949 the State Archives, and in 1953 the Yad Vashem archives. The enactment of an "Archives Law" by the Knesset in 1955, followed by a meeting of the Supreme Archives Council and the appointment of a State archivist, A. Bein, in August 1956, provided a new legal and operational basis for the functioning of an organized archives system. This was complemented by the establishment, in 1956, of the Israel Archives Association, a voluntary organization designed to promote cooperation among the country's archives.

The Archives Law had the following purposes: to provide the legal basis for the State Archives, which in fact had been created six years before, and to define the scope of its authority; to regulate the function of the registries in the government ministries, with special emphasis on the preservation or disposal of files; to organize and regulate the functioning of registries and archives by the local authorities; to supervise the work of historical archives maintained by nongovernmental organizations, recognized by the government as "public archives"; and to ensure the proper maintenance of historically valuable archives in private possession. The archives system is headed by the State archivist, who is also the head of the Supreme Archives Council, a body composed of representatives of government ministries and the public archives, and of experts in the field; the Council is a consultative body and, in certain instances, also serves as an appeals board. There are also various permanent committees assisting the State archivist and the Council, the most important of which are: the permanent committee on the disposal of archival material in government offices and in those of local authorities; the committee on professional terminology (relating to archives); and the coordination committee for public archives.

The following archives fall under the law:

Government Archives. The State Archives (see below) and the Army Archives (see below) are government controlled, with the latter being legally part of the State Archives, but administratively an independent unit under the Defense Ministry.

Archives of Local Authorities (municipal archives). As mentioned above, a great amount of files and documents have been accumulated in the various municipal units, which came into being as a result of their current operations; these archives represent valuable historical records, but thus far only a few have been organized into modern archives. Municipal archives have been established in Jerusalem and Tel Aviv, and beginnings have been made in Petaḥ Tikvah, Reḥovot, Afulah, Netanyah, and Ramat ha-Sharon. More substantial progress has been made in the organization of local archives in the kibbutzim. Also envisaged is the establishment of district archives. These would function as branches of the State Archives and would serve as the repository of the archival material from settlements which do not maintain any historical archives of their own.

Public Archives. These consist of the following: (1) the Central Zionist Archives (CZA) in Jerusalem; (2) the Labor Archives and Museum, Tel Aviv – the central archives of the *Histadrut, and its affiliated institutions; (3) the Central Archives for the History of the Jewish People (CAHJP); (4) the Yad Vashem archives; (5) the *Weizmann Archives, Reḥovot, established in 1951 as a part of Yad Chaim Weizmann (of special significance for the collection of Weizmann's letters now in the course of publication); (6) the Jabotinsky Institute, Tel Aviv, founded in 1933 as the Betar Museum, which took its present name in 1947, and whose task it is to collect material on the life and work of *Jabotinsky, youth movements and underground organizations founded or inspired by him; (7) Bet Aronson in Zikhron Ya'akov, which contains the private and public archives of Aaron *Aaronsohn, his brother Alexander, and his sister, Sarah; (8) the Archives of Religious Zionism, Jerusalem, which were established in 1953 as a part of the Mosad ha-Rav Kook (among its collections: the archives of the Mizrachi World Organization (1919–48), the archives of the Jerusalem branch of Ha-Po'el ha-Mizrachi (1930–48), and the private archive of Rabbi J.L. *Maimon); (9) the archives of Ha-Kibbutz ha-Arẓi of *Ha-Shomer ha-Ẓa'ir, Merḥavyah, which were established in 1937 as the first archive of a political movement in Ereẓ Israel and serves as the historical archive of Ha-Shomer ha-Ẓa'ir kibbutzim in Israel and of the Ha-Shomer ha-Ẓa'ir world movement (from 1911); (10) the archives of Ha-Kibbutz ha-Me'uḥad, in En-Harod, which were established in 1957; (11) The Isaac Katznelson Ghetto Fighters Museum Commemorating the Holocaust and the Resistance, which was founded in 1950 (includes the archives of the world He-Ḥalutz movement); (12) the archives of the Teachers' Association, Tel Aviv, which were established in 1959 to collect information on Hebrew education abroad and education in general in Israel; and (13) the Israel Film Art Archives, Haifa, which were founded in 1961 and collect significant Israel and Jewish films, as well as films that were inspired by Jewish life or are based on Jewish literary works.

Private Archives. The Archives Law provides for the listing by the State archivists of all private archives that are of value to the public. Some 200 such archives have been listed (numerous private archives, as well, have been deposited in government and public archives, esp. in the CZA). The archives maintained by political parties are also regarded as "private" archives (such as those of Mapai at Bet Berl, Tel Aviv, on its way to becoming a proper historical archive).

Important archival material is also at the National and University Library in Jerusalem, which before the establishment of special archives also served as the repository of the archives of public institutions and personalities. The material stored in the library is divided into the following groups: a section containing over 150 *pinkasim* of communities and institutions in Israel and abroad; the archives of outstanding personalities, especially scholars and writers, and which include the archives of Aḥad Ha-Am, Simḥa Assaf, Albert Einstein, Martin Buber, M.D. Gaon, J.L. Gordon, Eliahu Gutmacher, Joseph Klausner, J.L. Landau, Moritz Lazarus, Joseph Popper-Lynkeus, Stefan Zweig (letters he received from other authors), and Leopold Zunz; collections of letters of David Oppenheim, Akiva Eger, and J.L. Dukes, and of the early protagonists of the *Wissenschaft des Judentums*, as well as collections of letters concerning the history of Jewish settlement in Jerusalem; and a comprehensive collection of *autographs and portraits, founded by Abraham Schwadron-Sharon, which contains letters and documents of prominent Jews.

Genazim. The Asher Barash bio-bibliographical institute in Tel Aviv, was founded in 1953 by the Hebrew Writers' Association and contains the archives, manuscripts, and correspondence of Hebrew writers. There are also archives devoted to famous authors, such as Bet Bialik and Bet Shalom Aleichem in Tel Aviv (the latter also contains the archive of Y.D. Berkowitz, Shalom Aleichem's son-in-law and the Hebrew translator of his works).

A significant feature of the Israel Archives is the demarcation of the respective spheres of interest of the various archives and the coordination of their activities in order to avoid duplication and competition in the acquisition of material. The Israel Archives have organized professional courses at the Hebrew University, the graduates of which are awarded the designation of "archivist"; in addition, there are extension courses for the training of archives personnel. All the existing archives operate on the basis of approved statutes and are open to the public. Most of them follow the practice of the State Archives, whose files are made available for study after 20 years in the case of administrative files; 30 years, political files; or 50 years, security files and personal papers. In 1966 the Israel Archives Association published a guide (in Hebrew) to the historical archives of the country, which contains detailed lists of their contents.

[Alexander Bein]

MAJOR ISRAEL ARCHIVES. *The State (of Israel) Archives.* These archives were established in 1949 as part of the prime minister's office and were initially designed to collect documentary material – in manuscript, print, picture, and sound – relating to the history, organization, and operations of the state, and to conserve archival records of the Mandatory government departments which had remained in the country after its evacuation by the British. Even before the official establishment of the archives, the secretariat of the provisional government had taken care to assemble the files of the Mandate administration which had been found in the abandoned government offices. When the first archives director, Sophia Udin, was appointed in August 1949, the work of classifying and listing the large quantity of archival material was taken in hand. Special care was taken to collect the official publications of all state and local authorities. In 1953 the Knesset passed a law amending the Press Ordinance of 1933, which provided for the deposition in the State Archives of one copy of every publication appearing in Israel. In 1955 the Knesset passed the Archives Law, which provided the legal basis for the operation of the State Archives and the safeguarding of public records in the country. The law designates the State Archives as the sole repository of the historical records of all government departments and institutions, including the office of the state president, the Knesset, the Foreign Ministry and its missions abroad, and the police and the courts. In 1955 the State Archives were transferred from Tel Aviv to Jerusalem; this marked the conclusion of the first stage in their development. In 1957 P.A. Alsberg was appointed director of the State Archives.

The application of the Archives Law required certain changes in the definition of the State Archives' functions. Only such documentary material as is of sufficient value to be kept indefinitely would be deposited in the State Archives.

A special unit was established to supervise filing and archive operations in the government ministries and local authorities. Rules and regulations were published regarding the disposal of insignificant files, a prerequisite for the preservation of important archival material. In 1964 the Archives Law was amended to extend to governmental companies, and a Cabinet resolution (dated Nov. 22, 1959) charged the State Archives with the task of ensuring the exchange of official publications with foreign countries, as provided by the 1958 UNESCO convention. At the beginning of 1969, the State Archives contained deposits extending over approximately seven kilometers of shelf space (20,000 cu. ft.). Very little official material relating to the period of Ottoman rule is available; it consists of the lists of the censuses carried out between 1869 and 1917, and a limited amount of documents and registers from the office of the Jerusalem district governor relating to the period 1907–13. On the other hand, a great deal of material from the Mandatory period has been preserved; it consists of most of the files of the chief secretariat, the attorney general's office, the offices of the district commissioners, and a large part of the files of the various government departments. The number of files of Israel state and government institutions, which are deposited in the archives, has shown a steady rise. The president's office, the Knesset, and all ministries have made their first deposits of old files and documents of a special nature, such as credentials presented to the president, laws bearing the state seal, and special agreements. They are currently deposited with the archives. Large numbers of court files, dating back to the Mandatory government, are also stored because of their legal, sociological, and historical value.

These include the proceedings of trials that aroused special public interest and the proceedings of trials under the Law on the Punishment of Nazis and their Collaborators, including the files of the *Eichmann trial. Of special interest, from the point of view of historical research, are private archives and nongovernmental files. Among these are a great number of files from the German Consulate in Jerusalem (1839–1939), which were acquired by the State Archives when they were about to be disposed of as waste paper. Valuable Arab archives were found in abandoned houses and offices during the *War of Independence (1948), the *Sinai Campaign, and the *Six-Day War. In order to facilitate the use of its deposits, the State Archives publish series of reference guides. The first are: Herbert Samuel, a register of his papers; records of the chief secretary's office, 1918–1925; records of the Emergency Committee, 1947–1948; and records of the Prisoners' Welfare Society "Le-Assirenu," 1947–1949. The State Archives also publish "List of Government Publications" (Heb., from 1956 to 1965, quarterly, and since then annually). Other publications are designed to serve as instructions for operation of archives by the ministries and local authorities.

[Paul Awraham Alsberg]

Labor Archives (and Museum). They were established in 1932 by S. Eisenstadt, who was their director until 1941, and confirmed in 1962 by the Central Committee of the Histadrut as the central archives of all Histadrut institutions. The Labor archives contain complete or partial archives of various institutions, parties, and organizations in the Zionist labor movement in Israel and abroad, including those of the Agricultural Center, the Labor Councils of many towns and settlements, and the private archives and collections of the leading figures in the labor movement. Of special importance are the collections of periodicals published by the Labor movement in Israel and abroad.

Periodically, the archives issue *Asuppot*, which contains documents and articles; they have also published the anthology *Ha-Shomer* (1938).

Israel Defense Forces. The archives of the Israel Defense Forces (IDF), in Givatayim were established in 1948 on the instructions of the then defense minister David Ben-Gurion to R.R. Lev, who was its director until 1953. These archives developed rapidly under their second director M. Shilo who retired in 1968. Their task is to receive and preserve the documentary material of the Israel Defense Forces and the defense establishment and to prepare it for historical study. Owing to the special circumstances under which the various branches of the Army perform their function, the archives also have to receive and store comparatively recent files which are no longer in current use, even if they are not intended for permanent storage. They therefore serve both as a records center and as historical archives. When the Archives Law was passed, the Army archives were declared a part of the State Archives, but they have remained an administrative unit of the Ministry of Defense.

The voluminous documentary material in the Army archives covers the entire operations of the IDF and the defense establishment from their beginning. In view of the security classification of the material, the Army archives are, for the time being, not open to the public. A multi-storied building in Givatayim houses the archives.

The *Haganah Archives*, kept until 1969 at Bet Eliyahu, in Tel Aviv, the Haganah Museum, are now also attached to the Army archives. Their collection includes originals and photocopies of material pertaining to the Haganah organization in Palestine, its operations, and personalities, as well as the records of the Aliyah Bet (illegal immigration) organization. This collection will provide the basic material for a history of the Haganah.

[Alexander Bein]

BIBLIOGRAPHY: ANCIENT PERIOD: B. Meissner, *Babylonien und Assyrien*, 2 (1925), passim; G.R. Driver, *Semitic Writing* (1954), passim; Schneider, in: *Orientalia*, 9 (1940), 1ff.; Weitermeyer, in: *Libri*, 6 (1955–56), 217ff.; Burr, in: *Zeitschrift fuer Bibliothekwesen und Bibliographie*, 14 (1967), 154ff.; Goosens, in: RA, 46 (1952), 98; Otten, in: *Das Altertum*, 1 (1955), 67ff.; Papritz, in: *Archivalische Zeitschrift*, 55 (1959), 11–12; *Handbuch der Bibliothekwissenschaft*, 3, pt. 1 (1955); Leemans, in: RA, 48 (1954), 57ff.; Offner, in: ZA, 40 (1950), 133ff.; Kraus, in: JCS, 3 (1951), 122ff.; Weidner, in: AFO, 16 (1952–53), 198ff. GENERAL: Baron, Community, index; JSOS, 8 (1946), 5–103 (supplement); 10 (1948), 3–16 (supplement); Schwarzfuchs, in: *Archivum*, 4 (1954), 165ff.; Zivier, in: MGWJ, 49 (1905), 209ff.; A. Bein, *Al Atido shel Avarenu* (1963); Jones, in: *Archaeology*, 9 (1956), 16ff. ENGLAND: C. Roth, *Archives of the United Synagogue* (1930). FRANCE: Cahen, in: *Gazette des Archives*, 39 (1963), 177ff. AUSTRIA: A.F. Pribram, *Urkunden und Akten zur Geschichte der Juden in Wien*, 2 vols. (1918); B. Wachstein, *Urkunden und Akten…* (1926). On Holocaust, see *Holocaust, Sources and Literature. CAHJP: D.J. Cohen, in: YLBI, 1 (1956), 331ff.; 3 (1958), 3ff.; Ha-Ḥevrah ha-Ereẓ-Yisre'elit le-Historyah ve-Etnografyah, *Ha-Arkhiyyon ha-Kelali le-Toledot Yisrael* (1964), with selective list of archives and collections in Hebrew and English; Ha-Iggud ha-Arkhiyyoni be-Yisrael, *Madrikh la-Arkhiyyonim ha-Historiyyim be-Yisrael* (1966) 9ff.; *Archivum*, 15 (1965), 207ff.; Accounts of the archives' current acquisitions and activities are regularly appended to *Zion*, published by the Historical Society of Israel. CZA: Central Zionist Archives, *List of Archives and Collection of Documents…* (1965); Herzl Museum, *Guide and List of Exhibits*. ARCHIVES IN EREẒ ISRAEL: Bein, in: *Archivum*, 11 (1961), 171ff.; Alsberg et al., *ibid.*, 9 (1959), 101ff.; Bein, in: Israel Archives Association, *Archives in Israel* (1959); idem, *Ḥok ha-Arkhiyyonim u-Mashma'uto* (1957); idem, in: *Early History of Zionism in America* (1958), 109ff.; Bein and Heymann, in: *Zionist Year Book*, 8 (1959), 1ff.; idem, *Eser Shanim le-Vizu'o shel Ḥok ha-Arkhiyyonim* (1967); Israel Govt., *Laws of the State of Israel, Archives Law* (1955) and *Archives Regulations* (1967); Brilling, in: *Der Archivar*, 20 (1967), 399ff.; Karmish, in: *Yad Vashem Bulletin*, 16 (1965), 17ff. STATE ARCHIVES: IGYB, 3 (1951–). LABOR ARCHIVES: Histadrut ha-Ovedim…, *Shenaton ha-Histadrut*, 1 (1963–). ARKHIYYON ẒAHAL: IGYB, 2 (1950–).

ARCHIVOLTI, SAMUEL (ben Elhanan Jacob; 1515–1611), Italian author, grammarian, and poet. Archivolti was born in Cesena and in his youth studied with R. Meir *Katzenellenbogen. In 1563 Archivolti is known to have lived in Bologna; he visited Venice occasionally between 1565 and 1602, where he worked as a proof corrector. From 1568 he lived in Padua, where he served as secretary of the community, principal of a yeshivah, and *av bet din*. Leone *Modena was his pupil and so was Cardinal Marco Marini, who studied Hebrew with him. Modena and Archivolti contributed laudatory poems to Marini's *Arca Noae* (1593).

Archivolti's most important works are *He'arot le-Sefer he-Arukh*, supplying textual references on midrashic and talmudic passages cited in the *Arukh* of Nathan b. Jehiel of Rome (first printed in Venice, 1553; Basle, 1599); *Degel Ahavah*, an ethical work (Venice, 1551); *Ma'yan Gannim* (Venice, 1553), divided into "passages" containing 25 letters in metrical form designed to serve as models for students of this classic literary genre; and his major work, a Hebrew grammar, *Arugat ha-Bosem* (Venice, 1602; Amsterdam, 1730). This last work is divided into 32 chapters, beginning with the rudimentary usage of letters, nouns, and verbs (including a table of tenses and conjugations), and ending with an explanation of Hebrew accentuation, meter, and poetical form. Chapter 30 deals with Hebrew cryptography. Archivolti used his own poems as models to demonstrate 22 varying metrical forms. The Christian scholar Johannes *Buxtorf II translated the last section into Latin (1660), appending it to his Latin translation of the *Kuzari* of *Judah Halevi.

Archivolti also composed numerous poems and *piyyutim*, 76 of which have been printed. In 1988 D. Bregmann published 13 sonnets written by him. Like *Immanuel of Rome and Moses *Rieti, he circulated his works throughout the Italian communities. His achievements are noted by Modena, who complains that the study of Hebrew grammar was being neglected in his own day, in contrast to its cultivation at the time of Archivolti. Some of Archivolti's *piyyutim* appeared in prayer books of the Italian rite; especially well known are his *piyyut, Keḥi Kinnor*, and his poem, "*Arzei Levanon Yifraḥu*," on circumcision. Archivolti's poems reflect the state of contemporary Italian culture and the attitude of the Jews to their Christian neighbors. His responsa and letters, extant in manuscript, deal with halakhic questions such as the preparation of the *mikveh* and the prohibition of pictorial representations on synagogue walls. Modena composed an elegy on the death of his teacher, praising him as a light in Judaism, an erudite poet, and an expert in grammar and poetical craft.

BIBLIOGRAPHY: Kohut, Arukh, 1 (1926), LV, no. 4; Davidson, Oẓar, 4 (1933), 477; S. Bernstein, in: *Tarbiz*, 8 (1936/37), 55–68, 237; Schirmann, *Italya*, 251–5; Zinberg, *Sifrut*, 2 (1956), 305, 386; C. Roth, *Jews in the Renaissance* (1959), index; idem, Italy, 234–5; Zunz, Poesie, 417; Kaufmann, in: JQR, 9 (1896/97), 263–9; Kaufmann, *Schriften*, 1 (1908), 93–96; Hirschfeld, in: JQR, 14 (1901/02), 391, no. 182; Waxman, Literature, 2 (1960), 21–22, 82; S. Bernstein (ed.), *Divan of Leo de Modena* (1932), 93, 209. **ADD. BIBLIOGRAPHY:** Bregmann, in: *Italia*, 7:1-2 (1988), 29-65; Busi, *Il Succo dei Favi. Study sull'umanesimo ebraico* (1992).

[Yehoshua Horowitz]

ARCHON, communal officer for the independent Jewish community (*kehillah*) in the Greek and Roman period. The archons of the community constituted the executive committee of the council of elders (**gerusia*). Josephus mentions "the leaders of the council of elders" of Alexandria (Wars, 7:412), evidently the archons of the council who acted as its representatives vis-à-vis the people. The number of archons varied, probably relative to the size of the community. Thus an inscription from Berenice in Cyrenaica, records nine archons. In Rome there was at least one archon for each congregation. The archon was generally chosen for one year, and could be reelected for a second term, or even more. A passage in a Christian homily attributed to John Chrysostom, the Church Father, indicates that elections for the archons were held in the month of Tishri, i.e., at the beginning of the Jewish year. At this time the outgoing archons, or perhaps those assuming office, apparently participated in ceremonials which took place during the Feast of Tabernacles, such as one recorded in the Berenice inscription. Some inscriptions use the form *dis archon*, and sometimes *dia biou* (διά βίου; also *dia viu* in Latin inscriptions), evidently merely as an honorific title, indicating that the person so designated had been chosen as archon for life, although in practice he might only fulfill this function once or twice. This title probably was given to the archons held in highest esteem. The title occasionally appears to have been given to children, referred to as "the child archon," evidently children of notables. This may indicate that the office passed by inheritance in certain aristocratic families. The form μελλάρχων (future archon?) is also found, and may have designated younger members of distinguished and wealthy families of the community. The Talmud and Midrash frequently use the title "archon" although its implications are far from clear.

The sources show that there were archons in all the communities of the Diaspora, both East and West, including Syria, Egypt, Asia Minor and Greece, Italy, and Cyrenaica. The archon in Antioch, Syria, is mentioned by Josephus (Wars, 7:47). Archons in Alexandria are referred to by *Philo (*Against Flaccus*, 14:10). The above-mentioned inscription of Berenice (CIG, 5361) commemorates the Roman, Marcus Titius, son of Sextus of the Aemilia *tribus*, when he was honored on the Feast of Tabernacles in the year 55 according to the local calendar. This calendar apparently commenced in 67 B.C.E., so that the inscription dates from 13 B.C.E. In Rome there is an inscription mentioning the archon of the synagogue in the Suburra quarter (CIG, 6447). Other references to archons in Rome are to be found in the Garucchi collection of inscriptions from the Jewish cemetery in Vigna Randanini (pub. 1862, and in a supplement, 1865). The Roman inscriptions have been collected by Frey. For other parts of Italy, archons are recorded in Porto near Rome (Kaibel, *Inscriptiones Graeciae, Siciliae et Italiae*, no. 949), and Capua (T. Mommsen, *Inscriptiones Regni Neapolitani Latinae*, no. 3657; CIL, 10, pt. 1 (1883), 392, no. 3905).

BIBLIOGRAPHY: R. Garrucci, *Cimitero degli antichi Ebrei scoperto recentemente in Vigna Randanini* (1862); idem, *Dissertazioni archeologiche de vario argomento*, 2 (1865), 150–92; Schuerer, Gesch, 3 (1909[4]), 85 ff.; idem, *Die Gemeindeverfassung der Juden in Rom* (1879), 19 ff.; N. Mueller, *Die Inschriften der juedischen Katakombe am Monteverde zu Rom* (1919), index; idem, *Die juedische Katakombe am Monteverde zu Rom* (1912), 10 ff.; Frey, Corpus, 1 (1936), LXVIIff., s.v.

[Abraham Schalit]

ARCHPRESBYTER, PRESBYTER OF THE JEWS, title of the official representative of medieval English Jewry, designated in Latin as *Presbyter Judaeorum*. The first archpresbyter, Jacob le Prestre, is recorded in 1183. After the Exchequer of the Jews' foundation, c. 1190, he was to "reside there and advise its justices." In 1199 he accepted responsibility for "the Jewry's great debts from the reigns of Henry II and Richard I." His own tax he negotiated, personally, with the Crown. As the office carried risks as well as prestige, the king promised compensation would be paid, immediately, by any who transgressed against him. His own transgressions would be heard by the king or his chief justice. All Jacob's successors were eminent members of the Jewry. The great Rubigotsce's grandson, Josce, who retained the family's Rouen mansion, held office from 1207 to 1236 when Aaron of York, wealthiest of English magnates, replaced him. Elias l'Eveske, archpresbyter 1243–58, broke down under the pressure, accusing Henry III of exactions "for things we cannot give though he would put out our eyes and cut our throats after pulling off our skins," a few years later resigning, and converting to Christianity. Hagin, Master Moses' second son, succeeded in 1257, surrounded by persistent scandal, and intrigue. Imprisoned in 1280, he died the next year. The queen's puppet, Hagin "at her instance" was replaced by his nephew, Cok Hagin, who in 1275 had been excommunicated by his uncle, the great scholar Master Elias. At the Expulsion in 1290 the queen, whom Cok also had served for many years, granted him license to sell his properties.

BIBLIOGRAPHY: H.G. Richardson, *English Jewry under Angevin Kings* (1960), 117, 119–24; J. Hillaby, "The London Jewry: William I to John," in: JHSET, 33 (1993–34), 18–19, 36–39; idem, "London: The 13th-Century Jewry Revisited," in: JHSET, 32 (1990–92), 130–34, 137–46.

[Joe Hillaby (2nd ed.)]

ARCILA (**Asila** = ancient **Zilis**), port 27 mi. S. of Tangiers. Jews probably settled there in ancient times. When the Portuguese conquered the city in 1471, they seized 250 Jews and sold them as slaves in Portugal; they were ransomed by Isaac *Abrabanel. After 1492 Arcila was a disembarkation port for refugees from Spain and Portugal. The Portuguese governor Borba treated them inhumanly, but finally permitted their departure for Fez. When many of them returned, Borba forced their conversion. In 1510 a community was established. Ships from India and Brazil laden with spices, precious woods, and fabrics called at Arcila; cereals were exported, and much of this trade was in Jewish hands. The evacuation of the Jews of *Azemmour to Arcila was planned in 1541 and the following year they were given one month to leave for Fez. When the Portuguese were driven out in 1546, the Jews returned, lived among the Muslims, and paid an annual tax of 60 gold ducats. In the 19th century the very influential Levy-Benshetons were diplomatic representatives of England and the United States in Arcila. In 1940 the community numbered only 500. There was no organized community in 1968.

BIBLIOGRAPHY: D. Corcos, in: *Sefunot*, 10 (1966), 74; B. Meakin, *Land of the Moors* (1901), 221–6; Miège, Maroc, 2 (1961), 336, 385; Hirschberg, Afrikah, 1 (1965), 307, 314.

[David Corcos]

ARCO, GEORG WILHELM ALEXANDER HANS, GRAF VON (1869–1940), German inventor; son of a Jewish mother. Arco was a guards officer before attending a university. He was active in the early development of wireless telegraphy, and in 1898 participated in wireless transmission over 14 mi. (21 km.). In 1912 he invented a high-frequency machine for direct wireless telegraphy. From 1903 to 1931 he was director and chief engineer of the Gesellschaft fuer drahtlose Telegraphie m.b.h. System Telefunken, Berlin.

ARDASHIR (**Artaxata**), ancient capital of Armenia, situated on an island in the Aras (Araxes) River. According to the fifth-century Armenian chronicler Moses of Chorene, King Arsaces (85–127 C.E.) transplanted many Armenian Jews, originally captured in Palestine by King Tigranes during the years 83–69 B.C.E. from the city of Ernandi and resettled them in Ardashir. Another Armenian historian, Faustus of Byzantium, relates that the Persian king Shapur II (310–380 C.E.) deported a large number of Armenians to the provinces of Iran, among them 9,000 Jewish families from Ardashir.

BIBLIOGRAPHY: Faustus von Byzanz, *Geschichte Armeniens*, ed. by M. Lauer (1879), 137ff.; *Moses of Chorene, Histoire d'Arménie*, ed. by P.E. Le Vaillant de Florival, 3 (1841), 80ff.; Baron, Social, 2 (1952[2]), 204, 404–5.

[Isaiah Gafni]

°**ARDAVAN**, the name of five Parthian kings. The Ardavan mentioned in the Talmud is apparently Ardavan V, last of the Arsacid dynasty, who reigned from c. 213–26 C.E. He was defeated by Ardashir I, the founder of the Sassanid dynasty. The sparse talmudic references to Ardavan indicate that he was well-disposed toward the Jews. On hearing of his death, Rav exclaimed, "The bond has been sundered" (Av. Zar. 10b–11a). A king called Ardavan is mentioned in the Jerusalem Talmud (TJ, Pe'ah 1:1, 15d). He sent a valuable gift to "*Rabbenu ha-Kadosh*" ("our holy rabbi," the usual designation for *Judah ha-Nasi), and asked for a gift of similar value in return. The latter sent him a *mezuzah* which Ardavan returned, complaining that it could not be compared in value with the costly gift that he had sent. The rabbi replied, "You have sent me a gift which I am required to guard, whereas my gift will guard you."

BIBLIOGRAPHY: Graetz, Gesch, 4 (1908[4]), 257 (calls him Artaban III); Dubnow, Divrei, 3 (1958[6]), 90 (calls him Artaban IV). Numbering uncertain – see U. Kahrstedt, *Artabanos III und seine Erben* (1950), 11 n. 1; Neusner, Babylonia, 1 (1965), 85.

[Moshe Beer]

ARDIT, family of Sephardi rabbis, scholars, and philanthropists originating from Catalonia. After the expulsion from Spain a branch of the family settled in Salonika where it remained until the end of the 17th century when Abraham Ardit (d. 1729) moved to Smyrna. Among its notable members were (1) ḤAYYIM ABRAHAM BEN ISAAC (1735–1770), rabbi and exegete whose sermons and comments on Maimonides' *Mishneh Torah* appear in an appendage to Ephraim Ardit's *Matteh Efrayim* (Salonika, 1791). (2) ḤAYYIM MOSES ISAAC (1740–1800), scholar and philanthropist of Smyrna who financed the publication of the *Matteh Efrayim*. (3) ISAAC BEN SOLOMON (d. 1812), of Smyrna, author of a volume of sermons and a commentary on tractate *Arakhin, Yekar ha-Erekh* (Salonika, 1823). (4) One of Isaac's sons ḤAYYIM MOSES (d. 1846) was eulogized by Ḥayyim Palaggi and the other, Raphael Solomon (early 19th century), completed his father's book under the title *Paḥot Sheva Arakhin* (in: *Yekar ha-Erekh*). He published a commentary, *Shem Shelomo* (in *Yekar ha-Erekh*), which includes responsa, sermons, critical notes, and eulogies. (5) JOSHUA SOLOMON BEN JACOB NISSIM (d. 1876), rabbi of Smyrna and author of a book of sermons, *Ish Mevin* (Smyrna, 1894), and of a methodology on tractate *Ketubbot, Ḥina ve-Ḥisda* (3 vols.; Smyrna, 1864). (6) SOLOMON B. JACOB (mid-18th century) wrote two commentaries which were appended to various works by R. Meir Bakayam of Salonika: *Divrei Shelomo* (1747), a critical commentary on the *aggadah; Leḥem Shelomo* (1748), on Kabbalah. (7) RAPHAEL BEN SOLOMON (early 19th century), author of *Marpeh Lashon* (Salonika, 1826), a critical commentary to the *Mishneh Torah* of Maimonides and on tractate *Shevu'ot*.

BIBLIOGRAPHY: Joseph David ha-Kohen, *Yikra de-Shikhvi* (1774), nos. 6, 48, 62; Ḥ.J.D. Azulai, *Ḥayyim Sha'al* (1886), no. 72; Luncz, in: *Yerushalayim*, 4 (1892), 106; S. Ḥazzan, *Ha-Ma'alot li-Shelomo* (1894), 49b, no. 65, 61b, no. 18, 67b, no. 97; A. Freimann (ed.), *Inyanei Shabbetai Ẓevi* (1912), 141, no. 10, 147, nos. 158 and 160, 148, no. 161; B. Wachstein, *Mafte'aḥ ha-Hespedim*, 1 (1922), 50, 61, 63; 2 (1927), 15; 3 (1930), index viii; 4 (1932), index 5–6.

[Yehoshua Horowitz]

ARDIT, EPHRAIM BEN ABRAHAM (1700–1767), rabbi and preacher. He first engaged in business in his native Smyrna, but later studied there in the yeshivot, and was afterward appointed rabbi of Smyrna. He left manuscripts of glosses on the Talmud written by Spanish scholars; among them R. Jonah b. Abraham Gerondi's *Aliyyot* on *Bava Batra* which appeared in *Shitah Mekubbeẓet* (Salonika, 1791). These glosses were found by Ardit's grandson Isaac, author of *Sha'ar ha-Melekh*. Ephraim's family published *Matteh Efrayim* (1791), an anthology of his glosses and dialectic commentaries on Maimonides' halakhic writings, responsa, and sermons for the Sabbaths before the Day of Atonement, Passover, and Purim. A collection of Ephraim's homilies was extant in manuscript at Smyrna until World War I.

BIBLIOGRAPHY: J. Nuñez Belmonte, in: Bezalel Ashkenazi, *Shitah Mekubbeẓet al Massekhet Bava Batra* (Leghorn, 1774), introd.; Rosanes, Togarmah, 4 (1935), 289–90; A. Galante, *Histoire des Juifs d'Anatolie*, 1 (1937), 54.

[Yehoshua Horowitz]

ARDITI, ALBERT JUDAH (1891–1942), Greek socialist leader. Arditi, who was born in Salonika, was a paper merchant. He devoted his life to the Salonika socialist movement, the Salonikan Federation (the Socialist Labor Federation of Salonika), of which he was one of the founders in late spring 1909. He organized the city's trade union movement, contributed to the labor newspaper *La Solidaredad Obradera*, later called *Avanti*, and became its editor. He pulled the movement together when liberal criticism from Joseph *Nehama and former students of the Alliance Israélite Universelle within the Federation almost fragmented the movement. When movement leader Avraham *Ben-Aroya was exiled in 1912, Arditi filled in as editor-in-chief of *Avanti*. He was one of the Federation's foremost leaders, but yet a simple activist and devoted Socialist. In December 1912, after Salonika was captured by Greece, Arditi was sentenced to three years' imprisonment for insulting the Greek king in one of his newspaper's articles. In opposition to the collaboration of the Federation with the royalist conservative political establishment, Arditi, together with a small group of activists from the Federation, split off from the Federation in the summer of 1915. Arditi served as deputy mayor of Salonika and was a member of the Jewish Communal Council. A staunch fighter for his socialist ideals, he was outspoken and courageous in his public statements and was imprisoned by the authorities for his views. During World War II, Arditi, his wife, and children were deported to Birkenau and murdered by the Nazis.

ADD. BIBLIOGRAPHY: G.B. Leon, "The Greek Socialist Movement And The First World War: The Road To Unity," in: *Eastern European Quarterly* (1976), 26; D. Quataert, "The Workers of Salonica, 1850–1912," in: D. Quataert and Erik J. Zurcher (eds.), *Workers and the Working Class in the Ottoman Empire and the Turkish Republic 1839–1950* (1995), 59–74; DA. Recanati (ed.), *Zikhron Saloniki*, I (1972), 317–18.

[Baruch Uziel / Yitzchak Kerem (2nd ed.)]

ARDON, MORDECAI (1896–1992), Israeli painter. Ardon was born in Tuchow, Poland, as Max Bronstein, the eldest of the 12 children of Alexander Bronstein and Elisheva Buxbaum. His ḥasidic father sent his sons to study in a *bet midrash*. Influenced by his father's occupation as a watchmaker, Ardon uses images of the watch and of time to express his childhood memories (*Ascension of the Cuckoo Clock*, 1961, Private collection, Jerusalem).

From 1920 to 1925 Ardon studied at the Bauhaus under authoritative teachers such as Paul Klee, Wassily Kandinsky, Johannes Itten, and Lyonel Feininger. In Germany he was an enthusiastic Communist until 1933, when he escaped from the Nazis to Jerusalem. In 1936 he changed his name to the biblical Ardon. From 1935 he taught at the Bezalel Academy of Arts and Design in Jerusalem and was the director of the institute from 1940 to 1952. In 1963 he was awarded the Israel Prize.

The style of his early paintings was expressionistic, the landscapes and the portraits surrounded by darkness demonstrating his admiration for the Renaissance painter El Greco (*Self-Portrait*, 1938–39, Israel Museum, Jerusalem). His symbolic poetic style was shaped in the 1950s, becoming more abstract in the 1960s. Despite the abstraction, his paintings deal with historical and mystical subjects deriving from the Jewish world (*Train of Numbers*, 1962, Mishkan le-Omanut, Ein Harod).

In his unique way Ardon combined the modernism of the Bauhaus with traditional art. Tradition was expressed by the artistic technique and the choice of materials. Ardon did not use industrial paint, using instead ground powder, which enabled him to produce very light hues (*At the Gates of Jerusalem*, 1967, Israel Museum, Jerusalem). He used the triptych as a format in his most impressive works, influenced by the religious traditional meaning of it.

Ardon's most monumental work is the stained-glass window *Isaiah's Vision of Eternal Peace* (1992–94) at the Jewish National and University Library in Jerusalem. The triptych refers to the vision described on Isaiah 2:2–4. The verse "Come let us go up to the mountain of Lord …" is the theme of the left panel. It appears in several languages on symbolic white roads. The central panel describes the image of Jerusalem with motifs taken from the Dead Sea Scrolls, the view of the Walls of Jerusalem as well as kabbalistic symbols. The right panel depicts the verse "and they shall beat their swords into ploughshares"; spades hover above guns and shells. Due to Ardon's insistence on traditional technique he made the stained glass at Atelier Simon, Rheims, France.

BIBLIOGRAPHY: A. Schwartz, *Mordechi Ardon: The Colors of Time* (2003); M. Vishnym *Mordecai Ardon* (1974).

[Ronit Steinberg (2nd ed.)]

ARDUT (**Abenardut**), family of physicians in Aragon. ELEAZAR (ALAZAR) IBN ARDUT (d. c. 1350), born in Huesca, was adviser to Alfonso IV, who also used his services as a negotiator. At the beginning of the reign of Pedro IV, Eleazar was appointed chief justice for the Jewish communities of the kingdom. He evidently succeeded to the position formerly held by the *Alconstantini family. He was succeeded in this office by his brother, the court physician JOSEPH IBN ARDUT. In 1357 Joseph was directed to liquidate the debts owed by the communities of Aragon to Solomon Cresques.

BIBLIOGRAPHY: Baer, Spain, 2 (1966), 24, 28; Baer, Urkunden, index; Planas and Gallostra, in: *Sefarad*, 7 (1947), 303–48; del Arco and Balaguer, *ibid.*, 9 (1949), 355–8, 381.

ARÉGA, LÉON (1908–), French novelist. Born in Przasnysz (Poland), Aréga volunteered for the French Army on the outbreak of World War II, was captured, and made three escapes from German P.O.W. camps. After the Liberation he received a French decoration for his gallantry. Aréga began writing soon after the war and published *Comme si c'était fini* (1946), *A l'Essai* (1951), *Le même fleuve* (1954), *Pseudonymes* (1957), and *Aucune trace* (1963). He also wrote another novel, *La main sur la bouche* (1965), in collaboration with Thérèse Sandrau. In all of Aréga's stories, written in a rhythmic, musical style, the main theme is failure resulting from the unhappy circumstances which the author regards as universal. Only in the autobiographical *Comme si c'était fini* does this pervasive theme of failure assume a Jewish coloring. Here Aréga describes the fate of a typically Jewish hero, a foreign Jew living in France who volunteers for service in the French Army. No matter how hard he tries, the Jew is never accepted by his French comrades as one of themselves; nor, when he is taken prisoner, do the Germans regard him as a Frenchman.

[Arnold Mandel]

°**AREIOS** (**Areus**) **I** (309–265 B.C.E.), king of Sparta. According to Josephus, Areios wrote a letter to the high priest, Onias, telling of the discovery of a document proving "that the Jews and Spartans are of one race and are related by descent from Abraham." Josephus wrongly states that this high priest was Onias II (c. 170 B.C.E), but there is no doubt that it was Onias I. Many scholars are reluctant to accept that there was contact between the Spartan king and the obscure land of Judea but it is known that Areios cultivated many similar international relationships.

BIBLIOGRAPHY: I Macc. 12:5ff.; Jos., Ant., 12:225ff.; 13:167; Schuerer, Gesch, 1 (1901^4), 237, n. 33; M. Stern, *Ha-Te'udot le-Mered ha-Ḥashmona'im* (1965), 92, 111–6. For literature on Spartans and Jews see Josephus, *Works* (Loeb Classical Library), 7 (1943), 769.

[Isaiah Gafni]

ARENDA, Polish term designating the lease of fixed assets or of prerogatives, such as land, mills, inns, breweries, distilleries, or of special rights, such as the collection of customs duties and taxes. The term was adopted with the same meaning in Hebrew and Yiddish from the 16th century (with the lessee, in particular the small-scale lessee, being called the *arenda*). The *arenda* system was widespread in the economy of *Poland-Lithuania from the late Middle Ages.

I. Great Arenda

This term refers to the lease of public revenues and monopolies. The first leases to be held by Jews were of royal revenues and functions: the mint, salt mines, customs, and tax farming. Large-scale operations of this type were conducted by the Jews *Lewko (14th century) and Volchko (15th century). The number of Jewish lessees of central and regional customs duties and of salt mines increased in the 15th century, especially in the eastern districts. Often the same persons leased both the customs and the mines. In western Poland the nobility, possessing more capital, prevented Jews from leasing royal revenues, this being a highly lucrative activity. As the power of the nobility increased during the 16th and 17th centuries, they tried to obtain a monopoly on leasing the royal prerogatives. In 1538 the Polish *Sejm* (Diet) prohibited the lease of royal revenues to Jews. From fear of retaliation by the nobility, the Jewish autonomous body, the *Council of Four Lands, in 1580 forbade Jews to lease the great *arenda*. However, none of these enactments succeeded in eliminating Jewish enterprise completely from this sphere. Even where the nobility monopolized the lease of the royal prerogatives, there remained a broad field for Jewish enterprise and capital in the lease of revenues and functions from towns and private townships. These revenues were taxes on products and services, especially flour milling, potash and pitch, fish ponds, and alcoholic beverages (both production and sale); but sometimes the lease of whole estates was involved. All these types of lease were linked with the agricultural *arenda* (see below). Until the middle of the 16th century, Jews were among the chief lessees of the customs in the stations in Lithuania and White Russia. Some moved there from Poland for this purpose. In 1569 the Lithuanian *Sejm* accorded the nobility the monopoly on leases in Lithuania, which also included Belorussia and the Ukraine. The economic consequences of this prohibition would have been disastrous for Lithuanian Jewry, which felt strong enough to defy it openly. The Va'ad Medinat Lita (Lithuanian Council) therefore twice passed a resolution supporting the lease of customs and taxes by Jews, stating: "We have openly seen the great danger deriving from the operation of customs in Gentile hands; for the customs to be in Jewish hands is a pivot on which everything (in commerce) turns, since thereby Jews may exert control" (S. Dubnow, *Pinkas... Lita* (1925), 29, no. 123). In Lithuania, Jews openly held concessions for the great *arenda*, with the exception of the mint, until late in the 17th century.

In the 16th and 17th centuries the Jews in Red Russia also occupied a not insignificant place in the lease of customs, salt mines, taxes from drinks, etc. The lessees of these large economic undertakings often contracted them out to sublessees, mainly to Jews, as well. That Jews actually operated customs stations is attested by customs registers of 1580, written in mixed Hebrew and Yiddish, even where and when the prohibition on Jewish customs leasing formally remained in force. Jewish expertise and financial ability in this field were in demand. Jews are later found as silent partners of the nominal Christian lessees, often Armenians.

II. Agricultural Arenda

This term refers to the lease of landed estates or of specific branches (in agriculture, forestry, and processing), in which Jews gradually became predominant in eastern Poland during the 16th and 17th centuries. There were several reasons for this development. The increasing exports of agricultural products to Western Europe and the development of processing industries (especially of alcoholic beverages) led to the progressive commercialization of the landed estates, but the majority of the nobility had little interest in the actual administration of their vast (and remote) *latifundia*, as well as insufficient capital and commercial skills. Thus they turned to the capital, enterprise, and expertise of Jewish lessees. These, on the other hand, showed growing interest in this activity as a result of increasing competition and discrimination against Jews in the towns. Many a lease originated in a loan to the estate owner, who mortgaged the general or certain specific revenues from his land as security (*Zastaw*).

In Lithuania and Red Russia in this period Jews leased from the magnates not only single estates but also whole demesnes (*klucze*) and towns. In 1598 Israel of Zloczów leased the land owned by the Zloczów gentry, together with all the taxes, the monopoly on the taverns, and the corvée, for 4,500 zloty yearly. Jewish lessees played a central role in the colonization of the *Ukraine. The Jewish lessee frequently became the economic adviser and factotum of the Polish magnate. The Jewish sublessee could also exert considerable economic leverage and social influence from his position in the tavern, but his financial situation was not necessarily good.

Because of the importance of agricultural *arenda* in Jewish economic life, problems concerning this institution were often the subject of resolutions of the Councils of the Lands. One of the most far-reaching *takkanot* ("regulations") introduced by the Council was that of *ḥazakah* to prevent undercutting among Jews in this field. The regulation interdicted a Jew from attempting by any means to acquire a lease already held by another Jew for three years. Other *takkanot* dealt with problems of Sabbath observance or halakhic points arising in the course of management of estates with Christian owners. In southeastern Poland, Jewish lessees found themselves between the hammer and the anvil, under pressure from the extortionate nobility for whom they were agents, and hated by the peasantry. The attitude of the Jews themselves toward the peasants was often much more humane than that of the Polish landlords. A council of rabbis and communal leaders of Volhynia, a central district of the agricultural *arenda*, urged Jewish lessees in 1602 to forgo the work due from peasants on the Sabbath: "If the villagers are obliged to do the work on weekdays [i.e., Monday through Saturday]... let them forgo the Sabbath and [Jewish] holidays altogether. Living in exile and under the Egyptian yoke, our forefathers chose the Sabbath day for resting... Therefore also where Gentiles are under their hand [the Jews] are obliged to keep the Law... Let them not be ungrateful to the Giver of bounty, the very bounty given; let the name of the Lord be glorified through them" (Ben-Sasson, in: *Zion*, 21 (1956), 205). However, the Jews were frequently maligned. They were accused falsely of interfering in the affairs of Greek Orthodox (Pravoslav) churches in villages leased by them. All the Jews living in the southeastern parts of Poland were attacked and thousands massacred in the Cossack and peasant uprisings in the 17th century (see *Chmielnicki).

The last years of the Polish "republic of the nobility" (1648–c. 1772) were a period of economic and cultural decline accompanied by growing Catholic reaction to the Reformation. The central administrative authority progressively weakened and the nobility felt itself free to act unfettered by law. The conditions, character, and role of Jewish leaseholding changed for the worse in this situation. At that time in certain districts village Jews formed a third of the total Jewish population. The 1764 census shows that around 2% of the Jews in Poland were lessees (generally tavern keepers) in towns; in rural areas, while only a few were large-scale lessees on the magnates' estates, the number of Jewish lessees of taverns and inns had increased. In the district of Lublin at this date, 89% of the village Jews engaged in leaseholding operations were inn or tavern keepers. An insignificant number of larger-scale lessees held more than one inn or tavern. The rest, nearly 11%, leased mills and dairy processes. Petty lessees often combined trade with a craft, such as hatters, tailors, and pitch burners. Solomon *Maimon, in the late 18th century, depicts in his autobiography the poverty of the Jewish innkeeper who plied his trade in a smoky hut with peasants sitting on the floor and drinking vodka, while the Jewish teacher taught the half-naked children of the proprietor. The Polish poet Ignacy Krasicki describes an inn as a barn where the Jewish innkeeper had not even a bundle of straw to serve as a bed for his guests. Arbitrary arrests and humiliation were part of the lot of the Jews in these occupations. In the 18th century the petty squires and the general public demanded the expulsion of the Jews from the villages, especially the lessees of the taverns. During the period of the Partitions of Poland, the limitation which had been imposed on the lease of revenues and real property by Jews remained in force until the formal political emancipation of the Jews in each partition district.

The weight and importance of leaseholding in the occupational structure of Eastern European Jewry decreased in the 19th century with urbanization and industrialization and the process of Jewish migration to the cities and industrial and commercial centers. Formerly, the system of agricultural *arenda* had brought Jews to the villages and incorporated them in village life. It provided a broad area of settlement and sources of livelihood enabling the growth of the Jewish population in Poland-Lithuania. Even during its decline, and despite the tarnishing of its image from the 18th century, the *arenda* system for a considerable time played an important role in both Jewish and Polish economic and social life.

BIBLIOGRAPHY: Dubnow, Hist Russ, 3 (1920), index, s.v. *arendar*; idem, *Pinkas Va'ad ha-Kehillot be-Medinat Lita* (1925); R. Mahler, *Toledot ha-Yehudim be-Polin* (1946), index; S.B. Weinryb, *Neueste Wirtschaftsgeschichte der Juden in Russland und Polen* (1934), index; Halpern, Pinkas, s.v. Jurenda; H.H. Ben-Sasson, *Hagut ve-Hanhagah* (1959); idem, in: *Zion*, 21 (1956), 183–206; Ettinger, *ibid.*, 20 (1955), 128–52; 21 (1956), 107–42. **ADD. BIBLIOGRAPHY:** H.H. Ben-Sasson (ed.), *A History of the Jewish People* (1976); 641–44, index; J. Goldberg, "Wladza dominalna Zydow-arendarzy dobr ziemskich nad chlopami w XVII–XVIII w," in: *Przeglad Historyczny*, 1–2 (1990), 189–98.

[Abraham Wein]

ARENDT, HANNAH (1906–1975), political and social philosopher. Born in Hanover, Germany, she studied at the universities of Marburg, Freiburg, and Heidelberg. In the 1930s Arendt married Gunther Stern, a young Jewish philosopher. In 1933, fearing Nazi persecution, she fled to Paris, where she subsequently became friends with Walter *Benjamin and Raymond *Aron. In 1936, she met Heinrich Bluecher, a German political refugee whom she married in 1940, following her 1939 divorce from Stern. After the outbreak of war, and following detention as an "enemy alien," Arendt and Bluecher fled to the U.S. in 1941. From 1944 to 1948 she was successively research director of the Conference on Jewish Relations and chief editor of Schocken Books; from 1949 to 1952 she was executive director of Jewish Cultural Reconstruction. Arendt was professor at the University of Chicago from 1963 to 1967 and afterward at the New School for Social Research, New York.

An erudite, provocative, and penetrating writer, Arendt evaluated major developments in modern times. She believed that antisemitism contributed to totalitarianism which she saw as connected with the fall of the nation-state and to the change in the social structure. She advocated freedom based on public participation in politics, a tradition deriving from the Greco-Roman world, in contrast to freedom based on private interests. The former was furthered through revolutions, like the American, the latter through disastrous rebellions like the French. The dehumanizing and depoliticizing process of modern times have led away from genuine freedom to the evils of totalitarianism. Hannah Arendt covered the Eichmann trial for the *New Yorker* magazine and subsequently published as a book *Eichmann in Jerusalem: A Report on the Banality of Evil* (1963), which aroused violent controversy. In it she claimed that European Jewish leadership had failed, that the victims were partly responsible for the slaughter by their failure to resist, and that Eichmann represents the "banality of evil." Her other publications include *The Origins of Totalitarianism* (1951); *Rachel Varnhagen – The Life of a Jewess* (1957); *Between Past and Future* (1961); *On Revolution* (1963); and *Men in Dark Times* (1969). In 1970, Arendt presented a seminar on Kant's philosophy of judgment at New York City's New School (published posthumously as *Reflections on Kant's Political Philosophy* (1982)). She published "Thinking and Moral Considerations" in 1971, and the following year *Crisis of the Republic* (1972). In her final years, she worked on a projected three-volume work. Volumes 1 and 2 (*Thinking* and *Willing*) were published posthumously as *The Life of the Mind* (1981). Arendt died just as she was beginning work on the third and final volume, *Judging*.

In recent years, attention has focused on Arendt's intense intellectual and sexual relationship with German philosopher Martin Heidegger, whom she met at the University of Marburg in 1924 when she was an 18-year-old student and he was 35, married, and the father of two children. What is striking in this consistently unequal liaison is that it endured throughout Arendt's life, surviving a 17-year hiatus between 1933 and 1950, despite Arendt's knowledge that Heidegger stood accused of advancing the cause of Nazism in the academy and was banned in 1946 from the university of which he was rector. As Berel Lang has written, this lasting connection "overrode her recognition of his character – he had *no* character, she once concluded – [and] was so deep and constant that even love's blindness hardly explains it." At present, much of the correspondence between Arendt and Heidegger remains in sequestered archives. Certainty as to how the relationship evolved, its importance to Arendt and Heidegger over the course of half a century, and the extent to which their personal connection had an impact on Arendt's thinking will remain for future investigators to determine when the entire record is available.

ADD. BIBLIOGRAPHY: E. Ettinger, *Hannah Arendt/Martin Heidegger* (1995); B. Lang, "Snowblind: Martin Heidegger & Hannah Arendt," in: *The New Criterion*, 14:5 (1996); D. Villa (ed.), *The Cambridge Companion to Hannah Arendt* (2000); E. Young-Bruehl, *Hannah Arendt: For Love of the World* (2004^2).

[Richard H. Popkin / Judith R. Baskin (2nd ed.)]

ARENDT, OTTO (1854–1936), German economist and politician who sought radical changes in existing political and economic conditions in Germany. Arendt studied at the university of his native Berlin, but abandoned an academic career to engage in politics, aligning himself with the ultra-conservative Prussian elements. He became the foremost advocate of bimetallism and protective tariffs. In his main work, *Die vertragsmaessige Doppelwaehrung* (1880), he advocated the use of both gold and silver as legal tender at a fixed ratio to each other. He was also anxious to promote the interests of the land-owning population. He sat on the right wing of Parliament, as a member of the Free Conservatives in the Prussian Diet (1885–1918) and of the Reichspartei in the Reichstag (1898–1918). Arendt's polemical excesses frequently antagonized his adversaries. He was a cofounder of the German Colonial Society. In the *Deutsche Wochenblatt*, which he edited, he opposed democratic institutions and election by equal ballot to the Reichstag. Arendt's parliamentary career ended with the 1918 revolution. In 1935, as a Jew under the Hitler regime, he was deprived of his German citizenship, although he had converted to Protestantism long before. He married Olga, the daughter of the famous feminist Lina *Morgenstern.

BIBLIOGRAPHY: E. von Liebert, *Aus einem bewegten Leben* (1925); W. Liebe, *Die deutsch-nationale Volkspartei 1918–1924* (1956), 507, 509, 600; *Geschichte der Frankfurter-Zeitung* (1906), 565, 567ff., 667. **ADD. BIBLIOGRAPHY:** J. Baxa, in: NDB, 1 (1953), 345.

[*Encyclopaedia Hebraica*]

ARENS, MOSHE (1925–), Israeli politician and aeronautical engineer; member of the Ninth to Twelfth and Fifteenth Knessets. Arens was born in Kovno, Lithuania. He grew up in Riga in Latvia, and immigrated with his family to the United States in 1939, serving in the U.S. Army and graduating from MIT in engineering in 1947. He was Betar Commissioner in the U.S. in 1947–48, and immigrated to Israel in 1948. In the years 1948–49 he served as IZL emissary in Europe and North Africa. In 1949–51 he was a member of moshav Mevo'ot Betar, after which he continued his studies for a master's degree in aeronautical engineering at the California Institute of Technology until 1954. In the years 1954–57 he was employed in the development of jet engines at the Curtis Wright company, and in 1958 returned to Israel and was appointed an assistant professor of aeronautical engineering at the Technion in Haifa. From 1962 to 1971 he served as deputy director general of the Israel Aircraft Industry, involved in the development of the Aravah and the Kfir aircraft. In 1971 he received the Israel Security award. In the years 1972–77 he served as the director of the Cybernetics Company.

Arens was elected to the Ninth Knesset in 1977 as a representative of *Herut, and in the years 1977–78 was chairman of the Herut Party Center. Until the beginning of the Tenth Knesset he served as chairman of the Knesset Foreign Affairs and Defense Committee. He voted against the 1978 Camp David Agreements and the 1979 Peace Treaty with Egypt. In 1982, during Operation Peace for Galilee, Arens served as ambassador to Washington. He was recalled to Jerusalem after Ariel *Sharon was forced to resign from the Ministry of Defense following the publication of the Kahan Commission report on the Sabra and Shatila massacre, and was appointed minister of defense. In the National Unity Government formed in 1984 he was appointed minister without portfolio, and following the rotation in the premiership in October 1986, when Yitzhak *Shamir became prime minister, replaced Ezer *Weizman as minister in charge of minority affairs. While his positions regarding the Arab-Israeli conflict were always hawkish, with regards to the Arab citizens of Israel his positions were liberal. In September 1987 he resigned from the government in protest against the decision to discontinue the Lavi aircraft project for financial reasons, but returned to the government in April 1988. In the National Unity Government formed by Shamir in December 1988 Arens was appointed minister for foreign affairs, and in the government formed by Shamir in June 1990, after the Alignment left the government, was appointed once against minister of defense in place of Yitzhak *Rabin. Arens retired from politics following the defeat of the Likud in the elections to the Thirteenth Knesset and entered business. He was recalled by Prime Minister Binyamin *Netanyahu to the Ministry of Defense in January 1999, after Yitzhak Mordechai was forced to resign from the government, and remained in that post until Ehud *Barak formed his government in July of that year. Arens was reelected to the Fifteenth Knesset, serving in the Knesset Foreign Affairs and Defense Committee. He did not run for election to the Sixteenth Knesset. Among his writings are *Optimum Staging of Cruising Aircraft* (1959); *Some Requirements for the Efficient Attainment of Range by Air-borne Vehicles* (1959); and *Broken Covenant* (1995).

BIBLIOGRAPHY: S. Merrill, *Moshe Arens: Statesman and Scientist Speaks Out* (1988).

ARES (Αρης), god of war in Greek mythology, son of Zeus and Hera. The Greeks living in Ereẓ Israel during and after the Second Temple period associated several places with legends from their mythology. Thus the Greek designation for the city of Samaria (Σαμαρεία) was interpreted as denoting σᾶμα Αρεως "the sepulcher of Ares," or – more precisely – the tomb where Ares buried his son Asclepius. Similarly, Rabbath-Moab in Transjordan was called Areopolis, and coins struck by the town portray the deity. *Eusebius identifies Areopolis with the biblical Ariel (i.e., *Aryeh*; Isa. 15:9), and assumes that the inhabitants worshiped Ares, whom they also called *Aryeh*.

BIBLIOGRAPHY: Press, Ereẓ, 1 (1951), 34; Avi-Yonah, Land, 117; Pauly-Wissowa, 3 (1895), 641–2, and suppl., 3 (1918), 155.

°**ARETAS**, name of four *Nabatean kings. The sources relate little about the first two. ARETAS I (second century B.C.E.) is mentioned in II Maccabees 5:8 as the ruler with whom *Jason the high priest sought asylum. ARETAS II (first century B.C.E.) promised assistance to the people of *Gaza who were besieged by Alexander *Yannai.

Aretas III (85–60 B.C.E.) became involved in the war between the Seleucids Antiochus XII and Demetrius III in *Coele-Syria. When Antiochus fell in battle Aretas extended his rule to Coele-Syria and Damascus. He defeated Alexander Yannai at Addida. In the civil war between the two Hasmonean brothers, *Hyrcanus II and *Aristobulus II, Aretas III sided with Hyrcanus in exchange for a promise to restore to him 12 towns in Moab. Aretas laid siege to Aristobulus in the Temple Mount, but was forced to desist by Scaurus, the emissary of the Roman general *Pompey. After the conquest of Judea by Pompey in 63 B.C.E., Scaurus was sent against Aretas; but the difficulties of the terrain obliged the Romans to abandon the campaign, after exacting an indemnity of 300 talents.

Aretas IV (9 B.C.E.–40 C.E.), previously called Aeneas, was reluctantly recognized as king by *Augustus. His daughter married Herod Antipas, tetrarch of Galilee. She returned to her father, however, when Antipas married *Herodias, and a war broke out between Aretas and Antipas in which the latter was defeated. Antipas then appealed to the emperor *Tiberius, who ordered *Vittelius, governor of Syria, to attack Aretas. When Tiberius died, the campaign was abandoned. Aretas IV is also mentioned by Paul in connection with his visit to Damascus (II Cor. 11:32).

BIBLIOGRAPHY: Jos., index; Pauly-Wissowa, 3 (1895), 673–4, nos. 1–4, and suppl., 1 (1903), 125, no. 2; N. Glueck, *Deities and Dolphins* (1965), index; A. Kammerer, *Pétra et la Nabatène*, 1 (1929), index.

[Abraham Schalit]

ARETHUSA, town in Judea, probably located in the Shephelah. Arethusa is mentioned by Josephus (Ant., 14:75; Wars, 1:156) as one of the towns under Jewish rule that was returned to the Gentiles by Pompey. Its Greek inhabitants called it by the name of the Macedonian or Syrian town from which they came, which in turn was named after the famous source Arethusa in Sicily. It has been tentatively suggested to identify the place with the site of *Rosh ha-Ayin (Aphek, Antipatris) because of its rich water supply.

BIBLIOGRAPHY: Avi-Yonah, Geog, 129; E. Ciaceri, *Culti e miti nella storia dell'antica Sicilia* (1927[2]); V. Tcherikover, *Die hellenistischen Staedtegruendungen…* (1927), 63.

[Michael Avi-Yonah]

AREZZO, town in Tuscany, Italy. Jewish loan bankers were established in Arezzo from the close of the 14th century. At the beginning of 1406 their activities were suppressed, but reauthorized later that year. In the mid-15th century the da *Pisa family maintained a branch of their loan bank in Arezzo, as did the *Abrabanel family of Ferrara. Don Jacob Abrabanel lived in Arezzo for a time. When anti-Jewish reaction began in the Papal States, a number of refugees were allowed by Duke Cosimo I to settle in Arezzo in 1557. In 1570 Jewish loan banking in the city was prohibited and the Jews of the grand duchy, including those of Arezzo, were concentrated in the ghetto of *Florence. A small community was again established in Arezzo in the second half of the 18th century. It suffered when the anti-revolutionary Aretine mobs, sweeping through Tuscany in 1799, also attacked the Jews. The community came to an end in the 19th century.

BIBLIOGRAPHY: U. Cassuto, *Gli ebrei a Firenze nell'età del Rinascimento* (1918), passim; Margulies, in: RI, 3 (1906), 103–4.
ADD. BIBLIOGRAPHY: M.G. Cutini Gheri, *Le carte dei Monti Pii*

dell'Archivio di Stato di Arezzo; il prestito su pegno in città e nelle cortine (1986); R.G. Salvadori and G. Sacchetti, *Presenze ebraiche nell'aretino dal XIV al XX secolo* (1990); S. Duranti, "Federazioni di provincia; Arezzo, Grosseto, Pisa e Siena," in: E. Collotti (ed.), *Razza e fascismo; La persecuzione contro gli ebrei in Toscana (1938–1943)*, vol. 1 (1999), 325–66; idem, "Gli organi del GUF; Arezzo, Grosseto, Pisa e Siena," *ibid.*, 367–414.

[Cecil Roth / Manuela Consonni (2nd ed.)]

°**ARGENS, JEAN BAPTISTE DE BOYER (Marquis d'**; 1704–1771), French novelist and deist. Using the then current method of ascribing bold ideas to fictitious foreigners (as for example Montesquieu's *Lettres persanes*), Argens chose to couch his religious and social criticism in the form of an exchange of letters between three Jews who combined a general education with loyalty to Jewish tradition: *Lettres juives* (6 vols., 1736–38), *Lettres cabalistiques* (6 vols., 1737–41), and then *Lettres chinoises* (5 vols., 1739–40), were all published in The Hague, Holland, where he stayed for some time. The English edition appeared under the title *The Jewish Spy* (first 40 letters, London, 1739; complete in 5 vols., London, 1739–40; and many other editions). The "Jews" and "kabbalists" whom Argens introduces in his works are, in fact, "philosophers," who treat their religion lukewarmly and criticize its ritual and institutions. Argens confronts Judaism with Christianity, showing that mythological dogmas are absent from Judaism. However, in places his characters make remarks openly hostile to Judaism, in conformity with Argens' deistic views. He also had a personal grievance since the Jewish community of Amsterdam refused to grant him a subsidy (cf. his ironical dedication to this community in vol. 3 of his *Lettres juives*). After moving to Berlin, he became acquainted with Jewish scholars. A. *Gomperz, the teacher of Moses *Mendelssohn, was Argens' secretary for a time.

Argens is reported to have interceded with Frederick II of Prussia (being then his chamberlain) to grant Mendelssohn the protected status of a *Schutzjude*. He is quoted as having said, "A bad Catholic pleads with a bad Protestant for a bad Jew."

BIBLIOGRAPHY: E. Johnston, *Le marquis d'Argens* (1928); R.N. Bush, *Marquis d'Argens and his Philosophical Correspondence* (1953); Brav, in: SBB, 4 (1959/60), 133–41.

[Leon Poliakov]

ARGENTINA, South American Federal Republic, general population (2004) 39,150,000; Jewish population 190,000.

This entry is arranged according to the following outline:

COLONIAL PERIOD

After the temporary union of Spain and Portugal in 1580, Portuguese of Jewish descent began entering colonial Argentina. Thinly populated, the area served as a center of contraband trade in which silver from the Andes Mountains was exchanged for West African slaves, European textiles, and other imports. The area was also far removed from Lima, the seat of viceregal government and, from 1572, seat of the Inquisitional Tribunal (though a Portuguese inquisitor visited Buenos Aires in 1618). Arriving at Buenos Aires, or going by way of São Paulo and Paraguay, the Portuguese immigrants settled mainly in Buenos Aires, *Córdoba, and Tucumán. Throughout the next century, hostile reports (the only ones available) refer to the presence of "Jews," "Portuguese," and "merchants" – used as synonymous terms – and uniformly accuse them of "filling the land" and "monopolizing commerce." A decree of expulsion issued in 1602 also links "Portuguese" and "Judaizers" or *Crypto-Jews.

Actually, the number of people referred to in these accusations and the degree of their practice of Judaism are unknown. They themselves covered their tracks because of the Inquisition and the laws of Spain, which forbade the entry of any but "Old Christians" (see *New Christians). On the other hand, the inquisitors describe the faith of their Jewish victims in superficial stereotypes: the wearing of clean linen and abstention from work on their Sabbath, refusal to eat pork, and the denial of Christian tenets. The victims of the great Lima Auto-da-Fé of Jan. 23, 1639, included a native of Tucumán, the middle-aged surgeon Francisco *Maldonado de Silva, a man of mystic tendencies who had found his way back to the ancestral Jewish faith. Two other major figures of Jewish-Portuguese origin related to Argentina were Christians by persuasion: Francisco de *Vitoria, bishop of Tucumán (d. 1592), who was accused of Judaizing and was recalled to Spain, and the Córdoba-born jurist Antonio de León Pinelo, an important figure in South American literature (d. 1658), who brought an appeal against the fine imposed on resident Portuguese by the governor of Buenos Aires.

Few statistics are available on the activities of this period. Ninety-six Portuguese, among them 34 farmers, 25 artisans, and 14 sailors, have been identified out of a population of some 2,000 resident in Buenos Aires in about 1620; but the assumption that all Portuguese residents were Jewish is open to serious question. Probably fewer Crypto-Jews settled in the whole of Argentina than in the mining center of Potosí in modern Bolivia or in the colonial capital of Lima. Moreover, it is almost certain that their Judaism, such as it was, failed to take root. In the 18th century there are no trustworthy reports of Judaizing in Argentina, nor is it possible to verify reports that some local families were of Crypto-Jewish descent.

[Fred Bronner]

MODERN PERIOD

Legal Basis for Jewish Life

The Cabildo Abierto, whose convention in Buenos Aires on May 25, 1810, marked the beginning of Argentinean independence, did not abolish colonial legislation condemning non-Catholics to religious persecution. A circular of Dec. 3, 1810, signed by Mariano Moreno, secretary of the *Junta de Mayo*, extended an invitation to "British, Portuguese, and others not at war with us," while Bernardino Rivadavia's decree of Dec. 4, 1812, established freedom of immigration to Argentina for all nations, ensuring that their basic human rights were preserved. The Inquisition, however, was officially abolished only on March 24, 1813. On May 7, 1813, the Constitutional Assembly decided that foreigners would not be prevented from observing their religious rites if these were performed by individuals in their own homes. Following an 1825 agreement between the governments of Argentina and Great Britain, the Buenos Aires province extended religious freedom to all Protestants.

All these agreements, like that concerning non-Catholic wedding ceremonies promulgated in 1833, failed to take Jews into account. Only in the Constitution of 1853 did clauses appear which created the legal basis for Jewish life in Argentina. Complete religious freedom for all residents of Argentina, both nationals and foreign residents, was specifically laid down in paragraphs 14 and 20 of the constitution and is hinted at in paragraph 19. However, the legislation determines that the government must support Roman Catholic worship and decrees that the president and his deputy must be Roman Catholics (paragraphs 2, 76).

This constitution was passed as a result of pressure applied by liberal elements in the legislative assembly, who remained dominant in subsequent years. In 1876 they legislated a liberal immigration law, No. 817, which allowed immigration also to non-Catholics. During the 1880s, liberal politicians even created a conflict between the Argentinean government and the Catholic Church. Education Law No. 1420 of 1884 stipulated the secularization of official education, and that religious instruction in schools was to be given only before or after school hours and by clerics ordained by the various religious bodies and only to children of their respective faiths. This law, intended to eradicate church influence in state schools, naturally aroused opposition in conservative circles. In the same year another law, No. 1565, established the Registro Civil, requiring all citizens to register their civil status with the government, depriving the clergy of the sole right to register births, marriages, and deaths. When the Vatican representative intervened in the resulting controversy, Julio A. Roca's government severed relations with the Vatican, and these were resumed only in 1900.

This secular legislation was completed with the Civil Marriage Law of 1888. The liberal legislation naturally secured the legal status of non-Catholics, including Jews, and abolished all possible discrimination based on laws of civil status. Its importance diminished in the course of time, as conservative and nationalist elements ignored the liberal ideology that had promulgated the Argentinean constitution; but the religious freedom determined by the 1853 constitution was not abolished.

[Haim Avni]

History

EARLY JEWISH LIFE: 1840–1890. The foundations of contemporary Jewish life in Argentina were laid by immigrants from Western Europe. Some arrived in the 1840s, but the earliest recorded evidence of organized Jewish life was the first Jewish wedding, performed in 1860. A *minyan* that met for the High Holidays in 1862 developed into the Congregación Israelita de la República Argentina (CIRA) in 1868, concerned exclusively with serving the Buenos Aires community in matters such as marriage, burial in the cemetery of the dissidents, and, from 1874, circumcision. A permit to keep an official register of Jewish births, marriages, and deaths was at first denied to the president of the CIRA, Segismundo Auerbach (1877), under the pretext that this function was restricted to the clergy of each faith. Only when Henry Joseph (an intermarried English businessman who had some Jewish knowledge) was elected by the CIRA to serve as its rabbi and confirmed by the chief rabbi of the French Consistory in 1883 was the permit granted to the community.

The first Sephardim settled in Argentina in the early 1880s. They came from the northwestern coast of Morocco, mostly from Tetuán and Tangier, and in 1889 applied for permission to establish a synagogue according to the Hispanic-Portuguese rite. Many of the Moroccan Jews had formerly settled in Brazil, and upon their arrival in Argentina dispersed in the hinterland, forming chains of commercial enterprises, with branches in the main provincial cities.

Pogroms in Russia in 1881 led to the appointment of a government *ad honorem* immigration agent in Odessa to attract Russian Jewish immigrants. This decision prompted a vehement antisemitic attack in the press, which was boldly rejected by the leaders of the Jewish community. French antisemitism also influenced Julián Martel, who wrote *La Bolsa* (1891), a novel in which several antisemitic passages are taken almost verbatim from Edouard *Drumont's *La France Juive* (1886). Originally published by the influential newspaper *La Nación*, *La Bolsa* has been reedited and reprinted repeatedly until the present day and still serves widely as an historical source for the period. Although the 1887 census of Buenos Aires revealed only 366 Jews, it is believed that by 1889 between 1,500 and 2,000 Jews were living in the Argentine Republic.

[Victor A. Mirelman]

MASS MIGRATION: 1890–1918. Large-scale Jewish immigration to Argentina began only in the late 1880s, when echoes of Argentina's prodigious efforts to attract immigration reached Eastern Europe. Arriving singly at first, Jews later came in groups, the largest of which (820 immigrants arriving on the S.S. *Weser* on Aug. 14, 1889) laid the foundation for agricultural

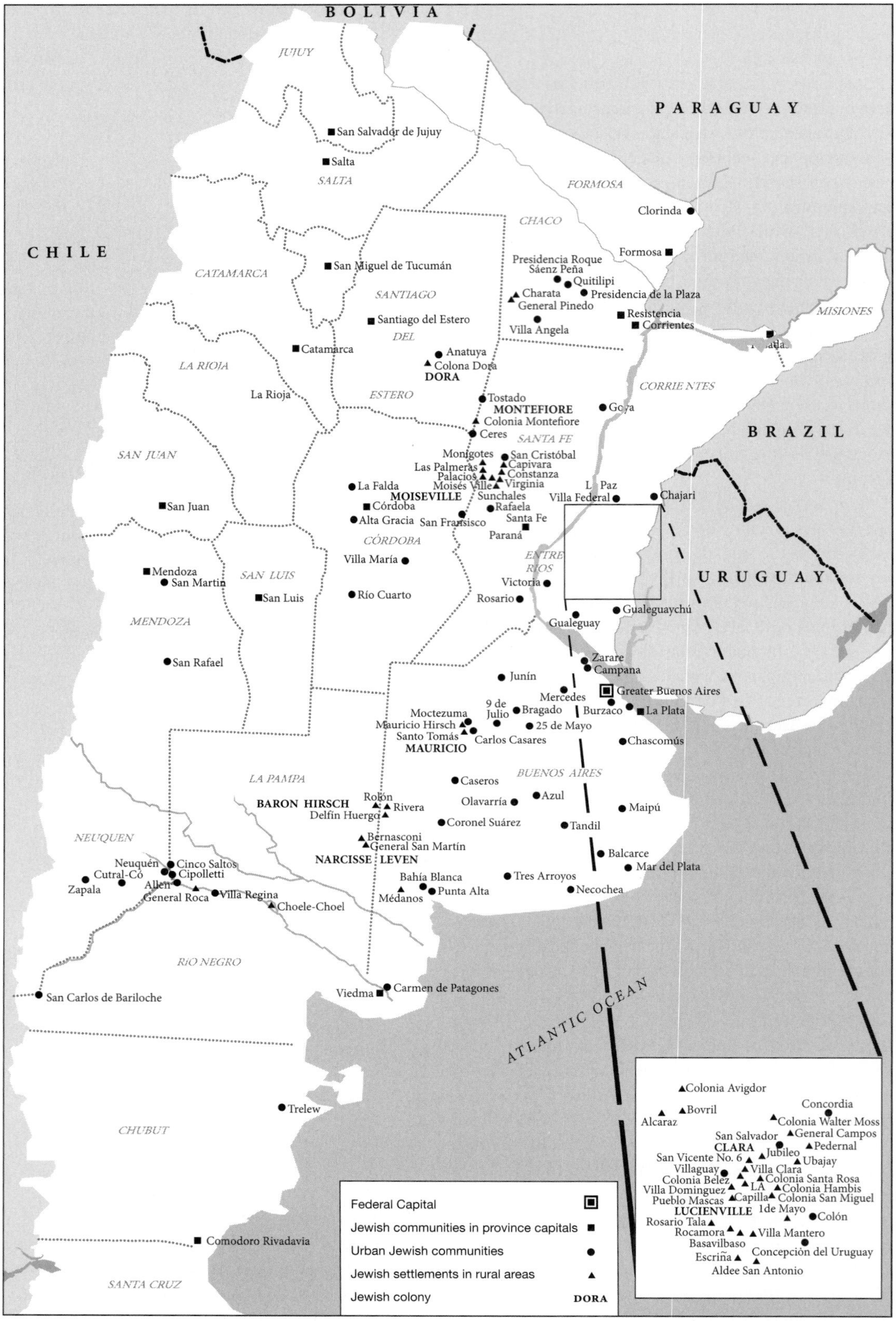
BOLIVIA
PARAGUAY
CHILE
BRAZIL
URUGUAY
ATLANTIC OCEAN
JUJUY
SALTA
FORMOSA
CHACO
CATAMARCA
SANTIAGO DEL ESTERO
MISIONES
LA RIOJA
CORRIENTES
SANTA FE
SAN JUAN
CÓRDOBA
ENTRE RIOS
SAN LUIS
MENDOZA
LA PAMPA
BUENOS AIRES
NEUQUEN
RIO NEGRO
CHUBUT
SANTA CRUZ
San Salvador de Jujuy
Salta
Clorinda
Formosa
San Miguel de Tucumán
Presidencia Roque Sáenz Peña
Quitilipi
Charata
Presidencia de la Plaza
General Pinedo
Santiago del Estero
Resistencia
Corrientes
Villa Angela
Catamarca
Anatuya
Colona Dora
DORA
La Rioja
Tostado
MONTEFIORE
Colonia Montefiore
Ceres
San Cristóbal
Monigotes
Capivara
Las Palmeras
Constanza
Palacios
Virginia
Moisés Ville
La Falda
MOISEVILLE
Sunchales
Villa Federal
Chajari
San Juan
Córdoba
Rafaela
Alta Gracia
San Fransisco
Santa Fe
Paraná
Villa María
Mendoza
San Martin
Victoria
San Luis
Río Cuarto
Rosario
Gualeguaychú
Gualeguay
San Rafael
Zarare
Campana
Junín
Greater Buenos Aires
Mercedes
9 de Julio
Bragado
Burzaco
La Plata
Moctezuma
Mauricio Hirsch
25 de Mayo
Santo Tomás
Carlos Casares
MAURICIO
Chascomús
Caseros
Rolón
Olavarría
Azul
BARON HIRSCH
Rivera
Maipú
Delfín Huergo
Coronel Suárez
Tandil
Bernasconi
General San Martín
Balcarce
NARCISSE LEVEN
Mar del Plata
Neuquén
Cinco Saltos
Cutral-Có
Cipolletti
Zapala
Allen
General Roca
Villa Regina
Choele-Choel
Bahía Blanca
Tres Arroyos
Médanos
Punta Alta
Necochea
San Carlos de Bariloche
Viedma
Carmen de Patagones
Trelew
Comodoro Rivadavia
Colonia Avigdor
Bovril
Alcaraz
Concordia
Colonia Walter Moss
San Salvador
General Campos
CLARA
Pedernal
Jubileo
San Vicente No. 6
Ubajay
Villaguay
Villa Clara
Colonia Belez
Colonia Santa Rosa
Villa Dominguez
LA
Colonia Hambis
Pueblo Mascas
Capilla
Colonia San Miguel
LUCIENVILLE
1de Mayo
Colón
Rosario Tala
Rocamora
Villa Mantero
Basavilbaso
Concepción del Uruguay
Escriña
Aldee San Antonio
Federal Capital
Jewish communities in province capitals
Urban Jewish communities
Jewish settlements in rural areas
Jewish colony
DORA

Jewish settlement in Argentina.

settlements (see below, Agricultural Settlement). Immigration to urban areas as well as to rural ones increased after the *Jewish Colonization Association (ICA) was established, reaching a peak of over 13,000 persons per year in 1906 and 1912. In the first 15 years 66% of the immigrants settled in agricultural colonies (in 1895, 4,000 of 6,000 Jews; in 1904, 12,000 out of a total population of 18,000). After 1905, urban immigration increased. In 1909 66% of the 55,000 Jews lived in cities and in 1919 80% of 125,000. Most of these immigrants were Ashkenazim, but also many groups of Sephardim came from the Ottoman Empire and North Africa, mainly from Syria, Turkey, Rhodes, and Spanish Morocco. In 1927 it was estimated that there were 20,000 Sephardim in Argentina.

Agricultural Settlement. Jewish agricultural settlement in Argentina began in 1888 under the auspices of the *Alliance Israélite Universelle. Of the 136 families who arrived on the SS *Weser* in 1889, about 40 acquired land from a landowner, Pedro Palacios, and set up the Moisesville colony. The settlers suffered from hunger and disease during the first months of their settlement, due to lack of equipment and financial means. Wilhelm Loewenthal, a Jewish physician and naturalist, was invited by the Argentine government to carry out a mission of inquiry in the latter half of 1889. On his way to Argentina, he was asked by Jewish leaders in Berlin and Paris, who had helped the immigrants on the *Weser*, to report on the settlers' condition. During his stay in Argentina, Loewenthal attempted to improve relations between Palacios and the settlers. He also set forth to the Alliance Israélite Universelle a long-range program for Jewish agricultural settlement in Argentina for the absorption of about 5,000 persons a year. Though the Alliance rejected his proposal, the idea was forwarded to Baron Maurice de *Hirsch, who decided to adopt the plan as he had completely abandoned his previous plans to improve the lot of Russian Jewry by establishing a network of schools in Russia.

In November 1890, Loewenthal was sent by Baron de Hirsch to Argentina at the head of an exploratory mission, and on April 28, 1891, the Baron appointed him director of his settlement project. Soon afterward, Baron de Hirsch decided that his plan would be the cornerstone of a comprehensive territorial project, which, within a relatively short period, would be a solution to the worsening condition of Russian Jewry. As a result, the first immigrants were sent to Argentina in July 1891. Negotiations were held with private individuals and with the Argentinean government for concessions and the acquisition of up to 3,750,000 hectares of land in Chaco. Negotiations were also held with the Russian government to allow the emigration of Jews and secure a permit to establish emigration agencies. The Russian government agreed to the request on May 20, 1892, assuming that in the ensuing 25 years 3,250,000 Jews would leave Russia. However, this grandiose scheme did not materialize. The Argentinean parliament did not approve the sale of large tracts of land, and Baron de Hirsch was persuaded that the climate and soil in the areas under consideration were unsuitable for Jewish colonization. The settlement of the first immigrants was beset by serious administrative and social difficulties, which Baron de Hirsch was unable to overcome even after Loewenthal was removed from his post and replaced by Colonel Albert E.W. Goldsmid. Baron de Hirsch continued to hope that he would find suitable locations and carry out a large and geographically concentrated project. In 1895 he admitted that his plans were unrealistic and tried to change the main objective of his activities from emigration and agricultural settlement to productive support of needy Jews in Europe and the Americas. On April 21, 1896, he died while in the midst of implementing the revised plan, which continued on a minor scale.

Instead of the mass project and the vast and concentrated territories, at the time of the Baron's death the Jewish Colonization Association (ICA) owned a total of only 302,736 hectares in the provinces of Buenos Aires, Entre Ríos, and Santa Fé with a total of 910 families (6,757 persons). Jewish colonization developed primarily in the 20 years after the Baron's death. The land area rose to 586,473 hectares on the eve of World War I, and from then on until ICA ceased its activity, it rose to only 617,468 hectares. The number of persons settled on the land reached 18,900 during this period, a figure only 1,428 short of the peak figure for 1925 (20,382 persons). Also during this period most of the cooperatives were formed in the colonies, and Alberto *Gerchunoff wrote his classic work, *Los Gauchos Judíos*.

Agricultural Cooperatives. The first agricultural cooperative in Argentina was established in the Jewish colony of Lucienville in the Entre Riós province. It was founded on Aug. 12, 1900, on the initiative of Leon Nemirovsky, agronomist and administrator of ICA under the name of Primera Sociedad Agrícola Israelita, and still exists under the name Sociedad Agrícola Lucienville. The cooperative's activities began with the purchase of seeds and supplies necessary for harvest, thus freeing its members from exploitation by merchants. Thereafter the following cooperatives were established with ICA's moral and financial support: Fondo Comunal in the Clara and San Antonio colonies (1904); Mutua Agrícola (Agricultural Mutual Fund) in Moisesville (1908); Barón Hirsch in Rivera (1910); and Unión Cooperativa Agrícola in Narcisse Leven (1910). In the course of time, all of these cooperatives developed many programs to protect the material interests of their members, satisfy their cultural and social needs, and represent them in conflicts with ICA. In 1910 a congress of the cooperatives' representatives was held in Buenos Aires. The congress laid the foundations of the Confederación Agrícola Israelita Argentina.

Immigration and Organization. The official attitude of Argentinean authorities toward Jewish immigration was based solely on the pertinent clauses of the national constitution. Thus, the committee responsible for immigration overruled the immigration officer's opposition to the admission of the Jews who had arrived on the *Weser*. It was argued even then, however, that immigration restrictions should be imposed to ensure the cultural homogeneity of Argentina, a view that was supported by the director of the Immigration Department. Public opinion and the authorities expected the immigrants to assimilate, and this feeling prompted a federal inquiry in 1908 into the cultural orientation of the schools in the Jewish colonies of the Entre Ríos province. Some Jewish schools in Buenos Aires were closed for a short period in January 1910 because it was believed that they were remiss in encouraging cultural integration and that the children did not attend public schools, and because of the poor condition of the school buildings. Nevertheless, the Jews in Argentina were living in an ethnically and culturally heterogeneous society, as demonstrated by the fact that in 1914 the country contained 2,358,000 immigrants in a total population of 7,885,000. More than one-third of the total population was foreign-born, while in the city of Buenos Aires the percentage was around 50%. The result of the immigration policy was reflected in the census of 1914, which showed that in 20 years the country's population had almost doubled (from approximately 3.9 million to about 7.9 million). As for the Jews, the rate of growth was several times higher, from 6,000 in 1895 to 125,000 in 1919. The agricultural colonies, where Jews formed an almost exclusively Jewish society, were an exception in this heterogeneous society, because of the high percentage of Jewish immigrants who settled there.

Despite the small size of their community, their feeling of transience (expressed by a certain degree of emigration back to Europe), and their poverty, by 1914 Argentinean Jewry had founded many organizations to fulfill religious and material needs and dispel a sense of cultural alienation in a strange land. Ashkenazim and Sephardim acted separately, according to the organizational and ideological experience they had brought with them. The Sephardim established small individual groups, organized on the basis of their geographical origin and designed to fulfill limited religious, welfare, and educational needs. These small institutions were gradually organized within four communal frameworks, each with its own cemetery: the Jews from Morocco founded the Congregación Israelita Latina in 1891; the Jews from Damascus founded their Bene Emet (Hijos de la Verdad) burial society in 1913, and two main synagogues, Agudat Dodim (1919) and Or Tora; the Jews from Aleppo founded their main religious organization, Yesod Hadat, in 1912 and their burial society, Chesed Shel Emet Sefaradit, acquired a cemetery in 1920; the Jews from Turkey, Rhodes, and the Balkan countries founded several small communities that were gradually consolidated around the Asociación Comunidad Israelita Sefaradí (ACIS), which was founded in 1914 by Jews from Smyrna. ACIS became the main communal framework for all the Sephardim of Ladino-speaking origin, when it acquired its cemetery in 1929.

The Ashkenazim, on the other hand, founded a network of religious, social, educational, cultural, and political organizations. The most prominent Ashkenazi religious and assistance organizations were the Burial Society (Chevra Keduscha Aschkenazi) founded in 1894, Bikkur Ḥolim (1896), and Ezrah (1900) – which provided medical aid, orphanages, homes for the aged, etc. The dominant political organizations were the various Zionist groups, founded as early as 1897 in the agricultural colonies and in Buenos Aires, which eventually imparted a strong Zionist orientation to the entire Jewish population of Argentina. Counteracting the Zionist organizations, including the *Po'alei Zion Party formed in 1909, were Bundist, anarchist, and communist groups. The Bund members tried to establish linguistically autonomous (Yiddish) sections within some of the general trade unions. The communists succeeded later in establishing a Jewish section (Yiddish-speaking) in the Communist Party. All organizations had varied cultural programs, which, except among the religious Zionists, emphasized a secular nationalist or cultural orientation toward Judaism. These activities included establishing libraries, schools, encouraging the development of a native literature, and experiments in theatrical production.

The immigrant colonists were accompanied by their *shoḥatim* and rabbis; the first of them was Rabbi Aaron Goldman of Moisesville. Religious life in the colonies at first followed traditional patterns, as exemplified by the foundation of a short-lived yeshivah in Colonia Belez (1907–08). However, isolation and lack of Jewish education combined with other factors to cause a decline in religious life. In Buenos Aires, where the Congregación Israelita de la República Argentina already existed, additional *minyanim* were organized: Po'alei Ẓedek, which established the first *talmud torah*; Maḥazikei Emunah, which brought the first official *shoḥet* to Buenos Aires in 1892 and built the first *mikveh* in 1893; and the Congregación Latina of the Jews of Morocco. Until 1897 Jews were buried in the Protestant cemetery; later, tombs had to be leased in a Catholic cemetery. It was only in 1910 that the Jews were able to overcome economic and legal difficulties and acquire their own cemetery. Although the white-slave traders already had a cemetery before 1910, none of the respectable Jews agreed to be buried in it.

The polarization of class and political opinion, the wide social and cultural gap between immigrants from Eastern and Western Europe, and personal ambition prevented the establishment of centralized organizations in Argentina during this period. The first attempt was made in 1909 with the establishment of the Federación Israelita Argentina, but this organization did not last after 1910. In 1915, when news of the fate of the Jews in war-stricken areas of Russia and in Palestine began to arrive, the Central Committee for the Jewish Victims of the War was established as the fundraising organ of the Argentinean Jewish community. In February 1916 the Congress of Argentinean Jewry was convened through the initiative of the Zionists and with the participation of all Jewish organizations, except those of the extreme left wing. The Congress declared the prime postwar demands of the Jewish nation to be equal rights for the Jews of the Diaspora and Jewish independence in Ereẓ Israel, and resolved to ask the Argentinean government to support these demands. When the *Jewish Legion was formed in 1917, several dozen young Jews volunteered and the enterprise was widely publicized by the Zionists.

Antisemitism was rare throughout this period. Nevertheless, when a Jewish anarchist, Simon Radowitzky, assassinated the chief of police, Ramón Falcón (Nov. 14, 1909), there were some repercussions against the Jewish population as such. Murders of Jewish settlers in the agricultural colonies resembled incidents between *gauchos* and settlers of other origins.

Cultural Life. At the beginning of the 20th century the cultural life of the Jewish community in Argentina was centered around the Jewish political parties, much as it had been in Eastern Europe. Thus, the founders of the first two Jewish libraries in Buenos Aires in 1905 – Biblioteca Rusa, and Ḥerut – had belonged to socialist organizations in czarist Russia. In addition to these libraries, cultural activities were sponsored by the Zionist organization Tiferet Sión, the anarchist group Arbayter Fraynd, and the Avangard. Another aspect of cultural life was the Yiddish theater, whose first performance was given in 1901. From that time onward, and especially after World War I, the Jewish theater became one of the central forces in Argentinean Jewish life. Its repertoire was mainly in Yiddish and the most outstanding actors in the Jewish dramatic world appeared on its stage. Individual actors and companies from Argentina visited Brazil, Uruguay, and other Latin American countries.

In 1898 the first three periodicals published in Yiddish in Argentina were *Der Vider-Kol*, edited by Mikhal Ha-Cohen Sinai; *Der Yidisher Fonograf*, edited by Fabian S. Halevi; and *Di Yidishe Folkshtime*, edited by Abraham Vermont. The first two publications were designed to serve as a forum for educated Jews, whereas *Di Yidishe Folkshtime* sought to serve the masses of Jewish immigrants and outlasted the former two by continued publication for 16 years. A host of short-lived periodicals also appeared during this period. At its end, in 1914, no less than 40 Jewish periodicals existed in Argentina. A fundamental change took place when the first daily, *Di Yidishe Tsaytung*, was published. The paper succeeded in overcoming its initial difficulties and presented a centrist middle-class political orientation. In 1918, a second daily newspaper, *Di Prese*, made its appearance. During the 1920s, *Di Prese* acquired a leftist orientation, which found its expression even in a change in the spelling of Hebrew words, imitating the communist transliteration. This leftist trend slackened off toward the end of the 1930s, and from the end of World War II and the establishment of the State of Israel, the paper also reinforced its ties with Zionism. Both newspapers were published until the 1970s. Other dailies were published in this period but were comparatively short lived (*Der Tog*, *Morgentsaytung*). Mention must also be made of *Kolonist Kooperator*, the organ of the Jewish colonists which first appeared in 1918 as a Yiddish-Spanish monthly and was published until the 1970s.

In 1913 the first attempt was made at organizing cultural activities in Argentina, and in 1915 the first conference of representatives of 25 libraries and other cultural institutions throughout the country was convened in La Plata without important results.

Jewish Education. The first Jewish school in Buenos Aires was a *talmud torah* – a traditional religious complementary school founded in 1891 by the Unión Po'alei Ẓedek. It had three teachers, who taught only religious subjects in Yiddish. In the mid-1890s the CIRA supported a Jewish experimental school with general and Jewish studies but it lasted no more than six months, after which it became a complementary *talmud torah*. In the first decade of the 20th century three or four new *talmudei torah* were established. The percentage of Jewish students who attended this complementary school was very low while almost 100% of the children attended public schools.

In 1892, at the start of agricultural settlement, the farmers set up *ḥadarim* for their sons, continuing to maintain them on a part-time basis even after ICA decided to establish its own school system in 1894. ICA schools followed the government syllabus with the addition of Hebrew and Jewish studies. Those were the only schools existing in the Jewish rural areas since the government did not have the infrastructure to fulfill the obligation established by Law No. 1420 to provide elementary education to all the population. These schools grew and multiplied as the number of settlers increased, with 50 schools attended by 3,538 pupils and a teaching staff of 155 in 1910. In 1911 the ICA and CIRA established a new organization to sustain the existing *talmudei torah* in the cities and to establish new traditional complementary schools, called Cursos Religiosos, in urban areas in Ashkenazi and Sephardi institutions.

In 1916, as a result of a diminishing budget and the interest of the ICA administrators in demonstrating to the authorities their patriotism and loyalty to the country, ICA handed over these schools, built and sustained by the settlers, to the local and national educational authorities. At the same time new complementary Jewish schools were established by the settlers and by ICA which gradually were supported and administrated by the Va'ad ha-Ḥinnukh ha-Roshi (Head Office of Education), founded on the initiative of ICA by the CIRA in 1917, which coordinated the Jewish education in rural areas until 1957.

All the schools established by the Cursos Religiosos and then by the Va'ad ha-Ḥinnukh ha-Roshi had a curriculum of Jewish studies with a religious orientation that aimed to suppress Jewish national values, teaching in Spanish and translating prayers and selected texts from the Pentateuch from Hebrew to Spanish. The official policy of this organization prohibited the teaching of Yiddish. Nevertheless, many teachers with the support of the settlers introduced national Jewish studies (history, Zionism, Ereẓ Israel) and Yiddish language.

THE RADICAL PERIOD: 1918–1930. The Russian Revolution increased the government's fear of similar revolutionary activity in Argentina. Since the Jews were generally identified as "rusos" (Russians), anti-revolutionary fervor developed into overt antisemitism. During the "Red-scare pogrom" known in Argentina as La Semana Trágica, January 7–13, 1919, a pogrom broke out following a general strike, which was organized after the brutal suppression of a strike in one factory. The general strike was portrayed by the authorities as a Bolshevik revolution in which a "shadow government" was being formed by the Jewish "dictator-president" Pinie Wald (a journalist at the daily *Di Prese*) to assume control of the country. Jews were beaten in the streets and their property was stolen and burned in full view of the police. These acts were about to be repeated in Rosario, and were even echoed in Montevideo (capital of Uruguay), when the heads of Jewish organizations published a desperate appeal, "150,000 Israelites – To the People of the Republic," and a deputation was received by the president of Argentina, Hipólito Yrigoyen. Liberal public opinion criticized the government and the president disassociated himself from the riots, but nevertheless expressed his displeasure at the fact that the deputation was presented in the name of the Jewish community and not individual Argentinean citizens.

The intense antagonism toward Jews, and particularly to "Russians," created administrative difficulties in Jewish immigration procedures in the 1920s. "Soprotimis," the organization dealing with immigrants, concluded special agreements with the Immigration Department in November 1921 and August 1924. In 1926, however, Jews were compelled to attempt illegal immigration, and, in at least one case, several of them drowned while crossing the Uruguay River. Concurrently, a strong feeling of nationalism, based on xenophobia and influenced by Mussolini's example in Italy, began to develop in Argentina.

Nevertheless, the 1920s saw a large increase in the Jewish population of Argentina. Around 79,000 immigrants arrived; the economic situation of veteran settlers continued to improve; 15 credit cooperatives were founded; charitable organizations expanded (the Jewish hospital opened its first building in 1921 and its second in 1928); and the Yiddish press, literature, and theater flourished. Simultaneously, the number of Argentinean-born Jews favoring comprehensive cultural integration increased, and they founded the organization Hebraica (see *Sociedad Hebraica Argentina). Political and institutional differences between various organizations, Zionist parties, and between the Zionists and left-wing groups became more pronounced during this decade and prevented attempts to form a central communal institution, the Alianza.

These differences, however, did not interfere with the general and determined fight against white-slave traders, the so-called "*Tmeim*" (unclean). A country that attracted predominantly male immigrants, Argentina had an unequal balance between the sexes and consequently drew representatives of the Jewish underworld of Eastern Europe beginning in the mid-1880s. The white-slave trade was a blot on the law-abiding Jewish public, and, despite the wealth of the traders, all Argentinean Jewish organizations imposed a comprehensive social ban on them, which was even specified in the statutes of most groups, from the 1890s onward. The matter became a violent public struggle during various periods, as in 1909 and 1913, and particularly in the 1920s. To compensate for their ostracism, the traders organized themselves into an official mutual aid organization known as Ẓvi Migdal, which was responsible for protecting them by bribing the authorities and for supplying religious services such as a separate synagogue and cemetery. From the 1890s onward, the London-based Jewish Association for the Protection of Girls and Women maintained a branch in Buenos Aires known as *Ezras Noshim*. It systematically dogged the footsteps of the "*Tmeim*" and provided as much assistance as possible to the victims, given an over-lenient law and the widespread bribing of government officials. The white-slave traders' association in Buenos Aires was not dissolved until 1930, when most of its members were either arrested or fled. The fight against and boycott of the remaining white-slave traders was continued and characterized the Jewish community as the only group in Argentina that eradicated slave trade in its own ranks.

Agricultural Settlement. The 15 years between 1919 and 1934 constitute the second stage in the history of colonization, during which the land area, the number of settlers, and the size of the non-agricultural population reached their peak. During this period, however, the deterioration of the settlement project began, with an increasing number leaving the land. Statistics do not show evidence of a drop in population, as new settlers came to replace those who left and the number of non-Jews in the colonies grew.

In 1925, following the critical years of 1911–16 and the subsequent increase in the number of cooperatives, delegates assembled and founded the Cooperativa de Cooperativas, later called Fraternidad Agraria (registered in 1931). Twenty-two cooperatives, including eight engaged in cattle breeding, were attached to the Fraternidad Agraria at the end of the 1960s, and though the Jewish agricultural population decreased and was replaced by non-Jewish colonists, the cooperatives were administered by Jews. All the cooperatives did their purchasing, modernized production methods, and marketed their products through the Fraternidad Agraria. The Jewish colonists had an important role in the Argentinean agricultural development. For example, the cultivation of sunflowers was introduced to Argentina by the Jews of the Mauricio colony. The first grain elevator of Entre Ríos province was built in 1931 by the Cooperativa Fondo Comunal in Domínguez. The cooperatives Granjeros Unidos (in Rivera), El Progreso (in Bernasconi), and La Mutua Agrícola (in Moisesville) were provided at the end of the 1960s with silos equipped with the most modern facilities to assure the greatest efficiency in handling, sorting, and storing grain. In Dominguez a vegetable oils factory named after Ingeniero Miguel Sajaroff was operated by Fondo Comunal together with the Federación Entrerriana de Cooperativas. It converts linen grains collected by the zone cooperatives into oil and by-products.

Eminent among the leaders of the agrarian cooperative movement in Argentina, together with Miguel Sajaroff, unquestionably the precursor and the mentor, are Adolfo Leibovich, Isaac Kaplan, Marcos Wortman, Miguel Kipen, Elias

Efron, and Francisco Loewy. The official organ of the Fraternidad Agraria, *El Colono Cooperativista* o *Kolonist Kooperator*, first appeared in 1918 and continued to be published monthly in Spanish and Yiddish until the mid-1970s. The impulse given by the Jewish colonists to the agrarian cooperative movement was fruitful. In 1937 only 3% of the country's producers were integrated into cooperatives; in the mid-1960s the number of farmers who sold their products through cooperatives increased to 63%.

Cultural Life. World War I caused a number of changes in the structure of the Jewish community of Argentina that were further augmented by a later wave of immigration. Many and varied cultural organizations, such as the Argentinean branch of *YIVO (1929), which established a central Jewish library and archives (dedicated mainly to the history of the community), were founded. A specific type of cultural activity was evidenced by the foundation of *Landsmanshaftn* (organizations of immigrants established according to countries and cities of origin) to aid the newcomers in their initial integration.

The outstanding characteristic of cultural life was that it was a microcosmic continuation of East European culture. Numerous organizations were built mainly around the Yiddish language and culture (such as the society of Jewish writers and journalists named after H.D. Nomberg, the Kultur Kongres, A. Zygielbojm Gezelshaft far Kultur un Hilf, Ringelblum Kultur-Tsenter, and Ratsionalistishe Gezelshaft). Cultural activity was also supported by circles that identified themselves with Bolshevism. On the other hand, activities in Hebrew were very limited. The first attempts to hold activities in Hebrew were made in 1911, when the organization Doverei Sefat-Ever was founded. In 1921 the first Hebrew periodical, *Ha-Bimah ha-Ivrit*, edited first by J.L. Gorelik and later by Tuvia Olesker, was published in Buenos Aires. Others soon followed, and in 1938 a Hebrew monthly, *Darom*, was founded by the Histadrut ha-Ivrit and has been published regularly until the 1970s.

Weeklies and monthlies in Spanish made their first appearance as early as 1911. *Juventud* was the first, followed by *El Israelita Argentino* (1913) and *Vida Nuestra* (1919). In 1917 the Spanish-language monthly *Israel* was established by a Moroccan Jew, Samuel A. Levi, and served mainly Sephardim. *Mundo Israelita* made its first appearance in 1923, followed by *La Luz*, a bi-monthly, edited first by David Elnecave and subsequently by his son Nissim and his grandson David, which also addressed itself to Sephardim, and literary periodicals such as *Shriftn* and *Davke*, devoted mainly to Jewish philosophy.

Religious Life. The period between the two World Wars marks the decline of religious life in Argentina. New immigration from Eastern Europe, especially from Poland, Lithuania, and Romania, introduced a strong anti-religious tradition, and there was a notable lack of religious authority and leadership. In 1928, Rabbi Shaul Sittehon Dabah of the Aleppan Jewish community, under the influence of Rabbi Aharon Halevi Goldman of Moisesville, and with his approval, published a ban against the performance of conversions to Judaism in the Argentine Republic. This prohibition, which is still maintained by the Orthodox communities in Argentina, was supported at the time by the chief rabbis of Ereẓ Israel, A.I. *Kook and Jacob *Meir, as well as by Rabbi Judah Leib *Zirelson of Kishinev and other authorities.

Jewish Education. Although efforts were made to establish secular schools before World War I, these schools only began operating from 1920 onward besides the *talmudei torah*. They were organized by activists, teachers, and to some extent by political parties such as the General Zionists, left-wing Po'alei Zion, the Bundists, Communists, and Anarchists. One of the accelerators of the establishment of independent and secular schools and the beginning of a modernization process was a teachers' strike declared by the teachers' organization Agudat Hamorim in the middle of 1920. Some of the schools recognized the right of the teachers to vacations and a decent salary. Others, supported by the Va'ad ha-Ḥinnukh ha-Roshi, had rejected the teachers' demands. Those schools continued their activities with traditional and less professional teachers.

THE SHADOW OF NATIONALISM: 1930–1946. The military coup d'état of 1930 introduced a period of political unrest in Argentina in which nationalist and antisemitic organizations played no small part. From 1933 on, nationalistic, xenophobic, and antisemitic activity increased, encouraged by German diplomatic institutions and by the local branch of the German Nazi Party, until it became a central problem for Argentinean Jewry. Also the Catholic Church, which was very close to the Vatican and Cardinal Pacelli (the future Pope *Pius XII), who visited Buenos Aires in 1934, was active in the dissemination of antisemitism. The leadership of the Church kept silent in its publications about the persecution and murder of the Jews in Europe. At the same time the lay Christians adopted an implicit or open antisemitic position in their periodicals and educational catechism material, and in lectures by their religious or lay leaders and teachers. The immigration decree of October 1938 increased discrimination against Jewish immigrants, and even Jewish farmers had great difficulty acquiring entry visas despite the preferential treatment for agricultural immigrants which even the drastic legislation on immigration provided. From 1933 to 1945 between 35,000 and 40,000 Jews entered Argentina by exploiting various loopholes in the law. About a third of them had to use illegal means to immigrate and their legal status was regulated only after a general amnesty was declared for illegal immigrants in 1948. When news of the Holocaust reached Argentina in 1943, Jewish organizations managed to convince the government to accept 1,000 Jewish children, but for various reasons, this rescue operation was never carried out.

The deteriorating security of Argentinean Jewry compelled all factions, Ashkenazi and Sephardi, to unite and form a federate defense organization. In 1933 they established the Committee Against the Persecutions of the Jews in Germany, which after two years of activity became known as *DAIA – Delegación de Asociaciones Israelitas Argentinas. Initially

DAIA provided representation for 28 institutions, while the communists and their sympathizers refused to be a part of this framework and (except for 1946–53) ran their own separate organization. With the aid of anti-Nazi publications and Argentinean democratic and socialist forces, Argentinean Jewry thus began to fight for equal rights and for freedom from persecution.

Economic and Social Stratification. During the first stage of Jewish settlement in Argentina up to 1914, there were four main sectors in Jewish society: (1) farmers – Jewish Colonization Association (ICA) settlers and permanently hired or seasonal laborers; (2) artisans in all branches – either self-employed, employed, or apprenticed; (3) peddlers selling goods on the installment plan (and therefore called "Cuenteniks"); and (4) shopkeepers dealing in supplying goods to meet daily needs. In addition to these groups were individuals who were among the first industrialists (in textiles, furniture, and in the extraction of tannin from the *quebracho* tree) and high officials, including managing directors, of large grain-export companies. In 1909 there were 90 Jews in Buenos Aires belonging to the liberal professions. Most of them were in the field of medicine and of the 60 students attending the university, 41 studied medicine or pharmacy.

Economic and professional development enabled many peddlers to become merchants, agricultural laborers to become farmers, and employed artisans to become independent. The occupations vacated by veteran settlers as they rose on the ladder of economic prosperity and social advancement were constantly filled by new waves of immigrants that continued to arrive until the outbreak of World War II. While the numbers of workers did not decrease to a great extent, the number of established merchants increased and a class of professional men developed. In 1934 the ICA director in Buenos Aires, Simon Weill, basing his report on figures submitted to ICA by towns throughout the country, estimated that 1,175 Jews were practicing in various branches of medicine and pharmacy, 190 in engineering and law, and many were writers, artists, and university lecturers.

During the period from 1918 to 1939, trade unions and economic associations were also formed. Carpenters, who organized a general strike in Jewish workshops in 1916, needle workers, bakers, and others maintained their own trade unions for a while, and in 1934 Jewish merchants and employers united under the Cámara Comercial e Industrial Israelita. The "Cuenteniks" formed two cooperatives that became important financial instruments. In urban centers and in some of the Jewish agricultural colonies cooperative credit banks flourished. In July 1940 the Asociación de Industriales de la Madera y del Hierro was established, incorporating the Jewish industrialists in the field of wood and iron furniture products.

Cultural Life. With the founding of the Sociedad Hebraica Argentina in 1926, which was preceded by Juventud and other groups before the outbreak of World War I, and Organización Hebrea Maccabi, Jewish cultural life expanded in the Spanish-speaking sphere. The cultural achievements of Hebraica are mainly in the fields of sports, art, and drama (its luxurious theater was dedicated in 1968). Its quarterly Spanish magazine *Davar*, to which the best Argentinean writers have contributed, has published more than 100 issues.

With the organization and strengthening of AMIA, most of the Jewish community's cultural activities were concentrated under its auspices. AMIA also subsidized the activities of other organizations and publishing houses. A large number of books on Jewish subjects (particularly in Yiddish) were published in Argentina, but only a minority of them were written by local authors. There were also a considerable number of monthlies and weeklies published primarily by various political parties and economic, social, and philanthropic organizations. The Jewish daily press played a decisive role in the consolidation of the community Jewish life. Efforts to establish a Jewish daily newspaper in Spanish had failed for financial reasons and lack of interest among the Jewish population. The *Juedische Wochenschau*, a German-language weekly with a Zionist orientation, was published from the end of the 1930s by Hardy Swarsensky (publication ceased in 1968 with the death of its editor).

Jewish Education. The Jewish educational network had to cope with the implementation of Catholic instruction in the official schools and consequently with the removal of non-Catholic pupils from such classes. Nevertheless, neither the overt public hostility, nor the occasional official prohibition of the use of Yiddish at public meetings arrested the development of the Jewish community. The Chevra Keduscha (which became in the 1940s AMIA) increased its communal activities and in 1935 founded in Buenos Aires the Va'ad ha-Ḥinnukh, a committee that centralized the educational system in Buenos Aires (with several dozen complementary schools), which had hitherto been promoted mainly by various synagogues, by some Zionist parties, and by the Zionist Teachers' Organization. From that time on the Jewish schools became one of the most vital forces enhancing Jewish socialization and community organization in Argentina, and they reflected the various streams of Jewish political views in the community. Until the late 1960s these schools functioned on a complementary basis, while the children were free from studies in the public schools, either in the morning shift or in the afternoon. The existing schools, for Ashkenazim and Sephardim, had many ideological trends: religious, traditional, leftist, secular, Zionist, non-Zionist, and anti-Zionist. The Va'ad ha-Ḥinnukh succeeded in 15 years of activity in bringing most of the schools to a minimal common curricula and in improving the physical conditions of the schools as well as the working conditions of the teachers. In the 1930s and the 1940s Yiddish was almost the only language of instruction for most Ashkenazi schools, even for the Zionist ones. The number of students in Jewish schools in Buenos Aires together with the schools coordinated by the Va'ad ha-Ḥinnukh Haroshi in the provinces rose from 5,300 in 1940 to more than 11,000 in 1950, more than 25% of the children of school age. This increase in the school population brought a rise in the demand for teachers. The Va'ad ha-Ḥinnukh of Buenos Aires responded to this situation by founding the Seminar Lemorim (Teacher's Seminar) in 1940 and five years later the CIRA founded the Machon Lelimudei Hayahaduth (Institute for Jewish Studies), which prepared teachers and functionaries for the Jewish religious establishment. The ideological map started to shift during these years, with the schools declaring a Zionist identification and adopting Hebrew as the language of instruction increasing. Jewish public institutions and cultural life continued to develop, and the recent arrivals from Central Europe founded their own communal and religious organizations, including the Asociación Filantrópica Israelita (1933), the Juedische Kulturgemeinschaft (1937), and both Orthodox and Liberal congregations.

Zionism. The Zionist movement in Argentina had changed in the 1930s and the 1940s from a conglomerate of organizations with disconnected activities to a stable federation called "Consejo Superior Sionista." The decision of the 19th Zionist Congress (1935) to promote the unification of the Zionist organizations, together with the impact of the Holocaust, brought the two main Zionist parties – General Zionist and Po'alei Zion (the Revisionists demurred) – to the realization that they had to work together under a common umbrella organization, although they kept their own identities within the Zionist framework.

The anti-Zionist left-wing organizations challenged the Zionists since they competed for the leadership of the communal institutions. This threat to their efforts to gain control over the main institutions, especially AMIA and DAIA, dictated the collaboration between the two Zionist parties.

Control of the National Funds – Keren Hayesod and Keren Kayemeth LeIsrael – was one of the ends that engendered competition between the different sectors in the community. In 1937, when a branch of the Jewish Agency for Ereẓ Israel was established in Argentina, the Zionist parties cooperated to avoid non-Zionist control of the Funds. During the second half of the 1940s circumstances were different and the Zionist parties competed with each other for the control of the National Funds and the appointment of their members as *shliḥim* (emissaries) of the Funds. The Zionist parties and the leaders of the National Funds tried to adhere to the policy established by the WZO and maintain the autonomy of both Funds. During the War of Independence (1948), however, Argentinean Jewry decided to declare a united campaign on behalf of Israel. The impressive results proved the extent of their identification with the Zionist cause, which went far beyond the politics of fundraising, leadership of organizations, parties, and *shliḥim*.

Until the middle of the 1940s the World Zionist Organization (WZO) believed that the most important activities of Zionism in Argentina were connected with fundraising. After WWII, when Argentina became relevant to the fight for the establishment of a Jewish state, the WZO changed its attitude and Argentinean Jewry was transformed into a partner in the political efforts to achieve international recognition.

The Zionist parties became dependent on their central organizations in Israel. Nevertheless, they believed that local activities within the framework of the Jewish communal organization were very important in themselves, also as a way to maintain their close ties with Zionism and Israel. The parties, especially the two trends of Po'alei Zion (right and left), made serious efforts to develop local activities. They were very active in formal education and maintained complementary Jewish schools like the Sholem Aleichem and Bialik school networks. All the parties were active in informal education and maintained pioneer youth movements like Ha-No'ar ha-Ẓiyyoni, Dror-Heḥalutz, Betar, Gordonia, Dror-Habonim, and Ha-Shomer ha-Ẓa'ir, which provided the first groups of *olim* with a strong ideological conviction in the second half of the 1940s and after the establishment of Israel.

The two major parties, General Zionists and Po'alei Zion, differed in their attitude to the desirable attitude of the Jews toward Argentina and its society. Both parties agreed that they had to respect the status of the Jews as Argentinean citizens. But while the General Zionists believed that Jews had to limit their organized activities as Jews to internal communal and Zionist matters, and that their activities in the general society was entirely a private matter, Po'alei Zion promoted organized Jewish action also in the general civil arena and politics. Actually, the latter's position failed.

The two parties also competed with each other for the leadership of the community's institutions and debated the organization and structure of DAIA. Po'alei Zion wanted a change in the electoral criteria and promoted the idea of general elections with the participation of all the Jews. The General Zionists supported the existing federative structure in which the board was elected by the representatives of the institutions which adhere to DAIA. While the latter's position prevailed, the discussion continued into the 21st century, even though there were different political trends now involved in DAIA.

Agricultural Settlement. Between 1936 and 1944, several hundred families who fled antisemitic persecution in Germany were absorbed into the settlement project. Many of them settled in Entre Ríos, where they founded the colony of Avigdor. In the succeeding period, however, more families left the land, and in 1962 there were fewer settlers than there had been in 1898 (5,907 compared to 6,755 at the earlier date). The families who remained in 1962 were smaller in size than those of 1898 (an average of less than three members as against over five to a family at the earlier date) and belonged to an older age group. On the other hand, the number of non-Jews in the colonies was almost double that of the Jewish colonists (about 10,220). In 1964 the number of Jewish farmers who lived on and cultivated their land in the colonies was estimated at 782 families.

The overall territory under Jewish ownership was 450,000 hectares. Despite the fact that there were Jewish farmers who were well established on their soil, especially in the south of Buenos Aires province, the future of the Jewish colonies was uncertain in the late 1960s.

Reasons for the Disintegration of the Agricultural Settlement Enterprise. The disintegration of ICA's farming project in Argentina can be attributed to a series of factors. One factor was the unfavorable location of a large proportion of the colonies on the margins of the "Wet Pampa," influenced mostly by droughts from the south and by almost annual invasions of locusts from the north. One of the colonies, Dora, was even located in an arid region, dependent on irrigation. Another basic factor was the extreme dependence on foreign markets and the inability of the Argentinean farmer to influence marketing conditions. In search of greater income, the settlers kept shifting from grain crops to cattle raising. Jewish agriculture, based on monoculture, was therefore extremely sensitive to the fluctuations of the markets and lacked stability. A third general factor was the extensive cultivation in Argentina, which necessitated large units of land, thus creating a low population density. This type of settlement, in which the farmer lives at the center of his property and far from his neighbors, was rejected by Jewish settlers from the outset because it obstructed the fulfillment of their religious, social, educational, and medical needs. Attempts to establish concentrated villages failed, however, and had to be abandoned. The fourth decisive factor was the attraction of the town as an easy and more secure source of employment, providing opportunities for rapid advancement for those with initiative. The town also provided a social center with well-developed educational, religious, and cultural services. Since the Perón government (1946–55) encouraged urbanization and the Jewish settler came from an urban background (some of his children had already left for the town, either to study or to engage in trade), the attraction of the town became especially strong. The overall increase in land values enabled him to sell his lands at a profit and arrive in the town with a large sum of money. ICA tried to counteract some of these disintegrating factors. For a long period it tried to prevent settlers from leaving the colonies by delaying absolving them of their debts. ICA exerted pressure on the settlers to diversify their farming, helped them to develop dairy herds and chicken farms, and experimented with new crops and modern methods of cultivation. It established an integral school system in the colonies that was financed by charging the settlers. ICA even tried to recruit settlers with previous agricultural experience from southern Russia and later from among agricultural laborers in her own colonies. However, the lack of flexibility in policy and the bureaucratic administrative structure, requiring the obedience and submission of the settlers, caused continual undermining of good relations in the colonies and the diminution of the moral influence of ICA on the settlers. ICA's bitter and prolonged refusal to recognize that the colony Narcisse Levin and part of Barón Hirsch, Montefiore, and Dora, located on the edge of the fertile regions, required larger areas of land, resulted in bitter and prolonged disputes. Moreover, ICA's prolonged opposition to facilitating the settlement of children near their parents' farms made it difficult for the younger generation to settle in the colonies. It was for the same reason, as well as to promote intensified farming of their own plots, that ICA refused to lease its vacant land to the settlers. All these factors led to the strengthening of the second central force in the colonies, the settlers' cooperatives (see below). Established and run with ICA's support, the cooperatives fought disintegration, but also became the settlers' chief weapon in fighting ICA. The steep decline in agricultural settlement brought about a concerted action by the two forces to preserve the existing state of affairs.

Independent Agricultural Settlements. Tensions between the settlers and the administration often resulted in large groups leaving to found independent settlements. In June 1901 about 40 families settled in Villa Alba (now called General San Martín) in the central Pampas after leaving the colonies of Entre Ríos. In 1906 about 20 families that left Moisesville, founded Médanos in the south of Buenos Aires province. In 1923, 80 families that left Narcisse Leven, Barón Hirsch, and Montefiore for the Chaco, as a result of the cotton boom, dispersed among settlements such as Charata and General Pinedo. In 1928, the settlers in Barón Hirsch acquired 8,653 hectares of land in order to settle their children and relatives and named their colony Akiva Ettinger. Other settlers in Entre Ríos and Santa Fé also bought land independently for settlement purposes.

The idealism and initiative of Isaac Losow brought about the settlement of 40 families in 1906 in General Roca in the heart of the uninhabited Río Negro territory. In 1941, despite its isolated location, 28 families were still living in the settlement. During the 1930s, the Asociación Filantrópica, composed of immigrants from Germany, established a farm on the island of Choele Choel in the Río Negro. Until it closed down c. 1941, it accepted about 150 young immigrants for training in fruit growing and afforestation. In 1941 the Fomento Agrario set up a fund to encourage agricultural settlement in the colony of Julio Levin in Buenos Aires province. The colony numbered about 20 families who had small holdings of 4½–7 hectares on which they grew vegetables and raised dairy cattle. However, the colony soon became a vacation center and some Zionist pioneer movements established training farms there.

Agricultural settlement outside the control of ICA, with the exception of Julio Levin, was even more geographically marginal than that of the ICA colonies. This was, of course, dictated by both the limited financial means at the disposal of the settlers and their strong idealism. In 1964 the number of agricultural settlers outside the ICA framework was estimated at 237. Despite the fact that by the 1960s the number of families whose source of income was the land had fallen to under 2,000, the large majority of whom were not living on their land, Jewish agricultural settlement had many positive achievements. Due to it a chain of small towns sprang up at the edge of the colonies as centers for trade and small industry, new crops were introduced, modern methods of cultivation were implemented, and the cooperative movement was developed. Agricultural settlements served as absorption centers for new immigrants and created areas of predominantly Jewish population from which many of the leaders and public figures of Argentinean Jewry emerged.

BETWEEN PERÓN AND ONGANÍA: 1946–1968. Juan Perón's accession to power prompted serious fears among the Jewish population because he had been aided by the Fascist organization Alianza Libertadora Nacionalista and was known to sympathize with the Nazi government in Germany. The establishment of the Registry of Non-Catholic Cults and the reaffirmation of Catholic religious instruction in the public schools introduced by the military, nationalistic, and Catholic government in December 31, 1943, increased these fears. Growing concern was partially dispelled by the introduction of a special clause (Clause 28) in the new constitution on March 16, 1949, forbidding racial discrimination and by Perón's declaration of sympathy for the rights of the Jews and for the State of Israel. Antisemitic attacks continued, however, and Buenos Aires became a center for antisemitic publications and neo-Nazi activity on an international scale. Jewish immigration was stopped entirely, while Argentina welcomed thousands of Nazis and their collaborators escaping from Europe. The protests of the DAIA and the efforts of the pro-Peronist Organización Israelita Argentina – OIA, based on Clause 28, were only partially successful. The overthrow of Perón (September 1955) and the election of a civil president Arturo Frondizi in 1958, was accompanied by an increase in antisemitic activities, especially by such antisemitic and nationalist movements as Tacuara and its various factions, which were further augmented after the capture of Adolf *Eichmann in May 1960 and his execution in June 1962. The senate's condemnation of antisemitism (September 1961) was not backed by any law-enforcement action, and even the outlawing of antisemitic organizations in May 1963 and especially November 1964 failed to wipe out antisemitism. After the revolution of June 1966, in which General Carlos Onganía seized power, antisemitic organizations became adherents of the new regime, and by 1967, despite the placatory declarations by the government, Argentina was a center of antisemitic activity. Of the 313 antisemitic incidents in the world recorded in 1967, 142 occurred in Argentina. Starting in the late 1950s, and particularly between 1963 and 1965, the antisemites were aided by representatives of the *Arab League in Buenos Aires. The penetration of antisemitism into the working classes, and especially the Peronist trade unions, was particularly significant as the Jewish working class had all but disappeared.

The increase in antisemitism heightened DAIA's activity, which reached a peak on June 28, 1962, with a general protest strike by Jewish merchants and businessmen. The annual ceremony commemorating the *Warsaw Ghetto uprising (with 20,000 participants in 1963 and 25,000 participants in 1968) organized by the DAIA gained a special significance and topicality.

In public life, the process of unification continued after 1948 and was greatly influenced by the establishment of the State of Israel. The Chevra Keduscha Aschkenazi became a central *kehillah* (whose political control was taken over by the Zionist parties after the democratic elections in 1949). The Zionists were organized into the Organización Sionista Argentina, which was the representative of the World Zionist Organization. In 1952 a Va'ad ha-Kehillot, established through the initiative of AMIA, united about 140 communities. Its objective was to provide help in improving religious, cultural, and educational services.

With the establishment of the State of Israel the Sephardi communities, which had had separate Sephardi Zionist frameworks since the 1930s, also deepened their interest in Zionism, and organized their own fundraising campaigns in two different organizations: the Arabic speakers (from the Damascene, Aleppan, and Moroccan communities) conducted their Zionist campaigns, from 1948, under the roof of the Comité Sefaradí Argentino, while the Ladino speakers withdrew from the joint Sephardi committee in 1949 and founded their own organization – DESA – Delegación de Entidades Sefardíes Argentinas. The Sephardim in Argentina, like those in other countries, were reluctant to join the Zionist parties, which embodied the traditions and ideologies of the Ashkenazim, and in 1963 they founded their own political entity – the Movimiento Sionista Sefaradí. After several years of conflict, the World Zionist Organization accepted the request of the Sephardim for separate representation and in 1972 they were able to found FESELA – Federación Sefaradí Latino Americana, which is still active as the umbrella organization of all the Sephardi Federations in Latin America. To coordinate the activities of the Sephardim in Argentina they formed ECSA – Ente Coordinador Sefaradí Argentino.

The Jewish educational system gradually became Israel- and Hebrew-oriented, and all Jewish organizations, including those that stressed their Argentinean character, actively identified with the State of Israel. For the large majority of Argentinean Jews identification with Israel constituted the basic means of Jewish identity, despite the fact that, from the beginning of the Perón regime, marked cultural and ethnic heterogeneity decreased and Argentinean nationalism grew. The clearest expression of this identification is the achievement of the pioneering youth movements and the trend of immigration to Israel. Beginning with a few pioneers who moved to Palestine-Ereẓ Israel in the pre-World War II period and a score more in 1945, *aliyah* increased after the establishment of the State of Israel and led to the founding of eight new kibbutzim (the first of which was Mefalsim in 1949). Smaller groups joined at least 15 other kibbutzim, while other groups founded and joined moshavim. A large number of economic enterprises and investment companies in Israel were also founded by Argentineans. By 1960 about 4,500 Argentineans had moved to Israel; *aliyah* increased considerably during Argentina's political and economic crisis of 1962–63 and after the *Six-Day War. The Argentinean Jewish community expressed its support for *aliyah* by granting special sums of money to the immigrants through AMIA. Nonetheless, the number of Jews who settled in Israel does not account for all Jewish emigrants from Argentina. In 1962–63 about 2,000 Argentinean Jews emigrated to the U.S. alone. In addition, difficulties of integration and absorption resulted in the return of a considerable number of Argentineans from Israel.

After the establishment of the State of Israel, estrangement increased between the Zionists and the communists, and in 1952, when the latter gave their unmitigated support to the Soviet government during the *Slansky Trials, the ties between the two groups were severed completely. The communists continued to develop their own institutions and educational system, press, and the IFT theater, while disassociating themselves from the State of Israel. Their negative attitude toward Israel grew stronger during the *Sinai Campaign and was maintained during the Six-Day War. But as a result, a considerable number of communists and their sympathizers seceded from their camp and many of them joined Zionist groups.

Despite the comprehensive character of organized Jewish life and the existence of antisemitism, Jews have been able to integrate. Many distinguished themselves in the arts and sciences and some even attained important positions in political life. During the presidency of Arturo Frondizi, two Jews became governors of provinces, and one, David Blejer, filled the post of minister of labor and social welfare. Since the 1960s assimilation of Argentinean Jewry has increased. The rate of mixed marriages has risen, although there are no exact statistics on this point, and Argentinean Jewish university youth participated more widely in non-Jewish activities (most of them left-wing) than in organized Jewish life. The Confraternidad Judeo-Cristiana, an organization of Catholics, Protestants, and Jews aimed at improving Judeo-Christian relations, was founded in 1958. After the Vatican Council II, the Catholic Church established an Ecumenical Office, which, together with other groups, maintained a religious dialogue with certain Jewish sectors, the benefits of which are limited both in the Jewish and Gentile communities.

Economy and Social Stratification. During World War II, growing industrialization in Argentina further encouraged the Jews to found new industries. The furniture, fur, and particularly the wool and textile industries, including the export of raincoats, woolens, and leather goods, were joined by enterprises in new fields such as plastics, the chemical and pharmaceutical industries, the automobile industry, electrical goods and electronics, and a large part of heavy industry. Jewish companies, often very large ones, existed within the new industries after World War II to supply the local market. Jews also engaged in all aspects of the building industry, played a significant role in the commerce that developed around the new branches of industry, and diversified their positions in the liberal professions.

The economic development of the Jewish population in the post-World War II era is also reflected in the considerable progress made by their financial institutions. Though the largest Jewish bank, the Banco Israelita del Río de la Plata, closed as a result of a financial scandal in 1963, other banks, such as the Banco Comercial de Buenos Aires and the Banco Mercantil Argentino, which served the general community, gained in status and the Cooperativas de Crédito also prospered. These cooperatives, which spread throughout Argentina, expanded especially among the Jewish population and in the late 1960s had many thousands of members – merchants, farmers, middle-class industrialists, and even salaried workers.

A small part of the large profits from the cooperatives' financial activities, which in fact include normal banking operations, was devoted to public and social purposes such as financing Jewish schools, cultural centers, and Jewish political activity, considerably influencing Jewish communal institutions. Thus Argentinean Jewry was greatly alarmed in 1966 when General Onganía's revolutionary government intended to limit or abolish the operations of the credit associations, and Jewish institutions suffered profoundly from the economic decline of the cooperatives after the bankruptcy of many of them at the beginning of the 1970s.

Economic changes naturally altered the social and economic class structure of Argentinean Jewry. There were fewer blue-collar workers, as more Jews entered the free and academic professions. By the early 1960s the socio-economic profile of the Jewish community was very different from that of the period of mass immigration. The relative proportion of blue-collar workers (in industries such as textiles, woodworking, leather goods, metalwork, and auto repair) declined to less than one-third of the total work force; the rest of the Jewish population was employed in commerce, clerical work, and the free professions. The percentage of farmers had already dwindled to almost zero. This process, which continued during the following decades, led to the concentration of the Jews at various levels of the middle class.

The status of Jews in the general population was exemplified by a census taken of the Jewish community in Quilmes, near Buenos Aires, in 1968. There were 1,169 Jews out of a total population of 317,783. In the economically viable portion of the Jewish population, only 26.7% were salaried workers, of whom 3.5% were laborers and the remainder were white-collar workers. The percentage of salaried workers in the general population was 81.2%, of whom at least half were laborers. On the other hand, 70.9% of the economically viable Jewish population were employers and self-employed, while the parallel figure for the general population was only 16.3%.

During this period, poverty was not eradicated among Argentinean Jewry, and AMIA alone spent some 6–7% of its budget in 1965–67 on supporting the poor (apart from the aid extended by other welfare associations). Nevertheless, the Jewish relationship to the Argentinean proletariat was becoming increasingly that of the employer to employees. Along with this, Jews were to a great extent absent from the upper and ruling echelons of society.

Religious Life. The period 1939–1968 was one of a limited religious renaissance, supported by a new wave of religious immigrants. New types of *talmudei torah* and yeshivot, both Ashkenazi and Sephardi, were founded. The most notable among them was the Yeshivah Gevohah that was maintained by AMIA, five graduates of which were ordained in Israel up to 1968. During this period various religious organizations, both political and apolitical, such as Mizrachi, Yavneh, Agudat Israel, and the Sephardi movement Shuvah Israel, were created. The rabbinate of the *kehillah* was institutionalized and developed during this period. In 1966, Rabbi David Kahana, former chief chaplain of the Israel Air Force, assumed the post of *av bet din* of the rabbinate of AMIA until the mid-1970s. In the Sephardi sector, the religious renaissance was manifested in the appointment of new spiritual leaders in each of the four communities and in the reinstatement of rabbinical authority, especially among the communities of Syrian origin. Conservative Judaism, represented only by the Congregación Israelita de la República Argentina (CIRA), led by Rabbi Guillermo Schlesinger, expanded during this period, when a few German-speaking Conservative congregations were established. In 1960 Rabbi Marshall Meyer was sent to CIRA from the Jewish Theological Seminary in New York. He founded Ramah as the youth section of CIRA with its own synagogue. In 1962, following his attempts to become the rabbi of CIRA, a schism ensued, and an important faction of CIRA established the Conservative Bet-El congregation under the leadership of Rabbi Meyer. Earlier that year, the Seminario Rabinico Latinoamericano was established, offering a preparatory course for advanced studies at the Jewish Theological Seminary of America in New York. This Conservative model of a congregation with many youth activities, a synagogue, and a *talmud torah* that in many cases became a day school, was adopted also by some of the Orthodox synagogues.

In 1964 Reform Judaism established its first congregation, Emanuel, in Buenos Aires. In 1968 Argentina had three Reform, seven Conservative, and fifteen Orthodox rabbis, ten of whom were Ashkenazi and five Sephardi; four other rabbis were practicing temporarily in Buenos Aires.

Jewish Education. The establishment of the State of Israel had a crucial impact on the character of the Jewish schools. All the schools that previously taught Yiddish started a transition to Hebrew, a process that ended with an overwhelming predominance of Hebrew in all the schools in the mid-1960s. Following the foundation of the Va'ad ha-Kehillot in 1952, the Va'ad ha-Ḥinnukh of the Chevra Kedusha – AMIA, and the Va'ad ha-Ḥinnukh ha-Roshi merged in 1957 to form the Va'ad ha-Ḥinnukh ha-Merkazi (Central Education Committee). All Jewish Ashkenazi schools, except those belonging to the Communists, were affiliated to this committee. Gradually most of the Sephardim and certain other communities (such as those of German origin), joined this Va'ad ha-Ḥinnukh. Until the end of the 1960s most Jewish schools provided supplementary education (20 hours weekly) for pupils attending public schools. This school structure was maintained, not only for economic reasons but also because of a deep concern to maintain close relations with the non-Jewish population. In 1966 the official schools gradually started introducing the long school day, which was a threat to the activities of the Jewish complementary schools. At the end of the 1960s the Jewish schools started to transform themselves into day schools to include the general Argentinean curriculum. In the mid-1970s the entire Jewish education network consisted of day schools; two of them had already existed from the beginning of the 1960s and were recognized as private schools. The budget required for building and maintaining such schools, however, was correspondingly much higher, and when public funds could not be acquired, parents of modest means were not able to afford to send their children to these schools. This problem was partially solved with special funds provided by community institutions and by the Jewish Agency which subsidized those students.

In 1968 the Jewish educational system of Greater Buenos Aires comprised the following: 5,065 children between the ages of two and five in 51 kindergartens; 8,900 pupils in 58 elementary schools (seven grades), eight of which were day schools and the rest supplementary schools; and 1,675 pupils in 13 high schools, four of which were yeshivot. In the rest of Argentina, there were 969 children in 33 kindergartens; 2,787 pupils in 52 elementary schools; and 633 pupils in eight high schools. These figures added up to 20,033 students in Jewish schools throughout Argentina; the students in the 5 to 12 age group comprised about 45% of the total Jewish population of this age. In spite of these relatively high rates of participation, there was considerable dropout from one year to the next, especially between elementary and secondary school. In 1967, in all the schools run by the Va'ad ha-Ḥinnukh in Buenos Aires, only 560 pupils finished elementary school and 126 graduated from secondary school.

In those years the division according to political trends diminished. All the schools, apart from the Communist schools, adopted Hebrew as the main language for Jewish studies (some kept Yiddish) and stressed the study of modern Israel and the development of Jewish national consciousness. The existing Communist schools in Buenos Aires, with several kindergartens, five primary schools, and two secondary schools were excluded from the Va'ad ha-Ḥinnukh in 1952 when all the Communist organizations were expelled from DAIA because of their refusal to condemn the antisemitic and anti-Zionist trials in Czechoslovakia and Russia. In 1953 they established an independent school network under the umbrella of the Jewish Communist central organization Yiddisher Cultur Farband – ICUF (Jewish Cultural Organization) with ten schools and close to 2,000 students all over the country. In the 1960s the number of these schools gradually diminished and by the end of the decade not one remained. The reasons for this development were the policy of the Communist Party to reduce the activities of the schools, the lack of interest among the parents (because of assimilation or transfer to the Zionist schools), and the decision of the leading school committees not to transform them into day schools.

From the 1960s most of the teachers in all the schools were Argentineans, trained in local seminaries. A new institution of higher Jewish education, Ha-Midrashah ha-Ivrit, was established in the mid-1950s by the State of Israel, with the cooperation of local individuals. It trained high school teachers, and by the end of the 1960s had close to 200 students.

Informal education activities organized by Zionist youth movements, social-sport organizations like Sociedad Hebraica Argentina, Maccabi and Hacoaj, and other communal institutions like the Conservative movement became more common and their activities attracted hundreds of children and adolescents. From 1962 AMIA and Hebraica, later with the support of the Youth Department of the World Zionist Organization, ran EDITTI, a school for youth leaders on the level of an institution of informal higher learning. Nevertheless the participation of youth in organizations of the Jewish communities was low and it became even lower among youth of university age. All the Jewish youth organizations were united in the Confederación Juvenil Judeo Argentina, which represented Argentinean Jewish youth locally, nationally, and internationally.

REPRESSION AND DEMOCRACY: 1968–2005. The attitude of non-Jewish Argentinean society towards the Argentinean Jews as individuals and the organized Jewish community as such is characterized by a certain ambivalence. Argentine society has never been, and is not today, a single ideological entity, being divided between nationalists with extreme xenophobic views and liberals with a pluralistic attitude toward other nations and peoples. But one idea is common to most of these points of view: the need for cultural and social uniformity to shape Argentina's immigrant society. This idea, which demanded complete integration and assimilation of the immigrants into the established culture was most strongly advocated by the Catholic, nationalistic right wing. This group seized power twice in the last third of the 20th century. The army, in which this ideology is predominant, installed itself in government in June 1966 by a coup d'état, which appointed general Juan Carlos Onganía as president. In the enactment of the Statute of the Revolution, which took precedence over the constitution, the Catholic nature of the State (already affirmed in the constitution of 1853) was further underscored with the Statute declaring that the State stood for a "Christian Western Civilization." As a result, many Jews employed as civil servants in the previous government were dismissed and Jewish professors who resigned in 1966, when university autonomy was abolished, experienced great difficulties in their attempts to be reinstated. The deposition of Onganía by a military junta and the appointment of General Roberto Marcelo Levingston (1970), and his deposition in turn by General Alejandro Agustín Lanusse (1971), did not change the Catholic nature of the government.

Raised in an acute form, in connection with the elections of March 1973 that brought to power the Peronist party and the president Héctor Cámpora, was the question of the relations of the Peronist regime when it was in power (1946–55), and of the Peronists, to the Jews and to the State of Israel. On the one hand, it was emphasized that Perón had often expressed his esteem for the Jewish community in Argentina and had established strong bonds with Israel; on the other hand, it was he who had permitted the mass immigration of Nazis to Argentina after World War II, at the same time restricting the entry of Jewish victims of the Holocaust. Antisemitic activities on the part of members of the Peronist party and the influence of Arab propaganda, which were a constant source of anxiety to the Jewish community in the 1960s, increased under the military regimes and reached their climax when one of the most prominent Peronist leaders, Andrés Framini, together with other Peronists, joined the pro-Arab Committee for a Free Palestine, of which Framini actually became head.

The increase in acts of terrorism and violence since 1966, culminating in the kidnapping and murder in 1970 of General Pedro Eugenio Aramburu, president after Perón's deposition, was accompanied by an increase in antisemitic violence. In addition to the previous extreme right-wing organizations, such as the Guardia Restauradora Nacionalista, pro-Arab leftist organizations supported this violence and all benefited from both the open and clandestine support of the Arab League and the Syrian and Egyptian embassies in Buenos Aires. The Arab community in Argentina, numbering several hundred thousand, supported the anti-Jewish activities, if only to a limited extent. Argentine Jewry was therefore forced to confront three hostile groups, who despite all their differences were united in their hostility to the Jews and to Israel. Bombs were placed in synagogues and Jewish communal buildings.

Widespread antisemitic propaganda also spread in Argentina, attempting to blame the Jews for the economic and social difficulties of the country. A certain innovation in this widely disseminated literature were the sensational revelations of the economist and university lecturer Professor Walter Beveraggi Allende, who accused "International Zionist Jewry" of a plan to impoverish Argentina in order to detach some provinces in the South and the Andes Mountains and establish a Jewish republic there. This accusation, which was included in the new edition of the *Protocols of the *Elders of Zion*, published in January 1972, had an effect on the public at large and was also evidenced in a more widespread slander campaign.

In September 1973 Héctor Cámpora resigned in favor of Perón who was elected by an enormous majority. During his brief reign of office, Cámpora nominated Jose Ber Gelbard (b. 1917), a Polish-born Jew, as minister of economy, and he retained his post after Perón's election.

In those years support for the exiled Perón had come not only from the right. After almost two decades of direct or indirect military regime, leftist intellectuals and students finally joined the working masses in demonstrating support for the general, amid manifestations of recurrent violence that undermined peaceful life and created a climate of uncertainty and fear for the future. Perón himself made public his views with regard to Jews and to Israel. Before his election, and soon after meeting in Madrid with a large group of Arab diplomats, he felt it proper, in the course of a meeting (also held in Madrid) with former Israel Ambassador Jacob *Tsur and other Israeli officials, to express his sympathy for Jews and for Israel.

Perón received a delegation from DAIA and the *kehillah* in Buenos Aires, at which he restated his opposition to antisemitism and proclaimed his neutrality in the Middle East conflict.

Perón died on July 1, 1974, and was succeeded by his wife María Estela (Isabel) Martínez de Perón, who had been vice president, but she could hardly confront the difficulties of a politically divided country and keep together the mass movement that had brought Perón back to power. From the middle of 1974 until his forced resignation in July 1975, the strongman in Argentina was José López Rega, minister of social welfare and advisor to the president. Perón's death was followed by a period of complete insecurity and terror. In November 1974 a state of siege was imposed; leftist guerrilla groups (Montoneros and Ejército Revolucionario del Pueblo – ERP) were outlawed, a fact that did not prevent them from spectacular acts of terror; thousands were arrested, and ultra-right paramilitary groups, allegedly supported from within the government and acting under the name Alianza Anticomunista Argentina (AAA), killed hundreds of persons, including prominent politicians, intellectuals, journalists, lawyers, trade-union leaders and students. Naturally, this situation had an impact on the Jewish community; and DAIA, the Latin American Jewish Congress, and also non-Jewish organizations and publications denounced the dangers inherent in the anti-Jewish aspects of the explosive situation.

A substantial change took place on March 24, 1976, when, in a bloodless coup, a military junta seized power, deposing President María Estela (Isabel) Martínez de Perón and appointing General Jorge Rafael Videla in her place. The junta had to confront a very difficult situation, characterized by economic chaos, enormous inflation, social unrest, terror, and violence. The junta, which suspended normal political and trade-union activities, at first had the support of wide middle class and liberal circles. They hoped that this time the military would restore order in the country. But they were very quickly disappointed. The military factions which took control of the country used extreme methods of terror and completely ignored civil rights and the rule of law. Thousands of people were kidnapped, tortured, and murdered and their bodies disappeared. Under this regime, xenophobic and antisemitic discourse became common, and when a Jew was incarcerated or kidnapped, his fate was bound to be far worse than that of a non-Jew. But at the same time the Jewish community as a whole went undisturbed and was able to conduct its social activities without impediment and administer its institutions democratically. Nevertheless antisemitic actions continued together with some violence against Jewish institutions and persons. A list of antisemitic incidents during the years 1975 and 1976 was published in Argentina and in the United States, together with the testimony by an American Jewish leader. The editor of the daily *La Opinion*, Jacobo *Timerman, was arrested and jailed in April 1977, and even though declared innocent by the Supreme Court, continued to be held and tortured by the army. In November 1977 Timerman was deprived of his civil rights and his property was placed in state custody. He was also accused of connections with David Graiver, a Jewish financier with alleged ties to the left wing Montoneros. Jewish, professional, and human rights organizations, and the diplomats of the State of Israel repeatedly urged the Argentine government to put an end to Timerman's detention, but it was not until September 1979 that he was released to Israel. Timerman stayed there about a year and then moved to the U.S.

There was also a sequence of anti-Jewish attacks, and antisemitic pamphlets, books, and magazines continued to appear. A prominent example of the anti-Jewish literature is the magazine *Cabildo*, which was temporarily banned under pressure from the U.S. and Israel. The government also closed down antisemitic publishing enterprises such as *Milicia, Odal*, and *Occidente*, but the dissemination of anti-Jewish literature was not stopped. The Graiver case and other economic scandals became a theme played up by the anti-Jewish publications.

In 1979, the government published a decree to the effect that all religions, except Roman Catholicism, must register with the State in order to establish "effective control" over non-Catholic religions.

Although traditional right-wing xenophobic groups were still the main source of anti-Jewish activity, on the left, anti-Zionist and anti-Israel agitation deteriorated usually into typical old-fashioned antisemitism. Special connections were established between anti-Israel Arabs and some leftist guerrilla groups which were received in military training camps of the PLO in Lebanon. There were also indications that the Arabs cooperated with other groups to create an anti-Jewish climate.

The Falklands (Malvinas) War against Great Britain (April–May 1982) and the consequences of Argentina's military defeat marked the beginning of the end for the regime installed by the military junta in 1976. During the hostilities in the south of Argentina, rabbis traveled to the war zone to serve as chaplains for the Jewish soldiers. In the following year, sectors of the community publicly supported the protests concerning the victims who had been arrested and disappeared during the repression practiced by the military junta. *Nunca Más* ("Never Again"), the report prepared by CONADEP (National Commission for the Missing Persons) published in 1985, revealed a special degree of atrocity in the treatment and torture of many Jewish citizens figuring in the dreadful lists: of the 10,000 to 15,000 "missing persons," about 1,500 were Jews. Some of the survivors testified to the pictures of Hitler and the antisemitic watchwords that formed the "habitual decor" of many torture rooms.

The establishment of a democratic regime after the free elections at the end of 1983 represented a relief for most Argentineans, including the Jews, many of whom became active participants in the Unión Cívica Radical (UCR), a party traditionally aligned with the middle classes.

From 1984 a new pluralistic attitude towards the different components of Argentinean society started to be felt, which gradually recognized and legitimized the right of the Jews, as an organized community and as individuals, to be different while part of Argentine society.

Raúl Alfonsín, a progressive and charismatic president, surrounded himself with many figures prominent in other spheres of life: Rabbi Marshall Meyer and Professor Gregorio Klimovsky joined CONADEP (chaired by writer Ernesto Sábato); Bernardo Grinspun became minister of the economy and Mario Brodersohn district secretary; Adolfo Gass obtained a seat in the Senate, Marcelo Stubrin and César Jaroslavsky (the latter, head of the district bank) entered the Chamber of Deputies and Jacobo Fiterman, ex-president of the Argentinean Zionist Organization, became secretary of public works in the Buenos Aires municipality. In the field of education and culture, traditionally a Catholic enclave, Marcos Aguinis became minister of national culture. Manuel Sadosky was minister of science and technology, and Oscar Shuberoff was appointed rector of Buenos Aires University. The Jewish Human Rights Movement was established, and the General San Martín Cultural Center of the City of Buenos Aires, seat of a hitherto unknown pluralism, inaugurated a Jewish Culture Sphere.

It may well have been this Jewish participation in public life that led Monsignor Antonio Plaza, spokesman of the most right-wing sectors of the Argentinean bishopric, to declare in March 1987 that "the government is full of Jews." A fresh antisemitic campaign throughout the initial democratic years of this regime, spoke of the "radical synagogue," a reference to the Jewish community's alleged influence. At the same time antisemitic incidents reappeared, probably as an instrument to discredit the democratic regime.

The trial of the leaders of the military junta, at the initiative of Alfonsín and many Argentineans, petered out as support for the government began to wane and economic problems worsened. The failure of the new economic plan and the return of inflation were accompanied by the opposition of the Peronist central trade union, which organized 14 general strikes during the Alfonsín regime.

The first counterattack by the army's "hardliners," led by the "carapintadas" (Aldo Rico and Mohamed Ali Seineldín, who had fought in the Falklands-Malvinas War), took place in April (Holy Week) 1987 and assumed the character of a military coup, that the civilian president had great difficulty in putting down. Successive concessions to the military disregarded the danger of institutional failure and put an end to trials of soldiers for human rights violations. The renewed insurgency of the "carapintadas" groups in 1988, although failing to obtain their objective, extended their base of support with sectors of the extreme right such as Alejandro Biondini's Nazi group. The precarious situation was further destabilized by the confused events of January 1989, when several score soldiers of the "Todos por la Patria" Movement, a heterogeneous national-Marxist group, influenced by surviving sectors of the guerrilla movement of the previous decade, tried to take by assault a military barracks at La Tablada (a province of Buenos Aires) and were wiped out after many hours of combat.

These episodes indirectly affected the Jewish community, since the "carapintada" sector leader, Colonel Mohamed Ali Seineldín was a fanatic Catholic and an avowed antisemite.

In November 1985 the Nazi war criminal Walter Kutschmann was arrested, but the extradition demand was delayed by legal appeals and Kutschmann died in prison in August 1986 without having been sent to Europe. In March 1986, a group of participants in a public meeting of the General Confederation of Labor (CGT) made antisemitic remarks that were later repudiated in a document issued by the Labor Central's governing board. The year 1987 saw continued anti-Jewish attacks, this time on the Sephardi Congregation and the AISA cemetery in Ciudadela. The Jewish community organized a mass demonstration at the central Houssay Square in Buenos Aires (November 1987), with the participation of Argentinean political, trade union, and religious leaders, to demand the speedy ratification of an anti-discrimination law to penalize any expression of antisemitism (this was achieved in the following year).

The social problems continued to increase. In early 1989 President Alfonsín fell victim to an "economic coup" engineered by the financial sectors, which unleashed a hyperinflation that culminated in pillaging of the supermarkets, general disturbances, and the early surrender of power (in July 1989) to the president-elect, Carlos Saúl Menem. The new president, who came from a Syrian Muslim family (although a convert to Catholicism), was very aware of the prejudices regarding his personal history (closely linked with the Argentinean Arab community), and to the prejudices of sectors of his "Justicialist" (Peronist) movement, which in the past had combined a degree of populism with a certain authoritarian tendency. His public acts soon allayed anxieties in these respects: he personally participated in the event organized by the Jewish community at the Congregación Israelita de la República Argentina synagogue to denounce the desecration of the Jewish cemetery of Carpentras in France. Nazi war criminal Joseph Schwamberger, commandant of a concentration camp in Poland (arrested in Córdoba in 1987), was extradited in 1989 to stand trial in Germany. In 1992 Menem announced the decision to "open the Nazi archives" to the investigators, a political measure of great significance (since Eichmann, Mengele, and dozens of other Nazi leaders resided in Argentina or had entered the country in the post-war period, under Perón's benevolent acquiescence) but with few practical results: the files now revealed contained carefully expurgated newspaper clippings, with almost no documental value. The Argentinean Foreign Ministry was pressured by the press and political figures to hand over the documents that certainly exist on the immigration of the Nazi criminals from Europe to Argentina.

The centenary of Jewish Settlement in Argentina (1889–1989) was celebrated by various events in the capital and in the rest of the country, with the participation of political authorities. In 1991, various celebrations marked the first centennial of the arrival of Jewish immigrants to Colonia Mauricio (Carlos Casares).

In general politics, Menem executed a dramatic volte-face when he pardoned the soldiers condemned for human rights violations and allied himself with representatives of business and financial sectors in order to commence privatization of state enterprises and introduced stringent economic regulations. Denouncing the failure by members of the Menem government to fulfill commitments, Colonel Seineldín headed a bloody "carapintada" uprising in December 1990 that ended with the defeat of this nationalist and antisemitic sector. While a ministerial reshuffle transferred science and education posts from Jewish to Catholic personalities participating in the new power alliance, no signs of particular discrimination were revealed and important posts went to personalities such as Moisés Ikonicoff (minister of planning), Enrique Kaplan (director of protocol), Néstor Perl (governor of Chubut), and Carlos Corach (presidential adviser). Argentinean citizens of Jewish origin participated together with their compatriots in various administrative and political posts, with some tacit restrictions in the armed forces, diplomacy, and the higher levels of the judiciary.

Jewish cemeteries were once more desecrated in 1992, in the province of Buenos Aires. A bus taking Jewish schoolchildren on a holiday trip came under fire in the province of Córdoba. In certain football clubs, groups of fans set fire to flags bearing swastikas and chanted anti-Jewish slogans. The fluctuations in antisemitism would seem to reflect an inherent tension between xenophobia and prejudice with the cosmopolitanism and culture expressions of Argentina's liberal urban society. Sociological studies carried out in Argentina have shown, for decades, the presence of a strong element of latent anti-Jewish prejudice, the magnitude and intensity of which grow in relation to the deterioration of the economic situation. At the end of the 1980s and beginning of the 1990s, Chinese and Korean immigrants, particularly in Buenos Aires, have in some cases replaced the Jews as the traditional scapegoat for Argentinean popular xenophobia. At the end of the 1990s their place was taken by immigrants from Bolivia.

Nevertheless, the new official and also popular pluralistic trend in Argentine society continued. In 1992 a public opinion survey commissioned by the American Jewish Committee and DAIA revealed more pluralistic attitudes among interviewees. For instance, 69% of respondents considered it better that Argentina's inhabitants had diverse origins, customs and religions, while 46% declared that Jews had made a positive contribution. Seven percent supported the notion that the country would be better off without Jews. While corroboration of such results would require the periodic holding of comparable polls, the outcome of this one can be reasonably attributed to changes going back to 1983.

But this pluralistic trend was challenged by two terror attacks against Israeli and Jewish targets. In March 1992, before the above-mentioned public opinion survey was made, a car bomb destroyed the Israeli embassy in Buenos Aires and 29 persons were killed. In July 1994 a second car bomb destroyed the community building of AMIA and DAIA killing 85 people. On the one hand, there was a spontaneous expression of popular solidarity in a rally of tens of thousands of people in the square in front of the Federal Congress, with the participation of President Menem and some of the leaders of the country. The government of Argentina gave the Jewish community, as a kind of reparation, $11 million for the expansion of Jewish cultural activity, including $1 million for the establishment of a Holocaust museum to be housed in a building provided to the community by the government. At the same time many groups turned a cold shoulder to the Jews and the investigation into the bombings led to no concrete result.

Nevertheless, the pluralistic process which also legitimized organized Argentinean Jewry as an integral part of Argentinean society was becoming stronger. One example of this trend was the approval in 1988, after a long debate in the two Chambers of Congress, of an anti-discrimination law. A draft bill prepared by the criminologist Dr. Bernardo Beiderman was sent by President Alfonsín to Congress and finally approved with some modifications with the support of the two main factions. Since then, Law 23,592 was applied in several circumstances against racial, religious, and other kinds of discrimination. Another important change was made by President Carlos Menem in his first term: the reform of the National Constitution in 1994. Best known for abolishing the ban on two consecutive terms in office for incumbents seeking reelection, and reducing the presidential term to four years, this also enfranchised non-Catholic aspirants to the leadership of state. The requirement of the original constitution that the chief executive and his deputy must be Catholic has now been dropped, with government support for the Catholic Church remaining in place. In spite of this constitutional change, the aforementioned 1992 opinion survey showed that 45% of respondents would not support a Muslim presidential candidate while 41 and 39% held similar views in respect of a Jew and a Protestant. If this is anything to go by, a sizable proportion of the Argentine public was not ready, when this change was made, for a non-Catholic head of state.

As another example of the official attitude towards Jews and pluralism, it could be mentioned that when in 1997 Argentina's National Institute Against Discrimination and Racism (INADI) was established in the Ministry of Justice, the DAIA was made part of its advisory council.

Economy and Social Stratification. The deep economic recession which affected Argentina in the last years of the 1990s produced great political upheavals. Fernando de la Rúa, the leader of the Radical Party, who became president in December 1999, resigned after two years because of economic instability, a big budget deficit, an external debt which he inherited from the former government, and violent popular opposition to his liberal economic policy as unemployment reached nearly a fifth of the workforce. Eduardo Duhalde, the leader of the Peronist party who had lost to de la Rúa in the 1999 elections, became president in January 2002. The radical economic measures instituted by his government brought about a serious deterioration of the situation: production declined by 16% and inflation reached 41%. The cost of basic products increased by 75% and unemployment reached 25%. This situation specially affected people belonging to the middle class: thousands of them lost almost everything they had or were reduced to living on charity. The difficult social and economic situation brought Duhalde to call for early elections. Néstor Kirchner was installed as president in May 2003 after former president Menem withdrew from a second-round runoff. By 2005 his administration had achieved a measure of stability. Kirchner also got international creditors to cancel 75% of Argentina's debt.

The trend toward industrialization of the Argentinean economy started in the 1930s had produced economic dividends until the 1950s that also benefited the Jewish population. Many Jews abandoned blue-collar employment and went into business while a large number entered the universities and acquired liberal professions. This development, which continued in the following decades, produced a concentration of the Jews at the different levels of the middle class.

The liberalization of the economy commenced at the beginning of the 1990s, which opened the local markets to international competition, the big cut in government spending, and the reduction of a national debt of a magnitude unknown until then, had an adverse effect on broad sectors of the populace and especially on the middle-class, to which Argentinean Jews belonged. The economic distress of the Jewish community became that much worse in 1998, when two banks owned by Jews, Mayo and Patricios, where money belonging to Jews and to Jewish institutions had been invested, went bankrupt. After the collapse of 2001 an estimated 30% of the Jews were unemployed and one-fourth lived below the poverty line, some of them subsisting only thanks to Jewish welfare organized by community agencies. Existing institutions like AMIA and the independent Tzedaka organization were the first organizations to assist the needy. They coordinated and channeled economic support from local Jewish sources, providing a wide spectrum of aid including distribution of food and clothing, housing, backing to new businesses, vocational training, etc. Many synagogues and community centers opened emergency kitchens and supported existing ones. These institutions were also supported by non-Argentinean Jewish organizations like the American Jewish Joint Distribution Committee and other North American organizations. Also the Inter-American Development Bank has supported the AMIA's job placement service.

The Jewish Agency also tried to help Argentinean Jews, classifying them, together with the Jews of France and South Africa, as being in danger. It stepped up its program to encourage *aliyah,* increasing the benefits already given to all immigrants. In the first four years of the 21st century close to 9,500 Jews immigrated to Israel. The peak was in 2002 with about 6,200 *olim*, while in 2001 and 2003 the number was about 1,400 each year and in 2004 approximately 400. This drop in *olim* could be explained by the relative economic stability in Argentina and the economic problems faced by immigrants in Israel together with the security situation and the difficulty of cultural adaptation.

Jews immigrated to other countries as well, and while there are no statistics, their number may be estimated at several thousand. HIAS (Hebrew Immigrant Aid Society), based in New York, helped Argentinean Jews by facilitating their emigration to different countries in addition to the U.S.

The economic crisis also affected the maintenance of Jewish institutions. The drop in the Jewish population and the consequent reduction in the school population, the collapse of the financial institutions that had supported communal activities, the decline of communal institutions because of changes in traditions like the use of Jewish cemeteries, which were one of the most important sources of income of the community, made community life and the maintenance of traditional ways more difficult. Among the most exposed institutions were the Jewish schools. In recent years they underwent major changes, including amalgamation for reasons of efficiency, serious student dropout, and a big reduction of the Jewish teacher's staff, with consequent unemployment. The community organized centralized projects to find answers to the needs of the schools, with the economic assistance of the Jewish Agency, the State of Israel, and the World Jewish Congress.

Community Organization. DAIA, the political representative of the Jewish community vis-à-vis society at large and the government, celebrated the 70th anniversary of its existence in 2005. All those years DAIA maintained its leading position in the community, through difficult periods of political, social, and economic upheaval, by adhering to a self-imposed restriction: no identification with any Argentinean party or political faction. This attitude during the first presidency of Juan Perón (1946–55), who pressured the community institutions to identify with him, endangered to some extent the freedom of action of DAIA when a competitive Peronist Jewish organization (Organización Israelita Argentina – OIA) was established by Jewish Peronists.

DAIA was sharply criticized for its position during the period of the military junta, 1976–83, when the regime acted criminally against the opposition and the civilian population in general. In those difficult years DAIA decided to maintain a low profile and avoid outright defiance of the junta that would make things even worse for the Jewish community. On the other hand, thousands of the victims and the families of the vanished Jews (at least a thousand), many members of the community, and some observers analyzing the events of that period, argue that DAIA did not speak out strongly enough against the cruel dictatorship and on behalf of the regime's Jewish victims.

The second umbrella organization founded in 1952, the Va'ad ha-Kehillot (Federation of Argentine Jewish Communities), included all the Jewish institutions in Argentina – Ashkenazi and Sephardi – on a federative basis. Nevertheless, AMIA, which was instrumental in organizing the federation, continued to play a dominant role. While constituents from the provinces sometimes complained that the Buenos Aires administration maintained excessive control, the federation remained the only body dealing with widely different services – spiritual and religious, culture, education, and social welfare – throughout the country. This supremacy of AMIA inspired the organization of a separate Sephardi umbrella organization, ECSA, and after its dismantlement in 1998, a new one was established in October 2002, the Federación Sefaradí de la República Argentina – FESERA – with the participation of 66 Sephardi institutions.

In the second half of the 20th century ideological trends changed. The left-wing non-Zionist movements, such as the Anarchists, the Bundists, and also the Jewish Communists, became irrelevant. With the establishment of the State of Israel, the antisemitic trials in Communist countries, and the Six-Day War (1967), many supporters of the Bund and the Communists crossed the lines and embraced Zionism, most of them in the left-wing factions. The traditional Zionist parties, whose roots were in the communities of origin, were close to the Israeli parties and sometimes became dependent on their political and financial support. The political leadership of the Ashkenazi community – AMIA, which was maintained in the 1940s by leaders of the financial institutions, and the *landsmanshaftn* together with the leftist anti-Zionist sector – was dominated by a coalition of the Zionist parties after the democratic elections of the beginning of the 1950s. This transition was felt in some way also in the Ladino-speaking Sephardi community and later in the Damascene community.

In the 1970s two new organizations emerged. One was based on sports and recreation organizations, including the four big clubs of Buenos Aires (Hebraica, Maccabi, Hakoach and the Sephardi Club CASA), a number of similar but smaller organizations in the Greater Buenos Aires area, and all the communal organizations in Argentina. These institutions, which grew to include social and family activities and some attempts at informal education, and embraced tens of thousands of Jews, enabled the leaders of the new organization to claim that they were representing most of the Jewish public. This organization was called FACCMA – Federación Argentina de Centros Comunitarios Macabeos – and was affiliated with the World Maccabi Organization based in Tel Aviv.

The second organization was the Conservative movement, which after 30 years of activity had become in the 1990s a well-established movement of more than 20 congregations with synagogues, social activities for youth and adults, and some of them maintaining day schools. These congregations had thousands of members in Buenos Aires and other cities in the country and a spiritual leadership from the graduates of the Seminario Rabínico Latinoamericano.

These two organizations cooperated to a certain degree and were instrumental in the creation in 1983 of a new group called Brerá – Movimiento de Integración y Renovación Comunitaria. The group was established to give voice to the new goals and views of the part of the community that was not connected to the existing Zionist parties, and to take part in the communal elections. In both the organizations that helped create Brerá, the inclusion of members of the various Jewish ethnic groups was more prominent. In the two AMIA elections in which Brerá ran (May 1984 and May 1987) it came in second to Avoda – the Zionist Labor Party. In the next election (May 1990) Brerá ran in the Lista Unidad Comunitaria, and in the election of May 1993 it did not run at all, claiming that the election procedures were fraudulent. In fact, the ranks of Brerá dwindled when the Conservative movement established its own party – Masorti – abandoning its alliance with Brerá and reaching an understanding with Avoda. In this manner, the latter maintained its hold on the community leadership.

In the middle of the 1990s a new political group, Menorah, began to emerge under the leadership of Rubén *Beraja. Because of his leading position in one of the foremost Jewish financial institutions of the 1980s and 1990s, Beraja enjoyed senior status in the community. Following his election as chairman of the DAIA, to a great extent due to the support of Brerá, Beraja, an active member of the community of Aleppo, became known even outside the boundaries of Argentina and was elected vice president of the World Jewish Congress and chairman of the Latin American Jewish Congress. In late 1998 and 1999, Beraja's standing was undermined by financial difficulties in the Banco Mayo, of which he was director and there were accusations of mismanagement. As a result, Beraja ceased all public activity and Menorah dissolved. Since then, the position of the representatives of the traditional Zionist parties has been reinforced. Nevertheless, in the elections of April 2005 only 3,000 of the approximately 13,000 members with voting rights out of a total of around 40,000 members participated.

Demography. The Jewish population of Argentina was estimated at about 187,000 in 2003. At its peak, in the 1960s, the community had numbered approximately 310,000, but had steadily declined since that time. The Jewish population – about 80% Ashkenazi – was mostly urban. Memories of Jewish agricultural settlement and the "Jewish gaucho" retained their places of honor in communal consciousness, reinforcing the idea that Jews were an old and legitimate element in the predominantly Catholic Argentine society, and in the Ar-

Jewish Population of Argentina, 1895–2004

Year	Total population	Estimated Jewish population	Jewish population(*)	Percent of the Jewish population
1895	3,954,911	6,085		
1900		6,700–15,600	14,700	
1905		22,500–25,400	24,700	
1910 (1911)	7,171,910	55,000–68,700	68,100	0.95
1914	7,885,273	100,000–116,300	115,600	1.47
1920 (1921)	8,698,516	120,000–126,900	126,700	1.46
1925	9,548,092	160,400–200,000	162,300	1.7
1930 (1928)	10,646,814	200,200–218,500	191,400	1.8
1935	12,227,761	226,400–253,500	218,000	1.78
1940 (1941)	13,320,641		254,400	1.9
1945		350,000	273,400	
1947	15,893,827	249,330–350,000	285,800	1.8
1950	16,109,000	360,000	294,000	1.83
1955	18,379,000	360,000	305,900	1.66
1960	20,008,945	291,877–450,000	310,000	1.55
1965	21,719,000	450,000	296,600	1.37
1970	23,983,000	500,000	286,300	1.19
1975	24,290,000	475,000	265,000	1.09
1980	26,060,000	300,000	242,000	0.93
1995	34,995,000	300,000	206,000	0.59
2001	37,032,000		197,000	0.53
2004	39,144,753		190,000	0.49

(*) Based on research by U. Schmelz, S. DellaPergola, and B. Bloch. See S. DellaPergola, "Demographic Trends of Latin American Jewry," in L. Laikin Elkin and G. Merkx (eds.), *The Jewish Presence in Latin America* (1987). See also S. DellaPergola in recent editions of the *American Jewish Yearbook*.

gentinean tourist industry, which was eager to exploit the image to get American Jews to come for a visit. But this image is divorced from contemporary reality. At present, the Jewish agricultural settlements and the Jewish communities in rural areas are almost nonexistent. More than 80% of the Jewish population lives in the urban area of the Autonomous City of Buenos Aires and its suburbs, and another 10% in cities of more than a million inhabitants (Córdoba, Rosario, Tucumán, and La Plata).

One reason for the constant demographic decline is the low birthrate. As in other urban and middle-class Jewish communities around the world, the low birthrate means an aging Jewish population. The average age, which was estimated at 25–27 in 1930, 31 in 1947, and 35 in 1960, jumped to over 40 in the 1970s and is continuously rising. The second reason is the growing number of Jews that abandon the community and assimilate into the majority society, many through exogamous marriages, which increase steadily. While no exact statistics are available, the intermarriage rate, approximately calculated in the mid-1930s to reach 1–5% and in the 1960s 20–25%, is now estimated at 40% and up. In addition, there is also a negative migratory balance. While in the period from the end of the 19th century until World War II Argentina was a receptive country for Jewish immigration, and in the Holocaust years – in spite of the restrictive legislation and the complete closure of the Argentinean borders to Jewish immigration after 1938 – about 40,000 Jews entered the country in legal and illegal ways. In 1945–50 about 1,500 Holocaust survivors immigrated to Argentina. The 1950s was the last decade with a positive migratory balance with the immigration of Jews from Hungary and Egypt. From the 1960s on, the community was characterized by emigration. The best statistically known destination of emigration was the State of Israel. The rate of *aliyah* was proportionally among the highest in the western Jewish Diaspora. Since the establishment of Israel close to 59,000 Jews from Argentina made *aliyah*. Zionism and antisemitism were important reasons for this emigration, but economic difficulties seemed to predominate, especially among the 9,500 Jews who emigrated in the first four years of the 21st century. This factor also motivated considerable immigration to the U.S., Canada, and other countries in Latin America, and, to a lesser extent, Western Europe. While it is almost impossible to measure this migration, it seems reasonable to assume that it affects many thousands of Argentinean Jews.

Cultural Life. In the second half of the 20th century and to a remarkable extent since the 1970s, Jews constituted an integral part of Argentine cultural life. Jewish participation was evident in every sphere of culture – teaching and research, literature, journalism, theater, cinema and television, the visual arts, and classical and popular music. The Jewish presence in these fields goes far beyond any discussion about the Jewish character of their cultural activity and should be considered Jewish creativity as such. While this multifaceted cultural creativity does in fact exhibit a profound connection with Jewish roots, there is at the same time rich cultural activity among Jews that entirely lacks Jewish particularity, being woven into the deepest layers of Argentinean culture, like the tango of Buenos Aires.

Jewish institutions have always been a vital outlet for this cultural activity. Literature, theater, music, lectures attracted the Jewish public throughout the 20th century and continue to do so today, despite the economic and social crisis that affected broad sectors of society. The cultural fare of the Jewish institutions is rich and is well received by the Jewish public. In place of the Editorial Israel, a joint cultural venture promoted by CIRA and a well-known Jewish family, which published many Jewish books from the 1940s to the 1960s, the Ashkenazi community AMIA established the Editorial Milá, which since 1986 has published hundreds of books, including literature, essays, testimonies, and research studies. In 2001–4 Milá published dozens of books, most of them in the original Spanish, as well as a number of translations, particularly from Yiddish.

In the provinces the situation is less encouraging, as these regions are to a large extent dependent upon events and activities organized by the Va'ad ha-Kehillot, whose headquarters are in Buenos Aires.

The change in the language used by Jews has been clearly reflected not just in the schools or in cultural and public activity but also in another dimension of cultural life – journalism. Since the 1970s Yiddish and German have almost disappeared from the print media in favor of Spanish. Arabic was common only on a colloquial level and periodicals in Hebrew were always a rare phenomenon. There are weekly or monthly publications like *Mundo Israelita* and *La Luz* – founded in the 1920s and 1930s, respectively – *Nueva Sión* (1948), *Comunidades* (1980s), and *La Voz Judía* (1990s). In recent years there were also daily news publications on the Internet like Iton Gadol and ShalomOnLine. In the 1990s Jewish TV cable and radio stations like Aleph and FM Jai were also established, of which only the latter still exists.

Religious Life. The Jewish community of Argentina is still overwhelmingly secular. For many, synagogue attendance on the Sabbath or Jewish holidays was not a religious act but instead a mode of social and national identification with the Jewish people and its culture. Yet even while the large majority of Jews and their leaders lived secular lives, the central institutions of AMIA Ashkenazi community remained officially Orthodox.

One controversial religious issue with potentially profound implications for Argentine Jewry as a whole was conversion. With the high rate of intermarriage, some non-Jewish spouses were willing to convert to Judaism, be formally incorporated into the community, and raise their children as Jews. From 1928 conversions in the country were prohibited by an Orthodox edict, but not every rabbinical authority abided by the ban. Today there are still many Jews in Argentina, including people who are not themselves religiously observant, who maintain that non-Jews converted by local rabbis are not yet Jews and will be recognized as Jews only after conversion by rabbinic courts in Israel, the U.S., or Europe.

The Masorti movement, which identifies with Conservative Judaism and has at present more than 20 affiliated congregations in Argentina, performs its own conversions. The Reform movement, which also performs conversions, has a very limited presence in Argentina and very few followers. Most Jews of Argentina, whose Judaism was a matter of social and ethnic identity and who emphasized active participation in Jewish life and the upbringing of children as members of the Jewish people rather than *halakhah*, were satisfied with Conservative and Reform conversions.

According to some estimates, about half of all the Jews in Argentina who maintained relatively continuous contact with a synagogue identified with the Masorti movement. In 2004, Masorti rabbis graduating from the Seminario Rabínico Latinoamericano in Buenos Aires served in Argentina and other communities in Latin America (more than 40), in the U.S. (more than 15), and in Israel (10).

In recent decades, certain groups of young people from various sectors of the Jewish population, in particular those who belong to the community of Aleppan origin and to some extent those of Damascene origin, as well as small groups of Ashkenazim, had "returned" to religious Orthodox observance. They observed Jewish law strictly and studied rabbinical literature in religious academies (yeshivot and *kolelim*). But this trend has very little impact on the broader community and is limited to a minority.

More significant was the growth of the Chabad-Lubavitch ḥasidic group. Chabad's entry into the Argentine Jewish community began in the late 1960s, and in 2005 the movement had approximately 20 centers in the country, two-thirds of them in the Buenos Aires metropolitan area. As a part of its worldwide strategy, also in Argentina Chabad established a public presence by celebrating holidays like Hanukkah, Sukkot, and Lag ba-Omer in public, non-Jewish spaces, and many Jews responded positively to such a demonstration of Jewish pride. Chabad's original appeal in Argentina was to the poorer Jews, a steadily growing group under the economic conditions of 2001–2, who appreciated the economic help this Orthodox movement furnished them. It also attracted a number of wealthy people to help support its activities. It was unclear, however, how many of those who identified with Chabad or received financial aid from it adopted the fully observant Chabad lifestyle, since the movement did not insist on strict conformity to *halakhah* on the part of those who found their way to them.

The Sephardi sector is characterized by the opposite trends of secularization and growing Orthodoxy. Secularization is more evident among the communities of Moroccans and Ladino speakers, whose ethnic identity has less of an appeal to the younger generation, which feels more at home among the Conservatives and joins the congregations of the Masorti. The two communities of Syrian origin – from Aleppo and Damascus – remain the stronghold of Orthodoxy among the Sephardim. During the last decades they strengthened their educational network, stressing the role of women in transmitting the Jewish tradition in the family. Many of their rabbis were born in Argentina and received their rabbinical education in yeshivot in Israel; they are influenced by the religious leadership of Rabbi Ovadiah *Yosef.

Jewish Education. When segments of the public educational system changed their schedule to a longer day in the late 1960s, leaving no time for the morning or afternoon complementary Jewish schools, the community transformed them into day schools offering both a general and a Jewish curriculum. This put pressure on the schools to excel in their general programs so that parents would not remove their children and send them to public or non-Jewish private schools. While tending to relegate the Jewish program to a secondary place, this strategy did succeed in retaining Jewish students. This change brought a solution to the above-mentioned dropout problem in the elementary schools and to some extent also at the secondary level. A survey carried out in 1997 found that nearly half of all Jewish children aged 13–17 and two-thirds of children aged 6–12 attended Jewish day schools. These schools taught the state curriculum along with a Jewish cultural program that took up between five and 20 hours per week. A total of 19,248 students attended classes in 56 kindergartens, 52 elementary schools, and 29 high schools.

By 2002, however, the numbers had dropped, showing just 14,700 students in 40 elementary schools and 22 high schools. Although the two surveys conducted five years apart had different methodologies and were therefore not necessarily comparable, it is likely that the difference reflected a real downturn, the natural result of the above-mentioned demographic processes: low birthrate, assimilation, and emigration. On the other hand, the economic situation which affected the middle-class Jewish population should be taken into account as well. The high tuition rates in these private schools were also a deterrent under the grim economic conditions, even though local Jewish institutions, the Jewish Agency, and Israel's Ministry of Education, together with the Joint Distribution Committee and World Jewish Congress, established financial aid programs.

In addition to formal Jewish education, Jewish schools offered an informal social framework with events connected to the Hebrew calendar and Israel-related activities such as dance groups and choirs. For students in the higher grades there was the opportunity for educational trips to Israel.

Another important contribution of the schools to Jewish life is the common framework they offer to thousands of young Jews, creating through them the opportunity to establish a connection with thousands of young families interested in a Jewish framework and being exposed to Jewish values.

Nevertheless socio-economic development since the 1990s imposed a revision of the existing model of Jewish schooling. Recognizing that other educational alternatives were necessary for those not in day schools, the community, in cooperation with the Jewish Agency, established a supplementary program called *Lomdim* for secondary level (with about 1,200 students in 2004) with classes two or three days (6–9 hours) a week. A second supplementary program, for elementary school children, called *Chalomot,* with 4–12 hours a week, has approximately 600 children. Chabad developed a similar strategy, offering children attending public school an enriched after-school program in computers, English, and other subjects, together with Jewish studies.

Teacher training suffered dramatically in this period. Such training was given in the 1940s and 1950s by certain secondary schools, in Buenos Aires mainly by the Seminar le-Morim of AMIA, the Machon le-Limudei ha-Yahaduth of CIRA, and the secondary school of the Sholem Aleichem Shul, and in Moisesville by the Seminar Yahaduth. Training was transferred to Ha-Midrashah ha-Ivrit in the mid-1960s. Students received training there as elementary school teachers in the first two years, and could became secondary school teachers after three additional years of study. At the beginning of the 1970s its name was changed to Michlelet Shazar (Shazar College) and received academic sponsorship from Tel Aviv University, which was withdrawn at the end of the 1980s. Many difficulties – academic, budgetary, and administrative, especially after the bombing of the community building in 1994 – led to a decline of its activities in the mid-1990s. In 1996 the Merkaz Rabin was established, which included the Michlelet Shazar and the Seminar Agnon for kindergarten teachers (established in the early 1960s). At the end of the 1990s, however, Shazar was closed, and today there is no teacher training institution in Argentina. The only institutions of higher Jewish studies are Orthodox yeshivot and the Seminario Rabínico Latinoamericano of Conservative orientation, in which there is also a section for non-rabbinic studies. All those institutions demand from their students one or more years of study at higher yeshivot or Jewish universities in Israel or the U.S. in order for them to receive a rabbinic degree.

Relations with Israel

Argentina has always had a significant place in Israel's foreign policy as a prominent Latin American country and a country with a very large Jewish community. From 1947, when Argentina abstained from voting for the UN Partition Plan for Palestine, relations were marked by steady progress. Argentina recognized Israel on Feb. 14, 1949, and diplomatic missions were established in Buenos Aires and Tel Aviv in August and September 1949, respectively.

Argentina's position varies on a number of issues affecting Israel. In the annually recurrent UN debates on Palestine refugees, Argentina has for years voted with Israel against attempts to appoint a UN property custodian, on the grounds that it would be an unacceptable interference with national sovereignty. Following the Six-Day War, Argentina was in the forefront of the Latin American nations that opposed Soviet and Arab efforts in the Emergency Session of the UN General Assembly to bring about an unconditional evacuation of the Israel-held territories. On the other hand, she has consistently favored the internationalization of Jerusalem, and after the Six-Day War voted against the municipal reunification of the city.

In 1960 the capture of Adolf Eichmann in Argentina caused a temporary crisis in relations, which returned to normal after some months. Commercial treaties exist between the two countries. In the 1960s the trade balance was overwhelmingly in favor of Argentina (due to meat exports that varied from $10 to 15 million a year). The trade balance remained disproportionate also in the 1970s (Israel's imports rose to $17.1 million while exports only reached $1.3 million). The balance changed radically in the 1980s ($42.7 and 35.4 million, respectively) and in the 1990s ($66.7 and 12.3 million). Since 2000 the total scope of bilateral trade was over $100 million a year, with the exception of 2002, when a deep crisis struck the Argentinean economy. The most remarkable year was 2004 with a total of $191.1 million ($136.3 and $54.8 million). Meat continues to be the principal Argentinean export product together with oil and processed food. The main goods exported by Israel are machinery and chemical products.

In 1957 a cultural exchange agreement was signed. An Israel-Argentina Cultural Institute has been active in Buenos Aires since the 1950s. The Argentina House was established in Jerusalem in 1967 as a result of a private initiative, offering cultural activities to the Israeli public. Technical cooperation between the two countries developed in fields, such as rural planning in semi-arid zones and the uses of water.

Since the establishment of diplomatic relations the Argentinean government has recognized the legitimacy of the special relationship between Israel and the Jews of Argentina. As an immigration country that legitimized the special ties of immigrants to their countries of origin, considered their "*madre patria*" (motherland), Israel was perceived as the *madre patria* of the Jews, although they had lived in Argentina at least 60 years before the creation of the State of Israel. This recognition was manifested when the government accepted the right of the Israeli ambassador to intervene on behalf of Argentinean Jewry, demanding that expressions of antisemitism should be stopped and prohibited.

After seven years of military rule, Argentina returned to democracy in 1973, with the victory of the Peronist party, which prevailed in free elections. Former President Juan Perón, who had been in exile since 1955, returned to Argentina and after a few months was elected president. During his year in office (he died on July 1974) and in the government headed by his wife, in which the strongman was Minister López Rega, antisemitism became more active in the streets as well as in official discourse. Moreover, López Rega strengthened relations with Arab countries, especially with Libya. He considered the establishment of diplomatic relations with the PLO and there were rumors that he was promoting the rupture of diplomatic relations with Israel. In those years of instability Israel protested many times against manifestations of antisemitism and against the anti-Israel policy. After the military coup d'état in March 1976, everyone thought that the generals would establish order in the country, but they abrogated all civil rights and instituted a reign of terror, tolerating no opposition.

Although antisemitism was not an official policy, antisemitic expressions were very frequent, also in the different ranks of the army, the government, and the forces of repression. In these circumstances Israel acted officially against antisemitism and interceded on behalf of incarcerated Jews and those who vanished (kidnapped and killed by the repressors). In the case of the former, the Argentinean government agreed to free from jail more than 55 persons. In the case of those who disappeared, Israel's intervention together with European public opinion and to some extent the U.S., succeeded in getting only one journalist freed – Jacobo *Timerman – under condition that he leave for Israel. Unofficially Israel evacuated from Argentina close to 500 Jews in danger and took them in. These activities on the part of the Israeli embassy, together with the Jewish Agency, were made possible because of the special position of Israel. On the one hand, the generals believed, as a part of their antisemitic perception, that through the Israeli embassy they could influence U.S. policy towards Argentina. On the other hand, Israel and officials of the embassy had had good relations since the beginning of the 1970s with military officers in charge of purchasing military equipment in Israel. Some of these officers occupied high posts in the government, like Minister of the Interior General Albano Harguindeguy, or Admiral Emilio Massera, commander-in-chief of the Navy and member of the first junta headed by General Jorge Videla. Although Israel continued to sell military equipment to the military government, the Israeli diplomats in Buenos Aires decided to avoid the use of these special relations as a means of putting diplomatic pressure on Argentina to change its position in matters of special interests for Israel, such as Argentina's consistent support of the Palestinian and Arab positions in the UN and in other international arenas, to improve economic and other bilateral relations that were unfavorable to Israel, and to obtain the release of the "vanished" Jews.

In 2000, by the request of the Knesset, the Israeli government established an Inter-Ministerial Commission with the objective of helping the Jewish families of the "vanished" in their demand of the Argentinean government to receive the bodies and to bring to trial those responsible for human rights violations in the dictatorship. This commission, composed of representatives of the Foreign and Justice Ministries and representatives of the public and of the families, presented its conclusions and recommendations in July 2003. As a result of the commission's report, the president of Israel and the government several times presented official requests supporting the demands of the families. Since then, the request to find and identify the bodies of the "vanished" Jews has been made in many meetings of Israeli and Argentinean officials.

In the first democratic government after the military dictatorship (1983–1989) Foreign Minister Caputo's foreign policy attempted to achieve an alliance both with Third World and developed countries at one and the same time. To these ends special attention was paid to the demands of the Arab bloc, while a cold but correct profile was maintained in relations with Israel. This in no way influenced the ideology of the ruling party (UCR), which was traditionally democratic and opposed to the nationalist right-wing groups. In 1992 then ex-president Alfonsín visited Israel, as did the possible radical candidate in the next presidential election, Fernando de la Rúa.

Relations between Argentina and Israel, despite the initial prejudices, were concretely upgraded after Menem came to power in 1989, together with a change toward a pro-North American policy in the international arena. The association between Argentina, Egypt, and Iraq for the construction of the Condor II missile was frozen and then disbanded. The missile was finally destroyed as a result of U.S. government pressure. Official visits at the highest level have increased: in late 1989 Israeli president Chaim Herzog visited Argentina, where he addressed the National Congress; in 1991 Menem became the first Argentine president to visit Israel. Before and after these visits, parliamentary and ministerial missions were exchanged between both countries for discussion of issues of mutual interest.

During the 1990 Persian Gulf crisis, the Argentinean government opposed the Iraqi invasion of Kuwait and sent two frigates to join the United Nations force that attacked the aggressor. This active position, consistent with the pro-American policy, was a source of controversy in Argentinean political sectors. In other aspects connected with the Middle East, the Alfonsín and Menem governments resisted PLO efforts to open an office in the country in order to obtain diplomatic recognition. In 1985 leaders of the Jewish community appealed to representatives of all the political streams to condemn UN General Assembly Resolution 3378 equating "Zionism" with "racism"; in the following years, the resolution was condemned by the Argentinean parliament (1990).

Moreover, the Argentinean chairman of the UN Commission on Human Rights convening in Durban in 2001 was very active in efforts to moderate anti-Israel resolutions.

The government headed by President Néstor Kirchner, elected in the fifth consecutive democratic elections in 2003, maintained good relations between the two countries. Politically, Argentina is against violent solutions to international conflicts and therefore supports the need of negotiations in the conflict between Israel and the Palestinians. Nevertheless the new administration changed its voting policy in the UN and is coming closer to that of the other Latin American countries: Argentinean votes against Israel or sometimes abstains.

In March 1992, the Israeli embassy in Buenos Aires was destroyed in a terrorist attack that left 20 dead and hundreds of injured, including passers-by and neighbors as well as embassy personnel. Following the July 1994 terrorist bombing of the central community building of AMIA, with 85 people killed and hundreds injured, President Menem called Israeli Prime Minister Yitzhak Rabin to express his condolences. After these events President Menem, his ministers, and representatives across almost the entire political, trade union, and intellectual spectrum participated together with tens of thousands of Argentinean citizens in expressing their solidarity with the Jews, in the first case visiting the ruins of the destroyed embassy and in the second in a mass demonstration a few days afterwards in the Plaza Congreso.

The subsequent investigations saw hard words and tensions between various sectors of the security forces, the law courts connected with the cases, politicians, including President Menem, the Israeli embassy, and the Jewish community. The investigations in both cases did not discover who was responsible for the attacks, despite a public trial of ten local suspects for collaboration with foreign terrorists. This trial began in September 2001 and was concluded at the end of 2004 with no convictions. Israel continued to demand that the government find the local perpetrators as well as take the necessary political steps against Iran.

[Haim Avni, Ignacio Klich / Efraim Zadoff (2nd ed.)]

BIBLIOGRAPHY: H.C. Lea, *Inquisition in the Spanish Dependencies* (1908); B. Lewin, *El Judio en la época colonial* (1939), includes bibliography; idem, *Los judios bajo la inquisición en Hispanoamérica* (1960); J. Monin, *Los Judíos en la America Española, 1492–1810* (1939).

ADD. BIBLIOGRAPHY: B. Ansel, "The Beginnings of the Modern Jewish Community in Argentina, 1852–1891" (Ph.D. dissertation: University of Kansas, 1969); H. Avni, *Argentina "Ha-Areẓ ha-Ye'uda" – Mifal ha-Hityashvut shel ha-Baron Hirsch be-Argentina* (1973); idem, *Argentina and the Jews: A History of Jewish Migration* (1991); idem, *Yahadut Argentina – Ma'amadah ha-Ḥevrati u-Demutah ha-Irgunit* (1972); G. Ben Dror, *Católicos, Nazis y judíos. La Iglesia Argentina en tiempos del Tercer Reich, 1933–1945* (2003); M. Braylan and A. Jmelnitzky, *Informe sobre antisemitismo en la Argentina 2000–2001* et seq. (2002, 2004); DAIA – Centro de Estudios Sociales, B. Gurevich, *Proyecto testimonio – revelaciones de los archivos argentinos sobre la política oficial en la era nazi-fascista, vols. I and II* (1998); S. Della Pergola, in: *American Jewish Yearbook* (2002, 2003); R. Feierstein and S. Sadow, *Recreando la cultura judeoargentina – 1894–2001: en el umbral del segundo siglo* (2002); I. Herschlag, D. Schers et al., *The Social Structure of Latin American Jewry – Final Report* (1975); J. Laikin Elkin and G.W. Merkxs (eds.), *The Jewish Presence in Latin America* (1987); J. Laikin Elkin, *The Jews of Latin America* (1998); V. Mirelman, *Jewish Buenos Aires, 1890–1930: In Search of an Identity* (1990); I. Rubel, *Las Escuelas Judías Argentinas (1985–1995) – Procesos de evolución y de involución* (1998); U.O. Schmelz and S. Della Pergola, *Ha-Demografiyah shel ha-Yehudim be-Argentina ve-Yeter Medinot America ha-Latinit* (1974); L. Senkman (ed.), *El Antisemitismo en la Argentina* (1989); idem, *Argentina, la Segunda Guerra Mundial y los refugiados indeseables, 1933–1945* (1991); L. Senkman and M. Sznajder (eds.), *El legado del autoritarismo* (1995); L. Slavsky, *La espada encendida – Un estudio sobre la muerte y la entidad étnica en el judaísmo* (1993); S. Schenkolewski-Kroll, *Ha-Tenu'ah ha-Ẓiyyonit ve-ha-Miflagot ha-Ẓiyyoniot be-Argentina, 1935–1948* (1996); Tel Aviv University, S. Roth Institute for the Study of Contemporary Antisemitism and Racism, *Anti-Semitism Worldwide* (yearbook); E. Zadoff, *Historia de la Educación Judía en Buenos Aires 1935–1957* (1994); idem, *A Century of Argentinean Jewry: In Search of a New Model of National Identity* (2000). **WEBSITES:** news.daia.org.ar; www.amia.org.ar; www.mfa.gov.il/desaparecidos.

ARGOB (Heb. אַרְגֹּב), region in northern Transjordan which was part of *Bashan and probably lay between Nahr al-Ruqād and Nahr al-ʿAlān. According to Thutmose III's geographical list (no. 126) and the el-Amarna letters, this region was heavily populated in the Late Bronze Age. At the time of the Israelite conquest Argob embraced "threescore cities… All these were fortified cities with high walls, gates, and bars; beside the unwalled towns, a great number" (Deut. 3:4–5). It was allotted by Moses to the half-tribe of Manasseh and was possibly settled by Jair (Deut. 3:13–14, but cf. I Kings 4:13). In Solomon's time the region was included in his sixth administrative district and its governor (the son of Geber) resided at Ramoth-Gilead (I Kings 4:13). In the Aramaic translations Argob is identified with the region which Josephus and the New Testament call Trachon or *Trachonitis (Targ. Onk.: Trakona; Targ. Yer.: Tragona), the basaltic highland desert now known as al-Lijā. This later tradition, however, is not consistent with the early sources.

BIBLIOGRAPHY: Bergman, in: JPOS, 16 (1936), 239; Albright, in: BASOR, 68 (1937), 21; de Vaux, in: *Vivre et Penser*, 1 (1941), 22; Mazar, in: JBL, 80 (1961), 16; EM, s.v.; Press, Ereẓ, 1 (1946), 36.

[Michael Avi-Yonah]

ARGOV, ALEXANDER (**Sasha**; 1914–1995), Israeli popular music composer. Argov was born in Moscow and immigrated to Palestine in 1934, where he changed his last name from Abramovich to Argov in 1946. His mother was a professional pianist and his father a dentist. Argov began to play the piano at the age of three and a half, and when he was six began composing songs which his mother wrote down for him. He had no formal training in music, and in his adult life music was not his main source of income; however, composing was always his mission in life. For over six decades he composed music in which he exhibited considerable originality.

He wrote over 1,000 songs, including songs for army and regular entertainment groups such as the Chizbatron (1948); Naḥal (1950–c. 1960); Batzal Yarok ("Green Onion," 1958–60); the Tarnegolim ("Roosters," 1961–63), as well as music for theater and film. He accompanied some performances of his songs, as the piano played an important part in his music. He ascribed considerable importance to the relationship between text and music and attempted to represent words in music using frequent changes of rhythm and meter. His songs range between art song and popular song. His most famous musical was *Shelomo ha-Melekh ve-Shalmai ha-Sandlar* ("King Solomon and Shalmai the Cobbler"), first performed in 1964.

Argov's music is distinguished by characteristics such as unexpected melodic leaps, chromaticisms, dissonances, complex harmonic progressions, and modulations to distant keys. His style had a far-reaching influence on the work of a younger generation of Israeli popular music composers. A selection of his songs was published in 1946. Argov published three others: *Kakhah Setam* (1979), *Et Ma she-Ratziti* (1983), and *Me-Ever la-Tekhelet* (2001). In 1988 he won the Israel Prize for his contribution to the Hebrew song.

BIBLIOGRAPHY: I. Vetzan, "Unique Musical Characteristics in the Songs of Sasha Argov," Ph.D. thesis, Hebrew University of Jerusalem (Hebrew, 2003).

[Gila Flam (2nd ed.)]

ARGOV (**Urkavi**), **ZOHAR** (1955–1987), Israeli popular singer in the Middle Eastern style. Born in the city of Rishon le-Zion into a Jewish Yemenite family, Argov was endowed with an innate musical talent and a naturally beautiful and expressive voice, and as a youngster started to sing in the local Yemenite synagogue. Lacking any formal musical training, he began to rise to stardom in the late 1970s and early 1980s, at a time when Middle Eastern singers were fighting for official recognition. Argov scored his breakthrough hit in 1982 with his song "*Peraḥ be-Ganni*" ("The Flower of my Garden"), composed by his close friend and supporter Avihu *Medina. The song won first place at the 1981 Oriental Song Festival sponsored by the Israel Broadcasting Authority. Achieving resounding success, it has been regarded as a paradigm of the so-called *zemer mizraḥi* (Oriental song) in its broadest socio-cultural context. It was indeed one of the most eloquent expressions of the initial stage of what may be called the trend toward "Israelization" that emerged among Oriental musicians in the early 1960s. It expressed above all an attempt to realize the ideal of the "Ingathering of the Exiles" by assimilating traditional musical styles to the predominant Israeli folk music and making their grievances heard in mainstream society. Argov's musical style indeed reflected both his Israeli and Yemenite heritage, combining stereotypical musical elements of both East and West with the prestigious vocal improvisation (*mawwal*) which derives from Arab art music.

On the heels of his meteoric rise to fame, Argov developed a serious drug habit that led to his premature tragic death by suicide in a prison cell. A play called "The King," as he was nicknamed by his numerous fans, was written and directed by dramatist Shmuel Hasfari, who describes Argov's life as the fundamental story of the struggle between two cultures.

[Amnon Shiloah (2nd ed.)]

ARḤA, ELIEZER BEN ISAAC (d. 1652), Ereẓ Israel kabbalist and physician. Arḥa was born in Safed, but moved to Hebron early in the 17th century to officiate as rabbi of the community. He studied with R. Abraham Azulai who wrote *Or ha-Ḥammah* ("The Light of the Sun") with Arḥa's assistance. According to R. Yom Tov Ẓahalon, Arḥa served as *dayyan* in the *bet din* in Gaza. It is possible that he was there only during the 1619 epidemic although he was certainly in Gaza in 1626. His name is also mentioned in an inscription on the walls of the reputed grave of Aaron on Mount Hor. In 1623 Arḥa and other scholars of Jerusalem recommended to the wealthy Jews of Constantinople the publication of Abraham Azulai's *Zohorei Ḥammah*. R. Isaiah *Horowitz appointed Arḥa executor of his estate. In about 1630 Arḥa had to leave Hebron and lived a wandering life. In 1648 he was in Jerusalem. His son Isaac Arḥa also figured among the scholars of Hebron. Eliezer Arḥa wrote extensively, but none of his works was published. The manuscripts extant include a volume of responsa (Ms. Oxford Mich. 291), sermons (Ms. Jerusalem 8⁰ 1300), a commentary on *Midrash Rabbah*, written between 1599 and 1639 in Hebron and Jerusalem, and a commentary on *Ein Ya'akov*. It is doubtful whether the annotations on Maimonides ascribed to Arḥa are actually his. In *Mavo le-She'elot u-Teshuvot Rabbeinu Eliezer ben Arḥa* (1978) Ezra Batzri has published 35 responsa of Arḥa; they were taken from a manuscript (Oxford 29 1). These responsa throw light on the relations between Jews and non-Jews in Israel. One of them discusses whether Jews are permitted to make clerical vestments for priests and another whether they are entitled to lend them money on interest, both of which Arḥa permits.

BIBLIOGRAPHY: M. Benayahu, in: *Yerushalayim*, 2 (1955), 151–4, 174–80; I. Ḥasida, in: J.L. Maimon (ed.), *Koveẓ ha-Rambam* (1955), 164–79.

[Yehoshua Horowitz (2nd ed.)]

ARIAS, JOSEPH SEMAH (or **Ẓemaḥ**; late 17th century), Marrano author. While serving in Brussels as a captain in the Spanish Army, Arias was adjutant to another Marrano writer, Nicolás de *Oliver y Fullana. A *décima burlesca* (ten-line humorous dedication) of Arias' has survived. It was printed in Miguel de *Barrios' *Flor de Apolo* (1665), 165. It seems likely that he and Barrios were friends during their military service in the Spanish Netherlands (c. 1665). Like Barrios and Oliver y Fullana, Arias eventually left the army and settled in Amsterdam, where he joined the Jewish community. In Amsterdam he published a Spanish translation of Josephus' *Contra Apionem*, the *Repuesta de Josepho contra Apión* (Amsterdam, 1687), which he dedicated to Isaac *Orobio de Castro.

BIBLIOGRAPHY: Kayserling, in: REJ, 18 (1889), 287; idem, Bibl, 13; idem, *Sephardim* (Ger., 1859), 251–2; Roth, Marranos, index.

[Kenneth R. Scholberg]

°**ARIAS MONTANO, BENITO** (1527–1598), one of the most eminent Bible scholars in Spain. Arias studied theology and Semitic languages in the University of Alacalá de Henares and was ordained a priest and became a member of the Order of Santiago. He was a vehement opponent of the Lutheran doctrines which he criticized with his profound erudition. He was one of the authors of the *Index*, the Catholic list of prohibited books. In 1568 King Philip II of Spain appointed him first director of the Escorial Library and chief editor of the second *Biblia Polyglotta* (the Hebrew Bible and New Testament in the original languages with translations), which was to supplant the first polyglot Bible (the *Complutensian* of 1514), also a product of Spanish scholarship. The second *Polyglotta*, known as the *Biblia Regia*, was published between 1569 and 1572 at the Plantin press, in Antwerp, in eight folio volumes. Volumes 1–4 include the Bible in Hebrew, along with the Aramaic Targums, the Septuagint, and the Peshitta (each with a Latin translation), as well as the Vulgate. The very scholarly qualities of the *Biblia Regia* put Arias in jeopardy for a prolonged period. Leon de Castro, professor of Hebrew at the University of Salamanca, who from motives of professional jealousy persecuted all Hebrew scholars of his day in Spain, denounced him to the Inquisition. He alleged that Arias had revealed a Judaizing tendency in the *Regia* in that he had given preference to the masoretic text and the Jewish translations over the Vulgate. After a trial that lasted some years, however, the Inquisition in Rome was persuaded by the scholarly defense of Juan de Mariana that Arias had not contradicted Catholic doctrine and acquitted him. In 1582–83 Arias served as the representative of Philip II at the Church Council in Toledo. He declined the offer of a bishopric and spent his last years in isolation in a monastery near Seville.

His writings (all in Latin, with the exception of a rhymed Spanish translation of the Song of Songs) include *Antiquitatum judaicarum libri IX* (Leyden, 1593); *Aaron sive sanctorum vestimentorum ornamentorumque descriptio* (1593); *Nehemias sive de antiquae Jerusalem situ* (1593); commentaries on various prophets; a collection of Latin hymns under the title *Hymni et Secula* (1593); rhymed translations of the Book of Psalms and various prophets; *Rhetorica* (in verse, 1569); a Latin translation of the travelog of Benjamin of Tudela, *Benjamini Tudelensis judaei itinerarium ex hebraeo latinum factum* (1575); *Historia naturalis* (1601, a description of the animal kingdom in which Arias greatly expanded the systematic classification of animals on the basis of their anatomic structure); and an extensive correspondence containing items of great interest (published in the *Colección de documentos inéditos para la historia de España*, vol. 41, pp. 127–418).

Despite the fact that Arias devoted himself to the study of the Hebrew language and that he was accused of harboring an inclination toward Judaism, it should not be assumed that he was descended from *Marranos. His admission to the Order of Santiago, which was most scrupulous in the matter of "racial purity," speaks strongly against such an assumption. The Institute Arias Montano de Estudios Hebraicos, established in Madrid in 1939 by the Supreme Council for Scientific Studies of the Spanish government, was named after him.

BIBLIOGRAPHY: B. Rekers, *Benito Arias Montano 1527–1598* (Dutch, 1961); F.G. Bell, *Benito Arias Montano* (1922); Lambert, in: DHGE, 4 (1930), 130–45 (incl. bibl.); EB, 2 (1969), 383. **ADD. BIBLIOGRAPHY:** A. Alcalá, in: *Cuadernos hispano-americanos*, 296 (1975), 347–78.

[Hiram Peri]

ARICHA, YOSEF (born **Dolgin**, pseudonym **Paziza**; 1907–1972), Hebrew writer. Aricha, who was born in Olevsk, Ukraine, lived in Ereẓ Israel from 1925, except for a stay in the United States (1929–32). Until his retirement in 1961, he was editor for the office of information of the Tel Aviv municipality. He wrote short stories, realistically depicting life in Israel and in the Diaspora, and tales for young people. In his novel *Ud Muẓẓal* ("The Survivor," 1937), Aricha describes the Ukrainian pogroms of 1919. Especially realistic is his collection of short stories, *Ba'alei Yeẓarim* ("Men of Passion," 1946), which contains scenes from the lives of Jewish butchers. In addition, Aricha wrote the novel *Leḥem ve-Ḥazon* ("Bread and Vision," 1933); *Kanfei Kesef* ("Silver Wings," stories for children, 1936); two historical novels, *Sanḥeriv bi-Yhudah* ("Sennacherib in Judah," 1958) and *Sofer ha-Melekh* ("The King's Scribe," 1966); and a historical play, *Mul Ḥerev* ("Facing the Sword," 1962). A collection of short stories, *Mivḥar Sippurim* (2–3 vols.), appeared in 1967. A list of his works and a bibliography are appended to his *Yom va-Laylah* ("Day and Night," 1963). Aricha and Y. Ogen edited *Dafdefet le-Sifrut Ivrit* (1952) and the literary magazine *Anakh*. An edition of his collected works appeared in 1963.

BIBLIOGRAPHY: Kressel, Leksikon, 1 (1965), 148–9; S. Kramer, *Ḥillufei Mishmarot be-Sifrutenu* (1959), 223–30.

[Haim Toren]

ARIDOR, YORAM (1933–), Israeli politician. Member of the Seventh to Eleventh Knessets. Yoram Aridor was born in Tel Aviv. He received his B.A. in economics and a second degree in law from the Hebrew University of Jerusalem. He joined the Ḥerut movement in 1961 and entered the Knesset in 1969 on the *Gaḥal list. In the years 1972–77 he was chairman of the Blue-White faction in the *Histadrut, associated with the Ḥerut movement. In the government established by Menaḥem *Begin in 1977 Aridor was appointed as the minister responsible for the portfolios that Begin held temporarily for the DMC, which joined the coalition in October. In 1978 he was the *Likud's candidate for treasurer of the Jewish Agency, but lost to the Labor candidate. In 1979 he was appointed chairman of the Ḥerut movement secretariat.

In January 1981 Aridor served for a short period as minister of communications following the resignation of Yitzḥak *Moda'i, but soon after he was appointed minister of finance, in place of Yigal *Hurwitz. In response to Hurwitz's "I haven't got a cent" policy, Aridor announced that he would implement a "correct economy," adopting the slogan "for the people." He tried to contend with the problem of rising inflation by introducing savings plans with attractive terms and reducing taxes on consumer goods and imports to lower their prices. He intended to cut taxes and improve the taxation system while gradually reducing the subsidies on basic products and services. However, with the rate of inflation continuing to rise, it was rumored in October 1983, around the time of the collapse of the bank share market, that he was considering a dollarization plan, introducing the U.S. dollar as legal tender in Israel, which aimed among other things at reducing Israel's deteriorating balance-of-payments deficit. As a consequence of these rumors Aridor was forced to resign. The 1986 Bejski Report on the collapse of the bank share market found that he had not acted to stop their manipulation by the banks, even when he realized the gravity of the situation.

In 1990 Aridor was appointed ambassador to the UN, but resigned after Labor won the 1992 elections. After retiring from politics, he served on the board of directors of numerous companies.

[Susan Hattis Rolef (2nd ed.)]

ARIE, RAFAEL (or **Rafaele**; 1922–1988), singer. Born in Sofia, Arie was a pupil of Brambaroff, the chief baritone of the Sofia Opera. He won first prize in the Geneva International Competition in 1946, and later sang leading basso roles at La Scala, Milan, and other European and American opera houses. In 1951 Igor Stravinsky chose him to sing at the Venice premiere of his opera *The Rake's Progress*. Arie visited Israel many times and eventually became an Israeli but continued his international concert career as one of the leading bassos of his generation.

ARIEL (Heb. אֲרִיאֵל). (1) The name given to Jerusalem in Isaiah 29:1–2, 7, where God will bring distress upon Ariel, and will make her like an *ariel* (for meaning, see below). *Ariel* in this sense is probably connected with the form *erellam* in Isaiah 33:7, understood as the plural form *arielim* ("Jerusalemites"), parallel to "messengers of Shalom" (i.e., of Jerusalem; cf. Gen. 14:18; Ps. 76:3). (2) A cultic object in Ezekiel 43:15–16, where it occurs in the forms *ariel* and *harel*. This is apparently an altar hearth superimposed upon the base of the altar, having horns at its four corners. Alternatively, it may be viewed as the top two sections of a three-tiered altar, again with the function of a hearth. This usage has been connected by some with the *ʾrʾl dwdh* which *Mesha of Moab dragged before *Chemosh from a captured town (*Mesha Stele*, 1:12). It may also be connected with II Samuel 23:20 = I Chronicles 11:22 "The two Ariels of Moab." (3) One of the chief men summoned by Ezra in Ezra 8:16 (cf. also Gen. 46:16; Num. 26:17). The etymology of this word is the subject of some dispute. Three principal modes of interpretation have been proposed: (a) from *ari-el*, "lion of God" or "Great Lion." This is the most probable derivation for the personal name in Ezra; (b) from a posited root *ari*, "to burn," with *lamed* afformative, thus meaning "hearth," similar to the Arabic *ʿiratun*, "hearth"; and (c) as a loanword from the Akkadian *arallû*-, the name for the netherworld and allegedly the world mountain. (In this view the altar is understood as a miniature ziggurat, which is taken to be the symbol of the world mountain.) However, *arallû* does not mean "mountain." In addition, the Akkadian, a loanword from Sumerian, would have not shown up in Hebrew in the form attested. Regardless of the ultimate derivation of the word, the meaning of Isaiah 29:1–2 seems to be that Jerusalem, here (prophetically?) called Ariel, is to become like the altar, i.e., a scene of holocaust.

BIBLIOGRAPHY: de Vaux, Anc Isr, 412–3; E. Kissane, *The Book of Isaiah*, 1 (1960), 362–3; EM, 1 (1955), 558–60. **ADD. BIBLIOGRAPHY:** J. Blenkinsopp, *Isaiah 1–39* (AB; 2000), 399–402; S. Muenger, in: DDD, 88–89.

[Tikva S. Frymer]

ARIEL (Heb. אֲרִיאֵל), town in Samaria, in the administered territories, 40 km. east of Tel Aviv and 65 km. from Jerusalem. Founded in 1978 by 40 families of defense and aviation industry workers, it received municipal status in 1998. In 1996 Ariel's population was approximately 14,200, increasing to 16,300 at the end of 2002, of whom 54% were recent immigrants, most from the Former Soviet Union. Its municipal area was 1.2 sq. mi. (3 sq. km.). The proximity to central Israel enabled the city to attract young families. Most residents are non-religious.

Mikhlelet Yehudah ve-Shomron (Judea and Samaria College) was founded in 1983 as a regional college-level academic institution under the auspices of Bar-Ilan University and had approximately 8,000 students. Ariel's industrial zone housed over 100 factories in the fields of electronics, food, metallurgy, computers, and aviation, employing 3,000 people. A technological park was established in 1992 and the 100-room Eshel Hashomron Hotel at the entrance to the city opened its doors in 1991. Ron Nachman served as mayor of Ariel for five consecutive terms from 1985, having served as chairman of the municipal council until that time. The peace talks which began in the 1990s cast a pall on the future of the city, and its inclusion inside the security fence built to protect Israel from Palestinian terrorist attacks became a heated issue in Israeli politics.

WEBSITE: www.ariel.muni.il.

[Shaked Gilboa (2nd ed.)]

ARIEL (Leibovitz), DOV (1860–1943), *Bilu pioneer. Ariel, who was born in the Kovno province, joined the first group of Bilu and acted as its propagandist in Russia. In 1884 he went to Ereẓ Israel and joined other Bilu members living in Jaffa and doing agricultural work at Mikveh Israel. Later that year he helped to found Gederah, the first Bilu colony. Ariel served for many years as chairman and secretary of the Gederah Committee, was its representative to the *yishuv* authorities, and published a booklet (*Ha-Moshavah Gederah*, 1900) and many articles about Gederah.

BIBLIOGRAPHY: Tidhar, 2 (1947), 722–4; S. Ben-Zion (Gutman), *Yissud Gederah* (1930).

[Benjamin Jaffe]

ARIEL (Fisher), JOSEPH (1893–1964), Israeli diplomat. Born in Odessa, Fisher was active in the Zionist movement from his early youth, and as a result of his activities in the Zionist student organization He-Ḥaver, he was imprisoned by the Czarist authorities. He immigrated to Ereẓ Israel in 1924 and, entering the service of the Jewish National Fund, was sent to Paris, where he directed the JNF until 1950. There he founded the bi-weekly *La Terre Retrouvée*, of which he was editor. After the Nazi occupation of France in 1940, Fisher maintained clandestine Zionist activities at Lyons. He was one of the active members of the Conseil Representatif des Juifs de France (C.R.I.F.) from its inception.

On returning to Israel in 1950, he was appointed Israeli ambassador to Belgium (1952–57), during which period he organized a visit to Israel by the Queen Mother Elisabeth of Belgium. In 1960, he was appointed director of the department of foreign relations of *Yad Vashem and engaged in research on the Holocaust in France. He contributed extensively to periodicals and wrote a number of books, including *Un Peuple Renaît* (1938) and memoirs of the Zionist movement in Russia during the period of the Bolshevik Revolution, which were published in *He-Avar*, a journal devoted to the history of the Jews in Russia.

[Jacob Tsur (2nd ed.)]

ARIELI, YEHOSHUA (Loebl; 1916–2002), Israeli historian. Born in Karlovy Vary (Carlsbad), Czechoslovakia, Arieli was taken to Ereẓ Israel in 1931. In 1933 he joined kibbutz Hefẓi Bah. In WWII he served in the British Army, was captured by the Germans, and was a prisoner of war for four years. In 1947 he joined the *Haganah, and was placed in charge of the Jerusalem Gadna (Youth Battalions). In 1953 he received his Ph.D. in American history from Harvard University. Arieli was appointed to the staff of the Hebrew University in 1966 and from 1967 served as chairman of the department of American studies. Between 1976 and 1991 he served as chairman and member of the board of directors of the Historical Society of Israel. Arieli's main fields of research and teaching were American history, historiography, and early modern history. Among his books is *Political Thought in the United States*, 2 vols. (1967–68). In 1993 he was awarded the Israel Prize for history.

ARIELI, YIẒḤAK (1898–1974), rabbi. Arieli was born in Jerusalem and studied in local yeshivot. He was one of the first heads of Yeshivat Merkaz ha-Rav in Jerusalem, founded by R. Abraham Isaac *Kook, where he served on the staff and was administrator for about 40 years. In 1924 he participated in the founding of the Jerusalem suburbs of Kiryat Shemuel and Neveh Sha'anan. In 1942 he was appointed rabbi of the Jerusalem suburb Keneset Israel. He represented the Chief Rabbinate on the government committee on autopsies. His works include *Einayim la-Mishpat* (1936–66), notes on, and a précis of, the methodology of the Babylonian and Jerusalem Talmuds; *Shirat ha-Geulah* (1956), on the month of Nisan and a commentary on the Passover *Haggadah*; and *Yeraḥ ha-Eitanim* (1964), on the month of Tishri. He was awarded the Israel Prize for rabbinical literature in 1966.

ARIKHA, AVIGDOR (1929–), Israeli painter. Arikha was born in Redauts, Bukovina, the second child of Haim-Karl and Perla Dlugacz. He discovered the power of his art in 1944, when his drawing ability helped get him released from a Romanian concentration camp, where he had been imprisoned from 1941. He escaped with his sister to Palestine, to kibbutz Ma'aleh ha-Ḥamishah, and joined the *Haganah. With support from Henrietta *Szold he studied at the Bezalel Academy of Art in Jerusalem under Mordecai *Ardon and Isidor *Aschheim. In 1949 Arikha began his studies in the Ecole Nationale des Beaux Arts in Paris, and from that time divided his life between Israel and Paris.

Arikha's preferred fields of art are drawing and book illustration. His illustrations for Samuel Beckett's *Nouvelles et Textes pour Rien* (1957) were the beginning of a long friendship. His main art style was figurative, but during the 1960s he tried abstraction. During the 1970s he improved his graphic and painting techniques and had many exhibitions in Europe and the United States. In 1981, on the recommendation of the Scottish National Portrait Gallery, he painted a portrait of Queen Elizabeth. During this time he created public works of art, such as stained-glass windows for the Bnei Israel Synagogue, Woonsocket, Rhode Island (1961) as well as at the City Council Hall of the Jerusalem Municipality (1972). During the 1980s Arikha became a curator and made five short films on famous artists (1985). In 1992 the BBC, produced a film about his work.

Arikha's art deals with everyday life. There are interior scenes, portraits of family members, and still lifes of his intimate surroundings and views of his studio. One can recognize a clear influence of photography in his work, but the complex compositions and vivid colors emphasize his abstract painting ability. In general his painted figures and objects are placed individually in the frame of the work, yet the artistic forms are complex and contribute to the interest of the whole (*Going Out*, 1981, Israel Museum, Jerusalem).

In his Jerusalem landscapes Arikha dealt with the subject of light (*Jerusalem Seen From the South*, 1980, Tate Gallery, London). He depicts the light as though from a mystical source, accenting the view. At the same time the dazzling power of light constitutes a technical challenge for him, which constitutes the difference between his Jerusalem drawings and those created in Europe.

In honor of his 70th birthday a retrospective exhibition was presented in Israel's two major museums, the Tel Aviv Museum of Art and the Israel Museum in Jerusalem.

BIBLIOGRAPHY: Israel Museum, *Avigdor Arikha – Selected Paintings 1953–1997* (1998); Tel Aviv Museum of Art, *Avigdor Arikha – Drawings* (1998).

[Ronit Steinberg (2nd ed.)]

ARIOCH (Heb. אַרְיוֹךְ). (1) A king of an unknown region, Ellasar, allied with *Chedorlaomer, king of Elam (Gen. 14:1ff.). (2) A captain of the guard in Babylon in the days of Nebuchadnezzar and Daniel (Dan. 2:14ff.). (3) A king of the Elymaeans (Elamites) in Judith 1:6. (4) An angel in II Enoch (the Slavonic Enoch) 33:11. While the first three cannot be identified with any independently attested persons, the name Arioch is probably identical with those of Arri(w)uk(i), a vassal of King Zimrilim of Mari (c. 1700 B.C.E.), and possibly related to Awariku king of the Danunians, and superior of Azatiwadda the author of the Phoenician-Hieroglyphic Luwian bilingual inscriptions of Karatepe (Adana, Turkey; first half of the first millennium B.C.E.).

BIBLIOGRAPHY: Koehler-Baumgartner, 87, 1054; H. Donner and W. Roellig, *Kanaanaeische und aramaeische Inschriften*, 2 (1963), 39; W. Baumgartner, *Hebraeisches und aramaeisches Lexikon zum Alten Testament*, 1 (1967), 85. **ADD. BIBLIOGRAPHY:** K. Younger, in: COS, 2, 148.

[Harold Louis Ginsberg]

ARIPUL, SAMUEL BEN ISAAC (1540?–after 1586), rabbinic scholar and preacher; probably born in Salonika. Although he was one of the greatest preachers in the 16th century, little is known about his life. From 1569 to 1571 he was seriously ill, and on his recovery wrote his book *Mizmor le-Todah* ("A Psalm of Thanksgiving"). Some time after 1571 he was in Constantinople. In 1576 he was in Venice where he undertook the publication of his works. It appears that he later settled in Safed for in the introduction to his *Ne'im Zemirot* he is referred to as "from the city of Safed." His books are rabbinical and philosophical commentaries on the Bible which emphasize its ethical message. He treats at length the problem of the redemption of Israel and quotes from the Zohar. At the beginning and end of each book he wrote poems on its contents. He printed the contents of his five books as a pamphlet, *Aggadat Shemu'el*, appended to *Mizmor le-Todah* which seems to be the earliest Hebrew book-prospectus to survive. This work contains panegyrics by two scholars of Salonika, where he evidently spent part of his adult life. Aripul previously had published *Zevaḥ Todah* (Constantinople, 1572), a homiletical exposition of Psalm 119 (also included as an introduction to his *Mizmor le-Todah*). His published books are (1) *Mizmor le-Todah* (Venice, 1576), on Psalms 112–34, the last section (on Psalms 120–34) being republished under the title *Ne'im Zemirot* (Cracow, 1576); (2) *Sar Shalom* (Safed, 1579) on the Song of Songs; and (3) *Lev Ḥakham* (Constantinople, 1586) on Ecclesiastes. His *Imrat Eloha* on the Pentateuch (mentioned in *Sar Shalom*) and his *Va'ad la-Ḥakhamim* on the liturgy (mentioned in *Lev Ḥakham*, p. 44b) have not been published.

BIBLIOGRAPHY: Rivkind, in: KS, 4 (1928/29), 279; A. Yaari, *Ha-Defus ha-Ivri be-Arẓot ha-Mizraḥ*, 1 (1936), 18.

ARISON, TED (1924–1998), Israeli shipping magnate. Arison was born in Zikhron Ya'akov and attended the Herzlia Gymnasia in Tel Aviv before studying for a year at the American University of Beirut. He fought in Italy and Germany in World War II as part of the Jewish Brigade of the British Army and again in Israel's War of Independence as a lieutenant colonel. After the war he set up a shipping agency but liquidated his operations in the early 1950s and moved to the United States, where he built up a major shipping business, culminating in 1972 when he started Carnival Cruise Lines for the holiday cruise trade. Under the aegis of the Carnival Corporation he acquired additional lines, such as Holland America and Cunard, becoming the biggest cruise line operator in the world with 46 ships. In 1990 he resigned as president of Carnival in favor of his son, MICKY, and in 1994 returned to Israel, setting up Arison Investments Ltd., which purchased a controlling interest in Bank Hapoalim for $1 billion as well as the Shikun u-Fittuaḥ construction company, both giants in the *Histadrut business empire.

A long-time resident of Miami, Arison established the National Foundation for the Advancement of the Arts there in 1981 as well as the New World Symphony Orchestra in 1987 with Michael Tilson Thomas. He was also instrumental in getting the city the NBA's Miami Heat. The Arison Foundation was active in philanthropical projects in both the United States and Israel. His personal fortune was estimated at as much as $10 billion.

Upon his death, his daughter, SHARI, took over the family's Israeli operations, including Bank Hapoalim, while Micky Arison continued to head Carnival from Miami. In 2005 she ranked 84th on the Forbes List, with an estimated worth of $5.5 billion, making her Israel's wealthiest citizen. In 1999 she founded Matan, a charity modeled on United Way.

ARISTEAS (Gr. Αριστέας; second or early first century B.C.E.), author of a history *On the Jews*, of which only one fragment consisting of about 16 lines survives. This summarizes the narrative portions of the book of Job and is inserted in an account of Genesis 36. Aristeas relates that Job was the son of Esau and his Edomite wife Bassarha, a native of Ausis, located between Idumea and Arabia. Formerly Job's name had been Jobab (Gen. 36:33). A just man, rich in cattle, God tried him by causing many misfortunes. Robbers drove away his cattle and later his camels, a fire from heaven burned his sheep together with the shepherds, the house fell down killing all of his children, ulcers covered his body. Eliphas, the king of the Themanites, Baldad, the tyrant of the Saucheans, and Sophar, the king of the Minneans, as well as Elihu, the son of Barachiel, the Zobite (read: Bozite), came to visit him. Job, however, rejected their consolations, saying that even without their help he would remain steadfast in his piety. God was pleased with Job and restored him to his former wealth.

Scholars generally agree that Aristeas is not identical with the author of the so-called Letter of *Aristeas to Philocrates; this opinion is chiefly based on stylistic differences. *Alexander Polyhistor, however, citing sections 88–90 of the Letter of Aristeas, which he names *On The Interpretation of Jewish Laws*, believed that its author also wrote the fragment on Job. Aristeas is clearly dependent on the Septuagint version of Job, but the postscript in the Septuagint (Job 42:17b–e) is in turn dependent on Aristeas. This postscript was taken from a passage dealing with Genesis 36 and apparently corrects Aristeas. Bassarha is said by Aristeas to have been Jobab's (Job's) mother because of a misunderstanding of Genesis 36:33, an error compounded by a slip which confused Bassarha with Basemath, which made Jobab (Job) the son of Esau. Septuagint, Job 42:17 corrects Aristeas' slip, but repeats his original error. There remains the problem of the meaning of the postscript in the Septuagint which alludes to a "Syriac Book." The allusion may be to a lost apocryphon to Job, echoes of which are possibly still discernible in the Testament of Job, *Bava Batra* 15b, Targum Job 2:9, and Jerome (on Gen. 22:21). Aristeas, too, may have been dependent on this Palestinian source.

BIBLIOGRAPHY: Eusebius, *Praeparatio Evangelica*, tr. by J. Gifford, 9 (1903), 25; G. Riessler, *Altjuedisches Schrifttum ausserhalb der Bibel* (1928), 178; Schuerer, Gesch, 3 (1909^4), 480; Ginzberg, Legends, 5 (1955), 384.

[Ben Zion Wacholder]

ARISTEAS, LETTER OF, Jewish-Alexandrian literary composition written by an anonymous Jew, in the form of a letter allegedly written to his brother Philocrates by Aristeas, a Greek in the court of Ptolemy II Philadelphus (285–246 B.C.E.). The contents of the book are as follows: On the advice of his courtiers, Demetrius of Phalerum and Aristeas, Ptolemy Philadelphus orders the sacred writings of the Jews to be translated for the library of Alexandria. The king writes to Eleazar, the high priest in Jerusalem, requesting that expert translators be sent to him. His letter is accompanied by a precious gift for the Temple. Aristeas at the head of an Egyptian delegation goes to Jerusalem and returns with a detailed description of Judea, Jerusalem, the Temple and its services, and his talks with Eleazar. Eleazar sends Ptolemy II 72 elders, six from each of the 12 tribes, who are well versed in both the Mosaic Law and in the customs of Greek society. The king gives them an elaborate reception and for ten days holds banquets in their honor in the course of which he discovers their great wisdom. They are then taken to the Island of Pharos and within 72 days they translate the Scripture into Greek. The translation is approved by the king and by the representatives of the Alexandrian Jewish community, and the translators are sent back home laden with gifts.

This story, based on a legend about the Septuagint current in Alexandria by the third century B.C.E., is more a historical romance than an accurate account. The author of the Letter used this legend as a framework which he filled with certain ideas that he wished to disseminate among his Jewish readers. He describes the Greeks as admirers of Judaism and pleads for the establishment of closer relations between the two peoples. He considers their idolatrous religion no barrier, since he believes that the Greeks too worship the one and only God under the name Zeus. He describes Judaism as pure monotheism which does not stand in conflict with the ideas accepted in Greek philosophy. This emerges in particular from the conversations with the 72 elders at the banquet. He gives a symbolic interpretation to the commandments as well as a rational explanation. A certain dualism thus underlies the outlook expressed in the Letter: on the one hand separation of Jews from non-Jews as a result of their religious observances, and on the other hand their approximation to Greek culture. This reflects the outlook of the upper class of the Alexandrian Jewish community, who though they mixed freely with the Greeks in business and were influenced by Greek culture, nevertheless adhered to the principles of Judaism on which the existence of the autonomous Alexandrian Jewish community depended.

The book is written in Hellenistic Greek, influenced by the official language in Ptolemaic Egypt. (For another account of the Septuagint Translation, see *Philo.) There is considerable disagreement among scholars as to the date of the Letter, and Elias Bickerman has attributed it to the late second century B.C.E.

BIBLIOGRAPHY: H.T. Andrews, in: R.H. Charles, *The Apocrypha and Pseudepigrapha of the Old Testament in English*, vol. 2 (1913), 83ff.; Wendland, in: E. Kautzsch, *Apocryphen und Pseudepigraphen*, 2 (1900), 1–31; H. St. John Thackeray, *Letter of Aristeas* (1918); Bickerman, in: ZNW, 29 (1930), 280ff.; M. Hadas, *Aristeas to Philocrates* (1951); R. Tramontano, *Lettera di Aristea a Filocrate* (1931); A. Tcherikover, *Ha-Yehudim ba-Olam ha-Yevani ve-ha-Romi* (1961), 316–18; idem, *Hellenistic Civilization and the Jews* (1959), 348. **ADD. BIBLI-**

OGRAPHY: S. Jellicoe, *The Septuagint and Modern Study* (1968); R.J. Shutt, "Letter of Aristeas (A New Translation and Introduction)," in: J.H. Charlesworth (ed.), *The Old Testament Pseudepigrapha.*, vol. 2 (1985); L.J. Greenspoon, "Truth and Legend about the Septuagint," in: *Approaches to the Bible. Vol. I: Composition, Transmission and Language* (1994), 184–96.

[Avigdor (Victor) Tcherikover]

ARISTOBULUS I (Judah), king of Judea 104–103 B.C.E.; eldest son of John *Hyrcanus I. According to his father's will Aristobulus was to become high priest while his mother was to receive the throne. However, not content merely with the priestly office, Aristobulus seized the throne, cast his mother in prison where she died of hunger, and incarcerated all his brothers, except *Antigonus, for whom he had a particular affection. According to Josephus, Aristobulus later had Antigonus put to death, following an allegation that Antigonus was plotting against his life. According to Josephus (Ant., 11:301), Aristobulus was the first of the Hasmoneans to adopt the title of king. The statement of Strabo, however (26:2, 40), that Alexander Yannai was the first, is more trustworthy since on extant coins Aristobulus is designated only as high priest while Alexander Yannai is specifically designated as king. Josephus also states that Aristobulus called himself "Philhellene." This title was assumed by other Eastern rulers who adopted Hellenistic culture. It is surprising however that Aristobulus should do so since the attitude of the Hasmoneans to the "Hellenes" was far from cordial. It is possible that it is a misreading for Philadelphus, which is the name he assumed as a sign of his affection for his brother Antigonus. But the use of the term is indicative of the extent of Hellenistic influence in his court. Aristobulus followed both the cultural and military policies of his father. The statement of Josephus that he conquered part of the territory of the Itureans, forcibly converting them to Judaism, probably refers to the conquest of Upper Galilee by his father, John Hyrcanus, since the Itureans inhabited the Lebanon. In this campaign it is possible that Aristobulus was in command of his father's army.

BIBLIOGRAPHY: Jos., Ant., 13:301ff.; Jos., Wars, 1:70ff.; Klausner, Bayit Sheni, 3 (1950²), 141ff.; Schuerer, Gesch, 3 (1904⁴), 273ff.; Graetz, Gesch, 3 (1905⁵), 118ff.; Meyer, Ursp, 2 (1921), 274 n. 4; A. Schalit, *Hordos ha-Melekh* (1964³), 107, 409 (esp. n. 183).

[Abraham Schalit]

ARISTOBULUS II (d. 49 B.C.E.), younger son of Alexander Yannai and Salome Alexandra. Aristobulus, who was the last independent Hasmonean king, reigned from 67 to 63 B.C.E. Toward the end of Salome's reign, Aristobulus made himself the spokesman of the Sadducees and complained of discrimination by the Pharisees who were in control of the royal council. When the queen was stricken by a fatal illness, he joined his Sadducee supporters who commanded the fortresses of Judea. With their aid he captured 28 strongholds and hired mercenaries from the Lebanon and Trachonitis in order to subdue the entire country and prevent his elder brother *Hyrcanus from seizing the throne. With the queen's consent, Aristobulus' wife and children were taken as hostages and confined to the citadel above the Temple in Jerusalem (Jos., Ant., 13:422–9). After Salome's death Aristobulus immediately declared war on Hyrcanus and won over most of his troops. He defeated Hyrcanus in a battle near Jericho and forced him to abdicate. But at the instigation of Hyrcanus' adviser, *Antipater II, *Aretas, king of the Nabateans, attacked Aristobulus with a large force and defeated him. Aristobulus fled and barricaded himself in the Temple area where he was besieged by Aretas and Hyrcanus (Jos., Ant., 14:4–21). When Scaurus, one of Pompey's generals, arrived in Damascus in 65 B.C.E. and heard of the fighting, he immediately left for Judea. He negotiated with the envoys of both brothers. Aristobulus offered him a large sum of money with the result that the Roman general decided to support him, and ordered Aretas to return home. Aretas obeyed. Aristobulus seized this opportunity to attack the withdrawing army and deal it a severe blow (*ibid.*, 29–33). Pompey arrived in Damascus in the spring of 63. He received delegations from the two brothers as well as one from the Jewish people. While the ambassadors of the brothers pleaded the cause of their masters, the people's emissaries urged that the country be freed of monarchical rule and restored to government by the high priest. Pompey deferred his decision (*ibid.*, 40–47). Aristobulus thereupon took the hasty and ill-advised decision to leave Pompey and return to Judea. Pompey, suspecting that he had embarked on an anti-Roman course, set out after him to the fortress of Alexandrium. The Roman commander demanded that Aristobulus surrender all the fortresses in Judea. After some hesitation he promised to accede. When he failed to do so, and continued on his way to Jerusalem, Pompey followed him to Jericho. Aristobulus returned to the Roman camp and promised to fulfill Pompey's terms. Pompey sent Gabinius to take over Jerusalem. However, Aristobulus' supporters resisted and closed the city gates. Pompey thereupon moved his entire force to Jerusalem. The peace party in the city gained the upper hand against Aristobulus' men, and the gates were opened. Aristobulus' men fled to the Temple area, and Pompey besieged the Temple fortifications. After a siege of three months, the Romans burst into the Temple precincts and inflicted heavy casualties. Pompey entered the inner sanctuary itself. With this, the Hasmonean kingdom ceased to exist (63 B.C.E.) and Aristobulus and his children were carried off as prisoners to Rome. In 56 B.C.E., however, Aristobulus and his son Antigonus succeeded in escaping and reached Jerusalem. He assembled a new army but was defeated and took refuge with the remnant of his troops in Machaerus. After two days' fighting the stronghold fell to a determined Roman onslaught. Aristobulus was again taken prisoner, sent to Rome in chains, and there imprisoned until Julius Caesar conquered the city in 49 B.C.E. Caesar planned to send him to Syria with two legions to fight Pompey's supporters, but Aristobulus was poisoned by Pompey's men before he was able to leave for the East. His body was later sent to Judea for burial.

BIBLIOGRAPHY: Jos., Ant., 14:48–79, 62–97, 123–4; Jos., Wars, 1:117–58, 171–4, 183–4; Klausner, Bayit Sheni, 3 (1950^2), 214–28, 238–40; A. Schalit, *Hordos ha-Melekh* (1964^3), 13 ff.; Schuerer, Gesch, 1 (1901^4), 291 ff., 341 ff.; Graetz, Hist, 2 (1893), 47, 56–57; F.M. Abel, *Histoire de la Palestine*, 1 (1952), 287 ff.

[Abraham Schalit]

ARISTOBULUS III (Hebrew name **Jonathan**; d. 35 B.C.E.), last Hasmonean high priest. His father was Alexander, son of *Aristobulus II, his mother was Alexandra, daughter of Hyrcanus II, and his sister *Mariamne the Hasmonean, wife of Herod. Aristobulus was due to become high priest, but Herod was afraid of Hasmonean influence on the people, and appointed the Babylonian *Hananel in his place. Mariamne and Alexandra considered this appointment discrimination against the Hasmonean dynasty. According to Josephus, Alexandra asked Cleopatra, queen of Egypt, to intercede with Mark Antony on her son's behalf. Antony ignored her request, but he summoned Aristobulus on the advice of Delius, a Roman who had visited Jerusalem and admired both the lad's good looks and the beauty of Mariamne. Herod feared that this visit might endanger his regime, and wrote to Antony that if Aristobulus left Judea, anti-Roman riots would ensue. Antony consequently canceled Aristobulus' visit. Most of this story about Delius is probably not authentic. It appears in part to have been the invention of Herod's sister, *Salome, who wished to incite Herod against Mariamne, and in part a story that developed as a result of Cleopatra's advice that Alexandra send her son to Antony. In any event, Herod did change his mind, dismissed Hananel, and appointed Aristobulus, hoping thereby to keep him under supervision. However, when Aristobulus appeared before the people for the first time, dressed in the ceremonial garb of the high priest, on the Feast of Tabernacles in 36 B.C.E., he was welcomed with cries of joy and undisguised affection. Herod again saw Aristobulus as a threat to his power and resolved to murder him. Aristobulus was drowned in the baths at Jericho by Herod's soldiers.

BIBLIOGRAPHY: Jos., Wars, 1:437; Jos., Ant., 15:21–64; 20:247 ff.; Klausner, Bayit Sheni, 4 (1950^2), 12–14; A.Schalit, *Hordos ha-Melekh* (1960), 61–66; A.H.M. Jones, *The Herods of Judaea* (1938), 37, 51–54.

[Abraham Schalit]

ARISTOBULUS (c. 35 B.C.E.–7 B.C.E.), son of *Herod and *Mariamne. Of Hasmonean lineage, both Aristobulus and his elder brother *Alexander were regarded as eventual heirs to the throne. The two were sent to Rome for their education. After his return to Judea, Aristobulus married Berenice, daughter of Herod's sister, Salome. Life at the court began with a long succession of slander against Aristobulus and his brother, who, though apparently more prudent, was still not beyond suspicion. Herod, although reluctant at first to believe all the stories about his sons, was eventually convinced of their treachery. This resulted in the reinstatement of Antipater, Herod's son by Doris, as heir to the throne (13 B.C.E.). Antipater and Salome went to great lengths to arouse the king's hatred toward his Hasmonean offspring, finally producing a forged letter as evidence of their plot to kill Herod. The youths fled to the fortress of Alexandrium, but they were seized and imprisoned despite their protestations of innocence. In a last desperate attempt, Aristobulus threatened to denounce Salome to the king as having communicated state secrets to his enemy, the Arab Syllaeus, if she did not come to the princes' aid. Salome, however, reported the incident to Herod, who thereupon ordered the youths to be confined separately in chains. Permission was obtained from Augustus to try the brothers, but before a joint council of the king's relatives and the provincial governors. At the trial, held at Berytus (Beirut), the princes were given no opportunity to defend themselves and were condemned. A dispute then ensued among the Roman officials as to the penalty to be administered, Saturninus, the presiding officer, recommending clemency, and the majority demanding the death sentence. The majority view finally prevailed and the brothers were executed by strangulation in Sebaste (Samaria). The bodies were sent to Alexandrium for burial near the grave of Alexander, the princes' maternal grandfather. Augustus, on learning of the execution, was reported as exclaiming "he would sooner be Herod's pig than Herod's son" (Macrobius, *Saturnalia* 2:4, no. 11).

By his marriage with Berenice, Aristobulus had three sons: Herod, Agrippa, and Aristobulus; and two daughters: Herodias and Mariamne. The children were cared for with great devotion by their grandfather, King Herod.

BIBLIOGRAPHY: Jos., Ant., 15:342; 16:11, 133, 193 ff.; 17:12 ff., 133 ff.; Jos., Wars, 1:445 ff.; Schuerer, Gesch, 1 (1901^4), 369–73, 407–11; Schuerer, Hist, 149–56; A. Schalit, *Hordos ha-Melekh* (1964), index.

[Isaiah Gafni]

ARISTOBULUS, brother of Agrippa I and youngest of the three sons of Aristobulus, the son of Herod, and Berenice. After executing their father on charges of treason in 7 B.C.E. Herod brought up the three children with great devotion. They married women of high rank, Aristobulus marrying Jotape, the daughter of King Sampsigeramus of Emesa. However, relations between the two younger brothers, Agrippa I and Aristobulus, became strained. Their mutual animosity was displayed before Flaccus, the governor of Syria (c. 32–35 C.E.). A boundary dispute between Damascus and Sidon had come before the governor, who at the time was entertaining Agrippa. The Damascenes offered Agrippa a large sum of money in return for his support. After learning of the incident, Aristobulus denounced his brother before the governor for accepting the bribe. Flaccus was thus forced to break off his friendship with Agrippa. In 40 C.E., Aristobulus was one of the Jewish leaders who appeared before Petronius, governor of Syria, appealing to him to prevent the erection of the statue in the Temple ordered by the emperor Caligula.

BIBLIOGRAPHY: Jos., Wars, 1:552; 2:221; Jos., Ant., 18: 133–5, 151–4, 273ff.; Schuerer, Gesch, 1 (1901[4]), 504; A.H.M. Jones, *The Herods of Judaea* (1938), 139, 186–7, 198.

[Isaiah Gafni]

ARISTOBULUS OF PANEAS (first half of second century B.C.E.), Jewish Hellenistic philosopher; one of the earliest allegorical interpreters of the Bible. The author of II Maccabees (1:10) describes Aristobulus as "the teacher of King Ptolemy," presumably Philometer VI (181–145 B.C.E.). Clement of Alexandria (middle of second century C.E.) in his *Stromata* (1:15; 5:14) and Eusebius (c. 260–c. 340) in his *Praeparatio evangelica* (8:9; 13:12) mention Aristobulus among the members of the Aristotelian school, but this cannot be taken too literally, since he undoubtedly was also influenced by Platonic and Stoic teachings. Clement of Alexandria also mentions that Aristobulus was the author of several works, but it appears that he had in mind one rather extensive work known to the Church Fathers and described by them as an exposition of the Mosaic law. Portions of this work, which was written in the form of a dialogue between King Ptolemy and Aristobulus, in which Aristobulus answers the king's questions concerning Scripture, have been preserved in books by Clement of Alexandria (*Stromata*, 1:22; 6:3) and Eusebius (*Historia ecclesiastica*, 7:32; *Praeparatio evangelica*, 7:14; 8:10; 13:12). These surviving fragments contain expositions of sections of Genesis and Exodus. A statement in the margin of the Florentine manuscript of Clement of Alexandria's *Stromata* dating from the 16th century (cf. Azariah dei Rossi, *Me'or Einayim* (1864–86), 146) to the effect that Aristobulus' writings were extant in their entirety at the time, is open to doubt.

Allegorical Interpretation

Aristobulus' fundamental premise in expounding the Pentateuch is that descriptions of the Deity must be interpreted in a manner appropriate to the nature of God; when Scripture applies to God expressions such as "hands," "feet," "arm," "face," and "walking," these are not to be understood literally. He appeals to the king not to fall into the error of comprehending divine matters anthropomorphically in the manner of mythology, but to endeavor to understand them in a manner commensurate with their exalted nature. The request of Aristobulus to the king may reflect the influence of Antisthenes the Cynic (born c. 444 B.C.E.) who taught that an understanding of the nature of cosmic being must be predicated upon the principle of the unity of the Deity. This supposition finds corroboration in the fact that Antisthenes' method of expounding Homer allegorically influenced Jewish allegorical methods in many ways. Aristobulus draws additional support for his argument by pointing to such linguistic usages as the Greek phrase μεγάλη χεὶρ ("the great hand"), which connotes "military power," stating that biblical terms such as "the hand of the Lord" were to be understood in a similar sense.

Of particular interest is the interpretation given by Aristobulus to the expressions "standing" and "descending" as applied to God in the Bible. "Standing," in his view, is a term connoting constancy or established order in natural phenomena, such as the regular succession of day and night, or of the seasons of the year. "Descending" signifies the revelation at Mt. Sinai, i.e., the manifestation of God's sublimity to human beings on earth.

In one of the fragments Aristobulus discusses the Hebrew calendar and establishes the rule that Passover always falls immediately after the vernal equinox.

In another discussion Aristobulus posits that portions of the Pentateuch had been rendered into Greek before it was translated in its entirety in the days of Ptolemy Philadelphus (see *Septuagint), and that these portions reached Pythagoras, Socrates, and Plato and formed the basis of their philosophical teachings. In developing their philosophical systems these Greek philosophers were influenced by the biblical account of creation. This makes it possible to understand why they say that they hear the voice of God when they delve deeply into the works of creation: they mean to say that they hear the echo of the cosmic harmony established by the Divine Will – just as the "voice of God" in the biblical account of creation, according to Aristobulus, denotes the manifestation of the Divine Power in the establishment of order and harmony in the world. The account of the six days of creation, Aristobulus explains, is not to be understood literally. The enumeration of six days is only for the purpose of fixing the sequence of the different phases of creation. Similarly, God's resting on the seventh day must not be understood as rest following laborious toil, but as the bestowal of a permanence upon the universe.

In Aristobulus' exposition of the account of creation the number seven is of great importance. Not only did God rest on the seventh day but also instituted the seventh day as a day of rest for man, in order that man would be free one day to contemplate the order and harmony of creation. This contemplation is accomplished by means of the intellect, man's seventh and most exalted faculty (the others being the five senses and the power of speech). Still further, the seven faculties of man correspond to the seven planets – evidence of the harmony between man and the universe as a whole. Aristobulus holds that the numerical symbolism which he finds in the biblical account of creation was the source of the Pythagorean theory of numbers.

In order to support his contention that the source of Greek philosophy lies in the Bible, Aristobulus, in his work, cites many passages from ancient Greek literature which to his mind reflect biblical ideas. There are indications that these citations were taken by Aristobulus from a collection of quotations that he had before him, which was used as a means for propagating the Jewish religion in the Hellenistic world.

BIBLIOGRAPHY: Schuerer, Gesch, 3 (1909[4]), 512ff.; D. Neumark, *Geschichte der juedischen Philosophie des Mittelalters*, 2 (1910), 386–90; W. Von Christ, et al., *Geschichte der griechischen Literatur*,

2 (1920[6]), 604–6; J. Gutmann, *Ha-Sifrut ha-Yehudit ha-Hellenistit*, 1 (1958), 186–220; Heinemann, in: *Mnemosyne*, 5 (1952), 130–8; N. Walter, *Thoraausleger Aristobulos* (1964).

[Joshua Gutmann]

ARISTON OF PELLA (mid-second century C.E.), Palestinian author of a lost dialogue between a Jew and a Jewish convert to Christianity which apparently discussed the question of messianic prophecies in the Old Testament. Whether this work contained the passage on the *Bar Kokhba rebellion cited by *Eusebius or whether Ariston wrote a separate monograph on this war is not known.

°**ARISTOTLE** (fourth century B.C.E.), Greek philosopher and founder of the peripatetic school. Aristotle achieved a unique rank in the estimation of Muslim and Jewish medieval philosophers, who often refer to him simply as "the philosopher." Maimonides stated that Aristotle had "reached the highest degree of intellectual perfection open to man, barring only the still higher degree of prophetic inspiration" (letter to Samuel ibn Tibbon, in: JQR, 25 (1934/35), 380; cf. Averroes, *Commentarium Magnum in Aristotelis De Anima* (1953), 3:2, 433). While Aristotelian influences made some inroads into medieval Jewish philosophy from its beginning (when it followed the teachings of the *Kalām and *Neoplatonism), Aristotelianism, in varying forms, became the predominant trend from Abraham *Ibn Daud (12th century) to the middle of the 17th century. As a reaction, a countermovement arose in traditionalist and kabbalistic circles from the 13th century onward, which included a critical evaluation of Aristotelian teachings, and can hence be considered a part of medieval Aristotelianism. Ḥasdai *Crescas was the most eminent philosophical critic in this movement.

Jewish Aristotelianism

Jewish Aristotelianism may be divided into two periods. From the ninth until the end of the twelfth century, Jews, living in the Muslim world and knowing Arabic, had available to them the Aristotelian literature existing in that language; from the thirteenth century on, Jews, living in the Christian world and using Hebrew for their philosophic writings, depended on Hebrew translations of Aristotelian works. During the first of these periods, the works of Aristotle (with the exception of the *Politics*, the *Eudemian Ethics, Magna Moralia*, and the *Dialogues*), together with many of the Greek commentaries on his works, became known through Arabic translations which were made between about 800 C.E. and 1000 C.E. (for the history of these translations see R. Walzer, *Greek into Arabic* (1962), 6–8, 60–113; in EIS, 1 (1960), 630ff., s.v. Arisṭūṭālīs). In addition, Jews became familiar with the teachings of Aristotle, at times interspersed with neoplatonic doctrines, through the summaries, commentaries, and independent works of such Islamic philosophers as al-*Fārābī (c. 870–950), *Avicenna (930–1037), and Ibn Bājja (*Avempace, d. 1138). In the Islamic world, Aristotelian studies were put on a firm footing as early as the tenth century when al-Fārābī, in his *The Philosophy of Plato and Aristotle*, outlined the differences between the two philosophers. The Aristotelian orientation established by al-Fārābī was shared by two tenth-century Jews of Mosul, Ibn Abi Saʿīd al-Mawṣilī and his pupil Bishr ibn Samʿān (see Pines, in: PAAJR, 24 (1955), 103–36); though, as has been noted, Jewish philosophy did not become predominantly Aristotelian until Abraham Ibn Daud. This philosopher, in his *Emunah Ramah*, attacked the neoplatonic metaphysics of Solomon ibn *Gabirol, and expounded an Aristotelianism derived from the teachings of Avicenna. During the Islamic period, Aristotelianism reached its highpoint with *Maimonides, who tended toward the teachings of al-Fārābī.

Hebrew Translations

The opening of the second period was marked by Hebrew translations, from the Arabic, of works by Aristotle, by Hellenistic commentators, and by Islamic commentators and compilers. These Hebrew translations brought about knowledge of the following works by Aristotle: the logical writings (*Organon*, lit. "instrument"; Heb. *keli*); *Physics* (*Ha-Shema ha-Tivi*); *De Caelo* (*Sefer ha-Shamayim ve-ha-Olam*); *De Generatione et Corruptione* (*Sefer ha-Havayah ve-ha-Hefsed*); *Meterologica* (*Otot ha-Shamayim*); *De Animalibus* (*Sefer Ba'alei Ḥayyim*); *De Anima* (*Sefer ha-Nefesh*); *De Sensu et Sensato* (*Sefer ha-Ḥush ve-ha-Muḥash*); *Metaphysica* (*Sefer Mah she-Aḥar ha-Teva*); and the *Nicomachean Ethics* (*Sefer ha-Middot*). (For a listing of manuscripts, see Steinschneider, and the catalogues of the major libraries possessing collections of Hebrew philosophical manuscripts.) Most of this literature exists only in manuscript form.

Of special attraction to Jewish translators, commentators, and philosophic authors were the works of *Averroes (1126–1198), most of whose commentaries on Aristotle were translated from Arabic into Hebrew between 1189 and 1337, some of them twice. In fact, the Hebrew translations of Averroes became the major source for the knowledge of Aristotle in Jewish circles.

In addition to Hebrew translations of genuine Aristotelian works, there also existed Hebrew translations of a number of works, which, though not written by Aristotle, were attributed to him. These were *Liber de Pomo* (*Sefer ha-Tappu'aḥ*), purporting to prove that Aristotle had changed his views in his old age (see below: Aristotle in Jewish Legend), which Maimonides rejected as spurious (see above; letter to Samuel ibn Tibbon); *Secretum Secretorum* (*Sod ha-Sodot*) or *Pseudo-Politics* (*Sefer ha-Hanhagah*, Hebrew version with an English translation in M. Gaster, *Studies and Texts*); *Liber de causis*, based on Proclus' *Elements of Theology*; and *Theology of Aristotle*, representing excerpts from Plotinus' *Enneads*, which, except for a few quotations, has been lost in Hebrew translation. The Aristotelian literature in Hebrew, in turn, gave rise to Hebrew commentaries and to summaries. In addition, independent works in Hebrew were based on it. Philosophers who contributed to the Aristotelian literature, at times as followers of Aristotle, at times as his critics, included, during the 13th and 14th centuries – Samuel ibn *Tibbon, Jacob *Anatoli, Shem Tov ibn *Falaquera, Levi b. Abraham of Villefranche, Joseph *Kaspi, Zerahiah b. Isaac *Gracian, *Hillel b. Samuel of Verona, Isaac *Albalag, Moses *Abulafia, *Moses b. Joshua of Narbonne, and *Levi b. Gershom (Gersonides), their most outstanding representative; from the 15th to the 17th century – Simeon b. Ẓemaḥ *Duran, Joseph *Albo, the brothers Joseph and Isaac *Ibn Shem Tov, Abraham *Bibago, *Judah b. Jehiel Messer Leon, Elijah *Delmedigo, Moses *Almosnino, and Joseph Solomon *Delmedigo. (The exact relation of these philosophers to Aristotle may be gathered from the entries appearing under their names.)

Issues in Jewish Aristotelianism

Jewish Aristotelianism is a complex phenomenon, the general trends of which can be seen from some of its characteristic discussions. Jewish Aristotelianism differs from the antecedent types of medieval Jewish philosophy in its heightened awareness of the boundaries of faith and reason (see *Belief). Jewish Kalām and Neoplatonism used a variety of rational arguments to establish the truth of revelation, without seeing, on the whole, any sharp boundaries between philosophy and religion. By contrast, Jewish Aristotelians held that philosophic speculations must proceed without any regard to theological doctrines. They recognized as valid only demonstrative arguments, that is to say, arguments based on the standards for such arguments laid down by Aristotle (see *Analytica posteriora*, 73a, 21ff., and passim). Once the content of faith and reason had been delineated independently, it could be asked how the two realms are related. According to one view, represented by Maimonides, the teachings of religion and philosophy could be harmonized only in part. For example, Maimonides maintains that while many doctrines, such as the existence of God and His unity, can be demonstrated scientifically, the doctrine of *creatio ex nihilo* cannot, and one therefore has to be guided by prophetic revelation (Guide, 2:15). By contrast, Jewish Averroists like Isaac Albalag, Joseph Kaspi, and Moses of Narbonne (Narboni) opposed the tendency to harmonize faith and reason. Thus, e.g., they accepted the doctrine of the eternity of the world, holding that it had been demonstrated by Aristotle. More than that, Kaspi and Narboni more or less openly alleged that Maimonides' defense of *creatio ex nihilo* was only apparent, i.e., exoteric, and that his real, i.e., esoteric, view agreed with Aristotle's (Kaspi, *Maskiyyot Kesef*, 99–101; Moses of Narbonne, *Commentary to the Guide*, 34a; see on the latter Joseph Solomon Delmedigo's *Epistle*, published by A. Geiger, in his *Melo Ḥofnajim*, Ger. pt. 18 and 65, n. 70). Using the terms of the Christian Averroists, Albalag opposes the way of faith based on the prophets (*ex prophetis*) to the way of reason (*via rationis*), the one being the way of miracle, the other the way of nature. The two realms, according to Albalag, are distinct and incompatible (see G. Vajda, *Isaac Albalag*, 153–7, 165–75, 251–66; and Ch. Touati, in: REJ, 1 (1962), 35–47). A central and most crucial issue in Jewish Aristotelianism was the question of *creation. Aristotle based his notion that the world is eternal on the nature of time and motion (*Physics*, 8:1–3; *Metaphysics*, 12:6, 1–2; *De Caelo*, 1:10–12) and on the impossibility of assuming a genesis of prime matter (*Physics*, 1:9). In contrast to the Kalām theologians, who maintained the doctrine of temporal creation, the medieval Muslim philosophers interpreted creation as eternal, i.e., as the eternal procession of forms which emanate from the active or creative knowledge of God (see *Emanation). The task with which the Jewish Aristotelians were faced was either to disprove or to accept the notion of the world's eternity. Maimonides offers a survey and refutation of Kalām proofs for creation and advances his own theory of temporal creation (Guide, 2:17), for which he indicates the theological motive that miracles are possible only in a universe created by a spontaneous divine will (2:25). He rejects the emanationist theory of the Muslim Aristotelians since it fails to account for the origin of matter (2:22). In the course of the subsequent discussion, the more radical Aristotelians veered toward the Muslim philosophers' position, namely, the doctrine of eternal creation. Isaac Albalag, echoing Avicenna, regarded eternal creation as much more befitting to God than temporal creation (see Vajda, loc. cit., 134ff.). Gersonides maintained the notion of creation in time, but denied the possibility of a temporal origination of prime matter (*Milḥamot*, 6:1, 7). Crescas, on the other hand, sought to combine the concept of *creatio ex nihilo* with that of eternal creation of the world by God's design and will (*Or Adonai*, 3:1, 4–5). For a survey of the problems involved and the main positions taken, see Isaac *Abrabanel, *Shamayim Ḥadashim*. In the period following Crescas, when there was greater emphasis on the possibility of miracles, the doctrine of temporal creation gained greater adherence. Closely allied to the problem of creation is that of divine *providence. The Muslim philosophers, who accepted the doctrine of eternal creation, understood Aristotle to teach that providence is identical with the operations of nature, which safeguards the permanence of the species, but is unconcerned with individuals. To bring the Aristotelian position more into harmony with the teachings of religion, Ibn Daud (*Emunah Ramah*, 6:2) makes the point, later elaborated by Maimonides (Guide, 2:17), that divine providence extends to individual men according to their degree of intellectual perfection. The question of divine providence and the related problem of God's knowledge gave rise to a concurrent problem, that of divine foreknowledge and man's *free will. Narboni shows that God's foreknowledge does not necessarily preclude man's free action (see Guttmann, Philosophies, 203–7). Crescas, on the other hand, adopts a determinist position, but states that this does not invalidate the divine commandments (*Or Adonai*, 2:5, 3; see Guttmann, op. cit., 238–40). The topic of providence is linked with that of *reward and punishment in the hereafter, which, in turn, raises the question of individual immortality. Since Jewish Aristotelianism inherited not only Aristotle's own rather ambiguous doctrine of the soul, but also the discussions of the Greek commentators and Muslim philosophers that revealed sharp disagreement in the interpretation of Aristotle, there was a division among the Jewish philosophers with relation to the soul's immortality, which stemmed from their differences of opinion with regard to the nature of man's material (potential) intellect at birth. Ibn Daud follows Avicenna in regarding the soul as an individual eternal immaterial substance capable of survival after death (*Emunah Ramah*, 1:7). Maimonides' position is somewhat ambiguous. He affirms, on the one hand, the immortality of the individual soul (Guide, 1:41, 70; 3:22, 27, 54), but adopts, on the other, the description of the material intellect at birth as a "mere disposition" (1:70) and also speaks of the numerical unity of all souls (1:74, 7), from which it would appear to follow that immortality is collective (see S. Pines, *Guide of the Perplexed* (1963), CII–CIV). In the post-Maimonides period, the discussion was dominated by Averroes' theory of the ultimate elimination of the individual coloring of intellect and the absorption of the individual intellect into the universal Agent Intellect. Gersonides, however, rejects the doctrine of the unity of souls and affirms the individual immortality of man's acquired intellect (*Milḥamot*, 1:1–14). The ultimate felicity of man, he says, consists in the enjoyment of the intellectual perfection achieved during life. No further increase of knowledge is possible after death. Crescas expresses the general mood of the anti-Aristotelianism of his period and attacks the intellectualist orientation in his statement that the ultimate felicity lies in the love of God (*Or Adonai*, 2:6, 1–2).

[Alexander Altmann]

Aristotle in Jewish Legend

In addition to his considerable influence upon medieval Jewish philosophy Aristotle also appears in Jewish literary works in which history and legend are found side by side. Aristotle as a legendary figure antedates Aristotle as an actual philosophical force in Jewish thought. The theme that all the Greek philosophers, including Aristotle, were influenced by Judaism first appeared in Hellenistic-Jewish literature. The most important specimen of this motif is the report in *Josephus' *Against Apion*. Josephus cites a passage from the lost treatise *On Sleep* of Clearchus, a pupil of Aristotle, where Aristotle meets a Jew and converses with him in Greek on philosophical topics. The report concludes with the remark that Aristotle learned more from the Jewish sage than conversely (Jos., Apion, 1:176–82; cf. Eusebius, *Praeparatio Evangelica*, 9:5; 13:12). As Aristotle's philosophical works were assimilated by the medieval Jewish philosophers, Aristotle's legendary status also grew, and in different directions. Utilizing the rabbinic accounts of the meeting between Alexander the Great, a pupil of Aristotle, and Simeon the Just (Yoma 69a), several medieval authors include Aristotle as a member of Alexander's entourage, and accuse him of plagiarizing from King Solomon's writings (M. *Aldabi, *Shevilei Emunah*, ch. 8). This story is a variation of the theme that Greek philosophy is Jewish in origin. Another recurring motif is the story of Aristotle's recantation of certain principles inimical to Judaism, and in some versions of his actual conversion to Judaism. Basing their accounts on the pseudo-Aristotelian treatises *De Pomo* and *Letter of Aristotle*, several medieval and Renaissance Jewish writers relate the story that as the result of his meeting with Simeon the Just Aristotle realized his mistakes, wrote a letter to Alexander the Great confessing his errors, and then converted to Judaism (Gedaliah ibn Yaḥya, *Shalshelet ha-Kabbalah* (1962), 241–43). The most fantastic story is the report of Abraham *Bibago that Aristotle was actually a Jew from the tribe of Benjamin. Bibago cites Eusebius' account of Josephus' aforementioned story as the source of his claim (*Derekh Emunah* (Constantinople, 1521), 46b). This theme is, however, rejected by Azariah dei Rossi, the great Renaissance Jewish historian; indeed dei Rossi is skeptical of the whole legendary history of Aristotle (*Me'or Einayim*, ch. 22). As the result of greater Jewish historical sophistication, of which dei Rossi is an example, and the decline of Aristotle's philosophical influence after the 16th century, the legendary Aristotle has virtually disappeared from Jewish literature.

[Seymour Feldman]

BIBLIOGRAPHY: Guttmann, Philosophies, 134–241; Husik, Philosophy, 197ff.; idem, *Philosophical Essays* (1952); G. Vajda, *Introduction à la pensée juive du moyen âge* (1947), 125–93; Munk, Mélanges; M. Steinschneider, in: HB, 15 (1857), 44–45; idem, in: MGWJ (1883), 89, 143–4; J.L. Teicher, in: *Homenaje a Millás-Vallicrosa*, 2 (1956), 403–44; H.A. Wolfson, *Crescas' Critique of Aristotle* (1929); idem, in: PAAJR, 11 (1941), 105–63; S. Horovitz, *Die Stellung des Aristoteles bei den Juden des Mittelalters* (1911); L. Strauss, *Philosophie und Gesetz* (1935); F. Bamberger, *Das System des Maimonides* (1935); H. Davidson, in: PAAJR, 31 (1963), 33–50; L. Berman, in: A. Altmann (ed.), *Jewish Medieval and Renaissance Studies* (1967). ARISTOTLE IN JEWISH LEGEND: Ginzberg, Legends, index; Steinschneider, Uebersetzungen, 229–75; E.N. Adler, in: REJ, 82 (1926), 91–102. **ADD. BIBLIOGRAPHY:** JEWISH ARISTOTELIANISM: A. Altmann, "Defining Maimonides' Aristotelianism," in: R.S. Cohen and Hillel Levine (eds.), *Maimonides and the Sciences* (2000), 1–7; L.V. Berman, "Greek into Hebrew: Samuel ben Judah, 14th Century Philosopher and Translator," in: A. Altmann (ed.), *Jewish Medieval and Renaissance Studies* (1967), 289–320; M. Fox, "The Doctrine of the Mean in Aristotle and Maimonides: A Comparative Study," in: S. Stern and R. Loewe (eds.), *Studies in Jewish Religious and Intellectual History* (1974), 93–120; D.H. Frank, "Maimonides and Medieval Jewish Aristotelianism," in: D.H. Frank and O. Leaman (eds.), *The Cambridge Companion to Medieval Jewish Philosophy* (2003), 136–56; R. Glasner, "Gersonides' Lost Commentary on the *Metaphysics*," in: *Medieval Encounters*, 4 (1998), 130–57; J. Guttmann, *Philosophies of Judaism*, 134–241; S. Horovitz, *Die Stellung des Aristoteles bei den Juden des Mittelalters* (1911); A. Hyman, "Demonstrative, Dialectical and Sophistic Arguments in Maimonides," in: Eric Ormsby (ed.), *Moses Maimonides and his Time* (1989), 35–51; J. Kraemer, "Maimonides' Use of (Aristotelian) Dialectic," in: R.S. Cohen and Hillel Levine (eds.), *Maimonides and the Sciences* (2000), 111–30; J.T. Robinson, "Hasdai Crescas and Anti-Aristotelianism," in: *The Cambridge Companion to Medieval Jewish Philosophy* (2003), 391–413; N.M. Samuelson, "Medieval Jewish Aristotelianism," in: D.H. Frank and O. Leaman (eds.), *History of Jewish Philosophy* (1997), 228–44; C. Sirat, *A History of Jewish Philosophy in the Middle Ages* (1990), 141–362; H. Wolfson, *Crescas' Critique of Aristotle* (1929); idem, "The Amphibilous Terms in Aristotle, Arabic Philosophy and Maimonides," in: *Harvard Theological Review*, 31 (1938), 151–73.

ARIZONA, state in the southwestern United States. Arizona had an estimated population in 2000 of 5,130,632, out of which 120,000 were Jews; of these 84,000 were in the *Phoenix metropolitan area and 25,000 in *Tucson. The Prescott Jewish community was estimated to be over 1,000. Organized Jewish congregations were also found in Flagstaff, Kingman, Lake Havasu, Sedona, and Yuma. In the latest demographic study (2002) Phoenix was ranked as the 13th largest Jewish community in the country and growing rapidly.

Permanent settlement of Arizona by Europeans occurred after the California Gold Rush of 1848–50. The discovery of gold in Arizona brought many new residents to the state from 1862 to 1864. Most of them came from California, and they included many Jewish businessmen. During the 1860s much of the retail business in the towns of La Paz, Wickenburg, Prescott, and Tucson was operated by Jews. The merchants and entrepreneurs who set up enterprises at the sites of new mines also included Jews. When the mines were exhausted or proved unprofitable, businesses and entire communities were abandoned. Consequently, the business population and its Jewish component fluctuated sharply. The opportunities for mercantile activity brought to Arizona such pioneer Jewish families as Goldberg, Goldman, Solomon, Drachman, Zeckendorf, Steinfeld, Mansfeld, Isaacson, and Frank. Michael Goldwater (grandfather of Senator Barry Goldwater who was not of the Jewish faith) was a government contractor and freighter as well as a wholesale and retail merchant, a mine operator, and a forwarding agent. His son Morris served 22 years as mayor of Prescott. Charles and Harry Lesinsky opened large copper mines near Clifton in the mid-1870s, and to serve that enterprise they built Arizona's first railroad. Michael Wormser was Arizona's leading farmer at the end of the 19th century.

Relations between Jews and Christians in pioneer Arizona were generally good; many well-known firms had Jewish and Christian partners. Only in rare instances did newspaper writers make disparaging remarks about Jews. Many Jews served in territorial and state legislatures. Jacob Weinberger was the youngest member of the state constitutional convention in 1910. Beginning in the 1880s, many easterners, especially those who suffered from tuberculosis, went to Arizona in hope of a cure. Some stayed on. During the mining boom in Tombstone (1881) the first organized Jewish community in the state emerged with Samuel Blace as president of the Jewish community. Newspapers reported Day of Atonement services that year, meeting in Turnverein Hall. A B'nai B'rith lodge was established in Tucson in 1882. From about the time of Arizona's statehood in 1912, an increasing number of Jews were in the professions, mainly law and medicine. The Jewish population grew rapidly after World War II. Houses of worship existed in Tucson, Phoenix, Mesa, and Scottsdale. Among the fields that Jews were most often found at the beginning of the 21st century were merchandising, the professions, technical fields, and service industries.

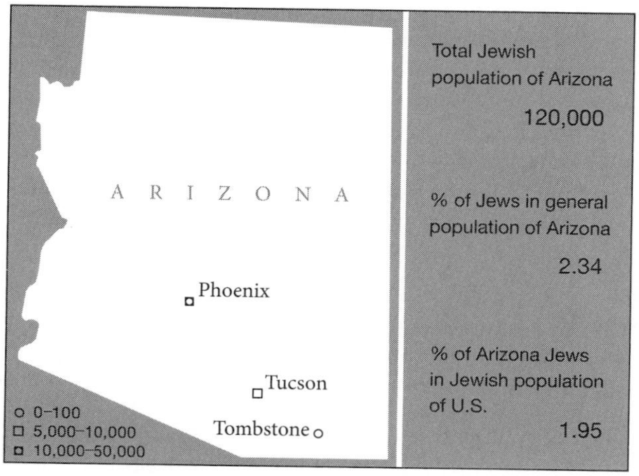

Jewish communities in Arizona. Population figures for 2001.

Among the leading Jewish officeholders of the state in the late 1960s were Justice Charles Bernstein of the State Supreme Court and Representative Sam Steiger of the third congressional district. Sam Coppersmith served in Congress in the 1980s. Andrew D Hurwitz and Stanley Feldman have served on the Arizona Supreme Court. There have been several Jewish mayors of Phoenix and Tucson in recent years.

BIBLIOGRAPHY: H. Parish, *History of Arizona*, 7 vols. (1915–18); F.S. Fierman, *Some Early Jewish Settlers in the South Western Frontier* (1960); idem, in: AJA, 16 (1964), 135–60; 18 (1966), 3–19; J.R. Marcus, *ibid.*, 10 (1958), 95–120; Aron, *ibid.*, 8 (1956), 94–98.

[Bert Fireman / Risa Mallin (2nd ed.)]

ARK, the receptacle in the synagogue in which the Torah scrolls are kept. Among Ashkenazim, it is generally called the *aron* or *aron kodesh* ("Holy Ark"; cf. II Chron. 35:3); among the Sephardim, it is known as the *heikhal* or sanctuary ("*Ehal*" among the Spanish and Portuguese communities of London, Amsterdam, etc.). The Ark is generally situated on the wall of the synagogue which in Israel faces the Temple Mount, and in other countries faces Israel. Thus in Babylonia the Ark was placed on the synagogue's western wall, while in the western world it is located on the wall facing east (see **Mizra*). In the Mishnah it is called *tevah* ("chest" or "box"; Ta'an. 2:1; Meg. 3:1; et al.). Thus the term "*yored lifnei ha-tevah*" ("go down before the Ark") means to lead the congregation in prayer, as the Ark was generally raised above the floor level on which the reader's lectern was set.

According to Jewish Law the Ark is the holiest part of the synagogue after the Torah scrolls themselves. It is permissible to sell the pews or the reading desk and apply the proceeds to the purchase of an Ark, because they have a lesser holiness, but it is forbidden to sell an Ark even in order to build a synagogue because "one may not descend in matters of holiness" (Meg. 26a and Rashi *ibid.*). It is forbidden to make any secular use of the Ark (Tosef., Meg. 3: 2); and when it is no longer usable it must be stored away (Tur., OH 154). One may not sleep in the vicinity of the Ark (Sh. Ar., OḤ 619), nor sit with one's back to it (Levush, OḤ 150). It is related that Jacob Segal Moellin (Maharil) used to bow three times to the Ark when he passed it on departing from the synagogue "like a disciple taking leave of his master" (Sh. Ar., OḤ 132, Magen Avraham, 6). The law is: "One must show great honor to the Torah scrolls and it is a *mitzvah* to set aside a special place for them, to honor that place, and to beautify it." (Sh. Ar., YD 282). It is said that the ignorant die because they refer to the Ark as *arana* (Aram. "box"), without the adjective "holy" (Shab. 32a).

The Mishnah records that on public fast days declared because of drought, the Ark was brought out into the town square and covered with ashes, and prayers were recited in front of it (Ta'an. 2:1). The ashes were symbolic of the unworthiness of the congregation (Ta'an. 16a; TJ, Ta'an. 11:1, 65a) or of the fact that God suffers with His people (Ta'an. 16a).

There are several widespread customs connected with the Ark. It is opened for certain prayers such as *Avinu Malkenu on fast days and during the *Ten Days of Penitence and for many of the *piyyutim* recited on the High Holy Day services. It is customary to stand while the Ark is open although there is no obligation to do so (Sh. Ar., YD 242:13). The accepted practice is not to leave the Ark empty. When all the Torah scrolls are taken out on Hoshana Rabba and Simḥat Torah, a lighted candle, symbolic of the "light" of the Torah, is often put there; however, halakhic objections have been raised to this custom (Sh. Ar., OḤ 154:7). The Ark usually has a curtain on it which is called *parokhet*. A lamp (**ner tamid*) is kept continually burning before it. It is not uncommon for men or women to open the Ark to offer private prayers for sick relatives or for other troubles. Generally, opening the Ark seems to stress the importance of the prayer.

Form of the Ark

The scrolls were originally kept in a movable receptacle which served both as their repository and as a pulpit. In the synagogue of Dura-Europos (c. 245 C.E.) a niche in the wall facing Jerusalem was fitted to receive the scrolls which are thought to have been placed in a low, wooden cabinet. Similar cabinets in ordinary use are pictured in Pompeian frescoes. Representations of the Ark are found in paintings and *grafitti* in the Jewish catacombs in Rome, as well as on the third- and fourth-century gold glasses from Jewish catacombs in that city. The scrolls are depicted lying on shelves in the open cabinets. In the Middle Ages, however, the Ark took the form of a taller niche or cabinet in which the scrolls stood upright, mounted, wrapped in cloth and sometimes topped with finials. This type is represented in 14th- and 15th-century illuminated Hebrew manuscripts of Spanish and German origin. In 15th-century Italian Hebrew manuscripts, a new type appears: the freestanding, tall, double-tiered cupboard, the upper tier fitted to take the scrolls and the lower one to contain ceremonial objects. A Gothic Ark from Modena from the year 1505, decorated with carved panels, is in the Musée Cluny, Paris. A more elaborate Renaissance Ark from Urbino with painted decorations (1550) is in the Jewish Museum in New York. The Sephardi synagogue in Amsterdam (1675) has a baroque Ark, occupying the whole width of the nave. Here a new feature is the twin tablets of the Ten Commandments set on top of the structure. This feature, taken over by the Sephardi synagogue in London in 1701, was later adopted generally.

A baroque structure, adorned with columns, pilasters, broken cornices, pediments, and vases became standard in German synagogues in the early 18th century. The style quickly spread to Eastern Europe, where it inspired Jewish wood and stone carvers to create their masterpieces of folk art. Lions, birds, dolphins, stags, and eagles intertwined with open-work scrolls covered the double-tiered Ark, with the door set into the lower story and the Decalogue into the upper level. The built-in Ark, such as the one of 1763 in the Touro Synagogue in Newport, Rhode Island, appeared in the late 18th century, as a product of the then dominant classicism. The cabinet is built into the wall and projects slightly. However, the most common type of Ark in the U.S. until the 1840s was a neoclassical structure with a curved, convex front and sliding doors. From the 1850s and 1860s the Arks of the Moorish style synagogues in Europe and America were designed in the Oriental style. They featured bulbous domes and horseshoe arches, and were covered with geometrical polychrome decorations. In 1925 an attempt was made to revive the old portable type of the Ark of the Tabernacle in Temple Emanu-el in San Francisco, California. Here the Ark, a house-like structure in cloisonné enamel with a double-pitched roof, resembles a Gothic jewel case or reliquary. It is placed sideways so that the *ḥazzan* taking out the scroll does not turn his back to the worshipers.

After World War II, the creation of Arks became an art form and many artists experimented with new and daring forms, and with the use of new materials, such as concrete and glass.

[Rachel Wischnitzer]

In Illuminated Manuscripts

In many 14th-century German *maḥzorim*, the first benediction in the morning prayer of the Day of Atonement is traditionally represented by the open Ark of the synagogue, since this prayer mentions the opening of the Gates of Mercy. Most of these Arks are gabled, with open doors revealing the decorated Torah scrolls within. In Spanish 14th-century *Haggadot* there is a similar open door Ark in illustrations of synagogue interiors (*Sarajevo Haggadah*, f. 34) Italian illustrations usually show the Ark with closed doors (Rothschild MS 24, Israel Museum; *Mishneh Torah* Heb., 4, 1193, fol. 33v, Jerusalem National Library) though occasionally there is an open Ark (BM Add. 26968, fol. 139v., Margoliouth, Cat. no. 616).

[Bezalel Narkiss]

BIBLIOGRAPHY: E.L. Sukenik, *Ancient Synagogues in Palestine and Greece* (1934); R. Wischnitzer, *Architecture of European Synagogues* (1964), index; idem, in: JBL, 60 (1941), 43–55; A. Kampf, *Contemporary Synagogue Art, Developments in the United States, 1945–65* (1966), index; R. Krautheimer, *Mittelalterliche Synagogen* (1927); G. Loukomski, *Jewish Art in European Synagogues* (1947); U. Nahon, *Scritti… S. Mayer* (It., 1956), 259–77; Roth, Art, index.

ARKANSAS, state in the south central part of the United States. It had an estimated Jewish population of 3,000 in 1967 out of a general population of 1,980,600 and 2,000 out of a total population of 2,673,400 in 2000. The first documented Jewish settler in Arkansas was Abraham Block, who came in 1823 and established a store at Washington, Arkansas (now known as Old Washington State Park), located on the Southwest Trail. He was a fairly wealthy man, husband of Frances "Fannie" Isaacs, whose father, Isaiah *Isaacs, was the initial Jewish settler in Richmond, Virginia. Block was acquainted with early Texas luminaries, such as Sam Houston, Davy Crockett, Stephen Austin, and Jim Bowie. Block's neighbor, smithy James Black, forged the famous Bowie knife. (Block's two-story home still stands.) He was followed to Arkansas by the brothers Jacob, Hyman, and Louis Mitchell, who immigrated to Hot Springs in 1830. They became successful merchants, conducting a large business between Fort Smith, Little Rock, and Hot Springs. In 1839 the eldest of the brothers, Jacob, organized a stagecoach line between Little Rock and Hot Springs. Samuel Adler, father of Cyrus *Adler, settled in Van Buren in the late 1850s.

From 1830 until the close of the Civil War Jews went to Arkansas sporadically. Some 200 Jewish merchants were in the state by 1860 and more than 70 served in the Confederate Army. Several were captured, and two lost their lives. Max Frauenthal, a Civil War hero, settled at Conway in 1872 and established what became one of the state's largest stores. After 1865 there was a large influx of Jews into the state. A number of towns were named for Jews, including such men as Louis and Joseph Altheimer, Adolph Felsenthal, J.D. Goldman, and Morris Levy, all of whom played vital roles in the state's history. Several sawmill towns were named for Jewish men, such as Henry Berger, Sol Bertig, and Victor Waldstein. At the close of the Civil War, the increase in the number of Jews led to the establishment of congregations throughout the state: Anshe Emeth in Pine Bluff and B'nai Israel in Little Rock formed congregations almost simultaneously in 1866–67; Beth El in Helena (1867); Beth El Emeth in Camden (1869); House of Israel in Hot Springs (1875); Mount Sinai in Texarkana (1876); Temple of Israel in Fort Smith (1880) merged with a second congregation and formed United Hebrew Congregation (1886); Orthodox Shul in Jonesboro (1892); Temple Israel in Jonesboro (1896); Agudath Achim in Little Rock (1904); Beth El in Newport (1904); Dermott Congregation in Dermott (1905); B'nai Israel in Pine Bluff (1907); Sheareth Israel in Hot Springs (1907); Bene Israel in Eudora (1912); B'rith Sholom in Osceola (1912); B'nai Israel in Fort Smith (1913); Tifereth Israel in Forrest City (1914); Marianna Congregation in Marianna (1914); Ahavah Achim in Wynne (1915); Ohev Zedek in El Dorado (1920s); Reform Congregation in El Dorado (1920s); Temple Israel in Pine Bluff (1921); Temple Israel in Blytheville (1936); Beth Israel in El Dorado (1940s); Meir Chayim in McGehee (1947); Beth Jacob in Hot Springs (1950); Temple Shalom in Fayetteville (1981); Lubavitch of Arkansas in Little Rock (1992). The Chabad-Lubavitch Hebrew Academy of Arkansas was opened in Little Rock in 2003 with 16 students. An outstanding

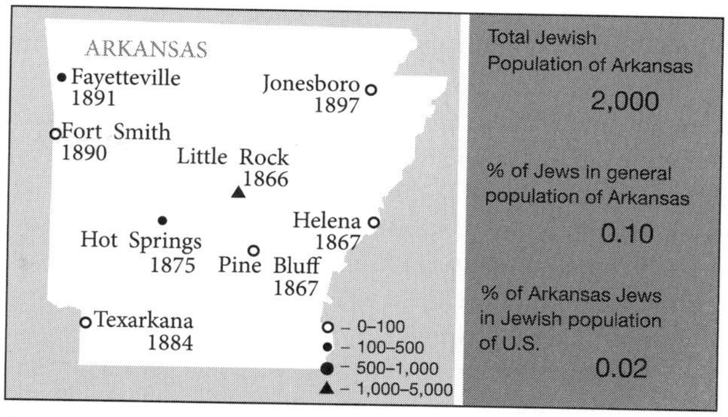

Jewish communities in Arkansas and dates of establishment. Population figures for 2001.

philanthropic institution is the Leo N. Levi Memorial Hospital (now Levi Hospital) established in 1914 in Hot Springs.

In 1931 the Jews of Arkansas formed a *Kehillah*-type organization, the Arkansas Jewish Assembly, which sought to strengthen the scattered Jews of the state. Supplying spiritual leaders to small congregations, promoting Jewish educational programs and youth groups, and holding yearly conventions, it was successful until 1951, when Jewish Federations began fulfilling such functions. Jews have occupied important government positions in Arkansas, including Jacob Trieber, United States District Court judge, 1900–27 (first Jewish Federal judge), and Sam Frauenthal, associate justice of the Arkansas Supreme Court. In 1997 Annabelle C. Imber, a Jew by choice, was the first woman elected to the Arkansas State Supreme Court. Many other Jewish citizens have served as mayors, aldermen, councilmen, and state senators and representatives.

Rabbi Ira E. Sanders, leader of Congregation B'nai Israel of Little Rock from 1926–63 (and as rabbi emeritus until his death in 1985), was an outspoken proponent of integration during the 1957 school crisis. He was followed in 1963 by Rabbi E.E. Palnick, who continued the civil rights efforts of his predecessor. Little Rock's Jewish women were prominent workers in the Women's Emergency Committee, which sought to reopen the city's high schools, which were closed by Gov. Orval Faubus after the desegregation order.

Of the 30 documented congregations established in the state between 1866 and 2004, only a few survive. Jewish communities with active congregations are located in Little Rock (3), Bentonville, Fayetteville, Fort Smith, Hot Springs, Jonesboro, and Helena (the latter two have but a handful of adherents).

BIBLIOGRAPHY: M.K. Bauman and B. Kalin, (eds.), *The Quiet Voices: Southern Rabbis and Black Civil Rights, 1880s to 1990s* (1997), 95–120; C.G. LeMaster, *A Corner of the Tapestry: A History of the Jewish Experience in Arkansas, 1820s–1990s* (1994), 3–12, 43–46, 51–93, 222–25, 309–31, 374–78; Sheppard, in: *Arkansas State Gazetteer* (1866), 319–21, 324–29; AJHSP, 3 (1893), 24, 38; 6 (1897), 144, 149, 150; 19 (1910), 96; Herndon, in: *Centennial History of Arkansas*, 2 (1922), 23, 100, 136, 396, 739, 895, 984; D.E. Wagoner, *Levi Arthritis Hospital: More Lasting Than Marble* OR *Stone* (1984).

[Carolyn G. LeMaster (2nd ed.)]

ARKIN, ALAN W. (1934–), U.S. actor. Born in New York City, Arkin began his career as a folk singer. As a founding member of the folk group The Tarriers, he co-composed the "The Banana Boat Song" (also known as "Day-o"), which Harry Belafonte later made a mega-hit. Arkin then became a founding member of Second City in Chicago, a troupe that specialized in improvisations. He appeared in Joseph Stein's comedy *Enter Laughing* (1963), for which he won a Tony award and became a star overnight. His next Broadway success was in Murray Schisgal's *Luv* (1964).

In the film industry, Arkin first starred in the comedy *The Russians Are Coming, The Russians Are Coming* in 1966 and won a Golden Globe award for best actor. Nominated as well for an Academy Award for best actor for the same role, Arkin is one of a handful of actors to receive such a nomination for a first screen appearance. His subsequent roles include *Wait until Dark* (1967); *The Heart Is a Lonely Hunter* (Oscar nomination for best actor, 1968); *Popi* (1969); *Catch 22* (1970); *Little Murders* (1971); *Last of the Red Hot Lovers* (1972); *Freebie and the Bean* (1974); *Hearts of the West* (1975); *The Seven-Per-Cent Solution* (as Sigmund Freud, 1976); *The Magician of Lublin* (1979); *The In-Laws* (1979); *Joshua Then and Now* (1985); *Edward Scissorhands* (1990); *Glengarry Glen Ross* (1992); *Mother Night* (1996); *Grosse Pointe Blank* (1997); *Gattaca* (1997); *Slums of Beverly Hills* (1998); *Jakob the Liar* (1999); *Noel* (2004); *Raising Flagg* (2003); and *Eros* (2004).

Arkin has made numerous television appearances as well, on both made-for-TV movies and popular series such as *100 Centre Street* and *St. Elsewhere.* In the riveting 1987 TV movie *Escape from Sobibor*, based on a true story, Arkin plays the lead role of Leon Feldhendler, the man who masterminded the escape plan for the 600 Jewish inmates of the Nazi death camp in Poland in 1944. He was nominated for a best actor Emmy for that performance.

In his real-life role as father, Arkin has three sons – Adam, Matthew, and Anthony – all of whom are actors as well. In fact, Arkin was nominated for another best actor Emmy for his appearance on the TV drama *Chicago Hope*, where he played the father of Dr. Aaron Shutt, the role performed by his son Adam Arkin.

In addition to his acting career, Arkin has directed projects for all media. His many directorial credits for the theater include several productions with Circle in the Square, including Jules *Feiffer's *The White House Murder Case*, which earned him an Obie award, and on Broadway *The Sunshine Boys*.

Arkin wrote and directed two short films, *T.G.I.F.* (1967) and *People Soup* (1969). The former opened the 1967 New York Film Festival; the latter received an Oscar nomination for Best Short Subject. Arkin went on to direct the feature film version of *Little Murders* (1971) as well as the films *Fire Sale* (1977), *Samuel Beckett Is Coming Soon* (1993), and *Arigo* (2000).

Also a writer of children's books, Arkin has authored *The Lemming Condition*; *The Clearing*; *Cassie Loves Beethoven*; *One Present from Flekman's*; and *Tony's Hard Work Day.*

Another book by Arkin, *Halfway through the Door: An Actor's Journey toward the Self* (1979), is autobiographical.

[Jonathan Licht and Ruth Beloff (2nd ed.)]

ARK OF THE COVENANT (Heb. אֲרוֹן הַבְּרִית, אֲרוֹן הָעֵדוּת (*aron ha-berit, aron ha-ʿedut*)), the chest which stood in the Holy of Holies, and in which "the tables of the covenant" were kept.

Designations

The modifying phrases qualifying the word "ark" are numerous: "the ark of YHWH" (Josh. 4:11; et al.); "the ark of YHWH, the Lord of all the earth" (Josh. 3:13); "the ark of the Lord YHWH" (I Kings 2:26); "the ark of God" (I Sam. 3:3; et al.); "the ark of YHWH your God" (Josh. 4:5); "the ark of the God of Israel" (I Sam. 5:8; et al. – the designation used by the Philistines); "the holy ark" (II Chron. 35:3). Especially important are the terms alluding to the religious and historical significance of the ark: "the ark of the pact" (Ex. 25:22; et al.); "the ark of the covenant" (Josh. 3:6; et al.); "the ark of the covenant of YHWH" (Num. 10:33; et al.); "the ark of the covenant of God" (Judg. 20:27; et al.); "the ark of the covenant of the Lord of all the earth" (Josh. 3:11); "the ark, wherein is the covenant of YHWH, which He made with our fathers…" (I Kings 8:21; "with the children of Israel" – II Chron. 6:11); "the ark of the covenant of YHWH of Hosts, who dwelleth between the cherubim" (see *Cherub; I Sam. 4:4); "the ark of God, whereupon is called the Name, even the Name of YHWH of Hosts who dwelleth between the cherubim" (II Sam. 6:2; very similar is I Chron. 13:6).

Description

According to the description contained in Exodus 25:10–22 and 37:1–9 (where *Bezalel, upon the instruction of *Moses, constructs the ark), the length of the ark was two and a half cubits (4 ft. 2 in.) and its width and height a cubit and a half (30 ins.); it was made of acacia wood and overlaid with pure gold both inside and out. A crown of gold surrounded it above, and four golden rings were attached to its feet, two on each side; into these were inserted the staves used for carrying the ark (see below). An ark cover (*kapporet*), which was made entirely of gold and the dimensions of which corresponded with those of the ark, covered the aperture on top. At the two ends of the ark cover were set two *cherubim that "screened," i.e., guarded or protected (cf. Gen. 3:24; Ps. 5:12; 91:4; et al.), as it were, the ark cover, as well as the tables of the covenant in the ark. The wings of the cherubim were outstretched and their faces were turned "one to another toward the ark cover." In the *Temple of Solomon there were apparently no cherubim on the ark cover, but two, ten cubits in height and made of olive wood overlaid with gold, stood on the floor in front of the ark. Each had two wings – each five cubits long – extending outward from the one wall to the wing of the other cherub, and they "covered the ark and the staves thereof above" (I Kings 6:23ff.; 8:6–9; II Chron. 3:10–13; 5:7–8).

The ark is depicted in the Torah as one object (Ex. 25:10–22; Deut. 10:1–5) (*kapporet* denoting simply "cover"), but according to traditions set in Solomonic times (I Kings 8:9), the cherubs were severed from the cover of the ark (see below). The cover (*kapporet*) with the cherubim symbolized the place of the manifestation of the Divinity in the Temple of Israel ("who dwelleth between the cherubim," I Sam. 4:4), whereas the ark contained underneath it "the tables of the covenant" or "the tables of the pact" (Ex. 25:21; 31:18; Deut. 10:3, 5; I Kings 8:9; II Chron. 5:10. In biblical Hebrew *ʿedut* is equivalent to Akkadian *adê* and Aramaic *ʿdy*, "pact," "treaty"), and served as a symbol of the covenant between God and His people. Some see in the cherubim "the chariots of God" (Ps. 68:18), symbolic of the celestial cherubim, upon which God manifests Himself to execute justice in the world and to bring salvation to His people (II Sam. 22:11; Ps. 18:11; Isa. 19:1; 66:15; Ps. 68:18, 34; 80:2; 99:1). Others again regard them as a kind of symbol for the clouds of heaven, which are similarly likened to God's chariot (cf. the epithet "that rideth upon the clouds," Ps. 68:5: *aravot*, "clouds," see also v. 34; cf. Ex. 13:21; Num. 10:34; 14:14). A later passage termed the ark cover together with the cherubim, "chariot" (I Chron. 28:18), but this may be a later adaptation (cf. Ezek. 1:26; 10:1–18: above the cherubim was the likeness of a throne and upon the throne a likeness as the appearance of the glory of the Lord). Similarly the ark was regarded, according to one view, as His footstool (cf. Ps. 99:5; Ps. 132:7–8; I Chron. 28:2; II Chron. 6:41). For this reason "the tables of the covenant" might have been placed in the ark in accordance with a custom, prevalent at the time, of placing documents and agreements between kingdoms "at the feet" of the god, the guardian of treaties and documents, who supervised their implementation (cf. I Sam. 10:25). Thus, for example, the pact between Ramses II and Hattusilis III was deposited at the feet both of the Hittite god Teshub and of the Egyptian god Ra. At all events, it is clear that the ark was regarded as the place of the manifestation of the Divine Presence and of God's will to His elect (Ex. 25:22; 30:6; Lev. 16:2, where God appeared between the two cherubim in "the cloud"; Num. 7:89). When the ark was conveyed elsewhere (see below), God also "journeyed" in a cloud over the Israelite host (Num. 10:34; 14:14; see also Ex. 33:7–11). Hence also the accounts of the miracles that occurred alongside the ark – the drying up of the waters of the Jordan when the ark preceded the people (Josh. 3–4) and the fall of the walls of Jericho after the ark had encircled them seven times (Josh. 6). Similarly, there was the stringent prohibition against touching the ark, the holiest of all the sacred appurtenances (Num. 4:15, 19, 20; cf. the narratives of the plagues among the Philistines after the capture of the ark (I Sam. 5); the smiting of the men of Beth-Shemesh "because they had gazed upon the ark of the Lord" (I Sam. 6:19); and the death of Uzzah (II Sam. 6:6–7). Even the high priest was to "come not at all times into the holy place within the veil, before the ark cover which is upon the ark; that he die not" (Lev. 16:2). When the high priest entered the Holy of Holies – once a year – he came with "the cloud of the incense," which was intended to shroud "the ark cover that is upon the pact, that he die not" (Lev. 16:13). In the period of the Second Temple, when the ark no longer existed, the high priest was still accustomed to hold "a feast for his friends for having come forth in peace from the Sanctuary" (Yoma 7:4).

History

During the period of the First Temple, a permanent place was allotted to the ark in the "Holy of Holies" (Ex. 26:34), but in times of need it was carried from place to place. The presence of the ark in the Israelite armed camp was believed to ensure God's help (cf. I Sam. 4:3). The Bible's writers project the movement of the ark into the legends of the Israelite journey from the desert of Sinai to the land of Israel (Num. 10:33; cf. 14:44) and into the legends of the conquest. In earliest Israel it was lodged at Shiloh (Josh. 18:1; I Sam. 3:3), but when great battles were fought, it was time and again brought from there to the front, as, for example, during the war against the Philistines near Eben-Ezer, which ended with the ark's falling into the hands of the Philistines (I Sam. 4). According to I Samuel 14:18, the ark also accompanied Saul during his first campaign against the Philistines; it was with the army during the siege of Rabbah in the days of David (II Sam. 11:11). The ark songs which are preserved in the Pentateuch belong to an early period, and were sung when the ark was borne to the battlefront. One such song is credited to Moses: "When the ark was to set out, Moses would say, 'Advance, O Lord! May Your enemies be scattered, and may Your foes flee before You!' And when it halted, he would say, 'Return, O Lord, You who are Israel's myriads of thousands'" (Num. 10:35–36; cf. Ps. 68:2; 132:8). The ark was always carried on shoulders, except for one occasion when it was conveyed in a cart (II Sam. 6:3), but when Uzzah, serving before the ark, died a sudden death, it was once more shoulder-borne (*ibid.* 6:6–15; cf. I Chron. 13:7ff.; 15:2ff.).

After the ark had been captured near Eben-Ezer and restored by the Philistines (I Sam. 4:11–6:11), it was at first transferred to Beth-Shemesh, because Shiloh had in the meantime been destroyed (Ps. 78:59–67; Jer. 26:6–9); but because a plague broke out in Beth-Shemesh, it was sent to Kiriath-Jearim, where it was placed in "the house of Abinadab in the hill, and [they] sanctified Eleazar his son to keep the ark of the Lord" (I Sam. 7:1). David, taking it from there, first deposited it in the house of Obed-Edom the Gittite (evidently from Gat-Rimmon – a levitic town), and after three months brought it to the city of David – Jerusalem – to a tent which he had pitched for it (II Sam. 6:2–17; I Chron. 13:5ff.; 15; 16:1, 4–6, 37–38). Psalm 132 (and perhaps also Ps. 24) probably refers to this event.

With the erection of the Temple in the reign of Solomon, the ark was placed in the Holy of Holies (I Kings 8:6; II Chron. 5:7), which consequently also came to be known, in the course of time, as "the place of the ark cover" (I Chron. 28:11; Tosef., Tem. 4:8; also in the Targum to the Prophets); but the cherubim were no longer attached to the ark cover (see above), and although the staves remained in position (I Kings 8:7–8), the

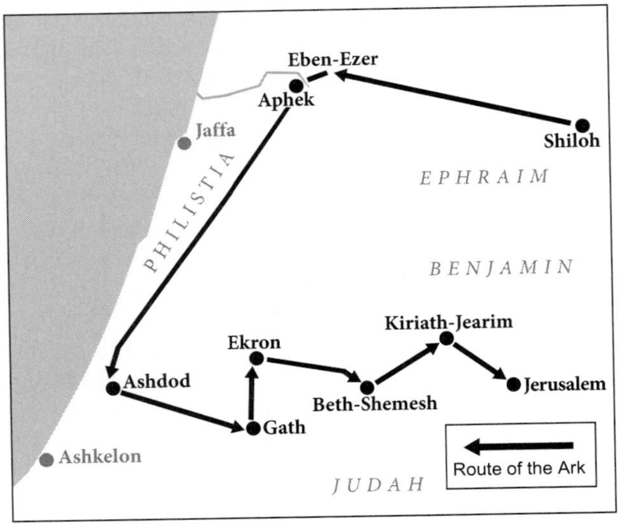

Route of the Ark of the covenant after it was brought from Shiloh, captured by the Philistines at Eben-Ezer, and eventually restored to Jerusalem.

practice of carrying the ark from place to place ceased. Henceforth, there is no information about the ark being taken to war or to celebrations, nor is its ultimate fate known. It may be assumed from Jeremiah's statement (3:16) that at the end of the period of the First Temple the ark was no longer in the Temple. It is not mentioned among the Temple vessels carried into exile or returned from Babylon. In talmudic times there was a widespread tradition that the ark had been hidden by Josiah "in its place," or beneath the woodshed (Shek. 6:1–2; Yoma 53b–54a). According to a legend in II Maccabees 2:1–7, the ark was concealed by Jeremiah on Mount Nebo. In the period of the Second Temple, at all events, the ark was no longer in the Temple (Yoma 5:2).

Sacred chests, containing holy objects or images of deities, are also to be found among other peoples, but they bear no conspicuous resemblance, either in appearance or in function, to the ark. A number of scholars have compared the ark to the *Markab* or *Atfah* (or *Utfah*, a type of elongated chest, adorned with ostrich feathers), to the *Maḥmal* (a pyramid-shaped box sent by Arab princes, with gifts, to a pilgrim procession to Mecca), or to the *Qubbah* (a kind of tent of the pre-Islamic period, tapering to a point and made of red leather), which is found among several Arabian tribes. All these are borne on camels and have a certain sanctity attributed to them. The *Atfah* – as in ancient times, the *Qubbah* – is generally brought to the camp only when decisive wars are being fought or when an enemy threatens grave danger. According to A. Musil, the *Atfah* – or at least that of the Rwalah, one of the ʿAnzah tribes of Transjordan – serves also as a guide, and predictions are made from the movement or swaying of its feathers. But according to the overwhelming evidence, including that of eyewitnesses, the *Atfah* – also that of the Rwalah tribe – functions chiefly as the seat for a young girl with uncovered hair and naked bosom, whose purpose is to incite the young men to conquer or die fighting. Clearly there is no resemblance between the ark and the *Atfah*, since the ark did not serve as a guide (even in Num. 10:33; Naḥmanides, *ibid.*) or as an instrument of divination. Unlike the ark, the *Maḥmal* is not taken out to war, while the *Qubbah* is, as previously stated, a tent. Some scholars have compared the ark to the chests (the lower parts of which were generally boat-shaped) which were brought out of the temple by the Egyptian priests at festivals and on which statues of the gods were placed. The motif of the cherub of human form with outstretched wings may also be fundamentally Egyptian, although the word cherub (*kurību*) is at present found only in Akkadian sources.

[Yehoshua M. Grintz]

In the *Aggadah*

The sanctuary in the wilderness contained among other things the Ark of the Covenant and the two stone tablets on which were inscribed the Ten Commandments (Ex. 25:10 ff.). The first tablets were broken and a second pair hewn out (*ibid.* 34:1, 4). According to one view there were two arks, one which housed the Torah (including the second tablets), while the other contained the fragments of the first tablets, and it was this ark that was taken out by the Israelites on various occasions. According to another view, both – the whole and the broken – tablets were contained in one ark, and from this the moral was drawn that a scholar who has forgotten his learning is still entitled to receive respect (Ber. 8b; BB 14b).

The ark traveled 2,000 cubits (the limits of a Sabbath journey) ahead of the Israelites in the wilderness, so that on the Sabbath they could go and pray there (Num. R. 2:9). Two fiery jets issued from between the cherubim above the ark, burning up snakes, scorpions, and thorns in its path, and destroying Israel's enemies (Tanḥ. Va-Yakhel 7).

When the Philistines returned the ark, which they had captured from the Israelites, the cows which drew the cart upon which it was placed burst into song (Av. Zar. 24b). Later, when Solomon brought it into the Temple, all the golden trees there yielded abundant fruit. This continued until Manasseh introduced into the Temple an image of an idol, whereupon the trees dried up and their fruit withered (Tanḥ. Terumah 11; Yoma 39b). It was housed in the Holy of Holies (I Kings 6:16–19). Miraculously, however, the ark did not diminish the area of the Holy of Holies in the least (BB 99a).

The ark was in the exact center of the whole world, and in front of it stood the *even shetiyyah ("foundation stone"), which was the starting point of the creation of the world (Tanḥ. Kedoshim 10). Opinions differ as to its subsequent fate. Some hold that it was taken to Babylon when the Temple was destroyed; others, that it was hidden in the Second Temple beneath the pavement in the wood storehouse. According to yet another tradition Josiah hid it, together with the other sacred utensils, to ensure that it would not be taken to Babylonia (Yoma 53b; TJ Shek. 6:1, 49c). A *baraita* quoted by Maimonides (Yad Hilkhot Beit ha-Beḥirah, 4:1) states that when Solomon built the Temple, he foresaw its destruction and built a deep secret cave, where Josiah ordered the ark to be hidden. In II Maccabees 2:4, it is stated that Jeremiah hid it in the cave of the mountain from which Moses had viewed the land of Israel prior to his death. In any case, it was not in evidence during the period of the Second Temple. With the ark were hidden the phial of manna, the phial of anointing oil, Aaron's staff, and the chest in which the Philistines sent a gift to the God of Israel (Yoma 52b).

[Harry Freedman]

BIBLIOGRAPHY: GENERAL: de Vaux, Anc Isr, 297–303, 591 (incl. bibl.); Tur-Sinai, in: EM, 1 (1965), 538–50 (incl. bibl.). HISTORY: Haran, in: IEJ, 13 (1963), 46–58; idem, in: BIES, 25 (1961), 211–23; Delcor, in: VT, 14 (1964), 136–54 (Fr.); Porter, in: JTS, 5 (1954), 161–73; Nielsen, in: VT supplement, 7 (1960), 61–74 (Eng.); Tur-Sinai, in: VT, 1 (1951), 275–86 (Eng.). FUNCTION AND SYMBOLIC SIGNIFICANCE: Bentaen, in: JBL, 67 (1948), 37–58; Haran, in: *Sefer Tur-Sinai* (1960), 2742; idem, in: *Sefer D. Neiger* (1959), 215–21; idem, in: IEJ, 9 (1959), 30–38, 89–94. **ADD. BIBLIOGRAPHY:** C.L. Seow, in: ABD, 1, 386–93; J. Fitzmyer, in: *The Aramaic Inscriptions of Sefire* (1995), 57–59; H. Niehr, in: K. van der Toorn (ed.), *The Image and the Book* (1996), 73–95; T. Mettinger, ibid., 173–204. AGGADAH: Ginzberg, *Legends*, index.

ARK OF MOSES (Heb. תֵּבָה, *tevah*; "box" or "basket"), the Hebrew word *tevah* occurs in the Bible only as a designation of the *ark of Noah (Gen. 6–9), and of the ark in which the infant *Moses was hidden by his mother (Ex. 2:2–6) in order to save him from Pharaoh's decree that every Hebrew male child should be killed (Ex. 1:22). According to the story, the basket was made of papyrus (Heb. *gome*) like the boats of the Egyptians (cf. Isa. 18:2), caulked with bitumen, and placed among the reeds on the bank of the Nile (models of vessels excavated in Ur are made of bitumen and dry, baked earth; finds in Egypt show the same use of bitumen). Exodus 2:6 implies that it had a lid. An analogous story is told about Sargon of Agade (in: COS, 1 461). Sargon was born in secret; he was enclosed in a basket made of rushes and bitumen, and furnished with a lid; and he was found and adopted by a stranger. In the Sargon story the basket containing the infant is actually allowed to drift, like Noah's ark. The river, in Sargon's case the Euphrates, carries the basket containing him down to where his future foster father, a drawer of water, is at work drawing water. Whereas in the Sargon legend the infant is cast adrift, apparently because his mother wishes to get rid of him without taking his life, in Egyptian mythology the goddess Isis places her child Horus in a reed boat and hides him in a papyrus thicket, where her sister (not that of the infant) spreads her mat over him, in order to save him from the god Seth. Despite the absence of the trait of adoption by a chance discoverer, this Egyptian tradition obviously has much more in common than the Sargon legend with the Exodus story about Moses; and the fact that the latter has Moses discovered and brought up – but without losing touch with his natural kin – by an Egyptian princess is probably independent of Mesopotamian influence. Nonetheless, the motif of overpopulation as a threat requiring drastic measures against humans, does have Mesopotamian parallels.

BIBLIOGRAPHY: Helck, in: VT, 15 (1965), 35–48; M. Greenberg, *Understanding Exodus* (1969), 40, 198–200; C.L. Woolley, *Ur Excavations*, 2 (1934), 145, 154, 232. **ADD. BIBLIOGRAPHY:** B. Lewis, *The Sargon Legend* (1980); W. Propp, *Exodus 1–18* (AB; 1998), 159–60.

ARK OF NOAH (Heb. תֵּבָה, *tevah*), the vessel built by *Noah at Divine command (Gen. 6:14–16). Its purpose was to preserve Noah, his family, and representatives of each species of living creature for a continuation of life after the *flood. The ark finally came to rest on the mountains of *Ararat (Gen. 8:4).

Built of gopher wood, conjectured to be of a resinous type, it was covered with pitch inside and out. The ark had three stories with an unspecified number of compartments. In addition, it was equipped with a skylight, which terminated a cubit from the top, a side door, and a window (Gen. 8:6). The dimensions recorded are 300 cubits in length, 50 in width, and 30 in height, corresponding approximately to 440 × 73 × 44 ft., and yielding a displacement of about 43,000 tons. The appearance as described is rectangular and box-like and was so interpreted by the Septuagint: κιβωτὸς; the Vulgate: *arca*; and Josephus: λάρναξ (Ant., 1:75ff.). The term *tevah* may be related to the Egyptian *db3t* ("chest," "box," "coffin"), a derivation appropriate to the only other occurrence of *tevah* in the Bible (Exodus 2:3–5), which describes the basket in which Moses was saved, but is less appropriate to the Noah story. In the earlier Mesopotamian Flood traditions the vessel is not an ark, but a "great ship," with a rudder. Tablet 11:60–62 of the Gilgamesh Epic describes an exact cube of 120 cubits on each side. It had seven stories, each with nine sections: a total of 63 compartments. It had a "strong cover," a door, and a window. Pitch served as one of the caulking compounds. These accounts speak variously of humans, living creatures, food, and a captain aboard; and refer to a divinely revealed blueprint similar to the detailed instructions to Noah. Josephus' description of the ark is closer to the Bible, whereas Berossus draws on native Babylonian traditions.

BIBLIOGRAPHY: J. Skinner, *Genesis* (ICC, 1930), 160–3; U. Cassuto, *A Commentary on the Book of Genesis*, 2 (1961), 55–71; E.A. Speiser, *Genesis* (1964), 47–56; N.M. Sarna, *Understanding Genesis* (1966), 37–59; Pritchard Texts, 42–44, 72–99, 104–6; A. Heidel, *The Gilgamesh Epic and Old Testament Parallels* (1946), 232–7; P. Schnabel, *Berossos und die babylonisch-hellenistische Literatur* (1923), 164ff. **ADD. BIBLIOGRAPHY:** C. Cohen, in: JANES, 4 (1972), 36–51.

[Michael Fishbane]

ARLEN, HAROLD (formerly **Hyman Arluck**; 1905–1986), American composer and one of the country's most important songwriters. Born in Buffalo, New York, Arlen was the son of a *ḥazzan*. He sang in the synagogue choir and worked as a ragtime pianist, dance band arranger, and singer in nightclubs and on river steamers. He first gained recognition as a songwriter with *Get Happy* (1928). In 1934 he turned to musical comedy and film scores as well as songs, which exemplify the trend of blending jazz with popular idioms. From 1931 to

1959, he composed eight musicals and from 1934 to 1963, 20 film scores. His successes include: "Stormy Weather" (1933); the music for the film *The Wizard of Oz* (1939), including the Academy Award-winning song "Over the Rainbow"; *Star-Spangled Rhythm* (1943); "That Old Black Magic" (1944); and the music for the film *Here Come the Waves* (1944). His musicals included *Bloomer Girl* (1944), *Country Girl* (1954), *Jamaica* (1957), and *Saratoga* (1959).

BIBLIOGRAPHY: Grove, s.v.; E. Jablonsky, *Harold Arlen: Rhythms, Ram Bows and Blues*, 1996.

[Amnon Shiloah (2nd ed.)]

ARLES (Heb. ארלי, ארלך, ארלאדי), town in France, 27 mi. (approx. 40 km.) south of Avignon. According to a Jewish legend, one of three rudderless ships bearing Jewish exiles arrived in Arles after the destruction of the Second Temple. It is said that Jews sang psalms at the funeral of Hilary, bishop of Arles, in 449. The first documented reference to Jews in the town (508) relates that defense of part of the wall was entrusted to them during a siege.

In 591 Archbishop Virgilius of Arles was rebuked by Pope *Gregory the Great for wishing to convert the Jews there by force. In 820, "a great number" of Jewish children from *Lyons, *Chalon-sur-Saone, *Mâcon, and *Vienne had to take refuge with the Jews of Arles to escape forcible conversion. The Jews of Arles were accused by *Agobard, archbishop of Lyons (c. 826–27), of having sold kidnapped Christian children into slavery. Jurisdiction over the Jews in the city was granted by Boso, count of Provence, to the archbishop of Arles in 879; the grant was renewed and ratified in 921, 1147, and 1154. A Hebrew copy of one of these documents, placed at the disposal of Archbishop Raymond (1142–57), mentions the first Jewish cemetery at the Montjuif, in the present Griffeville quarter, for which Jews made an annual payment of 44 sols to the archbishop. Twelfth century and later documents show that the Jews of Arles owned real estate. A record of 1170 shows that the archbishop shared the proceeds of the dues and taxes with a Jew. *Benjamin of Tudela, who visited Arles about this time, noted the existence of a community of 200. In 1215 the archbishop issued the Jewish community with its first constitution and delegated its administration to three elected "rectors." Jews were living in both the town and borough; later their main place of residence was on the Rue Neuve, near the church of the Jacobins. The present chapel of the *pénitents bleus* is said to stand on the site of the 13th-century synagogue.

During the 14th century the community was augmented by exiles from the kingdom of France, as well as through the incorporation into Arles of nearby Trinquetaille, with its considerable Jewish community. For the last quarter of the century the Jews of Arles paid directly to the count annual dues of 200 florins, formerly combined with the levy on the other Provençal communities. They also paid the Arles municipality an annual impost of 60 pounds of pepper. They renewed their association with the union of Jewish communities in Provence by 1420, in that year contributing 600 florins out of a total assessment for Provençal Jewry of 1,740 florins. The community maintained a charitable organization, founded in 1401. A school, founded at the end of the previous century and reorganized in 1407, provided instruction in both Bible and Talmud. At this time the communal administration included three *baylons*, eight councilors, and three auditors. There was a synagogue, ritual bathhouses, and a market. The cemetery in 1376 was situated at the present intersection of the Rue du Marché-Neuf and the Rue de la Rotonde. In 1434 it was replaced by sites at the Plan du Bourg and the Crau d'Arles. The Jews of Arles were mainly occupied in commerce, especially in brokerage. Their real property included numerous vineyards. More than 5% of the Jews appearing in the records (especially notarial ones) of the first half of the 15th century were doctors (*physicus*, *cirurgicus*, *medicus*). In 1425 a partnership of two Jews for the manufacture of soap is recorded.

Anti-Jewish outbreaks occurred in Arles in 1427, 1436, 1457, 1473, and 1480. The most violent attack took place on April 8, 1484, when bands of farm laborers from Dauphiné, Auvergne, and the Provençal highlands, assisted by citizens of Arles, invaded the Jewish street, looting and partially destroying it. Havoc was caused to the synagogue, already damaged by fire, possibly in 1457; two women were killed in the disorders and some 50 males were compelled to adopt Christianity. Similar disorders recurred in the following year but the municipal officers intervened to protect the Jews more effectively. In 1486 the Arles Jews contributed toward maintaining a police force for such contingencies. In 1493, however, soon after the acquisition of Provence by the French king (1481), the citizenry secured his consent to expel the Jews from Arles. The synagogue was now completely destroyed. The last Jews were expelled in September 1494. Some exiles who attempted to return in 1496 to settle their affairs were immediately expelled; certain Jews chose the alternative of conversion. Christian animosity toward these converts prompted the circulation of a literary forgery in the form of a purported exchange of correspondence between them and the Jews of Constantinople in which the latter advised their brethren in Arles to feign conversion.

Jews who passed through Arles in the 17th century were required to pay a crown impost, administered in 1658 by Levy of Arles, possibly himself a Jew. In 1775 a decree of the parliament of Provence ordered certain Jews who had tried to reestablish themselves in Arles to leave within eight days. In 1773, and again in 1775, trading in Arles was forbidden to Jews by the parliament of Provence. After the French Revolution, some Jews from the Comtat Venaissin settled in Arles. A few Jews were living in Arles in the late 1960s and the Municipal Museum possessed a rich collection of Jewish ritual objects and Jewish documents.

Jewish Scholarship and Translators

Arles, a center of Jewish scholarship, was also noted for the work of Jewish translators from the Arabic. The first known

Jewish scholar of Arles is R. Moses (c. 900). *Samuel ibn Tibbon, completed his translation of Maimonides' *Guide of the Perplexed* (1204) there. Other scholars in Arles included *Gershon b. Solomon of Arles (beginning of the 13th century); Joseph *Kaspi (c. 1317); Kalonymus b. Kalonymus (early 14th century); *Kalonymus b. David b. Todros (same period); Todros b. Meshullam of Arles, translated into Hebrew Averroes' "Middle Commentaries" on Aristotle's *Rhetoric* and *Poetics* (*Sefer ha-Meliẓah*) and *Sefer ha-Shir*; 1337); Isaac Nathan b. Kalonymus (middle 15th century) and Meir, known as Maestro Bendig, (second half of the 15th century).

BIBLIOGRAPHY: Blumenkranz, *Juifs et Chrétiens dans le monde occidental…* (1960), 35, 43, 105, 194; idem, *Auterus Chrétiens sur les juifs…* (1963), 15–16; Fassin, in: *Bulletin de la société des amis du vieil Arles*, 1 (1903–04), 30–33, 87–90; 6 (1909), 89–97; E. Engelmann, *Zur staedtischen Volks-Bewegung in Suedfrankreich…* (1959), 47–4, 60, 85–87; C. Arnaud, *Essai sur la condition des Juifs en Provence au moyen âge* (1879), 14, 19; Crémieux, in: REJ, 44 (1902), 301ff.; Gross, in: MGWJ, 27 (1878), 61ff.; 28 (1879); 29 (1880); 31 (1882); Gross, Gal Jud, 73ff.; Hildenfinger, in: REJ, 41 (1900), 62ff.; 47 (1903), 221ff.; 48 (1904), 48ff., 265ff.; Darmesteter, in: REJ, 1 (1880), 119ff.; Morel-Fatio, in: REJ, 1 (1880), 301ff.; Chotzner, in JQR, 13 (1901), 145–6; Gershon b. Solomon of Arles, *Gate of Heaven*, ed. and tr. by F.S. Bodenheimer (1953); Z. Szajkowski, *Franco-Judaica* (1963), 2, 31; Roth, Dark Ages, index.

[Bernhard Blumenkranz]

ARLOSOROFF, CHAIM (Victor; 1899–1933), Zionist statesman and leader of the Zionist labor movement. Arlosoroff was born in Romny, Ukraine, the grandson of a famous rabbi. He was taken to Germany by his parents in 1905 in the wake of a pogrom. In 1918 Arlosoroff joined the Zionist labor party Hitaḥadut (*Ha-Po'el ha-Ẓa'ir) and soon became one of its leaders. A pamphlet he wrote in 1919, "Jewish Popular Socialism," attempted to combine non-Marxist socialism with a practical approach to the problems of Jewish settlement in Palestine. He soon attracted attention by advocating new methods of financing Zionist settlement, especially through an international loan guaranteed by the League of Nations and the Mandatory power. He also expressed the belief that cooperation between the Arab and Jewish national movements was possible.

Arlosoroff settled in Palestine in 1924, after finishing his studies in economics at Berlin University. In 1926 he became a member of the *yishuv* delegation to the League of Nations Permanent Mandates Commission. In that year, and again in 1928–29, he visited the United States, publishing his impressions in a series of letters, *New York vi-Yrushalayim* (1929), which contain sociological and economic studies of American Jewry. With the founding of *Mapai in 1930, Arlosoroff became one of the party's leaders and spokesmen. A staunch supporter of Chaim *Weizmann's policies, Arlosoroff was elected a member of the Zionist and Jewish Agency Executive and head of its Political Department at the 17th Zionist Congress in 1931. Despite the friendly personal and political relations he established with the British High Commissioner in Palestine, Sir Arthur Wauchope, Arlosoroff began to doubt the durability of Britain's commitment to Zionism in view of its involvement in the Middle East. This was a reversal of his earlier conviction that the Zionist ideal could be fully implemented in cooperation with Britain. He also came to doubt the feasibility of a Jewish-Arab understanding in the foreseeable future. In a confidential letter to Weizmann, written in June 1932 (published in 1949), Arlosoroff discussed the possibility of an interim "revolutionary" period, in which a Jewish minority develop the country and save as many Jews as possible, as the approaching world war and emerging Arab nationalism might otherwise prevent the ultimate realization of Zionism. In 1933 Arlosoroff dedicated himself to organizing massive emigration of Jews from Nazi Germany and the transfer of their property to Palestine. In June 1933 he was assassinated by unknown assailants while walking with his wife on the seashore of Tel Aviv (see below).

Arlosoroff was a man of vision and action, a shrewd observer of sociological and economic processes, and a poet. A prolific writer, his works included political and economic analyses, a world history of colonization, research works, and poetry. His writings, *Kitvei Chaim Arlosoroff*, were published in seven volumes (1934–35), the last one containing his poetry. His highly informative diaries from the years 1931–33, *Yoman Yerushalayim*, were published in 1949 (ed. by Z. Sharef). In his "Selected Articles" (in Hebrew: *Mivḥar Ma'amarav*, 1944) there is a list of his works and writings about him. Kiryat Ḥayyim near Haifa, Kibbutz Givat Ḥayyim, and the village Kefar Ḥayyim in Emek Ḥefer, as well as streets in many towns, are named after him.

[Benjamin Jaffe]

The Arlosoroff Murder Trial

The Arlosoroff murder trial (1933–34) did not solve the mystery of the assassination but greatly exacerbated political relations in the *yishuv* and in the Zionist movement. Abba *Aḥimeir, the head of a clandestine "activist" group, "Berit ha-Biryonim," was charged by the Palestine police with plotting the murder. He was also a leader of an extremist *Revisionist faction, whose organ, *Ḥazit ha-Am*, violently attacked the Labor movement and the official Zionist leadership, including Arlosoroff. Two rank-and-file Revisionists, Abraham Stavsky and Ẓevi Rosenblatt, were arrested as the actual murderers, and were identified by Arlosoroff's widow. All three vehemently denied the accusation. The district court acquitted Aḥimeir and Rosenblatt but convicted Stavsky, who, however, was eventually acquitted by the Supreme Court for lack of corroborating evidence. The defense accused the police of manipulating the widow's testimony and other evidence for political reasons, and expounded the theory that the murder was connected with an intended sexual attack on Mrs. Arlosoroff by two young Arabs. One of these Arabs, in prison for another murder charge, twice confessed to having been involved in Arlosoroff's murder, but twice retracted his confession, accusing Stavsky and Rosenblatt of having bribed him to confess.

At the time, members of the Labor movement, with few exceptions, regarded the widow's testimony as proof of the existence of criminal fascist tendencies among Revisionists, while the Revisionists and most other non-labor circles, including Chief Rabbi *Kook, firmly maintained Stavsky's innocence, denouncing the affair as a blood libel of Jews against Jews.

[Binyamin Eliav]

BIBLIOGRAPHY: E. Biletzky, *Chaim Arlosoroff – Iyyunim be-Mishnato ha-Yehudit* (1966); A. Zweig, in: *Jewish Frontier* (June 1936). MURDER TRIAL: Dinur, Haganah, 2 pt. 1 (1959), 497–9; *Arlosoroff Murder Trial* (1934); A. Aḥimeir, *Ha-Mishpat* (1968); M. Sharett, *Orot she-Kavu* (1969), 30–38.

ARMAGEDDON, name of the site, in Christian eschatology, of the final battle between the forces of Good and Evil. The name Armageddon is not mentioned prior to the New Testament but is believed by some to be a corrupt spelling of *Megiddo, a city mentioned many times in Scripture. According to this explanation the first syllable *ar* would stand for *ir* ("city") or *har* ("mountain"). Indeed, the Valley of Megiddon (*bikat megiddon*) is referred to once in the Old Testament in the prophecies of Zechariah (12:11). Others suggest that Armageddon is a corruption of the Hebrew Har Mo'ed ("mount of assembly"; cf. Isa. 14:13) or of Har Migdo ("God's fruitful mountain") which is taken to refer to Mount Zion. This last suggestion is said by some to be supported by several passages in Revelations (9:13; 11:14; 14:14–20; 16:12–16), the imagery of which resembles that of Joel, who envisages the power of God proceeding from Mount Zion to battle against the forces of Evil (Joel 2:1–3; 3:16–17, 21). However, the author of Revelations was probably combining the strategic fame of Megiddo with the idea of an eschatological final conflict on the "mountains of Israel" (Ezek. 38:8, 21).

ARMENIA, in Transcaucasia. Historically its boundaries embraced a much wider area in different periods. The Armenian diaspora is scattered in many countries of the world and still identifies its past history and future aspirations with the wider connotations of the term Armenia. Jewish historical, exegetical, and descriptive sources reveal knowledge of the variations in geographical area and history of this remarkable people. The fate and modes of existence of the Armenians have been compared in some essential features to those of the Jews.

Much of the original Armenia is now the area of Kurdistan in Turkey. However, from the seventh to ninth centuries the Arab conquerors called by the name Armenia a province which included entire Transcaucasia, with the cities Bardhaʿa, now Barda in the present Azerbaijan, where the governors mostly resided, and *Tiflis (now Tbilisi, capital of Georgia). The province is also sometimes called Armenia in eastern sources. The *Khazars were sometimes credited with Armenian origin: this is stated by the seventh-century Armenian bishop and historian Sebeos, and the Arab geographer Dimashqī (d. 1327). In the 13th to 14th centuries the Crimea and the area to the east were known as Gazaria (Khazaria) to western authors, and as Maritime Armenia to Armenian authors. The term Armenia often included much of Anatolia, or otherwise referred to cities on the Syrian-Mesopotamian route (now Turkey, near the Syrian frontier) such as Haran (Ḥarrān), Edessa (Urfa), and Nisibis (Naṣībīn).

Identification of Armenia in Literature

In the past Armenia has been connected with the biblical Ashkenaz. The Armenians are termed "the Ashkenazi nation" in their literature. According to this tradition, the genealogy in Genesis 10:3 extended to the populations west of the Volga. In Jewish usage Ashkenaz is sometimes equated with Armenia; in addition, it sometimes covers neighboring *Adiabene (Targ. Jer. 51:27), and also Khazaria (David b. Abraham Alfasi, Ali ibn Suleiman; cf. S. Pinsker, *Likkutei Kadmoniyyot* (1860), 208; S.L. Skoss (ed.), *Hebrew-Arabic Dictionary of the Bible of David ben Abraham al-Fasi* (1936), 159), the Crimea and the area to the east (Isaac Abrabanel, Commentary to Gen. 10:3), the Saquliba (Saadiah Gaon, Commentary, *ibid.*), i.e., the territory of the Slavs and neighboring forest tribes, considered by the Arabs dependent of Khazaria, as well as Eastern and Central Europe, and northern Asia (cf. Abraham Farissol, *Iggeret Orḥot Olam* (Venice, 1587), ch. 3). In other expositions found in rabbinical works, Armenia is linked with *Uz. The anti-Jewish attitudes prevailing in eastern-Byzantine (Armenian) provinces made the *Targum identify it with the "daughter of Edom that dwellest in the land of Uz" (Lam. 4:21) or with "Constantina in the land of Armenia" (now Viransehir, between Urfa and Naṣībīn (*Nisibis). Hence Job's "land of Uz" is referred to as Armenia in some commentaries, for instance in those of Naḥmanides and Joseph b. David ibn Yaḥyā. The "Uz-Armenia" of Abraham Farissol is however the Anatolian region near Constantinople. Armenia is also sometimes called Amalek in some sources, and Jews often referred to Armenians as Amalekites. This is the Byzantine term for the Armenians. It was adopted by the Jews from the **Josippon* chronicle (tenth century, ch. 64). According to *Josippon*, Amalek was conquered by Benjaminite noblemen under Saul (*ibid.*, 26), and Benjaminites are already assumed to be the founders of Armenian Jewry in the time of the Judges (Judg. 19–21). Benjaminite origins are claimed by sectarian Kurds. The idea that Khazaria was originally Amalek helped to support the assumption that the Khazar Jews were descended from Simeon (1 Chron. 4:42–43; *Eldad ha-Dani*, ed. by A. Epstein (1891), 52; cf. Ḥisdai ibn Shaprut, *Iggeret*).

Armenia is sometimes identified in literature with the biblical Minni (Pal. Targ., 51:27), based on onomatopoeic exegesis of Armenia = *Har* ("Mountain") *Minni*; similarly, Harmon (*ha-Harmonah*, Amos 4:3) is understood in the Targum to denote the region where the Ten Tribes lived "beyond the mountains of Armenia." Rashi identified Harmon with "the Mountains of Darkness," the term used by medieval Jews for the Caspian Mountains, believed in the West to surround the kingdom of the Khazars (who were often taken for the Ten Lost Tribes) and to include the Caucasus. The reference in *Lamentations Rabbah* 1:14, no. 42, does not refer to the passage of the Tribes through Armenia as is usually claimed, but more probably to the Jerusalem exiles' easy (*harmonyah*, "harmonious") route.

Armenia has further been identified with the biblical Togarmah (Gen. 10:3). In Armenian tradition this genealogy has competed with the theory of Ashkenazi origins, and extended to the Scythians east of the Volga. The identification of Armenia as Aram (Gen. 10:22; 25:20; 28:5) is adopted by Saadiah Gaon and also occurs in Islamic literature.

In the biblical age Armenia was conceived as the mountainous expanse in the north dominating the route from Ereẓ Israel to Mesopotamia (via Haran or its neighborhood) and extending to (and beyond) the boundaries of the known world. The forested heights near the sources of the Euphrates and the Tigris stimulated Jewish commentators to develop geographical concepts concerning this area in regard to Paradise (Gen. 2:8ff.), the divine "mount of meeting" in the north (Isa. 14:13), the connection of the two (Ezek. 28:13–16), and the rebirth of mankind after the Flood (Gen. 8:4ff.). The name Ararat (Gen. 8:4; II Kings 19:37; Jer. 51:27) recalls the indigenous Armenian kingdom of Urartu, based on Lake Van.

Connections and Similarities Between Jewish and Armenian History in Premedieval Times

The Armenians had been formed as a people by 521 B.C.E. Both Armenia and Judea shared common overlords in the Persians, Alexander the Great, and the Seleucids, until their liberation during the Seleucid decline. The ancient kingdom of Armenia attained its apogee under Tigranes II. He invaded Syria, reached Acre, menaced the Hasmonean state, and then retreated because of the Roman attack on Armenia (69 B.C.E.). The medieval Armenian historian, Moses of Chorene, claims that Tigranes settled many Jewish captives in Armenian cities, a statement reflecting the idea that the growth of cities and trade under Tigranes was likely to attract Jews. In fact many Jews settled in the area. Vassal kings appointed there by the Romans included the Herodians Tigranes IV (c. 6 C.E.) and Tigranes V (60–61) in Greater Armenia, and Aristobulus (55–60) in the western borderland, or Lesser Armenia. Under the more autonomous Parthian dynasty (85–428/33), the Armenian cities retained their Hellenistic culture, as the excavations at Garni (the royal summer residence) have shown. The Jewish Hellenistic immigration continued, and by 360–370, when the Persian conqueror Shapur II reduced them by massive deportation to Iran, the cities were largely populated by Jews. The exaggerated figures recorded by the chronicler Faustus Byzantinus give 83,000 Jewish families deported from five cities, against 81,000 Armenian families; the Jews formed the majority of the exiles from the three cities of Eruandashat, Van, and Nakhichevan.

Halakhic studies never flourished in Greater Armenia, in contradistinction to the center at Nisibis; the scholar R. Jacob the Armenian (TJ, Git. 6:7, 48a) is exceptional. However, Armenia is mentioned in the aggadic Targums. The mention of two "mountains of Ararat" upon which Noah's ark stood (Targ. Yer., Gen. 8:4) indicates that the location of Armenia found in Jewish Hellenistic sources (roughly adopted by the Muslims) was now identified with a place further north, in conformity with the Christian Armenian tradition, which had won more general acceptance.

Medieval Times

Medieval Armenia consisted of a group of Christian feudal principalities, under foreign overlordship for most of the time. The cities were smaller, with a more ethnically homogeneous population than formerly, and generally excluded Jews. The Armenians joined the Monophysite current of Christianity, which here (as in Ethiopia) opposed the claims of the Byzantine church to hegemony by claiming closer connections with the ancient Israel. Moses of Chorene attributed a Hebrew origin to the Amatuni tribe and to the Bagratuni (Bagratid) feudal dynasty of Armenia. The Bagratids, who claimed King David as their ancestor, restored the Armenian kingdom, which lasted from 885 to 1045, when it fell to the Muslim invaders. The royal branch, whose descendants remained in Georgia until 1801, also spread the fashion of claiming Israelite genealogies and traditions in this Orthodox Christian territory. The downfall of the Armenian kingdom was followed by general decline. Many Armenians settled in Cilicia (a Byzantine province in Asia Minor) and founded the Kingdom of Lesser Armenia, an ally of the Latin Kingdom of Jerusalem, lasting until 1375, when it fell to the Mamluks. Armenian Jewry ultimately disappeared as a distinct entity, although a part was absorbed into Kurdish Jewry.

Armenia in Legend as the "Jewish Country"

Armenia figures prominently in tales from the medieval and early modern periods about the existence of autonomous settlements of "free Jews." The kingdom of the legendary Christian eastern emperor, Prester John, who was the overlord or neighbor of a Jewish land, is sometimes placed near Armenia. The 14th-century Ethiopic historical compendium *Kebra Negast* states that Ethiopia will assist "Rome" (Byzantium) in liquidating the rebel Jewish state "in Armenia" (Eng. tr. by E.A. Wallis Budge as *Queen of Sheba* (1922), 225–6). The 14th-century *Travels of Sir John Mandeville*, a geographical compilation, states that the Caspian Jews, the future Gog and Magog, are tributaries to the queen of Armony, Tamara of Georgia (1184–1212).

The Armenian diaspora is the closest historical parallel to the Jewish Diaspora, and a comparison of the two reveals much in common. Both suffered loss of statehood and underwent the process of urbanization. They traveled similar migrationary routes, adopted similar trades, received special charters of privilege, and established communal organizations. They also faced similar problems of assimilation, survival, and accusations made against a dispersed people, and underwent similar psychological stresses. In the Ukraine, both the Jews and the Armenians were accused of having destroyed the livelihood of indigenous merchants and artisans by the communal solidarity they manifested against competition. The massacres of the Armenians have also been explained as a revolt by the exploited masses. During the depopulation of Ottoman Armenia by the massacres and deportations of World War I, the Germans planned to "send Jewish Poles" to resettle the country. The Jewish population in Soviet Armenia numbered 10,000 in 1959. In the beginning of the 21st century the Jewish population of the Republic of Armenia (independent since 1991) was 500–1,000.

[Abraham N. Poliak]

In Israel

Mosaics with Armenian inscriptions point to an Armenian population in Jerusalem as early as the fifth century C.E., and scribal notes on manuscripts indicate a school of Armenian scribes of the same period. In Armenian history 21 bishops of Jerusalem are mentioned in the Arab period. In 1311 a certain Patriarch Sarkis preserved the independence of the patriarchate when Ereẓ Israel came under Mamluk rule. In the early 17th century the patriarchate was short of funds but Patriarch Krikor Baronder (1613–45) succeeded in raising large sums from Armenians in various parts the world over, and constructed an Armenian quarter in Jerusalem. There was a long dispute over the rights to use the monastery of St. James, and in 1813 the sultan Mahmud II granted it to the Armenians over the objection of the Greek Orthodox. In 1833 a printing press was founded which has published many liturgical and ritual books as well as a monthly periodical *Sion* (since 1866). In 1843 a theological seminary was founded. In the 20th century the community was centered around the patriarchate and the Monastery of St. James, and the Church of the Archangels, all in the Armenian quarter of the old city of Jerusalem, and the Church of St. Savior on Mt. Zion. These institutions have over the centuries inherited a large collection of manuscripts donated by bishops and pilgrims, firmans granted by sultans and caliphs, and specially commissioned religious articles for the services of the cathedral. The library of manuscripts in Jerusalem is exceeded in size only by the collection in Armenia. Though always available to scholars in the past, these treasures were exhibited to the general public for the first time in 1969. At the outset of the 21st century, around 3,000 Armenians were living in the State of Israel, which like certain other countries has never officially recognized the mass murder of the Armenians by the Turks in World War I as an act of genocide. Israel and Armenia maintained diplomatic relations but neither had an embassy in the other country.

BIBLIOGRAPHY: Baron, Social², index; A.N. Poliak, *Kazaryah* (Heb., 1951), index; J. Neusner, in: JAOS, 84 (1964), 230–40.

ARMILUS, legendary name of the Messiah's antagonist or anti-Messiah. Armilus appears frequently in the later Apocalyptic Midrashim, such as *Midrash Va-Yosha, Sefer Zerubbavel*, and *Nistarot shel R. Shimon b. Yoḥai*. He is also mentioned in the Targum pseudo-Jonathan, Isa. 11:14 and in the Targum Yerushalmi A (Deut. 34:3). Armilus is first mentioned otherwise in Saadiah Gaon's *Emunot ve-De'ot* (*Ma'amar* 8), apparently under the influence of *Sefer Zerubbavel*. The legend of Armilus thus originated not earlier than the beginning of the geonic period. Its basis, however, is the talmudic legend of Messiah the son of Joseph, who would be slain in the war between the nations prior to the redemption that would come through Messiah the son of David (Suk. 52a). In *Otot ha-Mashi'aḥ* (*Midreshei Ge'ullah*, p. 320), there is reference to "the Satan Armilus whom the Gentiles call Antichrist" but this is no proof of Christian influence.

Of the numerous conjectures about the origin of the name Armilus, the most probable is that it is derived from Romulus (founder of Rome, with Remus), although other suggestions are that it may be a corruption of Angra-Mainyu, the Persian god of evil, or from the Greek 'Αριμανος (Ahriman). The legend that he was born of a beautiful virgin (see below) likewise connects it with Rome. It is most likely that as a result of the sufferings of the Jews at the hands of the Romans at the time of the destruction of the Second Temple, and during and after the Bar Kokhba War, and especially after Christianity had conquered the Roman Empire and initiated a ruthless persecution of Judaism from which it had sprung, the Jews began to regard Rome, founded by Romulus, as the kingdom of Satan, the antithesis of the kingdom of Heaven. Hence they applied the name of Armilus to that diabolic power which had gained a transient, terrestrial victory (in contrast to the celestial and eternal kingdom of the Messiah).

Armilus and his evil deeds are described in detail only in the above-mentioned later Hebrew Midrashim now republished with detailed introduction and valuable notes, by J. Even Shemuel (Kaufmann) in his *Midreshei Ge'ullah* (1942, 1944²). Armilus is the least of the kings, the son of a bondwoman, and monstrous in appearance (*Midreshei Ge'ullah, Sefer Eliyahu*, 42; *Yemot ha-Mashi'aḥ*, 96–97; *Nistarot shel R. Shimon b. Yoḥai*, 4, 195; see also textual variants, 382b, 402). He is frequently referred to briefly as "the son of a stone." This brief reference is fully explained in a legend: "They tell that in Rome there is a marble statue of a beautiful maiden, fashioned not by human hand but by the Holy One blessed be He, who created it in His might. The wicked of the nations of the world, the sons of Belial, come and warm her and lie with her, and He preserves their seed within the stone from which He creates a being and forms it into a child, whereupon she splits asunder and there issues from her the likeness of a man whose name is the Satan Armilus, whom the Gentiles call Antichrist. He is 12 cubits tall and two cubits broad, there is a span between his eyes which are crooked and red, his hair is golden-colored, the soles of his feet are green, and he has two heads" (*Pirkei ha-Mashi'aḥ*, in *Midreshei Ge'ullah*, p. 320). This Armilus will deceive the whole world into believing that he is God and will reign over the entire world. He will come with ten kings and together they will fight over Jerusalem, and Armilus will slay Nehemiah b. Ḥushi'el, who is Messiah the son of Joseph, as well as many righteous men with him, and "Israel will mourn for him as one that is in bitterness for his only son" (cf. Zech. 12:9–12). Armilus will banish Israel "to the wilderness" and it will be a time of unprecedented distress for Israel: there will be increasing famine, and the Gentiles will expel the Jews from their lands, and they will hide in caves and towers. Armilus will conquer not only Jerusalem but also Antioch (the capital of Syria, where non-Jewish Christianity originated – Acts 11:26). "He will take the stone from which he was born" and make her "the chief of all idolatry." All the Gentiles will bow down to her, burn incense and pour out libations to her, "and whosoever will venture to look upon her will be unable to do so, for no man can look upon her face by reason of her beauty" (*Sefer Zerubbavel*, in *Midreshei Ge'ullah*, p. 80 ff.). The legendary "marble virgin" is based on the fable current in the Middle Ages, and associated with the name of Virgil, that in Rome there was a stone statue of a virgin with which the Romans had immoral relations, though it also probably contains elements of the immaculate conception and the Christian worship of images.

God will war against the host of Armilus (or of Gog and Magog), and all this host and all Judah's enemies will perish in the valley of Arbel. Five hundred men of Israel, with Nehemiah and Elijah at their head, will defeat 500,000 of the host of Armilus. Then there will be a great deliverance for Israel and the kingdom of Heaven will spread over all the earth.

These are the main features of the Armilus legend, as contained in *Sefer Zerubbavel*. In the other smaller Midrashim and in the works of Saadiah Gaon and Hai Gaon there are variants and addenda. All these legends, that embody the beautiful and the moral as well as the curious and the coarse, originated from an intermingling of Persian, Roman, and Christian beliefs with an ancient Jewish tradition concerning "messianic birthpangs" which would precede the messianic age and during which Messiah the son of Joseph would be killed by Romulus-Rome, even as Bar Kokhba was killed by Rome, which had adopted the belief, so strange in Jewish eyes, in a holy virgin and in beautiful stone images. The yearning for the downfall of Christian Rome, which persecuted Israel after adopting its Torah, gave rise to the legend of Armilus, the anti-Messiah, who would multiply evils upon Israel. But Messiah the son of David would vanquish him (that is, Romulus-Rome) and bring the kingdom of Heaven upon earth.

BIBLIOGRAPHY: M. Buttenwieser, *Outline of the Neo-Hebraic Apocalyptic Literature* (1901); M. Friedlaender, *Der Antichrist in den vorchristlichen juedischen Quellen* (1901), 125–9; J. Even Shemuel (Kaufmann), *Midreshei Ge'ullah* (1944^2); J. Klausner, *Messianic Idea in Israel* (1955), 313, 407, 496.

[Jacob Klatzkin]

ARMISTICE AGREEMENTS, ISRAEL-ARAB (1949), series of bilateral agreements concluded between Israel and Egypt (Rhodes, Feb. 24, 1949), Lebanon (Rosh ha-Nikrah, March 23, 1949), Jordan (Rhodes, April 3, 1949), and Syria (Maḥanayim, July 20, 1949), terminating the military phase of the *War of Independence.

The arbitrary character of the cease-fire lines of the second truce (July 15, 1948) rapidly became a source of dissatisfaction for all sides, leading to increased tension and outbreaks of heavy, if localized, fighting, especially in the Negev. A United Nations report of September, 1948 referred to an accumulated irritation of daily incidents and the danger that the truce, if too prolonged, would deteriorate into a virtual resumption of hostilities. On Oct. 19, 1948 the Security Council adopted a resolution envisaging negotiations for the settlement of outstanding problems. Shortly afterward UN Acting Mediator Ralph Bunche (subsequently awarded the Nobel Peace Prize) proposed that the parties should be required to enter into immediate negotiations aiming at a formal peace, or at least an armistice. On Nov. 4, 1948, the Security Council embodied this idea in a resolution relating to the Negev, and followed this with a general resolution on Nov. 16. The resolution urged that, in order to eliminate the threat to peace in Palestine and to facilitate the transition from truce to permanent peace, an armistice should be established in all sectors. To this end, it called upon the parties to seek agreement forthwith by negotiations conducted either directly or through the Acting Mediator. On Nov. 23, 1948 Israel indicated its preference for direct negotiations or, if that was impracticable, for negotiations through the United Nations. In December, Egypt, Jordan, and Lebanon also accepted the Nov. 16 resolution in principle, although they were not prepared to enter into negotiations immediately. Only after a further outbreak in the Negev at the end of December did Egypt decide to enter into immediate negotiations, which began at Rhodes on Jan. 12, 1949. The conferences with Lebanon and Jordan began on March 1. Syria did not agree to negotiate until March 21, 1949, the conference itself commencing on April 5. In each case the negotiations were terminated by the formal signing of a General Armistice Agreement.

Of the other Arab states involved in the War of Independence, Saudi Arabia formally notified the United Nations that it accepted the decisions of the Arab League on the Palestine situation, Yemen took no formal steps, and Iraq authorized Jordan to negotiate for the substantial Iraqi forces in its sector, which were to be withdrawn.

All four of these conferences followed a similar pattern, the framework of which was the Security Council's resolution of Nov. 16, 1948. Bunche was chairman of the conferences with Egypt and Jordan, and his personal deputy, Henri Vigier, chaired the conferences with Lebanon and Syria. They were assisted by the Chief of Staff of the UN Truce Supervision Organization (U.N.T.S.O.), Major General William E. Riley (U.S. Marine Corps). The negotiations proceeded both formally and informally, and frequently directly and not in the presence of the United Nations representatives. When the conference with Jordan encountered difficulties, the major issues were resolved directly between the two governments outside the conference. At one time, when the conference with Syria was on the point of breaking down, the general settlement of the issues of principle was negotiated by the governments directly, through UN Secretary-General Trygve Lie.

The four agreements also conform to a pattern. The Egyptian Agreement, being the first, constituted the model. In addition to two matters specifically mentioned in the Security Council resolution, namely, the establishment of the armistice itself and a withdrawal and reduction of the armed forces to insure its maintenance during the transition to permanent peace, they included provisions for the repatriation of prisoners of war. Each agreement provided for a bilateral Mixed Armistice Commission (M.A.C.), composed of representatives of the two sides under the chairmanship of the Chief of Staff of U.N.T.S.C.O. or his representative. At the armistice conferences, decisions could be reached only through the agreement of both parties; the M.A.C.s, however, operated by majority vote, the chairman also having a vote. The Egyptian Agreement contained provisions for an appeal committee from the M.A.C. but this was not followed in the other agreements. In practice, serious disputes not settled by the M.A.C. were left suspended or brought before the Security Council. The Demarcation Lines were determined primarily on the basis of local military needs, but subsequently, considerable difficulties arose in marking the lines on the ground.

As a result of the negotiations, Egypt was left in control of the Gaza Strip, but otherwise withdrew behind the previous frontier; Israeli forces withdrew from areas occupied in Lebanon, and the Demarcation Line followed the previous frontier; Jordan was left in control of a large bulge on the west bank of the Jordan River, including the Old City of Jerusalem; and Syrian armed forces withdrew to the Syria-Palestine international frontier, the areas between that line and the line of their forward advance in the War of Independence constituting a demilitarized zone which was also extended to the Ein Gev sector.

The agreements, both as originally conceived by the Security Council and as stated expressly in each of them, were provisional measures, not prejudicing the rights, claims, or positions of any party to facilitate the transition from the truce to permanent peace. They were hailed as such in the Security Council in August 1949 and were regarded by many representatives as virtually constituting non-aggression pacts between the parties. However, almost from the beginning, fundamental differences of opinion concerning their real purport became apparent and led to gradual loss of effectiveness on the part of the M.A.C. machinery. The Arab governments regarded the armistices as incidents in a war, which left intact their general belligerent rights. The most spectacular illustration of this was Egypt's refusal to raise the blockade of the Suez Canal and its later extension of the blockade to the Gulf of Akaba – actions which earned the censure of the Security Council in its resolution of Sept. 1, 1951. Israel, on the other hand, putting the agreements in the context of the United Nations Charter, considered that they terminated any possible state of war.

Although it was generally thought that the armistice would be of short duration and that the negotiations then being conducted through the Palestine Conciliation Commission would rapidly lead to a general peace settlement, such hopes were soon frustrated. After the final breakdown of the commission's negotiations in 1951, the stresses on the armistice increased. By 1955 it was becoming obvious that the agreements were wearing thin, and efforts were made by UN Secretary-General Dag Hammarskjold to arrest their deterioration, which was particularly marked in the case of the Egyptian and Syrian Agreements. In the *Sinai Campaign of Oct.–Nov. 1956 Israel announced that because of Egyptian belligerency and persistent violations of the armistice, the Egyptian Agreement was no longer serving any useful purpose and withdrew from further participation in that M.A.C.

The other agreements continued to function, although with varying degrees of difficulty and strain. However, toward the end of 1966, despite efforts by UN Secretary-General U Thant, tensions caused by Syrian encouragement of Arab terrorists, as well as direct encroachments on the Demilitarized Zone, led to the collapse of that agreement. The war of June 1967 swept away what was left of the armistice which was replaced by new cease-fire arrangements on the basis of the resolutions of the Security Council of June 1967.

BIBLIOGRAPHY: United Nations Treaty Series, 42 (1949); Sh. Rosenne, *Israel's Armistice Agreements with the Arab States* (1951); N. Bar-Yaacov, *Israel-Syrian Armistice, Problems of Implementation, 1949–1966* (1967); Israel Government, *Reshumot, Kitvei-Amanah*, 1 (1950), 3–63; D. Brook, *Preface to Peace* (1964).

[Shabtai Rosenne]

ARMLEDER, medieval German lawless bands, so called after the leather armpiece worn by the peasantry instead of the metal armor worn by knights; this served as a class label to denote the peasantry in particular during popular disturbances. The *Armleder* became identified with a gang of *Judenschlaeger* ("Jew-killers") who ranged Franconia and Alsace from 1336 to 1339. They were motivated by the feelings of hatred in which the Jews were held and the social tensions thus stimulated in Christian society in the first half of the 14th century. The preliminary band of *Judenschlaeger* was led through Franconia in 1336 by a nobleman claiming that an angel had called upon him to kill the Jews. The following year a tavernkeeper, John Zimberlin, claimed to be a prophet called upon to avenge Christ. He was assisted by a nobleman, Umbehoven of Dorlisheim. Zimberlin gathered together a gang of peasants armed with pitchforks and distinguished by leather armbands, and assumed the title Kunig (king) Armleder. The marauders overran Upper Alsace, and ravaged 120 communities; in many cities the populace handed over the Jewish residents. The Jews of Rouffach, Ensisheim, and Muelhausen (*Mulhouse) were massacred, their belongings in the two first cities confiscated by the bishop of Strasbourg, while the emperor Ludwig of Bavaria lent his tacit support to the crime by exonerating the city of Muelhausen from guilt in return for an indemnity of 1,000 pounds. The assault was repeated in Ribeauville, where it is said that about 1,500 Jews perished. During the prolonged siege of *Colmar the leading citizens refused to surrender the Jewish inhabitants, and on the arrival of imperial troops there

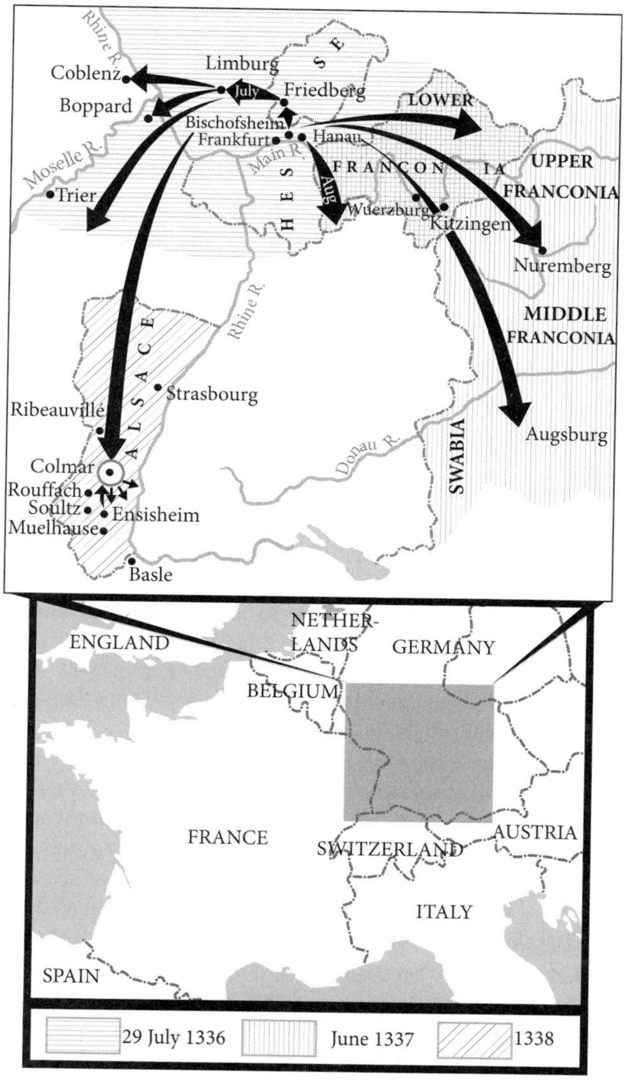

The Armleder Massacres.

"King Armleder" fled to France; Ludwig thereupon ceded the Jews to the city for 4,000 pounds, thus leaving them to the mercy of the populace. After Ludwig's departure Zimberlin returned to Alsace and continued his depredations. Before long, however, the *Armleder* began to menace the general peace and security, not confining their attacks to the Jewish population. On May 17, 1338, the bishop of Strasbourg made an agreement with several lords and 12 cities to end the raids and protect the Jews. On Aug. 28, 1339, a ten-year armistice was concluded with Zimberlin, who promised to refrain from further attacks. Additional *Landfrieden* ("alliances") were concluded to combat brigandage against both Jews and Christians in the Rhine Valley. The attacks persisted in certain districts of Alsace. The *Armleder* massacres were a prelude to the slaughter of the Jewish population during the *Black Death.

ADD. BIBLIOGRAPHY: F. Lotter, in: *Faelschungen im Mittelalter*, 5 (1988), 533–83; G. Mentgen, *Studien zur Geschichte der Juden im mittelalterlichen Elsass* (1995), 350–60; Ch. Cluse, in: *Liber amicorum necnon et amicarum für Alfred Heit* (1996), 371–92.

[Georges Weill]

°ARNALDO OF VILLANOVA (1240–1311), Spanish theologian, physician, and diplomat. Arnaldo taught medicine in Naples, Montpellier, and Paris. He studied Hebrew and Arabic, as well as talmudic and rabbinical literature under the guidance of Raymond *Martini. Although he aroused official anger by criticizing the superstitious and demonological elements in Christianity, Arnaldo followed common prejudice by ostracizing his Jewish colleagues. He attacked leading ecclesiastics for consulting Jewish physicians, and forbade laymen to do so. He proposed that the Jews should be offered the choice of conversion or exile. Jewish scholars, on their part, showed an unflagging interest in Arnaldo's scientific work and writings. More of his works were translated into Hebrew than of any other Christian physician in the Middle Ages. Several of these translations are extant in manuscript. One was translated under the title *Hanhagat ha-Beri'ut* ("Ways to Health") by Israel Kaslari in 1327; and another entitled *Ha-Parabolot* (345 medical aphorisms) by Abraham Avigdor in 1378. The original Latin text of Arnaldo's book on the use of drugs in digestive diseases was lost but the work survived in Hebrew translation (by Avigdor in 1381 and Todros b. Moses Yom Tov in 1394).

BIBLIOGRAPHY: Baer, Spain, index; M. Menéndez y Pelayo, *Historia de los heterodoxos españoles*, 1 (1956), 539–76; H. Friedenwald, *Jews in Medicine* (1967), index.

ARNDT, ADOLF (1849–1926), German jurist. He was born in Freienwalde, Pomerania, joined the administration of Mines in 1877 as legal adviser, and eventually became deputy director of the Mining Bureau in Halle. He taught at the universities of Halle and Koenigsberg, of which he became rector in 1904; after his retirement, he served as honorary professor at the universities of Frankfurt-on-Main and Marburg. Arndt also practiced criminal law and, together with Hellweg, edited *Deutsche Strafgesetzgebung* (German Criminal Law). He exercised considerable influence on the development of German constitutional and administrative law. His publications include *Die Verfassungsurkunde fuer den preussischen Staat…* (1886) and *Verfassung des Deutschen Reichs* (1895). His son, ADOLF ARNDT (1904–1974), was a jurist as well and a leading member of the German Social Democratic Party and a member of the German Bundestag from 1949 to 1964.

BIBLIOGRAPHY: *Deutsche Juristen-Zeitung*, 31 (1926), 660. **ADD. BIBLIOGRAPHY:** Heuer and Wolf (eds.), *Die Juden der Frankfurter Universitaet* (1997); D. Gosewinkel, *Adolf Arndt* (1991).

[B. Mordechai Ansbacher / Marcus Pyka (2nd ed]

°ARNDT, ERNST MORITZ (1769–1860), German antisemitic writer. Arndt, who was born in Schoritz (Ruegen), ranks among the fathers of modern journalism. He played a crucial part in the development of German nationalism, with a corollary of hostility to and fear of the Jews. He was one of the first exponents of racialism (see Theory of *Race). In his *Blick aus der Zeit auf die Zeit* (*noch etwas ueber die Juden*; 1814), Arndt considered that the Jews had become "a depraved and degenerate people, ... unfit to be full citizens in a Christian state" (p. 180–201). German-born Jews were less noxious and might be tolerated out of Christian charity, but those coming from Poland and elsewhere should not be permitted to enter Germany, lest the German stock should become tainted by admixture (*Mischung*).

BIBLIOGRAPHY: NDB, 1 (1953), 358–60; Schaefer and Schawe (eds.), *Ernst Moritz Arndt, ein bibliographisches Handbuch*, 1769–1969 (1969).

[Marcus Pyka (2nd ed.)]

ARNHEIM, FISCHEL (1812–1864), German politician and attorney. Arnheim was a well-known lawyer in his native Bayreuth and became interested in constitutional problems. In 1848 he was elected to the Bavarian *Landtag* (parliament), where by virtue of his legal training and political ability he played an active role in the drafting of important legislation. Arnheim fought for the fundamental rights of the Frankfurt *Nationalversammlung* (National Assembly) and, as an adherent of Hapsburg policy, supported the independence of Bavaria. He was active in the struggle for the abolition of capital punishment and the separation of the judicial branch of government from the executive branch. Arnheim strenuously combated antisemitism and the defamation of Jews. He was well versed in Jewish scholarship and engaged in a public debate with the Catholic theologian Doellinger. He devoted special efforts to the repeal of regulations designed to discriminate against Jews and curtail their rights (in particular the Matrikel Laws designed to limit the number of Jews in every town and village).

BIBLIOGRAPHY: AZDJ, 28 (1864), 115–16; A. Eckstein, *Beitraege zur Geschichte der Juden in Bayern* (1902), 7–16. **ADD. BIBLIOGRAPHY:** A. Eckstein, in: A. Chroust (ed.), *Lebenslaeufe aus Franken*, 7:2 (1922), 11–13.

[B. Mordechai Ansbacher / Marcus Pyka (2nd ed.)]

ARNHEIM, HEYMANN (1796–1869), German translator and grammarian. Arnheim taught himself German, French, English, Latin, and Greek, as well as some Arabic. After leading the unsettled life of a private tutor, he was appointed head of the Jewish school in Fraustadt/Wschowa. Three years later, in 1827, he became head of the Jewish school in Glogau (Lower Silesia), where he gave the first sermon in German. From 1849 to 1857 he also served as assessor for the rabbinate. His translation of and commentary on the Book of Job (1836) attracted the attention of Leopold Zunz, who commissioned him to translate a large number of books for his German Bible translation (1837–38; 17th ed., 1935). The Book of Jeremiah he translated in conjunction with Michael Sachs. Arnheim also published a translation of the *siddur*, including the *piyyutim* (*yoẓerot*) for all special Sabbaths and Purim (1839–40). His *Grammatik der hebraeischen Sprache* was edited by D. Cassel and published posthumously (1872). Arnheim also wrote for the *Hallesche Jahrbuecher*, the *Magazin fuer die Literatur des Auslands*, and other scholarly journals.

BIBLIOGRAPHY: M. Grunwald, in: *Festschrift Israel Lewy* (1911), 382–91. **ADD. BIBLIOGRAPHY:** C. Wilke, *Der Talmud und der Kant* (2003), 565–66; C. Wilke (ed.), *Biographisches Handbuch der Rabbiner*, part 1, 1 (2004), 145–46, bibl.

[Marcus Pyka (2nd ed.)]

ARNOLD, ABE (1922–), Canadian journalist, human rights advocate, and community leader. Arnold was born and educated in Montreal. After wartime service in the Canadian Army, he began a more than 50-year career combining journalism with Jewish community service. A man of deeply held progressive instincts, Arnold became English-language editor of the Toronto-based Yiddish-English weekly *Vochenblat* before he moved to Vancouver, where for almost 20 years he was editor and publisher of the *Jewish Western Bulletin*, the voice of western-Canadian Jewry.

Returning to Montreal in 1960, for five years he directed publicity and public relations for the Combined Jewish Appeal. He then moved to Winnipeg, where he served eight years as Western Regional Executive Director of the Canadian Jewish Congress in Winnipeg. Reflecting his passion for human rights Arnold was a founder and for a decade executive director of the Manitoba Association of Rights and Liberties. He had a hands-on role in drafting the Manitoba Human Rights Act of 1984, ensuring it was the strongest human rights legislation in Canada.

A self-taught historian, he was also instrumental in founding the Jewish Historical Society of Western Canada. He wrote several books and numerous articles on Canadian Jewish history. Recognizing his dedication to the community the Canadian government awarded him membership in the Order of Canada, the highest honor Canada can bestow on a citizen.

[Harold Troper (2nd ed.)]

ARNOLD, EVE (1913–), U.S. photographer. The first woman to be a member of the prestigious Magnum Photo Agency, Arnold was born in Philadelphia to Russian immigrants (her father, William Cohen, was a rabbi) and took up photography in 1946 after working at a photo-finishing plant in New York City. Her first picture was of a Bowery bum on the New York waterfront "sleeping off his excesses," she said. In 1948, she married Arnold Arnold, an industrial designer, and gave birth to their son, Frank. Arnold began her professional career while living on Long Island, near New York, in the 1950s. "People would come out to Long Island for me to photograph them on the beach," she recalled in an interview. "I took a series of Marilyn Monroe standing among the bulrushes. She was a beginning starlet and had seen photographs I'd done of Marlene Dietrich." She photographed Monroe in six formal sessions over a ten-year period. "Unschooled, clever, intuitive, very smart, she exuded fun and joy, and then as the years went by she became sad, withdrawn, and unhappy." Her pictures of movie stars and celebrities caught off guard resulted in memorable images: a slouchy Dietrich in a recording studio, Paul *Newman glued to a lecture at the Actors Studio, a 50-plus Joan Crawford in the nude, all shot in black and white. These photographs changed the nature of Hollywood photography from formal to informal and set the tone for the celebrity photos now common.

During that period, Arnold also photographed the first five minutes of a baby's life for *Life* magazine. "I photographed birth around the world, the last place Tibet. I photographed more deliveries than most doctors have delivered babies." She said the personal tragedy of losing a child had led her to this subject. "The only way I could lay that pain to rest was by going to the source."

Arnold became best known for her intimate photographs of Monroe on the set of the 1961 film *The Misfits*, which was written for her by her husband Arthur *Miller. The photographs, preserved in more than 200 contact sheets, are considered classics both for the photography and the emotion portrayed between Monroe and her husband. Arnold also photographed Malcolm X in Harlem in the early 1950s, seedy life in pre-Castro Cuba, and the dreadful life inside an insane asylum in Haiti. She additionally took candid shots of Senator Joseph R. McCarthy and Roy Cohn in their hearing room in 1954 as well as stark images of Khrushchev's Soviet Union. She was one of the first photojournalists to work in color, and she made lavish images of mainland China in the 1970s.

In 1962, Arnold moved to London to enroll her son at the boarding school where her husband had studied. The marriage fell apart, and Arnold lived in London and continued to photograph in places mostly closed to the rest of the world. She published 12 books and her work is included in most major museum collections. Her many honors include the Lifetime Achievement Award from the American Society of Magazine Photographers in 1980. In 1995, she was made a fellow of the Royal Photographic Society and was elected Master Photographer, the world's most prestigious photographic honor, by New York's International Center of Photography.

[Stewart Kampel (2nd ed.)]

ARNOLD, PAULA (1885–1968), Israeli columnist. Born in Vienna, the daughter of Leon *Kellner, Arnold taught at girls' high schools until 1933, when she settled in Palestine. She wrote *Austria of the Austrians* (1914) and translated novels and plays into German. For the centenary of the birth of Theodor *Herzl (1960), she prepared an English translation of his *Altneuland* ("Old-New Land") which was published in Israel in that year. She also wrote *Birds of Israel* (1962) and published *Israel Nature Notes* (1965), a selection of articles written for the *Jerusalem Post*.

ARNON (Heb. אַרְנוֹן; Ar. *al-Mawjib*), river in Transjordan having its source east of the al-Karak region and flowing south to north, then turning west for an overall distance of 50 mi. (80 km.). After the Jordan, it is one of the longest water courses in the Ereẓ Israel region. In its lower course it runs through a steep narrow valley and empties into the Dead Sea through a gateway 44 yd. (40 m.) wide of red and rose-colored layers of sandstone. The volume of its waters fluctuates considerably between the rainy season and the summer and autumn months; however, it is one of a few rivers in Israel that contains water all through the year. The average is estimated at 2 cu. m. per second, but due to the steepness of its banks they have so far not been exploited. When the Israelites reached the eastern side of the Jordan in the period of the Exodus, the Arnon marked the boundary between *Moab and the *Amorites (Num. 22:36). The Amorites had previously wrested the northern area from the Moabites (*ibid.* 21:13–15, 24–29). In their war against the Amorites, Moses and the Israelites had to cross the upper reaches of the Arnon (Deut. 2:24); they conquered the territory lying north of it up to the *Jabbok. This area was allotted by Moses (later confirmed by Joshua) to the tribe of *Reuben (Deut. 3:8, 12, 16; Josh. 12:1–2; 13:9, 16; Judg. 11:18, 26), making the Arnon its border with Moab. The border and the fort over the ravine were dominated by the city of *Aroer (Deut. 2:36; 3:12; 4:48; Josh. 12:2; 13:9, 16). In the ninth century B.C.E. Mesha, king of Moab, recovered part of the lands north of the Arnon, and in his inscription (line 26), speaks of the roads (*mesillot*) which he built across it. Moab, in fact, never accepted the Arnon as its northern border, although Jephthah describes it as the established northern frontier of Moab in his message to the Ammonite king (Judg. 11:26). The region north of the Arnon was conquered by Hazael of Damascus, from Jehu, and finally annexed by Tiglath-Pileser III of Assyria in 733 B.C.E. Both Isaiah (16:2) and Jeremiah (48:20) mention the Arnon in connection with Moab. The fords of the Arnon, referred to by Isaiah (16:2 – Mesha's *mesillot*), constituted an important link in the King's Highway connecting Elath with Damascus by way of Transjordan (Num. 20:17; 21:22; cf. 20:19). In Hasmonean times, when first John Hyrcanus and then Alexander Yannai subdued this region, the Arnon formed the border between their kingdoms and the *Nabateans (Jos., Ant., 13:254–55, 397). A legion stationed at "Castra Arnonensia" in Roman times guarded the road from Elath to Bozrah where it crossed the Arnon Valley. The Arab geographer al-Idrīsī speaks enthusiastically of the wildlife in the neighborhood of the Arnon ravine and of the abundance of fish in its waters. Rabbinic sources include the fords of the Arnon among the places at the sight of which the blessing "Blessed be He who performed miracles to our forefathers at this place" must be pronounced, and at the same time they describe the fantastic nature of these miracles performed in Moses' time (Ber. 54b; Tanḥ. B., Num. 127). An ancient road probably built by Mesha, king of Moab, which connected the southern parts of Moab to northern Moab, was discovered near the river.

BIBLIOGRAPHY: EM; Press, Ereẓ, 1 (1951), 38–39; G.A. Smith, *Historical Geography of the Holy Land* (1931[25]), 557ff.; Aharoni, Land, index; Ginzberg, Legends, 3 (1954), 337ff.; Abel, Geog, 1 (1933), 177, 487–9.

ARNON, ABRAHAM (1887–1960), educationalist. Arnon was born in Cherikov, Belorussia. He studied both in *ḥeder* and in the local secular Russian school, and in 1912 graduated in economics from the High School of Commerce and Economies in Kiev. In 1913 he immigrated to Ereẓ Israel and taught in Jerusalem and Tel Aviv. From 1922 to 1931 he was principal of the Laemel School in Jerusalem and active in the Hebrew Teachers' Association. In 1933 he was appointed inspector of schools and in 1948 chief inspector. On the establishment of the State he was appointed a member of the executive of the Ministry of Education and Culture, and from 1953 to 1955 was chief inspector for schools. He contributed numerous articles to pedagogical journals on topical problems of education. He was awarded the Israel Prize for education in 1960.

ARNON, DANIEL ISRAEL (1910–1994), U.S. biochemist. Born in Poland, Arnon received his B.Sc. in 1932 and his Ph.D. in plant physiology in 1936 from the University of California, Berkeley, where later he became professor of cell physiology and biochemistry. After military service in World War II, he set up and directed an experimental nutrient culture center on Ascension Island in the mid-Atlantic Ocean, for the United States Army Air Corps. Except for this military service and sabbatical leaves in England, Sweden, Germany, Switzerland, and Pacific Grove, California, he spent his entire career at Berkeley. His early research was concerned with the utilization of various trace elements by plants, and led to the elucidation of the role of such metals as molybdenum and vanadium. As a result, Arnon began his studies of photosynthesis in 1948. From 1951 until the end of his life, Arnon concentrated on photosynthesis. His major contribution to science dealt with the role of light, showing how light energy is converted by the green pigment (chlorophyll) in plants to chemical energy in the form of adenosine triphosphate (ATP) by a phenomenon which he called photophosphorylation (photosynthetic phosphorylation), and he was the first to demonstrate complete photosynthesis outside the living cell (*New York Times*, December 30, 1954). Arnon received many awards for his pioneering work with photosynthesis. These included membership in the U.S. National Academy of Sciences and Academy of Arts and Sciences, election as a fellow of the American Association for the Advancement of Science (1962), and membership in various international learned societies.

[Sharon Zrachya (2nd ed.)]

ARNON (Aharonowitz), ISAAC (1909–), agronomist. Arnon was born in Antwerp, Belgium, where he completed his studies as an engineer in agronomy in 1931, immigrating to Ereẓ Israel the following year. After working as an agricultural laborer, he was appointed inspector of the Agricultural Experimental Station of the Mandatory Government in Acre in 1933. In this capacity he established a chain of experimental services in settlements throughout Ereẓ Israel, and in 1945 was made responsible for all experimental stations for field crops. On the establishment of the State, he founded an experimental station at Neve Ya'ar in the Jezreel Valley. In 1958 he was appointed director of the Volcani Institute of Agricultural Research, and in 1964 associate professor of field crops at the Hebrew University. He resigned from the Volcani Institute in 1968 to devote himself to research on plant protection. He was sent to many countries on behalf of the United Nations as advisor on agricultural research and development and served as chairman of the World Food Organization. He also represented Israel on the Scientific Committee of the World Bromine Institute in Berne. Arnon published many books and articles in Hebrew and English about agriculture, including his autobiography, *My Life with Plants and Farmers, Memoirs of an Agronomist in Palestine (Ereẓ Israel), Israel and the Rest of the World* (2000). He was awarded the Israel Prize for agriculture in 1971.

ARNON, RUTH (1933–), Israeli biochemist and immunologist. Born in Israel, Arnon graduated from the Hebrew University of Jerusalem (M.Sc. in chemistry in 1955) and received her Ph.D. in biochemistry in 1960 from the Weizmann Institute. She served two years in the Israeli Navy as a second lieutenant (1955–56), beginning her scientific career as a Ph.D. student at the Weizmann Institute of Science under Ephraim *Katzir and Michael *Sela, in the field of chemical immunology. Pursuing her scientific career there, she contributed to the understanding of the chemical basis of antigenicity and to the elucidation of the immunochemistry of enzymes. She became a full professor in 1975 and continued her research in immunology, focusing on autoimmunity and multiple sclerosis as well as on the development of synthetic vaccines. At the Weizmann Institute she was head of the Department of Chemical Immunology (1973–74 and 1975–78), director of the MacArthur Center for Parasitology (1984–94), dean of biology (1985–88), vice president (1988–93), and vice president for international scientific relations (1995–97). Her scientific work led to her receipt of several prizes, including the German Robert Koch Prize in Medical Sciences (1979), the Spanish Jimenez Diaz Award (1986), the French Legion of Honor (1994), the Wolf Prize (1988), the Rothschild Prize (1988), and the Israel Prize (2001). She is an elected member of the European Molecular Biology Organization (EMBO) and was elected to the Israel Academy of Sciences and Humanities in 1990. At the academy she served as chairperson of the Sciences Division (1995–2001) and as vice president from 2004. In the international arena she served as president of the European Federation of Immunological Societies (EFIS) in 1983–86 and secretary-general of the International Union of Immunological Societies (IUIS) in 1989–93. Her name is linked with the drug to treat multiple sclerosis, which she invented at the Weizmann Institute and which was developed by TEVA Pharmaceutical Industries under the name Copaxone and is marketed worldwide. She was also involved in the development of an intranasal influenza vaccine and served as Advisor on Science and Technology to the president of Israel.

[Bracha Rager (2nd ed.)]

ARNONA (Heb. אַרְנוֹנָא, from Latin *Arnona*), annual crop tax. As in other Roman provinces the *arnona*, the duty to supply grain either for the Roman Army or for the city of Rome, was imposed in Judea. At the beginning of Roman rule there Julius Caesar made *Hyrcanus II responsible for remitting annually over 20,000 modii for the territory of Jaffa alone. The general tax due annually amounted to one quarter of the yield, but the Jews were exempt from the impost during the sabbatical year. The grain was collected in Sidon where the Roman warehouses for the *arnona* were situated. Information on the *arnona* in Ereẓ Israel in talmudic literature dates from the period after the destruction of the Second Temple.

During the third century C.E., with Ereẓ Israel constantly on the threshold of the arena of intermittent wars between Rome and Persia, taxes reached an intolerable level. This was especially the case with those used to supply the army, such as the *arnona militaris*, which toward the end of the third century, was the most important tax levied in the Roman Empire. It is this tax which is most often mentioned in rabbinic literature. The use of the term was extended to cover a tax not only on land, grain, and livestock, paid in kind (Tosef., Dem. 6:3), but also on bread, wine, meat, oil, clothing, etc. (ARN^{1}, 22, 71).

Furthermore, as part of this process of tax intensification, the exemption from the *arnona*, formerly granted for sabbatical years, was canceled in the third century. On one occasion, R. Yannai (c. 220–50) announced: "Go out and sow in the seventh year, because of the *arnona*," to aid the farmers in paying the heavy tax of the seventh year (Sanh. 26a; but cf. TJ, Sanh. 6:6, 21b). Isaac Nappaḥa (c. 250–320), extolling the virtues of one who observed the sabbatical laws, declared (Lev. R. 1:1)… "This man has left his field untilled and vineyard untended; yet he gives his *arnona* in silence [i.e., without complaint against God]. Is there one mightier than he?" (a reference to Ps. 103:20; but cf. Margulies ed. 4). However, when the burden became virtually unbearable, the patriarch Gamaliel III saw the need to legislate for a permanent easing of the sabbatical laws (Tosef., Shev. 1:1, 61; et al.; cf. Lieberman, *Tosefta ki-Feshutah*, 2 (1955) 482–3).

The *arnona militaris* was irregular and unpredictable, and therefore had halakhic implications. Thus, TJ, *Ḥallah* 3:4, 59a–b, explains why dough (*issah*) due to the *arnona* is nonetheless subject to the law of *ḥallah* (the removal of the priests' share of the dough) as follows: "In such a case [the dough] is still [considered to be] in the Jew's possession, as the Gentile may change his mind and not take it…" (cf. Lieberman, *ibid.*, 794). In the time of Diocletian (284–305) the *arnona* became a regular tax under a new name of *iugatio*. However, even afterward, it was sometimes levied unexpectedly on the population. Once, in the mid-fourth century Jonah had to order people to bake on the Sabbath in order to supply an *arnona* of bread (TJ, Shev. 4:2, 35a). In modern Israel *arnona* (*arnonah*) denotes municipal rates and property tax.

BIBLIOGRAPHY: Heichelheim, in: *An Economic Survey of Ancient Rome*, ed. by T. Frank, 4 (1938), 234–6, 241–2; Alon, Toledot^{2}, 1 (1958^{3}), 41; 2 (1961^{2}), 154–5, 185–6.

[Abraham Schalit / Daniel Sperber]

ARNSTADT, city in Thuringia, Germany. The Jews living in Arnstadt in the middle of the 13th century had close ties with the Jews of *Erfurt, to which many of them later migrated. Four anti-Jewish outbreaks between 1264 and 1466 resulted in massacres, and following the last the Jews were expelled from Arnstadt. A Jewish community was reestablished in the 19th century. It numbered 59 in 1880, 137 in 1910, 87 in 1933, and 39 in 1939. Before the rise of Nazism, most of the Jews living in Arnstadt were prosperous, their main occupations being cattle-dealing and banking. The synagogue, built in 1913, was burned down by the Nazis on Nov. 10, 1938. The Jews still in the city in 1942 were sent to the death camps of the east. The community was not reconstituted after World War II.

BIBLIOGRAPHY: Salfeld, Martyrol, 3, 19, 70; Germ Jud, 2 (1968), 21–23; PK. **ADD. BIBLIOGRAPHY:** Germ Jud, 3 (1987), 27–29.

ARNSTEIN (**Arnsteiner**), family of court purveyors and financiers in Vienna in the 18th and first half of the 19th centuries. The firm owned by the Arnsteins held a high place among the Viennese business houses until overtaken by that of Solomon *Rothschild in the 1820s. It cooperated with the *Fould brothers in France until its breakdown in 1859 and was liquidated in 1873. The Arnsteins became connected by marriage with other leading Jewish families, such as the *Itzig, *Mendelssohn, and *Pereira families. They achieved notable successes in Viennese society and in contemporary intellectual and cultural circles. The second generation tended to assimilate, several embracing Catholicism.

(1) ISAAC AARON (c. 1682–1744), founder of the family firm and fortune, arrived in Vienna in 1705 from Arnstein near Wuerzburg. Starting in the service of Samson *Wertheimer, he successfully negotiated a number of important financial transactions, including the redemption from pawn of the Spanish crown jewels. He later worked in partnership with Samson and Wolf *Wertheimer as well as independently on a large scale, becoming purveyor to the court and military establishment of Emperor Charles VI. He used his financial influence to avert the expulsion of Jews from Vienna in 1736.

(2) ADAM ISAAC (in Jewish sources: Asher Anshel; 1721–1785), son of Isaac Aaron, married Sibylle (Bella), a daughter of Bendit Gomperz-Nymwegen. Adam Isaac became head of the Arnstein firm. As purveyor to the consort of Empress Maria Theresa, from 1762 he was freed from some humiliating restrictions to which the Jews in Austria were then subjected, being exempted from wearing the yellow *badge

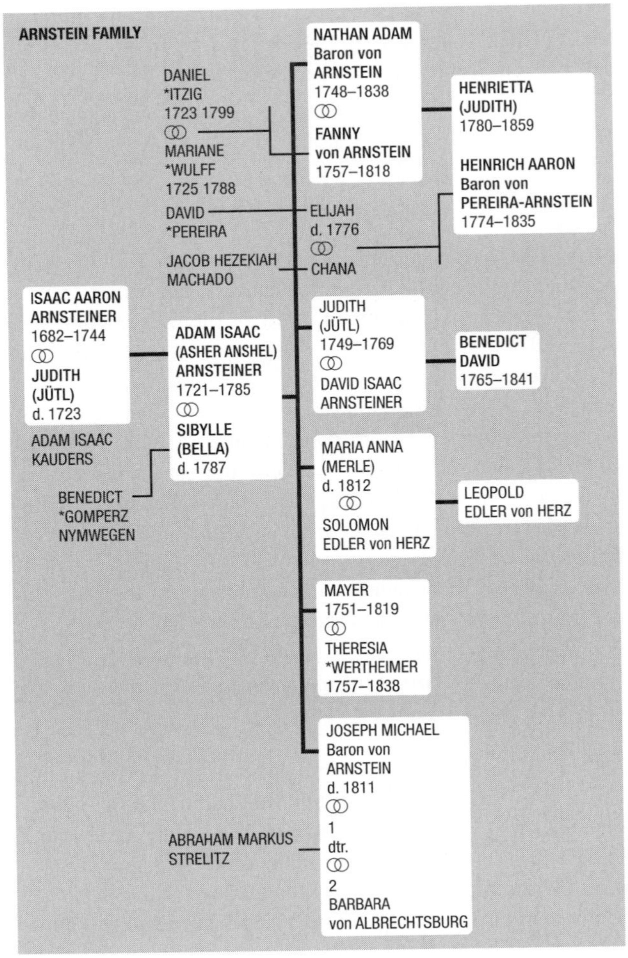

and permitted to wear a sword. He obtained more privileges in 1768 after threatening to leave Vienna for the Netherlands, but undertook not to ask for tax relief. Active in matters affecting the Vienna community, in 1744–45 he helped secure diplomatic intervention to prevent the expulsion of the Jews from Prague; he secured Austrian intercession with the government of Saxony and the Hamburg senate concerning Jewish rights. His favorite son, JOSEPH MICHAEL VON ARNSTEIN (d. 1811), became a Catholic in 1778, and married, for a second time, into the aristocracy. Joseph was ennobled in 1783, and had considerable social and business success. He was disowned in his father's will for having abandoned Judaism; Adam Isaac, however, had been made to pay him a compensatory sum at baptism.

(3) NATHAN ADAM (1748–1838), son of Adam Isaac, made large-scale loans to the government under *Joseph II. He and his brother-in-law and partner, Bernhard *Eskeles, expanded their business activities during the Napoleonic Wars. They financed inter alia the Tyrolese peasant revolt against the French and Bavarians, and a peak in the Alps was named "Arnstein-Spitze." Although little interested in Judaism, he subscribed to Moses *Mendelssohn's Bible translation and introduced Naphtali Hirz *Wessely to the Trieste community. During the Congress of Vienna (1814–15), he and other Jewish notables signed a petition to the emperor requesting civil rights for Austrian Jews. Historians differ as to the extent of his activities at the Congress on behalf of the Jews. His daughter HENRIETTA (Judith; 1780–1859) married Heinrich Pereira (1774–1835), reputedly a relative of Diego *d'Aguilar. They had their children baptized, and later followed suit themselves.

(4) FANNY (Franziska, Voegelchen; 1757–1818), daughter of Daniel *Itzig of Berlin, married Nathan Adam (see above) in 1776. At her famed salon, Fanny's artistic and cultural interests, together with her feminine charm, combined to attract many of the leading personalities of the day. Among them were the *Varnhagens and the *Schlegels, Mme. de Stael, and the Austrian writer Franz Grillparzer as well as the aristocracy, including Emperor Joseph II. Her sister Rebecca Ephraim, celebrated for her wit, and her niece Marianne Saaling (Salomon), famous for her beauty, enhanced her salon. A count of Lichtenstein was killed in a duel for Fanny's sake. She was a co-founder of the Music Society of Austria and for some time Mozart was on her payroll. Her social influence was greatest during the Congress of Vienna, and "the congress danced" mainly in her ballrooms. Most of the chief delegates, including Metternich, Hardenberg, and Talleyrand, attended her glittering receptions, which became a center of political intrigue. Fanny adopted the way of life, not to say libertine habits, of contemporary non-Jewish society. She had the first Christmas tree known in Vienna. However, she retained sentiments of loyalty to Judaism and felt it a duty to help needy Jews, principles which she tried to instill in her Catholic daughter in her wills of 1793 and 1806. Fanny died a Jewess, her final testament endowing equally the Jewish hospital and a home for aged Catholic priests. She was buried in Waehring cemetery and was eulogized by N.H. *Homberg; her husband gave an ark curtain to the synagogue in her memory.

(5) BENEDICT DAVID (1765–1841), dramatist and banker; grandson of Adam Isaac (2). His first publication, in dramatic form, *Eynige Juedische Familienscene bey Erblickung des Patents ueber die Freyheiten, welche die Juden in den Kayserlichen Staaten erhalten haben, von einem juedischen Juengling* (1782), describes the joy felt by Jewish families at the granting of Joseph II's **Toleranzpatent*. It was the first German work by a Jew published in Hapsburg territory. His later dramas were not concerned with Jewish themes, and he subsequently occupied himself in banking.

BIBLIOGRAPHY: N.M. Gelber, *Aktenstuecke zur Judenfrage am Wiener Kongress 1814–15* (1920), 10; H. Schnee, *Die Hoffinanz und der Preussische Staat*, 3 (1955), 245–6; 4 (1963), 328–30; 5 (1965), 232–6, 269; H. Spiel, *Fanny von Arnstein…* (1962), includes bibliography; idem, in: *Jews in Austria*, ed. by J. Fraenkel (1967), 97–110; Grunwald, in: YLBI, 12 (1967), 170, 206. **ADD. BIBLIOGRAPHY:** Burkhardt, in: Ries and Battenberg (ed.), *Hofjuden – Oekonomie und Interkulturalitaet* (2002), 71–86.

[Meir Lamed]

ARNSTEIN, WALTER LEONARD (1930–), U.S. historian. Born in Stuttgart, Germany, Arnstein immigrated to the United States in 1939 and became an American citizen in 1944. He served in Korea with the U.S. Army from 1951 to 1953 and earned his Ph.D. in 1961 at Northwestern University. He next taught at his alma mater as well as at Roosevelt University (1957–67). He was then appointed professor of history at the University of Illinois. Arnstein served as a member of the Department of History of the University of Illinois at Urbana-Champaign from 1968 to 1998, and holds the titles Professor of History Emeritus and Jubilee Professor of the Liberal Arts and Sciences Emeritus. He served for four years as department chair and for four years as department director of graduate studies. In 1987 he won the all-campus award for excellence in undergraduate teaching.

A specialist in British history, Arnstein wrote *The Bradlaugh Case: A Study in Late Victorian Opinion and Politics* (1965, 1984); *Britain, Yesterday and Today: 1830 to the Present* (1966, 2001^{8}); and *Queen Victoria* (2003). He also published two monographs on religious issues in Victorian England and 30 articles. Seven of the articles deal with Queen Victoria, whose papers he examined in the Royal Archives at Windsor.

Arnstein served as president of the Midwest Victorian Studies Association (1977–80), the Midwest Conference on British Studies (1980–82), and the North American Conference of British Studies (1995–97). In 1991 the annual Walter L. Arnstein Prize for Ph.D. students in Victorian Studies was established by the Midwest Victorian Studies Association.

[Ruth Beloff (2nd ed.)]

AROCH, ARIE (1908–1974), Israeli painter and diplomat. Aroch was born as Lyoba Niselevitch in Kharkov, Ukraine, the third child of Rivka Shulamit and Chaim. His father was a Zionist activist. In 1924 Aroch immigrated with his family to Ereẓ Israel, settling in Tel Aviv. He studied art at the Bezalel Academy of Arts and Design in Jerusalem and at the Colarossi Academy in Paris.

During the 1930s and 1940s Aroch had many one-man exhibitions and also participated in group exhibitions of young artists. His friendship with Avraham Halfi and other theater people led him to the design of stage sets. In 1942 he was inducted into the British Army. In the 1950s and the 1960s Aroch served in diplomatic posts in Argentina, Moscow, Brazil, and Stockholm (ambassador in the last two). In 1972 he was awarded the Israel Prize for art.

During the 1950s Aroch's artistic style changed from the figurative to the expressionistic, moving toward abstraction. In these years he developed his unique way of referring to Jewish motifs. He looked for a way to give them in modernist forms. He would thus quote from Jewish icons (for example from *The Sarajevo Haggadah*) but design them differently using a personal modernist method to create a completely new image out of the old icon (*Jewish Motif*, 1961, Tel Aviv Museum of Art).

His best-known art work is *Agrippas Street* (1964, The Israel Museum, Jerusalem). He began the creation of this work in Stockholm, where he painted abstractly his memories of and yearning for both his homes: the one in the Ukraine where he had spent his childhood and his home in Israel. To this end Aroch attached a "found object," which was an enamel street sign. The object integrates memories from his father's shoemaking workshop and from his student life in Jerusalem. The name of the street derives from the name of Jerusalem's market street and the name of the last Jewish governor appointed for Jerusalem in the years 41–44 C.E., referring to a period when Ereẓ Israel country was governed by scions of the Hasmonean dynasty. The linkage in this work between present and past, Israel and the Diaspora, as well as the dialogue between different modernist styles contributed to the fame of this work.

In general Aroch's art works are characterized by significant repetitive motifs, such as bus in the mountain, two cubes, angels, and boats, all of them with ambiguous and complex meanings.

BIBLIOGRAPHY: O. Mordechai (ed.), *Arie Aroch* (2003).

[Ronit Steinberg (2nd ed.)]

AROER (Heb. עֲרוֹעֵר, עֲרֹעֵר), (1) city on the northern bank of the Arnon River belonging to the domain of Sihon the Amorite king (Josh. 12:2), from whom Moses and the Israelites conquered it before they entered Canaan. It was then allotted to either the tribe of Reuben (Deut. 2:36; 3:12; 4:48; Josh. 12:2; Judg. 11:26) or to Gad (Num. 32:34; Josh. 13:9). Jephthah in his message to the Amorite king speaks of Israel as having "dwelt… in Aroer and its towns… 300 years" (Judg. 11:26) and he proceeded to defeat the Amorite cities from Aroer northward (*ibid.* 11:33). One of David's "mighty men," the Aroerite (I Chron. 11:44), may have come from this city (or perhaps from No. 3 below). Aroer was the southernmost city in Israel's territory east of the Jordan and the starting point of David's census (II Sam. 24:5). According to the inscription of Mesha, king of Moab, he fortified the city and also constructed the Arnon fort dominated by Aroer. It was captured by Hazael during the reign of Jehu (842–815 B.C.E.; see II Kings 10:33) and annexed by Tiglath-Pileser III in his campaign against Aram and Israel in 733 B.C.E. At about the same time, Isaiah (17:2) mentioned Aroer as belonging to Damascus, but the reading is doubtful (cf. Septuagint) and another place may be meant. Aroer is the present-day Khirbet Arair where excavations have uncovered a strong Iron Age fortress. (2) An unidentified city opposite the Ammonite capital of Rabbah (Josh. 13:25; Judg. 11:33). (3) Aroer was also the name of a city in the Negev, included among those to which David distributed the booty taken from Amalek (I Sam. 30:28). It is probably included in the southern district of Judah referred to in the corrupted form "Adadah" (Josh. 15:22). It is identified with Khirbet Arara, 12½ mi. (20 km.) southeast of Beersheba, a prominent tell with Iron Age remains, overlooking an important well.

BIBLIOGRAPHY: (1) Abel, Geog, 2 (1938), 250; Glueck, in: AASOR, 14 (1934), 49ff.; Aharoni, Land, index; Olávarri, in: RB, 72 (1965), 77–94. (3) Abel, Geog, 2 (1938), 250; N. Glueck, *Rivers in the Desert* (1959), 184ff.

[Michael Avi-Yonah]

AROLLIA, ISAAC BEN MOSES (16th century), Salonikan rabbi and author. Arollia was a disciple of Joseph *Taitaẓak. He is the author of *Beit Tefillah* (Salonika, 1583), a kabbalistic commentary on the liturgy; *Tanḥumot El* (*ibid.*, 1578), sermons on the Pentateuch; and *Makhil Kohelet* (*ibid.*, 1573), on Ecclesiastes. His halakhic decisions are cited in *Divrei Rivot* (*ibid.*, 1582) of Isaac Adarbi. The Arollia family is widespread in the Middle East, where many of its members are known as Aroyo, Alroy, and Ben Aroloyo.

BIBLIOGRAPHY: Conforte, Kore, 39b; Rosanes, Togarmah, 2 (1938), 68.

[Itzhak Alfassi]

AROM, SIMHA (1930–), Israeli-French ethnomusicologist. Arom studied the French horn at the Paris Conservatoire with Jean Devémy and received first prize there in 1954. From 1958 to 1963 he played horn in the Israel Broadcasting Authority Symphony Orchestra in Jerusalem. However, Arom received international recognition first of all as ethnomusicologist. In 1963, Arom was sent to the Central African Republic, where he did extensive fieldwork, founded the Musée National Boganda at Bangui, and was its director until 1967. Subsequently he studied musicology at the Sorbonne and received his Ph.D. in 1985 with a thesis on polyphony and polyrhythmic in the instrumental folk music of Central Africa, based on his African experience. After a long stint as researcher at the Centre national de la recherche scientifique (CNRS) in Paris, he was appointed Directeur de Recherche de Classe Exeptionelle there in 1993. In Israel he was made associate professor at Tel Aviv University (1979–83) and music director of the Israel Broadcasting Authority (1980–82).

Arom's main research interests are connected with Central Africa's folk music (polyphonic and polymetric structures) as well as with Jewish liturgical music of the Yemenite and Ethiopian communities. In 1972 he devised new methodological procedures for analytical recording of oral traditional music, enabling such music to be transcribed and analyzed; in 1989 he developed an interactive experimental method for the perception of the organization of musical scales in orally transmitted music. His fundamental monograph, *Polyphonies and Polyritmies instrumentales d'Afrique Centrale. Structure et méthodologie* (1985), was translated into English in 1991. Among his awards are the Grand Prix International du Disque de l'Académie Charles Cros (1971, 1978, and 1985), and the Silver Medal of the CNRS (1984). In 1992 he won the ASCAP Deems Taylor Award for excellence in music literature.

BIBLIOGRAPHY: NG²; MGG².

[Yulia Kreinin (2nd ed.)]

ARON, German family of medalists. PHILLIP ARON was active in the duchy of Mecklenburg-Schwerin, on the Baltic Sea, from about 1750 to 1787. Early in his career as medalist to the court, he struck an official medal for Duke Christian Ludwig II. He was followed by his younger brother ABRAHAM ARON (1744–1825), who worked first at Schwerin, up to 1776, as assistant to Phillip, then in Stockholm from 1776 to 1778, and then once more in Schwerin. His best known piece was struck to celebrate the accession of Frederick Franz I of Mecklenburg in 1785. This same duke also commissioned him to do a curious 50th anniversary medal of Olaus Gerhard *Tychsen, professor of Oriental languages in Mecklenburg, which shows both Hebrew and Arabic lettering at the foot of a palm tree.

[Daniel M. Friedenberg]

ARON, RAYMOND (1905–1983), French sociologist and writer. Aron, who was born in Paris, taught at Le Havre, Toulouse, Cologne, and Berlin. In 1956 he was appointed professor of sociology at the Sorbonne, and director of studies at the Ecole Pratique des Hautes Etudes in Paris in 1960. During World War II he was editor of *Free France – La France Libre*, published in London, and subsequently contributed both as writer and editor to *Combat, Le Figaro*, and the *European Journal of Sociology*, and other periodicals. In 1979 Aron was awarded the Goethe Prize of Frankfurt, a major literary award of West Germany. Philosophically, Aron was deeply influenced by the neo-Kantian Léon *Brunschvig and the phenomenologists Heidegger and *Husserl; in sociology he was influenced by Max Weber, and his critical study of several German sociologists, *Sociologie allemande contemporaine* (1936; *German Sociology*, 1957), reflects this influence. His most erudite and probing work is *Introduction à la philosophie de l'histoire* (1938; *Introduction to the Philosophy of History*, 1961), supplemented by *Les grandes doctrines de sociologie historique* (2 vols., 1960–62; *Main Currents in Sociological Thought*, 2 vols., 1965–67). In these works, Aron attempts to strike a balance between a humanistic sociology and a philosophically conceived treatment of the history of ideas, a combination of empiricism and phenomenology. His main interest was the analysis of modern industrial society which, in his opinion, is not so much defined by the class struggle as by the clash of competing political systems. Hence he was rather an exception among French thinkers of his time, and his commitment to liberal democracy set him apart from the then Marxist-dominated intellectual tendencies. Strongly opposed to Sartre's political views, he nevertheless joined him in the movement advocating the rights of Vietnamese refugees in the late 1970s. The return to pluralism and democracy in most French political philosophy in the 1980s and 1990s led to the rehabilitation of his works, which are now considered fundamental. He was a sophisticated commentator on the antecedents of modern society, on the dialectic between democracy and totalitarianism, on international relations, and on the terrifying issues raised by the cold war. Among his major works on these topics are *L'homme contre les tyrans* (1946); *L'Opium des intellectuels* (1955; *The Opium of the Intellectuals*, 1957); *Espoir et peur du siècle* (1957); *Le développement de la société industrielle et la stratification sociale* (2 vols., 1956–57); *Dimensions de la conscience historique* (1961); *Paix et guerre entre les nations* (1962); *Progress and Disillusion* (1968); *Histoire et dialectique de la violence* (1973); *Penser la guerre, Clausewitz* (1976; *Clausewitz, Philosopher of War*, 1983); *Plaidoyer pour l'Europe décadente* (1977; *In Defense of Decadent Europe*, 1984). His *Mémoires* were first published in 1983 (*Memoirs: Fifty Years of Political Reflection*, 1997).

Although not involved in Jewish affairs, Aron remained a conscious Jew. In a series of essays published as *De Gaulle, Israel and the Jews* (1969), he concluded that even if the French president was not himself an antisemite, his notorious press conference after the Six-Day War certainly encouraged the anti-Jewish elements in French society.

BIBLIOGRAPHY: M. Howard, in: *Encounter*, 30 (Feb. 1968), 55–59. **ADD. BIBLIOGRAPHY:** D.J. Mahoney, *The Liberal Political Science of Raymond Aron* (1992); N. Baverez, *Raymond Aron, un moraliste au temps des ideologies* (1993); S. Launay, *La pensée politique de Raymond Aron* (1995); B.C. Anderson, *Raymond Aron: The Recovery of the Political* (1998).

[Alvin Boskoff and Werner J. Cahnman / Dror Franck Sullaper (2nd ed.)]

ARON, ROBERT (1898–1975), French author. After completing classical studies and being wounded in World War I, he engaged in literary activity, as private secretary to the powerful critic R. Doumic and as a participant in the rising publishing enterprise NRF. His main interest was the reform of political life in a broad socialist, universalist, and ethical perspective, known as "personalism." He was active in the movement "Ordie Nouveau," which saw in federalism a remedy against fascism. With Arnaud Dandieu (1897–1933), Aron wrote *Décadence de la nation française* (1931), *Le Cancer américain* (1931), *La Révolution nécessaire* (1933), and (on his own) *La Fin de l'apres-guerre* (1938). Arrested as a Jew in occupied France during World War II and liberated as a result of the intervention of Vichy authorities, he joined the Resistance movement and remained in hiding until he reached free Algiers. There he worked for the provisional French government and returned to his beloved themes in writing: *Fraternité des Français* (1943), *Précis de l'unité française* (1945), and *Principes du fédéralisme* (1948, with Alexandre Marc).

After the liberation of France he devoted himself principally to contemporary and religious history. In addition to general studies on topical problems, *Les Origines de la Guerre d'Algérie* (1962), *Les Grands dossiers de l'histoire contemporaine* (1962), *Les Nouveaux grands dossiers de l'histoire contemporaine* (1963), *Le Socialisme français face au marxisme* (1971), he studied the internal rivalry which had divided the French people in World War II in his books *Le Piege ou nous a pris l'histoire* (1950), *Histoire de Vichy* (1954, with the half-Jewess Georgette Elgey [Lacour-Grayet]), *Histoire de la libération de la France* (1959), *Charles de Gaulle* (1964), and *Histoire de l'epuration* (four volumes, 1967–75). The tragedy of the fate of European Jewry awakened his Jewish consciousness, which he sought to confront with his Christian-based education in works such as *Retour a L'Eternel* (1946), *Portrait de Jésus* (1951), *Ce que je crois* (1958), *Les Années obscures de Jésus* (1960), the first volume of a *Histoire de Dieu* (1963), *Ainsi priait Jesus enfant* (1968), *Discours contre la methode* (1974), *Lettre ouverte a l'Eglise de France* (1975). Towards the end of his life he was reaching a neo-orthodox position – a living approach to the traditional teachings. His prestige in the world of literary criticism led to his election to the Académie française (1974), but he died a few days before the official ceremony.

BIBLIOGRAPHY: H. Smolowski, *R.A. est entré a l'Académie …* (T.J. Hebdo, 298, March 15–21, 1974); P. Viansson-Ponté, *La Mort de R.A.* (*Le Monde*, April 22, 1975).

[Moshe Catane]

ARONI (Aharoni), TSVI (1917–1990), cantor and professor of music and voice production. Born in Kalisch, Poland, he immigrated to Ereẓ Israel as a child with his parents. In Jerusalem he received his cantorial training under the distinguished cantor and composer Shmuel Kavetsky, whose two volumes of music were published and promoted by his protégé. He was imprisoned by the British as a member of the *Irgun Zeva'i Le'ummi. In 1947 he went to the United States and after holding several positions was appointed cantor of the Shaarey Zedek Synagogue in Manhattan in 1966. Together with Joseph Milo he founded the Manhattan School for Cantors which he directed from 1972. In 1976 he was appointed professor of music and voice production at Long Island University, New York. Later he held a cantorial position in Miami until his death. Besides specializing in the performance of works by Israel Alter, he was a renowned Yiddishist. After his death, his widow Chedva issued a commemorative series of five cassettes of his recordings and live performances. She later helped create the Tsvi Aroni Music Library, which contains sheet music and recordings of both sacred and secular music. This is part of the Molly S. Fraiberg Judaica Collection housed at Florida Atlantic University Libraries. As a concert artist, he performed both in the United States and Israel.

[Akiva Zimmerman / Raymond Goldstein (2nd ed.)]

ARONIUS, JULIUS (1861–1893), German historian. Aronius was born in Rastenberg, East Prussia, and studied history and philology at the universities of Berlin and Koenigsberg. He taught for a short time in the orphanage of the Berlin Jewish community. When the *Historische Commission fuer Geschichte der Juden in Deutschland* was founded in 1885, Aronius was invited to join its staff. In this capacity he gathered source material for the history of the Jews in medieval Germany. His collection, *Regesten zur Geschichte der Juden im fraenkischen und deutschen Reiche bis zum Jahre 1273* (1902), was the first source book on the history of German Jewry prepared according to scholarly principles and influenced similar works produced in other countries. After his early death his colleagues A. Dresdner and L. Lewinsky prepared for the press the last installment of the collection. The full work was published in 1902 (repr. 1970).

BIBLIOGRAPHY: Aronius, *Regesten*, "Vorbemerkung" by Bresslau.

[Zvi Avneri / Marcus Pyka (2nd ed.)]

ARONOVICH (Aranovich, Aharonovitch), YURI MIKHAYLOVICH (1932–2003), conductor. Born in St. Petersburg, he graduated from the St. Petersburg Conservatory, studying with N. Rabinovich, N. Rakhlin, and K. Zanderling. From 1957 to 1964 he was chief conductor of the Yaroslavl Symphony Orchestra and from 1964 to 1972 he was artistic director and chief conductor of the All-Union Radio and TV Symphony Orchestra in Moscow. Aronovich earned a reputation as an interpreter of contemporary music, introducing many new compositions. He also conducted many Jewish composers. In 1972 he immigrated to Israel, occasionally performing with the Israel Philharmonic and radio orchestras, and from 1975 he was chief conductor of the Stockholm Royal Symphony Orchestra and the Cologne Symphony Orchestra. He also conducted often in Frankfurt, performing Shostakovich, especially with the Leningrad Symphony.

BIBLIOGRAPHY: J. Soroker, *Rossiyskie muzykanty evrei, Bio-Bibliograficheskiy Lexikon*, part 1, Jerusalem (1992), 38.

[Marina Rizarev (2nd ed.)]

ARONOWITZ, BENJAMIN (1864–1945), rabbi. Aronowitz was born in Varzhan, Lithuania, and was a student and close disciple of Rabbi Meir Atlas of Shavel. He studied in Volozhin and Telshe. Married in 1885, he continued his studies in Volozhin until 1895, and then moved to Telshe as a *dayyan* (judge). He was ordained by Rabbi Naphtali Ẓevi *Berlin, Rabbi Yeruḥam Lieb of Minsk, and others. While at Telshe, he created preparatory programs for teenage students who wanted to advance their studies at the yeshivah. In 1906 he immigrated to the United States and served as a pulpit rabbi in Lowell, Mass.

In 1910, Aronowitz moved to New York and took a position at the Rabbi Isaac Elchanan Theological Seminary, where he became instrumental in developing Yeshiva University. A close associate of Bernard *Revel, who was also a student from Telshe, after 1915 he assumed an important role in determining the direction of the institution. Revel appointed him director of the rabbinical students and placed him on the ordination committee with Rabbis Moses *Soleveichik and Bernard Levinthal. He remained on the board for 35 years.

Aronowitz was also a supporter of the *Agudat Israel organization in Israel and worked to build the organization in America by helping to establish its branch in New York in 1939. He worked to make their programs successful in the early 1940s. He was a member of the Agudath ha-Rabbonim for almost 40 years and served as the president of the Vaad ha-Rabbonim of New York from 1935 to 1937. During his lifetime, he published a number of works about the Torah and Talmud in *Yagil Torah.*

BIBLIOGRAPHY: M. Sherman, *Orthodox Judaism in America: A Biographical Dictionary and Sourcebook* (1996), 20; B.Z. Eisenstadt, *Dorot ha-Aḥaronim* (1913), 44; *Who's Who in American Jewry* (1927), 26; *ibid.* (1938), 37; *Ha-Zedek, Yeshiva Student Publication* (Dec. 21, 1939), 2; *Morgen Journal* (Sept. 16, 1945), 1; *Yehadut Lita*, vol. 3 (1967), 24; A. Kahn (ed.), *Sefer Yeval ha-Yovelot* (1986), 208.

[Jeanette Friedman (2nd ed.)]

ARONS, LEO (1860–1919), German physicist and Social Democrat. The son of a wealthy Berlin banker, he became an assistant at the Institute of Physics and a *Privatdozent* in Strasbourg (1888–90) and Berlin (1890–1900). Because of his political convictions and his Jewish faith, he never obtained a professorship. In 1899, the Prussian Ministry of Public Education (Kultusministerium), considering his political activities incompatible with his academic duties, demanded his dismissal. When the faculty refused, the Prussian Diet passed a law ("Lex Arons") establishing the government as a body of appeal against disciplinary decisions of a faculty. Thereupon the faculty again confirmed unanimously its former decision, but the government, using the new law, dismissed Arons from his academic position.

In the area of physics, Arons devoted himself to empirical research on electric phenomena which fall under the Maxwell theory. One of his discoveries was the mercury vapor lamp, which was of considerable practical and scientific importance as a source of ultraviolet rays.

Arons belonged to the revisionist wing of his party. He was a city councilor of Berlin and interested himself mainly in educational matters, land reform, and consumers' cooperatives. He was financially independent and a generous donor, making possible the publication of the German bi-monthly, *Sozialistische Monatshefte*. The establishment of the Workers' Education School (Arbeiterbildungsschule) of the Social Democratic Party and the Trade Union Building in Berlin were also results of his contributions.

BIBLIOGRAPHY: *Sozialistische Monatshefte* (Nov. 7, 1919), 1058ff. (Albert Einstein, Paul Hirsch, and Wally Zepler as well as others), about the various aspects of Arons' person and work; U.V. Wilamowitz-Moellendorff, *Erinnerungen 1848–1914* (1928^2), 295.

[Ernest Hamburger]

ARONSON, ARNOLD (1911–1998), U.S. social activist. Aronson co-founded the pioneering Leadership Conference on Civil Rights (LCCR) and was a driving force behind the passage of the landmark civil rights legislation of the 1950s and 1960s. In addition to being president of the LCCR Education Fund until his death, he was also program director for the National Jewish Community Relations Council. His work was driven by the desire to further equality within the American social milieu and an aspiration to create bonds between peoples of differing ethnic backgrounds. Aronson fought for civil rights, civil liberties, immigration reform, and church-state separation. He was also committed to Soviet-Jewish immigration and support for Israel. He was a significant force in what became known as the "golden age" of *black-Jewish relations and one of its most creative figures.

Additionally, Aronson was a founding father of a number of other civil rights organizations including the National Urban Coalition, the National Committee Against Discrimination in Housing, and the National Association of Human Rights Workers. In January 1998, President William J. Clinton awarded Aronson the Presidential Medal of Freedom for his lifelong service.

His son BERNARD WILLIAM (1946–) was also a major public figure, serving as U.S. assistant secretary of state (1989–93). Bernard Aronson graduated from the University of Chicago with a B.A. in 1967 and later served in the U.S. Army Reserves. From 1973 through 1977, Aronson worked for the United Mine Workers, and in 1977 he became a special assistant and speechwriter for Vice President Walter Mondale. Subsequently, starting in 1982, he directed the Democratic National Strategy Council for two years until deciding to strike out on his own by starting a consulting firm, the Policy Project.

In 1989, Republican President George H.W. Bush appointed Aronson assistant secretary of state for inter-American affairs to replace the controversial Elliot *Abrams. Aronson (a Democrat) was chosen for the position in part to soften lingering Democratic Party criticism and skepticism surrounding the office in the wake of the Iran-Contra hearings.

Aronson's post entailed the coordination of U.S. foreign policy vis-à-vis the 34 nations of the Americas. Moreover, he was President Bush's principal foreign policy advisor on U.S. relations with Mexico, the Caribbean, and Central and South America.

Following President Bush's defeat in 1992, Aronson worked in the private sector with corporations like Goldman Sachs & Co., Liz Claiborne, and the Royal Caribbean Cruise Lines. He continued, however, to remain active in developing public policy, serving as a member of the Council of Foreign Relations and on the board of the National Democratic Institute for International Affairs. He also coauthored with William D. Rogers a report on "U.S.-Cuban Relations in the 21st Century." The report urged the U.S. to ease trade restrictions with Cuba and replace the outmoded trade embargo, a leftover from the Cold War, with more lenient policies.

BIBLIOGRAPHY: *American Jewish Yearbook*, Obituaries: United States (Arnold Aronson) (1999); L.S. Maisel and I. Forman, *Jews in American Politics* (2001).

[Yehuda Martin Hausman (2nd ed.)]

ARONSON, BORIS (1900–1980), U.S. stage designer and artist; son of Solomon *Aronson, chief rabbi of Kiev. Born in Kiev, Aronson was trained at the Kiev State Art School and spent five years in the Yiddish and other theaters in Moscow. From his exposure to the Russian experimental school, he began to formulate his theories of stage design: the set should allow varied movement; each scene should contain the mood of the whole play; and through the fusion of color and form, the setting should be beautiful in its own right. But, he added, "a set is only complete when the actors move through it."

Aronson studied in Berlin and Paris and wrote a book on Marc Chagall (1923). In New York he went to work for the small Unser Theater in the Bronx, and in 1925 designed the dream sets for *Bronx Express*. Thereafter, his rise was rapid, first at Maurice *Schwartz's Yiddish Art Theater and after 1930 on Broadway.

His innovations and his imaginative use of American ideas and fantasies in his sometimes surrealist sets made him the foremost American stage designer by the 1950s. He also held several exhibitions of his paintings and sculptures.

Broadway productions for which he designed the decor include *Walk a Little Faster* (1933), *Three Men on a Horse* (1935), *Battleship Gertie* (1935), *Awake and Sing!* (1935), *Paradise Lost* (1935), *Cabin in the Sky* (1940), *South Pacific* (1944), *Sadie Thompson* (1944), *The Bird Cage* (1950), *Season in the Sun* (1951), *The Country Girl* (1952), *The Rose Tattoo* (1952), *I Am a Camera* (1952), *The Crucible* (1953), *Bus Stop* (1955), *A View from the Bridge* (1955), *The Diary of Anne Frank* (1957), *A Hole in the Head* (1957), *JB* (1959), *Incident at Vichy* (1964), *Fiddler on the Roof* (1964), *Cabaret* (1969), *The Price* (1969), *Zorba* (1969), *Company* (1970), *Follies* (1972), *The Creation of the World and Other Business* (1972), *The Great God Brown* (1973), *A Little Night Music* (1973), *Sondheim: A Musical Tribute* (1973), *Dreyfus in Rehearsal* (1974), and *Pacific Overtures* (1976). His last set design was in 1976 for the ballet *The Nutcracker*, as choreographed by Mikhail Baryshnikov.

Aronson won eight Tony Awards and maintained an active career as a sculptor and painter until his death. His prodigious work in theater, opera (*Mourning Becomes Electra*), and ballet design proved that Aronson was a well-rounded set designer. His design of two synagogue interiors and his successful career as a painter and sculptor further distinguished him as one of the few leading figures in 20th-century scene design.

BIBLIOGRAPHY: W. George, *Boris Aronson et l'art du théâtre* (1928); C.A. Glassgold, in: *Art in the Theater*, 13 (1928), 46f. **ADD. BIBLIOGRAPHY:** F. Rich, *Boris Aronson: Stage Design as Visual Metaphor* (1989); idem, *The Theatre Art of Boris Aronson* (1987).

[Mark Perlgut / Ruth Beloff (2nd ed.)]

ARONSON, DAVID (1894–1988), U.S. rabbi; born in Ulla-Vitebsk, Russia, a descendant of the Gaon of Vilna. He immigrated to the United States and was educated at New York University (1916) and the Jewish Theological Seminary where he was ordained in 1919. He served as a chaplain in World War I and then at pulpits in Salt Lake City (1920–21) and Duluth, Minn. (1922–24). For 35 years he served as rabbi of the Conservative Beth El Synagogue in Minneapolis. He took an active role in public life, serving as associate editor of the *American Jewish World* and as a member of the Governor's Commission for Human Rights. After the establishment of Israel, he called for the standardization of the Jewish calendar by abolishing the second day of Jewish festivals in the Diaspora. In 1951 he posed a solution to the *agunah problem by allowing a Jewish court to initiate divorces. From 1959 Aronson was professor of rabbinics at the University of Judaism in Los Angeles. He was president of the Rabbinical Assembly from 1948 to 1950. He wrote *The Jewish Way of Life* (1946, 1957^2), *Torah, the Life of the Jew* (1964), and various articles, including a report on the Warsaw Jewish community, which he visited in 1927.

ARONSON, DAVID (1923–), U.S. painter. Born in Lithuania, Aronson taught at Boston University from 1955. His work, painting or drawing in several media, are often based on Jewish themes, such as Ḥasidim and kabbalists, the Ba'al Shem, and the dybbuk. His powerful figures stare from the pictures with sad, intense eyes in distorted faces.

ARONSON, GRIGORI (1887–1968), journalist, author, and public figure. Aronson, who was the nephew of Mordecai ben Hillel *Hacohen, was born in St. Petersburg and received a rudimentary traditional Jewish education in Gomel. As a youth, he was a Bolshevist, but in 1908 as a result of his growing Jewish awareness, joined the Bund. The following year, he became active in *ORT and the Society for Diffusion of Enlightenment. After the 1917 revolution he was active as a Menshevik and right-wing Bundist, particularly in Vitebsk. Aronson was permitted to leave the Soviet Union in 1922, after which he lived in Germany and France, and after 1940 in the United States. For some time he acted as general secretary of ORT in Berlin. He was engaged in the political activity of the Menshevik émigrés. Aronson's studies of Soviet Russia and Soviet Jewry include *Di Shpaltung fun Bund* (1920); *Di Yidishe Problem in Sovyet-Rusland* (1944); and *Anti-Semitism in Sovyet-Rusland* (1953). In 1966 he coedited a collection of essays, *Russian Jewry: 1860–1917*, with J. Frumkin and others.

BIBLIOGRAPHY: LNYL, 1 (1956), 169–70.

[Moshe Mishkinsky]

ARONSON, NAUM (1872/73–1943), graphic artist and sculptor. Aronson was born into a ḥasidic family in Kreslavka, Vitebsk province (today Kreslava, Latvia) and, as a child, received a traditional Jewish education. In 1889–91, he studied at the Vilna School of Drawing. Having settled in Paris in 1891, he worked as a stonemason at local sculpture workshops and studied both at École des Arts Décoratifs and at the F. Colarossi academy. In 1894, Aronson returned to Russia to serve in the army, but got an exemption and returned to France in 1896. In 1898, he joined the National Society for Fine Arts and participated in its exhibits as well as in exhibitions of other Paris salons. He exhibited his sculptures at the Berlin Secession and in London galleries. In 1900, he was awarded the second gold medal at the Paris World Show, and in 1905, the gold medal at the Liege International Show. He won a reputation as a leading impressionist sculptor. Residing mainly in France, Aronson remained active in Russian cultural life and regularly exhibited in Moscow and St. Petersburg. In 1901, he visited Yasnaya Polyana and did a bust of Leo Tolstoy and a number of portraits in graphics. In 1904, he was among the founders of the New Society of Artists in St. Petersburg. Prior to World War I, Aronson executed many sculptural portraits of prominent figures in Russian and European culture and politics. Many of his works treat "the Jewish theme," among them his composition *Kiddush ha-Shem* dedicated to the memory of victims of the *Kishinev pogrom. For all his fame and success in Europe, Aronson experienced antisemitism among art critics and was subjected to sanctions imposed by the authorities. The persecution only strengthened his national consciousness, which manifested itself in his active participation in Jewish cultural and public life. In 1912, in Paris, he helped a group of young Jewish artists from Russia; in 1915, he was among the founders and later a member of the Jewish Society for the Encouragement of the Arts and participated in its exhibit in 1916 in Petrograd. In 1917–22, Aronson executed a series of busts of Louis Pasteur that were domiciled in Paris and other European capitals and for which in 1924 he was awarded the National Order of the Legion of Honor (from 1938, Aronson was an officer of the Legion of Honor). His retrospective exhibition was held in 1926 in Paris. In the 1920s and 1930s, Aronson actively collaborated with Jewish cultural and public organizations in France. He showed his works at the Exhibition of Jewish Artists and Sculptors in 1924. From the late 1920s, he gave lecture courses on Jewish art at the Jewish People's University. From 1931, he was the chairman of the Union of Lithuanian Jews and participated in the World Congress of Jewish Art in Paris in 1937. In 1940, he fled occupied France to Portugal and later settled in the United States. From 1941, Aronson lived in New York, where he created a number of symbolic works dedicated to the historic fate of the Jewish people.

BIBLIOGRAPHY: *100 Contemporary* American *Jewish Painters and Sculptors* (1947), 8; O.L. Leykind, K.V. Makhrov, and D.J. Severiukhin, *Artists of Russian Diaspora: 1917–1939. Biographical Dictionary* (1991), 104–6 (Rus.).

[Hillel Kazovsky (2nd ed.)]

ARONSON, SOLOMON (1862–1935), chief rabbi of Tel Aviv and Zionist leader. Aronson was chief rabbi of Kiev, 1906–21, and was active in the Ḥovevei Zion movement, attending its conventions as a delegate. After the First Zionist Congress in 1897, Aronson published several articles in *Ha-Meliz*, defending political Zionism against the attacks of its ultra-Orthodox opponents. He later joined the Mizrachi organization. Aronson frequently interceded with the Czarist authorities on behalf of the Jews and helped in the legal defense of Mendel *Beilis in the blood libel of 1913. During World War I he worked for the relief of refugees from Galicia who had come to Kiev. After the Russian Revolution in 1917, he sponsored the national-religious Aḥdut Israel movement, which eventually merged into a nationwide federation. In 1921 he escaped to Berlin, serving as rabbi of the Russian community there until 1923, when he immigrated to Palestine. There he was appointed chief rabbi of the Tel Aviv-Jaffa community. Aronson founded and helped maintain various welfare institutions in Tel Aviv, including a society for the support of Russian refugees, established the Tel Aviv yeshivah, and took an active part in the Mizrachi movement, particularly in the field of education.

BIBLIOGRAPHY: *Enẓiklopedyah le-Ẓiyyonut*, 1 (1947), 14–15; Tidhar, 1 (1947), 164–5; EẒD, 1 (1958), 39–42 (includes bibliography).

[Zvi Kaplan]

ARPA, ABRAMO DALL' (**Abraham Levi**; c. 1542–c. 1577), Italian musician; the most outstanding of a Mantuan family whose members were known for their skill as musicians, chiefly harpists – hence their name.

A document from 1542 records the participation in a ducal spectacle of "a Jew playing the harp" and assuming the role of the god Pan. This may refer to Abramo, who appears as a musician on the payroll of Duke Guglielmo in 1553 and again in 1577. Between these two dates he got into trouble with the duke and was put into prison in 1566. It is also possible that he can be identified as "Abraham the musician of Mantua" whose presence is recorded in Rome in 1555. There is also record of a passport permitting residence in Vienna being granted to Abraham of Mantua, a harpist who gave music lessons to the children of Ferdinand I (M. Grunwald, *Vienna* (1936), p. 78). He may be identical with the Mantuan banker Abraham Levi, whose banking activities are recorded in 1544 and 1545 and who in 1561 was granted a ten-year monopoly for ritual slaughtering for the Mantuan Jewish community. The date of Abramo's death may be fixed between 1577 (the last mention of his name on the duke's payroll) and 1587, at which date his name appears in the *pinkas* (Ms. Kaufmann, no. 59, fol. 35, col. d) with the the words "may his memory be blessed."

Abramo dall'Arpa's fame as one of the outstanding harpists of his time is attested to by the painter, writer, and poet Giovanni Paolo Lomazzo. He mentions Abramo, together with his father "the Jew of Mantua" and the Neapolitan (non-Jewish) Giovanni Leonardo dall'Arpa, as the three most prominent harp players of their time. Abramo's nephew Abramino ("little Abraham") was also employed as a musician at the ducal court. In 1587 Abramino collaborated in an entertainment given on the lake of Mantua on occasion of a ducal baptism. The same year he followed the dying Duke Guglielmo to his palace at Goito to comfort him in his last days with music.

BIBLIOGRAPHY: A. d'Ancona, *Origini del teatro italiano* (1891^2), 400, 439; S. Simonsohn, *Toledot ha-Yehudim be-Dukkasut Mantovah*, 2 (1964), index; C. Roth, *Jews in the Renaissance* (1959), 283–4; Adler, in: *Taẓlil*, 9 (1969), 105–8.

[Israel Adler]

ARPAD (Heb. אַרְפָּד; in the Assyrian inscriptions **Ar-padda**), city in northern Syria, today Tell-Rifa'at, north of Aleppo; the capital city of the Aramean kingdom Bît-Aguši. Arpad is first mentioned in sources from the ninth century B.C.E. Archaeological excavations show the city to have been inhabited from the beginning of the Chalcolithic period, and that an Aramean population settled there as early as the last third of the second millennium B.C.E. In 858 B.C.E., Aramé, king of Arpad, dissociated himself from the alliance of north Syrian states against Assyria and paid a levy to Shalmaneser III. A few years later, Shalmaneser III conquered a few cities affiliated with Arpad, annexing them to Assyria. Arpad played an important political and military role in eighth-century Syria when it joined with other states and rose against Assyrian efforts to seize control of the area. The anti-Assyrian policy of the kings of Arpad is illustrated by the war of Ben-Hadad, son of Hazael, king of Aram-Damascus, against Hamath in the second quarter of the eighth century. Bargash, king of Arpad, allied himself with Ben-Hadad. In 754 B.C.E. Ashurnirari V of Assyria waged war against Arpad which was concluded by a treaty in which King Matiʾ-ilu of Arpad agreed to Assyrian suzerainty. In 745 Matiʾ-ilu signed a treaty with Bar-Ga'ayah, king of KTK, in which Matiʾ-ilu probably represented all the Syrian states from the Euphrates to Damascus. The alliance appears to have been made possible by the unified efforts of all the Syrian states to break the power of the Assyrian Empire and free themselves from its domination. In 743 Tiglath-Pileser III, king of Assyria, fought against Arpad, which was aided by the army of *Ararat. After four years of war and siege, Arpad fell and became an Assyrian province. Another attempt at rebellion was made in 720 when the city joined the abortive revolt of Hamath and other Syrian and Ereẓ Israel states against Sargon II. Echoes of the fall of Arpad and its destruction by Assyria are found in II Kings 18:34; 19:13; Isaiah 10:9; 36:19; 37:13; and Jeremiah 49:23. Archaeological data reveal that the place was not completely abandoned, but continued to be settled until the Roman period (fourth century C.E.).

[Bustanay Oded]

ʿARRĀBA (Ar. عرابة), Muslim-Arab village southwest of Jenin, on the rim of the Dothan Valley (called in Arabic Sahl ʿArrāba). In 1967 it had 4,231 inhabitants, increasing to 7,453 in 1997, among them 35% refugees. The economy was based on field and garden crops. It is generally identified with Aruboth (Heb. אֲרֻבּוֹת), the center of Solomon's Third Province (I Kings 4:10).

[Efraim Orni]

ARRABY MOOR (or **Rabbí Mór**), official title for the chief rabbi of *Portugal from the 13th century. A letter sent by Alfonso III to the municipal council of Braganza shows that this office existed at least from 1278. Duties of the *arraby moor* included supervision of the conduct of the rabbis and lay heads of the Jewish communities in Portugal. When he visited a community, any complaints made by its members were recorded in his presence. He was responsible for the property of orphans, whose guardians were answerable to him for any irregularities in their administration of the estates. The *ar-*

raby moor also examined the communal accounts and funds. To prevent dissension among the communal officers, his authority was restricted. He was prohibited from choosing rabbis for the communities, from using communal resources against the wishes of the community, and from issuing privileges such as grants of exemption from communal taxes or services. The *arraby moor* had his special seal, inscribed with the legend "Sello do Rabbí Mór de Portugal." His official staff included a chancellor, auditor, secretary, and "doorkeeper." In response to complaints lodged by the community of *Lisbon against the *arraby moor* Judah Cohen during the reign of John I (1385–1433) the king abrogated some of the privileges of the office. The last person to occupy it was Simon Maimi who died as a result of his sufferings at the time of the forced conversion of 1497.

BIBLIOGRAPHY: Baron, Community, 1 (1942), 285; 3 (1942), 65; Roth, Marranos, 60; J. Mendes dos Remedios, *Os Judeus em Portugal*, 1 (1895), 375–83,428–9.

[Joseph Kaplan]

ARRAGEL (Al-Ragil), MOSES (15th century), Spanish scholar of Guadalajara. In 1422 he settled in Maqueda and there Don Luis de Guzmán, grand master of the order of Calatrava invited him to translate the Bible into Spanish with a commentary. At first, he declined the offer, stating that a translation and commentary by a Jew would not be acceptable to Christian believers. His objections were finally overridden; and Arias de Enciena, *custos* of the Franciscan Order in Toledo, was attached as consultant. Moses completed the translation and commentary in 1433. His translation followed the *Vulgate version except where it departed from the Hebrew original. His commentaries show close knowledge of Jewish exegesis and familiarity with classical and Christian Latin literature. At times he emphasizes that in certain matters the Jewish version is different from the Christian. The correspondence between him, Don Guzmán, and other Franciscan scholars, concerning their common undertaking, precedes the translation. In these letters he lauded the superiority of Spanish Jews over all their brethren in "lineage, wealth, virtues, and wisdom." The original manuscript includes many illuminations. These come from Christian sources but often betray midrashic elements.

BIBLIOGRAPHY: Baer, Spain, 2 (1966), 251ff.; M. Golde, in: JJLG, 27 (1926), 9–33; Salvany, in: *Revista Española de Estudios Bíblicos*, 2 (1927), 139 46; D.S. Blondheim, *Gleanings from the Bible of Alva* (1927), 11, extract from *Medieval Studies… G.S. Loomis*; C.O. Nordström, *The Duke of Alba's Castilian Bible* (1967).

°ARRIAN (Flavius Arrianus; c. 96–c. 180 C.E.), Greek soldier, historian, and philosopher. Arrian is best known for his *Anabasis*, a history of Alexander the Great from his accession until his death, and *Parthica*, a history of the Parthians, of which only fragments have survived. In the former, Arrian recounts Alexander's capture of Gaza, though he is silent about Judea. On the other hand, in his *Parthica* (fragment 79), Arrian seems to have described in detail the suppression of the Jewish revolt in Mesopotamia in 116 C.E.

ARROW, KENNETH JOSEPH (1921–), U.S. economist and Nobel laureate. Arrow was born in New York and received his doctorate from Columbia University in 1951. He was appointed professor of economics and statistics at Stanford University, California, in 1953. Appointed in 1962 to the Council of Economic Advisors of the Executive Office of the President of the United States, he was a consultant for the RAND Corporation from 1948 on, which he refers to as "the heady days of emerging game theory and mathematical programming."

He received the John Bates Clark Medal of the American Economic Association in 1957 and was elected a member of the National Academy of Sciences and the American Philosophical Society. He was a fellow of Churchill College, Cambridge, in 1963–64 and 1970, and was appointed professor of economics at Harvard (1968–79). In 1979 he returned to Stanford University, where he held the title of Professor Emeritus in the Department of Economics.

His most significant works are his contributions to social choice theory, notably Arrow's "impossibility theorem," and his work on general equilibrium analysis. For his specialized work in welfare economics and general equilibrium theory, Arrow was awarded the 1972 Nobel Memorial Prize in economic sciences. His impossibility theorem, also known as "Arrow's paradox," shows the impossibility of designing rules for social decisionmaking that obey all of a number of "reasonable" criteria. The general equilibrium theory, a branch of theoretical microeconomics, seeks to explain production, consumption, and prices in a whole economy. It attempts to give an understanding of the whole economy using a bottom-up (as opposed to a Keynesian macroeconomic top-down) approach, starting with individual markets and agents. Working with Gerard Debreu (who won the Nobel Prize for this work in 1983), Arrow produced the first rigorous proof of the existence of a market-clearing equilibrium, given certain restrictive assumptions.

Among Arrow's numerous publications are *Social Choice and Individual Values* (1951); *Studies in Linear and Nonlinear Programming* (with L. Hurwicz and H. Uzawa, 1958); *A Time Series Analysis of Interindustry Demands* (with M. Hoffenberg, 1959); *Essays in the Theory of Risk-Bearing* (1971); *General Competitive Analysis* (1972); *The Limits of Organization* (1974); *The Economics of Information* (1984); *Handbook of Mathematical Economics* (1984); *General Equilibrium* (1984); *The Balance between Industry and Agriculture in Economic Development* (1988); *Barriers to Conflict Resolution* (1995); and *Saving Lives, Buying Time: Economics of Malaria Drugs in an Age of Resistance* (2004). Six volumes of his collected papers were published in 1984–85 and three volumes of essays in his honor (W.P. Heller, D.A. Starrett, and R.M. Starr, eds.) appeared in 1986, dealing, respectively, with equilibrium analysis, social choice and public decisionmaking, and uncertainty information and communications.

[Ruth Beloff (2nd ed.)]

ARROW CROSS PARTY (Hung. **Nyilaskeresztes Párt-Hungarista Mozgalom**), the most extreme of the Hungarian Fascist movements in the mid-1930s. The party consisted of several groups, though the name is now commonly associated with the faction organized by Ferenc *Szálasi and Kálmán Hubay in 1938. Following the Nazi pattern, the party promised not only the establishment of a fascist-type system including social reforms, but also the "solution of the Jewish question." The party's uniform was the green shirt, its badge a set of crossed arrows, a Hungarian version of the swastika based on the weapons of the old Magyar conquerors.

With financial and moral support from Nazi Germany, the Arrow Cross won 16.2% of the votes in the 1939 elections. From 1941 it lost many of its supporters and in August 1944 was dissolved along with all other parties. However, it continued secretly, under German guidance, to prepare a coup d'état against the government of Admiral Horthy. On October 15, 1944, when Horthy announced Hungary's withdrawal from the war, the Arrow Cross seized power with military help from the Germans. The Arrow Cross government ordered general mobilization and enforced a regime of terror which, though directed chiefly against the Jews, also inflicted heavy suffering upon the Hungarians. It was responsible for the deportation and death of tens of thousands of Jews. After the Soviet Army liberated the whole of Hungary by early April 1945, Szálasi and his Arrow Cross ministers were brought to trial and executed.

BIBLIOGRAPHY: J. Lévai, *Black Book on the Martyrdom of Hungarian Jewry* (1948), 335–421; idem, *Horogkereszt, kaszáskereszt, nyilaskereszt* (1945); A. Rozsnyai, *Nyilas rémuralom* (1962); M. Laczkó, in: *Századok*, 97:4 (1963), 782–809.

[Bela Adalbert Vago]

ART.

This article is arranged according to the following outline:

Antiquity to 1800

INTRODUCTION: JEWISH ATTITUDE TO ART. Whether there exists a form of art that can be described as "Jewish Art" has long been a matter for discussion. What is indisputable is that at every stage of their history the Jews and their ancestors of biblical times expressed themselves in various art forms which inevitably reflect contemporary styles and fashions and the environment in which they lived. For purposes of cult and of religious observance, as well as for household and personal adornment, Jews have constantly produced or made use of objects which appealed in some fashion to their aesthetic sense. In a famous passage (Shab. 133b), the rabbis, commenting on Exodus 15:2, prescribed that God should be "adorned" by the use of beautiful implements for the performance of religious observances. A problem exists, however, regarding the Jewish attitude toward figurative and representational art. The Pentateuchal code in many places (Ex. 20:4; Deut. 5:8 and in great detail 4:16–18) ostensibly prohibits, in the sternest terms, the making of any image or likeness of man or beast. In the context, this presumably implies a prohibition of such manufacture for the purposes of worship. But this reservation is not stated specifically in the text, and there is no doubt that at certain times the rigidity of the prohibition impeded or even completely prevented the development among the Jews of figurative art, and indeed of the visual arts generally, especially as far as representation of the human form or face was concerned. The inhibitions were stronger against the plastic arts (i.e., relief or sculpture) than against painting or drawing, because of the specific biblical reference to the "graven image." Nevertheless, at various periods and in various environments, in antiquity, as well as in modern times, these inhibitions were ignored. The meticulous obedience or relative neglect of the apparent biblical prohibition of representational art seems in fact to have been conditioned by external circumstances, and in two directions – revulsion, or attraction. In the later biblical period and throughout classical antiquity, in an environment in which the worship of images by their neighbors played a great part, the Jews reacted strongly against this practice and up to a point representational art was sternly suppressed. The same applied to a certain degree in the environment of Roman and Greek Catholicism in the Middle Ages. On the other hand, when the Jews were to some extent culturally assimilated, they began to share in the artistic outlook of their neighbors and the prejudice against representational art dwindled, and in the end almost disappeared. To this generalization, however, other factors must be added. Sometimes, the religious reaction of the Jews was influenced by political considerations. The almost frenzied Jewish opposition to images of any sort toward the close of the Second Temple period seems to have been prompted by the extreme nationalist elements, happy to find a point in which their political opposition could be based on a clear-cut religious issue. A few generations later, in an age of appeasement, their great-grandchildren could be, and were far more broadminded. But during periods of religious iconoclasm among their neighbors, the Jews – the classical iconoclasts – could not very well afford to be more compliant than others. Therefore, it seems, in the Byzantine Empire in the eighth and ninth centuries and in the Muslim world long after this, there ensued an interlude in which representational art was rigidly shunned even though the nonrepresentational made notable progress.

In certain areas during the Middle Ages and Ghetto period representational art, both pictorial and plastic, was tolerated even in connection with religious observances and with cult objects used in the synagogue. At the same period, in other areas, the inhibitions were so strong as to exclude such objects even from secular use. In more recent times, portrait painting and photography have come to be generally – though not quite universally – tolerated even among the extreme orthodox. The emergence of artists from the Jewish community similarly presents no clear-cut picture. The names are known of men active in representational art in the classical period, and there were a few in Christian Europe in the Middle Ages carrying out even ecclesiastical commissions. In the 18th century, Jewish painters and portraitists – artists in the modern sense – began to appear in several European countries. But it is not easy to explain the sudden emergence in recent generations of a flood of artists of outstanding genius, largely of Eastern European origin, in France, the United States, and elsewhere. Until the 19th century the Jewish attitude toward art was in fact not negative, but ambivalent.

BIBLICAL PERIOD. It is known that there was a relatively high development of art in Ereẓ Israel even before the coming of the Hebrews. In the Mesolithic period the inhabitants of the region that is now Wadi Natuf in Western Judea produced some carvings which, while intended for ritual purposes, show a love of full forms and beautiful shapes, a purity of line and balance of masses, which characterize naturalistic art at its best. The Jericho culture of the eighth to fifth millennia B.C.E. has a fresh aesthetic approach, and the clay masks found there, perhaps connected with ancestor worship, are among the chief works of ancient art in the Middle East. The carved bone and ivory figurines produced by the Beersheba culture of the fourth millennium are in advance both chronologically and qualitatively of the earliest productions of Egyptian art. The mysterious hoard of copper and ivory cult-objects of the Chalcolithic period found in 1961 in Naḥal Mishmar, not far from the Dead Sea, shows a sense of form and a high standard of execution. The Canaanite period which immediately preceded the Israelite conquest produced some significant religious art. Moreover, the invaders of Ereẓ Israel, whether Egyptians, Assyrians, or Hittites, all brought with them their own artistic conventions and left behind monuments or objects which inevitably affected the aesthetic conceptions of the inhabitants of the country. Hence the Hebrews arrived in a country which already had, if not an artistic tradition, at least a number of artistic expressions, most of them associated with cult purposes.

THE SANCTUARY AND FIRST TEMPLE PERIOD. According to the Pentateuch, there were among the Hebrews who left Egypt artificers of genius, capable "in all manner of workmanship, to devise curious works, to work in gold and in silver and in brass, and in the cutting of stones for setting, and in carving of wood, to make any manner of skillful work" (Ex. 35:31–35). The women were skilled in embroidery (*ibid.*, 25–26). The sanctuary in the wilderness, whose appurtenances and decoration were traditionally associated with the names of Bezalel son of Uri and Oholiab son of Ahisamach, was presumably designed in accordance with contemporary Egyptian artistic fashion. This fashion no doubt continued to exercise considerable influence on the Hebrews even after they entered Canaan. Artistically, the most memorable detail was the pair of *cherubim, apparently with human faces, whose wings extended over the Ark. The making of these has to be considered as art in the more restricted sense and not as mere skilled craftsmanship. These enigmatic figures, also a feature of the First *Temple until its destruction, were the outstanding exception which proved that the ancient Hebrews did not absolutely shun figurative and plastic art.

In addition to these and similar decorative cherubim, the great laver in Solomon's Temple, called the "molten sea," was supported on the backs of twelve oxen cast in bronze, a construction to which at some later age there were objections.

According to the detailed accounts in the books of Kings and Chronicles, the laver must have been both architecturally impressive and aesthetically memorable, especially in its decorative details.

It is not easy to discern the development of what may be termed native Hebrew art in the period of the Monarchy. Indeed, there is explicit information that the expert craftsmen employed in the construction of the Temple were Phoenicians from Tyre. The relatively few relics that have been preserved in Ereẓ Israel from this period, such as the not uncommon Astarte figurines, are mainly Canaanite in character. On the other hand, the plaques from the "House of Ivory" built in Samaria by King Ahab (876–853 B.C.E.), which show great taste and sensitivity, are under the influence of Phoenician art and were possibly executed by craftsmen introduced by Queen *Jezebel from her native Sidon. Similarly, the admirably executed Israelite *seals of the period are Egyptian or Assyrian both in character and in execution.

SECOND TEMPLE PERIOD. The situation continued into the period of the Second Temple. The handful of returned exiles lacked the conditions of political security and economic well-being that might have fostered the development of a native art. Any attempts in this direction must inevitably have been shaped at the beginning by Persian, and later by Greek, influences. With the Hellenization of the Middle East after the invasion of *Alexander the Great (333 B.C.E.), Greek art began to make its appearance throughout the region. Greek cities were constructed within the area of the historic Ereẓ Israel, with temples, baths, and statuary which inevitably became familiar to the Jewish population. *Antiochus IV's attempt to Hellenize Judea from 168 B.C.E. onward involved the forcible imposition of Greek standards and customs. These included the setting up throughout the land, and even in the Temple itself, not only of decorative statues, but also images for adoration. The religious reaction against this, under the Hasmoneans, inevitably fortified the Jewish opposition to any form of representational art. The latter Hasmonean rulers were nevertheless strongly affected by Hellenistic culture. Their buildings were constructed in accordance with Greek standards, with fine detail. The earliest Jewish *coins, produced in this period, are sometimes beautifully designed, with Greek symbols such as the star, cornucopia, and anchor, executed with great delicacy. It is significant, however, that the effigy of the ruler never figured in these coins, as might normally have been expected.

With the Roman occupation, and in particular under the House of *Herod, new attitudes began to emerge. Herod had no images in his remote, desert palace at *Masada; but he had no objection to the introduction of statues and images into the non-Jewish parts of his dominions, even where there may have been a considerable Jewish population. It is known, too, that even the more resolutely Jewish members of his household did not object to having their portraits painted. On the other hand, Jewish nationalist extremists seem to have found in the biblical prohibition of images, literally and rigidly interpreted, a useful pretext for or stimulus to their anti-Roman feelings. When Roman coins bearing the emperor's effigy circulated in Judea, many persons – patriots perhaps more than pietists – objected strongly and some even refused to handle them. It was natural that there should be frenzied objections when in 37 C.E. the emperor Caligula's statue was placed in the Temple for adoration, even though there was later to be no opposition to the patriotic placing of statues of the ruler in Babylonian synagogues. There was also a loud outcry against the bearing of standards with the imperial effigy by the Roman legionaries when they marched through Jerusalem. Similarly, Herod's placing of an eagle over the Temple gate as a symbol of Rome was the occasion for an incipient revolt – ostensibly on religious grounds, but obviously with patriotic motivation as well. But a talmudic source of a later period reveals a more tolerant attitude when it states (TJ, Av. Zar. 3:1, 42c) that all likenesses were to be found in Jerusalem (before the destruction of the Temple in 70 C.E.) except those of human beings. Although Herod's descendants would not use portraits in the coinage which they struck for Judea, they did not refrain from doing so for their possessions over the border. One of the Herodian palaces in Tiberias had figures of animals on the walls. No one appears to have objected to this until after the outbreak of the war against Rome in 66 C.E. when Josephus, as military governor of Galilee, led a campaign of competitive iconoclasm in order to demonstrate his zeal. There is some evidence that at this period patriotic religious fervor led to a decree forbidding all images. This temporarily stifled any artistic expression of the accepted type, precisely in an age of national resurgence when it might have been expected to flower. Architecture appears to have flourished in the Second Temple period around Jerusalem. Many ambitiously conceived funerary monuments are to be found, particularly in the *Kidron Valley, and a number of delicately decorated sarcophagi and *ossuaries have been unearthed. The Temple of Herod seems to have deserved its reputation as one of the architectural marvels of the Roman Empire.

AFTER THE FALL OF JERUSALEM. With the fall of Bethar in 135 C.E. and the acceptance of Roman rule by the Pharisee elements, conditions changed. Theoretically, the religious inhibitions remained in force, but there was an increasing tendency to interpret the biblical prohibition as applying only to imagery intended for adoration. Hence, in practice, greater tolerance came to be shown. Rabbis of the highest piety did not object to frequenting baths where there was a statue of a heathen deity, maintaining that it was placed there for decoration only. In addition to their architectural significance, the synagogue ruins dating from this period (second–fifth centuries) embody decorative carvings and symbols – including animal forms – which combine a high standard of craftsmanship with a well-developed aesthetic sense. In due course rabbinical pronouncements reflected the changed attitude: to this period belongs the statement quoted above that all images except the human were to be found in pre-Destruction Jerusalem.

In the third century R. *Johanan countenanced the painting of frescoes (TJ, Av. Zar. 3:3, 42d), while in the fifth century, according to a statement in the Jerusalem Talmud (Av. Zar. 4:1, 43d), R. *Abun permitted – or at least tolerated – decorated mosaics and wall frescoes even in synagogues. The sixth-century mosaic of the *Bet Alfa synagogue, vividly depicting the signs of the Zodiac, the Four Seasons, the Chariot of the Sun, and the sacrifice of Isaac, created a sensation when it was discovered in 1928. It is now realized, however, that there was nothing unusual about this form of decoration. Mosaics showing conventional figures and biblical scenes were a normal feature of synagogal decoration in Ereẓ Israel at the time. This is all the more remarkable in view of the fact that prostration in a synagogue on a figured floor would seem to be forbidden by the Bible (Lev. 26:1). Marianos and his son Ḥanina, who were responsible for the Bet Alfa mosaic, are the earliest Jewish artists in the modern sense known by name whose work has been preserved (though the epitaph of a Jewish painter named Edoxios has been found in the Jewish catacombs in Rome). More memorable from the artistic viewpoint are the magnificent third-century frescoes found in the synagogue at *Dura-Europos in Syria, preserved by what was no more than a lucky chance. These comprise an entire series of highly artistic wall paintings, executed in conventional Hellenistic style, which illustrate in great detail certain aspects of biblical history and prophecy. In these paintings the human face and form are lavishly represented. The lavish admission of figurative art to the synagogue, the very place of worship, is important. It is probable that this type of decoration was commonplace in synagogues of the period, even though the Dura specimen is the only one to have been preserved. It clearly represents a fairly long tradition of such art. Indeed, below the frescoes now revealed there have been discovered traces of others of a generation earlier, and these too, presumably, were no revolutionary innovation. Whether or not the Dura frescoes reflected, or were paralleled by, manuscript illuminations of Bible texts remains a problem. In view of the detailed regulations for the writing of the **Sefer Torah* such illuminations would of course be for domestic purposes only, and not for use in the synagogue. But it can be stated categorically that if human figures were tolerated on the walls of the synagogue before the worshiper's eyes, there is no reason why they should not have been permitted in codices or rolls studied in the home.

RELATION TO EARLY CHRISTIAN ART. The analogies between the Dura frescoes and early Christian art are in some cases obvious, and have given rise to the theory that the latter continued the tradition of an earlier Jewish book-art, though this remains a matter of speculation. Indeed, it has been suggested that the earliest specimens of Christian book illumination – the Vienna Genesis of the sixth century (going back probably to a fourth-century archetype), the Joshua Roll of the tenth, the Codex Amiatinus based on a sixth-century original – may be Jewish in origin, or copied from Jewish prototypes in the Diaspora. Three-dimensional figures were more objectionable religiously than two-dimensional ones. But the inhibitions were weakening, for in the catacombs of *Bet She'arim Greek coffins with crudely executed mythological figures in low relief were reused for Jewish burials. In the synagogues at Baram, Kefar Naḥum (Capernaum) and Chorazin in Ereẓ Israel there are fragmentary figures of lions in three dimensions. In Babylon, as has been mentioned, the statue of the ruler was admitted without protest, even in synagogues frequented by outstanding scholars (Av. Zar. 43b).

ART IN THE ROMAN EMPIRE. Clearly, the artistic traditions of the Palestinian and Near Eastern synagogues were imitated, perhaps with fewer inhibitions, in the Western Diaspora. The splendid architectural remains at *Ostia in Italy and *Sardis in Asia Minor show that monumental synagogues with fine attention to detail were common. Discoveries at Aegina in Greece and Hamam Lif in North Africa suggest that decorated floors were also usual. While no figurative art has yet been discovered in the Diaspora synagogues of the classical period (other than conventionally carved lions at Sardis), it is present in abundance on the wall frescoes of the Jewish catacombs in Rome. The emphasis, however, is on mythological figures, without the biblical reminiscences that might be expected. More remarkable are the lavishly decorated sarcophagi found in Rome, one at least bearing three-dimensional putti and other figures in high relief, by the side of the **menorah* or seven-branched candelabrum.

E.R. *Goodenough endeavored to demonstrate in his monumental work, *Jewish Symbols in the Graeco-Roman Period* (1953–65) and in a number of minor studies, that much of this representational art, in defiance of apparent rabbinic proscriptions, was the manifestation of a Jewish synthetic mystery religion. This popular religion was allied to, though not identical with, talmudic Judaism. But whether accepted or not, the theory cannot obscure the fact that within Judaism in the late classical period it was possible for figurative art in the fullest sense to develop.

The question remains, whether there was any continuity of tradition between the Jewish representational art centering in Bible illustration and the later version of the same art in Europe. There is unequivocal evidence of the former down to the sixth century at least, while the latter appeared, fully fledged but obviously of much earlier origin, from the 13th century onward.

Whatever the answer, the relative liberalism and normal development of art among the Jews in the late classical period subsequently received a check. To a certain extent this was the result of or paralleled the iconoclastic movement in the Byzantine Empire, which inevitably affected the Jews. There is evidence that at this time the figures in the Na'aran Synagogue mosaic were mutilated, and that a similar fate was suffered by some of the decorative carvings in other Galilean synagogues.

UNDER ISLAM. More decisive, naturally, was the spread of Islam, which became supreme for centuries in those areas where Jewish life flourished most. The new religion had, with certain exceptions, strong iconoclastic tendencies. Obviously the Jews could not afford to be more tolerant in this matter than their Muslim neighbors. Hence it appears that there was a revulsion in much of the Jewish world against the incipient representational art, and that this revulsion lingered in some vital areas even after the Islamic domination had receded.

The Spanish rabbis were outright in their opposition. The *Sefer ha-Ḥinnukh*, attributed to Aaron ha-Levi of Barcelona (39, 12), emphasized that it was forbidden to make likenesses of a human being out of any material, even for ornament. Maimonides, however, was somewhat more tolerant, forbidding (Yad. Av. Kokh. 3:10–11) only the human (not the animal) form in the round, and permitting it in painting and tapestries. Art expressed itself among the Jews, as among the Arabs, in nonrepresentational forms, making use of ornaments and arabesques, and exploiting to the full the decorative potentialities of the Hebrew alphabet and the patterning of minuscular characters. The exquisite decorations in the surviving medieval Spanish synagogues (especially at *Cordova and *Toledo), though somewhat later in date, are impressive examples of such work. More striking is the testimony of manuscript art. Throughout the Muslim world and the area under its influence, a new tradition established itself, highly Islamic in both feeling and conception. Illuminations in the accepted medieval sense – i.e., actual illustrations of the text – are ostentatiously absent. Instead, many pages are elaborately decorated – with carpet patterns, intricate geometrical designs, and the most skillful use of calligraphic characters both large and small, the last sometimes fashioned with consummate mastery into involved patterns of great ingenuity. Not infrequently, especially in biblical manuscripts, such decorative pages were deliberately and quite irrelevantly included at the beginning of the manuscript, and sometimes at the end as well, in great profusion, merely to enhance the beauty of the volume. The inclusion in the Bible manuscripts of highly stylized representations of the vessels of the Sanctuary seems, however, to form a link between these manuscripts and those of the now submerged tradition of the classical period. This method of Hebrew Bible illumination, divorced from the text, survived in some areas, or in some circles, as late as the second half of the 15th century. This is evidenced by the *Kennicott Bible* in Oxford illuminated by Joseph *Ibn Ḥayyim, and by the Hebrew Bible of the University of Aberdeen, completed in 1494.

NORTHERN EUROPE. Outside the Muslim orbit these inhibitions against representational art did not apply – at least not the same degree – and with the rise of the Jewish communities in Northern Europe, representational art began to reappear. Whether or not there was any direct link with the classical period remains a matter of dispute. Once again, there is a disparity between strict religious theory as reflected in the rabbinic texts and actuality as shown in surviving relics of the period. Although in the 12th century Eliakim b. Joseph of Metz ordered the removal of the stained glass windows from the synagogue of Mainz, his younger colleague *Ephraim b. Isaac of Regensburg permitted the painting of animals and birds on the walls. *Isaac b. Moses of Vienna recalled seeing similar embellishments in the place of worship he frequented at Meissen as a boy. The author of the *Sefer Ḥasidim* expressed his categoric disapproval of representations of animate beings in the synagogue. On the other hand, Rashi knew of, and apparently did not object to, wall frescoes – presumably in the home – illustrating biblical scenes, such as the fight between David and Goliath, with descriptive wording (in Hebrew?) below (Shab. 149a). On the surface, it seems that Rashi is referring to a practice current among the well-to-do Jews of his own circle in northern France and the Rhineland in the 11th century. In the 12th century, the French tosafists discussed and permitted even the three-dimensional representation of the human form, provided that it was incomplete. At the very same time, Jews living in England are known to have used signet rings that bore a human likeness on them.

The emergence at this period of Jewish mint-masters (see *Minting) presupposes some involvement in the production of coins bearing the ruler's head, a tradition which goes back to the activity of *Priscus, who was the court jeweler at the Frankish court during approximately the middle of the sixth century C.E.

ILLUMINATED MANUSCRIPTS. Hebrew manuscripts illuminated in the conventional sense, in accordance with European styles and techniques, began to emerge in Northern Europe not later than the 13th century. Certain inhibitions lingered as regards the human form, which in some manuscripts was quaintly provided with bird or animal heads (see color plate *Laud Maḥzor* vol. 11 between columns 812 and 813), thus observing at least marginally the biblical prohibition against representational art. Whether this indicates a stage in the decline of traditional inhibitions, or a momentary pietistic recession, is a matter for speculation. But toward the close of the Middle Ages the art of the illuminated manuscript – illuminated in the fullest sense – flourished in Northern Europe and spread to Italy. By the 14th century at the latest, the tradition had extended to Spain, where Christian rule was now in the ascendant. It is perhaps best exemplified in a fine series of illuminated **Haggadah* manuscripts, of which the *Sarajevo Haggadah* is the best known.

In some cases the artists were probably Jews (Nathan b. Simeon, *Joel b. Simeon, Meir Jaffe), while in others they were presumably Christians. But there is no need to assume that the work of the Jewish manuscript artists was necessarily restricted to Hebrew manuscripts and to a Jewish clientele. The work on mixing colors for manuscript illumination compiled in Judeo-Portuguese by Abraham ibn Ḥayyim suggests a degree of involvement in the illuminating craft in its wider sense, even though none of his own productions is known. His was certainly not an isolated case. The Catalan Atlas, executed in 1376/7 by Abraham *Cresques and his son Judah, is noteworthy artistically besides being an important monument to cartography and geographical science. Jewish professional painters who are mentioned in contemporary documents include Abraham b. Yom Tov de Salinas with his son Bonastruc (1406), and Moses ibn Forma of Saragossa (1438), as well as Vidal Abraham who, in 1330, was engaged to illuminate the *Book of Privileges of Majorca*.

CRAFTS. That Jews engaged in artistic craftsmanship even for Christian religious purposes is demonstrated by the bull of the anti-Pope *Benedict XIII of 1415, forbidding Jews to be employed in the making of ceremonial objects for Christian use such as chalices and crucifixes. In 1480, Isabella of Castile enjoined her court painter to ensure that no Jew be permitted to paint the figure of Jesus or the Virgin Mary. Official documents refer to Spanish Jews engaged in the manufacture of reliquaries and crucifixes and assisting sculptors of sacred images. It must be borne in mind that for the Middle Ages it is impossible to draw a sharp line of demarcation between the arts and the crafts because the craftsman in many branches was inevitably at the same time an artist in the modern sense. Bookbinding, for example, engaged Jewish craftsmen, even at the highly discriminating Papal court of Avignon; and, in Germany, Jewish experts such as the scribe-bookbinder, Meir Jaffe, mentioned above, were described as supreme artists in the execution of the difficult type of leather work known as *cuir cisélé*.

It must be emphasized that among the Jews pictorial art lacked one impetus which was potent in the outside world. The art of painting, especially frescoes, among Christians was stimulated by the fact that the Bible story was communicated to the almost illiterate common people by means of pictures on the walls of the churches. These served literally as the *Biblia pauperum*, the Bible of the Poor. For the Jews, with their high degree of literacy due to their almost universal system of education and their familiarity with the Scripture story, this was superfluous. Similarly, the cult of the saints rendered pictorial and plastic art essential in the church, whereas in the synagogue it was not needed. This is probably the reason for the late emergence of Jewish sculptors. It was not so much that Jews were opposed to art as that certain categories of art, essential in the world outside, were for them unnecessary.

THE RENAISSANCE PERIOD. In Italy, in the Renaissance period, Jews participated in every branch of activity, including the arts. Some of the most memorable illuminated Hebrew manuscripts belong to this epoch and there is good ground for believing that many of them came from unknown Jewish hands. Cases are recorded of Jews being admitted to the painters' guild, though none of their work can be identified. There were, however, some distinguished metal workers, such as Salomone da *Sessa (subsequently converted to Catholicism as Ercole de' Fedeli), who was in the service of Cesare Borgia. Da Sessa's swords and scabbards were among the finest of the period. His contemporary, Moses da *Castelazzo (d. 1527), was an engraver and medalist of some note. In the next century, Salvatore Rosa's assistant, Jonah Ostiglia of Florence (d. 1675), was proficient enough to be mentioned with deference by contemporary art chroniclers. A number of converted Italian artists of Jewish birth also achieved a reputation. Among them were Francesco Ruschi (c. 1640), a forerunner of the 18th century Venetian Renaissance, and Pietro Liberi (1614–1687), founder of the College of Artists in Venice. While names cannot be taken as conclusive evidence of origin, it must be noted that both in Spain and in Italy men named (de') Levi achieved artistic prominence in the 15th and 16th centuries.

RITUAL ART. It has already been mentioned that the Talmud has a general injunction that the glorification of God implies the use of the finest appurtenances in divine worship. There are ample descriptions both in the Bible and in Josephus of those used in the Temple. There are visual examples in the representations on the Arch of *Titus in Rome and in the synagogal and funerary art of the classical period. But there is no proof of a specifically Jewish ritual art for home and synagogue until a relatively late period. It is perhaps significant that among the many evidences of Jewish religious life around the beginning of the Christian era discovered in recent archaeological investigations, there is nothing with any specific bearing on the emergence of ritual art, even as regards manuscript decoration. Generally in ritual observances objects were used which were not specially manufactured for the purpose. The only exception was the *Ḥanukkah lamp which, because it had to have a definite number of burners – eight or sometimes nine – was from an early date specially manufactured, first in clay and later in stone. During the Middle Ages, however, it became established practice to create objects specifically for every form of ritual use, thus emphasizing the "glorification of the *mitzvah*" ("*hiddur mitzvah*"). The manufacturers were not always Jews. It is paradoxical that while in some areas Jewish craftsmen are to be found executing objects of the most sacred nature, such as crucifixes, for church use – which must, from certain points of view, have been highly objectionable on both sides – in others there is evidence of Christian craftsmen producing some of the commonplace ritual objects required by the Jewish community. Contracts survive relating to such work for Jews in Provence in the 15th century and Frankfurt on the Main in the 16th. It must be noted, however, that with the exception of Hanukkah lamps, virtually no specimens of Jewish ritual art of a date earlier than the end of the Middle Ages have been traced. The earliest positively identifiable is a pair of *rimmonim* (Torah finials) from Sicily, preserved in the Cathedral of Palma, Majorca. The favorite objects of Jewish ritual art were the *Torah ornaments, **Kiddush* cups, *Seder* plates, *Sabbath lamps, and spice boxes for the **Havdalah* ceremony on the conclusion of the Sabbath. It is possible that majolica *seder* plates originated in Spain before the Expulsion of 1492. An entire series was manufactured by several generations of two or three families of Italian-Jewish ceramists in the 17th and 18th centuries. Heavily embroidered brocades, with elaborate decorative inscriptions in gold and sometimes with human figures in stump-work, were used both in the synagogues, for the *Ark curtains, or for the wrappings of the Torah Scroll, and in the home, for Sabbath appurtenances and the like. Often these were made by the women of the community as a pious duty, but in due course a school of Jewish art embroiderers emerged. Certain branches of embroidery were indeed regarded as a Jewish specialty during the period of the Middle Ages.

FUNERARY ART. Surviving Jewish funerary art begins with the sepulchers and sarcophagi of the classical period in Palestine and the decorations in the catacombs of Rome and elsewhere. In the Middle Ages, Jewish tombstones in Europe were for the most part severely simple, owing whatever artistic quality they had to their shape and their impressive Hebrew lettering. After the Renaissance, funerary art began to take on some importance. Symbols indicating the name or profession of the person commemorated were carved above what were now highly ornamental inscriptions. In Italy, family badges – all but coats of arms – were added. In Central Europe, carvings denoting the calling or profession of the dead person were often incorporated. The most remarkable development was in some of the Sephardi communities of the Atlantic seaboard; such as Amsterdam and Curaçao, where the tombstone was enhanced by delicately executed carvings in relief. These generally depicted scenes in the life of the biblical personage whose name was borne by the dead person – for example, the call of Samuel, or the encounter between David and Abigail, or the death of Rachel. In some cases even the deathbed scene of the departed is shown, including, most amazingly, his actual likeness. The derivation of these artistic manifestations still needs investigation, but it seems at present that they were a purely spontaneous, native development in individual communities.

What is most significant is that here there are not flat surfaces but plastic art – precisely that which was most objectionable in talmudic law in its strict interpretation.

THE ART OF THE PRINTED BOOK. With the invention and spread of printing in the 15th and 16th centuries, a new area of artistic expression opened. The earliest printed books tried to imitate manuscript codices, and left space for illumination. This was the case with Hebrew works also, and there are some early examples which were embellished later by hand by skilled book-artists. In due course a genuine Jewish book art developed.

Early productions of the Hebrew printing press, especially of the *Soncino family, were decorated with elaborate borders on the opening pages. Sometimes these were borrowed or copied from non-Jewish productions; sometimes they were presumably original, perhaps in their turn to be copied by Christian printers. The early editions (Brescia, 1491, etc.) of the *Meshal ha-Kadmoni* by Isaac ibn *Sahula, following the example set by the 13th-century author, were accompanied by illustrations. Later on the practice was transmitted to other books of fables and similar literature. But as in the previous epoch, special care was lavished on the Passover **Haggadah*. At the beginning of the 16th century at the latest a fine series of illustrated editions, probably the work of Jewish hands, began to appear. These reached their apogee in the superb editions of Prague of 1526, Mantua of 1560 and 1568, Venice from 1609 onward, and finally the Amsterdam edition of 1695. When the first title pages appeared in printed books, early in the 16th century, these too received special attention.

It will by now have become apparent that it is no longer possible to maintain the commonly accepted generalization that Judaism was fundamentally opposed to representational art, or to give this as the reason for the late emergence of Jews as artists. The utmost that can be said is that in certain environments and at certain periods Jews either imitated the iconoclastic tendencies of their neighbors, as sometimes in Muslim countries, or, in revulsion against their iconolatry, as in some Catholic areas, developed a strong antipathy to such art. It is also true that Jews lacked the initial stimulus to artistic involvement which came to the Christian world from the lavish use of representational art for liturgical purposes in Roman Catholic churches. With these reservations, however, it can be said that Jews accepted representational art as a normal phenomenon of their lives, even in a religious context. They used it not only in the decoration of their homes (though curiously enough the evidence for this is somewhat thin), but in their liturgical manuscripts and printed books, especially the Passover *Haggadah*, and on cult objects such as Passover plates, Ḥanukkah lamps, spice boxes, and brocades. In some areas these representations were even introduced into the synagogue. Nor were representations of the human form restricted to plane surfaces: in metal work they were often three-dimensional. In some places in the Ashkenazi world, figures of Moses and Aaron were incorporated almost as a matter of convention in the appurtenances of the Torah – which was the central object of veneration in the synagogue – both in the brocade wrappings and in relief in the silver *breastplate which hung before the Scroll. Instances are known of such figures being included in the decoration of the Ark toward which the worshiper directed his devotions. Contrary to the universal belief, even the representation of the Deity was not entirely unknown. (See *Anthropomorphism in Jewish Art).

THE REVIVAL OF MANUSCRIPT ART. The art of illumination which had developed so promisingly in Spain, Italy, and Germany at the close of the Middle Ages did not die out. In the Italian Jewish upper classes and in the affluent circle of Court Jews which emerged in Germany in the 17th century, there was to be a notable renewal – it may be more correct to say perpetuation of the former tradition. There is some evidence that in the Middle Ages it was customary for Jews to insert illuminations in the *megillah* from which they followed the reading of the story of Esther in the synagogue on the uninhibited feast of Purim. It may also be significant that the scenes connected with this same story received disproportionate attention in the third-century frescoes of Dura-Europos. Every well-to-do householder now wished to have an illuminated *megillah*. Normally, though not invariably, these seem to have been executed by Jewish artists and some were of really high artistic merit. From the 17th century onward, elaborately engraved borders were provided by competent artists, such as Shalom *Italia, inside which the text would be written by hand. The case was similar with the marriage contract or **ketubbah*, expressing the joy implicit in the formation of a new family in the Jewish community. An isolated specimen has been preserved from the late 14th century, but from the 16th century these illuminated *ketubbot* became common especially in Italy, where some examples were veritable works of art. Some of the artists were probably Gentiles. Most were probably – and in a few cases provably – Jews. While in some countries and in some areas of ritual art the inhibition against the representation of the human figure was still rigorously applied, this was normally overlooked as far as the *megillah* and the *ketubbah* were concerned.

Apart from these and allied productions of illustrators and illuminators within the context of Jewish life, the art of Hebrew book-illumination was continued and in some cases revived in a remarkable fashion. Memorable Italian specimens of the 16th and 17th centuries have recently been brought to light, though in certain cases, the artists were almost certainly non-Jews. In the course of the 17th and 18th centuries, however, there grew up in Central and Northern Europe, especially in Moravia, Amsterdam, and Hamburg, an entire school of gifted Hebrew book-illuminators, who concentrated their attention on books of occasional prayers and benedictions (*Me'ah Berakhot*), circumcision rituals and similar works. The favorite was the Passover *Haggadah*. As in the Middle Ages, wealthy householders vied with one another in having these executed, sometimes as gifts for brides or newly married couples. They were often based on the older printed prototypes, especially of the Amsterdam *Haggadah* of 1695, but were sometimes rendered with a remarkable inventive power of reinterpretation and a fine sense of color. Outstanding among these manuscript artists were Samuel Dresnitz (1720), Aaron Wolf Herlingen of Gewitsch (c. 1700–c. 1768), and Moses Leib *Trebitsch (1723). In certain cases, as for example the Pinḥas family, this involvement in manuscript illumination led to a general training in art and the consequent emergence of artists in the conventional sense.

Meanwhile, in the Sephardi community of Amsterdam, a school of gifted *calligraphers was beginning to appear. The title pages executed for their finely written Spanish or Portuguese manuscripts, sometimes embodying charming vignettes, were works of art, and a few were in due course engraved.

[Cecil Roth]

NEW DEVELOPMENTS. From the 1970s there have been significant new developments in the field of Jewish art. Side by side with increased awareness of the role which the visual arts played in Jewish life, new discoveries have been made and a considerable number of previously little or unknown objects, images, and monuments have come to the fore. The major political events which took place during this period had their impact as well, adding new information and materials. Collections that had been unavailable for decades are now open to the public and accessible to scholars. Paralleling and supporting this growth is the increase in the scholarly publications in Jewish art, including the foundation of an important periodical (*Journal of Jewish Art*) by Bezalel *Narkiss in 1974; as well as growing public awareness in the field, expressed in interests in Judaic exhibitions, lectures, travels to Jewish monuments, and even the production and acquisition of contemporary Jewish art.

In the public arena, the most visible phenomenon concerns the growth of Jewish museums from the last quarter of the 20th century. New museums were established in many towns throughout the Jewish world – from Casablanca to Melbourne, and from Casale Monferrato, Italy, to Raleigh, North Carolina. The recent proliferation of Jewish museums is particularly noticeable in Germany, where many new museums opened towards the close of the 20th century, ranging from small display rooms (e.g., Bissingen, Creglingen) to impressive and sizeable buildings (Berlin, Frankfurt). Many of the small German museums are housed in former synagogues – nearly a hundred of them have been restored to date, especially after the reunification of Germany. In Israel the fashionable search for tangible personal and communal roots has led to the establishment of small "ethnic" museums – notably, Nahon Museum of Italian-Jewish Art in Jerusalem, Museum and Heritage Center of Babylonian Jewry in Or Yehudah, and the museum commemorating the heritage of the Jews from Cochin (Kochi), India, in Moshav Nevatim in the Negev. Along with the established institutions, the new museums play a vital role in increasing the awareness and knowledge of Jewish visual culture and encourage the collection and preservation of Judaic objects, whether from the remote past or the last generations. The stream of large and impressive catalogs that accompanied many of the exhibitions organized by the leading museums constitutes important sources for documentation and scholarly research in the field of Jewish art.

Even before the fall of the Soviet Union treasures hidden behind the Iron Curtain were displayed in the West. It took 15 years of private and public efforts on the highest levels before the Czechoslovak Socialist Republic allowed the landmark exhibition, "The Precious Legacy" – based on the collections of the Jewish Museum in Prague – to tour the United States in 1983. However, the Perestroika brought about many more opportunities for international partnerships and for presentations of significant collections of ceremonial, folk, and ethnographic Jewish art. Some of these collections, for example the collection of more than 400 silver ritual objects at the Museum of Historical Treasures of the Ukraine, Kiev – comprised largely of objects confiscated by the Soviets from many synagogues in the Ukraine in the 1920s and 1930s with the idea of melting them down for the silver – has been fully restored, displayed for the first time to the general public, traveled to capitals abroad, and been the subject of several catalogs. The opening of the borders has allowed, in addition, first hand documentation projects, chiefly conducted by the Center for Jewish Art, Jerusalem, which was founded in 1979 by Bezalel Narkiss with the purpose of documenting and publishing Jewish art treasures. The CJA's researchers have been documenting ceremonial objects, illuminated manuscripts, works by Jewish artists, and the architecture and interior decoration of synagogues, in Israel and abroad, often in locales that could not be visited earlier.

The hopes of scholars to unearth another ancient synagogue with painted walls have not materialized in the decades that have passed since the amazing discovery of the *Dura Europos synagogue in 1932. On the other hand, an exciting and unexpected discovery was made in the summer of 1993, when a well-preserved early fifth century synagogue was uncovered in the talmudic town of Sepphoris (Zippori). The synagogue nave's splendid floor mosaic, comprised of 14 richly decorated panels, has enriched Jewish iconography of the period and provided some new insights into the familiar motifs. Thus, for example, the ubiquitous zodiac cycle significantly deviates from its familiar depictions in the other five ancient synagogues, and exceptionally replaces the pagan sun god, Helios, with a non-figurative image of sun rays. Likewise, the popular Binding of Isaac scene, known from two other synagogues, presents some motifs and episodes in the story that are new to Jewish iconography of this period, though familiar from Christian art. The overall iconographic scheme of the floor has been interpreted as expressing the hope for redemption and the rebuilding of the Temple.

Another major development in the past decades concerns the growing attention to Jewish art and material culture emanating from Islamic lands. Prior to 1970, hardly any attention had been paid to this field of Jewish creativity, whether in the public at large, the world of Jewish museums, or even the scholarly community. Viewed as inferior to European Jewish art, little was done to either conduct fieldwork or save the art treasures from Arab lands before the mass immigration to Israel, and serious negligence followed the resettlement. This situation has changed from the last quarter of the 20th century, and especially in Israel considerable efforts have been made by museums and scholars to display and study the visual heritage of these communities. The Israel Museum in particular has been active in this field and its department of Jewish ethnography has mounted from the mid-1960s on major exhibits accompanied by large catalogs, each dedicated to a selected community. Starting in 1967, with a modest exhibition and catalog on the costumes and some artifacts of the Jews of Bukhara, there followed more comprehensive presentations on the communities of Morocco (1973), Kurdistan (1981), the Ottoman Empire (1990), India (1995), Afghanistan (1998), Yemen (2000), and the Mountain Jews of Azerbaijan (2001). Parallel to these exhibits, studies by local scholars as well as some Americans and Europeans, deal with the art and cultural context of the jewelry, costumes, domestic wares, ceremonial art, and manuscript illumination, in particular the figurative Judeo-Persian miniatures. A monograph by Bracha Yaniv was dedicated to the Torah case (*tik*) in Islamic lands (1997), while in Shalom Sabar's studies on the illustrated *ketubbah* the examples from Islamic lands are examined side by side with those from other parts of the Jewish world.

The monographs mentioned illustrate another recent trend. While most of the monographs in Jewish art in the past were dedicated to the study of selected Hebrew manuscripts, scholars have been focusing in addition on particular categories of Jewish art. In addition to the Torah case and *ketubbah*, mention should be made of Torah crowns (Grafman), Hanukkah lamps (Braunstein), *Shivviti* tablets (Juhasz), papercuts (Shadur), the Wimpel (various authors), synagogues in general and individual buildings in particular (Krinsky, Hubka). There are still, however, many categories missing from this list. Another direction of research, which more closely follows recent trends in the general scholarship of cultural studies, emerged in the 1990s, dealing with the visual experience in Jewish life and culture. Scholars like Richard Cohen, Barbara Kirschenblatt-Gimblett, Margaret Olin, and Kalman Bland, expanded the traditional methodological tools in which Jewish art has been examined, exploring issues such as Jewish art and social studies, historiography of Jewish art, collecting and exhibiting Jewish culture, Jewish attitudes to the visual, etc. Other studies explore the Jewish experience via folk art and daily artifacts, such as New Year cards or cans of Jewish food, as well as the interaction between sacred objects and the people who use them (Joselit, Sabar). The new studies have demonstrated the importance and relevance of the visual to the other, largely text-based, disciplines of Jewish studies, which would open the field to new stimulating cultural discourses.

ADD. BIBLIOGRAPHY: D. Altshuler (ed.), *The Precious Legacy: Judaic Treasures from the Czechoslovak State Collections* (1983); K.P. Bland, *The Artless Jew: Medieval and Modern Affirmations and Denials of the Visual* (2000); S. Braunstein, *Five Centuries of Hanukkah Lamps from the Jewish Museum* (2004); G. Cohen Grossman, *Jewish Museums of the World* (2003); R.I. Cohen, *Jewish Icons: Art and Society in Modern Europe* (1998); T. Hubka, *Resplendent Synagogues: Architecture and Worship in an Eighteenth Century Polish Community* (2003). J.W. Joselit, *The Wonders of America: Reinventing Jewish Culture, 1880–1950* (1995); E. Juhasz, "The "Shiviti-Menorah": A Representation of the Sacred – Between Spirit and Matter" (Ph.D. thesis, Hebrew University of Jerusalem, 2004); R. Grafman, *Crowning Glory: Silver Ornaments of the Jewish Museum* (1996); B. Kirshenblatt-Gimblett, *Destination Culture: Tourism, Museums, and Heritage* (1998); C.H Krinsky, *Synagogues of Europe: Architecture, History, Meaning*, Cambridge (1985); M. Olin, *The Nation Without Art: Examining Modern Discourses on Jewish Art* (2001); *Past Perfect: The Jewish Experience in Early 20th Century Postcards*, Library of the Jewish Theological Seminary, New York (1998); S. Sabar, *Ketubbah: Jewish Marriage Con-*

tracts of the Hebrew Union College Skirball Museum and Klau Library (1990); W. Seipel (ed.), *Thora und Krone: Kultgeraete der juedischen Diaspora in der Ukraine* (1993); Y. and J. Shadur, *Traditional Jewish Papercuts* (2002); A. Weber et al. (eds.), *Mappot ...blessed be who comes: The Band of Jewish Tradition* (1997); Z. Weiss, *The Sepphoris Synagogue: Deciphering an Ancient Message through Its Archaeological and Socio-Historical Contexts* (2005); B. Yaniv, *The Torah Case: Its History and Design* (Heb., 1997).

[Shalom Sabar (2nd ed.)]

Modern Jewish Art

The definition of Jewish art in the modern period is complex. Formerly, it consisted of objects made for Jewish use, but now it is rarely linked to the Jewish community. Instead, Jewish artists are fully integrated into secular international art and make major contributions to avant-garde movements. Some bow to the pressures of conformity and try to assimilate, and even if they express themselves as Jews, they do so in non-traditional ways. For many of them, the interplay between secular and Jewish factors in their art is problematic. This has led scholars to debate whether all Jews who are artists produce Jewish art or only those who stress their Jewish identity.

Furthermore, modern Jewish art developed parallel to the uneven process of Jewish emancipation that began in the United States and France in the late 18th century, spread through Western and Central Europe between the 1830s and 1870s, and reached Eastern Europe towards the end of the century. Due to this variable chronology, a "first generation" of emancipated Jewish artists continued to be produced into the 20th century, when those who arrived in the West from Eastern Europe faced the same problems that had confronted Jewish artists throughout the 19th century. To complicate matters, although the 18th and 19th centuries produced a few Jewish women artists, the majority began their careers only in the 20th century and were more concerned with problems of gender than of religion. Moreover, the return of Jews to Palestine and the establishment of the State of Israel produced artists who saw themselves as Israelis more than as Jews, while the emigration of Jewish artists from the former Soviet Union produced a reversed Emancipation, allowing them to express their Jewish identity freely. Finally, the gay liberation movement led some Jewish artists at the end of the 20th century to liken coming out of the closet as homosexuals to the problems involved in declaring Jewish identity in art.

In spite of this, modern Jewish art has certain basic characteristics. First of all, despite attempts to establish a "Jewish style," Jewish artists preferred to adopt normative styles in order to be accepted. At first they conformed to academic norms, but from the mid-19th century, they began to take part in avant-garde movements. Yet although they failed, the attempts to develop a "Jewish style" are instructive. In the 1870s Vladimir Stasov, a non-Jewish Russian critic, encouraged Mark *Antokolsky to develop a Jewish national art utilizing Jewish subject matter and an "eastern semitic" style. His ideas on this style are disclosed by his suggestion that the St. Petersburg synagogue be built in the "Arab-Moorish" style and his participation in publishing a book on the ornamental illumination of medieval Hebrew manuscripts from the Cairo Genizah. He thus proposed both the adoption of Near Eastern styles and a return to Oriental Jewish sources. Antokolsky did not agree to create a *Jewish school of art*, but he was stimulated to plan a *Jewish art school* to promulgate handicrafts that were widespread as folk art among Russian Jews. He felt that this education would expose Jews to art and provide them with a livelihood. He thus suggested that folk art was a form of national artistic expression.

Stasov's theories and Antokolsky's plans inspired two simultaneous movements: Russian artists created modern Jewish art based on folk art, and the *Bezalel School of Art was founded in Jerusalem and incorporated Oriental art into its style. These two trends expressed two views of the future: the first called for a continuation of Jewish culture in the Diaspora; the second for a new start to Jewish life in the Holy Land.

The Russian approach was also influenced by S. *An-Ski's idea that emancipated Jews could build a secular Jewish identity on Jewish folk culture. Marc *Chagall both welcomed this secular identity and felt close to folk art, claiming the painter of the Mogilev synagogue as his forefather. In St. Petersburg and Paris, he absorbed avant-garde art styles, one of which – Primitivism – acclaimed the aesthetic power of folk and tribal art. Chagall developed a style that translated Jewish themes into a folk art idiom, and later added Fauvist and Cubist elements to it. This union of Jewish folk art with modern styles was taken up by Nathan *Altman and Eliezar *Lissitzky, who joined Chagall in a Jewish art movement that reached its apogee directly after the Russian Revolution. The clearest expressions of this style are Chagall's murals for the State Jewish Chamber Theater in Moscow (1920) and Lissitzky's *Had Gadya* illustrations (1918–19).

Shortly thereafter, Lissitzky and Altman abandoned this style to join the Russian abstract artists in developing their own revolutionary style. Chagall, who left Russia in 1922, also abandoned this style, but retained a naïve quality in his art and occasionally incorporated folk art motifs into it.

In the mid-1920s, Soviet art enforced the use of Socialist Realism, but this type of Jewish art survived in Anatoli *Kaplan's copies of Jewish folk art in his illustrations. These inspired Michael Grobman in the 1960s to portray Russian and Jewish legends using strange creatures rendered in a folk art style. After Grobman moved to Israel in 1971, he began using bright colors, Hebrew and Russian texts, and kabbalistic symbols in his work. These elements also appear in the art of Grisha Bruskin, where traditional Jews stand beside strange monsters and angels on a background of Hebrew script which defines the figures in kabbalistic terms. He draws on medieval manuscripts, folk art, and Surrealism, blending them in a "naïve" manner. Whereas Grobman and Bruskin use folk art and modern styles in different ways than had Chagall, Lissitzky, and Altman, they are impelled by the same understanding of what Jewish national art should be and by the same need to stress their national identity.

The second movement began in 1906 when Boris *Schatz established the Bezalel School of Art in Jerusalem to teach local Jews to produce art. Influenced by Stasov, Schatz sought to create a Jewish art indigenous to the Near East that would visually express the Jews' return to their land. He united academic Jewish art with contemporary Oriental motifs, and used Oriental Jewish models clothed in Bedouin garb for biblical scenes as both were seen as authentic evidence of the biblical past. Schatz sent the European-born teachers to Istanbul, Damascus, and Cairo to learn Oriental crafts, employed Oriental Jews as experts to weave carpets designed by European students, and taught Yemenite jewelers an "improved" filigree technique. The resulting art was highly eclectic, and only the reaction against Bezalel by young artists in the 1920s would amalgamate these ideas into a coherent style.

These young artists revolted against Schatz's anti-modernist diktats, establishing a Hebrew (as opposed to a Jewish) Artists Association to stress their independence from the Diaspora, but they retained Schatz's ideas. They developed his Orientalist use of models into a cult of the Arab, and tried to create a Jewish national art by combining Near Eastern – i.e., ancient Egyptian, Assyrian, or Byzantine – modes of depiction with the contemporary classical styles of Henri Matisse and Pablo Picasso. They added a "childlike" quality they deemed appropriate to a newborn national art, turning for inspiration to the French naïve artist Henri Rousseau.

This synthesis is evident in Reuven *Rubin's *Dancers of Meron* (1926). The style of his ḥasidic Jews is based on "Eastern" Byzantine church murals from his native Romania; the inclined perspective and individually drawn plants recall naïve art; while the broad, almost flat planes of color were inspired by Matisse. Nahum *Gutman presented a different combination in his *Goatherd* (1926) whose stance is adapted from Egyptian art. Gutman uses this style to make the figure seem both archaic and continuously indigenous to the country, but the plasticity of the body and the childlike background also recall the art of Picasso and Rousseau.

During the 1930s, influenced by Arab onslaughts and the rise of Nazism in Europe, Palestinian Jewish artists rejected this style in favor of a specifically *Jewish* art. They turned to the Expressionism of the Jewish artists in Paris, an art that was Jewish only because of its authors' origins. At the end of the 1930s, Zionism again inspired artists to return to the ancient Near East in search of a national style, but this time they turned to the archeological excavations that were uncovering Jewish roots in Palestine. Yitzhak *Danziger based his sculpture *Nimrod* (1939) on ancient Near Eastern art. The very stone from which it is carved – Nubian sandstone from Petra – unites him with the land and its ancient peoples. Moshe *Castel based his pictographic style of the mid-1940s on the naïve figures in the *Sacrifice of Isaac* from the sixth century mosaic in the Bet Alpha synagogue, thus connecting modern art in Palestine with that practiced there by Jews in ancient times. Later, he used the ancient Hebrew alphabet and figures culled from Mesopotamian cylinder seals to create "ancient Jewish steles" made of colored ground basalt, a technique developed by the Spaniard Antoni Tápies. Rather than waiting for archeologists to uncover proof of Jewish residence in the land, he produced his own "documents" confirming it. Mordecai *Ardon was also influenced by Sumerian and Canaanite images, but turned as well to traditional Jewish sources, borrowing from medieval Hebrew manuscripts and using kabbalistic signs. He felt that the pagan elements in ancient Israelite life could not exist without a traditional Jewish mystical context, and that both must be incorporated into the new Israeli culture in order for it to survive.

Both the Russian and Israeli artists who wished to create a modern Jewish style blended elements from the Jewish past with those taken from contemporary art. Although both models presented viable options for a national style, they were not generally espoused. Even the idea of such a style was not accepted by most Jewish artists, who preferred to adopt the modern styles around them.

In like manner, Jewish artists often adopted contemporary subject matter. Whereas in the 19th century many of them expressed the problems they encountered in emerging from the ghetto and maintaining their Jewish identity in a Christian world, those who arrived from Eastern Europe in the 20th century often embraced secular Western art, preferring not to stress their Jewish roots. Moreover, those who had received a liberal education from emancipated parents preferred neutral subject matter and joined movements that stressed landscape and portrait painting in the 19th century and abstraction in the 20th century. Most of these artists believed that art was an international language and wanted to make their mark as individuals and not as Jews. This approach was also shared by Jewish photographers (e.g., Alfred *Stieglitz), gallery owners (e.g., Herwarth Walden), collectors (e.g., Joseph Hirshhorn), and art critics (e.g., Clement Greenberg). They all would have agreed with Greenberg's advice: "Jewishness, insofar as it has to be asserted in a predominantly Gentile world, should be a personal rather than a mass demonstration." At the same time, many Israelis opted for international styles and neutral subjects, espousing the Zionist desire for normalcy, "to be like unto the nations," while having a nation of their own.

Yet neutral subjects could be adapted to Jewish use. Thus Moritz *Oppenheim's portraits of converted Jews and of those who succeeded while remaining faithful to their religion, express the problems confronting Jews in 19th century Germany. In Russia during a year of pogroms Isaac *Levitan placed a *Jewish Tombstone* (1881) in a landscape. In like manner, Barnett *Newman and Ya'acov *Agam gave Jewish meaning to their abstract works through their theories and titles, although the latter have to be translated into Hebrew to be fully understood.

On the other hand, some Jewish artists sought to express their Judaism in their art, often as part of a dialogue with Christians. One method, the depiction of traditional Jewish life, developed three main approaches in the 19th century. On the one hand, artists such as Oppenheim and Isador *Kauffman painted cheerful scenes of ghetto life, stressing religious rites and a pleasant atmosphere. These works were intended to strengthen the roots of emancipated Jews by showing them nostalgic views of their grandparents' lifestyle which they had cast off, and to prove the inherent beauty of traditional Jewish life to Christians who were curious about the "exotic" Jews around them. Later artists, such as Yehuda Pen, inspired by a Romantic wish to return to their roots, turned from assimilation to depicting the lifestyle of the Orthodox Jewish community. Still later, nostalgic views of shtetl life, such as those by Chagall and *Mané-Katz, were used to memorialize a way of life that was slowly disappearing and was totally destroyed in the Holocaust.

The second, more pessimistic approach was developed in Eastern Europe by Antokolsky and Samuel *Hirszenberg who stressed the poverty and sufferings of the Jews to arouse pity and sympathy. Their works were inspired by the misery they saw around them and by the pogroms in Eastern Europe in the second half of the 19th century, both of which led to mass emigration. Their iconography influenced artists who depicted the hardships of traditional Jewish life during World War I and its destruction in World War II.

The third approach depicted tensions between Jews and Christians. In Oppenheim's *Lavater and Lessing Visit Moses Mendelssohn* (1856), Mendelssohn affirms Judaism despite Johann Caspar Lavater's demands that he convert. The intricacies of the dispute are suggested by the chessboard set between them, but the woman bringing in a tea tray suggests that all will end amicably. In contrast, in *The Spanish Inquisition Breaking in on a Marrano Seder* (1868), Antokolsky symbolized the fears of Jews in Russia where sudden arrest was common, and stated his belief that assimilation would not save Jews from persecution.

Whereas such problems continued to occupy Jews, some 20th century artists turned instead to confrontations within the Jewish community. Raphael *Soyer's *Dancing Lesson* (1926) sets portraits of the Orthodox Russian grandparents above the religious but modern parents, who worriedly regard the young couple attempting to assimilate into American life by dancing to the tune of the boy's harmonica.

A different dialogue with the Christian world utilized Christian themes such as the legend of Ahasver who – like the Jewish people – is doomed to eternal wandering for rejecting Jesus. Maurycy *Gottlieb gave this image a positive twist in 1876 by portraying himself in this role as a crowned prince. He thereby stressed pride in his Judaism, but his expression conveys his melancholy at being an outcast from Christian society. In contrast, Hirszenberg's *Exile* (1904) used this image to show the Jew as a modern refugee heading towards an unknown destination. Hirszenberg's denunciation of Christian antisemitism is even clearer in his rendering of Ahasver fleeing amidst a sea of crosses at the feet of which lie his massacred fellow Jews (1899).

The symbolic image that had the most impact on this type of dialogue was that of Jesus restored to his historical milieu. Antokolsky's *Ecce Homo* (1873) stressed Jesus' Judaism through his facial features, side locks, skullcap, and striped garment. Inspired by the Odessa pogrom, Antokolsky wanted his statue to remind Christians that persecuting Jesus's brothers perverted his teachings. The use of a Jewish Jesus to combat antisemitism became widespread in modern Jewish art, and Chagall's *White Crucifixion* (1938) used this imagery to symbolize Jewish victims in the Holocaust.

This dialogue, as well as problems within the Jewish community, led Jewish artists to inject new meanings into Old Testament themes. This practice began in the early 19th century in works by converted Jews. Thus Mendelssohn's grandson Philipp Veit and his fellow Nazarenes decorated the reception room of his converted relative, the Prussian consul Jacob Salomon Bartholdy, with the story of Joseph. This suggests that Bartholdy had a Jewish precedent both for his high office and for assuming the manners – and in his case, the religion – of a non-Jewish court. In a different vein, Eduard *Bendemann expressed the despair at Judaism's fate that led to his conversion by painting mournful scenes: *By the Waters of Babylon* (1832) and *Jeremiah on the Ruins of Jerusalem* (ca. 1834–35).

Early Zionist artists also turned to the Old Testament. Lesser *Ury's *Jerusalem* (1896) depicts the old exiles in Babylon sitting withdrawn or praying, while younger generations look past the river dreaming of the homeland, thus expressing the hope engendered in the young by Zionism. In like manner, Ephraim Moïse *Lilien depicted Theodor Herzl as Moses (1907–8), and created a parallel between the longing for the Promised Land of a Jew bound in slavery in Egypt and that of a European Jew trapped by thorns (1902). In the *Jerusalem River Project* (1970), Joshua Neustein, Gerard Marx, and Georgette Battle set loudspeakers along a *wadi* to bring the sound of rushing water to Jerusalem's dry environment, fulfilling the prophecy of Zechariah that when Israel is redeemed, "live waters will come forth out of Jerusalem."

Old Testament imagery was also used for personal expression. For instance, Simeon *Solomon used his illustrations to the *Song of Songs* (1857, 1865–68) to express his homosexuality and the despair it caused him, while Jacques *Lipchitz and Jacob *Epstein used their namesake, Jacob, wrestling with the angel to express their own struggles with inspiration during times of crisis (1932, 1940–41).

Biblical images were also employed to express the Holocaust and the birth of the State of Israel. Thus Lipchitz depicted David killing a Nazi Goliath (1933) to demonstrate Jewish resistance to the Nazis, and many artists utilized the Sacrifice of Isaac and Job to symbolize Holocaust victims. After the War of Independence, *Steinhardt used *Cain and Abel* to portray the war between brothers; *Jacob and Esau* embracing to express the coveted peace; and *Hagar* as an outcast Arab refugee. Recently, contemporary artists have been inspired by their times to develop new interpretations. For instance, before leaving Russia, Vitaly *Komar and Alexander *Melamid placed seven photographs of the first page of the text of the *Prophet Obadiah* (1976) in graded degrees of darkness, suggesting that they see their Jewish origins as fluctuating from readability to impenetrability. In like manner, in *The Liberation of God* (1990–96), Helene Aylon underlined all the places in the Old Testament in which the patriarchy was stressed as part of her feminist reassessment of Judaism.

After World War II, biblical imagery was also used to call for reconciliation between Judaism and Christianity. Chagall injected his crucified Jewish Jesus into Old Testament paintings that he wished to house in an interfaith chapel to promote peace by stressing Jesus' Jewish origins to members of both religions. In like manner, the Catholic Church began commissioning Jewish artists to decorate churches such as that at Assy, but the resulting works contain Jewish as well as Christian messages. Lipchitz's statue of the *Virgin* there shows an uninhabited mantle, with only the hands visible, brought down to earth by a dove. For a Catholic, this is a perfect rendering of the Immaculate Conception; for Lipchitz it was a way not to represent the Virgin. His inscription on the back dedicates the work to a better understanding between the two faiths. Chagall decorated the Assy Baptistery with a large *Crossing of the Red Sea*, a Christian prefiguration of baptism. However, at the top of the mural, a Wandering Jew leads the Exodus away from the crucified Christ towards Israel, symbolized by King David and the Tower of David. Such interplays remind us that in interfaith relations each side interprets events according to its own beliefs.

Jewish and Christian artists were also commissioned to produce art for the many synagogues and Jewish community centers that were built from 1945 on. Whereas most Christians produced art deemed appropriate for Jewish use, Jewish artists often felt free to express their own views. This is also true of Jewish book illustration: Arieh Allweil gave his *Haggadah* a Zionist reading (after 1948), while Leonard *Baskin infused his ambiguous feelings towards Judaism into the version he illustrated (1974).

Another common theme in the 19th century expressed the emancipated Jewish artists' feeling that due to their art they had no place in Jewish society: artists such as Gottlieb, Hirszenberg and Jacob Meyer *de Haan identified with outcasts such as Uriel Acosta and Baruch Spinoza. In the 20th century artists were more concerned with their tenuous place as Jews in contemporary society, and manifested this problem in various ways. Chagall hid his often sarcastic messages about the Christian world by translating Yiddish idioms into visual images that could only be understood by Yiddish speakers, and Ben *Shahn and Baskin incorporated Hebrew texts into their works that added dimensions of meaning that were not open to the general public. Many of R.B. *Kitaj's works deal with problems of non-belonging. He depicted himself symbolically as *Marrano (The Secret Jew)* (1976), and identified with all outsiders in his book *The First Diasporist Manifesto* (1989).

This outsider stance also connects Jews with other minorities, an identification espoused by Jewish artists with a strong social conscience. Josef *Israels and Max *Liebermann portrayed poor fishermen and peasants in Europe in the 19th century, while the Americans Max *Weber, the *Soyers, and Shahn depicted those rendered poor and homeless by the Depression. They and younger artists, such as Larry *Rivers, later identified with Afro-Americans, believing they were expressing the humanistic doctrines that they saw as Judaism's contribution to American life.

This affinity with the other assumed another dimension in Israeli art. In the 1920s, seeking to reconnect with the land, artists such as Rubin and Gutman identified with Arab fishermen and shepherds. This tendency stopped with the Arab attacks on Jews in 1929, but was revived in the 1950s in depictions of the Bedouin with whom Israel lived at peace, who were seen as living in harmony with the land. Steinhardt painted them, while Danzinger sculpted sheep to resemble Bedouin tents. Igael *Tumarkin developed this concept by adapting into his sculptures the way they tie material to trees in their sacred groves. All these works express a desire for peaceful coexistence, but Tumarkin also dealt with land as a holy object for which blood is shed. Another type of identification developed after 1967, when Tumarkin pointed out the similarity between the former situation of the Jews and that of present-day Palestinian refugees.

Identification with the other can also be linked to criticism of one's own group and even to self-hate. Whereas Alphonse Lévy portrayed Jews with ironic humor, Chagall criticized Jewish traditions. In *Sabbath* (1910) the colors and the expressions of the figures create a hellish atmosphere, while in *Succoth* (1914) the unconscious wish of the Jew who is about to enter a dark synagogue is expressed by a small figure on his head who turns to go the other way. Camille *Pissarro, who saw himself as a socialist-anarchist, depicted hook-nosed Jewish bankers carrying the Golden Calf in an 1890 drawing, and *Maryan Maryan who lost a leg in the Holocaust, portrayed repulsive Orthodox Jews. Chaim *Soutine displayed self-hate by making his own features as ugly as possible. In his series of slaughtered animals, he drenched their carcasses with blood to enrich their color, an action often interpreted as a willful violation of Jewish dietary laws.

In conclusion, the interplay between the personal and the historical has shaped the fabric of modern Jewish art: the artists' choices depend on their background, their attitude to the modern world, and that world's attitude to them. To be accepted in the Christian world they developed a number of strategies: some assimilated into the dominant culture, while others used both "normal" and Jewish subject matter, or expressed their identity in hidden ways. Some chose to be outsiders or had this status thrust upon them by antisemitism or by feelings that the Jewish community rejected them. At other times, they tried to use their art as a bridge between their two worlds, utilizing Christian imagery or socially relevant themes to this end. The creation of Israeli art did not change this situation, although it added its own variations to the characteristics of modern Jewish art. Despite a wish to participate in the international and secular character of modern art in which artists move easily from one country and culture to another, owing allegiance only to Art, many Jewish and Israeli artists at some point reconnected in their art with their Jewish identity.

BIBLIOGRAPHY: Z. Amishai-Maisels, "Jewish Artists from the 18th Century to the Present Day," in: G. Sed-Rajna et. al., *Jewish Art* (1997), esp. 325–36, 358–64, 494–96, 509; R. Apter-Gabriel (ed.), *Tradition and Revolution: The Jewish Renaissance in Russian Avant-Garde Art 1912–1928* (1987); M. Baigell, *Jewish Artists in New York: The Holocaust Years* (2002); M. Baigell and M. Heyd (eds.), *Complex Identities: Jewish Consciousness and Modern Art* (2001); R.I. Cohen, *Jewish Icons: Art and Society in Modern Europe* (1998); S.T. Goodman (ed.), *The Emergence of Jewish Artists in Nineteenth-Century Europe* (2001); idem (ed.), *Russian Jewish Artists in a Century of Change* (1995); M. Heyd, *Mutual Reflections: Jews and Blacks in American Art* (2001); A. Kampf, *Chagall to Kitaj: The Jewish Experience in 20th Century Art* (1990); N. Kleeblatt and S. Chevlowe, *Painting a Place in America: Jewish Artists in New York, 1900–1945* (1991); N. Kleeblatt (ed.), *Too Jewish? Challenging Traditional Identities* (1996); K.E. Silver, *Circle of Montparnasse: Jewish Artists in Paris, 1905–1945* (1985); C.M. Soussloff (ed.), *Jewish Identity in Modern Art History* (1999).

[Ziva Amishai-Maisels (2nd ed.)]

WESTERN EUROPE. *The 19th Century.* The removal of legal and social restrictions in the wake of Emancipation opened the way for West European Jews to engage in the arts. However, at first quite a few Jews chose to take up art as a civil profession. Among them was Moritz Daniel *Oppenheim (1800–1882). From the early stages of his career Oppenheim was aware of the bias between his own Jewish tradition, where the visual arts had played only a minor part so far, and the attitude of the surrounding society which considered art as a supreme expression of European culture. His first monumental painting, *Moses Holding the Tablets of the Law,* is like a manifesto of his self-awareness as a Jewish artist. After a brief acquaintance with the "Nazarene" movement in Rome, where he had been shunned as a "Jewish outsider" despite his obvious artistic talents, Oppenheim turned towards painting in a naturalist style. He acknowledged the need to accommodate himself to the requirements of an emerging German bourgeois society and became a successful genre painter, portraitist, and art dealer in Frankfurt, serving Jewish as well as non-Jewish clients. Committed to the progress of the Jewish cause throughout his life, he created several highly significant historical representations such as *The Return of the Jewish Volunteer* (1833), *Moses Mendelssohn Playing Chess with Lavater* (1856) and *Felix Mendelssohn-Bartholdy Playing for Goethe* (1864) to demonstrate Jewish civility but also his ability as a Jewish painter of history. Yet it was only in the mid-1860s that he gained lasting reputation as painter of the *Scenes from Traditional Jewish Family Life*, a series of genre scenes which conveyed religious traditions from the Age of the Ghetto as a source of cultural inspiration. In this case, the customers were foremost Jews, although the printed series had been prepared to address also a non-Jewish public. Subsequently Oppenheim was considered primarily as "the First Jewish painter," a specialist able to fulfil the specific needs of the emerging bourgeois Jewish public.

The career of Moritz Daniel Oppenheim offers a good insight in the kind of challenge that artists of Jewish origin encountered in the 19th century. They were facing not only increasing demands for diversion of a bourgeois society but also had to deal with their own Jewishness as the base of their artistic experience, and moreover were consistently exposed to latent antisemitic feelings.

The most radical solution of the problem was offered by conversion, and this was the case of Philipp Veit (1793–1877), a grandson of Moses Mendelssohn. After his conversion, he became one of the leading members of the Roman Catholic "Nazarene" group, whose rebellion against classicism led to an attempt to infuse a new style into European art on the base of a revival of Christian, i.e. medieval and Renaissance, painting. Veit's talents as a painter of the new style ensured him a successful public career, and eventually he was awarded the position of the director of the municipal Academy of the Arts in Frankfurt, a post never offered to Moritz Daniel Oppenheim. Somewhat similar was the case of Eduard *Bendemann (1811–1889) and Eduard *Magnus (1799–1872). Both came from apostate wealthy Jewish families and were celebrated painters of their time. Bendemann specialized in large historical compositions, obtained many public commissions and eventually followed Wilhelm Schadow as head of the Duesseldorf academy, while Eduard Magnus became a much sought-after portraitist of the Prussian Royal court and the Berlin "haute bourgeoisie."

As a British citizen, it seems to have been somewhat easier for Solomon Alexander *Hart (1806–1881) to ensure a successful public career without being forced to conceal or to defend incessantly his Jewish identity. His realistic paintings of *Interior of a Jewish Synagogue* and *The Feast of Rejoicing the Law* were well received and did not impair his election as a full member of the Royal Academy. However, he concentrated on presenting English historical and literary scenes, which were fashionable at the time, as he did not wish to be seen as "the painter merely of religious scenes." His compatriot Abraham Solomon (1823–1862) first presented some Jewish subjects, but later he and his sister Rebecca (1832–1886) painted small, brilliantly colored moral themes from 16th- and 17th- century dramas as well as genre scenes of mid-Victorian society. In the 1860s, both Rebecca and her younger brother Simeon *Solomon (1840–1905) became acquainted with the circle of Pre-Raphaelite artists, and Simeon soon established a reputation for his Jewish religious subjects such as *Carrying the Scrolls of the Law* painted in the Pre-Raphaelite style. Encouraged by Swinburne and Burne-Jones, he also created themes of Christian or classical pagan background and of religious mysticism sometimes figuring androgynous figures of an idealized male beauty. Arrested in 1873 and convicted for indecency, he was unable to pursue his artistic career and died in poverty.

Like Oppenheim, Solomon J. *Solomon (1860–1927) remained attached to Jewish affairs throughout his life and painted numerous biblical subjects as well as scenes of contemporary Anglo-Jewish life such as *High Tea in the Sukkah*. But this in no way hindered his success as a fashionable portrait painter for Edwardian society following the tradition of Joshua Reynolds and Lawrence. In 1894, he became a member of the Royal Academy. He was followed by Sir William *Rothenstein (1872–1945), an English impressionist who painted delicate landscapes and some remarkable synagogue interiors. In all, the first two generations of Anglo-Jewish painters were able to uphold their Jewish identity without impediment but chose to follow the artistic mainstream of their country which ensured a wider recognition of their artistic talents.

Likewise, the French painters Jacques-Emile-Edouard Brandon (1831–1897) and Edouard Moyse (1827–1908), both of the first generation of French-Jewish artists, also enjoyed freedom of choice regarding their careers. Like their English colleagues, they painted Jewish subjects alongside Christian ones in an academic style, although Brandon became acquainted with Corot, Degas, and Moreau. His initial success derived from a series of works depicting the life of Saint Brigitte, a subject highly fashionable in the time of Napoleon III. In later life, however, he concentrated on Jewish subjects like *A Synagogue Interior – "The Amidah."* Edouard Moyse shared an interest in Jewish subjects with Brandon and painted intimate portraits of rabbis as well as scenes from Jewish life in France at a time when Orientalist painters presented moments of Jewish life in North Africa as an exotic sensation. Like Alphonse Levy (1843–1918), Moyse produced nostalgic renderings of the Hebrew Bible and of the rural Jews from Alsace-Lorraine.

Manifesting his ethnic background in art however, was not of an issue for one of the greatest Impressionists of all, Camille *Pissarro (1830–1903), although he had studied first with the Danish-Jewish artist David Jacobsen. He met Cézanne and became a founding member of the Impressionists in 1874. Famous for his peasant scenes and landscape paintings, he turned to the representation of the modern city life of Paris after 1888. In 1894, however, Pissarro was deeply distressed about the *Dreyfus Affair and the antisemitic accusations of his colleagues Degas and Renoir. He reconsidered his identity but stated that "for a Hebrew, there is not much of that in me." This attitude was somewhat shared by Jules *Adler (1830–1903), who focused on representing the miserable life of the underclass in a naturalist style, a topic favored by many other Jewish painters in the late 19th century, for whom the subject was not alien, as it reminded them of their own backgrounds.

Pissarro's great Dutch contemporary, Jozef *Israels (1824–1911) was also concerned with the life of the poor, and he became internationally famous for his sympathetic renderings of the hard life of Dutch fishermen and peasants in a style which owed much to Rembrandt's somberness, tenderness, and humanity. He only occasionally turned to Jewish themes and personalities, as in *A Son of the Ancient Race*, but these few paintings became veritable icons in the eye of a Jewish public in quest of authentic Jewish art after the turn of the century. His son Isaac Israels (1865–1934) was a leading Dutch impressionist, known for his scenes from the lives of Paris working girls. Like Israels, the Dutch painter Jacob Meijer *de Haan (1852–1895) started from a traditional Jewish background and first painted some Jewish scenes and portraits but later on balked at this heritage and turned to secular painting. He became a close follower of Paul Gauguin in 1889 with a similar interest in painting landscapes and peasant scenes.

At the same time, a new generation of Jewish artists emerged in the Austrian-Hungarian Empire, among them the first Jewish sculptors. The Hungarian Jacob Guttmann (1815–1852), who made busts of the Austrian chancellor Metternich and of Pope Pius X, is now completely forgotten, as is his compatriot Jozsef *Engel (1815–1901), who portrayed Queen Victoria and the Prince Consort. Of sculptors of a later generation, the Austrian (Czech) Samuel Friedrich *Beer (1846–1912) is now remembered chiefly because Herzl sat for him and because he designed the medal for the first Zionist Congress at Basle in 1897.

In contrast, the work of Isidor *Kaufmann (1853–1921), Tina Blau (1845–1916), and Broncia Koller-Pinell (1863–1934) is still remembered today, because each of them made a substantial contribution to art in Austria. Isidor Kaufmann started as a genre painter and portraitist, but later turned to Jewish subjects and became the painter who documented the great heritage of ḥasidic life in Galicia and Moravia in a realist style. As a woman artist, Tina Blau became one of the leading Austrian impressionists, whereas Bianca Koller-Pinell was a major figure in the Viennese art nouveau movement. Both women showed little concern for their Jewish identity and converted later in life, though Blau painted the Jew's street of Amsterdam.

The secular approach to art was also favored by Italian-Jewish artists like Serafino da *Tivoli (1826–1890) and Vito d'*Ancona (1824–1884). Though ardent supporters of the Risorgimento, which led to the abolition of the Ghetto at last, they showed no interest in making their Jewish background artistically visible. Instead, they pursued secular painting and the latest currents of contemporary art. Serafino da Tivoli was the founder of the "Macchiaioli" school, which reacted against neoclassical formulae and applied paint in summary spots to gain an effect of spontaneity. One of the chief painters of this school was Vito d'Ancona, who executed fresh, lively landscapes and nudes and portraits in rich and luminous colors. Vittorio Matteo *Corcos (1859–1933) followed the Macchiaioli school at first, but became an internationally sought-after society portraitist after his marriage and conversion in 1886. Likewise the Swedish impressionist Ernst Josephson (1851–1906) worked also as a portraitist and his fresh, boldly executed portraits of a subject caught at a characteristic moment are among his best achievements.

In Germany, the second generation of Jewish artists like Max *Liebermann (1847–1935) and after him Lesser *Ury

(1861–1931) witnessed the emerging liberalism and became less preoccupied with manifesting their religious and ethnic status. Instead, dealing with the latest artistic trend and the search for pictorial truth prevailed. Max Liebermann as a socially conscious artist started to depict the harsh life of day laborers under the influence of the French Realists Courbet and Millet, thus setting a counterbalance to cozy Biedermeier genre scenes which dominated the German art market by then. However, when the artist sent his *Jesus in the Temple* to Munich in 1879, the public display of the painting set off vicious antisemitic criticism against an artist who had dared to show Jesus as a precocious Jewish boy surrounded by honest Jewish-looking rabbis. Irritated by the result, Liebermann refrained from painting biblical subjects and found his inspiration in the friendship with Jozef Israels and in the life of the small towns and villages of Holland. He adapted French impressionism and became himself the leading German impressionist and a most eminent portraitist. In addition, he made a major contribution to the development of the art of etching. As the founder of the Berlin Secession, Liebermann was elected president of the Prussian Academy of the Arts in the Weimar Republic, but during his entire career he had to withstand harsh attacks like those of the art historian Henry Thode in 1905, who chided him for his "un-German" character. It would seem to be no coincidence that Liebermann painted the famous *Jew's Street in Amsterdam* at that very time. At the end of his life he was confronted with the rise of Nazism and was forced to resign from the Prussian Academy.

Lesser Ury's artistic career resembled somewhat that of Liebermann's. He too started as an impressionist painter of rural life, but after he had settled in Berlin in 1887 he became the first artist to capture the vibrancy and the luster of the emerging modern metropolis in his Berlin cityscapes. At the very same time, he maintained a lifelong interest in the Bible and created many biblical paintings like *Jeremiah*, exhibited in one of the earliest shows of Jewish artists in Berlin in 1903. Alongside Israels, Lesser Ury was considered to be one of the first modern Jewish painters.

The 20th Century. With the 20th century, the general picture changed. Whereas hitherto Jewish artists had been few, now there was a sudden explosion of Jewish talent which left a permanent mark on artistic development. Not only from the teeming ghettos of Eastern Europe, but also from the Balkans and North Africa, from well-to-do homes in Germany, England, and America, a stream of Jewish artists emerged. In most cases their Mecca was Paris where they hoped to take up the latest art fashion. It was in the fruitful surroundings of the Fauves and Cubists that the School of Paris was formed which harbored such eminent artists as Soutine, Modigliani, Pascin, Mane-Katz, and especially Chagall. They played a highly significant role in modern painting and their contribution was so great as to be in some quarters considered dominant. Besides creating avant-garde art, some artists and critics of Jewish origin engaged also in discussing the possibility of establishing authentic Jewish art, but their attempt fell short as most of the members of the Paris School rejected the necessity of such a quest and favored the search for purely individual artistic expression instead. The best example is the Italian-Jewish painter Amedeo *Modigliani (1884–1920), who became famous only after his death for his sensual nudes and intimate portraits capturing the mood of loneliness and isolation of the sitter in simple elongated forms and iridescent colors.

However, the sense of loneliness and uprooting in the face of a modern world, where Jewish traditional life was threatened either by dissolution or deep change, could lead also to a new attempt to create an art based on Jewish themes. This was the case of a group of Anglo-Jewish artists like David *Bomberg (1890–1957), Mark *Gertler (1891–1939), and Jacob *Kramer (1892–1962). Mostly, they were born out of the first generation of East European immigrants centered in Whitechapel in the East End of London and educated at the London-based Slade School of Fine Arts. They started to document their Jewish surroundings, the Yiddish theater as the nucleus of culture or the archetypal Jewish family of immigrants, and tried to evoke tradition as with Jacob Kramer in his painting *Day of Atonement* of 1919.

In Germany, redefining Jewish art had became a major issue through the impact of Martin *Buber, who had proclaimed the necessity of a Jewish national art at the Fifth International Zionist Congress in 1901. Buber's cultural activities stimulated an entire generation of young German and Central European Jewish artists who became involved in creating the "Jewish Renaissance" which reached its climax in Berlin in the Weimar Republic. It was the first time in European art ever that Jewish artists developed their work first and foremost out of their consciousness of a distinct ethnic and religious background. Leading members were graphic artists like Moses Ephraim *Lilien (1874–1925), Herman *Struck (1876–1944), and Joseph *Budko (1888–1940), who leaned first toward art nouveau and later toward expressionism to create a whole new Jewish iconography ranging from Zionist symbols to representations of the world of the shtetl. Lilien's photo of *Herzl Overlooking the Rhine* became as much an icon as Struck's delicately etched portraits of Polish and Russian Jews in *Das Ostjuedische Antlitz*. This group was joined by a wide circle of artists, art historians, and critics like Max *Osborn, Rachel Wischnitzer, and Ernst *Cohn-Wiener. Among the artists were the expressionist painters Jakob *Steinhardt (1887–1968) and Ludwig *Meidner, who were already known for their cityscapes and biblical paintings foreshadowing imminent disaster like Meidner's *I and the City* of 1912 and Steinhardt's monumental *Prophet Jeremiah* of 1913. Of the same generation was the expressionist sculptor Arnold *Zadikow (1884–1943), who later created the portrait bust of Albert Einstein, and an entire group of avant-garde Polish and Russian Jewish artists such as Jankel *Adler, Issai Kulviansky, El *Lissitzky, and Issachar Ber *Ryback, to name but a few. Their art works contributed to Berlin's reputation as an international center for the creation of contemporary art.

At the same time, the ritual objects of the *Bezalel Art School founded in Jerusalem in 1906 had a major impact on the creation of modern European Judaica. This field had been largely neglected during the Age of Emancipation, and it was only in the later 19th century that manufacturers like Lazarus Posen started with mass-produced Judaica in the so called "antique silver style." In the early 20th century, however, a group of young artists emerged like Leo *Horovitz (1876–1961), Ludwig Wolpert (1900–1981), Friedrich Adler (1878–1942), and David Gumbel. They were trained as sculptors like Benno *Elkan (1877–1960), but in addition to secular art they started to create ritual objects under the influence of art nouveau at first and later under that of the Bauhaus.

Nevertheless German Jewish artists of the 1920s were not solely involved in the quest for an authentic Jewish art. Some of them formulated new aspects of art out of progressive political attitudes. Their left-wing views led them to defy the saturated bourgeois society, and they searched for new ways to express the human condition as marked by the vicissitudes of the Weimar Republic. This was the case with Otto *Freundlich (1878–1943), a painter, sculptor, and graphic artist who was attracted by the teachings of the Bauhaus during the Weimar Republic but lived predominantly in Paris. He sculpted a new image of man close to abstraction and engaged in painting of the pure form. Artists like John Heartfield (1891–1968) and Lea (1906–1977) and Hans (1901–1958) Grundig became members of the KPD (German Communist Party) and devoted their artistic talents exclusively to the service of the party by creating anti-fascist posters or presentations denouncing the living conditions of the proletariat. Political engagement was considered also a prerequisite of artistic creativity among the "Das Junge Rheinland" group," founded in 1919, where artists like Gert *Wollheim (1894–1970) and Arthur *Kaufmann (1888–1971) painted portraits and genre scenes denouncing the chaos of postwar life in a tortured and emotional late expressionist style, revealing the influence of the "Neue Sachlichkeit" and of Otto Dix. The Viennese painter Max Oppenheimer (1885–1954), who was influenced by Oskar Kokoschka, created portraits with deep psychological insight while Hanns Ludwig Katz (1892–1940), another late expressionist painter, who came under the influence of Max Beckmann in Frankfurt, followed a similar intention when he painted the portrait of Gustav Landauer in 1919/1920.

After the rise to power of the Nazi Party in 1933, all German Jewish artists were threatened by persecution, and later, during wartime, the entire generation of European Jewish artists born since the late 1880s was dispersed and many of them perished in death camps. The show "Degenerate Art" organized by the Nazi authorities in 1938 served as a prelude to annihilation. There, many of the avant-garde art works of Jews and non-Jews alike were publicly decried as "Jewish-Bolshevik botch" or as marks of insanity. However, artists did not simply give in to terror; they tried to resist by creating art. This was especially the case of Friedl *Dicker-Brandeis (1898–1944), who brought art to hundreds of children in the Theresienstadt concentration camp from 1942 until she was sent to Auschwitz in 1944. Charlotte *Salomon (1917–1943), Rudolf *Levy (1875–1944), and Felix Nussbaum (1904–1944) were among those who were persecuted and went into hiding but continued to work nevertheless. They all perished in the Holocaust, but their masterworks created while living under the most oppressive conditions offer a vivid testimony of humanity withstanding all odds. Felix Nussbaum revealed his feelings of solitude and despair in the face of imminent doom in his many self-portraits in a surrealist style and especially in the *Danse Macabre*, his last painting before deportation to the Auschwitz extermination camp.

While artists all over the world were deeply affected by the Holocaust, the experience of torture and humiliation, of persecution and exile, became a dominant subject for those who had survived. Yet, for many of the artists it was not only about documenting the actual horrors of the death camps but also of visualizing the abyss of human cruelty. Survivors like the Viennese artists Arik Brauer (1929–) and Fritz Hundertwasser (1928–2000) chose to depict scenes of Fantastic Realism in order to convey the inconceivable dimensions of the catastrophe. Other artists who survived in exile, like Jankel *Adler or Ludwig *Meidner, focused on presenting those who were barred from normal life or created monstrous apocalyptic scenes in order to express suffering.

Jankel Adler (1895–1949) was among those artists who could emigrate to England like Jacob *Bornfriend (1904–1976) and Joseph *Herman (1911–) but had a hard time supporting themselves as painters. They brought with them the figurative expressionist heritage from the Continent and continued to work in that style. A new style of painting, based as much on the aesthetic experience of expressionism as on abstract painting, emerged in the next generation of Anglo-Jewish artists with a refugee background. Today, the works of artists like Lucien *Freud (1922–), Leon *Kossoff (1926–), and Frank *Auerbach (1931–) are generally acknowledged as having a major impact on contemporary world art, while their ethnic and religious background is rarely stressed. Fascinated by the sheer physicality of the world, these London-based artists work as figurative painters and graphic artists who convey the vibrancy of life, especially the spirituality of human beings out of the materiality of the body in a sensuous, agitated style of brushwork. For them the visual reality offers the indispensable backdrop for exploring the metaphysical quality of life. They are joined in their efforts by the American born R.B. *Kitaj (1932–) who focuses on presenting the quest for a modern Jewish identity after the Holocaust in his paintings.

[Annette Weber (2nd ed.)]

EASTERN EUROPE. Jewish artists emerged in Eastern Europe, as well as in Western Europe, as a result of modernization and integration of a part of Jewry into European cultural and social life. It appears only natural, therefore, that the fist Jewish figures to appear on the artistic arena of Eastern Europe in the 1840s–1850s came from privileged circles of the

Jewish financial elite that was more prone, in comparison to other sectors of the Jewish community, to acculturation and even assimilation. The most prominent artists of this period (within the borders of the Austrian and the Russian Empire) are Barbu Iscovescu (Itskovich, 1816–1854) and Constantine Daniel Rosenthal (1820–1851) in Romania; Alexander Lesser (1814–1884) and Maximilian Fajans (1827–1890) in Poland.

Those artists' *Weltanschauung* was molded in the intellectual atmosphere of societies and salons of Jewish Reformist bourgeoisie and acculturated intelligentsia. An important element of the *Weltanschauung* was a firm belief that Jews were an integral part of the nations in whose midst they existed and whose historic destiny they thus shared. This belief inspired many works created by Jewish artists of the first generation, a striking example of which is Lesser's *The Funeral of Five Victims of the Warsaw Manifestation of 1861* (1866). The picture portrays the solemn ceremony of burying Polish patriots who were killed in the repression of the Russian imperial regime. Among the participants led by the Catholic archbishop of the Polish capital, Lesser included representatives of all the sectors and ethnic groups of the Warsaw population of the time, including an Orthodox rabbi and a reformist rabbi. The picture was to emphasize the unity of the Polish nation, composed of diverse ethnic groups including the Jews.

Jewish artists, as well as sections of Jewry they belonged to, identified themselves with the rest of the nation, and this feeling of unity brought about sympathy with the nationalist movements of their countries. Moreover, some Jewish artists were active participants in those movements, such as Iscovescu and Rosenthal, whose role in the 1848–49 revolution in Valakhia and Moldavia was quite prominent. Their art, which is believed to have established the foundations of the Romanian national school of painting, was a visual manifestation of the patriotic ideals of the Romanian nation then being in the process of formation (such as the painting by Rosenthal eloquently named *Romania Casting Off Her Handcuffs in the Liberty Camp*, 1849).

However, despite the fact that some Jewish artists of the first half of the 19th century had gained recognition, their works did not have a pronounced impact on the cultural transformation of East European Jewry. Being few in number and striving to merge into the national cultures of their countries, these artists remained at the periphery of contemporary Jewish society together with the thin social layer of Jewish intelligentsia whose ideas they expressed.

Owing to a number of political and cultural factors characterizing the evolution of East European Jewry (among them, complete or partial lack of emancipation, perpetuating the dominant role of the traditional culture, numerous Jews habitually living in mono-ethnic settlements, etc.), the process of modernization took specific forms and unfolded more slowly than in the countries of Western Europe. This is one of the reasons why the Jewish artistic presence in Eastern Europe did not become noticeable before the first decades of the second half of the 19th century, i.e., later than in the West.

In the specific historical conditions of Eastern Europe of that period, the new phenomenon of a professional Jewish artist needed certain legitimizing. Jewish traditionalists condemned the artistic trade, regarding it as breaking with the fundamental commandments of Judaism. The non-Jewish public mind shared a deeply rooted belief that Jews were not capable of creating original plastic art. This negative stereotype was also shared by some members of the Jewish intelligentsia. To overcome these prejudices, Jewish publicists came forth with the genre of art criticism and the esthetic essay. In the early 1880s, the pioneers in this genre were Nahum *Sokolow and Mordechai Zvi Mane (1859–1886), the latter being one of the first Jewish artists and a poet writing in Hebrew.

Despite the impeding factors and a certain "delay," in the early 1870s the Jewish presence in art was established by two outstanding names, those of Marc *Antokolsky, a sculptor living in Russia, and Maurycy *Gottlieb, a Polish painter, whose legacies in the art of their countries in particular and of Europe in general have been quite prominent. Some of their works, influenced by the *Haskalah, manifest a pioneering visual interpretation of images of early Christianity as part of the Jewish history, among them Antokolsky's *Ecce Homo* (1874) and Gottlieb's *Christ Preaching at Capernaum* (1878–79), where Jesus is portrayed, for the first time in the history of art, as a traditional Semitic Jew. Pioneering this interpretation, the artists tried to analyze anew the pattern of relationship between modern European civilization and Judaism and to demonstrate the universal contribution of Jews to the evolution of this civilization. At the same time, Antokolsky and Gottlieb managed to significantly expand the frames of "the Jewish theme" (depicting scenes of Jewish life and history), both in content and expression, having introduced historical and psychological elements and the cogency of realism. In fact, they turned these themes into a means of introspection revolving around the existential experience and national self-identity of a modern Jewish personality.

In Russia, Vladimir Stasov (1824–1906), a prominent art critic and one of the ideologists of liberal art, enthusiastically welcomed the advent of Jewish artists. Stasov was the first to encourage Antokolsky and later became his friend and patron; he authored a number of articles in which he came forward as an ardent apologist of Jewish creative artistic potential. Being a passionate advocate of the idea of creating a Russian national artistic school, Stasov viewed its emergence as a result of the common creative effort made by all the different peoples inhabiting the Russian empire, Jews in particular. He regarded national ("folk") art as a "truthful" portrayal of history and daily popular life, and urged Jewish artists to turn to Jewish national topics. This appeal elicited a response among several Jewish artists in Russia and Poland, who, being younger contemporaries of Antokolsky and Gottlieb, further developed their art in own manner and became active participants of the artistic life of the late 19th and the early 20th centuries. For a number of painters and sculptors, among them Isaac Asknasii, Moisei Maimon, Pinkhas Geller, Yehuda Pan, Yakov Kruger,

Naum *Aronson, and Yosif Gabovich (1862–1939) in Russia, and Lazar *Kreinstin, Mauricy *Trebacz, Artur *Markowicz, Leopold *Pilikhovsky and Hanoch *Glitzenstein in Poland, "the Jewish theme" became the focus of their creative work, notwithstanding all the differences in the artistic manner. They went into depth expressing the social meaning of Jewishness, imbued it with actual meaning, and made it serve as a tool of reflection and the search for solutions to national problems. Unlike those non-Jewish artists who chose to turn to "the Jewish theme," Jewish artists refrained from criticizing the Jewish people, seeing their mission rather in its apologia. At the same time, while portraying Jewish life in historic or genre paintings, the artists strove to embody novel esthetic and ethic national ideals expressed in the images they created.

Other artists were inspired by different goals while treating "the Jewish topic," such as Isidore *Kaufmann and Leopold *Horovitz, who both were of East European origin and lived in Austro-Hungary. Their works reflected nostalgia for the traditional "authentic" Jewish world lost by modernized Jewry. This tendency was especially pronounced in Kaufmann's works portraying an idealized image of the Galician Ḥasidism.

However, quite a few Jewish artists dedicated but a small fraction of their work to Jewish themes, or even chose to distance themselves completely from them, concentrating entirely on purely artistic goals. By the end of the 19th century, though, both groups of Jewish artists in Eastern Europe had gained celebrity and held prominent positions in the artistic life of their countries. In Russia, Asknasii and Maimon, as well as sculptor Ilya *Ginzburg were among the first Jews to become members of the Academy of Arts; Yuli Bershadsky (1869–1956) and Solomon Kishinevsky (1862–1942, died in the Odessa ghetto) were among the leaders of the Association of South Russian Artists in Odessa; Boris Anisfeld and Leon *Bakst were notable as leading pioneering artists who brought about dramatic innovation into the Russian stage design; Isaac *Levitan in Russia and Abraham Neumann in Poland were recognized as prominent masters of landscape painting.

At the same time, the ideologists of the Jewish national movement (mostly of East European origin, such as Martin *Buber) had "rehabilitated" art as an element within the set of national values and come to regarding it as an indispensable attribute of a "historical" nation. They envisioned the climax of Jewish national revival in the formation of the historical Jewish nation. This vision was the background against which the Jewish artistic milieu was formed in various centers of Eastern Europe, bringing together not only the artists but all Jewish intellectuals who shared the national ideas. It is within this milieu that an image of a Jewish artist was molded as someone who adhered to the national idea and by way of his creative work promoted the evolution of the national identification of his people.

The bond between the Jewish national ideology and art was strikingly reflected in the works of several artists connected to the Zionist movement, among them Wilhelm Wachtel from Galicia, Samuel *Hirshenberg from Poland, and especially Ephraim Moses *Lilien, a graphic artist from Austro-Hungary. The works of the latter, according to his contemporaries, provided visual means for "bridging" gaps in Zionist theory. Inspired by Zionist ideas and the mission of creating the national art, some of these artists moved to Ereẓ Israel, more precisely to Jerusalem, where in 1906 sculptor Boris *Shatz established "Betzalel," the Jewish school of arts.

The rise of the Jewish national movement, advancement of literature in both Yiddish and Hebrew, penetrated by modernist attitudes, the idea of creating "the New Jewish Culture," including "the New Jewish Art" as part of it – all these factors had an impact on evolution of the *Weltanschauung* of the new generation of Jewish artists. Being of East European origin, these artists emerged prior to World War I. For many of them, it was Paris that became the center of attraction, where they became acquainted with avant-garde art. Artists from Eastern Europe were a sizable and active part of the Parisian international artistic bohemia. In 1912, several young East European artists in La Rouche established the first Jewish artistic group "Makhmadim" ("The Precious Ones"), under the leadership of Leo Koenig (1889–1970), who later became a prominent art critic writing in Yiddish, Isaac Lichtenstein and Joseph Chaikov.

From the early 1910s, among the artists residing in Paris were Jacques *Lipchitz, Osip *Zadkine, Leon Indenbaum (1892–1981), Chana *Orloff, Chaim *Soutine, Pinchas Krémègne (1890–1981), originally from Russia; Henry *Epstein, Marek *Szwarz, Moïse *Kisling from Poland; Béla Czobel (1883–1976) from Hungary; and Jules *Pascin from Bulgaria, together with many other artists who had come from Eastern Europe. In this circle were such artists as Marc *Chagall, Nathan *Altman, and Robert *Falk, who had come from Russia and already gained celebrity, being regarded by art critics as the most prominent figures of "the New Jewish Art."

[Hillel Kazovsky (2nd ed.)]

MODERN EREẒ ISRAEL. Art in modern Ereẓ Israel can be dated from the first Zionist immigration to Palestine. Its evolution followed to a certain extent the pattern of the successive waves of immigration. One of the central questions concerning art in Ereẓ Israel, and later Israeli art, concerns identity, the question of assigning it precise defining characteristics that will distinguish it from the Jewish art of the Diaspora. The art in Ereẓ Israel of the first decades of the 20th century might be considered in terms of the continuity of the artistic and cultural traditions that the artists, who were all immigrants, had brought over with them. However, they also participated in the Zionist project of creating a new identity for an old nation creating itself anew. The creative awareness of artists of later generations fluctuated between, on the one hand, the desire to create a native art based on an indigenous independent language, an organic part of the land, and its physical and social conditions; and, on the other, the attraction to artistic developments overseas, which, particularly until the 1960s, were associated with Paris.

The Creation of the Bezalel School. The creation of new symbols of identity for the Jewish people in its ancient homeland was, indeed, at the heart of Boris *Schatz's life project. In 1906, Schatz (1867–1932) immigrated to Ereẓ Israel from Bulgaria. He was a painter and sculptor and had been head of the Royal Academy of Art in Sofia. In the year of his arrival he realized his dream of founding a school of arts and crafts in Jerusalem. He called it the *Bezalel School after the biblical architect of the Tabernacle. The founding of an art institute in Jerusalem in 1906 was an adventurous undertaking. The Jewish population of the Yishuv was small and the Orthodox were certain to protest vigorously against a school which might violate the biblical prohibition against the making of graven images. Nevertheless, Bezalel received the full backing of the Zionist Organization. The foundation of the school must be considered the beginning of genuine artistic activity. Until then the only art forms produced locally were by Arabs and the small Jewish communities of Jerusalem, Safed, and Tiberias. They consisted of arts and crafts and pictorial representations for devotional purposes. Schatz wanted to establish a cultural-artistic center that would advance the utopian vision of a Jewish homeland. He planned his school to train painters, sculptors, and craftsmen on two levels, which he was careful to define as the "technical level" and the "national level." The teachers he hired included local artisans (goldsmiths and Yemenite weavers) as well as Jewish artists who were already well established in Europe, such as Abel *Pann (1883–1963), Samuel *Hirshenberg (1865–1908), Ephraim Moses *Lilien (1874–1925), Zeev Raban (1890–1970), and Joseph *Budko (1888–1940). They all came from Eastern Europe and their artistic training had tended to lead them away from Judaism, but they had come to know both the horror of the pogroms and the nationalist revival in Europe. They now felt the need to use their academic knowledge to relate to the past as represented by the Bible and to the future as represented by the advent of Zionism. *The Wandering Jew* by Hirshenberg, the biblical pastels of Pann, and the reliefs of biblical figures and Zionist personalities by Schatz represented this outlook. In Lilien's illustrations and etchings, Yemenite Jews, Bedouins and Arabs in their traditional dresses served as models for images of biblical figures. The "Bezalel Style" was consequently quite eclectic, combining Oriental arabesques and Jugendstil flowing lines and decorative flatness. The themes combined biblical motifs, often in a Zionist perspective, and landscapes done in an idealist-utopian and Orientalist spirit. The products included jewelry, religious artifacts, ceramic tiles, postcards, illustrated books, and posters. Bezalel under the directorship of Schatz closed down in 1928 because of economic problems and because its generally conservative orientation seemed inimical to the modernist outlook. It reopened as the "New Bezalel" in the 1930s under the guidance of immigrant Jewish artists from Germany who oriented it toward the spirit of the Bauhaus School.

The 1920s. Early criticism of Bezalel is already in evident in the first important exhibition in Ereẓ Israel, organized in 1923 by the younger generation of Palestine artists. It was held in the so-called Tower of David in Jerusalem and included the work of Nahum *Gutman (1898–1980), Reuven *Rubin (1893–1974), Pinhas *Litvinovsky (1894–1985), and Israel *Paldi (1892–1979), all of whom had been pupils at the Bezalel. The work of newcomers such as Yossef *Zaritsky (1891–1985) was also shown. These young people had realized how anachronistic the style and ideas of their teachers had been and it was this group, who were mainly landscape artists, that formed the nucleus out of which Israeli art developed. With the new waves of immigration of 1919–25, Tel Aviv, a modern new city, became a lively cultural alternative to Jerusalem, drawing writers, artists, musicians, and theater people who felt the need to create a new local Hebrew culture. The three exhibitions of "Modern Artists" at the Ohel Theater during 1926–28 exhibited the modernist orientation of the young artists such as Nachum Gutman, Arieh Lubin (1897–1980), Moshe *Mokady (1902–1975), Israel Paldi, Reuven Rubin, Menachem *Shemi (1897–1951), Tziona *Tagger (1900–1988), Moshe *Castel (1909–1991), Yossef Zaritzky, and others.

The artistic alternatives these artists proposed were defined by a desire to become acculturated in the new Oriental surrounding and adopt the figure of the Arab as a model for the new "Hebrew." They went out to the landscapes in order to bring together the biblical past and the modern pioneers, the local Arabs, and the rooted Oriental Jews. Stylistically, they were guided by the need to create a national art, and, at the same time, to develop universal means of expression which would qualify them as modern artists. The conflict persisted throughout the 1920s and 1930s, even when definition of its components – national art, universalism – underwent slight alteration. Thus, in the 1920s, nationalism was equated with the ideals of pioneering and national renewal. The anti-Diaspora ideal and the demand for an original Hebrew culture found expression in stylistic primitivism (with affinity to the art of the Near and Far East) and exotic-naïve predilections which were realized in flattening and use of color planes with strong contours (corresponding, to some extent, to the expressionistic tendencies in European art which rejected the art of the museum and sought the roots of art in its primitive sources). At the same time, these artists showed a desire to belong to a modern artistic context as evinced by the borrowing of the trappings of modernism as represented by cubist and constructivist trends. These included simplification, even some distortion, and, to a certain degree, geometric construction of form, while preserving the realistic character of the work. Such artists as Tagger, Itzhak *Frenkel (1899–1981), and Mokady found the model in the work of André Derain, whose moderate modernism fitted the needs of a young art lacking in tradition.

The 1930s. In the late 1920s artists from Ereẓ Israel began flocking to Paris; this was accompanied by a tendency to abandon the former modernistic manifestations and folkloristic character and by an intensified desire to root art in an established artistic tradition, all the more so since France in those years was marked by the trend of reverting to traditional artistic values. Paris offered the Ereẓ Israel artists a wide range of choices. There was the French landscape tradition of the 19th century (Corot, Courbet) and various impressionist and post-impressionist trends (Cézanne, the "intimist" artists). The Jewish School of Paris artists (Soutine, Mintchine, Kremegne, Menkès) offered an expressionism based on a dark palette with the paint laid thickly as an element conveying atmosphere and feeling. Artists such as Haim *Atar (Apteker; 1902–1953), Mokady, Frenkel, and Moshe Castel were shaped by the extreme expressionist manifestations, as represented by Soutine. Others, such as Shemi, Haim Gliksberg (1904–1970), Avigdor *Stematsky (1908–1989), Eliahu Sigad (Sigard; 1909–1975), exhibit a more moderate expressionism together with post-impressionist influences.

From 1933, artists and architects who had fled the Nazis constituted an important element of the art scene in Palestine. Some of them were associated with German avant-garde expressionist groups; others studied at the Bauhaus under Itten, Kandinsky, Klee, and the architect Gropius. Jakob *Steinhardt (1887–1968), Mordecai *Ardon (1896– 1992), Miron *Sima (1902–1999), Isidor *Aschheim (1891–1968), and Shalom *Sebba (1897–1975) came in this wave of immigration. With the exception of Sebba, they all settled in Jerusalem. They created a "Jerusalem School" which was dominated by certain aspects of German expressionism. These artists were preceded by two Viennese painters, Anna *Ticho (1894–1980) and Leopold *Krakauer (1890–1954). By the mid-1930s, some of the painters of the first generation of Bezalel graduates had begun to lose their originality and vitality. The coming of new artists, in particular Ardon and Sebba, revived the artistic scene. Mordecai Ardon, a graduate of the Weimar Bauhaus, achieved this through his efficient teaching at the Bezalel School. Sebba aimed at applying a European archaistic-primitivist tendency to a "localism" associated with the figures of shepherds and exerted his influence through stage designs and the decoration of public buildings.

The 1940s. World War II brought about a feeling of isolation from the outside world for the younger artists of the period, but also an increasing sense of a local identity that was antithetical to the image of the Jew of the Diaspora. This trend was exemplified by a group of writers and poets – Amos *Kenan, Benjamin *Tammuz, Aharon *Amir, Jonathan *Ratosh – who became known as the "Canaanites." They called for a separation of the Hebrew identity from Judaism and for its re-attachment to the ancient land of Canaan and its culture. Artists such as Yitshak *Danziger (1916–1977) and Aharon *Kahana (1905–1967) adopted a primitivist-Oriental imagery and borrowed the myths of the Ancient East. Danziger's sculpture *Nimrod*, with its archaism, nudity, and non-Jewish connotations, became a manifesto and a model to young artists such as Yehiel *Shemi (1922–2003), Shoshana Heiman (1923–), and others. In the late 1950s, Danziger abandoned the "Canaanite" orientation and turned to abstract sculpture inspired by the Israeli landscape.

Alongside the "Canaanites," there was another group of artists whose orientation was geared to the expression of social issues. Among the "social realists" were kibbutz artists such as Yohanan Simon (1905–1976) and Shraga Weil (1918–), who endowed daily life in the kibbutz with a religious-mystical romantic mood. There were "engaged" artists, with pronounced socialist leanings, such as Avraham *Ofek (1935–1990), Naftali Bezem (1924–), Shimeon Tzabar (1926–), Moshe Gat (1935–), and others. In the 1950s, in the midst of the great waves of immigration to Israel, Ruth Schloss (1922–) Gerson Knispel (1932–), Bezem and Weil evoked in their works the hardships of the temporary homes for the immigrants in the *ma'barot*.

New Horizons. By 1945, Israel painters had become aware that the two Paris schools had ceased to exist. The Jewish painters had almost all disappeared. A younger generation of abstract painters had succeeded the post-cubist fauvist schools, and these painters now began to exercise a considerable influence on Israeli artists, including several veterans among them. The work of Aharon Giladi (1907–1993), Mordecai *Levanon (1901–1968), Litvinovsky, Paldi, and Frenkel evolved toward a more "modern" style, which in some cases resembled that of Rouault or Picasso, rather than that of the two Paris schools. The influence of Parisian abstraction could be seen in the work of Castel and Mokady. The most important event of this period was the creation of the New Horizons Group in 1947/48. The leaders were Zaritsky and Marcel *Janco (1895–1984), a painter of Romanian origin who had gained renown as a member of the dada movement in Zurich, and who arrived in Palestine in 1941. Around them were grouped Yeḥezkiel *Streichman (1906–1993) and Avigdor Stematsky. They all made a decisive contribution to the development of what became known as "lyrical abstraction," combining free, abstract style with a predilection for the expression of the light and color palate characterizing the local experience. Zaritsky followed his own path with some debt to Braque and French "intimisme"; Streichman and Stematsky were influenced by Picasso as well as by the lyrical trend in the School of Paris. They were joined by Avraham Naton (1906–1959), Kahana, and Yeḥiel Krize (1909–1968) who were still working on figurative though somewhat simplified themes; Jacob Wexler (1912–1995), Avshalom Okashi (1916–1980), Moshe Castel, Zvi *Mairovich (1909–1974), Arie *Aroch (1908–1974), and the sculptors Yitshak Danziger, Yeḥiel Shemi, and Moshe *Sternschuss (1903–1992). A little later the two leaders split over the choice of entries for Israel's first participation in the Venice Biennale. The reactions were so violent that Marcel Janco left the New Horizons Group after its first exhibition at the Tel Aviv Museum in 1949. Zaritsky inherited the leadership. Group exhibitions were held until 1963. Although certain members returned later to figurative work (Kahana), or geometric abstraction (Naton), the formation of the group marked the end of the expressionist phase in Israel art and opened the way to new ideas.

The 1960s. Lyrical abstraction dominated Israeli art until 1955. Streichman and Stematsky, both teachers at the Avni Institute in Tel Aviv, played an important role in the formation of a second generation of artists that took abstraction to new directions, at times more extreme than those of their teachers. Of this group should be singled out Lea *Nikel (1918–2005), whose work was highly abstract, sensual, lively, and colorful, and Moshe *Kupferman (1926–2003), a Holocaust survivor whose paintings might be seen as representing both formal abstract qualities and thematic connotations associated with his personal experiences. The way was already clear, however, for new experimenters. The most important of these was Arie Aroch, whose work may be associated with the spirit of the poetic revolution of the 1950s, embodied by Nathan *Zach, David *Avidan, Meir Wieseltier, and Dalia *Ravikovitch. Aroch proposed an alternative to lyrical abstraction by developing a calligraphy that was based on children's drawings, developing uncommon techniques (rubbing, erasing, scratching) and utilizing motifs and forms taken out of "non-artistic" sources (such as street signs), Jewish manuscripts, and other readymade forms. Aviva *Uri (1927–1989) chose to work with pencil, charcoal, and oil sticks and to develop an expressive line that reflected anxieties and emotional tensions. The third artist to work away from lyrical abstraction was Igael *Tumarkin (1933–), who in the early 1960s began making rather violent assemblages that combined readymade objects, expressionist brushwork, texts sprayed through matrices, art historical citations. These works, with their controversial political-social stand, echoed the new Pop Art and new Realism then current abroad. This new spirit, and the direct influence of Aroch and Uri, were seen in the work of several young painters, notably Rafi *Lavie (1937–), who formed the "Group of Ten." Lavie's work, in its connotation of a municipal billboard, with its torn posters and dynamic and haphazard piling up of images, evoked the essence of the spirit of Tel Aviv. An exhibition entitled "The Want of Matter – A Quality in Israeli Art," curated by Sara Breitberg-Semel at the Tel Aviv Museum in 1986, provided a major summing up of all these trends of the 1960s.

The 1970s. The "Group of Ten" reflected the beginning of the trend of the "Americanization" of Israeli art that was augmented by the greater exposure to American culture brought about by volunteers who flocked to Israel following the Six-Day War and by young Jewish-American artists such as Joshua *Neustein (1940–), who immigrated to Israel in 1964. The art of the 1970s mirrors American trends such as conceptual art, body art, performance, environmental art ("Earth Art"), and minimalist art. The years 1967–83, encompassing three wars, also brought about an eclipse of the former spirit of national identity, with the private identity replacing the collective dream. Michal Na'aman (1951–) searched the limits of language in their application to national or sexual identity; the works of Michael Druks (1940–), Motti Mizrahi (1946–), Yocheved Weinfeld (1947–), David Ginton (1947–), Gideon Gechtman (1942–), Moshe Gershuni (1936–), and Haim Maor (1951–) examine the human body and the limits of pain and suffering, at times in relation to war. Artists such as Avital *Geva (1941–), Micha *Ullman (1940–), Pinchas Cohen-Gan (1942–), Dov Or-Ner (1927–), Dganit Berest (1949–), Menashe Kadishman (1932–), Dov Heller (1937–), Dani *Karavan (1930–), and others, dealt with the question of borders, maps, environment and ecology. Alongside the trends that emphasized themes and contents, there was a more abstract trend, which engaged in examining minimalist form. This trend was amply reflected in the works of Yehiel Shemi, Michael *Gross (1920–2004), Nahum Tevet (1946–), Beni *Efrat (1936–), Rita Alima (1932–), and Ori *Reisman (1924–1991). It should be recalled that there were artists, such as Naftali Bezem (1924–) and Moshe Tamir (1924–2004), who remained figurative painters. A return to themes which were figurative and evocative of the Holocaust and to traditional Jewish subjects, first noticeable in the work of Ardon himself, is illustrated in various ways by Yossl *Bergner (1920–), Shmuel Boneh (1930–1999), and Shraga Weil.

The 1980s and After. Critical post-modernist attitudes, which became quite dominant in Israeli art in the 1980s, express a growing tendency to give voice to the "Other" – artists raised in immigrant families, homosexuals and lesbians, or artists belonging to minority groups. The "Israeli experience," based on a collective, monolithic memory, had fallen apart. The paintings of Yair *Garbuz (1945–), David Reeb (1952–), Tsivi Geva (1951–), and Avishai Eyal (1945–), or the photographs of Micha Kirshner (1947–), Michal Heyman (1954–), Shuka Glotman (1953–), and Adi Ness (1966–) are examples of a new critical and deconstructive examination of the Israeli experience, of local history and its visual representations, and of the manipulations of the collective-political memory. Various aspects of the post-modern condition gained in prominence in the course of the last two decades. These include an erasure of the borders separating illusion from reality (art based on the virtual worlds created in the cinema, for instance, as reflected in the paintings of Anat Ben Shaul; the sense of apocalyptic threat expressed in the works of Dorit Yacoby and Moshe Gershuni). The threat of loss of the family home or the national one is given form by the prominence of the "house" motif in the sculptures of Micha Ulman, Philip Renzer (1956–), Gideon Gechtman, and Buky Schwarz (1932–). For more than a decade now, there has been a growing emphasis on the Holocaust as one of the major constituents in defining the Israeli identity, especially on the part of artists such as Yocheved Weinfeld, Simcha Shirman (1947–), Haim Maor, and Uri Katzenshtein (1951–), who are second-generation survivors.

The particular problems of identity and the tensions surrounding the broad concept of the "Israeli experience" largely account for the development in the Israel of recent years of an art that is fully sensitive and attentive to what is happening both in the public sphere and in the private domain, and that has gained a prominent position in the global art scene, as evinced by the interest shown in exhibitions of Israeli art in various venues abroad.

[Haim Finkelstein and Haim Maor (2nd ed.)]

UNITED STATES. The term Jewish American art, like the more generalized Jewish art, is fraught with complications and variously understood. Critics debate whether Jewish American art need only be art made by a Jewish American, independent of content, or if both the artist's and the artwork's identity must be Jewish. Indeed, working in myriad styles and adopting both figuration and abstraction, some artists address Jewishness and the more specific Jewish American experience, while others make art indistinguishable in subject from their gentile counterparts. If a Jewish American artist should be defined sociologically or by theme remains an open question, and thus in this essay Jewish American artists are accepted by either criteria, leaving the matter for the reader to decide.

Before 1900. While Jews arrived in America as early as 1654, they did not enter the visual arts in a meaningful way until the 19th century. The freedoms accorded Jews enabled them to participate in the plastic arts, but the loosening of religious strictures as well as uneasiness about the respectability of an art career disappeared slowly. Hesitancy was often the result of the Second Commandment, the prohibition against graven images. Myer *Myers was an 18th-century silversmith who made both lay and religious objects for colonial merchants. He created *rimmonim* for several synagogues, including New York's Congregation Shearith Israel and the Yeshuat Israel Congregation in Newport, Rhode Island. In the 19th century, a handful of Jews painted portraits. Wealthy patrons commissioned the brothers Joshua and John Canter (or Canterson) to record their visages. Theodore Sidney *Moïse, Frederick E. Cohen, and Jacob Hart Lazarus are other 19th century Jewish portraitists of note.

Solomon Nunes *Carvalho is the best-known painter from this period. In addition to making portraits of members of the Jewish community, he did allegorical portraits, including one of Abraham Lincoln (1865). Carvalho created a few biblical paintings and landscapes as well, but his fame rests on his work as a daguerreotypist for John C. Frémont's 1853 exploratory expedition through Kansas, Utah, and Colorado. Max *Rosenthal was the official illustrator for the United States Military Commission during the Civil War. Later, Rosenthal painted *Jesus at Prayer* for a Protestant church in Baltimore, presenting Jesus with phylacteries on his forehead and right arm. The altarpiece was promptly rejected. Henry *Mosler began his career as an artist correspondent for *Harper's Weekly* during the Civil War. Like many non-Jewish artists, Mosler went to Europe for artistic training. He soon became a painter of genre scenes, frequently picturing peasant life in Brittany, France. His canvas *The Wedding Feast*, which was exhibited at the Paris Salon, records Breton marriage customs (c. 1892).

The eminent sculptor Moses Jacob *Ezekiel made numerous portrait heads, including a bronze bust of Isaac Mayer Wise in 1899. The B'nai B'rith commissioned Ezekiel's large marble group *Religious Liberty* for the Centennial Exhibition of 1876, and in 1888 he designed the seal for the recently established Jewish Publication Society of America. Ephraim Keyser created commemorative sculptures, for instance President Chester Arthur's tomb at the Rural Cemetery in Albany, New York. Katherine M. Cohen studied with the famous sculptor Augustus Saint-Gaudens and made portrait busts. These early painters and sculptors worked independently and were not readily known to each other. They created in relatively divergent styles along the same trends as the larger American community. It was not until the 20th century that Jewish American artists began interacting and taking art classes together.

1900–1945. Among the large 1880 to 1920 influx of immigrants to the United States were two million Jews. Mostly from poor communities in Eastern Europe, these immigrants were eager to assimilate. The Educational Alliance, a settlement house on the Lower East Side of New York City where many immigrants went to learn American manners and customs, offered art classes starting in 1895. Art classes were discontinued in 1905, resuming in 1917. From the school's reopening until 1955, Russian immigrant Abbo Ostrowsky served as director of the institution. Many well-known artists studied at the Alliance, including the sculptors Saul *Baizerman, Jo *Davidson, and Chaim *Gross, and the painters Philip Evergood, Barnett *Newman, and Moses *Soyer. The Alliance sponsored art exhibitions as did other Jewishly identified venues in New York. In 1912 the Ethical Culture Society's Madison House Settlement arranged a show of Jewish Russian immigrant artists, such as Samuel Halpert, in which Gentile artists also participated. The People's Art Guild held over 60 exhibitions from 1915 to 1918. In May 1917, 300 works by 89 artists were exhibited at the Forverts Building (the Yiddish daily newspaper the *Forward*), of which over half were Jewish. Well-known philanthropists Stephen Wise, Judah Magnes, and Jacob Schiff helped sponsor the exhibition. From 1925 to 1927 the Jewish Art Center, directed by Jennings Tofel and Benjamin *Kopman, held exhibitions focusing on Yiddish culture.

In the early decades of the 20th century some artists, such as Abraham *Walkowitz, William Meyerowitz, and Jacob *Epstein, began their nascent careers by picturing imagery of the Lower East Side. The gentile observer Hutchins Hapgood described East Side imagery in his 1902 text, "The Spirit of the Ghetto" as typically Jewish. Characterizing such work as "Ghetto art," Hapgood named Epstein, Bernard Gussow, and Nathaniel Loewenberg as exemplars of the mode. To illustrate Hapgood's evocation of the cultural and religious nature of the Jewish people, Epstein made 52 drawings and a cover design for the book. Epstein later became an expatriate, settling in London and gaining fame as a sculptor.

The photographer Alfred *Stieglitz championed modernism in the 1910s. While most of the artists that Stieglitz supported were not Jewish, the avant-garde painter and sculptor Max *Weber enjoyed his patronage. An underlying tone of antisemitism, or at least an intense nativism, pervaded some discussions of modernism at this time. The conservative critic Royal Cortissoz described modernism as "Ellis Island art," while others termed it the art of aliens. Indeed, modernism was frequently associated with Jews, a position later adopted by Hitler.

Many artists addressed political, social, and economic issues, especially during the Great Depression. It has been argued that traditions of social justice impel Jewish artists to create imagery of the underdog. Although secular in theme, these works – influenced by the Jewish experience – would be recognized as Jewish American art even by critics who define the term in its strictest sense. Working as Social Realists in the 1930s, the *Soyer brothers (Raphael, Moses, and Isaac) observed the mundane details of life, like waiting in an unemployment line, with gentleness and compassion. Peter *Blume and Ben *Shahn were more overtly politically committed; Shahn made over 20 images decrying the ethnically biased trial and execution of Italian American anarchists Nicola Sacco and Bartolomeo Vanzetti. William *Gropper expressed his political sympathies as a cartoonist for the left-wing publications *New Masses* and the Yiddish daily *Morning Freiheit*. Some artists' work appeared in the Yiddish journal *Schriftn* and in *The Menorah Journal*, a periodical devoted to Jewish culture that also attempted at various times to define Jewish art.

Louis *Lozowick, who worked as a Precisionist painter of city scenes and at times as a Social Realist, was also an art critic for *The Menorah Journal*. In a 1924 article on Jewish artists who recently exhibited in New York, Lozowick mentions Theresa *Bernstein, William Gropper, and William *Zorach, among others. Although few of the names devoted their art to Jewish themes (at least at that time), Lozowick's identification of the artists as Jewish indicates that he, like many critics, understood the term Jewish artist as connoting the ethnic identification of the artist rather than the artist's subject matter. A year later Peter Krasnow explicitly defined Jewish art in *The Menorah Journal* as any art produced by a Jew regardless of subject. In this early period of Jewish integration into America, most artists tried to avoid this kind of discourse, fearing that such categorization would pigeonhole their work as Other or parochial. There was, however, ambivalence on the part of many artists. To be sure, even if artists shied away from the classification "Jewish artist," several still displayed their work at the aforementioned Jewish Art Center and the Educational Alliance, among other Jewish locales. The art exhibitions of the Yiddisher Kultur Farband (YKUF), a Communist organization dedicated to fighting fascism, were also quite popular. Established in September 1937 by the World Alliance for Yiddish Culture, YKUF's first art exhibition was held in 1938. Minna *Harkavy, Lionel *Reiss, and Louis Ribak were among 102 artists who showed work on both Jewish and non-Jewish material.

In 1936, nine Jewish artists formed a group they dubbed "The Ten" (the tenth spot was reserved for a guest artist). *Ben-Zion, Ilya *Bolotowsky, Adolph *Gottlieb, Louis Harris, Jack Kufeld, Marcus Rothkowitz (Marc *Rothko), Louis *Schanker, Joseph Solman, and Nahum Tschacbasov exhibited together for four years. That the artists shared a Jewish background is typically understood as a coincidence. No common style or theme pervades the group's work, but most members were committed to modernist developments.

In the 1940s Jack *Levine worked as a Social Realist, although he painted more satirically and expressionistically than did the practitioners of the mode in the thirties. Beginning in 1941, Levine painted and made prints of biblical figures and stories in addition to his politically motivated art. After his first biblical painting, *Planning Solomon's Temple*, Levine rendered hundreds more images inspired by the Bible's narrative. Often employing Hebrew labels to identify figures, Levine's biblical works, he explained, attempt to augment Jewish pictorial expression, which he felt was hampered by the Second Commandment. The Boston-born Levine began a lifelong friendship with Hyman *Bloom when the pair started studying art together at a Jewish Community Center in their early teens. Bloom also retained the human figure in an increasingly abstract art world, painting secular and religious matter in brilliant colors.

1945–1990. A number of the leading Abstract Expressionists were Jewish. Adolph Gottlieb, Philip *Guston, Franz *Kline, Lee *Krasner, Barnett Newman, Ad Reinhardt, and Mark Rothko are among several artists who eschewed representation in the late 1940s and 1950s. The style(s) in which the artists worked are difficult to generalize, but they typically painted on large canvases and were interested in spontaneous expression. Although abstract, Newman's painting has been understood as shaped by his Jewish sensibilities, in part because of titles like *Covenant* and *The Name*, and also because, it has been argued, his knowledge of Kabbalah influenced his "zip paintings," which can be read as symbolic of God and Creation. Some second-generation Abstract Expressionists were also Jewish. Helen *Frankenthaler and Morris *Louis stained unprimed canvases with thinned color that seemed to float on and through the canvas. Louis named a series of his paintings with letters from the Hebrew alphabet. Clement *Greenberg and Harold *Rosenberg, two of the main art critics who promulgated abstraction, were Jewish.

Although better known for his criticism of contemporary art, Rosenberg also wrote one of the canonical articles on Jewish art. Published in *Commentary* in July 1966, Rosenberg's sarcastic and provocative essay "Is There a Jewish Art?" continues to serve as a springboard for scholarly discussions of Jewish art in America and abroad. Influenced in part by the formalist concerns of Abstract Expressionism, Rosenberg argued that an authentic Jewish art must be defined stylistically.

Artists who worked as Social Realists during the 1930s turned their sensibilities toward the civil rights movement of the 1960s. Raphael Soyer made a lithograph titled *Amos on Racial Equality* (1960s), which quotes Amos in Hebrew and English and depicts a white woman carrying a black infant. Ben Shahn's lithograph *Thou Shalt Not Stand Idly By* (1965) portrays an oversized interracial handshake. The title comes from Leviticus 19:16 and is printed in Hebrew and in English at the top of the image. Artists of the next generation also addressed social issues. After the fact, R.B. *Kitaj comments on the integration of blacks into professional baseball with his painting *Amerika* (*Baseball*) (1983–84). Jewish-black relations have become strained since the civil rights movement, a situation Art *Spiegelman tackled with his cover design of a black woman kissing a ḥasidic man for the February 1993 issue of the *New Yorker*.

Two Jewish artists initiated the Feminist Art Movement. At the height of the Women's Liberation Movement, Judy *Chicago and Miriam Schapiro jointly founded the Feminist Art Program at the California Institute of the Arts in 1971. Chicago is especially known for her enormous multimedia installation *The Dinner Party: A Symbol of Our Heritage* (1974–79). Made with over 400 collaborators, *The Dinner Party* was created to raise awareness of a forgotten women's history in a male-dominated society. Audrey Flack and Barbara *Kruger are also important feminist artists; Flack's photorealist paintings comment on stereotypes of femininity and Kruger deconstructs power relations in her photomontage images. Recent scholarship has argued that many of the early feminist artists were Jewish because as perennial outsiders and as the children or grandchildren of radical immigrants, fighting for justice and equality was a natural heritage. With such a link, feminist art by Jews would also be considered "Jewish Art" by critics who feel that elements of the Jewish experience, spiritual or secular, must be a prerequisite for art to receive this label.

In the 1960s, 1970s, and 1980s, Jewish artists worked in diverse manners. Jim *Dine and Roy *Lichtenstein engaged a Pop idiom in the vein of Andy Warhol during the 1960s. Emerging into the public eye in the 1970s, Philip *Pearlstein paints figures in a flat, unemotional style that treats the human form with the same objectivity as the inanimate objects surrounding the model. Also painting figuratively, Alex *Katz typically fills his large canvases with the flattened, simplified heads and shoulders of his sitters rendered in crisp color. Sol *LeWitt explored and wrote about Conceptual Art in addition to making Minimalist sculpture, and Jonathan *Borofsky continues to make multimedia site-specific installations using his own life as source material. In contrast, sculptor and Process artist Richard *Serra asserts that his focus on the physical qualities of material and the act of creation leave little room for expressions of the artist's personality.

Some artists who mostly worked akin to the mainstream for the majority of their careers became interested in Jewish matter later in life. Raphael Soyer illustrated two volumes of Isaac Bashevis Singer's memoirs (1978, 1981) and two short stories by Singer for the Limited Editions Club (1979). Larry *Rivers also illustrated a Singer story for the Limited Editions Club (1984) and painted an enormous three-paneled painting tackling the nearly four-millennia history of the Jews called *History of Matzah (The Story of the Jews)* (1982–84). Husband and wife William Meyerowitz and Theresa Bernstein traveled to Israel 13 times after 1948 and painted many images of the land after pursuing a more traditional American art trajectory before this time. Chaim Gross began sculpting Jewish subjects in the 1960s. While Ben Shahn and Leonard *Baskin explored some Jewish topics early on, they more consistently embraced Jewish identity in the visual arts as they aged, notably with *Haggadah* illustrations done in 1965 and 1974, respectively. Earlier in the century Saul *Raskin (1941) illustrated a *Haggadah* with woodcuts.

The Holocaust in Jewish American Art. Many Jewish American artists have treated the events of the Holocaust. Nahum Tschacbasov's 1936 canvas *Deportation* shows a crowd of emaciated deportees restrained by a fence. Ben-Zion was a poet who turned to painting because he felt that words could not adequately express the horrors of fascism and later the Shoah. Exhibited as a whole in 1946, the series *De Profundis (Out of the Depths): In Memory of the Massacred Jews of Nazi Europe* comprises 17 expressionistic works conveying the artist's distress at the events of the Holocaust that also pay homage to those who perished by Nazi hands. Leon *Golub's lithograph *Charnel House* (1946) and the *Burnt Man* series of the early 1950s vividly describe victims being exterminated.

Interest in the Holocaust as a subject for art has only increased in the years since artists felt the immediacy of the tragedy. Audrey Flack's photorealist canvas *World War II (Vanitas)* (1976–77) presents a still life in collage format, including a Jewish star from her key chain and a photograph of the 1945 liberation of Buchenwald taken by Margaret *Bourke-White. Alice Lok Cahana, a survivor of several concentration camps, uses the visual to work through her memories of the Holocaust in semi-abstract mixed media images. Cahana's art, she explains, is her *kaddish* for those who perished. The sculptor George *Segal symbolically employs the biblical figures Eve, Abraham, Isaac, and Jesus in his *Holocaust Memorial* (1983), which overlooks the Pacific Ocean in San Francisco's Legion of Honor Park. Another Holocaust sculpture group by Segal is at the Jewish Museum in New York (1982). Judy Chicago's enormous installation *Holocaust Project: From Darkness into Light* (1985–93) is anchored by a 4½ by 18 foot tapestry titled *The Fall*, which portrays the disintegration of rationality. While united by an interest in imaging the unthinkable, Holocaust works by Jewish American artists differ greatly in approach, conception, and style.

Last Decade of the Twentieth Century. In the last decade of the 20th century, Jewish identity became an increasing concern in the visual arts. New York City's Jewish Museum investigated this phenomenon in the 1996 exhibition *Too Jewish?: Challenging Traditional Identities*. Paralleling a larger interest in multicultural difference by other marginalized groups, the 18 artists in the show explored Jewish consciousness, while also testing the viewer's and the art world's (dis)comfort with what was perceived by some as excessively conspicuous Jewishness. These highly assimilated younger artists portray vastly different concerns than their immigrant and first-generation predecessors. Long after Andy Warhol, Deborah Kass appropriates Pop techniques and fascination with celebrity in her portraits of Barbra Streisand (1992) and Sandy Koufax (1994). Titling her Streisand silkscreens *Jewish Jackies* (playing on Warhol's iconic silkscreens of Jackie Kennedy), Kass proffers the ethnic star while subverting American norms of beauty. Also influenced by Warhol, Adam Rolston's *Untitled (Manischewitz American Matzos)* (1993) asserts ethnicity into a once "pure" American consumer culture. Dennis Kardon's installation *Jewish Noses* (1993–95) presents an array of noses sculpted from 49 Jewish models, destabilizing the notion that the Jew can be categorized as a monolithic type.

Indeed, just as Kardon demonstrates that the Jew's body cannot be homogenized, neither can Jewish American art. As this essay has described, Jewish American artists (defined broadly) have worked in manifold fashions, partly and sometimes entirely influenced by larger trends, and at the same time making significant contributions in style and content. Jewish American art is a nascent field, rich in material and long due for further exploration.

BIBLIOGRAPHY: Z. Amishai-Maisels, *Depiction and Interpretation: The Influence of the Holocaust on the Visual Arts* (1993); M. Baigell, *Jewish-American Artists and the Holocaust* (1997); M. Baigell, *Jewish Artists in New York: The Holocaust Years* (2002); S. Baskind, *Raphael Soyer and the Search for Modern Jewish Art* (2004); S. Goodman, *Jewish Themes/Contemporary American Artists* (1982); S. Goodman, *Jewish Themes/Contemporary American Artists II* (1986); J. Gutmann, "Jewish Participation in the Visual Arts of Eighteenth- and Nineteenth-Century America," in: *American Jewish Archives* (April 1963), 21–57; M. Heyd, *Mutual Reflections: Jews and Blacks in American Art* (1999); N. Kleeblatt and S. Chevlowe (eds.), *Painting a Place in America: Jewish Artists in New York, 1900–1945* (1991); N. Kleeblatt, *Too Jewish?: Challenging Traditional Identities* (1996); P. Krasnow, "What of Jewish Art?: An Artist's Challenge," in: *The Menorah Journal* (December 1925), 535–43; L. Lozowick, "Jewish Artists of the Season," in: *The Menorah Journal* (June-July 1924), 282–85; H. Rosenberg, "Is There a Jewish Art?," in: *Commentary* (July 1966), 57–60; O. Soltes, *Fixing the World: Jewish American Painters in the Twentieth Century* (2003); S. Zalkind, *Upstarts and Matriarchs: Jewish Women Artists and the Transformation of American Art* (2005).

[Samantha Baskind (2nd ed.)]

Art in the Ghettos and the Camps during the Holocaust

When the Nazis came to power in 1933, they banned all art which they regarded as subversive – i.e., modern, avant-garde, Communist, Jewish, Negro – or to use their term, *degenerate*. The fate of this art and its creators was very clear: both should be eliminated from society. *Degenerate* works of art were removed from museums, galleries, and other collections; Jewish artists were not allowed to pursue their careers, lost their teaching positions, and were permitted to display their works only in the premises of the *Juedischer Kulturbund. These degenerate works were assembled and put on show in Munich 1937 in the exhibition called "Degenerate Art" (*Entartete Kunst*), which was accompanied by vulgar and provocative quotations, accusing the artists of causing all the malaise of society and the world, thus warning the public of the dangers of such subversive artists.

Although Nazi laws should have been fully implemented in the concentration camp world, in many camps artistic creativity flourished and some of the works produced there were shown in exhibitions. Thus, ironically, the only place where these undesirable artists could produce and exhibit art was in their place of confinement.

During the Holocaust a tremendously rich variety of works of art were produced in the ghettos, hiding places, and camps of Nazi-occupied Europe. It was produced in extermination camps like Auschwitz, in the "model" camp of Theresienstadt, in transit camps like Westerbork in the Netherlands and Malines in Belgium, and in the network of camps set up throughout France, such as Drancy and Gurs. All these artists, whether professional or amateur, men or women, young or old, had one thing in common – they had been labeled *undesirables*, interned in the camps, cut off from society, and ordained to be victims of the Nazi Final Solution.

Artistic creation fulfilled many functions. It gave the artists a sense of self-assurance and allowed them to feel some connection with their past life as artists. It provided a way to pass the many hours of enforced idleness. It had barter value – the paintings that were commissioned by other inmates or by camp officials could be exchanged for food or other favors (such as smuggling out mail or some other improvement in conditions). Above all, art was the only means whereby the inmates could protest against their situation. They hoped that their protest would be heard beyond the barbed wire fences in the outside world, with the help of clandestine couriers mainly from the various welfare organizations and religious representatives who were permitted to enter the camp. Most of the paintings have documentary value, as the artists were aware of the necessity of recording for posterity the world in which they were imprisoned. Art, of course, does not merely portray an objective reflection of reality, but rather shows it through the personal prism of the artist. In other words, the works of art reflect the changing moods and feelings of the inmates/artists/witnesses.

Although the ghettos and the camps were isolated from each other certain themes were prevalent in these works of art. They include depictions of the barbed wire fences and the watchtowers, views of the camps, the daily routine, such as searching for food, attempts at personal hygiene, sickness and death, as well as landscapes and portraits. The common element in all these works is the need to portray and document in the closest detail the tragic and absurd circumstances in which the inmates found themselves. Such a situation was completely unforeseeable and the inmates were in no way prepared for this unimaginable nightmare which recurred in all the various ghettos and camps.

PORTRAITS AND "PRIVILEGED ARTISTS." The works that survived, frequently as the result of astounding resourcefulness, had these common themes regardless of whether they had been produced in Eastern or Western Europe, by professional artists or amateurs. About a quarter of the works are portraits, a fact that is not surprising. Portraying a face or a figure was in itself an act of commemoration, confirming the existence of the individual in a world where existence was so uncertain and arbitrary. These portraits were often used to send greetings to inmates' relatives, to show that they were alive and well. This explains why we frequently find the name of the subject of the picture next to the artist's signature, along with the date and place. It also explains why the figures in the portraits have a slightly better appearance than in reality, for the artist wanted to send a positive message and not show the misery of their situation. These portraits are in many cases the last record of people who soon afterwards were sent to their deaths.

Aizik-Adoplhe Féder (Odessa 1887–Auschwitz 1943) was interned in Drancy, on the outskirts of Paris, where he drew portraits of people from all walks of life who were interned in the camp – workers and intellectuals, observant Jews, women, teenagers, children and infants. Most of the inmates, especially the women, look well, and, except for the additional verbal information alongside the portrait – date and location of the work – there is no indication that the subjects are imprisoned in Drancy, a camp that was also known as the antechamber of Auschwitz.

Féder was part of the "Ecole de Paris," a group of artists, most of them Jews, who immigrated from Western Europe to Paris, hoping to establish their artistic careers there. Many of those artists such as *Benn (Ben-Zion Rabinowicz; Bialystok 1905–Paris 1989), Abraham-Joseph Berline (Niejine, Ukraine 1894–Auschwitz 1942), Jacques Gotko (Gotkowski; Odessa 1900–Auschwitz 1943), David Goychman (Bogopol, Ukraine 1900– Auschwitz 1942), Isis-Israel Kischka (Paris 1908–Paris 1973), Savely Schleifer (Odessa 1881–Auschwitz 1942), and Zber (Fiszel Zilberberg; Plock, Poland 1909–Auschwitz 1942) were interned in various French camps such as Compiègne, Beaune-la-Rolande, Pithiviers, and Drancy, where they portrayed their co-inmates as well as themselves. The portraits usually carry identifying inscriptions, such as Kischka's *Portrait of Uze, Internee in the Compiègne Camp, 29/3/42*, or *Portrait of Goychman by Kischka, 787122, 20/3/42*, giving the artist's camp identification number alongside his name as a signature. Some of the portraits bear moving dedications, which attest to their amicable relationship.

Malva Schalek (Prague 1882–Auschwitz 1944), a daughter of a well-to-do, cultured Jewish family in Prague, established her reputation as an artist in Vienna, specialized in portraits, and was interned in Theresienstadt, where she continued painting her fellow inmates. Many of the portraits Schalek produced in the camp were commissioned, and she received food in payment, a practice which was not uncommon. Artists were commissioned by both inmates and by camp and ghetto administrators, in most cases asked to copy portraits of relatives from photographs or do their own likeness. In turn they received favors like better food or smuggled clandestine letters. This was experienced and attested by many artists such as Halina Olomucki (Warsaw 1919–), who while interned in the Majdanek camp was commissioned by the head of the block to decorate the walls of the building. In return she received improved food rations. She used some of the materials she was given officially to paint her fellow women inmates clandestinely. From Majdanek she was transferred to Auschwitz-Birkenau, and there too she was a "commissioned artist" for the Germans. For this she received more substantial food, which helped her to survive. Esther Lurie (Liepaja, Latvia 1913–Tel Aviv 1998), while interned in the Kovno (Kaunas) ghetto, was commissioned by the Council of Elders (*Aeltestenrat*) to record ghetto life; to this end they arranged that she would not be engaged in any forced labor; later on when, while interned in Stutthof, the artist was asked by women inmates who had boyfriends to draw their portraits in return for a slice of bread. The painter-musician Isaac Schoenberg (Colmar, Alsace 1907–Auschwitz 1942), who was interned in Pithiviers, wrote to his beloved in Paris that he had to decline some of the inmates' requests to do their portraits, although he was paid more than the other artists in the camp, since he was engaged in producing her likeness from photographs, an activity which enabled him to endure life in the camp. Even amateur artists such as Etienne Rosenfeld (Budapest 1920–Paris 1995) were commissioned by their fellow inmates to draw their or their relatives' portraits, as is attested in his letters from the Drancy camp.

PORTRAYAL OF THE CAMPS. Another theme was the portrayal of the camps, particularly the barbed wire fences and watchtowers, which over time have become symbols of the Holocaust. They were part of the everyday experience of the prisoners, a constant reminder that they were confined in a closed camp, cut off from the society of which they had been an integral part up to a short while before. The barbed wire fences are a dominant element in many pictures. They appear in landscapes and genre paintings, while in some cases they have become the actual subject of the picture. Sometimes the fences are shown as a spider's web in which the figures are entangled, as, for example, in the aquarelle by Lou Albert-Lazard (Metz 1895–Paris 1969), depicting women imprisoned in the Gurs camp (France). Albert-Lazard, a German Jew who immigrated to Paris in the 1920s and was interned as a German alien, portrays the women as trapped by the barbed wire fence. Despite the delicacy of the painting, the barbed wire fence restricts their movements and closes in on them like a wall. The imprisoning barbed wire fence and the threatening watchtower, with an all-seeing eye at the top, are the central elements in the drawings and prints done by Jacques Gotko. At times, there is even an element of humor, with the artist painting laundry hung out to dry on the fence, as did the amateur artist Hanna Schramm (Berlin 1896– Paris 1978), a socialist activist who had sought refuge in France and was interned in Gurs on the outbreak of the war and depicted the miserable life there in ironic-humoristic drawings. But, however depicted, the prevalence of this motif stresses the sense of confinement the inmates experienced.

DAILY LIFE – INDOOR AND OUTDOORS SCENES. The forced communal life in ghettos and camps meant living in extremely crowded conditions with the need for privacy denied, no matter what race or sex the inmates were or what social standing they had enjoyed in their previous existence. The feeling of suffocation and the lack of private space is depicted by Malva Schalek in various aquarelles she produced in Theresienstadt. In many of her paintings she depicts the activity, or lack of it, in the camp. Sometimes she draws the interior as crowded and claustrophobic, with women and children lying or sitting on the triple-layered bunks, surrounded by bundles and suitcases. In others she portrays inmates reading or lying down. Similar depictions were produced by Osias Hofstaetter (Bochnia, Poland 1905–Ramat Gan, Israel 1994), who immigrated to Belgium, from where he was sent, after the Nazis invaded this country, to the French internment camps of Saint Cyprien and Gurs, where he depicted the forced idleness of men in and out of the barracks, as well as the overcrowdedness.

Some interior scenes, as those done by Jane Lévy (Paris 1884–Auschwitz 1943) in Drancy or Emmy Falck-Ettlinger (Lubeck 1882–Bet ha-Shtitah, Israel 1960) in Gurs, are characterized by extreme order and cleanliness. They depict kitchen utensils and personal items, a kind of desire to create a feeling of intimacy, warmth, and domesticity. Yet these works evoke a feeling of desolation and emptiness which even the domesticity of the interior cannot overcome.

Countless paintings show everyday, routine activities – bathing, washing one's hair, going to the toilet – since these basic human acts could no longer be taken for granted in the surroundings the inmates now found themselves in. Bathing was extremely difficult, as the water supply was completely inadequate for all the inmates and available only a few hours a day and often had to be done outdoors. Going to the toilet was no less embarrassing. The most intimate bodily functions had to be performed in public, adding to the dehumanization of the inmates. This may seem trifling compared to the acts of mass murder that were taking place at the time, but it should be remembered that the daily life of the inmates consisted in trying to meet the numerous "trifling" needs that are basic to civilized human life.

Many artists depict these activities, sometimes in humoristic drawings or aquarelles. Karl Schwesig (Gelsenkirchen, Germany, 1898–Duesseldorf 1955), a German communist who had fled from Germany after Hitler's rise to power and was a political refugee in Belgium, was interned in four different French camps. From his vast experience he depicted daily life, which became worse with the time. Many of his drawings illustrate the way the inmates were cooped up with a lack of hygienic facilities, as did other artists in the various camps – all attesting to the embarrassment and humiliation which accompanied these activities.

FOOD. The inmates suffered constantly from hunger, which weakened them both physically and mentally. Hunting for food was one of the main occupations of the camp inmates. Many paintings portray the subject of food, or the lack of food, ranging from lining up to get the daily rations (Leo Haas, Opava, Czechoslovakia 1901–Berlin 1983), to guarding a scrap of bread as though it were a treasure (Lili Rilik-Andrieux, Berlin 1914–San Diego 1996), to rummaging through the garbage to find a bite to eat that might ease the pangs of hunger (Karl Schwesig; Sigismond Kolos (Vary, Transylvania 1899–?)). Pictures of this last scene serve to illustrate again the degradation that was forced upon the camp inmates.

In the Auschwitz-Birkenau State Museum at Auschwitz, there is a *Memories Calendar (Kalendarz wspomnień)* comprising 22 small drawings (18 × 10 cm), produced in Auschwitz in 1944 by Ewa Gabanyi, prisoner no. 4739. Gabanyi was born in Czechoslovakia to a Jewish family and interned on April 3, 1942. The pictures in her calendar are mostly theatrical and fantastic – surrealistic dances and balls, elaborate costumes, weird animals, and exotic scenery. One picture stands out as completely different, as she depicts a woman prisoner in her striped dress eating soup, with the inscription *First soup in the camp (Zjada pierwswą Zoupkę Lagrową)*, dated April 27, 1942; hence her first hot meal came three weeks after her arrival in Auschwitz. A picture that seemed completely naturalistic turns out to have a surrealistic aspect in the world of the camps.

DEPORTATIONS. The huge numbers sent to camps and from there deported to the death camps were portrayed by various artists such as Dr. Karel Fleischmann (Klatovy, Czechoslovakia 1897–Auschwitz 1944) and Charlotte Buresova (Prague 1904–Prague 1983) in Thereisienstadt, David Brainin (Kharkov, Ukraine 1905–Auschwitz 1942) in Compiègne, Kurt-Connard Loew (Vienna 1914–Vienna 1980), and Julius-Collen Turner (Schivelbein, Germany 1881–?) in Gurs, and Leo Maillet (Leopold Mayer; Frankfurt-am-Main 1902–Switzerland 1990) in Les Milles. In these pictures the artists usually depict faceless masses rather than individuals being sent on their last journey. Yet in several pictures, amidst the endless lines of people stretching beyond the horizon, the artist reveals the face of one of the deportees, often a child clinging to its mother or a disabled old person guarded by soldiers with pointed weapons. These scenes depict with bitter irony the imbalance of power – the innocence and the helplessness of the deportees versus the power of the executioners.

LANDSCAPES. The camps were often situated in beautiful areas, with snow-covered mountains in the distance or picturesque seaside villages, which were in sharp contrast to the misery of the life within the barbed wire fences (e.g., Karel Fleischmann, Karl Schwesig, Lou Albert-Lazard). Many artists painted these views, which provided them with a kind of connection with the outside world. The colors of a beautiful sunset, while serving to remind them of ordinary life, also brought home the indifference of nature to their suffering.

ART AS A MEANS OF CONNECTION WITH THE OUTSIDE WORLD. Artists sought to use their work as means to make contact with the outside world and let people know what was happening "on the other side of the fence." They did this despite the danger inherent in such activity, as can be seen in the fate of Leo Haas and Dr. Karel Fleischmann, inmates of Theresienstadt, who paid a high price for their efforts to smuggle their works out of the ghetto. In preparation for a visit of the Red Cross in summer 1944, the Germans searched the artists' quarters. They did this because they realized that the truth about their "model ghetto" was likely to be revealed in paintings being smuggled out of Theresienstadt. The artists refused to talk and after being interrogated and tortured were taken to a Gestapo prison. Eventually they were deported to Auschwitz, where Fleischmann died.

Contact with the outside world was of tremendous importance to the camp inmates, and in many cases it was art that paved the way. In some camps, such as Gurs and Compiègne, exhibitions were held. These exhibitions were visited by the Nazi administration and, in some cases, members of the public from the surrounding area. The inmates felt, for a brief moment, as if they had broken through the fence and were involved in the outside world. It should be noted, however, that these events were not mentioned in the press, which used to stress that the camp inmates were parasites and profiteers. Presenting them as creative and productive would not have fit this negative stereotype.

Artists arrived in the camps from all over Europe, from cities, towns and villages and from all levels of society. As we have seen, despite the artistic variety of their work, one unifying factor was common to them all – they all portrayed the grim reality and their cruel experiences, with a sense of longing for their former world which had disintegrated so totally.

The art of the Holocaust is unique in the history of art. In a state of hunger and destitution, with death a constant part of their daily existence, hundreds of artists did not allow the spark of the human spirit to be extinguished. In the universal language of art they portrayed the images of one of the darkest periods in human history.

BIBLIOGRAPHY: Z. Amishai-Maisels, *Depiction and Interpretation: The Influence of the Holocaust on the Visual Arts* (1993); J. Blatter and S. Milton, *Art of the Holocaust* (1982); H. Fenster, *Nos artistes martyrs* (*Undzere Farpainikte Kinstler*) (Yid., 1951); M.S. Costanza, *The Living Witness: Art in the Concentration Camps and Ghettos* (1982); G. Green, *The Artists of Terezin* (1969); M. Novitch, *Spiritual Resistance: Art from Concentration Camps 1940–1945*. A selection of drawings and paintings from the collection of Kibbutz Loḥamei ha-Getta'ot, Israel. Union of American Hebrew Congregations, Philadelphia (1981); P. Rosenberg, *L'art des Indésirables: l'art dans les camps d'internement français 1939–1944* (2003).

[Pnina Rosenberg (2nd ed.)]

Art Influenced by the Holocaust

Reactions in the visual arts to the Nazi persecution of the Jews paralleled Adolf Hitler's rise to power and continue to this day. Unlike Holocaust Art – a name that designates the art produced by inmates in the ghettos and concentration camps (see above) – art that responded to the Holocaust has no clear name and its definition is highly complex. It was created by survivors as well as by refugees who fled to the free world before or during the war; by camp liberators who discovered the shocking truth of the Holocaust for themselves; by the children of survivors or refugees who carry in themselves the burden of memories, pain, and guilt transmitted to them from their parents; and by non-participants who may have lost relatives in the Holocaust or were simply shocked by it or by the idea that its lessons remain unlearned. Some artists reacted immediately, occasionally even anticipating events to come. Others – including survivors who had tried to turn their backs on their past – reacted to events that triggered their emotions: the discovery of the camps, the Eichmann trial, Israel's wars, or other examples of genocide. Such artists came from all religions – Jews, Christians, Muslims, Buddhists, etc. – and all nationalities, including Germans (e.g., Anselm Kiefer) who wish to express their own stance on the subject or to atone for the past. For some, the Holocaust was a specific event occurring in a set period of time; for others, it was an archetypal event which could be used to comment on other catastrophes – Hiroshima, genocide in Africa, or the Aids epidemic.

Moreover, artists had different motivations in using this subject. Some, such as Corrado *Cagli, documented the scenes on the spot or – like Audrey Flack and Nancy *Spero – on the basis of photographs, while others (for instance, William *Gropper and Leon *Golub) emotionally denounced cruelty and mass murder. Whereas survivors and their children often used art as therapy to recover from the past, most artists used it to make sure that the Holocaust would be remembered by memorializing it. Many reacted by affirming their Jewish identity, at first by depicting figures in prayer or the shtetl, as in the works of Max *Weber. More recently a few artists (such as Judy *Chicago) have begun to see the Holocaust itself as their sole means of Jewish identity. Still others, for example, Mark *Rothko and Karel Appel, responded in a highly personal manner by changing their style and subject matter in ways that are not self-evidently connected to the Holocaust but are revealed to be reactions to it on the basis of the artists' statements.

The artists' goals were often linked with the styles they chose to employ. For instance, Realism was used in witness reports as a means of confronting the spectator with the facts and convincing him of their truth, while Expressionism was used to express anger and heighten the denunciatory power of the work. Surrealism was often used to convey the idea that such events were taking place on "another planet," whereas Abstraction was a means of distancing the artist from the Holocaust and allowing it to be confronted from a safe place.

Although painters and sculptors had been working on the subject since 1933, it was the photographs and films taken by the liberators in 1944–45 that had the most immediate and lasting impact on the public at large. Appearing in magazines and newsreels, these reports turned everyone into a witness. It is for this reason that the most common images of the Holocaust in the public imagination are those they recorded: the mounds of corpses, the bald and emaciated survivors barely able to move, and the inmates crowded together behind barbed wire or in their bunks. Some of these images still inspire artists today (for instance, in the paintings of Natan Nuchi), but this source material has now been broadened to include the Nazis' own documentary snapshots of the ghettos, deportations, and executions as well as the identification photographs they took of the camp inmates, a type that influenced Aaron Gluska. Today new documentary photographs have been taken by artists who visit the camps. These images differ from the older ones in showing the camp as empty and clean, well-preserved monuments rather than the hellholes they were.

Several common motifs and themes run through all categories of Holocaust-related art. The primary image of the camp from the mid-1930s was of people behind barbed wire, an image used by John Heartfield because one of the few facts known then about the camps was that they were surrounded by barbed wire fences. This representation was reinforced after the camps were liberated, as photographers such as Margaret *Bourke-White took their stance outside the fence looking into the camp. The image was so pervasive and clearly understood that it could be suggested by including a single piece of barbed wire into an abstract composition, as was done by Igael *Tumarkin. Another primary symbol was the refugee, a subject documented by the refugees themselves (e.g., Marc *Chagall) and by those who wanted to state their plight. This image was transformed after the war by artists such as Lasar *Segall into that of the displaced person to represent survivors who were trying to find a place to stay. This subject slowly disappeared after 1948, as the State of Israel was seen as having solved this problem. It has recently been reinstated, as in a painting by Joan Snyder, in an attempt to identify Palestinian refugees with the victims of the Holocaust. Another image that was popular during the war was that of the Jewish partisan, especially those who participated in the Warsaw Ghetto uprising depicted in the monument by Nathan *Rapaport. Upheld at first as an image of Jewish pride in resistance to the Nazis, it was eventually supplanted by that of the Israeli soldier.

Other symbols became common only after the war, for instance the symbolic use of the crematorium chimney and the image of emaciated corpses or survivors, themes that grew out of the experience of liberating the camps and understanding what had happened there. Whereas the chimney and the survivors were relatively easy for Friedensreich Hundertwasser and George Grosz respectively to handle, the corpses were repugnant and many artists followed Pablo Picasso's lead in translating them into more stylized images. On the other hand, artists such as Zoran Music and Robert Morris later specifically portrayed the corpses in all their expressive reality to awaken the failed conscience of the modern world that continues to commit genocide.

All the above symbols were taken from the camp experience. But artists who were interested in learning moral lessons from the Holocaust also culled other images from religion and mythology to convey their ideas. Thus the victim can be portrayed through biblical symbols, such as the sacrifice of Isaac or Job who questions God, as in the works of Leonard *Baskin and Jakob *Steinhardt respectively. These subjects could also be used to vent anger against God for allowing the Holocaust to happen, as in the work of Mordecai *Ardon. Marc Chagall led the way in depicting the victims as the crucified Jewish Jesus, in an attempt to make Christians understand what was occurring. Resistance to Nazism was symbolized by Jacques *Lipchitz by means of David slaying a Nazi Goliath and Prometheus slaying the vulture.

The portrayal of the Nazis was more difficult: their portrayal as monsters or demons as in the works of Marcel *Janco ignores the fact that those who carried out the Holocaust were human beings. However, portraying them realistically as humans, as Gerhart Frankl did, underplays the horrific dimensions of their deeds. Beginning with Lipchitz, some artists concluded that the problem lay not only with the Nazis, and used their art to warn mankind that there is a beast lurking within us which must be tamed lest we cause other holocausts. Others, such as Matta and *Maryan Maryan, took a more pessimistic view of man's monstrous nature and portrayed ambiguous figures whose nature cannot be clearly defined as good or evil.

The Holocaust also prompted Jewish artists to take a renewed look at their Judaism. While some affirmed their faith and Jewish identity and others expressed their anger against God, a few stressed their lack of faith in the future of Judaism. Thus Samuel *Bak depicted a destroyed and patched-up Ten Commandments that will never be the same. Whereas the establishment of the State of Israel was at first seen by artists such as Chagall and Lipchitz as an answer to the Holocaust and a solution to the problems it caused, Israel's continuing wars – especially the threats to its existence in 1967, 1973, and 1991 – led artists such as Erich Brauer to see in each event a potential renewal of the Holocaust. Moreover, the resurgence of antisemitism in the 1980s caused R.B. *Kitaj and George *Segal to begin to deal with the Holocaust.

On the other hand, the conflicts between Israelis and Palestinians since 1967 have caused left-wing artists to adapt Holocaust imagery to this issue, with the Palestinians replacing the Jews. This generalization of Holocaust imagery is part of a wider phenomenon in which such images are applied to any current conflict in order to activate an inbred, unquestioning hatred against those who have been clothed in the despised Nazi imagery and an equally innate sympathy for those depicted as victims.

The newest developments in art inspired by the Holocaust can best be examined through three themes. First, children of survivors, such as Yocheved Weinfeld and Haim Maor, try to understand their parents' experiences by picturing themselves in their place and exploring how they would have reacted. The second theme – ghosts – is poignantly demonstrated by Shimon Attie's projections of old black and white photographs of the Jewish inhabitants of Berlin and Rome on the walls of these cities, so that they seem to be haunting their streets. The third subject is the expression of constant anxiety, a feeling Jonathan Borofsky explicitly connects with the Holocaust. Such new themes suggest that artists have not finished examining the Holocaust and that they will continue to find new means to express its relevance to the modern world.

BIBLIOGRAPHY: Z. Amishai-Maisels, *Depiction and Interpretation: The Influence of the Holocaust on the Visual Arts* (1993); M. Baigell, *Jewish-American Artists and the Holocaust* (1997); M. Bohm-Duchen, Monica (ed.), *Art after Auschwitz* (1995); S.C. Feinstein (ed.), *Absence/Presence: Critical Essays on the Artistic Memory of the Holocaust* (2005); idem, *Witness and Legacy: Contemporary Art about the Holocaust* (1995); S. Hornstein and F. Jacobowitz (eds.), *Image and Remembrance: Representation and the Holocaust* (2003); S. Hornstein, L. Levitt, and L.J. Silberstein. *Impossible Images: Contemporary Art after the Holocaust* (2003); D.G. Roskies, *Against the Apocalypse* (1984); Washington Project for the Arts. *Burnt Whole* (1994); J. Young, *At Memory's Edge: After-Images of the Holocaust in Contemporary Art and Architecture* (2000); idem, *Texture of Memory: Holocaust Memorials and Meanings* (1993).

[Ziva Amishai-Maisels (2nd ed.)]

ARTA, Greek town in southern Epirus. Jews were living there in the 11th century while the area was under Byzantine sovereignty. This early community later united around the synagogue known as Kehillat Kodesh Toshavim ("Congregation of the Inhabitants"). In 1167 *Benjamin of Tudela found about 100 Jews (or perhaps 100 families) in Arta. In the 15th century under Ottoman rule, the Jews of the city were relocated to the capital, Istanbul, in the *sorgun*. By the 16th century Jews had repopulated the town. In the 16th century after the arrival of exiles from southern Italy, several synagogues were founded in Arta by communities from various places of origin – Corfu, Sicily, Calabria, Apulia – each one jealously preserving its religious autonomy. The juxtaposition of such diverse cultural elements gave rise to conflicting concepts of ethics and customs, reflected in the numerous disputes and congregational regulations issued during the 16th and 17th centuries. One subject of heated controversy was whether a bridegroom is permitted to visit the home of his betrothed.

The Jews of Arta agreed in regarding the scholars of *Salonika as the highest religious authority, and the youth were sent there to study. *Benjamin Ze'ev b. Mattathias (author of *Binyamin Ze'ev*) was rabbi of the Corfu congregation in the 16th century, and other noted rabbis of the 16th century included Solomon ben Rabi Samuel Sefardi, and Caleb Ben Rabi Yohanan. Many Jews left Arta in the 17th century. The Jews of Arta were mainly merchants, or peddlers who traded in the villages. In the early 19th century, the famous Artan Jewish-born mathematician Hoca Yitzhak Effendi, a convert to Islam, was a translator for the Ottoman navy and Imperial divan, and occupied numerous important diplomatic positions from 1806 onward. In 1869 the Jewish population was estimated at 800. Local Jews were patrons and supporters of Skopos, a local literary-musical association founded in 1896. Thirty-six Artan Jews fought in the Balkan Wars of 1912–3. In 1915 the Zionist organization Mevakshei Zion was established. The bridge of Arta has been the focus of numerous Sephardi romances. In 1940 there were 384 Jewish inhabitants.

Under the Italian occupation during World War II relations between the Jewish community and the Italian authorities were good and life continued almost normally for nearly three years. However, on March 24, 1944 a detachment of Gestapo arrived in Arta, obtained the names and addresses of all Jewish families from the City Hall, and arrested 352 Jews. Only a few managed to escape. Together with the Jews of Preveza, they were taken to Athens (April 2, 1944) and after a few days sent to Auschwitz, where they were put to death. After the German defeat a few Jewish families returned to Arta. Joseph Zakar was a rare survivor among numerous Artan Jews who worked in the *Sonderkommando* in Birkenau. By 1948 there was an attempt to reorganize a Jewish community, but the number of Jews dwindled to only 20 in 1958.

BIBLIOGRAPHY: Rosanes, Togarmah, 1 (19302), 113–4, 155–60; 2 (1938), 41–42; 3 (1938), 78–79; 4 (1935), 35, 156–7; 276–7; 5 (1938), 54; Yaari, Sheluḥei, index; M. Franco, *Essai sur l'histoire des israélites de l'Empire Ottoman* (1897), 43–44; M. Molcho and J. Nehama, *Sho'at Yehudei Yavan* (1965), index. **ADD. BIBLIOGRAPHY:** L. Bornstein Makovetski, "Arta," in: *Pinkas Kehillot Yavan* (1999), 59–66; Y. Kerem, *The History of the Jews in Greece, 1821–1940*, I (1985), 99–112.

[Simon Marcus / Yitzchak Kerem (2nd ed.)]

ARTAPANUS (Ἀρτάπανος; second century B.C.E.), Hellenistic Jewish author. Artapanus wrote περὶ Ἰουδαίων ("On the Jews"), fragments of which are preserved in the writings of the Church Fathers. The purpose of this work was to prove that the foundations of Egyptian culture were laid by Abraham, Jacob, Joseph, and Moses. When Abraham came to Egypt, he taught the pharaoh (Pharethothes or Pharetones) the science of astrology. Jacob established the Egyptian temples at Athos and Heliopolis. Joseph was appointed viceroy of all Egypt and initiated Egyptian agrarian reforms to ensure that the powerful would not dispossess the weak and the poor of their fields. He was the first to divide the country and demarcate its various boundaries. He turned arid areas into arable land, distributed land among the priests, and also introduced standard measures for which he became popular among the Egyptians (Eusebius, *Praeparatio Evangelica*, 9:23). But the one who excelled all was Moses, whom Artapanus identifies with Musaeus, teacher of Orpheus, and with Hermes-Thoth, god of Egyptian writing and culture. The name Hermes was given to Moses by the priests who revered him for his wisdom and paid him divine homage. Moses founded the arts of building, shipping, and weaponry, as well as Egyptian religion and philosophy. He was also the creator of hieroglyphic writing. In addition, he divided the city into 36 wards and assigned to each its god for worship. Moses was the founder of the cult of Apis the Bull and of Ibis. All these accomplishments of Moses aroused the jealousy of King Kheneferis, father of Maris, Moses' foster mother. He tried to kill Moses, but failed. After the king's death, Moses was commanded by God to lead the Hebrews out of Egypt. In his story of the Exodus Artapanus generally follows the biblical narrative, although he expands and embellishes it (Eusebius, *ibid.*, 9:27). He devotes special attention to tales of Moses' battles against the Ethiopians and to events stemming from the personal rivalry between Moses and the king of Egypt. Similar accounts are to be found in Josephus (Ant., 2:242ff.), and it may well be that both used a common source. In view of the fact that, like Herodotus and Plato, Artapanus sees in Egyptian civilization the origin of all civilization, it may be said that he regards Moses as the father of universal civilization. It is indeed strange that a Jew should attribute to Moses the introduction of the idolatrous Egyptian rites. But Artapanus envisages Moses primarily as a "benefactor" (εὐεργέτης) in the Hellenistic sense of the word, that is, one who benefits all mankind without distinction of nationality or creed. In this way Artapanus wished to show that the lawgiver of the Jews was not a misanthrope as the enemies of the Jewish people claimed.

BIBLIOGRAPHY: Clement of Alexandria, *Stromata*, 1:23, 154; *Chronicon Paschale*, ed. Dindorf (1832), 117; J. Freudenthal, in: *Hellenistische Studien* (1875), 143ff., 215ff.; Pauly-Wissowa, 3 (1895), 1306; A. Gutschmid, *Kleine Schriften*, 2 (1890), 184–5; Schuerer, Gesch, 3 (1909^4), 477–80; A. Schalit (tr.), *Kadmoniyyot ha-Yehudim* (Heb. tr. of Josephus' *Antiquities*), 1 (1955^2), xlvii–xlix; J. Gutman, *Ha-Sifrut ha-Yehudit ha-Hellenistit*, 2 (1963), 109–35.

[Abraham Schalit]

ARṬAS, Muslim-Arab village in Judea, 2 mi. (3 km.) S.W. of Bethlehem. In 1967, it had 1,097 inhabitants, rising to 2,679 in 1997. Its economy was based on vineyards, deciduous fruit trees, vegetables, olives, and field crops. The important spring of Ein Etam is located near the village. During the Second Temple period its waters were led to Jerusalem through two aqueducts. British Mandate authorities attempted to pump these spring waters to Jerusalem through the adjacent Solomon's Pools. Arṭās has a Catholic convent, "Notre-Dame du Jardin Ferm" or "Hortus Conclusus," which maintains a girls' orphanage. The village's name may have its root in the Latin *hortus* ("garden").

[Efraim Orni]

°**ARTAXERXES** (Per. *Artakhshacha*; Gr. *Artaxerxes*; Heb. and Aram. אַרְתַּחְשַׁשְׂתְּא and אַרְתַּחְשַׁסְתְּא; in Heb. once also אַרְתַּחְשַׁשְׂתָּא; Aram. Papyri ארתחשסש), name of three Persian kings.

(1) Artaxerxes I was surnamed Makrokheir (Greek) or Longimanus (Latin), meaning "the long-handed." He reigned from 465 to 425 B.C.E. The first 16 years of his reign were troubled, with the Greeks attacking his northwestern holdings and supporting a revolt in Egypt which lasted from 460 to 454, and with Megabyzus, the satrap of Transeuphrates (embracing Syria, Palestine, and Transjordan) who reconquered Egypt for Artaxerxes, himself rebelling in 449–48. To end the war with the Greeks Artaxerxes was compelled to assent to the "peace of Callias" (449), which was a humiliation for Persia. It was probably during these troubled first three-fifths of his reign that the provincial authorities of *Samaria were able to persuade the king that the rebuilding of Jerusalem's walls by the Jews constituted a threat to his authority in the whole of Transeuphrates (Ezra 4:7–23 which belongs chronologically after Ezra 6). In the later, calmer years of his reign, he appointed *Nehemiah governor of Judah with authority to fortify Jerusalem. Regarding the identity of the Artaxerxes of Ezra 7:7, 11, 21; 8:1, who authorized the mission of *Ezra, opinions are divided over whether it was this monarch or the following one (2).

(2) Artaxerxes II, surnamed Mnemon (Gr. *Mnēmōn*, "the Rememberer"), reigned from 404 to 359 B.C.E. Artaxerxes II lost Egypt in 401 B.C.E. (the Jews of *Elephantine dated documents by his regnal years down to Jan. 18, 401 B.C.E.). So far from ever recovering it, he nearly lost all of Western Asia as well, since the revolting western satraps, relying on the Egyptian army which the Egyptian king Tachos led into Syria to aid them, invaded Mesopotamia. However, a revolt in Egypt compelled Tachos to abandon his allies and surrender, and Artaxerxes II reconquered the western satrapies. A growing number of scholars date Ezra's mission in the seventh year of his reign, 398/97 B.C.E.

(3) Artaxerxes III, a son of the preceding, surnamed Ochus by modern writers, because the Greeks, for some reason, refer to him as Okhos, reigned from 354 to 338 B.C.E. He had to quell revolts everywhere, and failure in his first attempt to reconquer Egypt (352–50) may have given the impetus to the revolt (350–45?) of King Tennes of Sidon. Artaxerxes burned the city down and put Tennes to death. In 344/43, a second attempt to reconquer Egypt was successful.

Several Church Fathers report that Ochus exiled a large number of Jews to Hyrcania, the region south of the Caspian Sea, and Paulus Orosius (fifth century), the author of a world history, and George the Syncellus (d. c. 810), a Byzantine chronicler, connect this action with his campaign against Egypt. It has naturally been surmised that this means the first campaign against Egypt and that the ensuing rebellion of Sidon also affected Palestine. D. Barag has sought confirmation for this hypothesis in the archaeology of Palestine and has called attention to seven sites, from Hazor in the north to Jericho in the south, the occupation of which was interrupted – in some cases, terminated – near the end of the Persian period. Although the archaeological evidence alone does not rule out the attribution of this abandonment to the advance of Alexander, hardly more than a dozen years later, the silence of the sources about any resistance to Alexander in Phoenicia apart from Tyre and in Palestine apart from Gaza seems to favor the earlier date for the depopulation, which perhaps partly accounts for the passivity toward Alexander.

A "Hyrcanian exile" such as is reported by the Church Fathers is unknown in Jewish tradition. Nevertheless, there may be a connection between it and the fact that the proper name Hyrcanus is attested among the Jews as early as the third century B.C.E. (II Macc. 3:11).

BIBLIOGRAPHY: N.C. Hirschy, *Artaxerxes III Ochus and his Reign* (1909); E. Drioton and J. Vandier, *Les peuples de l'orient méditerranéen*, 2 (1952[3]), 62; Barag, in: BASOR, 183 (1966), 6–12; Bright, Hist, 356–93; Noth, Hist Isr, 316–37; R.G. Kent, *Old Persian* (1953[2]), 153–6; R.N. Fyre, *The Heritage of Persia* (1962), index; H.T. Olmstead, *History of the Persian Empire* (1948), index.

[Harold Louis Ginsberg]

ART COLLECTORS AND ART DEALERS. Art collecting in the modern sense can be said to have originated during the period of the Renaissance in Italy, with the emergence on the one hand of individual artists from the anonymity of the Middle Ages, and on the other of families and individuals of wealth who eagerly sought to patronize and collect their work. Italian Jews of the Renaissance period inevitably patronized the arts to some degree, for their houses were furnished and decorated in much the same way as those of their gentile neighbors of the same social class. Jews at this time were active as art dealers as well, particularly as jewelers who bought and sold goldsmiths' work and as dealers in secondhand goods. In the 16th century Cosimo de' Medici, grand duke of Tuscany, bought antiques from Jewish merchants in Venice, while a few decades later David de' Cervi of Rome procured works of art for the dukes of Mantua. The first Jew known to have dealt specifically in paintings was also an Italian, the artist and art expert Jacob Carpi, who was in business in Amsterdam in the middle of the 18th century.

Here and there individual Jews continued to buy and sell objects of art for the next two centuries, but it is not until the early 19th century that one can begin to speak of Jewish art dealers and collectors in the proper sense of the word. In Fritz Lugt's comprehensive three-volume corpus (1938–64), which lists all public sales of art from 1600 on, it is only in the second quarter of the 19th century that the name of *Rothschild is first encountered in connection with an auction at Christie's in London; from this date on, however, art collecting cannot be thought of in England, France, and Germany, without reference to this great banking family. At approximately the same time, there developed other dynasties of Jewish collectors who often started out as bankers.

Among the many prominent 19th-century European collectors were Eduard Huldschinsky and James *Simon in Berlin (the latter's donations to the Kaiser Friedrich Museum, including the famous bust of Nefertiti, greatly enriched that collection); Georg Arnhold (1859–1926) in Dresden, whose son Hans followed him as a patron and collector of the arts; and Ludwig *Mond and Henry Oppenheimer (1859–1932) in England. Mond's collection of Italian paintings from the 15th to the 18th centuries went to the National Gallery in London; Oppenheimer specialized in applied and graphic arts. At the same time, the *Camondo Collection in Paris and the Franchetti Collection in Venice were being built up.

One of the most important modern personalities in international art collecting and dealing was Joseph *Duveen, who became the art consultant of a number of well-known Americans, such as J.P. Morgan, John D. Rockefeller, and Benjamin *Altman. Duveen achieved his reputation with the help of the art historian, connoisseur, and collector Bernard *Berenson, who advised him, especially on Italian art, from 1907 to 1936. Following Duveen's death in 1939, the House of *Wildenstein assumed the leading position in international art dealing.

After World War I the works of the impressionists and postimpressionists were especially collected and dealt in by Jews. The centers of this activity were Berlin, Munich, Vienna, Budapest, Paris, and London, although here interest in the Renaissance and Baroque periods continued. As a result of Jewish emigration from Europe following the Nazi rise to power, many valuable collections reached the United States, among them those of Jacob *Goldschmidt, whose treasures were auctioned after his death in 1955, and of Justin Thannhauser, who donated the greater part of his paintings to the Guggenheim Museum in New York, where they hang in a separate wing.

Among native Americans, Lessing *Rosenwald of Philadelphia collected one of the world's greatest collections of graphic arts. He presented the National Gallery in Washington, D.C., with some 25,000 drawings and etchings. The Cone Collection in Baltimore, which offers an excellent cross section of modern French art, was begun shortly after the turn of the century by the sisters Claribel and Etta *Cone, who acquired their paintings and drawings, particularly the work of Henri Matisse, through their close friendship with Leo and Gertrude *Stein. Instrumental in assembling the large collection of the *Guggenheim family were Solomon R. Guggenheim (d. 1949), whose treasures are housed in the museum in New York named after him, designed by Frank Lloyd Wright, and Peggy G. Guggenheim, whose palazzo in Venice contains many foremost works of surrealism and who was a great collector and friend of modern artists ever since she opened her first gallery in London in 1919. Also deserving of mention are the collections of Otto H. *Kahn, Michael Friedsam, and the Altman, *Lehmann, and *Blumenthal families.

Billy *Rose, the theatrical producer, gave his collection of modern sculpture to the Israel Museum in Jerusalem, where it is exhibited in a special garden that bears his name. The industrialist Joseph H. *Hirshhorn donated his collection of about 4,000 paintings and 1,600 sculptures to the nation, and it is on permanent public exhibit in Washington, D.C. Helena *Rubinstein, founder of the cosmetic enterprise, filled her homes with works of art and applied art and in Tel Aviv she built the Helena Rubinstein Pavilion. Norton Simon, California industrialist, attracted the attention of the international art market when he acquired Rembrandt's "Titus" at an auction in London (1965) and a Rembrandt self-portrait for more than $1,000,000 (1969).

[Lotte Pulvermacher-Egers]

One of the most remarkable art collections, that of Robert von Hirsch of impressionist and modern drawings and watercolors, was dispersed by public auction held in London, the proceeds of which were approximately $35 million. Von Hirsch, a German-born leather merchant, who died in Basel, Switzerland in November 1977 at the age of 94, accumulated his collection over a period of 70 years. It consisted of 608 articles, including superlative works of Cezanne, Van Gogh and Georges Seurat, and pieces of Meissen porcelain.

BIBLIOGRAPHY: A.B. Saarinen, *Proud Possessors* (1958); M. Rheims, *La vie étrange des objets* (1959) (= *Art on the Market*, 1961); P. Cabanne, *Great Collectors* (1963); S. Kaznelson (ed.), *Juden im deutschen Kulturbereich* (1962), 120–30; F. Lugt, *Repertoire des catalogues des ventes publiques*, 3 vols. (1938–46).

ARTEMION, leader of the Jewish uprising in Cyprus during the reign of Trajan (115–17 C.E.). According to Dio Cassius (the only author who actually refers to Artemion by name) the insurrection claimed 240,000 victims; other sources (Eusebius) allude to the total destruction of the capital, Salamis. With the suppression of the revolt, all Jews were prohibited on penalty of death to set foot on the island.

BIBLIOGRAPHY: Dio Cassius, *Historia Romana*, 68:32; Reinach, Textes, 196, no. 112; Schuerer, Hist, 292.

[Isaiah Gafni]

ARTEMOVSK (until 1923, **Bakhmut**), city in the Ukraine. Jewish settlement in Artemovsk dates from the late 18th century. The numbers increased as a result of immigration from Lithuania and Volhynia. In 1847, 496 Jews were registered in the community; in 1897, 3,259 (16.8% of the total population). In the early 20th century Jews owned big factories producing flour, beer, and soap, stone quarries, sawmills, and most of the oil storage facilities. Five hundred Jews worked in the garment industry. There were 11 *ḥadarim*, a *talmud torah*, and three public schools, one of them a vocational school for girls. In 1926, 6,631 (17.1%) Jews lived in the city and 17,622 (2.3%) in the Artemovsk district. Pogroms in October 1905 led to deaths and injuries and heavy damage to Jewish property. In the Soviet period Jewish sources of livelihood underwent a change: in 1926, 20% were blue-collar workers and clerks, 10% were artisans, 30% remained petty merchants, and the rest were without a defined profession. A Yiddish school with 400 pupils (in 1926) was in operation. The number of Jews dropped to 5,299 by 1939 (total population 55,409). The Germans occupied Artemovsk on October 31, 1941. On December 21, ten Jews were hanged. On January 5, 1942, 3,000 Jews were assembled and then held without food and water until February 15, when they were sealed off in one of the tunnels of the marble quarry and suffocated to death. In 1959, 1,800 Jews were registered in Artemovsk (30% of the total population); by 1979 the number had fallen to about 1,000. Most left in the 1990s.

BIBLIOGRAPHY: *Judenpogrome in Russland*, 2 (1909), 204–10. **ADD. BIBLIOGRAPHY:** PK Ukrainah, s.v.

[Yehuda Slutsky / Shmuel Spector (2nd ed.)]

ART HISTORIANS AND ART CRITICS. The discipline of art history first made its appearance in Germany, in the middle of the 18th century, but it was more than a hundred years before the lowering of the barriers that had excluded Jews from academic careers enabled them to enter this field. The Jewish inclination toward research and scholarship combined with a latent interest in the visual arts produced in Germany a large number of Jewish art historians, many of whom succeeded in continuing their work in other countries, especially in the United States, Britain, and Israel.

Jews were prominent as directors and founders of some of Germany's leading museums. Julius Friedlaender (1813–1884) and Julius Lessing (1843–1908) were both curators of the State Numismatic Museum in Berlin. Friedrich Lippmann (1838–1903) made the print department of the Berlin State Museum internationally important. One of his successors, Jacob Rosenberg (1893–1980), an authority on the work of Rembrandt and other Dutch artists, became professor of fine arts at Harvard University. Rosenberg's predecessor at Harvard, Paul Sachs (1878–1965), an American-born connoisseur and generous collector, was largely responsible for the university's collection of graphics. Two other art historians who made significant contributions to the history of the graphic arts were Max Lehrs (1855–1939), working in Dresden, Germany, and Franz Kristeller (1863–1931), who worked in Bologna, Italy. Their contribution to scholarship lay in the analytical description of works of art and the development of systems of organization and authentication. In the work of Bernard *Berenson the study and criticism of Italian art delved into the life and achievements of masters scarcely recognized before. Similar research into Dutch painting was undertaken by Max I. Friedlaender (1867–1958), director of the Berlin painting gallery until the advent of the Nazis. In the field of classical studies, the Anglo-American archaeologist Sir Charles Walston (formerly Waldstein; 1856–1927) supervised important excavations and wrote works on ancient Greek art. During the same period the French archaeologist Solomon *Reinach was combining his work on antiquity with a study of art generally. His *Apollo*, a collection of the lectures he delivered at the Ecole du Louvre in 1902–03, came to be for millions of readers the "manual of the history of art through the ages."

The Israel archaeologist Leo Aryeh *Mayer published works on Islamic architecture and archaeology. The art of Islam is also the field of research and teaching of Richard Ettinghausen (1906–1979), who was director of the Freer Gallery in Washington, D.C., and later connected with the Institute of Fine Arts of New York University. Alfred Salmony (1890–1958), formerly in Cologne, taught the history of Chinese art. A scholar in the same field, William Cohn (1880–1961), went from Berlin to Oxford, England. A great contribution to art history in general and to English architectural history in particular was made by Sir Nikolaus *Pevsner. Another noteworthy Anglo-German architectural writer was Helen Rosenau (c. 1910–). A scholar who concentrated on religious architecture was Richard Krautheimer (1897–), one of whose first books dealt with medieval German synagogues. He later wrote a standard work in many volumes on the early churches of Rome as well as a study of the Renaissance sculptor Ghiberti. Paul Frankl (1877–1962) was a thoughtful interpreter of Gothic architecture and Paul Zucker (1890–) related his experience as a Berlin architect to works – the later ones published after his emigration to the U.S. – on such varied subjects as the history of city planning, bridge architecture, and aesthetics. Important contributions to the history of painting and sculpture were made by Jewish scholars, who studied the problems of particular periods and styles. Walter Friedlaender (1873–1966), first in Freiburg, Germany, later in New York, helped to clarify 16th-century mannerism, while Werner Weisbach (1873–1953) enriched the concept of baroque art by relating it to the politico-theological problems of the following century. Many art historians have been influenced by the scholarship and teaching of Adolf Goldschmidt (1863–1944), who occupied the important chair of art history at Berlin University. He was a careful researcher, an exceptionally learned author, and a devoted teacher whose publications encompass many subjects, including medieval ivories, manuscripts, and bronze doors. Another German Jew who devoted himself to the medieval arts was George Swarzenski (1876–1957), whose connoisseurship and administrative skill were of considerable value to the museums of Frankfurt.

The Warburg Institute has had an intense impact on the ideas of art historians who went to the United States from Germany. Founded in Hamburg by Aby *Warburg (1866–1929), it moved to London in 1933. Under the direction of Warburg himself and of Fritz Saxl (1890–1948), the library became a center of humanistic studies and of publications in the field of "Kulturwissenschaft." Erwin *Panofsky, who became a member of the Institute of Advanced Studies at Princeton, transmuted iconography from an amalgam of auxiliary information into the science of iconology. In Panofsky the study of humanism underlying the philosophy of the Warburg Institute found its rich fulfillment. There were three other men with equally wide horizons of scholarship. One was the Russian-born Meyer Schapiro (1904–), whose analysis and interpretation of artists and their works stretches from the classical to the contemporary scene. In 1965 he became professor of art history at Columbia University. The others were Otto Kurz (1908–) and Rudolf Wittkower (1901–), a German by birth, who also held a chair at Columbia, specializing in Italian art of the baroque period. E.H. Gombrich (1909–), director of the Warburg Institute, was interested in the relationship between art and psychology. His *Story of Art* is a popular art history.

The following Italians should be mentioned: Igino Supino (b. 1858), an authority on restoration work; Ettore Modigliani (1873–1947), superintendent of ancient and modern work in Milan and founder of the Scala Theater Museum; and Paolo *d'Ancona (1878–1964), who wrote on Renaissance and modern art.

Since the establishment of the State of Israel and the founding of its Universities, all of the four major institutions have departments of art history, and many regional colleges have instituted instruction in art history as well. Israel's most prominent scholar of art history was Moshe *Barasch, who specialized in the Renaissance period.

Historians of Jewish Art

When the various fields of Jewish studies were defined by the scholars of the 19th century German movement *Wissenschaft des Judentums, Jewish art was not one of them. The prevalent notion in this period was that this aspect of Jewish life was not worthy of serious research since Judaism banned images and one should even question whether Jewish art ever existed. Actually, the first to deal with visual aspects of Jewish culture were Christian scholars, such as the French archeologist Louis-Félicien de Saulcy (1807–1880), who served as the consul of France in Jerusalem, and in 1858 published a book dealing with artistic creativity in biblical times (*Histoire de l'art judaïque*). The first Jewish scholar in the field was the Hungarian David *Kaufmann (1852–1899), who was actually interested in a vast spectrum of Jewish disciplines, including Jewish art and archeology. Kaufmann's seminal articles deal with the problem of art in rabbinical literature, synagogue interior decoration, ancient floor mosaics that were excavated during his lifetime, and Hebrew manuscript illumination. In 1898, Kaufmann collaborated with other scholars on the publication of the first monograph in the field, namely on the 14th-century Sephardi *Sarajevo Haggadah* (*Die Haggadah von Sarajevo: Eine spanisch-judische Bilderhandschrift des Mittelalters*, Vienna, 1898).

Toward the end of the 19th century scholarly attention was drawn for the first time to the study of Jewish ceremonial artistic objects. It was at this time that collections of ceremonial art were first established (e.g., that of Isaac Strauss in Paris), exhibited to the public (e.g., the Anglo-Jewish exhibition in London, 1887), and the first Jewish museums opened in some European-Jewish capitals (e.g., Vienna, 1897; Frankfurt, 1901). While some publications accompanied these events, the real impetus to scientific study of Jewish ceremonial art was given by yet another Christian scholar, the German Heinrich Frauberger (1845–1920). Frauberger served as the director of the Industrial and Crafts Museum (*Kunstgewerbemuseum*) in Duesseldorf, and his curiosity to investigate this topic was aroused when a local architect sought his advice on the design of a Jewish tombstone. In 1901 Frauberger established in Frankfurt the Gesellschaft zur Erforschung jueduscher kunstdenkmaeler, which engaged a number of Jewish scholars (mainly Rudolf Halo and Erich Toeplitz), and issued an illustrated periodical, edited and largely written by Frauberger himself.

The scholarly interest in Jewish art increased in German-speaking lands in the 1920s and 1930s. Some of the more prominent names include the curator of the Berlin Jewish Museum, Karl Schwarz (1885–1962), who was later invited by Meir Dizengoff to head the new Tel Aviv Museum. His most important work, *Die Juden in der Kunst*, which appeared in Berlin in 1928, dealt more with what he defined as "art of the Jews" rather than "Jewish art." A year later there appeared another important work, that of the German-Jewish art historian, Ernst *Cohn-Wiener (1882–1941), *Die judische Kunst: Ihre Geschichte von den Anfangen bis zur Gegenwart* (Berlin, 1929) – a serious attempt to systematically describe the development of Jewish art as it was known in those years.

While these scholars worked in relative isolation and did not endeavor to advance further research in the field, three other writers were more successful in promoting scholarly interest, as they published many more books and articles on many aspects of Jewish art, including ceremonial objects. The first of the three is the German-Jewish art historian Franz Landsberger (1883–1964), who turned to Jewish art only when the Nazis did not allow him to continue his work in general art at Breslau University. From 1935, when his first work on Jewish art appeared, until his death, he published numerous studies. In 1938 he fled Germany to England, and subsequently he was invited to lecture on Jewish art at the Hebrew Union College in Cincinnati and later also to serve as the director of the school's museum of Judaica. His essays and books, now published in English, include topics such as the *mezuzah* and its case, ancient Torah curtains, illuminated *ketubbot*, ritual implements for the Sabbath, Hanukkah lamps (a representative selection is presented in J. Gutmann (ed.), *Beauty in Holiness: Studies in Jewish Customs and Ceremonial Art*, Ktav, 1970).

The second scholar is Rachel Wischnitzer (1885–1989), who was born in Russia, educated in Heidelberg and Paris, established herself in Berlin, and then moved to the U.S., where she worked for many years and taught Jewish art (Stern College). Trained as an architect, Wischnitzer published two major books in English on synagogue architecture – one on American synagogues (1955), and the other on European synagogues (1964). Her third English book deals with the messianic symbolism in the paintings of the newly discovered third century *Dura Europos synagogue (1948). While she was still in Berlin, Wischnitzer co-edited *Rimon* (1922–24), a richly and beautifully illustrated periodical dedicated to the arts in Jewish life which appeared in both Hebrew and Yiddish (under the title *Milgroim*). In Berlin she also issued her first book, dealing with the meaning of Jewish symbols (*Symbole and Gestalten der juedishen Kunst*, 1934), a subject which underlined many of her studies. Her prolific writings in the field are still the basis for research on central issues of Jewish art, though her interpretations are not always accepted.

Mordechai *Narkiss (1897–1957), the last of the three, was actually the first scholar who worked in the Land of Israel and published most of his work in Hebrew. Following his immigration from Poland to Israel in 1920, he served as the chief assistant to Boris *Schatz, the founder of the *Bezalel School of Art in Jerusalem (1906). In 1925 Narkiss was appointed as the director of the newly established Bezalel Museum (later the Israel Museum). In this role Narkiss systematically acquired Judaic objects and Hebrew illuminated manuscripts (including the noted *Birds Head Haggadah*, and gradually devoted more and more time to research on Judaic objects. His education in a yeshivah, sound knowledge of the decorative arts, and mastery of several European languages undoubtedly provided him with the tools required for proper research in the field. Narkiss determined to write on Jewish art in a scientific manner differing from the "amateurish" writing of other scholars whose work he severely criticized in the several book reviews he published. His most important work is undoubtedly the monograph he dedicated to the history of the Hanukkah lamp (Jerusalem, 1939). This innovative work presented for the first time a thorough analysis of a single Jewish object, from its inception in the talmudic period until the modern period, and throughout the Jewish Diaspora. Living in Ereẓ Israel, Narkiss interacted with immigrant Jewish groups from different parts of the Jewish world, which led him to consider the visual heritage of the Jews from the lands of Islam – a subject almost entirely neglected by the scholars who preceded him. Notable in this respect is his short, pioneering book on the handicrafts of Yemenite Jews (Jerusalem, 1941), which paved the way and established the methodology for future studies on the material culture of the communities under Islamic rule.

In 1957, the year of Narkiss' untimely death, there appeared another major contribution, namely the book *Jewish Art*, edited by Cecil *Roth (1899–1970) and Zusia Efron (1916–2002). The first edition included 18 articles by various experts, who systematically discussed the development of Jewish art from biblical times to modern Israel. The book was first published in Hebrew, then translated into several languages, expanded, and given a set of new images (first English edition, 1961). Though a historian by training, Roth, whose name appeared on all the subsequent editions of the book, was attracted to Jewish art and published many articles on the subject but never made it his main field of research. However, unlike other historians of Judaism, he often drew attention to the visual world in his historical studies. Despite its many shortcomings, *Jewish Art* continues to be the standard textbook on the subject to this day.

In the 1950s and 1960s several other scholars joined the field, and made it their primary subject of research. The first is the American (non-Jewish) scholar Erwin Ramsdell *Goodenough (1893–1965), who devoted many years to the interpretation of visual symbols in the talmudic period. His massive 13-volume *Jewish Symbols in the Greco-Roman Period* (1953–65) exhibits nearly every Judaic object and work of art known at the time. While his methodology and conclusions have been generally rejected by scholars, his comprehensive volumes continue to be a major resource, and he is credited for drawing attention to the importance of visual culture in the talmudic period. Another American scholar, Joseph *Gutmann (1923–), dealt with nearly every aspect of Jewish art, including manuscript illumination, ceremonial objects and customs, and ancient synagogues as well as theoretical questions pertaining to the field. Gutmann's many books and articles have demonstrated the contribution of art to Jewish history and its interrelationships with Christian culture. In Europe, on the other hand, the leading scholars in the field have devoted their efforts mainly to book illumination (e.g., Thérèse and Mendel Metzger of Strasbourg, Gabrielle Sed-Rajana of Paris, and Luisa Mortara-Ottolenghi of Milan).

In Israel, Mordechai Narkiss' son, Bezalel *Narkiss (1926–), continued the work of his father. His publications centered on Hebrew book illumination, pointing to their visual sources in the art of the Christian and Islamic societies that hosted the Jewish communities. In 1974, Narkiss started the publication of the annual *Journal of Jewish Art* (from 1986/87 called *Jewish Art*), and in 1979 established the Center for Jewish Art. The center is chiefly active in documenting Jewish works of art, illuminated Hebrew manuscripts, ritual objects, synagogues, and cemeteries throughout the world. In addition, the center issues various publications in the field, and sponsors international conferences. Another institution is the Society for Jewish Art, which promotes the field in Israel and publishes *Rimonim*, the only periodical in Hebrew devoted to the subject. Recent volumes of *Rimonim* (edited by Shalom Sabar) have been devoted to art and objects connected to life cycle events.

The pioneering work of the above scholars showed the way and is being continued by a number of institutions and younger scholars in Israel, the United States, and Europe. At the Hebrew University of Jerusalem classes in Jewish art and material culture are offered by the departments of Art History and Jewish and Comparative Folklore, and both programs allow students to obtain the three academic degrees in the field. Other institutions include partial programs, such as Bar-Ilan University in Ramat Gan and the Jewish Theological Seminary of America in New York. Some of the scholars teaching in these and other schools include Vivian Mann (ceremonial art); Evelyn Cohen (Hebrew manuscript illumination), Bracha Yaniv (the Torah case and its appurtenances), and Shalom Sabar (ketubbot, Jewish folk art and rituals, magic and amulets, postcards, holy sites).

Important contributions to documentation and research of Judaica are also made by the curators of the Jewish museums around the world. The results of the fieldwork conducted by museum staffs culminate not only in a temporary exhibition but are best preserved in the accompanying catalog, often containing a number of pertinent essays. Some of the major exhibitions which pointed to new source materials and directions of research in the field include first and foremost the publications of the ethnography department at the Israel Museum, Jerusalem, and in particular the pioneering catalogs dealing with the arts and daily life of the Jews of Morocco (ed. Aviva Mueller-Lancet, 1973), Kurdistan (ed. Ora Schwartz-Be'eri, 1981), the Sephardim in the Ottoman Empire (ed. Esther Juhasz, 1990), India (ed. Orpah Slapak, 1995), Afghanistan (ed. No'am Bar'am-Ben Yossef, 1998), Yemen (Esther Muchawsky-Schnapper, 2000), and the Mountain Jews of Azerbaijan (ed. Leah Mikdash-Shmailov, 2001). Some of the Jewish museums in Europe and the United States embarked on similar projects. Noteworthy in this respect are the exhibition catalogs co-edited by Vivian B. Mann of the Jewish Museum, New York (for example, *A Tale of Two Cities: Jewish Life in Frankfurt and Istanbul 1750–1870* (1982) and *Gardens and Ghettos: The Art of Jewish Life in Italy* (1989)). In Europe we are witnessing a revival as well, and the leading Jewish museums sponsored major catalogs as well (for example, *Orphan Objects: Facets of the Textiles Collection* – The Jewish Historical Museum, Amsterdam, 1997; *Textiles Catalogue* – Jewish Museum, Prague, 2003).

Despite the significant development of research in Jewish art during the last decades, the tasks facing scholars are still major and require many more of years of groundwork before the foundations of the field are firm and solid. The investigation of art and material culture of the Jews differs from that of other nations and presents problems that are particular to the development of Judaism and Jewish history. Sincere and serious research should take into account the special circumstances in which the objects were created, the Jewish ideas and customs underlying their production and usage, and the influences of the host culture.

Historians of Modern Jewish Art

The bourgeoning field of artistic expression by Jews in the 20th century opened new avenues of research. Among notable scholars of contemporary Jewish Art are Avram Kampf (1919–), who was connected with the Jewish Museum in New York. He analyzed the renaissance of Jewish religious art in the United States in his *Contemporary Synagogue Art* and *From Chagall to Kitaj, Jewish Experience in Twentieth Century Art*. Other prominent scholars include Ziva *Amishai-Maisels (1939–), winner of the Israel Prize in 2004 for her groundbreaking scholarship on Holocaust art, as in *Depiction and Interpretation – the Influence of the Holocaust on the Visual Arts*, Monica Bohm-Duchen in England and Milly Heyd (1945–) of the Hebrew University, who together with Matthew Baigell (1933–) of Rutgers University, published *Complex identities: Jewish Consciousness and Modern Art*.

Jewish Art Critics

The influence on the appreciation of artists and art of Jewish critics writing in the daily press, in journals, and in magazines has grown appreciably since the beginning of the 20th century. Foremost among them were the German writers Max Osborn, from 1914 to 1933, art critic of the *Vossische Zeitung*, Lothar Brieger (1879–1949), and Carl Einstein (1885–1940), an authority on postimpressionism; and the Americans Harold Rosenberg (1906–1978), Clement Greenberg (1906–1994),

Hilton Kramer (1928–), art critic for the *New York Times* between 1965 and 1982, and Jed Perl (1951–), art critic for the *New Republic*. In Israel, the veteran artist and art critic Meir Ronnen wrote for the *Jerusalem Post* and Smadar Sheffi for *Haaretz*.

BIBLIOGRAPHY: S. Kaznelson, *Juden im deutschen Kulturbereich* (1959), 108–17; L. Venturi, *History of Art Criticism* (1964); Mayer, Art. **ADD. BIBLIOGRAPHY:** Bentwich, Norman *The Rescue and Achievement of Refugee Scholars* The Hague: 1953 Friedlander, Max *Reminiscences and Reflections* Greenwich: 1969 Goodwin, George M. "A New Jewish Elite: Curators, Directors, and Benefactors of American Art Museums" *Modern Judaism* – Volume 18, Number 1, February 1998, pp. 119–152 Hirschfeld, Gerhard "German Refugee scholars in Great Britain 1933–1945" in Anna C. Bramwell *Refugees in the Age of Total War* London: 1988, pp. 152–163 S. Kaznelson, *Juden im deutschen Kulturbereich* (1959), 108–17; L. Venturi, *History of Art Criticism* (1964); Mayer, Art. Meyer, Michael A. "The Refugee Scholars Project of the Hebrew Union College," in Bertram Wallace Korn,ed. *A Bicentennial Festschrift for Jacob Rader Marcus* New York: 1976, pp. 359–375 Michels, Karen "Art History, German Jewish Identity, and the Emigration of Iconology," in Catherine Soussloff. ed. *Jewish Identity in Modern Art History* Berkeley: 1999, pp. 167–179. Sabar, Shalom. "On the History of Research in the Field of Jewish Art," *Mahanaim*, 11, 1995, pp. 264–275 (in Hebrew). Soussloff, Catherine *Jewish Identity in Modern Art History* Berkeley:1999 Walfish, Barry D. "The Otto Schneid Archive of Jewish Art at the University of Toronto" *Proceedings of the 38th Annual Convention of the Association of Jewish Libraries (Toronto, ON – June 15–18, 2003)*, pp. 1–4. Wendland, Ulrike *Biographisches Handbuch deutschsprichiger Kunsthistoriker in Exil* Munich: 1999.

[Herman S. Gundersheimer /Shalom Sabar (2nd ed.)]

ARTHURIAN LEGENDS. The only Hebrew version of the perennially popular Arthurian legends was written in northern Italy in 1279. It was anonymously translated into Hebrew from an Italian source now lost. Found in a unique manuscript in the Vatican Library, the Hebrew text consists of two stories from the Arthurian cycle and an apology. The apology, directed toward the various authorities that condemned the reading of romances and tales in the vernacular, was needed in order that the translation of such obviously secular and even salacious material could be sanctioned. The translator also stressed the moral benefits to be derived from reading the legends. The two reasons he offers are to drive away melancholy and to induce sinners to repent and return to God. The first Arthurian episode (based ultimately on the Old French prose work *Merlin*) describes the seduction of Igerne by King Uther Pendragon with the aid of Merlin, and the conception of Arthur. The second story is an incomplete fragment from the *Mort Artu*, which, as is learned from the apology, the translator had intended to complete: it includes Lancelot's love affair with King Arthur's wife Guinevere, his meeting with the amorous Maid of Askalot, and his jousts at the tournaments at Winchester. At this point the Hebrew story abruptly and inexplicably breaks off.

The 13th-century Italian Jewish translator's literary methods are as fascinating as are the Arthurian stories in Hebrew dress. The scribe not only translates from Italian, as is evidenced by the gloss: *l'distruzion* for the Hebrew word *shemad* ("destruction"), and several Italian words in the manuscript, but he also changed and Judaized the story. The scribe's manner of Judaization is evident at the outset of the romance; the apology itself is filled with terms from a familiar Jewish world. Various citations from the Bible and the Talmud are used to support the reading of the fox fables: R. *Johanan b. Zakkai and his knowledge of fox fables (BB 134a), the rabbinic commentary on the beneficial uses of a minstrel (Pes. 66b), and the tales read to the high priest on the Day of Atonement (Yoma 1:6–7) are all mentioned for the express purpose of establishing the permissibility of the Hebrew translation, and for showing that diversion is only a means to a higher sacred purpose.

Instrumental to the Judaization of the Arthurian romance are the scribe's choice of plot (the seduction of Igerne by the king, with its parallels to the David-Bath-Sheba story), additions and omissions, use of language, and treatment of certain passages to stress Jewish ideas. For instance, the feast at which Uther meets Igerne is described in the Old French sources as a Christmas feast. In the Hebrew version, the statement "Then the king made a great feast for all the people and all the princes" (based on Esth. 2:18) conveys the aura of a Purim feast. Another example of such transference of concepts occurs when the translator takes the talmudic word *tamḥui* ("a charity bowl from which food was distributed to the needy"), with its uniquely Jewish associations, to describe the grail, an overtly Christian symbol. The constant use of well-known biblical phrases reminds the reader of religious literature and produces the effect of biblical scenes in the midst of the Arthurian narrative. In this fashion, then, the text and the language interact in polyphonic fashion.

The scribe through his translation introduced the Arthurian legends into Hebrew; in effect, however, Hebrew literature is the ultimate source for a number of Arthurian motifs. Many romance writers of the 12th and 13th centuries (see: *Fiction) were clerics who knew the Bible; there was also much contact and exchange of midrashic information between Jewish exegetes and their Christian counterparts, and there were, therefore, numerous channels of transmission for the Jewish tales. Many of the Arthurian motifs, drawn from the Bible and from the Midrash, polarize about the Arthur-David nexus; other Arthurian legends (the Tristan cycle) have many motifs parallel to the adventures of the young biblical heroes Joseph and David.

The Hebrew Arthurian romance is untitled and was first published by Abraham Berliner in 1885. Upon this inaccurate edition, Moses *Gaster in 1909 published an English translation which toned down the sexual elements, neglected the biblical nuances, and condensed the text. Moritz *Steinschneider called the translation *Melekh Artus* ("King Artus"), and considered it one of the great curiosities in Hebrew literature. An edition of the above manuscript, with an English translation facing the Hebrew text, was published in 1969.

BIBLIOGRAPHY: C. Leviant, *King Artus: A Hebrew Arthurian Romance of 1279* (1969); Berliner, in: *Oẓar Tov*, 8 (1885), 1–11; Steinschneider, Uebersetzungen, 967–9, no. 578; Gaster, in: *Folk Lore* (1909), 272–94.

[Curt Leviant]

ARTICLES OF FAITH. The term "dogma" which is well defined in Christianity has as such no place in Judaism. In Judaism the need for a profession of belief did not arise and rabbinic synods saw no necessity for drawing up concise formulas expressing Jewish beliefs. Theologically speaking, every Jew is born into God's covenant with the people of Israel, and membership in the community does not depend on credal affirmations of a formal character. Jewish beliefs are voiced in the form of prayer and in the twice-daily recital of the **Shema*.

In Rabbinic Literature

Outside the liturgy, formulations of specific aspects of the Jewish faith abound in rabbinic literature from the Mishnah onward. The need to define the Jewish position vis-à-vis heretical views (see *Heresy and Heretics) occasioned the statement of the Mishnah (Sanh. 10:1) that, while all Israelites have a share in the world to come, it is withheld from those who deny the resurrection of the dead, the divine origin of the Torah, and from the "*Epicurean." This statement comes close to formulating "dogmas" of Judaism, yet it is neither couched in the form of a credal affirmation nor is it comprehensive enough to serve as a total expression of Jewish beliefs. However, its insertion into the Mishnah invests it with authority, and it can readily be seen why Maimonides' famous formulation of 13 principles of Judaism was offered as a kind of elaboration of this particular passage. The formulation of articles of Jewish faith is largely a medieval development, even though *Philo (first century C.E.) had spoken of eight essential principles of scriptural religion: (1) existence of God; (2) His unity; (3) divine providence; (4) creation of the world; (5) unity of the world; (6) the existence of incorporeal ideas; (7) the revelation of the Law; and (8) its eternity (H.A. Wolfson, *Philo, Foundations of Religious Philosophy*, 1 (1947), 164ff.). In the Middle Ages it arose from the theological discussions which had started in Muslim **Kalām* and which then had spread to Jewish circles. The term *ikkarim* (lit. "roots"), the most widely used Hebrew term denoting the "principles" of Judaism, is a literal translation of the Arabic *uṣūl* denoting the "roots" of various disciplines (*Kalām*; the science of *Ḥadīth* or "tradition"; jurisprudence). The term *uṣūl al-din* ("the roots of religion") is synonymous with *Kalām*. In this sense Maimonides refers to the theologians employing the methods of *Kalām* as people concerned with *uṣūl al-dīn* (*ikkarei ha-dat*; Guide 3:51). Maimonides' formulation of articles of faith was not without precedent. *Hananel b. Hushi'el (in his commentary to Ex. 14:31) declared that faith is fourfold: belief (1) in God; (2) in the prophets; (3) in the world to come; and (4) in the advent of the Messiah. Among the Karaites the first enumeration of fundamental Jewish beliefs is found in Judah *Hadassi's (middle of the 12th century) *Eshkol ha-Kofer*. This author lists ten articles (*ishurim*) of faith: (1) God's unity and wisdom; (2) His eternity and unlikeness to any other being; (3) He is the Creator of the world; (4) Moses and the rest of the prophets were sent by God; (5) the Torah which has been given through Moses is true; (6) the Jews are obliged to study the Hebrew language in order to be able to understand the Torah fully; (7) the holy Temple in Jerusalem was chosen by God as the eternal dwelling place of His glory; (8) the dead will be resurrected; (9) there will be a Divine judgment; and (10) God will mete out reward and punishment. It is not clear whether Judah Hadassi offered this statement as an innovation on his part or whether he followed earlier authorities.

Maimonides

Maimonides' "Thirteen Principles" are set down in his commentary on the Mishnah by way of introducing his comments on *Sanhedrin* 10. Writing in Arabic, Maimonides presents these articles of faith as *uṣūl* ("roots") and *qawāʿid* ("fundamentals") of Jewish beliefs (*iʿtiqādāt*) and of the Law (*sharīʿa*). The Hebrew versions render *uṣūl* by *ikkarim* and *qawāʿid* by either *yesodot* or *ikkarim*. The term *uṣūl* acquires here a new meaning: it no longer denotes the topics of the *Kalām* investigations, but the fundamental tenets of faith or the concise abstracts of religion as seen through the eyes of a philosopher. Maimonides undertook such a presentation to teach the rank and file of the community the true spiritual meaning of the belief in the world to come (*ha-olam ha-ba*) and to disabuse their minds of crude, materialistic notions. Since the ultimate felicity of man depends on the possession of true concepts concerning God, the formulation and brief exposition of true notions in the realm of faith is meant to help the multitude to avoid error and to purify belief. The "fundamentals" listed by Maimonides are (1) the existence of *God which is perfect and sufficient unto itself and which is the cause of the existence of all other beings. (2) God's unity which is unlike all other kinds of unity. (3) God must not be conceived in bodily terms, and the anthropomorphic expressions applied to God in Scripture have to be understood in a metaphorical sense. (4) God is eternal. (5) God alone is to be worshiped and obeyed. There are no mediating powers able freely to grant man's petitions, and intermediaries must not be invoked. (6) *Prophecy. (7) *Moses is unsurpassed by any other prophet. (8) The entire *Torah was given to Moses. (9) Moses' Torah will not be abrogated or superseded by another divine law nor will anything be added to, or taken away from it. (10) God knows the actions of men. (11) God rewards those who fulfill the commandments of the Torah, and punishes those who transgress them (see *Reward and Punishment). (12) The coming of the *Messiah. (13) The *resurrection of the dead.

In a postscript Maimonides distinguishes between the "sinners of Israel" who, while having yielded to their passions, are not thereby excluded from the Jewish community or the world to come, and one who "has denied a root principle" (*kafar be-ikkar*). Such an individual has excluded himself from the community and is called a heretic (*min*) and Epicurean.

Maimonides thus attempted to invest his principles with the character of dogma, by making them criteria of orthodoxy and membership in the community of Israel; but it should be noted that his statement was a personal one and remained open to criticism and revision.

In their credal form ("I believe with perfect faith that…") Maimonides' "Thirteen Principles" appeared first probably in the Venice *Haggadah* of 1566. They are found in the Ashkenazi prayer book as an appendix to the regular morning service. Of the many poetic versions, the best known is the popular **Yigdal* hymn (c. 1300). This hymn has been adopted in practically all rites.

Maimonides' "Thirteen Principles" became the prototype of a succession of formulations of the Jewish creed which first merely varied in the number, order, and the articles of belief selected, but which eventually (in the 15th century) introduced methodological criteria for determining whether a certain belief could be regarded as fundamental. The discussion was at no time purely academic. It was stimulated by the controversy over the allegorical interpretations of traditional beliefs according to Aristotelian doctrine, and it focused on such articles of faith as *creatio ex nihilo*, individual providence, etc. The formulation of *ikkarim* was designed to accentuate the vital beliefs of Judaism and to strengthen Orthodoxy. It was also meant to define the position of the Jewish faith vis-à-vis Christianity.

Thirteenth and Fourteenth Centuries

In the 13th century David b. Samuel *Kokhavi and Abba Mari *Astruc b. Moses b. Joseph of Lunel offered fresh formulations of the creed. David Kokhavi in his (unpublished) *Migdal David* uses the term *ikkarim* to refer to the three elements of Judaism: (1) commandments; (2) beliefs; and (3) the duty to engage in philosophical speculation in order fully to understand the Torah (M. Steinschneider, *Hebr. Bibliographie*, 8 (1865), 63, 100–3). The "beliefs" are outlined in great detail under seven headings called "pillars" (*ammudim*) of the faith: (1) creation of the world; (2) freedom of the will; (3) divine providence; (4) divine origin of the Torah; (5) reward and punishment; (6) the coming of the Redeemer; and (7) resurrection. The author claims that these articles follow a logical order. Abba Mari, a defender of Orthodoxy in the Maimonidean controversy, arranged, in his *Minḥat Kena'ot* (ed. by M. Bisliches, 1838), Jewish beliefs under three principles: (1) God is eternal, incorporeal, and His unity is absolute simplicity (7–11); (2) *creatio ex nihilo* and its corollary, miracles (11–16); (3) God's individual providence (17–19). In the 14th century, Shemariah of Negropont (Crete), an Italian philosopher and exegete (d. after 1352), chiefly known for his efforts to reconcile Karaites and Rabbanites, presented five principles of Judaism relating to the existence of God: (1) incorporeality; (2) absolute unity; (3) creation; (4) creation in time; and (5) by a divine *fiat* (M. Steinschneider, *Catalogue… Muenchen*, no. 210). Another philosophical writer, David b. Yom Tov *Ibn Bilia of Portugal, in a treatise called *Yesodot ha-Maskil* (published in E. Ashkenazi's *Divrei Ḥakhamim* (1849), no. 8) supplemented Maimonides' 13 articles by 13 of his own. These additional principles include such dogmas as belief in angels, in the superiority of the Torah over philosophy, in the canonicity of the text of the Torah, and in good actions as a reward in themselves. In spite of their stress on the superiority of the Torah they bear a highly intellectual flavor.

Fifteenth and Sixteenth Centuries

The 15th century and the beginning of the 16th are particularly rich in works on Jewish dogmatics. Some of them are based on strictly methodological considerations, while others stress the purely revelational character of Jewish beliefs. To the first category belong the writings of Ḥasdai Crescas, Simeon b. Ẓemaḥ Duran, Joseph Albo, and Elijah del Medigo; to the second, those of Isaac Arama, Joseph Jabeẓ and Isaac Abrabanel.

HASDAI CRESCAS. Crescas' *Or Adonai* (completed in 1410) is essentially a treatise on dogmatics, the structure of which is determined by a sharp differentiation between various categories of belief. (1) The existence, (2) unity, and (3) incorporeality of God (1:3) form the three root principles (*shoresh vehatḥalah*) of Judaism. A second group of beliefs comprises the six fundamentals (*yesodot*) or pillars (*ammudim*) of the Jewish faith without whose recognition the concept of Torah loses its meaning (2:1–6): (1) God's knowledge of all beings; (2) His providence; (3) His omnipotence; (4) prophecy; (5) free will; and (6) the purpose of the Torah as instilling in man the love of God and thereby helping him to achieve eternal felicity. The third group represents true beliefs characteristic of Judaism and indispensable for Orthodoxy, yet not fundamental (3:1–8; part 2:1–3). Eight in number, they are (1) creation of the world; (2) immortality of the soul; (3) reward and punishment; (4) resurrection; (5) immutability of the Torah; (6) supremacy of Moses' prophecy; (7) divine instruction of the high priests by way of the Urim and Thummim; and (8) the coming of the Messiah. In addition there are three true beliefs connected with specific commandments: (1) prayers are answered by God; (2) repentance is acceptable to God; and (3) the Day of Atonement and the holy seasons are ordained by God. Finally Crescas lists 13 problems concerning which reason is the arbiter; these include such questions as: will the world last forever; are there more worlds than one; are the celestial spheres animate and rational; do the motions of the celestial bodies influence the affairs of men; are amulets and magic efficacious?

SIMEON BEN ZEMAH DURAN. Simeon b. Ẓemaḥ *Duran deals with the problem of dogmatics in his *Ohev Mishpat* (written in 1405; published, Venice, 1589) and *Magen Avot* (3 parts, Leghorn, 1785). He arranges Maimonides' 13 articles under three principles (*ikkarim*): (1) existence of God (implying His unity, incorporeality, eternity, and His being the only object of rightful worship); (2) revelation (implying prophecy, Moses' supremacy as a prophet, the divine origin of the Torah and its immutability); (3) reward and punishment (implying God's knowledge of things, providence, the coming of the

Messiah, resurrection). He finds these three dogmas indicated in the statement of the Mishnah *Sanhedrin* 10:1 (see above). He also mentions earlier attempts to reduce the dogmas to three, and draws a distinction between basic principles of the Torah and other beliefs, the denial of which do not constitute heresy but mere error.

JOSEPH ALBO. Albo's *Sefer ha-Ikkarim*, the most popular work on Jewish dogmatics, is indebted to both Crescas and Duran. Albo criticizes Maimonides' selection of principles, and finds some fault also with Crescas. Like Duran he finds his basic articles in three "root principles" (*ikkarim*): (1) existence of God; (2) divine origin of the Torah; and (3) reward and punishment. From these "root principles" stem derivative "roots" (*shorashim*) which, together with the former, constitute the divine Law. The existence of God implies His unity, incorporeality, independence of time, and freedom from defects. The divine origin of the Torah implies God's knowledge, prophecy, and the authenticity of divine messengers or lawgivers. Reward and punishment implies individual (in addition to general) providence (1:13–15). Of lower rank, although obligatory, are six beliefs (*emunot*), the denial of which does not constitute heresy: (1) the creation of the world in time and *ex nihilo*; (2) the supremacy of Moses' prophecy; (3) the immutability of the Torah; (4) the attainment of the bliss of the next world by the fulfillment of a single commandment; (5) resurrection; 6) coming of the Messiah (1:23).

ELIJAH DELMEDIGO. Elijah Delmedigo's *Beḥinat ha-Dat* (written in 1496; ed. by I.S. Reggio, 1833) is the last of the medieval works on Jewish dogmatics with a strong philosophic orientation. It reflects the doctrine of the "double truth" of the Christian Averroists (see *Averroes). Delmedigo distinguishes between basic dogmas (*shorashim*) which have to be accepted without interpretation (*perush; be'ur*) by masses and philosophers alike, and ramifications (*anafim*) which the masses must accept literally, while the philosophers are required to search for their deeper meaning. For Delmedigo Maimonides' 13 articles belong to the category of basic dogmas. Some of them he holds to be verifiable by reason (existence, unity and incorporeality of God), while the rest have to be taken on trust. The 13 articles are reducible to three: (1) existence of God; (2) prophecy; and (3) reward and punishment. Such topics as the "reasons of the commandments" belong to the category of ramifications as does the whole field of rabbinic *aggadah*. Here the philosopher must exercise great caution in publicizing his interpretations in areas where allegorizing may do harm to the unsophisticated.

ISAAC ARAMA. Isaac *Arama in his *Akedat Yizhak* criticizes Crescas and Albo who saw as the criterion for a "fundamental" of Judaism whether a certain belief was basic to the general concept of revelation, an approach which had tacitly equated Torah with revealed religion in a universal rational sense. According to Arama the Torah reveals principles above and supplementary to reason. Hence a belief in the existence, unity, eternity, and simplicity of God cannot rank as a principle of the Torah (Maimonides and his followers) nor can free will and purpose (Crescas). The principles (*ikkarim*) of the Torah have to be discovered in the Torah itself. They are embedded in the commandments (*mitzvot*), particularly in the laws relating to the Sabbath and the festivals. Arama counts six "principles of the faith" (*ikkarei ha-emunah*): (1) the createdness of the world (Sabbath); (2) God's omnipotence (Passover); (3) prophecy and divine revelation (Feast of Weeks); (4) providence (New Year); (5) repentance (Day of Atonement); (6) the world to come (Tabernacles; ch. 67; in ch. 55 the Sabbath is described as implying all the six principles). Arama lays particular stress on the dogma of creation as the essential dogma of the Torah (ch. 67).

JOSEPH JABEZ. Akin in spirit to Arama are his two contemporaries Joseph Jabez and Isaac Abrabanel. Jabeẓ wrote two small treatises on dogmatics, called *Ma'amar ha-Aḥdut* and *Yesod ha-Emunah* (first published together with his *Or ha-Ḥayyim* in Ferrara, 1554). In the first he rejects Maimonides', Crescas', and Albo's formulations of principles, substituting three of his own, all of which are explications of divine unity: (1) God alone is the Creator; (2) God alone is wondrously active in exercising providence; and (3) God alone will be worshiped in the messianic future. In the second he maintains that Maimonides' 13 principles are traceable to these three, but he now formulates them as: (1) createdness of the world (*ḥiddush ha-olam*); (2) providence; and (3) unity of God. The third dogma implies that God alone will be worshiped in the messianic future. In both treatises the belief in creation is considered the most fundamental principle.

ISAAC ABRABANEL. Isaac *Abrabanel's *Rosh Amanah* (written from 1499 to 1502; Eng. trans., M. Kellner, 1981) is a closely argued treatise on the "roots and principles" of the Jewish faith. Twenty-two of the work's 24 chapters are devoted to an analysis of Maimonides', Crescas', and Albo's respective positions. Abrabanel raises 28 "doubts" or objections to Maimonides' formulation of the creed, but, resolving these questions, he arrives at a complete vindication of Maimonides' views, while those of Crescas and Albo are found wanting. Abrabanel's own attitude, however, is close to Isaac Arama's. The search for "fundamental principles" has its place only in the human sciences which operate with "fundamental principles" that are either self-evident or borrowed from other, more fundamental, sciences. In the case of the Torah, divinely revealed, there is no exterior frame of reference that could furnish the fundamental principles of its laws and beliefs; everything contained therein has to be believed and there is no sense in trying to establish principles of Jewish belief. Were he to single out one principle of the divine Torah, Abrabanel states, he would select that of the createdness of the world (ch. 22).

Spinoza

The medieval Jewish philosophical tradition is still reflected in Spinoza who in his *Tractatus Theologico-Politicus* (publ.

1670) formulates seven "dogmas of universal faith" or "fundamental principles which Scripture as a whole aims to convey": (1) God's existence; (2) unity; (3) omnipresence; (4) supreme authority and power; (5) man's worship of Him in obedience; (6) the felicity of the obedient; (7) forgiveness of penitent sinners (ch. 14). Spinoza's scriptural religion stands between the "universal religion" of the philosopher and the "religion of the masses" (Introd.; chs. 4, 7).

Modern Period

Moses Mendelssohn, the pioneer of the modern phase in Judaism, formulates the following principles of the Jewish religion: (1) God, the author and ruler of all things, is one and simple; (2) God knows all things, rewards the good and punishes evil by natural and, sometimes, supernatural means; (3) God has made known His laws in the Scriptures given through Moses to the children of Israel. Mendelssohn rejects the Christian dogmas of the trinity, original sin, etc., as incompatible with reason, and stresses the harmony between religion and reason within Judaism (*Betrachtungen ueber Bonnets Palingenesie*, in: *Gesammelte Schriften*, 3 (1843), 159–66). The truths to be recognized by the Jew are identical with the eternal verities of reason, and they do not depend on a divine revelation. Only the laws of Judaism are revealed. Hence the Jewish religion does not prescribe belief nor does it lay down dogmas (symbols, articles of faith). The Hebrew term *emunah* means "trust" in the divine promises.

NINETEENTH AND TWENTIETH CENTURIES. Mendelssohn's distinction between the rational truths of Judaism and the revealed laws of the Torah did not appeal to the reformers of the 19th century, but it pervaded the catechisms and manuals of the Jewish religion written by the disciples of Mendelssohn in the early part of the century. It soon came up against opposition once the impact of *Kant's critique of rational theology made itself felt. Moreover, *Hegel's speculative interpretation of Christianity as the "absolute religion" was felt as a serious challenge. Solomon *Formstecher's *Religion des Geistes* (1841) and Samuel *Hirsch's *Religionsphilosophie der Juden* (1842) presented in their turn Judaism as the "absolute religion." In this changed climate of opinion Manuel *Joel (*Zur Orientierung in der Cultusfrage*, 1869) spoke of dogmas in Judaism as the essential prerequisite of its cult and ritual. Abraham *Geiger agreed with his repudiation of Mendelssohn and stressed the wealth of "ideas" with which Judaism entered history. He denied, however, the validity of the term "dogma" as applied to the Jewish religion, since the absence of ultimately fixed formulations of Jewish beliefs rendered the term "dogma" illegitimate. David *Einhorn, on the other hand, had no objection to using this term (*Das Prinzip des Mosaismus* (1854), 11–13). The same view was strongly expressed by Leopold Loew (*Juedische Dogmen* (1871), 138–49). The formulations of the Jewish creed by a number of Jewish theologians of the latter part of the 19th century manifest the strongly felt desire to offer some clear guidance on the essential affirmations of Judaism. To these belong Samuel Hirsch's *Systematischer Katechismus der israelitischen Religion* (1856); Solomon Formstecher's *Mosaische Religionslehre* (1860); and Joseph Aub's *Grundlage zu einem wissenschaftlichen Unterricht in der mosaischen Religion* (1865). The Orthodox creed found its powerful spokesman in Samson Raphael *Hirsch who in his *Choreb, Versuche ueber Jissroels Pflichten in der Zerstreuung* (1837; *Horeb: A Philosophy of Jewish Laws and Observances*, 1962) sought to interpret Judaism from within *halakhah*, expressing the view that "the catechism of the Jew is his calendar." Samuel David Luzzatto's *Yesodei ha-Torah* appeared in 1880, and Michael Friedlaender's *The Jewish Religion* in 1896. It was followed by Morris Joseph's *Judaism as Creed and Life* in 1903. Julien Weil wrote *La Foi d'Israel* (1926). Mordecai M. *Kaplan discussed "Creeds and Wants" in his *Judaism in Transition* (1941), 206–38. A later formulation of Jewish beliefs is given in the form of an epitome of Hermann Cohen's *Religion der Vernunft* in his *The Purpose and Meaning of Jewish Existence* (1964). A modification of Maimonides' creed in the light of modern biblical criticism is offered by Louis Jacobs in his *The Principles of Judaism* (1964).

BIBLIOGRAPHY: L. Loew, *Gesammelte Schriften*, 1 (1889), 31–52, 133–76; Jacob Guttmann, *Ueber Dogmenbildung im Judentum* (1894); S. Schechter, *Studies in Judaism* (1896, repr. 1945), 147–81; J. Holzer, *Zur Geschichte der Dogmenlehre…* (1901), 5–42 (contains also *Mavo le-Perek Ḥelek* in Arabic and Hebrew); Maimonides, *Commentary on Mishna*, ed. and tr. by Y. Kafaḥ (1965), 195–217; D. Neumark, *Toledot ha-Ikkarim be-Yisrael*, 2 vols. (1912); I. Scheftelowitz, in: MGWJ, 34 (1926), 65–75; L. Baeck, *ibid.*, 225–36; F. Goldmann, *ibid.*, 441–57; Julius Guttmann, *ibid.*, 35 (1927), 241–55; Guttmann, Philosophies, passim; A. Altmann, in: *Der Morgen* (Berlin-Amsterdam, 1937), 228–35; S. Heller-Wilensky, *Rabbi Yiẓḥak Arama u-Mishnato ha-Filosofit* (1956), 78–96; M. Goshen-Gottstein, in: *Tarbiz*, 26 (1957), 185–96; A. Hyman, in: A. Altmann (ed.), *Jewish Medieval and Renaissance Studies* (1967), 111–44; J. Petuchowski, in: A. Altmann (ed.), *Studies in Nineteenth Century Jewish Intellectual History* (1964), 47–64. **ADD. BIBLIOGRAPHY:** M. Kellner, *Dogma in Medieval Jewish Thought* (1986); H. Ben-Shammai, in: *Da'a*, 37 (1996), 11–26; M. Shapiro, *The Limits of Orthodox Theology: Maimonides' Thirteen Principles Reappraised* (2004).

[Alexander Altmann]

ARTIFICIAL INSEMINATION. Following earlier experiments on animals, the first human baby produced through artificial insemination on humans was born in the United States in 1866. Since then, particularly in recent decades, tens of thousands of children have been conceived artificially by a physician injecting the husband's or, more usually, a donor's semen into the mother's tract. Such operations are now commonplace, though mostly clandestine, in many countries, including Israel. They raise grave moral, religious, and legal problems. According to the preponderance of Christian teaching and of Western legislation as currently interpreted by the courts, a married woman's recourse to artificial insemination by donor constitutes adultery and any offspring so produced is illegitimate.

A major principle determining the attitude of a Jewish law is enshrined in a talmudic passage which is by far the first literary reference to the feasibility of an impregnation without any physical contact between the parents – a possibility evidently unknown to the Greeks or other nations of antiquity. Discussing the biblical law requiring a high priest to marry a virgin (Lev. 21:13), a third-century sage asked whether a pregnant virgin would be qualified for such a marriage, the pregnancy being explained as due to an accidental impregnation after she bathed in water previously fertilized by a male. The question is answered affirmatively (Ḥag. 15a). This indicates that a conception *sine concubito* does not compromise a woman's legal status as a virgin. Several medieval sources further imply that no bastardy (*mamzerut*) attaches to children born in this way of parents who, had they had normal relations with each other, would have committed adultery or incest (*Alfa Beta de-Ben Sira*, in J.D. Eisenstein (ed.), *Oẓar Midrashim* (1915), 43; and R. Perez of Corbeil, *Haggahot Semak*, see *Turei Zahav* on YD, 195:7). These references are so singular that one of them was quoted as "a legend of the rabbis" by the 16th-century physician *Amatus Lusitanus to clear a nun who had miscarried from the suspicion of fornication.

Following these precedents, virtually all rabbinic rulings on artificial insemination by a donor have refused to brand the act as adultery or the product as a bastard (**mamzer*), with the notable exception of the very first responsum on the subject dated 1930 (J.L. Zirelsohn, *Ma'arekhei Lev* (1932), no. 73). Nevertheless, rabbinic opinion utterly condemns the practice, mainly on moral rather than purely legal grounds. The Jewish conscience, it is emphasized in numerous responsa, recoils in horror from reducing human generation to such artificiality, arbitrariness, and public deceit, from placing into doubt the paternity of children (those conceived by artificial insemination being fraudulently registered in their putative fathers' names, thus investing all paternity claims with some uncertainty), from the resultant risk of incestuous marriages between blood-relations (conceived by a common donor) unknown to each other, from depriving fathers (i.e., the donors) and their natural children of their mutual rights and duties (e.g., maintenance, honor, inheritance), and from many other abuses which would inevitably become rampant.

On artificial insemination from the husband, usually indicated when some impediment in the wife renders a conception by the natural act impossible, most rabbinic authorities adopt a more lenient view, permitting the practice under certain conditions if the duty of procreation cannot otherwise be fulfilled.

The more recent issues of surrogacy and cloning present more complex problems that rabbinic thought is just beginning to contend with.

BIBLIOGRAPHY: I. Jakobovits, *Jewish Medical Ethics* (1966³), 244–50; idem, *Journal of a Rabbi* (1967²), 162–3; idem, in: *Essays… I. Brodie* (1967), 191–2; *Oẓar ha-Posekim, Even ha-Ezer*, 1 (1947), 11–12; M.S. Kasher (ed.), in: *No'am*, 1 (1958), 111–66; 6 (1963), 295–9; 10 (1967), 57–103, 314ff.; A. Joel, in: *Hebrew Medical Journal*, 26 pt. 2 (1953), 190ff.

[Immanuel Jakobovits]

ARTOM, Italian family originating from *Asti, Piedmont. The origin of the name is unknown but, like the rest of the Asti community, the family probably came from France. Various members of the family have achieved distinction, especially in politics, science, and literature. ISAAC (1829–1900) was a diplomat and writer. During the revolt against Austria in 1848, he fought in the students' battalion. On leaving the university, he joined the Foreign Office and in 1858 became private secretary to Count Cavour, who defended him against clerical opposition. After Cavour's death he was appointed minister plenipotentiary to Denmark (1862). He represented Italy during the 1866 peace negotiations with Austria and on the outbreak of the Franco-Prussian War was sent on a diplomatic mission to Vienna. Undersecretary of state for foreign affairs from 1870 to 1876, in 1877 he was elected to the senate of the kingdom, becoming the first Jewish member. He wrote several odes and poems and also published political, economic, and historical works. Isaac's grandson ALESSANDRO (1867–1927) was a physicist, specializing in radiotelegraphy. He invented the Artom system of telegraphy, and also made discoveries in dielectrics and meteorology. Alessandro was scientific advisor to the Italian navy, and was posthumously awarded the title of baron. A monument in his memory was erected in Asti. BENJAMIN (1835–79), a rabbi, was born in Asti. After occupying rabbinical posts in Italy he became haham of the Sephardi community in London (1866), where he was especially active in education. An eloquent preacher in English, he published a collection of sermons (1873) and also wrote odes and prayers in Hebrew and poems in Italian. ERNEST (1869–1935), diplomat and historian, was the nephew of Isaac. As a member of parliament, he supported a national expansionist policy, founding the Italian Colonial Institute in 1909 and inspiring the Italian Libyan campaign of 1911–12. In 1919 he was made a senator. Ernest published many historical studies on the Risorgimento and a monograph on Isaac, *L'opera politica del Senatore I. Artom* (1906). CAMILLO (b. 1886), a composer, was author of several musical works including the prize-winning *Variazioni sinfoniche*. His brother EUGENIO (b. 1896), attorney and author, rose to the rank of lieutenant colonel in World War I. In 1926 he was appointed attorney to the Supreme Court. An anti-Fascist liberal, he held important public positions (1943–46). In 1946 he became professor of history at Florence University and published several historical and political works. EMANUELE (1915–1944) was the author of an unfinished history of the Jews in Italy, published posthumously in *Rassegna Mensile di Israel* (vols. 15 and 16). He openly expressed anti-assimilationist views during the rise of the Fascists and later founded a resistance group (1943) but was captured and tortured by the Germans. His diary *Diari, gennaio 1940–febbraio 1944* (1966) is of special interest. Other important members of this family were the biologist Cesare *Artom and the scholar Elia Samuele *Artom.

BIBLIOGRAPHY: Milano, Bibliotheca, index; Milano, Italia, index; Roth, Italy, index; G. Bedarida, *Ebrei d'Italia* (1950); E. Artom, *Tre vite dell'ultimo '800 alla metà del '900: studi e memorie di Emilio, Emanuele, Ennio Artom* (1954), includes lists of works.

ARTOM, CESARE (1879–1934), Italian biologist. Artom was born in Asti and went to the university at Turin. In 1903 he was appointed assistant in zoology at the University of Cagliari. Here he acquired his lifelong interest in the biological problems presented by the brine-shrimp *Artemia salina*, which abounds in the nearby salt lake of San Bartolomeo. After a period of study in the Wuerzburg laboratory of Theodor Boveri (1908–12), Artom held academic posts at Genoa, Rome, Siena, and Sassari. In 1926 he was appointed to the chair of zoology and comparative anatomy at Pavia, which he held until his death. Apart from his writings on the brine-shrimp, he made more general contributions on the chromosomal and cellular aspects of heredity.

[Mordecai L. Gabriel]

ARTOM, ELIA SAMUELE (1887–1965), Italian rabbi and author. Born in Turin, Artom graduated from the Rabbinical College in Florence and served as rabbi in various communities, among them Tripoli (Libya, 1920–23) and Florence (1926–35), where he also taught at the university and at the Rabbinical College. He settled in Palestine in 1939, but from 1953 to 1965 he spent part of the year in Italy, teaching at the Rabbinical Schools of Turin and Rome. Among his many pupils was his son Emanuele (1916–). Artom's son Reuven was killed in action during the Israel War of Independence in 1948. A close friendship bound Artom to the distinguished scholar Umberto (M.D.) *Cassuto, who was his brother-in-law. Artom's work includes numerous biblical studies, and he also wrote on literature, grammar, history, *halakhah*, and Jewish thought. Artom's major work is a Hebrew commentary, with introduction, to the Bible (edited by M.D. Cassuto, 1952–57) and a Hebrew translation, commentary, and introduction to the Apocrypha (1958–67). His bibliography is contained in a posthumously published essay on the spiritual problems of modern Israel (*Ḥayyei Yisrael ha-Ḥadashim* 1966).

BIBLIOGRAPHY: *Israel*, 50 nos. 23–28 (1965); A. Segré, in: RMI, 31 (1965) 209–15, *Torath Chajim*, no. 53 (1970).

[Alfredo Mordechai Rabello]

ARTSCROLL, U.S. Judaica publishing house. Mesorah Publications, best known through its imprimatur, ArtScroll, was established in Brooklyn, New York, in 1976 by Rabbis Meir *Zlotowitz and Nosson *Scherman. It has since grown into one of the largest, most financially successful, and innovative Judaica publishing houses in the English-speaking world. It has well-established markets throughout the U.S., Canada, the U.K., Australia, and South Africa, as well as the anglophone community in Israel, and it enjoys a growing presence in French-, Spanish-, and Russian-language Judaica markets in the Former Soviet Union, France, Argentina, Mexico, and elsewhere. *ArtScroll* furnishes this international market with bilingual Bibles, liturgical and talmudic texts, *halakhic* commentaries, and various "non"-religious genres, including popular history books, biographies and memoirs, youth literature, novels, pop-psychology and self-help books, cookbooks, and curriculum materials for primary Jewish education.

Although *ArtScroll* defines itself as a totally independent Torah publisher, without ties to any of the major institutions of Jewish public life, its editors and authors are intimately related to the *ḥaredi yeshivah world. *ArtScroll*'s primary mission is to translate (in the sense of moving both from *leshon ha-kodesh* to English and from erudite to popular) Jewish canonical texts, supplanting what the press and its supporters regard as inadequate, distorted, or otherwise illegitimate representations of Jewish ritual practice, historical imagination, and theoretical knowledge, and replacing these with "corrected" editions. Eschewing many of the norms of translation and commentary familiar to other English-language publishers (such as the incorporation of philological and archaeological evidence from diverse sources), the *ArtScroll* cadre seeks a return to what it defines as "Torah-true" interpretations of Jewish texts, the authenticity of which is secured by *ArtScroll*'s close association with the *gedolim* of the yeshivah world. On these terms, *ArtScroll* functions as a vehicle for instilling a deeper understanding of Jewish tradition, a more intensive engagement with Jewish textual practice, and a greater observance of Jewish law, all defined from an unapologetically *ḥaredi* perspective.

ArtScroll has won the loyalty of a large, and apparently growing, constituency of readers and users of Jewish books – especially their *Siddur*, *Chumash*, and *Talmud*, which enjoy considerable appeal among both centrist (or "modern") and *ḥaredi* Orthodox Jews, as well as "Conservadox" Jews, who have become disaffected with the mainstream Conservative movement. Thus *ArtScroll* has effectively displaced many of the key liturgical works of English-speaking Orthodox Jews for the past two generations, such as the *Birnbaum Siddur*, the *Hertz Chumash*, and even the *siddurim* of De Sola Pool and Singer (in the U.K.). More broadly, the press has a commanding presence in Jewish libraries, bookstores, day schools, and community centers throughout the English-speaking world. In part, these successes can be attributed to *ArtScroll*'s distinct institutional structure (operating both as a nonprofit organization and as a business venture), the pool of authors and translators with whom the press works, and its keen marketing sense. *Artscroll*'s prayer books, for instance, are produced in various formats, including interlinear translations and transliterated versions, in different sizes, for daily or weekly usage, as well as slightly modified editions catering to specific clienteles. These include versions of the *ArtScroll Siddur* for Ashkenazi, ḥasidic, and Sephardi services, as well as versions specifically designed for the Orthodox Union, and – to the surprise of many observers – an arrangement with the *Rabbinical Council of America to produce a modified version of the *ArtScroll Siddur* bearing the RCA imprimatur, which included the prayer for the State of Israel, omitted from the standard, haredi version. *ArtScroll* has also embarked on large-scale translation projects that have had little precedent (and not much success) among other English-language Judaica publishers, such as in the case of their widely acclaimed, 73-volume *Schottenstein Talmud* (completed in 2005), which involved a remarkable array of sponsors, translators, and talmudic authorities from both within and outside the *ḥaredi* world.

Despite – or perhaps, because of – its considerable market successes, *ArtScroll* is no stranger to controversy. The press has in fact been a key touchstone in recent struggles among *ḥaredi* and non-*ḥaredi* Jews for authority to interpret the sources of legitimate knowledge and practice in Jewish texts and in public life. On the one hand, there exists a significant population for whom *ArtScroll* books are narrowly "ideological" and are seen to promulgate interpretations of Jewish tradition associated with what some describe as the demagoguery of the *ḥaredi* yeshivah world. *ArtScroll*'s detractors have thus expressed considerable indignation over the way the press translates Jewish texts, as well as its method of selecting commentaries from classical sources, and even the wording of *ArtScroll*'s own commentaries (a famous case is the debate over the translation of *Shir ha-Shirim*, which presents an allegorical rendering of God's relation to Israel rather than a literal, sensual translation). Others have criticized *ArtScroll* for legitimating the Jewish reader's reliance upon the English language at the expense of *leshon ha-kodesh*, enabling one to appear well versed in Jewish knowledge without having made the requisite effort to engage with the original sources. But for a much larger constituency, *ArtScroll* books are praised as instructive, meaningful, authentic, and even empowering. Its enthusiasts thus claim that an "*ArtScroll* revolution" has facilitated an unprecedented degree of access to Jewish knowledge and confidence in ritual performance among English-speaking Jews, forming a readership that extends from the erudite to the culturally illiterate and that transcends the traditional markers of institutional affiliation or local custom. At a further remove, *ArtScroll* has precipitated a reaction among its competitors that one is tempted to describe as an "ArtScrollification" of the Jewish liturgical field as a whole: most notably, with the recent publication of *Eitz Chaim* (the new Conservative *chumash*, designed explicitly to "respond" to *ArtScroll*'s success), and *Mishkan Tefillah* (the new Reform *siddur*, which incorporates many design elements, editorial structure, and instructional material found in *ArtScroll*). Whatever the position taken with regard to *ArtScroll*'s legitimacy as a translator, interpreter, and popularizer of Jewish literature, it would be difficult to ignore the cultural impact this press has had on the modern English-language Jewish public sphere.

[Jeremy Stolow (2nd ed.)]

ARTZI, SHLOMO (1949–), Israeli pop-rock singer-songwriter. Artzi was born at Alonei Abba in Galilee. He made his first public appearance as a singer as a high school student, at an international youth conference in Spain. Like many of his contemporaries Artzi began his musical career during his compulsory national service, though due to his high medical profile he initially began his three-year stint in the IDF as a regular serviceman. It was only a year later that he gained a slot in the Navy band.

In stark contrast with his later career, Artzi debuted with the Navy troupe as a backing vocalist but soon made an impact, becoming the band's soloist in their next show, "Rhapsody in Blue." Artzi's spots in the show included "*Ke-she-Ehyeh Gaddol*" ("When I'm Older"), "*Ha-Malakh Gavriel*" ("Angel Gabriel"), and "*Anshei Ha-Ẓefarde'a Anshei ha-Demamah*" ("The Frogmen, the Silent Ones"), all of which became hits on the pop charts and the road to Artzi's stardom was open. His stellar status was sealed when he won the National Song Festival in 1970, performing in his navy uniform, with a song called "*Pittom Akhshav, Pittom ha-Yom*" ("Suddenly Now, Suddenly Today"). Later that year he released his first solo record, *Shlomo Artzi, The First Record*, which included a new version of "*Pittom Akhshav, Pittom ha-Yom*," and received the prestigious David Harp's award. This was to be the first of many awards.

In 1971 he recorded his second solo effort, *Al Anashim* ("About People"), which primarily comprised original compositions, and took part in the musical movie *Ḥasamba ve-Na'arei ha-Hefker* ("Hasamba and the Gang"). The following year he teamed up with former Navy buddies Dadi Schlessinger and Etchie Stroh to form the Geverret Tapu'akh (Madam Apple) trio, which released four records between 1972 and 1975.

In 1975 it looked like Artzi was about to embark on an international career, when he recorded a single with German lyrics for Decca Telefunken. He was also asked by Switzerland to represent it at that year's Eurovision Song Contest, but ultimately represented Israel with "*At ve-Ani*" ("You and I"), which placed eleventh.

It was three years later that Artzi really hit the jackpot, with his 1978 album *Gever Holekh Le'Ibbud* ("A Man Loses His Way"), on which Artzi managed to lose his image as the baby-faced teen idol and take on a new angst-filled persona. It was an image that was to serve him well and almost all his releases to date have been big sellers.

After teaming up with producer Louis Lahav, in 1984, Artzi recorded *Tirkod* ("Dance") and was voted Singer of the Year. His 1988 release *Ḥom Yuli-August* ("July–August Heat") was the first double album ever made by an Israeli solo artist and, in 2000, his *Ahavtiḥem* CD became his biggest seller to date.

[Barry Davis (2nd ed.)]

ARTZI, YITZHAK (**Herzig**; 1920–2003), Zionist activist, Israeli politician, leader of Romanian Jewry in Israel. Born in Siret (Bukovina) into a ḥasidic family, Artzi received both a traditional and modern education, studying literature and philosophy at Onescu College for Jewish Students, Bucharest, Romania (1940–44). In 1931 he joined Pirḥei Agudat Israel, moving to Ha-No'ar ha-Ẓiyyoni in 1933 and becoming one of its leaders in 1940 after moving to Bucharest. In 1943 he was a member of Ezra (the commission for the aid and rescue of Jews deported to Transnistria) and in December 1943–January 1944 he was part of the official delegation sent to prepare the return of Transnistria orphans to Romania. After World War II he reorganized Ha-No'ar ha-Ẓiyyoni and became a member of the Zionist Executive of Romania. In September 1946 he and his wife left Romania as illegal emigrants to Palestine, but were arrested and sent to Cyprus. They entered Palestine in September 1947. In 1948 Artzi was among the founders of kibbutz Allonei Abba. In 1951 he moved to Tel Aviv and in 1953–57 studied at the School of Law and Economics there, where he became a lawyer. In 1952 he worked at the Ministry of Foreign Affairs and changed his name from Herzig to Artzi. From September 1953 to November 1955 he edited the Hebrew daily *Zemanim*. In 1958 he became general secretary of the Progressive Party, and after the founding of the Liberal Party (1961) became one of its two general secretaries. After the party split and the breakaway Independent Liberal Party was formed, Artzi became its general secretary (1965) and director of the Aliyat ha-No'ar Department of the Jewish Agency (1965–69). In 1974 he became deputy mayor and director of the Culture, Youth, and Sport Dept. of the Tel Aviv Municipality. Artzi remained a member of the Municipal Council of Tel Aviv until 1993. In 1984–88 he was a member of the Knesset. Artzi was active in the Claims Conference of the Jews against Germany. He encouraged the study of Romanian-Jewish history and the Holocaust, and was co-president of the Association of Romanian-born Jews in Israel; honorary president and columnist of the Romanian-language daily *Ultima Ora*, Tel Aviv; and president of the World Association of Bukovina-born Jews. In 1998 he published his memoirs in Hebrew, *Davka Ẓiyyoni*.

BIBLIOGRAPHY: Y. Artzi, *Siret Shelanu* (2003); Y. Govrin, in: *Ultima Ora* (Sept. 3, 2004), 9.

[Lucian-Zeev Herscovici (2nd ed.)]

ARUM, ROBERT (**Bob**; 1931–), U.S. boxing promoter, member of the International Boxing Hall of Fame. One of two dominant promoters of his era, Arum promoted more than 400 title fights. Arum was born in the Crown Heights section of Brooklyn and graduated from New York University in 1953 and cum laude from Harvard Law School in 1956. He was hired by Attorney General Robert Kennedy to work for the Justice Department, leaving in 1959 to become a partner in a private law firm. Arum met Muhammad Ali in 1966 and set up a company called Main Bout, Inc. to promote his first fight: Ali's title fight with George Chuvalo, the first fight Arum had ever seen in person. On September 15, 1978, Arum promoted a then record four world title bouts in one night at the Superdome. The boxers he promoted include Roberto Duran, Julio Cesar Chavez, Oscar De La Hoya, George Foreman, and Larry Holmes.

[Elli Wohlgelernter (2nd ed.)]

ARUNDI, ISAAC (**Ibn**; 14th century), philosophical writer, probably from Ronda (Lat. Arundi; Andalusia). He apparently lived in Italy and perhaps Provence. Arundi, who knew Arabic, wrote a commentary on Job, in which he frequently quotes Aristotle and his commentators Themistius and Averroes and in which he disputes the views of his contemporary Levi b. Gershom. A defective manuscript of the commentary is in Cambridge (S.M. Schiller-Szinessy, *Catalogue…*, vol. 1, no. 67) and there are copies at Paris and Oxford (Neubauer, Cat. 2279.4). Arundi also mentions a work entitled *Milḥamot Adonai*, which was directed against Levi ben Gershom's work bearing the same name.

ARUSI, ABRAHAM BEN MOSES HA-LEVI (1878–1934), prolific author and folklorist. Born in Kawkabān, north of San'a, Arusi immigrated to Ereẓ Israel in 1923 and settled in Maḥaneh Yehudah near Petaḥ Tikvah. In Yemen he had traveled from one place to another in order to look for employment. In this way he was able to collect traditional stories and legends about the first Jewish inhabitants of Yemen, of the miracles they had experienced throughout the generations and of Jewish historical personalities in general. After he immigrated to Israel he gathered 85 folklore stories as well as 300 Yemenite Jewish-Arabic proverbs in *Kore ha-Dorot* (Ben-Menaḥem, 1950; Ḥassid, 1956). On his way to Ereẓ Israel he had also stayed in Aden for a few years. His impressions also appeared as part of *Kore ha-Dorot* (Naḥum, 1986). He was talented not only in storytelling but in writing poetry as well, writing in the genre of traditional Yemenite poetry and Sephardi poetry. He left over 15 compositions, including numerous poems which were only partially published. He collected his poems in a special *dīwān* (manuscript), many of which were copied in other manuscripts. In his prose and poetry (detailed bibliography in Ratzaby, 1994, 401–2), Arusi tended to react to personal experience as well as to historical events such as the establishment of the Hebrew University in Jerusalem and the events of 1929 in Ereẓ Israel (*Dam Ẓaddikim*, 1930). He specifically wrote about the spiritual and social transformations which occurred in the Jewish settlement in Ereẓ Israel and especially among the Yemenite Jews. A significant part of his writings deal with the spiritual deterioration and secularization that became widespread among the Yemenite Jews who deserted their fathers' traditions (*Azharot Yegar Sahauta*, 1924). In spite of their importance, his essays were not used in the sociological research of the Yemenite Jewry of Ereẓ Israel.

BIBLIOGRAPHY: N. Ben-Menaḥem, in: *Minḥah li-Yehudah*, (1950), 141–61; Y. Ḥassid (ed.), *Kiẓẓat Yosef ha-Ẓaddik* (1956), 56–86; Y.L. Naḥum, *Mi-Yeẓirot Sifrutiyyot mi-Teiman* (1981), 118–59; Y. Ratzaby, in: *Yeda-Am*, 9 (1964), 127–31; idem, in: *Assufot*, 8 (1994), 399–423.

[Yosef Tobi (2nd ed.)]

ARVEY, JACOB M. (1893–1977), U.S. attorney and politician. Arvey was born in Chicago, qualified as a lawyer, and entered politics in 1918. In 1923 he was elected alderman from Chicago's heavily Jewish 24th ward, a position he held until 1941; from 1930 to 1934 he also served as master in chancery of the Cook County Court. Under the administration of Mayor Edward Kelly (1933–47), with whom he was closely associated,

Arvey rose to prominence in Chicago's powerful Democratic Party machine.

After service as colonel in the Judge Advocate General's Department in the Pacific during World War II, Arvey became a Democratic national committeeman from Illinois, a key post which enabled him to dominate local and state political life and to control the large Illinois delegation at national Democratic conventions over a period of 20 years. He was largely responsible for putting into office such figures as Chicago Mayor Martin H. Kennelly and Senator Paul Douglas. More than any other single individual, it was Arvey who masterminded the campaign that culminated in Stevenson's nomination for the presidency in 1952. His generally liberal outlook, his ability to adapt to changing times, and his eye for promoting individuals of unusual political intelligence and stature served to distinguish him from the ordinary political boss.

Throughout his career Arvey was highly active in Jewish life. He was chairman of the Israel Bond Campaign in Chicago. A Jewish National Fund reclamation project and a forest in Israel bear his name.

BIBLIOGRAPHY: J. Gunther, *Inside U.S.A.* (1951), 33, 400, 403; V.W. Peterson, *Barbarians in Our Midst* (1952), passim; *The Reporter* (June 7, 1949); *Collier's* (Feb. 1950); *New York Times Magazine* (Aug. 3, 1952).

[Hillel Halkin]

ARVIT (Heb. עַרְבִית; "evening" prayer), one of the three regular daily services. The popular name *Ma'ariv* (going back at least to the 16th century) is derived from the occurrence of this word at the beginning and end of the first blessing preceding the **Shema*. Its recital was originally regarded as optional (Ber. 27b, following R. Joshua against the view of Gamaliel II) since the evening service did not correspond to any set Temple sacrifice (unlike the morning and afternoon services). Tradition attributed the institution of *Arvit* to the patriarch Jacob (based on Gen. 28:11; cf. Ber. 26b). In the Talmud, opinions differ as to whether a third daily prayer is obligatory or optional but Psalms 55:18 and Daniel 6:11 are cited to support the view that prayers must be said three times daily. In common with the other services, its recital is the duty of the individual even outside the synagogue and congregational service.

In its present form the service consists chiefly of **Barekhu* (the invitation to congregational prayer), followed by the *Shema* and its framework of benedictions, and the **Amidah*. When *Arvit* is said after nightfall, the service generally opens with Psalms 134. On weekdays the service opens with Psalms 78:38 and 20:10. According to the Mishnah the reading of the *Shema* was obligatory at nighttime. This was based on the biblical phrase "when thou liest down" (Deut. 6:7; 11:19) and only the recital of its third section (Num. 15:37–41) was a matter of controversy (Ber. 1:5).

The theme of the first of the two blessings preceding the *Shema* is the incidence of evening and night. The second blessing is a thanksgiving for the love shown by God for Israel by revealing His Torah to them. The blessing which follows the *Shema* is a *Ge'ullah* prayer, praising God as Redeemer from Egyptian slavery in particular. The two blessings preceding the *Shema* and the one following it thus follow the pattern established in the morning prayer. They are followed by a night prayer *Hashkivenu* ("Grant us to lie down in peace"), imploring God's protection from a variety of dangers and mishaps. The final blessing existed in two versions, one Babylonian and one Palestinian. In the latter a prayer for peace and Zion-Jerusalem (*ha-pores sukkat shalom*; "who spreads the tabernacle of peace") replaces the more general formula (*shomer ammo Yisrael la-ad*; "who guards His people Israel forever"). The Babylonian version is now used on weekdays; the Palestinian on Sabbaths and festivals.

According to the Ashkenazi rite, a group of scriptural verses beginning with Psalms 89:53 (*barukh Adonai le-olam*; "blessed be the Lord for evermore"), and which originally may have numbered 18, is said between *Hashkivenu* and the *Amidah*. It is a late addition, not found in the Sephardi rite but given in **Maḥzor Vitry*. Later, an additional night prayer (*barukh Adonai ba-yom*; "blessed be the Lord by day") and a benediction expressing messianic hopes (*yiru einenu*; "may our eyes behold") were attached to this. Elijah of Vilna discontinued this custom and those who follow his *nusaḥ* (e.g., most Ashkenazim in Israel) omit the whole addition.

The *Amidah* is then read silently. This is the service to which the Mishnah and Talmud refer when they speak of *tefillat ha-erev* or *tefillat arvit* (Ber. 4:1; Ber. 27b). *Arvit* eventually came to be considered as a statutory prayer, though in token of its optional character, the *Amidah* is not repeated by the reader even in congregational prayer; further blessings could intervene between it, and the *Ge'ullah* blessing (cf. *ibid.* 4b, 9b) and the half *Kaddish* which originally marked the end of the service is recited before the *Amidah*.

The *Amidah* is followed by the full *Kaddish*. In post-talmudic times this was still preceded by **Taḥanun* and some other additions found in the morning service before the *Kaddish*. **Aleinu le-Shabbe'aḥ* concludes the service, though in some rites further psalms were added.

The evening service on Sabbaths and festivals differs in some details. Thus on Friday evening, the service is preceded by **Kabbalat Shabbat*, while the *Amidah* (which consists of the usual first and last three benedictions with a special Sabbath one between them) is followed by an abbreviated repetition consisting of Genesis 2:1–3, a shortened version of the *Avot* benediction, a summary of the seven benedictions of the *Amidah*, the middle (fourth) benediction in full, and *Kaddish*. On Sabbaths and festivals **Kiddush* is recited here in many rites (except on the first day(s) of Passover), originally for the benefit of wayfarers. The custom to follow *Hashkivenu* with Exodus 31:16–17 on Sabbath and similarly appropriate verses on the various festivals was abolished in the *nusaḥ* of Elijah of Vilna. On Sabbath and festivals the service ends with the singing of **Yigdal* or **Adon Olam*.

Arvit at the conclusion of the Sabbath follows the normal pattern except for the addition of a **Havdalah* formula to the fourth benediction of the *Amidah* and of sundry readings after its conclusion. These latter consist of biblical and talmudical passages of varying length and are not recited in all rites. At the conclusion of the Sabbath it is the general custom to preface the *Arvit* with the chanting of Psalms 144 and 67. Ideally, *Arvit* should be recited after nightfall and before dawn. It may, however, be recited after twilight and, to meet the convenience of worshipers, it is often immediately preceded by the *Minḥah* service on weekdays.

BIBLIOGRAPHY: Elbogen, Gottesdienst, 99–106, 109–12; Idelsohn, Liturgy, 118–21, 131–4; Abrahams, Companion, cvii–cxviii, cxxix–cxxxix; E. Munk, *The World of Prayer*, 1 (1954), 197–209; 2 (1963), 1–20.

[Alexander Carlebach]

ARYEH JUDAH HARARI (13th–14th centuries), *paytan*. The name Harari probably indicates that he lived in Montpellier. He wrote a three-part *Tokheḥah, Shifkhu be-Veit El Siḥah*, which is very similar to the *Tokheḥah, Ba'u Yemei Pekuddatkhem* by Aryeh Judah b. Levi ha-Yarḥi (i.e., of Lunel). It is possible that the two poets are identical and the difference in surnames is to be attributed to a change of residence. Harari may also have been the author of several poems which have his first name in acrostic: *Esh u-Mayim Eikh Davaku*, about the power of the elements and of love (printed with Gabirol's *Tikkun Middot ha-Nefesh*, ed. Lunéville (1807), 6); *Demut Kisse Kavod*, an introduction to *Nishmat* (published by S.D. Luzzatto, *Tal Orot* (1881), 45, no. 57, wrongly attributed by S. Philipp to Judah Halevi); *Ha-Parah Od Yegal El* also has the designation Halevi in the acrostic.

BIBLIOGRAPHY: Abraham Bedersi, *Ḥerev ha-Mithappekhet* (in his *Ḥotam Tokhnit*, 1885), verse 145; Zunz, Gesch, 469; Zunz, Lit Poesie, 405, 708; Luzzatto, in: *Oẓar Tov*, 3 (1880), 17; S. Philipp, *Kol Shirei R. Yehudah Halevi* (1898), 87; Steinschneider, Uebersetzungen, 381; Gross, Gal Jud, 323, 328; Davidson, Oẓar, 4 (1933), 370.

ARYEH JUDAH LEIB BEN EPHRAIM HA-KOHEN (1658–1720), Moravian rabbi. Aryeh was the younger son of Ephraim b. Jacob ha-Kohen, rabbi of Ofen. He studied under his father together with his nephew Ẓevi Hirsch *Ashkenazi (the Ḥakham Ẓevi). His elder brother Hezekiah died in the plague which broke out in Ofen in 1678 and Aryeh was taken ill. According to his own statement (introduction to the responsa *Sha'ar Efrayim*) his father prayed that he be taken instead of his son. Aryeh Leib recovered; but his father succumbed to the plague. Before he died, he ordered his son to publish his books. After the death of his mother in 1684, Aryeh Judah decided to immigrate to Ereẓ Israel with his family and they were joined by Aaron, son of his deceased brother Hezekiah. They arrived in Jerusalem in 1685. There he began to arrange his father's book for publication although he found the preparatory work difficult; "it involved much trouble because of the confusing handwriting and the loss of many pages." About a year later he returned to Prague and published it under the title *Sha'ar Efrayim* (Sulzbach, 1688). It comprises 150 responsa on the four parts of the Shulḥan Arukh. The end of the work contains *Kunteres Aḥaron* ("Last Pamphlet") consisting of Aryeh's explanatory notes on the Talmud and the *Tur, Ḥoshen Mishpat*. Aryeh later returned to Ereẓ Israel, where he died in Safed. His son Jedidiah, pupil and later son-in-law of Abraham Yiẓḥaki (the Sephardi rabbi of Jerusalem), also wrote responsa, only one of which was published.

BIBLIOGRAPHY: Michael, Or, 364, 510, 524, 946; S.J. Fuenn, *Kiryah Ne'emanah* (1860), 73–74; J. Emden, *Megillat Sefer*, ed. by D. Kahana (1896), 4ff.; D. Kaufmann, in: REJ, 21 (1890), 135; idem, *Die Erstuermung Ofens* (1895), 18–19, 22, 24, 26–27; idem, *Gesammelte Schriften*, 2 (1910), 303–5, 311–2; Frumkin-Rivlin, 2 (1928), 82–85.

[Yehoshua Horowitz]

ARYEH JUDAH LEIB (The "Mokhi'aḥ") OF POLONNOYE (d. 1770), ḥasidic exegete and popular preacher in Poland. Aryeh may have been the first of the early Ḥasidim to accept the charismatic leadership of *Israel b. Eliezer Ba'al Shem Tov, the founder of modern *Ḥasidism. As a preacher, he acquired considerable popular influence and traveled among the communities of the Ukraine and Galicia, which gave him opportunities to spread Ḥasidism. Most of his life was spent at Polonnoye. Aryeh's main theme was of moral exhortation to the simple religious life. He spoke out against overestimation of philosophical and casuistic methods in learning, emphasizing, as did the Ba'al Shem Tov, the primacy of prayer in the scale of religious values. Some of his sermons and exegetical commentaries were collected in *Kol Aryeh* (1798). In *Kol Aryeh*, several dicta of the Besht, unknown from other sources, have been preserved.

BIBLIOGRAPHY: S.A. Horodezky, in: *Ha-Ḥasidut*, 1 (1951), 135ff.; idem (ed.), *Shivḥei ha-Besht* (1814); Dubnow, Ḥasidut, 1 (1932), 104.

ARYEH LEIB BEN ELIJAH (1808–1888), Ukrainian rabbi and halakhist. Aryeh Leib was born in Satanov. For a time he engaged in trade, but before 1834, he was *av bet din* of Zaslav (now Izyaslav, Ukraine), a position he apparently held until his death. He corresponded on halakhic matters with leading authorities, including Solomon *Kluger. His works are *Arugat ha-Bosem* (1869), novellae on the *Yoreh De'ah* section of the Shulḥan Arukh (1–110), including some responsa; *Shem Aryeh* (1874), responsa to which were added two treatises later republished separately under the same title (1914). His works received the rare approbation of Joseph Saul *Nathanson. He used to sign his halakhic decisions "Aryeh Leibush Bolichover" (Bolichov was his father's birthplace).

BIBLIOGRAPHY: L. Ovchinskii, *Naḥalat Avot*, 1 (1894), 68; H. Brawermann, *Anshei-Shem* (1892), 96.

[Abraham David]

ARYEH LEIB BEN SAMUEL ẒEVI HIRSCH (1640–1718), Polish rabbi. Aryeh Leib was the grandson of Joel *Sirkes. He studied under his stepfather David ha-Levi, author of the *Turei Zahav*, and later under Joshua Hoeschel of Cracow. At the age of 23, he was appointed rabbi of Zwierz (in the district of Lemberg) and five years later of Kamorna. In 1666 his stepfather sent him and his stepbrother Isaiah ha-Levi to Constantinople to Shabbetai Ẓevi, who welcomed them and expressed his concern over the persecution of the Jews in 1648–51. Later he was rabbi of Stopnica (1677–78), Zamość (1682), Tiktin (1689), Cracow (1695), and Brest-Litovsk (1701–18). His responsa, entitled *Sha'agat Aryeh*, were published by his grandson Abraham Nathan Neta Meisels, who added his own responsa under the title of *Kol Shaḥal* (Neuwied, 1736; Salonika, 1746). Aryeh Leib also prepared a collection of his grandfather's responsa for publication. However, the work, *She'elot u-Teshuvot Ge'onei Batrai*, which includes three of his own responsa at the end, appeared (Turka, 1764) only after his death. In several responsa Aryeh Leib states that his halakhic decision is to be applied in practice subject to the agreement of his stepfather David ha-Levi, whose comment on these responsa was: "My stepson has determined the *halakhah* exactly."

BIBLIOGRAPHY: Michael, Or, no. 527; C.N. Dembitzer, *Kelilat Yofi*, 2 (1893), 61; B. Friedberg, *Luḥot Zikkaron* (1897), 24–25; Ẓ. Horowitz, *Kitvei ha-Ge'onim* (1928), 139; I. Halperin (ed.), *Pinkas Va'ad Arba Araẓot* (1945), 214, n. 3.

[Yehoshua Horowitz]

ARYEH LEIB OF OŻARÓW (d. 1833), ḥasidic *ẓaddik*, founder of the Ożarów dynasty of *ẓaddikim* in Poland. He was a pupil of *Jacob Isaac ha-Ḥozeh ("the seer") of Lublin and of his father-in-law Reuben ha-Levi of Dzierzgowice, author of *Duda'im ba-Sadeh* (1858). He became a *ẓaddik* in Ożarów in 1815 and later moved to Opole, but never gained a large following. His teachings are quoted by his grandson Aryeh Leib in *Birkat Tov* (1938). The Ożarów dynasty continued until World War II, when most of its members perished in the *Holocaust. One of his descendants was the rabbinical author MOSES JEHIEL EPSTEIN of Ożarów (d. 1971), who settled in Israel in 1953. He was awarded the Israel Prize of 1967 for his ten-volume series *Esh Dat* (1951), discourses on the ḥasidic approach to the concepts of "love of Israel" and "love of Torah," and *Be'er Moshe* (1964), a commentary on the Torah.

[Itzhak Alfassi]

ARYEH LEIB OF SHPOLA (1725–1812), ḥasidic **ẓaddik*, a popular miracle-worker and faith healer; known as the *Shpoler Zeide* (the "grandfather from Shpola"). Aryeh Leib belonged to the third generation of *Ḥasidim in the Ukraine, and was a disciple of Phinehas of Korets. While beadle in Zlatopol he became celebrated among the common people as a "saint" and a healer who helped the poor. Stories circulated about the numerous miracles he was said to have performed. Aryeh Leib was also active in communal affairs. He took part in the assembly of Jewish leaders which was held at the end of the 18th or beginning of the 19th century, probably at the initiative of *Levi Isaac of Berdichev, to discuss the anti-Jewish measures which the Russian government was considering. Aryeh Leib encountered opposition from *Baruch of Medzibezh, who despised Aryeh Leib for his affiliation with the common folk. When *Naḥman of Bratslav settled in Zlatopol, near Shpola, serious differences arose between the two ḥasidic leaders, both over matters of principle and out of personal rivalry. Aryeh Leib's simple, popular approach to religion in which he emphasized the importance of unsophisticated faith was incompatible with Naḥman's mode of leadership. Aryeh Leib's teachings show traces of the current messianic expectations that 1840 would be the year of redemption. None of his writings has been preserved. Tales of the miracles he reputedly performed were collected in *Tiferet ha-Maharal* (1914).

BIBLIOGRAPHY: Horodezky, Ḥasidut, 3 (1953⁴), 28–29, 155ff.; A.B. Gottlober, in: *Ha-Boker Or*, 5 (1881), 383–6; A.G. Duker, in: *J. Starr Memorial Volume* (1953), 191–201; Halpern, in: *Tarbiz*, 28 (1958/59), 90–98.

ARYEH LEIB SARAHS (i.e., son of Sarah; 1730–1791), semi-legendary ḥasidic **ẓaddik*. He was born in Rovno, Poland. Although his father's name was Joseph, Aryeh Leib was known as Leib Sarahs after his mother. This unusual form of identification may derive from a prayer in the mystical *Book of *Raziel*, which mentions a Leib b. Sarah. Aryeh Leib was the disciple of the *Maggid* *Dov Baer of Mezhirech. His saying: "I did not go to the *Maggid* of Mezhirech to learn Torah from him but to watch him tie his boot laces" emphasized that the *ẓaddik's* personality and conduct are of prime importance for *Ḥasidism. Aryeh Leib had the personality and popular status typical of the itinerant *ẓaddikim* who preceded *Israel b. Eliezer Ba'al Shem Tov, the founder of Ḥasidism. He wandered from place to place helping the needy, especially by securing the release of imprisoned debtors. His deeds are embellished by popular legend which relates that he came, while invisible, to the court of Emperor *Joseph II in Vienna, to obtain the abrogation of measures included in the **Toleranzpatent* (1782). Legends about Aryeh Leib Sarahs penetrated into Ukrainian folk literature. He died in Yaltushkov (Podolia).

BIBLIOGRAPHY: Dubnow, Ḥasidut, 176, 191–3; M. Bodek, *Sefer ha-Dorot he-Ḥadash*, 2 (1965), 43–49; Horodezky, Ḥasidut, 2 (1953⁴), 7–12; R. Margalioth, *Gevurat Ari* (1911).

[Avraham Rubinstein]

ARZIN, JOSEPH BEN JACOB (16th century), kabbalist of the Lurianic School. Arzin was third *ḥaver* ("member") in the "first class" among Isaac Luria's disciples. According to Ḥayyim *Vital's testimony, Joseph was older than Vital and was probably born before 1540. Ḥayyim Vital relates that Arzin quarreled with R. Elijah Falcon, one of Luria's disciples. Luria expelled Falcon from his group and considered dismissing Arzin, but refrained from doing so. Several of his sermons, as well as "special meditations" (*yiḥud*) which he received from Luria, are mentioned in Ḥayyim Vital's books. He was the author of a commentary on *Idra Rabba*. Arzin was among the 12 *ḥaverim* ("members") of Luria's school who signed a "writ of alliance" with Ḥayyim Vital to learn from him Luria's doctrines. In 1568 Arzin appeared in Salonika on behalf of the

Talmud Torah Association of Safed and the famous scholar R. Moses *Almosnino preached in honor of this mission. Arzin died young, when his father was still alive. In Saadiah Longo's eulogy for his father, the kabbalist Jacob Arzin, Joseph was also lamented. Joseph's son was probably R. Samuel Arizi, who in 1622 entered the meditative study circle of R. Samuel Noah of Safed.

BIBLIOGRAPHY: G. Scholem, in: *Zion*, 5 (1940), 143–4; M. Benayahu, in: *Sefunot*, 6 (1962), 22.

ARZT, MAX (1897–1975), U.S. Conservative rabbi. Arzt was born in Stanislav, Poland, and was brought to the U.S. at the age of four. He was ordained at the Jewish Theological Seminary (1921). During his college years, Arzt developed an interest in Zionism. After serving in Stamford, Conn. (1921–24), Arzt accepted the pulpit of Temple Israel in Scranton, Pa., where he remained for 15 years. The congregation became known as a laboratory for synagogue endeavor in many educational areas. In 1939 he became director of Field Service and Activities of the Jewish Theological Seminary and was a pioneer in educating laymen to support institutions of higher Jewish learning. He was named vice chancellor of the Seminary in 1951 and professor of practical theology in 1962. He wrote *Justice and Mercy, a Commentary on the New Year and the Day of Atonement* (1963) and various talmudic studies. Arzt was a member of the editorial committee of the Jewish Publication Society of America as well as of its translation committee preparing a new translation of the Bible. Other posts he held included president of the Rabbinical Assembly, and vice president of the Synagogue Council of America. *Joy and Remembrance: Commentary on the Sabbath Eve Liturgy* was published posthumously in 1979.

[Alvin Kass]

ASA (Heb. אָסָא; etymology uncertain), king of Judah, 908–867 B.C.E. According to I Kings 15:8 and II Chronicles 13:23, Asa was the son of *Abijah. *Maacah is listed in I Kings 15:2 as the mother of Asa and in II Chron. 15:16 as the mother of Abijah. Some scholars assume, therefore, that Asa and Abijah were brothers. Apparently, Asa acceded to the throne while still comparatively young, upon the death of Abijah; for some time Maacah, the queen mother, served as regent (cf. II Chron. 13:2). Upon reaching his majority, Asa removed her from the regency, along with her followers. The author of the book of Kings attributes this punishment by her son to her having made an image to an *Asherah (I Kings 15:11–13). According to II Chronicles 15:10–16, her removal was part of a general reform that reached its climax in the 15th year of his reign with an assembly in Jerusalem of the people who covenanted to "seek the Lord, the God of their fathers." It appears that Asa made genuine efforts to remove pagan influences and to restore the worship of the Lord in Jerusalem. It is also possible that the religious reformation in Judah resulted from a policy that sought to attract those circles in the kingdom of Israel who were favorable to the Temple in Jerusalem, and thus make possible the reunification of the two kingdoms. The beginning of Asa's reign was peaceful (II Chron. 13:23; 14:5), leaving him free to strengthen his position against possible attacks by outside enemies. He built fortified cities in Judah (14:5–6) adding to the chain of the kingdom's defenses which had been begun by his ancestors (see: *Rehoboam). The northern boundary of Judah had not been fortified at all prior to his reign.

After the years of quiet, Asa, like Rehoboam his grandfather, was faced with an incursion from the south which forced him to go to war. The invader was *Zerah the Nubian ("Cushite"; cf. 14:8–14) who acted either on his own initiative or in collaboration with *Baasha, king of Israel (900–877 B.C.E.). From the fortified border post of Mareshah (cf. 11:8), Asa pushed Zerah and his armies back as far as Gerar, capturing much spoil in the process. As a result of this victory, the tribe of Simeon was able to establish itself more fully in the Negev, seizing the most important wells and pasture lands. According to I Kings 15:16, there was warfare between the kingdoms of Judah and Israel during all of Asa's reign. Baasha evidently recovered most of the territory seized by *Abijah and proceeded to fortify Ramah (I Kings 15:16–22), only five miles north of Jerusalem, which was thus, so to speak, held in check. This threat caused Asa to turn to *Ben-Hadad I, son of Tabrimon, son of Hezion, king of *Aram (I Kings 15:18–19). In response, Ben-Hadad invaded Galilee from the north, breaking the defense chain of Naphtali from Ijon and Dan to the western shore of *Kinneret (cf. II Chron. 16:4). As a result of this two-front war, Israel probably lost northern Galilee and was compelled, in the south, to withdraw from the Ramah area, and Asa occupied Ramah, destroying its fortifications, reusing their materials to strengthen the defenses of Gibeah and Mizpah. In so doing he secured his northern boundary, removing the danger to the capital. H.L. Ginsberg is of the opinion that Asa understood that Judah could not expand northward at the expense of Israel in the foreseeable future. Further, it was clear to him that the new defense line represented a reasonable division between the two kingdoms. II Chronicles 15:8 and 17:2 seem to imply the contrary, but Rudolph has suggested an alternative interpretation.

See Rudolph also on the unfavorable picture of the final phase of Asa's reign that is painted by II Chronicles 15:19–16:12. It has long been suggested that the Chronicler's account of Asa's sin as a reliance on physicians rather than on YHWH (II Chronicles 16:12) resulted from a *Midrash on the name Asa, Aramaic for "physician."

In the *Aggadah*

During the early part of his reign, Asa performed many good deeds. Together with Jehoshaphat he destroyed all the idolatrous cults (Shab. 56b); and he refortified the cities of Lydda, Ono, and Gei ha-Harashim (Meg. 4a). As a reward, he was one of the four kings whose wish to defeat his enemies was immediately granted (Lam. R., introd. 30). The disease of his feet with which he was afflicted (I Kings 15:23), however, was his punishment for having pressed even students of the Law and newly marrieds into military service (Sot. 10a); his was the disease referred to in David's curse of Joab (II Sam. 3:29) "Let there not faileth from the house of Joab one… that leaneth on a staff" (Sanh. 48b). Although Asa retained the magnificent throne of Solomon from among the treasures which he took from Zerah the Ethiopian (Esth. R. 1:2), he gave the rest to Hadrimon the son of Tabrimon (Pes. 119a), which was accounted a grievous sin (SOR 17).

BIBLIOGRAPHY: Bright, Hist, 214–6, 220, 232; Albright, Arch Rel, 157ff.; J. Morgenstern, *Amos Studies* (1941), 224ff.; Noth, Hist Isr, index; Ginsberg, in: *Fourth World Congress of Jewish Studies*, 1 (1967), 91; Yeivin, in: BJPES, 10 (1944), 116ff.; Kittel, Gesch, index; W. Rudolph, *Chronikbuecher* (1955). **ADD. BIBLIOGRAPHY:** S. Japhet, *I & II Chronicles* (1993), 701–13; M. Cogan, I *Kings* (AB, 2000), 395–404.

A.S.A. The Academic Sports Association (A.S.A.) of Israel was established in 1952 by the Sports Committee of the Hebrew University, the Technion in Haifa, and the Tel Aviv School of Law and Economics, but subsequently students from other Israeli institutions of higher learning (in Tel Aviv, Haifa, Reḥovot, and Beersheba) also joined. The Association stimulates interest in sports in an age group which generally tends to show no special concern for physical activity and promotes physical exercise among Israeli academicians.

A.S.A. activity focuses on four areas: physical education classes in the universities for students and academic staff; team sports at the national league level; A.S.A. championship competitions in 15 different sports; and participation in international competitions. The Association is a member of national sports institutions in Israel and since 1953 has been a member of the International Federation of University Sportsmen (F.I.S.U.), and as such participates in the "Student Olympics" (the Universiada) every two years. Each year a different university is chosen to host the A.S.A. International Games (since 1969), and in addition there has been an international championship for windsurfing (since 1985) and winter games (since 1997) in Elath.

[Yehoshua Alouf (2nd ed.)]

ASAD, HAFEZ AL- (1930–2000), president of Syria. Asad was born in Qardaha, an Alawi village in northeast Syria, to a poor peasant family. Although born to the Alawi sect (a heterodox offspring of Shiʿa Islam, regarded as "heretic" by many Sunni Muslims), Asad was also educated as a Syrian-Arab nationalist in the predominantly Arab-Sunni town of Latakia. At the age of 17 he joined the newly formed Baʿth party and reportedly volunteered in 1948 to fight against the newborn State of Israel. Like many Alawi (and Druze) youngsters, Asad enlisted in the Syrian military in 1952, and in 1955 graduated with honors from the Air Force Academy in Aleppo. He was appointed a wing commander in the Syrian air force in 1957 after his party, the Baʿth, had mustered significant influence in the Syrian military and politics. Asad took an active part in the March 1963 revolution; and at the end of 1964 he was appointed commander of the air force with the rank of general. His rapid rise was not only a result of his Baʿthist affiliation but also of his unique qualities of leadership: ruthlessness, organization, manipulation, secrecy, patience, and coolness.

In February 1966, as number two to his fellow Alawi officer, Salah Jadid, Asad co-led the "neo-Baʿth" coup (the 13th coup in Syria) and was appointed also as minister of defense, a position which he used to strengthen his military power base. Despite the crushing defeat of the military in the 1967 war against Israel, Asad managed to shift the blame to the civilian Baʿthist leaders. Backed by the army command, he seized power in Damascus on November 16, 1970, deposing and jailing Jadid and his followers and thus opening a new era in Syrian history, politics, and society. On March 12, 1971, Asad was elected as Syria's president, by 99.2% of the vote in a national referendum, where he was the only candidate. He was subsequently reelected every seven years with 96% to 99% of the vote and served as president until his death on June 10, 2000.

Asad was the first Syrian ruler in modern Syrian history to dominate his country and people for 30 years. Establishing a personal-authoritarian regime, he was able to bring about significant achievements but also suffered major setbacks to Syria, in the domestic, regional, and international arenas.

First, he achieved unprecedented political stability in the country, which had been previously characterized by nearly nonstop military coups and countercoups. Yet this stability was realized not only through socio-political mobilization and cooptation, but also with an iron fist, mass arrests, and murder, torture, and other violations of human rights. The most notorious event was the Hama massacre of February 1982; at least 20,000 people were killed by the army, quelling a major rebellion by the "Muslim Brothers."

Asad's rule was also marked by significant socio-economic mobility of the lower, rural classes, notably the Alawi minority, and development of the educational and health systems as well as the economic infrastructure, but also by failure to solve the big problems of corruption, mismanagement, unemployment in the public sector, and tense intercommunal relations.

Asad succeeded in creating a powerful army and strong independent state, also exercising regional influence, particularly over Lebanon, which in 1989 become a de facto Syrian protectorate. Earlier, in 1980, Asad established a strategic alliance with the revolutionary Iranian Islamic regime. Asad backed Iran in the devastating war with Baʿthist Iraq (1980–88) and, from 1982, coordinated with Teheran support of Hizbullah's military struggle against Israel.

Asad was defeated in his wars with Israel in 1967, 1973, and 1982 (in Lebanon) and failed to reach a strategic balance with the Jewish state. During the 1990s, with American inducements, he was engaged in a peace process with Israel.

Though an agreement was not reached, Asad allowed Syrian Jews – approximately 5,000 – to emigrate after holding them as hostages but also protecting them.

Asad decreased Soviet influence in Syria, attempting to maneuver between the U.S.S.R. and the U.S. He backed the U.S. in its war against Saddam Hussein's Iraq in early 1991 after losing the military and diplomatic support of the U.S.S.R. under Gorbachev's leadership. He developed working relations with U.S. presidents Nixon, Carter, Bush, and Clinton, but failed to substantially improve Syrian-American relations. The relationship was aggravated on the ascendancy of Asad's son BASHAR (1965–) in June 2000. This was because of Syria's continued backing of Islamic terrorist groups – such as Hizbollah, Hamas, and Islamic Jihad, the de facto occupation of Lebanon, the development of chemical weapons, and particularly his opposition to the American attack and occupation of Iraq in March 2003. Domestically Bashar introduced some reforms in Syria's economic infrastructure, but not in the rigid political system.

BIBLIOGRAPHY: M. Ma'oz, *Asad – the Sphinx of Damascus, a Political Biography* (1988); P. Seale, *Asad – the Struggle for the Middle East* (1988); N. Van-Dam, *The Struggle for Power in Syria* (1979); E. Zissar, *Asad's Legacy: Syria in Transition* (2001).

[Moshe Ma'oz (2nd ed.)]

ASAEL, ḤAYYIM BEN BENJAMIN (1650–c. 1707), rabbi in Salonika and later an emissary from Jerusalem. Ḥayyim taught at the yeshivah of Solomon *Amarillo, the foremost house of study in Salonika, and also served as preacher to the Ashkenazi congregation in the city. After his father's death, in 1690, he moved to Jerusalem, where he remained for some years teaching at the yeshivah of "Pereyra" until his appointment as emissary to Turkey in 1704. He died in Smyrna. Ḥayyim wrote the *Sam Ḥayyei*, incorporating responsa given during the course of his travels and sermons. This work was published by his son, Benjamin Asael (Salonika, 1746). His responsa are also quoted elsewhere.

BIBLIOGRAPHY: Frumkin-Rivlin, 2 (1928), 164; Rosarnes, Togarmah, 4 (1935), 347; Yaari, Sheluḥei, 115, 352–3, 486, 888.

[Simon Marcus]

ASAHEL (Heb. עֲשָׂה־אֵל, עֲשָׂהאֵל; "God has made"), name of several biblical figures.

(1) Son of Zeruiah, sister of David (I Chron. 2:16), and one of the 30 heroes of David (II Sam. 23:24; I Chron. 11:26). After the defeat of the forces of Ish-Bosheth in Gibeon, Asahel pursued Abner (II Sam. 2:18–19) but was killed by him. The action brought about a blood revenge by the sons of Zeruiah, which led to the murder of Abner (II Sam. 3:27–30).

Asahel is listed among the officers of the monthly militia of David, as the commander of a division for the fourth month (I Chron. 27:7). This is problematical because he was killed early in the reign of David. Therefore, some scholars maintain that his name was added after his death to honor him; others challenge the historical accuracy of the list. Nonetheless, it was probably a prototype of the list of the Davidic militia, which was brought up to date by adding the name of Zebadiah, the son of Asahel and his successor in the same command (cf. I Chron. 12).

In the *Aggadah*

Asahel was so swift and light of foot that he could run over the ears of corn and leave them unbroken (Eccl. R. 9:11). The loss caused to David by the death of Asahel was equal to that caused by the death of the 19 men whom Abner killed at the same time (cf. II Sam. 2:30; Sif. Deut. 52).

(2) A Levite who, together with the high officials and priests of Judah, was sent by King *Jehoshaphat on a teaching mission to the cities of Judah (II Chron. 17:7–9). The purpose of the mission was to instruct the people in "the Law of Yahweh" (*ibid.* 9; cf. II Kings 23:2; Neh. 8:4–18).

BIBLIOGRAPHY: Yadin, in: J. Liver (ed.), *Historyah Ẓeva'it shel Ereẓ Yisrael* (1964), 355ff.; Mazar, in: *Sefer Ben Gurion* (1964), 248–67; de Vaux, Anc Isr, 214–8; Yadin, in: BJPES, 15 (1940), 86ff.

ASAPH (Heb. אָסָף), name of four biblical figures.

(1) The ancestor of one of the principal families of singers in the Temple. According to I Chronicles 6:24–26, Asaph himself, who is dated to the Davidic period, was descended from Gershom son of Levi (*ibid.*). The tradition of tracing families of singers back to eponymous ancestors of the age of David appears elsewhere in Chronicles and in Ezra-Nehemiah. Asaph is numbered among the levitical singers who participated in the bringing up of the Ark to Jerusalem (I Chron. 15:17, 19); David appointed him and his brother to serve before the Ark (I Chron. 16:37; cf. 25:1ff.). In many passages a special position is assigned to Asaph among the ancestors of families of singers, and he alone is mentioned in association with David (II Chron. 29:30; Neh. 12:46). Only singers of the family of Asaph appear in the register of the returnees from exile (Ezra 2:41; Neh. 7:44) and in other passages in Ezra-Nehemiah. It is only in the register of inhabitants of Jerusalem in the days of Nehemiah that singers of the descendants of Jeduthun are included along with the Asaphites (Neh. 11:17; I Chron. 9:15–16). Evidently the Asaphite singers, who possibly had already served in the first Temple since they are numbered among those returning from exile, played a leading part in the musical service of the Second Temple.

Asaph is designated in II Chronicles 29:30 as a seer (*ḥozeh*) and in I Chronicles 25:1–2 the musical function of the sons of Asaph was referred to as prophesying (cf. II Chron. 20:14–23). The institution of the levitical chanting of hymns is attributed to him in association with David (cf. Neh. 12:46). The psalms in the collection of Psalms 73–83, as also Psalm 50, have the caption "of Asaph." It is possible that this designation is based on a tradition which assigned their composition to him, although it is also possible that the purport of the caption was that the psalms in question pertained to a collection which the Asaphites used to sing, or perhaps that they were sung in a style peculiar to the Asaphites.

In the *Aggadah*

According to one view, Asaph was not the son of the wicked Korah, but merely a descendant of his branch of the tribe of Levi (Lev. R. 17:1); others, however, regard him as the son of Korah, and as an example of how the son of a wicked person can become religious through the study of the Torah (Song R. 4:4). He helped King David write the Book of Psalms (BB 14b). He sang while the Temple was burning, justifying his action, by stating: "I am happy that God has wrought His vengeance only on wood and stones" (Lam. R. 4:14). Even when God Himself wept at the destruction of the Temple, Asaph refused to do so, but instead exhorted Him to action with the words of Psalms 74:3: "Lift up Thy feet unto the perpetual desolations; even all that the enemy hath done wickedly in the sanctuary" (*Midrash Zuta*, Buber ed. (1894), Lam. 75, p. 166).

(2) The ancestor of a family of gatekeepers according to I Chronicles 26:1, but the name should probably be emended to Ebiasaph; cf. I Chronicles 9:19.

(3) The Father of Joah, "recorder" of King *Hezekiah (II Kings 18:18; Isa. 36:3).

(4) Keeper of the royal park of *Artaxerxes I, king of Persia (Neh. 2:8).

BIBLIOGRAPHY: J.W. Rothstein and J. Haenel, *Kommentar zum ersten Buch der Chronik* (1927), iii, 313ff., 345ff.; Albright, Arch Rel, 126ff.; de Vaux, Anc Isr, 382–5, 389, 392; S. Mowinckel, *The Psalms in Israel's Worship*, 2 (1962), 95ff.; EM, s.v. **ADD. BIBLIOGRAPHY:** S. Japhet, *I & II Chronicles* (1993), 294–96. AGADDAH: Ginzberg, *Legends*, 3, 462; 6, 105.

ASAPH HA-ROFE (i.e., Asaph the physician; also known as **Asaph ha-Yehudi**, **Rabbenu Asaph**, **Asaph ben Berechiah**, **Asaph ha-Yarhoni**; sixth century), physician who gave his name to a Hebrew book on medicine, *Sefer Asaf ha-Rofe*, written somewhere in the Middle East. As yet unpublished, it is extant in 16 manuscripts, some complete; it constitutes a source of information on ancient customs and Jewish medical ethics as well as of ancient Jewish remedies and Hebrew, Aramaic, Persian, Latin, and Greek medical terminology. Excerpts from Greek medical books, some of which have been lost and are not known from any other sources, appear in Hebrew in this book. The most complete manuscripts are in Munich, Oxford, Brit. Museum London, Florence, and Paris. The book was not written by Asaph himself, but by his disciples. They mention, as teachers, R. Johanan b. Zavda and R. Judah ha-Yarḥoni, as well as Asaph. Some sections of the book are very old, though others were written or translated from other languages as late as the seventh until the tenth century. The antiquity of the work is apparent from its style, similar to that of the older Midrashim, from its use of Persian (rather than Arabic) synonyms, and from the mention of weights current in Palestine during the talmudic period. The many sentences in the book which begin "And I shall teach you" indicate that its contents had, at one time, constituted oral medical teaching. Asaph's close connection with Babylonia, the cradle of astrology, is indicated by the surname Yarḥoni (i.e., one versed in the lunar calendar, or an astronomer) attributed to him, as well as by the nature of some of his medicaments and names of the scholars referred to as authorities. These facts denote that he lived somewhere between Upper Galilee and Babylonia. Since the book contains no indication of the influence of Arabic medicine and mentions pagan witch doctors, it can be assumed that Asaph lived before the Arab conquest of the Middle East.

Several early writers make direct or indirect reference to Asaph. The tenth-century grammarian, R. Judah *Ibn Quraysh, apparently refers to *Sefer Asaf* when he mentions a book of remedies bearing Aramaic names. In the commentary on *Tohorot*, attributed to *Hai Gaon, Asaph is mentioned by name. Al-Razi also mentions him, and in the Latin translation (1279) of his ninth- or tenth-century book, Asaph the Jew – "Judaeus" – is included among the famous medical authors. Ibn al-Gezzar (tenth century), a disciple of Isaac *Israeli, mentions Asaph b. Berechiah in his book *Ẓeidah li-Derakhim* and in its Greek translation, Asaph is referred to as "Ἀσιψ ὑιὸς Ιρακιου" *Naḥmanides refers to Asaph by name in *Sha'ar ha-Gemul*. *Sefer ha-Refu'ot shel Shem b. No'aḥ* quoted by R. *Solomon b. Jeroham (920) is apparently *Sefer Asaf ha-Rofe* which mentions Shem in its introduction. The same applies to *Sefer ha-Refu'ot* ("Book of Remedies") mentioned by Rashi (on Judges 15:5) and by *Nathan b. Jehiel of Rome, author of the *Arukh* (s.v. *vatan* which is a sinew mentioned in *Sefer ha-Refu'ot*).

In the introduction to the book, the editor refers to the pillars of medical science Hippocrates, Dioscorides, and Galen, and apparently considers their contemporary Asaph as their equal, referring to him as "the Jew." Asaph translated these Greek sources into idiomatic Hebrew and added commentaries. The book includes a Hebrew translation of the *Aphorisms* of Hippocrates with a short commentary on the first chapter entitled "*Ha-Midrash*." It notes the basic rules of medical science during the classical and medieval period. This is the first known Hebrew translation and commentary of any Greek medical work. There is also information derived from the lost *Pharmaceutics* of Hippocrates. Foremost among Hippocrates' writings which served Asaph as a model was the famous oath, in which he made basic changes. Although Asaph's medical teachings are fundamentally Hippocratic, they are also influenced by Rufus of Ephesus, Dioscorides, and to a lesser extent, Galen. The Greek influence is especially manifest in Asaph's theories on the nature of water and the Mediterranean climate and in his instructions on healing the poor. In anatomy, Asaph retains early Hebrew medical tradition and terminology. Blood vessels are called *gidim* ("sinews"), *mesillot meforadot* ("separate paths"), *te'alot* ("channels"); limbs are called *maḥlekot ha-guf* ("body parts"); and *ḥadrei ha-mo'aḥ* ("chambers of the brain") are discussed.

According to Asaph, the heart is the seat of the soul. The movement of the blood is explained as follows: "The pulsations of the blood vessels (the pulse) derive from the animating spirit; they originate from the heart, travel to the farthest extremities of the body, from which they return to the heart like water propelled by the wind…." Specific locations are assigned to the *sekhel* ("intellect"), *binah* ("understanding"), *da'at* ("knowledge"), and the *yeẓer* ("will"). "The spirit (*ru'aḥ*) resides in the head; understanding, in the heart; and fear, in the hidden recesses of the body." Asaph asserts that "melancholy is spiritual, not corporeal." He gives the number of bones (*evarim*) from the Talmud (Oho. 1:8; Mak. 23b) as 248, but adds 365 as the number of sinews corresponding to the days of the lunar year. The bones are fed by their marrow. From the Talmud, Asaph accepts the legend of the existence of an imperishable bone – the *luz* ("the nut of the spinal column"; *os resurrectionis*). He adopts the talmudic view that the embryo is completely shaped in its mother's womb 40 days after conception. The section "On the Influence of Diet" is based on Hippocrates, but Asaph devotes greater length to the various foods, drawing on the sayings of Jewish sages as well as on popular wisdom. He mentions only the meat of animals allowed under Jewish law. Asaph generally bases his treatment of illnesses on that of Hippocrates, though his is more comprehensive and is sometimes based on different points of view. He was the first medical writer to recognize the possibility of a hereditary factor in certain diseases.

Asaph's approach to pathology follows the theory of the four humors. Disease, according to this theory, involves a disturbance of the correct blending of the four elements (earth, air, fire, water), and of the four primary qualities (dryness, moisture, cold, heat) in the body. He also deals with prognosis, diagnosis, hygiene, and pharmacology. His rules for hygiene and diet in many cases parallel those of the Talmud. Asaph seeks primarily to prevent disease through a detailed and exact regimen which calls for physical exercise, baths, ointments, massage, sunshine, fresh air, clean water, various beverages, proper choice of foods, rules for sexual intercourse, cupping, blood-letting, and correct breathing. Most of his prescriptions are borrowed from the Greeks, but he also lists formulae from Babylonia, Persia, India, and Egypt; popular remedies from Ethiopia and Sudan; and ancient Hebrew medicaments which Asaph claims were used by *Samuel Yarḥinai and date back to "the days of the Judges, before a king ruled in Israel." Medicines took the forms of liquids, tablets, pills, gargles, eye-, ear-, and nose-drops, incense, ointment, suppositories, enemas, unguents, and oil-perfumes.

Asaph was deeply religious and tried to harmonize his faith and science. He believed that many diseases come as divine retribution for sins and that sincere prayer, together with repentance and charity, are important factors in healing. He saw the objective of the Bible's prohibitions of certain foods and in the distinction between clean and unclean animals, as the prevention of disease. He often emphasized that God is the only true healer and that physicians' first duties are to fear God and to practice virtue. Asaph's teachings reflect his scrupulous medical ethics. He vigorously attacked venality in physicians, bound his students to treat the poor without charge, and listed medicines easily procured or prepared at minimum cost. He addressed himself only to the well-trained professional physician and sharply censured quacks and amateurs who discredit true medicine. Asaph and his colleague, R. Johanan b. Zavda, required of the students whom they qualified as physicians a one-thousand word oath which evidenced the high ethical standards demanded: "… Take heed that ye kill not any man with the sap of a root; and ye shall not dispense a potion to a woman with a child by adultery to cause her to miscarry; and ye shall not lust after beautiful women to commit adultery with them; and ye shall not disclose secrets confided unto you…. Be strong and let not your hands slacken, for there is a reward for your labors. God is with you when ye are with Him. If ye will keep His covenant and walk in His statutes to cleave unto them, ye shall be as saints in the sight of all men and they shall say: 'Happy is the people that is in such a case; happy is that people whose God is the Lord.' … Ye shall not cause the shedding of blood by any manner of medical treatment. Take heed that ye do not cause malady to any man; and ye shall not cause any man injury by hastening to cut through flesh and blood with an iron instrument, or by branding, but shall first observe twice and thrice and only then shall ye give your counsel…."

An Israeli government hospital in Sarafand is named after Asaph ha-Rofe.

BIBLIOGRAPHY: H. Friedenwald, *Jews and Medicine*, 1 (1944), 147–8; S. Muntner, *Mavo le-Sefer Asaf ha-Rofe* (1957); idem, in: *Ha-Rofe ha-Ivri*, 20 (1947), 107–14; idem, in: S.R. Kagan (ed.), *Abraham Levinson Anniversary Volume* (1949), 247ff.; idem, in: *Bulletin of the History of Medicine*, 25 (1951), 101–31; S. Muntner and F. Rosner, in: *Journal of the American Medical Association*, 205 (1968), 912–13; L. Venetianer, *Asaf Judaeus*, 3 vols. (Ger., 1915–17).

[Suessmann Muntner]

ASARAMEL, word of doubtful meaning used in the description of *Simeon the Hasmonean's appointment as high priest and governor of the Jews in I Maccabees 14:27. It is stated there that these offices were conferred on Simeon the high priest ἐν ἀσαραμέλ. The meaning of the word ἀσαραμέλ has given rise to considerable speculation. Some consider it as a title and others as a place. Those who suggest that it is a title regard it as a transliteration of *sar am El* "a prince of the people of God" (Grimm and Kautsch) or, as the Syrian version has it *sar El* (Osterley). This interpretation is doubtful, however, since the name of God does not otherwise appear in I Maccabees, nor do they explain the preceding word ἐν. The suggestion of Geiger *aẓeret am El* ("the courtyard of the people of God") or the similar one of Ewald *ḥaẓar am El* meets this latter point but leaves the former unanswered. Schalit's emendation ἀσαραμέλ ἀσαρά μεγάλε ("in the great court") meets both difficulties and is the equivalent of the "*ha-azarah ha-Gedolah*" mentioned in II Chronicles 4:9.

BIBLIOGRAPHY: A. Schalit, *Koenig Herodes* (1969), 781–7; M. Stern, *Te'udot le-Mered ha-Ḥashmona'im* (1965), 134; Zeitlin, in: I Macc., ed. Dropsie College (1950), 44, 227, 248.

[Isaiah Gafni]

ASCAMA (pl. **Ascamot**), the normal transliteration among the Sephardim of Northern Europe (London, Amsterdam, etc.) of the Hebrew *haskamah*. The term was applied especially to the laws governing the internal organization and administration of the communities. The *Ascamot* of the Sephardi communities of London were drawn up in Portuguese in 1664 and translated into English only in the 19th century. The Reform controversy in London in 1840 revolved around *Ascama* No. 1 forbidding the establishment of a second synagogue. In the Ashkenazi communities the term **takkanot* was used to denote similar internal laws.

BIBLIOGRAPHY: A.M. Hyamson, *Sephardim of England* (1951[2]), index; L.D. Barnett, *El Livro de los Acuerdos* (1931).

ASCARELLI, DEVORA (16th century), Italian writer. Ascarelli may have been the first Jewish woman whose writings were published. Her book, containing translations of liturgical selections into Italian, as well as her own poetry in Italian, is the only source of information about her. According to the book's dedication, Devora and her husband, Joseph Ascarelli, lived in Rome; the family is associated with exiles from Spain and the leadership of the Catalan community of Rome. Ascarelli's book is usually identified by the title of its first selection, *L'abitacolo degli Oranti* or *Ma'on ha-Sho'alim*, "The Abode of the Supplicants," a translation into rhymed Italian of sections of a Hebrew liturgical poem. Prose translations include *Benedici il Signore o anima mia*, or *Barekhi Nafshi*, a *tokheḥah* prayer in the Roman rite by Rabbenu Baḥya ben Joseph the Pious (11th century) of Saragossa; *La Grande Confessione* by Rabbenu Nissim, identified as the head of the Babylonian Academy; and an *avodah* prayer for the Sephardi Yom Kippur service. The book also contains two of Ascarelli's sonnets, *Il Ritratto di Susanna*, "The Picture of Susannah," based on the apocryphal book *Susannah and the Elders, and *Quanto e' in me di Celeste*, "Whatever in me is of Heaven." The liturgical pieces appear both in Hebrew and Italian; they were apparently intended for liturgical use on Yom Kippur. The contents of the 31-page *L'abitacolo Degli Oranti* were probably completed between 1537 and 1540; the book was published in Venice in 1601, and with some differences in 1609; excerpts appear in A. Pesaro, "Alle Donne celebri Israelite," in *Il Vessilio Israelitico*, 29 (1881), 34–37 and 67–68 (reprinted with many modifications by Pellegrino Ascarelli, *Debora Ascarelli Poetessa*, Rome, 1925). Modern translations of Ascarelli's poems by Vladimir Rus appear in Sondra Henry and Emily Taitz, *Written Out of History: A Hidden Legacy of Jewish Women Revealed Through Their Writing And Letters* (1978), 130–31.

[Howard Tzvi Adelman (2nd ed.)]

ASCARELLI, TULLIO (1903–1959), Italian jurist, whose father, Attilio, was a scholar in forensic medicine. At the age of 23, Tullio Ascarelli was appointed to the chair of commercial law at the University of Ferrara and later taught at Cagliari, Catania, Parma, and Padua universities. Dismissed following Italy's adoption of racial laws in 1938, he left the country and, after a short period of teaching at the London School of Economics and at the Sorbonne, went to Brazil to teach at the University of São Paolo. He also served as juridical counselor to the Brazilian government. Returning to Italy after World War II, Ascarelli taught commercial law at the University of Bologna, and industrial law at the University of Rome. Shortly before his death he was appointed to the chair of commercial law at Rome. Author of essays on commercial, civil, maritime, and company law (collected in miscellaneous volumes published in 1949, 1952, and 1960), he also wrote basic works on commercial law subjects, among them *La moneta* (1928); *Il concetto di titolo di credito* (1932); and *Teoria della concorrenza e dei beni immateriali* (1960).

BIBLIOGRAPHY: *Dizionario Biografico degli Italiani*, 4 (1962), 371–2 (includes bibliography); Roth, Italy, index; Milano, Italia, 385.

[Giorgio Romano]

ASCETICISM. Rigorous abstention from any form of self-indulgence which is based on the belief that renunciation of the desires of the flesh and self-mortification can bring man to a high spiritual state. Asceticism never occupied an important place in the Jewish religion. Judaism did not believe that the freedom of man's soul could be won only by the subjugation of the flesh, a belief which was central in religions based upon anthropological dualism. Apart from the *Nazirites and the *Rechabites who constituted special groups, and the mortification practiced by Ezekiel (4:4–15) which was apparently to induce a vision, the only ascetic practice mentioned as of universal application is fasting which is called in the Bible "affliction of the soul" (Lev. 23:27; Isa. 58:3). In addition to the *Day of Atonement numerous fasts are mentioned as having been instituted on special occasions (see: *Fasting) but they are mostly expressions of remorse, sadness, and grief or acts to aid concentration in prayer rather than religious practices in their own right. The prophets emphasize over and over again the fact that fasting and mortification of the body by themselves do not please God. They are justified only if they help change man's moral actions.

The rabbis went even further; they consider asceticism and privation as a sin against the will of God, that people should enjoy the gift of life. Hillel considered taking care of and bathing the body a religious duty (Lev. R. 34:3). In practice, however, there were many ascetics among Jews during the period of the Second Temple. Y.F. Baer maintains (*Yisrael ba-Ammim* (1955), 22) that during this and the preceding period Judaism possessed a definite ascetic character and furthermore, the teachings of the first *tannaim* also leaned toward asceticism. This doctrine, though later rejected by the *halakhah*, according to him left its permanent traces in all the realms of *halakhah* and *aggadah* and in all spheres of Jewish life, and in it he sees the origin of the ascetic and monastic elements so prevalent in Christianity. Most other scholars disagree with this view. On the contrary Christian theologians (see e.g., Bousset-Gressman, *Die Religion des Judentums in spaethellenistischen Zeitalter* (1966), 428–29) saw in the fact that there is so little emphasis on asceticism in Judaism proof of the inferior religious quality of Judaism as compared with Christianity. This very point was used by Jewish apologists (e.g., M. Lazarus, *Die Ethik des Judenthums*, 1 (1904^2), 272–80) to demonstrate the higher standards of the Jewish religion. The entire subject of the attitude of early rabbinic Judaism to asceticism is summed up against its historical background, in a study by E.E. Urbach (*Y. Baer Jubilee Volume* (1960), 48–68). It maintains that the principal motive for Hellenistic asceticism in all its various manifestations, also found in Philo, does not occur in the Talmud, namely: the antithesis between the body and the soul, between the flesh and the spirit. The motivations for asceticism, according to Urbach, are fear of sin and a strong attraction to the sanctuary and sacrifices. Such cases of asceticism are included within the context of the *halakhah* dealing as it does with practical matters of the world. The heroic religious deeds of the *Ḥasidim during the rule of *Antiochus Epiphanes left no impression in this respect and did not give rise to ascetic ideals. Only the destruction of the Second Temple and the serious religious problems that arose with the cessation of the daily sacrifices gave rise to an ascetic movement and also endowed the fasts with a new significance. The scholars and leaders of that generation spared no effort to deprive this movement of its extremist character. The generation of *Jabneh witnessed its decline, but during the period of persecution and forced conversions that followed the movement spread and grew strong. The Jewish doctrine of **kiddush ha-Shem* crystallized at that time and the problems of theodicy were more deeply considered. Acts of asceticism and the acceptance of suffering were numerous, as evidenced by the fate of many of the sages in Ereẓ Israel and Babylonia. But even in the cases of these scholars, two phenomena generally typical of asceticism were missing: unusual acts of self-denial contradicting human nature, like total sexual deprivation or celibacy, and the establishment of a special caste and closed society of ascetics. The *Essenes and similar Jewish sects practiced austerity as conditional for a life of justice and purity; they did not however laud asceticism as a value in its own right. Instances of asceticism in the Talmud and the Midrashim are, according to Urbach, not remnants of a fanatical ascetic doctrine which degenerated, but the result of definite events in the history of the Jewish people at that time.

Motivations

In addition to historical circumstances, there are also personal motivations for asceticism within Judaism. Abstinence from pleasures in itself is not considered a way of religious worship of God. The characteristic of asceticism when found among the rabbis is not the pains and privations to which a man subjects himself, but the end which he proposes to achieve. Abstinence may be self-imposed as a penance for a mortal sin. In the Testament of the Twelve Patriarchs it is stated that for seven years Reuben drank no wine or other liquor, no flesh passed his lips, and he ate no appetizing food, but continued mourning over his great sin. In the fear of the Lord, Simeon afflicted his soul with fasting for two years for his hatred of Joseph. Judah, in repentance for his sin with Tamar, until his old age took neither wine nor flesh and saw no pleasure. That fasting has an expiatory value is distinctly expressed in the Bible (Isa. 58:3) as well as in the Psalms of Solomon (3:8–9): the righteous man continually investigates his household to remove the guilt incurred by transgression. He makes atonement for inadvertent sins by fasting, and afflicts his soul. R. Sheshet, a Babylonian *amora* of the third century, would have his fasting received as a substitute for sacrifice. When he was fasting he used to pray: "Lord of the Universe, Thou knowest that, while the Temple stood, if a man sinned he brought a sacrifice and they offered only the fat and the blood, and atonement was made for him. And now I have sat in fasting, and my fat and blood have been diminished; may it be Thy will that this diminution of my fat and blood be as though I had offered a sacrifice upon Thine altar, and be Thou gracious unto me" (Ber. 17a). It is perhaps in this aspect that fasting is associated with almsgiving (Ber. 6b; cf. Tob. 12:8).

The regulations of mourning do not prescribe fasting or other afflictions though in the interval between the death and the burial (except on Sabbath) the mourners must abstain from flesh and wine (MK 23b). Yet there is an aspect of fasting which is connected with the mourning for a national calamity, like the fast of the Ninth of Av. Fasting is always a potent auxiliary of prayer. "If a man prays and is not answered, he should fast, as it is written (Ps. 20:2) 'The Lord will answer thee in the day of distress'" (TJ, Ber. 4:3, 8a). Fasting is also mentioned as a preparation for revelation (Dan. 9:3, 20–22; 10:2 ff.; cf. Yoma 4b).

The destruction of the Temple in 70 C.E., the disastrous results of the widespread rising under Trajan, and the final catastrophe of the Bar Kokhba War, revived the temper in which the four memorial fasts in Zechariah had been kept (Zech. 7:3–5; 8:19). Private fasting also became more frequent. After the destruction of the Temple some altogether gave up eating meat and drinking wine, because the daily sacrifice and libation had ceased; some of the leading rabbis however disapproved their abstinence. R. *Joshua b. Hananiah pointed out to them that their logic would carry them much farther; they could not eat figs and grapes because the first fruits could no longer be brought, nor bread because there were no more "two loaves" and shewbread, and not drink water because there was no water libation at Tabernacles (Tosef., Sot. 15:11–12).

After the Bar Kokhba War R. Ishmael b. Elisha said: "From the day when the Temple was destroyed we should by right make a decree binding upon ourselves not to eat flesh nor drink wine, but it is a principle not to impose on the community a decree to which the majority of the community cannot adhere (Hor. 3b; Av. Zar. 36a). And from the triumph of the heathen empire which imposes upon us dire and cruel edicts and stops the study of the Law and fulfillment of the commandments, and does not let us circumcise our sons, we should by right make a decree for ourselves not to take a wife or beget sons, so that the seed of Abraham might come to its end in this way. Such a decree, however, would not be observed and the deliberate violation of it would be worse than marrying without seeing anything wrong in it" (BB 60b; cf. Shab 148b; Beẓah 30a).

Whether abstinence was a result of a national or a personal motivation, the rabbis disapproved of it. A vow of abstinence is an iron collar (such as is worn by prisoners) about a man's neck and one who imposes on himself a vow is like one who should find such a collar lying loose and stick his own head into it. Or, a man who takes a vow is like one who builds an illegal altar (*bamah*), and if he fulfills it, like one who sacrifices on such an altar (Ned. 22a). R. Isaac said: "Are not the things prohibited you in the Law enough for you that you want to prohibit yourself other things?" An ingenious interpretation of Numbers 6:11 discovers that the Nazirite had to make atonement by sacrifice for having sinned against his own soul by making himself miserable by abstaining from wine. Such a man is called (in the text) a sinner, and, a fortiori, if one who has denied himself the enjoyment of nothing more than wine is called a sinner, how much more one who denies himself the enjoyment of everything (Ta'an. 11a). In this spirit is also the saying of Rav: A man will have to give account on the judgment day of every good permissible thing which he might have enjoyed and did not (TJ, Kid. 4:12, 66d). For an apt summing up of this principle see Maimonides' *Mishneh Torah* (De'ot 3:1).

[Pinchas Hacohen Peli]

Sectarian Asceticism

In the postbiblical period the ascetic tradition, exemplified before the Exile in the Nazirites, Rechabites, etc., persisted as a "wilderness" tradition. From time to time, especially when conditions in the main centers of population seemed to become religiously or otherwise unbearable, pious Israelites withdrew to the wilderness to resume a more ascetic way of life. Such were the "many who were seeking righteousness and justice" who went down to the wilderness of Judea with their families and cattle to escape the intolerable conditions imposed by Antiochus Epiphanes but were pursued by the king's officers and massacred on the Sabbath (I Macc. 2:29–38). Similar movements in the Herodian period are reflected in apocalyptic works like the Assumption of *Moses, where a levite named Taxo and his seven sons fast for three days and then take up residence in a cave, ready to die there sooner than transgress God's Law (9:1–7), or the Martyrdom of Isaiah, where Isaiah is followed to his desert retreat by his disciples clothed in garments of hair (2:7–11).

The best-known instances of asceticism in the later years of the Second Temple are the *Qumran sect, the *Essenes, and the *Therapeutae. The first of these (c. 130 B.C.E.–70 C.E.), of which the *Zadokites who migrated to the region of Damascus formed a part, is treated in the articles on the Book of the Covenant of *Damascus, the *Dead Sea Scrolls, and *Yaḥad*.

The evidence for the Essenes is not entirely consistent: on the one hand they were to be found in considerable numbers in every city (Jos., Wars, 2:124), while on the other hand they are described by Philo and Pliny the Elder (and indeed by Josephus himself) in terms which strongly suggest a desert community. The situation probably was that the fully initiated members of the various Essene orders lived a communal and ascetic life in the wilderness, while they had sympathizers or "associate members" in most of the cities of Palestine, and perhaps of the Diaspora too. The Essene group which Pliny describes (Nat. Hist. 5:17) lived on the west shore of the Dead Sea; its headquarters are nowadays widely identified with the ruined buildings at Qumran. The Essenes maintained themselves by manual labor and were punctilious in their religious observances, which included communal prayer, Bible study, and frugal meals. Full members were bound by such strict oaths that even one who was expelled from the order could not bring himself to break them, and was liable to die of starvation in consequence. They had neither wives nor servants, although Josephus mentions one company of Essenes who, exceptionally, did marry for the sole purpose of begetting children (Wars 2:160f.).

The Therapeutae, of whom Philo speaks (Cont. 2ff.) immediately after his account of the Essenes, were a Jewish ascetic order comprising both men and women, living in the Egyptian desert on the landward side of Lake Mareotis, near Alexandria. Their designation is derived by Philo from the Greek verb *therapeuo*, but he is not sure whether it means primarily "healers" or "worshipers." If it is the former, it recalls a suggested derivation of "Essenes" from Aramaic *ʾāsyā* ("healer"). They lived in individual huts, giving themselves to contemplation, prayer, praise, and Bible study, in which they followed a traditional allegorical interpretation. Every seventh day they met in community to worship and eat. On other days they practiced extreme frugality in food (some even partaking only once a week), and even on the Sabbath their fare was as plain as possible. The weekly meal, according to Philo, was regarded as the eating of the showbread – which suggests a priestly character for their order. A noteworthy feature of their worship was their choral singing, which on the Sabbath eve followed their meal and lasted till dawn. What relation, if any, they bore to the Essenes or any other ascetic group in Israel is uncertain.

John the Baptist is not called an ascetic by Josephus (Ant., 18:116–9), but he is so described in the Gospel tradition. According to Mark (1:6) he wore camel's hair, girt with a leather belt, and lived on locusts and wild honey; according to Q (the non-Markan material common to Matthew and Luke) he ate no bread and drank no wine (Luke 7:33; cf. Matt. 11:18), which may be compared with what is said of the Rechabites in Jeremiah 35:6–10. The material special to Luke suggests rather that John was a lifelong Nazirite (Luke 1:15): he grows to manhood in the desert (1:80) and in his preaching urges his hearers to share their clothes and food with the destitute (3:11). Bannus, another ascetic of the wilderness with whom

Josephus spent some time (c. 55 C.E.), clothed himself with leaves or bark, ate food which grew naturally, and practiced frequent purifying ablutions, both by day and by night (Life, 11–12). The account in the Slavonic Josephus (between Wars 2:110 and 111) of a wild man of the woods who had a confrontation with Archelaus, ethnarch of Judea, seems to be based in part on the portrayals of John the Baptist and Bannus. In another Slavonic addition (after Wars, 2:168) John the Baptist avoids not only bread and wine but also the flesh of animals; here may be traced some influence on the tradition from the Encratites (the second-century ascetic Christian sect who abstained from meat, wine, and marriage). Some forms of wilderness asceticism toward the end of the Second Temple period probably arise from the self-denial imposed on those engaged in a holy war (Deut. 20); this appears in some of the Qumran texts (see *War Scroll).

[Frederick Fyvie Bruce]

In Medieval Jewish Philosophy

Among medieval religious philosophers, the general line of the talmudic approach to asceticism is maintained.

The medieval philosophical approaches to asceticism may be characterized by three stages: (a) a moderate approach, affirming the value of family and social life in accordance with the Aristotelian "golden mean" (Nicomachean Ethics 2:1; see on Maimonides, below); (b) limited asceticism, recognizing the need to sustain the body; (c) absolute asceticism and withdrawal from family and social life. The medieval philosophers regarded these stages as corresponding to levels of perfection: the first, moderate stage is that of the common people and of the first steps on the path to wisdom; the second stage of limited asceticism, making do with the minimum required for continued physical existence, characterizes a more perfect class of people; those who reach the highest level of perfection practice extreme asceticism.

*Saadiah Gaon mentions in his *Book of Beliefs and Opinions* (treatise 10), among the various conceptions of the ideal life, the way of asceticism. He finds it unacceptable as a correct way of life, since, if it were practiced by everyone, it would lead to the end of man's existence on earth. This would be counter to the will of God that the world be peopled and built up by men, who should carry out His commandments in life in this world. Saadiah states that man is constituted by both body and spirit; hence, both must be attended to.

On the other hand, *Baḥya ibn Paquda in his *Duties of the Hearts* prescribes a measure of regular fasting and other ascetic regimens as indispensable for the achievement of ethical perfection (part 9). Solomon ibn *Gabirol, while not advocating asceticism directly, presents a doctrine compatible with Neoplatonic philosophy, from which a proponent of asceticism might derive considerable comfort. According to Gabirol, the soul is the human being, and it should be the aim of man's life to prepare the soul for union with the world of its element. Thus, man's physical appetites are to be held in reign by reason (*Tikkun Middot ha-Nefesh*, passim).

*Judah Halevi in his *Kuzari* describes the righteous person as one who gives every part of his personality its due, thus decidedly protesting against the notion that inflicting mortifications on one's body is itself a virtuous act. "Our religion," says Halevi, "is divided among fear, love, and joy, by each of which one can approach God. Your contrition on a fast day is not more acceptable to Him than your joy on the Sabbath and holy days, if it is the outcome of a devout heart" (2:50; cf. 3:1ff.).

On the other hand, Halevi describes the perfect *ḥasid* as yearning for absolute asceticism and abandonment of social and family life, like the biblical *Enoch and *Elijah (3:1). For Halevi, then, the ideal of extreme asceticism is not desirable in our day because prophecy is no longer possible.

The most pronounced support for asceticism among the medieval philosophers came from *Abraham b. Ḥiyya, who actually advocates sexual abstinence as the ideal (*Meditation of the Sad Soul*, Eng. tr. (1969), 133). However, this view is strongly condemned in the treatise *Iggeret ha-Kodesh*, attributed to *Naḥmanides, where in a mystical vein sexual intercourse is exalted, when motivated by sacred intentions, as a lofty activity of men (see especially ch. 2).

*Maimonides' attitude is consistent with his philosophy of the "middle path." His emphasis on a contemplative, virtuous life naturally has as its corollary a depreciation of terrestrial pleasures; yet, he warns against the other extreme of complete abstinence. In his discussion of the topic in his introduction to the tractate *Avot* (4th chapter) and in his *Mishneh Torah* (*De'ot*, 3), he stresses that the Torah does not wish man to deprive himself of pleasures. God is not the enemy of man's body. The way of the golden mean calls for a conduct of life equidistant from the two extremes of overindulgence and self-deprivation.

While certain individuals may at certain times derive benefit for their moral constitution from a policy of extreme self-deprivation, this should not be made a general program of life. Such deprivation is like certain medicines that may be beneficial for certain sicknesses, but will harm the normal healthy person. Maimonides' interpretation in his introduction to *Avot* of Numbers 6:1, that the Nazirite must offer a sacrifice, because by refraining from such pleasures as wine he "sinned against his [own] soul," was opposed by Naḥmanides, who argued to the contrary that the Nazirite's sacrifice reflects atonement for leaving the higher sanctity of being a Nazirite in favor of returning to ordinary life. The dispute between them reflects talmudic discussions, with Naḥmanides following the opinion of Rabbi Eleazar (in *Ta'anit* 11a) and Maimonides following the view of the rabbis in *Nedarim* 10a.

In any event, in his *Guide for the Perplexed* Maimonides adopts a more pro-ascetic view and hints that extreme asceticism is the goal of such perfect persons as the prophets, and he accepts Aristotle's view that the sense of touch is the most repugnant of all the external senses, and accordingly regards sexual relations negatively.

*Abraham b. Moses b. Maimon expressed a positive attitude toward asceticism in his Arabic work *Kifāyat al-ʿĀbidīn* ("Comprehensive Guide for the Servants of God," Heb. ed. 1965), a philosophy reminiscent of Sufi views.

The ambivalent attitude towards asceticism, on the one hand rejecting it as the recommended moral way for the masses and on the other hand presenting it as an ideal of perfection, continued to permeate medieval Jewish thought. The radical rationalism of the 13th–15th centuries regarded conjunction with the Active Intellect – the beatitude sought by the philosopher – as attainable only after death. For the person who has reached perfection, matter becomes superfluous. Such rationalism led to idealizing extreme asceticism.

Extreme asceticism also came to be idealized as a repressed ideal of the religious Jew in other non-philosophical conceptions of human perfection, in the Kabbalah and in 12th–13th century German Ḥasidism (*Ḥasidut Ashkenaz*), which posit utter self-nullification and assimilation into the divine world.

Mystical tendencies towards asceticism took several forms. First, the mystical way leads to conjunction or communion (*devekut*) with the divine, and in some cases even to union with the divine world. Such views frequently result in an ascetic ethos. Second, the theurgic interest in Kabbalah focuses on repairing (*tikkun*) the divine world, with the result that the terrestrial dimension of physical life is rendered marginal. Third, certain trends, such as German Ḥasidism, developed a series of ascetic techniques in order to effect what was called a "counterbalance of repentance" (*teshuvat ha-mishkal*), namely, in order to attain perfection the penitent had to undergo suffering which would counterbalance his prior sinful pleasure. On the other hand, the movement's tendency towards asceticism was opposed by their concern for the sanctity of sex and for theurgic practices. Mystical attitudes towards asceticism thus remained mixed and complex.

Perhaps Moses Ḥayyim *Luzzatto best summarized the prevalent Jewish attitude toward asceticism. In *Mesillat Yesharim* (end of chapter 13) he explains that, while it is proper for a person to limit his superfluous enjoyments to guard against debasement of his character, it is wrong and sinful to deprive oneself of enjoyments in a manner that will cause one needless suffering and be detrimental to one's bodily and spiritual health.

Thus, while a moderate and balanced morality always dominated Jewish thought, the ascetic motif was never lacking.

[Jacob Haberman / Dov Schwartz (2nd ed.)]

Women and Asceticism

Biblical legislation places limits on ascetic practices women might take upon themselves. According to Numbers 30:4–17, a woman's vows and self-imposed obligations were valid only if her father or guardian, in the case of a minor, or husband, in the case of a married woman, did not object when he learned about them. The vows and self-imposed deprivations of a widow or divorced woman, however, were considered binding.

Issues connected with women's self-imposed ascetic vows are discussed in the Talmud (TB Ned. 81a–84a), including abstention from food, from bathing, from wearing certain clothes, and most importantly, from cohabitation and sexual relations. Following the model of biblical legislation, the rabbis affirmed that the male guardian or husband has the prerogative to annul all such vows as soon as he hears of them; however, if he delays significantly, he cannot annul them later. Generally, the rabbis disapproved of women who assumed obligations requiring extremes of self-denial and expressed particular disapproval of women who devoted themselves to excessive prayer and unusual degrees of fasting. Such a woman would be derelict in her central religious obligation, her domestic duties to her husband and family. Thus, TB *Sotah* 22a understands the "female 'pharisee' … who brings destruction upon the world" in R. Joshua's statement in *Sotah* 3:4, as "a maiden who gives herself up to prayer." In the parallel passage in TJ, the disapproval is extended to a woman "who gives herself up to fasting."

While celibacy and monastic living allowed a significant number of medieval Christian women, and to a certain extent, also, some Muslim women, to cross gender boundaries, engage in a variety of ascetic spiritual exercises, and secure a place alongside men as scholars, saints, and mystics, rabbinic insistence on universal marriage from early adolescence ruled out such life alternatives for medieval and early modern Jewish women. The effort to distance women from asceticism is also indicative of their absence in Jewish mystical life, where such practices were typical of the male elite.

The popular conception that East European Ḥasidism enabled a significant number of women to become mystical leaders with permitted access to the ascetic mortifications usually reserved for male leaders has been shown to be a 20th-century historiographical myth. It was only within the anti-nomian practices of the Shabbatean movement that gender barriers were removed sufficiently to allow for female participation in the spiritualization of physical existence and the advent of a new messianic reality.

[Judith R. Baskin (2nd ed.)]

BIBLIOGRAPHY: NON-TALMUDIC: M. Black, *The Scrolls and Christian Origins* (1961); H. Sérouya, *Les Esséniens* (1959); M. Simon, *Jewish Sects at the Time of Jesus* (1967); J. Steinmann, *St. John the Baptist and the Desert Tradition* (1958); J. Thomas, *Le mouvement baptiste en Palestine et Syrie* (1935). **ADD. BIBLIOGRAPHY:** RABBINIC: J. Baskin, *Midrashic Women: Formations of the Feminine in Rabbinic Literature* (2002); D. Boyarin, *Carnal Israel: Reading Sex in Talmudic Culture* (1993); E. Diamond, "Hunger Artists and Householders: The Tension between Asceticism and Family Responsibility among Jewish Pietists in Late Antiquity," in: *Union Seminary Quarterly Review*, 48 (1996), 28–47; S.D. Fraade, "Ascetical Aspects of Ancient Judaism," in: A. Green (ed.), *Jewish Spirituality* (1986), 253–88. MEDIEVAL: Guttmann, Philosophies, index; G. Vajda, *La théologie ascétique de Bahya ibn Paquda* (1947). **ADD. BIBLIOGRAPHY:** Kreisel, "Ascetism in the Thought of Bahya and Maimonides," *Da'at*, 21 (1988), V–XIII; A. Lazaroff, "Bahya's Ascetism against its Rabbinic and Islamic Background," JJS, 21 (1970), 11–38; S. Schwarzschild, "Moral Radicalism and Middlingness in the Ethics of Maimonides," in M. Kellner (ed.), *The Pursuit of the Ideal*, Albany (1990), 137–160. **ADD. BIBLIOGRAPHY:** D. Schwartz, "The Tension Between Moderate Ethics and Ascetic Ethics in Medieval Jewish Philosophy" (Heb.), in: D. Stitman and A. Sagi (eds.), *Between Religion and Ethics* (1993), 186–208. **ADD. BIBLIOGRAPHY:** WOMEN: A. Rapoport-Albert, "On Women in Hasidism, S.A. Horodecky and the Maid of Ludmir Tradition," in: A. Rapoport-Albert and S.J. Zipperstein (eds.), *Jewish History. Essays in Honour of Chimen Abramsky* (1988); idem, *Female Bodies, Male Souls: Asceticism and Gender in the Jewish Tradition* (2006).

ASCH, SHOLEM (1880–1957), Yiddish novelist and dramatist. Born in Kutno, Poland, to parents from scholarly Orthodox families, he was educated in traditional Jewish schools until the age of 17. He began to learn German with the aid of Moses Mendelssohn's Hebrew-alphabet German translation of the Psalms, later learning the Roman alphabet and immersing himself in German classics and Hebrew Haskalah literature. His parents' subsequent suspicions of heresy led him to move to the home of relatives in a Polish village, where he taught the children Torah. He later earned his living by writing letters for illiterate people in the town of Włocławek. Influenced by Hebrew, Yiddish, Russian, Polish, and German, Asch tried his hand at literary composition and, in 1900, took his first literary efforts (in Hebrew) to Warsaw where I.L. *Peretz advised him to concentrate on Yiddish. His early work is pervaded with the experiences of his youth and the influence of A. *Reisen and H.D. *Nomberg, his Warsaw roommates. A turning point in his life was his meeting with the Polish-Jewish writer, M.M. Shapiro, whose daughter Mathilde he married in 1900. His material needs provided for, Asch's literary achievements flourished correspondingly. In 1900 he published a Yiddish story, "Moyshele," and three years later his first book, a collection of Yiddish sketches, *In a Shlekhter Tsayt* ("In an Evil Time," 1903). With *A Shtetl* ("A Town," published in *Fraynd*, 1904–5), Asch introduced a new tone into his own works and into Yiddish literature as a whole; the former gloomy portrayal of Jewish life gave way to an awareness of its warmth and geniality; the work was received enthusiastically by readers. From this period date Asch's first friendships with Polish writers, among them Eliza Orzeszkowa, Stefan Żeromski, Maria Dąbrowska, and above all Stanisław Witkiewicz. His first play *Tsurikgekumen* ("The Return," 1904) (also published as *Mitn Shtrom*, "With the Current," 1909) won him further recognition. The most important of his dramas was *Got fun Nekome* ("God of Vengeance," 1907). In his psychological and socio-nationalist dramas, Asch tried to liberate himself from the spell of the *shtetl*. The same tendency is felt in his first novel, *Meri* (*Mary*, 1913), depicting the 1905 Revolution from a Jewish perspective, and its sequel, *Der Veg tsu Zikh* ("The Way to Oneself," 1914), both of which deal with worldwide Jewish problems and which were written after Asch had traveled in Europe and made journeys to Palestine (1908, which resulted in a collection of sketches, *Ereẓ Israel*, 1911) and the United States (1910), about which he wrote *Der Landsman* ("The Countryman," 1911) and *Amerike*. In 1912 Asch moved to France, and in 1913 he published *Reb Shloyme Nogid*, reverting to the world of the *shtetl* while bringing to the topic a new maturity of outlook; no longer content with lyrical description, he now wished to make a positive statement about this society. The story became the artistic yardstick by which he measured all his subsequent works, few of which reached the required standard. The same year Asch published his biblical stories for children, *Mayselekh fun Khumesh* ("Tale from the Pentateuch," 1913). In 1914 Asch made his second trip to Palestine and moved to New York, where he wrote a play, *Undzer gloybn* ("Our Faith," 1914) and other narratives that appeared in the *Forverts*. In 1915 he helped to raise funds for Jewish war victims. During this creative period he also published the social novel *Motke Ganev* ("Motke the Thief," 1916), a tale of the underworld, and *Onkl Mozes* (1918), which displays greater narrative unity and coherence, the scene now being an Americanized version of the Polish *shtetl* which, no longer the theme for a patriarchal idyll, verges on comedy. He was still more successful with *Kiddush ha-Shem* ("Martyrdom," 1919), one of the earliest historical novels in modern Yiddish literature; it represents Jewish martyrdom in mid-17th-century Ukraine and Poland, although its immediate motivation was the Ukrainian pogroms of 1918–19. In the spring of 1919 he traveled in Europe for the American Jewish Relief Committee. In the following year he became an American citizen, and on the occasion of his 40th birthday, a committee headed by J.L. *Magnes was founded in New York which published Asch's collected works in 12 volumes, with an introduction by S. *Niger. Asch's second grand historical novel, the somewhat melodramatic *Di Kishufmakhern fun Kastilyen* ("The Witch of Castile," 1921), is in spirit a continuation of *Kiddush ha-Shem*, telling of a beautiful girl's resolute death for her faith, contrasting the everyday world of Jewish life with the elevated spirit of the Sabbath, and outer servitude with inner freedom.

In 1924 Asch returned to Warsaw and wrote a social novel, *Di muter* ("The Mother," 1925), one part of which is about Polish Jewry, the other about the United States; *Toyt Urteyl* ("Death Sentence," 1924); and *Khaym Lederers Tsurikkumen* ("Chaim Lederer's Return," 1927), whose hero belongs to the typically Aschian characters who yearn for an ideal and search for faith. After the Polish coup d'état of 1926, Asch published in Warsaw's *Haynt* an open letter to Marshal Józef Piłsudski, which stirred controversy in Jewish circles. In the monumental trilogy, *Farn Mabl* ("Before the Flood," transl. as *Three Cities*): *Peterburg* ("St. Petersburg," 1929), *Varshe* ("Warsaw," 1930), and *Moskve* ("Moscow," 1931), he provides a broad panorama of Jewish life in Russia before and during the Revolution. In 1932 Asch moved to Nice and in the following year was elected honorary president of the Yiddish PEN Club. In the same year, he was awarded the medal *Polonia Restituta* by the Polish government and was nominated for the Nobel Prize in literature. After the monumental *Farn Mabl*, Asch published the less ambitious *Gots Gefangene* ("God's Captives," 1933),

Der Tilim Yid (1934, trans. as *Salvation*), *Bam Opgrunt* ("The Precipice," 1937), a novel about the years of rampant inflation in Germany before Hitler's rise to power, and *Dos Gezang fun Tol* ("The Song of the Valley," 1938), a poetic depiction of settlers' lives in Palestine. In 1937 Asch again toured the United States to raise funds for European Jews and received an honorary doctorate from the Jewish Theological Seminary. After 1938 he again made his home in the U.S.

His next group of books comprises his christological trilogy, which deal with the founders of Christianity: *Der Man fun Notseres* (1939, trans. as *The Nazarene*), *The Apostle* (1943), and *Mary* (1949) (the last two published only in English). In their psychological content, they develop directly from *Der Tilim Yid*, while the subject matter is connected with that of some of Asch's early stories. They were enthusiastically received by the English, but not by the Yiddish, press. The *Forverts*, to which Asch had hitherto contributed regularly, not only refused to publish the work, but openly attacked the author for encouraging heresy and conversion by preaching Christianity. Only a very few critics discussed the literary merits of the books, most of the Jewish press following the *Forverts'* lead in attacking Asch. The result was an estrangement between Asch and Yiddish literature and Jewish social life. His critics claimed to discern the missionary element in all the writing of the subsequent dozen or so years: his American-Jewish novel *Ist River* ("East River," 1946), his collection of ghetto stories about the Nazi period, *Der Brenendiker Dorn* ("The Burning Bush," 1946), and *Moyshe* ("Moses," 1951). In 1954 *Grosman un Zun* (trans. as *Passage in the Night*) appeared, and in 1955 Asch turned to the prophet Isaiah in *Der Novi* ("The Prophet"). As all his works, they reveal a first-rate storyteller who clothed romantic idealism in a realistic style. He stressed the individuality of his characters as well as their national and social environment, their moral deliberations, and their religious strivings. Controversial, aggressive, and tireless in his search for new horizons, Asch, who began as the poet of the *shtetl*, nevertheless liberated Yiddish literature from these narrow confines. Deeply attached to the legacy of the Jewish past, which he enshrined in novels and dramas of aesthetic beauty and moral grandeur, he connected the Yiddish world to the mainstream of European and American culture, becoming the first Yiddish writer to enjoy a truly international vogue.

In 1956, Asch settled in Tel Aviv, and in the following year he suffered a fatal stroke while in London. In accordance with Asch's request, his house in Bat Yam was converted into a Sholem Asch Museum. Of his notable collections of Jewish art objects, the accumulation of a lifetime, a valuable part is in Los Angeles, while the bulk of his library, containing rare Yiddish books and manuscripts, including the originals of some of his own works, is at Yale University.

BIBLIOGRAPHY: E.H. Jeshurin, *Sholem Ash Bibliografye* (1958); A. Cahan, *Sholem Ashs Nayer Veg* (1941); S. Niger, *Dertseylers un Romanistn*, 1 (1946), 320–530; H. Lieberman, *The Christianity of Sholem Asch* (1953); LNYL, 1 (1956), 183–92; I. Paner, *Sholem Ash in Zayn Letster Heym* (1958); S. Rosenberg, *Sholem Ash fun der Noent* (1958); S. Niger, *Sholem Ash, Zayn Lebn, Zayne Verk* (1960); L. Nemoy, *Catalogue of Hebrew and Yiddish Manuscripts and Books from the Library of Sholem Asch* (1945); C. Madison, *Yiddish Literature* (1968), 221–61; Waxman, Literature, 4 (1960), 526–43; S. Liptzin, *Flowering of Yiddish Literature* (1963), 178–89; N. Asch, in: *Commentary*, 39/1 (1965), 55–64. **ADD. BIBLIOGRAPHY:** S. Asch, *My Personal Faith* (1942); Y. Turkov-Grudberg, *Sholem Ashs Derekh in der Yidisher Eybikeyt. Monografye* (1967); B. Siegel, *The Controversial Sholem Asch. An Introduction to His Fiction* (1976); M. Tsanin (ed.), *Briv fun Sholem Ash* (1980); S. Liptzin, *A History of Yiddish Literature* (1985), 145–55; *American National Biography* (1999), 664; N. Stahl (ed.), *Sholem Asch Reconsidered* (2004).

[Shemuel Niger (Charney) / Magdalena Sitarz (2nd ed.)]

ASCHAFFENBURG, city in Bavaria, Germany. Jews are first mentioned as living in Aschaffenburg in 1147. Abraham, a scholar and colleague of *Meir b. Baruch of Rothenburg, lived there in the 13th century. A synagogue is mentioned in 1344. Outbreaks of anti-Jewish violence occurred in 1337 and in 1348–49 the Jews were expelled. They were readmitted in 1359, and granted protection by the archbishop of Mainz in 1384. During the 16th century three or four Jewish families were living in Aschaffenburg, which was the home of Simeon b. Isaac ha-Levi, author of *Devek Tov* (1588) and *Masoret ha-Mikra* (1572). The number of Jewish households increased to 15 by the end of the century, and to 20 by 1705. A new synagogue was built in 1698 and rebuilt in 1893. The Aschaffenburg community was under the jurisdiction of the *Mainz rabbinate during the early and mid-18th century. Isaac Saeckel Ethausen, author of *Or Ne'elam* (1765), officiated as rabbi in the early part of the period. A number of restrictions on Jewish trade in Aschaffenburg were abolished in 1732. The Aschaffenburg *kehillah* was the leading community in the area and regional assemblies of the communities were held there in 1753, 1770, and 1784 to deal with the establishment of Jewish schools. The Aschaffenburg cemetery (near Schweinheim) also served communities in the vicinity, which joined the **ḥevra kaddisha* (burial society) of Aschaffenburg in 1719. In 1807 permission was first granted to a Jew to become a tailor. Rabbis serving in Aschaffenburg in the 19th century include Hillel Wolf Sondheimer, who was assisted by Israel Wertheimer, Gabriel Loew Neuburger, Abraham Adler, and Simon Bamberger, and in the 20th century, Raphael Breuer. The Jewish population of Aschaffenburg totaled 35 families in 1803 and 46 in 1807; 172 persons in 1814–16, 286 in 1871, 604 in 1900, 670 in 1910, 643 in 1925, 700 in 1928 (2% of the total population), and 591 in 1933. The synagogue was destroyed in 1938. Around half the Jews emigrated between 1933 and 1941 and another 121 left for other German cities. The remaining 170 Jews of Aschaffenburg were deported to Izbica and Theresienstadt in 1942. Few Jews returned after the war. A park commemorating Aschaffenburg's former Jewish community was created on the site of the synagogue and a museum documenting local Jewish history was inaugurated in the former rabbinate building in 1984.

BIBLIOGRAPHY: Germ Jud, 1 (1963), 13–14; 2 (1968), 25–26 (includes bibliography); *Deutsches Staedtebuch*, 5 (1968), index. **ADD.**

BIBLIOGRAPHY: P. Körner, *Biographisches Handbuch der Juden in Stadt und Altkreis Aschaffenburg* (1993).

[Ze'ev Wilhem Falk / Stefan Rohrbacher (2nd ed.)]

ASCHAFFENBURG, GUSTAV (1866–1944), criminologist and psychiatrist. In 1899 he converted to Protestantism. Aschaffenburg was born in Zweibruecken, Germany. After an internship in psychiatry under Krafft-Ebing and Mynert in Vienna and under Ball, Charcot, and Pierre Marie in Paris, he became assistant to Kraepelin in Heidelberg, who encouraged him to follow his interests in criminology. In 1904 Aschaffenburg started teaching psychiatry at the Academy of Medicine in Cologne. When the University of Cologne was reestablished in 1919 after World War I he was appointed professor and director of the university's psychiatric clinic. Aschaffenburg, early in his career, turned his attention to the care of prisoners and endeavored to discover the causes of crime and methods of treatment. In *Das Verbrechen und seine Bekaempfung* (1903; 3rd ed. 1923), he described socio-environmental as well as physical, psychological, and the psychiatric factors in crime. He suggested progressive methods of treatment for offenders and stressed, in particular, society's duty to develop preventive measures, making him one of the founders of modern forensic psychiatry in Germany. In 1904 Aschaffenburg founded the *Monatsschrift fuer Kriminalpsychologie und Strafrechtsreform*, which he edited and wrote for until 1935. He also edited *Handbuch der Psychiatrie*. When the Nazi regime came to power, Aschaffenburg was dismissed from his many posts, and in 1939 immigrated to the U.S., where he became a professor at the Catholic University in Washington and subsequently Johns Hopkins in Baltimore.

BIBLIOGRAPHY: H. von Hentig, in: H. Mannheim (ed.), *Pioneers in Criminology* (1960), 327–34. **ADD. BIBLIOGRAPHY:** *Biographisches Handbuch der deutschsprachigen Emigration*, 2 (1983), 35–36.

[Zvi Hermon / Marcus Pyka (2nd ed.)]

ASCHER, SAUL (1767–1882), German author, philosopher, and pioneer of religious reform. Ascher was born in Berlin and was heavily influenced by the Kantian philosophy. His first work, *Bemerkungen ueber die buergerliche verbesserung der Juden, veranlasst durch die Frage: Soll der Jude Soldat werden* (1788), included a call to the Jews to relinquish their way of life and prejudices in order to obtain civic emancipation. Nevertheless he rejected military service as long as the Jews did not enjoy full emancipation and equality. In 1794 he published a polemical tract against the antisemitic opinions of Fichte, calling him a "second Eisenmanger" and criticizing some of his philosophical ideas. In his main work, *Leviathan, oder: ueber Religion in Ruecksicht des Judentums* (1792), in contradiction to Moses Mendelssohn Ascher considered religion a primary expression of human sentiment that leads to a specific world view and ideals. Judaism's uniqueness lies not in the practical commandments but in this specific world view, which he summed up in 14 dogmas basically corresponding to the 13 Articles of Faith of Maimonides. According to Ascher, the object of Jewish religious law is to stimulate the discernment of its philosophical kernel and should be reformed whenever necessitated by the social and spiritual conditions of the Jews.

ADD. BIBLIOGRAPHY: C. Schulte, "Saul Ascher's '*Leviathan*,' or the Invention of Jewish Orthodoxy in 1792," in: LBIYB, 54 (2000), 25–34; E. Schweid, *Toledot Philosofiyat ha-Dat ha-Yehudit ba-Zeman he-Ḥadash*, 1 (2001), 137–51; W. Grab, "Saul Ascher – ein jüdisch-deutscher Spaetaufklaerer zwischen Revulution und Restoration," in: *Jahrbuch des Instituts für Deutsche Geschichte*, 6 (1977), 131–79.

[Jacob S. Levinger / Yehoyada Amir (2nd ed.)]

ASCHERSON, PAUL FRIEDRICH AUGUST (1834–1913), German botanist. Born and educated in Berlin, Ascherson abandoned a medical practice to become involved in botanical research. He founded the Brandenburg botanical society and wrote the classic *Flora der Provinz Brandenburg* (1859–64) which was later expanded and published as *Flora des nordostdeutschen Flachlandes* (1898–99). He traveled widely, making botanical trips in Europe and North Africa. He made a special study of the coastal flora from Alexandria to El Arish and collaborated in G. Schweinfurth's *Illustration de la flore d'Egypte* (1887; suppl. 1889). He was appointed to Berlin University in 1863 and became a full professor in 1908. He and his pupil, Paul Graebner, completed seven volumes of *Synopsis der Mitteleuropaeischen Flora* (1896).

BIBLIOGRAPHY: A. Degen, in: *Ungarische botanische Blaetter*, 12, no. 1–5 (1913), 3–15; *Festschrift… P.F.A. Ascherson* (1904), includes bibliography; NDB.

[Mordecai L. Gabriel]

ASCHHEIM, ISIDOR (1891–1968), Israel painter. For most of the decade after 1940, Aschheim was practically the only Israel artist making etchings and lithographs and was mainly responsible for imparting these techniques to the new generation of Israel artists. Aschheim was born in Posen, Germany, and studied at the Breslau Art Academy under Otto Mueller, a member of Die Bruecke Group. He traveled in Italy and France, and upon his return to Breslau, devoted himself to painting, drawing, printmaking, and lithography. He arrived in Palestine in 1940, settled in Jerusalem, and from 1943 taught drawing at the Bezalel School of Art. Aschheim was a representative of the Jerusalem School, which was created by a group of artists who were refugees from the Nazi regime. Aschheim's work, which in Germany had been close to the moderate expressionism of Mueller, mellowed by contact with the Judean landscape. The importance of his work lies primarily in his printmaking. Aschheim won few prizes during his lifetime: the Diezengoff Prize in 1951 and the Jerusalem Art Prize in 1955. In 1956 he participated in the Venice Biennale. Two of his works, *Tiberias* (1949) and *Oriental Figure*, are on view in the Fine Art Museum at San Francisco.

[Yona Fischer]

ASCHNER, MANFRED (1901–1989), bacteriologist. Born in Ratibor, Germany, Aschner was a member of the Zionist *Blau-Weiss movement in his youth. He was educated at the School of Higher Agricultural Education in Berlin and immigrated to Ereẓ Israel in 1924, settling in kibbutz Yagur as part of the "Zvi group." In 1925, he joined the entomological station in Haifa to study the biology of malaria. In 1926 he was asked to join the Department of Bacteriology in the newly established Hebrew University at Mount Scopus, Jerusalem, and began his research on the symbiotic interaction between pathogenic parasites (Pupipara) and bacteria colonizing the parasites' gut. To complete his doctoral studies he went to the University of Breslau in 1929, returning to Palestine in 1930. In the mid-1940s he was approached by fish breeders from the Jordan Valley when a mysterious agent was causing the death of fish there and threatening to wipe out the entire fish industry in the north of the country. He found that a toxin produced by algae caused the death of the fish. He then developed a strategy for eradicating the algae and saved the fishponds. In 1952, he was appointed associate professor of bacteriology at the Hebrew University and in 1956 he was asked to head the newly established Department of Biotechnology at the Technion in Haifa. For discovering the cause of the fish epidemic and his contribution to the field of biological sciences he received the Israel Prize in 1956. He donated the prize money to a foundation devoted to the security of Israel (Keren ha-Magen). Aschner was a keen scientific observer, a devoted teacher and Zionist, and a pioneer in his field of research.

[Eitan Galun (2nd ed.)]

ASCOLI, Italian family, originating from the city of *Ascoli Piceno near Ancona. Members of the family are known from the 15th century. Among its members was JACOB BEN ABRAHAM OF ASCOLI (15th century), rabbi, physician, and liturgical poet. He wrote two introductions to *Nishmat Kol Ḥai*, one beginning *Yodu le-Shimkha Elyon*, for the Day of Atonement, and the other *Yifros Go'el Sukkat Shalom* for the Feast of Tabernacles. DAVID D'ASCOLI (mid-16th century) was the author of *Apologia Hebraeorum* (1559) in which he protested against the discriminatory anti-Jewish legislation of Pope Paul IV which enforced the Jewish *badge and established the ghetto system. As a result of his protest, David was imprisoned. A street in Ascoli has been named after him. ALBERT ABRAM (b. 1877) was a physician and educator. He was a pioneer in anti-tubercular vaccination and director of the Institute for Anti-Tubercular Vaccines in Milan (1924) as well as professor at Milan University. The author of some 180 publications, he received several decorations for his work. ALDO (b. 1882), a much decorated naval officer, rose to be commander of the Italian fleet in the Aegean (1930) but, after the racial laws came into effect, was forced to resign (1938). ALFREDO (1863–1942) was a jurist. He taught law at Messina, Pavia, and Rome. Alfredo also wrote numerous works, particularly on Roman law, and played a prominent part in elaborating the new Italian civil code. EMILIA (b. 1873) was the author and writer of fables. She wrote under the pseudonym Liana. Her works include *Favole* (1914) and *Canti Tricolori* (1917). GIULIO (1843–96) was a mathematician, and associate professor at the Politechnico in Milan from 1879. He introduced the concept of quasi-uniform convergence and dealt with the theory of functions and problems of calculation. His works appeared in Brioschi's *Annali di Matematica* and other scientific publications. GIULIO (1870–1916), a physicist, was born in Trieste. He was noted for his research on metabolism and uremia. GUIDO (1887–1957), a mathematician and educator, was professor of mathematics at the University of Pisa (1933–34), Milan (1934–38), and Turin (1949–57), specializing in analysis and geometry. MAURIZIO (1876–1958), a pathologist, taught at Palermo (1920–22), held the chair of pathology at the University of Catania (1911–20, 1922–27), and became director of its medical clinic (1927). Among his major contributions were studies on immunity to various diseases, the influence of irradiation on the endocrine gland function, and the effects of drugs. MOISE (1857–1921), a physician, born in Gorizia, was professor of technical physics at the University of Rome. He dealt with the properties of metals, magnetism, and electricity, and published numerous articles in scientific periodicals. VITTORIO (1863–1931), a pathologist, was director of the Clinica Medica Roma and was famous for his studies on malaria, diabetes, and tuberculosis. MAX (b. 1898), a jurist and author, was professor of law at the University of Genoa (1926–31). After the rise of Fascism he migrated to the U.S. where he lectured at the New School for Social Research, New York, and became a member of the "University in Exile." After World War II he participated in the restoration of artistic monuments damaged in the war. He was the author of several works on jurisprudence in Italian, and political writings, mainly on Fascism, in English. He was editor of the American weekly the *Reporter* (1949–68).

BIBLIOGRAPHY: Roth, Italy, index; Milano, Italia, index; G. Bedarida, *Ebrei d'Italia* (1950), index; *Dizionario biografico degli Italiani* (1962); *Nouvelle Biographie Universelle*, 3 (1852), 422–3; Vogelstein-Rieger, 2 (1895), 45, 111, 153; JQR, 14 (1901/02), 389–90; M. Steinschneider, in: MGWJ, 42 (1898), 263; A.G. Tiraboschi, *Storia della letteratura italiana* (Florence, 1805–1812³), index.

[Nathan H. Winter]

ASCOLI, ETTORE (1873–1943), Italian soldier. Ascoli, who was born in Ancona, was commissioned in the artillery in 1891. As a young man he took part in the African campaign of 1896, which ended in the defeat of Adua. He terminated his studies in 1902, and in 1905 he was appointed captain. For several years before World War I, from 1909 to 1915, he was a senior instructor at the Modena Military Academy.

In 1917 he was appointed colonel commander of the 7th Group of Artillery of the 26th Army Corps on Mount Podgora. He was then appointed divisional commander of Artillery. After the Austrian offensive of 1917, which terminated in the Italian defeat of Caporetto, Ascoli was appointed in June as commander of the Inter-Allied Artillery, which included British and French units.

He returned to instructional duties after the end of the war, by which time he had reached the rank of colonel and had been decorated several times, with the Bronze Medal, the War Cross, and the Knight's Cross of the Order of Savoy, and the Officer's Cross of the Order of Savoy. In 1924 he was appointed head of the Military Schools Service. Ascoli returned to the artillery in 1926, and in 1933, as a major general, was appointed deputy commander general of the Italian artillery. He was inspector of the military zone of Bologna from 1935 until 1937 when, as a lieutenant general, he was appointed an army corps commander. General Ascoli published various manuals for field artillery officers, as well as a book on Italian artillery during World War I.

Shortly before the outbreak of World War II when anti-Jewish legislation was enacted in Italy, Ascoli was compelled to leave the army. After September 1943, when the Germans invaded Italy, Ascoli joined the partisans, and was killed fighting against the Germans on December 14, 1943. He was buried in the cemetery of Cingoli.

BIBLIOGRAPHY: *Jewish Heroism in Modern Times* (1965); E. Rubin, *140 Jewish Marshals, Generals and Admirals* (1952), 179–80.

[Mordechai Kaplan]

ASCOLI, GRAZIADIO ISAIA (1829–1907), Italian philologist and linguist from *Gorizia. Ascoli was very closely connected with the Jewish cultural milieu of Abram Vita Reggio, Samuel David *Luzzatto, and Filosseno Luzzatto; from 1850 to 1852 he was president of the Jewish community of Gorizia. Ascoli devoted himself to the promotion of scientific philology in Italy. At the age of 16 he published *Sull'idioma friulano e sulla sua affinità con la lingua valaca. Schizzo storico-filologico* (1846), a comparative study of the Friulan dialect and the Wallachian tongue. In 1861, on the basis of his research on Turkish and Oriental languages, *Studii orientali e linguistici* (Gorizia, 1854–61), he was appointed professor of linguistics at the Regia Accademia Scientifico-Letteraria of Milan. He held the chair for over 40 years and influenced many Italian philologists of his own and succeeding generations. His *Lezioni di Fonologia Comparata del Sanscrito, del Greco e del Latino* (Turin, 1870) and *Studi critici* (Turin, 1877) wrought a revolution in comparative Indo-Germanic philology.

Ascoli made important contributions to the field of comparative linguistics, including the theory that the different Romance dialects had been influenced by Celtic dialects before the period of the Roman Empire and the spread of Latin. He was the first scholar to formulate many of the laws of phonetic change. His outstanding work on Romance philology, *Saggi ladini*, was published in the journal *Archivio glottologico italiano*, which he founded in 1873, and was awarded the Bopp Prize by the Berlin Academy in 1874.

In addition, Ascoli published *Die Ziegeuner in Europa und Asien* (Halle, 1865), *Studi Ario-Semitici* (1865), *Lettere Glottologiche* (1879–85), and *Il Codice irlandese dell'Ambrosiana* (Turin, 1877). Ascoli also devoted himself to Jewish historical research and published papers on the Hebrew, Latin, and Greek inscriptions on early medieval Jewish tombstones in southern Italy. The greater part of Ascoli's scientific papers were published in the *Archivio glottologico italiano*, of which 15 volumes had appeared up to 1900. Ascoli received many honors and scientific appointments in Italy and in Europe (mainly in Germany) and he was a member of the Academies of Science at Paris, Leningrad, Vienna, and Budapest and of the Italian Council for Higher Education. In 1889 he became a senator of the Italian Kingdom. His son, MOISÈ ASCOLI (1859–1921), was a distinguished physicist.

BIBLIOGRAPHY: M.E. Loricchio, *Graziadio Isaia Ascoli biografia di un intellettuale* (1999); A. Casella and G. Lucchini, *Graziadio e Moisè Ascoli. Scienza, cultura e politica nell'Italia liberale* (2002).

[Federica Francesconi (2nd ed.)]

ASCOLI PICENO, city in central Italy, south of Ancona. Ascoli Piceno was one of the first towns to authorize Jewish moneylending activities (in 1297). Jewish loan banks flourished there until this occupation was prohibited to Jews in 1458, when a *Monte di Pietà was set up. In 1470 Jewish moneylending was again permitted; other occupations were trade in cloth and agricultural produce. In 1502 the city came under pontifical rule, and so the Jews of Ascoli shared the vicissitudes of the other Jewries of the Papal States. In 1531 they were ordered by the bishop to wear the Jewish *badge. Their position deteriorated under Pope Paul IV. Jewish commerce was restricted, and they were confined to the ghetto. The physician David d'Ascoli was imprisoned for publishing his *Apologia Hebraeorum*, in protest against the restrictions. In 1569 the Jews were expelled from the town. In 1587 they were temporarily readmitted to the city, and in 1593 were again expelled. In 1604, some Jewish merchants were allowed to reopen their stores, but these were closed in 1678. Subsequently Jews were allowed to visit Ascoli only to take part in the three annual fairs. Ascoli Piceno is not to be confused with Ascoli Satriano in Apulia, where, in about 1165, *Benjamin of Tudela encountered 40 Jewish families.

BIBLIOGRAPHY: G. Fabiani, *Gli Ebrei e il Monte di Pietà in Ascoli* (1942); E. Loevinson, in: REJ, 93 (1932), 47.

[Attilio Milano]

ASEFAT ḤAKHAMIM (Heb. אֲסֵפַת חֲכָמִים; "Assembly of Sages"), Hebrew socialist monthly founded by M.L. Rodkinson in 1877 and published in Koenigsberg. *Asefat Ḥakhamim* was the second journal of its kind. It was a successor to A.S. *Liebermann's *Ha-Emet* ("The Truth") and propagated its ideology with mainly the same contributors. Eight issues were published between October 1877 and October 1878. A reprint of these appeared in one volume in 1967, *Asefat Ḥakhamim* (Hebrew University Press, Akademon). The prospectus published in the first issue stated that the journal would deal primarily with the "problem of existence," or the "spoon and fork" dilemma (the problem of earning one's daily bread). M. *Winchevsky, who was influenced by Liebermann, assumed active editorship and, under various pseudonyms, contributed most of the literary material appearing in the journal. The socialist and positivist tendency in his writings was inspired by the radical Russian writers D. Pisaryev and N. Chernyshevsky. Winchevsky's chief assistant, E.W. *Rabinowitz, wrote a series of articles for the journal on the "Problem of the Workers in the United States." Other contributors included Isaac Kaminer and M.L. Lilienblum. Publication ended after Winchevsky was arrested and expelled from Germany because of his political views.

BIBLIOGRAPHY: M. Winchevsky, *Gezamlte Verk*, 9 (1927), 182–316; Klausner, Sifrut, 6 (1958²), 289–301.

[Gedalyah Elkoshi]

ASENAPPER (Heb. אָסְנַפַּר), Mesopotamian king who deported several peoples – Babylonians, Elamites, and others – to Samaria, and elsewhere in Palestine-Syria (Ezra 4:10). Asenapper is commonly identified with Ashurbanipal, king of Assyria (668–c. 627 B.C.E.). Although there is no direct evidence that Ashurbanipal deported peoples to Palestine-Syria, it is plausible that he did – and actually from the very localities named in the text, since he crushed a revolt of southern Mesopotamia and liquidated the kingdom of Elam, which abetted the former. Furthermore, the name Asenapper can hardly be reconciled with that of any other king. The distortion of the name may have taken place with a supposed original Asurbanipal becoming Asurbanipar (*l* > *r* is a common phonetic shift), which then was abbreviated to As[ ]nipar, either through pronunciation or textual corruption. Some such process, if not precisely that one, must have led to the form Asenapper.

BIBLIOGRAPHY: M. Streck, *Assurbanipal*, 1 (Ger., 1916), ccclxivff.; B. Meisler (Mazar), in: EM, 1 (1965), 480–1 (incl. bibl.); Commentaries to Ezra 4:10.

[Jeffrey Howard Tigay]

ASENATH (Heb. אָסְנַת; meaning in Egyptian, "she belongs to, or is the servant of, [the goddess] Neith"), daughter of Poti-Phera, the high priest of On (Heliopolis). Asenath, at Pharaoh's instance, married Joseph (Gen. 41:45, et al.). She bore Joseph two sons, Manasseh and Ephraim, during the seven years of plenty (41:50; 46:20). For the rabbinic attitude to Asenath, see *Joseph (in *aggadah*).

BIBLIOGRAPHY: W. Spiegelberg, *Aegyptologische Randglossen zum Alten Testament* (1904), 18–19; J. Vergote, *Joseph en Egypte* (Fr., 1959), 148ff.; N.M. Sarna, *Understanding Genesis* (1966), 221. **ADD. BIBLIOGRAPHY:** D. Redford, *Egypt, Canaan, and Israel in Ancient Times* (1992), 424; V. Aptowitzer, in: HUCA, 1 (1924), 239–306.

[Nahum M. Sarna]

ASH (**Asch**; Heb. א"ש), abbreviation of various Hebrew words and transcriptions, later used as a name in its own right in Central and Eastern Europe. (1) Ash was the traditional Hebrew abbreviation of the city name *Eisenstadt. Meir b. Isaac *Eisenstadt is also known as "Maharam Ash"; "Ash" appears on a number of old Eisenstadt tombstones. Meir *Eisenstadter (Asch) made a pun from the Hebrew meaning of the word (אש, "fire") in the title of his work *Imrei Esh* (1852) and so did Abraham b. Joseph *Ash. (2) "Ash" is also used as an abbreviation for Alt-schul, the "old school" (synagogue) quarter of Prague, by Moses b. Ḥanokh *Altschul in the late 15th century; it was later found on tombstones of 1582 to 1727 in the old cemetery of Prague. (3) The Ash family of rabbis (descended from Moses b. Joseph of Mezhirech in Poland, who moved to Stargard in Pomerania), believing that their name literally signified "ash" (Asche in German), "retranslated" it into Hebrew as *Efer* (*Mishpaḥat Efer*), "ash" in Hebrew.

BIBLIOGRAPHY: H. Flesch, in: *Juedische Familien-Forschung*, 2, no. 4 (1926), 188; A. Berliner, *Zur Familiengeschichte Asch* (1913), 15; S. Hock, *Die Familien Prags* (1892), 16–19; B. Wachstein, *Die Grabinschriften des alten Judenfriedhofs in Eisenstadt* (1922), 660.

ASH, family which during the 18th and 19th centuries produced a number of distinguished rabbis, both in Poland and in Germany. These included:

(1) ABRAHAM ASH (18th century), rabbi and author who was born in Posen and became rabbi at Celle. He wrote *Torah Kullah* (Berlin, 1796), which comprises (a) *Yoreh De'ah*, a compendium of ethical essays based on the natural sciences; (b) *Yavin Shemu'ah*, statements from the Talmud and halakhic authorities opposing early burials; and (c) *Ḥerev la-Shem* – against Solomon *Pappenheim and in favor of delaying the interment of the dead. He proposed that "the very earliest rabbinic regulations" be reintroduced, that sepulchral chambers be built in every cemetery, where the deceased be placed and left for three days so that there can be no doubt of death.

(2) Abraham Joseph *Ash (1813–1888), rabbi and halakhic authority. Born at Siemiaticze, in the district of Grodno, he immigrated to New York in 1852 and was among the early founders of what came to be known as the Bet ha-Midrash ha-Gadol, where he was rabbi from 1860 until his death (except for intervals when he tried unsuccessfully to engage in business). He was regarded as an authority and rabbis in Europe paid special attention to him in religious matters. Ash was responsible for several new features relating to a *get* ("bill of divorce"): its text, the procedure of mailing it, its distinguishing marks, and the accepted spelling of American personal and place names. He was involved in halakhic controversies with Jacob *Ettlinger of Altona (*Binyan Ẓiyyon*, no. 63, dated 1858) and Isaac Elhanan *Spektor of Kovno. He wrote a protest against attempts of Reform rabbis to deliver sermons in Orthodox synagogues (1886).

(3) ABRAHAM BEN JOSEPH ASH (late 18th–early 19th century), rabbi and author. Born in Posen, he was rabbi at Zell, near Wuerzburg, in the *bet midrash* of Isaac Rans. He wrote

Mareh Esh ("The Appearance of Fire," "*Esh*" being a play on his surname), containing novellae on various talmudic themes and glosses on all the tractates of the Talmud (Berlin, 1803). The author's introduction includes his ethical will addressed to his son Moses Jacob who published his book.

(4) JOEL BEN MEIR JOSEPH ASH (1745–1811), rabbi and author. Born in Stargard, he studied in Berlin and Frankfurt on the Oder, and was appointed rabbi of Schoenlanke in 1779. He was the author of pilpulistic homilies on the Torah entitled *Yitedot Ohalim* (1788). His son Judah "he-Ḥasid" was rabbi at Samter (1814–1831).

BIBLIOGRAPHY: (1) ASH, ABRAHAM and (3) ASH, ABRAHAM B. JOSEPH: Steinschneider, Cat Bod, 666, no. 4184 (note), additions 87; Zedner, Cat, 56; Zeitlin, Bibliotheca, 6–7. (2) ASH, ABRAHAM JOSEPH: J.D. Eisenstein, in: AJHSP, 9 (1901), 64–71; 12 (1904), 145–6; I. Goldstein, *A Century of Judaism in New York* (1930), 145; P. Wiernik, *History of the Jews in America* (1931²), 189–91; H.B. Grinstein, *Rise of the Jewish Community of New York* (1945), 93, 253, 486, 488, n. 12. (4) ASH, JOEL B. MEIR B. JOSEPH: S. Wiener, *Kohelet Moshe*, 5 (1904), 629, no. 5134 A; M.L. Bamberger, *Geschichte der Juden in Schoenlanke* (1912), 16–17; A. Berliner, *Zur Familiengeschichte Asch* (1913), 7–13.

[Yehoshua Horowitz]

ASH, ABRAHAM JOSEPH (1813–1887), preacher, Talmud scholar. Ash was born in Semyatitch, Grodno region, Polish Russia, and immigrated to America around 1852. He was one of the founders of the Beth Hamidrash, New York's first Russian-Polish congregation.

Ash was often in disputes with fellow congregants and rabbis. Judah Mittelman, a learned Talmud scholar and founding member of the Beth Hamidrash, had gained the consent of several Galician rabbis to grant Aaron Zvi Friedman a permit to become a *shoḥet*. Ash disapproved of Friedman's appointment and refused to honor his permit to slaughter kosher animals. As a consequence, Mittelman and his followers seceded from the Beth Hamidrash in 1855 and started their own congregation, the Kalvarier Beth Hamidrash. A few years later, as a result of lingering disagreement with the president of the Beth Hamidrash, Ash led a group of his followers to secede from the Beth Hamidrash. In 1859, they established a new congregation, named the Beth Hamidrash Hagadol.

One of the few Talmud scholars in New York at the time, Ash taught advanced Talmud classes. He granted *shoḥetim* permits to slaughter animals for kosher meat and inspected their performance at several New York abattoirs. He prepared religious documents of divorce (*gittin*), which at times created problems for him with the civil courts. The Hebrew text for identifying the city of New York – on the Hudson River but not the East River – developed by Ash for documents of divorce set the standard for subsequent rabbis for more than a generation. He was frequently consulted on issues of practical Jewish law and periodically corresponded with European rabbis.

In the early 1870s, Ash started a business importing kosher wine from California. But Moses *Aaronsohn claimed that the wine Ash was importing was not kosher. As a consequence, Aaronsohn was excommunicated by both Rabbis Ash and Mittelman. When the business met with little success, Ash returned to his responsibilities as religious leader of the Beth Hamidrash Hagadol.

A staunch defender of Orthodox tradition, Ash not only opposed Reform Judaism but engaged in polemics against Reform notables regarding matters of Jewish theology. In particular, he criticized Orthodox synagogues that offered a platform to Reform spokesmen. He censured the Beth Midrash Anshei Suvalk, which in 1884 permitted Kaufman *Kohler, a well-known advocate of Reform, to address the congregation. In 1886 he wrote a satiric polemic against Kohler entitled *Ma le-Shor ha-Mazik be-Reshut ha-Nizuk* ("Regarding the Goring Bull on the Premises of the One Damaged"). On May 6, 1887, Ash died in New York City.

BIBLIOGRAPHY: *Jewish Messenger*, 61:19 (May 13, 1887), 2; J.D. Eisenstein, "The History of the First Russian-American Jewish Congregation," in: *Publications of the American Jewish Historical Society*, vol. 9 (1901), 64–71; B.Z. Eisenstadt, *Dorot Aḥaronim*, vol. 1 (1913), 43.

[Moshe Sherman (2nd ed.)]

ASHAMNU (Heb. אָשַׁמְנוּ; "we have trespassed" or "we are guilty"), opening word and hence the name of a formula of confession of sins which forms part of the *Day of Atonement and of other penitential services, such as **seliḥot*, the daily morning and afternoon prayers (according to most Sephardi and some Ashkenazi rites), and the prayer service recited on the day preceding the New Moon (*tefillat *Yom Kippur Katan*) according to the Ashkenazi rite. Its origin is in the confession recited by the high priest on the Day of Atonement (see *Avodah*). In later periods it was expanded in the more elaborate medieval style. The *Ashamnu* confession lists trespasses of a moral nature only and consists of 24 or more words in alphabetical order, the last letter of the Hebrew alphabet being repeated three times. In the Reform ritual *Ashamnu* appears in an abridged form. *Ashamnu* is also used as the form of confession at the approach of death as well as by the bridegroom and bride before their wedding, that day being considered a sort of "day of Atonement" for them (Shab. 32a; Sanh. 6:2; 43b).

BIBLIOGRAPHY: Elbogen, *Gottesdienst*, 149–51, 229.

ASHANSKI (Oshyanski), ABEL-AARON ITSKOVICH (1825–1899), Russian soldier, and the only Jew ever to reach the rank of regimental sergeant in the Czarist army. Ashanski was called up for service in an army labor battalion in 1846, but because of his good service and impressive physique he was transferred in 1863 to the czarina's own cavalry regiment. In 1874 he was promoted to regimental sergeant and served in this rank until 1896. Ashanski was given a state funeral, and was buried in the old Jewish cemetery of St. Petersburg.

ASHBEL, DOV (1895–1989), Israel meteorologist. Ashbel was born in Jerusalem. After serving in the Turkish Army in World War I he was a schoolteacher for some years before going to study at Berlin University. To study the basics of the Ereẓ Israel climate and particularly of the rains at the sources supplying water to the Jordan River, the Sea of Galilee, and the Dead Sea, Ashbel set up a network of gauging stations which soon covered the whole country up to the Negev. In 1928, Ashbel compiled a new rain map and in 1940, a rain map of the Near East. In 1930, Ashbel joined the Hebrew University in Jerusalem, and founded a department, which studied the various basic elements of climate in different parts of the country. He devoted most of his attention to solar radiation in general, and to the division of the spectrum.

One of the agricultural conclusions was the locating of sites where there was no fear of frost and freezing, for growing bananas and citrus. Hitherto, it had been considered that the Jordan Valley was the most suitable place for bananas, and the coastal plain was best suited to citrus groves. In 1950, Ashbel presented a proposal to plant these crops on the Carmel plain around Athlit, and on the plain at the foot of the hills of Western Galilee, around Nahariyyah. Thenceforward, these two areas were filled with plantations of these crops, which have proved to be among the most successful in Israel. At Ashbel's suggestion, a successful experiment was made to plant citrus crops in the western Negev. He was departmental editor of the *Encyclopaedia Judaica* for Jews in meteorology. His works include *Bio-Climatic Atlas of Israel and Neighbour Countries* (1951), *Regional Climatology of Israel* (1951), *Solar Radiation and Sunshine in Jerusalem* (1961), *Soil Temperature* (1965), *Climate of Israel* (1964–67), *Climate of the Near East* (1967, 1968), and *Snow and Rain in the Near East, Maps and Tables of Rainfall on both Banks of the Jordan* (1967).

ASHDOD (Heb. אַשְׁדּוֹד), city in the southern coastal plain of Ereẓ Israel; the ancient city was 3 mi. (4½ km.) from the sea, the modern city is on the seashore.

Ancient Ashdod

In the Late Canaanite period, it served as an important harbor city as is shown by archaeological finds and references to its maritime trade in the archives of *Ugarit. According to biblical tradition, it was a town of the ancient Anakim (lit. "giants"; Josh. 11:22). After its conquest by the *Philistines, it became one of their five chief cities and they erected a temple dedicated to the god Dagon at Ashdod (Josh. 13:3; 15:46; I Sam. 5:1–7; Amos 1:8). Uzziah, king of Judah, breached the fortifications of the town and built in the area (II Chron. 26:6). In 734 B.C.E. the city capitulated to Tiglath-Pileser III of Assyria and in 712 B.C.E. Sargon crushed a rebellion led by Ashdod which then became the capital of an Assyrian province (cf. Isa. 20:1). Although the city was situated on the *via maris*, the trade route near the sea, it was not directly on the coast but possessed an ancient port which was called Ashdod Yam ("Ashdod-on-the-Sea"). With the decline of Assyrian power, the Egyptian pharaoh Psammetichus I conquered the city after a siege of 29 years (according to Herodotus, 2:157). Ashdod was the Philistine capital in the post-Exilic period, so that in the days of Nehemiah, an "Ashdodite" was synonymous with a "Philistine" (Neh. 4:1; 13:24). Nehemiah fought against Ashdod's influence which extended as far as Jerusalem.

The town continued to be a district capital in the Hellenistic period when it was known as Azotus and it served as a Greek stronghold down to the days of the Hasmoneans (I Macc. 5:68). Its suburbs were burnt by Jonathan (I Macc. 10:84; 11:4) and the city was captured by John Hyrcanus (c. 165 B.C.E.; Jos., Ant., 13:324). Ashdod then remained in Hasmonean hands until its conquest by Pompey (63 B.C.E.). It was rebuilt by Gabinius (55 B.C.E.) and later changed hands several times, eventually becoming the property of Herod, who gave it to his sister Salome; she bequeathed it to Livia, the wife of Augustus Caesar, from whom it was inherited by the emperor Tiberius (*ibid.*, 14:75, 88; 17:189; 18:31). From the time of the Hasmoneans until the second century C.E., Ashdod appears to have been a Jewish town. It declined after Vespasian's conquest. In the Byzantine period, the Madaba Map distinguished between inland "Ashdod of the Horsemen" and the bigger coastal town "Ashdod-on-the-Sea." The discovery of a chancel screen of a synagogue at Ashdod-on-the-Sea (Mīnat al-Qalʿa) with a Greco-Jewish inscription gives evidence of a Jewish community there in the sixth century C.E. Part of the Muslim-Arab townlet of Isdūd, which was in existence until the end of the Mandate period, was built on a tell called al-Ra's on the site of the ancient city. Excavations conducted by the Israel Department of Antiquities near the new Ashdod port at Tell Mor (Tell Murra) uncovered remains of Canaanite and Israelite fortifications and a Hellenistic plant for extracting purple dye from murex. A joint Israel-American expedition (directed by Moshe Dothan and for the first two seasons also with David Noel Freedman) started excavating the mound in 1962. This is situated in the arable coastal plain of Philistia, and lies about 2.8 mi. (4.5 km.) from the sea and about 9.4 mi. (15 km.) northeast of Ashkelon. Stratigraphical evidence (22 strata were uncovered) shows nearly continuous occupation from the seventeenth century B.C.E. until the end of Byzantine times. The city was fortified from the end of the Middle Bronze II period onward until the Late Bronze Age (strata XXII–XIV). The Late Bronze Age city (mentioned frequently in Ugaritic texts) was destroyed by the Philistines and Ashdod became one of the cities of the Philistine Pentapolis. At least three Philistine strata have been uncovered (strata XIII–XI) revealing a rich material culture including seals inscribed in an unknown script. Cult objects, including a musicians' stand and many *kernoi* and offering tables, which attest to the local religious practices of the Iron Age II period, were probably manufactured in the potters' quarter of the lower city. The excavation verified the biblical tradition of destructions by Uzziah and by Sargon II of Assyria. After its complete destruction the city reached a new peak in Hellenistic times, afterward gradually declining to a small, unimportant village.

[Michael Avi-Yonah / Moshe Dothan]

Modern Period

During the War of Independence (1948–49), Egyptian forces entered Ashdod and advanced beyond it 6.3 mi. (10 km.) northward to the vicinity of Jabneh. In October 1948, the Egyptian forces were cut off in "Operation Ten Plagues" and they extricated themselves with great difficulty; the local Arab inhabitants abandoned the place with them. The modern city was founded in 1956 at the mouth of Naḥal Lachish, 4 mi. (7 km.) north of the mound of Philistine Ashdod. It received municipal status in 1968. Town planners envisaged Ashdod as Israel's second large port on the Mediterranean coast, thus shortening transport routes in the southern half of Israel, and as a major manufacturing center. The port was opened in 1965 and is biggest in the country. It has a long main breakwater and large-sized harbor basin and terrestrial area. It is linked to the country's railroad network by a trunk line and a gas refinery was later built nearby.

The town plan was based on the principle of self-contained neighborhood units, each with its own social, educational, and economic services; 16 such units were provided for in the Ashdod city plan. A large area was designated an industrial zone. Ashdod's first large industrial enterprise was the power station (a second was also built) which provided most of Israel's southern region with electricity. Large and medium-sized factories were also opened.

Ashdod's population grew rapidly from 200 in 1957 to 2,500 in 1959, 11,000 in 1963, and 30,000 in 1968. By the mid-1990s the population of Ashdod had reached 110,300, and at the end of 2002 there were 187,500 residents in the city, making it the fifth largest in Israel. Its municipal area extends over 23 sq. mi. (60 sq. km.). From the 1990s the city absorbed many new immigrants, who comprise 33% of the population. Of these, 88% are from the Former Soviet Union and the rest mainly from Ethiopia, France, and Latin America. Ashdod's population was fairly young, with nearly 130,000 of its residents below the age of 45.

[Efraim Orni / Shaked Gilboa (2nd ed.)]

BIBLIOGRAPHY: Schuerer, Gesch, 2 (1907⁴), 96ff.; Beyer, in: ZDPV, 56 (1933), 248; M. Dothan, in: IEJ, 4 (1954), 229–32; 13 (1963), 340–2; 14 (1964), 79–95; 15 (1965), 258–60; Dothan and Freedman, in: *Atiqot*, 7 (Eng., 1967); Dothan, in: D.N. Freedman and J.C. Greenfeld (eds.), *New Directions in Biblical Archeology* (1969), 15–24 (incl. bibl.). **ADD. BIBLIOGRAPHY:** Dothan, in, ABD 1:477–82. **WEBSITE:** www.ashdod.muni.il.

ASHDOT YA'AKOV (Heb. אַשְׁדּוֹת יַעֲקֹב), two kibbutzim in the central Jordan Valley in Israel, near the confluence of the Jordan and Yarmuk rivers. It was founded on PICA (*Palestine Jewish Colonization Association) land in 1933, by a group of Ha-Kibbutz ha-Me'uḥad members. The abundant water supply and warm climate enabled the kibbutz to develop highly intensive farming and to become one of the largest collective settlements in the country. In 1953, after the split in Ha-Kibbutz ha-Me'uḥad, Ashdot divided into two communes, one of them joining Iḥud ha-Kevuẓot ve-ha-Kibbutzim. The first settlers in both kibbutzim came mostly from Eastern and Central Europe, or were Israeli-born. In 1968 their economies were based on banana, grapefruit, and other tropical and subtropical plantations, irrigated field crops and fodder, carp ponds, and milch cattle as well as large metal workshops and other industries. They became partners in a large adjacent cellotex factory. The combined population of the two kibbutzim (1968) was 1,200, and in the mid-1990s it was around 1,000. In 2002 the population of Ashdot Ya'akov Iḥud was 564 and the population of Ashdot Ya'akov Me'uḥad was 336. In addition to farming, Ashdot Ya'akov Iḥud produced olive oil and ran a plastic products factory, and both kibbutzim had guest rooms. The name Ashdot ("Waterfalls") refers to the nearby Rutenberg Electricity Works, and Ya'akov to James de *Rothschild.

WEBSITE: www.ashdot.org.il.

[Efraim Orni / Shaked Gilboa (2nd ed.)]

ASHENDORF, ISRAEL (1909–1956), Yiddish poet, short story writer, and dramatist. Ashendorf grew up and lived in Lemberg (Lwow), Galicia (now Lviv, Ukraine), until World War II, when he fled to Uzbekistan. He spent five years in Paris and immigrated to Argentina in 1953. In Buenos Aires he served as supervisor of Jewish secular schools, taught Hebrew and Yiddish literature, and contributed to the *Yidishe Tsaytung*. His first poems were published in 1927, and thereafter he contributed to Yiddish periodicals in Europe, the Americas, and Israel. In 1929, he was co-editor of the literary journal *Tsushtayer*. Collections of his poetry were published in 1937, 1939, 1941, 1950, and 1956. His biblical dramas *Der Meylekh Shoel* ("King Saul," 1948) and *Der Meylekh Dovid* ("King David," 1956) express a pessimistic worldview. The posthumous collection *Letste Shriftn* ("Last Writings," 1958) includes his poems and short stories.

BIBLIOGRAPHY: LNYL, 1 (1956), 193–4; S. Bickel, *Shrayber fun Mayn Dor*, 1 (1958), 160–4; M. Ravitch, *Mayn Leksikon*, 1 (1945), 56ff.; J. Leftwich, *Golden Peacock* (1961).

[Shlomo Bickel]

ASHENHEIM, Jamaican family. LOUIS ASHENHEIM (1816–1858), born in Edinburgh, was one of the first Jewish graduates from a Scottish university. He immigrated to Jamaica about 1841. By profession a doctor, he was noted for his work in stemming a cholera epidemic. In Jamaica he helped edit a Jewish monthly entitled *Bikkure Hayam, The First Fruits of the West*. He was also the editor and proprietor of the newspaper *Daily Gleaner*. SIR NEVILLE NOEL ASHENHEIM (1900–1984), lawyer and politician, was born in Kingston, Jamaica. He practiced as a solicitor and in 1952 was appointed chairman of the Jamaican Industrial Development Corporation, a post he held until 1957. Ashenheim became a member of the Legislative Council in 1959 and was appointed minister without portfolio in 1962. He served as the first Jamaican ambassador to Washington from 1962 until 1967 and received a knighthood in 1963. In 1967 he was appointed to the Jamaican Senate as the leader of government business, and he was included in the Cabinet as minister of state for finance, serving until his party, the Jamaica Labor Party, was defeated in the elections of February 1973.

ASHER (Heb. אָשֵׁר). (1) Jacob's second son by Zilpah, Leah's handmaid (Gen. 30:12), and his eighth son (in the order of birth); eponymous ancestor of the tribe of Asher. (2) Tribe of Israel and its territory. The individual Asher was named by Leah who declared, "What fortune [*Be-oshri*]! Women will deem me fortunate [*ishruni*]" (30:13). It is thought, however, that the origin of the name is connected with the male counterpart of the goddess *Asherah. It is noteworthy that Zilpah's other son was also named after a heathen deity (see *Gad). Designating the eponym of the tribe as the son of a handmaid indicates a lesser standing for the tribe.

The Tribal Territory

According to Joshua (19:24–31), the tribe of Asher settled in northwest Canaan in the plain of Acre and in upper and lower west Galilee, as well as in the hinterland of Phoenician Tyre and Sidon, and in the westernmost part of the valley of Jezreel. The exact determination of the boundaries of Asher is complicated by two factors: (1) uncertainty as to the identification of several localities referred to in Joshua; and (2) the apparent confusion of two passages in that source, the one describing territorial limits, the other listing cities. In the course of time, the theoretical boundaries of Asher appear to have changed, a portion of its territory being annexed by the tribe of Zebulun, apparently shortly after Israel's successful war against Sisera (Judg. 4–5). The Zebulunites, having played a leading role in it, expanded westward. In the second half of the tenth century B.C.E. Solomon presented some of Asher's territory, "20 cities in the land of Galilee" (I Kings 9:11–13), to the king of Tyre in payment for the materials supplied by him for the Temple building operations. It seems that Solomon in compensation transferred Bealoth, a Naphtalite district, to Asher's territory (I Kings 4:16).

The History of the Tribe

Several genealogies of Asher are preserved in the Bible: Genesis 46:17; Numbers 26:44–46; I Chronicles 7:30–39. The last is the most detailed and much of it is found only in Chronicles. Noteworthy is the inclusion of the Egyptian name Harnepher as well as other foreign names. If historically reliable, the list indicates a "thorough mixture" (Japhet) of Israelite and non-Israelite elements. In addition, the list associates Asher with southern Mt. Ephraim as opposed to the western Galilee of the other biblical sources.

The people of Asher appear to be mentioned in an inscription of Seti I (c. 1291–1279) at the temple of Redeshiya and in an inscription in the temple of Rameses II (1279–1212) at Abydos. In Seti's list Asher appears in a geographical sequence between Kedesh on the Orontes and Megiddo, which would agree with those biblical references that locate Asher

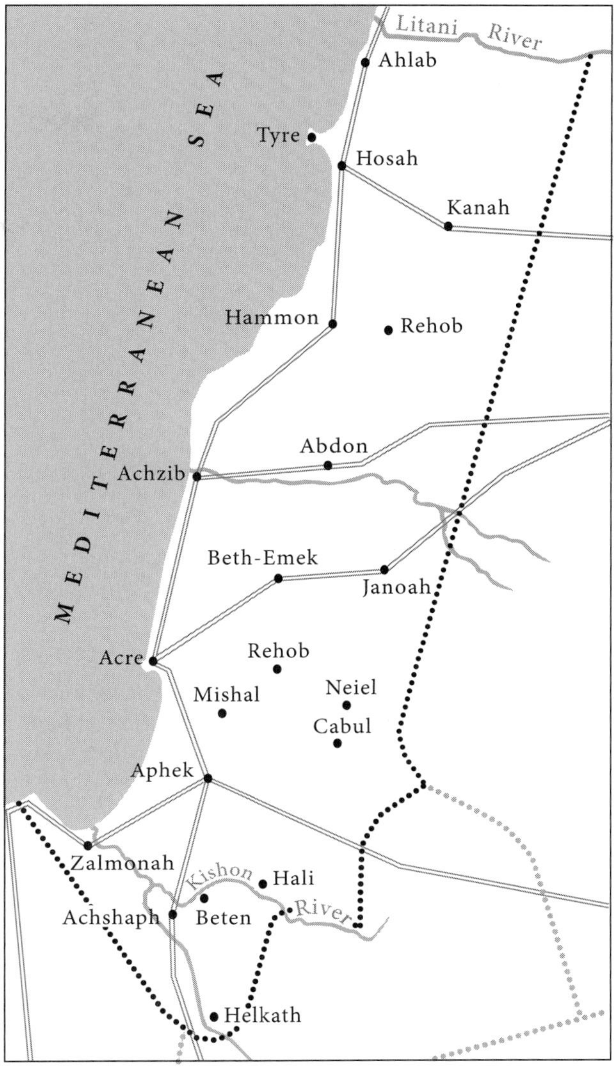

Territory of the tribe of Asher.

in the western Galilee. A satirical letter from the 13th century B.C.E. speaks of Qatsra-yadi ("I-am-Powerless," a seemingly fictitious mocking name), ruler of *ysr* or *ʾsr* which may reflect Asher (Papyrus Anastasi 1:23,6, in: COS, 3, 13). The ruler's name is clearly West Semitic. According to Gauthier, the name of Asher is also mentioned in a hitherto unpublished papyrus of the Golénischeff collection. Biblical references to Asher describe the fertility of its land (Gen. 49:20) and its economic potentialities (Deut. 33:24–5; Judg. 5:17). These permitted the tribe to develop in comparative tranquility, but at the same time also deprived it of the impetus and incentive for national activity and political leadership. Apart from Reuben and Simeon, who were afflicted with interminable conflicts over the southern boundaries of Israel, Asher was the only tribe that produced no national spokesman and leader in the period of the Judges. Apparently, at the beginning of the second decade of David's reign, the territorial association of the tribe of Asher with the kingdom of David was a close one. It was incorporated into the administrative division of the monarchy, and cities of the levites were appointed in its territory (see: *History; *David; *Priests and Priesthood). The four cities of Asher that were given to the levites were Mishal, Abdon (apparently the correct reading, and not Ebron mentioned in the passage defining Asher's territory (Josh. 19:28)), Helkath, and Rehob (Josh. 21:30–31; the parallel list in I Chron. 6:60 has, it is true, Hukok instead of Helkath, but this would appear to be a scribal error).

A short while before the destruction of the kingdom of Ephraim, Asher's landholdings were included in the Assyrian satrapy of Megiddo. From time to time, however, the kings of Judah attempted to extend their rule over them, as over other parts of the kingdom of Israel (II Chron. 30:10–12; cf. 34:6). After the return from the Babylonian exile, the Hasmoneans failed to incorporate Acre and the neighboring coastal plain within the confines of their kingdom. Most of the coast of Galilee was inhabited by a substantial non-Jewish population and was regarded, even from the halakhic point of view, as lying outside the limits of Israel.

In the *Aggadah*

The name Asher, meaning "praise," was chosen by Leah to indicate that all would praise her for the fact that, although already blessed with children, she was nevertheless unselfish enough to give her handmaid, Zilpah (Asher's mother) to Jacob (Mid. Hag. to Gen. 30:9); she also prophesied that in times to come, the sons of Asher would praise God for their fruitful possessions in Ereẓ Israel (Targ. Yer., Gen. 30:13). The soil of Asher's inheritance was so fertile that it sufficed to supply all Israel's needs (particularly olives; Sif. Deut. 355), even in a sabbatical year (Men. 85b). Asher himself was also blessed with riches. He never spent a night in an inn as he inherited lofty palaces throughout the world (Gen. R. 71:10). Such was the beauty of his daughters, that they all married high priests and kings (*ibid.*). When he informed his brothers of Reuben's sin against Bilhah, they reproached him (Sif. Deut. 355).

BIBLIOGRAPHY: H. Gauthier, *Dictionnaire des noms géographiques* …, 1 (1925), 105; Alt, in: ZAW, 45 (1927), 59–81; A.H. Gardiner, *Ancient Egyptian Onomastica*, 1 (1948), 191–3, no. 265; Mendenhall, in: JBL, 77 (1958), 52–66; Albright, in: JAOS, 74 (1954), 227–31; EM, 1 (1965), 777–86. **ADD. BIBLIOGRAPHY:** H.W. Fischer-Elfert, *Die satirische Streitschrift des Papyrus Anastasi I* (1986), 199–200; N. Na'aman, in: JSOT, 49 (1991), 99–111; D. Edelman, in: ABD, 1, 482–83; S. Japhet, *I & II Chronicles* (1993), 185–86; G. Ahlström, *The History of Ancient Palestine* (1993), 278–79; S. Ahituv, *Joshua* (Heb., 1995), 311–15. IN THE AGGADAH: Ginzberg, Legends, index; I. Ḥasida, *Ishei ha-Tanakh* (1964), 81.

ASHER, ABRAHAM (**Adolph**; 1800–1853), bookseller, publisher, and bibliographer. Asher founded the firm of Asher and Co. in 1830 in Berlin, which existed until the Nazi period. His main contribution to Jewish scholarship is his publication of *Benjamin of Tudela's *Itinerary*, including the text, Asher's English translation, critical notes by himself, L. Zunz, and S.J. Rapoport, and a geographical index (2 vols., 1842; repr., 1927). Steinschneider and Zedner cooperated with Asher in compiling important lists of books and manuscripts. Asher also published bibliographical studies on general subjects.

ADD. BIBLIOGRAPHY: Th. Keiderling, in: *Berlinische Monatsschrift*, 8 (1996), 55–60; D. Paisey, in: *British Library Journal*, 23:2 (1997), 131–53.

ASHER, ABRAHAM BEN GEDALIAH IBN (known also by the initials of Abraham Ben Asher as "**Aba**"; 16th century), talmudist and commentator on the Midrash. Abraham was apparently born in Safed. He was a disciple of Joseph *Caro and a colleague of Moses *Alshekh. Before 1566 he was serving as rabbi and head of the *bet din* of Aleppo. Asher's fame rests on his commentary to the **Midrash Rabbah*. He set himself the task of establishing the correct text of the Midrash by collating the various manuscripts, and clarifying the meaning by reference to parallel passages. The resultant work is one of the earliest and most valuable commentaries on the Midrash. It has the general title *Or ha-Sekhel*, but is generally known as "*Sefer Aba*." Each individual book of the Pentateuch and of the five scrolls has a separate title. The commentary on *Genesis Rabbah* called *Ma'adanei Melekh* was published by his brother-in-law Shneor b. Judah Falcon (Venice, 1567–68). It is accompanied by the text, and in addition has the commentary ascribed to Rashi, for which Asher prepared a critical edition based on two early manuscripts. The commentary on Exodus is extant in manuscript in Rome. From the eulogy on him by Saadiah Longo, it appears that he died in Ereẓ Israel.

BIBLIOGRAPHY: I. Theodor and Ch. Albeck, *Midrash Bereshit Rabbah*, 3 (1965^2), 132–34 ("*Mavo u-Mafteḥot*").

ASHER, DAVID (1818–1890), German philosophical writer and journalist. Born in Dresden, he went to England as a young man. There he published a catechism *Outlines of the Jewish Religion* (1845). He became headmaster of the Hebrew Association School of Manchester (1845) and later was tutor to the son of the chief rabbi, N.M. *Adler. Influenced to a mild degree by M. *Mendelssohn and thinkers of the Enlightenment (*Haskalah), Asher wrote a booklet on faith: *Der religioese Glaube: Eine psychologische Studie als Beitrag zur Psychologie und Religionsphilosophie*. By the time it appeared in 1860, he was mainly influenced by Schopenhauer, with whom he had been corresponding. Schopenhauer's non-belief in the immortality of the individual soul and his teachings on the Will to Live and the world-creating power of the Will, if not his pessimism, were in harmony with Mosaic concepts, argued Asher in *Das Endergebnis der Schopenhauer'schen Philosophie in seiner Uebereinstimmung mit einer der aeltesten Religionen* (1885). A few pages of this booklet are devoted to a refutation of antisemitism.

BIBLIOGRAPHY: JC (Dec. 5 and 12, 1890); Wininger, Biog, s.v.; AZDJ, 54 (1890), 609–10 (incl. bibl.).

[Otto Immanuel Spear]

ASHER, ISAIAH BEN MOSES HA-LEVI (1849–1912), traveler and Hebrew writer. Born in Galicia, Asher traveled throughout Europe in his youth and in 1873 set off on a journey to the Orient where he spent the rest of his life. Working as a shopkeeper and cobbler, he lived in Burma and Calcutta (1885–1900), then in 1902 moved to Darjeeling. He was a prolific writer of Hebrew poetry and prose, especially essays on psychology, history, and religion, including commentaries on the Psalms, Esther, and Song of Songs. All his works remain in manuscript form (Sassoon collection) except part of his autobiography (covering the years 1866–68) which was published in 1938.

BIBLIOGRAPHY: D.S. Sassoon, *Ohel Dawid*, 2 vols. (1932), index; idem, in: JC (July 25, 1930), supplement; A. Yaari (ed.), *Harpatka'otav shel Asher ha-Levi* (1938), 5–14.

[Walter Joseph Fischel]

ASHER, JOSEPH (1921–1990), U.S. Reform rabbi. Asher, born Joseph Ansbacher in Wiesbaden, Germany, was the scion of a line of Orthodox rabbis going back six generations. His father, Rabbi Jonah Ansbacher, learned in science and classics as well as Jewish law, broke with his traditional forebears by embracing the Neo-Orthodoxy of Samson Raphael *Hirsch. At age 17, shortly before *Kristallnacht*, Joseph fled to London, where he enrolled in the Orthodox Tree of Life Yeshiva. But he also gravitated toward Reform Judaism, influenced by Lily *Montagu who had founded the World Union of Progressive Judaism.

In 1940, Asher was interned by the British as a "friendly enemy alien," and endured abusive conditions aboard the HMT *Dunera*, which transported him and 2,000 other German-Jewish refugees to Australia. There he ultimately served as assistant rabbi in the Melbourne synagogue of Hermann Sanger, a German refugee who had established Liberal Judaism in Australia.

Asher, who had been ordained by the Tree of Life (having finished the course of study by correspondence), came to America in the late 1940s and attended Hebrew Union College in Cincinnati in order to familiarize himself further with the Reform movement. After pulpits in Florida and Alabama, he became the spiritual leader of Temple Emanuel of Greensboro, North Carolina, in 1958. He was active in the civil rights struggle, staunchly supporting the nation's first sit-ins held at that city's Woolworth's lunch counter. He became known outside the South with a highly controversial article in *Look* magazine in April 1965, urging reconciliation between Jews and Germans, which remained a lifelong preoccupation.

The quest for social justice at home and abroad characterized Asher's rabbinate at Congregation Emanu-El in San Francisco (1968–85), a synagogue with Gold Rush roots and the largest in Northern California. He opposed the Vietnam War, favored busing to achieve integration of the public schools, and highlighted such issues as world hunger, arms control, and the murder of thousands of Jehovah's witnesses in Africa. Appointed to the U.S. Holocaust Memorial Council by President Carter in 1980, and a close friend of its chairman, Elie *Wiesel, Asher emphasized the figure of 11 million people rather than six million Jews killed by Hitler.

The outspoken Asher was frequently embroiled in local controversies. He joined the national board of Breira, one of the few leading American pulpit rabbis to do so. The organization was sharply critical of Israel's policies toward the Palestinians. He also drew attention to many of the Jewish state's domestic problems, most notably the undue influence of its religious establishment. Yet Asher was decidedly conservative on American social and cultural issues and was offended by the irreverent youth culture and strident gay rights movement that took root in San Francisco in the late 1960s and 1970s. He also opposed and even ridiculed many of the alternative forms of American Judaism. Within Congregation Emanu-El, he and his cantor/educator, Joseph Portnoy, sought to preserve many aspects of the Classical Reform service and resisted attempts to bring the liturgy into the mainstream of Judaism even in the face of declining membership. Still, Asher was deeply respected by his flock and the larger community for the depth of his Jewish and secular learning, his masterfully crafted sermons, and his uncommon devotion to pastoral duties.

BIBLIOGRAPHY: F. Rosenbaum, *Visions of Reform: Congregation Emanu-El and the Jews of San Francisco, 1849-1999* (2000); M. Rischin and R. Asher (eds.), *The Jewish Legacy and the German Conscience: Essays in Memory of Rabbi Joseph Asher* (1991).

[Fred Rosenbaum (2nd ed.)]

ASHER, JOSEPH MICHAEL (1872–1909), rabbi and educator. Asher was born in Manchester, England, and studied at Trinity College, Cambridge, where he met Solomon *Schechter, who greatly stimulated his interest in the rabbinate and Jewish scholarship. He continued his studies in Europe and was ordained by David Tevel Katzenellenbogen of Suwalki, Russia. Asher returned to Manchester, where he organized *talmud torah* schools and for four years acted as *dayyan* for the Jewish cases at the Manchester courts.

In 1900 the B'nai Jeshurun congregation in New York City invited him to become its rabbi. From 1902, when the Jewish Theological Seminary was reorganized, until his death, he taught homiletics in that institution and headed its department of philosophy and ethics. From 1906 until his death he served as rabbi at the synagogue Orach Chaim. Asher earned a reputation as an eloquent orator because of his sermons and popular expositions on Jewish thinkers, which he delivered in Philadelphia and Baltimore as well as New York. He composed an evening service for the house of mourning.

BIBLIOGRAPHY: *American Hebrew* (Nov. 12, Dec. 24, 1909); DAB, 1 (1928), 388–9; I. Goldstein, *A Century of Judaism in New York: B'nai Jeshurun 1825–1925…* (1930), 222–5.

[Alvin Kass]

ASHERAH (Heb. אֲשֵׁרָה), in the Bible both a Canaanite goddess and a wooden cult object.

The Goddess

A Canaanite fertility and mother goddess. Asherah is now well known from the Ugaritic texts, where she is called *rabbatu atiratu yammi* ("Lady Athirat of the Sea"). The name is most probably to be understood as a feminine participle of the verb *ʾṯr* (Heb. *ʾshr* "to go, to tread"), thus meaning "The Lady who Treads upon the Sea." It is possible that the name goes back to some early myth in which Athirat defeated the rebellious Yamm, although in the Ugaritic text this deed was accomplished by Baal and in the Egyptian story by Astarte. Alternatively, it is possible that the name indicates some connection of Asherah with the sea. She has been identified by some with the Cyprian Aphrodite, the goddess intimately connected with harbors (as well as with love). Asherah is apparently (although not explicitly) the consort of El, the father and creator of the gods (she is called *qaniyatu el-îma*, "The Progenitress of the Gods"), who are accordingly called "the [70] children of Asherah." Similarly, the gods are also called "sons of *Qudšu*" ("holiness"), which, like *ʾelat* ("goddess"), is to be taken as an epithet of Asherah. The title "*Qudšu*" connects Asherah to the Egyptian figurines of nude goddesses commonly identified as fertility figurines. They show a nude goddess *en face*, frequently with a lion, and are inscribed QDŠ (*qudšu*).

Asherah was popular throughout the ancient Near East. In the Old Babylonian sources, Ašratum is listed as the consort of Amurru and occasionally of Anu (the Babylonian counterpart of El). In the el-Amarna letters, one of the kings of Amurru is known as ʿAbdi-Aširti ("the servant of Asherah"), and a letter from Tell Taanach from the 15th century B.C.E. refers to an *uban* (for *umman*) *Aširat* ("a sage of Aširat"). A Late Hittite tablet contains a myth in which Asherah tries unsuccessfully to seduce Baal and complains to Elkunirša (*El-qnhʾrs*; "El the world-Creator," cf. Gen. 14:19) that Baal has insulted her. In the Ugaritic Epic of Keret, Asherah is called "Asherah of the Sidonians, goddess of the Tyrians," and was thus intimately connected with the cities of the Phoenician coast. She was brought into the court worship of Israel by *Jezebel, the daughter of the king of Tyre, who also brought with her the cult of the Tyrian Baal. Thus it is related that Elijah vanquished the 450 prophets of Baal and the 400 prophets of Asherah who "dined off Jezebel's table" (I Kings 18:19). Earlier, Maacah, the mother of King *Asa, built an abominable image for Asherah (*la-Asherah*) and was therefore removed from the post of queen mother (I Kings 15:13; II Chron. 15:16). The last case of royal worship of Asherah was in the time of Manasseh, who placed an idol of Asherah in the Temple (II Kings 21:7), from which it was removed by Josiah (II Kings 23:6). During the Israelite period, the worship of Asherah was generally connected with the worship of Baal; the phrase "Baalim and Asheroth" is used to designate foreign gods in general (e.g., Judg. 3:7), and the term Asheroth is used as a synonym for "goddesses."

The Cult Object

There are also references in the Bible to some object called an Asherah which can be built, planted, erected, or constructed; is placed near the altar; and is destroyed by chopping it down and burning it. It therefore seems that Asherah, which is never described in the Bible, is some cult object made out of wood. The traditional explanation of the Asherah as a sacred grove can probably be rejected on the grounds that it seems to have been a man-made object. It is not known whether this object was an image of the goddess Asherah placed near the altar (no evidence at all exists for this), a sacred pole representing her, or an object of some other sort. These objects reportedly found during excavations at Qatna, Megiddo, and Ai are charred pieces of wood, and there is no proof of their identity. The use of the Asherah is found in both Israel and Judah, and is intimately connected with the use of *bamot* and *mazzevot* (I Kings 14:23) as one of the elements borrowed from the surrounding religions. It is probable that the use of the Asherah was originally connected with the worship of the goddess Airat. In the 1970s inscriptions from the ninth-century site of Kuntillet Ajrud in the Sinai and from the eighth-century site of Khirbet al-Qom on the West Bank were discovered. These mention *yhwh šmrm wʾšrth* and *yhwh tmn wʾšrth*. These phrases have been interpreted as "Yahweh of Samaria and his Ashera," and "Yahweh of Teman and his Asherah." On this interpretation Asherah would have been Yahweh's consort. Others have rendered *ʾšrth* as "his (Yahweh's) consort," arguing that the original divine name Asherah had become a common noun. Still others maintain that *ʾšr* represents an alternative form of the name of the goddess, either Ashirta, attested as a theophorous element in proper names, or Asheretah. Others have taken *ʾšrth* as a reference to the cultic object, translating "Yahweh of Samaria/Teman and its asherah" (II Kgs. 13:6).

BIBLIOGRAPHY: W.F. Albright, *Yahweh and the Gods of Canaan* (1968), index; Pope, in: H.W. Haussig (ed.), *Woerterbuch der Mythologie*, 1 (1965), 246–9 (incl. bibl.); Y. Yamashita, "The Goddess Asherah" (dissertation, Yale, 1963); W.L. Reed, *The Asherah in the Old Testament* (1949); IDB; Pritchard, Texts, 129–55. **ADD. BIBLIOGRAPHY:** J. Day, in: ABD, 1:483–87 (with bibliography); N. Wyatt, in: DDD, 99–105 (with bibliography).

[Tikva S. Frymer]

ASHER ANSHEL BEN ISAAC OF PRZEMYŚL (17th century), scholar and homiletic author. He is known almost exclusively through his popular collection of sermons *Shemenah Laḥmo* (Dessau, 1701; frequently reprinted). The first part of the work consists of seven major sermons devoted to the Sabbath and the major holidays. The second part consists of homilies on major events in the religious life of man: circumcision, bar mitzvah, marriage, burial, etc. The sermons begin with a series of questions, followed by *teʿamim* (homiletic interpretations). The theme of the last sermon in the book is resurrection.

BIBLIOGRAPHY: Steinschneider, Cat Bod, 748.

ASHER BEN DAVID (first half of the 13th century), Provence kabbalist of the second generation of kabbalists and author of the first "book" of any length intended for a wider audience. His grandfather, R. *Abraham b. David of Posquières, is considered the first known kabbalistic personality, although he refrained from acknowledging this status and from composing anything kabbalistic. His son, R. Isaac the Blind, uncle to R. Asher ben David, composed a highly enigmatic commentary to the *Book of Creation*, as he denied any literary activity in a celebrated letter to Nahmanides, in which he proclaimed allegiance to Nahmanides' stated policy of a complete reliance on oral transmission of kabbalistic secrets. R. Isaac suggests in this letter of defense that he has "no sign from heaven" to come himself to Spain and correct, or stop, the damage done by his students who were publicly disseminating texts or teachings, and mentions Asher as a possible emissary who could speak for his position on esotericism. We know, however, of no such visit by Asher, which would amount to an important and authorized link connecting the Provençal school directly with Spanish kabbalistic circles. Curiously, what has survived is a compendium of treatises edited into a lengthy work entitled *Sefer ha-Yiḥud*, the *Book of Unity*, in which Asher explains major kabbalistic concepts. It is unclear if this work was intended for the audience already exposed to ideas which emerged from Isaac's circle or whether it begins a new form of kabbalistic literature intended for other kabbalists. *Sefer ha-Yiḥud* is introduced by the first known kabbalistic poem. The treatises or chapters which comprise the book were often copied by kabbalists and survived in short and intermediate versions relative to the full length book, which may have been edited or expanded later by Asher or a student of the circle. A Latin translation of a section of *Sefer ha-Yiḥud* was prepared by Flavio Mithridates and survives in a single manuscript. An "epistle" attributed to Asher is now understood to be a collection of passages from his work. Finally, a highly popular *Commentary to the Account of Creation* is attributed to Asher, but his authorship of this work remains highly questionable, though it finds its place in a genre of literature which emerged from Provence. Asher makes one passing reference to an "*aggadah*," which might be from the *Sefer ha-*Bahir*, although it is clear that his Kabbalah is not based on the traditions of that work, like that of his teachers and family members in Provence. The Kabbalah of Asher is nevertheless significantly different from that of his contemporaries in Gerona, Ezra and Azriel, students of Isaac. His complete works have been edited in a single volume.

BIBLIOGRAPHY: D. Abrams, *R. Asher ben David. His Complete Works and Studies in his Kabbalistic Thought* (Heb., 1996); J. Dan and R. Elior, *Kabbalat R. Asher ben David*, Jerusalem (Heb., 1980); M. Rong-Wiznitzer, "Is Paris Ms. 767 Actually a Letter of Asher ben David," in: *Jerusalem Studies in Jewish Thought*, 3 (1982), 33–50 (Heb.); G. Scholem, *Origins of the Kabbalah* (1987), 93–94, 148–49, 171–74, 252–56, 303–7.

[Daniel Abrams (2nd ed.)]

ASHER BEN JEHIEL (also known as **Asheri** and **Rosh;** c. 1250–1327), talmudist. His first teachers were his father, one of the Ḥasidei Ashkenaz, who was a follower of *Judah b. Samuel he-Ḥasid, and his elder brother. He spent some time in France, apparently in Troyes, and then lived in Cologne and Coblenz. From there he moved to Worms, where his teacher *Meir b. Baruch of Rothenburg had been appointed rabbi in 1281. Meir esteemed his pupil, and appointed him a member of the local *bet-din*. After the imprisonment of Meir, Asher became the acknowledged leader of German Jewry and headed the unsuccessful efforts to obtain his master's release, toward which he was prepared to contribute a considerable portion of his assets. He distinguished himself for his activities during the period of the *Rindfleisch* massacres (1298) and for his decisions on matters arising from the resulting disruption of family and communal life. Fearing a similar fate to that of Meir of Rothenburg, Asher left Germany in 1303. The following year, he reached Barcelona, via north Italy and Provence, where he was welcomed with great honor by Solomon b. Abraham *Adret. In 1305 he accepted the position of rabbi in Toledo. His son, Judah, relates that shortly thereafter, Asher turned down a request of the German authorities that he return to his native country, for which they were prepared to provide an imperial letter of safe-conduct and an escort of 50 soldiers.

Asher was drawn into the contemporary conflict concerning the study of philosophy. In Provence he had found only "isolated individuals" engaged in exclusive study of the Torah, which fact he attributed to the widespread study of philosophy. From Barcelona he sent a letter of encouragement to Abba Mari *Astruc, a leader of the opponents of philosophy. Alive to the danger of discord, he proposed an intercommunal conference to reconcile the opposing views (*Minḥat Kena'ot*, 51). When Solomon Adret proposed a ban on the study of philosophy by anyone under the age of 25, Asher, already in Toledo, influenced the local leaders to support this ban. He criticized those who used positions of influence at court for their own advantage. He similarly opposed customs which had been influenced by the Christian environment, such as, granting equal rights of inheritance to husband and wife and bequeathing the whole estate to the oldest son, as was the custom among the nobility; chaining of debtors; and compelling a husband to grant his wife a divorce on her declaration of her unwillingness to live with him. His vast influence and moral stature enabled him to overcome the difficulties which he encountered in those activities, and his spiritual influence was acknowledged even by the Castilian queen, Maria de Molina.

His responsa sometimes reflect the modesty and humility that typified the German school, and at others, the firmness and authority of one speaking in the name of the supreme political and judicial body of Spanish Jewry. When the rabbi of Valencia insisted on his view in defiance of accepted practice and the opinion of Asher, the latter threatened him with capital punishment, if all the other deterrents enumerated in a letter to one of the scholars of the community should prove of no avail (*Responsa*, 107, 6). Despite his reservations and doubts as to the right of the rabbis to impose capital punishment, he nonetheless permitted them to act according to the custom prevalent in Spain, and consented to sentences of mutilation, particularly in the case of informers. Asher introduced into Spain the system of study of the *tosafists and tried to establish a German *minhag*. He is regarded as one of the outstanding halakhic authorities who put the final seal to the work of the German and French codifiers, joining to it the Spanish *halakhah*. True to the methods of the tosafists, he subjected the statements of the *rishonim* and *geonim* to a critical examination and did not hesitate to disagree with them whenever talmudic sources did not support their view and conclusions. Virtually all the communities of Spain referred their problems to him and students flocked to his yeshivah from all Europe, including Russia. When he encountered matters not specifically prohibited in the Torah, Asher was prepared to abandon his own opinion in the face of strong opposition, particularly for the sake of peace, but he never hesitated from taking a strong stand against undesirable developments in the communal life. In answer to a complaint that members of distinguished families had not been appointed as cantors, he stated forcibly that neither distinguished descent, nor the possession of a pleasant voice should be the criterion, but only moral standing (*ibid.*, 4:22).

His negative attitude toward philosophy did not extend to science generally, and he encouraged Isaac b. Joseph Israeli to write his *Yesod Olam*. He was familiar with German law and Spanish common law but his knowledge of Arabic was limited to the spoken language. Having lost all his property in Germany, he lived under conditions of financial stress, and his son notes that his father's assets at the time of his death were insufficient for the execution of his will. Asher nevertheless continued in Spain his ancestral custom of tithing all his income. His halakhic works are (1) *Piskei ha-Rosh* (also called *Hilkhot ha-Rosh, Sefer ha-Asheri*), modeled on that of *Alfasi. In it he sums up the decisions of the earlier codifiers and commentators. It covers most of the talmudic tractates to which are added the *Halakhot Ketannot*, such as *Seder Avodah, Tumah, Ẓiẓit, Tefillin, Mezuzah, Ḥaliẓah*, and *Milah*. Contrary to Alfasi, who primarily quotes the talmudic text, Asher discusses the halakhic issues raised by the Talmud and the earlier commentators, especially the tosafists. Rabbi Joseph *Caro considered *Piskei ha-Rosh* to be one of the three pillars (along with Alfasi and Maimonides) that form the foundation for his *Shulḥan Arukh. (2) Responsa (Constantinople, 1517). The extant collection numbers over 1,000 responsa, arranged in 108 chapters, subdivided into sections. They are of the utmost significance in the study of halakhic development and give an insight into the cultural life of Spanish and German Jewry. The collection of responsa, *Besamin Rosh*, has been forged under his name (see *Berlin, Saul b. Ẓevi Hirsch). In 1965 the Institute for Research in Jewish Law of the Hebrew University published a comprehensive index to Asher's responsa. The index includes lists of all biblical, talmudic, and post-talmudic sources quoted in the responsa. (3) Commentary on the Mishnayot to the orders of *Zera'im* (Altona, 1735; new edition, according to Ms., Jerusalem 1965/6) and *Tohorot* (also printed in the Vilna Talmud) being mainly an abridgment of the commentary of *Samson b. Abraham of Sens to these orders. Asher also made use of Maimonides' Mishnah commentary, translated for him by Israel b. Joseph. He also wrote commentaries on the tractates *Sotah* (in part), *Middot, Tamid* (Prague, 1725), and *Kinnim*. The full commentary to *Sotah* was published in Jerusalem, 1968. (4) *Tosafot*. The abridgment of the *tosafot* of Sens with the addition of Meir b. Baruch of Rothenburg's novellae and the opinions of Spanish scholars, was apparently the fruit of his instruction at the yeshivah and covered virtually all the tractates of the Babylonian Talmud (*Ber.* (Warsaw, 1863); *Shek.* (Jerusalem, 1943); *Meg.* (Leghorn, 1785); M.K. (Jerusalem, 1931); *Yoma* (N.Y., 1965); *Suk.* (Jerusalem, 1903); *Yev.* (Leghorn, 1776); *Ket.* (*ibid.*); *Git.* (Warsaw, 1927); *Kid.* (Pisa, 1806); *Ned.* (Vilna, Romm ed.); *Naz.* (*ibid.*); BM (Jerusalem, 1959); *Sot.* (see above); *Shevu.* (Leghorn, 1785); *Hor.* (Vilna, Romm ed.); *Nid.* (*ibid.*)). Many fragments to other tractates have been published. Only a part of his commentaries and *tosafot* have been published; the remainder is still in manuscript. His commentaries and *tosafot* were mainly studied in Spain where they were used almost exclusively, and were practically unknown in other countries. Asher apparently also wrote a commentary on the Pentateuch but the commentary printed in *Hadar Zekenim* (1840) was written by one of his German pupils, prior to 1327. Asher's piety and exemplary conduct are reflected in his celebrated work, known variously as *Hanhagot ha-Rosh, Orḥot Ḥayyim*, and *Ẓavva'at ha-Rosh* (Venice, 1579). It includes 131 ethical sayings grouped for each of the six weekdays, in which he details rules of conduct for a Jew in his private, family, and public life, and in relation to Jews and Gentiles. He demands integrity, courtesy, and sincerity in dealings with Gentiles. *Orḥot Ḥayyim*, a popular work throughout the centuries, was extensively studied in the Lithuanian *musar* yeshivot in the first half of the 20th century.

BIBLIOGRAPHY: Freimann, in: JJLG, 12 (1918), 237–317; 13 (1919), 142–254; Baer, Spain, 1 (1961), 297–301, 316–25; Faur, in: PAARJ, 33 (1965), 41–65 (Heb. part); Urbach, Tosafot, index; Epstein, in: *Tarbiz*, 12 (1940/41), 190–204; M. Elon (ed.), *Mafte'aḥ ha-She'elot ve-ha-Teshuvot… ha-Rosh* (1965). **ADD. BIBLIOGRAPHY:** J. Weisberg, "On the Political Thought of Rabbi Asher bar Yechiel," diss., Touro College (1998).

[*Encyclopaedia Hebraica* / David Derovan (2nd ed.)]

ASHER BEN MESHULLAM HA-KOHEN OF LUNEL (late 12th century), Provençal talmudist; known as the "Rosh of Lunel." He was the son of *Meshullam b. Jacob of Lunel and brother of *Aaron b. Meshullam of Lunel. He lived an ascetic life and was referred to as a *parush* ("hermit") by Benjamin of Tudela. Judah ibn Tibbon, who copied for Asher the *Tikkun Middot ha-Nefesh* of Ibn Gabirol (Steinschneider, *Oẓerot Ḥayyim*, 366), praised Asher for his positive attitude toward science and encouraged his son's friendship with Asher. Few of his responsa and decisions have been preserved in the works of others, and only fragments of his halakhic works have been preserved. Several talmudic comments quoted in the *Sefer ha-Hashlamah* of his nephew, *Meshullam b. Moses, are attributed to Asher, as well as a treatise on the laws of *niddui* and *ḥerem* ("banning and excommunication"). Asher was the author of *Sefer ha-Mattanot* (extracts of which were published by S. Assaf – see bibliography), a work which is modeled on the *Sefer ha-Mattanah* of Samuel b. Hophni. Asher apparently wrote a comprehensive work covering the whole of civil law of which *Sefer ha-Mattanot* formed only a part. The whole book was based on the *Sefer ha-Din* of Judah b. Barzillai al-Bargeloni.

BIBLIOGRAPHY: J. Lubetzky (ed.), *Sefer ha-Hashlamah*, 1 (1885), x–xii (pref.); S. Assaf, *Mi-Sifrut ha-Ge'onim* (1933), 1–31; Gross, Gal Jud, 280–1; E. Urbach, *Mazkeret ... Herzog* (1962), 411–3.

[Yehoshua Horowitz]

ASHER BEN SAUL (late 12th and early 13th centuries), one of the "sages of Lunel," later of Narbonne. Few biographical details are known about him and until recently many confused him with Asher b. Meshullam of Lunel. Asher was the younger brother of the kabbalist Jacob *Nazir. Asher's tendency toward mysticism can be detected in his writings. His principal teacher was Samuel b. David Provençal, but he was influenced by Abraham b. David of Posquières and Joseph b. Plat, although it is uncertain whether they were actually his teachers. Asher is the author of *Sefer ha-Minhagot* ("Book of Customs"), parts of which were first published from an incomplete manuscript by S. Assaf (see bibl.). It is the second book of its kind written in Europe (1205–10), having been preceded a few years earlier by the *Ha-Manhig* of Abraham b. Nathan ha-Yarḥi. Many customs were falling into neglect because of ignorance as to their origins. Asher sought to reinforce their observance by giving an extensive variety of sources. In addition to talmudic and midrashic material he quotes the Babylonian *geonim* and the rabbis of Spain and of northern and southern France. However, the only customs mentioned are those of Lunel and Narbonne. The *Minhagot* was well known by the codifiers and was used extensively, particularly by *Aaron b. Jacob of Lunel in his *Orḥot Ḥayyim*. The rest of his work is known only from quotations.

BIBLIOGRAPHY: M.B.Z. Benedikt, in: KS, 27 (1950/51), 240–1; I. Sonne, *ibid.*, 28 (1952/53), 416; S. Assaf, *Sifran shel Rishonim* (1935), 121–82; S. Schechter, in: JQR, 5 (1892/93), 18–23, 350ff.; A. Marx, in: REJ, 59 (1910), 204.

[Israel Moses Ta-Shma]

ASHI (d. 427 C.E.; pronounced by some with *hireq* under the *shin* and by others with *sere*); the most celebrated Babylonian *amora* of the sixth generation. Ashi, who lived in Mata Mehasya, is reported to be the son-in-law of Rami b. Abba (Ḥul. 111a). Ashi's teachers were Rav Papi I (RH 29b, et al.) and, even more so, Rav *Kahana of Pum Nahara (Ber. 39b et al.; see Cohen, *Ravina*, p.106–7). Ashi interacts with a large number of his contemporaries, but especially Ameimar, Mar Zutra, and *Ravina (Ber. 44a). Ashi had at least three children: Mar bar Rav Ashi, Rav Sama, and a daughter (Ket. 69a).

Ashi flourished during the reign of the Sassanian ruler Yazdigird I (399–421 C.E.). Yazdigird's general policy of tolerance for minorities extended to the Jews as well. The Talmud reports that Ashi met with Yazdigird together with Amemar and Mar Zutra. Ashi must have been wealthy for he possessed a forest, had a servant, and owned fancy utensils (MK 12b; Ned. 62b; Suk. 10b; Ber. 31a; Jacobowitz, p. 91). Aha bar Rava states that "from the time of Rabbi until R. Ashi we don't find anyone who was supreme both in Torah and in worldly affairs." Even the exilarch, Huna b. Nathan, accepted his authority (Git. 59a; Levin, p. 91). Ashi was responsible for several important innovations and was always concerned that a ruling should not cause embarrassment or monetary loss to people (Jacobowits). Among his sayings are "Everyone who is haughty will finally be humbled" (Sot. 5a); "Any scholar who is not as hard as iron is not a scholar" (Ta'an. 4a).

Nineteenth-century scholarship, following the opinion of Rashi (BM 86a) and Maimonides (Yad, Intro), thought that Ashi was the editor of the Babylonian Talmud. However, recent scholarship dates the editing of the Babylonian Talmud one to two centuries after the death of Ashi. The sources used by earlier scholars to prove that Ashi was the editor of the Babylonian Talmud are shown to be unconvincing upon critical analysis. The most important source quoted in this regard is the purported statement of the first-century *amora*, Samuel, who says he saw it written in the book of Adam that "Rebbi and Rav Natan are the end of the Mishnah; Rav Ashi and Ravina are the end of teaching (*hora'ah*)" (BM 86a). Besides the anachronism of Samuel (third cent.) speaking about Ashi and the legendary air of a book of Adam, the meaning of the term *hora'ah* is not at all clear. Early scholars thought *hora'ah* should be understood in parallelism with Mishnah and so must refer to the next major rabbinic compilation after the Mishnah, the Babylonian Talmud. However, *hora'ah* elsewhere simply means an authoritative ruling (Yev. 92a, et al.). The statement actually means that Ashi and Ravina mark the end of the amoraic period in that they are the last to teach in an apodictic style (Halivni) and the last to legislate with the authority of the *amoraim*.

*Sherira Gaon, who did equate the end of *hora'ah* with the end of the Talmud, could not accept that Ashi finished editing the Talmud since there are a number of Rabbis quoted in the Talmud who lived after Ashi such as Mar b. Rav Ashi and Rabba Tosfa'a. Sherirah therefore reads it as referring to Ravina b. Huna (Levin, p. 95) and Assi (ibid. p. 97; Spanish recension reads Yose), both seventh generation *amoraim*. The second major source for Ashi's editorial activity is the report of Ravina that Ashi taught a certain law one way in his first *mahadurah* and a different law in his last *mahadurah* (BB 157b). Early scholars understood the word *mahadurah* according to it modern usage to mean an edition of the Talmud. Sherirah explains, partly based on the customs of his day in the Geonic yeshivot, that Ashi taught for almost 60 years during which he reviewed two tractates each year during the two kallah sessions thus twice completing the 63 tractates of Mishnah (Levin, p. 93–94). However, *mahadurah* can simply mean a review of Ashi's personal teachings which has nothing to do with an official version of the Talmud.

Not only is there no good source for Ashi being the editor of the Babylonian Talmud, Ashi's activity and statements in the Talmud itself show that he could not have been its editor. Many passages in the Talmud cite and analyze sayings or practices of Ashi, which implies that a later group of editors received traditions from or about Ashi and discussed them just as they did for all previous *amoraim*. When Ashi remarks, "I have protected Mata Mehasya from being destroyed," an anonymous questioner says, "but it has been destroyed" (Shab 11a). The questioner here must have lived many years after Ashi. The Talmud is sometimes unsure of whether a certain statement was made by Ashi or someone else; other times it debates which source text was the subject of interpretation in a certain comment of Ashi. This would not occur if Ashi himself was the editor (Kaplan, 104–127).

Nevertheless, it is clear that Ashi contributed significantly to the substance of the Babylonian Talmud. The Talmud mentions Ashi's name well over a thousand times, often in the center of debate together with the illustrious names of his generation. Ashi, more so than other *amoraim*, frequently sits silently while subordinate scholars address arguments to him. Ashi is the dominant figure of his generation and the *amoraim* of his generation are more centralized than those of earlier generations (Kalmin, p. 125). Ashi's circle of students is referred to throughout the Talmud as "the rabbis of the house of Rav Ashi," a mark of distinction accorded to few others (Shab. 41a).

BIBLIOGRAPHY: Weiss, Dor, 3 (1904[4]), 184–8; S. Fink, *Die Juden in Babylonien*, 2 (1908), 98, 140 ff.; Hyman, Toledot, s.v.; Bacher, Bah Amor, 144–7; Bacher, Trad, index s.v.; Levin, *Iggeret Rab Sherira Gaon* (1920); Halevy, Dorot, 2 (1923), 536 ff.; J.S. Zuri, *Rav Ashi* (Heb., 1924); J. Kaplan, *Redaction of the Babylonian Talmud* (1933), index, s.v.; Z.W. Jawetz, *Toledot Yisrael*, 8 (19383), 128 ff.; A. Weiss *Hithavvut ha-Talmud bi-Shlemuto* (1943), pp. 245 ff.; Graetz, Hist, 2 (1949), 605–11; Albeck, in: *Sinai, Sefer Yovel* (1958), 73–79 (Heb.); idem. Mavo Latalmudim, 427–30; Baron, Social[2], index. **ADD. BIBLIOGRAPHY:** M. Feldblum, "Prof. Avraham Weiss: His Approach and Contributions to Talmudic Scholarship," in: *The Abraham Weiss Jubilee Volume* (1964), 43–48; T. Farhsel, "*Rav Ashi – Shin Haruqah O Seruyah*," in: *Hadoar*, 56 (1977), 104; J. Jacobowitz, "Aspects of the Economic and Social History of the Jews in Babylonia with Special Emphasis on the Teachings and Decisions of R. Ashi and the Sixth Generation of Amoraim" (Diss. New York University (1978)). Strack, Introduction, 98, 192–4; D. Halivni, *Mekorot u-Mesorot* (1968–); idem, *Midrash, Mishnah, and Gemara* (1986), 66–68; R. Kalmin, *The Redaction of the Babylonian Talmud* (1989); idem. *Sages, Stories, Authors and Editors in Rabbinic Babylonia* (1994), 111 – 25; A. Cohen, *Ravina and Contemporary Sages* (2001).

[Moshe Nahum Zobel]

ASHIMA (Heb. אֲשִׁימָא), deity worshiped by the people of Hamath in Syria, who were deported to Samaria and its environs to replace the Israelites, exiled in 722–21 B.C.E. (II Kings 17:30). Until recently no exact correspondent of the name Ashima was attested, and scholars attempted to identify Ashima with various deities from Phoenicia, Elephantine, and Mesopotamia having names similar to the biblical form. These attempts have been vitiated by the discovery of an Aramaic inscription from Teima in Arabia ca. 400 B.C.E. that refers to Ashima (אשימא) along with Sengalla (שנגלא) as "the gods of Teima (אלהי תימא)." The biblical association of Ashima with Hamath in Northern Syria versus his attestation at Teima may be explained by the gap of several centuries between the occurrences.

BIBLIOGRAPHY: M. Cogan and H. Tadmor, *II Kings* (AB; 1988), 211–12; M. Cogan, in: DDD, 105–6; A. Livingstone, in: M. Geller et al. (eds.), *Studia Aramaica* (1995), 133–43.

[S. David Sperling (2nd ed.)]

ASHINSKY, AARON MORDECAI HALEVI (1866–1954), U.S. rabbi and religious Zionist leader. Born in Rajgrod, Poland, he was ordained at an early age. In 1895 he went to the U.S., and first held rabbinical posts in Syracuse and Detroit. In 1898 he accepted a position in Montreal, where he organized Canada's first Zionist group and also served as chaplain to Jewish soldiers in the Canadian armed forces. Ashinsky subsequently became rabbi of the Beth Hamidrash Hagadol congregation in Pittsburgh, where he remained for 25 years until leaving for Brooklyn, a decision that was reversed when the congregation took him to a *din Torah*. He served in Pittsburgh for the rest of his life. Ashinsky was devoted to the cause of Jewish education and helped establish *talmud torah* schools in several of the cities where he served as rabbi. An able orator, he was among the founders of the Mizrachi Organization of America, of which he was vice president for many years. Ashinsky was also a founding member of the Union of Orthodox Rabbis of the United States and Canada and was very active in the aid and relief work of the Ezras Torah organization.

BIBLIOGRAPHY: *Enẓiklopedyah shel ha-Ẓiyyonut ha-Datit*, 1 (1958), 200–2. **ADD. BIBLIOGRAPHY:** I.A. Swiss and H.N. Shoop, *Rabbi Aron M. Ashinsky: Fifty Years of Study and Service* (1935).

[Aaron Lichtenstein]

ASHKANASY, MAURICE (1901–1971), Australian lawyer and communal leader. Born in London, Ashkanasy was taken to Australia as a child. He studied at the University of Melbourne, practiced law at the Victorian Bar, and was made a king's counsel in 1940. During World War II Ashkanasy served in the Australian Army in Malaya and New Guinea, rising to the rank of lieutenant-colonel. Subsequently he became chairman of the Victorian Bar Council (1952–55). Ashkanasy was a prominent figure in Jewish affairs; by 1945 he was the recognized lay leader of Australian Jewry. He was five times president of the Executive Council of Australian Jewry, president of the Victorian Jewish Board of Deputies, and a member of the executive of the World Jewish Congress. Ashkanasy was also an important figure in the Victorian branch of the Australian Labor Party, and sought election to Parliament, but was unsuccessful. He was a major force in reorienting Australian Jewry into a pro-Zionist direction and towards a greater willingness to assert its group identity forcefully, a path followed by all of his successors.

BIBLIOGRAPHY: *Australian Dictionary of Biography*, 13, 78–79; H.L. Rubinstein, *Australia*, 1, index.

[Isidor Solomon / William D. Rubinstein (2nd ed.)]

ASHKAVAH (Heb. אַשְׁכָּבָה; "laying to rest"; also *Hashkavah*), designation of memorial prayer in the Sephardi (Italian and Oriental) ritual. The *Ashkavah* is recited every Sabbath, on festivals, and on Mondays and Thursdays. It is said either after the Torah scroll has been returned to the Ark, or immediately after the Torah portion has been read, at the request of a mourner who had been called up to the Torah reading. After introductory verses from Psalms, Proverbs, etc., the *Ashkavah* continues: "May the repose which is prepared in the celestial abode under the wings of the Divine Presence… be the lot, dwelling, and the resting place of the soul of our deceased (so and so)…" and concludes with the phrase: "May he/she and all His people of Israel, who slumber in this dust, be included in mercy and forgiveness. May this be His will and let us say, Amen." For a deceased Torah scholar extra biblical verses are prefixed (Job 28:12; Ps. 25:12; 31:20; 36:8–9). A different text, opening with Proverbs 31:10–31, is used for women. A much shorter version is used by the Oriental Sephardim. The *Ashkavah* is also recited at the graveside as part of the funeral service. On the Day of Atonement, in many Sephardi congregations, the *Ashkavah* forms part of the evening service, and, as in the Ashkenazi ritual, the names of the deceased members of the community are read. The vows for charity in memory of the departed are, however, made the next day between *Musaf* and *Minḥah*. The full text of the *Ashkavah* may be found in M. Gaster, *The Book of Prayer* (1901), 200–01; De Sola Pool, *Book of Prayer* (1954), 206–7.

ASHKELON (Heb. אַשְׁקְלוֹן; Askelon, Ascalon).

Ancient Period

One of the five Philistine city-states and a seaport in the southern coastal plain of Ereẓ Israel situated 12 mi. (19 km.) north of Gaza and 10 mi. (16 km.) south of Ashdod. The etymology of the name Ashkelon is probably Western Semitic and may be derived from the root (*shkl*; "to weigh"), indicating thereby that it served as a center for mercantile activities. Ashkelon is first mentioned in the Egyptian Execration Texts of the 11th dynasty (c. 20th–19th centuries) as Asqanu. The city would appear to have been a Canaanite city-state under strong Egyptian influence throughout the 18th to 20th Dynasties. Ashkelon appears in several *El-Amarna letters (EA, 287, 320–2, 370). Although it seems to have remained loyal to Egypt on the whole (EA, 320, 322), Abdihiba, the ruler of Jerusalem, complained to Pharaoh that the people of Ashkelon helped the *Habiru, Egypt's enemy (EA, 287:14–16). About 1280 B.C.E., Ashkelon revolted against Ramses II, who put down the rebellion; the conquest is depicted on reliefs at the Karnak temple. It was again captured by Pharaoh *Merneptah approximately 1229 B.C.E., as indicated on his "Israel Stele." Ashkelon is also mentioned in an ivory tablet from *Megiddo. Toward the middle of the 12th century B.C.E. it was taken by the Philistines and was thereafter one of their Pentapolis (Josh. 13:3; I Sam. 6:17; II Sam. 1:20). According to Judges 1:18, the tribe of Judah conquered Ashkelon together with Gaza and Ekron (cf., however, Judg. 1:18 in the Septuagint, which states that Ashkelon, Gaza, and Ekron were not taken). Ashkelon is mentioned in connection with several details of the Samson stories (Judg. 14:19). During the period of the monarchy, it continued to be one of the main Philistine cities and ports (II Sam. 1:20), and Amos predicted its punishment (Amos 1:8). In the eighth century B.C.E. the size of its kingdom was substantially reduced by the Assyrians, who referred to it as Iskaluna or Askaluna, and it was eventually brought under their suzerainty by Tiglath-Pileser III in 734 B.C.E. A first unsuccessful rebellion by the King of Ashkelon against the Assyrians led a severe punishment in 732 B.C.E. Later, Sidqia, king of Ashkelon, became one of the participants in another rebellion against Assyria led by Hezekiah. In Sennacherib's account of his campaign in 701 B.C.E., he describes the capture of some of Sidqia's cities in the vicinity of Jaffa, Ashkelon's submission, and the deportation of its king (Sennacherib Prism, 1:50ff.). Tribute received from Ashkelon is mentioned in the inscriptions of the rulers Esarhaddon and Ashurbanipal. They used the city as a base for their campaigns against Egypt (end of the seventh and early sixth centuries B.C.E.) and the hardships that the city endured were mentioned by the prophets (e.g. Zeph. 2:4; Jer. 25:20). With the collapse of Assyrian rule, Ashkelon fell into the hands of Psammetichus and Necho of Egypt. The city was subdued and destroyed by Nebuchadnezzar (Jer. 47:5–7), who deported many of its inhabitants. In an Aramaic letter found in Egypt, which belongs to this period, a certain Adon, probably the king of Ashkelon, pleads for help, stating that the Babylonian king has reached *Aphek.

In the Persian period, Ashkelon was under the control of Tyre (according to Pseudo-Scylax, fourth century B.C.E.). With the division of Alexander's empire, Ashkelon – Ascalon as it was then known – was included in the Ptolemies' domain and it became a free port and an autonomous city. A Jewish community flourished in the city under their rule. Ashkelon subsequently fell into the hands of Antiochus III and became an important center of Greek civilization in Hellenistic times. In 111 B.C.E. it was minting its own coins. With the decline of the Seleucid kingdom, it regained its independence in 104 B.C.E., from which time it reckoned the beginning of its own era. Ashkelon maintained its independence throughout the reigns of the Hasmonean rulers John *Hyrcanus and Alexander *Yannai who were unsuccessful in their bids to conquer the city. In the Roman period it was considered a "free and allied city" (*Colonia Ascalon liberate et foederata*). Pagan cults included the worship of Isis, Apollo and Heracles, and of Atargatis/Derceto – a goddess with the face and upper body of a woman and the lower body and tail of a fish – whose temple contained pools for sacred fish (Diodorus, 2:4; Pausanias, 1:14, 16).Although not included in the territory ruled by Herod, he nevertheless built market places and public baths there and adorned the town with gardens – perhaps because it was his birthplace. During the war against the Romans (66 C.E), the Ashkelonites clashed with the Jews and defeated them. In the period of the Mishnah and the Talmud, Jews lived in Ashkelon, as the remains of a synagogue from that period show (see below). Talmudic sources mention its orchards and its fair (TJ, Shev. 6:1, 36c; Sif. Deut. 51). The orchards were incorporated within the boundaries of the Holy Land (set by the returnees from Babylonia) but not the city proper, and the latter was therefore exempted from the tithes and sabbatical year regulations (TJ, Shev. 6:1, 36c). In the early years of the Byzantine period, Ashkelon was the seat of a school of Hellenistic philosophy and was strongly opposed to Christianity.

Neolithic and Chalcolithic remains have been reported in the vicinity of Tel Ashkelon (Ar. Tell el-Hadr) and substantial Early Bronze Age I remains have been uncovered in the Afridar neighborhood of the modern city about a mile to the north of the ancient mound. Tel Ashkelon has been the focus of archaeological excavations ever since the first probes made there by W.J. Phythian-Adams and J. Garstang in 1920–21 that brought to light Hellenistic and Roman remains – including remains of a large building identified as a council-house (*bouleuterion*) or forum, as well as earlier Middle Bronze fortifications and pottery in fill layers indicating the links that the city had with Aegean and Cypriot cultures. During subsequent archaeological investigations a remarkable painted tomb was discovered by J. Ory bearing scenes of two nymphs in a Nilotic landscape, the god Pan playing a *syrinx*, a dog chasing a gazelle, a Gorgon mask, etc. Dating from the Byzantine period are the remains of a church and a synagogue with a chancel screen decorated with *menorot*. From 1985 large-scale excavations were initiated at Tel Ashkelon on a yearly basis by L.E. Stager. Apart from scanty remains from the Early Bronze II–III, an impressive Middle Bronze II defensive system and a well-preserved gate flanked by towers were uncovered. Nearby a small shrine (the "sanctuary of the silver calf") was uncovered. Late Bronze Age building remains and sunken burial vaults are known from the site. Philistine remains are represented by fortifications dated to 1100 B.C.E. The discovery of vats suggests that one of the occupations of the inhabitants was wine production. The Philistine city was destroyed in 604 B.C.E. Persian remains of the fifth century B.C.E. include the discovery of an unusual dog cemetery; the town was destroyed c. 300 B.C.E. In addition to these remains, signs of later occupation represented by public buildings and dwellings were also revealed from the Hellenistic, Roman, Byzantine, and Early Islamic periods. A bathhouse/brothel dating from the fourth century C.E. was found with the bones of hundreds of newborn babies in the underground sewers. A hexagonal Byzantine church with decorated mosaic floors has also been uncovered. An inscription from 1150 B.C.E. relates to the refortification of Ashkelon under the Fatimids. These walls, however, did not prevent the eventual capture of the site by the Crusaders.

[Michael Avi-Yonah / Shimon Gibson (2nd ed.)]

Medieval Period

Apparently a Jewish community existed in Ashkelon during the reign of the Abbasids. Under the Fatimids, Jews are mentioned in letters found in the Cairo *Genizah* as *kehal Ashkelon* ("the Ashkelon congregation") and *kahal kadosh* ("holy congregation").

In the first period of Crusader rule over Palestine, a yet unconquered Ashkelon sheltered a large number of refugees, including many Jews. The Jewish community became a sanctuary for those escaping from Jerusalem, and dealt with such matters as ransoming captives and buying ritual objects from looted synagogues in Jerusalem. At the same time, members of the community were in constant touch with Jewish centers abroad. For example in 1110, letters were sent to the head of the "Gaon Jacob Yeshivah," which was exiled from the country. After the Crusader conquest in 1153, part of the Jewish population remained in Ashkelon. *Benjamin of Tudela describes it as "a large and beautiful town, which contains two hundred Jews, and apart from them, several dozen Karaites and about three hundred Samaritans." In 1187 Saladin conquered it and in 1191 he destroyed its fortifications, (which were rebuilt later by Richard the Lion Heart). The town's Christian inhabitants, with the exception of one hundred merchants, were evacuated, and replaced by Muslims, and its Jewish population went to settle in Jerusalem. Judah *Al-Ḥarizi mentions that among the Jewish inhabitants of Jerusalem was "an excellent congregation from Ashkelon." In 1192 it was destroyed again and in 1240 built anew. In 1247 it passed to the rule of the Ayyub sultans and in 1270 Sultan Baybars destroyed it again.

Information also exists on the settlement of Samaritans in Ashkelon in the 13th century. Under Ottoman rule, Ashkelon was a small settlement, inhabited mainly by merchants and commercial agents who used its port. There was no Jewish community in Ashkelon throughout the Ottoman rule.

[Natan Efrati]

Modern Ashkelon

Modern Ashkelon is located 2 mi. (3.5 km.) northeast of the ruins of ancient Ashkelon. The Egyptian governor Ibrahim Pasha founded the town of Majdal (c. 1830) and settled Egyptian weavers there. Nearer the shore and the site of the antiquities was the fishing village of al-Jūra. During the Israel War of Independence (1948), the invading Egyptian army took Majdal but had to evacuate it by sea when Israel forces closed in on it from the land side (October 1948). Shortly after the war, the inhabitants of Majdal left the town for Gaza. After a short time, a Jewish settlement developed known as Migdal-Ashkelon. From 1949 on, Jewish immigrants from many countries settled there. In 1952, on the initiative of the South African Zionist Federation, the South African Jewish

War Appeal undertook the implementation of a planning program, based on the concept of self-contained neighborhood units, and in 1955 Ashkelon was granted city status. Its municipal boundaries, as then laid down, included an area of 17 sq. mi. (43 sq. km.), which subsequently increased to 21 sq. mi. (55 sq. km.). Its five neighborhoods were the town of Majdal (Migdal), which was the commercial and market center; the Afridar quarter, linking up with the hotel area near the bathing beach; the Southern Hills quarter of immigrant housing; the residential Shimshon (Samson) quarter; and the Barnea quarter. The industrial zone was located on the eastern fringe of the town. In 1969 an oil pipeline was constructed from Eilat to Ashkelon. Tourism and recreation, including a camp of the French Mediterranean Club, constituted an important part of the city's economy. In the beginning of the 21st century the city's economy was based on industry, administrative services, commerce, and tourism, employing some 40,000 people and making the city a regional center. About 40 factories and 1,000 workshops operated in the city's three industrial areas (which included an 8,000-acre industrial park), engaged in metalworking, plastics, wood, electronics, food, baked goods, chemicals, and prefab construction.

The city had a branch of *Bar-Ilan University with 180 students in attendance in 1968, which in 1990 became Ashkelon College, a regional institute. In 2000 the college was accredited academically, with a student body of approximately 6,000. The city's population rose from 38,000 in 1968 to 73,000 in the mid-1990s and 103,200 in 2002. Among Ashkelon's population, 33.5% were new immigrants, mainly from the former Soviet Union, with others from Ethiopia, France, and Latin America.

The area of ancient Ashkelon, including the archaeological findings, has been converted into a National Park.

[Efraim Orni / Shaked Gilboa (2nd ed.)]

BIBLIOGRAPHY: M. Ish-Shalom, *Masei Noẓerim le-Ereẓ Yisrael* (1965), 94–95, 97; Mann, Egypt, 2 (1922), 198–201; Ben-Zvi, Ereẓ Yisrael, index; *Sefer ha-Yishuv*, 2 (1944), 4–6; J. Prawer, in: *Eretz Israel*, 4 (1956), 231–42; 5 (1958), 224–37; B. Mazar, in: EM, 1 (1965), 769ff.; Schuerer, Gesch, 2 (1967^{4}), 119ff.; J. Garstang, *Joshua, Judges* (1931), 357ff.; idem, in: *PEFQS* (1923); J. Ory, in: *QDAP*, 8 (1939), 38ff.; Beyer, in: *ZDPV*, 56 (1933), 250ff.; Z. Vilnay, *Ashkelon ha-Ḥadashah ve-ha-Attikah* (1963). **ADD. BIBLIOGRAPHY:** W.J. Phythian-Adams, "History of Askalon," in: *PEFQS* (1921): 163–71; idem, in: "Report on the Stratification of Askalon," in: *PEFQS* (1923): 60–84; L. Stager, "Ashkelon," in: NEAEHL 1 (1993), 102–3; idem, in: *Biblical Archaeology Review*, 17 (1991); P. Wapnish and B. Hesse, "Pampered Pooches or Plain Pariahs," BA, 56 (1993), 55–80; B.L. Johnson and L.E. Stager, "Ashkelon: Wine Emporium of the Holy Land," in: S. Gitin (ed.), *Recent Excavations in Israel* (1995), 95–109. For a comprehensive list of later historical sources, see Y. Tsafrir, L. Di Segni, and J. Green, *Tabula Imperii Romani. Iudaea – Palaestina. Maps and Gazetteer* (1994), 68–70. **WEBSITE:** www.ashkelon.muni.il.

ASHKENAZ (Heb. אַשְׁכְּנַז), a people and a country bordering on Armenia and the upper Euphrates; listed in Genesis 10:3 and I Chronicles 1:6 among the descendants of *Gomer. The name Ashkenaz also occurs once in Jeremiah 51:27 in a passage calling upon the kingdoms of *Ararat, Minni, and Ashkenaz to rise and destroy Babylon. Scholars have identified the Ashkenaz as the people called Ashkuza (Ashguza, Ishguza) in Akkadian. According to Assyrian royal inscriptions the Ashkuza fought the Assyrians in the reign of Esharhaddon (680–669 B.C.E.) as allies of the Minni (Manneans). Since the Ashkuza are mentioned in conjunction with the Gimirrai-Cimmerians and the Ashkenaz with Gomer in Genesis, it is reasonable to infer that Ashkenaz is a dialectal form of Akkadian Ashkuza, identical with a group of Iranian-speaking people organized in confederations of tribes called Saka in Old Persian, whom Greek writers (e.g., Herodotus 1:103) called Scythians. They ranged from southern Russia through the Caucasus and into the Near East. Some scholars, however, have argued against this identification on philological grounds because of the presence of the "*n*" in the word Ashkenaz. In medieval rabbinical literature the name was used for Germany (see next entry).

BIBLIOGRAPHY: E.A. Speiser, *Genesis* (Eng., 1964), 66; U. Cassuto, *A Commentary on the Book of Genesis*, 2 (1964), 192; EM, 1 (1965), 762–3 (incl. bibl.). **ADD. BIBLIOGRAPHY:** W. Holladay, *Jeremiah, 2* (1989), 427; P. Briant, *From Cyrus to Alexander* (2002), 39.

[Yehoshua M. Grintz]

ASHKENAZ (אַשְׁכְּנַז), designation of the first relatively compact area of settlement of Jews in N.W. Europe, initially on the banks of the Rhine. The term became identified with, and denotes in its narrower sense, Germany, German Jewry, and German Jews ("Ashkenazim"), as well as their descendants in other countries. It has evolved a broader connotation denoting the entire Ashkenazi Jewish cultural complex, comprising its ideas and views, way of life and folk mores, legal concepts and formulations, and social institutions. The Ashkenazi cultural legacy, emanating from the center in northern France and Germany, later spread to Poland-Lithuania, and in modern times embraces Jewish settlements all over the world whose members share and activate it. The term "Ashkenaz" is used in clear contradistinction to *Sepharad, the Jewish cultural complex originating in Spain.

Terminology

It is difficult to determine when the term Ashkenaz was first applied to Germany. In the Babylonian Talmud (Yoma 10a) the biblical Gomer, the father of Ashkenaz, is rendered as "Germania," although in its original context the reference is to Germanikia in northwestern Syria (cf. Gen. R. 37:1; TJ, Meg. 1:11, 71b). In addition to this incorrect identification, a possible source of explanation may be in the name Scandza or Scanzia, the designation of Scandinavia in several sources, which was regarded as the cradle of some Germanic tribes. The association of Ashkenaz with Scandza is found as early as the sixth century in the Latin addendum to the chronology of Eusebius. According to another theory, the present connotation derives from the phonic resemblance of "Ashkenaz" to "Saxons" who during the period of Charlemagne constituted the predominant Germanic element in the Frankish kingdom. During the 11th and 12th centuries the province incorporating Mainz and Worms was still known as "Lothar" (Lotharingia; Rashi, *Sefer ha-Pardes*, 35:1; Tos. to BB 74a). The rabbis of Regensburg were referred to as "Rabbanei Reinus" (i.e., "of the Rhine"; Responsum of Eliezer b. Nathan, in: *She'elot u-Teshuvot Maharam mi-Rothenburg* (Lemberg, 1860), no. 81). At the same time, however, the term "Ashkenaz" established itself as the accepted Hebrew rendering of Germany. Thus in *Rashi's (1040–1105) commentary on the Talmud, German expressions appear as *leshon Ashkenaz* (Suk. 17a; Git. 55b; BM 73b). Similarly when Rashi writes: "But in Ashkenaz I saw…" (Ket. 77b) he no doubt meant the communities of Mainz and Worms in which he had dwelt. Thus also it is certain that such terms as *Ereẓ Ashkenaz* appearing in his commentaries (e.g., Ḥul. 93a) represent Germany. *Eliezer b. Nathan (early 12th century) distinguishes between Ẓarefatim (French) and Ashkenazim in reference to the crusaders as "a foreign people, a bitter and impetuous nation" (A.M. Habermann (ed.), *Gezerot Ashkenaz ve-Ẓarefat* (1946), 72). Letters from Byzantine and Syrian communities written during the First Crusade also refer to the crusaders as "Ashkenazim" (Mann, in: *Ha-Tekufah*, 23 (1925), 253, 256, 260).

The Cultural Complex

The use of the term "Ashkenazi Jewry" to denote a distinct cultural entity, comprising the communities of northern France and of the Slavonic countries previously known as *Ereẓ Kena'an*, can be discerned in sources dating from as early as the 14th century. *Asher b. Jehiel (d. 1327), who was born in western Germany, wrote after settling in Toledo: "I would not eat according to their [i.e., the Sephardi] usage, adhering as I do to our own custom and to the tradition of our blessed forefathers, the sages of Ashkenaz, who received the Torah as an inheritance from their ancestors from the days of the destruction of the Temple. Likewise the tradition of our forebears and teachers in France is superior to that of the sons of this land" (Responsa 20, 20).

While external influences are apparent in the Sephardi attitude toward religion, the Jews of Ashkenaz tended to be fundamentalist and rigorist, consonant mainly with internal Jewish sources, ideas, and customs. The Ashkenazi scholar's sphere of interest was circumscribed by study of the Bible and Talmud. He devoted more efforts to exegesis of the sacred text, rather than attempting a systematic codification of the *halakhah* or extracting general principles. The Ashkenazi and Sephardi cultural centers did, however, exert a reciprocal influence. The talmudic scholarship of early Ashkenazi authorities found its way into kabbalistic circles in Provence and Spain (see *Kabbalah). The approach of the Ashkenazi *tosafists to

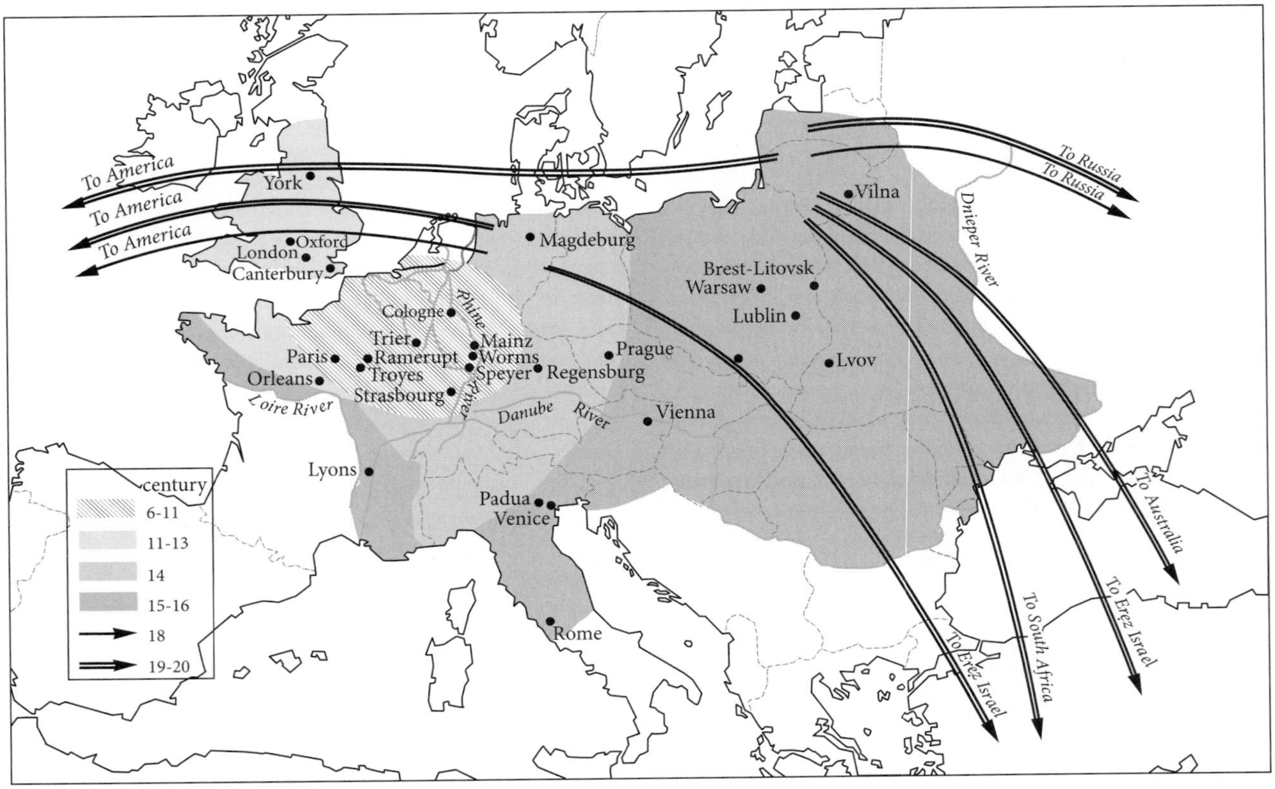

Areas of Ashkenazi settlement, 6th-16th centuries, and waves of Ashkenazi emigration, 18th-20th centuries.

the Talmud was adopted in Spain by *Naḥmanides and Solomon b. Abraham *Adret. The Ashkenazi Ḥasidim, who evolved original religious and social views, evinced an interest in the concepts of *Saadiah b. Joseph and *Maimonides.

Ashkenazi society was structured on the formally monogamic Jewish family, according to the *takkanah* of *Gershom b. Judah. Its leadership developed new and successful means of exercising *autonomy through the local community and synod. The Jews of Ashkenaz continued the hallowed tradition of **kiddush ha-Shem* ("martyrdom") as well as broadening its concept. Ashkenazi and Sephardi customs gradually established themselves as separate norms, expressed in differences in way of life, pronunciation of Hebrew, and the liturgical rite followed in the respective congregations (see *Liturgy). Ashkenazi scribes developed a distinctive script, and the illuminators of manuscripts, a specific style.

With the emigration of Ashkenazi Jewry from Western to Eastern Europe in the 15th and 16th centuries, the center of gravity shifted to *Bohemia, *Moravia, *Poland, and *Lithuania, developing in each place with local modifications. In the Slavonic territories their use of the Judeo-German language became a prominent distinguishing feature of Ashkenazi Jewry (see: *Yiddish Language). The Ashkenazi *maḥzor* included *seliḥot* and *piyyutim* composed by the liturgical poets of Germany and northern France. The Ashkenazi liturgical rite did not follow a uniform pattern. The southwestern Ashkenazi rite, similar to that followed by the communities of France and Holland, varied from that followed in the area west of the Elbe River; the *minhag* ("custom") of Bohemian Jewry differed from that of Lithuanian Jewry. However these divergences are insignificant as compared with the difference in the basic Ashkenazi and Sephardi rituals.

The parallel development of Sephardi and Ashkenazi religious and social usages was considerably influenced by the works of the codifiers Joseph *Caro on the one hand and Moses *Isserles on the other. Although Caro based his Shulḥan Arukh upon *Jacob b. Asher's *Sefer ha-Turim*, summarizing the *halakhah* of the Ashkenazi rabbinical authorities, Caro's decision in most cases favors the Sephardi codifiers (**posekim*). Isserles provided glosses to the Shulḥan Arukh wherever the Ashkenazi *posekim* disagreed with Caro's decision. Whereas the Ashkenazim accepted Isserles' decision, the Sephardim abided by the norms laid down by Caro.

From about the 17th century the significance of the Sephardi Jewry began to diminish as the Ashkenazim increased in number and importance. After the *Chmielnicki massacres in Poland in 1648, numbers of Ashkenazi Jews spread throughout Western Europe, some even crossing the Atlantic. After a few generations they were to outnumber the Sephardim in those lands. By the close of the 19th century, as a result of persecutions in *Russia, there was massive Ashkenazi emigration from Eastern Europe (see *United States). Ashkenazi Jewry then gained decisive numerical ascendancy in the Jewish communities of Europe, Australia, South Africa, the United States, and Ereẓ Israel. Sephardi Jewry maintained its preponderance only in North Africa, Italy, the Middle East, and wide areas of Asia. Before World War II Ashkenazi Jewry comprised 90% of the global total. The destruction of European Jewry drastically reduced their number and to some extent their proportionate preponderance. With the isolation of Russian Jews from world Jewry, the United States became the main center of Ashkenazi Jews.

Relations between Ashkenazim and Sephardim have varied from time to time and from one cultural region to another. In Holland and France the Sephardi communities excluded Ashkenazim from membership. An extreme example of such an attitude occurred in the Sephardi community of Bordeaux, which was empowered to expel undesired newcomers by a majority vote. In Italy, on the other hand, the contrast between the two was not so sharp and the Ashkenazi settlers adopted the characteristics of the native elements except in matters of ritual. The immigration of Ashkenazi Jews to Jerusalem in the 17th and 18th centuries strained relations with the Sephardim on economic grounds. At the beginning of the 19th century, efforts to obtain the sanction of the Turkish authorities for restoration of the Ashkenazi congregation in Jerusalem were aided by the Sephardim. The two communities existed side by side, each maintaining its own institutions. This division has established itself in the religious life of the present Jewish community in Israel, reflected in the composition of the Chief Rabbinate.

See also *Migration; *History; *Historiography.

BIBLIOGRAPHY: H.J. Zimmels, *Ashkenazim and Sephardim* (1958); Kraus, in: *Tarbiz*, 3 (1931/32), 423–35; Mann, *ibid.*, 4 (1932/33), 391–4; Zunz, Ritus, 66; *Germ Jud*, 1 (1963), index, s.v. *Deutschland*; 2 (1968), index, s.v. *Lothringen*, Baron, Community, 2 (1942), 19, 365; Wallach, in: MGWJ, 83 (1939), 302; Rosenthal, in: HJ, 5 (1943), 58–62. **ADD. BIBLIOGRAPHY:** I.G. Marcus, in: *Cultures of the Jews* (2002), 449–516.

[*Encyclopaedia Hebraica*]

ASHKENAZI, ABRAHAM BEN JACOB (1811–1880), Sephardi chief rabbi of Ereẓ Israel. Ashkenazi was born in Larissa, in Greece, but c. 1820 his family settled in Jerusalem where he studied under Samuel Arvaẓ, and was successively appointed a *dayyan* in the *bet din* of Benjamin Mordecai Navon, *av bet din* (1864), and *rishon le-Zion*, the title given to the Sephardi chief rabbi (1869). He was head of the Bet Jacob Pereira and the Tiferet Israel yeshivot. He was responsible for the purchase of the site of the traditional grave of Simeon ha-Ẓaddik in Jerusalem. During his years of office he introduced many important changes in the organization of the community. He was on friendly terms with the Greek patriarch. Ashkenazi was decorated by Emperor Franz Josef during the latter's visit to Jerusalem, and by the sultan. In 1847 he was sent on a mission to North Africa. Ashkenazi wrote approbations to many books. Some of his responsa have been published (chiefly in the responsa *Benei Binyamin* (1876–81) of Benjamin Navon, and the *Kappei Aharon* (1874–86) of Aaron Azriel); but most of them remained unpublished. Ashkenazi had a remarkable knowledge of halakhic literature and was said to know the responsa of Solomon b. Abraham *Adret by heart. Together with Jacob Kapiluto he edited *Takkanot Yerushalayim* on the regulations and customs of the city (1869). A ruling published under the title *Yismaḥ Moshe* (1874) upholding the will of the caid Nissim Samama of Tunis provoked considerable controversy, but the rabbis of Ereẓ Israel, Egypt, and Smyrna upheld his decision. Ashkenazi's most important work, an extensive commentary on the *Ḥukkat ha-Dayyanim* of Abraham b. Solomon ibn Tazrat, a disciple of Adret, has not been published. In it he assesses the views of the early and late halakhic authorities, particularly of Adret. The work is a real contribution to Jewish jurisprudence. Some of his essays and eulogies were published in *Ha-Levanon, Ḥavaẓẓelet, Yehudah vi-Yerushalayim*, etc. He had an intimate knowledge of the lives of the scholars of Jerusalem, and it was he who encouraged A.L. Frumkin to write his *Toledot Ḥakhmei Yerushalayim*. His son ISAAC, a well-known talmudist, was one of the leaders of the Jerusalem community (1908).

BIBLIOGRAPHY: A.M. Luncz (ed.), *Lu'aḥ Ereẓ Yisrael*, 13 (1908), 85–86; I. Badahab, *Ki be-Yiẓḥak Shenot Ḥayyim* (1928), 4–5, 24–27; M.D. Gaon, *Yehudei ha-Mizraḥ be-Ereẓ Yisrael*, 2 (1938), 121–2; S. Halevy, *Ha-Sefarim ha-Ivriyyim…* (1963), 66, 80–81, 85, index.

ASHKENAZI, BEḤOR (1840–1909), Turkish government official during the last days of the Ottoman Empire. Known as Beḥor Effendi, Ashkenazi was a member of the council of state from 1869 to 1899, when he became a member of the Ottoman parliament, representing the Jewish community. In 1908 he was made vice prefect of Constantinople and nominated to the Senate, the only Jew in the Ottoman upper chamber. In 1883 he served as vice president of the Jewish lay council of the Istanbul community, and in 1890, 1892, and 1898 he was president of the Jewish lay council.

ADD. BIBLIOGRAPHY: A. Levy, in: M. Rozen (ed.), *Yemei ha-Sahar* (1994), 257–61.

[Hayyim J. Cohen / Leah Bornstein-Makovetsky (2nd ed.)]

ASHKENAZI, BEZALEL BEN ABRAHAM (c. 1520–1591/94), talmudist and halakhic authority. Ashkenazi was born in Jerusalem or in Safed, where he studied in his youth under Israel di *Curiel. About 1540 he went to Egypt where he studied in Cairo under *David b. Solomon ibn Abi Zimra. Later he founded a yeshivah there which numbered among its scholars Isaac *Luria and Abraham *Monson. He was a good friend of the poet Israel *Najara. When David b. Solomon ibn Abi Zimra went to Ereẓ Israel (c. 1553), Ashkenazi succeeded him as head of the Egyptian rabbis. A bitter quarrel arose between him and *Jacob b. Ḥayyim Talmid, *nagid* of the Egyptian Jews, and Ashkenazi excommunicated him. Through the intervention of the local authorities, the office of *nagid* was abolished, and the head of the Jews given the title of "*chelebi*" (signifying dignitary in Turkish), with rather limited powers. It is highly probable that it was this quarrel which impelled him to leave Egypt. In 1587 he was head of the rabbis of Jerusalem, apparently succeeding Ḥayyim *Vital. Ashkenazi put new life into the Jerusalem community, instituting numerous communal enactments, exempting scholars from taxation, and persuading the Ashkenazi community to assist in bearing the burden of taxation, though most of them were officially exempt as aliens. He traveled as an emissary to a number of countries, collecting money for the community and encouraging immigration to the Land of Israel. He persuaded the Jews of various countries to set aside Purim as a special day for making contributions to the Land of Israel. Many students from the Diaspora, among them Solomon *Adani attended his yeshivah in Jerusalem. Ashkenazi visited Egypt again in 1591, and appears to have returned to Jerusalem.

Ashkenazi occupied himself a great deal with copying and editing old manuscripts, even hiring scribes to help him. He copied the novellae of the *geonim* and *rishonim* on the Babylonian Talmud, and these served as the basis for his classic *Asefat Zekenim*, better known as the *Shitah Mekubbeẓet*. Through this collection, much of the commentaries and responsa of R. *Gershom b. Judah, *Hananel, Joseph *Ibn Migash, Meir ha-Levi *Abulafia, and others, was preserved. The book in its different parts has been republished many times, and it serves as a supplement to the *tosafot, and the other classical *rishonim.

Much of the *Shitah Mekubbeẓet* is still in manuscript. Part of it has been lost, but is occasionally referred to in books by other authors. All of the available material on some tractates has been published; but only selections of others. The following commentaries under the title *Shitah Mekubbeẓet* have been published: *Berakhot*, the collection in *Berakhah Meshulleshet* (Warsaw, 1863), incorrectly attributed to Ashkenazi, and is most probably by *Yom Tov b. Abraham Ishbili; *Beẓah*, the collection attributed to Ashkenazi at the end of *Naḥalah li-Yhoshu'a* (Constantinople, 1731), of Joshua *Soncino is – according to Epstein's opinion – by a disciple of Nissim Gerondi; *Ketubbot* (Constantinople, 1738); it is doubtful whether *Nedarim* (Berlin, 1860) and *Nazir* (Leghorn, 1774) are by Ashkenazi; *Sotah* (Leghorn, 1800) is contained in *Yagel Ya'akov* of Jacob *Faitusi; *Bava Kamma* (Venice, 1762); *Bava Meẓi'a'* (Amsterdam, 1721); *Bava Batra* (Leghorn, 1774) up to page 133. The remainder was published under the title of *Shi'urei Shitah Mekubbeẓet* in the *Yad Ramah* (Salonika, 1790) of Meir ha-Levi Abulafia; *Sanhedrin* – sections in *Sha'ar ha-Melekh* (Salonika, 1771) of Isaac Nuñes Belmonte and in *Ḥamra ve-Ḥayyei* (Leghorn, 1802) of R. Ḥayyim *Benveniste; *Zevaḥim Bekhorot, Menaḥot*, and most of *Seder Kedoshim* in the Romm Talmud edition (first published in *Mizbaḥ Kapparah* by Jacob Faitusi (Leghorn, 1810) and other books). The *Shitah* to the smaller tractates of *Seder Kedoshim* is very much abbreviated.

Ashkenazi published glosses on the text of the Mishnah and the commentaries on the Mishnah of Samson of Sens and of *Maimonides. His glosses on Samson's commentary on *Pe'ah* and *Demai* were published by J.L. Maimon (*Sinai Jubilee Jubilee Volume* (1958), 102–25), as were his glosses to Maimonides' commentary on the Mishnah of *Zevaḥim* and *Menaḥot* in the same author's *Rabbi Moshe ben Maimon* (1960), 251–90. Ashkenazi also annotated the Babylonian and Jerusalem Talmuds, his glosses on *Yoma* being published by Aaron *Jellinek in *Kunteres ha-Mazkir* (1877), 20–26. *Derekh Tamim*, glosses on the works of Isaac *Alfasi and R. Nissim Girondi were published in *Tummat Yesharim* (Venice, 1622) of Benjamin Motal. His glosses on Books 9–13 of Maimonides' *Mishneh Torah* are in the library of the Jewish Theological Seminary (Ms. 825) in New York. Ashkenazi compiled *Kelalei ha-Talmud*, general rules of talmudic methodology excerpted from the *geonim* and *rishonim* (published by A. Marx in *Festschrift D. Hoffmann* (1914), Hebrew section 179–217). He also wrote responsa (Venice, 1595) and composed sermons and poems.

BIBLIOGRAPHY: Neubauer, Chronicles, 1 (1887), 116–7, 160; Conforte, Kore, 41a; Zomber, in: *Ha-Maggid*, 5 (1861), 287; Epstein, in: *Taḥkemoni*, 2 (1911), 33–36; Epstein, Mishnah, 1289–90; Lieberman, in: KS, 13 (1936/37), 105–12; Marx, in: *Festschrift... J. Freimann* (1937), 167–70; Rosanes, Togarmah, 2 (1938), 220–2; 3 (1938), 241–6; Frumkin-Rivlin, 1 (1928), 115–9; Freimann, in: *Sefer... L. Ginzberg* (1946), 334–54 (Heb. vol.); Yaari, Sheluḥei, 225–8; Benayahu, in: *Sinai*, 30 (1951/52), 66–67; Dimitrowski, in: *Zion*, 20 (1955), 175–9; Tamar, *ibid.*, 21 (1956), 236–7; Maimon, in: *Sinai Jubilee Volume* (1958), 89–125; Raphael, *ibid.*, 599–600.

[Abraham David]

ASHKENAZI, DAN (late 13th–early 14th centuries), German talmudist. No details are available of his life in Germany, which he left c. 1300 following the *Rindfleisch persecutions. He migrated to Spain and settled in Toledo, where he founded a yeshivah. He engaged in Kabbalah, and some of his sayings on the subject are preserved. He was among the believers in the "prophecy" of the pseudo-messiah, Abraham of Avila. His responsa are preserved in the works of Solomon b. Abraham *Adret and *Yom Tov b. Abraham Ishbili with whom he carried on a halakhic correspondence; they bear a novel character, departing from usual halakhic tradition. He cites halakhic decisions which are the opposite of all rulings by other halakhists, as Adret sharply comments in his responsa to Ashkenazi and his followers (1:529–530 et al.). Many of his readings of the Talmud bear the same unique and novel character. Some maintained that the statements ascribed to Ashkenazi were forgeries, while others held that he belonged to a group of scholars who were critical of *halakhah* and its recognized exponents. His unique "antinomistic" character tempted the famous forger, Saul *Berlin, to ascribe to him unusual customs, congruent to Berlin's desire to reform the *halakhah* (*Besamim Rosh*, 24). Adret nevertheless greatly esteemed Ashkenazi (responsa ascribed to Naḥmanides, 250 et al.) and *Nissim b. Reuben Gerondi (Responsa, 32) also wrote of him in the highest terms. Ashkenazi wrote commentaries on the Pentateuch; extracts are quoted in *Hadar Zekenim*, and in the commentary on the Pentateuch by *Baḥya b. Asher.

BIBLIOGRAPHY: Michael, Or, no. 787; Baer, in: *Zion*, 5 (1939/40), 41, n. 87; Rabbenu Bahya, *Be'ur al ha-Torah*, ed. by C.D. Shevel, 1 (1966), 10.

[Israel Moses Ta-Shma]

ASHKENAZI, ELIEZER BEN ELIJAH THE PHYSICIAN (1513–1586), rabbi and exegete. Eliezer's activities covered many of the Jewish centers of the 16th century. The influential position he held in widely scattered communities indicates the basic unity of Jewish society and culture in the period. A pupil of Joseph b. Solomon *Taitaẓak in Salonika, Eliezer went to Egypt when he was 26, and officiated as rabbi. *Elijah of Pesaro said he "judged all the community of Egypt for 22 years." While there, Eliezer was in contact with the *Safed community and its sages, including Joseph *Caro, who respected and consulted him. In 1561 Eliezer was compelled to leave Egypt, and settled at Famagusta in Cyprus. Elijah of Pesaro, who met him there in 1563, describes him as "well-versed in 12 languages... a sage in many general sciences and in the Talmud... he is wealthy." Azariah dei *Rossi called Eliezer "the greatest of the generation." In 1563 Eliezer was in *Venice; the following year he traveled to Prague, returned for a few years to Famagusta, and again went to Venice. From there he went to Cremona where in 1576 he published his commentary *Yosef Lekaḥ* on the book of Esther, dedicated to Joseph *Nasi. The same year he was invited to Poland as rabbi of Poznan; he was subsequently called to Gniezno, and thence to Cracow, where he died. In Poland his answers to legal queries were accepted as authoritative. Impartial in his decisions, he denied his support to the brother-in-law of Moses *Isserles, Joseph *Katz, who had referred to Eliezer in a discussion with his own pupils. Eliezer's main work, *Ma'aseh Adonai*, a commentary on the Torah, was completed in Gniezno in 1580 and printed in Venice in 1583. It follows the rationalist trend in rabbinical scholarship, calling for freedom in exegesis of the Scriptures: "Each and every one of us, our descendants too, to the end of all generations... is obliged to search for the meaning of the words of the Torah... to accept the truth from whoever says it, after we have understood it. Let us not permit the opinion of someone else – even if of an earlier generation – to hinder us from research... Research and choose: for that you have been created and reason has been given you from heaven" (*Ma'aseh Adonai*, 169). Eliezer suggests that irrational elements in Jewish tradition had accrued through copyists' errors, misunderstandings, and misreadings, or had been precipitated in times of trouble and expulsions, or even inserted by ill-disposed persons. In Joseph Solomon *Delmedigo's estimation "the *Ma'aseh Adonai* should be read in its entirety." He also records that Eliezer wrote a supercommentary on *Naḥmanides' commentary on the Torah and "a thousand refutations of the *Beit Yosef*" of Joseph Caro. Eliezer also wrote *seliḥot* and *piyyutim* printed at Cracow and in Lublin (1618). His glosses on the code of *Mordecai b. Hillel are included in *Gedulat Mordekhai* (Hanau, 1593).

BIBLIOGRAPHY: I.M. Jost, in: *Jahrbuch fuer die Geschichte der Juden* (1861), 30 ff.; H.H. Ben-Sasson, *Hagut ve-Hanhagah* (1959), index.

[Haim Hillel Ben-Sasson]

ASHKENAZI (Ulif), GERSHON (d. 1693), rabbi. His teachers were Joel *Sirkes and Menahem Mendel *Krochmal. While still young he was appointed a *dayyan* in Cracow, and afterward served as rabbi in Prossnitz (1650), in Hanau, and in Nikolsburg (Moravia) as chief rabbi of the province (*Landesrabbiner*) from 1661–62. He was then appointed chief rabbi of Austria, where he remained until the expulsion of the Jews from Vienna in 1670, and was noted for his fight against the Shabbateans. With the sanction of Louis XIV, Ashkenazi was appointed *av bet din* of Metz in 1671, remaining there until his death. In 1672 he was authorized by the civil authorities to establish a yeshivah. His responsa *Avodat ha-Gershuni* (1699) utilized the entire corpus of halakhic literature and talmudic commentaries. It is an important source for the *Chmielnicki massacres and the Thirty Years' War. He was renowned as a preacher, and a selection of his sermons, *Tiferet ha-Gershuni*, appeared in 1699. They include halakhic discussions. Ashkenazi, like Judah Rosanes in his *Parashat Derakhim*, frequently puts arguments on halakhic questions into the mouths of biblical personalities. In both works he treats kabbalistic subjects. His *Ḥiddushei ha-Gershuni* (Frankfurt, 1710) contains novellae and glosses on the Shulḥan Arukh. A collection of his responsa and sermons appeared in 1710, and a work on Alfasi and novellae on the Talmud remain in manuscripts. His students included David *Oppenheim.

BIBLIOGRAPHY: S.A. Horodezky, *Le-Korot ha-Rabbanut* (1911), 50ff.; idem, in: *Ha-Goren*, 3 (1907), 141ff.; D. Kaufmann, *Die letzte Vertreibung der Juden aus Wien* (1889), 84ff., 224ff.; H. Fleisch, in: *Juedische Familien-Forschung*, 2 (1930); Michael, Or, 305ff., no. 673; Freimann, in: JJLG, 15 (1923), 36; H. Gold (ed.), *Die Juden … Maehrens* (1929), 50; S.B. Freehof, *Responsa Literature* (1959), 196.

[Isaac Ze'ev Kahane]

ASHKENAZI, JONAH BEN JACOB (d. 1745), Hebrew printer in Turkey. Born in Zalośce (in the province of Lemberg), Poland, Ashkenazi immigrated to Turkey and settled in Constantinople. In 1710 he established a new printing press, using characters which he had engraved himself. Later he cast new ones, together with decorations for the title pages, and finally produced some beautiful books. During the first two years Ashkenazi was in partnership with another Polish emigrant, Naphtali b. Azriel of Vilna. He was compelled to leave Constantinople twice, continuing his work in the nearby village of Ortaköy. In 1720 a consignment of his books was lost at sea, and a dishonest agent of his fled to Poland. Ashkenazi followed him, and on his way back to Constantinople, stopped in Amsterdam. There, in 1721, he printed the *Shitah Mekubbeẓet* of Bezalel *Ashkenazi on *Bava Meẓ'ia* according to a manuscript which he had brought with him from Constantinople. On his return to Constantinople, he printed mainly the works of local rabbis. In 1714 he traveled to Egypt where he received several works of Egyptian rabbis for printing. There he found a manuscript of the *Tikkunei Zohar*, which had been corrected by Ḥayyim Vital, and which he published. In 1728 he established a branch of his press in Smyrna in partnership with R. David Ḥazzan, who later in 1739 immigrated to Palestine. The press then closed down.

During the 35 years of his activity in Constantinople and Smyrna, Ashkenazi printed 125 books. After his death in 1745, the press passed to his three sons: Reuben, Nissim, and Moses; later to his grandsons; and continued until 1778. In all 180 books were printed by three Ashkenazi generations. He printed in Ladino the Bible, a *siddur*, *Josippon*, and the first edition of *Me-Am Lo'ez*, as well as other works. Ashkenazi made Constantinople the metropolis of Hebrew printing in the Orient.

BIBLIOGRAPHY: Rosanes, Togarmah, 4 (1935), 391ff.; Yaari, in: KS, 14 (1937/38), 524ff.; 15 (1939), 97ff., 240ff.; idem, in: *Aresheth*, 1 (1959), 97ff.; H.B. Friedberg, *Toledot ha-Defus ha-Ivri be-Italyah* (1956^2), 127ff.; A. Yaari, *Ha-Defus ha-Ivri be-Kushta* (1967), index, s.v. *Yonah b. Ya'akov mi-Zalaziẓ.*

[Avraham Yaari]

ASHKENAZI, JOSEPH (1525–1577), annotator of and commentator on the Mishnah. Ashkenazi, known as "*ha-Tanna*" of Safed, was the son-in-law of R. Aaron b. Gershon Land, who was rabbi in Prague and later headed the *bet din* of the Poznan community. Ashkenazi fought fiercely against philosophy and theoretical-philosophical Kabbalah. At Prague he denounced Maimonides as a heretic and was threatened with excommunication by the rabbis of Prague if he did not desist. Abraham ha-Levi Horowitz wrote a polemical pamphlet against Ashkenazi's father-in-law, which was mainly directed against Ashkenazi himself. After his father-in-law's death (1560) he went to Verona but it would seem that he did not spend many years there and that he subsequently went on to Egypt where he taught at a yeshivah. Here he was friendly with Bezalel *Ashkenazi and probably also with Isaac *Luria. Perhaps his contacts with these two scholars, who devoted themselves to the study of variant readings of the Mishnah and Talmud as they occur in manuscripts, influenced Ashkenazi to accept the usage of the Egyptian scholars. In 1569/70 he went to Safed, where, as was his custom, he roused violent controversies. He demanded that tithes and *terumot* ("offerings") should be given from crops grown in Ereẓ Israel even when heaped by a Gentile (the obligation of tithing applying from the action of heaping) in contradiction to Joseph *Caro and the ordinance of 1572 which had ruled that these need not be tithed.

His opposition to philosophy in general is expressed in one of his works written in 1565 and preserved in manuscript (discovered by G. Scholem, Oxford Ms. 1664 and Budapest, Kaufmann Library, Ms. 290). Ashkenazi attacks Maimonides and his ideas; he opposes the use of allegory as well as the philosophic concept that "God is pure unchangeable intellect." According to Ashkenazi this heresy is the source of all other heresies. From it stem the denial of Providence; of reward and punishment; of the *mitzvot*; of resurrection in the world to come. His accusations are leveled mainly against Maimonides, Abraham *Ibn Ezra, *Levi b. Gershom, and

Joseph *Albo. Ashkenazi contends that the esoteric world is merely a dimension added to the exoteric one which applies to matters of the heavenly world; that the books of Kabbalah ascribed to the *tannaim* and *amoraim* are the true Kabbalah and must not be disputed. He sharply criticizes the kabbalists of the Middle Ages who tried to compromise with philosophy. According to him, even *Naḥmanides, Solomon b. Abraham *Adret, and *Baḥya b. Asher vacillated between true Kabbalah and philosophy. The authors of speculative kabbalism are "false kabbalists" and by this he means *Azriel of Gerona and Meir ibn *Gabbai. Manuscript copies of Ḥayyim *Vital's *Oẓerot Ḥayyim* contain kabbalistic sayings which Vital had heard from Ashkenazi and which resemble those of the late German Ḥasidim.

It was probably in Safed that he started to devote himself mainly to the textual criticism of the Mishnah. He annotated the complete Mishnah on the basis of various manuscripts. His annotations were widely used by students and commentators of the Mishnah.

BIBLIOGRAPHY: D. Kaufmann, in: MGWJ, 42 (1898), 38–46; O. Bloch, *ibid.*, 47 (1903), 153ff. (reprinted, Pressburg, 1903); Ẓevi ha-Levi Ish Hurwitz, in: *Sinai*, 7 (1940), 311ff.; J.N. Epstein, Mishnah, 2 (1948), 1284ff.; G. Scholem, in: *Tarbiz*, 28 (1958/59), 59–89, 201–35.

ASHKENAZI, JUDAH BEN JOSEPH (1730?–1791), rabbi and *rosh yeshivah* of Smyrna. Ashkenazi was a judge in matters of tax assessment and taught Talmud and codes in the city's yeshivot. Moses b. Joshua Soncino later financed the establishment of a yeshivah (Maḥazikei ha-Torah) for him. Ashkenazi's foremost pupil was Raphael Isaac Mayo, who later became chief rabbi of Smyrna. Another pupil, Ḥayyim Joshua Soncino, son of the yeshivah's founder, financed the publication of his teacher's first work. Ashkenazi wrote many works which were edited posthumously by his son, Raphael. *Maḥaneh Ye'udah* (Salonika, 1793) was originally intended as a commentary on the talmudic tractate *Bava Batra* but since it is essentially a clarification of the relevant *halakhah* in *Jacob b. Asher's Tur, it was rearranged and edited by his son as a commentary to the *Tur Ḥoshen Mishpat*. Among his other works are *Yad Ye'udah* (1816), on the tractate *Shevu'ot*, etc.; *Gevul Ye'udah* (1821), on tractate *Gittin*, etc.; *Kehal Ye'udah* (1825), on *Yoreh De'ah*, including a commentary to tractate *Beẓah; Seridei Ye'udah* (1831), homilies delivered at weddings, and eulogies, published by his grandson Abraham b. Raphael. Ashkenazi's first name appears in the title of all his works as "Ye'udah" in accordance with the pious custom of not writing the name as it is spelled since it contains the letters of the Tetragrammaton.

BIBLIOGRAPHY: R. Ashkenazi, *Mareh Einayim* (1816), 222a–b; idem, *Mareh ha-Gadol*, 2 (1831), 29a; R.I. Mayo, *Pe'at Yam* (1832), 23a; Azulai, 1 (1852), 38 no. 48.

ASHKENAZI, JUDAH BEN SIMEON (18th century), German codifier. Ashkenazi was born in Frankfurt on the Main where his father was a scribe and *parnas* of the community. Ashkenazi was serving as *dayyan* in Tiktin, Poland, before 1742. He wrote *Ba'er Heitev*, a brief commentary on Joseph Caro's Shulḥan Arukh. His commentary on *Oraḥ Ḥayyim* was published together with the text (Amsterdam, 1742); and on *Yoreh De'ah* (*ibid.*, 1736; with additions, 1777); on *Even ha-Ezer* (*ibid.*, 1739); *Ḥoshen Mishpat* was not published.

Three other works on the Shulḥan Arukh were published under the name *Ba'er Heitev*. These are not so much commentaries as résumés of the opinions of other codifiers. They are by Isaiah b. Abraham ha-Levi on *Oraḥ Ḥayyim* (*ibid.*, 1708); Moses b. Simeon Frankfurt on *Ḥoshen Mishpat* (*ibid.*, 1749); and by *Zechariah Mendel b. Aryeh Leib of Belz on *Yoreh De'ah* (*ibid.*, 1754) and *Ḥoshen Mishpat* (*ibid.*, 1764). In later editions of the Shulḥan Arukh the *Ba'er Heitev* of Ashkenazi on *Oraḥ Ḥayyim* and *Even ha-Ezer* are published, while those of *Yoreh De'ah* and *Ḥoshen Mishpat* are by Zechariah Mendel of Belz.

BIBLIOGRAPHY: Benjacob, Oẓar, 585–7; S.M. Chones, *Toledot ha-Posekim* (1910), 92–93; H. Tchernowitz, *Toledot ha-Posekim*, 2 (1947), 306–12. **ADD. BIBLIOGRAPHY:** M. Nadav, *Pinkas Kehal Tiktin*, 1 (1996), 22, 26, 43, 48, 51, 63.

[Abraham David]

ASHKENAZI, JUDAH SAMUEL (1780?–1849), Palestinian scholar. Ashkenazi went on a mission on behalf of the Tiberias community in 1820, probably to North Africa; visited Gibraltar and Italy; and paid a second visit to North Africa in 1833. Ashkenazi went to Leghorn c. 1842 in order to arrange for the publication of his works, but died there. The following are his most important works: (1) *Yissa Berakhah* (Leghorn, 1822), an exposition and halakhic clarification of section 22 of part 2 of the *Toledot Adam ve-Ḥavvah* of Jeroham b. Meshullam dealing with the laws of marriage. The continuation was not published. (2) *Geza Yishai*, a compendium of laws in alphabetical order (part 1, letters *Alef-Yod*, Leghorn, 1842). Ashkenazi was especially interested in the Sephardi prayer book. He assembled all the relevant rules and published them. (3) *Beit Oved* (1843), on prayers for weekdays; (4) *Beit Menuḥah* (1843), for the Sabbath; (5) *Beit Mo'ed*, part 1 (*Beit ha-Sho'evah* (Leghorn, 1849)) for Sukkot and Simḥat Torah. He died while the book was in the process of publication, and as a result of his death the manuscript of the remaining three sections on the other festivals was lost.

BIBLIOGRAPHY: Yaari, Sheluḥei, 644.

ASHKENAZI, LEON (1922–1996), French-Israeli educator and rabbi. Son of the last Great Rabbi of Algeria, Leon Ashkenazi once defined himself as "a son of Algeria, of Jewish denomination" and envisioned the course of own life, from Oran and Algiers to Paris and then Israel, as emblematic of the Jewish people's identity struggle and destiny. Raised in Oran in the specific cultural context of Algerian Jewry, where the Arab, Sephardi-Jewish, and French cultural worlds blended (Algerian Jews being largely assimilated and recognized as French citizens since the 1870 Crémieux Decree), Ashkenazi joined the Jewish Eclaireurs Israelites de France boy scout movement when it joined the Resistance against the Vichy government and the German presence in North Africa. The discriminatory laws promulgated by the Vichy regime, and the distressing fact that most of these laws remained in force for a while even after Algeria was liberated by Allied forces, and that Algerian Jewry did not immediately regain French citizenship, left Ashkenazi deeply affected, uncertain whether he could best define himself as "a Jew from Algeria and of French culture" or "a French Jew of Algerian culture." Mobilized in the French Foreign Legion, Ashkenazi was wounded near Strasbourg. After the war, he married the daughter of Holocaust victims and took part in the creation of the Ecole d'Orsay educational center devoted to the training of future Jewish teachers and to the spiritual rebirth of the French Jewish community. He was influenced by the teachings of Jacob *Gordin, who urged Ashkenazi to stay at Orsay and teach Judaism. Ashkenazi was appointed director of the school in 1949 and presided over the Union of France's Jewish Students (UEJF). This period deeply affected Ashkenazi's perception of Jewish identity: as a leader of Jewish youth and student movements, he was closely connected with the mainly Ashkenazi Jewry of France and became aware of the national, and not merely religious, dimension of the Jewish people, which eventually led him to adopt Zionist views. Besides, Gordin's teaching as well as his academic studies (ethnology and anthropology) led Ashkenazi to consider a new kind of relationship between Judaism and Western thought that can be defined as Modern Orthodox. His first visits to the State of Israel confirmed his conviction that Jews formed a national group and that their return to their Hebrew identity constituted a revolutionary change. In 1968, he immigrated to Israel, where he took part in the creation of several educational bodies, some of them for new immigrants, in the spirit of religious Zionism. In his Israeli years, he continued to be involved in Jewish education in France and in interreligious dialogue.

One of the most influential spiritual leaders of French and French-speaking Jewry, "Manitou" (his nickname from the boy scout period) personified, to a certain extent, the evolution of this community from a merely religious group of individuals to a community strongly linked to Zionism and the State of Israel.

BIBLIOGRAPHY: L. Ashkenazi and M. Goldman, *La parole et l' écrit: Penser la tradition juive aujourd'hui* (2000); idem, *Penser la vie juive aujourd'hui* (2005); M. Koginsky, *Un Hébreu d'origine juive* (1998).

[Dror Franck Sullaper (2nd ed.)]

ASHKENAZI, MALKIEL (d. c. 1620), kabbalist. He probably settled first at Safed, where he was close to the circle of Isaac *Luria's disciples, and subsequently in Hebron. He was probably the rabbi of Hebron and, according to reports that Ḥ.J.D. *Azulai heard from the elders of Hebron, Ashkenazi was responsible for consolidating Jewish settlement in Hebron. Ashkenazi had an important library at his house, including six scrolls of Lurianic Kabbalah corrected in Ḥayyim Vital's own hand (Ms. Montefiore 348). R. Solomon ha-Narboni of Hebron mentions a manuscript which was shown to him by "the accomplished scholar, pietist, and saint" (J. Kastaro, *Oholei Ya'akov* (1783), no. 113). R. Isaiah ha-Levi *Horowitz mentions in his book *Shenei Luḥot ha-Berit* (1648) the customs of Hebron according to R. Malkiel Ashkenazi. The impression left by Malkiel in the sources is of a learned man whose opinions were accepted; nevertheless none of his writings survived.

BIBLIOGRAPHY: Rosanes, Togarmah, 3 (1938), 306; M. Benayahu, *Sefer Ḥida* (1959), 69–70, 83, 89.

ASHKENAZI, MEIR BEN BENJAMIN WOLF (second half of the 17th century), German rabbi. Ashkenazi was the first appointed rabbi of the united communities of Altona, Hamburg, and Wandsbeck in 1664. He left his post in 1667, stipulating that he be reinstated within a given period. However, the Hamburg and Wandsbeck communities appointed another incumbent in his absence. Jacob *Sasportas, then *ḥakham* of the Sephardi community in Hamburg, arbitrated in the ensuing conflict in favor of the two communities. The union was temporarily dissolved and Ashkenazi remained rabbi of Altona until 1669.

BIBLIOGRAPHY: O. Wolfsberg (Aviad), *Die Drei-Gemeinde* (1960), 50–51.

ASHKENAZI, MORDECAI BEN ISAAC KOHEN (late 16th–early 17th century), rabbi and preacher in Syria. His major work *Rosh Mor Deror* (Venice, 1615), written in 1613, was influenced by his teacher and father-in-law, R. Samuel *Laniado. A collection of homilies on the Torah readings, written in the classical tradition of Jewish preaching, it treats the redemption, God's revenge on the Gentiles, and Israel's blessed condition after the coming of the Messiah. While Ashkenazi sometimes employed kabbalistic terms in his preaching, they are generally based directly on the Midrash.

BIBLIOGRAPHY: D.Z. Laniado, *Li-Kedoshim asher ba-Areẓ* (1952), 46ff. (second pagination).

ASHKENAZI, MOSES DAVID (c. 1780–1856), talmudist and author in Hungary and Ereẓ Israel. Ashkenazi was born in Galicia where his father Asher served as rabbi. From 1803 to 1843 he held the office of rabbi at Tolcsva, Hungary. Thereafter he settled in Ereẓ Israel where he became a rabbi of the Ashkenazi community in Safed, a position he held until his death. The following works of his have been published: (1) *Toledot Adam*, novellae to several talmudic tractates (Jerusalem, 1845); (2) *Be'er Sheva*, a collection of homiletical discussions of the Pentateuch (1853); (3) his will was printed as an addendum to *Shemen Rosh*, a responsa collection of his grandson Asher Anschel (1903). A responsum of Ashkenazi appears in the responsa *Heshiv Moshe* of Moses *Teitelbaum (2 (1866), no. 67). He also corresponded with Moses *Sofer.

BIBLIOGRAPHY: M. Sofer, *Ḥatam Sofer* (1858), *Even ha-Ezer* (1858), no. 29; Benjacob, Oẓar 65, no. 180; 618, no. 102; Z. Schwartz, *Shem ha-Gedolim me-Ereẓ Hagar*, 1, pt. 2 (1913), 12b, no. 190; 3 (1915), 8a, no. 9; 39a, no. 5.

ASHKENAZI, NAPHTALI BEN JOSEPH (c. 1540–1602), rabbi in Safed. Ashkenazi studied in the two great yeshivot of the Ashkenazi community in Safed and was later appointed preacher there. He suffered great privation as a result of the deterioration in the economic situation and in 1595 went to Egypt and then Italy. In Mantua he made the acquaintance of Moses *Berab. In 1601 he published in Venice *Imrei Shefer*, a volume of sermons which shows kabbalistic influence. Leone *Modena held Ashkenazi in high esteem and wrote a poem in praise of his book. In Venice, he was received with great honor and the *rosh yeshivah*, Ben Zion Ẓarefati, invited Ashkenazi to join his staff. During his stay in the city he was the guest of the wealthy Kalonymus Belgrado, founder of the yeshivah. He discovered the manuscripts of Solomon b. Abraham Adret's *Avodat ha-Kodesh* and Abraham b. David of Posquières' *Ba'alei Nefesh* and published them in Venice in 1602. He planned to return to Ereẓ Israel, but died in Venice. Leon Modena's eulogy of him was published in his *Midbar Yehudah* (78ff.).

BIBLIOGRAPHY: Ghirondi-Neppi, 273–5; L. Blau (ed.), *Leo Modenas Briefe und Schriftstuecke* (1905), 117; S. Bernstein, *The Divan of Leo di Modena* (1932), 73.

ASHKENAZI, NISSIM ABRAHAM BEN RAPHAEL (1790?–1860), *dayyan* and rabbi of Smyrna. Ashkenazi was taught by his father, and one of his first responsa, dated 1816, notes his father's approval of his ruling. He was appointed rabbi in 1838. Ashkenazi compiled *Neḥmad le-Mareh*, a commentary on the Jerusalem Talmud, in which he collected comments of the tosafists, the other early commentators, and, in particular, of later commentators. To these he added his own explanations of difficult passages. The work was published in four parts: *Zera'im* (Salonika, 1833), *Mo'ed* (*ibid.*, 1846), *Nashim* (Smyrna, 1857), *Nezikin ve-Niddah* (*ibid.*, 1861). His other published works are *Darash Avraham* (Salonika, 1841–48), in two parts, a collection of sermons arranged in the order of the Pentateuch (to which are appended his father's sermons, entitled *Mareh Adam*, with his notes); *Ma'aseh Avraham* (Smyrna, 1855), the first part of his two volumes of responsa; and *Na'eh le-Hodot* (Leghorn, 1865), a homiletical commentary on the Psalms. Ashkenazi also published his father's book, *Mareh ha-Gadol* (1820–31). Ashkenazi was known for his saintly ways and was a friend of the great sage, Ḥayyim Palaggi, whose eulogy to Ashkenazi is printed in his *Ḥelkam ba-Ḥayyim* (1874).

ASHKENAZI, SAMUEL JAFFE BEN ISAAC (16th century), rabbi in Constantinople. He wrote a number of works, some of which are still in manuscript. Most of them are homiletic commentaries on the major Midrashim: e.g., *Yefeh To'ar*, a homiletic exegesis on *Midrash Rabbah* (Genesis, Venice, 1597–1606; Exodus, *ibid.*, 1657; Leviticus, Constantinople, 1648), and *Yefeh Anaf* (Frankfurt, 1696), an exposition of the *Midrash Rabbah* on the five scrolls. Most of his writings in *halakhah* are unpublished. His responsa, however, were often quoted by 17th-century authorities.

BIBLIOGRAPHY: Azulai, 1 (1852), 175, no. 110, s.v. *Shemu'el Yafeh Ashkenazi*; Steinschneider, Cat Bod, 2427–28, no. 7037.

ASHKENAZI, SAUL BEN MOSES HA-KOHEN (c. 1470–1523), philosopher. Ashkenazi was born in Candia, Crete, and studied there with Elijah *Delmedigo. Later he lived in Constantinople. His best-known work is a set of 12 questions directed to Isaac *Abrabanel concerning the proper understanding of certain passages in Maimonides' *Guide of the Perplexed* and in works by the Muslim philosophers al-Ghazālī and Averroes. It was published under the title *She'elot ha-Ray Sha'ul ha-Kohen* (Venice, 1574; repr. Jerusalem, 1967–68) with Abrabanel's answers and some additions by other authors. Two other works of his are mentioned in his questions: *Ir Elohim* ("City of God") and *Yekholet Adonai* ("Power of the Lord"). Another of his works, *Sefer ha-Takhliyyot* ("Book of Goals"), devoted to problems of physics, is known to have been in the possession of Moses b. Samuel Kasani, who inherited his library.

In addition, Ashkenazi wrote glosses on Averroes' *Physics*. Reference is made to a syllogism composed by him. Finally, an epilogue he wrote to the book *Beḥinat ha-Dat* by his teacher Elijah Delmedigo is known. His opposition to the kabbalists drew the criticism of Joseph Solomon Delmedigo, who otherwise thought highly of him.

BIBLIOGRAPHY: A. Geiger, *Melo Ḥofnayim* (1840), xxii–xxiii, 23, 64, 66, 72; M. Steinschneider, *Catalog… Leiden* (1858), 107–8; Steinschneider, Cat Bod, 2507, no. 7098. **ADD. BIBLIOGRAPHY:** B. Netanyahu, *Don Isaac Abravanel* (1972), index.

[Jacob Haberman]

ASHKENAZI, SOLOMON (c. 1520–1602), Turkish physican and diplomat; born in Udine, northern Italy. His father Nathan apparently belonged to the *Basevi family, the name "Ashkenazi" indicating German origin. After studying medicine at Padua, Solomon went to Cracow, where he served for 16 years as court physician at the court of Sigismund II Augustus. In 1564, he settled in Constantinople, where he was physician and dragoman to Marcantonio Barbaro, the Venetian Bailo, and to the grand vizier, Mehmet Sokollu. During the war with Venice which broke out in 1570 (largely through the influence of Joseph *Nasi, duke of Naxos) Barbaro employed him for secret communications with the grand vizier, Nasi's political rival. After the Turkish disaster at Lepanto, Ashkenazi conducted the preliminary negotiations which led to the peace treaty of 1573. In the following year he was sent to Venice as the vizier's personal representative to propose an alliance to the Venetian government. It was determined that he should be treated as though he were an ambassador from the sultan, and he was formally received in this capacity by the doge and signoria in 1574. During the following decade, as "Aleman Oglou," Ashkenazi continued to wield great influence. He claimed to be responsible for the exertion of Turkish support when Henri de Valois was elected to the Polish throne in 1573, and when the Polish throne was again vacant in 1574–5 he promised to secure the support of the Sublime Porte for the duke of Ferrara. He advised the grand duke of Tuscany on procedure when the latter wished to resume diplomatic relations with Turkey in 1578. In 1583 his services were used to settle a minor dispute between the English and Venetian representatives. In 1586 he signed the preliminary articles of the treaty with Spain on behalf of the sultan. In 1591, he used his influence to secure the appointment as voivode of Moldavia of Emanuel Aron (who was probably of Jewish extraction). When he went to Jassy in 1593 in the hope of obtaining compensation for his efforts, he was handed over to the prince of Transylvania and thrown into jail; ultimately, the English ambassador in Constantinople secured his release. He died shortly afterwards. His final diplomatic activities took place under greatly changed circumstances during the reign of the Sultan Murad III, whose attitude to the Jews in the empire was negative.

His widow, Boula Eksati, inherited some of his medical secrets, and early in the 17th century cured the boy-sultan Ahmed I of smallpox. His son, Nathan Ashkenazi, likewise a physician, was officially received by the doge when he visited Venice in 1605, probably on a secret diplomatic mission, bringing letters of recommendation from the sultan.

BIBLIOGRAPHY: M. Brosch, *Geschichten aus dem Leben dreier Grosswesire* (Gotha, 1899), 34–42, passim; C. Roth, *The House of Naxos* (1948); M.A. Levy, *Don Joseph Nasi* (Ger., 1859); Rosanes, Togarmah, 3 (1938), 349–54; C. Roth, in: *Oxford Slavonic Papers*, 9 (1960), 8–20. **ADD. BIBLIOGRAPHY:** A. Galanté, ISIS, 9, 86–87; idem, in: *Sinai*, 3 (1940), 462–73; A. Aschkenasy, in: RHMH, 128 (1979), 5–10; S.W. Baron, *Social and Religious History*, 18, 130–31, 484–85; B. Arbel, in: G. Benzoni (ed.), *Gli ebrei e Venezia (secoli XIV–XVIII)* (1987); B. Arbel, in: *Il mondo ebraico* (1991), 105–28; M. Rozen, in: A. Rodrigue (ed.), *Ottoman and Turkish Jewry, Community and Leadership* (1992), 157; A. Levy, in: A. Levy (ed.), *The Jews of the Ottoman Empire* (1994), 76–77, 720; B. Arbel, *Jews and Venetians in the Early-Modern Eastern Mediterranean* (1995), 77–94.

[Cecil Roth / Leah Bornstein-Makovetsky (2nd ed.)]

ASHKENAZI, ẒEVI HIRSCH BEN JACOB (also known as the **Ḥakham Zevi**; 1660–1718), rabbi and halakhist. Both his father, Jacob Sak, a renowned scholar, and his maternal grandfather, *Ephraim b. Jacob ha-Kohen, had escaped from Vilna to Moravia during the 1655 Cossack uprising. It was there that Ashkenazi studied under them as a youth. He wrote his first responsa in 1676, about the time he was sent to the yeshivah of Elijah Covo in Salonika to study the Sephardi scholars' method of study. During his stay in Salonika (1676–78?) and Belgrade (1679), he adopted Sephardi customs and manners and, despite his Ashkenazi origin, assumed the title "*ḥakham*," the Sephardi title for a rabbi, and also the name "Ashkenazi." In 1680 he returned to Ofen and continued his studies. After his wife and daughter were killed during the siege of Ofen by the Imperial army of Leopold I, Ashkenazi escaped to Sarajevo where he was appointed *ḥakham* of the Sephardi community. His parents were taken prisoner by a Brandenburg regiment after the fall of Ofen and ransomed by Jews in Berlin. It seems that only much later Ashkenazi received the news that his parents were alive. He arrived in Berlin via Venice and Prague in 1689. There he married the daughter of Meshullam Zalman Neumark-Mirels, the *av bet din* of the "Three Communities" of Altona, Hamburg, and Wandsbeck. He later moved to Altona where for 18 years he devoted himself to teaching in the *Klaus*, which was founded for him by leading members of the congregation. On the death of his father-in-law (1707), he was elected rabbi of Hamburg and Wandsbeck, although he shared the position at Altona with Moses Rothenburg. It was eventually a violent controversy on a halakhic question between them (the "chicken without a heart," see below), which compelled him to resign his position in all three communities in 1709. He continued to act as the head of the yeshivah in the Altona *klaus* until invited to serve as rabbi of the Ashkenazi community in Amsterdam in 1710. There, Ashkenazi's relations were initially excellent. His responsa, published in Amsterdam in 1712, were highly regarded by the rabbis of the Portuguese (Sephardi) community there, and he was on intimate terms with the Sephardi rabbi, Solomon *Ayllon. This relationship, however, deteriorated with the arrival in Amsterdam of Nehemiah *Ḥayon, the emissary of *Shabbetai Ẓevi, who sought the help of the local Portuguese community in circulating his writings. Having been asked by the Portuguese elders (who did not rely on Ayllon) to rule on the matter, Ashkenazi and Moses *Ḥagiz – who was then in Amsterdam as a rabbinical emissary from Jerusalem – decided against Ḥayon and his writings and later excommunicated him. In revenge for not having been consulted about Ḥayyon's writings, Ayllon managed to transform the issue into one of supremacy of the old Portuguese community over the newcomers' Ashkenazi community. A new commission under Ayllon was appointed and found Ḥayon's writings to be in accordance with traditional Kabbalah. Upon Ashkenazi's refusal to apologize to Ḥayon, a bitter controversy took place between the Portuguese and Ashkenazi. As a result of his opponents' incessant personal attacks, Ashkenazi finally resigned his position in Amsterdam in 1714. After a brief stay in London (at the invitation of the Sephardi community), and a short sojourn in Emden, he proceeded to Poland and settled in Opatow. From there he was invited once more to Hamburg to take part in a complicated lawsuit. In the beginning of 1718 he was appointed rabbi of Lemberg, but he died there after a few months.

Ashkenazi's chief work is his collection of responsa *Ḥakham Ẓevi* (Amsterdam, 1712). These responsa reflect his stormy life and his many wanderings. Questions were addressed to him from all parts of Europe – from London to Lublin and from Hamburg to "Candia in Italy" – dealing in particular with problems which arose from the condition of the Jews in various countries. They shed light on the communal organization, its privileges and regulations (e.g., no. 131).

Three responsa (74, 76, 77) deal with the celebrated problem of the chicken which was allegedly found to have no heart. His decision that such a bird was *kasher* created a sensation in the rabbinic world, and was vigorously opposed by such leading rabbis as Moses Rothenburg, Naphtali Katz of Frankfurt, David Oppenheim, and Jonathan Eybeschuetz, who vehemently attacked the decision. He was supported by his son, Jacob *Emden. In one of his responsa (no. 93) Ashkenazi deals with the question of whether a golem could be counted in a *minyan* ("religious quorum"), one such being having been fashioned by his grandfather, Elijah of Chelm. Ashkenazi decided that a golem cannot be counted in a *minyan*. When in 1705 David Nieto of London expressed views which were deemed by his community to be heretical and bordering upon the doctrine of Spinoza, the matter was brought before Ashkenazi, who accepted Nieto's explanations (no. 8). The mutual relations between Ashkenazim and Sephardim are dealt with in a number of responsa (14, 38, 99). For example, on the question of whether it is permissible for Ashkenazim to use a Sephardi scroll, written in accordance with the views of Maimonides for the public reading of the Torah, he concludes that Ashkenazi and Sephardi scrolls are equally valid since the subdivision into sections is the same in both cases. As to the question of whether the Zohar should be given priority and relied upon in halakhic rulings, he declares emphatically that "even if the Zohar were to contradict the halakhic authorities we could not discard the opinions of the halakhic authorities in favor of what is written in the esoteric law; for in the laws and their practical application we are not concerned with mystic lore. But in cases where halakhic authorities differ, it is proper to follow the decision of the Zohar" (no. 36). In 1692 he published his glosses to the *Turei Zahav* on the *Ḥoshen Mishpat*. Opposed to *pilpul* in the study of the Talmud, he demanded a systematic and fundamental analysis of the subject matter. His son, Jacob Emden, praised him for his qualities of "abstinence, meticulousness, true saintliness, and inner reverence." One of his other sons, Abraham Meshullam Zalman, was *av bet din* in Ostrog from 1745. His son, Ẓevi Hirsch, published his father's responsa and novellae under the title *Divrei Meshullam* (1783).

BIBLIOGRAPHY: J. Emden, *Torat ha-Kena'ot* (Amsterdam, 1752), 33b; idem, *Megillat Sefer* (1897); Graetz-Rabbinowitz, 8 (1899), 370–6, 598–613, n. 6; C.N. Dembitzer, *Kelilat Yofi*, 1 (1888), 91–99; E. Duckesz, *Ivah le-Moshav* (1903), 11–17; S. Buber, *Anshei Shem* (1895), 187–92; S.M. Chones, *Toledot ha-Posekim* (1910), 557–9; Margolioth, in: *Sinai*, 29 (1951), 379–88; 31 (1952), 88–89; EG, 1 (1956), 405–7; D. Kaufmann, in: JJGL, 2 (1899), 123–47; idem, in: JHSET, 3 (1899), 102–25; Kaufmann, Schriften, 2 (1910), 303; A. Predmesky, *Life and Work of R. Ashkenazi* (1946); H.J. Zimmels, *Ashkenazim and Sephardim* (1958), 68–70, 297–9; M.M. Biber, *Mazkeret li-Gedolei Ostraha (Ostrog)* (1907), 106–10; Waxman, Literature, 2 (1960), 188–9. **ADD. BIBLIOGRAPHY:** M. Goldish, in: *Studia Rosenthaliana*, 27:1–2 (1993), 5–12; B. Sherwin, in: *Judaism*, 44:3 (1995), 314–22; J.J. Schacter, in: *Ashkenaz: The German Jewish Heritage* (1988), 69–78.

[Yehoshua Horowitz]

ASHKENAZY, VLADIMIR DAVIDOVICH (1937–), Russian-born pianist. His mother was Russian Orthodox, his father Jewish and himself a pianist. Ashkenazy made his first public appearance at the age of eight, in a performance of a Haydn piano concerto. He later studied at the Moscow Conservatory with Lev Oborin. In 1955 he was awarded second prize in the International Chopin piano competition in Warsaw and, the following year, first prize in the Queen Elizabeth international music competition in Brussels. In 1962 he shared the first prize in the Tchaikovsky competition with the British pianist John Ogdon. Ashkenazy's success in Brussels led to concert tours throughout the world. He soon achieved fame as a great virtuoso whose playing was marked by technical perfection, poetic expression, and a unique range of interpretation. He settled in England after a tour in 1963. He subsequently became a citizen of Iceland and was awarded the Icelandic Order of the Falcon. Ashkenazy served as music director of the London-based Royal Philharmonic Orchestra between 1987 and 1994 and of the Deutsches Symphonie-Orchester of Berlin from 1988. From 1998 he was director of the Czech Philharmonic Orchestra. He wrote an autobiography, *Beyond Frontiers* (with Jasper Parrott, 1984).

[Michael Goldstein / Rohan Saxena (2nd ed.)]

ASHKHABAD (formerly **Askhabad;** (1919–1927) **Poltoratsk**), capital of Turkmenistan. Jewish soldiers in the czarist army settled in Ashkhabad after the Russian conquest of the area in 1881, but they were expelled soon afterward by the governor-general of Turkestan. Later, Jewish artisans moved here from European Russia. By 1897, 310 Jews lived in the town (1.6% of the total population). At the end of the 1920s it served as a deportation center for Zionists exiled from European Russia. In 1939, 711 Jews (0.56% of the total) lived in the town and 1,202 in the entire district. In 1959 the Jewish population was 1,276. Around 600 remained in 2005.

[Yehuda Slutsky]

ASHLAG, YEHUDAH (1886–1954), Israeli kabbalist and rabbi. Ashlag, the most important 20th century kabbalist, who was born in Warsaw, was educated in ḥasidic schools. He was a disciple of Shalom Rabinowicz of Kalushin, and of his son Yehoshah Asher of Porissov. He also had a teacher of Kabbalah whose name, he maintained, he was not allowed to divulge. Ashlag immigrated to Palestine in 1920 and settled in the Old City of Jerusalem, where he established a yeshivah, named Bet Ulpena le-Rabbanim, and instructed his pupils in *halakhah* and Kabbalah. Between 1926 and 1928 he resided in London, where he wrote his first kabbalistic works, *Panim Me'irot* and *Panim Masbirot* (1927–30), a double commentary to the *Eẓ Ḥayyim* by Ḥayyim *Vital. In 1946 he moved to Tel Aviv. Ashlag wrote extensive commentaries to the Lurianic corpus and the Zohar. His writings include *Or Pashut*, a commentary to the Lurianic compilation *Beit Sha'ar Ha-Kavanot* (1941); *Talmud Eser Sefirot* (1955–67), on the kabbalistic doctrines of Isaac *Luria; *Ha-Sullam* ("The Ladder," 1945–60), a commentary on the entire *Zohar and *Zohar Ḥadash* (completed by his brother-in-law Yehuda Ẓevi *Brandwein). Apart from his kabbalistic writings, Ashlag published in 1933 a journal which included articles intended for the larger public. Other writings of Ashlag, letters to his disciples, commentaries, and homilies, were published posthumously in four volumes entitled *Peri Ḥakham* (1985–2003). Ashlag, who adopted socialist and communist ideas and integrated them in his kabbalistic systems, led discussions with various leaders of Israel's Labor Party, including Israel's first prime minister, David *Ben-Gurion.

In his extensive writings, Ashlag presents a highly complex and innovative kabbalistic doctrine. The central notion of his new kabbalistic system is that the Creator, who is defined as the infinite "will to bestow," created through a complex and dialectical process of emanation a "will to receive" the benefits bestowed by Him. Human beings stand at the end of the emanation process as a pure egoistic will to receive. Yet, recognizing their situation, human beings are able to change their nature, and try to transform their egoistic "will to receive" into a quasi-divine "will to bestow." As such a transformation is achieved, the gap between human and divine nature diminishes and man achieves spiritual perfection. This process also has a social feature, as the road to spiritual perfection is also the road to establishing a perfect, communist community in which every individual contributes according to his ability and receives according to his needs. Ashlag believed that Kabbalah should not be kept esoteric and attempted to disperse Kabbalah to the larger public through his popular treatises and his Zohar translation. After Ashlag's death, his kabbalistic doctrines were taught by his sons, R. Barukh Shalom and R. Shelomo Benjamin, and by his disciples, R. Levi Krakovsky and R. Yehuda Ẓevi *Brandwein. Various contemporary kabbalistic movements, including the Kabbalah Center headed by R. Philip *Berg and Bnei Baruch headed by R. Michael Leitman are based on the kabbalistic system of Yehudah Ashlag.

[Yehuda Ẓevi Brandwein / Boaz Huss (2nd ed.)]

ASHMAN, AHARON (1896–1981), Israeli playwright, poet, and editor. Ashman, who was born in Russia, was active in the Jewish self-defense units during the Petlyura pogroms in the Ukraine at the end of World War I. His literary career began after his arrival in Palestine in 1921. He wrote poems (some of which became popular when set to music) and dramas, including a biblical trilogy *Mikhal Bat Sha'ul* ("Saul's Daughter, Michal," 1956) and a play about *ḥalutzim*, *Ha-Adamah ha-Zot* ("This Earth," 1943). Ashman translated many librettos for the Palestinian opera. In addition to teaching, Ashman edited school textbooks for the study of Hebrew, such as *Aleh* and *Dabber Ivrit*. From 1956 to 1961 he was president of the Israel Authors and Composers Association.

[Getzel Kressel]

ASHREI (Heb. אַשְׁרֵי; "Happy are they"), the first word and the name of a reading from the Book of Psalms which occupies an important place in the liturgy. The reading consists of Psalms 84:5, 144:15, 145, and 115:18. The Talmud states that anyone who recites *Ashrei* three times a day is sure of life in the world to come (Ber. 4b), and therefore it is read twice in the morning service (in the *Pesukei de-Zimra* and toward the end), and at the commencement of the afternoon service. The addition of the first two verses is explained as a reference to the pious who arrive early before the start of the service proper (Ber. 32b; cf. Yal., II Sam. 146). *Ashrei* is recited before the *Seliḥot* of the months of Elul and Tishri. On the Day of Atonement the Sephardim recite it both at *Minḥah* and *Ne'ilah*, whereas the Ashkenazim say it only at *Ne'ilah*.

Psalm 145 is the only psalm to bear the title *tehillah* (literally "praise") from which the entire book of Psalms takes its Hebrew name, *Tehillim*. It is alphabetic with the strophe of the letter *nun* missing. A talmudic homily suggests that this is because the letter *nun* also begins a verse prophesying the destruction of Israel (Amos 5:2; Ber. 4b). However, in the Psalm Scroll discovered among the *Dead Sea Scrolls (ed. J.A. Sanders (1966), 64) there is a *nun* verse reading *ne'eman Elohim bi-devarav ve-ḥasid be-khol ma'asav* ("God is faithful in His words, and pious in all His works"). In the scrolls each line ends with the refrain *Barukh Adonai u-varukh shemo le-olam va-ed* ("Blessed is the Lord, and blessed be His name for evermore") which would indicate that the psalm was used liturgically as early as the Second Temple. In the psalm the author declares that he will praise God because He is "gracious," "merciful," "slow to anger," and "good"; "He supports the fallen" and gives mankind its "food in due season." God is close to all "who call upon His name in truth" and "preserves all who love Him."

Ashkenazim customarily touch the *tefillin* at verse 16: "Thou openest Thy hand, and satisfiest all living," whereas the Sephardim open their hands in symbolic gesture. In Reform synagogues *Ashrei* is recited in the vernacular; in many Conservative synagogues it is read responsively in Hebrew.

BIBLIOGRAPHY: *Oẓar ha-Tefillot* (Ashkenazi rite) (1923), 215; Elbogen, Gottesdienst, 85; Hertz, Prayer, 85ff.; E. Munk, *The World of Prayer* (1954), 73ff.

[Raphael Posner]

ASHRIKI, MORDECAI (second half of 18th century), known as Lahazan Bakha, personal adviser to the ruler of Morocco, Muhammad ibn Abdallah (1754–90) in Meknès. Ashriki was entrusted with important matters of administration, and was also a leader in the Meknès Jewish community; he tried to use his political position to improve the situation of his coreligionists. When Muhammad's son Yazīd tried to rebel against him, Ashriki advised the ruler to banish his son, fearing that the Jews would suffer under Yazīd. When Muhammad died, his son succeeded him. Yazīd (1790–92), in fact, hated the Jews and wanted to destroy them; and among his many Jewish victims was Ashriki, whom he ordered to be burned. Before the sentence was carried out, Ashriki was given the option of converting to Islam to stay alive, but he refused.

BIBLIOGRAPHY: S.A. Romanelli, *Massa be-Arav* (1834^2), 63–64, 81; J.M. Toledano, *Ner ha-Ma'arav* (1911), 165–8, 171; Hirschberg, *Afrikah*, 2 (1965), 292, 295–301.

ASHTAROTH, ASHTEROTH-KARNAIM, KARNAIM (Heb. עַשְׁתָּרוֹת, עַשְׁתְּרֹת־קַרְנַיִם, קַרְנַיִם; "horns"; Amos 6:13), Canaanite city in Bashan, named after the goddess *Ashtoreth. Ashtaroth is mentioned in the Egyptian Execration Texts (19th–18th centuries B.C.E.), in the inscriptions of Thutmosis III (No. 28 in his list), and in the El-Amarna letters (EA 197, 256). With the addition of neighboring *Karnaim, it appears in the list of *Chedorlaomer's conquests (Gen. 14:5). Together with *Edrei, Ashtaroth was the capital of Og, king of Bashan (Deut. 1:4), and after the Israelite conquest it was allotted to the tribe of *Manasseh (Josh. 13:31). It was a levitical city (I Chron. 6:56; Josh. 21:27 – "Beeshterah") and the home of Uzziah, one of David's "mighty men" (I Chron. 11:44). Ashtaroth was captured by Tiglath-Pileser III in 732 B.C.E.; a relief depicting the deportation of its inhabitants has been preserved. The temple of Atargatis there was stormed by Judah Maccabee (I Macc. 5:26, 43–44; II Macc. 12:21, 26). In talmudic literature it appears as Ashtor, a city of proselytes (TJ, Bik. 1:4, 64a). In the time of Eusebius (fourth century), two villages, one called Ashtaroth and the other Karnaim, still existed in the Bashan, nine (Roman) miles apart. It is identified with Tell Ashtareh, 21 mi. (34 km.) east of the Sea of Galilee.

BIBLIOGRAPHY: W.F. Albright, in: BASOR, 19 (1925), 15; A. Alt, in: PJB, 29 (1933), 21; Abel, Geog, 2 (1938), 255; Press, Ereẓ, 4 (1955), 760; Aharoni, Land, index.

[Michael Avi-Yonah]

ASHTOR (Strauss), ELIYAHU (1914–1984), Israel historian. Born and educated in Vienna, Ashtor went to Palestine in 1938. From 1939 until 1957 he served as librarian of the Oriental department of the Jewish National and University Library, Jerusalem. He taught from 1952 at the Hebrew University (later professor of Islamic civilization). In his programmatic *Prolegomena to the Medieval History of Oriental Jews* (JQR, 50 (1959)), he pointed out that it was the task of the historian to understand the Oriental Jewish communities as an integral element of Muslim society and at the same time to note their affinities with Jews from other countries and periods. Ashtor's *Toledot ha-Yehudim be-Miẓrayim ve-Suryah Taḥat Shilton ha-Mamlukim* ("History of the Jews in Egypt and Syria under the Rule of the Mamluks," 2 vols., 1944, 1951) reveals his familiarity with the relevant Muslim literature, much of which is still in manuscript, his apt use of the accounts of the European travelers, and of Jewish sources. He also wrote *Korot ha-Yehudim bi-Sefarad ha-Muslemit* ("History of the Jews in Muslim Spain," 2 vols., 1960, 1966). Ashtor made important contributions to Islamic social history and economic history in the Near East during the Middle Ages.

[Shelomo Dov Goitein]

ASHTORETH (Heb. עַשְׁתֹּרֶת), Canaanite goddess. Possibly, the deliberate corruption of the name *ʿštrt* (*ʿaštart* or *ʿašteret*) is meant to conform to the vocalization of the Hebrew word *boshet* ("shame"; see *Euphemism and Dysphemism). Ashtoreth is the preeminent goddess in the Bible, and the plural Ashtaroth is a generic term for goddesses, used together with *Baal(im) as a collective term for illicit worship (e.g., Judg. 2:13, "Baal and Ashtaroth"; I Sam. 7:3, "strange gods and Ashtaroth"; Judg. 10:6; I Sam. 7:4; 12:10, "Baalim and Ashtaroth"). In Israel, her worship is associated with the Sidonians, but Solomon in his later years went after "Ashtoreth, goddess of the Sidonians" (I Kings 11:5), and *Josiah destroyed the cult places which Solomon had built on the "Mount of Corruption (see: *Mount of Olives) for Ashtoreth, the abomination of the Sidonians" (II Kings 23:13). Ashtoreth (Greek *Astarté*) is known from the Ugaritic texts, where, however, her role is overshadowed by that of her alter ego, the goddess Anath. Both Astarte and Anath are the sisters and consorts of Baal and share the dual character of goddesses of love and of war; both are also associated with horses and the hunt. According to Ugaritic texts, Anath and Ashtoreth also share the same abode. It seems therefore that Anath and Ashtoreth are different aspects of the same goddess. This supposition is corroborated by the figure of the Aramaic goddess Atargatis, whose name results from a conflation of the names Astarte and Anath.

Astarte is a fierce warrior goddess and the goddess of sexual love (eros) and fertility. Like her Akkadian counterpart Ištar, she is an astral deity and is associated with the evening star. The name ʿAṯtart is a feminine form of the name ʿAṯtar, a god known from Ugarit and South Arabian sources, and associated with the morning star. The name is also known from the inscription of King *Mesha of Moab (1. 17, in: Pritchard, Texts, 320), where Ashtar-Chemosh occurs as a variant of Chemosh, the name of the national god of Moab. Since Ashtoreth as warrior goddess carries the full title *ʿAštart-šem-Baʿal* both in Ugarit (e.g., Pritchard, Texts, 130) and in the Eshmunazor (*ibid.*, 505, 1.18) inscriptions from Sidon 1,000 years later, it has been suggested that the name is derived ultimately from some root meaning "sparkle" and "splendor," but the evidence is far from conclusive. As the goddess of reproduction, her name became a common noun meaning "increase [of the flock]" in Deuteronomy 7:13; 28:4, 18, 51. (But it is possible that "increase," or "womb of flock," was the original meaning.) As witnessed by numerous personal names, Astarte was already popular in the Late Bronze Age. She played a large role in the cult at Ugarit, and her name appears often in ritual texts and sacrificial lists. From Egypt there is the Astarte papyrus (19th dynasty, in Pritchard, Texts, 17–18), an Egyptian recounting of the Canaanite myth of the revolt of the sea, in which Astarte is given as bride to the sea god Yamm, who is ultimately defeated. (In the Baal cycle from Ugarit, Astarte appears as the ally of Baal in his defeat of Yamm.) There are also numerous Egyptian representations of her as a naked young girl seated astride a stallion, carrying a bow and arrow or javelin and shield. The so-called Astarte Plaques, clay figurines of a mother goddess generally associated with the fertility cults, may be another representation of the goddess. She is most probably the "Queen of Heaven," for whom the women of Judah kneaded cakes, libated, and burned incense in order to assure fertility and plenty (Jer. 44:17–19; cf. Jer. 7:18).

BIBLIOGRAPHY: W.F. Albright, *Yahweh and the Gods of Canaan* (1968), 113–8; Albright, Arch Rel, 74–77; J. Leclant, in: *Syria*, 37 (1960), 1–67; A.H. Gardiner, in: *Studies… F. L Griffith* (1932), 74–85; M. Pope, in: H.W. Haussig (ed.), *Woerterbuch der Mythologie*, 1 (1965), 250–2 (incl. bibl.); J. Gray, in: IDB, 1 (1962), 255–6; Pritchard, Texts, 129–55; H. Gese et al., *Die Religionen Altsyriens, Altarabiens und der Manúäer* (*Die Religionen der Menschheit* 10.2) (1970), pp. 137ff. and 161ff. **ADD. BIBLIOGRAPHY:** N. Wyatt, DDD, 109–14

[Tikva S. Frymer]

ʿĀSHŪRĀʾ, the name of the fast of the tenth day of Muḥarram (the first month of the Muslim year), which according to ancient Islamic tradition was introduced by Muhammad when he came to Yathrib-Medina in 622. It is a fast from evening to evening, i.e., a full day. Both the name and the date of the fast are evidence that Muhammad based himself on the Day of Atonement (Lev. 16:29). Nearly a year and a half after he settled in Yathrib, however, as a result of a dispute with the Jewish community there, Muhammad abolished the ʿĀshūrāʾ and substituted for it the month-long fast of Ramadan (Koran, Sura 2:179–81). Nevertheless the instructions for this fast, both in the Koran and in Islamic tradition, show evidence of Jewish influence. Although ʿĀshūrāʾ thus ceased as a compulsory fast, the tenth of Muharram is still regarded as a most suitable day for voluntary fasting. In Shiʿite Islam this day enjoyed special historical importance as the day when Ḥusayn, the son of Ali, fell in the battle of Karbalaʾ in 650. Many processions are conducted since the previous day is a fast day for Shiʿite ascetics.

BIBLIOGRAPHY: EIS; EIS[2]; S.D. Goitein, *Studies in Islamic History and Institutions* (1966), 90–110.

[Haïm Z'ew Hirschberg]

ASIA.

History

Jewish history originated in this continent, in the Near-Eastern complex of the Fertile Crescent. The journeyings of the *Patriarchs led from *Ur of the Chaldees in present-day *Iraq through the Fertile Crescent to *Egypt. In antiquity, *Canaan controlled the highway linking Asia with Africa (Egypt). The crescent had ties with Hellenic Europe. These were initially established through *Crete, and somewhat later through the contact with the *Philistines and *Phoenicians. Despite the many ties with Egypt, few traces of Egyptian cultural influence are found in Ereẓ *Israel of the biblical period. The effects of this geopolitical background are, however, clearly discernible. The cultural differences existing between the kingdoms of *Israel and *Judah and their separate destinies largely resulted from the exposure of the northern kingdom to influences emanating from *Syria, Assyria, and *Babylonia, and its commercial or other ties with the Asiatic area of the crescent.

After the Assyrian conquest of the northern kingdom of Israel in 722 B.C.E., a considerable number of its population were deported further into the Asian interior. Thus began the myth of the Lost Tribes of Israel which was destined to have a pivotal role in the later development of relations between Jews and much of Asia. With the Babylonian conquest of Judea in 586 B.C.E., the transference of the center of Jewish life to *Mesopotamia was momentarily almost complete. Some historians believe that *monotheism crystallized in its pure form in Judaism from the impact of the Babylonian exile and the close confrontation with Babylonian paganism. Manifold religious and cultural concepts, the nomenclature of the months, the so-called Assyrian characters of the Hebrew script, were acquired in Mesopotamia and carried back to Ereẓ Israel. During the Second Temple period these became central and integral elements in Jewish mores, thought, and literature. A large proportion – possibly the bulk of Jewry – stayed on in Mesopotamia after the Return to Zion, often in flourishing trade centers such as Nippur. Thus Babylonia also became a Jewish national cultural center.

On the other hand, European influences began to penetrate Jewish life and culture with greater force after the conquests of *Alexander the Great. These emanated from Seleucid Syria in the north, as well as from Ptolemaic Egypt in the south. When acculturation was pressed by forcible measures under the Seleucid *Antiochus IV Epiphanes, the sharp Jewish reaction culminated in the *Hasmonean revolt. Jewish influence on its part was evident in some of the Asian principalities. The royal house of *Adiabene adopted Judaism. The Hasmonean revolt was the only instance of a religio-national uprising by an Asiatic society against Hellenistic domination. In the protracted Roman-Byzantine period (63 B.C.E.–641 C.E.) Jewish resistance to alien domination continued, erupting in the Jewish War of 66–73 and subsequent revolts (see *History of Israel, Second Temple Period; *Bar Kokhba). The Jewish image and the horizon of the Near East influenced the European conception of Asia until the modern era.

The Babylonian Jewish center, however, continued to develop independently under Arsacid Partho-Persian rule. The Jewish area of settlement expanded into Persia and toward Central Asia. Jewish settlements on the borders of the Roman and Persian empires in Asia developed a vital Jewish communal life and culture. Evidence of their exceptionally resplendent synagogue art is the *Dura-Europos synagogue and its paintings. The most important contribution of the Babylonian center for subsequent Jewish culture was evolved in the environment of the restored Sassanian Persian Empire. The Babylonian *Talmud exerted its powerful influence on Jewish life on all subsequent generations. Thus Sassanian cultural and folk elements absorbed into the Talmud were integrated into Jewish culture in addition to the former Babylonian and early Persian accretions.

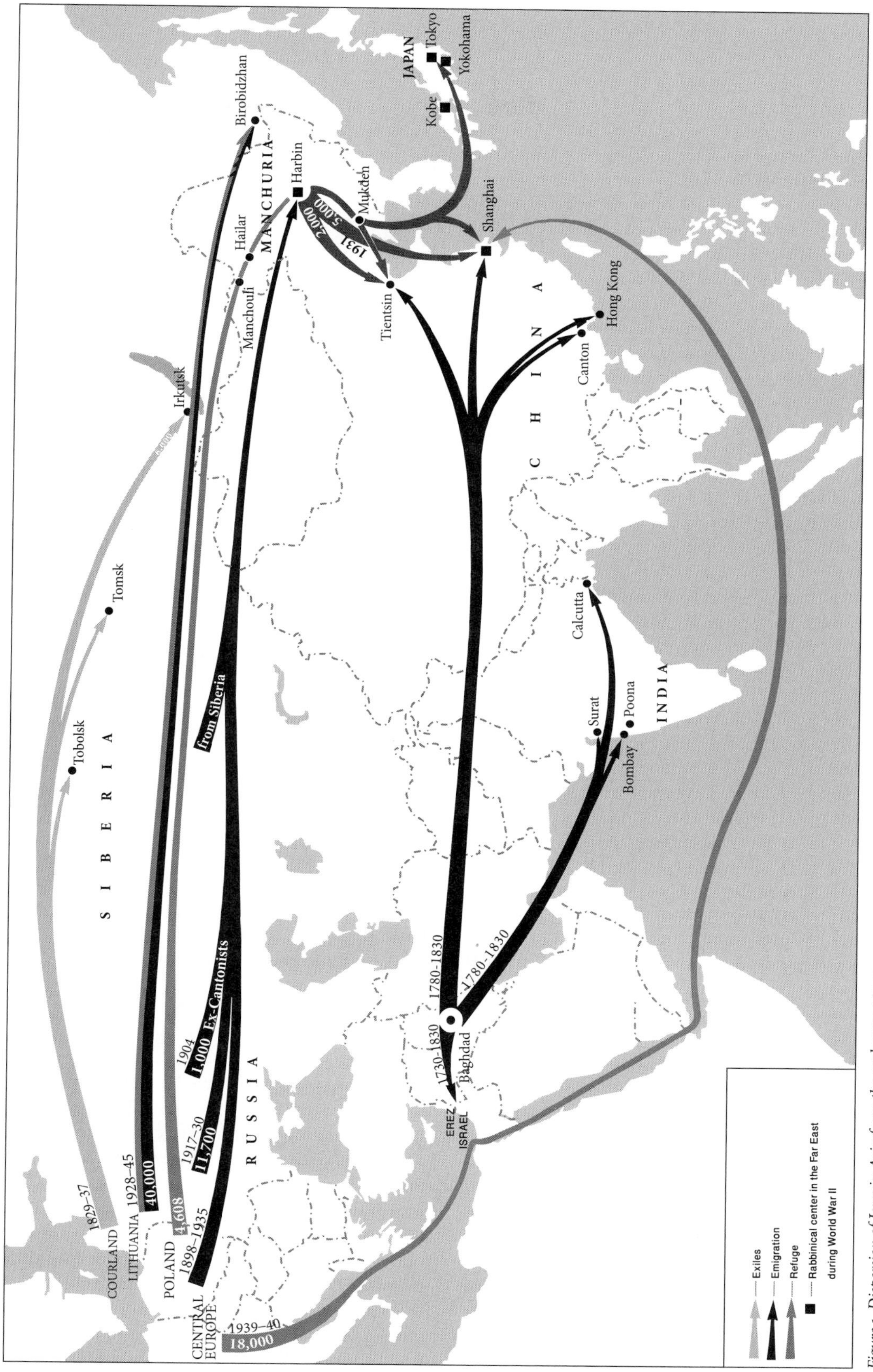

Figure 1. Dispersion of Jews in Asia from the early 1700s to 1945.

The Arab conquest of Ereẓ Israel, Mesopotamia, and the adjacent areas in the seventh and succeeding centuries brought the whole of North Africa, and for a time *Spain, within the sphere of influence of the Muslim caliphate. The fact that its center of gravity and seat of government lay in the Fertile Crescent (*Abbasids, *Umayyads, *Damascus) had an incalculably important effect on Jewish life for generations. The Mesopotamian scene under Arab rule centering on *Baghdad formed the background for an outstandingly creative period in Jewish history. This was the age of the *exilarchs and *geonim, lasting approximately from the seventh to the eleventh centuries. Meanwhile, the pax arabica enabled the area of Jewish settlement to extend increasingly farther eastward. The commercial and industrial revolution of the ninth century gave particular impetus to this advance. Trade with *India, where Jewish communities existed perhaps as early as the fifth century, was commonplace in the geonic period. The ancient Jewish settlement at *Kaifeng in China apparently owed its origin to the flourishing silk trade in about 1000. Jewish travelers of the 12th century, *Benjamin of Tudela and Pethahiah of Regensburg, reported dense and flourishing Jewish populations in most of the Near-Eastern areas. Source evidence from the Cairo *Genizah mirrored the diversified nature of Jewish international trading activities in the Indian Ocean in the 12th century. Links were established from the Near East and Egypt with the Far East via the staging post in *Yemen. The violence surrounding the *Crusades and the Tatar invasions of the 13th century critically endangered the Jewish communities throughout Western Asia. In Ereẓ Israel many Jews were massacred, and after the 11th century the Jewish settlement there stood in need of constant replenishment by immigration from the Diaspora. In the 13th century Mesopotamian Jewry was also almost annihilated though a remnant remained. Meanwhile the communities of Asia Minor had dwindled as a result of the traditional intolerance of the Byzantine rulers. However, a fairly robust Jewish society was flourishing in the areas comprised by the Ottoman *Empire in the second half of the 15th century. An isolated Arabized community of some numerical importance continued to exist in Yemen and the Arabian Peninsula, in conditions which remained largely unchanged for many centuries. In India the *Bene Israel of mysterious origin were settled in Bombay, in addition to the ancient communities in Cranganore (later transferred to *Kochi (Cochin)).

An important reinforcement of the Jewish existence in Asia was provided after the expulsion from Spain in 1492. Large numbers of Jewish exiles, followed later by Portuguese *Marranos, found new homes in various places within the Ottoman Empire. Their settlement was not confined to Ottoman territory in Europe, but also extended to Asia Minor, Syria, and other parts of Asia. The new immigration not only reinvigorated communities surviving from former days, but actually transformed their original character. Whereas these communities were formerly autochthonous, preserving an ancient native Jewish culture, they now assumed more European characteristics. They became largely Spanish speaking and followed the Spanish rite. Probably the former Jewish traditions were genuinely preserved only in Persia, in the Yemen, and in the small surviving Jewish community of Iraq. The post-expulsion period also witnessed a revival of Jewish settlement in Ereẓ Israel. The neo-kabbalistic school of *Safed (see *Kabbalah) renewed Palestinian cultural and religious influences in Jewish life after a recession of many centuries.

The record of Jewish life and creativity in Asia in the late medieval and early modern periods still awaits its definitive presentation. The state of research in modern Jewish historiography reflects its European focus. Numerically there was a Jewish decline in Asia and no certain data exist. Nevertheless the ancient matrix remained. In Yemen and in *Kurdistan Jewish creativity was manifested in specific folk art and customs. The national center of Ereẓ Israel drew to it devoted men and women in each generation. If the Asian communities failed to make their mark on European Jewry in the period, this was mainly the result of the general political predominance then achieved by Europe as a whole.

Two new waves of Jewish migration penetrated deep into Far Eastern Asia in the 19th century. Both were numerically small, but significant in their geographical scope and economic attainments. Both followed in the wake of European imperialism. The first was the considerable eastward emigration from Baghdad and other cities in Iraq, mainly to areas in the British sphere of influence. Small communities that were established in India and farther east, in points as far away as Hong Kong, became extremely affluent and correspondingly important. The second migratory wave to penetrate the fastnesses of Asia made the overland trek from Russia. Initially Jews went to live in *Siberia, mainly for trade for a limited period or when sentenced to exile. Others went on to *Manchuria, especially after World War I, and temporarily important communities were established in places like *Harbin. The industrialization of Asian regions of the Soviet Union, and the development of scientific centers there, again stimulated Jewish movement to Asia. Despite its failure, the autonomous Jewish region of *Birobidzhan, created on Far Eastern soil, still harbors a Jewish community.

With the commencement of Nazi persecution, a considerable increase in the number of Jews in Russian Asia was reported, although the actual figures are not known. World War II completely changed the Far Eastern picture. Many refugees from German-occupied countries and Russia escaped to territories under Japanese rule. The Japanese, although responsible for having introduced certain antisemitic measures, did not carry them out to the extreme. The communist victory in China after the war made it impossible for the Jews to continue there in their former occupations. The recently established communities disappeared. In the Middle East the reorganization of the Turkish state after World War I along nationalist lines and the changes in the Turkish economy had adverse effects on the local Jewish communities, which dwindled considerably. In Ereẓ Israel, however, new forces were at work. The rise of *Zionism revitalized the Jewish settlement. After the 1880s the yishuv played a role of increasing significance in world Jewry, growing rapidly in numbers and developing a character and culture of its own. Jewish settlement proceeded despite obstacles, and foundations were laid for state institutions. The achievements of the pioneers had their effect. By the *Balfour Declaration Ereẓ Israel became the declared Jewish national home. From 1920, after the *League of Nations gave the mandate for Palestine to Britain, an entirely new situation was created. Within the next few decades after the creation of the State of *Israel in 1948, almost all the Jews of the historic communities of Syria, Lebanon, Iraq, and the Yemen had emigrated to Israel. Only small communities remained. Israel also attracted numerous immigrants from other Asian countries, especially from those where economic conditions were poor, such as Turkey and Persia, as well as India. (See Table: Jewish Population of Asia.) The "black" Jews of Cochin, established on the Malabar coast from antiquity, migrated almost en masse. Scattered communities, however, continued to maintain themselves here and there in the Asian continent. In 1970 there were 2,518,000 Jews in the State of Israel, forming about 15% of world Jewry and the third largest Jewish concentration in the world. By the early 21st century it had passed the 5 million mark and constituted nearly 40% of the world Jewish population.

Demography and Statistics

The growth of the Jewish population on the Asian continent during a period of a bit more than 120 years, from 1840 to 1961, shows a steadily increasing tempo. This was, no doubt, in keeping with the general improvement in Asian health and hygienic standards, especially among urban populations, affected by the penetration of European influence. In the first 60 years (1840–1900) the Jewish population increased by only 70%; over the next 40 years (1900–40) it more than doubled, and in the next 21 years (1940–1961) the figure almost tripled, mainly due to the increase of the Jewish population in Ereẓ Israel. (See Table: Aliyah from Asian Countries.)

The drop in the ratio of Asian Jewry to total world Jewry during the first 60 years stemmed from the fact that population increase in Asia lagged considerably behind that in other continents. But the situation changed in the 20th century, and more especially in the period 1940–61, when the percentage more than tripled that at the outset of the period. This percentage increase, however, was not due solely to the absolute numerical growth of the Jewish population in Asia, since it was conditioned in the main by the annihilation of European Jewry, which changed the relative scale. By the 1970s Jews constituted everywhere barely a fraction of 1% of the total population. About 100,000 Jews were scattered over this gigantic continent (outside of Israel) as minority groups engulfed by overwhelming – and in the Arab countries, usually hostile – majorities and were thereby seriously exposed to various dangers. Complete assimilation threatened Asiatic Soviet Jewry, dispersed over the vast expanses of Asiatic Russia, among whom the rate of mixed marriages had been as high as 25–30% before World War II. Over the following decades, however, the trend continued. The various communities of Asia emigrated, often to Israel. Thus the remnant of the Yemeni and Syrian communities left and many thousands left Iran. There were still sizeable communities in Azerbaijan (6,000), Uzbekistan (7,000), Tajikistan (1,100) Kazakhstan (5,000), and Iran (11,500). However, the overall population of

Jewish Population of Asia in 1966 and in 2002 (excluding Israel)

	1966		2002	
Country	Total Population	Jewish Population	Total Population	Jewish Population
Far East				
Afganistan	15,352,000	800		
Burma	25,246,000	200		
China	700,000,000	20	1,287,900,000	1,000*
Hong Kong	3,836,000	200		
India	498,680,000	16,000	1,049,500,000	5,200
Indonesia	104,500,000	100		
Japan	97,960,000	1,000	127,096,000	1,000
Pakistan	105,044,000	300		
Philippines	33,477,000	500	80,000,000	100
Singapore	1,914,000	600	4,200,000	300
Near East				
Cyprus	603,000	30		
Iran	23,428,000	88,000	65,600,000	11,000
Iraq	8,262,000	2,500		
Lebanon	2,400,000	6,000		
Syria	5,399,000	3,000	17,200,000	100
Turkey	32,005,000	35,000	67,300,000	18,000

* Including Hong Kong.

Main Periods of *Aliyah* from Asian countries

Country	Main period of *Aliyah*	Number of Immigrants to Israel	Jewish Population in 1945
Turkey	1919–1950	37,000	80,000
Lebanon+Syria	1950–1955	12,000	25,000
Iraq*	1950–1951	106,662	90,000
Iran	1950–1965	18,000	50,000
Afganistan	1950	1,200	5,000
China	1949	5,000	9,000
Manchuria	1949	1,000	10,000
Japan			2,000
Philippine Islands	1950–1955	22	1,000
Pakistan	1949–1953	1,500	1,500
India	1950–1955	4,000	30,000
Indonesia	1950	20	2,000
Yemen	1948–1950	43,000	45,000
Aden	1950	2,825	6,000

* Iraq served as an assembly center for immigrants from other places. The high emigration figures do not indicate that all the Jews left Iraq in this period.

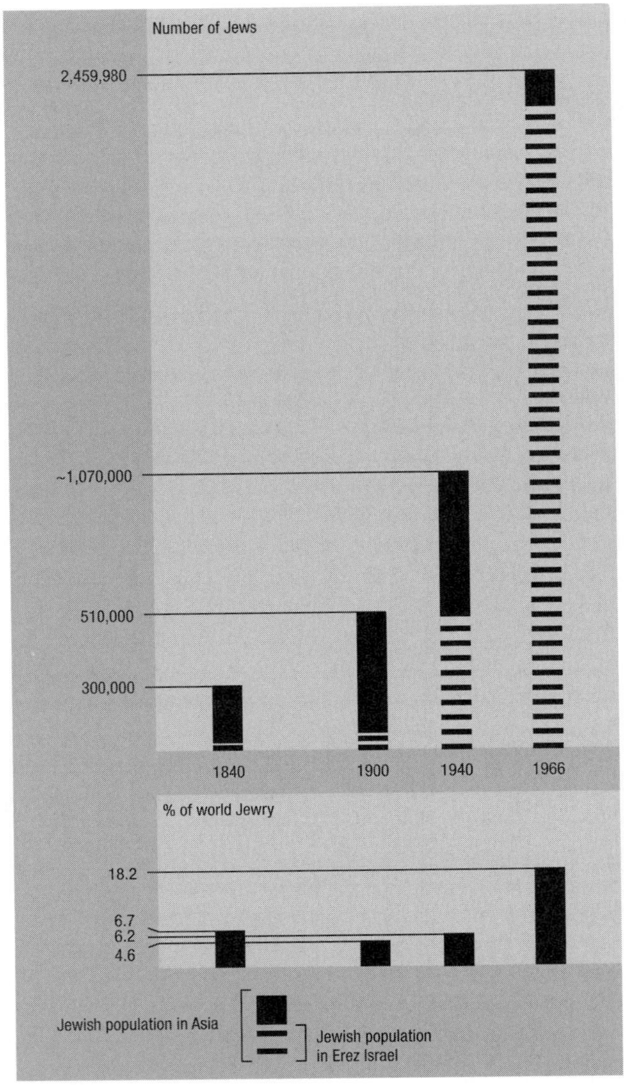

Figure 2. The growth of the Jewish population in Ereẓ Israel and its decrease in other parts of Asia from 1840 to 1966.

Jews in Asia (outside Israel) declined to no more than 47,000 in 2005. Over the same period Judaizing movements in *India and elsewhere did something to raise the total.

BIBLIOGRAPHY: E.N. Adler, *Jews in Many Lands* (1905), 173–244; I. Cohen, *Journal of a Jewish Traveller* (1925), 105–266; S.S. Mendelsohn, *Jews of Asia* (1930); J.J. Benjamin, *Eight Years in Asia and Africa* (1859); J. Saphir, *Even Sappir*, 2 vols. (1866); I. Ben Zvi, *The Exiled and the Redeemed* (1957); Fischel, Islam; H. Lord, *Jews in Indian and Far East* (1907); H. Dicker, *Wanderers and Settlers in the Far East: a Century of Jewish Life in China and Japan* (1962); S. Strizower, *Exotic Jewish Communities* (1962); Neusner, Babylonia; AJYB, passim. S.D. Goitein, *A Mediterranean Society: the Jewish Communities of the Arab World as Portrayed in the Documents of the Cairo Geniza*, 6 vols. (1967–1993); S.B. Isenberg, *India's Bene Israel: a Comprehensive Inquiry and Source Book* (1988); J.G. Roland, *Jews in British India: Identity in a Colonial Era* (1989); Thomas A. Triberg (ed.), *Jews in India* (1986); J.B.A. Segal, *A History of the Jews of Cochin* (1993); S.J. Shaw, *The Jews of the Ottoman Empire and the Turkish Republic* (1991); N.A. Stillman, *The Jews of Arab Lands* (1979). **ADD. BIBLIOGRAPHY:** T. Parfitt, *The Lost Tribes of Israel: the History of a Myth* (2002).

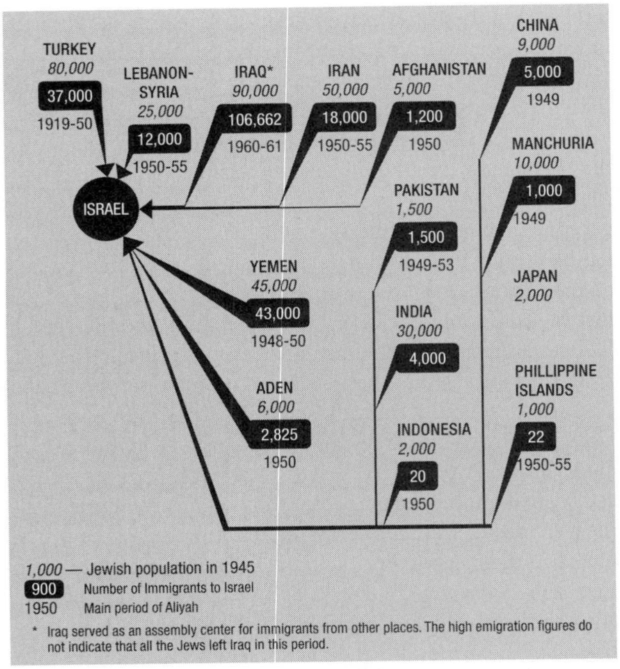

Figure 3. Figures for main periods of Aliyah *from Asian countries.*

ASIA MINOR. The westernmost peninsula of Asia, also known as Anatolia. There is no specific information as to when Jews first reached Asia Minor, but it was probably not later than the sixth century B.C.E. Evidence is found in Joel (4:4–6) which apparently refers to slave traders of the Phoenician coastal cities. In Isaiah (66:19) too, there is some evidence that Jews were living in certain regions of Asia Minor at that time. The Sepharad of Obadiah (1:20) is apparently *Sardis in Asia Minor. According to a report by Clearchus of Soli (mid-fourth century B.C.E.), a disciple of Aristotle, Aristotle met a Jew in Asia Minor who was "a Greek not only by speech but also in spirit." At the end of the third century B.C.E. *Antiochus III issued a command to transfer 2,000 Jewish families from Babylonia to *Phrygia and *Lydia in order to settle them in the fortified cities as garrisons. The first synagogues in Asia Minor were apparently built at that time. Important evidence of the distribution of Jews in Asia Minor has been preserved in the Roman circular of 139 B.C.E. to the Hellenistic cities and states. It mentions Caria, Pamphylia, and Lycia as places of Jewish settlement (I Macc. 15:23). Cicero's account of the confiscation of the money which the Jews of Pergamum, Adramythion, Laodicea, and Apamea had designated for the Temple in Jerusalem, during the governorship of L. Valerius Flaccus, provides additional evidence of the spread of Jews in Asia Minor. *Philo of Alexandria testifies that in his day in Asia Minor, as in Syria, there were many Jews. But the most extensive and detailed information on Jewish settlements throughout Asia Minor is furnished by numerous inscriptions and documents preserved by Josephus in *Antiquities* (book 14), and by accounts of the Jewish communities in the New Testament – in Acts and in Paul's Epistles. According to these inscriptions, Jews were settled in the following regions of Asia Minor: Ionia, Mysia, Lydia, Caria, Lycia, Phrygia, Lycaonia, Cappadocia, Galatia, Bithynia, Paphlagonia, Pisidia, Cilicia, and other localities. It may be assumed that the Jews in the cities of Asia Minor did not possess full citizenship, although probably many individuals enjoyed an exceptional status. Josephus states that Seleucus I Nicator (305–280 B.C.E.) had already given the Jews equal rights. But as the Jewish population grew in the cities of Ionia and in other regions, the hostility of the Greeks increased. In 14 B.C.E., the Jews of Ionia complained to Marcus Vipsanius *Agrippa, requesting that he confirm their special privileges. As a result of the intercession of Herod, who was staying with Agrippa at that time, these rights were confirmed. In this respect the numerous documents assembled in Josephus' *Antiquities* are of considerable importance. They include a defense of the Jewish religion from attacks by non-Jews in the Diaspora as well as resolutions of Greek cities (Sardis, Halicarnassus) on the need to guarantee the Jews their religious rights. There is reason to suppose that Jewish influence in Asia Minor was then considerable. Judaism attracted both the enlightened Gentiles and the masses. There is cogent proof of this at Apamea whose inhabitants associated the biblical story of the Deluge with legends connected with their city and inscribed Noah's ark on their coins. Jewish customs became popular throughout the towns of Asia Minor. Josephus reports that the kindling of Sabbath lights was customary among Gentiles. Many attended synagogues on Sabbaths and festivals. A movement of worshipers of the Supreme God, "God fearers" (σεβόμενοι, φοβούμενοι τὸν θεόν) was very popular throughout Asia Minor, and many groups of pagans practiced the cult of the "Supreme God" without renouncing their own religions. The fact that Jews were also conspicuously active in municipal government attests to their firm economic and social standing in Asia Minor.

BIBLIOGRAPHY: Jos., Ant., 12:119, 147ff.; 14:223ff., 234ff., 241ff.; 16:27; Jos., Apion, 1:176ff.; 2:39, 282; Cicero, *Pro Flacco*, 28:69; Philo, *De Legatione ad Gaium*, 33:245; 36:281; Klausner, Bayit Sheni, 3 (1950^2), 243–50; J. Klausner, *Mi-Yeshu ad Paulus*, 1 (1954^3), 18–59; Juster, Juifs, 1 (1914), 188–94; Frey, Corpus, 2 (1952), 8–54; A. Galanté, *Histoire des Juifs d'Anatolie*, 2 vols. (1937–39). On Jewish military colonies in Phrygia and Syria, see Schalit, in: JQR, 50 (1960/61), 289ff.

[Abraham Schalit]

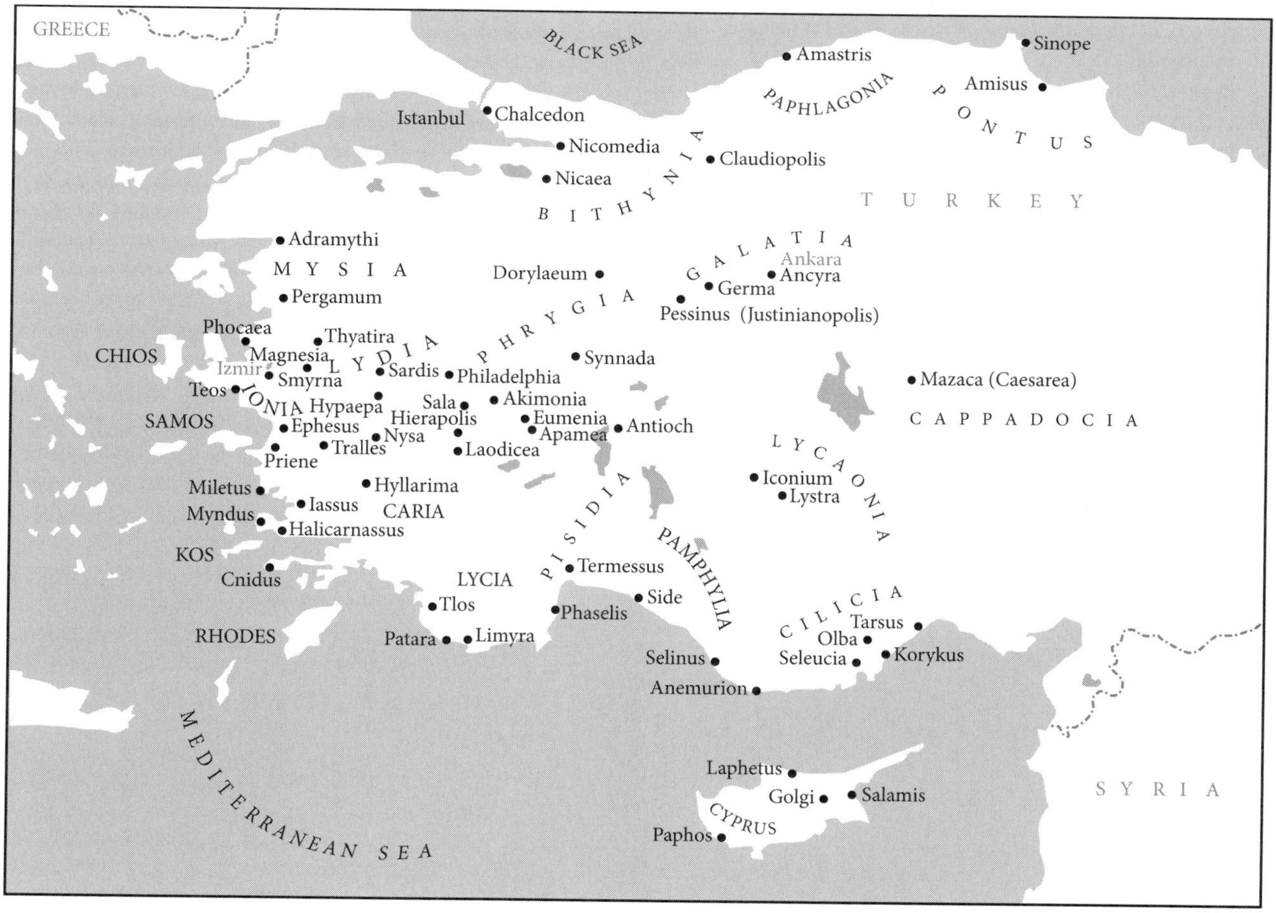

Ancient Jewish settlements in Asia Minor.

ASIMOV, ISAAC (1920–1992), U.S. biochemist and author of over 500 books. Born in Petrovichi, Russia, Asimov was raised in the U.S. from the age of three. He taught at Boston University's medical school, where he became associate professor of biochemistry in 1955. His work in enzymology was no less impressive than the many scientific books that he published from 1950. These include the textbook *Biochemistry and Human Metabolism* (1952, 1957²), *Life and Energy* (1962), and *Asimov's Biographical Encyclopedia of Science and Technology* (1964). He also wrote *The Wellsprings of Life* (1960) on evolutionary theory; popular guides to science *A Short History of Biology* (1964), *A Short History of Chemistry* (1965), and *Asimov's New Guide to Science* (1984); and science books for juveniles, including *Inside the Atom* (1956), *Breakthroughs in Science* (1959), *Of Time and Space and Other Things* (1965), and *Near East: 10,000 Years of History* (1968). His contributions to science notwithstanding, it was for his work as a science fiction writer that Asimov was best known. A member of Mensa and a prolific writer, Asimov was widely considered the father of modern science fiction. He wrote many novels that are considered classics in the field and countless short stories. Under the pseudonym Paul French, he wrote such sci-fi novels as *David Starr: Space Ranger* (1952) and several Lucky Starr novels, namely *Lucky Starr and the Pirates of the Asteroids* (1953); *Lucky Starr and the Oceans of Venus* (1954); *… the Big Sun of Mercury* (1956); *…the Moons of Jupiter* (1957); *…and the Rings of Saturn* (1958). Among Asimov's novels under his own name are *I, Robot* (1950), in which he first formulated the famous "Three Laws of Robotics"; *The Caves of Steel* (1954); *The End of Eternity* (1955); *A Whiff of Death* (1958); *Fantastic Voyage* (1966); *The Gods Themselves* (1972); *Foundation's Edge* (1982); *Foundation and Earth* (1986); *Fantastic Voyage II: Destination Brain* (1987); *Prelude to Foundation* (1988); *Nemesis* (1989); *Forward the Foundation* (1993). His *Foundation* trilogy (1951–53) was considered one of the most famous series of science fiction novels. In addition, his short story "Nightfall" was voted the most famous ever written in the genre. His short story collections include *Nine Tomorrows* (1959); *Asimov's Mysteries* (1968); *The Bicentennial Man and Other Stories* (1976); *Casebook of the Black Widowers* (1980); *The Complete Robot* (1982); *The Winds of Change and Other Stories* (1983); *The Best Mysteries of Isaac Asimov* (1986); *Azazel: Fantasy Stories* (1988); *Gold* (1995); and *Magic* (1996). He also edited collections of Soviet science fiction. Asimov published three autobiographical volumes: *In Memory Yet Green; In Joy Felt;* and *I. Asimov: A Memoir* (1994).

In 1986 he received the Science Fiction Writers of America Grand Master award, presented to a living author for a lifetime's achievement in science fiction and/or fantasy. He received a total of six Hugo awards, science fiction's most prestigious literary prize, for his novels *The Mule, The Gods Themselves,* and *Foundation's Edge*, as well as for his novelettes *The Bicentennial Man* and *Gold* and for his memoirs *I. Asimov: A Memoir.* He received Nebula awards for *The Gods Themselves* and *The Bicentennial Man.*

Although Asimov wrote about "the gods themselves," he regarded himself as an atheist. And although he penned story after story about the far-flung reaches of space and time, he was afraid of air travel and generally disliked travel of any kind. In fact, he had a penchant for confined spaces and liked to work in rooms that had no windows.

[Rohan Saxena / Ruth Beloff (2nd ed.)]

°**ASINIUS POLLIO, GAIUS** (76 B.C.E.–5 C.E.), Roman writer and political figure. Josephus cites him (Jos., Ant., 14:138) to show that the high priest Hyrcanus invaded Egypt in support of Julius *Caesar during the latter's Alexandrian campaign (48–47 B.C.E.). Asinius Pollio, like Caesar, may have been partial to the Jews. He may also have been in some way associated with Pollio the Pharisee (Jos., Ant., 15:1), who was probably identical with the sage Avtalion. But these are vague conjectures. Contrary to previous suggestions, it seems now unlikely that *Herod's sons lived in Asinius Pollio's home when they went to Rome in 24 B.C.E. (rather than 22) to complete their education (Jos., Ant., 15:343). Publius Vedius Pollio appears now to have been in a much better position: several amphora stamps bearing his name (PVE POL) have so far been found only in cities and residences built by Herod the Great (Caesarea, Sebastia, Masada, Herodium), clear evidence of amphorae having been derived from Vedius' estates in Chios. His career is paralleled by that of Herod and their paths may have crossed during their respective trips to western Asia Minor and to Rome. In any case, Asinius Pollio was only tolerated in the circle of Augustus at that time.

BIBLIOGRAPHY: Feldman, in: *Transactions and Proceedings of the American Philological Association*, 84 (1953), 73–80. **ADD. BIBLIOGRAPHY:** G. Finkielsztejn, in: *Grecs, Juifs, Polonais: à la recherche des racines de la civilisation européenne, dédié à Joseph Mélèze-Modrzejewski* (2005).

[Jacob Petroff / Gérald Finkielsztejn (2nd ed.)]

ASKENASY, EUGEN (1845–1903), German botanist. Born in Odessa, Russia, Askenasy was brought up in Dresden. While studying agriculture, Askenasy came under the influence of Julius von Sachs (1832–1897), the outstanding botanist and plant physiologist. Askenasy, who qualified in botany at Heidelberg University, was appointed to the staff in 1872 and became a full professor in 1891. His important contributions to the fields of algology and plant physiology include studies of chlorophyll and other plant pigments; physiology of growth and flowering; and the physical forces involved in the rise of water in plant stems. He wrote *Beitraege zur Kritik der Darwin'schen Lehre* (1872).

BIBLIOGRAPHY: M. Moebius, in: *Berichte der Deutschen Botanischen Gesellschaft*, 21 (Nov. 1903), 47–66, includes bibl.; NDB.

[Mordecai L. Gabriel]

ASKENASY, PAUL (1869–1934), German chemist and pioneer in the field of electrochemistry. Born in Breslau, Askenasy became professor of electrochemistry at the Technische Hochschule in Karlsruhe and an editor of the *Zeitschrift fuer Elektrochemie*. He took out some 50 patents, dealing with electrodes, industrial chemicals, and photographic materials. He also published papers in scientific and technical journals, dealing with electric furnaces, the production of potassium permanganate and of aluminum, arsenic acid, the fixation of atmospheric nitrogen by barium oxide and carbon, titanium, the oxidation of toluene, etc. His *Einfuehrung in die technische Elektrochemie* (2 vols., 1910–16) became a standard work.

[Samuel Aaron Miller]

AŠKENAZY, LUDVÍK (1921–1986), Czech author, playwright, and journalist. Born in Český Těšin and a Communist from his youth, Aškenazy joined the Czechoslovak Army brigade established in the U.S.S.R. during World War II. He adopted the principles of "socialist realism," which he expressed in his books, short stories, and radio plays. His works include *Ulice milá a jiné reportáže z Polska* ("Nice Street and Other Reports from Poland," 1950), *Německé jaro* ("German Spring," 1950), and his impressions of Austria, Greece, and other countries, *Všude jsem potkal lidi* ("I Met People Everywhere," 1955). In three volumes of short stories – *Sto ohňů* ("A Hundred Fires," 1952), *Vysoká politika* ("High Politics"; 1953), and *Květnové hvězdy* ("Stars in May," 1955) – Aškenazy repeatedly stresses the idea that the lives of ordinary people are influenced and determined by politics. A visit to Palestine with A. *Lustig in 1948 inspired *Kde teče krev a nafta* ("Where Blood and Oil Flow," 1948). In this Aškenazy gave expression to his anti-colonialism, showing scant sympathy for the emerging Jewish state.

Aškenazy often turned to the world of children and wrote some of his best stories about them, such as "Dětské etudy" ("Children's Etudes," 1955, 1966), "Ukradený měsíc" (1956, "The Stolen Moon"), also adapted for the stage as *Milenci z bedny* (1959, "Lovers from the Box"). Similarly he wrote the text for a book of photographs called *Černá bedýnka* (1960, "The Black Box") and published a collection of allegorical stories on animals for children, *Psí život* (1959, "The Dog's Life"). In the relatively liberal atmosphere of the 1960s he continued to write stories – *Vajíčko* (1963, "The Egg"), *Malá vánoční povídka* (1966, "A Small Christmas Story") – as well as fairy-tales for children – *Putování za švestkovou vůní* (1959, "Wandering toward the Plum's Scent"), *Osamělý létající talíř* (1963, "A Lonely Flying Saucer"), *Praštěné pohádky* (1966, "Dotty Fairy Tales"), *Pohádka na klíč* (1967, "Fairy Tale on Demand"), and *Cestopis s jezevčíkem* (1970, "Travel Story with a Dachshund"). In addition, he produced many radio and television scripts and was active as a playwright with *Host* (1960, "The Guest"), *Rasputin* (1967), etc. After the Soviet occupation of Czechoslovakia he left the country and lived in Germany, where he actively published his works in German after they were banned in Czechoslovakia. He died in Bolzano, Italy, and is buried in the Jewish cemetery there.

BIBLIOGRAPHY: J. Kunc, *Slovník českých spisovatelů beletristů* (1957). **ADD. BIBLIOGRAPHY:** *Slovník českých spisovatelů* ("Dictionary of Czech Writers," 1982); A. Mikulášek et al., *Literatura s hvězdou Davidovou* ("Literature with the Shield of David"), vol. 1.

[Avigdor Dagan / Milos Pohar (2nd ed.)]

ASKENAZY, SIMON (1867–1937), Polish historian. Askenazy studied at the universities of Warsaw and Goettingen and taught modern history at the University of Lemberg from 1897 to 1914, the last seven years as professor. During World War I he was a member of the Polish National Council in Switzerland. After the establishment of an independent Poland he served as its first representative at the League of Nations until 1923, when the National Democratic government dismissed him from his post because he was a Jew. From 1927 to 1937 he was a guest professor at the University of Warsaw. Askenazy's main historical studies dealt with the period from the partition of Poland in 1772 to the rebellion against Russia in 1863. His chief works were a monograph on Prince Joseph Poniatowski (1905) which was translated into English, French, and German; *Lukasinski* (1908); *Napoleon a Polska* (3 vols., 1918–19); *Uwagi* ("Notes on the Polish Problem," 1924); and *Gdansk a Polska* (1919; *Danzig and Poland*, 1921). He also wrote the chapters on Russia and Poland in the *Cambridge Modern History*. In 1929 he discovered manuscripts relating to Napoleon, which he published under the title *Rękopisy Napoleona, 1793–1795*. Askenazy raised a generation of students of Polish history who came to hold prominent positions in their country's cultural and political life. In 1912 a quarterly journal for the study of Jewish history in Poland, *Kwartalnik poświęcony badaniu przeszłości Żydów w Polsce*, was founded on his initiative. As a Jew, he was regarded as a spokesman for the assimilationists.

BIBLIOGRAPHY: M. Kukiel, *Szymon Askenazi* (Pol., 1935); J. Dutkiewicz, *Szymon Askenazy i jego szkoła* (1958); E. Kipa, in: *Studja i szkice historyczne* (1959), 183–97.

[Nathan Michael Gelber]

ASKNAZI, ISAAC LVOVICH (1856–1902), Russian painter. Born near Vitebsk (Belorussia) to a wealthy ḥasidic family, Asknazi attended the Academy of St. Petersburg where he formed a lifelong friendship with the sculptor Antokolski, whom he greatly admired. At the Academy he won a scholarship to study in Italy for four years. On his return from Italy he settled in St. Petersburg. Asknazi was a proud and observant Jew. As a student he was unique in being excused from attendance at the Academy on the Sabbath and Jewish holidays. He was reproached, however, by the Academy for his preoccupation with Jewish subjects, derived from the Bible, Jewish history, and the Jewish life of his day. A painstakingly academic artist, he made elaborate preparations for his compositions, including sculptures of the accessories. Some of his more important works are *Abraham Driving out Hagar and Ishmael*, *Moses in the Wilderness*, *Kohelet*, *The Death of Judah Halevi*, *A Jewish Wedding*, and *Sabbath Eve*.

BIBLIOGRAPHY: *Vyestnik Izyashchnykh Iskusstv* (1886), 418–9; D. Maggid, in: *Sefer ha-Shanah*, 2 (1901), 56–72.

ASKOWITH, DORA (1884–1958), U.S. scholar and college educator. Born in Kovno, Russia, in 1884, Askowith was brought to America that same year. After earning a B.A. at Barnard College in 1908, she entered Columbia University, where, in 1915, she earned her Ph.D. for her first book, *The Toleration and Persecution of the Jews in the Roman Empire: Part I: The Toleration of the Jews Under Julius Caesar and Augustus*. As the title suggests, Jewish history was and would remain her abiding passion, and she continued her studies at the American School for Oriental Research in Jerusalem, the American Academy in Rome, and New York's Jewish Institute of Religion.

Beginning in 1912 and continuing until 1957, just a year before her death, Askowith taught generations of New York's Hunter College female students ancient, medieval, and Renaissance history as well as comparative religion. In 1912, she founded the school's Menorah Society, a Jewish student organization. Askowith, who spent much of her career teaching in the college's evening and extension division, never acquired the regular faculty appointment she so desired. Nevertheless, she continued throughout her life to publish, writing more than a hundred articles on history, biography, and contemporary Jewish affairs. Her second book, *Three Outstanding Women* (1941), celebrated the achievements of the Zionist philanthropist Mary Fels, Jewish communal activist Rebekah Kohut, and Barnard College founder Annie Nathan *Meyer.

Askowith's interests in the Jewish people extended from the past to the present. A committed Zionist, she sat on Hadassah's Central Committee in its early years. She became national director of the Women's Organization for the American Jewish Congress in 1917. Her pamphlet *A Call to the Jewish Women of America* (c. 1917), urging America's Jewish women to turn out to vote for the Congress, revealed her fascination with Jewish women's history, a topic which surfaced in other of her writings and in her work with the Menorah Society. Askowith herself earned a place in that history when she tried, but failed, to be admitted as a regular student in the rabbinical program at the Jewish Institute of Religion in the 1930s.

BIBLIOGRAPHY: A.S. Miller, "Dora Askowith," in: P.E. Hyman and D. Dash Moore (eds.), *Jewish Women in America: An Historical Encyclopedia.*, vol. 1 (1997), 81–82; P.S. Nadell, *Women Who Would Be Rabbis: A History of Women's Ordination* (1998), 76–80, 106–8.

[Pamela S. Nadell (2nd ed.)]

°ASLAKSSEN, CORT (Conradus Aslacus Bergensis; 1564–1624), Scandinavian Hebraist. Born at Bergen, Aslakssen studied Hebrew and Aramaic in Germany with Johannes Piscator in Herborn and J. Buxtorf I in Basle. Eventually, he became professor of theology at Copenhagen. His Hebrew grammar (*Grammaticae Hebraeae libri duo*… (1606), including an analysis of Ps. 25), was the first printed in Scandinavia and was designed to replace that of Avenarius, considered too difficult for beginners; it was reprinted in 1608 (but not again in 1684 as erroneously reported by Steinschneider in *Zentralblatt fuer Bibliothekwesen*, 13 (1896), 353). Aslakssen was one of the founding fathers of Scandinavian Hebrew studies, most Danish and Norwegian 17th-century Hebraists being his direct or indirect pupils.

BIBLIOGRAPHY: J. Moller, *Bibliotheca septentrionis eruditi* (Leipzig, 1699), 52; A. Thurah, *Idea historiae litterariae Danorum* (Hamburg, 1723), 336; J. Brochmand, *Currus et equites Israelis* (Copenhagen, 1629), sig. G4v; C.J. Bartolocci, *Bibliotheca Magna Rabbinica*, 5 (Rome, 1694), 339, 539; O. Garstein, *Cort Aslakssøn: Studier*… (Oslo, 1953).

[Rafael Edelman]

ASMAKHTA (Aram. אַסְמַכְתָּא; "support," "reliance"), legal term with two connotations in the Talmud.

(1) In rabbinical exegesis it denotes the use of a biblical text merely as a "support" for a *halakhah* without suggesting that the *halakhah* is thus actually derived from this exegesis. Thus for the institution of the *prosbul* by Hillel for reasons which are explicitly given, the Talmud in addition gives Deuteronomy 15:9 as an *asmakhta* (TJ, Shev. 10:3, 39c). Its purpose was to give as much pentateuchal authority as possible to a purely rabbinic enactment but it was also used as a mnemotechnical aid (see: Herzog, Instit, 1 (1936), 2; Jastrow, Dict, s.v.).

(2) In civil law *asmakhta* is an important concept with regard to contracts and acquisition. It applies to such contracts in which one of the parties binds himself to an unreasonable penalty, which presumes that there was a lack of deliberate intention (*gemirat da'at*) on the part of the person entering into it. As a result the general rule is laid down that "an *asmakhta* does not give title" (BB 168a). It is only valid if it can be proved that the contract was regarded as binding (*semikhat da'at*).

Maimonides is of the opinion that every contract, even in writing, introduced by the conditional "if" constitutes an *asmakhta* and takes effect only from the time that the condition is fulfilled, since the person entering into the condition hopes that its nonfulfillment will nullify it. There is a difference of opinion as to the extent to which *asmakhta* applied to gambling and other games which depend upon chance. *Asmakhta* as a legal term is inherently connected with *semikhat da'at* ("mental reliance") and *gemirat da'at* ("perfect intention"), both highly significant concepts in the Jewish law of contract and acquisition. The underlying idea is that the validity of an obligation or a transaction depends on the confidence of one party that the other party's intention is serious, deliberate, and final. *Semikhat da'at* and *gemirat da'at* are complementary terms not only because most transactions impose reciprocal obligations, but also because, logically, no finality of intention can be presumed on either side as long as there might be reason that confident reliance is lacking on the part of one or the other. The connotation of "reliance" is evident in the word *asmakhta* from סמך, "to lean" (but see Gulak, Yesodei, 1 (1922), 68, especially n. 1) and, in the context of obligations or conveyance, it must originally have meant that in respect of that "reliance" the transaction was somehow problematic; eventually it came to be associated with transactions which were definitely defective in respect of reliance. It is clear that *asmakhta*, as a legal term, implies the absence of reliance. Thus, Gulak describes it as the absence of *gemirat da'at* and *semikhat da'at* (Gulak, loc. cit.). This description is much too wide as an exact definition of *asmakhta*. Firstly, the lack of *gemirat da'at* and *semikhat da'at* would undoubtedly invalidate the transaction, whereas there is a controversy in the Talmud as to whether or not *asmakhta* invalidates the transaction. *Asmakhta* must be seen as restricted, therefore, to cases where the question of finality of intention and reliance is debatable. Secondly, the cases in which the Talmud raises the question of *asmakhta* are all associated with conditional transactions (BM 48b; 66a–b; 109a–b; et al.). More precisely, the conditions visualized are suspensive conditions (conditions precedent) usually introduced simply by the word *im* ("if") which project the finalization of the obligation into the future in such a way that the obligation is not operative unless and until the condition is fulfilled, in contradiction to resolutive conditions (conditions subsequent) which allow for the immediate operation of the obligation (*me-akhshav*, "from now"), though the obligation may be reverted if the condition was not fulfilled. In fact, according to Jewish law, an obligation (or conveyance) would, as a rule, be valid only if it was immediately effective, by explicitly stipulating "from now," i.e., by letting the person obligated to take possession of the property in question actually or symbolically perform an act of *acquisition (*kinyan*), or the like. Maimonides (Yad, Mekhirah, 11, esp. para. 2 and 6) consequently draws the conclusion that all conditional transactions (i.e., not using the standard formulae of a condition such as *me-akhshav* (from the present moment) and *al-menat* (on condition that) but merely *im* (if)) are invalid on account of *asmakhta*, because the person obligating himself may be relying (*samkhah da'ato*) on the fact that the condition may not be fulfilled so that he will not be obligated. Since there has been no perfect intention of obligating oneself, the obligation is invalid *ab initio*, even if the condition were to be fulfilled.

Linking *asmakhta* with the rule of condition made the post-talmudic authorities introduce the whole range of the theory of condition into the discussion of *asmakhta*. There are, for example, fine distinctions between different conditions, the fulfillment of which is dependent on the person binding himself, on the other party or on both parties mutually, on a third person or on an accident. Rabbinic literature is replete with arguments showing how these and other distinctions may be of consequence in considering whether or not a certain transaction is defective on account of *asmakhta* (cf. glosses to Maim. Yad, Mekhirah and to Sh. Ar., ḤM 207). The linking of *asmakhta* with the problem of conventional penalties is particularly significant – this is emphasized by Solomon b. Abraham Adret (Resp. 1:933). Accordingly, the term *asmakhta* would be applicable to cases where a person promises to pay a conventional amount as a penalty, should there be a breach of a primary obligation. The validity of such a promise would be dependent on whether or not the penalty was "extravagant and unreasonable" and whether the fulfillment of the condition was dependent on the person binding himself, or on an accident, etc. The points involved here can be illustrated by the case presented in *Bava Batra* 168a. The Mishnah there speaks of a debtor who, while paying a part of his debt, allows the *shetar* ("bill of indebtedness") to be left in trust with a third person, with the instruction that the *shetar* for the full amount be handed to the creditor, in the event of the nonpayment of the balance at a time stipulated. The transaction comprises, in effect, two obligations, one relating to the actual debt (or rather to the outstanding balance) and the second to the payment of the penalty (the full amount of the *shetar* instead of the balance). It is clear that the minds of the parties were primarily set on the original obligation, whereas reliance and finality of intention may be in doubt over the matter of the penalty. The fulfillment of the condition is dependent on the person binding himself, which is to be viewed as diminishing reliance on the part of the person he is obligated to. In addition, the extravagance of the penalty is a relevant factor, unlike a case discussed in *Bava Meẓia* 104a–b, where in respect of land farmed on a percentage basis, the tenant obligates himself to pay a penalty if he lets the land lie fallow. Here the penalty is seen as justified, since it compensates the owner of the land for his damages (see: BM 109a, also Tos., Sanh. 24b–25a). There is a striking similarity to the differentiation in English law between "liquidated damages" and "penalty" proper (*in terrorem*, or extravagant and unconscionable). From the discussion in the Talmud (BB 168a) in the above quoted passage it would appear that such a penalty arrangement is invalid on account of *asmakhta*; on the other hand, from *Nedarim* 27b it appears that, if the arrangements were concluded with the due formalities of a *kinyan* before a recognized court, it is valid.

Thus already in talmudic times, remedies were sought to secure the validity of penalty clauses in practice, even though on principle they were defective because of *asmakhta*; this problem continued to occupy the post-talmudic authorities. The authorities in medieval Spain devised the following method to evade the pitfalls of *asmakhta*. *A* obligates himself to *B* to pay a penalty of 100 dinars if he does not fulfill a certain obligation on a stipulated day. A document is drawn up whereby *A* undertakes in absolute terms without a penalty clause to pay *B* 100 dinars. A separate document is then drawn up whereby *B* waives his claim to the 100 dinars, on condition that *A* fulfills his primary obligation on the stipulated day. Both documents are given to a third person to be handed over to *A* after he fulfills his primary obligation as stipulated, otherwise they are to be handed to *B*, who can then enforce his claim for 100 dinars on the strength of the first document (Maim. *ibid.*, 18, and see Isserles to Sh. Ar., ḤM 207:16).

It would appear that such arrangements were current in medieval England, at a time when finance was largely controlled by Jews, but later, the obligation to pay a certain amount and the conditional waiver came to be included in one document, now designated as a "conditional bond" (see:

J.J. Rabinowitz, EH, s.v. *asmakhta* and the literature indicated there).

It appears that this device was applied particularly to *shiddukhin* ("marriage contracts" – see: *Betrothal) in which were included very heavy penalties against breach of promise. The Ashkenazi authorities however tend to the opinion that the rule of *asmakhta* does not apply at all in this context, since the penalties may justifiably be considered as fair compensation for the damage, insult, and shame caused by a breach of promise (see Tos. to BM 66a; Sanh. 24b–25a and Sh. Ar., ḤM 207, 16). In the discussion whether and under what circumstances *asmakhta* applied to gambling contracts, the fact that the conditions are mutual and reciprocal is of significance (see: Sanh. 24b and Tos. in loc.). *Asmakhta* does not apply to a vow to *hekdesh* (Sh. Ar., YD 258:10); nor to any transaction strengthened by vow, oath, or handshake, even if it would otherwise be defective on account of *asmakhta* (ḤM 207:19). If *A* obligates himself unconditionally to *B*, there can be no question of *asmakhta*, and the obligation is valid, even if there was no actual justification for the obligation, as "*B* owed him nothing" (*ibid.* 20). The implication of this statement is twofold: (a) *asmakhta* relates to conditional transactions; and (b) although the defect of penalty arrangement is primarily that it is unjustified, lack of justification does not invalidate a promise, if it was absolute and unconditional. In the Jerusalem Talmud *asmakhta* is designated as *izzumin* (TJ, BB 10, 17c; Git. 5, 47b).

[Arnost Zvi Ehrman]

Another view explains *asmakhta* as a promise, having the same meaning as the term "utterance" (*devarim*). A promise is not binding (BM 66b), although not necessarily for the reason given by Maimonides, namely, the absence of a deliberate and final intention to be obligated thereby (*semikhut da'at*). Geonic literature draws a distinction between the two rationales. There are variant understandings of the difference between a binding and non-binding *asmakhta*, and inconsistent, contradictory explanations of the distinction between them. All these stem from a failure to distinguish between two basic positions: the position that denies any validity to promises as such; and that which views them as faulty due to the absence of full intent to be obligated thereby. A distinction must be made between these two positions. According to the former, the difficulty inherent in the promise can only be resolved by its conversion into a contemporaneous transaction – "from now" (*me-akhshav*). This is the rationale behind the mode of transaction known as *kinyan suddar* (acquisition affected through the (symbolic) raising of a small garment – (i.e., symbolic barter); cf. entries on *Contract and *Acquisition (*ḥalifin*), in which the party's obligation becomes effective immediately upon completion of the (symbolic) act of acquisition, by virtue of the undertaking to bind oneself).

A conditional transaction (of the kind which does not as a rule allow for its immediate validity as a transaction "from now") in which the condition is expressed using the phrase "on condition that," is a particular example of a promise to perform an act in the future.. The problem that arises regarding the absence of *semikhut da'at* is no more serious than in other cases in which the parties wish to perform an action in the future. To solve this problem, Maimonides proposed (*Yad, Hilkhot. Gerushin* 9:1–5) using the fixed rules governing "terminology of conditions" (see entry on *Conditions) to indicate a conditional transaction, which begins "now," thereby solving the problem of *asmakhta*, and remains in effect until the fulfillment of the condition.

[B. Lifshitz (2nd ed.)]

BIBLIOGRAPHY: Gulak, Yesodei, 1 (1922), 67–75; N. Wahrmann, *Die Bedingung (Tenai und Asmakhta) im juedischen Recht* (1938); ET, s.v.; B. Cohen, in: *H.A. Wolfson Jubilee Volume* (1965), 203–32; M. Elon, in: *Divrei ha-Congress ha-Olami ha-Revi'i le-Madda'ei ha-Yahadut*, 1 (1967), 201ff.; 268–9 (Eng. summ.); idem, in: ILR, 4 (1968), 435; idem, in: Mafteaḥ, 2ff. **ADD. BIBLIOGRAPHY:** M. Elon, *Ha-Mishpat Ha-lvri*, (1988), 1:106, 572f.; 2:895, 900f.; H1, 1343, 1532,; idem, *Jewish Law* (1994), 1:120; 2:584, 706, 1091; 3:1095f.; 4:1604, 1821; M. Elon and B. Lifshitz, *Mafte'aḥ ha-She'elot ve-ha-Teshuvot shel Ḥakhmei Sefarad u-Ẓefon Afrikah* (1986), 2:13–16; B. Lifshitz and E. Shohetman, *Mafte'aḥ. ha-She'elot ve-ha-Teshuvot shel Ḥakhmei Askenaz ve-Italyah* (1997), 11–14; B. Lifshitz, *Promise and Obligation in Jewish Law* (1998).

ASMODEUS (Ashmedai), an "evil spirit" or "evil demon." In the talmudic *aggadah*, Asmodeus is described as "king of the demons" (Pes. 110a). According to Rapoport, the concept of such a personage originated in Babylonian myth, though the name is Hebrew, derived from the root שמד, "to destroy." It is more likely, however, that the name derives from the Persian *aesma daeva* or *aesmadiv*, i.e., "the spirit of anger" which accompanies the god of evil.

Asmodeus first appears in the apocryphal book of Tobit (3:8, 17), which describes how in a fit of jealousy he slew the successive husbands of a young girl. He is again depicted as a malefactor – and in particular as the sower of discord between husband and wife – in the Testament of Solomon (first century C.E.). Throughout the later *aggadah*, however, Asmodeus is a gay creature, inclined at worst to drunkenness, mischief, and licentiousness. The Talmud nowhere identifies him as an evildoer, and in fact often assigns him the specific function of preserving the ethical order of the world. Asmodeus does, to be sure, usurp the throne of King Solomon in the celebrated talmudic account of his confrontation with the king (Git. 68a–b; Num. R. 11:3). But even here the demon is not vindictive: his actions are presented as opening the king's eyes to the emptiness and vanity of worldly possessions. What is more, the Asmodeus of this story is the source of considerable benefit to Solomon. He provides the king with the *shamir*, a worm whose touch cleaves rocks, and so enables Solomon's builders to hew stones for the Temple without the use of prohibited iron tools.

Asmodeus is described in the Talmud as "rising daily from his dwelling place on the mountain to the firmament," where he "studies in the academy on high" (Git. 68a). As a result of this practice, he possesses exact foreknowledge of the fate of human beings, knowledge which often prompts him to act in a seemingly inexplicable fashion. While on his way to Solomon, for example, Asmodeus weeps at the sight of a wedding party, only later explaining that the bridegroom has but a short time to live. Similarly, on the same journey, the demon goes out of his way to set a drunkard on the right path; "it was proclaimed in heaven," he later reveals, "that he is wholly wicked, and I have conferred a boon upon him in order that he may consume his share in the world to come in this world" (Git. 68b). Such stories of Asmodeus' enigmatic behavior provided the model for a long line of Jewish folktales, in which the apparently unjust acts of an angel or prophet are eventually justified by circumstances and thus demonstrate the infinite wisdom of God.

In Jewish folklore, though still the king of demons, Asmodeus often appears as a degraded hero – the butt of popular irony and humor. Typical stories relate how he is duped by the men with whom he enters into a partnership, or how his various lusts and loves on earth are exposed. For the most part, however, Asmodeus is regarded as a beneficent demon and a friend of man. He plays a similar role in the Kabbalah, where his name is frequently invoked in spells and incantations. The story of Asmodeus' enigmatic deeds and sayings (Git. 68a–b) are the narrative nucleus of the widespread international style type, known as "Angel and Hermit." The talmudic and the Jewish oral traditions of the Solomon-Asmodeus cycle penetrated the early Russian apocryphal literature and became the narrative archetype of the Solomon-Kitovras folk legends.

BIBLIOGRAPHY: Klausner, Bayit Sheni, 2 (1951^2), 59–60; M. Gaster, *Ilchester Lectures of Greco-Slavonic Literature* (1887), 40–44; A.A. Aarne, *Types of the Folktale*, ed. and tr. by S. Thompson (1961), no. 759; D. Noy, *Shivim Sippurim ve-Sippur mi-Pi Yehudai Luv* (1967), notes to nos. 37, 58; J.H. Moulton, *Early Zoroastrianism* (1926), 322–40; Meyer, Ursp, 2 (1925^4), 96; Scholem, in: *Tarbiz*, 19 (1947/48), 160–75; S.J.L. Rapoport, *Erekh Millin* (1914), 106 ff.

ASNER, EDWARD (1929–), U.S. actor. Born in Kansas City, Kansas, to an Orthodox Jewish family, Asner first gained attention as the gruff but gentle television station manager Lou Grant on the long-running sitcom *The Mary Tyler Moore Show* (1970–77). A spin-off from this successful production provided Asner with his own star vehicle, the drama series *Lou Grant* (1977–82).

Asner has received six Emmy Awards and five Golden Globe Awards for his TV performances on *Lou Grant*; *Roots*; *The Mary Tyler Moore Show*; and *Rich Man, Poor Man.* To date, Asner is the only actor to win Emmys for playing the same character (Lou Grant) in both a comedy and a drama series. A long-time political activist considered left of center, Asner accused the CBS network of canceling his show over his publicized disapproval of U.S. involvement in Central America. But he continued to prosper professionally after *Lou Grant.* Asner starred in many TV movies, had guest and repeat roles in a wide variety of TV dramas and comedies, and starred in two regular series, the sitcom *Off the Rack* and the drama *The Bronx Zoo*. He also appeared in the weekly sitcoms *Hearts Afire* and *Thunder Alley.*

In 1981 he had a starring role in the film *Fort Apache, The Bronx.* Other feature films include *O'Hara's Wife* (1982); *Daniel* (1983); *JFK* (1991); *The Golem* (1995); *The Fanatics* (1997); *The Bachelor* (1999); *Above Suspicion* (2000); *Bring Him Home* (2000); *Donzi: The Legend* (2001); *Academy Boyz* (2001); *The Commission* (2003); *Missing Brendan* (2003); and *Elf* (2003). In addition, Asner has lent his voice to a myriad of animated film and television characters.

Asner served two terms as president of the Screen Actors Guild (1981–85). In 1996 he was inducted into the TV Academy Hall of Fame, and in 2002 he was awarded the Life Achievement Award by the Screen Actors Guild.

[Ruth Beloff (2nd ed.)]

ASPER, ISRAEL H. (**Izzy**; 1932–2003), Canadian lawyer, politician, media magnate, philanthropist. Izzy Asper was born in the small community of Minnedosa, Manitoba, where his musician parents settled after immigrating to Canada from the Ukraine. The family moved to Winnipeg, where Asper's father ran several movie theaters. Izzy Asper began practicing tax law after graduating from the University of Manitoba in 1957. An up-by-the-bootstraps entrepreneur, in the early 1970s Asper and a partner founded an independent television station in Winnipeg, Also drawn to politics, Asper became Manitoba's Liberal Party leader in 1970, and in 1973 he was elected to the provincial legislature, heading a small opposition Liberal caucus of only five members.

Unhappy in opposition, in 1975 Asper withdrew from electoral politics and turned to building a media empire, CanWest. In 1974 he helped rescue the financially floundering Global Television in Toronto and began weaving Global together with a number of independent CanWest television stations across Canada into Global Television Network, Canada's second largest independent television network. CanWest's media investments eventually extended beyond Canada to include holdings in Australia, New Zealand, Chile, Ireland, and, more recently, Israel. In 2000 Asper's CanWest bought Conrad Black's Hollinger media holdings which gave Asper control of a number of Canadian newspapers, including the *National Post,* and several important off-shore newspapers and journals.

While Toronto had emerged as the undisputed center of media and investment in Canada, Asper, regarding himself as something of an establishment outsider, refused to move to Toronto. Instead he remained in Winnipeg, where he was a strong booster of western Canada and western Canadian Jewish life. Through the Asper Foundation which he established, he was generous in his support of Jewish and non-Jewish causes in western Canada, including the arts, education, and medical research. A jazz lover, Asper ensured that a jazz radio station broadcast in Winnipeg, and he was a patron of many western arts institutions, including the Royal Winnipeg Ballet. In recognition of his charitable contributions to the University of Manitoba, in 2000 the university's faculty of management was renamed the Asper School of Business. Asper also generously supported the medical research foundation at Winnipeg's St. Boniface Hospital. The recently opened Jewish community center in Winnipeg, which houses a Jewish community school, archives, museum, state-of-the-art athletic facilities, and meeting facilities, was also named in Asper's honor. Along with several honorary doctorates, in 1995, Asper was conferred with the Order of Canada, the highest award Canada can bestow on a citizen.

Izzy Asper was an outspokenly partisan supporter of Israel. This generated some controversy. Some media observers accused Asper of interfering in the editorial independence of CanWest publications, censoring out any criticism of Israel or its policies and, instead, dictating that CanWest publications tow a tight pro-Israel line. Asper, in turn, accused the media in general and Canada's public broadcaster, the CBC in particular, of anti-Israel bias.

All three of Asper's children are lawyers and even before Izzy Asper's death in 2003 they began taking on major responsibilities in managing CanWest's vast corporate empire.

[Harold Troper (2nd ed.)]

ASS (Heb. חֲמוֹר, *ḥamor*), in the Talmud the feminine form *ḥamorah* occurs, or *aton* whose colt is called *ayir*. The ass belongs to the genus *Equus* to which belong the horse and the wild ass. Various strains exist in Ereẓ Israel. The most common is small, usually brown in color (*ḥamor* is connected with Ar. *ḥamar*, "to be red"). However, other kinds exist such as the Damascus ass, which is tall, strong, and usually white or pale brown. This species is probably referred to in Judges 5:10 as ridden by the upper classes. Among other peoples the ass is regarded as a foolish animal; in ancient Jewish sources, however, it is the symbol of patience and understanding. Issachar, who chose the life of the modest farmer, is likened to a "strongboned ass" who bowed his shoulder to bear (Gen. 49:14–15). One of the best-known incidents associated with the animal is the story of *Balaam (Num. 22:22–30) whose ass sees an angel unperceived by his master and is given the power to speak in order to reprove Balaam for his obstinacy and quick temper. Unlike the horse which was regarded as a luxury or for war, the ass exemplifies the life of work and peace. The prophet Zechariah describes the savior of the people as "lowly and riding upon an ass, even upon a colt the foal of an ass [*aton*]." It is possible that the statement in the Talmud that "he who sees an ass in a dream should hope for salvation" (Ber. 56b) is connected with this passage. Today the ass is still employed in Israel as a beast of burden.

[Jehuda Feliks]

In Folklore

According to medieval bestiaries, the ass "has no sense at all" and this was the general attitude toward the domesticated ass in folkloric beliefs and tales, especially in Mediterranean countries. It played an essential role in the European medieval Feast of Fools; and in oral animal tales current among Jewish storytellers, it is the most foolish of all animals. The view of the ass in Jewish tradition stems from the aggadic fable of the lion, the fox, and the ass (Yal. 1:182; cf. Aesop-Chamdry, no. 199, ed. Span, no. 22), which ends with the statement of the ass "having no heart (brains)." The derogatory notion that the ass is the most stupid of all animals gave rise to the aggadic comparison of the Gentile to an ass (based on Gen. 22:3). The concept is relatively late, as the old aggadic attitude toward the ass was positive (see above). In Hebrew proverbial lore, the ass ascending a ladder denotes an incredible and impossible feat, such as the elephant "passing through the eye of a needle" mentioned in the Talmud (Ber. 55b; BM 38b), and the similar camel in the Synoptic Gospels (Matt. 19:24) and the Koran (7:40). It serves as a metaphor for the wisdom attributed to fools in medieval and later literature.

[Dov Noy]

BIBLIOGRAPHY: Aharoni, *Torat ha-Ḥai* (1923); S. Feigin, *Studies in Memory of Moses Schorr* (1944), 227; J. Feliks, *Animal World of the Bible*. IN FOLKLORE: Ginzberg, Legends, 7 (1936), 116; J.L. Zlotnik, *Midrash ha-Meliẓah* (1938), 62–64; Scheiber, in: *Folia Ethnographica*, 1 (Budapest, 1949), 1–3. **ADD. BIBLIOGRAPHY:** Feliks, Ha-Ẓome'aḥ, 232.

ASSAF, MICHAEL (1896–1983), Israeli author and specialist in Arab affairs. Born in Lodz, Poland, Assaf settled in Palestine in 1920 and became secretary of the cultural department of the Histadrut in 1921. He later went to Berlin to study Arabic and returned to edit the Arabic section of the Histadrut daily *Davar*. From 1937 he edited the paper's Arabic weekly, and from 1948 the Arabic daily *Al-Yom*. He published *Toledot ha-Araviyyim be-Ereẓ Yisrael* ("History of the Arabs in Ereẓ Israel"; 3 vols., 1935), and devoted himself to seeking understanding with the Arabs of Israel. For some time he was chairman of the Israel Journalists' Association.

ASSAF (Osofsky), SIMḤA (1889–1953), rabbinic scholar and Jewish historian. Assaf studied at the yeshivah in Telz and was ordained in 1910. He then served as rabbi in Luban and Minsk. From 1914 to 1919 he taught Talmud at the "modern" Odessa yeshivah founded by Chaim Tchernowitz and from 1915 to 1919 served as its director. When the yeshivah was closed by the government in 1919, he spent two years studying in France and Germany and at the end of 1921 went to Jerusalem as an instructor in Talmud at the Mizrachi Teachers' Seminary. When the first classes opened at the Hebrew University in 1925, Assaf was appointed lecturer on the geonic period and its literature; from 1929 he also taught rabbinic literature, becoming full professor in 1936. For many years he served the Hebrew University as a member of the executive board, as chairman of the Institute of Jewish Studies, as dean of the faculty of humanities, and from 1948 to 1950 as rector. From 1931 to 1943 he was a member of the Asefat ha-Nivḥarim and of the Va'ad Le'ummi, as well as chairman of its educational committee. After the establishment of the State of Israel, Assaf was appointed a member of the Supreme Court, although he was not a trained lawyer. Special retroactive legislation had to be passed in order to legalize his position. There was no sign of lack of legal training in his decisions, and his contribution was one of the greatest importance in introducing the concepts of rabbinic law into the legal system of the new state. He was active in many public and academic institutions. Assaf published articles and studies – almost all in Hebrew – on the literature of the *geonim*, the history of Jewish law, medieval Jewish culture, and the history of the Jewish community in Palestine. Some of them were collected in his *Be-Oholei Ya'akov* ("In the Tents of Jacob," 1943) and in *Mekorot u-Meḥkarim* ("Sources and Studies," 1946). In addition, in the same period, Assaf wrote important volumes based on source material, *Ha-Onshin Aḥarei Ḥatimat ha-Talmud* ("Penalties after the Redaction of the Talmud," 1922) and *Battei ha-Din ve-Sidreihem Aḥarei Ḥatimat ha-Talmud* ("Religious Courts and Their Procedures…," 1924). A comprehensive four-volume work, *Mekorot le-Toledot ha-Ḥinnukh be-Yisrael* ("Sources for the History of Jewish Education," 1925–43), is a remarkable anthology of sources relating to education which is at the same time a significant contribution to Jewish social history. Of outstanding importance are his critical editions of manuscripts and responsa of the geonic period (particularly from the *Genizah*) and the early codifiers. In collaboration with Israel Davidson and Issachar Joel, Assaf edited the *Seder R. Sa'adyah Ga'on* (1941) and, together with L.A. Mayer, he edited vol. 2 of the *Sefer ha-Yishuv* (*Mi-Ymei Kibbush Ereẓ Yisrael al Yedei ha-Aravim ad Masei ha-Ẓelav* "From the Arab Conquest to the Crusades," 1944), to which he wrote a comprehensive introduction. In his works Assaf combined a vast and expert knowledge of Jewish literature with a keen appreciation of the vital movements and characteristic features of the periods with which he dealt. This, added to his engaging personality, made him a popular and inspiring teacher. In 1955 Assaf's disciple, Mordecai Margalioth, edited a volume comprising lectures delivered by Assaf on the geonic period at the Hebrew University over a period of 27 years under the title *Tekufat ha-Ge'onim ve-Sifrutah*.

BIBLIOGRAPHY: Klausner, in: *Sefer Assaf* (1953), 7–11 (first pagination); Raphael, *ibid.*, 12–34 (first pagination); B. Dinur, *Benei Dori* (1965), 104–11; Margalioth, in: KS, 29 (1953/54), 257.

[Moshe Nahum Zobel]

ASSAULT, the infliction of any degree of violence on the body of another person, whether injury results or not. The biblical injunction, "he may be given up to 40 lashes but not more" (Deut. 25:3), which applies to *flogging by way of punishment, was interpreted as prohibiting, a fortiori, the nonauthorized flogging of an innocent person (Maim., Yad, Ḥovel u-Mazzik 5:1; Sh. Ar., ḤM 420:1). As it violated a negative biblical injunction for which no other penalty was prescribed, assault itself was punishable with flogging (Mak. 16a; Ket. 32b). Striking one's father or mother was an assault punishable with death (Ex. 21:15), but the capital offense was later restricted only to such blows as caused bodily injury (Sanh. 11:1). Criminal assaults, which result in any assessable injury and which also give rise to claims for damages, prompted the question of whether the civil or the criminal sanction was to prevail, it being common ground that for any one wrong not more than one sanction could be imposed (Mak. 4b; 13b). While as a general rule the lesser (civil) remedy would merge with the greater (criminal) remedy, so that the assailant would be liable to be flogged rather than held liable in damages, it was held that the sanction of payment of damages should prevail over the criminal sanction – for the practical reason (as distinguished from several hermeneutical ones) that having the assailant flogged would not relieve the victim's injury, and "the Torah has regard for the money of the injured" (Tos. to Ket. 32a). Thus, flogging came to be administered only where the assault had not caused any assessable injury (Ket. 32b; Maim., Yad, Ḥovel u-Mazzik 5:3; Sh. Ar., ḤM 420:2). This state of the law apparently failed to satisfy the rabbis, and in consequence they prescribed *fines for assaults which were insulting, but which had not caused substantial damage. The amounts of the fines were fixed, varying in accordance with the severity of the assault (e.g., kicking, slapping, punching, spitting, hair pulling, etc.) – always leaving it to the discretion of the court to increase or reduce the fine in special circumstances (BK 8:6; Maim., Yad, Ḥovel u-Mazzik 3:8–11; Sh. Ar., ḤM 420:41–43).

While criminal liability depended on the availability of sufficient evidence of warning previously administered to the assailant and of the act of the assault itself, liability for damages could be established on the strength of the assailant's own admission or other simplified modes of proof (Maim., Yad, Ḥovel u-Mazzik 5:4–8). Damages were to be estimated and assessed by the court, the biblical law of talion (Ex. 21:23–25; Lev. 24:19–20) being replaced for this purpose by an elaborate system of assessing the value of injured limbs in terms of money (BK 83b–86a).

Another distinction between criminal and civil assaults is that the criminal assault is deemed to be spiteful and malicious (Maim., Yad, Ḥovel u-Mazzik 5:1), whereas the civil assault might be unintentional: the warning, "nor must you show pity," given in connection with talion (Deut. 19:21), was interpreted so as to render even the unintentional assailant liable in damages (Maim., Yad, Ḥovel u-Mazzik 1:4), apart from the rule that the civil responsibility of a man never depends on the willfulness of his acts (BK 2:6). The amount of damages, however, would be reduced in cases of unintended assaults (see: *Damages). Mutual or anticipated assaults, as in boxing or wrestling matches, even if they result in grievous injury, do not give rise to claims for damages (Asher b. Jehiel, *She'elot u-Teshuvot* (1803), 1[a] (2nd pagination), no. 101:6; Sh. Ar., ḤM 421:5); but where two men assault each other maliciously, the one who suffered the greater injury has a claim for the damage suffered in excess of the damage inflicted by him (BK 3:8).

Assaults may be intentional, though not spiteful: for instance, if an injury results from surgical treatment, the surgeon – provided he was duly qualified – is not liable for damages (Tosef., BK 9:11). The same rule applies to a father beating his son, a teacher his pupil, and the messenger of the court assaulting a person in the course of duty (*ibid.*). In all those cases, liability may, however, be established by proving that the assailant exceeded the measure of violence necessary to achieve his legitimate purpose (*ibid.*). Still, if only by way of exhortation, assailants of this kind are warned that while they go free under the laws of men, they may yet be judged by the laws of Heaven (Tosef., BK 6:17). The assailant can only cite the consent of the victim to being assaulted if the victim has expressly waived beforehand any claim to damages, and if no grave injury was caused, for no man seriously consents to be injured (BK 8:7; BK 93a). The injunction, "nor must you show pity," was applied also where the assailant was indigent: that being no ground for reducing the damages (Maim., Yad, Ḥovel u-Mazzik 1:4). But, however generous the award might appear, where it was made according to the letter of the law, it was of no use when the victim could not collect the judgment debt, and, being practically unenforceable, did not provide any sanction against the assailant. Ways and means had to be found also to deter people who resorted to violence and against whom damages were no effective sanction: thus R. Huna is reported to have ordered the hand of one such recidivist to be cut off (Sanh. 58b) – a drastic measure which was sought to be justified by the extraordinary powers of the court to impose extralegal punishment in situations of emergency (Sanh. 46a), but also explained away as a mere curse which was not actually carried into effect (cf. Nid. 13b). The precedent of Huna was followed in Spain several centuries later, when an assailant who had attacked a rabbinical judge at night and wounded him badly, had both his hands cut off (Judah b. Asher, *Zikhron Yehudah* (Berlin, 1846), 6a, no. 36). Cutting off the hand that sinned is reminiscent of biblical law (Deut. 25:12), and it was used as a threat to a husband who habitually beat his wife and wounded her (Beit Yosef, Tur., EH 74, end). Huna, however, did not rely on the biblical law, but on the verse, "the high arm shall be broken" (Job 38:15), a precept which would scarcely warrant the hand being cut off. Indeed, in later sources the breaking of the hand is a punishment meted out to one who beat a rabbi with his fist (*Sefer Ḥasidim*, 631).

Jurisdiction in matters of personal injuries (*Dinei Ḥavalot*) is held not to have devolved on post-exilicy courts: these are regarded as "agents" of the ancient courts only in such common matters as contract and debt, but not in matters as rare and exceptional as personal injuries (BK 83b). This assumption of infrequency was disproved soon enough; and Jewish courts everywhere and at all times in effect assumed jurisdiction in personal injury cases, not only awarding discretionary damages, but also inflicting punishments, such as fines (e.g., Asher b. Jehiel, *She'elot u-Teshuvot* (1803), 13b, no. 13:14; Mordecai b. Hillel, *Sefer Mordekhai*, Kid. 554), and floggings (*Sha'arei Ẓedek*, 4:7:39; *Halakhot Pesukot min ha-Ge'onim*, 89; *Teshuvot ha-Ge'onim, Sha'arei Teshuvah*, 181; J. Weil, *She'elot u-Teshuvot* (1834), 8b–9b, no. 28; 23a–b, no. 87; et al.), as well as lesser penances such as fasting and beardshaving (Isaac b. Moses of Vienna, *Or Zaru'a* (1887); BK 51, no. 329; 52–53, no. 347). The legal basis for such punitive measures were normally **takkanot* or local custom (Asher b. Jehiel, *She'elot u-Teshuvot* (1803), 1[a] (2nd pagination), 101:1), but courts certainly followed also the precedents provided by the usage of earlier authorities. It is said that an ancient *ḥerem* ("*ḥerem kadmonim*") hangs over those who do violence to others (Moses Isserles and *Me'irat Einayim*, Sh. Ar., ḤM 420:1), and that, on the strength of that ban, they may not be admitted to communal worship or any matter of ritual, unless the *ḥerem* was first lifted from them by order of the court, after compliance with any judgment that may have been given against them (M. Sofer, *Ḥatam Sofer* to Sh. Ar., ḤM (1958), 68a–b, no. 182). Notwithstanding this preexisting *ḥerem*, both the imposition of and the threatening with bans and excommunication was a common measure against violence (Meir b. Baruch of Rothenburg, *She'elot u-Teshuvot Maharam...* (1895), 12a, no. 81; 129a, no. 927; et al.).

[Haim Hermann Cohn]

In the State of Israel

Harming (a person) as a civil wrong (assault) is defined in section 23 of the Torts Ordinance (New Version) 5728–1968, as consisting of the intentional application of force *of any kind* on a person's body.

Harming (a person) as a criminal offense is defined in the Penal Law 5733–1977, in sections 34(24), 327–344. The Law distinguishes between *grievous* harm, namely, harm that causes permanent disfigurement or injury to the victim's body, and *dangerous* harm, meaning harm that endangers the individual's life. The law further prescribes different rules for harm with aggravated *intent,* harm under aggravated *circumstances*, harm caused with particular *appurtenances*, and *negligent* harm.

IN THE SUPREME COURT. *Harm as an Act of Self-Defense.* An assailant's plea that he acted under the necessity of personal defense is discussed at length in the case of *Afanjar v. State of Israel* (33 (3) PD 141). The Supreme Court was required to resolve the question as to whether the *necessity defense* could be of avail to an accused who had used violence against policemen. The latter, dressed as civilians, had burst into an apartment in the dark of the night. The assailant claimed that he did not know that they were policemen and that he acted under the assumption that he was protecting the bodies and dignity of himself and his other friends in the apartment. The Supreme Court (Justice Elon) opened (pp. 150–51 of the judgment) with a discussion of the duty imposed upon every Jewish person to save another person from the hands of one who is pursuing him in order to kill him – a duty that appears in the Bible ("Do not stand idly by the blood of your fellow" – Lev 19:16) and in the Talmud (Sanh. 73a–74a) and is codified in the halakhah (Maim., Yad, *Hilkhot Roẓe'aḥ u-Shemirat ha-*

Nefesh, 1.6–16). The judgment then continues with a discussion of the right to protection against an assailant even when there is no threat to life, as expounded in the post-Maimonidean responsa literature: "If one sees a Jew attack his fellow and he cannot rescue him without hitting the attacker, even though his blow is not lethal, he can hit the attacker in order to prevent him from committing a crime" (*Piskei ha-Rosh, Baba Kamma*, Ch. 3, §13). This was also the view of R. Solomon *Luria (Poland, 16th century – *Yam shel Shelomo, Bava Kamma*, Ch. 3, §9).

Regarding the permissible degree of force, the Court cited, inter alia, the comments of Mordecai, a contemporary of Asheri: "Similarly, if people are engaged in a fight, one should not push them; rather, they should be gently restrained. If he did push, he is answerable to him in court" (*Mordekhai, Bava Kamma*, §38; cf Asheri, *ad loc.*; R. Israel Isserlein (Poland, 15th century), *Pesakim u-Ketavim* §208; *Teshuvot Maharam mi-Rothenburg*, quoted in *Mordekhai, Bava Kamma* §196). The Court summed up the discussion with the comments of R. Joseph *Caro:

> Where two people were fighting, if one person started, the second person is not liable, as he has the permission to injure him [the attacker] in order to save himself. However, it must be determined whether he could have saved himself by inflicting a minor injury but instead inflicted a major injury; [in such a case] he is liable. The same rule applies if one sees a Jew hitting his fellow and can only save him by hitting the attacker; in such a case, he can hit him in order to prevent him [the attacker] from committing the crime (Sh. Ar., ḤM 421:13) (*ibid.*, 153–54)

Justice Elon summed up the rules emerging from this analysis, ruling:

(1) Under Jewish law, every person is obligated to come to the aid of his fellow if the victim is pursued by one who is, in light of the circumstances, about to inflict a life-threatening injury. If the pursuit [involves the threat of] a lesser injury, most halakhic authorities take the view that there is no obligation [to aid], but one is permitted to rescue his fellow, even by injuring the pursuer. It goes without saying that in both cases, the pursued himself has the right to self-defense.

(2) The above-mentioned permission and obligation [to rescue] applies to every person and with regard to any victim – even one not related to the rescuer. *A fortiori*, it is not premised on any relationship between the rescuer and the victim in the framework of which the rescuer is legally responsible for his supervision or welfare.

(3) The above-mentioned permission and obligation [to rescue] only apply if, under the circumstances, they are required in order to protect the victim from the pursuer – that is, so long as there is a fear that the pursuer will continue his attack on the victim. They do not apply if, in light of the circumstances, it appears that the danger has passed and the intervention of the "defender" is no longer of a defensive nature, but is based on other motives.

(4) The basic rule is that the amount of force used by the intervener to rescue the pursued must be proportionate. His exemption from criminal liability is conditional upon his using only the minimal amount of force necessary to rescue the pursued – in talmudic terminology, "that he could have saved him [the victim] by maiming a limb [of the pursuer]." "If he fails to do so, he is criminally liable for the injury he inflicts on the pursuer, and he certainly bears criminal responsibility if he kills him…" (*ibid.*, 154).

This was the basis for the Court's acquittal of the appellant, and the Court stated that: "he was entitled under the principle of personal [self-]defense, to forcefully push the intruders through the door and out of the apartment. By doing so he sought, first of all, to prevent injury to himself … and the appellant could still claim that his actions were in the defense of others … to protect his 'pursued' friends from the two 'pursuers'… fearing injury or bodily harm to his friends" (*ibid.*, 157–58).

In discussing the question raised by the judgment, the Court further discussed the question of the appropriate construction of concepts rooted in public policy and in a moral and social world-view. Summing up, the Court observed:

> As we have seen, the principle of defending others involves concepts rooted in public policy and in a social and moral view of the duty to come to the aid of another person who is in danger of bodily injury. This conclusion is compelled by the logic and nature of civilized social life. We find this notion expressed by American and English legal scholars who see it as a matter of public policy and as "a peremotory response to injustice that the good man has ingrained," last and most important, this is the view reflected in the sources of Jewish law, in which the rule "Do not stand idly by the blood of your fellow" constitutes a basic principle of the world outlook of Judaism. In my opinion, fundamental concepts founded on moral attitudes and cultural values should be interpreted in the light of the moral and cultural heritage of Judaism (see also CA 461/62 *Zim v. Mazier* 17(2) PD 1319, 1332; CA 148/77 *Roth v. Yeshupe*, PD 33 (1) 617).

Harm Incidental to Medical Care – the Doctor's Liability in Negligence. Moral and legal questions arising in the area of medical practice have often been litigated from the perspective of the laws of causing harm, in both general and Jewish Law.

An example of this is provided by the case of *Levital v. Health Fund Center* (CA 552/66, 22 (2) PD 480) where the Supreme Court heard an appeal against the non-imposition of liability on a doctor in the wake of an injury caused during an operation. The Court cited the advice of Justice Denning, who warned against the imposition of exaggerated liability on surgeons, for reasons of public policy – i.e., to prevent a situation in which medical practitioners would be primarily concerned for their own welfare rather than that of the patient. The Israel Supreme Court (Justice Kister) added to this, ruling that Jewish Law distinguishes between an ordinary person who harms his fellow man – being forewarned by definition, and consequently liable even if acting inadvertently – and a doctor:

> Jewish Law recognizes the consideration of public policy in the context of medical practitioners – and surgeons in par-

> ticular. In principle, Jewish Law imposes liability on a person who harms his fellow man, even accidentally, because "a man is always forewarned," but liability was significantly reduced with respect to physicians engaged in their professions "with the court's permission"[i.e., in accordance with a license from a public authority]; that is to say – to the specific cases of negligence defined in the sources (Tos. BK 6:6, 9:3; Tos. Git. 3:13; these sources were the basis of *Nahmanides' ruling in *Torat Adam, Sha'ar ha-Sakanah* (…); Resp. Tashbez, vol. 3, 82; Sh. Ar. YD. 336).
>
> The physician's liability was limited for reasons of "public policy," as stated in the *Tosefta* and explained by Tashbez in the above-mentioned responsum, "for if we do not exempt him where there was an accident, people are liable to desist from healing." In his book *Torat Adam*, Naḥmanides sees an analogy between the role of the physician and that of the judge, who is commanded to adjudicate and to rule. On the one hand a judge must be cautious, and on the other hand he has nothing but the evidence before him. The same applies to the doctor, who is duty-bound to heal, and if he refrains from healing it is tantamount to bloodshed. Conversely, he must be cautious just as one must be "cautious in capital matters, and not cause harm by his negligence," but nevertheless, "it [treating patients] is not forbidden because of the fear of causing harm." Indeed, the physician is commanded to act in order to save the patient, and as such it would be injudicious of him to fear that he might fail, whether by dint of chance or accident, and avoid performing actions that he deems necessary in accordance with his evaluation of the circumstances. While it is true that science and technology have progressed since then, even today operations involve dangers, albeit of a lesser degree than in the past. Consequently, the doctor must occasionally operate even where it involves a certain degree of danger or the possibility of mistake or accident" (pp. 483–84 of judgment).

According to these principles, Justice Kister ruled that in the particular case the doctor's actions did not diverge from the boundaries of a reasonable mistake ("*sheggagah*") and liability should not be imposed.

Harm Incidental to Medical Act – Performance of Tissue Examination. Another medical matter adjudicated by the Supreme Court in which it relied on the principles of Jewish Law regarding harm is the *Sharon v. Levi* case (CA 548/78, 35 (1) PD 736).

The Supreme Court needed to decide whether a person may be compelled to perform a tissue test so as to clarify the paternity of a small child. The Court (Justice Elon) ruled that, in the absence of an explicit statutory provision, it was prohibited to compel a person to perform this kind of test, because it violates the basic right of every person to personal freedom, which includes the inviolability of his body. In substantiating its ruling, the Court invoked the provisions of Jewish Law, while discussing the boundaries of the prohibition on harming others, and the validity of a victim's consent [to be harmed]. "This basic right, as expressed in Jewish Law, is particularly instructive: 'he who strikes his neighbor with a blow inflicting less than a penny's worth of damage [i.e., without injuring him] transgresses a negative precept' (Sanh. 85b, Maim. Yad, *Hilkhot Ḥovel u-Mazik* 5:3). Moreover, even where the person being struck consents to it, his consent has no legal validity (BK 92a; Sh. Ar., ḤM. 420:1ff). What then is the legal source for permitting a person to let the blood (i.e., to wound) of another person in order to cure him? According to the amora Rav Matna (Sanh. 84b) this permission is not grounded in the patient's consent, whether express or implied, for, as stated above, his consent has no legal validity. The permission is derived, rather, from the verse "And thou shall love thy neighbor as thyself" (Lev 19:18) from which it is inferred, according to Rashi, that "Jews were only warned against doing the things to their fellow man that they would not want to do themselves" (Rashi, Sanh. 84b, s.v. *ve-ahavta;* cf. *Kitvei Ramban* (ed. Chavell, Jerusalem: Mosad Harav Kook, 1964))., Vol. II, *Torat ha-Adam,* 42ff.; M. Elon, "Halakhah and Modern Medicine" (Heb.), in: *Molad,* N.S. 4, 27 (5731–1971), 228, 232) (p. 755 of judgment).

A Wounded Person's Waiver Regarding Bodily Injuries. Another case in which the Supreme Court endorsed the approach of Jewish Law to bodily wounding was in *Lagil Trampoline v. Nachmias* (CA 285/73, 29 (1) 63). The case concerned a company operating a trampoline installation for sports purposes. The company claimed that it was not responsible for bodily damage caused to persons exercising on the installation, relying on a sign at the entry to the facilities that stated: "The company takes no responsibility for any accident, injury or wound caused to jumpers." Justice Kister invoked the approach of Jewish Law to the sanctity of life, and its implications: a person's obligation to take precautions so as not to cause injury to his fellow man (Tos. BK 23a); the duty to adopt measures to prevent injuries to others (Maim. Yad, Hilkhot Roẓe'aḥ u-Shemirat ha-Nefesh 11:1–4); the prohibition against a person injuring himself (Maim., *ibid.*, §5); and the presumption that a person cannot give a waiver in respect of damage to his own body (BK 93a) (p. 80 of judgment). According to these principles, the Court ruled that, even though a waiver and a release from liability clause for bodily injury are not invariably invalid, the circumstances in the particular case in question precluded the imposition of a duty of care on the individual exercising, and hence the exemption clause should be voided (pp. 481–83 of judgment).

[Menachem Elon (2nd ed.)]

BIBLIOGRAPHY: S. Assaf, *Ha-Onshin Aharei Hatimat ha-Talmud* (1922), index; s.v. *Hovel ba-Havero; ET* 7 (1956), s.v. *"Dinei Kenasot,"* 376–82, *ibid.*, 12 (1967) s.v. *Hovel,* 679–746; L. Finkelstein, *Middle Ages*, index. **ADD. BIBLIOGRAPHY:** M. Elon, *Ha-Mishpat ha-Ivri* (1988)1:9, 27, 97, 113, 130, 185, 405, 568, 637, 666; idem., *Jewish Law* (1994), I:8f, 29, 109, 127, 146, 207; 2:495, 698, 789, 823; idem., *Jewish Law (Cases and Materials)* (1999), 224–39; M. Elon and B. Lifshitz, *Mafte'aḥ ha-She'elot ve-ha-Teshuvot shel Ḥakhmei Sefarad u-Ẓefon Afrikah,* vol. 2., 334; B. Lifshitz and E. Shochetman, *Mafte'aḥ ha-She-elot ve-ha-Teshuvot shel Ḥakhmei Ashkenaz, Ẓarefat ve-Italyah* (1997), 230.

ASSCHER, ABRAHAM (1880–1955), Dutch Jewish leader, Zionist, and politician. He founded the largest diamond processing plant in his native Amsterdam, and, in 1907, served as president of the Amsterdam Chamber of Commerce. He was elected to the North Netherlands Provincial Council as a member of the Liberal State Party in 1917. Asscher was active in the affairs of the Amsterdam Jewish community from his youth and was elected to chair the Amsterdam Ashkenazi Community Council. In 1932 he became chairman of the Union of Dutch Ashkenazi Congregations (Nederlandsch-Israëlitisch Kerkgenootschap). In 1933 Asscher and David *Cohen founded the Comité voor Bijzondere Joodse Belangen ("Committee for Special Jewish Affairs") to combat Nazi antisemitism and policies, and to help refugees from Germany; for this purpose a special Sub-Committee for Jewish Refugees was established, which became one of the most powerful organizations in Dutch Jewry of the 1930s. In February 1941 Asscher and Cohen were charged by the German occupation authorities with the task of forming an Amsterdam Joodsche Raad ("Jewish Council"). This council utilized the personnel and administrative experience of the Jewish Refugees Committee, and its authority was soon extended by the Germans to include the whole of Dutch Jewry. Despite its intentions to help Jews, it became one of the tools of the Germans, first to control the Jewish population and later to deport it to the extermination camps (see *Netherlands, *Amsterdam). Asscher himself was arrested, and on September 23, 1943, was taken first to *Westerbork and then to *Bergen-Belsen. Asscher returned to Holland after the liberation (1945). There, he was denounced by some of the Jewish survivors. An honorary (Jewish) court of law condemned him, but Asscher rejected the court's verdict, and severed his connections with the Jewish community. After his death, he was buried in a non-Jewish cemetery. His and his colleague David Cohen's behavior has been a major theme of historiography and popular discussions of the fate of the Dutch Jews during the Holocaust.

BIBLIOGRAPHY: A.J. Herzberg, *Kroniek der Jodenvervolging* (1951); J. Presser, *Ashes in the Wind. The Destruction of Dutch Jewry* (1968). **ADD. BIBLIOGRAPHY:** A. Asscher, *Persoonlijkheden in het Koninkrijk der Nederlanden in Woord en Beeld* (1938); L. de Jong, *Het Koninkrijk der Nederlanden in de Tweede Wereldoorlog*, vols. 1, 4, 5, 6, 7, 14 (1969–89); D. Michman, "The Jewish Refugees from Germany in The Netherlands, 1933–1940," ch. 3 (Ph.D.-thesis, 1978) (Heb.); H. Knoop, *De Joodsche Raad. Het Drama van Abraham Asscher en David Cohen* (1983); N.K.C.A. in 't Veld, *De Joods Ereraad* (1989); W. Lindwer (with J. Houwink ten Cate), *Het fatale dilemma. De Joodsche Raad voor Amsterdam, 1941–1943* (1995); B. Moore, *Victims and Survivors. The Nazi Persecution of the Jews in the Netherlands, 1940–1945* (1997); J. Michman, H. Beem, and D. Michman, *Pinkas. Geschiedenis van de joodse gemeenschap in Nederland* (1999); N. van der Zee, *Um Schlimmeres zu verhindern. Die Ermordung der niederländischen Juden: Kollaboration und Widerstand* (1999); J.C.H. Blom, R.G. Fuks-Mansfeld, and I. Schöffer (eds.), *The History of the Jews in the Netherlands* (1992).

[Jozeph Michman / Dan Michman (2nd ed.)]

°**ASSEMANI**, Lebanese-Maronite family of Orientalists who were active in Italy. The most important member of the family, JOSEPH SIMON (1687–1768), was director of the Vatican Library. During two visits to Egypt and Syria, sponsored by Pope Clement XI, he bought thousands of manuscripts for the Vatican Library. Assemani edited a catalogue of Oriental manuscripts in the library, which was planned for 12 volumes, but because of a disastrous fire, only four volumes dealing with Syriac manuscripts were published (1719–28). STEPHANUS EVODIUS (1707–1782), his nephew, issued a catalogue of Oriental manuscripts in the Florence Library (1742) and with his uncle prepared a catalogue of all the manuscripts in the Vatican Library; but only the first part, a catalogue of Syriac and Hebrew manuscripts, appeared (3 vols., 1756–59). This was the main reference work for Hebrew manuscripts at the Vatican.

BIBLIOGRAPHY: P. Dib, *Joseph Simon Assémani et ses deux neveux: leurs testaments* (1939); *Catholic Encyclopedia*, index.

ASSEMBLY OF JEWISH NOTABLES, convocation of rabbis and Jewish communal leaders from the communities situated in the territories of the French Empire and the "Kingdom of Italy" convened by a decree of Napoleon *Bonaparte, issued in May 1806 to clarify the relations between the Napoleonic state and the Jews.

The process of Jewish adaptation to the conditions of the modern state and society had already begun before the Napoleonic era, after the granting of Jewish *Emancipation during the French Revolution. The Napoleonic regime attempted to subject all public activity to its authority, including the activities of the various religious denominations. Napoleon attained this objective in regard to the Catholics when he concluded the Concordat with the Pope in 1801. Later, government supervision was also extended over the Protestants. Attention was finally turned to the Jews, but this problem was more complicated because it was necessary to establish a central Jewish religious framework before subjecting it to the authority of the state. When early in 1806 complaints were made that the Jews of Alsace were engaging in usury, Napoleon accepted that there was ground for investigation, attributing this practice to a specifically separatist and undeniable Jewish character. He therefore passed consideration of the Jewish question to the Council of State. Subsequently its majority proposed either the adoption of general legislation against usury, or the expulsion of Jews from the country, if it became clear that they were unable for religious reasons to qualify as citizens of a non-Jewish state. Napoleon objected to the majority view, however, and decided to call a meeting of "Jewish estates" to clarify their situation for the benefit of both Jews and non-Jews. The decree of May 30, 1806, convening the Assembly of Jewish Notables, was issued on this basis. At the same time, the public debate in France about Jews and Judaism was resumed: in addition to the arguments of the rationalists, who advocated separating the "political," separatist, and harmful traits in Judaism

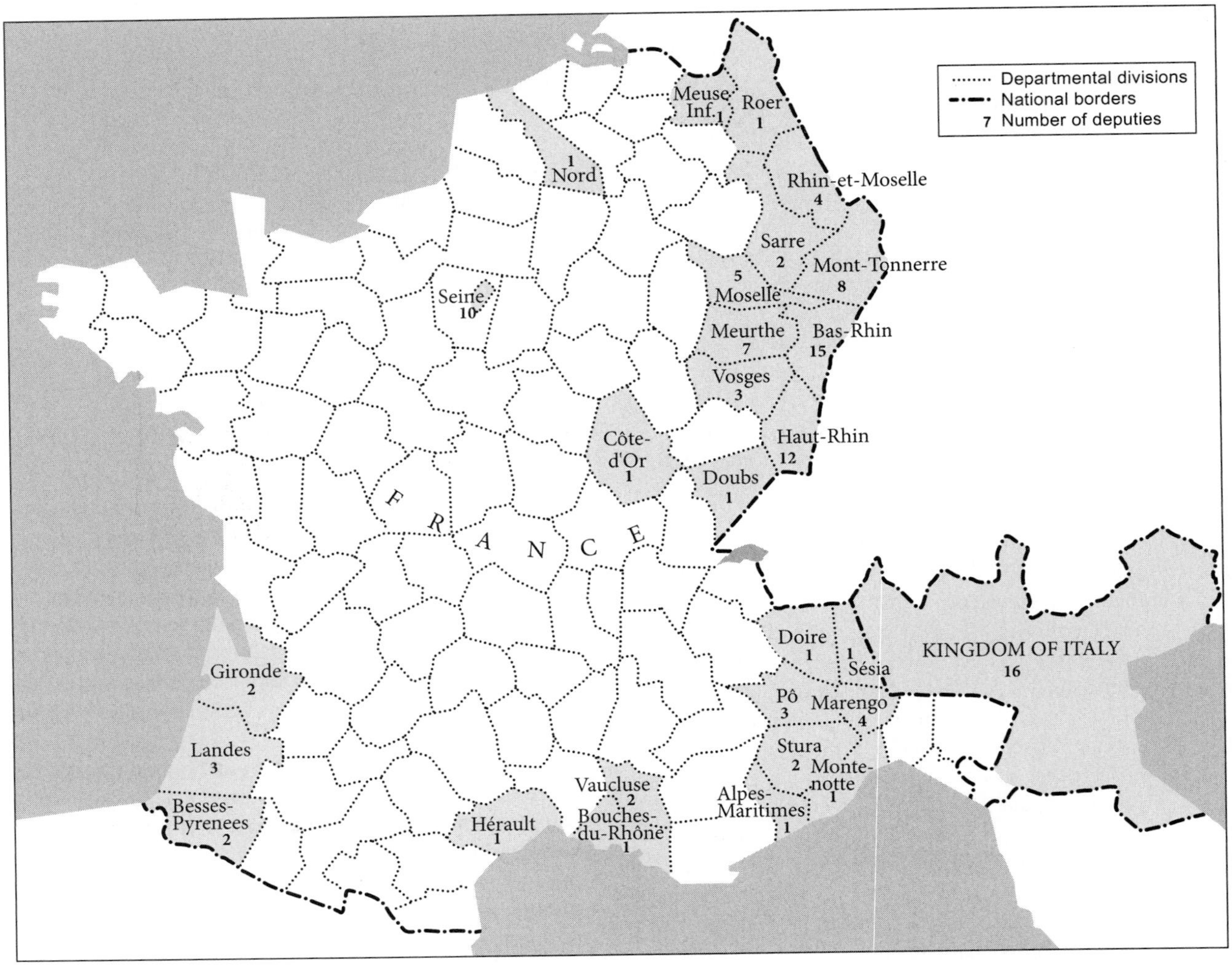

Delegations to the Assembly of Jewish Notables convened by Napoleonic decree in 1806.

from its "religious" aspects and abolishing the former, new arguments were advanced, typifying the Catholic-Romantic approach of intellectuals such as Louis-Gabriel-Ambroise *Bonald and Count Louis Matthieu Molé. Molé was the most active and influential of the three commissioners Napoleon appointed to the assembly and the expert in the Council of State on the Jewish question. The other two were Pasquier and Portalis junior.

The Assembly of Jewish Notables met on July 26, 1806. Its deliberations in plenary session and committees continued almost uninterruptedly to April 6, 1807; its final membership was 111. The delegates had been elected by local Jewish leaders, in consultation with the district prefects, on the basis of one representative to every 100–500 Jews. The assembly thus reflected most of the social patterns and attitudes of the Jewish communities of Central and Western Europe. The delegates from districts of overwhelmingly German Jewish culture, *Alsace-Lorraine, and other formerly-German areas which had been annexed to the empire, formed its largest group. Many of them were orthodox in outlook. The communities and "national organizations" in this area had been little affected by the upheavals that had taken place after the French Revolution. Some of the members from Alsace-Lorraine were disciples of Moses *Mendelssohn, of the conservative type and, while observant, would have liked to see social and educational reforms (for instance Berr Isaac *Berr). Only a small minority professed the radical ideas of the Enlightenment (see *Haskalah), such as Michel *Berr (son of Berr Isaac Berr). On the other hand, the Portuguese Jews from southern France and the Jews of Paris were largely radical. They were headed by Abraham *Furtado of Bordeaux, an adherent of Voltaire and a former Girondist, who was elected chairman of the assembly. The "Portuguese" delegates were few but, as the most radical upholders of the state views, they became the leaders of the assembly. The 16 representatives from Italy were mostly observant Jews, and members of organized communities anxious to preserve Jewish autonomy and traditional way of life, like Rabbi Jacob Israel Carmi (*Karmi) from Reggio (the exception being A. *Cologna). They included noted talmudic scholars, such as Hananel (Graziadio) *Neppi.

At the second session of the Assembly of Jewish Notables Molé presented 12 questions on four main aspects of social and political life:

A: THE CIVIL-MATRIMONIAL ASPECT.

(1) Is it lawful for Jews to marry more than one wife?

(2) Is divorce allowed by the Jewish religion? Is divorce valid when not pronounced by courts of justice, but by virtue of laws in contradiction to those of the French Code?

(3) Is intermarriage with Christians permitted to Jews or does the law allow the Jews to intermarry only among themselves?

B: THE POLITICAL-PATRIOTIC ASPECT.

(4) In the eyes of Jews, are Frenchmen considered as their brothers or are they considered as strangers?

(5) In either case, what line of conduct does their law prescribe toward Frenchmen not of their religion?

(6) Do Jews born in France and treated by the laws of French citizens, consider France as their country? Are they bound to defend it? Are they bound to obey the laws and to conform to the civil code?

C: THE FEAR OF A "STATE WITHIN STATE."

(7) Who appoints the rabbis?

(8) What police jurisdiction do rabbis exercise among Jews? What judicial power do they enjoy among themselves?

(9) Are the forms of choice of rabbis and their police judicial jurisdiction regulated by law, or are they only sanctioned by custom?

D: THE MORAL-SOCIO-ECONOMIC ASPECT.

(10) Are there professions which the law of the Jews forbids them from exercising?

(11) Does the law forbid the Jews to take usury from their brothers?

(12) Does it forbid or does it allow the taking of usury from strangers?

Formulation of the answers was entrusted to a "committee of twelve," headed by the halakhic scholar David *Sinzheim of Strasbourg. Sinzheim applied a remarkable degree of flexibility to his formulation, and while avoiding any infringement of halakhic principles, he was careful not to prejudice the civic status of French Jewry, which, it was thought, would be endangered should the answers fail to satisfy the emperor. Patriotic declarations were adopted unanimously at the plenary session in reply to questions 4 to 6, stating inter alia: "A French Jew considers himself in England as among strangers, although he may be among Jews... To such a pitch is this sentiment carried among them, that, during the last war, French Jews have been fighting desperately against other Jews, the subjects of countries then at war with France."

The answer to question 3 was fiercely disputed in the assembly. While the "progressives" favored mixed marriages, the upholders of orthodoxy insisted that such marriages had no validity from the religious point of view. The latter view was incorporated in the answers. Another difficulty arose, regarding questions 11–12 on usury, a problem widely disputed in Europe over many centuries. The answer stated that post-Mosaic Judaism, which no longer retains its egalitarian-agricultural character, permits "interest" (the assembly rejected the term "usury" for the Hebrew *neshekh*) to all alike, Jews as well as non-Jews. This is based on an apologetic definition, current from the 17th century, where in the biblical text "brother" denotes a citizen of the same state, whatever his religion may be, while "stranger" denotes a citizen of a foreign state. This point additionally reinforced the previous answers concerning civil brotherhood.

In reply to questions 7–9 the delegates stated inter alia that the rabbis had no authority over communal life. They also stressed that the communal authority had become impaired by lack of organization and lack of funds, after communal dues had become voluntary since the French Revolution and Emancipation.

An introduction to all 12 answers reiterated that according to *halakhah* the secular "prince" is the final authority in political or civil matters. Consequently, should their religious code, or its various interpretations, contain commands on civil or political matters at variance with those of the French code, those commands would, of course, cease to influence and govern them.

The content of these answers, as well as letters from the delegates of various countries, show that the majority of the assembly considered such statements to be a compromise, in form but not in substance, between the laws of the state and those of *halakhah*.

The deliberations of the assembly aroused interest among both Jewish and non-Jewish circles in Europe. Its "Transactions" consisting of the questions, answers, minutes (after internal censorship), and part of the public debates before and during the sessions, were published in French. They were republished the following year with the deliberations and decisions of the *Sanhedrin, and subsequently in English, Italian, and German at different times and places in varying versions.

The answers generally suited Napoleon. He decided to establish in accordance with their spirit an ecclesiastical organization to lead the Jews as French citizens of the Mosaic faith. The latter sessions of the assembly were therefore devoted to framing statutes to regulate the "ecclesiastical structure" of the Jewish religion. They provided for the abolition of communal organizations and establishment of the *Consistories, whose authority was limited to the appointment of rabbis, determination of their salaries, regulation of religious services, and the maintenance of synagogues; a central consistory was established in Paris. The budget was secured by a compulsory Jewish consistorial tax. The statutes were received with satisfaction by almost all participants. For the delegates from Alsace-Lorraine, they provided a setting for the continuation of their communal life with an assured budget, while other delegates welcomed the statutes as an expression of their own ideas for improving Jewish society. The sole exception was the

Italian delegates, who also wanted to include education and welfare in the jurisdiction of the consistories.

The answers of the assembly and the institutions it created have shaped the opinions and actions of certain Jewish circles confronted with the problem of regulating Jewish existence in a modern absolutist state. They furnished a rationale for conformity with the postulates of a modern centralized state and society which had already become, or were about to become, nationalist in character. The ad hoc answers of the assembly are, in historical perspective, a modern, if extreme, formulation of the old maxim "the Law of the land is [binding] Law" (BK 113a).

BIBLIOGRAPHY: Graetz, Hist, 5 (1949), 474ff.; Roth, Mag Bibl, 273, 397; Z. Szajkowski, in: SBB, 2 (1956), 107–52; R. Anchel, *Napoléon et les Juifs* (1928); E.A. Halphen, *Recueil des lois, decrets et ordonances concernant les Israélites depuis la Révolution* (1851); D. Tama, *Collection des écrits et des actes relatifs au dernier état des individus professant la religion hébraïque* (Paris, 1806); S. Romanelli, *Raccolta di inni ed ode de parechi Rabbini dell' Assemblea degli Ebrei e del Gran Sinedrio* (Mantua, 1807); J.I. Carmi, *All' Assemblea ed al Sinedrio di Parigi, 1806–1807; lettere…* ed. by A. Balletti (1905); B. Mevoraḥ (ed.), *Napoleon u-Tekufato* (1968).

[Baruch Mevorah]

ASSEO, DAVID (1914–2002), chief rabbi of Turkey. Born in Istanbul, Asseo first attended a religious school in Hasköy, then the Alliance Israélite school there. In 1928 he was sent on a scholarship of the Loge D'Orient Béné Berith to the Rhodes yeshivah. He studied there for six years and in 1933 returned to Istanbul. He started to work as a Hebrew teacher at the Jewish High School in Istanbul. In 1936 he became a member of the Bet Din. After Rafael Saban was elected chief rabbi in January 1953 he became his private secretary. In December 1961 he was elected chief rabbi, and served until October 2002, when he retired. He worked hard to keep the community together and represented it before the Turkish authorities with tact and dignity.

[Rifat Bali (2nd ed.)]

ASSER, family of lawyers and public figures in Holland. The founder of the family was MOSES SOLOMON ASSER (1754–1826), Amsterdam merchant and jurist. He was one of the protagonists of Jewish civic emancipation in the Netherlands after 1795 and a founder of *Felix Libertate, a society for attaining Jewish civic emancipation. He wrote many of its pamphlets and memoranda. In 1798 he became the first Jewish member of the Amsterdam district court. He took an active part in the constitution of the pioneering *Reform congregation in Amsterdam, Adath Jeshurun. He was appointed in 1808 to a commission to prepare the commercial code of the Bonapartist Kingdom of Holland, a work in which he laid the foundations of Dutch commercial law. His son CAREL (1780–1836), jurist, was one of the first Jews to practice law in Holland. He became secretary of the Department of Justice, and was responsible for much of the legislation of the Napoleonic period in the Netherlands and thereafter. Among the many government positions he filled, the most important were department head of the Council of State, secretary of the National Legislative Committee, and service as one of the authors of the Legal Code of 1830. He drew up the constitution of the Jewish *Consistory at the request of Louis Napoleon in 1808. From 1814 until his death, he was a member of the Supreme Committee on Israelite Affairs, of which he was appointed president in 1828. He was the founder of the Charity Board of the Ashkenazi community in Amsterdam. He wrote, among other things, a comparative study of the Dutch and French civil codes, *Het Nederlandsch Burgelijk Wetboek vergeleken met het Wetboek Napoleon* (1838), and, prompted by his sister-in-law, Rachel Varnhagen van *Ense (Lewin), a *Précis historique pour l'état des Israélites du Royaume des Pays-Bas* (1827, unpublished). Carel's brother, TOBIAS (1783–1847), was a lawyer as well. He married Caroline Itzig, the daughter of the prominent Berlin Jew Izak Daniel *Itzig. He succeeded his brother as a member of the Supreme Committee on Israelite Affairs (1836–47) and was chairman of the Charity Board. Tobias' son, CAREL DANIEL (1843–1898), jurist, was appointed judge at the district court of The Hague and subsequently professor of civil law at Leiden University. Later editions of his textbook on civil law, *Handleiding tot de beoefening van het Nederlandsch Burgelijk Recht* (5 vols., 1885–1915; in collaboration with Ph.W. van Heusde), are still in use at most Dutch universities. From his marriage with Rosette Godefroi, the sister of the first Jewish minister in the Netherlands, Michel Henry *Godefroi, TOBIAS MICHAËL CAREL (1838–1913) was born. He was a statesman and jurist specializing in international law. In 1860 he was appointed Dutch representative on the International Commission on the freedom of navigation in the Rhine. From 1862 to 1893 he was professor of commercial and private international law at the University of Amsterdam. Asser helped to found the Institut de droit international in 1873. In 1893 he was appointed a member of the Council of State, and in 1898 chairman of the royal commission on private international law. Asser participated in The Hague Peace Conferences of 1899 and 1907 and was appointed a member of The Hague Permanent Court of Arbitration in 1900, where he frequently arbitrated on international issues, such as the dispute between Russia and the United States over fishing rights in the Bering Straits. He shared with two others the Nobel Peace Prize in 1911. He was a member of the board of trustees of the Dutch Israelite Seminary (1882–87), but broke with Judaism around 1890. Asser was a cofounder and coeditor of the *Revue de droit international et de législation comparée* (1869). He wrote works on the codification of private international law (translated into French) and on Dutch commercial law, a standard work.

BIBLIOGRAPHY: I.H. van Eeghen (ed.), in: *Amstelodamum*, 55 (1955); Van Vollenhoven, in: *Jaarboeken der Koninklijke Akademie* (1914), on Tobias. **ADD. BIBLIOGRAPHY:** J. Michman, *Dutch Jewry during the Emancipation Period, Gothic Turrets on a Corinthian Building* (1995); P. Buijs, in: *Levend Joods Geloof*, 43 (1996), 14–17.

[Charles Boasson / Bart Wallet (2nd ed.)]

ASSI (late third and early fourth century C.E.), Palestinian *amora*. In the Jerusalem Talmud, he is also known as Issi, Yassi, and Assa; the name is probably a shortened form of Joseph. In both the Jerusalem and Babylonian Talmud, Assi is one of the most frequently mentioned *amoraim*, often together with his colleague, *Ammi. Assi, who was born in Babylonia, studied together with Ammi at Samuel's academy in Nehardea (cf. TJ, Shek. 2:5, 46d; Er. 6:8, 23d) and Huna's in Sura (MK 25a). As a result of a misunderstanding with his mother, he left for Ereẓ Israel (Kid. 31b). Here he attended lectures by such well-known *amoraim* as Ḥanina (Men. 50b) and *Joshua b. Levi (Ḥul. 28a). He settled in Tiberias, studying at the academy of *Johanan Nappaḥa in whose name he transmitted many halakhic sayings (Pes. 106a, Ḥul. 55b). Among Assi's colleagues in Tiberias was *Eleazar b. Pedat. It was the latter who succeeded Johanan as the head of the academy, although Assi possessed greater knowledge, especially in mysticism (Ḥag. 13a) and was lauded by Eleazar b. Pedat himself as "the prodigy of his generation" (Ḥul. 103b). Another of Assi's associates was *Ḥiyya b. Abba (Er. 32b, 65b, etc.). Assi, Ammi, and Ḥiyya were all priests who emigrated from Babylonia to Ereẓ Israel, and they are often mentioned together (e.g., Yoma 73a; TJ, Er. 4:6). *Judah III put them in charge of supervising schools in the country (TJ, Ḥag. 1:7, 76c). After the death of Eleazar b. Pedat (c. 279 C.E.) Ammi was appointed head of the Tiberian academy, Assi having declined to assume public office. He assisted Ammi, however, and taught with him "amid the pillars" of the Tiberian school (Ber. 8a). The two were held in highest esteem as the "distinguished priests of the Holy Land" (Meg. 22a) and were regarded as the most important "judges of the Land of Israel" (Sanh. 17b). Many of Assi's aggadic teachings were transmitted by his pupil *Avira (Ber. 20b, Pes. 119b, etc.). The son of Eleazar b. Pedat was his "*amora*" (TJ, Meg. 4:10, 75c). When Assi died in Tiberias, his death was likened to the collapse of a tower (TJ, Av. Zar. 3:1, 42c).

His Aggadic Teachings

He explained the practice of children beginning their Bible studies with Leviticus rather than with Genesis as a matter of the pure (i.e., the young) engaging in the study of the pure (i.e., the laws of purity in Leviticus (Lev. R. 7:3)). One of his famous teachings (based on Isa. 5:18) is that the evil inclination though initially fragile as a spider web, eventually attains the toughness of cart rope (Suk. 52a). Once, being reproached by his wife for siding with his maidservant rather than with her in a dispute, he justified his stand by quoting Job 31:13, "Did I despise the cause of my manservant or of my maidservant when they contended with me?" (Gen. R. 48:3). Among his sayings are: "The pangs of earning one's bread are twice as great as those of childbirth" (Gen. R. 20:9); "A man should eat and drink beneath his means, clothe himself in accordance with his means, and honor his wife and children beyond his means" (Ḥul. 84b). Assi is sometimes confused with the Babylonian *amora* of the same name.

BIBLIOGRAPHY: Bacher, Pal Amor, 2 (1896), 143ff.; Hyman, Toledot, 234–9; Halevy, Dorot, 2 (1923), 232ff.

[Meir Ydit]

ASSI, RAV (early third century), Babylonian *amora*. Assi was a contemporary of *Rav and *Samuel and a friend of R. Kahana. He lived in Huẓal near Nehardea and was wealthy (Ḥul. 105a). His authority was respected throughout Babylonia, and various regulations which he promulgated in Huẓal are referred to in the *halakhah* (Meg. 5b; Ḥul. 26b). While submitting to the authority of Rav in all that concerned traditions about the oral law which Rav had brought from Palestine, Assi freely contended with him on points of *halakhah*, in which he was no less conversant than Rav. His independent views were respected even by Rav (Sanh. 36b; Shab. 146b, etc.). Indeed, for fear that the opposing views of Assi might be correct, Rav preferred to conform to them in practice even though he personally differed from him (Kid. 44b, etc.). It would appear that Assi was considered greater than Samuel (BK 80a–b). In his controversies with Rav, he was not always successful in winning the majority of the scholars to his opinion. This was a source of contention between Assi and Rav's pupil Shila b. Avina (Nid. 36b) culminating in the excommunication of Shila by Assi. Assi's death, which apparently occurred not long after that of Rav in 246, was attributed by his colleagues to his excommunication of Shila (*ibid.*). When Assi was nearing death his nephew came to him and found him in tears. In answer to his question "Master why do you weep? Is there the least portion of Torah that you have not learned and have you not also taught many disciples? Is there any charity you have not performed? Have you not, despite all your virtues, always refused to sit in judgment and always refrained from accepting public office?" Assi replied, "My son, that is precisely what I bewail. Who knows if I shall not be made to answer for not having done what was in my power to regulate in the affairs of Israel?" (Tanḥ., Mishpatim, 2).

BIBLIOGRAPHY: Halevy, Dorot, 2 (1923), 228ff.; Hyman, Toledot, 232.

[Yitzhak Dov Gilat]

ASSIGNMENT (OF DEBT).

History and Development

Basically, Jewish law did not recognize the concept whereby personal rights or obligations (whether arising from contract or from a liability for damages in tort) could be legally assigned, either by the creditor or the debtor, to one who was not a party to the obligation itself. This was because a debt was considered intangible and therefore incapable of legal transfer (Rashi, Git. 13b; R. Gershom, BB 147b; Tos. to Ket. 55b). It was compared to the case of an object that was not yet in existence (*davar she-lo ba la-olam*) which also could not be transferred (see Tos. to BK 36b).

The development of commerce and its increasingly sophisticated requirements made it necessary however to overcome this difficulty in the law, and the assignment of debts, whether verbal or by deed, is already mentioned in the tannaitic period (Tosef., BM 4:3, et al.). Two principal methods of assignment were invented: (1) a form of novation, whereby an existing debt was canceled and an identical, but new debt created between the debtor and the creditor's assignee – all three parties consenting; and (2) a formula whereby the creditor appointed an agent to recover a debt on his behalf, but empowered the agent to retain the proceeds for himself. From these two methods were developed the two legal forms of assignment of debts dealt with in the Talmud, namely *Ma'amad Sheloshtan* (lit. "a meeting of the three") and *Mekhirat Shetarot* ("sale of bonds"). In addition, there was the *Shi'buda de Rabbi Natan* a process of legal execution entrusted to the court.

Ma'amad Sheloshtan, as an authorized legal transaction, is first mentioned by the early *amoraim* (Git. 13b). All three parties – the creditor, the debtor, and the assignee – being present together, the creditor would say to the debtor: "There is a debt owing to me by you; give it to – (the assignee)." On this simple oral declaration the assignee acquired good legal title to the debt and could claim it direct from the debtor. In the same way it was possible to transfer a pledge. The Talmud concludes that there was no legal reason for this arrangement, it having been evolved merely to facilitate commercial dealings (Tos. to Git. 14a).

However, some *amoraim* do suggest a legal basis for it. For example, Amemar opines that its legal justification rests on the assumption that, when the obligation first arises, the debtor is deemed to render himself liable not only to the principal creditor but to anyone claiming through him. On the other hand, R. Ashi takes the view that the benefit which the debtor enjoys from the cancellation of the original obligation to the creditor and the creation of a new one to the assignee, with a different date of payment, is itself sufficient to demonstrate, without further act or formality, the debtor's willingness to bind himself to the assignee as his new creditor. Relying on R. Ashi's reasoning, some held that the debtor's actual consent was required to complete a *Ma'amad Sheloshtan*, but others held that only his presence was necessary (*Ran* on *Rif*, Git. 13b). Thus, according to R. Ashi, the institution of *Ma'amad Sheloshtan* would appear to be equivalent to novation and it may be assumed that before *Ma'amad Sheloshtan* was recognized the assignment of debt was done by canceling the old debt and creating a new one through the formal act of *kinyan* ("acquisition"), constituting, in effect, a novation (Git. 14a).

Mekhirat Shetarot ("sale of bonds") was a method whereby a debt, embodied in a bond, was assigned by selling the bond and was effective when the bond was delivered to the assignee (BB 76a). However, although one opinion of the *tannaim* was that physical delivery was sufficient in the case of a bond, another opinion (by which the *halakhah* was ultimately decided) held that a further deed was required in the assignee's name, because whereas the act of delivery validly assigned the bond itself, i.e., the actual paper on which it was written, the debt, and the creditor's rights to the debt were not an intrinsic part of the paper and therefore not assigned with it. Accordingly, in the ancillary deed the creditor would confirm that the assignee should "acquire [the bond] and any rights contained therein" (BB 76b).

As to the sale of bonds, the *amora* Samuel stated: "If one sells a bond of indebtedness to another and then releases the debtor from his liability, the release is valid [and therefore binding on the assignee], and such release can even be given by the creditor's heir [with the same third-party consequences]" (Ket. 86a). The basis for this ruling was that since the initial premise (stated above) was that a debt was intangible and thus incapable of legal transfer, the creditor is really doing no more than giving the assignee a power of attorney to recover the debt and keep the proceeds. This is, in fact, the second of the two earlier methods of assignment already referred to. As the assignee is, from the strictly legal point of view, no more than an agent of the creditor, the latter remains competent to release the debtor or even to recover the debt himself. In such a case, however, it was accepted as the *halakhah* that the creditor would be liable to compensate the frustrated assignee for any loss he sustained.

As the *Ma'amad Sheloshtan*, unlike the sale of bonds, was not based on the principle of agency, it would seem that after its completion the original creditor could no longer give a valid release to the debtor (Tos. to Git. 13b). Nor could a *Ma'amad Sheloshtan* be used as a means of selling a bond (*Siftei Kohen*, no. 97 to Sh. Ar., ḤM 66:29), since being a form of novation whereby a new debt is substituted for an old one, the old debt ceases to exist and becomes valueless. The Talmud explains (Ket. 86a) that if a new bond is addressed to the assignee the original creditor is no longer competent to release the debtor – his debt having ceased to exist and there being no question of agency, as in the case of sale of bonds.

Other explanations have also been advanced to justify the validity of a release by the original creditor, even after he has sold his bond. One is that whereas the sale of bonds was *mi-de-rabbanan* ("instituted by the sages"), the legality of a release of a debt was *mi-de-orayta* ("stemming from biblical law"; Maim., Yad, Mekhirah 6:12; Tos. to BB 76b). This explanation is, however, questionable, as in other cases of sale instituted by rabbinical enactment (including the *Ma'amad Sheloshtan*) a subsequent release by the assignor was not recognized. Another explanation suggests that the original creditor has two rights from his debtor – one proprietary and the other personal, the latter being inalienable. This also presents difficulty since a debt itself is intangible and therefore inalienable; it is strange therefore that the idea of a personal right, which is not mentioned elsewhere, should be introduced here, when the general rule would be equally applicable. If the original creditor transferred a pledge he was holding to the purchaser he cannot then release the debtor (see *Pledge).

It may be assumed that in tannaitic times the assignment of debts, whether verbal or under bond, was also effected by means of a power of attorney proper, known in the Babylonian Talmud as *urkhata* (BK 70a). However, although tannaitic sources mention powers of attorney with regard to the assignment of debts (Rashi, Kid. 47b), in the Babylonian Talmud – where such a device is not recognized as applying to intangibles (such as debts) – the references mentioned are interpreted differently (Kid. 47b; *Or Zaru'a*, BK 296). Presumably the formula "institute proceedings, acquire and take for yourself," forming part of the text of a power of attorney, was a relic from the tannaitic period when the assignee was appointed as attorney to recover the debt and then retain the proceeds. In Babylonia this form of attornment was only used for the recovery of movables, not debts, and certainly not for the assignment of debts (BK 70a and Tos.), leaving unanswered the question of why this device was necessary in view of the well-established rule that "a man's agent is like himself" (*Yam shel Shelomo*, BK 7:12).

Assignment by the Debtor

Although the Babylonian Talmud does not mention the case of a debtor assigning his liability to another, reference to this can be found in the Mishnah (BM 9:12) and in the Jerusalem Talmud (cf. BM 4:1), but only in relation to a banker or shopkeeper, both commonly engaged in financial transactions (Gulak, in: *Tarbiz*, 2 (1930/31), 154–71). It is possible that assignments of this kind were effected by a means similar to the *Ma'amad Sheloshtan*, to which they are compared by the codifiers (Rif, *Halakhot*, BM 111a). Details of such assignments are unknown, however, particularly as the *Ma'amad Sheloshtan* is not mentioned in the Jerusalem Talmud.

Post-Talmudic Developments

In post-talmudic times the power of attorney was used for the recovery of debts, but not for their assignment (Tos. to BK 70a; Maim., Yad, Sheluḥin ve-Shutafin 3:7; see also *Attorney). Some authorities held that a bond of indebtedness, drawn in favor of the creditor and anyone claiming through him, enabled it to be assigned by mere delivery and thereafter precluded the original creditor from releasing the debtor; but others disagreed (Sh. Ar., ḤM 66:26). It was also customary to draw a bond in favor of "whomsoever may produce it"; this being assignable by mere delivery and precluding the debtor's release by the assignor (Responsa Rosh 68:9), and the bond thus became negotiable (cf. J.J. Rabinowitz, *Jewish Law* (1956), 342ff.). In Poland, from the 16th century onward, a bond drawn in favor of "whomsoever may produce it," bearing only the debtor's signature, the amount of the debt, and the date of payment, became customary. Such a bond was known as a "*Memoram*" and was, in effect, a negotiable instrument like a promissory note (*Levush*, Ir Shushan 48; *Sma* to ḤM 48:1).

Modern Israel Law

In the State of Israel the assignment of debts is governed by the Assignment of Obligations Law, 1969, under the provisions of which every obligation or any part of it can be assigned either by the creditor or by the debtor. The debtor's assignment can only be made with the agreement of the creditor. Promissory notes and checks are in common use and are governed by the Bills of Exchange Ordinance, 1929, which permits the assignment of a debt by the mere delivery of the relevant bill. According to some authorities, the assignment of debts, too, is given by an obligation in the form of "undertaking to bind himself" (*mesha'abbed nafsho*) (Git. 13b), in other words by obligating himself (see Lifshitz, Bibliography).

BIBLIOGRAPHY: Sh. Ar., ḤM 66 and 126; Gulak, Yesodei, 2 (1922), 96–104; A. Gulak, *Toledot ha-Mishpat be-Yisrael*, 1 (1939); *Ha-Ḥiyyuv ve-Shi'budav*, 96–104; Herzog, Instit, 1 (1936), 201–12; S. Albeck, in: *Tarbiz*, 26 (1956/57), 262–86; M. Elon, Mafteaḥ, 58–60. **ADD. BIBLIOGRAPHY:** B. Lifshitz, *Promise – Obligation and Acquisition in Jewish Law* (1988).

[Shalom Albeck]

ASSIMILATION. In general the sociocultural process in which the sense and consciousness of association with one national and cultural group changes to identification with another such group, so that the merged individual or group may partially or totally lose its original national identity. Assimilation can occur and not only on the unconscious level in primitive societies. It has been shown that even these societies have sometimes developed specific mechanisms to facilitate assimilation, e.g., adoption; mobilization, and absorption into the tribal fighting force; exogamic marriage; the client relationship between the tribal protector and members of another tribe. In more developed societies, where a stronger sense of cultural and historical identification has evolved, the mechanisms, as well as the automatic media of assimilation, become more complicated. The reaction of the assimilator group to the penetration of the assimilated increasingly enters the picture.

Various factors may combine to advance or hinder the assimilation process. Those actively contributing include the position of economic strength held by a group; the political advantages to be gained from adhesion or separation; acknowledged cultural superiority; changes in religious outlook and customs; the disintegration of one group living within another more cohesive group; the development of an "open society" by either group. Added to these are external factors, such as changes in the demographic pattern (mainly migration) or those wrought by revolution and revolutionary attitudes. Sociologists have described the man in process of assimilation as "the marginal man," both attracted and repelled by the social and cultural spheres in which he lives in a state of transition.

Antiquity and Middle Ages

Within its environment in antiquity, as far as known, the Jewish national and social group mainly operated as the assimilator, aided by the attraction of monotheism and exerting the power of its social cohesion and state mechanism. During the period of the conquest of Ereẓ Israel, Jewish society gradually absorbed many of the ethnic elements living there. The process continued well into the reigns of David and Solomon. While the prophets of the time deplored the cultural influence exerted by the assimilated group, they did not reject the end results of the process. The isolated yet striking instance of Naaman the Syrian demonstrates the element of partial assimilation into *Judaism. In Judaism the very concept of *proselytism involves readiness on the part of the Jews to accept and assimilate a group or an individual prepared to adopt the religion and become assimilated. The attitude of *Ezra and *Nehemiah, who opposed the assimilation of other ethnic elements, did not prevail. Some of the *Hasmonean rulers, John *Hyrcanus and Alexander *Yannai – adopted a clear-cut policy of forcible proselytization; the assimilation of the Idumeans was so complete that the last dynasty to rule the Jewish commonwealth in the Second Temple period was the Idumean house of *Herod, and some of the most devoted fighters in the war against Rome were Idumeans. Both Jewish and external sources yield plentiful information about groups and individuals living within the Roman Empire that had totally or partially adopted Judaism and assimilated the Jewish way of life. According to some scholars, the large number of Jews in the later period of the Roman Empire was the result of the assimilation of the Phoenician diaspora into the Jewish communities. On the other hand, sources dating from as early as the reign of *Antiochus Epiphanes (175–164 B.C.E.) mention the Hellenizers, a group wishing to accept the mode of life and culture of *Hellenism. *Tiberius Alexander, the nephew of Philo of *Alexandria, exemplifies assimilation by Jewish individuals of Hellenistic-Roman culture, particularly in the *Diaspora. To some degree the path of early Pauline *Christianity is viewed from the Jewish standpoint as a process of assimilation of the early Jewish Christian apostles and groups into the gentile ethnic identity and way of life.

In the course of Jewish history, processes that began as quasi-assimilatory were later transmuted to become hallmarks of continuing Jewish consciousness and identity. This applied to the adoption of the Greek language in the ancient period and of German and Spanish in the Middle Ages. As the alien language gained acceptance, it became not only a vehicle of Jewish cultural and religious creativity, but also gradually became converted into a specifically Jewish idiom and mark of Jewish identity that even formed barriers to later assimilation. *Yiddish became the idiom of East European Jewry amid a Slavic linguistic environment, and hence of Jewish emigrants from this area in the Anglo-Saxon countries. Similarly the Spanish Jews carried their language of Castile with them after the expulsion from Spain, developing it into *Ladino. During the Middle Ages the strength of Jewish cohesiveness was so powerful that only *apostates from Judaism became assimilated into the adopted environment, and not always even then (see **Anusim*; *Marranos).

From the Period of Enlightenment

Assimilation has been a major centrifugal force in Jewish life since the second half of the 18th century. It became an element of increasing magnitude in Jewish thought and society and helped to mold a new image of the Jew in literature and art, in which the problems it posed were reflected. Various factors combined to create this situation. The *Court Jews, their families, and social circle gradually, sometimes imperceptibly, assimilated the mores of the Christian court. The Enlightenment (*Haskalah) movement was accompanied by a certain readiness on the part of groups of Christian and Jewish intellectuals to create an "open society." The grant of civic *emancipation apparently premised that Jews could enter the emancipating society as equals if they relinquished their Jewish national cohesion. In rejecting the medieval system of corporation, the attitude of early capitalistic society militated against a continuance of Jewish *autonomy and its institutions. Similarly, the dictates of the modern state, postulating observance of a single legal code and an undifferentiated legal status for its citizens, militated against Jewish judicial autonomy while assisting Jewish emancipation. All these elements hastened the assimilatory process. As members of the upper strata of Jewish society in Central and Western Europe became assimilated, they left their positions of leadership in the autonomous Jewish body, thereby weakening it further. Other Jews in less influential positions followed their example. Jewish intellectuals who accepted the values and criteria of the Enlightenment and Christian culture and society tended to regard the Jewish counterpart as barren and primitive. Their attitude became devastatingly critical. They measured the Jewish past and culture by alien and historically inimical standards.

The first wave of assimilation carried Jews toward the ahistoric society envisioned by the 18th-century Enlightenment, a society that would not insist on national or religious definitions. For some Jews, assimilation served as a shortcut to attaining individual emancipation and advancement, hence there were many nominal apostates like Heinrich *Heine. Later, their admiration for the modern national state, a growing appreciation of the mores and social structure of the dominant nations, and the idea of progress combined to create the conception that the perpetuation of a Jewish national existence was obsolete. Such Jews also felt that they were guilty of intellectual and emotional dishonesty in cherishing Jewish messianic hopes. The evaluations, way of life, writings – both in German and in Hebrew – and influence of intellectuals like Moses *Mendelssohn and David Friedlaender, although formulating no clear-cut theory of assimilation, furthered the tendency. Socialite assimilation in the salons of Berlin and Vienna, fostering freedom in thought and with their romantic attractions, drew both the gifted and the wealthy away from the Jewish fold to a humanistic, cosmopolitan, and Christian allegiance. Rachel *Varnhagen-Levin saw her life vitiated by the blemish of her Jewish descent. Moses Mendelssohn's daughter, Dorothea *Schlegel, not only left her faith but also developed the feeling of self-hatred typical of many modern assimilated Jews. In 1802 she wrote to Friedrich Schleiermacher:

> … according to my own feeling, Protestant Christianity [is] much purer and to be preferred to the Catholic one. Catholicism has for me too much similarity to the old Judaism, which I greatly despise. Protestantism, though, seems to me to be the total religion of Jesus and the religion of civilization. In

> my heart I am completely, as far as I can understand from the Bible, a Protestant.

The ideology of assimilation gained momentum in the first half of the 19th century as it developed an eschatological message. This trend was part of the new direction which assimilation took when projected on the intense nationalistic society and state that prevailed in Europe with the romantic movement. The former nexus between the Jewish people and its religion and law was rejected; attempts were made to purge the Jewish religion of its nationalistic elements in order to relieve individual Jews in dispersion of the sense of being an alien and an exile. Instead of looking to Ereẓ Israel for redemption, the assimilationists stressed their attachment was to the land in which they and their forefathers had lived for generations. Nevertheless Jewish identity would be preserved in a redefinition as "Germans of Mosaic faith" or "Frenchmen of Mosaic faith," and so on.

The desire for emancipation blended with the will for religious reform and with revolutionary fervor for change at first in the liberal, and later in the socialist sense. The "messiah" envisaged by Leopold *Zunz was civic and political revolution in Germany and Europe, bearing on its wings freedom for mankind and equality for Jews. Derision of the former Jewish messianic hopes was intrinsic to burning faith in the new assimilationist form of existence. Thus in 1848, the year of the "Spring of Nations," Jews of the ancient community of Worms formulated the following program for religious reform, motivated by the ideal of assimilation:

> ...We have to aspire to truth and dignity in Divine worship, coordination between faith and life, to put away empty concepts and shape new institutions for the spirit of Judaism. We must no longer utter prayers for the return to Palestine while we are wholeheartedly attached to the German fatherland whose fate is indissolubly our fate; all that is beloved and dear to us is contained in this fatherland. We must not mourn in sackcloth and ashes the destruction of the Temple when we long ago came into the possession of a fatherland that has become so dear to us. We may commemorate yearly the destruction of the Temple, but why be in heavy mourning, which no longer comes from feelings of the heart, and sing songs of mourning about an historical fact, for which we praise the loving hand of God? We should not try to enlighten our children in the religious schools with facts that the living Jewish spirit looks upon as dead ballast, to be thrown overboard; no longer teach them to pray in a language that is dead, while the word and sound of our German mother tongue is understandable and dear to us and therefore is the only one fit to be raised in praise to our Creator. It is time to put a stop to this conflict, this sin of dishonesty in our midst.

Attachment to German soil, language, culture, and statehood was the compelling reason for effecting the change in prayer and its language, and for eradicating the hope for redemption in Ereẓ Israel. This attitude continued to persist in some circles; it led the British Liberal rabbi Israel Mattuck in 1939 to the conclusion that "the position which the Jews should seek and the world should give is one which combines separatism in religion with assimilation in all the other elements of national life, political, social, and cultural" (*What are the Jews?* (1939) 239).

The Late 19th and the 20th Century

Assimilation through the 19th and 20th centuries was not a unified process and was beset with a host of problems and complications. The position taken by assimilationists oscillated between the cosmopolitan and nationalist aspects of assimilation. Their theories clashed with the national spirit of exclusiveness of the assimilator group: Germans, Frenchmen, and others, resented the pollution of their race and culture by alien elements. Jews wishing to assimilate became involved in the array of conflicting assimilating nationalities and cultures within the same territorial arena. With the national awakening of the Czechs, the Jews of Prague, for instance, were confronted simultaneously by German and Czech demands for assimilation into one or the other national camp. The same conflict occurred between the demands of the Magyar and German cultures in Hungary; the Polish, German, and Russian cultures in Polish lands; the German, Polish, and Ukrainian cultures in East Galicia. In many countries the process of assimilation was deliberately assisted by social and educational measures. In Russia, *Nicholas I tried to promote assimilation of the Jewish youth through the mechanism of army mobilization (see *Cantonists). On the other hand the complications of the assimilation process itself necessarily acted to spur Jewish nationalism, and offered it a springboard. At the same time a school of historical thought that viewed each epoch and culture as a distinct phenomenon to be judged by its own system of values was gaining ascendancy. Thus, appreciation of the Jewish culture and history, achievements, values, and criteria strengthened, while the arrogance and ridicule on which the assimilationists based their arguments lost ground.

Assimilation into modern nationalities was described by Solomon *Schechter in 1901 upon viewing the disappointment that was felt when the concept of assimilation intrinsic to the hopes for a humanist, non-nationalistic society was definitively superseded by assimilation into different militarist, nationalist states. Schechter saw "... the ancient chosen people of God going about begging for a nationality – clamoring everywhere 'We are you!'... Using the last crumbs of the sacred language, in which God-Shalom addressed His children, to invoke His blessing upon the '*Mitrailleuse*,' the 'Krupp gun,' 'dum-dum' and 'Long Tom,' and other anti-messianic contrivances" ("Epistles to the Jews of England," in *Jewish Chronicle*, 1901). The disappointment at these developments in European society and the reaction that Jewish assimilation had provoked did not deter assimilationists from their beliefs. Even after World War II and the experience of the *Holocaust, and after his disillusionment with the Communist revolution, Boris *Pasternak clung to the Christian Orthodox faith and his Russian cultural identity. He dared to call upon Jews to assimilate as salvation from the fate which their nationality imposes. In the wake of the martyred Jews, he denied that there could be any sense in retaining a separate Jewish identity: "In whose interests is this voluntary martyrdom?... Dismiss this army which is forever fighting and being massacred, nobody knows for what?... Say to them: 'That's enough. Stop now. Don't hold on to your identity. Don't all get together in a crowd. Disperse. Be with all the rest.'" (*Dr. Zhivago* (1958) 117–8).

When this call for assimilation was pronounced, several years had elapsed since the suicide of a man who wrote at the beginning of Nazi rule and the end of the liberal German society of the early 20th century:

> I thought of my terrible joy when I realized that nobody would recognize me for a Jew; of the first day of the war and my passionate longing to prove that I was a real German by offering my life to my country; of my writing from the front to the authorities to say that they could strike my name from the list of the Jewish community. Had it all been for nothing? Had it all been wrong? Didn't I love Germany with all my heart? Had I not stood in the rich beauty of the Mediterranean landscape and longed for the austere pine woods, for the beauty of the still, secret lakes of north Germany? And wasn't the German language my language, the language in which I felt and thought and spoke, a part of my very being? But wasn't I also a Jew? A member of that great race that for centuries had been persecuted, harried, martyred and slain; whose prophets had called the world to righteousness, had exalted the wretched and the oppressed, then and for all time. A race who had never bowed their heads to their persecutors, who had preferred death to dishonor. I had denied my own mother, and I was ashamed. It is an indictment of society at large that a child should have thus been driven to deception. How much of me was German, how much Jewish? Must I then join the ranks of the bigoted and glorify my Jewish blood now, not my German? Pride and love are not the same thing, and if I were asked where I belonged I should answer that a Jewish mother had borne me, that Germany nourished me, that Europe had formed me, that my home was the earth and the world my fatherland (Ernst Toller, *I Was a German*, London, 1934, 280–2).

This anguished cry powerfully expresses the dynamics and problems that persisted after the doctrine of assimilation had been tested for over a century and a half. The assimilationist remained torn between his ideals and rejection by the assimilator society, between the allegiance he was seeking and the pride awakened by Jewish nationalism; he oscillated between the choice of assimilation into one nation and internationalist assimilation.

More recently the ideals of assimilation have assumed a different form. This has been determined by the combined impact of the Holocaust, the creation of the State of Israel and its struggle for survival, and the emergence of a monistic nationalism in Eastern and Central Europe. But if the advocates of assimilation have sometimes changed their formula, the substance of their arguments remains. This viewpoint clearly emerges in the evaluation of Jewish assimilation made by a philosopher of history hostile to Jewish nationalism, Arnold Toynbee. Toynbee regards assimilation and *intermarriage as beneficial and a natural process. By assimilating, a Jew is "deserting the Diaspora individually in order to lose himself in the ranks of a modern, Western, gentile, urban bourgeoisie. The liberal Jew [is]... assimilating himself to a gentile social milieu that had previously gone far, on its side, to assimilate itself socially and psychologically to the Jewish Disapora" (*Study of History*, 8 (1954), 310). Nevertheless, in volume 12 of the same study, published in 1961, Toynbee describes the solution he proposed for the Jews in 1954 as the fate of the Ten Tribes, who "lost their national identity through being assimilated. The Ten Tribes' way is passive, involuntary, and inglorious, and it is natural that the Jews should be on their guard against meeting the fate of their lost kinsmen." What he proposed in 1961 was that the Jews become "denationalized" without becoming totally assimilated. As an alternative to emigration to Israel he proposes that they "incorporate Gentiles in a Jewish religious community by converting them to the religion of Deutero-Isaiah" (p. 517). Thus, ideationally, the process has turned full circle. An opponent of *Zionism and the creation of the State of Israel, Toynbee proposed to the Jews of the Diaspora in 1961 that they undertake the conversion of the peoples in their environment to a non-national Jewish religion. For all practical purposes, however, the goal is the same: the abolition of Jewish national identity.

[Haim Hillel Ben-Sasson]

United States.

The term "assimilation" or "identification assimilation" is usually taken to mean the process by which members of an ethnic, religious, or national immigrant group takes on the identity of their host country or society, and simultaneously shed the identity of their "home" society. (Other forms of assimilation include "structural assimilation," which is the process by which immigrants enter into the structures – education, employment, political – of the host society; and "marital assimilation," which is intermarriage.) "Assimilation," which is about identity, is often confused with "acculturation" (or "cultural assimilation"), which is the process by which members of an immigrant group adopts aspects of the culture of the host society – modes of dress, language, cuisine, and so on – while retaining their ethnic, religious, or national identity.

The American Jewish community was created by three waves of immigration: the Sephardi-dominated handful of colonial times, several tens of thousands from Central Europe who arrived in the middle of the 19th century, and the mass of almost three million, mostly from Eastern Europe, who came between 1882 and 1914. The later and much smaller immigrations after both world wars and during the Hitler era have added certain colorations to the American Jewish scene, but the history of American Jewry and the changes in its modes of acculturation to the fluctuating composition of American society largely are the tale of these three immigration impulses.

There were so few Jews in the United States during colonial times (perhaps 2,000 at the time of the American Revolution) that they were regarded as exotics. Their acculturation was deep and broad, and their assimilation into the largely

English majority population was the result of neither conscious assimilationist pressure nor ideological choice. So small a Jewish population, with fewer women than men among it, inevitably had a considerable rate of intermarriage. A recent study of Jewish marriage before 1840 has shown that at least one in seven colonial Jews and their immediate descendants married unconverted Christians; after that year, in the fourth and fifth generations of colonial Jewish families, intermarriage was so dominant that most of these families disappeared from the Jewish community. Ideological factors were clearly secondary in this situation, for what increased assimilation was the family's length of the residence in a society almost totally open, at that point, to its handful of Jews. Isaac Harby, who led in the creation of a reformed synagogue in Charleston in 1824, wrote two years later that not all who agreed with him had joined his group, but that "the Jews born in Carolina are mostly of our way of thinking" and that the only consideration that kept them in the Orthodox synagogue was "a tender regard for the opinions and feelings of their parents."

The situation of the second major wave of Jewish immigration to the United States, which arrived in the middle of the 19th century, was significantly different. The American majority had crystallized as an assimilating force. Some of the rabbis among the Central European Jews who were then arriving in the United States had participated in the early stirrings of Reform Judaism in Europe; they believed in acculturation, even in religious practices, as a desirable value. Their efforts went unchecked by an entrenched Orthodox establishment. In the first generation after their arrival, many of these new immigrants lived out their secular lives not among the American majority, but in the more accessible environment of the gentile German immigrants; but this soon passed. Their American-born children looked to the world of their economic peers in American business for their social environment. The choice of life styles was not a problem until the 1870s, when the first signs of social antisemitism appeared. The Gentile *nouveau riche* were establishing their prestige on other than economic grounds, and they began by excluding the quite visible, even more recently enriched German Jews. In 1876 the first known advertisement by a resort hotel that it was barring Jews was printed in the *New York Tribune*, and in the next year the prominent banker Joseph Seligman was excluded as a Jew from the Grand Union Hotel in Saratoga. This kind of discrimination increased in the next several decades. Those Jews who remained identifiable as such turned to creating a network of social and philanthropic institutions within which they could live a life that largely paralleled that of their gentile peers. Their isolation, therefore, was partly willed and partly forced. This social ghetto was dominated by the ideals of middle class liberalism and by a special concern for the latest Jewish arrivals – those from Eastern Europe. The German-Jewish elite continued to dominate and to provide most of the social services for the American Jewish community during the period between 1881 and World War I, when almost three million Jews came to the United States from Eastern Europe. By the 1920s, however, the German group was clearly losing its hold for at least two reasons. The new immigrants and their children were losing their "strangeness," beginning to achieve some power in their own right, and growing ever less willing to accept the tutelage of the German-Jewish "Uptown." Some of the German-Jewish leadership associated itself within the new Jewish masses; larger numbers, however, were following after the pattern of the colonial Jews, so that by the third generation the rate of intermarriage was large enough as to bring into question the continued existence of many of these families as Jews. By the end of the 19th century, a new form of acculturation, leading to secular apostasy, had come into view. Thus it had become possible to vanish as a Jew without accepting any other religious identity.

The Eastern European Jewish immigrants brought with them the identity of a deprived national minority, sustained by great forces of religious, cultural, and communal cohesion. Political action in the name of Jewish interests, Jewish efforts toward social reform, pressure on society at large to regard the Jewish community as by right equal to all other communities, including the majority itself – in short, the total stance of a group fighting to express itself in all its peculiarities and to be accepted by society as such – all this became the new mode of American Jewish life among the immigrants and most of their children in the 20th century. The Yiddish language, socialism, union activities, Zionism, and orthodoxy in religion (locked in combat with other ideologies such as Marxism or atheism) composed the cultural temper of this mass community, which existed in large numbers in specific neighborhoods not only in New York, but also in most major American cities.

There were two contesting views on how to bring this community into the larger American society. Such thinkers as Horace *Kallen and Mordecai M. *Kaplan envisaged the American society of the future as one of cultural pluralism, in which the descendants of various European national traditions would retain their distinctiveness but have the ability to participate in an American society that is informed by many ethnic and religious groups. As such, they would retain and nurture substantial knowledge of their past and loyalty to it. This meant that American Jews would be able to exist as a separate community, as they would not be unique in this aspect; and that any group membership and association would be purely voluntary.

The counter theory was held by the dominant American Protestant cultural and political establishment; their vision was the model of the "melting pot," the notion that the ideal condition was one of complete assimilation in which all ethnic and religious differences would disappear. Upon arrival in the United States the new immigrant was to undergo the process of Americanization as rapidly as possible and surrender his foreignness, that is, he was to learn to behave and live in imitation of the dominant modes. The older American Jewish community was overwhelmingly committed to the second idea, and the institutions that it created to help the Jewish newcomers, such as the Educational Alliance on the lower

East Side of New York and the Yiddish newspaper *Forverts* (*Forward*), had as their primary purpose the Americanization of the immigrants. In the second generation, some younger Jewish intellectuals tried to live in both American and Jewish cultures with very complicated and often painful results. Because Jews remained in the position of a minority suffering from substantial disabilities until after World War II, some became an important part of reform and left-wing political movements. The overwhelming bulk of this generation, as was the case with its predecessors in the earlier migrations, simply tried to make their individual way in the American economy and society. In actual fact they had no choice but to adopt the way of life demanded by the "melting pot," while harboring very substantial Jewish emotions and commitments on a more personal level.

The ideal of bicultural existence in America was attacked by some of the American-born children of East European-Jewish immigrants as a form of schizophrenia. Jessie Bernard, writing as late as 1942, said that a child of immigrant parents "can never achieve complete oneness save he deliberately turn his back on one or the other [culture]." Kurt Lewin, a social theorist who arrived in the United States in those very years as a refugee from Hitler, had expressed the same insight in coining the phrase "marginal man" (see above). Both of them, however, offered different prescriptions for this discomfort: Bernard suggested conscious and total assimilation, and Lewin became a passionate believer in Zionism. The American Jewish community of the next generation did not follow either prescription. In the generation that followed after World War II, there was very little sign of any conscious assimilation. American society became more open to Jews than any country has ever been throughout the whole history of the Diaspora, and this acted to remove the need for any willed assimilation. The creation of the State of Israel and (after 1967) the Holocaust informed a reaffirmation on the part of many American Jews of their Jewish identity. The rapid economic rise of the bulk of the American Jewish community into the middle and upper-middle classes during the postwar period remade the lifestyle of American Jews, so that in many aspects Jews became part of the American establishment. This was particularly true in the realms of academic and artistic endeavor, where Jews became a dominant force during this era. It was thus no longer necessary to play down the fact of one's Jewishness or to make the defensive choice of highlighting it, because the open society, within which older traditions – including the dominant Christian one – were clearly under attrition, was then making no assimilatory demands in the name of an American ideology.

The behavior pattern of this post-World War II generation has been described in innumerable sociological studies. Jews associate socially overwhelmingly with other Jews, and the great majority of their children, in towns outside New York, receive some minimal amount of Jewish education. On the other hand, the rate of intermarriage has risen steadily, to the point at which it is between 40 and 50 percent for marriages started between 1985 and 2001, especially among the most highly educated. While Yiddish as a spoken language has experienced some measure of renaissance amongst academics, there has not been a revival of the language, and its use as a spoken language is limited to some sectarian Orthodox groups. In point of fact, English (and not Hebrew) has become the *lingua franca* of the Jewish people. The countertendencies to this pattern of non-ideological attrition are to be found in one or two social groups within American Jewry and in some of the work of the organized community as a whole. Jewish parochial schools have become the dominant form of education among the Orthodox and some of the Conservative Jews; such schools now contain a very large number of students. The postwar immigration from Europe reinforced pockets of Hasidic ghetto existence and created a number of new ethnic neighborhoods and enclaves, chiefly in New York. American Zionism had never had the fostering of *aliyah* to Israel as one of its prime purposes, and the increase in numbers who have chosen to immigrate to Israel from almost nothing in the early 1950s to more than 5,000 in 1969 was nonetheless relatively small. Yet there have been increased efforts on the part of almost every American Jewish body aimed at intensifying Jewish education and increasing the connection between American Jews and Israel.

The worsening of race relations in America in the 1960s and the concomitant tensions between Jews and blacks again posed the question of assimilation in an ideological way. Black emphasis on black identity has evoked much more identification with blacks among some younger Jews than with their own Jewish identity. In the 1960s and early 1970s the New Left tended to align itself with the "Third World," and thus sided with the Arabs against Israel. Many young Jews, heavily represented in these causes, tended to see their inherited Jewish identity as bourgeois and belonging to the camp of the oppressors, and thus need to be exorcised. During the *Six-Day War, however, the overwhelming majority of American Jewish youth were as involved as were their parents. Yet the emphasis on black identity also had a paradoxically important affect on American Jews, who felt free to emphasize their own Jewish experience in public and to proclaim it explicitly. Young Jews felt free to wear a "*yarmulke*" in public and Jewish stars as jewelry, an explicit affirmation of identity. On the university campuses, the introduction of Black (later Afro-American) Studies paved the way for the explosion of Jewish Studies, which soon became mainstream.

From the perspective of the history of Jewish assimilation in the United States, these ideological issues are quite secondary. The basic undertow continues to be the family's length of residence in the United States in a non-ghetto, middle class, Western educated milieu within a relatively open society. It is far from certain, even with the revived energy for Jewish particularists living in the United States that has recently been evoked, that the process of unreflective assimilation can be seriously checked. The minority of American Jews that is sectarian appears to be successful in surviving; so do those moving toward *aliyah* to Israel. Some sectarian Jews show remarkable degrees of acculturation. Chabad has mastered the American media and uses a telethon as an important means of fundraising. It also engages in two very American means of organizational management: charismatic leadership was replaced by management and marketing based on the charisma of the founder and local Chabad rabbis are franchises with assigned territories for their work. ArtScroll Publications with its contemporary designs and the emergence of a significant English-language ultra-Orthodox literature also indicates the emergence of English, not Yiddish and Hebrew, as a dominant language even among sectarian Jews.

Substantial numbers of American Jews, however, however, have not yet found an answer to the problem of how to continue to live permanently both within the mainstream of American life and within a Jewish community of their own.

[Arthur Hertzberg / Jerome A. Chanes (2nd ed.)]

In Other Western Countries

The major Jewish communities in this area, those in England and France, seemed on the surface to be going in different directions. In England an increasing rate of intermarriage, a birth rate so small that it was not adequate to maintain the size of the community, and substantial intellectual defection by the young were the marks of ongoing assimilation. On the other hand, Zionist consciousness remained high and the official establishment of Anglo-Jewry has consistently moved in more Orthodox directions (in the religious sense) for the last generation. In addition, Reform and Liberal judaism increasingly provided a set of Jewish religious institutions for non-Orthodox Jews and those not regarded as halakhichally Jewish by the Orthodox.

The so-called "remote" Jewish communities in the English-speaking world – Australia, South Africa, and New Zealand – all reflect a welcome departure from the picture of increased assimilation in the larger English-speaking communities. In Australia, Jewish numbers have steadily risen since World War II, and a range of Jewish institutions, especially a large day school system, has grown up since the late 1940s. More than one-half of school age Jews in Australia attend one or another of Australia's 19 Jewish day school, according to most estimates. Support for Israel and Zionism probably remain stronger and more central to Jewish identity among Australian Jewry than among American or British Jews. Intermarriage rates, too, are remarkably low by normal Diaspora standards and show little signs of rising. After many decades of decline, New Zealand Jewry also appears to be increasing in both size and Jewish identity, with the establishment in the recent past of two Jewish day schools. South African Jewry was long a by-word for an intensely committed, Zionistic Diaspora community, with a long-established range of institutions, including a major day school system in Cape Town, Johannesburg, and elsewhere. The traumas associated with the decline phase of the apartheid system and the institutionalization of a black majority government in the early 1990s of course shook South African Jewry to its core, and the community has declined in size by perhaps one-third, thanks to heavy emigration elsewhere, in the post-apartheid period. Nevertheless, the long-established core institutions of the South African Jewish community have remained intact.

In France, assimilation seemed even more advanced in the immediate aftermath of World War II, for organized Jewish life had been weak even before the Nazi occupation as the assimilating power of French culture had been, and remained, strong. With the end of the Algerian war, Jews were a significant element among the many hundreds of thousands of French citizens who chose to come to France rather than remain in Algeria. This element was far more religious and more consciously identified as Jews than was usual in France at the time. A number of moribund Jewish communities, especially in the south of France, were revived by their presence. The intensified connection with Israel however, was the factor that made the crucial difference in France. For more than a decade, from before the *Sinai Campaign of 1956 until the Six-Day War of 1967, France was Israel's major political and military ally. This relationship served to encourage the involvement of French Jews in affairs concerning Israel. De Gaulle's 1967 turnabout to the policy of arms embargo, followed soon thereafter by his remarks about the particularistic character of the Jews and his anger at their continued involvement with Israel after his policy had changed, acted, contrary to his will, to reinforce that very involvement. Among significant numbers of formerly alienated young people there arose a very visible tendency to study Hebrew, to reassert Jewish identity, and to settle in Israel.

In the ensuing years, the percentage of Jews identifying themselves as Sephardim (70 percent in 2002) continued to increase, indicating a decline through assimilation of the old Ashkenazi population. Though most of these French Jews were now French-born, they still had a strong sense of their Jewishness. According to a survey commissioned by the Fonds Social Juif Unifié and published in 2002, 80 percent of the Jews surveyed would choose to be born Jews, 70 percent had Jewish spouses (60 percent in the under-30 group), 86 percent considered Jewish education important, and 86 percent felt close to Israel. Half lit Sabbath candles and only 30 percent defined themselves as non-practicing Jews.

[Arthur Hertzberg / William D. Rubenstein and Fred Skolnik (2nd ed.)]

In the Soviet Union

After the October Revolution (1917), the Soviet government, under the leadership of *Lenin, was faced with a complicated Jewish problem. On the one hand, Bolshevik doctrine regarded the total assimilation of Jews as an essential feature of social progress and an indispensable prerequisite of the socialist order. On the other hand, the revolutionary regime found millions of Jews living in territorial concentration – mainly in the former *Pale of Settlement – with their own language, culture, and, for the most part, a strong sense of Jewish identity, either in its original religious form or in its national, or even

"Bundist" variation. Even Jews in the metropolitan centers and the large cities, who had embraced the Russian language and culture, were, in large measure, "Russians outside and Jews in their tents" (to adapt the famous phrase of J.L. Gordon). The new Soviet regime was therefore forced to regard the Jews as a "nationality" with its own linguistic and cultural character, similar to all the other ethnic groups ("nationalities") that the Revolution had promised to liberate from the forced Russification practiced under Czarist rule. Thus, a special Soviet system of Jewish education, press, literature, and theater – almost all in Yiddish – came into being, an "official" Soviet-Jewish culture which sought to dissociate itself from the prerevolutionary sources of the Hebrew language, Jewish culture, and historical consciousness. In spite of its official character, this Soviet-sponsored culture served hundreds of thousands of Jews and their children in the 1920s and early 1930s as the means of preserving their Jewish identity, while in their hearts many of them remained true to Hebrew language and the genuine Jewish culture.

Side by side with these efforts to retain some Jewish identity, many Soviet Jews streamed to the centers of government and constructive action and also sought to enter professions from which they had been barred in the Czarist past. Hundreds of thousands of Jews converged upon Moscow, Leningrad, and other urban centers, and a great many were absorbed in the government administration, the party apparatus, and in the economic, legal, and military professions. Although most of them made no attempt to hide their Jewish origin, they and their families quickly adopted the Russian culture and language, and their Jewish identity soon became devoid of any cultural content. Nevertheless, even these "assimilationists" could not call themselves "Russians," "Ukrainians," etc., for these terms define a person's ethnic origin. The Soviet Union does not use the word "Soviet" as a general term denoting national belonging, (the way "American" is used in the United States). Thus there were two parallel and seemingly contradictory processes at work; one being the development of an official Yiddish culture, and the other a drive toward rapid acculturation, especially among the masses of Jews who had left the Jewish towns for the metropolitan centers. Most of the latter regarded their Jewish "nationality" as a marginal detail, which in the course of time would be superseded by the emerging "supra-national" socialist society. Those who continued to adhere to Yiddish were able to express themselves as Jews, though only within the confines of official Yiddish culture. There was, however, a third kind of Jew, who, by semi-legal or illegal means, gave his children a Jewish religious education (especially among the Ḥasidim in Western Russia and the non-Ashkenazi Jewish communities in the Caucasus and in the Asian republics). Some even made efforts to foster Hebrew language and literature. The number of these Jews, however, was pitifully small, and they had little contact with one another.

The territorialist experiment of *Birobidzhan was too small and of too short a duration to have any effect upon these developments, for the entire project came to an abrupt end when the Jewish leadership of the "Autonomous Region" was liquidated in the great purges. The purges of the late 1930s also brought about the almost-complete liquidation of the institutions and machinery of Soviet Yiddish culture and deprived the great mass of nonassimilated Jews even of this tenuous official framework of Jewish life. Thus a new period was ushered in before World War II, in which the Jewish population was practically deprived of the last shreds of a legitimate Jewish culture and forced to assimilate to the majority i.e., Russian culture. Jews were, however, denied the possibility of a complete social assimilation and disappearance into the majority population for they continued to be identified as Jews "by nationality," in accordance with the traditional ethnic structure of East European society. The reintroduction at the end of 1932 of the czarist-style "passports" system, under which every Soviet citizen was obliged to have an identity card on his person, meant that every Jew, both of whose parents were Jewish, was marked in his personal documents as a Jew "by nationality." This greatly facilitated the various subtle methods of anti-Jewish discrimination employed by the Soviet authorites since the days of *Stalin; but it also served as a significant factor for the retention of Jewish consciousness by the Jews themselves, notwithstanding their deracination from all roots of Jewish religion and culture. During and after World War II Soviet Jews had twice a traumatic experience which shattered their belief in genuine equality and security under the Soviet regime, thus renewing and reinforcing their feelings of Jewish solidarity and identity: first, the fact that large segments of the Soviet population, including young people, actively helped the German occupants to exterminate their Jewish fellow citizens and that even army men and anti-German partisans often displayed hostile anti-Jewish attitudes; and later, Stalin's undisguised antisemitic policy in 1948–53, during the "anti-cosmopolitan" campaign and the "*Doctors' Plot" But even in normal times, the paradox between forced deracination and cultural assimilation, on one hand and official identification of Jews "by nationality," on the other, created a peculiar "Marrano" atmosphere among much of Soviet Jewry. This applied in particular to many of the young people who, unlike their parents in their youth, had no faith in any "supra-national" future socialist society. The increasing rebellion of Soviet Jewish youth against the humiliating discrimination contained in this paradox drew more and more upon a positive Jewish consciousness. This in turn, was based upon a profound emotional attachment to the State of Israel, which, for them, represented the "normal" and proud Jewish people. The rebellion expressed itself in a widespread search for the sources of genuine Jewish culture, in attempts to study the Hebrew language, and to acquire knowledge of Jewish history. The mass gatherings of Jewish youth around the synagogues, especially on Simḥat Torah in Moscow and Leningrad, became, in the late Soviet period, a demonstration of their identification with the Jewish people and with Israel and of their protest against the forced assimilation which singled out the Soviet Jew alone among more than 100 Soviet nationalites, to be deprived of his dignity as the son of a historical nation.

[Binyamin Eliav]

With the collapse of the Soviet Union, and even before under Gorbachev's liberalization policies, a great exodus of Soviet Jews commenced, paralleled in the former Soviet Union itself by a revival of communal Jewish life. Thus, in the 1990s, around a million immigrants arrived in Israel from the former Soviet Union. Large numbers also arrived in the United States, Germany (90,000), and Canada. In 2004, just 395,000 "core" Jews (identifying themselves as Jews in official questionnaires) remained in the former Soviet Union, of whom 243,000 lived in the Russian Federation and 89,000 in Ukraine.

In Israel a process of Israelification has definitely set in, most markedly, as was to be expected, among the young and those born to immigrant parents. Ironically, then, the same processes that have historically worked toward assimilation in other host countries, drawing the second generation of Jews away from its ethnic roots, serve to fortify the sense of Jewishness when the assimilation occurs in a Jewish state. To the extent that Russian immigrants cling to something in their past, it is to *Russian* culture and the Russian language.

In the former Soviet Union, a full range of community services under the auspices of the Federation of Jewish Communities, including an extensive educational system, has also fortified Jewish identity. In Germany too, active Jewish community life has been revived by the newcomers.

[Fred Skolnik (2nd ed.)]

In the modern era, acculturation of Jews to the dominant society has occurred quite rapidly whenever educational and economic opportunities have been even partially opened. Any prolonged period of such openness has universally produced substantial numbers of almost completely assimilated Jews. The forces which have fostered Jewish identity throughout this period have been the power of the religious tradition, especially of Jewish education; the repeated reappearances of antisemitism, with its climax in the Nazi era; the assertion of a Jewish national identity, through Zionism and its realization in the establishment of Israel in the last generation; and a growing weariness among some younger people at remaining Jews, marginal even under the best of circumstances, to the majority society. The ultimate result of these forces is an increasing polarization, in which part of world Jewry is quietly disappearing into various forms of secular apostasy and another part is evermore consciously affirming its Jewish character in increasing association with Israel. Each of these elements is presently growing at the expense of a rather tepid middle group, which remains very Jewish, especially in times of crisis, but is slowly evaporating. This middle group is still the majority of world Jewry.

[Arthur Hertzberg]

BIBLIOGRAPHY: E. Muehlmann, in: *Proceedings of the 14th International Congress of Sociology*, 2 (1951), 828–74 (Ger.); J. Frankel and S.J. Zipperstein (eds.), *Assimilation and Community: the Jews in Nineteenth Century Europe* (1991); E.V. Stonequist, *The Marginal Man* (1937); G. Rosen, *Juden und Phoenizier* (1929); Th. Lessing, *Der juedische Selbsthass* (1930); Y. Kaufman, *Golah ve-Nekhar*, 1 (1929), 171–207; 2 (1930), 5–102; M. Davis, in: JJSO, 10 no. 2 (1968), 177–220. IN U.S.A.: M.H. Stern, *Americans of Jewish Descent* (1960); Ch. Reznikoff and U.Z. Engelman, *The Jews of Charleston* (1950); I. Graeber and S.H. Britt (eds.), *Jews in a Gentile World* (1942); M. Sklare (ed.), *The Jews: Social Patterns of an American Group* (1958); C.B. Sherman, *The Jew within American Society* (1960); N. Glazer and D.P. Moynihan, *Beyond the Melting Pot* (1963); S. Esh (ed.), *Am Yisrael be-Dorenu* (1964); E. Rosenthal, in: AJYB, 64 (1963), 3–53; O. Janowsky (ed.), *The American Jew: a Reappraisal* (1964); M. Sklare, *Jewish Identity on the Suburban Frontier* (1967). IN U.S.S.R.: S.W. Baron, *Russian Jew under Tsars and Soviets* (1964); Benami (A. Eliav), *Between Hammer and Sickle* (1967); E. Wiesel, *Jews of Silence* (1966). **ADD. BIBLIOGRAPHY:** M. Tolts, "The Post-Soviet Jewish Population in Russia and the World," in: *Jews in Russia and Eastern Europe*, no. 1 (2004), 37–63. See also the ongoing annual accounts of all the Jewish communities in the world in the *American Jewish Year Book*.

ASSOCIATION FOR JEWISH STUDIES (AJS), U.S. learned society and professional organization, founded in 1969, that promotes and maintains teaching, research, and related endeavors in Jewish Studies in institutions of higher education. In the first decade of the 21st century, the AJS had a membership base of approximately 1,500 scholars, teachers, and graduate students, sponsored a well-attended annual conference each December, and published a scholarly journal, *The Association for Jewish Studies Review*, and a newsletter, *AJS Perspectives*. It also served as a focal point for filling academic positions in Jewish Studies. A constituent society of the American Council of Learned Societies since 1984, the AJS had offices at the Center for Jewish History in New York City.

The AJS was established to address the academic needs of its members throughout North America at a time when growing universities with increasingly diverse student populations were open to new academic disciplines. Its growth was stimulated by increasing interest in academic Jewish Studies, inspired in part by the Holocaust, the creation of the State of Israel, and the maturing of the Jewish community in the post-World War II era.

Under the leadership of its first president, Leon Jick, the AJS addressed issues connected with teaching Jewish Studies in secular institutions rather than in seminaries. The organization debated how Jewish Studies should relate to the general university curriculum and whether Jewish Studies should be taught in a separate department or if each subject area within Jewish Studies should be integrated within its academic discipline. Questions were also raised about whether the Jewish Studies professor should function solely as an academic scholar and teacher, or also serve as an adviser and mentor to the Jewish student body. The AJS attempted to delineate academic qualifications for positions in Jewish Studies and to develop guidelines for how and where professors of Jewish Studies might be trained. Many of these issues continue to be discussed almost four decades later.

The governance of the AJS was based on that of other American learned societies, with a president and executive committee, a board of directors, and an executive secretary. The annual conferences were organized to allow for intense scholarly discourse and personal communication. The AJS inaugurated a *Newsletter*, first edited by A.J. Band, designed to incorporate AJS business, abstracts of lectures, and reviews of scholarly books in the field. The Association also offered its services as a professional address for bringing together new positions and potential candidates for them. In the 1970s, Baruch Levine, the second president, secured a grant from the National Endowment for the Humanities to sponsor a series of regional conferences to bring accomplished scholars in a variety of areas to universities throughout the land. These events yielded both a host of lecture abstracts published in the *AJS Newsletter* and a series of five volumes of conference proceedings edited by S.D. Goitein (*Religion in a Religious Age*, 1974), J. Katz (*The Role of Religion in Modern Jewish History*, 1974), H. Paper (*Jewish Languages: Themes and Variation*, 1978), F. Talmage (*Studies in Jewish Folklore*, 1980), and J. Dan and F. Talmage (*Studies in Jewish Mysticism*, 1982).

These various undertakings, primarily performed by successive presidents with the crucial assistance of Charles Berlin, the third executive secretary (1973–95), propelled the AJS to the central position it obtained in the academic world. In the late 1990s, the title of executive secretary was changed to executive director, and the position was successively filled by Aaron Katchen (1995–2003) and Rona Sheramy (2003–).

Between 1973 and 1984, the *AJS Newsletter* (from 2000, *AJS Perspectives*) published conference abstracts, précis of selected papers from the annual conferences, and serious reviews of scholarly books in Jewish Studies. In 1976, publication of a scholarly journal, *The AJS* Review, was inaugurated, edited first by Frank Talmage (1976–83). An AJS website was established in the early 21st century.

The annual conferences developed from modest beginnings in 1969 and continued to expand in attendance and content throughout the next three and a half decades. By the mid-1980s a separate Conference Program was published; in 2004, the conference met for two and a half days, and offered more than 120 different panels, sessions, and other events of scholarly interest. The venue of the early conferences was not fixed; from the mid-1970s to the mid-1990s it convened at the Copley Plaza Hotel, Boston, before moving to other larger Boston locations. Beginning in 1999, the AJS began scheduling the annual conference in other cities, as well, including Washington, D.C., Chicago, Los Angeles, and San Diego.

Special interests sessions focusing on specific aspects of Jewish Studies were introduced by 1979. The most enduring of these has been the Women's Caucus, founded independently of AJS in 1986. The Caucus, which is now affiliated with AJS and open to all AJS members, sponsors a breakfast meeting at each year's conference, co-sponsors an academic session at each conference, and has prepared a syllabus collection and directories of its members to further academic and professional networking. While the first conference in 1969 was attended by only one female scholar, by the 1990s over one-third of participants were women.

AJS Review editors have been the following:

Frank Talmage, 1976–1983, I–VIII
Robert Chazan, 1984–1989, IX–XIV
Norman Stillman, 1990–1999, XV–XXIV
Jay M. Harris, 2000–2004, XXV–XXVIII, 1
Hillel Kieval and Martin Jaffee, 2004– , XXVIII, 2–

AJS Executive Secretaries/Directors have been the following:

Bernard Reisman, 1970–1971
Michael Fishbane, 1972
Charles Berlin, 1973–1995
Aaron Katchen, 1995–2004
Rona Sheremy, 2004–

AJS Presidents have been the following:

Leon Jick, 1969–1971
Baruch Levine, 1972
Arnold J. Band, 1973–1975
Marvin Fox, 1976–1978
Michael A. Meyer, 1979–1980
Jane Gerber, 1981–1983
Nahum Sarna, 1984–1985
Ruth R. Wisse, 1986–1988
Robert Chazan, 1989–1991
Herbert Paper, 1992–1994
Robert Seltzer, 1995–1997
David Berger, 1998–2000
Lawrence Schiffman, 2001–2003
Judith R. Baskin, 2004–

BIBLIOGRAPHY: A.J. Band. "Jewish Studies in American Liberal Arts Colleges and Universities," in: *American Jewish Yearbook*, 67 (1966); L. Jick. *The Teaching of Judaica in American Universities* (1970); J. Neusner. *The Academic Study of Judaism*, 2 vols. (1975; 1977). idem, *The New Humanities and Academic Disciplines. The Case of Jewish Studies* (1984); P. Ritterband, Paul and H.S. Wechsler. *Jewish Learning in American Universities* (1994).

[Arnold J. Band (2nd ed.)]

ASSOCIATION OF HOLOCAUST ORGANIZATIONS (**AHO**), organization established in 1985 to serve as an international network of organizations and individuals for the advancement of Holocaust programming, awareness, education, and research. Among its functions and services are annual conferences held every June, a winter seminar at the United States Holocaust Memorial Museum held every January, a listserv for members, a guide to curriculum evaluation, and a website (www.ahoinfo.org). There are also regional branches which meet independently. The AHO publishes an annual directory of its membership which is intended to facilitate the aims of the organization. It is distributed, free of charge, to all organizations and individuals who can make use of the information which it contains. The 1988 AHO Directory listed 48 members; the 2005 AHO Directory lists 231 full and affiliate members, representing a new type of organization, Holocaust museums, education, documentation and commemoration centers that have come into being from the late 1970s onward in the United States and increasingly throughout the world.

The AHO is governed by a nine-member board of directors, which is elected by and from the membership at its annual business meeting. The term of office is two years. The AHO is run on a volunteer basis. Membership dues cover the expenses of the organization.

[William Shulman (2nd ed.)]

ASSUMPÇÃO, DIOGO DA (1579–1603), Marrano martyr. Assumpção was born at Viana in Portugal. Only partly Jewish by descent, he was brought up as a devout Christian and became a Franciscan friar. His attention was directed to Judaism because of the ferocity with which it was persecuted, and in due course he made no secret of the fact that he accepted its tenets. Arrested by the Inquisition while attempting to escape abroad, he at first professed penitence, but later proudly confessed himself an adherent of the Law of Moses, "in which he lived and hoped to die, and to which he looked for salvation." Even in prison, he attempted to observe the Sabbath and dietary laws as he understood them, refused to take an oath on the Gospels, and argued vigorously against the theologians brought to convince him of his error. His execution by burning alive at the auto-da-fé held at Lisbon on Aug. 3, 1603, created a profound impression. He was considered one of the exemplary martyrs of the Inquisition by the communities abroad, and a number of elegies were composed in his honor. In Portugal, some devout Marranos formed a religious association in his memory, called the Brotherhood of S. Diogo in order to divert suspicion. His martyrdom inspired in particular the Marrano group in the University of Coimbra led by Antonio *Homem.

BIBLIOGRAPHY: Roth, Marranos, 149–51; Barnett, in: JQR, 15 (1924/25), 213–19; Archives of Torre do Tombo, Lisbon, *Inquisicão de Lisboa*, proc. no. 104 (in the course of publication).

[Cecil Roth]

ASSUR (Heb. אַשּׁוּר, Ashur), city situated on the west bank of the Tigris about two-thirds of the way between the confluence of the Great and Little Zab rivers; in the province of Mosul in northern Iraq. The ancient ruins are known as Qalʿat Sharqāt, which means "the Fortress of the Sharqātis." The Sharqātis are a local Arab tribe which, thanks to the experience acquired at this site, subsequently provided skilled labor for other excavations in the region. Reports about this imposing site overlooking the Tigris were brought back to the West by travelers early in the 19th century. Excavations were first undertaken by several British expeditions between 1847 and 1880 under the direction of A.H. Layard and H. Rassam, whose publications helped to arouse European interest in Assyriology. From 1903 to 1914 the site was systematically excavated by W.H. Andrae for the Deutsche Orientgesellschaft. That organization's reports provided a running account of the finds and furnished the definitive report on the site (W.H. Andrae, *Anu-Adad-Temple in Assur*, 1909). The statement in Genesis 2:14 that the river Tigris flows "east of Assur" is assumed by some to mean the city Assur rather than the country Assyria, since the Tigris actually passes west of the Assyrian cities named in Genesis 10:11–12. But the phrase may mean, rather, "in the eastern part of Assyria," since Assyria was often regarded as extending westward practically, or even actually, to the Euphrates (cf. Isa. 7:20; 8:7; 11:15–16).

BIBLIOGRAPHY: B. Mazar, in: EM, 1 (1965), 754–60 (incl. bibl.).

ASS WORSHIP. Numerous Greek and Latin writers allude to a widespread belief that Jews, and subsequently Christians, observed some form of ass worship. The earliest mention of this cult is by Mnaseas of Patras (third–second centuries B.C.E.) who, according to *Apion (Jos., Apion, 2:112ff.), refers to the "golden head of an ass" in the Temple sanctuary. Apion maintains that this ass's head was worshiped by the Jews, the fact coming to light "on the occasion of the spoliation of the Temple by Antiochus Epiphanes, when the head, made of gold and worth a high price, was discovered" (*ibid.*, 80). This account is similar to that of Posidonius of Apamea (c. 135–51 B.C.E.), who claims that Antiochus Epiphanes found in the Temple the statue of a bearded man, apparently Moses, sitting upon an ass and holding a book. Another Greek writer, Damocritus (first century B.C.E.–C.E.; see Suidas, *Lexicon*, ed. by A. Adler, 2 (1931), 5, no. 49, s.v. Δαμόκριτος), in his book "About the Jews" charges the Jews with sacrificing a human being to the head of a golden ass once every seven years. Suidas himself shortens the interval to three years (*ibid.*, 641, s.v. Ἰούδας καὶ Ἰουδαῖος). Plutarch (*Quaestiones convivales*, 4:5) also refers to the Jews' worship of the ass, giving it as a reason for their abstention from the flesh of the hare, whose flesh is similar to that of the ass. Tacitus (*Historiae*, 5:3ff.) tells of a herd of wild asses which led Moses and the Jews to a spring when they were sorely in need of water, the Jews, in consequence, elevating the ass to an object of worship (cf. Gen. 36:24).

The Christians apparently inherited the ass-cult accusation from the Jews. According to Tertullian (*Apologeticus* 16; *Ad Nationes* 1:2) the close relationship between Judaism and Christianity causes some people to believe that "an ass's head is our God." A presumably satiric graffito found in Rome in 1856 depicts a man with the head of an ass nailed to a cross. Christian Gnostic sects may indeed have observed some form of ass worship. In the Gnostic book Γέννα Μαρίας (Epiphanius of Salamis, *Adversus Haereses*, 26:10, 12) the spirit Sabaot is said to have had the form of an ass, and the prophet *Zechariah saw a man in similar form in the Temple of Jerusalem.

None of the above, however, solves the basic question of the origin of Jewish ass-worship legends. It has been pointed out that the Jewish religion was often identified with the Dionysus-Bacchus cult (see Frankel, in MGWJ, 9 (1860), 125ff.) which held the ass sacred, both Bacchus and his companion Silenus constantly riding upon an ass. Hence, Greek and Roman writers who were unfamiliar with Jewish worship may have associated the Jews with some form of ass worship. Another solution would associate the Jews with the Egyptian cult of Typhon-Seth, in which the ass played an important part (Tcherikover, *Hellenistic Civilization and the Jews* (1959), 365; Finkelstein, in HTR, 35 (1942), 301). It is interesting to note that the Septuagint translates *ḥamor* usually as ὄνος, but 12 times there is the uncommon ὑποζύγιον. It has been suggested that when the Scriptures deal with some aspect of religious belief, the translators of the Septuagint, in their awareness of the ass-worship accusations, attempted to eliminate any association with ὄνος (e.g., Zech. 9:9).

BIBLIOGRAPHY: J. Feliks, *Animal World of the Bible* (1962), 27; Y. Aharoni, *Torat ha-Ḥai* (1923), 99–100; S. Feigan, in: *Studies… M. Schorr* (1944), 227–40.

[Isaiah Gafni]

ASTI, city in Piedmont, N.W. Italy. Jews are mentioned in Asti in a document of 812, but its authenticity is doubtful. In the 14th century a number of Jews expelled from France found refuge in Asti, then an important commercial center, and neighboring towns. They retained the French rite, specifically for the New Year and the Day of Atonement: the "Apam" (properly "Afam") rite (מנהג אפם), so called after the Hebrew initials of the three towns Asti, Fossano, and Moncalvo (see *Liturgy). Now long relinquished, the prayers have been preserved in many manuscripts. There was a *blood libel accusation in 1553. The Regie Costituzioni of 1723 and 1729 established separate quarters for the Jews in all the royal domains. The ghetto became compulsory in 1730. Napoleon's decrees of December 1798 and February 1799 abolished the ghetto. It is difficult to establish the number of the Jews in Asti before the census ordered by King Carlo Emanuele III in 1761; in that year there were 38 families, numbering 196 Jews. In 1774 the number of Jews rose to 400. There were anti-Jewish riots in Asti in 1803. The *Artom family derived from here. During the Nazi persecution 51 members of the community were killed. In 1970 about 20 Jews lived in Asti. At the turn of the 20th century Asti no longer had a functioning Jewish community and was under the jurisdiction of the community of Turin, as were all the other nonfunctioning communities of Piedmont (Alessandria, Carmagnola, Cherasco, Cuneo, Mondovì, Saluzzo, and Ivrea).

BIBLIOGRAPHY: S. Foà, in: RMI, 27–28 (1961–62), passim; Goldschmidt, in: KS, 30 (1954/55), 118–36, 264–76; D. Disegni, in: *Scritti… S. Mayer* (1956), 78–81. **ADD. BIBLIOGRAPHY:** P. De Benedetti, "Gli ebrei di Asti e il loro rito," in: *Il Platano*, 4 (1977), 17–28; idem, "Ancora sugli ebrei di Asti," in: *Il Platano*, 5 (1979), 43–46; L. Voghera Luzzatto, "Ebrei ad Asti," in: *Il Torchio* (1979–80), 6–9; idem, "Emancipazione ebraica ad Asti," in: *Il Platano*, 2 (1980), 92–102; R. Segre and M.L. Giribaldi Sardi, *Il Ghetto, la Sinagoga. Viaggio attraverso la cultura ebraica di Asti* (1992); M.L. Giribaldi Sardi, *Scuola e vita nella comunità ebraica di Asti (1800–1930)* (1993); E. Rossi Artom, *Gli Artom – Storia di una famiglia della Comunità ebraica di Asti attraverso le sue generazioni (XVI–XX secolo)* (1997); M.L. Giribaldi Sardi, *Asti. Guida alla sinagoga, al museo e al cimitero ebraico* (1999).

[Attilio Milano / Manuela Consonni (2nd ed.)]

ASTORGA, city in the province of Leon, N.W. Spain. Jews were living in the fortified section of Astorga as early as the 11th century. Later they inhabited two quarters in the city. A street called the Garden (Paseo) of the Synagogue formerly ran beside the old city wall. Many Jews in Astorga were forcibly converted to Christianity in 1230–31. Although there is no record of the fate of the Jews of Astorga during the 1391 massacres, they suffered in the persecutions of 1412. At the synod held in *Valladolid in 1432, the Astorga community claimed privileges exempting them from payment of crown taxes. The community existed until the expulsion of the Jews from Spain in 1492.

BIBLIOGRAPHY: Baer, Spain, 2 (1966), index; Baer, Urkunden, 2 (1936), index; M. Rodríguez Díez, *Historia de Astorga* (1909); F. Cantera, *Sinagogas Españolas* (1955), 166–7; Suárez Fernández, Documentos, index.

ASTRAKHAN, Volga port, capital of Astrakhan district, Russia. The "Jewish Statute" of 1804 (see *Russia) included the province (*gubernia*) of Astrakhan in the *Pale of Settlement. However, in 1825 Jewish settlement in this government was prohibited. The "Jewish Statute" of 1835 excluded the province of Astrakhan from the Pale and the 49 Jews were ordered to leave. Shortly afterward a community was again established by Jewish soldiers stationed in the town. In 1850 Jewish merchants from the Caucasus obtained permission to visit Astrakhan twice yearly for a total of not longer than six months in the year. In the second half of the 19th century, Jews in categories with the right of domicile outside the Pale moved there. An Ashkenazi synagogue was established in 1866, and in 1879 the Oriental Jews, who used to visit Astrakhan on business, also founded a synagogue. In 1897 there were 2,164 Jews living in Astrakhan; in 1926, 5,904 (3.4% of the total population); and in 1939, 4,077 (1.61%). In 1970 there were 3,462 Jews in Astrakhan with a synagogue and a cemetery. The synagogue was attacked in 1964 and there were reports of Jews having been murdered. Hooligans were arrested but were not brought to trial. Jewish community life revived in the 1990s. The restored synagogue was reopened in 2003, and Shlomo Zalman Goldenberg became the first rabbi to serve the city in 70 years. The number of Jews was estimated at 3,000 in 2002.

[Eliyahu Feldman]

ASTROLOGY, the study of the supposed influence of the stars on human events and the predictions based on this study.

Bible and Apocrypha

There is no explicit mention of astrology in the Bible, but two biblical passages dealing with the diviner (*menaḥesh*) and soothsayer (*me'onen*; Lev. 19:26; Deut. 18:10) were understood by the rabbis as bearing relation to astrology (Sanh. 65b–66a; cf. Maim. Yad, Avodah Zarah 11:8, 9). The prophets were aware of the practices of "star-gazers" (*ḥoverei ha-shamayim*) among the Babylonians and other peoples but they scoffed at them

(Isa. 47:13; Jer. 10:2). In the book of Daniel the Babylonian astrologers are called *kasdim* (Chaldeans), and in Aramaic *kasda'ei* (2:2, 4, 5, 10; 4:14; 5:7, 11). *The Sibylline Oracles* (219–231) praise the Jewish people for refraining from astrology, which is a delusion. The Book of Jubilees (12:16–18) depicts the patriarch Abraham as overcoming the beliefs of the astrologers. The first Book of Enoch (8:3) includes astrology among the sins spread among mortals by the primeval giants (*nefilim*). Josephus, however, writes that astrology was common among the Jews in his days and that Jewish misinterpretation of celestial signs was partially responsible for the outbreak of the revolt against the Romans and its continuation for four years (Jos., Wars, 6:288ff.).

Talmud and the Midrash

In the Babylonian Talmud astrologers are known as *kaldiyyim* (Pes. 113b), Aramaic *kalda'ei* (Shab. 119a, 156b; Yev. 21b) – a term used by the Greeks, Romans, and Syrians. *Iẓtagninin* ("astrologers") and *iẓtagninut* ("astrology") were also common terms. In the Jerusalem Talmud and in Palestinian Midrashim *astrologos* and *astrologiyya* are the most frequent terms. The majority of the talmudic sages believed in the decisive role played by celestial bodies in determining human affairs in the sublunar world. On the one hand the patriarch Abraham and his descendants are spoken of as having been elevated beyond subjection to the stars (Gen. R. 44:12; Yal., Jer. 285), but on the other hand, the blessing bestowed on him in Genesis 24:1 is interpreted as the gift of astrology (Tosef., Kid. 5:17). Astrological consultation is one of the methods suggested by Jethro to Moses for governing the Children of Israel (Mekh., Amalek 2). Several instances are cited of astrologers whose predictions of future events came true (e.g., Shab. 119a). Gentile rulers were considered to have been especially well versed in astrology or to have consulted astrological experts; but knowledge of astrology was also attributed to King Solomon (Eccl. R. 7:23 no. 1). Nevertheless, the rabbis of the Talmud were skeptical of the astrologers' ability to interpret the stars correctly; they conceded the possibility that the astrologers might be able to predict the future by consulting the stars, but claimed that they err in understanding the contents of their forecasts. On the basis of the phrase in Isaiah 8:19, "the familiar spirits that chirp and mutter" (*ha-meẓafẓefim ve-ha-mahgim*), they developed the exegesis: "They gaze (*ẓofin*) and know not at what they gaze, they ponder (*mehaggin*) and know not what they ponder" (Sot. 12b). In several places in the Talmud it is stated that every man has a celestial body (*mazzal*), i.e., a particular star which is his patron from conception and birth (Shab. 53b; BK 2b) and which perceives things unknown to the man himself (Meg. 3a; Sanh. 94a). Two people born under the same star have a bodily and spiritual kinship (Ned. 39b; BM 30b). Not only human beings are influenced by the stars; but "there is not a blade of grass that has not its star in the heavens to strike it and say to it: grow!" Stars in certain constellations (the Pleiades, Orion, Ursa Major) were connected with the growth and ripening of fruits (Gen. R. 10:6).

As among most ancient peoples, eclipses were thought to be an evil portent, particularly for Jews, "because they are accustomed to calamities." According to another opinion, a solar eclipse was a bad omen for the Gentiles, a lunar eclipse for the Jews, since the Jews based their calendar on the moon, while the Gentiles based theirs on the sun (Suk. 29a).

Some held that there was a direct connection between the signs of the days of the week and the characters of those born on those days: a person born on Sunday would have one perfect attribute, either good or bad; a person born on Monday would be irascible, and so forth. According to another opinion, "it is not the sign of the day, but the sign of the hour, that determines." Thus, for example, he who was born under the rule of Venus would be rich and adulterous; he who was born under Saturn (Heb. *Shabbetai*) would have his plans annulled (*maḥshevotav yishbotu*); he who was born under Jupiter (Heb. *Ẓedek*) would be a righteous observer (*ẓidkan*) of the commandments (Shab. 156a).

A number of important *tanna'im* and *amora'im*, such as R. Akiva, R. Johanan, Mar Samuel, Rav Naḥman b. Isaac, were of the opinion that the power of the stars over ordinary mortals did not extend to the People of Israel. "R. Johanan said: there is no star (*mazzal*) for Israel" (Shab. 156a; cf. the statement by R. Samuel, 156b; also, Suk. 29a). R. Ḥanina b. Ḥama held the opposite opinion: "The stars make one wise, the stars make one rich, and there are stars for Israel" (*ibid.*, 156a). The rabbis were divided as to whether a fully virtuous person could transform and abrogate the decrees of the astral configurations for himself. Mar Samuel, who was an astrologer as well as an astronomer, formulated several rules of health and agriculture on the basis of astrological principles (Shab. 129b; Er. 56a); it was his opinion that "righteousness delivers from death" (Prov. 10:2) as it is ordained by the stars (Shab. 129b). Such deliverances were said to have been granted to R. Akiva's daughter and to R. Naḥman b. Isaac and his mother. The contrary position was upheld by Rava: "Life, children, and sustenance – these things depend not on merit, but on the stars" (MK 28a); by way of illustration he cited the histories of several great men of learning and faith. Because of the warnings of the "Chaldeans," R. Joseph refused appointment as head of a yeshivah (Ber. 64a); but R. Yose of Huẓal decreed that "one must not consult the Chaldeans" (Pes. 113b); cf. Rashi and Samuel b. Meir *ad loc.*

In several places in the Talmud (MK 27a; Ned. 56a; Sanh. 20a), one of the customs mentioned is clearly a survival of an ancient astrological belief: an unslept-in bed, called "the bed of Gad" (*arsa de-gadda*), would be kept in the house as a good luck charm. The astrological character of this custom was forgotten and the noun *gad*, originally the name of a star, came to mean simply "luck," as was eventually the case with the term *mazzal* ("star of luck") itself.

Dark Ages

During the eighth to the tenth centuries several famous Jewish astrologers lived in Islamic lands and wrote books on astronomy and astrology. First among these both in chronology and importance was Māshāʾallāh; of his many astrological treatises only two in Hebrew translation from the Arabic remain: *Sefer She'elot* ("Book of Queries") and *Sefer be-Kadrut ha-Levanah ve-ha-Shemesh* ("Book on the Lunar and Solar Eclipse"). Both were found among the astrological manuscripts of Ibn Ezra, and accordingly, it has been conjectured that Ibn Ezra himself was their translator. Second to Māshāʾallāh in time and rank was Sahl ibn Bishr, who wrote many books on astrology, at least one of which was translated into Hebrew under the title *Kelalim* ("Principles"). Toward the end of the Middle Ages the Hebrew translations of both these astrologers were translated into Latin and printed. Ibn Ezra refers several times to the Persian Jewish astrologer Andruzgar b. Zadi Faruk (ninth century). The Jewish astrologer Abu Dāʾūd, who lived in Baghdad at the beginning of the tenth century, composed the *Sefer Nevu'ot* ("Book of Prophecies") which also appeared in Arabic. Several astrological treatises in Arabic composed in the ninth and 11th centuries, some anonymous, were translated into Hebrew, and some of them, apparently by Jewish translators, into Spanish. Hebrew translations of Arabic version of the astrological works of Ptolemy, the *Tetrabiblos* and *Centiloquium*, have also been preserved.

Middle Ages

Among medieval Jewish scholars and philosophers who were versed in astrology and considered it to be a true science were *Saadiah Gaon, whose Arabic commentary on the *Sefer Yeẓirah* contains astrological material; Shabbetai *Donnolo, also the author of a commentary (*Ḥakhmoni* or *Taḥkemoni*) on the *Sefer Yeẓirah* possessing special importance for the histories of astronomy and astrology, and of a commentary on the *Baraita di-Shemu'el*, a type of Midrash on astronomy, astrology, and the science of intercalation; Samuel b. Joseph ha-Nagid; Solomon ibn *Gabirol, whose *Keter Malkhut* includes a detailed account of the influence of each of the seven planets on the events of the sublunar world, and who, according to Ibn Ezra (end of his commentary on Daniel), "wished to show that the end of days was dependent on a 'conjunction' of the two superior stars"; and Abraham *Ibn Daud, whose book *Emunah Ramah* argues that the positions of the stars were set at Creation and predictions can be made on the basis of them.

ABRAHAM BAR HIYYA. Abraham b. Ḥiyya and Abraham *Ibn Ezra took a positive position toward astrology. The former even based decisions in practical affairs on astrological considerations. He also undertook to prove from the Talmud that the rabbis of that time in their use of astrology agreed in principle with the gentile sages about the role played by the stars, differing only in that "they say that the power of the stars and the constellations is not a perfect power ... all being at the beck and call of God, who can at will set aside their rule and abrogate their decrees whenever He desires." The reason for prohibiting consultations with "Chaldeans" was that in talmudic times certain astrological techniques were compromised by idol worship. In his *Megillat ha-Megalleh* Abraham b. Ḥiyya predicted the date of the coming of the Messiah as 1358.

ABRAHAM IBN EZRA. Abraham ibn Ezra's reputation as a great student of astrology spread beyond Jewish circles. He believed that all beings in the sublunar world were influenced by the configurations of the stars and the zodiac, and that most men were entirely enslaved by the powers of the seven planets (Commentary on Ex. 23:28). Nonetheless, it is within the power of man to free himself of the dictates of the stars by perfecting himself spiritually. In his commentary on Deuteronomy 4:19 Ibn Ezra writes: "It is known from experience that every nation has its own star and constellation and similarly there is a constellation for every city; but God bestowed His greater favor on Israel by rendering them starless and Himself their adviser." In his commentaries on the Bible Ibn Ezra discusses astrological matters at length. To reconcile predestination by the stars and divine providence, he assigns an astrological significance to the two biblical names for God: *Elohim* refers to the Creator in His "natural" manifestations, revealed in conjunction with patterns of the stars, while the Tetragrammaton refers to the Creator as He is manifested miraculously, i.e., as "the pattern smasher." Ibn Ezra interpreted the word *mishpat* ("law") in the phrase *ḥoshen ha-mishpat* ("the breastplate of the Law" – Ex. 28:30) as an allusion to astrology (*mishpetei ha-kokhavim*), that is, to the prediction of events by means of contemplating the astral configurations. This accords with his opinion that the *Urim and Thummim of the high priest were an astrological instrument akin to the *astrolabe, and that by consulting them it was possible to read the future. Ibn Ezra composed a large number of astrological books; some of these were printed, but the majority are in manuscript. Most of these writings were translated into Latin at the close of the 13th century and were printed in 1507; several were also published in a French translation.

JUDAH HALEVI. Judah Halevi never took a definite stand concerning the value and reliability of astrology. He admitted (*Kuzari* 4:9) that the celestial bodies had an influence over terrestrial affairs, that terrestrial (sublunar) life was due to the changing constellations, and that all astrological sayings attributed to the rabbis of old were based on genuine traditions. At the same time, however, he rejected the astrologers' claim that it was possible to determine the exact influence of the stars on sublunar beings. Halevi complained that the Jewish people continued to be seduced by astrological charlatanry despite the biblical injunction to the contrary (*ibid.*, 4:23).

HASDAI CRESCAS AND JOSEPH ALBO. Ḥasdai *Crescas' attitude toward astrology was also skeptical. Inquiring whether the movements of celestial bodies really exercised "leadership and governance over the events of human life," he came to the conclusion that while there is no clear evidence rebutting the assumptions of the astrologers, in view of human free will and divine providence it is nevertheless impossible to attribute an absolutely decisive character to "the dictates of the configurations" (*Or Adonai* 4:4). Crescas' pupil Joseph *Albo followed his approach. He launched a series of attacks against the beliefs of the astrologers based not only on dogmatic considerations but on empirical events as well: many times thousands of people had perished by plague, in war, or had been drowned at sea, yet it was unimaginable that the horoscope of each should have been responsible for his untimely death in the general disaster. Accordingly, Albo fell back upon the opinion of Abraham ibn Ezra that there are several factors capable of annulling the destinies of private individuals (*Sefer Ikkarim* 4:4).

MAIMONIDES. Among the Jewish philosophers of the Middle Ages *Maimonides alone rejected astrology completely, referring to the astrologers' beliefs as vain superstitions unworthy to be called a science. Upon being asked by the rabbis of southern France whether it was possible to combine the theories of astrology with the principles of Judaism, Maimonides replied: "… This science, which is called the decree of the stars … is no science at all, but mere foolery … and it behooves us never to engage in it.… Those who composed treatises upon it… were the Chasdeans, the Chaldeans, the Canaanites, and the Egyptians … however, the wise men of Greece … scorned, mocked, and condemned these four nations… and compiled proofs to reject their notions completely… . I well know that you may seek and find in the Talmud and the Midrashim isolated sayings implying that the stars at the time of a man's birth will have a certain effect upon him… but this need not perplex you," inasmuch as "he is unworthy of pursuing knowledge … who would forsake it for the isolated saying of a rabbi of old who may perhaps have been mistaken…." Maimonides goes so far as to criticize the Jews of antiquity severely for their superstitious faith in astrology, as a result of which they brought upon themselves the destruction of the Temple and exile (Maimonides' epistle to *Jonathan b. David ha-Kohen of Lunel). He also ruled: "Who is a *me'onen* ["soothsayer"]? He who allots dates in the manner of the astrologers, who say … such-and-such a day … is good for performing such-and-such a task, such-and-such a year or month is bad for such-and-such… and even though he does nothing but tell lies, the foolish believe that his words are the truths of the wise. Thus, whosoever heeds the astrologers when he chooses to do something or go somewhere at a certain time, such a one should be punished by stripes, for it is written 'Ye shall not soothsay'" (Yad, Avodah Zarah 11:8–9). Similarly, in his commentary on the Mishnah he speaks of "the falsifying astrologers, who are wise and enlightened in their own eyes" (Sanh. 10 beginning).

Later Thinkers

Despite Maimonides' great prestige, his criticism of astrology had practically no influence on subsequent Jewish writers. With the exception of Joseph b. Judah ibn *Aknin and his enthusiastic admirer R. *Jedaiah ha-Penini (Bedersi), none of the Jewish philosophers of the succeeding generations opposed or deprecated astrology. Even the rationalistic *Levi b. Gershom maintained that the activities and events of a man's life were predestined by the positions and movements of celestial bodies. The astrologers fail, he asserted, first of all because of insufficient knowledge about the movements of the stars and the effects of their changed positions on sublunar beings, and secondly, because of the intervention of intellect and free will, "for the intellect and the will are empowered to carry us beyond the limitations imposed by the celestial bodies" (*Milḥamot Adonai* 2:2). Shem-Tov ibn *Falaquera also considered astrology a true science and made use of it. Many of the great rabbis, commentators, preachers, and ethical teachers dealt with astrology and were favorably disposed toward it; *Abraham b. David of Posquières, in his *Hassagot*, a commentary on Maimonides' *Mishneh Torah*; *Naḥmanides (Commentary on Gen. 1:16; Lev. 23:24, and passim) and his pupil Solomon b. Abraham *Adret (Responsa, no. 652); *Baḥya b. Asher (Commentary on Ex. 11:4; and passim); Isaac *Aboab (*Menorat ha-Ma'or*, 143; passim); Simeon b. Ẓemaḥ *Duran (*Magen Avot*, 72bff., and *Tashbeẓ*, no. 513); Isaac *Abrabanel, who cited many proofs "from the science of astronomy in regard to the celestial conjunctions" for his opinion that the redemption of Israel would begin in 1503 and come to completion in 1531 (*Ma'yenei ha-Yeshu'ah*, 12:2); Isaac *Arama (*Akedat Yiẓḥak*, 34, 56), though he disapproved of eschatological reckonings based on astrology; Moses b. Ḥayyim *Alshekh; *Judah Loew b. Bezalel (Maharal) of Prague, who is reputed to have practiced astrology in the company of his friend Tycho Brahe; David *Gans; Leone of *Modena; Joseph Solomon *Delmedigo of Candia, Jonathan *Eybeschuetz; and *Elijah, *Gaon* of Vilna (Commentary on *Sefer Yeẓirah*). A definitely negative attitude toward astrology was assumed by Azariah dei *Rossi (*Me'or Einayim*, 42, 43).

KABBALISTIC LITERATURE. The Sefer Yeẓirah contains several astrological passages concerning such topics as the relationship of the seven Hebrew consonants that take a *dagesh* to the seven planets and the seven days of the week, and the relationship of the 12 simple consonants to the 12 houses of the zodiac and the 12 months. In the *Sefer Razi'el ha-Malakh* ("Book of the Angel Raziel") the principle basis for a systematic astrology is found, for example: "How can the seers know what a man's life will be as soon as he is born? The ruling planet ascending in the East [at the hour of his birth] is his life's house. If the house of Saturn is in ascension, he will live to be 57, if it is the house of Jupiter, he will live 79 years, and so forth… Saturn presides over wealth, poverty, and the like… Jupiter presides over life, well-being, favorable circumstances, happiness, riches, honor, greatness, and royalty; Mars presides over blood, the sword, and the like… Venus presides over comeliness, grace, appetite… and the like."

The Zohar takes astrology for granted and in several places employs imagery and terminology that are clearly astrological (e.g., 3, *Ki Teẓe*, 281b. *Raya Meheimna*). It is stated explicitly: "All the stars and constellations in the heavens were appointed to be rulers and commandants over the world… there is not a single blade of grass in the entire world over which a star or a planet does not preside, and over that star one [angel] is appointed who serves in the presence of the Holy One Blessed Be He, each according to his merit" (2:171d; see *Mishnat ha-Zohar*, Tishbi-Lachower trans. vol. 1, 1957, 486). Astrological reasons for the commandments (*mitzvot*) are occasionally also given 3:251a–b, *Raya Meheimna*). On the whole, however, the Zohar's kabbalistic system deprives astrology and astrological beliefs of most of their relevance and importance. In Part 3 (*Pinḥas*, 216b, *Raya Meheimna*) it is stated that prior to the giving of the Torah all earthly creatures were dependent on the stars; after the revelation at Sinai, however, God exempted those children of Israel who studied and observed His Law from the rule of the stars, whereas the ignorant and the skeptical "were not absolved from the stars' jurisdictions." In the *Tikkunei Zohar* and other kabbalistic works the seven planets were linked with the seven days of the week and the seven nether spheres; the 12 houses of the zodiac were linked with the 12 months of the year, the 12 tribes of Israel, and the 12 permutations of the Tetragrammaton. According to the *Sefer ha-Peli'ah*, the higher powers descend on the seven planets from the divine name of 42 letters, each planet receiving the influx appropriate to it from six of the letters of that name.

Jewish Astrologers at the Courts of Christian Kings and Popes

Several Jewish astronomers and astrologers served in various royal capitals of Southern and Western Europe as court astrologers. Among them were Judah b. Moses ha-Kohen at the court of Alfonso x of Castile (1252–84); Jacob Alcorsono and Crescas de Vivers at the courts of Pedro iv (1336–87) and John i (1387–89) of Aragon; and Abraham *Zacuto (1450–1510), the author of the *Sefer Yuḥasin*, at the court of Manuel i of Portugal from 1494 until the expulsion of the Jews from Portugal in 1497. Jacob b. Emanuel Provinciale (Bonet de Lattes) served as physician and court astrologer to popes Alexander vi and Leo x. In his *Prognosticum*, dedicated to cardinals Valentiniani and Borgia, he expressed the opinion, based on the prophecies of Daniel and on a conjunction of Jupiter with Saturn in the house of Cancer due to take place on June 10, 1504, that the Messiah would appear in 1505.

Vestiges of Astrology in Jewish Folklore

In the Jewish religious literature of modern times there remain only vestiges of earlier astrological beliefs. On joyful occasions in individual and family life, Jews everywhere congratulate each other by saying *mazzal tov* ("good luck"). A successful person is popularly referred to as a *bar-mazzal* ("one of luck"), and a perennial failure is known as a *ra-mazzal* ("poor luck"; Yid., *shlimazl*; Aram., *bish-gadda*). It was customary in some parts to begin no new undertaking on Mondays or Wednesdays (Sh. Ar., YD 179:2, on the basis of the responsa of Naḥmanides, no. 242), since Mondays were ruled by the moon and nothing could be properly done on them, while Wednesdays were ruled by Mars, a hard patron. Another custom was to perform marriages only in the first half of the month while the moon was waxing (*ibid.*; Naḥmanides, responsum no. 282). R. Mordecai Jaffe explains the custom of fasting on the anniversary of a parent's death (Isserles to Sh. Ar., YD 402:12) as deriving from the belief that on that day the luck of the child is vulnerable. Until recently it was the custom in certain localities to prepare a bed (or table; see Isserles, *ibid.*, 65:11) in a mother's room on the eve of her son's circumcision so that the child should enjoy good luck (*ibid.*, 178:3).

BIBLIOGRAPHY: Ginzberg, Legends, index; R. Levy, *Astrological Works of A. Ibn Ezra* (1927); A. Ibn Ezra, *Beginning of Wisdom*, ed. by R. Levy and F. Cantera (1939); S. Sachs, *Ha-Yonah, Keneset Yisrael* (1851), 59ff.; S. Rubin, *Ma'aseh Ta'tu'im* (1887), 39ff.; Guttmann, Philosophies, 246 70; Steinschneider, Uebersetzungen, 186, 501ff.; Rosin, in: MGWJ, 42 (1898), 247ff.; Poznański, *ibid.*, 49 (1905), 45ff.; Marx, in; HUCA, 3 (1926), 311–42.

[Alexander Altmann]

ASTRONOMY.

In the Bible

Although the Bible contains no explicit mention of the science of astronomy, it nevertheless has many references to topics such as the laws of the heavens (Jer. 31:34 [35]; 33:25; Job 38:33) and the movements of the sun and the moon (Josh. 10:13; Ps. 19:6–7; Job 31:26; Eccles. 1:5–6).

The Israelites did not study the stars as did the Babylonians, Egyptians, and Greeks. They may have refrained from too close observation of the celestial bodies out of a fear of idolatry – "When you look up to the sky and behold the sun, and the moon, and the stars, the whole heavenly host, you must not be lured into bowing down to them or serving them…" (Deut. 4: 19). Nevertheless, some basic knowledge of astronomy was essential to fix the dates of festivals and holidays.

THE STARS AND THE PLANETS. The firmament or heavenly vault, the abode of the two "great lights" and the stars, was stretched between the waters above and the waters beneath (Gen. 1:14–18), and was rigid and strong "as a molten mirror" (Job 37:18). The stars of the heaven are as numerous "as the sands on the seashore" (Gen. 22:17); they are also frequently called "the host of heaven." The planets (*mazzalot*; II Kings 23:5) are, according to most biblical interpreters, in the twelve regions of the firmament which are later referred to as the signs of the *Zodiac. Other constellations, the five planets, the sun and the moon, and various individual stars are referred to in the Bible (e.g., cf. Job 38:31–32).

THE SUN AND THE MOON. The sun and the moon are frequently mentioned: the sun is referred to as *shemesh* (Ex. 22:2; Deut. 24:15), *ḥammah* (Isa. 24:23; Job 30:28), and *ḥarsah* (Judg. 14:18). The usual term for the moon *(yare'aḥ)* was also used to designate the lunar cycle (e.g., Ex. 2:2; Deut. 21:13; I Kings 6:37). The moon is also called *levanah* (Isa. 24:23; Song 6:10), and the full moon is called *kese(h)* (Ps. 81:4; Prov. 7:20). The word *ḥodesh* ("month") originally meant "the renewal of the moon," and described the day of the new moon (I Sam. 20:24, 34; Ezek. 26:1) and the length of its cycle (Gen. 29:14).

THE PLANETS SATURN AND VENUS. It is generally agreed that Chiun (Amos. 5:26) refers to Saturn (called *kaiwānu, kai[a]mānu* in Assyrian, and *kaivana* in Syrian). Lucifer (*Heilel*), the "son of the morning" is, according to most interpreters, the planet Venus that is visible at dawn (Isa. 14:12). In Arabic, Venus is called *al-Zuhara* ("the bright one.").

THE FIXED STARS. In the Bible *kesil* is mentioned four times (Isa. 13:10; Amos 5:8; Job. 9:9; 38:31). Views on its interpretation vary, but it is sometimes taken to represent Orion, which was considered to be one of the giant angels (Gen. 6:4). The Targum Jonathan rendered *kesil*, the "giant" (*nefila*; Job 9:9; 38:31); and in Isaiah 13:10 reference is made to "the stars of the heavens and their titans (*kesileihem*)." *Kimah* is, according to several interpreters, the constellation of the Pleiades. Other commentators identify it as Aldebaran, Arcturus, or Sirius. *Ash* (or *ayish*; Job 38:32) is mentioned with *kesil* and *kimah* (Job 9:9), and R. Judah b. Ezekiel claimed that it is the star called *Yuta*, "the lamb's tail," in Aramaic (Ber. 58b), which is probably Aldebaran. In the Vulgate, *ash* is translated as the Hyades, while the Septuagint gives it as "the Evening Star," i.e., Venus. *Ḥadrei-Teiman* (Job 9:9) is thought to represent the twinkling stars of the Southern firmament – the ship Argo, the Southern Cross, Centaurus and others – which could be observed in the land of Israel in the time of Job but cannot now, because of the precession of the equinoxes (that is, the slow westward movement of the earth's axis which makes the position of the stars change continuously), and thus the zodiac seems to change its position in relation to the horizon over hundreds of years. *Mezarim* in Job 37:9 is possibly a nickname for *mazzalot*, though according to some modern interpreters the *mezarim* are the Great Bear and the Little Bear.

In the Apocrypha

In the Book of Enoch several chapters are devoted to the courses of the heavenly bodies, to the fixing of the length of day and night in the different months, to the moon's course during the month, and to the difference between the solar and lunar years. These astronomical ideas, often inaccurate, were interspersed with legends about angels and spirits. Thus, the angels elevate Enoch through the various spheres of the heavens, and at the fourth he perceives the sun and the moon and a multitude of stars.

In the Talmud and Midrash

It is difficult to discuss fully the knowledge of astronomy in the talmudic period on the basis of the limited material in the Talmud and Midrashim. The knowledge of astronomy possessed by the *tannaim* and *amoraim* was not committed to paper, and only was recorded after its compilation by the *geonim*. The talmudic sages viewed astronomy – the computing of seasons and planets – and knowledge of the month order and the *calendar (intercalation) as important adjuncts to the study of the Torah. They attributed these studies to the ancients of the Bible, and interpreted the verse "And of the children of Issachar that had understanding of the times, to know what Israel ought to do" (I Chron. 12:33) as meaning that the children of Issachar knew how to compute the cycles of the planets in order to learn how Israel would determine the months and leap years. The study of this science was even considered an obligation for the talented person (Shab. 75a). Many of the *tannaim* and *amoraim* were experts in astronomy as, for example, *Johanan b. Zakkai (Suk. 28a), *Gamaliel II, and Joshua b. Hananiah. The last named knew of the existence of a comet which appeared once every seventy years and led mariners astray (Hor. 10a). This was probably Halley's Comet. Among the Babylonian *amoraim*, *Samuel was important in the field of astronomy. He claimed that he could calculate and adjust the festival calendar of the Diaspora, without recourse to an eyewitness' report of the new moon in Israel (RH 20b), and he even made intercalary calculations covering a period of years. The first generations of the *amoraim* were acquainted with a *baraita called "Secrets of Intercalation," in which were written precepts for the sanctification and intercalation of the month (RH 20b). In general, this knowledge was rarely committed to paper, being "secrets of the Torah not to be passed on to all and sundry" (Ket. 112a).

In the eyes of the talmudic sages the earth was the center of creation, with heaven as a hemisphere spread over it. The Midrash conceived the heavens as being made up of several spheres or vaults – the sun, moon, stars, and planets being fixed in the second one (Ḥag. 12b). Nevertheless, a knowledge of the order of the celestial bodies, their path and distances from the earth, existed alongside of the above mythological picture. At the horizon, the heaven and earth "kiss each other," and the earth's diameter from east to west is equivalent to the height of the heavens above the earth (Tam. 32a). The earth is usually described as a disk encircled by water. In the Midrash it is pictured as standing on twelve columns, for the tribes of Israel, or seven columns, for the pillars of wisdom. The columns rest upon water, the water upon mountains, the mountains upon the wind, the wind upon the storm, and the storm is dependent on the arm of the Almighty. Yet with all this there existed a clear recognition of the earth as a sphere (TJ, Av. Zar. 3:1, 42C; Num. R. 13; 14).

MOTIONS OF THE CELESTIAL BODIES. In one *baraita* (Pes. 94b) there are differing opinions regarding the circles of rotation and the planets. "The Jewish sages say 'The sun moves by day beneath the firmament, and by night above the firmament'; the learned of the nations say, 'The sun moves by day beneath the firmament and by night beneath the earth.'" This *baraita* is most important, as it is evidence of a serious interest in celestial mechanics, of an early knowledge of scientific concepts, and of an objective approach to the solution of astronomical problems. The daily changes in the positions of sunrise and sunset in the annual cycle of the sun were well known. These phenomena are explained by the existence of 365 windows in the firmament – 182 in the east, where the sun rises; and 182 in the west, where it sets; and one in the center of the firmament, the place of its first entrance at the time of the Creation (TJ, RH 2:5, 58a; Ex. R. 15:22). The distance traversed in 30 days by the sun, is traversed by the moon in two and one-half days. The sun is called the "Greater Light" and the moon, the "Lesser Light" because the solar year is longer than the lunar year by 11 days (Ex. R. ibid.). As for the courses of the planets, it is said (Gen. R. 10:4) " there is a planet that finishes its cycle in 12 years – that is Jupiter; and there is a planet which finishes its cycle in 30 years – that is Saturn; except for Venus and Mars that do not finish their cycles for 480 years." The figures given for Jupiter and Saturn are correct, according to the geocentric system of the motion of the planets, but the figures relating to Venus and Mars were wholly inaccurate and they seem to have been regarded as doubtful in quite early times.

A concept of the solar motions is found in the *baraita* (Ber. 59b), which is explained by a great cycle of 28 years, at the end of which the sun returns to its original position relative to the stars and planets. The *aggadah* even accurately works out the time of the start of both the solar and lunar cycles (Targ. Jon., Gen. 1:16). The great cycle of the moon is also mentioned, being 21 years (Pd–RE 7); there is also a possible hint of a cycle of 19 years (Targ. Jon., Gen. 1:14). This length of time is the basis for calendar calculation, having been fixed at a much later period, and it remains valid up to the present day. The monthly changes in the shape of the moon are also well described (Ex. R. 15:26), and it is clear that various writers on this problem were not too far from the truth.

THE FOUR SEASONS. (*Tekufot*). The change of season and the comparison of day and night are fairly well described: "there are four seasons of the year, from the Nisan season to the Tammuz season the day borrows from the night, and from the Tammuz season to the Tishri season the day repays the night; from the Tishri season to the Tevet season the night borrows from the day, and from the Tevet season to the Nisan season the night repays the day; during the Nisan season and Tishri season, neither one owes anything to the other" (Mid. Ps. 19:3). Samuel gives reasonably accurate figures regarding the periods between the seasons (Er. 56a), but when he discusses the fixing of the dates of the seasons, he allows imaginary bases to be included.

THE PLANETS, THE ZODIAC, STARS, AND COMETS. The names of the planets – Saturn, Jupiter, the Sun, Mars, Venus (or *Kokhevet*), Mercury (or *Kokhav Ḥammah*), and the Moon – are referred to collectively in an acrostic as שצ"מ הנכ"ל. The 12 signs of the Zodiac and their relation to the months of the year are Aries (Nisan), Taurus (Iyyar), Gemini (Sivan), Cancer (Tammuz), Leo (Av), Virgo (Elul), Libra (Tishri), Scorpio (Marḥeshvan), Sagittarius (Kislev), Capricorn (Tevet), Aquarius (Shevat), and Pisces (Adar). From the astrological viewpoint, the 12 signs of the Zodiac have different influences on the "four winds of heaven," and sometimes there is a symbolic connection with the 12 tribes of Israel (Yal., Ex. 418; Yal., I Kings 185). In addition to the stars mentioned in the Bible, there is also a reference to the Milky Way (Ber. 58b). The meteors mentioned in the Mishnah (Ber. 9:2) are comets (Ber. 58b), and Samuel admitted that he did not know their nature. The "*Baraita* of Samuel," which was traditionally written by the *amora* Samuel, is ascribed by some to the ninth century (see below).

Astronomy in the Middle Ages

The principal contributions of medieval Jewry to astronomy were the calculation of the Hebrew *calendar; the translation of Arabic works and the diffusion of knowledge from the Arabic world; and the compilation of astronomical tables for scientific and navigational purposes. *Ptolemy, the Alexandrian astronomer of the second century C.E., compiled the *Almagest (Syntaxis Mathematica)*, a long work in 13 books systematizing the structure of the universe and Greek astronomy. The *Almagest* dominated astronomical and astrological thought for 14 centuries, becoming the authority on astronomy and the major source for astronomical commentaries and translations in the medieval period. The Jews were of major importance to scholastic Europe and the beginning of the Renaissance, in that they provided a link between the Arabic translations, commentaries, and compilations of the *Almagest* and the Christian astronomers, mostly by means of their own translations and commentaries in Hebrew or Latin. One of the first Hebrew translations of the Arabic version of the *Almagest* was made by Jacob *Anatoli between the years 1231 and 1235 as *Ḥibbur ha-Gadol ha-Nikra al-Magesti*. Anatoli also translated *Averroes' summary of the *Almagest* under the title *Kiẓẓur al-Magesti*, and *Kitāb fial-Ḥarakāt al-Samāwiyya* ("The Book on the Heavenly Movements") by the ninth-century Arabic astronomer al-Farghānī (Alfraganus) under the title *Yesodot ha-Tekhunah*. The compendium of Ptolemy's *Almagest* in Arabic by Ibn Aflaḥ ha-Ishbili (the 12th-century Spanish astronomer), known also as Abu-Muhammad Jābir ibn Aflaḥ, is mentioned by *Maimonides in the *Guide of the Perplexed* (2:9). Ibn Aflaḥ's book (*Kitāb al-Hay'd*, "The Book of Astronomy") is important for its critical appraisal of the Ptolemaic system of the universe, and was translated into Hebrew in two versions: one by Moses ibn *Tibbon (the 13th-century French physician and translator in 1274), and another, apparently, by Jacob b. Machir ibn *Tibbon (Don Profiat), which was abridged by Samuel b. Judah of Marseilles (the 14th-century French physician) in 1335. Moses ibn Tibbon also translated *Eisagōgē eis ta Phainomena* ("Introduction to Celestial Phenomena") of the first-century B.C.E. Greek philosopher, Geminus, under the title of *Ḥokhmat ha-Kokhavim* or *Ḥokhmat Tekhunah ha-Kaẓar* or *Sefer ha-Ḥokhmah ha-Kaddurit*, in 1246 at Naples. He also translated *Kitâb al-Hay'a* ("The Book on Astronomy") by the Arab astronomer al-Biṭrūjī of Seville (d. 1185) under the title *Ma'amar bi-Tekhunah* in 1259. The latter work had a great influence on Jewish scholars up to the 16th century. Jacob b. Machir translated around 1271 *Fi-Hay'at al-ʿĀlam* ("On the Astronomy of the Universe" as *Sefer ha-Tekhunah*) by Abuʿali ibn al-Haytham (11th century), describing the quadrant and astronomy. Samuel b. Judah of Marseilles translated the treatise on the movement of the fixed stars (*Ma'amar bi-Tenu'at ha-Kokhavim ha-Kayyamim*), by Abu Isḥaq Ibrahim ibn Yaḥya al-Zarqālī (also known as Zarqāla or Zarqallah) of Cordova (second half of the 11th century). Moses b. Elijah the Greek (probably the 15th-century Moses Galeno) translated a study of astronomy by Omar ibn Muhammad under the title, *Sefer Mezukkak*. The Christian Jacob Christmann translated into Latin the Hebrew translations of the summary of the *Almagest* by Jacob Anatoli and al-Farghānī's book on astronomy (Frankfurt, 1590). Abraham de *Balmes (d. 1524) translated into Latin Moses ibn Tibbon's Hebrew translation of Geminus' work on astronomy (see above), under the mistaken title *Isagogicon Astrologiae Ptolemaei*, as well as Jacob b. Machir's Hebrew translation of the above work by Ibn al-Haytham, under the title *Liber de Mundo*.

The following are among those who published commentaries on the *Almagest*: Samuel ben Judah of Marseilles (14th century), David ibn *Naḥmias of Toledo (beginning of 14th century), and Elijah *Mizraḥi (d. 1525). Commentaries on the Hebrew translation of al-Farghānī's work were composed by Moses Handali (possibly 13th century), Isaac b. Samuel abu al-Khayr (c. 1340), Maimon of Montpellier (of unknown date; see *Montpellier), and Judah ibn Verga (1457). There exists a shortened version of the *Almagest* which was possibly written by Ḥayyim *Vital.

At the end of the Middle Ages books in Latin were also translated into Hebrew. The essay by the German astronomer, Johannes de Gamundia (1380–1442), "*De ratione componendi et usu novi instrumenti*" was translated by David Kalonymus b. Jacob Meir Kalonymus under the title *Marot ha-Kokhavim* (1466). *Theorica Planetarum* of Georg Peuerbach (1423–1461) was translated twice: once by Ephraim Mizraḥi, and a second time by Moses b. Baruch *Almosnino (1510–1580). John de Sacrobosco (John of Holywood, the Parisian mathematician and astronomer who died in 1256) wrote the famous *Tractatus de Sphaera*, which elucidated and incorporated Ptolemy's *Almagest* and the work of al-Farghānī (see above) and which soon replaced both these books. It was translated into Hebrew around 1399 by *Solomon b. Abraham (Avigdor) of Montpellier as the *Mareh ha-Ofannim*.

Several Arabic essays were translated into European languages, especially Latin and Spanish. These translations were, in fact, the main channels for the progress of astronomy in medieval Europe. In 1256 Judah b. Moses ha-Kohen of Toledo translated into Spanish the *Kitāb al-Kawākib* ("Book of the Stars") of ʿAbd al-Raḥmān al-Sūfī (tenth century) under the title *Libro de las figuras* and the astrological treatise *Kitāb al-Bārie* by Ibn Abu al-Rijāl (11th century) under the title *Libro complido*. Commentaries on the *Tractatus de Sphaera* by John de Sacrobosco were published in the 16th and 17th centuries by Moses b. Baruch Almosnino, Mattathias *Delacrut (1550), and Manoah Handil b. Shemariah (Polish author who died in 1612). A commentary on Georg Peuerbach's *Theorica Planetarum* was written by Moses *Isserles in the early 17th century.

In the Middle Ages Jews compiled most of the astronomical tables. Among these, the heretic Jew Sind ibn Ali (829–33) was a principal contributor to the astronomical tables of Caliph Maimun. *Abraham b. Ḥiyya ha-Nasi compiled (before 1136) tables called "*Luḥot ha-Nasi*" ("The Tables of the Prince or al-Battānī's *Tables*"), named after the Arab who died in 929, on whose calculations they were based. Al-Battānī had a great influence on astronomy; Maimonides relied on his tables for computing the sun's path, and his works were also mentioned by *Judah Halevi (12th-century), Abraham *Ibn Ezra (1092–1167), Isaac *Israeli (ninth to tenth century), and several other Hebrew authors. Abraham ibn Ezra compiled astronomical tables on the movements of the seven planets, and translated in 1160 the "Reasons for the al-Khwārizmī Tables" by Ahmad b. Elmenthi. Twelve Jewish astronomers, under the leadership of the Cordovan astronomer, Ibn Arzarkāli (Azarchel), helped to compile the "Toledo Tables" in the 12th century. In 1263 these were translated into Latin by John of Brescia and Jacob b. Machir ibn Tibbon, and later served as a basis in a Spanish version for the famous "Alphonsine Tables." These were prepared in 1272 by a group of astronomers, headed by Isaac *Ibn Sa'id (also Sid). The Latin Tables were translated into Hebrew in 1460 by Moses b. Abraham of Nimes, while a new corrected edition was made by Solomon Davin of Rodez. Commentaries were written by Moses Botarel Farissol in 1465 and Mattathias Delacrut in the 16th century.

Specially significant to the Hebrew astronomers were the "Persian Tables" in Greek, which were compiled late in the 14th century by Georgios Krisokaka. Solomon b. Elijah drew up (in about 1374) a set of astronomical tables with notes, the first section according to the Ptolemaic system and the second "in the manner of the Persians." Before 1525 Elijah Mizraḥi wrote a commentary on the tables "drawn up by the Persian sages."

Astronomical tables were also devised by *Levi b. Gershom (1288–1344), based on sources found in Persia, Egypt, etc. Isaac b. Solomon ibn Elhada (14th to 15th century) prepared tables for periods and seasons based on Ibn al-Raqqān, al-Battāni, and Ibn al-Kammād. Joseph b. Isaac b. Moses *Ibn Waqar, writing in Arabic in 1357, drew up tables for the years 720–840 of the Muslim calendar (i.e., 1342–1462) and in 1396 he translated his book into Hebrew with additions and alterations. Other tables were compiled by Jacob b. Machir (1300), Jacob b. David b. Yom Tov (1361), and Abraham *Zacuto, whose tables and *Almanach Perpetuum* in Latin and Spanish were used by Columbus on his voyages.

EARLY JEWISH ASTRONOMERS. There were comparatively few original works by medieval Jewish astronomers, but of these a number were equal to works of contemporary non-Jewish writers. Of importance was the group of men in the eighth and ninth centuries who took up astronomy professionally. Generally, they practiced as astrologers and their knowledge was derived from Greek and ancient Indian writers. Unfortunately, comparatively few of their writings have been preserved. Some were translated into Latin, and a few works have been found in Hebrew.

Māsha'allāh, whose Hebrew name was possibly Joab or Joel, lived during the second half of the eighth and the beginning of the ninth century, and served in the courts of the caliphs in Baghdad. His essay, *"Sefer be-Kadrut ha-Levanah ve-Ḥibbur ha-Kokhavim u-Tekufat ha-Shanim"* has been preserved in Hebrew. The Persian Jewish astronomer Andruzager b. Zadi Faruch, who lived in the ninth century, is often identified with the expert in intercalation Eliezer b. Faruch, to whom the Arab chronologist al-Bīrūnī (early 11th century) attributed the fixing of the Jewish calendar. The "Baraita of Samuel" which dealt with the secrets of intercalation, dates from the ninth century but was attributed to the *amora* Samuel; it is regarded by some as the first original Hebrew work on astronomy in the Middle Ages.

During the late tenth century Ḥasan ibn Ḥasan wrote three books on intercalation; unfortunately they have not been preserved, but reference to their contents was made by Abraham ibn Ezra and Isaac Israeli. Shabbetai *Donnolo (tenth century) wrote a commentary on the Sefer *Yeẓirah. Although they demonstrate the author's knowledge of the subject, the astronomical terms are confused with concepts belonging to astrology and mysticism. A calendar is given, showing the location of the heavenly bodies in 4706 (summer of 956). This work is important in that it constitutes the main source of *Rashi's astronomy.

The greatest of the Jewish astronomers who wrote in Hebrew at the beginning of the Spanish period was Abraham b. Ḥiyya ha-Nasi, whose works influenced generations of Jewish writers. Those of his works which were translated into Latin had an important influence on the development of European science. Apart from his astronomical calendars and Arabic astrological work which he translated into Latin, Abraham b. Ḥiyya wrote the following important works: *Ẓurat ha-Areẓ*, an astronomical-geographical text; *Sefer ha-Ibbur*, which included series of calculations of years, and determinations of new moons and cycles; *Ḥeshbon Mahalakhot ha-Kokhavim*, a book to which comments were added by Abraham ibn Ezra.

In his hymn, *"Keter Malkhut"* Solomon ibn *Gabirol describes the structure of the universe according to Aristotle and Ptolemy. This work contains detailed calculations of the length of the cycle of each star and its size in relation to the size of the earth.

Abraham Ibn Ezra, in addition to his works on astrology and his calendars and commentaries, wrote the following texts on theoretical astronomy: *Sefer ha-Ibbur* which is on the subject of cycles, new moons, seasons, and signs of the Zodiac; *Shalosh She'elot*, replies to three questions on intercalation posed by David b. Joseph of Narbonne (c. 1139); and *Kelei Neḥoshet* an explanation of the use of the instruments of the astrolabical type. This last was followed by *Kelei Neḥoshet ha-Sheni* which analyzes the fundamentals of intercalation and the sources of astronomy. It has been passed on by Maimonides who also gives a detailed description of the laws of the spheres (Yad. Yesodei ha-Torah, 3). He maintains (*ibid.*, 4:10) that it was to this that the talmudists referred in their commentaries on the creation (ch. 1). Maimonides' writings show him to have been a foremost astronomer of his time, and demonstrate a scientific approach in his analysis of apparent contradictory data.

The main Jewish astronomers of the 13th century were Judah b. Solomon ha-Kohen ibn Matkah of Toledo, the author of an encyclopedia, *Midrash ha-Ḥokhmah*, part of which consists of summaries of the great Greek and Muslim astronomers; *Gershom b. Solomon, whose work *Sha'ar ha-Shamayim* contains a section on the works of Ptolemy, Aristotle, Avicenna, and Averroes. This book was held in high esteem in the Middle Ages, and Meir *Aldabi (c. 1360) used it extensively in the astronomical section of his *Shevilei Emunah*.

In the *Zohar – probably a 13th-century Spanish composition – there is a passage which gives as a cause of the day's changing into night the revolution of the earth. Some 250 years before Copernicus the Zohar stated that "the whole earth spins in a circle like a ball; the one part is up when the other part is down; the one part is light when the other is dark, it is day in the one part and night in the other."

Of great importance is *Yesod Olam* by Isaac b. Joseph *Israeli. This work, written in 1310, includes a study of astronomy and cosmography. The author deals with the system of intercalation and with laws of the sanctification of the month according to Maimonides. He gives a method for calculating the parallax of the moon, the importance of which was appreciated up to the time of Kepler. This was the leading textbook on astronomy written during the Middle Ages, and was held in high esteem for hundreds of years. Commentaries and explanations to it were written by Isaac Alhadib, Elijah Mizraḥi, and others. In the yeshivot of the 19th century it was the main text for the study of the calendar. Isaac ben Solomon Israeli translated a summary of it into Hebrew entitled *Kiẓẓur Yesod Olam*. Isaac Israeli also wrote *Sha'ar ha-Shamayim* which dealt with the subject of periods and seasons and *Sefer Sha'ar ha-Millu'im* on the movement of the planets, their order, and positions.

The greatest of the Jewish astronomers of the Middle Ages was undoubtedly Levi b. Gershom. Curtze, the historian of astronomy, numbers him among the forerunners of Copernicus in that he pioneered new methods of research, from which evolved his own original system of astronomy. Levi b. Gershom was an independent and original scholar, and although he did not produce a work specifically devoted to astronomy, his knowledge of astronomy is clearly brought out in the first section of the fifth book of his *Milḥamot Adonai*. This section of the work was known to later generations as *Sefer ha-Tekhunah*. Levi b. Gershom explains in detail: a) his discovery, or improvement, of the cross-staff, a device for measuring angles and spherical distances. The inventor called it "the depth finder," while it became known in Europe as "Jacob's staff" (*baculus Jacobi*) b) his method of passing a light ray from a star through a small aperture in a darkened chamber on to a board. This is the first recorded use of the *camera obscura*. By these methods Levi b. Gershom carried out numerous measurements and rectified many erroneous conceptions regarding the position of the stars. Among his achievements was the measurement of the relationship of the diameters of the sun and the moon to the lengths of their apparent orbits, and the relationship between the parts of the surfaces covered during an eclipse, and the size of the total area. As a result of his corrections of the originally accepted distances and data, he was able to arrive at a new conception of the distances separating the bodies of the universe and their position in space, and hence (in ch. 9) at a rejection of the basic assumptions of the astronomy of Ptolemy and al-Biṭrūjī. Chapter 99 of the text contains his "Astronomical Tables" (*Luḥot*) on which commentaries have been written by Moses Botarel Farissol. The importance of the work may be gauged from the fact that part of the book was translated into Latin during the author's lifetime (in 1342). The entire book was not translated until the 15th century.

Other Jewish inventors of astronomical instruments in the later Middle Ages were Jacob b. Machir, who invented an angle measuring device, a quadrant, which he described in his work *Rova Yisrael*; Isaac b. Solomon b. Ẓaddik*Al Ḥadib (also al-Aḥdab) wrote *Keli ha-Mizzu'a* about his invention of a new instrument which was a combination of astrolabe and quadrant; Jacob (Bonet) de *Lattes (15th to 16th centuries) designed a device in the shape of a ring for measuring the height of the sun and the stars. His work on this was written in Latin (*De annuli astronomii utilitate*) and was reprinted no less than six times within 50 years. Immanuel b. Jacob *Bonfils (the 14th-century physician and astronomer of Tarascon) wrote many works on astronomy including one on the construction of the astrolabe, as well as tables of the determination of Venus from 1300 to 1357, and tables for the declination of the sun, etc.

Abraham Zacuto was an influential astronomer of the 16th century. His main work was originally written in Hebrew, but was very soon translated into Spanish, and the Latin synopsis of it, *Almanach Perpetuum* ("The Continual Almanac") was translated into Spanish and Arabic. All of Zacuto's works, his improved astrolabe, and his astronomical tables were of great importance, particularly in the voyages of discovery of the Spanish and Portuguese explorers.

Knowledge of Jewish medieval astronomy is limited to a very small part of the extensive writings on the subject. Much material remains undiscovered and most of what is available has yet to be studied carefully. Yet, over 250 Jewish astronomers are known to have lived before 1500.

Jewish Astronomy in the late Renaissance

The Jewish contribution to astronomy after Copernicus was relatively small. Most writers concerned themselves with transcriptions from old writings or with summarizing these. Thus, the writings on astronomy of the 18th century and in the rabbinical literature of the 19th century are basically derived from the Ptolemaic school.

In the 16th century *Judah Loew b. Bezalel had a high reputation as an astronomer. However, apart from his few astrological discussions, nothing can be found in his few writings to support this. Moses Isserles (d. 1573) showed a real knowledge of astronomy, particularly in his books *Torat ha-Olah* (Prague, 1569) and his commentary on *Theorica Planetarum*.

David *Gans was well acquainted with the development of astronomical knowledge. He was a colleague of Kepler and Tycho Brahe; for the latter he translated parts of the "Alphonsine Tables" into German. His most important astronomical work was *Neḥmad ve-Na'im* written in 1613 and published in Jessnitz, 1743, which presented the first Hebrew exposition of the Copernican system, but the author rejected it because of his traditional Ptolemaic outlook. Mordecai b. Abraham *Jaffe wrote *Levush Eder ha-Yakar* in *Levush Or Yekarot* (Lublin, 1594), which contains a commentary on Maimonides' laws of the sanctification of the month as well as a lesson on astronomy; his *Be'urei Yafeh* is a commentary on *Ẓurat ha-Areẓ* by Abraham b. Ḥiyya.

Joseph Solomon *Delmedigo was a pupil of Galileo. In his *Elim* two chapters are devoted to astronomy: the first, "The Laws of the Heavens" is an exposition of the first two chapters of the *Almagest*, the second, "The Mightiness of God," is devoted to an explanation of other parts of the *Almagest* and of writings by Copernicus and al-Battānī. Delmedigo was the first outstanding exponent of the Copernican theory in Hebrew literature within the framework of traditional Judaism. His method was to reply to questions from the viewpoint of the ancients, and from that of the astronomers who followed Copernicus.

Tobias *Cohn, the physician, remained faithful to the ancients, although he was quite familiar with the astronomy of Copernicus. In his *Ma'aseh Tuviyyah* (Venice, 1707–8) he analyzed the geocentric conception in its classic form, and in the one revised by Tycho Brahe. The heliocentric view is analyzed and rejected, mainly on religious and traditional grounds.

*Jonathan b. Joseph from Ruzhany, another commentator on *Ẓurat ha-Areẓ*, wrote *Yeshu'ah be-Yisrael* ("Salvation in Israel," Frankfurt, 1720), an explanation of Maimonides' laws of the sanctification of the month.

Raphael ha-Levi of Hanover (1685–1788) wrote *Tekhunat ha-Shamayim* (Amsterdam, 1756), a study of astronomy as related to Maimonides' law, and "Tables of Intercalation" (pt. 1, Leiden, 1756; pt. 2, Hanover, 1757).

Israel b. Moses ha-Levi of Zamosc in his book, *Neẓaḥ Yisrael* (Frankfurt on the Oder, 1741), classified certain obscure parts of the Talmud which dealt with engineering and astronomy. He also wrote a commentary on *Yesod Olam* by Isaac Israeli, and a textbook called *Arubbot ha-Shamayim. Shevilei de-Raki'a* (Prague, 1785) by Elijah b. Ḥayyim of Hochheim is devoted to an explanation of Maimonides' laws of the sanctification of the month. In it the author distinguishes between the geocentric assumptions of Maimonides, and the theories of the new astronomy. In the 19th century, Israel David b. Mordecai *Jaffe-Margoliot wrote *Ḥazon Mo'ed* (Pressburg, 1843), dealing with astronomy, the mathematics of intercalation, as well as with the additional day of festivals in the Diaspora.

Jews in Modern Astronomy

The frequently repeated statement that Sir William Herschel, astronomer to King George III and his sister Caroline, were of Jewish origin has been shown to be not in accordance with the facts. Among those who contributed to the development of astronomy in the 19th century were Wilhelm Beer (1797–1850), specialist in the mapping of the features of the moon; Hermann *Goldschmidt is especially noted for his work from 1852 to 1861 in discovering 14 new asteroids between Mars and Jupiter; Rudolph Wolf (1816–1893), at the turn of the century, organized systematic solar work at Zurich; Adolph Hirsch (1830–1901) conducted mainly geophysical work in Switzerland; Maurice *Loewy invented, at the Paris Observatory, the Coudé telescope; Edmund Weiss (1837–1917), was director of the Vienna Observatory in the mid-19th century; Friedrich Simon Archenhold (1861–1939) was a well-known writer of popular books on astronomy; Adolph Marcuse (1860–1930), participated in several astronomical expeditions; Fritz Cohen and Samuel Oppenheim conducted important work in celestical mechanics; as did Erwin Finlay *Freundlich, first in Berlin and then at St. Andrews in Scotland. During this century, Richard *Prager, at first at the University Observatory, Berlin, and from 1938 at the Harvard Observatory, worked on variable stars through the continuation of the *Geschichte und Literatur der Veraenderlichen Sterne*. Sir Arthur *Schuster, in England, founded in 1919 the forerunner of the International Astronomical Union, to whose subsequent rapid development was due much of the well-organized effort and success of present-day astronomy. Frank *Schlesinger, in the U.S.A., was the first to devise photographic methods for a large scale derivation of stellar distances ("parallax-determinations"). Karl *Schwarzchild, director of the Astrophysical Observatory in Potsdam, did fundamental work in many fields; for example, the laws of stellar motions, photometry, optics, the astrophysical application of atomic physics, and the theoretical exploration of stellar atmospheres. His son Martin *Schwarzschild, who taught at Princeton, U.S.A., was an expert in stellar evolution, and the design of satellite-borne telescopes. Albert *Einstein was noted also for his researches in astrophysics. Other contemporary American astronomers of Jewish origin were Luigi Jacchia (1911–1996), on solar-terrestrial relationships, and David Layzer (1925–), who researched in theoretical atomic astrophysics, both at Harvard University. At the University of Texas, Gerard de Vancouleurs (1918–1995) was involved in research into the structure and systems of extragalactic nebulae. Rudolph Minkowski (1895–1976) up to 1934 at Hamburg University, investigated at Pasadena the intricate problems of supernovae. Herbert A. *Friedman, at the U.S. Naval Research Laboratory in Washington, was a leader in the new field of outer-space spectroscopy. At Rochester University, Emil Wolf (1922–) was concerned with optical research with astrophysical applications. Leo Goldberg (1913–1987), at the Smithsonian Astrophysical Observatory, organized teamwork for the initiation of new solar and stellar space research. At the California Institute of Technology, Jesse L. Greenstein (1909–2002) carried out fundamental astrophysical work, particularly in high-dispersion spectroscopy.

Before going to Israel, George Alter (1890–1972) was at the University of Prague, and at the Sidmouth Observatory in England, where he was mainly concerned with problems of star clusters. Arthur Beer (1900–1980), formerly at Breslau and Hamburg, and, from 1934, at the Universities of London and Cambridge, investigated problems of spectroscopic binaries, new stars, stellar photometry, large-scale spectrophotometric determination of distances of stars in the outer regions of our galaxy, its spiral structure, and problems in the history of astronomy. At the Royal Greenwich Observatory, stellar evolution and the abundance of chemical elements in the stars were investigated by Bernard Pagel (1929–).

Modern cosmological theories, which began in the 1920s, have been developed by Thomas Gold (1920–2004), Hermann *Bondi, Dennis Sciama (1930–), Leon Mestel (1930–), and Franz Kahn (1926–1998).

Cosmological and other astronomical work of great originality and ingenuity was developed in Soviet Russia; outstanding among the researchers were Vitoli Lazarevich Ginzburg and Joseph S. Shklovski (d. 1985). Leading French astronomers included: the former general secretary of the International Astronomical Union, Jean-Claude Pecker (Observatoire de Paris), and Evry Schatzman (Institut d'Astrophysique, Paris), both active in studies of stellar evolution.

See also *Physics.

BIBLIOGRAPHY: G. Sarton, *Introduction to the History of Science*, 5 vols. (1927–48), indexes; C. Roth, *The Jewish Contribution to Civilisation* (19382), 67, 76, 80–81, 189–90; *Legacy of Israel* (19282), 173–314; G. Forbes, *History of Astronomy* (1909); M. Steinschneider, in: JQR, 13 (1900/01), 106–10; idem, *Jewish Literature from the 8th to the 18th Centuries* (1857); W.M. Feldman, *Rabbinical Mathematics and Astronomy* (1931), includes bibliography; O. Neugebauer, in: HUCA, 22 (1949), 321–63; J.B.J. Delambre, *Histoire de l'astronomie du moyen-âge* (1819, repr. 1965); C. Roth, in: JQR, 27 (1936/37), 233–6; A. Marx, in: *Essays and Studies… Linda R. Miller* (1938), 117–70; S. Gandz, *Studies in Hebrew Astronomy and Mathematics* (1970).

[Arthur Beer]

ASTRUC, ELIE-ARISTIDE (1831–1905), French rabbi and author. Astruc was born in Bordeaux and studied at the rabbinical college of Metz. He became assistant to the chief rabbi of Paris in 1857, chief rabbi of Belgium in 1866–79, and rabbi of Bayonne in 1887–91. He took part in the Rabbinical Synod of Leipzig in 1869. Astruc was a founder of the *Alliance Israélite Universelle. A successful writer, Astruc often shows originality and independence in his treatment of Jewish themes. His main works are *Histoire abrégée des juifs et de leurs croyances* (1869; 1880^2), a collection of sermons *Entretiens sur le juda-*

ïsme (1879), and *Origines et causes historiques de l'anti-sémitisme* (1884). He also composed *Olelot Eliyahu* (1865), a French metrical translation of the *piyyutim* of the Sephardi rite.

ASTRUC, JEAN (1684–1766), French physician and a founder of classical biblical criticism. The name Astruc was common among the Jews of southern France, and some have supposed that he was ultimately of Jewish extraction. Astruc learned Hebrew and Bible from his father, a former Huguenot preacher who had converted to Catholicism following the Edict of Nantes (1698). He served as professor of anatomy at Toulouse, Montpellier, and Paris. In 1729, he was court physician for a short time to King August II of Poland, and then to Louis XV of France. He wrote numerous tractates on medicine, the most important being his work on venereal diseases, *De morbis veneriis*, which appeared in 21 editions and numerous translations from 1736 onward.

Astruc is remembered principally as a Bible scholar who helped pioneer a method of biblical analysis which continues to hold an important place in biblical scholarship. The orthodox Astruc reacted to the criticism of freethinkers toward the Mosaic authorship of the Pentateuch. He published in Brussels (and secretly in Paris) an anonymous book entitled *Conjectures sur les mémoires originaux, dont il parait que Moyse s'est servi pour composer le livre de la Genèse* (1753) in which he attempted to show that Moses, the redactor of Genesis and the first two chapters of Exodus, made use of two parallel sources and ten fragments written before his time. The two primary sources can be distinguished by the fact that one refers to the deity as *YHWH* and the second as *Elohim*. Astruc assigned various repetitions, materials foreign to Hebrew history, glosses, and additions by later copyists to the ten fragments. He, however, was not aware of the work of H.B. Witter, *Jura Israelitarum in Palaestinam* (1711), which demonstrated that the first half of Genesis uses parallel sources and different divine names. The varying names for the deity had already been noted and discussed by older scholars such as Jean Le Clerc (Johannes Clericus) and Richard *Simon, but none of these went beyond the generalization that the Pentateuch was composed of different documents. Astruc's documentary hypothesis was received with ridicule in some circles and was unnoticed in others until J.G. *Eichhorn gave considerable attention to it, thus salvaging the theories of Astruc and Witter from oblivion.

BIBLIOGRAPHY: Lods, in: RHPR, 4 (1924), 109–32, 201–7; idem, in: ZAW, 43 (1925), 134–5; O'Doherty, in: CBQ, 15 (1953), 300–4; de Savignac, in: *La Nouvelle Clio*, 5 (1953), 138–47; de Vaux, in: VT, Suppl. 1 (1953), 182–98. **ADD. BIBLIOGRAPHY:** J.H. Hayes, in: DBI, 1:83.

[Moses Zevi (Moses Hirsch) Segal]

ASTRUC, SAUL HA-KOHEN (d. after 1395), physician and scholar. Astruc was the leader of a group which emigrated from Spain to Algeria before 1391. While physician to the ruler of Tlemcen, he generously supported the needy of all communities and was esteemed by both Jews and Gentiles. He was *dayyan* of Algiers, but ceded this position to R. Isaac *Bonastruc, when the latter arrived from Spain or Majorca, and Astruc gave him financial support. He was on friendly terms with R. *Isaac b. Sheshet Perfet, who was appointed chief *dayyan* of Algiers as a result of Astruc's intervention with the ruler of the Ziyānid dynasty.

BIBLIOGRAPHY: I. Epstein, *The Responsa of Rabbi Simeon b. Zemah Duran* (1930), 18, 19, 97, 99; A. Hershman, *Rabbi Isaac ben Sheshet Perfet and His Times* (1943), index. **ADD. BIBLIOGRAPHY:** H.Z. (J.W.) Hirschberg, *A History of the Jews in North Africa*, 1 (1974), 382.

[Abraham David]

ASTRUC, ZACHARIE (1839–1907), French sculptor, painter, and writer. Astruc went to Paris from Angers as a boy. He studied art there and while still a student founded the *Quart d'Heure: Gazette des Gens à Demi-Sérieux*. A member of the Society of French Artists, Astruc contributed sculptures and paintings to the Salon des Champs Elysées. He was very successful and received many awards. Some of his more celebrated sculptures are his bust of Manet, *Mars et Venus*, *Hamlet*, *Le Roi Midas*, and his copy of Alonzo Cano's statue of St. Francis of Assisi. Astruc was also a versatile writer who wrote art criticism, poems, novels, short stories, and plays. He published a novel and a book of poems in Spanish. Astruc was the author of a collection of art criticism, *Les Quatorze Stations du Salon de 1859*, with a preface by George Sand.

BIBLIOGRAPHY: *Dictionnaire biographique du départment de Marne-et-Loire* (1894).

ASTRUC HA-LEVI (end of 14th and beginning of 15th century), rabbi of *Alcañiz and vigorous representative of its community at the Disputation of *Tortosa (1413–14). A fellow townsman of Joshua *Lorki, Astruc took issue with him soon after Lorki's conversion to Christianity over a treatise he had directed against the Jews and Judaism. During the disputation, Astruc ably clarified the basic differences between the Jewish and Christian religions, as well as the futility of holding religious debates. Later, in 1414, he composed a joint memorandum with *Zeraḥiah b. Isaac ha-Levi of Saragossa, which formed the basis for the second half of the disputation. Although unyielding on questions of dogma, toward the end of the debate Astruc refused to continue the defense of the Talmud against allegations that it contained heresy and immorality, a course he undoubtedly pursued for reasons of policy. His close friend Solomon *da Piera addressed a number of poems to him.

BIBLIOGRAPHY: Baer, Spain, 2 (1966), 200–10, 228; S. Bernstein (ed.), *Divan Shelomo da Piera* (1942), XIV, 56–66; A. Pacios López, *La Disputa de Tortosa* (1957), index.

ASZÓD, town in Pest-Pilis-Solt-Kiskun county, Hungary, N.E. of Budapest. Jews, mostly of Moravian origin, settled in Aszód at the beginning of the 18th century. The first community was established in 1724. Between 1746 and 1784 the number of Jews increased from 60 to 395, largely due to the influx of Jews from Buda who were expelled by Maria Theresa in 1746. A burial society was founded in 1747 and a synagogue was built in 1757. By 1840, the town had a Jewish population of 530 (24% of the total population). The community organized itself on a Neolog (Conservative) basis. The community was joined by the small congregations from the neighboring villages, including Bag, Boldog, Dány, Domony, Galgamácsa, Héviz, Hévizgyörk, Iklad, Kartal, Ócsa, Tura, Újfalu, Váchartyán, Vácrátót, Vácszentlászló, Valkó, Veresegyház, Verseg, and Zsámbék.

During the Hungarian Revolution of 1848–49 against Austria, the community contributed a considerable sum to the fund for the militia. By the mid-19th century there were only 330 Jewish residents (21%). In 1908 the community erected an imposing new synagogue. After World War I the census recorded 311 Jewish residents (9.5%), occupied in commerce, crafts, and industry. Aszód was the birthplace of Simon Hevesi, Budapest's chief rabbi during the interwar period. During World War II Aszód served as a major recruitment center for Jewish males called up for labor service.

According to the census of 1941, the town had a Jewish population of 278 (4.9% of the total) and 19 (0.3%) converts or Christians identified as racially Jewish. In 1944, the community consisted of 230 Jews, led by Adolf Glück, a lawyer, Rabbi József Berg serving as spiritual leader. Rabbi Berg was preceded in that position by Benjamin Ze'ev Wolf *Boskowitz (1785); Samuel (Weisz) Budapitz (1789–1818), the founder of the local yeshivah; Ẓevi Isaac Hirsch Hirschfeld (1830–60); Mark Handler (1866–70), father of Simon *Hevesi; and Joseph L. Schreiber (1881–1921).

Shortly after the German occupation of Hungary on March 19, 1944, the Jews were first concentrated in a local ghetto and later transferred to Rákoscsaba, an assembly point. From there they were deported in early July 1944 together with the Jews from the neighboring communities in Aszód district, including Bag, Domony, Galgagyörk, Galgahéviz, Galgamácsa, Hévizgyörk, Kartal, Tura, and Verseg.

Only 21 Jews returned to Aszód – two survivors of concentration camps and 19 labor servicemen. Their number grew to 32 by 1949, but in the wake of the Communist anti-Jewish drive they all left by 1956. The synagogue was demolished in 1954.

BIBLIOGRAPHY: B. Vajda, *A zsidók története Abonyban* (1896), 13, 19–20; B. Bernstein, *Az 1848–49 i szabadságharc és a zsidók* (1898), 194, 269–71; M.M. Stein, *Magyar Rabbik*, 2 (1906), 10; 3 (1907), 6, 11; 4 (1908), 1–2, 4; 5 (1909), 3–6; E Karsai, *Fegyvertelen álltak az aknamezökön* (1962), 160; MHJ, 7 (1963), 91, 115–6, 430–2. **ADD. BIBLIOGRAPHY:** Braham, Politics; PK Hungaria, 160–61.

[Laszlo Harsanyi / Randolph Braham (2nd ed.)]

ASZOD, JUDAH BEN ISRAEL (1794–1866), Hungarian rabbi. Born in Aszód (Pest region), he studied at the yeshivah of Mordecai *Banet in Nikolsburg (Moravia). From 1826 to 1830 he served as *dayyan* in Dunaszerdahely (then Hungary), and later in other communities, and from 1853 he headed a large yeshivah there, which attracted hundreds of pupils. Aszod conducted halakhic correspondence with Moses *Sofer and with his son, as well as with other leading Hungarian rabbis of the time. He was a member of the Orthodox rabbinical delegation to the emperor Franz Joseph in Vienna in 1864, which appealed to him to cancel the proposed plan for a government-sponsored rabbinical seminary. The emperor requested his blessing, whereupon Aszod invoked on him the blessing of long life. His collection of responsa, *Teshuvot Maharia* (*Moreno ha-Rav Judah Aszod*), also called *Yehudah Ya'aleh* (pt. 1, (1873); pt. 2 (1880); repr. 1965), arranged according to the four divisions of the Shulḥan Arukh, is regarded as one of the best works of its kind. Of his other works there have been published *Ḥiddushei Maharia*, aggadic novellae on the Torah and some on talmudic themes (1912) and novellae to tractate Ketubbot (1913); *Divrei Maharia* (1931, with an additional part published in 1932), aggadic novellae on Torah and some sermons and eulogies, together with the novellae of his son Aaron Samuel Aszod. His novellae on Torah were published in the *Yalkut Efrayim* (1905). Judah was succeeded as rabbi of Dunaszerdahely by his son, Aaron Samuel Aszod (1830–1905).

BIBLIOGRAPHY: S. Buechler, *Die Lebensgeschichte des Rabbi Juda Aszód* (1933); Ben-Menahem, in: *Sinai*, 62 (1967/68), 268–77.

ATAKI (also **Otaci**), village in northern Moldavia (Bessarabia), on the River Dniester, opposite Mogilev-Podolski. During the Moldavian rule in Bessarabia (before 1812) Ataki was among the few settlements in the region where there was any trading activity and a regular market day. By the second half of the 18th century there was in Ataki a relatively large Jewish community. Its members traded in the village and had connections with other towns in Bessarabia and in the Ukraine. In 1817, 353 Jewish families were living in Ataki (out of a total of 773). The community grew during the first half of the 19th century, with the influx of Jews into Bessarabia, and in 1847 there were 559 Jewish families registered in Ataki. In 1897 the community counted 4,690 persons (67.2% of the total population) and in 1930 there were 2,781 Jews there (79.4% of the total population). A Jewish kindergarten and school run by the *Tarbut organization were established in the 1930s. In June 1940 Ataki together with all of Bessarabia was annexed to the Soviet Union and included in the Moldavian S.S.R. In the beginning of the German-Soviet war Ataki was taken by German and Romanian forces. The latter accused the Jews as being pro-Soviet and probably killed many of them.

[Eliyahu Feldman / Shmuel Spector (2nd ed.)]

No information is available on the fate of the Jews of Ataki during World War II. But situated as it was on the route taken by the deportation transports to *Transnistria, many thousands of Bessarabian and Bukovinan Jews were murdered at Ataki and thrown into the Dniester River. Probably the remaining Jews of Ataki were also murdered and deported to Transnistria. So far as is known, no Jews subsequently lived there.

[Jean Ancel / Shmuel Spector (2nd ed.)]

BIBLIOGRAPHY: BJCE; M. Carp, *Cartea Neagră*, 3 (1947), 155.

ATAR (also **Attar**, **Ibn Atar**, **Benatar**, **Abenatar**, **Abiatar**), family of Spanish origin. Many members of the Atar family left Spain during the persecutions of the 14th and 15th centuries. In the 17th century the name reappeared in Amsterdam, Turkey, and, particularly, Morocco, and afterward in Hamburg, London, and Curaçao. Many of the Abenatars in these communities were descended from Marranos; the family relationship among them is certain. ABRAHAM (I) BEN SOLOMON ABIATAR (17th–18th century) was a poet, talmudist, and kabbalist who lived in Fez, Morocco. ḤAYYIM (I) ABENATAR (same period) was a notable of the community there. Ḥayyim settled in Salé, founding and heading a yeshivah, where his distinguished grandson Ḥayyim Ben Moses (II) *Attar studied; his brother SHEM-TOV (d. 1701), a wealthy philanthropist, was *nagid* at Salé. Shem Tov's son MOSES (d. c. 1725) began his career as secretary-adviser to the viceroy of southern Morocco. He succeeded his father as *nagid*, directed the family's large commercial enterprises, and was appointed treasurer to King Mulay Ishmael. When Moses Mocatta of London failed to negotiate a peace treaty with Morocco on behalf of King George I of England, Moses Abenatar was chosen to replace him. He began by freeing English captives in Morocco and successfully concluded the treaty in 1721, introducing a clause stipulating that Moroccan Jews who had settled in the British Empire would be given the right to be judged in Jewish courts. However, his success aroused jealousy. Unjustly accused of embezzlement, he escaped death only by paying the king a huge fine. After the death of his rival, the *nagid* Abraham Maimaran in 1723, Moses was appointed *nagid* of all the Jews in the Sherifian Empire. Pious, generous, and learned, he built and maintained many schools for poor children. ABRAHAM (II) succeeded his brother Moses as *nagid*. Another brother, JACOB, became governor of the port of Tetuán. At the beginning of the 19th century JOSEPH ABENATAR represented Portugal and Denmark as consul in Rabat-Salé. His son ABRAHAM (III), *av bet din* in Mogador, composed religious poetry. His funeral oration was published under the title *Abi'a Ḥidot* (Leghorn, 1881).

BIBLIOGRAPHY: Baer, Urkunden, 1, pt. 2 (1936), 420–1; ESN, 182ff.; I.S. Emmanuel, *Precious Stones of the Jews of Curaçao* (1957), index; J. Abensur, *Mishpat u-Ẓedakah be-Ya'akov* (1894), nos. 14, 92, 201; SIHM, France, 2nd series, 6 (1960), 574–9; J. de la Faille, *Relation … Maroc* (1726), 27–28, 33–41; J. Windus, *A Journey to Mequinez* (London, 1725), 5–11, 89ff., 197–8, 219ff.; J.M. Toledano, *Ner ha-Ma'arav* (1911), 148, 154–5; Miège, *Maroc*, 2 (1961), 333, 561; Hirschberg, Afrikah, 2 (1965), 266, 273–6; H.Z. Hirschberg, in: *Essays … I. Brodie* (1967), 153–81.

[David Corcos]

ATAR (Aptheker), HAIM (1902–1953), Israeli painter and pioneer. Born in Zlatopol, Russia, Atar joined the "Flowers of Zion" Zionist youth organization and in 1919 became a member of the Jewish defense group set up to combat the pogroms that swept the Ukraine. In 1922 he went to Palestine and was a founder-member of kibbutz En Harod. In 1933 and 1937–38 he studied art in Paris, where he met some of the Jewish leading artists of the day. Atar was a socially committed artist and felt it his task to encourage the kibbutz to aspire to beauty. In 1948 he founded Art Center at En Harod, which he directed. In his own work he was influenced by *Soutine and other Jewish painters of the *Paris School as well as East European Jewish art. His paintings have an atmosphere of melancholy. He painted portraits, still-life subjects, and flowers. He left nearly 300 paintings and about 1,000 drawings, including a series of the members of the *Palmaḥ drawn at the British internment camp at Rafa. Some of his works are on view at the Haim Atar Hall in the En Harod's Art Center.

WEBSITE: www.museumeinharod.org.il.

ATAROT (Heb. עֲטָרוֹת; "crowns"), moshav, north of Jerusalem, evacuated and destroyed during the War of Independence (1948). A small group of laborers settled on the site in 1914 but had to abandon it in the course of World War I. Another group, of East European origin, established the moshav in 1922 and were joined in the 1930s by immigrants from Germany. The moshav withstood Arab assaults in the 1929 and 1936–39 riots. Atarot began to develop model hill culture but suffered a setback when its best lands were expropriated by the British authorities for the Jerusalem airport. During the first stages of the War of Independence, Atarot served crack *Palmaḥ units as a forward position, but on May 17, 1948, the isolated settlement had to be evacuated. A year later, the settlers founded Benei Atarot near Lydda (in 2002 it had a population of 548). Atarot remained in Jordanian territory and almost no trace was found of the settlement when Israeli soldiers captured the site during the Six-Day War (1967). Together with the adjoining airport, it was included in the municipal boundaries of united Jerusalem and an industrial area was developed there.

[Efraim Orni]

ATAROTH (Heb. עֲטָרוֹת), name of several biblical towns or settlements. (1) A city in the territory beyond the Jordan, conquered from the Amorites by Moses and the Israelites and allotted to Gad (Num. 32:3, 34), even though it was situated within the inheritance of Reuben (cf. Josh. 13:16). According to the Stele of Mesha, king of Moab, he captured the city from Israel: "Now the men of Gad had always dwelt in the land of Ataroth and the king of Israel had built Ataroth" (lines 10–11). It is now called Khirbat 'Attārūs, 8 mi. (13 km.) N.W. of Dibon (modern Dhībān) and about 10 mi. (16 km.) E. of the Dead Sea. Moabite, Nabatean, Roman, Byzantine, and Arab potsherds have been found there. (2) Atroth-Shophan

(עַטְרֹת שׁוֹפָן), a place in the vicinity of the above-mentioned Ataroth (Num. 32:35). (3) A city on the southern border of Ephraim (Josh. 16:2) which is perhaps identical with Atroth-Addar (עַטְרוֹת אַדָּר; Josh. 18:13). The Palestinian Targum translates Tomer Devorah ("palm tree of Deborah"; Judg. 4:5) as Atroth Devorah. A village with that name was located in this region in Byzantine times and is also mentioned in the Crusader period as Atarbereth (Atar Be'erot). (4) A city on the northern border of Ephraim (Josh. 16:7); its suggested identification is ʿAwja al-Fawqā or Tell Sheikh al-Dhiyāb, north of Jericho. (5) Atroth-Beth-Joab (עַטְרוֹת בֵּית יוֹאָב) in Judah (I Chron. 2:54) is unidentified.

BIBLIOGRAPHY: (1) Aharoni, Land, index; Avi-Yonah, Land, 152; Press, Ereẓ, 4 (1955), 693–4; Glueck, in: ASOR, 18–19 (1939), 135; idem, in: HUCA, 23 (1) (1950–51), 126ff. (2) Abel, Geog, 2 (1938), 255ff. (3) Alt, in: PJB, 21 (1925), 25; 22 (1926), 33; 23 (1927), 32; Elliger, in: ZDPV, 53 (1930), 279ff.

[Michael Avi-Yonah]

ATHALIAH (Heb. עֲתַלְיָה, עֲתַלְיָהוּ; perhaps: "Yahweh-is-lord"; cf. Akkadian *etellu*, "lord"), sole reigning queen of Judah (842–836 B.C.E.), daughter of *Ahab and *Jezebel (or perhaps a daughter of Omri) of Israel. Athaliah's marriage to *Jehoram (Joram), crown prince of Judah, sealed the alliance between Israel and Judah. It also led to the introduction of Baal (probably = Melqart) worship in Jerusalem alongside the worship of Yahweh, both during the period of her husband's rule and her son *Ahaziah's one-year reign (II Kings 8:16–18, 25–27; II Chron. 21:5ff.; 22:2–4). When Ahaziah was murdered by Jehu in the course of the anti-Omride revolt, Athaliah the queen-mother seized power, murdering all possible rivals in the royal family, just as her husband had done on his accession, possibly on her prompting. Only one infant son of Ahaziah, *Joash, escaped, saved by his aunt Jehosheba, the sister of the dead king and the wife of High Priest *Jehoiada (II Kings 9:27–28; 11:1–3; II Chron. 22:8–12). Six years later, Jehoiada carefully conspired to have Joash crowned in the Temple as the legitimate king, and Athaliah, who had hurried to the scene crying "treason," was led to the "horse entrance" ("The Horse Gate?"), where she was killed (II Kings 11:4–16; II Chron. 23:1–15). The Temple of Baal was destroyed and its priest Mattan, apparently a supporter of Athaliah, put to death (II Kings 11:18; II Chron. 23:17).

Athaliah's violent end was inevitable, as her reign must have been odious not only to the priesthood of the Yahweh Temple but also to the royal guard, who saw in her a foreign usurper and the murderer of the royal Davidic line. However, there is some reason to doubt that young Joash was really in danger, as he, a minor, would have given legitimacy to Athaliah's reign; there is also the suggestion that she herself placed him in the guardianship of the high priest.

In the *aggadah*, Athaliah is grouped with Jezebel, *Vashti, and Semiramis as one of the four women who achieved power in the world (Esth. R. 1:9).

[Hanoch Reviv]

In the Arts

Athaliah's violent career appealed to the taste of the late 17th-century theatergoer for grand and austerely moral themes. The outstanding treatment of her story was by the French dramatist Jean *Racine, whose *Athalie* (1691) became a classic tragedy. The part of the villainous queen was one of Sarah *Bernhardt's great roles. One of the play's many adaptations was *Gemul Atalyah* ("Athaliah's Revenge," 1770), a Hebrew version by the Dutch author David *Franco-Mendes.

Incidental music for the first performance of *Athalie* was written by J.B. Moreau and for later productions by F.A. Boieldieu (1809), Felix *Mendelssohn (1845), and Frank Martin (1946). Handel's oratorio *Athalia* (1733) was also based on Racine's play. Operas on the Athaliah theme were written by J.S. Mayr (1822) and Hugo *Weisgall (1964). Weisgall's work used some Jewish liturgical motifs to create a biblical atmosphere.

In Christian art, Athaliah's murder of the children of the House of David was treated as a prefiguration of Herod's "Massacre of the Innocents." There are interesting representations of Athaliah's story in the 14th-century Wenceslas Bible, the 15th-century Chaise-Dieu tapestry, Renaissance stained glass windows in Cologne and King's College Chapel, Cambridge, and some 15th-century French miniatures.

BIBLIOGRAPHY: BIBLE: Bright, Hist, 222, 233–4, 236; Katzenstein, in: IEJ, 5 (1955), 194ff.; J.A. Montgomery, *The Book of Kings* (ICC, 1951), 410–1; J. Gray, *I and II Kings* (1964), 510–1; Ginsberg, in: *Fourth World Congress of Jewish Studies*, 1 (1967), 91–93. ARTS: T. Ehrenstein, *Das Alte Testament im Bilde* (1923), 688, 696. **ADD. BIBLIOGRAPHY:** M. Cogan and H. Tadmor, *II Kings* (AB), 124–34.

ATHENS, city in Greece. In ancient Jewish history, Athens occupied a position of secondary importance, especially when compared to Alexandria, Antioch, Rome, even Cyrene, and other known cities in Asia Minor. Nevertheless, it must be noted that relations between Athens and Palestine can be traced as far back as the beginning of the sixth century B.C.E. Large quantities of Attic dark-visaged and red-visaged potsherds have been found in various places in the region which was exposed, during the Persian era, to the economic influence of Athens. Coins minted during the occupation of Judea by Persian governors were inscribed "Yahud," and had the image of an owl imprinted upon them, bearing a definite likeness to the Attic drachma.

After the conquest of Palestine by Alexander the Great, there was, apparently, an increase in the activities of the Athenians in the conquered land, though there is only limited information on this phase. The presence of an Athenian in Palestine is evidenced by a contract entered into by an Athenian in the purchase of a female slave in Transjordania, dating to the year 259 B.C.E. Among the signatories who witnessed the document, appears the name of "Heraklitus son of Phillip the Athenian" (Tcherikover, Corpus, 1 (1957), 119–20), who was in the service of Apollonius, minister of the treasury under Ptolemy II. There was an Athenian in command of the troops sent by Antiochus Epiphanes to Palestine to enforce his religious policies (II Macc. 6:1).

With the establishment of the Hasmonean state, Athens was one of the cities to enter into relations with the new state. Josephus records (Ant., 14:149 ff.) a resolution adopted by the Athenian people in honor of Hyrcanus the high priest, ethnarch of the Jews. The decree stated that Hyrcanus had always maintained friendly relations with the Athenians, and always received them cordially when they came to him, and therefore it was resolved to bestow upon him a crown of gold, and to place his statue in bronze in the temple of Demos and the Graces in the city. Josephus himself relates this document to Hyrcanus II, but most modern scholars are inclined to attribute it to Hyrcanus I, specifically to the year 106/5 B.C.E. (the year in which Agathocles served as archon in Athens). Herod also continued the traditional friendship with Athens, to the advantage of the city (Jos., Wars, 1:425). There are documents extant substantiating the existence of friendly relations between Athens and the House of Herod.

Concrete information about a Jewish community in Athens is available only from the beginning of the first century C.E. Agrippa I, in a letter to Gaius Caligula, mentions the land of Attica among other places inhabited by Jews (Philo, Legat., 281). Similarly, when Paul came to a synagogue in Athens, he found there, beside the Jews, many devout Gentiles who revered the Jewish religion (Acts, 17:17). Inscriptions testify that Samaritans lived at Athens (I.G., ed. minor, vol. 2–3, part 3/2, nos. 10219–22) as well as Jews (no. 12609) including one Jerusalemite (no. 8934).

Much attention has been lavished in Judeo-Hellenistic literature on Athens as the most celebrated city in Greek civilization. Philo refers to Athens with profound respect, in a style customary with Greek writers (see Prob. 140); he also mentions famous figures in the history of Athens, such as Solon (Spec. 3:22), as well as historic events relating to Athens, including the conflict between the Athenians and the Lacedaemonians (Spartans; Mos. 2:19). Josephus often refers to Athens and its customs especially in his *Contra Apionem*.

Athens also occupies a place in the talmudic-midrashic literature. The Midrash on Lamentations contains in its introduction many stories the intention of which is to emphasize the superior wit and wisdom of the Jerusalem Jews over the Athenians. Many such stories begin with the phrase: "An Athenian came to Jerusalem." The Babylonian Talmud relates the story of the *tanna*, Joshua b. Hananiah, who at the advice of the Roman emperor came to Athens and challenged the elders of the city to a dispute and defeated them (Bek. 8b).

[Menahem Stern]

Turkish Period and Greek Independence

After the Turkish conquest of Athens (1456) Muhammad II the Conqueror granted its inhabitants the right to prohibit Jewish residence. However, a number of exiles from Spain and their descendants took refuge there after 1492. In 1705 a French traveler found some 15–20 Jewish families living in Athens.

The Jewish community in Athens was one of those destroyed at the time of the Greek uprising against the Ottoman Empire (1821–29). A community with a corporate identity and interests developed after 1834, with the establishment of Athens as the capital of independent *Greece. A number of Jewish families from Germany were attracted to Athens; the financier Max de Rothschild was included in the retinue of the new king, Otto I. A large site for building a synagogue was acquired (1843) through the duchess of Plaisance, Sophie Barbé Marbois, who settled in Athens in 1831 and developed a deep sympathy for Judaism through her intensive Bible studies. In 1847 the Greek authorities banned a popular religious procession during which an effigy of Judas Iscariot was customarily burned, since it might have offended the Baron de Rothschild, then staying in Athens. In revenge, an angry mob sacked the house of David Pacifico, a British subject and honorary consul of Portugal, who was responsible for the completion of the duchess' plans. The British government pressed for his indemnification, and finally the foreign secretary, Lord Palmerston, sent a fleet to Piraeus in 1850, which seized a number of ships. In 1852 the municipality rescinded the gift of the site for the planned synagogue.

Jewish settlement in Athens increased from 60 in 1878 to about 250 in 1887. The Athens community was officially recognized in 1889. In 1890, Charles de Rothschild (1843–1918) became its president, and three small synagogues were established in Athens. In the first decade of the 20th century, as the Ottoman Empire deteriorated, economic decline set in, and there was a fear of political instability and eventual military conscription; many Jews migrated from Ioannina to Athens, eventually establishing their own synagogue.

As a result of the improved economic situation following the Balkan Wars (1912–13), a number of Jews from old Greece and Asia Minor – in particular from Salonika – moved to Athens. The migration increased after the great Salonika fire of 1917, and by the eve of World War II there were 3,000 Jews in Athens. Most of the wealthier businessmen were Ashkenazim while the Sephardi immigrants, originally from other parts of Greece and Turkey, were often peddlers, rag dealers, or small shopkeepers.

[Simon Marcus]

Holocaust and Postwar Period

The numbers of Jews in Athens increased with an influx of refugees from Salonika who fled the Italian air raids of 1940. When Germany invaded Greece in 1941, Greece was subdivided into German, Italian, and Bulgarian zones of occupation; Athens was under the relatively benign rule of the Italians, who, despite their alliance with Germany, were less interested and less disciplined about imposing the "Final Solution." After July 1942, when the Nazis carried out a manhunt of Jews in Salonika until August 1943, about 3,000 fled to Athens. Though Athens was under Italian occupation, the Gestapo began arrests of Jewish leaders in the city, expropriated the congregational records, and requested that the Italians surrender their authority over the Jewish inhabitants. The Italians, however, claimed their authority and tried to prevent Nazi persecution. After the fall of *Mussolini in September 1943, the Germans, having wiped out the congregations of Macedonia, began exterminating the Jews on the Greek mainland and in the islands, at which time Dieter Wisliceny, *Eichmann's assistant, arrived in Athens and tried to force Rabbi Elijah Barzilai to cooperate with him. The rabbi fled to Karpenisia in the mountains with the help of the leftist Communist-leaning ELAS-EAM Greek Resistance movement. Many Jews followed his example and were saved by the Greeks. A Council of Jews was set up by the Germans to organize the local Jewish community. On Oct. 7, 1943, General Jurgen *Stroop published an order dated October 3, ordering Athens Jews to register at the synagogue. The vast majority of them managed to go into hiding, aided by the Greek police and by the Greek Orthodox Church, on the instructions of Archbishop Damaskinos. The local Catholic Church assisted hundreds of Jews in Athens through its rescue stations and harbored Jews in monasteries, found them hiding places, and assisted them financially and with food. Hundreds of families escaped by means of small boats to the shores of Asia Minor, making their way from there to Palestine. However, a significant number did fall into Nazi hands. On March 24, 1944, a total of 800 Jews were captured by the Nazis in the vicinity of the Athens synagogue, after the Nazis had announced that flour for unleavened bread and sugar were to be distributed at the synagogue. They were interned in a camp at Haidari and on April 2 sent to Auschwitz along with other Jews who were caught in Athens. Most of the Jews sent from Athens arrived at Auschwitz; 155 Spanish nationals and 19 Portuguese nationals were sent to *Bergen-Belsen. A total of 1,500 Jews were sent from Athens.

When Greece was liberated from German occupation, about 4,500–5,000 Jews emerged from hiding to reassemble in Athens, but over 1,500 later immigrated to Ereẓ Israel in 1945–46 via illegal immigration boats from the Sounion coast. The Joint Distribution Committee enabled Athenian and Greek Jewry to recover economically from their losses in World War II. In 1957–58 there were over 2,500 Jews in Athens, and in 1968, 2,850, about half the total Jewish population of Greece. Many of those who returned were able to build themselves good positions in business, industry, and the professions. The community had a synagogue (Sephardi), a cemetery, a club, and an elementary school, and an ORT vocational school and welfare institute as well. In 1979, the Jewish Museum of Greece was established in Athens, and a Holocaust memorial was established in the late 20th century. At the outset of the 21st century there were about 3,000 Jews living in Athens.

[Joseph Nehama / Yitzchak Kerem (2nd ed.)]

BIBLIOGRAPHY: C.S. Clermont-Ganneau, *Recueil d'archéologie orientale* (1888), 9312–9900; L. Robert, in: *Hellenica*, 3 (Paris, 1946), 101; L.B. Urdahl, in: *Symbolic' Osloenses*, 43 (1968), 39ff.; Schuerer, Hist, index; Juster, Juifs, 1 (1914), 187; C. Bayet, *DeTitulis Atticae Christianis Antiquissimis…* (1878), 122ff.; H. Kastel, in: *Almanac Israelit* (1923), 49–58; Rosanes, Togarmah, 4 (1935), 37, 412; J. Nehama, *In Memoriam: Hommage aux victimes Juives des Nazis en Grèce*, 2 (1949), 155–7 and passim; M. Molcho, in: *J. Starr Memorial Volume* (1953), 231–9; Friedman, *ibid.*, 241–8. **ADD. BIBLIOGRAPHY:** Y. Kerem, "*Nisyonot Haẓalah be-Yavan be-Milḥemet ha-Olam ha-Sheniyah, 1941–1944*," in *Pe'amim*, 27 (1986), 77–109; B. Rivlin (ed.), *Pinkas Kehillot Yavan* (1999), 67–86.

AT(H)IAS. Sephardi family originating in Spain and later widely spread among the communities of Marrano origin, where it was divided among numerous branches such as Da Costa Athias, Athias Pereira, etc. Among the earliest prominent members was YOM TOV ATHIAS, formerly Jeronimo de Vargas, publisher of the Ferrara Bible (in Spanish) of 1553. MOSES ISRAEL (d. 1665) was the first reader and minister appointed by the Sephardi community of London in 1656, and served it until he died in the Great Plague. JACOB was rabbi in Bordeaux and preached the sermon (subsequently printed) for the restoration of the health of Louis XV in 1744. DAVID (d. 1806) was among his successors. SOLOMON DA COSTA (1690–1769), a London merchant and broker, in his youth an adherent of the Shabbatean movement, presented to the British Museum in 1759 a collection of Hebrew books formerly owned by Charles II, which formed the nucleus of its Hebrew library. DAVID ISRAEL (d. 1753) was *ḥakham* of the Sephardi community of Amsterdam for 25 years. MOSES (1898–) of Jerusalem made important contributions to Sephardi studies, including an edition of folk-ballads (*Romancero Sefaradi*, Jerusalem, 1956).

The family was prominent in Leghorn where, in the 17th century, JOSEPH ATHIAS was highly regarded in Christian literary circles for his scholarship, and MOSES composed in 1701 a discourse in celebration of the recent embellishments to the synagogue. He was possibly the father of DAVID BEN MOSES who, in consequence of his travels in the East as a merchant, became a master of many languages (including Turkish, Serbian, and Russian). He turned his knowledge to good account in his book in Ladino, *La guerta de oro* ("The Golden Garden"; Leghorn, 1778), comprising proverbs, fables, and sympathetic remedies, together with a treatise on physiognomy and a guide to rapid mastery of Greek and Italian, to which was incongruously appended the text of the "Letters Patent of the French Kings in favor of the Portuguese Jews," with a Ladino translation. The Athias mansion, in a central square in Leghorn, was one of the landmarks of the city.

The Athias family was memorable also in rabbinic scholarship, Hebrew printing (see Joseph *Athias), and the annals of Inquisitional martyrdom (Abraham Athias was burned at the stake in Cordova, 1665). It figured in America (Philadelphia, Savannah) from the mid-18th century.

BIBLIOGRAPHY: Roth, Marranos, index.

[Cecil Roth]

ATHIAS, JOSEPH and IMMANUEL (17th century), publishers and printers in Amsterdam. Joseph ben Abraham (Spain or

Portugal, 1634/35–Amsterdam, 1700) was a man of considerable learning. According to David Franco Mendes, the Dutch poet Joost van den Vondel sought the opinion of Joseph before publishing a political stage play.

He founded a printing house, producing works in many languages, especially in Hebrew, Yiddish, Portuguese, and Spanish, which proved successful. In 1681, after the death of Daniel Elsevier, Joseph bought the stock and equipment of Elsevier's publishing house, which also included the non-Hebrew type cut by Christoffel van Dijck. Where the Hebrew material came from is not clear. Probably the Hungarian typecutter Nikolas Kis worked for Joseph, who also experimented with stereotypy and textile printing.

Joseph's first book, a prayer book according to the Sephardi rite, was published in 1658. The famous Hebrew Bible he produced in 1661 was prepared under the editorial supervision of the distinguished scholar Johannes Leusden; a second edition appeared in 1667, for which the States General awarded him with a gold medal and chain. He also published translations of the Bible, and in 1687 he announced that he had printed more than a million Bibles for England and Scotland. Athias' designs were also copied elsewhere. Joseph was accused of appropriating long-term copyright and reprint privileges that had been given by the Polish Jewish authorities in order to produce a Yiddish translation of the Hebrew Bible.

On Joseph's death in 1700 his son Immanuel (Amsterdam, ca. 1664–1714), who had been a partner since 1685, took over the business. He completed the elegant four-volume edition of Maimonides' *Code* which the elder Athias had begun. This edition, of 1150 copies, was dedicated to Moses Machado, army purveyor for King William III of England, who had given economic support to the Athias business. After the completion of the *Code*, Immanuel began the production of Boton's commentary to it, the *Lehem Mishneh*, of which three volumes were published by the time of his death in 1709. Father and son published about 450 books.

The punches and matrices of the firm later passed into the possession of a distant relative of Immanuel, Abraham b. Raphael Hezkia (Amsterdam, ca. 1684–1746), who printed Hebrew books in Amsterdam from 1728. In 1761 the material was acquired by the Proops brothers, Joseph, Jacob, and Abraham, and used by them and successive members of this printing dynasty until 1917, when the so-called Athias Cabinet was sold by auction and acquired by the Tetterode firm (Typefoundry Amsterdam). In 2001 the Amsterdam University Library received the cabinet with its unique contents on permanent loan.

BIBLIOGRAPHY: H. Bloom, *Economic Activities of the Jews of Amsterdam* (1937), 48–52; J.S. da Silva Rosa, in: *Soncino Blaetter*, 3 (1930), 107–11; ESN, 1 (1949), 32–36; Roth, in: REJ, 100 (1936), 41–2. **ADD. BIBLIOGRAPHY:** I.H. van Eeghen, in: *Studia Rosenthaliana*, 2 (1968), 30–41; L. Fuks and R.G. Fuks-Mansfeld, *Hebrew Typography in the Northern Netherlands 1585–1815*, vol. 2 (1987), 286–339; R.G. Fuks-Mansfeld, in: *Een gulden kleinood. Liber amicorum D. Goudsmit* (1991), 155–64; A.K. Offenberg, in: *Lexikon des gesammten Buchwesens*, 1 (1986), 160; idem, in: *Studia Rosenthaliana*, 35 (2001), 100–2; Lane-Lommen, *Dutch Typefounders' Specimens* (1998), 301–5.

[Abraham Meir Habermann / A.K. Offenberg (2nd ed.)]

ATHLIT (Heb. עַתְלִית), ancient port on the Mediterranean coast of Ereẓ Israel, 19 mi. (31 km.) south of Cape Carmel; now site of a Jewish village. It has been identified with Kartha, a city of Zebulun, mentioned in some Greek versions of Joshua 21:34. The road station Certha was still mentioned in its vicinity in 333 C.E. Excavations have shown that the site was inhabited in the Iron Age, probably by Phoenicians. A colony of Greek mercenaries with Egyptian and native wives settled at Athlit in Persian-Hellenistic times. In 1217 Crusader pilgrims built a castle there called the Château des Pélerins (Castrum Peregrinorum); it was held by Templar knights. This served through most of the Crusader period as a kind of immigrants' hostel and absorption and clearing station for newly arrived knights of the Cross who were sent from here to their posts. It successfully resisted an attack by Sultan Baybars in 1264–65. Evacuated in 1291, a few months later than Acre, the fall of Athlit marked the final end of the Crusades. The castle was built on a promontory, jutting out into a bay which served it as a harbor. It was defended by a flooded fosse, a low outer wall, and an inner wall with two towers, 98 ft. high, one of which is still standing. Inside are vaulted store rooms, the foundations of an octagonal church, a vaulted refectory, and other ruins. A town with its own wall, church, and fort in the southeastern corner was attached to the castle; it contained a bath, and large smithies and stables. Near Athlit was a rock-cut passage (*Bāb al-Hawā*; in Latin: *Petra incisa* or *Destrictum*; now *Khirbat Duṣṭrī*) near which Baldwin I was attacked and wounded in 1103. The ruins of Athlit served as a quarry for the construction of Acre.

[Michael Avi-Yonah]

The modern village (moshavah) was founded in 1903 by Baron Edmond de *Rothschild's administration. Most of its lands were bought from Arab fishermen who had built their shacks among the Crusader ruins. One of the country's pioneer industrial enterprises, a plant for extracting table salt from sea water led into large evaporation pans, is located at Athlit. In 1911 an agricultural station was founded there by Aaron *Aaronsohn. In World War I it became a center of *Nili, the clandestine pro-British intelligence organization. During the Mandatory period, the British set up a prison there, and in the 1940s a detention camp for "illegal" immigrants (see *Immigration, "illegal"). A *Haganah raid on the camp in 1945 freed 200 inmates. After the establishment of the State of Israel in 1948 the camp became for a time a large immigrant reception center. In 1950 Athlit received municipal council status. In 1968 it had 2,110 inhabitants, increasing to 3,530 in the mid-1990s and 4,440 in 2002 on a municipal area of 5.5 sq. mi. (14 sq. km.).

In 1980 a bronze ram from a 2nd century B.C.E. warship was discovered about 200 yards off the coast of Athlit

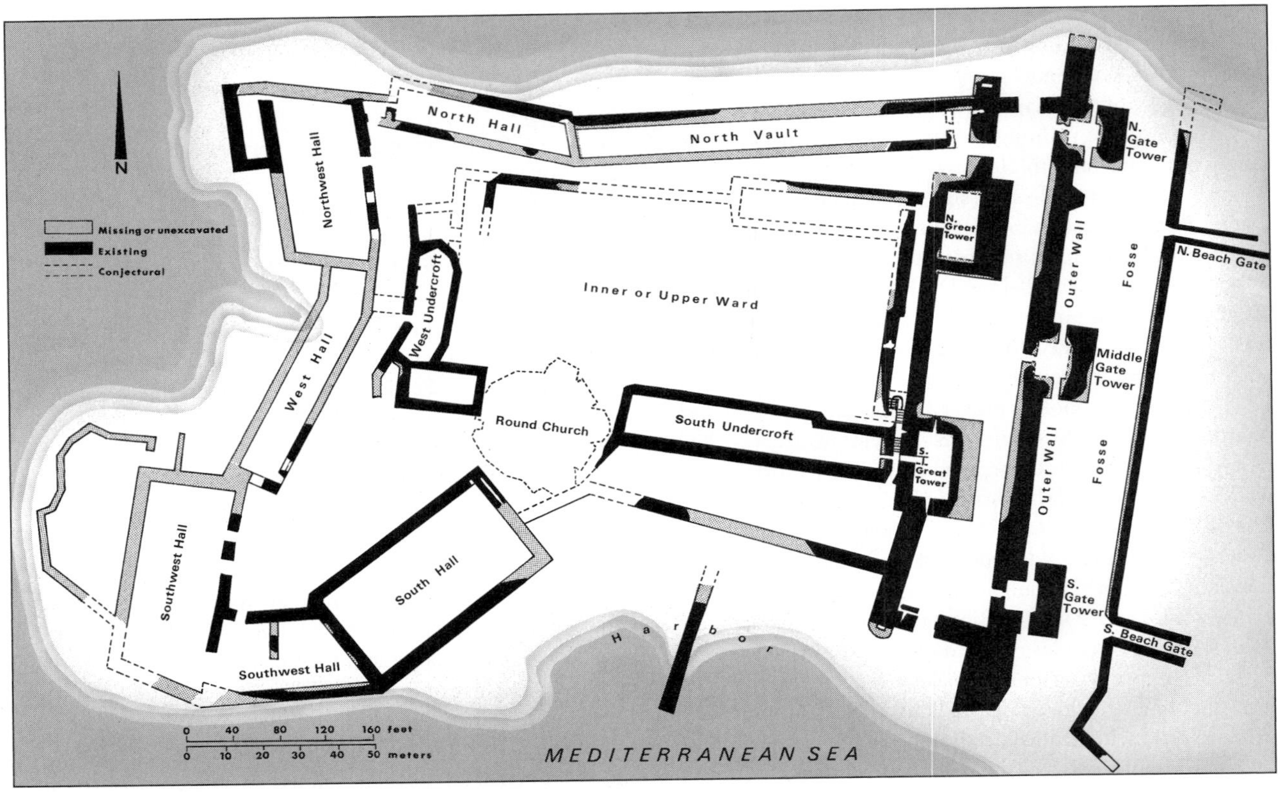

Plan of the 13th-century Crusader castle at Athlit.

(the "Athlit ram"), about 7.5 ft. long (2.26 m.) and weighing 1,000 lbs. (465 kg.). It is now on display at the Haifa Maritime Museum.

[Efraim Orni / Shaked Gilboa (2nd ed.)]

BIBLIOGRAPHY: Johns, in: QDAP, 1–6 (1932–38), excavation reports; S. Runciman, *History of the Crusades* (1965²), index; Prawer, Ẓalbanim, index.

ATHRIBIS, city in Lower Egypt on the Nile Delta, near the present Benha. Various inscriptions and papyri attest to a Jewish community in Athribis during the Ptolemaic and Roman periods. Two inscriptions dealt with a synagogue built there in the second or third century B.C.E. Jewish property in Athribis was confiscated by the Roman administration following the revolt of 115–17 C.E.

BIBLIOGRAPHY: Tcherikover, Corpus, 2 (1960), 255, no. 448; for a selective bibliography see Frey, Corpus, 2 (1952), 370–1, nos. 1443, 1444; W. Dittenberger, *Orientis Graeci Inscriptiones Selectae*, 1 (1903), 170, no. 96, and 177, no. 101; Schuerer, Gesch, 3 (1907⁴), 43.

[Isaiah Gafni]

ATHRONGES, shepherd, rebel, and pretender to the Judean throne following the death of Herod (4 B.C.E.). Athronges was known for "his great stature and feats of strength." After Herod's death, Athronges claimed the Judean throne. His claim was supported by his four brothers, each of whom led an armed band. The rebels began a campaign of terror and guerilla warfare that was originally aimed at Romans and royalists. Later, they mistreated all their captives without discrimination. The rebels' best-known feat was their attack near Emmaus (20 mi. west-northwest of Jerusalem) on a Roman company which was hauling grain and arms to the Roman Army. The rebels surrounded the Roman detachment and killed 40 soldiers and their commander, Arius, but Athronges' troops were driven off by counter-attacking royalist troops from Sebaste. Athronges and his brothers were finally subdued. However, it is not clear what happened to Athronges. Archelaus captured the eldest brother. Two other brothers were conquered by the troops of Ptolemy and Gratus. A fourth brother surrendered to Archelaus. An attempt has been made to identify Athronges with Ben-Batiaḥ, one of the heroes of the Jewish war against Rome (see S.J.L. Rapoport, *Erekh Millin* (1852), 257, s.v. *etrog*).

BIBLIOGRAPHY: Jos., Wars., 2:60ff.; Jos., Ant., 17:278ff.

[Isaiah Gafni]

ATIL or **ITIL** (Turkish "river"), the *Khazar capital on the Volga (itself also called Atil or Itil). According to the *Murūj al-Dhahab* of the Arab historian al-Masʿūdī, the Khazar capital was transferred from *Samandar to the site on the Volga during the first Arab invasions of the Caucasus (seventh century). Accounts of the Arab-Khazar wars in the seventh and eighth centuries refer to al-Bayḍāʿ, apparently the early Arabic name for the capital of the Volga. Surviving descriptions of Atil date from the ninth and tenth centuries. It was then a double town, the western part of which, on the right bank of the Volga, was walled, and consisted chiefly of felt tents with a few clay houses. Some accounts mention that the citadel stood on an island. The minaret of the Friday Mosque of the Muslims of Atil is said to have been higher than the castle. Numerous Christians lived in Atil, under the jurisdiction of their bishop. The eastern commercial part of the town, on the left bank of the Volga, is not described in detail. The double town is referred to by several Turkish names: Sarighshin (from which the later Saqsin is probably derived), the first part of which (cf. *sari*, "yellow") presumably refers to the same feature as indicated by the Arabic name al-Bayḍāʿ, "the white"; and, for the other half, Khanbaligh or Khamlikh (Khamlij). It appears a mistake to interpret the latter as "town of the Khan"; Sarighshin evidently refers to the western half and Khanbaligh to the eastern half of the town. The exact site of Atil cannot at present be determined, but it is placed by M. Artamonov at approximately 87 mi. (144 km.) above *Astrakhan in the region of Yenotayevka-Selitryanoye. L.N. Gumilev, who with others made an archaeological survey of this locality in 1959, found no traces of Atil.

BIBLIOGRAPHY: V. Minorsky, *Ḥudūd al-ʿĀlam* (1937), 451–4 (E.J.W. Gibb Memorial, 11); Dunlop, Khazars, index; A.N. Poliak, *Kazariyyah* (1951^3), 278–94 (includes bibliography); M.I. Artamonov, *Istoriya Khazar* (Rus., 1962), 385–99; G. Moravcsik, *Byzantinoturcica*, 2 (Ger., 1958), 78–79; Roth, Dark Ages, index.

[Douglas Morton Dunlop]

ATLAN, HENRI (1931–), French biologist and philosopher. Born in Algeria, Atlan became doctor of medicine and earned a Ph.D. in sciences. From 1966 to 1968, he was a research fellow in NASA's Ames Research Center and from 1970 to 1973 professor at the Weizmann Institute of Science in Reḥovot, Israel. In 1993, he was appointed to the French National Advisory Committee of Ethics for Sciences of Life and Health, remaining a member for seven years. He is emeritus professor of biophysics at the University of Paris VI and at the Hebrew University of Jerusalem, director of studies at the School of Higher Studies in Social Sciences (EHESS, Paris), and director of the Research Center in Human Biology at the Hadassah academic hospital of Jerusalem.

Atlan is a leading researcher in such fields as genetic applications of biophysics, cell biology, immunology, and artificial intelligence. He has notably developed a theory of complexity and self-organization in various fields, such as biophysics, and has devoted much thought to the philosophical implications of the development of biology, mainly in regard to ethical questions. He wrote *L'organisation biologique et la théorie de l'information* (1972); *Entre le cristal et la fumée* (1979); *A tort et à raison, intercritique de la science et du mythe* (1986); *Enlightenmen to Enlightenment: Intercritique of Science and Myth* (1993); *Tout, non, peut-être. Education et vérité* (1991); *La fin du tout génétique? Vers de nouveaux paradigmes* (1999); *Etincelles de hasard, T.1: Connaissance spermatique* (1999); *La science est-elle humaine?* (2002); and *Etincelles de hasard, T.2: Athéisme de l'écriture* (2003), an analysis of the relationship between science and ethics inspired by talmudic and kabbalistic sources as well as by Spinoza's philosophy.

Atlan has been awarded the highest French distinctions (Chevalier de la Légion d'honneur, Officier dans l'Ordre du Mérite, Officier dans l'Ordre des Arts et des Lettres), and, in 1999, the Prize of the Italian Senate Presidency.

BIBLIOGRAPHY: F. Fogelman-Soulié (ed.), *Les théories de la complexité: autour de l'œuvre d'Henri Atlan* (1991).

[Dror Franck Sullaper (2nd ed.)]

ATLAN, JEAN (1913–1960), French painter, one of France's leading abstract artists after World War II. Atlan, who was born in Constantine, Algeria, went to Paris in 1930 to study philosophy and remained a student there until the Nazi occupation. He took up painting after he was forced to hide from the Germans in a psychiatric hospital. Atlan believed that a painting should present a concept different from that of the external world, but equally organic and alive. Critics have detected various elements in his work forms, which are half vegetable and half animal, the influence of Afro-American sculpture, the art of pre-Columbian America, and the nonfigurative art of North Africa. He was fascinated by the primitive, the magical, and the erotic and was considered the most "mystical" among modern French abstract painters. His style developed gradually, reaching its fullest expression in the last five years of his life.

BIBLIOGRAPHY: B. Dorival, *Atlan* (Fr., 1963); A. Verdet, *Atlan* (Fr., 1957); M. Ragon, *Atlan* (Fr., 1962); Paris Musée National d'Art Moderne, *Exposition Jean Atlan* (1963) – catalogue.

ATLANTA, capital of the state of Georgia, U.S. General population of greater Atlanta: 4,400,000; Jewish population: 97,000. Atlanta was chartered in 1837 as Terminus and developed as an important transportation center. German Jews lived in the area starting in the early 1840s. The first Jew who lived in Atlanta was Jacob Haas; he opened a dry goods business with Henry Levi in 1846. Moses Sternberger, Adolph Brady, and David Mayer followed shortly as did Aaron Alexander and his family, who were American-born Sephardim from Charleston, South Carolina. The Hebrew Benevolent Society established in 1860 became the Hebrew Benevolent Congregation in 1867. This occurred following a visit by Rev. Isaac Leeser of Philadelphia, who came to conduct a wedding. Leeser was the *ḥazzan* of Mikveh Israel of Philadelphia in the middle of the 19th century. He established the monthly *Occident* newspaper in 1844 which became a major media vehicle for American Jewry. He stood for traditional Judaism as Isaac Mayer *Wise began to pioneer Reform Judaism in the U.S. Leeser urged the leadership to form an actual congregation which was incorporated that year. Later the synagogue came to be known as the "Temple." The first rabbi was appointed in 1869, and the first building was constructed in 1877. Although Reform from its inception, several of the rabbis in the late 1800s were more traditional, but with the arrival of Dr. David Marx in 1898, the character of the Temple became almost Radical Reform with even Sunday services substituted for Sabbath services from 1904 to 1908.

East Europeans emigrating in the late 1870s established several Orthodox congregations in the following decade. They merged into the Ahavath Achim synagogue in 1887. After several breakaway shuls were formed and then disappeared, the congregation built a synagogue in 1901. In 1896 a visitor from Palestine came to Atlanta to collect money to issue his new book. When it appeared in Jerusalem in 1898 as *Ẓir Ne'eman*, the author, Yehoshua Ze'ev Avner, listed the 18 Atlanta contributors, including the Moses Montefiore Relief Society and the Ahavath Achim congregation. The descendants of some of the contributors still lived in Atlanta in 2005. One of the early rabbis, Berachya Mayerowitz (1902–6), gave his sermons in English. He also led a major fundraising effort at the city's Bijou Theater for the survivors of the Kishniev pogrom in April 1903. On December 5–6, 1904, he welcomed Jacob deHaas, director of the Federation of American Zionists, on his boom trip of three weeks throughout the south. DeHaas characterized the members of the congregation as "muscular Jews committed to Zionism."

One of the breakaway Orthodox congregations in the early 20th century, Shearith Israel, was incorporated in 1904 and survived. Several others did not. In 1910 Rabbi Tobias *Geffen became the rabbi of the synagogue, which was seeking a rabbi with "outstanding learning credentials" and one whose "sermons could touch the hearts of the people." His 60-year career in Atlanta was a blend of Orthodoxy and modernism. His determination to raise the level of Jewish education succeeded when he and later his children personally taught in the Atlanta Jewish Preparatory School and Shearith Israel Sunday School. Nine Atlanta men and one Chattanooga individual, who boarded, became Orthodox and Conservative rabbis. In two areas, he was the authority not only for Atlanta but throughout the South. He was the *mesader gittin*, issuing Jewish divorces throughout his career, and he checked the *shoḥetim* in Atlanta and 15 other cities. In 1916 in Atlanta 48 Jewish families, who did not live in the "center of the Jewish community," petitioned Rabbi Geffen to permit a slaughterer of chickens to be available in their area, outside of his normal jurisdiction, once a week to do kosher killing at "five cents a chicken." Rabbi Geffen's most notable halakhic decision, giving a *hekhsher* to Coca-Cola, an Atlanta company, was made in 1934.

In 1919 Rabbi Tobias Geffen met with Bishop Warren Candler, chancellor of Emory, a Methodist college which had just moved to Atlanta from South Georgia. Geffen's concern about Saturday classes prompted Candler to permit observant Jewish students who attended Emory to be present on the Jewish Sabbath and holidays without having to take notes and stand for exams. (Rabbi) Joel *Geffen and (Professor) Moses *Hadas were the first two Jewish students in this category. After a decade the Saturday classes ended, which resolved the issue.

The Jewish student body at Emory remained small until the 1950s. Professor Nathan *Saltz, who graduated from the Emory medical school in 1940, made *aliyah* in 1949 and established the surgical systems for all the major hospitals in Israel. In 1998 he was awarded the Israel Prize in Medicine. In the 1950s the number of Jewish students in all the Emory University schools was between 150 and 175. By the 1970s Emory's reputation was attracting Jewish students from the entire United States. Hillel statistics in the 1990s suggested that between 30 to 40% of the 5,500 undergraduates were Jewish. Parallel to the student growth was the faculty growth both in academic Judaica and general academia. Professor David Blumenthal was given the Jay and Leslie Cohen chair in Jewish Thought in 1976 when it was established. When the Carter Center came into being in the early 1980s, Professor Ken Stein, a Middle East specialist, was chosen as the academic director. In 2004 there were 12 full-time faculty members teaching in all areas of Judaica. The Dorot Professor of Jewish History is the noted Holocaust specialist, Deborah Lipstadt. A masters program in Jewish Studies exists and a doctoral program was being planned. When Arthur *Blank of Home Depot gave Emory a major gift, the department was given Blank's spiritual leader's name, Rabbi Donald Tam Jewish Studies Department.

In addition to the thousands of new Judaic volumes in Hebrew, English, Yiddish, and many other languages purchased by the Woodruff Library of Emory in the last 25 years, the Special Collections department under the leadership of Dr. Linda Matthews, now head of all libraries at the school, began to receive diverse collections of Jewish interest. The Rabbi Jacob Rothschild papers, Holocaust collections from various sources, the Elliot Levitas papers (Rhodes Scholar and Georgia congressman), the Morris Abrams papers, the Geffen papers, and numerous other collections are all in Emory's Special Collections. Nineteenth century Judaica Americana has both been donated and purchased.

Atlanta's earliest Jews were mostly merchants. Some, primarily members of the Temple, were active in such fields as banking, brokerage, insurance, and real estate and pioneered in the manufacture of paper products and cotton bagging. The East European Jews had small stores, and a large number were pawnbrokers on Decatur Street in the heart of the city. Throughout the 1920s, Jewish lawyers and physicians were not allowed to join most law firms and could only practice at certain hospitals. Prior to World War II those barriers were broken down, and the number of Jewish professionals increased dramatically. The main department store in the city, founded in 1884, was Rich's until it was purchased by a conglomerate in 1991. In 2005 the name Rich's disappeared completely from the store's nomenclature. Starting with its arrival in Atlanta in 1987, the Home Depot became the major Jewish-owned firm in the city.

Jews have held public office in Atlanta since the post-Civil War era. Samuel Weil and Lewis Arnheim served in the Georgia legislature in 1869 and 1872. Aaron Haas became the city's mayor pro tem in 1875. Victor Kriegshaber was president of the Atlanta Chamber of Commerce from 1917 until 1922. A founding member of the Atlanta Board of Education, David Mayer, was known as the "father of public schools." In the 1930s Max Cuba, Charles Bergman, and Louis Geffen served on the Atlanta City Council and Board of Education. After being a vice mayor of Atlanta from 1961 to 1968, Sam *Massell Jr. ran for mayor against the candidate of the Atlanta power structure, labeled as antisemitic in the course of the campaign. He won the election with 20% of the white vote and 90% of the black vote. After a very successful four-year term, Massell lost to Maynard Jackson, the first black to be elected mayor of the city.

Elliot Levitas was elected to Congress for four terms, the first Jew from Georgia in the U.S. House of Representatives. Liane Levitan was the County Commissioner of DeKalb County for 20 years (1983–2003). The major electoral change in the Atlanta area was in Cobb County. There in 1915 Leo *Frank was lynched by vigilantes in the town of Marietta near the home of the young white Protestant girl whom he was convicted of murdering by circumstantial evidence. Few Jews lived in Marietta and Cobb County until the 1980s. In 2000 Sam Olens, an attorney and active Conservative Jew, was elected chairman of the Cobb County Council. After his reelection in 2004, he was chosen chairperson of the Atlanta Regional Planning Board. Two other Marietta Jews were elected as judges in the county judicial system and statewide to the Georgia Court of Appeals.

Dr. David Marx (1872–1962) was rabbi of the Temple for 52 years. A leader in interfaith activities, Marx was extremely anti-Zionist, helping to found the American Council for Judaism. In 1945 his Yom Kippur sermon was a "tirade against the establishment of a Jewish state." He was challenged publicly by one of his own members, Albert Freedman, director of the Southeastern Region of the Zionist Organization of America. When Dr. Jacob *Rothschild succeeded Marx in 1947, he brought a deep commitment to social justice and also became a Zionist advocate. Rothschild was so outspoken for the civil rights of blacks that in 1958 the Temple was bombed, fortunately when no one was in the building. From the Atlanta mayor to the Georgia governor to President Eisenhower, strong support poured out against the perpetrators of this act. Ralph McGill, editor of the *Atlanta Constitution* and a visitor to Palestine and Israel in 1946 and 1950, won a Pulitzer Prize for his moving editorials condemning the bombing. In the 1960s Rothschild worked closely with Dr. Martin Luther King Jr. as new federal legislation was passed assuring American blacks their rights. When King was awarded the Nobel Prize, Rothschild organized the dinner in King's honor in Atlanta. Rothschild died a very young man and was succeeded by his associate Dr. Alvin Sugarman, an Atlanta native. Sugarman took the lead in the Atlanta Jewish community in regard to developing closer relations between the blacks and the Jews. The Rich's store, whose owners belonged to the Temple, was the first major Atlanta store to allow its cafeteria to be integrated. Many Jewish firms hired blacks for administrative positions prior to such hiring becoming widespread in the general community. The Anti-Defamation League's southeast region office in Atlanta and the American Jewish Committee's regional office worked diligently to aid blacks in court and through demonstrations. The changing attitude of the blacks toward American Jews was influenced by funding from Muslim groups and anti-Israel propaganda, which reached deeply into the South in general and Atlanta in particular.

From 1928 until 1982 Dr. Harry *Epstein served as the rabbi of Ahavath Achim. Ordained at the Hebron Yeshiva in 1925, where his brother was killed in the 1929 riots, Epstein possessed all the training necessary to be an Orthodox rabbi but chose to move his congregation into the Conservative movement after World War II. A marvelous orator in English and Yiddish, Epstein was the key Zionist leader in Atlanta and attended national conferences in major American cities where the foundation of the State of Israel was forged during World War II. He and Rothschild traveled to Israel together in 1950. On their return, they co-chaired the annual Welfare Fund Drive. In 1953 Epstein joined the Rabbinical Assembly and brought his congregation into the United Synagogue of Conservative Judaism. He was most adept at training individuals to be communal and synagogue leaders. Once he moved his synagogue to the Northside of the city where most of his members lived, the congregation grew to over 2,000 families. From 1971 until 1995, Cantor Isaac Goodfriend, a Holocaust survivor, served as the cantor of Ahavath Achim. Goodfriend developed a full-scale music program at Ahavath Achim. In addition he became a community leader in his own right. He campaigned throughout the United States in 1976 for President Jimmy Carter, and he was asked to sing "The Star-Spangled Banner" at the Inauguration in Washington. Once elected, Carter appointed Stuart *Eizenstat his domestic policy advisor and attorney Robert Lifshitz, as White House counsel. Eizenstat played a major role in the legislation for the Holocaust Memorial in Washington and Cantor Goodfriend served on the first Holocaust Memorial Commission. Lifshitz was a significant figure in the negotiations between Menahem Begin and Anwar Sadat, which led to the Camp David agreements in 1979.

Epstein was succeeded by Dr. Arnold Goodman, who led Ahavath Achim for the last 20 years of the 20th century. He taught at one of the black colleges in Atlanta and was an outspoken advocate for Israel.

In the period just after World War II the only synagogue facility available on the north side of Atlanta was the educational building of Ahavath Achim. A group of Orthodox Jews established in 1947 a small congregation, Beth Jacob, on

Boulevard in that area. There was no way of predicting how this synagogue would change the Jewish character of Atlanta. In 1951 Dr. Emanuel Feldman came from the Ner Israel Yeshiva in Baltimore to be Beth Jacob's rabbi. His commitment to Orthodoxy helped develop the congregation into the first of a string of Orthodox congregations and day schools. This growth coincided both with the **Ba'al Teshuvah* movement in Judaism and the evangelical revival in American Christianity. Feldman was an outstanding speaker, had the knowledge to give *shi'urim*, and had a very fine secular education. Once Beth Jacob moved to the Toco Hills area near Emory University, Rabbi Feldman was able to build a community of Sabbath observers, many of whom taught at the university and worked at what is now known as the Centers for Disease Control and Prevention. His experience as a congregational rabbi was so successful that he wrote a "love letter to his congregation," a rare document in the American Jewish rabbinate. His son Ilan Feldman succeeded him as rabbi in 1995, and Rabbi Emanuel Feldman and his wife moved to Jerusalem.

The Sephardi congregation, Or VeShalom, was founded in 1914. The majority of the early Sephardi Jews in Atlanta, who arrived in the first decade of the 20th century, were from Rhodes. Rabbi Joseph Cohen, a Hebraic scholar and a *sofer*, was the spiritual leader of the congregation from the mid-1930s until 1973. Under his leadership the synagogue built a new building in the Toco Hills area in 1968.

In 1904 the Reform and Orthodox Jews formed the YMHA. By 1908 it had become the Jewish Educational Alliance, and by 1911 a building was completed on Capitol Avenue. In 1954 the Alliance moved to Peachtree Street as the Jewish Community Center. As the Jewish community began to grow beyond the perimeter highway, a satellite facility of the JCC was built in 1979 in the Dunwoody area. Then the community in Cobb County expanded into a new center of Jewish life, and another satellite facility of the JCC was constructed in Marietta in 1989. Because the JCC locale in Dunwoody had major acreage, the leadership decided to sell the intown facility and build a new campus. In 1995 the JCC and adjacent Federation facilities were closed. The campus in Dunwoody was named for Bernard Marcus, who gave a major gift to the $60 million capital campaign. In the early years of the 21st century the JCC grew from 10,000 units to over 26,000 units. At the Marcus JCC campus programming is provided for all ages with athletic facilities, a professional theater, a children's discovery museum, and a kosher cafeteria.

Two organizations, the Moses Montefiore Relief Society (1896) and the Free Kindergarten and Social Settlement (1903), merged into the Federation of Jewish Charities in 1912. In 1924 the Jewish Social Services evolved out of the Federation. In 1928 Ed Kahn came to Atlanta as the head of Social Services. Then in 1936 Harold Hirsch, a noted leader in the Jewish and Atlanta legal community, pioneered the establishment of the Jewish Welfare Fund for combined fundraising, headed by Ed Kahn until 1960. He was succeeded by Mike Gettinger, an Orthodox Jew who broadened the scope of the Federation and brought in major donors from different sectors of the community. Gettinger was followed by David Sarnat, who took over in 1984.

At the end of 1984 the Metropolitan Atlanta Jewish Population Study pointed to the growth of the Jewish population from 9,630 at the end of World War II to 59,084. Affiliation with synagogues had dropped from 90% in 1947 to 44% in 1984. The key to the future of Atlanta Jewry lay in the fact that a quarter of the population were 18 and below; 22% were in the 30–39 age bracket and only 12.6% were above 60. The Jews had moved, according to the study, to suburban areas north of Atlanta in Gwinett and Cobb counties. Because of the needs of youth and younger parents, five synagogues had been formed in these counties. In total there were 15 synagogues in the Atlanta area in 1984. In 2005 there were 34 synagogues in the Greater Atlanta area; six of which were Chabad, six Orthodox, one Gay, and the rest Reform and Conservative. In the 1984 study number 23 on the priority agenda for community needs were Jewish educational programs. Once that became known to the Federation leadership changes began to occur.

In 1985 the Torah Day School joined the Greenfield Academy (1953), Yeshiva High School (1970), and Epstein Solomon Schechter School (1973). Since then the Davis Academy (Reform) (1992), Temima Girls High School (1996), Weber Community High School (1997), and Yeshiva Ohr Yisrael (2002) have been established. There is a Tichon Communal High School for all students who are graduates of elementary day school programs and congregational religious schools. There are active Jewish educational programs at all 34 synagogues as well as afternoon Hebrew schools and Sunday schools in some congregations. The Jewish Community Center has many Jewish educational programs and lectures including the largest Melton program in the United States.

In November 1983 the General Assembly of the Jewish Federations was held in Atlanta. Featured at the newly opened Schatten Gallery in the Woodruff Library at Emory University was an exhibit on the history of Georgia Jewry from 1733 to 1983. That exhibit proved to be a key step in the founding of the Breman Jewish Museum. The Museum and Archives were established in 1996 after a major exhibit on Atlanta Jewry at the Atlanta History Center's new annex. The Breman Museum has two permanent displays: one on the Holocaust and the other on Atlanta Jewry. The Museum has been quite active, and new exhibits have been created just for display. Other traveling exhibits have also been shown at the Museum. As an archival center, the Breman Museum has major collections on Atlanta Jews and communal institutions. In addition archival material from various parts of the South is now being housed at the Museum.

The Jewish Federation of Greater Atlanta acquired its new name in 1997. Since that time the Federation's professional leadership went from David Sarnat to Steve Rakkitt. The endowment program of the Federation now contains over $125 million. The Federation is the major initiator of programs for the Jewish community, although it does not provide any grants for synagogue programs. The Federation has seen a major age change in the Jewish community, so in 1998 a new Jewish Home was constructed on the campus where the older Jewish Home stood and the Jewish Tower. The Jewish Home built in 1975 was renovated and became an assisted living facility. The campus gives senior citizens the opportunity to move from one facility to the other as per their needs.

The entrepreneurial skills of Atlanta Jewish merchants were evident in the Dalton Carpet Mart Centers, Home Depot, and dot.com startup companies. The heads of these companies, Nate Lipson, Arthur *Blank, and Bernard Marcus, have become major donors in the community. Arthur Blank purchased the Atlanta Falcons Professional Football team; Bernard Marcus was building a $250 million Aquarium in the center of Atlanta. Many other communal projects are under Jewish leadership.

When Atlanta won the right to host the Summer Olympics in 1996, the leadership of the Jewish Federation of Greater Atlanta allied itself with the Southeastern Office of the Israel Consul based in Atlanta to ensure that during the Games the martyred Munich 11 were remembered. Negotiations occurred for several years, and the Olympics Board was trying to avoid this public type of memorial. Steve Selig, at the time of the Olympics in 1996, worked incessantly until the breakthrough occurred. On the site of the Federation Offices, the Selig Center, there was a public dedication of a memorial to the Munich 11. The international president of the Modern Olympics participated in the moving event along with the families of the Munich martyrs who came from Israel to be at the Games and a very large group of Jewish Olympians from all over the world.

Atlanta has always had Anglo-Jewish papers from early in its history. There were four different English papers and one in Yiddish prior to World War I. In 1925 the *Southern Israelite* moved from Augusta to Atlanta and became the only weekly southern Jewish paper aside from the *Baltimore Jewish Comment*, which became the current *Baltimore Jewish Times*. The *Southern Israelite*, now the *Atlanta Jewish Times*, had three notable editors: Adolph Rosenberg, Vida Goldgar, and Neil Rubin. In the early 21st century the paper was owned by Jewish Renaissance Publications headed by Michael Steinhardt.

A writer and a playwright have helped to enlighten the American Jewish community and the world Jewish community about Atlanta Jewry. Eli Evans published *The Provincials* in 1973, the first book on the Jews in the South. The popularity of the book has kept it in print since then. The revised edition has several illuminating chapters on Atlanta Jewry through the year 2000. The playwright Alfred Uhry made Atlanta Jewry come to life in his award-winning play *Driving Miss Daisy*. Uhry captures the spirit of the Atlanta Temple crowd through the interaction of Miss Daisy and her chauffeur Hoke. The play has been produced in many languages and was an Oscar award-winning movie with Jessica Tandy and Morgan Freeman. Alfred Uhry has donated his papers to Special Collections at Emory University.

BIBLIOGRAPHY: S. Hertzberg, *Strangers Within the Gate City* (1978); M.K. Bauman, "Centripetal and Centrifugal Forces Facing the People of Many Communities: Atlanta Jewry from the Frank Case to the Great Depression," in: *The Atlanta Historical Journal*, vol. 23 (1979), 25–54; E. Evans, *The Provincials* (1997²); L. Dinnerstein, *The Leo Frank Case* (1968); *Creating Community* (Breman Museum, 1994), essays on Atlanta Jewry for the exhibit at the Atlanta Historical Center 1994–95; *The Southern Israelite – Atlanta Jewish Times* (1925–).

[David Geffen (2nd ed.)]

ATLANTIC CANADA, designation for the Canadian provinces of New Brunswick, Nova Scotia, Prince Edward Island, and Newfoundland. The Jewish communities of Atlantic Canada often are overlooked in discussions of Canadian Jewry or simply lumped together with other small Jewish communities. Sometimes they even take on an exotic quality, as if there were something mystical about Jewish existence in Atlantic Canada. Yet Jewish life in the region continues to exist, and although it may not be as vibrant as in others, some communities in fact are thriving.

History

The Jewish community of Atlantic Canada is one of the oldest in Canada. In New Brunswick, Jewish settlement is traced back to Solomon Hart, who came to Saint John from England in 1856. Over the next decades this community grew and became a center of Jewish life in New Brunswick. The Moncton Jewish community was established by 22 families from Durbonne, Lithuania, who immigrated at or about the same time, while the Fredericton community is much more recent (the first family arrived around 1912).

The beginnings of a Jewish community in Nova Scotia can be traced back to the mid-1700s when there were approximately 30 Jews in Halifax. This small community disappeared by the mid-19th century and was not re-established until the 1880s. Halifax emerged during this period as the center of Jewish population in Nova Scotia. Halifax was also one of the major debarkation points for thousands of Jewish immigrants coming from Europe throughout the 20th century. There are very few Canadian Jews whose families did not arrive through Pier 21 in Halifax. For many, it was off the ships and onto the trains to destinations west.

The other area of significant Jewish settlement in Nova Scotia was Cape Breton, with Jewish communities in Sydney, Glace Bay, New Waterford, and Whitney Pier. Prince Edward Island never had more than a handful of Jews most of whom arrived after the 1920s. Their numbers limit Jewish organization there. Newfoundland's population, largely concentrated in St. John's, is more recent.

Demography

The Jewish population of Atlantic Canada is small, numbering only 3,915 persons in 2001 and constituting only 1.1% of the Jewish population of Canada. The vast majority (71%) of Jews in the region resided in Nova Scotia (2,780). The remaining Jewish population was distributed as follows: New Brunswick, 21.5%; Newfoundland and Labrador, 4.9%; and Prince Edward Island, 2.7%.

Over half of Atlantic Canadian Jews resided in Halifax. Pockets of Jewish population were found in the smaller cities (Fredericton, 290; Moncton, 265; Cape Breton, 235; St. John's, 145; and St. John, 135). These smaller communities, however, experienced population decline in the late 1990s, particularly Saint John, while Halifax experienced increases in Jewish population. Communities also varied greatly by age. For example, the median age in Saint John and Cape Breton was 57.1 and 62.0 respectively, while the median age for Halifax was 41.1. Half of Cape Breton's Jewish population – but only 16% of Halifax's population – was 65 years of age or older. As these demographics suggest, Halifax has become an important center for Jewish life in the region.

The viability of the region's Jewish communities must be set in the context of these demographic factors. Not only does Nova Scotia have the largest Jewish population of the region, it is the only Atlantic Province that has experienced positive growth in the last number of decades, growing by 21.1% since 1971. The Jewish populations of New Brunswick and Newfoundland, on the other hand, declined by 27.6% and 28.3% respectively. These demographics have important repercussions as they impact on mechanisms for Jewish identity such as visibility, integration, and institutional support structures.

Community Life

Because of their numbers, Atlantic Canada Jews cannot be identified as living in certain residential areas or belonging to certain social clubs. Even in Halifax there are no homogenous Jewish neighborhoods. This lack of a critical mass means that Atlantic Jews lack collective visibility and also have become integrated into the larger society. While integration occurs everywhere in Canada, in Atlantic Canada, Jews participate not only in the impersonal aspects of the larger society such as politics and economics, but also in the more personal areas such as friendship networks and kinship ties through intermarriage. In the smaller communities of the region this participation is further encouraged by the limited number of fellow Jews.

One does not find in the smaller Jewish communities in Atlantic Canada the panoply of Jewish support systems, both religious and secular, that are found in metropolitan centers, e.g., synagogues, Jewish Ys, community centers, and day schools. In Atlantic Canada, there are synagogues only in a few communities. Only Moncton, Fredericton, and Halifax have both synagogues and rabbis (Halifax has two synagogues as well as Lubavitch activity). Cape Breton, Saint John, and St. John's synagogues do not have rabbis.

These factors would lead one to conclude that Jewish life in Atlantic Canada is highly precarious. While this is possibly true for centers with declining and aging Jewish populations, it is important to understand that the differences among the communities are not only quantitative differences but translate into qualitative differences in the struggle for viability of the Jewish communities. What supports this struggle and how are these differences manifested?

Mechanisms for Survival

(1) THE SYNAGOGUE. For religiously affiliated Jews in Atlantic Canada, synagogues, where they exist, are important conservers of Jewish life. The synagogue, as well as the rabbi, takes on a much more critical role in organized Jewish life than in larger centers where there are a variety of Jewish institutional connections. Communities where there are no synagogues and/or rabbis are less likely to grow and survive than those communities with active synagogues. Halifax has the most developed (but still limited) religious institutional base for maintaining Jewish identity. It is, however, difficult for the synagogue alone to address all aspects of Jewish identity. Nor does the synagogue address the needs of secular Jews. There are, however, a number of other mechanisms that reinforce Jewish life.

(2) THE ATLANTIC JEWISH COUNCIL (AJC). The AJC, created in 1975, serves as an umbrella organization for Jewish activities in the entire region, offering a range of services such as youth programming, campus services, young leadership, seniors' programming, conferences, chaplaincy, and Camp Kadimah (a Jewish Zionist camp in Nova Scotia). It not only affords a secular focus for Jewish identity, but also is an important link to the external Jewish community. The AJC's participation in national organizations such as the Canadian Jewish Congress, the United Israel Appeal, and Canada-Israel Committee reinforces the region's sense of belonging to the Canadian Jewish community. As such, the parameters of the Jewish community have grown beyond the geographical boundaries of Atlantic Canada. Aided by advanced communication and transportation, community can be disentangled from spatial constraints. Through participation in activities such as national organizations, national newspapers, and the Internet, important mechanisms for preservation of Jewish identity have been developed.

(3) INTERPERSONAL SUPPORTS. In addition to these structural and institutional supports, there are unique interpersonal supports that are important in maintaining Jewish identity. In Atlantic Canada, Jews include all Jews in their communities and are friendly and welcoming to everyone. Whether this is necessitated by small numbers, or reflects the larger regional culture of hospitality, the result is the same – a better integration of Jews into the Jewish community. Having to rely on one's fellow Jews for services such as a *minyan* or *shiva* meals creates a sense of community that is not found in metropolitan centers. Jewishness cannot be taken for granted when one is not surrounded by Jews.

Postscript

It is often surprising for Jews from other regions to recognize that there is Jewish life in Atlantic Canada. While some communities are aging and declining, and one is pessimistic about their future, for others there remains limited but ongoing Jewish life. Yet, often one hears from larger centers that if Jewish survival is important, Atlantic Jews should simply pack their bags and move west.

Advocates for a continued presence have responded to this challenge. They argue that Atlantic Jewry must be maintained and supported for reasons that go beyond the economic impracticability of relocation. Firstly, there is the Jewish responsibility that the entire Jewish community is obligated to help fellow Jews survive (both physically and spiritually). Secondly, there is much about Atlantic Jewry that is worthwhile maintaining, for example, the friendliness, national participation, and sense of community discussed earlier. Finally, Jews in Atlantic Canada carry the larger Canadian Jewish agenda to their communities. If there were no Jews in Moncton or Halifax to carry the torch for Jewish causes (e.g., Israel, antisemitism, etc.), then non-Jews in these cities would know nothing about Jewish issues. Because they are often friends and neighbors of political decision makers, they can carry the torch more successfully than Jews in larger communities. The Jewish community of Atlantic Canada, it is hoped, will remain a vital piece in the Canadian Jewish mosaic.

[Sheva Medjuck (2nd ed.)]

ATLANTIC CITY, one of the most frequently visited tourist sites on the East Coast of the United States, located off the southern New Jersey coast and part of a two-county area rich in Jewish culture and identity opportunity. At the outset of the 21st century, over 15,000 year-round Jewish residents lived in the Atlantic/Cape May bi-county area, which more than triples in population in the summer months. The gaming mecca with its nearby historic Boardwalk exists basically on Absecon Island, which includes Atlantic City, Ventnor, Margate, and the downbeach community of Longport. The area has various synagogues of most denominations including two thriving Reform congregations, several well-attended Conservative congregations, and a small but growing Orthodox population. Wildwood, part of Cape May County, is home to another Conservative congregation.

The first Jewish settlers arrived in 1880, when the city was already a summer resort for Philadelphians. Ten years later the first congregation, Beth Israel (Reform), was founded, followed by Rodef Sholom (Orthodox) in 1896. From the outset Jews gravitated to the tourist-oriented industries. They have continued in this capacity and in the professions, while also playing a leading role in the city's cultural and philanthropic activities. Jewish organizational life developed gradually. As precursors to what now exists a Young Men's Hebrew Association was founded in 1911, and in 1916 the Hebrew Sheltering Home was founded to provide a temporary haven for indigent persons needing food and lodging. This then evolved into the 155-bed Hebrew Old Age Center, now formally known as Seashore Gardens Living Center, providing geriatric care. From the Montefiore True Sisters, who provided food baskets to the needy, evolved the Federation of Jewish Agencies, founded in 1923 to coordinate all fundraising, budgeting, and community planning for local, national, and overseas agencies. There was a community weekly, the *Jewish Record*, founded in 1939, which existed until the early 1990s. As with many northeastern cities and even the famed Catskill Resort area in New York, during the middle of the 20th century, Atlantic City underwent a decline. With the advent of air conditioning and with non-Jewish hotels ending their policy of excluding Jews, the Jewish hotels declined and went out of business. The introduction of gaming was intended to revive investment in the city and to make it a tourist destination once again. By then many Jews and most Jewish institutions had left the city. By the turn of the 20th century Atlantic and Cape May counties rather than Atlantic City had become the center of Jewish life.

Atlantic County boasts two popular kosher restaurants, two day schools (Jewish Community Day School of Atlantic and Cape May Counties, housed in a new building in Northfield, and the Trocki Hebrew Academy, which is located in Egg Harbor Township), a *mikveh*, and a newly expanded network of social service agencies. They include the brand new Katz Jewish Community Center and Jewish Family Service, both housed as part of the "community campus" environment in Margate City. Also part of the campus is the Jewish Federation of Atlantic and Cape May Counties as well as the local Board of Jewish Education. During the summer season the well-known Camp By the Sea is a thriving area for local and summer youth held at the JCC.

Atlantic City is home to the Jewish Older Adult Services agency and in nearby Galloway Township the Seashore Gardens Living Center accommodates both assisted living and long-term care in a magnificent facility opened in 2003. Seashore Gardens offers kosher living to all of its residents. Nearby Cape May is a peaceful paradise for summer and year-round visitors who want pristine beaches, a beautiful walkway, lots of hotels, and bed and breakfast choices along with top-notch restaurants. A newspaper, the *Jewish Times*, located in Pleasantville, serves the local community with its weekly publication.

The Richard Stockton College of New Jersey, a growing college in the New Jersey State Higher Education system, is also the center for the Holocaust Resource Center. Here those interested in this academic area find a study environment conducive to this highly regarded program. The RSCNJ campus offers a myriad of degree choices, including a baccalaureate degree in Jewish Studies and a masters degree program in Holocaust and Genocide Studies.

[Linda S. Kulp (2nd ed.)]

ATLAS, mountain range in Morocco and Algeria.

History

Arabic literary sources tell of some *Berber tribes in the Atlas Mountains which observed the tenets of Judaism: e.g., the Jarawa in the Aurès Mountains of eastern Algeria (see *Kahina), the Nafusa, the Fandalawa, and Madyuna (west Algerian tribes), and the Bahlula, the Ghayata, and the Fazaz in the Moroccan Atlas. The Islamization of these tribes is ascribed to Idris the Great (ninth century). It is significant that in Jewish sources there is no mention of these tribes. The *Almohads did not succeed in conquering the Atlas tribes and, apparently, many Jews found shelter among them during the persecutions. Until 1956, many Jewish *mellahs* existed in the Atlas Mountains and on their slopes. Situated on the main communication routes in their quarters near the Berber villages, these small isolated communities remained closely attached to their faith and traditions. Their primary occupations included small business, peddling, metal crafts (silversmiths and blacksmiths), and wine production. According to legends, these tribes had once been strong enough to sustain themselves and to aid the Berbers in their internecine struggles. Many Jews in the Middle Atlas and in Sous Valley either converted voluntarily to Islam or were forced to convert during the *marabout* movement in the 16th century. During the 19th century the Atlas communities were finally subjugated and sometimes reduced to semi-slavery. The Jewish communities of the Atlantic Atlas disappeared. Throughout the Atlas region old Jewish cemeteries and sanctuaries served as shrines for both Jews and Muslim Berbers.

[David Corcos]

In Recent Times

In 1948 there were about 10,000 Jews living in the Atlas Mountains area of Morocco. About half were peddlers and artisans, while some engaged in agriculture. They were scattered in many settlements, in which there were often no more than a few dozen families. These Jews were observant, although the majority were illiterate. They lacked teachers in their villages, and frequently they had no contact even with Jewish communities in the area. Some of the villages were so isolated that their very existence was unknown, until they were discovered in the 1950s when the exodus to Israel began. Between 1952 and 1955 dozens of villages in the area were abandoned. In the largest of these, Tamzert, there were 68 families consisting of 340 persons. During this period a total of 532 families (2,914 persons) went to Israel from the Atlas Mountains, the rest, some 5,000 persons, migrating there later. The fact that they possessed no property facilitated their migration, for even the farmers among them did not own land but were tenants in exchange for a quarter of the crops. On the other hand, they were in need of basic medical attention, since many suffered from skin diseases, and from partial or total blindness resulting from trachoma. Almost all immigrants from the Atlas Mountains settled in cooperative villages in Israel and engaged in agriculture.

[Haim J. Cohen]

BIBLIOGRAPHY: N. Slouschz, *Travels in North Africa* (1927), 295ff., 306ff.; R. Montagne, *Berbères et le Makhzen* (1930), 45–46, 66–68, 76–77; L. Poinot, *Pélerinages judéomusulmans du Maroc* (1948), passim; A.N. Chouraqui, *Between East and West* (1968), passim; P. Flamand, *Diaspora en terre d'Islam* (1956), 67–105; Hirschberg, in: *Journal of African History*, 4 (1963), 313–39; Hirschberg, Afrikah, passim; Corcos, in: *Sefunot*, 10 (1966), 77, 80ff., 93ff.; Minkovitz, in: JJSO, 9 (1967), 191–208; Kohls, in: *Megamot*, 7 (1956), 345–76 (Eng. summ.).

ATLAS, DAVID (1924–), U.S. meteorologist. Born in New York, Atlas joined the Air Force Cambridge Research Laboratory in 1948, and became chief of the weather radar branch. In 1965 he accepted a professorship at the University of Chicago's Department of Geophysical Sciences. Atlas was active in the field of meteorology for six decades. He is best known for his research in the field of radar technology. Other dimensions to Atlas' career are those of inventor, educator at the University of Chicago, laboratory director at the Air Force Cambridge Research Laboratory, division director at the National Center for Atmospheric Research, and laboratory director at the Goddard Laboratory for Atmospheric Science. He served the AMS in many capacities, including the position of president. In recognition of his accomplishments, Atlas received the AMS Meisinger, Charney, and Rossby awards. He is also a member of the National Academy of Engineering.

Atlas has had a profound influence on meteorology in general through his research and through the people with whom he worked and whom he touched as a mentor. Atlas' contributions to aviation safety include a device for detecting severe storms, which was adopted by all major commercial airlines, based upon the use of the Doppler effect in radar systems to comprehend the structure of the tornado as well as devices for the automatic plotting of wind velocity at set altitudes within storms. He made further major contributions to radar meteorology by inventing a method for the measurement of atmospheric turbulence and also by developing means of detecting the sea breeze and the echoes of lightning channels descending from the tops of thunderstorms. His recognition of the exceptionally wide radar reflections received from hailstones enabled pilots to detect hail conditions in advance and to avoid them. The safety of modern air travel is largely due to these contributions to radar research, which have also greatly helped the science of agrometeorology.

BIBLIOGRAPHY: *The Newton Graphic* (August 12, 1966).

[Dov Ashbel / Bracha Rager (2nd ed.)]

ATLAS, ELEAZAR (1851–1904), Hebrew scholar and critic. He was born in Beisagola (district of Kovno) and educated at the yeshivah of Zager, where under the influence of *maskilim* he secretly devoted himself to the study of Jewish history and literature. His literary work was first published in *Ha-Karmel* (1875); later he became a principal contributor to *Ha-Ẓefirah* and published critical essays on important works on Jewish history in *Ha-Asif*; these included discussions of the works of A.H. Weiss, Graetz, and others. In 1888 he published *Ha-Kerem* in which leading Hebrew writers were to participate; it was intended to be a periodical, but only one issue appeared. Financial difficulties forced him to move from place to place, until he settled in Bialystok in 1895 and became a bookkeeper. His severe criticism of the growing political Zionist movement, Herzl, Aḥad Ha-Am, and of new trends in Hebrew literature is contained in a collection of articles, *Mah le-Fanim u-Mah le-Aḥor* ("What is Progressive and What is Retrogressive," 1898). During his later years he served as a private tutor in Moscow and wrote articles on the history of the Jews in Poland. These were stolen from him shortly before his death, while on a journey to Bialystok, to which he was compelled to return when Jews were no longer permitted to live in Moscow.

BIBLIOGRAPHY: Hirschberg, in: *Ha-Ẓefirah* (1904), literary supplement, 263–5; Kressel, in: *Me'assef le-Divrei Sifrut*, 3 (1962), 439–54; P. Kaplan, *Eleazar Atlas* (Heb., 1907); B. Kadar, *E. Atlas, Zayn Leben, Zayn Shafn, Zayn Kamf* (1949).

[Getzel Kressel]

ATLAS, JECHEZKIEL (1913–1942), physician and a leader of Jewish partisans fighting the Nazis in Poland. Atlas was born in Rawa-Mazowiecka, Poland, and studied medicine in France and Italy. With the German invasion of Poland in September 1939 Atlas and his parents were in Kozłowszczyzna, an area under Soviet occupation. When the Germans invaded the Soviet Union in June 1941, they sent *Einsatzgruppen* to murder Jews, Soviet commissars, and gypsies. Ghettoization followed the murder. Atlas' parents and sister died in the ghetto on November 24, 1941. He remained alone and like so many partisans without the bonds of family. He went to serve as a doctor in the village of Wielka-Wola and as a physician to Soviet troops who had escaped to the forests. Atlas organized young Jews who had managed to escape from the nearby Dereczyn ghetto on the day of its liquidation as a partisan group. He obtained weapons for them and became their commander under the authority of a Soviet partisan commander. The Soviets initially wanted his services as a physician, but as he was a skilled tactician, the partisans insisted that he lead a combat team. Atlas initiated attacks on the German garrisons in Dereczyn in August 1942, in Kozłowszczyzna in September killing 44 policemen, and in Ruda-Jaworska in October of that year, killing 127 Germans, capturing 75, and seizing much needed arms and ammunition. He headed a sabotage team which blew up a train on the Lida-Grodno line, and which burned a strategic bridge on the Niemen (Neman) River. He also led his fighters into battle when the Germans carried out a reprisal against the partisans (Sept. 15, 1942) and captured a German plane that had made a forced landing in the area (Oct. 2, 1942). Atlas was wounded in the battle at Wielka-Wola, dying from his wounds in December 1942.

BIBLIOGRAPHY: Tushnel, in: Y. Suhl (ed.), *They Fought Back* (1967), 253–9; Bornstein, in: *Extermination and Resistance*, publ. by the Ghetto Fighters House, 1 (1958), 121–8; idem, in: M. Barkai (ed.), *Fighting Ghettos* (1962), 217–40; idem, *Peluggat ha-Doktor Atlas* (1965^2); M. Kahanovich, *Milḥemet ha-Partizanim ha-Yehudim be-Mizraḥ Eiropah* (1954); Y. Granestein and M. Kahanovich, *Leksikon ha-Gevurah* (1965), 52–54; *Yad Vashem Bulletin*, no. 8–9 (1961), 41–43; N. Levin, *The Holocaust* (1968), 368–70.

[Michael Berenbaum (2nd ed.)]

ATLAS, SAMUEL (1899–1977), philosopher and talmudist. Born in Kamai, Lithuania, Atlas studied at rabbinic schools there and afterward at universities in Russia and Germany. He taught in Warsaw and in England before going to the United States in 1942. He joined the faculty of the Hebrew Union College in Cincinnati as professor of philosophy and Talmud, and from 1951 taught in its New York school. Despite his Reform institutional affiliation, Atlas retained a life-long, intimate friendship with the outstanding Orthodox rabbinic scholar, Jehiel Jacob *Weinberg. Atlas was essentially a follower of Hermann *Cohen's critical idealism, in the light of which he pursued his studies in both Jewish legal and philosophical thought. For Atlas, God is the idea of the ultimate coincidence of the "ought" and the "is" that occurs only in infinity. Until then all action and thought strive toward this noumenal goal; these strivings constitute, respectively, human ethical history and the history of philosophy. However, as opposed to Cohen who held that God "guarantees" the ultimate consummation, Atlas stressed that God only assures "the possibility of its realization," and it is up to man to bring about the realization ("Man and the Ethical Idea of God," in: the *Central Conference of American Rabbis Journal*, 15 (1968), no. 1, 40–53). Atlas wrote *From Critical to Speculative Idealism: The Philosophy of Solomon Maimon* (1965), a series of monographs, especially on Maimonides and Maimon, and was the editor of texts from medieval Jewish legal literature. He published an annotated edition of R. Abraham b. David's (Ravad's) novellae to the Talmud on tractate *Bava Kamma*, and miscellaneous chapters of Maimonides' *Yad*. Atlas' *Netivim ba-Mishpat ha-Ivri* (1978) was published posthumously.

ADD. BIBLIOGRAPHY: S. Atlas, "Portrayal of the Gaon Rabbi Jehiel Jacob Weinberg" (Heb.), in: *Sinai*, 58 (1966), 281–92; M. Shapiro, "Scholars and Friends: Rabbi Jehiel Jacob Weinberg and Professor Samuel Atlas," in: *Torah u-Madda Journal*, 7 (1997), 105–21.

[Steven S. Schwarzschild / Marc B. Shapiro (2nd ed.)]

ATOMISM, theory that physical bodies consist ultimately of minute, irreducible, and homogeneous particles called atoms (Greek *atomos/atomon* = indivisible). In medieval Arabic and Hebrew works atomism derives from Greek (Democritus, Epicurus) and Indian sources. Common Hebrew terms for the atom are: "*ha-ḥelek she-eino mitḥallek*" ("indivisible particle") or simply "*ḥelek*"; "*ha-eẓemha-pirdi*" ("separate substance") or simply "*eẓem*"; in Karaite texts also "*ḥatikhah*" = "*juz*'," "*ḥelek*," and "*dak*" ("minute [body]"). The majority of Jewish thinkers rejected atomism, except for Karaite authors who adhered to the *Mu'tazilite* system of *Kalām, along with its atomism; e.g., Joseph al-Basir (11th century), his pupil *Jeshua b. Judah, and *Aaron b. Elijah of Nicomedia (14th century; *Eẓ Ḥayyim*, ed. by F. Delitzch (1841), 12ff.). Judah Hadassi (12th century) is a prominent exception (*Eshkol ha-Kofer* (1836), ch. 28, 19b). While propounding a Mu'tazilite-type system, Saadiah Gaon (tenth century) rejected its atomism, and affirmed the virtual infinite divisibility of matter (*Beliefs and Opinions*, tr. by S. Rosenblatt (1948), 45, 50ff.). Objections to atomism are also raised by Saadiah's contemporary, the Neoplatonist Isaac b. Joseph *Israeli (*Sefer ha-Yesodot*, ed. Fried, ch. 2, pp. 43ff.), and by the later Neoplatonist, Solomon ibn *Gabirol (11th century; *Fons Vitae*, ed. by C. Baeumker (1895), 52, 57–58). *Maimonides (12th century) followed the physics of Aristotle with its rejection of atomism (*Guide of the Perplexed*, tr. by Pines, 1 (1963), 51, 112). In a historically significant context, Maimonides criticized the atomism of the later Ashʿarite Kalām, maintaining that its doctrine of constant creation of new atoms by God and rejection of natural causality was induced by preconceived religious opinions concerning creation (*ibid.*, 177ff., 194ff.). Aaron b. Elijah defended the Kalām by arguing that atomism is necessitated by reason and is neutral per se with respect to the question of creation, as is evident from its advocacy by Epicurus, who viewed atoms as primordial. Maimonides' strictures were accentuated by later Aristotelians, e.g., *Levi b. Gershom (14th century; *Milḥamot Adonai* (1560), pt. 6, 1; ch. 3), who also gives a sophisticated explanation of the infinite divisibility of extension (*ibid.*, pt. 6:1, ch. 11). Ḥasdai *Crescas (14th–15th century), a critic of the Aristotelian system, defended the atomistic theory (H.A. Wolfson, *Crescas' Critique of Aristotle* (1929), 121, 569–70).

BIBLIOGRAPHY: C. Bailey, *Greek Atomists and Epicurus* (1928); I. Efros, *Problem of Space in Jewish Mediaeval Philosophy* (1917); idem, *Ha-Pilosofiyyah ha-Yehudit bi-Ymei ha-Beinayim* (1964), index; Guttmann, Philosophies, index; Husik, Philosophy, index; S. Pines, *Beitraege zur islamischen Atomenlehre* (1936); M. Schreiner, *Der Kalām in der juedischen Literatur* (1895).

[Joel Kraemer]

ATONEMENT (Heb. כִּפֻּרִים, *kippurim*, from the verb כפר). The English word atonement ("at-one-ment") significantly conveys the underlying Judaic concept of atonement, i.e., reconciliation with God. Both the Bible and rabbinical theology reflect the belief that as God is holy, man must be pure in order to remain in communion with Him. Sin and defilement damage the relationship between creature and Creator, and the process of atonement – through *repentance and reparation – restores this relationship.

In the Bible

The basic means of atonement is the sacrificial rite, which functions to purify man from both sin and uncleanliness (e.g., Lev. 5; Pederson, pp. 358–64). In its most spiritualized aspect, however, the sacrificial rite is only the outward form of atonement, and in order for it to be effective, man must first purify himself. This was the constantly reiterated message of the prophets during periods when Israel came close to viewing the atoning efficacy of the rite as automatic (Isa. 1:11–17; see de Vaux, Anc Isr, 454ff.). Fasting and prayer are also specified as means of atonement (Isa. 58:1–10; Jonah 3; see *Kipper).

In Rabbinic Literature

After the destruction of the Temple and the consequent cessation of sacrifices, the rabbis declared: "Prayer, repentance, and charity avert the evil decree" (TJ, Ta'an. 2:1, 65b). Suffering is also regarded as a means of atonement and is considered more effective than sacrifice to win God's favor (Ber. 5a). Exile and the destruction of the Temple (Sanh. 37b, Ex. R. 31:10) were also reputed to bring about the same effect. Above all, death is the final atonement for sins (Mekh. Jethro 7); "May my death be an expiation for all my sins" is a formula recited when the end is near (Sanh. 6:2). Atonement for some sins is achieved immediately after the individual repents, while for others repentance alone does not suffice. If a person transgresses a positive commandment and repents, he is immediately forgiven (Yoma 85b). For a negative commandment, repentance suspends the punishment, and the Day of Atonement procures atonement: "For on this day shall atonement be made for you… from all your sins" (Lev. 16:30). For a graver sin, punishable by death or extirpation, repentance and the Day of Atonement suspend the punishment and suffering completes the atonement (cf. Ps. 89:33). If one has been guilty of profaning the Divine Name, however, penitence, the Day of Atonement, and suffering merely suspend punishment, and death procures the final atonement: "The Lord of hosts revealed Himself in my ears; surely this iniquity shall not be expiated by you till ye die" (Isa. 22:4; Yoma 86a).

Atonement is only efficacious in the above way if the sin concerned does not involve suffering or material injury to a second party. If it did, full restitution must be made to the wronged party and his pardon must be sought. This law was derived from the verse "… all your sins before the Lord…" (Lev. 16:30), i.e., the Day of Atonement is effective for transgressions between man and God, but for sins against a fellow man, restitution and forgiveness are also necessary (Yoma 8:9). The general rabbinic approach was to deritualize atonement and center it more on the personal religious life of the individual in his relationship to God: "Now that we have no prophet or priest or sacrifice, who shall atone for us? In our hands is left only – prayer" (Tanḥ. Va-Yishlaḥ. 10). A similar idea is found in the dictum that after the destruction of the Temple a man's table atones in place of the altar, i.e., his everyday behavior is all important. Although a rite analogous to that of sacrificial atonement is found in the post-talmudic custom of slaughtering a cock on the eve of the Day of Atonement, as a symbolic replacement for the sinner himself (*kapparot*), this practice was not universally accepted (Sh. Ar., OH 605).

BIBLIOGRAPHY: J. Pederson, *Israel*, 2 vols. (1940), index; G.F. Moore, *Judaism in the First Centuries of the Christian Era*, 1 (1927; repr. 1966), 445–546; S.R. Hirsch, *Judaism Eternal*, 1 (1956), 3–14, 142–52; S. Schechter, *Some Aspects of Rabbinic Theology* (1909), 293–343; A. Buechler, *Studies in Sin and Atonement in the Rabbinic Literature of the First Century* (1928); Faur, in: *Sinai*, 61 (1967), 259–66.

ATRAN, FRANK Z. (1885–1952), U.S. businessman and philanthropist. Atran was born in Russia. He immigrated to Belgium in the wake of the Russian Revolution and established a textile business there. Subsequently he moved the firm to France and then to New York City, where it was highly successful. Toward the end of his life Atran contributed generously to various charitable causes and Jewish organizations, particularly to the Jewish Labor Committee, which established the Atran Jewish Culture House. In 1950 he contributed a million dollars for a laboratory building for Mount Sinai Hospital. Several months before his death he established a chair in Yiddish Language, Literature, and Culture at Columbia University.

[Hillel Halkin]

ATTAH EḤAD (Heb. אַתָּה אֶחָד; "Thou art One"), name of the central section of the Sabbath afternoon **Amidah*. The prayer emphasizes the Oneness of God: "Thou art One, Thy Name is One," and the uniqueness of Israel: "and who is like Thy people Israel, a nation one on earth" (I Chron. 17:21). In the prayer, the Sabbath is called "a crown of distinction and salvation" which God gave to His people as a day of rest and holiness. The patriarchs Abraham, Isaac, and Jacob all found joy and rest on the Sabbath. The prayer closes with the invocation: "May Thy children know that from Thee cometh their rest, and by their rest they hallow Thy name." This prayer, which originated with the *geonim* (eighth–tenth century C.E.), is based upon the Midrash (cf. Tos. Ḥag. 3b) that God, Israel, and the Sabbath mutually testify to the Oneness of God, the peerlessness of Israel His people, and the uniqueness of the Sabbath as a day of holy rest.

ATTAH HORETA LADA'AT (Heb. אַתָּה הָרְאֵתָ לָדַעַת; "Unto thee [Israel] it was shown"), verses recited responsively on *Simḥat Torah before the Scrolls of the Law are taken out of the Ark to be carried in a procession in the synagogue. The verses occur in different order in the southern Ashkenazi and Polish rites. Sephardim also recite a shorter collection of verses on Sabbaths and holiday mornings when the Scrolls are taken from the Ark. The prayer is named after its introductory verse (Deut. 4:35) which is followed by 15 others, glorifying God, etc., and invoking His acceptance of prayers.

ATTAH ZOKHER (Heb. אַתָּה זוֹכֵר; "Thou rememberest"), opening words of the **Zikhronot* section of the Additional Service of *Rosh Ha-Shanah. This prayer is designated as "*Teki'ata de-Vei Rav*," since its authorship is ascribed to the third century C.E. Babylonian *amora* *Rav. The prayer starts by emphasizing the character of Rosh Ha-Shanah as a "Day of Remembrance" from Creation onward. Ten verses from Scripture are quoted describing God as remembering His creatures, especially Israel. The prayer closes with the benediction: "Blessed art Thou, O Lord, who rememberest the Covenant."

BIBLIOGRAPHY: Davidson, *Oẓar*, 1 (1924), 398.

ATTALI, BERNARD (1943–), French civil servant and businessman, twin brother of Jacques *Attali. Born in Algeria, Bernard Attali studied law and political science in Paris. In 1966, he entered the prestigious Ecole Nationale d'Administration (ENA), France's major school for the civil service, and two years later began his career as a high-level civil servant, occasionally working for private and semi-private companies. From 1988 to 1993, he served as managing director of Air France, and eventually published a book about the evolution of French civil aviation in this same period (*Les guerres du ciel*, 1994).

Attali was honored with the highest French distinctions, Officier de la Legion d' Honneur and Commandeur de l'Ordre National du Mérite.

[Dror Franck Sullaper (2nd ed.)]

ATTALI, JACQUES (1943–), French economist and special adviser to President Mitterrand. Attali was born in Algiers and was educated there and in France. In 1981 he was appointed special adviser to President Mitterrand and in that capacity was influential on both internal and foreign issues and was sent on several highly confidential missions. In addition to being an economist (he holds a Ph.D. in economics among many other high-level degrees from prestigious French academic institutions), he is a philosopher and has written a number of works which include *Analyse économique de la vie politique* (1973), *Modèles politiques* (1973), *L'Anti-économique* (1974), *La parole et l'Outil* (1975), *La Nouvelle economie française* (1978), and *Les Trois Mondes* (1981). Before taking office in the Socialist government, Attali was very active in Jewish affairs and held the post of vice president of the Fonds Social Juif.

In 1990 Attali was appointed to a four-year term as president of the European Bank for Reconstruction and Development (BERD) with headquarters in London. From 1993 he was chairman of A&A, an international consulting firm, and in 1998 founded Planet Finance, an international non-profit organization devoted to fighting poverty through the development of microfinance. His wide knowledge in numerous fields combined with his interest in the evolution of civilizations led him to write essays on futurology such as *Lignes d'horizons* (1990) and *L'Homme nomade* (2003) as well as novels, from science fiction (*La vie éternelle*, 2000) to historical novels (*La Confrérie des Eveillés*, 2004). In 2001, he analyzed from an historical perspective the relationships between Jews and money in *Les Juifs, le monde et l'argent*.

[Gideon Kouts / Dror Franck Sullaper (2nd ed.)]

ATTAR, ḤAYYIM BEN MOSES (IBN) (1696–1743), rabbi and kabbalist. Born in Salé, Morocco, he received his early education from his grandfather, Ḥayyim *Atar. Attar settled in Meknes after the death of his great-uncle Shem Tov in order to manage his business in partnership with Shem Tov's son, whose daughter he married. There he studied and taught but the deterioration of the economic and political situation in Morocco and his belief that redemption was imminent induced him to settle in Ereẓ Israel. He was encouraged in this decision when he learned that Ḥayyim *Abulafia had renewed the community of Tiberias. Desirous of establishing a college in Ereẓ Israel to which Diaspora students would flock in order to hasten the redemption, he set out for Ereẓ Israel together with his closest disciples, among whom were David

Ḥasan and Shem Tov Gabbai, reaching Leghorn in 1739. There Attar's saintly nature soon earned him an eager audience. His home in Leghorn became a center for students who gathered to study under him, and there he preached to large audiences, urging them to repent. R. Moses *Franco states that "all the people used to come early in order to find seats and it became impossible to enter because of the multitude." Groups were organized to assist his yeshivah and philanthropists financed the publication of some of his works. He sent proclamations to Jewish communities throughout Italy, urging immigration to Ereẓ Israel, and for that purpose he traveled extensively, visiting Venice, Ferrara, Modena, Reggio, and Mantua. Learning about the epidemics in Ereẓ Israel, some of his disciples became hesitant about making the journey to the Holy Land, but Ḥayyim declared: "It is immaterial to me who comes and who remains; he who has ideals will immigrate and inherit the Land."

In 1741, Attar with a group of 30, including Jews from Morocco and young rabbis from Italy, set sail from Leghorn. Moses Franco and Abraham Ishmael Sangvinetti describe the voyage in their writings. The group reached Acre in the late summer. Hearing of the epidemics raging in Jaffa and Jerusalem, Attar decided to establish a temporary yeshivah in Acre which continued for nearly a year. He then decided to move to Peki'in, attributing the deaths of two of his disciples to the fact that Acre, according to the Talmud, was not within the historic boundaries of Ereẓ Israel. During a visit to Tiberias Ḥayyim Abulafia urged him to reestablish his school there, but when the epidemic subsided, the group set out for Jerusalem.

There Attar established the Midrash Keneset Israel Yeshivah, which had one division for advanced and one for young scholars. He acted as head of the former division which did not study the Talmud with the commentaries, but concentrated on the codes and their connection with the talmudic sources. Special attention was paid to reconciling the decisions of Maimonides with the Talmud. *Rishon le-Ẓiyyon* (Constantinople, 1750), whose author was apparently David Ḥasan, is the fruit of those researches. It contains novellae on the Shulḥan Arukh, *Yoreh De'ah*, and Maimonides, as well as a commentary on the Prophets, the five scrolls, and Psalms, Proverbs, and Job. The students indulged in ascetic practices, spending their nights in supplication and prayer for the redemption and peace of Diaspora Jewry. The group also used to prostrate themselves in prayer on holy graves in supplication for the Jewish community. Ḥ.J.D. *Azulai, who studied at the "Midrash," describes it in reverential terms, and in his works he gives details of Attar's customs as well as sermons and explanations which he heard from him. Attar died approximately a year after settling in Jerusalem.

His first work was the *Ḥefeẓ Adonai* (Amsterdam, 1742) on the Talmud. His best-known and most important work is the *Or ha-Ḥayyim* (Venice, 1742), a commentary on the Pentateuch, often republished with the biblical text. It had an extensive circulation in Germany and Poland especially among the Ḥasidim. In many communities it was read along with the weekly portion of the Torah. Only one of his responsa has been published (in *Benei Yehudah*, Leghorn, 1758, of Judah Ayyash, no. 47, pp. 115–9) and a few still exist in manuscript (*Malkhei Rabbanan*, 35). In his halakhic work, the *Peri To'ar* on the Shulḥan Arukh, *Yoreh De'ah* (Amsterdam, 1742), he does not hesitate to contradict his predecessors. He is particularly critical of the *Peri Ḥadash* of *Hezekiah da Silva. He laid great store by his own ideas, suggesting that he was divinely guided in reaching them. Many tales about him have been preserved. A ḥasidic legend relates that *Israel Ba'al Shem Tov attempted to go to the Holy Land to have the merit of studying under him.

BIBLIOGRAPHY: B. Klar, *Rabbi Ḥayyim ibn Attar, Aliyyato le-Ereẓ Yisrael* (1951); J. Nacht, *Mekor Ḥayyim* (1898); J.M. Toledano, *Oẓar Genazim* (1960), 62–66; idem, *Ner ha-Ma'arav* (1911), 154–7; R. Margaliot, *Toledot Rabbenu Ḥayyim ibn Attar* (1918); J.H. Illos, *Yalkut Yosef* (1924), 62–69; Mann, in: *Tarbiz*, 7 (1935/36), 74–101; Frumkin-Rivlin, 3 (1929), 9; J. Ben-Naim, *Malkhei Rabbanan* (1931), 34b–36a; Benayahu, in: *Hed ha-Mizraḥ*, 2 (1943/44), nos. 4–7; idem, in: *Yerushalayim*, 2 (1949), 103–31; idem, *Rabbi Ḥ.J.D. Azulai* (1959), 335–7.

ATTAR, JUDAH BEN JACOB (IBN) (known as "Rabbi al-Kabbir" (the great teacher); 1655–1733), talmudic scholar in Morocco. Attar was born in Fez and at a young age he was appointed head of the Moroccan *dayyanim*, after refusing to accept any remuneration for this function. He earned his living in trade and devoted his life to the well-being of his coreligionists. In collaboration with his disciple, Jacob Abensur, he published the *takkanot* of the first Spanish exiles in Fez and drew up new regulations which continued to serve as the basis of Judeo-Moroccan jurisprudence. His published works include *Minḥat Yehudah* on the Pentateuch (1940); customs and practices of Fez regarding *terefot* published in *Mekor Ḥayyim* (1897). Many responsa were published in *Mishpat u-Ẓedakah le-Ya'akov* (pt. 1–1894, pt. 2–1903) and others appear in works of various Moroccan rabbis. Many of Attar's writings still exist in manuscript including a commentary on *Midrash Rabbah*. Attar's grandson, JUDAH B. OBED (1725–1812), was a *dayyan* in Fez and among other works wrote *Zikkaron li-Venei Yisrael*, on the persecution of the Jews in Morocco during 1790–1792. Several excerpts from this work have been published.

BIBLIOGRAPHY: Azulai, 1 (1852), 67, no. 55, s.v. *Yehudah Attar*; J.M. Toledano, *Ner ha-Ma'arav* (1911), passim; J. Ben-Naim, *Malkhei Rabbanan* (1931), 46–50; Judah Attar, *Minḥat Yehudah* (1940), preface; G. Vajda, *Recueil de textes historiques judéo-marocains* (1951), 79–96.

[David Obadia]

ATTELL, ABRAHAM WASHINGTON (**Abe**; "The Little Hebrew," "The Little Champ"; 1884–1970), U.S. boxer, underworld figure; world featherweight champion for 11 years (career record 107–16–19, with 53 knockouts); member of Boxing Hall of Fame and International Boxing Hall of Fame. Considered one of the greatest pound-for-pound fighters in history at 5′4″, 122-pounds, Attell was born February 22 – hence the middle name Washington – the 16th of 19 children to a poor family in San Francisco, and learned to fight as a kid on the streets of his Irish neighborhood. His father abandoned the family when Attell was 13, and he had to find a job selling newspapers to support his family.

Attell fought his first professional fight at age 16 on August 19, 1900, winning a $15 purse with a KO in the second round over Kid Lennett. He promised his mother it would be his "first and last fight," but after he came home with the $15, his mother encouraged his career and even bet on him. Attell won his first ten fights by knockout, and 23 of his first 29. On October 28, 1901, Attell won the disputed world featherweight title by defeating George Dixon in 15 rounds, and won the undisputed world championship on his 22nd birthday in 1906, beating Jimmy Walsh in a 15-round decision. Attell lost a 20-round decision to Johnny Kilbane in 1912 on his 28th birthday – becoming the only boxer to win and lose championships on his birthday – ending an 11-year reign as world champion. He fought sparingly afterward for five years, with his final bout on January 8, 1917. Attell claimed to have fought 365 times, and although his official record indicates less than half that number, the little pugilist was known to have fought as often as three times a week, often giving away as many as 25 pounds to an opponent.

Attell's story does not end there. Involved with mobsters during his boxing career and part of the entourage of renowned gambler Arnold Rothstein, he allegedly was the bagman between *Rothstein and players of the Chicago White Sox in the fix of the 1919 World Series known as the Black Sox scandal. Attell was indicted after several Chicago White Sox players testified before an Illinois grand jury that he was involved in fixing the games. Attell claimed that it was a different Abe Attell, and the charges against him were subsequently dropped because of insufficient evidence.

MONTE (The "Nob Hill Terror"; 1885–1960), Abe's younger brother, fought from 1903 to 1916, winning the world bantamweight title on June 19, 1909, when he defeated Frankie Neil. It was the first time brothers held world titles simultaneously. He fought and won seven more times in seven months following his title win, until losing the championship to Frankie Conley on February 22, 1910. Monte left the ring in 1916 because of an eye infection, which eventually led to blindness. He finished with a record of 24–20–17, with 10 KOs. An older brother, CAESAR (1880–1979), fought from 1902 to 1906, compiling a record of 5–6–1 with three KOs.

[Elli Wohlgelernter (2nd ed.)]

ATTIA, ISAAC BEN ISAIAH (18th–19th century), rabbi in Aleppo. He served as *dayyan* and taught in the yeshivah in Aleppo. Attia's wife and children perished in the plague of 1787. He was in halakhic communication with the scholars of Aleppo and also in 1790 with Ḥayyim Joseph David *Azulai. In c. 1814 he set out on a journey which lasted more than seven years. Attia traveled from Syria to Ereẓ Israel and then to Egypt, France, and Italy, staying in Leghorn for at least five years. There he published many of his books. Among his works are (1) *Zera Yiẓḥak* (Leghorn, 1793), sermons on Genesis. The book also included *Yekara de-Ḥayyei*, eulogies, as well as *Pilpelet Kol she-Hu*, on the tractate *Sukkah*; (2) *Rov Dagan* (Leghorn, 1818), on the Babylonian Talmud together with *Ot le-Tovah*, responsa and halakhic novellae in alphabetical order; (3) *Eshet Ḥayil* (Leghorn, 1821), on the last chapter of Proverbs; (4) *Zekhut Avot* (Leghorn, 1821), on *Avot*; (5) *Mesharet Moshe* (Leghorn, 1821), on Maimonides' *Yad*, to which is appended a collection of articles on the Shulḥan Arukh; (6) *Va-Yikra Yiẓḥak* (Leghorn, 1825), a homiletical commentary on Leviticus, Numbers, Deuteronomy, and the five scrolls. Included with it are *Doresh Tov*, on Genesis and Exodus and *Ekev Anavah*, sermons and eulogies; (7) *Tanna ve-Shiyyer; Penei ha-Mayim* (Leghorn, 1831), responsa, and novellae on the Talmud, together with a commentary on Rashi and Elijah *Mizraḥi.

BIBLIOGRAPHY: M. Benayahu, *Rabbi Ḥ.Y.D. Azulai*, 1 (1959), 109, 218.

ATTIA, SHEM TOV (c. 1530–after 1601), rabbi and kabbalist. He lived in Salonika but settled in Safed before 1570. Attia was one of the 12 disciples of Isaac *Luria who requested Ḥayyim *Vital to reveal to them the secrets of the Kabbalah which he had learned from their master. His only extant halakhic work is his responsa on the laws of the sabbatical year, published in the responsa *Avkat Rokhel* (1791, no. 25) of Joseph Caro. Nathan Shapira included Attia's responsum on wine made by Gentiles in the introduction to his book, *Yayin ha-Meshummar* (Venice, 1660). In Safed he gave an approbation to the responsa of Moses *Galante and was a signatory to the regulation passed by the scholars of Safed exempting rabbis from taxation. Apparently, Attia left Safed, for in 1591 he was mentioned among the scholars of Adrianople. In 1601 he was again in Safed where he headed the Bet Va'ad (the local community council). In this capacity, his signature appears first among the 20 leading scholars of Safed.

BIBLIOGRAPHY: Tamar, in: *Tarbiz*, 27 (1957/58), 108–10.

°ATTLEE, CLEMENT RICHARD, EARL (1883–1967), British Labour Party leader (1935–55), deputy prime minister in Churchill's war cabinet (1940–45), and prime minister (1945–51). As a social worker in London's East End in the 1920s, Attlee had contact with Jewish labor organizations. Before he became prime minister, he expressed sympathy for the Jewish cause in Palestine and opposed the 1939 White Paper (see *Israel, Historical Survey). In December 1944 Attlee supported Labour's official pronouncement in favor of a Jewish majority in Palestine. As prime minister, however, he gave full support to the policy of his foreign secretary, Ernest *Bevin, which involved Britain in a violent conflict with the Jews in Palestine in their struggle for full-scale immigration, especially of the survivors of the Holocaust, and for Jewish independence in Palestine. As Attlee was a Fabian socialist, the ideological basis of Zionism had no appeal for him. Later, Attlee defended his policy in Palestine, claiming that incompatible assurances had been given to Arabs and Jews and blaming American "irresponsibility." His government recognized Israel in January 1949.

BIBLIOGRAPHY: C.R. Attlee, *As It Happened* (1954); Hugh Dalton, *Memoirs (1945–1960)* (1962), index. **ADD. BIBLIOGRAPHY:** K. Harris, *Attlee* (1995); M. Jones, *Failure in Palestine* (1986), index; ODNB online.

ATTORNEY. Biblical law requires that "the two parties to the dispute shall appear before the Lord, before the priests or magistrates" (Deut. 19:17), i.e., in person and not by proxy. It was considered essential that the court should hear all pleadings and arguments, as well as all testimony, directly from the mouths of litigants or witnesses; even interpreters were not to be admitted (Mak. 1:9; Maim., Yad, Sanhedrin 21:8). While legal and economical developments subsequently necessitated changes in the practice of the courts, the prejudice against proxies could never be eradicated, and the courts which admitted advocates did so only by way of accommodation to a necessary evil (Meir b. Baruch of Rothenburg, *Responsa* (1895), 67b, no. 357). This prejudice was enhanced by the fact that those who acted as spokesmen for litigants were often found to be sly and untruthful (Isaac b. Sheshet, *Responsa* (1805), 125, no. 235). The Talmud applies the verse "oppressors and robbers who did that which is not good among his people" (Ezek. 18:18) to attorneys (Shevu. 31a). Furthermore, there were legal difficulties to contend with: e.g., a debtor was presumed never to be impertinent enough to prevaricate in the presence of his creditor (BK 107a, et al.), but there could not be any such presumption in the face of the creditor's attorney; or a party may have to take an *oath, which could not be administered to his proxy. The general rule that "a man's agent is as himself" (Kid. 42a) was not applied to agents for litigants – an anomaly which it has been found difficult to justify but which can be explained only by the overriding desire "to discourage litigation by outsiders" (Herzog, Instit, 1 (1936), 203ff.).

However, ways had to be found to enable plaintiffs to be represented if injustice was to be avoided – e.g., where the plaintiff himself was absent, or where he was weak and timid and the defendant violent and powerful (Tos. to Shevu. 31a; Tur, ḤM 123:16 and Beit Yosef *ibid.*). Nevertheless, talmudic jurists still would not accept a power of attorney in favor of another, unless the plaintiff had therein transferred his rights in the chose in action to the attorney, so that the attorney in effect claimed in his own right (BK 70a) – not unlike the *mandatum in res suam* of Roman law. The result of this rule in the past was that a defendant was unable to appoint an attorney on his behalf, as he had no chose in action to transfer (Asher b. Jehiel, *Tosefei Rabbenu Asher*, Shevu. 30a, Sh. Ar., ḤM 124). Gulak has shown that the rule is of Babylonian origin and influenced by Babylonian laws; but it became Jewish law (Sh. Ar., ḤM 122–23). The requirements for such a transfer to be inserted in powers of attorney were in the course of time radically mitigated and Maimonides expressed regret at reforms by which purely fictitious transfers were admitted to validate powers of attorney (Maim., Yad, Sheluḥin ve-Shutafin 3:7). While transfers continued to be inserted in all powers of attorney, they were nearly always fictitious: anything the attorney recovered by virtue thereof, although ostensibly for himself, would have to be accounted for immediately to his principal (3:1).

With regard to the representation of defendants, there is a tradition in the Jerusalem Talmud that the high priest, when sued in court, could appoint an attorney (*entelar*) to represent him (TJ, Sanh. 2:1, 19d). Whether it was this tradition or the pressure of changing conditions, attorneys for defendants were soon admitted into the courts, and instead of powers of attorney containing the formal transfer, even oral authorization of the attorney by the defendant before the court was accepted as sufficient (Menahem b. Solomon ha-Me'iri, *Beit ha-Beḥirah* to Sanh. 18a). Where the parties were present in person and the court could, if necessary, administer oaths directly to them and perceive their bearing and demeanor, their being assisted by skilled pleaders was not considered too reprehensible and could even be useful (cf. *Urim ve-Tummim* and J.H. Epstein, *Arukh ha-Shulḥan* to ḤM 124). The rule then evolved that a plaintiff, by presenting his claim, submitted to the court's jurisdiction and thus also by implication submitted to its procedure, including any customary or equitable admission of defendants' attorneys (cf. *Siftei Kohen*, Sh. Ar., ḤM 124). But apart from custom (and equity), the purely legal position has never been resolved (see Bezalel Ashkenazi, *Shitah Mekubbeẓet* to BK 70a).

The stipulation of fees was regarded as an assurance of the attorney's good faith (Isaac Alfasi, *Responsa* (1954), 98, no. 157; *Be'er Heitev* to Sh. Ar., ḤM 123:10, 11), eliminating the suspicion that he might engage in champerty or unlawful enrichment. Such stipulations were usually very generously enforced by the courts (Solomon b. Abraham Adret, *Responsa* 2 (1811), 56a (erroneously 58), no. 393; 3 (1812), 21a, no. 141; 5 (1884), 123, no. 287.

BIBLIOGRAPHY: Rav Ẓa'ir (Tchernowitz), in: *Ha-Shilo'aḥ*, 3 (1898), 418–22; Gulak, Yesodei, 4 (1922), 54–64; idem, Oẓar, 272–9; idem, *Das Urkundenwesen im Talmud* (1935), 137–47; S. Assaf, *Battei ha-Din ve-Sidreihem Aḥarei Ḥatimat ha-Talmud* (1924), 95–99; Herzog, Instit, 1 (1936), 202–11; Lipkin, in: *Sinai*, 30 (1951/52), 46–61; 31 (1951/52), 265–83; ET, 4 (1952), 101–4, s.v. *Ba'al Din*; 11 (1965), 44–48, s.v. *Harsha'ah*.

[Haim Hermann Cohn]

ATZMON, MOSHE (1931–), Israeli conductor. Atzmon was born in Hungary and immigrated to Israel in 1944. He studied piano and horn and graduated in composition and conducting in Tel Aviv (1962) and at the Guildhall in London. He won several international prizes such as the GSM school's conducting prize (1963) and the international conducting competition sponsored by the Royal Liverpool PO (1964). From 1969 to 1971, he was chief conductor of the Sydney Symphony Orchestra (Australia), and in 1972 he became chief conductor of the Hamburg (NDR) Radio Symphony Orchestra and of the Basel Symphony Orchestra. Later he was a musical adviser for the Tokyo Metropolitan SO (1978–82), served as principal conductor of the American Symphony Orchestra (1982–84), and was the permanent conductor of the Nagoya Philharmonic Orchestra, Japan (1986–92). In 1991 he was appointed Generalmusikdirektor at Dortmund. His operatic debut occurred in October 1969 with Rossini's *La Cenerentola* at the Deutsche Oper, Berlin. His first recording was as conductor of the New Philharmonia Orchestra in 1968.

BIBLIOGRAPHY: Grove online.

[Israela Stein (2nd ed.)]

AUB, JOSEPH (1805–1880), German moderate Reform rabbi. Aub was rabbi in Bayreuth from 1830 to 1850, in Mainz, and in Berlin from 1865. He was among the first rabbis in Bavaria to preach in German. Aub published a polemical tract on the Bavarian edict regarding rabbinical qualifications (*Betrachtungen und Widerlegungen*, 2 vols., 1839), a weekly periodical *Sinai* (1846), a prayer book (1866), and a religious educational textbook *Biblisches Spruchbuch* (1868); he collaborated in the writing of periodicals published by A. *Geiger. He participated in the rabbinical synods of 1869 and 1871. HIRSCH AUB, Joseph's cousin (1796–1876), was rabbi of Munich from 1827 to 1876. Aub acted as mediator, keeping peace between the Reform and Orthodox wings. He was largely responsible for the abolition of the restrictions on the number of Jewish marriages in Bavaria by the *Matrikelgesetz*.

BIBLIOGRAPHY: AZDJ, 44 (1880), 359; D. Philipson, *Reform Movement in Judaism* (1967^3), index; W.G. Plaut, *Rise of Reform Judaism* (1963), 217–9; J.J. Petuchowski, *Prayerbook Reform in Europe* (1968), index.

AUB, MAX (1903–1972), Spanish poet, novelist, and playwright. Aub was born in Paris of a German father and a French mother, but on the outbreak of World War I the family moved to Valencia and he eventually took Spanish citizenship. A staunch anti-Fascist, Aub fled to France after the Spanish Civil War. After the defeat of France in 1940, he was imprisoned in several concentration camps. The last of these was Djelfa, in North Africa. In 1942 he escaped from Djelfa to Mexico, where most of his writing was done. Aub's first play, *Narciso*, written under the influence of the Vanguardist movement, appeared in 1928 and his first novel, *Geografía*, in 1929. His best-known works, while difficult to classify, deal primarily with the political and social realities of contemporary life. The novels *Campo Cerrado* (1944), *Campo de Sangre* (1946), *Campo Abierto* (1951), and *Campo del Moro* (1963) are based on the Spanish Civil War. *La Calle de Valverde* (1961) recreates the artistic and literary life of pre-war Madrid. Aub's bitter three-act tragedy, *San Juan* (1943), is about some Jewish refugees on an old cargo ship in the Mediterranean who are refused permission to land anywhere. *Diario de Djelfa* (1944) is a poetic account of Aub's internment in North Africa. *Jusep Torres Campalans* (1958) is a light-hearted literary hoax about a Catalan painter invented by Aub.

BIBLIOGRAPHY: *Primer Acto*, no. 52 (May, 1964), 6–41; *Manual de Historia de la Literatura Española*, 1 (1966), contains bibliography.

[Kenneth R. Scholberg]

AUCKLAND, largest city in *New Zealand, situated in the North Island. The Auckland community was founded by David Nathan (a Londoner who removed from northern Kororareka in 1840) with the assistance of other Jewish traders. By 1842 a crown grant of land had been obtained for a cemetery, and in 1855 the congregation, now called Beth Israel, leased a wooden synagogue building. A breakaway congregation called "Gates of Hope," with Rev. J.E. Myers of London as minister, existed briefly in 1859. The congregation developed vigorously under the lay leadership of P.S. Solomon (later an outstanding Fijian lawyer and legislator) and Rev. Moses Elkin (1864–79). From 1880 to 1934, the Auckland community was under the spiritual leadership of Rabbi S.A. Goldstein. He was assisted until 1931 by Rabbi Solomon Katz, and then by Rabbi Alexander Astor (d. 1988). David Nathan, by then a business magnate, lived to open the Prince's St. Synagogue in 1885. He and his sons, L.D. and N.A. Nathan, were the community's lay leaders almost continuously during the period that Goldstein served as minister. The present synagogue and community center were dedicated in 1968.

The Auckland community is vigorous and prosperous. It provides many Jewish educational, cultural, social, and welfare amenities. Strong support has always been in evidence for Zionism and Israel, and Jewish education fostered. A Liberal community was formed in 1959. Auckland Jews have played a notable part in the city's banking, commercial, and industrial life as well as in the legal and medical professions. The many Jewish benefactors include members of the Myers, Davis, and Nathan families. There have been six Jewish mayors of Auckland, including P.A. Philips, H. Isaacs, Sir Arthur *Myers, Sir E.H. Davis, and D.M. Robinson. In 1967 the Jewish population numbered about 2,000 but by 2004 it had grown to about 3,100 (of a total population of 1.1 million), thanks to immigration from Russia, South Africa, and elsewhere.

BIBLIOGRAPHY: L.M. Goldman, *History of the Jews in New Zealand* (1958), index. **ADD. BIBLIOGRAPHY:** A. & L. Gluckman, *Auckland Jewry Past and Present* (1994).

[Maurice S. Pitt]

AUER, LEOPOLD (1845–1930), Hungarian violinist and teacher. Born in Veszprém, Auer studied at the Budapest, Vienna, and Paris conservatoires and with Josef *Joachim. In 1868 he was appointed soloist of the Russian Imperial Orchestra and professor at the conservatoire in St. Petersburg. His baptism into the Russian Orthodox Church probably took place shortly before this time. In 1895 he was ennobled by the czar. He left Russia in 1918 and ultimately settled in New York, but he died in Germany. Auer was one of the greatest violinists and teachers of his time, renowned for his nobility of interpretation and for fostering the individuality of his pupils. These included Joseph Achron, Mischa Elman, Jascha Heifetz, and Nathan Milstein. Auer's works for the violin included cadenzas, études, and arrangements. His *Graded Course of Violin Playing* was published in 1926–27. He also wrote three books on his life and work: *Violin Playing as I Teach It* (1921); *Violin Master Works and Their Interpretation* (1925); and *My Long Life in Music* (1923).

BIBLIOGRAPHY: Riemann-Gurlitt; Grove, Dict; Baker, Biog Dict; Sendrey, Music.

[Bathja Bayer]

AUERBACH, German rabbinical family. The Austrian branch of the family was also known as Wolf. MESHULLAM ZALMAN B. SHALOM (d. Vienna, 1622) belonged to the Wolf branch of the family which later became known as Auerbach-Fischhof. There were also other branches of the family in Vienna at that time: Linz-Auerbach and Metzlein-Auerbach. MOSES AUERBACH was court Jew to the bishop of Regensburg in 1497. SIMEON WOLF was a rabbi at Lublin (1578–84), Przemysl, Poznan (1625–29), Vienna, and finally Prague. His tombstone mentions his writings which, however, remained unpublished. SAMUEL OF LUBLIN, grandson of Simeon Wolf, wrote *Ḥesed Shemu'el* (1699) on the Pentateuch, which also contains a short account of the *Chmielnicki massacres in Poland. MESHULLAM ZALMAN FISCHHOF, son of Simeon Wolf and head of the Vienna community, was expelled from the city in 1670 and died in Mikulov (Nikolsburg). Simon (1611–1638), son of Meshullam, lived in Cracow. At the age of 23 he composed a *seliḥah* to commemorate an epidemic that ravaged Vienna in 1634. This poem was published posthumously in 1639 in Cracow, went through several editions, and was republished with a commentary as *Rav Shalom* (1712), by his grandson, MESHULLAM ZALMAN FISCHHOF II, who was martyred in Lublin in 1692.

MENAHEM MENDEL (1620–1689), considered the founder of the Polish branch of the family, was *dayyan* in Cracow in 1665, and also served as the rabbi of Prausnitz (Prusice) and Krotoszyn. He wrote *Ateret Zekenim*, a commentary on *Oraḥ Ḥayyim* of the Shulḥan Arukh. His grandson MENAHEM MENDEL BEN MOSES (d. 1732) succeeded him as rabbi of Krotoszyn, and was a leader of the *Council of the Lands. Responsa and 12 approbations of his are extant. PHINEHAS, son of Simeon Wolf, who had succeeded his father as *av bet din* of Cracow, left Poland for Frankfurt in 1714 and died in Vienna. His *Halakhah Berurah* on the Shulḥan Arukh was published in 1891; the part on *Oraḥ Ḥayyim* was published in 1717. NATHAN of Satanov, son of MOSES, who was Simeon Wolf's brother, had three sons: JACOB, *maggid* in Haissin (Podolia); JUDAH, rabbi of Glogory, near Lvov; and SELIG, *av bet din* in Gorokhow. ẒEVI BENJAMIN (HIRSCH; 1690–1778), son of Selig and *dayyan* in Brody in 1710, moved to Vienna and later to Worms, where he was appointed rabbi in 1763. His son SELIG AVI'EZRI (1726–1767?), was rabbi of Edenkoben, near Worms, in 1750, and Buxweiler, Alsace, in 1763. His son *Abraham was a noted rabbi and author.

The Auerbach family had other noteworthy rabbis among its members. ABRAHAM BEN ISAAC was rabbi of Coesfeld, Westphalia (17th century). When he was slandered by an apostate, Abraham's fortune was confiscated and he and his family expelled in 1674. He took refuge in Amsterdam but was later reinstated. In 1677 on the eve of the execution of the slanderous apostate he initiated a fast in his community with the recitation of *seliḥot*, which he composed. ARYEH LEIBUSH BEN MORDECAI MARDUSH (c. 1740), rabbi of Stanislav, Ukraine, was the uncle and teacher of Meyer Margulies, author of the responsa *Me'ir Netivim*. His great-grandson was ISRAEL MATTATHIAS (b. 1838), *av bet din* of Bauska, Latvia, and rabbi of Ciechanow, Poland. He wrote seven halakhic works.

ḤAYYIM BEN ISAAC (1755–1840) was born in Leszno, Poland, and served there as *dayyan*. He was rabbi of Leczyca, Poland, from 1818. He wrote *Divrei Mishpat* (1835), glosses on the *Ḥoshen Mishpat* with those by his sons Menahem and Isaac. At the end of his son Isaac Itzik's *Divrei Ḥayyim* there is a selection of Ḥayyim's glosses on the *Oraḥ Ḥayyim* and *Yoreh De'ah* called *Mayim Ḥayyim*. MENAHEM BEN ḤAYYIM (1773–1848) was rabbi of Ostrow, Poland, in 1822. He wrote the introduction to his father's *Divrei Mishpat* and appended to it some interpretations of the Pentateuch. ISAAC ITZIK BEN ḤAYYIM (19th century) was rabbi of Dobra, Plock, and, after his father's death, of Leczyca. His responsa, *Divrei Ḥayyim* (1851–52), were published posthumously by his son Meir Ben Isaac *Auerbach, together with some glosses by his brother. MENAHEM ẒEVI HIRSCH BEN MENAHEM (b. Ḥayyim) was rabbi of Leszno and Konin. He wrote *Divrei ha-Torah* on Shulḥan Arukh *Ḥoshen Mishpat* (1881).

ELIEZER BEN ḤAYYIM, known as Reb Leizerl of Kalisz, wrote *Migdanot Eli'ezer* (1911), a commentary on Esther and Psalms. PEREZ BEN MENAHEM NAHUM (18th century) wrote *Pe'er Halakhah* (1738), glosses to the Talmud and Maimonides' Code. JUDAH LEIB BEN ISRAEL was rabbi of Torchin in 1801 and Wiszmowice from 1807–08. He wrote *Meḥokek Yehudah* (1792), on the Passover laws.

[Yehoshua Horowitz]

After 1763 the Auerbach family was mainly concentrated in Germany and Alsace where its members served as rabbis, becoming prominent in the German Orthodox rabbinate, as well as in Jewish scholarship. The modern line of the family began with Abraham, who had 15 children, the oldest of whom was ẒEVI BENJAMIN (HIRSCH; 1808–1872), a rabbi and rabbinical scholar. He belonged to the first generation of German rabbis with a university education. Ẓevi Benjamin's first rabbinate was Darmstadt (1831–57), where he preached in High German; selections of his sermons were published in 1834 and 1837. He resigned on account of his disagreement with leaders of the congregation, who wished to introduce Reform, and settled in Frankfurt, where he devoted his time to research and

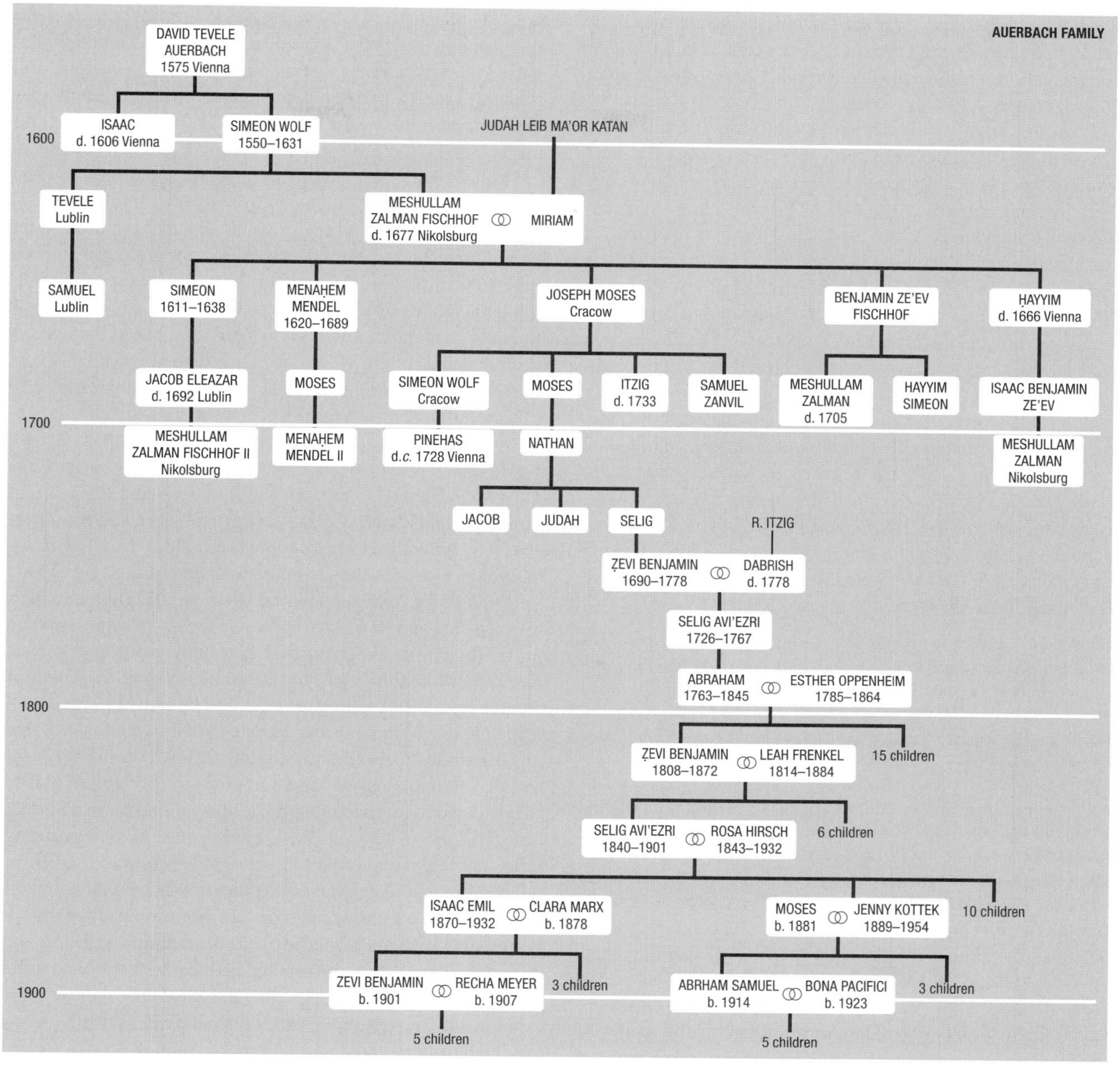

writing. In 1863 he became rabbi at Halberstadt. In 1868–69 Auerbach published the 12th-century halakhic compendium *Sefer ha-Eshkol* by *Abraham b. Isaac of Narbonne with a commentary, *Naḥal Eshkol* (repr. 1962). In 1909 Shalom *Albeck published an "Open Letter" accusing Auerbach of forgery. He maintained that the Old Spanish manuscript on which Auerbach said he based his edition did not exist and that Auerbach, while in Frankfurt, had copied from the Carmoly manuscript, but with alterations and additions of his own. J. Schorr, H. Ehrentreu, D. Hoffmann, and A. Berliner wrote *Ẓidkat ha-Ẓaddik* (1910) in defense of Auerbach; Albeck wrote *Kofer ha-Eshkol* (1910) in reply. Albeck's own edition of the *Sefer ha-Eshkol* (1910, completed by his son Ḥanokh, 1935–38) shows wide divergences from Auerbach's edition. The alleged Spanish manuscript has never been found. Among Auerbach's other works are *Berit Avraham* (1880), on the liturgy of circumcision; *Mishnat R. Natan* (1862; repr. 1962), on Nathan *Adler's *Seder Zera'im* (1862; repr. 1962); *Torat Emet* (1893^3), a manual of the Jewish religion; and *Ha-Ẓofeh al-Darkhei ha-Mishnah* (1861), a polemic against Z. Frankel's *Darkhei ha-Mishnah*, whose orthodoxy he questioned together with S.R. *Hirsch and G. Fischer (see Hirsch's *Jeschurun*, 7, 1861).

SELIG AVI'EZRI AUERBACH (1840–1901), son of Ẓevi Benjamin, was a rabbi and educator. After serving as head of the Jewish High School at Fuerth, he succeeded his father as rabbi at Halberstadt. His son ISAAC EMIL (1870–1932) succeeded his father and directed the local Jewish school. For many years he was chairman of the Association of Orthodox Congregations (*Halberstaedter Verband*) and of the German *Agudat Israel.

MOSES (1881–1976) was rabbi, educator, and historian. He went to Palestine from 1909 to 1917 to direct the network of schools established by Orthodox German Jews (*Freie Vereinigung*), including the Neẓaḥ Yisrael school in Petaḥ Tikvah. Moses then served for a short time as principal of the Ḥavaẓẓelet Girls' School in Warsaw but left to teach at the Cologne Talmud Torah under his brother-in-law Benedict (Pinḥas) Wolf. In 1934 he returned to Palestine and once more became principal of Neẓaḥ Yisrael. In 1947–48 he and his son ABRAHAM SAMUEL reorganized Jewish schools in Tripoli. In 1949 he began lecturing at the Beth Jacob Seminary in Tel Aviv. Among his published writings are the following: on Jewish history, *Der Streit zwischen Saadiah Gaon und dem Exilarchen David b. Zakkai* (1928); *Zur politischen Geschichte der Juden unter Hadrian* (in: Wohlgemuth's *Jeschurun*, 10 (1923), 398ff.; 11 (1924), 59ff., 161ff.); *Toledot Am Yisrael* (4 vols., 1944–62); and on education, *Torat ha-Ḥinnukh* (1958). Auerbach was the last chairman of the *Juedische Literarische Gesellschaft and last editor of its *Jahrbuch*.

[Alexander Carlebach]

BIBLIOGRAPHY: S.M. Auerbach, *The Auerbach Family* (1957); K. Lieben, *Gal-Ed* (1856), 75–76, no. 149; B.H. Auerbach, *Geschichte der israelitischen Gemeinde Halberstadt* (1866), 83f., 222; Bloch, in: *Kaufmann-Gedenkbuch* (1900), 318–24; L. Lewin, *Geschichte der Juden in Lissa* (1904), 233–5, 323; B. Wachstein, *Inschriften des alten Judenfriedhofes in Wien*, 1 (1912), index, 545f.; idem, *Grabschriften des alten Judenfriedhofes in Eisenstadt* (1922), 26, 84; idem, *Urkunden und Akten zur Geschichte der Juden in Eisenstadt* (1926), 12, 25, 30f.; G. Klemperer, in: HJ, 12 (1950), 143–5; J. Hirsch, *R. Benjamin Hirsch... Korot Bet Hirsch... ve-Auerbach* (1948), 63ff.; H. Schwab, *History of Orthodox Jewry in Germany* (1950), index; idem, *Ḥakhmei Ashkenaz* (1964), 15ff.; *Sefer Przemysl* (1964), 57.

AUERBACH, ABRAHAM BEN SELIG AVI'EZRI (1763–1845), Alsatian rabbi. Auerbach, a nephew of David *Sinzheim, was born in Bouxwiller. He was in charge of the affairs of the Strasbourg community, subsequently serving as rabbi of Forbach (Alsace), Neuwied, Coblenz, and Bonn. During the Reign of Terror Auerbach was arrested in Strasbourg and imprisoned for a year because of his connection with Herz *Cerfberr, who was suspected of royalist sympathies. He composed prayers and a poem commemorating the abolition in 1784 of the Jewish poll tax, in which Cerfberr was instrumental, and wrote the preface to the second edition of Sinzheim's responsa *Yad David* (1799).

BIBLIOGRAPHY: Fuenn, Keneset, 277; AZDJ, no. 98 (1839), 593.

AUERBACH, BEATRICE FOX (1887–1968), U.S. retail pioneer, philanthropist. Beatrice Fox was born in Hartford, Connecticut, part of an affluent family steeped in the retail business. As president of G. Fox & Co. for almost three decades, she was one of the leading merchants in the United States, one of the few women to achieve such a lofty position, and she established a pattern of labor reforms for her employees that became a model for the industry. What is even more remarkable, she did not begin her retail career until she was in her middle years. Her parents were Teresa and Moses Fox and both sets of her grandparents – German-Jewish immigrants – had already established their own stores in the United States by the time she was born. Gerson Fox, her grandfather, built his establishment in Hartford in 1845, a one-room shop selling fancy goods. It would eventually become a 14-story New England landmark known as G. Fox & Co., one of the nation's premier department stores. When Fox died (1880), his son, Moses, took over and embarked on a series of buying trips to Europe, often accompanied by his family, including his daughter Beatrice. On one such trip she met a retailer named George S. Auerbach. They were married in 1911 and settled in Salt Lake City, Utah, where Auerbach's family operated a department store. Six years later, G. Fox was gutted by fire and the Auerbachs returned to Hartford to help rebuild it. Moses Fox appointed his son-in-law secretary-treasurer of the new G. Fox, while Beatrice continued raising their two daughters. In 1927, George died and Beatrice – at the age of 40 – became involved in the business, slowly at first and then more intensely as her father's health began to fail. In 1938, upon the death of Moses Fox, she became president and launched a significant expansion program. Under her stewardship, annual volume grew tenfold to about $60 million. G. Fox became the largest privately owned department store in the United States. Beatrice Fox Auerbach had more than a sharp eye for what merchandise would sell. She was also a visionary, instituting a series of fair employment practices for her more than 3,500 employees that were unusual for the times. G. Fox staffers enjoyed retirement plans, a five-day, 40-hour week, interest-free loans, and non-profit medical and lunchroom facilities. She was one of the first white retailers to hire African-Americans for meaningful jobs. G. Fox also provided free delivery service, a toll-free telephone order department, and fully automated billing. In 1965, Mrs. Auerbach stepped down as president, selling the company to May Department Stores Co. for $40 million. For the remaining few years of her life, she was actively involved in philanthropy and civic affairs, serving on numerous hospital, educational, and cultural committees and boards. She launched the Beatrice Fox Auerbach Foundation to help college students. She also founded the Service Bureau for Women's Organizations in Hartford, a clearinghouse for charitable and civic organizations that became the host organization for the U.S. State Department's foreign visitor program.

BIBLIOGRAPHY: S. Brody, *Jewish Heroes and Heroines of America: 150 True Stories of American Jewish Heroism* (1996); *New York Times* (Dec. 1, 1968).

[Mort Sheinman (2nd ed.)]

AUERBACH, BERTHOLD (1812–1882), German author and a leader of Jewish emancipation. His work is marked by the constant attempts to reconcile his different identities as a religiously free-thinking Jew, as a writer from southwest Germany with strong regional bonds, and as a liberal *kleindeutsch*-borussian patriot. Born at Nordstetten in Wuerttemberg, Auerbach, after some initial training for the rabbinate at Hechingen (1825–27), became interested in law and philosophy and continued his studies at the universities of Tuebingen, Munich, and Heidelberg. As a *Burschenschafter* he was persecuted by the authorities and arrested for two months at the Hohenasperg stronghold, where he wrote his first novel, *Spinoza, Ein Denkerleben* (1837). Four years later, Auerbach published his five-volume translation of the philosopher's works. In this early period of his work, he tried to establish himself as a firmly Jewish author, e.g., in his pamphlet *Das Judentum und die neueste Literatur* (1836). In this he criticized the "Junges Deutschland" authors like Heine as well as their German nationalist opponents gathered around the influential editor, Wolfgang Menzel, but he also recognized the ambivalence of many liberal non-Jewish authors in their attitude towards Jews. Nevertheless Auerbach stressed in his second historical novel (*Dichter und Kaufmann* (1840), about the German-Jewish poet Ephraim Moses *Kuh) the importance of *Bildung* as the only means for full bourgeois emancipation. The failure of his Jewish writings made Auerbach turn to a more general discussion on *Heimat* in his popular *Schwarzwaelder Dorfgeschichten* (1843–54). After the failure of the revolution of 1848, Auerbach wrote several long social novels, *Auf der Hoehe* (3 vols., 1864, popular in English as *On the Heights*), *Das Landhaus am Rhein* (5 vols., 1869), and *Waldfried* (3 vols., 1874), whose old-fashioned esthetics let their popularity soon decline.

Auerbach fervently strove for a reconciliation of Jewish emancipation and the German national movement. Judaism meant to him a rather ethical monotheism ("Mosaism"), probably one of the reasons for his popularity among a broad educated public. His specific point of view, however, was denounced by Reform rabbi and journalist Ludwig Philippson as "lack of religion" ("Confessionslosigkeit," AZDJ, 39 (1875), 466). In private letters to his relative Jakob Auerbach (*Briefe*, 2 vols., 1884), the author shows full awareness of the threat to the position of Jews in German society by the newly emerging antisemitism.

BIBLIOGRAPHY: E. Wolbe, *Berthold Auerbach* (Ger., 1907); A. Bettelheim, *Berthold Auerbach* (Ger., 1907); M.I. Zwick, *Berthold Auerbachs sozialpolitischer und ethischer Liberalismus* (1933). **ADD. BIBLIOGRAPHY:** J.S. Skolnik, in: *Prooftexts*, 19:2 (1999), 101–25; Th. Scheuffelen, *Berthold Auerbach* (Ger., 1986); H.O. Horch, in: A. Kilcher (ed.), *Metzler Lexikon der deutsch-juedischen Literatur* (2000), 19–23.

[Marcus Pyka (2nd ed.)]

AUERBACH, CARL A. (1915–), U.S. law professor. Born in New York, Auerbach graduated from Long Island University in 1935 and from Harvard Law School in 1938. He then took a position on the legal staff of the Department of Labor's Wage and Hour Division, followed by positions in the National Defense Commission and the Office of Price Administration (O.P.A.). In the latter agency he served as assistant general counsel. For two of the war years he served in the army, and then reentered federal government service, where he held important legal positions, including that of general counsel of the O.P.A. From 1947 to 1961 he was a professor at the University of Wisconsin Law School and then served for 25 years as a professor at the University of Minnesota Law School. As a law teacher and legal scholar, Auerbach selected as his chief subjects administrative law, constitutional law, civil rights, legal education, and law and the social sciences. Auerbach obtained a Fulbright Advanced Research Award at the London School of Economics and Political Science (1953–54), and then became a fellow with Stanford University's Center for Advanced Study in the Behavioral Sciences (1958–59). In 1972 Auerbach was appointed acting dean at Minnesota, and was dean from 1973 to 1979.

Auerbach is the author or co-author of several books on the regulation of transportation and on the legal process. He identified himself with the mainstream of American liberal thought, with the reform-liberal program and policies of Hubert Humphrey; he was one of the founders of Americans for Democratic Action. He believed that the best critical legal thought should have a bearing on important social and political issues and policies. His writings contributed to the planning that resulted in the civil rights legislation of Congress; and while he questioned the wisdom of the Communist Control Act of 1954, he defended its constitutionality. He has also written numerous articles in the areas of administrative law, civil rights, constitutional law, legal education, and law and the social sciences. Since 1985, Auerbach has been distinguished professor at the University of San Diego School of Law. As an eminent scholar in administrative law and constitutional law, Auerbach was the 1994 recipient of the American Bar Foundation Award for outstanding research in law and government. He is a member of the American Law Institute and the American Academy of Arts and Sciences.

[Milton Ridvas Konvitz and Ruth Beloff (2nd ed.)]

AUERBACH, ELIAS (1882–1971), Israeli physician, biblical scholar, and historical writer. Auerbach emigrated from Berlin to Ereẓ Israel in 1909 and settled in Haifa. He published *Die Juedische Rassenfrage; Palaestina als Judenland* (1912); *Joab, ein Heldenleben* (1920), a novel; *Die Prophetie* (1920), a psychological probe into the nature of prophecy based mainly on the religious experience of Jeremiah; and *Wueste und Gelobtes Land* (2 vols., 1938^2), his main work, which also appeared in Hebrew as *Ha-Midbar ve-Ereẓ ha-Beḥirah* (2 vols., 1957–62), a history of Israel from its beginning until the period of the return from Babylon. From 1950 he lectured on biblical subjects and the history of Israel at various European universities.

Auerbach was heavily influenced by Eduard *Meyer. On the occasion of his 70th birthday a volume of essays was published in his honor by the Ḥevrah le-Ḥeker ha-Mikra be-Yisrael, *Sefer Auerbach*, ed. by A. Biram (1955). Auerbach's autobiography up to 1918 has appeared under the title *Pionier der Verwirklichung* (1969).

BIBLIOGRAPHY: Luschan, in: *Archiv fuer Rassen-und Gesellschaftbiologie*, 4 (1907), 362–73; R. Weltsch, in: *Haaretz* (Dec. 5, 1969).

AUERBACH, EPHRAIM (1892–1973), Yiddish poet and essayist. Born in Belz, Bessarabia, Auerbach began publishing in Russian and Hebrew, but turned to Yiddish after 1909. In 1912 he worked in various colonies in Palestine. Expelled by the Turkish authorities at the outbreak of World War I, he joined the Jewish Legion and took part in the Gallipoli campaign. In 1915, he immigrated to the United States and worked as a teacher in Yiddish schools. For 50 years he was associated with New York Yiddish dailies and among other public functions was president of the League for the Rights of Yiddish in Palestine. He published numerous volumes: *Oyfn Shvel* ("On the Threshold," 1915); *Karavanen* ("Caravans," 1918) describes his experiences in Palestine and Gallipoli; *Di Vayse Shtot* ("The White City," 1952) and *Vakh iz der Step* ("The Steppe is Awake," 1963) treat, respectively, the experiences of Jews on Israel's first Independence Day, and memories of Bessarabia; *Loyter iz der Alter Kval* ("The Ancient Spring Is Pure," 1940); *Yankevs Getseltn* ("Jacob's Tents," 1945); and *Gildene Shkie* ("Golden Sunset," 1959). A Hebrew translation of Auerbach's poems by Eliahu Meitus appeared in 1966. His memoirs of the Second Aliyah appeared in Hebrew (1954), the prose translated by Y. Twersky, and the lyrics by Avigdor Hameiri.

BIBLIOGRAPHY: LNYL, 1 (1956), 31–33; J. Glatstein, *In Tokh Genumen* (1956), 480–5; S. Bickel, *Shrayber fun Mayn Dor*, 1 (1958), 98–107; 2 (1965), 49–54; A. Glanz-Leyeles, *Velt un Vort* (1958), 199–209; M. Gross-Zimmerman, *Intimer Videranand* (1964), 227–36. **ADD. BIBLIOGRAPHY:** D. Sadan, in: *Avnei Miftan*, 2 (1970), 98–119.

[Shlomo Bickel]

AUERBACH, ERICH (1892–1957), literary critic. Auerbach is remembered foremost for his innovative book *Mimesis*, a survey of what he defined as "the representation of reality in Western literature" (1946), which he wrote during his exile years in Istanbul. The book was gradually appreciated as the most valuable contribution to the field of literary criticism in the 20th century, especially in the English-speaking world.

Auerbach was born in Berlin and first took a degree in law before changing over to Romance studies. After his doctorate he was appointed in 1929 as ordinarius university professor in Marburg. In 1936 he left Germany for Turkey and taught there at Istanbul State University until 1947. He then lectured in several American universities before he was appointed Sterling Professor at Yale, a year before his death. His other books include *Dante, Poet of the Secular World* (trans. Ralph Manheim, 1961), and *Scenes from the Drama of European Literature* (1984).

Although he lacked an adequate library during his exile in Istanbul, he managed to write an introduction for his Turkish students called *Introduction to Romance Languages and Literature*, as well as further articles. He never mentioned being a Jew in his writings. His ten years of Turkish exile and then the several universities in the U.S. where he taught made him a symbol of the wandering Jewish scholar who had fled Nazi Germany. His intimate self-reflective linguistic and stylistic examination of diverse texts ranging back almost 3,000 years has made his work indispensable for critics and scholars of Western culture. In his efforts to explain the workings of literary allegory in European literature he coined the word "Figura." This could be summarized as a personage or event that prefigures or signifies another. Both are distinct historical personages or incidents, related to each other in many ways.

In 1993, on the 50th anniversary of *Mimesis*, Edward Said, who recognized Auerbach as a fellow-émigré, wrote an introduction to the new edition of this essential work.

BIBLIOGRAPHY: S. Lerer (ed.), *Literary History and the Challenge of Philology. The Legacy of Erich Auerbach* (1996); "Auerbach-Alphabet," Karlheinz (Carlo) Barck zum 70. Geburtstag, in: *Trajekte* (special edition, 2004); D. Caroll, "Mimesis Reconsidered: Literature, History, Ideology," in: *Diacritics* (1975), 5–12.

[Ittai Joseph Tamari (2nd ed.)]

AUERBACH, FRANK (1931–), English artist. Auerbach was sent to London from Berlin by his parents at the age of eight; he never saw them again. Auerbach studied in London at the St. Martin's School of Art and the Royal College of Art, and also attended classes held by David *Bomberg, who influenced his work. Auerbach held his first exhibition in 1956. His work is expressionist, showing delicate care in composition and sound draftsmanship, and often evokes a sense of tragedy. He is also known for his figurative paintings, often of his friends, and for his urban landscapes. Major exhibitions of his works were held at the Hayward Gallery in London in 1978, the National Gallery in 1995, and the Royal Academy in 2002. In 2000 the Tate Modern opened a room devoted to his works. Auerbach is regarded as one of the most important and influential contemporary expressionistic artists. He has worked from the same studio in Camden, London, for more than 50 years, painting every day.

ADD. BIBLIOGRAPHY: R. Hughes, *Frank Auerbach* (1990); C. Lampert, N. Rosenthal, and I. Carlisle, *Frank Auerbach: Paintings and Drawings, 1945–2001* (2001).

AUERBACH, ISAAC EISIG BEN ISAIAH (also known as **Reis**; early 18th century), German grammarian and commentator. Auerbach's father was known as "*ha-kadosh*" ("the martyr"). Ignorant of grammar, Auerbach was unable to understand Rashi's commentary and as a result became interested in philology. The scholars of Fuerth (his place of residence) ridiculed this interest. Auerbach thereupon went to Amsterdam where he studied Hebrew grammar under Samuel Posen and wrote a Hebrew grammar entitled *Girsa de-Yenuka* ("A Schoolboy's Study," 1718). The book consists of excerpts from grammar books and the principles of grammar. The popularity of the work in Frankfurt, where Auerbach had settled, encouraged him to write another Hebrew grammar, *Shuta de-Yenuka* ("Schoolboy's Talk," 1725). Having meanwhile devoted himself "to interpreting and explaining ... Rashi's grammatical comments on the Pentateuch," he published his work, *Be'er Reḥovot* (Sulzbach, 1730; a supercommentary on Rashi's commentary on the Pentateuch). In his introduction, Auerbach states that he followed in the footsteps of Elijah *Mizraḥi and that his purpose was not "to criticize the great scholars but rather to comprehend and understand the literal and true meaning of Rashi's grammatical comments." He also translated into Yiddish *Jedaiah ha-Penini's *Beḥinat Olam* under the title of *Ẓafenat Pa'ne'aḥ* (1743).

BIBLIOGRAPHY: Benjacob, Oẓar, 65, no. 174; A. Walden, *Shem ha-Gedolim he-Ḥadash*, 2 (1864), 5b, no. 11; Fuenn, Keneset, 589; Steinschneider, Cat Bod, 908–9, no. 4910.

[Yehoshua Horowitz]

AUERBACH, ISAAC LEVIN (1791–1853), German preacher and pioneer of the *Reform movement. From 1815 Auerbach served as preacher in the Berlin synagogue established by Israel *Jacobson; he was co-founder of the *Verein fuer Kultur und Wissenschaft des Judentums, taught for some years at a girl's school, and for 25 years, until 1851, was preacher in Leipzig. Auerbach, as an advocate of Reform, preached in German and wrote a thesis using talmudic argumentation justifying the use of German in divine service (1818). He also published sermons on contemporary problems (1828), a call for tolerance (1833), and for Reform based on historical grounds (1845). His attitude to assimilation and religion can be discerned in his sermon on the *Damascus Affair; while not especially identifying himself with his coreligionists in the East, he defended the Jewish religion against the degradation it had suffered. His brother BARUCH AUERBACH (1793–1864) founded the Berlin Jewish Orphanage in 1833, directing it until his death.

BIBLIOGRAPHY: H.G. Reissner, *Eduard Gans* (Ger., 1965), index; Altmann, in: YLBI, 6 (1961), 4–16; Ottenheimer, in: MGWJ, 78 (1934), 481–8.

AUERBACH, ISRAEL (1878–1956), Zionist writer. Auerbach was born in Wissek, Posen province (then Germany). He joined the Zionist group at the University of Berlin, together with his brother Elias *Auerbach, his two brothers-in-law, Arthur *Hantke and Heinrich *Loewe, and Alfred *Klee, all of whom became leaders of German Zionism. Auerbach was active in Zionist circles in Berne where he became a teacher. From 1908 until 1920 Auerbach directed the educational network in Constantinople of the *Hilfsverein der Juden. He enlisted the sympathies of many influential personalities for the Zionist cause. After returning to Berlin in 1920, he became secretary-general of the Hochschule fuer die Wissenschaft des Judentums. Auerbach directed the *Keren Hayesod office in France from 1933 to 1936, and its Jerusalem office from 1936. Auerbach contributed articles to the Zionist and Jewish press, outstanding of which are his reports from Constantinople written for the central Zionist organ, *Die Welt*. He also published poetry, essays, and a play, *Mose* (1925, in German), which was performed on the occasion of the 14th Zionist Congress.

BIBLIOGRAPHY: *Davar* (June 18, 1956); MB (June 8, 1956).

[Getzel Kressel]

AUERBACH, LEOPOLD (1828–1897), German physician and biologist; one of the pioneers of modern embryology. Auerbach was born in Breslau and studied there and at Leipzig and Berlin. From 1863 until his death he held teaching posts at Breslau University, being appointed assistant professor of biology and histology in 1877, but because he was Jewish never becoming a full professor. Auerbach pursued research in almost every field of botany and biology, but his major achievements lay in the investigation of cell division and embryonic development in animals. In his *Organologische Studien* (1874) he provided a basis for the new science of cellular biology. He was ahead of his time in concluding that differences in the cells of the embryo are the result of differences in the various parts of the organism to which they belong. He was also among the first to realize that during cell division the nucleus does not disintegrate, but merely changes its form and structure. The lymphatics in the intestinal walls are named after him.

BIBLIOGRAPHY: B. Kisch, *Forgotten Leaders in Modern Medicine* (1954).

[Joshua O. Leibowitz]

AUERBACH, MEIR BEN ISAAC (1815–1878), rabbi of Jerusalem. Auerbach was born in Dobra, central Poland, and served as rabbi of the Polish towns of Kowal, Kolo, and Kalish (Kalisz). In 1860 he migrated to Jerusalem where, at the request of Samuel *Salant, one of the leading Jerusalem rabbis, he was elected rabbi of the Ashkenazi congregation. He refused to accept a salary, living on the great wealth he had brought with him. "The rabbi of Kalish," as he was usually called in Jerusalem, was noted for his efforts to develop Jewish settlement in Ereẓ Israel and to extend and strengthen the Jewish settlement in Jerusalem. He headed a society which attempted unsuccessfully to purchase land in Jericho for an agricultural settlement. In Jerusalem he gave generous aid to various charitable institutions and supported such projects as arranging the affairs of the **ḥalukkah*, founding the general council of Keneset Yisrael, and the yeshivah Ohel Ya'akov. One of the founders of the Me'ah She'arim quarter, he was a vigilant defender of tradition, and fought vehemently against reformers, especially the supporters of secular education in Jerusalem. He was author of *Imrei Binah*, novellae on the Shulḥan Arukh and responsa on *Oraḥ Ḥayyim* and on *Ḥoshen Mishpat* (pts. 1, 2, Jerusalem, 1869–76); part 3, novellae to *Even* *ha-Ezer*, and part 4, glosses on the Talmud and on Maimonides' *Mishneh Torah*, as well as sermons, were not published. His glosses to Aryeh Leib Ginsburg's *Turei Even* were published along with that work in 1860. His will was published by A. Yaari (see bibl.).

BIBLIOGRAPHY: Rivlin, in: *Ha-Devir*, 1–2 (1919), 72–75; 3–4 (1919), 12–16 (second pagination); 4–6 (1920), 36–40; 7–9 (1920), 42–44; 10–12 (1920), 55–60; 1–3 (1920), 50–55; Tidhar, 3 (1949), 1103–04; I.Y. Fraenkel (ed.), *Sefer Lintshiz* (1953), 79–86; Yaari, in: KS, 34 (1958/59), 371, 379–81. **ADD. BIBLIOGRAPHY:** J. Kaniel, *Ba-Ma'avar* (2000), index.

[Abraham David]

AUERBACH, PHILIPP (1906–1952), German-Jewish political activist. Born in Hamburg, Auerbach received a traditional Jewish education and began an apprenticeship in the chemical export and import business of his father. During the Weimar Republic he was actively engaged in the Liberal Party (DDP). After a brief detention in 1933 he immigrated to Belgium in 1934, where he established a successful chemical business. His father was murdered in the concentration camp of Fuhlsbuettel in July 1938. Auerbach was arrested by German occupation forces on the day of their capture of Antwerp. After internment in various French camps he was brought to a Berlin prison in 1942 and deported to Auschwitz in January 1944. After the war, he was accused of mistreatment of other camp inmates, but the ensuing investigations were suspended with no proof of his misbehavior.

After his liberation, Auerbach soon rose to become the most prominent political spokesman of the reconstituted German-Jewish community. His political career began in the British Occupied Zone as a high official for the affairs of those persecuted under Nazi rule. Suspended from his office by the British authorities a few months later, he was employed by the Bavarian government as "State Commissioner for Racial, Religious, and Political Persecution" and was responsible for the establishment of the Bavarian Office for Restitution. He established the Union of Jewish Communities in the North Rhine Province in December 1945 and, following his move to Munich, was the leader of the Bavarian Jewish community and one of the chairpersons of the Central Council of Jews in Germany founded in 1950. He was an outspoken advocate of immediate financial restitution to Nazi victims and total exposure of Nazi crimes. His activities were recorded with much interest and often opposition by the German public.

In 1949 allegations were made by Bavarian government ministers against Auerbach concerning the misuse of his office, fraud, and the illegal use of an academic title. He was arrested in early 1951. The trial of August 1952 resulted in his acquittal of the most serious allegations, but he was found guilty of corruption, attempted blackmail, perjury, and the illegal use of his academic title. He was sentenced to two and a half years in prison. The following night, Auerbach committed suicide, convinced of his innocence. His activities are still disputed. While most historians agree that he did not mishandle money for personal use, they also stress his unorthodox political style.

BIBLIOGRAPHY: C. Goschler, "Der Fall Auerbach. Wiedergutmachung in Bayern," in: L. Herbst and C. Goschler (eds.), *Wiedergutmachung in der Bundesrepublik Deutschland* (1989), 77–89; W. Kraushar, "Zur Virulenz des Antisemitismus in den Gruenderjahren der Bundesrepublik Deutschland," in: *Menora*, 6 (1995), 319–43; W. Bergmann, "Philipp Auerbach – Wiedergutmachung war, nicht mit normalen Mitteln durchzusetzen," in: C. Froehlich and M. Kohlstruck (eds.), *Engagierte Demokraten* (1999), 57–70.

[Michael Brenner (2nd ed.)]

AUERBACH, "RED" (**Arnold Jacob**; 1917–2006), U.S. basketball coach and executive, member of the Basketball Hall of Fame. Auerbach was born in the Williamsburg section of Brooklyn, New York. He was a star at Eastern District High School and after graduating from George Washington University in 1941 with a master's degree, he coached high school basketball for three years in the Washington, D.C. area and played a year (1942–43) in the American Basketball League with the Harrisburg Senators. Following a three-year tour of duty in the Navy, Auerbach began his professional coaching career in 1946 with the newly formed Basketball Association of America, later to be renamed the National Basketball Association (NBA). Auerbach coached the Washington Capitols to a league-best 49–11 record his first year, but lost in the playoff semifinals to the Chicago Stags. He went to the finals two years later in 1949, where he lost to the Minneapolis Lakers, 4–2. He then left to coach the Tri-Cities Blackhawks for one season, posting the only losing season in his career with a 29–35 record. Auerbach then moved to the Boston Celtics, and history was about to be made. Inheriting a team that had a 22–46 record the previous season, the Celtics then went 39–30 in his first year with the help of rookie guard and future Hall of Famer Bob Cousy.

Five years later, Auerbach made the first of many shrewd trades for which he would become famous, landing Bill Russell with the second pick of the 1956 NBA draft. After winning the NBA championship in Russell's rookie season, the Celtics lost in the NBA finals in 1958 when Russell was injured. Boston won the next eight NBA titles, a record streak that remains unmatched in the history of any American professional sport. Auerbach popularized the concept of the role player and the "sixth man," providing his teams with an added boost from the bench with an established player. Auerbach was famous for his habit of lighting up a cigar on the bench when he felt his team was assured of victory.

When Auerbach retired, he was the first coach to exceed 1,000 wins, finishing with a combined BAA/NBA record of 938–479 in the regular season for a .661 percentage, and 99–69 (.589) in the playoffs for an overall record of 1,037–548. He also coached 11 future Hall of Famers. Auerbach remained Boston's general manager when he retired and named Russell as the team's player-coach, the first African-American head coach in NBA history. Auerbach rebuilt the Celtics as general manager as well, winning two titles in the 1960s and 1970s before drafting Hall of Famers Larry Bird and Kevin McHale and trading for Robert Parish, which led to three more titles in the 1980s. Auerbach was replaced as president in 1997, but returned as team president in 2001. Overall, he won nine NBA titles as a coach and seven more as Boston's GM. He was named NBA Coach of the Year in 1965, NBA Executive of the Year in 1980, the NBA's 25th Anniversary All-Time Team coach, and the greatest coach in NBA history by the Professional Basketball Writers Association of America (PBWAA) in 1980. The Red Auerbach Trophy is now presented each year to the NBA's Coach of the Year. Auerbach is the author of *Basketball for the Player, the Fan and the Coach* (1953) and, with co-author Paul Sann, *Winning the Hard Way* (1966).

[Elli Wohlgelernter (2nd ed.)]

AUERBAKH, ROKHL (**Rachel**; 1903–1976), prolific Yiddish and Polish author, historian, and essayist. Born in Lanovtsy (Galicia), in the prewar period Auerbakh founded and edited the literary journal *Tsushtayer* in Lemberg (Lvov). In Warsaw from 1933, she published in the central Yiddish and Polish Jewish press on literature, education, psychology, folklore, art, linguistics, and theater. Under German occupation, she was active in the underground archives of the Warsaw ghetto and served in Jewish self-help organizations. In postwar Poland, she worked to document and collect testimonial accounts and materials and was co-founder of the Central Jewish Historical Commission in Lodz. In Israel from 1950, she collected testimony from survivors and published her Holocaust period writings and testimonial memoirs in various forms. She was founder and director of the Department for the Collection of Witness Testimony at *Yad Vashem; her personal archives are classified as Inventory no. P-16, Yad Vashem. Her publications include *Oyf di Felder fun Treblinke* (1947); *Der Yidisher Oyfshtand: Varshe 1943* (1948); *Undzer Kheshbn mitn Daytshn Folk* (1952); *Behutsot Varsha 1939–1943* (1954); *Varshever Tsavoes* (1974); *Baym Letsten Veg: In Geto Varshe un oyf der Arisher Zayt* (1977).

[Carrie Friedman-Cohen (2nd ed.)]

AUERNHEIMER, RAOUL (1876–1948), Austrian author (pseudonyms **R. Heimern, R. Othmar**). Auernheimer was born in Vienna, where he studied law (Ph.D., 1904). Under the aegis of his mother's cousin, Theodor *Herzl, he became editor of the Viennese *Neue Freie Presse*. A minor member of the "Young Vienna" group of writers, Auernheimer gained prominence with his numerous plays, novels, and books on historical and social themes. These works include *Talent* (1899), *Das Paar nach der Mode* (1913), *Casanova in Wien* (1924), *Gewitter auf dem Rigi* (1932), and *Wien* (1938). His many volumes of short stories are reminiscent of the impressionistic style of Arthur *Schnitzler. From 1922, he was vice president of Austrian PEN. After internment in the Dachau concentration camp (Feb.–Aug. 1938), Auernheimer immigrated to the U.S., settling in Hollywood, where he wrote biographies of Metternich and of the Austrian dramatist Franz Grillparzer (1948). His autobiography, *Das Wirtshaus zur verlorenen Zeit*, was published posthumously (1948).

BIBLIOGRAPHY: H. Zohn, *Wiener Juden in der deutschen Literatur* (1964), 49–51. **ADD. BIBLIOGRAPHY:** *Biographisches Handbuch der deutschsprachigen Emigration*, 2 (1983), 41, bibl.

[Harry Zohn / Marcus Pyka (2nd ed.)]

AUFRUFEN (Yid. "call up"), traditionally a designation among Ashkenazim for the honor bestowed upon a groom to ascend the *bimah* for the reading of the Torah at a synagogue service (see Reading of the *Torah) on the Sabbath prior to his wedding. He may be called up with a special chant (*reshut*). In some congregations the groom receives the *maftir aliyah* and reads the prophetic portion (*haftarah*). There may be a similar celebratory Torah honor on the first Sabbath after the wedding called *Shabbat Kallah* marking the change in status of the bride. Among Sephardi Jews this custom is called *Shabbat Ḥatan* (the bridegroom's Sabbath) and takes place the Sabbath after the wedding. This public recognition of change of status was originally based on a talmudic tradition that King Solomon built a special gate through which bridegrooms would pass on the Sabbath and be greeted by family and friends. After the destruction of the Second Temple, the custom was moved to the synagogue.

In recent decades, brides within the Conservative, Reform, and Reconstructionist movements have begun to share these honors with their bridegrooms or have their own Torah honors. In some modern Orthodox congregations, the bride may be called to the Torah before her wedding at a special women's prayer group (*tefillah*). The bride and groom may be showered with sweets and the rabbi will express the good wishes of the community to the couple through a *Mi she-berakh* (May the One who blessed our ancestors, bless this bride and groom) prayer.

BIBLIOGRAPHY: Eisenstein, Dinim, 322; I.G. Marcus, *The Jewish Life Cycle – Rites of Passage from Biblical to Modern Times* (2004), 152, 185.

[Rela Mintz Geffen (2nd ed.)]

AUGSBURG, city in Bavaria, Germany; a free imperial city from 1276 to 1806. Documentary evidence of Jews living in Augsburg dates from 1212. Records from the second half of the 13th century show a well-organized community, and mention the *Judenhaus* (1259), the synagogue and cemetery (1276), the ritual bathhouse, and "dancehouse" for weddings (1290). The Jews were mainly occupied as vintners, cattledealers, and moneylenders. The Augsburg municipal charter of 1276, determining the political and economic status of the Jewish residents, was adopted by several cities in south Germany. Regulation of the legal status of Augsburg Jewry was complicated by the rivalry between the episcopal and municipal powers. Both contended with the emperor for jurisdiction over the Jews and enjoyment of the concomitant revenues. Until 1436 lawsuits between Christians and Jews were adjudicated before a mixed court of 12 Christians and 12 Jews. In 1298 and 1336 the Jews of Augsburg were saved from massacre through the intervention of the municipality. During the *Black Death (1348–49), many were massacred and the remainder expelled from the city. The emperor granted permission to the bishop and burghers to readmit them in 1350 and 1355, and the community subsequently recovered to some extent. Later, however, it became so impoverished by the extortions of the emperor that the burghers could no longer see any profit in tolerance. In 1434–36 Jews in Augsburg were forced to wear the yellow *badge. The community, then numbering about 300 families, dissolved within a few years; by 1340 the last Jews had left Augsburg. The Augsburg town council paid Albert II of Austria 900 gulden to compensate him for the loss of his *servi camerae*. Thereafter Jews were only permitted to visit Augsburg during the day on business. They were also granted the right of asylum in times of war. From the late 16th century Jewish communities existed in the close-by villages Pfersee, Kriegshaber, and, temporarily, Oberhausen.

In the late Middle Ages the Augsburg yeshivah made an important contribution to the development of the **pilpul* method of study and analysis of the Talmud. The variant of the *pilpul* method evolved in Augsburg is referred to as the "Augsburg *ḥillukim*." The talmudist Jacob *Weil lived in Augsburg between 1412 and 1438. While some Hebrew pamphlets were printed in Augsburg by Erhard Oeglin as early as 1514 on the initiative of the apostate J. Boeschenstein, a Hebrew press was established in 1532 by Ḥayyim b. David Shaḥor, the wandering printer from Prague, together with his son Isaac and son-in-law Joseph b. Yakar who had learned printing in Venice. Between that year and 1540 nine books appeared including Rashi's Pentateuch commentary (1533); an illustrated Passover *Haggadah* (1534); Jacob b. Asher's *Turim* (1536); a *Melokhim Buch*, in Yiddish (1543); a *maḥzor*; and a *siddur*. In 1530 *Joseph Joselmann of Rosheim convened a synod of German community representatives in Augsburg, the seat of the Reichstag (see *Germany). An organized Jewish community was again established in Augsburg in 1803. Jewish bankers settled there by agreement with the municipality in an endeavor to redress the city's fiscal deficit. In practice, the anti-Jewish restrictions in Augsburg were eliminated in 1806, with the abrogation of the city's special status and its incorporation into Bavaria; however, the new Jewish civic status was not officially recognized until 1861. In 1871 Augsburg was the meeting place of a rabbinical assembly dealing with liturgical reform. The Jewish population increased from 56 in 1801 to 1,156 in 1900. It numbered 1,030 in 1933. In 1938, the magnificent synagogue, dedicated in 1917, was burned down by the Nazis. In late 1941, after emigration and flight to other German cities, the last 170 Jews were herded into a ghetto, with 129 of them sent to Piaski in Poland in April 1942 and the rest mostly to the Riga ghetto and Theresienstadt. In the immediate postwar period, a camp was established in Augsburg to house displaced Jews. A few weeks after the liberation, services were resumed in the badly damaged synagogue by survivors of the Holocaust and Jewish soldiers of the U.S. Army, and the community was eventually reestablished. The synagogue was restored and rededicated in 1985. As a result of the immigration of Jews from the Former Soviet Union, the number of community members rose from 199 in 1989 to 1,619 in 2003.

BIBLIOGRAPHY: R. Gruenfeld, *Ein Gang durch die Geschichte der Juden in Augsburg* (1917); R. Strauss, *Regensburg and Augsburg* (1939), includes bibliography; H. Rinn (ed.), *Augusta* 955–1955 (Ger., 1955); M. Steinschneider, in: ZGJD, 1 (1887), 282–7; *German Jewry* (Wiener Library, Catalogue, series 3, 1958), 35; A.M. Habermann, in: KS, 31 (1955/56), 483–500; *Monumenta Judaica*, 2 vols. (1963–64); Germ Jud, 1 (1963), 14–16; 2 (1968), 30–41; A.M. Habermann, *Ha-Sefer ha-Ivri be-Hitpatteḥuto* (1968), 127ff.; A. Marx, *Studies in Jewish History and Booklore* (1944), 329ff. **ADD. BIBLIOGRAPHY:** M.N. Rosenfeld, *Der juedische Buchdruck in Augsburg in der ersten Haelfte des 16. Jh.* (1985); H. Kuenzl, in: *Judentum im deutschen Sprachraum* (1991), 382–405; P. Boettger, in: *Denkmaeler juedischer Kultur in Bayern* (1994), 75–90; S. Muetschele, "Juden in Augsburg 1212–1440" (Diss., 1996); S. Ullmann, *Nachbarschaft und Konkurrenz* (1999); J. Spokojny, in: *Geschichte und Kultur der Juden in Schwaben*, 2 (2000), 413–21.

[Zvi Avneri / Stefan Rohrbacher (2nd ed.)]

°**AUGUSTINE** (354–430), bishop of Hippo (North Africa) and outstanding *Church Father of Western Christianity. Born in Tagaste in North Africa to mixed Christian/pagan parentage, Augustine was educated at the University of Carthage, abandoned his faith temporarily and fathered a son, was eventually ordained and became the bishop of Hippo in 395. As an influential ecclesiastic and prolific theological writer, Augustine attacked various Christian sects and heresies and also took issue with Judaism. His religious and philosophical views reveal the influence of a great variety of spiritual movements and trends (Neo-Platonism, Manichaeism, the Stoics, Cicero, Aristotle, etc.) but most of his major doctrines are completely foreign and indeed opposed to traditional Jewish teaching (e.g., his concepts of the innate sinfulness of man, and predestination). Nevertheless, Jewish influences are also discernible, though these are mainly derived from the common biblical background and from Hellenistic Jewish philosophy (Philo of Alexandria), the Neoplatonic character of which had an obvious affinity with Augustine's own thinking. Thus Augustine's emphasis upon the absolute transcendence and unity of God is such that the doctrine of the Trinity assumes a relatively secondary importance. His theology of history, as developed in his *City of God*, has Jewish overtones only in the sense that its historical perspective contains some traditional eschatological and apocalyptic elements and insists on Israel's universal religious mission in history. In spite of his unequivocal rejection of post-Christian Judaism (e.g., in his *Tractatus adversus Judaeos*) – in keeping with the basic tenets of Christian thinking – Augustine evinces in some of his writings (e.g., in his commentary on the Psalms), and quite unlike the violently anti-Jewish diatribes of his contemporary, John Chrysostom, a positive (i.e., missionary attitude) to the Jewish people as being destined ultimately to join in the fullness of the Divine promise as realized in the church. The definitely anti-Jewish tracts circulating in the Middle Ages under the name of Augustine are later compositions wrongly attributed to him.

More than any other Church Father of his time, Augustine studied the "Old Testament," quoted from it and commented upon it. Biblical history, as the history of Israel, the people of God, formed the basis of Augustine's philosophy of history, and his division of world history into periods was derived from it. His method of interpreting the Bible is partly rationalistic, partly allegorical and mystical. Augustine had little or no knowledge of Hebrew, although he was probably familiar with the rudiments of the related Punic language. In order to overcome this handicap he occasionally consulted African Jews. Two legends (that of Adam's second wife and of Abraham in the furnace) are explicitly quoted by him as of Jewish origin but he often mentions rabbinic opinions without quoting their source. In his work *De doctrina christiana* (ch. XXXIV, col. 15–122), Augustine seeks to establish guidelines for biblical exegesis and states that a knowledge of Hebrew was essential for the understanding of Scripture. At the same time he regarded the Vulgate text as authentic from the point of view of the church and attacked Jerome for embarking upon a new Bible translation from the Hebrew. His opposition to Jerome's work, which was only temporary, may have resulted from his hostility to Judaism and to Jews in general, whom he accused of failing to understand the Bible, or deliberately misunderstanding it (*Tractatus adversus Judaeos*).

There has been no noticeable influence of Augustine's doctrines upon Jewish religious philosophy. The attacks of Saadiah Gaon on the concept of the Trinity and of God as a hypostasis of three attributes – being, living, and knowing (*Emunot ve-De'ot*, ch. 2; cf. *De libero arbitrio*, ch. II, 3 no. 7) were surely directed at Christianity as such and not specifically at Augustine. Like Augustine, Saadiah taught that time was created by God, but this doctrine has its roots in the philosophy of Plato (*Timaeus*) and was also accepted by Philo. There are similarities in the doctrine of God's will and of Divine omniscience as propounded by Augustine, Saadiah, and Maimonides, respectively (Kaufmann). Jewish authors who mentioned Augustine in their writings are Judah Romano, in the notes to his translation of Averroes' *De substantia orbis (Eẓem ha-Shamayim)*; Isaac Abrabanel, who according to Joseph Delmedigo took considerable interest in Augustine; Hillel b. Samuel of Verona, in his work *Tagmulei ha-Nefesh*; and several anonymous authors, such as *Sefer Ḥokhmah Kelalit*, the translation of a pseudo-Aristotelian work.

There is an incomplete translation into Hebrew of Augustine's *Confessions* by Paul Levertoff ("*Vidduyei Augustinus*," 1908).

BIBLIOGRAPHY: D. Kaufmann, *Geschichte der Attributenlehre* (1877), 41, 72, 304, 307; B. Blumenkranz, *Die Judenpredigt Augustins* (1946); H.A. Wolfson, *The Philosophy of the Church-Fathers I* (1956), index. **ADD. BIBLIOGRAPHY:** St. Augustine, *Confessions*, ed. and tr. H. Chadwick (1991); H. Chadwick, *Augustine* (1986); P. Brown, *Augustine of Hippo* (1967).

[Jacob Klatzkin / Shimon Gibson (2nd ed.)]

AUGUSTOW, district town in Bialystok province, Poland. Jewish inhabitants are mentioned for the first time in 1630 and numbered 239 in 1765. Many were occupied in the local lumber industry, rafting logs to Danzig. The Russian limitations on Jewish settlement in border towns, in operation from 1823 to 1862, barred further Jewish settlement in Augustow in this period, although the community did not decrease until the regulations were stringently enforced. The Jewish population numbered 3,764 in 1860 (45% of the total), and 3,637 in 1897 (28.5%). The first synagogue was founded in the 1840s. There were five synagogues in Augustow by the beginning of the 20th century. During World War I, Augustow was heavily damaged and the community diminished, in 1921 numbering 2,261 (25.8%) members, mainly employed in ready-made tailoring.

[Nathan Michael Gelber]

Holocaust Period

Nearly 4,000 Jews were living in Augustow prior to the outbreak of World War II. On Sept. 20, 1939, the Soviet Army entered the town. Jewish political parties were outlawed and a few local leaders arrested, but the cultural and religious institutions continued to function. On June 22, 1941, the German Army captured the town. Shortly after, about 1,000 Jewish males rounded up in the town were concentrated in the forest near Szczebre and executed. In October 1941 a ghetto was established. In June 1942 all the remaining Jews, mostly women and children, were deported to the camp in Bogusze, near *Grajewo, where about 7,000 Jews from the vicinity were concentrated. Within a few weeks about 1,700 of them died of hunger and disease. In August 1942 the German and Polish police conducted an *Aktion*. The Bogusze camp was liquidated and all its Jewish prisoners deported to *Treblinka and *Auschwitz death camps, where all but a few were put to death.

[Stefan Krakowski]

BIBLIOGRAPHY: *Sefer Yizkor li-Kehillat Augustow ve-ha-Sevivah* (1966, Heb. and partly Yid.; incl. bibl.).

°AUGUSTUS (Caius Julius Caesar Octavianus; 63 B.C.E.–14 C.E.), first Roman emperor (27 B.C.E.). The policies of Augustus toward the Jews of the Roman Empire in general, and the inhabitants of Judea in particular, followed the favorable line established by Julius *Caesar. But with respect to Judea, the emperor's personal friendship with Herod probably played the decisive role. Herod's rule in Judea (37–4 B.C.E.) was contemporaneous with the rule of Augustus, and a close relationship existed between the two monarchs. It was Augustus, together with Mark Antony, who had been instrumental in the Senate's appointment of Herod as ruler of Judea (Jos., Ant., 14:383; Wars, 1:283–5). After the defeat of Antony at Actium (31 B.C.E.), Herod had been summoned by Augustus to Rhodes to explain his relations with the defeated Antony, and had succeeded in gaining the favor and friendship of the new emperor. After Augustus had confirmed his rule, and occupied

Egypt, he annexed to Herod's kingdom "the territory which Cleopatra had earlier appropriated [in 34 B.C.E., i.e., mainly the territory of Jericho] with the addition of Gadara, Hippos, and Samaria and the maritime towns of Gaza, Anthedon, Jaffa, and Strato's Tower [later Caesarea]" (Wars, 1:396; Ant., 15:217). Aware of Herod's difficulties within his realm, Augustus did everything to support him in his effort to fulfill his obligations as a faithful vassal of the Roman Empire. Augustus thought highly of Herod's ability as a ruler and valued his personal friendship. He approved of Herod's efforts to introduce Roman culture into Judea and for this reason paid little heed to the claims of Herod's enemies, foreign and domestic. The deterioration of their relationship toward the end of Herod's reign was only a minor interlude, after which the friendship was restored. Knowing the Jewish aversion to pork, it is reported that Augustus, on hearing of Herod's execution of his own son *Antipater, made the pun that he would rather be Herod's pig (Greek: ὑς) than Herod's son (ὑιος). In spite of this friendship, Herod's rule as a Roman vassal was never changed by Augustus. After Herod's death in 4 B.C.E. Augustus did not confirm his will but divided the country among the king's three sons. Archelaus was appointed to rule over Judea, Idumea, and Samaria, but only as ethnarch and not as king, as had been the will of Herod. The two other sons, Herod Antipas and Philip, were assigned tetrarchies in the north of the country. The Hellenistic cities of Gaza, Gadara, and Hippos were detached from the territory by Augustus. Archelaus failed to live up to the hopes reposed in him, and in 6 C.E. Augustus accepted the demands of two embassies from Judea, both urging abolition of the monarchy, as a result of which Archelaus was banished and Judea came under direct Roman rule.

Jews throughout the Diaspora were favorably treated by Augustus. In one edict the rights of Jews in Asia Minor were upheld, including the privilege of sending money to the Temple treasury (Ant., 16:102 ff.). Augustus also issued decrees in favor of the Jews of Cyrene (*ibid.*, 169 ff.). He also ensured the "inviolability of their sacred books and synagogues" and exempted them from the need to give bond to appear in court on the Sabbath or Friday after the ninth hour. The emperor's praise of his grandson, Gaius, for not worshiping in Jerusalem (Suetonius, *De Vita Caesarum*, 2:93) does not imply antagonism toward the Jews, but reflects his rejection, in general, of the Eastern religious rites which were penetrating Rome at that time. Probably in Augustus' lifetime, several synagogues were founded in Rome (cf. the Synagog Augustasion).

BIBLIOGRAPHY: Vogelstein-Rieger, 1 (1895), 11 ff.; Juster, Juifs, 1 (1914), 149 ff.; Schuerer, Hist, index; Schuerer, Gesch, index, s.v. *Octavianus Ausgustus*; A. Schalit, *Hordos ha-Melekh* (1964^3), 507.

[Isaiah Gafni]

AUMMAN, ROBERT J. (**Yisrael**; 1930–), Israeli mathematician, Nobel Prize laureate in economics. Aumman was born in Frankfurt, Germany, and immigrated with his family to New York in 1938. He studied mathematics, and graduated from the City College of New York in 1950 and received his M.A. and Ph.D. in mathematics from MIT in 1955. In 1956 he immigrated to Israel and joined the Institute of Mathematics at the Hebrew University of Jerusalem, where he taught until his retirement. After completing his Ph.D. he shifted his interest to practical science and began to study game theory, then a novel scientific discipline, at Princeton (1960–61). From 1966 until 1968 he was the chairman of the Institute of Mathematics and in 1968 became a professor. Aumman was the first to conduct a full-fledged formal analysis of so-called infinitely repeated games. His research identified exactly what outcomes can be maintained over time in long-run relations. He introduced measure theory into the analysis of economies with an infinite number of agents, where each agent has little influence on the end result. Aumman also applied game theory to political conflicts, such as the Israeli-Palestinian conflict. During his long academic career, he wrote about 100 articles and six books and was a visiting professor a many universities. He received several prizes for his research: Harvey Prize in Science and Technology (1983), the Israel Prize in economics (1994), Lanchester Prize in Operations Research (1995), Erwin Plein Nemmers Prize in Economics (awarded by Northwestern University, 1988), and EMET prize in economics (2002). In 2005 he received the Nobel Prize with Thomas C. Schelling for their contribution to conflict solution in fields such as commerce and war.

BIBLIOGRAPHY: Y. Melaman, and T. Traubman, "Nobel Prize in Economics To Be Given to an Israeli, Prof. Yisrael Aumman of the Hebrew University," in: *Haaretz* (Oct. 11, 2005).

[Shaked Gilboa (2nd ed.)]

AURICH, town near Hanover, Germany. Jews from Italy apparently first settled in Aurich around 1378 by invitation of the ruler of the region; this community came to an end in the 15th century. In 1592 two Jews were permitted to perform as musicians in the villages around Aurich. A new community had formed by 1647 when the *Court Jew Samson Calman settled there. Aurich was the seat of the *Landparnass* and *Landrabbiner* (see **Landesjudenschaft*) of East Friesland from 1686 until 1813, when it was transferred to *Emden. Under Dutch rule (1807–15) the Jews enjoyed the civil rights which they had lost in 1744 during Prussian rule. A cemetery was established in Aurich in 1764; the synagogue was consecrated in 1811. The Jews in Aurich numbered 14 in 1708, 166 in 1804, 420 in 1900 (7% of the total), and 398 in 1933. The synagogue was burned down on *Kristallnacht* (Nov. 9–10, 1938). In 1940 the remaining 155 Jews in Aurich fled to other German towns before a rumored evacuation. About 150 had managed to emigrate, and in all, about 160 died.

BIBLIOGRAPHY: K. Anklam, in: MGWJ, 71 (1927), 194–206; PK (Germanyah); EJ, 3 (1929), 697. **ADD. BIBLIOGRAPHY:** H. Reyer (ed.), *Die Juden in Aurich* (1992).

AURUM CORONARIUM (Latin "gold for the crown"), term for two separate taxes paid in ancient times.

(1) It was originally a voluntary gift donated by the provinces to victorious Roman generals and later to emperors upon accession. The gift had the form of a golden crown. In time it became a mandatory tax, collected by every new emperor. When, from the third century C.E., Roman rule changed hands every two or three years, it became a heavy burden. It is not surprising, therefore, that Romans and Jews alike tried to evade payment of the tax. The Talmud tells of "the crown for which the inhabitants of Tiberias were called upon to find money." After demanding that R. Judah ha-Nasi, who was apparently responsible for transfer of the money, distribute the heavy burden equally among all residents, half the citizens of Tiberias finally fled to avoid payment (BB 8a).

(2) For the Jews, however, *aurum coronarium* took on another meaning, namely the voluntary contributions of world Jewry to support the Patriarchate in Palestine. These funds, called *Demei Kelila* (דְּמֵי כְּלִילָא) in rabbinic sources (BB 143a), were collected by official messengers (ἀπόστολοι) of the patriarch, and as a result were also known as *apostolé*. According to Epiphanius (Adv. haereses 1:30, 3–12) these emissaries were of the highest rank and participated in the patriarch's councils. A similar description appears in the letter of authorization given to R. Ḥiyya b. Abba: "We are sending you a great man, our messenger, who shall be treated on a par with ourselves until he returns to us" (TJ, Ḥag. 1:8, 76d; TJ, Ned. 10:10, 42b). The emperor Julian, probably in an attempt to secure the good will of those Jewish communities who were forced to carry the burden, ordered the discontinuation of the Jewish tax (362–3 C.E.). This pause however, was only temporary (as was a similar one in 399–404 C.E.) and collection of the *aurum coronarium* continued until 429 C.E. After the suppression of the Patriarchate in 425 C.E., the funds were delivered to the Palestinian academies. In an edict dated May 30, 429 C.E., the *aurum coronarium* was officially converted by the emperors Theodosius II and Valentinian III into a special Jewish tax to the state treasury (*Codex Theod.* 16, 8:29).

BIBLIOGRAPHY: Lacombrade, in: *Revue des études anciennes*, 51 (1949), 54–59; Alon, Toledot, 1 (1953), 147, 156ff.; Baron, Social, 2 (1952^2), 194–5; Juster, Juifs, 1 (1914), 385.

[Isaiah Gafni]

AUSCHWITZ (Oświęcim), Nazi Germany's largest concentration and extermination camp. The word "Auschwitz" has become a metaphor for the Holocaust in general, and the phrase "after Auschwitz" has come to signify the great historical rupture wrought by the murder of six million Jews.

These meanings often overshadow the particular and specific history of Auschwitz. Founded by German settlers and known to them as Auschwitz and to the Poles as Oświęcim, the town of Auschwitz/Oświęcim has existed since 1270 (see *Oswiecim). Since World War II, however, the name Auschwitz refers to the concentration and annihilation camp the Germans established in spring 1940. This camp, which came to encompass a whole complex of sections and sub-camps, remained in operation until January 27, 1945, when the Red Army arrived.

The character and scope of the atrocities that took place in Auschwitz fully justify the identification of the camp as the symbolic center of the Holocaust. It was there that the single largest group of Jews was murdered: over one million men, women, and children; in total more than 90 percent of the 1.1 million Jews deported to the camp. To put this number in perspective: 750,000 Jews were murdered at the death camp of Treblinka; nearly 500,000 at Belzec; 200,000 at Sobibor; and 150,000 at Kulmhof (Chelmno). Jewish citizens from more European countries (at least 12) were deported to Auschwitz than to any other camp. Thus the history of Auschwitz also testifies to the pan-European character of the Holocaust. Then too the Germans killed more than 100,000 non-Jews at Auschwitz: 75,000 Poles (or some 50 percent of the 150,000 Poles deported to the camp), at least 18,000 Sinti and Roma (about 80 percent of the 23,000 imprisoned there), 15,000 Soviet prisoners of war (nearly 100 percent of those in the camp), and some 15,000 others (or 60 percent of that group). Auschwitz therefore testifies as well to the often forgotten Nazi aim to create a "New Order." This German plan called for the total annihilation of the Jews and the genocide of other groups, including selected population strata of the Slavs, undesirable Sinti and Roma, and the mentally ill and physically handicapped.

Finally, Auschwitz holds a key place in history because its technology and organization were so thoroughly "modern." With its central location in the European railway infrastructure, its business relationships with many large and small industries that relied on slave labor, its medical experiments conducted by highly qualified physicians working in collaboration with distinguished research institutions, and its large and efficient crematoria equipped with logically designed killing installations for those deemed "unfit for labor," Auschwitz stands for industrial civilization. In its use of gas chambers, it stands, too, for the deliberate nature of the genocide of which it became a center. People shot with rifles, or even machine guns, are killed with arms designed, manufactured, and purchased for use in combat. The use of these weapons to massacre civilians is an aberration. Like the gallows, the guillotine, and the electric chair, gas chambers are designed and built to kill non-combatants. Unlike these other means of execution, gas chambers permit many people to be executed, anonymously, at the same time. The 52 ovens built in the five crematoria of Auschwitz, with a total incineration capacity of 4,756 corpses per day, testify to the genocidal purpose of the Nazi state.

Located in the historical borderland between Germany and Poland, the town of Auschwitz was established by Germans in the 13th century, became a Polish fief called Oświęcim in the 15th century, merged into the Hapsburg patrimony as part of Austrian Galicia in the First Polish Partition (1772), and, with the collapse of the Austro-Hungarian Empire (1918), become part of the Polish Republic. After their conquest of Poland in 1939, the Germans annexed Oświęcim to the Reich, and called it Auschwitz once again. They designated eastern Upper Silesia, the region in which the town was located, a high-priority area for political, social, and economic development. For the Germans, Auschwitz signified a return to the pristine, lost past of medieval German achievement: it betokened opportunity and promise to new generations.

Reichsführer-SS Heinrich *Himmler acquired responsibility for the redevelopment of eastern Upper Silesia, as well as of the other annexed territories (Wartheland, Danzig-West Prussia) in his role of Reich Commissioner for the Consolidation of the German Nation. Himmler initiated a policy of ethnic cleansing in the annexed territories, deporting Poles and Jews and bringing in ethnic Germans from the Baltic countries, the part of Poland annexed by the Soviet Union, and Romania. Population transfers proceeded smoothly in the predominantly rural areas of the Wartheland and Danzig-West Prussia, but proved more difficult in eastern Upper Silesia. This area was heavily industrialized, and its mainly Polish workers could not be deported without crippling production in the area. Aiming to intimidate the hostile population, Himmler decided (April 27, 1940) to transform a former Polish military base, located in the Zasole suburb of Auschwitz, into a concentration camp. He appointed SS-Captain Rudolf *Hoess as its first Kommandant, and sent him off to Auschwitz to build the camp.

Hoess chose five SS men to assist him, obtained 15 SS men stationed in Cracow to serve as guards, and selected 30 German common criminals imprisoned in Sachsenhausen to be transferred to Auschwitz as prisoner functionaries and 40 Polish inmates from Dachau as a construction crew.

Refurbishing the former military base to fulfill its new function as a concentration camp to incarcerate recalcitrant Poles proved laborious. The army barracks were in poor condition, and Hoess had great difficulty obtaining barbed wire for fences and building materials for repairs and construction. Inmates were used as construction laborers, mainly in excavation works, transportation, demolishing nearby houses, leveling the roll-call area, paving roads, and as skilled workers. The first transport of 728 Polish prisoners arrived from Tarnow on June 14, followed by a transport of 313 on June 20. The reasons for their arrest varied: some of them had tried to cross the border, others were resistance organizers, political activists, member of the intelligentsia, and Jews. By July 6, the camp counted 1,282 inmates. Tadeusz Wiejowski escaped that day, and the SS punished all the inmates by forcing them to stand for roll call for 20 hours. One inmate, David Wongczewski, did not survive the ordeal. He was the first Auschwitz inmate to die. Significantly, Wongczewski was a Jew.

The camp grew rapidly throughout the summer; on September 22 prisoner number 5,000 was issued, and by year's end 7,879 inmates had been registered. Many were victims of random street roundups in Warsaw. Witold Pilecki, by contrast, had voluntarily joined a group of men seized during such a *Razzia*. A prominent resistor, Pilecki sought to set up a resistance organization within Auschwitz. One of his goals was to improve living conditions in the camp. This was necessary: within six months, almost 1,900 men had died from exhaustion, deprivation, beatings, and execution.

Populated primarily by Poles, whom the Germans considered disposable, Auschwitz was a particularly violent place even by concentration camp standards. If in the camps in the Reich proper the *Arbeit Macht Frei* ("work will set you free") motto inscribed above the gate of Dachau carried at least an echo of the idea that the camps were meant not only to paralyze opposition to the regime but also to bring the "politically misguided" or "asocials" back to the true German community, in Auschwitz this ideology did not apply – despite the fact that Hoess hoisted the same motto above a camp gate. Poles could never be part of the German community. With no restraint imposed by ideology, the judiciary, or public opinion, Auschwitz quickly became a closed universe in which inmates had no rights at all. Tadeusz Borowski described the total and unremitting domination to which he and his fellow inmates were subjected in intimate detail.

> If the barrack walls were suddenly to fall away, many thousands of people, packed together, squeezed tightly in their bunks, would remain suspended in mid-air. Such a sight would be more gruesome than the medieval paintings of the last Judgment. For one of the ugliest sights to a man is that of another man sleeping on his tiny portion of the bunk, of the space which he must occupy, because he has a body – a body that has been exploited to the utmost: with a number tattooed on it to save on dog tags, with just enough sleep at night to work during the day, and just enough time to eat. And just enough food so it will not die wastefully. As for actual living there is only one place for it – a piece of bunk. The rest belongs to the camp, the Fatherland. But not even this small space, not the shirt you wear, nor the space you work with are your own. If you get sick, everything is taken away from you: your clothes, your camp, your "organized" scarf, your handkerchief. If you die – your gold teeth, already recorded in the camp inventory, are extracted. Your body is burned, and your ashes are used to fertilize fields, or fill in the ponds. Although in fact so much fat and bone is wasted in the burning, so much flesh, so much heat.

Living on a starvation diet, without warm clothes or shoes, with little sleep, no privacy, subject to an arbitrary regime imposed by the SS and prisoner functionaries such as the Kapos, and exhausted by 12 hours of hard labor, every inmate struggled to survive each day. Most of the work involved outdoor construction. In the fall and winter, exposure, exhaustion, and malnutrition led to quick physical decline. Inmates called a prisoner who began to slip a *Muselmann* (Muslim). A breathing corpse, unable to keep himself clean, indifferent to his surroundings, and only dreaming about food, a *Muselmann* became a burden on the lives of other inmates. Inhabiting a limbo between life and death, the *Muselmaenner* document the triumph of total power over human beings and the negation of dignity. All prisoners faced the prospect of becoming *Muselmaenner.* But those assigned to the penal company were likely to end that way. Established in August 1940, this especially punitive work detail comprised those who broke camp rules, all Catholic priests, and all Jews.

The high mortality at Auschwitz called for a crematorium to dispose of corpses. The former ammunition depot served. In summer 1940 the SS took delivery of one double-muffle oven manufactured by the Topf company in Erfurt. Its official incineration capacity of over 100 corpses per day proved insufficient, and in fall 1940 the Auschwitz SS ordered a second double-muffle oven. A third (summer 1941) brought the official daily cremation capacity to 340 corpses. Clearly, the SS perceived murder to be a growth industry in Auschwitz. While many of the dead were registered inmates, the camp also functioned (from November 1940) as an execution site of prisoners of the Gestapo office in Kattowitz, the provincial capital of Upper Silesia. These people were transported to Auschwitz for court-martial and summary execution in the courtyard of Block 11, the camp prison. They were not registered into the camp.

While death had become common and killing a daily occurrence, the SS initially remained somewhat squeamish about conducting the mass killings that characterized Auschwitz later that year. When the SS selected 573 invalid and chronically ill inmates for execution in July 1941 as part of the so-called 14f13 program, they did not kill them in Auschwitz but transported them by train to Sonnenstein asylum. There the victims were killed in carbon-monoxide gas chambers constructed in the T4 program initiated two years earlier to "eliminate" the insane, the handicapped, and others deemed "unworthy of life." This inefficient solution of shipping inmates to a mass murder facility prompted SS-Captain Dr. Friedrich Entress to experiment in cheap ways to kill by means of injection. After trying hydrogen and gasoline, Entress settled on phenol. From September 1941 to April 1943 this became the preferred way of killing *Muselmaenner* who refused to die quickly enough, or inmates who were to be liquidated on orders of the so-called Political Department, the camp Gestapo. The task to kill by injection usually fell to SS medics like the notorious SS-Sergeant Josef Klehr. Assuming the crucial role of executioner, Entress set an important precedent in Auschwitz. He and the other SS physicians working in the camp were central to the annihilation system at Auschwitz, selecting inmates for death and selecting new arrivals "unable to work" for immediate dispatch to the gas chambers. Entress and his colleagues, all of whom had sworn the Hippocratic Oath, condemned a million people, mostly Jews, to death.

In the fall of 1940 the camp acquired two economic functions: to provide prisoners to work in adjacent gravel pits owned and exploited by the SS company DEST, and to serve Himmler's policy of ethnic cleansing. Poles living in the rural areas immediately south of Auschwitz were targeted for deportation, and ethnic Germans from Romania were to move into the area. In order to provide practical support to help the new arrivals establish economically viable farms, Himmler made the concentration camp the center of a huge agricultural experiment estate. The camp claimed ever larger territories for its new role as a scientific farm. Himmler began to envision a different future for Auschwitz than he had originally intended. As a concentration camp, Auschwitz would be a temporary facility; as an agricultural estate it claimed permanence. Much labor was needed to create drainage canals to improve the land, build dikes along the Vistula, and clean the large fishponds. By August 1941, some 20,000 inmates had been admitted into the camp. Of these, 12,000 were still alive. Yet Himmler was pleased with Hoess' performance as Kommandant. In recognition of his achievements, the latter was promoted to SS-Major.

Originally a small compound surrounded by a double barbed wire fence, the camp had grown by the beginning of 1941 to include a 15-square-mile SS "Zone of Interests." Himmler needed an enormous influx of money and building materials to develop this zone and he therefore sought to generate income by attracting the huge chemical conglomerate, IG Farben, to Auschwitz. The terms of the bargain were that the camp would grow to 30,000 inmates to supply labor to construct Farben's synthetic rubber ("Buna") plant. A new satellite to the concentration camp, Birkenau, to be populated initially by 100,000 Soviet prisoners of war (a number increased to 125,000 in the fall of 1941), was to provide labor to transform the town of Auschwitz into a handsome, 60,000-German-strong city worthy of an IG Farben enterprise and exemplary of Himmler's ambitions in the East. In return, IG Farben was to finance and supply building materials for Himmler's Germanization project in the area. This included the expansion of the concentration camp and the construction of an idyllic village for the SS guards.

The designs for the new town showed that the German inhabitants of Auschwitz were to get the very best: beautiful houses, elegant shops, restaurants, cinemas, and hotels to house tourists. The slave workers to actualize these dreams received the worst. The German government did not feel obliged to treat the Soviet prisoners of war according to the Geneva Convention. Under direction of SS-Captain Karl Bischoff, the chief architect of the Auschwitz *Zentralbauleitung* (Central Construction Agency), the young Bauhaus-trained architect SS-Second Lieutenant Fritz Ertl designed an enormous compound subdivided into three large sections by barbed wire (named *Bauabschnitt* (Building Sector) I, II, and III, or BA I, BA II, and BA III), which were in turn divided up into smaller compounds (BA Ia–b, BA IIa–f, etc). Ertl's housing plan consisted of rows upon rows of the most primitive brick barracks. Heated by two tiny stoves and with no washing or toilet facilities of any kind, each barrack was designed to house 748 men on three tiers of shelves, four to each shelf of 2 × 2 meters. The living conditions of these barracks were infinitely worse than those of the barracks of concentration camps such as Dachau, Buchenwald, and Sachsenhausen, and considerably worse than the overcrowded barracks in the Auschwitz main camp. In the end, only 30 of these barracks were built in BA Ia and Ba Ib, but the alternative, wooden horse stables designed and manufactured for the army which filled the compounds of BA II, was not much better. While these horse stables could be built quickly, they proved stiflingly hot in the summer and bitterly cold in the winter.

The SS expected many deaths from endemic and epidemic disease in Birkenau, with its targeted population of 125,000 Soviet POWs, and in the main camp located in a suburb of Auschwitz called Zasole, where 30,000 Polish prisoners were to be interned. The existing crematorium capacity of 340 corpses per day was deemed insufficient. The SS commissioned (fall 1941) a very large, state-of-the-art crematorium that could manage 1,440 corpses per day. The initial design was worked out between Bischoff, Topf engineer Kurt Pruefer, and the architect Georg Werkmann, who was employed in SS headquarters in Berlin. The main features of their plan were a large incineration hall with five triple-muffle ovens above ground, and two large morgues below ground. The main access to the morgues was by means of a corpse-slide – a feature that had become standard in concentration camp underground morgues. It was to be built in the main camp, right next to the existing crematorium, but to service Birkenau. This staggering cremation capacity was considered appropriate to cope with the anticipated "normal" mortality of the 155,000 slave laborers to be worked to death. Given the rapidity with which the 9,890 Soviet prisoners of war who had been brought to Auschwitz since October had died, the dimensions of the crematorium did not seem out of place: 1,255 Soviet prisoners of war died as the result of deprivation or killings by phenol injections or beatings in October; 3,726 in November; and 1,912 in December. The crematorium did not provide execution facilities. Nothing in the original conceptual sketches of the crematorium, nor in the worked-out blueprints which date from January 1942, suggests homicidal gas chambers, or their use in what the Nazis called the "Final Solution to the Jewish Problem." When large-scale mass murder of Jews began in the summer and fall of 1941 in the wake of Operation Barbarossa, the *Kommandantur* in Auschwitz was still fully focused on Himmler's project to develop the town and the region.

Step by step, however, the camp at Auschwitz became part of the Nazis' genocidal apparatus. The SS began to send Soviet POWs they considered "commissars" to be executed in Auschwitz in addition to POWs for forced labor. Initially these men were executed by rifle and machine gun in the DEST gravel pits. In August 1941, camp officials considered whether a more efficient and – for the SS – less disturbing manner of execution could be found. They settled on the use of a gas chamber.

Gas chambers had been used in animal pounds to kill stray dogs and cats since the 1880s. Persuaded that gassing would cause a quick and merciful death, the state of Nevada installed a gas chamber in 1924 to execute convicted criminals. By the end of the 1930s, eight American states had followed Nevada's example. Besides its allegedly humane procedure, gas chamber executions were popular with the prison authorities because they were effective (unlike failed hangings or failed electrocutions, there is no record of a failed gassing) and clean: no blood, and no sudden evacuations of the bowels or bladder.

Unlike in the United States, gas chambers did not gain a foothold in the Third Reich as a means to execute those convicted to death by regular courts. In prisons, guillotines chopped off the heads of the "legally" condemned and, from 1943 onwards, gallows were used for multiple executions. In the fall of 1939 German officials began to construct gas chambers in selected asylums to kill groups of mentally ill and handicapped patients (T4 program) and, from 1941 on, groups of selected concentration camp inmates (14f13 program) by bottled carbon monoxide. When the Auschwitz SS considered gas chambers as a tool of mass execution, they followed the precedent of the T4 chambers, but decided to use Zyklon B instead of carbon monoxide.

Zyklon B was the commercial name of a fumigation agent that had been developed by Drs. Bruno Tesch and Gerhard Peters at the Kaiser Wilhelm Institute in Berlin with the support of IG Farben. The active ingredient of Zyklon B was hydrogen cyanide, which was mixed with an irritant tear gas to serve as a "warning," and which was soaked at a ratio of 1:2 in diatomaceous earth, a porous, highly absorbent material. The resulting mixture consisted of solid granules that could be packed in tins of 200, 500, 1,000, and 1,500 grams. When the tins were opened and the granules exposed to air, the hydrogen cyanide evaporated from the diatomaceous earth. Safe to transport, Zyklon B proved a very efficient agent for the fumigation of whole buildings, ships, and railroad cars without damaging the contents. An important characteristic of Zyklon B was that, upon opening the tin, the granules "degassed" for a 24-hour period – important when seeking to kill lice and other vermin, which can survive up to 14 hours in a highly toxic environment.

Zyklon B was patented by IG Farben, which assigned the patent and the production license to its (partial) subsidiary Degesch, the Deutsche Gesellschaft fuer Schaedlingsbekaempfung (German Society for the Destruction of Vermin). In turn, Degesch used two companies, the Dessauer Werke and the Kalin Werke at Kolin, for the production of the solution. The sale of Zyklon B was highly regulated both because of the nature of the product and the various special permissions needed to obtain the product in a time of rationing. To take the administrative pressure off Degesch, a pest control company created in 1923 by Dr. Tesch and a certain Paul Stabenow, known as Tesch and Stabenow (TeSta), was appointed to act as a general clearing-house for all Zyklon B orders east of the Elbe River. TeSta thus oversaw the purchase of Zyklon B for Auschwitz.

Developed to kill lice and other insects, Zyklon B proved its versatility when the city of Vienna adopted it (1938) as the preferred means to kill pigeons, praising its "easy and inconspicuous practicality offering the possibility to conduct mass exterminations in the shortest possible time." In early September 1941, the Auschwitz SS expanded on the Vienna example and used Zyklon B on people. They packed 600 Soviet prisoners of war and 250 Polish inmates behind barred gates in the basement of Block 11 and, protected by gas masks, opened tins with Zyklon B in full view of the inmates and emptied a tin with pellets on the floor. Hoess claimed after the war that he had adopted Zyklon B because it ensured a quick and easy death for the victims. He lied. It took some of the Soviet prisoners more than a day of terrible agony to die.

The poison had been effective, but the SS had difficulty ventilating the basement of Block 11 after the killing, and this impeded the clean-up procedure. The SS therefore decided to move the killing operation to the crematorium, and they transformed the morgue adjacent to the room with the ovens into a Zyklon gas chamber. This morgue had already been used for some time for the execution of people convicted by the Gestapo summary court from Kattowitz, and so the precedent for killing people in the morgue had been established. As the morgue had a flat roof, it was easy to create holes in the roof that allowed camp personnel to drop Zyklon pellets into the gas chamber below. An existing ventilation system, created at the request of Gestapo executioners nauseated when shooting their prisoners in the foul-smelling morgue, ensured that the hydrogen cyanide could be removed easily after everyone had died. A gas chamber thus in place, the Auschwitz crematorium became a small but efficient "factory of death," with killing and incineration facilities under one roof. This killing installation, later called crematorium 1, was not meant to operate on a continuous basis, however. It was too visible. Located right next to the main camp, neither the building nor the arrival of victims to be killed inside its gas chambers were screened or hidden.

The creation of the new killing installation proves that murder had become important business in Auschwitz. But it does not establish whether, in the late summer of 1941, Himmler intended Auschwitz to have a central role in the murder of Jews. Two statements made by Hoess after the war suggest that Himmler had already designated Auschwitz as a death camp for Jews as early as June 1941 and that the killing experiments with Zyklon B were preparatory to their anticipated arrival. Hoess' statements are not supported by other evidence, however. Given what we know about the origins of the "Final Solution," it is clear that in the early summer of 1941 the Germans had not yet envisioned the total annihilation of the Jewish people. To be sure, wide-scale murder of Jews by *Einsatzgruppen* in the East had begun in July and become policy in August, but the Nazi leadership had not adopted those actions as a model for the fate of all of Europe's Jews. While Germans experimented in the late summer with gas vans to lighten the burden on killing squads, the concept of mass killing installations with stationary gas chambers evolved only in the late fall of 1941, after they had embraced the policy to kill all Jews. Thus, Hoess' postwar statements conflict with the history of the Final Solution.

They conflict, too, with the history of the Germans' designs for Auschwitz. Though planning for the large new crematorium with a daily incineration capacity of 1,440 corpses began in fall 1941, the drawings for this building do not show any accommodation for gas chambers, and the anticipated location of the new crematorium in a tight but very public place right next to the main camp is such that it would not physically accommodate the smooth arrival, selection, and killing of great numbers of Jews, nor provide camouflage. There is evidence, however, that crematorium 1 was used in early 1942 to kill small groups of Jews from Upper Silesia who had been sent to forced-labor camps run by the so-called Organization Schmelt.

Established by SS-Major-General Albrecht Schmelt, this organization oversaw the forced labor of 50,000 Jews in Upper Silesia. In early 1942, Schmelt decided that Jews "unfit for work" should be killed, and he got Hoess to agree to do the dirty work for him. These murders were not part of the Europe-wide policy of concentration, deportation, and killing overseen by the Reich Security Main Office which brought more than 1.1 million Jews to Auschwitz between March 1942 and November 1944. It appears likely that when Hoess made his statement after the war, he conflated three separate events: the development of the Zyklon gas chamber in the summer of 1941, the killing of the Schmelt Jews in early 1942, and the arrival and killing of Jews pursuant to the Nazis' policy of genocide in the summer of 1942.

Himmler, in short, did not designate Auschwitz as an annihilation camp for Jews in June 1941. It was only when Reichsmarshall Hermann *Goering, who was in charge of the war economy, directed Soviet POWs from Auschwitz to German armament factories in January 1942 that Himmler began to consider how he could use the emerging "Final Solution" policy to promote his "Auschwitz Project." Committed to Auschwitz as the centerpiece of his racial utopia, he now turned to the use of Jewish slave laborers instead of Soviet POWs. At the *Wannsee Conference in January 1942, Heydrich secured for Himmler the power he needed to negotiate with German and foreign civilian authorities for the transfer of Jews to his SS empire. SS headquarters informed Hoess immediately after the conference that transports of Jews would be sent to Auschwitz. The Soviet prisoner-of-war camp was officially dissolved on March 1. Of the 10,000 Soviet prisoners sent to Auschwitz, 945 survived and they merged into the general camp population that then counted 11,500 inmates.

The SS did not lack for trapped Jews to send. The Germans had incarcerated almost 9,000 Jews in occupied France since May 1941, most of them refugees. Section IV-B4 of the Reich Security Main Office, the Gestapo Bureau for Jewish Affairs headed by SS-Major Adolf *Eichmann, saw these Jews as a source of slave labor for Auschwitz, and dispatched 1,112 in March. But France was far from Auschwitz; Slovakia was much nearer.

Established in the wake of the German occupation of the Czech lands in 1939, Slovakia was a German satellite state. The Slovak government had agreed to send 120,000 workers to the labor-strapped Reich, but they soon regretted their decision. When the Germans insisted in summer 1941, the Slovaks offered to send 20,000 young Jews. The Germans declined: they were not interested in bringing Jewish forced laborers into the Reich. But when the SS looked for a new supply of labor for Auschwitz in January 1942, they remembered the Slovak offer and negotiations began that ended in an agreement to ship 10,000 Jews to Auschwitz and 10,000 to *Majdanek, another camp that was to have had Soviet POWs. Once again, the Slovak government had second thoughts: sending those who were young and fit to the camps would leave children and old people as a burden on the state. When the Slovak government then suggested that Himmler also take Jews unfit for labor, he dispatched SS Construction Chief SS-Brigadier General Hans Kammler to Auschwitz. Kammler toured Birkenau, identified a peasant cottage close to the northern boundary of the prisoner compound, and ordered the building department to transform it into a gas chamber. It was to be known as "The Little Red House," or "The Bunker." During that same visit, he also ordered that the large crematorium then in design for the main camp was to be erected in Birkenau close to the bunker. Kammler's command reflects the leadership's intent to hide the annihilation program. Upon his return to SS headquarters in Berlin, Kammler reported that Auschwitz would be prepared to receive Jews both fit and unfit for work. Berlin then concluded a deal with Bratislava to take all its Jews. The Slovak government paid 500 marks in cash for every Jew deported. They raised the funds by seizing Jewish property. Section IV-B4 of the Reich Security Main Office organized the transports.

The bunker was brought into operation on March 20. No Slovak transports had arrived yet. A small group of Schmelt Jews was brought to the bunker and killed. Prisoners buried the bodies nearby and were brought in turn to the infirmary, where they were killed by phenol injection.

The first transport with 999 female Slovak Jews arrived in Auschwitz on March 26. As all of these women were considered fit for labor, they were not subjected to a selection. Sent to a section of the main camp in Zasole separated from the rest by a barbed-wire fence, they were the first inmates of the women's camp. In the next five months, 17,000 women were imprisoned in that sub-camp, 5,000 of whom died. The surviving 12,000 women were brought to Birkenau in August and imprisoned in compound BA Ia. As the women's camp expanded, it needed more space, and in July 1943 a new sector, BA Ib, was added. The women's camp was run by Johanna Lagerfeld (until October 1942), Maria Mandel (October 1942–November 1944), and Elisabeth Volkerrath (November 1944–January 1945). In 1942, 28,000 women were admitted, of whom 5,000 were alive at the end of the year; in 1943, 56,000, of whom 28,000 died; and in 1944 some 47,000 were admitted. Of the 131,000 women prisoners, 82,000 were Jews and 31,000 Poles.

All 9,000 Slovak Jews who arrived in March, April, and June 1942 were considered fit for labor and were admitted into the camp. But the SS put the bunker to use. Impatient with the slow death of some 1,200 ill inmates in the medical isolation ward in Birkenau, the SS transported some 1,000 selected by a medical officer and brought them to the bunker. From then (May 4) on, inmates selected for death were killed by phenol injection and, if a gas chamber was available, by gas. More transports of Jews from the local area were brought to Auschwitz that May and, without selection, some 5,200 people were killed in the bunker. While the murder of Jews was still secret, information about Auschwitz leaked out on July 1 when an article in the *Polish Fortnightly Review*, an English-language newspaper published by the Polish government-in-exile, mentioned it as a particularly violent concentration camp where inmates were gassed. Events had gone far beyond the scope of this news: the article referred to the experiments of fall 1941.

As the bunker created to cope with the deportation of the Slovakian Jews was already in full use before any Slovakian transport with "unfit" Jews had arrived, the SS converted a second peasant house into a killing installation. It was known as the "Little White House," or bunker 2. The "Little Red House" was now renamed bunker 1.

The first transport of Jews from Slovakia that included children and the elderly arrived on July 4, 1942. Unloading the train on a makeshift platform between Auschwitz and Birkenau, SS men separated the men from the women and children and an SS doctor selected 264 able-bodied men and 108 women for work. The elderly, children, mothers with children, and pregnant women were loaded onto trucks and brought to bunker 1, where they were killed. As before, prisoners were forced to empty the bunker and bury the bodies. Unlike their predecessors, who had been killed after each "action," the prisoners who did the work on July 4 were not murdered. Imprisoned in a special barrack in Birkenau, they lived totally isolated from the rest of the inmates. Assigned the designation *Sonderkommando* (Special Squad), they became the specialists assigned to operate the killing machine. And as the killing machine became more sophisticated, their tasks increased. By the time the crematoria came into operation, it was they who gave instructions to the victims in the undressing room, maintained order and led them to the gas chamber, dragged out the corpses, checked body orifices for valuable objects, extracted gold teeth and cut women's hair, brought the corpses to the incineration rooms, and cremated the bodies – day in, day out. After three months of work, the *Sonderkommandos* were murdered and a new special squad was assigned. Their first task was to cremate the remains of their predecessors. In Auschwitz, in survivor (and chemist and author) Primo *Levi's view, the National Socialists' most demonic crime was the conception and organization of the *Sonderkommando*.

These procedural steps – selection on arrival and the establishment of the *Sonderkommando* – moved the annihilation of Jews at Auschwitz from "incidental" practice (the murder of the Schmelt Jews from Upper Silesia) into what one could call "continuing" practice. But it had not yet become policy. The bunkers were still a particular solution to a situation created by the collision of Slovak unwillingness to provide for old and very young Jews and German greed for labor and money.

The turning point in the history of Auschwitz as an annihilation camp came when Himmler acquired responsibility (around mid-July 1942) for German settlement in Russia. He had coveted that authority for more than a year, and he turned his attention to the vast possibilities this promised. His Auschwitz Project was no longer of interest to him. The camp could be used for the systematic killing of Jews. Practice became policy. Transports from ever-farther destinations arrived in Auschwitz on a daily basis. Regular trains began to arrive from France in June, from Holland in July, and from Belgium and Yugoslavia in August. Throughout the summer an average of 1,000 deportees arrived every day at the so-called *Judenrampe* located between the main camp and Birkenau. A quick selection by a cadre of SS physicians found most of them "unfit for work." Loaded on trucks and brought to bunkers 1 and 2, they were forced to undress and were killed.

Himmler visited the camp on July 17 and 18. There were various items on his agenda. Discussions with Albert Speer, the newly appointed minister for armaments and war production, had led to an agreement to employ 25,000 inmates at Auschwitz and four other camps to produce carbines. Himmler ordered the expansion of Birkenau to accommodate 200,000 inmates and instructed Eichmann to fill the camp with Jews able to work. He then checked on the construction progress and toured the grounds. At Birkenau, he watched the selection of a transport of 2,000 Dutch Jews at the *Judenrampe*, the killing in Bunker 2 of 449 of them considered unfit for work, and the burial of the corpses. According to Hoess, "Himmler very carefully observed the whole process of annihilation.... He did not complain about anything." Himmler also visited IG Farben. The next day he returned to the camp, and told Hoess that Auschwitz would become a major destination for Europe's Jews. "Eichmann's program will continue," he announced, "and will be accelerated every month from now on. See to it that you move ahead with the completion of Birkenau. The gypsies are to be exterminated. With the same relentlessness you will exterminate those Jews who are unable to work." To bolster Hoess' motivation, Himmler promoted him to SS-Lieutenant-Colonel.

The architects at Auschwitz got to work. So did Kurt Pruefer at Topf and Sons. In addition to building the large crematorium, commissioned in late 1941 for the main camp, they were to add its mirror image in Birkenau. These were to be known as crematoria 2 and 3, while the crematorium in the main camp was now called crematorium 1. The original design, sketched in October 1941 and drafted in great detail in early 1942, did not show gas chambers. Now the design team moved to include homicidal gas chambers. Walther Dejaco transformed the basement plan, adding new stairs that allowed for easy access below and removing the corpse-slide. He changed the larger of the two underground morgues into an undressing room and the smaller, which already was planned to have a powerful ventilation system in its wall and ceiling, into a gas chamber which could hold up to 2,000 victims at one time. He reversed the swing of the chamber door to open outwards, not inwards, to allow access to the room after a gassing. He also equipped each gas chamber with four so-called gas columns – hollowed-out, wire mesh columns with a kind of basket in the center that could be lowered down into the gas chamber or hoisted up through an opening in the ceiling. This simple mechanism not only allowed for the easy introduction of Zyklon pellets into the crowded room but also for the quick removal of the still degassing pellets when all the victims had died 20 minutes later. Once the pellets were removed and the ventilators turned on, the gas was cleared from the room in half an hour, allowing for corpse cremation in the 15 large ovens to begin without delay. In this manner, one "load" of victims could be killed and cremated in a 24-hour period. This streamlined murder system facilitated a regular daily schedule of arrivals, selections, and killings.

Efficient as crematoria 2 and 3 were, they were also large, expensive, and unwieldy. Underground gas chambers created many problems that required complex solutions: the mechanical ventilation system, the gas columns, and an elevator to move the corpses to the incineration ovens on the main floor. The camp administration's experience with the bunkers had shown that primitive gas chambers could work very efficiently and that combining simple above-ground gas chambers without mechanical ventilation and with an adjacent undressing room and an incineration facility provided a simple, functional killing installation. Following these principles, the camp architects and Pruefer developed a design for a crematorium with an incineration capacity of 768 corpses per day, an undressing room that also could function as a morgue, and three homicidal gas chambers in a lower annex. This design, euphemistically referred to in the architects' meeting minutes as "Bath Installations for Special Actions," became crematoria 4 and 5, built near the bunkers.

Killing hundreds of thousands of people created problems the Auschwitz administrators did not anticipate. Decomposing corpses in mass graves near the bunkers began to pollute the ground water. Kommandant Hoess and architect Dejaco traveled (September 16) to the annihilation camp at *Chelmno to examine open-air incinerators constructed by SS-Colonel Paul Blobel. Back in Auschwitz, Dejaco built copies near the bunkers. Beginning September 21, 1,400 inmates began to exhume the bodies from the mass graves and burn the corpses. It was a wretched and dangerous job. With bare hands, standing knee-deep in decomposing flesh, the prisoners emptied the pits. The bodies of those killed thereafter were burned on these pyres immediately after gassing. By November a total of 107,000 corpses had been incinerated in this manner, including all 1,400 inmates who had done the work, killed on the job or upon completion of the work. Primitive as this method of corpse disposal may have been, it did not limit the rate of murder: in 1942, some 200,000 Jews were killed in Auschwitz.

The Germans sent most Jews to their death upon arrival. But not all. They continued to admit worker Jews into the camp. By December 1942, the inmate population had grown to 30,000 and, four months later, to 50,000, the majority of whom were Jews. Auschwitz had become the largest camp in the SS concentration camp system, and the only one that had a large Jewish inmate population. According to an order of Himmler, the other camps in the Reich had been made "Jew-free."

If Jews comprised the great majority of the inmates, they also sat at the bottom of the camp pyramid of privilege. Auschwitz had been an extraordinarily violent camp from the outset, and that violence intensified over time. What Polish inmates had suffered in the first two years was a pale foreshadowing of the fate of Jewish inmates. Most Polish prisoners could be reasonably sure that their families were alive. Most Jews arrived with their families, were torn from them during selection, and knew that their loved ones had been killed in the gas chambers. They also knew, for certain, that they had been given only a reprieve from death, and that every day could be their last. In addition to this crushing emotional burden, the living and working conditions of Jewish inmates were even harsher than those of Polish inmates. If a significant proportion of Polish inmates had been fated to become the nameless and emaciated *Muselmaenner,* amongst the Jews they were the majority. According to Primo Levi, they were "an anonymous mass, continually renewed and always identical, of non-men who march and labor in silence, the divine spark dead in them, already too empty to really suffer. One hesitates to call them living: one hesitates to call their death death."

The SS did not expect any of the Jews to survive. On September 26, 1942, the chief of the SS Economic Administrative Office, SS-Lieutenant General Oswald Pohl, instructed Hoess that the belongings of the deportees were not to be stored in view of a possible release, as was the practice in "normal" concentration camps. Hoess was to ship currency, valuables, and precious metals to SS headquarters in Berlin; rags and unusable clothes to the Reich Ministry of Economy for use as raw materials in industrial production; and all usable garments, shoes, blankets, bed linens, quilts, and household utensils to the Ethnic German Liaison Office (VOMI) for distribution among ethnic German settlers. The yield was enormous. In an interim report Pohl submitted to Himmler on February 6, 1943, he noted that 824 boxcars of goods had left Auschwitz: 569 to the Reich Ministry of Economy, 211 to VOMI, and 44 to other concentration camps, various other Nazi organizations, and the IG Farben works at the other end of town.

These mass murders and massive distribution of goods could not be kept secret. The Polish resistance well knew that Auschwitz had become a central site for the annihilation of Jews. In March 1943, a secret radio station operated by the Polish resistance broadcast that 65,000 Poles, 26,000 Soviet prisoners of war, and more than 520,000 Jews had been killed in the camp. The figures were inflated, but the basic message was correct: Jews had become the main victim group in the camp.

The broadcast did not mention the Roma and Sinti, perhaps because they were recent arrivals. Just a month earlier, the SS had established the so-called gypsy camp in section BA IIe of Birkenau in response to a Reich Security Main Office decree (January 1943) that all German Roma and Sinti were to be deported to Auschwitz. In total, 32 transports arrived from Germany, four from Bohemia and Moravia, three from Poland, one from Yugoslavia, and four mixed transports, bringing 23,000 Roma and Sinti to the camp. No selections took place upon arrival. The Roma and Sinti families remained intact, housed together in the so-called gypsy camp. Some 10,000 died from illness, deprivation, and individual murders. Another 2,700 sick with typhoid were gassed in two actions in 1943. At least 3,000 Roma and Sinti were gassed when the Germans liquidated the gypsy camp in 1944. More than 4,000 of the remaining 7,000 Roma and Sinti merged with the general camp population and at least 2,500 were transferred to Buchenwald and Ravensbrueck. Few survived.

In the late winter and early spring of 1943, when the killing reached 800 people per day, the first of the new crematoria in Birkenau came into operation. In their final form, all the crematoria provided for murder and corpse disposal. People walked in, and exited the building as smoke through the chimneys and ashes that were dumped in the nearby Vistula River. Between entrance and exit the Germans built a logical sequence that included undressing rooms, gas chambers of different sizes, places to cut women victims' hair for industrial use and to extract gold tooth crowns from men and women, and fuel-efficient ovens that allowed for high-rate multiple corpse incinerations. The official total incineration capacity of the four large crematoria in Birkenau was 4,416 corpses per day. In 30 adjacent storehouses, nicknamed "Canada" for the wealth they contained, inmates sorted and packaged arrivals' belongings. All usable items were shipped back to the Reich for the use of less fortunate Germans. Most importantly, the new crematoria offered the SS the opportunity to kill anonymously. The SS doctors who undertook the selection of the victims could tell themselves that, as all Jews who arrived at Auschwitz were a priori condemned, they actually saved the lives of those whom they chose as slave laborers. The SS medics who introduced the Zyklon B into the gas chambers never saw their victims. In the case of crematoria 2 and 3, they just opened some vents that emerged from the grass, emptied a can of Zyklon into the hole, and closed the top. The dying below was invisible to them and everyone else. Jewish *Sonderkommandos* cleaned the gas chambers after the killing and incinerated the corpses: Germans were not involved.

Oddly enough, upon their completion, the crematoria appeared superfluous. The Holocaust itself had peaked when all four crematoria were ready for use in the summer of 1943. The genocide had begun in 1941, and the Germans had killed some 1.1 million Jews that year. In 1942 they murdered another 2.7 million Jews, of whom less than 10 percent died in Auschwitz. The year the crematoria of Auschwitz came into operation the number of victims dropped to 500,000, half of whom were killed in Auschwitz. All the Jews whom the Germans had been able to catch easily had been trapped. In June and July 1943 average daily transports brought 275 Jews into the camp. The crematoria could easily keep up, despite the fact that crematoria 2 and 4 were out of commission because of technical difficulties. This lull gave the Germans the opportunity to liquidate the nearby Sosnowiec Ghetto in August. It was in Sosnowiec that, two years earlier, the Oświęcim Jewish community had been imprisoned to make space for German settlers and IG Farben personnel. The camp numbered 74,000 inmates that month, or one-third of the total prisoner population of the entire German concentration camp system. In the fall and winter the number of arrivals dropped again to some 250 people per day.

Almost all transports were still subjected to selection. A train of 5,006 Jews of all ages from Theresienstadt on September 9 was a notable exception. The Theresienstadt Jews were allowed to keep their clothes and hair, and they were quartered in section B IIb of Birkenau, the so-called Czech family camp. This unusual event occurred again on December 16, when 2,491 Jews arrived from Terezin, and on December 20 with another transport of 2,471 Jews. Everyone was registered into the camp. In the context of Auschwitz, this seemed to be a stable situation, so stable that the well-known educator Freddy Hirsch established a children's program in Block 31. But nothing in Auschwitz was secure. On March 7, all those who had come on the first transport were forced to write postcards to their family and friends in Theresienstadt. Then they were killed. The Germans had waited six months to murder them because the Red Cross had visited Theresienstadt and the SS wanted to be able to prove to that charitable organization that inmates shipped from Theresienstadt to Auschwitz were alive and well. They could have saved themselves the trouble: the Red Cross never asked what happened to deported Jews.

As killing abated in the fall of 1943, the regime in the camp became less violent. An SS judge, Konrad Morgen, initiated an investigation into corruption and theft of valuables in the camp, and he focused on the head of the camp Gestapo, SS-Second Lieutenant Maximilian Grabner. Morgen ordered Grabner's arrest in October for corruption and for having exceeded the boundaries of his authority in killing at least 2,000 prisoners "beyond the general guidelines." Morgen did not bring a case against Hoess, but he was sufficiently implicated to be relieved of his duties as Kommandant in November 1943 and transferred to Berlin. His successor was SS-Lieutenant Colonel Arthur Liebehenschel, a manager in SS headquarters who had never worked in a concentration camp. In an attempt to improve the situation for the inmates, Liebehenschel abolished the selection of the *Muselmaenner* and somewhat lightened the regime in the main camp. He also reorganized the camps administratively. Auschwitz, Birkenau, and Monowitz became separate camps, known as Auschwitz I, II, and III. Liebehenschel took control of Auschwitz I and appointed SS-Major Friedrich Hartjenstein as Kommandant of Auschwitz II. SS-Captain Heinrich Schwartz took charge of Auschwitz III.

The major project of the Auschwitz SS at this time was to foster an increasingly lucrative collaboration between German industry in Upper Silesia and the camp. They established three satellite camps in 1942 to provide slave labor to the IG Farben synthetic rubber and fuel plant in Monowitz, the coal mines in nearby Jawischowitz, and German industry in Chelmek; in 1943, five more satellite camps were set up; and in 1944, another 19. In 1942, 4,600 prisoners (of 24,000) worked for outside firms; in 1943 the number had increased to 15,000 (of 88,000); and in 1944 some 37,000 (of 105,000). When the camp was evacuated in early 1945, more than half the prisoners provided slave labor outside of the camp. The rest worked in the construction and maintenance of the camp, in SS-owned companies, and in the amelioration of the 15-square-mile estate around the camp. All of it – the outside firms, SS-owned companies, mines, factories, construction, and fieldwork – was lethal. Prisoners worked long hours on starvation diets, with insufficient clothing in the winter, no safety protections, and subject to brutal treatment by supervisors and guards. Regular selections ensured that any prisoner who could not keep the pace was sent to the gas chambers.

Prisoners were not dispatched as slave laborers alone. They were also given to physicians as guinea pigs. Doctors experimented on concentration camp inmates from the beginning of the war. In Dachau, recent medical graduates of the SS medical academy in Graz were offered inmates for surgery practice. In the same camp, Dr. Claus Carl Schilling injected inmates with live malaria cells, assuming they would develop resistance to it. Hundreds died. Testing the survival chances of airmen who had to bail out of planes at high altitude, or sailors on the open sea, physicians put Dachau inmates into low-pressure low-oxygen chambers, submerged them for long periods in ice-cold water, or gave them seawater to drink. They died horrible deaths. "Research" in Auschwitz concentrated on mass sterilization of able-bodied Jews without impairing their ability to work. One professor of medicine, Dr. Carl Clauberg, subjected women inmates to massive doses of x-rays in Block 10 of the main camp, which killed many.

The most assiduous and notorious medical "researcher," Jozef *Mengele, arrived in Auschwitz on May 30, 1943. His interests grew out of his work at the Kaiser Wilhelm Institute in Berlin, where he had served as research assistant to Otmar von Verschuer, a pioneer in the study of inherited diseases through research with twins. Mengele well knew that comparative autopsies on twins would provide ideal study conditions, but twins rarely died simultaneously and at a convenient location for the researcher. Auschwitz offered him an opportunity to do what was impossible elsewhere. He set up a block for twins in the gypsy camp where he conducted brazenly diabolical "experiments." Interested in eye color, he injected dye into the eyes of his human subjects. Curious about the course of infectious disease and resistance to it, he inoculated inmates with infectious agents. Fecundity, sterility, and gender fascinated Mengele. He conducted sex change operations, castrating boys to transform them into girls; he burned the uteri of girls to sterilize them, and he forced incestuous impregnations. One twin served as the control while the other underwent medicalized torture. If one twin died during surgery, the other was killed by phenol injection and comparative autopsies were performed. Mengele's zeal to identify twins on arriving transports prompted him to volunteer regularly to conduct selections. His became the face of the SS physician conducting selections on the arrivals ramp.

For Jews continued to arrive. By the end of 1943 the Germans closed down the death camps built specifically for annihilation: Chelmno, Sobibor, Belzec, and Treblinka. Auschwitz remained to mop up the remnants of the Jewish communities of Poland, Italy, France, the Netherlands, and the rest of occupied Europe. In 1944 another 600,000 Jews were killed in Auschwitz, most of them Hungarians. By that time, information about the role of Auschwitz as an annihilation center was available as the result of the successful escape of two young Slovak Jews, Rudolf Vrba and Alfred Wetzler. With a lot of planning and even more luck, Vrba and Wetzler managed to slip out of Auschwitz on April 10, 1944. They had been imprisoned for two years and they fled to Slovakia in the hope of warning the Jews of Hungary, the last large community of Jews. The Jewish underground debriefed them and their information yielded the first substantial report on the use of Auschwitz as a death factory. But it did not reach the Hungarians in time.

As the camp prepared for new heights of murderous activity, SS headquarters transferred Liebehenschel to Lublin. He was considered too soft on the inmates of the main camp and not tough enough to conduct the planned Hungarian Action. Hartjenstein was also relieved of his duties in Birkenau. He was blamed for delays in the construction of the railway spur into the camp. Knowing that in the midst of the Hungarian Action a new Kommandant would not have time to ease into the job, Himmler dispatched Hoess to Auschwitz to run both the main camp and Birkenau. Hoess appointed SS-Master Sergeant Otto Moll as head of the crematoria. Under Moll's direction, crematoria 4 and 5 were brought back into operation, as was bunker 2, closed down since the spring of 1943. The number of *Sonderkommando* was increased to 1,000.

In the months of May and June almost 7,000 Hungarian Jews arrived in Auschwitz every day, and nearly all were killed on arrival. The crematoria could not keep up, and once again large pyres disposed of many corpses. Most able-bodied deportees were registered and admitted to the camp, but at least 30,000 of them were not tattooed with an identification number. These "transit Jews" were temporarily held in Auschwitz to be shipped to other camps as slave laborers. Hitler had decided earlier that year to allow Jews into the officially "Jew-free" but labor-strapped Reich – but only as slave workers in concentration camps.

Hungarian transit Jews were not the only ones sent to the Reich. The SS combed the camps for other able-bodied Jews. Most of the inmates were already deployed, but the Czech family camp in Birkenau held many able-bodied men and women who had arrived on the December transports from Theresienstadt and had survived. Some 3,000 of them were now prepared for transport to other concentration camps. The remaining 3,000 women and children who were considered of no use to the German economy were brought to the crematoria on July 10. The Czech family camp was closed.

The Vrba-Wetzler report reached Switzerland as the murders continued unabated, and by the middle of June various copies were in circulation. By the beginning of July, the British and American governments had summaries of the Vrba-Wetzler report which stated explicitly: "authors set number of Jews gassed and burned in B[irkenau] between April 1942 and April 1944 at from 1.5 to 1.75 million." The *New York Times* had already run a substantial story on Auschwitz under the heading "Inquiry Confirms Nazi Death Camps," subtitled "1,715,000 Jews Said to Have Been Put to Death by the Germans Up to April 15."

By the time the *New York Times* had published the news, the king of Sweden, the Pope, and the chairman of the Red Cross had approached the Hungarian regent Miklos Horthy. He realized Germany had lost the war and he had credible information about the fate of Hungarian citizens in Auschwitz. Unable to claim ignorance, he fired the main supporters of the deportations in the government. Within days, the Hungarian government assured ambassadors of neutral countries that the *Aktionen* would cease. And the trains stopped, leaving 260,000 Jews who had been destined for Auschwitz in limbo in Budapest. According to a report by the German plenipotentiary in Hungary, a total of 437,402 Jews had been taken "to their destination" – Auschwitz.

The suspension of deportations also brought some relief in the offices of the American and British air forces. Requests to bomb the railway lines that carried the transports had been made from early June onwards. The generals dragged their feet. The American military believed it to be "impracticable," and British Bomber Command pleaded that it was "out of bounds of possibility" because of the distance and the fact that the British bombed at night. When Hungarian deportations stopped, the generals and their civilian superiors in the American War Department and the British Air Ministry felt they were no longer under any obligation to do anything (see *Auschwitz, Bombing Controversy).

Hoess' tour of duty at Auschwitz now came to an end. The Hungarian transports had ceased in mid-July and Hoess handed over a camp of 100,000 inmates to SS-Major Richard Baer at the end of the month. Over a third of the camp population, 37,000 inmates, slaved for German companies, with IG Farben as the largest employer.

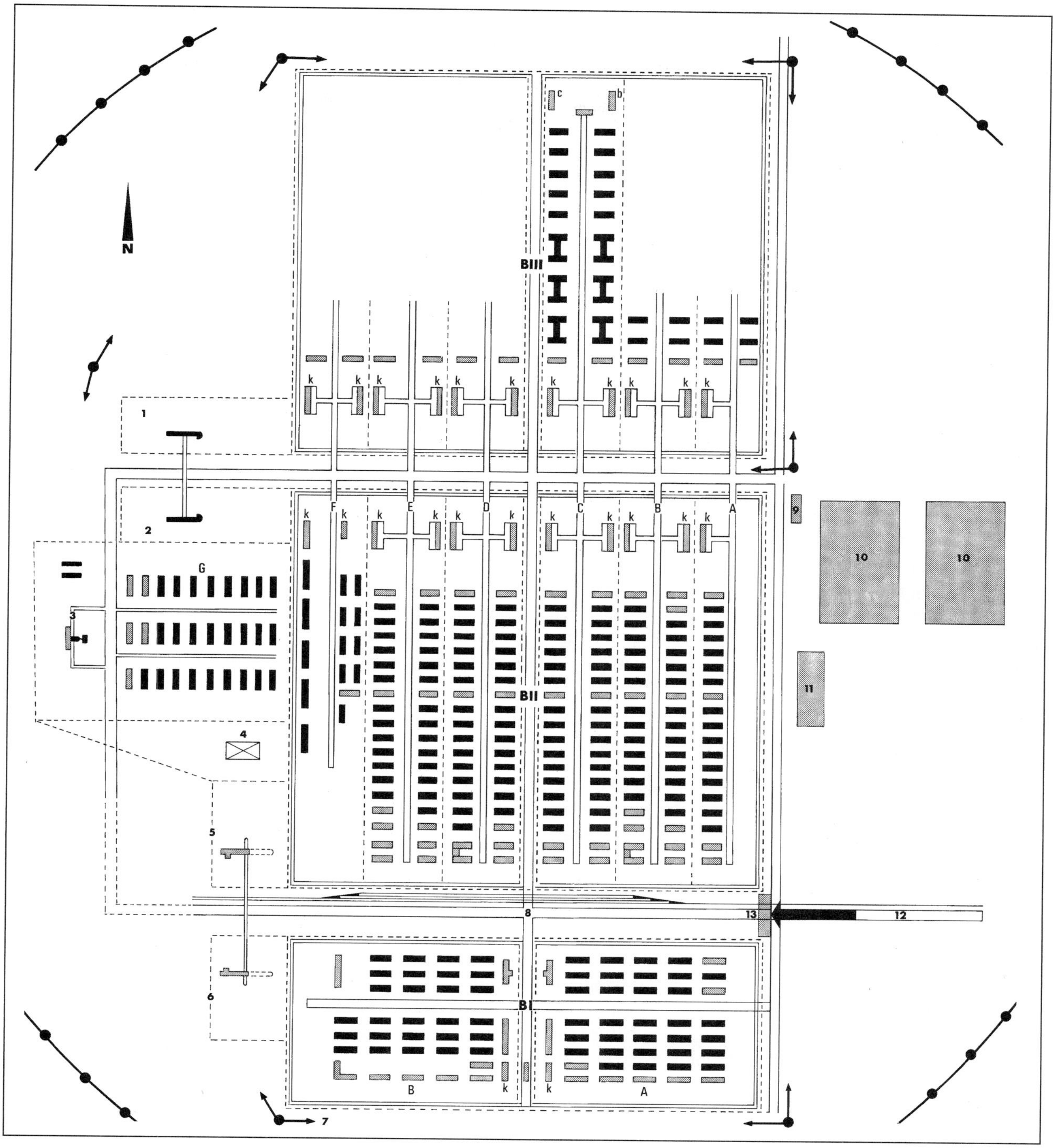

1. Crematory 4
2. Crematory 3
3. Disinfection Station
4. Cleansing Station
5. Crematory 2
6. Crematory 1
7. Guard Posts
8. Railway Station
9. Headquarters

10. Military Camp, SS Hospital
11. Water Supply
12. Road to Auschwitz
13. Main Entrance

K Kitchen
(shaded) Administration and Service Facilities
---- Barbed Wire Fence
BI A. Women's Isolation Camp and Hospital
BI B. Women's Forced Labor Camp

BII A. Men's Isolation Camp
BII B. Family Camp for Jews from Czechoslovakia
BII C. Camp for Hungarian Women
BII D. Main Men's Camp
BII E. Family Camp for Gypsies
BII F. Hospital Camp for Men
BII G. Storage Camp ("Kanada")
BIII b. Bunker no. 4
BIII c. Bunker no. 5

Plan of the Birkenau camp.

The last large group to arrive at Auschwitz came from Lodz, which had survived, a remnant of itself, as a labor camp until August 1944. Baer oversaw the murder of nearly 65,000 Lodz Jews in a few short weeks.

Shortly thereafter, a number of Jewish and gentile prisoners began to prepare a general uprising in the camp. Perhaps they knew that Germany had lost the war and they believed their tormenters would kill every inmate before surrender. Or perhaps, given the enormous mortality rate at Auschwitz, it was only then that the inmates were able to develop a resistance organization committed to uprising. One of the resisters, 23-year-old Rosa Robota, recruited women working in the Union Munitions Plant, a factory operating within the camp, to smuggle gunpowder off the premises. Robota passed the explosives to Borodin, a Russian technician, who carried it to the *Sonderkommando* of the crematorium. But the planned general uprising went awry. The *Sonderkommando* heard that the slave workers of crematoria 4 and 5 were going to be gassed, and they revolted sooner than anticipated, on October 7. They killed three SS men, wounded 12, blew up crematorium 4, and attempted to break out. Some made it as far as a barn in nearby Rajsko. But none escaped, and in total 451 members of the *Sonderkommando* were killed. In the subsequent investigation, the camp Gestapo identified Rosa Robota and three other Jewish women, Regina Sapirstein, Ala Gartner, and Esther Weisblum. After weeks of torture, they were publicly hanged in the women's camp on January 6, 1945.

Himmler, too, knew Germany had lost the war, but he believed that, were it not for the image of the camps in the foreign press, he could have an honorable future in Germany after military collapse. The Red Army had liberated Majdanek on July 23 and by the end of August articles published by the Allies provided horrifying accounts by journalists who had visited the camp. "I have just seen the most terrible place on the face of the earth – the German concentration camp at Maidanek, which was a veritable River Rouge for the production of death," wrote journalist Bill Lawrence in his article on "Nazi Mass Killing Laid Bare in Camp," which ran on the front page of the *New York Times* of August 30. *Time* published a full-page article called "Murder, Inc." A joint Soviet-Polish forensic commission issued a report in October that described a "huge death factory" at Majdanek. Himmler considered all of this "a public relations" disaster and was determined that it would not continue. As he had "solved" the "Jewish Question" as far as it had been in his power to do, he ordered the SS to cease gassings in Auschwitz and to dismantle the gas chambers in the crematoria. Inmates continued to die, but from shootings, starvation, and disease.

The Red Army began its winter offensive on January 10, 1945. The SS prepared to evacuate the remaining prisoners at Auschwitz. When the Red Army reached the outskirts of Cracow on January 17, the SS held a last roll call. They counted 15,317 male prisoners and 26,577 female prisoners in Auschwitz and Birkenau and 33,023 male and 2,095 female prisoners in Monowitz and the 23 other satellite camps. The total came to a little over 67,000. A day later the death march began. Everyone well enough to walk out of the camp was forced to leave. The SS kept a brutal pace. Prisoners who fell behind were shot. The 52,000 survivors arrived in Loslau, some 45 miles (70 km.) west of Auschwitz, and then were transported in open freight cars to camps in the west. Many froze to death. An SS squad in Auschwitz blew up the last remaining crematorium, number 5, on January 26. The next day, units of the 28th and 106th Corps of the First Ukrainian Front liberated the Auschwitz camps. They found 600 sick inmates in Monowitz, the slave labor camp attached to the IG Farben Buna works; 1,200 in the Auschwitz main camp; and 5,800 in Birkenau. The Soviets also found the blown-up remains of the four crematoria in Birkenau and a large compound with 32 burned storage houses. The four huts that were not utterly destroyed were filled with 5,525 pairs of women's shoes; 38,000 pairs of men's shoes; 348,820 men's suits; 836,255 women's garments; 13,964 carpets; 69,848 dishes; huge quantities of toothbrushes, shaving brushes, glasses, crutches, false teeth; and seven tons of hair.

With more than 1.1 million victims, of whom one million were Jews, Auschwitz had become the most lethal death camp of all by the end of the war. But Auschwitz was also the camp with the greatest number of survivors. Only a few people survived Belzec, and a couple of hundred people survived Sobibor and Treblinka. Those camps were annihilation centers. Auschwitz had other functions and ultimately served as an enormous slave labor pool. Many more inmates thus survived Auschwitz than any of the other death camps. Of the 1.1 million Jews deported to Auschwitz, some 100,000 Jews left the camp alive, either in 1944 as transit Jews, or in the death march of 1945. Many of those survivors died or were shot on the long way to the west, or during their imprisonment in spring 1945 in concentration camps like Buchenwald and Bergen-Belsen. Yet tens of thousands saw liberation and testified about their ordeal after the war. Some 100,000 Gentiles, 75,000 of whom were Poles, survived Auschwitz and they too bore witness to the camp as an annihilation center for Jews. These testimonies, and the testimony given by Hoess in Nuremberg and during his own trial in Warsaw, ensured that Auschwitz would figure prominently in the memory of the Holocaust.

The survival of significant parts of the camp also has ensured the continued importance of Auschwitz in the collective memory of the Western world. Visitors to Treblinka, Belzec, and Sobibor, where 1.5 million Jews were murdered, will see nothing of the original arrangement. In Auschwitz, by contrast, much remains, due largely to the preservation efforts of the State Museum Auschwitz-Birkenau, established in 1947 when the Polish Parliament adopted the law "Commemorating the Martyrdom of the Polish Nation and other Nations in Oświęcim."

BIBLIOGRAPHY: T. Borowski, *This Way for the Gas, Ladies and Gentlemen* (1976); D. Czech, *Auschwitz Chronicle* (1990); W. Dlugoborski and F. Piper, *Auschwitz 1940–1945*, 5 vols. (2000); D. Dwork and R.J. van Pelt, *Auschwitz: 1270 to the Present* (1986); Y. Gutman and M. Berenbaum, *Anatomy of the Auschwitz Death Camp* (1994);

R. Hoess, *Death Dealer: The Memoirs of the SS Kommandant at Auschwitz* (1992); P. Levi, *Survival in Auschwitz: The Nazi Assault on Humanity* (1958); R.J. van Pelt, *The Case for Auschwitz: Evidence from the Irving Trial* (2001).

[Deborah Dwork and Robert Jan Van Pelt (2nd ed.)]

AUSCHWITZ BOMBING CONTROVERSY. The debate over whether the Allies could have bombed the gas chamber-crematoria complexes of *Auschwitz-Birkenau, or the rail lines leading to them, had its origins in 1944. Jewish groups appealed to the U.S. and British governments to do something in the face of the Nazis' frighteningly rapid concentration and deportation of Hungarian Jews that quickly followed the German occupation of Hungary, a shaky ally of Hitler's Reich, beginning on March 19. Word of the preparations in Auschwitz for a major new gassing campaign reached the Slovakian resistance in late April with the escape of two Slovakians from the camp, Rudolf Vrba, a name he assumed – his original name was Walter Rosenberg – and Alfred Wetzler. The so-called Vrba-Wetzler Report was smuggled through underground channels and reached Allied representatives and Jewish groups in Switzerland only in June. Earlier in May, the mass deportations began, leading to specific Slovakian requests for the Allies to bomb two rail lines leading to Auschwitz in order to disrupt these movements. These requests, followed by summary versions of the report, filtered to the top of the U.S. War Department in late June, where they met a chilly reception. Requests to divert military resources to "rescue" operations were viewed unsympathetically by Assistant Secretary John McCloy as only likely to slow victory at a time of climactic battles in Europe.

On June 11, 1944, the Jewish Agency in Jerusalem, in a meeting chaired by David *Ben-Gurion, voted against requesting that Auschwitz be bombed. Their reasoning: "It is forbidden for us to take responsibility for a bombing that could very well cause the death of even one Jew." Early in July 1944, presumably after the Vrba-Wetzler report informed the Jewish leadership of the true nature of Auschwitz, two leaders of the Jewish Agency in Palestine, Chaim *Weizmann and Moshe *Shertok, went to London to appeal to the British government. Although Prime Minister Winston *Churchill subsequently told Foreign Secretary Anthony *Eden "to get anything out of the Air Force you can and invoke me if necessary," the idea of attacking the rail lines or crematoria met bureaucratic resistance in the Air Ministry. Inertia only increased when word leaked out that the Hungarian regent, Admiral Horthy, ordered a stop to the deportations on July 7, following Allied air raids on Budapest mistakenly interpreted as punishment for the Holocaust. Renewed appeals to the U.S. government during the summer and fall also got nowhere. McCloy's claims that such air attacks were unfeasible, however, is belied by the fact that U.S. four-engine heavy bombers based in Italy attacked the IG Farben plant at Auschwitz III-Monowitz, only 5 mi. (8 km.) from the gas chambers, on August 25. A follow-up raid on September 13 damaged Auschwitz SS barracks as an accidental by-product, and two further raids against Monowitz took place in December, after the gassing operations had already stopped at Birkenau. In the interim, however, trains full of Jews from all parts of Europe had continued to roll toward Auschwitz, if with less frequency than during the Hungarian campaign.

The futile attempt to get Allied air power to intervene in mid- to late 1944, the only time when U.S. or British bombers had the realistic capability to attack the extermination camps, had been carried out almost entirely through secret government channels and was little known after the war. Combined with the fact that public interest in and understanding of the Holocaust rose only rather slowly through the 1960s, it is perhaps not surprising that the "bombing of Auschwitz controversy" did not erupt until 1978. The catalyst was the publication of an article by the historian David A. Wyman. He summarized powerfully the futile appeals to the U.S. government in 1944, and presented four possible scenarios for attacking the Birkenau crematoria or the rail lines leading to them: (1) a diversion of U.S. B-17 and B-24 heavy bombers from IG Farben to the crematoria; (2) the employment of two-engine B-25 medium bombers, which would presumably bomb more accurately from a lower altitude; (3) a dive-bombing raid by two-engine P-38 fighters, such as the U.S. Army Air Forces carried out on the Romanian oil complex of Ploesti on June 10, 1944; (4) a special mission by Royal Air Force Mosquito two-engine bombers, like the ones executed against Gestapo prisons and headquarters in Western Europe. In 1979, CIA photo-analysts Dino Brugioni and Robert Poirier reinforced Wyman's arguments by presenting to the public dramatic aerial reconnaissance photos of Auschwitz taken by Allied aircraft in 1944 and early 1945, showing prisoners being marched to the gas chambers, albeit through the use of magnification unavailable to Allied photo-interpreters 35 years earlier. Allied intelligence had photos of the Auschwitz-Birkenau complex, but ignored them because no priority was placed on a bombing mission, and because camps were viewed only as places to avoid in an attack.

Wyman's arguments in the American media drew only scattered opposition at the time, mostly from veterans who pointed out that bombing accuracy left much to be desired in 1944. Knowledge of the appeals to Britain, which greatly expanded in the late 1970s and early 1980s, notably through the publication of Martin *Gilbert's *Auschwitz and the Allies*, only seemed to strengthen the Wyman case. Scholarly replies were slow to appear, in part because the military history community was mostly dismissive of ex post facto hypothetical arguments for a raid. Retired physician Richard Foregger wrote the first articles in the 1980s against the Wyman thesis, and was reinforced in the 1990s by James Kitchens, an Air Force archivist writing unofficially, and by Richard Levy, a retired engineer, both of whom published articles in scholarly journals. Their major arguments were (1) that bombing accuracy of heavy bombers was indeed often poor in World War II, and such a raid on Birkenau might have led to untold prisoner deaths in the barracks while failing to put any or most of the crematoria out of order; (2) that B-25 range was marginal and accuracy was no better, and that the P-38 raid on Ploesti was such a disaster that U.S. Army Air Force leaders had been scarcely likely to try that method again; (3) that Wyman consistently underestimated the effectiveness of German fighter and antiaircraft artillery defenses and overestimated Allied intelligence knowledge of Auschwitz-Birkenau; (4) that breaking rail lines through bombing was difficult to do, especially from high-altitude bombers, and breaks were easy to repair; (5) that RAF Mosquitoes in the Mediterranean theater were the wrong type of aircraft for a precision raid and the elite squadron used for the raids in northern Europe would not likely have been diverted south for such a mission.

Stuart Erdheim, a theologian and filmmaker, in turn defended Wyman, responding in detail to the above arguments, and a U.S. Air Force officer, Rondall Rice, independently published a detailed analysis of bombing accuracy and types of missions, arguing for the feasibility of attacking the Birkenau crematoria. Others have noted that Soviet air forces were much closer, but in view of Josef *Stalin's indifference to the Holocaust, this attack scenario has not received close attention. In 2002, after examining the actual and hypothetical response of the Auschwitz SS to air raids, Joseph Robert White concluded, however, that they would likely have found ways to continue the killing even after the complete destruction of the Birkenau crematoria complexes.

As the debate is by its very nature hypothetical, it can never be settled, but a few conclusions can be reached: (1) a raid or raids on Birkenau were certainly feasible, but it remains debatable whether such attacks would have been effective in taking out the gas chambers, and what the cost would have been in prisoner lives; (2) such raids were only possible in late spring 1944 at the earliest, at a rather late stage of the Holocaust; (3) bombing railroads at the long ranges needed for such missions was indeed very unlikely to succeed; (4) the use of U.S. heavy bombers, being the smallest diversion from the practice of the Army Air Forces in the summer of 1944, is a historically much more likely scenario than others presented by Wyman; (5) that sustained pressure from top Allied leaders, most notably President *Roosevelt and Prime Minister Churchill, would have been required to overcome the inertia of the Allied military command, which was tasked with winning a gigantic war with resources that were always less than ideal. It appears, however, that Roosevelt was unsympathetic to the idea and most appeals never reached him anyway; Churchill did not sustain his interest. Ultimately, the failure to give much consideration to bombing Auschwitz in 1944 is symbolic of the Western Allies' failure to do anything except verbally denounce the genocide. A raid would likely have had a strong symbolic value even if it was unlikely to actually save many lives.

BIBLIOGRAPHY: M.J. Neufeld and M. Berenbaum (eds.), *The Bombing of Auschwitz: Should the Allies Have Attempted It?* (2000); D.A. Wyman, "Why Auschwitz Was Never Bombed," in: *Commentary*, 65 (May 1978), 37–46; idem, *The Abandonment of the Jews: America and the Holocaust 1941–1945* (1984); D.A. Brugioni and R.G. Poirier, *The Holocaust Revisited: A Retrospective Analysis of the Auschwitz-Birkenau Extermination Complex*, CIA Report 79-10001 (1979); M. Gilbert, *Auschwitz and the Allies* (1981); J.R. White, "Target Auschwitz: Historical and Hypothetical Responses to Allied Attack," in: *Holocaust and Genocide Studies* 16:1 (Spring 2002), 54–76.

[Michael J. Neufeld (2nd ed.)]

AUSCHWITZ CONVENT. In 1984 Cardinal Macharski, archbishop of Cracow, announced the establishment of a Carmelite convent in Auschwitz in a building on the camp periphery which had originally been a theater but was utilized during World War II to store the poison gas used in the Auschwitz-Birkenau crematoria. When a Catholic organization called Aid to the Church in Distress issued an appeal to mark the pope's visit to the Benelux countries in 1985 under the slogan "Your gift to the Pope – a convent in Auschwitz," the Jewish community – initially in Belgium – reacted with outrage. They were joined in their protest by leading Catholic dignitaries in Western Europe. Jews stressed that although others had suffered there, Auschwitz had become a symbol of Jewish martyrdom and while not objecting to a convent devoted to commemoration of Catholic suffering in Auschwitz, it should not be situated within the boundaries of the camp. Although similar Christian institutions existed in other camp sites, Auschwitz, it was felt, was different. The presence of the convent would contribute to the minimization of the Jewish aspect, already scarcely mentioned in the official communist era descriptions on the site as prepared by the Polish government. One reaction in Polish circles was to emphasize the theme of the fate of Poles for whom Auschwitz was also "a synonym for martyrdom and extermination." The issue energized the Jewish world and became the major subject in Jewish-Catholic discussions, overshadowing all other aspects of the ongoing dialogue.

Two top-level meetings in Geneva in 1986 and 1987 (attended on the Catholic side by four cardinals and on the Jewish side by West European leaders) led to the undertaking by the Catholics to create a new "center of information, education, meeting, and prayer outside the area of the Auschwitz-Birkenau camps" with the Carmelite convent transferred to this new area. Cardinal Macharski, who was one of the participants, agreed that the nuns would be moved to the new site within two years.

The issue then dropped to the background and only came again to the fore as the two-year deadline approached and there was still no sign of progress and indications that the Catholics were not fulfilling the Geneva promises. Macharski claimed that the problems encountered with the Polish authorities over the new site made postponement inevitable. Moreover the nuns in the convent and some elements in the Polish Catholic Church were opposed to the move. Tensions rose as the Catholics announced a delay, and the Jews complained that no indication was being given for the fulfillment of the original agreement. Jews were further incensed by reports that a large cross had been erected on the grounds of the convent. Protests and demonstrations were held in various countries. A French-Belgian delegation attempted to deliver a petition signed by 800 Belgian Catholics requesting the removal of the convent but were not received by the nuns. On the other side, over a thousand inhabitants of the town of Oświęcim (Auschwitz) protested "the illegal demands of the Jews to ruthlessly carry out an unwarranted eviction of the nuns," while other anti-Jewish reactions were reported from elsewhere in Poland.

As the new deadline of July 22, 1989, approached, tensions rose still higher. One indication was the call of the Board of Deputies of British Jews for prayers to be recited in all synagogues in Britain calling for the removal of the convent. The Catholics restated that they intended to keep the agreement but that an educational program had first to be implemented in Poland. The situation reached a flashpoint when an American rabbi, Avraham "Avi" Weiss, and six colleagues dressed in concentration camp garb scaled the walls of the convent blew a *shofar*, and screamed "Nazi antisemites." Polish workmen at the site demanded that they leave and then poured paint and water on the protesters and physically removed them from the site. Reactions were divided in the Jewish world to the demonstration, but Polish sources portrayed it as an attempted attack on the nuns. The deadline passed with a march around the convent by 300 European Jewish students, to the sound of the *shofar*. In August Cardinal Macharski announced that in reaction to the Jewish campaign, the agreement was to be canceled and the nuns would remain where they were.

At this time the archbishop of Warsaw, Cardinal Glemp, delivered a sermon in Czestochowa to a congregation of 100,000 including the Polish premier, which was seen as antisemitic when he called on the Jews "not to talk to us from the position of a superior nation and do not dictate terms that cannot be fulfilled.... Your strength is in the mass media, at your disposal in many countries. Do not use it to spread anti-Polonism." Glemp's remarks were condemned not only by Jews but also in Polish quarters, with Lech Walesa calling them "a shame and a disgrace." Glemp's attacks on the Geneva agreement were also seen as revealing a rift with his fellow prelate, Cardinal Macharski, and indicating a division in the Polish Catholic hierarchy and also divisions between those Poles who sought a pro-Western orientation and hence friendlier relations with the Jews and those who sought to build Polish nationalism in another way. The three Western cardinals who had signed the agreement – Cardinal Decourtray of Lyons, Cardinal Lustiger of Paris, and Cardinal Daneels of Brussels – also publicly opposed Glemp.

The convent controversy revealed the conflicting claims to Auschwitz. When Jews heard the word Auschwitz, they naturally thought of Auschwitz-Birkenau, the death camps, which were the site of the murder of some one million Jews, or Auschwitz III (Buna Monowitz), the work camp where many Jews were worked to death or to near death before they were sent to the gas chambers. They thought of Auschwitz in purely Jewish terms. They did not think of Auschwitz I, the prison camp, which had been the site of Polish incarceration, torture, and death. For Poles of a certain generation reared on the notion of Auschwitz as the site of Polish martyrdom, Auschwitz was a sacred site of Polish nationalism, as they had been taught; they believed four million had been murdered at Auschwitz, two million Jews and two million Poles. Consequently, they confidently advanced the notion of this site as a Roman Catholic, Polish national site. It took time – much time – for the revised figures of the dead at Auschwitz, 1.1 million, 90% of them Jews, to seep into Polish culture and Polish consciousness. The number of people killed at Auschwitz was a figure determined by chief historian Franciszek Piper of the post-Communist Auschwitz State Museum, who dramatically revised the figures; the perceptions of what happened at Auschwitz I, II, and III took a much longer time to change.

Shortly thereafter the Vatican spoke out for the first time, supporting the relocation of the convent in order to restore good relations with the Jews, and even expressed its willingness to contribute financially to the project. Cardinal Glemp, who was then visiting England, executed a volte-face and two days after delivering a speech calling the agreement "a form of wishful thinking," he wrote a letter (the Vatican statement had appeared in the meanwhile) stating that the convent should be moved as soon as possible. With this the crisis was defused.

Although the original deadline for the new complex, set in 1990, proved overly optimistic, work progressed on the interfaith center and the convent, which was ready in 1993. Nevertheless the nuns continued to be reluctant to leave the old building, and this was only accomplished in the summer of 1993 following a letter from the pope and pressure from the Polish Bishops' Conference. Seven of the 14 nuns agreed to move to the new convent, the others going elsewhere. Jewish-Catholic relations returned to normal and the dialogue was resumed. In particular Jews were encouraged by the understanding that had been evinced towards Jewish sensibilities by many Catholic quarters.

Jewish sensitivity to Auschwitz was also recognized by the new Polish regime, which succeeded the communists, and a special commission was set up, with the participation of Jewish scholars, to prepare completely new texts for the information and inscriptions presented in Auschwitz-Birkenau and the literature available there, in which due prominence would be given to the Jewish aspects of the site and to the fact that of the then current figures of 1,100,000 victims at Auschwitz, 90% were Jews (the others being approximately 83,000 Poles, 19,000 gypsies, and 12,000 Soviet prisoners of war).

ADD. BIBLIOGRAPHY: J. Huener, *Auschwitz, Poland and the Politics of Commemoration, 1945–1979* (2003); I. Gutman and M. Berenbaum (eds.), *Anatomy of the Auschwitz Death Camp* (1994).

[Geoffrey Wigoder (2nd ed.)]

AUSCHWITZ TRIALS. In the Moscow Declaration of October 30, 1943, the Allied Powers agreed that Germans guilty of war crimes would be extradited to the country which had been the scene of their activities. Accordingly, Germans arrested in connection with the Auschwitz issue were handed over to Poland. On April 2, 1947, Rudolf Hoess, the first commandant of the camp, was sentenced to death in Warsaw and hung on a gallows adjacent to the gas chamber at Auschwitz I. This was followed by a trial in Cracow, at which 23 SS members were condemned to death. Twenty-one of the sentences were carried out, including those of Arthur Liebehenschel, Hoess' successor as commandant of the camp, Maximilian Grabner, and the camp leaders Hans Aumeier and Maria Mandel. Two of the accused, camp doctors Johann Paul Kremer and Arthur Breitwieser, had their sentences commuted to prison terms. Sixteen of the accused were given prison terms ranging from three years to life, and one Hans Munch, an official of the Hygiene Institute in Rajsko, was acquitted. At a later stage, a long series of minor trials connected with Auschwitz was held in Poland, bringing the total up to at least 617 defendants, of whom 34 were sentenced to death.

By no means did these trials bring to justice all those, or even most of those, men and women who served at Auschwitz. And the Ukrainians on the grounds were also never brought to trial. Historians at the Auschwitz State Museum estimate that the SS staff of Auschwitz numbered approximately 700 people in 1941, 2,000 in 1942, 3,000 in April 1944, and reached its peak with the evacuation in January 1945, with 4,415 SS men and 71 SS women overseers. Between 7,000 and 7,200 people served on the staff of Auschwitz at one time or another according to the card files of personnel.

SS men from Auschwitz were also tried by the tribunals of other countries; according to available information, there were 11 such trials held by British, American, Soviet, French, and Czech courts, culminating in 24 convictions, with sentences ranging from prison terms to death. At the trial for the mass murders committed at *Bergen-Belsen, the sentences also took into consideration crimes committed at Auschwitz, since many of the accused had been transferred to Belsen when Auschwitz was evacuated (on January 18, 1945). There is no information available on the summary trials held by Soviet military tribunals. The trials against officials of the firms IG Farben-Werke and Krupp were in some respects also Auschwitz trials, for the indictment included crimes committed against Auschwitz prisoners whom these firms had used as forced labor. Bruno Tesch, who built the crematoria at Auschwitz, was sentenced to death in Hamburg. Gerhard Peters, general manager of Degesch Company, which had supplied the poison gas to Auschwitz, was acquitted at his Frankfurt trial. After 1951 all the *laender* (states of the German Federal Republic) commuted the prison terms that had earlier been passed by Allied tribunals.

Until 1960 the only trials by German and Austrian courts on record were one against seven SS men from Auschwitz, as well as those of several Auschwitz inmates who became functionaries in the camp. It was not until 1958 that German courts began a systematic inquiry into the Auschwitz issue, prompted by complaints submitted by camp survivors as well as by the investigations carried out by the newly established central office for the prosecution of Nazi criminals (*Zentralstelle der Landesjustizverwaltungen* – "central agency of the ministries of justice of the *laender*" – in Ludwigsburg). First to stand trial in November 1960 in Muenster was the camp doctor Kremer, who had been released from his Polish prison. He was sentenced to ten years' imprisonment, but his Polish prison term was taken into account and he did not have to serve any further sentence. The trial of Carl Clauberg, the gynecologist, who had been sentenced in Russia and later released, came to an abrupt end when the defendant died in jail.

On December 20, 1963, after 5½ years of preparation, the lengthy Auschwitz trial began in Frankfurt lasting 183 sessions and ending on August 20, 1965. Six of the accused were given maximum sentences (life imprisonment), three were acquitted, two were released because of ill health, and the rest received prison terms ranging from 3¼ to 14 years. The verdict was appealed to the Federal Supreme Court, and with one exception all appeals were rejected.

Simultaneously with the German Auschwitz trial, investigations of SS men from Auschwitz were also initiated in Austria, on the basis of complaints lodged by survivors. However, no indictment was issued. In East Germany inquiries started at a later date. In the summer of 1965 camp doctor Horst Fischer, who until then had been permitted to carry on his practice under his own name, was arrested and, after a brief show trial, sentenced to death and executed. On completion of the major trial, several minor trials were held at Frankfurt: the second Auschwitz trial (with three defendants) from December 14, 1965, to September 16, 1966; and the third Auschwitz trial, which began on August 30, 1967, and ended on June 14, 1968. More trials were in the stage of preparation. Some of the guilty men of Auschwitz committed suicide after the war; others managed to escape. One of the latter was Horst Schumann who, like Clauberg, had carried out sterilization experiments at Auschwitz, and who found refuge in Ghana until November 1966, when he was extradited to Germany.

In total no more than 15% of the Auschwitz concentration camp staff ever stood before the bar of justice in any country. Yet the percentage tried because of their work at Auschwitz is significantly larger than at any other camps, perhaps owing to the emblematic nature of Auschwitz as the epicenter of the Holocaust.

The Auschwitz trials formed the subject of a play by Peter *Weiss which was performed in several countries.

BIBLIOGRAPHY: Naumann, *Auschwitz* (Eng., 1966); H. Langbein, *Der Auschwitz-Prozess: eine Documentation*, 2 vols. (1965); Brand, in: *Yad Vashem Bulletin*, 15 (1964), 43–117. **ADD. BIBLIOGRAPHY:** *Auschwitz 1940–1945: Central Issue in the History of the Camp, Volume V: Epilogue* (2000).

[Hermann Langbein]

AUSLAENDER, NAHUM (**Nokhem Oyslender**; 1893–1962), Soviet Yiddish critic, literary historian, and writer. Auslaender, who was born near Kiev, studied medicine in Berlin and Kiev, was drafted into the Red Army as a physician in 1919, and settled in Moscow in 1921. He early became a leading figure of the Yiddish literary criticism and research. From 1917, when his first volume of poetry, *Lider* ("Poems"), appeared, he published in various Soviet Yiddish journals – poetry, prose, and especially critical essays dealing with the classics of Yiddish literature, as well as with contemporary writers. After teaching Yiddish at the Moscow Western University, he headed the Yiddish literature section at the Belorussian Academy of Sciences in Minsk from 1926 to 1928 and the literature section at the Institute for Jewish Proletarian Culture of the Ukrainian Academy of Science, Kiev, from 1928 to 1931, institutions most active in studying and editing Yiddish texts. In 1946, he was on the historical commission of the anti-Fascist committee but was spared during the purges of 1948 to 1953. He was on the editorial staff of *Sovetish Heymland* from its launching in Moscow in 1961 until his death. His most important studies are *Grundshtrikhn fun Yidishn Realizm* ("Main Characteristics of Jewish Realism," Kiev (1919; Vilna, 1928)); *Veg Ayn, Veg Oys* ("Through All Pathways," 1924); *Goldfaden, Materialn far a Biografie* ("Goldfaden: Materials for a Biography," together with U. Finkel, 1926); *Der Yunger Sholem-Aleykhem un Zayn Roman "Stempenyu"* ("The Younger Sholem Aleichem and His Novel *Stempenyu*," 1928); *Yidisher Teater* ("Yiddish Theater," 1940).

BIBLIOGRAPHY: LNYL, 1 (1956), 30–1; *Sovetish Heymland*, 6 (1962), 120. **ADD. BIBLIOGRAPHY:** U. Finkel, in: *Shtern* (Minsk), 2 (1941), 63–76; *Kratkaya Yevreiskaya Entsiklopediya*, 6 (1992), 143; M.D. Kiel, in: *Yivo-Bleter*, 4 (2003), 259–70.

[Shlomo Bickel]

AUSLAENDER, ROSE (**Rosalie Scherzer**; 1901–1988), German poet. Born and raised in Czernowitz, Auslaender emigrated in 1921 and settled with her husband Ignaz Auslaender in New York, where she worked mainly as an editor of several German-language journals and also started publishing her first poems. Although granted American citizenship in 1926, Auslaender returned to Bukovina five years later and finally settled in Bucharest in 1933, earning her living as an English secretary in an oil company. After publishing her first lyric anthology, *Der Regenbogen*, she returned to New York in the face of the coming German invasion of Romania in October 1939. Concern for her mother led her to return to Czernowitz at the end of the year despite her premonition that this would mean a fight for her life.

Under the German occupation, Auslaender was forced into slave labor. Later she went into hiding with her mother until Czernowitz was taken by the Russian Army in 1944. During this time of suffering, she wrote her famous cycle *Gettomotive* and met Paul *Celan, with whom she built up a literary circle following the liberation. When the Soviet Union annexed Bukovina, she fled to Bucharest, ultimately deciding to go back to New York, where she joined "The New Yorkers," a circle of German-speaking Jewish survivors. Subsequently, she began to write poetry in English. She regained her American citizenship in 1948. Auslaender's return to the German language came with a visit to Europe in 1957, when she met Celan again in Paris. In 1963, she settled in Vienna. From there she took several trips with stops in France, Italy, Spain, and Israel, which was remembered in her second book, *Blinder Sommer* (1956), as the "forthcoming / myland yourland" (*das "zukuenftige / Meinland Deinland"*). The fate of Jewry, the experience of persecution as well as the hope of Jerusalem, and a narrator in a dialogue with thousands of years of tradition remained recurring motifs in Auslaender's poetry henceforth, but did not dominate her poetics. As characteristic one might stress the pneumatological aspect of Auslaender's use of language, since time and again the poems appear to be celebrations of world creation by words – it is a language that calls its speaker into being. (A conceptual background to her poetics can be found in the philosophy of Constantin *Brunner, to whom Auslaender referred for a long time as her "*Meister*.")

In 1971 Auslaender moved to Duesseldorf, Germany, where she spent the rest of her life in a nursing home; despite progressing frailty that confined her to bed, she continued to dictate poems and completed almost 2,500 of them before her death in 1988.

She was awarded the Droste-Preis (1967), the Andreas-Gryphius-Preis (1977), and the Grosses Verdienstkreuz des Verdienstordens der Bundesrepublik Deutschland (1984).

BIBLIOGRAPHY: C. Helfrich, *"Es ist ein Aschensommer in der Welt": Rose Auslaender* (1995); H. Braun, *"Ich bin fünftausend Jahre jung": Rose Ausländer – zu ihrer Biographie* (1999).

[Phillipp Theisohn (2nd ed.)]

AUSLANDER, JOSEPH (1897–1965), poet. Born in Philadelphia, Auslander published *Sunrise Trumpets* (1924), poems on romantic figures and exotic themes, five other volumes of verse, two poetry anthologies, and translations from Petrarch and La Fontaine. Auslander became editor of the *North American Review* in 1936.

AUSPITZ, Moravian family connected with the *Gomperz and Lieben families. The name is derived from the German name of the Moravian town Hustopeče. ABRAHAM SHAYE AUSPITZ was *Judenrichter* (Jewish judge) in 1755 and *Landesaeltester* (head) of the Bruenn district from 1769. He was instrumental in curtailing the powers of the *Landesrabbiner* (chief rabbi) of Moravia by an imperial decree, issued in 1776. In 1781 SAMSON was elected *Landesaeltester*. Abraham Shaye's son LAZAR (1772–1853) established the textile industry in Bruenn and was the first to export wool from Moravia to England. With M.L. *Biedermann he was instrumental in transferring the center of the wool trade from Budapest to Vienna. In 1815 he signed the petition for Jewish rights in Austria with Nathan *Arnstein, but himself broke with Jewish tradition. His only son SAMUEL moved to Vienna and opened a bank. Samuel left two sons, KARL, EDLER VON ARTENEGG (1824–1912), an art patron, and RUDOLF (1837–1906), one of the leading beet sugar manufacturers in Moravia. With his cousin Richard Lieber, Rudolf published a highly regarded book on price theory (*Untersuchungen ueber die Theorie des Preises,* 1889; repr. 1993). He entered the Moravian Diet in 1871 and the Austrian Parliament in 1873, and became spokesman of the German Liberal Party. From 1900 he was a member of the Vienna communal board. Rudolf was a member of the parliamentary commission investigating the antisemitic riots of *Holesov in 1899. HEINRICH (1835–1886), who was baptized, was also a member of this family. He taught medicine at Vienna University, was a dermatologist, and wrote many works on the subject.

BIBLIOGRAPHY: T. Gomperz, *Essays und Erinnerungen* (1905), 4–6; W. Mueller, *Urkundliche Beitraege zur Geschichte der maehrischen Judenschaft* (1903), 13–22; J. Winter, *Fuenfzig Jahre eines Hauses* (1934); Schumpeter, in: ESS, 2 (1930), 317. **ADD. BIBLIOGRAPHY:** J. Niehans and St. Jaeggi, *Rudolf Auspitz und Richard Lieben…* (1993).

[Meir Lamed / Marcus Pyka (2nd ed.)]

AUSTER, DANIEL (1893–1962), Israeli lawyer and mayor of Jerusalem. Auster, who was born in Stanislav (then Western Galicia), studied law in Vienna, graduated in 1914, and moved to Palestine. During World War I he served in the Austrian expeditionary force headquarters in Damascus, where he assisted Arthur *Ruppin in sending financial help from Constantinople to the starving *yishuv.* After the war he established a law practice in Jerusalem that represented several Jewish-Arab interests, and served as secretary of the Legal Department of the Zionist Commission (1919–20). In 1934 Auster was elected a Jerusalem councillor; in 1935 he was appointed deputy mayor of Jerusalem; and in 1936–38 and 1944–45 he was acting mayor. Auster represented the Jewish case against the internationalization of Jerusalem brought before the United Nations in 1947–48. In 1948 Auster (who represented the Progressive Party) was elected mayor of Jerusalem, the first to hold that office in an independent Israel. Auster held the post until 1951. He also served as a member of the Provisional Council of Israel in 1948. He headed the Israel United Nations Association from its inception until his death.

BIBLIOGRAPHY: Tidhar, 1 (1947), 165–6.

[Isaac Abraham Abbady]

AUSTER, PAUL (1947–), U.S. writer. Born in New Jersey, Auster studied at Columbia University, and after receiving his M.A. became a merchant seaman, spending the years from 1971 to 1974 in France. His early notable work encompasses translations and poetry, for example, *A Little Anthology of Surrealist Poems* (1972) and *Unearth: Poems, 1970–1972* (1974). Auster – as well as critics – has pointed out his multiple literary heritages: Jabes, Kafka, Blanchot (whom Auster translated), Hawthorne, and Hamsun, to name but a few. Running throughout most of his works is a quest for certainty, and if not that, at least the demarcation of a figure or event bestowing a putative coherence upon history and memory.

He recounted to Adam Begley, in the latter's "Case of the Brooklyn Symbolist" (*New York Times*, August 30, 1992), that 1979 was a shattering year: "I had run into a wall with my work. I was blocked and miserable, my marriage was falling apart, I had no money, I was finished." The death of Auster's father opened up, for the "blocked" author, both the possibilities of writing a memoir as well as questions about fiction's capacity to recount the world by accounting for itself. His search for his father's self, and the recovery of the past, is found in *The Invention of Solitude* (1982), which suggest the roles that chance, the violation of expectation, and the power of memory play in literature's creation of order which is, nonetheless, paradoxical. Heraclitus provided Auster's epigraph as well as a clue to much of his later writing: "In searching out the truth be ready for the unexpected, for it is difficult to find and puzzling when you find it."

Auster's novels, making much of the self in its relation to others, as well as to its own nature, offer dazzling inventiveness, a taste for a metaphysical playfulness, and often despair regarding the limits of writing and cognition. His major works are "The New York Trilogy" consisting of *City of Glass* (1985), *Ghosts* (1986), and *The Locked Room* (1986); *The Music of Chance* (1990); *Leviathan* (1992); and *Mr. Vertigo* (1994). His screenplays can be found in *Three Films: Smoke, Blue in the Face, and Lulu on the Bridge* (2003). His *Collected Prose* appeared in 2003; his *Collected Poems* in 2004.

BIBLIOGRAPHY: C. Springer, *A Paul Auster Sourcebook* (2001); I. Shiloh, *Paul Auster and Postmodern Quest* (2002); J. Tabbi, *Cognitive Fictions* (2002); H. Bloom (ed.), *Paul Auster* (2004).

[Lewis Fried (2nd ed.)]

AUSTERLITZ (Cz. **Slavkov u Brna**; also **Nové Sedlice**; Ger. **Neu-Sedlitz**), town in S. Moravia, now the Czech Republic, famous as the site of Napoleon's victory in 1806. Its Jewish community was one of the oldest in Moravia. It had a cemetery dating from the 12th century and is first mentioned as the place of origin of Moses b. Tobiah, whose *Sefer ha-Minhagim* is dated 1294; about the same time the existence of a yeshivah there is mentioned. In 1567 the sale of houses between Jews and Gentiles was prohibited, and its Jews owned fields. There were 65 houses in Jewish ownership in Austerlitz before the Thirty Years' War (1618–48), and 30 after it. In 1662 and 1722 the Moravian synod (see *Landesjudenschaft) convened there, and the "*shai*" (311 = שי״א) *takkanot* were signed there. At the end of the 17th century the destruction of the Jewish cemetery was ordered. Most of the Jewish quarter, with the synagogue, was burnt down in 1762 and all the Moravian communities contributed toward its reconstruction. Seventy-two families were authorized to reside in Austerlitz in 1798 (see *Familiants). A new synagogue was built in 1857, at which time the Jewish population was 544. In 1905 there was an outbreak of antisemitic riots. There were only 66 Jews living in Austerlitz in 1930. Under the Nazi occupation they were deported to Theresienstadt in 1942, and from there to Auschwitz. Synagogue equipment was sent to the Central Jewish Museum in Prague. The Jewish quarter is preserved in its original form.

Austerlitz gave its name to several Jewish families who are found in Central Europe.

BIBLIOGRAPHY: H. Gold (ed.), *Die Juden und Judengemeinden Maehrens* (1929), 111–6; Flesh, in: JJV (1924–25), 564–616; B. Bretholz, *Geschichte der Juden in Maehren* (1934), index; I. Halpern, *Takkanot Medinat Mehrin* (1942), 114–8, 212–8; S. Hock, *Die Familien Prags* (1892), index; B. Wachstein, *Die Inschriften des alten Judenfriedhofes in Wien*, 1 (1912), index; idem, *Die Grabschriften des alten Judenfriedhofes in Eisenstadt* (1922), index. **ADD. BIBLIOGRAPHY:** J. Fiedler, *Jewish Sights of Bohemia and Moravia* (1991), 164.

AUSTIN, geographic and political center of Texas and the state's capital, with a Jewish population of around 13,500 in 2001. Jewish settlers arrived as early as the 1840s. The first well-known Jewish settler was Phineas de Cordova, born in Philadelphia and grandson of a 1749 Amsterdam immigrant to Curaçao, Netherlands West Antilles. De Cordova arrived in Texas sometime after 1848 with his wife, Jemimina Delgado. During a brief time in Galveston and Houston, he formed a land company and newspaper publishing business with his brother Jacob de Cordova, then settled in Austin at the request of Governor P.H. Bell in 1850.

Once in Austin, Phineas de Cordova published a weekly, the *Southwestern American*, for two years. As the de Cordova land agency grew, he became an expert in Texas land laws and published a topographical map of Austin in 1872. He developed a number of political associations, and served in the Texas Senate for three terms during the Civil War years. Other notable Jewish families in Austin during this period included the family of Henry Hirshfeld, who fought for the Confederacy during the Civil War.

Hirshfeld, de Cordova, and a handful of other Jewish pioneers met in the mayor's office of the City of Austin to organize its first congregation, Temple Beth Israel, in 1876. Chartered by the State of Texas in 1879, the congregation built its first house of worship in 1884 on the corner of 11th and San Jacinto streets in the heart of downtown Austin.

As Austin grew through the end of the 19th and into the beginning of the 20th century, its Jewish population grew slowly relative to other Texas cities, and unlike places such as Dallas, Houston, San Antonio, and Waco, a merchant prince who was philanthropist or benefactor never emerged. The Jewish population included peddlers who eventually founded small Main Street types of businesses and intellectuals drawn to teach or study at the University of Texas at Austin. Temple Beth Israel remained the cornerstone of the organized Jewish community until 1924, when the Federation of Jewish Charities was formed.

Orthodox Jews formed a *minyan* as early as 1914, which was chartered to become Austin's second congregation, Congregation Agudas Achim, in 1924. In 1931, the congregation built its first building at 909 San Jacinto, and occupied this location for more than 30 years. The members affiliated with the Conservative Jewish movement in 1948. Among the founders was Jim Novy, whose longstanding relationship with President Lyndon Baines Johnson served as a springboard of congregational growth. In the early 1960s, Johnson helped Novy trade the synagogue's land downtown for an easement along the Missouri Pacific railroad, in an expanding and newer part of Austin. The site of the old synagogue became the site of Austin's Federal building, a move that helped ensure the financial viability of the congregation for years to come.

In 1963, the congregation moved, but its dedication ceremony, which was to include then Vice President Johnson, had to be postponed in the wake of the assassination and mourning of President John F. Kennedy. On December 30, 1963, President Johnson returned to Austin, and in his first non-official address as president, dedicated the new synagogue, the second time in U.S. history for a sitting U.S. president to do so.

Austin's beginnings as a center of high technology began shortly after the Great Depression. The city grew steadily through the World War II years, and by the 1950s, several research laboratories and think tanks had been founded. As these formed and began to draw innovative thinkers and high-tech companies to the area, the Jewish population grew as Jewish engineers, doctors, intellectuals, and inventors followed the trend. Rapid growth in the 1970s contributed to more political activity, this time at the local level.

During the 1970s, local Jews contributed to the growth and development of the state's cultural and political life. Michael R. Levy founded *Texas Monthly* magazine, and Austin's first Jewish mayor, Jeff Friedman (also the youngest ever to hold that position, and fondly known as "the hippie mayor"), was elected in 1975. Also during the 1970s, local philanthropist Helen Smith became the first Texan to serve as international president of B'nai B'rith Women. Helen's husband, Milton Smith, was among those responsible for purchasing land to move Congregation Beth Israel from its downtown location to the suburbs in the 1960s.

While Austin's Jewish population steadily rose and remained at about 1% of the total population of Austin for over a century, its communal growth trajectory differed from most Texas Jewish communities. Unlike Houston, Dallas, San Antonio, and other cities, the concept of a united Jewish community was slow to catch on, and support for Zionism was fairly limited. From the late 1970s to the 1990s, the Austin Jewish Federation had a small community center located in an old church and small trailer park. During the late 1970s and 1980s, signs of communal growth manifested itself through a preschool of about 100 children, a Jewish Book Fair, and a Jewish Family Service.

The high technology boom of the 1990s caused an unexpected influx of hundreds if not thousands of new Jewish families to Austin and stretched the longtime traditional bi-congregational infrastructure to the breaking point. In addition to the hi-tech think tanks and start-up shops, Dell Computers, founded by a member of Austin's Jewish community, Michael Dell, also played a large part in the community's growth. As a member of the community, Dell became Austin's first major Jewish philanthropist.

The tone of the community changed dramatically in response to population growth in the 1990s, and new members called for organizations and structures from the Jewish community that had never before existed. Perhaps most emblematic of its unique hi-tech tone was the innovative consolidation of the Austin Jewish Federation and Jewish Community Center. Michael Dell and his wife, Susan Lieberman Dell, purchased and donated a 40-acre site in central Austin, which has become the Jewish Community Association of Austin's Dell Jewish Community Campus. Ground was broken in December 1996 for the new campus facility, which would house Congregation Agudas Achim, a community center, and space that allows for the operation of the Austin Jewish Academy, Early Childhood Program, and a number of youth and family programs. While the campus has become the physical center of Austin's burgeoning Jewish community, the community's growth since 1997 has also spawned two new Reform congregations, as well as growth of its existing Conservative and Orthodox *minyans*.

The innovative "campus" approach to Jewish communal life has set the tone for the second century of Jewish life in Austin and is actively watched by other mid-sized communities throughout the United States as a model for operating Jewish communities in dynamic and changing times.

BIBLIOGRAPHY: R. Winegarten and C. Schechter, *Deep in the Heart: The Lives & Legends of Texas Jews, a Photographic History* (1990). **WEBSITE:** www.jcaaonline.com for Dell Jewish Community Campus and JCAA.

[Cathy Schechter (2nd ed.)]

AUSTRALIA, island continent, within the British Commonwealth. At least six Jewish convicts who arrived at Botany Bay, New South Wales, in 1788 were later among the first settlers, including John Harris who, when freed, became the first policeman in Australia. The first *minyan* and burial society date from 1817, and the 1828 census records about 100 Jews in New South Wales and 50 in Van Diemen's Land (Tasmania). In the 1830s Jews arrived in increasing numbers, mainly from England, and by 1841 Jews had also settled in Victoria, South Australia, and Western Australia, bringing the total in the continent to 1,183 (0.57% of the whole population). The number of Jews in Australia reached 59,343 by 1961. (For updated information, see below.) Australian censuses trace the increase in the Jewish population, showing the rise and fall in each state and the percentage of Jews in the total population. (See Table: Australian Jewish Population and Table: Australasia Age Distributions.)

There were several waves of immigration – in the 1850s due to the prosperity following the discovery of gold; from 1891 to 1911 an influx of Eastern European Jews fleeing from pogroms; in the 1930s German refugees; and in the post-World War II period the displaced *persons who survived the Holocaust in Europe.

Nineteenth Century

In 1828 Philip Joseph Cohen was authorized by England's chief rabbi to perform marriages. R. Aaron Levy (Levi), a member of the London *bet din*, paid a visit in 1830 to arrange a divorce. The first synagogue in *Sydney was constructed in 1844. Organized communities were established in Hobart (1845), Launceston (1846), *Melbourne (1841), and *Adelaide (1848). Several small communities which came into being during the gold rushes had all but disappeared in the 1960s: Forbes, Goulburn, Maitland, Tamworth, Bendigo, Geelong, Kalgoorlie, Toowoomba, and Launceston (see Map: Australian Jewry). Economic conditions made the country towns most attractive to the new Jewish settlers who came with little money, but fear of assimilation induced many to move to larger urban centers as soon as their material situation permitted. In the 1860s almost one-quarter of all Jews lived in country towns (14%) and rural areas (10%), whereas the 1961 census showed that 96.4% lived in the six large cities, 2.7% in small towns, and 0.9% in rural areas. Jacob *Saphir of Jerusalem, who visited Australia in 1862, gives an interesting account of Jewish conditions in his *Even Sappir.*

Australian Jewry in this early period was numerically small and scattered and consequently in danger of assimilation. Ministers and teachers were scarce, and religious observance was lax. The shortage of Jewish women (in 1881 there were only 78 women to every 100 men) led to a high rate of intermarriage. Many, however, still maintained their Jewish observances, often traveling hundreds of miles to take part in religious services or to have a child circumcised. Nor did they fail in charitable and social endeavor, and several Australian Jewish philanthropic institutions have a history of well over a century. Until free and compulsory state education was introduced in the last quarter of the 19th century, the Jewish communities maintained their own Hebrew day schools. The early Jewish settlers made a considerable impact on the colony's development, in the civic, and in some instances agricultural, spheres. Religious life was based on the English-Jewish tradition, which remained dominant, and the authority of the British chief rabbinate was respected. Civil rights and the right of Jews to vote and sit in Parliament were never subject to restrictions. The government acceded to Jewish requests for land for cemeteries, synagogues, schools, and ministers' residences, and limited subsidies were granted at different periods for Jewish religious establishments.

The synagogue was the focal point of communal life. Jews were generally highly respected; Judaism was recognized as a "denomination"; and the rabbinical office enjoyed a prestige seldom found in other lands. It is characteristic that throughout Australian Jewish history many Jews who were prominent in public life, at times occupying some of the highest positions in the land, were also active in the congregation. These include Sir Saul *Samuel, minister of the crown in New South Wales and president of the Sydney Great Synagogue; Sir Benjamin Benjamin (1836–1905), lord mayor of Melbourne and president

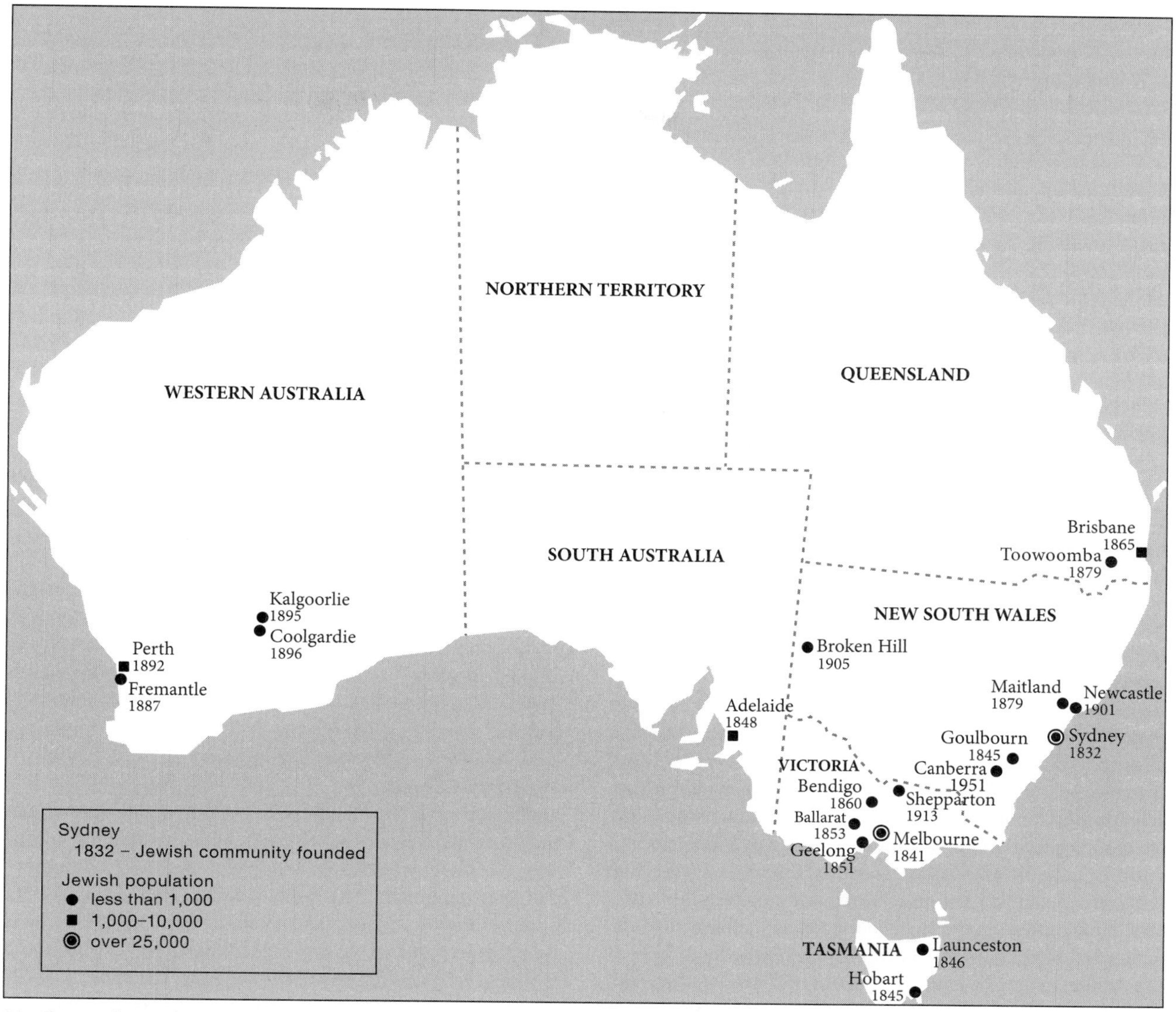

Distribution of Australian Jewry, giving date when the communities were organized.

of the Melbourne Hebrew Congregation; Sir Julian Emanuel Salamons (1835–1909), solicitor general in New South Wales; Sir Daniel *Levy, speaker of the House of Representatives and editor of *The Australian Hebrew*; Vabian Louis *Solomon, premier of South Australia and leader of the community there; George Judah Cohen, a leader in commerce and president of the Great Synagogue from 1878; and Sir Archie Michaelis (1889–1975), speaker of the Victorian parliament and president of the St. Kilda Synagogue. Other Jews who achieved prominence were Barnett Levy, founder of the first theater in Australia, and the composer Isaac *Nathan, described as the "father of Australian music." The historian Joseph *Jacobs and the philosopher Samuel *Alexander were also Australians. The close integration of the Jews in Australian life is exemplified in the careers of Sir Isaac Alfred *Isaacs, the first Australian-born governor-general, and General Sir John *Monash, who commanded the Australian forces in France in World War I.

[Israel Porush / Yitzhak Rischin]

Role of Sephardi Jewry

Two of the convicts in the First Fleet which arrived in Australia in 1788 were apparently Sephardi Jews. A. Aaron estimates that at least 30 of the 384 Jewish convicts transported to Australia by 1830 were of Sephardi origin.

During the 19th century, representatives of several Sephardi mercantile families from Britain were prominent among free settlers. Solomon Mocatta operated a shipping agency; Benjamin Mendes da Costa and his sister Louisa bequeathed substantial property to a private school and public hospital in Adelaide; Alfred Mendoza served as choirmaster to the Melbourne Synagogue. Edward Cohen was elected to the Parliament in Victoria in 1861 and served for a time as a

Australian Jewish Population

Year	New South Wales	Victoria	Queensland	South Australia	Western Australia	Tasmania	Northern Territory	Total	% of Total Population
1841	856	57		10*	1*	259		1,183*	0.57
1851	979	354		100*	9*	435		1,887*	0.47
1861	1,759	2,903	49	420*	12*	343		5,486*	0.48
1871	2,395	3,751	291	435	22	232		6,946*	0.42
1881	3,266	4,330	457	762	27*	282	1	9,125*	0.41
1891	5,484	6,459	809	840	130	84	3	13,809	0.43
1901	6,447	5,907	733	786	1,259	107		15,239	0.40
1911	7,660	6,270	672	765	1,790	130		17,287	0.38
1921	10,150	7,677	1,003	743	1,919	121	1	21,615	0.40
1933	10,305	9,500	1,041	528	2,105	70		23,553	0.36
1947	13,194	14,910	1,011	454	2,294	123	7	32,019	0.42
1954	19,583	24,016	1,340	722	2,555	158	8	48,436	0.56
1961	24,026	29,932	1,334	985	2,782	136	23	59,329	0.57
1971	25,971	30,117	1,491	1,137	3,102	98	46	61,962	0.48
1986	28,197	32,358	2,631	1,144	3,919	160	98	68,507	0.43
2001	34,345	38,374	4,271	1,072	5,072	180	149	83,463	0.43

* approximate figure

member of cabinet. In 1864, Charles Dyte won a seat in the Victorian Parliament; Maurice Salom entered the South Australian Parliament in 1882; and Jacob Levi Montefiore served in the Parliament of New South Wales (NSW).

The Montefiores were closely associated with progress in Australia throughout the century. Jacob Montefiore was one of the commissioners appointed to establish the first non-penal colony, South Australia, in 1836. His brother Joseph Barrow Montefiore became the president of the first formal Jewish congregation on the continent, founded in Sydney in 1832 and run according to Ashkenazi rites. He was a businessman with interests in the various colonies and a cofounder of several banks. Eliezer Levi Montefiore was instrumental in the formation of the Jewish community in Adelaide, promoted the establishment of lending libraries and art galleries, and served as the first director of the Art Gallery of NSW from 1892 until his death in 1894.

In 1854 and 1855 Sephardi Jews in Melbourne held Rosh ha-Shanah and Yom Kippur services according to their tradition in a classroom of the Melbourne synagogue. The synagogue management complained that a number of Ashkenazi Jews had joined the Sephardi *minyan* to avoid paying pew rent required in the main synagogue, so the next year the Sephardim held their services in a private home and applied to the Spanish and Portuguese congregation in London for assistance to form a separate Sephardi community. However, they returned to the synagogue in 1857 and maintained a Sephardi *minyan* until 1873. This folded when a quorum of Sephardi worshipers could no longer be found.

The Sephardi Jews in Australia in the 20th century (estimated at 6,000 in 1970) are not the descendants of the 19th-century Spanish and Portuguese Jews from Britain but largely immigrants who have arrived since World War II. The main sources of immigration were Egypt and Jews of Iraqi origin who had resided in India and Britain's prewar colonies in the Far East. Smaller numbers also came from southern Europe, Turkey, and North Africa. From the 1960s there was a steady inflow from Israel, of all backgrounds, but particularly Iraqi Jews. The main centers of settlement were Sydney and Melbourne.

[Meyer Samra]

Twentieth Century

At the end of the 19th and the beginning of the 20th centuries Australian Jewry was reinforced by further immigration, mainly from Europe. The *Perth and *Brisbane communities were firmly established, and additional synagogues were founded in Sydney and Melbourne. In 1878 the Great Synagogue of Sydney was opened. Notable leadership in the sphere of religious affairs was provided by such rabbis as Alexander B. *Davis of the Sydney Synagogue (1862–78) and of the Great Synagogue (1878–1903); Joseph Abrahams of the Melbourne Hebrew Congregation (1883–1919); Abraham Tobias *Boas of Adelaide (1870–1918); David Isaac Freedman of Perth (1897–1939); Francis Lyon Cohen of the Great Synagogue (1905–34); Jacob *Danglow (1905–60); and Israel *Brodie of the Melbourne Hebrew Congregation (1922–37), who was later chief rabbi of the United Hebrew Congregation of the British Commonwealth.

The periods immediately before World War I and between the two world wars brought a number of Eastern European Jews to Australia and also some from Palestine who settled in Perth. Mass immigration followed the rise of Hitler. Although the Australian authorities were at first reluctant to encourage non-British immigration, at the *Evian Conference in 1938 the Australian government allotted 15,000 entry permits to victims of oppression. The outbreak of war in 1939, however, prevented the complete realization of this scheme, but some 7,000 refugees, almost all Jews, settled in Australia between 1935 and 1940. In the 1920s Australian Jewry was in danger of losing its identity and becoming fully assimilated into Australian life when judged by the high incidence of intermarriage, poor synagogue attendance, lack of knowledge of the Hebrew language and Jewish studies, and inadequate educational facilities. Jewish cultural life and Zionism were practically nonexistent. (The Zionist Federation of Australia was founded in 1927 with Israel Brodie as its first president and Sir John Monash as its honorary president.) At the most there were a few social and philanthropic institutions and even these activities were uncoordinated. There was no united body to represent or speak in the name of the whole community. Community affairs were largely in the hands of the Australian-born segment whose activities centered around the synagogues and who had little or no experience of the organization or the vast range of cultural activities known to the European *kehillot*. They deemphasized elements of Jewish distinctiveness and group particularism, believing that in this way it would be easier to integrate into Australian society. Feeling that Jews should maintain a few basic religious differences but not be socially segregated or institutionally isolated, they formed State Advisory Boards with only the synagogues represented.

The newer immigrants from Europe brought with them deep religious convictions, Hebrew and Jewish scholarship, Yiddish culture, and Zionist sentiments. During the late 1930s a struggle for community control was launched by these new elements. Their impact on community life brought into being state Boards of Deputies on which not only the synagogues but all major organizations (secular, Zionist, cultural) were represented. The Board of Deputies in each state could speak in the name of the whole community. The state Boards of Deputies amalgamated in 1944 to form the Executive Council of Australian Jewry to represent the community on all federal matters and in world Jewish organizations. These new bodies embarked on programs in the spheres of education, Zionism, the combating of antisemitism, and Jewish immigration into Australia with remarkable results, stemming the tide of assimilation and building up a virile Jewish community life. As a result the large majority of Australian Jews adhered moderately to Jewish rituals, was strongly opposed to intermarriage, supported the Jewish day schools, and had strong sympathies with Israel.

The Executive Council of Australian Jewry in 1946 dissociated the community from the anti-Zionist views of Sir Isaac Isaacs and wholeheartedly supported the demands for a Jewish state and free immigration to Palestine. From 1945 it strongly influenced the Australian immigration policy, obtaining many concessions from Arthur A. Calwell, minister for immigration, to admit Jews on humanitarian grounds. Later it kept a vigilant eye on the entry of Germans to Australia, ensuring there would be adequate screening to prevent the entry of former Nazis. From the 1950s it succeeded in its efforts to secure Australian government support for the rights of Jews in the U.S.S.R.

[Israel Porush / Yitzhak Rischin]

Demography

Australia's Jewish community more than doubled in size between 1933 and 1954 (increasing from 23,553 to 48,436 persons), as a result of both natural increase and of an immigration policy favorable toward Jewish refugees from Europe. The 1966 census indicated that 63,271 persons had registered as Jews, whereas informed estimates calculated the actual number of Jews in 1968 at 70,000 (constituting 0.5% of the total population). In the last third of the 20th century, Australia was one of the few Diaspora societies whose Jewish population continued to rise steadily, thanks to continuing immigration, low rates of intermarriage and assimilation, and a relatively high birthrate. Our knowledge of Australia's Jewish population derives primarily from the Australian census, which is held every five years and always includes an optional religious question. In 1971, the declared Jewish population of Australia, according to the census of that year, was 62,208. This figure rose to 69,088 in 1986, to 74,386 in 1991, 79,805 in 1996, and 83,993 in 2001, an increase of 35 percent in 30 years. This steady increase has shown little sign of leveling off, with Australian Jewry experiencing an increase of 5.2 percent in the five years between 1996 and 2001 alone. These figures are, moreover, widely regarded as underestimates, since, as noted, the census question of religious identity is optional. In 2001, 27.92 percent of the Australian population stated they were of "no religion" or declined to answer the religious question ("religion not stated"). Assuming that the Jewish population's non-response rate is similar to that of the general population, the actual number of Jews in Australia was about 116,527 in 2001. Most demographers regard the actual figure as in the range of 110–115,000. There is, however, some evidence that even this figure is too low. The Melbourne Jewish Welfare Society maintains a master list of all Jews in the state of Victoria (which includes Melbourne) that is constantly updated. In the early 1990s it contained about 48,000 names, over 40 percent in excess of the census figure of about 34,000.

Most Australian Jews continue to live in the two principal centers of Jewish life, Melbourne (in Victoria) and Sydney (in New South Wales). Both contain a wide range of Jewish institutions – often seen by visitors to Australia as extraordinary in their scope for so remote a community – especially an extensive Jewish day school system. In 1971 the census Jewish population of Victoria was 30,117. This grew to 32,358 in 1986, 35,963 in 1996, and 38,374 in 2001. The rise in the declared Jewish population of New South Wales was as follows: 1971: 25,971; 1986: 28,197; 1996: 32,652; 2001: 34,345. Jewish communities exist in all other states, with the Jewish population of Perth (Western Australia) and the Gold Coast, a resort area in Queensland, having increased significantly during the past 30 years. On the other hand, the smaller Jewish communities have not experienced much growth. The Jewish populations of the smaller states in 1971, 1986, and 2001 were as follows: Queensland – 1971: 1,491; 1986: 2,631; 2001: 4,271; South Australia (Adelaide) – 1971: 1,137; 1986: 1,144; 2001: 1,072; Western Australia – 1971: 3,102; 1986: 3,919; 2001: 5,072; Tasmania – 1971: 98; 1986: 160; 2001: 180; Northern Territory – 1971: 46; 1986: 98; 2001: 149; Australian Capital Territory (Canberra) –1971: 251; 1986: 501; 2001: 529. Within the largest centers of Jewish life there are a number of heavily Jewish areas, especially Caulfield-East St. Kilda in Melbourne, Bondi-Randwick and the North Shore in Sydney, and Dianella in Perth. By and large, these have been notably stable during the past 40 years, with few new Jewish areas of heavy settlement established outside them.

During the past 35 years, Jewish immigration to Australia has come from a number of main sources, especially the Former Soviet Union and South Africa, as well as from a steady stream of migrants for normal professional reasons from the English-speaking world, particularly Britain, and smaller numbers from Israel and elsewhere. Probably the largest single source of recent Jewish immigration to Australia has been the Former Soviet Union. An estimated 25,000 Soviet Jews have come to Australia since 1970 (many of whom are probably not included in the census figures). In 1971, of Australia's total of 62,208 declared Jews, 41.7 percent (25,964) were born in Australia, 9,302 (15.0%) in Poland, 5,663 (9.1%) in Britain, 3,506 (5.6%) in Hungary, 3,303 (5.3%) in Germany, and 3,081 (5.0%) in Israel and "other Asia." In 1986, 31,619 (45.8%) of the declared Jewish population of 69,088 were born in Australia, with the largest foreign-born sources being Poland– 6,663 (9.6%); Britain – 5,135 (7.49%); the U.S.S.R. – 3,611 (5.2%); and South Africa – 3,420 (4.0%). In 2001, 46.4 percent (38,940) of Australia's 83,993 Jews were born in Australia, followed by South Africa – 10,473 (12.5%); the former U.S.S.R. – 6,751 (8.0%); Britain – 4,329 (5.2%); Israel – 3,886 (4.6%); and Poland – 3,838 (4.6%).

Intermarriage rates among Australian Jews were, by other Diaspora standards, extremely low, and declined significantly between the 1933 Census and the 1961 Census, consistent with the arrival in Australia of the Holocaust survivors, and a greater sense of Jewish identity. In 1961, 6.3 percent of Jewish wives were married to a non-Jewish husband, and 12.3 percent of Jewish husbands to a non-Jewish wife. In 1981 (Victoria and New South Wales only) these figures were respectively 11.2 percent and 14.0 percent; in 2001, these figures were 11.2 percent and 15.6 percent. The 2001 statistics were, specifically, for women and men married to adherents of another religion. Several thousand other Jews were married to spouses giving "no religion" or "religion not stated" in response to the census question, many of whom are believed to be Jewish. Additionally, many Jews married to non-Jews are believed to be divorced (or widowed) and remarried, often late in life. Intermarriage rates were consistently lower in Victoria than in New South Wales, which were in turn lower than in the smaller states. It seems reasonable to conclude that Australia, especially in its main centers of Jewish life, has managed to avoid the disturbing rates of intermarriage found elsewhere in the Diaspora, especially the United States. While one can debate the reasons for this, observers pointed to the high levels of attendance at Jewish day schools and to the fact that in Australia, unlike the United States and other Diaspora societies, university students generally live at home, attending a local college, and thus often continue to draw their associational networks from among their school friends.

Australian Jews are, for the most part, situated in the upper middle classes, with relatively high income levels and socio-economic attainments. Plainly, not all Australian Jews share in high income levels, although the community has no obvious and well-defined areas of poverty, except among recent immigrants and the elderly. As elsewhere in the Diaspora, Australian Jewry contains a disproportionate number of elderly persons, with 18.97 percent of those declaring themselves to be Jewish by religion in 2001 aged 70 or more, compared with 11.51 percent of the whole Australian population. (On the other hand, it should be noted that the Australian Jewish percentage of children was not much lower than the whole Australian population, with 17.22 percent of Jews aged 0–14 in 2001, compared with 21.7 percent of the whole Australian population.)

Community Life

The great influx of Jewish immigrants rejuvenated community life in the 1950s. This trend sharply contrasted with the diminishing influence of Jewish communal life and the typical rising intermarriage rates of the previous decade. Synagogues, centers, and schools sprang up in the suburbs of the capital cities. By the end of the 1960s a number of day schools and over 45 synagogues existed throughout Australia. Brisbane, Adelaide, and other communities with small Jewish populations carried on religious and Jewish cultural activities. In the new federal capital, Canberra, the Jewish community was granted a site for a synagogue. An estimated 55–65% of the adult members of the communities were members of synagogues, 80% of them Orthodox and 20% Liberal. The first Sephardi synagogue was established in Sydney in 1962. The congregations' rabbinical courts were located in Melbourne and Sydney. The Orthodox congregations in Sydney were organized in the United Synagogues of New South Wales. All six Liberal congregations, which were first introduced in 1935, were affiliated with the Australian Union for Progressive Judaism.

Between 1970 and 2004 the Australian Jewish community grew and developed on the foundations of community life which had been, for the most part, laid between about 1935 and 1955, when the community was transformed by the arrival of refugees and migrants from Europe and the institutional bases of the community were altered to a considerable extent. The Australian Jewish community has remained centered on much the same framework of communal governing bodies, synagogues, day schools, and even areas of neighborhood residency as 40 years earlier. This stability probably accounts for its relative success. Australian Jewry remains notably pro-Zionist, while Australia's mainstream political culture has been generally favorable to Israel and the West. The growth and development of the community which has occurred during the past 45 years has generally come by additions and extensions of the institutional framework which developed in the c. 1935–55 period rather than through any sharp break with the past. For instance, in recent decades, Sydney Jewry has become more like Melbourne Jewry in its patronage of Jewish day schools and its religious Orthodoxy, while most new Jewish immigrants to Australia have chosen to live in or near existing Jewish neighborhoods where this has been financially possible. There are no signs that this is likely to change in the near future.

Education

One of the most notable features of the modern Australian Jewish community is the extent of its Jewish day school system, which is arguably without parallel in the Diaspora with the possible exception of South Africa. In 2004, 15 full-time Jewish day schools existed throughout Australia, attended by an estimated 60 percent of Australian Jewish children. Most of these were founded between 1949 and about 1970, although some schools have been established since. In Melbourne and Sydney, Jewish day schools were established by different religious and secular factions within the overall community, whose outlook was not, in their view, well-served by any existing Jewish school. Eight Jewish day schools exist in Melbourne: Mount Scopus (Orthodox Zionist), Bialik (secular Zionist), Sholem Aleichem (secular Yiddish), Leibler Yavneh (Mizrachi), Adass (non-Lubavitcher Strictly Orthodox), Yeshivah College (boys' Lubavitcher), Beth Rivkah (girls' Lubavitcher), and King David (Liberal Judaism). All take students from ages 5–18 except for Sholem Aleichem, which is only a primary school. For many decades, Mount Scopus, the oldest of these day schools, was regarded as the largest day school in the Diaspora, although in recent years its numbers have declined slightly, from about 2,200 students in the 1980s to about 1,700 in 2004. Overall, about 6,000 students attend these Melbourne day schools.

In Sydney, there are six Jewish day schools: Moriah (Orthodox), Yeshivah College (Lubavitcher), Yeshivah Girls' High School (Lubavitcher), Masada College (Orthodox, on Sydney's North Shore), Mount Sinai College (Orthodox, in Sydney's south), and Emanuel College (Liberal Judaism). Throughout most of the period since the first of these schools, Moriah College, was founded in 1951, a lower percentage of Jewish students have attended a Jewish day school in Sydney than in Melbourne, although the percentage gap has narrowed since the 1980s. There are also three Jewish day schools in other Australian cities: Carmel College (Orthodox) in Perth, Western Australia; Sinai College in Brisbane; and Massada College, a primary school, in Adelaide.

Jewish children who do not receive a full-time Jewish education often attend a Jewish Sunday school or receive tuition from United Jewish Education Boards which exist in Melbourne and Sydney. There have been many concerns that, in very recent years, the high cost of education at Jewish day schools – in 2004 up to A $20,000 (U.S. $13,000) per year for senior students – is driving students into the state sector, although the number of students at Australia's Jewish day schools continues to grow.

While there has been a growth in Jewish-interest courses at the university level in Australia in recent years, these have certainly not kept pace with the growth of "Jewish studies" at college level in America and elsewhere. Monash University in Melbourne and Sydney and New South Wales universities do offer sequences in Jewish studies. It should be pointed out that courses in Australia last for three years (not four) and are more career-oriented than in American institutions of higher education. An Australian Association for Jewish Studies was founded in 1987. It holds well-attended annual conferences and publishes the *Australian Journal of Jewish Studies*. Hillel organizations exist on some campuses. There are also a number of *kolelim* conducted by Orthodox synagogues. It might also be noted that Australian Jewish millionaires have been notably more reluctant to fund university chairs and research compared with their equivalents elsewhere.

Congregations

The broadening and extension of the religious bases of Australian Jewish life, which also began in the 1935–55 period, has continued into the 21st century. Most Australian Jews who are affiliated to a synagogue are Orthodox, with a minority as members of Progressive (Liberal) (affiliated to the World Union for Progressive Judaism) congregations. Recently, a small Conservative (Masorti) movement, unknown before the 1990s, has emerged in Melbourne. By 2004, there were 50 synagogues in Melbourne, 34 of which were Orthodox, of which eight were Strictly Orthodox – seven Lubavitcher and one Adass, non-Lubavitcher Strictly Orthodox – one Mizrachi, and two Sephardi; the others were mainstream Orthodox representing both British United Synagogue and European origins. Four Melbourne synagogues were Progressive, one Masorti, and one Independent. Another Orthodox synagogue also existed in Ballarat, Victoria, about 100 miles (160 km.) north of Melbourne. In Sydney, there were 19 synagogues, with the same denominational breakdown: three were Progressive, two Sephardi, the rest Ashkenazi Orthodox, of which four or five were Strictly Orthodox. Two synagogues existed in New South Wales outside of Sydney, in Byron Bay and Newcastle. Among the smaller states, there were five synagogues (four Orthodox, one Progressive) in Perth, Western Australia; five in Queensland (two Orthodox, three Progressive); three in Tasmania (all Orthodox); as well as both Orthodox and Progressive services at the Jewish community center in Canberra. There were thus approximately 87 synagogues in Australia in 2004. Some, especially the Great Synagogue in central Sydney and the Melbourne Hebrew Congregation near central Melbourne, are historically important or architecturally distinguished. Both the Orthodox and Progressive movements held national rabbinical conferences. Orthodox and Progressive *battei din* existed in Melbourne and Sydney, with Melbourne's Orthodox Beth Din involved in controversy over its structure from the 1990s on. A number of postwar Australian rabbis have become nationally known, among them Yitzhak Groner, Chaim *Gutnick, Israel *Porush, Raymond *Apple, and Ronald Lubofsky among the Orthodox rabbinate and Herman Sanger and John S. *Levi among Progressive rabbis. Several Progressive synagogues appointed women rabbis, the first (Karen Soria) in Melbourne in 1981. Relations between the Orthodox and Progressive movements have, with some striking exceptions, been notably bad, with animosity between the two surfacing at regular intervals. As in Britain, it is probably fair to say that congregational growth during the past generation has come at the extremes, among Strictly Orthodox and Progressive synagogues, while moderate Orthodoxy has, in the main, not grown as rapidly.

Community Organization and Services

The Australian Jewish community has evolved a recognized structure of bodies who are entitled to speak on its behalf on public issues, make representations to the government, liaise with the media, and so on. Each state has a local Board of Deputies (which, in Victoria, has since 1988 been known as the Jewish Community Council of Victoria) headed by a president and other office holders, and composed of delegates from affiliated Jewish bodies, including most synagogues. In New South Wales (but not elsewhere) there is a measure of direct election of delegates from the Jewish community. Nationally, the Jewish community's central body is the Executive Council of Australian Jewry (ECAJ), whose president usually serves for a two-year term, the post normally rotating between a leading figure in Melbourne and Sydney. Among the presidents of the ECAJ, Maurice *Ashkanasy, Syd *Einfeld, Jeremy Jones, and, in particular, Isi *Leibler, have been recognized as influential spokesmen for the Australian Jewish community. Before making *aliyah* in 1998, Isi Leibler had unquestionably been the dominant Jewish lay leader in Australia during the previous quarter-century. Australia also contains a strong Zionist movement, based in organizations in each state and a national Zionist Federation of Australia (ZFA). *WIZO, with 3,000 members, is a particularly strong component, which also includes *Po'alei Zion, *Mizrachi, *Revisionists, and youth groups. The ZFA has often lobbied politicians as equal partners with the ECAJ, often to good effect, especially under the presidency of Mark *Leibler in the 1980s and 1990s.

Since 1976, the Australian Zionist movement has been associated with a well-known semi-independent bimonthly magazine, known until the late 1990s as *Australia-Israel Review* and, since then, as *The Review*. Apart from publishing pro-Israel material, it examines antisemitic and anti-Zionist extremists in Australia. In 1996 *The Review* received considerable publicity in the mainstream media for publishing a list of financial donors to One Nation, a right-wing anti-Asian, anti-Aboriginal party, an act which was widely criticized as an invasion of privacy. Since 1983 its editor has been Dr. Colin Rubenstein (1942–), formerly an academic at Monash University.

Since 1968, when the *Australian Jewish Herald* ceased publication, the Australian Jewish community has had one weekly community newspaper, the *Australian Jewish News*, published in both Melbourne and Sydney editions with the same national news but different local coverage. A high-quality, wide-ranging paper, it was edited in the 1980s and 1990s by Sam Lipski (1936–), a respected communal figure and formerly the Washington correspondent of *The Australian*. Its Sydney edition was edited by Susan Bures. In the early 21st century the newspaper was edited by Dan Goldberg. Until the early 1990s, it also contained a weekly Yiddish supplement, *Die Yiddishe Naes*, which ceased publication due to the decline in the number of Yiddish speakers. A number of other Australian Jewish publications have existed, such as *The Bridge*, a quarterly which existed in the 1960s; *Generation*, another quarterly journal of commentary and fiction, edited in the 1980s and 1990s by Melbourne historian and novelist Mark Baker; and the *Melbourne Chronicle*, a Yiddish-English quarterly edited by Melbourne writer Serge *Liberman. Unfortunately none of these publications became a permanent fixture. The Australian Jewish Historical Society, founded in 1938, has, however, published a continuing *Journal* since the 1950s, which, since 1988, has appeared twice annually, with its Melbourne and Sydney committees each producing an annual issue. The *Australian Jewish Historical Society Journal* has also included memoirs and commentary.

Welfare provisions in the Australian Jewish community are, for the most part, in the hands of the Australian Jewish Welfare Society (known since 1999 as Jewish Care). The Welfare Society was founded in Melbourne and Sydney in the 1930s as an immigrants' aid society, specifically to assist German Jewish refugees. It remained mainly a refugees' aid society until the 1970s and helped to bring thousands of former Soviet Jews to Australia then and after the collapse of the USSR. Since the 1970s, it has chiefly functioned as a welfare society in the more normal sense, assisting the disabled, the elderly, and other disadvantaged groups.

Many other Jewish groups exist, especially in Melbourne and Sydney, including women's groups such as the National Council of Jewish Women and WIZO, youth groups, and Hillel on campuses. From about 1983 until 1998 the Australian Institute of Jewish Affairs existed, headed by Isi Leibler. It conducted significant research, brought well-known overseas speakers to Australia, and published a journal, *Without Prejudice*, designed to combat antisemitism. Australia is also home to a significant *B'nai B'rith movement, which is particularly well known for combating antisemitism. Virtually all are pro-Zionist, with support for Israel unusually strong. A number of left-wing groups, critical of right-wing Israeli policies, and with a progressive agenda on such issues as Aboriginal rights, exist, most notably the Jewish Democratic Society.

From the early 1940s until about 1970 a controversial but, in its early phase, very influential body existed, the Jewish Council to Combat Fascism and Antisemitism. From the late 1940s it was accused by conservative sources of being a

Communist front group, and lost much of its influence. Three Jewish museums were founded in Australia in the 1980s, the A.M. Rosenblum Jewish Museum in Sydney, founded in 1982, which includes exhibits on Australian Jewish history and the Holocaust; the Jewish Museum of Australia in Melbourne, also founded in 1982; and the Holocaust Museum and Research Centre, also in Melbourne, founded in 1984, whose guides are mainly Holocaust survivors.

Jews in Public Life

Fewer Jews have been elected to public office in contemporary Australia than in many other Diaspora societies. Nine Jews have served as members of the federal Parliament since World War II, most notably Peter *Baume, Moss *Cass, Barry *Cohen, Sam *Cohen, and Michael *Danby. On the other hand, one of Australia's most distinguished Jews, Sir Zelman *Cowen, served as governor-general of Australia in 1977–82.

Jews are prominent in the spheres of business and professional life, with an estimated 15–20 percent of Australia's annual "rich lists" being Jewish, mainly Melbourne Holocaust survivors and their relatives. Jews also comprise a disproportionate percentage of Australia's lawyers and doctors, especially in Melbourne and Sydney. Jews are not as numerous in academic and cultural life as in other societies, with only a handful of Jewish "public intellectuals," such as Frank Knopfelmacher (1923–95), a right-wing political commentator; Robert Manne (1947–), an academic political commentator; Dennis Altman (1947–), a well-known social critic and advocate of gay rights; and Peter Singer, internationally known for his views on animal rights. In general, however, Jews are much less publicly visible as opinion leaders and trendsetters than elsewhere. It is perhaps indicative of this that unquestionably the Australian work about Jews which has had the greatest international impact was written by a non-Jew: *Schindler's Ark*, by gentile Australian writer Thomas Keneally, which formed the basis for Steven *Spielberg's famous film, *Schindler's List*.

Australia-Israel Relations

In general, relations between Australia and Israel have been unusually good, a continuation of a trend which began with the foundation of the State of Israel. Most Australian governments have consistently sided with the small minority of states of the U.N. and other bodies which have supported Israel when anti-Israel measures were proposed. Australia sent troops to the *Sinai MFO in the 1980s to enforce the peace treaty between Israel and Egypt. Trade between the two states, despite their geographic remoteness, is not inconsiderable and an Australia-Israel Chamber of Commerce has existed since the 1950s. The absence of a direct air link between Israel and Australia as of 2004 (travelers must change at Bangkok or some other midway point) remains a barrier to increasing tourism.

There has only been one notable exception to this pattern of bilateral friendliness, the Whitlam government of 1972–75, which went out of its way to stress its pro-Third World credentials and alienated many Jews. In contrast, Malcolm Fraser (Australia's prime minister in 1975–83), Bob Hawke (prime minister in 1983–91), and John Howard (prime minister from 1996) have been notable supporters of Israel, with Hawke's warm backing for Israel being legendary. It is, however, probably accurate to state that most Australian governments, especially its Australian Labor Party administrations, are much happier with a Labor government in power in Israel than with a Likud government and also that, as everywhere, the left and the organs of opinion it controls or influences have turned sharply against Israel in recent decades.

Antisemitism, Anti-Zionism, War Crimes

Australia has also been relatively free of extreme right-wing antisemitic groups or activists. On the far right, the best-known continuing antisemitic group is the League of Rights, loosely related to the Social Credit movement. Individual antisemitic activists and local "Holocaust deniers" exist, and some antisemitic attacks occur periodically. On the far left, Australia has long had a series of extremist anti-Zionist activists. From 1978 until the late 1980s very extreme anti-Zionist groups had air time on Radio 3CR, a Melbourne "community radio" station dominated by the extreme left, especially the far left of the Victorian branch of the ALP. In 1978–80 the local Jewish community appealed to the Australian Broadcasting Tribunal to remove these programs from the air, with mixed success at the time, although they largely disappeared by about 1990. More recently, several left-wing members of the Australian Parliament, particularly from Sydney seats with high concentrations of Muslims, have caused concern. The number of Muslims in Australia rose from 100,000 to 300,000 during the period from 1970 through 2001. Most were Turks or east Asians rather than Arabs. Nevertheless, antisemitic extremism from Muslim fundamentalists, especially from Sheik Taj El-Hilaly of Sydney, has caused considerable concern to Australian Jews.

From the mid-1980s, efforts were made to bring to justice former Nazi war criminals who, it was widely believed, migrated to Australia after World War II. Most were Balts or Ukrainians. The effort was chiefly sparked by a series of radio broadcasts in 1985 by Mark Aarons, an investigative journalist. After a full investigation by a Government Commission, which found that up to 50 serious Nazi war criminals had migrated to Australia, in 1989 Australia's Parliament, after bitter discussion, passed a War Crimes Act allowing alleged Nazi war criminals to be tried in Australia. For a variety of reasons, especially the lack of interest by Paul Keating, Australia's prime minister, 1991–96, in pursuing these efforts, no prosecutions have ever been commenced, and it is now most unlikely that any ever will.

Summary

In many respects, Australia is a model Diaspora community; if any Diaspora Jewish community has a viable future, it is Australia's. This has probably been due, in part, to the concentration of resources on what some sociologists describe as the "bottom half" of the community, especially the Jewish day school system, rather than on the "top half," on the college-educated or cultural sector, or in grandiose monuments. If anything the past 45 years have seen a considerable strengthening of the Australian Jewish community, which has managed to escape many of the problems found elsewhere in the Diaspora.

[Israel Porush and Yitzhak Rischin / William D. Rubinstein (2nd ed.)]

BIBLIOGRAPHY: H.L. Rubinstein and W.D. Rubinstein, *The Jews in Australia: A Thematic History* (2 vols., 1991); S. Rutland, *Edge of the Diaspora* (2001²); H.L. Rubinstein, *Chosen: The Jews in Australia* (1987); M. Turnbull (ed.), *Safer Haven: Records of the Jewish Experience in Australia* (1999); S. Liberman and L. Gallon (eds.), *Bibliography of Australian Jewry* (1991); S. Rutland, *Pages of History: A Century of Australian Jewish Press* (1995); W.D. Rubinstein (ed.), *Jews in the Sixth Continent* (1986); P.Y. Medding (ed.), *From Assimilation to Group Survival* (1968); C.A. Price, *Jewish Settlers in Australia* (1968); B. Hyams, *History of the Australian Zionist Movement* (1998); H.L. Rubinstein, *The Jews in Victoria, 1935–1985* (1986); D. Mossenson, *Hebrew, Israelite, Jew: A History of the Jews in Western Australia* (1990); H. Munz, *The Jews in South Australia, 1836–1936* (1936); M. Gordon, *The Jews of Van Diemen's Land* (1965); A. Aaron, *The Sephardi Jews of Australia and New Zealand* (1979); J.S. Levi and G.F.J. Bergman, *Australian Genesis: Jewish Convicts and Settlers, 1788–1860* (2002²;); I. Getzler, *Neither Toleration Nor Favour: The Australian Chapter of Emancipation* (1970); P.R. Bartrop, *Australia and the Holocaust, 1933–1945* (1995); J. Foster (ed.), *Community of Fate: Memoirs of German Jews in Melbourne* (1986); J.E. Berman, *Holocaust Remembrance in Australian Jewish Communities, 1945–2000* (2001); A. Andgel, *Fifty Years of Caring: A History of the Australian Jewish Welfare Society, 1936–1986* (1988); R. Benjamin, *A Serious Influx of Jews: A History of Jewish Welfare in Victoria* (1998); R. Gouttman, *Bondi in the Sinai: Australia, the MFO, and the Politics of Participation* (1996); G.F. Levey and P. Mendes (eds.), *Jews and Australian Politics* (2004); Y. Aron and J. Arndt, *The Enduring Remnant: The First 150 Years of the Melbourne Hebrew Congregation* (1992); I. Porush, *House of Israel: A Study of Sydney Jewry from its Foundations … and a History of the Great Synagogue of Sydney* (1997); J.S. Levy, *Rabbi Jacob Danglow: "The Uncrowned Monarch of Australian Jews"* (1995); D.J. Elazar, *Jewish Communities in Frontier Societies: Argentina, Australia, South Africa* (1983). The *Australian Jewish Historical Society Journal* appears twice annually and should be consulted by anyone interested in the history of Australian Jewry.

AUSTRIA, country in Central Europe.

Middle Ages

Jews lived in Austria from the tenth century. However the history of the Jews in Austria from the late Middle Ages was virtually that of the Jews in *Vienna and its environs. In the modern period, Austrian Jewish life was interwoven with that of other parts of the Hapsburg Empire. Austria's position as the bulwark of the Holy Roman Empire against the Turks, as a transit area between Europe and the Middle East, and later as a center attracting East European Jewry, conferred on Austrian Jewry, and on legal formulations of their status, an importance far beyond its size and its national boundaries.

According to legend, a Jewish kingdom named *Judaesaptan was founded in the territory in times before recorded history. Jews apparently arrived in Austria with the Roman legions. They are mentioned in the Raffelstatten customs ordinance (c. 903–06) among traders paying tolls on slaves and merchandise. The earliest Jewish tombstone in the region, found near St. Stephan (Carinthia), dates from 1130. The first reliable evidence of a permanent Jewish settlement is the appointment (1194) of Shlom the Mintmaster. During the reign of Frederick I of Babenberg (1195–98) there was an influx of Jews from Bavaria and the Rhineland. A synagogue is recorded in Vienna in 1204. By then, Jews were also living in *Klosterneuburg, *Krems, Tulln, and *Wiener Neustadt. In the 13th century, Austria became a center of Jewish learning and leadership for the German and western Slavonic lands. Prominent scholars included *Isaac b. Moses, author of *Or Zaru'a*, *Avigdor b. Elijah ha-Kohen, and Moses b. Ḥasdai *Taku. At this time, Jews held important positions, administering the taxes and mints, and in trade. *Frederick II of Hohenstaufen granted the Jews of Vienna a charter in 1238. In 1244 Duke Frederick II of Babenberg granted the charter known as the "Fredericianum" to the Jews in the whole of Austria. It became the model for similar *privilegia* granted to the Jews of Bohemia, Hungary, and Poland during the 13th century. *Rudolph of Hapsburg confirmed the charter in 1278, in his capacity as Holy Roman Emperor. It was ratified by the emperors Ludwig IV of Bavaria in 1330 and Charles IV in 1348. Although Jews were excluded by the charter from holding public office, two are mentioned as royal financiers (*comites camerae*) in 1257. Immigration from Germany increased in the second half of the 13th century, but meanwhile the Jews encountered growing hostility, fostered by the church (for example, by the ecclesiastical Council of Vienna, 1267). Four instances of *blood libel occurred. The massacres of Jews in Franconia instigated by *Rindfleisch spread to Austria. Some protection was afforded by Albert I, who in 1298 endeavored to suppress the riots and imposed a fine on the town of St. Poelten. However, in 1306, he punished the Jews in *Korneuburg on a charge of desecration of the *Host. *Frederick I (1308–30) canceled a debt owed by a nobleman to a Jewish moneylender, thus introducing the usage of the pernicious *Toetbrief*. He also prohibited Jews in his domains from manufacturing or selling clothes. Under *Albert II wholesale massacres of Jews followed the host libel in *Pulkau. A fixed Jewish tax is mentioned for the first time in 1320. Rudolph IV (1358–65), who unified all the legal codes then extant, retained the former enactments granting Jewish judicial autonomy, and took measures to prevent Jews from leaving Austria. The position of the Jews became increasingly precarious during the reigns of *Albert III and Leopold III. Cancellation of debts owed to Jews, confiscations of their property, and economic restrictions multiplied. In consequence, they became greatly impoverished. Their wretchedness culminated when *Albert V ordered the arrest of all the Jews after the host libel in Enns (1420); 270 Jews were burnt at the stake that year, a calamity remembered in Jewish annals as the **Wiener gesera*. The rest were expelled and the property of the victims was confiscated. Austria became

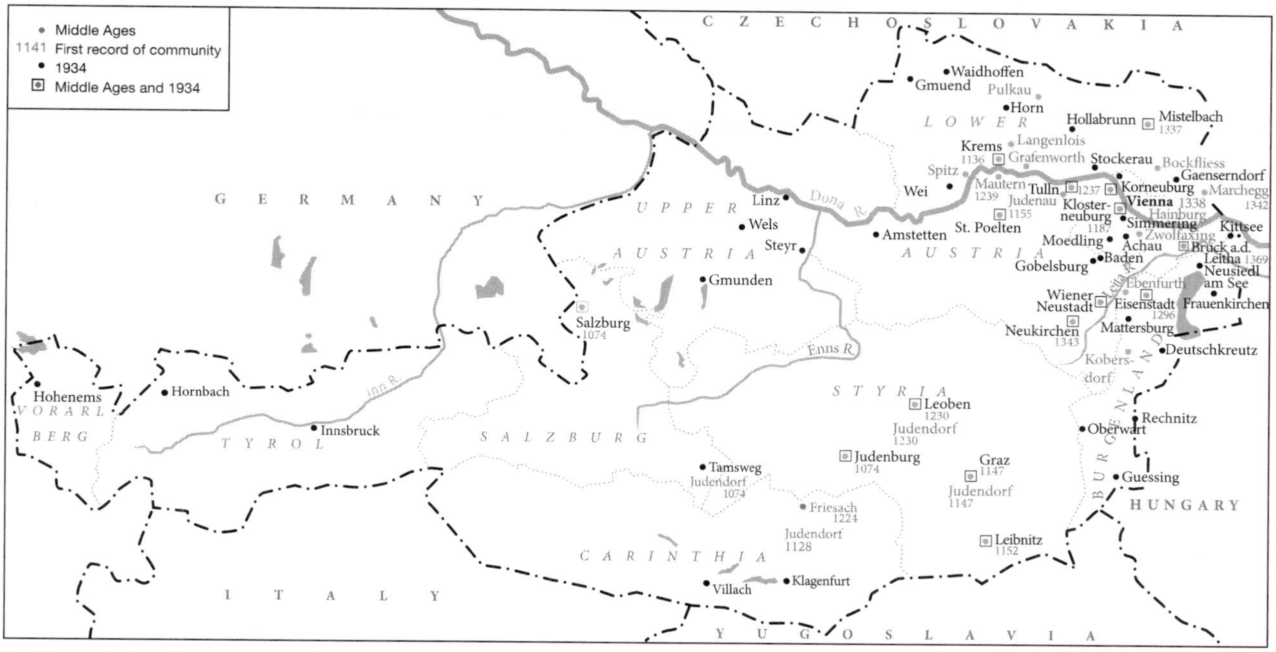

Jewish population of Austria in Middle Ages and 1934.

notorious among Jewry as "*Ereẓ ha-Damim*" ("the bloodstained land").

Jewish settlement was subsequently renewed, and despite the persecutions, Austria became a center of spiritual leadership and learning for the Jews in southern Germany and Bohemia. The teachings of its sages and usages followed in its communities were accepted by Jews in many other countries. Austrian usage helped to determine the form of rabbinical ordination *(*semikhah*), mainly owing to the authority of R. *Meir b. Baruch ha-Levi. His colleague R. Abraham *Klausner compiled *Sefer Minhagim*, a Jewish custumal, which was widely used.

During the reign of Ladislaus (1440–57), the Franciscan John of *Capistrano incited popular feelings against the Jews, leading to the expulsion of almost all of them from Austria proper. Under *Frederick III (1440–93) the position improved; with papal consent he gave protection to Jewish refugees and permitted them to settle in *Styria and *Carinthia. Yeshivot were again established, and under the direction of Israel *Isserlein, the yeshivah in Wiener Neustadt provided guidance for distant communities. Hostility to the Jews on the part of the Estates caused Emperor *Maximilian I (1493–1519) to expel the Jews from Styria and Carinthia in 1496, after receiving a promise from the Estates that they would reimburse him for the loss of his Jewish revenues. However, he permitted the exiles to settle in Marchegg, *Eisenstadt, and other towns then annexed from Hungary. A few Jews, including Meyer *Hirshel, to whom the emperor owed money, settled in Vienna.

*Ferdinand I (1521–64) agreed only in part to requests by the Estates to expel the Jews, ordering their exclusion only from towns holding the "privilege" *de non tolerandis Judaeis*, i.e., the right to exclude Jews. Ferdinand employed a Jew in the mint. In 1536 a statute regulating the Jewish status (*Judenordnung*) was published, which included a clause enforcing the wearing of the yellow *badge on their garments.

Counter-Reformation to 19th Century

In the period of the Counter-Reformation, during the reigns of Maximilian II (1564–76), *Rudolph II (1576–1612), and Matthias (1612–19), there were frequent expulsions and instances of oppression. Under Rudolph the Jewish population in Vienna increased; certain families enjoying special court privileges ("*hofbefreite Juden*") moved there and were permitted to build a synagogue.

In 1621 *Ferdinand II allotted the Jews of Vienna a new quarter outside the city walls. In the rural areas the jurisdiction over the Jews and their exploitation for fiscal purposes increasingly passed to the local overlords. Important communities living under the protection of the local lordships existed in villages such as Achau, Bockfliess, Ebenfurth, Gobelsburg, Grafenwoerth, Langenlois, Marchegg, Spitz, Tribuswinkel, and Zwoelfaxing. In Vienna also, *Ferdinand III (1637–57) temporarily transferred Jewish affairs to the municipality. The *Chmielnicki massacres in Eastern Europe (1648–49) brought many Jewish refugees to Austria, among them important scholars. The situation of the Jews deteriorated under *Leopold I (1657–1705). In 1669 a commission for Jewish affairs was appointed, in which the expulsion of the Jews from Vienna and the whole of Austria was urged by Bishop Count Kollonch. In the summer of that year, 1,600 Jews from the poorer and middle classes had to leave Vienna within two weeks; and in 1670 the wealthy Jews followed. The edict of expulsion remained nominally in force until 1848, although sometimes transvened. A number of *Court Jews in particular, such as Samuel *Oppenheimer, Samson *Wertheimer, Simon Michael, and Joseph von Geldern, were permitted to live in Vienna. Their households included Jewish clerks and servants. In 1752 it is estimated that there were 452 Jews living in Vienna, all of whom were connected with 12 tolerated families. Restrictive legislation was enforced in most localities in the Hapsburg Empire; often Jews were segregated from Christians. In 1727, in order to limit the Jewish population, the *Familiants laws were introduced, allowing only the oldest son of a Jewish family to marry. They remained in force until 1848. By the peace treaty of Passarowitz between Austria and Turkey (1718), Jews who were Turkish subjects were permitted to live and trade freely in Austria. Their position was thus more favorable than that of Jews who were Austrian subjects. In 1736, Diego d'*Aguilar founded the "Turkish community" in Vienna.

The Jewish policy of Maria Theresa (1740–80) wavered between the mercantilism which stood to gain from increased settlement of wealthy Jews and their participation in economic activities, and her own deeply ingrained enmity toward the Jews. A special decree was issued in 1749 encouraging Jews to found manufacturing establishments. The *Judenordnung* of 1753 regulated all aspects of Jewish public and private life, and was based on full judicial autonomy for the communities. At this time some Jewish financiers and industrialists, such as Nathan von *Arnstein, Lazar Auspitz, Bernhard *Eskeles, Israel *Hoenigsberg, and Abraham *Wetzlar, moved to Vienna, having the status of "*Tolerierte*" (tolerated) Jews. Some of them received titles for activities benefiting the Hapsburg Empire; many of their descendants left Judaism. The annexation of *Galicia in 1772 more than doubled the Jewish population of the monarchy, and inaugurated a continuous stream of migration from there, mainly to Vienna.

From the end of the 18th century, with the growing centralization of the government of the empire and new political developments, the position of the Jews in Austria proper became increasingly linked with the history of the empire as a whole. As part of his endeavors to modernize the empire, *Joseph II (1780–90) attempted to make the Jews into useful citizens by introducing reforms of their social mores and economic practices and abolishing many of the measures regulating their autonomy and separatism. Although not altering the legal restrictions on Jewish residence (mainly affecting Vienna) or marriage, he abolished in 1781 the wearing of the yellow badge and the poll tax hitherto levied on Jews. Joseph II's *Toleranzpatent*, issued in 1782, in which he summarized his previous proposals, is the first enactment of its kind in Europe. Jews were directed to establish German-language elementary schools for their children, or if their number did not justify this, to send them to general schools. Jews were encouraged to engage in agriculture and ordered to discontinue the use of Hebrew and Yiddish for commercial or public purposes. It became official policy to facilitate Jewish contacts with general culture in order to hasten assimilation. Jews were permitted to engage in handicrafts and to attend schools and universities. Jewish judicial autonomy was abolished in 1784. Jews were also inducted into the army, which in due course became one of the careers where Jews in Austria enjoyed equal opportunities, at least in the lower commissioned ranks. The "tolerated" Jews in Vienna and the intellectuals who, influenced by the enlightenment movement (see *Haskalah), tended toward assimilation, accepted the *Toleranzpatent* enthusiastically. The majority, however, considered that it endangered their culture and way of life without giving them any real advantages. The implementation of these measures promoted the assimilation of increasingly broader social strata within Austrian Jewry. In 1792 the Jewish Hospital was founded in Vienna, which benefited Jews throughout the empire for many years. In 1803, there were 332 Jewish families living in Austria proper (including Vienna), and approximately 87,000 families throughout the Hapsburg Empire.

19th Century

The position of the Jews in Austria deteriorated after the death of Joseph II, though the *Toleranzpatent* remained in force. Francis I (1792–1835) introduced the Bolletten-tax (see *Taxation), and ordered that measures should be taken against "Jewish superstitions" and "vain rabbinical argumentation." Efforts to "enlighten" the Jews during his reign included the activities of Herz *Homberg, whose catechism "Benei Zion" was introduced into schools for the teaching of religion. Until 1856, Jews were compelled to pass an examination in it before they were permitted to marry. A decree issued in 1820 required all rabbis to study philosophy, and to use only the "language of the state" for public prayers; Jewish children were required to attend Christian schools. The period between the issue of the *Toleranzpatent* and 1848 saw further fundamental changes in Jewish life. A number of Jews were instrumental in the expansion and modernization of industry, transportation, commerce, and banking in the Hapsburg Empire. Lazar Auspitz, Michael *Biedermann, and Simon von *Laemel developed the textile industry; Salomon Mayer *Rothschild built the first railway; the Rothschilds, Arnstein-Eskeles, and *Koenigswarters were the outstanding bankers and were on the board of the newly founded National Bank. Many Jews had a university education and became prominent in journalism and German literature. Prominent among them were Moritz *Saphir, Ludwig August *Frankl, Moritz *Hartmann, and Leopold *Kompert. The less wealthy classes of Jews also prospered, opening workshops, or selling and peddling products of the developing industries. Their heightened awareness of human dignity evoked by their economic and cultural attainments and the relaxation of humiliating restrictions emphasized the basic inequality of their status, even among the wealthy and the nobility. It was even more bitterly resented on the background of Jewish emancipation in France, the liberalizing edict passed in Prussia in 1812, and the budding liberal, revolutionary, and nationalist ideologies in Europe.

During the Congress of Vienna (1814–15), Nathan von Arnstein with other Jewish notables applied unsuccessfully to the emperor for the conferment of civil rights on Austrian Jewry. Joseph von *Wertheimer's anonymously published work on the status of Austrian Jewry (1842) advocated extensive reforms. In 1846 the humiliating *oath *more Judaico* was abolished. The number of Jews actively participating in the 1848 revolution, such as Adolf Fischhof, Joseph Goldmark, Ludwig August Frankl, Hermann *Jellinek (the brother of Adolf *Jellinek and later executed) – some of whom fell victims in the street fighting, among them Karl Heinrich *Spitzer – in part reflected the spread of assimilation among Jews who identified themselves with general political trends, and in part expressed the bitterness of those already assimilated. The new election law passed in 1848 imposed no limitation on the franchise and eligibility to elective offices. Five Jewish deputies, Fischhof and Goldmark from Vienna, Abraham Halpern of Stanislavov, Dov Berush *Meisels of Cracow, and Isaac Noah *Mannheimer of Copenhagen, were elected to the revolutionary parliament meeting at Kromeriz (Kremsier; 1848–49). On the other hand, the revolution resulted in anti-Jewish riots in many towns, and the newly-acquired freedom of the press produced venomous antisemitic newspapers and pamphlets (see Q. *Endlich, S. *Ebersberg, S. *Brunner). Isidor *Busch published his short-lived but important periodical *Oesterreichisches Central-Organ fuer Glaubensfreiheit, Cultur, Geschichte und Literatur des Judenthums*, in which Leopold Kompert was the first to advocate emigration as a solution of the Jewish problem in Austria (and initiated the Auf nach Amerika! ("Forward to America!") movement). After the revolution the specifically Jewish taxes were abolished by parliament. The imposed constitution ("*Octroyierte Verfassung*") of 1849 abrogated discrimination on the basis of religion. The hated *Familiantengesetz* became ineffective. Freedom of movement in the empire was granted. As a result old communities were dissolved and new ones emerged. Some Jews were admitted to state service. On Dec. 31, 1851, the imposed constitution was revoked. Although religious freedom was retained in principle, Jews were again required to obtain marriage licenses from the authorities, even if the number of marriages was no longer limited. The right of Jews to acquire real estate was suspended. Other restrictions were introduced up to 1860. In 1857 the establishment of new communities was prohibited in Lower Austria. Attempts were made to expel Jews from cities, based on the rights afforded by medieval charters. In 1860 a new, more liberal, legislation was promulgated, although in some parts of Austria Jews still were unable to hold real estate. In general, however, the position of the Jews was now improved. Jewish financiers in partnership with members of the nobility founded new industries and banks, outstanding among them the Creditanstalt. Jews founded leading newspapers and many became journalists. In 1862 Adolf *Jellinek, the successor of Isaac Noah Mannheimer, founded his modernized *bet ha-midrash* in Vienna. The new constitution of Austria-Hungary of Dec. 21, 1867, again abolished all discrimination on the basis of religion. The Vienna community then rapidly grew, attracting Jews from all parts of the monarchy. Jews increasingly entered professions hitherto barred to them and assimilation also increased. Communal organization remained, based on laws of 1789; in towns where there had not formerly been a Jewish community, only a "congregation for worship" (**Kultusverein*) could be established. A law issued in 1890 authorized the existence of one undivided community in each locality, supervising all religious and charitable Jewish institutions in the area, and entitled to collect dues; only Austrian citizens were eligible for election to the communal board. In 1893 a rabbinical seminary, the *Israelitisch-Theologische Lehranstalt, was founded which also provided instruction for teachers of religion, and received aid from the authorities.

The upper strata of Austrian Jewry identified themselves with German culture and liberal trends. This was reflected in the views of Jewish members in both houses of parliament such as Ignaz *Kuranda, Heinrich Jacques, Rudolph *Auspitz, Moritz von *Koenigswarter, and Anselm von *Rothschild. The German Schulverein (Association for German minority schools) supported Jewish schools in non-German towns.

ANTISEMITISM. Toward the latter part of the 19th century, antisemitism rapidly developed in the Austro-Hungarian Empire, the blood libel case of *Tisza-Eszlar being followed by rioting and other false accusations. Antisemitism manifested two tendencies. The Catholic-religious form later found expression through Karl *Lueger and his *Christian-Social party; and in its pan-Germanic nationalistic form it was expressed by Georg von *Schoenerer and his party (see *antisemitic political parties). The government, however, opposed antisemitic propaganda. The manifestation of antisemitism brought a change in ideological attitude on the part of the Jews, strengthening the national elements. Efforts were made to combat antisemitism in Austro-Hungary by Joseph Samuel *Bloch with the help of his weekly *Oesterreichische Wochenschrift* (founded 1884) and the Oesterreichisch-Israelitische Union (later *Union Oesterreichischer Juden), founded in 1885. An association to combat antisemitism ("Verein zur Abwehr des Antisemitismus"), consisting of members of the higher strata of Austrian society, was founded in 1891 under the presidency of Arthur Gundaccar Freiherr von Suttner (1850–1902). The historian Heinrich *Friedjung continued to urge complete Jewish integration into the German nation. Some Jews ascribed the wave of anti-Jewish hostility to the immigration at this period of masses of "uncultured" Jews from Eastern Europe. In opposition to the assimilationist Oesterreichisch-Israelitische Union a Juedisch-politischer Verein (later Juedisch-nationale Partei) advocated an independent Jewish policy. Jewish nationalist ideology penetrated Austrian circles through the influence of Perez *Smolenskin, Leon *Pinsker, and Nathan *Birnbaum. The first Jewish national students' society, *Kadimah, was founded in Vienna in 1882.

ZIONISM. Vienna was the city of Theodor *Herzl, and the Zionists combined to strengthen the Jewish national viewpoint and opposition to assimilation. Herzl was opposed not only by the majority of the Jewish community executive and by his employees, the prestigious "*Neue Freie Presse*," but also by Chief Rabbi Moriz Guedemann, the successor of Adolf Jellinek. After the passage of the General Franchise Law in 1907, four representatives of the Jewish National Party were elected to parliament. They founded a Jewish *"Parlamentsklub." In the 1911 elections the Jewish national candidates were not returned. The Zionist influence in Jewish public life increased during World War I and was significantly reinforced after Hirsch (Zevi) Perez *Chajes became chief rabbi of Vienna in 1918.

During the war, 36,000 Jewish refugees arrived in Vienna from Galicia and Bukovina alone. The *Zentralstelle fuer juedische Kriegsfluechtlinge was formed to provide them with social assistance. The Zionist social worker and politician Anitta Mueller Cohen founded numerous social institutions to support the refugees. Many stayed on after the war and influenced the revival of Jewish culture and life in hitherto stagnant communities. In 1918 there were 300,000 Jews in 33 communities in the Austrian Republic, with 200,000 Jews living in Vienna in 1919. Distribution of the communities was as follows: ten in Burgenland, one in Carinthia, sixteen in Lower Austria, one in Salzburg, one in Styria, one in Tyrol, two in Upper Austria, one in Vorarlberg. (See Table: Jews in Austrian Provinces.)

Jews in Austrian Provinces

Province	1910	1934
Burgenland	4,837	3,632
Carinthia	339	269
Lower Austria	9,287	7,716
Salzburg	285	239
Styria	2,708	2,195
Tyrol	469	365
Vienna	175,318	176,034
Vorarlberg	126	42
Total	193,369	190,492

After 1918

JEWISH RIGHTS AND POLITICAL ACTIVITY. The Treaty of St. Germain (1919) guaranteed the Jews *minority rights. The Zionists founded a Jewish National Council (Juedischer Nationalrat). On November 5 they forced Alfred Stern, a former city councillor and the assimilationist president of the Jewish community since 1903, to resign. Stern died on December 1 at age 88. His successor became in 1920 the *Generaloberstabsarzt* (senior medical officer of the Austrian-Hungarian army) Alois Pick, who remained in office until 1932. A Jewish militia (Juedische Stadtschutzwache) was founded and protected Jews in the postwar unrests.

The Zionist Robert *Stricker was elected to the first Austrian National Assembly in February 1919. In October 1920, due to a change of the election law, he was not reelected. Besides his political involvement as board member and later vice president of the Jewish community Stricker also edited the *Juedische Zeitung*, the daily the *Wiener Morgenzeitung*, and the *Neue Welt*. Three Zionists (Jakob Ehrlich, Bruno Pollack-Parnau, and Leopold Plaschkes) were also elected to the Vienna city parliament. Jews who had settled in Austria after the outbreak of the war were deprived of the right to vote, and the reorganization of the Vienna electoral districts also adversely affected the Jewish voting strength. Special measures disqualifying the war refugees from becoming Austrian citizens were introduced in 1921. In the postwar era, many Zionist youths intending to immigrate to Ereẓ Israel passed through Austria. In 1919 therefore the first Palaestinaamt (Palestine Office) was founded in Vienna, directed by Emil Stein and Egon Michael Zweig. Among Jews, chiefly in Vienna, the Social-Democratic Party gained many supporters, attracting the lower-middle-class electorate. Some of its leaders of Jewish descent, such as Otto *Bauer and Julius Deutsch, were widely popular; in Jewish affairs they adhered to a policy of assimilation. Their leading positions, however, drew antisemitic invective. The Social Democrats were careful to avoid the label of a Jewish party and the display of too many Jews in prominent positions.

In the period 1919–1939, a number of Jewish educational institutions opened their doors to students. These included the Jewish Realgymnasium (since 1927 named Chajesgymnasium), the Paedagogium (a Hebrew teachers' seminary), and a seminary for religion teachers. The Jewish community maintained a museum – the oldest Jewish museum worldwide, opened in 1896 – a famous library, which was directed by the historian Bernhard Wachstein, and a renowned historical commission. In 1927 Chief Rabbi Chajes died; he was succeeded in 1932 by David Feuchtwang, who also was the honorary head of the Vienna Mizrachi. After Feuchtwang's death in 1936 the scholar Israel Taglicht became chief rabbi. In addition, youth movements had many supporters. Reforms were introduced in communal institutions and new ones were established. These included the Organisation fuer juedische Wanderfuersorge ("Organization for the Care of Jewish Migration"), established in 1930 to cope with the huge transitory Jewish migration, which became even greater with the influx of emigrants from Germany after 1933. From 1932 until 1938 the Zionists formed the majority in the executive of the Vienna Jewish community.

After the suppression of the Social Democrats in 1934, the Jewish situation declined, mainly through an insidious discrimination. Jews were quietly deprived of their means of existence under various pretexts while the authorities continued to emphasize that all citizens had equal civic status. In schools Jewish and non Jewish pupils were segregated. Jews were permitted to join the Vaterlaendische Front which in 1934 replaced the political parties. In January 1938 it was proposed that Jewish youth should be organized in a separate subdivision of the youth division of the Front. This the Zionists accepted willingly, but it angered those in favor of assimilation.

The Christlich-Soziale Partei (*Christian Social Party), which formed the majority of the governments in Austria, under Ignaz Seipel, Engelbert *Dollfuss, and Kurt von Schuschnigg, was not racist antisemitic; the dependence of Austria on the League of Nations and the Western powers, and the growing menace of National Socialism, made the government play down antisemitism and seek Jewish support.

Federal Chancellor Schuschnigg sent Desider *Friedmann, the president of the Vienna community from 1932 until 1938, on a mission abroad to mobilize support for the Austrian currency. There was a wide discrepancy between the attitude of the government and of the Austrian public toward the Jews. When, for instance, Schuschnigg congratulated Sigmund *Freud on his birthday in 1936, the letter was not published in the press. On the other hand, the official policy to emphasize everything specifically Austrian enhanced the reputation of writers and intellectuals of Jewish origin living there. Outstanding were the writers Franz *Werfel, Stefan *Zweig, Arthur Schnitzler, Richard Beer-Hofmann, Felix *Salten, Hermann Broch, Peter *Altenberg, and Alfred *Polgar, the musicians Bruno *Walter and Arnold *Schoenberg, and the theatrical producer Max *Reinhardt.

In 1932 the Austrian association of Jewish frontline fighters (Bund Juedischer Frontsoldaten Österreichs) was founded. It was headed by Major-General Emil von *Sommer and later by Captain Sigmund Edler von Friedmann and had about 20,000 members. Efforts to combat antisemitism, including reminders of the part played by Jewish soldiers in World War I, could do nothing to counter the violent hatred against the Jews ingrained in wide sectors of the Austrian population. Many Jews, outstanding among them Emil von Sommer – who founded in 1934 the monarchist association of Jewish frontline fighters (Legitimistische Jüdische Frontkämpfer) – yearning for Hapsburg rule, became monarchists.

[Nathan Michael Gelber and Meir Lamed / Evelyn Adunka (2nd ed.)]

The Holocaust

1938–1939. The liquidation of Austrian Jewry began with the *Anschluss* (annexation) to Germany on March 13, 1938. According to the Israelitische Kultusgemeinde, the Jewish community of Vienna, there were at the time 181,778 Jews in Austria, of whom 91.3% (165,946) were living in Vienna. According to Himmler's statistics, however, the number of Austrian Jews persecuted under the *Nuremberg Laws reached 220,000; in addition, tens of thousands of persons of Jewish descent were affected by the racial laws. The new Nazi regime immediately introduced decrees and perpetrated acts of violence of an even greater scope and cruelty than those then practiced in the Reich itself. The Jews were denied basic civil rights, and they and their property were at the mercy of organized and semi-organized Nazi gangs. The activities of Jewish organizations and congregations were forbidden. Many Jewish leaders were imprisoned, and several were murdered in *Dachau concentration camp. A fine of 800,000 schillings ($30,800) was levied on the Jewish communities. At the same time, the first pogroms took place in Vienna and in the provinces, and synagogues, including the Great Synagogue of Vienna, were desecrated and occupied by the German Army. The main victims of systematic terrorization were the Austrian Jewish intelligentsia and property owners. The former were immediately banned from any public activity, from educational and scientific institutions and from the arts. Many of them – including Sigmund Freud, Stefan Zweig, and Hermann *Broch – were among the first Austrian Jewish refugees. Freud left for London by plane but before he left he gathered his disciples, pioneers of psychoanalysis, and invoked the memory of Rabban *Johanan ben Zakkai, who after the destruction of the Temple in Jerusalem made the Torah portable. The biggest property owners were arrested by the Gestapo and forced to turn over their property, most especially their artworks. Some of those who refused were murdered and many others were sent to Dachau, where they were either killed or committed suicide. In addition, street attacks and brutal persecution became daily occurrences in the lives of Austrian Jews of all social classes. The dramatic change in circumstances led to great despair among Austrian Jews. In March alone, 311 cases of suicide were registered in the Viennese community, and in April, 267. During these two months, at least 4,700 Jews escaped from Austria. Systematic deportation of Jews and the confiscation of their property began in several Austrian provinces. The ancient Jewish communities of *Burgenland were deported over the Czech border. A group of 51, which was returned to Austria, was sent up and down the Danube for four months and denied entry to all the countries bordering on the river. As a result of the persecutions, a stream of Jews from the provinces, most of them destitute, began to flow to Vienna. In May 1938 the Viennese Jewish community renewed its activities and several of its leaders were released from prison in order to help organize mass emigration which the Nazi authorities encouraged. The Zionist Palestine Office in Vienna was permitted to organize both legal and "illegal" immigration to Palestine. In the same month, the Nuremberg Laws were officially enforced in Austria. In August 1938, under *Eichmann's aegis, the "Zentralstelle fuer juedische Auswanderung" was established in Vienna, headquartered in a confiscated Rothschild palace. This organization was to be responsible for the "solution of the Jewish problem" in Austria. Its "efficient" methods of persecution and deportation were later copied in Germany and in several of the German-occupied countries. A special body, the Vermoegensverkehrsstelle, was responsible for the transfer of Jewish property to non-Jews. With the help of the major Jewish welfare organizations in the world, the community and the Palestine Office were able to assist in the emigration of thousands of Jews. The importance of this aid grew with the straitened circumstances of Austrian Jewry; as against 25% of the emigrants who needed financial assistance in May and July 1938, 70% needed assistance in July and August 1939. Between July and September 1938 emigration reached a monthly average of 8,600. Hundreds of training courses were organized to prepare emigrants for new occupations in the countries of immigration. (In Vienna, these had 31,306 participants up to the end of 1939.) Thousands of young people received agricultural training at the farm owned by the *He-Ḥalutz Zionist movements (in August 1939, there were 1,801 people in 18 training camps) and *Youth Aliyah wards received special agricultural and technical training. The community also took care of those whose education had been interrupted by their expulsion from educational institutions, and of the thousands of Jews whose livelihoods had been taken from them and who were in urgent need of assistance. In October 1938 antisemitic riots again broke out and Jews were once more deported from various places. On the eve of the Day of Atonement (October 5) thousands of Jewish families were evicted from their homes in certain districts of Vienna and elsewhere, and ordered to leave the country, though this decree was subsequently canceled through the intervention of Eichmann. On October 10, Hitler gave personal instructions "to act for the deportation of 27,000 Viennese Jews of Czech nationality." On October 28, thousands of Jews who were Polish nationals were deported into the no-man's-land on the German-Polish border. Of these, only 1,300 were able to cross the frontier. The rest remained in Austria as stateless persons (see *Germany). During the pogroms of November 9–11 (see **Kristallnacht*), approximately 8,000 Jews were arrested, and of these 5,000 were sent to Dachau. Six hundred and eighty others committed suicide or were murdered that single night. In Vienna alone, 42 synagogues were burned and 4,038 Jewish shops were looted. Almost all Jewish homes were destroyed and cemeteries desecrated. Synagogues were also destroyed in Graz, Salzburg, Klagenfurt, Linz, Innsbruck, Baden, Eisenstadt, Berndorf, and Bad Voeslau. In Linz, all the Jewish inhabitants were arrested, and all Jews in the district were ordered to move to Vienna within three days. The president of the Innsbruck Jewish community, Richard Berger, was murdered and the chief rabbi of Graz and Styria, David Herzog, was almost beaten to death. He was able to immigrate to England, where he wrote his memoirs (published in 1995). One-third of the fine of a billion marks ($83,300,000) imposed on the whole of the German Reich Jewry was levied on Austrian Jews. During the November pogroms employees of the Jewish community and the Palestine Office were released from prison and ordered to continue organizing emigration. In February 1939 began the publication of the official Jewish newspaper, *Juedisches Nachrichtenblatt*, under the supervision of the Gestapo. The paper appeared until the end of 1943, and was intended to inform the Jewish public of official decrees. Most of those arrested during the pogroms were released before the end of April 1939, having agreed to leave the country as soon as possible. At the end of April 1939, under a special law, almost all Austrian Jews were evicted from their homes, and most were gathered into certain streets in selected districts of Vienna. By the eve of World War II, 109,060 had succeeded in emigrating and only 66,260 Jews were left in Austria. Only 438 still lived outside Vienna while whole regions, such as Salzburg and Carinthia, were devoid of Jews. With the exception of isolated cases, all were deprived of a livelihood and all 25,898 factories and places of business belonging to Jews had been confiscated and shut. With the outbreak of war in September 1939, emigration opportunities lessened, and 17,000 Jews possessing entry visas to enemy countries were forbidden to use them. In the new wave of arrests, hundreds of Austrian Jews were sent to concentration camps. All Jews lived under martial law and additional restrictions were imposed upon them. On October 20, 922 Viennese Jews were exiled to Nisko on the San River. (Some of the Nisko deportees succeeded in crossing the border into the Soviet Union; the remaining 152 were returned to Vienna in April 1940.) In November 1939 Eichmann informed the leaders of the community that all Jews who did not emigrate within one year would be exiled to occupied Poland. During the first four months of the war, 11,240 Jews succeeded in immigrating to neutral countries. Of the 53,403 persons registered with the Viennese community at the end of 1939, 45,140 were dependent on social welfare. However, the community continued to arrange technical training in preparation for emigration, and 5,017 children of school age studied in its 14 educational institutions. Among the community's projected activities for 1940 was its own gradual dissolution, so that, by the end of that year, it would be merely an institution for the care of 24,000 aged and infirm, who were unable to emigrate.

1940–1945. Between February and March 1941, desperate attempts to continue limited emigration resulted in the deportation of 5,000 Jews to five places in the *Lublin district. It is assumed that all met their death within the year, being murdered either locally or in the gas chambers of *Belzec. From October to the beginning of November, another 5,486 Jews were deported to the *Lodz Ghetto. After the official prohibition on emigration, there remained approximately 40,000 Austrian Jews. Very few could leave the country after this date. Of the 128,500 who had emigrated up to that time, 30,800 had gone to England, 24,600 to other European countries, 28,600 to the United States, 9,200 to Palestine, and 39,300 to 54 other countries. At the end of 1941, with the Nazi occupation of territories in the Soviet Union, 3,000 Austrian Jews were deported to the ghettos of Riga, Minsk, and Kovno; many were put to death upon arrival in the vicinity of these ghettos. After the Wannsee Conference, Eichmann announced to the Viennese community his general *Aussiedlung* ("evacuation") program under which 3,200 more Austrian Jews were deported to Riga, 8,500 to Minsk, and 6,000 to Izbica and several other places in the Lublin region. This last group was almost entirely exterminated. Between June and October, 13,900 people were deported to *Theresienstadt, most of them aged 65 and over. On Oct. 10, 1942, the last transport of 1,300 persons left for Theresienstadt. There still remained 7,000 Jews in Austria (about 8,000 according to the Nuremberg Laws). The majority were spared because they were married to non-Jews. All able-bodied persons were compelled to do forced labor. On November 1, 1942, the Israelitische Kultusgemeinde was dissolved and the Aeltestenrat der Juden in Wien took over its remaining duties. It represented Austrian Jewry in dealings with the authorities, and was responsible for running the Jewish hospital, the home for the aged, the soup kitchen, and burying the dead. This council was headed by Josef Loewenherz (the former Zionist vice president and executive director of the Vienna Jewish community) from 1938 until the end of the war. In 1942 Desider Friedmann and Robert Stricker were deported to Theresienstadt; from there they were taken to Auschwitz in autumn 1944 and murdered after their arrival.

Loewenherz's deputy was the former community rabbi and lecturer at the Israelitisch-theologische Lehranstalt Benjamin Murmelstein. In January 1943 he was deported to the ghetto Theresienstadt. In December 1944 he became the "*Judenaelteste*" (Elder of the Jews) of Theresienstadt after Jakob Edelstein and Paul Eppstein. In June 1945 Murmelstein was arrested by the Soviet authorities. He was imprisoned in Leitmeritz and accused of collaboration with the Nazis. After 18 months the Czechoslovak prosecutor released him for lack of evidence. Murmelstein later went to Italy; he lived in Rome as a businessman and private scholar, researching in the Vatican library, until his death in 1989.

Isolated deportation continued from January 1943 until March 1945, and consisted of not more than a hundred persons in each transport. At least 216 Jews were sent to *Auschwitz and 1,302 Jews to Theresienstadt. Most of the victims were former communal workers, and Jews whose non-Jewish spouses had died.

In the summer of 1943, there were still approximately 800 Jews left in Vienna. They had gone underground and were secretly helped by members of the community and the Budapest Jewish rescue committee (*Va'adat ha-Hazzalah*). A few managed to escape to Hungary, but many others were caught by the Gestapo and sent to Auschwitz. Some managed to stay underground until Vienna fell to the Soviet Army. In July and December 1944, approximately 60,000 Hungarian Jews were deported to Vienna and Lower Austria, to be employed by the Nazis in building fortifications. A few were permitted to receive treatment at the Vienna Jewish hospital. Just before Vienna was liberated, 1,150 were deported to Theresienstadt. During the last months of the war, thousands of Jewish evacuees from various concentration camps crossed Austria. A few remained in Vienna and the Vienna district or were transferred to Austrian camps. The remnant of the Viennese Jewish community organized itself into a committee to save the victims, and extended help to them in conjunction with the International Red Cross and Jewish welfare organizations. A report by the Red Cross representative described the last synagogue in the Third Reich located in the cellar of the Viennese Jewish hospital. Of the approximately 50,000 Jews deported from Austria to ghettos and extermination camps only 1,747 returned to Austria at the end of the war. (The largest group of survivors, which numbered 1,293, was liberated from the Theresienstadt Ghetto.) Among the Austrian victims of the Holocaust there were over 20,000 Austrian Jews who had migrated to other European countries later conquered by the Nazis. The number of Austrian Jewish victims of the Holocaust is estimated at 65,000. One of the largest and most terrible of concentration camps, *Mauthausen, where thousands of European Jews met their death, was situated in Austria. A large part in the campaigns to exterminate European Jewry was played by Austrian Nazis, including Eichmann, *Globocnik, *Kaltenbrunner and Hitler himself. In 1946, a documentation committee (Juedisch historische Dokumentation) was set up in Vienna by Tuvia Friedman for the tracing and prosecution of Nazi war criminals.

[Dov Kulka]

Early Postwar Period

At the end of World War II, there were many displaced persons in Austria, most of them from Hungary. They had been sent to Austrian concentration camps during the last two years of the war. Their number was then estimated at about 20,000. Though some returned to their countries of origin after the liberation, postwar Austria had one of the largest concentrations of still unsettled Jewish displaced persons. It was the main transit country for Jewish refugees from Poland, Hungary, Romania, and other East European countries, on their way to Palestine or to the main concentration of refugees in the American Zone of Germany. The number of displaced persons reached its peak in late 1946, when it was estimated at 42,500, of whom over 35,000 were in the American-occupied area of Austria, i.e., in the western part of the country. The most important and biggest displaced persons' camp in Vienna was the "Rothschildspital," the former hospital of the Jewish community, which was later sold and demolished in 1960. Head of the committee of former concentration camp prisoners and Jewish refugees was Bronislaw Teichholz. The number of the refugees later dropped, particularly as a result of mass emigration following the establishment of the State of Israel in 1948. By 1953 only 949 refugees were left in displaced persons camps.

In May 1945 Josef Loewenherz was arrested by the Soviet occupation authorities and taken to Czechoslovakia. After several weeks he was released. With the help of his family he immigrated via London to the United States, where he died in 1960. The same as Murmelstein, he never came to Vienna again.

The secretary of state of the new Austrian government, who was responsible for the Jewish community, the prominent Communist writer Ernst Fischer, appointed in summer 1945 the 75-year-old well known physician Dr. Heinrich Schur, who had survived, because he was married to a non-Jewess, as the first provisional chairman of the Jewish community. After complaints about Schur's age and inability to cope with the many problems of the community Fischer appointed in September 1945 as Schur's successor the Communist journalist David Brill, who had worked as a journalist and private secretary of the chairman of the Communist party in Austria, Johann Koplenig. Brill organized, together with other party members, the first free elections of the community executive, for which only one party, called "Unity" (Einigkeit), stood, and where Brill was confirmed as community president. His group also founded in January 1946 the first Jewish newspaper, called *Der Neue Weg* (The New Way). Brill bitterly complained there that the Jewish survivors of the concentration camps were treated as if they were criminals and he actually wrote that the Jews in Austria at that time were really not allowed to live. In February 1946 he stated in an unpublished report that all the Jews in Vienna were filled with disgust for the present and the future. Both the Jewish community and the reports of mainly Jewish visitors and correspondents from abroad, which were published in the Jewish press worldwide, warned Austrian Jews against returning. In the first years the Jewish community lived from the American Care parcels, and from the contributions of the American Joint Distribution Committee, which lasted until the 1960s.

In 1946 the community celebrated the 120-year-jubilee of the only surviving synagogue, the famous Stadttempel in the Seitenstettengasse, which was built in the backyard of other houses, because of the Austrian law in the 19th century. Nevertheless provisional benches could only be erected in 1947. The temple could be restored to its former glory only in 1963. It took some three years, until 1948, until a new chief rabbi, Akiba Eisenberg, the former rabbi of the city of Györ in Hungary, could be found for the spiritually deserted Jewish community. Eisenberg was a very outspoken person and a strong Zionist. He remained chief rabbi until his death in 1983.

After the second elections for the community executive in 1948, in which several parties stood for election, the blind lawyer David Schapira, a survivor of Theresienstadt and devoted Labour Zionist (of the Poale Zion), became president. He was the head of the so-called Jewish Federation and was strongly supported by Ernest Stiassny, the director of the Vienna office of the World Jewish Congress, who founded an association of Austrian Jews as a counter-institution against the then Communist-led Jewish community. During Schapira's term of office, in August 1949, the remains of Theodor Herzl were transferred to the State of Israel according to his last will. The ceremony and the surrounding festivities were the biggest and most impressive demonstration of the existence and will to survive of the Viennese Jewish community after the Shoah. The State of Israel sent the then 78-year-old Isidor Schalit, once a close collaborator of Herzl and a member of the famous student union Kadimah, to Vienna. The various Zionist associations organized 14 events. This was only one example of the many activities of the Zionist movement (that included the always quarreling Zionist Federation, the Landesverband, the Poale Zion, the General Zionists, the Revisionists, the Mizrachi, the WIZO, and the youth organizations) until the late 1960s. They organized many lectures and courses as well as convening large conferences three times. The Zionist Federation was strongly supported by the two emissaries S.J. Kreutner and Aron Zwergbaum from the Organization Department of the World Zionist Organization in Jerusalem. Their aim was not only *aliyah*, but also education, fostering of Jewish identity, and a democratic takeover of the Jewish community executive, at which they were no longer successful after 1952. A Hebrew school, which was supported by the Zionists, had to close down in 1967 because of lack of pupils and funding. The culmination of the community's support of Israel was reached when after Israel's Six-Day War, in a financially strained situation, the Jewish community sent a check of ATS 10 million to Israel with the help of a bank credit.

After two short and turbulent presidencies of the General Zionist Wolf Hertzberg and the Communist Kurt Heitler, both of them lawyers, there began in 1952 the long era of the rule of the Social Democratic party Bund werktaetiger Juden (Union of Working Jews). They stood for an assimilationist and strongly anti-Communist policy. Their first president was the lawyer Emil Maurer, who had been governor (*Bezirksvorsteher*) of the seventh district of Vienna until 1934, had been imprisoned in the concentration camps Dachau and Buchenwald in 1938, and had immigrated to Britain in 1939. Although Maurer was on good terms with several prominent Socialist Austrian politicians, the Jewish community did not succeed in achieving a satisfying result for the restitution of property. Maurer's successor in 1963 was Ernst Feldsberg, a bank official and survivor of Theresienstadt. In the 1930s he had been a board member of the Union Oesterreichischer Juden and a member of the executive of the Jewish community. Feldsberg was undoubtedly the most active functionary of the Jewish community in many of its bodies both before and after the Shoah.

In the 1960s the building of a community center failed because of lack of funding, although the cornerstone was laid in a public ceremony in the presence of prominent politicians. Community plans to erect a Jewish museum, for which a provisional room was opened in 1964 and closed a few years later, and to reorganize and open the library, failed. In 1966 the Jewish community opened a youth center. In 1967 the ceremonial hall in the main Jewish cemetery was built. In June 1975 the cornerstone was laid for a monument to the Jewish victims of the Holocaust at the site of the former concentration camp of Mauthausen.

The Jewish community published from 1958 the monthly *Die Gemeinde*. The Association of Jewish Students began, in 1952, to publish an outstanding cultural journal, *Das Juedische Echo*, which continued as an annual. Among its founders was Leon Zelman, who from 1978 was the director of the Jewish Welcome Service. The General Zionists published *Die Stimme* (from 1947 until 1963), the revisionist Zionists publish *Heruth* (1957–) and *Die Neue Welt und Judenstaat* (from 1948 until 1952). It was continued as a cultural Jewish journal under the name *Die Neue Welt* and from 1974 it has appeared as *Illustrierte Neue Welt*, edited by Joanna Nittenberg.

In 1967 Desider Stern of the Vienna B'nai B'rith lodge Zwi Perez Chajes organized an exhibition of 400 books by German Jewish authors and published an expanded catalogue in 1970 with 700 entries, which became one of the most important reference works for the studies of literature in exile. The exhibition was later also shown in Germany and South America, but the Hebrew University was not interested in it.

In 1961 Simon *Wiesenthal settled in Vienna. As in Linz he directed the documentation center for Nazi criminals, first as an official of the association of Austrian Jewish communities. After a conflict with the executive director of the Vienna Jewish community Wilhelm Krell he left this position and founded the "Bund juedischer Verfolgter des Naziregimes" (Union of the Jewish Persecuted of the Nazi Regime). The Bund also stood for the elections to the board of the Jewish community, tried in vain to break the majority, and published in its journal – *Der Ausweg* (The Way Out) – numerous reports about its defects and its cold, bureaucratic character.

Feldsberg's successor was the lawyer Anton Pick. In the interwar years he was a functionary of the Socialist Democratic Party, close to their leader Otto Bauer, and had spent time in Palestine, where he published articles in *Davar.* In 1976 younger members of the community founded a new party, called the "Alternative." Their aim was the renewal of the Jewish community and their most important reproach concerned the selling of a great deal of real estate at cheap prices to the city of Vienna, which began in the 1960s and which the opposition, the group of Simon Wiesenthal and the Zionists, polemically called the "second Aryanization." They and a second list, called the "Young Generation" (Junge Generation), eventually gained the majority of the community board and produced the next two presidents, the lawyer Ivan Hacker from 1981 until 1987 and the furrier Paul Grosz.

The number of Jews living in Austrian communities rose with the return of several thousand Jews from camps in Eastern Europe, from the countries to which they had fled (mainly Great Britain, China, and Palestine), and from their hiding places. A small percentage of displaced persons settled in Austrian towns. The number of Jews in these communities reached a peak in 1950 with 13,396 registered. As in the past, the large majority lived in Vienna (12,450), and the rest in the capitals of the provinces (*Laender*) of Graz, Linz, Salzburg, and Innsbruck. From 1950 their number began to decrease. In 1965, 9,537 persons were registered as members of the community, of whom 8,930 lived in Vienna. It is estimated that another 2,000 Jews, not registered as community members, lived in the country. Thereafter the number of Jews remained more or less stable, with a slight tendency to fall. The ancient communities of Burgenland, on the Austro-Hungarian border, which before the *Anschluss* had numbered about 4,000 persons, were not rebuilt. In 1968 nearly 65% of Austrian Jewry was aged 50 and over. Austria became a country of transit for the Jewish migration from Eastern Europe to Israel and the West. In general, these travelers spent only a few days in Austria, in camps in and around Vienna. However, after the Hungarian Revolution of 1956, about 20,000 Jewish refugees fled to Austria. Most continued on their way after a short while, between 200 and 300 remaining in Austria.

ANTISEMITISM. The tradition of antisemitism was not uprooted in Austria, nor confined to ex-Nazis or neo-Nazis, who found sanctuary in the Freiheit (Freedom) Party. Only a few months after the end of World War II, a leader of the large Christian Party (the People's Party), Leopold Kunschak, declared that he had always been antisemitic. This did not prevent his being elected president of Parliament. The universities were often the scene of antisemitic demonstrations. There was the case of the Austrian university professor Taras Borodajkewycz, who boasted about his Nazi past and made vicious antisemitic remarks during his lectures. A demonstration with about 6,000 students against and 1,000 for him escalated into a street riot. In the course of it an elderly demonstrator was mortally beaten by a neo-Nazi student, who was later sentenced to ten months' imprisonment. Borodajkewycz was suspended on most of his pay.

The official attitude toward Nazi criminals, when brought to trial, was generally lenient; among the cases that aroused international indignation was the acquittal of the brothers Johann and Wilhelm Mauer, accused of mass murder in the Stanislaw Ghetto. Public pressure caused their retrial and sentence. In 1964 Franz Murer, who was responsible for the murder of the Jews of Vilna, was acquitted. Although the Austrian Supreme Court quashed this verdict, Murer was not tried again.

There was an antisemitic campaign against Bruno *Kreisky, leader of the Social Democratic Party, of Jewish origin, who served for several years as foreign minister. After an election victory in 1970 Kreisky became federal chancellor (prime minister), the first Jew to hold this high office. Kreisky's governments from 1970 until 1983 included six former Nazis, for which he was publicly attacked by Simon Wiesenthal. In the 1970s Bruno Kreisky made libelous vicious lying attacks on Wiesenthal. The Kreisky-Wiesenthal affair was followed by a series of court actions, in which Kreisky and the Austrian journalist Peter Michael Lingens, who attacked the chancellor, were eventually found guilty. Only in the 1990s did the climate change and many official Austrian honors bestowed on Wiesenthal.

Negotiations between the executive committee for Jewish claims on Austria, headed by Nahum *Goldmann, and the Austrian government started in 1953, but the process of legislation on the return of property and the payment of indemnification to victims of Nazi persecution was concluded only in 1962 and was considered inadequate. No satisfactory progress was made with regard to the solution of problems stemming from the Nazi period. Legislation on indemnification to victims of Nazi persecution did not satisfy the most elementary demands and could not compare with that of West Germany. On the other hand, Austria showed a humanitarian approach in granting transit facilities or temporary residence for Jews and as a result played a major role in enabling Soviet Jews to leave the country when they received permission to immigrate to Israel. They were first housed in Schoenau Castle, but it was closed as a result of a terrorist attack in September

1973. Two armed Arab terrorists took three Russian-Jewish immigrants and an Austrian customs official hostage, and the government succumbed to their demands to close the transit camp. After the Yom Kippur War, however, the emigration of Russian Jews from the U.S.S.R. attained unprecedented proportions and Austria continued to grant them facilities in a former army camp in Woellersdorf starting in December, and in September 1974 the camp site was again moved to Simmering, near Vienna.

[Chaim Yahil / Evelyn Adunka (2nd ed.)]

The 1980s

It was estimated that no less than 90% of the Jews of Austria resided in Vienna at the end of the 1970s, the remainder being in small communities in Salzburg, Linz, and Graz. Some 7,500 Jews were registered members of the Jewish community of Vienna, and it was estimated that there were between 3,000 and 4,000 who were not registered. More than two-thirds of the community was over the age of 60 and the major share of the communal budget was expended on aid to the aged, of whom nearly 1,000 were supported from communal funds.

On August 29, 1981, Arab terrorists attacked the Seitenstettengasse synagogue in Vienna, killing two and wounding 18. Police who were guarding the synagogue apprehended the perpetrators (police guards had been on duty at the synagogue from 1979 when an Arab terrorist group claimed it was responsible for causing an explosion on the synagogue grounds).

In 1985 the first conference of the World Jewish Congress in Vienna was overshadowed by the populist Freedom Party's defense minister's act of sending his official helicopter to pick up the Nazi war criminal Walter Reder when he was released from an Italian prison. (He had slaughtered 1,500 Italian civilians.)

The year 1986 was dominated by the election of President Kurt Waldheim – the most important event of the 1980s for the Austrian state and the Jewish community, causing a most serious crisis for both. The World Jewish Congress charged Waldheim with wartime involvement in Nazi activities in the Balkans as a staff member of General Löhr, who was executed as a war criminal by the Yugoslavs in 1947. During Waldheim's election campaign strong antisemitic feelings were openly expressed by parts of the population, and also by several politicians and the media, especially by the two dailies, *Die Presse* and *Die Neue Kronen Zeitung*. The latter, which had a circulation of 1.5 million in a country of 7 million, had already published in 1974 a notorious series about the Jews by Viktor Reimann which was strongly attacked as antisemitic and discontinued. Waldheim's election was opposed by many intellectuals and artists, who formed a new club called "New Austria" and organized demonstrations, symposia, vigils, press conferences, and publications in order to recall Austria's responsibility for the Nazi crimes. Many Jews considered emigrating and felt homeless again. Israel recalled its ambassador and replaced him by a chargé d'affaires. The coolness between the two countries lasted until Waldheim left the presidency in 1992.

Because of the Waldheim affair the so-called "*Bedenkjahr*" (year of commemoration), which in 1988 marked the 50th anniversary of the "*Anschluss*" of Austria to Nazi Germany, was taken very seriously. At the state ceremony and the festive event in Parliament on March 11 the leading role was played by the socialist Austrian chancellor Franz Vranitzky. Whole series of symposia, exhibitions, lectures, discussion groups, etc., were organized, especially at universities and schools (including many events fostering Christian-Jewish dialogue). This was a new experience for Austria, at last confronting historic truth. In June 1988 the heads of the Austrian Jewish community, Chief Rabbi Chaim Eisenberg and President Paul Grosz, were received by Pope John Paul II during his visit to Vienna. In July Helmut Zilk, the mayor of Vienna, commissioned from the sculptor Alfred Hrdlicka a monument to commemorate "the victims of war and fascism" in the center of Vienna. It shows a kneeling Jew being forced by the Nazis to clean the streets in 1938. This caused great controversy in the Jewish community because of the Jew's humiliating posture.

In June 1987 the deputy mayor of Linz, Carl Hoedl, wrote an open letter to Edgar *Bronfman, head of the *World Jewish Congress, comparing his attitude to Waldheim with the "show trial of the Jews about Jesus." In November of that year Michael Graff, the general secretary of the People's Party, resigned after saying: "As long as there is no proof that Waldheim strangled six Jews with his own hands, there will be no problem"; however, he remained active in politics.

COMMUNAL AND CULTURAL LIFE. In September 1981, the Austrian Constitutional Law amended the *Israelitengesetz* of 1890 after an application by Benjamin Schreiber, the head of the Vienna Agudah. The amendment allowed more than one *Kultusgemeinde* in any geographic region.

In 1982 the Austrian Jewish museum in Eisenstadt near Vienna – the first in Austria – was opened. It was initiated by Kurt Schubert, the founder of the institute of Jewish studies of the University of Vienna. Its director is Johannes Reiss.

In 1983 the late Chief Rabbi Akiba Eisenberg was succeeded by his son Chaim Eisenberg, who was still serving in 2005. In 1988 he was appointed chief rabbi of Austria, a title which did not exist before the Holocaust.

In 1984 a series of events called "*Versunkene Welt*" on the lost culture of Eastern Jewry was organized by Leon Zelman's Jewish Welcome Service. In 1984 the Art Nouveau Synagogue in St. Poelten was renovated and in its building was established a new Institute for the History of the Jews of Austria. It was directed until 2004 by Klaus Lohrmann; his successor was Martha Keil.

In 1983 the city of Vienna began inviting former Jewish citizens to visit their old home for a week. Organized by the Jewish Welcome Service, headed by Leon Zelman, several thousand Viennese Jews returned to Vienna in the framework of the program.

Several new institutions were built or founded, among others the Jewish community center in 1980, the Jewish High

School (the Chajesgymnasium) in 1984, a second Jewish high school by Chabad in 1987, and a Jewish trade school in 1997. In 1999 the Lauder Chabad Campus was opened. It was named after Ronald *Lauder, the former U.S. ambassador to Vienna, who financed it. The square in front of it was named for the Lubavitcher Rebbe Menachem Mendel *Schneersohn. (He is the only rabbi after whom a square or street has been named in Vienna.)

In 1988 the home for the care of the aged was enlarged and named after Maimonides (Maimonides Zentrum). The historic Stadttempel, the main synagogue of Vienna, was reopened after its renovation in the presence of Chancellor Vranitzky, who in 1989 received the gold medal of the Austrian Zwi Perez Chajes B'nai B'rith lodge. In 1988 the Vienna yeshivah was founded; it included a boarding school and was praised in 1991 by the well-known former Viennese rabbi Schmuel (Schmelke) Pinter from London in the highest terms. In 1989 the Jewish Institute of Adult Education was founded by Kurt Rosenkranz. It also organized guest performances of Yiddish theater groups from Tel Aviv, Montreal, and Bucharest. After ten years, in 1998, it published a Festschrift.

The 1990s and After

From 1990 a Liberal Jewish congregation called Or Chadasch functioned in Vienna. Its president from the beginning through the year 2005 was the dermatologist Theodor Much. It had many visiting and some permanent rabbis; amongst the latter were Michael Koenig, Walter Rothschild, Robert L. Lehmann, Eveline Goodman-Thau, and in 2004/5 Irit Shillor. In February 2004 it opened its own synagogue and community center, with the financial help of the city of Vienna and the Austrian government, in rent-free premises belonging to the Jewish community.

In 1992 President Klestil opened the Sephardi Center with two synagogues, a Bukharian and a Georgian one. In March 1993 the newly built synagogue of Innsbruck – which had about 40 members – was consecrated.

In June 1993 the Vienna Jewish community organized a large-scale commemoration of Aaron Menczer, the charismatic leader of Viennese Youth Aliyah, who was murdered in 1943 in Auschwitz. His surviving pupils unveiled a large memorial to Menczer in the foyer of the Stadttempel.

After the retirement of Chief Cantor Abraham Adler in 1993 the Jewish community took on Israeli-born Shmuel Barzilai, another first-rate chief cantor.

In September 1994, the Vienna Jewish community opened the Esra psychological and social case center, an outpatient center particularly for people suffering from the so-called Holocaust syndrome. In 2004 it celebrated its first ten years of existence with a main speech given by the new Social-Democrat Austrian president Heinz Fischer and publication of a Festschrift.

In June 1991 Vranitzky made a speech in Parliament, in which he fully acknowledged Austria's moral guilt and responsibility for the Nazi crimes – the first such speech by the head of an Austrian government. In 1993 an Austrian *Gedenkdienst* was founded, which gave young Austrians the opportunity to work at Holocaust memorial sites instead of doing compulsory military or civilian service. Up to 2002 about 150 young men and some women had worked in the framework of this service in 15 countries.

In 2001 the Archive for the Austrian Resistance (Dokumentationsarchiv des oesterreichischen Widerstands) finished a project to document the Austrian victims of the Holocaust. The names and data of 62,000 victims were published on their website and on a CD-ROM.

In 1998 the Austrian Parliament decided to inaugurate a commemoration day for the victims of racism and violence. The day is commemorated around May 5, the day of the liberation of the Austrian concentration camp Mauthausen.

The real estate tycoon Ariel Muzicant initiated the Austrian Historical Commission of the Republic of Austria. It was founded in 1998, headed by the distinguished judge and head of the Administrative Court Clemens Jabloner, and operated until 2003. In 47 projects, 160 historians were asked "to investigate and report on the whole complex of expropriation in Austria during the Nazi regime and on restitution and/or compensation (including other financial or social benefits) after 1945 by the Republic of Austria." All the reports were published by the German publisher Oldenbourg.

In several official statements the Austrian Republic promised – at last – to pay adequate compensation to the surviving Austrian victims of National Socialism. In summer 1995 a National Fund was established by the Austrian Parliament, which was endowed with 500 million ATS. It was directed by Hannah Lessing and paid about 20,000 Austrian victims of National Socialism 70,000 ATS as individual compensation and 80,000 ATS for stolen property and apartments.

In 1996 more than 600 art objects, whose owners could not be identified, were at last paid for by the Republic of Austria to the Jewish community. They were sold at the internationally acclaimed Mauerbach auction by Christie's (named for the former monastery where they were hidden). The proceeds of 155 million ATS were given to Jewish and some non-Jewish Holocaust victims.

In April 1998 Ariel Muzicant was elected president of the Vienna Jewish community. He was the first president born after the Holocaust. In 2002 he was reelected.

In November 1998 the synagogue of Vienna's Josefstadt district in the Neudeggergasse was reproduced in full size for six weeks in commemoration of the pogrom in November 1938. Former Jewish residents of the district were invited, a book was published, and a film was made by the Austrian filmmaker Käthe Kratz.

In June 1999 the Vienna Jewish community celebrated the 150th anniversary of its existence with a gathering of 1,300 people in the Vienna Burgtheater.

In October 2000 a monument to the Austrian victims of the Shoah, showing a stylized library of untitled books in a 70-sq.-m. space, designed by the British artist Rachel

Whiteread and initiated by Simon Wiesenthal, was unveiled on the historic Judenplatz in the heart of the city of Vienna. The Vienna Jewish museum opened a branch in the historic Mizrachi building on the Judenplatz. It showed a multimedia reconstruction of the Vienna Or Sarua synagogue, which was destroyed in the **Wiener Gesera* in 1420 and which was discovered in the course of the excavation of the monument. In 2000 the Mizrachi published a Festschrift about its first 100 years; in 2001 it began to organize a series of symposia on the history of the Jews of Vienna, in the course of which the first volume of the new edition of the talmudic commentary *Or Zaru'a* by Rabbi *Isaac ben Moses of Vienna was launched.

In November 2000 the newly built synagogue of Graz, the second largest city of Austria, was consecrated.

The square in front of the synagogue was named after Chief Rabbi David Herzog. The Graz Jewish community then had 135 members. At the University of Graz a Center for Jewish Studies was established.

In January 2001 the Vienna Jewish community celebrated the 175th anniversary of the historic Stadttempel together with President Thomas Klestil and tenor Neil Shicoff. In contrast to the jubilees in 1976 and 1988 they did not publish a Festschrift.

In June 2001 the Jewish community of Salzburg – which had 70–80 members – celebrated its 100th jubilee together with President Thomas Klestil. In 2004, at the University of Salzburg, a Center for Jewish Cultural Studies was founded.

In 1999 the Jewish community founded a Holocaust victim's information and support center. In 2000 the Austrian Reconciliation Fund was created in order to compensate forced laborers in the NS era. In January 2001 U.S. President Bill Clinton's deputy secretary of finance and chief negotiator for restitution Stuart *Eizenstat and the Austrian government agreed on the sum of $360 million. With this money the General Settlement Fund, which is administered by the National Fund, was created. The Fund received about 20,000 applications, but was still not effective. Austria demanded a legally binding guarantee that no further legal action would be taken by anyone for restitution, which was not possible because of several ongoing class actions in the U.S. In June 2002 the Jewish communities signed an agreement with the Austrian federal provinces, which pledged to pay 18.2 million Euro in the next five years as restitution for stolen community property. The city of Vienna promised to rebuild the premises of the historic Jewish Ha-Koaḥ sports club.

From 1945 until 1980 the community had to sell 170 of its 230 real estate properties in order to cover its deficit. After 1980 it had to apply for bank credit in order to cover its expenses. In 2003 the financial situation of the community became extremely difficult. Reports in the national and international press spoke about the possible closing down of the Jewish community. In the end the insolvency of the Jewish community was prevented through an advance payment of half of the Austrian provincial restitution money. Finally, in May 2005 an agreement was reached for payment of 18.2 million Euro by the Republic of Austria to the Vienna Jewish community, which therefore withdrew its applications to the General Settlement Fund.

Beginning in the 1980s, in Vienna and in the provinces a number of plaques or monuments commemorating destroyed synagogues or Jewish communities were erected. In November 2002 Austrian President Thomas Klestil unveiled a monument in memory of the 65,000 Austrian Holocaust victims in the hall of the Stadttempel.

In 2001 a Center for Austrian Studies, financed by the Austrian Society of the Friends of the Hebrew University, was opened at the Hebrew University. Its academic chair was Robert S. Wistrich; its first director was Professor Hanni Mittelmann.

In autumn 2003 the federal land of Lower Austria, the city of Baden, and the Jewish community of Vienna decided to finance the renovation of the historic synagogue in Baden near Vienna.

In February 2004 a rabbinical conference of the Chabad movement was held in Vienna, with more than a hundred rabbis participating. The guest of honor was Romano Prodi, head of the EU commission, who was personally blessed by the Ashkenazi chief rabbi of Israel, Yonah Metzger.

In July 2004 a square on the Vienna park ring was named after Theodor Herzl. Austria, Hungary, and Israel issued, uniquely, a joint and identical stamp with the portrait of Herzl. The city of Vienna held its fifth international Herzl Symposium.

In autumn 2004 the statutes of the Vienna Jewish community were changed and the federal association of the Austrian Jewish communities (Bundesverband der israelitischen Kultusgemeinden) became the Israelitische Religionsgesellschaft. This meant that instead of being an association it was now a state corporation (Koerperschaft des oeffentlichen Rechts).

In November 2004 the Vienna Jewish community had 6,894 members. It was estimated that altogether about 14,000 Jews lived in Austria.

COMMUNAL AND CULTURAL LIFE. From 1990 Chief Rabbi Chaim Eisenberg organized an annual cantorial concert with distinguished international cantors. In 1993 and 1994 they took place in the former synagogues of Mikulov (Nikolsburg) and Trebitsch in Moravia in order to help with their renovations. In spring 1992 a week of Jewish culture was for the first time part of the Vienna "*Festwochen*." It was organized in collaboration with the city of Vienna, and attracted over 10,000 people. From 1990 Vienna also had a Jewish street festival and annual Jewish film festival.

In 1991 a Jewish museum opened in Hohenems in the Austrian province of Vorarlberg; its director was Hanno Loewy. In November 1993 the Jewish Museum of the city of Vienna, which was initiated by the Vienna mayor Helmut Zilk, was opened in the historic Palais Eskeles in the heart of Vienna by the Vienna-born mayor of Jerusalem, Teddy Kollek. Its first director was the German-Jewish historian Julius H. Schoeps; his successor in 1998 was Karl-Albrecht Weinberger. The city of Vienna bought the famous Judaica collection of Max Berger for the museum. In November 1994 the library of the Vienna Jewish community (with 30,000 volumes) was reopened. It could be made public only with the aid of the Vienna Jewish Museum, which had the library on permanent loan.

ANTISEMITISM. When in October 1991 the Jewish cemetery of Vienna was desecrated, 10,000 people took part in a silent march against antisemitism in Vienna. In October 1992, the Jewish cemetery of Eisenstadt was desecrated and Chancellor Vranitzky and Paul Grosz attended a commemorative ceremony.

In spring 1991 Jörg Haider, the populist leader of the Freedom Party, praised the "decent and proper employment policies" in Nazi Germany, for which he was voted out of office as governor of Carinthia. A year later a committee of prominent artists and publicists organized a "concert for Austria" on the Heldenplatz in Vienna against rightist tendencies in Austrian politics. Elie *Wiesel was invited to speak from the huge balcony, the first person since Hitler to speak from there. Even more people – about 250,000 – took part in a "sea of lights" in January 1993 opposing a petition of Haider's Freedom Party against the immigration of foreigners, which was signed by 417,000 people, far fewer than expected.

In May 1992 the popular columnist of the country's most widely read daily *Neue Kronen Zeitung*, Richard Nimmerrichter, published two articles in which he asserted that relatively few Jews had been gassed and that anyone who survived Hitler would also survive Mr. Grosz, the president of the Vienna Jewish community. The Jewish community and Paul Grosz subsequently sued Nimmerrichter, winning partial victories in eight trials and getting the newspaper to moderate its tone.

In 1995 German television showed a video of a meeting of former SS-men in the Austrian village of Krumpendorf with Heinrich Himmler's daughter as guest of honor. At the meeting Jörg Haider praised the SS-men for having remained decent and despite enormous pressures loyal to their convictions until today.

Opinion polls throughout these years showed that the number of antisemites in the Austrian population can be estimated at 20%.

In 1994 and 1995, Austria was shocked by several neo-Nazi terrorist bombings. In December 1993, a letter bomb was sent to the popular Social Democrat mayor of Vienna, Helmut Zilk, which cost him his left hand and almost killed him. In the same week, letter bombs were sent to several politicians, journalists, and other people working for the integration of foreigners; three of them were injured. The letter bombs were sent by the mentally ill Austrian neo-Nazi and antisemite Franz Fuchs. He also planted a bomb which killed four gypsies. He was sentenced to life imprisonment and committed suicide.

In 1997 the monthly magazine *Wiener* published an article by Thomas Köpf entitled "Scandal in the Jewish Community, Good Business with a Bad Conscience," which was full of antisemitic stereotypes and phrases and illustrated with a red Magen David composed of bank notes. The Jewish community responded with a press conference and a court order and received an apology.

[Evelyn Adunka (2nd ed.)]

Austria-Israel Relations

The establishment of relations between Austria and Israel was involved with the question of whether the 1938 *Anschluss*, by which Austria became part of Nazi Germany, should influence the relations between the two countries. The government of Israel adopted the thesis that was at the basis of the Austrian "State Treaty"; that is, that Austria was the victim of Nazi aggression in 1938. However, the adoption of this policy encountered obstacles of public opinion in Israel arising out of Austria's identification with Germany. Great significance was ascribed to Austria's unsatisfactory response to Jewish claims for restitution and indemnification for crimes committed by the Nazi regime in Austria. This situation gradually changed as a result of Austria's friendly attitude to Israel in the context of the implementation of the "State Treaty," which imposed complete neutrality upon her. Austria's political stand at the UN, as well as in other international arenas, and her support of Israel during the *Six-Day War, contributed much to the development of friendly ties. Relations were established on a consular level almost immediately after the formation of the State of Israel. From 1956, normal diplomatic relations existed, which soon were on the ambassadorial level. Friendship leagues exist in the two states, as well as mutual chambers of commerce. Trade between Israel and Austria steadily increased since 1948. In 1968 Israel exported $6.8 million worth of goods to Austria, headed by citrus fruits (of which Israel was the main supplier to Austria) and phosphates and chemicals. Austria exported $6.2 million worth of goods to Israel, chiefly timber and machinery. By 2002 the figures had risen to $68 million (mostly manufactured goods) and $154 million, respectively.

[Yohanan Meroz]

Austria declared itself in favor of Security Council Resolution 242 of November 1967. It voted for the right of Yasser Arafat, then leader of the PLO, to address the United Nations General Assembly, but the Austrian delegation abstained on the vote to grant the PLO observer status at the UN.

The visit of Israel foreign minister Shimon Peres in November 1992 and his official invitation to President Klestil and Chancellor Vranitzky to Israel, together with the inauguration of several Austrian-Israeli projects, marked a new era in the relationship of the two countries.

In 1994 four leading Austrian politicians – President Thomas Klestil, Chancellor Franz Vranitzky, Vice Chancellor Erhard Busek, and the president of Parliament, Heinz Fischer – visited Israel. This demonstrated the excellent relations between Austria and Israel since Kurt Waldheim's presidency ended in 1992 (see above). In his capacity as Austria's science minister, Busek inaugurated a new chair for Austrian culture and history at the Hebrew University, named after the former archbishop of Vienna, Cardinal Franz Koenig. Vranitzky was awarded an honorary doctorate from the Hebrew University. In May 1995 a multifunctional encounter hall in the renovated high school in Reḥavia in Jerusalem was opened, which was financed by the Austrian branch of the Jerusalem Foundation on the initiative of Professor Leon Zelman of the Jewish Welcome Service. An Austrian committee for the support of Amcha, an organization for the psychological and social treatment of victims of the Holocaust, collected money for Simon Wiesenthal House in Ramat Gan.

In 1997 Prime Minister Benjamin Netanjahu visited Austria. During his visit in the Stadttempel he appealed to the Jews of Austria to immigrate to Israel.

In 2002 the Austrian minister for foreign affairs Benita Ferrero-Waldner and the secretary of state for the arts Franz Morak and the then president of Parliament Heinz Fischer visited Israel. In December 2003 the charge d'affaires of the state of Israel Avraham Toledo was appointed ambassador. (In 2000 Israel formerly withdrew its ambassador because of the inclusion of Jörg Haider's Freedom Party in the Austrian government.) In October 2004 the first state visit of an Israeli president took place in Austria. During four days President Moshe *Katzav visited amongst other places the Stadttempel and the Mauthausen concentration camp.

[Evelyn Adunka (2nd ed.)]

BIBLIOGRAPHY: J. Fraenkel (ed.), *The Jews of Austria. Essays on their Life, History and Destruction* (1967), includes bibliography; S. Eidelberg, *Jewish Life in Austria in the XVth Century…* (1962); D. van Arkel, *Anti-semitism in Austria* (1966); P.G.J. Pulzer, *Rise of Political Anti-semitism in Germany and Austria* (1964); idem, in: *Journal of Central European Affairs*, 23 (1963), 131–42; R.A. Kann, *Study in Austrian Intellectual History* (1960); idem, in; JSOS, 10 (1948), 239–56; Silberner, in: HJ, 13 (1951), 121–39; J.S. Bloch, *Reminiscences* (1927); Freud, in: BLBI, 3 (1960), 80–100; J. von Wertheimer, *Juden in Oesterreich*, 2 vols. (1892); J.E. Scherer, *Rechtsverhaeltnisse der Juden in den deutsch-oesterreichischen Laendern* (1901); N.M. Gelber, *Aus zwei Jahrhunderten* (1924); S. Baron, *Judenfrage auf dem Wiener Kongress* (1920); M.J. Kohler, *Jewish Rights at the Congress of Vienna…* (1918); S. Krauss, *Wiener Geserah vom Jahre 1421* (1920); L. Moses, *Juden in Niederoesterreich* (1935); *Festschrift zur Feier des 50jährigen Bestandes der Union oesterreichischer Juden* (1937); I. Smotricz, *Mahpekhat 1848 be-Ostriyyah* (1957); Y. Toury, *Mahpekhah u-Mehumah be-1848* (1967), index. HOLOCAUST: T. Guttmann, *Dokumentenwerk…*, 2 vols. (1943–45); O. Karbach, in: JSOS, 2 (1940), 255–78; H. Rosenkranz, in: *Yad Vashem Bulletin*, 14 (1964), 35–43; idem: *Kristallnacht in Oesterreich* (1968); H. Gold, *Geschichte der Juden in Wien* (1966); H. Gold, *Geschichte der Juden in Oesterreich* (1971); G. Reitlinger, *The Final Solution* (1953), index; R. Hilberg, *Destruction of the European Jews* (1961), index; H.G. Adler, *Theresienstadt* (Ger., 1960[2]); I. Friedmann, in: JSOS, 27 (1965), 147–67, 236, 249; J. Moser, *Die Judenverfolgung in Oesterreich 1938–1945* (1966). POSTWAR PERIOD: F. Wilder-Okladek, *The Return-Movement of Jews to Austria after the Second World War* (1969); A. Tartakower, *Shivtei Yisrael*, 2 (1966), 315–23; Y. Bauer, *Flight and Rescue* (1970); L.O. Schmelz, in: *Deuxième colloque sur la vie juive dans l'Europe contemporaire* (Eng. 1967). **ADD. BIBLIOGRAPHY:** T. Albrich, *Wir lebten wie sie. Juedische Lebensgeschichten aus Tirol und Vorarlberg* (1999); H. Brettl, *Die juedische Gemeinde von Frauenkirchen* (2003); D.A. Binder, G. Reitter, and H. Ruetgen, *Judentum in einer antisemitischen Umwelt. Am Beispiel der Stadt Graz 1918–1938* (1988); K.H. Burmeister (ed.), *Rabbiner Dr. Aron Tänzer. Gelehrter und Menschenfreund 1871–1937* (1987); D. Ellmauer, H. Embacher, and A. Lichtblau (eds.), *Geduldet, geschmaeht und vertrieben. Salzburger Juden erzählen* (1998); H. Embacher (ed.), *Juden in Salzburg. History, Cultures, Facts* (2002); M.M. Feingold (ed.), *Ein Ewiges Dennoch. 125 Jahre Juden in Salzburg* (1993); D. Herzog, *Erinnerungen eines Rabbiners 1882–1940* (1995); Israelitische Kultusgemeinde Graz, *Geschichte der Juden in Suedost-Oesterreich* (1988); R. Kropf (ed.), *Juden im Grenzraum* (1993); G. Lamprecht (ed.), *Juedisches Leben in der Steiermark* (2004); A. Lang, B. Tobler, and G. Tschoegl (eds.), *Vertrieben. Erinnerungen burgenlaendischer Juden und Juedinnnen* (2004); E. Lappin (ed.), *Juedische Gemeinden. Kontinuitaeten und Brueche* (2202); A. Lichtblau (ed.), *Als haetten wir dazugehoert. Oesterreichisch-juedische Lebensgeschichten aus der Habsburgermonarchie* (1999); C. Lind, *…es gab so nette Leute dort. Die zerstoerte juedische Gemeinde St. Poelten* (1998); idem, *…sind wir doch in unserer Heimat als Landmenschen aufgewachsen…. Der Landsprengel der Israelitischen Kultusgemeinde St. Poelten* (2002); idem, *Der letzte Jude hat den Tempel verlassen. Juden in Niederoesterreich 1938–1945* (2004); G. Milchram, *Heilige Gemeinde Neunkirchen* (2000); P. Schwarz, *Tulln ist judenrein!* (1997); W. Neuhauser-Pfeiffer and K. Ransmaier, *Vergessene Spuren. Die Geschichte der Juden in Steyr* (1993); F. Polleroß (ed.), *Die Erinnerung tut zu weh. Juedisches Leben uns Antisemitismus im Waldviertel* (1996); J. Reiss (ed.), *Aus den sieben Gemeinden* (1997); W. Sotill, *Es gibt nur einen Gott und eine Menschheit. Graz und seine juedischen Mitbuerger* (2001); S. Spitzer (ed.), *Beitraege zur Geschichte der Juden im Burgenland* (1994); S. Spitzer, *Die juedische Gemeinde von Deutschkreuz* (1995); S. Spitzer, *Bne Chet. Die oesterreichischen Juden im Mittelalter* (1997); R. Streibel, *Ploetzlich waren sie alle weg. Die Juden der ‚Gauhauptstadt Krems' und ihre Mitbuerger.* (1991); W. Wadl, *Geschichte der Juden in Kaernten in Mittelalter* (1981); A. Walzl, *Die Juden in Kärnten und das Dritte Reich* (1987).

For further bibliography see *Vienna.

AUSUBEL, DAVID PAUL (1918–), U.S. educator and psychiatrist, who contributed significantly to the study of psychological factors in the development of ethnic culture. Born in Brooklyn, New York, Ausubel began his career as a practicing physician and psychiatrist, especially concerned with drug addiction; he became senior psychiatrist at Buffalo State Hospital in 1947. He taught psychology at Long Island University and psychiatry at Yeshiva University. In 1950 he became head of the Bureau of Educational Research at the University of Illinois. In 1957 Ausubel was awarded a Fulbright research grant for study in New Zealand. There he continued his work in psychological development by comparative cross-cultural research on the Maori ethnic minority. The resulting books, *The Fern and the Tiki, an American View of New Zealand* (1960) and *Maori Youth, a Psychoethnological Study of Cultural Deprivation* (1961), expressed his belief that educational malfunctioning could result from cultural deprivation, and that the systematic use of culture as a variable in psychological research is of primary significance.

Ausubel developed the theory of significant learning, one of the basic concepts of modern constructivism. It applies to the cognitive concept of learning, where a person interacts with his or her surroundings and tries to give meaning to what he or she perceives.

BIBLIOGRAPHY: In 1963 he wrote *The Psychology of Meaningful Verbal Learning*. Other books by Ausubel include *School Learning* (1969); *Ego Psychology and Mental Disorder* (1977); *Theory and Problems of Adolescent Development* (1978); *What Every Well-Informed Person Should Know about Drug Addiction* (1980); and *The Acquisition and Retention of Knowledge* (2000).

[Ronald E. Ohl / Ruth Beloff (2nd ed.)]

AUSUBEL, NATHAN (1899–1986), U.S. author and folklorist. Born in Galicia, he went to the U.S. as a small child. Ausubel published anthological works. His popular collection, *A Treasury of Jewish Folklore* (1948), went through over 20 editions, and was followed by further anthologies, all of which included useful contributions in the form of prefaces, summaries, and notes by the editor. Among his many compilations are *A Treasury of Jewish Humor* (1951) and *A Pictorial History of the Jewish People* (1953). He wrote *The Book of Jewish Knowledge* (1964).

[David Niv]

AUTHORITY, RABBINICAL, the authority of the halakhic scholars in maintaining the creativeness and development of Jewish law, by means of its legal sources.

Development of the Law

An important tenet of Judaism and a guiding principle of the halakhists is that, together with the Written Law (*Torah she-bi-khetav*), Moses received also the *Oral Law (*Torah she-be-al peh*) (Meg. 19b), the latter, within its wider meaning, embracing all the *halakhah* not explicit in the Written Law (Sifra Beḥukotai 8:12). However, the talmudic sages themselves clearly distinguished between that part of the Oral Law based on a tradition handed down from generation to generation, from the time of Moses who received it from God Himself (Avot 1:1; ARN[1] 1:1; Maim., Yad, Mamrim 1:1–2), and the other parts of the Oral Law, created and developed by the halakhic scholars. The sages of the Midrash in answer to the question whether Moses learned the whole Torah in 40 days while he was on Mt. Sinai, answered that "God taught Moses the principles" (Ex. R. 41:6). These words are interpreted by Joseph *Albo to mean that "the law of God cannot be (given) in complete form so as to be adequate for all times… and therefore at Sinai Moses was given general principles… by means of which the sages in every generation may formulate the details as they present themselves" (*Ikkarim*, 3:23). A study of the statements of the halakhic scholars reveals that just as they emphasized in unequivocal terms the supra-human and divine nature of the source of *halakhah*, so too – and with the same degree of emphasis – they insisted upon the human element, the exclusive authority of the halakhic scholars to continue to develop and shape the *halakhah*. This dual image of *halakhah* finds expression in two basic and apparently contradictory dicta: on the one hand, the basic tenet that "the Torah is from Heaven" (*Torah min ha-Shamayim*) – on the other, the principle that "the Torah is not in Heaven" (*Torah lo ba-Shamayim*; BM 59b based on Deut. 30:12; Maim., Yad, Yesodei ha-Torah 9:4). In other words, the source of the *halakhah* is divine, but its place, its life, development, and formation, is with mankind, in the life of society. The halakhic scholars saw no inconsistency in these two principles, believing as they did that in their exegesis, enactments, innovations, and creativeness, they were merely giving practical expression to a further unfolding of the revelation at Sinai, destined from the beginning for the needs of each particular generation (Ex. R. 28:6; Tanḥ. Yitro 11).

Authority of the Halakhic Scholars

Even in the written law problems are encountered to which no solutions are given within the framework of the existing law – such as the case of the blasphemer (Lev. 24:10–16), the gatherer of sticks on the Sabbath (Num. 15:32–36), and the inheritance of the daughters of Zelophehad (Num. 27:1–11; 36:1–10) – but are explicitly made known by God to Moses. On the other hand, a number of biblical passages, particularly Deuteronomy 17:8–13, enjoin that a decision for every future problem, whether arising from a precept governing man's relationship with the Divine, or with his fellow man, must be sought at the hands of "the priest, the levite, and the judge," sitting at the particular time in the midst of the people, in judgment over them. This combination of priest, levite, and judge was designed to ensure, according to the halakhic interpretation, that the law should be determined by teachers and judges deciding according to their human knowledge and understanding, since the function of the priest and levite was to instruct and teach the people (cf. Deut. 33:10; Ezek. 44:23–24; Mal. 2:7; Josephus' reference to the prophet (Ant., 4:218) within the context of Deuteronomy 17:9 is contrary to the plain meaning of the text). Hence, when in the course of time the teaching of the law ceased to be the exclusive function of the priests and levites, it was decided that while it was proper for priests and levites to be members of the *bet din*, their absence would not affect its competence (Sif. Deut. 153).

Authority in Deciding the *Halakhah*

The prophet in his function as a bearer of the divine vision is assigned no part in determining the *halakhah*. "'These are the commandments – henceforth a prophet may no longer make any innovations" (Sifra 27:34). A halakhic rule that is forgotten may not be recalled by means of "divine spirit" but by way of study and logical reasoning (Tem. 16a; see Maim., intro. to Comm. to the Mishnah).

The sages of the Talmud carried this basic conception concerning the exclusive authority to interpret the Torah and continue its development to an extreme but inevitable conclusion – "even if they tell you that left is right and right is left – hearken unto their words" (Comm. on Deut. 17:10,

11; Mid. Tan. to *ibid.*; Sif. Deut. 154 et al.; cf. the version in TJ, Hor. 1:1, 45d: "until they tell you that right is right and left is left." For a reconciliation between the texts see Abrabanel to Deut. *ibid.; Divrei David* (of David b. Samuel ha-Levi, author of the *Turei Zahav*) ad loc.; D. Hoffman, in Bibliography. It is possible that the two versions are related to the conflicting views between R. Kahana and R. Eliezer concerning the **Zaken Mamre* (Sanh. 88a)). Thus the *halakhah* is so identified with its scholars and tradents that even their errors are binding as *halakhah* – a notion clearly expressed by Naḥmanides (Comm. on Deut. *ibid.*; see also Nissim Girondi, *Derashot ha-Ran*, nos. 7 and 11). This twofold principle of the exclusive authority of the halakhic scholars and of excluding any supra-human influence on the determination of the *halakhah* is vividly exemplified in the well-known *aggadah* of the dispute between R. Eliezer b. Hyrcanus and R. Joshua b. Hananiah and his colleagues concerning the "oven of Aknai" (BM 59b). Although a heavenly voice (*bat kol*) came forth to confirm the correctness of the former's minority opinion, R. Joshua refused to concede, countering with the argument that the Torah "is not in Heaven," "the Torah has already been given… embracing the rule that the majority must be followed" (Ex. 23:2). The *aggadah* concludes that even God accepted the majority view, and "rejoiced that His children had vanquished Him." Thus the absolute truth may be according to the opinion of an individual and the majority may err, but the halakhic truth lies with the majority opinion, since the *halakhah* was entrusted to the scholars, whose decision is accepted, as it were, by the Lawgiver Himself. It is true that some scholars took a contrary view, attributing a certain influence to supra-human authority in the determination of the *halakhah*, particularly with regard to the visions of the prophets, whose halakhic statements were interpreted as the Torah itself. Even after prophecy had ceased there were scholars who attached significance to supra-human influence, as illustrated in the *aggadot* of the *bat kol* intervening in the above-mentioned dispute and in that between Bet Hillel and Bet Shammai (Er. 13b). These must be seen, however, as the opinion of individual scholars, and it is clear that the opinion of Joshua prevailed, that "no attention is paid to a *bat kol*" (Ber. 52a; Pes. 114a). Maimonides (introd. to Yad.) assigns to the prophets and their courts an honorable place as links in the chain of tradition of halakhic transmission, stressing however that this was by virtue of the prophets' functioning as scholars and not in the role of prophets, and he explains that "the prophet does not come to make law but to command about the precepts of the Torah, to warn people that they shall not transgress them." A prophet who claimed divine instruction as to what was law or the *halakhah*, was to be branded "a false prophet" (Yad., Yesodei ha-Torah 9:1–4), from which it follows that "even if a thousand prophets, all of them equal to Elijah and Elisha, should hold to a reasoned opinion, and a thousand and one scholars reason otherwise, the majority must yet be followed" and the *halakhah* decided according to the words of the latter (Yad. introd.). Some seven centuries later Aryeh Leib b. Joseph ha-Kohen succinctly summarized the matter, stating: "The Torah was not given to the angels, but to man who possesses human intelligence… the Torah was given to be determined by human intelligence, even if human intelligence errs… and the truth is determined by the agreement of the sages by using human intelligence" (introd. to *Keẓot ha-Ḥoshen* to Sh. Ar., ḤM).

Authority in Every Generation

This guiding principle in the *Weltanschauung* of the halakhists dictated the development of the *halakhah* in all its history. From time to time there emerged new spiritual centers of the Jewish people. When Jabneh became such a center, after the destruction of the Temple, it was laid down that the court there was to be the central determining authority (Sif. Deut. 153), and Yose ha-Gelili explains the words "in those days" in that verse (Deut. 17:9) as referring to "a competent judge functioning at the particular time" (Sif. Deut. 153). The possibility is recognized that future scholars might not be as wise as their predecessors; nevertheless contemporary scholars and judges should be regarded with the same esteem as those of past generations and "whoever is appointed leader of the community, even if he be the least worthy, is to be regarded with the same esteem as the mightiest of earlier generations." Moreover, "Say not, 'How was it that the former days were better than these?' for it is not out of wisdom that you enquire concerning this" (RH 25b based on Eccles. 7:10; Tosef. RH 2:3). The enduring continuity and vitality of the *halakhah* dictate that the scholars of each generation exercise the authority conferred on them in the cause of its continued creativity and development, and to refrain from using such authority, or to question it, on the grounds that the wisdom of later scholars does not match that of their precursors, would show lack of understanding.

Evolution of the *Halakhah*

The halakhic scholars exercised the authority given them by the basic norms of the *halakhah* – i.e., Written Torah, in certain established ways, recognized by the halakhic system itself for the purpose of its own evolution, i.e., by utilizing *halakhah's* legal sources. The primary legal source is *Midrash (i.e., interpretation and construction), various modes of which were employed to find solutions to new problems, first by interpretation of the written law and thereafter of the Mishnah and successive halakhic sources (see *Interpretation). When interpretation offered no means of a solution, or the proffered solution provided no answer to contemporary requirements, a second legal source was used: namely, legislation or enactment by way of the *takkanah* and *gezerah* (see **Takkanot*). Other legal sources employed were **minhag* (custom), *ma'aseh* (precedent), and *sevara* (legal logic). In pursuing, by means of the above-mentioned legal sources, their task of fashioning the *halakhah* – which gave order to daily vicissitudes of life, while itself being shaped by them – the halakhic scholars clung to a twofold objective. On the one hand they maintained an unswerving concern for the continued evolution and development of the *halakhah*, and, on the other, for the great and onerous responsibility of preserving its spirit, orientation, and continuity.

The Rule of "*Hilkheta Ke-Vatra'ei*"

The substantive rule of "*hilkheta ke-vatra'ei*" (i.e., that "the law is according to later halakhic scholars") was a development of the post-talmudic period, endorsed by the fundamental principle of the halakhic scholars' authority. In the history of the *halakhah*, the terms "*rishonim*" and "*aḥaronim*" are commonly accepted as signifying the scholars from the middle of the 11th to the 16th centuries and those from the 16th century onward, respectively. These terms, however, are also applied to halakhic scholars prior to the 11th century to indicate not only their chronological order but also the greater authority halakhically attributed to earlier scholars as compared with later ones. R. Johanan stated: "The hearts of the *rishonim* were like the door of the *ulam* ('the larger hall of the Temple') and those of the *aḥaronim* like the door of the *heikhal* ('the smaller hall') but ours are like the eye of a fine needle." *Abbaye, *Rava, and Rav *Ashi compared with even more modesty their own standing with that of earlier scholars (Er. 53a). **Amoraim* were not permitted to dispute statements of the **tannaim*, a relationship of deference preserved in turn by the **geonim* and the *rishonim* and *aḥaronim* of the rabbinic period toward their respective predecessors.

The high regard paid to the statements of earlier scholars did not prevent Jewish law from developing in the course of time an important rule, essential for the purpose of bestowing authority on contemporary scholars to decide the *halakhah* according to the prevailing circumstances and problems of their time. This rule – that the law is according to later scholars – dates from the geonic period. It laid down that until the time of Abbaye and Rava, i.e., the middle of the fourth century C.E., the *halakhah* – in case of any difference of opinion among the scholars – was to be decided according to the views of the earlier scholars rather than those of later dissenting scholars; from the time of Abbaye and Rava onward and also in case of disputes among the post-talmudic scholars, the opinions of later scholars would prevail over the contrary opinions of an earlier generation in deciding the *halakhah* (Asher b. Jehiel, *Piskei ha-Rosh*, BM 3:10; 4:21; Shab. 23:1). Certain sources render this rule applicable also to the period preceding Abbaye and Rava (see L. Ginzberg, *Geonica*, 2 (1909), 21–22, 32). The principle of *hilkheta ke-vatra'ei* is applicable also when a pupil dissents from his teacher (Resp. Maharik, 84; Malachi b. Jacob ha-Kohen, *Yad Malakhi*, no. 17) and even when an individual disputes the views of a number of earlier scholars (*Yad Malakhi*, no. 169; *Pitḥei Teshuvah* no. 8, Sh. Ar., ḤM 25).

Among the reasons advanced for this rule are those of Asher ben Jehiel. "All matters not elucidated in the Talmud, as compiled by Rav Ashi and Ravina, may be controverted and reconstructed even when the statements of the *geonim* are dissented from… The statements of later scholars carry primary authority because they knew the reasoning of earlier scholars as well as their own, and took it into consideration in making their decision" (*Piskei ha-Rosh*, Sanh. 4:6; idem, 55:9); Joseph *Colon gives the somewhat similar reason that since the later scholars knew of the statements of earlier scholars and deliberated them, yet did not heed them, "it is a sign that they knew that the statements of earlier scholars were not to be relied upon in the particular matter" (Resp. Maharik, 84). So, too, various reasons were given as to why this rule was only relevant from the time of Abbaye and Rava onward, one view being that from their time onward pupils learned not only the system of their own teacher but other systems as well, and therefore the pupils' decision was to be preferred (Colon, *ibid.*); in the *tosafot* (Kid. 45b) the view is given that later scholars "took greater pains to present the *halakhah* in a sound form."

It follows from the above-mentioned reasons that the rule of *hilkheta ke-vatra'ei* only applied when the later scholar had considered the statements of his predecessor, and, after weighing them, was able to prove the correctness of his opposing view in ways acceptable to his contemporaries (*Piskei ha-Rosh, ibid.*; Resp. Maharik, 94). Thus, too, the rule was accepted by *Isserles as a guiding principle in deciding Jewish law (to Sh. Ar., ḤM 25:2). Some of the scholars, particularly among the *aḥaronim*, laid down several additional reservations concerning the operation of the rule. The rule should not be understood as diminishing in any way the esteem in which scholars of an earlier generation were held by later ones, but rather as inspiring the later **posek* (decider) to reach his decision with a sense of responsibility, awe, and humility, once having reached his conclusion, the *halakhah* was as he and not as earlier scholars had decided.

On the meaning of the rule that "a *bet din* may not set aside the ruling of another *bet din* unless it exceeds the latter in wisdom and standing," and the resultant conclusions, see **Takkanot*.

BIBLIOGRAPHY: Z.H. Chajes, *Torat ha-Nevi'im* (1836), ch. 1 = his: *Kol Sifrei Mahariẓ Ḥayyut*, 1 (1958); D. Hoffmann, *Der Oberste Gerichtshof…* (1878), 9–13; M. Tchernowitz, *Toledot ha-Halakhah*, 1, pt. 1 (1934), 67–111; ET, 9 (1959), 341–5; Urbach, in: *Tarbiz*, 18 (1946/47), 1–27; Elon, in: ILR, 2 (1967), 550–61.

[Menachem Elon]

AUTO DA FÉ ("Act of Faith"), name given in Portugal to the ceremony of the pronouncing of judicial sentence by the Inquisition and the "reconciliation" of penitents: the corresponding Spanish form is "Auto de Fé," the Italian "Atto di Fede," etc. While the torture, the trial, and the testimony of the Inquisition were conducted in complete secrecy, the auto de fé ceremony was generally held with great pomp in a principal church or central square, in the presence of the chief dignitaries and great crowds (for further details see *Inquisition). Such an auto de fé was called *Auto público general*. At the *Auto particular* only the inquisitors were present. Other types of autos de fé were *Auto singular*, involving one individual, and the *Autillo*, which was held on the site of the Inquisition, in the presence of the Inquisitors and some special guests. The

Inquisition imposed a variety of punishments, ranging from imprisonment, confiscation of property, and death. The burning of heretics did not strictly form part of the auto da fé, since the church did not desire to be formally associated with the shedding of blood. Those adjudged guilty were instead "relaxed" (i.e., handed over) to the secular authorities who were responsible for their execution at the place of burning (*quemadero*), sometimes outside the town. The condemned persons were dressed in special garb, the *sanbenito*. A procession was formed which moved to the location of the auto de fé. A feature of the autos was the delivery of vituperative sermons by some eminent cleric; these were frequently published and 70 are extant that were delivered in Portugal alone between 1612 and 1749. In Portugal the programs of the autos with names of those who appeared in them (*listas*) were published in uniform quarto form: in Spain, less regularly, and mainly in octavo. The earliest auto of the Spanish Inquisition took place in Seville in 1481, the latest recorded in Valencia in 1826. All told, some 2,000 autos took place in the Peninsula and its dependencies between these two dates. The total number of those who appeared runs into hundreds of thousands, many of whom were however charged with offenses carrying less stringent penalties, such as bigamy. Those who suffered the death penalty have been reckoned at upward of 30,000. These however, include not only *Marranos and Crypto-Jews, but also Protestants, Crypto-Muslims, and others.

BIBLIOGRAPHY: H.C. Lea, *History of the Inquisition of Spain*, 4 vols. (1906–08); E.N. Adler, *Auto de fé and Jew* (1908); Glaser, in: HUCA, 27 (1956), 327–85; Shunami, Bibl, nos. 1392, 2435–36, 2478; Roth, Marranos, passim.

[Cecil Roth / Yom Tov Assis (2nd ed.)]

AUTOGRAPHS. Jews occupy a prominent place among founders and owners of autograph collections. Although collections of Hebrew manuscripts, and of manuscripts of Jewish contents in other languages, have been in existence for many centuries, a special systematic Jewish autograph collection is of fairly recent origin. Its creation is largely the work of Avraham Sharon (Schwadron), who spent some 30 years on it, and by 1928 had succeeded in establishing a universal Jewish collection, consisting of over 2,900 autographs of c. 1,950 prominent personalities of Jewish origin. This collection covers, approximately, the period from 1480 to the present. In 1927 it was presented as a gift to the Jewish National and University Library in Jerusalem, which then proceeded to open an autograph and portrait section. The collection represents a valuable source for Jewish graphology, especially of the Hebrew script, and it contains documents which by their contents are of great significance for Jewish cultural history. Today the collection contains more than 12,000 autographs and 700 portraits.

The scientific value of a Jewish autograph collection is to be found in the means that it provides for the identification of manuscripts whose authors are unknown, as well as of forgeries (the latter being quite frequent in the case of rabbinical and ḥasidic autographs). Special difficulties were encountered in locating the autographs of Jewish personalities of Eastern Europe, particularly those whose activities were restricted to the Jewish sphere; among other reasons the reluctance to part with such autographs stems from the belief that a letter of a great rabbi or *ẓaddik* has the power of warding off evil, and often such a document would be buried with its owner. Autographs of the early Jewish socialists and revolutionaries in Eastern Europe are also very rare, as they were frequently destroyed, either out of fear of the police, or by the police itself. Older manuscripts originating in Eastern Europe, insofar as they have come to light, are usually in a poor condition. In the West, on the other hand, the systematic collection of autographs and the trade in them have tended to ensure their retention and proper preservation.

BIBLIOGRAPHY: EIV, 1 (1962), 758ff.; EJ, 3 (1929), 748ff.; B. Wachstein, in: *Menorah* (Vienna), 5 (1927), 689–94; A. Schwadron, *Ketuvim* (1927), nos. 29–31; idem, in: *New Palestine*, 14, no. 2 (1928), 35–36.

[Abraham Schwadron (Sharon)]

AUTONOMISM. A term coined by Simon *Dubnow in 1901 to designate a theory and conception of Jewish nationalism in the Diaspora, based on a specific view of Jewish history. This gave rise to a program for the future of the Jews, who were to be politically and territorially members of the states in which they were dispersed but at the same time exist as a national-cultural entity.

The Theory

At the basis of Autonomism is the view that in "the evolution of national types… we can distinguish the following stages…: (1) the tribal…; (2) the territorial-political…; (3) the cultural, historical, or spiritual…" (S. Dubnow, *Nationalism and History…* (1958), 76). The Jewish nation is regarded as exemplifying the development of this third stage: "This people, after it had passed through the stages of tribal nationalism, ancient culture, and political territory, was able to establish itself and fortify itself on the highest stage, the spiritual and historical-cultural, and succeeded in crystallizing itself as a spiritual people that draws the sap of its existence from a natural or intellectual 'will to live'" (*ibid.*, 84–85). In the view of the Autonomists, this development within Jewry has a general historical significance, for to reach this third stage and continue to exist in it is a "rigid test for the maturity of a nation…. Such a people has reached the highest stage of cultural-historical individuality and may be said to be indestructible, if only it cling forcefully to its national will…. We find only one instance… of a people that has survived for thousands of years despite dispersion and loss of homeland. This unique people is the people of Israel" (*ibid.*, 80).

The survival of the Jewish people in this "third and ultimate stage" of national existence was brought about in the Diaspora through the strength of "the chain of *autonomy – the essential source of power of the Jewish communities in all lands. Were it not for this chain… Israel would not have survived all these generations after the destruction of its state and its land. The secret of national survival is dependent on the positive command of the ancient prophecy, 'the scepter shall not depart from Judah' (Gen. 49:10). It is indeed possible to say that kingship never ceased in Israel. It merely shed one form to assume another.... The state is destroyed and the national body separates into its parts – the communities. In this way the people build for themselves in every place something like a kingdom in miniature. Our enemies... in modern times... call it 'a state within a state.' But the congregation of Israel goes on in its historical path and says: 'Indeed, a state within a state,' an internal autonomous group within an external political group and the nature of things sanctions it" (*ibid.*, 48–49). On this basis Dubnow insisted – in opposition to both the Zionist view as he understood it and to the assimilationist view – that it is only "the Autonomists [who] recognize Jewry, not only as a nation of the past or of the future, but also as a nation that is of the present, which has never ceased to exist and which will never cease to exist in time to come" (*ibid.*, 167). The Autonomists conceive that Jewry is a nation in spite of and in the fact of its dispersion throughout many countries and amid many peoples.

Although the Autonomist theory is based on an overall view of Jewish history, its application and even its theoretical premises are in reality limited by the European outlook of its founders. This is apparent in the intrinsic nexus between Autonomism and *Yiddish. Dubnow stated that "among the forces which are the basis of our autonomy in the Diaspora I also set aside a place for the powerful force of the folk language used by seven million Jews in Russia and Galicia.... Insofar as we recognize the merit of national existence in the Diaspora, we must also recognize the merit of Yiddish as one of the instruments of autonomy, together with Hebrew and the other factors in our national culture" (*ibid.*, 51). In practice, Yiddish was the only cultural factor stressed by most Autonomists and in the main they were concerned solely with Jewish problems in Europe.

The Program

The European centrism of the Autonomists was also conditioned by the fact that even their theory was founded on their prognosis for the future development of states within Europe, particularly those areas where the greatest masses of Jews were then concentrated. They believed that the concept of statehood in Europe must logically lead to the autonomy of various nationalities within the framework of a "multinational state," such as was bound to evolve from the struggle for cohesion within the vast complexes of *Austro-Hungary and czarist *Russia. In its resolution of 1890 the "Austrian school of Social Democracy" formulated a program for an autonomous coexistence of the separate nationalities within Austro-Hungary. Otto *Bauer stated the theoretical foundation of this policy in his *Die Nationalitaetenfrage und die Sozialdemokratie* (Vienna, 1907). This is the background to Dubnow's affirmation "that Jewish nationalism... is concerned with only one thing: protecting the national individuality [of the Jewish people] and safeguarding its autonomous development in all states" (*ibid.*, 97). On the basis of what he considered the immanent tendency of the past and the victorious trend of the future, Dubnow thought that "the chief axiom of Jewish autonomy may thus be formulated as follows: Jews in each and every country who take an active part in civic and political life enjoy all rights given to the citizens, not merely as individuals but also as members of their national groups" (*ibid.*, 137). Since it was impossible to evade the fact that the Jews did not live in a single compact territory even within one state, the Autonomists had to insist on "personal autonomy" to be granted to the communities scattered throughout a given state.

The policy of the Autonomists was accepted by the Folkspartei, the Sejmists and, after lengthy hesitation, by the *Bund. Although Zionism never accepted the Autonomist doctrine, in its program of "*Gegenwartsarbeit*" (as formulated at the *Helsingfors Conference, 1906) – especially in Eastern Europe – the movement shared most of the goals of its policy.

After World War I the realization of Autonomist hopes seemed ensured by the affirmation of *minority rights by the peace treaties and the autonomous institutions established in the Baltic states and the U.S.S.R. The blatant infringement of these rights, however, in the 1930s and later the *Holocaust put an end to the existential foundation of Autonomism. Theoretically the philosophy is as valid or invalid as before; in practice neither the philosophy nor the policies based on it have any force in the thinking or the aspirations of the Jewish people today.

BIBLIOGRAPHY: K. Pinson, in: S. Dubnow, *Nationalism and History* (1958), 3–65.

[Haim Hillel Ben-Sasson]

AUTONOMY, the religious, legal, social, and cultural self-sufficiency of the Jewish community within the sovereign non-Jewish state or its subdivision; Jewish self-government. Jewish autonomy was conditioned by both external and internal forces. By definition it did not exist during the periods of political sovereignty in the days of the Jewish independent states. During the periods of Persian and Greco-Roman subjugation the Jews enjoyed considerable self-government, especially in the form of *polyteuma*, an autonomous community within the Hellenistic city, as in *Alexandria. Throughout the Middle Ages, when European society generally was constituted of distinct corporate groups each with its own way of life, the Jews were also governed by their own laws and institutions. The Christian authority in the lands of Europe, whether emperor, king, pope, duke, or municipality, as well as the Muslim caliph or other ruler, granted them various privileges of serf-rule. These dealt mainly with their rights of commerce, moneylending, or litigation with Gentiles. The internal political and social life of the Jews was left inviolate. The basic Christian legal concept permitted the Jews to live according to their law (*secundum legem eorum vivere*). In Islam the very idea of the "People of the Book" predicated the toleration of Jews and Christians to live according to their respective sacred scriptures. The trend toward civic emancipation and the onset of the Enlightenment (*Haskalah) movement within Judaism in the 18th century tended to curtail group autonomy in favor of the rights of the individual. The tendency was afforded external stimulus by the insistence of the modern state on the complete allegiance of its citizens, demanding the elimination of corporations. The 20th century has seen brief experimentation with a special form of self-rule based on *minority rights, only to witness the dissolution of Jewish autonomy in its traditional form in many places. In countries with a pluralistic society, such as the United States, a new, voluntary Jewish internal leadership structure is emerging.

Throughout more than 2½ millennia powerful internal forces bolstered the Jewish autonomous institutions. Most pronounced were the religious element and national cohesion. From their law the Jews evolved a unique way of living, a regimen of holiness and pietism; the freedom to practice it was cherished above life. The messianic hope for eventual political sovereignty was never abandoned. The Jews clung to the eschatological vision of redemption from **galut* ("exile") and of national revival and reunification in Ereẓ Israel. The basic institutions of Jewish self-government were developed in ancient times: the congregation, which enabled ten adult males anywhere to form a viable group; the association (see **Ḥevrah*); the court of justice; and self-taxation. According to the formulation of *Saadiah b. Joseph, the Jews formed "a nation by virtue of their laws." No matter how far the Jews exerted themselves to observe the talmudic rule that "the law of the land is law" (BK 113a), they still clung tenaciously to their autonomous institutions. They also preferred physical segregation from the other religious, ethnic, and professional groups among whom they lived. Topographical isolation enabled them to enjoy the religious, educational, and social advantages of contiguous living. Moreover, the instinct for self-preservation dictated communal solidarity, a united front to face the often hostile outside world. Finally, the sense of alienation from the surrounding population engendered primary loyalty to their own community. With all the structural and functional diversity occasioned by the manifold conditions in the countries of dispersion, the autonomous Jewish community succeeded in maintaining a continuity with the past and an essential unity with far-flung Jewry.

Three main instruments of Jewish self-government have been the national or regional agency, the local community, and the association.

Centralization

When the Arabs conquered Persia in 637 C.E., they maintained there the hereditary exilarchate in its traditional glory (see *Exilarch, **Geonim*, *Academies). The Jews were responsible for the collection of the poll and land taxes demanded from them by the central government. Otherwise, they were free to govern themselves. They levied taxes for internal needs, regulated imposts on ritually slaughtered meat, and appointed judges. Government of the community was aristocratic. All communal affairs were guided by the leadership strata constituted roughly of (1) a hereditary aristocracy of scholarly families, institutionalized in the academies; (2) the "Davidic" dynasty of the exilarchs; (3) from the tenth century, wealthy and influential court bankers. During most of the Islamic period, Ereẓ Israel formed a kind of center of Jewish autonomy, with *geonim* of its own; later, with the breakup of the caliphate, provincial leaders, such as the **nagid*, made their appearance.

Medieval European society was structured into corporate groups, each governed by its own laws. Noblemen and serfs in the feudal system, burghers and guild members in the municipality, the clergy and religious orders within the church, all enjoyed some degree of autonomy. The corporate body in turn owed fealty to a more embracing power. Jews were generally under the direct protection of the monarch; they were, therefore, often exempt from obligations to intermediate powers. Christendom kept the Jews apart and in subjection to remain as visible witnesses testifying to the truth and victory of Christianity. These factors favored Jewish autonomy. The synagogues and Jewish cemeteries were protected; litigation among Jews was left to the rabbinical courts, while the community as a whole had powers of taxation, excommunication, and, in some cases, capital punishment. The greater the fiscal contribution to the state by the Jews in comparison to that of the Christian population, the more the rulers tended to rely on the Jewish autonomous organization as their fiscal agents.

Jews enjoyed considerable autonomy in the *Byzantine Empire. In Christian *Spain self-rule achieved heights rivaled only in the Muslim lands and by the Councils of the Lands of Poland-Lithuania. In order to foster strong communal cohesion, the Jewish authorities in Spain were granted wide powers to deal with informers, including the imposition of capital punishment. Jewish autonomy in Spain attained its peak in the 13th century. In Germany, France, England, and the Netherlands the institution of the corporation was particularly developed and powerful. The Jews were increasingly placed outside the framework of Christian society, more so than in Spain. Within this political framework, and against this social and legal background, therefore, the Jewish community in Northern Europe, as in the south, acquired the status of a corporation. The individual communities were governed by a variety of privileges granted by imperial, royal, ducal, episcopal, or municipal rulers. The similar institutions in Poland and Lithuania were patterned after those of Central Europe. Early legislation was modeled on privileges granted to the Jews in neighboring Austria and Bohemia. Gradually, the Polish king expanded the autonomy granted to the Jews. Sigismund II, for example, decreed in 1551 that any Jew who resists "the censures and bans imposed upon him by the rabbi, judge, or other Jewish elders… shall be beheaded." After a certain point in the second half of the 16th century, Jewish autonomy in Poland-Lithuania developed in explicit recognition by the monarch of the fiscal functions of central organs and tacit acceptance of their activities in other fields as well (see *Councils of the Lands). However, in 1764 the Jewish self-governing agencies were abolished on the express order of the disintegrating Polish state.

Central Organs of Self-Rule

The European communities in medieval and early modern times did not perpetuate the hereditary exilarchate, or patriarchate, or the geonate of the earlier period. Central organs of self-rule, however, developed as a result of two factors: (1) the built-in ideological and practical endeavors of the Jews to preserve an inclusive national unity, as far as communications and the respective political framework permitted; and (2) the practice of rulers of imposing a lump sum of taxes upon the Jews of a country. Central agencies were formed in order to distribute the fiscal burden among the provinces and communities. In addition to functioning as an arm of the state, these agencies also regulated the internal affairs of their constituents.

The Jewish striving for a central, national, autonomous leadership often took the form of *synods. Recourse was also made to the personal authority of a great rabbi, such as Jacob b. Meir *Tam. In addition, institutional authority was delegated through the representatives of the leading communities and the congregation of many scholars combined in them. They usually sought some form of confirmation of their resolutions by the secular ruler. The earliest Jewish synods on record are those held by the French and Rhenish communities; they were later convened from time to time in various countries and in various periods from the Middle Ages to early modern times. The synods generally attempted to deal with the whole gamut of problems relevant at their time of meeting, even though a single central problem often seemed to dominate their deliberations. Sometimes the synods were coterminous with a national framework and boundaries (see *Bohemia-Moravia; *Aragon; *Italy); sometimes they were regional only (see *Germany). (In the modern period the synod form of communal leadership has been revived by the Jewish *Reform movement.)

The Local *Community (Heb. קְהִלָּה, *kehillah*)

The *kehillah*, the cell of Jewish societal life and leadership, was based on the concept of partnership shared by the Jews as inhabitants of a certain locality. Much as the individual Jew was affected by his national or regional autonomous institutions, he enjoyed the fruits of self-government directly only through his own local community and the various associations within it. The foundations of the local community are to be found in the early days of the Second Temple, when the congregation took root and every town had its administrative machinery. The hallmarks of community life evolved as communal prayer, charity, mutual aid, a judiciary, and the power to enforce communal decisions. The *kehillah* did not figure prominently in the days when the exilarchs and *geonim* appointed local functionaries. It came into its own again in North African and Spanish communities and in those on the Rhine in the second half of the tenth century. The *kehillah* acquired a legal character with the right to judge and to impose taxes. The rabbis of that age reinterpreted talmudic law in the responsa to strengthen the autonomous institutions by giving them authority over the individual.

In time, marked similarities developed in the widely scattered communities in regard to both structure and function. Nearly every *kehillah* possessed written *takkanot*, many of them of a constitutional character. There were regularly scheduled meetings of the entire membership, as well as of the elected elders to the *kahal* ("community board"), who were usually drawn from the aristocracy of wealth or learning. The elders were designated by a variety of titles in Hebrew or in the local vernacular. Each community was served by paid communal officials, such as the rabbi, *dayyan*, or preacher, who offered religious, educational, judicial, financial, and welfare services to the residents. Notwithstanding the underlying uniformity of autonomous practices in the countries of the dispersal, the councils, *kehalim*, and associations were not all of one cloth. In Central and Eastern Europe there was only one *kahal* for every local community. On the other hand, the advent of refugees from Spain in Italy, Holland, and the Ottoman Empire sometimes produced differentiation within each community on the basis of the country or city of origin, or by Sephardi or Ashkenazi descent. On the other hand, in some places the various elements, while maintaining separate religious institutions, were treated as a corporate body vis-à-vis the outside world in relations with the government.

The Association

The smallest cell of Jewish communal life was the local association (*ḥevrah*). Whereas the community board had powers of taxation and legal standing, the association was a voluntary membership group. Throughout the Middle Ages it was controlled by the *kahal* to serve the public weal. As the *kahal* dissolved in the Emancipation era, the association often took over its essential functions. A major characteristic of most *ḥavarot* was the assurance to every member that upon his death the survivors would intercede before God for his soul through prayer and study.

The four major categories of associations were (1) religious, to maintain synagogues or chapels, or for worship or mystical activities; (2) educational, for provision of school facilities for the poor, or adult study groups; (3) philanthropic, for visiting the sick, or care of paupers; and (4) vocational, mainly consisting of craft guilds. Outstanding among the philanthropic associations was the burial society, **ḥevrah kaddisha gomelei ḥasadim*, which often achieved wide powers through its monopoly over the cemetery, a major source of secured income. In Central and South America the *ḥevrah kaddisha gomelei ḥasadim* for many years also controlled most other communal activities. In the United States it lost its power as two of its functions were commercialized; funeral parlors passed to private ownership and cemeteries to **Landsmanschaften* and congregations.

Decline of Autonomy

The era of civic emancipation ushered in a gradual dissolution of the self-governing community. The evolution of centralized monarchies, the crumbling of the medieval social structure, the harnessing of Jewish leadership in the service of the state, Enlightenment as an inner solvent, early capitalism with its emphasis on individualism, loss of status of the rabbinical courts, financial bankruptcy – these were some of the powerful internal and external factors that spelled the doom of Jewish autonomy. Many declared that emancipation and autonomy were inherently contradictory; that once the individual Jew is granted equal civic rights he can no longer claim group privileges.

Between the two world wars, efforts were made in Eastern European countries to grant Jews, along with other nationalities, certain *minority rights. In Russia, Alexander Kerensky's short-lived provisional government of 1917 stirred Jewish hopes for national self-determination. Upon seizing power the Soviets too proclaimed the rights to autonomy of territorial nationalities. For a while autonomous regions and soviets enjoyed linguistic, judicial, and educational self-rule. *Birobidzhan was proclaimed such a region. However, atheistic and assimilationist trends as well as the incipient anti-Jewishness gradually eradicated Jewish communal life. The claim for minority rights was based on the ideology of Diaspora nationalism, or *Autonomism, which demanded from the state group rights along with individual equality. The experiment did not last long. Intense nationalism among the ruling states and the force of economic rivalry between the Jews and the local populations tended to shatter all good intentions. In Ereẓ Israel the central and local self-government granted by Turkey and by the Mandatory power offered the Jewish community wide autonomy, which was used constructively to help prepare for eventual independence. Only one community, the Keneset Israel, was recognized, the exception being the separate Orthodox community network (see *Agudat Israel).

The Voluntary Post-Emancipation Community

Hardly any trace is left in the post-World War II period of either state-enforced group autonomy or of the minority rights program. Emancipated Jewry developed wholly voluntary associations and communal organs. These serve a wide variety of purposes, mainly religious and social organizations abound for cultural, recreational, and social services. There have also arisen societies for the defense of Jewish rights and for developing institutions that serve both the Jewish and non-Jewish residents of the state on a non-sectarian basis, such as hospitals, recreational centers, and universities, as well as employment and vocational agencies. The *Board of Deputies of British Jews, the *American Jewish Committee, the *American Jewish Congress, and many other national bodies specialize in defense or in broader community services. The Orthodox, Conservative, and Reform religious groups in Western Europe and the United States each have their own network of local congregations and of regional and national institutions.

See also sections on Minority Rights in articles on various European countries.

BIBLIOGRAPHY: Baron, Community (1942), includes bibliography; Finkelstein, Middle Ages; Baer, Spain, 1–2; M. Wischnitzer, *History of Jewish Crafts and Guilds* (1965); I. Levitats, *Jewish Community in Russia, 1772–1844* (1943); M. Burstein, *Self-Government of the Jews in Palestine since 1900* (1934); J. Katz, *Tradition and Crisis* (1961), 79–134, 157–67.

[Isaac Levitats]

AUTONOMY, JUDICIAL, the right granted to Jews under non-Jewish rule to administer justice and to execute judgment according to their own law and by their own judges. The practical administration of justice in the Jewish society of the Diaspora was conditioned by the general socio-political conditions and government legislation; but Jewish factors also played an important role in obtaining and maintaining legal status for the Jewish judicature.

Certain general trends in Jewish autonomy are apparent throughout Diaspora history despite persistent exceptions and a variety of practices. Religious and family matters were subject exclusively to Jewish jurisdiction. Civil and often criminal cases involving Jews only were also the sole domain of the Jewish court. Sometimes the privileges granted to the communities in Europe in the Middle Ages allowed a Christian to cite a Jewish defendant only in cases tried by Jewish judges. In mixed cases involving both Christians and Jews an equal number of Christian and Jewish witnesses (e.g., three of each, as stipulated in some grants of privileges) or an equal number of judges was often stipulated. The *bet din* followed Jewish law, except in such matters as taxes or pledges on loans, which were often disposed of according to the law of the land. In several countries the Jewish legal system was under the jurisdiction of a chief rabbi. The Jews sometimes resisted the imposition of such authority from the outside. In England the *Presbyter Judaeorum* (see *Archpresbyter) seems to have exercised judicial functions only in matters affecting the royal exchequer; he was mainly an administrative officer.

From an early period of the Jewish settlement in Europe, the consensus of Jewish society insisted on recourse both to its own law and to its own judges. A responsum delivered by a rabbi of the Rhine district in the 11th century (in *Ma'aseh ha-Ge'onim*) concerns a case in which Jewish litigants "came before the *camerarius* (chamberlain) of the Gentiles; and he ordered Jews – as the case was brought before him – to judge them according to [Jewish] law." The Christian official then pronounced judgment as his Jewish advisers had counseled. Although the successful litigant thought that he had won his suit "according to [the law of] both Jews and Gentiles," the rabbi decided "that what has been adjudged to him by Jews through the Gentile court is null and void"; a Jewish judge had to consider the matter.

Long before municipalities originated in Europe, the Jews had more than a millennium of experience in self-government. Nor were they subject to irrational procedures. The rules of evidence in Jewish law were rational. They admitted the testimony of witnesses or legal documents only. Thus as early as the days of the Carolingian Empire, Jews were granted exemption from the ordeals of fire and scalding water.

Judicial autonomy was stipulated in privileges issued by kings and lesser authorities. Only in the *Byzantine Empire were Jews sometimes denied their own tribunals. In Muslim countries the *exilarchs and *geonim* supervised local Jewish courts, which enjoyed extensive jurisdiction. Jewish courts were generally free to use their own system of sanctions and punishment; in Christian Spain they had the right to impose capital punishment against informers. A pronouncement of the *ḥerem* ("excommunication") by Jewish courts was not usually interfered with by the authorities, who often had recourse to it for their own purposes.

As early as 1084 Bishop *Ruediger of Speyer granted the Jews within his diocese the right to try suits between Jews in a Jewish court. A Christian plaintiff against a Jewish defendant also had to take his case to this court. If the court found itself unable to pass judgment, the suit might come for decision before the bishop or his chamberlain. The privilege granted by Emperor Henry IV to the Jews of Worms in 1090 became the model for many subsequent documents of this sort. It states: "… not the bishop, nor the chamberlain, nor the count, nor the bailiff, nor anyone else, shall presume to interfere in any judicial issue arising between Jews, or with Jews as defendants, but [such matters shall be treated] only by the person elected by them [i.e., the Jews] and appointed by us to exercise authority" in matters of justice among Jews according to Jewish law. The same attitude is found in the oldest code of Castile, that of Alfonso VI (c. 1042–1109). The principle was confirmed with slight variations by succeeding emperors, princes, and municipal authorities throughout medieval Christian Europe. In several cities, however, such as Zurich and Nuremberg, attempts were made to compel Jews to bring their suits before municipal courts.

In Spain – both in Aragon and in Castile – the exercise of maximum Jewish judicial autonomy found confirmation not only in the various grants of privileges and laws but also through long-established precedent. Capital punishment was sometimes meted out in the 13th and 14th centuries, and even in the 15th, by Jewish rabbis. Their procedure, however, was often modeled on that of the Christian courts rather than on strict talmudic rules. Pedro III of Aragon (1276–85) ordered Solomon b. Abraham *Adret and Jonah b. Abraham *Gerondi, the two most respected rabbis of Catalonia, to pass judgment on an informer accused by the communities of Aragon, and urged them to arrive at a decision. They finally informed the king "that he may proceed according to his law; that we have found him deserving of the death penalty, if he should wish to put him to death." The informer was publicly executed.

From the end of the 13th century a trend to limit Jewish judicial autonomy in Christian Spain began, particularly in criminal matters, and became increasingly pronounced during the 14th and 15th centuries. Jewish jurisdiction in criminal cases was abolished in Castile in 1380 by Juan I, although reinstated in 1432. In 1412 a decree of Juan II of Castile abolished Jewish judges for both civil and criminal cases. Evidently shelved for a time, the decree was renewed and extended to all Spain by Ferdinand and Isabella in 1476.

In Poland–Lithuania the Jewish community exercised considerable judicial autonomy; in the first half of the 16th century the kings even granted the chief rabbis appointed by them the sanction of capital punishment for "… any Jew who ventures to take censures and bans lightly." The courts of the *Councils of the Lands and of single communities administered and executed justice, but capital punishment is rarely mentioned in the sources.

Referring to the Jews of the territories annexed from Poland in 1772, Catherine II of Russia decreed that "the administration of law and justice by Jews shall continue to be vested in their present tribunals." However, as early as 1786 such autonomy was withdrawn and the statute of 1804 states that "Jews, too, in their lawsuits… shall seek law and justice in the general courts." The *bet din* was recognized only as a court of arbitration. In this decision Russian absolutism reflected the general trend in Europe commencing with the *Haskalah movement against the exercise of Jewish judicial autonomy within the state.

In practice, the Jews of Russia, and all other countries where there was a vibrant Jewish life, jealously guarded their judicial autonomy and in the majority of cases prevented Jews from appearing in non-Jewish courts. The case of *Novaya Ushica (Russia), where, as late as 1836, rabbis sentenced two informers to death, exemplifies the strength of the Jewish determination to be governed by Jewish law.

BIBLIOGRAPHY: Baron, Community, 2 (1942), 208–45; 3 (1942), bibliography; Kisch, Germany, 172ff.; Finkelstein, Middle Ages; Baer, Spain, 2 (1966), index; I. Levitats, *Jewish Community in Russia 1772–1884* (1943); M. Elon, in: ILR (1967), 515–40; (1968) 119–26, 416–42.

[Isaac Levitats]

AUTOPSIES AND DISSECTION. Respect for the dead, and the utmost reverence for the human body after death are enjoined by both Jewish law and custom. The rabbis deduce the prohibition of the desecration of the corpse (*nivvul ha-met*) as well as the duty of the reverent disposal of the body by burial as soon as possible after death from Deuteronomy 21:22, 23. Mutilation of the body, whether for anatomical dissection or for post-mortem examination, would appear to violate the respect due to the dead and is consequently to be forbidden. Reverence for the corpse (*kevod ha-met*) must yield, however, to the superior value of life and its preservation. In fact, the duty of saving and maintaining life (**pikku'aḥ nefesh*), which includes even cases of a doubtful nature, overrides all but three commandments of the Torah. Hence the question of the permissibility of the dissection of human bodies for the study of medicine, and of autopsies for the purpose of establishing the cause of death and for the development of medical research revolves therefore round the interpretations of the two principles: *nivvul ha-met* and *pikku'aḥ nefesh*. For while any tampering with the corpse comes under the former category and is therefore prohibited, it can be argued that as a result of dissections and autopsies the lives of others can be saved or prolonged, and hence the prohibition of *nivvul ha-met* would be overridden by the prime commandment of *pikku'aḥ nefesh*.

In the Bible there would appear to be two clear instances of the dissection of the body of a deceased person: the embalming of Jacob (Gen. 50:2–3) and of his son Joseph (*ibid*., 26). According to all evidence the process of *embalming as practiced by the ancient Egyptians consisted of disemboweling the body and filling the cavity with certain unguents. The view was put forward in a question addressed to Ezekiel *Landau (see below), that this act should be permitted since it was performed out of the principle of respect for the dead, and what is done out of respect for the dead cannot be considered as *nivvul ha-met*, which is essentially disrespect for the dead. This principle is explicitly laid down in the Talmud to justify certain cases of postponement of burial so that proper respect may be shown to the dead (Sanh. 47a), and it has been advanced again as an argument in favor of permitting autopsies.

In the Talmud there are two noteworthy references to the possibility of autopsies, each for different reasons. One (Ḥul. 11b) clearly states that an autopsy may be performed on the victim of a murder in order to establish whether he was viable at the time of the assault. Were he not, no charge of murder could be laid against the assailant. This case would come within the framework of permissibility of *pikku'aḥ nefesh*. Such a consideration, however, does not apply to the second instance. The question was raised, in an actual incident, whether the corpse of a boy could be exhumed for examination to ascertain whether he was a major or a minor at the time of death, the question of the disposition of an estate being involved. In this case the exhumation was forbidden, but only because it would have had to be performed by relatives, who stood in a special category with regard to the deceased, and because of the possibility of changes having taken place in the corpse after burial, thus rendering the examination inconclusive. The whole discussion, however, suggests the possibility of the examination of a body for reasons not connected with *pikku'aḥ nefesh* (BB 154a–b). There are in the Talmud various instances of the dissection of human bodies for anatomical research (cf., e.g., Bek. 45a), but in all these instances it would appear that the corpses of non-Jews were employed.

It was not until the 18th century, when human bodies began to be used systematically for medical research as a regular practice, that the permissibility of autopsies for medical research and saving lives became a practical question of *halakhah*. A query addressed from London to Ezekiel Landau, of Prague, inquired as to the possibility of performing an autopsy on the body of a Jew, in order to reveal the cause of death and thus find a cure for others suffering from the same malady. The questioner gave his reasons for permitting this, citing, inter alia, the embalming of Jacob. Landau dismissed his arguments but conceded that, should there be at the time of death, in the same hospital, another patient suffering from the same symptoms, so that the autopsy could immediately help, it could be permitted on the grounds of *pikku'aḥ nefesh*. Strictly limited though this permission was, it was the first clear, recorded ruling permitting autopsies in the interest of the living, and all subsequent discussions on the subject have used it as their starting point (responsa *Nodabi-Yhudah, Mahadurah Tinyana*, YD 310).

The problem became an acute and practical one with the establishment of the Medical School of the Hebrew University in Jerusalem. It was obvious that bodies would have to be made available for the study of anatomy and that the cause of medical research would necessitate autopsies. Chief Rabbi A.Y. *Kook, usually liberal in his approach, entirely forbade the use of Jewish bodies for such purposes (*Da'at Kohen*, 199), but in 1944, his successor, Rabbi I.H. *Herzog, and Ẓevi Pesaḥ *Frank, chief rabbi of Jerusalem, reached an agreement with Dr. H. Yasski on behalf of the Hadassah Hospital, permitting autopsies in the following cases: (1) when the civil law demanded it in cases of crime and accidental death; (2) to establish the cause of death when it was doubtful; (3) in order to save lives; and (4) in cases of hereditary disease. The authority to perform such autopsies was made conditional upon the signatures of three doctors. All organs dissected were to be handed over for burial after the necessary examinations had been performed. This agreement was the basis for the Law of Anatomy and Pathology passed by the Knesset in 1953.

The Sephardi Chief Rabbi B.M. *Ouziel devoted two responsa to the halakhic basis of the question (*Mishpetei Uziel* (1935), 1:28 and 29; cf. 11 (1952), no. 110). Arguing that dissection of the body for anatomical study and autopsies in the interests of the advancement of medicine did not constitute *nivvul ha-met*, Ouziel ruled that "the essence of the prohibition of *nivvul ha-met* is that it refers specifically to cases where there is a deliberate intention to desecrate a body or to treat it with disrespect without any advantage to others. Whenever others can benefit, however, and most certainly when there is a possibility of thereby saving life, the prohibition does not apply. Anyone with a knowledge of the development and progress of medicine will not for a moment doubt the benefits which accrue from autopsies and dissections. Autopsies are of inestimable value in establishing the cause of the ailment and its effect upon other organs of the body. In addition, where the preservation of life and the interests of the living are concerned, there is neither *nivvul ha-met* nor desecration of the body."

Other rabbinic authorities (e.g., Rabbi I. *Jakobovits), taking modern developments into account, suggest that autopsies, especially in cases of heart disease and cancer, not only belong to the category of *pikku'aḥ nefesh* in a general way, but are even sometimes imperative, especially in connection with determining the effects of new medicines. "As it is the duty of the rabbi to prevent autopsies where no *pikku'aḥ nefesh* is involved, so is it his duty to insist on it where there is the slightest possibility of it being of benefit" (R. Isaac Arieli, in: *Torah she-be-al Peh* (1964), 66).

In 1965, following allegations of widespread abuse of the safeguards contained in the Law of Anatomy and Pathology, certain Orthodox circles in Israel agitated to have the law amended by reverting to the strictly limited permission given by Ezekiel Landau. A ruling to this effect was issued under the signatures of the two chief rabbis (Y. *Nissim and I.Y. *Unterman) and the heads of yeshivot.

Although from the halakhic point of view the objections that apply to autopsies also apply to dissection for the purpose of anatomical study, enough people bequeath their bodies for this purpose so that the religious opposition has been confined largely to autopsies, despite the fact that the halakhic permission for such bequests is doubtful. Similarly, there has been a universal consensus of opinion permitting autopsies in the case of violent or accidental death or where crime is suspected. In such cases the talmudic precedents quoted above would apply. Most of those who oppose autopsies made an exception in the case of corneal transplants which restore sight to a blind person. In this specific instance Rabbi Unterman stated that the deceased would consider it an honor for his eye to be used for such a purpose, thus overcoming the prohibition of *nivvul ha-met*., In the same responsum, Rabbi Unterman put forward the interesting view that an organ from a deceased person is "revived" when successfully grafted on to a living person and ceases to be regarded as part of a corpse. Though resistance to transplants remains widespread, there has been a tendency to greater leniency, as in the case of heart transplants where the position has shifted from total opposition to conditional consent.

BIBLIOGRAPHY: M. Greiber, *Nittu'aḥ Metim le-Ẓorkhei Limmud ve-Ḥakirah* (1943); I. Jakobovits, *Jewish Medical Ethics* (1956), 144–56; idem, *Jewish Law Faces Modern Problems* (1965); I.Y. Unterman, *Shevet mi-Yhudah* (1945), 317–22; *Torah she-be-Al Peh* (Proceedings from the Sixth Annual Conference on Oral Law, 1964), 39–73, 81–86; K. Kahana, *Nittuḥei Metim ba-Halakhah* (1967), bibliography of Hebrew works.

[Louis Isaac Rabinowitz]

AUVERGNE, former French province including the present departments of Cantal, Puy-de-Dôme, and part of Haute-Loire. The presence of Jews in Auvergne is known from the end of the fifth century. In the second half of the 13th century they were settled in the localities of Auzon, Clermont, Ennezat, Langeac, Monton, Oilac, Peissin, Pont-du-Château, Puy-Roger, Ris, Rochefort, Taleine, Veyre, and Vichy. Banished together with the other Jews of France in 1306, they returned after 1359 to settle in Ennezat, Lignat, and Montaigut-en-Combraille until the expulsion of the Jews from the kingdom in 1394.

BIBLIOGRAPHY: A. Tardieu, in: *Dépêche du Puy-de-Dôme* (Sept. 15, 1891); P. Andigier, *Histoire d'Auvergne*, 1 (1899), 14; A. Molinier (ed.), *Correspondance administrative d'Alfonse de Poitiers*, 1 (1894), 402–4 and passim; P. Fournier and P. Guébin (eds.), *Enquêtes administratives d'Alfonse de'Poitiers…* (1959), passim.

[Bernhard Blumenkranz]

AUXERRE, capital of the department of Yonne, north central France. The first reference to the presence of Jews in Auxerre is found in a responsum addressed by *Rashi to the scholars of this area. Representatives of the Auxerre community took part in the *synod which met at Troyes around 1160. Jurisdiction over the Jews was divided between the count, the cathedral chapter, and the abbey of Saint-Germain of Auxerre. One of the Jewish quarters was situated near the Féchelle gate; the former Rue du Puits des Juifs is today included in the Rue du Pont. A wall of the clock tower has a stone bearing the Hebrew inscription: "Meir son of R. Solomon the valiant," perhaps referring to a Jew who had been imprisoned there. An anonymous 12th-century work, dedicated to a certain Count Guillaume (perhaps Guillaume II) of Auxerre, deals mainly with circumcision, and supplies the count with arguments for use in religious *disputations with Jews. The Jews were expelled from Auxerre by Count Pierre, between 1184 and 1206. Letters addressed to the bishop of Auxerre and the count of Nevers by Pope *Innocent III in 1207 and 1208, complain that the Jews of Auxerre had refused to pay the ecclesiastical tithe on their fields and vineyards, and that they sold so much of the surplus wine they produced to Christians that the latter were using it for the sacrament of the Mass. The Jews were again expelled in 1306, returning to Auxerre in 1315, and in 1322, returning in 1359. In 1393 the city of Auxerre turned to the authorities in Paris to expedite the expulsion of Jews from its territory. It is not known whether this was effected immediately or in conjunction with the general expulsion of the Jews from France which took place the following year. It was not until 1398 that a royal ordinance declared null and void all the debts owing to Jews by Christian debtors of Auxerre. At the beginning of World War II there were 70 Jews living in Auxerre, most of them refugees from Nazi persecution. There is no Jewish community in Auxerre today.

BIBLIOGRAPHY: Gross, Gal Jud, 60–62; Abbé Leboeuf, *Mémoires concernant l'histoire d'Auxerre*, 3 (1855); S. Grayzel, *Church and the Jews* (1966^2), 125–6, 128–9; Dondenne and Molard, in: *Bulletin de la société des sciences historiques et naturelles… Yonne*, 47 (1893), 573–4; Z. Szajkowski, *Analytical Franco-Jewish Gazetteer* (1966), 290.

[Bernhard Blumenkranz]

AV (Heb. אָב), post-Exilic name of the fifth month in the Jewish year. Occurring in Assyrian inscriptions, in *Megillat Ta'anit*, and all later branches of rabbinic literature but nowhere in the Bible, it is etymologically connected with *abib* (or *aviv*; "spring"), the pre-Exilic biblical name of the first month (Nisan); the verbal root *v'v* denoting "fresh growth." The zodiacal sign of this month is Leo. In the present fixed Jewish calendar it invariably consists of 30 days, the first of Av never falling on Sunday, Tuesday, or Thursday. In the 20th century, Av in its earliest occurrence, extended from July eighth to August sixth and in its latest, from August seventh to September fifth. Traditional days in Av comprise: (a) First of Av, the anniversary of the death of Aaron according to Numbers 33:38

(in the masoretic text and all the ancient versions, except the Syriac), once observed as a fast (Meg. Ta'an., last chapter, Neubauer). (b) The Ninth of *Av, still observed as the strictest of the four fasts commemorating the destruction of the Temple, is the culmination of a period of nine days of semi-mourning. Connected with it are two special Sabbaths, the one preceding the fast called *Shabbat Ḥazon* (cf. Isa. ch. 1) and the one following the fast called *Shabbat Naḥamu* (cf. Isa. 40) after the respective Sabbath *haftarah* readings. (c) The Fifteenth of *Av, once a joyous popular festival, the main day of wood offering to the altar (Ta'an. 4:5, 8; Jos., Wars, 2:17). (d) The Eighteenth of Av, once observed as a fast commemorating the quenching of the Eternal Light in the Temple in the reign of King Ahaz (Meg. Ta'an., loc. cit.). Predominantly joyful in Temple times, with the fifth, seventh, tenth, and twentieth of Av as additional festive days of wood offering (Ta'an. 4:5, 8), this month's character became increasingly somber after the Romans' destruction of the Temple and as more and more national catastrophes occurred (or were held to have occurred) in it, with increasing restrictions on sundry expressions of joy, in keeping with the mishnaic ruling "When Av comes in, gladness is diminished" (*ibid.* 4:6).

BIBLIOGRAPHY: Eisenstein, Dinim, 1; Guttmann, Mafte'aḥ, 1 (1906), 70f.; ET, 1 (1947), 9–10.

[Ephraim Jehudah Wiesenberg]

AV, THE FIFTEENTH OF (Heb. ט"ו בְּאָב, Tu be-Av), minor holiday in the days of the Second Temple, marking the beginning of the vintage in ancient Palestine. According to the Mishnah, on this day (as well as on the *Day of Atonement) the daughters of Jerusalem dressed in white raiments (which they borrowed that "none should be abashed which had them not") and went forth to dance in the vineyards chanting songs (Ta'an. 4:8; TB, *ibid.* 31a). This was also the day of the wood offering when all people brought kindling wood for the Temple altar (see: Neh. 10:35). This festival was instituted by the Pharisees who, according to Graetz, celebrated their victory over the Sadducees on this day (Graetz, Gesch, 3 (1960^5), 460, 572). Josephus, however, gives the 14th of Av as the date of this holiday (Wars, 2:6). The Talmud (Ta'an. 30b–31a; BB 121a, b; TJ, Ta'an. 4:11, 69c) gives six more events that occurred on this date as reasons for this minor holiday: (1) the tribes were allowed to intermarry (Num. 36:8ff.); (2) the Benjamites were readmitted into the community (Judg. 21:18ff.); (3) the death of the Israelites in the Sinai Desert for their sin regarding the report of the spies to Canaan ceased (Num. 14:32); (4) the last king of the Israelite kingdom, *Hosea b. Elah, removed the checkposts which *Jeroboam I installed to prevent the Israelites from making their pilgrimage to Jerusalem (I Kings 12:29; II Kings 18:4); (5) the Romans permitted the burial of the soldiers who fell in the defense of Bar Kokhba's last stronghold, *Bethar; and (6) from this day onward no more wood was chopped for the Temple because the sun was no longer strong enough to dry it. Since this holiday was celebrated by torches and bonfires some scholars believe that it originated in a pagan festival of the summer solstice (such as the 15th of Shevat which falls on the day of winter solstice). On Av the Fifteenth the **Taḥanun* prayer is omitted and there are no eulogies at burials.

BIBLIOGRAPHY: J.T. Lewinski (ed.), *Sefer ha-Mo'adim*, 6 (1956), 481–531; Gutmann, Mafte'ah, s.v. *"Av-[4]"*; ET, s.v. *"Av-[4]"*; L. Finkelstein, *The Pharisees*, 1 (1946), 54–56.

AV, THE NINTH OF (Heb. תִּשְׁעָה בְּאָב, Tishah be-Av), traditional day of mourning for the destruction of the Temples in Jerusalem.

Historical Background

The First Temple, built by King Solomon, was destroyed by the Babylonian king Nebuchadnezzar in 586 B.C.E. on the 10th of Av, according to Jeremiah 3:12, whereas in the corresponding record in II Kings 25:8–9, the date is given as the 7th of Av. The Tosefta *Ta'anit* 4:10 (also Ta'an. 29a) explains this discrepancy by stating that the destruction of the outer walls and of the courtyard started on the 7th of Av while the whole edifice was destroyed on the 10th of Av. R. Johanan declared that he would have fixed the fast on the 10th of Av because it was on that day that the greater part of the calamity happened. The rabbis however decided that it is more fitting to commemorate the "beginning of the calamity."

The Second Temple was destroyed by the Romans in 70 C.E., on the 10th of Av, according to the historian Josephus (Wars, 6:249–50). This day is still observed as a day of mourning by the Karaites. The Talmud (Ta'an. 29a), however, gives the date as the 9th of Av, which became accepted as the anniversary of both destructions.

The Talmud justifies the 9th of Av as the major day of mourning because a series of calamities occurred on this day throughout Jewish history. The Mishnah (Ta'an. 4:6) enumerates five disasters: (1) on the 9th of Av it was decreed that the Children of Israel, after the Exodus from Egypt, should not enter the Promised Land; (2) the First and (3) the Second Temples were destroyed; (4) Bethar, the last stronghold of the leaders of the *Bar Kokhba war, was captured in 135 C.E.; and (5) one year later, in 136, the Roman emperor Hadrian established a heathen temple on the site of the Temple and rebuilt Jerusalem as a pagan city which was renamed *Aelia Capitolina* and which the Jews were forbidden to enter.

The expulsion of the Jews from Spain in 1492 is said also to have occurred on the 9th of Av.

The 9th of Av thus became a symbol for all the persecutions and misfortunes of the Jewish people, for the loss of national independence and the sufferings in exile. The massacres of whole communities during the Crusades intensified this association.

Mourning Rites

It is uncertain whether or how the 9th of Av was observed as a day of mourning before 70 C.E. in memory of the destruction of the First Temple. In Zechariah 7:5 such an enquiry is quoted and the prophet's answer is that instead of fasting they should love truth and peace, as a result of which the former days of fast and mourning would become days of joy and gladness (*ibid.* 8:16–19). The Talmud tells that R. Eliezer b. Zadok, who lived before and after the destruction of the Second Temple, did not fast on the 9th of Av, which was deferred because of the Sabbath to the following day since it was his family's traditional holiday of "wood-offerings" for the altar (Ta'an. 12a; TJ, Ta'an. 4:4; also Tosef., Ta'an. 4:6). This would indicate that fasting on the 9th of Av was observed during the period of the Second Temple too. In any case, fasting on the 9th of Av was observed in the mishnaic period (RH 1:13). Some rabbis advocated permanent abstention from wine and meat in memory of the destruction of the Temple, but this was regarded as an excessive demand (BB 60b; Tosef., Sot. 15:11ff.). The general rule in the Talmud for the mourning rites of Tishah be-Av is that a person is obliged to observe on it all mourning rites which apply in the case of the death of a next of kin (Ta'an. 30a). These mourning rites have to be observed from sunset to sunset (Pes. 54b). Some mourning rites are already observed during the weeks prior to Tishah be-Av, from the fast of the 17th of Tammuz (see *Three Weeks). On the 1st of Av, the mourning rites are intensified. On the eve of Tishah be-Av, at the final meal before the fast, one may neither partake of two cooked dishes nor eat meat nor drink wine. It is customary to eat a boiled egg at this meal as a symbol of mourning, and to sprinkle ashes on it. Grace after this meal is said individually and silently.

The following rules are observed on the fast of Tishah be-Av: (1) Complete abstention from food and drink. (2) Bathing is strictly forbidden. Washing of the face and hands is permissible for cleansing purposes only (Ta'an. 13a). (3) The use of any oils for anointing and the application of perfumes are forbidden, as is sexual intercourse. (4) It is forbidden to put on footwear made of leather. Therefore the tenth blessing in the Morning Benedictions, originally recited when putting on shoes, is omitted. (5) One must sit either on the ground or on a low stool. (6) It is customary to abstain from work and business because Tishah be-Av was regarded as an inauspicious day. A person who works on the 9th of Av would derive no benefit from his efforts (Ta'an. 30b). (7) The study of Torah is forbidden because it is a source of joy, except for the reading of the Scroll of *Lamentations and its Midrash (*Lamentations Rabbah*), the Book of Job, the curses in Leviticus (26:14–42), some chapters in Jeremiah (e.g., 39), the aggadic tales in the Talmud describing the destruction of Jerusalem (e.g., Git. 55b–58a), and similar texts.

On the night of Tishah be-Av the pious used to sleep on the floor with a stone as a pillow. Many fasted until noon of the 10th of Av. Meat and wine may not be consumed until the afternoon of the 10th of Av, although some of the mourning rites are lessened from Tishah be-Av afternoon onward based on the belief that Tishah be-Av will again be a holiday since the Messiah will be born then (TJ, Ber. 2:4). Toward the end of the 17th century strict observance of Tishah be-Av also became a mark of adherence to Orthodox rabbinic Judaism, after the pseudo-messiah, Shabbetai *Ẓevi, had abolished the fast of Tishah be-Av and turned it into a day of rejoicing.

In Liturgy and Synagogue Ceremonial

The mourning rites of Tishah be-Av are reflected in the following changes in the synagogue liturgy and usage: (1) the lights in the synagogue are dimmed and only a few candles are lit, as a symbol of the darkness which has befallen Israel. In some rites (Sephardi, Yemenite), it is customary to extinguish all lights immediately after the conclusion of the evening service prior to the reading of the *Kinot* (Dirges), and the oldest member of the congregation or the *ḥazzan* then announces: "This year is the… so and so… since the destruction of the Holy Temple." Afterward he addresses the congregation with words of chastisement and repentance in the spirit of the saying: "Each generation in which the Temple is not rebuilt should regard itself as responsible for its destruction." This is answered by wailing and crying. Then the lights are lit again. (2) The curtain of the Ark is removed in memory of the curtain in the Holy of Holies in the Temple which, according to talmudic legend, was stabbed and desecrated by Titus. In some Sephardi synagogues where the Ark normally has no curtain, a black curtain is hung and the Torah scrolls themselves are draped in black mantles. (3) The congregants sit on low benches, footstools, or on the floor as mourners do during the *shivah* period. (4) The *ḥazzan* recites the prayers in a monotonous and melancholy tune. (5) Some people change their customary seats in the synagogue. (6) In some congregations the Torah scroll is placed on the floor and ashes put on it while the congregants recite the words "the crown is fallen from our head" (Lam. 5:16), or other appropriate verses (see Sof. 18:7). (7) The prayer service is the regular weekday service, with the following changes: In the evening, the Scroll of Lamentations (*Eikhah*) is followed by special dirges, *Kinot*. In the Sephardi rite the Song of Moses, Deuteronomy 32, is substituted for the Song of Moses, Exodus 15, which is normally recited after the morning Psalms. After the main part of the morning service *Kinot* are recited commemorating many of the tragic events in Jewish history (in the Sephardi rite they are recited before the Reading of the Torah). In the Ashkenazi rite these include *Sha'ali Serufah be-Esh* by R. Meir of Rothenburg (occasioned by the burning of the Talmud in Paris in 1242), *Arzei ha-Levanon* (commemorating the death of the "Ten Martyrs"), the Odes to Zion, beginning with the famous *Ẓiyyon ha-lo Tishali* of Judah Halevi and concluding with *Eli Ẓiyyon ve-Areha* sung to a special melody (see *Eli Ẓiyyon*). The Sephardi *Kinot* differ from the Ashkenazi and do not include those mentioned. There is, however, one which is based upon the Four Questions of the Passover Seder, the opening stanza of which is "I will ask some questions of the holy congregation: How is this night different from other nights? Why on Passover eve do we eat *mazzah* and bitter herbs, while this night all is bitterness…?" (8) During the reader's repetition of the *Amidah* the *Anenu* prayer is inserted between the seventh and eighth benedictions as on all fast days. In the silent *Amidah* it is recited in the 16th benediction of the afternoon service and in the Sephardi and Yemenite rites at all services. The Italian rite recites it in the morning and afternoon services. In the afternoon service a special prayer *Naḥem* is added to the benediction for the restoration of Jerusalem. (9) From the Middle Ages it became customary except among certain Oriental communities not to wear *tallit* and *tefillin* during the morning service. (They are considered to be ornaments, and the *tefillin* in particular are held to be Israel's "crown of glory.") They are worn instead during the afternoon service. (Thus the blessing "who crowns Israel with glory" is omitted from the Morning Benedictions, because it refers to the *tefillin*.) (10) The morning service as well as the afternoon service include readings from the Torah. In the morning the reading is Deuteronomy 4:24–40, and the *haftarah* Jeremiah 8:13–9:23; in the afternoon service Exodus 32:11–14 and 34:1–10, and, as *haftarah*, Isaiah 55:6; 56:8 as on all fast days. The Sephardi *haftarah* is Hosea 14:2–9. In some rituals the person called up to the Torah says: "Blessed be the righteous Judge" – the verse by which mourners are greeted. (11) Some people sprinkle ashes on their head as a symbol of mourning. In Jerusalem it is customary to visit the Western Wall on Tishah be-Av, where Lamentations and the *Kinot* are recited by the different communities according to their rites. There are many other local mourning customs. Visits to cemeteries, especially to the graves of martyrs and pious men, were frequent, in order to implore the deceased to intercede for the speedy redemption of Israel. Schoolchildren used to throw seed-burrs of plants at each other in Poland and in Russia. The *shofar* was blown in Algiers in memory of the ancient fast day ceremonies in the time of the Temple. Women anointed themselves with fragrant oils and perfumes on the afternoon of Tishah be-Av, for they believed that the Messiah would be born (or appear) on this day and it would become a great holiday (Egypt). In the evening after the fast, some people greet each other with the formula: "You shall soon enjoy the comfort of Zion."

In Modern Israel

Beside the special synagogue services for Tishah be-Av, public places of entertainment and restaurants are closed on the eve of Tishah be-Av. The *Eikhah* dirges and talks about the significance of the day replace music or entertainment on the radio. Newspapers devote articles and pictures to the Old City of Jerusalem, the Western Wall, the Mount of Olives, and other holy places. With the reoccupation of the Old City of Jerusalem in 1967, the problem arose as to whether the mourning practices for the destruction of Jerusalem should be modified. A modified ritual, based upon a passage in the Talmud envisaging a situation in which Jews in Ereẓ Israel would not be oppressed, but the Temple still not rebuilt, is advocated by some.

Reform Judaism and the Ninth of Av

Classical Reform Judaism of the 19th century did not observe the mourning ritual of Tishah be-Av. The rationale for the abolishment of these rites was summed up by David *Einhorn (*Olat Tamid*, prayer book, p. 100) as follows: "Reform Judaism beholds in the cessation of the sacrificial services, the termination of a special nationality, and the scattering of the Jews among all nations, the fundamental conditions for the fulfillment of their mission among mankind. Only after the destruction of Jerusalem was it possible for Israel to become a kingdom of priests and a holy nation, a conception which even in the Talmud is intimated in the saying: 'On the day of the destruction of the Temple the Messiah was born.'" In the last decades, however, Reform circles have come to feel that Tishah be-Av should not be ignored but rather that it should be reinterpreted to make it relevant and meaningful in modern times. This conforms to the practice of Reform Judaism with regard to all festivals whose original symbolism was reinterpreted.

The laws and customs of the Tishah be-Av ritual are to be found in Maimonides (Yad, Ta'anit, ch. 5), and in Sh. Ar., OḤ 549–61.

BIBLIOGRAPHY: Zunz, Ritus, 88ff.; Elbogen, Gottesdienst, 128ff., 229ff.; H. Schauss, *Jewish Festivals* (1938), 96–105; J.T. Lewinski, *Sefer ha-Mo'adim*, 7 (1957), 97–417; S.R. Hirsch, *Horeb, a Philosophy of Jewish Laws and Observances*, 1 (1962), 141–50; D. Goldschmidt (ed.), *Kinot Ashkenaziyyot* (1968).

[Meir Ydit]

AV BET DIN (Heb. אַב בֵּית דִּין; "father of the law court"), title of (a) one who presided over a Jewish ecclesiastical court (**bet din*); (b) the vice president of the *Bet Din ha-Gadol* ("Supreme Court of Justice") during the Second Temple period. The origin and history of the office are obscure. It is first mentioned in the Mishnah which states that, while one of the (pairs of sages listed in Mishnah *Avot* 1) was the **nasi* (president) of the court, the second held the office of *av bet din* (Ḥag. 2:2). The Talmud quotes a tradition that even as early a personality as King Saul was the *nasi*, and his son Jonathan the *av bet din* (MK 26a). According to some scholars, however, the institution originated at the beginning of the Hasmonean period, when the high priest was the *nasi*; as he was not usually a great scholar, he needed an assistant to act as the effective president of the Sanhedrin. Indeed, the main duty of the *av bet din* was evidently to superintend the administration of the court; and it was an official position even in the Lesser Sanhedrin of 23 members found in every city (Ruth R. 2; et al.). A body of regulations affecting the *av bet din* of the Great (and, according to some opinions, also of a Lesser) Sanhedrin was gradually established by the *halakhah*. His appointment was to be made orally (TJ, Hor. 3:2 end, 47a). He could not decide a law in the presence of the *nasi* (Ḥag 16b). The scholars were to rise before him and honor him in the street and on his entry to the Sanhedrin (Kid. 33b; Hor. 13b). Everyone had to rend his garments on the death of an *av bet din* (MK 26a). At *Usha, it was enacted that if an *av bet din* was guilty of an offense he was not to be placed under a ban but was to be told: "Preserve your honor and remain at home" (*ibid.* 17a).

During the geonic period, the term was used to designate the deputy to the principal, *gaon*, of the academies of Babylonia and Ereẓ Israel. Usually the *av bet din* was also the heir-designate of the *gaon*, generally his son. The deputies are also referred to as *rabbenu ha-av* ("our rabbi the father"), or simply *av* ("father").

In the 14th and 15th centuries, the title *av bet din* was occasionally employed by communities as a synonym for the local rabbi. The title appears more frequently in the communal documents of Poland-Lithuania during the 16th and 17th centuries, and of Russia in the 19th century. *Av bet din* then designated the principal of the yeshivah who promulgated halakhic rulings and took part in the communal administration; in particular it was used as the title of the district rabbi of a large community. A rabbi who presided over a *bet din* was termed *rav av bet din* (abbreviated as ראב"ד *ravad*). This traditional connotation has remained. In the State of Israel, *av bet din* also designates the chairman of a civil or a rabbinical court.

BIBLIOGRAPHY: A. Buechler, *Das Synedrion in Jerusalem…* (1902); L. Ginzberg, *Perushim ve-Ḥiddushim be-Yerushalmi*, 3 (1941), 208–20; H. Tchernowitz, *Toledot ha-Halakhah*, 4 (1950), 262–76; Alon, *Meḥkarim*, 2 (1958²), 22–23, no. 37; H. Mantel, *Studies in the History of the Sanhedrin* (1961), 102–29, contains detailed bibliography; ET, 1 (1955), 10–11; Assaf, Ge'onim, 44; H.H. Ben-Sasson, *Hagut ve-Hanhagah* (1959), index; Weiss, in: JJS, 1 (1948), 172–7.

AVDAN (also known as **Avidan**, **Abba Dan**, **Abba Yudan**; c. 200 C.E.), pupil and *amora* ("interpreter") of *Judah ha-Nasi. Avdan lived in Ereẓ Israel during the transition from the tannaitic to the amoraic period (late second and early third centuries C.E.), and his duty was to convey to the student assembly the teachings which Judah ha-Nasi whispered to him (TJ, Ber. 4:1, 7c). In the Talmud, some of his teacher's *halakhot* are cited in his name (Ber. 27b). The Talmud (Yev. 105b) describes an incident in which Avdan was involved. On one occasion R. *Ishmael b. Yose, who was rather corpulent, was still making slow progress to his seat in the academy of Judah ha-Nasi after the latter had already arrived, and the rest of the audience had already seated themselves. Avdan pointedly enquired, "Who is it that steps over the heads of the holy people (in order to get to his seat)?" The reply was "I am Ishmael ben Yose, come to learn Torah from Rabbi (Judah ha-Nasi)." Avdan then asked him, "And are you fit to learn Torah from Rabbi?" Ishmael continued the exchange by enquiring, "Was Moses worthy to learn from the Almighty?" "And are you Moses?" rejoined Avdan. "And is your master the Almighty?" retorted Ishmael. While this exchange was going on, a certain matter was brought before Judah ha-Nasi, and he sent Avdan to clarify an attendant point. Ishmael b. Yose, however, cited a ruling on the subject, which Judah ha-Nasi accepted, making Avdan's mission unnecessary. He thereupon instructed him to return to his place for which purpose he was obliged to make his way over the assembled students. Ishmael thereupon exclaimed, "He of whom the holy people have need may step over (their) heads, but how dare he of whom the holy people have no need step over (their) heads?" "Remain where you are!" said Judah ha-Nasi to Avdan. Legend relates that at that instant Avdan was stricken with leprosy and two of his sons were drowned. This led R. *Naḥman b. Isaac to comment: "Blessed be the All-Merciful, who put Avdan to shame in this world [so that his share in the world to come remains undiminished]."

BIBLIOGRAPHY: Hyman, Toledot, 62.

[Zvi Kaplan]

AVDIMI (Dimi) BAR ḤAMA (probably of the third–fourth century), *amora*. Avdimi is mentioned only in the Babylonian Talmud and is best known for his aggadic interpretation of Exodus 19:17: "The Holy One, blessed be He, overturned the mountain (Sinai) over them (Israel) like an inverted bowl and said to them: 'If you accept the Torah, it is well; but if not, here shall be your burial place'" (Shab. 88a). Aḥa b. Jacob observed (*ibid.*) that since this implied duress, it could provide an excuse for the nonobservance of the Torah. On the verse "But his delight is in the law of the Lord" (Ps. 1:2) he commented that God fulfills the desires of whosoever engages in the study of the Torah (Av. Zar. 19a). A halakhic statement of his is quoted in *Horayot* 10a.

BIBLIOGRAPHY: Hyman, Toledot, s.v.; Bacher, Pal Amor; Z.W. Rabinowitz, *Sha'arei Torat Bavel* (1961), 327.

[Zvi Kaplan]

AVDIMI (Avdimai, Avdima, Avudama, Dimi) OF HAIFA (c. 400 C.E.), Palestinian *amora*. His teachers were *Levi b. Sisi and Resh Lakish (see *Simeon b. Lakish; TJ, Ber. 2, 4, 4d; TJ, Kil. 4, 4, 29b). He apparently possessed compilations of *beraitot* since he refers to "my Mishnah" (i.e., a collection of Mishnayot not included in that of Judah ha-Nasi; Tanḥ., Ẓav, 12; et al.). Several of his aggadic remarks have mystical content (Yal. Ps. 751; et al.). Avdimi is the author of a statement dealing with the proper respect to be shown to a *nasi*, an *av bet din*, and an ordinary scholar respectively (Kid. 33b). His sayings include: "From the day the Temple was destroyed prophecy was taken from the prophets and given to the wise" (BB 12a), and "Before a man eats and drinks he has two hearts [i.e., he is at odds with himself], but after he has eaten and drunk he has only one" (*ibid.*, 12b). According to tradition, Avdimi was buried in Haifa, where his grave is venerated to this day.

BIBLIOGRAPHY: Z. Vilnay, *Maẓẓevot Kodesh be-Ereẓ Yisrael* (1963), 378; Hyman, Toledot, 60–61; Bacher, Pal Amor.

[Yitzhak Dov Gilat]

AVEDAT (**Ovdat**; Ar. "Abde") (Heb. עֲבְדַת), former town in the central Negev, probably named after the deified Nabatean king Obodas; a UNESCO World Heritage Site. It is referred to in ancient sources as Oboda (*tabula Peutingeriana*) Eboda (Ptolemaeus 5:16, 4), and Oboda (Stephanus Byzantinus s.v.).

The site was discovered and mapped in 1870 by E.H. Palmer and C.F. Tyrwhitt-Drake, while a more detailed survey was made by A. Musil in 1902. Survey expeditions conducted

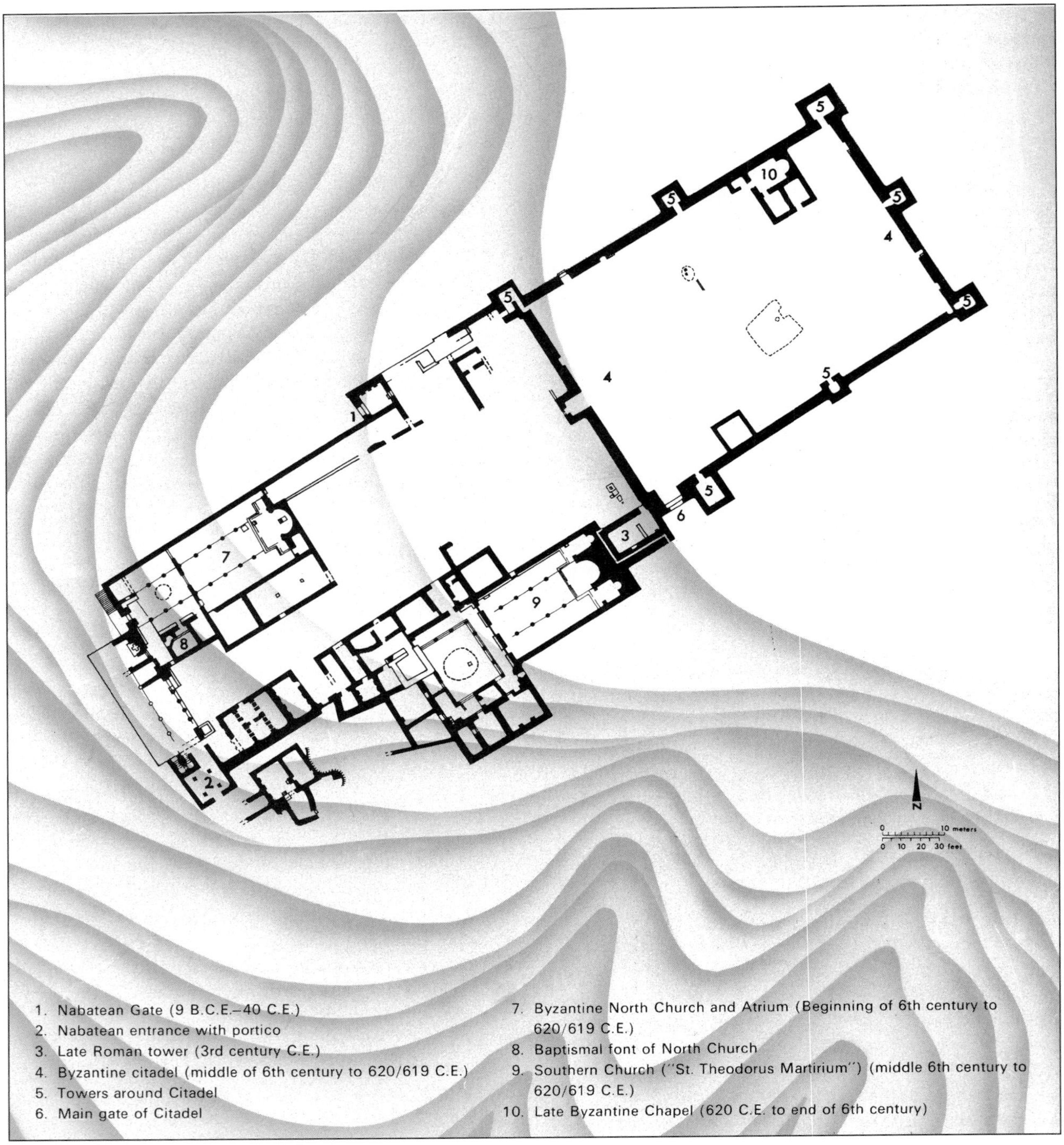

Plan of the reconstructed city of Avedat.

more detailed investigations in 1904 (A. Jaussen, R. Savignac, and H. Vincent) and 1913/14 (C.L. Woolley and T.E. Lawrence), with trial digs at the site by D.H. Colt in 1937. Large-scale excavations were undertaken in the 1950s directed by Michael Avi-Yonah (1958) and Avraham Negev (1959–60). Negev resumed excavations in the 1970s (with R. Cohen) and later in 1989 excavated on the acropolis. More recent excavations were conducted at the site by T. Erickson-Gini (1999–2000). Avedat is situated near the point where the two main routes from *Petra and *Elath converge to form one road leading north to Ḥaluẓah and the Mediterranean coast. Here, in the third century B.C.E., the *Nabateans established a road station for the supply of their caravans with water and food (campsites existed to the north and east of the acropolis), as is shown by the pottery and coins dating back to that period. The diverse nature of the archaeological finds indicates that Avedat occupied a position of great importance in Indo-Arabian commerce. Little more is known of the first few centuries of the city's existence, but it is clear that the site was abandoned at the beginning of the first century B.C.E., perhaps as a result of Alexander Jannaeus' (*Yannai's) conquests in the central Negev. A road leading to Oboda was established in the late first century C.E. and was guarded by a series of small forts. The Nabatean settlement reached its zenith during the reign of Aretas IV (9 B.C.E.–40 C.E.), when a large temple was apparently built on the city's acropolis, though very few remains of it have survived. The Nabatean town appears to have extended over the northern part of the mountain ridge at the edge of which the acropolis was situated. A Roman army camp, situated north of the city, has the remains of a Nabatean building of the first century C.E., on its western side under the *principia*. A Nabatean fort dating to the first and second centuries C.E. was also excavated at En Avdat not far to the southwest of Oboda. A building built of fine ashlars which has been identified as a temple was unearthed to the northwest of the town. In the days of Aretas IV, Avedat was the site of a flourishing ceramic industry. A potter's workshop for the manufacture of the thin painted Nabatean ware was excavated in the eastern part of the city.

By the mid-first century C.E. the Nabatean trade diminished and Avedat began to decline. The Roman conquest in 106 C.E. and the city's annexation to the Roman Empire produced little change. Thamudic and Safa'itic tribes intruded into the area at the beginning of the second century C.E. and scores of inscriptions in their dialects have been found at Avedat. They indicate that these tribes were responsible for the city's destruction sometime after 126 C.E. In about the mid-third century the Romans incorporated southern Ereẓ Israel and Transjordan into their chain of defenses to protect the Empire's southern frontier. Avedat, situated on this line, became a settlement for discharged soldiers who received land grants and other benefits in return for guaranteed military service in times of emergency. A new residential quarter was established on the southern end of the mountain ridge at Oboda. It was not fortified, but consisted of a number of well-built houses along two short roads. A temple dedicated to Zeus-Obodas and to Aphrodite was built, or rebuilt, on the acropolis. A burial cave on the southwestern slope also dates to this period. The Roman settlement was short-lived and the latest Roman epigraphic remains are from the end of the third century. The houses of the residential quarter close to the North Tower were rebuilt c. 300 C.E. and were still in use at time the site was rocked by an earthquake in the early fifth century C.E.

Avedat flourished in the Byzantine period (in the early sixth century). On the acropolis a large citadel, two churches, and a monastery were built. The settlement itself moved down to the western slopes of the mountain ridge. The Byzantine dwellings consisted of houses erected over rock-hewn caves. These caves served for storing and processing agricultural produce. A small bath-house which drew its water from a nearby well was built in the valley west of the city. Extensive remains of dams, irrigation canals, and the many other water-storage installations, as well as winepresses and fruit-drying apparatus, all demonstrate that in the Byzantine period Avedat's economy was based mainly on agriculture and wine production.

The citadel and two churches were razed and the city itself suffered partial destruction in the Persian invasion in 614. Twenty years later, the Arab invaders found there hardly more than a village. While there is evidence of partial rebuilding and repair, the total absence of early Arabic pottery indicates that after the middle of the seventh century the city was completely deserted.

The ancient city of Avedat has been reconstructed by the Israel Department for Landscaping and Preservation of Historic Sites and is open to visits by the general public. An experimental agricultural station was established in 1959 near Avedat, with research conducted on methods of ancient desert agriculture, under the direction of Michael *Evenari. The farm was based on methods presumed to have been used by the builders of the ancient terraces and runoff systems in the Negev. The farm made use of field walls and installations that had been preserved at that location since ancient times.

BIBLIOGRAPHY: N. Glueck, *Deities and Dolphins* (1965), index; A. Negev, *Arim ba-Midbar* (1966); idem, in: IEJ, 11 (1961), 127–38; 13 (1963), 113–24; idem, in: *Sefer Eilat* (1963), 118–48; idem, *Avedat* (Heb., 1962); idem, in: *Archaeology*, 14 (1961), 122–36; Palmer, in: PEFQS (1871), 1–80; A. Musil, *Arabia Petraea*, 2 (Ger., 1908), 106–51; Janssen et al., in: RB, 13 (1904), 404–24; 14 (1905), 74–89, 235–44; Woolley and Lawrence, in: *Palestine Exploration Fund, Annual*, 3 (1914–15), 93–107. **ADD. BIBLIOGRAPHY:** M. Evenari, L. Shanan, and N. Tadmor, *The Negev: The Challenge of a Desert* (1971); Y. Tsafrir and Z. Meshel, *Archaeological Survey at En Avdat* (1977); A. Negev, *The Masters of the Desert* (1983), s.v. Eboda; Y. Tsafrir, L. Di Segni, and J. Green, *Tabula Imperii Romani. Iudaea – Palaestina. Maps and Gazetteer.* (1994), 114–15; A. Negev, "Obodas the God in a Nabatean-Arabic Inscription from the Vicinity of Oboda and a Review of Other Nabatean Inscriptions," in: R. Rosenthal-Heginbottom, *The Nabateans in the Negev* (2003).

[Avraham Negev / Shimon Gibson (2nd ed.)]

AVEDON, RICHARD (1923–2004), U.S. photographer. Born in New York City, the son of a Russian-Jewish immigrant, Avedon carved out a long and successful career as a photographer of fashion models and celebrities, becoming the first staff photographer of the influential magazine the *New Yorker*, in 1992. He studied philosophy at Columbia University in 1941–42, before entering the U.S. Merchant Marine during World War II, where he served in the photography section until 1944. He studied photography in New York at the New School for Social Research, where one of his teachers was Alexey Brodovitch, the influential art director of *Harper's Bazaar* magazine. Avedon became Brodovitch's protégé, and he made his first photographs for the fashion magazine at 21.

In 1946 he established the Richard Avedon Studio in New York. He remained a staff photographer for *Harper's Bazaar* until 1966, during which time his fresh energetic photographs created a "democratic" vision of high fashion, with his models, often clothed by Dior, strolling down the streets of Paris and chatting with shopkeepers and street performers. He virtually reinvented portraiture as a photographic genre, making arresting, though not always flattering, images of the country's cultural elite (artists, fashion designers, writers, actors) and culturally destitute (drifters and carnival workers he photographed in the western United States in the early 1980s). Posing his subjects against empty white backdrops and removing the descriptive devices of setting and props, Avedon called attention to the subject's gesture and expression, to the drama and psychology revealed in that person's gaze or the lines of his or her face. He worked as an advertising photographer, director, and visual consultant for film and television. One of his most famous fashion photographs, made in 1995 in Paris, shows the then famous model Dovina, in a gown by Dior, before several live elephants. The 1957 film *Funny Face*, with Fred Astaire and Audrey Hepburn, was loosely based on his life. In 1959 Avedon's first book of photographs, designed by Brodovitch, with a text by Truman Capote, was published under the title *Observations*. He joined *Vogue*, a rival fashion magazine to *Harper's Bazaar*, in 1966.

Traveling widely, Avedon produced several notable bodies of work. In 1963 he went to the American South and photographed the civil rights movement, collaborating with James Baldwin on the book *Nothing Personal*. In the late 1960s and 1970s he photographed antiwar demonstrators, and in 1971 he went to Vietnam to document military leaders and war victims. From 1985 to 1992 his editorial work appeared exclusively in *Egoiste*, the French literary and art magazine.

His work is in the permanent collections of major museums, and he has been the subject of numerous solo exhibitions, including a display of his fashion photography at the Metropolitan Museum of Art in New York in 1978. He was also the recipient of numerous honors, including an honorary doctorate from London's Royal College of Art in 1989, the International Photography Prize from the Erna and Victor Hasselblad Foundation in 1991, and the Master of Photography Award from the International Center of Photography in 1993, the year his book, *An Autobiography*, was published.

"A portrait is not a likeness," Avedon said. "The moment an emotion or fact is transformed into a photograph it is no longer a fact but an opinion. There is no such thing as inaccuracy in a photograph. All photographs are accurate. None of them is the truth."

Avedon once described himself as "completely agnostic, someone who doesn't believe in anything." John Avedon, his son, described his father in a film about him, similarly, and with affection and a bit of humor. "My father, who has absolutely no religious sentiment of any kind, and has no cultural sentiment in terms of Jewish culture, has a very standard Jewish personality, if that's not too big a generalization to make. And by that I mean he thrives on anxiety. It's a way of life."

In *Richard Avedon: Darkness and Light*, a documentary produced in 1995, Avedon, who considered himself unequivocally secular, said his Jewishness was "connected to something pure in the genes, something in me that was a Jew." He tells of an intimate revelation with his experience of touching an ancient Torah in a synagogue in Europe. "I was shaking," he said. "I can't explain it."

[Stewart Kampel (2nd ed.)]

°AVÉ-LALLEMANT, FRIEDRICH CHRISTIAN BENEDICT (1809–1892), German criminologist and writer. Avé-Lallemant was a senior police official in Luebeck from 1843 to 1868 who studied the psychopathology of criminals and wrote novels about the underworld. In his studies of the language of the underworld, he had noted the large proportion of Yiddish words in the vocabulary, chiefly derived from Hebrew and Aramaic and therefore unintelligible to police and criminologists. He therefore included a translation and analysis of approximately 8,000 words and idiomatic expressions, an elucidation of 1,200 abbreviations, a basic Yiddish grammar, and illustrative texts. In 1889 the linguistic section was reprinted under the title *Dolmetsch der Geheimsprache* as a manual for court officials and was recommended for businessmen. The nonlinguistic sections were reprinted in 1914.

BIBLIOGRAPHY: Rejzen, Leksikon, 1 (1926), 48–50; F. Avé-Lallemant, *Das deutsche Gaunerthum* (1914), v–xi (introd.); NDB, 1 (1953), 465; *Algemeyne Entsiklopedye*, 1 (1934), 175–6.

[Sol Liptzin]

AVELEI ZION (Heb. אֲבֵלֵי צִיּוֹן; "Mourners of Zion," based on Isa. 61:3), groups of Jews devoted to mourning the destruction of the Temple and to praying for the redemption of Zion. The customs of this group can be traced to the period immediately following the destruction of the Second Temple. Perhaps the group itself arose in Jerusalem. The Babylonian Talmud (BB 60b) mentioned that after the destruction of the Temple many became *perushim* (ascetics) and abstained from meat and wine as a sign of mourning. Rabbis such as Joshua b. Hananiah and Ishmael, while sympathizing with their sentiments, felt that these customs could not be universally applied. After the Bar Kokhba War (132–5) Jews were no longer allowed to live in Jerusalem and could only visit it on the Ninth of *Av. After the Arab conquest, however, the Jewish community resettled in Jerusalem and this led to the revival of the Avelei Zion. They were obviously inspired by mystical and messianic ideas which found expression in writings such as the *Orot ha-Mashi'aḥ, Nistarot de-R. Shimon b. Yoḥai*, and the *Tefillot R. Shimon b. Yoḥai*. The ninth-century author of the *Pesikta Rabbati* may have belonged to the group: he praises them highly, although they were held in ridicule by the community at large (158a/b).

The Avelei Zion would not engage in either commerce or trade and therefore lived in great poverty; for their meager subsistence they depended on the charity of Diaspora communities and pilgrims. The Chronicle of Ahimaaz reports a donation of 1,000 dinars pledged by Paltiel in Fostat (c. 969) for the benefit of the *Avelei Beit Olamim*. After Paltiel's death, his son reinterred him and his wife in Jerusalem and donated a considerable sum for the *Avelei ha-Heikhal*. Both these terms are evidently identical with Avelei Zion. Avelei Zion is mentioned for the first time in the *Halakhot Keẓuvot* (Italy, first half of the ninth century) where it is incorporated into a prayer of consolation as part of the grace recited in the home of a mourner ("Comfort, O Lord our God, the mourners of Zion and the mourners of Jerusalem"). This phrase was also included in the prayer *Naḥem* of the afternoon service on the Ninth of Av, although it is not mentioned either in the order of prayers in the Jerusalem Talmud (Ber. 4:3, 8a) or in *Seder Rav Amram*. The new formula is found in *Maḥzor Vitry*, 269.

Groups of Avelei Zion existed also in Germany, Italy, Yemen, and other Oriental countries. In Germany, one of the prominent members of this group was the liturgical poet *Meir b. Isaac, a contemporary of Rashi. With the conquest of Palestine by the Seljuks (1071) and by the Crusaders (1099) the Avelei Zion disappeared from Jerusalem, though *Benjamin of Tudela, who visited the city about 1179, talked to "R. Abraham Alcostantini, the saintly ascetic, who was one of the mourners of Jerusalem." Benjamin also heard of Avelei Zion in Yemen "who live in caves or secluded houses and fast every day except for Sabbaths and holidays and pray to God to have mercy upon dispersed Israel," and of others like them in Germany.

Most of the Karaites who settled in Jerusalem in the first half of the ninth century ordered their lives according to the customs of the Avelei Zion. Their scholars, for example, Daniel al-Kumisi and *Sahl b. Maẓli'aḥ, sent messages to the Karaites in the Diaspora calling upon them to abandon the vanities of this world and go to Jerusalem to spend their days there in prayer for the redemption of Israel. Some scholars believed, in fact, that the Avelei Zion were a Karaite sect, but this can hardly be maintained as they seem to have developed before the emergence of Karaism. Possibly the Karaite scholars Tobias b. Moses (11th century), who lived in Jerusalem for a time, and Judah Hadassi (12th century) of Constantinople belonged to the Avelei Zion.

BIBLIOGRAPHY: Mann, in: JQR, 12 (1920), 271; S. Schechter, *Studies in Judaism*, 3 (1924), 6–7; Baron, Social, 2:5 (1957), 185, index; Zucker, in: *Sefer ha-Yovel… Ch. Albeck* (1963), 378 ff.

[Zvi Avneri]

AVELIM or **OVELIM** and other variants (Heb. אֲבֵלִים or אוֹבְלִים; "vale" or "pasture"), a valley and village in Galilee, about 7½ mi. (12 km.) northwest of Sepphoris. It was inhabited in the Late Bronze Age and rebuilt in Roman times. The *tannaim* Yose b. Peredah and Eliezer b. Judah lived in Avelim (Tosef., Er. 1:1; Er. 11b; Tosef., Ma'as. Sh. 1:9). One of the caravan routes leading from Egypt to Damascus and Mesopotamia passed near it, as did the Roman road connecting Acre and Sepphoris. According to the *amora* Abba b. Kahana (c. 400), Job's oxen and asses were stolen by marauders (Job 1:14) in the valley of Avelim (PdRK 66; et al.), which may reflect the insecurity of the region in his own time. Avelim is the present-day village of Ibillīn, with a population of about 1,500 in 1970 (60% Christian and 40% Muslim). In 2002 the population was over 10,000 (55% Muslim and 45% Christian). Income was about half the national average.

Relics from several periods have been discovered in the area. From the Roman period there is a *mikveh*, from the Byzantine period a dwelling, and a wall dating to the Crusaders period was also found. A synagogue of the talmudic period, including part of a decorative lintel with an Aramaic inscription and a stone decorated with a *menorah*, was found at Khirbat 'Ibillīn.

BIBLIOGRAPHY: Press, Erez, 1 (1951^2), 4; S. Klein, *Sefer ha-Yishuv*, 1 (1939), 1; S.J.L. Rapoport, *Erekh Millin*, 1 (1914), 4; Neubauer, Géogr., 259–60; Press, in: *Jeschurun*, 17 (1930), 261–7; J. Braslavi (Braslavski), *Le Heker Arzenu* (1954), 74, 277–80; Ginsberg and Klein, in BJPES, 2, nos. 3–4 (1935), 47–48 (inscription not in Frey, Corpus).

[Michael Avi-Yonah / Shaked Gilboa (2nd ed.)]

°**AVEMPACE** (**Abu Bakr Muhammad ibn Yahya ibn Bajja**, called **Ibn al-Ṣā'igh**; d. 1138), Muslim philosopher, born in Saragossa; lived in Seville, Granada, and Fez where he died supposedly as the result of an accusation of heresy. He was a celebrated philosopher, mathematician, musician, poet, and served as vizier. His influence on Spanish philosophical studies was profound and continued the tradition of *al-Fārābī. Through the writings of *Averroes, he influenced the whole later Jewish philosophical school, writing in Hebrew, in Spain, Southern France, and Italy until the 16th century. His *Governance of the Solitary* was summarized by *Moses b. Joshua of Narbonne and, until the publication of the original Arabic text in 1946, the Hebrew summary was the only source for the knowledge of Avempace's political thought. He describes the way of life the philosopher ought to follow in the existing corrupt communities in order to achieve union with the Active *Intellect. Perhaps under the impact of the chaotic conditions then existing in Spain and North Africa, he seems to counsel the sage to withdraw from society rather than to attempt to influence it toward a more philosophic course. In this he influenced Maimonides in his *Guide of the Perplexed* which at times also seems to suggest that the solitary way is the best. His *Epistle of Farewell*, translated into Hebrew in the first half of the 14th century by Ḥayyim ibn Vivas, may be considered a summary of Aristotle's *Nicomachean Ethics*. It contains his doctrine of the immortality of the intellect which can be achieved only through philosophic study, not through mystical exercises. He later developed this theme at greater length in his *Epistles of Conjunction*. Excerpts from these works were translated by Shem Tov ibn *Falaquera in his philosophical source book to *Maimonides' *Guide of the Perplexed* entitled

Moreh ha-Moreh. In general, Avempace influenced the Jewish world through Maimonides and Averroes in the field of political theory and the doctrine of the immortality of the intellect. In addition he was also known for his views on physics and astronomy (Maimonides, *Guide*, 2:9, 24; 3:29). Ḥasdai *Crescas frequently refers to him in connection with the interpretation of certain passages of Aristotle's *Physics*. Crescas' knowledge derives from quotations of Avempace's views by Averroes.

BIBLIOGRAPHY: R. Lerner and M. Mahdi, *Medieval Political Philosophy* (1963), 122–33; Aṣín Palacios, in: *Al-Andalus*, 7 (1942), 1–47; 8 (1943), 1–87; Schreiner, in: *Mi-Mizraḥ u-mi-Ma'arav*, 1 (1895), 96–106; 4 (1899), 26–39; Shem Tov Ibn Falaquera, *Moreh ha-Moreh* (1837), 135–8 and passim; Maimonides, *Guide*, ciii–cviii (introd.); H.A. Wolfson, *Crescas' Critique of Aristotle* (1929), index. **ADD. BIBLIOGRAPHY:** EIS², 3 (1971), s.v. Badjdja (includes bibliography).

[Lawrence V. Berman]

AVENARY, HANOCH (formerly **Herbert Loewenstein**; 1908–1994), musicologist. Born in Danzig, he immigrated to Palestine in 1936. He studied musicology, literature, and art history at the universities of Leipzig, Munich, Frankfurt, and Koenigsberg (Kaliningrad). His musicological work centered on the history of Jewish music from the Middle Ages to the 19th century. After serving as a major in the research department of the Israeli Air Force from 1948 to 1965, he became a lecturer and research fellow at the Hebrew University (1965–72) and senior lecturer at Tel Aviv University. He was appointed professor in 1972 and was a guest professor in Vienna (1973) and Heidelberg (1982–83). In 1994 he received the Israel Prize for his achievements in Jewish music research. His scientific editions include *Il primo libro delle canzonette* (1975) and *Il secondo libro de madrigali* (1989) of S. Rossi. His publications include *Wort und Ton bei Oswald von Wolkenstein* (1932); *Formal Structure of Psalms and Canticles in Early Jewish and Christian Chant* (1953); *Studies in the Hebrew, Syrian and Greek Liturgical Recitative* (1963); *The Cantorial Fantasia of the 18th and 19th Centuries* (1968); *The Ashkenazi Tradition of Biblical Chant between 1500 and 1900* (1978); *Encounters of East and West in Music* (1979); *Kantor Salomon Sulzer und seine Zeit: Eine Dukumentation* (1985); *The Aspects of Time and Environment in Jewish Traditional Music* (1987); and several articles on Jewish music for encyclopedias, including *Juedische Musik* in *MGG VII* (1957) and the section on music (from the Middle Ages to the present) in the *Encyclopedia Judaica*. His personal archive is at the JNUL Music Department.

ADD. BIBLIOGRAPHY: Grove online; MGG².

[Gila Flam and Israela Stein (2nd ed.)]

AVENDAUTH (**Avendeuth**, **Avendeath**; mid-12th century), translator active in Toledo, Spain, in 1135–53. His activities took place mainly under the patronage of Archbishop Raimundode la Sauvetat. Later generations thought him to have been a convert to Christianity, and he was identified by some scholars with John Hispanus, a translator of considerable importance. It has been suggested that not only was he a loyal Jew throughout his life, but, on the basis of an analysis of the introduction to the *De Anima*, that he is also probably the well-known philosopher and historian Abraham *Ibn Daud (c. 1110–80). A thorough examination and investigation by the French scholar Mme. M.T. d'Alverny of the manuscripts containing the rendering into Latin of *Avicenna's *De Anima*, and of the dedicatory preface found in many of them, made her realize that Jourdain, the first bibliographer to call attention to this work, had erroneously supplied the translator with the first name John; in so doing, he had prepared the ground for the alleged change of faith and the assumptions and conjectures of subsequent scholars. The correct reading of the dedication is *reverendissimo Toletanae episcopo Johanni*, not Johannes. The work, it follows, was dedicated to John, archbishop of Toledo (1151–66), and not to his predecessor Raymond, as had been thought from the time of Jourdain. In this introduction, and in others, the translator is identified as "Avendehut Israelita philosophus," or simply "Avendeuth Israelita"; the name John does not appear in any of them. Besides the introduction to the *De Anima*, the first chapters of Avicenna's *Shifa'* in Latin begin with *Verba Avendeuth Israelitae*; a small part of the work, bearing the title *De Universalibus*, also has in the manuscripts the name Avendeuth or Avendeath. He translated philosophical and scientific works. In his work, Avendauth collaborated with Dominicus Gundisalvi. It is doubtful that the latter, a well-known scholar who was instrumental in the transmission of Arabic culture to Europe, knew the original language of the works that he rendered into Latin. Painstaking study of the style and terminology are needed before a conclusive statement can be made; it may, however, be that Ibn Daud was the intermediary between the Arabic and the Latin version. He was the author of *Epitome totius astrologie*.

BIBLIOGRAPHY: Ibn Daud, Tradition, xxvi–xxvii; M. Steinschneider, *Die Hebraeischen Uebersetzungen des Mittelalters* (1893), 20–23; D'Alvery, in: *Homenaje a Millás-Vallicrosa*, 1 (1954), 19–43. **ADD. BIBLIOGRAPHY:** D. Romano, *La ciencia hispanojudía* (1992), 113–22; idem, in: H. Beinart (ed.), *The Sephardi Legacy*, 1 (1992), 252.

[Abraham Solomon Halkin]

AVERAH (Heb. עֲבֵרָה; "transgression"), term used in rabbinic literature to designate a transgression of the *halakhah*. It is also used as the opposite of *mitzvah*.

AVERBAKH, LEOPOLD LEONIDOVICH (1903–1938?), Soviet Russian critic and the leading spirit of the Russian Association of Proletarian Writers (RAPP), which dominated the Soviet literary scene from 1929 to 1932. A fanatical, dogmatic Communist, Averbakh, unlike the later exponents of socialist realism, claimed that the regime had nothing to fear from the truth and did not flinch from writing about the more unpleasant aspects of Soviet life. After the dissolution of RAPP and the establishment of the even more strictly regimented Union of Soviet Writers, Averbakh was accused of a multitude of crimes, ranging from Trotskyism to the fact that he was a brother-in-law of the disgraced secret police chief Yagoda.

These attacks on Averbakh had a strongly antisemitic flavor. He disappeared during the purges in the late 1930s.

BIBLIOGRAPHY: H. Borland, *Soviet Literary Theory and Practice During the First Five-Year Plan 1928–1932* (1950); E.J. Brown, *Proletarian Episode in Russian Literature 1928–1932* (1953).

[Maurice Friedberg]

°**AVERROES (Abu al-Walid Muhammad ibn Rushd**; 1126–1198), qadi, jurist, noted physician, and one of the greatest Islamic philosophers. Averroes, who lived in Spain, is best known as the outstanding commentator of the medieval period on Aristotle's works. He commented on most of Aristotle's works and on five of them composed three different kinds of commentaries – long, middle, and short or epitome. He also wrote a commentary on Plato's *Republic* (trans. R. Lerner, 1974), an epitome of Ptolemy's *Almagest*, and commentaries or paraphrases on logical, scientific, and medical writings of authors such as *Galen, *Alexander of Aphrodisias, al-*Farabi, and *Avicenna, and on a book on the principles of Islamic jurisprudence by al-*Ghazālī. His major independent work was *Tahāfut al-Tahāfut* ("The Incoherence of the Incoherence," trans. S. van den Bergh, 1954), a defense of Islamic Aristotelian philosophy against the attacks made on it by al-Ghazālī in his *Tahāfut al-Falāsifa* ("The Incoherence of the Philosophers," trans. M.E. Marmura, 1997). In addition he wrote short treatises on the relationship of philosophy, religion, and society (see G.F. Hourani (trans.), *Averroes on the Harmony of Religion and Philosophy*, 1961); some medical works; and works on astronomy and Islamic law.

Philosophic Teachings

Averroes' views on the position of the philosopher in society account for some of the main characteristics of his writings. He holds that it is incumbent upon philosophers to observe the religious law; but this law contains pointers to philosophic truths which they, and only they, are capable of understanding. They must hide this knowledge from the generality of people, i.e., the masses, and they may reveal it only to the chosen few, whose intellectual ability and philosophic training enable them to understand it. With other Islamic philosophers, Averroes shared the vision of an ideal state ruled by philosophers (patterned after Plato's *Republic*). However, unlike them, he does not expect that political revolution will bring this state into being in the near future, though he does not altogether exclude the possibility that a succession of enlightened rulers may bring it about. The absence of the ideal state in the present does not bring Averroes to Ibn Bājja's (*Avempace) position that the philosopher should live as a solitary stranger within the community in which he finds himself. Instead Averroes advocates that the philosopher should live within the state as an integral part, working for its welfare. At the same time, the philosopher must pursue his philosophic studies by himself or with likeminded people, but not propagate philosophy, since the public teaching of philosophy destroys the community. In his commentaries Averroes endeavors to grasp the intentions and conceptions of Aristotle, whom he calls "the perfect man." As part of his exposition he polemicizes against *Avicenna who, according to his view, had compromised some Aristotelian teachings by capitulating to theological concerns. Averroes sometimes resorts to philological methods to establish the text on which he comments and, not knowing Greek, he compares the Arabic versions. While a number of Averroes' interpretations deal with fine points of Aristotelian philosophy, there are major doctrines which serve to determine his position. Thus he objects to Avicenna's view that essence and existence are ontologically distinct, that is to say, that existence is an accident superadded to essence, holding instead that they are merely analytic distinctions within individual substances. Differing once again with Avicenna who considers God an intelligence apart from the world, Averroes inclines to identify God with the mover of the first celestial sphere. Whereas for Avicenna the essential attributes of God must be understood negatively, for Averroes they have a positive meaning. Considering the origin of the world, Averroes rejects the Neoplatonic doctrine of emanation, holding instead that the world is eternal. In psychology Averroes changed his views over time, but his final position on the intellect seems to be a doctrine of the unity of the material intellect in all human beings, from which it follows that human immortality is collective rather than individual. All in all, while Avicenna's interpretation of Aristotle had a certain theological bent, Averroes' was more naturalistic. While Averroes had little influence on Islamic thought, Latin and Hebrew translations of his works made him a central figure in Christian and Jewish philosophy from the 13th century on.

Role in Jewish Philosophy

In late medieval Jewish philosophy, Averroes became, next to Maimonides, the most important influence. He arrived at this stature as a result of Maimonides' high recommendation of him and by means of the many Hebrew translations of his works, especially of the commentaries. Jewish philosophers describe him by such appellations as "the great sage," "the chief of the commentators [on Aristotle]," and "the soul and the intellect of Aristotle." Among Jewish philosophers (as among Christians) there were some who tried to harmonize Averroes' teachings with those of Judaism, while there were others who had a purely philosophic interest in his views. Since Maimonides and Averroes disagreed on certain philosophic topics, some Jewish philosophers also attempted to reconcile their divergent views. Nearly all of Averroes' commentaries and independent works were translated into Hebrew, many of them more than once, but most of these translations exist at present only in manuscript form. Critical editions of the Arabic, Hebrew, and Latin versions of Averroes' commentaries, as well as modern translations of them, have appeared under the collective title *Corpus Commentariorum Averrois in Aristotelem* (see H.A. Wolfson, in: *Speculum*, 6 (1931) and 37 (1963), and G. Endress, "Averrois Opera," in: Endress and Aertsen, *Averroes and the Aristotelian Tradition* (1999)).

Hebrew Translations of His Works

The range of the translations of the commentaries may be gathered from the following partial list: Jacob b. Abba Mari *Anatoli translated in 1232 the middle commentary on Porphyry's *Isagoge* and those on the first four books of Aristotle's *Organon*; Moses b. Samuel ibn *Tibbon translated between 1244 and 1258 almost all of the epitomes of Aristotle's works on natural science and metaphysics, and in 1261 the middle commentary on the *De Anima*; Zerahiah b. Shealtiel Hen (*Gracian) translated in 1284 the middle commentaries on the *Physics* and the *Metaphysics*; Jacob b. Machir translated in 1289 the epitome of the *Organon*, and in 1302 the epitome of part of the *De Animalibus*; Kalonymus b. Kalonymus of Arles translated between 1313 and 1317 the middle commentaries on the *Topics, Sophistical Refutations, Physics, On Generation and Corruption, Meteorology*, and *Metaphysics*, as well as the long commentaries on the *Posterior Analytics* and, it seems, the *Physics* and *Metaphysics*; Samuel b. Judah of Marseilles translated in 1320–22 the middle commentary on the *Nicomachean Ethics* and the commentary on Plato's *Republic*; Todros Todrosi of Arles translated in 1337 the middle commentaries on the *Rhetoric* and *Poetics*.

In addition to the commentaries on Aristotle, Averroes' independent works were also translated into Hebrew. The *Tahāfut al-Tahāfut* was translated twice: once under the title *Happalat ha-Happalah* by *Kalonymus b. David b. Todros, who completed his translation in 1328; a second time anonymously under the title *Sefer ha-Tekumah*. The anonymous translation was used by *Moses b. Joshua of Narbonne. There also exist medieval Hebrew translations of the *Fasl al-Maqāl* (the treatise on the connection between religion and philosophy); of logical, physical, and metaphysical questions; the treatises on the conjunction of the hylic and the active intellects, and the *De Substantia Orbis*. The Hebrew translations of Averroes' commentaries, in turn, gave rise to supercommentaries on these works. The most famous of the authors of the supercommentaries was *Levi b. Gershom (Gersonides) (see R. Glasner, in: JQR, 86 (1995), 51ff.). Other commentators on the commentaries by Averroes include *Jedaiah ha-Penini, Solomon of Urgul, R.S. ha-Levi, Isaac Albalag, Judah b. Isaac ha-Kohen of Provence (second half of the 14th century), Moses of Narbonne, Joseph *Kaspi, Abraham *Avigdor, Mordecai Natan, Abraham *Bibago, Isaac *Ibn Shem Tov, Shem Tov ben Joseph *Ibn Shem Tov, *Judah b. Jehiel (Messer Leon), Eli Habillo, and Elijah *Delmedigo. In addition, Levi b. Gershom, Moses of Narbonne, Joseph *Ibn Shem Tov, and Elijah Delmedigo also wrote commentaries on some of Averroes' original works.

Influence on Jewish Philosophy

Since Averroes and Maimonides were both born in Cordova, some historians (for example, Leo Africanus) assumed that the two were close to one another; it has even been maintained that Maimonides was a pupil of Averroes. Some have found Averroes' views in the *Guide* (for example, Isaac Abrabanel in his commentary on *Guide* 1:51). However, all of these conjectures are incorrect, for, while some of Maimonides' views appear to be similar to those of Averroes, it seems certain that Maimonides was not familiar with Averroes' commentaries when he wrote the *Guide* (S. Pines (trans.), *Guide of the Perplexed* (1963), CVIII–CXXIII; H.A. Wolfson, *Crescas' Critique of Aristotle* (1929), 323). Maimonides mentions Averroes' works in two letters. In 1190, when Maimonides had completed at least some portions of the *Guide*, he wrote to his pupil Joseph b. Judah Ibn Shem Tov that he had received only recently Averroes' commentaries with the exception of the one on *De sensu et sensato*. He also wrote that, while he had not had time to study them carefully, he was favorably impressed by their content (*Iggerot ha-Rambam*, ed. I. Shailat (1995), I, 299, 313). Similarly, in a letter to Samuel ibn Tibbon, the translator of the *Guide*, in 1199, Maimonides strongly recommends the commentaries of Averroes as an aid for understanding Aristotle (ibid., II, 552–53). As a result perhaps of Maimonides' high praise for Averroes' commentaries, they became in Hebrew translation the prime source for studying Aristotelian science, supplanting even the works of the Stagirite himself. Among the philosophers of the 13th and 14th centuries, Levi b. Gershom and Moses of Narbonne are usually considered faithful followers of Averroes. However, this applies only to Moses of Narbonne, whose commentary on Maimonides' *Guide* is pervaded by Averroes' ideas (see esp. on 1:68 and 1:70), not to Gersonides. While the latter accepts a number of Averroes' teachings, e.g., the eternity of the world (but only partially); that the existence of a thing is identical with its essence, not something superadded to it; that God can be described through positive attributes; he differs from him on a number of others (*Milhamot Adonai*, passim). R. Glasner has shown in several studies that in his supercommentaries on Averroes' epitomes and middle commentaries on Aristotle's books on natural science, Gersonides rejects certain fundamental Aristotelian positions presented therein, such as the Aristotelian accounts of natural motion and violent motion (see, e.g., Glasner, in C. Sirat et al. (eds.), *Les méthodes de travail de Gersonide* (2003), 90–103, esp. 98–101). Averroes' commentaries served as the principle source for the first two 13th-century encyclopedias of science and philosophy, the *Midrash ha-Ḥokhmah* by Judah b. Solomon ha-Kohen ibn *Matkah and the *De'ot ha-Filosofim* (ascribed incorrectly in the manuscripts to Samuel ibn Tibbon) by Shem Tov b. Joseph ibn *Falaquera. While the *Midrash ha-Ḥokhmah* presents a much abridged version of Averroes' commentaries, the *De'ot ha-Filosofim* quotes them at length, often blending sections of the various commentaries together for the sake of clarification and comprehensiveness. Falaquera explains his reliance on Averroes in his introduction where he states: "All that I write are the words of Aristotle as explained in the commentaries of the scholar Averroes, for he was the last of the commentators and he incorporated what was best from the [earlier] commentaries." This view of Averroes is explicitly shared by another 13th-century encyclopedist, Levi ben Hayyim of Villefranche, who writes that "the books of Aristotle are better than the books of anyone else" and the "commentaries of Averroes are superior to all other commentaries." Falaquera in another work, his commentary on Maimonides' *Guide*, writes that Averroes "inclines toward the views of our sages" (*Moreh ha-Moreh*, ed., Y. Shiffman (2001), intro., 116), and he cites him in his commentary over 80 times. In his *Iggeret ha-Vikku'aḥ*, he bases his own attempt to harmonize philosophy and religion on that of Averroes' *Fasl al-Maqāl*. Gershom b. *Solomon, the author of the popular late 13th-century encyclopedia, *Sha'ar ha-Shamayim*, also cites many of Averroes' views, although he generally does not incorporate his commentaries on Aristotle. Other philosophers influenced by Averroes include Isaac Albalag, Jedaiah ha-Penini, Joseph Kaspi, Nissim of Marseilles, and Moses ben Judah Nogah. *Hillel b. Samuel of Verona in his *Tagmulei ha-Nefesh* follows Averroes in teaching that there exists only one universal soul (1:5) and that the human intellect is ultimately united with the cosmic active intellect (1:6), but, contrary to Averroes, he holds that the human intellect is part of the individual human soul and that it is subject to reward and punishment in the hereafter (2). Many of Averroes' opinions are also cited by the 14th-century Karaite philosopher *Aaron b. *Elijah in his *Eẓ Ḥayyim*, though this philosopher opposes Averroes on the whole. Ḥasdai *Crescas was very familiar with Averroes' commentaries, in particular those on Aristotle's natural science, and relies on them for his knowledge of Aristotelian science. While a severe opponent and learned critic of Averroes, he accepts his view that God can be described by means of positive attributes, a view also accepted by Abraham *Shalom in his *Neveh Shalom*. During the late Middle Ages, which saw the gradual decline of Jewish philosophy, there still existed Jewish philosophers who studied Averroes and followed his teachings. Simeon *Duran uses Averroes' treatises on philosophy and religion in his *Keshet u-Magen* (directed against Islam), while he attacks his system in his *Magen Avot*. Even Averroes' opponents accepted his views on theologically neutral topics, which were not in conflict with religious teachings, for example in logic, or in instances in which his views supported Jewish teachings. Judah b. Jehiel (Messer Leon), who commented on Averroes' logic, also followed him in his *Mikhlal Yofi*, a compendium on logic. Obadiah *Sforno, who in his *Or Ammim* defends Jewish tradition against Aristotle (interpreted according to Averroes), accepts some of Averroes' views concerning God's knowledge and will, as set down in his *Tahāfut al-Tahāfut*. Joseph b. Shem Tov, who composed commentaries on Averroes' treatises on the material intellect and on conjunction, cites, in his *Kevod Elohim*, many of Averroes' views even though, in general, he is against philosophy and the "stubborn" Averroes. The last important Jewish Averroist was Elijah Delmedigo, who, in 1482, composed a work concerning the intellect and prophecy according to the teachings of Averroes and who used Averroes' *Fasl al-Maqāl* in his treatise on faith and reason, *Beḥinat ha-Dat*. Elijah was a faithful student of Averroes and was very familiar with Averroes' philosophic works, some of which he translated into Latin, some of which he commented upon, and many of which he used in his independent treatises on psychology, metaphysics, and especially natural science. In the 15th century when Jewish thought assumed a more conservative theological character, Jewish thinkers gradually moved away from the radical theological teachings of Averroes. Thus Isaac *Abrabanel, who at times bases himself on Averroes in his commentary on Maimonides' *Guide*, polemicizes against him in his *Shamayim Hadashim* and in other works. Similarly Abraham *Bibago, who wrote commentaries on several of Averroes' writings, including one on Averroes' middle commentary on the *Metaphysics* (in which he also refers to Averroes' short and long commentaries), attacks him in his *Derekh Emunah*. For a variety of reasons Averroes' scientific commentaries also became less popular, although, as is evident also from the many Hebrew copies of them written in the 16th century, they continued to be studied. However, by the mid-16th century, their impact seems to have become minimal.

Medical Writings

Among Averroes' medical works, the most important is *Kitāb al-Kullīyāt fī al-Tibb*, a seven-book summary of the medicine of his day. This work was translated into Latin under the title *Colliget* in 1255 in Padua by Jacob Bonacosa, and was printed many times (1490, 1496, 1497, 1514, 1531, and 1533). Jacob *Mantino translated the fifth book of the *Kullīyāt* (on special drugs) into Latin. This translation was made from the first (?) Hebrew translation and also printed a number of times. On Averroes' approach to pharmacology, as expressed in the fifth book of the *Kullīyāt*, and the contexts through which his famous medical work should be understood, see T. Langermann's suggestive study, "Another Andalusian Revolt?" (in: J.P. Hogendijk and A.I. Sabra, *The Enterprise of Science in Islam* (2003)).

There are two Hebrew translations of the *Kullīyāt* extant in manuscript. The first one, by Solomon b. Abraham ibn Daud (beginning of 14th century), is called *Mikhlal* (Bodleian Library, Ms. Opp. 176; Paris, Ms. Heb. 1172). Another copy was found by S. Muntner (Rome, Bibl. Casenateanse, Ms. 2762; also Ms. Jerusalem). The second translation, at one time thought to be an anonymous one, was apparently made by *Jacob ha-Katan in Provence as is evident from the separate use of medical terms in Provençal and Hebrew.

Averroes' *Kullīyāt* is mentioned by a number of Jewish authors. Shem Tov b. Joseph ibn Falaquera cites the work and praises it as follows: "The *Kullīyāt* is small and good and has no impurities, and all its words are true and of much use." Gershom b. Solomon mentions the work in his encyclopedia, *Sha'ar ha-Shamayim*. Samuel ibn *Zarza, who lived in the 14th century, refers to the *Kullīyāt* in his philosophical commentary on the Pentateuch and, a century later, Abraham Bibago mentions that he had composed a commentary on the *Kullīyāt*, but this is lost. Isaac Abrabanel writes in his commentary on the Bible (Lev. 15, beginning), when speaking of the three digestive systems in the living body: "… and the third digestion is in the organs and that is the true opinion as written by Averroes in the book *al-Kullīyāt* and not as written by Maimonides that the third digestion is in the openings of the veins and the fourth digestion is the organs." In addition to the *Kullīyāt*, there are Hebrew translations of other medical works of Averroes, among them that of Moses ibn Tibbon of Averroes' commentary on the *Urjūza* of Avicenna.

BIBLIOGRAPHY: E. Renan, *Averroès et l'averroïsme* (1852, 1861, and many reprints and republications); Munk, Mélanges, 418–58, 461–511; Steinschneider, Hebr. Uebersetzungen, index; Baer, Spain, index; E. Gilson, *History of Christian Philosophy in the Middle Ages* (1955). **ADD. BIBLIOGRAPHY:** G. Endress and J.A. Aertsen (eds.), *Averroes and the Aristotelian Tradition* (1999); M. Cruz Hernández, *Averroes: Vida, obra, pensamiento, influencia* (1986, 1997^2); R.C. Taylor, in: P. Adamson and Taylor (eds.), *Cambridge Companion to Arabic Philosophy* (2005); A. Hasnaoui (ed.), *La pensée philosophique et scientifique d'Averroès dans son temps* (2005); *Multiple Averroès* (1978); S. Harvey, in: JSQ, 7 (2000); D.H. Frank and O. Leaman (eds.), *Cambridge Companion to Medieval Jewish Philosophy* (2003), index; G. Tamari and M. Zonta, *Aristoteles Hebraicus* (1997); S. Harvey (ed.), *The Medieval Hebrew Encyclopedias of Science and Philosophy* (2000); M.C. Vázquez de Benito, *Obra médica Averroes* (1998).

[Shlomo Pines, Bernard Suler, and Suessmann Muntner / Steven Harvey (2nd ed.)]

AV HA-RAḤAMIM (Heb. אַב הָרַחֲמִים; "Merciful Father"), memorial prayer for Jewish martyrs and martyred communities. This prayer, by an unknown author, was composed in memory of the martyrs massacred in Germany during the First Crusade. It is first known from a prayer book dated 1290. The prayer emphasizes the merit of the martyrs who died for *kiddush ha-Shem*. Several scriptural verses (Deut. 32:43; Joel 4:21; Ps. 79:10; 9:13; 110:6, 7) are quoted, and God is asked to remember the martyrs, to avenge them, and to save their offspring. The wording of the last part of the prayer, invoking Divine retribution on the persecutors, has undergone many changes. Originally this prayer was recited in southern Germany only on the Sabbaths preceding Shavuot and the Ninth of Av and at the conclusion of the *Hazkarat Neshamot* (*Yizkor*) memorial service. In the Ashkenazi ritual it became part of the Sabbath morning service. In the Polish rite it is recited either every Sabbath (except when the Prayer for the *New Moon is said, Sabbath falls on a New Moon, or a circumcision takes place), or only on all the Sabbaths of the *Omer* period between Passover and Shavuot, and on those of the Three Weeks between the Fast of Tammuz and the Ninth of Av. The prayer is recited after the Torah reading before the scroll is returned to the Ark (see *Magen Avraham*, Sh. Ar., OH 284:7). Another short prayer of the same name "May the Father of mercy have mercy upon a people that has been borne by Him," etc., is recited in Orthodox synagogues immediately before the reading from the Torah.

BIBLIOGRAPHY: Hertz, Prayer, 482–3, 510–5; Elbogen, Gottesdienst, 203; Davidson, Oẓar, 1 (1924), 3, no. 40.

AVIA (fourth century), Babylonian *amora*. Avia studied in Pumbedita under R. *Joseph b. Ḥiyya (Ber. 28b). He appears to have been a colleague as well as a disciple for R. Joseph addressed a problem to him (Shab. 63a). He married the sister of Rami b. Ḥama (Ket. 56b–57a) and was a colleague of Rabbah b. Rav Hanan (Kid. 39a). Avia once visited *Rava who wished to trap him with difficult halakhic problems, but Avia avoided the pitfalls, whereupon R. *Naḥman b. Isaac remarked, "Blessed be the All-merciful that Rava did not put Avia to shame" (Shab. 46a–b). Avia settled in Ereẓ Israel and studied under R. *Ammi in Caesarea, later transmitting his teachings (Ḥul. 50a). Avia's teachings in *halakhah* are recorded in many passages in the Talmud (e.g., Shab. 23a; BK 35a). The *amoraim*, R. Adda, R. Aḥa, and R. Hilkiah, were apparently his sons.

BIBLIOGRAPHY: Hyman, Toledot, 107; Margalioth, Ḥakhmei, 1 (1964), 61f.

[Zvi Kaplan]

AVIAD, YESHAYAHU (**Wolfsberg, Oscar**; 1893–1957), author and leader of religious Zionism. Aviad, who was born in Hamburg, studied at the universities of Heidelberg, Wuerzburg, and Berlin. After serving as medical officer on the Eastern Front during World War I, he settled in Berlin where he practiced as a pediatrician. Aviad became a member of the central committee of the Mizrachi movement in Germany, edited its organ *Juedische Presse*, and was a delegate to many Zionist Congresses. In 1926 he was elected president of Mizrachi in Germany. Settling in Palestine in 1933, Aviad continued in medical practice there. He became a leading member of Ha-Po'el ha-Mizrachi, as well as a member of the executive of Mosad ha-Rav Kook, of Brit Ivrit Olamit ("World Hebrew Union"), and of the Court of Honor of the World Zionist Organization. One of the founders of the religious youth village Kefar ha-No'ar ha-Dati near Haifa (1938), he was also its spiritual mentor. He served as Israeli envoy in Scandinavia in 1948–49, and in 1956 was Israeli minister in Switzerland, where he died. His principal works are *Theory of Evolution and the Faith of the Jews* (1927); *Zur Zeit-und Geistesgeschichte des Judentums* (1938); *Yahadut ve-Hoveh* ("Judaism and the Present," 1962); a collection of essays, *Ba-Perozedor* ("In the Corridor," 1943); *She'arim* ("Gateways," 1948); and *Iyyunim be-Yahadut* ("Studies in Judaism," 1955). He also wrote books on the philosophy of history and profiles of prominent Jewish personalities. A list of his works appears in *Shai li-Yshayahu* (1956), 47–63.

BIBLIOGRAPHY: EẒD, 1 (1958), 12–18; Kressel, Leksikon, 1 (1965), 9f.

[Yosef Burg]

AVI AVI (Heb. אָבִי אָבִי; "My father, My father"), refrain of "*Bore ad anna*," *kinah* by a certain Benjamin sung on the Ninth of *Av in the Sephardi rite. The fifth verse of the original version makes a derogatory reference to the Trinity, and was modified in some western communities. The tune, though substantially the same from Aleppo to London, exhibits interesting local variations. The European-Sephardi style is illustrated best by the Bayonne version: most of the typical Sephardi characteristics disappeared, however, in the London variant. The Oriental versions are in the *maqām Bayāt-Nawā* and combine the melodic phrases at random to form a typical Eastern "endless melody." In some communities the hymn is sung in *Ladino under the title "La paloma" ("The Dove").

BIBLIOGRAPHY: M.J. Benharoche-Baralia, *Chants hébraiques traditionnels … de Bayonne* (1961), 98–99, no. 131; E. Aguilar and D.A. de Sola, *Sephardi Melodies* (1931), 53, no. 59; Idelsohn, Melodien, 4 (1923), 168, no. 135; 179, no. 177.

[Hanoch Avenary]

°**AVICENNA**, as he is known in the West, or **Abu Ali al-Hussein ibn ʿAbdallah ibn Sīnā** (980–1037), physician, scientist, statesman, and one of the greatest Islamic philosophers.

His writings cover a wide range of topics. His encyclopedic work *Kitāb Shifa-a'l Nafs* ("The Book Concerning the Healing of the Soul") is a magisterial summary of the kind of Neoplatonized Aristotelianism which at that time dominated philosophy in the Islamic East. Divided into four parts, dealing, respectively, with logic, physics, mathematics, and metaphysics, the work contains summaries, analyses, and reconceptualizations of those Aristotelian doctrines that appeared sound to Avicenna. In his expositions Avicenna was influenced by Aristotle and his Greek interpreters, Neoplatonic thinkers and writings (some of which were incorrectly ascribed to Aristotle), and by earlier Islamic philosophers, primarily, al-*Fārābī. Avicenna later composed an abridgment of the *Shifaʿ*, entitled *Kitāb al-Najat* ("Book of Deliverance"). His *Isharat wa-al-Tanbihat* ("Pointers and Reminders"), however, is generally regarded as his most mature work and the last major statement of his philosophy.

Avicenna wrote on all the branches of Aristotelian philosophy, but was primarily a metaphysician. As such, he maintained that in all beings other than God their essence or quiddity (e.g., horseness) is ontologically distinct from *both* their concrete existence (e.g., this white horse beside me) and from the universal concept of it (horse) that can be predicated of all instances. Thus, from *what* a thing is (its essence or quiddity), we cannot infer *that* it is, i.e., that it exists concretely, because existence is not a constituent part of its essence. We can infer only that its existence is possible. Assuming that the essence is internally consistent and that a concrete instance of it does exist, however, some other thing external to the essence would be necessary to cause it to exist concretely in space and time. In that respect, existence would have to be an accident added to essence. Closely related to this analysis is Avicenna's more general distinction between contingent and necessary being, according to which the world and everything in it are contingent (possible in themselves, and, if they exist concretely, necessary through some other being or beings acting as their cause), while God is the only being who does not depend on anything external to bring about or assure His existence because God is necessary through Himself. This is to say that God's essence is identical with His existence. This distinction between necessary and contingent being led Avicenna to formulate his famous metaphysical proof for the existence of God (later used by *Maimonides, Thomas *Aquinas, and others), according to which the existence of God as a being necessary through Himself can be demonstrated from the contingent nature of the world. For the actual existence of the world and any thing within it, which are possible in themselves, cannot be caused or explained by other beings that are *only* possible in themselves, for these might or might not exist. Rather, such beings must be "specified" to exist by external, necessitating causes. Since there cannot be an infinite number of such causes coexisting through time, there must be one that is necessary, not through yet another cause, but through itself. This Necessary Existent is God. In his description of God, Avicenna was the champion of the theory of negative attributes, according to which, essential attributes applied to God, such as existing, being one, and being wise, do not have a positive meaning but must be understood as denying the opposite characteristics of God. To explain creation Avicenna turned to the Neoplatonic theory of *emanation. From God's contemplative activity there emanates a series of intelligences, souls, celestial bodies, and finally the sublunar world of generation and corruption. The intelligences, ten in number, are hierarchically ordered; and the tenth intelligence, according to Avicenna, fulfills a dual function. As the "Giver of the forms" (a distinctively Avicennian notion), it provides sublunar matter with the all of the various forms that characterize concrete particulars, while as the "Agent Intellect" it is the decisive cause in producing actual knowledge within suitably prepared individual minds. It should be noted, however, that Avicenna understood this entire emanative process as atemporal and ongoing, which is to say that the world, according to him, is co-eternal with, yet dependent on, God. In human psychology, Avicenna maintained that each human soul is a simple, independent substance, created by God, and by nature immortal. In his political thought, Avicenna emphasized the social nature of man and the need for both laws and a legislator, who, in the best case, is a prophet. In addition to other works, Avicenna also wrote philosophical allegories, chief among them *Ḥayy Ibn Yaqẓan* ("The Recital of Ḥayy Ibn Yaqẓan," in: H. Corbin, *Avicenna and the Visionary Recital*, 1960). This latter work served as a model for similarly entitled works by Ibn Tufayl and Abraham *Ibn Ezra.

Influence on Jewish Philosophy

The influence of Avicenna on Jewish philosophy remains largely to be studied. While it is quite clear that he influenced a number of Jewish philosophers, it is often difficult to determine just what his influence was. When Jews used Arabic as the language of philosophy, they had direct access to Avicenna's writings; but when the language of philosophy became Hebrew, they had to rely on Hebrew translations of his works, and on accounts of his teachings in other works available in Hebrew. Only a few of Avicenna's philosophical works were translated into Hebrew, and most of these, according to Steinschneider, were based on Latin translations. A work by

Avicenna entitled *Sefer ha-Shamayim ve-ha-Olam* (*De caelo et mundo*) was widely read, as the number of extant manuscripts testifies. This work, apparently part of the *Shifaʿ*, was translated by Solomon b. Moses of Melgueuil (middle or second half of 13th century), most likely from the Latin. Solomon translated, from the Latin, a treatise *Ha-Shenah ve-ha-Yekiẓah* (*De somno et Vigilia*) attributed to Aristotle, but probably written by Avicenna. Todros Todrosi, between the years 1330 and 1340, translated Avicenna's *Najāt* under the title *Hazzalat ha-Nefesh*, though the one extant manuscript (Paris, Bibliothèque Nationale, Cod. Hebr. 1023) contains only the physical and metaphysical sections of the work. There also exists a Hebrew translation of *Ḥayy Ibn Yaqẓan* together with a commentary (ed. by D. Kaufmann, 1886). Avicenna's views became known, also, through al-Ghazālī's *Maqāṣid al-Falāsifa* ("Intentions of the Philosophers"), Hebrew translations of which circulated widely in the Jewish world during the late Middle Ages.

Influence on Maimonides

Among Jewish philosophers, Maimonides made use of certain Avicennian doctrines, but it would be false to describe his philosophy as essentially Avicennian. In a famous letter to Samuel ibn *Tibbon (Marx, in: JQR, 25 (1934–35), 380), Maimonides registers some reservations about Avicenna's philosophical views. A number of Maimonidean teachings that medieval and modern commentators on the *Guide of the Perplexed* attribute to Avicenna, are, in fact, already found in al-Fārābī. Nevertheless, some typical Avicennian doctrines are found in the *Guide* (see S. Pines, *Guide of the Perplexed* (1963), XCIII–CIII (introduction)). In metaphysics, Maimonides accepts the Avicennian distinctions between essence and existence, and between necessary and contingent beings. He holds, with Avicenna, that God's essential attributes are to be understood negatively and he uses the Avicennian proof for the existence of God, known as the proof from necessity and contingency. In politics, Maimonides agrees with Avicenna that man must live in a community, and that prophets are needed to establish the law of the community. Maimonides further agrees with Avicenna that the appearance of prophets is due to teleological provisions of nature. Avicennian influences also seem to be at work in Maimonides' contention that prophets can reach knowledge of reality without having previously grasped the theoretical premises for such knowledge, and in his view that meditation is superior to worship.

Prior to Maimonides, Abraham *Ibn Daud in his *Emunah Ramah* was strongly influenced by Avicenna's views, so much so, that certain sections of the work seem to be almost a compendium of Avicenna's views. Ibn Daud follows Avicenna in his psychology and often makes use of Avicenna's demonstrations. From Avicenna, Ibn Daud takes the proof of the existence of God as a necessary being, and the proof that there can be only one such being. *Judah Halevi who, in his *Kuzari*, polemicizes against Neoplatonic Aristotelian philosophy, presents as its spokesman a philosopher whose views show many connections with the teachings of Avicenna (*Kuzari*, 1:1). However, Halevi returns to several of these themes much later in the dialogue (*Kuzari*, 5:12), when he has his own principal spokesman, the Jewish sage, present Avicenna's views on the soul, its faculties, and the possibility of conjunction with the Agent Intellect after death much more sympathetically. Abraham *Ibn Ezra (commentary on Genesis 18:21) and *Levi b. Gershom (*Milḥamot*, 3:5) adopt Avicenna's view that God knows only universals, not individuals. Similarly, Ibn Ezra's view that God exercises His providence by means of the separate intelligences and the celestial spheres (commentary on Ex. 20:2) is probably also derived from Avicenna. Shem Tov *Falaquera based his *Sefer ha-Nefesh* on Avicenna's views (chapter 18 is an almost literal translation from the *Najāt*), and he accepted in his *Moreh ha-Moreh* (1:34) Avicenna's view that singular individuals receive illumination through the "holy intelligence." Avicenna's psychology also influenced the authors of the philosophical compendium *Ru'aḥ Ḥen*, as well as *Hillel b. Samuel of Verona in his *Tagmulei ha-Nefesh*. Avicennian influences are found in Hillel's proof of the existence of the soul (ch. 1) and in his contention that the soul is not body, property, or accident but substance and form (ch. 2). Avicenna's influence on Simeon b. Ẓemaḥ *Duran is evident in the latter's description of the internal senses and their position in the brain (*Magen Avot*, 4:21, 4:22, 5:1, 5:7, 5:8). The "Physics" of *al-Shif'a*, in particular the "Meteorology," was used by Samuel ibn Tibbon in his *Yikkavu ha-Mayim*. In this work he also cites Avicenna's view that it is possible that man may be generated from earth, a view for which *Immanuel of Rome (c. 1268–c. 1328) in his *Maḥberet ha-Tofet ve-ha-Eden*, the last section of his *Maḥbarot*, assigns Avicenna to hell.

[Shlomo Pines]

Medical Writings

Among Avicenna's medical writings, his greatest work is his *al-Qānūn fī al-Ṭibb* ("Canon of Medicine," called Avicenna's Canon). Divided into five books, the work deals with such topics as the description of the human body, the causes and complications of common ailments, treatment of diseases, the diseases that affect only parts of the body, diseases which affect the body as a whole, and pharmacology. Basing himself on Hippocrates and Galen and drawing on his own extensive experience, Avicenna is mainly concerned with practical matters rather than with theoretical discussions. The work achieved world fame and was accepted as authoritative not only by Muslim physicians, but also by Jews and Christians. The popularity of the work is attested to by the fact that many manuscript copies (in the Arabic original, and in Hebrew and Latin translations) are still extant. The work has been published, at different times, in Arabic, Hebrew, and Latin, and is still considered authoritative in parts of the Muslim world.

The principal Hebrew translation of the Canon (books 2–5) was made by Nathan ha-Me'ati (1279); printed at Naples in 3 vols. (1491–92). A beautifully illustrated manuscript of this translation exists at Bologna, Italy (Cod. 2197). Parts of the work were also translated by Zerahiah b. Isaac b. Shealtiel

*Gracian (1249), and by Joseph b. Joshua Lorki (1408, book 1, included in the Naples edition). There exists also an abridged version in ten tractates of the Canon prepared by someone other than Avicenna (Arabic original in single manuscript, Ms. Escurial 863) which was translated into Hebrew twice: once by Moses ibn *Tibbon (*Ha-Seder ha-Katan*, 1272), a second time by an anonymous translator who entitled his translation *Olam Katan* (see Steinschneider, Uebersetzungen, p. 696). The anonymous translation has been preserved in many manuscripts (e.g., Bodleian Library, Ms. Mich. Add. 17).

Like other authors, Avicenna also composed a medical treatise in verse entitled *Manẓūma* (or *Urjūza*) *fī al-Ṭibb*. Averroes wrote a commentary to one version of this poem. The poem with its commentary was translated into Hebrew, in prose form, once by Moses ibn Tibbon (1260) and a second time by an anonymous translator (apparently by *Jacob ha-Katan). Solomon ibn Ayyūb of Granada (1261) and the physician Ḥayyim Yisra'eli (1320) prepared a Hebrew verse translation of the work. Another medical work by Avicenna entitled *al-Adwiya al-Qalbiyya* ("On Remedies for the Heart") was translated into Hebrew twice: once under the title *Sammim Libbiyyim*, a second time under the title *Sefer ha-Refu'ot ha-Libbiyyot*. Baruch ibn Ya'ish ibn Isaac composed a commentary on the first one (c. 1485, Italy) as did an anonymous commentator (Oxford, Bodleian Library, Ms. Mich. Add. 15, fol. 122).

[Bernard Suler]

BIBLIOGRAPHY: A.J. Arberry, *Avicenna on Theology* (1951); A. Hyman and J.J. Walsh, *Philosophy in the Middle Ages* (1967); Pines, in: *Archives d'histoire doctrinale et littéraire du moyen âge*, 19 (1952), 5–37; 21 (1954), 21–98; Husik, Philosophy, index; Guttmann, Philosophies, index. **ADD. BIBLIOGRAPHY:** L.E. Goodman, *Avicenna* (1992); D. Gutas, *Avicenna and the Aristotelian Tradition* (1988); H.A. Davidson, *Alfarabi, Avicenna, and Averroes on Intellect* (1992); S.H. Nasr, *An Introduction to Islamic Cosmological Doctrines* (1964); S. Kemal, *The Poetics of Alfarabi and Avicenna* (1991); P. Heath, *Allegory and Philosophy in Avicenna* (1992); D. Black, *Logic and Aristotle's Rhetoric and Poetics in Medieval Arabic Philosophy* (1990), 279–86, 677–702; M.E. Marmura, in: *Journal of the American Oriental Society*, 82 (1962), 299–312; idem, in: *Mediaeval Studies*, 42 (1980), 337–52; S.J.L. Janssens, *An Annotated Bibliography on Ibn Sina* (1991); H.A. Davidson, *Moses Maimonides: The Man and His Works* (2005), index; N. Samuelson and G. Weiss, *Abraham ibn Daud: The Exalted Faith* (1986), index; R. Jospe, *Torah and Sophia* (1988), index; A.W. Hughes, *The Texture of the Divine* (2004), index; C. Sirat, *A History of Jewish Philosophy in the Middle Ages* (1985), index; D.H. Frank and O. Leaman, *History of Jewish Philosophy* (1997), index.

AVIDA (Zlotnick), YEHUDA LEIB (1887–1962), communal worker, rabbi, and writer. Born in Plock, Avida studied in the yeshivah of Volozhin. During World War I he was held hostage by the local Russian commander against possible spy activities by members of his community. He was a founder (1917) and general secretary of *Mizrachi in Poland until 1920. Ordained in 1910, he was appointed rabbi of the city of Gabin (Gombin), Poland (1911–19). In 1920 he went to Canada and successively held positions as Jewish National Fund director for Canada, director of Montreal Hebrew schools, and rabbi in Vancouver. In 1938 he immigrated to South Africa, where as director of the South African Board of Jewish Education he substantially strengthened the Hebrew educational structure by establishing a seminary for teacher training later called in his name, a model nursery school, and the beginnings of a day school. In 1949 he immigrated to Jerusalem where he spent the rest of his life. His wide-ranging personality is reflected not only by the breadth of his activities in Zionism, education, and religion but also by his prolific literary activities in Hebrew, Yiddish, and English as a Zionist publicist, philologist, folklorist, and ethnologist. His first contributions in these fields appeared in 1917, when he was still rabbi in Gabin. He wrote under the pen name Yehuda Elzet (formed from the initials of his name Leib Zlotnik), fearing that the common people, who could not appreciate the importance of such studies, would deem them unworthy of a rabbi. In his latter days he served as president of the Israel Institute of Folklore and Ethnology. Outstanding in Yiddish philology is his *Vunder Oytser fun der Yudisher Shprakh* (4 vols., 1918–20). His *Koyheles, der Mentsh un dos Bukh* (1929) is another well-known work of his Yiddish period. During his South African period he favored Hebrew. At that time he produced such works as *Bereshit ba-Meliẓah ha-Ivrit* (1938) and *Ma'amarim mi-Sefer Midrash ha-Meliẓah ha-Ivrit* (1939). He also wrote *Koso shel Eliyahu ha-Navi* (1958). The Hebrew periodical of Jewish folklore *Edot* (April–June 1947) was dedicated to him on his 60th birthday. For a complete list of Avida's works see S. Assaf, et al. (eds.), *Minḥah li-Yhudah… Zlotnick* (1950).

BIBLIOGRAPHY: Rejzen, Leksikon, 1 (1928), 1090–94; *Tidhar*, 4 (1950), 1915–17 (portrait).

AVIDAN, DAVID (1934–1995), Israeli poet. Avidan was born in Tel Aviv. During his student years at the Hebrew University (1952–54) he became intimate with the group of poets called *Li-Kra'at* ("Towards") after the journal of that name which they published and to which Yehuda *Amichai and Nathan *Zach belonged. Like theirs, his first volume, *Berazim Arufei Sefatayim* (1954), was unfavorably reviewed, though it was to transpire that these poets contributed more than others to the transformation which took place in the new Hebrew poetry and they are today considered the characteristic representatives of the poetry of the 1950s. Their poetry represents a reaction against the poetry of Abraham *Shlonsky and Nathan *Alterman and their followers of the "Palmaḥ generation." They attempted to reflect the problems associated with the existence of the individual, seen both in their subjects and in their vocabulary and images, which were less literary and closer to the realities and landscape (particularly the urban settings) of Israel.

Unlike the majority of them, however, Avidan continued to develop and change, a fact which is closely connected with his poetics. His early poetry was social, under the clear influence of communist ideology, but he abandoned it at an early age and social revolution gave way to individual revolution, with contempt for social and poetic conventions. Characteristic is his mockery of the masses and accepted social norms with an emphasis on the individuality of the poet. More than any other contemporary poet he abandoned the usual poetic language and coined new words, and did not hesitate to describe his own and other thought processes in an almost detached manner. This refusal to follow conventional paths brought in its train a fear of old age and death, as well as a profound interest in science and technology of the future. These subjects already appear in various forms in his earliest poetry.

In addition to the volume mentioned he published *Be'ayot Ishiyot* ("Personal Problems," 1957), *Sikkum Benayim* ("Interim," 1960), *Shirei Laḥaz* (1962), *Ma-she-hu Bishevil Mi-she-hu* ("Something for Somebody," 1964), *Shirim Bilti Efshari'im* and *Doaḥ Ishi al Masa* L.S.D. ("Impossible Poems," one volume, 1970), *Shirim Ḥizoni'im* ("External Poems," 1970), *Shirim Shimushi'im* ("Practical Poems," 1973), *Shirei Milḥamah ve-Meḥa'ah* ("Poems of War and Protest," 1976), *Shirim Ekroniyim* ("Axiomatic Poems," 1978), *Avidaniyum 20* (1987), and the collection *Berazim Arufei Sefatayim*, which appeared posthumously (2001). He also published a play, *David Avidan Magish Te'atron Mufshat* (1965).

A selection of his poems written between 1952 and 1966 has appeared in English translation (mostly by himself) under the title *Megaovertone*.

Towards the end of the 1960s Avidan applied himself to other artistic pursuits, holding a number of exhibitions and producing short films, but without the success which accompanied his poetry. During his last years, Avidan, one of the best-known bohemian figures on the artistic scene of Tel Aviv, suffered from severe asthma attacks and lived in abject poverty. M. Ben published a long interview with him, which comes close to a biographical portrait, entitled *David Avidan* (2003).

BIBLIOGRAPHY: G. Moked, in: *Mevo'ot*, 4 (Dec. 9, 1954); idem, in: *Ha'arez* (July 21, 1961). **ADD. BIBLIOGRAPHY:** Idem, *Ḥoveret ha-Mukdeshet le-David Avidan* (1995); H. Shaham, *Hedim shel Niggun: Shirat Dor ha-Palmaḥ ve- Ḥavurat Likrat be-Zikatah le-Shirat Alterman* (1997). **WEBSITE:** www.ithl.org.il.

[Abraham Balaban]

AVIDOM (Mahler-Kalkstein), MENAHEM (1908–1995), Israeli composer. Avidom, who was born in Stanislav, Poland, immigrated to Palestine in 1925. He went to Paris to study music and was a music teacher in Tel Aviv from 1935 to 1946. From 1945 to 1952 he was general secretary of the Israel Philharmonic Orchestra and from 1952 to 1955 an adviser on the arts to the Ministry of Tourism. From 1955 to 1980 he was director-general of the Israel Performing Rights Society (ACUM) and chairman of the Israel Composers' League. As a composer, Avidom, using modern techniques, succeeded in interweaving Oriental musical elements – rhythmic, melodic, and stylistic – with Israeli dance rhythms. His works include

ten symphonies; a concerto for flute and strings and a violin concerto; two string quartets, a brass quartet, and *Enigma* for five wind instruments, percussion, and piano; seven operas, including *Alexandra* and *In Every Generation*; and an opera buffa, *The Crook*. Avidom's more recent works include *The Pearl and the Coral*, ballet music for ten instruments written for the Inbal Theater (1972); *Passacaglia for Piano* (1973); *Hommage à Rubinstein*, six inventions on his name, commissioned for the 1973 International Rubinstein Competition; *Yemenite Wedding Suite*, for piano (1973), commissioned by Gerick Edition, Germany; an overture (*Spring*), commissioned by the Jerusalem (Radio) Symphony Orchestra (1973); and *The Farewell* or *Louise*, a radiophonic opera (1969). He was awarded an Israel Prize in 1961.

BIBLIOGRAPHY: P. Gradenwitz, *Music and Musicians in Israel* (1959), 83–88; A. Holde, *Jews in Music* (1959), 319; A.M. Rothmueller, *Music of the Jews* (1954), 204 and index.

[Herzl Shmueli]

AVIDOV, ZVI (formerly **Henry Klein**; 1896–1984), Israeli agricultural entomologist. Avidov was born in Znin, Germany, into an Orthodox Jewish family. While in high school, he joined the Blau Weiss Zionist youth movement which duly oriented him in the direction of agriculture as the first step toward the realization of his idealistic aspirations, namely, to immigrate to Palestine and become a farm worker in the Land of Israel. In 1916 Avidov was drafted into the German Army and served for two years in the Signal Corps on both the Eastern and Western fronts of World War I. In 1921 he immigrated to Palestine, where he worked as a farm laborer in Galilee and the Sharon regions. In 1923 he accepted an offer to join F.S. *Bodenheimer as a field entomologist of the Agricultural Experiment Station established in Tel Aviv by the Palestine Zionist Executive (later the Volcani Institute in Reḥovot). During their 30 years of collaboration, Bodenheimer and Avidov laid the foundation and built the structure of the science of agricultural entomology in Israel. In 1958 he joined the Hebrew University and was appointed professor of agricultural entomology at the Faculty of Agriculture at Reḥovot, where he was credited with the training of a whole new generation of specialists in the field of applied entomology. Avidov's contribution to entomological research in Israel was particularly prominent in the field of pest control, a field he pioneered. Apart from being instrumental in the training of the first cadres of practitioners and instructors, Avidov also established and headed the Department of Entomology at the Hebrew University's Faculty of Agriculture. During 1959–62 he served as dean of the Faculty of Agriculture, an office which provided him with the opportunity to make unique contributions to shaping the country's higher education and research programs, not only in entomology but also in agriculture as a whole. Even after retiring from university teaching and administrative chores in 1965, Avidov continued full time with an intensive research program and supervision of graduate student work, concentrating mainly on the biology of natural enemies of citrus scale insects and the development of methods for their mass rearing. He edited *Studies in Agricultural Entomology and Plant Pathology* (1966) and wrote several books, including *Plant Pests of Israel* (1969) with I. Harpaz which is still the standard manual on the subject. In 1977 Avidov received the Israel Prize in agriculture.

BIBLIOGRAPHY: Hebrew University of Jerusalem, *Faculty of Agriculture* (1958), 179–82 (list of Avidov's publications).

[Isaac Harpaz / Sharon Zrachya (2nd ed.)]

AVIGAD (formerly **Reiss**), **NAḤMAN** (1905–1992), Israeli archaeologist. Avigad was born in Zawalow in the Ukraine (then Austria) and studied architecture at the University of Brno, Czechoslovakia, before immigrating to Palestine in 1925. In 1928 he joined the Hebrew University of Jerusalem and over the years participated in numerous excavations, some conducted by E.L. *Sukenik, including the Ophel, Beth Alpha, Hammath Gader, Samaria (joint expedition), Tel Jerishe, Afulah, and others, as well as participating in hikes, as part of a youth group, to historical sites around the country. As a result of his earlier architectural training, Avigad had become an accomplished draftsman and graphic artist, and many excavation drawings in publications of the 1930s to 1940s were his work. Avigad's first article in English, on a seal of a slave-girl, was published in the *Palestine Exploration Quarterly* in 1946. Avigad began his formal studies in archaeology in 1941 and in 1952 completed his Ph.D. and his thesis, *Ancient Monuments in the Kidron Valley*, was published in 1954. It was at this point that he was appointed lecturer in archaeology in the Department (later Institute) of Archaeology at the Hebrew University. Throughout his subsequent career, Avigad divided his scholarly interests between archaeology and Hebrew and Aramaic epigraphy. Avigad was the coauthor (with Yigael *Yadin) of *A Genesis Apocryphon. A Scroll from the Wilderness of Judea* (1956). From 1953 to 1958 he directed the excavations at Bet She'arim, where he uncovered a subterranean necropolis of the second and third centuries C.E. He also participated in the 1955 survey of Masada and in two expeditions to the Judean Desert caves (1960–61). A specialist in Hebrew epigraphy, he deciphered a number of important inscriptions, notably the "Epitaph of a Royal Steward" at Silwan in the Kidron Valley (see *Shebna), inscriptions on the synagogue lintel at *Kefar Neburaya, and additional inscriptions in Jason's tomb, Jerusalem. He was awarded the Israel Prize for Jewish studies in 1977. Between 1969 and 1982 Avigad conducted a series of important excavations in the Jewish Quarter in Jerusalem. Hillel Geva, his assistant on the excavations, wrote that "despite his advanced age, Avigad spent many hours at the excavations every day during the hot summer months and showed no signs of tiring as the years passed. He did not neglect the opportunity to excavate in any area in which excavation was possible and would climb down into the deep pits to personally examine details of the architectural remains and stratigraphy. It is no exaggeration to say that the excavations in the Jewish Quarter rejuvenated him." Among his many archaeological achievements, Avigad will always be remembered for the three very important archaeological discoveries he made in Jerusalem: the finding of the Israelite "broad wall" of the city, the fire-blackened "burnt house" dating from the time of the Roman destruction of the city in 70 C.E., and the uncovering of the main street (*cardo*) of the Byzantine city. His popular account of these excavations appeared in a book entitled *Discovering Jerusalem* (1983).

BIBLIOGRAPHY: H. Geva, (ed.), *Jewish Quarter Excavations in the Old City of Jerusalem. Conducted by Nahman Avigad, 1969–1982* (2000); "Professor Nahman Avigad, 1905–1992: In Memoriam," in: *Israel Exploration Journal*, 42 (1992), 1–3; S. Gibson, "Obituary: Nahman Avigad, 1905–1992," in: *Bulletin of the Anglo-Israel Archaeological Society* (1992–93), 83.

[Shimon Gibson (2nd ed.)]

AVIGDOR (Heb. אֲבִיגְדוֹר), moshav in the southern coastal plain of Israel near Kiryat Malakhi. It was founded in 1950 by ex-servicemen of the British Army's World War II Jewish Transport Unit (Yael), who had first attempted to settle with the veteran farmers at Menaḥemiyyah. Its economy was based on intensive field crops, milch cattle, and citrus. Large pecan nut plantations existed nearby. In 2002 the population of Avigdor was 615. The settlement was named after the English Zionist Sir Osmond *d'Avigdor-Goldsmid and his son Henry.

[Efraim Orni]

AVIGDOR, ABRAHAM, also known as **Abram Bonet Avigdor** and **Bonet Ben Meshullam Ben Solomon Avigdor** (second half 14th century), French physician, translator from Latin to Hebrew, and philosophic author. Avigdor was born in Arles, Provence, of a distinguished family of physicians. Abraham spent 12 years in Montpellier, where he pursued medical and philosophical studies. He is the first Jewish writer to mention his studies in this well-known School of Medicine. It is not excluded that he even taught there. He settled in Arles, where he practiced medicine.

Avigdor's only independent work is *Sefer Segullat Melakhim*, which he composed in 1367 at the age of 17 as a student in Montpellier. Written in rhymed prose, the work is influenced by al-*Ghazālī's *Maqāṣid al-Falāsifa*. In it Avigdor emphasizes the importance of logic and complains that the natural philosophers do not esteem this discipline highly enough. Statements dispersed throughout the work disclose that Avigdor was a pious Jew. In spite of his love of science and philosophy he takes to task those scholars who through imprecision of expression foster error and heresy. His work echoes the controversy between the followers and opponents of philosophy that had engaged the Jews of southern France in the 13th century (Mss. Paris Cod. Hebr. 990; Munich 44, 1; and Parma, de'Rossi, 402, 3; 1342, 2). Avigdor also composed a supercommentary on Averroes' middle commentary on the first three sections of Aristotle's *Organon* (Ms. Munich 63, 3–5). His translations from the Latin include (1) *Higgayon* or *Higgayon*

Kaẓer or *Trattato*, a translation of Peter of Spain's *Summulae logicales*. The translation is precise, though the order of the chapters is changed at times and there are occasional additions and deletions (Bodleian Library, Ms. Mich, 280; Bodl. 56); (2) *Mavo bi-Melakhah*, a translation of Bernard Alberti's *Introductorium in practicam pro provectis in theorica*. It is a work devoted to medicines and based on the fourth book of Avicenna's *Canon* (Mss. Berlin, Or. Qu. 544; Munich 297, 2; Paris, Cod. Hebr. 1054, 12; (3) *Mevo ha-Ne'arim* is the wrong name, preserved in many manuscripts, of the Hebrew translation of two parts of a well-known medical textbook written by Gerard de Solo, a prominent 14th century professor, the *Tractatus de febrivus*. Avigdor finished it in 1379, and it was preserved in no fewer than 21 manuscripts (Mss. Hamburg 308, 4; Munich 296, 297; Parma, de'Rossi 399; Bodleian, Mich. 135; etc.). Lola Ferre edited the Latin text and the Hebrew translation (*Miscelánea de Estudios Árabes y Hebreos*, secc. Hebr., 45 (1996) 149–83); (4) *Be'ur*, a commentary also by Gerard de Solo on *Ad Almansorem*, a Latin translation of part of al-Rāzī's *Kitāb al-Manṣūrī*, to which Avigdor added valuable comments (Munich, 296, 1); (5) *Pirkei Arnau*, a translation of the *Medicationis parabolae* or *Regulae generales* written in 1300 by Arnoldus de Villanova (Arnau de Vilanova), a famous Spanish physician. It was finished around 1388, and has been preserved in seven manuscripts (Munich, Cod. Hebr. 286; Firenze Pl. 88, c. 36, f. 15; London, Brit. Libr., Or. 10507; Macerata, Bibl. Com. 310, 2; Hamburg 308, 3; Munich, Cod. Hebr. 297; Milano 137). The work has been published by Lola Ferre, based on Munich, Cod. Hebr. 286, in: J.A. Paniagua, L. Ferre, E. Feliú: *Medicationis parabole. Pirqé Arnau de Vilanova*, AVOMO, Vol. VL, 1, Barcelona: Universidad de Barcelona, 1990; (6) *Megillah*, translated in 1380, a reference book dealing with digestive and purgative drugs, the *Practica* by Johannes of Parma, extant in seven manuscripts (Paris, Bibl. Nat. 1054, 11 and 1128, 10; Hamburg 308, 2; London, Brit. Libr., Or. 1036; Berlin, Staatsbibliothek 71, 3 and 245; Jerusalem, NUL B 1, 8º 85 B 140), edited, translated and studied by Lola Ferre (*Práctica de Johannes de Parma*, Granada: Univ. de Granada, 2002).

Avigdor also aided his son Solomon in translating an astronomical work by Arnoldus de Villanova entitled *De judiciis astronomiae* or *Capitula astrologiae*, whose title in the Hebrew translation was *Panim ba-Mishpat*.

BIBLIOGRAPHY: G. Sarton, *Introduction to the History of Science*, 3, pt. 2 (1948), 1380–82; E. Carmoly, *Histoire des médecins juifs* (1844); Renan, Ecrivains, 717–21; Steinschneider, Uebersetzungen, index, s.v. *Abraham Abigedor, Bonet*; H. Friedenwald, *Jews and Medicine* (1944), 685–9; Gross, Gal Jud, 333–4. **ADD. BIBLIOGRAPHY:** L. Ferre, "La version hebrea del Tratado De Febribus de Gerard de Solo," in: *Miscelánea de Estudios Árabes y Hebreos*, secc. Hebr., 45 (1996), 149–83.

[I.M. Salkind / Angel Saenz-Badillos (2nd ed.)]

AVIGDOR BEN ELIJAH HA-KOHEN (c. 1200–1275), talmudic scholar in Italy and Austria. Avigdor was born in Italy and studied under Eleazar b. Samuel of Verona, Isaac of Verona, and later Simḥah b. Samuel of Speyer. For a number of years Avigdor lived in northern Italy in Ferrara, in Mantua, and in Verona. Students flocked to his school at Verona, among them members of the distinguished Anav family of Rome, including Zedekiah b. Abraham *Anav. For a time Avigdor lived in Halle, Germany, from where he conducted halakhic correspondence with *Hezekiah b. Jacob of Magdeburg concerning a letter of divorce. On the death of *Isaac b. Moses Or Zaru'a of Vienna, Avigdor was invited to succeed him at Vienna. For about 25 years he was the central rabbinic figure in Austria, and transplanted the talmudic scholarship of Italo-German Jewry to Austria, which eventually became the most important center of Ashkenazi Jewry. Both Isaac Or Zaru'a and Abraham of Pesaro referred to him as one of "the greatest scholars of our generation." He was one of the teachers of *Meir b. Baruch of Rothenburg. His responsa are included in the responsa of Meir of Rothenburg, in the *Haggahot Maimoniyyot*, in *Mordekhai*, in the responsa of R. Asher b. Jehiel and of Ḥayyim b. Isaac of Vienna, and in the *Shibbolei ha-Leket*. His *tosafot* to the talmudic tractates of *Ketubbot* and *Eruvin* have survived, as well as a commentary on the Pentateuch and the Five Scrolls.

BIBLIOGRAPHY: S. Buber (ed.), *Shibbolei ha-Leket* (1886), 8 (introd.); J. Hamburger, *Avigdor Kohen Ẓedek* (Mainz, 1900); Zimmels, in: HHY, 15 (1931), 110–26; Urbach, Tosafot, 442, n. 4; I.A. Agus, *Teshuvot Ba'alei ha-Tosafot* (1954), 199–204; S.K. Mirsky (ed.), *Shibbolei ha-Leket* (1966), 13–25; Germ Jud, 1 (1934), 410–3, no. 5.

[Irving A. Agus]

AVIGDOR BEN JOSEPH ḤAYYIM (18th–19th centuries), rabbi in Poland, one of the leading opponents of *Ḥasidism in Poland-Lithuania in the late 18th century. In 1785 he became rabbi of Pinsk and its district, but through the influence of the Ḥasidim he was dismissed in 1794, two years before the end of his term. He lodged a complaint with the civil courts, claiming the balance of his salary and damages resulting from loss of office. He also took up the matter with government officials in St. Petersburg. During the six years of embittered litigation with the leaders of the community, Avigdor embarked on a campaign of denunciation against Ḥasidism. He lodged a second complaint in 1800 with the office of Czar Paul I containing charges against Ḥasidism in which he brought arguments from Scripture to prove that it was a heretical sect in conflict with the accepted values of religion, morality, and the laws of the state, and that it continued to adhere to the beliefs of the pseudo-messiah, *Shabbetai Ẓevi. When, on investigation, the authorities failed to find anything exceptional in the behavior of the Ḥasidim, Avigdor did not relax his efforts and as a result of his denunciations *Shneur Zalman of Lyady, the founder of Ḥabad Ḥasidism, was reimprisoned. Avigdor subsequently drew up 19 questions accusing Shneur Zalman, in which he continued to denounce the Ḥasidim as disloyal both to the state and to Judaism. In December 1800 he lodged another accusation before the government in which he cited extracts from Shneur Zalman's *Sefer ha-Tanya*, in an attempt to prove that Ḥasidism was inimical to Christianity.

BIBLIOGRAPHY: Z.W. Rabinowitsch, *Ha-Ḥasidut ha-Lita'it* (1961), 39–47, 51–55; Dubnow, Ḥasidut, 265–78; M. Teitelbaum, *Ha-Rav mi-Lyady u-Mifleget Ḥabad* (1914), 90–121, 185–202; Ḥ.M. Hilman, *Beit Rabbi* (1965), 54–60 (Arabic numerals).

AVIGDOR BEN SIMḤAH HA-LEVI OF GLOGAU (or **Glogauer**; pseudonym **Alem**; c. 1725–1810), teacher and author. In his youth he was one of the *maskilim* of Moses *Mendelssohn's circle in Berlin. He later (1768) moved to Prague where he wrote a short Hebrew grammar, *Davar Tov*, which he published together with the treatise *Marpe Lashon* by R. Moses b. Ḥaviv (Prague, 1783). Avigdor also published a collection of Mendelssohn's letters to him, *Iggerot Remad* (in two pamphlets, Vienna, 1792, 1797), in one of which Mendelssohn explains his purpose in translating the Pentateuch into German. The second volume also contains a selection of Avigdor's poems entitled *Ḥotam Tokhnit*. In 1802 he published Mendelssohn's Pentateuch with German translation, adding a preface.

ADD. BIBLIOGRAPHY: B. Nosek, in: *Judaica Bohemiae*, 25 (1989), 14–30; 26 (1990), 102–18; 27 (1991), 31–44; 30–31 (1996), 72–90.

AVIGNON (sometimes called in Hebrew *Ir ha-gefanim* "city of grapes"; *gefen* = vigne, i.e., vine), capital of the department of Vaucluse, southeastern France, formerly part of *Provence. Avignon was the residence of the popes for some years after 1309. In 1348 Joanna, countess of Provence, sold the city to Pope Clement VI and it belonged to the French states of the Holy See until the French Revolution. In consequence the Jews were permitted to remain there and in the adjacent area of the *Comtat-Venaissin even when they were excluded from the rest of France. According to legend the Jews took part in a revolt against Bishop Stephen of Avignon in 390. The first archaeological evidence of their presence there dates from the fourth century and is given by a stamp with the five-branched *menorah* and the inscription: *Avin* (*ionnensis*); the first written evidence dates from 1178 when Emperor Frederick I entrusted the protection of the Jews of Avignon to Bishop Pons. The Jewish quarter was at first situated at the present Vieille Juiverie street. About 1221 it was transferred to the neighborhood of the Church of St. Peter. Its location is marked by Rue Jacob and the former Place Jérusalem (today Place Victor-Basch). The old synagogue which stood on this site was destroyed by fire in 1845 and replaced on the same spot by the existing circular synagogue in the Roman manner. Near the synagogue, or *escole*, there was also a wedding hall, a butchery, and the oven for baking unleavened bread. The Jewish quarter, or *carrière des Juifs*, was surrounded by walls and closed by three gates. The Jews of Avignon were obliged to pay a tax to the collegiate chapter of St. Peter's (Arch. départ. G IX. 10). Although covering an area of approximately 100 yards by 100 yards, the quarter nevertheless housed over 1000 persons in 1358. One of the cemeteries was located on the site formerly called La Pignotte.

The statutes of the city of Avignon of 1243 mention the *Communitas Iudeorum* several times. It was specifically laid down (art. 84) that animals killed according to Jewish ritual were not to be sold outside the carrière. Jewish commerce flourished during the period of papal residence in Avignon, supplying the papal court with victuals, bed and table linen, horses, perfumes, coral and pearls for rosary beads, parchment, and other commodities. The tailor of Gregory XI was a Jew, as was the papal bookbinder. The less wealthy Jews generally engaged in brokerage. In 1374, 87 of 94 textile dealers and 41 of 62 timber merchants were Jews. In the 14th century, Jewish moneylending on interest, practically nonexistent in the previous century, gradually developed, although limited in scale. At the time of the *Black Death in 1348 a massacre of the Jews was prevented by the energetic intervention of Pope *Clement VI and the city councilors; nevertheless two or three Jews were burned by the populace. After the popes returned to Rome, the attitude of the populace and the civic authorities became increasingly hostile to the Jews.

The first evidence of ordinances promulgated by the Jewish community dates from 1413. Its administration already comprised *baylons*, or delegates, and a council. The first extant ordinances date from 1452. They include a detailed tariff of dues of the charity fund, or *hekdesh*. The 1558 ordinances show the financial organization: community members were divided into three categories, or *mains* ("hands"), according to financial status. The "manifest," or tax declaration, was based on property, not on income. The officials and administrators of the community were members of the council which included the various *baylons*, notably those in charge of the manifest, charity, the sick, study, etc., and the secretary, cantor, preacher, translator of services into the vernacular for women, and beadle. The police regulations of the city of Avignon of 1458 prohibited Jews from keeping their shops open or transacting business on Christian holy days, and from accepting as pledges church ornaments or Christian religious objects. Restrictions were imposed on Jewish trade in textiles and clothing. A bull of Pope Sixtus IV (Aug. 1, 1479), relatively favorable to the Jews, was annulled at the beginning of 1480 after opposition from the city council and guilds of Avignon. During the anti-Jewish disturbances at *Tarascon and *Arles in 1484, the town council of Avignon took security measures. These precautions prevented more violent outbursts when students and artisans attacked the Jews in Avignon in May of the following year. In 1486, after refugees from anti-Jewish violence in other towns of Provence had begun to arrive in Avignon, the municipal councilors demanded their expulsion. In 1493 they again asked for measures to be taken against the influx of Jews from other parts. It was then that Jews expelled from Spain also began to take refuge there.

From the end of the 15th century, the Jewish community of Avignon undertook to pay annuities or allowances to wealthy Christian families against the deposit of capital sums of various sizes ranging from 40 to 500 florins. This was probably not only a way of coping with temporary financial difficulties, but also of interesting influential citizens of Avignon in maintaining the Jewish right of residence. The policy bore fruit in 1500 when Pope *Alexander VI imposed a tax of 1/20 of Jewish property; the inhabitants of Avignon managed to enlist the opposition of the pontifical governor to this levy until a formal order from Rome confirmed it. Such an exceptional levy was in addition to the regular dues and taxes required from Jewish residents beside their share of the general charges. In 1510 the archbishop and papal legate in Avignon granted the Jewish community a comparatively favorable constitution. This confirmed that the *baylons* could not be arrested for debt during their period of office, modified the former regulations which imposed the wearing of the Jewish *badge, and obliged the Jews to attend only one compulsory missionary sermon a year. From the 17th century the main occupations of Avignon Jewry were dealing in second hand goods, horses and mules, and peddling. From the beginning of the 18th century many left Avignon and emigrated to Paris, Bordeaux, and Bayonne.

In September 1791 Avignon ceased to be a papal possession (together with the adjacent Comtat-Venaissin) and was united with France. The Jews of Avignon were granted full civil rights in June 1791. The egalitarian aspirations of the new regime were not without influence on the inner structure of the Jewish community. In October 1790 the rabbi Elie Vitte Spire maintained in a sermon that in conformity with the new principles the syndics should no longer be elected to represent the existing groups of taxpayers. This marked the end of the old system of minority control. Following the Napoleonic decree of 1808 on the organization of the Jewish *consistoire, the community was included in the regional consistory of Marseilles. However the cultural level of the Jews seems to have suffered from these changes, and, from 1789, to have reflected the activities of single individuals rather than a communal entity. The number of Jews in Avignon dwindled to 149 (54 families) in 1892 and thereafter communal life almost ceased until somewhat revived by North African immigration.

Avignon Jewry had its own rite of prayers, similar to, though not identical with, that which was followed in *Carpentras and the other two "Holy Communities" of the Comtat-Venaissin: the volumes for the New Year, Day of Atonement, and Penitential Prayers only were published (Amsterdam, 1765, 1766, 1763). In addition, the daily prayers (*Seder ha-Tamid*) were published for all four communities (2 vols., Avignon, 1767) along with occasional prayers and hymns (*Seder ha-Kunteres*; Avignon, 1765). Many manuscripts of the ritual according to the Avignon rite are extant in various libraries. For the specific nature of the rite see *Comtat-Venaissin. Avignon Jewry shared also the peculiar Hebrew pronunciation, Judeo-Provençal patois, synagogue architecture, and folklore common to the other communities of the region.

A local Purim was observed at Avignon on the 8th of Shevat to celebrate a providential escape of the community in 1757.

Notable among the many Jewish scholars and writers born or living in Avignon were Mordecai b. Joseph, Joseph Samuel b. Abraham b. Joseph b. Abraham Baruch b. Neriah, *Kalonymus b. Kalonymus, *Levi b. Gershom, *Jacob b. Ḥayyim, Israel b. Joseph ha-Levi (Crescas Caslari), Judah b. Solomon Nathan (Maestro Bonjudas Nathan), Abraham b. Mordecai Farissol, and *Joseph ha-Kohen. The first Hebrew printing venture was attempted at Avignon in 1446 when the Jew Davin de Caderousse acquired Hebrew characters from the Prague engraver Procop Waldfoghel against an obligation to teach him the craft of cloth dyeing. Davin's failure to do so involved him in a lawsuit, and he had to return the type. The early prayer books of Avignon were, however, printed in Holland, and a Hebrew press did not function in Avignon until 1765 when the *Seder ha-Kunteres* was published. The Jewish religious periodicals *La Loi Divine* and *La Famille de Jacob* were published there in the second half of the 19th century.

During World War II, many Jewish refugees, especially from Alsace, settled in Avignon. According to a census of June 1941, 300 Jews were living there. But on April 17, 1943, several Jewish families were arrested and deported.

[Bernhard Blumenkranz]

Since World War II

North African Jews brought the Jewish population to 500 in 1960 and to almost 2,000 in 1968. There is a synagogue of mixed rite, Ashkenazi and Sephardi, and various communal and educational institutions. Avignon is the seat of the Consistoire Israélite de Vaucluse, which covers the department comprised of the ancient communities of the Comtat Venaissin – Cavaillon, *Carpentras, and L'Isle-sur-Sorgue (no Jewish population today).

[Georges Levitte]

BIBLIOGRAPHY: REJ, 50 (1905), index to volumes 1–50; B. Blumenkranz, in: Comptes-Rendus … Académie des Inscríptions … (1969); A. Mossé, *Histoire des Juifs d' Avignon* … (1934), includes bibliography; E. Triolet, *Les Amants d' Avignon* (1943); B. Guillemain, *La Cour Pontificale d'Avignon* (1962), 642–53; L.H. Labande, *Avignon au XVe siècle* (1920), 278f., 416–8; Gross, Gal Jud, 1–17; Grayzel, in: HJ, 2 (1940), 1–12; Roth, in: JJB, 1 (1939), 99–105; Z. Szajkowski, *Franco-Jewish Gazeteer* (1966), 282; P. Prévot, *A travers la carrière des Juifs d'Avignon*, 2 vols. (1942); *Guide Juif de France* (1968), 144–6; A. Hertzberg, *The French Enlightenment and the Jews* (1968), index.

AVIGUR (Meirov), SHAUL (1899–1978), key figure in the *Haganah. Avigur was born in Dvinsk, Russia. He went to Ereẓ Israel in 1912 and, six years later, became a member of the *kevuẓah* Kinneret, participating in the defense of *Tel Ḥai in 1920. Later he took charge of the Haganah's central arms depot in Kinneret. He was an active member of the *Aḥdut ha-Avodah Party and then of *Mapai. From 1922 Avigur was a member of the national committee of the Haganah. He devoted himself to purchasing arms, to underground arms manufacture, and to the organization of the Haganah's intelligence service (Sherut Yedi'ot). During World War II Avigur was active in organizing "illegal" *aliyah* from Middle Eastern countries. When the war ended, he headed the vast underground operation for the transportation of the survivors of European Jewry (Ha-Mosad le-Aliyah Bet; see *Immigration, "Illegal"), working from Paris in close contact with the *Beriḥah ("Escape") organization. In 1948, during the Israeli War of Independence, Avigur was in charge of the purchase of arms in Europe. Until the mid-1950s he was a chief assistant to Minister of Defense David Ben-Gurion, and thereafter served in special capacities on behalf of the Ministry for Foreign Affairs and the Prime Minister's Office. He was a member of the editorial board of *Sefer Toledot ha-Haganah* ("The History of the Haganah"), and published a book of reminiscences, *Im Dor ha-Haganah* ("With the Haganah Generation"), 1962.

Avigur was a central figure in the fight for emigration of Soviet Jewry. He was the recipient of the Israel Prize in 1973.

BIBLIOGRAPHY: Dinur, Haganah, 2, pt. 3 (1964^2); part 3 (1972), index; Tidhar, 4 (1950), 2648–50.

[Yehuda Slutsky]

AVIGUR-ROTEM, GABRIELA (1946–), Israeli novelist. Avigur-Rotem was born in Buenos Aires, Argentina, and came to Israel in 1950. She studied Hebrew and English literature and worked for several years as a high school teacher. Later she worked as an editor at the Haifa University Publishing House. Following the publication of two poetry collections (1980; *Ḥomot ve-Keisarim*, 1990), Avigur-Rotem published in 1992 her first novel, *Moẓart lo Hayah Yehudi* ("Mozart Wasn't a Jew"; Italian, 1997) and was awarded the Peter Schwisert Prize for Young Writers. The novel, which was highly praised by critics and readers alike, is a family saga set against the historical backdrop of early Zionism, Baron Hirsch's support of a Jewish colony in Argentina, and, later, the Spanish Civil War and World War II. Leon Gidekel has to give up his dream of becoming a great singer, transferring his hopes of musical success to his nine children, for each of whom he buys a piano. Avigur-Rotem unfolds an exuberant epic tapestry, displaying a fine touch for nuanced characterization and a sensitive ear for various layers of Hebrew. In 2001, Avigur-Rotem published a second novel, *Ḥamsin ve-Ẓipporim Meshuga'ot* ("Heatwave and Crazy Birds"; Italian, 2004; French, 2005), the story of Loya Kaplan who at the age of 48 tries to uncover the story of her family. Her journey into the past discloses the fate of her parents during the Holocaust and brings her finally to her elderly mother, who had chosen to return to Czechoslovakia for ideological reasons. Undoubtedly one of the most interesting voices in contemporary Hebrew literature, Avigur-Rotem was twice awarded the Prime Minister's Prize for Literature as well as the President's Prize (2002).

BIBLIOGRAPHY: Y. Orian, "*Hi Tiheyeh Soferet Gedolah Me'od*," in: *Yedioth Ahronoth* (1992); M. Shaked, "*Panim Ḥadashot: Ha-Roman ha-Akhshavi al Toledot Mishpaḥah*," in: *Itton*, 77:153 (1993), 22–27; A. Holtzman, "*Me'od Yisraeli*," in: *Yedioth Ahronoth* (May 4, 2001).

[Anat Feinberg (2nd ed.)]

AVIḤAYIL (Heb. אֲבִיחַיִל; "father of strength"), moshav in central Israel, N.E. of Netanyah. In 1921 veterans of the *Jewish Legion of World War I settled on desert land allocated to it by the British Mandatory government in the northeastern Negev, near Tel Arad. This effort failed when no water was found. On July 19, 1932, they founded Aviḥayil on a wasteland stretch of sand dunes in the Ḥefer Plain. In 1946 Aviḥayil merged with the neighboring moshav, Ein ha-Oved. Its settlers were from Ereẓ Israel, Russia, the United States, Canada, and other countries. In 1967 there were 605 inhabitants. The economy was based on intensive mixed farming including citrus. In the mid-1990s the population of Aviḥayil was approximately 880, increasing to 1,090 in 2002. It established "Bet ha-Gedudim," a museum of the Jewish Legion and clubhouse for veterans.

[Efraim Orni]

ÁVILA, city in Castile, central Spain. Jews are mentioned there in 1085. The first documentary evidence of a Jewish community is from 1144. In 1176 the king granted one-third of the taxes levied on the Jews to the bishop of Ávila. However, they evidently refused to pay it to him, although ordered to do so by the crown in 1285 and again in 1293. By the end of the 13th century the community was one of the largest in Castile. Among some of its leading members was Yuc'af de Ávila, a very important tax collector under Sancho IV. In 1303 the community numbered about 50 families, or about 250 people, occupying 40 houses on diocesan land. The majority were artisans and shopkeepers, some were moneylenders, and others engaged in farming and sheep- and cattle-raising. Prominent were "R. Judah the dyer" and Yuc'af de Ávila, mentioned in 1285 as tax-collector for the province of Ávila, and owner of several houses in the city. By the end of the 13th century Ávila had become a center of mysticism and messianic activities (see Ávila, Prophet *of). Yuc'af was a patron of mystics and scholars. The famous kabbalist *Moses de Leon resided for a while in the city. During the civil war in Castile, when a moratorium was imposed on debts to Jews in 1366, the Jews in Ávila and other communities were attacked by rioters who seized their promissory notes and securities. The Jews of Ávila were forced to attend a religious disputation in church between the apostate *Juan de Valladolid and *Moses ha-Kohen of Tordesillas in 1375. Nothing is known of the fate of Ávila Jewry during the 1391 massacres. In the 15th century the community was still important and consisted of 107 families, more than 500 Jews, constituting some 8% of the city population. In 1474 the community had to pay taxes amounting to 12,000 maravedis, and in 1489 a war levy of 86,900 maravedis. Abraham Melamed of Ávila farmed various taxes in this period. *Anusim* ("forced converts") were already living in Ávila in the 15th century. During the reign of Ferdinand and Isabella a number of restrictive measures were imposed, and in 1480 the Jews were segregated into a separate quarter of the city. In 1490 the *La Guardia blood libel trial was transferred from Segovia to Ávila. The proceedings so inflamed the populace that after the accused had been burned at the stake a Jew was stoned to death. Later a royal order of protection was issued. After the expulsion of the Jews from Spain, the two synagogues of Ávila were sold and the Jewish cemetery was given to a monastery in 1494. An inquisitional tribunal was set up in Ávila in 1490. In 1499, 75 victims were burned at the stake, as well as the bones of 26 who had already died "in sin."

A document from 1303 shows that the Jews of Ávila lived then with Christians in different parts of the city. Many, however, were concentrated in the area of the *Mercado Grande* and the *Mercado Chico* (today's Reyes Católicos and Vallespín). Near the San Vicente church the Jews had a synagogue and a slaughterhouse. In 1412 the Jews had to live within a *judería* situated on the southwest part of the city wall, in the Santo Domingo quarter. In 1481 the *judería* was completely enclosed. Another Jewish quarter was on the east side of the wall. The documents refer to many synagogues in Ávila.

BIBLIOGRAPHY: P.L. Tello, *Judíos de Ávila* (1963); Baer, Spain, 2 (1966), index; idem, in: *Zion*, 5 (1940), 1–44; Beinart, in: *Tarbiz*, 26 (1957), 76; L. Suárez Fernández, *Documentos acerca de la Expulsión de los Judíos* (1964), index; Scholem, in: *Madda'ei ha-Yahadut*, 1 (1926), 17–18; Baer, Urkunden, 2 (1936), index. **ADD. BIBLIOGRAPHY:** M.A. Martín Sánchez, in: *El Olivo*, 7/8 (1978), 73–88; J. Belmonte Díaz, *Judíos e Inquisición en Ávila* (1989); J. Bilinkoff, *The Avila of Saint Teresa.*, (1989); J.L. Lacave, *Juderías y sinagogas españolas*, (1992), 214–8.

[*Encyclopaedia Hebraica* / Yom Tov Assis (2nd ed.)]

AVILA, DE, Sephardi family. Several of its members held prominent positions in Spain, both when professing Jews and after they became ostensibly converted to Catholicism, in the 15th century. From the second half of the 17th century the family appears in Morocco, England, and later in the United States. The most notable member living in Spain was the Converso DIEGO ARIAS DE AVILA, secretary and auditor of the royal accounts, one of the most disliked courtiers of his day. The marriage of his son into the nobility was the subject of a satire. His enemies dwelt on his depravity and asserted that he sucked the blood of his country. His son PEDRO succeeded to his father's post, while another son, JUAN ARIAS D'AVILA (Dávila) became bishop of Segovia and was subjected to the persecution of the Inquisition. Among the members of the family in Morocco were ISAAC (d. 1717), MEIR B. JOSEPH (c. 1724), author of responsa, in Rabat-Salé, and MOSES (d. 1725), philanthropist and talmudist in Meknès, author of responsa (preserved in Berdugo's *Mishpatim Yesharim*, 1 (Amsterdam, 1891), 93a, 94a). Moses was the father of Samuel *Avila and grandfather of Eliezer *Avila. SOLOMON DE AVILA (d. after 1791), son-in-law of Eliezer, talmudist and *dayyan* in Rabat, was also the banker and adviser of the sultan Muhammad ben Abdullah. Under the reign of Moulay Yazid, Solomon was cruelly persecuted. His son SAMUEL (d. after 1810) was the author of *Oz ve-Hadar* (Leghorn, 1855).

BIBLIOGRAPHY: Baer, Urkunden, 2 (1936), 106, 181–4, 424; Baer, Spain, index; J. Abensur, *Mishpat u-Ẓedakah be-Ya'akov*, 1 (1894), 17, 90, 261; S. Romanelli, *Massa be-Arav* (1834), 38, 59ff.; J.M. Toledano, *Ner ha-Ma'arav* (1911), 167; Azulai, 1 (1852), 23, 59; 2 (1852), 77.

[David Corcos]

AVILA, ELIEZER BEN SAMUEL BEN MOSES DE (known from the initials of his name as "**Rav Adda**"; 1714–1761), Moroccan rabbinical scholar; son of Samuel *Avila, born in Salé, Morocco. His commentaries on the Talmud, written while he was still a youth, are noteworthy for their acumen and independence. His works, published posthumously, are *Magen Gibborim*, on the Talmud (2 vols., Leghorn, 1781–85); *Milḥemet Mitzvah*, also on the Talmud (Leghorn, 1805) and including sermons entitled *Ḥesed ve-Emet; Be'er Mayim Ḥayyim*, responsa (Leghorn, 1806); *Ma'yan Gannim*, on the *Turim*. Another part of his responsa, entitled *She'elot u-Teshuvot de-Rav Adda*, and a work on the Bible, remain in manuscript. His responsa are a valuable source of information on the condition of the Jews of Morocco in the 18th century. He died in Rabat. To this day the Jews of Morocco go on pilgrimage to his grave.

BIBLIOGRAPHY: Azulai, 1 (1852), no. 42; 2 (1852), 77, no. 56; J.M. Toledano, *Ner ha-Ma'arav* (1911), 191; J. Ben-Naim, *Malkhei Rabbanan* (1931), 226.

AVILA, PROPHET OF, name given to a seer who declared himself at Avila, Spain, in 1295. The prophet, an illiterate man, purportedly experienced visions through the medium of an angel, who "dictated" to him a Book of Wondrous Wisdom, on which the seer immediately compiled a detailed commentary. A synopsis of 50 chapters was forwarded to R. Solomon ibn *Adret, who treated the matter with reserve (Resp. 1:548). The work has not been preserved, but evidently resembled the Christian mystical prophecies of this type common in the 13th and 14th centuries. The prophet of Avila is also mentioned by the apostate *Abner of Burgos, who records that a prophet announced that the ram's horn of the Messiah would be blown on the last day of the month of Tammuz. The Jews of the district prepared themselves by prayer and fasting, and on the appointed day gathered in the synagogue robed in white, whereupon crosses suddenly appeared on their garments. The community was panic-stricken; some were induced to adopt Christianity.

BIBLIOGRAPHY: Baer, Spain, 1 (1961), 278–81, 288, 439; idem, in: *Zion*, 5 (1939–40), 40.

AVILA, SAMUEL BEN MOSES (b. 1688), talmudic scholar in Morocco. Born in Meknès, Avila studied under Ḥayyim ibn Attar (the First), whose granddaughter he married, and under Joseph b. Bahatit. He began preaching publicly when he was about 20 years old. An affluent merchant, he left Meknès for Salé and Rabat because of the excessive taxes levied upon him by the community. Part of his work, *Keter Torah* (Amsterdam, 1725), which he calls "a guide for scholars and for the conduct of communal affairs," was written to prove that scholars should be exempt from communal taxation, probably as a result of his own experiences. At the end of this work is his commentary to tractate *Nazir*. He also wrote *Ozen Shemu'el* (Amsterdam, 1715), homilies and eulogies; and *Me'il Shemu'el*, still in manuscript.

BIBLIOGRAPHY: Steinschneider, Cat Bod, 2409, no. 7011; J.M. Toledano, *Ner ha-Ma'arav* (1911), 148 ff.; J. Ben-Naim, *Malkhei Rabbanan* (1931), 123b.

AVIMI (second half of the third century C.E.), Babylonian *amora*. He was the teacher of R. *Ḥisda who declared: "Many times I have been vanquished by Avimi," referring to a *halakhah* which Avimi had taught him (Ar. 22a). However, when Avimi forgot the tractate *Menaḥot*, he went to the *bet midrash* of R. Ḥisda his pupil, to be reminded. Avimi took the trouble to go to him personally, rather than sending for him, believing that in this way he would the better succeed in his purpose. This was in keeping with the statement, "I have toiled and achieved," meaning that he had gone out of his way and this had proved worthwhile (Men. 7a, and Rashi, *ibid.*). R. Ḥisda transmitted many *halakhot* in the name of Avimi (Suk. 16b; Ket. 71b, 100b; et al.), and also the *aggadah* that after the First Temple was built, the Tent of Meeting was stored away beneath the crypts of the Temple (Sot. 9a).

BIBLIOGRAPHY: Hyman, Toledot, 87–88.

[Zvi Kaplan]

AVIMI BEN ABBAHU (beginning of the fourth century C.E.), Palestinian *amora*. He had commercial contacts with Babylonia (Ket. 85a). Of his teachings almost nothing has been preserved, but he is held up as an exemplar of filial respect, his father himself praising him highly in this regard. The Talmud relates that although Avimi had five grown-up sons, when his father R. Abbahu (whose identity is a subject of dispute) would visit him, he would rush to open the door himself. Once, R. Abbahu, after asking Avimi to bring him some water to drink, fell asleep. Avimi waited at his side until he awoke (Kid. 31b). Avimi said: "One son may give his father pheasants to eat, and yet be driven from the world if he does so grudgingly, while another son may cause him to grind in a mill, and yet be brought to the world to come if he does so respectfully and solicitously" (see *ibid.*, 31a–b). He is said to have stated: "The days of Israel's Messiah will be 7,000 years, as it is written (Isa. 62:5): 'As the bridegroom rejoiceth over the bride, so shall thy God rejoice over thee'" (Sanh. 99a, and Rashi *ibid.*, the bridegroom's rejoicing being seven days, and God's day a thousand years).

BIBLIOGRAPHY: Bacher, Pal Amor; Hyman, Toledot, 88; Frankel, Mevo, 60.

[Zvi Kaplan]

AVIN (**Ravin**, **Avun**, **Bun**), variations of the same name. Ravin, an elision of R. (or Rav) Avin, occurs in the Babylonian Talmud, Avun and Bun in the Jerusalem Talmud and Avin in both. Many *amoraim* were called by this name, mostly with the addition of their patronymic but also without it, thus making it at times impossible to identify the author of a halakhic or aggadic statement.

(1) Babylonian *amora*, c.300. Emigrating to Ereẓ Israel where he met R. Johanan and Resh Lakish, he studied under Abbahu in Caesarea, R. Zeira in Tiberias, and R. Ilai. He was one of the *naḥutei*, i.e., sages who journeyed from Ereẓ Israel to Babylonia or vice versa, conveying to the scholars of one the teachings of the other. Hence the frequent statement in the Talmud: "When Ravin came" (i.e., from Ereẓ Israel to Babylonia). With the increased persecution in Ereẓ Israel after the Edict of Milan, the *naḥutei* settled in Babylonia. Ravin went to live in Pumbedita where he was a close associate of *Abbaye, the head of the local academy.

(2) Palestinian *amora* of the fourth century, apparently the son of the above, according to the tradition that "on the day Avin died, Avun his son was born" (Gen. R. 58:2; cf. TJ, Kid. 1:7, 61b). He was a colleague of R. Mana, the head of the yeshivah of Sepphoris, with whom he was involved in many halakhic controversies. Once when Avun built gates for a large *bet midrash* and joyfully showed them to R. Mana, the latter, quoting the verse "For Israel hath forgotten his Maker, and builded palaces" (Hos. 8:14), replied that it would be preferable if he had occupied himself with obtaining support for students (TJ, Shek. 5:4, 49b). A parable quoted in the name of Avun (either 1 or 2) is directed against the various Christian sects who were then arguing among themselves as to which of them represented the spiritual continuity of Israel. It is to the effect that the straw, the chaff, and the stubble disputed with one another, each contending that on its account the earth was sown. The wheat said to them: "Wait until the harvest, when we shall know on whose account the field was sown." When the crop was harvested and the owner came to winnow it, the chaff was blown away by the wind, the straw was thrown to the ground, the stubble burnt and the wheat heaped up. It is so with the various nations of the world who claim: "We are Israel and on our account the world was created." Israel said to them: "Wait until the coming of the day of the Lord. Then we shall indeed know on whose account the world was created" (Song R. 7:3).

BIBLIOGRAPHY: Frankel, Mevo, 60b; Hyman, Toledot, 89–93; Bacher, Pal Amor.

[Yitzhak Dov Gilat]

AVINA (third–fourth century), amora. Avina was a Babylonian who later emigrated to Ereẓ Israel. In Babylon he studied under R. *Huna (Git. 66a) and transmitted *halakhot* in the names of R. Jeremiah b. Abba (Shab. 137b), R. *Ḥisda (Pes. 59a), and *Rav (TJ, Ket. 13:4, 36a). He was friendly with Geniva, the opponent of the exilarch, Mar Ukva, and when Geniva was sentenced to death by the civil authorities, he gave instructions that 400 zuz from his estate should be given to Avina (Git. 65b). In Ereẓ Israel he became the colleague of R. Imi, R. Zeira, and R. *Jacob b. Aḥa, with whom he held halakhic discussions, and they transmitted his statements (TJ,

Shev. 4:2, 35a; Pes. 5:5, 32c). The Talmud also relates an argument between Avina and a sectarian (Sanh. 39a–b).

BIBLIOGRAPHY: Hyman, Toledot, 97ff.

[Yitzhak Dov Gilat]

AVINERI, SHLOMO (1933–), Israeli political scientist and educator. Born in Bielsko, Poland, Avineri arrived in Palestine in 1939 with his family who settled in Herzliyya. Avineri studied political science and history at the Hebrew University of Jerusalem, and received his doctorate for a thesis "The Concept of Revolution."

Avineri has served on the academic faculty of the Hebrew University since 1959. In 1974 he became professor and in 1975–76 he served as dean of the Faculty of Social Sciences. In 1999–2001 he was director of the Institute for European Studies and in 2001 became professor emeritus. Over the years he was also a visiting professor in universities in the U.S. and Britain.

His research work was initially an extension of his doctoral thesis, dealing with the social and political thought of Karl Marx. It was connected to the discovery and publication of the philosophical manuscripts of the young Karl Marx. His research addressed the relationship between the philosophical, humanistic, and anthropological writings of the young Marx and his economically-orientated later writings. He claimed there was a degree of continuity in Marx's thought and that the mature Marx cannot be understood without the presuppositions of earlier thought. This research led Avineri to consider the philosophy of Hegel and its relationship with modern totalitarianism (of the left and the right). His research showed that the view presented by Karl Popper of Hegelian philosophy as a form of modern totalitarianism did not present an adequate picture of the Hegelian philosophy and its heritage. Avineri was awarded the Rubin Prize in 1969 for his research, the Naftali Prize in 1971, and the Present Tense Award (American Jewish Communities) in 1982. In 1996 he received the Israel Prize for political science.

In 1970 Avineri published an article in *Commentary* calling for a dialogue with the Palestinians. In the following year he edited a book *Israel and the Palestinians*, which explored the possibility of negotiations with the PLO. When he was appointed director-general of the Foreign Ministry by Foreign Minister Yigal Allon, the Likud opposition took exception to Avineri's statements calling for the establishment of a Palestinian state in the West Bank and tried unsuccessfully to block his appointment by a parliamentary motion.

After his year in the Foreign Ministry, Avineri devoted himself to researching the intellectual origins of Zionism. He tried to place Zionism in the context of 19th-century socialism and nationalistic movements. He has taken a deep interest in recent developments in East Europe where he was one of the first Israeli academics to be invited to give talks in seminars in the Soviet Academy of Sciences in the U.S.S.R., Poland, Hungary, and the former German Democratic Republic. He was an observer to the 1989 elections in Hungary and Czechoslovakia.

His books include several works on Marx and Marxism as well as *The Making of Modern Zionism* (1982), *Moses Hess: Prophet of Communism and Zionism* (1985), *Arlosoroff: An Intellectual Biography* (1989), *Communitarianism and Individualism* (with De-Shalit, eds., 1992), *Jews of the Former Soviet Union: Yesterday, Today and Tomorrow* (with Chelnov and Gitelman, 1997), *Integration and Identity: Challenges to Europe and Israel* (with Weidenfeld, eds., 1999), and *Politics and Identities in Transformation: Europe and Israel* (with Weidenfeld, eds., 2001).

[Elaine Hoter / Shaked Gilboa (2nd ed.)]

AVINERI, YITZḤAK (1900–1977), Israeli grammarian and philologist. Avineri was born in the Ukraine and first came to Ereẓ Israel in 1913, and studied at the Herzliyyah Hebrew Gymnasia. He returned to Europe, however, to study in Berlin and Paris, and after graduating from the Sorbonne in mathematics, he took up permanent residence in Ereẓ Israel in 1926. Despite his proficiency in mathematics he devoted himself entirely to research in the Hebrew language, and his encyclopedic knowledge of sources made him an outstanding expert in his field.

His major work *Heikhal ha-Mishkalim*, on which he worked for 40 years, garnered him the Prize of the Academy of the Hebrew Language, but his four-volume *Heikhal Rashi* is regarded as his most important work. He was engaged in the preparation of a revised edition at the time of his death. His book *Yad ha-Lashon* is a collection of the numerous articles he published in the course of his life, arranged alphabetically as an encyclopedia of modern Hebrew linguistics and grammar.

AVIN THE CARPENTER, man of outstanding piety in Babylon in the third century C.E. R. *Huna said to him that as a reward for his piety, two great men would emerge from his home. This prophecy was fulfilled in the person of his sons, the two *amoraim* R. *Idi b. Avin and R. *Ḥiyya b. Avin (Shab. 23b). In the printed text of the Talmud he is given the title *Rav* but this is omitted in some manuscripts, thus suggesting that he was not a scholar.

BIBLIOGRAPHY: Hyman, Toledot, 96–97; Rabinovitz, Dik Sof, 7 (1875), 44.

[Yitzhak Dov Gilat]

AVINOAM (Grossman), REUVEN, (1905–1974), poet and translator. Avinoam, who was born in Chicago and educated in New York, received a thorough Hebrew education fostered by his father, a Hebrew writer. In 1929 he immigrated to Palestine and taught English language and literature at the Herzliyyah High School in Tel Aviv. In 1950 he was appointed supervisor of English studies at the Israel Ministry of Education and Culture. On behalf of Israel's Ministry of Defense, he published the literary remains of the young men – including his own son, Noam – who had fallen in the Israeli War of Independence, under the title *Gevilei Esh* (3 vols., 1952–61). Excerpts were published in English under the title *Such Were Our Fighters …* (1965). Avinoam's literary contributions have appeared in many Hebrew periodicals. Several volumes of his poetry, a volume of stories on Jewish life in America, and translations from the work of Jack London, Edgar Allan Poe, H.G. Wells, Israel Zangwill, and Ludwig Lewisohn were published in Israel. Avinoam also translated Tennyson's *Enoch Arden*, Thoreau's *Walden*, and Shakespeare's *Romeo and Juliet, King Lear*, and *Anthony and Cleopatra.* He edited a Hebrew anthology of English verse. Avinoam and H. Sachs compiled a Hebrew–English dictionary which was revised and edited by M.H. Segal (Tel Aviv, 1938).

BIBLIOGRAPHY: R. Wallenrod, *The Literature of Modern Israel* (1956), 243–5.

[Eliezer Schweid]

AVINU MALKENU (Heb. אָבִינוּ מַלְכֵּנוּ; "Our Father, our King"), a litany recited during the *Ten Days of Penitence and, in some rites, on fast days. Each line begins with the words *Avinu Malkenu* and ends with a petition. The number and order of the verses vary considerably in the different rites: in *Seder Rav Amram Ga'on* there are 25 verses, in the Sephardi rite 29, 31, and 32, the German 38, the Polish 44, and in that of Salonika 53. According to Jacob b. Asher (Tur, Sh. Ar., OḤ 602), Amram Gaon's *Avinu Malkenu* consisted of 22 verses arranged in alphabetical order. It became the Ashkenazi custom to recite them each morning and evening during the Ten Days of Penitence after the *Amidah*. The prayer is not found in the prayer books of Saadiah Gaon and Maimonides. The origin of *Avinu Malkenu* is R. Akiva's prayer on a fast day proclaimed because of a drought: "*Avinu Malkenu*, we have no King but Thee; *Avinu Malkenu*, for Thy sake have compassion upon us" (Ta'an. 25b). Other such litanies containing some of the same petitions but opening with *"*Avinu she-ba-Shamayim*" ("Our Father who art in Heaven") are still in use in some rites. *Avinu Malkenu* now opens, in the Ashkenazi rite, with "Our Father, our King, we have sinned before Thee" and contains petitions such as "Inscribe us in the book of good life; inscribe us in the book of redemption and salvation; inscribe us in the book of prosperity and sustenance." In the *Ne'ilah* service of the Day of Atonement "seal us" is substituted for "inscribe us," and on fast days "remember us" is used. In the Ashkenazi rite *Avinu Malkenu* is not recited on the Sabbath, since supplications should not be presented on that day (Tur, Sh. Ar., OḤ 602; cf. TJ Shab. 15b). If the Day of Atonement occurs on a Sabbath, *Avinu Malkenu* is recited only during the *Ne'ilah* service. In Spain, though, it was the custom to recite it on the Sabbath of the Ten Days of Penitence, presumably on the grounds that this was warranted by the gravity of the period (Tur, *ibid.*, and *Beit Yosef*, ad loc.; cf. Ta'an. 19a and Rashi ad loc.). Originally, the words *Avinu Malkenu* were chanted by the congregation and the rest of each verse was recited by the Reader who could add verses freely. It became the custom for the congregation to recite the whole prayer in an undertone except for some of the middle verses, which are repeated individually after the Reader. In many congregations the last verse is sung to a popular tune. The ark is opened for the prayer. The opening appeal to God as both "Our Father" and "Our King" expresses two complementary aspects of the relationship between God

'AVINU MALKÉNU 1.

'AVINU MALKÉNU 2.

and man, striking a balance between the intimacy of the one and the awe of the other.

BIBLIOGRAPHY: Hertz, Prayer, 161; Abrahams, *Companion*, lxxiiif.; Elbogen, Gottesdienst, 147–8, 223–4; J. Heinemann, *Ha-Tefillah bi-Tekufat ha-Tanna'im ve ha-Amora'im* (1966²), 95–96.

AVINU SHE-BA-SHAMAYIM (Heb. אָבִינוּ שֶׁבַּשָּׁמַיִם; "Our Father in Heaven"), form of adoration frequently found at the beginning of prayers of petition, based on the rabbinic epithet of God as "Father in Heaven." The description of God as "Father" occurs in the Bible, e.g., "Thou art our Father…" (Isa. 63:16), or "O Lord, Thou art our Father; we are the clay, and Thou our potter" (*ibid.* 66:8), and the prayer of David in I Chronicles 29:10, "Blessed be Thou, O Lord, the God of Israel, our Father for ever and ever." The tendency to describe God's relationship to Israel as analogous to the intimate father-child relationship was balanced by the desire to emphasize God's sovereignty and transcendence. Consequently, the rabbis of the talmudic period in formulating prayers preferred formulae in which God's position as King and Ruler is stressed as much as the father-child relationship. Piety and observance of the Law are described in early rabbinic parlance as "doing the will of our Father in heaven." The intimate relationship with God, as cultivated in particular by Eastern European Ḥasidism, found expression in the Yiddish language too, where, especially in private petitions and prayers, reference to God as "Father in Heaven" (*"foter in himl," "tate in himl"*) was common.

BIBLIOGRAPHY: J. Heinemann, *Ha-Tefillah bi-Tekufat ha-Tanna'im ve-ha-Amora'im* (1966²), 116, 120.

AVIRA.

(1) Palestinian *amora* of the third and fourth century. Avira was a colleague of R. *Ḥelbo and R. Yose b. Ḥanina. He frequented the *bet ha-midrash* of Judah II where he held the office of *"maftir kenesiyyot"* (according to Rashi, supervising the assembly and dismissal of the students). Avira went to Babylon in the time of Abbaye and transmitted *halakhot* in the name of R. Judah II (Ḥul. 51a) and *aggadah* in the names of R. Ammi and R. Assi, e.g., "A man should always eat and drink for less than his means allow, clothe himself in accordance with his means, and honor his wife and children beyond his means for they depend upon him, while he depends upon God" (Ḥul. 84b).

(2) A fourth century, Babylonian *amora*, Avira, transmitted *halakhot* in the name of *Rava (BB 131b; Ḥul. 55a). He discussed halakhic problems with Ravina (Pes. 73a; Ket. 103a). His son was Aḥa (Ber. 44a).

BIBLIOGRAPHY: Hyman, Toledot, 970.

[Zvi Kaplan]

AVIRAM, JOSEPH (1917–), director of the *Israel Exploration Society (IES) in Jerusalem, which has been at the forefront of Israeli archaeological activity especially since the 1950s. Born in Suwalki, Poland, Aviram completed his studies at the Tarbut Hebrew Teachers Seminary in Vilna in 1936, immigrating that year to Palestine and subsequently furthering his studies in the Bible and Hebrew Literature departments of the Hebrew University of Jerusalem. Prior to the War of Independence in 1948, Aviram worked as an elementary school teacher. After serving as an officer in the Israel Defense Forces, he was appointed as deputy director of the *Youth Aliyah organization. Between the years 1955 and 1969 Aviram served as the academic secretary of the Faculty of Humanities at the Hebrew University of Jerusalem, and in 1969–1983 he was the director of the Institute of Archaeology.

Serving first as the honorary secretary of the Israel Exploration Society in 1940, then as an Executive Board member, and eventually as its director from 1983, Aviram was the guiding light of the Society. During his time many major excavation projects were sponsored by the IES, with Aviram taking an integral part in their administration, notably at Beth Shearim, Hazor, Masada, the Judean Desert Cave surveys (1960–61), and in different parts of Jerusalem (the Temple Mount, Jewish Quarter, and City of David projects). The IES was also the publisher of numerous publications of very high scientific quality, overseen by Aviram himself. These include the *Israel Exploration Journal*, *Qadmoniot* (in Hebrew), the *New Encyclopedia of Archaeological Excavations in the Holy Land*, the *Ancient Pottery of Israel and Its Neighbors from the Neolithic through the Hellenistic Periods,* and the final reports on Beth Shearim (3 vols.), the Judean Desert (3 vols.), the Jewish Quarter (2 vols.), Jericho (3 vols.), Yokne`am (3 vols.), Dor (2 vols.), Masada (6 vols.), and Arad (3 vols.), among other sites.

Aviram was the recipient of many awards and distinctions, notably the prestigious Israel Prize (together with the Israel Exploration Society) in 1989 and the P. Schimmel Prize of the Israel Museum in 1990. The 25th volume of the *Eretz-Israel* scholarly series was dedicated as a *Festschrift* to Aviram in 1996 in recognition of his important services to the field of archaeology in Israel.

[Shimon Gibson (2nd ed.)]

AVI-SHAUL (Mandel), MORDEKHAI (1898–1988), writer and translator. Avi-Shaul, who was born in Szolnok, Hungary, studied at yeshivot and at the Budapest rabbinical seminaries. He went to Palestine in 1921 and was a teacher until 1948. He was active in Berit Shalom and pro-Communist organizations. Avi-Shaul's writings include *Ha-Maḥarozet* and *Bein Iyyim* (plays, 1928); *Ba-Azikin* (poems, 1932); *Yugurnat* (poems, 1945); *Ha-Melekh Karakash u-She'ar Ḥullin* (stories, 1965); *Kevarim Li* (a novel about the Holocaust, 1968); and various articles on current affairs. He also wrote pacifist literature, *Baladah al Shalom* being one such work. He edited the literary and social science anthology *Temurot* (1951–52), and translated the works of Thomas Mann, Goethe, Feuchtwanger (*Jew Suess,* which he also dramatized), Stefan Zweig, Bertolt Brecht, Jaroslav Hašek, Joseph Conrad, and others.

ADD. BIBLIOGRAPHY: E. Ben Ezer, in: *Yedioth Ahronoth* (April 21, 1967).

[Getzel Kressel]

°**AVITUS** (sixth century), bishop of *Clermont-Ferrand, France. Following a series of missionary sermons Avitus had addressed to the Jews, one of them accepted baptism on Easter Day, 576. The convert was subsequently insulted by a Jew and Avitus restrained the Christians from taking revenge at the time, but on May 14 (Ascension Day) they destroyed the synagogue. He then issued an ultimatum to the Jews, ordering them to convert to Christianity or leave Clermont. More than 500 submitted and were baptized at Pentecost. Those who refused took refuge in *Marseilles.

BIBLIOGRAPHY: B. Blumenkranz, *Les auteurs chrétiens latins...* (1963), 64ff., 70.

[Bernhard Blumenkranz]

AVITZUR, SHMUEL (1908–1999), geographer and specialist in cultural studies. Avitzur was born in Russia and immigrated to Ereẓ Israel in 1931. He early evinced an interest in the geography of Ereẓ Israel, on which he taught and lectured and in which he undertook research. His main area of study was the history of daily life in the past and especially methods of work, housing, clothes, food, utensils, and equipment. For that purpose he established a special museum in Tel Aviv, which was the first historical museum in Israel. Avitzur published more than 300 papers, including an atlas on the history of work, equipment, and production facilities in Ereẓ Israel. He was involved in the Sites and Buildings Restoration Council and participated in the establishment of many museums and sites. In 1977 he was awarded the Israel Prize for geography and cultural studies.

AVIV, HAIM (**Greenshpan**; 1940–), Israeli scientist. Aviv was born in Arad, Romania, and immigrated to Israel at the age of ten. He received his B.Sc. (1962) and M.Sc. (1965) in agriculture from the Hebrew University of Jerusalem and his Ph.D. in molecular biology from the Weizmann Institute, Rehovot (1970). His work as a postdoctoral fellow at the U.S. National Institutes of Health (1970–73) and at Weizmann (1973–80) led to the introduction of new probes for isolating genes and their cloning. This work has had important applications in the study of gene regulation and recombinant DNA technology. Aviv is prominent in Israel's biotechnology industry and academic biotechnology institutions, including Ben-Gurion University, as a board member, and Yeda, the commercial arm of the Weizmann Institute; he has served as chairman of Israel's National Biotechnology Committee and other public functions in the bio arena in Israel and is a recipient of the Israel Biochemistry Society Prize. Aviv is a scholar in Judaic studies and ethical issues in the life sciences.

[Michael Denman (2nd ed.)]

AVI-YITZHAK, DAN (1936–), Israeli attorney. Born in Jerusalem, Avi-Yitzhak graduated magna cum laude from the Hebrew University law faculty in 1957. He was admitted to the Israeli bar in 1959 and was a lecturer at the law faculty of the Hebrew University of Jerusalem and its Tel Aviv branch in 1957–70 in family law, estates, and principles of jurisprudence. From 1965 to 1975 he held key positions in the Israeli Bar Association. In 1975–78 he was a member of the Judges Appointment Committee.

For 45 years, Avi-Yitzhak engaged in active private law practice, appearing in a series of lengthy and complex criminal and civil cases. Several (civil) cases led to important legal principles in Israel law, such as Knesset Member Pinḥasi v. Knesset, in which the Supreme Court adopted new criteria for review of Knesset decisions and in regard to substantive immunity of Knesset members. Criminal defendants whom he represented in high-profile public interest cases include the "Jewish underground," Interior Minister Aryeh *Deri, and *Maariv* newspaper publisher Ofer *Nimrodi. He provided legal opinions of public interest and frequent legal commentary and declined several requests by the Israeli government to serve as attorney general.

[Leon Fine (2nd ed.)]

AVI-YONAH, MICHAEL (1904–1974), Israeli classical historian, historical geographer, and archaeologist; remembered for his extraordinary breadth of knowledge and didactic approach to scholarship. A native of Galicia from the Polish city of Lemberg, then in Austria, Avi-Yonah came from a very creative family. He wrote: "My father, who was a lawyer by profession, played the violin to orchestral standards, would enthusiastically attend operas and concerts, and became one of the founders of the local Jewish Society of Music. Both he and my mother appreciated paintings and sculpture, and, whenever possible, they would commission pictures from young Jewish painters who came to our house...." Avi-Yonah left for Palestine in 1921 and worked as Records Officer of the Palestine Department of Antiquities from 1931 to 1948. In 1931 he assisted L.A. *Mayer, the librarian of the PDA, with the task of editing the *Quarterly of the Department of Antiquities of Palestine* (QDAP). Eventually he took over the editing of QDAP between 1933 to 1950 and some of his most important articles were published within its pages: on mosaic pavements, on lead coffins, and on the map of Roman Palestine. Avi-Yonah became the scientific secretary of the Israel Department of Antiquities, serving from 1948 to 1953, at which point he was appointed professor of classical archaeology and the history of art at the Hebrew University of Jerusalem. Avi-Yonah later received a doctorate from the University of London in recognition of his major contribution to scholarship. He participated in numerous archaeological excavations at Avdat, Ḥusifa, Beth-Shean, Nahariyyah, Bet Yeraḥ, and Caesarea and was a member of the Masada Survey (1955). There were many scholarly subjects that Avi-Yonah had an interest in, but one subject in particular that always fascinated him was the study of the history and archaeology of Jerusalem, and one result of his endeavors in this field was undoubtedly the Holy Land Model of Second-Temple Period Jerusalem, which was built under his supervision (and later relocated to the grounds of the Israel Museum). He was a very prolific writer and among his works (some in Hebrew) may be counted *In the Days of Rome and Byzantium* (1946, 1962^3), *The Madaba Mosaic Map* (1954), *The Antiquities of Israel* (1955, with S. Yeivin and M. Stekelis), *Oriental Art in Roman Palestine* (1961), *Our Living Bible* (1962, with E. Kraeling), *The Holy Land From the Persian to the Arab Conquests (536 B.C. to A.D. 640). A Historical Geography* (1966), *Carta's Atlas of the Period of the Second Temple, the Mishna and the Talmud* (1966), and *Gazetteer of Roman Palestine* (1976). For many decades Avi-Yonah served as the editor of the leading scholarly journal *Israel Exploration Journal* and participated in the editing of a number of books and encyclopedias, including *Sefer Yerushalayim* (*The Book on Jerusalem*, vol. 1, 1956) and the *Encyclopedia of Archaeological Excavations in the Holy Land*. He also contributed numerous entries on archaeological and historical-geographical subjects to editions of the *Encyclopedia Hebraica*, the *Encyclopaedia Judaica*, and the *Atlas of Israel*. His *Illustrated Encyclopedia of the Classical World* (edited with Israel Shatzman) appeared not long after his death.

BIBLIOGRAPHY: M. Avi-Yonah, "Things Professor Avi-Yonah Said About Himself," in: *Qadmoniot*, 7:25–26 (1974), 67–68 (Hebrew); M.C. Salzmann, "Bibliography of M. Avi-Yonah," in: *Israel Exploration Journal*, 24 (1974), 287–311; B. Mazar, D. Barag, and Y. Tsafrir, "In Memoriam Michael Avi-Yonah," in: *Qadmoniot*, 7:25–26 (1974), 65–67 (Hebrew).

[Shimon Gibson (2nd ed.)]

AVNERY (Ostermann), URI (Helmut; 1923–), Israeli journalist, writer, and peace activist. Member of the Sixth, Seventh, and Ninth Knessets. Avnery was born in Beckum, Westphalia, in Germany. His father was a private banker and financial advisor. Avnery immigrated to Eretz Israel with his family in 1933. Owing to the family's financial difficulties, he left school at the age of 14 to go to work, turning to journalism at 18. At the age of 15 he joined the *Irgun Tzeva'i Le'ummi, remaining a member until 1942. In 1946 he founded a group called Eretz Yisrael Hatze'irah, which argued that the Jewish community in Palestine constituted a "new Hebrew nation" within the Jewish people and was part of Asia and a natural ally of the Arab nation. Avnery advocated turning the Middle East into a "Semitic region."

In the War of Independence he served in the Givati Brigade, and later volunteered for the famous Shu'alei Shimshon commando unit that fought on the southern front, being badly wounded toward the end of the war.

While on active service Avnery reported from the front to the *Ha'aretz* daily. In 1949–50 he was on the *Ha'aretz* editorial board but left due to his radical views on such issues as the expropriation of Arab land after the war. He then purchased a failing magazine called *Ha-Olam ha-Zeh*, which he soon turned into a popular weekly tabloid combining sensationalism with serious writing on issues that no other paper in Israel dared touch, especially corruption in government. Consequently he gathered around him a large group of admirers while provoking the wrath of the establishment. From 1950 to 1990 he served as both publisher and editor-in-chief of *Ha-Olam ha-Zeh*, whose name David *Ben-Gurion could not bring himself to pronounce.

In 1956 Avnery established, together with Nathan *Yellin-Mor, a political group called Ha-Pe'ullah ha-Shemit ("Semitic Action"). In 1965 he formed a party by the name of Ha-Olam ha-Zeh–Ko'aḥ Ḥadash ("This World–New Force") and ran in the elections to the Sixth Knesset, winning a single seat. In the elections to the Seventh Knesset, which took place after the Six-Day War, his party won two seats but soon split in two. In the Knesset Avnery was one of the most prolific speakers, holding forth on a large variety of topics, including the two-state solution to the Israeli-Palestinian conflict. Following the Yom Kippur War, after he lost most of his radical voters to the new Ratz party, and consequently lost his Knesset seat, Avnery turned to extra-parliamentary political activity, advocating direct contacts with the PLO. In 1975 he was one of the founders of the Israeli Council for Israeli-Palestinian Peace, and was part of a secret dialogue that began between Israeli personalities and PLO representatives Sa'id Hamami and Issam Sartawi, both of whom were eventually assassinated by fellow Palestinians for their meetings with Israelis. In the elections to the Ninth Knesset in 1977, Avnery ran within the framework of a new radical party called Sheli, serving in the Knesset for a short period between 1979 and 1981. In July 1982, during the Israeli siege of Beirut, which ended with the departure of the PLO leadership from Lebanon to Tunisia, Avnery met with *Arafat in the Lebanese capital, and was thus the first Israeli to openly meet with the Palestinian leader. In 1983 he established a new party called Alternativah, which joined the Progressive List for Peace – a joint Jewish-Arab party – the following year. Avnery became the chairman of the new party, which won two seats in the Eleventh Knesset, but he himself did not run for election, and in 1988 left party politics altogether.

After *Ha-Olam ha-Zeh* closed down in 1990, Avnery continued to write as a columnist in *Ma'ariv*, and to participate in demonstrations and other protest activities against the Israeli occupation and in favor of a two-state solution. In 1993 he was one of the founders of a peace movement called Gush Shalom. Later he published a regular column on the Internet. Avnery has received numerous prizes abroad for his peace and human rights activities.

His writings include *Bisdot Pleshet: Yoman Kravi* ("In the Fields of the Philistines," 1948), an account of the War of Independence; *Ha-Ẓad ha-Sheni shel ha-Matbe'a* ("The Other Side of the Coin," 1950); *Ẓelav ha-Kerres: Eichmann – Ish u-Tekufato* ("The Swastika: Eichmann – the Man and His Time," 1961); *Israel without Zionists: A Plan for Peace in the Middle East* (1968); *Milḥemet ha-Yom ha-Shevi'i* ("The War of the Seventh Day," 1969); *My Friend the Enemy* (1986); *Lenin Lo Gar Po Yotter* ("Lenin Doesn't Live Here Anymore," 1992).

BIBLIOGRAPHY: Zichroni (ed.), *1 mul 119: Uri Avnery Ba-Knesset* (1969); A. Bechar, *Hanidon: Uri Avnery – Dyokan Politi*

(1968); *Die Jerusalemfrage: Israelis und Palaestinenser im gespraech* (1996).

[Susan Hattis Rolef (2nd ed.)]

AVNET, JON (1949–), U.S. producer, director. Born in Brooklyn, New York, Avnet grew up in Great Neck, Long Island. He began his entertainment career directing off-Broadway theater productions before winning a directing fellowship at the American Film Institute that steered him towards filmmaking. Avnet's early success in the film industry came as a producer. In 1977, he received his first feature film producing credits as an associate producer of *Checkered Flag or Crash* and *Outlaw Blues*. The same year, he co-founded Tisch/Avnet Productions with producer Steve Tisch. The fruitful Avnet/Tisch partnership produced films such as *Risky Business* (1983), which launched Tom Cruise's career, and the made-for-television success *The Burning Bed* (1984), starring Farrah Fawcett in a breakthrough performance. In 1986 Avnet joined forces with former ABC executive Jordan Kerner to found the Avnet/Kerner Company. The Avnet/Kerner Company's first feature production was *Less Than Zero* (1987), adapted from the Bret Easton Ellis novel of the same name. After his success in the 1980s as a producer, Avnet made his directorial feature film debut with the surprise hit *Fried Green Tomatoes* (1991). Avnet continued to juggle his producing and directing efforts throughout the 1990s, directing *The War* (1994), *Up Close and Personal* (1996), and the acclaimed television miniseries about the Warsaw Ghetto, *Uprising* (2001). His notable credits as a producer included the popular *Mighty Ducks* trilogy, *George of the Jungle* (1997), and *Inspector Gadget* (1999). More recently, Avnet produced the television series *Boomtown* (2002), directing the show's pilot episode, and the sci-fi thriller *Sky Captain and the World of Tomorrow* (2004).

[Walter Driver (2nd ed.)]

AVNI, AHARON (1906–1951), Israel painter. Born in Yekaterinoslav in the Ukraine, Avni studied art at the Art Academy of Moscow. He arrived in Palestine in 1925 and continued his studies at the *Bezalel School of Art, Jerusalem, until 1928. He traveled widely before settling in Tel Aviv in 1929. Between 1930 and 1932 he was in Paris. In 1936, Avni founded the Histadrut Seminary for Painting and Sculpture in Tel Aviv and remained its director for 15 years. In 1948 he founded the College of Art Teachers and taught architecture and mathematics. He worked as an architect at the Jaffa municipality. Avni was at first influenced by the work of Cézanne, but later his style became more expressionistic. He painted members of the Haganah underground movement, in which he took part, and during the War of Independence he portrayed soldiers on the battlefield. Paintings such as *Visit to a Wounded Soldier* bear witness to his warm sense of humanity and patriotism. Avni won the Histadrut Prize in 1935 and the Dizengoff Prize in 1947–48.

AVNI, HAIM (**Steindling**; 1930–), historian of Latin American and contemporary Spanish Jewry. Born in Vienna, Avni immigrated with his family to Israel in 1933. He became acquainted with Latin America through his educational work with leaders of youth movements at the Institute for Young Leaders from Abroad (Makhon Le-Madrikhei Ḥuẓ La-Areẓ) of the World Zionist Organization in Jerusalem. He studied at the Hebrew University and wrote his master's thesis on the attitude of Franco's Spain towards Jewish refugees during the Holocaust and his Ph.D. dissertation on the Jewish agricultural colonization promoted by the Baron Maurice de *Hirsch in Argentina. Avni served as head of the Division of Latin America, Spain, and Portugal at the Institute of Contemporary Jewry of the Hebrew University from its establishment in 1967. In the years 1983–95 he was the co-director of the Graduate Jewish Studies Program of the Universidad Iberoamericana, Mexico City. After his retirement in 1999 he became (in 2000) the academic director of the Central Zionist Archives.

Avni bases his studies of the Jews in Spanish-speaking countries on a thorough analysis of the host societies as well as on the broad Jewish context, emphasizing the relevance of Latin American cases both to the local arena and to general Jewish history. Among his major publications are *Argentina "The Promised Land"* (Heb., 1973), *Spain, the Jews and Franco* (1982), *Argentina and the Jews: A History of Jewish Migration* (1991), *Emancipation and Jewish Education* (Heb., 1986), and *Judíos en América: cinco siglos de historia* (1992). He was the editor of the entries on Latin America in the first edition of the *Encyclopaedia Judaica* (1971).

Avni's studies on Latin American Jewry opened a new field of research in contemporary Jewry. In 1982 he took part in the foundation of LAJSA – Latin American Jewish Studies Association.

[Margalit Bejarano (2nd ed.)]

AVNI, TZEVI (1927–), Israeli composer. Avni was born in Saarbruecken, Germany, and immigrated to Eretz Israel in 1935. He studied theory and composition with Paul *Ben-Haim, *Ehrlich, and *Seter and graduated from the Academy of Music in Tel Aviv. From 1962 to 1964 he studied music librarianship in the U.S. and branched into electronic music under Vladimir Ussachewsky. Avni was director of the Central Music Library in Tel Aviv; editor of *Guitite*, the journal of the "*Jeunesses musicales*" in Israel; and chairman of the Rubinstein International Piano Contest (1989). He was the recipient of the ACUM, Engel, and Lieberson *Kurstermeier* composition prizes, and he was awarded the Israel Prize in 1998.

Avni was appointed professor of musical theory and composition at the Rubin Academy of Music in Jerusalem in 1976, a position he held until his retirement. There, he developed an advanced studio for electro-acoustic music. In 1977 he was appointed general secretary of the National Music Council, and in 1978 chairman of the Executive of the Festival of Contemporary Music.

His diversified style ranges from folk-like choral songs, such as *Psalms*, to the austere contrapuntal texture of the String Quartet *Summer Strings*. After his studies in the U.S. he turned to large-scale orchestral forms, marked by his powerful *Meditation on a Drama*, in which he reached a synthesis of influences ranging from Arnold *Schoenberg to Edgar Varese. The same pluralistic tendencies were even more prominent in his *Programme Music* (1980). In *Ecce Homo* to an Italian text by Primo Levi for soprano and orchestra, Avni reached an apex of poignant expression. In his more experimental electronic music he retained traditional elements, as in *Vocalise*, in which the pure soprano sounds of the singer Pnina (1927–73), Avni's first wife, are electronically worked out and elaborated with synthesized sounds. Avni regularly collaborated with the leading dance troupes in Israel (*Bat-Sheva, Bat-Dor, Kol Demama) for whom he composed both electronic music and instrumental scores.

ADD. BIBLIOGRAPHY: Grove online.

[Uri (Erich) Toeplitz / Jehoash Hirshberg (2nd ed.)]

AVODAH (Heb. עֲבוֹדָה; literally "service"), name for *Temple ritual, applied to the central part of the *Musaf* liturgy on the *Day of Atonement. This poetically recounts the sacrificial ritual in the Temple on the Day of Atonement. The ritual, based on Leviticus 16, is described in detail in Mishnah *Yoma* (chs. 1–7) and in the talmudic tractate of that name.

After the destruction of the Second Temple, the description of this ancient ritual became the core of the *Musaf* service on the Day of Atonement. In early times it was also recited during *Shaḥarit* and *Minḥah* (cf. *Siddur* of Saadiah Gaon). The Day of Atonement was the only occasion during the year when the high priest entered the Holy of the Holies in the Temple, and he had to make special preparations for the ritual. Seven days prior to the Day of Atonement, the high priest was moved to a special apartment in the Temple court (*palhedrin*) where he studied with the elders every detail of the sacrificial cult for the Day of Atonement. A deputy priest was appointed to take the place of the high priest should he be prevented by defilement or death from performing his duties. The day before the Day of Atonement, the high priest was escorted by the elders to his chamber in the Temple compound where he joined the other priests. The elders earnestly entreated him to perform all the minutiae of the sacrificial cult carefully as interpreted by the Pharisaic school, and took leave of him. On the Day of Atonement, the high priest himself performed the offering of the daily sacrifice, the incense offering, and the other sacred duties. After a series of immersions and ablutions he offered a bull as his personal sin-offering. He confessed his own and his family's sins, the sins of the tribe of Aaron (the priests), and those of all Israel (Lev. 16:6). Every time he uttered the holy name of God, the Tetragrammaton which was uttered only on the Day of Atonement, the people prostrated themselves and responded: "Blessed be His Name whose glorious kingdom is forever and ever" (see Tosef., Sot. 13:8; Yoma 39b). During the service of the high priest, this procedure was repeated ten times (Tosef., Yoma 2:2), or, according to another source (TJ, Yoma 3:7), 13 times.

The high priest then drew two lots from a wooden box, one inscribed "For *Azazel" and the other "A sin-offering for the Lord." The role of each of two he-goats participating in the ritual was determined by the lots. The high priest sent the goat "For Azazel" into the desert and he offered the other as a sin-offering. After a special incense-offering in the Holy of the Holies, the high priest recited a prayer (Yoma 5:1) that the climate in the coming year be moderate, neither too hot nor too wet; that the sovereignty of Judah be preserved; that Israel be prosperous (Yoma 53b; Ta'an. 24b); and that no earthquake harm the inhabitants of the Sharon Plain.

This traditional, and to some extent idealized, account of the ceremony served as the base for the subsequent development of the *Musaf* liturgy of the Day of Atonement. Originally, the *Avodah* was of a simple nature, being an unadorned description of the Temple service following the Mishnah *Yoma*. The main section was composed, at latest, in the fourth century C.E. but was enriched in the Middle Ages by elaborate *piyyutim*, most of them of an acrostic pattern. The *Avodah* texts currently in use contain compositions by Yose b. Yose, Solomon ibn Gabirol, Judah Halevi, and Moses ibn Ezra. The *Avodah* service, according to the Sephardi rite, opens with the *piyyut "Attah Konanta Olam"* by an unknown *paytan*, or with an introductory poem *"Be-Or Divrei Nekhoḥot"* (Roman rite), followed by a series of acrostics where the initial letter is repeated up to eight or even 16 times. The Piedmont rite opens with another *piyyut* entitled *"Attah Konanta Olam"* by Yose b. Yose. The Yemenite *Avodah* is similar to the Piedmont rite. In the Ashkenazi rite the *Avodah* opens with an introductory *piyyut*, *"Amiẓ Ko'aḥ"* by the poet Meshullam b. Kalonymus, which gives a short account of biblical history, the creation of the world, the sinfulness of the early generations, the election of the Patriarchs and of Israel, up to the priestly ritual of atonement in the Holy of Holies in the Temple. These themes are found in all of the later *Avodah* services. Next follow detailed descriptions of the sacrificial cult on the Day of Atonement in the Temple. There is also an opening *Avodah piyyut*, entitled *"Asoḥe'aḥ Nifle'otekha,"* found in the ancient French rite and attributed to Meshullam b. Kalonymus. In both the Ashkenazi and the Sephardi rite (but not the Yemenite), the order of the confession of the high priest is recited three times as is the response of the people: "And when the priests and the people that stood in the court (of the Temple) heard the glorious Name (of God) pronounced out of the mouth of the high priest, in holiness and purity, they knelt and prostrated themselves, and made acknowledgment to God, falling on their faces and saying: Blessed be His name, whose glorious kingdom is forever and ever." This response is recited a fourth time in the Sephardi rite. At this passage, it is still customary in the Orthodox Ashkenazi rite and in some Sephardi communities for worshipers to prostrate themselves on the floor of the synagogue.

Other parts of the *Avodah* (e.g., "*Tikkanta Kol Elleh li-Khevod Aharon*" ("All this didst Thou establish for the glory of Aaron") in the Sephardi and Yemenite rites) then describe in great detail the high priest's actions, including the counting of the blood-sprinklings of the sacrifices, which are recited in solemn melody "And thus he counted: One, One and One, One and Two…" etc.

This elaborate poetic description of the sacrificial cult of the Day of Atonement closes with an account of the festivity which the high priest arranged for his friends in gratitude for the successful performance of the Day of Atonement ritual "in peace and without harm" (Yoma 7:4). After a free poetic rendition of the high priest's prayer for the welfare of the people of Israel, this section of the *Avodah* closes with the nostalgic *piyyut*, "*Ashrei Ayin Ra'atah Kol Elleh*" ("Happy is the eye that saw these glorious services…"), based on a hymn in Ben Sira 50.

This is followed by a series of acrostic *piyyutim* deploring the misfortune of Israel, now deprived of the Temple and its sacred cult, and subjected to the sufferings and persecutions of exile. This cycle of *piyyutim*, which closes with an ardent prayer for the reestablishment of the Holy Temple, its cult and institutions, destroyed because of the sins of Israel, is immediately followed by the penitential *Seliḥot* prayers of *Musaf*, thus linking up again with the main motif of the Day of Atonement service.

In the Reform ritual, only the confession of the high priest "*Anna Adonai Kapper Na*," is recited, in Hebrew and the vernacular. The details of the ancient sacrificial cult are not dwelt upon and the congregation does not prostrate itself during the service. In that ritual the prayers inserted instead of the traditional *Avodah* emphasize the moral duties to which Israel has to consecrate itself anew to bring about the kingdom of God among all mankind. The last Hebrew poet to compose an entire *Avodah* was S.D. *Luzzatto in his *Kinnor Na'im* (1913), 341–62 (this was not composed for synagogue use). In the Conservative ritual, most parts of the traditional Hebrew *Avodah* service are retained, but, instead of their exact rendition in English, new meditations and prayers of contemporary relevance are inserted as well as modern interpretations of the symbolism of the ancient sacrificial cult.

[Meir Ydit]

Musical Settings

The descriptions and emotional content of the *Avodah* have always been a challenge to musical inventiveness. It was set to especially solemn melodies in many Jewish communities, for example that of Rome. The most distinguished *Avodah* tunes, however, can be heard in Ashkenazi synagogues. These possess a uniform tradition for the chapter *Ve-ha-kohanim ve-ha-am*; less distinctive tunes are given to the texts *Ve-khakh hayah Omer* and *Ve-khakh hayah moneh*. In addition, the cantors of Eastern Europe used to perform their own versions of sections such as *Amiẓ Ko'aḥ* (*Bachmann), *Nilvim elav nevonim* (*Abrass), or the elegiac *U-mi-she-ḥarav Beit Mikdashenu* (Bezalel Shulsinger).

The *Ve-ha-kohanim* tune is common to all Ashkenazi communities, both eastern and western, and belongs to the cycle of unchangeable *Mi-Sinai* melodies. Its musical character is that of a "cantorial fantasia," in which sustained passages of vocalize are inserted between short groups of words. In *Ve-ha-kohanim*, the brief textual statements are interrupted by almost explosive coloraturas which are intended to give expression to the vision of the overwhelming power of the former atonement ritual.

The traditional Ashkenazi *Ve-ha-kohanim* tune comprises nine themes, the majority extended vocalizes, each attached to one word or at most a few words of the text. The complete series of themes is repeated three times. The musical substance of these themes has to be sought for in a melodic idea which is conceived only as a general outline; auditory shape and final elaboration are provided by the individual performer. Thus there are as many "realizations" of the fundamental idea as there are written (and recorded) versions, but all of them remain closely related to an imagined archetype.

The unending process of variation can be illustrated by samples taken from four Ashkenazi versions, two eastern and two western. The examples demonstrate Theme VII of the *Avodah* melody (which follows *Shome'im et ha-Shem*). The first western version changes from E-flat major to F minor, and the second one remains in the major key, while the eastern versions are in the characteristic scale of a **Shtayger*. Nevertheless their common origin is clearly perceptible. Western Ashkenazi cantors generally tend to favor diatonic progression of the coloraturas and to curtail or even omit some of the longer vocalizes. The *Ve-ha-kohanim* tune remains, however, one of the most grandiose creations of Ashkenazi synagogue song.

[Hanoch Avenary]

BIBLIOGRAPHY: AVODAH: *Union Prayerbook*, 2 (1928), 262–75; M. Silverman, *High Holiday Prayerbook* (1939), 368–79; *High Holiday Prayerbook* (Reconstructionist), 2 (1948), 366–85; Elbogen, Gottesdienst, 216–7; idem, *Studien zur Geschichte des juedischen Gottesdienstes* (1907), 49–190; E. Levy, *Yesodot ha-Tefillah* (1963), 259–61. For *piyyutim* and *seliḥot* see: Davidson, Oẓar, 1 (1924), 221 (nos. 4805, 4806, 4808, 4809), 223 (nos. 4838, 4843), 260 (no. 5703), 381 (no. 8430); 2 (1929), 462 (no. 6), 490 (no. 574); 3 (1930), 93 (no. 540), 534 (no. 401), 535 (no. 423). For *Ve-ha-Kohanim* see music examples, and also: Idelsohn, *Melodien* 6 pt. 2 (1932), no. 7; 7 pt. 1 (1932), no. 234; pt. 2, no. 204; M. Deutsch, *Vorbeterschule* (1871), nos. 429–31; M. Wodak, *Hamnazeach* (1898), nos. 760–2; Ch. Vinaver, *Anthology of Jewish Music* (1955), no. 33–34. FOR OTHER PARTS OF THE AVODAH SEE: Ephros, Cant, 2 (1940), 265–90; Vinaver, no. 35; O. Abrass, *Simrat-Joh* (n.d.), no. 34; J. Bachmann, *Schirat Jacob* (1884), no. 133–5; EJ, 1 (1925[8]), 353–6; Idelsohn, in: *Zeitschrift fuer Musikwissenschaft*, 8 (1926), 449–72; Avenary, in: *Yuval*, 1 (1968), 65–85.

AVODAH ZARAH (Heb. עֲבוֹדָה זָרָה; "Idolatrous Worship"), tractate of the Mishnah, Tosefta, and Jerusalem and Babylonian Talmuds in the order of *Nezikin*; its name is already referred to in the Babylonian Talmud (Av. Zar. 56b). The tractate was assigned to the order of *Nezikin*, since it is linked with the tractates *Sanhedrin* and *Makkot* which include some laws on idolatry (cf. Tos. Av. Zar. 2a).

The Mishnah, which consists of five chapters, treats of the following subjects: (1) prohibitions concerning dealings with Gentiles (who are presumed to be idolaters) in their festival periods; objects which may not be sold or hired to Gentiles as they may be required for idol worship; objects which may not be sold to Gentiles as they may cause public damage (e.g., arms); prohibitions of sale or lease of real estate in Ereẓ Israel to Gentiles (chapter 1); (2) prohibitions arising from Gentiles being suspected of incest and murder (2:1–2); (3) laws concerning articles belonging to Gentiles – differentiating between those which are entirely prohibited for benefit, or only for food, since they may be offered up in idolatrous worship, and those which are entirely permitted (2:3–7); (4) the prohibition of actual idolatrous objects (images, shrines, etc.) and the ways in which they are to be abolished or destroyed (3:1–4:7); (5) laws about wine produced or handled by non-Jews, which is presumed to have been used, or intended for use, as a libation before an idol; the procedure of making utensils that have been bought from a Gentile fit for use (4:8–5:12).

The Mishnah (4:7) contains a question asked by "philosophers" of some sages, apparently R. Gamaliel, R. Joshua, and R. Eleazar b. Azariah, when they were in Rome:

"If [your God] does not want idolatry, why does He not abolish it?"

The sages answered: "If something is worshiped which the world has no need of, He would abolish it. But the sun, the moon, and the stars are worshiped. Should God, then, destroy His world because of fools?"

"If so, He should destroy what the world has no need of, and leave what is essential for the world."

"We would then merely be strengthening the hands of those worshiping these things, since they would say, 'See, these are deities, for they have not been destroyed.'"

The Tosefta of the tractate has eight chapters, is longer and much fuller than the Mishnah, and contains quite a few aggadic matters. The redactor of the Tosefta used not only *beraitot* which complement the Mishnah but also parallel sources as well as various others which deal with subjects not mentioned in the Mishnah. The relation between the different sections of the Tosefta also differs from that of the Mishnah, half of the former (its first four and a half chapters) being devoted to subjects which occupy only a quarter of the latter (1:1–2:2). The first two chapters of the Tosefta correspond to the first chapter of the Mishnah, while the third and first half (1–6) of the fourth chapter of the Tosefta correspond to the Mishnah (2:1–2); these *halakhot* in the Tosefta treat, in passing, of laws concerning Cutheans (Samaritans), of dealings with an **am ha-areẓ*, of one who purchases a slave from gentiles or sells his slave to them or abroad, as well as laws which apply specifically to Ereẓ Israel and to Syria and which conclude with the duty to live in Ereẓ Israel. The rest of the fourth chapter (7–13) of the Tosefta corresponds to the Mishnah 2:3–7; chapters 5–6 of the Tosefta correspond to the Mishnah 3:1–4:7, while Tosefta 7:1–8:3 corresponds to the final part of the Mishnah. The final part of the Tosefta (8:4–8), which is completely unconnected with the Mishnah, is devoted to the seven Noachian commandments, which include the prohibition against idolatry.

An examination of the names of the sages mentioned in the Mishnah and the Tosefta shows that most of these belong to the period after the Bar Kokhba revolt. One passage in the Mishnah (2:6) mentions Rabbi and his *bet din*. The parallel text in the Tosefta (4:11) reads R. Judah, which is understood by some to refer to Judah Nesia II and his *bet din*. If this understanding is correct, then this is a late addition to the text of the Mishnah in line with the *baraita* in the Tosefta.

The tractate in the two Talmuds contains much aggadic material, important historical traditions, especially on the relations between Jews and non-Jews in general and between Jews and non-Jewish authorities in particular. It also conveys much information on idolatrous, including Oriental, religions, on Christianity, and Gnosticism. The Babylonian Talmud deals also with the Persian religion. Nonetheless the Babylonian *amoraim* admitted that not everything in the Mishnah was clear to them: "R. Ḥisda said to Avimi: There is a tradition that the (tractate) *Avodah Zarah* of our father Abraham consisted of four hundred chapters. We have learnt only five, and yet we do not know what we are saying" (Av. Zar. 14b). It is doubtful if parallels between the Mishnah of *Avodah Zarah* and Tertullian's *de idolatria* indicate an influence of Jewish *halakhah* on Christianity in this sphere.

Copies of the tractate were rare even at an early period, probably because in the course of the centuries it suffered greatly at the hands of Christian censors. This led many Jewish scholars to issue apologetic declarations to the effect that the statements in the tractate are directed only against the nations of antiquity, and to adopt a lenient attitude to some of its prohibitions (see Meiri, *Beit ha-Beḥirah* on Av. Zar., 53).

BIBLIOGRAPHY: Ch. Albeck, *Shishah Sidrei Mishnah, Seder Nezikin* (1953), 321–4, 491; idem, *Meḥkarim bi-Veraita ve-Tosefta* (1944), 142–3; S. Abramson (ed.), *Massekhet Avodah Zarah Ketav Yad shel Beit ha-Midrash la-Rabbanim be-New-York* (1957); S. Lieberman, *Hellenism in Jewish Palestine* (1950), 115–52; IEJ, (1959), 149–65, 229–45.

[Moshe David Herr]

AVOT (Heb. אָבוֹת), a tractate of the Mishnah, is the most popular rabbinic composition of all time. Its timeless lessons and uncomplicated language have made the work accessible to vast audiences beyond the learned few who traditionally were well versed in the rhyme and reason of rabbinic discourse. The custom of studying *Avot* on the Sabbath, which spread from geonic Babylonia to Jewish communities all over the globe, enhanced the public profile of the work and led to *Avot*'s mass circulation in the Siddur. Over the centuries, *Avot* inspired hundreds of commentaries and was translated into many languages such as Latin, Greek, English, German, French, Italian, and Spanish. No other rabbinic composition has sustained such widespread interest and popular appeal.

Structure

The first four of *Avot*'s five chapters present an anthology of wisdom sayings attributed to rabbinic (and proto-rabbinic) sages and the central principle structuring these chapters is the chain of transmission. This chain is prominently introduced in the opening statement of *Avot* 1:1, a statement that constructs the earliest stages of the transmission of the Torah from its initial reception on Mt. Sinai until the early Second Temple period: "Moses received the Torah from Sinai and passed it on to Joshua, and Joshua to the elders, and the elders to the prophets, and the prophets passed it on to the Men of the Great Assembly." *Avot* 1:2 states that Simeon the Just was of the remnants of the Great Assembly and 1:3–12 states that Antigonus of Sokho and then five pairs of leading sages from Second Temple times each received the Torah from their predecessors. The frequent repetition of the keyword "received," "קִבֵּל," conveys the impression that each sage received the Torah from his predecessor in the chain and chronological gaps are thereby glossed over. After the fifth pair of sages receives the tradition, however, the teacher-disciple pattern is disrupted and a genealogy of the patriarch's family is introduced without any explicit mention of their "receiving" the Torah (see *Patriarch). The shift from the teacher-disciple chain to a familial genealogy reflects a literary rift in the text and the significance of the location of this genealogy will be discussed below. The teacher-disciple chain resumes in 2:8, after the presentation of the genealogy of the patriarchate, with Rabban Johanan ben Zakkai "receiving" the Torah from Hillel and Shammai, the final pair of sages from Second Temple times. Chapter two continues with literary material that focuses on five disciples of Rabban Johanan ben Zakkai, and then concludes with two sayings attributed R. Tarfon, another disciple of Rabban Johanan ben Zakkai. Thus, the chain of transmission in the first two chapters of *Avot* constructs the history of the Torah's reception from biblical times until the early tannaitic period. Though commentators have often assumed that the Torah under discussion is the "Oral Torah," this rabbinic term, which refers to an oral Torah delivered to Moses on Sinai, probably postdates the original formulation of *Avot*'s chain of transmission. On the other hand it seems unlikely that a chain of transmission would have been employed solely to defend the veracity of a written corpus, i.e., Scripture, and indeed, the three other chains of transmission in the Mishnah all relate to specific extra-biblical materials (see Yadayim 4:3; Pe'ah 2:6; Eduyyot 8:7). Thus, it seems that the Torah of *Avot*'s chain of transmission included extra-biblical traditions though these traditions were apparently envisioned as natural offshoots of Scripture.

Chapters three and four also adhere to a chronological structure though they are structured by a generational rather than by a teacher-disciple schema. Chapter three opens with statements attributed to sages from the end of the Second Temple period such as Akavyah ben Mahalalel and R. Hananiah deputy of the priests, and then cites sages from the first three generations of the tannaitic period with only a few minor exceptions. Chapter four picks up with a few sages from the third generation of *tannaim* such as Ben Zoma and Ben Azzai, and then records statements, attributed, for the most part, to sages from the fourth and fifth generation of *tannaim*. This rough, generational schema suggests that chapters three and four were designed to continue the chain of transmission down through the tannaitic period. Thus, a bird's eye view of the text notes the continuous historical theme of the first four chapters of *Avot* while a closer examination reveals that this historical theme is developed in two ways; the explicit transmission of the Torah in the first two chapters and the implicit transmission in the latter two chapters.

Earlier Jewish literature certainly records familial genealogies, but there is no pre-rabbinic precedent for a teacher-disciple chain of transmission extending over a number of generations. Rather, *Avot*'s chain of transmission is most closely akin to the contemporary successions genre that was common in the Graeco-Roman world. Successions, which emerged within philosophical academies during the second century B.C.E., ascribed the origin of a philosophical school to a legendary sage from the past and then portrayed each successive "scholarch" as the disciple of his immediate predecessor. Successions were scholastic (or doctrinal) in nature, since they outlined the transmission of proper doctrine over the course of time and thereby served to ground the traditions of a school in the hallowed past. Yet, since the links in succession lists were "scholarchs," i.e., the heads of philosophical academies, successions were also supposed to reflect the line of the legitimate institutional authority of an academy. In time, successions spread beyond philosophy to other intellectual traditions such as law, medicine, and Christianity while becoming in the process a standard element in the construction of the history of an intellectual discipline in the Graeco-Roman world.

The similarities between *Avot* and successions suggest that this Graeco-Roman literary genre was introduced into the Jewish setting in order to construct the history of the rabbinic academy. Like successions, *Avot*'s chain of transmission opens with a legendary sage of the past and then traces the transmission of Torah through a list of successors portrayed within a teacher-disciple framework. Moreover, like successions, *Avot*'s chain is not a straightforward reflection of historical reality but rather a rhetorical construct designed to demonstrate the continuity of a school and thereby ground its current teachings within the ancient past. By legitimating one particular school, *Avot* rejected the claims of all other competing groups, at least implicitly.

The institutional and scholastic dimensions of successions appear to be intertwined in the earliest stratum of the rabbinic chain of transmission but then separate as the chain is developed in two distinct trajectories. The earliest stratum of the chain which comprises the teacher-disciple chain from Moses until Rabban Johanan ben Zakkai consists of personalities who were both tradents in the history of the transmission of the Torah and leaders of the Jewish people. Like scholarchs in successions, they represented both continuous scholastic tradition and legitimate leadership. The scholastic dimension of this early stratum finds its continuation amongst the students of Rabban Johanan ben Zakkai who appear in chapter two and the sages of the implicit chain of transmission in chapters three and four. These sages represent the continuation of Jewish scholarship throughout the early rabbinic period and through them the tannaitic movement is portrayed as the preserver of authentic Torah knowledge. In contrast, the institutional dimension of the early stratum finds its continuation in the genealogy of the patriarchate of chapters one and two. The genealogy of the patriarchate was juxtaposed to the earliest stratum of *Avot* in order to portray the patriarchs as the proper heirs to the Jewish leadership of earlier eras. Thus the genealogy of the patriarchate and the implicit chain of transmission both seek to present the rightful heirs of Hillel and Shammai during the tannaitic period though from two different perspectives; the former focusing on the institutional dimension of successions and the latter on the scholastic.

Content

The sayings attributed to the sages in the first four chapters of *Avot* are quite unlike the halakhic materials that comprise the core of the Mishnah. Instead, they are akin to the contents and style of wisdom literature, a literature which includes such works as Proverbs, Ecclesiastes and Ben-Sira. *Avot* 4:4 paraphrases Ben-Sira 7:17, *Avot* 4:19 cites Proverbs 24:17, and other *Avot* sayings employ literary techniques often employed in wisdom literature such as riddles, numerical sayings, lists, anadiplosis, dialogue and metaphor. Moreover, the hallmark of Hebrew wisdom, the bipartite proverb, leaves traces throughout *Avot* as attested by the following examples: "Make for yourself a master and possess for yourself a comrade" (1:6); "Love work and hate mastery" (1:10); "He who makes his name great, loses his name," (1:13); "Say little and do much" (1:15); "And not study is the essential thing but action" (1:17); "Everything is seen (or: foreseen) and free will is granted" (3:15); "Be a tail to lions and not a head to foxes" (4:15); "Look not at the pitcher but at what is in it" (4:20). Numerous themes that appear in ancient wisdom literature also surface in *Avot* such as the search for life's secrets, reward and punishment, groping after order, self-evident intuitions about mastering life, and a bias against women. It is especially noteworthy that ethics receives more attention than any other traditional wisdom theme. *Avot* portrays kindness as one of the three pillars of the world; extols disinterested righteousness; exhorts the opening of one's house to the poor; urges one to select worthy companions and a virtuous way of life; commends truthful testimony; praises the pursuit of peace and love of humanity; counsels how to avoid transgression; cautions one to cherish the honor and property of others; and calls upon one to receive every person with joy and a pleasant countenance. In short, since *Avot* expresses wisdom themes by means of artistic literary forms it should be considered a member in the trajectory of Hebrew wisdom.

The prominence of Torah in *Avot* sayings, however, is unparalleled in earlier wisdom compositions. Although Torah plays a role in post-biblical wisdom, *Avot* elevates Torah to new heights by establishing the study of Torah and the observance of its precepts as fundamental Jewish values. *Avot* depicts Torah as a pillar of the world and the instrument through which it was created; as a crown of the Jewish people and the purpose of their creation. Torah is not to be viewed as an inheritance that is acquired without effort, rather it is to be toiled after constantly, sought even in distant places, established in one's home, discussed at one's dinner table, studied on the road and carefully preserved in one's memory. Torah is to be honored, cherished and implemented meticulously, and *Avot* guarantees that knowledge and observance of Torah will be rewarded in this world and in the world to come. Through this depiction of Torah, *Avot* transforms and updates the traditional understanding of wisdom by identifying wisdom with the tannaitic conception of Torah and rabbinic notions of religious piety.

Like wisdom literature and rabbinic thought, the Graeco-Roman literary setting also provides, at times, an illuminating backdrop for the contents of *Avot*'s sayings. For example, the counter-intuitive definitions of wisdom, strength, wealth and honor attributed to Ben Zoma in *Avot* 4:1 are highly reminiscent of well known Stoic paradoxes. In a related vein, the five-part saying attributed to R. Tarfon, "The day is short, and the work is great, and the laborers are sluggish, and the recompense is great, and the master of the house is urging" (2:15) is extraordinarily similar to Hippocrates's five-part aphorism, "Life is short, the Art long, opportunity fleeting, experiment treacherous, judgment difficult" (*Aphorisms* 1.1) The literary similarities between these two statements suggest that the short *mashal* attributed to R. Tarfon is a variation on a well-known aphorism of the period, while their differences contrast the world-views of a Greek physician and a rabbinic sage. Whereas Hippocrates bemoaned the difficulty of acquiring medical knowledge during the course of a human's short lifetime, *Avot* stressed the temporal limitations that bound and challenge the *homo religiosus*.

Saying Collections

The collection of attributed wisdom sayings in chapters one through four is unusual for a Hebrew wisdom composition since collections of multiple author named-sayings simply do not appear in the Hebrew and ancient Near Eastern wisdom tradition. In Graeco-Roman antiquity, however, collections of proverbs and aphorisms were very popular and one type of Greek saying, the chreia, was technically defined as an attributed maxim. This distinctive feature of the chreia is precisely what also distinguishes the attributed sayings in *Avot* and therefore it appears that *Avot* sayings should be viewed as chreiai (despite the differences in content and tone between chreiai and rabbinic sayings). Many chreiai were both attributed to and collected by philosophers and therefore it is highly likely that chreiai collections served to preserve and propagate the teachings of philosophical schools. Moreover, chreiai were aggregated in various sorts of sayings collections including successions and thus the synthesis of the chain of transmission and attributed sayings in *Avot* was apparently modeled on the succession literary genre, a genre which included both chreiai and a succession list. In other words, the idea of conjoining a teacher-disciple chain with collected chreiai diffused into the rabbinic world from the overarching Graeco-Roman environment. In the wider Graeco-Roman setting as in *Avot*, the joint succession list-chreiai collection was apparently designed to legitimate and preserve the teachings of a scholastic tradition.

The Fifth Chapter of Avot

Chapter 5 is the only chapter of *Avot* that is not structured by an explicit or implicit chain of transmission. Instead, the chapter employs a descending numerical framework for the ordering of its mostly anonymous materials. This numerical structure commences with eleven lists of ten items apiece (5:1–6), continues with two lists of seven (5:7–8) and seven lists of four (5:9–15) and concludes with four bipartite sayings (5:16–19). The first ten lists are also chronologically ordered and run from creation until the period of the Temple. This historical overview suggests perhaps that chapter five provided the historical backdrop for the chain of transmission and, more generally, that *Avot* was designed to offer a chronology of Jewish experience from creation through the tannaitic period. In any event, the contents of these anonymous materials are in keeping with the spirit of the contents of the other chapters. After the numerical sayings, two sayings are attributed to Judah ben Tema (5:20) and, as the only attributed sayings in chapter five, these sayings supply a stylistic link to the first four chapters of *Avot*. It is possible that *Avot* originally concluded with Judah ben Tema's first saying, but the prayer of *Avot* 5:20 which beseeches God to grant his people a portion in his Torah is also well attested and provides a fitting conclusion for the tractate as a whole. In short, *Avot* encouraged the observance and study of rabbinic Torah traditions by developing a theological vision of a God who prizes adherence to the Torah, by demonstrating the sagacity of the rabbis via their sayings and by offering an historical justification for rabbinic authority.

After the redaction of *Avot*, some mishnayot were appended to chapter five and a sixth chapter called *Kinyan Torah*, also found in *Kallah Rabbati* and *Seder Eliahu Zuta*, was attached to the end of the tractate during the Geonic period. Furthermore, siddurim in the Sephardic tradition, assorted *genizah* fragments and the commentary attributed to R. Nathan b. Abraham Av ha-Yeshivah omit various *mishnayot* found in most versions of *Avot*. This shorter version of the tractate has been interpreted as an abridged version of an originally longer tractate or as an alternate and perhaps even more original version of the tractate.

Date of Redaction

The prominent role of the genealogy of the patriarchate in *Avot* suggests that a member of the patriarch's circle, if not the patriarch himself, redacted this treatise. Indeed, R. Judah ha-Nasi, the famous patriarch and editor of the Mishnah, strikingly appears in the opening mishnah of chapter two (in parallel position to Moses at the beginning of chapter one) within the context of the genealogy of the patriarchate. This genealogy establishes his family credentials and his authority is further legitimated by the institutional dimension of the succession in chapters one and two. R. Judah ha-Nasi appears for a second time in *Avot* 4:17 (though not according to certain Sephardic siddurim) where he functions as the penultimate tradent in the scholastic chain of transmission, a position which perhaps intimates that he should also be viewed as heir to the scholastic traditions of the past. Thus, the resounding recommendation of R. Judah ha-Nasi and the *tannaim* in *Avot* suggests that with the publication of the Mishnah or shortly thereafter, *Avot* was designed to legitimate the Mishnah and to justify the authority of its editor and his family. It should be noted, however, that some scholars prefer to date *Avot* to the fourth century or later.

Title

Since the Middle Ages, *Avot* has frequently been called *Pirkei Avot*, "the chapters of the fathers," but its name in earlier periods was simply, Avot. This title is often thought to be a shortened form of "*avot ha-olam*" ("the fathers of the universe") or "*avot ha-rishonim*" ("the first fathers"). In either case, *Avot* translates as "Fathers" and apparently refers to the many sages included in the tractate. An alternative interpretation suggests that the name of the treatise should be translated as 'Essentials' or 'First Principles'. According to this interpretation, the name refers to the wisdom of the sages, the fundamental principles of rabbinic Judaism expressed in the sayings of the tractate. This alternative interpretation has the added advantage of belonging to a literary practice in the Graeco-Roman world attested, for example, by the *Kyriai Doxai* ("Crucial Principles") of the Epicureans and the *Regulae Iuris* (Rules of law) of Roman law; similar literary collections which were also designed to describe the world-view of their respective intellectual traditions. The ambiguity of the title *Avot* is fortuitous and perhaps even intentional since it highlights the importance of both the structure, i.e. the sages of the chain of transmission, and the contents of the composition.

Location in the Mishnah

Avot is the penultimate tractate in the fourth order of the Mishnah, Seder Nezikin, and lacks both a companion Tosefta and talmudic commentary (though see *Avot de Rabbi Nathan*). The inclusion of *Avot* within an order that discusses civil law, criminal law and the judiciary process, led Maimonides to conclude that *Avot* was designed to legitimate the authority of rabbinic magistrates and to complement the legal code with a moral and spiritual guide (cf. Ex. 22:20–23:9).

Others have suggested that *Avot* be viewed as an epilogue to the Mishnah since *Nezikin* may have once been the last order in the Mishnah or at least the final order to be studied. This suggestion is striking in light of the similar placement of *Regulae Iuris* at the end of Justinian's Digest and *Kyriai Doxai* at the end of Diogenes Laertius's *Lives of Eminent Philosophers*. It is possible that just as the abstract and general format of the *Regulae Iuris* and *Kyriae Doxai* made them suitable conclusions for larger compositions, *Avot*'s survey of rabbinic principles and the transmission of the Torah made it a suitable epilogue for the Mishnah as a whole.

Commentaries

As noted above, classical and modern translations and commentaries to *Avot* abound. For lists of classical and select modern commentaries, see Cohen, Kasher-Mandelbaum, Kohn and Lerner. S. Sharvit deserves special mention due to his investigations into the language and style of *Avot* and the recent publication of his critical edition of the tractate.

BIBLIOGRAPHY: E. Bikerman [Bickerman], in: *Revue Biblique*, 59 (1952), 44–54; J.J. Cohen, in: KS, 40 (1964–5), 104–17, 277–85 (Hebrew); L. Finkelstein, *Introduction to the Treatises Abot and Abot of Rabbi Nathan* (Heb., 1950); H.A. Fischel, *Rabbinic Literature and Greco-Roman Philosophy: A Study of Epicurea and Rhetorica in Early Midrashic Writings* (1973); D.E. Gershenson, in: *Grazer Beiträge*, 19 (1993), 207–19; I.B. Gottlieb, in: VT, 40 (1990), 152–64; R.T. Herford, *Pirke Aboth* (1925); M.M. Kasher and J.B. Mandelbaum, *Sarei ha-Elef*, 2 vols. (1978); P.J. Kohn, *Oẓar ha-Be'urim ve-ha-Perushim* (1952); M. Kister, *Studies in Avot de-Rabbi Nathan: Text, Redaction and Interpretation* (Heb., 1998); M.B. Lerner, in: S. Safrai (ed.), *The Literature of the Sages* (1987), 263–76; J. Kapah (trans.), *Mishnah with Commentary of Maimonides: Zeraim* (Heb., 1963); A.J. Saldarini, *Scholastic Rabbinism: A Literary Study of the Fathers According to Rabbi Nathan* (1982); S. Sharvit, "Textual Variants and Language of the Treatise Abot and Prolegomena to a Critical Editions" (Diss, Bar-Ilan Univ., 1976) (Hebrew); idem, *Tractate Avot Through the Ages: A Critical Edition, Prolegomena and Appendices* (Heb., 2004); A. Tropper, *Wisdom, Politics, and Historiography: Tractate Avot in the Context of the Graeco-Roman Near East* (2004). See also bibliography to *Avot de-Rabbi Nathan.

[Amram Tropper (2nd ed.)]

AVOT DE-RABBI NATHAN (Heb. אָבוֹת דְּרַבִּי נָתָן; "The Fathers according to Rabbi Nathan"), a commentary on, and an elaboration of, the mishnaic tractate *Avot*. The work contains many ethical sayings, but also historical traditions, stories and bits of folklore. The work has come down to us in two highly different versions, customarily termed Version A (40 chapters) and B (49 chapters). It was known and used by many rabbinic authorities throughout the Jewish world in the middle ages. Version A has been included among the so-called "minor tractates" of the Talmud in printed editions of the Talmud since 1550. It should be emphasized, however, that the work was never considered part of "minor tractates" before the printed publication of the Babylonian Talmud. Version B was first published by Solomon Schechter (1887, together with a critical edition of Version A). The two versions seem to be two distinct forms (and the only forms known at least since the Middle Ages) of an earlier work.

ARN consists of three different sections in both versions, reflecting the varying character of the five chapters of *Avot* in the Mishnah: (a) a detailed *commentary* on most of the sayings in Mishnah *Avot* 1:1–2:12, except 1:16–2:7 (see below); (b) *supplementary* material to Mishnah *Avot* chapter 3–4, consisting of diverse sayings of Tannaim; (c) an *elaboration* of the numerical sayings in Mishnah *Avot* chapter 5. Versions A and B both follow this threefold division: neither version includes any commentary on the sayings of the two students of Rabban Johanan ben Zakkai cited in Mishnah *Avot* 2:13–14 and neither version comments on Avot 1:16–2:7. These features, as well as others, shared by both versions, indicate that both must have evolved from one source. Indeed, they basically share the same core of material throughout the work, although the wording in each version is unique, and each contains additional material unparalleled in the other.

ARN is probably not to be attributed to Rabbi Nathan (late 2nd century C.E.), but its name cannot be easily explained according to the texts as we have them. The skipping of *Avot* 1:16–2:7 in the first section of both versions indicates that the text of the mishnaic tractate *Avot* did not yet include this section (which is a later interpolation designed to introduce sayings by members of the Patriarch's family up to Rabbi Yehuda ha-Nasi's grandson Hillel). To be sure, parallel sayings of these same sages, who flourished at the beginning of the amoraic period, are included elsewhere in ARN in both versions. However, no other sayings attributed to later *amoraim* are to be found in either version.

From these data one may conclude that the earliest form of ARN goes back to a time not much later than the first half of the 3rd century C.E. However, a detailed comparison of the material in *Avot de-Rabbi Nathan* (in both versions) with the parallel material in other compositions of the talmudic literature leads to the conclusion that the present form of the two versions of ARN is post-talmudic. The *terminus post quem* for the final redaction of the work is thus after the redaction of the Babylonian Talmud (5th century C.E. [?]) and the *terminus ante quem* is probably sometime in the 8th century, since the earliest manuscripts of ARN are from the 9th century, or somewhat earlier. In several cases it can be demonstrated that an older form of a story was replaced (sometimes in both versions) by a newer, more elaborate one. Moreover, traditions known from elsewhere are frequently paraphrased in ARN, thereby distorting their original form. The two versions seem to be basically of Palestinian provenance, but at least in Version A there are evident indications of secondary Babylonian coloring. The general outlines (but usually not the wording) of a common core, from which the two versions evolved, can often be reconstructed by careful comparison between them. This also means that each version is frequently unintelligible by itself. By and large, it seems that Version A tends to be more remote from the common source of the two versions than is Version B; yet, there are many examples in which one must rely on Version A in order to make sense of Version B. This complex history of composition and transmission was noted by Schechter, the first editor of both versions, but was subsequently played down in research. Kister has strongly emphasized that both Version A and Version B are post-talmudic works, although there are certainly ancient elements in the traditions included in them.

The textual transmission of *Avot de-Rabbi Nathan* is also problematic. According to Kister, the textual witnesses (manuscripts and testimonia of ARN in the writings of medieval rabbinic authorities) of Version A fall into two principal branches, but often the original reading is contained in neither of them. An acquaintance with the two textual families, however, enables one in many cases to suggest, through cautious philological analysis, what the original reading might have been. An early *genizah* fragment (9th century?) of Version A seems not to represent an entirely new branch of that version, as suggested by some scholars, but rather a secondary text which attempted to reckon with textual defects found in the manuscript from which it was copied, defects that occur in later manuscripts of Version A (Kister). Only a few manuscripts of Version B survive, most of them stemming from a single, rather late, medieval copy. Errors in this manuscript cannot often be corrected without conjecture.

Current research into ARN owes much to S.Z. Schechter, who published the two versions, with *variae lectiones*, notes, and a general introduction. Schechter's edition was a pioneering philological achievement in his time. Although it does not conform to the prevailing standards of modern philology, his notes are of durable importance for the student. A synopsis, and eventually also a new critical edition, are being prepared for publication by Menahem Kister.

BIBLIOGRAPHY: L. Zunz, *Die gottesdienstlichen Vorträge der Juden, historisch entwickelt* (1832), 108ff. (Zunz-Albeck, 50–51); S.Z. Schechter, *Aboth de-Rabbi Nathan* (Heb., 1887); L. Finkelstein, *Mavo le-Massektot Avot ve-Avot d'Rabbi Natan* (Heb., 1950); J. Goldin, *The Fathers according to Rabbi Nathan* (1955); J. Goldin, *Studies in Midrash and Related Literature* (1988); A.J. Saldarini, *The Fathers according to Rabbi Nathan, Version B* (1975); M.B. Lerner, "Minor Tractates," in: *The Literature of the Sages* (1987), 369ff.; M. Kister, *Studies in Avot de-Rabbi Nathasn: Text, Redaction and Interpretation* (Heb., 1998); M. Kister, "Prolegomenon," *Avoth de-Rabbi Nathan Solomon Schechter Edition with References to Parallels in the two versions and to the Addenda in the Schechter's Edition* (Heb., 1997); M. Kister, "Legends of the Destruction of the Second Temple in Avot de-Rabbi Nathan," in: *Tarbiz* 67 (1998), 483–529 (in Heb.); M. Kister, "Avot de-Rabbi Nathan Chapter 17: Redaction and Transfigured Traditions," in: *Meḥkerei Talmud*, 3 (2005), 703–39 (in Heb.)

[Menahem Kister (2nd ed.)]

AVOT NEZIKIN (Heb. אֲבוֹת נְזִיקִין; lit. "Fathers of Damage"), the classification of *torts. Certain passages in the Pentateuch (Ex. 21–22) have been expounded in the Talmud to form the basis on which tortious liability in Jewish law can be classified. The Mishnah (BK 1, 1) classifies the tort-feasors into four categories: ox, pit, grazing, fire. Basically, three sources of common danger – (1) animals, (2) pits, and (3) fire – have been developed as the principal categories of the talmudic law of torts.

1) Animals

The Talmud distinguishes between two kinds of damage that an animal can cause – habitual or common damage, termed *shen*, (Heb. שֵׁן, "a tooth") and *regel* (Heb. רֶגֶל, "a foot"); and unusual or uncommon damage, termed *keren* (Heb. קֶרֶן "a horn"). These terms are derived from instances of damage by animals referred to in the Torah (*ibid.*).

(a) SHEN AND REGEL: the former refers to acts of damage caused by an animal while grazing, while the latter refers to acts of damage caused by an animal while walking, i.e., both occurring during the course of an animal's normal activities. The fact that *shen* and *regel* torts result from an animal's normal activities distinguishes them from *keren* – the abnormal, unexpected act of an animal, such as goring, biting, or kicking. In cases of *shen* and *regel* damage is presumed to be foreseeable and the owner is therefore required to take suitable precautions, and, if negligent, is held fully liable for the damage caused. However, such liability is limited in that it attaches only when the damage is caused on the premises of the injured party or in any other place not commonly frequented by the animal. When the damage occurs on the owner's premises, or in the public domain, or in any other place commonly frequented by animals, the owner is exempt from *shen* or *regel* liability on the grounds that he is entitled to expect that the injured party would take reasonable precautions to protect himself against such foreseeable risks. Furthermore, the owner is also exempt from liability where the damage occurs in a place which neither the animal nor the injured party commonly frequent, since the presence of either of them there (especially the injured party) was not foreseeable (BK, 14a).

(b) KEREN: this term covers an animal's unexpected, vicious acts; i.e., goring, biting, or kicking, as mentioned above. The ox was the popular beast of burden and thus was frequently encountered in public places. Its nature and propensities made it a common cause of damage and the term *keren* was extended to include all the unforeseeable acts of an animal. Unlike *shen* and *regel* acts, *keren* damage is not the result of an animal's normal behavior, and since it is accordingly unforeseeable the owner cannot be accused of negligence. On the other hand, *keren* is not so uncommon as to exclude negligence altogether and exempt the owner from liability entirely. In fact, *keren* was deemed to be midway between negligence and inevitable accident and the authorities differed as to whether it should be included as a tort of negligence or not. Whatever the viewpoint adopted, however, all agreed that the owner should be liable for half the cost of the damage caused – this being regarded according to the accepted opinion as a fine to encourage the owner to take greater care in preventing his animal from causing even unusual (*keren*) damage. The owner is exempt from all liability, however, where the injury caused by a *keren* act was completely unforeseeable, e.g., where his ox gored a pregnant woman, causing her to miscarry – this being an unexpected degree of damage (as far as the miscarriage is concerned). Similarly, the owner is not liable for acts of *keren* committed on his own premises – there being no negligence on his part – but such acts committed anywhere else, including the public domain, result in his being liable for half the damage caused.

This "half-damages" liability was deemed a charge on the carcass of the offending animal, so that the owner did not have to make up any shortfall. This was not interpreted, however, as implying that the animal itself was "liable," since the law is that a person who acquired an animal that had committed an act of *keren* while it was ownerless was exempt from the charge. The *tannaim* disputed the question whether the injured party's right was a lien on the carcass or created a part-ownership therein.

The first two times an animal commits an act of *keren* the damage is called *keren tammah* (i.e., caused by an animal considered harmless), but after the third such act (witnesses having duly testified to the facts before the court so that the owner was made fully aware of the position), the animal becomes *mu'ad* ("forewarned") and the damage is called *keren mu'edet* – the owner thereafter being liable for all further damage caused by similar acts of the animal, even if committed in the public domain. But the animal becomes a *mu'ad* only for the same kind of act, remaining a *tam* ("innocent") in respect of any other unusual act causing damage. For example, an ox *mu'ad* to gore other oxen is not *mu'ad* to bite a person; if he does, it is a *tam* with regard to that act unless and until it commits it three times as well. A *mu'ad* can be restored to the status of *tam* if it can be proved that it has ceased displaying the particular propensity that made it a *mu'ad* – although three further acts of the same kind would result in the status of *mu'ad* again. Wild animals are always regarded as *mu'ad* and their owners fully liable in all cases. After the talmudic period, *keren* liability, whether of the *tam* or *mu'ad* variety, was not enforced because of its rarity; instead, the owner of the offending animal was placed under a ban until he came to terms with the injured party (Maim. Yad, Sanhedrin, 5:17; see also *Damages).

(c) *Ẓerorot* (צְרוֹרוֹת; "pebbles"): this is the talmudic term for damage caused by an animal without bodily contact – the term being derived from the most common form of this type of damage, namely when an animal dislodges pebbles or the like which fall and break something. This category was extended to cover the case of a cock shattering a glass with the resonance of its crowing. Where *ẓerorot* damage is common, it is treated as a form of *regel* and where it is uncommon, it is treated as a form of *keren*. It appears that the Palestinian Talmud rendered the owner fully liable in the former case (*regel*), but only half liable in the latter case (*keren*; TJ, BK 2:1, 2d). The Babylonian Talmud discusses whether the owner is fully or only half liable, but the dispute seems to center on whether *ẓerorot* is as common as *regel*. The *halakhah* accords with the view of Rava that in the case of common damage the owner is liable for half, while in the case of uncommon *ẓerorot* damage there is doubt whether he pays half or only quarter damages (BK 17b–19b).

(d) KILLING A HUMAN BEING: an animal which kills a human being, whether it is a *tam* or a *mu'ad*, is stoned to death. Some regard this as a punishment for the animal, while others are of the opinion that it is simply to eliminate a public menace. A third view is that, as an animal has no mind, it cannot be subjected to punishment and its execution is therefore a punishment for the owner. If the animal was *mu'ad* as a killer, its owner had to indemnify the victim's heirs (*ibid.*, 41a), since he was negligent in failing to guard his animal properly. It follows, therefore, that such liability would not result from a killing that occurred on the owner's premises, as presumably there was there no negligence on his part (*ibid.*, 23b).

2) Pit (בּוֹר, *bor*)

This is the name given to another leading category of tort and covers cases where an obstacle is created by a person's negligence and left as a hazard by means of which another is injured. The prime example is that of a person who digs a pit, leaves it uncovered, and another person or an animal falls into it. Other major examples would be leaving stones or water unfenced and thus potentially hazardous. The common factor is the commission or omission of something which brings about a dangerous situation and the foreseeability of damage resulting. A person who fails to take adequate precautions to render harmless a hazard under his control is considered negligent, since he is presumed able to foresee that damage may result, and he is therefore liable for any such subsequent damage.

If the *bor* (i.e., the hazard) is adequately guarded or left in a place where persons or animals do not normally pass, such as one's private property, no negligence or presumed foreseeability can be ascribed and no liability would arise (BK 49b, 52a). Furthermore, no liability attaches to a person whose property became a public hazard through no fault of his and he had abandoned it, e.g., where by an inevitable accident a vessel breaks and the owner abandons the broken pieces, which subsequently cause damage (Rif, *Halakhot*, BK 29a, 31a) – just as a mere passerby is under no legal obligation to render harmless a hazard he happens to encounter. A person is not liable for a *bor* he creates if he could not have foreseen that it would not have been rendered harmless before it was likely to cause injury; e.g., where he digs a well in a public place and then entrusts it to the proper public authority (BK 50a), or where he is the part-owner of a well and he leaves it uncovered while it is still being used by his co-owner (51a–b). In these cases, the lack of any negligence absolves him.

One who commits the tort of *bor* is liable for foreseeable damage, but not for unusual or unforeseeable damage. Thus, if one digs a pit and leaves it uncovered in the daytime in a place where it is clearly visible, he would not be liable because persons or animals passing by are expected to be able to look where they are going. It is thought by most authorities that this rule also applies to cases where vessels are dropped into and damaged by the *bor*, since a similar standard of care is expected from those who carry such vessels (52a, 53b). Furthermore, no liability attaches in the case where a *bor* causes damage or injury to someone or something for whom or for which it would not normally be considered a hazard (48b). On the other hand, a *bor* that is not a hazard by day may become one at night, or may not be a hazard to big animals but one to young animals, who may not be so capable of guarding against such dangers. There would also be liability in respect of a *bor* that could only cause injury to human beings, but not death, as people do not usually pay much attention to such minor hazards (28b). If an animal dies from falling into a pit less than ten handbreadths deep there is no liability, for such a small pit is not normally expected to cause death (3a). Where two people create a *bor* jointly, or where one enlarges a *bor* created by another, each is liable for half the resulting damage – if liability attaches at all under the rules outlined above.

3) Fire (**אֵשׁ**, Esh)

The third leading category of tort covers damage caused by a hazard, such as fire, that can spread if not adequately contained or guarded. A person is liable for such damage if it is caused by his own negligence, but not otherwise. Accordingly, he is liable for damage caused by fire carried by a normal wind (which he should have foreseen), but not if the wind was exceptional (BK 60a). Similarly, he is liable if the fire spread over a foreseeable distance, but not if it spread further than could reasonably have been anticipated (61a–b). Yet another example given is the sending of fire or burning objects in the hands of an imbecile, for which the sender would be liable if damage resulted – but not if he sent a mere flickering coal, which is presumed harmless (59b). Thus the underlying rule is that the tort-feasor is liable for foreseeable damage – because he is negligent if he does not prevent it – but not where the damage was unforeseeable and thus no negligence was involved.

One who is negligent in guarding a fire created by him is only liable to the extent of foreseeable damage. For example, a fire that consumes hidden articles would not render the tort-feasor liable for them, whereas he would be liable in respect of exposed articles, damage to them being foreseeable. However, the *tanna* R. Judah extended the liability to cover hidden articles as well, on the grounds that it should have been foreseen that articles may have been hidden (61b). Some scholars interpret this discussion as being a question of evidence only, i.e., the acceptability of the plea that the articles have been there (*Siftei Kohen* to Sh. Ar., ḤM, 388:6).

The Talmud records a dispute over the substantive nature of damage caused by fire, i.e., whether it is to be considered as damage caused by a person's property (*ke-mamono*) like damage caused by his animal, or as damage caused by the person himself (*ke-gufo*) as if he had shot an arrow. The difference is relevant in determining the measure of compensation, since higher damages are payable for damage caused directly by one person to another (*ke-gufo*). The conclusion seems to be that even those who consider *esh* to be a tort *ke-gufo* concede that sometimes it can only justly be regarded as a tort *ke-mamono*, thus incurring a lower measure of damages (BK 22a–b, 23a).

State of Israel

The Civil Wrongs Ordinance, 1944, makes no substantive distinction between liability for damage caused by animals or obstacles or fire and damage caused in other ways; in all cases there is liability if there has been negligence. However, if damage is caused by a dangerous animal or by a dangerous explosion or fire, the onus is on the possessor to prove that there was no negligence on his part.

BIBLIOGRAPHY: Maimonides, Yad, Nizkei Mammon; Sh. Ar., ḤM, 389–418; Gulak, Yesodei, 2 (1922), 227–37; ET, s.v. *Avot Nezikin, Esh, Bor, Hefker*; S. Albeck, *Pesher Dinei ha-Nezikin ba-Talmud* (1965), 93–172.

[Shalom Albeck]

AVRIEL (Ueberall), EHUD (1917–1980), Israeli diplomat. Born in Vienna, Avriel settled in Palestine in 1939 and became a member of kibbutz Ne'ot Mordekhai. During World War II he was active in the *Haganah rescue of European Jews. From 1942 to 1944 he was stationed in Istanbul. In 1948 he went to Czechoslovakia to purchase arms. Avriel was Israel's first minister to Czechoslovakia and Hungary (1948), and was later minister to Romania (1950). From 1955 to 1957 he was a *Mapai member of Knesset. He later served as ambassador to Ghana, Congo (Leopoldville), and Liberia (1957–60). From 1961 to 1965 Avriel was deputy director general of the Foreign Ministry, in charge of African affairs, and one of the pioneers of Israel's policy of developing close ties with the new African nations. From 1965 to 1968 he was ambassador to Italy. At the 27th Zionist Congress in 1968 he was elected chairman of the General Zionist Council. His autobiography, *Open the Gates*, appeared in 1975.

[Benjamin Jaffe]

AVRUNIN, ABRAHAM (1869–1957), Hebrew philologist and grammarian. Born in Russia, he joined the Ḥibbat Zion movement there and became an ardent Zionist. From 1898 he taught Hebrew in Minsk and devoted himself to the study of Hebrew philology. In 1910 Avrunin settled in Ereẓ Israel, where he taught in public schools in Tel Aviv and at the college for kindergarten teachers founded by Yeḥiel *Halperin who had been one of Avrunin's students in his youth. Avrunin fought for the use of pure and correct Hebrew and reintroduced archaic idioms. He wrote etymological and linguistic studies, poems and epigrams, a Hebrew grammar *Netivot ha-Dikduk* (together with A. Pepper, 1922), edited the linguistic column of the newspaper *Ha'aretz*, and was coeditor of the periodical of *Va'ad ha-Lashon*, *Leshonenu la-Am* (see *Academy of the Hebrew Language). His works include a commentary on the Book of Job (with A.Z. Rabinowitz, 1916); a study on Hebrew medieval poetry (1929); philological studies on Bialik and Y.L. Gordon (1943); and an edition of Judah Al-Ḥarizi's *Sefer ha-Anak* with an introduction and notes (1945).

BIBLIOGRAPHY: *Moznayim*, 28 (1957), 60ff.; D. Sadan, in: *Leshonenu la-Am*, 7 (1957), 223–7; M. Shamir, *Be-Kulmos Mahir* (1960), 356–60.

AVRUTICK, ABRAHAM N. (1909–1982), U.S. Orthodox rabbi and communal leader. Born in Russia, he received his early education in Montreal and rabbinical ordination from the Isaac Elchanan Theological Seminary of Yeshiva University in 1936. He held pulpits in Fitchburg, Mass. (1936–38), Newburgh, N.Y. (1938–46), and at Congregation Agudas Achim in Hartford, Conn. (1946–82). One the unique characteristics of the Hartford area in the post-World War II era was that its rabbinical leadership in all denominations served for decades at a time and the synagogues enjoyed uniquely stable leadership. He was a leader during a time of transition, when American Orthodoxy was moving from a European-educated Yiddish-speaking rabbinate to American-educated, English-speaking rabbis who appealed to the young. He was instrumental in establishing a Va'ad Hakashruth in Hartford, which established one standard of *kashrut* for the community, was a long-time vice president of the Yeshiva of Hartford (later known as the Bess and Paul Sigel Hebrew Academy of Greater Hartford), and active on many communal Jewish Boards of Directors, including the Federation, Hebrew Home, and Mikveh. Nationally, he held every office in the *Rabbinical Council of America (RCA) including president (1962–64), was a founder and the first president (1951) of the Rabbinical Council of Connecticut, a member of the national board of the *Union of Orthodox Jewish Congregations of America, and, as a life-long, passionate Zionist, was active in the Mizrachi Organization. In 1976, together with other rabbinic colleagues, he traveled to the Soviet Union to meet and encourage a group of refuseniks. He was honored by Yeshiva University with a Distinguished Alumnus Award and an honorary Doctor of Divinity degree (1965) and by the Union of Orthodox Jewish Congregations with a National Award for Outstanding Rabbinic Leadership (1964). He attracted a large and devoted following because of his high religious and ethical standards combined with a pleasant demeanor, unusual sensitivity, and an ability to see God's reflection in all human beings, even those he disagreed with.

BIBLIOGRAPHY: D.G. Dalin, J. Rosenbaum, and D.C. Dalin, *Making a Life Building a Community: A History of the Jews of Hartford* (1997).

AVSHALOMOV, AARON (1894–1965), composer, father of Jacob *Avshalomov. Born in Siberia, Avshalomov was almost an autodidact in composition (except for one term of study at the Zurich Conservatoire). In around 1917 he settled in China, remaining there for 30 years and working as librarian of the Municipal Library of Shanghai (1928–43) and conductor of the Shanghai Symphonic Orchestra (1943–46). In 1947 he immigrated to the United States. In his compositions he strove to create an Oriental atmosphere by incorporating Chinese motifs and rhythms into European music. Among his works are three operas, *Kuan Yin* (Beijing, 1925), *The Twilight Hour of Yan Kuei Fei* (1933), and *The Great Wall* (Shanghai, 1945, later produced in Nanjing, under the sponsorship of Mmes. Sun Yat Sen and Chiang Kaishek); a ballet, *The Soul of the Ch'in* (1933); a symphonic poem, *Peiping Hutungs* (1933); three symphonies (conducted by Leopold Stokowski, Pierre Monteux, and Artur Rodzinski); and concertos for piano, violin, and flute.

ADD. BIBLIOGRAPHY: *American Composers Alliance Bulletin*, X/2 (1962), 18–19.

[Marina Rizarev (2nd ed.)]

AVSHALOMOV, JACOB (1919–), U.S. composer; son of the Russian composer Aaron *Avshalomov. Jacob Avshalomov was born in China and immigrated to the U.S. in 1937. He studied there with Ernst Toch in Los Angeles and with Aaron *Copland at Tanglewood (1947). At Columbia University, where he taught from 1946 to 1954, he conducted the university chorus and orchestra and performed with them in the American premieres of Bruckner's *Mass in D minor*, Tippet's *A Child of our Time*, and Handel's *The Triumph of Time and Truth*. In 1968, President Johnson appointed him to the National Council of the Humanities. His compositions are marked by Asian sonorities absorbed at an early age in China and his predilection for Renaissance counterpoint. His many vocal works include *Inscriptions at the City of Brass* (1964) and more than 30 songs. His instrumental output comprises a "Sinfonietta" (1946); a symphony, *The Oregon* (1962); and *Open Sesame* (1984).

BIBLIOGRAPHY: Grove online.

[Amnon Shiloah (2nd ed.)]

AVTALYON (late first century B.C.E.), colleague of *Shemaiah. Together Shemaiah and Avtalyon constitute the fourth of the *zugot ("pairs"), receiving the tradition from *Judah b. Tabbai and *Simeon b. Shetaḥ. Shemaiah was *nasi* and Avtalyon *av bet din*. Like Shemaiah, Avtalyon is said to have been a descendant of proselytes (Git. 57b; Sanh. 96b). Avtalyon and Shemaiah were called "the two great men of their generation" (Pes. 66a), and "great sages and interpreters" (*ibid.*, 70b), and the people held them in higher esteem than the high priest (Yoma 71b). In the earliest dispute recorded in the Talmud, concerning the laying of hands on the head of a festal sacrifice (see **Semikhah* of sacrifice), Avtalyon's views coincided with those of the *nesi'im* who preceded him viz., that it "may not be performed" (Ḥag. 2:2). It was from Avtalyon and Shemaiah that *Hillel learned that the paschal sacrifice is offered even on the Sabbath (Pes. 66a). Avtalyon's decisions are also quoted in *Eduyyot* (1:3; 5:6).

Some scholars identify Avtalyon with the Pollio mentioned by Josephus as one of the Pharisaic leaders in the days of *Herod (Ant. 15:1–4, 370). According to a manuscript variant to *Antiquities* 14:172, it was Pollio, and not Samaias, as in the printed text, who was "the upright man and for that reason superior to fear" who denounced Hyrcanus and his colleagues in the Sanhedrin for their cowardice in refusing to judge Herod. Avtalyon on that occasion prophesied the bitter fate that awaited them. He persuaded the people to accept Herod and to open the gates of Jerusalem to him. Consequently Herod favored him when he became king.

Some hold that Avtalyon's exhortation, "Scholars be careful with your words, lest you incur the penalty of exile and be banished to a place of evil waters (heretical teachings), and the disciples who follow you into exile are likely to drink of them and die" (Avot. 1:11), reflects contemporary conditions and refers to the punishment of expulsion meted out by the regime. The allusion seems to be to Avtalyon's teachers, who fled to Alexandria during the reign of Alexander Yannai, and it may also refer to the Herodian persecution in Avtalyon's time.

BIBLIOGRAPHY: Feldman, in: JQR, 49 (1958), 53–62; Ḥ. Albeck, *Shishah Sidrei Mishnah, Seder Nezikin* (1952), 494; Solberg, in: Doron, *Essays... A.I. Katsh* (1965), 21–24.

[Bialik Myron Lerner]

AVTINAS, family in charge of mixing the incense in the Temple (Shek. 5:1). Originally the sages denounced the house of Avtinas for refusing to teach the manufacture of the incense (Yoma 3, 11). They sent for skilled perfumers from Alexandria, but when the column of smoke from their incense did not rise in a straight shaft, as that produced by the Avtinas family, the sages reached an agreement with them and doubled their remuneration (Yoma 38a; TJ, Yoma 41a; Tosef., Yoma 2:6–7), which was paid from the public treasury (Tosef., Shek. 2:6). Later generations did not agree with the censure. It was explained that the reason for their refusal to disclose their secret formula was that they had a tradition that the Temple would soon be destroyed, and if their formula became known, the incense would be used for idol worship. The *aggadah* relates that an old man of the Avtinas family gave Johanan b. Nuri a written recipe for the incense, and when Akiva heard this, he said, "We need no longer mention them with censure" (Yoma 38a). They also were praised because they did not permit their wives to perfume themselves, lest they be accused of using the incense as ointment. The Mishnah mentions the upper chamber of the house of Avtinas where the high priest was brought during the days preceding the Day of Atonement. This was where members of the house of Avtinas prepared the incense which was guarded by the priests (Yoma 1:5; Tam. 1:1).

BIBLIOGRAPHY: Schuerer, Gesch, 2 (1907[4]), 333; Klein, in: *Leshonenu*, 1 (1928/29), 347; Derenbourg, in: REJ, 6 (1883), 49; ET, 3 (1951), 149–50.

[Lea Roth]

AVVIM (Heb. עַוִּים): (1) a people who dwelt in "villages near Gaza," and were conquered and displaced by the Caphtorim (Philistines; Deut. 2:23). The difficult verse Joshua 13:3 may indicate that they were still living in the Philistine region at the time of the Conquest. (2) The Avvim in II Kings 17:31 were a group brought by the king of Assyria from their homeland Avva, perhaps the Elamite city Ama, and resettled in Samaria.

BIBLIOGRAPHY: Aharoni, Land, 216; Speiser, in: AASOR, 13 (1933), 30, n. 67. **ADD. BIBLIOGRAPHY:** M. Cogan and H. Tadmor, *II Kings* (AB; 1998), 212; M. Weinfeld, *Deuteronomy 1–11* (AB; 1991), 164; S. Ahituv, *Joshua* (1995), 212.

[Tikva S. Frymer]

AX, EMANUEL (1949–), U.S. pianist of Polish birth. After World War II, the Ax family immigrated to Canada, moving to New York in 1961. Ax's first teacher was his father, a coach at the Lvov Opera. In 1966 he begun his studies with M. Münz at the Juilliard School of Music and also attended Columbia University (B.A. 1970). Ax had already received several honors in competitions and made his New York debut in 1973. In 1974 he won the first Arthur Rubinstein International Piano Competition in Tel Aviv. The following year he received the Young Concert Artists' Michaels Award and in 1979 he won the Avery Fisher Prize. Ax developed an international career that brought him acclaim in equal measure for his concert, chamber, and recital performances. He appeared in the U.S. (Philadelphia Orchestra, New York PO, and the LPO) and abroad with major orchestras. In 1991 he made his debut at the Proms in London, performing Brahms' First Piano Concerto. Devoted to chamber music literature, Ax regularly performed with artists such as Young Uck Kim, Yo-Yo Ma, and Jaime Laredo and was a frequent collaborator with the late Isaac *Stern. In addition, he made regular festival appearances at Aspen, Blossom, and Tanglewood. Acclaimed for his poetic lyricism, brilliant dramatic technique, and dynamic control, Ax is noted for his playing of the Classic and Romantic repertoire. As a particular supporter of 20th-century composers, he gave several world premieres of their work, including *Century Rolls* by John Adams (1997), *Seeing* by Christopher Rouse (1999), and *Resurrection* by Krzysztof Penderecki. He also performed works by Tippett, Hans Werner Henze, Hindemith, and Piazzolla. Many of his recordings won top honors.

BIBLIOGRAPHY: Grove online; MGG 2; D. Dubal, *Reflections from the Keyboard: The World of the Concert Pianist* (1984), 44–49.

[Naama Ramot (2nd ed.)]

AXEL, RICHARD (1946–), U.S. medical scientist and Nobel laureate in medicine. Axel was born in New York City and graduated with a B.A. from Columbia University (1967) and an M.D. from Johns Hopkins University School of Medicine, Baltimore (1970). He was a professor at Columbia University from 1978 and a researcher at Howard Hughes Medical Institute from 1984. Axel's research interests concern the interpretation of sensory signals by the brain. He was awarded the Nobel Prize (2004) jointly with Linda Buck for their work on the olfactory system. They showed that there is only one type of receptor cell for odors in the nose and that these recognize a very limited number of odors. The nerve fibers of individual cells transmit signals to discrete regions of the olfactory bulb (glomeruli) in the brain where they activate receptors on cells controlled by many different genes, up to 1,000 in some species. Signals from these cells are relayed to different parts of the brain and processed to allow a wide range of odors to be recognized. Thus the olfactory and visual systems have many common features. Axel's many honors include election to the U.S. National Academy of Sciences (1983) and the Gairdner Award (2003).

[Michael Denman (2nd ed.)]

AXELRAD, AVRAM (**Adolf**; 1879–1963), Romanian poet and publicist, editor, teacher of literature in Jewish schools. Axelrad was born in Barlad, where he finished his schooling. In 1900 he edited the literary review *Aurora* in Barlad and then moved to Bucharest. The poems in his first collection, *Spre rasarit* ("Eastward," 1900), were inspired by Jewish emigration by foot (the "*Fussgeyers*") from Romania on the way to America (1900); while those of his second, *Ladita cu necazuri* ("Box of Troubles," 1919), bewailed Jewish homelessness. The latter collection was republished in 1945 under the title *La raul Babilonului* ("Near the River of Babylon") with new poems on the Holocaust of the Romanian Jews. Although his poems are not of great literary value, written in popular form they were disseminated among simple people. Axelrad was called the "poet of Jewish suffering." As a publicist he edited some popular science reviews, such as *Revista ideilor* ("Review of Ideas") and *Oameni si idei* ("People and Ideas"), under the pseudonym A.A. Luca. Axelrad also managed a small publishing house, Lumen (1908), publishing popular editions of translations of classical philosophical works. He also translated parts of the Book of Psalms and Ecclesiastes into Romanian.

BIBLIOGRAPHY: A. Mirodan, *Dictionar neconventional,* 1 (1986), 81–4; A.B. Yoffe, *Bisdot Zarim* (1996), 158–69, 439.

[Lucian-Zeev Herscovici (2nd ed.)]

AXELROD, ALBERT (**Albie**; 1921–2004), U.S. fencer; one of the greatest American fencers in history, competing in five consecutive Olympics from 1952 to 1968, winning the bronze in 1960. Axelrod was ranked no. 1 in the U.S. in 1955, 1958, 1960, and 1970 (at age 49), no. 2 nine times, no. 3 twice, and among the U.S. top ten from 1942–70, except for three years during World War II. Axelrod was a member of five National Foil Team Championships (1940, 1950, 1952, 1954, 1958), and five times a member of the National Three-Weapon team championship (1949, 1952, 1954, 1962, 1963).

Born in New York to Russian immigrants, Axelrod learned to fence at Stuyvesant High School and continued fencing at City College after naval service in the Pacific. He won the U.S. Intercollegiate Foil Championship and led CCNY to the National Team Foil Championship in 1948.

At the 1956 Olympics, Axelrod competed on a U.S. foil team that was entirely Jewish – Axelrod, Daniel Bukantz, Harold Goldsmith, Nathaniel Lubell, and Byron Krieger. At the 1960 Olympics, when he won his bronze medal at age 39, he defeated 79 opponents in a seven-hour competition held in a heat wave. It was only the fourth-ever individual Olympic fencing medal won by an American and the last in foil through 2004.

Axelrod won two gold medals (1959, 1963) in team foil at the Pan Am Games and is the only men's foil fencer in U.S. history to make the finals of the world championships. He competed in six consecutive *Maccabiah Games from 1957 to 1977. Axelrod also served as U.S. head coach in 1981 and as manager of the team in 1985.

[Elli Wohlgelernter (2nd ed.)]

AXELROD, GEORGE (1922–2003), U.S. comedy writer, movie director, and producer. Axelrod, who was born in New York City, was the son of silent film actress Betty Carpenter. He started out writing scripts for radio and television. He wrote several successful plays – *The Seven Year Itch* (1953), *Will Success Spoil Rock Hunter?* (1955), *Bus Stop* (1956), *Once More, with Feeling* (1958), *Goodbye Charlie* (1964) – and began his film career writing the adaptations for *The Seven Year Itch* (1955) and *Bus Stop* (1956). Associated with several films as co-writer and co-producer, including *A Visit to a Small Planet* (1957), *Breakfast at Tiffany's* (1961), *Paris When It Sizzles* (1964), and *How to Murder Your Wife* (1965), he also wrote the screenplays for *Phffft!* (1954), *The Manchurian Candidate* (1962), *The Lady Vanishes* (1979), *The Holcroft Covenant* (1985), and *The Fourth Protocol* (1987). He wrote, directed, and produced *Lord Love a Duck* (1966) and *The Secret Life of an American Wife* (1968). For his work on *Breakfast at Tiffany's*, Axelrod won the Writer's Guild of America award for Best Written American Comedy and was nominated for an Academy Award for his screen adaptation. In 1971 he wrote the novel *Where Am I Now When I Need Me?*

At the outset of his career as a playwright, Axelrod specialized in blending sex farce with social satire, though the film versions of his works had to be toned down to get past the censors. But he was very adept at writing for the screen and was at one point the highest-paid scriptwriter in Hollywood. *The Manchurian Candidate* is regarded as one of the best film dramas of all time, albeit, as Axelrod once commented, "It broke every rule. It's got dream sequences, flashbacks, narration out of nowhere … everything in the world you're told not to do."

[Ruth Beloff (2nd ed.)]

AXELROD, JULIUS (1912–), U.S. biochemist, pharmacologist, and Nobel Prize laureate. Born in New York City, the son of Polish immigrants, he obtained his B.Sc. in 1933 from New York's City College, his M.A. in 1941 from New York University, and his Ph.D. in 1955 from George Washington University. In 1949 he joined the staff of the National Heart Institute, Bethesda, Maryland, and in 1954 he was invited to establish a pharmacology section and was appointed chief of the section, Laboratory of Clinical Science, National Institute of Mental Health (NIMH). In 1957 he began his most famous research project which focused on the activity of neurotransmitter hormones. Axelrod specialized in the field of biochemical mechanisms, drug and hormone actions, and glandular research. His achievement was based on Euler's discovery of noradrenaline (norepinephrine), a chemical substance that transmits nerve impulses. Axelrod identified the mechanisms that regulate the formation of noradrenaline in nerve cells as well as the mechanisms in its inactivation. He discovered the enzyme that neutralizes noradrenaline by an enzyme, and named it catechol-o-methyl transferase. The enzyme was shown to be useful in dealing with the effects of certain psychotropic drugs and in research on hypertension and schizophrenia. Axelrod's work enabled researchers during the 1970s to develop a new class of antidepressant medication such as Prozac. Over the next 30 years, until his retirement in 1984, he worked on many research projects in pharmacology. He shared the 1970 Nobel Prize for physiology and medicine with the British biophysicist Sir Bernard *Katz and the Swedish physiologist Ulf von Euler. Axelrod remained an active scientist and researcher and distinguished lecturer throughout the 1970s. He was the recipient of many awards and a member of many editorials boards and committees of scientific journals. In 1984 he formally retired from NIMH and was named Scientist Emeritus of the National Institute of Health in 1996.

[Gali Rotstein (2nd ed.)]

AXELROD, LUBOV (**Esther**; pseudonym **Otodox**; 1868–1946), Russian revolutionary and philosopher. Axelrod was born in Dunilovichi (Lithuania). From the age of 16 she was a member of the Narodnaya Volya revolutionary organization, propagating its ideas in workers' circles and traveling around the country with illegal literature. In 1887 she was compelled to leave for France and later settled in Switzerland. In 1892 she turned to Marxism, joined the Osvozhdzenie Truda (Freedom for Labor) group, and became the closest adviser of its leader, P. Plekhanov. In 1900 she received her Ph.D. from Bern University and her thesis on Tolstoy was published in German in Stuttgart in 1902. She was one of the major contributors to the newspapers *Iskra* and *Zaria*. In 1906 she returned to Russia, and became the leading authority on Marxist philosophy (after Plekhanov). In the same year she published an anthology on the subject, criticizing Berdyaev, Struve, Kant, and others. In social-democrat circles, she earned a reputation as the defender of the "pure" Marxist philosophy. Probably because of this, she did not have to pay the price of being a member of the Central Committee of the Menshevik Party after the Bolshevik October Revolution of 1917, even after she sharply criticized Lenin's *Materialism and Empirio-Criticism*. In the 1920s she lectured in various academic institutes. She published several books, but in the beginning of the 1930s she was included in the "*makhanisty*" group of philosophers, and banned from teaching, publishing, etc., and forgotten. When she had left Russia in 1887 she cut off all her ties with her rabbinical family and with Jewish life.

[Shmuel Spektor (2nd ed.)]

AXELROD, MEYER (1902–1970), Russian painter, graphic artist, and stage designer. Axelrod was born in Molodechno, Vilna province, Belorussia. As a child, he received a traditional Jewish education. During World War I, the family lived in Tambov, where he attended N. Perelman's private art studio. In 1918–19 he lived in Minsk, where he finished a technical school and made advertisement boards for Minsk movie theaters. He was drafted and served in the army in 1919–20. Serving in Smolensk, he attended the local Proletkult ("Proletarian Culture") Art Studio and occasionally visited Vitebsk, where he took painting classes with Y. Pan. In 1921, he displayed his works at the First All-Belorussia Exhibition in Minsk. From his earliest works and throughout his life, Axelrod was keenly interested in Jewish themes, depicting scenes and characters from the Belorussian shtetl as well as capturing the trauma of pogroms. In 1921–27, Axelrod studied at the Faculty of Graphics at the High Arts and Technical Workshops (VHUTEMAS) in Moscow. He was a member of the "4 Arts" group and participated in its exhibits. In the 1920s and 1930s, he regularly exhibited in Moscow and Minsk and worked for various publishers, mainly designing books written in Yiddish or translated from Yiddish into Russian. In the early 1930s, Axelrod paid several visits to Jewish kolkhozes in the Crimea and executed a series of paintings portraying the life of Jewish agriculturists. From 1932, he worked for theaters, mostly Jewish, in Moscow, Belorussia, and the Ukraine, designing sets for several productions. In 1941–43, he lived in Alma-Ata, where he had a one-man show in 1942. In the 1940s, Axelrod continued to work as a set designer for Jewish theaters and designed editions of Yiddish literary classics. In the 1960s, he created a series of paintings called "Memories of the Old Minsk" and "The Ghetto." In 1968, he had a one-man exhibition in Rostov-on-Don.

BIBLIOGRAPHY: G. Fiodorov, *Meer Akselrod* (Rus., 1982); E. Akselrod, *Meer Akselrod* (Rus., 1993).

[Hillel Kazovsky (2nd ed.)]

AXELROD, PAVEL BORISOVICH (1850–1928), Russian revolutionary, one of the founders of the Russian Social Democratic party. He was born in a small village in the province of Chernigov and spent his childhood in great poverty. While still at school, he published his first article on the condition of the Jewish poorer classes. He started his revolutionary activity in 1872 among Jewish students in Kiev where, attracted by anarchist ideas, he was anxious to work among Russian peasants and workers. In 1874, during a period of severe czarist repression, he escaped abroad and lived for a while in Berlin, where he studied the German socialist movement. He later settled in Geneva and married Nadezhda, daughter of the socialist Hebrew poet Isaac *Kaminer. Living at starvation level, Axelrod continued his revolutionary activity both in Russia and abroad. He maintained close contact with the "Land and Liberty" movement (Zemlya i Volya), editing its organ of that name, but left because of his opposition to the use of terror advocated by most of its members. Together with George Plekhanov, he founded the "Chorny peredel" group, which favored distributing the nobility's landholdings among the peasants.

In 1881, during the anti-Jewish pogroms in southern Russia, Axelrod was briefly attracted by the ideas of Ḥibbat Zion and prepared a pamphlet describing the disillusionment of young Jewish radicals with the attitude of the revolutionary movement to the specific problems of Russian Jewry. His ideas found little response among his closest friends, however, and he became a Marxist and an opponent of both the Bund and Zionism. In 1883 he was one of the founders of the "Liberation of Labor" (Osvobozhdeniye Truda) movement, which was to develop into the Russian Social Democratic party, and he edited the movement's newspaper, *Iskra* ("The Spark"). When in 1903 the party divided into Bolsheviks and Mensheviks, he became one of the Menshevik leaders, and from 1913 represented the party at socialist conferences. Axelrod returned to Russia in 1917 but after the October Revolution went to live in Germany. Later he took part in congresses of the Socialist International and was a member of its international bureau. He was an uncompromising opponent of the communist regime. Axelrod was the author of several works on social democratic ideology and tactics; his memoirs, *My Life and Thoughts*, appeared in 1922.

BIBLIOGRAPHY: L. Deutsch, *Yidn in der Rusisher Revolutsie* (1924); L.S. Dawidowicz (ed.), *Golden Tradition* (1967), 405–10.

[Simha Katz]

AXELROD, SELIK (1904–1941), Soviet Yiddish poet. Born in Molodetchno, Vilna province, Axelrod lived in Tambov during the war, then studied literature in Moscow. He began to publish poetry in 1920 and contributed to various Yiddish journals in the Soviet Union, especially *Royte Velt* (Kharkov, 1925–26) and *Shtern* (Minsk, 1927–40). He also wrote parodies and translated Russian and Belorussian poets. His own lyrics gained much appreciation, and two collections of his poetry appeared in Russian (1937, 1939). Some Soviet Jewish critics, however, complained of his continued attachment to existential themes. In 1939 Axelrod went from Minsk to Bialystok and Vilna in the newly occupied Soviet territories to meet with refugee Jewish writers from Poland. After his return, he was arrested in June 1941 and executed shortly before German troops occupied Minsk. He published *Tsapl* ("Quiver," 1922); *Lider* ("Poems," 1932); *Un Vider Lider* ("And More Poems," 1935); *Oyg oyf Oyg* ("Eye-to-Eye," 1937), *Roytarmeyishe Lider* ("Red Army Poems," 1939). A selection of his poems, *Lider*, with an introduction by Nakhman Mayzl, was published in New York (1961). In Moscow a collection of his poems in Russian translation by the poet Elena Axelrod (1963) and a volume in Yiddish, *Lider* (1980), were published.

BIBLIOGRAPHY: LNYL, 1 (1956), 159–60; *Pismeniki Sovetskoy Belorusi* (1959), 31–32. **ADD. BIBLIOGRAPHY:** R. Rubin, in: *Sovetish Heymland*, 1 (1963), 105–9; Ch. Shmeruk (ed.), *A Shpigl oyf a Shteyn* (1964, 1987^2), 767–70.

[Elias Schulman]

AXENFELD, ISRAEL (1787–1866), pioneering Yiddish novelist and dramatist. He was born in Nemirov and was originally a follower of the ḥasidic rabbi *Naḥman of Bratslav, in Podolia, Ukraine, but after traveling through Germany as a supplier of the Russian Army in 1812–13 and coming into contact with the early *maskilim* of Brody, Galicia, Axenfeld became staunchly anti-ḥasidic. In 1824 he settled in Odessa as merchant and attorney. Two years before his death he moved to Paris, to join his sons, Auguste Alexander (1825–76), professor of internal pathology at the Sorbonne, and Henri, a painter who frequently exhibited in Paris and London.

Axenfeld completed 30 novels and plays in which he portrayed Jewish life according to a realist esthetic (analyzed by Dan Miron). In the cause of Enlightenment, he satirized ḥasidic beliefs, ridiculed ḥasidic rabbis, and sought to improve his readers' manners, etiquette, and morals. He contrasted Jewish life in Poland and the Ukraine with "civilized" life in Western Europe, often exaggerating the backwardness of the *shtetl*. Though his characters are alive and convincing, his plots are often melodramatic. The only two printing presses then allowed in Russia refused to publish his works because of their anti-ḥasidic bias; they were therefore circulated in manuscript form. Only his novel *Dos Shterntikhl* ("The Head-Band," 1861) and the drama *Der Ershter Yidisher Rekrut* ("The First Jewish Recruit," 1861) appeared during his lifetime. The latter deals with the confusion caused by the Czar's edict to draft Jews for the army. A modernized version by Aaron Kushnirov was staged in the 1930s in Russia, Poland, and the U.S.A. His plays *Man un Vayb* ("Husband and Wife") and *Di Genarte Velt* ("The Foolish World"), and his story *Noch Tsvey Hozn* ("Two More Hares," retranslated by L. Reznik from the Russian) appeared posthumously. The rest of his valuable writings have disappeared. Whatever was extant was reprinted in two volumes (1, Kiev, 1931; 2, Moscow, 1938).

BIBLIOGRAPHY: LNYL, 1 (1956), 159–63; Z. Rejzen, *Fun Mendelssohn biz Mendele* (1923), 355–418; M. Wiener, in: *I. Axenfelds Verk*, 1 (1931), v–xvi, 3–142; S. Niger, *Dertseylers un Romanistn*, 1 (1946), 52–60; I. Zinberg, *Geshikhte fun der Literatur bay Yidn*, 8:2 (1937), 172–202. **ADD. BIBLIOGRAPHY:** M. Wiener, in: *Tsu der Geshikhte fun der Yidisher Literatur in 19stn Yorhundert* (1945), 65–204; D. Miron, *A Traveler Disguised* (1973, 1996^2).

[Elias Schulman]

AYALON, AMI (1945–), Israeli soldier and security services chief. Ayalon was born in kibbutz Ma'agan. He received a B.A. degree in social sciences from Bar-Ilan University and an M.A. in public administration from Harvard University. In 1963 he joined the commando unit of the Israeli navy. In 1969 he was honored for bravery for his actions in the Green Island raid in Egypt. He also received a citation from the army chief of staff for carrying out 22 actions as a commander without casualties. In 1992 he became commander of the navy, retiring from the IDF in 1995. After the murder of Prime Minister Yitzhak *Rabin in 1995, he became head of Israel's general security services (the Shin Bet or Shabak), rehabilitating the organization after what was perceived as a breakdown in security at the time of the assassination. After leaving the Shin Bet in 2000 he became chairman of Netafim, a successful kibbutz plant for irrigation equipment. In 2003 he sponsored with Dr. Sari Nusseibeh, president of Al-Quds University, the "People's Voice" peace initiative aimed to advance the peace process between Israel and the Palestinians. Their well-publicized peace plan was based on the idea of two states for two nations and the relinquishment by the Palestinians of the right of return. In 2004 Ayalon registered with the Labor Party and announced his intention to enter politics.

[Shaked Gilboa (2nd ed.)]

AYALON (formerly **Neustadt**), **DAVID** (1914–1998), Israeli Arabist and historian, specializing in the social and military history of the medieval and early modern Muslim world. Born in Haifa, Ayalon studied at the Hebrew University, as well as a year at the American University of Beirut, receiving his Ph.D. in 1946. During World War II he served in the British Army, and subsequently worked in the political department of the Jewish Agency. After the establishment of the State of Israel, he was employed at the Foreign Ministry until 1950, when he joined the staff of the Hebrew University as lecturer in the history of the Islamic peoples. He became a professor in 1959 and in 1962–66 served as director of the university's Institute of Asian and African Studies. Ayalon's early publications were in the field of medieval Jewish history, but he soon turned to the study of *Mamluk military and social history as well as other topics in pre-modern Islamic history. His many publications included *Gunpowder and Firearms in the Mamluk Kingdom: A Challenge to a Medieval Society* (1956; Hebrew translation 1994), several volumes of collected studies published in the 1970s to 1990s, and the posthumous *Eunuchs, Caliphs and Sultans: A Study in Power Relationships* (1999). His series of essays on "The Great Yasa of Chingiz Khan: A Re-examination" (published 1970–73) was a major contribution to the study of Mongol history. In 1947, together with the Arabist Pesaḥ Schusser (later Shinar), Ayalon published an Arabic-Hebrew dictionary, which for five decades was the mainstay of teaching Arabic among Hebrew speakers in Israel. Subsequently its revision and expansion were undertaken by the scholars of the Institute of Asian and African Studies. Ayalon was awarded the Israel Prize for humanities in 1972.

ADD. BIBLIOGRAPHY: R. Amitai, "David Ayalon, 1914–1998," in: *Mamluk Studies Review*, 3 (1999), 1–12 (with a complete list of publications); Heb. version in *Ha-Mizraḥ he-Ḥadash*, 41 (2000), 3–5.

[Norman Itzkowitz / Reuven Amitai (2nd ed.)]

AYALTI (Klenbart), HANAN J. (1910–1992), Yiddish writer and cultural activist. At the age of 19, Ayalti left Bialystok for Palestine. In 1933 he went to Paris to study at the Sorbonne. During World War II he escaped from occupied France, lived in Uruguay 1942–46, and subsequently moved to New York, where he became editorial secretary for the Zionist publication *Der Yidisher Kemfer*. After a first novel in Hebrew (1934), he turned to writing in Yiddish: short stories, novels, travel sketches, and a collection of proverbs. Some of these works were translated into Hebrew, English, and Spanish. His best-known novel is *Tate un Zun* ("Father and Son," 1943). His experiences during the Spanish Civil War in 1936 as a war correspondent are reflected in his novel *Der Hotel Vos Ekzistirt Nit* ("The Non-Existent Hotel," 2 vols., 1944). Ayalti's literary work generally gives a detailed description of the social milieu and is characterized by his skeptical analysis of ideologies, his distrust of his heroes, a tendency to see the darker sides of ideas and personalities, and the exaltation of physical love. Translations of his stories appeared in such significant American journals as *Commentary* and *Midstream*; several were gathered into a volume entitled *The Presence Is in Exile, Too* (1997).

BIBLIOGRAPHY: LNYL, 1 (1956), 43–4; J. Glatstein, *In Tokh Genumen* (1956), 448–52; S. Bickel, *Shrayber fun Mayn Dor*, 2 (1965), 402–8; Kressel, Leksikon, 1 (1965), 94.

[Shlomo Bickel / Alan Astro (2nd ed.)]

AYANOT (Heb. עֲיָנוֹת; "springs"), agricultural school in central Israel, near Nes Ẓiyyonah. Founded in 1930 by *WIZO as an agricultural training farm, Ayanot initially absorbed immigrant girls only, but later also accepted Israeli-born girls. In 1947 Ayanot became a coeducational school. Vocational training and secondary school education included the Ministry of Education curriculum. Subsequently Ayanot operated as an agricultural boarding school. Students were new immigrants who came to Israel on their own from Brazil and the former Soviet Union. Intensive farming included a computerized dairy. In the mid-1990s there were approximately 340 inhabitants in Ayanot, increasing to 399 in 2002.

[Efraim Orni / Shaked Gilboa (2nd ed.)]

AYASH (Ayyash), family of rabbis and scholars. JUDAH AYASH (d. 1760), son of the widely revered Algiers rabbi Isaac (d. 1727), was himself one of the most famous rabbis of Algiers. As *av bet din* (1728–56) all disputes were referred to him and he carried on a voluminous correspondence with the rabbinical authorities of Morocco, Italy, and Egypt. He had gathered many pupils and his Sabbath sermons drew crowds of listeners. In 1756 Ayash decided to go to Palestine and devote himself entirely to study. He visited Leghorn in 1756 and then reached Jerusalem. Judah Ayash's works (published in Leghorn) include *Leḥem Yehudah*, notes on Maimonides (1745); *Beit Yehudah* (1746); responsa followed by *Minhagim*, customs of Algiers from the 15th century (1746); *Benei Yehudah* (1758); *Ve-Zot li-Yhudah* (1760); commentaries on the *halakhah; Matteh Yehudah* and *Shevet Yehudah* (1783), critical notes on the code of Joseph Caro; and *Afra di-Ara* (1783). Judah's son JACOB MOSES (c. 1750–1817) returned to Algiers in 1783 as a fundraising agent for the *kolel* of Jerusalem. He went to Leghorn and eventually settled in Ferrara where he became chief rabbi of the community there. Jacob had many famous disciples. He was the compiler of *Derekh Ḥayyim*

(Leghorn, 1790), and also edited his father's *Matteh Yehudah* and *Shevet Yehudah*. Judah's second son JOSEPH edited *Kol Yehudah* (1793). A third son, ABRAHAM (d. 1791), traveled to Leghorn to publish *Ve-Zot li-Yhudah* (1790). JUDAH-LEON (d. 1846) was an officer-interpreter in the French Army, who showed great courage in the campaign against Abd-el Kader. He died of wounds received in action.

BIBLIOGRAPHY: Prefaces to Judah Ayash's works mentioned above; I. Bloch, *Inscriptions Tumulaires ... d'Alger* (1888), 74–78; Yaari, Sheluḥei.

[David Corcos]

AYDAN, DAVID (1873–1954), Tunisian rabbi and printer. Aydan was born in Djerba and was a founder of the Zionist movement Ateret Zion (1919). He acquired a printing press in Tunis, and in 1912 founded the first Hebrew printing press at Djerba, to which he gave the name Defus Ziyyoni (Zion Press). The first work which came off this press was *Me'il Ya'akov* by R. Jacob ha-Kohen. He opened two more presses in Djerba, publishing more than 1,000 works by rabbis from Djerba, Tunis, and the rest of North Africa. One of these presses was still functioning in the late 1960s.

BIBLIOGRAPHY: S. and Ḥ. Aydan, *Mazkeret Neẓaḥ* (1956).

[Robert Attal]

AYDIN, capital city of Aydin province in western Turkey. Population (2004): 156,600. There was a Jewish community in Aydin (then called *Tralles*) from the Roman era until the Ottoman period. At the beginning of the 20th century the community numbered approximately 3,000. The community was led by a rabbi, who together with a number of its members formed a communal council. The community had three synagogues, a hospital, charitable institutions, a *talmud torah*, and a yeshivah. In 1894 an Alliance Israélite Universelle school for boys was founded and in 1904, one for girls. The Jews were primarily engaged in import and export trade. The community, however, gradually declined and virtually ceased to exist after World War I, mainly because of the Greek invasion of western Turkey. Some of the Jews moved to Smyrna (Izmir), others to Rhodes, and about 200 families to South America.

BIBLIOGRAPHY: A. Galanté, *Histoire des Juifs d'Anatolie*, 2 (1939), 127–42; EIS^2, 1 (1960), 782–3 (includes bibliography). **ADD. BIBLIOGRAPHY:** P.R. Trebilco, *Jewish Communities in Asia Minor* (1987).

[Abraham Haim / David Kushner (2nd ed.)]

'AYIN (Heb. עַיִן ;ע) (fricative pharyngeal), the 16th letter of the Hebrew alphabet; its numerical value is 70. Its earliest representation is the acrophonic pictograph of an eye (*ʿayin*) ⊙. The pupil of the eye disappears already in the early evolution of the letter. In the later Proto-Canaanite, Phoenician, Hebrew, and Samaritan on the one hand and in South-Arabic and Ethiopic on the other, though with variations, the *ʿayin* has a circular shape. Thus also in Greek and Latin, in which the consonantal value of the letter turns into the vowel "o".

In the Aramaic script as early as the seventh century B.C.E. the top of the circle opens: ᴗ (compare with *bet, dalet,* and *resh*). It is written mainly with two bars (first the left and then the right) meeting at the base v. As there is a cursive tendency to draw the pen toward the next letter, the right bar becomes longer and longer v → y → y, and thus the classical shape of this letter develops, which is known in the Jewish scripts until the present: ע. The Nabatean and Palmyrene scripts also adopt this Aramaic letter: the Arabic ع develops through the Nabatean cursive y → y → y → y, and the Syriac ܥ through the Palmyrene cursive y → y → y → y. The Ashkenazic Jewish cursive develops as follows: y → y → ɣ → ɣ. See *Alphabet, Hebrew.

[Joseph Naveh]

AYLLON, SOLOMON BEN JACOB (c. 1655–1728), rabbi and kabbalist. Ayllon was born in Salonika, and received his rabbinical training there. As a young man he joined the followers of *Shabbetai Ẓevi and was in personal contact with *Nathan of Gaza. The accusation made by Ayllon's opponents that he was among those followers of Shabbetai who had adopted Islam (*Doenmeh) and the insinuation that his first wife had not been properly divorced from her first husband, have never been proved. He seems, in fact, to have belonged to those moderate Shabbateans who remained faithful to rabbinical tradition. After 1680 he settled in Safed in Ereẓ Israel, spending several years there, and later went to Europe as an emissary of the Safed community. In 1688 he arrived in Leghorn and established close ties with the Italian followers of Shabbetai Ẓevi. In 1689 he went to London and was appointed haham of the Jewish community, although not without opposition, which was further aggravated when his earlier connections with Shabbetai Ẓevi became known.

In 1700 he was appointed rabbi of the Portuguese community at Amsterdam, a post he occupied until his death, and was greatly respected there. Ayllon supported efforts to print one of the most important works of the Shabbatean Abraham Miguel *Cardoso, declaring that in his opinion the work was above suspicion from the theological point of view. Nonetheless, the book was burned as heretical in accordance with the contrary opinions of learned authorities in Smyrna. During the summer of 1713 Ayllon, together with the president of the Portuguese community, came into serious conflict with Ẓevi *Ashkenazi, who had in the meantime been appointed chief rabbi of the Amsterdam Ashkenazi community. The dispute started when the Shabbatean author Nehemiah Ḥiyya *Ḥayon came to Amsterdam and requested Ayllon's approval to distribute his book *Oz le-Elohim*. It was clear that he looked upon Ayllon as a secret fellow believer, despite the fact that Ayllon in his Amsterdam years had behaved most cautiously in matters that concerned the Shabbateans. Before Ayllon and six other scholars from his community had had an opportunity to examine the book, Ẓevi Ashkenazi and Moses *Ḥagiz issued a ban on Ḥayon forbidding him to publish or disseminate his book, which they declared a Shabbatean work. In this case, they were undoubtedly right. Ayllon and his community, however, saw in Ashkenazi's ban a slur upon their authority and placed themselves on the side of Ḥayon. They declared his book a mere kabbalistic work, and although they objected to certain passages, they declared that they found nothing heretical in it. The official defense, part of which was doubtless written by Ayllon himself, appeared in Amsterdam in 1714 in Hebrew as *Kosht Imrei Emet* ("Certainty of the Words of Truth"), and in Spanish as *Manifesto*. The dispute caused much excitement in Amsterdam and in other communities as well, especially in Italy. Much correspondence and many pamphlets and tracts testify to the furor raised. Ayllon and the council of his community applied to the magistrate of Amsterdam and forced both Ẓevi Ashkenazi and Ḥayon to leave Amsterdam. Later Ayllon avoided Ḥayon, and when the latter reappeared in Amsterdam in 1726 Ayllon refused to receive him.

Ayllon died shortly afterward. A collection of his responsa is preserved in manuscript no. 125 of the London *bet ha-midrash* and in the Ets Ḥayim Library in Amsterdam. A few responsa of his have been printed in various other collections of contemporary rabbis. There remains a complete treatise of his kabbalistic writings, probably written before his arrival in London, as well as a large number of separate pronouncements and explanations, in two manuscripts. Their Shabbatean character is evident; it is not certain whether in his later years Ayllon entirely relinquished his Shabbatean views or whether he continued to hold these convictions secretly.

BIBLIOGRAPHY: M. Gaster, *History of the Ancient Synagogue of the Spanish and Portuguese Jews in London* (1901), 22–30; Nadav, in: *Sefunot*, 3–4 (1959–60), 301–47 (with detailed bibliography); Emmanuel, in: *Sefunot*, 9 (1965), 209–46 (Documents from the Archives of the Portuguese Community of Amsterdam).

[Gershom Scholem]

AYRTON, HERTHA (née **Marks**; 1854–1923), British physicist of Jewish parentage. She married Professor W.E. Ayrton, whom she greatly assisted in his research, especially on the electric arc. She later established the laws that govern the behavior of the electric arc. She presented many papers on this and other subjects before the Royal Society of London and other scientific bodies. During World War I, she invented an anti-gas fan which was distributed to thousands of British troops. Ayrton explained the formation of sand ripples on the seashore and, at the time of her death, was investigating the transmission of coal gas. She was the first woman to become a member of the Institution of Electrical Engineers and in 1902 was nominated for election as a Fellow of the Royal Society. However, the election of a woman to the society was impossible at the time. She played a militant role in the campaign for woman's suffrage. Hertha Ayrton had two daughters, one of whom was the wife of Israel Zangwill and the other, BARBARA AYRTON GOULD (d. 1950), was a Labour member of Parliament and chairman of the Labour Party (1939–40), and a forceful supporter of the Zionist cause in the House of Commons. Her son was the painter and sculptor, MICHAEL AYRTON (1921–1975).

[J. Edwin Holmstrom]

AYYELET HA-SHAḤAR (Heb. אַיֶּלֶת הַשַּׁחַר; "Morning Star," deriving from the Arabic name for the site, Nijmat-al-Ṣubḥ), kibbutz in northern Israel, near ancient *Hazor. Ayyelet ha-Shaḥar, affiliated with Iḥud ha-Kevuẓot ve-ha-Kibbutzim, was founded in 1918 by Second Aliyah pioneers who were joined by members of *Gedud ha-Avodah to secure exposed land holdings of *ICA and increase food production for the Jewish urban population which during World War I suffered severe hunger. The existence of Ayyelet ha-Shaḥar, together with *Tel Ḥai and *Kefar Giladi, resulted in the inclusion of the Ḥuleh Valley in the borders of Palestine after World War I. The kibbutz economy was based on intensive mixed farming – industrial field crops, fodder, dairy cattle, carp ponds, and particularly fruit (mainly apple) orchards. It operated a museum of the findings from nearby Hazor and a popular guest house. Its population in 1967 was 710, increasing to 925 in the mid-1990s and 1,270 in 2002.

[Efraim Orni]

AYYUBIDS, dynasty of sultans in Egypt and Syria (1171–1250). The founder of the Kurdish family of Ayyūb was one of the commanders of Zangī, a freed Turkish slave and one of the greatest emirs in the court of Malik Shāh the Seljuk (1072–92). His son *Saladin Yusuf, who was educated in Syria in the Turkish-Seljuk military tradition, succeeded in founding the Ayyubid dynasty in 1171, in conquering Jerusalem in 1187, and expanding his country from Egypt to East Asia in the east and Yemen to the south. Even before his death Saladin divided his country between his sons and his brothers. One of his sons, al-Malik al-Afḍal, received Damascus in 1186 and Ereẓ Israel, but his uncle ʿAdil took Damascus from him in 1196. The second son, al-Malik al-Ẓāhir (1186–1216), received Aleppo. But ʿAdil, the brother of Saladin, succeeded in the early 13th century in uniting most of the areas under him. After his death in 1218, the Ayyubid rulers were compelled to fight harsh wars with the Crusaders, losing Safed, Tiberias, and Ashkelon. In 1229 ʿAdil's son, the sultan Kamil (1218–38), who ruled in Egypt and in Ereẓ Israel, gave Emperor Frederick II Jerusalem and Bethlehem, as well as a corridor of free passage to them from Jaffa. In 1244 with the aid of the Khwārizmis Jerusalem was returned to Ṣāliḥ the Ayyubid (1240–49), the ruler of Egypt and Syria. An energetic sultan, Ṣāliḥ succeeded in uniting almost all the kingdom of Saladin under him. His death and the murder of his son al-Muʿazzam Tūrān Shāh put an end to the Ayyubid dynasty, and after ten years of changes of succession, the Mamluks established their reign in Egypt (Baybars, 1260). Ayyubid rule only lasted about 80 years and was accompanied by many wars. Despite this, the Ayyubid reign was a period of cultural development. Their devotion to orthodox *sunna* Islam, their war against the sects of the *shiʿa*, and their concern for the spread of learning did not affect their tolerance toward Jews and Christians. Saladin opened Jerusalem to the Jews in 1190, and the number of Jews in Ereẓ Israel increased under the Ayyubids. *Egyptian Jewry also benefited from the stable regime and Jewish scholars from Christian countries settled in Egypt.

BIBLIOGRAPHY: Mann, Egypt, 1 (1920), 255–8; Mann, Texts, 1 (1931), 412–34; Ashtor, Toledot, 1 (1944), 46f., 117–24; EIS; EIS³. **ADD. BIBLIOGRAPHY:** N.A. Stillman, "The Non-Muslim Communities: The Jewish Community" and M. Chamberlain, "The Crusader Era and the Ayyubid Dynasty," in: *The Cambridge History of Egypt*, vol. 1; Petry, C.F. (ed.), *Islamic Egypt, 640–1517* (1998), 198–211, 211–42.

[Haïm Z'ew Hirschberg]

AẒANCOT, Moroccan family. SADIA BEN LEVI AẒANCOT (early 17th century) of Marrakesh taught in Holland and published a paraphrase of the Book of Esther in rhymed prose (*Iggeret ha-Purim*, Amsterdam, 1647). He transcribed *Maimonides' *Guide of the Perplexed* into Arabic characters for the Orientalist Jacob Golius. From 1600 to 1770, several members of this family were leaders of the Marrakesh community. Deprived of their possessions by the sultan, they eventually settled in Tangier and played a diplomatic role during the bombardments of Tangier (1844) and the war with Spain (1859–60). MOSES AẒANCOT (19th century) was kidnapped by the Franciscan mission at the age of nine and was converted in Madrid, his godfather being Fernando VII. Moses became a tutor to the future Alfonso XII, and his daughter was lady of honor to Isabella II. His brother DAVID (19th century) was a diplomat and an antiquarian. In Tangier he received Delacroix who painted many portraits of his family, and in 1846 he was host to Alexandre Dumas who wrote at length about him in his *Impressions de Voyage*.

BIBLIOGRAPHY: Benjacob, Oẓar, 13; Neubauer, Cat, nos. 1240, 1438; J.M. Toledano, *Ner ha-Ma'arav* (1911), 137; I. Larédo, *Memorias de un viejo Tangerino* (1935), 97–108.

[David Corcos]

AZARIAH (end of the first century C.E.), one of the first generation of *tannaim* after the destruction of the Second Temple. His son was the *tanna* *Eleazar b. Azariah (Yev. 16a). An affluent merchant, Azariah supported his brother Simeon, also a *tanna*, so that he might devote himself to his study. It was because of this that Simeon was referred to as "the brother of Azariah" (Zev. 1:2; see Sot. 21a and Rashi, *ibid.*).

BIBLIOGRAPHY: Frankel, Mishnah, 69, 105ff.; Hyman, Toledot, 980.

[Zvi Kaplan]

AZARIAH (early fourth century C.E.), Palestinian *amora*. He is believed to have been the pupil of R. *Mana, in whose name he transmitted *halakhot* (e.g., TJ, Shab. 7:1, 9b). Some scholars have identified him with the *amora* Ezra, but erroneously, since they flourished in different generations. Azariah is often quoted in the *aggadah* of the Palestinian Talmud and even more often in midrashic literature where he transmits *aggadot* in the names of R. *Aḥa (Gen. R. 39:6), R. *Joshua b. Levi (Gen. R. 15:7), and Yudan b. Simeon (Gen. R. 39:8).

Azariah himself was a prolific and versatile aggadist. He explains the verse "As an apple tree among the trees of the wood, so is my beloved among the sons" (Song 2:3): As the apple ripens only in the month of Sivan, so Israel emitted a sweet fragrance in the month of Sivan (i.e., at the giving of the Torah at Sinai); and as there are 50 days between the budding and the ripening of its fruit, so did Israel take 50 days between the Exodus and the giving of the Torah (Song R., to 2:3). In the word אֶשֶׁל (*eshel*, "tamarisk"), which Abraham planted at Beer-Sheba (Geb. 21:33), Azariah sees an allusion to the three duties of hospitality toward guests, who must be provided with food (אֲכִילָה; *akhilah*), drink (שְׁתִיָּה; *shetiyyah*), and escort (לְוָיָה, *levayah*; Mid. Ps. 110:1, ed. Buber, 465, n. 4). The reading "lodging" (לִינָה; *linah*) for the last does not appear in ancient texts.

BIBLIOGRAPHY: Bacher, Pal Amor; Hyman, Toledot, 980.

AZARIAH BEN ELIYAH (d. after 1838), one of the leaders of the Karaite community in Chufut-Kale and its chronicler. Very little is known about his life. He signed a letter (1810) from the community of Chufut-Kale to that of Constantinople, concerning financial support for the Karaite community in Jerusalem. He wrote an important chronicle in which he describes the events of the civil war in the Crimea during the Russian invasion (1777–83) and the rule of the last Crimean Khan, Shahin Giray. As an eyewitness Azariah depicts the suffering of the population of the Crimea, including Karaites. He gives unique information about the events in the Crimea in general, and in particular about the Karaite communities of Chufut-Kale and Eupatoria (Yevpatoriya), the relations between Karaites and Rabbanites and other communities of the Crimea, the rates of taxation levied on the Karaites, etc. This work, with many biblical citations incorporated into the text, is written in a very lively and fascinating way. It was published twice in the Russian translation of A. *Firkovich and recently in the Hebrew original text.

BIBLIOGRAPHY: G. Akhiezer, "*Ha-Me'ora'ot she-Hitraḥashu bi-Krim bi-Tekufat Malkhuto shel Shahin Giray Khan:* The Historical Chronicle by R. Azaryah ben Eliya the Karaite" (M.A. thesis, Heb. Univ. of Jerusalem, 2000); idem, in: M. Polliack (ed.), *Karaite Judaism* (2003), 730, 734–35, 738, 748, 751–52; Azarija ben Elija (trans. A. Firkovich), in: *Vremennik imperatorskago moskovskago obshchestva istorii i drevnostei rossiiskix*, 24 (1854), 101–34; K. zh. V–VI (1911), 52–77.

[Golda Akhiezer (2nd ed.)]

AZARIAH BEN SOLOMON (late 10th–early 11th centuries), exilarch in Babylonia after 953. Azariah's father, Solomon, was the son of Josiah (Ḥasan) but nevertheless supported by *Saadiah Gaon against Josiah's brother *David b. Zakkai. From documents of the Cairo *Genizah*, it is known that Solomon held office during the years 951–53. His precise term of office is, however, unknown. It seems that his son Azariah succeeded to his position. The latter was the founder of several families of *nesi'im* in various countries. One of Azariah's sons, Zakkai, settled in Mosul and his descendants were *nesi'im* for several generations. His second son, Daniel, was *gaon* and *nasi* in Palestine from 1051 to 1062 and is mentioned in the Scroll of *Abiathar as well as in letters and other documents. His third son, Solomon, seems to have settled in Aleppo, where he established a dynasty of *nesi'im* which was still in existence in the 14th century.

BIBLIOGRAPHY: J. Mann, in: *Sefer Zikkaron... S. Poznański* (1927), 19–21; Assaf, *Ge'onim*, 35–36. **ADD. BIBLIOGRAPHY:** M. Gil, *Be-Malkhut Ishmael*, 1 (1997), 109–10.

[Abraham David]

AZARKH, RAÏSA MOYSEYEVNA (1897–1971), author. Azarkh was a Bolshevik commissar during the civil war and fought with the International Brigade in Spain, where she organized the Republican army's medical corps. She survived the purges of the 1930s and post-World War II era, publishing reminiscences of the civil wars in Russia and Spain, *Doroga chesti* ("The Path of Honor," 1956–59).

ADD. BIBLIOGRAPHY: K.J. Cottam, *Women in War and Resistance: Selected Biographies of Soviet Women Soldiers* (1998).

AZAZEL (Heb. עֲזָאזֵל), name of the place or the "power" (see below) to which one of the goats in the Temple service of the *Day of Atonement was sent. There is a great deal of confusion regarding the exact meaning of the word. The name appears in Leviticus (16:8–10): "And Aaron shall cast lots upon the two goats; one lot for the Lord, and the other lot for Azazel. And Aaron shall present the goat upon which the lot fell for the Lord, and offer him for a sin-offering. But the goat, on which the lot fell for Azazel, shall be set alive before the Lord, to make atonement over him, to send him away for Azazel into the wilderness."

The goat which was dispatched to Azazel was not a sacrifice since it was not slaughtered. From the actual verses themselves it is not even certain whether the goat was killed; thus it seems that the two goats can be compared to the two birds used in the purification ritual of the leper. Just as there one of the birds is set free to fly over the field (Lev. 14:4–7), so here too the goat of Azazel was sent into the wilderness. The goat was dispatched in order to carry the sins of Israel into the wilderness, i.e., to cleanse the people of their sins. This is also the reason why the ritual took place on the Day of Atonement.

The idea that the goat was loaded with the sins of Israel is expressed in the Mishnah (Yoma 6:4) which relates that the Babylonians (or the Alexandrians) used to pluck the hair of the goat and proclaim "Take and go" which is explained as meaning "why is this goat waiting here when the sins of the generation are many and are upon them" (Yoma 66b., cf. the text cited by R. Hananel ad loc.).

A detailed description of the ritual in the Second Temple is found in the Mishnah in the general description of the **avodah* of the Day of Atonement: the high priest cast lots – upon one the word *L*-YHWH ("For the Lord") was written and upon the other *La-'Azazel* ("For Azazel"). Afterward he drew lots and on the head of the goat chosen for Azazel he bound a thread of crimson wool and stood the animal opposite the gate through which it would ultimately be taken (Yoma 4:1–2). After the high priest had performed several other rituals he returned to the goat, placed his hands on it and confessed: "O God, Thy people, the house of Israel, has sinned and transgressed before Thee…." He then handed the goat over to the person who was going to take it, called *I'sh 'Itti* (Lev. 16:21), i.e., the man who had been prepared for that time (*et*). Although any Jew was qualified to fulfill this function, the high priests did not allow non-priests to do it (Yoma 6:3). When the *I'sh 'Itti* reached the cliff, he pushed the goat over it backward and it hardly reached the halfway mark in its descent before it was completely dismembered (Yoma 6:2–6).

It seems that even in the time of the Second Temple when they used to kill the goat, its actual death was not considered indispensable since, as soon as the goat reached the desert, the high priest was permitted to continue with the divine service and was not required to wait until the goat was killed. It is possible that the goat was killed in order to ensure that it would not return – laden with the sins – to inhabited places.

There have been efforts to compare the ritual of the goat to several customs of the ancient world. In Babylonia, for instance, it was customary on the festival of *Akītu* (the New Year) to give a goat as a substitute for a human being (*pūḫ*) to Ereshkigal (the goddess of the abyss). In an Akkadian magical inscription from the city of Assur which deals with the cure for a man who is unable to eat and drink, it is prescribed that a goat should be tied to his bed and that thus the sickness will pass to the goat. On the following morning, the goat is to be taken to the desert and decapitated. Its flesh is then cooked and put in a pit together with honey and oil, perhaps as an offering to the demons. During plagues, the Hittites used to send a goat into enemy territory in order that it should carry the plague there. On the head of the goat they would bind a crown made of colored wool, comparable perhaps to the thread of crimson wool which was tied to the head of the goat in the Second Temple period (Yoma 4:2). In the Hellenistic world there were also "scapegoat" rituals, but they had the custom to take a man as "scapegoat" and not an animal. In some places these rituals were performed in times of trouble, in others at fixed appointed times of the year. However, in the Hellenistic world the important part of the ceremony was not the killing of the "scapegoat," but its being sent out of the city and indeed, in some places, it was not even killed.

The exact meaning of Azazel was a point of dispute already in the times of the talmudic sages: some held that it is the name of the place to which the goat was sent, while others believed that it was the name of some "power." According to the first opinion, the word Azazel is a parallel to "a land which is cut off" (Lev. 16:22), meaning (according to the rabbinic interpretation) an area of rocks and cliffs, i.e., inaccessible. The word Azazel is also interpreted as meaning strong and hard as though it were written עזז אל, namely, hardest of the mountains (Yoma 63b; cf. Sifra Aḥarei Mot 2:8; Targum Jonathan to Lev. 16:10). It does appear, however, that this is an attempt to reconcile the meaning of the word Azazel with the actual usage in the time of the Second Temple, namely to bring the goat to a cliff and to push it over. The interpretation does not quite fit the written form of the word עזאזל. The second opinion, which sees Azazel as a supernatural power, also treats the word as though it were written עֲזָזְאֵל. This opinion is based on Leviticus (16:8): "One lot for the Lord and the other lot for Azazel," i.e., just as the first goat is set aside for the Lord so the second is set aside for Azazel, Azazel being a parallel to the Lord (cf. PdRE ch. 46, p. 111a). God gets a burnt offering while Azazel gets a sin offering. This view is reinforced by the widespread belief that the wilderness was the habitat of demons (see Lev. 13:21; 34:14; esp. Lev. 17:7). The demonic identification would indicate that the original purpose of the ritual was to get rid of the evil by banishing it to its original source.

Ibn Ezra and Naḥmanides both interpret Azazel as the name of the goat and this view is also found in the Talmud: "The school of Rabbi Ishmael explained it is called Azazel because it atones for the acts of the fallen *angels *Uzza and Azael" (Yoma 67b, cf. Targ. Jon., Gen. 6:1; Deut. R. 11:10). In the various Greek translations of the Bible and the Vulgate the word Azazel is interpreted in a different form – as being made up of the word עז ("goat") and the Aramaic root אזל ("to go") thus making "the goat which goes." The Septuagint has χίμαρον... ἐπ᾽ αὐτὸν ὁ κλῆρος τοῦ ἀποπομπαίου (Lev. 16:10, cf. 8, i.e., the goat on which went the lot of dismissal); also, verse 26, i.e., the goat which goes free. Symmachus has τράγως ἀπερχόμενος and the Vulgate *caper emissarius*.

David Kimḥi in his *Book of Roots* explains the word as being the name of the mountain to which the goat was taken and the mount was so called because the goat was taken there. Latterly N.H. Tur *Sinai has explained the word as meaning a wild goat.

In the retelling of the story of the sons of God and daughters of men (Gen. 6:1–4) in the First Book of Enoch, Azazel (or Azael) is one of the leaders of the angels who desired the daughters of men (6:4), and it was he who taught human beings how to manufacture weapons and ornaments (8:1–2). The identification of this Azazel with the biblical Azazel is clear from the continuation of the story, as the angel Raphael is commanded to "bind the hands and feet of Azazel and cast him into the darkness. Make an opening to the wilderness which is in Dudael and cast him there. Put upon him hard sharp rocks" (10:4–5). Dudael is the Bet Hadudo (or Bet Harudo) which is mentioned in the Mishnah (Yoma 6:8) and the association is certainly with the cliff from which the goat was cast. The remnant of a *pesher* (commentary) on Azazel and the angels found in Cave 4 at Qumran resembles the account in the Book of Enoch. Although the remnant is deficient, it is possible to learn from it that the *pesher* is dealing with Azazel and the angels who lusted after the daughters of men so that they might bear them strong men, and that Azazel taught human beings how to deal wickedly. Azael is also identified with Azazel in several late Midrashim (cf. Yalkut Shimoni, Gen. 44; Jellinek, *Beit ha-Midrash*, vol. 4, p. 127). Azazel also appears in the Apocalypse of *Abraham where he takes the form of a fallen angel.

BIBLIOGRAPHY: J.E. Harrison, *Prolegomena to the Study of Greek Religion* (1922³), 95–109; J. Pederson, *Israel, Its Life and Culture*, 3–4 (1940), 454, 712; L. Rost, in: ZDPV, 66 (1943), 213–4; W. Gipsen, in: *Orientalia Neerlandica* (1948), 156–61 (Eng.); E. Kutsch, in: RGG³, 6 (1962), 506–7; *Oxford Classical Dictionary*, s.v. *Pharmakos, Sacrifice* and *Thargelia*; C. Lattey, in: VT, 1 (1951), 272; S. Hooke, *ibid.*, 2 (1952), 8–10; O.R. Gurney, *The Hittites* (1952), 162; Pritchard, Texts, 347; W.F. Albright, in: VT Supplement, 4 (1956), 245–6; G.R. Driver, in: JSS, 1 (1956), 97–98; C.L. Finberg, in: *Bibliotheca Sacra*, 115 (1958), 320–3; de Vaux, Anc Isr, 508–9; W. Eichrodt, *Theology of the Old Testament*, 2 (1967), 224–6; M.H. Segal, in JQR, 53 (1962/63), 248–51; H. Wohlstein, in: ZDMG, 113 (1963), 487–9; J.G. Frazer, in: T.H. Gaster (ed.), *The New Golden Bough* (1964), xviii, xxiii, 609–23, 638–40; H.M. Kuemmel, in: ZAW, 80 (1968), 290–318; J.M. Allegro, *Qumrân Cave 4* (1968), 78.

[Shmuel Ahituv]

AZEFF, YEVNO FISHELEVICH (1869–1918), agent of the czarist secret police and simultaneously a leader of the Russian social revolutionary movement. Azeff was born in Lyskovo, Russia, into a poor family and studied in Rostov-on-Don until the age of 21. He wandered from one unremunerative job to another. In 1892, faced with arrest for alleged revolutionary activities, he fled to Germany. Azeff enrolled as a student at the Polytechnic in Karlsruhe, where he became a member of a socialist group. Reduced to poverty, he wrote a letter to the Russian secret police offering his services, and thus began his double life as a secret informer and an ardent advocate of the revolutionary struggle among Russian students abroad. In 1899, on receiving his diploma in electrical engineering at Darmstadt University, Azeff returned to Russia. During the 15 years that he was in the pay of the czarist secret police (1893–1908) he betrayed many revolutionaries. At the same time he acquired a reputation as a courageous leader of the Social Revolutionary Party and its "fighting organization." He planned a number of assassinations, including that of the Russian minister of the interior, von Plehve, in 1904. Though Azeff usually tended to ignore his Jewish background, he blamed von Plehve for the notorious Kishinev pogrom. In 1902 rumors of his double dealing began to circulate, but it was not until 1908 that his activities were revealed before a party court. This was the result of long investigations by V.L. Burtsev, a socialist historian of the revolutionary movement, who managed to obtain the testimony of Lopukhin, former director of the Russian secret police. Azeff fled abroad, and went into hiding. He was sentenced to death *in absentia*. In World War I he was incarcerated in a German prison as a dangerous revolutionary, and died there in April 1918.

BIBLIOGRAPHY: R. Seth, *Russian Terrorists* (1966), index; B. Nikolaevsky, *Aseff: the Russian Judas* (1934).

°AZEGLIO, MASSIMO TAPARELLI, MARCHESE D' (1798–1866), Italian statesman and writer; prominent figure in the Italian National Revival. D'Azeglio was born in Turin, the son of the Marchese Cesare d'Azeglio and of the Cristina Marozzo di Bianzé. Driven from his youth by intense and eclectic interests and traveling with his father, a diplomat of the Piedmontese court, he had a chance to frequent the literary and artistic clubs of different Italian cities, being especially interested in painting. It was, however, as a novelist that d'Azeglio won fame among his contemporaries, mostly owing to the publication in 1833 of the novel *Ettore Fieramosca o la Disfida di Barletta*, a real bestseller at the time. A keen advocate of the civil emancipation of the Regno di Piemonte's religious minorities (Hebrews and Protestants), d'Azeglio played a leading role both in the preliminary ideological stage (with the 1844 political pamphlet *I casi di Romagna*) and in the political stage of the 1848 uprisings (the first Italian War of Independence). After the defeat of the Piedmontese army at Novara, d'Azeglio was appointed prime minister of the Kingdom of Piedmont through the Austrians on May 7, 1849. In this role he instituted a judicious and balanced reform of public institutes. With the abrogation of ecclesiastic jurisdiction in 1850, d'Azeglio began the transformation of Piedmont into a liberal, secular, and modern state. He resigned as prime minister in 1852 and was replaced by Cavour but continued holding positions of political importance, without ever abandoning his literary interests. He died while at work on his autobiography (*I miei ricordi*), one of the most interesting literary works on the Italian National Revival.

BIBLIOGRAPHY: *Dizionario Biografico Italiano*, 4 (1962), 746–52, including bibliography.

[Massimo Longo Adorno (2nd ed.)]

AZEKAH (Heb. עֲזֵקָה), biblical town in the Shephelah on the road leading north from Lachish to Beth-Horon. Eusebius describes Azekah (Onom. 18:10–12) as a village situated between Eleutheropolis (Bet-Guvrin) and Jerusalem. After the second battle of Ai, Joshua pursued the fleeing Canaanites down the ascent of the Beth-Horon road to Azekah and a hailstorm wrought havoc among them as far as Azekah (Josh. 10:10, 11). The town was included in the northern district of Judah (*ibid.* 15:35). In the days of Saul the border between Israel and Philistia ran between Socoh and Azekah in the valley of Elah and it was here that the armies of the two peoples were drawn up during the battle between David and Goliath (I Sam. 17:2). The town was fortified by Rehoboam to protect Judah against Egypt and the Philistine cities (II Chron. 11:9). Because of Judah's involvement in the Ashdod-led rebellion of 713–12 B.C.E., a part of the Assyrian army invading Philistia in 712 attacked and captured Azekah which lay close to the Philistine border and almost due east of Ashdod (Sargon II Inscription). A reference to this attack, which probably resulted in Judah's submission, may be contained in Isaiah 20ff. In 588 B.C.E. Lachish and Azekah were the last two provincial fortresses of Judah to hold out against Nebuchadnezzar (Jer. 34:7). A passage in a Lachish ostracon which dates from this period seems to imply that Lachish was still standing after Azekah had fallen. The campaigns of both Sargon II and Nebuchadnezzar indicate that Azekah lay astride the approach road to Jerusalem. After the fall of Jerusalem Azekah continued to be a Jewish town (cf. Neh. 11:30). It is generally identified with Tell Zakariyeh where excavations carried out in 1899–1900 uncovered remains of a rectangular fortress with square towers from the period of the Kingdom of Judah. Azekah is possibly mentioned in a *baraita* (Dem. 5:2, 53; Yev. 122a) as a place producing quality fruit, although the meaning of the passage is uncertain.

BIBLIOGRAPHY: F.J. Bliss and R.A.S. Macalister, *Excavations in Palestine* (1902), 12–27; Tadmor, in: BIES, 24 (1960), 24; idem, in: *Journal of Cuneiform Studies*, 12 (1958), 80–83; Abel, Geog, 2 (1938), 257; Z. Vilnay, *Israel Guide* (1961), 167–8; Aharoni, Land, index.

[Michael Avi-Yonah]

AZEMMOUR, city on the Atlantic coast of Morocco. In the 15th century Azemmour was a free city with 20,000 inhabitants, of whom 2,500 were Jews, mainly occupied as fishermen and craftsmen, and including wealthy merchants. Exiles from Portugal in 1496 found refuge there. It was subsequently raided by the Spanish, but the Jews were afforded protection by the Portuguese, who occupied Azemmour in 1513 without bloodshed. A grant of privileges was conferred on the Jews on June 14, 1514, which also fixed their annual tax payment. Joseph Adibe was appointed rabbi of Azemmour and invested with wide powers (c. 1512). The community flourished and prominent members included the families of Adibe, *Roti, Valensi, Buros, Rodrigues, and Cordilha. Numerous *Marranos were welcomed in Azemmour and enabled to go to the interior where they could return to the Jewish faith. The community supported financially and diplomatically the pretensions of David Ha-*Reuveni when he arrived in Portugal in 1525. Azemmour was captured by the Moors in 1541; during the siege John III ordered the evacuation of all Jewish noncombatants to Arzila, and compensated them for the losses they had incurred. A community was reestablished in 1780. Most of the more wealthy members immigrated to Mazagan c. 1820, after the sultan ʿAbd al-Raḥmān ibn Hishām permitted Jews to trade there. Only the Jewish craftsmen remained in Azemmour, which continued to have a Jewish population until the emigration from Morocco after 1948. In 1968 there were no Jewish inhabitants in the town.

BIBLIOGRAPHY: D. Corcos, in: *Sefunot*, 10 (1966), 63–69; *Villes et tribus du Maroc*, 2 (1932), 34, 40–48, 51–53, 56, 64; Hirschberg, Afrikah, 1 (1965), 311–3, 332; A. Baião, *Inquisição em Portugal* (1921), 128 and passim.

[David Corcos]

AZENBERG, EMANUEL (1934–), U.S. theatrical producer. Born in a Yiddish-speaking household in the Bronx to Joshua Charles Azenberg, the manager of a Labor-Zionist organization, and Hannah Kleiman Azenberg, he attended New York

University and served in the United States Army . He said he first became interested in theater when he went to see his uncle portray a rabbi in a play with John *Garfield in 1948 called *Skipper Next to God.* Azenberg worked for David *Merrick, a prolific Broadway producer, on 22 shows and for Alexander *Cohen before teaming with Eugene Wolsk in 1966 to produce *The Lion in Winter* with Robert Preston and Rosemary Harris. That was followed almost immediately by *Mark Twain Tonight!* with Hal Holbrook. Both were successes.

In 1972 Azenberg produced his first Neil *Simon play, *Sunday in New York,* which was followed by 60 other Broadway stage productions, including virtually all of Simon's 30 comedies, among them: *The Sunshine Boys, Chapter Two, They're Playing Our Song, Brighton Beach Memoirs, Biloxi Blues, Broadway Bound,* and *Lost in Yonkers,* all major successes. In addition Azenberg produced for Broadway *Ain't Misbehavin', Children of a Lesser God, Master Harold ... and the Boys, The Real Thing, A Moon for the Misbegotten, Sunday in the Park With George, Long Day's Journey Into Night,* and *The Iceman Cometh.* He received 134 Tony nominations and won 41 Tony Awards. He also taught at Duke University from 1985.

In Azenberg's office are reminders of his commitment to Jewish causes, including photographs with Israeli notables. He said he was pulled out of school in 1948 to meet Chaim *Weizmann when he traveled to New York as the first president of the new Jewish state. Azenberg spent most of his childhood summers at Camp Kinderwelt, a Labor-Zionist retreat in Highland Mills, New York. Kinderwelt left a strong enough impression on him that a camp photograph from 1948 adorned his office. His fellow campers included the novelist Leonard Michaels, the sculptor Chaim *Gross, and the film directors Martin *Ritt and Sidney *Lumet. "All of Manny's ethical values he learned at camp," said a long-time friend. "Manny is the epitome of Yiddishe neshuma."

[Stewart Kampel (2nd ed.)]

AZERBAIJAN, one of the independent states of the C.I.S.; formerly part of Persia and the Soviet Union. It gained its independence with the breakup of the U.S.S.R.

Persian

Former northwestern province of Iran. There have been Jewish settlements in Azerbaijan ever since Jews first settled in Persia. However, their presence is attested by documentary evidence only from the 12th century. *Benjamin of Tudela (c. 1165) refers in his *Travels* to a chain of "more than a hundred congregations in the Haftan mountains up to the frontiers of Media," which included Persian Azerbaijan. *Samuel b. Yaḥyā al-Maghribī relates that David *Alroy (12th century) found adherents for his messianic movement in such cities as Khoi, Salmas, *Tabriz, Maragha, and Urmia (*Rizaiyeh).

When after 1258 Hūlāgū Khān established his residence in Tabriz, the new center attracted many Jewish settlers. Saʿad al-Dawla (d. 1291) made his career there as courtier. Tabriz, Sulṭāniyya, and other places in Azerbaijan continued to be a scene of Jewish events in the 13th and 14th centuries. Azerbaijan was also a *Karaite center. Under the Safavids, Jews are mentioned in several districts.

The Jews in Azerbaijan survived persecutions in the 17th century. Between 1711 and 1713 an emissary (*shali'aḥ*) from Hebron, Judah b. Amram Dīwān, visited many communities in Azerbaijan. The sufferings of the Jews under the Kajar dynasty (from 1794) in Maragha, Urmia, Salmas, and Tabriz is graphically described by Christian missionaries and various travelers of the 19th century, including *David d'Beth Hillel. The dialect of the Jews in various communities in Azerbaijan has been the object of investigations by western scholars such as *Noeldecke, Socin, Duval, *Gottheil, Maclean, and J.J. *Rivlin.

[Walter Joseph Fischel]

Russian

Soviet Socialist Republic, eastern Transcaucasia, from 1921. It was ceded to Russia in 1813 and finally incorporated in it in 1828; before the 1917 Revolution it formed the governments of (provinces) *Baku and Yelizavetpol. Up to the late Middle Ages this region was called Albania, Azerbaijan then comprising only the present Persian area. When the region was first annexed by Russia the Jewish population mainly consisted of Tat-speaking *Mountain Jews. Their main centers were the city of *Kuba and district as well as the villages of Miudji and Miudji-Aftaran in the government of Baku, and the village of Vartashen in the government of Yelizavetpol. The Jewish residents in Kuba and district numbered 5,492 in 1835, of whom 2,718 lived in the city itself, which had a separate Jewish quarter. In 1866 a Jewish traveler reported 952 Jewish households in Kuba, 145 in Miudji, and 190 in Vartashen, while a Russian traveler recorded that year 6,282 Jews in Kuba, 957 in Miudji, and 1,396 in Vartashen. The Jews of Azerbaijan generally engaged in agriculture, petty trade, and manual labor; on average, their economic position was poor. They also suffered from persecution by the local Muslim population, and were often the victims of violent attacks. The region was closed to residence for Jews from European Russia during the czarist regime (see *Pale of Settlement). With Baku's rapid growth as an oil-producing center, however, a considerable number of European Jews took an active part in developing the industry. The census of 1897 records 12,761 Jewish residents in Baku government and 2,031 in Yelizavetpol. The largest urban communities were in Kuba (6,662 Jewish residents) and Baku (2,341). A secular Jewish-Russian school was opened in Kuba in 1908.

During the civil war following the 1917 revolution and in subsequent years, many Jews in Azerbaijan left their villages, mainly for Baku, which also attracted Jews from European Russia. Miudji was completely deserted, and about 3,500 Jews left Kuba; Baku then became the most important Jewish center in Azerbaijan. After the establishment of the Soviet regime, all Jewish traditional schools were closed and government schools were opened for the Jewish population. By the end of the 1920s there was a Turkish-Jewish school in Vartashen and a school for Mountain Jews in Baku; a Jewish club was functioning in Kuba, and a group of Tat-speaking writers was active in Kuba and in Baku. Attempts were made to settle Jews on the land, and 250 Jewish families were occupied in agriculture by the end of 1927. The census of 1926 recorded 19,000 European Jews and 7,500 Mountain Jews in Azerbaijan, and that of 1959 showed 40,204 Jews in Azerbaijan (1.1% of the total population); of the 38,917 living in urban communities, 29,197 were settled in Baku and its environs; 8,357 declared Tat their mother tongue and 6,255 Yiddish. A religious congregation was reported to exist in Baku in 1955, and a congregation of Mountain Jews was active in Kuba in 1964, but the synagogue was then under threat of closure. In 1959 one Jew was serving on the Supreme Soviet of the Republic (out of 325 members).

[Yehuda Slutsky / Eliyahu Feldman]

C.I.S. Republic

In 1970 there were 41,288 Jews in the Azerbaijan S.S.R. and in 1989 30,800 (of whom 22,700 were Ashkenazi Jews living in Baku). In the wake of the continuing warfare between Azerbaijan and Armenia over Nagorno-Karabakh in 1989, 1,981 Jews (97.5%, or 1,933 of them, from Baku) emigrated. In 1990, 7,673 Jews emigrated to Israel from Azerbaijan and in 1991 5,968 (with 5,513 of them coming from Baku). Baku had a Jewish culture club, called "Alef." In 1992 Azerbaijani Jews began issuing the newspaper *Aziz* (an abbreviation of "Azerbaijan-Israel"). In deference to local nationalism, the newspaper published anti-Armenian articles. The government and the Popular Front of Azerbaijan publicly condemned antisemitism and the Jewish Agency was allowed to operate openly in Baku.

[Michael Beizer]

In June 1993, as a result of a coup, Geidar Aliev, a former top Communist Party official, became president. Aliev's relatively favorable stance vis-à-vis Iran resulted in an increased number of Iran-financed periodicals, including *Islamic World* and *Word of Truth*, with antisemitic and anti-Israel contents. In October 1993 the newspaper *And* launched a series of articles signed by a certain Eloglu (The Nation's Son), the first of which attributed the problems of Azerbaijan to the "Jewish mafia, Armenians, and the Russian Empire." Antisemitism, however, did not constitute a problem in the country.

There were an estimated 17,300 Jews in Azerbaijan at the end of 1993. The rate of emigration from Azerbaijan to Israel continued to be high, with an estimated 7,500 Jews remaining in 2003.

[Daniel Romanowski (2nd ed.)]

BIBLIOGRAPHY: Fischel, Islam, passim; idem, in: PAAJR, 22 (1953), 1–21; Lowenthal, in: HJ, 14 (1952), 61–62; J.J. Chorny, *Sefer ha-Massa'ot* (1884), 106–25, 263–4, 324–31; Benyamini, in: *Aḥdut*, 3 (1912), 14–15, 47–48; V.F. Miller, *Materialy dlya izucheniya yevreysko-tatarskogo yazyka* (1892), includes bibliography. **ADD. BIBLIOGRAPHY:** U. Schmelz and S. DellaPergola, in: AJYB, 95 (1995), 478; AJYB, 103 (2003); *Supplement to the Monthly Bulletin of Statistics*, 2 (1995); Institute of Jewish Affairs, *Antisemitism World Report 1994*, 137–38.

AẒERET (Heb. עֲצֶרֶת), word used in the Bible to convey "a general assembly" (Amos 5:21) or a "concluding celebration" (II Chron. 7:9). In the Torah, *aẓeret* refers to the final (seventh) day of *Passover (Deut. 16:8) and to the concluding celebration which takes place on the eighth day of Sukkot (Lev. 23:33ff.; Num. 29:35ff.). The Jewish religious calendar considers Sukkot as one seven-day festival, and *aẓeret* (see Feast of *Sukkot) as a separate celebration with a distinct ritual. In the Second Temple period, however, *aẓeret* was used exclusively to designate the third pilgrim festival, *Shavuot. Shavuot is closely related to Passover (Lev. 23:15ff.), and so rabbinic literature treated it as the *aẓeret*, the "concluding celebration," of that festival.

AZEVEDO (D'Azevedo), Portuguese Sephardi family whose members were found in N. Africa as *Marranos in the 16th century, and from the 17th century in Amsterdam, where they reverted to Judaism; a branch of the family moved to London. MELCHIOR (BELCHIOR) VAZ, born in Arzila (Morocco; 16th century), Marrano diplomat and sea captain, was appointed by the king of Navarre as an emissary to conclude a peace treaty with the ruler of Morocco in 1559. He commanded the corsair ships which attacked Spanish galleons returning from America, and established contact with Queen Elizabeth's minister Cecil. On his return from a visit to London, Azevedo brought a ship with a large cargo of Bibles and Hebrew works for Jews living in Morocco; the Portuguese ambassador in Paris was dispatched to England to protest against this traffic, which the Catholics regarded as harmful to Christianity. Azevedo was twice denounced to the Inquisition for practicing Judaism. FRANCISCO LOPES (alias Abraham Farrar; c. 1650) was the London agent of the *Spinoza family in Holland. HENRICO (c. 1661) was one of the first ambassadors of Holland to the dey of Algiers. The same position was held by LOUIS (c. 1675). DAVID SALOM (d. 1699), minister-resident of the dey of Algiers in Amsterdam; he concluded a commercial treaty between Holland and Algiers, and was on the building committee of the Great Synagogue of the Portuguese communities in Amsterdam. MOSES RAPHAEL SALOM (d. 1703), son of Louis, was a physician in Amsterdam. JOSEPH COHEN (d. 1705), of London, a notorious speculator, was a director of the Scottish East India Company, later suppressed.

BIBLIOGRAPHY: SIHM, France, 1 (1905), 177–221; Angleterre, 1 (1918), 27–40, 44–49; Portugal, 5 (1953), 50–54, 84–85; T.S. Williams, *Studies in Elizabethan Foreign Trade* (1959), 107–8; A. Baião, *Inquisição em Portugal* (1921), 183; D.H. de Castro, *Keur van Grafsteenen-Auswahl von Grabsteinen* (Dutch and Ger., 1883), 89–90, 97–98; J.S. da Silva Rosa, *Geschiedenis der portugesche Joden te Amsterdam* (1925), 100; Hirschberg, Afrikah, 1 (1965), 321; 2 (1965), 50.

[David Corcos]

AZEVEDO (Ferme), MOSES COHEN D' (1720–1784), English rabbi. Azevedo, who was born into a rabbinic family in Holland, immigrated to London, where he married in 1749 the daughter of haham Moses Gomes De *Mesquita. His appointment to the **bet din* in 1757 led to the resignation from the rabbinate of Isaac *Nieto; after a four-year interval Azevedo was appointed haham. On the public fast day of December 13, 1776, marking the revolt of the American colonies, he preached the sermon, which was published both in English and in Spanish.

BIBLIOGRAPHY: A.M. Hyamson, *Sephardim of England* (1951), 182–3; M. Gaster, *History of the Ancient Synagogue of the Spanish and Portuguese Jews* (1901), 131–41; Roth, Mag Bibl, 312, 324, 325.

[Cecil Roth]

AZHAROT, AZHARAH (Heb. אַזְהָרוֹת sing. אַזְהָרָה; "warning"), category of liturgical poems for the Feast of Weeks (Shavuot) in which are enumerated the 613 *Commandments. The term originates from the opening of the early *piyyut*, *"Azharah reshit le-ammekha nattata"* ("Thou gavest thy people a preliminary warning"); and also because the numerical value of the word *azharot* is 613. At first, the style of the *azharot* was simple and devoid of psalmodic embellishments, but with time they were infused with the spirit of *piyyut*. First mentioned by R. *Natronai Gaon, the *azharot* were already accepted in his day, even though there were some who, then and later, opposed them. One reason for this opposition was that the composers were *paytanim* and not halakhists.

Occasionally the poems dealt with subjects other than the 613 commandments, e.g., the number of Mishnayot, the 70 names of God, etc. Since no composer's name is found on the early *azharot* they are known as *azharot de-rabbanan* (*azharot* of the rabbis) or *azharot de-metivta kaddisha de-rabbanim de-Pumbedita* (the *azharot* of the holy yeshivah of the rabbis of Pumbedita). *Azharot* are known in the liturgy of Ereẓ Israel, Babylonia, Spain, Italy, Germany, Provence, and Romania (i.e., Byzantium), and have also been included in other liturgies. *Saadiah Gaon, two of whose *azharot* were printed in his *Siddur*, wrote in his introduction that he composed his *azharot* because his contemporaries were accustomed to such poems, in particular *"attah hinḥalta"* ("Thou hast bequeathed"), and also because the existing *azharot* did not mention all the 613 commandments and were repetitious and long-winded. Subsequent *azharot* were composed by the outstanding poets, including Joseph ibn Abitur, Solomon ibn *Gabirol, and Isaac b. Reuben *al-Bargeloni. In later generations, introductions to *azharot* were also composed; and, since the language of the *azharot* was often difficult and complicated, scholars wrote commentaries on them. *Azharot* were usually said at the *Shaḥarit* or at the *Musaf* Services, while among northern Sephardim they were also said at the *Minḥah* Service. Beside the *azharot* for the Feast of Weeks which include the 613 commandments, there are *azharot* for other times of the year, e.g., for the Sabbath before Sukkot, the Sabbath before Shavuot, the Great Sabbath (the Sabbath before Passover), and also Rosh Ha-Shanah, Ḥanukkah, Purim, and New Moon. These include sections pertaining to their particular season. In most Ashkenazi rites, *azharot* are not recited at all, even though they are printed in the festival prayer book. The Sephardim and Yemenites recite the *azharot* by Solomon ibn Gabirol – on the first day of Shavuot, the positive commandments, and on the second day, the negative commandments. Over 60 *azharot* are known.

BIBLIOGRAPHY: Gaguin, in: *Essays… J.H. Hertz* (1942), 45–51 (Heb.); Zunz, Lit Poesie, 21, 35, 127; Elbogen, Gottesdienst, 217–9, 558; Benjacob, Oẓar, 32, no. 635; Davidson, Oẓar, 4 (1933), 493, no. 3; Idelsohn, Liturgy, 42, 197.

[Abraham Meir Habermann]

AZIKRI, ELEAZAR BEN MOSES (sometimes mispronounced **Azkari**; 1533–1600), kabbalist, talmudist, preacher, and poet. He was born in Ereẓ Israel and studied under Joseph Sagis and Moses *Cordovero in Safed. In 1596 he was ordained by Jacob *Berab II. His mystical diary, which has survived in his own handwriting (New York, J.T.S.A., Ms. Adler 74; published in M. Pachter's *From Safed's Hidden Treasures*, Jerusalem, 1994, pp. 121–186), contains meditations, revelations, and dreams, jotted down in the course of mystical experience, in a brief and obscure manner, lacking all order and unity. It covers the period from 1564 until close to his death, and reveals the inner world of an ecstatic kabbalist, whose sole aim was repentance (*teshuvah*), self-purification, spiritual ascent, and communion (*devekut*) with God. In 1571 he divided his day: one-third to be devoted to writing, and two-thirds – to a quiet, if peculiar, meditation. During this time he would not even study, but would sit in awed silence, without moving, his phylacteries on him and his eyes incessantly "focused upon God." During the following years in which he continued to practice asceticism and spiritual solitude while adhering to this behavior, he advanced in the stages of *devekut*. At the same time he was very active as the founder and spiritual leader of two groups (*ḥavurot*) of mystics and ascetics, called "*ḥaverim makshivim*" ("the hearkening companions") and "*sukkat shalom*" ("The tabernacle of peace"). In 1575 he drew up a "deed of association" with the members of (apparently) the first group for the purpose of spiritual partnership and cooperation. The partners undertook "not to relinquish the Law of God," to refrain from all worldly activity, commerce, and work, and to devote all their time to the study of the Torah and the worship of God. In another deed which they (or perhaps the members of the second group) drew up in 1588, the following rules are specified: unity of the group, love of people, not to judge anyone and to respect everyone; to accept the law of the Torah without reservations, to study it with fervor and to study the Mishnah; to constantly concentrate their thoughts on God and the **Shekhinah* and to pray with zeal and awe. The members of both groups did not accept any public function and did not officiate as rabbis. They appeared in public only in order to exhort the people to repent. This was also Azikri's main, if not sole, purpose in his public activity which culminated in the authorship of his ethical-kabbalistic treatise *Sefer Ḥaredim* (Venice, 1601). This classic of ethical-kabbalistic literature, the composition of which was completed by Azikri in 1588, actually reflects the ethos and worldview of the two groups over which he presided. Thus it includes four of Azikri's poems which were recited by the members of the groups as love poems to God; the best known is the poem "*Yedid Nefesh*" ("Faithful friend"), called by him "prayer for union and the desire of love." This *piyyut* was accepted in all Jewish communities and is printed in the prayer book (Eng. tr. in JQR, 9 (1896/97), 290). Furthermore, the most important and influential part of *Sefer Ḥaredim*, the section called *Divrei Kibbushin*, is actually a compilation of chapters from *Milei De-Shemaya*, originally composed by Azikri as a collection of ethical-kabbalistic directives and rules of conduct toward God and fellow men for his personal use and the use of his companions in the two groups. In writing *Sefer Ḥaredim* Azikri probably saw the completion of his public activity and from 1578 until his death he retreated more and more into his seclusion and solitude with God. He only thought of means by which he would entrust to God his spirit and soul, and apparently in 1589 he drew up a "deed of association" with God, in the form of a legal document, the witnesses being Heaven and Earth. In it he totally subdued himself to God. In 1601 he died childless after a lifelong yearning for children (his two sons apparently died as young children at the beginning of 1573 or a little before that).

Azikri wrote:

(1) Comments on the Jerusalem Talmud; his commentary on tractate *Berakhot* was first printed together with the Zhitomir Jerusalem Talmud (1860); and since then in all editions (Bodleian Library, Ms. Mich. 199), and the commentary on *Beẓah* (New York, 1967) was completed in 1577.

(2) Commentary on the Babylonian Talmud. This was not printed, and only preliminary notes on certain subjects have survived. His comments on the tractate *Nedarim, Peri Megadim,* are in manuscript (Ms. Adler 74, fols. 28–58).

(3) A homiletic commentary on the Pentateuch (*ibid.*).

(4) Commentary on Lamentations (published under the title *Kol Bokhim* (Venice, 1589).

(5) A commentary, *Ahasuerus Scroll*, passages from which are found at the beginning of Ms. Adler 74.

(6) *Milei de-Shemaya* (*ibid.*; published and edited with introduction and notes by M. Pachter, Tel Aviv, 1991).

(7) *Sefer Ḥaredim* (Venice, 1601). This book had a wide circulation and was printed in over 27 editions. It was also abridged, and a commentary was added to it.

(8) Responsa (in responsa of Moses di Trani, 1 (1768), no. 235; Responsa of Joseph di Trani, 1 (1768), no. 17).

BIBLIOGRAPHY: S. Lieberman, in: *Sefer ha-Yovel... A. Marx* (1950), 304–13; M. Benayahu, in: *Sefer Yovel... Y. Baer* (1961), 262; J. Franzos (ed.), *Talmud Yerushalmi, Beẓah*, with commentary by R. Eleazar Azikri (1967), introd.; M. Pachter (ed.), *Milei de-Shemaya* (1991), intro.

[Mordechai Pachter (2nd ed.)]

AẒILUT (Heb. אֲצִילוּת), a short treatise schematizing the theories of the older Kabbalah, written in the style of a *baraita*. The significance and age of this small volume are matters of controversy. In various passages the author appears as Elijah b. Joseph, but further on, with reference to a Midrash on the name Elijah (Ex. R. 40), also as Jaareshiah b. Joseph, Zechariah b. Joseph, and Jeroham b. Joseph. According to A. *Jellinek (see bibliography) the reference is to the prophet Elijah who thus appears as the pseudepigraphical author of the book. Jellinek's opinion, adopted by D. *Neumark, was that it was written by Jacob *Nazir, to whom, according to old traditions, the prophet Elijah first disclosed the Kabbalah; in consequence, Jellinek dates it to the first half of the 12th century. The definite statement, "ben Joseph," in connection with the prophet Elijah, whose father is never mentioned by name, is quite inexplicable, as well as the whole of the style which nowhere gives the impression of a revelation from on high. It points rather to a certain person of that name. The factual author, Elijah b. Joseph, was manifestly fond of replacing his name by synonyms, as is often done by Abraham *Abulafia. Jellinek thought that he had found a quotation from the book in a **piyyut* by Jacob *Tam, but the relevant passage is already found in the *Heikhalot*.

The treatise contains general thoughts on esoteric doctrines, a great deal about *angelology and *demonology, as well as the teaching of the four worlds: *Aẓilut*, the world of divine emanation (*pleroma*); *Beri'ah*, the world of the throne and the seven palaces; *Yeẓirah*, the world of the divine chariot (*Merkabah) and the ten angel choirs; *Asiyyah*, the world of the lower angels and the good and evil spirits, which here, however, is not in any way identical with the terrestrial sensual world. Finally, in connection with I Chronicles 29:11, the system of the ten *Sefirot* conceived both as modes and instruments of divine activity is developed. An explanation of the relationship of the ten *Sefirot* to the four worlds is not given. Neumark (see bibliography) considered the book to be "the first classic of the Kabbalah" which supplied the pattern for the book **Bahir*. P. *Bloch (see bibliography) discerned the superficial nature of the book's schematization and dated it in the first half of the 13th century (as did Karppe). The work was not significant for the development of Kabbalah; it came into being most probably at the end of the 13th or the beginning of the 14th century. The linguistic usage and terminology of the work are certainly influenced by the *Zohar and even by its latest parts. From it, for instance, come the use of אוליפנא (*olifna*) in the sense of "we learn" instead of "we teach," the names of the seven palaces of the world of creation, and the description of the four worlds which corresponds exactly with that of the *Ra'aya Meheimna* (Zohar, 2, 43). Noteworthy, in connection with the corresponding theme in the Zohar, is also the teaching that "Darkness," the veiled power of the demonic which punishes evildoers, is none other than the rudiment of the destroyed primeval worlds left by the withdrawal of the divine light. The angelology, and especially the demonology of the book also point decisively to the period around 1300.

The stress laid here on the secrecy of the teaching is no proof of the early date of the book but accords with the literary style of the older Kabbalah well into the 14th century.

The work *Aẓilut* does not appear in kabbalistic literature and is nowhere quoted; nor is any manuscript of it now in existence. Abraham, son of *Elijah b. Solomon Zalman, the Gaon of Vilna, first published it in 1802 from a manuscript (now lost; at the end of the edition of the *Aggadat Bereshit*). Isaac Chower wrote a commentary to it, entitled *Ginzei Meromim*, which was published by N.H. Herzog in *Yalkut ha-Ro'im* (1885, p. 11–39). The text was published by Jellinek in his *Auswahl kabbalistischer Mystik* (1853).

BIBLIOGRAPHY: A. Jellinek, *Auswahl kabbalistischer Mystik* (1853), 1–9 (Germ. sec.), 1–8 (Heb. sec.); P. Bloch, *Geschichte der Entwickelung der Kabbalah und der juedischen Religionsphilosophie* (1894), 45; S. Karppe, *Etude sur les Origines et la Nature du Zohar* (1901), 251–5; D. Neumark, *Geschichte der juedischen Philosophie des Mittelalters*, 1 (1907), 195–7; idem, *Toledot ha-Filosofyah be-Yisrael*, 1 (1921), 179–81, 260f.

[Gershom Scholem]

°**AZIZ**, king of Emesa in Syria (d. 54 C.E.). Aziz succeeded Sampigermos, who had diplomatic and family relationships with *Agrippa I, king of Judea. These ties were strengthened when Aziz married Drusilla, Agrippa II's sister, and even agreed to undergo circumcision. The marriage did not last long, for *Felix, the procurator of Judea, was infatuated with her and married her. Aziz died in the first year of Nero's reign and was succeeded by his brother Soemis.

BIBLIOGRAPHY: Jos., Ant., 18:135; 19:338; 20:139ff., 158; J. Marquardt, *Roemische Staatsverwaltung*, 1 (1881), 403–4; Schuerer, Gesch 1 (1904⁴), 537, n. 2, 573, 591.

[Lea Roth]

AZMON (Heb. עַצְמוֹן), a point on the southern boundary of Ereẓ Israel between Hazar-Addar and the Brook of Egypt (Wadi al-ʿArīsh; Num. 34:4–5; cf. Josh. 15:4). In the *Targumim* it is called קֵיסָם or קְסָם. *Abel has identified it with Ayn al-Quṣayma but exploration of the Kadesh Oasis has suggested a height nearer Be'erotayim (Bīr (Biʿr) Bīrayn). Azmon is mentioned by Eusebius (Onom. 14:14) and also appears on the Madaba Map, south of Elusa. Azmon is also the name of a mountain near Sepphoris to which the Jewish rebels fled at the approach of *Cestius Gallus and his army during the Jewish War in 66 C.E. (Jos., Wars, 2:511). Mt. Azmon (Arab: Jebel al-Daydaba) is 1,798 ft. (548 m.) high, composed of dolomitic and chalky rock. The name Azmon was erroneously applied to Mt. Meron.

BIBLIOGRAPHY: Abel, Geog, 1 (1933), 79, 306; 2 (1938), 47; Avi-Yonah, *Madaba Map* (1954), 100; Avi Yonah, Geog, 135; Aharoni, Land, 63, 65.

[Michael Avi-Yonah]

AZNOTH-TABOR (Heb. אַזְנוֹת תָּבוֹר), place on the southern boundary of the tribe of Naphtali (Josh. 19:34). Its suggested identification is with Khirbat Umm-Jubayl, north of Mt. Tabor, where potsherds of the Israelite period have been found.

BIBLIOGRAPHY: Aharoni, Land, 239; EM, s.v.; A. Saarisalo, *Boundary between Issachar and Naphtali* (1927), 127; Alt, in: PJB, 23 (1927), 42. **ADD. BIBLIOGRAPHY:** R. Frankel, in: ABD, 1:540.

[Michael Avi-Yonah]

AZOR (Heb. אָזוֹר), a place southeast of Tel Aviv-Jaffa on the road to Jerusalem.

Ancient Period

Azor is not mentioned in the masoretic text of the Bible but the Septuagint adds the name to the list of cities in Danite territory together with Jehud, *Bene-Berak, and *Gath-Rimon (Josh. 19:45). It also appears in the Annals of Sennacherib as one of the cities he conquered on his march south against Egypt together with Beth-Dagon, Jaffa, and Bene-Berak. The name has been preserved at Yāzūr where remains from the Canaanite and Israelite periods have been discovered.

A collective burial tomb from the Late Chalcolithic period (c. 3500–3100 B.C.E.) was accidentally discovered at Azor in 1957. The tomb consisted of an egg-shaped chamber 36 ft. (11 m.) long and 26 ft. (8 m.) wide cut deeply into the hard sandstone layers; access was through a circular shaft on the side. Inside, clay ossuaries had been deposited containing the desiccated bones of the dead in a secondary type of burial. The Azor *ossuaries belong to a culture remains of which were found at Teleilat Ghassl, in the Jordan Valley, and at Beer-Sheba.

Four groups of ossuaries were distinguished: (1) simple chests; (2) jar-shaped ossuaries, with rounded tops and openings on the shoulders; (3) clay chests in the shape of animals (sheep or dogs) or monsters; (4) house-shaped receptacles, the most prevalent type. The normal type of this group is a box-like clay chest, approximately 2 ft. (60 cm.) long, 1 ft. (30 cm.) wide, and 2 ft. (50 cm.) high, with a rounded top and projecting front and back walls at each end. A square opening in the upper part of the facade, sometimes closed by a door, served to introduce the skull. Above this entrance is often found a schematic human or owl-like figure, which could have had some prophylactic purpose. Some of the ossuaries resemble models of houses, with gabled roofs, walls pierced by windows, and imitations of protruding wooden beams used in a decorative way. Some of the "houses" are mounted on an imitation of piles. The painted ornamentation on the walls and roofs utilizes motifs (palms, lattices) which recall vegetal materials used in buildings. In the Crusader period Richard Coeur-de-Lion built at Azor (Yāzūr) a small fort, Casal des Plains (1191), which served as a meeting place with Muslim representatives. The remains of this tower are still visible inside the old village.

[Jean Perrot]

Modern Period

Modern Azor is a small town 3 mi. (5 km.) southeast of Tel Aviv. Before 1948 this was an Arab village (Yāzūr, يازور) which enjoyed prosperity thanks to Tel Aviv's growth, but during the 1936–39 riots, Arabs in Yāzūr repeatedly attacked adjoining *Mikveh Israel as well as traffic on the highway which passes through it to Jerusalem and the South. In the 1948 War of Independence, the highway was blocked by Arabs who killed a detachment of seven Jews (who were commemorated in the neighboring moshav, Mishmar ha-Shivah, "Guard of the Seven," founded in 1949). In the ensuing battles the Arabs fled, and after the end of 1949 the place was settled by Jewish immigrants. In 1951 Azor received municipal council status, forming part of the Tel Aviv conurbation, whose largest industrial zone, Ḥolon-Azor, bordered on it. The town's area was 1.1 sq. mi. (2.9 sq. km.). By 1968 its population had reached 5,100 and in 2002 it was 9,670.

[Efraim Orni / Shaked Gilboa (2nd ed.)]

BIBLIOGRAPHY: ANCIENT PERIOD: Aharoni, Land, index; Abel, Geog, 2 (1938), 258; Perrot, in: *Attiqot*, 3 (1961), 1–83. **ADD. BIBLIOGRAPHY:** S.S. Ahituv, *Joshua* (1995), 322.

AZORES, archipelago in the N. Atlantic; Portuguese possession. *New Christians from Portugal presumably settled in the Azores in the 16th and 17th centuries, but there is no consistent record of them. The first known settlement of Jews in the islands began in 1818 with the arrival of five merchants from Morocco. By 1848 the Jews in the Azores numbered 250; several small communities had been established, the most important being in Ponta Delgada (founded in 1836) where there were 150 Jews. Among the founders were several members of the *Bensaude family, whose descendants became influential in international commerce, banking, and philanthropy. The number of Jews in the islands has dwindled steadily in recent years.

Bibliography: Amzalak, in: *Revista de Estudios Hebraícos*, 1 (1928), 239–40. **ADD. BIBLIOGRAPHY:** I. Da R. Pereira, in: *Arquipélago* 1 (1979), 181–201; 2 (1980), 143–87; 3 (1981), 167–85; A.M. Mendes, in: *Boletim* (Instituto Histórico da Ilha Terceira), 40 (1982), 673–92.

AZRIELI, DAVID (1922–), architect, property developer, philanthropist. Azrieli was born in Makow, Poland. In 1939 he escaped the Nazi invasion of Poland, journeying east into Central Asia before arriving in British Mandate Palestine. Azrieli began architectural studies at the Technion in Haifa but left the program to fight in Israel's 1948 War of Independence.

In 1954 he moved to Montreal. Encouraged by Canada's postwar construction boom, in 1958 Azrieli built four duplexes in suburban Montreal. Thus began what grew into a major development company, Canpro Investments, with commercial holdings across North America and Israel. Azrieli revolutionized shopping in Israel by building Israel's first North American-style mall and transformed urban skylines with state-of-the-art skyscrapers, including Tel Aviv's Azrieli Center and a commercial development in *Modi'in, a planned community between Tel Aviv and Jerusalem.

At 73 Azrieli returned to university, earning a master's degree in architecture from Ottawa's Carlton University. Azrieli extended his philanthropic support to architectural and Jewish studies in North America and Israel. Concordia University, Carlton University, Yeshiva University, the Technion, and Tel Aviv University have all benefited from Azrieli's generosity. He was honored with Israel's Jubilee Award and the Order of Canada, the highest award Canada can bestow upon a citizen.

BIBLIOGRAPHY: D. Azrieli, *One Step Ahead* (2001).

[Harold Troper (2nd ed.)]

AZRIEL OF GERONA (early 13th century), one of the outstanding members of the kabbalist center in Gerona, Spain. Azriel is not to be confused with his older contemporary *Ezra b. Solomon, also of Gerona; this mistake has repeatedly been made from the 14th century onward. *Graetz's opinion, that as far as the history of Kabbalah is concerned the two are to be regarded as one, has lost its validity since the works of both authors have been more closely studied. No details of his life are known. In a letter to Gerona that has been preserved, his teacher, *Isaac the Blind, seems to have opposed his open propagation of kabbalistic doctrines in wider circles (*Sefer Bialik* (1934), 143–8). The poet Meshullam Dapiera of Gerona in various poems hailed him as a leader of kabbalists in Gerona and as his teacher. An Oxford manuscript found by S. Sachs containing his alleged discussions with philosophic opponents of the Kabbalah is the plagiarization of a genuine Azriel manuscript by an anonymous author of a century later, who prefixed it with his own autobiography.

The clear separation of the works of Ezra from those of Azriel is largely the achievement of I. *Tishby. Azriel's works have a characteristic style and a distinctive terminology. All, without exception, deal with kabbalistic subjects. They include (1) *Sha'ar ha-Sho'el* ("The Gate of the Enquirer"), an explanation of the doctrine of the ten *Sefirot* ("Divine Emanations") in question and answer form, with the addition of a sort of commentary by the author himself. It was first printed in Berlin as an introduction to a book by Meir ibn *Gabbai, *Derekh Emunah*, "The Way of Belief" (1850); (2) commentary on the *Sefer *Yeẓirah*, printed in the editions of this book but ascribed to *Naḥmanides; (3) a commentary to the talmudic *aggadot*, a critical edition of which was published by Tishby in Jerusalem in 1943. This commentary represents a revision and, partly, an important expansion of the commentary of Ezra b. Solomon, particularly clarifying the differences from the version of his older colleague; (4) a commentary on the liturgy; actually a collection of instructions for mystical meditations on the most important prayers; it generally appears under the name of Ezra in the extant manuscripts. Large sections are quoted under Azriel's name in the prayer book of Naphtali Hirz Treves (Thiengen, 1560); (5) a long letter sent by Azriel from Gerona to Burgos in Spain, dealing with kabbalistic problems. In some manuscripts, this letter is wrongly ascribed to *Jacob b. Jacob ha-Kohen of Soria; it was published by Scholem in *Madda'ei ha-Yahadut*, 2 (1927), 233–40; (6) a number of shorter treatises, the most important of which is a large section of a partly-preserved work, *Derekh ha-Emunah ve-Derekh ha-Kefirah* ("The Way of Belief and the Way of Heresy"), as well as essays on the mysticism of prayer (published by Scholem in *Studies in Memory of A. Gulak and S. Klein*, (1942), 201–22), as well as the yet unpublished treatise on the mystical meaning of sacrifice, *Sod ha-Korban*.

Azriel is one of the most profound speculative thinkers in kabbalistic mysticism. His work most clearly reflects the process whereby Neoplatonic thought penetrated into the original kabbalistic tradition, as it reached Provence in the *Sefer ha-*Bahir*. He was acquainted with various sources of Neoplatonic literature, from which he quotes many passages directly. It is as yet impossible to say how he became acquainted with concepts belonging to the philosophy of Solomon ibn *Gabirol and the Christian Neoplatonic thinker John Scotus Erigena; but, somehow, Azriel must have come into contact with their way of thinking. Most significantly, the status and importance of the will of God as the highest potency of the deity, surpassing all other attributes, closely associated with God and yet not identical with Him, corresponds to the doctrine of Gabirol. Other points such as the coincidence of opposites in the divine unity, which plays a special role in Azriel's work, appear to come from the Christian Neoplatonic tradition. Azriel particularly stresses the disparity of the Neoplatonic idea of God, which may be formulated only in negatives, and that of the biblical God, about whom positive assertions may be made and to whom attributes may be ascribed. The former is *Ein-Sof*, the Infinite; the other is represented by the world of the *Sefirot*, which in various emanations reveals the creative movement of the divine unity. The logic, by which Azriel established the need for the assumption that the existence of the *Sefirot* is an emanation of divine power, is entirely Neoplatonic. Yet, in contrast with the doctrine of Plotinus, these emanations are processes taking place within the deity, and not extra-divine steps intermediate between God and the visible creation. Rather, the process takes its course in God Himself, namely between His hidden being, about which nothing positive can actually be said, and His appearance as Creator to which the Bible is testimony. In probing the mysteries of this world of the *Sefirot*, Azriel displays great daring. The same boldness is exhibited in those theosophical speculations which he carries into the talmudic *aggadah*. The Kabbalah of Azriel knows nothing of a true creation from nothingness although he uses this formula emphatically. However, he changes its meaning entirely: the "nothingness" out of which everything was created is here (as with Erigena) only a symbolic designation of the Divine Being, which surpasses all that is comprehensible to man, or of the Divine Will, which in itself has no beginning.

BIBLIOGRAPHY: I. Tishby, in: *Zion*, 9 (1944), 178–85; idem, in: *Sinai*, 16 (1945), 159–78; idem, in: *Minḥah li-Yhudah (Zlotnick)* (1950, jubilee volume… J.L. Zlotnik), 170–4; G. Scholem, *Ursprung und Anfaenge der Kabbala* (1962), ch. 4.

[Gershom Scholem]

AZ ROV NISSIM (Heb. אָז רוֹב נִסִּים; "Then many miracles"), alphabetical acrostic by the early *paytan* *Yannai (sixth century). Its theme is the events which, according to the Midrash, took place on the night of Passover (cf. Num. R. 20:12, Tanḥ. B., Num. 69). Since the 13th century it has been included as the first of the hymns and folk songs in the final section of the Passover *Haggadah*. The *piyyut* consists of seven stanzas, each concluding with the refrain "and it came to pass at midnight" (Ex. 12:29). The first six are of three lines each; the last verse, of four lines, is a prayer for the advent of the messianic age. The song formed part of the *kerovah* prayer *Onei Pitrei Raḥamatayim*, found in the Western (Ashkenazi) rite for the Sabbath before Passover. *Az Rov Nissim* passed also into the Eastern (Polish) rite.

BIBLIOGRAPHY: Davidson, Oẓar, 1 (1924), 102, no. 2175; Baer S., Seder, 705ff.; M. Zulay, *Piyyutei Yannai* (1938), 92; D. Goldschmidt (ed.), *Haggadah* (1960), 96, 106–7. **ADD. BIBLIOGRAPHY:** Tz.M. Rabinovits, *Maḥzor Piyyutei Rabbi Yanai la-Torah ve-la-Mo'adim* (1985); Sh. Spiegel, *Avot ha-Piyyut* (1996); N.M. Bronznick, *Piyyutei Yanai* (2000).

[*Encyclopaedia Hebraica*]

AZUBIB, Algerian rabbinical family prominent in the 17th and 18th centuries.

JOSEPH BEN NEHORAI AZUBIB was in Alexandria in 1665. The following year he wrote to Moses Tardiola, an emissary from Jerusalem in Tripoli, informing him of the appearance of *Shabbetai Ẓevi and giving him important information about *Nathan of Gaza. SAADIAH BEN NEHORAI (late 17th–early 18th centuries), younger brother of Joseph, was the head of the Algerian community during a period of exceptional economic hardship and stern decrees on the part of the local authorities, among them an order for the destruction of all the city's synagogues (1706). Only the intervention of "leading courtiers" brought about the repeal of this decree. Saadiah was author of *Tokhaḥat Musar* (Leghorn, 1871), a commentary on Proverbs, and of *Limmudei Adonai*, an unpublished commentary on Psalms (Mss. Ginsburg, no. 26, Moscow). His novellae on the Talmud are referred to by Judah Ayyash in *Leḥem Yehudah* (1745). Saadiah was among those who banned the books of Nehemiah *Ḥayon, the follower of Shabbetai Ẓevi. A copy of the ban, with his name at the head of the Algerian signatories, is published in the *Milḥamah la-Adonai* of Moses *Ḥagiz (Amsterdam, 1714, 51b). NEHORAI BEN SAADIAH (d. c. 1785), nephew of the brothers, compiled a short commentary on an anthology of *piyyutim* according to the Algerian rite (Leghorn, 1793), and *Purim Tammuz shel Algir* (1775), thanksgiving prayers to commemorate the departure of the Spanish Army from Algiers. JOSEPH BEN NEHORAI (1740?–1794), disciple of his father, and of Judah Ayyash. He was appointed assistant to his father in the rabbinate and their names appear together with those of other Algerian rabbis on commendations to the *Matteh Yehudah* (1783) of Judah Ayyash and the *Zera Ya'akov* (1784) of Jacob b. Na'im. Joseph succeeded his father in 1784. A most erudite scholar and an influential speaker, he had many disciples. He published *Yamim Aḥadim* (Leghorn, 1794), sermons on Sabbaths and festivals, and his talmudic novellae are quoted by Abraham Bushʿara in *Berit Avraham* (1791). He died at Blida.

BIBLIOGRAPHY: I. Bloch, *Inscriptions tumulaires* (1881), 66–68, 83–85; Davidson, Oẓar, 4 (1933), 452; Scholem, Shabbetai Ẓevi, 1 (1957), 163, n. 1,230, n. 1,263; idem, in: *Zion*, 6 (1940/41), 85–87; 19 (1953/54), 16, n. 53; Hirschberg, Afikah, 2 (1965), 53, 187.

AZUBY, ABRAHAM (1738–1805), first paid minister (rabbi-*ḥazzan*) of K.K. Beth Elohim Congregation in Charleston, South Carolina. Born in Amsterdam, Azuby went to Charleston in 1784 with a knowledge of Hebrew and synagogal experience in the Sephardi rite as practiced in the Dutch city, which was also the practice at Beth Elohim. He was engaged in 1785 to succeed Abraham *Alexander, Sr.

BIBLIOGRAPHY: B.A. Elzas, *The Jews of South Carolina* (1905), passim; C. Reznikoff and U.Z. Engelman, *The Jews of Charleston* (1950), 113, 245f., 284. **ADD. BIBLIOGRAPHY:** J.W. Hagy, *This Happy Land: The Jews of Colonial and Antebellum Charleston* (1993), 68.

[Thomas J. Tobias]

AZULAI, Italian family of makers of majolica; active from the early 16th to the early 18th centuries. The Azulais were of Spanish origin. Together with the *Cohen family, the Azulai family was noteworthy for having produced most of the majolica *seder* dishes that have come down from Renaissance Italy. The first name recorded is that of Jacob Azulai, who worked in Padua. His *seder* dish, made in 1532, was formerly in the Jewish Museum in Vienna, but is no longer in existence and is known from photographs. Isaac, who lived in Faenza, was another 16th-century member of the family. Two other members of the family, named Jacob, lived in Pesaro. There is in existence a *seder* dish by Jacob Azulai II dated 1652 and another by Jacob Azulai III dated 1732.

AZULAI, family of scholars and kabbalists of Castilian origin which settled in Fez, Hebron, and Jerusalem after the expulsion from Spain.

ABRAHAM BEN MORDECAI *AZULAI (1570–1643), the kabbalist, is the first of the family whose works are known. His son, Isaac (17th century), born in Hebron, was also a kabbalist and achieved a reputation as a wonder-worker. There is extant a manuscript pamphlet by him in which each of the letters of the books of Ecclesiastes and Ruth is turned into a word. It was written in 1652 and echoes the controversy over the Hebron rabbinate which took place at that time. Ḥayyim Joseph David Azulai mentions his *Zera Yiẓḥak*, which is no longer extant. He also wrote *Segullot Neḥmadot* (of which fragments are in the Benayahu collection). He was the teacher of Israel Ze'evi, his sister's son, later rabbi of Hebron. He died in Constantinople while on a visit there as an emissary. His son Isaiah, a disciple of Hezekiah da Silva, died in Jerusalem in 1732. Isaac Zerahiah ben Isaiah (1702–65), grandson of Isaac b. Abraham, born in Jerusalem, was a halakhist, kabbalist, and rabbinic emissary. He was a member of the *bet ha-midrash*, Bet Ya'akov; headed the Gedulat Mordecai yeshivah; was a member of the *bet din* of Eliezer Nahum, and later of that of Meyouhas b. Samuel Meyouhas. In 1741, when the Jerusalem community was heavily burdened by debt, he was chosen, together with Abraham Asher, to visit Turkey and Europe on its behalf. While in Constantinople he became ill and returned to Jerusalem. It was at that time that the name Raphael was added to his original names. In 1758 he was one of the scholars in the yeshivah of Jacob Pereira. He was considered one of the seven greatest scholars in Jerusalem and, together with the others, signed the communal *takkanot* between 1749 and 1762. His son, the famous scholar Ḥayyim Joseph David *Azulai, published four of his father's responsa and refers to his writings in his books.

RAPHAEL ISAIAH AZULAI (1743–1826), the son of Ḥayyim Joseph David Azulai, was a talmudist and emissary. He accompanied his father on his mission to Constantinople in 1764. In 1774 he visited Smyrna, possibly as an emissary for Ereẓ Israel, and three years later was in Leghorn. In 1782 he was again in Italy, this time as an emissary for Tiberias. Apparently, he also visited Germany. After completing his assignment as an emissary to Amsterdam in 1783, he stayed on there until 1787, engaging in the book trade. From 1788 until

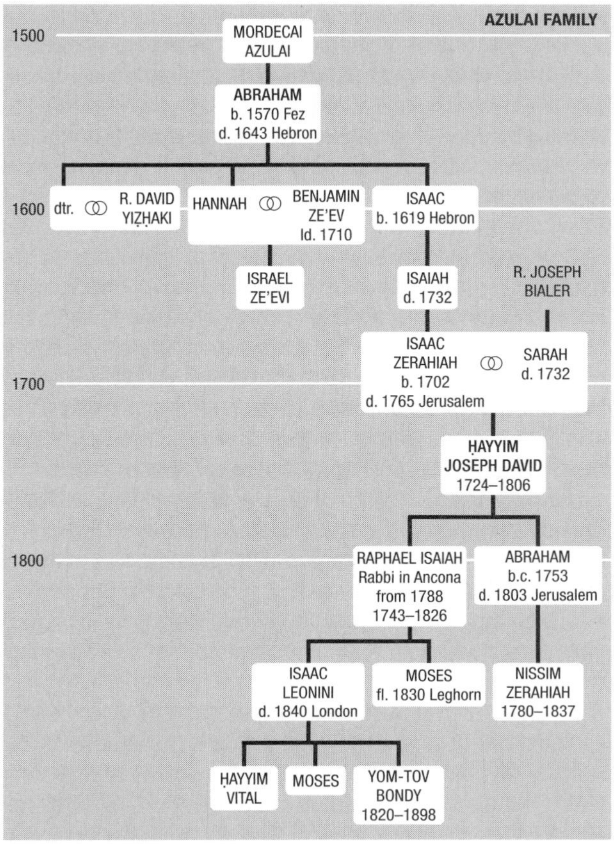

his death he served as rabbi of Ancona. His son Moses (19th century) published his responsa, *Imrei No'am*, under the title *Tiferet Moshe* at the end of *Zikhron Moshe,* pt. 1 (Leghorn, 1830). Raphael Isaiah's responsa and novellae are quoted in the works of his father.

ABRAHAM (before 1753–?1803), another son of Ḥayyim Joseph David Azulai, was a talmudist and emissary. Born in Jerusalem, he accompanied his father to Egypt (1765–69), and returned with him to Hebron. In 1778 he was one of the seven community leaders of Hebron. From 1782 to 1795 he was in Europe and North Africa as an emissary. An account of his mission to Poland in 1791 is extant (Ms., J.T.S.A., New York). He died in Jerusalem.

Abraham's son, NISSIM (before 1780–1837), was born in Jerusalem. He was in Leghorn in 1803, and the following year is mentioned as one of the scholars of Jerusalem. Nissim traveled to Turkey and was appointed head of the *bet din* of Magnesia, near Smyrna. He was in Smyrna in 1811 and appears also to have been in Baghdad. He visited Safed in 1831 and there published the prayer book according to the Sephardi rite *Sefat Emet*, with an introduction, commentary, and regulations. He visited Damascus in 1835 and the following year published his *Shulḥan ha-Tahor* in Safed. Nissim was a victim of the great Safed earthquake of 1837.

BIBLIOGRAPHY: Yaari, Sheluḥei, index; M. Benayahu, *Rabbi Ḥ.Y.D. Azulai* (1959); idem, in: *Aresheth*, 4 (1966), 273 ff., 281 ff.; Brilling, in: M. Benayahu (ed.), *Sefer ha-Ḥida* (1959), 141–77.

AZULAI, ABRAHAM BEN ISRAEL (c. 1660–c. 1741), kabbalist. Azulai was born in Marrakesh. He was related to R. Abraham b. Mordecai *Azulai, and was the disciple of R. Isaac de-Levayah and a friend of R. Solomon Amar II and R. Abraham ibn Musa. He lived for some time in Tetuan and in 1724 he was in Meknès, Morocco. R. Ḥayyim b. *Attar knew him and praised his erudition in Kabbalah. He told Ḥ.J.D. *Azulai that Abraham b. Israel used to write amulets for sick people, but without writing any of the names of God on them. There were many legends about him in Morocco. He wrote a commentary on the Zohar, extracts from which are quoted by his disciple R. Solomon *Buzaglo in *Mikdash Melekh.* Azulai also wrote annotations and corrections to R. Ḥayyim *Vital's *Oẓerot Ḥayyim* (Leghorn, 1854). His responsa are scattered in various manuscripts; one of them was published in the collection of responsa *Mishpat u-Ẓedakah be-Ya'akov*, by R. Jacob b. Ẓur (paragraph 161). His most notable disciples were R. Jacob Pinto and R. Isaiah ha-Kohen.

BIBLIOGRAPHY: Azulai, s.v. *Avraham Azulai*; J. Ben-Naim, *Malkhei Rabbanan* (1931), 11a.

AZULAI, ABRAHAM BEN MORDECAI (c. 1570–1643), kabbalist. Azulai, who was born in Fez, first mastered the study of the Talmud and philosophic literature and then Kabbalah. He did not agree with the interpretations of the Zohar which his teachers provided, and he did not really enter this subject until he obtained Moses *Cordovero's *Pardes Rimmonim.* Thereafter, he was preoccupied with the question of the relation between Kabbalah and philosophy, until he forsook philosophy and dedicated himself entirely to Kabbalah. He decided to go to the center of kabbalism in Ereẓ Israel, but did not realize his wish until after he had lost all his wealth during the anti-Jewish persecutions in Morocco (1610–13). He drifted between Hebron, Jerusalem, and Gaza during the epidemic of 1619, and finally settled in Hebron where kabbalists from Safed had congregated and where he found all the books of Cordovero and the majority of Isaac *Luria's works in Ḥayyim *Vital's version. R. Eliezer b. Arḥa became his friend there.

Azulai's numerous writings were not published during his lifetime. Those books he had written while still in Fez, were lost at sea. He wrote three treatises on the Zohar: (1) *Or ha-Levanah* ("The Light of the Moon"), annotations and textual corrections based sometimes on conjecture and sometimes on early manuscripts (1899); (2) *Or ha-Ḥammah* ("The Light of the Sun"), a complete commentary on the Zohar (completed 1619 and published 1896–98), based mainly on Cordovero's book and also on Luria's commentary, and on a commentary on the Zohar by Ḥayyim Vital written before he knew Luria, and marginal notes on the Zohar by an unknown author. Azulai abbreviated Cordovero's phraseology; occasionally he quoted statements by Cordovero and added his own interpretations. The result is a comprehensive and important commentary to the Zohar; (3) *Or ha-Ganuz* ("The Hidden Light"), an explanation of the profound expressions in the Zohar, which was never published. To these three works he gave the all-inclusive title *Kiryat Arba*, alluding to the four above-mentioned commentators and the city of Hebron. In 1622, Azulai abridged R. Abraham *Galante's (Cordovero's disciple) commentary on the Zohar, *Yare'aḥ Yakar,* under the title *Zoharei Ḥammah* (Gen., 1655; Ex., 1882). His book *Ḥesed le-Avraham* (Amsterdam, 1685) is devoted to a thorough analysis of the principles of the Kabbalah in the spirit of Cordovero with his own and Luria's additions, as well as to a refutation of the arguments of the philosophers.

Azulai adhered to Lurianic kabbalism and believed that it superseded Cordovero's system. He reedited the Lurianic *Sefer ha-Kavvanot* ("The Book of Intentions") and wrote two books based on it: *Kenaf Renanim* and *Ma'aseh Ḥoshev* (1621/2; in Mss.). He also wrote a commentary on the Bible in a somewhat mystical style, entitled *Ba'alei Berit Avraham* (1873), and a commentary on the Mishnah, *Ahavah be-Ta'anugim*, in manuscripts. The part on *Avot* was printed in Jerusalem, 1910.

BIBLIOGRAPHY: G. Scholem, *Kitvei Yad ba-Kabbalah* (1930), 144; M. Benayahu (ed.), *Aggadot Zacut* (1955), 151–2; M. Benayahu, *Rabbi Ḥ.J.D. Azulai*, (Heb, 1959), 275–7.

AZULAI, ḤAYYIM JOSEPH DAVID (known by his Hebrew acronym **Ḥida, Ḥayyim Yoseph David Azulai**; 1724–1806), halakhist, kabbalist, emissary, and bibliographer. Azulai was born in Jerusalem; he was descended on his father's side from a prominent family of rabbis and kabbalists from Spain while his mother was a daughter of Joseph Bialer who had gone to Ereẓ Israel with *Judah Ḥasid in 1770. He studied under some of the outstanding Jewish scholars of his age including Jonah *Navon, Isaac ha-Kohen *Rapoport, and Ḥayyim ibn *Attar. Azulai attained early eminence in Jewish studies and was regarded by the Jewry of the Ottoman Empire and of Italy as the leading scholar of his generation. He was highly esteemed, too, by the Jews of Germany, especially after the publication of his works.

Possessed of great intellectual powers and many-faceted talents, he combined a religious and mystical ardor with an insatiable intellectual curiosity. Added to these were critical ability, a facile pen, and a boundless capacity for work. He spent most of his active years traveling abroad as an emissary of the communities of Ereẓ Israel for the collection of funds for the upkeep of the academies and scholars. Between 1753 and 1758 he visited Italy, Germany, Holland, France, and England as *shali'aḥ* of the Hebron Yeshivah. During these travels he refused the call to become *ḥakham* of the Sephardim in Amsterdam. On his return to Jerusalem, where he remained for some seven years, he served as *dayyan* and engaged in communal activities. He also became a member of Shalom *Sharabi's esoteric group of kabbalists, Ahavat Shalom. He left Ereẓ Israel again in 1764, having been delegated to travel to Constantinople to intercede on behalf of the scholars in their disputes with the communal leaders, but learning *en route* that the communal leaders had triumphed in the dispute and of the consequent futility of his proceeding on his mission, he remained in Cairo where he served briefly as rabbi. Azulai returned in 1769 and settled in Hebron where he was held in high esteem. In 1772 he again went abroad as the emissary of Hebron, this time devoting most of his efforts to Italy where, on his earlier visit, he had gained many admirers. Having sent a large sum of money to Hebron which relieved the financial difficulties of its community, he ended his mission in 1778 in Leghorn, where he spent the rest of his life.

During his highly successful missions, Azulai earned a great reputation for his involvement in communal activities. Once, when he was taken to the court of Versailles, he attracted royal attention through his striking appearance. At Leghorn, for his annual discourse, the streets were crowded with admirers who wished to catch a glimpse of his person. Azulai devoted himself, however, also to writing, study, and research. He exchanged views with Jewish as well as non-Jewish scholars and investigated scholarly literature. Everywhere he went he visited libraries, both private and public, and noted down their rarities, both in early printed books and also in manuscripts, almost as Moritz *Steinschneider, the father of Jewish scientific bibliography, was to do in the following century.

In his literary diary *Ma'agal Tov* (Good Path) which covers the years 1753–78, with some later jottings (full ed. by A. Freimann, 1921–34), he entered every idea and novel thought in the field of Jewish scholarship, history, and folklore which occurred to him on his travels. This diary is an invaluable source of information regarding not only his own experiences but also the circumstances, personalities, and bibliographical treasures of the places which Azulai visited, in particular in Italy, Holland, and France. From this diary he later drew the material for his numerous works on a variety of subjects to which he devoted the latter part of his life. His chief claims to fame as a halakhist rest on his glosses to the Shulḥan Arukh, contained in his *Birkei Yosef* (1774), *Maḥazik Berakhah* (1785), and *Shiyyurei Berakhah* (1771–76), which complemented Ḥayyim *Benveniste's *Keneset ha-Gedolah* with citations from later halakhic works and from numerous manuscripts. In his books *Va'ad la-Ḥakhamim* (1796) and *Shem ha-Gedolim* (1, 1774; 2, 1786; scholarly ed., 1853), Azulai followed in the footsteps of Shabbetai *Bass, adding 1,300 bibliographical references to the approximately 2,200 already contained in the *Siftei Yeshenim*.

Azulai seems to have been the first Hebrew writer to be interested in collecting Jewish folk-stories in a systematic way. In his *Zikhron Ma'asiyyot ve-Nissim* he listed hundreds of these; in most cases he wrote down only a detail or two, to identify them, whereas less famous stories were given in greater detail or in full.

Many stories were related of the wonders and miracles Azulai performed. Pilgrimages were made to his tomb at Leghorn until, some 150 years after his death, in 1960, his remains were reinterred in Jerusalem.

BIBLIOGRAPHY: Toaff, in: L. Jung (ed.), *Guardians of Our Heritage* (1958), 155–64; M. Benayahu, *R. Ḥayyim Yosef David Azulai* (1959); idem (ed.), *Sefer ha-Ḥida* (1959); idem, *Ha-Ḥida* (1960); KS, 35 (1959–60), 285–9, nos. 1612, 1616; Yaari, Sheluḥei.

[Moshe Shraga Samet]

AZULAI, MASʿUD (17th century), kabbalist and rabbi; also called **Masʿūd *Ma'aravi*** ("the Westerner") and **Masʿūd *Saggi-Nahor*** (euphemism for "the blind"). Azulai, who went from Safed to Morocco, was a kabbalist ascetic and in 1601 he became a member of the Beit ha-Va'ad ("The Academy of Scholars") in Safed. About 1612 he was among the six Safed scholars who ordained R. Azriel b. Meir ha-Levi Ashkenazi, one of the Ashkenazi scholars in Salonika. He was still alive in 1621. His disciples included R. Solomon Shlomel Dreznitz, about whom Azulai wrote, in a letter dated 1607, that he had read all Isaac *Luria's writings three times and was as familiar with them as with the letters of the alphabet. No writings of Azulai are known, except MS. Guenzberg 1760, the contents of which are described as "Sermons of R. Mas'oud Saggi Nahor" (66 folios).

BIBLIOGRAPHY: S. Assaf, *Iggerot mi-Ẓefat* (1940), 125–7; M. Benayahu, in: *Sefer Yovel … Y. Baer* (1960), 268–9.

ABBREVIATIONS

GENERAL ABBREVIATIONS

This list contains abbreviations used in the Encyclopaedia (apart from the standard ones, such as geographical abbreviations, points of compass, etc.). For names of organizations, institutions, etc., in abbreviation, see Index. For bibliographical abbreviations of books and authors in Rabbinical literature, see following lists.

*	Cross reference; i.e., an article is to be found under the word(s) immediately following the asterisk (*).
°	Before the title of an entry, indicates a non-Jew (post-biblical times).
‡	Indicates reconstructed forms.
>	The word following this sign is derived from the preceding one.
<	The word preceding this sign is derived from the following one.

ad loc.	*ad locum*, "at the place"; used in quotations of commentaries.
A.H.	*Anno Hegirae*, "in the year of Hegira," i.e., according to the Muslim calendar.
Akk.	Addadian.
A.M.	*anno mundi*, "in the year (from the creation) of the world."
anon.	anonymous.
Ar.	Arabic.
Aram.	Aramaic.
Ass.	Assyrian.
b.	born; *ben, bar.*
Bab.	Babylonian.
B.C.E.	Before Common Era (= B.C.).
bibl.	bibliography.
Bul.	Bulgarian.
c., ca.	Circa.
C.E.	Common Era (= A.D.).
cf.	*confer*, "compare."
ch., chs.	chapter, chapters.
comp.	compiler, compiled by.
Cz.	Czech.
D	according to the documentary theory, the Deuteronomy document.
d.	died.
Dan.	Danish.
diss., dissert,	dissertation, thesis.
Du.	Dutch.
E.	according to the documentary theory, the Elohist document (i.e., using Elohim as the name of God) of the first five (or six) books of the Bible.
ed.	editor, edited, edition.
eds.	editors.
e.g.	*exempli gratia*, "for example."
Eng.	English.
et al.	*et alibi*, "and elsewhere"; or *et alii*, "and others"; "others."
f., ff.	and following page(s).
fig.	figure.
fl.	flourished.
fol., fols	folio(s).
Fr.	French.
Ger.	German.
Gr.	Greek.
Heb.	Hebrew.
Hg., Hung	Hungarian.
ibid	*Ibidem*, "in the same place."
incl. bibl.	includes bibliography.
introd.	introduction.
It.	Italian.
J	according to the documentary theory, the Jahwist document (i.e., using YHWH as the name of God) of the first five (or six) books of the Bible.
Lat.	Latin.
lit.	literally.
Lith.	Lithuanian.
loc. cit.	*loco citato*, "in the [already] cited place."
Ms., Mss.	Manuscript(s).
n.	note.
n.d.	no date (of publication).
no., nos	number(s).
Nov.	Novellae (Heb. *Ḥiddushim*).
n.p.	place of publication unknown.
op. cit.	*opere citato*, "in the previously mentioned work."
P.	according to the documentary theory, the Priestly document of the first five (or six) books of the Bible.
p., pp.	page(s).
Pers.	Persian.
pl., pls.	plate(s).
Pol.	Polish.
Port.	Potuguese.
pt., pts.	part(s).
publ.	published.
R.	Rabbi or Rav (before names); in Midrash (after an abbreviation) – *Rabbah.*
r.	recto, the first side of a manuscript page.
Resp.	Responsa (Latin "answers," Hebrew *She'elot u-Teshuvot* or *Teshuvot),* collections of rabbinic decisions.
rev.	revised.

Rom.	Romanian.
Rus(s).	Russian.
Slov.	Slovak.
Sp.	Spanish.
s.v.	*sub verbo, sub voce*, "under the (key) word."
Sum	Sumerian.
summ.	Summary.
suppl.	supplement.
Swed.	Swedish.
tr., trans(l).	translator, translated, translation.
Turk.	Turkish.
Ukr.	Ukrainian.
v., vv.	*verso*. The second side of a manuscript page; also verse(s).
Yid.	Yiddish.

ABBREVIATIONS USED IN RABBINICAL LITERATURE

Adderet Eliyahu, Karaite treatise by Elijah b. Moses *Bashyazi.
Admat Kodesh, Resp. by Nissim Ḥayyim Moses b. Joseph |Mizraḥi.
Aguddah, Sefer ha-, Nov. by *Alexander Suslin ha-Kohen.
Ahavat Ḥesed, compilation by *Israel Meir ha-Kohen.
Aliyyot de-Rabbenu Yonah, Nov. by *Jonah b. Avraham Gerondi.
Arukh ha-Shulḥan, codification by Jehiel Michel *Epstein.
Asayin (= positive precepts), subdivision of: (1) *Maimonides, *Sefer ha-Mitzvot;* (2) *Moses b. Jacob of Coucy, *Semag.*
Asefat Dinim, subdivision of *Sedei Ḥemed* by Ḥayyim Hezekiah *Medini, an encyclopaedia of precepts and responsa.
Asheri = *Asher b. Jehiel.
Aeret Ḥakhamim, by Baruch *Frankel-Teomim; pt, 1: Resp. to Sh. Ar.; pt2: Nov. to Talmud.
Ateret Zahav, subdivision of the *Levush*, a codification by Mordecai b. Abraham (Levush) *Jaffe; *Ateret Zahav* parallels Tur. YD.
Ateret Ẓevi, Comm. To Sh. Ar. by Ẓevi Hirsch b. Azriel.
Avir Ya'akov, Resp. by Jacob Avigdor.
Avkat Rokhel, Resp. by Joseph b. Ephraim *Caro.
Avnei Millu'im, Comm. to Sh. Ar., EH, by *Aryeh Loeb b. Joseph ha-Kohen.
Avnei Nezer, Resp. on Sh. Ar. by Abraham b. Ze'ev Nahum Bornstein of *Sochaczew.
Avodat Massa, Compilation of Tax Law by Yoasha Abraham Judah.
Azei ha-Levanon, Resp. by Judah Leib *Zirelson.

Ba'al ha-Tanya – *Shneur Zalman of Lyady.
Ba'ei Ḥayyei, Resp. by Ḥayyim b. Israel *Benveniste.
Ba'er Heitev, Comm. To Sh. Ar. The parts on OḤ and EH are by Judah b. Simeon *Ashkenazi, the parts on YD AND ḤM by *Zechariah Mendel b. Aryeh Leib. Printed in most editions of Sh. Ar.
Baḥ = Joel *Sirkes.
Baḥ, usual abbreviation for *Bayit Ḥadash*, a commentary on Tur by Joel *Sirkes; printed in most editions of Tur.
Bayit Ḥadash, see *Baḥ*.
Berab = Jacob Berab, also called Ri Berav.
Bedek ha-Bayit, by Joseph b. Ephraim *Caro, additions to his *Beit Yosef* (a comm. to Tur). Printed sometimes inside *Beit Yosef*, in smaller type. Appears in most editions of Tur.
Be'er ha-Golah, Commentary to Sh. Ar. By Moses b. Naphtali Hirsch *Rivkes; printed in most editions of Sh. Ar.
Be'er Mayim, Resp. by Raphael b. Abraham Manasseh Jacob.
Be'er Mayim Ḥayyim, Resp. by Samuel b. Ḥayyim *Vital.
Be'er Yiẓḥak, Resp. by Isaac Elhanan *Spector.
Beit ha-Beḥirah, Comm. to Talmud by Menahem b. Solomon *Meiri.
Beit Me'ir, Nov. on Sh. Ar. by Meir b. Judah Leib Posner.
Beit Shelomo, Resp. by Solomon b. Aaron Ḥason (the younger).
Beit Shemu'el, Comm. to Sh. Ar., EH, by *Samuel b. Uri Shraga Phoebus.
Beit Ya'akov, by Jacob b. Jacob Moses *Lorberbaum; pt.1: Nov. to Ket.; pt.2: Comm. to EH.
Beit Yisrael, collective name for the commentaries *Derishah, Perishah*, and *Be'urim* by Joshua b. Alexander ha-Kohen *Falk. See under the names of the commentaries.
Beit Yiẓḥak, Resp. by Isaac *Schmelkes.
Beit Yosef: (1) Comm. on Tur by Joseph b. Ephraim *Caro; printed in most editions of Tur; (2) Resp. by the same.
Ben Yehudah, Resp. by Abraham b. Judah Litsch (ליטש) Rosenbaum.
Bertinoro, Standard commentary to Mishnah by Obadiah *Bertinoro. Printed in most editions of the Mishnah.
[Be'urei] Ha-Gra, Comm. to Bible, Talmud, and Sh. Ar. By *Elijah b. Solomon Zalmon (Gaon of Vilna); printed in major editions of the mentioned works.
Be'urim, Glosses to Isserles *Darkhei Moshe* (a comm. on Tur) by Joshua b. Alexander ha-Kohen *Falk; printed in many editions of Tur.
Binyamin Ze'ev, Resp. by *Benjamin Ze'ev b. Mattathias of Arta.
Birkei Yosef, Nov. by Ḥayyim Joseph David *Azulai.
Ha-Buẓ ve-ha-Argaman, subdivision of the *Levush* (a codification by Mordecai b. Abraham (Levush) *Jaffe); *Ha-Buẓ ve-ha-Argaman* parallels Tur, EH.

Comm. = Commentary

Da'at Kohen, Resp. by Abraham Isaac ha-Kohen. *Kook.
Darkhei Moshe, Comm. on Tur Moses b. Israel *Isserles; printed in most editions of Tur.
Darkhei No'am, Resp. by *Mordecai b. Judah ha-Levi.
Darkhei Teshuvah, Nov. by Ẓevi *Shapiro; printed in the major editions of Sh. Ar.
De'ah ve-Haskel, Resp. by Obadiah Hadaya (see *Yaskil Avdi).*

Derashot Ran, Sermons by *Nissim b. Reuben Gerondi.
Derekh Ḥayyim, Comm. to *Avot* by *Judah Loew (Lob., Liwa) b. Bezalel (Maharal) of Prague.
Derishah, by Joshua b. Alexander ha-Kohen *Falk; additions to his *Perishah* (comm. on Tur); printed in many editions of Tur.
Derushei ha-Ẓelaḥ, Sermons, by Ezekiel b. Judah Halevi *Landau.
Devar Avraham, Resp. by Abraham *Shapira.
Devar Shemu'el, Resp. by Samuel *Aboab.
Devar Yehoshu'a, Resp. by Joshua Menahem b. Isaac Aryeh Ehrenberg.
Dikdukei Soferim, variae lections of the talmudic text by Raphael Nathan*Rabbinowicz.
Divrei Emet, Resp. by Isaac Bekhor David.
Divrei Ge'onim, Digest of responsa by Ḥayyim Aryeh b. Jeḥiel Ẓevi *Kahana.
Divrei Ḥamudot, Comm. on *Piskei ha-Rosh* by Yom Tov Lipmann b. Nathan ha-Levi *Heller; printed in major editions of the Talmud.
Divrei Ḥayyim several works by Ḥayyim *Halberstamm; if quoted alone refers to his Responsa.
Divrei Malkhi'el, Resp. by Malchiel Tenebaum.
Divrei Rivot, Resp. by Isaac b. Samuel *Adarbi.
Divrei Shemu'el, Resp. by Samuel Raphael Arditi.

Edut be-Ya'akov, Resp. by Jacob b. Abraham *Boton.
Edut bi-Yhosef, Resp. by Joseph b. Isaac *Almosnino.
Ein Ya'akov, Digest of talmudic *aggadot* by Jacob (Ibn) *Habib.
Ein Yiẓḥak, Resp. by Isaac Elhanan *Spector.
Ephraim of Lentshitz = Solomon *Luntschitz.
Erekh Leḥem, Nov. and glosses to Sh. Ar. by Jacob b. Abraham *Castro.
Eshkol, Sefer ha-, Digest of *halakhot* by *Abraham b. Isaac of Narbonne.
Et Sofer, Treatise on Law Court documents by Abraham b. Mordecai *Ankawa, in the 2nd vol. of his Resp. *Kerem Ḥamar.*
Etan ha-Ezraḥi, Resp. by Abraham b. Israel Jehiel (Shrenzl) *Rapaport.
Even ha-Ezel, Nov. to Maimonides' *Yad Ḥazakah* by Isser Zalman *Meltzer.
Even ha-Ezer, also called *Raban* of *Ẓafenat Pa'ne'aḥ,* rabbinical work with varied contents by *Eliezer b. Nathan of Mainz; not identical with the subdivision of Tur, Shulḥan Arukh, etc.
Ezrat Yehudah, Resp. by *Isaar Judah b. Nechemiah of Brisk.

Gan Eden, Karaite treatise by *Aaron b. Elijah of Nicomedia.
Gersonides = *Levi b. Gershom, also called Leo Hebraecus, or Ralbag.
Ginnat Veradim, Resp. by *Abraham b. Mordecai ha-Levi.

Haggahot, another name for *Rema.*
Haggahot Asheri, glosses to *Piskei ha-Rosh* by *Israel of Krems; printed in most Talmud editions.
Haggahot Maimuniyyot, Comm,. to Maimonides' Yad Ḥazakah by *Meir ha-Kohen; printed in most eds. of Yad.
Haggahot Mordekhai, glosses to *Mordekhai* by Samuel *Schlettstadt; printed in most editions of the Talmud after *Mordekhai.*
Haggahot ha-Rashash on Tosafot, annotations of Samuel *Strashun on the Tosafot (printed in major editions of the Talmud).
Ha-Gra = *Elijah b. Solomon Zalman (Gaon of Vilna).
Ha-Gra, Commentaries on Bible, Talmud, and Sh. Ar. respectively, by *Elijah b. Solomon Zalman (Gaon of Vilna); printed in major editions of the mentioned works.
Hai Gaon, Comm. = his comm. on Mishnah.
Ḥakham Ẓevi, Resp. by Ẓevi Hirsch b. Jacob *Ashkenazi.
Halakhot = Rif, *Halakhot.* Compilation and abstract of the Talmud by Isaac b. Jacob ha-Kohen *Alfasi; printed in most editions of the Talmud.
Halakhot Gedolot, compilation of *halakhot* from the Geonic period, arranged acc. to the Talmud. Here cited acc. to ed. Warsaw (1874). Author probably *Simeon Kayyara of Basra.
Halakhot Pesukot le-Rav Yehudai Ga'on compilation of *halakhot.*
Halakhot Pesukot min ha-Ge'onim, compilation of *halakhot* from the geonic period by different authors.
Ḥananel, Comm. to Talmud by *Hananel b. Ḥushi'el; printed in some editions of the Talmud.
Harei Besamim, Resp. by Aryeh Leib b. Isaac *Horowitz.
Ḥassidim, Sefer, Ethical maxims by *Judah b. Samuel he-Ḥasid.
Hassagot Rabad on Rif, Glosses on Rif, *Halakhot,* by *Abraham b. David of Posquières.
Hassagot Rabad [on Yad], Glosses on Maimonides, *Yad Ḥazakah,* by *Abraham b. David of Posquières.
Hassagot Ramban, Glosses by Naḥmanides on Maimonides' *Sefer ha-Mitzvot;* usually printed together with *Sefer ha-Mitzvot.*
Ḥatam Sofer = Moses *Sofer.
Ḥavvot Ya'ir, Resp. and varia by Jair Ḥayyim *Bacharach
Ḥayyim Or Zaru'a = *Ḥayyim (Eliezer) b. Isaac.
Ḥazon Ish = Abraham Isaiah *Karelitz.
Ḥazon Ish, Nov. by Abraham Isaiah *Karelitz
Ḥedvat Ya'akov, Resp. by Aryeh Judah Jacob b. David Dov Meisels (article under his father's name).
Heikhal Yiẓḥak, Resp. by Isaac ha-Levi *Herzog.
Ḥelkat Meḥokek, Comm. to Sh. Ar., by Moses b. Isaac Judah *Lima.
Ḥelkat Ya'akov, Resp. by Mordecai Jacob Breisch.
Ḥemdah Genuzah, , Resp. from the geonic period by different authors.
Ḥemdat Shelomo, Resp. by Solomon Zalman *Lipschitz.
Ḥida = Ḥayyim Joseph David *Azulai.
Ḥiddushei Halakhot ve-Aggadot, Nov. by Samuel Eliezer b. Judah ha-Levi *Edels.
Ḥikekei Lev, Resp. by Ḥayyim *Palaggi.
Ḥikrei Lev, Nov. to Sh. Ar. by Joseph Raphael b. Ḥayyim Joseph Ḥazzan (see article *Ḥazzan Family).
Hil. = Hilkhot … (e.g. *Hilkhot Shabbat).*
Ḥinnukh, Sefer ha-, List and explanation of precepts attributed (probably erroneously) to Aaron ha-Levi of Barcelona (see article **Ha-Ḥinnukh*).
Ḥok Ya'akov, Comm. to Hil. Pesaḥ in Sh. Ar., OḤ, by Jacob b. Joseph *Reicher.
Ḥokhmat Sehlomo (1), Glosses to Talmud, *Rashi* and Tosafot by Solomon b. Jehiel "Maharshal") *Luria; printed in many editions of the Talmud.
Ḥokhmat Sehlomo (2), Glosses and Nov. to Sh. Ar. by Solomon b. Judah Aaron *Kluger printed in many editions of Sh. Ar.
Ḥur, subdivision of the *Levush,* a codification by Mordecai b. Abraham (Levush) *Jaffe; *Hur (or Levush ha-Hur)* parallels Tur, OḤ, 242–697.
Ḥut ha-Meshullash, fourth part of the *Tashbeẓ* (Resp.), by Simeon b. Zemaḥ *Duran.

Ibn Ezra, Comm. to the Bible by Abraham *Ibn Ezra; printed in the major editions of the Bible *("Mikra'ot Gedolot")*.
Imrei Yosher, Resp. by Meir b. Aaron Judah *Arik.
Ir Shushan, Subdivision of the *Levush*, a codification by Mordecai b. Abraham (Levush) *Jaffe; *Ir Shushan* parallels Tur, ḤM.
Israel of Bruna = Israel b. Ḥayyim *Bruna.
Ittur. Treatise on precepts by *Isaac b. Abba Mari of Marseilles.

Jacob Be Rab = *Be Rab.
Jacob b. Jacob Moses of Lissa = Jacob b. Jacob Moses *Lorberbaum.
Judah B. Simeon = Judah b. Simeon *Ashkenazi.
Judah Minz = Judah b. Eliezer ha-Levi *Minz.

Kappei Aharon, Resp. by Aaron Azriel.
Kehillat Ya'akov, Talmudic methodology, definitions etc. by Israel Jacob b. Yom Tov *Algazi.
Kelei Ḥemdah, Nov. and *pilpulim* by Meir Dan *Plotzki of Ostrova, arranged acc. to the Torah.
Keli Yakar, Annotations to the Torah by Solomon *Luntschitz.
Keneh Ḥokhmah, Sermons by Judah Loeb *Pochwitzer.
Keneset ha-Gedolah, Digest of *halakhot* by Ḥayyim b. Israel *Benveniste; subdivided into annotations to *Beit Yosef* and annotations to Tur.
Keneset Yisrael, Resp. by Ezekiel b. Abraham Katzenellenbogen (see article *Katzenellenbogen Family).
Kerem Ḥamar, Resp. and varia by Abraham b. Mordecai *Ankawa.
Kerem Shelmo. Resp. by Solomon b. Joseph *Amarillo.
Keritut, [Sefer], Methodology of the Talmud by *Samson b. Isaac of Chinon.
Kesef ha-Kedoshim, Comm. to Sh. Ar., ḤM, by Abraham *Wahrmann; printed in major editions of Sh. Ar.
Kesef Mishneh, Comm. to Maimonides, *Yad Ḥazakah*, by Joseph b. Ephraim *Caro; printed in most editions of *Yad Ḥazakah*.
Keẓot ha-Ḥoshen, Comm. to Sh. Ar., ḤM, by *Aryeh Loeb b. Joseph ha-Kohen; printed in major editions of Sh. Ar.
Kol Bo [*Sefer*], Anonymous collection of ritual rules; also called *Sefer ha-Likkutim*.
Kol Mevasser, Resp. by Meshullam *Rath.
Korban Aharon, Comm. to *Sifra* by Aaron b. Abraham *Ibn Ḥayyim; pt. 1 is called: *Middot Aharon*.
Korban Edah, Comm. to Jer. Talmud by David *Fraenkel; with additions: *Shiyyurei Korban*; printed in most editions of Jer. Talmud.
Kunteres ha-Kelalim, subdivision of *Sedei Ḥemed*, an encyclopaedia of precepts and responsa by Ḥayyim Hezekiah *Medini.
Kunteres ha-Semikhah, a treatise by *Levi b. Ḥabib; printed at the end of his responsa.
Kunteres Tikkun Olam, part of *Mispat Shalom* (Nov. by Shalom Mordecai b. Moses *Schwadron).

Lavin (negative precepts), subdivision of: (1) *Maimonides, *Sefer ha-Mitzvot;* (2) *Moses b. Jacob of Coucy, *Semag*.
Leḥem Mishneh, Comm. to Maimonides, *Yad Ḥazakah*, by Abraham [Ḥiyya] b. Moses *Boton; printed in most editions of *Yad Ḥazakah*.
Leḥem Rav, Resp. by Abraham [Ḥiyya] b. Moses *Boton.
Leket Yosher, Resp and varia by Israel b. Pethahiah *Isserlein, collected by *Joseph (Joselein) b. Moses.
Leo Hebraeus = *Levi b. Gershom, also called Ralbag or Gersonides.
Levush = Mordecai b. Abraham *Jaffe.
Levush [Malkhut], Codification by Mordecai b. Abraham (Levush) *Jaffe, with subdivisions: *[Levush ha-] Tekhelet* (parallels Tur OḤ 1–241); *[Levush ha-] Ḥur* (parallels Tur OḤ 242–697); *[Levush] Ateret Zahav* (parallels Tur YD); *[Levush ha-Buẓ ve-ha-Argaman* (parallels Tur EH); *[Levush] Ir Shushan* (parallels Tur ḤM); under the name *Levush* the author wrote also other works.
Li-Leshonot ha-Rambam, fifth part (nos. 1374–1700) of Resp. by *David b. Solomon ibn Abi Zimra (Radbaz).
Likkutim, Sefer ha-, another name for *[Sefer] Kol Bo*.

Ma'adanei Yom Tov, Comm. on *Piskei ha-Rosh* by Yom Tov Lipmann b. Nathan ha-Levi *Heller; printed in many editions of the Talmud.
Mabit = Moses b. Joseph *Trani.
Magen Avot, Comm. to *Avot* by Simeon b. Ẓemaḥ *Duran.
Magen Avraham, Comm. to Sh. Ar., OḤ, by Abraham Abele b. Ḥayyim ha-Levi *Gombiner; printed in many editions of Sh. Ar., OḤ.
Maggid Mishneh, Comm. to Maimonides, *Yad Ḥazakah*, by *Vidal Yom Tov of Tolosa; printed in most editions of the *Yad Ḥazakah*.
Maḥaneh Efrayim, Resp. and Nov., arranged acc. to Maimonides' *Yad Ḥazakah* , by Ephraim b. Aaron *Navon.
Maharai = Israel b. Pethahiah *Isserlein.
Maharal of Prague = *Judah Loew (Lob, Liwa), b. Bezalel.
Maharalbaḥ = *Levi b. Ḥabib.
Maharam Alashkar = Moses b. Isaac *Alashkar.
Maharam Alshekh = Moses b. Ḥayyim *Alashekh.
Maharam Mintz = Moses *Mintz.
Maharam of Lublin = *Meir b. Gedaliah of Lublin.
Maharam of Padua = Meir *Katzenellenbogen.
Maharam of Rothenburg = *Meir b. Baruch of Rothenburg.
Maharam Shik = Moses b. Joseph Schick.
Maharash Engel = Samuel b. Ze'ev Wolf Engel.
Maharashdam = Samuel b. Moses *Medina.
Maharḥash = Ḥayyim (ben) Shabbetai.
Mahari Basan = Jehiel b. Ḥayyim Basan.
Mahari b. Lev = Joseph ibn Lev.
Mahari'az = Jekuthiel Asher Zalman Ensil Zusmir.
Maharibal = *Joseph ibn Lev.
Mahariḥ = Jacob (Israel) *Ḥagiz.
Maharik = Joseph b. Solomon *Colon.
Maharikash = Jacob b. Abraham *Castro.
Maharil = Jacob b. Moses *Moellin.
Maharimat = Joseph b. Moses di Trani (not identical with the Maharit).
Maharit = Joseph b. Moses *Trani.
Maharitaẓ = Yom Tov b. Akiva Ẓahalon. (See article *Ẓahalon Family).
Maharsha = Samuel Eliezer b. Judah ha-Levi *Edels.
Maharshag = Simeon b. Judah Gruenfeld.
Maharshak = Samson b. Isaac of Chinon.
Maharshakh = *Solomon b. Abraham.
Maharshal = Solomon b. Jeḥiel *Luria.
Mahasham = Shalom Mordecai b. Moses *Sschwadron.
Maharyu = Jacob b. Judah *Weil.
Maḥazeh Avraham, Resp. by Abraham Nebagen v. Meir ha-Levi Steinberg.
Maḥazik Berakhah, Nov. by Ḥayyim Joseph David *Azulai.

*Maimonides = Moses b. Maimon, or Rambam.
*Malbim = Meir Loeb b. Jehiel Michael.
Malbim = Malbim's comm. to the Bible; printed in the major editions.
Malbushei Yom Tov, Nov. on *Levush,* OḤ, by Yom Tov Lipmann b. Nathan ha-Levi *Heller.
Mappah, another name for *Rema.*
Mareh ha-Panim, Comm. to Jer. Talmud by Moses b. Simeon *Margolies; printed in most editions of Jer. Talmud.
Margaliyyot ha-Yam, Nov. by Reuben *Margoliot.
Masat Binyamin, Resp. by Benjamin Aaron b. Abraham *Slonik
Mashbir, Ha- = *Joseph Samuel b. Isaac Rodi.
Massa Ḥayyim, Tax *halakhot* by Ḥayyim *Palaggi, with the subdivisions *Missim ve-Arnomiyyot* and *Torat ha-Minhagot.*
Massa Melekh, Compilation of Tax Law by Joseph b. Isaac *Ibn Ezra with concluding part *Ne'ilat She'arim.*
Matteh Asher, Resp. by Asher b. Emanuel Shalem.
Matteh Shimon, Digest of Resp. and Nov. to Tur and *Beit Yosef,* ḤM, by Mordecai Simeon b. Solomon.
Matteh Yosef, Resp. by Joseph b. Moses ha-Levi Nazir (see article under his father's name).
Mayim Amukkim, Resp. by Elijah b. Abraham *Mizraḥi.
Mayim Ḥayyim, Resp. by Ḥayyim b. Dov Beresh Rapaport.
Mayim Rabbim, , Resp. by Raphael *Meldola.
Me-Emek ha-Bakha, , Resp. by Simeon b. Jekuthiel Ephrati.
Me'irat Einayim, usual abbreviation: *Sma* (from: *Sefer Me'irat Einayim*); comm. to Sh. Ar. By Joshua b. Alexander ha-Kohen *Falk; printed in most editions of the Sh. Ar.
Melammed le-Ho'il, Resp. by David Ẓevi *Hoffmann.
Meisharim, [*Sefer*], Rabbinical treatise by *Jeroham b. Meshullam.
Meshiv Davar, Resp. by Naphtali Ẓevi Judah *Berlin.
Mi-Gei ha-Haregah, Resp. by Simeon b. Jekuthiel Ephrati.
Mi-Ma'amakim, Resp. by Ephraim Oshry.
Middot Aharon, first part of *Korban Aharon,* a comm. to *Sifra* by Aaron b. Abraham *Ibn Ḥayyim.
Migdal Oz, Comm. to Maimonides, *Yad Ḥazakah,* by *Ibn Gaon Shem Tov b. Abraham; printed in most editions of the *Yad Ḥazakah.*
Mikhtam le-David, Resp. by David Samuel b. Jacob *Pardo.
Mikkaḥ ve-ha-Mimkar, Sefer ha-, Rabbinical treatise by *Hai Gaon.
Milḥamot ha-Shem, Glosses to Rif, *Halakhot,* by *Naḥmanides.
Minḥat Ḥinnukh, Comm. to *Sefer ha-Ḥinnukh,* by Joseph b. Moses *Babad.
Minḥat Yiẓḥak, Resp. by Isaac Jacob b. Joseph Judah Weiss.
Misgeret ha-Shulḥan, Comm. to Sh. Ar., ḤM, by Benjamin Ze'ev Wolf b. Shabbetai; printed in most editions of Sh. Ar.
Mishkenot ha-Ro'im, Halakhot in alphabetical order by Uzziel Alshekh.
Mishnah Berurah, Comm. to Sh. Ar., OḤ, by *Israel Meir ha-Kohen.
Mishneh le-Melekh, Comm. to Maimonides, *Yad Ḥazakah,* by Judah *Rosanes; printed in most editions of *Yad Ḥazakah.*
Mishpat ha-Kohanim, Nov. to Sh. Ar., ḤM, by Jacob Moses *Lorberbaum, part of his *Netivot ha-Mishpat;* printed in major editions of Sh. Ar.
Mishpat Kohen, Resp. by Abraham Isaac ha-Kohen *Kook.
Mishpat Shalom, Nov. by Shalom Mordecai b. Moses *Schwadron; contains: *Kunteres Tikkun Olam.*
Mishpat u-Ẓedakah be-Ya'akov, Resp. by Jacob b. Reuben *Ibn Ẓur.
Mishpat ha-Urim, Comm. to Sh. Ar., ḤM by Jacob b. Jacob Moses *Lorberbaum, part of his *Netivot ha-Mishpat*; printed in major editons of Sh. Ar.
Mishpat Ẓedek, Resp. by *Melammed Meir b. Shem Tov.
Mishpatim Yesharim, Resp. by Raphael b. Mordecai *Berdugo.
Mishpetei Shemu'el, Resp. by Samuel b. Moses *Kalai (Kal'i).
Mishpetei ha-Tanna'im, Kunteres, Nov on *Levush,* OḤ by Yom Tov Lipmann b. Nathan ha-Levi *Heller.
Mishpetei Uzzi'el (Uziel), Resp. by Ben-Zion Meir Hai *Ouziel.
Missim ve-Arnoniyyot, Tax *halakhot* by Ḥayyim *Palaggi, a subdivision of his work *Massa Ḥayyim* on the same subject.
Mitzvot, Sefer ha-, Elucidation of precepts by *Maimonides; subdivided into *Lavin* (negative precepts) and *Asayin* (positive precepts).
Mitzvot Gadol, Sefer, Elucidation of precepts by *Moses b. Jacob of Coucy, subdivided into *Lavin* (negative precepts) and *Asayin* (positive precepts); the usual abbreviation is *Semag.*
Mitzvot Katan, Sefer, Elucidation of precepts by *Isaac b. Joseph of Corbeil; the usual, abbreviation is *Semak.*
Mo'adim u-Zemannim, Rabbinical treatises by Moses Sternbuch.
Modigliano, Joseph Samuel = *Joseph Samuel b. Isaac, Rodi (Ha-Mashbir).
Mordekhai (Mordecai), halakhic compilation by *Mordecai b. Hillel; printed in most editions of the Talmud after the texts.
Moses b. Maimon = *Maimonides, also called Rambam.
Moses b. Naḥman = Naḥmanides, also called Ramban.
Muram = Isaiah Menahem b. Isaac (from: Morenu R. Mendel).

Naḥal Yiẓḥak, Comm. on Sh. Ar., ḤM, by Isaac Elhanan *Spector.
Naḥalah li-Yhoshu'a, Resp. by Joshua Ẓunẓin.
Naḥalat Shivah, collection of legal forms by *Samuel b. David Moses ha-Levi.
*Naḥmanides = Moses b. Naḥman, also called Ramban.
Naẓiv = Naphtali Ẓevi Judah *Berlin.
Ne'eman Shemu'el, Resp. by Samuel Isaac *Modigilano.
Ne'ilat She'arim, concluding part of *Massa Melekh* (a work on Tax Law) by Joseph b. Isaac *Ibn Ezra, containing an exposition of customary law and subdivided into *Minhagei Issur* and *Minhagei Mamon.*
Ner Ma'aravi, Resp. by Jacob b. Malka.
Netivot ha-Mishpat, by Jacob b. Jacob Moses *Lorberbaum; subdivided into *Mishpat ha-Kohanim,* Nov. to Sh. Ar., ḤM, and *Mishpat ha-Urim,* a comm. on the same; printed in major editions of Sh. Ar.
Netivot Olam, Saying of the Sages by *Judah Loew (Lob, Liwa) b. Bezalel.
Nimmukei Menaḥem of Merseburg, Tax *halakhot* by the same, printed at the end of Resp. Maharyu.
Nimmukei Yosef, Comm. to Rif. *Halakhot,* by Joseph *Ḥabib (Ḥabiba); printed in many editions of the Talmud.
Noda bi-Yhudah, Resp. by Ezekiel b. Judah ha-Levi *Landau; there is a first collection *(Mahadura Kamma)* and a second collection *(Mahadura Tinyana).*
Nov. = Novellae, Ḥiddushim.

Ohel Moshe (1), Notes to Talmud, *Midrash Rabbah,* Yad, *Sifrei* and to several Resp., by Eleazar *Horowitz.

Ohel Moshe (2), Resp. by Moses Jonah Zweig.
Oholei Tam. Resp. by *Tam ibn Yaḥya Jacob b. David; printed in the rabbinical collection *Tummat Yesharim.*
Oholei Ya'akov, Resp. by Jacob de *Castro.
Or ha-Me'ir Resp by Judah Meir b. Jacob Samson Shapiro.
Or Same'aḥ, Comm. to Maimonides, *Yad Ḥazakah,* by *Meir Simḥah ha-Kohen of Dvinsk; printed in many editions of the *Yad Ḥazakah.*
Or Zaru'a [the father] = *Isaac b. Moses of Vienna.
Or Zaru'a [the son] = *Ḥayyim (Eliezer) b. Isaac.
Or Zaru'a, Nov. by *Isaac b. Moses of Vienna.
Orah, Sefer ha-, Compilation of ritual precepts by *Rashi.
Oraḥ la-Ẓaddik, Resp. by Abraham Ḥayyim Rodrigues.
Oẓar ha-Posekim, Digest of Responsa.

Paḥad Yiẓḥak, Rabbinical encyclopaedia by Isaac *Lampronti.
Panim Me'irot, Resp. by Meir b. Isaac *Eisenstadt.
Parashat Mordekhai, Resp. by Mordecai b. Abraham Naphtali *Banet.
Pe'at ha-Sadeh la-Dinim and Pe'at ha-Sadeh la-Kelalim, subdivisions of the *Sedei Ḥemed,* an encyclopaedia of precepts and responsa, by Ḥayyim Hezekaih *Medini.
Penei Moshe (1), Resp. by Moses *Benveniste.
Penei Moshe (2), Comm. to Jer. Talmud by Moses b. Simeon *Margolies; printed in most editions of the Jer. Talmud.
Penei Moshe (3), Comm. on the aggadic passages of 18 treatises of the Bab. and Jer. Talmud, by Moses b. Isaiah Katz.
Penei Yehoshu'a, Nov. by Jacob Joshua b. Ẓevi Hirsch *Falk.
Peri Ḥadash, Comm. on Sh. Ar. By Hezekiah da *Silva.
Perishah, Comm. on Tur by Joshua b. Alexander ha-Kohen *Falk; printed in major edition of Tur; forms together with *Derishah* and *Be'urim* (by the same author) the *Beit Yisrael.*
Pesakim u-Khetavim, 2nd part of the *Terumat ha-Deshen* by Israel b. Pethahiah *Isserlein' also called *Piskei Maharai.*
Pilpula Ḥarifta, Comm. to *Piskei ha-Rosh, Seder Nezikin,* by Yom Tov Lipmann b. Nathan ha-Levi *Heller; printed in major editions of the Talmud.
Piskei Maharai, see *Terumat ha-Deshen,* 2nd part; also called *Pesakim u-Khetavim.*
Piskei ha-Rosh, a compilation of *halakhot,* arranged on the Talmud, by *Asher b. Jehiel (Rosh); printed in major Talmud editions.
Pitḥei Teshuvah, Comm. to Sh. Ar. by Abraham Hirsch b. Jacob *Eisenstadt; printed in major editions of the Sh. Ar.

Rabad = *Abraham b. David of Posquières (Rabad III.).
Raban = *Eliezer b. Nathan of Mainz.
Raban, also called *Ẓafenat Pa'ne'aḥ* or *Even ha-Ezer,* see under the last name.
Rabi Abad = *Abraham b. Isaac of Narbonne.
Radad = David Dov. b. Aryeh Judah Jacob *Meisels.
Radam = Dov Berush b. Isaac Meisels.
Radbaz = *David b Solomon ibn Abi Ziumra.
Radbaz, Comm. to Maimonides, *Yad Ḥazakah,* by *David b. Solomon ibn Abi Zimra.
Ralbag = *Levi b. Gershom, also called Gersonides, or Leo Hebraeus.
Ralbag, Bible comm. by *Levi b. Gershon.
Rama [da Fano] = Menaḥem Azariah *Fano.
Ramah = Meir b. Todros [ha-Levi] *Abulafia.
Ramam = *Menaham of Merseburg.
Rambam = *Maimonides; real name: Moses b. Maimon.
Ramban = *Naḥmanides; real name Moses b. Naḥman.
Ramban, Comm. to Torah by *Naḥmanides; printed in major editions. ("Mikra'ot Gedolot").
Ran = *Nissim b. Reuben Gerondi.
Ran of Rif, Comm. on Rif, *Halakhot,* by Nissim b. Reuben Gerondi.
Ranaḥ = *Elijah b. Ḥayyim.
Rash = *Samson b. Abraham of Sens.
Rash, Comm. to Mishnah, by *Samson b. Abraham of Sens; printed in major Talmud editions.
Rashash = Samuel *Strashun.
Rashba = Solomon b. Abraham *Adret.
Rashba, Resp., see also; *Sefer Teshuvot ha-Rashba ha-Meyuḥasot le-ha-Ramban,* by Solomon b. Abraham *Adret.
Rashbad = Samuel b. David.
Rashbam = *Samuel b. Meir.
Rashbam = Comm. on Bible and Talmud by *Samuel b. Meir; printed in major editions of Bible and most editions of Talmud.
Rashbash = Solomon b. Simeon *Duran.
*Rashi = Solomon b. Isaac of Troyes.
Rashi, Comm. on Bible and Talmud by *Rashi; printed in almost all Bible and Talmud editions.
Raviah = Eliezer b. Joel ha-Levi.
Redak = David *Kimḥi.
Redak, Comm. to Bible by David *Kimḥi.
Redakh = *David b. Ḥayyim ha-Kohen of Corfu.
Re'em = Elijah b. Abraham *Mizraḥi.
Rema = Moses b. Israel *Isserles.
Rema, Glosses to Sh. Ar. by Moses b. Israel *Isserles; printed in almost all editions of the Sh. Ar. inside the text in Rashi type; also called *Mappah* or *Haggahot.*
Remek = Moses Kimḥi.
Remakh = Moses ha-Kohen mi-Lunel.
Reshakh = *Solomon b. Abraham; also called Maharshakh.
Resp. = Responsa, *She'elot u-Teshuvot.*
Ri Berav = *Berab.
Ri Escapa = Joseph b. Saul *Escapa.
Ri Migash = Joseph b. Meir ha-Levi *Ibn Migash.
Riba = Isaac b. Asher ha-Levi; Riba II (Riba ha-Baḥur) = his grandson with the same name.
Ribam = Isaac b. Mordecai (or: Isaac b. Meir).
Ribash = *Isaac b. Sheshet Perfet (or: Barfat).
Rid= *Isaiah b. Mali di Trani the Elder.
Ridbaz = Jacob David b. Ze'ev *Willowski.
Rif = Isaac b. Jacob ha-Kohen *Alfasi.
Rif, *Halakhot,* Compilation and abstract of the Talmud by Isaac b. Jacob ha-Kohen *Alfasi.
Ritba = Yom Tov b. Abraham *Ishbili.
Riẓbam = Isaac b. Mordecai.
Rosh = *Asher b. Jehiel, also called Asheri.
Rosh Mashbir, Resp. by *Joseph Samuel b. Isaac, Rodi.

Sedei Ḥemed, Encyclopaedia of precepts and responsa by Ḥayyim Ḥezekiah *Medini; subdivisions: *Asefat Dinim, Kunteres ha-Kelalim, Pe'at ha-Sadeh la-Dinim, Pe'at ha-Sadeh la-Kelalim.*
Semag, Usual abbreviation of *Sefer Mitzvot Gadol,* elucidation of precepts by *Moses b. Jacob of Coucy; subdivided into *Lavin* (negative precepts) *Asayin* (positive precepts).
Semak, Usual abbreviation of *Sefer Mitzvot Katan,* elucidation of precepts by *Isaac b. Joseph of Corbeil.

Sh. Ar. = *Shulḥan Arukh,* code by Joseph b. Ephraim *Caro.
Sha'ar Mishpat, Comm. to Sh. Ar., ḤM. By Israel Isser b. Ze'ev Wolf.
Sha'arei Shevu'ot, Treatise on the law of oaths by *David b. Saadiah; usually printed together with Rif, *Halakhot;* also called: *She'arim of R. Alfasi.*
Sha'arei Teshuvah, Collection of resp. from Geonic period, by different authors.
Sha'arei Uzzi'el, Rabbinical treatise by Ben-Zion Meir Ha *Ouziel.
Sha'arei Ẓedek, Collection of resp. from Geonic period, by different authors.
Shadal [or Shedal] = Samuel David *Luzzatto.
Shai la-Moreh, Resp. by Shabbetai Jonah.
Shakh, Usual abbreviation of *Siftei Kohen*, a comm. to Sh. Ar., YD and ḤM by *Shabbetai b. Meir ha-Kohen; printed in most editions of Sh. Ar.
Sha'ot-de-Rabbanan, Resp. by *Solomon b. Judah ha-Kohen.
She'arim of R. Alfasi see *Sha'arei Shevu'ot.*
Shedal, see Shadal.
She'elot u-Teshuvot ha-Ge'onim, Collection of resp. by different authors.
She'erit Yisrael, Resp. by Israel Ze'ev Mintzberg.
She'erit Yosef, Resp. by *Joseph b. Mordecai Gershon ha-Kohen.
She'ilat Yavez, Resp. by Jacob *Emden (Yavez).
She'iltot, Compilation arranged acc. to the Torah by *Aḥa (Aḥai) of Shabḥa.
Shem Aryeh, Resp. by Aryeh Leib *Lipschutz.
Shemesh Ẓedakah, Resp. by Samson *Morpurgo.
Shenei ha-Me'orot ha-Gedolim, Resp. by Elijah *Covo.
Shetarot, Sefer ha-, Collection of legal forms by *Judah b. Barzillai al-Bargeloni.
Shevut Ya'akov, Resp. by Jacob b. Joseph Reicher.
Shibbolei ha-Leket Compilation on ritual by Zedekiah b. Avraham *Anav.
Shiltei Gibborim, Comm. to Rif, *Halakhot,* by *Joshua Boaz b. Simeon; printed in major editions of the Talmud.
Shittah Mekubbeẓet, Compilation of talmudical commentaries by Bezalel *Ashkenazi.
Shivat Ẓiyyon, Resp. by Samuel b. Ezekiel *Landau.
Shiyyurei Korban, by David *Fraenkel; additions to his comm. to Jer. Talmud *Korban Edah;* both printed in most editions of Jer. Talmud.
Sho'el u-Meshiv, Resp. by Joseph Saul ha-Levi *Nathanson.
Sh[ulḥan] Ar[ukh] [of Ba'al ha-Tanyal], Code by *Shneur Zalman of Lyady; not identical with the code by Joseph Caro.
Siftei Kohen, Comm. to Sh. Ar., YD and ḤM by *Shabbetai b. Meir ha-Kohen; printed in most editions of Sh. Ar.; usual abbreviation: *Shakh.*
Simḥat Yom Tov, Resp. by Tom Tov b. Jacob *Algazi.
Simlah Ḥadashah, Treatise on *Sheḥitah* by Alexander Sender b. Ephraim Zalman *Schor; see also *Tevu'ot Shor.*
Simeon b. Ẓemaḥ = Simeon b. Ẓemaḥ *Duran.
Sma, Comm. to Sh. Ar. by Joshua b. Alexander ha-Kohen *Falk; the full title is: *Sefer Me'irat Einayim;* printed in most editions of Sh. Ar.
Solomon b. Isaac ha-Levi = Solomon b. Isaac *Levy.
Solomon b. Isaac of Troyes = *Rashi.

Tal Orot, Rabbinical work with various contents, by Joseph ibn Gioia.
Tam, Rabbenu = *Tam Jacob b. Meir.
Tashbaẓ = Samson b. Zadok.
Tashbeẓ = Simeon b. Zemaḥ *Duran, sometimes also abbreviation for Samson b. Zadok, usually known as Tashbaẓ.
Tashbeẓ [Sefer ha-], Resp. by Simeon b. Ẓemaḥ *Duran; the fourth part of this work is called: *Ḥut ha-Meshullash.*
Taz, Usual abbreviation of *Turei Zahav,* comm., to Sh. Ar. by *David b. Samnuel ha-Levi; printed in most editions of Sh. Ar.
(Ha)-Tekhelet, subdivision of the *Levush* (a codification by Mordecai b. Abraham (Levush) *Jaffe); *Ha-Tekhelet* parallels Tur, OḤ 1-241.
Terumat ha-Deshen, by Israel b. Pethahiah *Isserlein; subdivided into a part containing responsa, and a second part called *Pesakim u-Khetavim* or *Piskei Maharai.*
Terumot, Sefer ha-, Compilation of *halakhot* by Samuel b. Isaac *Sardi.
Teshuvot Ba'alei ha-Tosafot, Collection of responsa by the Tosafists.
Teshjvot Ge'onei Mizraḥ u-Ma'aav, Collection of responsa.
Teshuvot ha-Geonim, Collection of responsa from Geonic period.
Teshuvot Ḥakhmei Provinzyah, Collection of responsa by different Provencal authors.
Teshuvot Ḥakhmei Ẓarefat ve-Loter, Collection of responsa by different French authors.
Teshuvot Maimuniyyot, Resp. pertaining to Maimonides' *Yad Ḥazakah;* printed in major editions of this work after the text; authorship uncertain.
Tevu'ot Shor, by Alexander Sender b. Ephraim Zalman *Schor, a comm. to his *Simlah Ḥadashah,* a work on *Sheḥitah.*
Tiferet Ẓevi, Resp. by Ẓevi Hirsch of the "AHW" Communities (Altona, Hamburg, Wandsbeck).
Tiktin, Judah b. Simeon = Judah b. Simeon *Ashkenazi.
Toledot Adam ve-Ḥavvah, Codification by *Jeroham b. Meshullam.
Torat Emet, Resp. by Aaron b. Joseph *Sasson.
Torat Ḥayyim, , Resp. by Ḥayyim (ben) Shabbetai.
Torat ha-Minhagot, subdivision of the *Massa Ḥayyim* (a work on tax law) by Ḥayyim *Palaggi, containing an exposition of customary law.
Tosafot Rid, Explanations to the Talmud and decisions by *Isaiah b. Mali di Trani the Elder.
Tosefot Yom Tov, comm. to Mishnah by Yom Tov Lipmann b. Nathan ha-Levi *Heller; printed in most editions of the Mishnah.
Tummim, subdivision of the comm. to Sh. Ar., ḤM, *Urim ve-Tummim* by Jonathan *Eybeschuetz; printed in the major editions of Sh. Ar.
Tur, usual abbreviation for the *Arba'ah Turim* of *Jacob b. Asher.
Turei Zahav, Comm. to Sh. Ar. by *David b. Samuel ha-Levi; printed in most editions of Sh. Ar.; usual abbreviation: *Taz.*

Urim, subdivision of the following.
Urim ve-Tummim, Comm. to Sh. Ar., ḤM, by Jonathan *Eybeschuetz; printed in the major editions of Sh. Ar.; subdivided in places into *Urim* and *Tummim.*

Vikku'aḥ Mayim Ḥayyim, Polemics against Isserles and Caro by Ḥayyim b. Bezalel.

Yad Malakhi, Methodological treatise by *Malachi b. Jacob ha-Kohen.

Yad Ramah, Nov. by Meir b. Todros [ha-Levi] *Abulafia.
Yakhin u-Vo'az, Resp. by Ẓemaḥ b. Solomon *Duran.
Yam ha-Gadol, Resp. by Jacob Moses *Toledano.
Yam shel Shelomo, Compilation arranged acc. to Talmud by Solomon b. Jehiel (Maharshal) *Luria.
Yashar, Sefer ha-, by *Tam, Jacob b. Meir (Rabbenu Tam); 1st pt.: Resp.; 2nd pt.: Nov.
Yaskil Avdi, Resp. by Obadiah Hadaya (printed together with his Resp. *De'ah ve-Haskel).*
Yaveẓ = Jacob *Emden.
Yehudah Ya'aleh, Resp. by Judah b. Israel *Aszod.
Yekar Tiferet, Comm. to Maimonides' *Yad Ḥazakah,*by David b. Solomon ibn Zimra, printed in most editions of *Yad Ḥazakah.*
Yere'im [ha-Shalem], [Sefer], Treatise on precepts by *Eliezer b. Samuel of Metz.
Yeshu'ot Ya'akov, Resp. by Jacob Meshullam b. Mordecai Ze'ev *Ornstein.
Yiẓhak Rei'aḥ, Resp. by Isaac b. Samuel Abendanan (see article *Abendanam Family).
Ẓafenat Pa'ne'aḥ (1), also called *Raban* or *Even ha-Ezer,* see under the last name.
Ẓafenat Pa'ne'aḥ (2), Resp. by Joseph *Rozin.
Zayit Ra'anan, Resp. by Moses Judah Leib b. Benjamin Auerbach.
Ẓeidah la-Derekh, Codification by *Menahem b. Aaron ibn Zerah.
Ẓedakah u-Mishpat, Resp. by Ẓedakah b. Saadiah Huẓin.
Zekan Aharon, Resp. by Elijah b. Benjamin ha-Levi.
Zekher Ẓaddik, Sermons by Eliezer *Katzenellenbogen.
Ẓemaḥ Ẓedek (1) Resp. by Menaham Mendel Shneersohn (see under *Shneersohn Family).
Zera Avraham, Resp. by Abraham b. David *Yiẓḥaki.
Zera Emet Resp. by *Ishmael b. Abaham Isaac ha-Kohen.
Ẓevi la-Ẓaddik, Resp. by Ẓevi Elimelech b. David Shapira.
Zikhron Yehudah, Resp. by *Judah b. Asher
Zikhron Yosef, Resp. by Joseph b. Menahem *Steinhardt.
Zikhronot, Sefer ha-, Sermons on several precepts by Samuel *Aboab.
Zikkaron la-Rishonim . . ., by Albert (Abraham Elijah) *Harkavy; contains in vol. 1 pt. 4 (1887) a collection of Geonic responsa.
Ẓiẓ Eliezer, Resp. by Eliezer Judah b. Jacob Gedaliah Waldenberg.

BIBLIOGRAPHICAL ABBREVIATIONS

Bibliographies in English and other languages have been extensively updated, with English translations cited where available. In order to help the reader, the language of books or articles is given where not obvious from titles of books or names of periodicals. Titles of books and periodicals in languages with alphabets other than Latin, are given in transliteration, even where there is a title page in English. Titles of articles in periodicals are not given. Names of Hebrew and Yiddish periodicals well known in English-speaking countries or in Israel under their masthead in Latin characters are given in this form, even when contrary to transliteration rules. Names of authors writing in languages with non-Latin alphabets are given in their Latin alphabet form wherever known; otherwise the names are transliterated. Initials are generally not given for authors of articles in periodicals, except to avoid confusion. Non-abbreviated book titles and names of periodicals are printed in *italics.* Abbreviations are given in the list below.

AASOR	*Annual of the American School of Oriental Research* (1919ff.).
AB	*Analecta Biblica* (1952ff.).
Abel, Géog	F.-M. Abel, *Géographie de la Palestine,* 2 vols. (1933–38).
ABR	*Australian Biblical Review* (1951ff.).
Abr.	Philo, *De Abrahamo.*
Abrahams, Companion	I. Abrahams, *Companion to the Authorised Daily Prayer Book* (rev. ed. 1922).
Abramson, Merkazim	S. Abramson, *Ba-Merkazim u-va-Tefuẓot bi-Tekufat ha-Ge'onim* (1965).
Acts	Acts of the Apostles (New Testament).
ACUM	*Who is who in ACUM [Aguddat Kompozitorim u-Meḥabbrim].*
ADAJ	*Annual of the Department of Antiquities, Jordan* (1951ff.).
Adam	Adam and Eve (Pseudepigrapha).
ADB	*Allgemeine Deutsche Biographie,* 56 vols. (1875–1912).
Add. Esth.	The Addition to Esther (Apocrypha).
Adler, Prat Mus	1. Adler, *La pratique musicale savante dans quelques communautés juives en Europe au XVIIe et XVIIIe siècles,* 2 vols. (1966).
Adler-Davis	H.M. Adler and A. Davis (ed. and tr.), *Service of the Synagogue, a New Edition of the Festival Prayers with an English Translation in Prose and Verse,* 6 vols. (1905–06).
Aet.	Philo, *De Aeternitate Mundi.*
AFO	*Archiv fuer Orientforschung* (first two volumes under the name *Archiv fuer Keilschriftforschung)* (1923ff.).
Ag. Ber	*Aggadat Bereshit* (ed. Buber, 1902*).*
Agr.	Philo, *De Agricultura.*
Ag. Sam.	*Aggadat Samuel.*
Ag. Song	*Aggadat Shir ha-Shirim* (Schechter ed., 1896).
Aharoni, Ereẓ	Y. Aharoni, *Ereẓ Yisrael bi-Tekufat ha-Mikra: Geografyah Historit* (1962).
Aharoni, Land	Y. Aharoni, *Land of the Bible* (1966).

Ahikar	Ahikar (Pseudepigrapha).
AI	*Archives Israélites de France* (1840–1936).
AJA	*American Jewish Archives* (1948ff.).
AJHSP	*American Jewish Historical Society – Publications* (after vol. 50 = AJHSQ).
AJHSQ	*American Jewish Historical (*Society) *Quarterly* (before vol. 50 =AJHSP).
AJSLL	*American Journal of Semitic Languages and Literature* (1884–95 under the title *Hebraica,* since 1942 JNES).
AJYB	*American Jewish Year Book* (1899ff.).
AKM	Abhandlungen fuer die Kunde des Morgenlandes (series).
Albright, Arch	W.F. Albright, *Archaeology of Palestine* (rev. ed. 1960).
Albright, Arch Bib	W.F. Albright, *Archaeology of Palestine and the Bible* (1935^{3}).
Albright, Arch Rel	W.F. Albright, *Archaeology and the Religion of Israel* (1953^{3}).
Albright, Stone	W.F. Albright, *From the Stone Age to Christianity* (1957^{2}).
Alon, Meḥkarim	G. Alon, *Meḥkarim be-Toledot Yisrael bi-Ymei Bayit Sheni u-vi-Tekufat ha-Mishnah ve-ha Talmud,* 2 vols. (1957–58).
Alon, Toledot	G. Alon, *Toledot ha-Yehudim be-Ereẓ Yisrael bi-Tekufat ha-Mishnah ve-ha-Talmud,* I (1958^{3}), (1961^{2}).
ALOR	Alter Orient (series).
Alt, Kl Schr	A. Alt, *Kleine Schriften zur Geschichte des Volkes Israel,* 3 vols. (1953–59).
Alt, Landnahme	A. Alt, *Landnahme der Israeliten in Palaestina* (1925); also in Alt, Kl Schr, 1 (1953), 89–125.
Ant.	Josephus, *Jewish Antiquities* (Loeb Classics ed.).
AO	*Acta Orientalia* (1922ff.).
AOR	*Analecta Orientalia* (1931ff.).
AOS	American Oriental Series.
Apion	Josephus, *Against Apion* (Loeb Classics ed.).
Aq.	Aquila's Greek translation of the Bible.
Ar.	*Arakhin* (talmudic tractate).
Artist.	Letter of Aristeas (Pseudepigrapha).
ARN^{1}	*Avot de-Rabbi Nathan,* version (1) ed. Schechter, 1887.
ARN^{2}	*Avot de-Rabbi Nathan,* version (2) ed. Schechter, 1945^{2}.
Aronius, Regesten	I. Aronius, *Regesten zur Geschichte der Juden im fraenkischen und deutschen Reiche bis zum Jahre 1273* (1902).
ARW	*Archiv fuer Religionswissenschaft* (1898–1941/42).
AS	*Assyrological Studies* (1931ff.).
Ashtor, Korot	E. Ashtor (Strauss), *Korot ha-Yehudim bi-Sefarad ha-Muslemit,* 1(1966^{2}), 2(1966).
Ashtor, Toledot	E. Ashtor (Strauss), *Toledot ha-Yehudim be-Miẓrayim ve-Suryah Taḥat Shilton ha-Mamlukim,* 3 vols. (1944–70).
Assaf, Ge'onim	S. Assaf, *Tekufat ha-Ge'onim ve-Sifrutah* (1955).
Assaf, Mekorot	S. Assaf, *Mekorot le-Toledot ha-Ḥinnukh be-Yisrael,* 4 vols. (1925–43).
Ass. Mos.	Assumption of Moses (Pseudepigrapha).
ATA	Alttestamentliche Abhandlungen (series).
ATANT	Abhandlungen zur Theologie des Alten und Neuen Testaments (series).
AUJW	*Allgemeine unabhaengige juedische Wochenzeitung* (till 1966 = AWJD).
AV	Authorized Version of the Bible.
Avad.	*Avadim* (post-talmudic tractate).
Avi-Yonah, Geog	M. Avi-Yonah, *Geografyah Historit shel Ereẓ Yisrael* (1962^{3}).
Avi-Yonah, Land	M. Avi-Yonah, *The Holy Land from the Persian to the Arab conquest (536 B.C. to A.D. 640)* (1960).
Avot	*Avot* (talmudic tractate).
Av. Zar.	*Avodah Zarah* (talmudic tractate).
AWJD	*Allgemeine Wochenzeitung der Juden in Deutschland* (since 1967 = AUJW).
AZDJ	*Allgemeine Zeitung des Judentums.*
Azulai	Ḥ.Y.D. Azulai, *Shem ha-Gedolim,* ed. by I.E. Benjacob, 2 pts. (1852) (and other editions).
BA	*Biblical Archaeologist* (1938ff.).
Bacher, Bab Amor	W. Bacher, *Agada der babylonischen Amoraeer* (1913^{2}).
Bacher, Pal Amor	W. Bacher, *Agada der palaestinensischen Amoraeer* (Heb. ed. *Aggadat Amora'ei Ereẓ Yisrael),* 2 vols. (1892–99).
Bacher, Tann	W. Bacher, *Agada der Tannaiten* (Heb. ed. *Aggadot ha-Tanna'im,* vol. 1, pt. 1 and 2 (1903); vol. 2 (1890).
Bacher, Trad	W. Bacher, *Tradition und Tradenten in den Schulen Palaestinas und Babyloniens* (1914).
Baer, Spain	Yitzhak (Fritz) Baer, *History of the Jews in Christian Spain,* 2 vols. (1961–66).
Baer, Studien	Yitzhak (Fritz) Baer, *Studien zur Geschichte der Juden im Koenigreich Aragonien waehrend des 13. und 14. Jahrhunderts* (1913).
Baer, Toledot	Yitzhak (Fritz) Baer, *Toledot ha-Yehudim bi-Sefarad ha-Noẓerit mi-Teḥillatan shel ha-Kehillot ad ha-Gerush,* 2 vols. (1959^{2}).
Baer, Urkunden	Yitzhak (Fritz) Baer, *Die Juden im christlichen Spanien,* 2 vols. (1929–36).
Baer S., Seder	S.I. Baer, *Seder Avodat Yisrael* (1868 and reprints*).*
BAIU	*Bulletin de l'Alliance Israélite Universelle* (1861–1913*).*
Baker, Biog Dict	*Baker's Biographical Dictionary of Musicians,* revised by N. Slonimsky (1958^{5}; with Supplement 1965).
I Bar.	I Baruch (Apocrypha).
II Bar.	II Baruch (Pseudepigrapha).
III Bar.	III Baruch (Pseudepigrapha).
BAR	*Biblical Archaeology Review.*
Baron, Community	S.W. Baron, *The Jewish Community, its History and Structure to the American Revolution,* 3 vols. (1942).

Baron, Social	S.W. Baron, *Social and Religious History of the Jews,* 3 vols. (1937); enlarged, 1-2(1952^{2}), 3-14 (1957–69).
Barthélemy-Milik	D. Barthélemy and J.T. Milik, *Dead Sea Scrolls: Discoveries in the Judean Desert,* vol. 1 *Qumram Cave* I (1955).
BASOR	*Bulletin of the American School of Oriental Research.*
Bauer-Leander	H. Bauer and P. Leander, *Grammatik des Biblisch-Aramaeischen* (1927; repr. 1962).
BB	(1) *Bava Batra* (talmudic tractate). (2) *Biblische Beitraege* (1943ff.).
BBB	Bonner biblische Beitraege (series).
BBLA	*Beitraege zur biblischen Landes- und Altertumskunde* (until 1949–ZDPV).
BBSAJ	*Bulletin,* British School of Archaeology, Jerusalem (1922–25; after 1927 included in PEFQS).
BDASI	*Alon* (since 1948) or *Hadashot Arkhe'ologiyyot* (since 1961), bulletin of the Department of Antiquities of the State of Israel.
Begrich, Chronologie	J. Begrich, *Chronologie der Koenige von Israel und Juda* (1929).
Bek.	*Bekhorot* (talmudic tractate).
Bel	Bel and the Dragon (Apocrypha).
Benjacob, Oẓar	I.E. Benjacob, *Oẓar ha-Sefarim* (1880; repr. 1956).
Ben Sira	see Ecclus.
Ben-Yehuda, Millon	E. Ben-Yedhuda, *Millon ha-Lashon ha-Ivrit,* 16 vols (1908–59; repr. in 8 vols., 1959).
Benzinger, Archaeologie	I. Benzinger, *Hebraeische Archaeologie* (1927^{3}).
Ben Zvi, Eretz Israel	I. Ben-Zvi, *Eretz Israel under Ottoman Rule* (1960; offprint from L. Finkelstein (ed.), *The Jews, their History, Culture and Religion* (vol. 1).
Ben Zvi, Ereẓ Israel	I. Ben-Zvi, *Ereẓ Israel bi-Ymei ha-Shilton ha-Ottomani* (1955).
Ber.	*Berakhot* (talmudic tractate).
Beẓah	*Beẓah* (talmudic tractate).
BIES	Bulletin of the Israel Exploration Society, see below BJPES.
Bik.	*Bikkurim* (talmudic tractate).
BJCE	Bibliography of Jewish Communities in Europe, catalog at General Archives for the History of the Jewish People, Jerusalem.
BJPES	Bulletin of the Jewish Palestine Exploration Society – English name of the Hebrew periodical known as: 1. *Yedi'ot ha-Ḥevrah ha-Ivrit la-Ḥakirat Ereẓ Yisrael va-Attikoteha* (1933–1954); 2. *Yedi'ot ha-Ḥevrah la-Ḥakirat Ereẓ Yisrael va-Attikoteha* (1954–1962); 3. *Yedi'ot ba-Ḥakirat Ereẓ Yisrael va-Attikoteha* (1962ff.).
BJRL	*Bulletin of the John Rylands Library* (1914ff.).
BK	*Bava Kamma* (talmudic tractate).
BLBI	*Bulletin of the Leo Baeck Institute* (1957ff.).
BM	(1) *Bava Meẓia* (talmudic tractate). (2) *Beit Mikra* (1955/56ff.). (3) British Museum.
BO	*Bibbia e Oriente* (1959ff.).
Bondy-Dworský	G. Bondy and F. Dworský, *Regesten zur Geschichte der Juden in Boehmen, Maehren und Schlesien von 906 bis 1620,* 2 vols. (1906).
BOR	*Bibliotheca Orientalis* (1943ff.).
Borée, Ortsnamen	W. Borée *Die alten Ortsnamen Palaestinas* (1930).
Bousset, Religion	W. Bousset, *Die Religion des Judentums im neutestamentlichen Zeitalter* (1906^{2}).
Bousset-Gressmann	W. Bousset, *Die Religion des Judentums im spaethellenistischen Zeitalter* (1966^{3}).
BR	*Biblical Review* (1916–25).
BRCI	*Bulletin of the Research Council of Israel* (1951/52–1954/55; then divided).
BRE	*Biblical Research* (1956ff.).
BRF	*Bulletin of the Rabinowitz Fund for the Exploration of Ancient Synagogues* (1949ff.).
Briggs, Psalms	Ch. A. and E.G. Briggs, *Critical and Exegetical Commentary on the Book of Psalms,* 2 vols. (ICC, 1906–07).
Bright, Hist	J. Bright, *A History of Israel* (1959).
Brockelmann, Arab Lit	K. Brockelmann, *Geschichte der arabischen Literatur,* 2 vols. 1898–1902), supplement, 3 vols. (1937–42).
Bruell, Jahrbuecher	*Jahrbuecher fuer juedische Geschichte und Litteratur,* ed. by N. Bruell, Frankfurt (1874–90).
Brugmans-Frank	H. Brugmans and A. Frank (eds.), *Geschiedenis der Joden in Nederland* (1940).
BTS	*Bible et Terre Sainte* (1958ff.).
Bull, Index	S. Bull, *Index to Biographies of Contemporary Composers* (1964).
BW	*Biblical World* (1882–1920).
BWANT	*Beitraege zur Wissenschaft vom Alten und Neuen Testament* (1926ff.).
BZ	*Biblische Zeitschrift* (1903ff.).
BZAW	*Beihefte zur Zeitschrift fuer die alttestamentliche Wissenschaft,* supplement to ZAW (1896ff.).
BŻIH	*Biuletyn Zydowskiego Instytutu Historycznego* (1950ff.).
CAB	*Cahiers d'archéologie biblique* (1953ff.).
CAD	*The* [*Chicago*] *Assyrian Dictionary* (1956ff.).
CAH	*Cambridge Ancient History,* 12 vols. (1923–39)
CAH^{2}	*Cambridge Ancient History,* second edition, 14 vols. (1962–2005).
Calwer, Lexikon	*Calwer, Bibellexikon.*
Cant.	Canticles, usually given as Song (= Song of Songs).

Cantera-Millás, Inscripciones	F. Cantera and J.M. Millás, *Las Inscripciones Hebraicas de España* (1956).
CBQ	*Catholic Biblical Quarterly* (1939ff.).
CCARY	Central Conference of American Rabbis, *Yearbook* (1890/91ff.).
CD	*Damascus Document* from the Cairo *Genizah* (published by S. Schechter, *Fragments of a Zadokite Work*, 1910).
Charles, Apocrypha	R.H. Charles, *Apocrypha and Pseudepigrapha . . .*, 2 vols. (1913; repr. 1963–66).
Cher.	Philo, *De Cherubim.*
I (or II) Chron.	Chronicles, book I and II (Bible).
CIG	*Corpus Inscriptionum Graecarum.*
CIJ	*Corpus Inscriptionum Judaicarum,* 2 vols. (1936–52).
CIL	*Corpus Inscriptionum Latinarum.*
CIS	*Corpus Inscriptionum Semiticarum* (1881ff.).
C.J.	Codex Justinianus.
Clermont-Ganneau, Arch	Ch. Clermont-Ganneau, *Archaeological Researches in Palestine*, 2 vols. (1896–99).
CNFI	*Christian News from Israel* (1949ff.).
Cod. Just.	Codex Justinianus.
Cod. Theod.	Codex Theodosinanus.
Col.	Epistle to the Colosssians (New Testament).
Conder, Survey	Palestine Exploration Fund, *Survey of Eastern Palestine*, vol. 1, pt. I (1889) = C.R. Conder, *Memoirs of the . . . Survey.*
Conder-Kitchener	Palestine Exploration Fund, *Survey of Western Palestine*, vol. 1, pts. 1-3 (1881–83) = C.R. Conder and H.H. Kitchener, *Memoirs.*
Conf.	Philo, *De Confusione Linguarum.*
Conforte, Kore	D. Conforte, *Kore ha-Dorot* (1842^{2}).
Cong.	Philo, *De Congressu Quaerendae Eruditionis Gratia.*
Cont.	Philo, *De Vita Contemplativa.*
I (or II) Cor.	Epistles to the Corinthians (New Testament).
Cowley, Aramic	A. Cowley, *Aramaic Papyri of the Fifth Century B.C.* (1923).
Colwey, Cat	A.E. Cowley, *A Concise Catalogue of the Hebrew Printed Books in the Bodleian Library* (1929).
CRB	*Cahiers de la Revue Biblique* (1964ff.).
Crowfoot-Kenyon	J.W. Crowfoot, K.M. Kenyon and E.L. Sukenik, *Buildings of Samaria* (1942).
C.T.	Codex Theodosianus.
DAB	*Dictionary of American Biography* (1928–58).
Daiches, Jews	S. Daiches, *Jews in Babylonia* (1910).
Dalman, Arbeit	G. Dalman, *Arbeit und Sitte in Palaestina,* 7 vols.in 8 (1928–42 repr. 1964).
Dan	Daniel (Bible).
Davidson, Oẓar	I. Davidson, *Oẓar ha-Shirah ve-ha-Piyyut,* 4 vols. (1924–33); Supplement in: HUCA, 12–13 (1937/38), 715–823.
DB	J. Hastings, *Dictionary of the Bible,* 4 vols. (1963^{2}).
DBI	F.G. Vigoureaux et al. (eds.), *Dictionnaire de la Bible,* 5 vols. in 10 (1912); Supplement, 8 vols. (1928–66)
Decal.	Philo, *De Decalogo.*
Dem.	*Demai* (talmudic tractate).
DER	*Derekh Ereẓ Rabbah* (post-talmudic tractate).
Derenbourg, Hist	J. Derenbourg *Essai sur l'histoire et la géographie de la Palestine* (1867).
Det.	Philo, *Quod deterius potiori insidiari solet.*
Deus	Philo, *Quod Deus immutabilis sit.*
Deut.	Deuteronomy (Bible).
Deut. R.	*Deuteronomy Rabbah.*
DEZ	*Derekh Ereẓ Zuta* (post-talmudic tractate).
DHGE	*Dictionnaire d'histoire et de géographie ecclésiastiques,* ed. by A. Baudrillart et al., 17 vols (1912–68).
Dik. Sof	*Dikdukei Soferim,* variae lections of the talmudic text by Raphael Nathan Rabbinovitz (16 vols., 1867–97).
Dinur, Golah	B. Dinur (Dinaburg), *Yisrael ba-Golah,* 2 vols. in 7 (1959–68) = vols. 5 and 6 of his *Toledot Yisrael,* second series.
Dinur, Haganah	B. Dinur (ed.), *Sefer Toledot ha-Haganah* (1954ff.).
Diringer, Iscr	D. Diringer, *Iscrizioni antico-ebraiche palestinesi* (1934).
Discoveries	*Discoveries in the Judean Desert* (1955ff.).
DNB	*Dictionary of National Biography,* 66 vols. (1921–222) with Supplements.
Dubnow, Divrei	S. Dubnow, *Divrei Yemei Am Olam,* 11 vols (1923–38 and further editions).
Dubnow, Ḥasidut	S. Dubnow, *Toledot ha-Ḥasidut* (1960^{2}).
Dubnow, Hist	S. Dubnow, *History of the Jews* (1967).
Dubnow, Hist Russ	S. Dubnow, *History of the Jews in Russia and Poland,* 3 vols. (1916 20).
Dubnow, Outline	S. Dubnow, *An Outline of Jewish History,* 3 vols. (1925–29).
Dubnow, Weltgesch	S. Dubnow, *Weltgeschichte des juedischen Volkes* 10 vols. (1925–29).
Dukes, Poesie	L. Dukes, *Zur Kenntnis der neuhebraeischen religioesen Poesie* (1842).
Dunlop, Khazars	D. H. Dunlop, *History of the Jewish Khazars* (1954).
EA	El Amarna Letters (edited by J.A. Knudtzon), *Die El-Amarna Tafel,* 2 vols. (1907 14).
EB	*Encyclopaedia Britannica.*
EBI	*Estudios biblicos* (1941ff.).
EBIB	T.K. Cheyne and J.S. Black, *Encyclopaedia Biblica,* 4 vols. (1899–1903).
Ebr.	Philo, *De Ebrietate.*
Eccles.	Ecclesiastes (Bible).
Eccles. R.	*Ecclesiastes Rabbah.*
Ecclus.	Ecclesiasticus or Wisdom of Ben Sira (or Sirach; Apocrypha).
Eduy.	*Eduyyot* (mishanic tractate).

EG	*Enziklopedyah shel Galuyyot* (1953ff.).
EH	*Even ha-Ezer.*
EHA	*Enziklopedyah la-Ḥafirot Arkheologiyyot be-Ereẓ Yisrael,* 2 vols. (1970).
EI	*Enzyklopaedie des Islams,* 4 vols. (1905–14). Supplement vol. (1938).
EIS	*Encyclopaedia of Islam,* 4 vols. (1913–36; repr. 1954–68).
EIS^{2}	*Encyclopaedia of Islam, second edition (1960–2000).*
Eisenstein, Dinim	J.D. Eisenstein, *Oẓar Dinim u-Minhagim* (1917; several reprints).
Eisenstein, Yisrael	J.D. Eisenstein, *Oẓar Yisrael* (10 vols, 1907–13; repr. with several additions 1951).
EIV	*Enziklopedyah Ivrit* (1949ff.).
EJ	*Encyclopaedia Judaica* (German, A-L only), 10 vols. (1928–34).
EJC	*Enciclopedia Judaica Castellana,* 10 vols. (1948–51).
Elbogen, Century	I Elbogen, *A Century of Jewish Life* (1960^{2}).
Elbogen, Gottesdienst	I Elbogen, *Der juedische Gottesdienst ...* (1931^{3}, repr. 1962).
Elon, Mafte'aḥ	M. Elon (ed.), *Mafte'aḥ ha-She'elot ve-ha-Teshuvot ha-Rosh* (1965).
EM	*Enziklopedyah Mikra'it* (1950ff.).
I (or II) En.	I and II Enoch (Pseudepigrapha).
EncRel	*Encyclopedia of Religion,* 15 vols. (1987, 2005^{2}).
Eph.	Epistle to the Ephesians (New Testament).
Ephros, Cant	G. Ephros, *Cantorial Anthology,* 5 vols. (1929–57).
Ep. Jer.	Epistle of Jeremy (Apocrypha).
Epstein, Amora'im	J N. Epstein, *Mevo'ot le-Sifrut ha-Amora'im* (1962).
Epstein, Marriage	L M. Epstein, *Marriage Laws in the Bible and the Talmud* (1942).
Epstein, Mishnah	J. N. Epstein, *Mavo le-Nusaḥ ha-Mishnah,* 2 vols. (1964^{2}).
Epstein, Tanna'im	J. N. Epstein, *Mavo le-Sifruth ha-Tanna'im.* (1947).
ER	*Ecumenical Review.*
Er.	*Eruvin* (talmudic tractate).
ERE	*Encyclopaedia of Religion and Ethics,* 13 vols. (1908–26); reprinted.
ErIsr	*Eretz-Israel,* Israel Exploration Society.
I Esd.	I Esdras (Apocrypha) (= III Ezra).
II Esd.	II Esdras (Apocrypha) (= IV Ezra).
ESE	*Ephemeris fuer semitische Epigraphik,* ed. by M. Lidzbarski.
ESN	*Encyclopaedia Sefaradica Neerlandica,* 2 pts. (1949).
ESS	*Encyclopaedia of the Social Sciences,* 15 vols. (1930–35); reprinted in 8 vols. (1948–49).
Esth.	Esther (Bible).
Est. R.	*Esther Rabbah.*
ET	*Enziklopedyah Talmudit* (1947ff.).
Eusebius, Onom.	E. Klostermann (ed.), *Das Onomastikon* (1904), Greek with Hieronymus' Latin translation.
Ex.	Exodus (Bible).

Ex. R.	*Exodus Rabbah.*
Exs	Philo, *De Exsecrationibus.*
EẒD	*Enziklopeday shel ha-Ẓiyyonut ha-Datit* (1951ff.).
Ezek.	Ezekiel (Bible).
Ezra	Ezra (Bible).
III Ezra	III Ezra (Pseudepigrapha).
IV Ezra	IV Ezra (Pseudepigrapha).
Feliks, Ha-Ẓome'aḥ	*J. Feliks, Ha-Ẓome'aḥ ve-ha-Ḥai ba-Mishnah* (1983).
Finkelstein, Middle Ages	L. Finkelstein, *Jewish Self-Government in the Middle Ages* (1924).
Fischel, Islam	W.J. Fischel, *Jews in the Economic and Political Life of Mediaeval Islam* (1937; reprint with introduction "The Court Jew in the Islamic World," 1969).
FJW	*Fuehrer durch die juedische Gemeindeverwaltung und Wohlfahrtspflege in Deutschland* (1927/28).
Frankel, Mevo	Z. Frankel, *Mevo ha-Yerushalmi* (1870; reprint 1967).
Frankel, Mishnah	Z. Frankel, *Darkhei ha-Mishnah* (1959^{2}; reprint 1959^{2}).
Frazer, Folk-Lore	J.G. Frazer, *Folk-Lore in the Old Testament,* 3 vols. (1918–19).
Frey, Corpus	J.-B. Frey, *Corpus Inscriptionum Iudaicarum,* 2 vols. (1936–52).
Friedmann, Lebensbilder	A. Friedmann, *Lebensbilder beruehmter Kantoren,* 3 vols. (1918–27).
FRLT	*Forschungen zur Religion und Literatur des Alten und Neuen Testaments* (series) (1950ff.).
Frumkin-Rivlin	A.L. Frumkin and E. Rivlin, *Toledot Ḥakhmei Yerushalayim,* 3 vols. (1928–30), Supplement vol. (1930).
Fuenn, Keneset	S.J. Fuenn, *Keneset Yisrael,* 4 vols. (1887–90).
Fuerst, Bibliotheca	J. Fuerst, *Bibliotheca Judaica,* 2 vols. (1863; repr. 1960).
Fuerst, Karaeertum	J. Fuerst, *Geschichte des Karaeertums,* 3 vols. (1862–69).
Fug.	Philo, *De Fuga et Inventione.*
Gal.	Epistle to the Galatians (New Testament).
Galling, Reallexikon	K. Galling, *Biblisches Reallexikon* (1937).
Gardiner, Onomastica	A.H. Gardiner, *Ancient Egyptian Onomastica,* 3 vols. (1947).
Geiger, Mikra	A. Geiger, *Ha-Mikra ve-Targumav,* tr. by J.L. Baruch (1949).
Geiger, Urschrift	A. Geiger, *Urschrift und Uebersetzungen der Bibel* 1928^{2}).
Gen.	Genesis (Bible).
Gen. R.	*Genesis Rabbah.*
Ger.	*Gerim* (post-talmudic tractate).
Germ Jud	M. Brann, I. Elbogen, A. Freimann, and H. Tykocinski (eds.), *Germania Judaica,* vol. 1 (1917; repr. 1934 and 1963); vol. 2, in 2 pts. (1917–68), ed. by Z. Avneri.

GHAT	*Goettinger Handkommentar zum Alten Testament* (1917–22).
Ghirondi-Neppi	M.S. Ghirondi and G.H. Neppi, *Toledot Gedolei Yisrael u-Ge'onei Italyah ... u-Ve'urim al Sefer Zekher Ẓaddikim li-Verakhah* . . .(1853), index in ZHB, 17 (1914), 171–83.
Gig.	Philo, *De Gigantibus.*
Ginzberg, Legends	L. Ginzberg, *Legends of the Jews,* 7 vols. (1909–38; and many reprints).
Git.	*Gittin* (talmudic tractate).
Glueck, Explorations	N. Glueck, *Explorations in Eastern Palestine,* 2 vols. (1951).
Goell, Bibliography	Y. Goell, *Bibliography of Modern Hebrew Literature in English Translation* (1968).
Goodenough, Symbols	E.R. Goodenough, *Jewish Symbols in the Greco-Roman Period,* 13 vols. (1953–68).
Gordon, Textbook	C.H. Gordon, *Ugaritic Textbook* (1965; repr. 1967).
Graetz, Gesch	H. Graetz, *Geschichte der Juden* (last edition 1874–1908).
Graetz, Hist	H. Graetz, *History of the Jews,* 6 vols. (1891–1902).
Graetz, Psalmen	H. Graetz, *Kritischer Commentar zu den Psalmen,* 2 vols. in 1 (1882–83).
Graetz, Rabbinowitz	H. Graetz, *Divrei Yemei Yisrael,* tr. by S.P. Rabbinowitz. (1928 1929^{2}).
Gray, Names	G.B. Gray, *Studies in Hebrew Proper Names* (1896).
Gressmann, Bilder	H. Gressmann, *Altorientalische Bilder zum Alten Testament* (1927^{2}).
Gressmann, Texte	H. Gressmann, *Altorientalische Texte zum Alten Testament* (1926^{2}).
Gross, Gal Jud	H. Gross, *Gallia Judaica* (1897; repr. with add. 1969).
Grove, Dict	*Grove's Dictionary of Music and Musicians,* ed. by E. Blum 9 vols. (1954^{5}) and suppl. (1961^{5}).
Guedemann, Gesch Erz	M. Guedemann, *Geschichte des Erziehungswesens und der Cultur der abendlaendischen Juden,* 3 vols. (1880–88).
Guedemann, Quellenschr	M. Guedemann, *Quellenschriften zur Geschichte des Unterrichts und der Erziehung bei den deutschen Juden* (1873, 1891).
Guide	Maimonides, *Guide of the Perplexed.*
Gulak, Oẓar	A. Gulak, *Oẓar ha-Shetarot ha-Nehugim be-Yisrael* (1926).
Gulak, Yesodei	A. Gulak, *Yesodei ha-Mishpat ha-Ivri, Seder Dinei Mamonot be-Yisrael, al pi Mekorot ha-Talmud ve-ha-Posekim,* 4 vols. (1922; repr. 1967).
Guttmann, Mafte'aḥ	M. Guttmann, *Mafte'aḥ ha-Talmud,* 3 vols. (1906–30).
Guttmann, Philosophies	J. Guttmann, *Philosophies of Judaism* (1964).
Hab.	*Habakkuk* (Bible).
Ḥag.	*Ḥagigah* (talmudic tractate).
Haggai	*Haggai* (Bible).
Ḥal.	*Ḥallah* (talmudic tractate).

Halevy, Dorot	I. Halevy, *Dorot ha-Rishonim,* 6 vols. (1897–1939).
Halpern, Pinkas	I. Halpern (Halperin), *Pinkas Va'ad Arba Araẓot* (1945).
Hananel-Eškenazi	A. Hananel and Eškenazi (eds.), *Fontes Hebraici ad res oeconomicas socialesque terrarum balcanicarum saeculo XVI pertinentes,* 2 vols, (1958–60; in Bulgarian).
HB	*Hebraeische Bibliographie* (1858–82).
Heb.	Epistle to the Hebrews (New Testament).
Heilprin, Dorot	J. Heilprin (Heilperin), *Seder ha-Dorot,* 3 vols. (1882; repr. 1956).
Her.	Philo, *Quis Rerum Divinarum Heres.*
Hertz, Prayer	J.H. Hertz (ed.), *Authorised Daily Prayer Book* (rev. ed. 1948; repr. 1963).
Herzog, Instit	I. Herzog, *The Main Institutions of Jewish Law,* 2 vols. (1936–39; repr. 1967).
Herzog-Hauck	J.J. Herzog and A. Hauch (eds.), *Real-encyklopaedie fuer protestantische Theologie* (1896–1913^{3}).
HḤY	*Ha-Ẓofeh le-Ḥokhmat Yisrael* (first four volumes under the title *Ha-Ẓofeh me-Ereẓ Hagar)* (1910/11–13).
Hirschberg, Afrikah	H.Z. Hirschberg, *Toledot ha-Yehudim be-Afrikah ha-Zofonit,* 2 vols. (1965).
HJ	*Historia Judaica* (1938–61).
HL	*Das Heilige Land* (1857ff.)
ḤM	*Ḥoshen Mishpat.*
Hommel, Ueberliefer.	F. Hommel, *Die altisraelitische Ueberlieferung in inschriftlicher Beleuchtung* (1897).
Hor.	*Horayot* (talmudic tractate).
Horodezky, Ḥasidut	S.A. Horodezky, *Ha-Ḥasidut ve-ha-Ḥasidim,* 4 vols. (1923).
Horowitz, Ereẓ Yis	I.W. Horowitz, *Ereẓ Yisrael u-Shekhenoteha* (1923).
Hos.	Hosea (Bible).
HTR	*Harvard Theological Review* (1908ff.).
HUCA	*Hebrew Union College Annual* (1904; 1924ff.)
Ḥul.	*Ḥullin* (talmudic tractate).
Husik, Philosophy	I. Husik, *History of Medieval Jewish Philosophy* (1932^{2}).
Hyman, Toledot	A. Hyman, *Toledot Tanna'im ve-Amora'im* (1910; repr. 1964).
Ibn Daud, Tradition	Abraham Ibn Daud, *Sefer ha-Qabbalah – The Book of Tradition,* ed. and tr. By G.D. Cohen (1967).
ICC	International Critical Commentary on the Holy Scriptures of the Old and New Testaments (series, 1908ff.).
IDB	*Interpreter's Dictionary of the Bible,* 4 vols. (1962).
Idelsohn, Litugy	A. Z. Idelsohn, *Jewish Liturgy and its Development* (1932; paperback repr. 1967)
Idelsohn, Melodien	A. Z. Idelsohn, *Hebraeisch-orientalischer Melodienschatz,* 10 vols. (1914 32).
Idelsohn, Music	A. Z. Idelsohn, *Jewish Music in its Historical Development* (1929; paperback repr. 1967).

IEJ — *Israel Exploration Journal* (1950ff.).
IESS — *International Encyclopedia of the Social Sciences* (various eds.).
IG — *Inscriptiones Graecae,* ed. by the Prussian Academy.
IGYB — *Israel Government Year Book* (1949/50ff.).
ILR — *Israel Law Review* (1966ff.).
IMIT — *Izraelita Magyar Irodalmi Társulat Évkönyv* (1895 1948).
IMT — International Military Tribunal.
INB — *Israel Numismatic Bulletin* (1962–63).
INJ — *Israel Numismatic Journal* (1963ff.).
Ios — Philo, *De Iosepho.*
Isa. — Isaiah (Bible).
ITHL — Institute for the Translation of Hebrew Literature.
IZBG — *Internationale Zeitschriftenschau fuer Bibelwissenschaft und Grenzgebiete* (1951ff.).

JA — *Journal asiatique* (1822ff.).
James — Epistle of James (New Testament).
JAOS — *Journal of the American Oriental Society* (c. 1850ff.)
Jastrow, Dict — M. Jastrow, *Dictionary of the Targumim, the Talmud Babli and Yerushalmi, and the Midrashic literature,* 2 vols. (1886 1902 and reprints).
JBA — *Jewish Book Annual* (19242ff.).
JBL — *Journal of Biblical Literature* (1881ff.).
JBR — *Journal of Bible and Religion* (1933ff.).
JC — *Jewish Chronicle* (1841ff.).
JCS — *Journal of Cuneiform Studies* (1947ff.).
JE — *Jewish Encyclopedia,* 12 vols. (1901–05 several reprints).
Jer. — Jeremiah (Bible).
Jeremias, Alte Test — A. Jeremias, *Das Alte Testament im Lichte des alten Orients* 1930[4]).
JGGJČ — *Jahrbuch der Gesellschaft fuer Geschichte der Juden in der Čechoslovakischen Republik* (1929–38).
JHSEM — Jewish Historical Society of England, *Miscellanies* (1925ff.).
JHSET — Jewish Historical Society of England, *Transactions* (1893ff.).
JJGL — *Jahrbuch fuer juedische Geschichte und Literatur* (Berlin) (1898–1938).
JJLG — *Jahrbuch der juedische-literarischen Gesellschaft* (Frankfurt) (1903–32).
JJS — *Journal of Jewish Studies* (1948ff.).
JJSO — *Jewish Journal of Sociology* (1959ff.).
JJV — *Jahrbuch fuer juedische Volkskunde* (1898–1924).
JL — *Juedisches Lexikon,* 5 vols. (1927–30).
JMES — *Journal of the Middle East Society* (1947ff.).
JNES — *Journal of Near Eastern Studies* (continuation of AJSLL) (1942ff.).
J.N.U.L. — Jewish National and University Library.
Job — Job (Bible).
Joel — Joel (Bible).
John — Gospel according to John (New Testament).
I, II and III John — Epistles of John (New Testament).
Jos., Ant — Josephus, *Jewish Antiquities* (Loeb Classics ed.).
Jos. Apion — Josephus, *Against Apion* (Loeb Classics ed.).
Jos., index — *Josephus Works,* Loeb Classics ed., index of names.
Jos., Life — Josephus, *Life* (ed. Loeb Classics).
Jos, Wars — Josephus, *The Jewish Wars* (Loeb Classics ed.).
Josh. — Joshua (Bible).
JPESB — Jewish Palestine Exploration Society Bulletin, see BJPES.
JPESJ — Jewish Palestine Exploration Society Journal – Eng. Title of the Hebrew periodical *Kovez ha-Ḥevrah ha-Ivrit la-Ḥakirat Erez Yisrael va-Attikoteha.*
JPOS — *Journal of the Palestine Oriental Society* (1920–48).
JPS — Jewish Publication Society of America, *The Torah* (1962, 1967[2]); *The Holy Scriptures* (1917).
JQR — *Jewish Quarterly Review* (1889ff.).
JR — *Journal of Religion* (1921ff.).
JRAS — *Journal of the Royal Asiatic Society* (1838ff.).
JHR — *Journal of Religious History* (1960/61ff.).
JSOS — *Jewish Social Studies* (1939ff.).
JSS — *Journal of Semitic Studies* (1956ff.).
JTS — *Journal of Theological Studies* (1900ff.).
JTSA — Jewish Theological Seminary of America (also abbreviated as JTS).
Jub. — Jubilees (Pseudepigrapha).
Judg. — Judges (Bible).
Judith — Book of Judith (Apocrypha).
Juster, Juifs — J. Juster, *Les Juifs dans l'Empire Romain,* 2 vols. (1914).
JYB — *Jewish Year Book* (1896ff.).
JZWL — *Juedische Zeitschift fuer Wissenschaft und Leben* (1862–75).

Kal. — *Kallah* (post-talmudic tractate).
Kal. R. — *Kallah Rabbati* (post-talmudic tractate).
Katz, England — *The Jews in the History of England, 1485-1850 (1994).*
Kaufmann, Schriften — D. Kaufmann, *Gesammelte Schriften,* 3 vols. (1908 15).
Kaufmann Y., Religion — Y. Kaufmann, *The Religion of Israel* (1960), abridged tr. of his *Toledot.*
Kaufmann Y., Toledot — Y. Kaufmann, *Toledot ha-Emunah ha-Yisre'elit,* 4 vols. (1937 57).
KAWJ — *Korrespondenzblatt des Vereins zur Gruendung und Erhaltung der Akademie fuer die Wissenschaft des Judentums* (1920 30).
Kayserling, Bibl — M. Kayserling, *Biblioteca Española-Portugueza-Judaica* (1880; repr. 1961).
Kelim — *Kelim* (mishnaic tractate).
Ker. — *Keritot* (talmudic tractate).
Ket. — *Ketubbot* (talmudic tractate).

Kid.	*Kiddushim* (talmudic tractate).
Kil.	*Kilayim* (talmudic tractate).
Kin.	*Kinnim* (mishnaic tractate).
Kisch, Germany	G. Kisch, *Jews in Medieval Germany* (1949).
Kittel, Gesch	R. Kittel, *Geschichte des Volkes Israel,* 3 vols. (1922–28).
Klausner, Bayit Sheni	J. Klausner, *Historyah shel ha-Bayit ha-Sheni,* 5 vols. (1950/512).
Klausner, Sifrut	J. Klausner, *Historyah shel haSifrut ha-Ivrit ha-Ḥadashah,* 6 vols. (1952–582).
Klein, corpus	S. Klein (ed.), *Juedisch-palaestinisches Corpus Inscriptionum* (1920).
Koehler-Baumgartner	L. Koehler and W. Baumgartner, *Lexicon in Veteris Testamenti libros* (1953).
Kohut, Arukh	H.J.A. Kohut (ed.), *Sefer he-Arukh ha-Shalem,* by Nathan b. Jehiel of Rome, 8 vols. (1876–92; Supplement by S. Krauss et al., 1936; repr. 1955).
Krauss, Tal Arch	S. Krauss, *Talmudische Archaeologie,* 3 vols. (1910–12; repr. 1966).
Kressel, Leksikon	G. Kressel, *Leksikon ha-Sifrut ha-Ivrit ba-Dorot ha-Aḥaronim,* 2 vols. (1965–67).
KS	*Kirjath Sepher* (1923/4ff.).
Kut.	*Kuttim* (post-talmudic tractate).
LA	Studium Biblicum Franciscanum, *Liber Annuus* (1951ff.).
L.A.	Philo, *Legum allegoriae.*
Lachower, Sifrut	F. Lachower, *Toledot ha-Sifrut ha-Ivrit ha-Ḥadashah,* 4 vols. (1947–48; several reprints).
Lam.	Lamentations (Bible).
Lam. R.	*Lamentations Rabbah.*
Landshuth, Ammudei	L. Landshuth, *Ammudei ha-Avodah* (1857–62; repr. with index, 1965).
Legat.	Philo, *De Legatione ad Caium.*
Lehmann, Nova Bibl	R.P. Lehmann, *Nova Bibliotheca Anglo-Judaica* (1961).
Lev.	Leviticus (Bible).
Lev. R.	*Leviticus Rabbah.*
Levy, Antologia	I. Levy, *Antologia de liturgia judeo-española* (1965ff.).
Levy J., Chald Targ	J. Levy, *Chaldaeisches Woerterbuch ueber die Targumim,* 2 vols. (1967–68; repr. 1959).
Levy J., Nuehebr Tal	J. Levy, *Neuhebraeisches und chaldaeisches Woerterbuch ueber die Talmudim . . .,* 4 vols. (1875–89; repr. 1963).
Lewin, Oẓar	Lewin, *Oẓar ha-Ge'onim,* 12 vols. (1928–43).
Lewysohn, Zool	L. Lewysohn, *Zoologie des Talmuds* (1858).
Lidzbarski, Handbuch	M. Lidzbarski, *Handbuch der nordsemitischen Epigraphik,* 2 vols (1898).
Life	Josephus, *Life* (Loeb Classis ed.).
LNYL	*Leksikon fun der Nayer Yidisher Literatur* (1956ff.).
Loew, Flora	I. Loew, *Die Flora der Juden,* 4 vols. (1924 34; repr. 1967).
LSI	*Laws of the State of Israel* (1948ff.).
Luckenbill, Records	D.D. Luckenbill, *Ancient Records of Assyria and Babylonia,* 2 vols. (1926).
Luke	Gospel according to Luke (New Testament)
LXX	Septuagint (Greek translation of the Bible).
Ma'as.	*Ma'aserot* (talmudic tractate).
Ma'as. Sh.	*Ma'ase Sheni* (talmudic tractate).
I, II, III, and IVMacc.	Maccabees, I, II, III (Apocrypha), IV (Pseudepigrapha).
Maimonides, Guide	Maimonides, *Guide of the Perplexed.*
Maim., Yad	Maimonides, *Mishneh Torah (Yad Ḥazakah).*
Maisler, Untersuchungen	B. Maisler (Mazar), *Untersuchungen zur alten Geschichte und Ethnographie Syriens und Palaestinas,* 1 (1930).
Mak.	*Makkot* (talmudic tractate).
Makhsh.	*Makhshrin* (mishnaic tractate).
Mal.	Malachi (Bible).
Mann, Egypt	J. Mann, *Jews in Egypt in Palestine under the Fatimid Caliphs,* 2 vols. (1920–22).
Mann, Texts	J. Mann, *Texts and Studies,* 2 vols (1931–35).
Mansi	G.D. Mansi, *Sacrorum Conciliorum nova et amplissima collectio,* 53 vols. in 60 (1901–27; repr. 1960).
Margalioth, Gedolei	M. Margalioth, *Enẓiklopedyah le-Toledot Gedolei Yisrael,* 4 vols. (1946–50).
Margalioth, Ḥakhmei	M. Margalioth, *Enẓiklopedyah le-Ḥakhmei ha-Talmud ve-ha-Ge'onim,* 2 vols. (1945).
Margalioth, Cat	G. Margalioth, *Catalogue of the Hebrew and Samaritan Manuscripts in the British Museum,* 4 vols. (1899–1935).
Mark	Gospel according to Mark (New Testament).
Mart. Isa.	Martyrdom of Isaiah (Pseudepigrapha).
Mas.	Masorah.
Matt.	Gospel according to Matthew (New Testament).
Mayer, Art	L.A. Mayer, *Bibliography of Jewish Art* (1967).
MB	*Wochenzeitung* (formerly *Mitteilungsblatt*) *des Irgun Olej Merkas Europa* (1933ff.).
MEAH	*Miscelánea de estudios drabes y hebraicos* (1952ff.).
Meg.	Megillah (talmudic tractate).
Meg. Ta'an.	*Megillat Ta'anit* (in HUCA, 8 9 (1931–32), 318–51).
Me'il	*Me'ilah* (mishnaic tractate).
MEJ	*Middle East Journal* (1947ff.).
Mehk.	*Mekhilta de-R. Ishmael.*
Mekh. SbY	*Mekhilta de-R. Simeon bar Yoḥai.*
Men.	*Menaḥot* (talmudic tractate).
MER	*Middle East Record* (1960ff.).
Meyer, Gesch	E. Meyer, *Geschichte des Alterums,* 5 vols. in 9 (1925–58).
Meyer, Ursp	E. Meyer, *Urspring und Anfaenge des Christentums* (1921).
Mez.	*Mezuzah* (post-talmudic tractate).
MGADJ	*Mitteilungen des Gesamtarchivs der deutschen Juden* (1909–12).
MGG	*Die Musik in Geschichte und Gegenwart,* 14 vols. (1949–68).

MGG^2	*Die Musik in Geschichte und Gegenwart, 2nd edition (1994)*
MGH	*Monumenta Germaniae Historica* (1826ff.).
MGJV	*Mitteilungen der Gesellschaft fuer juedische Volkskunde* (1898–1929); title varies, see also JJV.
MGWJ	*Monatsschrift fuer Geschichte und Wissenschaft des Judentums* (1851–1939).
MHJ	*Monumenta Hungariae Judaica,* 11 vols. (1903–67).
Michael, Or	H.Ḥ. Michael, *Or ha-Ḥayyim: Ḥakhmei Yisrael ve-Sifreihem,* ed. by S.Z. Ḥ. Halberstam and N. Ben-Menahem (1965^2).
Mid.	*Middot* (mishnaic tractate).
Mid. Ag.	*Midrash Aggadah.*
Mid. Hag.	*Midrash ha-Gadol.*
Mid. Job.	*Midrash Job.*
Mid. Jonah	*Midrash Jonah.*
Mid. Lek. Tov	*Midrash Lekaḥ Tov.*
Mid. Prov.	*Midrash Proverbs.*
Mid. Ps.	*Midrash Tehillim* (Eng tr. *The Midrash on Psalms* (JPS, 1959).
Mid. Sam.	*Midrash Samuel.*
Mid. Song	*Midrash Shir ha-Shirim.*
Mid. Tan.	*Midrash Tanna'im* on Deuteronomy.
Miége, Maroc	J.L. Miège, *Le Maroc et l'Europe,* 3 vols. (1961 62).
Mig.	Philo, *De Migratione Abrahami.*
Mik.	*Mikva'ot* (mishnaic tractate).
Milano, Bibliotheca	A. Milano, *Bibliotheca Historica Italo-Judaica* (1954); supplement for 1954–63 (1964); supplement for 1964–66 in RMI, 32 (1966).
Milano, Italia	A. Milano, *Storia degli Ebrei in Italia* (1963).
MIO	*Mitteilungen des Instituts fuer Orientforschung* 1953ff.).
Mish.	Mishnah.
MJ	*Le Monde Juif* (1946ff.).
MJC	see Neubauer, Chronicles.
MK	*Mo'ed Katan* (talmudic tractate).
MNDPV	*Mitteilungen und Nachrichten des deutschen Palaestinavereins* (1895–1912).
Mortara, Indice	M. Mortara, *Indice Alfabetico dei Rabbini e Scrittori Israeliti ... in Italia ...* (1886).
Mos	Philo, *De Vita Mosis.*
Moscati, Epig	S, Moscati, *Epigrafia ebraica antica* 1935–1950 (1951).
MT	Masoretic Text of the Bible.
Mueller, Musiker	[E.H. Mueller], *Deutisches Musiker-Lexikon* (1929)
Munk, Mélanges	S. Munk, *Mélanges de philosophie juive et arabe* (1859; repr. 1955).
Mut.	Philo, *De Mutatione Nominum.*
MWJ	*Magazin fuer die Wissenshaft des Judentums* (18745 93).
Nah.	Nahum (Bible).
Naz.	*Nazir* (talmudic tractate).
NDB	*Neue Deutsche Biographie* (1953ff.).
Ned.	*Nedarim* (talmudic tractate).
Neg.	*Nega'im* (mishnaic tractate).
Neh.	Nehemiah (Bible).
NG^2	*New Grove Dictionary of Music and Musicians* (2001).
Nuebauer, Cat	A. Neubauer, *Catalogue of the Hebrew Manuscripts in the Bodleian Library ...,* 2 vols. (1886–1906).
Neubauer, Chronicles	A. Neubauer, *Mediaeval Jewish Chronicles,* 2 vols. (Heb., 1887–95; repr. 1965), Eng. title of *Seder ha-Ḥakhamim ve-Korot ha-Yamim.*
Neubauer, Géogr	A. Neubauer, *La géographie du Talmud* (1868).
Neuman, Spain	A.A. Neuman, *The Jews in Spain, their Social, Political, and Cultural Life During the Middle Ages,* 2 vols. (1942).
Neusner, Babylonia	J. Neusner, *History of the Jews in Babylonia,* 5 vols. 1965–70), 2nd revised printing 1969ff.).
Nid.	*Niddah* (talmudic tractate).
Noah	Fragment of Book of Noah (Pseudepigrapha).
Noth, Hist Isr	M. Noth, *History of Israel* (1958).
Noth, Personennamen	M. Noth, *Die israelitischen Personennamen.* ... (1928).
Noth, Ueberlief	M. Noth, *Ueberlieferungsgeschichte des Pentateuchs* (1949).
Noth, Welt	M. Noth, *Die Welt des Alten Testaments* (1957^3).
Nowack, Lehrbuch	W. Nowack, *Lehrbuch der hebraeischen Archaeologie,* 2 vols (1894).
NT	New Testament.
Num.	Numbers (Bible).
Num R.	*Numbers Rabbah.*
Obad.	Obadiah (Bible).
ODNB online	*Oxford Dictionary of National Biography.*
OḤ	*Oraḥ Ḥayyim.*
Oho.	*Oholot* (mishnaic tractate).
Olmstead	H.T. Olmstead, *History of Palestine and Syria* (1931; repr. 1965).
OLZ	*Orientalistische Literaturzeitung* (1898ff.)
Onom.	Eusebius, *Onomasticon.*
Op.	Philo, *De Opificio Mundi.*
OPD	*Osef Piskei Din shel ha-Rabbanut ha-Rashit le-Ereẓ Yisrael, Bet ha-Din ha-Gadol le-Irurim* (1950).
Or.	*Orlah* (talmudic tractate).
Or. Sibyll.	Sibylline Oracles (Pseudepigrapha).
OS	*L'Orient Syrien* (1956ff.)
OTS	*Oudtestamentische Studien* (1942ff.).
PAAJR	*Proceedings of the American Academy for Jewish Research* (1930ff.)
Pap 4QS^e	A papyrus exemplar of IQS.
Par.	*Parah* (mishnaic tractate).
Pauly-Wissowa	A.F. Pauly, *Realencyklopaedie der klassichen Alertumswissenschaft,* ed. by G. Wissowa et al. (1864ff.)

PD	*Piskei Din shel Bet ha-Mishpat ha-Elyon le-Yisrael* (1948ff.)
PDR	*Piskei Din shel Battei ha-Din ha-Rabbaniyyim be-Yisrael.*
PdRE	*Pirkei de-R. Eliezer* (Eng. tr. 1916. (1965^{2}).
PdRK	*Pesikta de-Rav Kahana.*
Pe'ah	*Pe'ah* (talmudic tractate).
Peake, Commentary	A.J. Peake (ed.), *Commentary on the Bible* (1919; rev. 1962).
Pedersen, Israel	J. Pedersen, *Israel, Its Life and Culture,* 4 vols. in 2 (1926–40).
PEFQS	*Palestine Exploration Fund Quarterly Statement* (1869–1937; since 1938–PEQ).
PEQ	*Palestine Exploration Quarterly* (until 1937 PEFQS; after 1927 includes BBSAJ).
Perles, Beitaege	J. Perles, *Beitraege zur rabbinischen Sprach- und Alterthumskunde* (1893).
Pes.	*Pesaḥim* (talmudic tractate).
Pesh.	Peshitta (Syriac translation of the Bible).
Pesher Hab.	Commentary to Habakkuk from Qumran; see 1Qp Hab.
I and II Pet.	Epistles of Peter (New Testament).
Pfeiffer, Introd	R.H. Pfeiffer, *Introduction to the Old Testament* (1948).
PG	J.P. Migne (ed.), *Patrologia Graeca,* 161 vols. (1866–86).
Phil.	Epistle to the Philippians (New Testament).
Philem.	Epistle to the Philemon (New Testament).
PIASH	*Proceedings of the Israel Academy of Sciences and Humanities* (1963/7ff.).
PJB	*Palaestinajahrbuch des deutschen evangelischen Institutes fuer Altertumswissenschaft,* Jerusalem (1905–1933).
PK	*Pinkas ha-Kehillot,* encyclopedia of Jewish communities, published in over 30 volumes by Yad Vashem from 1970 and arranged by countries, regions and localities. For 3-vol. English edition see Spector, *Jewish Life.*
PL	J.P. Migne (ed.), *Patrologia Latina* 221 vols. (1844–64).
Plant	Philo, *De Plantatione.*
PO	R. Graffin and F. Nau (eds.), *Patrologia Orientalis* (1903ff.)
Pool, Prayer	D. de Sola Pool, *Traditional Prayer Book for Sabbath and Festivals* (1960).
Post	Philo, *De Posteritate Caini.*
PR	*Pesikta Rabbati.*
Praem.	Philo, *De Praemiis et Poenis.*
Prawer, Ẓalbanim	J. Prawer, *Toledot Mamlekhet ha-Ẓalbanim be-Ereẓ Yisrael,* 2 vols. (1963).
Press, Ereẓ	I. Press, *Ereẓ-Yisrael, Enẓiklopedyah Topografit-Historit,* 4 vols. (1951–55).
Pritchard, Pictures	J.B. Pritchard (ed.), *Ancient Near East in Pictures* (1954, 1970).
Pritchard, Texts	J.B. Pritchard (ed.), *Ancient Near East Texts* ... (1970^{3}).
Pr. Man.	Prayer of Manasses (Apocrypha).
Prob.	Philo, *Quod Omnis Probus Liber Sit.*
Prov.	Proverbs (Bible).
PS	*Palestinsky Sbornik* (Russ. (1881 1916, 1954ff).
Ps.	Psalms (Bible).
PSBA	*Proceedings of the Society of Biblical Archaeology* (1878–1918).
Ps. of Sol	Psalms of Solomon (Pseudepigrapha).
IQ Apoc	The *Genesis Apocryphon* from Qumran, cave one, ed. by N. Avigad and Y. Yadin (1956).
6QD	*Damascus Document* or *Sefer Berit Dammesk* from Qumran, cave six, ed. by M. Baillet, in RB, 63 (1956), 513–23 (see also CD).
QDAP	*Quarterly of the Department of Antiquities in Palestine* (1932ff.).
4QDeut. 32	Manuscript of Deuteronomy 32 from Qumran, cave four (ed. by P.W. Skehan, in BASOR, 136 (1954), 12–15).
4QEx^{a}	Exodus manuscript in Jewish script from Qumran, cave four.
4QEx$^{\alpha}$	Exodus manuscript in Paleo-Hebrew script from Qumran, cave four (partially ed. by P.W. Skehan, in JBL, 74 (1955), 182–7).
4QFlor	*Florilegium,* a miscellany from Qumran, cave four (ed. by J.M. Allegro, in JBL, 75 (1956), 176–77 and 77 (1958), 350–54).).
QGJD	*Quellen zur Geschichte der Juden in Deutschland* 1888–98).
IQH	*Thanksgiving Psalms* of *Hodayot* from Qumran, cave one (ed. by E.L. Sukenik and N. Avigad, *Oẓar ha-Megillot ha-Genuzot* (1954).
IQIs^{a}	Scroll of Isaiah from Qumran, cave one (ed. by N. Burrows et al., *Dead Sea Scrolls ...,* 1 (1950).
IQIs^{b}	Scroll of Isaiah from Qumran, cave one (ed. E.L. Sukenik and N. Avigad, *Oẓar ha-Megillot ha-Genuzot* (1954).
IQM	The *War Scroll* or *Serekh ha-Milḥamah* (ed. by E.L. Sukenik and N. Avigad, *Oẓar ha-Megillot ha-Genuzot* (1954).
4QpNah	Commentary on Nahum from Qumran, cave four (partially ed. by J.M. Allegro, in JBL, 75 (1956), 89–95).
IQphyl	Phylacteries *(tefillin)* from Qumran, cave one (ed. by Y. Yadin, in *Eretz Israel,* 9 (1969), 60–85).
4Q Prayer of Nabonidus	A document from Qumran, cave four, belonging to a lost Daniel literature (ed. by J.T. Milik, in RB, 63 (1956), 407–15).
IQS	*Manual of Discipline* or *Serekh ha-Yaḥad* from Qumran, cave one (ed. by M. Burrows et al., *Dead Sea Scrolls ...,* 2, pt. 2 (1951).

IQS[a]	The *Rule of the Congregation or Serekh ha-Edah* from Qumran, cave one (ed. by Burrows et al., *Dead Sea Scrolls* ..., 1 (1950), under the abbreviation IQ28a).
IQS[b]	*Blessings* or *Divrei Berakhot* from Qumran, cave one (ed. by Burrows et al., *Dead Sea Scrolls* ..., 1 (1950), under the abbreviation IQ28b).
4QSam[a]	Manuscript of I and II Samuel from Qumran, cave four (partially ed. by F.M. Cross, in BASOR, 132 (1953), 15–26).
4QSam[b]	Manuscript of I and II Samuel from Qumran, cave four (partially ed. by F.M. Cross, in JBL, 74 (1955), 147–72).
4QTestimonia	Sheet of Testimony from Qumran, cave four (ed. by J.M. Allegro, in JBL, 75 (1956), 174–87).).
4QT.Levi	*Testament of Levi* from Qumran, cave four (partially ed. by J.T. Milik, in RB, 62 (1955), 398–406).
Rabinovitz, Dik Sof	See Dik Sof.
RB	*Revue biblique* (1892ff.)
RBI	*Recherches bibliques* (1954ff.)
RCB	*Revista de cultura biblica* (São Paulo) (1957ff.)
Régné, Cat	J. Régné, *Catalogue des actes . . . des rois d'Aragon, concernant les Juifs* (1213–1327), in: REJ, vols. 60 70, 73, 75–78 (1910–24).
Reinach, Textes	T. Reinach, *Textes d'auteurs Grecs et Romains relatifs au Judaïsme* (1895; repr. 1963).
REJ	*Revue des études juives* (1880ff.).
Rejzen, Leksikon	Z. Rejzen, *Leksikon fun der Yidisher Literature,* 4 vols. (1927–29).
Renan, Ecrivains	A. Neubauer and E. Renan, *Les écrivains juifs français* ... (1893).
Renan, Rabbins	A. Neubauer and E. Renan, *Les rabbins français* (1877).
RES	*Revue des étude sémitiques et Babyloniaca* (1934–45).
Rev.	Revelation (New Testament).
RGG[3]	*Die Religion in Geschichte und Gegenwart,* 7 vols. (1957–65^{3}).
RH	*Rosh Ha-Shanah* (talmudic tractate).
RHJE	*Revue de l'histoire juive en Egypte* (1947ff.).
RHMH	*Revue d'histoire de la médecine hébraïque* (1948ff.).
RHPR	*Revue d'histoire et de philosophie religieuses* (1921ff.).
RHR	*Revue d'histoire des religions* (1880ff.).
RI	*Rivista Israelitica* (1904–12).
Riemann-Einstein	*Hugo Riemanns Musiklexikon,* ed. by A. Einstein (1929^{11}).
Riemann-Gurlitt	*Hugo Riemanns Musiklexikon,* ed. by W. Gurlitt (1959–67^{12}), Personenteil.
Rigg-Jenkinson, Exchequer	J.M. Rigg, H. Jenkinson and H.G. Richardson (eds.), *Calendar of the Pleas Rolls of the Exchequer of the Jews,* 4 vols. (1905–1970); cf. in each instance also J.M. Rigg (ed.), *Select Pleas* ... (1902).
RMI	*Rassegna Mensile di Israel* (1925ff.).
Rom.	Epistle to the Romans (New Testament).
Rosanes, Togarmah	S.A. Rosanes, *Divrei Yemei Yisrael be-Togarmah,* 6 vols. (1907–45), and in 3 vols. (1930–38^{2}).
Rosenbloom, Biogr Dict	J.R. Rosenbloom, *Biographical Dictionary of Early American Jews* (1960).
Roth, Art	C. Roth, *Jewish Art* (1961).
Roth, Dark Ages	C. Roth (ed.), *World History of the Jewish People,* second series, vol. 2, *Dark Ages* (1966).
Roth, England	C. Roth, *History of the Jews in England* (1964^{3}).
Roth, Italy	C. Roth, *History of the Jews in Italy* (1946).
Roth, Mag Bibl	C. Roth, *Magna Bibliotheca Anglo-Judaica* (1937).
Roth, Marranos	C. Roth, *History of the Marranos* (2nd rev. ed 1959; reprint 1966).
Rowley, Old Test	H.H. Rowley, *Old Testament and Modern Study* (1951; repr. 1961).
RS	*Revue sémitiques d'épigraphie et d'histoire ancienne* (1893/94ff.).
RSO	*Rivista degli studi orientali* (1907ff.).
RSV	Revised Standard Version of the Bible.
Rubinstein, Australia I	*H.L. Rubinstein, The Jews in Australia, A Thematic History, Vol. I (1991).*
Rubinstein, Australia II	*W.D. Rubinstein, The Jews in Australia, A Thematic History, Vol. II (1991).*
Ruth	Ruth (Bible).
Ruth R.	*Ruth Rabbah.*
RV	Revised Version of the Bible.
Sac.	Philo, *De Sacrificiis Abelis et Caini.*
Salfeld, Martyrol	S. Salfeld, *Martyrologium des Nuernberger Memorbuches* (1898).
I and II Sam.	Samuel, book I and II (Bible).
Sanh.	*Sanhedrin* (talmudic tractate).
SBA	Society of Biblical Archaeology.
SBB	*Studies in Bibliography and Booklore* (1953ff.).
SBE	*Semana Biblica Española.*
SBT	*Studies in Biblical Theology* (1951ff.).
SBU	*Svenkst Bibliskt Uppslogsvesk,* 2 vols. (1962–63^{2}).
Schirmann, Italyah	J.Ḥ. Schirmann, *Ha-Shirah ha-Ivrit be-Italyah* (1934).
Schirmann, Sefarad	J.Ḥ. Schirmann, *Ha-Shirah ha-Ivrit bi-Sefarad u-vi-Provence,* 2 vols. (1954–56).
Scholem, Mysticism	G. Scholem, *Major Trends in Jewish Mysticism* (rev. ed. 1946; paperback ed. with additional bibliography 1961).
Scholem, Shabbetai Ẓevi	G. Scholem, *Shabbetai Ẓevi ve-ha-Tenu'ah ha-Shabbeta'it bi-Ymei Ḥayyav,* 2 vols. (1967).
Schrader, Keilinschr	E. Schrader, *Keilinschriften und das Alte Testament* (1903^{3}).
Schuerer, Gesch	E. Schuerer, *Geschichte des juedischen Volkes im Zeitalter Jesu Christi,* 3 vols. and index-vol. (1901–11^{4}).

Schuerer, Hist	E. Schuerer, *History of the Jewish People in the Time of Jesus,* ed. by N.N. Glatzer, abridged paperback edition (1961).
Set. T.	*Sefer Torah* (post-talmudic tractate).
Sem.	*Semaḥot* (post-talmudic tractate).
Sendrey, Music	A. Sendrey, *Bibliography of Jewish Music* (1951).
SER	*Seder Eliyahu Rabbah.*
SEZ	*Seder Eliyahu Zuta.*
Shab	*Shabbat* (talmudic tractate).
Sh. Ar.	J. Caro Shulḥan Arukh. OḤ – *Oraḥ Ḥayyim* YD – *Yoreh De'ah* EH – *Even ha-Ezer* ḤM – *Ḥoshen Mishpat.*
Shek.	*Shekalim* (talmudic tractate).
Shev.	*Shevi'it* (talmudic tractate).
Shevu.	*Shevu'ot* (talmudic tractate).
Shunami, Bibl	S. Shunami, *Bibliography of Jewish Bibliographies* (1965^{2}).
Sif.	*Sifrei Deuteronomy.*
Sif. Num.	*Sifrei Numbers.*
Sifra	*Sifra* on Leviticus.
Sif. Zut.	*Sifrei Zuta.*
SIHM	Sources inédites de l'histoire du Maroc (series).
Silverman, Prayer	M. Silverman (ed.), *Sabbath and Festival Prayer Book* (1946).
Singer, Prayer	S. Singer *Authorised Daily Prayer Book* (1943^{17}).
Sob.	Philo, *De Sobrietate.*
Sof.	*Soferim* (post-talmudic tractate).
Som.	Philo, *De Somniis.*
Song	Song of Songs (Bible).
Song. Ch.	Song of the Three Children (Apocrypha).
Song R.	*Song of Songs Rabbah.*
SOR	*Seder Olam Rabbah.*
Sot.	*Sotah* (talmudic tractate).
SOZ	*Seder Olam Zuta.*
Spec.	Philo, *De Specialibus Legibus.*
Spector, Jewish Life	*S. Spector (ed.), Encyclopedia of Jewish Life Before and After the Holocaust (2001).*
Steinschneider, Arab lit	M. Steinschneider, *Die arabische Literatur der Juden* (1902).
Steinschneider, Cat Bod	M. Steinschneider, *Catalogus Librorum Hebraeorum in Bibliotheca Bodleiana,* 3 vols. (1852–60; reprints 1931 and 1964).
Steinschneider, Hanbuch	M. Steinschneider, *Bibliographisches Handbuch ueber die . . . Literatur fuer hebraeische Sprachkunde* (1859; repr. with additions 1937).
Steinschneider, Uebersetzungen	M. Steinschneider, *Die hebraeischen Uebersetzungen des Mittelalters* (1893).
Stern, Americans	M.H. Stern, *Americans of Jewish Descent* (1960).
van Straalen, Cat	S. van Straalen, *Catalogue of Hebrew Books in the British Museum Acquired During the Years 1868–1892* (1894).
Suárez Fernández, Docmentos	L. Suárez Fernández, *Documentos acerca de la expulsion de los Judios de España* (1964).
Suk.	*Sukkah* (talmudic tractate).
Sus.	Susanna (Apocrypha).
SY	*Sefer Yeẓirah.*
Sym.	Symmachus' Greek translation of the Bible.
SZNG	*Studien zur neueren Geschichte.*
Ta'an.	*Ta'anit* (talmudic tractate).
Tam.	*Tamid* (mishnaic tractate).
Tanḥ.	*Tanḥuma.*
Tanḥ. B.	*Tanḥuma.* Buber ed (1885).
Targ. Jon	Targum Jonathan (Aramaic version of the Prophets).
Targ. Onk.	Targum Onkelos (Aramaic version of the Pentateuch).
Targ. Yer.	Targum Yerushalmi.
TB	Babylonian Talmud or Talmud Bavli.
Tcherikover, Corpus	V. Tcherikover, A. Fuks, and M. Stern, *Corpus Papyrorum Judaicorum,* 3 vols. (1957–60).
Tef.	*Tefillin* (post-talmudic tractate).
Tem.	*Temurah* (mishnaic tractate).
Ter.	*Terumah* (talmudic tractate).
Test. Patr.	Testament of the Twelve Patriarchs (Pseudepigrapha). Ash. – Asher Ben. – Benjamin Dan – Dan Gad – Gad Iss. – Issachar Joseph – Joseph Judah – Judah Levi – Levi Naph. – Naphtali Reu. – Reuben Sim. – Simeon Zeb. – Zebulun.
I and II	Epistle to the Thessalonians (New Testament).
Thieme-Becker	U. Thieme and F. Becker (eds.), *Allgemeines Lexikon der bildenden Kuenstler von der Antike bis zur Gegenwart,* 37 vols. (1907–50).
Tidhar	D. Tidhar (ed.), *Enẓiklopedyah la-Ḥalutẓei ha-Yishuv u-Vonav* (1947ff.).
I and II Timothy	Epistles to Timothy (New Testament).
Tit.	Epistle to Titus (New Testament).
TJ	Jerusalem Talmud or Talmud Yerushalmi.
Tob.	Tobit (Apocrypha).
Toh.	*Tohorot* (mishnaic tractate).
Torczyner, Bundeslade	H. Torczyner, *Die Bundeslade und die Anfaenge der Religion Israels* (1930^{3}).
Tos.	*Tosafot.*
Tosef.	Tosefta.
Tristram, Nat Hist	H.B. Tristram, *Natural History of the Bible* (1877^{5}).
Tristram, Survey	Palestine Exploration Fund, *Survey of Western Palestine,* vol. 4 (1884) = *Fauna and Flora* by H.B. Tristram.
TS	*Terra Santa* (1943ff.).

TSBA	*Transactions of the Society of Biblical Archaeology* (1872–93).
TY	*Tevul Yom* (mishnaic tractate).
UBSB	United Bible Society, *Bulletin.*
UJE	*Universal Jewish Encyclopedia,* 10 vols. (1939–43).
Uk.	*Ukẓin* (mishnaic tractate).
Urbach, Tosafot	E.E. Urbach, *Ba'alei ha-Tosafot* (1957^2).
de Vaux, Anc Isr	R. de Vaux, *Ancient Israel: its Life and Institutions* (1961; paperback 1965).
de Vaux, Instit	R. de Vaux, *Institutions de l'Ancien Testament,* 2 vols. (1958 60).
Virt.	Philo, *De Virtutibus.*
Vogelstein, Chronology	M. Volgelstein, *Biblical Chronology (1944).*
Vogelstein-Rieger	H. Vogelstein and P. Rieger, *Geschichte der Juden in Rom,* 2 vols. (1895–96).
VT	*Vetus Testamentum* (1951ff.).
VTS	*Vetus Testamentum* Supplements (1953ff.).
Vulg.	Vulgate (Latin translation of the Bible).
Wars	Josephus, *The Jewish Wars.*
Watzinger, Denkmaeler	K. Watzinger, *Denkmaeler Palaestinas,* 2 vols. (1933–35).
Waxman, Literature	M. Waxman, *History of Jewish Literature,* 5 vols. (1960^2).
Weiss, Dor	I.H. Weiss, *Dor, Dor ve-Doreshav,* 5 vols. (1904^4).
Wellhausen, Proleg	J. Wellhausen, *Prolegomena zur Geschichte Israels* (1927^6).
WI	*Die Welt des Islams* (1913ff.).
Winniger, Biog	S. Wininger, *Grosse juedische National-Biographie ...,* 7 vols. (1925–36).
Wisd.	Wisdom of Solomon (Apocrypha)
WLB	*Wiener Library Bulletin* (1958ff.).
Wolf, Bibliotheca	J.C. Wolf, *Bibliotheca Hebraea,* 4 vols. (1715–33).
Wright, Bible	G.E. Wright, *Westminster Historical Atlas to the Bible* (1945).
Wright, Atlas	G.E. Wright, *The Bible and the Ancient Near East* (1961).
WWWJ	*Who's Who in the World Jewry* (New York, 1955, 1965^2).
WZJT	*Wissenschaftliche Zeitschrift fuer juedische Theologie* (1835–37).
WZKM	*Wiener Zeitschrift fuer die Kunde des Morgenlandes* (1887ff.).
Yaari, Sheluḥei	A. Yaari, *Sheluḥei Ereẓ Yisrael* (1951).
Yad	Maimonides, *Mishneh Torah (Yad Ḥazakah).*
Yad	*Yadayim* (mishnaic tractate).
Yal.	*Yalkut Shimoni.*
Yal. Mak.	*Yalkut Makhiri.*
Yal. Reub.	*Yalkut Reubeni.*
YD	*Yoreh De'ah.*
YE	*Yevreyskaya Entsiklopediya,* 14 vols. (c. 1910).
Yev.	*Yevamot* (talmudic tractate).
YIVOA	*YIVO Annual of Jewish Social Studies* (1946ff.).
YLBI	*Year Book of the Leo Baeck Institute* (1956ff.).
YMḤEY	See BJPES.
YMḤSI	*Yedi'ot ha-Makhon le-Ḥeker ha-Shirah ha-Ivrit* (1935/36ff.).
YMMY	*Yedi'ot ha-Makhon le-Madda'ei ha-Yahadut* (1924/25ff.).
Yoma	*Yoma* (talmudic tractate).
ZA	*Zeitschrift fuer Assyriologie* (1886/87ff.).
Zav.	*Zavim* (mishnaic tractate).
ZAW	*Zeitschrift fuer die alttestamentliche Wissenschaft und die Kunde des nachbiblishchen Judentums* (1881ff.).
ZAWB	*Beihefte* (supplements) to ZAW.
ZDMG	*Zeitschrift der Deutschen Morgenlaendischen Gesellschaft* (1846ff.).
ZDPV	*Zeitschrift des Deutschen Palaestina-Vereins* (1878–1949; from 1949 = BBLA).
Zech.	Zechariah (Bible).
Zedner, Cat	J. Zedner, *Catalogue of Hebrew Books in the Library of the British Museum* (1867; repr. 1964).
Zeitlin, Bibliotheca	W. Zeitlin, *Bibliotheca Hebraica Post-Mendelssohniana* (1891–95).
Zeph.	Zephaniah (Bible).
Zev.	*Zevaḥim* (talmudic tractate).
ZGGJT	*Zeitschrift der Gesellschaft fuer die Geschichte der Juden in der Tschechoslowakei* (1930–38).
ZGJD	*Zeitschrift fuer die Geschichte der Juden in Deutschland* (1887–92).
ZHB	*Zeitschrift fuer hebraeische Bibliographie* (1896–1920).
Zinberg, Sifrut	I. Zinberg, *Toledot Sifrut Yisrael,* 6 vols. (1955–60).
Ẓiẓ.	*Ẓiẓit* (post-talmudic tractate).
ZNW	*Zeitschrift fuer die neutestamentliche Wissenschaft* (1901ff.).
ZS	*Zeitschrift fuer Semitistik und verwandte Gebiete* (1922ff.).
Zunz, Gesch	L. Zunz, *Zur Geschichte und Literatur* (1845).
Zunz, Gesch	L. Zunz, *Literaturgeschichte der synagogalen Poesie* (1865; Supplement, 1867; repr. 1966).
Zunz, Poesie	L. Zunz, *Synogogale Posie des Mittelalters,* ed. by Freimann (1920^2; repr. 1967).
Zunz, Ritus	L. Zunz, *Ritus des synagogalen Gottesdienstes* (1859; repr. 1967).
Zunz, Schr	L. Zunz, *Gesammelte Schriften,* 3 vols. (1875–76).
Zunz, Vortraege	L. Zunz, *Gottesdienstliche vortraege der Juden ...* 1892^2; repr. 1966).
Zunz-Albeck, Derashot	L. Zunz, *Ha-Derashot be-Yisrael,* Heb. Tr. of Zunz Vortraege by H. Albeck (1954^2).

TRANSLITERATION RULES

HEBREW AND SEMITIC LANGUAGES:

	General	*Scientific*
א	not transliterated[1]	ʾ
בּ	b	b
ב	v	v, b̲
גּ	g	g
ג		ḡ
דּ	d	d
ד		d̲
ה	h	h
ו	v – when not a vowel	w
ז	z	z
ח	ḥ	ḥ
ט	t	ṭ, t
י	y – when vowel and at end of words – i	y
כּ	k	k
כ, ך	kh	kh, k̲
ל	l	l̲
מ, ם	m	m
נ, ן	n	n
ס	s	s
ע	not transliterated[1]	ʿ
פּ	p	p
פ, ף	f	p, f, ph
צ, ץ	ẓ	ṣ, ẓ
ק	k	q, k
ר	r	r
שׁ	sh[2]	š
שׂ	s	ś, s
תּ	t	t
ת		t̲
ג׳	dzh, J	ğ
ז׳	zh, J	ž
צ׳	ch	č
ָ		å, o, ȯ (short) â, ā (long)
ַ	a	a
ֲ		a, ^{a}
ֵ		e, ẹ, ē
ֶ	e	æ, ä, ȩ
ֱ		œ, ĕ, ^{e}
ְ	only *sheva na* is transliterated	ə, ĕ, e; only *sheva na* transliterated
ִ, ִי	i	i
ֹ, וֹ	o	o, o, o
ֻ, וּ	u	u, ŭ û, ū
ֵי	ei; biblical e	
‡		reconstructed forms of words

1. The letters א and ע are not transliterated.
An apostrophe (’) between vowels indicates that they do not form a diphthong and are to be pronounced separately.
2. *Dagesh ḥazak* (forte) is indicated by doubling of the letter, except for the letter שׁ.
3. Names. Biblical names and biblical place names are rendered according to the Bible translation of the Jewish Publication Society of America. Post-biblical Hebrew names are transliterated; contemporary names are transliterated or rendered as used by the person. Place names are transliterated or rendered by the accepted spelling. Names and some words with an accepted English form are usually not transliterated.

YIDDISH

א	not transliterated
אַ	a
אָ	o
בּ	b
בֿ	v
ג	g
ד	d
ה	h
ו, וּ	u
וו	v
וי	oy
ז	z
זש	zh
ח	kh
ט	t
טש	tsh, ch
י	(consonant) y (vowel) i
יִ	i
יי	ey
ײַ	ay
כּ	k
כ, ך	kh
ל	l
מ, ם	m
נ, ן	n
ס	s
ע	e
פּ	p
פֿ, ף	f
צ, ץ	ts
ק	k
ר	r
שׁ	sh
שׂ	s
תּ	t
ת	s

1. Yiddish transliteration rendered according to U. Weinreich's Modern *English-Yiddish Yiddish-English* Dictionary.
2. Hebrew words in Yiddish are usually transliterated according to standard Yiddish pronunciation, e.g., חזנות = *khazones.*

LADINO

Ladino and Judeo-Spanish words written in Hebrew characters are transliterated phonetically, following the General Rules of Hebrew transliteration (see above) whenever the accepted spelling in Latin characters could not be ascertained.

ARABIC

ا ء	a[1]	ض	ḍ
ب	b	ط	ṭ
ت	t	ظ	ẓ
ث	th	ع	c
ج	j	غ	gh
ح	ḥ	ف	f
خ	kh	ق	q
د	d	ك	k
ذ	dh	ل	l
ر	r	م	m
ز	z	ن	n
س	s	ه	h
ش	sh	و	w
ص	ṣ	ي	y
ـَ	a	ـَا ى	ā
ـِ	i	ـِي	ī
ـُ	u	ـُو	ū
ـَو	aw	ـِيّ	iyy[2]
ـَي	ay	ـُوّ	uww[2]

1. not indicated when initial
2. see note (f)

a) The EJ follows the *Columbia Lippincott Gazetteer* and the *Times Atlas* in transliteration of Arabic place names. Sites that appear in neither are transliterated according to the table above, and subject to the following notes.

b) The EJ follows the *Columbia Encyclopedia* in transliteration of Arabic names. Personal names that do not therein appear are transliterated according to the table above and subject to the following notes (e.g., Ali rather than ʿAlī, Suleiman rather than Sulayman).

c) The EJ follows the *Webster's Third International Dictionary, Unabridged* in transliteration of Arabic terms that have been integrated into the English language.

d) The term "Abu" will thus appear, usually in disregard of inflection.

e) Nunnation (end vowels, *tanwīn*) are dropped in transliteration.

f) Gemination (*tashdīd*) is indicated by the doubling of the geminated letter, unless an end letter, in which case the gemination is dropped.

g) The definitive article *al-* will always be thus transliterated, unless subject to one of the modifying notes (e.g., El-Arish rather than al-ʿArīsh; modification according to note (a)).

h) The Arabic transliteration disregards the Sun Letters (the antero-palatals (*al-Ḥurūf al-Shamsiyya*).

i) The *tā-marbūṭa* (o) is omitted in transliteration, unless in construct-stage (e.g., *Khirba* but *Khirbat Mishmish*).

These modifying notes may lead to various inconsistencies in the Arabic transliteration, but this policy has deliberately been adopted to gain smoother reading of Arabic terms and names.

GREEK

Ancient Greek	*Modern Greek*	*Greek Letters*
a	a	*Α; α; ᾳ*
b	v	*Β; β*
g	gh; g	*Γ; γ*
d	dh	*Δ; δ*
e	e	*Ε; ε*
z	z	*Ζ; ζ*
e; e	i	*Η; η; ῃ*
th	th	*Θ; θ*
i	i	*Ι; ι*
k	k; ky	*Κ; κ*
l	l	*Λ; λ*
m	m	*Μ; μ*
n	n	*Ν; ν*
x	x	*Ξ; ξ*
o	o	*Ο; ο*
p	p	*Π; π*
r; rh	r	*Ρ; ρ; ῥ*
s	s	*Σ; σ; ς*
t	t	*Τ; τ*
u; y	i	*Υ; υ*
ph	f	*Φ; φ*
ch	kh	*Χ; χ*
ps	ps	*Ψ; ψ*
o; ō	o	*Ω; ω; ῳ*
ai	e	*αι*
ei	i	*ει*
oi	i	*οι*
ui	i	*υι*
ou	ou	*ου*
eu	ev	*ευ*
eu; ēu	iv	*ηυ*
–	j	*τζ*
nt	d; nd	*ντ*
mp	b; mb	*μπ*
ngk	g	*γκ*
ng	ng	*νγ*
h	–	ʽ
–	–	ʼ
w	–	*Ϝ*

RUSSIAN

А	A
Б	B
В	V
Г	G
Д	D
Е	E, Ye[1]
Ё	Yo, O[2]
Ж	Zh
З	Z
И	I
Й	Y[3]
К	K
Л	L
М	M
Н	N
О	O
П	P
Р	R
С	S
Т	T
У	U
Ф	F
Х	Kh
Ц	Ts
Ч	Ch
Ш	Sh
Щ	Shch
Ъ	omitted; see note [1]
Ы	Y
Ь	omitted; see note [1]
Э	E
Ю	Yu
Я	Ya

1. Ye at the beginning of a word; after all vowels except ***Ы***; and after ***Ъ*** and ***Ь***.
2. O after ***Ч***, ***Ш*** and ***Щ***.
3. Omitted after ***Ы***, and in names of people after ***И***.

A. Many first names have an accepted English or quasi-English form which has been preferred to transliteration.
B. Place names have been given according to the *Columbia Lippincott Gazeteer.*
C. Pre-revolutionary spelling has been ignored.
D. Other languages using the Cyrillic alphabet (e.g., Bulgarian, Ukrainian), inasmuch as they appear, have been phonetically transliterated in conformity with the principles of this table.

GLOSSARY

Asterisked terms have separate entries in the Encyclopaedia.

Actions Committee, early name of the Zionist General Council, the supreme institution of the World Zionist Organization in the interim between Congresses. The Zionist Executive's name was then the "Small Actions Committee."

***Adar**, twelfth month of the Jewish religious year, sixth of the civil, approximating to February–March.

***Aggadah**, name given to those sections of Talmud and Midrash containing homiletic expositions of the Bible, stories, legends, folklore, anecdotes, or maxims. In contradistinction to **halakhah.*

***Agunah**, woman unable to remarry according to Jewish law, because of desertion by her husband or inability to accept presumption of death.

***Aharonim**, later rabbinic authorities. In contradistinction to **rishonim* ("early ones").

Ahavah, liturgical poem inserted in the second benediction of the morning prayer *(*Ahavah Rabbah)* of the festivals and/or special Sabbaths.

Aktion (Ger.), operation involving the mass assembly, deportation, and murder of Jews by the Nazis during the *Holocaust.

***Aliyah**, (1) being called to Reading of the Law in synagogue; (2) immigration to Ereẓ Israel; (3) one of the waves of immigration to Ereẓ Israel from the early 1880s.

***Amidah**, main prayer recited at all services; also known as *Shemoneh Esreh* and *Tefillah.*

***Amora** (pl. **amoraim**), title given to the Jewish scholars in Ereẓ Israel and Babylonia in the third to sixth centuries who were responsible for the **Gemara.*

Aravah, the *willow; one of the *Four Species used on *Sukkot ("festival of Tabernacles") together with the **etrog, hadas,* and **lulav.*

***Arvit**, evening prayer.

Asarah be-Tevet, fast on the 10th of Tevet commemorating the commencement of the siege of Jerusalem by Nebuchadnezzar.

Asefat ha-Nivḥarim, representative assembly elected by Jews in Palestine during the period of the British Mandate (1920–48).

***Ashkenaz**, name applied generally in medieval rabbinical literature to Germany.

***Ashkenazi** (pl. **Ashkenazim**), German or West-, Central-, or East-European Jew(s), as contrasted with *Sephardi(m).

***Av**, fifth month of the Jewish religious year, eleventh of the civil, approximating to July–August.

***Av bet din**, vice president of the supreme court (*bet din ha-gadol*) in Jerusalem during the Second Temple period; later, title given to communal rabbis as heads of the religious courts (see **bet din*).

***Badḥan**, jester, particularly at traditional Jewish weddings in Eastern Europe.

***Bakkashah** (Heb. "supplication"), type of petitionary prayer, mainly recited in the Sephardi rite on Rosh Ha-Shanah and the Day of Atonement.

Bar, "son of . . . "; frequently appearing in personal names.

***Baraita** (pl. **beraitot**), statement of **tanna* not found in *Mishnah.

***Bar mitzvah**, ceremony marking the initiation of a boy at the age of 13 into the Jewish religious community.

Ben, "son of . . . ", frequently appearing in personal names.

Berakhah (pl. **berakhot**), *benediction, blessing; formula of praise and thanksgiving.

***Bet din** (pl. **battei din**), rabbinic court of law.

***Bet ha-midrash**, school for higher rabbinic learning; often attached to or serving as a synagogue.

***Bilu**, first modern movement for pioneering and agricultural settlement in Ereẓ Israel, founded in 1882 at Kharkov, Russia.

***Bund**, Jewish socialist party founded in Vilna in 1897, supporting Jewish national rights; Yiddishist, and anti-Zionist.

Cohen (pl. **Cohanim**), see Kohen.

***Conservative Judaism**, trend in Judaism developed in the United States in the 20th century which, while opposing extreme changes in traditional observances, permits certain modifications of *halakhah* in response to the changing needs of the Jewish people.

***Consistory** (Fr. *consistoire*), governing body of a Jewish communal district in France and certain other countries.

***Converso(s)**, term applied in Spain and Portugal to converted Jew(s), and sometimes more loosely to their descendants.

***Crypto-Jew**, term applied to a person who although observing outwardly Christianity (or some other religion) was at heart a Jew and maintained Jewish observances as far as possible (see Converso; Marrano; Neofiti; New Christian; Jadīd al-Islām).

***Dayyan**, member of rabbinic court.

Decisor, equivalent to the Hebrew *posek* (pl. **posekim*), the rabbi who gives the decision (*halakhah*) in Jewish law or practice.

***Devekut**, "devotion"; attachment or adhesion to God; communion with God.

***Diaspora**, Jews living in the "dispersion" outside Ereẓ Israel; area of Jewish settlement outside Ereẓ Israel.

Din, a law (both secular and religious), legal decision, or lawsuit.

Divan, diwan, collection of poems, especially in Hebrew, Arabic, or Persian.

Dunam, unit of land area (1,000 sq. m., c. ¼ acre), used in Israel.

Einsatzgruppen, mobile units of Nazi S.S. and S.D.; in U.S.S.R. and Serbia, mobile killing units.

***Ein-Sof**, "without end"; "the infinite"; hidden, impersonal aspect of God; also used as a Divine Name.

***Elul**, sixth month of the Jewish religious calendar, 12th of the civil, precedes the High Holiday season in the fall.

Endloesung, see *Final Solution.

***Ereẓ Israel**, Land of Israel; Palestine.

***Eruv**, technical term for rabbinical provision permitting the alleviation of certain restrictions.

***Etrog**, citron; one of the *Four Species used on *Sukkot together with the **lulav, hadas,* and *aravah.*

Even ha-Ezer, see Shulḥan Arukh.

***Exilarch**, lay head of Jewish community in Babylonia (see also *resh galuta*), and elsewhere.

***Final Solution** (Ger. *Endloesung*), in Nazi terminology, the Nazi-planned mass murder and total annihilation of the Jews.

***Gabbai**, official of a Jewish congregation; originally a charity collector.

***Galut**, "exile"; the condition of the Jewish people in dispersion.

*Gaon (pl. geonim), head of academy in post-talmudic period, especially in Babylonia.

Gaonate, office of *gaon.

*****Gemara**, traditions, discussions, and rulings of the **amoraim*, commenting on and supplementing the *Mishnah, and forming part of the Babylonian and Palestinian Talmuds (see Talmud).

*****Gematria**, interpretation of Hebrew word according to the numerical value of its letters.

General Government, territory in Poland administered by a German civilian governor-general with headquarters in Cracow after the German occupation in World War II.

*****Genizah**, depository for sacred books. The best known was discovered in the synagogue of Fostat (old Cairo).

Get, bill of *divorce.

*****Ge'ullah**, hymn inserted after the **Shema* into the benediction of the morning prayer of the festivals and special Sabbaths.

*****Gilgul**, metempsychosis; transmigration of souls.

*****Golem**, automaton, especially in human form, created by magical means and endowed with life.

*****Ḥabad**, initials of *ḥokhmah, binah, da'at*: "wisdom, understanding, knowledge"; ḥasidic movement founded in Belorussia by *Shneur Zalman of Lyady.

Hadas, *myrtle; one of the *Four Species used on Sukkot together with the **etrog*, **lulav*, and *aravah*.

*****Haftarah** (pl. **haftarot**), designation of the portion from the prophetical books of the Bible recited after the synagogue reading from the Pentateuch on Sabbaths and holidays.

*****Haganah**, clandestine Jewish organization for armed self-defense in Ereẓ Israel under the British Mandate, which eventually evolved into a people's militia and became the basis for the Israel army.

*****Haggadah**, ritual recited in the home on *Passover eve at seder table.

Haham, title of chief rabbi of the Spanish and Portuguese congregations in London, England.

*****Hakham**, title of rabbi of *Sephardi congregation.

*****Hakham bashi**, title in the 15th century and modern times of the chief rabbi in the Ottoman Empire, residing in Constantinople (Istanbul), also applied to principal rabbis in provincial towns.

Hakhsharah ("preparation"), organized training in the Diaspora of pioneers for agricultural settlement in Ereẓ Israel.

*****Halakhah** (pl. **halakhot**), an accepted decision in rabbinic law. Also refers to those parts of the *Talmud concerned with legal matters. In contradistinction to **aggadah*.

Ḥaliẓah, biblically prescribed ceremony (Deut. 25:9–10) performed when a man refuses to marry his brother's childless widow, enabling her to remarry.

*****Hallel**, term referring to Psalms 113-18 in liturgical use.

*****Ḥalukkah**, system of financing the maintenance of Jewish communities in the holy cities of Ereẓ Israel by collections made abroad, mainly in the pre-Zionist era (see *kolel*).

Ḥalutz (pl. **ḥalutzim**), pioneer, especially in agriculture, in Ereẓ Israel.

Ḥalutziyyut, pioneering.

*****Ḥanukkah**, eight-day celebration commemorating the victory of *Judah Maccabee over the Syrian king *Antiochus Epiphanes and the subsequent rededication of the Temple.

Ḥasid, adherent of *Ḥasidism.

*****Ḥasidei Ashkenaz**, medieval pietist movement among the Jews of Germany.

*****Ḥasidism**, (1) religious revivalist movement of popular mysticism among Jews of Germany in the Middle Ages; (2) religious movement founded by *Israel ben Eliezer Ba'al Shem Tov in the first half of the 18th century.

*****Haskalah**, "enlightenment"; movement for spreading modern European culture among Jews c. 1750–1880. See *maskil*.

*****Havdalah**, ceremony marking the end of Sabbath or festival.

*****Ḥazzan**, precentor who intones the liturgy and leads the prayers in synagogue; in earlier times a synagogue official.

*****Ḥeder** (lit. "room"), school for teaching children Jewish religious observance.

Heikhalot, "palaces"; tradition in Jewish mysticism centering on mystical journeys through the heavenly spheres and palaces to the Divine Chariot (see Merkabah).

*****Ḥerem**, excommunication, imposed by rabbinical authorities for purposes of religious and/or communal discipline; originally, in biblical times, that which is separated from common use either because it was an abomination or because it was consecrated to God.

Ḥeshvan, see Marḥeshvan.

*****Ḥevra kaddisha**, title applied to charitable confraternity (**ḥevrah*), now generally limited to associations for burial of the dead.

*****Ḥibbat Zion**, see Ḥovevei Zion.

*****Histadrut** (abbr. For Heb. **Ha-Histadrut ha-Kelalit shel ha-Ovedim ha-Ivriyyim be-Ereẓ Israel**). Ereẓ Israel Jewish Labor Federation, founded in 1920; subsequently renamed Histadrut ha-Ovedim be-Ereẓ Israel.

*****Holocaust**, the organized mass persecution and annihilation of European Jewry by the Nazis (1933–1945).

*****Hoshana Rabba**, the seventh day of *Sukkot on which special observances are held.

Ḥoshen Mishpat, see Shulḥan Arukh.

Ḥovevei Zion, federation of *Ḥibbat Zion, early (pre-*Herzl) Zionist movement in Russia.

Illui, outstanding scholar or genius, especially a young prodigy in talmudic learning.

*****Iyyar**, second month of the Jewish religious year, eighth of the civil, approximating to April-May.

I.Ẓ.L. (initials of Heb. ***Irgun Ẓeva'i Le'ummi**; "National Military Organization"), underground Jewish organization in Ereẓ Israel founded in 1931, which engaged from 1937 in retaliatory acts against Arab attacks and later against the British mandatory authorities.

*****Jadīd al-Islām** (Ar.), a person practicing the Jewish religion in secret although outwardly observing Islām.

*****Jewish Legion**, Jewish units in British army during World War I.

*****Jihād** (Ar.), in Muslim religious law, holy war waged against infidels.

*****Judenrat** (Ger. "Jewish council"), council set up in Jewish communities and ghettos under the Nazis to execute their instructions.

*****Judenrein** (Ger. "clean of Jews"), in Nazi terminology the condition of a locality from which all Jews had been eliminated.

*****Kabbalah**, the Jewish mystical tradition:
Kabbala iyyunit, speculative Kabbalah;
Kabbala ma'asit, practical Kabbalah;
Kabbala nevu'it, prophetic Kabbalah.

Kabbalist, student of Kabbalah.

*****Kaddish**, liturgical doxology.

Kahal, Jewish congregation; among Ashkenazim, *kehillah*.

*Kalām (Ar.), science of Muslim theology; adherents of the Kalām are called *mutakallimūn*.

***Karaite**, member of a Jewish sect originating in the eighth century which rejected rabbinic (*Rabbanite) Judaism and claimed to accept only Scripture as authoritative.

***Kasher**, ritually permissible food.

Kashrut, Jewish *dietary laws.

***Kavvanah**, "intention"; term denoting the spiritual concentration accompanying prayer and the performance of ritual or of a commandment.

***Kedushah**, main addition to the third blessing in the reader's repetition of the *Amidah* in which the public responds to the precentor's introduction.

Kefar, village; first part of name of many settlements in Israel.

Kehillah, congregation; see *kahal*.

Kelippah (pl. **kelippot**), "husk(s)"; mystical term denoting force(s) of evil.

***Keneset Yisrael**, comprehensive communal organization of the Jews in Palestine during the British Mandate.

Keri, variants in the masoretic (*masorah) text of the Bible between the spelling (*ketiv*) and its pronunciation (*keri*).

***Kerovah** (collective plural (corrupted) from **kerovez̧**), poem(s) incorporated into the **Amidah*.

Ketiv, see *keri*.

***Ketubbah**, marriage contract, stipulating husband's obligations to wife.

Kevuz̧ah, small commune of pioneers constituting an agricultural settlement in Erez̧ Israel (evolved later into *kibbutz).

***Kibbutz** (pl. **kibbutzim**), larger-size commune constituting a settlement in Erez̧ Israel based mainly on agriculture but engaging also in industry.

***Kiddush**, prayer of sanctification, recited over wine or bread on eve of Sabbaths and festivals.

***Kiddush ha-Shem**, term connoting martyrdom or act of strict integrity in support of Judaic principles.

***Kinah** (pl. **kinot**), lamentation dirge(s) for the Ninth of Av and other fast days.

***Kislev**, ninth month of the Jewish religious year, third of the civil, approximating to November-December.

Klaus, name given in Central and Eastern Europe to an institution, usually with synagogue attached, where *Talmud was studied perpetually by adults; applied by Ḥasidim to their synagogue ("*kloyz*").

***Knesset**, parliament of the State of Israel.

K(c)ohen (pl. **K(c)ohanim**), Jew(s) of priestly (Aaronide) descent.

***Kolel**, (1) community in Erez̧ Israel of persons from a particular country or locality, often supported by their fellow countrymen in the Diaspora; (2) institution for higher Torah study.

Kosher, see *kasher*.

***Kristallnacht** (Ger. "crystal night," meaning "night of broken glass"), organized destruction of synagogues, Jewish houses, and shops, accompanied by mass arrests of Jews, which took place in Germany and Austria under the Nazis on the night of Nov. 9–10, 1938.

***Lag ba-Omer**, 33rd (Heb. **lag**) day of the **Omer* period falling on the 18th of *Iyyar; a semi-holiday.

Leḥi (abbr. For Heb. ***Loḥamei Ḥerut Israel**, "Fighters for the Freedom of Israel"), radically anti-British armed underground organization in Palestine, founded in 1940 by dissidents from *I.Z.L.

Levir, husband's brother.

***Levirate marriage** (Heb. *yibbum*), marriage of childless widow (*yevamah*) by brother (*yavam*) of the deceased husband (in accordance with Deut. 25:5); release from such an obligation is effected through *ḥaliz̧ah*.

LHY, see Leḥi.

***Lulav**, palm branch; one of the *Four Species used on *Sukkot together with the **etrog*, *hadas*, and *aravah*.

***Ma'aravot**, hymns inserted into the evening prayer of the three festivals, Passover, Shavuot, and Sukkot.

Ma'ariv, evening prayer; also called **arvit*.

***Ma'barah**, transition camp; temporary settlement for newcomers in Israel during the period of mass immigration following 1948.

***Maftir**, reader of the concluding portion of the Pentateuchal section on Sabbaths and holidays in synagogue; reader of the portion of the prophetical books of the Bible (**haftarah*).

***Maggid**, popular preacher.

***Maḥzor** (pl. **maḥzorim**), festival prayer book.

***Mamzer**, bastard; according to Jewish law, the offspring of an incestuous relationship.

***Mandate, Palestine**, responsibility for the administration of Palestine conferred on Britain by the League of Nations in 1922; mandatory government: the British administration of Palestine.

***Maqāma** (Ar. pl. **maqamāt**), poetic form (rhymed prose) which, in its classical arrangement, has rigid rules of form and content.

***Marḥeshvan**, popularly called Ḥeshvan; eighth month of the Jewish religious year, second of the civil, approximating to October–November.

***Marrano(s)**, descendant(s) of Jew(s) in Spain and Portugal whose ancestors had been converted to Christianity under pressure but who secretly observed Jewish rituals.

Maskil (pl. **maskilim**), adherent of *Haskalah ("Enlightenment") movement.

***Masorah**, body of traditions regarding the correct spelling, writing, and reading of the Hebrew Bible.

Masorete, scholar of the masoretic tradition.

Masoretic, in accordance with the masorah.

Meliz̧ah, in Middle Ages, elegant style; modern usage, florid style using biblical or talmudic phraseology.

Mellah, *Jewish quarter in North African towns.

***Menorah**, candelabrum; seven-branched oil lamp used in the Tabernacle and Temple; also eight-branched candelabrum used on *Ḥanukkah.

Me'orah, hymn inserted into the first benediction of the morning prayer (*Yoz̧er ha-Me'orot*).

***Merkabah**, *merkavah*, "chariot"; mystical discipline associated with Ezekiel's vision of the Divine Throne-Chariot (Ezek. 1).

Meshullaḥ, emissary sent to conduct propaganda or raise funds for rabbinical academies or charitable institutions.

***Mezuzah** (pl. **mezuzot**), parchment scroll with selected Torah verses placed in container and affixed to gates and doorposts of houses occupied by Jews.

***Midrash**, method of interpreting Scripture to elucidate legal points (*Midrash Halakhah*) or to bring out lessons by stories or homiletics (*Midrash Aggadah*). Also the name for a collection of such rabbinic interpretations.

***Mikveh**, ritual bath.

***Minhag** (pl. **minhagim**), ritual custom(s); synagogal rite(s); especially of a specific sector of Jewry.

***Minḥah**, afternoon prayer; originally meal offering in Temple.

*Minyan, group of ten male adult Jews, the minimum required for communal prayer.

*Mishnah, earliest codification of Jewish Oral Law.

Mishnah (pl. mishnayot), subdivision of tractates of the Mishnah.

Mitnagged (pl. *Mitnaggedim), originally, opponents of *Ḥasidism in Eastern Europe.

*Mitzvah, biblical or rabbinic injunction; applied also to good or charitable deeds.

Mohel, official performing circumcisions.

*Moshav, smallholders' cooperative agricultural settlement in Israel, see moshav ovedim.

Moshavah, earliest type of Jewish village in modern Ereẓ Israel in which farming is conducted on individual farms mostly on privately owned land.

Moshav ovedim ("workers' moshav"), agricultural village in Israel whose inhabitants possess individual homes and holdings but cooperate in the purchase of equipment, sale of produce, mutual aid, etc.

*Moshav shittufi ("collective moshav"), agricultural village in Israel whose members possess individual homesteads but where the agriculture and economy are conducted as a collective unit.

Mostegab (Ar.), poem with biblical verse at beginning of each stanza.

*Muqaddam (Ar., pl. muqaddamūn), "leader," "head of the community."

*Musaf, additional service on Sabbath and festivals; originally the additional sacrifice offered in the Temple.

Musar, traditional ethical literature.

*Musar movement, ethical movement developing in the latter part of the 19th century among Orthodox Jewish groups in Lithuania; founded by R. Israel *Lipkin (Salanter).

*Nagid (pl. negidim), title applied in Muslim (and some Christian) countries in the Middle Ages to a leader recognized by the state as head of the Jewish community.

Nakdan (pl. nakdanim), "punctuator"; scholar of the 9th to 14th centuries who provided biblical manuscripts with masoretic apparatus, vowels, and accents.

*Nasi (pl. nesi'im), talmudic term for president of the Sanhedrin, who was also the spiritual head and later, political representative of the Jewish people; from second century a descendant of Hillel recognized by the Roman authorities as patriarch of the Jews. Now applied to the president of the State of Israel.

*Negev, the southern, mostly arid, area of Israel.

*Ne'ilah, concluding service on the *Day of Atonement.

Neofiti, term applied in southern Italy to converts to Christianity from Judaism and their descendants who were suspected of maintaining secret allegiance to Judaism.

*Neology; Neolog; Neologism, trend of *Reform Judaism in Hungary forming separate congregations after 1868.

*Nevelah (lit. "carcass"), meat forbidden by the *dietary laws on account of the absence of, or defect in, the act of *sheḥitah* (ritual slaughter).

*New Christians, term applied especially in Spain and Portugal to converts from Judaism (and from Islam) and their descendants; "Half New Christian" designated a person one of whose parents was of full Jewish blood.

*Niddah ("menstruous woman"), woman during the period of menstruation.

*Nisan, first month of the Jewish religious year, seventh of the civil, approximating to March-April.

Niẓoẓot, "sparks"; mystical term for sparks of the holy light imprisoned in all matter.

Nosaḥ (nusaḥ) "version"; (1) textual variant; (2) term applied to distinguish the various prayer rites, e.g., *nosaḥ Ashkenaz*; (3) the accepted tradition of synagogue melody.

*Notarikon, method of abbreviating Hebrew works or phrases by acronym.

Novella(e) (Heb. *ḥiddush (im)*), commentary on talmudic and later rabbinic subjects that derives new facts or principles from the implications of the text.

*Nuremberg Laws, Nazi laws excluding Jews from German citizenship, and imposing other restrictions.

Ofan, hymns inserted into a passage of the morning prayer.

*Omer, first sheaf cut during the barley harvest, offered in the Temple on the second day of Passover.

Omer, Counting of (Heb. *Sefirat ha-Omer*), 49 days counted from the day on which the *omer* was first offered in the Temple (according to the rabbis the 16th of Nisan, i.e., the second day of Passover) until the festival of Shavuot; now a period of semi-mourning.

Oraḥ Ḥayyim, see Shulḥan Arukh.

*Orthodoxy (Orthodox Judaism), modern term for the strictly traditional sector of Jewry.

*Pale of Settlement, 25 provinces of czarist Russia where Jews were permitted permanent residence.

*Palmaḥ (abbr. for Heb. *peluggot maḥaz*; "shock companies"), striking arm of the *Haganah.

*Pardes, medieval biblical exegesis giving the literal, allegorical, homiletical, and esoteric interpretations.

*Parnas, chief synagogue functionary, originally vested with both religious and administrative functions; subsequently an elected lay leader.

Partition plan(s), proposals for dividing Ereẓ Israel into autonomous areas.

Paytan, composer of *piyyut* (liturgical poetry).

*Peel Commission, British Royal Commission appointed by the British government in 1936 to inquire into the Palestine problem and make recommendations for its solution.

Pesaḥ, *Passover.

*Pilpul, in talmudic and rabbinic literature, a sharp dialectic used particularly by talmudists in Poland from the 16th century.

*Pinkas, community register or minute-book.

*Piyyut, (pl. piyyutim), Hebrew liturgical poetry.

*Pizmon, poem with refrain.

Posek (pl. *posekim), decisor; codifier or rabbinic scholar who pronounces decisions in disputes and on questions of Jewish law.

*Prosbul, legal method of overcoming the cancelation of debts with the advent of the *sabbatical year.

*Purim, festival held on Adar 14 or 15 in commemoration of the delivery of the Jews of Persia in the time of *Esther.

Rabban, honorific title higher than that of rabbi, applied to heads of the *Sanhedrin in mishnaic times.

*Rabbanite, adherent of rabbinic Judaism. In contradistinction to *Karaite.

Reb, rebbe, Yiddish form for rabbi, applied generally to a teacher or ḥasidic rabbi.

*Reconstructionism, trend in Jewish thought originating in the United States.

*Reform Judaism, trend in Judaism advocating modification of *Orthodoxy in conformity with the exigencies of contemporary life and thought.

Resh galuta, lay head of Babylonian Jewry (see exilarch).

Responsum (pl. ***responsa**), written opinion (*teshuvah*) given to question (*she'elah*) on aspects of Jewish law by qualified authorities; pl. collection of such queries and opinions in book form (*she'elot u-teshuvot*).

***Rishonim**, older rabbinical authorities. Distinguished from later authorities (**aḥaronim*).

***Rishon le-Zion**, title given to Sephardi chief rabbi of Ereẓ Israel.

***Rosh Ha-Shanah**, two-day holiday (one day in biblical and early mishnaic times) at the beginning of the month of *Tishri (September–October), traditionally the New Year.

Rosh Hodesh, *New Moon, marking the beginning of the Hebrew month.

Rosh Yeshivah, see *Yeshivah.

***R.S.H.A.** (initials of Ger. *Reichssicherheitshauptamt*: "Reich Security Main Office"), the central security department of the German Reich, formed in 1939, and combining the security police (Gestapo and Kripo) and the S.D.

***Sanhedrin**, the assembly of ordained scholars which functioned both as a supreme court and as a legislature before 70 C.E. In modern times the name was given to the body of representative Jews convoked by Napoleon in 1807.

***Savora** (pl. **savoraim**), name given to the Babylonian scholars of the period between the **amoraim* and the **geonim*, approximately 500–700 C.E.

S.D. (initials of Ger. *Sicherheitsdienst*: "security service"), security service of the *S.S. formed in 1932 as the sole intelligence organization of the Nazi party.

Seder, ceremony observed in the Jewish home on the first night of Passover (outside Ereẓ Israel first two nights), when the *Haggadah is recited.

***Sefer Torah**, manuscript scroll of the Pentateuch for public reading in synagogue.

***Sefirot, the ten**, the ten "Numbers"; mystical term denoting the ten spheres or emanations through which the Divine manifests itself; elements of the world; dimensions, primordial numbers.

Selektion (Ger.), (1) in ghettos and other Jewish settlements, the drawing up by Nazis of lists of deportees; (2) separation of incoming victims to concentration camps into two categories – those destined for immediate killing and those to be sent for forced labor.

Seliḥah (pl. ***seliḥot**), penitential prayer.

***Semikhah**, ordination conferring the title "rabbi" and permission to give decisions in matters of ritual and law.

Sephardi (pl. ***Sephardim**), Jew(s) of Spain and Portugal and their descendants, wherever resident, as contrasted with *Ashkenazi(m).

Shabbatean, adherent of the pseudo-messiah *Shabbetai Ẓevi (17th century).

Shaddai, name of God found frequently in the Bible and commonly translated "Almighty."

***Shaḥarit**, morning service.

Shali'aḥ (pl. **sheliḥim**), in Jewish law, messenger, agent; in modern times, an emissary from Ereẓ Israel to Jewish communities or organizations abroad for the purpose of fund-raising, organizing pioneer immigrants, education, etc.

Shalmonit, poetic meter introduced by the liturgical poet *Solomon ha-Bavli.

***Shammash**, synagogue beadle.

***Shavuot**, Pentecost; Festival of Weeks; second of the three annual pilgrim festivals, commemorating the receiving of the Torah at Mt. Sinai.

***Sheḥitah**, ritual slaughtering of animals.

***Shekhinah**, Divine Presence.

Shelishit, poem with three-line stanzas.

***Sheluḥei Ereẓ Israel** (or **shadarim**), emissaries from Ereẓ Israel.

***Shema** ([Yisrael]; "hear… [O Israel]," Deut. 6:4), Judaism's confession of faith, proclaiming the absolute unity of God.

Shemini Aẓeret, final festal day (in the Diaspora, final two days) at the conclusion of *Sukkot.

Shemittah, *Sabbatical year.

Sheniyyah, poem with two-line stanzas.

***Shephelah**, southern part of the coastal plain of Ereẓ Israel.

***Shevat**, eleventh month of the Jewish religious year, fifth of the civil, approximating to January–February.

***Shi'ur Komah**, Hebrew mystical work (c. eighth century) containing a physical description of God's dimensions; term denoting enormous spacial measurement used in speculations concerning the body of the **Shekhinah*.

Shivah, the "seven days" of *mourning following burial of a relative.

***Shofar**, horn of the ram (or any other ritually clean animal excepting the cow) sounded for the memorial blowing on *Rosh Ha-Shanah, and other occasions.

Shoḥet, person qualified to perform **sheḥitah*.

Shomer, *Ha-Shomer, organization of Jewish workers in Ereẓ Israel founded in 1909 to defend Jewish settlements.

***Shtadlan**, Jewish representative or negotiator with access to dignitaries of state, active at royal courts, etc.

***Shtetl**, Jewish small-town community in Eastern Europe.

***Shulḥan Arukh**, Joseph *Caro's code of Jewish law in four parts:
Oraḥ Ḥayyim, laws relating to prayers, Sabbath, festivals, and fasts;
Yoreh De'ah, dietary laws, etc;
Even ha-Ezer, laws dealing with women, marriage, etc;
Ḥoshen Mishpat, civil, criminal law, court procedure, etc.

Siddur, among Ashkenazim, the volume containing the daily prayers (in distinction to the **maḥzor* containing those for the festivals).

***Simḥat Torah**, holiday marking the completion in the synagogue of the annual cycle of reading the Pentateuch; in Ereẓ Israel observed on Shemini Aẓeret (outside Ereẓ Israel on the following day).

***Sinai Campaign**, brief campaign in October–November 1956 when Israel army reacted to Egyptian terrorist attacks and blockade by occupying the Sinai peninsula.

Sitra aḥra, "the other side" (of God); left side; the demoniac and satanic powers.

***Sivan**, third month of the Jewish religious year, ninth of the civil, approximating to May–June.

***Six-Day War**, rapid war in June 1967 when Israel reacted to Arab threats and blockade by defeating the Egyptian, Jordanian, and Syrian armies.

***S.S.** (initials of Ger. *Schutzstaffel*: "protection detachment"), Nazi formation established in 1925 which later became the "elite" organization of the Nazi Party and carried out central tasks in the "Final Solution."

***Status quo ante** community, community in Hungary retaining the status it had held before the convention of the General Jewish Congress there in 1868 and the resultant split in Hungarian Jewry.

***Sukkah**, booth or tabernacle erected for *Sukkot when, for seven days, religious Jews "dwell" or at least eat in the *sukkah* (Lev. 23:42).

***Sukkot**, festival of Tabernacles; last of the three pilgrim festivals, beginning on the 15th of Tishri.

Sūra (Ar.), chapter of the Koran.

Ta'anit Esther (Fast of *Esther), fast on the 13th of Adar, the day preceding Purim.

Takkanah (pl. ***takkanot**), regulation supplementing the law of the Torah; regulations governing the internal life of communities and congregations.

***Tallit (gadol)**, four-cornered prayer shawl with fringes (*ẓiẓit*) at each corner.

***Tallit katan**, garment with fringes (*ẓiẓit*) appended, worn by observant male Jews under their outer garments.

***Talmud**, "teaching"; compendium of discussion on the Mishnah by generations of scholars and jurists in many academies over a period of several centuries. The Jerusalem (or Palestinian) Talmud mainly contains the discussions of the Palestinian sages. The Babylonian Talmud incorporates the parallel discussion in the Babylonian academies.

Talmud torah, term generally applied to Jewish religious (and ultimately to talmudic) study; also to traditional Jewish religious public schools.

***Tammuz**, fourth month of the Jewish religious year, tenth of the civil, approximating to June-July.

Tanna (pl. ***tannaim**), rabbinic teacher of mishnaic period.

***Targum**, Aramaic translation of the Bible.

***Tefillin**, phylacteries, small leather cases containing passages from Scripture and affixed on the forehead and arm by male Jews during the recital of morning prayers.

Tell (Ar. "mound," "hillock"), ancient mound in the Middle East composed of remains of successive settlements.

***Terefah**, food that is not **kasher*, owing to a defect on the animal.

***Territorialism**, 20th century movement supporting the creation of an autonomous territory for Jewish mass-settlement outside Ereẓ Israel.

***Tevet**, tenth month of the Jewish religious year, fourth of the civil, approximating to December–January.

Tikkun ("restitution," "reintegration"), (1) order of service for certain occasions, mostly recited at night; (2) mystical term denoting restoration of the right order and true unity after the spiritual "catastrophe" which occurred in the cosmos.

Tishah be-Av, Ninth of *Av, fast day commemorating the destruction of the First and Second Temples.

***Tishri**, seventh month of the Jewish religious year, first of the civil, approximating to September–October.

Tokheḥah, reproof sections of the Pentateuch (Lev. 26 and Deut. 28); poem of reproof.

***Torah**, Pentateuch or the Pentateuchal scroll for reading in synagogue; entire body of traditional Jewish teaching and literature.

Tosafist, talmudic glossator, mainly French (12–14th centuries), bringing additions to the commentary by *Rashi.

***Tosafot**, glosses supplied by tosafist.

***Tosefta**, a collection of teachings and traditions of the *tannaim*, closely related to the Mishnah.

Tradent, person who hands down a talmudic statement on the name of his teacher or other earlier authority.

***Tu bi-Shevat**, the 15th day of Shevat, the New Year for Trees; date marking a dividing line for fruit tithing; in modern Israel celebrated as arbor day.

***Uganda Scheme**, plan suggested by the British government in 1903 to establish an autonomous Jewish settlement area in East Africa.

***Va'ad Le'ummi**, national council of the Jewish community in Ereẓ Israel during the period of the British *Mandate.

***Wannsee Conference**, Nazi conference held on Jan. 20, 1942, at which the planned annihilation of European Jewry was endorsed.

Waqf (Ar.), (1) a Muslim charitable pious foundation; (2) state lands and other property passed to the Muslim community for public welfare.

***War of Independence**, war of 1947–49 when the Jews of Israel fought off Arab invading armies and ensured the establishment of the new State.

***White Paper(s)**, report(s) issued by British government, frequently statements of policy, as issued in connection with Palestine during the *Mandate period.

***Wissenschaft des Judentums** (Ger. "Science of Judaism"), movement in Europe beginning in the 19th century for scientific study of Jewish history, religion, and literature.

***Yad Vashem**, Israel official authority for commemorating the *Holocaust in the Nazi era and Jewish resistance and heroism at that time.

Yeshivah (pl. ***yeshivot**), Jewish traditional academy devoted primarily to study of rabbinic literature; *rosh yeshivah*, head of the yeshivah.

YHWH, the letters of the holy name of God, the Tetragrammaton.

Yibbum, see levirate marriage.

Yiḥud, "union"; mystical term for intention which causes the union of God with the **Shekhinah*.

Yishuv, settlement; more specifically, the Jewish community of Ereẓ Israel in the pre-State period. The pre-Zionist community is generally designated the "old yishuv" and the community evolving from 1880, the "new yishuv."

Yom Kippur, Yom ha-Kippurim, *Day of Atonement, solemn fast day observed on the 10th of Tishri.

Yoreh De'ah, see Shulḥan Arukh.

Yoẓer, hymns inserted in the first benediction (*Yoẓer Or*) of the morning **Shema*.

***Ẓaddik**, person outstanding for his faith and piety; especially a ḥasidic rabbi or leader.

Ẓimẓum, "contraction"; mystical term denoting the process whereby God withdraws or contracts within Himself so leaving a primordial vacuum in which creation can take place; primordial exile or self-limitation of God.

***Zionist Commission (1918)**, commission appointed in 1918 by the British government to advise the British military authorities in Palestine on the implementation of the *Balfour Declaration.

Ẓyyonei Zion, the organized opposition to Herzl in connection with the *Uganda Scheme.

***Ẓiẓit**, fringes attached to the **tallit* and **tallit katan*.

***Zohar**, mystical commentary on the Pentateuch; main textbook of *Kabbalah.

Zulat, hymn inserted after the **Shema* in the morning service.